Official 1995 National Football League Record & Fact Book

A National Football League Book.
Workman Publishing Co., New York.

NATIONAL FOOTBALL LEAGUE, 1995

410 Park Avenue, New York, N.Y. 10022 (212) 758-1500

Commissioner: Paul Tagliabue
President: Neil Austrian

Executive Vice President & League Counsel: Jay Moyer
Executive Vice President-Labor Relations/Chairman NFLMC: Harold Henderson
Senior Vice President-Communications & Government Affairs: Joe Browne
Senior Vice President-League & Football Development: Roger Goodell
Senior Vice President-Broadcasting & Network Television: Val Pinchbeck, Jr.
Chief Financial Officer: Tom Spock

COMMUNICATIONS
Director of Communications: Greg Aiello
Director of International Public Relations: Pete Abitante
Director of Information, AFC: Leslie Hammond
Director of Information, NFC: Reggie Roberts
Director of Corporate Communications: Chris Widmaier

BROADCASTING
Director of Broadcasting Services: Dick Maxwell
Director of Broadcasting Research: Joe Ferreira

LEAGUE AND FOOTBALL DEVELOPMENT
Director of Club Relations/Stadium Management: Joe Ellis
Director of Officiating: Jerry Seeman
League Secretary: Jan Van Duser
Director of Football Development: Gene Washington
Director of Security: Warren Welsh

SPECIAL EVENTS
Executive Director of Special Events: Jim Steeg
Director of Special Events Operations: Don Renzulli
Director of Special Events Planning: Sue Robichek

MANAGEMENT COUNCIL
Vice President-General Counsel: Dennis Curran
Vice President-Operations & Compliance: Peter Ruocco
Director of Player Programs: Lem Burnham
Director of Player Personnel/Football Operations: Joel Bussert
Director of Compliance: William Duffy
Director of Labor Operations: Peter Hadhazy
Director of Labor Relations: Lal Heneghan

FINANCE AND ADMINISTRATION
Vice President-Internal Audit: Tom Sullivan
Director of Administration: John Buzzeo
Controller: Richard Iandoli
Treasurer: Joe Siclare
Director of Systems & Information Processing: Mary Oliveti
Director of Planning: Swan Paik
Director, Financial Planning & Analysis: Ken Saunders

NFL Internet Address: http://nflhome.com

NFL ENTERPRISES
President: Ron Bernard
Vice President-Programming/Media Development: Ann Kirschner
Vice President-International TV Distribution: Robert Miller
Vice President-Marketing & Sales: Tola Murphy-Baran

NFL FILMS
President: Steve Sabol
Vice President-Cinematography: Steve Andrich
Vice President-Marketing & Sales: John Collins
Vice President-In Charge of Production: Jay Gerber
Vice President-Video Operations: Jeff Howard
Vice President-Editor-in-Chief: Bob Ryan
Vice President-Special Projects: Phil Tuckett
Vice President-Finance & Administration: Barry Wolper

NFL PROPERTIES
President: Sara Levinson
Vice President-Retail Sales: Roger Atkin
Vice President-Advertising: Bruce Burke
Vice President-Retail Licensing: Jim Connelly
Vice President-Business Development/Special Events: Don Garber
Vice President-Legal/Business Affairs & General Counsel: Gary Gertzog
Vice President-Marketing: Howard Handler
Vice President-Club Marketing: Mark Holtzman
Vice President-Corporate Sponsorships: Jim Schwebel
Vice President-Publishing: John Wiebusch

Cover Photograph by Greg Trott.

Printed in the United States of America.

A National Football League Book.
Compiled by the NFL Communications Department and Seymour Siwoff, Elias Sports Bureau.

Edited by Chris Hardart, NFL Communications Department and Chuck Garrity, Jr., NFLP Publishing.
Statistics by Elias Sports Bureau.
Produced by NFL Properties, Inc., Publishing Group, Los Angeles.

Workman Publishing Co.
708 Broadway, New York, N.Y. 10003
Manufactured in the United States of America.
First printing, July 1995.
10 9 8 7 6 5 4 3 2 1

INDEX

1995 SCHEDULE AND NOTE CALENDAR

(All times local except Tokyo, which is EDT.)
Nationally televised games in parentheses.

PRESEASON/FIRST WEEK

Saturday, July 29	Pro Football Hall of Fame Game at Canton, Ohio		
	Carolina ____ vs. Jacksonville ____	(ABC)	2:30
	Buffalo ____ at Dallas ____		8:00
	San Francisco ____ at Denver ____		7:00
Friday, August 4	Carolina ____ at Chicago ____		7:30
	Cincinnati ____ at Indianapolis ____		7:30
	Detroit ____ at New England ____		7:00
	Jacksonville ____ at Miami ____		7:00
	Pittsburgh ____ at Buffalo ____		7:30
Saturday, August 5	American Bowl at Tokyo		
	Denver ____ vs. San Francisco ____	(ESPN)	10:00 *
	Arizona ____ at Houston ____		7:00
	Atlanta ____ at Philadelphia ____		7:30
	Los Angeles ____ at Dallas ____		8:00
	New Orleans ____ vs. Green Bay ____ at Madison, Wis.		12:00
	New York Jets ____ at Tampa Bay ____		7:30
	St. Louis ____ at Seattle ____		7:00
	Washington ____ at Kansas City ____		7:00
Sunday, August 6	New York Giants ____ at Cleveland ____	(NBC)	4:00
Monday, August 7	Minnesota ____ at San Diego ____	(ABC)	5:00

* Tokyo game actual kickoff 11:00 A.M., August 6.

PRESEASON/SECOND WEEK

Thursday, August 10	Jacksonville ____ at Detroit ____		7:30
Friday, August 11	Kansas City ____ at Arizona ____		7:30
	Miami ____ at Atlanta ____		7:30
	New Orleans ____ at New York Giants ____		8:00
	Tampa Bay ____ at Cincinnati ____		7:30
Saturday, August 12	American Bowl at Toronto		
	Buffalo ____ vs. Dallas ____	(FOX)	8:00
	Denver ____ at Carolina ____		7:30
	Houston ____ vs. Washington ____ at Knoxville, Tenn.		8:00
	Indianapolis ____ at Seattle ____		7:00
	Minnesota ____ at New England ____		8:00
	New York Jets ____ vs. Philadelphia ____ at Jackson, Miss.		8:00
	St. Louis ____ at Los Angeles ____		TBA
Sunday, August 13	Green Bay ____ at Pittsburgh ____	(NBC)	1:00
	San Francisco ____ at San Diego ____	(TNT)	5:00
Monday, August 14	Chicago ____ at Cleveland ____	(ABC)	8:00

PRESEASON/THIRD WEEK

Thursday, August 17	Cincinnati ____ at Detroit ____		7:30
	New England ____ at Philadelphia ____	(TNT)	8:00
Friday, August 18	Los Angeles ____ at Minnesota ____	(FOX)	7:00
	St. Louis ____ at Jacksonville ____		7:00
Saturday, August 19	Buffalo ____ at Kansas City ____	(ESPN)	7:00
	Carolina ____ at San Francisco ____		5:00
	Cleveland ____ at Atlanta ____		7:00
	Indianapolis ____ at Green Bay ____		12:00
	New York Jets ____ at New York Giants ____		8:00
	Pittsburgh ____ at Tampa Bay ____		7:30
	San Diego ____ at Houston ____		7:30
	Washington ____ at Miami ____		7:00
Sunday, August 20	Arizona ____ at Chicago ____	(TNT)	7:00
	Seattle ____ at New Orleans ____		12:00
Monday, August 21	Dallas ____ at Denver ____	(ABC)	6:00

PRESEASON/FOURTH WEEK	**Thursday, August 24**	Chicago _____ at Indianapolis _____		7:30
		Philadelphia _____ at Pittsburgh _____	(ESPN)	8:00
	Friday, August 25	Atlanta _____ at Buffalo _____		7:30
		Cleveland _____ at Arizona _____		7:30
		Denver _____ at Jacksonville _____		7:00
		Detroit _____ at New Orleans _____		7:00
		Miami _____ vs. Tampa Bay _____ at Orlando, Fla.		8:00
		New England _____ at Los Angeles _____		6:00
		New York Jets _____ at Cincinnati _____		7:30
		St. Louis _____ at San Diego _____		7:30
		Washington _____ at Green Bay _____		6:00
	Saturday, August 26	Dallas _____ vs. Houston _____ at San Antonio, Tex.		7:00
		Kansas City _____ at Minnesota _____	(NBC)	12:30
		New York Giants _____ at Carolina _____		4:00
		Seattle _____ at San Francisco _____	(FOX)	5:00
FIRST WEEK	**Sunday, September 3 (FOX-TV National Weekend)**	Arizona _____ at Washington _____		4:00
		Carolina _____ at Atlanta _____		1:00
		Cincinnati _____ at Indianapolis _____		12:00
		Cleveland _____ at New England _____		1:00
		Detroit _____ at Pittsburgh _____		1:00
		Houston _____ at Jacksonville _____		1:00
		Kansas City _____ at Seattle _____		1:00
		Minnesota _____ at Chicago _____		3:00
		New York Jets _____ at Miami _____		4:00
		St. Louis _____ at Green Bay _____		12:00
		San Diego _____ at Los Angeles _____		1:00
		San Francisco _____ at New Orleans _____		12:00
		Tampa Bay _____ at Philadelphia _____		1:00
	Sunday Night	Buffalo _____ at Denver _____	(TNT)	6:00
	Monday, September 4	Dallas _____ at New York Giants _____	(ABC)	9:00
SECOND WEEK	**Sunday, September 10 (NBC-TV National Weekend)**	Atlanta _____ at San Francisco _____		1:00
		Carolina _____ at Buffalo _____		1:00
		Denver _____ at Dallas _____		3:00
		Detroit _____ at Minnesota _____		12:00
		Indianapolis _____ at New York Jets _____		4:00
		Jacksonville _____ at Cincinnati _____		4:00
		Los Angeles _____ at Washington _____		1:00
		Miami _____ at New England _____		1:00
		New Orleans _____ at St. Louis _____		12:00
		New York Giants _____ at Kansas City _____		12:00
		Pittsburgh _____ at Houston _____		12:00
		Seattle _____ at San Diego _____		1:00
		Tampa Bay _____ at Cleveland _____		1:00
	Sunday Night	Philadelphia _____ at Arizona _____	(TNT)	5:00
	Monday, September 11	Green Bay _____ at Chicago _____	(ABC)	8:00
THIRD WEEK	**Sunday, September 17 (NBC-TV National Weekend)**	Arizona _____ at Detroit _____		1:00
		Atlanta _____ at New Orleans _____		12:00
		Chicago _____ at Tampa Bay _____		4:00
		Cincinnati _____ at Seattle _____		1:00
		Cleveland _____ at Houston _____		12:00
		Indianapolis _____ at Buffalo _____		1:00
		Jacksonville _____ at New York Jets _____		4:00
		Los Angeles _____ at Kansas City _____		12:00
		New England _____ at San Francisco _____		1:00
		New York Giants _____ at Green Bay _____		12:00
		St. Louis _____ at Carolina _____		1:00
		San Diego _____ at Philadelphia _____		1:00
		Washington _____ at Denver _____		2:00
	Sunday Night	Dallas _____ at Minnesota _____	(TNT)	7:00
	Monday, September 18	Pittsburgh _____ at Miami _____	(ABC)	9:00

1995 SCHEDULE AND NOTE CALENDAR

FOURTH WEEK
Open Dates: Buffalo, Carolina, Indianapolis, Miami, New England, Seattle

Date	Game		Time
Sunday, September 24 (FOX-TV National Weekend)	Arizona ___ at Dallas ___		3:00
	Chicago ___ at St. Louis ___		12:00
	Denver ___ at San Diego ___		1:00
	Houston ___ at Cincinnati ___		4:00
	Kansas City ___ at Cleveland ___		4:00
	Minnesota ___ at Pittsburgh ___		1:00
	New Orleans ___ at New York Giants ___		1:00
	New York Jets ___ at Atlanta ___		4:00
	Philadelphia ___ at Los Angeles ___		1:00
	Washington ___ at Tampa Bay ___		1:00
Sunday Night	Green Bay ___ at Jacksonville ___	(TNT)	8:00
Monday, September 25	San Francisco ___ at Detroit ___	(ABC)	9:00

FIFTH WEEK
Open Dates: Chicago, Detroit, Green Bay, Minnesota

Date	Game		Time
Sunday, October 1 (NBC-TV National Weekend)	Dallas ___ at Washington ___		1:00
	Denver ___ at Seattle ___		1:00
	Jacksonville ___ at Houston ___		3:00
	Kansas City ___ at Arizona ___		1:00
	Miami ___ at Cincinnati ___		1:00
	New England ___ at Atlanta ___		1:00
	New York Giants ___ at San Francisco ___		1:00
	Philadelphia ___ at New Orleans ___		12:00
	St. Louis ___ at Indianapolis ___		12:00
	San Diego ___ at Pittsburgh ___		4:00
	Tampa Bay ___ at Carolina ___		1:00
Sunday Night	Los Angeles ___ at New York Jets ___	(TNT)	8:00
Monday, October 2	Buffalo ___ at Cleveland ___	(ABC)	9:00

SIXTH WEEK
Open Dates: Atlanta, New Orleans, St. Louis, San Francisco

Date	Game		Time
Sunday, October 8 (NBC-TV National Weekend)	Arizona ___ at New York Giants ___		4:00
	Carolina ___ at Chicago ___		12:00
	Cincinnati ___ at Tampa Bay ___		1:00
	Cleveland ___ at Detroit ___		4:00
	Green Bay ___ at Dallas ___		12:00
	Houston ___ at Minnesota ___		12:00
	Indianapolis ___ at Miami ___		4:00
	New York Jets ___ at Buffalo ___		1:00
	Pittsburgh ___ at Jacksonville ___		1:00
	Seattle ___ at Los Angeles ___		1:00
	Washington ___ at Philadelphia ___		1:00
Sunday Night	Denver ___ at New England ___	(TNT)	8:00
Monday, October 9	San Diego ___ at Kansas City ___	(ABC)	8:00

SEVENTH WEEK
Open Dates: Cincinnati, Cleveland, Houston, Pittsburgh

Date	Game		Time
Thursday, October 12	Atlanta ___ at St. Louis ___	(TNT)	7:00
Sunday, October 15 (FOX-TV National Weekend)	Chicago ___ at Jacksonville ___		1:00
	Dallas ___ at San Diego ___		1:00
	Detroit ___ at Green Bay ___		12:00
	Miami ___ at New Orleans ___		3:00
	Minnesota ___ at Tampa Bay ___		1:00
	New England ___ at Kansas City ___		12:00
	New York Jets ___ at Carolina ___		4:00
	Philadelphia ___ at New York Giants ___		1:00
	San Francisco ___ at Indianapolis ___		12:00
	Seattle ___ at Buffalo ___		1:00
	Washington ___ at Arizona ___		1:00
Monday, October 16	Los Angeles ___ at Denver ___	(ABC)	7:00

EIGHTH WEEK
Open Dates: Arizona, Dallas, New York Giants, Philadelphia

Date	Game		Time
Thursday, October 19	Cincinnati ___ at Pittsburgh ___	(TNT)	8:00
Sunday, October 22 (NBC-TV National Weekend)	Atlanta ___ at Tampa Bay ___		1:00
	Detroit ___ at Washington ___		1:00
	Houston ___ at Chicago ___		12:00
	Indianapolis ___ at Los Angeles ___		1:00
	Jacksonville ___ at Cleveland ___		1:00
	Kansas City ___ at Denver ___		2:00
	Miami ___ at New York Jets ___		1:00
	Minnesota ___ at Green Bay ___		12:00
	New Orleans ___ at Carolina ___		1:00
	San Diego ___ at Seattle ___		1:00

		San Francisco ____ at St. Louis ____		3:00
	Monday, October 23	Buffalo ____ at New England ____	(ABC)	9:00
NINTH WEEK **Open Dates: Denver, Kansas City, Los Angeles, San Diego**	**Sunday, October 29** **(FOX-TV National Weekend)**	Buffalo ____ at Miami ____		4:00
		Carolina ____ at New England ____		1:00
		Cleveland ____ at Cincinnati ____		1:00
		Dallas ____ at Atlanta ____		1:00
		Green Bay ____ at Detroit ____		1:00
		Jacksonville ____ at Pittsburgh ____		1:00
		New Orleans ____ at San Francisco ____		1:00
		New York Jets ____ at Indianapolis ____		1:00
		St. Louis ____ at Philadelphia ____		1:00
		Seattle ____ at Arizona ____		2:00
		Tampa Bay ____ at Houston ____		3:00
	Sunday Night	New York Giants ____ at Washington ____	(TNT)	8:00
	Monday, October 30	Chicago ____ at Minnesota ____	(ABC)	8:00
TENTH WEEK **Open Dates: Jacksonville, Tampa Bay**	**Sunday, November 5** **(NBC-TV National Weekend)**	Arizona ____ at Denver ____		2:00
		Buffalo ____ at Indianapolis ____		1:00
		Carolina ____ at San Francisco ____		1:00
		Detroit ____ at Atlanta ____		1:00
		Green Bay ____ at Minnesota ____		12:00
		Houston ____ at Cleveland ____		1:00
		Los Angeles ____ at Cincinnati ____		4:00
		New England ____ at New York Jets ____		1:00
		New York Giants ____ at Seattle ____		1:00
		Pittsburgh ____ at Chicago ____		3:00
		St. Louis ____ at New Orleans ____		12:00
		Washington ____ at Kansas City ____		12:00
	Sunday Night	Miami ____ at San Diego ____	(ESPN)	5:00
	Monday, November 6	Philadelphia ____ at Dallas ____	(ABC)	8:00
ELEVENTH WEEK **Open Dates: New York Jets, Washington**	**Sunday, November 12** **(FOX-TV National Weekend)**	Atlanta ____ at Buffalo ____		1:00
		Carolina ____ at St. Louis ____		12:00
		Chicago ____ at Green Bay ____		12:00
		Cincinnati ____ at Houston ____		12:00
		Indianapolis ____ at New Orleans ____		12:00
		Kansas City ____ at San Diego ____		1:00
		Los Angeles ____ at New York Giants ____		1:00
		Minnesota ____ at Arizona ____		2:00
		New England ____ at Miami ____		1:00
		San Francisco ____ at Dallas ____		3:00
		Seattle ____ at Jacksonville ____		1:00
		Tampa Bay ____ at Detroit ____		1:00
	Sunday Night	Denver ____ at Philadelphia ____	(ESPN)	8:00
	Monday, November 13	Cleveland ____ at Pittsburgh ____	(ABC)	9:00
TWELFTH WEEK	**Sunday, November 19** **(FOX-TV National Weekend)**	Arizona ____ at Carolina ____		1:00
		Buffalo ____ at New York Jets ____		4:00
		Dallas ____ at Los Angeles ____		1:00
		Detroit ____ at Chicago ____		12:00
		Green Bay ____ at Cleveland ____		1:00
		Indianapolis ____ at New England ____		1:00
		Jacksonville ____ at Tampa Bay ____		1:00
		New Orleans ____ at Minnesota ____		3:00
		New York Giants ____ at Philadelphia ____		1:00
		Pittsburgh ____ at Cincinnati ____		1:00
		St. Louis ____ at Atlanta ____		1:00
		San Diego ____ at Denver ____		2:00
		Seattle ____ at Washington ____		1:00
	Sunday Night	Houston ____ at Kansas City ____	(ESPN)	7:00
	Monday, November 20	San Francisco ____ at Miami ____	(ABC)	9:00

1995 SCHEDULE AND NOTE CALENDAR

THIRTEENTH WEEK	**Thursday, November 23**	Kansas City ____ at Dallas ____	(NBC) 3:00
		Minnesota ____ at Detroit ____	(FOX) 12:30
	Sunday, November 26	Atlanta ____ at Arizona ____	2:00
	(NBC-TV National Weekend)	Chicago ____ at New York Giants ____	1:00
		Cincinnati ____ at Jacksonville ____	1:00
		Denver ____ at Houston ____	3:00
		Miami ____ at Indianapolis ____	1:00
		New England ____ at Buffalo ____	1:00
		New York Jets ____ at Seattle ____	1:00
		Philadelphia ____ at Washington ____	1:00
		Pittsburgh ____ at Cleveland ____	4:00
		St. Louis ____ at San Francisco ____	1:00
		Tampa Bay ____ at Green Bay ____	12:00
	Sunday Night	Carolina ____ at New Orleans ____	(ESPN) 7:00
	Monday, November 27	Los Angeles ____ at San Diego ____	(ABC) 6:00
FOURTEENTH WEEK	**Thursday, November 30**	New York Giants ____ at Arizona ____	(ESPN) 6:00
	Sunday, December 3	Atlanta ____ at Miami ____	1:00
	(FOX-TV National Weekend)	Cincinnati ____ at Green Bay ____	12:00
		Cleveland ____ at San Diego ____	1:00
		Houston ____ at Pittsburgh ____	1:00
		Indianapolis ____ at Carolina ____	1:00
		Jacksonville ____ at Denver ____	2:00
		Kansas City ____ at Los Angeles ____	1:00
		New Orleans ____ at New England ____	1:00
		Philadelphia ____ at Seattle ____	1:00
		St. Louis ____ at New York Jets ____	1:00
		Tampa Bay ____ at Minnesota ____	12:00
		Washington ____ at Dallas ____	3:00
	Sunday Night	Buffalo ____ at San Francisco ____	(ESPN) 5:00
	Monday, December 4	Chicago ____ at Detroit ____	(ABC) 9:00
FIFTEENTH WEEK	**Saturday, December 9**	Arizona ____ at San Diego ____	(FOX) 1:00
		Cleveland ____ at Minnesota ____	(NBC) 11:30
	Sunday, December 10	Buffalo ____ at St. Louis ____	12:00
	(NBC-TV National Weekend)	Chicago ____ at Cincinnati ____	1:00
		Dallas ____ at Philadelphia ____	1:00
		Detroit ____ at Houston ____	12:00
		Indianapolis ____ at Jacksonville ____	1:00
		New Orleans ____ at Atlanta ____	1:00
		New York Jets ____ at New England ____	1:00
		Pittsburgh ____ at Los Angeles ____	1:00
		San Francisco ____ at Carolina ____	1:00
		Seattle ____ at Denver ____	2:00
		Washington ____ at New York Giants ____	4:00
	Sunday Night	Green Bay ____ at Tampa Bay ____	(ESPN) 8:00
	Monday, December 11	Kansas City ____ at Miami ____	(ABC) 9:00
SIXTEENTH WEEK	**Saturday, December 16**	Green Bay ____ at New Orleans ____	(FOX) 3:00
		New England ____ at Pittsburgh ____	(NBC) 12:30
	Sunday, December 17	Arizona ____ at Philadelphia ____	1:00
	(FOX-TV National Weekend)	Atlanta ____ at Carolina ____	1:00
		Cincinnati ____ at Cleveland ____	1:00
		Denver ____ at Kansas City ____	3:00
		Jacksonville ____ at Detroit ____	1:00
		Miami ____ at Buffalo ____	1:00
		New York Giants ____ at Dallas ____	3:00
		New York Jets ____ at Houston ____	12:00
		San Diego ____ at Indianapolis ____	4:00
		Tampa Bay ____ at Chicago ____	12:00
		Washington ____ at St. Louis ____	12:00
	Sunday Night	Los Angeles ____ at Seattle ____	(ESPN) 5:00
	Monday, December 18	Minnesota ____ at San Francisco ____	(ABC) 6:00

SEVENTEENTH WEEK

Saturday, December 23	Detroit ____ at Tampa Bay ____	(FOX)	4:00
	San Diego ____ at New York Giants ____	(NBC)	12:30
Saturday Night	New England ____ at Indianapolis ____	(ESPN)	8:00
Sunday, December 24	Carolina ____ at Washington ____		4:00
(NBC-TV National Weekend)	Cleveland ____ at Jacksonville ____		1:00
	Denver ____ at Los Angeles ____		1:00
	Houston ____ at Buffalo ____		1:00
	Miami ____ at St. Louis ____		3:00
	Minnesota ____ at Cincinnati ____		1:00
	New Orleans ____ at New York Jets ____		1:00
	Philadelphia ____ at Chicago ____		12:00
	Pittsburgh ____ at Green Bay ____		12:00
	San Francisco ____ at Atlanta ____		1:00
	Seattle ____ at Kansas City ____		12:00
Monday, December 25	Dallas ____ at Arizona ____	(ABC)	7:00

Wild Card Playoff Games
Site Priorities
Three Wild Card teams (division non-champions with best three records) from each conference and the division champion with the third-best record in each conference will enter the first round of the playoffs. The division champion with the third-best record will play host to the Wild Card team with the third-best record. The Wild Card team with the best record will play host to the Wild Card team with the second-best record. There are no restrictions on intra-division games.

Saturday, December 30, 1995
American Football Conference
________ at ________ (ABC)
National Football Conference
________ at ________ (ABC)

Sunday, December 31, 1995
American Football Conference
________ at ________ (NBC)
National Football Conference
________ at ________ (FOX)

Divisional Playoff Games
Site Priorities
In each conference, the two division champions with the highest won-lost-tied percentage during the regular season will play host to the Wild Card winners. The division champion with the best record in each conference is assured of playing the Wild Card survivor with the poorest record. There are no restrictions on intra-division games.

Saturday, January 6, 1996
American Football Conference
________ at ________ (NBC)
National Football Conference
________ at ________ (FOX)

Sunday, January 7, 1996
American Football Conference
________ at ________ (NBC)
National Football Conference
________ at ________ (FOX)

Championship Games
Site Priorities
for Championship Games
The home teams will be the surviving playoff winners with the best won-lost-tied percentage during the regular season. A Wild Card team cannot play host unless two Wild Card teams are in the game, in which case the Wild Card team with the best record will play host.

Sunday, January 14, 1996
American Football Conference
________ at ________ (NBC)
National Football Conference
________ at ________ (FOX)

Super Bowl XXX

Sunday, January 28, 1996
Super Bowl XXX at Sun Devil Stadium, Tempe, Arizona
________ at ________ (NBC)

AFC-NFC Pro Bowl

Sunday, February 4, 1996
AFC-NFC Pro Bowl at Honolulu, Hawaii
AFC ________ at NFC ________ (ABC)

POSTSEASON AND NATIONALLY TELEVISED GAMES

POSTSEASON GAMES

Saturday, Dec. 30	AFC and NFC Wild Card Playoffs (ABC)
Sunday, Dec. 31	AFC and NFC Wild Card Playoffs (NBC and FOX)
Saturday, January 6	AFC and NFC Divisional Playoffs (NBC and FOX)
Sunday, January 7	AFC and NFC Divisional Playoffs (NBC and FOX)
Sunday, January 14	AFC and NFC Championship Games (NBC and FOX)
Sunday, January 28	Super Bowl XXX at Sun Devil Stadium, Tempe, Arizona (NBC)
Sunday, February 4	AFC-NFC Pro Bowl at Honolulu, Hawaii (ABC)

1995 NATIONALLY TELEVISED GAMES

Regular Season

Sunday, September 3	Minnesota at Chicago (day, FOX) Buffalo at Denver (night, TNT)
Monday, September 4	Dallas at New York Giants (night, ABC)
Sunday, September 10	Denver at Dallas (day, NBC) Philadelphia at Arizona (night, TNT)
Monday, September 11	Green Bay at Chicago (night, ABC)
Sunday, September 17	New England at San Francisco (day, NBC) Dallas at Minnesota (night, TNT)
Monday, September 18	Pittsburgh at Miami (night, ABC)
Sunday, September 24	Arizona at Dallas (day, FOX) Green Bay at Jacksonville (night, TNT)
Monday, September 25	San Francisco at Detroit (night, ABC)
Sunday, October 1	San Diego at Pittsburgh (day, NBC) Los Angeles at New York Jets (night, TNT)
Monday, October 2	Buffalo at Cleveland (night, ABC)
Sunday, October 8	Indianapolis at Miami (day, NBC) Denver at New England (night, TNT)
Monday, October 9	San Diego at Kansas City (night, ABC)
Thursday, October 12	Atlanta at St. Louis (night, TNT)
Sunday, October 15	Dallas at San Diego (day, FOX)
Monday, October 16	Los Angeles at Denver (night, ABC)
Thursday, October 19	Cincinnati at Pittsburgh (night, TNT)
Sunday, October 22	Kansas City at Denver (day, NBC)
Monday, October 23	Buffalo at New England (night, ABC)
Sunday, October 29	New Orleans at San Francisco (day, FOX) New York Giants at Washington (night, TNT)
Monday, October 30	Chicago at Minnesota (night, ABC)
Sunday, November 5	Pittsburgh at Chicago (day, NBC) Miami at San Diego (night, ESPN)
Monday, November 6	Philadelphia at Dallas (night, ABC)
Sunday, November 12	San Francisco at Dallas (day, FOX) Denver at Philadelphia (night, ESPN)
Monday, November 13	Cleveland at Pittsburgh (night, ABC)
Sunday, November 19	Dallas at Los Angeles (day, FOX) Houston at Kansas City (night, ESPN)
Monday, November 20	San Francisco at Miami (night, ABC)
Thursday, November 23	Minnesota at Detroit (day, FOX) Kansas City at Dallas (day, NBC)
Sunday, November 26	Pittsburgh at Cleveland (day, NBC) Carolina at New Orleans (night, ESPN)
Monday, November 27	Los Angeles at San Diego (night, ABC)
Thursday, November 30	New York Giants at Arizona (night, ESPN)
Sunday, December 3	Washington at Dallas (day, FOX) Buffalo at San Francisco (night, ESPN)
Monday, December 4	Chicago at Detroit (night, ABC)
Saturday, December 9	Cleveland at Minnesota (day, NBC) Arizona at San Diego (day, FOX)
Sunday, December 10	Pittsburgh at Los Angeles (day, NBC) Green Bay at Tampa Bay (night, ESPN)
Monday, December 11	Kansas City at Miami (night, ABC)
Saturday, December 16	New England at Pittsburgh (day, NBC) Green Bay at New Orleans (day, FOX)
Sunday, December 17	New York Giants at Dallas (day, FOX) Los Angeles at Seattle (night, ESPN)
Monday, December 18	Minnesota at San Francisco (night, ABC)
Saturday, December 23	San Diego at New York Giants (day, NBC) Detroit at Tampa Bay (day, FOX) New England at Indianapolis (night, ESPN)
Sunday, December 24	Denver at Los Angeles (day, NBC)
Monday, December 25	Dallas at Arizona (night, ABC)

NATIONAL PRIMETIME TELEVISION GAMES AT A GLANCE

(All times local; Sunday/Thursday/Saturday on TNT and ESPN, Monday on ABC; all on CBS radio)

Sunday, September 3	Buffalo at Denver (TNT)	6:00
Monday, September 4	Dallas at New York Giants (ABC)	9:00
Sunday, September 10	Philadelphia at Arizona (TNT)	5:00
Monday, September 11	Green Bay at Chicago (ABC)	8:00
Sunday, September 17	Dallas at Minnesota (TNT)	7:00
Monday, September 18	Pittsburgh at Miami (ABC)	9:00
Sunday, September 24	Green Bay at Jacksonville (TNT)	8:00
Monday, September 25	San Francisco at Detroit (ABC)	9:00
Sunday, October 1	Los Angeles at New York Jets (TNT)	8:00
Monday, October 2	Buffalo at Cleveland (ABC)	9:00
Sunday, October 8	Denver at New England (TNT)	8:00
Monday, October 9	San Diego at Kansas City (ABC)	8:00
Thursday, October 12	Atlanta at St. Louis (TNT)	7:00
Monday, October 16	Los Angeles at Denver (ABC)	7:00
Thursday, October 19	Cincinnati at Pittsburgh (TNT)	8:00
Monday, October 23	Buffalo at New England (ABC)	9:00
Sunday, October 29	New York Giants at Washington (TNT)	8:00
Monday, October 30	Chicago at Minnesota (ABC)	8:00
Sunday, November 5	Miami at San Diego (ESPN)	5:00
Monday, November 6	Philadelphia at Dallas (ABC)	8:00
Sunday, November 12	Denver at Philadelphia (ESPN)	8:00
Monday, November 13	Cleveland at Pittsburgh (ABC)	9:00
Sunday, November 19	Houston at Kansas City (ESPN)	7:00
Monday, November 20	San Francisco at Miami (ABC)	9:00
Sunday, November 26	Carolina at New Orleans (ESPN)	7:00
Monday, November 27	Los Angeles at San Diego (ABC)	6:00
Thursday, November 30	New York Giants at Arizona (ESPN)	6:00
Sunday, December 3	Buffalo at San Francisco (ESPN)	5:00
Monday, December 4	Chicago at Detroit (ABC)	9:00
Sunday, December 10	Green Bay at Tampa Bay (ESPN)	8:00
Monday, December 11	Kansas City at Miami (ABC)	9:00
Sunday, December 17	Los Angeles at Seattle (ESPN)	5:00
Monday, December 18	Minnesota at San Francisco (ABC)	6:00
Saturday, December 23	New England at Indianapolis (ESPN)	8:00
Monday, December 25	Dallas at Arizona (ABC)	7:00

1995

July 5	Claiming period of 24 hours begins in waiver system. All waiver requests for the rest of the year are no-recall and no-withdrawal.
July 12	The Indianapolis Colts are first team to open training camp. Veteran players cannot be required to report earlier than 15 days prior to club's first preseason game or July 15, whichever is later.
July 15	Signing period ends at 4 P.M., Eastern Daylight Time, for Unrestricted Free Agents to whom June 1 tender was made by Old Club, and for Transition Players and Franchise Players who are subject to the rules for Transition Players. After this date and through 4 P.M., Eastern Daylight Time, on November 7, Old Club has exclusive negotiating rights with its unsigned Unrestricted Free Agents.
July 29	Hall of Fame Game, Canton, Ohio: Carolina vs. Jacksonville.
August 4	If a drafted rookie has not signed with his club by this date, he may not be traded to any other club in 1995.
August 4	Deadline for players under contract to report in order to earn a season of free agency credit.
August 5	American Bowl, Tokyo, Japan: Denver vs. San Francisco.
August 12	American Bowl, Toronto, Canada: Buffalo vs. Dallas.
August 22	Roster cutdown to maximum of 60 players on Active List by 4 P.M., Eastern Daylight Time. Carolina and Jacksonville are permitted to retain 65 players.
August 27	Roster cutdown to maximum of 53 players on Active/Inactive List by 4 P.M., Eastern Daylight Time. Clubs may dress minimum of 42 and maximum of 45 players and third quarterback for each regular-season and postseason game. Carolina and Jacksonville are permitted to retain 56 players until after their third regular-season game.
August 28	After 4 P.M., Eastern Daylight Time, clubs may establish a Practice Squad of five players by signing free agents who do not have an accrued season of free-agency credit, unless that season was achieved by spending an entire regular season on Reserve/Injured or Reserve/Physically Unable to Perform.
September 1	All clubs are required to identify their 49-player Active List by 7:00 P.M., Eastern Daylight Time, on this Friday and thereafter on each Friday before a regular-season Sunday game. No later than one hour and 30 minutes prior to kickoff, clubs must identify their 45-player Active List and third quarterback, if any.
September 3-4	Regular season opens.
September 18	Carolina and Jacksonville are required to reduce their Active/Inactive Lists to 53 players.
September 19	Priority on multiple waiver claims is now based on the current season's standing.
October 10	All trading ends at 4 P.M., Eastern Daylight Time.
October 11	Players with at least four previous pension-credited seasons are subject to the waiver system for the remainder of the regular season and postseason.
November 7-8	NFL Fall Meeting, Dallas, Texas.
November 7	Deadline for clubs to sign by 4 P.M., Eastern Daylight Time, their Franchise and Transition players. If still unsigned after this date, such players are prohibited from playing in NFL in 1995.
November 7	Deadline for clubs to sign by 4 P.M., Eastern Daylight Time, their Unrestricted and Restricted Free Agents to whom June 1 tender was made. If still unsigned after this date, such players are prohibited from playing in NFL in 1995.
November 7	Deadline for clubs to sign drafted players by 4 P.M., Eastern Daylight Time. If such players remain unsigned, they are prohibited from playing in NFL in 1995.
November 25	Deadline for reinstatement of players in Reserve List categories of Retired and Did Not Report.
December 22	Deadline for waiver requests in 1995, except for "special waiver requests" which have a 10-day claiming period, with termination or assignment delayed until after the Super Bowl.
December 26	Clubs may begin signing free-agent players for the 1996 season.
December 30-31	Wild Card Playoff Games.

1996

January 6-7	Divisional Playoff Games.
January 14	AFC and NFC Championship Games.
January 28	Super Bowl XXX at Sun Devil Stadium, Tempe, Arizona.
February 4	AFC-NFC Pro Bowl, Honolulu, Hawaii.
February 5	Waiver system begins for 1996. Players with at least four previous pension-credited seasons that a club desires to terminate are not subject to the waiver system until after the trading deadline.
February 8-12	Combine Timing and Testing, RCA Dome, Indianapolis, Indiana.
February 15	Deadline for clubs to designate Franchise and Transition Players.
February 15	Expiration date of all player contracts due to expire in 1996.
February 16	Free Agency period begins.
February 16	Trading period begins for 1996 after expiration of all 1995 contracts.
March 10-15	NFL Annual Meeting, West Palm Beach, Florida.
April 15	Deadline for signing of Offer Sheets by Restricted Free Agents.
April 20-21	Annual player selection meeting, New York, New York.
May 21-22	NFL Spring Meeting, Charlotte, North Carolina.
June 1	Deadline for Old Club to send tender to its unsigned Restricted Free Agents or to extend Qualifying Offer, whichever is greater, in order to retain rights.
June 1	Deadline for Old Club to send tender to its unsigned Unrestricted Free Agents to retain rights if player is not signed by another club by July 15.
*July 27	Hall of Fame Game, Canton, Ohio.
*September 1-2	Regular season opens.
*December 28-29	Wild Card Playoff Games.

1997

*January 4-5	Divisional Playoff Games.
*January 12	AFC and NFC Championship Games.
*January 26	Super Bowl XXXI, Superdome, New Orleans, Louisiana.
*February 2	AFC-NFC Pro Bowl, Honolulu, Hawaii.

**Tentatively scheduled.*

WAIVERS

The waiver system is a procedure by which player contracts or NFL rights to players are made available by a club to other clubs in the League. During the procedure, the 29 other clubs either file claims to obtain the players or waive the opportunity to do so—thus the term "waiver." Claiming clubs are assigned players on a priority based on the inverse of won-and-lost standing. In 1995, Carolina and Jacksonville will have priority on claiming players through the third weekend of the regular season. If both expansion clubs claim the same player, priority shall be determined by coin toss, with the teams alternating priority thereafter. The claiming period normally is 10 days during the offseason and 24 hours from early July through December. In some circumstances, another 24 hours is added on to allow the original club to rescind its action (known as a recall of a waiver request) and/or the claiming club to do the same (known as withdrawal of a claim). If a player passes through waivers unclaimed and is not recalled by the original club, he becomes a free agent. All waivers from July through December are no recall and no withdrawal. Under the Collective Bargaining Agreement, from the beginning of the waiver system each year through the trading deadline (October 10, 1995), any veteran who has acquired four years of pension credit is not subject to the waiver system if the club desires to release him. After the trading deadline, such players are subject to the waiver system.

ACTIVE/INACTIVE LIST

The Active/Inactive List is the principal status for players participating for a club. It consists of all players under contract who are eligible for preseason, regular-season, and postseason games. In 1995, teams will be permitted to open training camp with no more than 80 players under contract and thereafter must meet two mandatory roster reductions prior to the season opener. Teams will be permitted an Active List of 45 players and an Inactive List of eight players for each regular-season and postseason game during the 1995 season. Provided that a club has two quarterbacks on its 45-player Active List, a third quarterback from its Inactive List is permitted to dress for the game, but if he enters the game during the first three quarters, the other two quarterbacks are thereafter prohibited from playing. Teams also are permitted to establish Practice Squads of up to five players who are eligible to participate in practice, but these players remain free agents and are eligible to sign with any other team in the league.

August 22 ....Roster reduction to 60 players
August 27 ....Roster reduction to 53 players
August 28 ....Teams establish a Practice Squad of up to five players

In addition to the squad limits described above, the overall roster limit of 80 players remains in effect throughout the regular season and postseason. The overall limit is applicable to players on a team's Active, Inactive, and Exempt Lists, and any players on the Practice Squad and on the Reserve List as Injured, Physically Unable to Perform, Non-Football Illness/Injury, and Suspended by Club.

In 1995, Carolina and Jacksonville are permitted to have 90 players under contract until August 22, when the two expansion clubs must reduce their roster to 65 players. On August 27, Carolina and Jacksonville must establish an Active/Inactive List of 56 players, which will be in effect for the first three weekends of the regular season, after which they must be in compliance with the 53-player roster limit. Gameday roster limits are the same as for the other clubs.

RESERVE LIST

The Reserve List is a status for players who, for reasons of injury, retirement, military service, or other circumstances, are not immediately available for participation with a club. Players on Reserve/Injured are not eligible to practice or return to the Active/Inactive List in the same season that they are placed on Reserve. Players in the category of Reserve/Retired or Reserve/Did Not Report may not be reinstated during the period from 30 days before the end of the regular season through the postseason.

TRADES

Unrestricted trading between the AFC and NFC is allowed in 1995 through October 10, after which trading will end until 1996.

ANNUAL ACTIVE PLAYER LIMITS

NFL

Year(s)	Limit
1991-95	45**
1985-90	45
1983-84	49
1982	45†-49
1978-81	45
1975-77	43
1974	47
1964-73	40
1963	37
1961-62	36
1960	38
1959	36
1957-58	35
1951-56	33
1949-50	32
1948	35
1947	35*-34
1945-46	33
1943-44	28
1940-42	33
1938-39	30
1936-37	25
1935	24
1930-34	20
1926-29	18
1925	16

**45 plus a third quarterback
† 45 for first two games
* 35 for first three games

AFL

Year(s)	Limit
1966-69	40
1965	38
1964	34
1962-63	33
1960-61	35

The following procedures will be used to break standings ties for postseason playoffs and to determine regular-season schedules.

TO BREAK A TIE WITHIN A DIVISION

If, at the end of the regular season, two or more clubs in the same division finish with identical won-lost-tied percentages, the following steps will be taken until a champion is determined.

TWO CLUBS

1. Head-to-head (best won-lost-tied percentage in games between the clubs).
2. Best won-lost-tied percentage in games played within the division.
3. Best won-lost-tied percentage in games played within the conference.
4. Best won-lost-tied percentage in common games, if applicable.
5. Best net points in division games.
6. Best net points in all games.
7. Strength of schedule.
8. Best net touchdowns in all games.
9. Coin toss.

THREE OR MORE CLUBS

(Note: If two clubs remain tied after third or other clubs are eliminated during any step, tiebreaker reverts to step 1 of the two-club format).

1. Head-to-head (best won-lost-tied percentage in games among the clubs).
2. Best won-lost-tied percentage in games played within the division.
3. Best won-lost-tied percentage in games played within the conference.
4. Best won-lost-tied percentage in common games.
5. Best net points in division games.
6. Best net points in all games.
7. Strength of schedule.
8. Best net touchdowns in all games.
9. Coin toss.

TO BREAK A TIE FOR THE WILD CARD TEAM

If it is necessary to break ties to determine the three Wild Card clubs from each conference, the following steps will be taken.

1. If the tied clubs are from the same division, apply division tiebreaker.
2. If the tied clubs are from different divisions, apply the following steps.

TWO CLUBS

1. Head-to-head, if applicable.
2. Best won-lost-tied percentage in games played within the conference.
3. Best won-lost-tied percentage in common games, minimum of four.
4. Best average net points in conference games.
5. Best net points in all games.
6. Strength of schedule.
7 Best net touchdowns in all games.
8. Coin toss.

THREE OR MORE CLUBS

(Note: If two clubs remain tied after third or other clubs are eliminated, tiebreaker reverts to step 1 of applicable two-club format.)

1. Apply division tiebreaker to eliminate all but the highest ranked club in each division prior to proceeding to step 2. The original seeding within a division upon application of the division tiebreaker remains the same for all subsequent applications of the procedure that are necessary to identify the three Wild Card participants.
2. Head-to-head sweep. (Applicable only if one club has defeated each of the others or if one club has lost to each of the others).
3. Best won-lost-tied percentage in games played within the conference.
4. Best won-lost-tied percentage in common games, minimum of four.
5. Best average net points in conference games.
6. Best net points in all games.
7. Strength of schedule.
8. Best net touchdowns in all games.
9. Coin toss.

When the first Wild Card team has been identified, the procedure is repeated to name the second Wild Card, i.e., eliminate all but the highest-ranked club in each division prior to proceeding to step 2, and repeated a third time, if necessary, to identify the third Wild Card. In situations where three or more teams from the same division are involved in the procedure, the original seeding of the teams remains the same for subsequent applications of the tiebreaker if the top-ranked team in that division qualifies for a Wild Card berth.

OTHER TIE-BREAKING PROCEDURES

1. Only one club advances to the playoffs in any tie-breaking step. Remaining tied clubs revert to the first step of the applicable division or Wild Card tiebreakers. As an example, if two clubs remain tied in any tie-breaker step after all other clubs have been eliminated, the procedure reverts to step one of the two-club format to determine the winner. When one club wins the tie-breaker, all other clubs revert to step 1 of the applicable two-club or three-club format.
2. In comparing division and conference records or records against common opponents among tied teams, the best won-lost-tied percentage is the deciding factor since teams may have played an unequal number of games.
3. To determine home-field priority among division titlists, apply Wild Card tiebreakers.
4. To determine home-field priority for Wild Card qualifiers, apply division tiebreakers (if teams are from the same division) or Wild Card tiebreakers (if teams are from different divisions).

TIE-BREAKING PROCEDURE FOR SELECTION MEETING

If two or more clubs are tied in the selection order, the strength-of-schedule tie-breaker is applied, subject to the following exceptions for playoff clubs:

1. The Super Bowl winner is last and the Super Bowl loser next-to-last.
2. Any non-Super Bowl playoff club involved in a tie shall be assigned priority within its segment below that of non-playoff clubs and in the order that the playoff clubs exited from the playoffs. Thus, within a tied segment a playoff club that loses in the Wild Card game will have priority over a playoff club that loses in the Divisional playoff game, which in turn will have priority over a club that loses in the Conference Championship game. If two tied clubs exited the playoffs in the same round, the tie is broken by strength-of-schedule.

If any ties cannot be broken by strength-of-schedule, the divisional or conference tie-breakers, whichever are applicable, are applied. Any ties that still exist are broken by a coin flip.

FIGURING THE 1996 SCHEDULE

At the conclusion of the 1995 NFL regular season, it will be possible to determine the 1996 opponents of the 30 teams.

Each 1995 team schedule is based on a "common-opponent" formula initiated for the 1978 season and most recently modified in 1995. Under the common-opponent format, all teams in a division play at least 11 of their 16 games the following season against common opponents. It is not a position scheduling format in which the strong play the strong and the weak play the weak.

In creating a schedule, the NFL seeks an easily understood and balanced formula that provides both competitive equality and a variety of opponents. Under the rotation scheduling system in effect from 1970-77, non-division opponents were determined by a pre-set formula. This often resulted in competitive imbalances.

With common opponents as the basis for scheduling, a more competitive and equitable method of determining division champions and postseason playoff representatives has developed. Teams battling for a division title are playing more than two-thirds of their games against common opponents.

In 1987, NFL owners passed a bylaw proposal designed to modify the common-opponent scheduling format and create greater equity. And in 1995, with the addition of two expansion teams, the 1987 changes were modified to include fifth-place teams in the common-opponent scheduling format for each division. The following chart shows a history of the pairings in non-division games within the conference since the change to a common-opponent format in 1978:

Prior Year's Finish in Division	Current Pairings in Non-Division Games Within Conference	Previous Pairings 1987-94	Previous Pairings 1978-86
1	1-1-2-3	1-1-2-3	1-1-4-4
2	1-2-2-4	1-2-2-4	2-2-3-3
3	1-3-3-5	1-3-3-4	2-2-3-3
4	2-4-4-5	2-3-4-4	1-1-4-4
5	3-4-5-5		

Under the common-opponent format, schedules of all NFL teams are figured according to the following formula. (The reference point for the figuring is the team's final division standing. Ties in divisions are broken according to the tie-breaking procedures outlined on page 13.)

1. Home-and-away round-robin **within the division** (8 games).
2. In the **interconference games,** each team plays four teams in a division of the other conference (4 games). In 1996, the AFC East will play the NFC East, the AFC Central will play the NFC West, and the AFC West will play the NFC Central (see chart on following page).
3. **Within the conference,** the first-place team plays the first-place teams in the other divisions plus a second- and third-place team in the conference. The second-place team plays the second-place teams in the other divisions plus a first- and fourth-place team in the conference. The third-place team plays the third-place teams in the other divisions plus a first- and fifth-place team in the conference. The fourth-place team plays the fourth-place teams in the other divisions plus a second- and fifth-place team in the conference. The fifth-place team plays the fifth-place teams in the other divisions plus a third- and fourth-place team in the conference (4 games, see chart).

This completes the 16-game schedule.

The 1996 Opponent Breakdown chart on the following page does not include the round-robin games within the division. Those are automatically scheduled on a home-and-away basis.

NOTES

1995 NFL Standings

AFC

EAST AE

1 ______
2 ______
3 ______
4 ______
5 ______

CENTRAL AC

1 ______
2 ______
3 ______
4 ______
5 ______

WEST AW

1 ______
2 ______
3 ______
4 ______
5 ______

NFC

EAST NE

1 ______
2 ______
3 ______
4 ______
5 ______

CENTRAL NC

1 ______
2 ______
3 ______
4 ______
5 ______

WEST NW

1 ______
2 ______
3 ______
4 ______
5 ______

A Team's 1996 Schedule

______
Team Name

OPPONENTS

1 ______
2 ______
3 ______
4 ______
5 ______
6 ______
7 ______
8 ______
9 ______
10 ______
11 ______
12 ______
13 ______
14 ______
15 ______
16 ______

1996 Non-Divisional Opponent Breakdown (Combined Intraconference and Interconference)

American Football Conference

AFC East

	Home	Away
AE1	AW 1	AC 1
	AC 2	AW 3
	NE 1	NE 2
	NE 3	NE 4
AE2	AW 2	AC 2
	AC 4	AW 1
	NE 2	NE 1
	NE 5	NE 3
AE3	AW 3	AC 3
	AC 1	AW 5
	NE 1	NE 2
	NE 4	NE 5
AE4	AW 4	AC 4
	AC 5	AW 2
	NE 3	NE 1
	NE 5	NE 4
AE5	AW 5	AC 5
	AC 3	AW 4
	NE 2	NE 3
	NE 4	NE 5

AFC Central

	Home	Away
AC1	AE 1	AW 1
	AW 2	AE 3
	NW 1	NW 2
	NW 3	NW 4
AC2	AE 2	AW 2
	AW 4	AE 1
	NW 2	NW 1
	NW 5	NW 3
AC3	AE 3	AW 3
	AW 1	AE 5
	NW 1	NW 2
	NW 4	NW 5
AC4	AE 4	AW 4
	AW 5	AE 2
	NW 3	NW 1
	NW 5	NW 4
AC5	AE 5	AW 5
	AW 3	AE 4
	NW 2	NW 3
	NW 4	NW 5

AFC West

	Home	Away
AW1	AC 1	AE 1
	AE 2	AC 3
	NC 1	NC 2
	NC 3	NC 4
AW2	AC 2	AE 2
	AE 4	AC 1
	NC 2	NC 1
	NC 5	NC 3
AW3	AC 3	AE 3
	AE 1	AC 5
	NC 1	NC 2
	NC 4	NC 5
AW4	AC 4	AE 4
	AE 5	AC 2
	NC 3	NC 1
	NC 5	NC 4
AW5	AC 5	AE 5
	AE 3	AC 4
	NC 2	NC 3
	NC 4	NC 5

National Football Conference

NFC East

	Home	Away
NE1	NC 1	NW 1
	NW 2	NC 3
	AE 2	AE 1
	AE 4	AE 3
NE2	NC 2	NW 2
	NW 4	NC 1
	AE 1	AE 2
	AE 3	AE 5
NE3	NC 3	NW 3
	NW 1	NC 5
	AE 2	AE 1
	AE 5	AE 4
NE4	NC 4	NW 4
	NW 5	NC 2
	AE 1	AE 3
	AE 4	AE 5
NE5	NC 5	NW 5
	NW 3	NC 4
	AE 3	AE 2
	AE 5	AE 4

NFC Central

	Home	Away
NC1	NW 1	NE 1
	NE 2	NW 3
	AW 2	AW 1
	AW 4	AW 3
NC2	NW 2	NE 2
	NE 4	NW 1
	AW 1	AW 2
	AW 3	AW 5
NC3	NW 3	NE 3
	NE 1	NW 5
	AW 2	AW 1
	AW 5	AW 4
NC4	NW 4	NE 4
	NE 5	NW 2
	AW 1	AW 3
	AW 4	AW 5
NC5	NW 5	NE 5
	NE 3	NW 4
	AW 3	AW 2
	AW 5	AW 4

NFC West

	Home	Away
NW1	NE 1	NC 1
	NC 2	NE 3
	AC 2	AC 1
	AC 4	AC 3
NW2	NE 2	NC 2
	NC 4	NE 1
	AC 1	AC 2
	AC 3	AC 5
NW3	NE 3	NC 3
	NC 1	NE 5
	AC 2	AC 1
	AC 5	AC 4
NW4	NE 4	NC 4
	NC 5	NE 2
	AC 1	AC 3
	AC 4	AC 5
NW5	NE 5	NC 5
	NC 3	NE 4
	AC 3	AC 2
	AC 5	AC 4

NFL PASSER RATING SYSTEM

The NFL rates its passers for statistical purposes against a fixed performance standard based on statistical achievements of all qualified pro passers since 1960. The current system replaced one that rated passers in relation to their position in a total group based on various criteria. The current system, which was adopted in 1973, removes inequities that existed in the former method and, at the same time, provides a means of comparing passing performances from one season to the next.

It is important to remember that the system is used to rate **passers,** not **quarterbacks.** Statistics do not reflect leadership, play-calling, and other intangible factors that go into making a successful professional quarterback. Four categories are used as a basis for compiling a rating:

—Percentage of touchdown passes per attempt
—Percentage of completions per attempt
—Percentage of interceptions per attempt
—Average yards gained per attempt

The **average** standard, is 1.000. The bottom is .000. To earn a 2.000 rating, a passer must perform at exceptional levels, i.e., 70 percent in completions, 10 percent in touchdowns, 1.5 percent in interceptions, and 11 yards average gain per pass attempt. The **maximum** a passer can receive in any category is 2.375.

For example, to gain a 2.375 in completion percentage, a passer would have to complete 77.5 percent of his passes. The NFL record is 70.55 by Ken Anderson (Cincinnati, 1982). To earn a 2.375 in percentage of touchdowns, a passer would have to achieve a percentage of 11.9. The record is 13.9 by Sid Luckman (Chicago, 1943). To gain 2.375 in percentage of interceptions, a passer would have to go the entire season without an interception. The 2.375 figure in average yards is 12.50, compared with the NFL record of 11.17 by Tommy O'Connell (Cleveland, 1957).

In order to make the rating more understandable, the point rating is then converted into a scale of 100. For instance, if a passer completes 11 of 23 passes for 114 yards, with one touchdown and no interceptions, the four components would be:

—**Percentage of Completions**—11 of 23 is 47.8 percent. The point rating is 0.890.

—**Percentage of Touchdown Passes**—1 touchdown in 23 attempts works out to 4.3 percent for a rating of 0.860.

—**Percentage of Interceptions**—You can't do better than zero, so the passer receives a maximum rating of 2.375.

—**Average Yards Gained Per Attempt**—114 yards divided by 23 attempts equals 4.96 yards per attempt for a corresponding rating of 0.490.

The sum of the four components is 4.615, which converts to a rating of 76.9. In order for a passer to achieve 100, his points would have to total 6.000. In rare cases, where statistical performance has been superior, it is possible for a passer to surpass 100.

The following is a list of qualifying passers who had a single-season passer rating of 100 or higher:

Player, Team	Season	Rating	Att.	Comp.	Pct.	Yds.	Avg.	TD	TD Pct.	Int.	Int. Pct.
Steve Young, San Francisco	1994	112.8	461	324	70.3	3,969	8.61	35	7.6	10	2.2
Joe Montana, San Francisco	1989	112.4	386	271	70.2	3,521	9.12	26	6.7	8	2.1
Milt Plum, Cleveland	1960	110.4	250	151	60.4	2,297	9.19	21	8.4	5	2.0
Sammy Baugh, Washington	1945	109.9	182	128	70.3	1,669	9.17	11	6.0	4	2.2
Dan Marino, Miami	1984	108.9	564	362	64.2	5,084	9.01	48	8.5	17	3.0
Sid Luckman, Chicago Bears	1943	107.5	202	110	54.5	2,194	10.86	28	13.9	12	5.9
Steve Young, San Francisco	1992	107.0	402	268	66.7	3,465	8.62	25	6.2	7	1.7
Bart Starr, Green Bay	1966	105.0	251	156	62.2	2,257	8.99	14	5.6	3	1.2
Roger Staubach, Dallas	1971	104.8	211	126	59.7	1,882	8.92	15	7.1	4	1.9
Y.A. Tittle, N.Y. Giants	1963	104.8	367	221	60.2	3,145	8.57	36	9.8	14	3.8
Bart Starr, Green Bay	1968	104.3	171	109	63.7	1,617	9.46	15	8.8	8	4.7
Ken Stabler, Oakland	1976	103.4	291	194	66.7	2,737	9.41	27	9.3	17	5.8
Joe Montana, San Francisco	1984	102.9	432	279	64.6	3,630	8.40	28	6.5	10	2.3
Charlie Conerly, N.Y. Giants	1959	102.7	194	113	58.2	1,706	8.79	14	7.2	4	2.1
Bert Jones, Baltimore	1976	102.5	343	207	60.3	3,104	9.05	24	7.0	9	2.6
Joe Montana, San Francisco	1987	102.1	398	266	66.8	3,054	7.67	31	7.8	13	3.3
Steve Young, San Francisco	1991	101.8	279	180	64.5	2,517	9.02	17	6.1	8	2.9
Len Dawson, Kansas City	1966	101.7	284	159	56.0	2,527	8.90	26	9.2	10	3.5
Steve Young, San Francisco	1993	101.5	462	314	68.0	4,023	8.71	29	6.3	16	3.5
Jim Kelly, Buffalo	1990	101.2	346	219	63.3	2,829	8.18	24	6.9	9	2.6

ACTIVE COACHES' CAREER RECORDS (Order Based on Career Victories)

Start of 1995 Season

Coach	Team(s)	Regular Season Yrs.	Won	Lost	Tied	Pct.	Postseason Won	Lost	Tied	Pct.	Career Won	Lost	Tied	Pct.
Don Shula	Baltimore Colts, Miami Dolphins	32	319	149	6	.679	19	16	0	.543	338	165	6	.670
Dan Reeves	Denver Broncos, New York Giants	14	130	85	1	.604	8	7	0	.533	138	92	1	.600
Marv Levy	Kansas City Chiefs, Buffalo Bills	14	117	90	0	.565	10	6	0	.625	127	96	0	.570
Marty Schottenheimer	Cleveland Browns, Kansas City Chiefs	11	103	63	1	.620	5	9	0	.357	108	72	1	.599
Bill Parcells	New York Giants, New England Patriots	10	92	66	1	.582	8	4	0	.667	100	70	1	.588
Jim Mora	New Orleans Saints	9	84	59	0	.587	0	4	0	.000	84	63	0	.571
George Seifert	San Francisco 49ers	6	75	21	0	.781	9	3	0	.750	84	24	0	.778
Sam Wyche	Cincinnati Bengals, Tampa Bay Buccaneers	11	77	98	0	.440	3	2	0	.600	80	100	0	.444
Ted Marchibroda	Baltimore-Indianapolis Colts	8	62	60	0	.508	0	3	0	.000	62	63	0	.496
Wayne Fontes	Detroit Lions	6	51	50	0	.505	1	3	0	.250	52	53	0	.495
Buddy Ryan	Philadelphia Eagles, Arizona Cardinals	6	51	43	1	.542	0	3	0	.000	51	46	1	.526
Rick Kotite	Philadelphia Eagles, New York Jets	4	36	28	0	.563	1	1	0	.500	37	29	0	.561
Bill Cowher	Pittsburgh Steelers	3	32	16	0	.667	1	3	0	.250	33	19	0	.635
Bobby Ross	San Diego Chargers	3	30	18	0	.625	3	2	0	.600	33	20	0	.623
Bill Belichick	Cleveland Browns	4	31	33	0	.484	1	1	0	.500	32	34	0	.485
Dennis Green	Minnesota Vikings	3	30	18	0	.625	0	3	0	.000	30	21	0	.588
Mike Holmgren	Green Bay Packers	3	27	21	0	.563	2	2	0	.500	29	23	0	.558
Dave Wannstedt	Chicago Bears	2	16	16	0	.500	1	1	0	.500	17	17	0	.500
Barry Switzer	Dallas Cowboys	1	12	4	0	.750	1	1	0	.500	13	5	0	.722
Dave Shula	Cincinnati Bengals	3	11	37	0	.229	0	0	0	.000	11	37	0	.229
Mike Shanahan	Los Angeles Raiders, Denver Broncos	2	8	12	0	.400	0	0	0	.000	8	12	0	.400
June Jones	Atlanta Falcons	1	7	9	0	.438	0	0	0	.000	7	9	0	.438
Norv Turner	Washington Redskins	1	3	13	0	.188	0	0	0	.000	3	13	0	.188
Jeff Fisher	Houston Oilers	1	1	5	0	.167	0	0	0	.000	1	5	0	.167
Rich Brooks	Los Angeles Rams	0	0	0	0	.000	0	0	0	.000	0	0	0	.000
Dom Capers	Carolina Panthers	0	0	0	0	.000	0	0	0	.000	0	0	0	.000
Tom Coughlin	Jacksonville Jaguars	0	0	0	0	.000	0	0	0	.000	0	0	0	.000
Dennis Erickson	Seattle Seahawks	0	0	0	0	.000	0	0	0	.000	0	0	0	.000
Ray Rhodes	Philadelphia Eagles	0	0	0	0	.000	0	0	0	.000	0	0	0	.000
Mike White	Los Angeles Raiders	0	0	0	0	.000	0	0	0	.000	0	0	0	.000

COACHES WITH 100 CAREER VICTORIES (Order Based on Career Victories)

Start of 1995 Season

Coach	Team(s)	Regular Season Yrs.	Won	Lost	Tied	Pct.	Postseason Won	Lost	Tied	Pct.	Career Won	Lost	Tied	Pct.
Don Shula	Baltimore Colts, Miami Dolphins	32	319	149	6	.679	19	16	0	.543	338	165	6	.670
George Halas	Chicago Bears	40	318	148	31	.671	6	3	0	.667	324	151	31	.671
Tom Landry	Dallas Cowboys	29	250	162	6	.605	20	16	0	.556	270	178	6	.601
Earl (Curly) Lambeau	Green Bay Packers, Chicago Cardinals, Washington Redskins	33	226	132	22	.624	3	2	0	.600	229	134	22	.623
Chuck Noll	Pittsburgh Steelers	23	193	148	1	.566	16	8	0	.667	209	156	1	.572
Chuck Knox	Los Angeles Rams, Buffalo Bills, Seattle Seahawks	22	186	147	1	.558	7	11	0	.389	193	158	1	.550
Paul Brown	Cleveland Browns, Cincinnati Bengals	21	166	100	6	.621	4	8	0	.333	170	108	6	.609
Bud Grant	Minnesota Vikings	18	158	96	5	.620	10	12	0	.455	168	108	5	.607
Steve Owen	New York Giants	23	151	100	17	.595	2	8	0	.200	153	108	17	.581
Joe Gibbs	Washington Redskins	12	124	60	0	.674	16	5	0	.762	140	65	0	.683
Dan Reeves	Denver Broncos, New York Giants	14	130	85	1	.604	8	7	0	.533	138	92	1	.600
Hank Stram	Kansas City Chiefs, New Orleans Saints	17	131	97	10	.571	5	3	0	.625	136	100	10	.573
Weeb Ewbank	Baltimore Colts, New York Jets	20	130	129	7	.502	4	1	0	.800	134	130	7	.507
Marv Levy	Kansas City Chiefs, Buffalo Bills	14	117	90	0	.565	10	6	0	.625	127	96	0	.570
Sid Gillman	Los Angeles Rams, Los Angeles-San Diego Chargers, Houston Oilers	18	122	99	7	.550	1	5	0	.167	123	104	7	.541
George Allen	Los Angeles Rams, Washington Redskins	12	116	47	5	.705	2	7	0	.222	118	54	5	.681
Don Coryell	St. Louis Cardinals, San Diego Chargers	14	111	83	1	.572	3	6	0	.333	114	89	1	.561
Mike Ditka	Chicago Bears	11	106	62	0	.631	6	6	0	.500	112	68	0	.622
John Madden	Oakland Raiders	10	103	32	7	.750	9	7	0	.563	112	39	7	.731
Marty Schottenheimer	Cleveland Browns, Kansas City Chiefs	11	103	63	1	.620	5	9	0	.357	108	72	1	.599
Ray (Buddy) Parker	Chicago Cardinals, Detroit Lions, Pittsburgh Steelers	15	104	75	9	.577	3	1	0	.750	107	76	9	.581
Tom Flores	Oakland-Los Angeles Raiders, Seattle Seahawks	12	97	87	0	.527	8	3	0	.727	105	90	0	.538
Vince Lombardi	Green Bay Packers, Washington Redskins	10	96	34	6	.728	9	1	0	.900	105	35	6	.740
Bill Walsh	San Francisco 49ers	10	92	59	1	.609	10	4	0	.714	102	63	1	.617
Bill Parcells	New York Giants, New England Patriots	10	92	66	1	.582	8	4	0	.667	100	70	1	.588

Active coaches in bold.

AFC ACTIVE STATISTICAL LEADERS

TOP ACTIVE PASSERS, AMERICAN FOOTBALL CONFERENCE

1,000 or more attempts

	Yrs.	Att.	Comp.	Pct. Comp.	Yards	Avg. Gain	TD	Pct. TD	Had Int.	Pct. Int.	Rating Pts.
Dan Marino, Mia.	12	6049	3604	59.6	45173	7.47	328	5.4	185	3.1	88.2
Jim Kelly, Buff.	9	3942	2397	60.8	29527	7.49	201	5.1	143	3.6	85.8
Bernie Kosar, Mia.	10	3225	1896	58.8	22394	6.94	120	3.7	82	2.5	81.8
Jeff Hostetler, Raiders	9	1506	864	57.4	10985	7.29	54	3.6	38	2.5	81.7
Boomer Esiason, N.Y.J.	11	4291	2440	56.9	31874	7.43	207	4.8	153	3.6	81.6
Neil O'Donnell, Pitt.	4	1455	823	56.6	9897	6.80	51	3.5	32	2.2	80.1
John Elway, Den.	12	5384	3030	56.3	37736	7.01	199	3.7	177	3.3	76.8
Jim Harbaugh, Ind.	8	1961	1148	58.5	13007	6.63	59	3.0	62	3.2	75.4
Stan Humphries, S.D.	5	1397	796	57.0	9652	6.91	49	3.5	51	3.7	74.8
Bubby Brister, N.Y.J.	9	1862	1008	54.1	12516	6.72	67	3.6	63	3.4	73.1
Drew Bledsoe, N.E.	2	1120	614	54.8	7049	6.29	40	3.6	42	3.8	70.3
Chris Chandler, Hou.	9	1242	693	55.8	8121	6.54	41	3.3	50	4.0	70.1
Mike Tomczak, Pitt.	10	1511	785	52.0	10632	7.04	57	3.8	68	4.5	68.5
Vinny Testaverde, Clev.	8	2766	1463	52.9	19192	6.94	107	3.9	139	5.0	67.0
Billy Joe Tolliver, Hou.	6	1124	578	51.4	6740	6.00	39	3.5	43	3.8	65.5
Vince Evans, L.A.	14	1215	604	49.7	8249	6.79	46	3.8	66	5.4	61.8

TOP ACTIVE RUSHERS, AFC

2,000 or more yards

	Yrs.	Att.	Yards	TD
1. Marcus Allen, K.C.	13	2485	10018	98
2. Thurman Thomas, Buff.	7	2018	8724	48
3. Earnest Byner, Clev.	11	1737	6882	50
4. Marion Butts, N.E.	6	1274	5000	39
5. John L. Williams, Pitt.	9	1216	4896	18
6. Lorenzo White, Clev.	7	1000	4079	29
7. Johnny Johnson, N.Y.J.	5	1046	4078	21
8. Chris Warren, Sea.	5	846	3658	20
9. Reggie Cobb, Jax.	5	1031	3640	24
10. Kenneth Davis, Buff.	9	823	3513	27
Other Leading Rushers				
Harold Green, Cin.	5	797	3066	6
Keith Byars, Mia.	9	833	3005	22
Rod Bernstine, Den.	8	647	2914	21
John Elway, Den.	12	596	2670	26
Brad Baxter, N.Y.J.	6	694	2632	34
Derrick Fenner, L.A.	6	691	2617	28
Ronnie Harmon, S.D.	9	525	2420	8
Tom Rathman, L.A.	9	544	2020	26

TOP ACTIVE PASS RECEIVERS, AFC

275 or more receptions

	Yrs.	No.	Yards	TD
1. Andre Reed, Buff.	10	676	9536	66
2. Gary Clark, Mia.	10	662	10331	63
3. Ernest Givins, Jax.	9	542	7935	46
4. Marcus Allen, K.C.	13	522	4845	21
John L. Williams, Pitt.	9	522	4529	18
6. Irving Fryar, Mia.	11	500	8006	50
7. Webster Slaughter, Hou.	9	489	7070	38
8. Keith Byars, Mia.	9	481	4563	21
9. Andre Rison, Clev.	6	475	6453	60
10. Ronnie Harmon, S.D.	9	459	4718	17
Other Leading Receivers				
Anthony Miller, Den.	7	434	6689	42
Brian Blades, Sea.	7	416	5560	26
Earnest Byner, Clev.	11	400	3713	12
Thurman Thomas, Buff.	7	345	3402	18
Kelvin Martin, Jax.	8	325	4182	14
Tim McGee, Cin.	9	321	5203	28
Tom Rathman, L.A.	9	320	2684	8
Tim Brown, L.A.	7	316	4734	36
Ricky Proehl, Sea.	5	287	3840	21

TOP ACTIVE SCORERS, AFC

250 or more points

	Yrs.	TD	FG	PAT	TP
1. Nick Lowery, N.Y.J.	16	0	349	512	1559
2. Gary Anderson, Pitt.	13	0	309	416	1343
3. Matt Bahr, N.E.	20	0	277	495	1326
4. Al Del Greco, Hou.	13	0	177	335	866
5. Dean Biasucci, Ind.	10	0	176	255	783
6. Marcus Allen, K.C.	13	120	0	1	722
7. Jeff Jaeger, L.A.	7	0	153	222	681
8. Pete Stoyanovich, Mia.	6	0	149	209	656
9. John Carney, S.D.	9	0	131	163	556
10. Steve Christie, Buff.	5	0	109	166	493
Other Leading Scorers					
Andre Reed, Buff.	10	67	0	0	402
Thurman Thomas, Buff.	7	66	0	0	396
Gary Clark, Mia.	10	63	0	0	378
Earnest Byner, Clev.	11	63	0	0	378
Matt Stover, Clev.	4	0	79	130	367
Andre Rison, Clev.	6	60	0	1	362
Irving Fryar, Mia.	11	54	0	2	328
Ernest Givins, Jax.	9	48	0	0	288
Anthony Miller, Den.	7	45	0	1	272
Keith Byars, Mia.	9	43	0	0	258

TOP ACTIVE INTERCEPTORS, AFC

20 or more interceptions

	Yrs.	No.	Yards	TD
1. Ronnie Lott, K.C.	14	63	730	5
2. Eugene Robinson, Sea.	10	41	554	0
3. Albert Lewis, L.A.	12	38	329	0
4. Lionel Washington, Den.	12	33	357	3
5. Rod Woodson, Pitt.	8	32	658	4
6. Dennis Smith, Den.	14	30	431	0
7. Eugene Daniel, Ind.	11	29	246	1
8. Cris Dishman, Hou.	7	27	324	1
9. Maurice Hurst, N.E.	6	26	263	1
Nate Odomes, Sea.	7	26	224	1
Other Leading Interceptors				
Louis Oliver, Mia.	6	24	495	2
Gene Atkins, Mia.	8	24	348	0
James Hasty, K.C.	7	24	251	1
Don Griffin, Clev.	9	24	51	0
Terry McDaniel, L.A.	7	22	411	3
Brian Washington, K.C.	6	21	310	3
Darren Carrington, Jax.	6	20	339	1
Tyrone Braxton, Den.	8	20	268	2

TOP ACTIVE PUNT RETURNERS, AFC

40 or more punt returns

	Yrs.	No.	Yards	Avg.	TD
1. Darrien Gordon, S.D.	2	67	870	13.0	2
2. Mel Gray, Hou.	9	181	2084	11.5	3
3. David Meggett, N.E.	6	202	2230	11.0	6
4. Tim Brown, L.A.	7	233	2447	10.5	2
5. Dexter Carter, N.Y.J.	5	72	732	10.2	1
6. Irving Fryar, Mia.	11	206	2055	10.0	3
7. Glyn Milburn, Den.	2	81	804	9.9	0
8. Kelvin Martin, Jax.	8	203	1980	9.8	3
9. Dale Carter, K.C.	3	81	769	9.5	2
10. Jeff Query, Cin.	6	76	712	9.4	0
Other Leading Punt Returners					
Rod Woodson, Pitt.	8	257	2362	9.2	2
O.J. McDuffie, Mia.	2	60	545	9.1	2
Don Griffin, Clev.	9	74	667	9.0	1
Chris Warren, Sea.	5	94	819	8.7	1
Troy Brown, N.E.	2	49	426	8.7	0
Scott Miller, Mia.	4	53	436	8.2	0
Ernest Givins, Jax.	9	56	397	7.1	1

TOP ACTIVE QUARTERBACK SACKERS, AFC (since 1982)

50 or more sacks

	Yrs.	No.
1. Bruce Smith, Buff.	10	116.0
2. Kevin Greene, Pitt.	10	99.0
3. Jim Jeffcoat, Buff.	12	94.5
4. Leslie O'Neal, S.D.	8	93.0
5. Simon Fletcher, Den.	10	92.5
6. Pat Swilling, L.A.	9	86.5
7. Derrick Thomas, K.C.	6	77.0
8. Ray Childress, Hou.	10	74.5
9. Freddie Joe Nunn, Ind.	10	67.5
Neil Smith, K.C.	7	67.5
Other Leading Sackers		
Jeff Cross, Mia.	7	53.5
Michael Dean Perry, Den.	7	51.5
Cornelius Bennett, Buff.	8	50.5
Duane Bickett, Sea.	10	50.0

TOP ACTIVE KICKOFF RETURNERS, AFC

40 or more kick returns

	Yrs.	No.	Yards	Avg.	TD
1. Andre Coleman, S.D.	1	49	1293	26.4	2
2. Tim Brown, L.A.	7	47	1204	25.6	1
3. Anthony Miller, Den.	7	50	1269	25.4	2
4. Mel Gray, Hou.	9	309	7650	24.8	6
5. Jon Vaughn, K.C.	6	103	2390	23.2	4
6. Corey Harris, Sea.	5	78	1791	23.0	0
7. Raghib Ismail, L.A.	2	68	1528	22.5	0
8. O.J. McDuffie, Mia.	2	68	1522	22.4	0
9. Rod Woodson, Pitt.	8	220	4894	22.2	2
10. Tim McGee, Cin.	9	58	1249	21.5	0
Eric Ball, L.A.	6	115	2474	21.5	0
Other Leading Kickoff Returners					
Dexter Carter, N.Y.J.	5	153	3276	21.4	2
Gene Atkins, Mia.	8	71	1508	21.2	0
Chris Warren, Sea.	5	86	1794	20.9	0
Steve Tasker, Buff.	12	43	898	20.9	0
David Meggett, N.E.	6	146	2989	20.5	1
Harvey Williams, L.A.	4	56	1135	20.3	0
Desmond Howard, Jax.	3	43	867	20.2	0
Fred McAfee, Pitt.	6	55	1100	20.0	0
Glyn Milburn, Den.	2	49	981	20.0	0
Ray Crittenden, N.E.	2	47	938	20.0	0
Michael Bates, Sea.	2	56	1111	19.8	0
Aaron Craver, Den.	3	40	789	19.7	0
Ronnie Harmon, S.D.	9	67	1305	19.5	0
Kelvin Martin, Jax.	8	56	1065	19.0	0
Todd McNair, Hou.	6	57	1079	18.9	0
Kenneth Davis, Buff	9	42	707	16.8	0

TOP ACTIVE PUNTERS, AFC

50 or more punts

	Yrs.	No.	Avg.	LG
1. Tom Rouen, Den.	2	143	43.9	62
2. Rohn Stark, Pitt.	13	985	43.8	72
3. Rick Tuten, Sea.	6	398	43.1	65
4. Rich Camarillo, Hou.	14	950	42.9	76
5. Brian Hansen, N.Y.J.	10	773	42.2	73
6. Lee Johnson, Cin.	14	686	42.1	70
7. Jeff Gossett, L.A.	15	850	41.4	65
8. Bryan Barker, Jax.	5	338	41.3	67
9. Pat O'Neill, N.E.	1	69	41.2	67
10. John Kidd, Mia.	13	729	40.8	67
Other Leading Punters				
Bryan Wagner, S.D.	8	469	40.7	71
Tom Tupa, Clev.	6	86	40.6	65
Chris Mohr, Buff.	6	339	40.5	71
Louie Aguiar, K.C.	5	295	40.3	71
Chris Gardocki, Ind.	4	235	39.8	61

TOP ACTIVE PASSERS, NATIONAL FOOTBALL CONFERENCE

1,000 or more attempts

	Yrs.	Att.	Comp.	Pct. Comp.	Yards	Avg. Gain	TD	Pct. TD	Had Int.	Pct. Int.	Rating Pts.
Steve Young, S.F.	10	2429	1546	63.6	19869	8.18	140	5.8	68	2.8	96.8
Dave Krieg, Ariz.	15	4390	2562	58.4	32114	7.32	231	5.3	166	3.8	83.0
Brett Favre, G.B.	4	1580	983	62.2	10412	6.59	70	4.4	53	3.4	82.2
Troy Aikman, Dall.	6	2281	1424	62.4	16303	7.15	82	3.6	78	3.4	81.6
Warren Moon, Minn.	11	5147	3003	58.3	37949	7.37	214	4.2	185	3.6	80.3
Randall Cunningham, Phil.	10	3241	1805	55.7	22272	6.87	147	4.5	100	3.1	79.4
Mark Rypien, St.L.	7	2335	1303	55.8	16622	7.12	105	4.5	78	3.3	79.3
Jim Everett, N.O.	9	3817	2193	57.5	27613	7.23	164	4.3	141	3.7	79.0
Bobby Hebert, Atl.	9	2588	1517	58.6	18218	7.04	111	4.3	98	3.8	78.8
Jim McMahon, Ariz.	13	2568	1488	57.9	18103	7.05	100	3.9	90	3.5	78.1
Wade Wilson, Dall.	13	2244	1281	57.1	16130	7.19	91	4.1	94	4.2	75.7
Jeff George, Atl.	5	2056	1196	58.2	13285	6.46	64	3.1	64	3.1	74.9
Chris Miller, St.L	8	2406	1302	54.1	16170	6.72	103	4.3	86	3.6	74.6
Rodney Peete, Phil.	6	1181	674	57.1	8634	7.31	42	3.6	50	4.2	74.3
Steve Beuerlein, Jax.	6	1283	681	53.1	9090	7.08	49	3.8	45	3.5	74.0
Don Majkowski, Det.	8	1783	986	55.3	11985	6.72	62	3.5	64	3.6	72.8
Steve Walsh, Chi.	7	1191	658	55.2	7368	6.19	40	3.4	39	3.3	71.5
Jack Trudeau, Car.	9	1627	862	53.0	10143	6.23	42	2.6	66	4.1	63.9

TOP ACTIVE RUSHERS, NFC

2,000 or more yards

	Yrs.	Att.	Yards	TD
1. Barry Sanders, Det.	6	1763	8672	62
2. Herschel Walker, N.Y.G.	11	1907	7996	60
3. Emmitt Smith, Dall.	5	1630	7183	71
4. Rodney Hampton, N.Y.G.	5	1241	4807	37
5. Randall Cunningham, Phil.	10	656	4384	32
6. Barry Foster, Car.	5	915	3943	26
7. Leonard Russell, St.L.	4	879	3057	22
8. Steve Young, S.F.	10	489	2969	27
9. Mark Higgs, Ariz.	9	794	2959	14
10. Ricky Watters, Phil.	3	653	2840	25
Other Leading Rushers				
Craig Heyward, Atl.	7	683	2798	20
Cleveland Gary, St.L.	6	674	2645	24
Jerome Bettis, St.L.	2	613	2454	10
Lewis Tillman, Chi.	6	630	2305	12
Brad Muster, N.O.	7	520	2231	24
Eric Metcalf, Atl.	6	592	2229	11

TOP ACTIVE PASS RECEIVERS, NFC

275 or more receptions

	Yrs.	Att.	Yards	TD
1. Jerry Rice, S.F.	10	820	13275	131
2. Henry Ellard, Wash.	12	667	11158	54
3. Herschel Walker, N.Y.G.	11	460	4387	18
4. Cris Carter, Minn.	8	449	5833	49
5. Michael Irvin, Dall.	7	416	6935	40
6. Mark Carrier, Car.	8	393	6216	35
7. Keith Jackson, G.B.	7	388	4636	38
8. Rodney Holman, Det.	13	360	4736	36
9. Jay Novacek, Dall.	10	360	3925	25
10. Mark Bavaro, Phil.	9	351	4733	39
Other Leading Receivers				
Jessie Hester, St.L.	9	343	5451	26
Michael Haynes, N.O.	7	331	5051	38
Pete Metzelaars, Car.	13	329	3225	26
John Taylor, S.F.	8	318	5211	41
Rob Moore, Ariz.	5	306	4258	22
Brett Perriman, Det.	7	298	3688	15
Eric Metcalf, Atl.	6	297	2732	15
Brent Jones, S.F.	8	295	3789	27

TOP ACTIVE SCORERS, NFC

250 or more points

	Yrs.	TD	FG	PAT	TP
1. Eddie Murray, Phil.	17	0	298	465	1359
2. Morten Andersen, N.O.	13	0	302	412	1318
3. Norm Johnson, Atl.	13	0	243	476	1205
4. Kevin Butler, Chi.	10	0	220	342	1002
5. Tony Zendejas, St.L.	10	0	183	311	860
6. Jerry Rice, S.F.	10	139	0	1	836
7. Fuad Reveiz, Minn.	11	0	162	323	809
8. Chip Lohmiller, Wash.	7	0	175	262	787
9. Greg Davis, Ariz.	10	0	142	197	623
10. Chris Jacke, G.B.	6	0	135	207	612
Other Leading Scorers					
Herschel Walker, N.Y.G.	11	80	0	0	480
Emmitt Smith, Dall.	5	75	0	0	450
Barry Sanders, Det.	6	68	0	0	408
Henry Ellard, Wash.	12	58	0	0	348
John Kasay, Car.	4	0	82	95	341
Jason Hanson, Det.	3	0	73	97	316
Cris Carter, Minn.	8	50	0	2	304
John Taylor, S.F.	8	44	0	0	264

TOP ACTIVE INTERCEPTORS, NFC

20 or more interceptions

	Yrs.	No.	Yards	TD
1. Darrell Green, Wash.	12	37	308	3
2. Eric Allen, N.O.	7	34	482	5
3. Kevin Ross, Atl.	11	33	577	2
4. Deion Sanders, S.F.	6	30	823	6
Vencie Glenn, N.Y.G.	11	30	453	1
Scott Case, Atl.	11	30	267	1
7. Tim McKyer, Car.	9	29	136	1
8. Mike Prior, G.B.	9	28	352	1
9. Tim McDonald, S.F.	8	25	417	2
10. Donnell Woolford, Chi.	6	22	154	0
Other Leading Interceptors				
Terry Taylor, Atl.	11	22	228	3
Thomas Everett, T.B.	8	21	255	0
Seth Joyner, Ariz.	9	20	288	2
Aeneas Williams, Ariz.	4	20	261	1
Greg Jackson, Phil.	6	20	200	1

TOP ACTIVE PUNT RETURNERS, NFC

40 or more punt returns

	Yrs.	No.	Yards	Avg.	TD
1. Henry Ellard, Wash.	12	135	1527	11.3	4
Darrell Green, Wash.	12	51	576	11.3	0
3. Tyrone Hughes, N.O.	2	58	646	11.1	2
4. Brian Mitchell, Wash.	5	147	1623	11.0	5
5. John Taylor, S.F.	8	138	1461	10.6	2
Eric Metcalf, Atl.	6	127	1341	10.6	5
7. Kevin Williams, Dall.	2	75	730	9.7	3
8. Johnny Bailey, St.L.	5	146	1378	9.4	2
Anthony Parker, St.L.	6	46	431	9.4	0
10. Clifford Hicks, S.F.	10	138	1284	9.3	0
Clarence Verdin, T.B.	9	178	1650	9.3	4
Other Leading Punt Returners					
Jeff Sydner, Phil.	3	47	433	9.2	0
Terance Mathis, Atl.	5	50	445	8.9	1
Robert Brooks, G.B.	3	67	589	8.8	1
Mike Prior, G.B.	9	42	368	8.8	0
Vernon Turner, Car.	7	89	778	8.7	1
Tony Smith, Car.	3	56	485	8.7	0
Deion Sanders, S.F.	6	93	789	8.5	2
Vince Buck, N.O.	5	70	569	8.1	0
Dewell Brewer, Car.	1	42	339	8.1	1

TOP ACTIVE QUARTERBACK SACKERS, NFC (since 1982)

50 or more sacks

	Yrs.	No.
1. Reggie White, G.B.	10	145.0
2. Sean Jones, G.B.	11	99.0
3. Chris Doleman, Atl.	10	95.5
4. Charles Haley, Dall.	9	86.0
5. Clyde Simmons, Ariz.	9	82.0
6. William Fuller, Phil.	9	68.5
7. Clay Matthews, Atl.	17	63.0
8. Ken Harvey, Wash.	7	61.0
9. Henry Thomas, Det.	8	56.0

TOP ACTIVE KICKOFF RETURNERS, NFC

40 or more kick returns

	Yrs.	No.	Yards	Avg.	TD
1. Tyrone Hughes, N.O.	2	93	2309	24.8	3
Kevin Williams, Dall.	2	74	1837	24.8	1
3. Robert Brooks, G.B.	3	50	1209	24.2	2
4. Tony Smith, Car.	3	61	1453	23.8	1
5. Herschel Walker, N.Y.G.	11	97	2257	23.3	2
6. Deion Sanders, S.F.	6	147	3388	23.0	3
Nate Lewis, Atl.	5	127	2921	23.0	1
8. Randy Baldwin, Car.	5	83	1886	22.7	1
9. Brian Mitchell, Wash.	5	161	3596	22.3	0
Charles Wilson, T.B.	5	92	2048	22.3	1
Other Leading Kickoff Returners					
Qadry Ismail, Minn.	2	77	1709	22.2	0
Alexander Wright, St.L.	7	79	1681	21.3	2
Johnny Bailey, St.L.	5	110	2323	21.1	0
Leonard Harris, Atl.	9	59	1240	21.0	0
Clarence Verdin, T.B.	9	237	4930	20.8	1
Alton Montgomery, Atl.	5	65	1351	20.8	0
Marc Logan, Wash.	8	85	1760	20.7	1
Eric Metcalf, Atl.	6	139	2806	20.2	2
David Lang, Dall.	4	52	1048	20.2	0
Jeff Sydner, Phil.	3	46	918	20.0	0
Vernon Turner, Car.	7	117	2303	19.7	0
Don Beebe, Car.	6	51	983	19.3	0
Dwight Stone, Car.	8	109	2086	19.1	1
Terance Mathis, Atl.	5	107	1980	18.5	0
Vince Workman, T.B.	6	61	980	16.1	0
Mark Ingram, G.B.	8	48	742	15.5	0

TOP ACTIVE PUNTERS, NFC

50 or more punts

	Yrs.	No.	Avg.	LG
1. Greg Montgomery, Det.	7	373	43.7	77
2. Sean Landeta, St.L.	12	646	43.5	71
Reggie Roby, T.B.	12	715	43.5	77
4. Tommy Barnhardt, Car.	10	454	42.9	65
5. Mike Horan, N.Y.G.	12	686	42.2	75
6. John Jett, Dall.	2	126	41.9	59
7. Mike Saxon, Minn.	10	741	41.8	67
8. Harold Alexander, Det.	2	143	41.6	75
9. Craig Hentrich, G.B.	1	81	41.4	70
10. Mark Royals, Det.	8	426	41.0	64
Other Leading Punters				
Klaus Wilmsmeyer, N.O.	3	145	40.5	61
Jeff Feagles, Ariz.	7	576	40.5	77
Dan Stryzinski, Atl.	5	378	39.8	63

DRAFT LIST FOR 1995

60th Annual NFL Draft, April 22-23, 1995
*Denotes Compensatory Selection

ARIZONA CARDINALS
(Drafted alternately 16-15)
1. Choice to N.Y. Jets
2. Frank Sanders—47, WR, Auburn
3. Stoney Case—80, QB, New Mexico
4. Choice to Buffalo
5. Cedric Davis—150, DB, Tennessee State
   *Lance Scott—165, C, Utah
   *Tito Paul—167, DB, Ohio State
6. Choice to Detroit
   *Anthony Bridges—205, DB, North Texas
7. Billy Williams—212, WR, Tennessee, from Washington
   Wesley Leasy—224, LB, Mississippi State
   *Chad Eaton—241, DT, Washington State

ATLANTA FALCONS
(Drafted alternately 10-14-13-12-11)
1. Choice to San Francisco through Cleveland
   Devin Bush—26, DB, Florida State, from Cleveland
2. Ronald Davis—41, DB, Tennessee, from Tampa Bay through Dallas
   Choice to Dallas
3. Lorenzo Styles—77, LB, Ohio State
4. Choice to Dallas
5. Roell Preston—145, WR, Mississippi
6. Travis Hall—181, DT, Brigham Young
7. Choice to Denver
   *John Burrough—245, DE, Wyoming

BUFFALO BILLS
(Drafted alternately 14-13-12-11-10)
1. Ruben Brown—14, G, Pittsburgh
2. Todd Collins—45, QB, Michigan
3. Marlon Kerner—76, DB, Ohio State
   *Damien Covington—96, LB, North Carolina State
4. Ken Irvin—109, DB, Memphis State
   Justin Armour—113, WR, Stanford, from Arizona
   *Tony Cline—131, TE, Stanford
5. John Holecek—144, LB, Illinois
6. Shannon Clavelle—185, DE, Colorado
7. Tom Nutten—221, C, Western Michigan
   *Darick Holmes—244, RB, Portland State

CAROLINA PANTHERS
(Drafted alternately 1-2, 32-31)
1. Choice to Cincinnati
   Kerry Collins—5, QB, Penn State, from Cincinnati
   Tyrone Poole—22, DB, Ft. Valley State, from Green Bay
   Blake Brockermeyer—29, T, Texas, from San Diego
   Choice to Green Bay
2. Choice to San Diego
   Shawn King—36, DE, Northeast Louisiana, from Cincinnati
   Forfeited
3. Choice to Green Bay
   Choice to San Diego
4. Choice to San Diego
   Frank Garcia—132, C, Washington
5. Michael Senters—135, DB, Northwestern
   Andrew Peterson—171, T, Washington
6. Choice to Green Bay
   Steve Strahan—188, DT, Baylor, from Green Bay
   Jerry Colquitt—191, QB, Tennessee, from Kansas City
   Forfeited
7. Chad Cota—209, DB, Oregon
   Michael Reed—249, DB, Boston College

CHICAGO BEARS
(Drafted alternately 21-20-19-18-17-22)
1. Rashaan Salaam—21, RB, Colorado
2. Patrick Riley—52, DE, Miami
   Todd Sauerbrun—56, P, West Virginia, from Miami
3. Sean Harris—83, LB, Arizona
   Evan Pilgrim—87, G, Brigham Young, from Miami
4. Jack Jackson—116, WR, Florida
5. Choice to Pittsburgh
6. Kenny Gales—193, DB, Wisconsin
   Carl Reeves—198, DE, North Carolina State, from Dallas
7. Jamal Cox—229, LB, Georgia Tech

CINCINNATI BENGALS
(Drafted alternately 5-4)
1. Ki-Jana Carter—1, RB, Penn State, from Carolina
   Choice to Carolina
2. Choice to Carolina
3. Melvin Tuten—69, T, Syracuse
4. Sam Shade—102, DB, Alabama
5. David Dunn—139, WR, Fresno State
6. Ryan Grigson—175, T, Purdue
7. John Walsh—213, QB, Brigham Young

CLEVELAND BROWNS
(Drafted 26)
1. Choice to Atlanta
   Craig Powell—30, LB, Ohio State, from San Francisco
2. Choice to Philadelphia
3. Eric Zeier—84, QB, Georgia, from Green Bay
   Choice to Green Bay
   Mike Frederick—94, DE, Virginia, from San Francisco
4. Choice to Jacksonville
5. Tau Pupua—136, DT, Weber State, from Jacksonville
   Mike Miller—147, WR, Notre Dame, from Philadelphia
   Choice to Green Bay
6. Choice to San Diego
7. A.C. Tellison—231, WR, Miami, from New England
   Choice to New England

DALLAS COWBOYS
(Drafted alternately 28-27)
1. Choice to Tampa Bay
2. Sherman Williams—46, RB, Alabama, from Atlanta
   Kendell Watkins—59, TE, Mississippi State
   *Shane Hannah—63, G, Michigan State, from Philadelphia through Tampa Bay
3. Charlie Williams—92, DB, Bowling Green
4. Eric Bjornson—110, WR, Washington, from Atlanta
   Choice to Denver through St. Louis
   *Alundis Brice—129, DB, Mississippi
   *Linc Harden—130, LB, Oklahoma State
5. Choice exercised in 1994 Supplemental Draft
   *Edward Hervey—166, WR, Southern California
   *Dana Howard—168, LB, Illinois
6. Choice to Chicago
7. Oscar Sturgis—236, DE, North Carolina

DENVER BRONCOS
(Drafted alternately 11-10-14-13-12)
1. Choice to Minnesota through Atlanta
2. Choice to Minnesota
3. Choice to Philadelphia
4. Choice to Minnesota
   Jamie Brown—121, T, Florida A&M, from Minnesota
   Ken Brown—124, LB, Virginia Tech, from Dallas through St. Louis
5. Phil Yeboah-Kodie—146, LB, Penn State
6. Fritz Fequiere—182, G, Iowa
   Terrell Davis—196, RB, Georgia, from Minnesota
7. Steve Russ—218, LB, Air Force
   Byron Chamberlain—222, WR, Wayne State, Neb., from Atlanta

DETROIT LIONS
(Drafted alternately 20-19-18-17-22-21)
1. Luther Elliss—20, DT, Utah
2. Choice to San Diego
3. David Sloan—70, TE, New Mexico, from St. Louis
   Choice to St. Louis
4. Choice to St. Louis
5. Stephen Boyd—141, LB, Boston College, from Seattle
   Kez McCorvey—156, WR, Florida State
   Ronald Cherry—163, T, McNeese State, from San Francisco
6. Kevin Hickman—186, TE, Navy, from Arizona
   Cory Schlesinger—192, RB, Nebraska
7. Hessley Hempstead—228, G, Kansas

GREEN BAY PACKERS
(Drafted alternately 22-21-20-19-18-17)
1. Choice to Carolina
   Craig Newsome—32, DB, Arizona State, from Carolina
2. Choice to Miami
3. Darius Holland—65, DT, Colorado, from Carolina
   William Henderson—66, RB, North Carolina, from Jacksonville
   Brian Williams—73, LB, Southern California, from Seattle
   Choice to Cleveland
   Antonio Freeman—90, WR, Virginia Tech, from Cleveland
4. Jeff Miller—117, T, Mississippi
5. Choice to Washington through L.A. Raiders
   Jay Barker—160, QB, Alabama, from Cleveland
   Travis Jervey—170, RB, Citadel, from Jacksonville
6. Charlie Simmons—173, WR, Georgia Tech, from Carolina
   Choice to Carolina
7. Adam Timmerman—230, G, South Dakota State

HOUSTON OILERS
(Drafted 3)
1. Steve McNair—3, QB, Alcorn State
2. Anthony Cook—35, DT, South Carolina State
3. Chris Sanders—67, WR, Ohio State
   Rodney Thomas—89, RB, Texas A&M, from Minnesota
   *Torey Hunter—95, DB, Washington State
4. Michael Roan—101, TE, Wisconsin
5. Choice to Washington
   Gary Walker—159, DE, Auburn, from New England
6. Hicham El-Mashtoub—174, C, Arizona
7. C.J. Richardson—211, DB, Miami

INDIANAPOLIS COLTS
(Drafted alternately 15-16)
1. Ellis Johnson—15, DT, Florida
2. Ken Dilger—48, TE, Illinois
3. Zack Crockett—79, RB, Florida State
4. Ray McElroy—114, DB, Eastern Illinois
5. Derek West—149, T, Colorado
6. Brian Gelzheiser—187, LB, Penn State
7. Jessie Cox—223, LB, Texas Southern

JACKSONVILLE JAGUARS
(Drafted alternately 2-1, 31-32)
1. Tony Boselli—2, T, Southern California
   James Stewart—19, RB, Tennessee, from Kansas City
   Choice to Kansas City
2. Choice to N.Y. Jets
   Brian DeMarco—40, T, Michigan State, from N.Y. Jets
   Bryan Schwartz—64, LB, Augustana, S.D.
3. Choice to Green Bay
   Chris Hudson—71, DB, Colorado, from N.Y. Jets
   Choice to Kansas City
4. Rob Johnson—99, QB, Southern California
   Mike Thompson—123, DT, Wisconsin, from Cleveland
   Choice to Kansas City
5. Choice to Cleveland
   *Ryan Christopherson—169, RB, Wyoming, from Philadelphia
   Choice to Green Bay
6. Marcus Price—172, T, Louisiana State
   Choice to Philadelphia
7. Choice to Philadelphia
   Curtis Marsh—219, WR, Utah, from Philadelphia
   Choice to Philadelphia

KANSAS CITY CHIEFS
(Drafted alternately 19-18-17-22-21-20)
1. Choice to Jacksonville
   Trezelle Jenkins—31, T, Michigan, from Jacksonville
2. Choice to Philadelphia
3. Tamarick Vanover—81, WR, Florida State
   Troy Dumas—97, LB, Nebraska, from Jacksonville
4. Choice to Philadelphia through San Francisco and Cleveland
   Steve Stenstrom—134, QB, Stanford, from Jacksonville
5. Mike Pelton—155, DT, Auburn
   *Jerrott Willard—164, LB, California
6. Choice to Carolina
   *Bryan Proby—202, DT, Arizona State
   *Tom Barndt—207, C, Pittsburgh
7. Choice to Tampa Bay

LOS ANGELES RAIDERS
(Drafted alternately 18-17-22-21-20-19)
1. Napoleon Kaufman—18, RB, Washington
2. Barret Robbins—49, C, Texas Christian
3. Joe Aska—86, RB, Central State, Okla.
4. Mike Morton—118, LB, North Carolina
5. Matt Dyson—138, LB, Michigan, from Washington
   Jeff Kysar—154, T, Arizona State
6. Eli Herring—190, T, Brigham Young
7. Choice to Washington

MIAMI DOLPHINS
(Drafted alternately 25-24-23)
1. Billy Milner—25, T, Houston
2. Andrew Greene—53, G, Indiana, from Green Bay
   Choice to Chicago
3. Choice to Chicago
4. Pete Mitchell—122, TE, Boston College
5. Norman Hand—158, DT, Mississippi
6. Jeff Kopp—194, LB, Southern California
7. Corey Swinson—233, DT, Hampton
   *Shannon Myers—246, WR, Lenoir-Rhyne

MINNESOTA VIKINGS
(Drafted alternately 24-23-25)
1. Derrick Alexander—11, DE, Florida State, from Denver through Atlanta
   Korey Stringer—24, T, Ohio State
2. Orlanda Thomas—42, DB, Southwestern Louisiana, from Denver
   Corey Fuller—55, DB, Florida State
3. Choice to Houston
4. Chad May—111, QB, Kansas State, from Denver
   Choice to Denver
5. James Stewart—157, RB, Miami
6. John Solomon—189, LB, Sam Houston State, from N.Y. Giants
   Choice to Denver
7. Jose White—232, LB, Howard
   *Jason Fisk—243, DT, Stanford

NEW ENGLAND PATRIOTS
(Drafted alternately 23-25-24)
1. Ty Law—23, DB, Michigan
2. Ted Johnson—57, LB, Colorado
3. Curtis Martin—74, RB, Pittsburgh, from Philadelphia
   Jimmy Hitchcock—88, DB, North Carolina
4. Dave Wohlabaugh—112, C, Syracuse, from Philadelphia through Kansas City
   Choice to Pittsburgh
5. Choice to Houston
6. Dino Philyaw—195, RB, Oregon
7. Choice to Cleveland
   Carlos Yancy—234, DB, Georgia, from Cleveland

NEW ORLEANS SAINTS
(Drafted alternately 13-12-11-10-14)
1. Mark Fields—13, LB, Washington State
2. Ray Zellars—44, RB, Notre Dame
3. Mike Verstegen—75, T, Wisconsin
4. Dameian Jeffries—108, DE, Alabama
5. William Strong—148, DB, North Carolina State
6. Lee DeRamus—184, WR, Wisconsin
7. Choice to St. Louis
   *Travis Davis—242, DB, Notre Dame

NEW YORK GIANTS
(Drafted alternately 17-22-21-20-19-18)
1. Tyrone Wheatley—17, RB, Michigan
2. Scott Gragg—54, T, Montana
3. Rodney Young—85, DB, Louisiana State
4. Choice exercised in 1994 Supplemental Draft
   *Rob Zatechka—128, G, Nebraska
   *Ben Talley—133, LB, Tennessee
5. Roderick Mullen—153, DB, Grambling State
6. Choice to Minnesota
   *Jamal Duff—204, DE, San Diego State
   *Charles Way—206, RB, Virginia
7. Bryne Diehl—225, P, Alabama

NEW YORK JETS
(Drafted alternately 9-8-7)
1. Kyle Brady—9, TE, Penn State
   Hugh Douglas—16, DE, Central State, Ohio, from Arizona
2. Matt O'Dwyer—33, T, Northwestern, from Jacksonville
   Choice to Jacksonville
3. Choice to Jacksonville
4. Melvin Hayes—106, T, Mississippi State, from Seattle through Arizona
   Tyrone Davis—107, WR, Virginia
5. Carl Greenwood—142, DB, UCLA
6. Eddie Mason—178, LB, North Carolina
7. Curtis Ceaser—217, WR, Grambling State

PHILADELPHIA EAGLES
(Drafted alternately 12-11-10-14-13)
1. Mike Mamula—7, DE, Boston College, from Tampa Bay
   Choice to Tampa Bay
2. Choice to Tampa Bay
   Bobby Taylor—50, DB, Notre Dame, from Kansas City
   Barrett Brooks—58, T, Kansas State, from Cleveland
   *Choice to Dallas through Tampa Bay
3. Greg Jefferson—72, DE, Central Florida, from Tampa Bay
   Choice to New England
   Chris T. Jones—78, WR, Miami, from Denver
4. Choice to New England through Kansas City
   Dave Barr—119, QB, California, from Kansas City through San Francisco and Cleveland
5. Choice to Cleveland
   Choice to Jacksonville
6. Choice to San Diego
   Fred McCrary—208, RB, Mississippi State, from Jacksonville
7. Kevin Bouie—210, RB, Mississippi State, from Jacksonville
   Choice to Jacksonville
   Howard Smothers—248, T, Bethune-Cookman, from Jacksonville

PITTSBURGH STEELERS
(Drafted alternately 27-28)
1. Mark Bruener—27, TE, Washington
2. Kordell Stewart—60, QB, Colorado
3. Brenden Stai—91, G, Nebraska
4. Oliver Gibson—120, DE, Notre Dame, from New England
   Donta Jones—125, LB, Nebraska
5. Choice to Pittsburgh from Chicago
   Lethon Flowers—151, DB, Georgia Tech, from Chicago
   Lance Brown—161, DB, Indiana
6. Barron Miles—199, DB, Nebraska
7. Henry Bailey—235, WR, Nevada-Las Vegas
   *Cole Ford—247, K, Southern California

ST. LOUIS RAMS
(Drafted 6)
1. Kevin Carter—6, DE, Florida
2. Zach Wiegert—38, T, Nebraska
   Jesse James—62, G, Mississippi State, from San Francisco
3. Choice to Detroit
   Steve McLaughlin—82, K, Arizona, from Detroit
4. Choice to San Diego
   Lovell Pinkney—115, TE, Texas, from Detroit
5. Mike Scurlock—140, DB, Arizona
6. Choice to San Diego
7. Gerald McBurrows—214, DB, Kansas
   Herman O'Berry—220, DB, Oregon, from New Orleans
   *Bronzell Miller—239, DE, Utah
   *Johnny Thomas—240, WR, Arizona State

SAN DIEGO CHARGERS
(Drafted 29)
1. Choice to Carolina
2. Terrance Shaw—34, DB, Stephen F. Austin, from Carolina
   Terrell Fletcher—51, RB, Wisconsin, from Detroit
   Jimmy Oliver—61, WR, Texas Christian
3. Don Sasa—93, DT, Washington State
   Preston Harrison—98, LB, Ohio State, from Carolina
4. Chris Cowart—100, LB, Florida State, from Carolina
   Aaron Hayden—104, RB, Tennessee, from St. Louis
   Choice to Seattle
5. 'OMar Ellison—162, WR, Florida State
6. Troy Sienkiewicz—177, G, New Mexico State, from St. Louis
   Brandon Harrison—183, WR, Howard Payne, from Philadelphia
   Craig Whelihan—197, QB, Pacific, from Cleveland
   Tony Berti—200, T, Colorado
7. Mark Montreuil—237, DB, Concordia, Canada

SAN FRANCISCO 49ERS
(Drafted 30)
1. J.J. Stokes—10, WR, UCLA, from Atlanta through Cleveland
   Choice to Cleveland
2. Choice to St. Louis
3. Choice to Cleveland
4. Tim Hanshaw—127, G, Brigham Young
5. Choice to Detroit
6. Antonio Armstrong—201, DE, Texas A&M
7. Herbert Coleman—238, DE, Trinity, Illinois.

SEATTLE SEAHAWKS
(Drafted alternately 8-7-9)
1. Joey Galloway—8, WR, Ohio State
2. Christian Fauria—39, TE, Colorado
3. Choice to Green Bay
4. Choice to N.Y. Jets through Arizona
   Jason Kyle—126, LB, Arizona State, from San Diego
5. Choice to Detroit
6. Henry McMillian—180, DT, Florida
   *Eddie Goines—203, WR, North Carolina State
7. Keif Bryant—216, DE, Rutgers

TAMPA BAY BUCCANEERS
(Drafted alternately 7-9-8)
1. Choice to Philadelphia
   Warren Sapp—12, DT, Miami, from Philadelphia
   Derrick Brooks—28, LB, Florida State, from Dallas
2. Choice to Atlanta through Dallas
   Melvin Johnson—43, DB, Kentucky, from Philadelphia
3. Choice to Philadelphia
4. Jerry Wilson—105, DB, Southern
5. Clifton Abraham—143, DB, Florida State
6. Wardell Rouse—179, LB, Clemson
7. Steve Ingram—215, G, Maryland
   Jeff Rodgers—227, DE, Texas A&M-Kingsville, from Kansas City

DRAFT LIST FOR 1995

WASHINGTON REDSKINS

(Drafted alternately 4-5)

1. Michael Westbrook—4, WR, Colorado
2. Cory Raymer—37, C, Wisconsin
3. Darryl Pounds—68, DB, Nicholls State
4. Larry Jones—103, RB, Miami
5. Jamie Asher—137, TE, Louisville, from Houston
   Choice to L.A. Raiders
   Rich Owens—152, DE, Lehigh, from Green Bay through L.A. Raiders
6. Brian Thure—176, T, California
7. Choice to Arizona
   Scott Turner—226, DB, Illinois, from L.A. Raiders

NUMBER OF PLAYERS DRAFTED

BY POSITION:

Defensive Backs	44
Linebackers	34
Wide Receivers	31
Running Backs	25
Tackles	25
Defensive Ends	22
Defensive Tackles	17
Quarterbacks	14
Guards	13
Tight Ends	12
Centers	8
Kickers	2
Punters	2
Kick Returners	0
Nose Tackles	0

BY COLLEGE:

Colorado	10
Florida State	10
Ohio State	8
Miami	7
Nebraska	7
Wisconsin	7
Mississippi State	6
Southern California	6
Tennessee	6
Alabama	5
Arizona State	5
Brigham Young	5
Michigan	5
North Carolina	5
Notre Dame	5
Penn State	5
Washington	5
Arizona	4
Boston College	4
Florida	4
Illinois	4
Mississippi	4
North Carolina State	4
Stanford	4
Utah	4
Washington State	4
Auburn	3
California	3
Georgia	3
Georgia Tech	3
Oregon	3
Pittsburgh	3
Virginia	3
Grambling State	2
Indiana	2
Kansas	2
Kansas State	2
Louisiana State	2
Michigan State	2
New Mexico	2
Northwestern	2
Syracuse	2
Texas	2
Texas A&M	2
Texas Christian	2
UCLA	2
Virginia Tech	2
Wyoming	2
Air Force	1
Alcorn State	1
Augustana, S.D.	1
Baylor	1
Bethune-Cookman	1
Bowling Green	1
Central Florida	1
Central State, Ohio	1
Central State, Okla.	1
Citadel	1
Clemson	1
Concordia, Canada	1
Eastern Illinois	1
Florida A&M	1
Ft. Valley State	1
Fresno State	1
Hampton	1
Houston	1
Howard	1
Howard Payne	1
Iowa	1
Kentucky	1
Lehigh	1
Lenoir-Rhyne	1
Louisville	1
Maryland	1
McNeese State	1
Memphis	1
Montana	1
Navy	1
Nevada-Las Vegas	1
New Mexico State	1
Nicholls State	1
North Texas	1
Northeast Louisiana	1
Oklahoma State	1
Pacific	1
Portland State	1
Purdue	1
Rutgers	1
Sam Houston State	1
San Diego State	1
South Carolina State	1
South Dakota State	1
Southern	1
Southwestern Louisiana	1
Stephen F. Austin	1
Tennessee State	1
Texas A&M-Kingsville	1
Texas Southern	1
Trinity, Ill	1
Wayne State, Neb.	1
Weber State	1
West Virginia	1
Western Michigan	1

BY CONFERENCE:

Big 10	37
Pac 10	36
SEC	34
ACC	27
Big 8	22
Big East	20
WAC	16
Independent	13
SWC	8
Southland	6
SWAC	5
Big West	4
MEAC	4
Big Sky	2
Lone Star	2
MAC	2
NCC	2
CIAA	1
Gateway	1
OVC	1
Patriot	1
SAC	1
SIAC	1
Southern	1
TIAA	1

The **Chicago Bears**, the all-time winningest team in NFL history with a 596-392-42 record, can win their 600th game with 4 victories in 1995.

The **New England Patriots** ended the 1994 season with 7 consecutive regular-season victories and can set a club record with a win in their first game of 1995.

Wayne Fontes, Detroit, needs 4 wins to become the Lions' all-time winningest coach, surpassing George Wilson (55). Fontes has recorded 52 victories in seven seasons as Lions head coach.

Dan Marino, Miami, needs 1,830 yards to surpass Fran Tarkenton with 47,003 yards as the NFL's all-time leading passer. Marino has thrown for 45,173 yards in 12 NFL seasons.

Marino needs 15 touchdown passes to move past Tarkenton (342) into first on the all-time list. Marino has 328 career touchdown passes.

Marino needs 83 completions and 419 attempts to surpass Tarkenton's all-time records of 3,686 completions and 6,467 attempts. Marino has completed 3,604 of 6,049 attempts.

Jerry Rice, San Francisco, needs 730 yards to pass James Lofton (14,004) as the NFL's all-time leader in receiving yards. Rice has 13,275 yards in 10 NFL seasons.

Rice needs 80 catches to become the second player to reach 900 career receptions, joining Art Monk (934).

Warren Moon, Minnesota, needs 2,051 yards to become the sixth quarterback in history to reach 40,000 passing yards, joining Fran Tarkenton (47,003), Dan Marino (45,173), Dan Fouts (43,040), Joe Montana (40,551), and Johnny Unitas (40,239). Moon has 37,949 yards in 11 NFL seasons. (See Elway note).

John Elway, Denver, needs 2,264 yards to become the sixth quarterback in history to reach 40,000 passing yards, joining Fran Tarkenton (47,003), Dan Marino (45,173), Dan Fouts (43,040), Joe Montana (40,551), and Johnny Unitas (40,239). Elway has 37,736 yards in 12 NFL seasons. (See Moon note).

Steve Young, San Francisco, can extend his NFL-record streak of 4 consecutive seasons leading the NFL in passer rating and also his NFL-record streak of 4 consecutive seasons with a passer rating of at least 100.

With 31 rushing yards, Young can become the fourth quarterback in history to rush for 3,000 yards. He has 2,969 rushing yards in 10 NFL seasons.

Rodney Hampton, New York Giants, needs 490 yards to move past Joe Morris (5,296), as the Giants' all-time rushing leader. Hampton has 4,807 yards in five NFL seasons.

Jerome Bettis, St. Louis Rams, can join Eric Dickerson as the only two players in Rams history to rush for 1,000 yards in each of their first three seasons. Bettis rushed for 1,025 yards in 1994 and 1,429 yards in 1993.

John L. Williams, Pittsburgh, needs 45 catches to surpass Roger Craig (566) as the NFL's all-time leading receiver for running backs. Williams has 522 receptions in nine NFL seasons.

Andre Reed, Buffalo, the Bills' all-time receiver with 676 catches in 10 seasons, needs 24 receptions to become the sixth player in history with 700 receptions, joining Art Monk (934), Jerry Rice (820), Steve Largent (819), James Lofton (764), and Charlie Joiner (750). (See Ellard note).

Henry Ellard, Washington, needs 33 receptions to become the sixth player in history with 700 receptions, joining Art Monk (934), Jerry Rice (820), Steve Largent (819), James Lofton (764), and Charlie Joiner (750). (See Reed note).

Michael Irvin, Dallas, needs 74 receptions to move past Drew Pearson (489 career catches) and become the Cowboys' all-time leading receiver. Irvin has 416 catches in seven NFL seasons.

With 1,054 yards, Irvin also will surpass Tony Hill with 7,988 yards as the team's all-time leader in receiving yards. Irvin has 6,935 yards.

Jim Kelly, Buffalo, needs 473 yards to become the seventeenth player in NFL history to pass for 30,000 yards. Kelly has passed for 29,527 yards in nine NFL seasons. (See Everett note).

Jim Everett, New Orleans, needs 2,387 yards to become the seventeenth player in NFL history to pass for 30,000 yards. Everett has accumulated 27,613 yards in nine NFL seasons. (See Kelly note).

Randall Cunningham, Philadelphia, needs 284 completions to surpass Ron Jaworski's club-record of 2,088. Cunningham has 1,805 completions in 10 NFL seasons.

Emmitt Smith, Dallas, needs 12 touchdowns to exceed Tony Dorsett's club-record 86 touchdowns. Smith has 75 touchdowns in five NFL seasons.

Jackie Slater, St. Louis Rams, needs to play in six games to pass Jan Stenerud for third place on the NFL's all-time service chart behind George Blanda (340) and Jim Marshall (282). Slater has played in 258 games in 19 NFL seasons.

Thurman Thomas, Buffalo, needs 5 touchdowns to surpass O.J. Simpson with 70 and become the Bills' all-time touchdown scorer. Thomas has 66 touchdowns in seven NFL seasons.

Thomas also needs 2 100-yard rushing performances to exceed Simpson's club record 41 100-yard rushing games. Thomas has rushed for more than 100 yards in 40 games.

With 1,000 rushing yards, Thomas can become the second player in history to rush for 1,000 yards in seven consecutive seasons, joining Eric Dickerson. (See Sanders note).

Barry Sanders, Detroit, can become the second player in history to rush for 1,000 yards in seven consecutive seasons, joining Eric Dickerson. (See Thomas note).

Errict Rhett, Tampa Bay, gained 1,011 rushing yards in his rookie season. Rhett can become the first Buccaneers rusher to gain more than 1,000 yards in each of his first two NFL seasons and the first to post consecutive 1,000-yard seasons since James Wilder in 1984 and 1985.

Morten Andersen, New Orleans, needs to score in each of the first 13 games to break Jim Breech's NFL record of 186 consecutive games scoring a point.

Fuad Reveiz, Minnesota, needs 2 field goals to break John Carney's NFL-record 29 consecutive field goals made.

Nick Lowery, New York Jets, needs 25 field goals to pass Jan Stenerud (373) and move into first place on the all-time field goal list. Lowery has 349 field goals in 15 NFL seasons.

Gary Anderson, Pittsburgh, needs 27 field goals to move past George Blanda (335) in third place on the all-time field goal list behind Jan Stenerud (373) and Nick Lowery (349). Anderson has 309 field goals in 13 NFL seasons.

Eddie Murray, Philadelphia, needs 112 points to move past Pat Leahy (1,470) into fourth place on the NFL's all-time scoring list. Murray has 1,359 points in 15 NFL seasons.

Pete Stoyanovich, Miami, needs 17 field goals to break the Dolphins' team record of 165 set by Garo Yepremian. Stoyanovich has 149 field goals in six NFL seasons.

John Carney, San Diego, needs 18 field goals to surpass Rolf Benirschke's club-record 146 field goals. Carney has 129 field goals in five NFL seasons.

Steve Christie, Buffalo, needs 25 field goals to become the Bills' all-time leading field-goal kicker, surpassing Scott Norwood's 133. Christie has 109 field goals in three seasons with the Bills.

Matt Bahr, New England, needs 74 points to become the seventh player in NFL history to score 1,400 points. Bahr has 1,326 points in 16 NFL seasons.

Kevin Greene, Pittsburgh, and **Sean Jones,** Houston, each need 1 sack to become the seventh player in NFL history to have at least 100 career sacks.

Ben Coates, New England, needs a reception in 10 consecutive games to break the Patriots' all-time record of 42 consecutive games with a catch set by Jim Colclough.

Brian Mitchell, Washington, needs 858 yards to break the team's all-time return-yardage record held by Mike Nelms with 6,076 yards. Mitchell has 5,219 return yards (1,623 on punt returns, 3,596 on kick returns) in five NFL seasons.

Clarence Verdin, Tampa Bay, needs 70 yards to become the sixth player to reach 5,000 career kickoff-return yards. Verdin has 4,930 yards on 237 kickoff returns in nine NFL seasons.

The AFC

BUFFALO BILLS

American Football Conference
Eastern Division
Team Colors: Royal Blue, Scarlet Red, and White
One Bills Drive
Orchard Park, New York 14127-2296
Telephone: (716) 648-1800

CLUB OFFICIALS

President: Ralph C. Wilson, Jr.
Exec. V.P./General Manager: John Butler
Corporate V.P.: Linda Bogdan
V.P./Head Coach: Marv Levy
Treasurer: Jeffrey C. Littmann
Director of Administration/Ticket Sales: Jerry Foran
Asst. G.M./Business Operations: Bill Munson
Director of Business Operations: Jim Overdorf
Director of Marketing and Sales: John Livsey
Director of Merchandising: Christy Wilson Hofmann
Director of Player Personnel: Dwight Adams
Director of Pro Personnel: A.J. Smith
Director of Player/Alumni Relations: Jerry Butler
Director of Public/Community Relations: Denny Lynch
Director of Media Relations: Scott Berchtold
Director of Stadium Operations: George Koch
Stadium Operations Supervisor: Pete Reidy
Director of Security: Bill Bambach
Ticket Director: June Foran
Equipment Manager: Dave Hojnowski
Strength/Conditioning Coordinator: Rusty Jones
Trainers: Ed Abramoski, Bud Carpenter, Bill Ford
Video Director: Henry Kunttu
Scouts: Tom Beck, Doug Majeski, Buddy Nix, Bob Ryan, George (Chink) Sengel, David G. Smith, David W. Smith
Stadium: Rich Stadium • **Capacity:** 80,091
One Bills Drive
Orchard Park, New York 14127-2296
Playing Surface: AstroTurf
Training Camp: Fredonia State University
Fredonia, New York 14063

1995 SCHEDULE

PRESEASON

July 29	at Dallas	8:00
Aug. 4	**Pittsburgh**	7:30
Aug. 12	vs. Dallas at Toronto	8:00
Aug. 19	at Kansas City	7:00
Aug. 25	**Atlanta**	7:30

REGULAR SEASON

Sept. 3	at Denver	6:00
Sept. 10	**Carolina**	1:00
Sept. 17	**Indianapolis**	1:00
Sept. 24	Open Date	
Oct. 2	at Cleveland (Monday)	9:00
Oct. 8	**New York Jets**	1:00
Oct. 15	**Seattle**	1:00
Oct. 23	at New England (Monday)	9:00
Oct. 29	at Miami	4:00
Nov. 5	at Indianapolis	1:00
Nov. 12	**Atlanta**	1:00
Nov. 19	at New York Jets	4:00
Nov. 26	**New England**	1:00
Dec. 3	at San Francisco	5:00
Dec. 10	at St. Louis	12:00
Dec. 17	**Miami**	1:00
Dec. 24	**Houston**	1:00

RECORD HOLDERS

INDIVIDUAL RECORDS—CAREER

Category	Name	Performance
Rushing (Yds.)	O.J. Simpson, 1969-1977	10,183
Passing (Yds.)	Jim Kelly, 1986-1994	29,527
Passing (TDs)	Jim Kelly, 1986-1994	201
Receiving (No.)	Andre Reed, 1985-1994	676
Receiving (Yds.)	Andre Reed, 1985-1994	9,536
Interceptions	George (Butch) Byrd, 1964-1970	40
Punting (Avg.)	Paul Maguire, 1964-1970	42.1
Punt Return (Avg.)	Keith Moody, 1976-79	10.5
Kickoff Return (Avg.)	Wallace Francis, 1973-74	27.2
Field Goals	Scott Norwood, 1985-1991	133
Touchdowns (Tot.)	O.J. Simpson, 1969-1977	70
Points	Scott Norwood, 1985-1991	670

INDIVIDUAL RECORDS—SINGLE SEASON

Category	Name	Performance
Rushing (Yds.)	O.J. Simpson, 1973	2,003
Passing (Yds.)	Jim Kelly, 1991	3,844
Passing (TDs)	Jim Kelly, 1991	33
Receiving (No.)	Andre Reed, 1994	90
Receiving (Yds.)	Andre Reed, 1989	1,312
Interceptions	Billy Atkins, 1961	10
	Tom Janik, 1967	10
Punting (Avg.)	Billy Atkins, 1961	44.5
Punt Return (Avg.)	Keith Moody, 1977	13.1
Kickoff Return (Avg.)	Ed Rutkowski, 1963	30.2
Field Goals	Scott Norwood, 1988	32
Touchdowns (Tot.)	O.J. Simpson, 1975	23
Points	O.J. Simpson, 1975	138

INDIVIDUAL RECORDS—SINGLE GAME

Category	Name	Performance
Rushing (Yds.)	O.J. Simpson, 11-25-76	273
Passing (Yds.)	Joe Ferguson, 10-9-83	419
Passing (TDs)	Jim Kelly, 9-8-91	6
Receiving (No.)	Andre Reed, 11-20-94	15
Receiving (Yds.)	Jerry Butler, 9-23-79	255
Interceptions	Many Times	3
	Last time by Jeff Nixon, 9-7-80	
Field Goals	Pete Gogolak, 12-5-65	5
	Scott Norwood, 9-25-88	5
	Steve Christie, 9-18-94	5
Touchdowns (Tot.)	Cookie Gilchrist, 12-8-63	5
Points	Cookie Gilchrist, 12-8-63	30

COACHING HISTORY

(254-278-8)

1960-61	Buster Ramsey	11-16-1
1962-65	Lou Saban	38-18-3
1966-68	Joe Collier*	13-17-1
1968	Harvey Johnson	1-10-1
1969-70	John Rauch	7-20-1
1971	Harvey Johnson	1-13-0
1972-76	Lou Saban**	32-29-1
1976-77	Jim Ringo	3-20-0
1978-82	Chuck Knox	38-38-0
1983-85	Kay Stephenson***	10-26-0
1985-86	Hank Bullough****	4-17-0
1986-94	Marv Levy	96-54-0

*Released after two games in 1968
**Resigned after five games in 1976
***Released after four games in 1985
****Released after nine games in 1986

RICH STADIUM

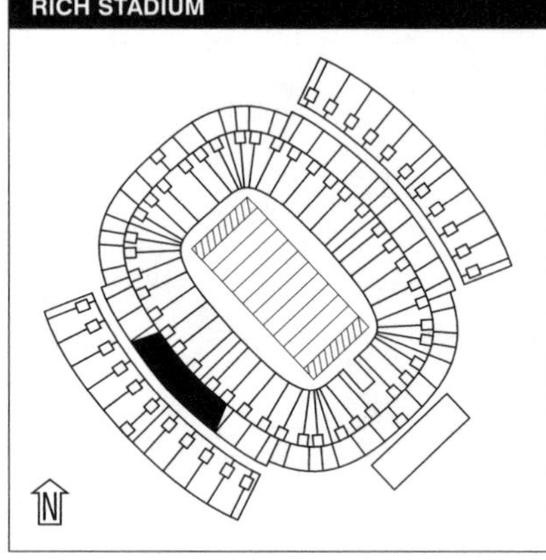

1994 TEAM RECORD

PRESEASON (3-1)

Date	Result		Opponent
8/8	W	13-11	Washington
8/12	L	7-27	at Atlanta
8/20	W	18-16	vs. Houston at San Antonio
8/26	W	24-3	Kansas City

REGULAR SEASON (7-9)

Date	Result		Opponents	Att.
9/4	L	3-23	N.Y. Jets	79,460
9/11	W	38-35	at New England	60,274
9/18	W	15- 7	at Houston	55,424
9/26	W	27-20	Denver	75,373
10/2	L	13-20	at Chicago	62,406
10/9	W	21-11	Miami	79,491
10/16	L	17-27	Indianapolis	79,404
10/30	W	44-10	Kansas City	79,501
11/6	L	17-22	at N.Y. Jets	66,949
11/14	L	10-23	at Pittsburgh	59,019
11/20	W	29-20	Green Bay	79,029
11/24	L	21-35	at Detroit	75,672
12/4	W	42-31	at Miami	69,358
12/11	L	17-21	Minnesota	66,501
12/18	L	17-41	New England	56,784
12/24	L	9-10	at Indianapolis	38,458

(OT) Overtime

SCORE BY PERIODS

Bills	82	120	69	69	0	—	340
Opponents	46	115	87	108	0	—	356

ATTENDANCE

Home 595,543 Away 487,560 Total 1,083,103
Single-game home record, 80,366 (9-29-91)
Single-season home record, 635,899 (1991)*
*NFL record

1994 TEAM STATISTICS

	Bills	Opp.
Total First Downs	319	294
Rushing	107	82
Passing	181	199
Penalty	31	13
Third Down: Made/Att	96/222	91/217
Third Down Pct.	43.2	41.9
Fourth Down: Made/Att	5/16	12/18
Fourth Down Pct.	31.3	66.7
Total Net Yards	5244	5175
Avg. Per Game	327.8	323.4
Total Plays	1066	1007
Avg. Per Play	4.9	5.1
Net Yards Rushing	1831	1515
Avg. Per Game	114.4	94.7
Total Rushes	483	447
Net Yards Passing	3413	3660
Avg. Per Game	213.3	228.8
Sacked/Yards Lost	41/301	25/152
Gross Yards	3714	3812
Att./Completions	542/342	535/314
Completion Pct.	63.1	58.7
Had Intercepted	21	16
Punts/Avg.	67/41.8	69/42.3
Net Punting Avg.	67/36.0	69/34.1
Penalties/Yards Lost	92/631	101/770
Fumbles/Ball Lost	30/13	23/12
Touchdowns	38	40
Rushing	14	10
Passing	23	26
Returns	1	4
Avg. Time of Possession	29:21	30:39

1994 INDIVIDUAL STATISTICS

PASSING	Att.	Comp.	Yds.	Pct.	TD	Int.	Tkld.	Rate
Kelly	448	285	3114	63.6	22	17	34/244	84.6
Reich	93	56	568	60.2	1	4	7/57	63.4
Reed	1	1	32	100.0	0	0	0/0	118.8
Bills	542	342	3714	63.1	23	21	41/301	81.2
Opponents	535	314	3812	58.7	26	16	25/152	84.4

SCORING	R	TD P	TD Rt	TD PAT	FG	Saf	PTS
Christie	0	0	0	38/38	24/28	0	110
T. Thomas	7	2	0	0/0	0/0	0	54
Reed	0	8	0	0/0	0/0	0	48
Metzelaars	0	5	0	0/0	0/0	0	30
Beebe	0	4	0	0/0	0/0	0	24
Gardner	4	0	0	0/0	0/0	0	24
Bi. Brooks	0	2	0	0/0	0/0	0	12
K. Davis	2	0	0	0/0	0/0	0	12
Copeland	0	1	0	0/0	0/0	0	6
Kelly	1	0	0	0/0	0/0	0	6
Lodish	0	0	1	0/0	0/0	0	6
Turner	0	1	0	0/0	0/0	0	6
Bills	14	23	1	38/38	24/28	1	340
Opponents	10	26	4	34/36	26/30	0	356

2-Point conversions: 0. Team: 0-0.

RUSHING	Att.	Yds.	Avg.	LG	TD
T. Thomas	287	1093	3.8	29	7
K. Davis	91	381	4.2	60	2
Gardner	41	135	3.3	13	4
Reed	10	87	8.7	20	0
Kelly	25	77	3.1	18	1
Jourdain	17	56	3.3	16	0
Beebe	2	11	5.5	6	0
Turner	2	4	2.0	4	0
Reich	6	3	0.5	5	0
Copeland	1	-7	-7.0	-7	0
Mohr	1	-9	-9.0	-9	0
Bills	483	1831	3.8	60	14
Opponents	447	1515	3.4	28	10

RECEIVING	No.	Yds.	Avg.	LG	TD
Reed	90	1303	14.5	83t	8
T. Thomas	50	349	7.0	28	2
Metzelaars	49	428	8.7	35t	5
Bi. Brooks	42	482	11.5	32	2
Beebe	40	527	13.2	72t	4
Copeland	21	255	12.1	35	1
K. Davis	18	82	4.6	12	0
Gardner	11	89	8.1	21	0
Jourdain	10	56	5.6	18	0
Marrow	5	44	8.8	14	0
L. Johnson	3	42	14.0	21	0
D. Thomas	2	31	15.5	17	0
Turner	1	26	26.0	26t	1
Bills	342	3714	10.9	83t	23
Opponents	314	3812	12.1	57	26

INTERCEPTIONS	No.	Yds.	Avg.	LG	TD
Darby	4	20	5.0	20	0
Washington	3	63	21.0	36	0
Jones	2	45	22.5	45	0
Burris	2	24	12.0	24	0
M. Patton	2	8	4.0	8	0
Maddox	1	11	11.0	11	0
T. Smith	1	4	4.0	4	0
B. Smith	1	0	0.0	0	0
Bills	16	175	10.9	45	0
Opponents	21	262	12.5	37t	2

PUNTING	No.	Yds.	Avg.	In 20	LG
Mohr	67	2799	41.8	13	71
Bills	67	2799	41.8	13	71
Opponents	69	2916	42.3	19	67

PUNT RETURNS	No.	FC	Yds.	Avg.	LG	TD
Burris	32	6	332	10.4	57	0
Copeland	1	2	11	11.0	11	0
Bills	33	8	343	10.4	57	0
Opponents	38	11	324	8.5	31	0

KICKOFF RETURNS	No.	Yds.	Avg.	LG	TD
Jourdain	27	601	22.3	42	0
Copeland	12	232	19.3	32	0
Beebe	12	230	19.2	35	0
Bu. Brooks	9	162	18.0	25	0
Turner	6	102	17.0	23	0
Pike	2	9	4.5	9	0
Gardner	1	6	6.0	6	0
Tasker	1	2	2.0	2	0
J. Patton	1	1	1.0	1	0
K. Davis	1	0	0.0	0	0
Bills	72	1345	18.7	42	0
Opponents	72	1455	20.2	45	0

SACKS	No.
B. Smith	10.0
Hansen	5.5
Bennett	5.0
Wright	2.0
Barnett	1.0
Jones	1.0
Washington	0.5
Bills	25.0
Opponents	41.0

1995 DRAFT CHOICES

Round	Name	Pos.	College
1	Ruben Brown	G	Pittsburgh
2	Todd Collins	QB	Michigan
3	Marlon Kerner	DB	Ohio State
	Damien Covington	LB	North Carolina State
4	Ken Irvin	DB	Memphis
	Justin Armour	WR	Stanford
	Tony Cline	TE	Stanford
5	John Holecek	LB	Illinois
6	Shannon Clavelle	DE	Colorado
7	Tom Nutten	C	Western Michigan
	Darick Holmes	RB	Portland State

BUFFALO BILLS

1995 VETERAN ROSTER

No.	Name	Pos.	Ht.	Wt.	Birthdate	NFL Exp.	College	Hometown	How Acq.	'94 Games/ Starts
97	Bennett, Cornelius	LB	6-2	238	8/25/65	9	Alabama	Birmingham, Ala.	T(Ind)-'87	16/16
81	Brooks, Bucky	WR	6-0	190	1/22/71	2	North Carolina	Raleigh, N.C.	D2a-'94	3/0
96	Brown, Monty	LB	6-0	228	4/13/70	3	Ferris State	Bridgeport, Mich.	FA-'93	3/0
22	Burris, Jeff	CB-S	6-0	204	6/7/72	2	Notre Dame	Rock Hill, S.C.	D1-'94	16/0
2	Christie, Steve	K	6-0	185	11/13/67	6	William & Mary	Oakville, Canada	PB(TB)-'92	16/0
87	Coons, Rob	TE	6-5	249	9/18/69	2	Pittsburgh	Brea, Calif.	FA-'95	0*
85	Copeland, Russell	WR	6-0	200	11/4/71	3	Memphis State	Tupelo, Miss.	D4-'93	15/4
43	Darby, Matt	S	6-1	200	11/19/68	4	UCLA	Virginia Beach, Va.	D5-'92	16/16
23	# Davis, Kenneth	RB	5-10	208	4/16/62	10	Texas Christian	Temple, Tex.	PB(GB)-'89	16/1
62	Devlin, Mike	G-C	6-1	293	11/16/69	3	Iowa	Marlton, N.J.	D5a-'93	16/0
70	Fina, John	T-G	6-4	285	3/11/69	4	Arizona	Tucson, Ariz.	D1-'92	12/12
35	Gardner, Carwell	RB	6-2	244	11/27/66	6	Louisville	Louisville, Ky.	D2-'90	16/7
90	Hansen, Phil	DE	6-5	278	5/20/68	5	North Dakota State	Ellendale, N.D.	D2-'91	16/16
76	Hoyem, Steve	T	6-7	287	11/12/70	2	Stanford	Boise, Idaho	FA-'94	6/0
67	Hull, Kent	C	6-5	284	1/13/61	10	Mississippi State	Greenwood, Miss.	FA-'86	16/16
26	Humphrey, Bobby	RB	6-1	201	10/11/66	6	Alabama	Birmingham, Ala.	FA-'95	0*
77	Jeffcoat, Jim	DE	6-5	280	4/1/61	13	Arizona State	Cliffwood, N.J.	UFA(Dall)-'95	16/0*
84	Johnson, Lonnie	TE	6-3	230	2/14/71	2	Florida State	Miami, Fla.	D2b-'94	10/1
20	Jones, Henry	S	5-11	197	12/29/67	5	Illinois	St. Louis, Mo.	D1-'91	16/16
30	Jourdain, Yonel	RB	5-11	204	4/20/71	2	Southern Illinois	Evanston, Ill.	FA-'93	9/0
12	Kelly, Jim	QB	6-3	226	2/14/60	10	Miami	East Brady, Pa.	D1b-'83	14/14
68	Lacina, Corbin	T-G	6-4	297	11/2/70	2	Augustana, S.D.	Woodbury, Minn.	D6-'93	11/10
29	Lang, Le-Lo	CB	5-11	185	1/23/67	5	Washington	Los Angeles, Calif.	FA-'95	0*
63	Lingner, Adam	C	6-4	268	11/2/60	13	Illinois	Rock Island, Ill.	PB(KC)-'89	16/0
72	Louchiey, Corey	T	6-7	305	10/10/71	2	South Carolina	Greenville, S.C.	D3b-'94	0*
55	Maddox, Mark	LB	6-1	233	3/23/68	5	Northern Michigan	Milwaukee, Wis.	D9-'91	15/14
9	Mohr, Chris	P	6-5	215	5/11/66	6	Alabama	Thomson, Ga.	FA-'91	16/0
86	Ofodile, A.J.	TE	6-7	260	10/9/73	2	Missouri	Detroit, Mich.	D5-'94	0*
74	Parker, Glenn	G-T	6-5	305	4/22/66	6	Arizona	Huntington Beach, Calif.	D3-'90	16/16
99	Patton, James	DE-NT	6-3	287	1/5/70	4	Texas	Houston, Tex.	D2-'92	11/0
95	Paup, Bryce	LB	6-5	247	2/29/68	6	Northern Iowa	Jefferson, Iowa	UFA(GB)-'95	16/16*
58	Perry, Marlo	LB	6-4	250	8/25/72	2	Jackson State	Forest, Miss.	D3a-'94	2/0
75	Philion, Ed	NT	6-2	273	3/27/70	2	Ferris State	Essex, Canada	FA-'94	4/0
94	Pike, Mark	DE	6-4	272	12/27/63	10	Georgia Tech	Villa Hills, Ky.	D7b-'86	16/0
83	Reed, Andre	WR	6-2	190	1/29/64	11	Kutztown	Allentown, Pa.	D4a-'85	16/16
59	Rogers, Sam	LB	6-3	245	5/30/70	2	Colorado	Pontiac, Mich.	D2c-'94	14/0
24	Schulz, Kurt	S	6-1	208	12/28/68	4	Eastern Washington	Yakima, Wash.	D7-'92	16/0
78	Smith, Bruce	DE	6-4	273	6/18/63	11	Virginia Tech	Norfolk, Va.	D1a-'85	15/15
28	Smith, Thomas	CB	5-11	188	12/5/70	3	North Carolina	Gates, N.C.	D1-'93	16/16
11	Strom, Rick	QB	6-2	197	3/11/65	6	Georgia Tech	Pittsburgh, Pa.	UFA(Pitt)-'94	0*
89	Tasker, Steve	WR	5-9	181	4/10/62	11	Northwestern	Leoti, Kan.	W(Hou)-'86	14/0
82	Thomas, Damon	WR	6-2	215	12/15/70	2	Wayne State	Clovis, Calif.	FA-'94	3/0
34	Thomas, Thurman	RB	5-10	198	5/16/66	8	Oklahoma State	Missouri City, Tex.	D2-'88	15/15
21	Turner, Nate	RB	6-1	255	5/28/69	4	Nebraska	Chicago, Ill.	D6-'92	13/0
92	Washington, Ted	NT	6-4	315	4/13/68	5	Louisville	Tampa, Fla.	UFA(Den)-'95	15/15*
50	White, David	LB	6-2	235	2/27/70	2	Nebraska	New Orleans, La.	FA-'95	0*
18	Williams, Tyrone	WR	6-5	220	3/26/70	2	Western Ontario	Halifax, Nova Scotia	FA-'95	0*

* Coons missed '94 season because of injury; Humphrey last on injured reserve with Miami in '93; Jeffcoat played 16 games with Dallas in '94; Lang last active with Denver in '93; Louchiey inactive for 4 games; Ofodile missed '94 season because of injury; Paup played 16 games with Green Bay; Strom active for 2 games but did not play; Washington played 15 games with Denver; White last active with New England in '93; Williams last active with Dallas in '93.

\# Unrestricted free agent; subject to developments.

† Restricted free agent; subject to developments.

Players lost through free agency (10): DE Oliver Barnett (SF; 16 games in '94), WR Don Beebe (Car; 13), S Mike Dumas (Jax; 14), CB Jerome Henderson (Phil; 12), NT Mike Lodish (Den; 15), TE Pete Metzelaars (Car; 16), LB Marvcus Patton (Wash; 16), QB Frank Reich (Car; 16), LB Darryl Talley (Atl; 16), CB Mickey Washington (Jax; 16).

Players lost through Expansion Draft (2): LB Keith Goganious (Jax; 16 games in '94), TE Vince Marrow (Car; 10).

Also played with Bills in '94—WR Bill Brooks (16 games), T Jerry Crafts (16), G John Davis (16), NT Jeff Wright (12).

COACHING STAFF

Head Coach,
Marv Levy

Pro Career: Begins his ninth full season as Bills head coach. Led Bills to four consecutive AFC Championships in 1990-93. Under Levy, the Bills recorded 13-3 records in 1990 and 1991, the best regular-season marks in club history. He guided the Bills to their second consecutive AFC East title with a 9-7 record in 1989. Finished 1988 season with a 12-4 record and a berth in the AFC Championship Game. In his first full year with Bills in 1987, he led team to a 7-8 record. Replaced Hank Bullough on November 3, 1986, and compiled a 2-5 record over the final seven weeks of the season. Previously served as head coach of the Kansas City Chiefs from 1978-1982 and produced a 31-42 mark. Levy began his pro coaching career in 1969 as an assistant with the Philadelphia Eagles. He joined George Allen and the Los Angeles Rams as an assistant one-year later and followed Allen to Washington, where he remained with the Redskins through the 1972 season when Washington played in Super Bowl VII. He was named head coach of the Montreal Alouettes (CFL) in 1973 and posted a 50-34-4 record and two Grey Cup victories (1974, 1977) in five seasons in Canada. After two seasons away from football, he became head coach of the Chicago Blitz of the USFL in 1984. No pro playing experience. Career record: 127-96.

Background: Running back at Coe College 1948-50. Coached at high school level for two years before returning to alma mater from 1953-55. Joined New Mexico staff in 1956 and served as head coach there in 1958-59. Head coach at California from 1960-63 before becoming head coach at William & Mary from 1964-68.

Personal: Born August 3, 1928, Chicago, Ill. Levy was Phi Beta Kappa at Coe College and earned master's degree in English history from Harvard. He lives with his wife Mary Frances in Hamburg, N.Y.

ASSISTANT COACHES

Tom Bresnahan, offensive coordinator-offensive line; born January 21, 1935, Springfield, Mass., lives in Orchard Park, N.Y. Tackle Holy Cross 1953-55. No pro playing experience. College coach: Williams 1963-67, Columbia 1968-72, Navy 1973-80. Pro coach: Kansas City Chiefs 1981-82, New York Giants 1983-84, St. Louis/Phoenix Cardinals 1986-88, joined Bills in 1989.

Ted Cottrell, linebackers; born June 13, 1947, Chester, Pa., lives in Orchard Park, N.Y. Linebacker Delaware Valley College 1966-68. Pro linebacker Atlanta Falcons 1969-70, Winnepeg Blue Bombers (CFL) 1971. College coach: Rutgers 1973-80, 1983. Pro coach: Kansas City Chiefs 1981-82, New Jersey Generals (USFL) 1983-84, Buffalo Bills 1986-89, Arizona Cardinals 1990-94, rejoined Bills in 1995.

Bruce DeHaven, special teams; born September 6, 1952, Trousdale, Kan., lives in East Aurora, N.Y. No college or pro playing experience. College coach: Kansas 1979-81, New Mexico State 1982. Pro coach: New Jersey Generals (USFL) 1983, Pittsburgh Maulers (USFL) 1984, Orlando Renegades (USFL) 1985, joined Bills in 1987.

Charlie Joiner, receivers; born October 14, 1947, Many, La., lives in Orchard Park, N.Y. Wide receiver Grambling 1965-68. Defensive back-wide receiver Houston Oilers 1969-72, Cincinnati Bengals 1972-75, San Diego Chargers 1976-86. Pro coach: San Diego Chargers 1987-91, joined Bills in 1992.

Rusty Jones, strength and conditioning; born August 14, 1953, Berwick, Maine, lives in Hamburg, N.Y. No college or pro playing experience. College coach: Springfield 1978-79. Pro coach: Pittsburgh Maulers (USFL) 1983-84, joined Bills in 1985.

Don Lawrence, offensive quality control-tight ends; born June 4, 1937, Cleveland, Ohio, lives in Orchard Park, N.Y. Offensive-defensive lineman Notre Dame 1957-58. Pro offensive-defensive lineman Washington Redskins 1959-61. College coach: Notre Dame 1961-63, Kansas State 1964-65, Cincinnati 1966, Virginia 1970-73 (head coach 1971-73), Texas Christian 1974-75, Missouri 1976-77. Pro coach: British Columbia Lions (CFL) 1978-79, Kansas City Chiefs 1980-82, 1987-88, Buffalo Bills 1983-84, Tampa Bay Buccaneers 1985-86, Winnipeg Blue Bombers (CFL) 1989, rejoined Bills in 1990.

Chuck Lester, administrative assistant to head coach, assistant linebackers coach; born May 18, 1955, Chicago, Ill., lives in Orchard Park, N.Y. Linebacker Oklahoma 1974. No pro playing experience. College coach: Iowa State 1980-81, Oklahoma 1982-84. Pro coach: Kansas City Chiefs 1984-86 (scout), joined Bills in 1987.

Wade Phillips, defensive coordinator; born June 21, 1947, Orange, Tex., lives in Orchard Park, N.Y. Linebacker Houston 1966-68. No pro playing experience. College coach: Houston, 1969, Oklahoma State 1973-74, Kansas 1975. Pro coach: Houston Oilers 1976-80, New Orleans Saints 1981-85 (head coach last four games of 1985), Philadelphia Eagles 1986-88, Denver Broncos 1989-94 (head coach 1993-94), joined Bills in 1995.

Elijah Pitts, assistant head coach-running backs; born February 3, 1938, Mayflower, Ark., lives in Orchard Park, N.Y. Running back Philander Smith 1957-60. Pro running back Green Bay Packers 1961-69, 1971, Los Angeles Rams 1970, Chicago Bears 1970, New Orleans Saints 1970. Pro coach: Los Angeles Rams 1974-77, Buffalo Bills 1978-80, Houston Oilers 1981-83, Hamilton Tiger-Cats (CFL) 1984, rejoined Bills in 1985.

Dick Roach, defensive backs; born August 23, 1937, Rapid City, S.D., lives in Orchard Park, N.Y. Defensive back Black Hills State 1952-55. No pro playing experience. College coach: Montana State 1966-69, Oregon State 1970, Wyoming 1971-72, Fresno State 1973, Washington State 1974-75. Pro coach: Montreal Alouettes (CFL) 1976-77, Kansas City Chiefs 1978-80, New England Patriots 1981, Michigan Panthers (USFL) 1983-84, Tampa Bay Buccaneers 1985-86, joined Bills in 1987.

Dan Sekanovich, defensive line; born July 27, 1933, West Hazelton, Pa., lives in Depew, N.Y. End Tennessee 1951-53. Pro defensive end Montreal Alouettes (CFL) 1954. College coach: Susquehanna 1961-63, Connecticut 1964-67, Pittsburgh 1968, Navy 1969-70, Kentucky 1971-72. Pro coach: Montreal Alouettes (CFL) 1973-76, New York Jets 1977-82, Atlanta Falcons 1983-85, Miami Dolphins 1986-91, joined Bills in 1992.

Jim Shofner, quarterbacks; born December 18, 1935, Grapevine, Tex., lives in Depew, N.Y. Running back Texas Christian 1955-57. Pro defensive back Cleveland Browns 1958-63. College coach: Texas Christian 1964-66, 1974-76 (head coach). Pro coach: San Francisco 49ers 1967-73, 1977, Cleveland Browns 1978-80, 1990-91 (head coach last 7 games in 1990, director of player personnel in 1991), Houston Oilers 1981-82, Dallas Cowboys 1983-85, St. Louis/Phoenix Cardinals 1986-89, joined Bills in 1992.

1995 FIRST-YEAR ROSTER

Name	Pos.	Ht.	Wt.	Birthdate	College	Hometown	How Acq.
Anderson, Jason	WR	6-0	175	9/11/71	Eastern Washington	Hoquiam, Wash.	FA
Armour, Justin	WR	6-4	221	1/1/73	Stanford	Colorado Springs, Colo.	D4b
Bender, Carey	RB	5-8	185	1/28/72	Coe College	Marion, Iowa	FA
Brown, Ruben	T	6-3	304	2/13/70	Pittsburgh	Lynchburg, Va.	D1
Clavelle, Shannon	DE	6-2	283	12/12/73	Colorado	Lafayette, La.	D6
Cline, Tony	TE	6-4	251	11/24/71	Stanford	Davis, Calif.	D4c
Collins, Todd	QB	6-4	224	11/5/71	Michigan	Walpole, Mass.	D2
Counts, Eric	NT	6-2	275	1/11/72	North Carolina State	Medford, N.J.	FA
Covington, Damien	DE-DT	5-11	236	12/4/72	North Carolina	Berlin, N.J.	D3b
Damas, Herve'	LB	6-0	235	2/16/72	Hofstra	New York, N.Y.	FA
Evans, Greg (1)	S	6-1	217	6/28/71	Texas Christian	Daingerfield, Tex.	FA
Evans, Randall	WR	5-11	190	10/26/70	St. Augustines	Virginia Beach, Va.	FA
Foster, Che'	FB	6-2	240	1/16/73	Michigan	Edmond, Okla.	FA
Glass, Myron	CB	5-8	170	1/10/73	Northern Iowa	Cedar Falls, Iowa	FA
Harvey, Steve	LB	6-3	230	4/21/71	Kansas	Leavenworth, Kan.	FA
Hendricks, Michael	DB	6-0	190	2/24/73	Texas A&M	San Antonio, Tex.	FA
Hill, Adrian	WR	6-2	180	10/14/72	North Carolina State	Asheville, N.C.	FA
Holecek, John	LB	6-2	238	5/7/72	Illinois	Steger, Ill.	D5
Holmes, Darick	RB	6-0	226	7/1/71	Portland State	Pasadena, Calif.	D7b
Irvin, Ken	CB	5-10	182	7/11/72	Memphis State	Rome, Ga.	D4a
Johnson, Filmel (1)	CB-S	5-10	187	12/24/70	Illinois	Detroit, Mich.	FA
Kerner, Marlon	CB	5-10	187	3/18/73	Ohio State	Columbus, Ohio	D3a
Nutten, Tom	C-G	6-4	276	6/8/71	Western Michigan	Mangog, Canada	D7a
Ostroski, Jerry (1)	G	6-4	310	7/12/70	Tulsa	Collegeville, Pa.	FA
Quinn, Terry	S	6-0	200	1/15/70	Louisville	Port St. Joe, Fla.	FA
Sheldon, Michael	G	6-4	278	6/8/73	Grand Valley State	Villa Park, Ill.	FA
Tindale, Tim (1)	RB	5-10	220	4/15/71	Western Ontario	London, Canada	FA
Van Pelt, Alex (1)	QB	6-1	219	5/1/70	Pittsburgh	Pittsburgh, Pa.	FA

The term NFL Rookie is defined as a player who is in his first season of professional football and has not been on the roster of another professional football team for any regular-season or postseason games. A Rookie is designated by an "R" on NFL rosters. Players who have been active in another professional football league or players who have NFL experience, including either preseason training camp or being on an Active List or Inactive List, or on Reserve/Injured or Reserve/Physically Unable to Perform for fewer than six regular-season games, are termed NFL First-Year Players. An NFL First-Year Player is designated by a "1" on NFL rosters. Thereafter, a player is credited with an additional year of experience for each season in which he accumulates six games on the Active List or Inactive List, or on Reserve/Injured or Reserve/Physically Unable to Perform.

NOTES

CINCINNATI BENGALS

American Football Conference
Central Division
Team Colors: Black, Orange, and White
200 Riverfront Stadium
Cincinnati, Ohio 45202
Telephone: (513) 621-3550

CLUB OFFICIALS

President/General Manager: Michael Brown
Vice President: John Sawyer
Assistant General Manager/Director of Player Personnel: Pete Brown
Secretary/Treasurer: Katherine Blackburn
Assistant Secretary/Treasurer; Scouting: Paul Brown
Scouting/Personnel: Jim Lippincott
Business Manager: Bill Connelly
Public Relations Director: Jack Brennan
Accountants: Jay Reis, Bill Scanlon
Ticket Manager: Paul Kelly
Consultant: John Murdough, Bill Johnson
Trainer: Paul Sparling
Assistant Trainer: Rob Recker
Equipment Manager: Tom Gray
Video Director: Al Davis
Stadium: Riverfront Stadium • **Capacity:** 60,389
200 Riverfront Stadium
Cincinnati, Ohio 45202
Playing Surface: AstroTurf-8
Training Camp: Wilmington College
Wilmington, Ohio 45177

1995 SCHEDULE

PRESEASON

Aug. 4	at Indianapolis	7:30
Aug. 11	**Tampa Bay**	7:30
Aug. 17	at Detroit	7:30
Aug. 25	**New York Jets**	7:30

REGULAR SEASON

Sept. 3	at Indianapolis	12:00
Sept. 10	**Jacksonville**	4:00
Sept. 17	at Seattle	1:00
Sept. 24	**Houston**	4:00
Oct. 1	**Miami**	1:00
Oct. 8	at Tampa Bay	1:00
Oct. 15	Open Date	
Oct. 19	at Pittsburgh (Thursday)	8:00
Oct. 29	**Cleveland**	1:00
Nov. 5	**Los Angeles**	4:00
Nov. 12	at Houston	12:00
Nov. 19	**Pittsburgh**	1:00
Nov. 26	at Jacksonville	1:00
Dec. 3	at Green Bay	12:00
Dec. 10	**Chicago**	1:00
Dec. 17	at Cleveland	1:00
Dec. 24	**Minnesota**	1:00

RECORD HOLDERS

INDIVIDUAL RECORDS—CAREER

Category	Name	Performance
Rushing (Yds.)	James Brooks, 1984-1991	6,447
Passing (Yds.)	Ken Anderson, 1971-1986	32,838
Passing (TDs)	Ken Anderson, 1971-1986	197
Receiving (No.)	Cris Collinsworth, 1981-88	417
Receiving (Yds.)	Isaac Curtis, 1973-1984	7,101
Interceptions	Ken Riley, 1969-1983	65
Punting (Avg.)	Dave Lewis, 1970-73	43.9
Punt Return (Avg.)	Mitchell Price, 1990-92	10.4
Kickoff Return (Avg.)	Lemar Parrish, 1970-77	24.7
Field Goals	Jim Breech, 1980-1992	225
Touchdowns (Tot.)	Pete Johnson, 1977-1983	70
Points	Jim Breech, 1980-1992	1,151

INDIVIDUAL RECORDS—SINGLE SEASON

Category	Name	Performance
Rushing (Yds.)	James Brooks, 1989	1,239
Passing (Yds.)	Boomer Esiason, 1986	3,959
Passing (TDs)	Ken Anderson, 1981	29
Receiving (No.)	Dan Ross, 1981	71
	Carl Pickens, 1994	71
Receiving (Yds.)	Eddie Brown, 1988	1,273
Interceptions	Ken Riley, 1976	9
Punting (Avg.)	Dave Lewis, 1970	46.2
Punt Return (Avg.)	Mike Martin, 1984	15.7
Kickoff Return (Avg.)	Lemar Parrish, 1970	30.2
Field Goals	Doug Pelfrey, 1994	28
Touchdowns (Tot.)	Pete Johnson, 1981	16
Points	Jim Breech, 1985	120

INDIVIDUAL RECORDS—SINGLE GAME

Category	Name	Performance
Rushing (Yds.)	James Brooks, 12-23-90	201
Passing (Yds.)	Boomer Esiason, 10-7-90	490
Passing (TDs)	Boomer Esiason, 12-21-86	5
	Boomer Esiason, 10-29-89	5
Receiving (No.)	James Brooks, 12-25-89	12
Receiving (Yds.)	Eddie Brown, 11-6-88	216
Interceptions	Many times	3
	Last time by David Fulcher, 12-16-89	
Field Goals	Doug Pelfrey, 11-6-94	6
Touchdowns (Tot.)	Larry Kinnebrew, 10-28-84	4
Points	Larry Kinnebrew, 10-28-84	24

COACHING HISTORY

(187-212-1)

1968-75	Paul Brown	55-59-1
1976-78	Bill Johnson*	18-15-0
1978-79	Homer Rice	8-19-0
1980-83	Forrest Gregg	34-27-0
1984-91	Sam Wyche	64-68-0
1992-94	Dave Shula	11-37-0

*Resigned after five games in 1978

RIVERFRONT STADIUM

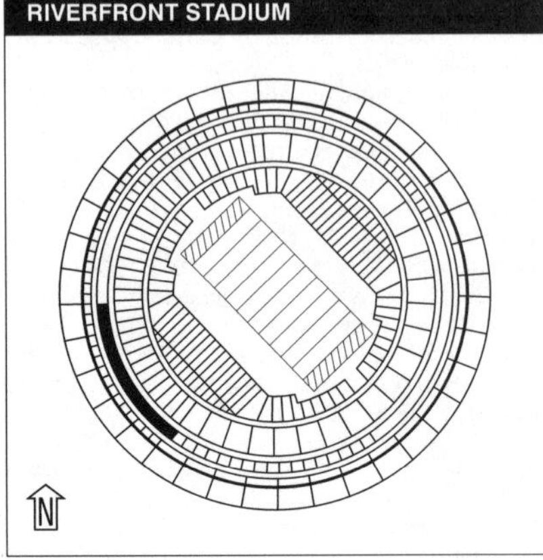

1994 TEAM RECORD

PRESEASON (1-3)

Date	Result		Opponent
8/6	L	16-17	at Tampa Bay
8/13	L	21-26	Indianapolis
8/20	L	7-17	at Philadelphia
8/26	W	38-14	Detroit

REGULAR SEASON (3-13)

Date	Result		Opponents	Att.
9/4	L	20-28	Cleveland	52,778
9/11	L	10-27	at San Diego	53,217
9/18	L	28-31	New England	46,640
9/25	L	13-20	at Houston	44,253
10/2	L	7-23	Miami	55,056
10/16	L	10-14	at Pittsburgh	55,353
10/23	L	13-37	at Cleveland	77,588
10/30	L	20-23	Dallas	57,096
11/6	W	20-17	at Seattle (OT)	46,630
11/13	W	34-31	Houston	54,908
11/20	L	13-17	Indianapolis	55,566
11/27	L	13-15	at Denver	69,714
12/4	L	15-38	Pittsburgh	53,401
12/11	L	20-27	at N.Y. Giants	67,530
12/18	L	7-28	at Arizona	50,110
12/24	W	33-30	Philadelphia	39,923

(OT) Overtime

SCORE BY PERIODS

Bengals	58	66	53	96	3	—	276
Opponents	85	149	79	93	0	—	406

ATTENDANCE

Home 415,368 Away 464,395 Total 879,763
Single-game home record, 60,284 (10-17-71)
Single-season home record, 473,288 (1990)

1994 TEAM STATISTICS

	Bengals	Opp.
Total First Downs	267	310
Rushing	84	126
Passing	158	168
Penalty	25	16
Third Down: Made/Att	66/213	92/231
Third Down Pct.	31.0	39.8
Fourth Down: Made/Att	12/22	4/8
Fourth Down Pct.	54.5	50.0
Total Net Yards	4792	5154
Avg. Per Game	299.5	322.1
Total Plays	990	1053
Avg. Per Play	4.8	4.9
Net Yards Rushing	1556	1906
Avg. Per Game	97.3	119.1
Total Rushes	404	517
Net Yards Passing	3236	3248
Avg. Per Game	202.3	203.0
Sacked/Yards Lost	44/305	31/210
Gross Yards	3541	3458
Att./Completions	542/289	505/294
Completion Pct.	53.3	58.2
Had Intercepted	19	10
Punts/Avg.	80/43.3	87/40.6
Net Punting Avg.	80/35.3	87/34.4
Penalties/Yards Lost	90/618	99/861
Fumbles/Ball Lost	31/22	26/8
Touchdowns	27	45
Rushing	5	16
Passing	21	22
Returns	1	7
Avg. Time of Possession	27:11	32:49

1994 INDIVIDUAL STATISTICS

PASSING	Att.	Comp.	Yds.	Pct.	TD	Int.	Tkld.	Rate
Blake	306	156	2154	51.0	14	9	19/120	76.9
Klingler	231	131	1327	56.7	6	9	24/165	65.7
Hollas	2	0	0	0.0	0	1	1/20	0.0
L. Johnson	1	1	7	100.0	1	0	0/0	135.4
Scott	1	1	53	100.0	0	0	0/0	118.8
Broussard	1	0	0	0.0	0	0	0/0	39.6
Bengals	542	289	3541	53.3	21	19	44/305	72.0
Opponents	505	294	3458	58.2	22	10	31/210	85.4

SCORING	TD R	TD P	TD Rt	PAT	FG	Saf	PTS
Pelfrey	0	0	0	24/25	28/33	0	108
Pickens	0	11	0	0/0	0/0	0	66
Scott	0	5	0	0/0	0/0	0	30
Broussard	2	0	0	0/0	0/0	0	14
Fenner	1	1	0	0/0	0/0	0	12
Green	1	1	0	0/0	0/0	0	12
Blake	1	0	0	0/0	0/0	0	8
Cothran	0	1	0	0/0	0/0	0	6
Ti. McGee	0	1	0	0/0	0/0	0	6
To. McGee	0	1	0	0/0	0/0	0	6
Sawyer	0	0	1	0/0	0/0	0	6
A. Williams	0	0	0	0/0	0/0	1	2
Bengals	5	21	1	24/25	28/33	1	276
Opponents	16	22	7	41/41	31/35	0	406

2-Point conversions: Blake, Broussard. Team: 2-2.

RUSHING	Att.	Yds.	Avg.	LG	TD
Fenner	141	468	3.3	21	1
Broussard	94	403	4.3	37t	2
Green	76	223	2.9	22	1
Blake	37	204	5.5	16	1
Scott	10	106	10.6	23	0
Klingler	17	85	5.0	15	0
Cothran	26	85	3.3	13	0
Ball	2	0	0.0	1	0
Ti. McGee	1	-18	-18.0	-18	0
Bengals	404	1556	3.9	37t	5
Opponents	517	1906	3.7	40	16

RECEIVING	No.	Yds.	Avg.	LG	TD
Pickens	71	1127	15.9	70t	11
Scott	46	866	18.8	76	5
To. McGee	40	492	12.3	54	1
Fenner	36	276	7.7	29	1
Broussard	34	218	6.4	25	0
Green	27	267	9.9	34	1
Ti. McGee	13	175	13.5	25	1
Sadowski	11	54	4.9	11	0
Query	5	44	8.8	14	0
Cothran	4	24	6.0	8	1
Ball	1	4	4.0	4	0
Klingler	1	-6	-6.0	-6	0
Bengals	289	3541	12.3	76	21
Opponents	294	3458	11.8	81	22

INTERCEPTIONS	No.	Yds.	Avg.	LG	TD
Oliver	3	36	12.0	19	0
Brim	2	72	36.0	49	0
D. Williams	2	45	22.5	33	0
Sawyer	2	0	0.0	0	0
Tovar	1	14	14.0	14	0
Bengals	10	167	16.7	49	0
Opponents	19	176	9.3	41	2

PUNTING	No.	Yds.	Avg.	In 20	LG
L. Johnson	79	3461	43.8	19	64
Bengals	80	3461	43.3	19	64
Opponents	87	3528	40.6	30	60

PUNT RETURNS	No.	FC	Yds.	Avg.	LG	TD
Sawyer	26	16	307	11.8	82t	1
Pickens	9	2	62	6.9	16	0
D. Williams	1	0	4	4.0	4	0
Rog. Jones	1	0	0	0.0	0	0
Bengals	37	18	373	10.1	82t	1
Opponents	43	12	459	10.7	92t	2

KICKOFF RETURNS	No.	Yds.	Avg.	LG	TD
Ball	42	915	21.8	43	0
Scott	15	342	22.8	34	0
Hardy	8	185	23.1	42	0
Broussard	7	115	16.4	24	0
Green	5	113	22.6	31	0
Hill	4	97	24.3	40	0
Stegall	1	16	16.0	16	0
Sawyer	1	14	14.0	14	0
Tovar	1	8	8.0	8	0
To. McGee	1	4	4.0	4	0
Shaw	1	1	1.0	1	0
Bengals	86	1810	21.0	43	0
Opponents	61	1408	23.1	94t	2

SACKS	No.
A. Williams	9.5
Wilkinson	5.5
Francis	4.5
Tovar	3.0
Rucker	2.0
Rog. Jones	1.5
Copeland	1.0
Krumrie	1.0
McDonald	1.0
Oliver	1.0
D. Williams	1.0
Bengals	31.0
Opponents	44.0

1995 DRAFT CHOICES

Round	Name	Pos.	College
1	Ki-Jana Carter	RB	Penn State
3	Melvin Tuten	T	Syracuse
4	Sam Shade	DB	Alabama
5	David Dunn	WR	Fresno State
6	Ryan Grigson	T	Purdue
7	John Walsh	QB	Brigham Young

CINCINNATI BENGALS

1995 VETERAN ROSTER

No.		Name	Pos.	Ht.	Wt.	Birthdate	NFL Exp.	College	Hometown	How Acq.	'94 Games/ Starts
21		Bieniemy, Eric	RB	5-7	198	8/15/69	5	Colorado	New Orleans, La.	UFA(SD)-'95	16/0*
8		Blake, Jeff	QB	6-0	202	12/4/70	4	East Carolina	Sanford, Fla.	W(NYJ)-'94	10/9
74		Braham, Rich	T	6-4	290	11/6/70	2	West Virginia	Morgantown, W. Va.	W(Ariz)-'94	3/0
58	#	Braxton, David	LB	6-2	230	5/26/65	7	Wake Forest	Jacksonville, N.C.	UFA(Ariz)-'94	9/0
65		Brilz, Darrick	G	6-3	287	2/14/64	9	Oregon State	Pinole Valley, Calif.	UFA(Sea)-'94	15/15
43		Brim, Mike	CB	6-0	192	1/23/66	8	Virginia Union	Danville, Va.	UFA(NYJ)-'93	16/16
33		Broussard, Steve	RB	5-7	201	2/22/67	6	Washington State	Los Angeles, Calif.	FA-'94	13/3
72		Brumfield, Scott	T	6-8	320	8/19/70	3	Brigham Young	Spanish Fork, Utah	FA-'94	2/0
68		Cadigan, Dave	G	6-4	285	4/6/65	8	Southern California	Newport Beach, Calif.	FA-'94	13/13
55		Collins, Andre	LB	6-1	231	5/4/68	6	Penn State	Cinaminson, N.J.	FA-'95	16/16*
92		Copeland, John	DE	6-3	286	9/20/70	3	Alabama	Lanett, Ala.	D1-'93	12/12
46		Cothran, Jeff	RB	6-1	249	6/28/71	2	Ohio State	Middletown, Ohio	D3-'94	14/4
96		Flores, Mike	DE	6-3	256	12/1/66	5	Louisville	Youngstown, Ohio	UFA(Phil)-'95	15/2*
50	†	Francis, James	LB	6-5	252	8/4/68	6	Baylor	Houston, Tex.	D1-'90	16/16
83		Frisch, David	TE	6-7	260	6/22/70	3	Colorado State	House Springs, Mo.	FA-'93	16/0
28		Green, Harold	RB	6-2	222	1/29/68	6	South Carolina	Ladson, S.C.	D2-'90	14/11
45		Hardy, Adrian	CB	5-11	194	8/16/70	3	Northwestern Louisiana	New Orleans, La.	W(SF)-'94	16/0*
51		Hollinquest, Lamont	LB	6-3	245	10/24/70	3	Southern California	Downey, Calif.	W(Wash)-'94	14/0*
57		Jefferson, Kevin	LB	6-2	232	1/14/74	2	Lehigh	Greensburg, Pa.	FA-'94	6/0
11		Johnson, Lee	P-K	6-2	200	11/27/61	11	Brigham Young	Conroe, Tex.	W(Clev)-'88	16/0
66		Jones, Dan	T	6-7	298	7/22/70	3	Maine	Maiden, Mass.	FA-'93	14/0
25		Jones, Rod	CB	6-0	185	3/31/64	10	Southern Methodist	Dallas, Tex.	T(TB)-'90	16/16
24		Jones, Roger	CB	5-9	175	4/22/69	5	Tennessee State	Nashville, Tenn.	W(TB)-'94	16/0
32		Joseph, James	RB	6-2	222	10/28/67	5	Auburn	Phenix City, Ala.	UFA(Phil)-'95	14/5*
7		Klinger, David	QB	6-2	205	2/17/69	4	Houston	Stratford, Tex.	D1a-'92	10/7
64		Kozerski, Bruce	G	6-4	287	4/2/62	12	Holy Cross	Plains, Pa.	D9-'84	16/16
56	†	McDonald, Ricardo	LB	6-2	235	11/8/69	4	Pittsburgh	Kingston, Jamaica	D4-'92	13/13
85		McGee, Tim	WR	5-10	183	8/7/64	10	Tennessee	Cleveland, Ohio	FA-'94	14/1
82		McGee, Tony	TE	6-3	246	4/21/71	3	Michigan	Terre Haute, Ind.	D2-'93	16/16
60	#	Moore, Eric	G	6-5	290	1/21/65	8	Indiana	Berkeley, Mo.	UFA(NYJ)-'94	6/6
73	#	Moyer, Ken	C	6-7	297	11/19/66	6	Toledo	Temperance, Mich.	FA-'89	16/14
93		Parten, Ty	DE	6-4	272	10/13/69	3	Arizona	Washington, D.C.	D3a-'93	14/4
9		Pelfrey, Doug	K	5-11	185	9/25/70	3	Kentucky	Ft. Thomas, Ky.	D8-'93	16/0
81		Pickens, Carl	WR	6-2	206	3/23/70	4	Tennessee	Murphy, N.C.	D2-'92	15/15
76		Pollard, Trent	T	6-4	304	11/20/72	2	Eastern Washington	Seattle, Wash.	D5-'94	8/0
89		Query, Jeff	WR	6-0	165	3/7/67	7	Millikin	Maroa, Ill.	W(Hou)-'92	10/4
95		Rucker, Keith	DT	6-4	340	11/20/68	4	Ohio Wesleyan	University Park, Ill.	FA-'94	16/14
87		Sadowski, Troy	TE	6-5	250	12/8/65	6	Georgia	Atlanta, Ga.	UFA(NYJ)-'94	15/1
77		Sargent, Kevin	T	6-6	284	3/31/69	4	Eastern Washington	Bremerton, Wash.	FA-'92	15/15
23		Sawyer, Corey	CB	5-11	171	10/4/71	2	Florida State	Key West, Fla.	D4-'94	15/0
86		Scott, Darnay	WR	6-1	180	7/7/72	2	San Diego State	St. Louis, Mo.	D2-'94	16/12
52		Shine, Steve	LB	6-6	232	11/28/70	2	Northwestern	Kokomo, Ind.	D3a-'94	0*
70		Smith, Artie	DE	6-4	285	5/15/70	3	Louisiana Tech	Stillwater, Okla.	W(SF)-'94	9/0*
79		Stallings, Ramondo	DE	6-7	285	11/21/71	2	San Diego State	Winston-Salem, N.C.	D7-'94	6/0
58		Tovar, Steve	LB	6-3	244	4/25/70	3	Ohio State	Elyria, Ohio	D3-'93	16/16
59		Truitt, Greg	LS	6-0	235	12/8/65	2	Penn State	Sarasota, Fla.	FA-'94	16/0
34	#	Vinson, Fernandus	S	5-10	197	11/3/68	5	North Carolina State	Montgomery, Ala.	D7-'91	16/4
67		von Oelhoffen, Kimo	DT	6-4	300	1/30/71	2	Boise State	Molokai, Hawaii	D6-'94	7/0
27		Walker, Bracey	S	5-10	200	10/28/70	2	North Carolina	Pine Forest, N.C.	W(KC)-'94	9/0*
91		Wallerstedt, Brett	LB	6-1	240	11/24/70	3	Arizona State	Manhattan, Kan.	FA-'94	10/0
63		Walter, Joe	T	6-7	292	6/18/63	11	Texas Tech	Dallas, Tex.	D7a-'85	0*
88		Ware, Derek	TE	6-2	255	9/17/67	4	Central State, Ohio	Sacramento, Calif.	W(Ariz)-'94	15/12*
37		Wheeler, Leonard	CB	5-11	189	1/15/69	4	Troy State	Toccoa, Ga.	D3-'92	0*
4		Wilhelm, Erik	QB	6-3	217	11/9/65	6	Oregon State	Lake Oswego, Ore.	FA-'94	1/0
99		Wilkinson, Dan	DT	6-5	313	3/13/73	2	Ohio State	Dayton, Ohio	D1-'94	16/14
94	#	Williams, Alfred	DE	6-6	265	11/6/68	5	Colorado	Houston, Tex.	D1-'91	16/16
31		Williams, Darryl	S	6-0	191	1/7/70	4	Miami	Miami, Fla.	D1a-'92	16/16

* Bieniemy played 16 games with San Diego in '94; Collins played 16 games with Washington; Flores played 15 games with Philadelphia; Hardy played 2 games with San Francisco, 14 games with Cincinnati; Hollinquest played 14 games with Washington; Joesph played 14 games with Philadelphia; Shine, Walter, and Wheeler missed '94 season because of injury; Smith played 2 games with San Francisco, 7 games with Cincinnati; Walker played 2 games with Kansas City, 7 games with Cincinnati; Ware played 15 games with Arizona.

Unrestricted free agent; subject to developments.

† Restricted free agent; subject to developments.

Players lost through free agency (2): RB Derrick Fenner (Raid; 16 games in '94), QB Don Hollas (Det, 2).

Players lost through Expansion Draft (2): RB Eric Ball (Car; 16 games in '94), LB Santo Stephens (Jax; 14).

Also played with Bengals in '94—T Mark Dennis (7 games), S Forey Duckett (2), DE Mike Frier (1), WR Jeff Hill (1), LB John Johnson (5), DT Tim Krumrie (16), DE Kanavis McGhee (1), S Louis Oliver (12), LB Eric Shaw (3), WR Milt Stegall (1).

COACHING STAFF

Head Coach,
Dave Shula

Pro Career: Shula is in his fourth year as head coach of the Cincinnati Bengals. He became the sixth head coach in Bengals history on December 27, 1991. Shula was offensive coordinator and quarterbacks coach for Dallas in 1989-90 before joining Cincinnati in 1991 as receivers coach. Shula began his coaching career with the Miami Dolphins in 1982. In 1988, Shula was named assistant head coach with the Dolphins. He was a wide receiver and kick return specialist with the Baltimore Colts in 1981. Career record: 11-37.

Background: Outstanding wide receiver at Dartmouth where he was a two-time All-Ivy League selection.

Personal: Born May 28, 1959, Lexington, Ky. Dave and his wife, Leslie, live in Cincinnati, and have three sons—Daniel, Christopher, and Matthew.

ASSISTANT COACHES

Paul Alexander, offensive line; born February 12, 1960, Rochester, N.Y., lives in Cincinnati. Tackle Cortland State 1979-81. No pro playing experience. College coach: Penn State 1982-84, Michigan 1985-86, Central Michigan 1987-91. Pro coach: New York Jets 1992-93, joined Bengals in 1994.

Jim Anderson, running backs; born March 27, 1948, Harrisburg, Pa., lives in Cincinnati. Linebacker-defensive end Cal Western (U.S. International) 1967-70. No pro playing experience. College coach: Cal Western 1970-71, Scottsdale, Ariz., Community College 1973, Nevada-Las Vegas 1974-75, Southern Methodist 1976-80, Stanford 1981-83. Pro coach: Joined Bengals in 1984.

Ken Anderson, quarterbacks; born February 15, 1949, Batavia, Ill., lives in Lakeside Park, Ky. Quarterback Augustana (Ill.) 1967-70. Pro quarterback Cincinnati Bengals 1971-86. Pro coach: Joined Bengals in 1992.

Bruce Coslet, offensive coordinator-tight ends; born August 5, 1946, Oakdale, Calif., lives in Cincinnati. Tight end University of Pacific 1965-67. Pro tight end Cincinnati Bengals 1969-76. Pro coach: San Francisco 49ers 1980, Cincinnati Bengals 1981-89, New York Jets (head coach) 1990-93, rejoined Bengals in 1994.

Bobby DePaul, defensive line; born January 24, 1963, Bowie, Md., lives in Cincinnati. Linebacker Maryland 1981-84. No pro playing experience. College coach: Catholic University 1986-88. Pro coach: Washington Redskins 1989-93, joined Bengals in 1994.

John Garrett, offensive assistant; born March 2, 1965, Danville, Pa., lives in Cincinnati. Wide receiver Columbia 1983-84, Princeton 1987. Pro wide receiver Cincinnati Bengals 1989, San Antonio Riders (World League) 1991. Pro coach: Tampa Bay Buccaneers 1992-94 (Pro Personnel Assistant), joined Bengals in 1995.

Tim Krumrie, defensive assistant, born May 20, 1960, Menomonie, Wis., lives in Cincinnati. Defensive tackle Wisconsin 1979-82. Pro defensive tackle Cincinnati Bengals 1983-94. Pro coach: Joined Bengals in 1995.

Ron Meeks, defensive backfield; born August 27, 1954, Jacksonville, Fla., lives in Cincinnati. Defensive back Arkansas State 1975-76. Pro defensive back Hamilton Tiger-Cats (CFL) 1977-79, Ottawa Roughriders (CFL) 1979, Toronto Argonauts (CFL) 1980-81. College coach: Arkansas State 1984-85, Miami 1986-87, New Mexico State 1988, Fresno State 1989-90. Pro coach: Dallas Cowboys 1991, joined Bengals in 1992.

Joe Pascale, linebackers; born April 4, 1946, New York, N.Y., lives in Cincinnati. Linebacker Connecticut 1963-66. No pro playing experience. College coach: Connecticut 1967-68, Rhode Island 1969-73, Idaho State 1974-76 (head coach 1976), Princeton 1977-79. Pro coach: Montreal Alouettes (CFL) 1980-81. Ottawa Rough Riders (CFL) 1982-83, New Jersey Generals (USFL) 1984-85, St. Louis/Phoenix Cardinals 1986-93, joined Bengals in 1994.

Larry Peccatiello, defensive coordinator; born December 21, 1937, Newark, N.J., lives in Cincinnati. Receiver William & Mary 1955-58. No pro playing experience. College coach: William & Mary 1961-68, Navy 1969-70, Rice 1971. Pro coach: Houston Oilers 1972-75, Seattle Seahawks 1976-80, Washington Redskins 1981-93, joined Bengals in 1994.

Joe Wessel, special teams; born January 5, 1962, Miami, Fla., lives in Cincinnati. Quarterback-safety Florida State 1981-84. No pro playing experience. College coach: Louisiana State 1985-90, Notre Dame 1991-93. Pro coach: Joined Bengals in 1994.

Kim Wood, strength; born July 12, 1945, Barrington, Ill., lives in Cincinnati. Running back Wisconsin 1965-68. No pro playing experience. Pro coach: Joined Bengals in 1975.

1995 FIRST-YEAR ROSTER

Name	Pos.	Ht.	Wt.	Birthdate	College	Hometown	How Acq.
Bailey, Thomas	WR	6-0	196	12/6/71	Auburn	Dallas, Tex.	FA
Brown, Anthony	T	6-5	310	11/6/72	Utah	Salt Lake City, Utah	FA
Burns, Jason	RB	5-7	195	11/27/72	Wisconsin	Chicago, Ill.	FA
Carter, Ki-Jana	RB	5-10	227	9/12/73	Penn State	Westerville, Ohio	D1
Collins, Gerald	LB	6-2	250	2/13/71	Vanderbilt	St. Loius, Mo.	FA
Dickerson, Bryan	RB	6-1	260	3/22/72	Eastern Kentucky	Louisville, Ky.	FA
Dunn, David	WR	6-3	210	6/10/72	Fresno State	San Diego, Calif.	D5
Forsythe, Ray	G	6-3	310	2/13/72	Central Florida	Oakland, Fla.	FA
Grigson, Ryan	T	6-6	290	2/23/72	Purdue	Highland, Ind.	D6
Hill, Jeff (1)	WR	5-11	178	9/24/72	Purdue	Cincinnati, Ohio	FA
Joseph, Sherrard	T	6-5	304	7/27/72	Connecticut	Farmingdale, N.Y.	FA
Rhodes, David	WR	6-1	200	3/15/72	Central Florida	Mulberry, Fla.	FA
Rowlett, J.J.	WR	6-3	212	10/15/72	Texas-El Paso	San Diego, Calif.	FA
Shade, Sam	S	6-1	191	6/14/73	Alabama	Birmingham, Ala.	D4
Shelling, Chris	CB	5-10	180	11/13/72	Auburn	Columbus, Ga.	FA
Stewart, Vince	DT	6-4	295	5/7/72	Penn State	Shirley, N.Y.	FA
Toomer, Donald	CB	6-1	180	8/10/72	Utah State	Berkeley, Calif.	FA
Tuten, Melvin	T	6-6	305	11/11/71	Syracuse	Washington, D.C.	D3
Walsh, John	QB	6-4	215	12/12/72	Brigham Young	Torrance, Calif.	D7
Yurkiewicz, Rich	LB	6-3	220	5/2/73	Kent State	Parma, Ohio	FA

The term NFL Rookie is defined as a player who is in his first season of professional football and has not been on the roster of another professional football team for any regular-season or postseason games. A Rookie is designated by an "R" on NFL rosters. Players who have been active in another professional football league or players who have NFL experience, including either preseason training camp or being on an Active List or Inactive List, or on Reserve/Injured or Reserve/Physically Unable to Perform for fewer than six regular-season games, are termed NFL First-Year Players. An NFL First-Year Player is designated by a "1" on NFL rosters. Thereafter, a player is credited with an additional year of experience for each season in which he accumulates six games on the Active List or Inactive List, or on Reserve/Injured or Reserve/Physically Unable to Perform.

NOTES

CLEVELAND BROWNS

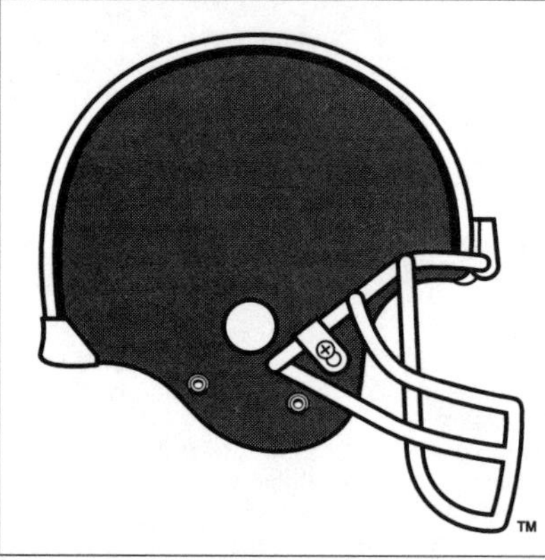

American Football Conference
Central Division
Team Colors: Seal Brown, Orange, and White
80 First Avenue
Berea, Ohio 44017
Telephone: (216) 891-5000

CLUB OFFICIALS

President and Owner: Arthur B. Modell
Executive Vice President/Legal and Administration: Jim Bailey
Vice President/Assistant to President: David Modell
Vice President/Public Relations: Kevin Byrne
Director of Player Personnel: Michael Lombardi
Director of Pro Personnel: Ozzie Newsome
Treasurer: Mike Srsen
Director of Operations/Information: Bob Eller
Director of Business Operations: Pat Moriarty
Assistant Director of Public Relations: Francine Lubera
Player Relations/Media Services: Dino Lucarelli
Scouts: Tom Dimitroff, Ron Marciniak, Terry McDonough, Vince Newsome, Ernie Plank, Ellis Rainsberger, Phil Savage, Bill Shunkwiler, Lionel Vital
Head Trainer: Bill Tessendorf
Facilities Manager: Charley Cusick
Equipment Manager: Ed Carroll
Stadium: Cleveland Stadium • **Capacity:** 78,512
West 3rd Street
Cleveland, Ohio 44114
Playing Surface: Grass
Training Camp: 80 First Avenue
Berea, Ohio 44017

1995 SCHEDULE

PRESEASON

Aug. 6	**New York Giants**	4:00
Aug. 14	**Chicago**	8:00
Aug. 19	at Atlanta	7:00
Aug. 25	at Arizona	7:30

REGULAR SEASON

Sept. 3	at New England	1:00
Sept. 10	**Tampa Bay**	1:00
Sept. 17	at Houston	12:00
Sept. 24	**Kansas City**	4:00
Oct. 2	**Buffalo** (Monday)	9:00
Oct. 8	at Detroit	4:00
Oct. 15	Open Date	
Oct. 22	**Jacksonville**	1:00
Oct. 29	at Cincinnati	1:00
Nov. 5	**Houston**	1:00
Nov. 13	at Pittsburgh (Monday)	9:00
Nov. 19	**Green Bay**	1:00
Nov. 26	**Pittsburgh**	4:00
Dec. 3	at San Diego	1:00
Dec. 9	at Minnesota (Saturday)	11:30
Dec. 17	**Cincinnati**	1:00
Dec. 24	at Jacksonville	1:00

RECORD HOLDERS

INDIVIDUAL RECORDS—CAREER

Category	Name	Performance
Rushing (Yds.)	Jim Brown, 1957-1965	12,312
Passing (Yds.)	Brian Sipe, 1974-1983	23,713
Passing (TDs)	Brian Sipe, 1974-1983	154
Receiving (No.)	Ozzie Newsome, 1978-1990	662
Receiving (Yds.)	Ozzie Newsome, 1978-1990	7,980
Interceptions	Thom Darden, 1972-74, 1976-1981	45
Punting (Avg.)	Horace Gillom, 1950-56	43.8
Punt Return (Avg.)	Greg Pruitt, 1973-1981	11.8
Kickoff Return (Avg.)	Greg Pruitt, 1973-1981	26.3
Field Goals	Lou Groza, 1950-59, 1961-67	234
Touchdowns (Tot.)	Jim Brown, 1957-1965	126
Points	Lou Groza, 1950-59, 1961-67	1,349

INDIVIDUAL RECORDS—SINGLE SEASON

Category	Name	Performance
Rushing (Yds.)	Jim Brown, 1963	1,863
Passing (Yds.)	Brian Sipe, 1980	4,132
Passing (TDs)	Brian Sipe, 1980	30
Receiving (No.)	Ozzie Newsome, 1983	89
	Ozzie Newsome, 1984	89
Receiving (Yds.)	Webster Slaughter, 1989	1,236
Interceptions	Thom Darden, 1978	10
Punting (Avg.)	Gary Collins, 1965	46.7
Punt Return (Avg.)	Leroy Kelly, 1965	15.6
Kickoff Return (Avg.)	Billy Reynolds, 1954	29.5
Field Goals	Matt Bahr, 1984	24
	Matt Bahr, 1988	24
Touchdowns (Tot.)	Jim Brown, 1965	21
Points	Jim Brown, 1965	126

INDIVIDUAL RECORDS—SINGLE GAME

Category	Name	Performance
Rushing (Yds.)	Jim Brown, 11-24-57	237
	Jim Brown, 11-19-61	237
Passing (Yds.)	Bernie Kosar, 1-3-87	489
Passing (TDs)	Frank Ryan, 12-12-64	5
	Bill Nelsen, 11-2-69	5
	Brian Sipe, 10-7-79	5
Receiving (No.)	Ozzie Newsome, 10-14-84	14
Receiving (Yds.)	Ozzie Newsome, 10-14-84	191
Interceptions	Many times	3
	Last time by Frank Minnifield, 11-22-87	
Field Goals	Don Cockroft, 10-19-75	5
Touchdowns (Tot.)	Dub Jones, 11-25-51	*6
Points	Dub Jones, 11-25-51	36

*NFL Record

COACHING HISTORY

(380-274-10)

1950-62	Paul Brown	115-49-5
1963-70	Blanton Collier	79-38-2
1971-74	Nick Skorich	30-26-2
1975-77	Forrest Gregg*	18-23-0
1977	Dick Modzelewski	0-1-0
1978-84	Sam Rutigliano**	47-52-0
1984-88	Marty Schottenheimer	46-31-0
1989-90	Bud Carson***	12-14-1
1990	Jim Shofner	1-6-0
1991-94	Bill Belichick	32-34-0

*Resigned after 13 games in 1977
**Released after eight games in 1984
***Released after nine games in 1990

CLEVELAND STADIUM

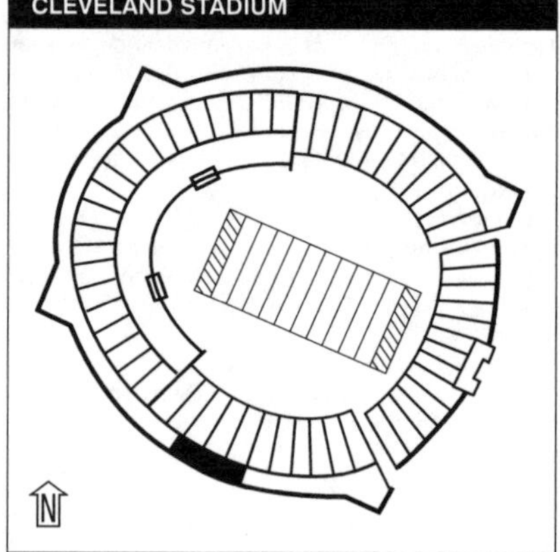

1994 TEAM RECORD

PRESEASON (3-1)

Date	Result		Opponents
8/6	W	24-15	at N.Y. Giants
8/13	W	16-7	Detroit
8/19	W	28-7	Atlanta
8/25	L	7-24	at Indianapolis

REGULAR SEASON (11-5)

Date	Result		Opponents	Att.
9/4	W	28-20	at Cincinnati	52,778
9/11	L	10-17	Pittsburgh	77,774
9/18	W	32- 0	Arizona	62,818
9/25	W	21-14	at Indianapolis	55,821
10/2	W	27- 7	N.Y. Jets	76,188
10/13	W	11- 8	at Houston	50,364
10/23	W	37-13	Cincinnati	77,588
10/30	L	14-26	at Denver	73,190
11/6	W	13- 6	New England	73,878
11/13	W	26- 7	at Philadelphia	65,233
11/20	L	13-20	at Kansas City	69,121
11/27	W	34-10	Houston	65,088
12/4	L	13-16	N.Y. Giants	72,068
12/10	W	19-14	at Dallas	64,826
12/18	L	7-17	at Pittsburgh	60,808
12/24	W	35- 9	Seattle	54,180

POSTSEASON (1-1)

1/1	W	20-13	New England	77,452
1/7	L	9-29	at Pittsburgh	58,185

(OT) Overtime

SCORE BY PERIODS

Browns	65	121	55	99	0	—	340
Opponents	52	58	28	66	0	—	204

ATTENDANCE

Home 559,582 Away 492,141 Total 1,051,723

Single-game home record, 85,073 (9-21-70)

Single-season home record, 620,496 (1980)

1994 TEAM STATISTICS

	Browns	Opp.
Total First Downs	273	304
Rushing	80	98
Passing	161	173
Penalty	32	33
Third Down: Made/Att	69/204	83/242
Third Down Pct.	33.8	34.3
Fourth Down: Made/Att	4/12	7/18
Fourth Down Pct.	33.3	38.9
Total Net Yards	4832	4826
Avg. Per Game	302.0	301.6
Total Plays	970	1090
Avg. Per Play	5.0	4.4
Net Yards Rushing	1657	1669
Avg. Per Game	103.6	104.3
Total Rushes	449	465
Net Yards Passing	3175	3157
Avg. Per Game	198.4	197.3
Sacked/Yards Lost	14/94	38/268
Gross Yards	3269	3425
Att./Completions	507/266	587/325
Completion Pct.	52.5	55.4
Had Intercepted	21	18
Punts/Avg.	80/40.1	97/40.0
Net Punting Avg.	80/35.4	97/33.0
Penalties/Yards Lost	113/969	129/1139
Fumbles/Ball Lost	26/14	26/13
Touchdowns	37	22
Rushing	12	9
Passing	20	13
Returns	5	0
Avg. Time of Possession	28:44	31:16

1994 INDIVIDUAL STATISTICS

PASSING	Att.	Comp.	Yds.	Pct.	TD	Int.	Tkld.	Rate
Testaverde	376	207	2575	55.1	16	18	12/83	70.7
Rypien	128	59	694	46.1	4	3	2/11	63.7
Jackson	2	0	0	0.0	0	0	0/0	39.6
Metcalf	1	0	0	0.0	0	0	0/0	39.6
Browns	507	266	3269	52.5	20	21	14/94	68.6
Opponents	587	325	3425	55.4	13	18	38/268	67.1

SCORING	TD R	TD P	TD Rt	PAT	FG	Saf	PTS
Stover	0	0	0	32/32	26/28	0	110
Hoard	5	4	0	0/0	0/0	0	54
Metcalf	2	3	2	0/0	0/0	0	42
Carrier	1	5	0	0/0	0/0	0	36
Alexander	0	2	0	0/0	0/0	0	14
Byner	2	0	0	0/0	0/0	0	12
Jackson	0	2	0	0/0	0/0	0	12
Testaverde	2	0	0	0/0	0/0	0	12
Baldwin	0	0	1	0/0	0/0	0	6
Hartley	0	1	0	0/0	0/0	0	6
Hill	0	0	1	0/0	0/0	0	6
Kinchen	0	1	0	0/0	0/0	0	6
Reeves	0	1	0	0/0	0/0	0	6
Tupa	0	0	0	0/0	0/0	0	6
Turner	0	0	1	0/0	0/0	0	6
Vardell	0	1	0	0/0	0/0	0	6
Browns	12	20	5	32/32	26/28	0	340
Opponents	9	13	0	19/19	17/26	0	204

2-Point conversions: Tupa (3), Alexander. Team: 4-5.

RUSHING	Att.	Yds.	Avg.	LG	TD
Hoard	209	890	4.3	39	5
Metcalf	93	329	3.5	37t	2
Byner	75	219	2.9	15	2
Baldwin	23	78	3.4	16	0
Vardell	15	48	3.2	9	0
Alexander	4	38	9.5	25	0
Testaverde	21	37	1.8	12	2
Carrier	1	14	14.0	14t	1
Rypien	7	4	0.6	2	0
J. Jones	1	0	0.0	0	0
Browns	449	1657	3.7	39	12
Opponents	465	1669	3.6	41	9

RECEIVING	No.	Yds.	Avg.	LG	TD
Alexander	48	828	17.3	81t	2
Metcalf	47	436	9.3	57t	3
Hoard	45	445	9.9	65t	4
Carrier	29	452	15.6	43	5
Kinchen	24	232	9.7	38	1
Jackson	21	304	14.5	30	2
Vardell	16	137	8.6	19	1
Byner	11	102	9.3	30	0
McCardell	10	182	18.2	34	0
Reeves	6	61	10.2	22	1
Baldwin	3	15	5.0	15	0
Hartley	3	13	4.3	8	1
Smith	2	61	30.5	50	0
J. Jones	1	1	1.0	1	0
Browns	266	3269	12.3	81t	20
Opponents	325	3425	10.5	44	13

INTERCEPTIONS	No.	Yds.	Avg.	LG	TD
Turner	9	199	22.1	93t	1
Jacobs	2	9	4.5	8	0
Griffin	2	2	1.0	2	0
Langham	2	2	1.0	2	0
Stams	1	7	7.0	7	0
Booth	1	4	4.0	4	0
Caldwell	1	0	0.0	0	0
Browns	18	223	12.4	93t	1
Opponents	21	225	10.7	49	0

PUNTING	No.	Yds.	Avg.	In 20	LG
Tupa	80	3211	40.1	27	65
Browns	80	3211	40.1	27	65
Opponents	97	3880	40.0	24	59

PUNT RETURNS	No.	FC	Yds.	Avg.	LG	TD
Metcalf	35	6	348	9.9	92t	2
Carrier	9	1	112	12.4	60	0
Caldwell	1	0	2	2.0	2	0
Turner	1	0	0	0.0	0	0
Browns	46	7	462	10.0	92t	2
Opponents	38	15	220	5.8	31	0

KICKOFF RETURNS	No.	Yds.	Avg.	LG	TD
Baldwin	28	753	26.9	85t	1
Metcalf	9	210	23.3	32	0
Kinchen	3	38	12.7	15	0
Hoard	2	30	15.0	20	0
Browns	42	1031	24.5	85t	1
Opponents	71	1372	19.3	54	0

SACKS	No.
Burnett	10.0
Pleasant	4.5
Griffin	4.0
Perry	4.0
J. Jones	3.0
Footman	2.5
P. Johnson	2.5
Stams	2.0
Banks	1.5
Dixon	1.0
B. Johnson	1.0
Thompson	1.0
Turner	1.0
Browns	38.0
Opponents	14.0

1995 DRAFT CHOICES

Round	Name	Pos.	College
1	Craig Powell	LB	Ohio State
3	Eric Zeier	QB	Georgia
	Mike Frederick	DE	Virginia
5	Tau Pupua	DT	Weber State
	Mike Miller	WR	Notre Dame
7	A.C. Tellison	WR	Miami

CLEVELAND BROWNS

1995 VETERAN ROSTER

No.		Name	Pos.	Ht.	Wt.	Birthdate	NFL Exp.	College	Hometown	How Acq.	'94 Games/ Starts
85		Alexander, Derrick	WR	6-2	195	11/6/71	2	Michigan	Detroit, Mich.	D1b-'94	14/2
70		Arvie, Herman	T	6-4	305	10/12/70	3	Grambling State	Opelousas, La.	D5-'93	16/1
97		Bandison, Romeo	DT	6-5	290	2/12/71	2	Oregon	Mill Valley, Calif.	D3-'94	0*
58		Banks, Carl	LB	6-4	235	8/29/62	12	Michigan State	Flint, Mich.	FA-'94	16/15
71		Bedosky, Mike	G	6-4	290	2/13/71	2	Missouri	Jefferson City, Mo.	W(Atl)-'94	0*
89	t-	Bishop, Harold	TE	6-4	254	4/8/70	2	Louisiana State	Tuscaloosa, Ala.	T(TB)-'95	6/0*
36		Booth, Isaac	CB-S	6-3	190	5/23/71	2	California	Indianapolis, Ind.	D5-'94	16/1
77		Brown, Orlando	T	6-7	325	12/12/70	3	South Carolina State	Washington, D.C.	FA-'93	14/8
90		Burnett, Rob	DE	6-4	280	8/27/67	6	Syracuse	Coram, N.Y.	D5-'90	16/16
21		Byner, Earnest	RB	5-10	215	9/15/62	12	East Carolina	Milledgeville, Ga.	UFA(Wash)-'94	16/1
56		Caldwell, Mike	LB	6-2	235	8/31/71	3	Middle Tennessee State	Oak Ridge, Tenn.	D3-'93	16/1
26		Cecil, Chuck	S	6-0	190	11/8/64	7	Arizona	San Diego, Calif.	FA-'95	0*
72		Dahl, Bob	G	6-5	310	11/5/68	4	Notre Dame	Chagrin Falls, Ohio	FA-'92	15/15
69	#	Dawson, Doug	G	6-3	288	12/27/61	9	Texas	Houston, Tex.	FA-'94	12/9
51		Dixon, Gerald	LB	6-3	250	6/20/69	4	South Carolina	Rock Hill, S.C.	D3b-'92	16/0
91		Dixon, Ronnie	DE-DT	6-3	292	5/10/71	2	Cincinnati	Clinton, N.C.	FA-'95	0*
16		Ethridge, Ray	WR	5-10	180	9/11/68	3	Pasadena City College	San Diego, Calif.	FA-'95	0*
61		Everitt, Steve	C	6-5	290	8/21/70	3	Michigan	Miami, Fla.	D1-'93	15/15
78		Footman, Dan	DE	6-5	290	1/13/69	3	Florida State	Tampa, Fla.	D2-'93	16/2
73		Goad, Tim	NT	6-3	280	2/28/66	8	North Carolina	Stuart, Va.	UFA(NE)-'95	13/13*
8		Goebel, Brad	QB	6-3	214	10/13/67	5	Baylor	Cuero, Tex.	FA-'93	1/0
28		Griffin, Don	CB	6-0	176	3/17/64	10	Middle Tennessee State	Camilla, Ga.	UFA(SF)-'94	15/15
31		Hairston, Stacey	CB	5-9	185	8/16/67	3	Ohio Northern	Columbus, Ohio	FA-'93	15/0
25		Hall, Dana	S	6-2	206	7/8/69	4	Washington	Diamond Bar, Calif.	FA-'95	16/4*
48		Hartley, Frank	TE	6-2	268	12/15/67	2	Illinois	Chicago, Ill.	FA-'94	10/5
93		Hill, Travis	LB	6-2	240	10/3/69	3	Nebraska	Houston, Tex.	D7-'93	14/0
33		Hoard, Leroy	RB	5-11	225	5/15/68	6	Michigan	New Orleans, La.	D2-'90	16/12
81		Jackson, Michael	WR	6-4	195	4/12/69	5	Southern Mississippi	Kentwood, La.	D6-'91	9/7
41		Jacobs, Tim	CB	5-10	185	4/5/70	3	Delaware	Landover, Md.	FA-'93	9/1
96		Johnson, Bill	DE-DT	6-4	290	12/9/68	4	Michigan State	Chicago, Ill.	D3a-'92	14/13
68		Johnson, Mario	DE-DT	6-3	288	1/30/70	3	Missouri	Florissant, Mo.	FA-'95	0*
52		Johnson, Pepper	LB	6-3	248	7/29/64	10	Ohio State	Detroit, Mich.	FA-'93	16/16
24		Jones, Reginald	CB-S	6-1	202	1/11/69	5	Memphis State	West Memphis, Ark.	T(NO)-'94	1/1*
66		Jones, Tony	T	6-5	295	5/24/66	8	Western Carolina	Cannesville, Ga.	FA-'95	16/16
88		Kinchen, Brian	TE	6-2	240	8/6/65	8	Louisiana State	Baton Rouge, La.	FA-'91	16/11
38		Langham, Antonio	CB	6-0	180	7/31/72	2	Alabama	Town Creek, Ala.	D1a-'94	16/16
95		Lyle, Rick	DE-DT	6-5	275	2/26/71	2	Missouri	Kansas City, Mo.	FA-'94	3/0
87		McCardell, Keenan	WR	6-1	175	1/6/70	4	Nevada-Las Vegas	Houston, Tex.	FA-'93	13/3
27		Moore, Stevon	S	5-11	210	2/9/67	7	Mississippi	Wiggins, Miss.	FA-'92	16/16
98		Pleasant, Anthony	DE	6-5	280	1/27/68	6	Tennessee State	Century, Fla.	D3-'90	14/14
86		Reeves, Walter	TE	6-4	270	12/16/65	7	Auburn	Eugaula, Ala.	UFA(Ariz)-'94	5/5
42		Riddick, Louis	S	6-2	215	3/15/69	4	Pittsburgh	Quakertown, Pa.	FA-'93	16/0
80		Rison, Andre	WR	6-1	188	3/18/67	7	Michigan State	Flint, Mich.	UFA(Atl)-'95	15/14*
75		Sagapolutele, Pio	DE-DT	6-6	297	11/28/69	5	San Diego State	Honolulu, Hawaii	D4-'91	11/0
79		Schad, Mike	G	6-5	290	10/2/63	10	Queens College, Canada	Bellville, Canada	FA-'94	0*
84		Smith, Rico	WR	6-0	185	1/14/69	4	Colorado	Paramount, Calif.	D6a-'92	5/4
3		Stover, Matt	K	5-11	178	1/27/68	6	Louisiana Tech	Dallas, Tex.	PB(NYG)-'91	16/0
54		Sutter, Ed	LB	6-3	235	10/3/69	3	Northwestern	Peoria, Ill.	W(NE)-'93	16/0
12		Testaverde, Vinny	QB	6-5	215	11/13/63	9	Miami	Floral Park, N.Y.	UFA(TB)-'93	14/13
40		Thomas, Johnny	CB	5-9	191	8/3/64	8	Baylor	Houston, Tex.	UFA(Wash)-'95	16/0*
55		Thomas, Marquise	LB	6-4	255	5/25/71	2	Mississippi	Fresno, Calif.	FA-'95	0*
37		Thompson, Bennie	S	6-0	214	2/10/63	6	Grambling State	New Orleans, La.	FA-'94	16/0
7		Tupa, Tom	P	6-4	230	2/6/66	7	Ohio State	Brecksville, Ohio	FA-'94	16/0
29		Turner, Eric	S	6-1	207	9/20/68	5	UCLA	Ventura, Calif.	D1-'91	16/16
44		Vardell, Tommy	RB	6-2	230	2/20/69	4	Stanford	El Cajon, Calif.	D1-'92	5/5
74		Webster, Larry	DT	6-5	288	1/18/69	4	Maryland	Elkton, Md.	FA-'95	16/7*
34		White, Lorenzo	RB	5-11	222	4/12/66	8	Michigan State	Ft. Lauderdale, Fla.	UFA(Hou)-'95	15/8*
62		Williams, Gene	T-G	6-2	305	10/14/68	5	Iowa State	Omaha, Neb.	T(Mia)-'93	15/9
63		Williams, Wally	C	6-2	300	2/19/71	3	Florida A&M	Tallahassee, Fla.	FA-'93	11/7

* Bandison inactive for 16 games in '94; Bedosky inactive for 11 games; Bishop played 6 games with Tampa Bay; Cecil last active with Phoenix in '93; R. Dixon last active with New Orleans in '93; Ethridge last on injured reserve with San Diego in '92; Goad played 13 games with New England; Hall played 16 games with San Francisco; M. Johnson last active with New England in '93; R. Jones played 1 game with New Orleans; Rison played 15 games with Atlanta; Schad missed '94 season because of injury; J. Thomas played 16 games with Washington; M. Thomas last active with Indianapolis in '93; Webster played 16 games with Miami; White played 15 games with Houston.

Unrestricted free agent; subject to developments.

† Restricted free agent; subject to developments.

Traded—RB Eric Metcalf to Atlanta.

t- Browns traded for Bishop (Tampa Bay).

Players lost through free agency (3): RB Randy Baldwin (Car; 16 games in '94), DT James Jones (Den; 16), LB Frank Stams (Car; 16).

Players lost through Expansion Draft (1): WR Mark Carrier (Car; 16 games in '94).

Also played with Browns in '94—WR Thomas McLemore (2 games), RB Eric Metcalf (16), WR Pat Newman (1), DT Michael Dean Perry (15), QB Mark Rypien (6), S Del Speer (8).

COACHING STAFF

Head Coach,
Bill Belichick

Pro Career: Became the Browns' eight full-time head coach on February 5, 1991. Belichick formerly was defensive coordinator of the New York Giants, which defeated the Buffalo Bills 20-19 in Super Bowl XXV. He also coordinated the Giants' defense that won Super Bowl XXI in 1986. Began coaching career at 23 as a special assistant to Ted Marchibroda with the Baltimore Colts in 1975. He tutored the Detroit Lions' tight ends, wide receivers, and special teams in 1976-77, before joining the Denver Broncos in 1978. He joined the Giants in 1979 as a defensive assistant and special teams coach, moved to linebackers in 1981-82, and became defensive coordinator in 1983. Career record: 32-34.

Background: Attended Annapolis (Maryland) High School and Phillips Academy in Andover, Mass. Played football and lacrosse at Wesleyan (Conn.) University. Earned a bachelor's degree in economics from Wesleyan in 1975.

Personal: Born April 16, 1952, in Nashville, Tenn. Bill and his wife, Debby, live in Brecksville, Ohio, and have three children—Amanda, Stephen, and Brian.

ASSISTANT COACHES

Ernie Adams, special assignments; born March 31, 1953, Waltham, Mass., lives in Lakewood, Ohio. No college or pro playing experience. Pro coach: New England Patriots 1975-78, New York Giants 1979-81 (Pro Personnel Director 1982-85), joined Browns in 1991.

Jim Bates, secondary; born May 31, 1946, Pontiac, Mich., lives in Strongsville, Ohio. Linebacker Tennessee 1964-67. No pro playing experience. College coach: Tennessee 1968, 1989, Southern Mississippi 1972, Villanova 1973-74, Kansas State 1975-76, West Virginia 1977, Texas Tech 1978-83, Florida 1990. Pro coach: San Antonio Gunslingers (USFL) 1984-85 (head coach 1985), Arizona Wranglers (USFL) 1986, Detroit Drive (Arena Football) 1988, Cleveland Browns, 1991-93, Atlanta Falcons 1994, rejoined Browns in 1995.

Chuck Bresnahan, linebackers; born September 8, 1960, Springfield, Mass., lives in Strongsville, Ohio. Linebacker Navy 1981-82. No pro playing experience. College coach: Navy 1986-87, Georgia Institute of Technology 1987-91, Maine 1992-94. Pro coach: Joined Browns in 1995.

Jacob Burney, defensive line; born January 24, 1959, Chattanooga, Tenn., lives in Twinsburg, Ohio. Defensive tackle Tennessee-Chattanooga 1977-80. No pro playing experience. College coach: New Mexico 1983-86, Tulsa 1987, Mississippi State 1988, Wisconsin 1989, UCLA 1990-92, Tennessee 1993. Pro coach: Joined Browns in 1994.

Steve Crosby, offensive coordinator; born July 3, 1950, Great Bend, Kan., lives in Strongsville, Ohio. Running back Fort Hays State 1969-72. Pro running back New York Giants 1974-76. Pro coach: Miami Dolphins 1979-82, Atlanta Falcons 1983-84, 1986-89, Cleveland Browns 1985, New England Patriots 1990, rejoined Browns in 1991.

Kirk Ferentz, offensive line; born August 1, 1955, Royal Oak, Mich., lives in North Royalton, Ohio. Linebacker Connecticut 1973-76. No pro playing experience. College coach: Connecticut 1977, Pittsburgh 1980, Iowa 1981-89, Maine 1990-92 (head coach). Pro coach: Joined Browns in 1993.

Pat Hill, tight ends-assistant offensive line; born December 17, 1951, Los Angeles, Calif., lives in Berea, Ohio. Center California-Riverside 1971-73. No pro playing experience. College coach: Los Angeles Valley Junior College 1974-76, Utah 1977-80, Nevada-Las Vegas 1981-82, Fresno State 1985-89, Arizona 1990-91. Pro coach: Calgary Stampeders (CFL) 1983-84, joined Browns in 1992.

Scott O'Brien, special teams; born June 25, 1957, Superior, Wis., lives in Strongsville, Ohio. Defensive end Wisconsin-Superior 1975-78. Pro defensive end Green Bay Packers 1979, Toronto Argonauts (CFL) 1979. College coach: Wisconsin-Superior 1980-82, Nevada-Las Vegas 1983-85, Rice 1986, Pittsburgh 1987-90. Pro coach: Joined Browns in 1991.

John Settle, offensive assistant; born June 2, 1965, Reidsville, N.C., lives in North Olmsted, Ohio. Running back Appalachian State 1983-86. Pro running back Atlanta Falcons 1987-90, Washington Redskins 1991-92. College coach: Appalachian State 1994. Pro coach: Joined Browns in 1995.

Mike Sheppard, receivers; born October 29, 1951, Tulsa, Okla., lives in Strongsville, Ohio. Wide receiver Cal Lutheran 1969-72. No pro playing experience. College coach: Cal Lutheran 1974-76, Brigham Young 1977-78, U.S. International 1979, Idaho State 1980-81, Long Beach State 1982, 1984-86 (head coach), Kansas 1983, New Mexico 1987-91 (head coach), California 1992. Pro coach: Joined Browns in 1993.

Jerry Simmons, strength and conditioning; born June 15, 1954, Elkhart, Kan., lives in Strongsville, Ohio. Linebacker Fort Hays State 1976-77. No pro playing experience. College coach: Fort Hays State 1978, Clemson 1980, Rice 1981-82, Southern California 1983-87. Pro coach: New England Patriots 1988-90, joined Browns in 1991.

Rick Venturi, defensive coordinator; born February 23, 1946, Taylorville, Ill., lives in North Olmstead, Ohio. Quarterback-defensive back Northwestern 1965-67. No pro playing experience. College coach: Northwestern 1968-72, 1978-80 (head coach), Purdue 1973-76, Illinois 1977. Pro coach: Hamilton Tiger-Cats (CFL) 1981, Indianapolis Colts 1982-93 (interim head coach 1991), joined Browns in 1994.

1995 FIRST-YEAR ROSTER

Name	Pos.	Ht.	Wt.	Birthdate	College	Hometown	How Acq.
Adams, Vashon	CB-S	5-10	196	9/12/73	Eastern Michigan	Aurora, Colo.	FA
Brady, Donny	CB-S	6-2	195	11/24/73	Wisconsin	North Bellmore, N.Y.	FA
Cates, Toby	WR	6-1	194	3/3/72	South Carolina	Chapman, S.C.	FA
DeLong, Greg	TE	6-4	245	4/3/73	North Carolina	Orefield, Pa.	FA
Devries, Jed (1)	G-T	6-5	282	1/6/71	Utah State	Ogden, Utah	FA
Fleming, Joe	DE-DT	6-3	291	12/5/71	New Hampshire	Wellesley, Mass.	FA
Fortune, Elliott	DE-DT	6-4	275	5/28/74	Georgia Tech	Roosevelt, N.Y.	FA
Frederick, Mike	DE	6-5	280	8/6/72	Virginia	Neshaminy, Pa.	D3b
Hickson, Don	LB	6-2	238	7/13/72	Georgia Tech	Blackwood, N.J.	FA
Hunter, Ernest	RB	5-8	201	12/21/70	Southeast Oklahoma	Longview, Tex.	FA
Isaia, Sale	G-T	6-5	315	6/13/72	UCLA	Oceanside, Calif.	FA
McKenzie, Rich (1)	LB	6-2	240	4/15/71	Penn State	Ft. Lauderdale, Fla.	D6-'93
Miller, Mike	WR	5-7	160	6/9/72	Notre Dame	Sugar Land, Tex.	D5b
Neal, Randy	LB	6-3	236	12/29/72	Virginia	Hackensack, N.J.	FA
Neujahr, Quenton (1)	G-T	6-4	285	1/30/71	Kansas State	Seward, Neb.	FA
Poumele, Pulu	G-T	6-3	300	1/31/72	Arizona	Oceanside, Calif.	FA
Powell, Craig	LB	6-4	230	11/13/71	Ohio State	Youngstown, Ohio	D1
Powers, Ricky (1)	RB	6-0	213	11/30/70	Michigan	Akron, Ohio	FA
Pupua, Tau	DT	6-5	290	8/24/71	Weber State	Salt Lake City, Utah	D5a
Royal, Andre	LB	6-2	220	12/1/72	Alabama	Tuscaloosa, Ala.	FA
Schade, Tim	QB	6-5	228	9/3/71	Minnesota	Pekin, Ill.	FA
Senior, Mike	WR	6-1	195	1/4/72	Nevada-Reno	Richmond, Calif.	FA
Smigiel, Joe	G-T	6-4	305	12/31/71	Arizona	Newbury Park, Calif.	FA
Smith, Avrom	RB	5-10	191	3/13/72	New Hampshire	Cross River, N.Y.	FA
Strait, Robert (1)	RB	6-1	230	11/14/69	Baylor	Cuero, Tex.	FA
Tellison, A.C.	WR	6-3	208	9/5/71	Miami	Bay City, Tex.	D7
Thomas, Marquis	LB	6-3	255	2/25/69	Mississippi	Tigard, Ore.	FA
Williams, Mike	CB-S	6-3	201	7/7/71	Alabama State	Columbus, Ga.	FA
Zeier, Eric	QB	6-0	205	9/6/72	Georgia	Marietta, Ga.	D3a

The term NFL Rookie is defined as a player who is in his first season of professional football and has not been on the roster of another professional football team for any regular-season or postseason games. A Rookie is designated by an "R" on NFL rosters. Players who have been active in another professional football league or players who have NFL experience, including either preseason training camp or being on an Active List or Inactive List, or on Reserve/Injured or Reserve/Physically Unable to Perform for fewer than six regular-season games, are termed NFL First-Year Players. An NFL First-Year Player is designated by a "1" on NFL rosters. Thereafter, a player is credited with an additional year of experience for each season in which he accumulates six games on the Active List or Inactive List, or on Reserve/Injured or Reserve/Physically Unable to Perform.

NOTES

DENVER BRONCOS

American Football Conference
Western Division
Team Colors: Orange, Royal Blue, and White
13655 Broncos Parkway
Englewood, Colorado 80112
Telephone: (303) 649-9000

CLUB OFFICIALS

President-Chief Executive Officer: Pat Bowlen
General Manager: John Beake
Head Coach: Mike Shanahan
Director of Player Personnel: Bob Ferguson
Controller: Alex Rohr
Director of Ticket Operations/Business Development: Rick Nichols
Executive Assistant to the President: Yolanda Saltus
Director of Media Relations: Jim Saccomano
Stadium Operations Manager: Gail Stuckey
Director of Operations: Bill Harpole
Director of Marketing: Rosemary Hanratty
Assistant to the General Manager/Community Relations: Fred Fleming
Director of Player Relations: Bill Thompson
Community Relations Coordinator: Steve Sewell
Trainer: Steve Antonopulos
Equipment Manager: Doug West
Video Director: Kent Erickson
Stadium: Denver Mile High Stadium
•**Capacity:** 76,273
1900 West Eliot
Denver, Colorado 80204
Playing Surface: Grass (PAT)
Training Camp: University of Northern Colorado
Greeley, Colorado 80639

1995 SCHEDULE

PRESEASON

July 29	**San Francisco**	7:00
Aug. 5	vs. San Francisco at Tokyo	10:00
Aug. 12	at Carolina	7:30
Aug. 21	**Dallas**	6:00
Aug. 25	at Jacksonville	7:00

REGULAR SEASON

Sept. 3	**Buffalo**	6:00
Sept. 10	at Dallas	3:00
Sept. 17	**Washington**	2:00
Sept. 24	at San Diego	1:00
Oct. 1	at Seattle	1:00
Oct. 8	at New England	8:00
Oct. 16	**Los Angeles** (Monday)	7:00
Oct. 22	**Kansas City**	2:00
Oct. 29	Open Date	
Nov. 5	**Arizona**	2:00
Nov. 12	at Philadelphia	8:00
Nov. 19	**San Diego**	2:00
Nov. 26	at Houston	3:00
Dec. 3	**Jacksonville**	2:00
Dec. 10	**Seattle**	2:00
Dec. 17	at Kansas City	3:00
Dec. 24	at Los Angeles	1:00

RECORD HOLDERS

INDIVIDUAL RECORDS—CAREER

Category	Name	Performance
Rushing (Yds.)	Floyd Little, 1967-1975	6,323
Passing (Yds.)	John Elway, 1983-1994	37,736
Passing (TDs)	John Elway, 1983-1994	199
Receiving (No.)	Lionel Taylor, 1960-66	543
Receiving (Yds.)	Lionel Taylor, 1960-66	6,872
Interceptions	Steve Foley, 1976-1986	44
Punting (Avg.)	Jim Fraser, 1962-64	45.2
Punt Return (Avg.)	Rick Upchurch, 1975-1983	12.1
Kickoff Return (Avg.)	Abner Haynes, 1965-66	26.3
Field Goals	Jim Turner, 1971-79	151
Touchdowns (Tot.)	Floyd Little, 1967-1975	54
Points	Jim Turner, 1971-79	742

INDIVIDUAL RECORDS—SINGLE SEASON

Category	Name	Performance
Rushing (Yds.)	Otis Armstrong, 1974	1,407
Passing (Yds.)	John Elway, 1993	4,030
Passing (TDs)	John Elway, 1993	25
Receiving (No.)	Lionel Taylor, 1961	100
Receiving (Yds.)	Steve Watson, 1981	1,244
Interceptions	Goose Gonsoulin, 1960	11
Punting (Avg.)	Jim Fraser, 1963	46.1
Punt Return (Avg.)	Floyd Little, 1967	16.9
Kickoff Return (Avg.)	Bill Thompson, 1969	28.5
Field Goals	Jason Elam, 1994	30
Touchdowns (Tot.)	Sammy Winder, 1986	14
Points	Gene Mingo, 1962	137

INDIVIDUAL RECORDS—SINGLE GAME

Category	Name	Performance
Rushing (Yds.)	Otis Armstrong, 12-8-74	183
Passing (Yds.)	Frank Tripucka, 9-15-62	447
Passing (TDs)	Frank Tripucka, 10-28-62	5
	John Elway, 11-18-84	5
Receiving (No.)	Lionel Taylor, 11-29-64	13
	Bobby Anderson, 9-30-73	13
Receiving (Yds.)	Lionel Taylor, 11-27-60	199
Interceptions	Goose Gonsoulin, 9-18-60	*4
	Willie Brown, 11-15-64	*4
Field Goals	Gene Mingo, 10-6-63	5
	Rich Karlis, 11-20-83	5
Touchdowns (Tot.)	Many times	3
	Last time by Shannon Sharpe, 12-12-93	
Points	Gene Mingo, 12-10-60	21

*NFL Record

COACHING HISTORY

(257-268-10)

1960-61	Frank Filchock	7-20-1
1962-64	Jack Faulkner*	9-22-1
1964-66	Mac Speedie**	6-19-1
1966	Ray Malavasi	4-8-0
1967-71	Lou Saban***	20-42-3
1971	Jerry Smith	2-3-0
1972-76	John Ralston	34-33-3
1977-80	Robert (Red) Miller	42-25-0
1981-92	Dan Reeves	117-79-1
1993-94	Wade Phillips	16-17-0

*Released after four games in 1964
**Resigned after two games in 1966
***Resigned after nine games in 1971

DENVER MILE HIGH STADIUM

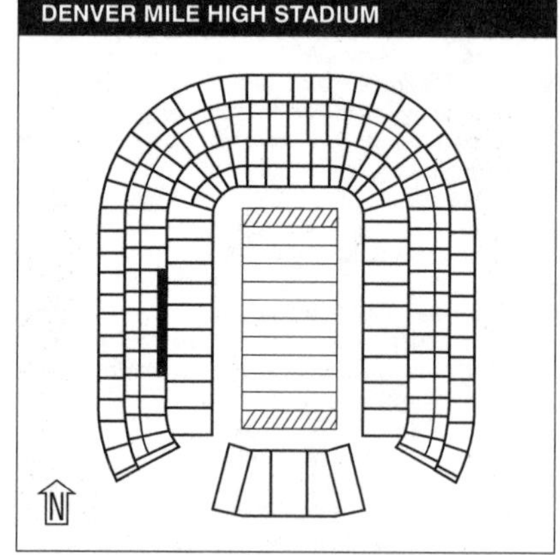

1994 TEAM RECORD

PRESEASON (2-3)

Date	Result		Opponents
7/31	L	22-25	vs. L.A. Raiders at Barcelona
8/6	W	37-16	Atlanta
8/12	L	3-20	at San Francisco
8/21	L	10-34	at Dallas
8/25	W	30-21	Arizona

REGULAR SEASON (7-9)

Date	Result		Opponents	Att.
9/4	L	34-37	San Diego	74,032
9/11	L	22-25	at N.Y. Jets (OT)	73,436
9/18	L	16-48	L.A. Raiders	75,764
9/26	L	20-27	at Buffalo	75,373
10/9	W	16- 9	at Seattle	63,872
10/17	L	28-31	Kansas City	75,151
10/23	W	20-15	at San Diego	61,626
10/30	W	26-14	Cleveland	73,190
11/6	L	21-27	at L.A. Rams	48,103
11/13	W	17-10	Seattle	71,290
11/20	W	32-28	Atlanta	70,594
11/27	W	15-13	Cincinnati	69,714
12/4	W	20-17	at Kansas City (OT)	77,631
12/11	L	13-23	at L.A. Raiders	60,016
12/17	L	19-42	at San Francisco	64,884
12/24	L	28-30	New Orleans	64,445

(OT) Overtime

SCORE BY PERIODS

Broncos	53	96	102	93	3	—	347
Opponents	64	148	77	104	3	—	396

ATTENDANCE

Home 574,180 Away 524,941 Total 1,099,121
Single-game home record, 76,105 (1-4-87)
Single-season home record, 598,224 (1981)

1994 TEAM STATISTICS

	Broncos	Opp.
Total First Downs	346	303
Rushing	105	86
Rushing	101	103
Passing	202	182
Penalty	43	18
Third Down: Made/Att	87/231	86/217
Third Down Pct.	37.7	39.6
Fourth Down: Made/Att	7/17	3/10
Fourth Down Pct.	41.2	30.0
Total Net Yards	5487	5907
Avg. Per Game	342.9	369.2
Total Plays	1112	1023
Avg. Per Play	4.9	5.8
Net Yards Rushing	1470	1752
Avg. Per Game	91.9	109.5
Total Rushes	431	432
Net Yards Passing	4017	4155
Avg. Per Game	251.1	259.7
Sacked/Yards Lost	55/366	23/141
Gross Yards	4383	4296
Att./Completions	626/388	568/322
Completion Pct.	62.0	56.7
Had Intercepted	13	12
Punts/Avg	76/42.9	76/43.5
Net Punting Avg.	76/37.1	76/35.8
Penalties/Yards Lost	101/865	134/1031
Fumbles/Ball Lost	27/18	24/14
Touchdowns	37	43
Rushing	19	12
Passing	18	28
Returns	0	3
Avg. Time of Possession	30:58	29:02

1994 INDIVIDUAL STATISTICS

PASSING	Att.	Comp.	Yds.	Pct.	TD	Int.	Tkld.	Rate
Elway	494	307	3490	62.1	16	10	46/303	85.7
Millen	131	81	893	61.8	2	3	9/63	77.6
Rivers	1	0	0	0.0	0	0	0/0	39.6
Broncos	626	388	4383	62.0	18	13	55/366	83.8
Opponents	568	322	4296	56.7	28	12	23/141	88.5

SCORING	TD R	TD P	TD Rt	PAT	FG	Saf	PTS
Elam	0	0	0	29/29	30/37	0	119
L. Russell	9	0	0	0/0	0/0	0	54
Miller	0	5	0	0/0	0/0	0	32
Sharpe	0	4	0	0/0	0/0	0	28
Elway	4	0	0	0/0	0/0	0	24
Milburn	1	3	0	0/0	0/0	0	24
Clark	3	0	0	0/0	0/0	0	18
Evans	0	2	0	0/0	0/0	0	12
Rivers	2	0	0	0/0	0/0	0	12
Campbell	0	1	0	0/0	0/0	0	6
Pritchard	0	1	0	0/0	0/0	0	6
D. Russell	0	1	0	0/0	0/0	0	6
Tillman	0	1	0	0/0	0/0	0	6
Broncos	19	18	0	29/29	30/37	0	347
Opponents	12	28	3	35/35	31/37	0	396

2-Point conversions: Sharpe (2), Miller. Team: 3-8.

RUSHING	Att.	Yds.	Avg.	LG	TD
L. Russell	190	620	3.3	22t	9
Elway	58	235	4.1	22	4
Milburn	58	201	3.5	20	1
Clark	56	168	3.0	12	3
Bernstine	17	91	5.4	24	0
Rivers	43	83	1.9	11	2
Millen	5	57	11.4	24	0
D. Russell	1	6	6.0	6	0
Campbell	2	6	3.0	6	0
Miller	1	3	3.0	3	0
Broncos	431	1470	3.4	24	19
Opponents	432	1752	4.1	36	12

RECEIVING	No.	Yds.	Avg.	LG	TD
Sharpe	87	1010	11.6	44	4
Milburn	77	549	7.1	33	3
Miller	60	1107	18.5	76	5
L. Russell	38	227	6.0	19	0
Tillman	28	455	16.3	63	1
D. Russell	25	342	13.7	43	1
Rivers	20	136	6.8	25	0
Pritchard	19	271	14.3	50t	1
Evans	13	127	9.8	20t	2
Bernstine	9	70	7.8	16	0
Clark	9	47	5.2	10	0
Kimbrough	2	20	10.0	12	0
Campbell	1	22	22.0	22t	1
Broncos	388	4383	11.3	76	18
Opponents	322	4296	13.3	75t	28

INTERCEPTIONS	No.	Yds.	Avg.	LG	TD
Jones	2	9	4.5	9	0
Hilliard	2	8	4.0	8	0
Crockett	2	6	3.0	6	0
Atwater	1	24	24.0	24	0
Washington	1	5	5.0	5	0
Fletcher	1	4	4.0	4	0
Alexander	1	2	2.0	2	0
B. Smith	1	0	0.0	0	0
Williams	1	-3	-3.0	-3	0
Broncos	12	55	4.6	24	0
Opponents	13	288	22.2	99t	3

PUNTING	No.	Yds.	Avg.	In 20	LG
Rouen	76	3258	42.9	23	59
Broncos	76	3258	42.9	23	59
Opponents	76	3303	43.5	21	62

PUNT RETURNS	No.	FC	Yds.	Avg.	LG	TD
Milburn	41	4	379	9.2	44	0
Broncos	41	4	379	9.2	44	0
Opponents	39	13	275	7.1	29	0

KICKOFF RETURNS	No.	Yds.	Avg.	LG	TD
Milburn	37	793	21.4	40	0
By'Not'e	24	545	22.7	41	0
D. Russell	5	105	21.0	34	0
Clark	3	34	11.3	20	0
Campbell	3	24	8.0	11	0
Swann	1	16	16.0	16	0
Evans	1	6	6.0	6	0
Carswell	1	0	0.0	0	0
Broncos	75	1523	20.3	41	0
Opponents	70	1396	19.9	62	0

SACKS	No.
Fletcher	7.0
Dronett	6.0
Washington	2.5
Hasselbach	2.0
Mecklenburg	1.5
Alexander	1.0
Bradford	1.0
Robinson	1.0
D. Smith	1.0
Broncos	23.0
Opponents	55.0

1995 DRAFT CHOICES

Round	Name	Pos.	College
4	Jamie Brown	T	Florida A&M
	Ken Brown	LB	Virginia Tech
5	Phil Yeboah-Kodie	LB	Penn State
6	Fritz Fequiere	G	Iowa
	Terrell Davis	RB	Georgia
7	Steve Russ	LB	Air Force
	Byron Chamberlain	WR	Wayne State, Neb.

DENVER BRONCOS

1995 VETERAN ROSTER

No.	Name	Pos.	Ht.	Wt.	Birthdate	NFL Exp.	College	Hometown	How Acq.	'94 Games/ Starts
57	Aldridge, Allen	LB	6-1	245	5/30/72	2	Houston	Houston, Tex.	D2-'94	16/2
58	Alexander, Elijah	LB	6-2	230	8/8/70	4	Kansas State	Ft. Worth, Tex.	W(TB)-'93	16/16
27	Atwater, Steve	S	6-3	217	10/28/66	7	Arkansas	Chicago, Ill.	D1-'89	14/14
33	Bernstine, Rod	RB	6-3	238	2/8/65	9	Texas A&M	Bryan, Tex.	UFA(SD)-'93	3/3
23	Bradford, Ronnie	CB	5-10	188	10/1/70	3	Colorado	Commerce City, Colo.	FA-'93	12/0
34	Braxton, Tyrone	S	5-11	185	12/17/64	9	North Dakota State	Parker, Colo.	FA-'95	16/0*
56	Burns, Keith	LB	6-1	233	5/16/72	2	Oklahoma State	Greelyville, S.C.	D7a-'94	11/1
28	By'not'e, Butler	CB	5-9	160	9/29/72	2	Ohio State	St. Louis, Mo.	D7b-'94	9/0
86	Campbell, Jeff	WR	5-8	167	3/26/68	6	Colorado	Vail, Colo.	UFA(Det)-'94	16/1
20	Canley, Sheldon	RB	5-9	195	4/19/68	2	San Jose State	Santa Barbara, Calif.	FA-'95	0*
43	Clark, Derrick	RB	6-3	230	5/4/71	2	Evangel	Orlando, Fla.	FA-'94	16/4
29	Craver, Aaron	RB	6-0	220	12/18/68	5	Fresno State	Compton, Calif.	UFA(Mia)-'95	8/0*
39	Crockett, Ray	CB	5-10	185	1/5/67	7	Baylor	Dallas, Tex.	UFA(Det)-'94	14/14
99	Dronett, Shane	DE	6-6	275	1/12/71	4	Texas	Orange, Tex.	D2-'92	16/15
1	Elam, Jason	K	5-11	192	3/8/70	3	Hawaii	Ft. Walton Beach, Fla.	D3b-'93	16/0
7	Elway, John	QB	6-3	215	6/28/60	13	Stanford	Port Angeles, Wash.	T(Balt)-'83	14/14
88	Evans, Jerry	TE	6-4	250	9/28/68	3	Toledo	Lorain, Ohio	FA-'93	16/11
73	Fletcher, Simon	LB	6-5	240	2/18/62	11	Houston	Bay City, Tex.	D2b-'85	16/16
24	Fuller, Randy	CB	5-9	173	6/2/70	2	Tennessee State	Griffin, Ga.	D4-'94	10/1
75	Habib, Brian	G	6-7	292	12/2/64	8	Washington	Ellensburg, Wash.	UFA(Minn)-'93	16/16
54	Hager, Britt	LB	6-1	225	2/20/66	7	Texas	Odessa, Tex.	UFA(Phil)-'95	16/5*
40	Hall, Darryl	S	6-2	210	8/1/66	3	Washington	Oscoda, Mich.	FA-'93	16/3
96	Hasselbach, Harald	DE	6-6	280	9/22/67	2	Washington	Amsterdam, Holland	FA-'94	16/9
37	Hauck, Tim	S	5-10	185	12/20/66	6	Montana	Big Timber, Mont.	UFA(GB)-'95	13/3*
21	Hilliard, Randy	CB	5-11	165	2/6/67	6	Northwestern Louisiana	Metairie, La.	FA-'94	15/6
50	Jacobs, Ray	LB	6-2	244	8/18/72	2	North Carolina	Hamstead, N.C.	FA-'94	16/0
82	Johnson, Vance	WR	5-11	185	3/13/63	10	Arizona	Trenton, N.J.	FA-'95	0*
93	Jones, James	DT	6-2	290	2/6/69	5	Northern Iowa	Davenport, Iowa	UFA(Clev)-'95	16/5*
31	Jones, Rondell	S	6-2	210	5/7/71	3	North Carolina	Sunderland, Mass.	D3a-'93	16/3
72	Kartz, Keith	C	6-4	270	5/5/63	9	California	Las Vegas, Nev.	FA-'95	0*
80	Kimbrough, Tony	WR	6-2	192	9/17/70	3	Jackson State	Weir, Miss.	D7b-'93	12/0
62	Lewis, Bill	C	6-6	290	7/12/63	9	Nebraska	Sioux City, Iowa	FA-'95	0*
97	Lodish, Mike	DT	6-3	280	8/11/67	6	UCLA	Birmingham, Mich.	UFA(Buff)-'95	15/5*
87	McCaffrey, Ed	WR	6-5	215	8/17/68	5	Stanford	Allentown, Pa.	UFA(SF)-'95	16/0*
68	McElroy, Reggie	T	6-6	290	3/4/60	12	West Texas State	Beaumont, Tex.	FA-'95	10/0*
61	Meeks, Bob	G	6-2	279	5/28/69	4	Auburn	Andulusia, Ala.	D10-'92	0*
22	Milburn, Glyn	RB	5-8	177	2/19/71	3	Stanford	Santa Monica, Calif.	D2-'93	16/3
36	Miles, Ostell	RB	6-0	227	8/6/71	3	Cincinnati	Denver, Colo.	FA-'95	0*
17	Millen, Hugh	QB	6-5	216	11/22/63	10	Washington	Des Moines, Iowa	FA-'94	5/2
83	Miller, Anthony	WR	5-11	190	4/15/65	8	Tennessee	Pasadena, Calif.	RFA(SD)-'94	16/15
14	Musgrave, Bill	QB	6-2	205	11/11/67	5	Oregon	Grand Junction, Colo.	UFA(SF)-'95	0*
66	Nalen, Tom	C	6-2	280	5/13/71	2	Boston College	Foxboro, Mass.	D7c-'95	7/1
91	Oshodin, Willie	DE	6-4	260	9/16/69	3	Villanova	Benn City, Nigeria	FA-'92	13/0
95	Perry, Michael Dean	DT	6-1	285	8/27/65	8	Clemson	Aiken, S.C.	FA-'95	15/14*
81	Pritchard, Mike	WR	5-10	190	10/26/69	5	Colorado	Las Vegas, Nev.	T(Atl)-'94	3/0
38	Rivers, Reggie	RB	6-1	215	2/22/68	5	Southwest Texas State	Dayton, Ohio	FA-'91	16/1
94	Robinson, Jeff	DE	6-4	265	2/20/70	3	Idaho	Kennewick, Wash.	D4-'93	16/0
16	Rouen, Tom	P	6-3	215	6/9/68	3	Colorado	Hindsdale, Ill.	FA-'93	16/0
69	Schlereth, Mark	G	6-3	278	1/25/66	7	Idaho	Anchorage, Alaska	UFA(Wash)-'95	16/6*
74	Schultz, Bill	T	6-5	305	5/1/67	6	Southern California	Granada Hills, Calif.	UFA(Hou)-'95	0*
84	Sharpe, Shannon	TE	6-2	230	6/26/68	6	Savannah State	Glennville, Ga.	D7-'90	15/13
26	Thomas, Eric	CB	5-11	184	9/11/64	9	Tulane	Tucson, Ariz.	UFA(NYJ)-'95	1/0*
76	Thompson, Broderick	T	6-5	295	8/14/60	10	Kansas	Cerritos, Calif.	FA-'95	14/14*
46	Wainright, Frank	TE	6-3	245	10/10/67	5	Northern Colorado	Peoria, Ill.	UFA(NO)-'95	0*
48	Washington, Lionel	CB	6-0	185	10/21/60	13	Tulane	Lutcher, La.	UFA(Raid)-'95	11/7*
90	Williams, Dan	DE	6-4	290	12/15/69	3	Toledo	Ypsilanti, Mich.	D1-'93	12/7
92	Wyman, Dave	LB	6-2	248	3/31/64	9	Stanford	San Diego, Calif.	UFA(Sea)-'93	4/0
65	Zimmerman, Gary	T	6-6	294	12/13/61	10	Oregon	Walnut, Calif.	T(Minn)-'94	16/16

* Braxton played 16 games with Miami in '94; Canley last active with N.Y. Jets in '92; Craver played 8 games with Miami; Hager played 16 games with Philadelphia; Hauck played 13 games with Green Bay; Johnson last active with Denver in '93; J. Jones played 16 games with Cleveland; Kartz inactive for 11 games; Lewis last active with New England in '93; Lodish played 15 games with Buffalo; McCaffrey played 16 games with San Francisco; McElroy played 10 games with Minnesota; Meeks missed '94 season because of injury; Miles last active with Cincinnati in '93; Musgrave inactive for 16 games with San Francisco; Perry played 15 games with Cleveland; Schlereth played 16 games with Washington; Schultz active for 5 games with Houston but did not play; Thomas played 1 game with N.Y. Jets; Thompson played 14 games with Philadelphia; Wainright missed '94 season with New Orleans because of injury; Washington played 11 games with L.A. Raiders.

\# Unrestricted free agent; subject to developments.

† Restricted free agent; subject to developments.

Players lost through free agency (5): LB Mitch Donahue (Atl; 3 games in '94), LB Richard Harvey (NO; 16), T Kirk Scrafford (SF; 16), NT Ted Washington (Buff; 15), G Dave Widell (Jax; 16).

Players lost through Expansion Draft (2): WR Charles Swann (Car; 13 games in '94), WR Cedric Tillman (Jax; 16).

Also played with Broncos in '94—WR Melvin Bonner (0 games), TE Dwayne Carswell (4), LB Mike Croel (13), T Russell Freeman (13), T Ken Lanier (4), T Don Maggs (9), LB Karl Mecklenburg (16), G Jon Melander (15), WR Derek Russell (12), RB Leonard Russell (14), LB Glenell Sanders (1), CB Ben Smith (14), S Dennis Smith (12), RB Deon Strother (2).

COACHING STAFF

Head Coach,
Mike Shanahan

Pro Career: Became the eleventh head coach in Broncos history on January 31, 1995, coming to Denver from the world champion San Francisco 49ers, where he served as offensive coordinator from 1992-94. San Francisco's three-year average under Shanahan's direction was the most-productive offense in the history of pro football. His three-year averages included being number one in total points (an average of 470 per year), total touchdowns (61), rushing touchdowns (24), passing touchdowns (32), third-down efficiency (49%), total offense (an average of 6,225 yards annually), and average yards per play (6.2 yards per attempt). San Francisco's quarterback Steve Young re-wrote many NFL passing records and was named the NFL most valuable player twice in his three years under Shanahan's guidance, in addition to throwing for six touchdowns and earning Super Bowl XXIX most valuable player honors. During his NFL career, Shanahan has been a part of teams that have played in seven AFC or NFC Championship Games, in addition to his four Super Bowl appearances, three with Denver and Super Bowl XXIX with San Francisco. In his 20 seasons coaching in the NFL and at the college level, Shanahan's teams have participated in postseason playoffs or bowl games 15 times. A driving force behind the Broncos' offense for all three of the team's most recent Super Bowl appearances (following the 1986, 1987, and 1989 seasons), he first came to Denver in 1984 as wide receivers coach. Shanahan was Broncos' offensive coordinator from 1985-87, and then returned to Denver as quarterbacks coach on October 16, 1989, after serving as head coach of the Los Angeles Raiders in 1988 and through the first four games of the 1989 campaign. His record with the Raiders was 8-12. Career record: 8-12.

Background: Shanahan began his coaching career at Oklahoma in 1975-76, also coaching at Northern Arizona (1977), Eastern Illinois (1978), and Minnesota (1979), before moving on to Florida (1980-83), where he led the Gators to an NCAA-record 4,540 yards as assistant head coach in 1983. During his tenure on the college level, Shanahan's teams had a combined record of 77-29-3 (.720), including national championship seasons at Oklahoma in 1975 and at Eastern Illinois in 1978.

Personal: Shanahan was born in Oak Park, Illinois, on August 24, 1952. He attended East Leyden High School in Franklin Park and was a wishbone quarterback/defensive back at Eastern Illinois, graduating in 1974 with a degree in physical education. He earned a master's degree there in 1975. Mike and his wife Peggy have two children, son Kyle and daughter Krystal.

ASSISTANT COACHES

Frank Bush, linebackers; born January 10, 1963, Athens, Ga., lives in Englewood, Colo. Linebacker North Carolina State 1981-84. Pro linebacker Houston Oilers 1985-86. Pro coach: Houston Oilers 1992-94, joined Broncos in 1995.

Barney Chavous, assistant offensive line-assistant strength and conditioning; born March 22, 1951, Aiken, S.C., lives in Englewood, Colo. Defensive end South Carolina State 1969-72. Pro defensive end Denver Broncos 1973-85. Pro coach: Joined Broncos in 1989.

Rick Dennison, offensive assistant; born June 22, 1958, in Kalispel, Mont., lives in Englewood, Colo. Tight end Colorado State 1976-79. Pro linebacker Denver Broncos 1982-90. Pro coach: Joined Broncos in 1995.

Ed Donatell, defensive backs; born February 4, 1957, Akron, Ohio, lives in Littleton, Colo. Safety Glenville State 1975-78. No pro playing experience. College coach: Kent State 1979-80, Washington 1981-82, Pacific 1983-85, Idaho 1986-88, Cal State-Fullerton 1989. Pro coach: New York Jets 1990-94, joined Broncos in 1995.

George Dyer, defensive line; born May 4, 1940, Alhambra, Calif., lives in Aurora, Colo. Center-linebacker U.C. Santa Barbara 1961-63. No pro playing experience. College coach: Humboldt State 1964-66, Coalinga (Calif.) J.C. 1967 (head coach), Portland State 1968-71, Idaho 1972, San Jose State 1973, Michigan State 1977-79, Arizona State 1980-81. Pro coach: Winnipeg Blue Bombers (CFL) 1974-76, Buffalo Bills 1982, Seattle Seahawks 1983-91, Los Angeles Rams 1992-94, joined Broncos in 1995.

Alex Gibbs, assistant head coach-offensive line; born February 11, 1941, Morganton, N.C., lives in Greenwood Village, Colo. Running back-defensive back Davidson College 1959-63. No pro playing experience. College coach: Duke 1969-70, Kentucky 1971-72, West Virginia 1973-74, Ohio State 1975-78, Auburn 1979-81, Georgia 1982-83. Pro coach: Denver Broncos 1984-87, Los Angeles Raiders 1988-89, San Diego Chargers 1990-91, Indianapolis Colts 1992, Kansas City Chiefs 1993-94, rejoined Broncos in 1995.

Mike Heimerdinger, wide receivers; born October 13, 1952, DeKalb, Ill., lives in Englewood, Colo. Wide receiver Eastern Illinois 1970-74. No pro playing experience. College coach: Florida 1980, Air Force 1981, North Texas State 1982, Florida 1983-87, Cal State-Fullerton 1988, Rice 1989-93, Duke 1994. Pro coach: Joined Broncos in 1995.

Gary Kubiak, offensive coordinator-quarterbacks; born August 15, 1961, Houston, Tex., lives in Englewood, Colo. Quarterback Texas A&M 1979-82. Pro quarterback Denver Broncos 1983-91. College coach: Texas A&M 1992-93. Pro coach: San Francisco 49ers 1994, joined Broncos in 1995.

Brian Pariani, tight ends; born July 2, 1965, San Francisco, Calif., lives in Castle Pines, Colo. No college or pro playing experience. College coach: UCLA 1989. Pro coach: San Francisco 49ers 1991-94, joined Broncos in 1995.

Al Reynolds, defensive assistant-assistant defensive backs; born June 24, 1959, Pineville, La., lives in Aurora, Colo. Safety Indiana State 1978-81. No pro playing experience. College coach: Indiana State 1982-92. Pro coach: Joined Broncos in 1993.

Greg Robinson, defensive coordinator; born October 9, 1951, Los Angeles, Calif., lives in Aurora, Colo. Linebacker-tight end Pacific 1972-74. No pro playing experience. College coach: Pacific 1975-76, Cal State-Fullerton 1977-79, North Carolina State 1980-81, UCLA 1982-89. Pro coach: New York Jets 1990-94, joined Broncos in 1995.

Greg Saporta, assistant strength and conditioning; born February 2, 1957, New York, N.Y., lives in Englewood, Colo. Wide receiver Buffalo State 1977-79. No pro playing experience. College coach: Florida 1981-88, 1993-94, North Carolina 1989-92. Pro coach: Joined Broncos in 1995.

Richard Smith, special teams; born October 17, 1955, Los Angeles, Calif., lives in Larkspur, Colo. Offensive lineman Rio Hondo (Calif.) J.C. 1975-76, Fresno State 1977-78. No pro playing experience. College coach: Rio Hondo (Calif.) J.C. 1979-80, Cal State-Fullerton 1981-83, California 1984-86, Arizona 1987. Pro coach: Houston Oilers 1988-92, joined Broncos in 1993.

Bobby Turner, running backs; born May 6, 1949, East Chicago, Ind., lives in Englewood, Colo. Defensive back Indiana State 1968-71. No pro playing experience. College coach: Indiana State 1975-82, Fresno State 1983-88, Ohio State 1989-90, Purdue 1991-94. Pro coach: Joined Broncos in 1995.

Rich Tuten, strength and conditioning; born December 30, 1953, Columbia, S.C., lives in Englewood, Colo. Nose guard Clemson 1976-78. No pro playing experience. College coach: Florida 1979-88, 1993-94, North Carolina 1989-92. Pro coach: Joined Broncos in 1995.

1995 FIRST-YEAR ROSTER

Name	Pos.	Ht.	Wt.	Birthdate	College	Hometown	How Acq.
Brown, Jamie	T	6-8	300	4/24/72	Florida A&M	Miami, Fla.	D4a
Brown, Ken	LB	6-1	235	5/5/71	Virginia Tech	Richmond, Va.	D4b
Burch, Joe (1)	C	6-2	280	8/8/71	Texas Southern	Dallas, Tex.	FA
Carswell, Dwayne (1)	TE	6-3	261	1/18/72	Liberty	Jacksonville, Fla.	FA
Chamberlain, Byron	WR	6-1	225	10/17/71	Wayne State, Neb.	Ft. Worth, Tex.	D7b
Davis, Terrell	RB	5-11	200	10/28/72	Georgia	San Diego, Calif.	D6b
Diaz-Infante, David (1)	G-T	6-3	292	3/31/64	San Jose State	San Jose, Calif.	FA
Farquhar, John	TE	6-6	263	3/22/72	Duke	Stanford, Calif.	FA
Fequiere, Fritz	G	6-2	289	1/31/72	Iowa	Uniondale, N.Y.	D6a
Hall, Kenny (1)	G-T	6-3	315	7/15/71	Fresno State	Pomona, Calif.	FA
Hoffman, Jim	DE-DT	6-4	290	12/14/72	Arizona	Spring Valley, Calif.	FA
Hunter, Brad (1)	P	6-5	260	8/16/68	Brigham Young	North Bend, Ore.	FA
Ivlow, John (1)	RB	5-10	210	1/26/70	Colorado State	Joliet, Colo.	FA
Jackson, Larry	DE-DT	6-3	262	10/7/71	Texas A&M	Rockdale, Tex.	FA
Jasper, Shane	LB	6-2	256	12/23/71	UCLA	Troup, Tex.	FA
McCoy, Mike	QB	6-2	204	4/1/72	Utah	Novato, Calif.	FA
Pearson, Malcolm X.	S	6-0	208	6/4/72	Miami	Ft. Lauderdale, Fla.	FA
Russ, Steve	LB	6-4	237	9/16/72	Air Force	Stetsonville, Wis.	D7a
Small, Errol	LB	6-2	220	6/17/72	Southern California	Los Angeles, Calif.	FA
Smith, Rod (1)	WR	6-0	183	5/15/70	Missouri Southern	Texarkana, Ark.	FA
Strother, Deon (1)	RB	5-11	213	4/12/72	Southern California	Saginaw, Mich.	FA
Tanuvasa, Maa (1)	DT	6-2	277	11/6/70	Hawaii	Mililani, Hawaii	FA
Taylor, Eddie (1)	CB-S	5-11	188	10/12/68	San Jose State	San Diego, Calif.	FA
Yeboah-Kodie, Phil	LB	6-2	220	1/22/71	Penn State	Montreal, Canada	D5

The term NFL Rookie is defined as a player who is in his first season of professional football and has not been on the roster of another professional football team for any regular-season or postseason games. A Rookie is designated by an "R" on NFL rosters. Players who have been active in another professional football league or players who have NFL experience, including either preseason training camp or being on an Active List or Inactive List, or on Reserve/Injured or Reserve/Physically Unable to Perform for fewer than six regular-season games, are termed NFL First-Year Players. An NFL First-Year Player is designated by a "1" on NFL rosters. Thereafter, a player is credited with an additional year of experience for each season in which he accumulates six games on the Active List or Inactive List, or on Reserve/Injured or Reserve/Physically Unable to Perform.

NOTES

HOUSTON OILERS

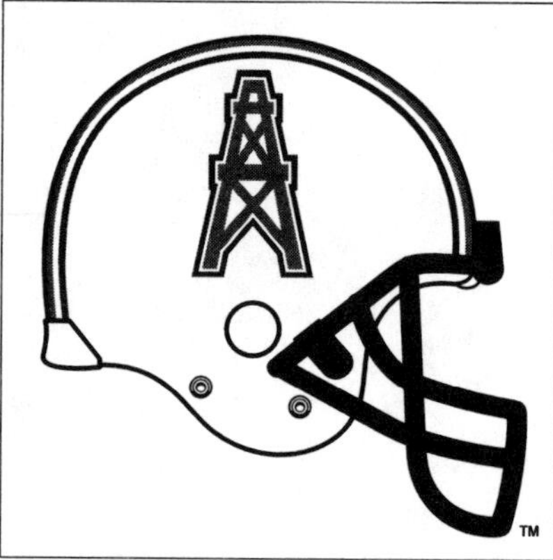

American Football Conference
Central Division
Team Colors: Columbia Blue, Scarlet, and White
6910 Fannin Street
Houston, Texas 77030
Telephone: (713) 797-9111

CLUB OFFICIALS

President: K.S. (Bud) Adams, Jr.
Exec. V.P./General Manager: Floyd Reese
Exec. V.P./Administration: Mike McClure
Exec. V.P./Finance: Scott Thompson
Exec. Assistant to President: Thomas S. Smith
Vice President/General Counsel: Steve Underwood
Vice President/Player Personnel and Scouting: Mike Holovak
Senior Vice President//Marketing and Broadcasting: Don MacLachlan
Director of Pro Personnel: Rich Snead
Director of Business Operations: Lewis Mangum
Director of Media Services: Dave Pearson
Director of Public and Community Relations: Rod St. Clair
Director of Ticket Administration Services: Mike Mullis
Assistant Ticket Manager: Ralph Stolarski
Director of Security: Grady Sessums
Director of Player Relations: Willie Alexander
Head Trainer: Brad Brown
Assistant Trainer: Don Moseley
Equipment Manager: Dan Murray
Video Coordinator: Ken Sparacino
Stadium: Astrodome • **Capacity:** 59,969
8400 Kirby Drive
Houston, Texas 77054
Playing Surface: AstroTurf-8
Training Camp: Prassel Residence Hall
Trinity University
San Antonio, Texas 78212

1995 SCHEDULE

PRESEASON

Aug. 5	**Arizona**	7:00
Aug. 12	vs. Washington at Knoxville, Tenn.	8:00
Aug. 19	**San Diego**	7:30
Aug. 26	vs. Dallas at San Antonio, Tex.	7:00

REGULAR SEASON

Sept. 3	at Jacksonville	1:00
Sept. 10	**Pittsburgh**	12:00
Sept. 17	**Cleveland**	12:00
Sept. 24	at Cincinnati	4:00
Oct. 1	**Jacksonville**	3:00
Oct. 8	at Minnesota	12:00
Oct. 15	Open Date	
Oct. 22	at Chicago	12:00
Oct. 29	**Tampa Bay**	3:00
Nov. 5	at Cleveland	1:00
Nov. 12	**Cincinnati**	12:00
Nov. 19	at Kansas City	7:00
Nov. 26	**Denver**	3:00
Dec. 3	at Pittsburgh	1:00
Dec. 10	**Detroit**	12:00
Dec. 17	**New York Jets**	12:00
Dec. 24	at Buffalo	1:00

RECORD HOLDERS

INDIVIDUAL RECORDS—CAREER

Category	Name	Performance
Rushing (Yds.)	Earl Campbell, 1978-1984	8,574
Passing (Yds.)	Warren Moon, 1984-1993	33,685
Passing (TDs)	Warren Moon, 1984-1993	196
Receiving (No.)	Ernest Givins, 1986-1994	542
Receiving (Yds.)	Ernest Givins, 1986-1994	7,935
Interceptions	Jim Norton, 1960-68	45
Punting (Avg.)	Greg Montgomery, 1988-1993	43.6
Punt Return (Avg.)	Billy Johnson, 1974-1980	13.2
Kickoff Return (Avg.)	Bobby Jancik, 1962-67	26.5
Field Goals	Tony Zendejas, 1985-1990	117
Touchdowns (Tot.)	Earl Campbell, 1978-1984	73
Points	George Blanda, 1960-66	596

INDIVIDUAL RECORDS—SINGLE SEASON

Category	Name	Performance
Rushing (Yds.)	Earl Campbell, 1980	1,934
Passing (Yds.)	Warren Moon, 1991	4,690
Passing (TDs)	George Blanda, 1961	36
Receiving (No.)	Charlie Hennigan, 1964	101
Receiving (Yds.)	Charlie Hennigan, 1961	*1,746
Interceptions	Fred Glick, 1963	12
	Mike Reinfeldt, 1979	12
Punting (Avg.)	Greg Montgomery, 1992	46.9
Punt Return (Avg.)	Billy Johnson, 1977	15.4
Kickoff Return (Avg.)	Ken Hall, 1960	31.3
Field Goals	Al Del Greco, 1993	29
Touchdowns (Tot.)	Earl Campbell, 1979	19
Points	Al Del Greco, 1993	126

INDIVIDUAL RECORDS—SINGLE GAME

Category	Name	Performance
Rushing (Yds.)	Billy Cannon, 12-10-61	216
Passing (Yds.)	Warren Moon, 12-16-90	527
Passing (TDs)	George Blanda, 11-19-61	*7
Receiving (No.)	Charlie Hennigan, 10-13-61	13
	Haywood Jeffires, 10-13-91	13
Receiving (Yds.)	Charlie Hennigan, 10-13-61	272
Interceptions	Many times	3
	Last time by Marcus Robertson, 11-21-93	
Field Goals	Skip Butler, 10-12-75	6
Touchdowns (Tot.)	Billy Cannon, 12-10-61	5
Points	Billy Cannon, 12-10-61	30

*NFL Record

COACHING HISTORY

(245-287-6)

1960-61	Lou Rymkus*	12-7-1
1961	Wally Lemm	10-0-0
1962-63	Frank (Pop) Ivy	17-12-0
1964	Sammy Baugh	4-10-0
1965	Hugh Taylor	4-10-0
1966-70	Wally Lemm	28-40-4
1971	Ed Hughes	4-9-1
1972-73	Bill Peterson**	1-18-0
1973-74	Sid Gillman	8-15-0
1975-80	O.A. (Bum) Phillips	59-38-0
1981-83	Ed Biles***	8-23-0
1983	Chuck Studley	2-8-0
1984-85	Hugh Campbell****	8-22-0
1985-89	Jerry Glanville	35-35-0
1990-94	Jack Pardee#	44-35-0
1994	Jeff Fisher	1-5-0

*Released after five games in 1961
**Released after five games in 1973
***Resigned after six games in 1983
****Released after 14 games in 1985
#Released after 10 games in 1994

ASTRODOME

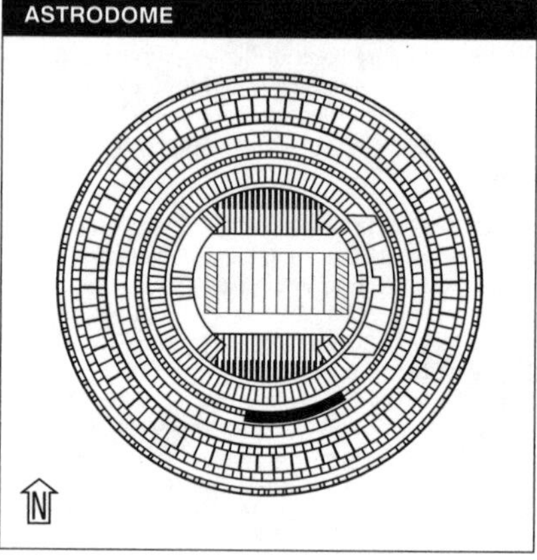

1994 TEAM RECORD

PRESEASON (2-3)

Date	Result		Opponents
7/31	L	17-24	at Kansas City
8/6	W	31-3	vs. San Diego at San Antonio
8/15	W	6-0	vs. Dallas at Mexico City
8/20	L	16-18	vs. Buffalo at San Antonio
8/27	L	23-24	L.A. Raiders

REGULAR SEASON (2-14)

Date	Result		Opponents	Att.
9/4	L	21-45	at Indianapolis	47,372
9/11	L	17-20	at Dallas	64,402
9/18	L	7-15	Buffalo	55,424
9/25	W	20-13	Cincinnati	44,253
10/3	L	14-30	at Pittsburgh	57,274
10/13	L	8-11	Cleveland	50,364
10/24	L	6-21	at Philadelphia	65,233
10/30	L	14-17	at L.A. Raiders	40,473
11/6	L	9-12	Pittsburgh (OT)	47,822
11/13	L	31-34	at Cincinnati	54,908
11/21	L	10-13	N.Y. Giants	53,201
11/27	L	10-34	at Cleveland	65,088
12/4	L	12-30	Arizona	39,821
12/11	L	14-16	Seattle	31,453
12/18	L	9-31	at Kansas City	74,474
12/24	W	24-10	N.Y. Jets	31,176

(OT) Overtime

SCORE BY PERIODS

Oilers	45	56	25	100	0	—	226
Opponents	57	122	60	110	3	—	352

ATTENDANCE

Home 353,514 Away 469,224 Total 822,738
Single-game home record, 63,705 (9-6-92)
Single-season home record, 494,447 (1992)

1994 TEAM STATISTICS

	Oilers	Opp.
Total First Downs	278	275
Rushing	97	112
Passing	158	132
Penalty	23	31
Third Down: Made/Att	78/224	80/218
Third Down Pct.	34.8	36.7
Fourth Down: Made/Att	9/18	3/10
Fourth Down Pct.	50.0	30.0
Total Net Yards	4481	4915
Avg. Per Game	280.1	307.2
Total Plays	1036	971
Avg. Per Play	4.3	5.1
Net Yards Rushing	1682	2120
Avg. Per Game	105.1	132.5
Total Rushes	417	540
Net Yards Passing	2799	2795
Avg. Per Game	174.9	174.7
Sacked/Yards Lost	65/417	31/168
Gross Yards	3216	2963
Att./Completions	554/274	399/221
Completion Pct.	49.5	55.3
Had Intercepted	17	14
Punts/Avg.	96/42.9	82/42.0
Net Punting Avg.	96/36.4	82/36.9
Penalties/Yards Lost	115/959	102/807
Fumbles/Ball Lost	42/25	20/12
Touchdowns	25	37
Rushing	10	17
Passing	13	18
Returns	2	2
Avg. Time of Possession	29:06	30:54

1994 INDIVIDUAL STATISTICS

PASSING	Att.	Comp.	Yds.	Pct.	TD	Int.	Tkld.	Rate
Tolliver	240	121	1287	50.4	6	7	27/166	62.6
Richardson	181	94	1202	51.9	6	6	23/136	70.3
Carlson	132	59	727	44.7	1	4	15/115	52.2
Camarillo	1	0	0	0.0	0	0	0/0	39.6
Oilers	554	274	3216	49.5	13	17	65/417	62.5
Opponents	399	221	2963	55.4	18	14	31/168	79.6

SCORING	TD R	TD P	TD Rt	PAT	FG	Saf	PTS
Del Greco	0	0	0	18/18	16/20	0	66
Jeffires	0	6	0	0/0	0/0	0	42
G. Brown	4	1	0	0/0	0/0	0	30
White	3	1	0	0/0	0/0	0	24
Givins	0	1	1	0/0	0/0	0	12
Slaughter	0	2	0	0/0	0/0	0	12
Tolliver	2	0	0	0/0	0/0	0	12
Carter	0	1	0	0/0	0/0	0	6
Coleman	0	1	0	0/0	0/0	0	6
Dishman	0	0	1	0/0	0/0	0	6
Richardson	1	0	0	0/0	0/0	0	6
R. Brown	0	0	0	0/0	0/0	0	2
Lathon	0	0	0	0/0	0/0	1	2
Oilers	10	13	2	18/18	16/20	1	226
Opponents	17	18	2	34/35	30/31	1	352

2-Point conversions: Jeffires (3), R. Brown.
Team: 4-7.

RUSHING	Att.	Yds.	Avg.	LG	TD
White	191	757	4.0	33	3
G. Brown	169	648	3.8	18	4
Richardson	30	217	7.2	18	1
Tolliver	12	37	3.1	10	2
Carlson	10	17	1.7	6	0
Tillman	2	12	6.0	9	0
Coleman	1	2	2.0	2	0
Wellman	1	-3	-3.0	-3	0
Givins	1	-5	-5.0	-5	0
Oilers	417	1682	4.0	33	10
Opponents	540	2120	3.9	52	17

RECEIVING	No.	Yds.	Avg.	LG	TD
Slaughter	68	846	12.4	57	2
Jeffires	68	783	11.5	50	6
Givins	36	521	14.5	76t	1
White	21	188	9.0	41	1
Coleman	20	298	14.9	81	1
G. Brown	18	194	10.8	24	1
Carter	11	74	6.7	19	1
Wellman	10	112	11.2	25	0
McNair	8	78	9.8	21	0
R. Lewis	4	48	12.0	19	0
R. Brown	4	34	8.5	11	0
Hannah	3	24	8.0	11	0
Maston	2	12	6.0	10	0
Mills	1	4	4.0	4	0
Oilers	274	3216	11.7	81	13
Opponents	221	2963	13.4	55	18

INTERCEPTIONS	No.	Yds.	Avg.	LG	TD
D. Lewis	5	57	11.4	20	0
Dishman	4	74	18.5	38	1
Robertson	3	90	30.0	41	0
Bishop	1	21	21.0	21	0
St. Jackson	1	0	0.0	0	0
Oilers	14	242	17.3	41	1
Opponents	17	188	11.1	41	0

PUNTING	No.	Yds.	Avg.	In 20	LG
Camarillo	96	4115	42.9	34	58
Oilers	96	4115	42.9	34	58
Opponents	82	3443	42.0	31	56

PUNT RETURNS	No.	FC	Yds.	Avg.	LG	TD
Givins	37	9	210	5.7	78t	1
Hannah	9	0	58	6.4	13	0
Coleman	2	2	13	6.5	10	0
Dishman	1	0	0	0.0	0	0
Robertson	1	1	0	0.0	0	0
Oilers	50	12	281	5.6	78t	1
Opponents	50	16	438	8.8	82t	1

KICKOFF RETURNS	No.	Yds.	Avg.	LG	TD
McNair	23	481	20.9	44	0
Mills	15	282	18.8	34	0
St. Jackson	14	285	20.4	40	0
White	8	167	20.9	28	0
Hannah	5	116	23.2	39	0
Tillman	4	51	12.8	19	0
Bishop	2	18	9.0	11	0
Teeter	2	9	4.5	9	0
Givins	1	27	27.0	27	0
Oilers	74	1436	19.4	44	0
Opponents	48	832	17.3	35	0

SACKS	No.
Lathon	8.5
Childress	6.0
Davidson	6.0
Montgomery	3.0
Barrow	2.5
A. Smith	2.5
Bishop	1.5
St. Jackson	1.0
Oilers	31.0
Opponents	65.0

1995 DRAFT CHOICES

Round	Name	Pos.	College
1	Steve McNair	QB	Alcorn State
2	Anthony Cook	DT	So. Carolina State
3	Chris Sanders	WR	Ohio State
	Rodney Thomas	RB	Texas A&M
	Torey Hunter	DB	Washington State
4	Michael Roan	TE	Wisconsin
5	Gary Walker	DE	Auburn
6	Hicham El-Mashtoub	C	Arizona
7	C.J. Richardson	DB	Miami

HOUSTON OILERS

1995 VETERAN ROSTER

No.	Name	Pos.	Ht.	Wt.	Birthdate	NFL Exp.	College	Hometown	How Acq.	'94 Games/ Starts
56	Barrow, Micheal	LB	6-1	236	4/19/70	3	Miami	Homestead, Fla.	D2-'93	16/16
23	Bishop, Blaine	S	5-9	197	7/24/70	3	Ball State	Indianapolis, Ind.	D8-'93	16/13
59	† Bowden, Joe	LB	5-11	230	2/25/70	4	Oklahoma	Mesquite, Tex.	D5a-'92	14/1
33	Brown, Gary	RB	5-11	233	7/1/69	5	Penn State	Williamsport, Pa.	D8-'91	12/8
89	Brown, Reggie	WR	6-1	195	5/5/70	3	Alabama State	Miami, Fla.	FA-'93	4/0
16	Camarillo, Rich	P	5-11	202	11/29/59	15	Washington	Pico Rivera, Calif.	UFA(Ariz)-'94	16/0
14	Carlson, Cody	QB	6-3	202	11/5/63	9	Baylor	San Antonio, Tex.	D3-'87	5/5
85	# Carter, Pat	TE	6-4	258	8/1/66	8	Florida State	Sarasota, Fla.	UFA(Rams)-'94	16/13
17	Chandler, Chris	QB	6-4	225	10/12/65	8	Washington	Everett, Wash.	UFA(Rams)-'95	12/6*
79	Childress, Ray	DT	6-6	272	10/20/62	11	Texas A&M	Richardson, Tex.	D1a-'85	16/16
87	# Coleman, Pat	WR	5-7	176	4/8/67	5	Mississippi	Cleveland, Miss.	FA-'91	10/2
90	Davidson, Kenny	DE	6-5	288	8/17/67	6	Louisiana State	Shreveport, La.	UFA(Pitt)-'94	16/16
3	Del Greco, Al	K	5-10	202	3/2/62	12	Auburn	Coral Gables, Fla.	FA-'91	16/0
28	Dishman, Cris	CB	6-0	188	8/13/65	8	Purdue	Louisville, Ky.	D5a-'88	16/16
77	Donnalley, Kevin	G-T	6-5	305	6/10/68	5	North Carolina	Raleigh, N.C.	D3b-'91	13/11
58	# Faryniarz, Brett	LB	6-3	230	7/23/65	6	San Diego State	Rancho Cordova, Calif.	FA-'94	16/0
55	Flannery, John	G-C	6-3	304	1/13/69	5	Syracuse	Pottsville, Pa.	D2c-'91	16/16
92	Ford, Henry	DE	6-3	284	10/30/71	2	Arkansas	Ft. Worth, Tex.	D1-'94	11/0
21	Gray, Mel	KR-WR	5-9	171	3/16/61	10	Purdue	Williamsburg, Va.	UFA(Det)-'95	16/0*
82	Hannah, Travis	WR	5-7	161	1/31/70	3	Southern California	Hawthorne, Calif.	D4-'93	9/0
72	Hopkins, Brad	T	6-3	306	9/5/70	3	Illinois	Moline, Ill.	D1-'93	16/15
24	Jackson, Steve	CB	5-8	182	4/8/69	5	Purdue	Houston, Tex.	D3a-'91	11/0
29	Lewis, Darryll	CB	5-9	183	12/16/68	5	Arizona	La Puente, Calif.	D2b-'91	16/15
49	Lewis, Roderick	TE	6-5	254	6/9/71	2	Arizona	Dallas,Tex.	D5a-'94	3/1
74	# Matthews, Bruce	C	6-5	298	8/8/61	13	Southern California	Arcadia, Calif.	D1-'83	16/16
37	McNair, Todd	RB	6-1	202	10/7/65	7	Temple	Camden, N.J.	FA-'94	16/1
48	Mills, John Henry	RB-TE	6-0	222	10/31/69	3	Wake Forest	Tallahassee, Fla.	D5-'93	16/1
94	Montgomery, Glenn	DT	6-0	282	3/31/67	7	Houston	Gretna, La.	D5-'89	14/14
64	Norgard, Erik	C-G	6-1	282	11/4/65	7	Colorado	Arlington, Wash.	FA-'90	16/7
93	Nunley, Jeremy	DE	6-5	278	9/19/71	2	Alabama	Winchester, Tenn.	D2-'94	12/0
7	Richardson, Bucky	QB	6-1	228	2/7/69	4	Texas A&M	Baton Rouge, La.	D8-'92	7/4
31	Robertson, Marcus	S	5-11	197	10/2/69	5	Iowa State	Pasadena, Calif.	D4b-'91	16/16
50	† Robinson, Eddie	LB	6-1	245	4/13/70	4	Alabama State	New Orleans, La.	D2-'92	15/15
83	Seabron, Malcolm	WR	6-0	194	12/29/72	2	Fresno State	Sacramento, Calif.	D3-'94	13/0
84	Slaughter, Webster	WR	6-1	175	10/19/64	10	San Diego State	Stockton, Calif.	FA-'92	16/12
54	Smith, Al	LB	6-1	244	11/26/64	9	Utah State	Los Angeles, Calif.	D6a-'87	16/16
53	Stepnoski, Mark	C	6-2	269	1/20/67	7	Pittsburgh	Erie, Pa.	UFA(Dall)-'95	16/16*
70	Thomas, Stan	T	6-5	295	10/28/68	5	Texas	San Diego, Calif.	FA-'93	16/0
88	† Wellman, Gary	WR	5-9	173	8/9/67	4	Southern California	Westlake Hills, Calif.	D5-'91	8/0
73	Williams, David	T	6-5	292	6/21/66	7	Florida	Lakeland, Fla.	D1-'89	16/16
10	Williamson, Lee	QB	6-4	206	8/10/68	2	Presbyterian	Marietta, Ga.	FA-'94	0*
52	Wortham, Barron	LB	5-11	244	11/1/69	2	Texas-El Paso	Everman, Tex.	D6b-'94	16/1

* Chandler played 12 games with L.A. Rams in '94; Gray played 16 games with Detroit; Stepnoski played 16 games with Dallas; Williamson inactive for 7 games.

Unrestricted free agent; subject to developments.

† Restricted free agent; subject to developments.

Players lost through free agency (5): LB Lamar Lathon (Car; 16 games in '94), S Bo Orlando (SD; 16), DE Tim Roberts (NE; 12), G Bill Schultz (Den; 0), RB Lorenzo White (Clev; 15).

Players lost through Expansion Draft (3): CB Mike Davis (Jax; 16 games in '94), LB Le 'Shai Maston (Jax; 5), DT-DE Mike Teeter (Car; 14).

Also played with Oilers in '94—CB Tomur Barnes (1 game), WR Ernest Givins (16), WR Haywood Jeffires (16), DE Keith McCants (4), S Bubba McDowell (9), RB Spencer Tillman (16), QB Billy Joe Tolliver (10).

COACHING STAFF

Head Coach,
Jeff Fisher

Pro Career: Officially named as Oilers' fifteenth head coach on January 5, 1995. Was elevated to head coach-defensive coordinator on November 14, 1994, after head coach Jack Pardee and assistant head coach-offense Kevin Gilbride were relieved of their duties. Took over a 1-9 team and guided them through the final six games of the season, picking up his first victory against the New York Jets in the season finale. Originally joined the Oilers on February 9, 1994, as defensive coordinator after spending two seasons as defensive backs coach for the San Francisco 49ers (1992-93). Prior to stint with the 49ers, worked as defensive coordinator for the Los Angeles Rams (1991). From 1986-1990, was an assistant for Buddy Ryan's Philadelphia Eagles, serving as defensive backs coach from 1986-88 before becoming the NFL's youngest defensive coordinator in 1989. Drafted by Chicago in seventh round in 1981, spent five seasons as a cornerback and kick returner for the Bears (1981-85). Did not play in Bears' 1985 Super Bowl championship season after being placed on injured reserve with an ankle injury. That season he assisted defensive coordinator Buddy Ryan. Career record: 1-5.

Background: Played at Southern California (1977-1980) for John Robinson in a star-studded defensive backfield that included Ronnie Lott, Dennis Smith, and Joey Browner. Member of the USC team that won the national championship in 1978. Also served as the Trojans' backup placekicker and was a Pac-10 All-Academic selection in 1980.

Personal: Born February 25, 1958, in Culver City, Calif. Jeff and his wife Juli have three children, sons Brandon and Trenton, and daughter Tara. The family resides in Sugar Land, Tex.

ASSISTANT COACHES

Larry Beightol, offensive line; born November 21, 1942, Morrisdale, Pa., lives in Sugar Land, Tex. Guard-linebacker Catawba College 1961-63. No pro playing experience. College coach: William & Mary 1968-71, North Carolina State 1972-75, Auburn 1976, Arkansas 1977-78, 1980-82, Louisiana Tech 1979 (head coach), Missouri 1983-84. Pro coach: Atlanta Falcons 1985-86, Tampa Bay Buccaneers 1987-88, San Diego Chargers 1989, New York Jets 1990-94, joined Oilers in 1995.

Dick Coury, offensive assistant; born September 29, 1929, Athens, Ohio, lives in Pearland, Tex. No pro playing experience. College coach: Southern California 1967-69, Cal State-Fullerton 1970-71 (head coach). Pro coach: Denver Broncos 1972-73, Portland Storm (WFL) 1974 (head coach), San Diego Chargers 1975, Philadelphia Eagles 1976-81, Boston/New Orleans/Portland Breakers (USFL) 1983-85 (head coach), Los Angeles Rams 1986-90, New England Patriots 1991-92, Minnesota Vikings 1993, joined Oilers in 1994.

Mike Munchak, offensive assistant-quality control; born March 5, 1960, Scranton, Pa., lives in Sugar Land, Tex. Guard-tackle Penn State 1979-81. Pro guard Houston Oilers 1982-93. Pro coach: Joined Oilers in 1994.

Rex Norris, defensive line; born December 10, 1939, Tipton, Ind., lives in Sugar Land, Tex. Linebacker San Angelo (Tex.) J.C. 1959-60, East Texas State 1961-62. No pro playing experience. College coach: Navarro (Tex.) J.C. 1970-71, Texas A&M 1972, Oklahoma 1973-83, Arizona State 1984, Florida 1988-89, Tennessee 1990-91, Texas 1992-93. Pro coach: Detroit Lions 1985-87, Denver Broncos 1994, joined Oilers in 1995.

Clancy Pendergast, defensive assistant-quality control; born November 29, 1967, Phoenix, Ariz., lives in Houston, Tex. No college or pro playing experience. College coach: Mississippi State 1991, Southern California 1992, Oklahoma 1993-94. Pro coach: Joined Oilers in 1995.

Rod Perry, defensive backs; born September 11, 1953, Fresno, Calif., lives in Sugar Land, Tex. Defensive back Colorado 1972-74. Pro cornerback Los Angeles Rams 1975-82, Cleveland Browns 1983-84. College coach: Columbia 1985, Fresno City College 1986, Fresno State 1987-88. Pro coach: Seattle Seahawks 1989-91, Los Angeles Rams 1992-94, joined Oilers in 1995.

Russ Purnell, special teams; born June 12, 1948, Chicago, Ill., lives in Sugar Land, Tex. Center Orange Coast (Calif.) J.C. 1966-67, Whittier College 1968-69. No pro playing experience. College coach: Whittier College 1970-71, Southern California 1982-84. Pro coach: Seattle Seahawks 1986-94, joined Oilers in 1995.

Jerry Rhome, offensive coordinator; born March 6, 1942, Dallas, Tex., lives in Lake Olympia, Tex. Quarterback Southern Methodist 1960-61, Tulsa 1963-64. Pro quarterback Dallas Cowboys 1965-68, Cleveland Browns 1969, Houston Oilers 1970, Los Angeles Rams 1971-72. College coach: Tulsa 1973-75. Pro coach: Seattle Seahawks 1976-82, Washington Redskins 1983-87, San Diego Chargers 1988, Dallas Cowboys 1989, Phoenix Cardinals 1990-93, Minnesota Vikings 1994, joined Oilers in 1995.

Steve Sidwell, defensive coordinator; born August 30, 1944, Winfield, Kan., lives in Sugar Land, Tex. Linebacker Colorado 1962-65. No pro playing experience. College coach: Colorado 1966-73, Nevada-Las Vegas 1974-75, Southern Methodist 1976-81. Pro coach: New England Patriots 1982-84, Indianapolis Colts 1985, New Orleans Saints 1986-94, joined Oilers in 1995.

Sherman Smith, running backs; born November 1, 1954, Youngstown, Ohio, lives in Missouri City, Tex. Quarterback Miami, Ohio 1972-75. Pro running back Seattle Seahawks 1976-82, San Diego Chargers 1983-84. College coach: Miami, Ohio 1990-91, Illinois 1992-94. Pro coach: Joined Oilers in 1995.

Les Steckel, wide receiver-tight ends; born July 1, 1946, North Hampton, Pa., lives in Sugar Land, Tex. Running back Kansas 1964-68. No pro playing experience. College coach: Colorado 1972-76, 1991-92, Navy 1977, Brown 1989. Pro coach: San Francisco 49ers 1978, Minnesota Vikings 1979-84 (head coach, 1984), New England Patriots 1985-88, Denver Broncos 1993-94, joined Oilers in 1995.

Steve Watterson, strength and rehabilitation; born November 27, 1956, Newport, R.I., lives in Sugar Land, Tex. Attended Rhode Island. No college or pro playing experience. Pro coach: Philadelphia Eagles 1984-85 (assistant trainer), joined Oilers in 1986 (strength and rehabilitation coordinator), named assistant coach in 1988.

Gregg Williams, linebackers; born July 15, 1958 in Excelsior Springs, Mo., lives in Katy, Tex. Quarterback Northeast Missouri State 1976-79. No pro playing experience. College coach: Houston 1988-89. Pro coach: Joined Oilers in 1990 (quality control coordinator), named assistant coach in 1993.

1995 FIRST-YEAR ROSTER

Name	Pos.	Ht.	Wt.	Birthdate	College	Hometown	How Acq.
Barnes, Tomur	CB	5-10	188	9/8/70	North Texas	McNair, Tex.	FA
Cook, Anthony	DT-DE	6-3	293	5/30/72	South Carolina State	Bennettsville, S.C.	D2
El-Mashtoub, Hicham	C	6-2	288	5/11/72	Arizona	Laval, Canada	D6
Hall, Lemanski (1)	LB	6-0	229	11/24/70	Alabama	Valley, Ala.	D7-'94
Hunt, Purvis	G	6-4	378	11/25/70	Mississippi State	Ruston, La.	FA
Hunter, Torey	CB	5-9	176	2/10/72	Washington State	Tacoma, Wash.	D3c
Jackson, Sean (1)	RB	6-1	222	2/6/71	Florida State	New Orleans, La.	D4b-'94
Lewis, Scotty	DE	6-3	266	12/30/71	Baylor	Sulphur Springs, Tex.	FA
Logan, James	LB	6-2	210	12/6/72	Memphis State	Opp, Ala.	FA
Lundy, Dennis	RB	5-9	190	7/6/72	Northwestern	Tampa, Fla.	FA
McNair, Steve	QB	6-2	224	2/14/73	Alcorn State	Mt. Olive, Miss.	D1
Neal, Keith	WR	6-2	183	7/26/71	Idaho	Los Angeles, Calif.	FA
Reid, Jim (1)	T	6-6	306	2/13/71	Virginia	Newport News, Va.	D5b-'94
Richardson, C.J.	S	5-10	209	6/10/72	Miami	Dallas, Tex.	D7
Roan, Michael	TE	6-3	251	8/29/72	Wisconsin	Iowa City, Iowa	D4
Saenz, Richard	C	6-4	284	5/5/73	Vanderbilt	Houston, Tex.	FA
Sanders, Chris	WR	6-0	184	5/8/72	Ohio State	Denver, Colo.	D3a
Sharkey, Neal	G	6-2	297	6/27/72	Northwestern Louisiana	Greenville, Miss.	FA
Terrell, George	TE	6-4	275	3/21/71	Florida A&M	Lakeland, Fla.	FA
Thomas, Rodney	RB	5-10	213	3/30/73	Texas A&M	Groveton, Tex.	D3b
Walker, Gary	DT-DE	6-2	285	2/28/73	Auburn	Lavonia, Ga.	D5

The term NFL Rookie is defined as a player who is in his first season of professional football and has not been on the roster of another professional football team for any regular-season or postseason games. A Rookie is designated by an "R" on NFL rosters. Players who have been active in another professional football league or players who have NFL experience, including either preseason training camp or being on an Active List or Inactive List, or on Reserve/Injured or Reserve/Physically Unable to Perform for fewer than six regular-season games, are termed NFL First-Year Players. An NFL First-Year Player is designated by a "1" on NFL rosters. Thereafter, a player is credited with an additional year of experience for each season in which he accumulates six games on the Active List or Inactive List, or on Reserve/Injured or Reserve/Physically Unable to Perform.

NOTES

INDIANAPOLIS COLTS

American Football Conference
Eastern Division
Team Colors: Royal Blue and White
P.O. Box 535000
Indianapolis, Indiana 46253
Telephone: (317) 297-2658

CLUB OFFICIALS

President-Treasurer: Robert Irsay
Vice President-General Manager: James Irsay
Vice President-Director of Football Operations: Bill Tobin
Vice President-General Counsel: Michael G. Chernoff
Assistant General Manager: Bob Terpening
Director of Pro Player Personnel: Clyde Powers
Director of College Player Personnel: George Boone
Controller: Kurt Humphrey
Director of Operations: Pete Ward
Director of Public Relations: Craig Kelley
Ticket Manager: Larry Hall
Director of Sales: Rene Longoria
Assistant Director of Public Relations: Todd Stewart
Purchasing Administrator: David Filar
Administrative Assistant: Nicole Kucharski
Equipment Manager: Jon Scott
Assistant Equipment Manager: Mike Mays
Video Director: Marty Heckscher
Assistant Video Director: John Starliper
Head Trainer: Hunter Smith
Assistant Trainer: Dave Hammer
Team Physician and Orthopedic Surgeon: K. Donald Shelbourne
Orthopedic Surgeon: Arthur C. Rettig
Physician: Douglas Robertson
Stadium: RCA Dome • **Capacity:** 60,272
100 South Capitol Avenue
Indianapolis, Indiana 46225
Playing Surface: AstroTurf
Training Camp: Anderson University
Anderson, Indiana 46011

1995 SCHEDULE

PRESEASON

Aug. 4	**Cincinnati**	7:30
Aug. 12	at Seattle	7:00
Aug. 19	at Green Bay	12:00
Aug. 24	**Chicago**	7:30

REGULAR SEASON

Sept. 3	**Cincinnati**	12:00
Sept. 10	at New York Jets	4:00
Sept. 17	at Buffalo	1:00
Sept. 24	Open Date	
Oct. 1	**St. Louis**	12:00
Oct. 8	at Miami	4:00
Oct. 15	**San Francisco**	12:00
Oct. 22	at Los Angeles	1:00
Oct. 29	**New York Jets**	1:00
Nov. 5	**Buffalo**	1:00
Nov. 12	at New Orleans	12:00
Nov. 19	at New England	1:00
Nov. 26	**Miami**	1:00
Dec. 3	at Carolina	1:00
Dec. 10	at Jacksonville	1:00
Dec. 17	**San Diego**	4:00
Dec. 23	**New England** (Saturday)	8:00

RECORD HOLDERS

INDIVIDUAL RECORDS—CAREER

Category	Name	Performance
Rushing (Yds.)	Lydell Mitchell, 1972-77	5,487
Passing (Yds.)	Johnny Unitas, 1956-1972	39,768
Passing (TDs)	Johnny Unitas, 1956-1972	287
Receiving (No.)	Raymond Berry, 1955-1967	631
Receiving (Yds.)	Raymond Berry, 1955-1967	9,275
Interceptions	Bob Boyd, 1960-68	57
Punting (Avg.)	Rohn Stark, 1982-1994	43.8
Punt Return (Avg.)	Wendell Harris, 1964	12.6
Kickoff Return (Avg.)	Jim Duncan, 1969-1971	32.5
Field Goals	Dean Biasucci 1984, 1986-1994	176
Touchdowns (Tot.)	Lenny Moore, 1956-1967	113
Points	Dean Biasucci, 1984, 1986-1994	783

INDIVIDUAL RECORDS—SINGLE SEASON

Category	Name	Performance
Rushing (Yds.)	Eric Dickerson, 1988	1,659
Passing (Yds.)	Johnny Unitas, 1963	3,481
Passing (TDs)	Johnny Unitas, 1959	32
Receiving (No.)	Reggie Langhorne, 1993	85
Receiving (Yds.)	Raymond Berry, 1960	1,298
Interceptions	Tom Keane, 1953	11
Punting (Avg.)	Rohn Stark, 1985	45.9
Punt Return (Avg.)	Clarence Verdin, 1989	12.9
Kickoff Return (Avg.)	Jim Duncan, 1970	35.4
Field Goals	Raul Allegre, 1983	30
Touchdowns (Tot.)	Lenny Moore, 1964	20
Points	Lenny Moore, 1964	120

INDIVIDUAL RECORDS—SINGLE GAME

Category	Name	Performance
Rushing (Yds.)	Norm Bulaich, 9-19-71	198
Passing (Yds.)	Johnny Unitas, 9-17-67	401
Passing (TDs)	Gary Cuozzo, 11-14-65	5
	Gary Hogeboom, 10-4-87	5
Receiving (No.)	Lydell Mitchell, 12-15-74	13
	Joe Washington, 9-2-79	13
Receiving (Yds.)	Raymond Berry, 11-10-57	224
Interceptions	Many times	3
	Last time by Mike Prior, 12-20-92	
Field Goals	Many times	5
	Last time by Dean Biasucci, 9-25-88	
Touchdowns (Tot.)	Many times	4
	Last time by Eric Dickerson, 10-31-88	
Points	Many times	24
	Last time by Eric Dickerson, 10-31-88	

COACHING HISTORY

BALTIMORE 1953-1983
(297-310-7)

1953	Keith Molesworth	3-9-0
1954-62	Weeb Ewbank	61-52-1
1963-69	Don Shula	73-26-4
1970-72	Don McCafferty*	26-11-1
1972	John Sandusky	4-5-0
1973-74	Howard Schnellenberger**	4-13-0
1974	Joe Thomas	2-9-0
1975-79	Ted Marchibroda	41-36-0
1980-81	Mike McCormack	9-23-0
1982-84	Frank Kush***	11-28-1
1984	Hal Hunter	0-1-0
1985-86	Rod Dowhower****	5-24-0
1986-91	Ron Meyer#	36-36-0
1991	Rick Venturi	1-10-0
1992-94	Ted Marchibroda	21-27-0

*Released after five games in 1972
**Released after three games in 1974
***Resigned after 15 games in 1984
****Released after 13 games in 1986
#Released after five games in 1991

RCA DOME

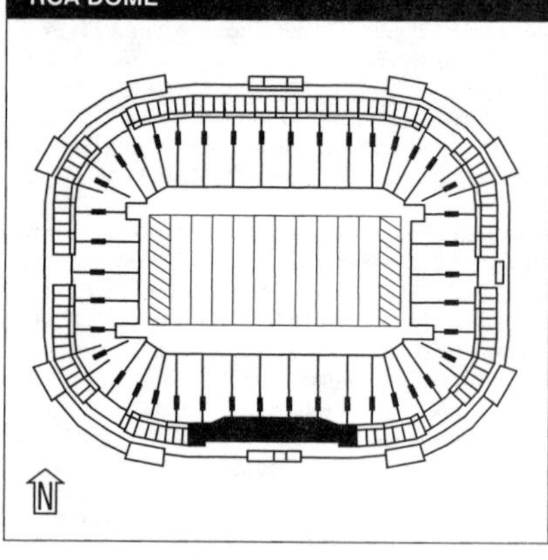

1994 TEAM RECORD

PRESEASON (4-0)

Date	Result		Opponents
8/5	W	13-9	Seattle
8/13	W	26-21	at Cincinnati
8/20	W	17-14	at Pittsburgh
8/25	W	24-7	Cleveland

REGULAR SEASON (8-8)

Date	Result		Opponents	Att.
9/4	W	45-21	Houston	47,372
9/11	L	10-24	at Tampa Bay	36,631
9/18	L	21-31	at Pittsburgh	54,040
9/25	L	14-21	Cleveland	55,821
10/2	W	17-15	Seattle	49,876
10/9	L	6-16	at N.Y. Jets	64,934
10/16	W	27-17	at Buffalo	79,404
10/23	L	27-41	Washington	57,879
10/30	W	28-25	N.Y. Jets	44,350
11/6	L	21-22	at Miami	67,863
11/20	W	17-13	at Cincinnati	55,566
11/27	L	10-12	New England	43,839
12/4	W	31-19	at Seattle	39,574
12/11	L	13-28	at New England	57,656
12/18	W	10- 6	Miami	58,867
12/24	W	10- 9	Buffalo	38,458

(OT) Overtime

SCORE BY PERIODS

Colts	82	86	73	66	0	—	307
Opponents	48	81	59	132	0	—	320

ATTENDANCE

Home 396,462 Away 455,668 Total 852,130
Single-game home record, 61,479 (11-13-83)
Single-season home record, 481,305 (1984)

1994 TEAM STATISTICS

	Colts	Opp.
Total First Downs	252	311
Rushing	108	98
Passing	126	192
Penalty	18	21
Third Down: Made/Att	70/198	115/251
Third Down Pct.	35.4	45.8
Fourth Down: Made/Att	12/17	13/23
Fourth Down Pct.	70.6	56.5
Total Net Yards	4413	5325
Avg. Per Game	275.8	332.8
Total Plays	899	1090
Avg. Per Play	4.9	4.9
Net Yards Rushing	2060	1646
Avg. Per Game	128.8	102.9
Total Rushes	495	463
Net Yards Passing	2353	3679
Avg. Per Game	147.1	229.9
Sacked/Yards Lost	28/166	29/218
Gross Yards	2519	3897
Att./Completions	376/217	598/354
Completion Pct.	57.7	59.2
Had Intercepted	14	18
Punts/Average	74/41.8	72/42.2
Net Punting Avg.	74/34.1	72/35.6
Penalties/Yards	82/658	110/824
Fumbles/Ball Lost	30/17	21/10
Touchdowns	37	34
Rushing	15	8
Passing	15	24
Returns	7	2
Possession Avg.	28:31	31:29

1994 INDIVIDUAL STATISTICS

PASSING	Att.	Comp.	Yds.	Pct.	TD	Int.	Tkld.	Rate
Harbaugh	202	125	1440	61.9	9	6	17/72	85.8
Majkowski	152	84	1010	55.3	6	7	9/76	69.8
Nagle	21	8	69	38.1	0	1	2/18	27.7
Warren	1	0	0	0.0	0	0	0/0	39.6
Colts	376	217	2519	57.7	15	14	28/166	75.9
Opponents	598	354	3897	59.2	24	18	29/218	79.4

SCORING	TD R	TD P	TD Rt	PAT	FG	Saf	PTS
Biasucci	0	0	0	37/37	16/24	0	85
Faulk	11	1	0	0/0	0/0	0	72
Turner	0	6	0	0/0	0/0	0	36
Dawkins	0	5	0	0/0	0/0	0	30
Buchanan	0	0	3	0/0	0/0	0	18
Majkowski	3	0	0	0/0	0/0	0	18
Potts	1	1	0	0/0	0/0	0	12
Bennett	0	0	1	0/0	0/0	0	6
Brewer	0	0	1	0/0	0/0	0	6
Cash	0	1	0	0/0	0/0	0	6
Coryatt	0	0	1	0/0	0/0	0	6
Humphrey	0	0	1	0/0	0/0	0	6
Jackson	0	1	0	0/0	0/0	0	6
Colts	15	15	7	37/37	16/24	0	307
Opponents	8	24	2	29/29	27/34	1	320

2-Point conversions: 0. Team: 0-0.

RUSHING	Att.	Yds.	Avg.	LG	TD
Faulk	314	1282	4.1	52	11
Potts	77	336	4.4	52	1
Harbaugh	39	223	5.7	41	0
Humphrey	18	85	4.7	27	0
Warren	18	80	4.4	34	0
Majkowski	24	34	1.4	10	3
Nagle	1	12	12.0	12	0
Toner	1	11	11.0	11	0
Turner	3	-3	-1.0	5	0
Colts	495	2060	4.2	52	15
Opponents	463	1646	3.6	40	8

RECEIVING	No.	Yds.	Avg.	LG	TD
Turner	52	593	11.4	28	6
Faulk	52	522	10.0	85t	1
Dawkins	51	742	14.5	49	5
Potts	26	251	9.7	30	1
Cash	16	190	11.9	24	1
Jackson	8	97	12.1	22	1
Warren	3	47	15.7	29	0
Humphrey	3	19	6.3	12	0
Bailey	2	30	15.0	23	0
Baker	2	15	7.5	10	0
Arbuckle	1	7	7.0	7	0
Etheredge	1	6	6.0	6	0
Colts	217	2519	11.6	85t	15
Opponents	354	3897	11.0	65t	24

INTERCEPTIONS	No.	Yds.	Avg.	LG	TD
Buchanan	8	221	27.6	90t	3
Tate	3	51	17.0	30	0
Ambrose	2	50	25.0	42	0
Daniel	2	6	3.0	6	0
Belser	1	31	31.0	31	0
Humphries	1	1	1.0	1	0
Watts	1	0	0.0	0	0
Colts	18	360	20.0	90t	3
Opponents	14	174	12.4	39	2

PUNTING	No.	Yds.	Avg.	In 20	LG
Stark	73	3092	42.4	22	60
Colts	74	3092	41.8	22	60
Opponents	72	3039	42.2	16	71

PUNT RETURNS	No.	FC	Yds.	Avg.	LG	TD
Brewer	42	8	339	8.1	75t	1
Colts	42	8	339	8.1	75t	1
Opponents	40	9	366	9.2	38	0

KICKOFF RETURNS	No.	Yds.	Avg.	LG	TD
Humphrey	35	783	22.4	95t	1
Brewer	18	358	19.9	34	0
Warren	2	56	28.0	38	0
Etheredge	2	23	11.5	14	0
Radecic	1	17	17.0	17	0
Toner	1	8	8.0	8	0
Jackson	1	5	5.0	5	0
Mahlum	0	4	—	4	0
Colts	60	1254	20.9	95t	1
Opponents	65	1316	20.2	47	0

SACKS	No.
Bennett	9.0
McCoy	6.0
Siragusa	5.0
Alberts	2.0
Buchanan	1.0
Coryatt	1.0
Emtman	1.0
Herrod	1.0
McDonald	1.0
Noga	1.0
Nunn	1.0
Colts	29.0
Opponents	28.0

1995 DRAFT CHOICES

Round	Name	Pos.	College
1	Ellis Johnson	DT	Florida
2	Ken Dilger	TE	Illinois
3	Zack Crockett	RB	Florida State
4	Ray McElroy	DB	Eastern Illinois
5	Derek West	T	Colorado
6	Brian Gelzheiser	LB	Penn State
7	Jessie Cox	LB	Texas Southern

INDIANAPOLIS COLTS

1995 VETERAN ROSTER

No.		Name	Pos.	Ht.	Wt.	Birthdate	NFL Exp.	College	Hometown	How Acq.	'94 Games/ Starts
51		Alberts, Trev	LB	6-4	243	8/8/70	2	Nebraska	Cedar Falls, Iowa	D1b-'94	5/0
33		Ambrose, Ashley	CB-S	5-10	185	9/17/70	4	Mississippi Valley State	New Orleans, La.	D2-'92	16/4
84		Anderson, Willie	WR	6-0	175	3/7/65	8	UCLA	Paulsboro, N.J.	UFA(Rams)-'95	16/16*
81		Arbuckle, Charles	TE	6-3	248	9/13/68	5	UCLA	Beaumont, Tex.	FA-'94	7/1
80		Bailey, Aaron	WR	5-10	184	10/24/71	2	Louisville	Ann Arbor, Mich.	FA-'94	13/0
83		Banta, Bradford	TE	6-6	255	12/14/70	2	Southern California	Baton Rouge, La.	D4-'94	16/0
29		Belser, Jason	CB-S	5-9	187	5/28/70	4	Oklahoma	Kansas City, Mo.	D8a-'92	13/12
56		Bennett, Tony	LB	6-2	243	7/1/67	6	Mississippi	Clarksdale, Miss.	UFA(GB)-'94	16/15
4	#	Biasucci, Dean	K	6-0	190	7/25/62	11	Western Carolina	Niagara Falls, N.Y.	FA-'86	16/0
34		Buchanan, Ray	CB-S	5-9	193	9/29/71	3	Louisville	Chicago, Ill.	D3-'93	16/16
3		Cofer, Mike	K	6-1	190	2/19/64	7	North Carolina State	Charlotte, N.C.	FA-'95	0*
55		Coryatt, Quentin	LB	6-3	250	8/1/70	4	Texas A&M	St. Croix, Virgin Islands	D1b-'92	16/16
39		Covington, John	CB-S	6-0	198	4/22/72	2	Notre Dame	Winter Haven, Fla.	D5-'94	3/0
38		Daniel, Eugene	CB-S	5-11	188	5/4/61	12	Louisiana State	Baton Rouge, La.	D8-'84	16/15
87		Dawkins, Sean	WR	6-4	210	2/3/71	3	California	Red Bank, N.J.	D1-'93	16/16
69	#	Dixon, Randy	G	6-3	305	3/12/65	9	Pittsburgh	Clewiston, Fla.	D4-'87	14/14
90		Emtman, Steve	DE	6-4	300	4/16/70	4	Washington	Spokane, Wash.	D1a-'92	4/0
7	t-	Erickson, Craig	QB	6-2	205	5/17/69	4	Miami	West Palm Beach, Fla.	T(TB)-'95	15/15*
28		Faulk, Marshall	RB	5-10	200	2/26/73	2	San Diego State	New Orleans, La.	D1a-'94	16/16
17		Gardocki, Chris	P	6-1	196	2/7/70	5	Clemson	Stone Mountain, Ga.	UFA(Chi)-'95	16/0*
59		Grant, Stephen	LB	6-0	242	12/23/69	4	West Virginia	Miami, Fla.	D10-'92	16/12
30		Gray, Derwin	CB-S	5-11	198	4/9/71	3	Brigham Young	San Antonio, Tex.	D4a-'93	16/2
12		Harbaugh, Jim	QB	6-3	215	12/23/63	9	Michigan	Ann Arbor, Mich.	FA-'94	12/9
54		Herrod, Jeff	LB	6-0	249	7/29/66	8	Mississippi	Birmingham, Ala.	D9-'88	15/15
25		Humphrey, Ronald	RB	5-10	211	3/3/69	3	Mississippi Valley State	Marland, Tex.	FA-'93	15/0
23		Humphries, Leonard	CB-S	5-9	180	6/19/70	2	Penn State	Akron, Ohio	FA-'94	13/0
84		Jackson, Mark	WR	5-9	180	7/13/63	10	Purdue	Chicago, Ill.	FA-'94	12/0
63		Lowdermilk, Kirk	C	6-4	280	4/10/63	11	Ohio State	Canton, Ohio	UFA(Minn)-'93	16/16
65		Mahlum, Eric	G	6-4	285	12/6/70	2	California	San Diego, Calif.	D2-'94	16/2
74		Mathews, Jason	T	6-5	284	2/9/71	2	Texas A&M	Orange, Tex.	D3-'94	10/0
61	†	McCoy, Tony	NT	6-0	279	6/10/69	4	Florida	Orlando, Fla.	D4b-'92	15/15
57		McDonald, Devon	LB	6-4	248	11/8/69	3	Notre Dame	Kingston, Jamaica	D4b-'93	16/3
47		McLemore, Thomas	TE	6-5	250	3/14/70	4	Southern	Shreveport, La.	FA-'95	2/1*
18		Nagle, Browning	QB	6-3	225	4/29/68	5	Louisville	Philadelphia, Pa.	FA-'94	1/1
93	#	Nunn, Freddie Joe	DE	6-5	255	4/9/62	11	Mississippi	Noxubee, Miss.	FA-'94	11/6
42		Potts, Roosevelt	RB	6-0	245	1/8/71	3	Northeast Louisiana	Rayville, La.	D2-'93	16/15
97		Radecic, Scott	LB	6-3	240	6/14/62	12	Penn State	Pittsburgh, Pa.	FA-'94	16/1
52		Ratigan, Brian	LB	6-4	241	12/27/70	3	Notre Dame	Council Bluffs, Iowa	FA-'93	14/0
58		Sanders, Glenell	LB	6-1	236	11/4/66	2	Louisiana Tech	New Orleans, La.	FA-'95	1/0*
98		Siragusa, Tony	DT	6-3	315	5/14/67	6	Pittsburgh	Kenilworth, N.J.	FA-'90	16/16
86		Stablein, Brian	WR	6-1	191	4/14/70	2	Ohio State	Erie, Pa.	FA-'94	0*
79		Staysniak, Joe	G	6-4	302	12/8/66	5	Ohio State	Elyria, Ohio	FA-'92	16/16
49	#	Tate, David	CB-S	6-1	200	11/22/64	8	Colorado	Buffalo Grove, Ill.	FA-'94	16/8
88		Turner, Floyd	WR	5-11	198	5/29/66	7	Northwestern Louisiana	Shreveport, La.	UFA(NO)-'94	16/16
21		Warren, Lamont	RB	5-11	194	1/4/73	2	Colorado	Indianapolis, Ind.	D6-'94	11/0
36		Watts, Damon	CB-S	5-10	173	4/8/72	2	Indiana	Indianapolis, Ind.	FA-'94	16/8
85		West, Ed	TE	6-1	245	8/2/61	12	Auburn	Leighton, Ala.	UFA(GB)-'95	14/12*
95		Whittington, Bernard	DE	6-6	257	8/20/71	2	Indiana	St. Louis, Mo.	FA-'94	13/8
67		Wolford, Will	T	6-5	300	5/18/64	10	Vanderbilt	Louisville, Ky.	RFA(Buff)-'93	16/16

* Anderson played 16 games with L.A. Rams in '94; Cofer last active with San Francisco in '93; Erickson played 15 games with Tampa Bay; Gardocki played 16 games with Chicago; McLemore played 2 games with Cleveland; Sanders played 1 game with Denver; Stablein active for 2 games but did not play; West played 14 games with Green Bay.

\# Unrestricted free agent; subject to developments.

† Restricted free agent; subject to developments.

t- Colts traded for Erickson (Tampa Bay).

Players lost through free agency (6): TE Kerry Cash (Raid; 16 games in '94), T Cecil Gray (Raid; 16), QB Don Majkowski (Det; 9), T Zefross Moss (Det; 11), DT Tom Sims (Minn; 16), P Rohn Stark (Pitt; 16).

Players lost through Expansion Draft (2): RB Dewell Brewer (Car; 16 games in '94), LB Paul Butcher (Car; 13).

Also played with Colts in '94—WR Shannon Baker (4 games), TE Carlos Etheredge (9), DE Jon Hand (5), DT Garry Howe (1), DE Al Noga (4), CB-S Robert O'Neal (2), DE-DT Lance Teichelman (1), RB Ed Toner (9).

COACHING STAFF

Head Coach,
Ted Marchibroda

Pro Career: Marchibroda ranks as the second-winningest head coach in Colts history with a 62-63 record. His 125 total games coached are a franchise record. He returned to the Colts on January 28, 1992, after serving as head coach with the team from 1975-79. Marchibroda's first tenure produced a 41-36 overall record and three AFC Eastern Divisional titles (1975, 10-4; 1976, 11-3; and 1977, 10-4). He took over a Colts team that was 2-12 in 1974 and produced an eight-game improvement, then the best one-season turnaround in NFL history. It marked the first time a coach had taken a team from last to first place in one season. Marchibroda authored a 9-7 record three years ago, thus his 1975 and 1992 Colts squads posted two of the four eight-game seasonal turnarounds in NFL history. The Colts were 8-8 in 1994. His three divisional championships represent the most titles won by a Colts head coach. Prior to returning to the Colts, Marchibroda served five years as an assistant with the Buffalo Bills, the last three as offensive coordinator. Marchibroda began his career as backfield coach with the Washington Redskins in 1961. He joined George Allen's staff with the Los Angeles Rams in 1966. He moved with Allen to the Redskins in 1971, where he served as offensive coordinator through the 1974 season. After his stint with the Colts, Marchibroda served as quarterback coach with Chicago in 1981, then moved on to Detroit as offensive coordinator from 1982-83. He served in that same role in Philadelphia from 1984-85 before joining Buffalo in 1987. Marchibroda was the first draft pick of the Pittsburgh Steelers in 1953 and played one year before serving in the Army. He returned to Pittsburgh for the 1955-56 seasons. His top year was 1956, completing 124 of 275 passes for 1,585 yards and 12 touchdowns. Marchibroda's playing career ended with the Chicago Cardinals in 1957. Career record: 62-63.

Background: Quarterback at St. Bonaventure 1950-51 and University of Detroit 1952. Led nation in total offense at Detroit. He was a football, basketball (all-state selection), and baseball player at Franklin (Pa.) High School.

Personal: Born March 15, 1931, Franklin, Pa. Ted and his wife, Ann, reside in Indianapolis. They have two daughters, Jodi and Lonni, and two sons, Ted, Jr. and Robert.

1995 FIRST-YEAR ROSTER

Name	Pos.	Ht.	Wt.	Birthdate	College	Hometown	How Acq.
Anderson, Phil	WR	5-11	190	5/20/72	Delaware State	Wilmington, Del.	FA
Berry, Mike	DT	6-4	268	2/13/69	Valdosta State	Warner Robins, Ga.	FA
Biggens, Wilbert	CB-S	5-8	187	12/24/72	Texas A&M	Dallas, Tex.	FA
Bronson, Ben	WR	5-10	165	9/9/72	Baylor	Jaspar, Tex.	FA
Clarks, Conrad	CB-S	5-10	212	4/21/69	Northeast Louisiana	Franklin, La.	FA
Conway, Duane	C	6-2	288	8/24/72	Eastern Illinois	Bolingbrook, Ill.	FA
Copher, Chad	DT	6-7	265	12/1/71	Illinois	East Dundee, Ill.	FA
Cox, Jessie	LB	6-2	222	9/8/71	Texas Southern	Long Beach, Calif.	D7
Craft, Douglas (1)	CB-S	6-0	190	7/23/68	Southern	Bossier City, La.	FA
Crockett, Zack	RB	6-2	244	12/2/72	Florida State	Pompano Beach, Fla.	D3
Dilger, Ken	TE	6-5	249	2/2/71	Illinois	Mariah Hill, Ind.	D2
Duggins, Brent	T	6-4	288	1/19/72	Southern Mississippi	Carrolton, Ga.	FA
Edwards, Jason	DE	6-5	263	4/9/72	Illinois	Evansville, Ind.	FA
Gelzheiser, Brian	LB	6-1	235	2/12/72	Penn State	Pittsburgh, Pa.	D6
Groce, Clif	RB	5-11	244	7/30/72	Texas A&M	College Station, Tex.	FA
Hardin, Steve	G	6-7	310	12/30/71	Oregon	Snohomish, Wash.	FA
Harris, Lamar	RB-TE	6-2	255	5/19/72	Arizona	Tucson, Ariz.	FA
Hill, Aubrey	WR	5-11	169	2/2/72	Florida	Miami, Fla.	FA
Johnson, Ellis	DE-DT	6-2	290	10/30/73	Florida	Wildwood, Fla.	D1
Johnson, Eric	RB	5-10	200	6/7/71	Central Michigan	Grand Rapids, Mich.	FA
Jones, Tyronne	WR	5-8	165	9/12/71	Grambling State	New Orleans, La.	FA
Justin, Paul (1)	QB	6-4	202	5/19/68	Arizona State	Schaumburg, Ill.	FA
Marshall, Marvin	WR	5-10	175	6/21/72	South Carolina State	Hephzibah, Ga.	FA
McElroy, Ray	CB-S	5-11	188	7/31/72	Eastern Illinois	Bellwood, Ill.	D4
Morrison, Steve	LB	6-3	238	12/28/71	Michigan	Birmingham, Mich.	FA
Patrick, Garin (1)	G-T	6-3	265	8/31/71	Louisville	Canton, Ohio	FA
Pollard, Marcus	TE	6-4	248	2/8/72	Bradley	Valley, Ala.	FA
Smith, Carl	CB-S	6-0	199	3/12/73	Virginia	Richmond, Va.	FA
Smith, Terry (1)	WR	6-0	200	4/20/71	Clemson	Clemson, S.C.	FA
Smith, Warner	G	6-2	291	3/30/73	Arizona	San Manual, Ariz.	FA
Stevenson, Jon	G	6-3	270	2/23/73	Alabama	Memphis, Tenn.	FA
Vickers, Kipp (1)	G-T	6-2	288	8/27/69	Miami	Holiday, Fla.	FA
West, Derek	T	6-8	298	3/28/72	Colorado	Denver, Colo.	D5
West, Royal	DT	6-3	265	7/8/71	Texas Christian	Tyler, Tex.	FA
Wilmot, Trevor	LB	6-2	220	10/30/72	Indiana	Evanston, Ill.	FA

The term NFL Rookie is defined as a player who is in his first season of professional football and has not been on the roster of another professional football team for any regular-season or postseason games. A Rookie is designated by an "R" on NFL rosters. Players who have been active in another professional football league or players who have NFL experience, including either preseason training camp or being on an Active List or Inactive List, or on Reserve/Injured or Reserve/Physically Unable to Perform for fewer than six regular-season games, are termed NFL First-Year Players. An NFL First-Year Player is designated by a "1" on NFL rosters. Thereafter, a player is credited with an additional year of experience for each season in which he accumulates six games on the Active List or Inactive List, or on Reserve/Injured or Reserve/Physically Unable to Perform.

NOTES

ASSISTANT COACHES

Tom Batta, tight ends-quality control; born October 6, 1942, Youngstown, Ohio, lives in Indianapolis. Offensive-defensive line Kent State 1961-63. No pro playing experience. College coach: Akron 1973, Colorado 1974-78, Kansas 1979-82, North Carolina State 1983. Pro coach: Minnesota Vikings 1984-93, joined Colts in 1994.

Greg Blache, defensive line; born March 9, 1949, New Orleans, La., lives in Indianapolis. No college or pro playing experience. College coach: Notre Dame 1973-75, 1981-83, Tulane 1976-80, Southern University 1986, Kansas 1987. Pro coach: Jacksonville Bulls (USFL) 1984-85, Green Bay Packers 1988-93, joined Colts in 1994.

Ron Blackledge, offensive line; born April 15, 1938, Canton, Ohio, lives in Indianapolis. Tight end-defensive end Bowling Green 1957-59. No pro playing experience. College coach: Ashland 1968-69, Cincinnati 1970-72, Kentucky 1973-75, Princeton 1976, Kent State 1977-81 (head coach 1979-81). Pro coach: Pittsburgh Steelers 1982-91, joined Colts in 1992.

Fred Bruney, defensive assistant; born December 30, 1931, Martins Ferry, Ohio, lives in Indianapolis. Running back-defensive back Ohio State 1950-52. Pro defensive back San Francisco 49ers 1953-56, Pittsburgh Steelers 1957, Los Angeles Rams 1958, Boston Patriots 1960-62. College coach: Ohio State 1959. Pro coach: Boston Patriots 1962-63, Philadelphia Eagles 1964-68, 1977-85, Atlanta Falcons 1969-76, 1986-89, Tampa Bay Buccaneers 1990, New York Giants 1991-92, joined Colts in 1993.

Gene Huey, running backs; born July 20, 1947, Uniontown, Pa., lives in Indianapolis. Defensive back-wide receiver Wyoming 1966-69. No pro playing experience. College coach: Wyoming 1970-74, New Mexico 1975-77, Nebraska 1978-87, Ohio State 1988-91. Pro coach: Joined Colts in 1992.

Lindy Infante, offensive coordinator; born May 27, 1940, Miami, Fla., lives in Indianapolis. Running back Florida 1959-62. Pro running back Hamilton Tiger-Cats (CFL) 1963. College coach: Florida 1966-71, Memphis State 1972-73, Tulane 1976, 1979. Pro coach: Charlotte Hornets (WFL) 1975, New York Giants 1977-78, Cincinnati Bengals 1980-82, Jacksonville Bulls (USFL) 1984-85 (head coach), Cleveland Browns 1986-87, Green Bay Packers 1988-91 (head coach), joined Colts in 1995.

Jim Johnson, linebackers; born May 26, 1941, Maywood, Ill., lives in Indianapolis. Quarterback Missouri 1959-62. Pro tight end Buffalo Bills 1963-64. College coach: Missouri Southern 1967-68 (head coach), Drake 1969-72, Indiana 1973-76, Notre Dame 1977-80. Pro coach: Oklahoma Outlaws (USFL) 1984, Jacksonville Bulls (USFL) 1985, Phoenix Cardinals 1986-93, joined Colts in 1994.

Hank Kuhlmann, special teams; born October 6, 1937, Webster Groves, Mo., lives in Indianapolis. Running back Missouri 1956-59. No pro playing experience. College coach: Missouri 1962-71, Notre Dame 1975-77. Pro coach: Green Bay Packers 1972-74, Chicago Bears 1978-82, Birmingham Stallions (USFL) 1983-85, Phoenix Cardinals 1986-90 (scout, 1990), Tampa Bay Buccaneers 1991, joined Colts in 1994.

Jimmy Robinson, wide receivers; born January 3, 1953, Atlanta, Ga., lives in Indianapolis. Wide receiver Georgia Tech 1972-74. Pro wide receiver Atlanta Falcons 1975, New York Giants 1976-79, San Francisco 49ers 1980, Denver Broncos 1981. College coach: Georgia Tech 1986-89. Pro coach: Memphis Showboats (USFL) 1984-85, Atlanta Falcons 1990-93, joined Colts in 1994.

Pat Thomas, secondary; born September 1, 1954, Plano, Tex., lives in Indianapolis. Cornerback Texas A&M 1972-75. Pro cornerback Los Angeles Rams 1976-82. College coach: Houston 1987-89. Pro coach Houston Gamblers (USFL) 1984-85, Houston Oilers 1990-92, joined Colts in 1994.

Vince Tobin, defensive coordinator; born September 29, 1943, Burlington Junction, Mo., lives in Indianapolis. Defensive back-running back Missouri 1961-64. No pro playing experience. College coach: Missouri 1967-76. Pro coach: British Columbia Lions (CFL) 1977-82, Philadelphia/Baltimore Stars (USFL) 1983-85, Chicago Bears 1986-92, joined Colts in 1994.

Tom Zupancic, strength and conditioning; born September 14, 1955, Indianapolis, lives in Indianapolis. Defensive tackle-offensive tackle Indiana Central 1975-78. No pro playing experience. Pro coach: Joined Colts in 1984.

JACKSONVILLE JAGUARS

American Football Conference
Central Division
Team Colors: Teal, Black, and Gold
One Stadium Place
Jacksonville, Florida 32202
Telephone: (904) 633-6000

CLUB OFFICIALS

Chairman and Chief Executive Officer: Wayne Weaver
President and Chief Operating Officer: David Seldin
Head Coach: Tom Coughlin
Vice President/Football Operations: Michael Huyghue
General Counsel: Paul Vance
Senior Vice President/Marketing: Dan Connell
Vice President/Ticket Operations: Judy Seldin
Vice President/Broadcasting & Creative Services: Peter Scheurmier
Executive Director of Communications: Dan Edwards
Executive Director of Administration: John Jones
Director of Pro Personnel: Ron Hill
Director of College Scouting: Rick Reiprish
Director of Finance: David Blasic
Director of Special Events & Promotions: Ann Carroll
Director of Corporate Sponsorship: David Rowan
Director of Facilities: Jeff Cannon
Director of Computer Services: Bruce Swindell
Director of Player Programs: Paul Lankford
Head Athletic Trainer: Mike Ryan
Video Director: Mike Perkins
Equipment Manager: Bob Monica

Chair & Chief Executive Officer, Jaguars Foundation: Delores Barr Weaver
President, Jaguars Foundation: Dr. Gregory Gross
Stadium: A New Stadium for Jacksonville
•**Capacity:** 73,000
One Stadium Place
Jacksonville, Florida 32202
Playing Surface: Grass
Training Camp: University of Wisconsin-Steven's Point
Steven's Point, Wisconsin 54481

FORMULATION OF JACKSONVILLE JAGUARS

The player access plan for the expansion Carolina Panthers and Jacksonville Jaguars was announced jointly by the NFL and the NFL Players Association on September 29, 1994. Under the plan, Carolina and Jacksonville were given three ways to acquire players:

1. Veteran Allocation Draft—On February 15, 1995, the expansion teams selected from a list of six veteran players submitted by each of the 28 existing NFL teams. Carolina and Jacksonville had to select at least 30 players but no more than 42. An existing club had to recall a player from its list each time one of its players was selected. The expansion teams could select a maximum of three players from each of the other clubs. Jacksonville had the first pick and selected 31 players. Carolina chose 35.
2. College Player Draft—In addition to their regular selections, each expansion team received a total of 14 extra picks in the 1995 and 1996 college drafts. For the 1995 draft, Carolina and Jacksonville were awarded the first two choices in all seven rounds. The picks were allotted in rotating order with Carolina given the first choice in round one, Jacksonville the first in round two, etc. Carolina won the right to select first via a coin flip with Jacksonville at the 1994 draft. In addition to their picks at the top of each round, the expansion teams received seven additional 1995 selections each, one at the end of rounds one through seven.

   In the 1996 draft, both the Panthers and Jaguars will receive an extra choice after each of their original picks in rounds three through five, plus two extra picks each after their original selections in rounds six and seven. The additional picks will fall 15 selections after the team's original choice in those rounds.
3. Free Agency—The clubs signed veteran free agents between February and July, 1995, under the same terms as the league's current 28 clubs.

1995 SCHEDULE

PRESEASON

July 29	vs. Carolina at Canton, Ohio	2:30
Aug. 4	at Miami	7:00
Aug. 10	at Detroit	7:30
Aug. 18	**St. Louis**	7:00
Aug. 25	**Denver**	7:00

REGULAR SEASON

Sept. 3	**Houston**	1:00
Sept. 10	at Cincinnati	4:00
Sept. 17	at New York Jets	4:00
Sept. 24	**Green Bay**	8:00
Oct. 1	at Houston	3:00
Oct. 8	**Pittsburgh**	1:00
Oct. 15	**Chicago**	1:00
Oct. 22	at Cleveland	1:00
Oct. 29	at Pittsburgh	1:00
Nov. 5	Open Date	
Nov. 12	**Seattle**	1:00
Nov. 19	at Tampa Bay	1:00
Nov. 26	**Cincinnati**	1:00
Dec. 3	at Denver	2:00
Dec. 10	**Indianapolis**	1:00
Dec. 17	at Detroit	1:00
Dec. 24	**Cleveland**	1:00

1995 DRAFT CHOICES

Round	Name	Pos.	College
1	Tony Boselli	T	Southern California
	James Stewart	RB	Tennessee
2	Brian DeMarco	T	Michigan State
	Bryan Schwartz	LB	Augustana, S.D.
3	Chris Hudson	DB	Colorado
4	Rob Johnson	QB	Southern California
	Mike Thompson	DT	Wisconsin
5	Ryan Christopherson	RB	Wyoming
6	Marcus Price	T	Louisiana State
7	Curtis Marsh	WR	Utah

A NEW STADIUM FOR JACKSONVILLE

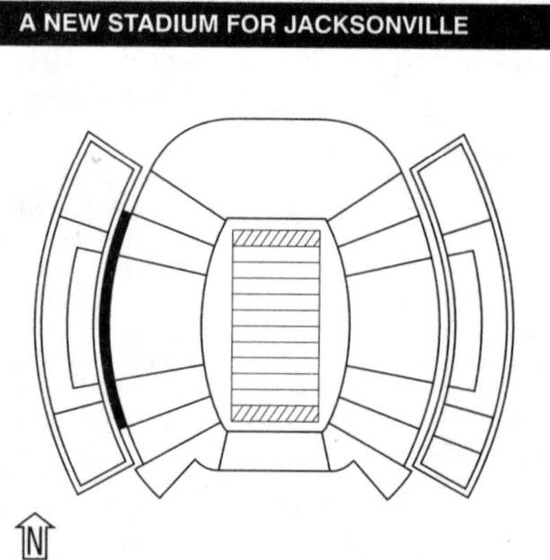

JACKSONVILLE JAGUARS CHRONOLOGY

August 17, 1989
Touchdown Jacksonville!, a partnership to lead the community effort to win an NFL franchise is formed. Jacksonville businessman Tom Petway heads the group.

April 4, 1990
National Football League Commissioner Paul Tagliabue announces that the league will expand by two teams no later than the 1993 season.

July 26, 1990
The NFL Realignment and Expansion Committee recommends that the NFL expand by two teams for the 1993 season.

February 12, 1991
In a unanimous vote, the Jacksonville City Council votes to commit $60 million to renovate the Gator Bowl contingent upon the city being awarded an NFL expansion football team.

May 15, 1991
The NFL Realignment and Expansion Committee recommends that the league expand by two teams for the 1994 season.

May 22, 1991
At the NFL meetings in Minneapolis, a plan is approved that will add two expansion teams to the league for the 1994 season.

May 30, 1991
Florida Governor Lawton Chiles signs into law the Professional Sports Facilities Program, a state statute that provides state funding of up to $2 million for 30 years for funding new sports facilities that operate in the state of Florida.

July 17, 1991
The NFL announces that it will accept applications for expansion teams.

September 16, 1991
The city of Jacksonville files an expansion application with the NFL, one of 11 cities to apply.

October 1, 1991
Touchdown Jacksonville!, Ltd. submits its ownership application to the NFL. The nine-member partnership includes local businessman and Touchdown Jacksonville!, Ltd. general partner Tom Petway. J. Wayne Weaver is one of the eight limited partners, along with Jeb Bush, Lawrence DuBow, Earl Hadlow, Preston Haskell, Sandy McArthur, Charles Towers, and Ron Weaver.

October 24, 1991
David Seldin is named president and chief operating officer of Touchdown Jacksonville!, Ltd.

December 6, 1991
Touchdown Jacksonville!, Ltd. announces that the team name will be the Jacksonville Jaguars if an expansion team is awarded.

December 10, 1991
Touchdown Jacksonville!, Ltd. and city officials make the group's first presentation to Commissioner Tagliabue and other NFL officials in New York.

March 17, 1992
At the NFL's annual winter meeting in Phoenix, the list of expansion candidate cities is cut from eleven to seven. Jacksonville is one of the seven, while Nashville, San Antonio, Raleigh-Durham, and Honolulu are eliminated.

May 19, 1992
The five finalists in the expansion race are named: Jacksonville, Charlotte, Baltimore, Memphis, and St. Louis. Sacramento and Oakland are eliminated.

October 20, 1992
Citing complications surrounding the ongoing labor situation, the NFL votes to delay the expansion announcement to the 1993 fall meeting in Chicago, and for expansion teams to begin play in 1995.

January 6, 1993
A seven-year Collective Bargaining Agreement is reached between the NFL and its players. With the labor situation resolved, a new expansion timetable is expected in March, 1993.

March 18, 1993
J. Wayne Weaver is introduced as managing general partner of Touchdown Jacksonville!, Ltd.

April 12, 1993
After a tour with Touchdown Jacksonville, Ltd. representatives, NFL officials indicate that additional renovations beyond those already planned would be necessary to renovate the Gator Bowl to NFL standards.

August 21, 1993
Mayor Austin and Touchdown Jacksonville!, Ltd. reach an agreement on a stadium lease capping stadium renovation cost at $121 million, with $53 million to come from city funds and $68 million from team and team-related sources. As project manager, Touchdown Jacksonville!, Ltd. assumes responsibility for cost overruns.

August 23, 1993
Jacksonville City Council votes 14-4 to approve the new lease.

September 21, 1993
Weaver and other Touchdown Jacksonville!, Ltd. officials make their presentation to the NFL finance and expansion committees.

October 26, 1993
In Chicago, League owners select the Carolinas for an expansion team but delay the announcement of the second expansion city.

November 30, 1993
In Chicago, Jacksonville is awarded the thirtieth franchise in the National Football League.

December 1, 1993
"Victory" celebration in the Gator Bowl. Twenty-five thousand Jaguars fans battle cold and rain to welcome Wayne Weaver, Jaguars officials, and community leaders upon their return from Chicago.

January 3, 1994
Demolition of the Gator Bowl begins.

January 6, 1994
The Jaguars announce a season-ticket sellout for their first three seasons. More than 56,000 season tickets are sold through December 31, just one month after the awarding of the team.

February 21, 1994
Tom Coughlin is hired as head coach of the Jaguars. The former Boston College head coach brings six of his assistants with him.

November 2, 1994
Commissioner Tagliabue slots the Jaguars in the AFC Central Division.

December 15, 1994
The Jaguars sign their first 10 players: Wide receiver Shannon Baker, linebacker Hillary Butler, defensive tackle Ferric Collins, guard Greg Huntington, running back Randy Jordan, defensive end Ernie Logan, tackle Rickie Shaw, defensive end Jason Simmons, defensive tackle Ricky Sutton, and defensive tackle Chris Williams.

February 15, 1995
The Jaguars draft 31 veteran players in the expansion draft, with Arizona Cardinals quarterback Steve Beuerlein the first player selected overall.

April 22, 1995
The Jaguars make Southern California offensive tackle Tony Boselli their first selection in the college draft.

JACKSONVILLE JAGUARS

1995 VETERAN ROSTER

No.	Name	Pos.	Ht.	Wt.	Birthdate	NFL Exp.	College	Hometown	How Acq.	'94 Games/ Starts
83	Baker, Shannon	WR	5-10	190	7/20/70	2	Florida State	Lakeland, Fla.	FA-'94	4/0*
4	Barker, Bryan	P	6-1	187	6/28/64	6	Santa Clara	Miramonte, Calif.	UFA(Phil)-'95	11/0*
7	Beuerlein, Steve	QB	6-3	210	3/7/65	9	Notre Dame	Hollywood, Calif.	ED(Ariz)-'95	9/7*
66	Bouwens, Shawn	G	6-4	290	5/25/68	5	Nebraska-Wesleyan	Lincoln, Neb.	UFA(Det)-'95	16/16*
52	Boyer, Brant	LB	6-0	237	6/27/71	2	Arizona	Ogden, Utah	ED(Mia)-'95	14/0*
36	Boykin, Deral	S	5-11	196	9/2/70	3	Louisville	Kent, Ohio	FA-'94	12/0*
86	Brown, Derek	TE	6-6	260	3/31/70	4	Notre Dame	Fairfax, Va.	ED(NYG)-'95	13/0*
8	t- Brunell, Mark	QB	6-1	208	9/17/70	3	Washington	Santa Maria, Caif.	T(GB)-'95	2/0*
29	Carrington, Darren	S	6-2	200	10/10/66	7	Northern Arizona	Bronx, N.Y.	ED(SD)-'95	16/16*
95	Carthen, Jason	LB	6-3	255	11/16/70	2	Ohio	Toledo, Ohio	FA-'94	1/0*
69	Chung, Eugene	G	6-4	295	6/14/69	4	Virginia Tech	Oakton, Va.	ED(NE)-'95	3/0*
59	Clark, Reggie	LB	6-2	225	10/17/67	2	North Carolina	Charlotte, N.C.	FA-'95	5/0*
27	Clark, Vinnie	CB	6-0	192	1/22/69	5	Ohio State	Cincinnati, Ohio	UFA(NO)-'95	16/15*
34	Cobb, Reggie	RB	6-0	215	7/7/68	6	Tennessee	Knoxville, Tenn.	ED(GB)-'95	16/13*
24	Colon, Harry	S	6-0	203	2/14/69	5	Missouri	Kansas City, Kan.	ED(Det)-'95	16/0*
89	Davenport, Charles	WR	6-3	216	11/22/68	4	North Carolina State	Fayetteville, N.C.	ED(Pitt)-'95	7/0*
92	Davey, Don	DT	6-4	270	4/8/68	5	Wisconsin	Manitowoc, Wis.	UFA(GB)-'95	16/2*
30	Davis, Michael	CB	6-1	192	1/14/72	2	Cincinnati	Springfield, Ohio	ED(Hou)-'95	16/0*
96	Duff, John	DE	6-7	250	7/31/67	2	New Mexico	Tustin, Calif.	ED(Raid)-'95	4/0*
38	Dumas, Mike	S	5-11	181	3/18/69	5	Indiana	Lowell, Mich.	UFA(Buff)-'95	14/0*
97	Etheredge, Carlos	TE	6-5	259	8/10/70	2	Miami	Albuquerque, N.M.	FA-'94	9/0*
91	Frase, Paul	DT	6-5	260	5/5/65	7	Syracuse	Barrington, N.H.	ED(NYJ)-'95	16/5*
58	Freeman, Reggie	LB	6-2	233	5/8/70	2	Florida State	Clewiston, Fla.	FA-'94	0*
54	† Goganious, Keith	LB	6-2	239	12/7/68	4	Penn State	Virginia Beach, Va.	ED(Buff)-'95	16/1*
26	Green, Rogerick	CB	6-0	184	12/14/69	4	Kansas State	San Antonio, Tex.	ED(TB)-'95	11/0*
48	Griffith, Rich	TE	6-5	252	7/31/69	2	Arizona	Tucson, Ariz.	FA-'95	0*
28	Grow, Monty	S	6-3	214	9/4/71	2	Florida	Inverness, Fla.	ED(KC)-'95	15/0*
81	Howard, Desmond	WR	5-9	180	5/15/70	4	Michigan	Cleveland, Ohio	ED(Wash)-'95	16/15*
68	Huntington, Greg	G	6-3	295	9/22/70	2	Penn State	Cincinnati, Ohio	FA-'94	0*
47	Jackson, Al	CB	6-0	182	9/7/71	2	Georgia	Pensacola, Fla.	ED(Phil)-'95	11/0*
80	Jackson, Willie	WR	6-1	205	8/16/71	2	Florida	Gainesville, Fla.	ED(Dall)-'95	0*
23	Jordan, Randy	RB	5-10	208	6/6/70	2	North Carolina	Manson, N.C.	FA-'94	0*
56	Lageman, Jeff	DE	6-5	266	7/18/67	7	Virginia	Sterling, Va.	UFA(NYJ)-'95	16/16*
93	Logan, Ernie	DE	6-4	280	5/18/68	4	East Carolina	Fayetteville, N.C.	FA-'94	0*
35	Maston, Le'Shai	RB	6-1	232	10/7/70	3	Baylor	Dallas, Tex.	ED(Hou)-'95	5/1*
98	Mayfield, Corey	DT	6-3	290	2/25/70	2	Oklahoma	Tyler, Tex.	FA-'95	0*
22	McNabb, Dexter	RB	6-2	245	7/9/69	3	Florida	DeFuniak Springs, Fla.	FA-'94	0*
50	Myslinski, Tom	G	6-2	289	12/7/68	3	Tennessee	Rome, N.Y.	ED(Chi)-'95	4/0*
67	Novak, Jeff	T	6-5	295	7/27/67	2	Southwest Texas State	Cook County, Ill.	ED(Mia)-'95	6/0*
94	Pritchett, Kelvin	DT	6-2	281	10/24/69	5	Mississippi	Atlanta, Ga.	UFA(Det)-'95	16/15*
39	† Raymond, Corey	CB	5-11	185	7/28/69	4	Louisiana State	New Iberia, La.	ED(NYG)-'95	16/12*
43	Robinson, Frank	CB	5-11	180	1/11/69	3	Boise State	Novato, Calif.	FA-'95	0*
31	Royster, Mazio	RB	6-1	200	8/3/70	4	Southern California	Pomona, Calif.	ED(TB)-'95	14/1*
74	Shaw, Rickie	T	6-5	305	12/26/69	2	North Carolina	Whiteville, N.C.	FA-'94	0*
76	Siever, Paul	G	6-6	294	8/10/69	3	Penn State	Downingtown, Pa.	FA-'94	0*
37	Simmons, Marcello	CB	6-1	180	8/8/71	2	Southern Methodist	Tomball, Tex.	FA-'94	0*
9	Sisson, Scott	K	6-0	197	7/21/71	2	Georgia Tech	Marietta, Ga.	FA-'95	0*
99	Smeenge, Joel	DE	6-5	250	4/1/68	6	Western Michigan	Grand Rapids, Mich.	UFA(NO)-'95	16/2*
82	Smith, Jimmy	WR	6-1	205	2/9/69	2	Jackson State	Jackson, Miss.	FA-'95	0*
53	Stephens, Santo	LB	6-4	232	6/16/69	3	Temple	Capital Heights, Md.	ED(Cin)-'95	14/3*
41	Thomas, Dave	CB	6-2	205	8/25/68	3	Tennessee	Miami, Fla.	ED(Dall)-'95	16/0*
87	Tillman, Cedric	WR	6-2	204	7/22/70	4	Alcorn State	Gulfport, Miss.	ED(Den)-'95	16/4*
75	Tucker, Mark	C	6-3	290	4/29/68	3	Southern California	Los Angeles, Calif.	ED(Ariz)-'95	16/3*
11	Ware, Andre	QB	6-2	220	7/31/68	5	Houston	Dickinson, Tex.	FA-'95	0*
25	Washington, Mickey	CB	5-9	191	7/8/68	5	Texas A&M	Beaumont, Tex.	UFA(Buff)-'95	16/16*
79	Widell, Dave	G-C	6-6	292	5/14/65	8	Boston College	Hartford, Conn.	UFA(Den)-'95	16/16*
90	Williams, James	LB	6-0	230	10/10/68	6	Mississippi State	North Natchez, Miss.	ED(NO)-'95	16/7*
51	Williams, Mark	LB	6-3	240	5/17/71	2	Ohio State	Upper Marlboro, Md.	ED(GB)-'95	16/0*
88	Williams, Mike	WR	5-11	187	10/9/66	4	Northeastern	Katonah, N.Y.	FA-'95	15/0*
21	Wilson, Marcus	RB	6-1	215	4/16/68	4	Virginia	Rochester, N.Y.	ED(GB)-'95	12/0*

* Baker played 4 games with Indianapolis in '94; Barker played 11 games with Philadelphia; Beuerlein played 9 games with Arizona; Bouwens played 16 games with Detroit; Boyer played 14 games with Miami; Boykin played 12 games with Washington; Brown played 13 games with N.Y. Giants; Brunnell played 2 games with Green Bay; Carrington played 16 games with San Diego; Carthen played 1 game with New England; Chung played 3 games with New England; R. Clark played 5 games with Pittsburgh; V. Clark played 11 games with Atlanta, 5 games with New Orleans; Cobb played 16 games with Green Bay; Colon played 16 games with Detroit; Davenport played 7 games with Pittsburgh; Davey played 16 games with Green Bay; Davis played 16 games with Houston; Duff played 4 games with L.A. Raiders; Dumas played 14 games with Buffalo; Etheredge played 9 games with Indianapolis; Frase played 16 games with N.Y. Jets; Freeman last active with New Orleans in '93; Goganious played 16 games with Buffalo; Green played 11 games with Tampa Bay; Griffith last active with New England in '93; Grow played 15 games with Kansas City; Howard played 16 games with Washington; Huntington last active with Washington in '93; A. Jackson played 11 games with Philadelphia; W. Jackson inactive for 16 games with Dallas; Jordan last active with L.A. Raiders in '93; Lageman played 16 games with N.Y. Jets; Logan last active with Atlanta in '93; Maston played 5 games with Houston; Mayfield last active with Tampa Bay in '92; McNabb last active with Green Bay in '93; Myslinski played 4 games with Chicago; Novak played 6 games with Miami; Pritchett played 16 games with Detroit; Raymond played 16 games with N.Y. Giants; Robinson last active with Denver in '93; Royster played 14 games with Tampa Bay; Shaw last active with Seattle in '93; Siever last active with Washington in '93; Simmons last active with Cincinnati in '93; Sisson last active with New England in '93; Smeenge played 16 games with New Orleans; Smith last active with Dallas in '92; Stephens played 14 games with Cincinnati; Thomas played 16 games with Dallas; Tillman played 16 games with Denver; Tucker played 16 games with Arizona; Ware last active with Detroit in '93; Washington played 16 games with Buffalo; Widell played 16 games with Denver; J. Williams played 16 games with New Orleans; Ma. Williams played 16 games with Green Bay; Mi. Williams played 15 games with Miami; Wilson played 12 games with Green Bay.

† Restricted free agent; subject to developments.

t- Jaguars traded for Brunell (Green Bay).

COACHING STAFF

Head Coach,
Tom Coughlin

Pro Career: Became the first head coach of the NFL's newest franchise on February 21, 1994, following a successful three seasons as head coach at Boston College. A veteran of 25 years in coaching, including 17 at the collegiate level and seven as an NFL assistant, Coughlin previously coached wide receivers for the Philadelphia Eagles (1984-85), Green Bay Packers (1986-87), and New York Giants (1988-1990). He was a member of the Giants' Super Bowl XXV champion coaching staff prior to being named head coach at Boston College in 1991. In three seasons at Boston College, he turned a struggling program into a top-20 team, posting a 21-13-1 record. His final season at Boston College was highlighted by eight consecutive wins, including a 41-39 victory over top-ranked Notre Dame, and a 9-3 finish. Despite an 0-2 start to the season, Boston College ranked thirteenth in the *Associated Press* poll and twelfth in the *USA Today/CNN* coaches poll at the end of the 1993 season. Coughlin's previous 14 seasons as a college coach were at Rochester Institute of Technology 1970-73 (head coach), Syracuse 1974-1980, and Boston College 1981-83.

Background: Played wingback for Syracuse from 1965-67 under legendary coach Ben Schwartzwalder, along with teammates Larry Czonka and Floyd Little. Received Syracuse 1967 Orange Key Award as outstanding scholar athlete, and graduated in 1968 with bachelor's degree in education. Received master's degree in education from Syracuse in 1969.

Personal: Born August 31, 1947, Waterloo, N.Y. Was standout scholastic star for Waterloo Central High School. Tom and his wife Judy reside in Jacksonville. They have two daughters, Keli and Katie, and two sons, Tim and Brian.

ASSISTANT COACHES

Joe Baker, assistant special teams; born June 29, 1969, Glen Ridge, N.J., lives in Jacksonville. Wide receiver Princeton 1987-90. No pro playing experience. College coach: Samford 1993. Pro coach: Joined Jaguars in 1995.

Pete Carmichael, wide receivers; born March 4, 1941, North Plainfield, N.J., lives in Jacksonville. Quarterback Dayton 1961, Montclair State College 1962-63. No pro playing experience. College coach: Virginia Military 1965-66, New Hampshire 1967, Boston College 1968-72, 1981-93, Trenton State College 1973 (head coach), Columbia 1974-77, Merchant Marine Academy 1977-80 (head coach). Pro coach: Joined Jaguars in 1995.

Randy Edsall, secondary; Born August 27, 1958, Glen Rock, Pa., lives in Jacksonville. Quarterback Syracuse 1976-79. No pro playing experience. College coach: Syracuse 1983-90, Boston College 1991-93. Pro coach: Joined Jaguars in 1995.

Kevin Gilbride, offensive coordinator; born August 27, 1951, New Haven, Conn., lives in Jacksonville. Quarterback-tight end Southern Connecticut State 1970-73. No pro playing experience. College coach: Idaho State 1974-75, Tufts 1976-77, American International 1978-79, Southern Connecticut State 1980-84 (head coach), East Carolina 1987-88. Pro coach: Ottawa Rough Riders (CFL) 1985-86, Houston Oilers 1989-94, joined Jaguars in 1995.

Jerald Ingram, running backs; born December 24, 1960, Beaver, Pa., lives in Jacksonville. Fullback Michigan 1979-84. No pro playing experience. College coach: Ball State 1985-90, Boston College 1991-93. Pro coach: Joined Jaguars in 1995.

Dick Jauron, defensive coordinator; born October 7, 1950, Peoria, Ill., lives in Jacksonville. Defensive back Yale 1970-72. Pro defensive back Detroit Lions 1973-77, Cincinnati Bengals 1978-80. Pro coach: Buffalo Bills 1985, Green Bay Packers 1986-94, joined Jaguars in 1995.

Mike Maser, offensive line; born March 2, 1947, Clayton, N.Y., lives in Jacksonville. Guard Buffalo 1967-70. No pro playing experience. College coach: Marshall 1973, Bluefield State College 1974-78, Maine 1979-80, Boston College 1981-93. Pro coach: Joined Jaguars in 1995.

Nick Nicolau, tight ends; born May 5, 1933, New York, N.Y., lives in Jacksonville. Running back Southern Connecticut State 1957-59. No pro playing experience. College coach: Southern Connecticut State 1960, Springfield 1961, Bridgeport 1962-69 (head coach 1965-69), Massachusetts 1970, Connecticut 1971-72, Kentucky 1973-75, Kent State 1976. Pro coach: Hamilton Tiger-Cats (CFL) 1977, Montreal Alouettes (CFL) 1978-79, New Orleans Saints 1980, Denver Broncos 1981-87, Los Angeles Raiders 1988, Buffalo Bills 1989-91, Indianapolis Colts 1992-94, joined Jaguars in 1995.

Jerry Palmieri, strength and conditioning; born October 30, 1958, Englewood, N.J., lives in Jacksonville. No college or pro playing experience. College coach: Oklahoma State 1984-87, Kansas State 1988-92, Boston College 1993-94. Pro coach: Joined Jaguars in 1995.

Larry Pasquale, special teams coordinator; born April 21, 1941, Brooklyn, N.Y., lives in Jacksonville. Quarterback Bridgeport 1961-63. No pro playing experience. College coach: Slippery Rock State 1967, Boston University 1968, Navy 1969-70, Massachusetts 1971-75, Idaho State 1976. Pro coach: Montreal Alouettes (CFL) 1977-78, Detroit Lions 1979, New York Jets 1980-89, San Diego Chargers 1990-91, Philadelphia Eagles 1992-94, joined Jaguars in 1995.

John Pease, defensive line; born October 14, 1943, Pittsburgh, Pa., lives in Jacksonville. Wingback Utah 1963-64. No pro playing experience. College coach: Fullerton, Calif., J.C. 1970-73, Long Beach State 1974-76, Utah 1977, Washington 1978-83. Pro coach: Philadelphia/Baltimore Stars (USFL) 1983-85, New Orleans Saints 1986-94, joined Jaguars in 1995.

Lucious Selmon, outside linebackers; born March 15, 1951, Muskogee, Okla., lives in Jacksonville. Defensive tackle Oklahoma 1970-73. Pro defensive tackle Memphis Southmen (WFL) 1974-75. College coach: Oklahoma 1976-94. Pro Coach: Joined Jaguars in 1995.

Steve Szabo, inside linebackers; born September 11, 1943, Chicago, Ill., lives in Jacksonville. Halfback/defensive back Navy 1961-64. No pro playing experience. College coach: Johns Hopkins 1969, Toledo 1970, Iowa 1971-73, Syracuse 1974-76, Iowa State 1977-78, Ohio State 1979-81, Western Michigan 1982-84, Edinboro 1985-87 (head coach), Northern Iowa 1988, Colorado State 1989-90, Boston College 1991-93. Pro coach: Joined Jaguars in 1995.

1995 FIRST-YEAR ROSTER

Name	Pos.	Ht.	Wt.	Birthdate	College	Hometown	How Acq.
Bech, Brett	WR	6-1	184	8/20/71	Louisiana State	Slidell, La.	FA
Boselli, Tony	T	6-7	323	4/17/72	Southern California	Boulder, Colo.	D1a
Brown, Kendall	DE	6-3	267	9/12/71	Louisville	Detroit, Mich.	FA
Brown, Leon (1)	RB	5-10	190	5/16/70	Eastern Kentucky	Jacksonville, Fla.	FA
Butler, Hillary (1)	LB	6-2	250	1/5/71	Washington	Tacoma, Wash.	FA
Christopherson, Ryan	RB	5-11	238	7/26/72	Wyoming	Glendale, Ariz.	D5
Collins, Ron (1)	G-T	6-5	289	9/30/71	Fresno State	San Bernardino, Calif.	FA
Dausin, Chris (1)	C	6-5	285	12/18/69	Texas A&M	San Antonio, Tex.	FA
DeMarco, Brian	T	6-5	314	4/9/72	Michigan State	Lorain, Ohio	D2a
Dillard, Ivory (1)	G-T	6-3	299	8/15/71	Florida A&M	Dallas, Tex.	FA
Floyd, Gonzalo (1)	DE	6-3	260	9/2/71	Texas-El Paso	Orange Park, Fla.	FA
Hall, Matt	WR	6-4	215	9/22/72	Murray State	Tallahassee, Fla.	FA
Hall, Ray (1)	DT	6-4	267	3/2/71	Washington State	Seattle, Wash.	FA
Harris, Willie (1)	WR	6-2	196	11/8/70	Mississippi State	Moss Point, Miss.	FA
Hollis, Mike	K	5-7	165	5/5/72	Idaho	Spokane, Wash.	FA
Hudson, Chris	S	5-9	195	10/6/71	Colorado	Houston, Tex.	D3
Johnson, Rob	QB	6-3	220	3/18/73	Southern California	El Toro, Calif.	D4a
Johnson, Tommy	CB	5-10	180	12/5/71	Alabama	Niceville, Fla.	FA
Laro, Gordon	TE	6-3	257	4/17/72	Boston College	Lynn, Mass.	FA
Marsh, Curtis	WR	6-1	212	11/24/70	Utah	Simi Valley, Calif.	D7
Mason, Andy (1)	LB	6-2	228	8/31/71	Washington	Longview, Wash.	FA
McCoy, Ryan (1)	LB	6-2	237	3/13/72	Houston	Beaumont, Tex.	FA
McManus, Tom (1)	LB	6-2	240	7/30/70	Boston College	Edgewater, Fla.	FA
Meinert, Ben	LB	6-3	245	11/10/72	Northeast Oklahoma	Hobart, Okla.	FA
Mills, Vidal (1)	S	5-11	190	7/21/72	Bethune-Cookman	Tampa, Fla.	FA
Moore, Andrew	T	6-5	300	12/22/72	Sonoma State	Crawford, Calif.	FA
Morton, John (1)	WR	6-0	185	9/24/69	Western Michigan	Auburn Hills, Mich.	FA
Price, Marcus	T	6-5	303	3/3/72	Louisiana State	Port Arthur, Tex.	D6
Schorp, Greg (1)	TE	6-3	242	9/6/71	Texas A&M	San Antonio, Tex.	FA
Schwartz, Bryan	LB	6-3	256	12/5/71	Augustana, S.D.	St. Lawrence, S.D.	D2b
Simmons, Jason (1)	DE	6-5	250	12/20/70	Ohio State	Akron, Ohio	FA
Smalley, Rod	LB	6-4	235	12/8/71	UCLA	Solvang, Calif.	FA
Stewart, James	RB	6-1	222	12/27/71	Tennessee	Morristown, Tenn.	D1b
Thompson, Mike	DT	6-3	276	12/22/72	Wisconsin	Portage, Wis.	D4b
Williams, Chris (1)	DT	6-3	281	8/8/70	Hampton	Houston, Tex.	FA

The term NFL Rookie is defined as a player who is in his first season of professional football and has not been on the roster of another professional football team for any regular-season or postseason games. A Rookie is designated by an "R" on NFL rosters. Players who have been active in another professional football league or players who have NFL experience, including either preseason training camp or being on an Active List or Inactive List, or on Reserve/Injured or Reserve/Physically Unable to Perform for fewer than six regular-season games, are termed NFL First-Year Players. An NFL First-Year Player is designated by a "1" on NFL rosters. Thereafter, a player is credited with an additional year of experience for each season in which he accumulates six games on the Active List or Inactive List, or on Reserve/Injured or Reserve/Physically Unable to Perform.

NOTES

KANSAS CITY CHIEFS

American Football Conference
Western Division
Team Colors: Red, Gold, and White
One Arrowhead Drive
Kansas City, Missouri 64129
Telephone: (816) 924-9300

CLUB OFFICIALS

Founder: Lamar Hunt
Chairman of the Board: Jack Steadman
President/General Manager and Chief Executive Officer: Carl Peterson
Executive Vice President and Chief Operating Officer: Tim Connolly
Vice President/Player Personnel: Lynn Stiles
Assistant General Manager: Dennis Thum
Vice President of Sales and Marketing: Dennis Watley
Secretary: Jim Seigfreid
Director of Finance/Treasurer: Dale Young
Director of Public Relations: Bob Moore
Director of Operations: Jeff Klein
Director of Development: Ken Blume
Director of Sales: Wallace Bennett
Assistant Director of Public Relations: Jim Carr
Director of Promotions: Phil Thomas
Community Relations Manager: Brenda Sniezek
Director of Ticket Operations: Doug Hopkins
Equipment Manager: Mike Davidson
Asst. Equipment Managers: Allen Wright, Darin Kerns
Trainer: Dave Kendall
Assistant Trainer: Bud Epps
Video Coordinator: Mike Dennis
Assistant Video Coordinators: Mike Kirk, Mike Portz
Stadium: Arrowhead Stadium • **Capacity:** 79,101
One Arrowhead Drive
Kansas City, Missouri 64129
Playing Surface: Grass
Training Camp: University of Wisconsin-River Falls
River Falls, Wisconsin 54022

1995 SCHEDULE

PRESEASON

Aug. 5	**Washington**	7:00
Aug. 11	at Arizona	7:30
Aug. 19	**Buffalo**	7:00
Aug. 26	at Minnesota	12:30

REGULAR SEASON

Sept. 3	at Seattle	1:00
Sept. 10	**New York Giants**	12:00
Sept. 17	**Los Angeles**	12:00
Sept. 24	at Cleveland	4:00
Oct. 1	at Arizona	1:00
Oct. 9	**San Diego** (Monday)	8:00
Oct. 15	**New England**	12:00
Oct. 22	at Denver	2:00
Oct. 29	Open Date	
Nov. 5	**Washington**	12:00
Nov. 12	at San Diego	1:00
Nov. 19	**Houston**	7:00
Nov. 23	at Dallas (Thursday)	3:00
Dec. 3	at Los Angeles	1:00
Dec. 11	at Miami (Monday)	9:00
Dec. 17	**Denver**	3:00
Dec. 24	**Seattle**	12:00

RECORD HOLDERS

INDIVIDUAL RECORDS—CAREER

Category	Name	Performance
Rushing (Yds.)	Christian Okoye, 1987-1992	4,897
Passing (Yds.)	Len Dawson, 1962-1975	28,507
Passing (TDs)	Len Dawson, 1962-1975	237
Receiving (No.)	Henry Marshall, 1976-1987	416
Receiving (Yds.)	Otis Taylor, 1965-1975	7,306
Interceptions	Emmitt Thomas, 1966-1978	58
Punting (Avg.)	Jerrel Wilson, 1963-1977	43.5
Punt Return (Avg.)	J.T. Smith, 1979-1984	10.6
Kickoff Return (Avg.)	Noland Smith, 1967-69	26.8
Field Goals	Nick Lowery, 1980-1993	329
Touchdowns (Tot.)	Otis Taylor, 1965-1975	60
Points	Nick Lowery, 1980-1993	1,466

INDIVIDUAL RECORDS—SINGLE SEASON

Category	Name	Performance
Rushing (Yds.)	Christian Okoye, 1989	1,480
Passing (Yds.)	Bill Kenney, 1983	4,348
Passing (TDs)	Len Dawson, 1964	30
Receiving (No.)	Carlos Carson, 1983	80
Receiving (Yds.)	Carlos Carson, 1983	1,351
Interceptions	Emmitt Thomas, 1974	12
Punting (Avg.)	Jerrel Wilson, 1965	46.0
Punt Return (Avg.)	Abner Haynes, 1960	15.4
Kickoff Return (Avg.)	Dave Grayson, 1962	29.7
Field Goals	Nick Lowery, 1990	34
Touchdowns (Tot.)	Abner Haynes, 1962	19
Points	Nick Lowery, 1990	139

INDIVIDUAL RECORDS—SINGLE GAME

Category	Name	Performance
Rushing (Yds.)	Barry Word, 10-14-90	200
Passing (Yds.)	Len Dawson, 11-1-64	435
Passing (TDs)	Len Dawson, 11-1-64	6
Receiving (No.)	Ed Podolak, 10-7-73	12
Receiving (Yds.)	Stephone Paige, 12-22-85	309
Interceptions	Bobby Ply, 12-16-62	*4
	Bobby Hunt, 12-4-64	*4
	Deron Cherry, 9-29-85	*4
Field Goals	Many times	5
	Last time by Nick Lowery, 9-20-93	
Touchdowns (Tot.)	Abner Haynes, 11-26-61	5
Points	Abner Haynes, 11-26-61	30

*NFL Record

COACHING HISTORY

DALLAS TEXANS 1960-62
(272-249-12)

1960-74	Hank Stram	129-79-10
1975-77	Paul Wiggin*	11-24-0
1977	Tom Bettis	1-6-0
1978-82	Marv Levy	31-42-0
1983-86	John Mackovic	30-35-0
1987-88	Frank Gansz	8-22-1
1989-94	Marty Schottenheimer	62-41-1

*Released after seven games in 1977

ARROWHEAD STADIUM

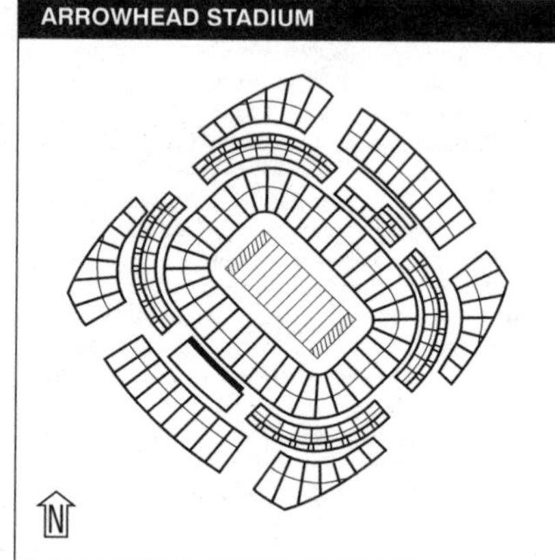

1994 TEAM RECORD

PRESEASON (2-3)

Date	Result		Opponents
7/31	W	24-17	Houston
8/6	L	9-17	vs. Minnesota at Tokyo
8/12	W	17-14	at Washington
8/22	L	18-21	Chicago
8/26	L	3-24	at Buffalo

REGULAR SEASON (9-7)

Date	Result		Opponents	Att.
9/4	W	30-17	at New Orleans	69,362
9/11	W	24-17	San Francisco	79,907
9/18	W	30-10	at Atlanta	67,357
9/25	L	0-16	L.A. Rams	78,184
10/9	L	6-20	at San Diego	62,923
10/17	W	31-28	at Denver	75,151
10/23	W	38-23	Seattle	78,847
10/30	L	10-44	at Buffalo	79,501
11/6	W	13- 3	L.A. Raiders	78,709
11/13	L	13-14	San Diego	76,997
11/20	W	20-13	Cleveland	69,121
11/27	L	9-10	at Seattle	54,120
12/4	L	17-20	Denver (OT)	77,631
12/12	L	28-45	at Miami	71,578
12/18	W	31- 9	Houston	74,474
12/24	W	19- 9	at L.A. Raiders	64,130

POSTSEASON (0-1)

12/31	L	17-27	at Miami	67,487

(OT) Overtime

SCORE BY PERIODS

Chiefs	52	92	79	96	0	—	319
Opponents	40	84	72	99	3	—	298

ATTENDANCE

Home 613,870 Away 544,122 Total 1,157,992
Single-game home record, 82,094 (11-5-72)
Single-season home record, 613,870 (1994)

1994 TEAM STATISTICS

	Chiefs	Opp.
Total First Downs	322	289
Rushing	97	93
Passing	211	164
Penalty	14	32
Third Down Made/Att	94/238	80/212
Third Down Pct.	39.5	37.7
Fourth Down: Made/Att	12/23	8/14
Fourth Down Pct.	52.2	57.1
Total Net Yards	5692	5000
Avg. Per Game	355.8	312.5
Total Plays	1098	989
Avg. Per Play	5.2	5.1
Net Yards Rushing	1732	1734
Avg. Per Game	108.3	108.4
Total Rushes	464	446
Net Yards Passing	3960	3266
Avg. Per Game	247.5	204.1
Sacked/Yards Lost	19/132	39/234
Gross Yards	4092	3500
Att./Completions	615/366	504/300
Completion Pct.	59.5	59.5
Had Intercepted	14	12
Punts/Average	85/42.1	85/45.0
Net Punting Avg.	85/34.5	85/38.9
Penalties/Yards	127/911	119/925
Fumbles/Ball Lost	21/12	36/26
Touchdowns	34	35
Rushing	12	11
Passing	20	23
Returns	2	1
Avg. Time of Possession	30:55	29:05

1994 INDIVIDUAL STATISTICS

PASSING	Att.	Comp.	Yds.	Pct.	TD	Int.	Tkld.	Rate
Montana	493	299	3283	60.6	16	9	19/132	83.6
Bono	117	66	796	56.4	4	4	0/0	74.6
Blundin	5	1	13	20.0	0	1	0/0	0.0
Chiefs	615	366	4092	59.5	20	14	19/132	80.8
Opponents	504	300	3500	59.5	23	12	39/234	85.9

SCORING	TD R	TD P	TD Rt	PAT	FG	Saf	PTS
Elliott	0	0	0	30/30	25/30	0	105
Allen	7	0	0	0/0	0/0	0	44
W. Davis	0	5	0	0/0	0/0	0	32
Birden	0	4	0	0/0	0/0	0	26
Anders	2	1	0	0/0	0/0	0	18
Bennett	2	0	0	0/0	0/0	0	12
Cash	0	2	0	0/0	0/0	0	12
Dawson	0	2	0	0/0	0/0	0	12
Valerio	0	2	0	0/0	0/0	0	12
D. Walker	0	2	0	0/0	0/0	0	12
Collins	0	0	1	0/0	0/0	0	6
Greene	0	1	0	0/0	0/0	0	6
Hill	1	0	0	0/0	0/0	0	6
Martin	0	1	0	0/0	0/0	0	6
Vaughn	0	0	1	0/0	0/0	0	6
Thomas	0	0	0	0/0	0/0	1	2
Chiefs	12	20	2	30/30	25/30	2	319
Opponents	11	23	1	30/30	18/23	0	298

2-Point conversions: Allen, Birden, W. Davis. Team: 3-4.

RUSHING	Att.	Yds.	Avg.	LG	TD
Allen	189	709	3.8	36t	7
Hill	141	574	4.1	20	1
Anders	62	231	3.7	19	2
Bennett	46	178	3.9	17	2
Dawson	3	24	8.0	13	0
Montana	18	17	0.9	13	0
Dickerson	1	0	0.0	0	0
Bono	4	-1	-0.2	2	0
Chiefs	464	1732	3.7	36t	12
Opponents	446	1734	3.9	60	11

RECEIVING	No.	Yds.	Avg.	LG	TD
Anders	67	525	7.8	30	1
W. Davis	51	822	16.1	62t	5
Birden	48	637	13.3	44	4
Allen	42	349	8.3	38	0
Dawson	37	537	14.5	50	2
D. Walker	36	382	10.6	57t	2
Martin	21	307	14.6	61	1
Cash	19	192	10.1	31	2
Hill	16	92	5.8	21	0
Hughes	7	80	11.4	22	0
Bennett	7	53	7.6	15	0
Greene	6	69	11.5	20	1
Penn	3	24	8.0	13	0
Dickerson	2	11	5.5	6	0
Johnson	2	7	3.5	5	0
Valerio	2	5	2.5	4t	2
Chiefs	366	4092	11.2	62t	20
Opponents	300	3500	11.7	72t	23

INTERCEPTIONS	No.	Yds.	Avg.	LG	TD
Mincy	3	49	16.3	31	0
Collins	2	83	41.5	78t	1
Carter	2	24	12.0	24	0
White	2	0	0.0	0	0
Smith	1	41	41.0	41	0
Grow	1	21	21.0	21	0
Taylor	1	0	0.0	0	0
Chiefs	12	218	18.2	78t	1
Opponents	14	217	15.5	76t	1

PUNTING	No.	Yds.	Avg.	In 20	LG
Aguiar	85	3582	42.1	15	61
Chiefs	85	3582	42.1	15	61
Opponents	85	3822	45.0	28	64

PUNT RETURNS	No.	FC	Yds.	Avg.	LG	TD
Hughes	27	9	192	7.1	43	0
Carter	16	4	124	7.8	42	0
Chiefs	43	13	316	7.3	43	0
Opponents	50	13	506	10.1	60	0

KICKOFF RETURNS	No.	Yds.	Avg.	LG	TD
Vaughn	15	386	25.7	91t	1
Dickerson	21	472	22.5	62	0
Penn	9	194	21.6	34	0
Hughes	9	190	21.1	32	0
Anders	2	36	18.0	19	0
Booker	2	10	5.0	10	0
Bennett	1	12	12.0	12	0
Chiefs	59	1300	22.0	91t	1
Opponents	66	1447	21.9	41	0

SACKS	No.
Smith	11.5
Thomas	11.0
Mickell	7.0
Phillips	3.0
Collins	2.0
McDaniels	2.0
Jamison	1.0
Saleaumua	1.0
Williams	0.5
Chiefs	39.0
Opponents	19.0

1995 DRAFT CHOICES

Round	Name	Pos.	College
1	Trezelle Jenkins	T	Michigan
3	Tamarick Vanover	WR	Florida State
	Troy Dumas	LB	Nebraska
4	Steve Stenstrom	QB	Stanford
5	Mike Pelton	DT	Auburn
	Jerrott Willard	LB	California
6	Bryan Proby	DT	Arizona State
	Tom Barndt	C	Pittsburgh

KANSAS CITY CHIEFS

1995 VETERAN ROSTER

No.		Name	Pos.	Ht.	Wt.	Birthdate	NFL Exp.	College	Hometown	How Acq.	'94 Games/ Starts
5		Aguiar, Louie	P	6-2	222	6/30/66	5	Utah State	Livermore, Calif.	FA-'94	16/0
56		Ale, Arnold	LB	6-3	234	6/17/70	2	UCLA	Carson, Calif.	FA-'94	2/0
32		Allen, Marcus	RB	6-2	210	3/26/60	14	Southern California	San Diego, Calif.	UFA(Raid)-'93	13/13
76		Alt, John	T	6-8	307	5/30/62	12	Iowa	Columbia Heights, Minn.	D1b-'84	13/13
38		Anders, Kimble	RB	5-11	230	9/10/66	5	Houston	Galveston, Tex.	FA-'91	16/13
44		Anderson, Darren	CB	5-10	180	1/11/69	3	Toledo	Cincinnati, Ohio	T(TB)-'94	15/1
85	t-	Bailey, Victor	WR	6-2	196	7/3/70	3	Missouri	Ft. Worth, Tex.	T(Phil)-'95	16/0*
30		Bennett, Donnell	RB	6-0	241	9/14/72	2	Miami	Ft. Lauderdale, Fla.	D2-'94	15/0
14		Blundin, Matt	QB	6-6	233	3/7/69	4	Virginia	Ridley, Pa.	D2-'92	1/0
13		Bono, Steve	QB	6-4	215	5/11/62	11	UCLA	Norristown, Pa.	T(SF)-'94	7/2
99		Booker, Vaughn	DE	6-5	283	2/24/68	2	Cincinnati	Cincinnati, Ohio	FA-'94	13/0
4		Carroll, Wesley	WR	6-2	183	9/6/67	4	Miami	Cleveland, Ohio	FA-'95	0*
34		Carter, Dale	CB	6-1	188	11/28/69	4	Tennessee	Covington, Ga.	D1-'92	16/16
89		Cash, Keith	TE	6-4	248	8/7/69	4	Texas	San Antonio, Tex.	PB(Pitt)-'92	6/5
25		Collins, Mark	CB	5-10	196	1/16/64	10	Cal State-Fullerton	San Bernardino, Calif.	UFA(NYG)-'94	14/13
69		Criswell, Jeff	T	6-7	291	3/7/64	8	Graceland, Iowa	Searsboro, Iowa	UFA(NYJ)-'95	15/15*
50		Davis, Anthony	LB	6-0	231	3/7/69	2	Utah	Pasco, Wash.	FA-'94	5/0
84		Davis, Willie	WR	6-0	181	10/10/67	4	Central Arkansas	Altheimer, Ark.	FA-'92	14/13
80		Dawson, Lake	WR	6-1	204	1/2/72	2	Notre Dame	Federal Way, Wash.	D3a-'94	12/6
23		Dickerson, Ron	RB	6-0	225	8/13/71	3	Arkansas	State College, Pa.	FA-'93	9/0
2		Elliott, Lin	K	6-0	182	11/11/68	3	Texas Tech	Waco, Tex.	FA-'94	16/0
59		Fields, Jaime	LB	5-11	236	8/28/70	3	Washington	Lynwood, Calif.	D4-'93	11/2
12		Gannon, Rich	QB	6-3	208	1/20/66	8	Delaware	Philadelphia, Pa.	FA-'95	0*
87		Greene, Tracy	TE	6-5	282	11/5/72	2	Grambling State	Grambling, La.	D7b-'94	7/2
61		Grunhard, Tim	C	6-2	299	5/17/68	6	Notre Dame	Chicago, Ill.	D2-'90	16/16
53		Hamilton, Rick	LB	6-2	241	4/19/70	2	Central Florida	Inverness, Fla.	FA-'94	3/0*
40		Hasty, James	CB	6-0	201	5/23/65	8	Washington State	Seattle, Wash.	UFA(NYJ)-'95	16/16*
29		Hill, Greg	RB	5-11	205	2/23/72	2	Texas A&M	Dallas, Tex.	D1-'94	16/1
83		Hughes, Danan	WR	6-2	206	12/11/70	3	Iowa	Bayonne, N.J.	D7-'93	16/0
57		Jamison, George	LB	6-1	235	9/30/62	10	Cincinnati	Bridgeton, N.J.	FA-'94	13/12
93		Johnson, John	LB	6-3	247	5/8/68	4	Clemson	La Grange, Ga.	FA-'95	5/0*
65		Knapp, Lindsay	G-T	6-6	290	2/25/70	3	Notre Dame	Deerfield, Ill.	D5-'93	2/0
88		LaChapelle, Sean	WR	6-3	205	7/29/70	2	UCLA	Napa, Calif.	FA-'95	0*
42		Lott, Ronnie	S	6-1	203	5/8/59	15	Southern California	Rialto, Calif.	UFA(NYJ)-'95	15/15*
51		Manusky, Greg	LB	6-1	233	8/12/66	8	Colgate	Dallas, Pa.	FA-'94	16/2
77		McDaniels, Pellom	DE	6-3	275	2/21/68	3	Oregon State	San Jose, Calif.	FA-'93	12/3
92		Mickell, Darren	DE	6-4	284	8/3/70	4	Florida	Miami, Fla.	SD2-'92	16/13
81		Penn, Chris	WR	6-0	198	4/20/71	2	Tulsa	Lenapah, Okla.	D3b-'94	8/0
75		Phillips, Joe	DT	6-5	300	7/15/63	9	Southern Methodist	Vancouver, Wash.	FA-'92	16/16
52		Rogers, Tracy	LB	6-2	241	8/13/67	6	Fresno State	Taft, Calif.	FA-'90	14/3
97		Saleaumua, Dan	DT	6-0	300	11/25/64	9	Arizona State	San Diego, Calif.	PB(Det)-'89	14/14
91		Shaw, Eric	LB	6-3	247	9/17/71	3	Louisiana Tech	Pensacola, Fla.	FA-'95	3/0*
68		Shields, Will	G	6-3	300	9/15/71	3	Nebraska	Lawton, Okla.	D3-'93	16/16
66		Siglar, Ricky	T	6-7	307	6/14/66	4	San Jose State	Manzano, N.M.	FA-'93	16/8
54		Simien, Tracy	LB	6-1	250	5/21/67	5	Texas Christian	Bay City, Tex.	FA-'91	15/15
90		Smith, Neil	DE	6-4	273	4/10/66	8	Nebraska	New Orleans, La.	D1-'88	14/13
79		Szott, Dave	G	6-4	290	12/12/67	6	Penn State	Clifton, N.J.	D7-'90	16/16
24		Terry, Doug	S	5-11	204	12/12/69	4	Kansas	Liberal, Kan.	FA-'92	10/1
58		Thomas, Derrick	LB	6-3	247	1/1/67	7	Alabama	Miami, Fla.	D1-'89	16/15
94		Traylor, Keith	DT	6-2	295	9/3/69	4	Central Oklahoma	Malvern, Ark.	FA-'95	0*
73		Valerio, Joe	G-C	6-5	295	2/11/69	5	Pennsylvania	Ridley, Pa.	D2-'91	16/1
72		Villa, Danny	G	6-5	308	9/21/64	9	Arizona State	Nogales, Ariz.	UFA(Phx)-'93	14/0
98		Waldrop, Rob	NT	6-1	276	12/1/71	2	Arizona	Scottsdale, Ariz.	D5b-'94	3/0
82		Walker, Derrick	TE	6-0	244	6/23/67	6	Michigan	Chicago Heights, Ill.	FA-'94	15/11
62		Ware, David	T	6-5	290	2/21/70	2	Virginia	Roanoke, Va.	FA-'94	0*
48		Washington, Brian	S	6-1	210	9/10/65	7	Nebraska	Richmond, Va.	FA-'95	15/15*
26		Watson, Tim	S	6-1	215	8/13/70	3	Howard	Ft. Valley, Ga.	FA-'93	1/0
35		White, William	S	5-10	200	2/19/66	8	Ohio State	Lima, Ohio	FA-'94	15/14

* Bailey played 16 games with Philadelphia in '94; Carroll last active with Cincinnati in '93; Criswell played 15 games with N.Y. Jets; Gannon last active with Washington in '93; Hamilton played 1 game with Washington, 2 games with Kansas City; Hasty played 16 games with N.Y. Jets; Johnson played 5 games with Cincinnati; LaChapelle last active with L.A. Rams in '93; Lott played 15 games with N.Y. Jets; Shaw played 3 games with Cincinnati; Traylor last active with Green Bay in '93; Ware inactive for 3 games with Miami; Washington played 15 games with N.Y. Jets.

\# Unrestricted free agent; subject to developments.

† Restricted free agent; subject to developments.

t- Chiefs traded for Bailey (Philadelphia).

Retired—Joe Montana, 16-year quarterback, 14 games in '94.

Players lost through free agency (3): WR J.J. Birden (Atl; 13 games in '94), T Derrick Graham (Car; 16), S Charles Mincy (Minn; 16).

Players lost through Expansion Draft (2): CB-S Monty Grow (Jax; 15 games in '94), NT Greg Kragen (Car; 16).

Also played with Chiefs in '94—S Matt Gay (2 games), TE Jimmie Johnson (7), RB Victor Jones (1), WR Eric Martin (10), TE Tommie Stowers (1), CB Jay Taylor (16), RB Jon Vaughn (3), S Bracey Walker (2), S David Whitmore (12), LB Jerrol Williams (6), WR Michael Young (2).

COACHING STAFF

Head Coach,
Marty Schottenheimer

Pro Career: In six seasons as head coach of the Kansas City Chiefs, Schottenheimer has established the highest winning percentage in franchise history (.620). He has directed the Chiefs to six of their eight winning seasons since 1974 and has led the club to five consecutive postseason berths, the longest current streak of any NFL club. In 1994, Schottenheimer became the first coach in NFL history to direct two clubs (Chiefs and Cleveland Browns) to five-year playoff streaks and also became the twentieth NFL coach to register 100 regular-season wins. He also is the only coach to take his teams to the playoffs nine times since 1985. As head coach of the Cleveland Browns from midseason in 1984 through 1988, he led the club to four playoff berths, three AFC Central Division titles, two AFC Championship Game appearances, and captured AFC coach of the years honors (1986). He first joined the Browns in 1980 as defensive coordinator after serving as linebackers coach of the Detroit Lions in 1978-79. His first NFL coaching job came with the New York Giants, where he was linebackers coach and later defensive coordinator from 1975-77. He also served as an assistant coach with the Portland Storm (WFL) in 1974. A seventh-round draft choice of the Buffalo Bills in 1965, he played linebacker with the Bills until 1968 and finished his pro playing career with the Boston Patriots in 1969-70. Career record: 108-72-1.

Background: Schottenheimer was an All-America linebacker at the University of Pittsburgh 1962-64. Following his retirement from pro football, he worked as a real estate developer in both Miami and Denver from 1971-74.

Personal: Born September 23, 1943, Canonsburg, Pa. Marty and his wife, Patricia, live in Overland Park, Kan., and have one daughter, Kristen, and one son, Brian.

ASSISTANT COACHES

Russ Ball, assistant strength and conditioning; born August 28, 1959, Moberly, Mo., lives in Kansas City. Center Central Missouri State 1977-80. No pro playing experience. College coach: Missouri 1981-88. Pro coach: Joined Chiefs in 1989.

John Bunting, linebackers; born July 15, 1950, Portland, Me., lives in Kansas City. Linebacker North Carolina 1968-71. Pro linebacker Philadelphia Eagles 1972-82, Philadelphia Stars (USFL) 1983-84. College coach: Brown 1986, Rowan College 1987-92 (head coach 1988-92). Pro coach: Baltimore Stars (USFL) 1985, joined Chiefs in 1993.

Gunther Cunningham, defensive coordinator; born December 6, 1944, Munich, Germany, lives in Kansas City. Linebacker-placekicker Oregon 1966-68. No pro playing experience. College coach: Oregon 1969-71, Arkansas 1972, Stanford 1973-76, California 1977-80. Pro coach: Hamilton Tiger-Cats (CFL) 1981, Baltimore/Indianapolis Colts 1982-84, San Diego Chargers 1985-90, Los Angeles Raiders 1991-94, joined Chiefs in 1995.

Jim Erkenbeck, tight ends-offensive assistant; born September 10, 1933, Los Angeles, Calif., lives in Kansas City. Linebacker-end San Diego State 1949-51. No pro playing experience. College coach: San Diego State 1961-63, Grossmont (Calif.) J.C. 1964-67 (head coach), Utah State 1968, Washington State 1969-71, California 1972-76. Pro coach: Winnepeg Blue Bombers (CFL) 1977, Montreal Alouettes (CFL) 1978-81, Calgary Stampeders (CFL) 1982, Philadelphia/Baltimore Stars (USFL) 1983-85, New Orleans Saints 1986, Dallas Cowboys 1987-88, Kansas City Chiefs 1989-91, Los Angeles Rams 1992-94, rejoined Chiefs in 1995.

Paul Hackett, offensive coordinator; born July 5, 1947, Burlington, Vt., lives in Overland Park, Kan. Quarterback Cal-Davis 1965-68. No pro playing experience. College coach: Cal-Davis 1970-71, California 1972-75, Southern California 1976-80, Pittsburgh 1989-92 (head coach 1990-92). Pro coach: Cleveland Browns 1981-82, San Francisco 49ers 1983-85, Dallas Cowboys 1986-88, joined Chiefs in 1993.

Carl Hairston, defensive line; born December 15, 1952, Martinsville, Va., lives in Kansas City. Defensive end-linebacker Maryland-Eastern Shore 1972-75. Pro defensive end Philadelphia Eagles 1976-83, Cleveland Browns 1984-89, Phoenix Cardinals 1990. Pro scout: Phoenix Cardinals 1991-93, Kansas City Chiefs 1994. Pro coach: Joined Chiefs in 1995.

Woodrow Lowe, defensive assistant-assistant special teams; born June 9, 1954, Columbus, Ga., lives in Kansas City. Linebacker Alabama 1973-75. Pro linebacker San Diego Chargers 1976-86. Pro coach: Joined Chiefs in 1995.

Mike McCarthy, quarterbacks; born November 10, 1963, Pittsburgh, Pa., lives in Overland Park, Kan. Tight end Baker University 1985-86. No pro playing experience. College coach: Fort Hays State 1987-88, Pittsburgh 1989-92. Pro coach: Joined Chiefs in 1993.

Jimmy Raye, running backs; born March 26, 1946, Fayetteville, N.C., lives in Kansas City. Quarterback Michigan State 1965-67. Pro defensive back Philadelphia Eagles 1969. College coach: Michigan State 1971-75, Wyoming 1976. Pro coach: San Francisco 49ers 1977, Detroit Lions 1978-79, Atlanta Falcons 1980-82, 1987-89, Los Angeles Rams 1983-84, 1991, Tampa Bay Buccaneers 1985-86, New England Patriots 1990, joined Chiefs in 1992.

Dave Redding, strength and conditioning; born June 14, 1952, North Platte, Neb., lives in Kansas City. Defensive end Nebraska 1972-75. No pro playing experience. College coach: Nebraska 1976, Washington State 1977, Missouri 1978-81. Pro coach: Cleveland Browns 1982-88, joined Chiefs in 1989.

Al Saunders, assistant head coach-receivers; born February 1, 1947, London, England, lives in Kansas City. Defensive back San Jose State 1966-68. No pro playing experience. College coach: Southern California 1970-71, Missouri 1972, Utah State 1973-75, California 1976-81, Tennessee 1982. Pro coach: San Diego Chargers 1983-88 (head coach 1986-88), joined Chiefs in 1989.

Kurt Schottenheimer, defensive backs; born October 1, 1949, McDonald, Pa., lives in Kansas City. Defensive back Miami 1969-70. No pro playing experience. College coach: William Patterson 1974, Michigan State 1978-82, Tulane 1983, Louisiana State 1984-85, Notre Dame 1986. Pro coach: Cleveland Browns 1987-88, joined Chiefs in 1989.

Art Shell, offensive line; born November 26, 1946, Charleston, S.C., lives in Kansas City. Offensive-defensive tackle Maryland State 1965-67. Pro offensive tackle Oakland/Los Angeles Raiders 1968-82. Pro coach: Los Angeles Raiders 1983-94 (head coach 1989-94), joined Chiefs in 1995.

Mike Stock, special teams; born September 29, 1939, Barberton, Ohio, lives in Kansas City. Fullback Northwestern 1957-60. Pro running back Saskatchewan Roughriders (CFL) 1961. College coach: Northwestern 1961, Buffalo 1966-67, Navy 1968, Notre Dame 1969-74, Wisconsin 1975-78, Eastern Michigan 1979-83 (head coach), Notre Dame 1984-86, Ohio State 1992-94. Pro coach: Cincinnati Bengals 1987-91, joined Chiefs in 1995.

Darvin Wallis, special assistant-quality control; born February 14, 1949, Ft. Branch, Ind., lives in Overland Park, Kan. Defensive end Arizona 1970-71. No pro playing experience. College coach: Adams State 1976-77, Tulane 1978-79, Mississippi 1980-81. Pro coach: Cleveland Browns 1982-88, joined Chiefs in 1989.

1995 FIRST-YEAR ROSTER

Name	Pos.	Ht.	Wt.	Birthdate	College	Hometown	How Acq.
Barndt, Tom	C	6-3	290	3/14/72	Pittsburgh	Mentor, Ohio	D6b
Bonds, Byron (1)	DT	6-3	290	4/21/72	Southern Methodist	Cooper, Tex.	FA
Carter, Perry (1)	CB	5-11	194	8/15/71	Southern Mississippi	McComb, Miss.	FA
Childs, Ron	LB	5-11	212	9/18/71	Washington State	Kennewick, Wash.	FA
Crocker, Sean (1)	CB	5-9	191	6/14/71	North Carolina	Wakefield, Va.	FA
DeGraffenreid, Allen (1)	WR	6-2	210	5/1/70	Ohio State	Cincinnati, Ohio	FA
Dumas, Troy	LB	6-3	233	9/30/72	Nebraska	Cheyenne, Wyo.	D3b
Florine, Ron	T	6-6	297	9/27/71	Central Missouri State	Marceline, Mo.	FA
Houston, Harrison (1)	WR	5-9	180	1/26/72	Florida	Pensacola, Fla.	FA
Jenkins, Trezelle	T	6-7	322	3/13/73	Michigan	Chicago, Ill.	D1
Layton, Gary	P	6-1	205	9/28/72	Miami, Ohio	St. Joseph, Mich.	FA
Matthews, Steve (1)	QB	6-3	209	10/13/70	Memphis State	Tullahoma, Tenn.	D7a-'94
Pay, Garry (1)	C	6-4	285	1/20/68	Brigham Young	Glendale, Ariz.	FA
Pelton, Mike	DT	6-2	284	12/13/71	Auburn	Goshen, Ala.	D5a
Proby, Bryan	DT	6-5	283	11/30/71	Arizona State	Los Angeles, Calif.	D6a
Reece, John (1)	CB	6-0	203	1/24/71	Nebraska	Houston, Tex.	FA
Richardson, Terry (1)	RB	6-0	204	10/8/71	Syracuse	Ft. Lauderdale, Fla.	FA
Richardson, Tony (1)	RB	6-1	224	12/17/71	Auburn	Daleville, Ala.	FA
Scott, Sean	WR-KR	6-3	204	5/23/73	Pittsburg State	Tulsa, Okla.	FA
Smith, J.J.	RB	6-0	207	10/14/72	Kansas State	Kansas City, Mo.	FA
Stenstrom, Steve	QB	6-2	200	12/23/71	Stanford	El Toro, Calif.	D4
Tate, Willy	TE	6-3	240	8/7/72	Oregon	Elk Grove, Calif.	FA
Vanover, Tamarick	WR-KR	5-11	213	2/25/74	Florida State	Tallahassee, Fla.	D3a
Washington, Michael	RB	6-0	266	1/3/72	Missouri	Monroe City, Mo.	FA
Willard, Jerrott	LB	6-1	233	7/11/72	California	Newport Beach, Calif.	D5b
Williams, Robert	TE	6-3	240	2/1/72	Valdosta State	Washington, Ga.	FA
Woolfork, Ronnie (1)	LB	6-3	254	12/21/70	Colorado	Detroit, Mich.	FA

The term NFL Rookie is defined as a player who is in his first season of professional football and has not been on the roster of another professional football team for any regular-season or postseason games. A Rookie is designated by an "R" on NFL rosters. Players who have been active in another professional football league or players who have NFL experience, including either preseason training camp or being on an Active List or Inactive List, or on Reserve/Injured or Reserve/Physically Unable to Perform for fewer than six regular-season games, are termed NFL First-Year Players. An NFL First-Year Player is designated by a "1" on NFL rosters. Thereafter, a player is credited with an additional year of experience for each season in which he accumulates six games on the Active List or Inactive List, or on Reserve/Injured or Reserve/Physically Unable to Perform.

NOTES

LOS ANGELES RAIDERS

American Football Conference
Western Division
Team Colors: Silver and Black
332 Center Street
El Segundo, California 90245
Telephone: (310) 322-3451

CLUB OFFICIALS

President of the Managing General Partner: Al Davis
Executive Assistant: Al LoCasale
Pro Football Scout: George Karras
Legal Affairs: Jeff Birren, Amy Trask
Senior Assistant: Bruce Allen
Finance: Tom Blanda
Senior Administrator: Morris Bradshaw
Business Manager: John Novak
Senior Executive: John Herrera
Publications: Mike Taylor
Community Relations: Gil Lafferty-Hernandez
Administrative Assistants: Mario Perez, Marc McKinney
Ticket Operations: Peter Eiges
Trainers: H. Rod Martin, Jonathan Jones
Equipment Manager: Richard Romanski
Assistant Equipment Manager: Bob Romanski
Stadium: Los Angeles Memorial Coliseum
•**Capacity:** 67,800
3911 South Figueroa Street
Los Angeles, California 90037
Playing Surface: Grass
Training Camp: Radisson Hotel
Oxnard, California 93030

1995 SCHEDULE

PRESEASON

Aug. 5	at Dallas	8:00
Aug. 12	**St. Louis**	TBA
Aug. 18	at Minnesota	7:00
Aug. 25	**New England**	6:00

REGULAR SEASON

Sept. 3	**San Diego**	1:00
Sept. 10	at Washington	1:00
Sept. 17	at Kansas City	12:00
Sept. 24	**Philadelphia**	1:00
Oct. 1	at New York Jets	8:00
Oct. 8	**Seattle**	1:00
Oct. 16	at Denver (Monday)	7:00
Oct. 22	**Indianapolis**	1:00
Oct. 29	Open Date	
Nov. 5	at Cincinnati	4:00
Nov. 12	at New York Giants	1:00
Nov. 19	**Dallas**	1:00
Nov. 27	at San Diego (Monday)	6:00
Dec. 3	**Kansas City**	1:00
Dec. 10	**Pittsburgh**	1:00
Dec. 17	at Seattle	5:00
Dec. 24	**Denver**	1:00

RECORD HOLDERS

INDIVIDUAL RECORDS—CAREER

Category	Name	Performance
Rushing (Yds.)	Marcus Allen, 1982-1992	8,545
Passing (Yds.)	Ken Stabler, 1970-79	19,078
Passing (TDs)	Ken Stabler, 1970-79	150
Receiving (No.)	Fred Biletnikoff, 1965-1978	589
Receiving (Yds.)	Fred Biletnikoff, 1965-1978	8,974
Interceptions	Willie Brown, 1967-1978	39
	Lester Hayes, 1977-1986	39
Punting (Avg.)	Ray Guy, 1973-1986	42.5
Punt Return (Avg.)	Claude Gibson, 1963-65	12.6
Kickoff Return (Avg.)	Jack Larscheid, 1960-61	28.4
Field Goals	George Blanda, 1967-1975	156
Touchdowns (Tot.)	Marcus Allen, 1982-1992	98
Points	George Blanda, 1967-1975	863

INDIVIDUAL RECORDS—SINGLE SEASON

Category	Name	Performance
Rushing (Yds.)	Marcus Allen, 1985	1,759
Passing (Yds.)	Ken Stabler, 1979	3,615
Passing (TDs)	Daryle Lamonica, 1969	34
Receiving (No.)	Todd Christensen, 1986	95
Receiving (Yds.)	Art Powell, 1964	1,361
Interceptions	Lester Hayes, 1980	13
Punting (Avg.)	Ray Guy, 1973	45.3
Punt Return (Avg.)	Claude Gibson, 1964	14.4
Kickoff Return (Avg.)	Harold Hart, 1975	30.5
Field Goals	Jeff Jaeger, 1993	*35
Touchdowns (Tot.)	Marcus Allen, 1984	18
Points	Jeff Jaeger, 1993	132

INDIVIDUAL RECORDS—SINGLE GAME

Category	Name	Performance
Rushing (Yds.)	Bo Jackson, 11-30-87	221
Passing (Yds.)	Jeff Hostetler, 10-31-93	424
Passing (TDs)	Tom Flores, 12-22-63	6
	Daryle Lamonica, 10-19-69	6
Receiving (No.)	Dave Casper, 10-3-76	12
Receiving (Yds.)	Art Powell, 12-22-63	247
Interceptions	Many times	3
	Last time by Terry McDaniel, 10-9-94	
Field Goals	Jeff Jaeger, 12-11-94	5
Touchdowns (Tot.)	Art Powell, 12-22-63	4
	Marcus Allen, 9-24-84	4
Points	Art Powell, 12-22-63	24
	Marcus Allen, 9-24-84	24

*NFL Record

COACHING HISTORY

OAKLAND 1960-1981
(334-207-11)

1960-61	Eddie Erdelatz*	6-10-0
1961-62	Marty Feldman**	2-15-0
1962	Red Conkright	1-8-0
1963-65	Al Davis	23-16-3
1966-68	John Rauch	35-10-1
1969-78	John Madden	112-39-7
1979-87	Tom Flores	91-56-0
1988-89	Mike Shanahan***	8-12-0
1989-94	Art Shell	56-41-0

*Released after two games in 1961
**Released after five games in 1962
***Released after four games in 1989

LOS ANGELES MEMORIAL COLISEUM

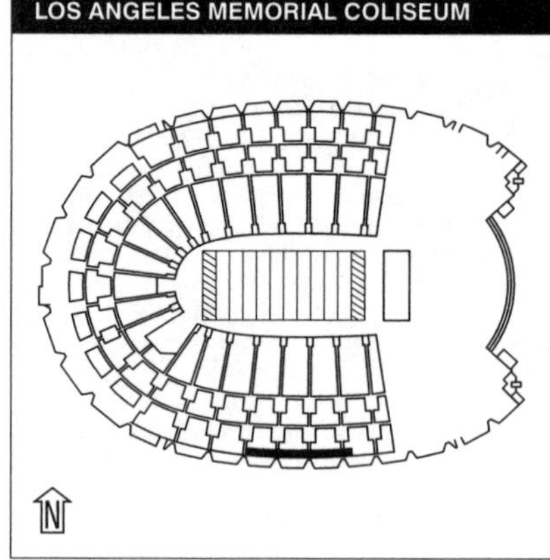

1994 TEAM RECORD

PRESEASON (4-1)

Date	Result		Opponents
7/31	W	25-22	vs. Denver at Barcelona
8/7	W	27-19	at Dallas
8/13	L	17-29	at Pittsburgh
8/20	W	29-20	at L.A. Rams
8/27	W	24-23	at Houston

REGULAR SEASON (9-7)

Date	Result		Opponents	Att.
9/5	L	14-44	at San Francisco	68,032
9/11	L	9-38	Seattle	47,319
9/18	W	48-16	at Denver	75,764
9/25	L	24-26	San Diego	55,385
10/9	W	21-17	at New England	59,889
10/16	L	17-20	at Miami (OT)	69,380
10/23	W	30-17	Atlanta	42,192
10/30	W	17-14	Houston	40,473
11/6	L	3-13	at Kansas City	78,709
11/13	W	20-17	at L.A. Rams	65,208
11/20	W	24-19	New Orleans	41,722
11/27	L	3-21	Pittsburgh	58,327
12/5	W	24-17	at San Diego	63,012
12/11	W	23-13	Denver	60,016
12/18	W	17-16	at Seattle	53,301
12/24	L	9-19	Kansas City	64,130

(OT) Overtime

SCORE BY PERIODS

Raiders	62	94	61	86	0	—	303
Opponents	72	87	52	113	3	—	327

ATTENDANCE

Home 409,564 Away 533,295 Total 942,859
Single-game home record, 91,494 (9-29-91)
Single-season home record, 516,205 (1986)

1994 TEAM STATISTICS

	Raiders	Opp.
Total First Downs	267	303
Rushing	87	94
Passing	158	176
Penalty	22	33
Third Down: Made/Att	82/208	90/233
Third Down Pct.	39.6	38.6
Fourth Down: Made/Att	3/12	15/24
Fourth Down Pct.	25.0	62.5
Total Net Yards	4779	4943
Avg. Per Game	298.7	308.9
Total Plays	965	1046
Avg. Per Play	5.0	4.7
Net Yards Rushing	1512	1543
Avg. Per Game	94.5	96.4
Total Rushes	428	444
Net Yards Passing	3267	3400
Avg. Per Game	204.2	212.5
Sacked/Yards Lost	50/289	38/284
Gross Yards	3556	3684
Att./Completions	487/281	564/306
Completion Pct.	57.7	54.3
Had Intercepted	16	12
Punts/Avg.	77/43.9	84/40.6
Net Punting Avg.	77/35.2	84/32.0
Penalties/Yards Lost	156/1186	113/823
Fumbles/Ball Lost	22/14	26/13
Touchdowns	34	38
Rushing	7	11
Passing	22	24
Returns	5	3
Avg. Time of Possession	29:30	30:30

1994 INDIVIDUAL STATISTICS

PASSING	Att.	Comp.	Yds.	Pct.	TD	Int.	Tkld.	Rate
Hostetler	454	263	3334	57.9	20	16	41/232	81.0
Evans	33	18	222	54.5	2	0	9/57	95.8
Raiders	487	281	3556	57.7	22	16	50/289	82.0
Opponents	564	306	3684	54.3	24	12	38/284	79.8

SCORING	TD R	TD P	TD Rt	PAT	FG	Saf	PTS
Jaeger	0	0	0	31/31	22/28	0	97
Brown	0	9	0	0/0	0/0	0	54
H. Williams	4	3	0	0/0	0/0	0	44
Ismail	0	5	0	0/0	0/0	0	30
McDaniel	0	0	3	0/0	0/0	0	18
Glover	0	2	0	0/0	0/0	0	12
Hostetler	2	0	0	0/0	0/0	0	12
Wright	0	2	0	0/0	0/0	0	12
McCallum	1	0	0	0/0	0/0	0	6
Montgomery	0	1	0	0/0	0/0	0	6
A. Smith	0	0	1	0/0	0/0	0	6
Washington	0	0	1	0/0	0/0	0	6
Raiders	7	22	5	31/31	22/28	0	303
Opponents	11	24	3	34/35	21/29	1	327

2-Point conversions: H. Williams. Team: 1-3.

RUSHING	Att.	Yds.	Avg.	LG	TD
H. Williams	282	983	3.5	28	4
Hostetler	46	159	3.5	14	2
Rathman	28	118	4.2	14	0
Montgomery	36	97	2.7	15	0
C. Jones	22	93	4.2	10	0
Ismail	4	31	7.8	13	0
Evans	6	24	4.0	23	0
McCallum	3	5	1.7	3	1
K. Smith	1	2	2.0	2	0
Raiders	428	1512	3.5	28	7
Opponents	444	1543	3.5	33t	11

RECEIVING	No.	Yds.	Avg.	LG	TD
Brown	89	1309	14.7	77t	9
H. Williams	47	391	8.3	27t	3
Ismail	34	513	15.1	42	5
Glover	33	371	11.2	27t	2
Rathman	26	194	7.5	18	0
Wright	16	294	18.4	76t	2
Jett	15	253	16.9	54	0
Montgomery	8	126	15.8	65t	1
Hobbs	5	52	10.4	14	0
J. Williams	3	25	8.3	16	0
Bender	2	14	7.0	7	0
C. Jones	2	6	3.0	4	0
K. Smith	1	8	8.0	8	0
Raiders	281	3556	12.7	77t	22
Opponents	306	3684	12.0	69t	24

INTERCEPTIONS	No.	Yds.	Avg.	LG	TD
McDaniel	7	103	14.7	35	2
Washington	3	65	21.7	31t	1
Biekert	1	11	11.0	11	0
Frank	1	8	8.0	8	0
Raiders	12	187	15.6	35	3
Opponents	16	202	12.6	78t	1

PUNTING	No.	Yds.	Avg.	In 20	LG
Gossett	77	3377	43.9	19	65
Raiders	77	3377	43.9	19	65
Opponents	84	3414	40.6	17	64

PUNT RETURNS	No.	FC	Yds.	Avg.	LG	TD
Brown	40	14	487	12.2	48	0
Raiders	40	14	487	12.2	48	0
Opponents	38	5	366	9.6	90t	1

KICKOFF RETURNS	No.	Yds.	Avg.	LG	TD
Ismail	43	923	21.5	51	0
Wright	10	282	28.2	55	0
H. Williams	8	153	19.1	24	0
J. Williams	1	0	0.0	0	0
Raiders	62	1358	21.9	55	0
Opponents	65	1406	21.6	68	0

SACKS	No.
McGlockton	9.5
A. Smith	6.0
Harrison	5.0
Ball	3.0
Fredrickson	3.0
Anderson	2.0
Moss	2.0
Wallace	2.0
White	2.0
Biekert	1.5
Lewis	1.0
Trapp	1.0
Raiders	38.0
Opponents	50.0

1995 DRAFT CHOICES

Round	Name	Pos.	College
1	Napoleon Kaufman	RB	Washington
2	Barret Robbins	C	Texas Christian
3	Joe Aska	RB	Central State, Okla.
4	Mike Morton	LB	North Carolina
5	Matt Dyson	LB	Michigan
	Jeff Kysar	T	Arizona State
6	Eli Herring	T	Brigham Young

LOS ANGELES RAIDERS

1995 VETERAN ROSTER

No.	Name	Pos.	Ht.	Wt.	Birthdate	NFL Exp.	College	Hometown	How Acq.	'94 Games/ Starts
33	Anderson, Eddie	S	6-1	210	7/22/63	10	Ft. Valley State	Warner Robins, Ga.	FA-'87	14/14
45	Ball, Eric	RB	6-2	220	7/1/66	7	UCLA	Ypsilanti, Mich.	FA-'95	16/0*
93	Ball, Jerry	DT	6-1	315	12/15/64	9	Southern Methodist	Beaumont, Tex.	UFA(Clev)-'94	16/14
24	Bates, Patrick	S	6-3	215	11/27/70	3	Texas A&M	Galveston, Tex.	D1-'93	16/9
49	Bender, Wes	RB	5-10	235	8/2/70	2	Southern California	Burbank, Calif.	FA-'94	9/0
54	Biekert, Greg	LB	6-2	235	3/14/69	3	Colorado	Longmont, Colo.	D7-'93	16/14
89	Bobo, Phillip	WR	5-11	186	12/6/71	2	Washington State	Moreno Valley, Calif.	FA-'95	0*
97	Broughton, Willie	DT	6-5	285	9/9/64	9	Miami	Ft. Pierce, Fla.	FA-'95	0*
81	Brown, Tim	WR	6-0	195	7/22/66	8	Notre Dame	Dallas, Tex.	D1-'88	16/16
56	Bruce, Aundray	DE	6-5	260	4/30/66	8	Auburn	Montgomery, Ala.	PB(Atl)-'92	16/0
88	Cash, Kerry	TE	6-4	250	8/7/69	5	Texas	San Antonio, Tex.	UFA(Ind)-'95	16/16*
70	Davis, Scott	DE	6-7	285	7/8/65	6	Illinois	Plainfield, Ill.	D1-'88	14/1
58	Dinkins, Howard	LB	6-1	230	4/26/69	3	Florida State	Jacksonville, Fla.	FA-'95	0*
11	# Evans, Vince	QB	6-2	215	6/14/55	15	Southern California	Greensboro, N.C.	FA-'92	9/0
34	Fenner, Derrick	RB	6-3	230	4/6/67	7	North Carolina	Oxon Hill, Md.	UFA(Cin)-'95	16/13*
55	Folston, James	LB	6-3	235	8/14/71	2	Northeast Louisiana	Cocoa, Fla.	D2-'94	7/0
53	Fredrickson, Rob	LB	6-4	240	5/13/71	2	Michigan State	St. Joseph, Mich.	D1-'94	16/12
87	Glover, Andrew	TE	6-6	245	8/12/67	5	Grambling State	Geismar, La.	D10-'91	16/16
66	Gogan, Kevin	G	6-7	315	11/2/64	9	Washington	San Francisco, Calif.	UFA(Dall)-'94	16/16
7	Gossett, Jeff	P	6-2	190	1/25/57	14	Eastern Illinois	Charleston, Ill.	T(Hou)-'88	16/0
8	Graham, Jeff	QB	6-5	220	2/5/66	3	Long Beach State	Costa Mesa, Calif.	FA-'95	0*
75	Gray, Cecil	T	6-4	305	2/16/68	6	North Carolina	Norfolk, Va.	UFA(Ind)-'95	16/5*
74	Harrison, Nolan	DE	6-5	285	1/25/69	5	Indiana	Flossmoor, Ill.	D6-'91	16/16
80	Hobbs, Daryl	WR	6-2	175	5/23/68	3	Pacific	Los Angeles, Calif.	FA-'93	10/0
9	Hobert, Billy Joe	QB	6-3	220	1/8/71	3	Washington	Puyallup, Wash.	D3-'93	0*
57	Holmberg, Rob	LB	6-3	225	5/6/71	2	Penn State	Mt. Pleasant, Pa.	D7-'94	16/0
20	Hoskins, Derrick	S	6-2	200	11/14/70	4	Southern Mississippi	Philadelphia, Miss.	D5-'92	15/9
15	Hostetler, Jeff	QB	6-3	215	4/22/61	12	West Virginia	Davidsville, Pa.	UFA(NYG)-'93	16/16
86	Ismail, Raghib	WR	5-11	175	11/18/69	3	Notre Dame	Wilkes-Barre, Pa.	D4-'90	16/0
18	Jaeger, Jeff	K	5-11	190	11/26/64	9	Washington	Kent, Wash.	PB(Clev)-'89	16/0
64	Jenkins, Robert	T	6-5	295	12/30/63	10	UCLA	Dublin, Calif.	FA-'94	10/4
82	Jett, James	WR	5-10	165	12/28/70	3	West Virginia	Kearneysville, W. Va.	FA-'93	16/1
27	Jones, Calvin	RB	5-11	205	11/27/70	2	Nebraska	Omaha, Neb.	D3-'94	7/0
84	Jones, Hassan	WR	6-0	208	7/2/64	9	Florida State	Clearwater, Fla.	FA-'95	0*
52	Jones, Mike	LB	6-1	230	4/15/69	5	Missouri	Kansas City, Mo.	FA-'91	16/1
25	Land, Dan	S	6-0	195	7/3/65	7	Albany State	Donalsonville, Ga.	FA-'89	16/0
29	Lewis, Albert	CB	6-2	195	10/6/60	13	Grambling State	Mansfield, La.	UFA(KC)-'94	14/9
36	McDaniel, Terry	CB	5-10	180	2/8/65	8	Tennessee	Saginaw, Mich.	D1-'88	16/16
91	McGlockton, Chester	DT	6-4	315	9/16/69	4	Clemson	Whiteville, N.C.	D1-'92	16/16
21	Montgomery, Tyrone	WR	6-0	190	8/3/70	3	Mississippi	Greenville, Miss.	FA-'93	6/6
72	Mosebar, Don	C	6-6	295	9/11/61	13	Southern California	Visalia, Calif.	D1-'83	16/16
48	Mustafaa, Najee	CB	6-1	190	6/20/64	8	Georgia Tech	East Point, Ga.	FA-'95	0*
71	Perry, Gerald	T	6-6	290	11/12/64	8	Southern	Columbia, S.C.	UFA(Rams)-'93	12/12
39	Pickens, Bruce	CB	5-11	190	5/9/68	4	Nebraska	Kansas City, Mo.	FA-'95	0*
44	Rathman, Tom	RB	6-1	230	10/7/62	10	Nebraska	Grand Island, Neb.	UFA(SF)-'94	16/16
95	Robbins, Austin	DT	6-6	290	3/1/71	2	North Carolina	Washington, D.C.	D4-'94	2/0
28	Robinson, Greg	RB	5-10	200	8/7/69	3	Northeast Louisiana	Grenada, Miss.	D8-'93	0*
78	Skrepenak, Greg	T	6-6	300	1/31/70	4	Michigan	Wilkes-Barre, Pa.	D2-'92	12/10
94	Smith, Anthony	DE	6-3	260	6/28/67	6	Arizona	Elizabeth City, N.C.	D1-'90	16/16
83	Smith, Kevin	TE	6-4	255	7/25/69	3	UCLA	Oakland, Calif.	FA-'95	3/0
77	Stephens, Rich	T	6-7	305	1/1/65	3	Tulsa	House Springs, Mo.	FA-'92	0*
56	Swilling, Pat	LB	6-3	242	10/25/64	10	Georgia Tech	Toccoa, Ga.	FA-'95	16/7*
37	Trapp, James	CB	6-0	180	12/28/69	3	Clemson	Lawton, Okla.	D3-'93	16/2
67	Turk, Dan	C	6-4	290	8/25/62	11	Wisconsin	Milwaukee, Wis.	FA-'89	16/0
51	Wallace, Aaron	DE	6-3	240	4/17/67	6	Texas A&M	Dallas, Tex.	D2-'90	16/5
96	White, Alberto	DE	6-3	245	4/8/71	2	Texas Southern	Miami, Fla.	FA-'94	8/0
68	# Wilkerson, Bruce	T	6-5	295	7/28/64	9	Tennessee	Philadelphia, Tenn.	D2-'87	11/6
22	Williams, Harvey	RB	6-2	210	4/22/67	5	Louisiana State	Hempstead, Tex.	UFA(KC)-'94	16/10
88	# Williams, Jamie	TE	6-4	250	2/25/60	13	Nebraska	Davenport, Iowa	UFA(SF)-'94	16/0
76	Wisniewski, Steve	G	6-4	285	4/7/67	7	Penn State	Houston, Tex.	D2-'89	16/16

* Ball played 16 games with Cincinnati in '94; Bobo last on injured reserve with L.A. Rams in '93; Broughton inactive for 9 games with L.A. Raiders, 5 games with Miami; Cash played 16 games with Indianapolis; Dinkins last active with Atlanta in '93; Fenner played 16 games with Cincinnati; Graham inactive for 3 games with Seattle; Gray played 16 games with Indianapolis; Hobert inactive for 16 games; H. Jones last active with Kansas City in '93; Mustafaa active for 1 game with Miami but did not play; Pickens last active with Kansas City in '93; Robinson missed '94 season because of injury; Stephens active for 1 game but did not play; Swilling played 16 games with Detroit.

Unrestricted free agent; subject to developments.

† Restricted free agent; subject to developments.

Retired—G Max Montoya, 16-year veteran, 13 games in '94.

Players lost through free agency (4): CB Donald Frank (Minn; 16 games in '94), LB Winston Moss (Sea; 16), CB Lionel Washington (Den; 11), WR Alexander Wright (Rams; 16).

Players lost through Expansion Draft (2): S Cary Brabham (Car; 7 games in '94), TE-DE John Duff (Jax; 4).

Also played with Raiders in '94—RB Jarrod Bunch (3 games), RB Napoleon McCallum (1).

COACHING STAFF

Head Coach,
Mike White

Pro Career: Named tenth head coach in Raiders history on February 2, 1995, after five years as an assistant coach with the organization. First joined Raiders in 1990 as quarterback coach. In 1992, he became offensive line coach. During these five seasons Raiders were 47-33 in league play and made AFC playoffs three times (1990, 1991, 1993). First came into pro coaching as an assistant with San Francisco 49ers in 1978-79 on Bill Walsh's staff.

Background: Offensive end at California 1955-57. Also lettered in basketball and track while earning degree in business. Began a 37-year coaching career at California as an assistant coach in 1958. He then joined staff at Stanford University as an assistant coach in 1964, remaining there through 1972, including Rose Bowl seasons of 1970 and 1971. In 1973, was named head coach at California where he remained through 1977, building 31-23-0 record. Was named college football coach-of-the-year in 1975. In 1980, was selected as head coach at Illinois, serving in that capacity through 1987 with a record of 47-38-3, earning berths in the Rose Bowl, Liberty Bowl, and Peach Bowl. He also coached in 11 college all-star games—two East-West Shrine Games, two Hula Bowls, two Blue-Grey games, and five Japan Bowls. Leaving college coaching after the 1987 season, he spent the next two years with the National Football League helping to plan and organize the World League of American Football before coming to the Raiders in April, 1990.

Personal: Born January 4, 1936, Berkeley, Calif. Mike and wife Marilyn, live in Newport Beach, Calif. Their family includes daughter Carrie and sons Chris and Matt.

ASSISTANT COACHES

Fred Biletnikoff, quality control-offense; born February 23, 1943, Erie, Pa., lives in El Segundo, Calif. Wide receiver Florida State 1962-64. Pro wide receiver Oakland Raiders 1965-78, Montreal Alouettes (CFL) 1980. College coach: Palomar, (Calif.), J.C. 1983, Diablo Valley, (Calif.), J.C. 1984, 1986. Pro coach: Oakland Invaders (USFL) 1985, Calgary Stampeders (CFL) 1987-88, joined Raiders in 1989.

Willie Brown, squad development; born December 2, 1940, Yazoo City, Miss., lives in Lomita, Calif. Defensive back Grambling 1959-62. Pro defensive back Denver Broncos 1963-66, Oakland Raiders 1967-78. College coach: Long Beach State 1990-91 (head coach 1991). Pro coach: Oakland/Los Angeles Raiders 1979-88, re-joined Raiders in 1995.

Joe Bugel, assistant head coach-offense; born March 10, 1940, Pittsburgh, Pa., lives in Palos Verdes, Calif. Offensive guard at Western Kentucky 1960-62. No pro playing experience. College coach: Western Kentucky 1964-68, Navy 1969-72, Iowa State 1973, Ohio State 1974. Pro coach: Detroit Lions 1975-76, Houston Oilers 1977-80, Washington Redskins 1981-89, Phoenix Cardinals 1990-93 (head coach), joined Raiders in 1995.

Jim Fassel, quarterbacks; born August 31, 1949, Anaheim, Calif., lives in Manhattan Beach, Calif. Quarterback Southern California 1969-70, Long Beach State 1971. Pro quarterback Chicago Bears 1972, Houston Oilers 1972, San Diego Chargers 1972. College coach: Fullerton (Calif.) J.C. 1973, Utah 1976, 1985-89 (head coach), Weber State 1977-78, Stanford 1979-83. Pro coach: Hawaii (WFL) 1974, Portland Breakers (USFL) 1984, New York Giants 1991-92, Denver Broncos 1993-94, joined Raiders in 1995.

John Fox, defensive coordinator; born February 8, 1955, Virginia Beach, Va., lives in Palos Verdes, Calif. Defensive back San Diego State 1975-77. No pro playing experience. College coach: U.S. International 1979, Boise State 1980, Long Beach State 1981, Utah 1982, Kansas 1983, 1985, Iowa State 1984, Pittsburgh 1986-88. Pro coach: Los Angeles Express (USFL) 1985, Pittsburgh Steelers 1989-91, San Diego Chargers 1992-93, joined Raiders in 1994.

1995 FIRST-YEAR ROSTER

Name	Pos.	Ht.	Wt.	Birthdate	College	Hometown	How Acq.
Aska, Joe	RB	5-11	230	7/14/72	Central Oklahoma	Putnam City, Okla.	D3
Baker, Jon (1)	DT	6-7	280	3/6/68	Pittsburgh	San Rafael, Calif.	FA
Bobo, Phillip (1)	WR	5-11	185	12/6/71	Washington State	Moreno Valley, Calif.	FA
Caswell, A.C. (1)	WR	5-9	165	9/17/68	Glendale, Ariz., J.C.	Glendale, Ariz.	FA
Dyson, Matt	LB	6-3	280	8/1/72	Michigan	La Plata, Md.	D5a
Foster, Sean (1)	WR	6-0	190	12/22/67	Long Beach State	Los Angeles, Calif.	FA
Herpin, John	CB	5-11	185	3/25/72	Southern California	La Porte, Tex.	FA
Hinton, Marcus	TE	6-4	255	12/27/71	Alcorn State	Wiggins, Miss.	FA
Kaufman, Napoleon	RB	5-9	185	6/7/73	Washington	Lompoc, Calif.	D1
Kysar, Jeff	T	6-7	320	6/14/72	Arizona State	San Diego, Calif.	D5b
Mason, Kevin	QB	6-3	200	9/25/72	Syracuse	Cheektowaga, N.Y.	FA
McCullough, Russ (1)	T	6-9	315	10/31/68	Missouri	Olathe, Kan.	FA
Moncanto, Vic	WR-P	6-2	195	3/19/71	Fairleigh Dickinson	Sussex, N.J.	FA
Moore, Josh	S	6-1	200	9/29/72	San Diego State	Torrance, Calif.	FA
Morton, Mike	LB	6-4	235	3/28/72	North Carolina	Kannapolis, N.C.	D4
Raney, Len	CB	5-11	185	9/17/72	Northern Arizona	Fresno, Calif.	FA
Robbins, Barret	C	6-3	305	8/26/73	Texas Christian	Houston, Tex.	D2
Robsock, Tom	G	6-4	275	12/1/71	West Virginia	Berwick, Pa.	FA
Smith, Al	WR	5-9	165	10/5/68	Idaho State	Stockton, Calif.	FA
Stubbins, Willie (1)	T	6-5	290	5/23/67	Texas Southern	Tifton, Ga.	FA
Wright, Claudius	CB	5-11	180	7/10/72	Arizona	West Covina, Calif.	FA

The term NFL Rookie is defined as a player who is in his first season of professional football and has not been on the roster of another professional football team for any regular-season or postseason games. A Rookie is designated by an "R" on NFL rosters. Players who have been active in another professional football league or players who have NFL experience, including either preseason training camp or being on an Active List or Inactive List, or on Reserve/Injured or Reserve/Physically Unable to Perform for fewer than six regular-season games, are termed NFL First-Year Players. An NFL First-Year Player is designated by a "1" on NFL rosters. Thereafter, a player is credited with an additional year of experience for each season in which he accumulates six games on the Active List or Inactive List, or on Reserve/Injured or Reserve/Physically Unable to Perform.

NOTES

Garrett Giemont, strength and conditioning; born August 31, 1957, Fullerton, Calif., lives in Hermosa Beach, Calif. No college or pro playing experience. Pro coach: Los Angeles Rams 1990-91, joined Raiders in 1995.

John Guy, defensive assistant; born May 26, 1951, Greensboro, N.C., lives in El Segundo, Calif. Defensive back-kicker North Carolina A&T 1969-72. No pro playing experience. College coach: North Carolina 1973-77, Virginia Tech 1978, Duke 1978-80, Georgia Tech 1981-86, Alabama 1987-89, Kentucky 1990-91. Pro coach: Pittsburgh Steelers 1992-93, joined Raiders in 1995.

Bishop Harris, running backs; born November 23, 1941, Phenix City, Ala., lives in Redondo Beach, Calif. Running back and defensive back North Carolina College 1960-63. No pro playing experience. College coach: Duke 1972-75, North Carolina State 1977-79, Louisiana State 1980-83, Notre Dame 1984-85, Minnesota 1986-90, North Carolina Central 1991-92 (head coach). Pro coach: Denver Broncos 1993-94, joined Raiders in 1995.

Bill Meyers, tight ends; born October 8, 1946, Chippewa Falls, Wis., lives in Surfside, Calif. Tackle Stanford 1970-71. No pro playing experience. College coach: California 1972-73, 1977-78, Santa Clara 1974-76, Notre Dame 1979-81, Missouri 1985-86, Pittsburgh 1987-92. Pro coach: Green Bay Packers 1982-83, Pittsburgh Steelers 1984, joined Raiders in 1993.

Floyd Peters, defensive line; born May 21, 1936, Council Bluffs, Iowa, lives in Long Beach, Calif. Defensive lineman San Francisco State 1954-57. Defensive tackle Baltimore Colts 1958, Cleveland Browns 1959-62, Detroit Lions 1963, Philadelphia Eagles 1964-69, Washington Redskins 1970. Pro coach Miami Dolphins 1971-73, New York Giants 1974-75, San Francisco 49ers 1976-77, Detroit Lions 1978-81, St. Louis Cardinals 1982-85, Minnesota Vikings 1986-90, Tampa Bay Buccaneers 1991-94, joined Raiders in 1995.

Steve Shafer, defensive backs; born December 8, 1940, Glendale, Calif., lives in El Segundo, Calif. Quarterback-defensive back Utah State 1961-62. Pro defensive back British Columbia Lions (CFL) 1963-67. College coach: San Mateo (Calif.) J.C. 1968-74 (head coach 1973-74), San Diego State 1975-82, 1994. Pro coach: Los Angeles Rams 1983-90, Tampa Bay Buccaneers 1991-93, joined Raiders in 1995.

Kevin Spencer, special teams; born November 2, 1953, Queens, N.Y., lives in Redondo Beach, Calif. No college or pro playing experience. College coach: State University of New York 1975-76, Cornell 1979-80. Ithaca 1981-86, Wesleyan 1987-91 (head coach). Pro coach: Cleveland Browns 1991-94, joined Raiders in 1995.

Fred Whittingham, linebackers; born February 4, 1939, Boston, Mass., lives in El Segundo, Calif. Tight end-linebacker Brigham Young 1957-58, Cal Poly-SLO 1961-62. Pro linebacker Los Angeles Rams 1963-64, Philadelphia Eagles 1965-66, 1971, New Orleans Saints 1967-70. College coach: Brigham Young 1973-81, Utah 1992-94. Pro coach: Los Angeles Rams 1982-91, joined Raiders in 1995.

Mike Wilson, wide receivers; born December 19, 1958, Los Angeles, Calif., lives in Manhattan Beach, Calif. Wide receiver Washington State 1977-80. Pro wide receiver San Francisco 49ers 1981-90. College coach Stanford 1992-94. Pro coach: Joined Raiders in 1995.

MIAMI DOLPHINS

American Football Conference
Eastern Division
Team Colors: Aqua, Coral, and White
7500 S.W. 30 Street
Davie, Florida 33314
(305) 452-7000

CLUB OFFICIALS

President/Chief Executive Officer: H. Wayne Huizenga
Executive Vice President/General Manager: Eddie J. Jones
Vice President/Head Coach: Don Shula
Vice President-Administration: Bryan Wiedmeier
Vice President-Finance: Jill R. Strafaci
Vice President-Player Personnel: Tom Heckert
Director of College Scouting: Tom Braatz
Director of Pro Scouting: Tom Heckert, Jr.
Director of Media Relations: Harvey Greene
Media Relations Coordinator: Mike Hanson
Director of Publications: Scott Stone
Marketing Director: David Evans
Community Relations Director: Fudge Browne
Ticket Director: Bill Galante
Player Relations Director: Liffort Hobley
Trainer: Ryan Vermillion
Equipment Manager: Tony Egues
Stadium: Joe Robbie Stadium • **Capacity:** 74,916
2269 N.W. 199th Street
Miami, Florida 33056
Playing Surface: Grass (PAT)
Training Camp: Nova University
7500 S.W. 30th Street
Davie, Florida 33314

1995 SCHEDULE

PRESEASON

Aug. 4	**Jacksonville**	7:00
Aug. 11	at Atlanta	7:30
Aug. 19	**Washington**	7:00
Aug. 25	vs. Tampa Bay at Orlando, Fla	8:00

REGULAR SEASON

Sept. 3	**New York Jets**	4:00
Sept. 10	at New England	1:00
Sept. 18	**Pittsburgh** (Monday)	9:00
Sept. 24	Open Date	
Oct. 1	at Cincinnati	1:00
Oct. 8	**Indianapolis**	4:00
Oct. 15	at New Orleans	3:00
Oct. 22	at New York Jets	1:00
Oct. 29	**Buffalo**	4:00
Nov. 5	at San Diego	5:00
Nov. 12	**New England**	1:00
Nov. 20	**San Francisco** (Monday)	9:00
Nov. 26	at Indianapolis	1:00
Dec. 3	**Atlanta**	1:00
Dec. 11	**Kansas City** (Monday)	9:00
Dec. 17	at Buffalo	1:00
Dec. 24	at St. Louis	3:00

RECORD HOLDERS

INDIVIDUAL RECORDS—CAREER

Category	Name	Performance
Rushing (Yds.)	Larry Csonka, 1968-1974, 1979	6,737
Passing (Yds.)	Dan Marino, 1983-1994	45,173
Passing (TDs)	Dan Marino, 1983-1994	328
Receiving (No.)	Mark Clayton, 1983-1992	550
Receiving (Yds.)	Mark Duper, 1982-1992	8,869
Interceptions	Jake Scott, 1970-75	35
Punting (Avg.)	Reggie Roby, 1983-1992	43.3
Punt Return (Avg.)	Freddie Solomon, 1975-77	11.4
Kickoff Return (Avg.)	Mercury Morris, 1969-1975	26.5
Field Goals	Garo Yepremian, 1970-78	165
Touchdowns (Tot.)	Mark Clayton, 1983-1992	82
Points	Garo Yepremian, 1970-78	830

INDIVIDUAL RECORDS—SINGLE SEASON

Category	Name	Performance
Rushing (Yds.)	Delvin Williams, 1978	1,258
Passing (Yds.)	Dan Marino, 1984	*5,084
Passing (TDs)	Dan Marino, 1984	*48
Receiving (No.)	Mark Clayton, 1988	86
Receiving (Yds.)	Mark Clayton, 1984	1,389
Interceptions	Dick Westmoreland, 1967	10
Punting (Avg.)	Reggie Roby, 1991	45.7
Punt Return (Avg.)	Freddie Solomon, 1975	12.3
Kickoff Return (Avg.)	Duriel Harris, 1976	32.9
Field Goals	Pete Stoyanovich, 1991	31
Touchdowns (Tot.)	Mark Clayton, 1984	18
Points	Pete Stoyanovich, 1992	124

INDIVIDUAL RECORDS—SINGLE GAME

Category	Name	Performance
Rushing (Yds.)	Mercury Morris, 9-30-73	197
Passing (Yds.)	Dan Marino, 10-23-88	521
Passing (TDs)	Bob Griese, 11-24-77	6
	Dan Marino, 9-21-86	6
Receiving (No.)	Jim Jensen, 11-6-88	12
Receiving (Yds.)	Mark Duper, 11-10-85	217
Interceptions	Dick Anderson, 12-3-73	*4
Field Goals	Garo Yepremian, 9-26-71	5
Touchdowns (Tot.)	Paul Warfield, 12-15-73	4
Points	Paul Warfield, 12-15-73	24

*NFL Record

COACHING HISTORY

(280-178-4)

1966-69	George Wilson	15-39-2
1970-94	Don Shula	265-139-2

JOE ROBBIE STADIUM

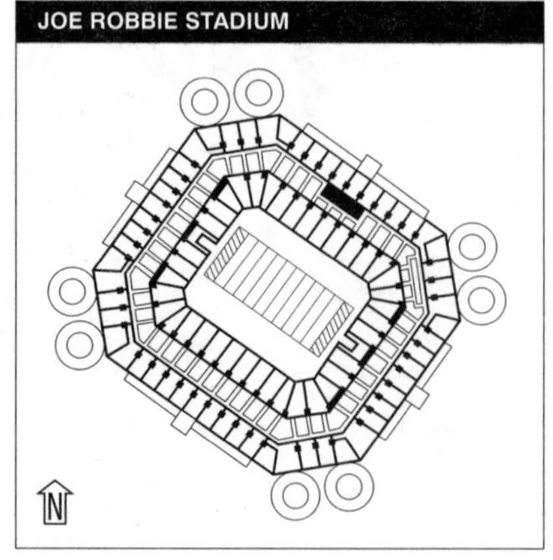

1994 TEAM RECORD

PRESEASON (3-2)

Date	Result		Opponents
7/30	W	20-19	at N.Y. Giants
8/6	W	24-14	Pittsburgh
8/13	W	31-24	vs. Green Bay at Milw.
8/20	L	14-29	Tampa Bay
8/26	L	16-31	at Minnesota

REGULAR SEASON (10-6)

Date	Result		Opponents	Att.
9/4	W	39-35	New England	71,023
9/11	W	24-14	at Green Bay	55,011
9/18	W	28-14	N.Y. Jets	68,977
9/25	L	35-38	at Minnesota	64,035
10/2	W	23- 7	at Cincinnati	55,056
10/9	L	11-21	at Buffalo	79,491
10/16	W	20-17	L.A. Raiders (OT)	70,112
10/30	W	23- 3	at New England	59,167
11/6	W	22-21	Indianapolis	71,158
11/13	L	14-17	Chicago	64,871
11/20	L	13-16	at Pittsburgh (OT)	59,148
11/27	W	28-24	at N.Y. Jets	75,606
12/4	L	31-42	Buffalo	69,358
12/12	W	45-28	Kansas City	71,578
12/18	L	6-10	at Indianapolis	58,867
12/25	W	27-20	Detroit	70,980

POSTSEASON (1-1)

Date	Result		Opponents	Att.
12/31	W	27-17	Kansas City	69,757
1/8	L	21-22	at San Diego	63,381

(OT) Overtime

SCORE BY PERIODS

Dolphins	22	135	105	124	3	—	389
Opponents	85	52	87	100	3	—	327

ATTENDANCE

Home 551,970 Away 506,381 Total 1,058,351
Single-game home record, 72,161 (12-5-93)
Single-season home record, 551,970 (1994)

1994 TEAM STATISTICS

	Dolphins	Opp.
Total First Downs	344	305
Rushing	109	85
Passing	220	195
Penalty	15	25
Third Down: Made/Att	101/219	76/197
Third Down Pct.	46.1	38.6
Fourth Down: Made/Att	17/25	8/22
Fourth Down Pct.	68.0	36.4
Total Net Yards	6078	5224
Avg. Per Game	379.9	326.5
Total Plays	1078	1000
Avg. Per Play	5.6	5.2
Net Yards Rushing	1658	1430
Avg. Per Game	103.6	89.4
Total Rushes	433	394
Net Yards Passing	4420	3794
Avg. Per Game	276.3	237.1
Sacked/Yards Lost	17/113	29/160
Gross Yards	4533	3954
Att./Completions	627/392	577/334
Completion Pct.	62.5	57.9
Had Intercepted	18	23
Punts/Average	60/40.2	68/41.7
Net Punting Avg.	60/32.5	68/36.4
Penalties/Yards	92/747	82/653
Fumbles/Ball Lost	28/14	29/9
Touchdowns	45	42
Rushing	13	14
Passing	31	23
Returns	1	5
Avg. Time of Possession	31:46	28:14

1994 INDIVIDUAL STATISTICS

PASSING	Att.	Comp.	Yds.	Pct.	TD	Int.	Tkld.	Rate
Marino	615	385	4453	62.6	30	17	17/113	89.2
Kosar	12	7	80	58.3	1	1	0/0	71.5
Dolphins	627	392	4533	62.5	31	18	17/113	88.8
Opponents	577	334	3954	57.9	23	23	29/160	75.6

SCORING	TD R	TD P	TD Rt	PAT	FG	Saf	PTS
Stoyanovich	0	0	0	35/35	24/31	0	107
Fryar	0	7	0	0/0	0/0	0	46
K. Jackson	0	7	0	0/0	0/0	0	44
Parmalee	6	1	0	0/0	0/0	0	44
Byars	2	5	0	0/0	0/0	0	42
Ingram	0	6	0	0/0	0/0	0	36
McDuffie	0	3	0	0/0	0/0	0	18
Kirby	2	0	0	0/0	0/0	0	14
Spikes	2	0	0	0/0	0/0	0	12
Baty	0	1	0	0/0	0/0	0	6
Marino	1	0	0	0/0	0/0	0	6
Miller	0	1	0	0/0	0/0	0	6
Vincent	0	0	1	0/0	0/0	0	6
Craver	0	0	0	0/0	0/0	0	2
Dolphins	13	31	1	35/35	24/31	0	389
Opponents	14	23	5	40/40	11/18	0	327

2-Point conversions: Fryar (2), Craver, K. Jackson, Kirby, Parmalee. Team: 6-10.

RUSHING	Att.	Yds.	Avg.	LG	TD
Parmalee	216	868	4.0	47t	6
Spikes	70	312	4.5	40	2
Kirby	60	233	3.9	30	2
Higgs	19	68	3.6	21	0
Byars	19	64	3.4	12	2
Craver	6	43	7.2	19	0
McDuffie	5	32	6.4	12	0
Kosar	1	17	17.0	17	0
Saxon	8	16	2.0	7	0
Gary	7	11	1.6	4	0
Marino	23	-6	-0.3	10	1
Dolphins	434	1658	3.8	47t	13
Opponents	394	1430	3.6	45	14

RECEIVING	No.	Yds.	Avg.	LG	TD
Fryar	73	1270	17.4	54t	7
K. Jackson	59	673	11.4	35	7
Byars	49	418	8.5	34	5
Ingram	44	506	11.5	64t	6
McDuffie	37	488	13.2	30	3
Parmalee	34	249	7.3	22	1
Saxon	27	151	5.6	25	0
Craver	24	237	9.9	28	0
M. Williams	15	221	14.7	29	0
Kirby	14	154	11.0	26	0
Miller	6	94	15.7	27	1
Spikes	4	16	4.0	9	0
R. Williams	2	26	13.0	17	0
Gary	2	19	9.5	11	0
Baty	2	11	5.5	8	1
Dolphins	392	4533	11.6	64t	31
Opponents	334	3954	11.8	83t	23

INTERCEPTIONS	No.	Yds.	Avg.	LG	TD
Vincent	5	113	22.6	58t	1
Brown	3	82	27.3	38	0
Atkins	3	24	8.0	18	0
Stewart	3	11	3.7	11	0
Braxton	2	3	1.5	3	0
Beavers	2	0	0.0	0	0
Hollier	1	36	36.0	36	0
Veasey	1	7	7.0	7	0
Cross	1	0	0.0	0	0
Malone	1	0	0.0	0	0
Oliver	1	0	0.0	0	0
Dolphins	23	276	12.0	76t	1
Opponents	18	190	10.6	28t	1

PUNTING	No.	Yds.	Avg.	In 20	LG
Arnold	46	1810	39.3	14	53
Kidd	14	602	43.0	2	58
Dolphins	60	2412	40.2	16	58
Opponents	68	2834	41.7	18	64

PUNT RETURNS	No.	FC	Yds.	Avg.	LG	TD
McDuffie	32	15	228	7.1	26	0
Miller	1	2	13	13.0	13	0
Dolphins	33	17	241	7.3	26	0
Opponents	32	6	324	10.1	75t	1

KICKOFF RETURNS	No.	Yds.	Avg.	LG	TD
McDuffie	36	767	21.3	46	0
Spikes	19	434	22.8	34	0
R. Williams	2	25	12.5	15	0
M. Williams	2	9	4.5	9	0
Parmalee	2	0	0.0	0	0
Braxton	1	34	34.0	34	0
Miller	1	13	13.0	13	0
Saxon	1	12	12.0	12	0
Baty	1	0	0.0	0	0
Ingram	1	0	0.0	0	0
Dolphins	66	1294	19.6	46	0
Opponents	74	1549	20.9	93t	2

SACKS	No.
Cross	9.5
Coleman	6.0
Bowens	3.0
Cox	3.0
Veasey	2.5
Singleton	2.0
Atkins	1.0
Smith	1.0
Dolphins	29.0
Opponents	17.0

1995 DRAFT CHOICES

Round	Name	Pos.	College
1	Billy Milner	T	Houston
2	Andrew Greene	G	Indiana
4	Pete Mitchell	TE	Boston College
5	Norman Hand	DT	Mississippi
6	Jeff Kopp	LB	Southern California
7	Corey Swinson	DT	Hampton
	Shannon Myers	WR	Lenoir-Rhyne

MIAMI DOLPHINS

1995 VETERAN ROSTER

No.		Name	Pos.	Ht.	Wt.	Birthdate	NFL Exp.	College	Hometown	How Acq.	'94 Games/ Starts
92	t-	Armstrong, Trace	DE	6-4	265	10/5/65	7	Florida	Birmingham, Ala.	T(Chi)-'95	15/15*
28		Atkins, Gene	S	5-11	201	11/22/64	9	Florida A&M	Tallahassee, Fla.	UFA(NO)-'94	15/15
53		Beavers, Aubrey	LB	6-3	231	8/30/71	2	Oklahoma	Houston, Tex.	D2a-'94	16/10
95		Bowens, Tim	NT	6-4	310	2/7/73	2	Mississippi	Okolona, Miss.	D1-'94	16/15
77		Brothen, Kevin	G-C	6-1	293	11/16/69	3	Vanderbilt	Chicago, Ill.	FA-'94	0*
37		Brown, J.B.	CB	6-0	191	1/5/67	7	Maryland	Washington, D.C.	D12-'89	16/16
27	t-	Buckley, Terrell	CB	5-9	176	7/7/71	4	Florida State	Pascagoula, Miss.	T(GB)-'95	16/16*
54		Bullough, Chuck	LB	6-1	238	3/3/69	2	Michigan State	Orchard Park, N.Y.	FA-'93	1/1
41		Byars, Keith	RB	6-1	255	10/14/63	10	Ohio State	Dayton, Ohio	UFA(Phil)-'93	9/9
84		Clark, Gary	WR	5-9	173	5/1/62	11	James Madison	Dublin, Va.	FA-'95	15/2*
90		Coleman, Marco	DE	6-3	267	12/18/69	4	Georgia Tech	Dayton, Ohio	D1b-'92	16/16
51		Cox, Bryan	LB	6-4	248	2/17/68	5	Western Illinois	East St. Louis, Ill.	D5a-'91	16/16
91		Cross, Jeff	DE	6-4	280	3/25/66	8	Missouri	Blythe, Calif.	D9-'88	13/10
57		Foxx, Dion	LB	6-3	250	6/11/71	2	James Madison	Richmond, Va.	FA-'94	16/0
80		Fryar, Irving	WR	6-0	200	9/28/62	12	Nebraska	Mt. Holly, N.J.	T(NE)-'93	16/16
93		Gaines, William	NT	6-5	294	6/20/71	2	Florida	Jackson, Miss.	D5-'94	7/0
62		Gray, Chris	G-T	6-4	292	6/19/70	3	Auburn	Birmingham, Ala.	D5-'93	16/2
42	#	Green, Chris	S	5-11	198	2/26/68	5	Illinois	Lawrenceburg, Ind.	D7-'91	16/1
86		Green, Eric	TE	6-5	280	6/22/67	6	Liberty	Savannah, Ga.	UFA(Pitt)-'95	15/14*
73		Heller, Ron	T	6-6	290	8/25/62	12	Penn State	Farmingdale, N.Y.	UFA(Phil)-'93	16/16
89		Hill, Randal	WR	5-10	180	9/21/69	5	Miami	Miami, Fla.	UFA(Ariz)-'95	14/14*
31		Hill, Sean	CB	5-10	179	8/14/71	2	Montana State	Ft. Carson, Colo.	D7-'94	16/1
50		Hollier, Dwight	LB	6-2	250	4/21/69	4	North Carolina	Hampton, Va.	D4-'92	11/7
17		Kidd, John	P	6-3	214	8/22/61	12	Northwestern	Findlay, Ohio	FA-'94	6/0*
43		Kirby, Terry	RB	6-1	218	1/20/70	3	Virginia	Tabb, Va.	D3-'93	4/4
99		Klingbeil, Chuck	NT	6-1	301	11/2/65	5	Northern Michigan	Houghton, Mich.	FA-'91	16/15
19		Kosar, Bernie	QB	6-5	214	11/25/63	11	Miami	Boardman, Ohio	UFA(Dall)-'94	2/0
13		Marino, Dan	QB	6-4	224	9/15/61	13	Pittsburgh	Pittsburgh, Pa.	D1-'83	16/16
81		McDuffie, O.J.	WR	5-10	188	12/2/69	3	Penn State	Gates Mills, Ohio	D1-'93	15/3
11		McGwire, Dan	QB	6-8	239	12/18/67	5	San Diego State	Claremont, Calif.	UFA(Sea)-'95	7/3*
83		Miller, Scott	WR	5-11	185	10/20/68	5	UCLA	El Toro, Calif.	FA-'94	9/0
25		Oliver, Louis	S	6-2	224	3/9/66	7	Florida	Belle Glade, Fla.	FA-'95	12/12*
30		Parmalee, Bernie	RB	5-11	196	9/16/67	4	Ball State	Jersey City, N.J.	FA-'92	15/10
61		Ruddy, Tim	C	6-3	290	4/27/72	2	Notre Dame	Scranton, Pa.	D2b-'94	16/0
69		Sims, Keith	G	6-3	309	6/17/67	6	Iowa State	Watchung, N.J.	D2-'90	16/16
55		Singleton, Chris	LB	6-2	246	2/20/67	6	Arizona	Parsippany, N.J.	FA-'93	11/11
29		Smith, Frankie	CB	5-9	182	10/8/68	3	Baylor	Groesbeck, Tex.	FA-'93	13/2
40		Spikes, Irving	RB	5-8	206	12/21/70	2	Northeast Louisiana	Ocean Springs, Miss.	FA-'94	12/1
35		Stewart, Michael	S	5-11	202	7/12/65	9	Fresno State	Bakersfield, Calif.	UFA(Rams)-'94	16/16
10		Stoyanovich, Pete	K	5-11	195	4/28/67	7	Indiana	Dearborn Heights, Mich.	D8-'89	16/0
23		Vincent, Troy	CB	6-0	184	6/8/70	4	Wisconsin	Trenton, N.J.	D1a-'92	13/12
78		Webb, Richmond	T	6-6	303	1/11/67	6	Texas A&M	Dallas, Tex.	D1-'90	16/16
60	#	Weidner, Bert	G-C	6-2	295	1/20/66	6	Kent State	Eden, N.Y.	D11-'89	14/14
85		Williams, Ronnie	TE	6-3	258	1/19/66	4	Oklahoma State	North Natchez, Miss.	FA-'93	14/0
49		Wilson, Robert	RB	6-0	255	1/13/69	3	Texas A&M	Houston, Tex.	FA-'94	4/0*

* Armstrong played 15 games with Chicago in '94; Brothen inactive for 9 games; Buckley played 16 games with Green Bay; Clark played 15 games with Arizona; E. Green played 15 games with Pittsburgh; R. Hill played 14 games with Arizona; Kidd played 2 games with San Diego, 4 games with Miami; McGwire played 7 games with Seattle; Oliver played 12 games with Cincinnati; Wilson played 2 games with Dallas, 2 games with Miami.

\# Unrestricted free agent; subject to developments.

† Restricted free agent; subject to developments.

Traded—WR Mark Ingram to Green Bay, TE Keith Jackson to Green Bay.

t- Dolphins traded for Armstrong (Chicago), Buckley (Green Bay).

Players lost through free agency (3): RB Aaron Craver (Den; 8 games in '94), C Jeff Dellenbach (NE; 16), RB Cleveland Gary (Rams; 2).

Players lost through Expansion Draft (3): LB Brant Boyer (Jax; 14 games in '94), G-T Jeff Novak (Jax; 6), QB Doug Pederson (Car; 0).

Also played with Dolphins in '94—P Jim Arnold (12 games), TE Greg Baty (16), S Tyrone Braxton (16), RB Mark Higgs (5), G Houston Hoover (3), T Tim Irwin (5), CB-S Calvin Jackson (2), LB Tyoka Jackson (1), CB Darrell Malone (5), CB David Pool (1), RB James Saxon (16), LB Jesse Solomon (6), NT Craig Veasey (12), DE-NT Larry Webster (16), WR Mike Williams (15).

COACHING STAFF

Head Coach,
Don Shula

Pro Career: Begins his thirty-third season as an NFL head coach, and twenty-sixth with the Dolphins. Miami has won or shared first place in the AFC East in 15 of his 25 years and has earned 15 playoff berths in that span. Has most wins (338) in NFL history, surpassing George Halas's 324 in 1993. Captured back-to-back NFL championships, defeating Washington 14-7 in Super Bowl VII and Minnesota 24-7 in Super Bowl VIII. Lost to Dallas 24-3 in Super Bowl VI, to Washington 27-17 in Super Bowl XVII, and to San Francisco 38-16 in Super Bowl XIX. His 17-0 team in 1972 is the only team in NFL history to go undefeated throughout the regular season and postseason. Started his pro playing career with Cleveland Browns as defensive back in 1951. After two seasons with Browns, spent 1953-56 with Baltimore Colts and 1957 with Washington Redskins. Joined Detroit Lions as defensive coach in 1960 and was named head coach of the Colts in 1963. Baltimore had a 13-1 record in 1968 and captured NFL championship before losing to New York Jets in Super Bowl III. Career record: 338-165-6

Background: Outstanding offensive player at John Carroll University in Cleveland before becoming defensive specialist as a pro. His alma mater awarded him a doctorate in humanities in May, 1973. Served as assistant coach at Virginia in 1958 and at Kentucky in 1959.

Personal: Born January 4, 1930, in Painesville, Ohio. Don and his wife, Mary Anne, live in Miami. He has five children—Dave, Donna, Sharon, Annie, and Mike. Dave is Cincinnati's head coach and Mike is tight ends coach with Chicago.

ASSISTANT COACHES

Monte Clark, offensive line; born January 24, 1937, Fillmore, Calif., lives in Miami. Offensive lineman Southern California 1956-58. Pro offensive-defensive tackle San Francisco 49ers 1959-61, Dallas Cowboys 1962, Cleveland Browns 1963-69. College coach: Stanford 1993-94. Pro coach: Miami Dolphins 1970-75, San Francisco 49ers 1976 (head coach), Detroit Lions 1978-84 (head coach), Miami Dolphins 1990 (director of pro personnel), rejoined Dolphins in 1995.

Joel Collier, staff assistant; born December 25, 1963, Buffalo, N.Y., lives in Miami. Linebacker Northern Colorado 1984-87. No pro playing experience. College coach: Syracuse 1988-89. Pro coach: Tampa Bay Buccaneers 1990, New England Patriots 1991-93, joined Dolphins in 1994.

John Gamble, strength; born June 26, 1957, Richmond, Va., lives in Miami. Linebacker Hampton Institute 1975-78. No pro playing experience. College coach: Virginia 1982-93. Pro coach: Joined Dolphins in 1994.

Joe Greene, defensive line; born September 24, 1946, Temple, Tex., lives in Miami. Defensive tackle North Texas State 1966-68. Pro defensive tackle Pittsburgh Steelers 1969-81. Inducted into Pro Football Hall of Fame in 1987. Pro coach: Pittsburgh Steelers 1987-91, joined Dolphins in 1992.

George Hill, linebackers; born April 28, 1933, Bay Village, Ohio, lives in Miami. Tackle-fullback Denison 1954-57. No pro playing experience. College coach: Findlay 1959, Denison 1960-64, Cornell 1965, Duke 1966-70, Ohio State 1971-78. Pro coach: Philadelphia Eagles 1979-84, Indianapolis Colts 1985-88, joined Dolphins in 1989.

Rich McGeorge, assistant offensive line-tight ends; born September 14, 1948, Roanoke, Va., lives in Miami. Tight end Elon College 1966-69. Pro tight end Green Bay Packers 1970-78. College coach: Duke 1981-82, 1987-89, Florida 1990-92. Pro coach: Birmingham Stallions (USFL) 1983-84, Tampa Bay Bandits (USFL) 1985, joined Dolphins in 1993.

Tony Nathan, offensive backs; born December 14, 1956, Birmingham, Ala., lives in Miami. Running back Alabama 1975-78. Pro running back Miami Dolphins 1979-87. Pro coach: Joined Dolphins in 1988.

1995 FIRST-YEAR ROSTER

Name	Pos.	Ht.	Wt.	Birthdate	College	Hometown	How Acq.
Albright, Ethan (1)	T	6-5	292	5/1/71	North Carolina	Greensboro, N.C.	FA
Bender, Jason	P	6-2	212	8/14/71	Georgia Tech	Pittsburgh, Pa.	FA
Bonner, Sherdrick	QB	6-5	225	10/19/68	Cal State-Northridge	Azusa, Calif.	FA
Caesar, Mark (1)	NT	6-2	295	1/12/70	Miami	Newark, N.J.	FA
Carter, Ontiwaun	RB	5-8	175	7/3/72	Arizona	Granada Hills, Calif.	FA
Cooper, Travis	LB	6-2	242	12/16/73	Central Florida	Miami, Fla.	FA
Crawford, Melvin	S	5-11	176	2/18/73	Hampton	Germantown, Md.	FA
Dar Dar, Kirby	RB	5-9	183	3/27/72	Syracuse	Tampa, Fla.	FA
Davis, Michael	RB	5-11	230	7/7/71	Mississippi State	Morton, Miss.	FA
Dittman, Seth	T	6-7	273	7/23/72	Stanford	Tigard, Ore.	FA
Dotson, Dewayne (1)	LB	6-1	256	6/10/71	Mississippi	Hendersonville, Tenn.	FA
Fayak, Craig (1)	K	6-1	188	7/22/72	Penn State	Belle Vernon, Pa.	FA
Gatewood, Randy	WR	6-0	180	1/31/73	Nevada-Las Vegas	Wichita Falls, Tex.	FA
Glenn, Maurice	S	6-1	184	10/7/73	Richmond	Virginia Beach, Va.	FA
Greene, Andrew	G	6-3	304	9/24/69	Indiana	Kingston, Jamaica	D2
Hack, Dave	G	6-6	285	4/22/72	Maryland	Holland, N.Y.	FA
Hand, Norman	NT	6-3	329	9/4/72	Mississippi	Walterboro, S.C.	D5
Hawthorne, Ed	NT	6-1	305	7/30/70	Minnesota	St. Louis, Mo.	FA
Jackson, Calvin (1)	CB	5-9	185	10/28/72	Auburn	Ft. Lauderdale, Fla.	FA
Jackson, Tyoka (1)	DE	6-2	266	11/22/71	Penn State	Forestville, Md.	FA
James, Jason	C	6-4	302	12/15/71	Fresno State	Buena Park, Calif.	FA
Johnson, Demeris (1)	WR	6-0	182	8/26/69	Western Illinois	Detroit, Mich.	FA
Johnson, Deon	S	6-0	214	9/25/71	Michigan	Detroit, Mich.	FA
Johnson, Pat (1)	S	6-1	204	6/10/72	Purdue	Mineral Point, Mo.	FA
Kennedy, Larry	S	5-10	190	7/28/71	Florida	Sarasota, Fla.	FA
Kopp, Jeff	LB	6-3	243	7/8/71	Southern California	Danville, Calif.	D6
Lynch, Tarrant	RB	5-11	226	1/28/72	Alabama	Hazelwood, Ala.	FA
McClinton, Lee	RB	5-11	252	8/2/72	New Hampshire	Highland, N.Y.	FA
Milner, Billy	T	6-5	293	6/21/72	Houston	Atlanta, Ga.	D1
Mitchell, Pete	TE	6-2	243	10/9/71	Boston College	Birmingham, Mich.	D4
Moss, Brent	RB	5-8	211	1/30/72	Wisconsin	Racine, Wis.	FA
Myers, Shannon	WR	6-0	171	6/16/73	Lenior-Rhyne	Salisbury, N.C.	D7b
Needham, Gary (1)	G	6-3	352	8/28/67	Eastern Washington	Beaverton, Ore.	FA
Nelson, Chico (1)	S	6-0	198	12/25/69	Tennessee	Miami, Fla.	FA
Perkins, Steve	DE	6-2	250	12/21/71	West Virginia	Ft. Lauderdale, Fla.	FA
Planansky, Joe	TE	6-4	250	10/21/71	Chadron State	Hemingford, Neb.	FA
Seigler, Dexter (1)	CB	5-9	179	1/11/72	Miami	Avon Park, Fla.	FA
Smith, Kwame (1)	CB	5-9	172	1/1/71	West Virginia	Miami, Fla.	FA
Swinson, Corey	NT	6-5	334	12/15/69	Hampton	Bayshore, N.Y.	D7a
Thornton, Burt	WR	6-1	202	1/30/72	Purdue	Akron, Ohio	FA
Whittemore, Mark	WR	5-9	170	4/18/73	Central Florida	Gainesville, Fla.	FA
Wilkerson, Rodney	LB	6-2	233	10/18/72	Georgia Tech	Franklin, Ga.	FA

The term NFL Rookie is defined as a player who is in his first season of professional football and has not been on the roster of another professional football team for any regular-season or postseason games. A Rookie is designated by an "R" on NFL rosters. Players who have been active in another professional football league or players who have NFL experience, including either preseason training camp or being on an Active List or Inactive List, or on Reserve/Injured or Reserve/Physically Unable to Perform for fewer than six regular-season games, are termed NFL First-Year Players. An NFL First-Year Player is designated by a "1" on NFL rosters. Thereafter, a player is credited with an additional year of experience for each season in which he accumulates six games on the Active List or Inactive List, or on Reserve/Injured or Reserve/Physically Unable to Perform.

NOTES

Tom Olivadotti, defense; born September 22, 1945, Long Branch, N.J., lives in Cooper City, Fla. Defensive back-wide receiver Upsala 1963-66. No pro playing experience. College coach: Princeton 1975-77, Boston College 1978-79, Miami 1980-83. Pro coach: Cleveland Browns 1985-86, joined Dolphins in 1987.

Mel Phillips, defensive backs; born January 6, 1942, Shelby, N.C., lives in Miami Lakes, Fla. Defensive back-running back North Carolina A&T 1964-65. Pro defensive back San Francisco 49ers 1966-77. Pro coach: Detroit Lions 1980-84, joined Dolphins in 1985.

Larry Seiple, wide receivers; born February 14, 1945, Allentown, Pa., lives in Miami Lakes, Fla. Running back-receiver-punter Kentucky 1964-66. Pro punter-tight end-receiver-running back Miami Dolphins 1967-77. College coach: Miami 1978-79. Pro coach: Detroit Lions 1980-84, Tampa Bay Buccaneers 1985-86, joined Dolphins in 1988.

Gary Stevens, offense-quarterbacks; born March 19, 1943, Cleveland, Ohio, lives in Kendall, Fla. Running back John Carroll 1963-65. No pro playing experience. College coach: Louisville 1971-74, Kent State 1975, West Virginia 1976-79, Miami 1980-88. Pro coach: Joined Dolphins in 1989.

Junior Wade, conditioning; born February 2, 1947, Bath, S.C., lives in Miami. South Carolina State 1969. No college or pro playing experience. Pro coach: Joined Dolphins in 1975, coach since 1983.

Mike Westhoff, special teams; born January 10, 1948, Pittsburgh, Pa., lives in Ft. Lauderdale, Fla. Center-linebacker Wichita State 1967-69. No pro playing experience. College coach: Indiana 1974-75, Dayton 1976, Indiana State 1977, Northwestern 1978-80, Texas Christian 1981. Pro coach: Baltimore/Indianapolis Colts 1982-84, Arizona Outlaws (USFL) 1985, joined Dolphins in 1986.

NEW ENGLAND PATRIOTS

American Football Conference
Eastern Division
Team Colors: Blue, Red, Silver, and White
Foxboro Stadium
60 Washington Street
Foxboro, Massachusetts 02035
Telephone: (508) 543-8200

CLUB OFFICIALS

President/Chief Executive Officer: Robert K. Kraft
Vice President-Owner's Repesentative: Jonathan A. Kraft
Vice President-Business Operations: Andrew Wasynczuk
Vice President-Finance: James Hausmann
Vice President-Event Management: Brian O'Donovan
Corporate Marketing and Sales: Daniel A. Kraft
Director of Public and Community Relations: Donald Lowery
Director of Media Relations: Stacey James
Director of Player Resources: Andre Tippett
Controller: Virginia Widman
Director of Pro Personnel: Bobby Grier
Director of College Scouting: Charles Armey
Director of Data Processing: Peg Myers
Director of Ticketing: Mike Nichols
Director of Sales: Mitch Hardin
Operations Manager: Dan Murphy
Building Services Manager: Bernie Reinhart
Head Trainer: Ron O'Neil
Equipment Manager: Don Brocher
Video Director: Ken Deininger
Stadium: Foxboro Stadium • **Capacity:** 60,292
60 Washington Street
Foxboro, Massachusetts 02035
Playing Surface: Grass
Training Camp: Bryant College
Route 7
Smithfield, Rhode Island 02917

1995 SCHEDULE

PRESEASON

Aug. 4	**Detroit**	7:00
Aug. 12	**Minnesota**	8:00
Aug. 17	at Philadelphia	8:00
Aug. 25	at Los Angeles	6:00

REGULAR SEASON

Sept. 3	**Cleveland**	1:00
Sept. 10	**Miami**	1:00
Sept. 17	at San Francisco	1:00
Sept. 24	Open Date	
Oct. 1	at Atlanta	1:00
Oct. 8	**Denver**	8:00
Oct. 15	at Kansas City	12:00
Oct. 23	**Buffalo** (Monday)	9:00
Oct. 29	**Carolina**	1:00
Nov. 5	at New York Jets	1:00
Nov. 12	at Miami	1:00
Nov. 19	**Indianapolis**	1:00
Nov. 26	at Buffalo	1:00
Dec. 3	**New Orleans**	1:00
Dec. 10	**New York Jets**	1:00
Dec. 16	at Pittsburgh (Saturday)	12:30
Dec. 23	at Indianapolis (Saturday)	8:00

RECORD HOLDERS

INDIVIDUAL RECORDS—CAREER

Category	Name	Performance
Rushing (Yds.)	Sam Cunningham, 1973-79, 1981-82	5,453
Passing (Yds.)	Steve Grogan, 1975-1990	26,886
Passing (TDs)	Steve Grogan, 1975-1990	182
Receiving (No.)	Stanley Morgan, 1977-1989	534
Receiving (Yds.)	Stanley Morgan, 1977-1989	10,352
Interceptions	Raymond Clayborn, 1977-1989	36
Punting (Avg.)	Rich Camarillo, 1981-87	42.6
Punt Return (Avg.)	Mack Herron, 1973-75	12.0
Kickoff Return (Avg.)	Allen Carter, 1975-76	27.2
Field Goals	Gino Cappelletti, 1960-1970	176
Touchdowns (Tot.)	Stanley Morgan, 1977-1989	68
Points	Gino Cappelletti, 1960-1970	1,130

INDIVIDUAL RECORDS—SINGLE SEASON

Category	Name	Performance
Rushing (Yds.)	Jim Nance, 1966	1,458
Passing (Yds.)	Drew Bledsoe, 1994	4,555
Passing (TDs)	Vito (Babe) Parilli, 1964	31
Receiving (No.)	Ben Coates, 1994	96
Receiving (Yds.)	Stanley Morgan, 1986	1,491
Interceptions	Ron Hall, 1964	11
Punting (Avg.)	Rich Camarillo, 1983	44.6
Punt Return (Avg.)	Mack Herron, 1974	14.8
Kickoff Return (Avg.)	Raymond Clayborn, 1977	31.0
Field Goals	Tony Franklin, 1986	32
Touchdowns (Tot.)	Steve Grogan, 1976	13
	Stanley Morgan, 1979	13
Points	Gino Cappelletti, 1964	155

INDIVIDUAL RECORDS—SINGLE GAME

Category	Name	Performance
Rushing (Yds.)	Tony Collins, 9-18-83	212
Passing (Yds.)	Drew Bledsoe, 11-13-94	426
Passing (TDs)	Vito (Babe) Parilli, 11-15-64	5
	Vito (Babe) Parilli, 10-15-67	5
	Steve Grogan, 9-9-79	5
Receiving (No.)	Ben Coates, 11-27-94	12
Receiving (Yds.)	Stanley Morgan, 11-8-81	182
Interceptions	Many times	3
	Last time by Roland James, 10-23-83	
Field Goals	Gino Cappelletti, 10-4-64	6
Touchdowns (Tot.)	Many times	3
	Last time by Stanley Morgan, 9-21-86	
Points	Gino Cappelletti, 12-18-65	28

*NFL Record

COACHING HISTORY

BOSTON 1960-1970
(235-283-9)

1960-61	Lou Saban*	7-12-0
1961-68	Mike Holovak	53-47-9
1969-70	Clive Rush**	5-16-0
1970-72	John Mazur***	9-21-0
1972	Phil Bengtson	1-4-0
1973-78	Chuck Fairbanks****	46-41-0
1978	Hank Bullough-Ron Erhardt#	0-1-0
1979-81	Ron Erhardt	21-27-0
1982-84	Ron Meyer##	18-16-0
1984-89	Raymond Berry	51-41-0
1990	Rod Rust	1-15-0
1991-92	Dick MacPherson	8-24-0
1993-94	Bill Parcells	15-18-0

*Released after five games in 1961
**Released after seven games in 1970
***Resigned after nine games in 1972
****Suspended for final regular-season game in 1978
#Co-coaches
##Released after eight games in 1984

FOXBORO STADIUM

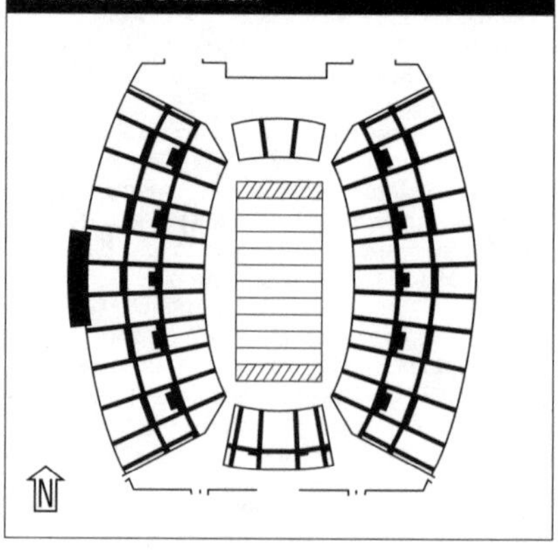

1994 TEAM RECORD

PRESEASON (3-1)

Date	Result		Opponents
8/5	W	24-6	New Orleans
8/13	W	28-10	at L.A. Rams
8/18	W	27-17	Washington
8/26	L	20-24	at Green Bay

REGULAR SEASON (10-6)

Date	Result		Opponents	Att.
9/4	L	35-39	at Miami	69,613
9/11	L	35-38	Buffalo	60,274
9/18	W	31-28	at Cincinnati	46,640
9/25	W	23-17	at Detroit	59,618
10/2	W	17-16	Green Bay	57,522
10/9	L	17-21	L.A. Raiders	59,889
10/16	L	17-24	at N.Y. Jets	71,123
10/30	L	3-23	Miami	59,167
11/6	L	6-13	at Cleveland	73,878
11/13	W	26-20	Minnesota (OT)	58,382
11/20	W	23-17	San Diego	59,690
11/27	W	12-10	at Indianapolis	43,839
12/4	W	24-13	N.Y. Jets	60,138
12/11	W	28-13	Indianapolis	57,656
12/18	W	41-17	at Buffalo	56,784
12/24	W	13- 3	at Chicago	60,178

POSTSEASON (0-1)

1/1	L	13-20	at Cleveland	77,452

(OT) Overtime

SCORE BY PERIODS

Patriots	46	95	94	110	6	—	351
Opponents	53	133	56	70	0	—	312

ATTENDANCE

Home 472,718 Away 481,673 Total 954,391
Single-game home record, 61,457 (12-5-71)
Single-season home record, 482,572 (1986)

1994 TEAM STATISTICS

	Patriots	Opp.
Total First Downs	348	280
Rushing	83	86
Passing	243	173
Penalty	22	21
Third Down: Made/Att	106/257	72/215
Third Down Pct.	41.2	33.5
Fourth Down: Made/Att	18/35	6/16
Fourth Down Pct.	51.4	37.5
Total Net Yards	5776	5207
Avg. Per Game	361.0	325.4
Total Plays	1199	1006
Avg. Per Play	4.8	5.2
Net Yards Rushing	1332	1760
Avg. Per Game	83.3	110.0
Total Rushes	478	422
Net Yards Passing	4444	3447
Avg. Per Game	277.8	215.4
Sacked/Yards Lost	22/139	39/290
Gross Yards	4583	3737
Att./Completions	699/405	545/298
Completion Pct.	57.9	54.7
Had Intercepted	27	22
Punts/Average	69/41.2	83/40.2
Net Punting Avg.	69/35.7	83/34.6
Penalties/Yards	78/597	111/795
Fumbles/Ball Lost	28/11	34/18
Touchdowns	39	36
Rushing	12	11
Passing	25	21
Returns	2	4
Avg. Time of Possession	32:08	27:52

1994 INDIVIDUAL STATISTICS

PASSING	Att.	Comp.	Yds.	Pct.	TD	Int.	Tkld.	Rate
Bledsoe	691	400	4555	57.9	25	27	22/139	73.6
Zolak	8	5	28	62.5	0	0	0/0	68.8
Patriots	699	405	4583	57.9	25	27	22/139	73.5
Opponents	545	298	3737	54.7	21	22	39/290	72.2

SCORING	TD R	TD P	TD Rt	PAT	FG	Saf	PTS
Bahr	0	0	0	36/36	27/34	0	117
Butts	8	0	0	0/0	0/0	0	48
Coates	0	7	0	0/0	0/0	0	42
Thompson	2	5	0	0/0	0/0	0	42
Brisby	0	5	0	0/0	0/0	0	30
Crittenden	0	3	0	0/0	0/0	0	18
Timpson	0	3	0	0/0	0/0	0	18
Turner	1	2	0	0/0	0/0	0	18
Reynolds	0	0	2	0/0	0/0	0	12
Thomas	1	0	0	0/0	0/0	0	6
O'Neill	0	0	0	0/0	0/1	0	0
Patriots	12	25	2	36/36	27/35	0	351
Opponents	11	21	4	32/33	20/25	0	312

2-Point conversions: 0. Team: 0-2.

RUSHING	Att.	Yds.	Avg.	LG	TD
Butts	243	703	2.9	26	8
Thompson	102	312	3.1	13	2
Turner	36	111	3.1	13	1
Gash	30	86	2.9	10	0
Thomas	19	67	3.5	13	1
Bledsoe	44	40	0.9	7	0
Timpson	2	14	7.0	10	0
Coates	1	0	0.0	0	0
Zolak	1	-1	-1.0	-1	0
Patriots	478	1332	2.8	26	12
Opponents	422	1760	4.2	52	11

RECEIVING	No.	Yds.	Avg.	LG	TD
Coates	96	1174	12.2	62t	7
Timpson	74	941	12.7	37	3
Thompson	65	465	7.2	27t	5
Brisby	58	904	15.6	43	5
Turner	52	471	9.1	32	2
Crittenden	28	379	13.5	32	3
Burke	9	86	9.6	17	0
Gash	9	61	6.8	19	0
Butts	9	54	6.0	15	0
Hawkins	2	22	11.0	14	0
Thomas	2	15	7.5	9	0
Harris	1	11	11.0	11	0
Patriots	405	4583	11.3	62t	25
Opponents	298	3737	12.5	65t	21

INTERCEPTIONS	No.	Yds.	Avg.	LG	TD
Hurst	7	68	9.7	24	0
H. Barnett	3	51	17.0	24	0
V. Brown	3	22	7.3	12	0
Guyton	2	18	9.0	15	0
Smith	2	10	5.0	10	0
Sabb	2	6	3.0	5	0
Whigham	1	21	21.0	21	0
Reynolds	1	11	11.0	11t	1
Ray	1	2	2.0	2	0
Patriots	22	209	9.5	24	1
Opponents	27	252	9.3	90t	2

PUNTING	No.	Yds.	Avg.	In 20	LG
O'Neill	69	2841	41.2	25	67
Patriots	69	2841	41.2	25	67
Opponents	83	3333	40.2	21	53

PUNT RETURNS	No.	FC	Yds.	Avg.	LG	TD
T. Brown	24	10	202	8.4	38	0
Crittenden	19	6	155	8.2	26	0
Harris	3	0	26	8.7	12	0
Patriots	46	16	383	8.3	38	0
Opponents	34	9	260	7.6	30	0

KICKOFF RETURNS	No.	Yds.	Avg.	LG	TD
Crittenden	24	460	19.2	36	0
Thompson	18	376	20.9	30	0
Croom	10	172	17.2	24	0
Thomas	3	40	13.3	16	0
Burke	3	11	3.7	6	0
Timpson	1	28	28.0	28	0
T. Brown	1	14	14.0	14	0
DeOssie	1	14	14.0	14	0
Gash	1	9	9.0	9	0
Guyton	1	-1	-1.0	-1	0
Patriots	63	1123	17.8	36	0
Opponents	63	1375	21.8	80t	1

SACKS	No.
Slade	9.5
M. Jones	6.0
McGinest	4.5
A. Jones	4.0
Sabb	3.5
Goad	3.0
Hurst	2.0
Reynolds	2.0
V. Brown	1.5
T. Barnett	1.0
Pitts	1.0
Agnew	0.5
Smith	0.5
Patriots	39.0
Opponents	22.0

1995 DRAFT CHOICES

Round	Name	Pos.	College
1	Ty Law	DB	Michigan
2	Ted Johnson	LB	Colorado
3	Curtis Martin	RB	Pittsburgh
	Jimmy Hitchcock	DB	North Carolina
4	Dave Wohlabaugh	C	Syracuse
6	Dino Philyaw	RB	Oregon
7	Carlos Yancy	DB	Georgia

NEW ENGLAND PATRIOTS

1995 VETERAN ROSTER

No.		Name	Pos.	Ht.	Wt.	Birthdate	NFL Exp.	College	Hometown	How Acq.	'94 Games/ Starts
50		Abrams, Bobby	LB	6-3	230	4/12/67	6	Michigan	Detroit, Mich.	UFA(Minn)-'95	16/0*
78		Armstrong, Bruce	T	6-4	284	9/7/65	9	Louisville	Miami, Fla.	D1-'87	16/16
65		Arthur, Mike	C	6-3	280	5/7/68	5	Texas A&M	Houston, Tex.	W(Cin)-'93	12/11
3		Bahr, Matt	K	5-10	175	7/6/56	17	Penn State	Langhorne, Pa.	W(Phil)-'93	16/0
98		Barnett, Troy	DE	6-4	280	5/24/71	2	North Carolina	Jacksonville, N.C.	FA-'94	14/0
11		Bledsoe, Drew	QB	6-5	233	2/14/72	3	Washington State	Walla Walla, Wash.	D1-'93	16/16
82		Brisby, Vincent	WR	6-2	188	1/25/71	3	Northeast Louisiana	Lake Charles, La.	D2c-'93	14/11
30		Brown, Corwin	S	6-1	200	4/25/70	3	Michigan	Chicago, Ill.	D4b-'93	16/0
86		Brown, Troy	WR	5-9	190	7/2/71	3	Marshall	Blackville, S.C.	FA-'94	9/0
59		Brown, Vincent	LB	6-2	245	1/9/65	8	Mississippi Valley State	Decatur, Ga.	D2-'88	16/16
85		Burke, John	TE	6-3	255	9/7/71	2	Virginia Tech	Holmdel, N.J.	D4-'94	16/6
44	#	Butts, Marion	RB	6-1	248	8/1/66	7	Florida State	Sylvester, Ga.	T(SD)-'94	16/15
87		Coates, Ben	TE	6-5	245	8/16/69	5	Livingstone College	Greenwood, S.C.	D5b-'91	16/16
54		Collins, Todd	LB	6-2	242	5/27/70	4	Carson-Newman	New Market, Tenn.	D3a-'92	7/7
81		Crittenden, Ray	WR	6-1	188	3/1/70	3	Virginia Tech	Washington, D.C.	FA-'93	16/2
26		Croom, Corey	RB	5-11	208	5/22/71	3	Ball State	Sandusky, Ohio	FA-'93	16/0
64		Dellenbach, Jeff	C	6-6	300	2/14/63	11	Wisconsin	Wausau, Wis.	UFA(Mia)-'95	16/16*
99		DeOssie, Steve	LB	6-2	248	11/22/62	12	Boston College	Roslindale, Mass.	UFA(NYJ)-'94	16/0
84		Ellis, Elbert	WR	6-5	216	6/23/69	2	Pittsburgh	Durham, N.C.	FA-'94	0*
33		Gash, Sam	RB	5-11	224	3/7/69	4	Penn State	Hendersonville, N.C.	D8b-'92	13/6
67		Gisler, Mike	G-C	6-4	300	8/26/69	3	Houston	Range, Tex.	FA-'93	15/5
29		Guyton, Myron	S	6-1	205	8/26/67	7	Eastern Kentucky	Thomasville, Ga.	UFA(NYG)-'94	16/16
		Hand, Jon	DE	6-7	310	11/13/63	10	Alabama	Sylacauga, Ala.	FA-'95	5/3*
77		Harlow, Pat	T	6-6	290	3/16/69	5	Southern California	Norco, Calif.	D1a-'91	16/16
37		Hurst, Maurice	CB	5-10	185	9/17/67	7	Southern	New Orleans, La.	D4a-'89	16/16
97		Jones, Aaron	DE	6-5	267	12/18/66	8	Eastern Kentucky	Orlando, Fla.	UFA(Pitt)-'93	16/0
96		Jones, Mike	DE	6-4	295	8/25/69	5	North Carolina State	Columbus, S.C.	FA-'94	16/16
61		Kratch, Bob	G	6-3	288	1/6/66	7	Iowa	Mahwah, N.J.	UFA(NYG)-'94	16/16
68		Lane, Max	T	6-6	295	2/22/71	2	Navy	Norborne, Mo.	D6b-'94	14/0
19		Lee, Kevin	WR	6-1	194	1/1/71	2	Alabama	Mobile, Ala.	D2-'94	0*
35		Legette, Burnie	RB	6-1	243	12/5/70	3	Michigan	Colorado Springs, Colo.	FA-'93	3/0
43		Lewis, Vernon	CB	5-10	192	10/27/70	3	Pittsburgh	Houston, Tex.	FA-'93	11/0
55		McGinest, Willie	LB	6-5	252	12/11/71	2	Southern California	Long Beach, Calif.	D1-'94	16/7
22		Meggett, Dave	RB	5-7	195	4/30/66	7	Towson State	Charleston, S.C.	UFA(NYG)-'95	16/3*
70		Moore, Brandon	T	6-6	295	6/21/70	3	Duke	Bowling Springs, Pa.	FA-'93	4/0
58		Moore, Marty	LB	6-1	244	3/19/71	2	Kentucky	Ft. Thomas, Ky.	D7b-'94	16/4
5		O'Neill, Pat	P-K	6-1	200	2/9/71	2	Syracuse	Harrisburg, Pa.	D5-'94	16/0
93		Pitts, Mike	DE	6-5	277	9/25/60	13	Alabama	Baltimore, Md.	UFA(Phil)-'93	16/16
23		Ray, Terry	S	6-1	205	10/12/69	4	Oklahoma	Killeen, Tex.	W(Atl)-'93	16/0
21		Reynolds, Ricky	CB	5-11	190	1/19/65	9	Washington State	Sacramento, Calif.	UFA(TB)-'94	15/10
94		Roberts, Tim	DE	6-6	318	4/14/69	4	Southern Mississippi	Atlanta, Ga.	RFA(Hou)-'95	12/2*
71		Rucci, Todd	G	6-5	291	7/14/70	3	Penn State	Upper Darby, Pa.	D2b-'93	13/10
95		Sabb, Dwayne	LB	6-4	248	10/9/69	4	New Hampshire	Union, N.J.	D5-'92	16/8
74		Skene, Doug	G	6-6	295	6/17/70	3	Michigan	Fairview, Tex.	FA-'93	6/6
53		Slade, Chris	LB	6-4	232	1/30/71	3	Virginia	Newport News, Va.	D2a-'93	16/16
63		Stanley, Sylvester	NT	6-2	286	5/14/70	2	Michigan	Youngstown, Ohio	FA-'94	7/0
36	#	Thompson, Leroy	RB	5-11	216	2/3/68	5	Penn State	Knoxville, Tenn.	T(Pitt)-'94	16/1
7		Walker, Jay	QB	6-3	232	1/24/72	2	Howard	Los Angeles, Calif.	D7a-'94	0*
25		Whigham, Larry	S	6-2	202	6/23/72	2	Northeast Louisiana	Hattiesburg, Miss.	FA-'94	12/0
90		White, Reggie	DE-DT	6-4	300	3/22/70	4	North Carolina A&T	Baltimore, Md.	FA-'95	11/0*
27	#	Wren, Darryl	CB	6-1	188	1/25/67	5	Pittsburg State	Tulsa, Okla.	W(Buff)-'93	8/0
16		Zolak, Scott	QB	6-5	222	12/13/67	5	Maryland	Monogahela, Pa.	D4-'91	16/0

* Abrams played 16 games with Minnesota in '94; Dellenbach played 16 games with Miami; Ellis inactive for 6 games; Hand played 5 games with Indianapolis; Lee missed '94 season because of injury; Meggett played 16 games with N.Y. Giants; Roberts played 12 games with Houston; Walker inactive for 16 games; White played 11 games with San Diego.

Unrestricted free agent; subject to developments.

† Restricted free agent; subject to developments.

Players lost through free agency (5): DE Ray Agnew (NYG; 11 games in '94), S Harlon Barnett (Minn; 16), NT Tim Goad (Clev; 13), WR Michael Timpson (Chi; 15), RB Kevin Turner (Phil; 16).

Players lost through Expansion Draft (3): G Eugene Chung (Jax; 3 games in '94), WR Steve Hawkins (Car; 7), CB Rod Smith (Car; 16).

Also played for Patriots in '94—LB David Bavaro (9 games), LB Jason Carthen (1), WR Ronnie Harris (1), RB Blair Thomas (4).

COACHING STAFF

Head Coach,
Bill Parcells

Pro Career: On January 21, 1993, Parcells became the franchise's thirteenth head coach since the Patriots' inception in 1960. It took Parcells just two seasons to resurrect the 2-14 team he inherited in 1992 into a playoff team in 1994. The Patriots finished 1994 with seven consecutive victories to tie a franchise record and qualified for the playoffs with a 10-6 regular-season record. Parcells made his NFL coaching debut with the New England Patriots as the linebackers coach on Ron Erhardt's staff in 1980. He accepted the same position on the New York Giants staff in 1981 and was named the Giants head coach in 1983. In eight seasons at the helm of the Giants, Parcells led his teams to two Super Bowl championships. His first title came in 1986, with a 39-20 victory over the Denver Broncos. Four years later, the Giants claimed another championship with a 20-19 victory over the Buffalo Bills. On May 15, 1991, health concerns caused Parcells to resign from the Giants. During his two seasons away from coaching, Parcells entertained football audiences from the broadcast booth, in 1991 as a studio analyst and in 1992 as a color commentator for NBC Sports. Career record: 100-70-1.

Background: Linebacker at Wichita State 1961-63. College assistant Hastings (Neb.) 1964, Wichita State 1965, Army 1966-69, Florida State 1970-72, Vanderbilt 1973-74, Texas Tech 1975-77, Air Force 1978 (head coach).

Personal: Born August 22, 1941, Englewood, N.J. Bill and his wife, Judy, live in Foxboro, Mass., and have three daughters—Suzy, Jill, and Dallas.

ASSISTANT COACHES

Maurice Carthon, offensive assistant fullbacks/special teams; born April 24, 1961, Chicago, Ill., lives in Foxboro, Mass. Running back Arkansas State 1979-82. Pro running back New Jersey Generals (USFL) 1983-85, New York Giants 1985-91, Indianapolis Colts 1992. Pro coach: Joined Patriots in 1994.

Romeo Crennel, defensive line; born June 18, 1947, Lynchburg, Va., lives in Walpole, Mass. Defensive tackle, linebacker Western Kentucky 1966-69. No pro playing experience. College coach: Western Kentucky 1970-74, Texas Tech 1975-77, Mississippi 1978-79, Georgia Tech 1980. Pro coach: New York Giants 1981-92, joined Patriots in 1993.

Al Groh, defensive coordinator-linebackers; born July 13, 1944, New York, N.Y. Defensive end Virginia 1964-67. No pro playing experience. College coach: Army 1968-69, Virginia 1970-72, North Carolina 1973-77, Air Force 1978-79, Texas Tech 1980, Wake Forest 1981-86 (head coach), South Carolina 1988. Pro coach: Atlanta Falcons 1987, New York Giants 1989-91, Cleveland Browns 1992, joined Patriots in 1993.

Fred Hoaglin, offensive line; born January 28, 1944, Alliance, Ohio, lives in Cumberland, R.I. Center Pittsburgh 1962-65. Pro center Cleveland Browns 1966-72, Baltimore Colts 1973, Houston Oilers 1974-75, Seattle Seahawks 1976. Pro coach: Detroit Lions 1978-84, New York Giants 1985-92, joined Patriots in 1993.

Chris Palmer, wide receivers; born September 23, 1949, Mt. Kisco, N.Y., lives in Foxboro, Mass. Quarterback Southern Connecticut State 1968-71. No pro playing experience. College coach: Connecticut 1972-74, Lehigh 1975, Colgate 1976-82, New Haven 1986-87 (head coach), Boston University 1988-89 (head coach). Pro coach: Montreal Concordes (CFL) 1983, New Jersey Generals (USFL) 1984-85, Houston Oilers 1990-92, joined Patriots in 1993.

Johnny Parker, strength and conditioning; born February 1, 1947, Greenville, S.C., lives in Foxboro, Mass. Graduate of Mississippi, master's degree from Delta State University. No college or pro playing experience. College coach: South Carolina 1974-76, Indiana 1977-79, Louisiana State 1980, Mississippi 1981-83. Pro coach: New York Giants 1984-92, joined Patriots in 1993.

1995 FIRST-YEAR ROSTER

Name	Pos.	Ht.	Wt.	Birthdate	College	Hometown	How Acq.
Adams, Daniel	WR	6-0	185	1/16/72	Houston	Schulenburg, Tex.	FA
Alford, Eric	TE	6-1	232	8/12/72	Nebraska	High Point, N.C.	FA
Andrews, David	WR	6-2	174	11/11/71	Angelo State	Beaumont, Tex.	FA
Bowden, Andre (1)	LB	6-3	240	4/4/68	Fayetteville State	Faquay Varina, N.C.	FA
Bullard, Kendricke	WR	6-1	170	4/30/72	Arkansas State	Pine Bluff, Ark.	FA
Cade, Eddie	S	6-0	206	8/4/73	Arizona State	Eloy, Ariz.	FA
Catanho, Alcides	LB	6-3	216	1/20/72	Rutgers	Elizabeth, N.J.	FA
Francisco, Paul (1)	TE	6-6	236	10/14/69	Boston University	Dorchester, Mass.	FA
Gaines, Stephen	DT	6-2	314	9/28/72	Texas Tech	Electra, Tex.	FA
Graham, Hason	WR	5-10	176	3/21/71	Georgia	Decatur, Ga.	FA
Grant, Rupert	RB	6-1	233	11/5/73	Howard	Washington, D.C.	FA
Green, David	RB	5-11	193	4/18/72	Boston College	Mt. Kisco, N.Y.	FA
Gregory, James (1)	DE	6-3	310	7/26/71	Alabama	St. Louis, Mo.	FA
Henry, Mario (1)	WR	6-1	187	9/14/71	Rutgers	Medford, N.J.	FA
Hitchcock, Jimmy	CB	5-10	188	11/9/71	North Carolina	Concord, N.C.	D3b
Holcomb, Sean	DE	6-3	250	3/9/71	Texas A&M-Kingsville	Midland, Tex.	FA
Johnson, Ted	LB	6-3	240	12/4/72	Colorado	Carlsbad, Calif.	D2
Landry, Greg	G	6-4	295	8/5/72	Boston College	Lynn, Mass.	FA
Law, Ty	CB	6-0	201	2/10/74	Michigan	Aliquippa, Pa.	D1
Martin, Curtis	RB	5-11	197	5/1/73	Pittsburgh	Pittsburgh, Pa.	D3a
Moore, Will (1)	WR	6-2	180	2/21/70	Texas Southern	Dallas, Tex.	FA
Parker, Jeff	LB	6-0	252	7/9/71	Albany State	Warthen, Ga.	FA
Philyaw, Dino	RB	5-10	192	10/30/70	Oregon	Dudley, S.C.	D6
President, Andre	TE	6-3	255	6/16/71	Angelo State	Ft. Worth, Tex.	FA
Provo, Dwayne	CB-S	5-9	180	10/7/70	St. Mary's, Canada	N. Preston, Nova Scotia	FA
Ray, Jr., Leonard (1)	DE	6-3	297	1/21/69	Louisville	Port St. Joe, Fla.	FA
Suarez, Mike	T	6-5	290	3/6/72	Illinois	DePue, Ill.	FA
Tylski, Rich (1)	C	6-4	289	2/27/71	Utah State	San Diego, Calif.	FA
White, Brian	S	6-0	190	4/21/73	Dartmouth	Newton, Mass.	FA
Wohlabaugh, Dave	C-G	6-3	304	4/13/72	Syracuse	Hamburg, N.Y.	D4
Wright, Byron	LB	6-4	245	3/24/72	Texas Tech	Wichita Falls, Tex.	FA
Yancy, Carlos	CB	6-2	190	6/26/70	Georgia	Sarasota, Fla.	D7

The term NFL Rookie is defined as a player who is in his first season of professional football and has not been on the roster of another professional football team for any regular-season or postseason games. A Rookie is designated by an "R" on NFL rosters. Players who have been active in another professional football league or players who have NFL experience, including either preseason training camp or being on an Active List or Inactive List, or on Reserve/Injured or Reserve/Physically Unable to Perform for fewer than six regular-season games, are termed NFL First-Year Players. An NFL First-Year Player is designated by a "1" on NFL rosters. Thereafter, a player is credited with an additional year of experience for each season in which he accumulates six games on the Active List or Inactive List, or on Reserve/Injured or Reserve/Physically Unable to Perform.

NOTES

Ray Perkins, offensive coordinator-quarterbacks, born November 6, 1941, Mount Olive, Miss., lives in Foxboro, Mass. Wide receiver Alabama 1964-66. Pro receiver Baltimore Colts 1967-71. College coach: Mississippi State 1973, Alabama 1983-86 (head coach), Arkansas State 1992 (head coach). Pro coach: New England Patriots 1974-77, San Diego Chargers 1978, New York Giants 1979-82 (head coach), Tampa Bay Buccaneers 1987-90 (head coach), rejoined Patriots in 1993.

Michael Pope, tight ends; born March 15, 1942, Monroe, N.C., lives in Foxboro, Mass. Quarterback Lenoir Rhyne 1962-64. No pro playing experience. College coach: Florida State 1970-74, Texas Tech 1975-77, Mississippi 1978-82. Pro coach: New York Giants 1983-91, Cincinnati Bengals 1992-93, joined Patriots in 1994.

Dante Scarnecchia, defensive assistant-linebackers; born February 15, 1948, Los Angeles, Calif., lives in Wrentham, Mass. Center-guard California Western 1968-70. No pro playing experience. College coach: California Western (now U.S. International) 1970-72, Iowa State 1973, Southern Methodist 1975-76, 1980-81, Pacific 1977-78, Northern Arizona 1979. Pro coach: New England Patriots 1982-89, Indianapolis Colts 1990, rejoined Patriots in 1991.

Mike Sweatman, special teams, born October 23, 1947, Kansas City, Mo., lives in Foxboro, Mass. Linebacker Kansas 1964-67. No pro playing experience. College coach: Kansas 1973-74, 1979-82, Tulsa 1977-78, Tennessee 1983. Pro coach: Minnesota Vikings 1984, New York Giants 1985-92, joined Patriots in 1993.

Bob Trott, defensive backs, born March 19, 1954, Kannapolis, N.C., lives in Franklin, Mass. Defensive back North Carolina 1973-75. No pro playing experience. College coach: North Carolina 1976-77, Air Force 1978-83, Arkansas 1984-89, Clemson 1990. Pro coach: New York Giants 1990-92, joined Patriots in 1993.

Charlie Weis, running backs, born March 30, 1956, Trenton, N.J., lives in Foxboro, Mass. Graduate of Notre Dame. No college or pro playing experience. College coach: South Carolina 1985-88. Pro coach: New York Giants 1990-92, joined Patriots in 1993.

NEW YORK JETS

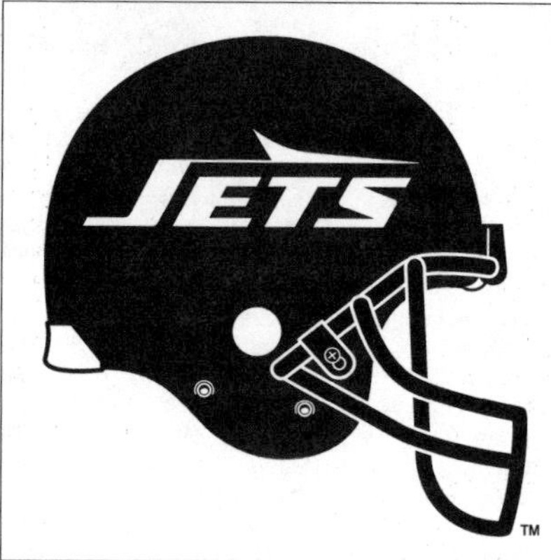

American Football Conference
Eastern Division
Team Colors: Kelly Green and White
1000 Fulton Avenue
Hempstead, New York 11550
Telephone: (516) 538-6600

CLUB OFFICIALS

Chairman of the Board: Leon Hess
President: Steve Gutman
V.P./General Manager: Dick Steinberg
Director of Player Personnel: Dick Haley
Assistant General Manager: James Harris
Director of Player Administration: Pat Kirwan
Talent Scouts: Sid Hall, Jesse Kaye, Marv Sunderland
College Scouting Coordinator: John Griffin
Director of Public Relations: Frank Ramos
Asst. Director of Public Relations: Brooks Thomas
Public Relations Assistants: Ken Ilchuk, Sharon Czark
Public Relations Assistant/Community Affairs: Doug Miller
Travel Coordinator: Kevin Coyle
Treasurer & C.F.O.: Mike Gerstle
Controller: Mike Minarczyk
Director of Operations: Mike Kensil
Exec. Director of Business Operations: Bob Parente
Marketing Manager: Beth Conroy
Director of Ticket Operations: John Buschhorn
Assistant Director of Ticket Operations: Gerry Parravano
Video Director: Jim Pons
Assistant Video Director: John Seiter
Head Trainer: Bob Reese
Assistant Head Trainer: Joe Patten
Assistant Trainer: Darryl Conway
Equipment Manager: Bill Hampton
Equipment Director: Clay Hampton
Stadium: Giants Stadium • **Capacity:** 77,716
East Rutherford, New Jersey 07073
Playing Surface: AstroTurf
Training Center: 1000 Fulton Avenue
Hempstead, New York 11550

1995 SCHEDULE

PRESEASON

Aug. 5	at Tampa Bay	7:30
Aug. 12	vs. Philadelphia at Jackson, Miss.	8:00
Aug. 19	at New York Giants	8:00
Aug. 25	at Cincinnati	7:30

REGULAR SEASON

Sept. 3	at Miami	4:00
Sept. 10	**Indianapolis**	4:00
Sept. 17	**Jacksonville**	4:00
Sept. 24	at Atlanta	4:00
Oct. 1	**Los Angeles**	8:00
Oct. 8	at Buffalo	1:00
Oct. 15	at Carolina	4:00
Oct. 22	**Miami**	1:00
Oct. 29	at Indianapolis	1:00
Nov. 5	**New England**	1:00
Nov. 12	Open Date	
Nov. 19	**Buffalo**	4:00
Nov. 26	at Seattle	1:00
Dec. 3	**St. Louis**	1:00
Dec. 10	at New England	1:00
Dec. 17	at Houston	12:00
Dec. 24	**New Orleans**	1:00

RECORD HOLDERS

INDIVIDUAL RECORDS—CAREER

Category	Name	Performance
Rushing (Yds.)	Freeman McNeil, 1981-1992	8,074
Passing (Yds.)	Joe Namath, 1965-1976	27,057
Passing (TDs)	Joe Namath, 1965-1976	170
Receiving (No.)	Don Maynard, 1960-1972	627
Receiving (Yds.)	Don Maynard, 1960-1972	11,732
Interceptions	Bill Baird, 1963-69	34
Punting (Avg.)	Curley Johnson, 1961-68	42.8
Punt Return (Avg.)	Dick Christy, 1961-63	16.2
Kickoff Return (Avg.)	Bobby Humphery, 1984-89	22.8
Field Goals	Pat Leahy, 1974-1991	304
Touchdowns (Tot.)	Don Maynard, 1960-1972	88
Points	Pat Leahy, 1974-1991	1,470

INDIVIDUAL RECORDS—SINGLE SEASON

Category	Name	Performance
Rushing (Yds.)	Freeman McNeil, 1985	1,331
Passing (Yds.)	Joe Namath, 1967	4,007
Passing (TDs)	Al Dorow, 1960	26
	Joe Namath, 1967	26
Receiving (No.)	Al Toon, 1988	93
Receiving (Yds.)	Don Maynard, 1967	1,434
Interceptions	Dainard Paulson, 1964	12
Punting (Avg.)	Curley Johnson, 1965	45.3
Punt Return (Avg.)	Dick Christy, 1961	21.3
Kickoff Return (Avg.)	Bobby Humphery, 1984	30.7
Field Goals	Jim Turner, 1968	34
Touchdowns (Tot.)	Art Powell, 1960	14
	Don Maynard, 1965	14
	Emerson Boozer, 1972	14
Points	Jim Turner, 1968	145

INDIVIDUAL RECORDS—SINGLE GAME

Category	Name	Performance
Rushing (Yds.)	Freeman McNeil, 9-15-85	192
Passing (Yds.)	Joe Namath, 9-24-72	496
Passing (TDs)	Joe Namath, 9-24-72	6
Receiving (No.)	Clark Gaines, 9-21-80	17
Receiving (Yds.)	Don Maynard, 11-17-68	228
Interceptions	Many times	3
	Last time by Marcus Turner, 11-20-94	
Field Goals	Jim Turner, 11-3-68	6
	Bobby Howfield, 12-3-72	6
Touchdowns (Tot.)	Wesley Walker, 9-21-86	4
Points	Wesley Walker, 9-21-86	24

COACHING HISTORY

New York Titans 1960-62
(232-287-8)

1960-61	Sammy Baugh	14-14-0
1962	Clyde (Bulldog) Turner	5-9-0
1963-73	Weeb Ewbank	73-78-6
1974-75	Charley Winner*	9-14-0
1975	Ken Shipp	1-4-0
1976	Lou Holtz**	3-10-0
1976	Mike Holovak	0-1-0
1977-82	Walt Michaels	41-49-1
1983-89	Joe Walton	54-59-1
1990-93	Bruce Coslet	26-39-0
1994	Pete Carroll	6-10-0

*Released after nine games in 1975
**Resigned after 13 games in 1976

GIANTS STADIUM

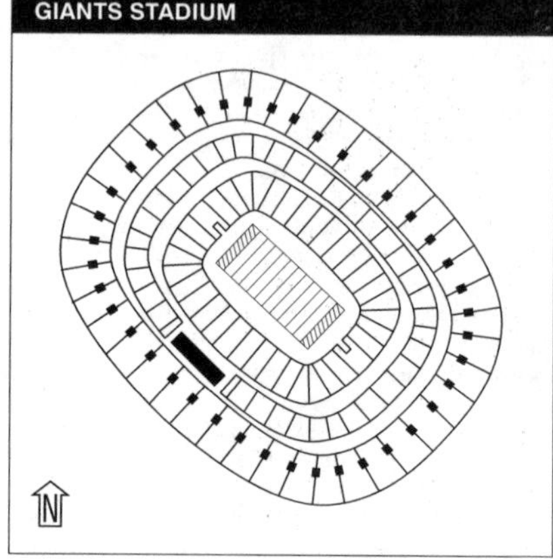

1994 TEAM RECORD

PRESEASON (3-1)

Date	Result		Opponents
8/5	L	13-26	at Detroit
8/13	W	34-24	at Philadelphia
8/20	W	13-10	N.Y. Giants
8/26	W	10-9	at Tampa Bay

REGULAR SEASON (6-10)

Date	Result		Opponents	Att.
9/4	W	23- 3	at Buffalo	79,460
9/11	W	25-22	Denver (OT)	73,436
9/18	L	14-28	at Miami	68,192
9/25	L	7-19	Chicago	70,806
10/2	L	7-27	at Cleveland	76,188
10/9	W	16- 6	Indianapolis	64,934
10/16	W	24-17	New England	71,123
10/30	L	25-28	at Indianapolis	44,350
11/6	W	22-17	Buffalo	66,949
11/13	L	10-17	at Green Bay	58,307
11/20	W	31-21	at Minnesota	60,687
11/27	L	24-28	Miami	75,606
12/4	L	13-24	at New England	60,138
12/10	L	7-18	Detroit	56,080
12/18	L	6-21	San Diego	48,213
12/24	L	10-24	at Houston	31,176

(OT) Overtime

SCORE BY PERIODS

Jets	40	112	51	58	3	— 264
Opponents	54	111	72	83	0	— 320

ATTENDANCE

Home 527,147 Away 478,498 Total 1,005,645
Single-game home record, 75,945 (9-20-92)
Single-season home record, 603,619 (1992)

1994 TEAM STATISTICS

	Jets	Opp.
Total First Downs	265	315
Rushing	90	105
Passing	164	189
Penalty	11	21
Third Down: Made/Att	76/219	83/208
Third Down Pct.	34.7	39.9
Fourth Down: Made/Att	12/27	12/24
Fourth Down Pct.	44.4	50.0
Total Net Yards	4703	5338
Avg. Per Game	293.9	333.6
Total Plays	983	1014
Avg. Per Play	4.8	5.3
Net Yards Rushing	1566	1809
Avg. Per Game	97.9	113.1
Total Rushes	416	463
Net Yards Passing	3137	3529
Avg. Per Game	196.1	220.6
Sacked/Yards Lost	28/186	29/201
Gross Yards	3323	3730
Att./Completions	539/310	522/333
Completion Pct.	57.5	63.8
Had Intercepted	18	17
Punts/Average	84/42.1	62/43.1
Net Punting Avg.	84/36.1	62/36.3
Penalties/Yards	95/754	63/489
Fumbles/Ball Lost	28/10	30/21
Touchdowns	29	37
Rushing	8	17
Passing	18	19
Returns	3	1
Avg. Time of Possession	29:54	30:06

1994 INDIVIDUAL STATISTICS

PASSING	Att.	Comp.	Yds.	Pct.	TD	Int.	Tkld.	Rate
Esiason	440	255	2782	58.0	17	13	19/134	77.3
Trudeau	91	50	496	54.9	1	4	9/52	55.9
Foley	8	5	45	62.5	0	1	0/0	38.0
Jets	539	310	3323	57.5	18	18	28/186	72.9
Opponents	522	333	3730	63.8	19	17	29/201	83.6

SCORING	TD R	TD P	TD Rt	PAT	FG	Saf	PTS
Lowery	0	0	0	26/27	20/23	0	86
Moore	0	6	0	0/0	0/0	0	40
J. Johnson	3	2	0	0/0	0/0	0	30
B. Baxter	4	0	0	0/0	0/0	0	24
Mitchell	0	4	0	0/0	0/0	0	24
Monk	0	3	0	0/0	0/0	0	18
R. Anderson	1	1	0	0/0	0/0	0	12
Lewis	0	0	2	0/0	0/0	0	12
F. Baxter	0	1	0	0/0	0/0	0	6
Turner	0	0	1	0/0	0/0	0	6
Yarborough	0	1	0	0/0	0/0	0	6
Jets	8	18	3	26/27	20/23	0	264
Opponents	17	19	1	31/32	21/27	0	320

2-Point conversions: Moore (2). Team: 2-2.

RUSHING	Att.	Yds.	Avg.	LG	TD
J. Johnson	240	931	3.9	90	3
R. Anderson	43	207	4.8	55	1
B. Baxter	60	170	2.8	13	4
Murrell	33	160	4.8	19	0
Esiason	28	59	2.1	15	0
Trudeau	6	30	5.0	15	0
A. Johnson	5	12	2.4	5	0
Moore	1	-3	-3.0	-3	0
Jets	416	1566	3.8	90	8
Opponents	463	1809	3.9	37t	17

RECEIVING	No.	Yds.	Avg.	LG	TD
Moore	78	1010	12.9	41t	6
Mitchell	58	749	12.9	55	4
Monk	46	581	12.6	69	3
J. Johnson	42	303	7.2	24	2
R. Anderson	25	212	8.5	27t	1
Thornton	20	171	8.6	25	0
B. Baxter	10	40	4.0	7	0
S. Anderson	9	90	10.0	17	0
Murrell	7	76	10.9	20	0
Yarborough	6	42	7.0	12	1
A. Johnson	5	31	6.2	9	0
F. Baxter	3	11	3.7	6	1
Parker	1	7	7.0	7	0
Jets	310	3323	10.7	69	18
Opponents	333	3730	11.2	60t	19

INTERCEPTIONS	No.	Yds.	Avg.	LG	TD
Turner	5	155	31.0	90t	1
Hasty	5	90	18.0	40	0
Lewis	4	106	26.5	67t	2
B. Washington	2	-3	-1.5	0	0
M. Washington	1	7	7.0	7	0
Jets	17	355	20.9	90t	3
Opponents	18	232	12.9	32	1

PUNTING	No.	Yds.	Avg.	In 20	LG
Hansen	84	3534	42.1	25	64
Jets	84	3534	42.1	25	64
Opponents	62	2675	43.1	15	70

PUNT RETURNS	No.	FC	Yds.	Avg.	LG	TD
Hicks	38	5	342	9.0	26	0
A. Johnson	1	0	3	3.0	3	0
Jets	39	5	345	8.8	26	0
Opponents	38	12	260	6.8	31	0

KICKOFF RETURNS	No.	Yds.	Avg.	LG	TD
Glenn	27	582	21.6	45	0
Prior	16	316	19.8	27	0
Murrell	14	268	19.1	37	0
R. Anderson	3	43	14.3	18	0
Hicks	2	30	15.0	16	0
F. Baxter	1	20	20.0	20	0
Clifton	1	13	13.0	13	0
Cadrez	1	10	10.0	10	0
Thornton	1	0	0.0	0	0
Jets	66	1282	19.4	45	0
Opponents	61	1195	19.6	52	0

SACKS	No.
Lageman	6.5
Lewis	6.0
Houston	3.5
Hasty	3.0
M. Washington	3.0
Casillas	1.5
Barber	1.0
Frase	1.0
Green	1.0
Lott	1.0
Evans	0.5
Jones	0.5
Oglesby	0.5
Jets	29.0
Opponents	28.0

1995 DRAFT CHOICES

Round	Name	Pos.	College
1	Kyle Brady	TE	Penn State
	Hugh Douglas	DE	Central State, Ohio
2	Matt O'Dwyer	T	Northwestern
4	Melvin Hayes	T	Mississippi State
	Tyrone Davis	WR	Virginia
5	Carl Greenwood	DB	UCLA
6	Eddie Mason	LB	North Carolina
7	Curtis Ceaser	WR	Grambling State

NEW YORK JETS

1995 VETERAN ROSTER

No.	Name	Pos.	Ht.	Wt.	Birthdate	NFL Exp.	College	Hometown	How Acq.	'94 Games/ Starts
20	Anderson, Richie	RB	6-2	225	9/13/71	3	Penn State	Sandy Spring, Md.	D6-'93	13/5
88	Anderson, Stevie	WR	6-5	215	5/12/70	2	Grambling State	Jonesboro, La.	FA-'93	10/0
98	Barber, Kurt	DE	6-4	249	1/5/69	4	Southern California	Paducah, Ky.	D2-'92	15/0
30	Baxter, Brad	RB	6-1	235	5/5/67	6	Alabama State	Slocomb, Ala.	FA-'89	15/9
84	Baxter, Fred	TE	6-3	260	6/14/71	3	Auburn	Brundidge, Ala.	D5a-'93	11/1
78	Benfatti, Lou	DT	6-4	278	3/9/71	2	Penn State	Green Pond, N.J.	D3-'94	7/0
6	Brister, Bubby	QB	6-3	207	8/15/62	10	Northeast Louisiana	Monroe, La.	UFA(Phil)-'95	7/2*
94	Brock, Matt	DT	6-5	290	1/14/66	7	Oregon	San Diego, Calif.	UFA(GB)-'95	5/0*
76	Brown, James	T	6-6	321	1/3/70	3	Virginia State	Philadelphia, Pa.	W(Ind)-'92	16/6
50	Cadrez, Glenn	LB	6-3	245	1/2/70	4	Houston	El Centro, Calif.	D6a-'92	16/0
35	Carter, Dexter	RB-KR	5-9	170	1/15/67	6	Florida State	Baxley, Ga.	UFA(SF)-'95	16/0*
92	Casillas, Tony	DT	6-3	278	10/26/63	10	Oklahoma	Tulsa, Okla.	FA-'94	12/11
59	Clifton, Kyle	LB	6-4	236	8/23/62	12	Texas Christian	Bridgeport, Tex.	D3-'84	16/5
52	Dixon, Cal	C-G	6-4	292	10/11/69	4	Florida	Merritt Island, Fla.	D5-'92	15/0
62	Duffy, Roger	G-C	6-3	294	7/16/67	6	Penn State	Canton, Ohio	D8-'90	16/14
7	Esiason, Boomer	QB	6-5	224	4/17/61	12	Maryland	East Islip, N.Y.	T(Cin)-'93	15/14
66	Evans, Donald	DT-DE	6-2	282	3/14/64	8	Winston-Salem State	Raleigh, N.C.	UFA(Pitt)-'94	16/16
4	Foley, Glenn	QB	6-2	205	10/10/70	2	Boston College	Cherry Hill, N.J.	D7-'94	1/0
31	Glenn, Aaron	CB-KR	5-9	185	7/16/72	2	Texas A&M	Aldine, Tex.	D1-'94	15/15
21	Green, Victor	CB	5-9	195	12/8/69	3	Akron	Americus, Ga.	FA-'93	16/0
11	Hansen, Brian	P	6-4	215	10/26/60	11	Sioux Falls	Hawarden, Iowa	UFA(Clev)-'94	16/0
55	Houston, Bobby	LB	6-2	245	10/26/67	5	North Carolina State	Hyattsville, Md.	PB(Atl)-'91	16/16
74	Howard, Erik	DE-DT	6-4	275	11/12/64	10	Washington State	San Jose, Calif.	UFA(NYG)-'95	16/16*
39	Johnson, Johnny	RB	6-3	220	6/11/68	6	San Jose State	Santa Cruz, Calif.	T(Phx)-'93	16/14
26	Jones, Gary	S	6-1	217	11/30/67	6	Texas A&M	Dallas, Tex.	UFA(Pitt)-'95	14/0*
54	Jones, Marvin	LB	6-2	249	6/28/72	3	Florida State	Miami, Fla.	D1-'93	15/11
57	Lewis, Mo	LB	6-3	250	10/21/69	5	Georgia	Peachtree, Ga.	D3-'91	16/16
8	Lowery, Nick	K	6-4	205	5/27/56	16	Dartmouth	Washington, D.C.	FA-'94	16/0
75	Malamala, Siupeli	T	6-5	315	1/15/69	4	Washington	Kalaheo, Hawaii	D3-'92	12/10
74	McIver, Everett	G	6-6	315	8/5/70	2	Elizabeth City State	Fayetteville, N.C.	FA-'93	4/0
86	Mitchell, Johnny	TE	6-3	241	1/20/71	4	Nebraska	Chicago, Ill.	D1-'92	16/14
33	t- Moore, Ron	RB	5-10	220	11/26/70	3	Pittsburg State	Spencer, Okla.	T(Ariz)-'95	16/16*
29	Murrell, Adrian	RB	5-11	212	10/16/70	3	West Virginia	Wahiawa, Hawaii	D5b-'93	10/1
95	Oglesby, Alfred	DT	6-4	276	1/27/67	5	Houston	Weimer, Tex.	FA-'94	15/1
89	Parker, Orlando	WR-KR	5-11	190	3/7/72	2	Troy State	Montgomery, Ala.	D4-'94	2/0
37	Prior, Anthony	CB-S	5-11	185	3/27/70	3	Washington State	Riverside, Calif.	FA-'93	13/0
38	Scott, Todd	S	5-10	207	1/23/68	5	Southwestern Louisiana	Galveston, Tex.	UFA(Minn)-'95	15/15*
45	Smith, Otis	CB	5-11	190	10/22/65	6	Missouri	New Orleans, La.	FA-'95	16/2*
27	Terrell, Pat	S	6-2	210	3/18/68	6	Notre Dame	St. Petersburg, Fla.	UFA(Rams)-'94	16/2
23	Turner, Marcus	CB-S	6-0	190	1/13/66	7	UCLA	Long Beach, Calif.	PB(Phx)-'92	16/1
97	Washington, Marvin	DE	6-6	272	10/22/65	7	Idaho	Dallas, Tex.	D6a-'89	15/15
77	Willig, Matt	T	6-8	305	1/21/69	3	Southern California	La Mirada, Calif.	FA-'92	16/3
87	Yarborough, Ryan	WR	6-2	190	4/26/71	2	Wyoming	Park Forest, Ill.	D2-'94	13/0

* Brister played 7 games with Philadelphia in '94; Brock played 5 games with Green Bay; Carter played 16 games with San Francisco; Howard played 16 games with N.Y. Giants; G. Jones played 14 games with Pittsburgh; Moore played 16 games with Arizona; Scott played 15 games with Minnesota; Smith played 16 games with Philadelphia.

\# Unrestricted free agent; subject to developments.

† Restricted free agent; subject to developments.

Retired—Bill Pickel, 12-year defensive tackle, 11 games in '94.

Traded—WR Rob Moore to Arizona.

t- Jets traded for Moore (Arizona).

Players lost through free agency (8): T Jeff Criswell (KC; 15 games in '94), CB James Hasty (KC; 16), CB Clifford Hicks (SF; 16), RB Anthony Johnson (Chi; 15), DE Jeff Lageman (Jax; 16), S Ronnie Lott (KC; 15), CB Eric Thomas (Den; 1), G Dwayne White (Rams; 16).

Players lost through Expansion Draft (2): DT-DE Paul Frase (Jax; 16 games in '94), QB Jack Trudeau (Car; 5).

Also played with Jets in '94—LB Tuineau Alipate (8 games), WR Rob Carpenter (3), DT-DE Mark Gunn (3), WR Art Monk (16), WR Rob Moore (16), C Jim Sweeney (16), TE James Thornton (15), S Brian Washington (15).

COACHING STAFF

Head Coach,
Rich Kotite

Pro Career: Became New York's tenth head coach on January 10, 1995. Kotite rejoins the Jets after spending five years with the Philadelphia Eagles (1990-94), the last four as head coach. Under difficult circumstances, Kotite led the Eagles to a 36-28 regular-season record and guided them to their first playoff victory since 1980 when they defeated New Orleans 36-20 in the 1992 NFL Wild Card game. In his first year as a head coach, Kotite led Philadelphia to 10 wins despite losing Randall Cunningham, the starting quarterback, in the first game and playing the rest of the season with four other quarterbacks. The second year, the Eagles won 12 games including a playoff win, despite losing one of their best players, Jerome Brown, in a car crash. In 1993, the Eagles lost 15 starters and still won eight games and went down to the final game of the season before missing the playoffs. As the Eagles' offensive coordinator in 1990, Kotite's squad led the NFL in rushing and topped the NFC in scoring and touchdown passes. Kotite had served previously as the Jets' offensive coordinator and receivers coach from 1985-89 after originally joining the club as receivers coach in 1983. In each of Kotite's years at the helm of the New York offense, the Jets finished near the top in the AFC in total offense, including a third-place ranking in 1985. Kotite began his pro coaching career with New Orleans in 1977 before joining Cleveland as a receivers coach from 1978-1982. He aided in the development of perennial all-pro tight end Ozzie Newsome while with the Browns. During his playing days, Kotite was known as a tenacious tight end and outstanding special teams performer with the New York Giants (1967 and 1969-72) and Steelers (1968). Career record: 37-29.

Background: Attended Poly Prep in Brooklyn, N.Y. After a brief boxing career at the University of Miami where he was the school's heavyweight champion, he served as a sparring partner for Cassius Clay, later known as Muhammad Ali. Kotite became a Little All-America tight end at Wagner College on Staten Island, N.Y.

Personal: Born in Brooklyn on October 13, 1942. He and his wife, Elizabeth, live on Staten Island and have one daughter, Alexandra.

ASSISTANT COACHES

Zeke Bratkowski, offensive coordinator-quarterbacks; born October 20, 1931, Danville, Ill., lives on Long Island, N.Y. Quarterback Georgia 1951-1953. Pro quarterback Chicago Bears 1954, 1957-60, Los Angeles Rams 1961-63, Green Bay Packers 1963-68, 1971. Pro coach: Green Bay Packers 1969-70, 1975-81, Chicago Bears 1972-74, Baltimore-Indianapolis Colts 1982-84, New York Jets 1985-89, Cleveland Browns 1990, Philadelphia Eagles 1991-1994, rejoined Jets in 1995.

Chip Falivene, assistant to the head coach; born March 10, 1953, Schenectady, N.Y., lives on Long Island, N.Y. Center Baldwin-Wallace College 1972-74. No pro playing experience. No college coaching experience. Pro coach: Joined Jets in 1995.

Tom Gamble, defensive assistant-quality control; born February 14, 1963, Woodbury, N.J. No college or pro playing experience. Pro coach: Joined Jets in 1995.

Peter Giunta, defensive secondary; born August 11, 1956, Salem, Mass., lives on Long Island, N.Y. Running back-defensive back Northeastern 1974-77. No pro playing experience. College coach: Penn State 1981-83, Brown 1984-87, Lehigh 1988-90. Pro coach: Philadelphia Eagles 1991-1994, joined Jets in 1995.

Ray Hamilton, defensive line; born January 20, 1951, Omaha, Neb., lives on Long Island, N.Y. Nose tackle Oklahoma 1969-72. Pro nose tackle-defensive end New England Patriots 1973-81. College coach: Tennessee 1992. Pro coach: New England Patriots 1985-89, Tampa Bay Buccaneers 1991, Los Angeles Raiders 1993-94, joined Jets in 1995.

1995 FIRST-YEAR ROSTER

Name	Pos.	Ht.	Wt.	Birthdate	College	Hometown	How Acq.
Allen, Alan (1)	WR	6-1	186	8/9/71	Idaho	Tacoma, Wash.	FA
Askew, Chad	WR	6-4	200	1/27/72	Pittsburgh	Aliquippa, Pa.	FA
Baczek, Todd	G	6-3	297	2/1/72	Northwestern	Graylake, Ill.	FA
Ball, LaVar (1)	TE	6-5	263	10/23/68	Cal St.-Los Angeles	Canoga Park, Calif.	FA
Bazile, Wilky	DT	6-3	271	11/21/71	Syracuse	Spring Valley, N.Y.	FA
Brady, Kyle	TE	6-6	260	1/14/72	Penn State	New Cumberland, Pa.	D1a
Burke, Paul (1)	TE	6-3	244	2/16/69	Idaho	Detroit, Mich.	FA
Cascadden, Chad	LB	6-1	225	5/14/72	Wisconsin	Chippewa Falls, Wis.	FA
Ceaser, Curtis	WR	6-2	185	8/11/72	Grambling State	Beaumont, Tex.	D7
Chrebet, Wayne	WR	5-10	180	8/14/73	Hofstra	Garfield, N.J.	FA
Connealy, Terry	DT	6-5	278	6/10/72	Nebraska	Hyannis, Neb.	FA
Cronin, Colin	G	6-6	285	10/15/71	Michigan State	St. Joseph, Mich.	FA
Davis, Don	LB	6-1	239	12/17/72	Kansas	Olathe, Kan.	FA
Davis, Tyrone	WR	6-4	229	6/30/72	Virginia	Halifax, Va.	D4b
Douglas, Hugh	DE	6-2	255	8/23/71	Central State, Ohio	Mansfield, Ohio	D1b
Garlick, Tom (1)	WR	5-11	180	9/22/71	Fordham	Philadelphia, Pa.	FA
Greenwood, Carl	CB	5-11	186	3/11/72	UCLA	Corpus Christi, Tex.	D5
Hayes, Melvin	T	6-6	329	4/28/73	Mississippi State	New Orleans, La.	D4a
Jerich, Mike	T	6-5	295	7/10/72	Stanford	LaGrange, Ill.	FA
Joseph, Vance	CB-S	6-0	202	9/20/72	Colorado	Marrero, La.	FA
Knutson, Jon	LB	6-3	249	5/31/73	Colorado	Great Falls, Mont.	FA
Lamb, Marc	C	6-5	292	5/4/72	Montana	Yorba Linda, Calif.	FA
Lester, Fred (1)	RB	6-0	232	8/1/71	Alabama A&M	Miami, Fla.	D6-'94
Marsh, Erik	RB	5-10	195	5/2/73	Lafayette	Hellertown, Pa.	FA
Mason, Eddie	LB	6-0	230	1/9/72	North Carolina	Siler City, N.C.	D6
May, Sheriden	RB	6-0	215	8/10/73	Idaho	Tacoma, Wash.	FA
O'Dwyer, Matt	G	6-5	308	9/1/72	Northwestern	Lincolnshire, Ill.	D2
Rhoades, Elton	CB	6-1	196	5/22/72	Central Oklahoma St.	Guthrie, Okla.	FA
Sacca, John	QB	6-2	203	12/12/71	Eastern Kentucky	Delran, N.J.	FA
Sallee, Brian	WR	6-2	194	5/12/72	Missouri	Jackson, Tenn.	FA
Seapker, Jason	S	6-3	193	11/28/71	Northeastern	Wexford, Pa.	FA
Wisdom, Terrence (1)	G	6-4	300	12/4/71	Syracuse	Brooklyn, N.Y.	FA

The term NFL Rookie is defined as a player who is in his first season of professional football and has not been on the roster of another professional football team for any regular-season or postseason games. A Rookie is designated by an "R" on NFL rosters. Players who have been active in another professional football league or players who have NFL experience, including either preseason training camp or being on an Active List or Inactive List, or on Reserve/Injured or Reserve/Physically Unable to Perform for fewer than six regular-season games, are termed NFL First-Year Players. An NFL First-Year Player is designated by a "1" on NFL rosters. Thereafter, a player is credited with an additional year of experience for each season in which he accumulates six games on the Active List or Inactive List, or on Reserve/Injured or Reserve/Physically Unable to Perform.

NOTES

Richard Mann, receivers; born April 20, 1947, Aliquippa, Pa., lives on Long Island, N.Y. Wide receiver Arizona State 1966-68. No pro playing experience. College coach: Arizona State 1974-79, Louisville 1980-81. Pro coach: Baltimore-Indianapolis Colts 1982-84, Cleveland Browns 1985-93, joined Jets in 1994.

Bill Muir, offensive line; born Ocrtober 26, 1942, Pittsburgh, Pa., lives on Long Island, N.Y. Tackle Susquehanna 1962-64. No pro playing experience. College coach: Susquehanna 1965, Delaware Valley 1966-67. Rhode Island 1970-71, Idaho State 1972-73, Southern Methodist 1976-77. Pro coach: Orlando (Continental Football League) 1968-69, Houston-Shreveport Steamer (WFL) 1975, New England Patriots 1982-84, Detroit Lions 1985-88, Indianapolis Colts 1989-91, Philadelphia Eagles 1992-1994, joined Jets in 1995.

Ken Rose, special teams; born June 9, 1962, Sacramento, Calif. lives on Long Island, N.Y. Linebacker Nevada-Las Vegas 1979-82. Pro linebacker Saskatchewan Rough Riders (CFL) 1983-84, Tampa Bay Bandits (USFL) 1986, New York Jets 1987-89, Cleveland Browns 1990, Philadelphia Eagles 1990-94. Pro coach: Joined Jets in 1995.

Jim Vechiarella, defensive coordinator-linebackers; born February 20, 1937, Youngstown, Ohio, lives on Long Island, N.Y. Linebacker Youngstown State 1955-57. No pro playing experience. College coach: Youngstown State 1964-74, Southern Illinois 1976-77, Tulane 1978-80. Pro coach: Charlotte (WFL) 1975, Los Angeles Rams 1981-82, Kansas City Chiefs 1983-85, New York Jets 1986-89, Cleveland Browns 1990, Philadelphia Eagles 1991-94, rejoined Jets in 1995.

Jim Williams, strength and conditioning; born March 29, 1948, Kingston, Pa., lives on Long Island, N.Y. No college or pro playing experience. College coach: Nebraska 1972-74, Arkansas 1974-77, Wyoming 1977-79. Pro coach: New York Giants 1979-81, New York Jets 1982-89, Philadelphia Eagles 1991-1994, rejoined Jets in 1995.

Dick (Richard) Wood, running backs; born February 2, 1936, Lanett, Ala., lives on Long Island, N.Y. Quarterback Auburn 1956-59. Pro quarterback Baltimore Colts 1960-61, San Diego Chargers 1962, Denver Broncos 1962, New York Jets 1963-64, Oakland Raiders 1965, Miami Dolphins 1966. College coach: Georgia 1967-68, Mississippi 1971-73, Auburn 1986. Pro coach: Oakland Raiders 1969-70, Cleveland Browns 1974, New Orleans Saints 1976-77, Atlanta Falcons 1978-82, Philadelphia Eagles 1983, 1991-94, Kansas City Chiefs 1987-88, New England Patriots 1989-90, joined Jets in 1995.

PITTSBURGH STEELERS

American Football Conference
Central Division
Team Colors: Black and Gold
Three Rivers Stadium
300 Stadium Circle
Pittsburgh, Pennsylvania 15212
Telephone: (412) 323-1200

CLUB OFFICIALS

President: Daniel M. Rooney
Vice President: John R. McGinley
Vice President: Arthur J. Rooney, Jr.
Secretary and Counsel: Arthur J. Rooney II
Administration Advisor: Charles H. Noll
Director of Communications: Joe Gordon
Public Relations Coordinator: Rob Boulware
P.R. Assistant/Community Relations: Ron Miller
Controller: Michael J. Hagan
Assistant Controller: Dan Ferens
Assistant Controller: Jim Ellenberger
Director of Football Operations: Tom Donahoe
Football Business Manager: James A. Boston
College Personnel Coordinator: Tom Modrak
Pro Personnel Coordinator: Charles Bailey
College Scouts: Phil Kreidler, Bob Lane, Max McCartney, Bob Schmitz
Ticket Sales Manager: Geraldine R. Glenn
Player Development Coordinator: Anthony Griggs
Trainers: John Norwig, Rick Burkholder
Equipment Manager: Anthony Parisi
Field Manager: Rodgers Freyvogel
Stadium: Three Rivers Stadium
•**Capacity:** 59,600
300 Stadium Circle
Pittsburgh, Pennsylvania 15212
Playing Surface: AstroTurf
Training Camp: St. Vincent College
Latrobe, Pennsylvania 15650

1995 SCHEDULE

PRESEASON

Aug. 4	at Buffalo	7:30
Aug. 13	**Green Bay**	1:00
Aug. 19	at Tampa Bay	7:30
Aug. 24	**Philadelphia**	8:00

REGULAR SEASON

Sept. 3	**Detroit**	1:00
Sept. 10	at Houston	12:00
Sept. 18	at Miami (Monday)	9:00
Sept. 24	**Minnesota**	1:00
Oct. 1	**San Diego**	4:00
Oct. 8	at Jacksonville	1:00
Oct. 15	Open Date	
Oct. 19	**Cincinnati** (Thursday)	8:00
Oct. 29	**Jacksonville**	1:00
Nov. 5	at Chicago	3:00
Nov. 13	**Cleveland** (Monday)	9:00
Nov. 19	at Cincinnati	1:00
Nov. 26	at Cleveland	4:00
Dec. 3	**Houston**	1:00
Dec. 10	at Los Angeles	1:00
Dec. 16	**New England** (Saturday)	12:30
Dec. 24	at Green Bay	12:00

RECORD HOLDERS

INDIVIDUAL RECORDS—CAREER

Category	Name	Performance
Rushing (Yds.)	Franco Harris, 1972-1983	11,950
Passing (Yds.)	Terry Bradshaw, 1970-1983	27,989
Passing (TDs)	Terry Bradshaw, 1970-1983	212
Receiving (No.)	John Stallworth, 1974-1987	537
Receiving (Yds.)	John Stallworth, 1974-1987	8,723
Interceptions	Mel Blount, 1970-1983	57
Punting (Avg.)	Bobby Joe Green, 1960-61	45.7
Punt Return (Avg.)	Bobby Gage, 1949-1950	14.9
Kickoff Return (Avg.)	Lynn Chandnois, 1950-56	29.6
Field Goals	Gary Anderson, 1982-1994	309
Touchdowns (Tot.)	Franco Harris, 1972-1983	100
Points	Gary Anderson, 1982-1994	1,343

INDIVIDUAL RECORDS—SINGLE SEASON

Category	Name	Performance
Rushing (Yds.)	Barry Foster, 1992	1,690
Passing (Yds.)	Terry Bradshaw, 1979	3,724
Passing (TDs)	Terry Bradshaw, 1978	28
Receiving (No.)	John Stallworth, 1984	80
Receiving (Yds.)	John Stallworth, 1984	1,395
Interceptions	Mel Blount, 1975	11
Punting (Avg.)	Bobby Joe Green, 1961	47.0
Punt Return (Avg.)	Bobby Gage, 1949	16.0
Kickoff Return (Avg.)	Lynn Chandnois, 1952	35.2
Field Goals	Gary Anderson, 1985	33
Touchdowns (Tot.)	Louis Lipps, 1985	15
Points	Gary Anderson, 1985	139

INDIVIDUAL RECORDS—SINGLE GAME

Category	Name	Performance
Rushing (Yds.)	John Fuqua, 12-20-70	218
Passing (Yds.)	Bobby Layne, 12-3-58	409
Passing (TDs)	Terry Bradshaw, 11-15-81	5
	Mark Malone, 9-8-85	5
Receiving (No.)	J.R. Wilburn, 10-22-67	12
Receiving (Yds.)	Buddy Dial, 10-22-61	235
Interceptions	Jack Butler, 12-13-53	*4
Field Goals	Gary Anderson, 10-23-88	6
Touchdowns (Tot.)	Ray Mathews, 10-17-54	4
	Roy Jefferson, 11-3-68	4
Points	Ray Mathews, 10-17-54	24
	Roy Jefferson, 11-3-68	24

*NFL Record

COACHING HISTORY

Pittsburgh Pirates 1933-1940
(403-431-20)

1933	Forrest (Jap) Douds	3-6-2
1934	Luby DiMelio	2-10-0
1935-36	Joe Bach	10-14-0
1937-39	Johnny Blood (McNally)*	6-19-0
1939-40	Walt Kiesling	3-13-3
1941	Bert Bell**	0-2-0
	Aldo (Buff) Donelli***	0-5-0
1941-44	Walt Kiesling****	13-20-2
1945	Jim Leonard	2-8-0
1946-47	Jock Sutherland	13-10-1
1948-51	Johnny Michelosen	20-26-2
1952-53	Joe Bach	11-13-0
1954-56	Walt Kiesling	14-22-0
1957-64	Raymond (Buddy) Parker	51-48-6
1965	Mike Nixon	2-12-0
1966-68	Bill Austin	11-28-3
1969-91	Chuck Noll	209-156-1
1992-94	Bill Cowher	33-19-0

*Released after three games in 1939
**Resigned after two games in 1941
***Released after five games in 1941
****Co-coach with Earle (Greasy) Neale in Philadelphia-Pittsburgh merger in 1943 and with Phil Handler in Chicago Cardinals-Pittsburgh merger in 1944

THREE RIVERS STADIUM

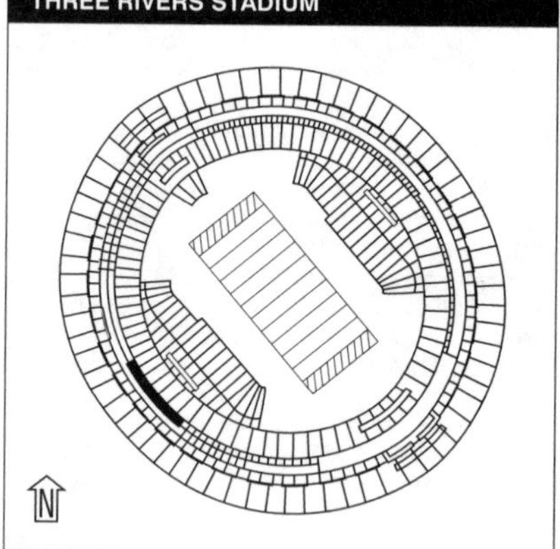

1994 TEAM RECORD

PRESEASON (1-3)

Date	Result		Opponents
8/6	L	14-24	at Miami
8/13	W	29-17	L.A. Raiders
8/20	L	14-17	Indianapolis
8/26	L	21-22	at Washington

REGULAR SEASON (12-4)

Date	Result		Opponents	Att.
9/4	L	9-26	Dallas	60,156
9/11	W	17-10	at Cleveland	77,774
9/18	W	31-21	Indianapolis	54,040
9/25	L	13-30	at Seattle	59,637
10/3	W	30-14	Houston	57,274
10/16	W	14-10	Cincinnati	55,353
10/23	W	10- 6	at N.Y. Giants	71,819
10/30	L	17-20	at Arizona (OT)	65,690
11/6	W	12- 9	at Houston (OT)	47,822
11/14	W	23-10	Buffalo	59,019
11/20	W	16-13	Miami (OT)	59,148
11/27	W	21- 3	at L.A. Raiders	58,327
12/4	W	38-15	at Cincinnati	53,401
12/11	W	14- 3	Philadelphia	55,474
12/18	W	17- 7	Cleveland	60,808
12/24	L	34-37	at San Diego	58,379

POSTSEASON (1-1)

1/7	W	29- 9	Cleveland	58,185
1/15	L	13-17	San Diego	61,545

(OT) Overtime

SCORE BY PERIODS

Steelers	64	106	20	120	6	—	316
Opponents	50	86	31	64	3	—	234

ATTENDANCE

Home 461,272 Away 492,849 Total 954,121
Single-game home record, 60,808 (12-18-94)
Single-season home record, 471,306 (1992)

1994 TEAM STATISTICS

	Steelers	Opp.
Total First Downs	307	262
Rushing	138	76
Passing	148	156
Penalty	21	30
Third Down: Made/Att	89/228	72/225
Third Down Pct.	39.0	32.0
Fourth Down: Made/Att	4/10	11/19
Fourth Down Pct.	40.0	57.9
Total Net Yards	5144	4326
Avg. Per Game	321.5	270.4
Total Plays	1048	1008
Avg. Per Play	4.9	4.3
Net Yards Rushing	2180	1452
Avg. Per Game	136.3	90.8
Total Rushes	546	421
Net Yards Passing	2964	2874
Avg. Per Game	185.3	179.6
Sacked/Yards Lost	39/283	55/382
Gross Yards	3247	3256
Att./Completions	463/266	532/280
Completion Pct.	57.5	52.6
Had Intercepted	9	17
Punts/Avg.	97/39.7	97/42.2
Net Punting Avg.	97/35.7	97/37.0
Penalties/Yards Lost	119/974	91/763
Penalties/Yards Lost	18/8	31/14
Touchdowns	35	23
Rushing	15	7
Passing	17	12
Returns	3	4
Avg. Time of Possession	31:58	28:02

1994 INDIVIDUAL STATISTICS

PASSING	Att.	Comp.	Yds.	Pct.	TD	Int.	Tkld.	Rate
O'Donnell	370	212	2443	57.3	13	9	35/250	78.9
Tomczak	93	54	804	58.1	4	0	4/33	100.8
Steelers	463	266	3247	57.5	17	9	39/283	83.3
Opponents	532	280	3256	52.6	12	17	55/382	65.6

SCORING	TD R	TD P	TD Rt	PAT	FG	Saf	PTS
Anderson	0	0	0	32/32	24/29	0	104
Morris	7	0	0	0/0	0/0	0	42
Foster	5	0	0	0/0	0/0	0	30
Green	0	4	0	0/0	0/0	0	24
Thigpen	0	4	0	0/0	0/0	0	24
Johnson	0	3	0	0/0	0/0	0	18
J. Williams	1	2	0	0/0	0/0	0	18
Hastings	0	2	0	0/0	0/0	0	12
Woodson	0	0	2	0/0	0/0	0	12
Hayes	0	1	0	0/0	0/0	0	6
McAfee	1	0	0	0/0	0/0	0	6
Mills	0	1	0	0/0	0/0	0	6
O'Donnell	1	0	0	0/0	0/0	0	6
G. Williams	0	0	1	0/0	0/0	0	6
Stone	0	0	0	0/0	0/0	0	2
Steelers	15	17	3	32/32	24/29	0	316
Opponents	7	12	4	22/22	24/29	0	234

2-Point conversions: Stone. Team: 1-3.

RUSHING	Att.	Yds.	Avg.	LG	TD
Foster	216	851	3.9	29t	5
Morris	198	836	4.2	20	7
J. Williams	68	317	4.7	23	1
O'Donnell	31	80	2.6	18	1
McAfee	16	56	3.5	13	1
Tomczak	4	22	5.5	13	0
Mills	3	18	6.0	17	0
Stone	2	7	3.5	4	0
Avery	2	4	2.0	5	0
Anderson	1	3	3.0	3	0
Johnson	4	-1	-0.2	7	0
Royals	1	-13	-13.0	-13	0
Steelers	546	2180	4.0	29t	15
Opponents	421	1452	3.4	46	7

RECEIVING	No.	Yds.	Avg.	LG	TD
J. Williams	51	378	7.4	23	2
Green	46	618	13.4	46	4
Johnson	38	577	15.2	84t	3
Thigpen	36	546	15.2	60t	4
Morris	22	204	9.3	49	0
Hastings	20	281	14.1	46	2
Foster	20	124	6.2	27	0
Mills	19	384	20.2	43	1
Stone	7	81	11.6	25	0
Hayes	5	50	10.0	17	1
Avery	1	2	2.0	2	0
Keith	1	2	2.0	2	0
Steelers	266	3247	12.2	84t	17
Opponents	280	3256	11.6	76t	12

INTERCEPTIONS	No.	Yds.	Avg.	LG	TD
Perry	7	112	16.0	42	0
Woodson	4	109	27.3	37t	2
Kirkland	2	0	0.0	0	0
Brown	1	9	9.0	9	0
Lloyd	1	8	8.0	8	0
Lake	1	2	2.0	2	0
G. Jones	1	0	0.0	0	0
Steelers	17	240	14.1	42	2
Opponents	9	106	11.8	35t	1

PUNTING	No.	Yds.	Avg.	In 20	LG
Royals	97	3849	39.7	35	64
Steelers	97	3849	39.7	35	64
Opponents	97	4096	42.2	31	59

PUNT RETURNS	No.	FC	Yds.	Avg.	LG	TD
Woodson	39	9	319	8.2	42	0
Johnson	15	7	90	6.0	15	0
Hastings	2	0	15	7.5	12	0
Steelers	56	16	424	7.6	42	0
Opponents	39	23	263	6.7	19	0

KICKOFF RETURNS	No.	Yds.	Avg.	LG	TD
Johnson	16	345	21.6	71	0
Woodson	15	365	24.3	54	0
Stone	11	182	16.5	31	0
Thigpen	5	121	24.2	31	0
Morris	4	114	28.5	45	0
Zgonina	2	8	4.0	8	0
Mills	2	6	3.0	6	0
Steelers	55	1141	20.7	71	0
Opponents	68	1530	22.5	95t	2

SACKS	No.
Greene	14.0
Lloyd	10.0
Brown	8.5
Seals	7.0
Kirkland	3.0
Woodson	3.0
Buckner	2.0
Gildon	2.0
Steed	2.0
G. Williams	1.5
Figures	1.0
Lake	1.0
Steelers	55.0
Opponents	39.0

1995 DRAFT CHOICES

Round	Name	Pos.	College
1	Mark Bruener	TE	Washington
2	Kordell Stewart	QB	Colorado
3	Brenden Stai	G	Nebraska
4	Oliver Gibson	DE	Notre Dame
	Donta Jones	LB	Nebraska
5	Lethon Flowers	DB	Georgia Tech
	Lance Brown	DB	Indiana
6	Barron Miles	DB	Nebraska
7	Henry Bailey	WR	Nevada-Las Vegas
	Cole Ford	K	Southern California

PITTSBURGH STEELERS

1995 VETERAN ROSTER

No.		Name	Pos.	Ht.	Wt.	Birthdate	NFL Exp.	College	Hometown	How Acq.	'94 Games/ Starts
1	#	Anderson, Gary	K	5-11	179	7/16/59	14	Syracuse	Durban, South Africa	W(Buff)-'82	16/0
43		Avery, Steve	RB	6-2	233	8/18/66	2	Northern Michigan	Oconomowoc, Wis.	FA-'93	14/1
80		Barnes, Johnnie	WR	6-1	185	7/21/68	4	Hampton	Suffolk, Va.	FA-'94	11/0*
40		Bell, Myron	S	5-11	203	9/15/71	2	Michigan State	Toledo, Ohio	D5a-'94	15/0
94		Brown, Chad	LB	6-2	236	7/12/70	3	Colorado	Altadena, Calif.	D2-'93	16/16
96		Buckner, Brentson	DE	6-2	305	9/30/71	2	Clemson	Columbus, Ga.	D2-'94	13/5
63		Dawson, Dermontti	C	6-2	286	6/17/65	8	Kentucky	Lexington, Ky.	D2-'88	16/16
78		Faumui, Taase	DE-DT	6-3	278	3/19/71	2	Hawaii	Honolulu, Hawaii	D4-'94	5/0
21		Figures, Deon	CB	6-0	203	1/20/70	3	Colorado	Compton, Calif.	D1-'93	16/15
60		Gammon, Kendall	C	6-4	288	10/23/68	4	Pittsburg State	Wichita, Kan.	FA-'95	16/0
92		Gildon, Jason	LB	6-3	237	7/31/72	2	Oklahoma State	Altus, Okla.	D3a-'94	16/1
91		Greene, Kevin	LB	6-3	247	7/31/62	11	Auburn	Oxford, Ala.	UFA(Rams)-'93	16/16
88		Hastings, Andre	WR	6-0	190	11/7/70	3	Georgia	Atlanta, Ga.	D3-'93	16/8
85		Hayes, Jonathan	TE	6-5	248	8/11/62	11	Iowa	Oxford, Ala.	FA-'94	16/6
76		Henry, Kevin	DE	6-4	270	10/23/68	3	Mississippi State	Mound Bayou, Miss.	D4-'93	16/5
65		Jackson, John	T	6-6	297	1/4/65	8	Eastern Kentucky	Cincinnati, Ohio	D10-'88	16/16
81		Johnson, Charles	WR	6-0	189	1/3/72	2	Colorado	San Bernardino, Calif.	D1-'94	16/9
62		Kalis, Todd	G	6-6	296	5/10/65	8	Arizona State	Phoenix, Ariz.	UFA(Minn)-'94	11/11
87		Keith, Craig	TE	6-3	264	4/27/71	3	Lenoir-Rhyne	Raleigh, N.C.	D7b-'93	16/1
99		Kirkland, Levon	LB	6-1	252	2/17/69	4	Clemson	Lamar, S.C.	D2-'92	16/15
37	†	Lake, Carnell	S	6-1	210	7/15/67	7	UCLA	Inglewood, Calif.	D2-'89	16/16
95		Lloyd, Greg	LB	6-2	226	5/26/65	9	Ft. Valley State	Ft. Valley, Ga.	D6b-'87	15/15
56		Mack, Rico	LB	6-4	242	2/22/71	3	Appalachian State	Statham, Ga.	FA-'93	0*
28		Mays, Alvoid	CB-S	5-9	172	7/10/66	6	West Virginia	Bradenton, Fla.	UFA(Wash)-'95	2/0*
2		Mays, Damon	WR	5-9	170	5/20/68	3	Missouri	Phoenix, Ariz.	FA-'95	0*
25		McAfee, Fred	RB	5-10	193	6/20/68	5	Mississippi	Philadelphia, Miss.	FA-'94	13/0*
16		Miller, Jim	QB	6-2	226	2/9/71	2	Michigan State	Waterford, Mich.	D6a-'94	0*
89		Mills, Ernie	WR	5-11	192	10/28/68	5	Florida	Dunnellon, Fla.	D3-'91	15/6
33		Morris, Byron "Bam"	RB	6-0	235	1/13/72	2	Texas Tech	Cooper, Tex.	D3b-'94	15/6
66		Newberry, Tom	G	6-2	285	12/20/62	10	Wisconsin-La Crosse	Onalaska, Wis.	UFA(Rams)-'95	15/14*
14		O'Donnell, Neil	QB	6-3	230	7/3/66	6	Maryland	Madison, N.J.	D3a-'90	14/14
24		Oldham, Chris	CB	5-9	183	10/28/68	5	Oregon	Sacramento, Calif.	UFA(Ariz)-'94	11/1*
55		Olsavsky, Jerry	LB	6-1	221	3/29/67	7	Pittsburgh	Youngstown, Ohio	FA-'94	1/0
66		Palelei, Siulagi	G	6-3	320	10/15/70	3	Nevada-Las Vegas	Nu'uuli, American Samoa	D5a-'93	0*
79		Parrish, James	T	6-6	320	5/19/68	3	Temple	Jessup, Md.	FA-'95	0*
20		Pegram, Erric	RB	5-9	188	1/7/69	5	North Texas	Dallas, Tex.	UFA(Atl)-'95	13/5*
39	†	Perry, Darren	S	5-11	196	12/29/68	4	Penn State	Deep Creek, Va.	D8a-'92	16/16
84		Rasby, Walter	TE	6-3	247	9/7/72	2	Wake Forest	Washington, N.C.	FA-'94	2/0
57		Ravotti, Eric	LB	6-3	254	3/16/71	2	Penn State	Freeport, Pa.	D6b-'94	2/0
51		Robinson, Ed	LB	6-0	228	12/7/70	2	Florida	DeFuniak Springs, Fla.	FA-'94	16/0
97		Seals, Ray	DE	6-3	309	6/17/65	8	No College	Syracuse, N.Y.	UFA(TB)-'94	13/11
72		Searcy, Leon	T	6-3	304	12/21/69	4	Miami	Orlando, Fla.	D1-'92	16/16
69		Solomon, Ariel	C-G	6-5	290	7/16/68	5	Colorado	Boulder, Colo.	D10-'91	16/0
3		Stark, Rohn	P	6-3	203	5/4/59	14	Florida State	Minneapolis, Minn.	UFA(Ind)-'95	16/0*
93		Steed, Joel	NT	6-2	295	2/17/69	4	Colorado	Denver, Colo.	D3-'92	16/16
73		Strzelczyk, Justin	G-T	6-6	295	8/18/68	6	Maine	Seneca, N.Y.	D11-'90	16/5
82		Thigpen, Yancey	WR	6-1	208	8/15/69	4	Winston-Salem State	Tarboro, N.C.	FA-'92	15/6
48		Thompson, Craig	TE	6-2	250	1/13/69	3	North Carolina A&T	Hartsville, S.C.	FA-'94	0*
18		Tomczak, Mike	QB	6-1	207	10/23/62	11	Ohio State	Calumet City, Ill.	UFA(Clev)-'93	6/2
44		Toner, Ed	RB	6-0	240	3/22/68	4	Boston College	Lynn, Mass.	FA-'95	9/0*
22		Williams, John L.	RB	5-11	231	11/23/64	10	Florida	Palatka, Fla.	UFA(Sea)-'94	15/12
26		Woodson, Rod	CB	6-0	200	3/10/65	9	Purdue	Ft. Wayne, Ind.	D1-'87	15/15
90		Zgonina, Jeff	NT	6-1	287	5/24/70	3	Purdue	Lake Grove, Ill.	D7a-'93	16/0

* Barnes played 11 games with San Diego in '94; Mack missed '94 season because of injury; A. Mays played 2 games with Washington; D. Mays last active with Houston in '93; McAfee played 7 games with Arizona, 6 games with Pittsburgh; Miller and Palelei inactive for 16 games; Newberry played 15 games with L.A. Rams; Oldham played 11 games with Arizona; Parrish inactive with Dallas for 1 game; Pegram played 13 games with Atlanta; Stark played 16 games with Indianapolis; Thompson last active with Cincinnati in '93; Toner played 9 games with Indianapolis.

\# Unrestricted free agent; subject to developments.

† Restricted free agent, subject to developments.

Traded—RB Barry Foster to Carolina.

Players lost through free agency (6): TE Eric Green (Mia; 15 games in '94), S Gary Jones (NYJ; 14), G Duval Love (Ariz; 16), P Mark Royals (Det; 16), WR Dwight Stone (Car; 15), DE Gerald Williams (Car; 11).

Players lost through Expansion Draft (3): WR Charles Davenport (Jax; 7 games in '94), CB-S Fred Foggie (Car; 3), CB Tim McKyer (Car; 16).

Also played with Steelers in '94—LB Reggie Clark (5 games), RB Randy Cuthbert (1), RB Anthony Daigle (1), RB Barry Foster (11), RB Victor Jones (10), P Mark Royals (16), G-C Tim Simpson (4), WR Dwight Stone (15).

COACHING STAFF

Head Coach,
Bill Cowher

Pro Career: Became the fifteenth head coach in Steelers' history on January 21, 1992, succeeding the retired Chuck Noll. Cowher is the second-youngest head coach in the NFL. Named *AP* NFL Coach of the Year in 1992, after becoming one of only 12 coaches in NFL history to win 11 games in his first season. Began his NFL career as a free agent linebacker with the Philadelphia Eagles in 1979, and then signed with the Cleveland Browns the following year. Cowher played three seasons (1980-82) in Cleveland before being traded back to the Eagles, where he played two more years (1983-84). Cowher began his coaching career in 1985 at age 28 under Marty Schottenheimer with the Cleveland Browns. He was the Browns' special teams coach in 1985-86 and secondary coach in 1987-88 before following Schottenheimer to the Kansas City Chiefs in 1989 as defensive coordinator. Career record: 33-19.

Background: Excelled in football, basketball, and track for Carlynton High in Crafton, Pa. Was a three-year starter at linebacker for North Carolina State, serving as captain and earning team MVP honors as senior. Graduated in 1979 with education degree.

Personal: Born in Pittsburgh, Pa., on May 8, 1957. His wife Kaye, also a North Carolina State graduate, played professional basketball for the New York Stars of the Women's Professional Basketball League with twin sister Faye. Bill and Kaye live in Pittsburgh and have three daughters—Meagan Lyn, Lauren Marie, and Lindsay Morgan.

ASSISTANT COACHES

Bobby April, Jr., special teams; born April 15, 1953, New Orleans, La., lives in Pittsburgh. Defensive end/linebacker Nicholls State 1972-75. No pro playing experience. College coach: Tulane 1979, Arizona 1980-86, Southern California 1987-90. Pro coach: Atlanta Falcons 1991-93, joined Steelers in 1994.

Ron Erhardt, offensive coordinator; born February 27, 1931, Mandan, N.D., lives in Pittsburgh. Quarterback Jamestown (N.D.) College 1951-54. No pro playing experience. College coach: North Dakota State 1963-72 (head coach 1966-72). Pro coach: New England Patriots 1973-81 (head coach 1979-81), New York Giants 1982-91, joined Steelers in 1992.

Chan Gailey, wide receivers; born January 5, 1952, Gainesville, Ga., lives in Pittsburgh. Quarterback Florida 1970-73. No pro playing experience. College coach: Troy State 1976-78, 1983-84, Air Force 1979-82, Samford (head coach) 1992. Pro coach: Denver Broncos 1985-90, Birmingham Fire (WL) 1991-92, joined Steelers in 1994.

Dick Hoak, running backs; born December 8, 1939, Jeannette, Pa., lives in Greensburg, Pa. Halfback-quarterback Penn State 1958-60. Pro running back Pittsburgh Steelers 1961-70. Pro coach: Joined Steelers in 1972.

Pat Hodgson, tight ends; born January 30, 1944, Columbus, Ga., lives in Pittsburgh. Tight end Georgia 1963-65. Pro tight end Washington Redskins 1966, Minnesota Vikings 1967. College coach: Georgia 1968-70, 1972-77, Florida State 1971, Texas Tech 1978. Pro coach: San Diego Chargers 1978, New York Giants 1979-87, joined Steelers in 1992.

Dick LeBeau, defensive coordinator; born September 9, 1937, London, Ohio, lives in Pittsburgh. Defensive back-offensive back Ohio State 1954-57. Pro cornerback Detroit Lions 1959-72. Pro coach: Philadelphia Eagles 1972-75, Green Bay Packers 1976-79, Cincinnati Bengals 1980-91, joined Steelers in 1992.

Marvin Lewis, linebackers; born September 23, 1958, McDonald, Pa., lives in Pittsburgh. Linebacker Idaho State 1977-80. No pro playing experience. College coach: Idaho State 1981-84, Long Beach State 1985-86, New Mexico 1987-89, Pittsburgh 1990-91. Pro coach: Joined Steelers in 1992.

Tim Lewis, defensive backs; born December 18, 1961, Quakertown, Pa., lives in Pittsburgh. Defensive back Pittsburgh 1979-82. Pro cornerback Green Bay Packers 1983-86. College coach: Texas A&M 1987-88, Southern Methodist 1989-92, Pittsburgh 1993-94. Pro coach: Joined Steelers in 1995.

John Mitchell, defensive line; born October 14, 1951, Mobile, Ala., lives in Pittsburgh. Defensive end Eastern Arizona J.C. 1969-70, Alabama 1971-72. No pro playing experience. College coach: Alabama 1973-76, Arkansas 1977-82, Temple 1986, Louisiana State 1987-90. Pro coach: Birmingham Stallions (USFL) 1983-85, Cleveland Browns 1991-1993, joined Steelers in 1994.

Kent Stephenson, offensive line; born February 4, 1942, Anita, Iowa, lives in Pittsburgh. Guard-nose tackle Northern Iowa 1962-64. No pro playing experience. College coach: Wayne State 1965-68, North Dakota 1969-71, Southern Methodist 1972-73, Iowa 1974-76, Oklahoma State 1977-78, Kansas 1979-82. Pro coach: Michigan Panthers (USFL) 1983-84, Seattle Seahawks 1985-91, joined Steelers in 1992.

1995 FIRST-YEAR ROSTER

Name	Pos.	Ht.	Wt.	Birthdate	College	Hometown	How Acq.
Bailey, Henry	WR-KR	5-8	176	2/28/73	Nevada-Las Vegas	Chicago, Ill.	D7a
Black, Greg	DT	6-4	306	9/14/73	North Carolina	Gastonia, N.C.	FA
Brown, Lance	CB-S	6-0	200	2/2/72	Indiana	Jacksonville, Fla.	D5b
Bruener, Mark	TE	6-4	250	9/16/72	Washington	Aberdeen, Wash.	D1
Coleman, LaMonte	RB	5-10	227	6/24/71	Slippery Rock	Pittsburgh, Pa.	FA
Daigle, Anthony (1)	RB	5-10	203	4/5/70	Fresno State	Benicia, Calif.	FA
Dinkins, Vincent	C	6-1	291	4/10/72	South Carolina	Columbia, S.C.	FA
Ellis, Joey	CB-S	5-8	194	4/6/73	Texas	Tyler, Tex.	FA
Esters, Jeff (1)	NT	6-2	300	7/6/69	Pittsburgh	Hollywood, Fla.	FA
Flowers, Lethon	CB-S	6-0	202	1/14/73	Georgia Tech	Spring Valley, N.C.	D5a
Ford, Cole	K	6-2	195	12/31/72	Southern California	Tucson, Ariz.	D7b
Gibson, Oliver	DT	6-2	283	3/15/72	Notre Dame	Romeoville, Ill.	D4a
Grant, Doug	WR	5-8	171	2/7/68	Savannah State	Atlanta, Ga.	FA
Greene, Tirrell	G	6-2	305	5/15/72	Miami	Pittsburgh, Pa.	FA
Holden, Germaine	DE	6-3	268	1/17/73	Notre Dame	Anderson, S.C.	FA
Holliday, Corey (1)	WR	6-2	208	1/31/71	North Carolina	Richmond, Va.	FA
Ingrassia, Anthony	T	6-2	313	5/28/72	Florida	Warren, N.J.	FA
Jones, Donta	LB	6-2	226	8/27/72	Nebraska	Pomfret, Md.	D4b
Mays, Damon (1)	WR	5-9	170	5/20/68	Missouri	Phoenix, Ariz.	FA
Miles, Barron	CB-S	5-8	165	1/1/72	Nebraska	Roselle, N.J.	D6
Parrish, James (1)	G-T	6-6	320	5/19/68	Temple	Jessup, Md.	FA
Patillo, Tim	CB-S	5-10	179	5/24/72	Ohio State	Aliquippa, Pa.	FA
Phillips, Kiefer	LB	6-0	264	9/11/72	Grambling State	Baton Rouge, La.	FA
Simpson, Tim (1)	G-C	6-2	284	3/5/69	Illinois	Peoria, Ill.	FA
Stai, Brenden	G	6-4	305	3/30/72	Nebraska	Anaheim, Calif.	D3
Stewart, Kordell	QB	6-1	212	10/16/72	Colorado	Marrero, La.	D2
Stewart, Ty	K	5-11	194	9/13/71	Iowa State	Omaha, Neb.	FA

The term NFL Rookie is defined as a player who is in his first season of professional football and has not been on the roster of another professional football team for any regular-season or postseason games. A Rookie is designated by an "R" on NFL rosters. Players who have been active in another professional football league or players who have NFL experience, including either preseason training camp or being on an Active List or Inactive List, or on Reserve/Injured or Reserve/Physically Unable to Perform for fewer than six regular-season games, are termed NFL First-Year Players. An NFL First-Year Player is designated by a "1" on NFL rosters. Thereafter, a player is credited with an additional year of experience for each season in which he accumulates six games on the Active List or Inactive List, or on Reserve/Injured or Reserve/Physically Unable to Perform.

NOTES

SAN DIEGO CHARGERS

American Football Conference
Western Division
Team Colors: Navy Blue, White, and Gold
San Diego Jack Murphy Stadium
P.O. Box 609609
San Diego, California 92160-9609
Telephone: (619) 280-2111

CLUB OFFICIALS

Chairman of the Board: Alex G. Spanos
President-Vice Chairman: Dean A. Spanos
Executive Vice President: Michael A. Spanos
General Manager: Bobby Beathard
Vice President-Finance: Jeremiah T. Murphy
Assistant General Manager: Dick Daniels
Director of Player Personnel: Billy Devaney
Director of Pro Personnel: Rudy Feldman
Coordinator of Football Operations: Marty Hurney
Business Manager: John Hinek
Director of Public Relations: Bill Johnston
Chief Financial Officer: Jeanne Bonk
Director of Marketing: Rich Israel
Director of Ticket Operations: Ron Tuck
Video Director: Gene Leff
Head Trainer: Keoki Kamau
Equipment Manager: Sid Brooks
Stadium: San Diego Jack Murphy Stadium
Capacity: 60,794
9449 Friars Road
San Diego, California 92108
Playing Surface: Grass
Training Camp: University of California-San Diego
Third College
La Jolla, California 92037

1995 SCHEDULE

PRESEASON

Aug. 7	**Minnesota**	5:00
Aug. 13	**San Francisco**	5:00
Aug. 19	at Houston	7:30
Aug. 25	**St. Louis**	7:30

REGULAR SEASON

Sept. 3	at Los Angeles	1:00
Sept. 10	**Seattle**	1:00
Sept. 17	at Philadelphia	1:00
Sept. 24	**Denver**	1:00
Oct. 1	at Pittsburgh	4:00
Oct. 9	at Kansas City (Monday)	8:00
Oct. 15	**Dallas**	1:00
Oct. 22	at Seattle	1:00
Oct. 29	Open Date	
Nov. 5	**Miami**	5:00
Nov. 12	**Kansas City**	1:00
Nov. 19	at Denver	2:00
Nov. 27	**Los Angeles** (Monday)	6:00
Dec. 3	**Cleveland**	1:00
Dec. 9	**Arizona** (Saturday)	1:00
Dec. 17	at Indianapolis	4:00
Dec. 23	at New York Giants (Saturday)	12:30

RECORD HOLDERS

INDIVIDUAL RECORDS—CAREER

Category	Name	Performance
Rushing (Yds.)	Paul Lowe, 1960-67	4,963
Passing (Yds.)	Dan Fouts, 1973-1987	43,040
Passing (TDs)	Dan Fouts, 1973-1987	254
Receiving (No.)	Charlie Joiner, 1976-1986	586
Receiving (Yds.)	Lance Alworth, 1962-1970	9,585
Interceptions	Gill Byrd, 1983-1992	42
Punting (Avg.)	Ralf Mojsiejenko, 1985-88	42.9
Punt Return (Avg.)	Leslie (Speedy) Duncan, 1964-1970	12.3
Kickoff Return (Avg.)	Leslie (Speedy) Duncan, 1964-1970	25.2
Field Goals	Rolf Benirschke, 1977-1986	146
Touchdowns (Tot.)	Lance Alworth, 1962-1970	83
Points	Rolf Benirschke, 1977-1986	766

INDIVIDUAL RECORDS—SINGLE SEASON

Category	Name	Performance
Rushing (Yds.)	Natrone Means, 1994	1,350
Passing (Yds.)	Dan Fouts, 1981	4,802
Passing (TDs)	Dan Fouts, 1981	33
Receiving (No.)	Kellen Winslow, 1980	89
Receiving (Yds.)	Lance Alworth, 1965	1,602
Interceptions	Charlie McNeil, 1961	9
Punting (Avg.)	Dennis Partee, 1969	44.6
Punt Return (Avg.)	Leslie (Speedy) Duncan, 1965	15.5
Kickoff Return (Avg.)	Keith Lincoln, 1962	28.4
Field Goals	John Carney, 1994	34
Touchdowns (Tot.)	Chuck Muncie, 1981	19
Points	John Carney, 1994	135

INDIVIDUAL RECORDS—SINGLE GAME

Category	Name	Performance
Rushing (Yds.)	Gary Anderson, 12-18-88	217
Passing (Yds.)	Dan Fouts, 10-19-80	444
	Dan Fouts, 12-11-82	444
Passing (TDs)	Dan Fouts, 11-22-81	6
Receiving (No.)	Kellen Winslow, 10-7-84	15
Receiving (Yds.)	Wes Chandler, 12-20-82	260
Interceptions	Many times	3
	Last time by Pete Shaw, 11-2-80	
Field Goals	John Carney, 9-5-93	6
	John Carney, 9-18-93	6
Touchdowns (Tot.)	Kellen Winslow, 11-22-81	5
Points	Kellen Winslow, 11-22-81	30

COACHING HISTORY

(263-259-11)

1960-69	Sid Gillman*	83-51-6
1969-70	Charlie Waller	9-7-3
1971	Sid Gillman**	4-6-0
1971-73	Harland Svare***	7-17-2
1973	Ron Waller	1-5-0
1974-78	Tommy Prothro****	21-39-0
1978-86	Don Coryell#	72-60-0
1986-88	Al Saunders	17-22-0
1989-91	Dan Henning	16-32-0
1992-94	Bobby Ross	33-20-0

*Retired after nine games in 1969
**Resigned after 10 games in 1971
***Resigned after eight games in 1973
****Resigned after four games in 1978
#Resigned after eight games in 1986

SAN DIEGO JACK MURPHY STADIUM

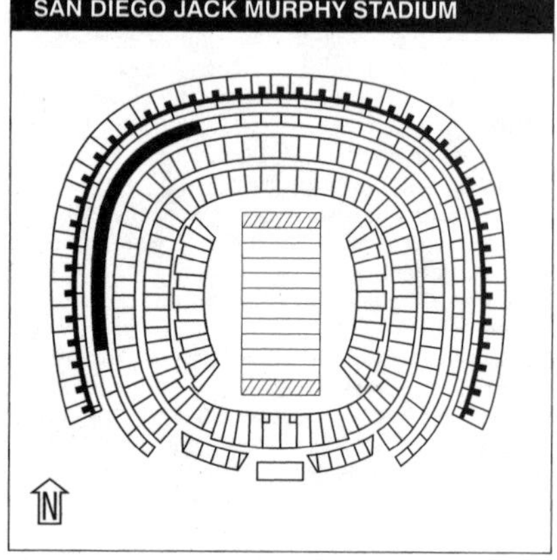

1994 TEAM RECORD

PRESEASON (1-4)

Date	Result		Opponents
7/30	L	17-21	vs. Atlanta at Canton
8/6	L	3-31	vs. Houston at San Antonio
8/13	L	20-28	vs. N.Y. Giants at Berlin
8/18	L	24-30	San Francisco
8/25	W	24-6	L.A. Rams

REGULAR SEASON (11-5)

Date	Result		Opponents	Att.
9/4	W	37-34	at Denver	74,032
9/11	W	27-10	Cincinnati	53,217
9/18	W	24-10	at Seattle	65,536
9/25	W	26-24	at L.A. Raiders	55,385
10/9	W	20- 6	Kansas City	62,923
10/16	W	36-22	at New Orleans	50,565
10/23	L	15-20	Denver	61,626
10/30	W	35-15	Seattle	59,001
11/6	L	9-10	at Atlanta	59,217
11/13	W	14-13	at Kansas City	76,997
11/20	L	17-23	at New England	59,690
11/27	W	31-17	L.A. Rams	59,579
12/5	L	17-24	L.A. Raiders	63,012
12/11	L	15-38	San Francisco	62,105
12/18	W	21- 6	at N.Y. Jets	48,213
12/24	W	37-34	Pittsburgh	58,379

POSTSEASON (2-1)

1/8	W	22-21	Miami	63,381
1/15	W	17-13	at Pittsburgh	61,545
1/29	L	26-49	San Francisco	74,107

(OT) Overtime

SCORE BY PERIODS

Chargers	52	134	95	100	0	—	381
Opponents	51	104	46	105	0	—	306

ATTENDANCE

Home 479,842 Away 489,635 Total 969,477
Single-game home record, 64,411 (12-15-84)
Single-season home record, 494,103 (1988)

1994 TEAM STATISTICS

	Chargers	Opp.
Total First Downs	311	308
Rushing	102	89
Passing	181	191
Penalty	28	28
Third Down: Made/Att	88/223	77/210
Third Down Pct.	39.5	36.7
Fourth Down: Made/Att	10/17	13/25
Fourth Down Pct.	58.8	52.0
Total Net Yards	5220	5062
Avg. Per Game	326.3	316.4
Total Plays	1033	1005
Avg. Per Play	5.1	5.0
Net Yards Rushing	1852	1404
Avg. Per Game	115.8	87.8
Total Rushes	482	385
Net Yards Passing	3368	3658
Avg. Per Game	210.5	228.6
Sacked/Yards Lost	29/251	43/253
Gross Yards	3619	3911
Att./Completions	522/305	577/363
Completion Pct.	58.4	62.9
Had Intercepted	14	17
Punts/Avg.	72/41.0	76/43.3
Net Punting Avg.	72/35.0	76/36.0
Penalties/Yards Lost	96/875	109/989
Fumbles/Ball Lost	19/9	29/15
Touchdowns	40	34
Rushing	13	11
Passing	20	20
Returns	7	3
Average Time of Possession	30:19	29:41

1994 INDIVIDUAL STATISTICS

PASSING	Att.	Comp.	Yds.	Pct.	TD	Int.	Tkld.	Rate
Humphries	453	264	3209	58.3	17	12	25/223	81.6
Gilbert	67	41	410	61.2	3	1	4/28	87.3
Martin	1	0	0	0.0	0	1	0/0	0.0
Means	1	0	0	0.0	0	0	0/0	39.6
Chargers	522	305	3619	58.4	20	14	29/251	81.3
Opponents	577	363	3911	62.9	20	17	43/253	82.0

SCORING	TD R	TD P	TD Rt	PAT	FG	Saf	PTS
Carney	0	0	0	33/33	34/38	0	135
Means	12	0	0	0/0	0/0	0	72
Martin	0	7	0	0/0	0/0	0	42
Seay	0	6	0	0/0	0/0	0	36
Harmon	1	1	0	0/0	0/0	0	18
Jefferson	0	3	0	0/0	0/0	0	18
Coleman	0	0	2	0/0	0/0	0	12
Gordon	0	0	2	0/0	0/0	0	12
Pupunu	0	2	0	0/0	0/0	0	12
Richard	0	0	2	0/0	0/0	0	12
Vanhorse	0	0	1	0/0	0/0	0	6
D. Young	0	1	0	0/0	0/0	0	6
Chargers	13	20	7	33/33	34/38	0	381
Opponents	11	20	3	30/30	22/27	0	306

2-Point conversions: Harmon (3). Team: 3-7.

RUSHING	Att.	Yds.	Avg.	LG	TD
Means	343	1350	3.9	25	12
Bieniemy	73	295	4.0	36	0
Harmon	25	94	3.8	15t	1
Culver	8	63	7.9	22	0
Jefferson	3	40	13.3	22	0
Humphries	19	19	1.0	8	0
Hendrickson	1	3	3.0	3	0
Gilbert	8	-3	-0.4	5	0
Martin	2	-9	-4.5	4	0
Chargers	482	1852	3.8	36	13
Opponents	385	1404	3.6	24	11

RECEIVING	No.	Yds.	Avg.	LG	TD
Seay	58	645	11.1	49t	6
Harmon	58	615	10.6	35	1
Martin	50	885	17.7	99t	7
Jefferson	43	627	14.6	52t	3
Means	39	235	6.0	22	0
Pupunu	21	214	10.2	25	2
D. Young	17	217	12.8	31	1
Mitchell	11	105	9.5	36	0
Bieniemy	5	48	9.6	25	0
May	2	22	11.0	18	0
Barnes	1	6	6.0	6	0
Chargers	305	3619	11.9	99t	20
Opponents	363	3911	10.8	84t	20

INTERCEPTIONS	No.	Yds.	Avg.	LG	TD
Richard	4	224	56.0	99t	2
Gordon	4	32	8.0	23	0
Carrington	3	51	17.0	32	0
Harper	3	28	9.3	15	0
Vanhorse	2	56	28.0	50t	1
Griggs	1	11	11.0	11	0
Chargers	17	402	23.6	99t	3
Opponents	14	233	16.6	90t	2

PUNTING	No.	Yds.	Avg.	In 20	LG
Wagner	65	2705	41.6	20	59
Kidd	7	246	35.1	1	53
Chargers	72	2951	41.0	21	59
Opponents	76	3290	43.3	19	62

PUNT RETURNS	No.	FC	Yds.	Avg.	LG	TD
Gordon	36	19	475	13.2	90t	2
Chargers	36	19	475	13.2	90t	2
Opponents	38	14	348	9.2	44	0

KICKOFF RETURNS	No.	Yds.	Avg.	LG	TD
Coleman	49	1293	26.4	90t	2
Harmon	9	157	17.4	25	0
Martin	8	167	20.9	29	0
Mitchell	1	18	18.0	18	0
Parker	1	1	1.0	1	0
Chargers	68	1636	24.1	90t	2
Opponents	79	1740	22.0	93t	1

SACKS	No.
O'Neal	12.5
Mims	11.0
Lee	6.5
Seau	5.5
White	2.0
Johnson	1.5
Parrella	1.0
L. Young	1.0
R. Davis	0.5
L. Miller	0.5
Chargers	43.0
Opponents	29.0

1995 DRAFT CHOICES

Round	Name	Pos.	College
2	Terrance Shaw	DB	Stephen F. Austin
	Terrell Fletcher	RB	Wisconsin
	Jimmy Oliver	WR	Texas Christian
3	Don Sasa	DT	Washington State
	Preston Harrison	LB	Ohio State
4	Chris Cowart	LB	Florida State
	Aaron Hayden	RB	Tennessee
5	'OMar Ellison	WR	Florida State
6	Troy Sienkiewicz	G	New Mexico State
	Brandon Harrison	WR	Howard Payne
	Craig Whelihan	QB	Pacific
	Tony Berti	T	Colorado
7	Mark Montreuil	DB	Concordia, Canada

SAN DIEGO CHARGERS

1995 VETERAN ROSTER

No.	Name	Pos.	Ht.	Wt.	Birthdate	NFL Exp.	College	Hometown	How Acq.	'94 Games/ Starts
39	Allred, Brian	CB	5-10	180	3/16/69	2	Sacramento State	Washington, D.C.	FA-'94	0*
50	Binn, David	TE	6-3	240	2/6/72	2	California	San Mateo, Calif.	FA-'94	16/0
67	Brock, Stan	T	6-6	295	6/8/58	16	Colorado	Portland, Ore.	UFA(NO)-'93	16/16
11	Brohm, Jeff	QB	6-1	200	4/24/71	2	Louisville	Louisville, Ky.	FA-'94	0*
58	Bush, Lewis	LB	6-2	245	12/2/69	3	Washington State	Tacoma, Wash.	D4b-'93	16/0
3	Carney, John	K	5-11	170	4/20/64	6	Notre Dame	West Palm Beach, Fla.	FA-'90	16/0
44	Castle, Eric	S	6-3	212	3/15/70	3	Oregon	Lebanon, Ore.	D6-'93	16/1
31	Clark, Willie	CB	5-10	186	1/6/72	2	Notre Dame	Wheatland, Calif.	D3b-'94	6/0
68	Cocozzo, Joe	G	6-4	300	8/7/70	3	Michigan	Mechanicville, N.Y.	D3-'93	13/13
83	Coleman, Andre	WR-KR	5-9	165	1/18/71	2	Kansas State	Hermitage, Pa.	D3a-'94	13/0
35	Culver, Rodney	RB	5-9	224	12/23/69	4	Notre Dame	Detroit, Mich.	W(Ind)-'94	3/0
73	Davis, Isaac	G	6-3	320	4/8/72	2	Arkansas	Malvern, Ark.	D2a-'94	13/2
93	Davis, Reuben	DT	6-5	320	5/7/65	8	North Carolina	Greensboro, N.C.	UFA(Ariz)-'94	16/16
60	Engel, Greg	C	6-3	285	1/18/71	2	Illinois	Bloomington, Ill.	FA-'94	0*
23	Gayle, Shaun	S	5-11	202	3/8/62	12	Ohio State	Bethel, Va.	UFA(Chi)-'95	16/16*
57	Gibson, Dennis	LB	6-2	240	2/8/64	9	Iowa State	Ankeny, Iowa	UFA(Det)-'94	16/15
13	Gilbert, Gale	QB	6-3	209	12/20/61	10	California	Red Bluff, Calif.	UFA(Buff)-'94	15/1
21	Gordon, Darrien	CB	5-11	182	11/14/70	3	Stanford	Shawnee, Okla.	D1-'93	16/16
66	Greene, Earnest	T	6-5	308	2/25/71	2	Savannah State	Savannah, Ga.	FA-'94	0*
92	Griggs, David	LB	6-3	250	2/5/67	6	Virginia	Miami Beach, Fla.	UFA(Mia)-'94	16/15
53	Hall, Courtney	C	6-1	281	8/26/68	7	Rice	Wilmington, Calif.	D2a-'89	15/15
33	Harmon, Ronnie	RB	5-11	207	5/7/64	10	Iowa	Queens, N.Y.	PB(Buff)-'90	16/0
28	Harper, Dwayne	CB	5-11	175	3/29/66	8	South Carolina State	Orangeburg, S.C.	UFA(Sea)-'94	16/16
37	Harrison, Rodney	S	6-0	201	12/15/72	2	Western Illinois	Marion, Ill.	D5b-'94	15/0
34	# Hendrickson, Steve	LB	6-0	250	8/30/66	7	California	Napa, Calif.	FA-'94	16/0
12	Humphries, Stan	QB	6-2	223	4/14/65	7	Northeast Louisiana	Shreveport, La.	T(Wash)-'92	15/15
80	Jefferson, Shawn	WR	5-11	180	2/22/69	5	Central Florida	Jacksonville, Fla.	T(Hou)-'91	16/16
99	Johnson, Raylee	DE-DT	6-3	265	6/1/70	3	Arkansas	Fordyce, Ark.	D4a-'93	15/0
74	† Jonassen, Eric	T	6-5	310	8/16/68	4	Bloomsburg College	Glen Burnie, Md.	D5c-'92	16/0
56	Krein, Darren	LB	6-4	272	7/7/71	2	Miami	Aurora, Colo.	D5c-'94	0*
84	Laing, Aaron	TE	6-3	264	7/19/71	2	New Mexico State	Houston, Tex.	D5a-'94	5/1
98	Lee, Shawn	DT	6-2	300	10/24/66	8	North Alabama	Brooklyn, N.Y.	FA-'92	15/15
81	Martin, Tony	WR	6-0	181	9/5/65	6	Mesa, Colo.	Miami, Fla.	T(Mia)-'94	16/1
88	May, Deems	TE	6-4	263	3/6/69	4	North Carolina	Lexington, N.C.	D7-'92	5/2
20	Means, Natrone	RB	5-10	245	4/26/72	3	North Carolina	Harrisburg, N.C.	D2-'93	16/16
71	# Milinichik, Joe	G	6-5	300	3/30/63	10	North Carolina State	Emmaus, Pa.	UFA(Rams)-'93	16/16
94	Mims, Chris	DE	6-5	290	9/29/70	4	Tennessee	Los Angeles, Calif.	D1-'92	16/16
89	Mitchell, Shannon	TE	6-2	245	3/28/72	2	Georgia	Alcoa, Tenn.	FA-'94	16/6
77	Moten, Eric	G-T	6-2	306	4/11/68	5	Michigan State	Cleveland Heights, Ohio	D2c-'91	0*
91	O'Neal, Leslie	DE	6-4	265	5/7/64	10	Oklahoma State	Little Rock, Ark.	D1a-'86	16/16
26	Orlando, Bo	S	5-10	180	4/3/66	6	West Virgina	Berwick, Pa.	UFA(Hou)-'95	16/0*
70	Parker, Vaughn	T	6-3	296	6/5/71	2	UCLA	Buffalo, N.Y.	D2b-'94	6/0
97	Parrella, John	DT	6-3	290	11/22/69	3	Nebraska	Topeka, Kan.	FA-'94	13/1
27	Pool, David	CB	5-9	184	12/20/66	5	Carson-Newman	Cincinnati, Ohio	FA-'95	1/0*
86	Pupunu, Alfred	TE	6-2	265	10/17/69	4	Weber State	Salt Lake City, Utah	W(KC)-'92	13/10
55	Seau, Junior	LB	6-3	250	1/19/69	6	Southern California	Oceanside, Calif.	D1-'90	16/16
82	Seay, Mark	WR	6-0	175	4/11/67	3	Long Beach State	San Bernardino, Calif.	W(SF)-'93	16/14
72	Swayne, Harry	T	6-5	295	2/2/65	9	Rutgers	Philadelphia, Pa.	PB(TB)-'91	16/16
79	Thomas, Cornell	DE	6-3	270	11/11/72	2	West Georgia	Norcross, Ga.	FA-'94	0*
75	Vander Poel, Mark	T	6-7	303	3/6/68	5	Colorado	Upland, Calif.	UFA(Ariz)-'95	0*
9	# Wagner, Bryan	P	6-2	200	3/28/62	8	Cal State-Northridge	Chula Vista, Calif.	FA-'94	14/0
87	Young, Duane	TE	6-1	270	5/29/68	5	Michigan State	Kalamazoo, Mich.	D5-'91	14/14

* Allred last active with Seattle in '93; Brohm, Engel, and Thomas inactive for 16 games in '94; Gayle played 16 games with Chicago; Greene, Krein, and Moten missed '94 season because of injury; Orlando played 16 games with Houston; Pool played 1 game with Miami; Vander Poel active with Arizona for 2 games but did not play.

Unrestricted free agent; subject to developments.

† Restricted free agent; subject to developments.

Players lost through free agency (2): RB Eric Bieniemy (Cin; 16 games in '94), S Stanley Richard (Wash; 16).

Players lost through Expansion Draft (2): S Darren Carrington (Jax; 16 games in '94), C Curtis Whitley (Car; 12).

Also played with Chargers in '94—WR Johnnie Barnes (12 games), P John Kidd (2), LB Doug Miller (15), DE-DT Les Miller (4), CB Sean Vanhorse (16), DT Reggie White (12), DT Blaise Winter (2), S Lonnie Young (12).

COACHING STAFF

Head Coach,
Bobby Ross

Pro Career: Begins fourth season as San Diego's head coach. In 1994, led the Chargers to an 11-5 regular-season record, second AFC Western Division title in the last three years, and first-ever AFC Championship. Named ninth head coach in Chargers' history on January 2, 1992. Ross began his pro coaching career in 1978 as an assistant with the Kansas City Chiefs, where he coached special teams and defense in 1978-79 and offensive backs in 1980-81. No pro playing experience. Career record: 33-20.
Background: Played quarterback and defensive back for Virginia Military Institute. Began coaching career in 1965 at VMI. Moved on as an assistant at William & Mary 1967-70, Rice 1971, and Maryland 1972. Head coach at The Citadel 1973-77. Compiled 39-19-1 (.672) record as he led Maryland (1982-86) to three Atlantic Coast Conference titles and made four bowl game appearances in five seasons. Guided Georgia Tech (1987-91) to first ACC title in school history. Under Ross, the Yellow Jackets won first national championship as country's only undefeated team (11-0-1) in 1990. Named consensus national coach of the year in 1990. Career collegiate head coaching record: 94-76-2.
Personal: Born December 23, 1936, Richmond, Va. Bobby and wife, Alice, live in San Diego and have five children—Chris, Kevin, Robbie, Mary, and Teresa.

ASSISTANT COACHES

Dave Adolph, defensive coordinator; born June 6, 1937, Akron, Ohio, lives in San Diego. Guard-linebacker Akron 1955-58. No pro playing experience. College coach: Akron 1963-64, Connecticut 1965-68, Kentucky 1969-72, Illinois 1973-76, Ohio State 1977-78. Pro coach: Cleveland Browns 1979-84, 1986-88, San Diego Chargers 1985, Los Angeles Raiders 1989-91, Kansas City Chiefs 1992-94, rejoined Chargers in 1995.
Greg Brown, secondary; born October 10, 1957, Denver, Colo., lives in San Diego. Defensive back Texas-El Paso 1978-79. No pro playing experience. College coach: Wyoming 1987-88, Purdue 1989-90, Colorado 1991-93. Pro coach: Denver Gold (USFL) 1983-84, Tampa Bay Buccaneers 1984-86, Atlanta Falcons 1994, joined Chargers in 1995.
Sylvester Croom, offensive backs; born September 25, 1954, Tuscaloosa, Ala., lives in San Diego. Center Alabama 1971-74. Pro center New Orleans Saints 1975. College coach: Alabama 1976-86. Pro coach: Tampa Bay Buccaneers 1987-90, Indianapolis Colts 1991, joined Chargers in 1992.
John Dunn, strength and conditioning; born July 22, 1956, Hillsdale, N.Y., lives in San Diego. Guard Penn State 1974-77. No pro playing experience. College coach: Penn State 1978. Pro coach: Washington Redskins 1984-86, Los Angeles Raiders 1987-89, joined Chargers in 1990.
Frank Falks, H-Backs-tight ends; born March 9, 1943, Tampa, Fla., lives in San Diego. Linebacker Joplin (Missouri) J.C. 1963-64, Parsons College 1965-66. No pro playing experience. College coach: Parsons College 1967-69, Kansas State 1970-72, Arkansas 1973-77, Wyoming 1978-79, San Diego State 1980, Oklahoma State 1981-82, Southern California 1983-86, Arizona State 1987-91, Ohio State 1992-93. Pro coach: Joined Chargers in 1994.
Ralph Friedgen, offensive coordinator; born April 4, 1947, Harrison, N.Y., lives in San Diego. Guard Maryland 1967-68. No pro playing experience. College coach: The Citadel 1973-79, William & Mary 1980, Murray State 1981, Maryland 1982-86, Georgia Tech 1987-91. Pro coach: Joined Chargers in 1992.
Dale Lindsey, linebackers; born January 18, 1943, Bedford, Ind., lives in San Diego. Linebacker Western Kentucky 1961-64. Pro linebacker Cleveland Browns 1965-73. College coach: Southern Methodist 1988-89. Pro coach: Cleveland Browns 1974, Portland Storm (WFL) 1975, Toronto Argonauts (CFL) 1979-82, Boston Breakers (USFL) 1983, New Jersey Generals (USFL) 1984-85, Green Bay Packers 1986-87, New England Patriots 1990, Tampa Bay Buccaneers 1991, joined Chargers in 1992.
Carl Mauck, offensive line; born July 7, 1947, McLeansboro, Ill., lives in San Diego. Linebacker-center Southern Illinois 1966-68. Pro center Baltimore Colts 1969, Miami Dolphins 1970, San Diego Chargers 1971-74, Houston Oilers 1975-81. Pro coach: New Orleans Saints 1982-85, Kansas City Chiefs 1986-88, Tampa Bay Buccaneers 1991, joined Chargers in 1992.
John Misciagna, quality control; born December 11, 1954, Brooklyn, N.Y., lives in San Diego. Guard Dickinson College 1973-76. No pro playing experience. College coach: Indiana (Pa.) University 1977, Columbia 1978-79, Maryland 1980-88, Georgia Tech 1989-91. Pro coach: Joined Chargers in 1992.
Dennis Murphy, defensive line; born October 22, 1940, Endicott, N.Y., lives in San Diego. Tight end-defensive lineman Notre Dame 1959-61. No pro playing experience. College coach: Notre Dame 1968-74, Colgate 1975, Holy Cross 1976-77, Eastern Michigan 1978-81, Maryland 1982-91, Navy 1992-93. Pro coach: Joined Chargers in 1994.
Dwain Painter, quarterbacks; born February 13, 1942, Monroeville, Pa., lives in San Diego. Quarterback-defensive back Rutgers 1961-64. No pro playing experience. College coach: San Jose State 1971-72, UCLA 1976-78, Northern Arizona 1979-81 (head coach), Georgia Tech 1982-85, Texas 1986, Illinois 1987. Pro coach: Pittsburgh Steelers 1988-91, Indianapolis Colts 1992-93, joined Chargers in 1994.
Chuck Priefer, special teams; born July 26, 1943, Cleveland, Ohio, lives in San Diego. No college or pro playing experience. College coach: Miami (Ohio) 1977, North Carolina 1978-83, Kent State 1986, Georgia Tech 1987-91. Pro coach: Green Bay Packers 1984-85, joined Chargers in 1992.
Jerry Sullivan, wide receivers; born July 13, 1944, Miami, Fla., lives in San Diego. Quarterback Florida State 1963-64. No pro playing experience. College coach: Kansas State 1971-72, Texas Tech 1973-75, South Carolina 1976-82, Indiana 1983, Louisiana State 1984-90, Ohio State 1991. Pro coach: Joined Chargers in 1992.

1995 FIRST-YEAR ROSTER

Name	Pos.	Ht.	Wt.	Birthdate	College	Hometown	How Acq.
Araguz, Leo (1)	P	6-0	185	1/18/70	Stephen F. Austin	Harlingen, Tex.	FA
Bennett, Darren (1)	P	6-5	235	1/9/65	No College	Western, Australia	FA
Berti, Tony	T	6-5	287	6/21/72	Colorado	Thornton, Colo.	D6d
Brown, Charlie	RB	5-9	200	10/22/71	Utah	San Diego, Calif.	FA
Campbell, David	DT	6-0	280	1/16/73	Oklahoma	Terrell, Tex.	FA
Cavil, Ben	G	6-2	310	1/31/72	Oklahoma	LaMarque, Tex.	FA
Cowart, Chris	LB	6-2	232	6/14/71	Florida State	New Orleans, La.	D4a
Edwards, Vernon	DE	6-4	255	6/23/72	Southern Methodist	Houston, Tex.	FA
Ellison, 'OMar	WR	6-1	200	10/8/71	Florida State	Griffin, Ga.	D5
Fletcher, Terrell	RB	5-8	196	9/14/73	Wisconsin	St. Louis, Mo.	D2b
Harrell, Maurice	TE	6-4	245	4/10/72	Georgia	Eastman, Ga.	FA
Harrison, Brandon	WR	5-10	181	9/10/71	Howard Payne	Dallas, Tex.	D6b
Harrison, Preston	LB	6-4	243	9/14/71	Ohio State	Columbus, Ohio	D3b
Hayden, Aaron	RB	6-0	218	4/13/73	Tennessee	Detroit, Mich.	D4b
Hendrix, David	S	6-1	213	5/29/72	Georgia Tech	Norcross, Ga.	FA
Holland, Melvin	S	6-2	180	9/2/72	Florida State	Miami, Fla.	FA
Huzzie, Tracy	DT	6-4	300	5/24/70	Georgia	La Grange, Ga.	FA
Kahl, Kent	RB	6-1	217	9/21/71	Iowa	Ft. Morgan, Colo.	FA
Montgomery, Bill	S	6-0	186	12/23/70	Georgia	Carrollton, Ga.	FA
Montreuil, Mark	CB	6-2	200	12/29/71	Concordia, Canada	Montreal, Canada	D7
Oliver, Jimmy	WR	5-10	173	1/30/73	Texas Christian	Dallas, Tex.	D2c
Parker, Riddick	DT	6-3	274	11/20/72	North Carolina	Southhampton, Va.	FA
Proctor, Basil (1)	LB	6-3	243	10/6/67	West Virginia	Miami, Fla.	FA
Sasa, Don	DT	6-3	286	9/16/72	Washington State	Long Beach, Calif.	D3a
Shaw, Terrance	CB	5-11	190	11/11/73	Stephen F. Austin	Marshall, Tex.	D2a
Sienkiewicz, Troy	T	6-4	300	5/27/72	New Mexico State	Alamogordo, N.M.	D6a
Simon, Damon	DE	6-5	251	6/16/70	Missouri	Cerritos, Calif.	FA
Slovacek, Gerald	C	6-1	282	6/26/72	New Mexico State	Dallas, Tex.	FA
Thymes, Derrick	WR	5-11	180	1/14/72	Louisiana State	North Iberville, La.	FA
Watkins, Michael	WR	5-9	173	12/28/71	Northeast Louisiana	Hickory, N.C.	FA
Whelihan, Craig	QB	6-5	204	4/15/71	Pacific	San Jose, Calif.	D6c
Young, Glen (1)	LB	6-3	240	5/2/69	Syracuse	Scarboro, Canada	FA

The term NFL Rookie is defined as a player who is in his first season of professional football and has not been on the roster of another professional football team for any regular-season or postseason games. A Rookie is designated by an "R" on NFL rosters. Players who have been active in another professional football league or players who have NFL experience, including either preseason training camp or being on an Active List or Inactive List, or on Reserve/Injured or Reserve/Physically Unable to Perform for fewer than six regular-season games, are termed NFL First-Year Players. An NFL First-Year Player is designated by a "1" on NFL rosters. Thereafter, a player is credited with an additional year of experience for each season in which he accumulates six games on the Active List or Inactive List, or on Reserve/Injured or Reserve/Physically Unable to Perform.

NOTES

SEATTLE SEAHAWKS

American Football Conference
Western Division
Team Colors: Blue, Green, and Silver
11220 N.E. 53rd Street
Kirkland, Washington 98033
Telephone: (206) 827-9777

CLUB OFFICIALS

Owner: Ken Behring
President: David Behring
Executive Vice President: Mickey Loomis
Vice President/Administration and Communications: Gary Wright
Player Personnel Director: Mike Allman
Public Relations Director: Dave Neubert
Community Relations Director: Sandy Gregory
Sales and Marketing Director: Reggie McKenzie
Assistant Public Relations Director: Steve Wright
Information Systems Director: Sterling Monroe
Ticket Manager: James Nagaoka
Trainer: Jim Whitesel
Equipment Manager: Terry Sinclair
Team Physicians: Dr. Kevin Auld, Dr. Stan Herring, Dr. Pierce Scranton, Dr. James Trombold
Stadium: Kingdome • **Capacity:** 66,400
201 South King Street
Seattle, Washington 98104
Playing Surface: AstroTurf
Training Camp: 11220 N.E. 53rd Street
Kirkland, Washington 98033

1995 SCHEDULE

PRESEASON

Aug. 5	**St. Louis**	7:00
Aug. 12	**Indianapolis**	7:00
Aug. 20	at New Orleans	12:00
Aug. 26	at San Francisco	5:00

REGULAR SEASON

Sept. 3	**Kansas City**	1:00
Sept. 10	at San Diego	1:00
Sept. 17	**Cincinnati**	1:00
Sept. 24	Open Date	
Oct. 1	**Denver**	1:00
Oct. 8	at Los Angeles	1:00
Oct. 15	at Buffalo	1:00
Oct. 22	**San Diego**	1:00
Oct. 29	at Arizona	2:00
Nov. 5	**New York Giants**	1:00
Nov. 12	at Jacksonville	1:00
Nov. 19	at Washington	1:00
Nov. 26	**New York Jets**	1:00
Dec. 3	**Philadelphia**	1:00
Dec. 10	at Denver	2:00
Dec. 17	**Los Angeles**	5:00
Dec. 24	at Kansas City	12:00

RECORD HOLDERS

INDIVIDUAL RECORDS—CAREER

Category	Name	Performance
Rushing (Yds.)	Curt Warner, 1983-89	6,705
Passing (Yds.)	Dave Krieg, 1980-1991	26,132
Passing (TDs)	Dave Krieg, 1980-1991	195
Receiving (No.)	Steve Largent, 1976-1989	819
Receiving (Yds.)	Steve Largent, 1976-1989	13,089
Interceptions	Dave Brown, 1976-1986	50
Punting (Avg.)	Rick Tuten, 1991-94	43.7
Punt Return (Avg.)	Paul Johns, 1981-84	11.4
Kickoff Return (Avg.)	Bobby Joe Edmonds, 1986-88	22.1
Field Goals	Norm Johnson, 1982-1990	159
Touchdowns (Tot.)	Steve Largent, 1976-1989	101
Points	Norm Johnson, 1982-1990	810

INDIVIDUAL RECORDS—SINGLE SEASON

Category	Name	Performance
Rushing (Yds.)	Chris Warren, 1994	1,545
Passing (Yds.)	Dave Krieg, 1984	3,671
Passing (TDs)	Dave Krieg, 1984	32
Receiving (No.)	Brian Blades, 1994	81
Receiving (Yds.)	Steve Largent, 1985	1,287
Interceptions	John Harris, 1981	10
	Kenny Easley, 1984	10
Punting (Avg.)	Rick Tuten, 1993	44.5
Punt Return (Avg.)	Bobby Joe Edmonds, 1987	12.6
Kickoff Return (Avg.)	Al Hunter, 1978	24.1
Field Goals	John Kasay, 1991	25
Touchdowns (Tot.)	David Sims, 1978	15
	Sherman Smith, 1979	15
	Derrick Fenner, 1990	15
Points	Norm Johnson, 1984	110

INDIVIDUAL RECORDS—SINGLE GAME

Category	Name	Performance
Rushing (Yds.)	Curt Warner, 11-27-83	207
Passing (Yds.)	Dave Krieg, 11-20-83	418
Passing (TDs)	Dave Krieg, 12-2-84	5
	Dave Krieg, 9-15-85	5
	Dave Krieg, 11-28-88	5
Receiving (No.)	Steve Largent, 10-18-87	15
Receiving (Yds.)	Steve Largent, 10-18-87	261
Interceptions	Kenny Easley, 9-3-84	3
	Eugene Robinson, 12-6-92	3
Field Goals	Norm Johnson, 9-20-87	5
	Norm Johnson, 12-18-88	5
Touchdowns (Tot.)	Daryl Turner, 9-15-85	4
	Curt Warner, 12-11-88	4
Points	Daryl Turner, 9-15-85	24
	Curt Warner, 12-11-88	24

COACHING HISTORY

(136-163-0)

1976-82	Jack Patera*	35-59-0
1982	Mike McCormack	4-3-0
1983-91	Chuck Knox	83-67-0
1992-94	Tom Flores	14-34-0

*Released after two games in 1982

KINGDOME

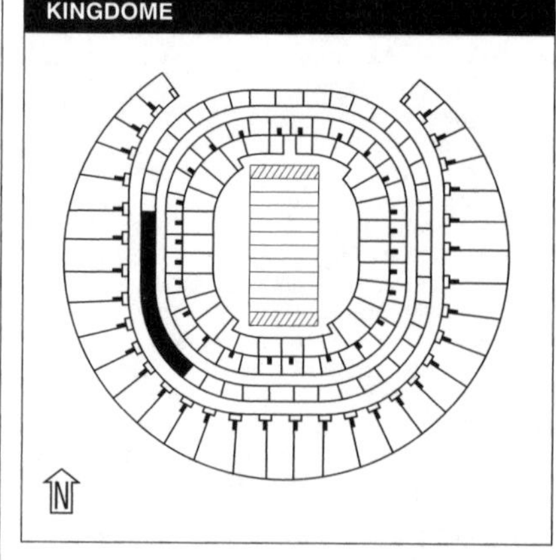

1994 TEAM RECORD

PRESEASON (2-2)

Date	Result		Opponents
8/5	L	9-13	at Indianapolis
8/13	W	29-6	Tampa Bay
8/20	W	30-19	Minnesota
8/26	L	9-13	at San Francisco

REGULAR SEASON (6-10)

Date	Result		Opponents	Att.
9/4	W	28- 7	at Washington	52,930
9/11	W	38- 9	at L.A. Raiders	47,319
9/18	L	10-24	San Diego	65,536
9/25	W	30-13	Pittsburgh	59,637
10/2	L	15-17	at Indianapolis	49,876
10/9	L	9-16	Denver	63,872
10/23	L	23-38	at Kansas City	78,847
10/30	L	15-35	at San Diego	59,001
11/6	L	17-20	Cincinnati (OT)	46,630
11/13	L	10-17	at Denver	71,290
11/20	W	22-21	Tampa Bay	37,466
11/27	W	10- 9	Kansas City	54,120
12/4	L	19-31	Indianapolis	39,574
12/11	W	16-14	at Houston	31,453
12/18	L	16-17	L.A. Raiders	53,301
12/24	L	9-35	at Cleveland	54,180

(OT) Overtime

SCORE BY PERIODS

Seahawks	53	74	49	111	0	— 287
Opponents	48	98	65	109	3	— 323

ATTENDANCE

Home 420,136 Away 444,896 Total 865,032

Single-game home record, 65,536 (9-18-94, Husky Stadium)

Single-season home record, 514,984 (1992)

1994 TEAM STATISTICS

	Seahawks	Opp.
Total First Downs	285	318
Rushing	114	122
Passing	143	178
Penalty	28	18
Third Down: Made/Att	89/235	83/224
Third Down Pct.	37.9	37.1
Fourth Down: Made/Att	10/19	8/20
Fourth Down Pct.	52.6	40.0
Total Net Yards	4652	5349
Avg. Per Game	290.8	334.3
Total Plays	1018	1077
Avg. Per Play	4.6	5.0
Total Net Yards	2084	1952
Avg. Per Game	130.3	122.0
Total Rushes	480	511
Net Yards Passing	2568	3397
Avg. Per Game	160.5	212.3
Sacked/Yards Lost	40/241	29/206
Gross Yards	2809	3603
Att./Completions	498/253	537/313
Completion Pct.	50.8	58.3
Had Intercepted	9	19
Punts/Avg.	91/42.9	78/40.9
Net Punting Avg.	91/36.7	78/35.5
Penalties/Yards Lost	114/898	103/773
Fumbles/Ball Lost	31/19	21/11
Touchdowns	32	34
Rushing	16	15
Passing	13	15
Returns	3	4
Avg. Time of Possession	28:35	31:25

1994 INDIVIDUAL STATISTICS

PASSING	Att.	Comp.	Yds.	Pct.	TD	Int.	Tkld.	Rate
Mirer	381	195	2151	51.2	11	7	27/145	70.2
McGwire	105	51	578	48.6	1	2	13/96	60.7
Gelbaugh	11	7	80	63.6	1	0	0/0	115.7
Tuten	1	0	0	0.0	0	0	0/0	39.6
Seahawks	498	253	2809	50.8	13	9	40/241	69.1
Opponents	537	313	3603	58.3	15	19	29/206	73.2

SCORING	TD R	TD P	TD Rt	PAT	FG	Saf	PTS
Kasay	0	0	0	25/26	20/24	0	85
C. Warren	9	2	0	0/0	0/0	0	68
Blades	0	4	0	0/0	0/0	0	26
Vaughn	1	1	1	0/0	0/0	0	20
S. Smith	2	1	0	0/0	0/0	0	18
Johnson	2	0	0	0/0	0/0	0	12
Strong	2	0	0	0/0	0/0	0	12
Bates	0	1	0	0/0	0/0	0	6
Green	0	1	0	0/0	0/0	0	6
Junkin	0	1	0	0/0	0/0	0	6
Martin	0	1	0	0/0	0/0	0	6
McKnight	0	1	0	0/0	0/0	0	6
Watters	0	0	1	0/0	0/0	0	6
Wooden	0	0	1	0/0	0/0	0	6
Tuten	0	0	0	0/0	0/0	0	2
Seahawks	16	13	3	25/26	20/24	1	287
Opponents	15	15	4	28/28	27/33	1	323

2-Point conversions: Blades, Tuten, Vaughn, C. Warren. Team: 4-6.

RUSHING	Att.	Yds.	Avg.	LG	TD
C. Warren	333	1545	4.6	41	9
Mirer	34	153	4.5	14	0
Strong	27	114	4.2	14	2
Vaughn	27	96	3.6	16	1
S. Smith	26	80	3.1	12	2
Johnson	12	44	3.7	14	2
Blades	2	32	16.0	40	0
T. Warren	3	15	5.0	11	0
Gelbaugh	1	10	10.0	10	0
B. Bryant	1	6	6.0	6	0
L. Smith	2	-1	-0.5	0	0
Bates	2	-4	-2.0	7	0
McGwire	10	-6	-0.6	2	0
Seahawks	480	2084	4.3	41	16
Opponents	511	1952	3.8	45t	15

RECEIVING	No.	Yds.	Avg.	LG	TD
Blades	81	1086	13.4	45	4
Martin	56	681	12.2	32	1
C. Warren	41	323	7.9	51	2
Green	30	208	6.9	20	1
S. Smith	11	142	12.9	25	1
Johnson	10	91	9.1	17	0
Edmunds	7	43	6.1	8	0
Bates	5	112	22.4	40t	1
Thomas	4	70	17.5	35	0
Strong	3	3	1.0	5	0
Crumpler	2	19	9.5	12	0
McKnight	1	25	25.0	25t	1
Vaughn	1	5	5.0	5t	1
Junkin	1	1	1.0	1t	1
Seahawks	253	2809	11.1	51	13
Opponents	313	3603	11.5	99t	15

INTERCEPTIONS	No.	Yds.	Avg.	LG	TD
Hunter	3	85	28.3	51	0
Wooden	3	78	26.0	69t	1
Watters	3	39	13.0	35t	1
E. Robinson	3	18	6.0	18	0
Gray	2	0	0.0	0	0
Porter	1	33	33.0	33	0
Blackmon	1	24	24.0	24	0
Spitulski	1	7	7.0	7	0
R. Robinson	1	0	0.0	0	0
Taylor	1	0	0.0	0	0
Seahawks	19	284	14.9	69t	2
Opponents	9	210	23.3	73t	2

PUNTING	No.	Yds.	Avg.	In 20	LG
Tuten	91	3905	42.9	33	64
Seahawks	91	3905	42.9	33	64
Opponents	78	3188	40.9	25	64

PUNT RETURNS	No.	FC	Yds.	Avg.	LG	TD
Martin	33	20	280	8.5	23	0
McCloughan	3	3	26	8.7	16	0
B. Bryant	1	0	31	31.0	31	0
Seahawks	37	23	337	9.1	31	0
Opponents	43	21	426	9.9	78t	1

KICKOFF RETURNS	No.	Yds.	Avg.	LG	TD
Bates	26	508	19.5	38	0
Vaughn	18	443	24.6	93t	1
T. Warren	14	350	25.0	47	0
B. Bryant	7	136	19.4	38	0
Martin	2	30	15.0	16	0
Seahawks	67	1467	21.9	93t	1
Opponents	61	1229	20.1	45	0

SACKS	No.
Sinclair	4.5
Adams	4.0
Kennedy	4.0
Spitulski	3.0
Edwards	2.5
Stephens	2.5
Nash	2.0
McCrary	1.5
Porter	1.5
Wooden	1.5
E. Robinson	1.0
Williams	1.0
Seahawks	29.0
Opponents	40.0

1995 DRAFT CHOICES

Round	Name	Pos.	College
1	Joey Galloway	WR	Ohio State
2	Christian Fauria	TE	Colorado
4	Jason Kyle	LB	Arizona State
6	Henry McMillian	DT	Florida
	Eddie Goines	WR	North Carolina State
7	Keif Bryant	DE	Rutgers

SEATTLE SEAHAWKS

1995 VETERAN ROSTER

No.		Name	Pos.	Ht.	Wt.	Birthdate	NFL Exp.	College	Hometown	How Acq.	'94 Games/ Starts
98		Adams, Sam	DT	6-3	285	6/13/73	2	Texas A&M	Houston, Tex.	D1-'94	12/7
74		Atkins, James	T	6-6	303	1/28/70	2	Southwestern Louisiana	Amite, La.	FA-'93	4/2
66		Baldinger, Rich	G-T	6-4	293	12/31/59	13	Wake Forest	Long Island, N.Y.	FA-'95	0*
75		Ballard, Howard	T	6-6	332	11/3/63	8	Alabama A&M	Ashland, Ala.	UFA(Buff)-'94	16/16
81		Bates, Michael	WR	5-10	196	12/19/69	3	Arizona	Tucson, Ariz.	D6-'92	15/0
20		Bellamy, Jay	S	5-11	193	7/8/72	2	Rutgers	Aberdeen, N.J.	FA-'94	3/0
50		Bickett, Duane	LB	6-5	245	12/1/62	11	Southern California	Glendale, Calif.	FA-'94	7/1
25		Blackmon, Robert	S	6-0	203	5/12/67	6	Baylor	Van Vleck, Tex.	D2b-'90	15/15
69		Blackshear, Jeff	G	6-6	323	3/29/69	3	Northeast Louisiana	Ft. Pierce, Fla.	D8a-'93	16/16
89		Blades, Brian	WR	5-11	186	7/24/65	8	Miami	Ft. Lauderdale, Fla.	D2-'88	16/16
51		Brandon, David	LB	6-4	240	2/9/65	9	Memphis State	Memphis, Tenn.	FA-'93	13/0
29		Brown, Tony	CB	5-9	183	5/15/70	4	Fresno State	Granada Hills, Calif.	FA-'94	13/5
27		Covington, Tony	S	5-11	195	12/26/67	5	Virginia	Winston-Salem, N.C.	UFA(TB)-'95	14/2*
48		Crumpler, Carlester	TE	6-6	255	9/5/71	2	East Carolina	Greenville, N.C.	D7-'94	9/4
23		Duckett, Forey	S	6-3	195	2/5/70	3	Nevada	Pinole, Calif.	FA-'94	7/0*
67		Edwards, Antonio	DE	6-3	271	3/10/70	3	Valdosta State	Moultrie, Ga.	D8b-'93	15/14
17		Friesz, John	QB	6-4	220	5/19/67	6	Idaho	Coeur d'Alene, Idaho	UFA(Wash)-'95	16/4*
18		Gelbaugh, Stan	QB	6-3	215	12/4/62	7	Maryland	Mechanicsburg, Pa.	PB(Phx)-'92	1/0
26		Gray, Carlton	CB	6-0	196	6/26/71	3	UCLA	Cincinnati, Ohio	D2-'93	11/11
87	†	Green, Paul	TE	6-3	230	10/8/66	4	Southern California	Clovis, Calif.	FA-'92	16/11
64		Hamilton, Bobby	DE	6-4	269	7/1/71	2	Southern Mississippi	Columbia, Miss.	FA-'94	0*
30		Harris, Corey	CB	5-11	190	10/25/69	4	Vanderbilt	Indianapolis, Ind.	RFA(GB)-'95	16/2*
76		Hitchcock, Bill	G	6-6	306	8/26/65	5	Purdue	Kirkland, Canada	FA-'91	5/5
47	#	Jackson, Kirby	CB	5-10	176	2/2/65	9	Mississippi State	Sturgis, Miss.	FA-'91	0*
43		Johnson, Tracy	RB	6-0	242	11/29/66	7	Clemson	Kannapolis, N.C.	PB(Atl)-'92	16/10
83		Junkin, Trey	TE	6-2	241	1/23/61	13	Louisiana Tech	North Little Rock, Ark.	FA-'90	16/0
65		Kegarise, Mike	G	6-5	300	6/19/70	2	Edinboro	Milan, Ohio	FA-'94	0*
78		Keim, Mike	T	6-7	302	11/12/65	4	Brigham Young	Springerville, Ariz.	FA-'92	16/0
96		Kennedy, Cortez	DT	6-3	293	8/23/68	6	Miami	Wilson, Ark.	D1-'90	16/16
34		Lambert, Dion	S	6-1	190	2/12/69	3	UCLA	Granada Hills, Calif.	FA-'94	1/1
52		Mawae, Kevin	G	6-4	288	1/23/71	2	Louisiana State	Leesville, La.	D2-'94	14/11
99		McCrary, Michael	DE	6-4	267	7/7/70	3	Wake Forest	Vienna, Va.	D7-'93	16/0
3		Mirer, Rick	QB	6-2	211	3/19/70	3	Notre Dame	Goshen, Ind.	D1-'93	13/13
55		Moss, Winston	LB	6-3	240	12/24/65	9	Miami	Miami, Fla.	FA-'95	16/15*
72	#	Nash, Joe	DT	6-3	278	10/11/60	14	Boston College	Boston, Mass.	FA-'82	16/15
37		Odomes, Nate	CB	5-10	188	8/25/65	8	Wisconsin	Columbus, Ga.	UFA(Buff)-'94	0*
82	t-	Proehl, Ricky	WR	6-0	190	3/7/68	6	Wake Forest	Hillsborough, N.J.	T(Ariz)-'95	16/16
73		Roberts, Ray	T	6-6	308	6/3/69	4	Virginia	Asheville, N.C.	D1-'92	14/14
41		Robinson, Eugene	S	6-0	195	5/28/63	11	Colgate	Hartford, Conn.	FA-'85	14/14
21		Robinson, Rafael	S	5-11	195	6/19/69	4	Wisconsin	Jefferson, Tex.	FA-'92	16/1
70		Sinclair, Michael	DE	6-4	271	1/31/68	4	Eastern New Mexico	Beaumont, Tex.	D6-'91	12/2
36		Smith, Lamar	RB	5-11	224	11/29/70	2	Houston	Ft. Wayne, Ind.	D3-'94	2/0
35		Smith, Steve	RB	6-1	242	8/30/64	9	Penn State	Hyattsville, Md.	FA-'94	16/0
28		Speer, Del	S	6-0	200	2/1/70	3	Florida	Miami, Fla.	FA-'94	9/0*
58	†	Spitulski, Bob	LB	6-3	246	9/10/69	4	Central Florida	Orlando, Fla.	D3-'92	16/1
59		Stowe, Tyronne	LB	6-2	250	5/30/65	9	Rutgers	Passaic, N.J.	FA-'95	16/15*
38		Strong, Mack	RB	6-0	222	9/11/71	2	Georgia	Columbus, Ga.	FA-'93	8/1
53		Sweeney, Jim	C	6-4	284	8/8/62	12	Pittsburgh	Pittsburgh, Pa.	FA-'95	16/16*
86	#	Thomas, Robb	WR	5-11	175	3/29/66	7	Oregon State	Corvallis, Ore.	FA-'92	16/1
56		Tofflemire, Joe	C	6-2	277	7/7/65	7	Arizona	Post Falls, Idaho	D2-'89	1/0
14		Tuten, Rick	P	6-2	218	1/5/65	6	Florida State	Ocala, Fla.	FA-'91	16/0
42		Warren, Chris	RB	6-2	225	1/24/67	6	Ferrum	Burke, Va.	D4-'90	16/15
88		Warren, Terrence	WR	6-1	205	8/2/69	3	Hampton	Suffolk, Va.	D5-'93	14/0
31		Watters, Orlando	CB	5-11	173	10/26/71	2	Arkansas	Anniston, Ala.	FA-'94	16/8
95		Wells, Dean	LB	6-3	242	7/20/70	3	Kentucky	Louisville, Ky.	D4-'93	15/0
61		Werner, Matt	DT	6-3	262	6/14/71	2	UCLA	Anaheim, Calif.	FA-'94	0*
93		Williams, Brent	DE	6-4	283	10/23/64	10	Toledo	Flint, Mich.	UFA(NE)-'94	10/9
90		Wooden, Terry	LB	6-3	239	1/14/67	6	Syracuse	Farmington, Conn.	D2a-'90	16/15

* Baldinger last active with New England in '93; Covington played 14 games with Tampa Bay in '94; Duckett played 2 games with Cincinnati, 3 games with Green Bay, and 2 games with Seattle; Friesz played 16 games with Washington; Hamilton, Jackson, Kegarise, and Odomes missed '94 season because of injury; Harris played 16 games with Green Bay; Moss played 16 games with L.A. Raiders; Speer played 8 games with Cleveland, 1 game with Seattle; Stowe played 16 games with Washington; Sweeney played 16 games with N.Y. Jets; Werner active for 5 games but did not play.

\# Unrestricted free agent; subject to developments.

† Restricted free agent; subject to developments.

t- Seahawks traded for Proehl (Arizona).

Players lost through free agency (7): C Ray Donaldson (Dall; 16 games in '94), CB Patrick Hunter (Ariz; 5), K John Kasay (Car; 16), QB Dan McGwire (Mia; 7), LB Rufus Porter (NO; 16), LB Rod Stephens (Wash; 16), CB Terry Taylor (Atl; 5).

Players lost through Expansion Draft (2): WR Kelvin Martin (Jax; 16 games in '94), DE Tyrone Rodgers (Car; 5).

Also played with Seahawks in '94—RB Beno Bryant (2 games), TE Ferrell Edmunds (7), DT Mike Frier (3), WR Ronnie Harris (1), S Dave McCloughan (13), WR James McKnight (2), RB Jon Vaughn (9).

COACHING STAFF

Head Coach, Dennis Erickson

Pro Career: Named the fifth head coach in franchise history on January 12, 1995. Quarterback at Montana State from 1966-68.

Background: Started his coaching career at Montana State as a graduate assistant in 1969. Also served as a graduate assistant at Washington State in 1970. Was an assistant at Montana State, Idaho, and Fresno State before becoming the head coach at Idaho in 1982. Twice advanced to NCAA I-AA playoffs and was a two-time All-Big Sky Conference coach of the year. Head coach one season (1986) at Wyoming before moving to Washington State in 1987. Took Cougars to their first bowl game since 1981 and postd their first bowl game win in 72 years in 1988. Finished the season with a national ranking of sixteenth, the school's best ever. Spent the last six seasons at the University of Miami, where he won national championships in 1989 (his first season) and in 1991, compiling an undefeated (12-0) record. Played in six New Year's Day bowl games, including five with national championship implications. Twice finished third in the country and once sixth in addition to the two national titles. Posted an NCAA-best 63-9 record during tenure at Miami and reached 100 career wins in just 137 games, the fourth fastest among Division I coaches active in 1994. Was 35-2 at the Orange Bowl, including being part of an NCAA-record 58-game winning streak. Career record: 137-40-1.

Personal: Born March 24, 1947, in Everett, Washington. Graduated from Montana State with a bachelor of arts degree in Physical Education. Dennis and his wife, Marilyn, have two sons, Bryce and Ryan, and live in Redmond, Washington.

ASSISTANT COACHES

Dave Arnold, special teams; born September 18, 1944, Jackson, Mich., lives in Bellevue, Wash. Tight end Drake 1963-66. No pro playing experience. College coach: Michigan State 1980-81, Montana State 1982-86 (head coach 1983-86), Washington State 1987-88, Miami 1989-94. Pro coach: Joined Seahawks in 1995.

Tommy Brasher, defensive line; born December 30, 1940, El Dorado, Ark., lives in Redmond, Wash. Linebacker Arkansas 1962-63. No pro playing experience. College coach: Arkansas 1970, Virginia Tech 1971, Northeast Louisiana 1974, 1976, Southern Methodist 1977-81. Pro coach: Shreveport Steamer (WFL) 1975, New England Patriots 1982-84, Philadelphia Eagles 1985, Atlanta Falcons 1986-89, Tampa Bay Buccaneers 1990, joined Seahawks in 1992.

Bob Bratkowski, offensive coordinator-wide receivers; born December 2, 1955, San Angelo, Tex., lives in Redmond, Wash. Wide receiver Washington State 1974, 1976-77. No pro playing experience. College coach: Missouri 1978-80, Weber State 1981-85, Wyoming 1986, Washington State 1987-88, Miami 1989-91. Pro coach: Joined Seahawks in 1992.

Dave Brown, defensive assistant; born January 16, 1953, Akron, Ohio, lives in Woodinville, Wash. Defensive back Michigan 1972-74. Pro defensive back Pittsburgh Steelers 1975, Seattle Seahawks 1976-86, Green Bay Packers 1987-90. Pro coach: Joined Seahawks in 1992.

Tom Catlin, quality control; born September 8, 1931, Ponca City, Okla., lives in Redmond, Wash. Center-linebacker Oklahoma 1950-52. Pro linebacker Cleveland Browns 1953-54, 1957-58, Philadelphia Eagles 1959. College coach: Army 1956. Pro coach: Dallas Texans-Kansas City Chiefs 1960-65, Los Angeles Rams 1966-77, Buffalo Bills 1978-82, joined Seahawks in 1983.

Ned James, offensive staff assistant; born January 18, 1964, Syracuse, N.Y., lives in Kirkland, Wash. Quarterback New Mexico 1965-66. Pro quarterback Montreal Alouettes (CFL) 1987, Dallas Texans (Arena Football) 1990. College coach: Arizona State 1987-88, Long Beach State 1988-89, Texas Christian 1989-90, Winona State 1992-94. Pro coach: London Monarchs (World League) 1991-92, joined Seahawks in 1995.

Dana LeDuc, strength and conditioning; born March 22, 1953, Tacoma, Wash., lives in Bellevue, Wash. No college or pro playing experience. College coach: Texas 1977-92, Miami 1993-94. Pro Coach: Joined Seahawks in 1995.

Arnie Matsumoto, defensive staff assistant; born December 18, 1962, Isesaki, Gumma, Japan, lives in Kirkland, Wash. No college or pro playing experience. Pro coach: Joined Seahawks in 1989.

Greg McMakin, defensive coordinator; born April 24, 1947, Springfield, Ore., lives in Redmond, Wash. Defensive back Southern Oregon 1964-68. No pro playing experience. College coach: Arizona 1968-69, Western Oregon State 1973-76, Idaho 1976-78, San Jose State 1978-85, Stanford 1984-85, Oregon Tech 1986-90, Utah 1990-92, Miami 1993-94. Pro coach: Denver Gold (USFL) 1985-86, joined Seahawks in 1995.

Howard Mudd, offensive line; born February 10, 1942, Midland, Mich., lives in Kirkland, Wash. Guard Hillsdale College 1961-63. Pro guard San Francisco 49ers 1964-69, Chicago Bears 1969-71. College coach: California 1972-73. Pro coach: San Diego Chargers 1974-76, San Francisco 49ers 1977, Seattle Seahawks 1978-82, Cleveland Browns 1983-88, Kansas City Chiefs 1989-92, rejoined Seahawks in 1993.

Mike Murphy, linebackers; born September 25, 1944, New York City, N.Y., lives in Bellevue, Wash. Guard-linebacker Huron College 1963-1965. No pro playing experience. College coach: Vermont 1970-73, Idaho State 1974-76, Western Illinois 1977-78. Pro coach: Saskatchewan Roughriders (CFL) 1979, Chicago Blitz (USFL) 1984, Detroit Lions 1985-89, Arizona Cardinals 1990-93, joined Seahawks in 1995.

Rich Olson, quarterbacks; born July 7, 1948, Wilmington, Calif., lives in Bellevue, Wash. Quarterback/free safety Washington State 1968-69. No pro playing experience. College coach: Washington State 1970, Fresno State 1976, Southern California 1977, Southern Methodist 1978-80, Arkansas 1981-83, Fresno State 1984-91, Miami 1992-94. Pro coach: Joined Seahawks in 1995.

Willy Robinson, defensive backs; born February 10, 1956, Fort Carson, Colo., lives in Bellevue, Wash. No college or pro playing experience. College coach: Fresno State 1978, 1980-83, San Jose State 1979, Miami 1994. Pro coach: Joined Seahawks in 1995.

Clarence Shelmon, running backs; born September 17, 1952, Bossier City, La., lives in Kirkland, Wash. Running back Houston 1971-75. No pro playing experience. College coach: Army 1978-80, Indiana 1981-83, Arizona 1984-86, Southern California 1987-90. Pro coach: Los Angeles Rams 1991, joined Seahawks in 1992.

Gregg Smith, assistant head coach-tight ends; born October 28, 1946, Oklahoma City, Okla., lives in Bellevue, Wash. Tight end Idaho 1965-66. No pro playing experience. College coach: Idaho 1967-68, 1982-85, Wyoming 1986, Washington State 1987-88, Miami 1989-94. Pro coach: Joined Seahawks in 1995.

1995 FIRST-YEAR ROSTER

Name	Pos.	Ht.	Wt.	Birthdate	College	Hometown	How Acq.
Allen, Ernest	DT	6-2	289	3/11/73	Cincinnati	South Bend, Ind.	FA
Anderson, Kelvin	RB	5-8	198	2/4/72	S.E. Missouri State	New Madrid, Miss.	FA
Ariail, Mills	T	6-3	288	5/17/73	Davidson	Greenville, N.C.	FA
Baldwin, Robert	RB	6-0	230	9/1/72	Duke	Deland, Fla.	FA
Barber, Michael	LB	6-1	247	11/9/71	Clemson	Edgemore, S.C.	FA
Bledsoe, Jerrick	CB	5-10	180	7/1/72	Texas Southern	Texas City, Tex.	FA
Bryant, Beno (1)	RB	5-9	170	1/1/71	Washington	Los Angeles, Calif.	FA
Bryant, Keif	DE	6-4	275	3/12/73	Rutgers	Largo, Fla.	D7
Davis, Judd	K	6-1	186	8/28/71	Florida	Ocala, Fla.	FA
Dye, Tyree	RB	6-0	210	11/19/72	Ferris State	Jackson, Mich.	FA
Fauria, Christian	TE	6-4	245	9/22/71	Colorado	Northridge, Calif.	D2
Galloway, Joey	WR	5-11	188	11/20/71	Ohio State	Bellair, Ohio	D1
Goines, Eddie	WR	6-0	186	8/16/72	North Carolina State	Lakeland, Fla.	D6b
Harris, Ronnie (1)	WR	5-11	180	6/4/70	Oregon	San Jose, Calif.	FA
Heath, Bryan	C	6-2	288	7/17/72	Virginia	Kernersville, N.C.	FA
Joyce, Matt (1)	G	6-7	283	3/30/72	Richmond	St. Petersburg, Fla.	FA
Kyle, Jason (1)	LB	6-3	240	5/12/72	Arizona State	Tempe, Ariz.	D4b-'94
McKeehan, James	TE	6-3	251	8/9/73	Texas A&M	Willis, Tex.	FA
McKnight, James (1)	WR	6-0	186	6/17/72	Liberty	Apopka, Fla.	FA
McMillian, Henry	DT	6-3	275	10/17/71	Florida	Folkston, Ga.	D6a
Moody, Mike (1)	T	6-7	305	5/6/69	Southern California	San Francisco, Calif.	FA
Peterson, Todd (1)	K	5-10	175	2/4/70	Georgia	Valdosta, Ga.	FA
Pickens, Joe	QB	6-3	221	2/11/72	Duke	Brooklyn, Ohio	FA
Pollack, Kris	G	6-4	290	12/21/71	Southern California	Clovis, Calif.	FA
Shelman, Anthony	RB	6-3	214	6/21/71	Louisville	Bradenton, Fla.	FA
Willis, Donald	G	6-3	330	7/15/73	North Carolina A&T	Lompoc, Calif.	FA
Wilson, Chad	CB	5-11	178	5/23/72	Miami	Canyon Springs, Calif.	FA
Woods, Manley	WR	6-2	169	7/28/72	New Mexico	Gardena, Calif.	FA

The term NFL Rookie is defined as a player who is in his first season of professional football and has not been on the roster of another professional football team for any regular-season or postseason games. A Rookie is designated by an "R" on NFL rosters. Players who have been active in another professional football league or players who have NFL experience, including either preseason training camp or being on an Active List or Inactive List, or on Reserve/Injured or Reserve/Physically Unable to Perform for fewer than six regular-season games, are termed NFL First-Year Players. An NFL First-Year Player is designated by a "1" on NFL rosters. Thereafter, a player is credited with an additional year of experience for each season in which he accumulates six games on the Active List or Inactive List, or on Reserve/Injured or Reserve/Physically Unable to Perform.

NOTES

The NFC

ARIZONA CARDINALS

National Football Conference
Eastern Division
Team Colors: Cardinal Red, Black, and White
P.O. Box 888
Phoenix, Arizona 85001-0888
Telephone: (602) 379-0101

CLUB OFFICIALS

President: William V. Bidwill
Head Coach and General Manager: Buddy Ryan
Vice President: Larry Wilson
Vice President of Sales and Marketing: John Shean
Secretary and General Counsel: Thomas J. Guilfoil
Treasurer and Chief Financial Officer: Charley Schlegel
Assistant to the General Manager: Joe Woolley
Public Relations Director: Paul Jensen
Media Coordinator: Greg Gladysiewski
Director of Community Relations: Adele Harris
Director of Marketing: Joe Castor
Business Manager: Steve Walsh
Ticket Manager: Steve Bomar
Trainer: John Omohundro
Assistant Trainers: Jim Shearer, Jeff Herndon
Equipment Manager: Mark Ahlemeier
Assistant Equipment Manager: Steve Christensen
Stadium: Sun Devil Stadium • **Capacity:** 73,400
Fifth Street
Tempe, Arizona 85287
Playing Surface: Grass
Training Camp: Northern Arizona University
Flagstaff, Arizona 86011

1995 SCHEDULE

PRESEASON

Aug. 5	at Houston	7:00
Aug. 11	**Kansas City**	7:30
Aug. 20	at Chicago	7:00
Aug. 25	**Cleveland**	7:30

REGULAR SEASON

Sept. 3	at Washington	4:00
Sept. 10	**Philadelphia**	5:00
Sept. 17	at Detroit	1:00
Sept. 24	at Dallas	3:00
Oct. 1	**Kansas City**	1:00
Oct. 8	at New York Giants	4:00
Oct. 15	**Washington**	1:00
Oct. 22	Open Date	
Oct. 29	**Seattle**	2:00
Nov. 5	at Denver	2:00
Nov. 12	**Minnesota**	2:00
Nov. 19	at Carolina	1:00
Nov. 26	**Atlanta**	2:00
Nov. 30	**New York Giants** (Thursday)	6:00
Dec. 9	at San Diego (Saturday)	1:00
Dec. 17	at Philadelphia	1:00
Dec. 25	**Dallas** (Monday)	7:00

RECORD HOLDERS

INDIVIDUAL RECORDS—CAREER

Category	Name	Performance
Rushing (Yds.)	Ottis Anderson, 1979-1986	7,999
Passing (Yds.)	Jim Hart, 1966-1983	34,639
Passing (TDs)	Jim Hart, 1966-1983	209
Receiving (No.)	Roy Green, 1979-1990	522
Receiving (Yds.)	Roy Green, 1979-1990	8,497
Interceptions	Larry Wilson, 1960-1972	52
Punting (Avg.)	Jerry Norton, 1959-1961	44.9
Punt Return (Avg.)	Charley Trippi, 1947-1955	13.7
Kickoff Return (Avg.)	Ollie Matson, 1952, 1954-58	28.5
Field Goals	Jim Bakken, 1962-1978	282
Touchdowns (Tot.)	Roy Green, 1979-1990	70
Points	Jim Bakken, 1962-1978	1,380

INDIVIDUAL RECORDS—SINGLE SEASON

Category	Name	Performance
Rushing (Yds.)	Ottis Anderson, 1979	1,605
Passing (Yds.)	Neil Lomax, 1984	4,614
Passing (TDs)	Charley Johnson, 1963	28
	Neil Lomax, 1984	28
Receiving (No.)	J.T. Smith, 1987	91
Receiving (Yds.)	Roy Green, 1984	1,555
Interceptions	Bob Nussbaumer, 1949	12
Punting (Avg.)	Jerry Norton, 1960	45.6
Punt Return (Avg.)	John (Red) Cochran, 1949	20.9
Kickoff Return (Avg.)	Ollie Matson, 1958	35.5
Field Goals	Jim Bakken, 1967	27
Touchdowns (Tot.)	John David Crow, 1962	17
Points	Jim Bakken, 1967	117
	Neil O'Donoghue, 1984	117

INDIVIDUAL RECORDS—SINGLE GAME

Category	Name	Performance
Rushing (Yds.)	John David Crow, 12-18-60	203
Passing (Yds.)	Neil Lomax, 12-16-84	468
Passing (TDs)	Jim Hardy, 10-2-50	6
	Charley Johnson, 9-26-65	6
	Charley Johnson, 11-2-69	6
Receiving (No.)	Sonny Randle, 11-4-62	16
Receiving (Yds.)	Sonny Randle, 11-4-62	256
Interceptions	Bob Nussbaumer, 11-13-49	*4
	Jerry Norton, 11-20-60	*4
Field Goals	Jim Bakken, 9-24-67	*7
Touchdowns (Tot.)	Ernie Nevers, 11-28-29	*6
Points	Ernie Nevers, 11-28-29	*40

*NFL Record

COACHING HISTORY

Chicago 1920-1959, St. Louis 1960-1987
(394-534-39)

1920-22	John (Paddy) Driscoll	17-8-4
1923-24	Arnold Horween	13-8-1
1925-26	Norman Barry	16-8-2
1927	Guy Chamberlin	3-7-1
1928	Fred Gillies	1-5-0
1929	Dewey Scanlon	6-6-1
1930	Ernie Nevers	5-6-2
1931	LeRoy Andrews*	0-1-0
1931	Ernie Nevers	5-3-0
1932	Jack Chevigny	2-6-2
1933-34	Paul Schissler	6-15-1
1935-38	Milan Creighton	16-26-4
1939	Ernie Nevers	1-10-0
1940-42	Jimmy Conzelman	8-22-3
1943-45	Phil Handler**	1-29-0
1946-48	Jimmy Conzelman	27-10-0
1949	Phil Handler-Buddy Parker***	2-4-0
1949	Raymond (Buddy) Parker	4-1-1
1950-51	Earl (Curly) Lambeau****	7-15-0
1951	Phil Handler-Cecil Isbell#	1-1-0
1952	Joe Kuharich	4-8-0
1953-54	Joe Stydahar	3-20-1
1955-57	Ray Richards	14-21-1
1958-61	Frank (Pop) Ivy##	17-29-2
1961	Chuck Drulis-Ray Prochaska-Ray Willsey###	2-0-0
1962-65	Wally Lemm	27-26-3
1966-70	Charley Winner	35-30-5
1971-72	Bob Hollway	8-18-2
1973-77	Don Coryell	42-29-1
1978-79	Bud Wilkinson####	9-20-0
1979	Larry Wilson	2-1-0
1980-85	Jim Hanifan	39-50-1
1986-89	Gene Stallings@	23-34-1
1989	Hank Kuhlmann	0-5-0
1990-93	Joe Bugel	20-44-0
1994	Buddy Ryan	8-8-0

* Resigned after one game in 1931
** Co-coach with Walt Kiesling in Chicago Cardinals-Pittsburgh merger in 1944
*** Co-coaches for first six games in 1949
**** Resigned after 10 games in 1951
\# Co-coaches
\## Resigned after 12 games in 1961
\### Co-coaches
\#### Released after 13 games in 1979
@ Released after 11 games in 1989

SUN DEVIL STADIUM

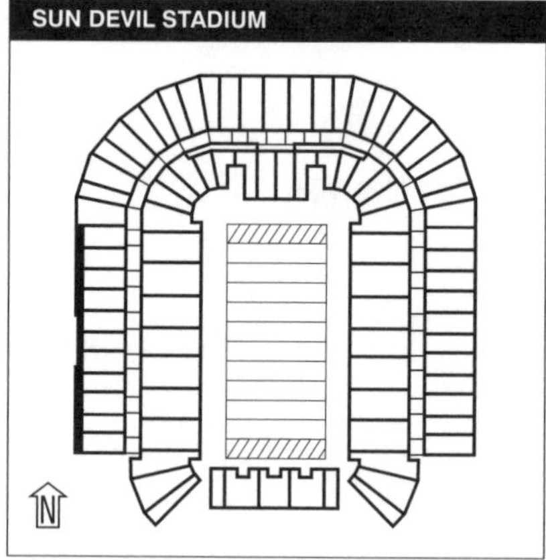

1994 TEAM RECORD

PRESEASON (1-3)

Date	Result		Opponents
8/5	W	17-7	San Francisco
8/13	L	0-16	Chicago
8/19	L	16-24	at Detroit
8/25	L	21-30	at Denver

REGULAR SEASON (8-8)

Date	Result		Opponents	Att.
9/4	L	12-14	at L.A. Rams	32,969
9/11	L	17-20	N.Y. Giants	60,066
9/18	L	0-32	at Cleveland	62,818
10/2	W	17- 7	Minnesota	67,950
10/9	L	3-38	at Dallas	64,518
10/16	W	19-16	at Washington (OT)	50,019
10/23	L	21-28	Dallas	71,023
10/30	W	20-17	Pittsburgh (OT)	65,690
11/6	L	7-17	at Philadelphia	64,952
11/13	W	10- 9	at N.Y. Giants	71,719
11/20	W	12- 6	Philadelphia	62,779
11/27	L	16-19	Chicago (OT)	65,922
12/4	W	30-12	at Houston	39,821
12/11	W	17-15	Washington	53,790
12/18	W	28- 7	Cincinnati	50,110
12/24	L	6-10	at Atlanta	35,311

(OT) Overtime

SCORE BY PERIODS

Cardinals	41	66	18	104	6	—	235
Opponents	74	83	62	45	3	—	267

ATTENDANCE

Home 497,330 Away 422,127 Total 919,457
Single-game home record, 71,628 (11-22-92)
Single-season home record, 497,330 (1994)

1994 TEAM STATISTICS

	Cardinals	Opp.
Total First Downs	287	245
Rushing	90	71
Passing	169	144
Penalty	28	30
Third Down: Made/Att	75/228	52/187
Third Down Pct.	32.9	27.8
Fourth Down: Made/Att	5/14	4/10
Fourth Down Pct.	35.7	40.0
Total Net Yards	4607	4408
Avg. Per Game	287.9	275.5
Total Plays	1052	909
Avg. Per Play	4.4	4.8
Net Yards Rushing	1560	1370
Avg. Per Game	97.5	85.6
Total Rushes	480	409
Net Yards Passing	3047	3038
Avg. Per Game	190.4	189.9
Sacked/Yards Lost	34/237	35/272
Gross Yards	3284	3310
Att./Completions	538/287	465/234
Completion Pct.	53.3	50.3
Had Intercepted	19	23
Punts/Avg	98/40.8	90/40.9
Net Punting Avg.	98/36.0	90/35.7
Penalties/Yards Lost	128/1090	108/800
Fumbles/Ball Lost	25/10	28/13
Touchdowns	24	31
Rushing	12	7
Passing	11	19
Returns	1	5
Avg. Time of Possession	32:37	27:23

1994 INDIVIDUAL STATISTICS

PASSING	Att.	Comp.	Yds.	Pct.	TD	Int.	Tkld.	Rate
Beuerlein	255	130	1545	51.0	5	9	20/129	61.6
Schroeder	238	133	1510	55.9	4	7	11/85	68.4
McMahon	43	23	219	53.5	1	3	3/23	46.6
Hearst	1	1	10	100.0	1	0	0/0	147.9
R. Moore	1	0	0	0.0	0	0	0/0	39.6
Cardinals	538	287	3284	53.3	11	19	34/237	64.1
Opponents	465	234	3310	50.3	19	23	35/272	66.7

SCORING	TD R	TD P	TD Rt	PAT	FG	Saf	PTS
Davis	0	0	0	17/17	20/26	0	77
Centers	5	2	0	0/0	0/0	0	42
R. Moore	4	1	0	0/0	0/0	0	32
Proehl	0	5	0	0/0	0/0	0	30
Peterson	0	0	0	4/4	2/4	0	10
Beuerlein	1	0	0	0/0	0/0	0	6
Clark	0	1	0	0/0	0/0	0	6
Hearst	1	0	0	0/0	0/0	0	6
McAfee	1	0	0	0/0	0/0	0	6
McCants	0	0	1	0/0	0/0	0	6
Reeves	0	1	0	0/0	0/0	0	6
Ware	0	1	0	0/0	0/0	0	6
Swann	0	0	0	0/0	0/0	1	2
Cardinals	12	11	1	21/21	22/30	1	235
Opponents	7	19	5	28/29	15/24	3	267

2-Point conversions: R. Moore. Team: 1-3.

RUSHING	Att.	Yds.	Avg.	LG	TD
R. Moore	232	780	3.4	24	4
Centers	115	336	2.9	17	5
Hearst	37	169	4.6	36	1
Higgs	43	127	3.0	16	0
Schroeder	16	59	3.7	16	0
Beuerlein	22	39	1.8	19	1
McMahon	6	32	5.3	17	0
Levy	3	15	5.0	22	0
Feagles	2	8	4.0	12	0
Samuels	1	1	1.0	1	0
Reeves	1	-1	-1.0	-1	0
McAfee	2	-5	-2.5	2t	1
Cardinals	480	1560	3.3	36	12
Opponents	409	1370	3.3	26	7

RECEIVING	No.	Yds.	Avg.	LG	TD
Centers	77	647	8.4	36	2
Proehl	51	651	12.8	63	5
Clark	50	771	15.4	45	1
R. Hill	38	544	14.3	51	0
Ware	17	171	10.1	33	1
Reeves	14	202	14.4	33	1
Fann	12	96	8.0	16	0
Samuels	8	57	7.1	17	0
R. Moore	8	52	6.5	18	1
Hearst	6	49	8.2	29	0
Levy	4	35	8.8	15	0
Robinson	1	5	5.0	5	0
McAfee	1	4	4.0	4	0
Cardinals	287	3284	11.4	63	11
Opponents	234	3310	14.1	85t	19

INTERCEPTIONS	No.	Yds.	Avg.	LG	TD
A. Williams	9	89	9.9	43	0
J. Williams	4	48	12.0	29	0
Hoage	3	64	21.3	41	0
Joyner	3	2	0.7	2	0
Lynch	2	35	17.5	23	0
McCants	1	46	46.0	46t	1
Swann	1	0	0.0	0	0
Marshall	0	13	---	13	0
Cardinals	23	297	12.9	46t	1
Opponents	19	262	13.8	93t	3

PUNTING	No.	Yds.	Avg.	In 20	LG
Feagles	98	3997	40.8	33	54
Cardinals	98	3997	40.8	33	54
Opponents	90	3677	40.9	29	58

PUNT RETURNS	No.	FC	Yds.	Avg.	LG	TD
Robinson	41	12	285	7.0	23	0
Reeves	1	1	1	1.0	1	0
Cardinals	42	13	286	6.8	23	0
Opponents	40	22	270	6.8	16	0

KICKOFF RETURNS	No.	Yds.	Avg.	LG	TD
Levy	26	513	19.7	31	0
Robinson	12	231	19.3	33	0
McAfee	7	113	16.1	29	0
Henesey	6	108	18.0	25	0
Reeves	3	83	27.7	53	0
Higgs	2	25	12.5	17	0
Samuels	1	6	6.0	6	0
Cardinals	57	1079	18.9	53	0
Opponents	53	1214	22.9	87t	1

SACKS	No.
Swann	7.5
Bankston	6.5
Joyner	6.0
Simmons	6.0
Miller	3.0
E. Hill	1.5
Hoage	1.0
Marshall	1.0
McCants	1.0
Wilson	1.0
Lynch	0.5
Cardinals	35.0
Opponents	34.0

1995 DRAFT CHOICES

Round	Name	Pos.	College
2	Frank Sanders	WR	Auburn
3	Stoney Case	QB	New Mexico
5	Cedric Davis	DB	Tennessee State
	Lance Scott	C	Utah
	Tito Paul	DB	Ohio State
6	Anthony Bridges	DB	North Texas
7	Billy Williams	WR	Tennessee
	Wesley Leasy	LB	Mississippi State
	Chad Eaton	DT	Washington State

ARIZONA CARDINALS

1995 VETERAN ROSTER

No.	Name	Pos.	Ht.	Wt.	Birthdate	NFL Exp.	College	Hometown	How Acq.	'94 Games/ Starts
46	Alexander, Brent	CB-S	5-10	184	7/10/71	2	Tennessee State	Gallatin, Tex.	FA-'95	16/7
63	Bankston, Michael	DT-DE	6-3	280	3/12/70	4	Sam Houston State	East Bernard, Tex.	D4b-'92	16/16
73	Barrie, Sebastian	DT	6-2	280	5/26/70	3	Liberty	Dallas, Tex.	FA-'94	10/0
78	Brown, Chad	DE	6-7	265	7/9/71	3	Mississippi	Thomasville, Ga.	FA-'95	8/2
16	Buck, Mike	QB	6-3	227	4/22/67	5	Maine	Sayville, N.Y.	FA-'95	0*
37	Centers, Larry	RB	5-11	215	6/1/68	6	Stephen F. Austin	Tatum, Tex.	D5-'90	16/5
62	Coleman, Ben	T-G	6-6	335	5/18/71	3	Wake Forest	South Hill, Va.	D2-'93	15/13
79	† Cunningham, Ed	C	6-3	285	8/17/69	4	Washington	Alexandria, Va.	D3-'92	16/16
5	Davis, Greg	K	6-0	205	10/29/65	8	Citadel	Atlanta, Ga.	PB(Atl)-'91	14/0
64	Dukes, Jamie	C-G	6-1	285	6/14/64	10	Florida State	Orlando, Fla.	FA-'95	6/6*
26	Dunson, Walter	RB	5-9	173	10/24/70	2	Middle Tennessee State	Carrollton, Ga.	FA-'95	0*
65	Dye, Ernest	G	6-6	325	7/15/71	3	South Carolina	Greenwood, S.C.	D1b-'93	16/16
83	Edwards, Anthony	WR	5-10	190	5/26/66	7	New Mexico Highlands	Casa Grande, Ariz.	FA-'91	0*
92	England, Eric	DE	6-2	283	3/25/71	2	Texas A&M	Sugar Land, Tex.	D3b-'94	11/1
80	Fann, Chad	TE	6-3	250	6/7/70	3	Florida A&M	Jacksonville, Fla.	FA-'93	16/9
10	Feagles, Jeff	P	6-1	205	3/7/66	8	Miami	Scottsdale, Ariz.	UFA(Phil)-'94	16/0
89	Gaines, Wendall	DT-TE	6-4	293	1/17/72	2	Oklahoma State	Frederick, Okla.	FA-'94	0*
31	# Harris, Odie	S	6-0	190	4/1/66	8	Sam Houston State	Bryan, Tex.	W(Clev)-'92	13/0
23	Hearst, Garrison	RB	5-11	215	1/4/71	3	Georgia	Lincolnton, Ga.	D1a-'93	8/0
22	Higgs, Mark	RB	5-7	199	4/11/66	8	Kentucky	Owensboro, Ky.	FA-'94	11/1*
58	Hill, Eric	LB	6-2	255	11/14/66	7	Louisana State	Galveston, Tex.	D1-'89	16/15
34	Hoage, Terry	S	6-2	210	4/11/62	12	Georgia	Huntsville, Tex.	FA-'94	16/16
24	Hunter, Patrick	CB	5-11	186	10/24/64	10	Nevada-Reno	San Francisco, Calif.	UFA(Sea)-'95	5/5*
56	Irving, Terry	LB	6-0	224	7/3/71	2	McNeese State	Galveston, Tex.	D4c-'94	16/0
53	Jax, Garth	LB	6-2	250	9/16/93	10	Florida State	Houston, Tex.	PB(Dall)-'89	16/0
61	Jones, Todd	C	6-3	295	7/3/67	3	Henderson State	Little Rock, Ark.	FA-'95	0*
59	Joyner, Seth	LB	6-2	235	11/18/64	10	Texas-El Paso	Spring Valley, N.Y.	UFA(Phil)-'94	16/16
57	Kirk, Randy	LB	6-2	231	12/27/64	8	San Diego State	San Diego, Calif.	UFA(Cin)-'94	16/0
17	Krieg, Dave	QB	6-1	202	10/20/58	16	Milton	Schofield, Wis.	UFA(Det)-'95	14/7*
4	Levy, Chuck	RB-QB	6-0	197	1/7/72	2	Arizona	Torrance, Calif.	D2-'94	11/0
67	Love, Duval	G	6-3	288	6/24/63	11	UCLA	Fountain Valley, Calif.	UFA(Pitt)-'95	16/16*
29	Lynch, Lorenzo	S	5-11	200	4/6/63	9	Cal State-Sacramento	Oakland, Calif.	PB(Chi)-'90	15/15
50	Merritt, David	LB	6-1	237	9/8/71	3	North Carolina State	Raleigh, N.C.	FA-'93	16/0
95	Miller, Jamir	LB	6-4	242	11/19/73	2	UCLA	Oakland, Calif.	D1-'94	16/0
85	t- Moore, Rob	WR	6-3	205	9/27/68	6	Syracuse	Hempstead, N.Y.	T(NYJ)-'95	16/16*
61	Nix, Roosevelt	DE	6-6	292	4/17/67	4	Central State, Ohio	Toledo, Ohio	FA-'95	2/0*
60	Redmon, Anthony	G	6-4	308	4/6/71	2	Auburn	Brewton, Ala.	D5b-'94	6/5
80	Reeves, Bryan	WR	5-11	195	7/10/70	2	Nevada-Reno	Los Angeles, Calif.	FA-'94	14/0
44	Samuels, Terry	TE	6-2	254	9/27/70	2	Kentucky	Louisville, Ky.	D6-'94	16/6
11	# Schroeder, Jay	QB	6-4	215	6/28/61	12	UCLA	Pacific Palisades, Calif.	FA-'94	9/8
96	Simmons, Clyde	DE	6-6	280	6/16/60	10	Western Carolina	Wilmington, N.C.	UFA(Phil)-'94	16/16
98	Swann, Eric	DT	6-5	295	8/16/70	5	No College	Swann Station, N.C.	D1-'91	16/16
71	Tharpe, Larry	T	6-4	299	11/19/70	4	Tennessee State	Macon, Ga.	RFA(Det)-'95	0*
35	Williams, Aeneas	CB	5-10	190	1/29/69	5	Southern	New Orleans, La.	D3-'91	16/16
94	Wilson, Bernard	DT	6-2	295	8/17/70	3	Tennessee State	Nashville, Tenn.	W(TB)-'94	13/12
68	# Wolf, Joe	G-T	6-6	296	12/28/66	7	Boston College	Allentown, Pa.	D1b-'89	7/6

* Buck last active with New Orleans in '93; Dukes played 16 games with Green Bay in '94; Dunson last on injured reserve with San Diego in '93; Edwards missed '94 season because of injury; Gaines inactive for 7 games; Higgs played 5 games with Miami, 6 games with Arizona; Hunter played 5 games with Seattle; Jones last active with New England in '93; Krieg played 14 games with Detroit; Love played 16 games with Pittsburgh; Moore played 16 games with N.Y. Jets; Nix played 2 games with Minnesota; Tharpe active for 1 game with Detroit but did not play.

Unrestricted free agent; subject to developments.

† Restricted free agent; subject to developments.

Traded—RB Ron Moore to N.Y. Jets, WR Ricky Proehl to Seattle.

t- Cardinals traded for Moore (N.Y. Jets).

Players lost through free agency (6): T Pat Cunningham (Minn; 11 games in '94), WR Randal Hill (Mia; 14), DE Keith McCants (Rams; 12), CB Chris Oldham (Pitt; 11), T Mark Vander Poel (SD; 0), CB James Williams (Car; 15).

Players lost through Expansion Draft (2): QB Steve Beuerlein (Jax; 9 games in '94), C Mark Tucker (Jax; 16).

Also played with Cardinals in '94—DE Michael Brandon (1 game), WR Gary Clark (15), CB-S Herschel Currie (1), DT Karl Dunbar (4), RB Frank Harvey (2), RB Brian Henesey (3), WR Kevin Knox (2), LB Wilber Marshall (15), RB Fred McAfee (7), QB Jim McMahon (2), K Todd Peterson (2), WR Patrick Robinson (15), T Luis Sharpe (11), TE Derek Ware (15), S Andre Waters (12), RB Barry Word (1).

COACHING STAFF

Head Coach,
Buddy Ryan

Pro Career: Named head coach and general manager on February 3, 1994. Became thirty-second head coach in the history of the franchise dating back to 1920. Cardinals made noticeable strides in 1994, Ryan's first season in Arizona, with an 8-8 record that translated into the franchise's first nonlosing season and highest victory total since 1984. Known as one of the game's top defensive minds, he devised the "46 defense" with its multiple variations of alignments and coverages. Served as defensive coordinator for Houston Oilers' in 1993. Defense set a club record with 52 quarterback sacks and ranked first in the league in both rushing defense (79.6 yards per game) and interceptions (26). Posted 43-35-1 record as head coach for Philadelphia Eagles from 1986-1990, a span which included consecutive playoff berths his final three seasons with records of 10-6, 11-5, and 10-6, highlighted by the NFC East title in 1988, the Eagles' first divisional crown since 1980. Defensive coordinator of the Chicago Bears from 1978-1985 as the Bears' defense set an NFL record with 72 quarterback sacks in 1984, then a year later led the league in nine defensive categories. In Chicago's Super Bowl XX victory over New England, Chicago held the Patriots to a Super Bowl record fewest first downs (7) and fewest rushing first downs (1), while allowing just 123 total yards. En route to the Super Bowl, Chicago posted playoff shutouts against the Los Angeles Rams and New York Giants, an unprecedented accomplishment in NFL postseason annals. Served as defensive line coach for Bud Grant's Minnesota Vikings in 1976-77 as the "Purple People Eaters" line of Carl Eller, Alan Page, and Jim Marshall helped the Vikings reach Super Bowl XI. Ryan was a member of the New York Jets defensive staff from 1968-1975 under Hall of Fame coach Weeb Ewbank, when Jets upset heavily-favored Baltimore Colts in Super Bowl III. Career record: 51-43-1.

Background: Ryan was a four-year letterman at Oklahoma State from 1952-55 as a guard. While serving in the U.S. Army in Korea, Ryan played on the Fourth Army championship team in Japan. He began his coaching career at the high school level in Texas at Gainesville (1957-59) and Marshall (1960), then was a college assistant at Buffalo (1961-65), Vanderbilt (1966), and Pacific (1967). Has a master's degree in education from Middle Tennessee State.

Personal: Born February 17, 1934, in Frederick, Oklahoma. Buddy and his wife, Joan, live in Phoenix and have three sons—twins Rex and Rob, and Jim.

ASSISTANT COACHES

David Atkins, offensive coordinator; born May 18, 1949, Victoria, Tex., lives in Phoenix. Running back Texas-El Paso 1970-72. Pro running back San Francisco 49ers 1973, Honolulu (WFL) 1974, San Diego Chargers 1975. College coach: Texas-El Paso 1979-80, San Diego State 1981-85. Pro coach: Philadelphia Eagles 1986-92, New England Patriots 1993, joined Cardinals in 1994.

Matt Cavanaugh, quarterbacks; born October 27, 1956, Youngstown, Ohio, lives in Phoenix. Quarterback Pittsburgh 1974-77. Pro quarterback New England Patriots 1978-82, San Francisco 49ers 1983-85, Philadelphia Eagles 1986-89, New York Giants 1990-91. College coach: Pittsburgh 1993. Pro coach: Joined Cardinals in 1994.

Ronnie Jones, defensive coordinator; born October 17, 1955, Dumas, Tex., lives in Phoenix. Running back Northwestern Oklahoma, State 1974-77. No pro playing experience. College coach: Northeastern Oklahoma State 1979-83, Tulsa 1984, Arizona State 1985-86. Pro coach: Philadelphia Eagles 1987-90, Los Angeles Rams 1991, Los Angeles Raiders 1992, Houston Oilers 1993, joined Cardinals in 1994.

George Martinez, running backs; born August 5, 1961, Fort Bragg, N.C., lives in Phoenix. Quarterback Northwestern Oklahoma State 1969-72. No pro playing experience. College coach: East Central Oklahoma 1981-87, Panhandle State 1988, New Mexico Highlands 1989-91 (head coach). Pro coach: Joined Cardinals in 1994.

Dan Neal, offensive line; born August 30, 1949, Corbin, Ky., lives in Phoenix. Center Kentucky 1970-72. Pro center Baltimore Colts 1973-74, Chicago Bears 1975-83. Pro coach: Philadelphia Eagles 1986-91, joined Cardinals in 1994.

Ted Plumb, receivers-tight ends; born August 20, 1939, Reno, Nev., lives in Phoenix. Wide receiver Baylor 1960-61. Pro wide receiver Buffalo Bills 1962. College coach: Cerritos, Calif., J.C. 1966-67, Texas Christian 1968-70, Tulsa 1971, Kansas 1972-73. Pro coach: New York Giants 1974-76, Atlanta Falcons 1977-79, Chicago Bears 1980-85, Philadelphia Eagles 1986-89, joined Cardinals in 1990.

Al Roberts, special teams; born January 6, 1944, Fresno, Calif., lives in Phoenix. Running back Washington 1964-65, Puget Sound 1967-68. No pro playing experience. College coach: Washington 1977-82, Purdue 1986, Wyoming 1987. Pro coach: Los Angeles Express (USFL) 1983-84, Houston Oilers 1984-85, Philadelphia Eagles 1988-90, New York Jets 1991-93, joined Cardinals in 1994.

Bob Rogucki, strength and conditioning; born September 27, 1953, Clarksburg, W. Va., lives in Phoenix. No college or pro playing experience. College coach: Penn State 1981, Weber State 1982, Army 1983-89. Pro coach: Joined Cardinals in 1990.

Rex Ryan, linebackers; born December 13, 1962, Ardmore, Okla., lives in Phoenix. Defensive end Southwest Oklahoma State 1983-86. No pro playing experience. College coach: Eastern Kentucky 1987-88, New Mexico Highlands 1989, Morehead State 1990-93. Pro coach: Joined Cardinals in 1994.

Robert Ryan, defensive backs; born December 13, 1962, Ardmore, Okla., lives in Phoenix. Defensive end-linebacker Southwest Oklahoma State 1983-86. No pro playing experience. College coach: Western Kentucky 1987, Ohio State 1988, Tennessee State 1989-93. Pro coach: Joined Cardinals in 1994.

Jim Stanley, defensive line; born June 22, 1934, Dunham, Ky., lives in Phoenix. Guard-defensive tackle Texas A&M 1954-57. No pro playing experience. College coach: Southern Methodist 1961, Texas El Paso 1962, Oklahoma State 1963-68, 1972-78 (head coach 1973-78), Navy 1969-70. Pro coach: Winnipeg Blue Bombers (CFL) 1971, New York Giants 1979, Atlanta Falcons 1980-82, Michigan Panthers (USFL) 1983-84 (head coach), Tampa Bay Buccaneers 1986, Houston Oilers 1990-94, joined Cardinals in 1995.

1995 FIRST-YEAR ROSTER

Name	Pos.	Ht.	Wt.	Birthdate	College	Hometown	How Acq.
Askin, Mark	T	6-4	295	8/1/71	Kentucky	Louisville, Ken.	FA
Bonds, John (1)	QB	6-4	230	12/6/70	Northern Arizona	Phoenix, Ariz.	FA
Booth, Blayne	T	6-4	259	5/27/70	Texas-El Paso	Midland, Tex.	FA
Bowens, Larry	CB-S	6-0	166	8/10/72	Mississippi Valley St.	Decatur, Ga.	FA
Bridges, Anthony	CB	5-9	181	1/1/73	North Texas	Moultrie, Ga.	D6
Brooks, Carlos	CB-S	6-0	200	5/8/71	Bowling Green	Middletown, Ohio	FA
Brown, Michael	WR	6-2	183	9/27/72	Langston	Detroit, Mich.	FA
Burke, Patrick (1)	CB	5-11	180	11/6/68	Fresno, Calif., J.C.	Toronto, Canada	FA
Caflisch, Andy	P	6-2	190	8/7/70	Wisconsin-Stout	River Falls, Wis.	FA
Case, Stoney	QB	6-2	206	7/7/72	New Mexico	Odessa, Tex.	D3
Davidson, Will	G-T	6-4	298	1/26/72	Baylor	Pleasanton, Tex.	FA
Davis, Cedric	CB	5-9	170	9/7/72	Tennessee State	Brandon, Fla.	D5a
Dominick, Brandon	DT	6-1	310	5/19/71	Mississippi Valley St.	Memphis, Tenn.	FA
Drake, Jerry	DE	6-4	292	7/9/69	Hastings College	Kingston, N.Y.	FA
Eaton, Chad	DT	6-4	292	4/6/72	Washington State	Puyallup, Wash.	D7c
Frazier, Lamont	TE	6-2	245	3/23/72	Missouri	Charleston, Mo.	FA
Gillock, Mike	CB-S	5-10	175	5/20/72	Indianapolis College	Greenwood, Ind.	FA
Gray, Oscar	RB	6-1	265	9/25/72	Arkansas	Cincinnati, Ohio	FA
Hardy, Darryl (1)	LB-TE	6-2	220	11/22/68	Tennessee	Cincinnati, Ohio	FA
Hardy, Sam	G	6-2	280	8/7/72	Carson-Newman	Nashville, Tenn.	FA
Harper, Jermaine	LB	6-1	235	9/11/71	Northeast Oklahoma	Oklahoma City, Okla.	FA
Hooks, Bryan (1)	DE	6-3	286	9/15/70	Arizona State	Tempe, Ariz.	FA
Howard, Ed	WR	6-4	195	1/14/73	Rice	Huntsville, Tex.	FA
Knox, Kevin (1)	WR	6-3	195	1/20/71	Florida State	Niceville, Fla.	FA
Lassiter, Kwamie	CB-S	5-11	180	12/3/69	Kansas	Newport News, Va.	FA
Leasy, Wesley	LB	6-2	234	9/7/71	Mississippi State	Greenville, Miss.	D7b
Lopez, Justin	DE-DT	6-4	300	3/18/71	Pittsburgh	Pinebush, N.Y.	FA
Maston, Richard	K	5-11	195	6/2/72	Temple	Atco, N.J.	FA
McBride, Oscar	TE	6-5	266	7/23/72	Notre Dame	Chiefland, Fla.	FA
Meyer, Pat	DE-DT	6-0	274	4/5/72	Colorado State	Girard, Ohio	FA
Morris, Horace (1)	LB	6-2	230	5/29/71	Tennessee	Miami, Fla.	FA
Paul, Tito	CB-S	6-0	195	5/24/72	Ohio State	Kissimmee, Fla.	D5c
Rivers, Terrance	RB	5-9	183	2/10/72	Citadel	Jacksonville, Fla.	FA
Sanders, Frank	WR	6-1	202	2/17/73	Auburn	Ft. Lauderdale, Fla.	D2
Scott, Lance	C	6-3	285	2/15/72	Utah	Salt Lake City, Utah	D5b
Shanks, Simon	LB	6-1	215	10/16/71	Coahoma, Miss., J.C.	Laurel, Miss.	FA
Terry, Ryan	RB	5-11	203	9/20/71	Iowa	Steubenville, Ohio	FA
Truitt, Leroy (1)	T	6-4	310	5/23/69	Houston	LaMarque, Tex.	FA
Turner, Cornelius	WR	6-0	176	1/4/72	Mississippi Valley St.	Birmingham, Ala.	FA
West, Franky	CB-S	5-10	170	3/21/72	Illinois State	St. Louis, Mo.	FA
Williams, Billy	WR	5-11	175	6/7/71	Tennessee	Alcoa, Tenn.	D7a

The term NFL Rookie is defined as a player who is in his first season of professional football and has not been on the roster of another professional football team for any regular-season or postseason games. A Rookie is designated by an "R" on NFL rosters. Players who have been active in another professional football league or players who have NFL experience, including either preseason training camp or being on an Active List or Inactive List, or on Reserve/Injured or Reserve/Physically Unable to Perform for fewer than six regular-season games, are termed NFL First-Year Players. An NFL First-Year Player is designated by a "1" on NFL rosters. Thereafter, a player is credited with an additional year of experience for each season in which he accumulates six games on the Active List or Inactive List, or on Reserve/Injured or Reserve/Physically Unable to Perform.

NOTES

ATLANTA FALCONS

National Football Conference
Western Division
Team Colors: Black, Red, Silver, and White
One Falcon Place
Suwanee, Georgia 30174
Telephone: (770) 945-1111

CLUB OFFICIALS

Chairman of the Board: Rankin M. Smith, Sr.
President: Taylor Smith
Vice President & Chief Financial Officer: Jim Hay
Vice President of Player Personnel: Ken Herock
Vice President of Administration: Rob Jackson
Director of Public Relations: Charlie Taylor
Asst. Director of Public Relations: Frank Kleha
Public Relations Assistant: Gary Glenn
Sales & Marketing: Todd Marble, John Knox, Trisha Williamson
Director of Community Relations: Carol Breeding
Director of Player Programs: Billy Johnson
Director of Ticket Operations: Jack Ragsdale
Asst. Director of Ticket Operations: Mike Jennings
Administrative Asst./Finance: Kevin Anthony
Administrative Asst./Player Personnel: Danny Mock
Scouts: Bill Baker, Scott Campbell, Dick Corrick, Elbert Dubenion, Bill Groman
Director of Pro Personnel: Chuck Connor
Director of Player Development: Tommy Nobis
Controller: Wallace Norman
Trainer: Ron Medlin
Assistant Trainers: Arnold Gamber, Matt Smith
Equipment Manager: Craig Campanozzi
Senior Equipment Manager: Horace Daniel
Video Director: Tom Atcheson
Stadium: Georgia Dome • **Capacity:** 71,280
One Georgia Dome Drive
Atlanta, Georgia 30313
Playing Surface: Artificial turf
Training Camp: One Falcon Place
Suwanee, Georgia 30174

1995 SCHEDULE

PRESEASON

Aug. 5	at Philadelphia	7:30
Aug. 11	**Miami**	7:30
Aug. 19	**Cleveland**	7:00
Aug. 25	at Buffalo	7:30

REGULAR SEASON

Sept. 3	**Carolina**	1:00
Sept. 10	at San Francisco	1:00
Sept. 17	at New Orleans	12:00
Sept. 24	**New York Jets**	4:00
Oct. 1	**New England**	1:00
Oct. 8	Open Date	
Oct. 12	at St. Louis (Thursday)	7:00
Oct. 22	at Tampa Bay	1:00
Oct. 29	**Dallas**	1:00
Nov. 5	**Detroit**	1:00
Nov. 12	at Buffalo	1:00
Nov. 19	**St. Louis**	1:00
Nov. 26	at Arizona	2:00
Dec. 3	at Miami	1:00
Dec. 10	**New Orleans**	1:00
Dec. 17	at Carolina	1:00
Dec. 24	**San Francisco**	1:00

RECORD HOLDERS

INDIVIDUAL RECORDS—CAREER

Category	Name	Performance
Rushing (Yds.)	Gerald Riggs, 1982-88	6,631
Passing (Yds.)	Steve Bartkowski, 1975-1985	23,468
Passing (TDs)	Steve Bartkowski, 1975-1985	154
Receiving (No.)	Andre Rison, 1990-94	423
Receiving (Yds.)	Andre Rison, 1990-94	5,635
Interceptions	Rolland Lawrence, 1973-1980	39
Punting (Avg.)	Rick Donnelly, 1985-89	42.6
Punt Return (Avg.)	Al Dodd, 1973-74	11.8
Kickoff Return (Avg.)	Tony Smith, 1992-94	24.9
Field Goals	Mick Luckhurst, 1981-87	115
Touchdowns (Tot.)	Andre Rison, 1990-94	56
Points	Mick Luckhurst, 1981-87	558

INDIVIDUAL RECORDS—SINGLE SEASON

Category	Name	Performance
Rushing (Yds.)	Gerald Riggs, 1985	1,719
Passing (Yds.)	Steve Bartkowski, 1981	3,830
Passing (TDs)	Steve Bartkowski, 1980	31
Receiving (No.)	Terance Mathis, 1994	111
Receiving (Yds.)	Alfred Jenkins, 1981	1,358
Interceptions	Scott Case, 1988	10
Punting (Avg.)	Billy Lothridge, 1968	44.3
Punt Return (Avg.)	Gerald Tinker, 1974	13.9
Kickoff Return (Avg.)	Sylvester Stamps, 1987	27.5
Field Goals	Nick Mike-Mayer, 1973	26
	Norm Johnson, 1993	26
Touchdowns (Tot.)	Andre Rison, 1993	15
Points	Mick Luckhurst, 1981	114

INDIVIDUAL RECORDS—SINGLE GAME

Category	Name	Performance
Rushing (Yds.)	Gerald Riggs, 9-2-84	202
Passing (Yds.)	Steve Bartkowski, 11-15-81	416
Passing (TDs)	Wade Wilson, 12-13-92	5
Receiving (No.)	William Andrews, 11-15-81	15
Receiving (Yds.)	Alfred Jackson, 12-2-84	193
	Andre Rison, 9-4-94	193
Interceptions	Many times	2
	Last time by Vinnie Clark, 10-9-94	
Field Goals	Norm Johnson, 11-13-94	6
Touchdowns (Tot.)	Many times	3
	Last time by Andre Rison, 9-19-93	
Points	Norm Johnson, 11-13-94	20

COACHING HISTORY

(165-268-5)

1966-68	Norb Hecker*	4-26-1
1968-74	Norm Van Brocklin**	37-49-3
1974-76	Marion Campbell***	6-19-0
1976	Pat Peppler	3-6-0
1977-82	Leeman Bennett	47-44-0
1983-86	Dan Henning	22-41-1
1987-89	Marion Campbell****	11-32-0
1989	Jim Hanifan	0-4-0
1990-93	Jerry Glanville	28-38-0
1994	June Jones	7-9

*Released after three games in 1968
**Released after eight games in 1974
***Released after five games in 1976
****Retired after 12 games in 1989

GEORGIA DOME

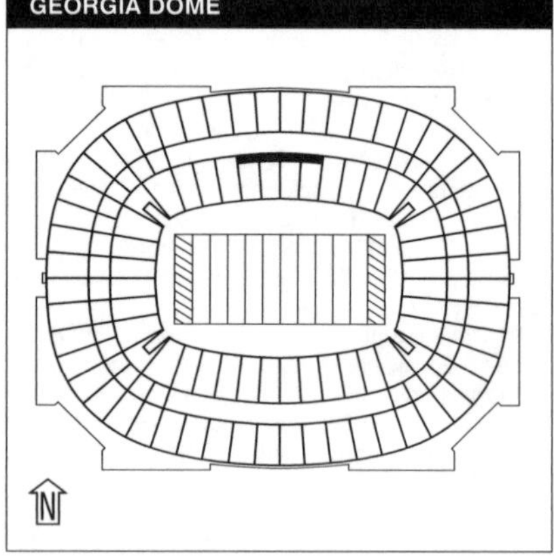

1994 TEAM RECORD

PRESEASON (3-2)

Date	Result		Opponents
7/30	W	21-17	vs. San Diego at Canton
8/6	L	16-37	at Denver
8/12	W	27-7	Buffalo
8/19	L	7-28	at Cleveland
8/26	W	20-12	Philadelphia

REGULAR SEASON (7-9)

Date	Result		Opponents	Att.
9/4	L	28-31	at Detroit (OT)	60,740
9/11	W	31-13	L.A. Rams	55,378
9/18	L	10-30	Kansas City	67,357
9/25	W	27-20	at Washington	53,238
10/2	W	8- 5	at L.A. Rams	34,599
10/9	W	34-13	Tampa Bay	52,633
10/16	L	3-42	San Francisco	67,298
10/23	L	17-30	at L.A. Raiders	42,192
11/6	W	10-9	San Diego	59,217
11/13	L	32-33	at New Orleans	60,313
11/20	L	28-32	at Denver	70,594
11/27	W	28-21	Philadelphia	60,008
12/4	L	14-50	at San Francisco	60,549
12/11	L	20-29	New Orleans	61,307
12/18	L	17-21	at Green Bay	54,885
12/24	W	10- 6	Arizona	35,311

(OT) Overtime

SCORE BY PERIODS

Falcons	93	76	61	87	0	—	317
Opponents	61	110	82	129	3	—	385

ATTENDANCE

Home 458,509 Away 437,110 Total 895,619
Single-game home record, 69,898 (11-9-92)
Single-season home record, 553,979 (1992)

1994 TEAM STATISTICS

	Falcons	Opp.
Total First Downs	302	330
Rushing	63	107
Passing	218	201
Penalty	21	22
Third Down: Made/Att	76/204	84/205
Third Down Pct.	37.3	41.0
Fourth Down: Made/Att	4/9	9/20
Fourth Down Pct.	44.4	45.0
Total Net Yards	5361	5829
Avg. Per Game	335.1	364.3
Total Plays	996	1038
Avg. Per Play	5.4	5.6
Net Yards Rushing	1249	1693
Avg. Per Game	78.1	105.8
Total Rushes	330	426
Net Yards Passing	4112	4136
Avg. Per Game	257.0	258.5
Sacked/Yards Lost	37/232	32/229
Gross Yards	4344	4365
Att./Completions	629/374	580/364
Completion Pct.	59.5	62.8
Had Intercepted	25	22
Punts/Avg.	79/39.5	62/42.9
Net Punting Avg.	79/34.5	62/38.6
Penalties/Yards Lost	119/934	111/853
Fumbles/Ball Lost	28/11	20/11
Touchdowns	36	44
Rushing	8	16
Passing	25	26
Returns	3	2
Avg. Time of Possession	29:10	30:50

1994 INDIVIDUAL STATISTICS

Passing	Att.	Comp.	Yds.	Pct.	TD	Int.	Tkld.	Rate
J. George	524	322	3734	61.5	23	18	32/206	83.3
Hebert	103	52	610	50.5	2	6	3/17	51.0
Emanuel	1	0	0	0.0	0	1	0/0	0.0
Klein	1	0	0	0.0	0	0	2/9	39.6
Falcons	629	374	4344	59.5	25	25	37/232	77.1
Opponents	580	364	4365	62.8	26	22	32/229	84.9

SCORING	TD R	TD P	TD Rt	PAT	FG	Saf	PTS
N. Johnson	0	0	0	32/32	21/25	0	95
Mathis	0	11	0	0/0	0/0	0	70
Rison	0	8	0	0/0	0/0	0	50
Heyward	7	1	0	0/0	0/0	0	48
Emanuel	0	4	0	0/0	0/0	0	24
Jack	0	0	1	0/0	0/0	0	6
Pegram	1	0	0	0/0	0/0	0	6
Sanders	0	1	0	0/0	0/0	0	6
C. Smith	0	0	1	0/0	0/0	0	6
Walker	0	0	1	0/0	0/0	0	6
Falcons	8	25	3	32/32	21/25	0	317
Opponents	16	26	2	39/40	26/33	1	385

2-Point conversions: Mathis (2), Rison. Team: 3-4.

RUSHING	Att.	Yds.	Avg.	LG	TD
Heyward	183	779	4.3	17	7
Pegram	103	358	3.5	25	1
J. George	30	66	2.2	10	0
Hebert	9	43	4.8	20	0
Emanuel	2	4	2.0	2	0
Alexander	1	0	0.0	0	0
J. Anderson	2	-1	-0.5	0	0
Falcons	330	1249	3.8	25	8
Opponents	426	1693	4.0	91t	16

RECEIVING	No.	Yds.	Avg.	LG	TD
Mathis	111	1342	12.1	81	11
Rison	81	1088	13.4	69t	8
Sanders	67	599	8.9	28	1
Emanuel	46	649	14.1	85t	4
Heyward	32	335	10.5	34	1
Pegram	16	99	6.2	28	0
Harris	9	113	12.6	26	0
Lyons	7	54	7.7	10	0
Mims	3	14	4.7	6	0
Spencer	2	51	25.5	40	0
Falcons	374	4344	11.6	85t	25
Opponents	364	4365	12.0	78t	26

INTERCEPTIONS	No.	Yds.	Avg.	LG	TD
D. Johnson	5	0	0.0	0	0
Clark	4	119	29.8	74	0
Walker	3	105	35.0	44t	1
Ross	3	26	8.7	16	0
Case	2	12	6.0	12	0
C. Smith	1	36	36.0	36t	1
Harper	1	22	22.0	22	0
Doleman	1	2	2.0	2	0
Phillips	1	0	0.0	0	0
Tuggle	1	0	0.0	0	0
Falcons	22	322	14.6	74	2
Opponents	25	419	16.8	93t	1

PUNTING	No.	Yds.	Avg.	In 20	LG
Alexander	71	2836	39.9	12	61
Tyner	8	285	35.6	2	46
Falcons	79	3121	39.5	14	61
Opponents	62	2661	42.9	27	67

PUNT RETURNS	No.	FC	Yds.	Avg.	LG	TD
Verdin	23	13	113	4.9	29	0
T. Smith	8	3	75	9.4	20	0
Falcons	31	16	188	6.1	29	0
Opponents	31	16	273	8.8	26	0

KICKOFF RETURNS	No.	Yds.	Avg.	LG	TD
Verdin	44	1026	23.3	69	0
T. Smith	16	333	20.8	31	0
Pegram	9	145	16.1	35	0
Montgomery	2	58	29.0	37	0
Harris	2	47	23.5	30	0
J. Anderson	1	11	11.0	11	0
Heyward	1	7	7.0	7	0
Falcons	75	1627	21.7	69	0
Opponents	66	1328	20.1	39	0

SACKS	No.
C. Smith	11.0
Geathers	8.0
Doleman	7.0
Archambeau	2.0
Harper	1.0
Matthews	1.0
Ross	1.0
Walker	1.0
Falcons	32.0
Opponents	37.0

1995 DRAFT CHOICES

Round	Name	Pos.	College
1	Devin Bush	DB	Florida State
2	Ronald Davis	DB	Tennessee
3	Lorenzo Styles	LB	Ohio State
5	Roell Preston	WR	Mississippi
6	Travis Hall	DT	Brigham Young
7	John Burrough	DE	Wyoming

ATLANTA FALCONS

1995 VETERAN ROSTER

No.		Name	Pos.	Ht.	Wt.	Birthdate	NFL Exp.	College	Hometown	How Acq.	'94 Games/ Starts
68		Agee, Mel	DT	6-5	295	11/22/68	4	Illinois	Chicago, Ill.	FA-'92	16/6
32		Anderson, Jamal	RB	5-10	240	3/6/72	2	Utah	El Camino, Calif.	D7-'94	3/0
92		Archambeau, Lester	DE	6-5	275	6/27/67	6	Stanford	Montville, N.J.	T(GB)-'93	16/12
80		Birden, J.J.	WR	5-9	170	6/16/65	7	Oregon	Portland, Ore.	UFA(KC)-'95	13/13*
19		Dixon, Corey	WR	5-7	155	2/16/72	2	Nebraska	Dallas, Tex.	FA-'94	0*
56		Doleman, Chris	DE	6-5	275	10/16/61	11	Pittsburgh	York, Pa.	T(Minn)-'94	14/7
54		Donahue, Mitch	LB	6-2	254	2/4/68	5	Wyoming	Billings, Mont.	UFA(Den)-'95	3/0*
20		Edwards, Brad	S	6-2	207	3/22/66	7	South Carolina	Fayetteville, N.C.	FA-'94	4/0
87		Emanuel, Bert	WR	5-10	175	10/27/70	2	Rice	Houston, Tex.	D2-'94	16/16
65		Fortin, Roman	G-C	6-5	295	2/26/67	6	San Diego State	Ventura, Calif.	PB(Det)-'92	16/16
67		Gardner, Moe	NT	6-2	265	8/10/68	5	Illinois	Indianapolis, Ind.	D4-'91	16/16
97		Geathers, Jumpy	DT	6-7	290	6/26/60	12	Wichita State	Georgetown, S.C.	UFA(Wash)-'93	16/1
1		George, Jeff	QB	6-4	210	12/8/67	6	Illinois	Indianapolis, Ind.	T(Ind)-'94	16/16
50		George, Ron	LB	6-2	225	3/20/70	3	Stanford	Heidelberg, Germany	D5-'93	16/9
53		Gordon, Dwayne	LB	6-1	240	11/2/69	3	New Hampshire	LaGrangeville, N.Y.	FA-'93	16/0
47		Harper, Roger	S	6-2	223	10/26/70	3	Ohio State	Columbus, Ohio	D2-'93	10/10
82		Harris, Leonard	WR	5-8	162	11/27/60	10	Texas Tech	McKinney, Tex.	FA-'94	8/2
3		Hebert, Bobby	QB	6-4	215	8/19/60	10	Northwestern Louisiana	Mandeville, La.	UFA(NO)-'93	8/0
34		Heyward, Craig	RB	5-11	265	9/26/66	8	Pittsburgh	Passaic, N.J.	FA-'94	16/11
95		Holt, Pierce	DT	6-4	275	1/1/62	8	Angelo State	Marlin, Tex.	RFA(SF)-'93	12/12
39		Jack, Eric	CB	5-10	177	4/19/72	2	New Mexico	El Paso, Tex.	FA-'94	16/0
44		Johnson, D.J.	CB	6-0	190	7/14/66	7	Kentucky	Lexington, Ky.	UFA(Pitt)-'94	16/16
9		Johnson, Norm	K	6-2	203	5/31/60	14	UCLA	Garden Grove, Calif.	FA-'91	16/0
8		Jones, Preston	QB	6-3	223	7/3/70	2	Georgia	Anderson, S.C.	FA-'94	0*
66		Kennedy, Lincoln	G-T	6-6	350	2/12/71	3	Washington	San Diego, Calif.	D1-'93	16/2
7		Klein, Perry	QB	6-2	218	3/25/71	2	C.W. Post	Santa Monica, Calif.	D4-'94	2/0
88		Le Bel, Harper	TE	6-4	255	7/14/63	7	Colorado State	Sherman Oaks, Calif.	PB(Phil)-'91	16/0
80		Lewis, Nate	WR	5-11	198	10/19/66	6	Oregon Tech	Moultrie, Ga.	UFA(Chi)-'95	13/0*
86		Lyons, Mitch	TE	6-4	265	5/13/70	3	Michigan State	Grand Rapids, Mich.	D6-'93	7/2
81		Mathis, Terance	WR	5-10	175	6/7/67	6	New Mexico	Stone Mountain, Ga.	UFA(NYJ)-'94	16/16
57		Matthews, Clay	LB	6-2	245	3/15/56	18	Southern California	Los Angeles, Calif.	FA-'94	15/15
21	t-	Metcalf, Eric	RB-WR	5-10	190	1/23/68	7	Texas	Arlington, Va.	T(Clev)-'95	16/8*
38		Miano, Rich	S	6-1	200	9/3/62	11	Hawaii	Honolulu, Hawaii	UFA(Phil)-'95	16/0*
22		Montgomery, Alton	S	6-0	205	6/16/68	6	Houston	Griffin, Ga.	T(Den)-'93	2/1
96		Pahukoa, Jeff	G-T	6-2	298	2/9/69	4	Washington	Vancouver, Wash.	FA-'95	0*
26		Phillips, Anthony	CB	6-2	207	10/5/70	2	Texas A&M	Galveston, Tex.	D3-'94	5/0
51	#	Ritcher, Jim	G	6-3	273	5/21/58	16	North Carolina State	Raleigh, N.C.	FA-'94	2/0
36		Ross, Kevin	S	5-9	185	1/16/62	12	Temple	Mickleton, N.J.	UFA(KC)-'94	16/16
83	#	Sanders, Ricky	WR	5-11	180	8/30/62	10	Southwest Texas State	Temple, Tex.	FA-'94	14/12
74		Selby, Rob	G	6-3	286	10/11/67	5	Auburn	Birmingham, Ala.	UFA(Phil)-'95	2/0*
37		Shelley, Elbert	CB	5-11	190	12/24/64	9	Arkansas State	Tyronza, Ark.	D11-'87	16/0
90	†	Smith, Chuck	DE	6-2	257	12/21/69	4	Tennessee	Athens, Ga.	D2-'92	15/10
84		Spencer, Darryl	WR	5-8	172	3/21/70	2	Miami	Merritt Island, Fla.	FA-'94	8/0
4		Stryzinski, Dan	P	6-2	200	5/15/65	6	Indiana	Indianapolis, Ind.	UFA(TB)-'95	16/0*
99		Talley, Darryl	LB	6-4	235	7/10/60	13	West Virginia	Cleveland, Ohio	UFA(Buff)-'95	16/16*
24		Taylor, Terry	CB-S	5-10	185	7/18/61	10	Southern Illinois	Warren, Ohio	UFA(Sea)-'95	5/3*
52		Tippins, Ken	LB	6-1	235	7/22/66	7	Middle Tennessee State	Adel, Ga.	FA-'90	16/7
61		Tobeck, Robbie	C	6-4	287	3/6/70	2	Washington State	Tarpon Springs, Fla.	FA-'93	5/0
58		Tuggle, Jessie	LB	5-11	230	2/14/65	9	Valdosta State	Spalding, Ga.	FA-'87	16/16
2		Tyner, Scott	K	6-1	189	4/11/72	2	Oklahoma State	Edgewood, Tex.	FA-'94	6/0
45		Walker, Darnell	CB	5-8	168	1/17/70	3	Oklahoma	St. Louis, Mo.	D7-'93	16/5
46	#	Washington, Charles	S	6-1	214	10/8/66	7	Cameron	Dallas, Tex.	FA-'93	16/1
70		Whitfield, Bob	T	6-5	300	10/18/71	4	Stanford	Carson, Calif.	D1a-'92	16/16
72		Zandofsky, Mike	C-G	6-2	305	11/30/65	7	Washington	Corvallis, Ore.	UFA(SD)-'94	16/16

* Birden played 13 games with Kansas City in '94; Dixon missed '94 season because of injury; Donahue played 3 games with Denver; Jones last active with Philadelphia in '93; Lewis played 13 games with Chicago; Metcalf played 16 games with Cleveland; Miano played 16 games with Philadelphia; Pahukoa last active with L.A. Rams in '93; Selby played 2 games with Philadelphia; Stryzinski played 16 games with Tampa Bay; Talley played 16 games with Buffalo; Taylor played 5 games with Seattle.

\# Unrestricted free agent; subject to developments.

† Restricted free agent; subject to developments.

Traded—P Harold Alexander to Detroit, DT Ferric Collons to Green Bay.

t- Falcons traded for Metcalf (Cleveland).

Players lost through free agency (4): S Brett Maxie (Car; 4 games in '94), RB Erric Pegram (Pitt; 13), WR Andre Rison (Clev; 15), WR-KR Clarence Verdin (TB; 12).

Players lost through Expansion Draft (2): DT Bill Goldberg (Car; 5 games in '94), WR David Mims (Car; 2).

Also played with Falcons in '94—P Harold Alexander (15 games), S Scott Case (15), CB Vinnie Clark (11), T Irv Eatman (4), LB Darryl Ford (15), T Mike Kenn (15), G Dave Richards (15), RB Tony Smith (4).

COACHING STAFF

Head Coach,
June Jones

Pro Career: Became the eighth head coach in Falcons history on January 24, 1994, succeeding Jerry Glanville. Most recently was Falcons' assistant head coach-offense since 1991. He played five seasons (1977-1981) in NFL mainly as a backup quarterback to Falcons' all-time leading passer Steve Bartkowski. He was a member of the Falcons' first-ever playoff team in 1978. Jones began his coaching career as wide receivers coach of Houston Gamblers of the USFL in 1984. He became the offensive coordinator of the Denver Gold (USFL) in 1985 and then moved on to Ottawa Roughriders of the CFL in 1986. He was quarterbacks coach of the Houston Oilers in 1987-89. Was the quarterbacks and receivers coach for Detroit Lions in 1989-90.

Background: Guided Portland State to back-to-back 8-3 seasons, serving as team captain during his senior year, after also playing at Hawaii and Oregon. Jones and new Redskins head coach, Norv Turner, were backups to Hall of Famer quarterback Dan Fouts at Oregon. Jones has been to a Grey Cup final in the CFL, a division title with Jim Kelly in the USFL, and has advanced to the postseason in both NFL conferences.

Personal: Born on February 19, 1953, in Portland, Oregon. June and his wife, Diane, live in Lake Lanier, Ga., and have three daughters—Jennifer, Kelli, Nicole, and son June, IV.

ASSISTANT COACHES

Keith Armstrong, defensive assistant; born December 15, 1963, Philadelphia, Pa., lives in Duluth, Ga. Running back Temple 1983-86. No pro playing experience. College coach: Akron 1989, Oklahoma State 1990-92, Notre Dame 1993. Pro coach: Joined Falcons in 1994.

Darrell (Mouse) Davis, quarterbacks; born September 6, 1932, Palouse, Wash., lives in Alpharetta, Ga. Quarterback Western Oregon State 1952-55. No pro playing experience. College coach: Portland State 1974-80 (head coach 1975-80). Pro coach: Toronto Argonauts (CFL) 1982-83, Houston Gamblers (USFL) 1984, Denver Gold (USFL) 1985, Detroit Lions 1989-90, NY/NJ Knights (WL) 1991-92, joined Falcons in 1994.

Frank Gansz, assistant head coach-offense; born November 22, 1938, Altoona, Pa., lives in Braselton, Ga. Center-linebacker Navy 1957-59. No pro playing experience. College coach: Air Force 1964-66, Colgate 1968, Navy 1969-72, Oklahoma State 1973, 1975, Army 1974, UCLA 1976-77. Pro coach: San Francisco 49ers 1978, Cincinnati Bengals 1979-80, Kansas City Chiefs 1981-82, 1986-88 (head coach 1987-88), Philadelphia Eagles 1983-85, Detroit Lions 1989-93, joined Falcons in 1994.

Joe Haering, defensive coordinator; born February 1, 1946, Pittsburgh, Pa., lives in Lawrenceville, Ga. Linebacker Bucknell 1961-65. No pro playing experience. College coach: Bucknell 1969, Kentucky 1970-72, Boston University 1973-74, Kent State 1975-77. Pro coach: New York Jets 1978-79, Hamilton Tiger-Cats (CFL) 1980, Chicago Blitz (USFL) 1982-83, Pittsburgh Maulers (USFL) 1984, Denver Gold (USFL) 1985, NY/NJ Knights (WL) 1992, joined Falcons in 1994.

Milt Jackson, receivers; born October 16, 1943, Groesbeck, Tex., lives in Suwanee, Ga. Defensive back Tulsa 1965-66. Pro defensive back San Francisco 49ers 1967. College coach: Oregon State 1973, Rice 1974, California 1975-76, Oregon 1977-78, UCLA 1979. Pro coach: San Francisco 49ers 1980-82, Buffalo Bills 1983-84, Philadelphia Eagles 1985, Houston Oilers 1986-88, Indianapolis Colts 1989-91, Los Angeles Rams 1992-93, joined Falcons in 1994.

Tim Jorgensen, strength and conditioning; born April 21, 1955, St. Louis, Mo., lives in Snellville, Ga. Guard Southwest Missouri State 1974-76. No pro playing experience. College coach: Southwest Missouri State 1977-78, Alabama 1979, Louisiana State 1980-83. Pro coach: Philadelphia Eagles 1984-86, joined Falcons in 1987.

Bill Kollar, defensive line; born November 27, 1952, Warren, Ohio, lives in Duluth, Ga. Defensive end Montana State 1971-74. Pro defensive end Cincinnati Bengals 1974-76, Tampa Bay Buccaneers 1977-81. College coach: Illinois 1985-87, Purdue 1988-89. Pro coach: Tampa Bay Buccaneers 1984, joined Falcons in 1990.

Will Lewis, defensive assistant; born January 16, 1958, Quarkerstown, Pa., lives in Suwanee, Ga. Defensive back Millersville State 1976-79. Pro defensive back Seattle Seahawks 1980-81, Kansas City Chiefs 1981, Houston Gamblers (USFL) 1984-86, Ottawa Roughriders (CFL) 1986-88, Hamilton Tiger-Cats (CFL) 1989. College coach: Houston 1989, Lock Haven 1990-91, Millersville State 1992-93, Maine 1994. Pro coach: New York/New Jersey Knights (World League) 1991-92, joined Falcons in 1995.

Bob Palcic, offensive line; born July 2, 1948, Gowanda, N.Y., lives in Lawrenceville, Ga. Linebacker Dayton 1968-70. No pro playing experience. College coach: Dayton 1974-75, Ball State 1976-77, Wisconsin 1978-81, Arizona 1984-85, Ohio State 1986-91, Southern California 1992, UCLA 1993. Pro coach: Joined Falcons in 1994.

Rod Rust, defensive assistant; born August 2, 1928, Cedar Rapids, Iowa, lives in Lawrenceville, Ga. Center-linebacker Iowa State 1947-49. No pro playing experience. College coach: New Mexico 1960-62, Stanford 1963-66, North Texas State 1967-72 (head coach). Pro coach: Montreal Alouettes 1973-75, Philadelphia Eagles 1976-77, Kansas City Chiefs 1978-82, 1988, New England Patriots 1983-87, 1990 (head coach), Pittsburgh Steelers 1989, New York Giants 1992, Winnepeg Blue Bombers (CFL) 1994, joined Falcons in 1995.

Ollie Wilson, running backs; born March 31, 1951, Worcester, Mass., lives in Roswell, Ga. Wide receiver Springfield 1971-73. No pro playing experience. College coach: Springfield 1975, Northeastern 1976-82, California 1983-90. Pro coach: Joined Falcons in 1991.

1995 FIRST-YEAR ROSTER

Name	Pos.	Ht.	Wt.	Birthdate	College	Hometown	How Acq.
Anderson, Dunstan (1)	DE	6-4	254	12/31/70	Tulsa	Ft. Worth, Tex.	FA
Brewer, George (1)	DT	6-5	295	6/11/69	Savannah State	West Point, Ga.	FA
Brown, Tyrone	WR	5-11	164	1/3/73	Toledo	Cincinnati, Ohio	FA
Burrough, John	DT	6-5	265	5/17/72	Wyoming	Pinedale, Wyo.	D7
Bush, Devin	S	5-11	208	7/3/73	Florida State	El Paso, Tex.	D1
Ceasar, Ricky	DE	6-2	252	11/10/70	Northeast Oklahoma St.	Houston, Tex.	FA
Davis, Ronald	CB	5-10	190	2/24/72	Tennessee	Bartlett, Tenn.	D2
Etheridge, Alonzo	DE	6-4	255	2/2/72	Auburn	Selma, Ala.	FA
Evans, Bobby (1)	CB-S	6-2	200	12/2/67	Southern Arkansas	Haynesville, La.	FA
Evans, Stacy	DE	6-2	265	7/28/72	South Carolina	Laurens, S.C.	FA
Gary, Kyle	WR	5-9	177	3/2/73	Idaho	Portland, Ore.	FA
Hall, Travis	DE	6-5	278	8/3/72	Brigham Young	Kenai, Alaska	D6
Hamilton, Brian	DE	6-3	278	3/22/72	Notre Dame	Chicago, Ill.	FA
Jackson, Abdul	LB	6-1	236	7/5/72	Mississippi	Atlanta, Ga.	FA
Miller, Maurice (1)	LB	6-3	220	9/6/69	Wake Forest	Richmond, Va.	FA
Norman, Todd (1)	T	6-5	300	9/11/71	Notre Dame	Huntington Beach, Calif.	FA
Preston, Roell	WR	5-10	187	6/23/72	Mississippi	Miami, Fla.	D5
Pruitt, Brian	RB	5-9	205	1/16/73	Central Michigan	Saginaw, Mich.	FA
Purdie, Aaron	T	6-6	280	6/6/72	Kentucky	Toledo, Ohio	FA
Purgason, Roger	T	6-5	286	10/18/71	North Carolina	Charlotte, N.C.	FA
Rogers, Joe (1)	WR	5-7	161	5/23/71	Texas Southern	Miami, Fla.	FA
Schulte, Ross	P-K	6-5	190	8/14/72	Western Illinois	Fowler, Ill.	FA
Styles, Lorenzo	LB	6-1	244	1/31/74	Ohio State	Columbus, Ohio	D3
Vaitai, Anolo	G	6-2	284	12/5/71	Texas-El Paso	Dallas, Tex.	FA
Vinson, Tony (1)	RB	6-1	229	3/13/71	Towson State	Denbigh, Va.	FA
Williams, Thomas (1)	DE	6-3	274	12/19/70	Wyoming	Pueblo, Colo.	FA

The term NFL Rookie is defined as a player who is in his first season of professional football and has not been on the roster of another professional football team for any regular-season or postseason games. A Rookie is designated by an "R" on NFL rosters. Players who have been active in another professional football league or players who have NFL experience, including either preseason training camp or being on an Active List or Inactive List, or on Reserve/Injured or Reserve/Physically Unable to Perform for fewer than six regular-season games, are termed NFL First-Year Players. An NFL First-Year Player is designated by a "1" on NFL rosters. Thereafter, a player is credited with an additional year of experience for each season in which he accumulates six games on the Active List or Inactive List, or on Reserve/Injured or Reserve/Physically Unable to Perform.

NOTES

CAROLINA PANTHERS

National Football Conference
Western Division
Team Colors: Black, Panther Blue, and Silver
227 West Trade Street, Suite 1600
Charlotte, North Carolina 28202
Telephone: (704) 358-7000

CLUB OFFICIALS

Founder/Owner: Jerry Richardson
President: Mike McCormack
General Manager: Bill Polian
Director of Business Operations: Mark Richardson
Director of Stadium Operations: Jon Richardson
Assistant Director of Business Operations: Charles Waddell
Counsel: Richard Thigpen, Jr.
Chief Financial Officer: Dave Olsen
Controller: Lisa Garber
Assistant General Manager: Joe Mack
Director Player Personnel: Dom Anile
Pro Scout: Chris Polian
Regional Scouts: Jack Bushofsky, Ralph Hawkins
Area Scouts: Hal Athon, Boyd Dowler, Bob Guarini, Jerry Hardaway, Tony Softli
Scouting Assistant: Steve Hinshaw
Director of Communications: Charlie Dayton
Media Relations Assistant: Lex Sant
Media Relations and Marketing Assistant: Bruce Speight
Director of Ticket Sales: Phil Youtsey
Assistant Ticket Manager: Kati Hynes
Director of Community Affairs/Player Relations: Donnie Shell
Director of Family Programs: B.J. Waymer
Director of Special Events: Leslie Matz
Director of Information Systems: Roger Goss
Video Director: Dave Sutherby
Assistant Video Director: Mark Hobbs
Head Trainer: John Kasik
Assistant Trainer: Al Shuford
Equipment Manager: Jackie Miles
Assistant Equipment Managers: Don Toner, Mitchell Harper
Director of Football Administration: Steve Champlin
Director of Football Security: Ed Stillwell
Office Manager: Jackie Jeffries
1995 Stadium: Clemson Memorial Stadium
•**Capacity:** 76,055
Williamson Road
Clemson, South Carolina 28633
Playing Surface: Grass
Stadium Beginning 1996: Carolinas Stadium
•**Capacity:** 72,500
Charlotte, North Carolina 28202
Training Camp: Wofford College
Spartanburg, South Carolina 29303

FORMULATION OF CAROLINA PANTHERS

The player access plan for the expansion Carolina Panthers and Jacksonville Jaguars was announced jointly by the NFL and the NFL Players Association on September 29, 1994. Under the plan, Carolina and Jacksonville were given three ways to acquire players:

1. Veteran Allocation Draft—On February 15, 1995, the expansion teams selected from a list of six veteran players submitted by each of the 28 existing NFL teams. Carolina and Jacksonville had to select at least 30 players but no more than 42. An existing club had to recall a player from its list each time one of its players was selected. The expansion teams could select a maximum of three players from each of the other clubs. Jacksonville had the first pick and selected 31 players. Carolina chose 35.
2. College Player Draft—In addition to their regular selections, each expansion team received a total of 14 extra picks in the 1995 and 1996 college drafts. For the 1995 draft, Carolina and Jacksonville were awarded the first two choices in all seven rounds. The picks were allotted in rotating order with Carolina given the first choice in round one, Jacksonville the first in round two, etc. Carolina won the right to select first via a coin flip with Jacksonville at the 1994 draft. In addition to their picks at the top of each round, the expansion teams received seven additional 1995 selections each, one at the end of rounds one through seven.

   In the 1996 draft, both the Panthers and Jaguars will receive an extra choice after each of their original picks in rounds three through five, plus two extra picks each after their original selections in rounds six and seven. The additional picks will fall 15 selections after the team's original choice in those rounds.
3. Free Agency—The clubs signed veteran free agents between February and July, 1995, under the same terms as the league's current 28 clubs.

1995 SCHEDULE

PRESEASON

July 29	vs. Jacksonville at Canton, Ohio	2:30
Aug. 4	at Chicago	7:30
Aug. 12	**Denver**	7:30
Aug. 19	at San Francisco	5:00
Aug. 26	**New York Giants**	4:00

REGULAR SEASON

Sept. 3	at Atlanta	1:00
Sept. 10	at Buffalo	1:00
Sept. 17	**St. Louis**	1:00
Sept. 24	Open Date	
Oct. 1	**Tampa Bay**	1:00
Oct. 8	at Chicago	12:00
Oct. 15	**New York Jets**	4:00
Oct. 22	**New Orleans**	1:00
Oct. 29	at New England	1:00
Nov. 5	at San Francisco	1:00
Nov. 12	at St. Louis	12:00
Nov. 19	**Arizona**	1:00
Nov. 26	at New Orleans	7:00
Dec. 3	**Indianapolis**	1:00
Dec. 10	**San Francisco**	1:00
Dec. 17	**Atlanta**	1:00
Dec. 24	at Washington	4:00

1995 DRAFT CHOICES

Round	Name	Pos.	College
1	Kerry Collins	QB	Penn State
	Tyrone Poole	DB	Ft. Valley State
	Blake Brockermeyer	T	Texas
2	Shawn King	DE	Northeast Louisiana
4	Frank Garcia	C	Washington
5	Michael Senters	DB	Northwestern
	Andrew Peterson	T	Washington
6	Steve Strahan	DT	Bayor
	Jerry Colquitt	QB	Tennessee
7	Chad Cota	DB	Oregon
	Michael Reed	DB	Boston College

CLEMSON MEMORIAL STADIUM

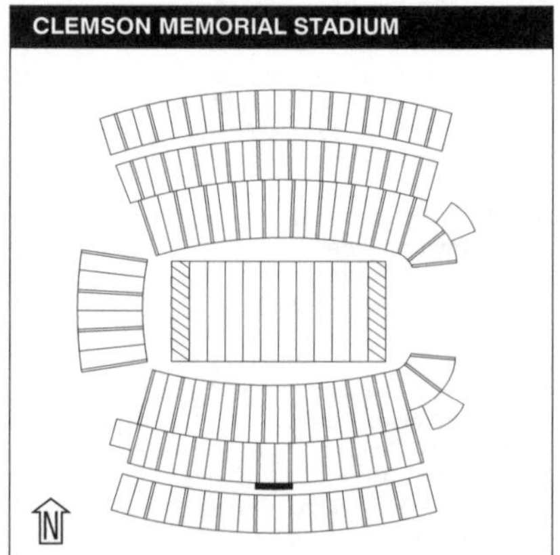

CAROLINAS STADIUM

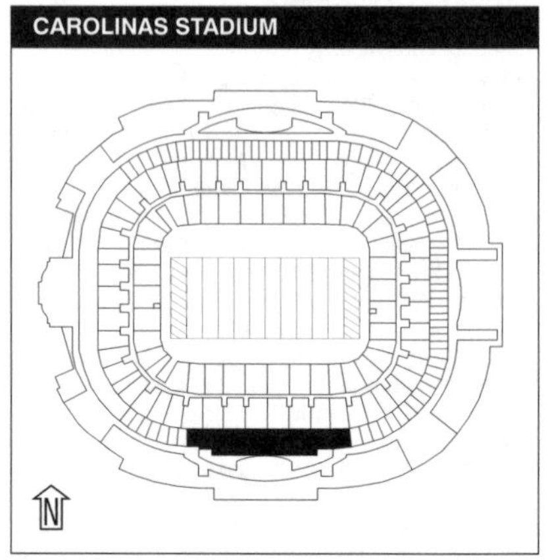

CAROLINA PANTHERS CHRONOLOGY

July 16, 1987
Jerry and Mark Richardson; NationsBank Chairman and Chief Executive Officer Hugh McColl, Jr.; attorney Richard Thigpen, Jr.; Max Muhleman of Muhleman Marketing; and John Lewis of Arthur Andersen and Company meet in Charlotte to discuss the feasibility of entering a multi-city competition for two NFL expansion franchises.

December 15, 1987
Jerry Richardson officially announces an NFL franchise bid and stadium effort for the Carolinas.

April 11, 1989
Mike McCormack, Pro Football Hall of Fame lineman and former president, general manager, and head coach of the Seattle Seahawks, joins Richardson Sports as executive consultant for its expansion effort.

August 20, 1989
At "Carolinas Kickoff '89," a sellout crowd of 52,855 in Raleigh, North Carolina's Carter-Finley Stadium watches the New York Jets play the Philadelphia Eagles.

April 4, 1990
National Football League Commissioner Paul Tagliabue announces that the league will expand by two teams no later than the 1993 season.

July 26, 1990
The NFL Realignment and Expansion Committee recommends that the NFL expand by two teams for the 1993 season.

August 11, 1990
"Carolinas Kickoff II" at Kenan Stadium in Chapel Hill, North Carolina, features the Washington Redskins and the Atlanta Falcons before a sellout crowd of 52,036.

May 15, 1991
The NFL Realignment and Expansion Committee recommends that the league expand by two teams for the 1994 season.

May 22, 1991
At the NFL meetings in Minneapolis, a plan is approved that will add two expansion teams to the league for the 1994 season.

June 26, 1991
South Carolina governor Carroll Campbell and North Carolina governor Jim Martin officially announce their support of NFL expansion in the Carolinas.

July 17, 1991
The NFL announces that it will accept applications for expansion teams.

August 24, 1991
69,117 fans cram Williams-Brice Stadium in Columbia, South Carolina, for "Carolinas Kickoff III."

September 13, 1991
Richardson Sports submits a formal community application for Carolinas NFL franchise along with $100,000 deposit.

December 10, 1991
Richardson Sports representatives make a presentation to NFL Commissioner Paul Tagliabue and members of the NFL staff in New York.

March 17, 1992
At the NFL's annual winter meeting in Phoenix, the list of expansion candidate cities is cut from eleven to seven. Charlotte is one of the seven, while Nashville, San Antonio, Raleigh-Durham, and Honolulu are eliminated.

May 19, 1992
At a league meeting in Pasadena, California, the NFL cuts the list of expansion hopefuls to five communities: Charlotte, Jacksonville, Baltimore, Memphis, and St. Louis. Sacramento and Oakland are eliminated.

September 1, 1992
Jerry and Mark Richardson present a stadium financing plan to NFL officials.

October 20, 1992
At the NFL owners meeting in Chicago, league officials delay expansion until 1995 because of a labor dispute involving a new collective bargaining agreement.

January 6, 1993
A seven-year Collective Bargaining Agreement is reached between the NFL and its players. With the labor situation resolved, a new expansion timetable is expected in March, 1993.

July 1, 1993
Sale of luxury suites, club seats, and Personal Seat Licenses (PSL) officially begins.

September 13, 1993
Richardson Sports and Clemson University announce the terms of an agreement in which the Panthers would play the 1995 season in Clemson Memorial Stadium.

September 22, 1993
Richardson Sports makes its presentation to the NFL Expansion and Finance Committees and league officials.

October 26, 1993
At a league meeting in Chicago, NFL owners unanimously select the Carolinas as the twenty-ninth NFL franchise.

January 12, 1994
Veteran NFL executive Bill Polian is hired as general manager and Mike McCormack is promoted to club president.

April 22, 1994
Construction begins on Carolinas Stadium, which is expected to take 27 months to complete.

April 24, 1994
Carolina wins the first selection in the 1995 NFL Draft by winning a coin toss with the Jacksonville Jaguars at the 1994 draft in New York.

May 3, 1994
Wofford College in Spartanburg, South Carolina, is chosen as the team's training camp site.

May 26, 1994
Carolina and Jacksonville are named participants in the 1995 Hall of Fame game.

October 5, 1994
The first free-agent workout at Winthrop University in Rock Hill, South Carolina.

November 2, 1994
Commissioner Tagliabue slots the Carolina Panthers in the NFC Western Division.

December 15, 1994
The Panthers sign their first 10 free-agent players.

January 23, 1995
Dom Capers, the defensive coordinator for the Pittsburgh Steelers, is named the Panthers' first head coach.

February 15, 1995
The expansion draft held in New York City is held. The Panthers select 35 players.

April 22, 1995
The NFL college draft is held. The Panthers trade their number-one pick to Cincinnati and choose Penn State quarterback Kerry Collins with the fifth overall selection.

CAROLINA PANTHERS

1995 VETERAN ROSTER

No.		Name	Pos.	Ht.	Wt.	Birthdate	NFL Exp.	College	Hometown	'94 Games/ How Acq.	Starts
54		Bailey, Carlton	LB	6-3	235	12/15/64	8	North Carolina	Baltimore, Md.	FA-'95	16/11*
23		Baldwin, Randy	RB	5-10	216	8/19/67	5	Mississppi	Griffin, Ga.	UFA(Clev)-'95	16/0*
6		Barnhart, Tommy	P	6-2	207	6/11/63	9	North Carolina	China Grove, N.C.	UFA(NO)-'95	16/0*
82		Beebe, Don	WR	5-11	180	12/18/64	7	Chadron State	Sugar Grove, Ill.	UFA(Buff)-'95	13/11*
77		Boatswain, Harry	T	6-4	295	6/26/69	5	New Haven	Brooklyn, N.Y.	ED(SF)-'95	13/4*
40		Brabham, Cary	CB-S	6-0	195	8/11/70	2	Southern Methodist	Hughes Springs, Tex.	ED(Raid)-'95	7/0*
26		Brewer, Dewell	RB	5-8	199	5/22/70	2	Oklahoma	Lawton, Okla.	ED(Ind)-'95	16/0*
11		Buchanan, Richard	WR	5-10	178	5/8/69	3	Northwestern	Maywood, Ill.	ED(Rams)-'95	3/0*
53		Butcher, Paul	LB	6-0	240	11/8/63	8	Wayne State	Dearborn, Mich.	ED(Ind)-'95	13/0*
83		Carrier, Mark	WR	6-0	185	10/28/65	9	Nicholls State	Church Point, La.	ED(Clev)-'95	16/6*
44		Christian, Bob	RB	5-10	225	11/14/68	3	Northwestern	Florissant, Mo.	ED(Chi)-'95	12/0*
56		Conner, Darion	LB	6-2	242	9/28/67	6	Jackson State	Noxubee, Miss.	UFA(NO)-'95	16/13*
43		Cuthbert, Randy	RB	6-2	224	1/16/70	2	Duke	Doylestown, Pa.	FA-'95	1/0*
52		Elliott, Matt	C-G	6-3	294	10/1/68	3	Michigan	Carmel, Ind.	FA-'95	0*
79		Finn, Mike	T	6-5	275	9/26/67	3	Arkansas-Pine Bluff	Texarkana, Tex.	FA-'95	0*
36		Foggie, Fred	CB-S	6-0	200	6/10/69	2	Minnesota	Laurens, S.C.	ED(Pitt)-'95	3/0*
29	t-	Foster, Barry	RB	5-10	217	12/8/68	6	Arkansas	Duncanville, Tex.	T(Pitt)-'95	11/10*
93		Fox, Mike	DE	6-6	288	8/5/67	6	West Virginia	Akron, Ohio	UFA(NYG)-'95	16/16*
34		Fuller, Eddie	RB	5-9	198	6/22/68	5	Louisiana State	Leesville, La.	FA-'95	0*
74		Graham, Derrick	T	6-4	315	3/18/67	6	Appalachian State	Groveland, Fla.	UFA(KC)-'95	16/11*
86		Green, Willie	WR	6-4	188	4/2/66	6	Mississippi	Clarke, Ga.	FA-'95	5/0*
33		Griffith, Howard	RB	6-0	226	11/17/67	3	Illinois	Chicago, Ill.	ED(Rams)-'95	16/10*
84		Guliford, Eric	WR	5-8	165	10/25/69	3	Arizona State	Peoria, Ariz.	ED(Minn)-'95	7/1*
24		Haller, Alan	CB	5-11	185	8/9/70	2	Michigan State	Lansing, Mich.	FA-'95	0*
8		Hawkins, Steve	WR	6-5	210	3/16/71	2	Western Michigan	Detroit, Mich.	ED(NE)-'95	7/0*
89		Haws, Kurt	TE	6-5	248	9/25/69	2	Utah	Mountain View, Ariz.	ED(Wash)-'95	6/0*
4		Kasay, John	K	5-10	189	10/27/69	5	Georgia	Athens, Ga.	UFA(Sea)-'95	16/0*
71		Kragen, Greg	NT	6-3	265	3/1/62	11	Utah State	Pleasanton, Calif.	ED(KC)-'95	16/2*
25		Lassic, Derrick	RB	5-10	188	1/26/70	3	Alabama	Haverstraw, N.Y.	ED(Dall)-'95	0*
57		Lathon, Lamar	LB	6-3	252	12/23/67	6	Houston	Wharton, Tex.	UFA(Hou)-'95	16/15*
27		Lofton, Steve	CB	5-9	180	11/26/68	4	Texas A&M	Jacksonville, Fla.	FA-'95	0*
87		Marrow, Vince	TE	6-3	251	8/17/68	2	Toledo	Youngstown, Ohio	ED(Buff)-'95	10/0*
39		Maxie, Brett	S	6-2	194	1/13/62	11	Texas Southern	Dallas, Tex.	UFA(Atl)-'95	4/2*
25		McDowell, Bubba	S	6-1	198	11/4/66	7	Miami	Merritt Island, Fla.	FA-'95	9/3*
22		McKyer, Tim	CB	6-0	178	9/5/63	10	Texas-Arlington	Port Arthur, Tex.	ED(Pitt)-'95	16/2*
88		Metzelaars, Pete	TE	6-7	254	5/24/60	14	Wabash	Portage, Mich.	UFA(Buff)-'95	16/16*
51		Mills, Sam	LB	5-9	225	6/3/59	10	Montclair State	Long Branch, N.J.	UFA(NO)-'95	16/16*
81		Mims, David	WR	5-8	191	7/7/70	3	Baylor	Daingerfield, Tex.	ED(Atl)-'95	2/2*
76		Moore, Darryl	G	6-3	293	1/27/69	3	Texas-El Paso	Minden, La.	FA-'95	0*
31		O'Neal Brian	RB	6-0	233	2/25/70	2	Penn State	Cincinnati, Ohio	ED(Phil)-'95	14/0*
55		Powell, Andre	LB	6-1	235	6/5/69	3	Penn State	York, Pa.	ED(NYG)-'95	1/0*
92		Price, Shawn	DE	6-5	260	3/28/70	3	Pacific	North Tahoe, Nev.	ED(TB)-'95	6/0*
14		Reich, Frank	QB	6-4	210	12/4/61	11	Maryland	Lebanon, Pa.	UFA(Buff)-'95	16/2*
63		Rodenhauser, Mark	C	6-5	280	6/1/61	8	Illinois State	Addison, Ill.	ED(Det)-'95	16/0*
90		Rodgers, Tyrone	DT	6-3	276	4/27/69	4	Washington	Longview, Tex.	ED(Sea)-'95	5/0*
72		Rollins, Baron	G	6-4	335	7/23/70	2	Louisiana Tech	Winnsboro, La.	ED(NO)-'95	0*
15		Ryans, Larry	WR	5-11	182	7/28/71	2	Clemson	Greenwood, S.C.	ED(Det)-'95	0*
58		Sims, William	LB	6-3	265	12/30/70	2	Southwestern Louisiana	Brooks County, Ga.	ED(Minn)-'95	8/0*
21		Smith, Rod	CB	5-11	187	3/12/70	4	Notre Dame	St. Paul, Minn.	ED(NE)-'95	16/7*
28		Smith, Tony	RB	6-1	212	6/29/70	3	Southern Mississippi	Vicksburg, Miss.	FA-'95	4/0*
50		Stams, Frank	LB	6-2	240	7/17/66	7	Notre Dame	Akron, Ohio	UFA(Clev)-'95	16/15*
80		Stone, Dwight	WR	6-0	194	1/28/64	8	Middle Tennessee State	Florala, Ala.	UFA(Pitt)-'95	15/1*
91	†	Teeter, Mike	DT	6-3	272	10/4/67	4	Michigan	Fruitport, Mich.	ED(Hou)-'95	14/0*
75		Thomas, Mark	DE	6-5	273	5/6/69	4	North Carolina State	Lilburn, Ga.	ED(SF)-'95	9/0*
85		Tillman, Lawyer	TE	6-5	254	5/20/66	6	Auburn	Mobile, Ala.	FA-'95	0*
10		Trudeau, Jack	QB	6-3	227	9/9/62	10	Illinois	Livermore, Calif.	ED(NYJ)-'95	5/2*
30		Turner, Vernon	RB	5-8	185	1/6/67	5	Carson-Newman	Staten Island, N.Y	UFA(TB)-'95	12/1*
64		Whitley, Curtis	C	6-1	288	5/10/69	4	Clemson	Smithfield, N.C.	ED(SD)-'95	12/2*
98		Williams, Gerald	DE	6-3	293	9/8/63	10	Auburn	Valley, Ala.	UFA(Pitt)-'95	11/11*
20		Williams, James	CB	5-10	190	3/30/67	6	Fresno State	Coalinga, Calif.	UFA(Ariz)-'95	15/7*

* Bailey played 16 games with N.Y. Giants in '94; Baldwin played 16 games with Cleveland; Barnhardt played 16 games with New Orleans; Beebe played 13 games with Buffalo; Boatswain played 13 games with San Francisco; Brabham played 7 games with L.A. Raiders; Brewer played 16 games with Indianapolis; Buchanan played 3 games with L.A. Rams; Butcher played 13 games with Indianapolis; Carrier played 16 games with Cleveland; Christian played 12 games with Chicago; Conner played 16 games with New Orleans; Cuthbert played 1 game with Pittsburgh; Elliott last on injured reserve with Washington in '93; Finn active for 2 games with Philadelphia but did not play; Foggie played 3 games with Pittsburgh; Fox played 16 games with N.Y. Giants; Fuller last active with Buffalo in '93; Graham played 16 games with Kansas City; Green played 5 games with Tampa Bay; Griffith played 16 games with L.A. Rams; Guliford played 7 games with Minnesota; Haller last active with Pittsburgh in '93; Hawkins played 7 games with New England; Haws played 6 games with Washington; Kasay played 16 games with Seattle; Kragen played 16 games with Kansas City; Lassic inactive for 12 games with Dallas; Lathon played 16 games with Houston; Lofton last active with Phoenix in '93; Marrow played 10 games with Buffalo; Maxie played 4 games with Atlanta; McDowell played 9 games with Houston; McKyer played 16 games with Pittsburgh; Metzelaars played 16 games with Buffalo; Mills played 16 games with New Orleans; Mims played 2 games with Atlanta; Moore last active with Washington in '93; O'Neal played 14 games with Philadelphia; Powell played 1 game with N.Y. Giants; Price played 6 games with Tampa Bay; Reich played 16 games with Buffalo; Rodenhauser played 16 games with Detroit; Rodgers played 5 games with Seattle; Rollins active for 3 games with New Orleans but did not play; Ryans active for 1 game with Detroit but did not play; Sims played 8 games with Minnesota; R. Smith played 16 games with New England; T. Smith played 4 games with Atlanta; Stams played 16 games with Cleveland; Teeter played 14 games with Houston; Thomas played 9 games with San Francisco; Tillman last active with Cleveland in '93; Trudeau played 5 games with N.Y. Jets; Turner played 12 games with Tampa Bay; Whitley played 12 games with San Diego; G. Williams played 11 games with Pittsburgh; J. Williams played 15 games with Arizona.

† Restricted free agent; subject to developments.

t- Panthers traded for Foster (Pittsburgh).

COACHING STAFF

Head Coach,
Dom Capers

Pro Career: Named first head coach of the Carolina Panthers on January 23, 1995. Capers came to the Panthers after spending the past three seasons as defensive coordinator for the Pittsburgh Steelers where he oversaw a unit that allowed the fewest points in the league over the past three seasons. His 1994 defense was the best overall in the AFC for the second consecutive year and second best in the league. The Steelers led the league in sacks and finished second in points allowed, opponents average gain per play, first downs allowed, and opponents' third-down efficiency. In addition to leading the league in overall defense in 1993, Capers' unit led all teams in forced fumbles, finished second with an opponents passer rating of 64.9, tied for second in interceptions, and ranked third in rushing yards allowed. In 1992, the Pittsburgh defense led the NFL in takeaways, fumble recoveries, tied for the league lead in touchdowns allowed, while ranking second in points allowed. Capers only has experienced one losing season in 11 years as an assistant coach on the professional level and four overall in 24 years of coaching. Capers entered the professional coaching ranks in 1984 as an assistant under Jim Mora with the USFL Baltimore/Philadelphia Star where he helped them earn championships in 1984 and 1985. He then moved with Mora to the New Orleans Saints where he coached the secondary from 1986-1991.

Background: Capers played defensive back for Mount Union College under Ron Lynn, who now is the Washington Redskins' defensive coordinator. He entered the coaching ranks as a graduate assistant at Kent State before taking a graduate assistant position at the University of Washington with Mora. Capers also served full-time coaching stints at Hawaii (1975-76), San Jose State (1977), California (1978-79), Tennessee (1980-81), and Ohio State (1982-83).

Personal: Born August 5, 1950, in Cambridge, Ohio, Capers and his wife, Karen, were married in June, 1994.

ASSISTANT COACHES

Don Breaux, tight ends; born August 3, 1940, Jennings, La., lives in Charlotte, N.C. Quarterback McNeese State 1959-61. Pro quarterback Denver Broncos 1963, San Diego Chargers 1964-65. College coach: Florida State 1966-67, Arkansas 1968-71, 1977-80, Florida 1973-74, Texas 1975-76. Pro coach: Houston Oilers 1972, Washington Redskins 1981-1993, New York Jets 1994, joined Panthers in 1995.

George Catavolos, defensive backs; born May 8,1945, Chicago, Ill., lives in Charlotte, N.C. Defensive back Purdue 1963-67. No pro playing experience. College coach: Purdue 1967-68, 1971-76, Middle Tennessee State 1969, Louisville 1970, Kentucky 1977-81, Tennessee 1982-83. Pro coach: Indianapolis Colts 1984-93, joined Panthers in 1995.

Billy Davis, outside linebackers; born November 5, 1965, Youngstown, Ohio, lives in Charlotte, N.C. Quarterback Cincinnati 1984-88. No pro playing experience. College coach: Michigan State 1990-91. Pro coach: Pittsburgh Steelers 1992-94, joined Panthers in 1995.

Vic Fangio, defensive coordinator; born August 22, 1958, Dunmore, Pa., lives in Charlotte, N.C. Defensive back East Stroudsburg State 1976-78. No pro playing experience. College coach: North Carolina 1983. Pro coach: Philadelphia/Baltimore Stars (USFL) 1984-85, New Orleans Saints 1986-94, joined Panthers in 1995.

Cary Goodette, defensive line; born March 20, 1954, New Bern, N.C., lives in Charlotte, N.C. Defensive end East Carolina 1973-76. No pro playing experience. College coach: East Carolina 1977-79, 1990-91, Wyoming 1980-82, Cincinnati 1983-88, Georgia Tech 1992-93, North Carolina State 1994. Pro coach: Joined Panthers in 1995.

Chick Harris, running backs; born September 21, 1945, Durham, N.C., lives in Charlotte, N.C. Running back Northern Arizona 1966-69. No pro playing experience. College coach: Colorado State 1970-72, Long Beach State 1973-74, Washington 1975-80. Pro coach: Buffalo Bills 1981-82, Seattle Seahawks 1983-91, Los Angeles Rams 1992-94, joined Panthers in 1995

Jim McNally, offensive line; born December 13, 1943, Buffalo, N.Y., lives in Charlotte, N.C. Guard Buffalo 1961-65. No pro playing experience. College coach: Buffalo 1966-69, Marshall 1973-75, Boston College 1976-78, Wake Forest 1979. Pro coach: Cincinnati Bengals 1980-94, joined Panthers in 1995.

Chip Morton, strength and conditioning; born November 27, 1962, Hamden, Conn., lives in Charlotte, N.C. No college or pro playing experience. College coach: Ohio State 1985-86, Penn State 1987-91. Pro coach: San Diego Chargers 1992-94, joined Panthers in 1995.

Joe Pendry, offensive coordinator; born August 5, 1947, Matheny, W. Va., lives in Charlotte, N.C. Tight end West Virginia 1966-67. No pro playing experience. College coach: West Virginia 1967-74, 1976-77, Kansas State 1975, Pittsburgh 1978-79, Michigan State 1980-81. Pro coach: Philadelphia Stars (USFL) 1983, Pittsburgh Maulers (USFL) 1984 (head coach), Cleveland Browns 1985-88, Kansas City Chiefs 1989-92, Chicago Bears 1993-94, joined Panthers in 1995.

Brad Seely, special teams; born September 6, 1956, Vinton, Iowa, lives in Charlotte, N.C. Tackle-guard South Dakota State 1974-77. No pro playing experience. College coach: Colorado State 1980, Southern Methodist 1981, North Carolina State 1982, Pacific 1983, Oklahoma State 1984-88. Pro coach: Indianapolis Colts 1989-93, New York Jets 1994, joined Panthers in 1995.

John Shoop, quality control-offense; born August 1, 1969, Pittsburgh, Pa., lives in Charlotte, N.C. Quarterback University of the South 1987-91. No pro playing experience. College coach: Dartmouth 1991, Vanderbilt 1992-94. Pro coach: Joined Panthers in 1995.

Kevin Steele, linebackers; born March 17, 1958, La Jolla, Calif., lives in Matthews, N.C. Linebacker Tennessee 1976-79. No pro playing experience. College coach: Tennessee 1981-82, 1987-88, New Mexico State 1983, Oklahoma State 1984-86, Nebraska, 1989-94. Pro coach: Joined Panthers in 1995.

Richard Williamson, wide receivers; born April 13, 1941, Ft. Deposit, Ala., lives in Charlotte, N.C. Receiver Alabama 1961-62. No pro playing experience. College coach: Alabama 1963-67, 1970-71, Arkansas 1968-69, 1972-74, Memphis State 1975-80 (head coach). Pro coach: Kansas City Chiefs 1983-86, Tampa Bay Buccaneers 1987-91 (interim head coach final three games of 1990 season, head coach 1991), Cincinnati Bengals 1992-94, joined Panthers in 1995.

1995 FIRST-YEAR ROSTER

Name	Pos.	Ht.	Wt.	Birthdate	College	Hometown	How Acq.
Brockermeyer, Blake	T	6-4	305	4/11/73	Texas	Ft. Worth, Tex.	D1c
Brookins, Willie	LB	6-2	240	8/14/72	East Carolina	West Palm Beach, Fla.	FA
Campbell, Matthew (1)	TE	6-4	257	7/14/72	South Carolina	North Augusta, S.C.	FA
Clifton, Greg (1)	WR	6-0	178	2/6/68	Johnson C. Smith	Charlotte, N.C.	FA
Collins, Kerry	QB	6-5	240	12/30/72	Penn State	Lancaster, Pa.	D1a
Colquitt, Jerry	QB	6-4	208	6/28/72	Tennessee	Oak Ridge, Tenn.	D6b
Cota, Chad	S	6-1	195	8/31/71	Oregon	Ashland, Ore.	D7a
Farkas, Kevin (1)	T	6-9	375	2/4/71	Appalachian State	Richmond, Va.	FA
Feighery, Kevin	P	6-4	215	12/2/73	Merchant Marine Acad.	Carmel, N.Y.	FA
Fields, Jeff (1)	NT	6-3	320	7/3/67	Arkansas State	Jackson, Miss.	FA
Frazier, Daryl (1)	WR	6-1	181	1/23/71	Florida	Winter Haven, Fla.	FA
Garcia, Frank	C	6-1	290	1/28/72	Washington	Phoenix, Ariz.	D4
Garrett, Judd (1)	RB	6-1	214	6/25/67	Princeton	Cleveland, Ohio	FA
Hayes, Brandon	T	6-4	315	3/11/73	Central State, Ohio	Muncie, Ind.	FA
Jones, Tony	S	6-4	200	3/2/72	Syracuse	Tampa, Fla.	FA
King, Shawn	DE	6-3	280	6/24/72	Northeast Louisiana	Monroe, La.	D2
Larramore, Leonard (1)	NT	6-2	310	4/24/70	So. Mississippi	Jacksonville, Fla.	FA
Lauder, David	K	6-2	210	2/18/69	Brigham Young	Centreville, Utah	FA
Leomiti, Carlson (1)	G	6-3	380	1/10/71	San Diego State	Wilmington, Calif.	FA
Martin, Emerson (1)	G	6-2	297	5/6/70	Hampton	Elizabethtown, N.C.	FA
Mitchell, Billy	CB-S	5-11	185	12/15/70	Texas A&M	DeSoto, Tex.	FA
Peterson, Andrew	T	6-5	310	6/11/72	Washington	Port Orchard, Wash.	D5b
Poole, Tyrone	CB	5-8	185	2/3/72	Ft. Valley State	La Grange, Ga.	D1b
Reed, Michael	CB	5-9	177	8/16/72	Boston College	Wilmington, Del.	D7b
Rose, Barry (1)	WR	5-11	183	7/28/68	Wis.-Steven's Point	Woodville, Wis.	FA
Scott, Patrick (1)	LB	6-4	241	6/4/71	South Carolina State	Durham, N.C.	FA
Senters, Mike	CB	5-11	173	12/14/71	Northwestern	Dallas, Tex.	D5a
Strahan, Steve	NT	6-1	298	10/29/72	Baylor	Houston, Tex.	D6a
Stuart, Ed	LB	6-0	221	3/2/72	Nebraska	Carmel, Ind.	FA
Wier, Eric (1)	WR	6-2	175	7/15/70	Vanderbilt	Houston, Tex.	FA
Wiggins, Brian (1)	WR	5-11	183	6/14/68	Texas Southern	New Rochelle, N.Y.	FA
Williams, Allen	RB	5-9	202	9/17/72	Maryland	Thomasville, Ga.	FA

The term NFL Rookie is defined as a player who is in his first season of professional football and has not been on the roster of another professional football team for any regular-season or postseason games. A Rookie is designated by an "R" on NFL rosters. Players who have been active in another professional football league or players who have NFL experience, including either preseason training camp or being on an Active List or Inactive List, or on Reserve/Injured or Reserve/Physically Unable to Perform for fewer than six regular-season games, are termed NFL First-Year Players. An NFL First-Year Player is designated by a "1" on NFL rosters. Thereafter, a player is credited with an additional year of experience for each season in which he accumulates six games on the Active List or Inactive List, or on Reserve/Injured or Reserve/Physically Unable to Perform.

NOTES

CHICAGO BEARS

National Football Conference
Central Division
Team Colors: Navy Blue, Orange, and White
Halas Hall, 250 North Washington
Lake Forest, Illinois 60045
Telephone: (708) 295-6600

CLUB OFFICIALS

Chairman of the Board: Edward W. McCaskey
President and CEO: Michael B. McCaskey
Secretary: Virginia H. McCaskey
Vice President: Tim McCaskey
Vice President of Operations: Ted Phillips
Director of Player Personnel: Rod Graves
Director of Administration: Tim LeFevour
Director of Community Relations: Pat McCaskey
Player Liaison: Brian McCaskey
Director of Marketing/Communications: Ken Valdiserri
Manager of Promotions: John Bostrom
Manager of Sales: Jack Trompeter
Director of Public Relations: Bryan Harlan
Asst. Director of Public Relations: Doug Green
Ticket Manager: George McCaskey
Computer Systems: Greg Gershuny
Controller: Scott Worthen
Video Director: Dean Pope
Trainer: Fred Caito
Strength Coordinator: Clyde Emrich
Physical Dev. Coordinator: Russ Reiderer
Equipment Manager: Gary Haeger
Assistant Equipment Manager: Tony Medlin
Scouts: Gary Smith, Jeff Shiver, Charlie Mackey, Bobby Riggle, Mike McCartney, Charles Garcia
Stadium: Soldier Field • **Capacity:** 66,944
425 McFetridge Place
Chicago, Illinois 60605
Playing Surface: Grass
Training Camp: University of Wisconsin-Platteville
Platteville, Wisconsin 53818

1995 SCHEDULE

PRESEASON

Aug. 4	**Carolina**	7:30
Aug. 14	at Cleveland	8:00
Aug. 20	**Arizona**	7:00
Aug. 24	at Indianapolis	7:30

REGULAR SEASON

Sept. 3	**Minnesota**	3:00
Sept. 11	**Green Bay** (Monday)	8:00
Sept. 17	at Tampa Bay	4:00
Sept. 24	at St. Louis	12:00
Oct. 1	Open Date	
Oct. 8	**Carolina**	12:00
Oct. 15	at Jacksonville	1:00
Oct. 22	**Houston**	12:00
Oct. 30	at Minnesota (Monday)	8:00
Nov. 5	**Pittsburgh**	3:00
Nov. 12	at Green Bay	12: 00
Nov. 19	**Detroit**	12: 00
Nov. 26	at New York Giants	1:00
Dec. 4	at Detroit (Monday)	9:00
Dec. 10	at Cincinnati	1:00
Dec. 17	**Tampa Bay**	12:00
Dec. 24	**Philadelphia**	12:00

RECORD HOLDERS

INDIVIDUAL RECORDS—CAREER

Category	Name	Performance
Rushing (Yds.)	Walter Payton, 1975-1987	*16,726
Passing (Yds.)	Sid Luckman, 1939-1950	14,686
Passing (TDs)	Sid Luckman, 1939-1950	137
Receiving (No.)	Walter Payton, 1975-1987	492
Receiving (Yds.)	Johnny Morris, 1958-1967	5,059
Interceptions	Gary Fencik, 1976-1987	38
Punting (Avg.)	George Gulyanics, 1947-1952	44.5
Punt Return (Avg.)	Ray (Scooter) McLean, 1940-47	14.8
Kickoff Return (Avg.)	Gale Sayers, 1965-1971	30.6
Field Goals	Kevin Butler, 1985-1994	220
Touchdowns (Tot.)	Walter Payton, 1975-1987	125
Points	Kevin Butler, 1985-1994	1,002

INDIVIDUAL RECORDS—SINGLE SEASON

Category	Name	Performance
Rushing (Yds.)	Walter Payton, 1977	1,852
Passing (Yds.)	Bill Wade, 1962	3,172
Passing (TDs)	Sid Luckman, 1943	28
Receiving (No.)	Johnny Morris, 1964	93
Receiving (Yds.)	Johnny Morris, 1964	1,200
Interceptions	Mark Carrier, 1990	10
Punting (Avg.)	Bobby Joe Green, 1963	46.5
Punt Return (Avg.)	Harry Clark, 1943	15.8
Kickoff Return (Avg.)	Gale Sayers, 1967	37.7
Field Goals	Kevin Butler, 1985	31
Touchdowns (Tot.)	Gale Sayers, 1965	**22
Points	Kevin Butler, 1985	**144

INDIVIDUAL RECORDS—SINGLE GAME

Category	Name	Performance
Rushing (Yds.)	Walter Payton, 11-20-77	*275
Passing (Yds.)	Johnny Lujack, 12-11-49	468
Passing (TDs)	Sid Luckman, 11-14-43	*7
Receiving (No.)	Jim Keane, 10-23-49	14
Receiving (Yds.)	Harlon Hill, 10-31-54	214
Interceptions	Many times. Last time by Mark Carrier, 12-9-90	3
Field Goals	Roger LeClerc, 12-3-61	5
	Mac Percival, 10-20-68	5
Touchdowns (Tot.)	Gale Sayers, 12-12-65	*6
Points	Gale Sayers, 12-12-65	36

*NFL Record
**NFL Rookie Record

COACHING HISTORY

Decatur Staleys 1920,
Chicago Staleys 1921
(596-392-42)

1920-29	George Halas	84-31-19
1930-32	Ralph Jones	24-10-7
1933-42	George Halas*	88-24-4
1942-45	Hunk Anderson-Luke Johnsos**	24-12-2
1946-55	George Halas	76-43-2
1956-57	John (Paddy) Driscoll	14-10-1
1958-67	George Halas	76-53-6
1968-71	Jim Dooley	20-36-0
1972-74	Abe Gibron	11-30-1
1975-77	Jack Pardee	20-23-0
1978-81	Neill Armstrong	30-35-0
1982-92	Mike Ditka	112-68-0
1993-94	Dave Wannstedt	17-17

*Retired after five games to enter U.S. Navy
**Co-coaches

SOLDIER FIELD

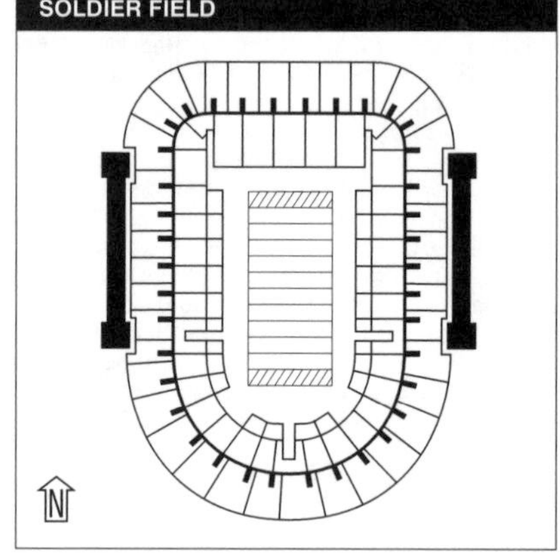

1994 TEAM RECORD

PRESEASON (4-0)

Date	Result		Opponents
8/5	W	12-6	Philadelphia
8/13	W	16-0	at Arizona
8/22	W	21-18	at Kansas City
8/27	W	27-21	N.Y. Giants

REGULAR SEASON (9-7)

Date	Result		Opponents	Att.
9/4	W	21- 9	Tampa Bay	61,844
9/12	L	22-30	at Philadelphia	64,890
9/18	L	14-42	Minnesota	61,073
9/25	W	19- 7	at N.Y. Jets	70,806
10/2	W	20-13	Buffalo	62,406
10/9	W	17- 7	New Orleans	63,822
10/23	L	16-21	at Detroit	73,574
10/31	L	6-33	Green Bay	47,381
11/6	W	20- 6	at Tampa Bay	60,821
11/13	W	17-14	at Miami	65,006
11/20	W	20-10	Detroit	55,035
11/27	W	19-16	at Arizona (OT)	65,922
12/1	L	27-33	at Minnesota (OT)	61,483
12/11	L	3-40	at Green Bay	57,927
12/18	W	27-13	L.A. Rams	56,276
12/24	L	3-13	New England	60,178

POSTSEASON (1-1)

1/1	W	35-18	at Minnesota	60,347
1/7	L	15-44	at San Francisco	64,644

(OT) Overtime

SCORE BY PERIODS

Bears	40	61	61	106	3	—	271
Opponents	44	116	67	74	6	—	307

ATTENDANCE

Home 468,015 Away 520,429 Total 988,444
Single-game home record, 66,900 (9-5-93)
Single-season home record, 528,465 (1992)

1994 TEAM STATISTICS

	Bears	Opp.
Total First Downs	274	275
Rushing	88	100
Passing	165	163
Penalty	21	12
Third Down: Made/Att	97/232	81/218
Third Down Pct.	41.8	37.2
Fourth Down: Made/Att	9/16	8/17
Fourth Down Pct.	56.3	47.1
Total Net Yards	4679	5009
Avg. Per Game	292.4	313.1
Total Plays	1014	982
Avg. Per Play	4.6	5.1
Net Yards Rushing	1588	1922
Avg. Per Game	99.3	120.1
Total Rushes	487	432
Net Yards Passing	3091	3087
Avg. Per Game	193.2	192.9
Sacked/Yards Lost	25/139	28/175
Gross Yards	3230	3262
Att./Completions	502/308	522/295
Completion Pct.	61.4	56.5
Had Intercepted	16	12
Punts/Avg.	76/37.8	72/39.0
Net Punting Avg.	76/32.4	72/34.9
Penalties/Yards Lost	65/503	80/645
Fumbles/Ball Lost	21/10	29/10
Touchdowns	30	31
Rushing	10	10
Passing	19	16
Returns	1	5
Avg. Time of Possession	31:37	28:23

1994 INDIVIDUAL STATISTICS

PASSING	Att.	Comp.	Yds.	Pct.	TD	Int.	Tkld.	Rate
Walsh	343	208	2078	60.6	10	8	11/52	77.9
Kramer	158	99	1129	62.7	8	8	14/87	79.9
Conway	1	1	23	100.0	1	0	0/0	158.3
Bears	502	308	3230	61.4	19	16	25/139	79.4
Opponents	522	295	3262	56.5	16	12	28/175	75.9

SCORING	TD R	TD P	TD Rt	PAT	FG	Saf	PTS
Butler	0	0	0	24/24	21/29	0	87
Tillman	7	0	0	0/0	0/0	0	42
Graham	0	4	1	0/0	0/0	0	32
Gedney	0	3	0	0/0	0/0	0	18
Jennings	0	3	0	0/0	0/0	0	18
Conway	0	2	0	0/0	0/0	0	14
Green	0	2	0	0/0	0/0	0	12
Cook	0	1	0	0/0	0/0	0	6
Harris	1	0	0	0/0	0/0	0	6
Lewis	0	1	0	0/0	0/0	0	6
McMurtry	0	1	0	0/0	0/0	0	6
Waddle	0	1	0	0/0	0/0	0	6
Walsh	1	0	0	0/0	0/0	0	6
Wetnight	0	1	0	0/0	0/0	0	6
Worley	1	0	0	0/0	0/0	0	6
Bears	10	19	1	24/24	21/29	0	271
Opponents	10	16	5	25/26	30/41	0	307

2-Point conversions: Conway, Graham. Team: 2-6.

RUSHING	Att.	Yds.	Avg.	LG	TD
Tillman	275	899	3.3	25t	7
Harris	123	464	3.8	13	1
Green	25	122	4.9	14	0
Conway	6	31	5.2	12	0
Christian	7	29	4.1	8	0
Hoge	6	24	4.0	8	0
Worley	9	17	1.9	4	1
Walsh	30	4	0.1	12	1
Kramer	6	-2	-0.3	2	0
Bears	487	1588	3.3	25t	10
Opponents	432	1922	4.4	90	10

RECEIVING	No.	Yds.	Avg.	LG	TD
Graham	68	944	13.9	76t	4
Conway	39	546	14.0	85t	2
Harris	39	236	6.1	18	0
Tillman	27	222	8.2	39	0
Waddle	25	244	9.8	22	1
Green	24	199	8.3	39t	2
Cook	21	212	10.1	34	1
Gedney	13	157	12.1	37t	3
Hoge	13	79	6.1	11	0
Wetnight	11	104	9.5	19	1
Jennings	11	75	6.8	23t	3
McMurtry	8	112	14.0	30	1
Primus	3	25	8.3	12	0
Christian	2	30	15.0	21	0
Lewis	2	13	6.5	8	1
Carter	1	24	24.0	24	0
Worley	1	8	8.0	8	0
Bears	308	3230	10.5	85t	19
Opponents	295	3262	11.1	65t	16

INTERCEPTIONS	No.	Yds.	Avg.	Long	TD
Woolford	5	30	6.0	25	0
Gayle	2	33	16.5	33	0
Carrier	2	10	5.0	7	0
Spellman	1	31	31.0	31	0
Douglass	1	18	18.0	18	0
Lincoln	1	5	5.0	5	0
Bears	12	127	10.6	33	0
Opponents	16	335	20.9	81t	3

PUNTING	No.	Yds.	Avg.	In 20	LG
Gardocki	76	2871	37.8	23	57
Bears	76	2871	37.8	23	57
Opponents	72	2808	39.0	27	61

PUNT RETURNS	No.	FC	Yds.	Avg.	LG	TD
Graham	15	5	140	9.3	61t	1
Conway	8	9	63	7.9	24	0
Waddle	3	3	8	2.7	6	0
Lewis	1	3	7	7.0	7	0
Bears	27	20	218	8.1	61t	1
Opponents	26	18	225	8.7	57	0

KICKOFF RETURNS	No.	Yds.	Avg.	LG	TD
Lewis	35	874	25.0	55	0
Conway	10	228	22.8	34	0
Carter	6	99	16.5	26	0
Green	6	77	12.8	16	0
Worley	4	52	13.0	25	0
Flanigan	2	26	13.0	14	0
Woolford	1	28	28.0	28	0
Harris	1	18	18.0	18	0
Thierry	1	0	0.0	0	0
Bears	66	1402	21.2	55	0
Opponents	65	1271	19.6	102t	1

SACKS	No.
Armstrong	7.5
Spellman	7.0
Zorich	5.5
A. Fontenot	4.0
Douglass	1.5
Epps	1.0
Smith	1.0
Mangum	0.5
Bears	28.0
Opponents	25.0

1995 DRAFT CHOICES

Round	Name	Pos.	College
1	Rashaan Salaam	RB	Colorado
2	Patrick Riley	DE	Miami
	Todd Sauerbrun	P	West Virginia
3	Sean Harris	LB	Arizona
	Evan Pilgrim	G	Brigham Young
4	Jack Jackson	WR	Florida
6	Kenny Gales	DB	Wisconsin
	Carl Reeves	DE	North Carolina State
7	Jamal Cox	LB	Georgia Tech

CHICAGO BEARS

1995 VETERAN ROSTER

No.	Name	Pos.	Ht.	Wt.	Birthdate	NFL Exp.	College	Hometown	How Acq.	'94 Games/ Starts
72	Adams, Scott	G-T	6-5	293	9/28/66	4	Georgia	Lake City, Fla.	FA-'95	11/0*
70	Auzenne, Troy	T	6-7	300	6/26/69	4	California	Baldwin Park, Calif.	D2-'92	11/3
91	Baker, Myron	LB	6-1	228	1/6/71	3	Louisiana Tech	Haughton, La.	D4b-'93	16/3
52	Bass, Robert	LB	6-1	239	11/10/70	2	Miami	Tilden, N.Y.	FA-'94	0*
63	Burger, Todd	G	6-3	296	3/20/70	2	Penn State	Clark, N.J.	FA-'93	4/0
35	Burton, James	CB	5-9	181	4/22/71	2	Fresno State	Long Beach, Calif.	FA-'94	13/1
6	Butler, Kevin	K	6-1	205	7/24/62	11	Georgia	Redan, Ga.	D4-'85	15/0
59	Cain, Joe	LB	6-1	237	6/11/65	7	Oregon Tech	Compton, Calif.	RFA(Sea)-'93	16/15
20	Carrier, Mark	S	6-1	190	4/28/68	6	Southern California	Long Beach, Calif.	D1-'90	16/15
23	Carter, Marty	S	6-1	200	12/27/69	5	Middle Tennessee State	La Grange, Ga.	UFA(TB)-'95	16/14*
30	Carter, Tony	RB	5-11	216	8/23/72	2	Minnesota	Columbus, Ohio	FA-'94	14/0
43	Cobb, Trevor	RB	5-9	209	11/20/70	3	Rice	Pasadena, Calif.	FA-'94	1/0
80	Conway, Curtis	WR-KR	6-0	193	3/13/71	3	Southern California	Hawthorne, Calif.	D1-'93	13/12
54	Cox, Ron	LB	6-2	235	2/27/68	6	Fresno State	Fresno, Calif.	D2b-'90	15/3
37	Eilers, Pat	CB-S	5-11	197	9/3/66	5	Notre Dame	St. Paul, Minn.	UFA(Wash)-'95	16/0*
68	Flanigan, Jim	DT	6-2	280	8/27/71	2	Notre Dame	Green Bay, Wis.	D3-'94	14/0
96	Fontenot, Albert	DE	6-4	272	9/17/70	3	Baylor	Houston, Tex.	D4c-'93	16/8
67	Fontenot, Jerry	G-C	6-3	285	11/21/66	7	Texas A&M	Lafayette, La.	D3-'89	16/16
84	Gedney, Chris	TE	6-5	265	8/9/70	3	Syracuse	Liverpool, N.Y.	D3-'93	7/7
81	Graham, Jeff	WR	6-2	196	2/14/69	5	Ohio State	Kettering, Ohio	T(Pitt)-'94	16/15
22	Green, Robert	RB	5-8	212	9/10/70	4	William & Mary	Ft. Washington, Md.	W(Wash)-'93	15/0
29	Harris, Raymont	RB	6-0	225	12/23/70	2	Ohio State	Lorain, Ohio	D4-'94	16/11
74	Hawkins, Garland	DE	6-3	253	2/19/70	2	Syracuse	Washington, D.C.	FA-'94	0*
64	Heck, Andy	T	6-6	296	1/1/67	7	Notre Dame	Fairfax, Va.	RFA(Sea)-'94	14/14
85	Jennings, Keith	TE	6-4	270	5/19/66	6	Clemson	Summerville, S.C.	FA-'91	9/1
25	Johnson, Anthony	RB	6-0	222	10/25/67	6	Notre Dame	South Bend, Ind.	UFA(NYJ)-'95	15/0*
12	Kramer, Erik	QB	6-1	200	11/6/64	7	North Carolina State	Burbank, Calif.	UFA(Det)-'94	6/5
58	Leeuwenburg, Jay	G-C	6-3	290	6/18/69	4	Colorado	Kirkwood, Mo.	W(KC)-'92	16/16
39	† Lincoln, Jeremy	CB	5-10	180	4/7/69	4	Tennessee	Toledo, Ohio	D3-'92	15/14
26	Mangum, John	S	5-10	192	3/16/67	6	Alabama	Magee, Miss.	D7-'90	16/3
9	Matthews, Shane	QB	6-3	196	6/1/70	3	Florida	Pascagoula, Fla.	FA-'93	0*
88	McMurtry, Greg	WR	6-2	210	10/15/67	6	Michigan	Brockton, Mass.	FA-'94	9/4
24	Miniefield, Kevin	CB-S	5-9	180	3/2/70	3	Arizona State	Phoenix, Ariz.	FA-'93	12/0
92	Minter, Barry	LB	6-2	239	1/28/70	3	Tulsa	Mt. Pleasant, Tex.	T(Dall)-'93	13/1
83	Obee, Terry	WR	5-10	189	6/15/68	3	Oregon	Richmond, Calif.	UFA(Minn)-'93	0*
75	Perry, Todd	G	6-5	310	11/28/70	3	Kentucky	Elizabethtown, Ky.	D4a-'93	15/4
18	Primus, Greg	WR	5-11	190	10/20/70	2	Colorado State	Denver, Colo.	FA-'94	3/1
19	Shedd, Kenny	WR	5-9	171	2/14/71	2	Northern Iowa	Davenport, Iowa	FA-'94	0*
98	Simpson, Carl	DT	6-2	285	4/18/70	3	Florida State	Appling County, Ga.	D2-'93	15/8
55	Smith, Vinson	LB	6-2	247	7/3/65	8	East Carolina	Statesville, N.C.	T(Dall)-'93	12/10
76	Spears, Marcus	T	6-4	300	9/28/71	2	Northwestern State, La.	Baton Rouge, La.	D2-'94	0*
90	Spellman, Alonzo	DE	6-4	285	9/27/71	4	Ohio State	Rancocas, N.J.	D1-'92	16/16
94	Thierry, John	DE	6-4	260	9/4/71	2	Alcorn State	Opelousas, La.	D1-'94	16/1
33	Thompson, Darrell	RB	6-1	217	11/23/67	6	Minnesota	Rochester, Minn.	UFA(GB)-'95	8/0*
27	Tillman, Lewis	RB	6-0	204	4/16/66	7	Jackson State	Hazelhurst, Miss.	UFA(NYG)-'94	16/15
86	Timpson, Michael	WR	5-10	180	6/6/67	7	Penn State	Miami Lakes, Fla.	UFA(NE)-'95	15/14
4	Walsh, Steve	QB	6-3	200	12/1/66	7	Miami	St. Paul, Minn.	FA-'94	12/11
89	Wetnight, Ryan	TE	6-2	235	11/5/70	3	Stanford	Fresno, Calif.	FA-'93	11/0
71	Williams, James	T	6-7	335	3/29/68	5	Cheyney State	Allerdice, Pa.	FA-'91	16/15
21	Woolford, Donnell	CB	5-9	188	1/6/66	7	Clemson	Byrd, N.C.	D1a-'89	16/16
97	Zorich, Chris	DT	6-1	277	3/13/69	5	Notre Dame	Chicago, Ill.	D2-'91	16/16

* Adams played 11 games with New Orleans in '94; Bass, Hawkins, and Obee missed '94 season due to injury; M. Carter played 16 games with Tampa Bay; Eilers played 16 games with Washington; Johnson played 15 games with N.Y. Jets; Matthews active for 2 games but did not play; Shedd inactive with N.Y. Jets for 2 games, and inactive with Chicago for 9 games; Spears inactive for 16 games; Thompson played 8 games with Green Bay.

Unrestricted free agent; subject to developments.

† Restricted free agent; subject to developments.

Retired—RB Merril Hoge, 8-year veteran, 5 games in '94.

Traded—DE Trace Armstrong to Miami.

Players lost through free agency (6): S Maurice Douglass (NYG; 16 games in '94), DT Tory Epps (NO; 5), P Chris Gardocki (Ind; 16), S Shaun Gayle (SD; 16), WR Nate Lewis (Atl; 13), WR Tom Waddle (Cin; 9).

Players lost through Expansion Draft (2): RB Bob Christian (Car; 12 games in '94), G Tom Myslinski (Jax; 4).

Also played with Bears in '94—DE Trace Armstrong (15 games), G Mark Bortz (12), TE Marv Cook (16), RB Merril Hoge (5), LB Darwin Ireland (2), CB Keshon Johnson (6), LB Dante Jones (15), CB-S Anthony Marshall (3), RB Tim Worley (5).

COACHING STAFF

Head Coach,
Dave Wannstedt

Pro Career: Led Bears to a 9-7 regular-season record in 1994, which qualified Chicago for the playoffs. Chicago had a 7-9 record in his rookie season. Named Chicago's head coach on January 19, 1993. He was an integral part of one of the most successful turnarounds in NFL history, helping to turn the 1989 Dallas Cowboys, which finished the season 1-15, into Super Bowl champions four years later. In January, 1992, he was named Dallas's assistant head coach and defensive coordinator. He was the defensive coordinator for the Cowboys in 1989. Selected by the Green Bay Packers in the fifteenth round of the 1974 draft, but spent the entire season on injured reserve. Career record: 17-17.
Background: Played offensive tackle at the University of Pittsburgh from 1970-73. Began coaching career at Pittsburgh in 1975 and was part of the staff that led the Panthers to a 12-0 record and the NCAA championship in 1976. In 1979, he took a job with Jimmy Johnson at Oklahoma State as defensive line coach. After two seasons, he was promoted to defensive coordinator. In 1983, Wannstedt was the defensive line coach for Southern California before rejoining Johnson at the University of Miami as the Hurricanes' defensive coordinator. In his first year (1986), Miami went 11-0 before losing to Penn State in the Fiesta Bowl. The following season Miami was crowned NCAA champion with a perfect 12-0 record.
Personal: Born May 21, 1952, Pittsburgh, Pa. Dave and his wife, Jan, live in Lake Forest, Ill. and have two children—Keri and Jami.

ASSISTANT COACHES

Danny Abramowicz, special teams; born July 13, 1945, Steubenville, Ohio, lives in Lake Forest, Ill. Wide receiver Xavier 1964-66. Pro wide receiver New Orleans Saints 1967-73, San Francisco 49ers 1973-74. Pro coach: Joined Bears in 1992.

Clarence Brooks, defensive line; born May 20, 1951, New York, N.Y., lives in Lake Forest, Ill. Guard Massachusetts 1970-73. No pro playing experience. College coach: Massachusetts 1976-80, Syracuse 1981-89, Arizona 1990-92. Pro coach: Joined Bears in 1993.

Ivan Fears, wide receivers; born November 15, 1954, Portsmouth, Va., lives in Lake Forest, Ill. Running back William and Mary 1973-75. No pro playing experience. College coach: William and Mary 1977-80, Syracuse 1981-90. Pro coach: New England Patriots 1991-92, joined Bears in 1993.

Carlos Mainord, defensive assistant; born August 26, 1944, Greenville, Tex., lives in Lake Forest, Ill. Linebacker Navarro (Tex.) Junior College 1962-63, McMurry College 1964-65. No pro playing experience. College coach: McMurry College 1966-68, Texas Tech 1969, 1983-85, 1987-92, Ranger (Tex.) Junior College 1970-71, 1972-77 (head coach), Rice 1978-82, Miami 1986. Pro coach: Joined Bears in 1993.

David McGinnis, linebackers; born August 7, 1951, Independence, Kan., lives in Lake Forest, Ill. Defensive back Texas Christian 1970-72. No pro playing experience. College coach: Texas Christian 1973-74, 1982, Missouri 1975-77, Indiana State 1978-81, Kansas State 1983-85. Pro coach: Joined Bears in 1986.

Willie Peete, running backs; born July 14, 1937, Mesa, Ariz., lives in Chicago. Fullback Arizona 1956-59. No pro playing experience. College coach: Arizona 1960-62, 1971-82. Pro coach: Kansas City Chiefs 1983-86, Green Bay Packers 1987-91, Tampa Bay Buccaneers 1992-94, joined Bears in 1995.

Mike Shula, tight ends; born June 23, 1965, Baltimore, Md., lives in Lake Forest, Ill. Quarterback Alabama 1984-87. Pro quarterback Tampa Bay Buccaneers 1987. Pro coach: Tampa Bay Buccaneers 1988-90, Miami Dolphins 1991-92, joined Bears in 1993.

Bob Slowik, defensive coordinator-defensive backs; born May 16, 1954, Pittsburgh, Pa., lives in Lake Forest, Ill. Cornerback Delaware 1973-76. No pro playing experience. College coach: Delaware 1977, Florida 1978-81, Drake 1982, Rutgers 1983, East Carolina 1984-91. Pro coach: Dallas Cowboys 1992, joined Bears in 1993.

Ron Turner, offensive coordinator-quarterbacks; born December 5, 1953, Martinez, Calif., lives in Lake Forest, Ill. Running back-defensive back Pacific 1973-76. No pro playing experience. College coach: Pacific 1977, Arizona 1978-80, Northwestern 1981-82, Pittsburgh 1983-84, Southern California 1985-87, Texas A&M 1988, Stanford 1989-91, San Jose State 1992 (head coach). Pro coach: Joined Bears in 1993.

Tony Wise, assistant head coach-offensive line; born December 28, 1951, Albany, N.Y., lives in Lake Forest, Ill. Offensive lineman Ithaca College 1971-72. No pro playing experience. College coach: Albany State 1973, Bridgeport 1974, Central Connecticut State 1975, Washington State 1976, Pittsburgh 1977-78, Oklahoma State 1979-83, Syracuse 1984, Miami 1985-88. Pro coach: Dallas Cowboys 1989-92, joined Bears in 1993.

1995 FIRST-YEAR ROSTER

Name	Pos.	Ht.	Wt.	Birthdate	College	Hometown	How Acq.
Bownes, Fabien	WR	5-11	180	2/29/72	Western Illinois	Aurora, Ill.	FA
Collier, Ervin (1)	DT	6-3	290	5/12/71	Florida A&M	Jacksonville, Fla.	FA
Cox, Jamal	LB	6-1	240	1/21/72	Georgia Tech	Baltimore, Md.	D7
Crumpton, Robert	S	6-0	191	2/14/72	Illinois	Florissant, Mo.	FA
Forbes, Marlon	CB	6-1	202	12/25/71	Penn State	Long Island, N.Y.	FA
Gales, Kenny	CB	5-11	173	4/1/72	Wisconsin	Bayside, N.Y.	D6a
Gavin, Lauren	LB	6-1	230	8/5/72	Jackson State	Laurel, Miss.	FA
Greeley, Bucky	C	6-2	280	7/30/72	Penn State	Wilkes-Barre, Pa.	FA
Harris, Sean	LB	6-3	244	2/25/72	Arizona	Tucson, Ariz.	D3a
Ireland, Darwin (1)	LB	5-11	240	5/26/71	Arkansas	Pine Bluff, Ark.	FA
Jackson, Jack	WR	5-8	171	11/11/72	Florida	Moss Point, Miss.	D4
Joseph, Dwayne (1)	CB	5-9	180	6/2/72	Syracuse	Carol City, Fla.	FA
Kaplan, Scott (1)	K	6-0	195	2/17/70	Pittsburgh	Coral Springs, Fla.	FA
Kmet, Frank (1)	G-T	6-3	300	3/13/70	Purdue	Arlington Heights, Ill.	FA
Krichbaum, Mark	DT	6-5	283	8/8/72	Virginia	Ridgefield, Conn.	FA
Lewis, Tim	T	6-4	300	4/24/71	Northern Illinois	Chicago, Ill.	FA
Lumelski, Zev	T	6-8	304	4/14/72	Miami	Miami, Fla.	FA
Marshall, Anthony (1)	S	6-1	205	9/16/70	Louisiana State	Mobile, Ala.	FA
McNerney, Pat	TE	6-3	260	1/3/71	Weber State	Ontario, Canada	FA
Pilgrim, Evan	G	6-4	300	8/14/72	Brigham Young	Antioch, Calif.	D3b
Polk, Octus	G	6-3	340	9/17/71	Stephen F. Austin	Sulfur Springs, Tex.	FA
Primus, Greg (1)	WR	5-11	188	10/20/70	Colorado State	Denver, Colo.	FA
Reeves, Carl	DE	6-4	247	12/17/71	North Carolina State	Durham, N.C.	D6b
Riley, Pat	DE	6-5	285	3/8/72	Miami	Marrero, La.	D2a
Salaam, Rashaan	RB	6-1	226	10/8/74	Colorado	La Jolla, Calif.	D1
Sauerbrun, Todd	P-K	5-10	206	1/20/71	West Virginia	Setauket, N.Y.	D2b
Tobias, Michael	DT	6-1	282	4/29/71	Southern Mississippi	Jefferson, La.	FA
Walker, Cedric (1)	S	6-0	205	2/16/71	Stephen F. Austin	Lufkin, Tex.	FA

The term NFL Rookie is defined as a player who is in his first season of professional football and has not been on the roster of another professional football team for any regular-season or postseason games. A Rookie is designated by an "R" on NFL rosters. Players who have been active in another professional football league or players who have NFL experience, including either preseason training camp or being on an Active List or Inactive List, or on Reserve/Injured or Reserve/Physically Unable to Perform for fewer than six regular-season games, are termed NFL First-Year Players. An NFL First-Year Player is designated by a "1" on NFL rosters. Thereafter, a player is credited with an additional year of experience for each season in which he accumulates six games on the Active List or Inactive List, or on Reserve/Injured or Reserve/Physically Unable to Perform.

NOTES

DALLAS COWBOYS

National Football Conference
Eastern Division
Team Colors: Royal Blue, Metallic Silver Blue, and White
Cowboys Center
One Cowboys Parkway
Irving, Texas 75063
Telephone: (214) 556-9900

CLUB OFFICIALS

Owner/President/General Manager: Jerry Jones
Vice President-Player Personnel: Stephen Jones
Vice President: Mike McCoy
Vice President/Marketing: George Hays
Marketing and Special Events Coordinator: Charlotte Anderson
Public Relations Director: Rich Dalrymple
Assistant Director of Public Relations: Brett Daniels
Director of College and Pro Scouting: Larry Lacewell
Director of Operations: Bruce Mays
Ticket Manager: Carol Padgett
Trainer: Kevin O'Neill
Equipment Manager: Mike McCord
Video Director: Robert Blackwell
Cheerleader Director: Kelli McGonagill
Stadium: Texas Stadium • **Capacity:** 65,812 Irving, Texas 75062
Playing Surface: Texas Turf
Training Camp: St. Edward's University Austin, Texas 78704

1995 SCHEDULE

PRESEASON

July 29	**Buffalo**	8:00
Aug. 5	**Los Angeles**	8:00
Aug. 12	vs. Buffalo at Toronto	8:00
Aug. 21	at Denver	6:00
Aug. 26	vs. Houston at San Antonio, Tex.	7:00

REGULAR SEASON

Sept. 4	at New York Giants (Monday)	9:00
Sept. 10	**Denver**	3:00
Sept. 17	at Minnesota	7:00
Sept. 24	**Arizona**	3:00
Oct. 1	at Washington	1:00
Oct. 8	**Green Bay**	12:00
Oct. 15	at San Diego	1:00
Oct. 22	Open Date	
Oct. 29	at Atlanta	1:00
Nov. 6	**Philadelphia** (Monday)	8:00
Nov. 12	**San Francisco**	3:00
Nov. 19	at Los Angeles	1:00
Nov. 23	**Kansas City** (Thursday)	3:00
Dec. 3	**Washington**	3:00
Dec. 10	at Philadelphia	1:00
Dec. 17	**New York Giants**	3:00
Dec. 25	at Arizona (Monday)	7:00

RECORD HOLDERS

INDIVIDUAL RECORDS—CAREER

Category	Name	Performance
Rushing (Yds.)	Tony Dorsett, 1977-1987	12,036
Passing (Yds.)	Roger Staubach, 1969-1979	22,700
Passing (TDs)	Danny White, 1976-1988	155
Receiving (No.)	Drew Pearson, 1973-1983	489
Receiving (Yds.)	Tony Hill, 1977-1986	7,988
Interceptions	Mel Renfro, 1964-1977	52
Punting (Avg.)	Mike Saxon, 1985-1992	41.5
Punt Return (Avg.)	Bob Hayes, 1965-1974	11.1
Kickoff Return (Avg.)	Mel Renfro, 1964-1977	26.4
Field Goals	Rafael Septien, 1978-1986	162
Touchdowns (Tot.)	Tony Dorsett, 1977-1987	86
Points	Rafael Septien, 1978-1986	874

INDIVIDUAL RECORDS—SINGLE SEASON

Category	Name	Performance
Rushing (Yds.)	Emmitt Smith, 1992	1,713
Passing (Yds.)	Danny White, 1983	3,980
Passing (TDs)	Danny White, 1983	29
Receiving (No.)	Michael Irvin, 1991	93
Receiving (Yds.)	Michael Irvin, 1991	1,523
Interceptions	Everson Walls, 1981	11
Punting (Avg.)	Sam Baker, 1962	45.4
Punt Return (Avg.)	Bob Hayes, 1968	20.8
Kickoff Return (Avg.)	Mel Renfro, 1965	30.0
Field Goals	Eddie Murray, 1993	28
Touchdowns (Tot.)	Emmitt Smith, 1994	22
Points	Emmitt Smith, 1994	132

INDIVIDUAL RECORDS—SINGLE GAME

Category	Name	Performance
Rushing (Yds.)	Emmitt Smith, 10-31-93	237
Passing (Yds.)	Don Meredith, 11-10-63	460
Passing (TDs)	Many times	5
	Last time by Danny White, 10-30-83	
Receiving (No.)	Lance Rentzel, 11-19-67	13
Receiving (Yds.)	Bob Hayes, 11-13-66	246
Interceptions	Herb Adderley, 9-26-71	3
	Lee Roy Jordan, 11-4-73	3
	Dennis Thurman, 12-13-81	3
Field Goals	Roger Ruzek, 12-21-87	5
	Eddie Murray, 10-3-93	5
Touchdowns (Tot.)	Many times	4
	Last time by Emmitt Smith, 11-18-90	
Points	Many times	24
	Last time by Emmitt Smith, 11-18-90	

COACHING HISTORY

(334-220-6)

1960-88	Tom Landry	270-178-6
1989-93	Jimmy Johnson	51-37-0
1994	Barry Switzer	13-5-0

TEXAS STADIUM

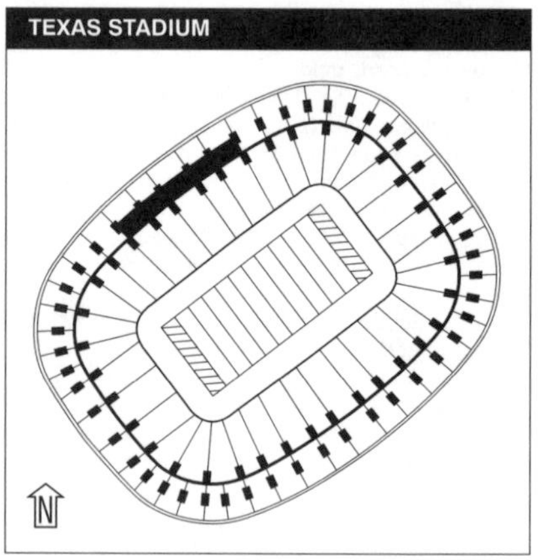

1994 TEAM RECORD

PRESEASON (2-3)

Date	Result		Opponents
7/31	W	17-9	Minnesota
8/7	L	19-27	L.A. Raiders
8/15	L	0-6	vs. Houston at Mexico City
8/21	W	34-10	Denver
8/25	L	10-28	at New Orleans

REGULAR SEASON (12-4)

Date	Result		Opponents	Att.
9/4	W	26- 9	at Pittsburgh	60,156
9/11	W	20-17	Houston	64,402
9/19	L	17-20	Detroit (OT)	64,102
10/2	W	34- 7	at Washington	55,394
10/9	W	38- 3	Arizona	64,518
10/16	W	24-13	Philadelphia	64,703
10/23	W	28-21	at Arizona	71,023
10/30	W	23-20	at Cincinnati	57,096
11/7	W	38-10	N.Y. Giants	64,836
11/13	L	14-21	at San Francisco	69,014
11/20	W	31- 7	Washington	64,644
11/24	W	42-31	Green Bay	64,597
12/4	W	31-19	at Philadelphia	65,974
12/10	L	14-19	Cleveland	64,826
12/19	W	24-16	at New Orleans	67,323
12/24	L	10-15	at N.Y. Giants	66,943

POSTSEASON (1-1)

Date	Result		Opponents	Att.
1/8	W	35- 9	Green Bay	64,745
1/15	L	28-38	at San Francisco	69,125

(OT) Overtime

SCORE BY PERIODS

	1	2	3	4	OT		Total
Cowboys	100	122	104	88	0	—	414
Opponents	34	93	46	72	3	—	248

ATTENDANCE

Home 516,628 Away 512,923 Total 1,029,551
Single-game home record, 80,259 (11-24-66)
Single-season home record, 516,628 (1994)

1994 TEAM STATISTICS

	Cowboys	Opp.
Total First Downs	322	273
Rushing	136	86
Passing	160	157
Penalty	26	30
Third Down: Made/Att	93/209	91/229
Third Down Pct.	44.5	39.7
Fourth Down: Made/Att	6/7	8/17
Fourth Down Pct.	85.7	47.1
Total Net Yards	5321	4313
Avg. Per Game	332.6	269.6
Total Plays	1018	1006
Avg. Per Play	5.2	4.3
Net Yards Rushing	1953	1561
Avg. Per Game	122.1	97.6
Total Rushes	550	437
Net Yards Passing	3368	2752
Avg. Per Game	210.5	172.0
Sacked/Yards Lost	20/93	47/299
Gross Yards	3461	3051
Att./Completions	448/282	522/269
Completion Pct.	62.9	51.5
Had Intercepted	14	22
Punts/Avg	70/41.9	84/43.3
Net Punting Avg.	70/35.4	84/36.8
Penalties/Yards Lost	100/895	102/826
Fumbles/Ball Lost	22/10	15/9
Touchdowns	50	27
Rushing	26	8
Passing	19	19
Returns	5	0
Avg. Time of Possession	31:35	28:25

1994 INDIVIDUAL STATISTICS

PASSING	Att.	Comp.	Yds.	Pct.	TD	Int.	Tkld.	Rate
Aikman	361	233	2676	64.5	13	12	14/59	84.9
Peete	56	33	470	58.9	4	1	4/21	102.5
Garrett	31	16	315	51.6	2	1	2/13	95.5
Cowboys	448	282	3461	62.9	19	14	20/93	87.8
Opponents	522	269	3051	51.5	19	22	47/299	64.0

SCORING	TD R	TD P	TD Rt	PAT	FG	Saf	PTS
E. Smith	21	1	0	0/0	0/0	0	132
Boniol	0	0	0	48/48	22/29	0	114
Harper	0	8	0	0/0	0/0	0	48
Irvin	0	6	0	0/0	0/0	0	36
Johnston	2	2	0	0/0	0/0	0	24
Novacek	0	2	0	0/0	0/0	0	12
K. Williams	0	0	2	0/0	0/0	0	12
B. Thomas	1	0	0	0/0	0/0	0	6
Aikman	1	0	0	0/0	0/0	0	6
Coleman	1	0	0	0/0	0/0	0	6
D. Smith	0	0	1	0/0	0/0	0	6
Tolbert	0	0	1	0/0	0/0	0	6
Woodson	0	0	1	0/0	0/0	0	6
Cowboys	26	19	5	48/48	22/29	0	414
Opponents	8	19	0	24/24	20/25	1	248

2-Point conversions: 0. Team: 0-2.

RUSHING	Att.	Yds.	Avg.	LG	TD
E. Smith	368	1484	4.0	46	21
Coleman	64	180	2.8	13	1
Johnston	40	138	3.5	9t	2
B. Thomas	24	70	2.9	11	1
Aikman	30	62	2.1	13	1
K. Williams	6	20	3.3	8	0
Agee	5	4	0.8	3	0
Wilson	1	-1	-1.0	-1	0
Garrett	3	-2	-0.7	0	0
Peete	9	-2	-0.2	2	0
Cowboys	550	1953	3.6	46	26
Opponents	437	1561	3.6	40	8

RECEIVING	No.	Yds.	Avg.	LG	TD
Irvin	79	1241	15.7	65t	6
E. Smith	50	341	6.8	68	1
Novacek	47	475	10.1	27	2
Johnston	44	325	7.4	24	2
Harper	33	821	24.9	90	8
K. Williams	13	181	13.9	29	0
Coleman	8	46	5.8	14	0
Galbraith	4	31	7.8	15	0
B. Thomas	2	1	0.5	5	0
Agee	1	2	2.0	2	0
Kennard	1	-3	-3.0	-3	0
Cowboys	282	3461	12.3	90	19
Opponents	269	3051	11.3	67t	19

INTERCEPTIONS	No.	Yds.	Avg.	LG	TD
Woodson	5	140	28.0	94t	1
Washington	5	43	8.6	25	0
Brown	4	21	5.3	14	0
D. Smith	2	13	6.5	13t	1
K. Smith	2	11	5.5	11	0
Tolbert	1	54	54.0	54t	1
Marion	1	11	11.0	11	0
Haley	1	1	1.0	1	0
Gant	1	0	0.0	0	0
Holmes	0	3	—	3	0
Cowboys	22	297	13.5	94t	3
Opponents	14	180	12.9	56	0

PUNTING	No.	Yds.	Avg.	In 20	LG
Jett	70	2935	41.9	26	58
Cowboys	70	2935	41.9	26	58
Opponents	84	3637	43.3	31	80

PUNT RETURNS	No.	FC	Yds.	Avg.	LG	TD
K. Williams	39	13	349	8.9	83t	1
Holmes	5	1	55	11.0	19	0
Cowboys	44	14	404	9.2	83t	1
Opponents	36	14	378	10.5	58	0

KICKOFF RETURNS	No.	Yds.	Avg.	LG	TD
K. Williams	43	1148	26.7	87t	1
Holmes	4	89	22.3	32	0
Marion	2	39	19.5	21	0
Jones	1	8	8.0	8	0
Cowboys	50	1284	25.7	87t	1
Opponents	82	1709	20.8	67	0

SACKS	No.
Haley	12.5
Jeffcoat	8.0
Hennings	7.0
Tolbert	5.5
Lett	4.0
D. Smith	4.0
Maryland	3.0
Bates	1.0
Edwards	1.0
Marion	1.0
Cowboys	47.0
Opponents	20.0

1995 DRAFT CHOICES

Round	Name	Pos.	College
2	Sherman Williams	RB	Alabama
	Kendell Watkins	TE	Mississippi State
	Shane Hannah	G	Michigan State
3	Charlie Williams	DB	Bowling Green
4	Eric Bjornson	WR	Washington
	Alundis Brice	DB	Mississippi
	Linc Harden	LB	Oklahoma State
5	Edward Hervey	WR	Southern California
	Dana Howard	LB	Illinois
7	Oscar Sturgis	DE	North Carolina

DALLAS COWBOYS

1995 VETERAN ROSTER

No.		Name	Pos.	Ht.	Wt.	Birthdate	NFL Exp.	College	Hometown	How Acq.	'94 Games/ Starts
34	#	Agee, Tommie	RB	6-0	235	2/22/64	9	Auburn	Maplesville, Ala.	FA-'93	15/0
8		Aikman, Troy	QB	6-4	228	11/21/66	7	UCLA	Henryetta, Okla.	D1-'89	14/14
73		Allen, Larry	G-T	6-3	325	11/27/71	2	Sonoma State	Napa, Calif.	D2-'94	16/10
56		Barnes, Reggie	LB	6-1	240	1/23/69	2	Oklahoma	Grand Prairie, Tex.	FA-'95	0*
40		Bates, Bill	S	6-1	210	6/6/61	13	Tennessee	Knoxville, Tenn.	FA-'83	15/0
18		Boniol, Chris	K	5-11	159	12/9/71	2	Louisiana Tech	Alexandria, La.	FA-'94	16/0
24		Brown, Larry	CB	5-11	186	11/30/69	5	Texas Christian	Los Angeles, Calif.	D12-'91	15/15
96		Carver, Shante	DE	6-5	242	2/12/71	2	Arizona State	Stockton, Calif.	D1-'94	10/0
44		Coleman, Lincoln	RB	6-1	239	8/12/69	3	Baylor	Dallas, Tex.	FA-'94	11/0
68	#	Cornish, Frank	C-G	6-4	287	9/24/67	6	UCLA	Chicago, Ill.	FA-'94	7/0*
53		Donaldson, Ray	C	6-3	300	5/18/58	16	Georgia	Rome, Ga.	UFA(Sea)-'95	16/16*
58		Edwards, Dixon	LB	6-1	225	3/25/68	5	Michigan State	Cincinnati, Ohio	D2-'91	16/15
23		Fields, Floyd	S	6-1	200	1/7/69	4	Arizona State	South Holland, Ill.	FA-'95	0*
46	#	Fishback, Joe	S	6-0	212	11/29/67	6	Carson-Newman	Knoxville, Tenn.	FA-'94	12/0
82		Fleming, Cory	WR	6-1	216	3/19/71	2	Tennessee	Nashville, Tenn.	FA-'94	2/0
17		Garrett, Jason	QB	6-2	195	3/28/66	3	Princeton	Chagrin, Ohio	FA-'93	2/1
94		Haley, Charles	DE	6-5	255	1/6/64	10	James Madison	Campbell County, Va.	T(SF)-'92	16/16
69		Hegamin, George	T	6-7	338	2/14/73	2	North Carolina State	Camden, N.J.	D3-'94	2/0
70		Hellestrae, Dale	G-C	6-5	286	7/11/62	11	Southern Methodist	Scottsdale, Ariz.	T(Raid)-'90	16/0
95		Hennings, Chad	DT	6-6	288	10/20/65	4	Air Force	Elberon, Iowa	D11-'88	16/0
47		Holmes, Clayton	CB	5-10	181	8/23/69	4	Carson-Newman	Florence, S.C.	D3a-'92	16/1
88		Irvin, Michael	WR	6-2	205	3/5/66	8	Miami	Ft. Lauderdale, Fla.	D1-'88	16/16
19		Jett, John	P	6-0	194	11/11/68	3	East Carolina	Reedville, Va.	FA-'93	16/0
48		Johnston, Daryl	RB	6-2	242	2/10/66	7	Syracuse	Youngstown, N.Y.	D2-'89	16/16
55		Jones, Robert	LB	6-2	237	9/27/69	4	East Carolina	Nottoway, Va.	D1b-'92	16/16
38		Lang, David	RB	5-11	210	3/28/68	5	Northern Arizona	Rialto, Calif.	UFA(Rams)-'95	13/0*
78		Lett, Leon	DE-DT	6-6	288	10/12/68	5	Emporia State	Fair Hope, Ala.	D7-'91	16/16
31		Marion, Brock	S	5-11	189	6/11/70	3	Nevada-Reno	Bakersfield, Calif.	D7-'93	14/1
67		Maryland, Russell	DT	6-1	279	3/22/69	5	Miami	Chicago, Ill.	D1a-'91	16/16
99		McCormack, Hurvin	DT	6-5	274	4/6/72	2	Indiana	Brooklyn, N.Y.	FA-'94	4/0
98		Myles, Godfrey	LB	6-1	242	9/22/68	5	Florida	Miami, Fla.	D3a-'91	15/0
61		Newton, Nate	G	6-3	320	12/20/61	10	Florida A&M	Orlando, Fla.	FA-'86	16/16
84		Novacek, Jay	TE	6-4	234	10/24/62	11	Wyoming	Gothenburg, Neb.	PB(Phx)-'90	16/14
76		Reynolds, Jerry	T	6-6	315	4/2/70	2	Nevada-Las Vegas	Ft. Thomas, Ky.	FA-'94	0*
52	t-	Schwantz, Jim	LB	6-2	232	1/23/70	2	Purdue	Palatine, Ill.	T(Chi)-'94	7/0
59		Smith, Darrin	LB	6-1	230	4/15/70	3	Miami	Miami, Fla.	D2b-'93	16/16
22		Smith, Emmitt	RB	5-9	209	5/15/69	6	Florida	Escambia, Fla.	D1-'90	15/15
26		Smith, Kevin	CB	5-11	184	4/7/70	4	Texas A&M	Orange, Tex.	D1a-'92	16/16
65		Stone, Ron	G	6-5	309	7/20/71	3	Boston College	West Roxbury, Md.	D4b-'93	16/0
92		Tolbert, Tony	DE	6-6	263	12/29/67	7	Texas-El Paso	Englewood, N.J.	D4-'89	16/16
71		Tuinei, Mark	T	6-5	305	3/31/60	13	Hawaii	Honolulu, Hawaii	FA-'83	15/15
79		Williams, Erik	T	6-6	322	9/7/68	5	Central State, Ohio	Philadelphia, Pa.	D3c-'91	7/7
85		Williams, Kevin	WR	5-9	195	1/25/71	3	Miami	Dallas, Tex.	D2a-'93	15/2
11		Wilson, Wade	QB	6-3	206	2/1/59	15	East Texas State	Commerce, Tex.	FA'95	4/0*
28		Woodson, Darren	S	6-1	215	4/25/69	4	Arizona State	Phoenix, Ariz.	D2b-'92	16/16

* Barnes last active with Pittsburgh in '93; Cornish played 7 games with Minnesota in '94; Donaldson played 16 games with Seattle; Fields last active with San Diego in '93; Lang played 13 games with L.A. Rams; Reynolds active for one game but did not play; Wilson played 4 games with New Orleans.

\# Unrestricted free agent; subject to developments.

† Restricted free agent; subject to developments.

t- Cowboys traded for Schwantz (Chicago).

Players lost through free agency (9): LB Darrick Brownlow (Wash; 16 games in '94), TE Scott Galbraith (Wash; 16), S Kenneth Gant (TB; 16), WR Alvin Harper (TB; 16), DE Jim Jeffcoat (Buff; 16), QB Rodney Peete (Phil; 7), C Mark Stepnoski (Hou; 16), LB Matt Vanderbeek (Wash; 12), S James Washington (Wash; 16).

Players lost through Expansion Draft (3): WR Willie Jackson (Jax; 0 games in '94), RB Derrick Lassic (Car; 0); CB Dave Thomas (Jax; 16).

Also played with Cowboys in '94—G Derek Kennard (16 games), RB Blair Thomas (2), RB Robert Wilson (2).

COACHING STAFF

Head Coach,
Barry Switzer

Pro Career: Led Cowboys to NFC Championship Game and NFC East title in 1994 with a 12-4 regular season record. Named the third head coach in Cowboys history on March 30, 1994. No pro playing experience. Career record: 13-5.

Background: Played at Arkansas from 1955-59 before beginning his assistant coaching career at his alma mater in 1962. Moved on to Oklahoma in 1966, and was named the Sooners' offensive coordinator in 1967. As head coach at Oklahoma from 1973-88, Switzer registered a career record of 157-29-4. His .837 winning percentage at Oklahoma is the fourth highest mark in college history, behind only Notre Dame's Knute Rockne (.881) and Frank Leahy (.864) and Carlisle's George Woodruff (.846). He guided the Sooners to 28 consecutive wins from 1973-75 and went 37 straight games without a defeat. Switzer's Oklahoma teams won national championships (1974, 1975, and 1985) and 12 Big Eight Conference championships.

Personal: Born October 5, 1937, Crossett, Arkansas. Switzer lives in Irving, Texas. He has two sons—Greg and Doug and one daughter Kathy.

ASSISTANT COACHES

Hubbard Alexander, wide receivers; born February 14, 1939, Winston-Salem, N.C., lives in Coppell, Tex. Center Tennessee State 1958-61. No pro playing experience. College coach: Tennessee State 1962-63, Vanderbilt 1974-78, Miami 1979-88. Pro coach: Joined Cowboys in 1989.

Joe Avezzano, special teams; born November 17, 1943, Yonkers, N.Y., lives in Coppell, Tex. Guard Florida State 1961-65. Pro center Boston Patriots 1966. College coach: Florida State 1968, Iowa State 1969-72, Pittsburgh 1973-76, Tennessee 1977-79, Oregon State 1980-84 (head coach), Texas 1985-88. Pro coach: Joined Cowboys in 1990.

John Blake, defensive line; born March 6, 1961, Sand Springs, Okla., lives in Irving, Tex. Nose tackle Oklahoma 1980-83. No pro playing experience. College coach: Oklahoma 1986-87, 1989-92, Tulsa 1988. Pro coach: Joined Cowboys in 1993.

Joe Brodsky, running backs; born June 9, 1934, Miami, Fla., lives in Coppell, Tex. Fullback-linebacker Florida 1953-56. No pro playing experience. College coach: Miami 1978-88. Pro coach: Joined Cowboys in 1989.

Dave Campo, defensive coordinator; born July 18, 1947, New London, Conn., lives in Coppell, Tex. Defensive back Central Connecticut State 1967-70. No pro playing experience. College coach: Central Connecticut State 1971-72, Albany State 1973, Bridgeport 1974, Pittsburgh 1975, Washington State 1976, Boise State 1977-79, Oregon State 1980, Weber State 1981-82, Iowa State 1983, Syracuse 1984-86, Miami 1987-88. Pro coach: Joined Cowboys in 1989.

Jim Eddy, linebackers; born May 2, 1939, Checotah, Okla., lives in Carrollton, Tex. Defensive back-running back New Mexico State 1956-59. No pro playing experience. College coach: New Mexico State 1965-70, Texas El-Paso 1971-72, Houston 1987-89. Pro coach: Saskatchewan Rough Riders (CFL) 1974-78 (head coach 1977-78), Hamilton Tiger Cats (CFL) 1979-80, Montreal Alouettes (CFL) 1981 (head coach), Toronto Argonauts (CFL) 1982-83, Houston Gamblers (USFL) 1984-85, Houston Oilers 1990-92, joined Cowboys in 1993.

Robert Ford, tight ends; born June 21, 1951, Belton, Tex., lives in Coppell, Tex. Wide receiver Houston 1970-72. No pro playing experience. College coach: Western Illinois 1974-76, New Mexico 1977-79, Oregon State 1980-81, Mississippi State 1982-83, Kansas 1986, Texas Tech 1987-88, Texas A&M 1989-90. Pro coach: Houston Gamblers (USFL) 1985, joined Cowboys in 1991.

Steve Hoffman, kickers-research and development; born September 8, 1958, Camden, N.J., lives in Coppell, Tex. Quarterback-running back-wide receiver Dickinson College 1979-82. Pro punter Washington Federals (USFL) 1983. College coach: Miami 1985-87. Pro coach: Joined Cowboys in 1989.

Hudson Houck, offensive line; born January 7, 1943, Los Angeles, Calif., lives in Irving, Tex. Center Southern California 1962-64. No pro playing experience. College coach: Southern California 1970-72, 1976-82, Stanford 1973-75. Pro coach: Los Angeles Rams 1983-91, Seattle Seahawks 1992, joined Cowboys in 1993.

Mike Woicik, strength and conditioning; born September 26, 1956, Westwood, Mass., lives in Coppell, Tex. Boston College 1974-78. No college or pro playing experience. College coach: Springfield 1978-80, Syracuse 1980-89. Pro coach: Joined Cowboys in 1990.

Ernie Zampese, offensive coordinator; born March 12, 1936, Santa Barbara, Calif., lives in Mission Viejo, Calif. Halfback Southern California 1956-58. No pro playing experience. College coach: Hancock, Calif., J.C. 1962-65, Cal Poly-SLO 1966, San Diego State 1967-75. Pro coach: San Diego Chargers 1976, 1979-86, New York Jets 1977-78 (scout), Los Angeles Rams 1987-93, joined Cowboys in 1994.

Mike Zimmer, defensive backs; born June 5, 1956, Peoria, Ill., lives in Irving, Tex. Quarterback-linebacker Illinois State 1974-76. No pro playing experience. College coach: Missouri 1979-80, Weber State 1981-88, Washington State 1989-93. Pro coach: Joined Cowboys in 1994.

1995 FIRST-YEAR ROSTER

Name	Pos.	Ht.	Wt.	Birthdate	College	Hometown	How Acq.
Anderson, John	S	5-10	186	11/30/71	Oklahoma	Sugar Land, Tex.	FA
Baker, Jon	K	6-1	170	8/13/72	Arizona State	Bakersfield, Calif.	FA
Batiste, Michael (1)	DT	6-3	295	12/24/70	Tulane	Beaumont, Tex.	FA
Bjornson, Eric	TE	6-4	215	12/15/71	Washington	Oakland, Wash.	D4a
Brice, Alundis	CB	5-10	178	5/1/70	Mississippi	Brookhaven, Miss.	D4b
Coger, Freddie	LB	6-2	248	2/9/70	Georgia Tech	Pittsburgh, Pa.	FA
Davis, Billy	WR	6-1	199	7/6/72	Pittsburgh	El Paso, Tex.	FA
Davis, John (1)	TE	6-4	257	5/14/73	Emporia State	Jasper, Tex.	FA
Dickson, Wayne (1)	DE	6-3	265	11/27/67	Oklahoma	Borger, Tex.	FA
Edwards, Demetrius	DT	6-3	287	3/25/72	Fresno State	East Palo Alto, Calif.	FA
Evans, Josh	DT	6-2	283	9/6/72	Alabama-Birmingham	West Shawmut, Ala.	FA
Gadsden, Oronde	WR	6-3	218	8/20/71	Winston-Salem State	Charleston, S.C.	FA
Goosby, Michael	WR	6-3	207	10/15/70	North Texas	Arlington, Tex.	FA
Graham, Roger	RB	5-10	212	11/8/72	New Haven	Spring Valley, N.Y.	FA
Gruttadauria, Mike	C	6-3	273	12/6/72	Central Florida	Palm Harbor, Fla.	FA
Hannah, Shane	G	6-5	345	10/21/71	Michigan State	Germantown, Ohio	D2c
Harden, Linc	LB	6-3	238	4/9/72	Oklahoma State	Galveston, Tex.	D4c
Harris, Rodney	WR	6-5	207	12/1/71	Kansas	Kansas City, Kan.	FA
Hervey, Edward	WR	6-3	179	5/4/73	Southern California	Compton, Calif.	D5a
Hmielewski, Jim	T	6-5	314	2/13/72	Kansas State	Franklin Park, Ill.	FA
Houston, Artis	CB	5-7	179	11/29/72	California	Compton, Calif.	FA
Howard, Dana	LB	6-0	238	2/25/72	Illinois	East St. Louis, Mo.	D5b
Johnson, Curtis	RB	5-9	204	11/11/71	North Carolina	Greensboro, N.C.	FA
Jones, John	G	6-1	309	12/8/72	Kansas	Los Angeles, Calif.	FA
McClenton, Michael	RB	5-11	252	12/9/69	North Alabama	Tallahassee, Fla.	FA
McCord, Paul	P	6-6	229	9/23/71	Western Maryland	Wilmington, Del.	FA
McGrath, Ryan	TE	6-5	255	8/23/72	Southwest Louisiana	Granada Hills, Calif.	FA
McGuire, Stephen	RB	5-11	215	11/20/69	Miami	Brooklyn, N.Y.	FA
Ross, Dominique	RB	6-0	203	1/12/72	Valdosta State	Jacksonville, Fla.	FA
Semptimphelter, Scott	QB	6-2	199	5/15/72	Lehigh	Florence, N.J.	FA
Studstill, Darren (1)	S	6-1	186	8/9/70	West Virginia	Palm Beach Garden, Fla.	FA
Stugis, Oscar	DE	6-5	280	1/12/71	North Carolina	Hamlet, N.C.	D7
Tagoai, Mu	G	6-3	305	4/10/72	Arizona	Honolulu, Hawaii	FA
Thomas, Jeff	WR	6-0	192	1/13/72	Georgia	Valdosta, Ga.	FA
Tremble, Greg (1)	S	5-11	188	4/16/72	Georgia	Warner Robins, Ga.	FA
Vaughn, DeMario	T	6-5	283	3/21/72	Arizona State	Lynwood, Calif.	FA
Watkins, Kendell	TE	6-1	305	3/8/73	Mississippi State	Jackson, Miss.	D2b
Williams, Charlie	S	6-0	190	2/2/72	Bowling Green	Detroit, Mich.	D3
Williams, Germaine (1)	RB	5-10	228	2/4/71	Louisiana State	Donaldsonville, La.	FA
Williams, Sherman	RB	5-8	190	8/13/73	Alabama	Mobile, Ala.	D2a

The term NFL Rookie is defined as a player who is in his first season of professional football and has not been on the roster of another professional football team for any regular-season or postseason games. A Rookie is designated by an "R" on NFL rosters. Players who have been active in another professional football league or players who have NFL experience, including either preseason training camp or being on an Active List or Inactive List, or on Reserve/Injured or Reserve/Physically Unable to Perform for fewer than six regular-season games, are termed NFL First-Year Players. An NFL First-Year Player is designated by a "1" on NFL rosters. Thereafter, a player is credited with an additional year of experience for each season in which he accumulates six games on the Active List or Inactive List, or on Reserve/Injured or Reserve/Physically Unable to Perform.

NOTES

DETROIT LIONS

National Football Conference
Central Division
Team Colors: Honolulu Blue and Silver
Pontiac Silverdome
1200 Featherstone Road
Pontiac, Michigan 48342
Telephone: (810) 335-4131

CLUB OFFICIALS

President-Owner: William Clay Ford
Vice Chairman: William Clay Ford, Jr.
Executive Vice President and Chief Operating Officer: Chuck Schmidt
Vice President of Administration and Communications: Bill Keenist
Vice President-General Counsel: David Potts
Director of Player Personnel: Ron Hughes
Director of Pro Scouting: Kevin Colbert
Director of Player Programs/Pro Scouting Assistant: Larry Lee
Scouts: Milt Davis, Dirk Dierking, Thomas Dimitroff, Allen Hughes, Scott McEwen, Jim Owens, Rick Spielman, John Trump
Controller: Tom Lesnau
Director of Marketing: Steve Harms
Director of Media Relations: Mike Murray
Media Relations Assistant: James Petrylka
Director of Sales and Ticket Operations: Fred Otto
Director of Community Relations and Detroit Lions Charities: Tim Pendell
Community Relations Assistant: Kim French
Promotions Manager: Paula Buckhaulter
Head Athletic Trainer: Kent Falb
Equipment Manager: Dan Jaroshewich
Video Director: Steve Hermans
Stadium: Pontiac Silverdome • **Capacity:** 80,368
1200 Featherstone Road
Pontiac, Michigan 48342
Playing Surface: AstroTurf
Training Camp: Pontiac Silverdome
1200 Featherstone Road
Pontiac, Michigan 48342

1995 SCHEDULE

PRESEASON

Aug. 4	at New England	7:00
Aug. 10	**Jacksonville**	7:30
Aug. 17	**Cincinnati**	7:30
Aug. 25	at New Orleans	7:00

REGULAR SEASON

Sept. 3	at Pittsburgh	1:00
Sept. 10	at Minnesota	12:00
Sept. 17	**Arizona**	1:00
Sept. 25	**San Francisco** (Monday)	9:00
Oct. 1	Open Date	
Oct. 8	**Cleveland**	4:00
Oct. 15	at Green Bay	12:00
Oct. 22	at Washington	1:00
Oct. 29	**Green Bay**	1:00
Nov. 5	at Atlanta	1:00
Nov. 12	**Tampa Bay**	1:00
Nov. 19	at Chicago	12:00
Nov. 23	**Minnesota** (Thursday)	12:30
Dec. 4	**Chicago** (Monday)	9:00
Dec. 10	at Houston	12:00
Dec. 17	**Jacksonville**	1:00
Dec. 23	at Tampa Bay (Saturday)	4:00

RECORD HOLDERS

INDIVIDUAL RECORDS—CAREER

Category	Name	Performance
Rushing (Yds.)	Barry Sanders, 1989-1994	8,672
Passing (Yds.)	Bobby Layne, 1950-58	15,710
Passing (TDs)	Bobby Layne, 1950-58	118
Receiving (No.)	Charlie Sanders, 1968-1977	336
Receiving (Yds.)	Gail Cogdill, 1960-68	5,220
Interceptions	Dick LeBeau, 1959-1972	62
Punting (Avg.)	Yale Lary, 1952-53, 1956-1964	44.3
Punt Return (Avg.)	Jack Christiansen, 1951-58	12.8
Kickoff Return (Avg.)	Pat Studstill, 1961-67	25.7
Field Goals	Eddie Murray, 1980-1991	243
Touchdowns (Tot.)	Barry Sanders, 1989-1994	68
Points	Eddie Murray, 1980-1991	1,113

INDIVIDUAL RECORDS—SINGLE SEASON

Category	Name	Performance
Rushing (Yds.)	Barry Sanders, 1994	1,883
Passing (Yds.)	Gary Danielson, 1980	3,223
Passing (TDs)	Bobby Layne, 1951	26
Receiving (No.)	James Jones, 1984	77
Receiving (Yds.)	Pat Studstill, 1966	1,266
Interceptions	Don Doll, 1950	12
	Jack Christiansen, 1953	12
Punting (Avg.)	Yale Lary, 1963	48.9
Punt Return (Avg.)	Jack Christiansen, 1952	21.5
Kickoff Return (Avg.)	Tom Watkins, 1965	34.4
Field Goals	Jason Hanson, 1993	34
Touchdowns (Tot.)	Barry Sanders, 1991	17
Points	Jason Hanson, 1993	130

INDIVIDUAL RECORDS—SINGLE GAME

Category	Name	Performance
Rushing (Yds.)	Barry Sanders, 11-13-94	237
Passing (Yds.)	Bobby Layne, 11-5-50	374
Passing (TDs)	Gary Danielson, 12-9-78	5
Receiving (No.)	Cloyce Box, 12-3-50	12
	James Jones, 9-28-86	12
Receiving (Yds.)	Cloyce Box, 12-3-50	302
Interceptions	Don Doll, 10-23-49	*4
Field Goals	Garo Yepremian, 11-13-66	6
Touchdowns (Tot.)	Dutch Clark, 10-22-34	4
	Cloyce Box, 12-3-50	4
	Barry Sanders, 11-24-91	4
Points	Dutch Clark, 10-22-34	24
	Cloyce Box, 12-3-50	24
	Barry Sanders, 11-24-91	24

*NFL Record

COACHING HISTORY

Portsmouth Spartans 1930-33 (418-429-32)

1930	Hal (Tubby) Griffen	5-6-3
1931-36	George (Potsy) Clark	49-20-6
1937-38	Earl (Dutch) Clark	14-8-0
1939	Elmer (Gus) Henderson	6-5-0
1940	George (Potsy) Clark	5-5-1
1941-42	Bill Edwards*	4-9-1
1942	John Karcis	0-8-0
1943-47	Charles (Gus) Dorais	20-31-2
1948-50	Alvin (Bo) McMillin	12-24-0
1951-56	Raymond (Buddy) Parker	50-24-2
1957-64	George Wilson	55-45-6
1965-66	Harry Gilmer	10-16-2
1967-72	Joe Schmidt	43-35-7
1973	Don McCafferty	6-7-1
1974-76	Rick Forzano**	15-17-0
1976-77	Tommy Hudspeth	11-13-0
1978-84	Monte Clark	43-63-1
1985-88	Darryl Rogers***	18-40-0
1988-94	Wayne Fontes	52-53-0

*Released after three games in 1942
**Resigned after four games in 1976
***Released after 11 games in 1988

PONTIAC SILVERDOME

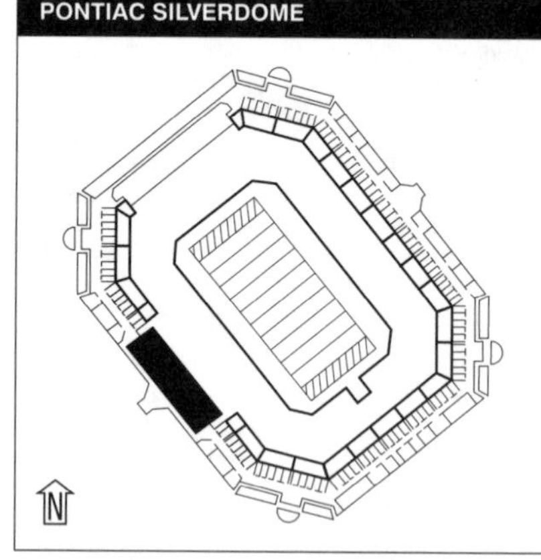

DETROIT LIONS

1994 TEAM RECORD

PRESEASON (2-2)

Date	Result		Opponents
8/5	W	26-13	N.Y. Jets
8/13	L	7-16	at Cleveland
8/19	W	24-16	Arizona
8/26	L	14-38	at Cincinnati

REGULAR SEASON (9-7)

Date	Result		Opponents	Att.
9/4	W	31-28	Atlanta (OT)	60,740
9/11	L	3-10	at Minnesota	57,349
9/19	W	20-17	at Dallas (OT)	64,102
9/25	L	17-23	New England	59,618
10/2	L	14-24	at Tampa Bay	38,012
10/9	L	21-27	San Francisco	77,340
10/23	W	21-16	Chicago	73,574
10/30	W	28-25	at N.Y. Giants (OT)	75,124
11/6	L	30-38	at Green Bay	54,995
11/13	W	14- 9	Tampa Bay	50,814
11/20	L	10-20	at Chicago	55,035
11/24	W	35-21	Buffalo	75,672
12/4	W	34-31	Green Bay	76,338
12/10	W	18- 7	at N.Y. Jets	56,080
12/17	W	41-19	Minnesota	73,881
12/25	L	20-27	at Miami	70,980

POSTSEASON (0-1)

12/31	L	12-16	at Green Bay	58,125

(OT) Overtime

SCORE BY PERIODS

Lions	45	130	82	91	9	— 357
Opponents	60	148	72	62	0	— 342

ATTENDANCE

Home 547,977 Away 471,677 Total 1,019,654

Single-game home record, 80,444 (12-20-81)

Single-season home record, 622,593 (1980)

1994 TEAM STATISTICS

	Lions	Opp.
Total First Downs	280	326
Rushing	94	131
Passing	164	169
Penalty	22	26
Third Down: Made/Att	75/188	112/231
Third Down Pct.	39.9	48.5
Fourth Down: Made/Att	5/12	10/20
Fourth Down Pct.	41.7	50.0
Total Net Yards	5002	5405
Avg. Per Game	312.6	337.8
Total Plays	891	1086
Avg. Per Play	5.6	5.0
Net Yards Rushing	2080	1859
Avg. Per Game	130.0	116.2
Total Rushes	406	512
Net Yards Passing	2922	3546
Avg. Per Game	182.6	221.6
Sacked/Yards Lost	26/163	27/199
Gross Yards	3085	3745
Att./Completions	459/250	547/370
Completion Pct.	54.5	67.6
Had Intercepted	14	12
Punts/Avg.	64/43.5	66/44.9
Net Punting Avg.	64/34.2	66/37.4
Penalties/Yards Lost	109/781	130/1036
Fumbles/Ball Lost	26/10	34/11
Touchdowns	43	40
Rushing	12	15
Passing	24	21
Returns	7	4
Avg. Time of Possession	26:06	33:54

1994 INDIVIDUAL STATISTICS

PASSING	Att.	Comp.	Yds.	Pct.	TD	Int.	Tkld.	Rate
Mitchell	246	119	1456	48.4	10	11	12/63	62.0
Krieg	212	131	1629	61.8	14	3	14/100	101.7
Perriman	1	0	0	0.0	0	0	0/0	39.6
Lions	459	250	3085	54.5	24	14	26/163	80.2
Opponents	547	370	3745	67.6	21	12	27/199	90.6

SCORING	TD R	TD P	TD Rt	PAT	FG	Saf	PTS
Hanson	0	0	0	39/40	18/27	0	93
H. Moore	0	11	0	0/0	0/0	0	66
Sanders	7	1	0	0/0	0/0	0	48
Perriman	0	4	0	0/0	0/0	0	28
D. Moore	4	0	0	0/0	0/0	0	24
Carter	0	3	0	0/0	0/0	0	18
Gray	0	0	3	0/0	0/0	0	18
Matthews	0	3	0	0/0	0/0	0	18
Morton	0	1	1	0/0	0/0	0	12
Clay	0	0	1	0/0	0/0	0	6
Conover	0	1	0	0/0	0/0	0	6
Johnson	0	0	1	0/0	0/0	0	6
Mitchell	1	0	0	0/0	0/0	0	6
Spielman	0	0	1	0/0	0/0	0	6
Lions	12	24	7	39/40	18/27	1	357
Opponents	15	21	4	37/38	21/28	0	342

2-Point conversions: Perriman (2). Team: 2-3.

RUSHING	Att.	Yds.	Avg.	LG	TD
Sanders	331	1883	5.7	85	7
Perriman	9	86	9.6	25	0
D. Moore	27	52	1.9	12	4
Krieg	23	35	1.5	15	0
Mitchell	15	24	1.6	7	1
Lynch	1	0	0.0	0	0
Lions	406	2080	5.1	85	12
Opponents	512	1859	3.6	32	15

RECEIVING	No.	Yds.	Avg.	LG	TD
H. Moore	72	1173	16.3	51t	11
Perriman	56	761	13.6	39	4
Sanders	44	283	6.4	22	1
Matthews	29	359	12.4	33	3
Holman	17	163	9.6	18	0
Hall	10	106	10.6	18	0
Carter	8	97	12.1	18	3
Hallock	7	75	10.7	21	0
Morton	3	39	13.0	18t	1
Lynch	2	18	9.0	12	0
D. Moore	1	10	10.0	10	0
Conover	1	1	1.0	1t	1
Lions	250	3085	12.3	51t	24
Opponents	370	3745	10.1	76t	21

INTERCEPTIONS	No.	Yds.	Avg.	LG	TD
Massey	4	25	6.3	17	0
Clay	3	54	18.0	28t	1
Johnson	1	48	48.0	48t	1
McNeil	1	14	14.0	14	0
Colon	1	3	3.0	3	0
Blades	1	0	0.0	0	0
Mack	1	0	0.0	0	0
Lions	12	144	12.0	48t	2
Opponents	14	154	11.0	38	1

PUNTING	No.	Yds.	Avg.	In 20	LG
Montgomery	63	2782	44.2	19	64
Lions	64	2782	43.5	19	64
Opponents	66	2963	44.9	20	67

PUNT RETURNS	No.	FC	Yds.	Avg.	LG	TD
Gray	21	11	233	11.1	24	0
Clay	3	0	20	6.7	12	0
Massey	1	0	3	3.0	3	0
Lions	25	11	256	10.2	24	0
Opponents	36	9	431	12.0	80t	2

KICKOFF RETURNS	No.	Yds.	Avg.	LG	TD
Gray	45	1276	28.4	102t	3
D. Moore	10	113	11.3	19	0
Lynch	9	105	11.7	16	0
Morton	4	143	35.8	93t	1
Malone	3	38	12.7	20	0
Lions	71	1675	23.6	102t	4
Opponents	65	1572	24.2	96t	1

SACKS	No.
Thomas	7.0
Pritchett	5.5
Owens	3.0
Porcher	3.0
Scroggins	2.5
Swilling	2.5
Johnson	1.5
Blades	1.0
Hayworth	1.0
Lions	27.0
Opponents	26.0

1995 DRAFT CHOICES

Round	Name	Pos.	College
1	Luther Elliss	DT	Utah
3	David Sloan	TE	New Mexico
5	Stephen Boyd	LB	Boston College
	Kez McCorvey	WR	Florida State
	Ronald Cherry	T	McNeese State
6	Kevin Hickman	TE	Navy
	Cory Schlesinger	RB	Nebraska
7	Hessley Hempstead	G	Kansas

DETROIT LIONS

1995 VETERAN ROSTER

No.	Name	Pos.	Ht.	Wt.	Birthdate	NFL Exp.	College	Hometown	How Acq.	'94 Games/ Starts
5	t- Alexander, Harold	P	6-2	224	10/20/70	3	Appalachian State	Pickens, S.C.	T(Atl)-'95	15/0*
48	Beer, Tom	LB	6-1	237	3/27/69	2	Wayne State	Bayport, Mich.	D7-'94	9/0
36	Blades, Bennie	S	6-1	221	9/3/66	8	Miami	Ft. Lauderdale, Fla.	D1-'88	16/16
96	Bonham, Shane	DE-DT	6-4	260	10/18/70	2	Tennessee	Fairbanks, Alaska	D3-'94	15/1
27	Borgella, Jocelyn	CB	5-10	180	8/26/71	2	Cincinnati	Miami, Fla.	D6-'94	4/0
75	† Brown, Lomas	T	6-4	275	3/30/63	11	Florida	Miami, Fla.	D1-'85	16/16
68	Burton, Leonard	C	6-3	275	6/18/64	9	South Carolina	Memphis, Tenn.	FA-'94	0*
81	# Carter, Anthony	WR	5-11	181	9/17/60	11	Michigan	Riviera Beach, Fla.	FA-'94	4/1
32	Clay, Willie	S	5-9	184	9/5/70	4	Georgia Tech	Pittsburgh, Pa.	D8-'92	16/16
77	Compton, Mike	C-G	6-6	297	9/18/70	3	West Virginia	Richland, Va.	D3b-'93	2/0
76	Conover, Scott	T	6-4	285	9/27/68	5	Purdue	Freehold, N.J.	D5-'91	11/0
53	Glover, Kevin	C	6-2	282	6/17/63	11	Maryland	Upper Marlboro, Md.	D2-'85	16/16
89	Hall, Ron	TE	6-4	245	3/15/64	9	Hawaii	Escondido, Calif.	UFA(TB)-'94	13/10
49	Hallock, Ty	TE	6-3	249	4/30/71	3	Michigan State	Greenville, Mich.	D7-'93	15/10
4	Hanson, Jason	K	5-11	183	6/17/70	4	Washington State	Spokane, Wash.	D2b-'92	16/0
99	Hayworth, Tracy	LB	6-3	260	12/18/67	6	Tennessee	Franklin, Tenn.	D7-'90	9/1
12	Hollas, Don	QB	6-3	215	11/22/67	5	Rice	Rosenberg, Tex.	UFA(Cin)-'95	2/0*
82	Holman, Rodney	TE	6-3	238	4/20/60	14	Tulane	Ypsilanti, Mich.	UFA(Cin)-'93	15/7
25	Jeffries, Greg	CB	5-9	184	10/16/71	3	Virginia	High Point, N.C.	D6-'93	16/1
33	Johnson, Keshon	CB	5-10	185	7/17/70	3	Arizona	Fresno, Calif.	W(GB)-'95	13/0*
59	Johnson, Mike	LB	6-1	230	11/26/62	10	Virginia Tech	Hyattsville, Md.	UFA(Clev)-'94	16/16
57	# Jones, Victor	LB	6-2	250	10/19/66	8	Virginia Tech	Rockville, Md.	FA-'89	16/0
52	Kowalkowski, Scott	LB	6-2	228	8/23/68	5	Notre Dame	Orchard Lake, Mich.	FA-'94	16/0
55	London, Antonio	LB	6-2	234	4/14/71	3	Alabama	Tullahoma, Tenn.	D3a-'93	16/0
16	# Long, Chuck	QB	6-4	217	2/18/63	9	Iowa	Wheaton, Ill.	FA-'94	0*
73	Lutz, David	G-T	6-6	305	12/20/59	13	Georgia Tech	Peachland, N.C.	UFA(KC)-'93	16/16
26	Lynch, Eric	RB	5-10	224	5/16/70	2	Grand Valley State	Woodhaven, Mich.	FA-'93	12/3
24	# Mack, Milton	CB	5-11	195	9/20/63	9	Alcorn State	Jackson, Miss.	FA-'94	16/3
1	Majkowski, Don	QB	6-3	208	2/25/64	9	Virginia	Depew, N.Y.	UFA(Ind)-'95	9/6*
39	Malone, Van	S	5-11	186	7/1/70	2	Texas	Houston, Tex.	D2-'94	16/0
40	Massey, Robert	CB	5-11	195	2/16/67	7	North Carolina Central	Charlotte, N.C.	UFA(Ariz)-'94	16/15
83	Matthews, Aubrey	WR	5-7	165	9/15/62	10	Delta State	Pascaguola, Miss.	FA-'90	14/3
47	McNeil, Ryan	CB	6-2	192	10/4/70	3	Miami	Ft. Pierce, Fla.	D2-'93	14/13
19	Mitchell, Scott	QB	6-6	230	1/2/68	6	Utah	Springville, Utah	UFA(Mia)-'94	9/9
9	# Montgomery, Greg	P	6-4	215	10/29/64	8	Michigan State	Red Bank, N.J.	UFA(Hou)-'94	16/0
84	Moore, Herman	WR	6-3	210	10/20/69	5	Virginia	Danville, Va.	D1-'91	16/16
87	Morton, Johnnie	WR	6-0	190	10/7/71	2	Southern California	Torrance, Calif.	D1-'94	14/0
71	Moss, Zefross	T	6-6	324	8/17/66	7	Alabama State	Tuscaloosa, Ala.	UFA(Ind)-'95	11/11*
90	Owens, Dan	DE-DT	6-3	280	3/16/67	6	Southern California	Whittier, Calif.	D2-'90	16/8
80	Perriman, Brett	WR	5-9	180	10/10/65	8	Miami	Miami, Fla.	T(NO)-'91	16/14
91	Porcher, Robert	DE	6-3	283	7/30/69	4	South Carolina State	Wando, S.C.	D1-'92	15/15
	Royals, Mark	P	6-5	215	6/22/65	6	Appalachian State	Mathews, Va.	UFA(Pitt)-'95	16/0*
20	Sanders, Barry	RB	5-8	203	7/16/68	7	Oklahoma State	Wichita, Kan.	D1-'89	16/16
38	# Scott, Kevin	CB	5-9	175	5/19/69	5	Stanford	Phoenix, Ariz.	D4-'91	0*
97	† Scroggins, Tracy	LB	6-2	255	9/11/69	4	Tulsa	Checotah, Okla.	D2a-'92	16/9
62	Semple, Tony	G	6-4	286	12/20/70	2	Memphis State	Lincoln, Ill.	D5-'94	0*
54	Spielman, Chris	LB	6-0	247	10/11/65	8	Ohio State	Massillon, Ohio	D2b-'88	16/16
98	Thomas, Henry	DE-DT	6-2	277	1/12/65	9	Louisiana State	Houston, Tex.	UFA(Minn)-'95	16/16*
13	Torretta, Gino	QB	6-2	215	8/10/70	3	Miami	Pinole Valley, Calif.	FA-'94	0*
29	Vanhorse, Sean	CB-S	5-10	180	7/22/68	6	Howard	Baltimore, Md.	FA-'95	16/1*
95	Wells, Mike	DE	6-3	287	1/6/71	2	Iowa	Arnold, Mo.	W(Minn)-'94	4/0
67	Widell, Doug	G	6-4	280	9/23/66	7	Boston College	Hartford, Conn.	UFA(GB)-'94	16/16

* Alexander played 15 games with Atlanta in '94; Burton inactive for 16 games; Hollas played 2 games with Cincinnati; K. Johnson played 6 games with Chicago, 7 games with Green Bay; Long active for 7 games but did not play; Majkowski played 9 games with Indianapolis; Moss played 11 games with Indianapolis; Royals played 16 games with Pittsburgh; Scott and Semple missed '94 season because of injury; Thomas played 16 games with Minnesota; Torretta inactive for 7 games; Vanhorse played 16 games with San Diego.

\# Unrestricted free agent; subject to developments.

† Restricted free agent; subject to developments.

Traded—RB Derrick Moore to San Francisco.

t- Lions traded for Alexander (Atlanta).

Players lost through free agency (7): G Shawn Bouwens (Jax; 16 games in '94), WR-KR Mel Gray (Hou; 16), QB Dave Krieg (Ariz; 14), DE Kelvin Pritchett (Jax; 16), NT Marc Spindler (TB; 9), T Larry Tharpe (Ariz; 0), LB Broderick Thomas (Minn; 16).

Players lost through Expansion Draft (3): S Harry Colon (Jax; 16 games in '94), C Mark Rodenhauser (Car; 16), WR Larry Ryans (Car; 0).

Also played with Lions in '94—RB Derrick Moore (16 games), LB Pat Swilling (16).

COACHING STAFF

Head Coach,
Wayne Fontes

Pro Career: Became the Lions' seventeenth head coach on December, 22, 1988, after serving five weeks as interim head coach (2-3 record). Has led the Lions to two Central Division championships and three playoff appearances in the last four seasons. In 1994, the Lions earned a Wild Card spot, but failed to advance beyond the first round of the playoffs. The Lions captured the NFC Central title with a 10-6 record in 1993, but were eliminated in the first round of the playoffs. Detroit finished 5-11 in 1992. In 1991, Fontes led the Lions to a 12-4 record and the team's first NFC Central Division title since 1983. The Lions notched their first playoff victory since 1957 and reached the NFC Championship Game in 1991. The Lions were 6-10 in 1990. In 1989, Fontes's first full season, the Lions finished 7-9, including five consecutive season-ending wins. He began the 1988 season as Detroit's defensive coordinator and secondary coach, following a nine-year stint with the Tampa Bay Buccaneers. A former defensive back with the New York Jets, Fontes advanced from secondary coach to defensive coordinator to assistant head coach of the Buccaneers during his years with Tampa Bay. As a player with the Jets, his brief pro career was cut short by a broken leg after two seasons (1963-64). However, his 83-yard interception return against Houston (12-15-63) did stand as the Jets' team record until it was broken in 1989 by Erik McMillan's 93-yard return. Career record: 52-53.

Background: A former two-sport star (football and baseball) at Michigan State, Fontes earned all-Big Ten honors at defensive back for the Spartans. He earned his bachelor's degree in education and biological science and later earned his master's degree in administration, all from Michigan State. Fontes became defensive backfield coach at Dayton in 1968. He also served in the same capacity at Iowa (1969-71) and Southern California (1972-75).

Personal: Born February 17, 1939, New Bedford, Mass. Fontes and his wife, Evelyn, live in Rochester Hills, Mich., and have three children—Mike, Scott, and Kim.

ASSISTANT COACHES

Paul Boudreau, offensive line; born December 30, 1949, Somerville, Mass., lives in Rochester Hills, Mich. Guard Boston College 1971-73. No pro playing experience. College coach: Boston College 1974-76, Maine 1977-78, Dartmouth 1979-81, Navy 1983. Pro coach: Edmonton Eskimos (CFL) 1983-86, New Orleans Saints 1987-93, joined Lions in 1994.

Don Clemons, linebackers; born February 15, 1954, Newark, N.J., lives in Rochester, Mich. Defensive end Muehlenberg College 1973-76. No pro playing experience. College coach: Kutztown State 1977-78, New Mexico 1979, Arizona State 1980-84. Pro coach: Joined Lions in 1985.

John Fontes, defensive backs; born June 24, 1949, New Bedford, Mass., lives in Rochester Hills, Mich. Defensive back Iowa 1969-70. No pro playing experience. College coach: Iowa 1971-72, Oregon State 1976-80, Northwestern 1985, Miami 1986, Louisiana State 1987-89. Pro coach: Tampa Bay Storm (Arena League) 1991, Sacramento Surge (World League) 1992, joined Lions in 1992.

Mo Forte, running backs; born March 1, 1947, Hannibal, Mo., lives in Rochester Hills, Mich. Running back Minnesota 1965-68. No pro playing experience. College coach: Minnesota 1970-75, Duke 1976-77, Michigan State 1978-79, Arizona State 1980-81, North Carolina A&T 1982-87 (head coach). Pro coach: Denver Broncos 1988-94, joined Lions in 1995.

Bert Hill, strength and conditioning-defensive assistant; born January 25, 1958, Montgomery, Ala., lives in Rochester Hills, Mich. Linebacker Marion (Ala.) Military Institute 1976-77, Wichita State 1978. No pro playing experience. College coach: Nicholls State 1981-82, Auburn 1983, Texas A&M 1984-88, Ohio State 1989. Pro coach: Joined Lions in 1989.

Steve Kazor, tight ends-offensive assistant; born February 24, 1948, New Kensington, Pa., lives in Oxford, Mich. Nose tackle Westminster College 1967-70. No pro playing experience. College coach: Emporia State 1973 (head coach), Texas Arlington 1974, Colorado State 1975, Wyoming 1976, Texas 1977-78, Texas-El Paso 1979-80, Iowa Wesleyan 1993 (head coach). Pro coach: Chicago Bears 1982-92, joined Lions in 1994.

Greg Landry, quarterbacks; born December 18, 1946, Nashua, N.H., lives in Rochester Hills, Mich. Quarterback Massachusetts 1965-67. Pro quarterback Detroit Lions 1968-78, Baltimore Colts 1979-81, Chicago Blitz/Arizona Wranglers (USFL) 1983-84, Chicago Bears 1984. College coach: Illinois 1993-94. Pro coach: Cleveland Browns 1985, Chicago Bears 1986-92, joined Lions in 1995.

Dave Levy, assistant head coach; born October 25, 1932, Carrollton, Mo., lives in Southfield, Mich. Guard UCLA 1952-53. No pro playing experience. College coach: UCLA 1954, Long Beach City College 1955, Southern California 1960-75. Pro coach: San Diego Chargers 1980-88, joined Lions in 1989.

Tom Moore, offensive coordinator; born November 7, 1938, Owatanna, Minn., lives in Rochester Hills, Mich. Quarterback Iowa 1957-60. No pro playing experience. College coach: Iowa 1961-62, Dayton 1965-68, Wake Forest 1969, Georgia Tech 1970-71, Minnesota 1972-73, 1975-76. Pro coach: New York Stars (WFL) 1974, Pittsburgh Steelers 1977-89, Minnesota Vikings 1990-93, joined Lions in 1994.

Frank Novak, special teams; born May 18, 1938, Worcester, Mass., lives in Rochester Hills, Mich. Quarterback Northern Michigan 1959-61. No pro playing experience. College coach: Northern Michigan 1966-72, East Carolina 1973, Virginia 1974-75, Western Illinois 1976-77, Holy Cross 1978-83, Massachusetts 1986, Missouri 1988. Pro coach: Oklahoma Outlaws (USFL) 1984, Birmingham Stallions (USFL) 1985, Houston Oilers 1989-94, joined Lions in 1995.

Herb Paterra, defensive coordinator; born November 8, 1940, Glassport, Pa., lives in Rochester Hills, Mich. Offensive guard-linebacker Michigan State 1960-62. Pro linebacker Buffalo Bills 1963-64, Hamilton Tiger-Cats (CFL) 1965-68. College coach: Michigan State 1969-71, Wyoming 1972-74. Pro coach: Charlotte Hornets (WFL) 1975, Hamilton Tiger-Cats (CFL) 1978-79, Los Angeles Rams 1980-82, Edmonton Eskimos (CFL) 1983, Green Bay Packers 1984-85, Buffalo Bills 1986, Tampa Bay Buccaneers 1987-88, joined Lions in 1989.

Charlie Sanders, receivers; born August 25, 1946, Greensboro, N.C., lives in Rochester, Mich. Tight end Minnesota 1966-67. Pro tight end Detroit Lions 1968-77. Pro coach: Joined Lions in 1989.

John Teerlinck, assistant head coach-defense; born April 9, 1951, Rochester, N.Y., lives in Rochester Hills, Mich. Defensive lineman Western Illinois 1970-73. Pro defensive tackle San Diego Chargers 1974-76. College coach: Iowa Lakes (Iowa) J.C. 1977, Eastern Illinois 1978-79, Illinois 1980-82. Pro coach: Chicago Blitz (USFL) 1983, Arizona Wranglers/Outlaws (USFL) 1984-85, Cleveland Browns 1989-90, Los Angeles Rams 1991, Minnesota Vikings 1992-94, joined Lions in 1995.

Howard Tippett, outside linebackers; born September 23, 1938, Tallassee, Ala., lives in Rochester Hills, Mich. Quarterback-safety East Tennessee State 1956-58. No pro playing experience. College coach: Tulane 1963-65, West Virginia 1966, 1970-71, Houston 1967-69, Wake Forest 1972, Mississippi State 1973, 1979, Washington State 1976, Oregon 1977-78, UCLA 1980, Illinois 1987. Pro coach: Jacksonville Express (WFL) 1974-75, Tampa Bay Buccaneers 1981-86, Green Bay Packers 1988-91, Los Angeles Rams 1992-93, joined Lions in 1994.

1995 FIRST-YEAR ROSTER

Name	Pos.	Ht.	Wt.	Birthdate	College	Hometown	How Acq.
Bevill, Bryce	CB	5-9	185	7/27/72	Syracuse	Hyattsville, Md.	FA
Bowers, Brad	DE	6-6	264	5/30/72	California	San Jose, Calif.	FA
Boyd, Stephen	LB	6-0	247	8/22/72	Boston College	Valley Stream, N.Y.	D5a
Boyd, Tommy	WR	6-0	195	12/21/71	Toledo	Lansing, Mich.	FA
Cherry, Ronald	T	6-4	300	4/15/72	McNeese State	New Orleans, La.	D5c
Coleman, Mill	WR	5-9	175	6/19/72	Michigan State	Farmington, Mich.	FA
Dixson, Kevin	WR	5-8	166	3/14/72	Illinois State	Pontiac, Mich.	FA
Elliss, Luther	DE	6-5	291	3/22/73	Utah	Mancos, Colo.	D1
Hatfield, Mark	T	6-6	305	8/21/70	Bishop's, Canada	Gloucester, Canada	FA
Heinrich, Josh	DE	6-7	260	5/13/72	Northeastern	Yarmouth, Mass.	FA
Hempstead, Hessley	G	6-1	295	1/29/72	Kansas	Upland, Calif.	D7
Hickman, Kevin	TE	6-4	258	8/20/71	Navy	Delran, N.J.	D6a
Jones, Jeff	T	6-6	310	5/30/72	Northeastern	Killeen, Tex.	FA
Major, Darryl	LB	6-1	240	12/24/72	Missouri	St. Louis, Mo.	FA
McCorvey, Kez	WR	6-0	180	1/23/72	Florida State	Pascagoula, Miss.	D5b
Nonhoff, Randy	G	6-5	305	10/12/70	California	Moreno Valley, Calif.	FA
Pooler, Kyle	K	5-11	202	5/29/72	Missouri	Phoenix, Ariz.	FA
Rice, Ron	S	6-1	206	11/9/72	Eastern Michigan	Detroit, Mich.	FA
Rivers, Ron (1)	RB	5-8	205	11/13/71	Fresno State	Highland, Calif.	FA
Schlesinger, Cory	RB	6-0	230	6/23/72	Nebraska	Duncan, Neb.	D6b
Sloan, David	TE	6-6	254	6/8/72	New Mexico	Tollhouse, Calif.	D3
Smith, Willie	LB	6-1	225	2/13/73	Penn State	Ft. Pierce, Fla.	FA
Williams, Earnest	RB	5-11	185	7/29/72	Ft. Hayes State	Aurora, Colo.	FA
Wilson, James (1)	DE	6-3	253	1/10/70	Tennessee	Hampton, Va.	FA
Woodley, Richard (1)	WR	5-9	180	1/13/72	Texas Christian	Texas City, Tex.	FA

The term NFL Rookie is defined as a player who is in his first season of professional football and has not been on the roster of another professional football team for any regular-season or postseason games. A Rookie is designated by an "R" on NFL rosters. Players who have been active in another professional football league or players who have NFL experience, including either preseason training camp or being on an Active List or Inactive List, or on Reserve/Injured or Reserve/Physically Unable to Perform for fewer than six regular-season games, are termed NFL First-Year Players. An NFL First-Year Player is designated by a "1" on NFL rosters. Thereafter, a player is credited with an additional year of experience for each season in which he accumulates six games on the Active List or Inactive List, or on Reserve/Injured or Reserve/Physically Unable to Perform.

NOTES

GREEN BAY PACKERS

National Football Conference
Central Division
Team Colors: Dark Green, Gold, and White
1265 Lombardi Avenue
Green Bay, Wisconsin 54304
Telephone: (414) 496-5700

CLUB OFFICIALS

President, CEO: Robert E. Harlan
Vice President: John Fabry
Secretary: Peter M. Platten III
Treasurer: John R. Underwood
Vice President-Administration/CFO: Michael R. Reinfeldt
Exec. V.P. and General Manager: Ron Wolf
Exec. Assistant to the President: Phil Pionek
General Legal Counsel: Lance Lopes
Exec. Director of Public Relations: Lee Remmel
Director of Marketing: Jeff Cieply
Assistant Director of Public Relations: Jeff Blumb
Assistant Director of Public Relations/Travel Coordinator: Mark Schiefelbein
Director of Pro Personnel: Ted Thompson
Director of College Scouting: John Math
Ticket Director: Mark Wagner
Accountants: Duke Copp, Vicki Vannieuwenhoven
Dir. of Computer Operations: Wayne Wichlacz
Video Director: Al Treml
Trainer: Pepper Burruss
Equipment Manager: Gordon Batty
Corporate Security Officer: Jerry Parins
Stadium Supervisor: Ted Eisenreich
Stadium: Lambeau Field • **Capacity:** 60,790
1265 Lombardi Avenue
Green Bay, Wisconsin 54304
Playing Surface: Grass
Training Camp: St. Norbert College
West De Pere, Wisconsin 54115

1995 SCHEDULE

PRESEASON

Aug. 5	vs. New Orleans at Madison, Wis.	12:00
Aug. 13	at Pittsburgh	1:00
Aug. 19	Indianapolis	12:00
Aug. 25	**Washington**	6:00

REGULAR SEASON

Sept. 3	**St. Louis**	12:00
Sept. 11	at Chicago (Monday)	8:00
Sept. 17	**New York Giants**	12:00
Sept. 24	at Jacksonville	8:00
Oct. 1	Open Date	
Oct. 8	at Dallas	12:00
Oct. 15	**Detroit**	12:00
Oct. 22	**Minnesota**	12:00
Oct. 29	at Detroit	1:00
Nov. 5	at Minnesota	12:00
Nov. 12	**Chicago**	12:00
Nov. 19	at Cleveland	1:00
Nov. 26	**Tampa Bay**	12:00
Dec. 3	**Cincinnati**	12:00
Dec. 10	at Tampa Bay	8:00
Dec. 16	at New Orleans (Saturday)	3:00
Dec. 24	**Pittsburgh**	12:00

RECORD HOLDERS

INDIVIDUAL RECORDS—CAREER

Category	Name	Performance
Rushing (Yds.)	Jim Taylor, 1958-1966	8,207
Passing (Yds.)	Bart Starr, 1956-1971	23,718
Passing (TDs)	Bart Starr, 1956-1971	152
Receiving (No.)	Sterling Sharpe, 1988-1994	595
Receiving (Yds.)	James Lofton, 1978-1986	9,656
Interceptions	Bobby Dillon, 1952-59	52
Punting (Avg.)	Dick Deschaine, 1955-57	42.6
Punt Return (Avg.)	Billy Grimes, 1950-52	13.2
Kickoff Return (Avg.)	Travis Williams, 1967-1970	26.7
Field Goals	Chris Jacke, 1989-1994	135
Touchdowns (Tot.)	Don Hutson, 1935-1945	105
Points	Don Hutson, 1935-1945	823

INDIVIDUAL RECORDS—SINGLE SEASON

Category	Name	Performance
Rushing (Yds.)	Jim Taylor, 1962	1,474
Passing (Yds.)	Lynn Dickey, 1983	4,458
Passing (TDs)	Brett Favre, 1994	33
Receiving (No.)	Sterling Sharpe, 1993	112
Receiving (Yds.)	Sterling Sharpe, 1992	1,461
Interceptions	Irv Comp, 1943	10
Punting (Avg.)	Jerry Norton, 1963	44.7
Punt Return (Avg.)	Billy Grimes, 1950	19.1
Kickoff Return (Avg.)	Travis Williams, 1967	*41.1
Field Goals	Chester Marcol, 1972	33
Touchdowns (Tot.)	Jim Taylor, 1962	19
Points	Paul Hornung, 1960	*176

INDIVIDUAL RECORDS—SINGLE GAME

Category	Name	Performance
Rushing (Yds.)	Jim Taylor, 12-3-61	186
Passing (Yds.)	Lynn Dickey, 10-12-80	418
Passing (TDs)	Many times.	5
	Last time by Lynn Dickey, 9-4-83	
Receiving (No.)	Don Hutson, 11-22-42	14
Receiving (Yds.)	Bill Howton, 10-21-56	257
Interceptions	Bobby Dillon, 11-26-53	*4
	Willie Buchanon, 9-24-78	*4
Field Goals	Chris Jacke, 11-11-90	5
Touchdowns (Tot.)	Paul Hornung, 12-12-65	5
Points	Paul Hornung, 10-8-61	33

*NFL Record

COACHING HISTORY

(518-436-36)

1921-49	Earl (Curly) Lambeau	212-106-21
1950-53	Gene Ronzani*	14-31-1
1953	Hugh Devore- Ray (Scooter) McLean**	0-2-0
1954-57	Lisle Blackbourn	17-31-0
1958	Ray (Scooter) McLean	1-10-1
1959-67	Vince Lombardi	98-30-4
1968-70	Phil Bengtson	20-21-1
1971-74	Dan Devine	25-28-4
1975-83	Bart Starr	53-77-3
1984-87	Forrest Gregg	25-37-1
1988-91	Lindy Infante	24-40-0
1992-94	Mike Holmgren	29-23-0

*Resigned after 10 games in 1953
**Co-coaches

LAMBEAU FIELD

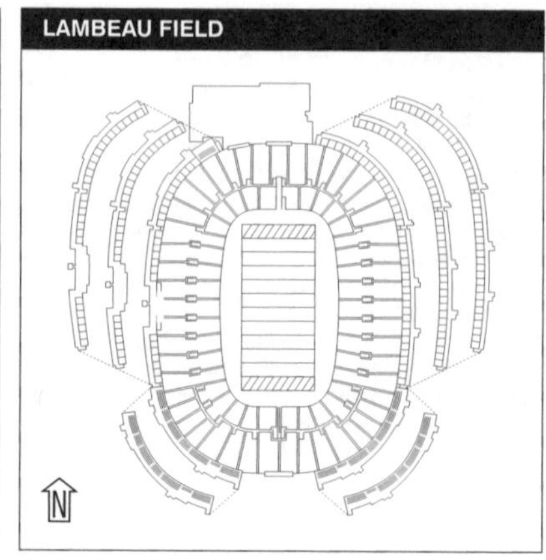

1994 TEAM RECORD

PRESEASON (3-1)

Date	Result		Opponents
8/6	W	14-6	vs. L.A. Rams at Madison
8/13	L	24-31	vs. Miami at Milwaukee
8/19	W	13-10	at New Orleans
8/26	W	24-20	New England

REGULAR SEASON (9-7)

Date	Result		Opponents	Att.
9/4	W	16-10	Minnesota	59,487
9/11	L	14-24	Miami	55,011
9/18	L	7-13	at Philadelphia	63,922
9/25	W	30- 3	Tampa Bay	58,551
10/2	L	16-17	at New England	57,522
10/9	W	24-17	L.A. Rams	58,911
10/20	L	10-13	at Minnesota (OT)	63,041
10/31	W	33- 6	at Chicago	47,381
11/6	W	38-30	Detroit	54,995
11/13	W	17-10	N.Y. Jets	58,307
11/20	L	20-29	at Buffalo	79,029
11/24	L	31-42	at Dallas	64,597
12/4	L	31-34	at Detroit	76,338
12/11	W	40- 3	Chicago	57,927
12/18	W	21-17	Atlanta	54,885
12/24	W	34-19	at Tampa Bay	65,076

POSTSEASON (1-1)

Date	Result		Opponents	Att.
12/31	W	16-12	Detroit	58,125
1/8	L	9-35	at Dallas	64,745

(OT) Overtime

SCORE BY PERIODS

	1	2	3	4	OT		Total
Packers	89	129	92	72	0	—	382
Opponents	40	96	65	83	3	—	287

ATTENDANCE

Home 458,074 Away 516,906 Total 974,980
Single-game home record, 59,487 (9-4-94)
Single-season home record, 458,074 (1994)

1994 TEAM STATISTICS

	Packers	Opp.
Total First Downs	314	281
Rushing	88	82
Passing	205	182
Penalty	21	17
Third Down: Made/Att	97/225	79/222
Third Down Pct.	43.1	35.6
Fourth Down: Made/Att	6/14	9/18
Fourth Down Pct.	42.9	50.0
Total Net Yards	5316	4764
Avg. Per Game	332.3	297.8
Total Plays	1059	1023
Avg. Per Play	5.0	4.7
Net Yards Rushing	1543	1363
Avg. Per Game	96.4	85.2
Total Rushes	417	381
Net Yards Passing	3773	3401
Avg. Per Game	235.8	212.6
Sacked/Yards Lost	33/204	37/276
Gross Yards	3977	3677
Att./Completions	609/375	605/337
Completion Pct.	61.6	55.7
Had Intercepted	14	21
Punts/Avg.	81/41.4	88/39.7
Net Punting Avg.	81/35.5	88/33.8
Penalties/Yards Lost	85/760	82/675
Fumbles/Ball Lost	25/8	32/12
Touchdowns	47	32
Rushing	11	9
Passing	33	20
Returns	3	3
Avg. Time of Possession	30:56	29:04

1994 INDIVIDUAL STATISTICS

PASSING	Att.	Comp.	Yds.	Pct.	TD	Int.	Tkld.	Rate
Favre	582	363	3882	62.4	33	14	31/188	90.7
Brunell	27	12	95	44.4	0	0	2/16	53.8
Packers	609	375	3977	61.6	33	14	33/204	89.1
Opponents	605	337	3677	55.7	20	21	37/276	70.4

SCORING	TD R	TD P	TD Rt	PAT	FG	Saf	PTS
Sharpe	0	18	0	0/0	0/0	0	108
Jacke	0	0	0	41/43	19/26	0	98
Bennett	5	4	0	0/0	0/0	0	54
Brooks	0	4	2	0/0	0/0	0	36
Cobb	3	1	0	0/0	0/0	0	24
Morgan	0	4	0	0/0	0/0	0	24
West	0	2	0	0/0	0/0	0	14
Favre	2	0	0	0/0	0/0	0	12
Brunell	1	0	0	0/0	0/0	0	6
Paup	0	0	1	0/0	0/0	0	6
Packers	11	33	3	41/43	19/26	0	382
Opponents	9	20	3	24/24	21/25	1	287

2-Point conversion: West. Team: 1-4

RUSHING	Att.	Yds.	Avg.	LG	TD
Bennett	178	623	3.5	39t	5
Cobb	153	579	3.8	30	3
Favre	42	202	4.8	36t	2
L. Johnson	26	99	3.8	43	0
Sharpe	3	15	5.0	8	0
Levens	5	15	3.0	5	0
Brunell	6	7	1.2	5t	1
Jordan	1	5	5.0	5	0
Brooks	1	0	0.0	0	0
Thompson	2	-2	-1.0	2	0
Packers	417	1543	3.7	43	11
Opponents	381	1363	3.6	63	9

RECEIVING	No.	Yds.	Avg.	LG	TD
Sharpe	94	1119	11.9	49	18
Bennett	78	546	7.0	40	4
Brooks	58	648	11.2	35	4
Cobb	35	299	8.5	37t	1
West	31	377	12.2	26	2
Morgan	28	397	14.2	47t	4
Chmura	14	165	11.8	27	0
L. Johnson	13	168	12.9	33	0
Lewis	7	108	15.4	38	0
R. Johnson	7	79	11.3	24	0
Wilner	5	31	6.2	9	0
Mickens	4	31	7.8	11	0
Levens	1	9	9.0	9	0
Packers	375	3977	10.6	49	33
Opponents	337	3677	10.9	68	20

INTERCEPTIONS	No.	Yds.	Avg.	LG	TD
Buckley	5	38	7.6	26	0
Butler	3	68	22.7	51	0
Paup	3	47	15.7	30	1
Teague	3	33	11.0	16	0
Willis	2	20	10.0	17	0
McGill	2	16	8.0	16	0
Strickland	1	7	7.0	7	0
K. Johnson	1	3	3.0	3	0
Evans	1	0	0.0	0	0
Packers	21	232	11.0	51	1
Opponents	14	193	13.8	36	0

PUNTING	No.	Yds.	Avg.	In 20	LG
Hentrich	81	3351	41.4	24	70
Packers	81	3351	41.4	24	70
Opponents	88	3491	39.7	21	60

PUNT RETURNS	No.	FC	Yds.	Avg.	LG	TD
Brooks	40	13	352	8.8	85t	1
Prior	8	4	62	7.8	16	0
Jordan	1	1	0	0.0	0	0
Packers	49	18	414	8.4	85t	1
Opponents	36	10	272	7.6	25	0

KICKOFF RETURNS	No.	Yds.	Avg.	LG	TD
Harris	29	618	21.3	59	0
Brooks	9	260	28.9	96t	1
Jordan	5	115	23.0	33	0
Thompson	4	67	16.8	19	0
Jurkovic	4	57	14.3	16	0
Levens	2	31	15.5	16	0
M. Wilson	2	14	7.0	14	0
Davey	1	6	6.0	6	0
Packers	56	1168	20.9	96t	1
Opponents	75	1380	18.4	91t	1

SACKS	No.
Jones	10.5
White	8.0
Paup	7.5
Gi. Brown	3.0
McMichael	2.5
Davey	1.5
Butler	1.0
Evans	1.0
Koonce	1.0
Wilkins	1.0
Packers	37.0
Opponents	33.0

1995 DRAFT CHOICES

Round	Name	Pos.	College
1	Craig Newsome	DB	Arizona State
3	Darius Holland	DT	Colorado
	William Henderson	RB	North Carolina
	Brian Williams	LB	Southern California
	Antonio Freeman	WR	Virginia Tech
4	Jeff Miller	T	Mississippi
5	Jay Barker	QB	Alabama
	Travis Jervey	RB	Citadel
6	Charlie Simmons	WR	Georgia Tech
7	Adam Timmerman	G	South Dakota State

GREEN BAY PACKERS

1995 VETERAN ROSTER

No.	Name	Pos.	Ht.	Wt.	Birthdate	NFL Exp.	College	Hometown	How Acq.	'94 Games/ Starts
51	Alipate, Tuineau	LB	6-2	245	8/21/67	2	Washington State	Union City, Calif.	FA-'95	8/0*
48	Bartrum, Mike	TE	6-5	243	6/23/70	2	Marshall	Pomeroy, Ohio	FA-'95	0*
34	Bennett, Edgar	RB	6-0	224	2/15/69	4	Florida State	Jacksonville, Fla.	D4-'92	16/15
61	Bollinger, Brian	G	6-5	290	11/21/68	4	North Carolina	Melbourne, Fla.	FA-'95	7/0*
87	† Brooks, Robert	WR	6-0	175	6/23/70	4	South Carolina	Greenwood, S.C.	D3-'92	16/16
71	Brown, Gary	T	6-4	290	6/25/71	2	Georgia Tech	Brentwood, N.Y.	W(Pitt)-'94	1/0
93	Brown, Gilbert	DT	6-2	330	2/22/71	3	Kansas	Detroit, Mich.	W(Minn)-'93	13/1
36	Butler, LeRoy	S	6-0	197	7/19/68	6	Florida State	Jacksonville, Fla.	D2-'90	13/13
28	Chaffey, Pat	RB	6-2	225	4/9/67	4	Oregon State	Aurora, Ore.	FA-'95	0*
89	Chmura, Mark	TE	6-5	245	2/22/69	4	Boston College	South Deerfield, Mass.	D6-'92	14/4
95	t- Collons, Ferric	DT	6-6	300	12/4/69	2	California	Sacramento, Calif.	T(Atl)-'95	0*
77	Crafts, Jerry	T	6-6	350	1/6/68	4	Louisville	Tulsa, Okla.	FA-'95	16/7*
45	Crawford, Keith	CB	6-2	188	11/21/70	2	Howard Payne	Palestine, Tex.	FA-'94	0*
11	Detmer, Ty	QB	6-0	186	10/30/67	4	Brigham Young	San Antonio, Tex.	D9a-'92	0*
29	Dixon, Rickey	CB-S	5-11	184	12/15/65	7	Oklahoma	Dallas, Tex.	FA-'95	0*
72	Dotson, Earl	T	6-4	310	12/17/70	3	Texas A&I	Beaumont, Tex.	D3-'93	4/0
33	Evans, Doug	CB	6-1	188	5/13/70	3	Louisiana Tech	Haynesville, La.	D6a-'93	16/15
4	Favre, Brett	QB	6-2	222	10/10/69	5	Southern Mississippi	Kiln, Miss.	T(Atl)-'92	16/16
76	Galbreath, Harry	G	6-1	285	1/1/65	8	Tennessee	Clarksville, Tenn.	UFA(Mia)-'93	16/16
58	Hamilton, Ruffin	LB	6-1	230	3/2/71	2	Tulane	Zachary, La.	FA-'94	5/0
17	Hentrich, Craig	P	6-3	200	5/18/71	2	Notre Dame	Alton, Ill.	FA-'93	16/0
70	Hope, Charles	G	6-3	303	3/12/70	2	Central State, Ohio	New Castle, Del.	FA-'94	6/0
67	Hutchins, Paul	T	6-5	335	2/11/70	3	Western Michigan	Chicago, Ill.	FA-'93	16/2
82	t- Ingram, Mark	WR	5-11	194	8/23/65	9	Michigan State	Flint, Mich.	T(Mia)-'95	15/13*
13	Jacke, Chris	K	6-0	200	3/12/66	7	Texas-El Paso	Richardson, Tex.	D6-'89	16/0
88	t- Jackson, Keith	TE	6-2	258	4/9/65	8	Oklahoma	Little Rock, Ark.	T(Mia)-'95	16/16*
42	Johnson, LeShon	RB	5-11	200	1/15/71	2	Northern Illinois	Haskell, Okla.	D3-'94	12/0
96	Jones, Sean	DE	6-7	275	12/19/62	12	Northeastern	Montclair, N.J.	UFA(Hou)-'94	16/16
80	Jordan, Charles	WR	5-10	175	10/9/69	3	Long Beach City College	Inglewood, Calif.	T(Raid)-'94	10/0
64	Jurkovic, John	NT	6-2	290	8/18/67	4	Eastern Illinois	Calumet City, Ill.	FA-'91	16/15
53	† Koonce, George	LB	6-1	240	10/15/68	4	East Carolina	Vanceboro, N.C.	FA-'92	16/16
97	LaBounty, Matt	DE	6-4	268	1/3/69	3	Oregon	San Marin, Calif.	W(SF)-'93	0*
16	Lamb, Brad	WR	5-10	175	10/7/67	4	Anderson, Ind.	Springboro, Ohio	FA-'95	0*
25	Levens, Dorsey	RB	6-1	235	5/21/70	2	Georgia Tech	Syracuse, N.Y.	D5b-'94	14/0
22	McGill, Lenny	CB	6-2	194	5/31/71	2	Arizona State	Escondido, Calif.	FA-'94	6/0
60	McGuire, Gene	C	6-4	300	7/17/70	3	Notre Dame	Lynn Haven, Fla.	FA-'95	0*
62	# McIntyre, Guy	G	6-3	275	2/17/61	12	Georgia	Thomasville, Ga.	FA-'94	10/10
85	Mickens, Terry	WR	6-1	200	2/21/71	2	Florida A&M	Tallahassee, Fla.	D5a-'94	12/0
81	Morgan, Anthony	WR	6-1	195	11/15/67	5	Tennessee	Cleveland, Ohio	W(Chi)-'93	16/0
39	Prior, Mike	S	6-0	215	11/14/63	10	Illinois State	Chicago Heights, Ill.	UFA(Ind)-'93	16/0
12	Rubley, T.J.	QB	6-3	205	11/29/68	4	Tulsa	Davenport, Iowa	FA-'95	0*
75	Ruettgers, Ken	T	6-6	290	8/20/62	11	Southern California	Bakersfield, Calif.	D1-'85	16/16
59	Simmons, Wayne	LB	6-3	245	12/15/69	3	Clemson	Hilton Head, S.C.	D1a-'93	12/1
44	Stegall, Milt	WR	6-0	185	1/25/70	4	Miami, Ohio	Cincinnati, Ohio	FA-'95	1/0*
55	Strickland, Fred	LB	6-2	250	8/15/66	8	Purdue	Wanaque, N.J.	FA-'94	16/14
73	Taylor, Aaron	G-T	6-4	300	11/14/72	2	Notre Dame	Concord, Calif.	D1-'94	0*
31	Teague, George	S	6-1	190	2/18/71	3	Alabama	Montgomery, Ala.	D1b-'93	16/16
49	Thomason, Jeff	TE	6-5	245	12/30/69	3	Oregon	Newport Beach, Calif.	FA-'95	0*
23	Walker, Sammy	CB	5-11	200	1/20/69	5	Texas Tech	McKinney, Tex.	FA-'93	0*
92	White, Reggie	DE	6-5	295	12/19/61	11	Tennessee	Chattanooga, Tenn.	UFA(Phil)-'93	16/15
24	White, Russell	RB	5-11	220	12/15/70	2	California	Encino, Calif.	FA-'95	0*
98	Wilkins, Gabe	DT-DE	6-5	300	9/1/71	2	Gardner-Webb	Spartanburg, S.C.	D4-'94	15/0
57	Williams, Jerrol	LB	6-4	245	7/5/67	7	Purdue	Las Vegas, Nev.	FA-'95	6/0*
56	Willis, James	LB	6-2	238	9/2/72	3	Auburn	Huntsville, Ala.	D5b-'93	12/0
83	Wilner, Jeff	TE	6-5	250	12/31/71	2	Wesleyan, Conn.	Exeter, N.H.	FA-'94	11/1
35	Wilson, Ray	S	6-1	204	8/26/71	2	New Mexico	Panama City, Fla.	FA-'94	3/0
52	Winters, Frank	C	6-3	290	1/23/64	9	Western Illinois	Union City, N.J.	PB(KC)-'92	16/16

* Alipate played 8 games with N.Y. Jets in '94; Bartrum last active with Kansas City in '93; Bollinger played 7 games with San Francisco; Chaffey last active with N.Y. Jets in '93; Collons last active with Raiders in '93; Crafts played 16 games with Buffalo; Crawford inactive for 4 games; Detmer active for 5 games but did not play; Dixon last active with L.A. Raiders in '93; Ingram played 15 games with Miami; Jackson played 16 games with Miami; LaBounty, Rubley, Taylor, and Walker missed '94 season because of injury; Lamb last active with Buffalo in '93; McGuire last active with Chicago in '93; Stegall played 1 game with Cincinnati; Thomason last active with Cincinnati in '93; Ru. White last active with L.A. Rams in '93; Williams played 6 games with Kansas City.

\# Unrestricted free agent; subject to developments.

† Restricted free agent; subject to developments.

Traded—QB Mark Brunell to Jacksonville, CB Terrell Buckley to Miami.

t- Packers traded for Collons (Atlanta), Ingram (Miami), Jackson (Miami).

Players lost through free agency (9): DT Matt Brock (NYJ; 5 games in '94), DE Don Davey (Jax; 16), CB Corey Harris (Sea; 16), S Tim Hauck (Den; 13), TE Reggie Johnson (Phil; 9), LB Bryce Paup (Buff; 16), G Joe Sims (Phil; 15), RB Darrell Thompson (Chi; 8), TE Ed West (Ind; 14).

Players lost through Expansion Draft (3): Reggie Cobb (Jax; 16 games in '94), LB Mark Williams (Jax; 16), RB Marcus Wilson (Jax; 12).

Also played with Packers in '94—QB Mark Brunell (2 games), CB Terrell Buckley (16), CB Forey Duckett (3), C Jamie Dukes (6), CB Keshon Johnson (7), WR Ron Lewis (6), DT Steve McMichael (16), CB Roland Mitchell (1), WR Sterling Sharpe (16).

COACHING STAFF

Head Coach,
Mike Holmgren

Pro Career: Became Packers' eleventh head coach on January 11, 1992. He led team to three consecutive winning seasons (identical 9-7 records in 1992, 1993, and 1994) for the first time since 1965, 1966, and 1967 and first back-to-back playoff berths (1993-94) since 1966-67. Holmgren was offensive coordinator for the San Francisco 49ers under George Seifert (1989-91) after spending three previous seasons (1986-88) as quarterbacks coach under Bill Walsh. During his six-year tenure with San Francisco, the 49ers won five consecutive NFC Western Division championships (1986-1990) and back-to-back Super Bowls (XXIII and XXIV). In that span, San Francisco compiled the NFL's best overall record (71-23-1, a .753 percentage). The 49ers never ranked lower than third overall in his three years as offensive coordinator. Career record: 29-23.

Background: Quarterback at Southern California (1966-69) and was drafted by the St. Louis Cardinals in the eighth round of the 1970 NFL draft. He served as an assistant coach at San Francisco State (1981) and Brigham Young (1982-85) before his tenure with the 49ers. Earned his bachelor of science degree in business finance at Southern California (1970).

Personal: Born June 15, 1948, in San Francisco. He and his wife, Kathy, live in Green Bay and have four daughters—Calla, Jenny, Emily, and Gretchen.

ASSISTANT COACHES

Larry Brooks, defensive line; born June 10, 1950, Prince George, Va., lives in Green Bay. Defensive lineman Virginia State 1968-71. Pro defensive tackle Los Angeles Rams 1972-82. College coach: Virginia State 1992-93. Pro coach: Los Angeles Rams 1983-90, joined Packers in 1994.

Nolan Cromwell, special teams; born January 30, 1955, Smith Center, Kan., lives in Green Bay. Quarterback-safety Kansas 1973-76. Pro defensive back Los Angeles Rams 1977-87. Pro coach: Los Angeles Rams 1991, joined Packers in 1992.

Gil Haskell, wide receivers; born September 24, 1943, San Francisco, Calif., lives in Green Bay. Defensive back San Francisco State 1961, 1963-65. No pro playing experience. College coach: Southern California 1978-82. Pro coach: Los Angeles Rams 1983-91, joined Packers in 1992.

Johnny Holland, defensive assistant-quality control; born March 11, 1965, Hempstead, Tex., lives in Green Bay. Linebacker Texas A&M 1983-86. Pro linebacker Green Bay Packers 1987-1993. Pro coach: Joined Packers in 1995.

Kent Johnston, strength and conditioning; born February 21, 1956, Mexia, Tex., lives in Green Bay. Defensive back Stephen F. Austin 1974-77. No pro playing experience. College coach: Northwestern State (Louisiana) 1979, Northeast Louisiana 1980-81, Alabama 1983-86. Pro coach: Tampa Bay Buccaneers 1987-91, joined Packers in 1992.

Sherman Lewis, offensive coordinator; born June 29, 1942, Louisville, Ky., lives in Green Bay. Running back Michigan State 1961-63. Pro running back Toronto Argonauts (CFL) 1964-65, New York Jets 1966. College coach: Michigan State 1969-82. Pro coach: San Francisco 49ers 1983-91, joined Packers in 1992.

Jim Lind, linebackers; born November 11, 1947, Isle, Minn., lives in Green Bay. Linebacker Bethel College 1965-66; defensive back Bemidji State 1971-72. No pro playing experience. College coach: St. Cloud State 1977-78, St. John's (Minn.) 1979-80, Brigham Young 1981-82, Minnesota-Morris 1983-86 (head coach), Wisconsin-Eau Claire 1987-91 (head coach). Pro coach: Joined Packers in 1992.

Tom Lovat, offensive line; born December 28, 1938, Bingham, Utah, lives in Green Bay. Guard-linebacker Utah 1958-60. No pro playing experience. College coach: Utah 1967, 1972-76 (head coach 1974-76), Idaho State 1968-70, Stanford 1977-79, Wyoming 1989. Pro coach: Saskatchewan Roughriders (CFL) 1971, Green Bay Packers 1980, St. Louis-Phoenix Cardinals 1981-84, 1990-91, Indianapolis Colts 1985-88, rejoined Packers in 1992.

Steve Mariucci, quarterbacks; born November 4, 1955, Iron Mountain, Mich., lives in Green Bay. Quarterback Northern Michigan 1974-77. No pro playing experience. College coach: Northern Michigan 1978-79, Cal State-Fullerton 1980-82, Louisville 1983-84, Southern California 1986, California 1987-91. Pro coach: Orlando Renegades (USFL) 1985, Los Angeles Rams 1985, joined Packers in 1992.

Marty Mornhinweg, offensive assistant-quality control; born March 29, 1962, Edmond, Okla., lives in Green Bay. Quarterback Montana 1981-84. Pro quarterback Denver Dynamite (Arena Football) 1986. College coach: Montana 1985, Texas-El Paso 1986-87, Northern Arizona 1988, Southeast Missouri State 1989-90, Missouri 1991-93, Northern Arizona 1994. Pro coach: Joined Packers in 1995.

Andy Reid, tight ends assistant-offensive line; born March 19, 1958, Los Angeles, Calif., lives in Green Bay. Offensive tackle-guard Brigham Young 1978-80. No pro playing experience. College coach: Brigham Young 1982, San Francisco State 1983-85, Northern Arizona 1986, Texas-El Paso 1987, Missouri 1988-91. Pro coach: Joined Packers in 1992.

Fritz Shurmur, defensive coordinator; born July 15, 1932, Riverview, Mich., lives in Green Bay. No pro playing experience. College coach: Albion 1956-61, Wyoming 1962-74 (head coach 1971-74). Pro coach: Detroit Lions 1975-77, New England Patriots 1978-81, Los Angeles Rams 1982-90, Phoenix Cardinals 1991-93, joined Packers in 1994.

Harry Sydney, running backs; born June 26, 1959, Petersburg, Va., lives in Green Bay. Quarterback/running back Kansas 1978-81. Pro running back Denver Gold (USFL) 1983-84, Memphis Showboats (USFL) 1985, Montreal Alouettes (CFL) 1986, San Francisco 49ers 1987-91, Green Bay Packers 1992. Pro coach: Joined Packers in 1994.

Bob Valesente, defensive backs; born July 19, 1940, Seneca Falls, N.Y., lives in Green Bay. Halfback Ithaca College 1958-61. No pro playing experience. College coach: Cornell 1964-74, Cincinnati 1975-76, Arizona 1977-79, Mississippi State 1980-81, Kansas 1984-87 (head coach 1986-87), Maryland 1988, Pittsburgh 1989. Pro coach: Baltimore Colts 1982-83, Pittsburgh Steelers 1990-91, joined Packers in 1992.

1995 FIRST-YEAR ROSTER

Name	Pos.	Ht.	Wt.	Birthdate	College	Hometown	How Acq.
Barker, Jay	QB	6-3	215	7/20/72	Alabama	Trussville, Ala.	D5a
Becton, Lee	RB	5-11	194	2/11/73	Notre Dame	Vanceboro, N.C.	FA
Bergman, Jeff	S	6-0	186	2/24/73	Northern Arizona	Bakersfield, Calif.	FA
Borgognone, Dirk (1)	K	6-2	225	1/9/68	Pacific	Reno, Nev.	FA
Brock, Randy	DE	6-6	267	11/21/71	Brigham Young	Rexburg, Idaho	FA
Carter, Bernard (1)	LB	6-3	237	8/22/71	East Carolina	Tallahassee, Fla.	FA
Dorsett, Matthew	CB	5-11	188	8/23/73	Southern	New Orleans, La.	FA
Fagan, Tommy (1)	DE	6-5	265	3/26/71	Northeast Louisiana	Monticello, Fla.	FA
Freeman, Antonio	WR	6-1	185	5/27/72	Virginia Tech	Baltimore, Md.	D3d
Goheen, Justin	LB	6-2	239	8/16/73	Notre Dame	Wexford, Pa.	FA
Hampton, Andre	LB	6-0	227	6/4/71	Valdosta State	Valdosta, Ga.	FA
Harris, Bernardo (1)	LB	6-2	283	10/15/71	North Carolina	Chapel Hill, N.C.	FA
Henderson, William	RB	6-2	245	2/19/71	North Carolina	Chester, Va.	D3b
Henley, Steve	S	6-0	220	8/30/71	Mankato State	Ford Heights, Ill.	FA
Hogan, Chauncey (1)	RB	6-3	175	12/24/72	Southern	Zachary, La.	FA
Holland, Darius	DT	6-5	303	11/10/73	Colorado	Las Cruces, N.M.	D3a
Holt, Reggie (1)	S	5-11	202	2/18/71	Wisconsin	Miami, Fla.	FA
Jervey, Travis	RB	6-0	219	5/5/72	Citadel	Isle of Palms, S.C.	D5b
Kuberski, Bob (1)	DE-DT	6-5	295	4/5/71	Navy	Folsom, Pa.	D7-'93
Miller, Jeff	T	6-4	300	11/23/72	Mississippi	Vero Beach, Fla.	D4
Nedney, Joe	K	6-5	205	3/22/73	San Jose State	San Jose, Calif.	FA
Newsome, Craig	CB	6-0	185	8/10/71	Arizona State	Rialto, Calif.	D1
Satterfield, Brian (1)	RB	6-0	215	12/22/69	North Alabama	Blue Ridge, Ga.	FA
Sauders, Mike (1)	RB	6-0	212	10/3/69	Iowa	Milton, Wis.	FA
Schroeder, Bill (1)	WR	6-2	195	1/9/71	Wisconsin-LaCrosse	Sheboygan, Wis.	FA
Simmons, Charlie	WR	6-3	215	8/25/72	Georgia Tech	Macon, Ga.	D6
Timmerman, Adam	G	6-4	289	8/14/71	South Dakota State	Cherokee, Iowa	D7
Wagner, Keith (1)	T	6-4	300	1/22/70	Abilene Christian	Corpus Christi, Tex.	FA
Williams, Brian	LB	6-2	238	12/17/72	Southern California	Dallas, Tex.	D3c
Wilson, Oscar	DT	6-2	298	12/6/70	Cal State-Northridge	Santa Ana, Calif.	FA

The term NFL Rookie is defined as a player who is in his first season of professional football and has not been on the roster of another professional football team for any regular-season or postseason games. A Rookie is designated by an "R" on NFL rosters. Players who have been active in another professional football league or players who have NFL experience, including either preseason training camp or being on an Active List or Inactive List, or on Reserve/Injured or Reserve/Physically Unable to Perform for fewer than six regular-season games, are termed NFL First-Year Players. An NFL First-Year Player is designated by a "1" on NFL rosters. Thereafter, a player is credited with an additional year of experience for each season in which he accumulates six games on the Active List or Inactive List, or on Reserve/Injured or Reserve/Physically Unable to Perform.

NOTES

MINNESOTA VIKINGS

National Football Conference
Central Division
Team Colors: Purple, Gold, and White
9520 Viking Drive
Eden Prairie, Minnesota 55344
Telephone: (612) 828-6500

CLUB OFFICERS

Chairman of the Board: John C. Skoglund
Vice Chairmen: Jaye F. Dyer, Philip S. Maas
Directors: N. Bud Grossman, Roger L. Headrick, James R. Jundt, Elizabeth MacMillan, Carol S. Sperry, Wheelock Whitney

CLUB OFFICIALS

President/CEO: Roger L. Headrick
Vice President Administration/Team Operations: Jeff Diamond
Vice President Player Personnel: Frank Gilliam
Vice President of Marketing and Business Development: Stew Widdess
Assistant General Manager/National Scouting: Jerry Reichow
Assistant General Manager/Pro Personnel: Paul Wiggin
Director of Finance: Nick Valentine
Director of Research and Dev.: Mike Eayrs
Director of Marketing: Kernal Buhler
Director of Public Relations: David Pelletier
Director of Team Operations: Breck Spinner
Ticket Manager: Harry Randolph
Director of Security: Steve Rollins
Player Personnel Coordinator: Scott Studwell
Equipment Manager: Dennis Ryan
Trainer: Fred Zamberletti
Video Director: Larry Kohout
Stadium: Hubert H. Humphrey Metrodome
•**Capacity:** 64,035
500 11th Avenue South
Minneapolis, Minnesota 55415
Playing Surface: AstroTurf
Training Camp: Mankato State University
Mankato, Minnesota 56001

1995 SCHEDULE

PRESEASON

Aug. 7	at San Diego	5:00
Aug. 12	at New England	8:00
Aug. 18	**Los Angeles**	7:00
Aug. 26	**Kansas City**	12:30

REGULAR SEASON

Sept. 3	at Chicago	3:00
Sept. 10	**Detroit**	12:00
Sept. 17	**Dallas**	7:00
Sept. 24	at Pittsburgh	1:00
Oct. 1	Open Date	
Oct. 8	**Houston**	12:00
Oct. 15	at Tampa Bay	1:00
Oct. 22	at Green Bay	12:00
Oct. 30	**Chicago** (Monday)	8:00
Nov. 5	**Green Bay**	12:00
Nov. 12	at Arizona	2:00
Nov. 19	**New Orleans**	3:00
Nov. 23	at Detroit (Thursday)	12:30
Dec. 3	**Tampa Bay**	12:00
Dec. 9	**Cleveland** (Saturday)	11:30
Dec. 18	at San Francisco (Monday)	6:00
Dec. 24	at Cincinnati	1:00

RECORD HOLDERS

INDIVIDUAL RECORDS—CAREER

Category	Name	Performance
Rushing (Yds.)	Chuck Foreman, 1973-79	5,879
Passing (Yds.)	Fran Tarkenton, 1961-66, 1972-78	33,098
Passing (TDs)	Fran Tarkenton, 1961-66, 1972-78	239
Receiving (No.)	Steve Jordan, 1982-1994	498
Receiving (Yds.)	Anthony Carter, 1985-1993	7,636
Interceptions	Paul Krause, 1968-1979	53
Punting (Avg.)	Harry Newsome, 1990-93	43.8
Punt Return (Avg.)	Tommy Mason, 1961-66	10.4
Kickoff Return (Avg.)	Bob Reed, 1962-63	27.1
Field Goals	Fred Cox, 1963-1977	282
Touchdowns (Tot.)	Bill Brown, 1962-1974	76
Points	Fred Cox, 1963-1977	1,365

INDIVIDUAL RECORDS—SINGLE SEASON

Category	Name	Performance
Rushing (Yds.)	Terry Allen, 1992	1,201
Passing (Yds.)	Warren Moon, 1994	4,264
Passing (TDs)	Tommy Kramer, 1981	26
Receiving (No.)	Cris Carter, 1994	*122
Receiving (Yds.)	Cris Carter, 1994	1,256
Interceptions	Paul Krause, 1975	10
Punting (Avg.)	Bobby Walden, 1964	46.4
Punt Return (Avg.)	Leo Lewis, 1987	12.5
Kickoff Return (Avg.)	John Gilliam, 1972	26.3
Field Goals	Fuad Reveiz, 1994	34
Touchdowns (Tot.)	Chuck Foreman, 1975	22
Points	Chuck Foreman, 1975	132
	Fuad Reveiz, 1994	132

INDIVIDUAL RECORDS—SINGLE GAME

Category	Name	Performance
Rushing (Yds.)	Chuck Foreman, 10-24-76	200
Passing (Yds.)	Tommy Kramer, 11-2-86	490
Passing (TDs)	Joe Kapp, 9-28-69	*7
Receiving (No.)	Rickey Young, 12-16-79	15
Receiving (Yds.)	Sammy White, 11-7-76	210
Interceptions	Many times	3
	Last time by Jack Del Rio, 12-5-93	
Field Goals	Rich Karlis, 11-5-89	*7
Touchdowns (Tot.)	Chuck Foreman, 12-20-75	4
	Ahmad Rashad, 9-2-79	4
Points	Chuck Foreman, 12-20-75	24
	Ahmad Rashad, 9-2-79	24

*NFL Record

VIKINGS COACHING HISTORY

(285-239-9)

1961-66	Norm Van Brocklin	29-51-4
1967-83	Bud Grant	161-99-5
1984	Les Steckel	3-13-0
1985	Bud Grant	7-9-0
1986-91	Jerry Burns	55-46-0
1992-94	Dennis Green	30-21-0

METRODOME

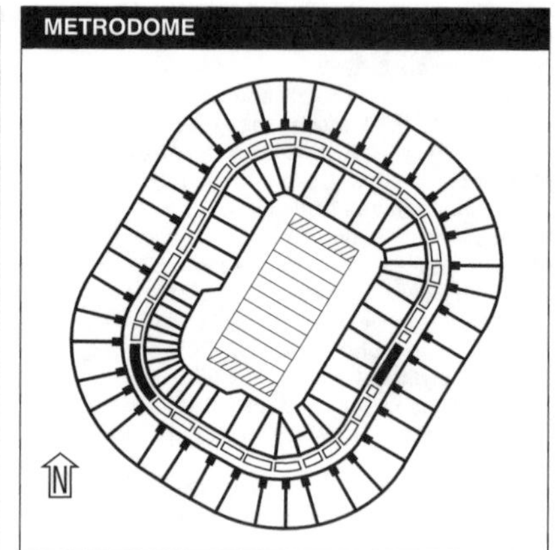

1994 TEAM RECORD

PRESEASON (3-2)

Date	Result		Opponents
7/31	L	9-17	at Dallas
8/6	W	17-9	vs. Kansas City at Tokyo
8/13	W	21-17	New Orleans
8/20	L	19-30	at Seattle
8/26	W	31-16	Miami

REGULAR SEASON (10-6)

Date	Result		Opponents	Att.
9/4	L	10-16	at Green Bay	59,487
9/11	W	10- 3	Detroit	57,349
9/18	W	42-14	at Chicago	61,073
9/25	W	38-35	Miami	64,035
10/2	L	7-17	at Arizona	67,950
10/10	W	27-10	at N.Y. Giants	77,294
10/20	W	13-10	Green Bay (OT)	63,041
10/30	W	36-13	at Tampa Bay	42,110
11/6	W	21-20	New Orleans	57,564
11/13	L	20-26	at New England (OT)	58,382
11/20	L	21-31	N.Y. Jets	60,687
11/27	L	17-20	Tampa Bay (OT)	47,259
12/1	W	33-27	Chicago (OT)	61,483
12/11	W	21-17	at Buffalo	66,501
12/17	L	19-41	at Detroit	73,881
12/26	W	21-14	San Francisco	63,326

POSTSEASON (0-1)

1/1	L	18-35	Chicago	60,347

(OT) Overtime

SCORE BY PERIODS

Vikings	74	116	75	82	9	—	356
Opponents	51	80	74	100	9	—	314

ATTENDANCE

Home 474,744 Away 506,678 Total 981,422
Single-game home record, 64,035 (9-25-94)
Single-season home record, 485,616 (1992)

1994 TEAM STATISTICS

	Vikings	Opp.
Total First Downs	325	287
Rushing	92	65
Passing	215	195
Penalty	18	27
Third Down: Made/Att	99/241	78/215
Third Down Pct.	41.1	36.3
Fourth Down: Made/Att	7/16	7/15
Fourth Down Pct.	43.8	46.7
Total Net Yards	5848	4742
Avg. Per Game	365.5	296.4
Total Plays	1123	988
Avg. Per Play	5.2	4.8
Net Yards Rushing	1524	1090
Avg. Per Game	95.3	68.1
Total Rushes	419	355
Net Yards Passing	4324	3652
Avg. Per Game	270.3	228.3
Sacked/Yards Lost	31/246	36/250
Gross Yards	4570	3902
Att./Completions	673/409	597/368
Completion Pct.	60.8	61.6
Had Intercepted	20	18
Punts/Avg.	77/42.9	86/40.5
Net Punting Avg.	77/36.2	86/36.1
Penalties/Yards Lost	112/880	83/614
Fumbles/Ball Lost	32/14	25/16
Touchdowns	36	37
Rushing	11	9
Passing	18	25
Returns	7	3
Avg. Time of Possession	32:06	27:54

1994 INDIVIDUAL STATISTICS

PASSING	Att.	Comp.	Yds.	Pct.	TD	Int.	Tkld.	Rate
Moon	601	371	4264	61.7	18	19	29/235	79.9
Johnson	37	22	150	59.5	0	0	1/5	68.5
Salisbury	34	16	156	47.1	0	1	1/6	48.2
Saxon	1	0	0	0.0	0	0	0/0	39.6
Vikings	673	409	4570	60.8	18	20	31/246	77.6
Opponents	597	368	3902	61.6	25	18	36/250	82.1

SCORING	TD R	TD P	TD Rt	PAT	FG	Saf	PTS
Reveiz	0	0	0	30/30	34/39	0	132
Allen	8	0	0	0/0	0/0	0	50
Carter	0	7	0	0/0	0/0	0	46
Ismail	0	5	0	0/0	0/0	0	30
Reed	0	4	0	0/0	0/0	0	24
Parker	0	0	3	0/0	0/0	0	18
Washington	0	0	3	0/0	0/0	0	18
Graham	2	0	0	0/0	0/0	0	12
Lee	0	2	0	0/0	0/0	0	12
J. Harris	0	0	1	0/0	0/0	0	6
R. Smith	1	0	0	0/0	0/0	0	6
A. Jordan	0	0	0	0/0	0/0	0	2
Vikings	11	18	7	30/30	34/39	0	356
Opponents	9	25	3	31/31	19/30	0	314

2-Point conversions: Carter (2), Allen, A. Jordan. Team: 4-5.

RUSHING	Att.	Yds.	Avg.	LG	TD
Allen	255	1031	4.0	45	8
Graham	64	207	3.2	11	2
R. Smith	31	106	3.4	14t	1
Lee	29	104	3.6	16	0
Moon	27	55	2.0	12	0
Evans	6	20	3.3	8	0
Salisbury	3	2	0.7	5	0
Palmer	1	1	1.0	1	0
Saxon	1	0	0.0	0	0
Johnson	2	-2	-1.0	-1	0
Vikings	419	1524	3.6	45	11
Opponents	355	1090	3.1	64t	9

RECEIVING	No.	Yds.	Avg.	LG	TD
Carter	122	1256	10.3	65t	7
Reed	85	1175	13.8	59	4
Ismail	45	696	15.5	65t	5
Lee	45	368	8.2	35	2
A. Jordan	35	336	9.6	25	0
Cooper	32	363	11.3	34	0
Allen	17	148	8.7	31	0
R. Smith	15	105	7.0	15	0
Palmer	6	90	15.0	39	0
S. Jordan	3	23	7.7	10	0
Novoselsky	2	7	3.5	4	0
Evans	1	2	2.0	2	0
Graham	1	1	1.0	1	0
Vikings	409	4570	11.2	65t	18
Opponents	368	3902	10.6	62t	25

INTERCEPTIONS	No.	Yds.	Avg.	LG	TD
Parker	4	99	24.8	44t	2
Glenn	4	55	13.8	32	0
Washington	3	135	45.0	81t	2
Del Rio	3	5	1.7	5	0
Boyd	1	22	22.0	15	0
J. Harris	1	21	21.0	21	0
McGriggs	1	1	1.0	1	0
E. McDaniel	1	0	0.0	0	0
Vikings	18	338	18.8	81t	4
Opponents	20	292	14.6	90t	1

PUNTING	No.	Yds.	Avg.	In 20	LG
Saxon	77	3301	42.9	28	67
Vikings	77	3301	42.9	28	67
Opponents	86	3485	40.5	25	57

PUNT RETURNS	No.	FC	Yds.	Avg.	LG	TD
Palmer	30	9	193	6.4	20	0
Guliford	5	6	14	2.8	12	0
Parker	4	1	31	7.8	25	0
Vikings	39	16	238	6.1	25	0
Opponents	44	10	410	9.3	61t	1

KICKOFF RETURNS	No.	Yds.	Avg.	LG	TD
Ismail	35	807	23.1	61	0
R. Smith	16	419	26.2	45	0
Lee	3	42	14.0	26	0
Novoselsky	2	10	5.0	10	0
A. Jordan	1	8	8.0	8	0
Walsh	1	6	6.0	6	0
Evans	1	4	4.0	4	0
Garnett	1	0	0.0	0	0
Vikings	60	1296	21.6	61	0
Opponents	83	1843	22.2	98t	1

SACKS	No.
Randle	13.5
Thomas	7.0
Barker	3.5
J. Harris	3.0
Del Rio	2.0
R. Harris	2.0
E. McDaniel	1.5
Glenn	1.0
Jenkins	1.0
Sheppard	0.5
Vikings	36.0
Opponents	31.0

1995 DRAFT CHOICES

Round	Name	Pos.	College
1	Derrick Alexander	DE	Florida State
	Korey Stringer	T	Ohio State
2	Orlanda Thomas	DB	Southwestern Louisiana
	Corey Fuller	DB	Florida State
4	Chad May	QB	Kansas State
5	James Stewart	RB	Miami
6	John Solomon	LB	Sam Houston State
7	Jose White	LB	Howard
	Jason Fisk	DT	Stanford

MINNESOTA VIKINGS

1995 VETERAN ROSTER

No.		Name	Pos.	Ht.	Wt.	Birthdate	NFL Exp.	College	Hometown	How Acq.	'94 Games/ Starts
63		Alex, Keith	G	6-4	307	6/9/69	2	Texas A&M	Beaumont, Tex.	FA-'94	0*
92		Barker, Roy	DE	6-4	285	2/14/69	4	North Carolina	New York, N.Y.	D4-'92	16/15
42		Barnett, Harlon	S	5-11	200	1/2/67	6	Michigan State	Cincinnati, Ohio	UFA(NE)-'95	16/16*
96		Boudreaux, Frank	DT	6-5	263	6/20/70	2	Northwestern	Honolulu, Hawaii	FA-'94	0*
36		Boyd, Malik	CB	5-10	176	11/5/70	2	Southern	Houston, Tex.	FA-'94	16/1
57		Brady, Jeff	LB	6-1	238	11/9/68	5	Kentucky	Melbourne, Ky.	UFA(TB)-'95	16/0*
52		Brown, Richard	LB	6-3	240	9/21/65	7	San Diego State	Westminster, Calif.	FA-'94	3/0
80		Carter, Cris	WR	6-3	202	11/25/65	9	Ohio State	Middletown, Ohio	W(Phil)-'90	16/16
62		Christy, Jeff	C	6-3	290	2/3/69	3	Pittsburgh	Freeport, Pa.	FA-'93	16/16
87		Cooper, Adrian	TE	6-5	268	4/27/68	5	Oklahoma	Denver, Colo.	T(Pitt)-'94	12/11
67		Cunningham, Rick	T	6-6	307	1/4/67	5	Texas A&M	Los Angeles, Calif.	UFA(Ariz)-'95	11/10*
75		Dafney, Bernard	T	6-5	329	11/1/68	4	Tennessee	Los Angeles, Calif.	FA-'92	16/16
34	#	Davis, Brian	CB	6-2	187	8/31/63	9	Nebraska	Phoenix, Ariz.	FA-'94	9/0
55		Del Rio, Jack	LB	6-4	246	4/4/63	11	Southern California	Hayward, Calif.	PB(Dall)-'92	16/16
71		Dixon, David	G	6-5	354	1/5/69	2	Arizona State	Auckland, New Zealand	FA-'94	1/0
29		Evans, Charles	RB	6-1	232	4/16/67	3	Clark	Augusta, Ga.	FA-'93	14/0
38		Frank, Donald	CB	6-0	192	10/24/65	6	Winston-Salem State	Tarboro, N.C.	UFA(Raid)-'95	16/0*
46		Gerak, John	G	6-3	284	1/6/70	3	Penn State	Struthers, Ohio	D3a-'93	13/3
31		Graham, Scottie	RB	5-9	217	3/28/69	3	Ohio State	Long Island, N.Y.	FA-'93	16/0
24		Griffith, Robert	CB-S	5-11	189	11/30/70	2	San Diego State	San Diego, Calif.	FA-'94	15/0
99		Harris, James	DE	6-6	255	5/13/68	3	Temple	East St. Louis, Ill.	FA-'93	16/16
91		Harrison, Martin	DE	6-5	240	9/20/67	5	Washington	Bellevue, Wash.	FA-'94	13/0
78		Hinton, Chris	T	6-4	300	7/31/61	13	Northwestern	Chicago, Ill.	UFA(Atl)-'94	16/16
82		Ismail, Qadry	WR	6-0	191	11/8/70	3	Syracuse	Wilkes-Barre, Pa.	D2-'93	16/3
25		Jackson, Alfred	CB-S	6-0	185	7/10/67	5	San Diego State	Tulare, Calif.	FA-'95	0*
14		Johnson, Brad	QB	6-5	220	9/13/68	4	Florida State	Black Mountain, N.C.	D9a-'92	4/0
53		Jones, Donald	LB	6-0	232	3/26/69	3	Washington	Lynchburg, Va.	FA-'94	0*
89		Jordan, Andrew	TE	6-4	262	6/21/72	2	Western Carolina	Charlotte, N.C.	D6-'94	16/12
83	#	Jordan, Steve	TE	6-3	240	1/10/61	13	Brown	Phoenix, Ariz.	FA-'94	4/1
32		Lee, Amp	RB	5-11	198	10/1/71	4	Florida State	Chipley, Fla.	FA-'94	13/0
61		Lindsay, Everett	G	6-4	301	9/18/70	3	Mississippi	Raleigh, N.C.	D5-'93	0*
58		McDaniel, Ed	LB	5-11	231	2/23/69	4	Clemson	Battesburg, S.C.	D5-'92	16/16
64		McDaniel, Randall	G	6-3	274	12/19/64	8	Arizona State	Avondale, Ariz.	D1-'88	16/16
37	#	McGriggs, Lamar	S	6-3	218	5/9/68	5	Western Illinois	Harvey, Ill.	FA-'93	16/1
33		Mincy, Charles	S	5-11	197	12/16/69	5	Washington	Los Angeles, Calif.	UFA(KC)-'95	16/7*
1		Moon, Warren	QB	6-3	219	11/18/56	12	Washington	Los Angeles, Calif.	T(Hou)-'94	15/15
68		Morris, Mike	C	6-5	277	2/22/61	9	Northeast Missouri State	Centerville, Iowa	FA-'91	16/0
74		Nelson, Royce	G-T	6-4	315	8/9/70	2	Nicholls State	New Orleans, La.	FA-'95	0*
85	#	Novoselsky, Brent	TE	6-2	237	1/8/66	8	Pennsylvania	Niles, Ill.	FA-'89	12/0
22		Palmer, David	RB	5-8	167	11/19/72	2	Alabama	Birmingham, Ala.	D2a-'94	13/1
93		Randle, John	DT	6-1	272	12/12/67	6	Texas A&I	Hearne, Tex.	FA-'90	16/16
86		Reed, Jake	WR	6-3	217	9/28/67	5	Grambling State	Covington, Ga.	D3b-'91	16/16
7		Reveiz, Fuad	K	5-11	227	2/24/63	11	Tennessee	Miami, Fla.	FA-'90	16/0
65	#	Ruether, Mike	G-C	6-4	286	9/20/62	10	Texas	Shawnee Mission, Kan.	FA-'94	0*
12	#	Salisbury, Sean	QB	6-5	217	3/9/63	8	Southern California	Escondido, Calif.	FA-'94	1/1
4		Saxon, Mike	P	6-3	205	7/10/62	11	San Diego State	Whittier, Calif.	FA-'94	16/0
59		Sheppard, Ashley	LB	6-3	240	1/21/69	3	Clemson	North Pitt, N.C.	D4-'93	7/0
94		Sims, Tom	DT	6-2	308	4/18/67	6	Pittsburgh	Detroit, Mich.	UFA(Ind)-'95	16/1*
95		Smith, Fernando	DE	6-6	276	8/2/71	2	Jackson State	Flint, Mich.	D2b-'94	7/0
26		Smith, Robert	RB	6-0	197	3/4/72	3	Ohio State	Euclid, Ohio	D1-'93	14/0
73		Steussie, Todd	T-G	6-6	304	12/1/70	2	California	Canoga Park, Calif.	D1b-'94	16/16
51		Thomas, Broderick	LB	6-4	242	2/20/67	7	Nebraska	Houston, Tex.	UFA(Det)-'95	16/16*
98		Tuaolo, Esera	DT	6-2	263	7/11/68	5	Oregon State	Chino, Calif.	FA-'92	16/0
81		Walsh, Chris	WR	6-1	193	12/12/68	3	Stanford	Concord, Calif.	FA-'94	10/0
20		Washington, Dewayne	CB	5-11	189	12/27/72	2	North Carolina State	Durham, N.C.	D1a-'94	16/16

* Alex last active with Atlanta in '93; Barnett played 16 games with New England in '94; Boudreaux, Jones, and Lindsay missed '94 season because of injury; Brady played 16 games with Tampa Bay; Cunningham played 11 games with Arizona; Frank played 16 games with L.A. Raiders; Jackson last active with Cleveland in '92; Mincy played 16 games with Kansas City; Nelson last on injured reserve with New Orleans in '93; Ruether active for 7 games but did not play; Sims played 16 games with Indianapolis; Thomas played 16 games with Detroit.

\# Unrestricted free agent; subject to developments.

† Restricted free agent; subject to developments.

Traded—S Vencie Glenn to N.Y. Giants.

Players lost through free agency (7): LB Bobby Abrams (NE; 16 games in '94), DE Robert Harris (NYG; 11), LB Carlos Jenkins (Rams; 16), T Reggie McElroy (Den; 10), CB Anthony Parker (Rams; 15), S Todd Scott (NYJ; 15), DT Henry Thomas (Det; 16).

Players lost through Expansion Draft (3): LB Dave Garnett (Car; 9 games in '94), WR Eric Guliford (Car; 7), LB William Sims (Car; 8).

Also played with Vikings in '94—RB Terry Allen (16 games), G Frank Cornish (7), S Vencie Glenn (16), DE Roosevelt Nix (2).

COACHING STAFF

Head Coach

Dennis Green

Pro Career: Named the fifth head coach in Vikings history on January 10, 1992, Green is one of only seven people in the history of the league to lead his team to the playoffs in each of his first three seasons as an NFL head coach. Last season, he led the Vikings to a 10-6 record and their second NFC Central title in three seasons. In 1994, NFL Commissioner Paul Tagliabue appointed Green to the league's Competition Committee. His best coaching job may have come in 1993, when the Vikings qualified as a wild-card entrant with a 9-7 mark and won their final three regular-season games for the first time since 1974. In '92, Green led the Vikings to their best record (11-5) and first division title under a first-year head coach. He earned NFL coach of the year honors from the Washington Touchdown Club and NFC coach of the year honors from *United Press International* and *College & Pro Football Newsweekly*. As receivers coach at San Francisco from 1986-89, Green developed Pro Bowl players Jerry Rice and John Taylor. Green's first pro coaching opportunity came as special teams coach for the 49ers in 1979. Green briefly played defensive back with British Columbia (CFL) in 1971. Career record: 30-21.

Background: A running back at Iowa from 1968-70, Green began his coaching career as a graduate assistant for Iowa in 1972. He coached running backs and receivers at Dayton in 1973 then running backs and receivers at Iowa from 1974-76. Green worked with running backs at Stanford in 1977-78. He returned to Stanford as offensive coordinator in 1980 then was head coach at Northwestern from 1981-85. Green was named Big Ten coach of the year in 1982. As head coach at Stanford from 1989-91, he led the school to the 1991 Aloha Bowl, its first bowl game since 1986.

Personal: Born February 17, 1949 in Harrisburg, Pa., Green earned his degree in recreation from Iowa. He lives in Wayzata, Minn., and has two children, Patti and Jeremy.

ASSISTANT COACHES

Mark Asanovich, assistant strength and conditioning; born May 20, 1959, Duluth, Minn., lives in Coon Rapids, Minn. No college or pro playing experience. College coach: Ohio State 1984-85, Citadel 1986. Pro coach: Joined Vikings in 1995.

Brian Billick, offensive coordinator; born February 28, 1954, Redlands, Calif., lives in Eden Prairie, Minn. Tight end Brigham Young 1974-76. Pro tight end Dallas Cowboys 1977. College coach: Brigham Young 1978, Redlands 1979, San Diego State 1981-85, Utah State 1986-88, Stanford 1989-91. Pro coach: Joined Vikings in 1992.

Tony Dungy, defensive coordinator; born October 6, 1955, Jackson, Mich., lives in Eden Prairie, Minn. Quarterback Minnesota 1973-76. Pro safety Pittsburgh Steelers 1977-78, San Francisco 49ers 1979. College coach: Minnesota 1980. Pro coach: Pittsburgh Steelers 1981-88, Kansas City Chiefs 1989-91, joined Vikings in 1992.

Foge Fazio, inside linebackers; born February 28, 1939, Dawmont, W.Va., lives in Eden Prairie, Minn. Linebacker-center Pittsburgh 1957-60. No pro playing experience. College coach: Boston University 1967, Harvard 1968, Pittsburgh 1969-72, 1977-81, 1982-85 (head coach), Cincinnati 1973-76, Notre Dame 1986-87. Pro coach: Atlanta Falcons 1988-89, New York Jets 1990-94, joined Vikings in 1995.

Chris Foerster, tight ends, offensive line assistant; born October 12, 1961, Milwaukee, Wis., lives in Maple Grove, Minn. Center Colorado State 1979-82. No pro playing experience. College coach: Colorado State 1983-87, Stanford 1988-91, Minnesota 1992. Pro coach: Joined Vikings in 1993.

Carl Hargrave, running backs; born November 8, 1954, Frankfurt, Germany, lives in Eden Prairie, Minn. Defensive back Upper Iowa 1972-75. No pro playing experience. College coach: Upper Iowa 1977-80, Northwestern 1981-85, Pittsburgh 1986, Houston 1987-91, Iowa 1992-93. Pro coach: Joined Vikings in 1994.

John Levra, defensive line; born October 2, 1937, Arma, Kan., lives in Eden Prairie, Minn. Guard-linebacker Pittsburg (Kan.) State 1963-65. No pro playing experience. College coach: New Mexico Highlands 1966-70, Stephen F. Austin 1971-74, Kansas 1975-78, North Texas State 1979. Pro coach: British Columbia Lions (CFL) 1980, New Orleans Saints 1981-85, Chicago Bears 1986-92, Denver Broncos 1993-94, joined Vikings in 1995.

Chip Myers, wide receivers; born July 9, 1945, Panama City, Fla., lives in Eden Prairie, Minn. Receiver Northwestern Oklahoma 1964-66. Pro receiver San Francisco 49ers 1967, Cincinnati Bengals 1969-76. College coach: Illinois 1980-82. Pro coach: Tampa Bay Buccaneers 1983-84, Indianapolis Colts 1985-88, New York Jets 1990-93, New Orleans Saints 1994, joined Vikings in 1995.

Keith Rowen, offensive line; born September 2, 1952, New York, N.Y., lives in Eden Prairie, Minn. Offensive tackle Stanford 1972-74. No pro playing experience. College coach: Stanford 1975-76, Long Beach State 1977-78, Arizona 1979-82. Pro coach: Boston/New Orleans Breakers (USFL) 1983-84, Cleveland Browns 1984, Indianapolis Colts 1985-88, New England Patriots 1989, Atlanta Falcons 1990-93, joined Vikings in 1994.

Ray Sherman, quarterbacks; born November 27, 1951, Berkeley, Calif., lives in Eden Prairie, Minn. Wide receiver Laney (Calif.) J.C. 1969-70, Fresno State 1971-72. Pro defensive back Green Bay Packers 1973. College coach: San Jose State 1974, California 1975, 1981, Michigan State 1976-77, Wake Forest 1978-80, Purdue 1982-85, Georgia 1986-87. Pro coach: Houston Oilers 1988-89, San Francisco 49ers 1991-93, New York Jets 1994, joined Vikings in 1995.

Richard Solomon, defensive backs; born December 8, 1949, New Orleans, La., lives in Eden Prairie, Minn. Running back-defensive back Iowa 1970-73. No pro playing experience. College coach: Dubuque 1973-75, Southern Illinois 1976, Iowa 1977-78, Syracuse 1979, Illinois 1980-86. Pro coach: New York Giants 1987-91 (scout), joined Vikings in 1992.

Trent Walters, outside linebackers; born November 20, 1943, Knoxville, Tenn., lives in Eden Prairie, Minn. Defensive back Indiana 1963-65. Pro defensive back Edmonton Eskimos (CFL) 1966-67. College coach: Indiana 1968-71, Louisville 1972, Indiana 1973-80, Washington 1981-83, Pittsburgh 1985, Louisville 1986-90, Texas A&M 1991-93. Pro coach: Cincinnati Bengals 1984, joined Vikings in 1994.

Steve Wetzel, strength and conditioning; born May 11, 1963, Washington D.C., lives in Eden Prairie, Minn. No college or pro playing experience. College coach: Maryland 1985-89, George Mason 1990. Pro coach: Washington Redskins 1990-91, joined Vikings in 1992.

Gary Zauner, special teams; born November 2, 1950, Milwaukee, Wis., lives in Eden Prairie, Minn. Kicker Wisconsin-LaCrosse 1968-72. No pro playing experience. College coach: Brigham Young 1979-80, San Diego State 1981-86, New Mexico 1987-88, Long Beach State 1990-91. Pro coach: Joined Vikings in 1994.

1995 FIRST-YEAR ROSTER

Name	Pos.	Ht.	Wt.	Birthdate	College	Hometown	How Acq.
Alexander, Derrick	DE	6-4	276	11/3/73	Florida State	Jacksonville, Fla.	D1a
Bercich, Pete (1)	LB	6-1	236	12/23/71	Notre Dame	Joliet, Ill.	D7-'94
Buffaloe, Jeff (1)	P	6-1	194	9/18/70	Memphis State	Memphis, Tenn.	FA
Burmeister, Paul	QB	6-3	215	3/10/71	Iowa	Iowa City, Iowa	FA
Fisk, Jason	DT	6-3	286	9/4/72	Stanford	Davis, Calif.	D7b
Fuller, Corey	CB	5-10	197	5/11/71	Florida State	Rickards, Fla.	D2b
Hammonds, Shelly (1)	CB	5-10	182	2/13/71	Penn State	Barnwell, S.C.	D5-'94
Johnson, Chris (1)	S	6-0	205	8/7/71	San Diego State	San Diego, Calif.	FA
Kirchoff, Jay (1)	K	6-4	198	5/28/70	Arizona	Plymouth, Minn.	FA
May, Chad	QB	6-1	219	9/28/71	Kansas State	LaVerne, Calif.	D4
Solomon, John	LB	6-3	233	11/10/73	Sam Houston State	Houston, Tex.	D6
Stewart, James	RB	6-2	245	12/8/71	Miami	Vero Beach, Fla.	D5
Stringer, Korey	T	6-4	332	5/8/74	Ohio State	Warren, Ohio	D1b
Thomas, Orlanda	S	6-1	209	10/21/72	S.W. Louisiana	Crowley, La.	D2a
White, Jose	LB	6-3	261	2/2/73	Howard	Washington, D.C.	D7a

The term NFL Rookie is defined as a player who is in his first season of professional football and has not been on the roster of another professional football team for any regular-season or postseason games. A Rookie is designated by an "R" on NFL rosters. Players who have been active in another professional football league or players who have NFL experience, including either preseason training camp or being on an Active List or Inactive List, or on Reserve/Injured or Reserve/Physically Unable to Perform for fewer than six regular-season games, are termed NFL First-Year Players. An NFL First-Year Player is designated by a "1" on NFL rosters. Thereafter, a player is credited with an additional year of experience for each season in which he accumulates six games on the Active List or Inactive List, or on Reserve/Injured or Reserve/Physically Unable to Perform.

NOTES

NEW ORLEANS SAINTS

National Football Conference
Western Division
Team Colors: Old Gold, Black, and White
6928 Saints Drive
Metairie, Louisiana 70003
Telephone: (504) 733-0255

CLUB OFFICIALS

Owner: Tom Benson
Executive Vice President: Jim Miller
Vice President/Football Operations: Bill Kuharich
Vice President/Head Coach: Jim Mora
Vice President/Marketing: Greg Suit
Director of Pro Personnel: Chet Franklin
Director of College Scouting: Bruce Lemmerman
Treasurer: Bruce Broussard
Administrative Coordinator: Austin Dejan
Comptroller: Charleen Sharpe
Director of Corporate Sales: Bill Ferrante
Director of Media Relations: Rusty Kasmiersky
Assistant Director of Media Relations: Neal Gulkis
Data Processing Manager: Jay Romig
Director of Travel/Entertainment/Special Projects: Barra Birrcher
Director of Community Relations: Chanel Lagarde
Player Personnel Scouts: Bill Baker, Hamp Cook, Hokie Gajan, Tom Marino, Carmen Piccone
Director of Ticket Sales: Sandy King
Trainer: Dean Kleinschmidt
Equipment Manager: Dan Simmons
Video Director: Albert Aucoin
Stadium: Louisiana Superdome
•**Capacity:** 69,056
1500 Poydras Street
New Orleans, Louisiana 70112
Playing Surface: AstroTurf
Training Camp: University of Wisconsin-La Crosse
La Crosse, Wisconsin 54601

1995 SCHEDULE

PRESEASON

Aug. 5	vs. Green Bay at Madison, Wis.	12:00
Aug. 11	at New York Giants	8:00
Aug. 20	**Seattle**	12:00
Aug. 25	**Detroit**	7:00

REGULAR SEASON

Sept. 3	**San Francisco**	12:00
Sept. 10	at St. Louis	12:00
Sept. 17	**Atlanta**	12:00
Sept. 24	at New York Giants	1:00
Oct. 1	**Philadelphia**	12:00
Oct. 8	Open Date	
Oct. 15	**Miami**	3:00
Oct. 22	at Carolina	1:00
Oct. 29	at San Francisco	1:00
Nov. 5	**St. Louis**	12:00
Nov. 12	**Indianapolis**	12:00
Nov. 19	at Minnesota	3:00
Nov. 26	**Carolina**	7:00
Dec. 3	at New England	1:00
Dec. 10	at Atlanta	1:00
Dec. 16	**Green Bay** (Saturday)	3:00
Dec. 24	at New York Jets	1:00

RECORD HOLDERS

INDIVIDUAL RECORDS—CAREER

Category	Name	Performance
Rushing (Yds.)	George Rogers, 1981-84	4,267
Passing (Yds.)	Archie Manning, 1971-1982	21,734
Passing (TDs)	Archie Manning, 1971-1982	115
Receiving (No.)	Eric Martin, 1985-1993	532
Receiving (Yds.)	Eric Martin, 1985-1993	7,854
Interceptions	Dave Waymer, 1980-89	37
Punting (Avg.)	Tommy Barnhardt, 1987, 1989-1994	43.0
Punt Return (Avg.)	Mel Gray, 1986-88	13.4
Kickoff Return (Avg.)	Walter Roberts, 1967	26.3
Field Goals	Morten Andersen, 1982-1994	302
Touchdowns (Tot.)	Dalton Hilliard, 1986-1993	53
Points	Morten Andersen, 1982-1994	1,318

INDIVIDUAL RECORDS—SINGLE SEASON

Category	Name	Performance
Rushing (Yds.)	George Rogers, 1981	1,674
Passing (Yds.)	Jim Everett, 1994	3,855
Passing (TDs)	Archie Manning, 1980	23
Receiving (No.)	Eric Martin, 1988	85
Receiving (Yds.)	Eric Martin, 1989	1,090
Interceptions	Dave Whitsell, 1967	10
Punting (Avg.)	Tommy Barnhardt, 1992	44.0
Punt Return (Avg.)	Mel Gray, 1987	14.7
Kickoff Return (Avg.)	Don Shy, 1969	27.9
Field Goals	Morten Andersen, 1985	31
Touchdowns (Tot.)	Dalton Hilliard, 1989	18
Points	Morten Andersen, 1987	121

INDIVIDUAL RECORDS—SINGLE GAME

Category	Name	Performance
Rushing (Yds.)	George Rogers, 9-4-83	206
Passing (Yds.)	Archie Manning, 12-7-80	377
Passing (TDs)	Billy Kilmer, 11-2-69	6
Receiving (No.)	Tony Galbreath, 9-10-78	14
Receiving (Yds.)	Wes Chandler, 9-2-79	205
Interceptions	Tommy Myers, 9-3-78	3
	Dave Waymer, 10-6-85	3
	Reggie Sutton, 10-18-87	3
	Gene Atkins, 12-22-91	3
Field Goals	Morten Andersen, 12-1-85	5
	Morten Andersen, 11-15-87	5
	Morten Andersen, 12-3-92	5
	Morten Andersen, 12-11-94	5
Touchdowns (Tot.)	Many times	3
	Last time by Mario Bates, 12-4-94	
Points	Many times	18

COACHING HISTORY

(167-250-5)

1967-70	Tom Fears*	13-34-2
1970-72	J.D. Roberts	7-25-3
1973-75	John North**	11-23-0
1975	Ernie Hefferle	1-7-0
1976-77	Hank Stram	7-21-0
1978-80	Dick Nolan***	15-29-0
1980	Dick Stanfel	1-3-0
1981-85	O.A. (Bum) Phillips****	27-42-0
1985	Wade Phillips	1-3-0
1986-94	Jim Mora	84-63-0

*Released after seven games in 1970
**Released after six games in 1975
***Released after 12 games in 1980
****Resigned after 12 games in 1985

LOUISIANA SUPERDOME

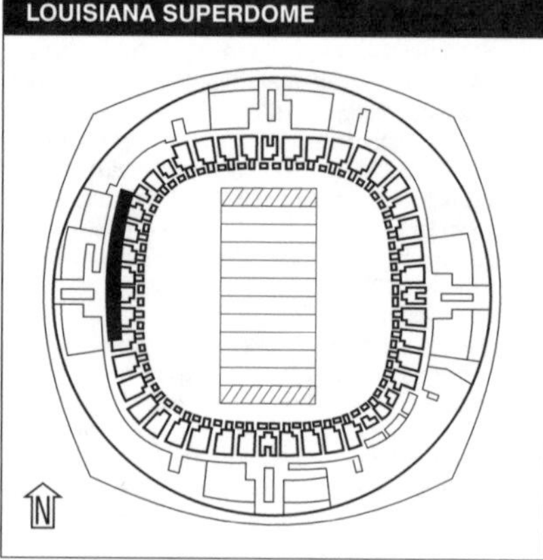

1994 TEAM RECORD

PRESEASON (1-3)

Date	Result		Opponents
8/5	L	6-24	at New England
8/13	L	17-21	at Minnesota
8/19	L	10-13	Green Bay
8/25	W	28-10	Dallas

REGULAR SEASON (7-9)

Date	Result		Opponents	Att.
9/4	L	17-30	Kansas City	69,362
9/11	L	24-38	Washington	58,049
9/18	W	9- 7	at Tampa Bay	45,522
9/25	L	13-24	at San Francisco	63,971
10/2	W	27-22	N.Y. Giants	55,076
10/9	L	7-17	at Chicago	63,822
10/16	L	22-36	San Diego	50,565
10/23	W	37-34	L.A. Rams	47,908
11/6	L	20-21	at Minnesota	57,564
11/13	W	33-32	Atlanta	60,313
11/20	L	19-24	at L.A. Raiders	41,722
11/28	L	14-35	San Francisco	61,304
12/4	W	31-15	at L.A. Rams	34,960
12/11	W	29-20	at Atlanta	61,307
12/19	L	16-24	Dallas	67,323
12/24	W	30-28	at Denver	64,445

(OT) Overtime

SCORE BY PERIODS

Saints	42	132	77	97	0	— 348
Opponents	82	120	83	122	0	— 407

ATTENDANCE

Home 469,900 Away 433,313 Total 903,213
Single-game home record, 70,940 (11-4-79)
Single-season home record, 548,655 (1991)

1994 TEAM STATISTICS

	Saints	Opp.
Total First Downs	308	337
Rushing	78	106
Passing	203	208
Penalty	27	23
Third Down: Made/Att	71/199	91/210
Third Down Pct.	35.7	43.3
Fourth Down: Made/Att	8/16	11/19
Fourth Down Pct.	50.0	57.9
Total Net Yards	5182	5569
Avg. Per Game	323.9	348.1
Total Plays	966	1053
Avg. Per Play	5.4	5.3
Net Yards Rushing	1336	1758
Avg. Per Game	83.5	109.9
Total Rushes	373	458
Net Yards Passing	3846	3811
Avg. Per Game	240.4	238.2
Sacked/Yards Lost	24/181	36/196
Gross Yards	4027	4007
Att./Completions	569/366	559/353
Completion Pct.	64.3	63.1
Had Intercepted	18	17
Punts/Avg.	67/43.6	60/42.6
Net Punting Avg.	67/33.5	60/37.4
Penalties/Yards Lost	88/678	105/922
Fumbles/Ball Lost	22/14	28/14
Touchdowns	38	45
Rushing	11	10
Passing	22	28
Returns	5	7
Avg. Time of Possession	29:04	30:56

1994 INDIVIDUAL STATISTICS

PASSING	Att.	Comp.	Yds.	Pct.	TD	Int.	Tkld.	Rate
Everett	540	346	3855	64.1	22	18	21/164	84.9
W. Wilson	28	20	172	71.4	0	0	3/17	87.2
Barnhardt	1	0	0	0.0	0	0	0/0	39.6
Saints	569	366	4027	64.3	22	18	24/181	84.9
Opponents	559	353	4007	63.1	28	17	36/196	88.6

SCORING	TD R	TD P	TD Rt	PAT	FG	Saf	PTS
Andersen	0	0	0	32/32	28/39	0	116
Bates	6	0	0	0/0	0/0	0	36
Small	0	5	0	0/0	0/0	0	32
Haynes	0	5	0	0/0	0/0	0	30
Walls	0	4	0	0/0	0/0	0	26
Brown	3	1	0	0/0	0/0	0	24
Early	0	4	0	0/0	0/0	0	24
Hughes	0	0	4	0/0	0/0	0	24
Smith	0	3	0	0/0	0/0	0	18
Muster	1	0	0	0/0	0/0	0	6
Neal	1	0	0	0/0	0/0	0	6
J. Williams	0	0	1	0/0	0/0	0	6
Saints	11	22	5	32/32	28/39	0	348
Opponents	10	28	7	41/41	30/37	0	407

2-Point conversions: Small, Walls. Team: 2-6.

RUSHING	Att.	Yds.	Avg.	LG	TD
Bates	151	579	3.8	40	6
Brown	146	489	3.3	16	3
Neal	30	90	3.0	12	1
Haynes	4	43	10.8	15	0
Ned	11	36	3.3	15	0
Everett	15	35	2.3	14	0
Barnhardt	1	21	21.0	21	0
W. Wilson	7	15	2.1	9	0
Early	2	10	5.0	8	0
Dunbar	3	9	3.0	3	0
Hughes	2	6	3.0	7	0
Muster	1	3	3.0	3t	1
Saints	373	1336	3.6	40	11
Opponents	458	1758	3.8	25t	10

RECEIVING	No.	Yds.	Avg.	LG	TD
Early	82	894	10.9	33	4
Haynes	77	985	12.8	78t	5
Small	49	719	14.7	75t	5
Brown	44	428	9.7	37	1
Smith	41	330	8.0	19	3
Walls	38	406	10.7	31	4
Ned	13	86	6.6	19	0
Muster	10	88	8.8	21	0
Bates	8	62	7.8	14	0
Neal	2	9	4.5	5	0
Mitchell	1	13	13.0	13	0
W. Williams	1	7	7.0	7	0
Saints	366	4027	11.0	78t	22
Opponents	353	4007	11.4	59	28

INTERCEPTIONS	No.	Yds.	Avg.	LG	TD
Spencer	5	24	4.8	11	0
J. Williams	2	42	21.0	33t	1
Hughes	2	31	15.5	31	0
Lee	2	3	1.5	3	0
Conner	1	56	56.0	56	0
Clark	1	30	30.0	30	0
Mills	1	10	10.0	10	0
Lumpkin	1	1	1.0	1	0
Buck	1	0	0.0	0	0
Tubbs	1	0	0.0	0	0
Saints	17	197	11.6	56	1
Opponents	18	386	21.4	74t	3

PUNTING	No.	Yds.	Avg.	In 20	LG
Barnhardt	67	2920	43.6	14	57
Saints	67	2920	43.6	14	57
Opponents	60	2558	42.6	22	63

PUNT RETURNS	No.	FC	Yds.	Avg.	LG	TD
Hughes	21	8	143	6.8	35	0
Mitchell	3	2	9	3.0	5	0
Legette	1	0	0	0.0	0	0
Saints	25	10	152	6.1	35	0
Opponents	40	8	495	12.4	103t	2

KICKOFF RETURNS	No.	Yds.	Avg.	LG	TD
Hughes	63	1556	24.7	98t	2
Ned	7	77	11.0	19	0
Mitchell	6	129	21.5	30	0
Smith	2	10	5.0	10	0
Dunbar	1	28	28.0	28	0
Bates	1	20	20.0	26	0
Neal	1	17	17.0	15	0
Brown	1	3	3.0	3	0
Saints	82	1840	22.4	98t	2
Opponents	63	1493	23.7	86	0

SACKS	No.
Conner	10.5
Martin	10.0
Turnbull	6.0
Warren	4.0
J. Johnson	1.5
Buck	1.0
Legette	1.0
Mills	1.0
Tubbs	1.0
Saints	36.0
Opponents	24.0

1995 DRAFT CHOICES

Round	Name	Pos.	College
1	Mark Fields	LB	Washington State
2	Ray Zellars	RB	Notre Dame
3	Mike Verstegen	T	Wisconsin
4	Dameian Jeffries	DE	Alabama
5	William Strong	DB	North Carolina State
6	Lee DeRamus	WR	Wisconsin
7	Travis Davis	DB	Notre Dame

NEW ORLEANS SAINTS

1995 VETERAN ROSTER

No.		Name	Pos.	Ht.	Wt.	Birthdate	NFL Exp.	College	Hometown	How Acq.	'94 Games/ Starts
21		Allen, Eric	CB	5-10	180	11/22/65	8	Arizona State	San Diego, Calif.	RFA(Phil)-'95	16/16*
7		Andersen, Morten	K	6-2	221	8/19/60	14	Michigan State	Indianapolis, Ind.	D4-'82	16/0
24		Bates, Marlo	RB	6-1	217	1/16/73	2	Arizona State	Tucson, Ariz.	D2-'94	11/7
50		Bavaro, David	LB	6-1	237	3/27/67	4	Syracuse	Danvers, Mass.	FA-'95	9/5*
9		Blanchard, Cary	K	6-1	225	11/5/68	3	Oklahoma State	Hurst, Tex.	FA-'95	0*
20		Brown, Derek	RB	5-9	197	4/15/71	3	Nebraska	Anaheim, Calif.	D4b-'93	16/9
26		Buck, Vince	CB-S	6-0	198	1/12/68	6	Central State, Ohio	Owensboro, Ky.	D2-'90	16/16
74		Carroll, Herman	DE	6-4	265	6/20/71	2	Mississippi State	North Natchez, Miss.	D5a-'94	4/0
71		Cooper, Richard	T	6-5	290	11/1/64	6	Tennessee	Memphis, Tenn.	FA-'89	14/14
76	#	Davidson, Jeff	C-G	6-5	305	10/3/67	5	Ohio State	Westerville, Ohio	FA-'94	0*
56		Dixon, Ernest	LB	6-1	250	10/17/71	2	South Carolina	Ft. Mill, S.C.	FA-'94	15/1
72		Dombrowski, Jim	G	6-5	300	10/19/63	10	Virginia	Williamsville, N.Y.	D1-'86	16/16
32	†	Dunbar, Vaughn	RB	5-10	204	9/4/68	4	Indiana	Ft. Wayne, Ind.	D1-'92	8/0
89		Early, Quinn	WR	6-0	188	4/13/65	8	Iowa	South Great Neck, N.Y.	PB(SD)-'91	16/13
79		Epps, Tory	DT	6-1	280	5/28/67	6	Memphis State	Uniontown, Pa.	UFA(Chi)-'95	5/0*
17		Everett, Jim	QB	6-5	212	1/3/63	10	Purdue	Albuquerque, N.M.	T(Rams)-'94	16/16
91		Goff, Robert	DE	6-3	280	10/2/65	8	Auburn	Bradenton, Fla.	T(TB)-'90	16/0
30		Gunn, Lance	S	6-3	222	1/9/70	2	Texas	Houston, Tex.	FA-'95	0*
98		Hanna, Jim	DT	6-4	275	8/10/71	2	Louisville	West Palm Beach, Fla.	FA-'94	7/0
52		Harvey, Richard	LB	6-1	242	9/11/66	6	Tulane	Pascagoula, Miss.	UFA(Den)-'95	16/1*
81		Haynes, Michael	WR	6-0	184	12/24/65	8	Northern Arizona	New Orleans, La.	RFA(Atl)-'94	16/16
14		Hodson, Tommy	QB	6-3	195	1/28/67	4	Louisiana State	Matthews, La.	FA-'95	0*
33		Hughes, Tyrone	CB	5-9	175	1/14/70	3	Nebraska	New Orleans, La.	D5-'93	15/5
94		Johnson, Joe	DT	6-4	285	7/11/72	2	Louisville	St. Louis, Mo.	D1-'94	15/14
80		Johnson, Tyrone	WR	5-11	171	9/4/71	2	Western State, Colo.	Aurora, Colo.	FA-'94	1/0
27	†	Jones, Selwyn	CB	6-0	185	5/13/70	4	Colorado State	Missouri City, Tex.	W(Clev)-'94	5/1
43	†	Legette, Tyrone	CB	5-9	177	2/15/70	4	Nebraska	Columbia, S.C.	D3-'92	15/2
46	†	Lumpkin, Sean	S	6-0	206	1/4/70	4	Minnesota	St. Louis Park, Minn.	D4b-'92	16/15
93		Martin, Wayne	DE	6-5	275	10/26/65	7	Arkansas	Cherry Valley, Ark.	D1-'89	16/16
44		McCleskey, J.J.	S	5-7	177	4/10/70	2	Tennessee	Knoxville, Tenn.	FA-'94	13/0
67		McCollum, Andy	C-G	6-4	270	6/6/70	2	Toledo	Akron, Ohio	FA-'94	0*
88		Mitchell, Derrell	WR	5-9	190	9/16/71	2	Texas Tech	Miami, Fla.	D6-'94	14/0
25		Muster, Brad	RB	6-4	235	4/11/65	8	Stanford	Santa Rosa, Calif.	FA-'93	7/1
22		Neal, Lorenzo	RB	5-11	240	12/27/70	3	Fresno State	Lemoore, Calif.	D4a-'93	16/7
36		Ned, Derrick	RB	6-1	210	1/5/69	3	Grambling State	Eunice, La.	FA-'92	16/1
60		Novitsky, Craig	C-T	6-5	295	5/12/71	2	UCLA	Dumfries, Va.	D5b-'94	9/1
13		Nussmeier, Doug	QB	6-3	211	12/11/70	2	Idaho	Lake Oswego, Ore.	D4-'94	0*
35		Pahukoa, Shane	S	6-2	202	11/25/70	2	Washington	Marysville, Wash.	FA-'94	0*
70		Port, Chris	G-T	6-5	295	11/2/67	5	Duke	Wanaque, N.J.	FA-'90	16/16
59		Porter, Rufus	LB	6-1	230	5/18/65	8	Southern	Baton Rouge, La.	UFA(Sea)-'95	16/15*
84		Rhem, Steve	WR	6-2	212	11/9/71	2	Minnesota	Ocala, Fla.	FA-'94	7/0
77		Roaf, William	T	6-5	300	4/18/70	3	Louisiana Tech	Pine Bluff, Ark.	D1a-'93	16/16
3		Rosenbach, Timm	QB	6-1	215	10/27/66	5	Washington State	Pullman, Wash.	FA-'95	0*
78		Roth, Tom	C-G	6-5	285	9/19/68	2	Southern Illinois	Godfrey, Ill.	FA-'94	0*
83		Small, Torrance	WR	6-3	201	9/6/70	4	Alcorn State	Tampa, Fla.	D5-'92	16/0
82		Smith, Irv	TE	6-3	246	10/13/71	3	Notre Dame	Pemberton, N.J.	D1b-'93	16/16
37		Spencer, Jimmy	CB	5-9	180	3/29/69	4	Florida	South Bay, Fla.	FA-'92	16/16
99		Tuatagaloa, Natu	DE	6-4	275	5/25/66	6	California	San Rafael, Calif.	FA-'95	0*
54		Tubbs, Winfred	LB	6-4	250	9/24/70	2	Texas	Fairfield, Tex.	D3-'94	13/7
97		Turnbull, Renaldo	DE	6-4	255	1/5/66	6	West Virginia	St. Thomas, Virgin Islands	D1-'90	16/16
62		Uhlenhake, Jeff	C	6-3	284	1/28/66	7	Ohio State	Newark, Ohio	UFA(Mia)-'94	16/15
85		Walls, Wesley	TE	6-5	250	3/26/66	7	Mississippi	Pontotoc, Miss.	UFA(SF)-'94	15/7
65		Williams, Willie	T	6-6	295	8/6/67	4	Louisiana State	Houston, Tex.	FA-'94	16/5
10		Wilmsmeyer, Klaus	P	6-1	210	12/4/67	4	Louisville	Toronto, Canada	FA-'95	16/0*

* Allen played 16 games with Philadelphia in '94; Bavaro played 9 games with New England; Blanchard last active with N.Y. Jets in '93; Davidson inactive for 7 games; Epps played 5 games with Chicago; Gunn last active with Cincinnati in '93; Harvey played 16 games with Denver; Hodson inactive for 1 game with Dallas; McCollum active for 1 game but did not play; Nussmeier inactive for 16 games; Pahukoa missed '94 season because of injury; Porter played 16 games with Seattle; Rosenbach last active with Phoenix in '92; Roth active for 8 games but did not play; Tuatagaloa last active with Seattle in '93; Wilmsmeyer played 16 games with San Francisco.

Unrestricted free agent; subject to developments.

† Restricted free agent; subject to developments.

Players lost through free agency (7): P Tommy Barnhardt (Car; 16 games in '94), CB Vinnie Clark (Jax; 5), LB Darion Conner (Car; 16), DT Mark Gunn (Phil; 0), LB Sam Mills (Car; 16), LB Joel Smeenge (Jax; 16), TE Frank Wainwright (Den; 0).

Players lost through Expansion Draft (3): CB-S Othello Henderson (Jax; 16 games in '94), G Baron Rollins (Car; 0), LB James Williams (Jax; 16).

Also played with Saints in '94—G Scott Adams (11 games), TE Kirk Botkin (3), CB Israel Byrd (3), CB Reginald Jones (1), CB Carl Lee (12), NT Les MIller (8), LB Mike Stonebreaker (2), DE Frank Warren (16), S Ray Wilson (3), QB Wade Wilson (4), LB DeMond Winston (3).

COACHING STAFF

Vice President-Head Coach, Jim Mora

Pro Career: Begins tenth year as an NFL head coach. Led Saints to a 12-4 record and their third straight playoff appearance in 1992. Guided Saints to an 11-5 mark and the club's first-ever NFC West title in 1991. Was named 1987 NFL coach of the year after leading Saints to a 12-3 record and the team's first playoff appearance. Came to New Orleans following a three-year career as the winningest coach in USFL history as head coach of the Philadelphia/Baltimore Stars. Directed Stars to championship game in each of his three seasons and won league championship in 1984 and 1985. He won USFL coach of the year honors following the 1984 season. Mora began his pro coaching career in 1978 as defensive line coach of the Seattle Seahawks. In 1982, he became defensive coordinator of the New England Patriots and played a vital role in the Patriots' march to the playoffs that year. No pro playing experience. Career record: 84-63.

Background: Played tight end and defensive end at Occidental College. Assistant coach at Occidental from 1960-63 and head coach from 1964-66. Linebacker coach at Stanford (1967) on a staff that included former Eagles head coach Dick Vermeil. Defensive assistant at Colorado 1968-73. Linebacker coach under Vermeil at UCLA 1974. Defensive coordinator at Washington 1975-77. Received bachelor's degree in physical education from Occidental in 1957. Also holds master's degree in education from Southern California.

Personal: Born May 24, 1935, in Glendale, Calif. Jim and his wife, Connie, live in Metairie, La., and have three sons—Michael, Stephen, and Jim (defensive backs coach for the Saints).

ASSISTANT COACHES

Jim Haslett, linebackers; born December 9, 1955, Pittsburgh, Pa., lives in Destrehan, La. Defensive end Indiana University (Pa.) 1975-78. Linebacker Buffalo Bills 1979-86, New York Jets 1987. College coach: Buffalo 1988-90. Pro coach: Sacramento Surge (World League) 1991-92, Los Angeles Raiders 1993-94, joined Saints in 1995.

Larry Kennan, tight ends; born June 13, 1944, Pomona, Calif., lives in Mandeville, La. Quarterback La Verne College 1962-65. No pro playing experience. College coach: Colorado 1969-71, Nevada-Las Vegas 1973-75, Southern Methodist 1976-78, Lamar 1978-81 (head coach). Pro coach: Los Angeles Raiders 1982-87, Denver Broncos 1988, Indianapolis Colts 1989-90 (offensive coordinator), London Monarchs (World League) 1991 (head coach), Seattle Seahawks 1992-94, joined Saints in 1995.

Monte Kiffin, defensive coordinator; born February 29, 1940, Lexington, Neb., lives in Kenner, La. Offensive-defensive tackle Nebraska 1958-61. Pro defensive end Winnipeg Blue Bombers (CFL) 1965. College coach: Nebraska 1966-76, Arkansas 1977-79, North Carolina State 1980-82 (head coach). Pro coach: Green Bay Packers 1983, Buffalo Bills 1984-85, Minnesota Vikings 1986-89, 1991-94, New York Jets 1990, joined Saints in 1995.

Joe Marciano, tight ends-special teams; born February 10, 1954, Scranton, Pa., lives in Kenner, La. Quarterback Temple 1972-75. No pro playing experience. College coach: East Stroudsburg 1977, Rhode Island 1978-79, Villanova 1980, Penn State 1981, Temple 1982. Pro coach: Philadelphia/Baltimore Stars (USFL) 1983-85, joined Saints in 1986.

John Matsko, offensive line; born February 2, 1951, Cleveland, Ohio, lives in Mandeville, La. Fullback Kent State 1970-73. No pro playing experience. College coach: Kent State 1973, Miami, Ohio 1974-75, 1977, North Carolina 1978-84, Navy 1985, Arizona 1986, Southern California 1987-91. Pro coach: Phoenix Cardinals 1992-93, joined Saints in 1994.

Jim Mora, defensive backs; born November 19, 1961, Los Angeles, Calif., lives in New Orleans. Defensive back Washington 1980-83. No pro playing experience. College coach: Washington 1984. Pro coach: San Diego Chargers 1985-91, joined Saints in 1992.

Wayne Nunnely, defensive line; born March 29, 1952, Los Angeles, Calif., lives in Kenner, La. Fullback Nevada-Las Vegas 1972-75. No pro playing experience. College coach: Nevada-Las Vegas 1976, 1982-89 (head coach 1986-89), Cal Poly-Pomona 1977-78, Cal State-Fullerton 1979, Pacific 1980-81, Southern California 1991-92, UCLA 1993-94. Pro coach: Joined Saints in 1995.

Russell Paternostro, strength and conditioning; born July 21, 1940, New Orleans, La., lives in Covington, La. San Diego State. No college or pro playing experience. Pro coach: Joined Saints in 1981.

Jim Skipper, running backs; born January 23, 1949, Breaux Bridge, La., lives in Kenner, La. Defensive back Whittier College 1971-72. No proplaying experience. College coach: Cal Poly-Pomona 1974-76, San Jose State 1977-78, Pacific 1979, Oregon 1980-82. Pro coach: Philadelphia/Baltimore Stars (USFL) 1983-85, joined Saints in 1986.

Carl Smith, offensive coordinator-quarterbacks; born April 26, 1948, Wasco, Calif., lives in Kenner, La. Defensive back Cal Poly-SLO 1968-70. No pro playing experience. College coach: Cal Poly-SLO 1971, Colorado 1972-73, Southwestern Louisiana 1974-78, Lamar 1979-81, North Carolina State 1982. Pro coach: Philadelphia/Baltimore Stars (USFL) 1983-85, joined Saints in 1986.

Steve Trimble, defensive assistant; born May 11, 1958, Cumberland, Md., lives in Destrehan, La. Defensive back Maryland 1976-80. Pro defensive back Denver Broncos 1981-83, Denver Gold (USFL) 1984-85, Chicago Bears 1987. College coach: New Mexico Highlands 1986-87, Colorado 1988-90, Howard 1991-92. Pro coach: Detroit Drive (Arena Football) 1988-89, Cincinnati Rockers (Arena League) 1993, New York Jets 1994, joined Saints in 1995.

Steve Walters, wide receivers; born June 16, 1948, Jonesboro, Ark., lives in Destrehan, La. Quarterback-defensive back Arkansas 1967-70. No pro playing experience. College coach: Tampa 1973, Northeast Louisiana 1974-75, Morehead State 1976, Tulsa 1977-78, Memphis State 1979, Southern Methodist 1980-81, Alabama 1985. Pro coach: New England Patriots 1982-84, joined Saints in 1986.

1995 FIRST-YEAR ROSTER

Name	Pos.	Ht.	Wt.	Birthdate	College	Hometown	How Acq.
Botkin, Kirk (1)	TE	6-3	245	3/19/71	Arkansas	Baytown, Tex.	FA
Bravy, Brian	G	6-4	332	12/3/71	Georgia Tech	Lake Ronkonkoma, N.Y.	FA
Byrd, Israel (1)	CB	5-11	184	2/1/71	Utah State	St. Louis, Mo.	FA
Davis, Travis	S	6-0	200	1/10/73	Norte Dame	Wilmington, Calif.	D7
Dawkins, Ralph (1)	RB	5-8	195	10/20/70	Louisville	Jacksonville, Fla.	FA
DeRamus, Lee	WR	6-0	191	8/24/72	Wisconsin	Sicklerville, N.J.	D6
Farrell, Derrick	DE	6-5	290	1/10/72	Louisiana State	Brooklyn, N.Y.	FA
Fields, Mark	LB	6-2	244	11/9/72	Washington State	Cerritos, Calif.	D1
Gaines, Kevin	CB	6-0	181	8/7/71	Louisville	Euclid, Ohio	FA
Goo, Kendall	G	6-6	286	2/5/72	Hawaii	Kapaa, Hawaii	FA
Henry, Adam (1)	WR	6-1	184	4/27/72	McNeese State	Beaumont, Tex.	FA
Ingram, Kelvin	DE	6-5	276	10/25/70	Oklahoma State	Ft. Pierce, Fla.	FA
Jeffries, Dameian	DE	6-4	277	5/7/73	Alabama	Sylacauga, Ala.	D4
Jones, Terrence (1)	WR	6-1	210	6/18/66	Tulane	Lutcher, La.	FA
Kline, Alan (1)	T	6-5	277	5/25/71	Ohio State	Tiffin, Ohio	FA
Latson, Lawann (1)	WR	5-8	170	3/11/71	N.W. Louisiana	Shreveport, La.	FA
Moore, Travis (1)	WR	6-0	187	8/5/70	Ball State	Los Angeles, Calif.	FA
Nesbitt, Mike (1)	P	6-2	180	2/3/71	New Mexico	Delen, N.M.	FA
Pahukoa, Shane (1)	S	6-2	202	11/25/70	Washington	Marysville, Calif.	FA
Palermo, Mike	T	6-5	290	10/10/70	Gannon College	Erie, Pa.	FA
Roberson, James	LB	6-3	244	5/3/71	Florida State	Lake Wales, Fla.	FA
Stanley, Israel (1)	DT	6-3	260	4/21/70	Arizona State	San Diego, Calif.	FA
Strong, William	CB	5-10	191	11/3/71	North Carolina State	Lewisville, S.C.	D5
Verstegen, Mike	T	6-6	311	10/24/71	Wisconsin	Kimberly, Wis.	D3
Zellars, Ray	RB	5-11	221	3/25/73	Notre Dame	Pittsburgh, Pa.	D2

The term NFL Rookie is defined as a player who is in his first season of professional football and has not been on the roster of another professional football team for any regular-season or postseason games. A Rookie is designated by an "R" on NFL rosters. Players who have been active in another professional football league or players who have NFL experience, including either preseason training camp or being on an Active List or Inactive List, or on Reserve/Injured or Reserve/Physically Unable to Perform for fewer than six regular-season games, are termed NFL First-Year Players. An NFL First-Year Player is designated by a "1" on NFL rosters. Thereafter, a player is credited with an additional year of experience for each season in which he accumulates six games on the Active List or Inactive List, or on Reserve/Injured or Reserve/Physically Unable to Perform.

NOTES

NEW YORK GIANTS

National Football Conference
Eastern Division
Team Colors: Blue, Red, and White
Giants Stadium
East Rutherford, New Jersey 07073
Telephone: (201) 935-8111

CLUB OFFICIALS

President/Co-CEO: Wellington T. Mara
Chairman/Co-CEO: Preston Robert Tisch
Executive Vice President/General Counsel: John K. Mara, Esq.
Treasurer: Jonathan Tisch
Vice President-General Manager: George Young
Assistant General Manager: Ernie Accorsi
Special Assistant to the General Manager: Harry Hulmes
Controller: John Pasquali
Director of Player Personnel: Tom Boisture
Director of Pro Personnel: Tim Rooney
Assistant Director of Player Personnel: Rick Donohue
Director of Administration: Tom Power
Senior Director of Marketing: Rusty Hawley
Director of Promotion: Frank Mara
Ticket Manager: John Gorman
Director of Public Relations: Pat Hanlon
Assistant Controller: Christine Prokops
Assistant Director of Public Relations: Aaron Salkin
Assistant Director of Marketing: Bill Smith
Head Trainer: Ronnie Barnes
Assistant Trainers: John Johnson, Michael Colello, Steve Kennelly
Equipment Manager: Ed Wagner, Jr.
Stadium: Giants Stadium • **Capacity:** 78,148
East Rutherford, New Jersey 07073
Playing Surface: AstroTurf
Training Camp: Fairleigh Dickinson-Madison
Florham Park, N.J. 07932

1995 SCHEDULE

PRESEASON

Aug. 6	at Cleveland	4:00
Aug. 11	**New Orleans**	8:00
Aug. 19	**New York Jets**	8:00
Aug. 26	at Carolina	4:00

REGULAR SEASON

Sept. 4	**Dallas** (Monday)	9:00
Sept. 10	at Kansas City	12:00
Sept. 17	at Green Bay	12:00
Sept. 24	**New Orleans**	1:00
Oct. 1	at San Francisco	1:00
Oct. 8	**Arizona**	4:00
Oct. 15	**Philadelphia**	1:00
Oct. 22	Open Date	
Oct. 29	at Washington	8:00
Nov. 5	at Seattle	1:00
Nov. 12	**Los Angeles**	1:00
Nov. 19	at Philadelphia	1:00
Nov. 26	**Chicago**	1:00
Nov. 30	at Arizona (Thursday)	6:00
Dec. 10	**Washington**	4:00
Dec. 17	at Dallas	3:00
Dec. 23	**San Diego** (Saturday)	12:30

RECORD HOLDERS

INDIVIDUAL RECORDS—CAREER

Category	Name	Performance
Rushing (Yds.)	Joe Morris, 1982-88	5,296
Passing (Yds.)	Phil Simms, 1979-1993	33,462
Passing (TDs)	Phil Simms, 1979-1993	199
Receiving (No.)	Joe Morrison, 1959-1972	395
Receiving (Yds.)	Frank Gifford, 1952-1960, 1962-64	5,434
Interceptions	Emlen Tunnell, 1948-1958	74
Punting (Avg.)	Don Chandler, 1956-1964	43.8
Punt Return (Avg.)	David Meggett, 1989-1994	11.0
Kickoff Return (Avg.)	Rocky Thompson, 1971-72	27.2
Field Goals	Pete Gogolak, 1966-1974	126
Touchdowns (Tot.)	Frank Gifford, 1952-1960, 1962-64	78
Points	Pete Gogolak, 1966-1974	646

INDIVIDUAL RECORDS—SINGLE SEASON

Category	Name	Performance
Rushing (Yds.)	Joe Morris, 1986	1,516
Passing (Yds.)	Phil Simms, 1984	4,044
Passing (TDs)	Y.A. Tittle, 1963	36
Receiving (No.)	Earnest Gray, 1983	78
Receiving (Yds.)	Homer Jones, 1967	1,209
Interceptions	Otto Schnellbacher, 1951	11
	Jim Patton, 1958	11
Punting (Avg.)	Don Chandler, 1959	46.6
Punt Return (Avg.)	Merle Hapes, 1942	15.5
Kickoff Return (Avg.)	John Salscheider, 1949	31.6
Field Goals	Ali Haji-Sheikh, 1983	35
Touchdowns (Tot.)	Joe Morris, 1985	21
Points	Ali Haji-Sheikh, 1983	127

INDIVIDUAL RECORDS—SINGLE GAME

Category	Name	Performance
Rushing (Yds.)	Gene Roberts, 11-12-50	218
Passing (Yds.)	Phil Simms, 10-13-85	513
Passing (TDs)	Y.A. Tittle, 10-28-62	*7
Receiving (No.)	Mark Bavaro, 10-13-85	12
Receiving (Yds.)	Del Shofner, 10-28-62	269
Interceptions	Many times	3
	Last time by Terry Kinard, 9-27-87	
Field Goals	Joe Danelo, 10-18-81	6
Touchdowns (Tot.)	Ron Johnson, 10-2-72	4
	Earnest Gray, 9-7-80	4
Points	Ron Johnson, 10-2-72	24
	Earnest Gray, 9-7-80	24

*NFL Record

COACHING HISTORY

(516-421-32)

1925	Bob Folwell	8-4-0
1926	Joe Alexander	8-4-1
1927-28	Earl Potteiger	15-8-3
1929-30	LeRoy Andrews*	24-5-1
1930	Benny Friedman	2-0-0
1930-53	Steve Owen	155-108-17
1954-60	Jim Lee Howell	55-29-4
1961-68	Allie Sherman	57-54-4
1969-73	Alex Webster	29-40-1
1974-76	Bill Arnsparger**	7-28-0
1976-78	John McVay	14-23-0
1979-82	Ray Perkins	24-35-0
1983-90	Bill Parcells	85-52-1
1991-92	Ray Handley	14-18-0
1993-94	Dan Reeves	21-13-0

*Released after 15 games in 1930
**Released after seven games in 1976

GIANTS STADIUM

N

1994 TEAM RECORD

PRESEASON (1-4)

Date	Result		Opponents
7/30	L	19-20	Miami
8/6	L	15-24	Cleveland
8/13	W	28-20	vs. San Diego at Berlin
8/20	L	10-13	at N.Y. Jets
8/27	L	21-27	at Chicago

REGULAR SEASON (9-7)

Date	Result		Opponents	Att.
9/4	W	28-23	Philadelphia	76,130
9/11	W	20-17	at Arizona	60,066
9/18	W	31-23	Washington	77,298
10/2	L	22-27	at New Orleans	55,076
10/10	L	10-27	Minnesota	77,294
10/16	L	10-17	at L.A. Rams	40,474
10/23	L	6-10	Pittsburgh	71,819
10/30	L	25-28	Detroit (OT)	75,124
11/7	L	10-38	at Dallas	64,836
11/13	L	9-10	Arizona	71,719
11/21	W	13-10	at Houston	53,201
11/27	W	21-19	at Washington	43,384
12/4	W	16-13	at Cleveland	72,068
12/11	W	27-20	Cincinnati	67,530
12/18	W	16-13	at Philadelphia	64,540
12/24	W	15-10	Dallas	66,943

(OT) Overtime

SCORE BY PERIODS

Giants	64	106	39	70	0	—	279
Opponents	44	100	77	81	3	—	305

ATTENDANCE

Home 583,857 Away 453,645 Total 1,037,502
Single-game home record, 77,356 (1-2-94)
Single-season home record, 608,706 (1992)

1994 TEAM STATISTICS

	Giants	Opp.
Total First Downs	263	280
Rushing	103	92
Passing	136	166
Penalty	24	22
Third Down: Made/Att	76/220	86/209
Third Down Pct.	34.5	41.1
Fourth Down: Made/Att	5/10	5/13
Fourth Down Pct.	50.0	38.5
Total Net Yards	4316	4950
Avg. Per Game	269.8	309.4
Total Plays	976	973
Avg. Per Play	4.4	5.1
Net Yards Rushing	1754	1728
Avg. Per Game	109.6	108.0
Total Rushes	525	447
Net Yards Passing	2562	3222
Avg. Per Game	160.1	201.4
Sacked/Yards Lost	46/285	26/169
Gross Yards	2847	3391
Att./Completions	405/226	500/289
Completion Pct.	55.8	57.8
Had Intercepted	18	16
Punts/Avg.	89/40.2	69/40.5
Net Punting Avg.	89/35.0	69/33.7
Penalties/Yards Lost	92/818	130/1122
Fumbles/Ball Lost	28/7	25/16
Touchdowns	30	31
Rushing	12	11
Passing	16	16
Returns	2	4
Avg. Time of Possession	30:28	29:32

1994 INDIVIDUAL STATISTICS

PASSING	Att.	Comp.	Yds.	Pct.	TD	Int.	Tkld.	Rate
Da. Brown	350	201	2536	57.4	12	16	42/248	72.5
Graham	53	24	295	45.3	3	2	2/22	66.2
Meggett	2	1	16	50.0	1	0	1/7	116.7
Marshall	0	0	0	—	0	0	1/8	—
Giants	405	226	2847	55.8	16	18	46/285	72.5
Opponents	500	289	3391	57.8	16	16	26/169	75.8

SCORING	TD R	TD P	TD Rt	PAT	FG	Saf	PTS
Treadwell	0	0	0	22/23	11/17	0	55
Daluiso	0	0	0	5/5	11/11	0	38
Hampton	6	0	0	0/0	0/0	0	38
Meggett	4	0	2	0/0	0/0	0	36
Sherrard	0	6	0	0/0	0/0	0	36
Cross	0	4	0	0/0	0/0	0	24
Pierce	0	4	0	0/0	0/0	0	24
Da. Brown	2	0	0	0/0	0/0	0	12
Calloway	0	2	0	0/0	0/0	0	12
Giants	12	16	2	27/28	22/28	2	279
Opponents	11	16	4	30/30	29/34	1	305

2-Point conversions: Hampton. Team: 1-2.

RUSHING	Att.	Yds.	Avg.	LG	TD
Hampton	327	1075	3.3	27t	6
Meggett	91	298	3.3	26t	4
Da. Brown	60	196	3.3	21	2
Calloway	8	77	9.6	20	0
Downs	15	51	3.4	8	0
Rasheed	17	44	2.6	6	0
Graham	2	11	5.5	9	0
Marshall	2	8	4.0	6	0
Elias	2	4	2.0	5	0
Sherrard	1	-10	-10.0	-10	0
Giants	525	1754	3.3	27t	12
Opponents	447	1728	3.9	62	11

RECEIVING	No.	Yds.	Avg.	LG	TD
Sherrard	53	825	15.6	55	6
Calloway	43	666	15.5	51t	2
Meggett	32	293	9.2	34	0
Cross	31	364	11.7	40	4
Pierce	20	214	10.7	29	4
Marshall	16	219	13.7	34	0
Hampton	14	103	7.4	17	0
Rasheed	10	97	9.7	22	0
Lewis	4	46	11.5	23	0
Downs	2	15	7.5	10	0
Kozlowski	1	5	5.0	5	0
Giants	226	2847	12.6	55	16
Opponents	289	3391	11.7	93	16

INTERCEPTIONS	No.	Yds.	Avg.	LG	TD
Booty	3	95	31.7	36	0
Sparks	3	4	1.3	4	0
J. Williams	2	10	5.0	10	0
Miller	2	6	3.0	6	0
Campbell	2	3	1.5	2	0
Brooks	1	10	10.0	10	0
Armstead	1	0	0.0	0	0
Randolph	1	0	0.0	0	0
Raymond	1	0	0.0	0	0
Giants	16	128	8.0	36	0
Opponents	18	299	16.6	48t	3

PUNTING	No.	Yds.	Avg.	In 20	LG
Horan	85	3521	41.4	25	63
Da. Brown	2	57	28.5	1	33
Giants	89	3578	40.2	26	63
Opponents	69	2792	40.5	19	55

PUNT RETURNS	No.	FC	Yds.	Avg.	LG	TD
Meggett	26	14	323	12.4	68t	2
Lewis	5	2	64	12.8	35	0
Marshall	1	1	1	1.0	1	0
Giants	32	17	388	12.1	68t	2
Opponents	39	14	307	7.9	52	0

KICKOFF RETURNS	No.	Yds.	Avg.	LG	TD
Meggett	29	548	18.9	30	0
Lewis	26	509	19.6	36	0
Marshall	15	249	16.6	30	0
Kozlowski	2	21	10.5	14	0
De. Brown	1	1	1.0	1	0
Giants	73	1328	18.2	36	0
Opponents	44	923	21.0	42	0

SACKS	No.
Hamilton	6.5
Howard	6.5
Strahan	4.5
Armstead	3.0
Dillard	1.5
Beamon	1.0
Brooks	1.0
Fox	1.0
Widmer	1.0
Giants	26.0
Opponents	46.0

1995 DRAFT CHOICES

Round	Name	Pos.	College
1	Tyrone Wheatley	RB	Michigan
2	Scott Gragg	T	Montana
3	Rodney Young	DB	Louisiana State
4	Rob Zatechka	G	Nebraska
	Ben Talley	LB	Tennessee
5	Roderick Mullen	DB	Grambling State
6	Jamal Duff	DE	San Diego State
	Charles Way	RB	Virginia
7	Bryne Diehl	P	Alabama

NEW YORK GIANTS

1995 VETERAN ROSTER

No.		Name	Pos.	Ht.	Wt.	Birthdate	NFL Exp.	College	Hometown	How Acq.	'94 Games/ Starts
93		Agnew, Ray	DT	6-3	295	12/9/67	6	North Carolina State	Winston-Salem, N.C.	UFA(NE)-'95	11/3*
98		Armstead, Jessie	LB	6-1	228	10/26/70	3	Miami	Dallas, Tex.	D8-'93	16/0
21		Beamon, Willie	CB	5-11	175	6/14/70	3	Northern Iowa	Riviera Beach, Fla.	FA-'93	15/0
78		Bishop, Greg	T	6-5	295	5/2/71	3	Pacific	Lodi, Calif.	D4-'93	16/1
41	#	Booty, John	S	6-0	180	10/9/65	8	Texas Christian	Deberry, Tex.	FA-'94	16/9
77		Bratzke, Chad	DE	6-4	262	9/15/71	2	Eastern Kentucky	Brandon, Fla.	D5-'94	2/0
94		Brooks, Michael	LB	6-1	235	3/2/64	9	Louisiana State	Ruston, La.	UFA(Den)-'93	16/16
17		Brown, Dave	QB	6-5	225	2/25/70	4	Duke	Westfield, N.J.	SD1-'92	15/15
55		Buckley, Marcus	LB	6-3	235	2/3/71	3	Texas A&M	Ft. Worth, Tex.	D3-'93	16/1
80		Calloway, Chris	WR	5-10	185	3/29/68	6	Michigan	Chicago, Ill.	FA-'92	16/14
37		Campbell, Jesse	S	6-1	215	4/11/69	5	North Carolina State	Vanceboro, N.C.	FA-'92	14/10
51		Croel, Mike	LB	6-3	240	6/6/69	5	Nebraska	Detroit, Mich.	FA-'95	13/12*
87		Cross, Howard	TE	6-5	258	8/8/67	7	Alabama	Huntsville, Ala.	D6-'89	16/16
3		Daluiso, Brad	K	6-2	215	12/31/67	5	UCLA	San Diego, Calif.	FA-'93	16/0
62		Davis, Scott	G	6-3	289	1/29/70	3	Iowa	Glenwood, Iowa	D6-'93	15/4
71	†	Dillard, Stacey	DT	6-5	292	9/17/68	4	Oklahoma	Clarksville, Tex.	D6-'92	16/0
82		Douglas, Omar	WR	5-10	170	6/3/72	2	Minnesota	New Orleans, La.	FA-'94	6/0
24		Douglass, Maurice	CB	5-11	202	2/12/64	9	Kentucky	Dayton, Ohio	UFA(Chi)-'95	16/4*
45		Downs, Gary	RB	6-0	212	6/28/71	2	North Carolina State	Columbus, Ga.	D3-'94	14/0
20		Elias, Keith	RB	5-9	191	2/3/72	2	Princeton	Lacey Township, N.J.	FA-'94	2/0
76		Elliott, John	T	6-7	308	4/1/65	8	Michigan	Lake Ronkonkoma, N.Y.	D2-'88	16/15
25	t-	Glenn, Vencie	S	6-0	201	10/26/64	10	Indiana State	Silver Spring, Md.	T(Minn)-'95	16/16*
10	†	Graham, Kent	QB	6-5	236	11/1/68	4	Ohio State	Wheaton, Ill.	D8-'92	13/1
75		Hamilton, Keith	DE	6-6	290	5/25/71	4	Pittsburgh	Lynchburg, Va.	D4-'92	15/15
27		Hampton, Rodney	RB	5-11	230	4/3/69	6	Georgia	Houston, Tex.	D1-'90	14/13
97		Harris, Robert	DE	6-4	290	6/13/69	4	Southern	Riviera Beach, Fla.	RFA(Minn)-'95	11/1*
2		Horan, Mike	P	5-11	188	2/1/59	11	Long Beach State	Orange, Calif.	FA-'93	16/0
85		Kozlowski, Brian	TE	6-3	250	10/4/70	2	Connecticut	Rochester, N.Y.	FA-'94	16/2
81		Lewis, Thomas	WR	6-1	185	1/10/72	2	Indiana	Akron, Ohio	D1-'94	9/0
86	†	Marshall, Arthur	WR	5-11	178	4/29/69	4	Georgia	Hephzibah, Ga.	T(Den)-'94	16/0
99		Maumalanga, Chris	DT	6-2	288	12/15/71	2	Kansas	Redwood City, Calif.	D4-'94	7/0
57		Miller, Corey	LB	6-2	255	10/25/68	5	South Carolina	Pageland, S.C.	D6-'91	15/13
84		Pierce, Aaron	TE	6-5	248	9/6/69	4	Washington	Seattle, Wash.	D3-'92	16/11
23		Randolph, Thomas	CB	5-9	176	10/5/70	2	Kansas State	Norfolk, Va.	D2a-'94	16/10
44		Rasheed, Kenyon	RB	5-10	235	8/23/70	3	Oklahoma	Kansas City, Mo.	FA-'93	16/7
63		Reese, Darren	G	6-4	285	10/25/70	2	Ohio	Elida, Ohio	FA-'94	0*
72		Riesenberg, Doug	T	6-5	280	7/22/65	9	California	Moscow, Idaho	D6a-'87	16/16
91		Rudolph, Coleman	DE	6-4	270	10/22/70	3	Georgia Tech	Valdosta, Ga.	FA-'94	12/2
67		Schreiber, Adam	C	6-4	290	2/20/62	11	Texas	Galveston, Tex.	FA-'94	16/2
31		Sehorn, Jason	S	6-2	212	4/15/71	2	Southern California	Mt. Shasta, Calif.	D2b-'94	8/0
88		Sherrard, Mike	WR	6-2	187	6/21/63	10	UCLA	Los Angeles, Calif.	UFA(SF)-'93	16/14
61		Smith, Lance	G	6-3	290	1/1/63	11	Louisiana State	Kannapolis, N.C.	UFA(Ariz)-'94	13/13
22		Sparks, Phillippi	CB	5-11	190	4/15/69	4	Arizona State	Glendale, Calif.	D2-'92	11/11
92		Strahan, Michael	DE	6-4	270	11/21/71	3	Texas Southern	Westbury, Tex.	D2-'93	15/15
34		Walker, Herschel	RB	6-1	225	3/3/62	10	Georgia	Wrightsville, Ga.	FA-'95	16/14*
8		White, Stan	QB	6-2	202	8/14/71	2	Auburn	Birmingham, Ala.	FA-'94	0*
90		Widmer, Corey	LB	6-3	250	12/25/68	4	Montana State	Bozeman, Mont.	D7-'92	16/5
59		Williams, Brian	C	6-5	300	6/8/66	7	Minnesota	Mt. Lebanon, Pa.	D1-'89	14/14
68		Winrow, Jason	G	6-4	321	1/16/71	2	Ohio State	Bridgeton, N.J.	D6-'94	0*
29		Wooten, Tito	S	6-0	181	12/12/71	2	Northeast Louisiana	Goldsboro, N.C.	SD4-'94	16/2

* Agnew played 11 games with New England in '94; Croel played 13 games with Denver; Douglass played 16 games with Chicago; Glenn played 16 games with Minnesota; Harris played 11 games with Minnesota; Reese active for 1 game but did not play; Walker played 16 games with Philadelphia; White inactive for 16 games; Winrow active for 2 games but did not play.

Unrestricted free agent; subject to developments.

† Restricted free agent; subject to developments.

t- Giants traded for Glenn (Minnesota).

Players lost through free agency (3): DE MIke Fox (Car; 16 games in '94), DT Erik Howard (NYJ; 16), RB David Meggett (NE; 16).

Players lost through Expansion Draft (3): TE Derek Brown (Jax; 13 games in '94), LB Andre Powell (Car; 1), CB Corey Raymond (Jax; 16).

Also played with Giants in '94—LB Carlton Bailey (16 games), WR Mark Jackson (2), G William Roberts (16), K David Treadwell (13), S Jarvis Williams (13).

COACHING STAFF

Head Coach,
Dan Reeves

Pro Career: At the end of last season, head coach Dan Reeves told the New York writers, "If you take away the seven-game losing streak, we would have been undefeated." That statement was made after the Giants up-and-down year ended on an "up" note. Reeves and his staff were faced with many questions before the start of the 1994 season, not the least of which was what kind of production they would get from a young, inexperienced quarterback and secondary. Following a 3-0 start, Reeves' Giants suffered the seven-game losing streak, the longest of Reeves' 29-year NFL career. The Giants then won their final six games to get back into playoff contention and finish the year with a 9-7 record. After being named the fourteenth head coach in New York Giants history on January 27, 1993, Reeves led his squad to an 11-5 record and a berth in the playoffs as a Wild Card team in his first season with the Giants. Reeves's regular-season record of 11-5 was the best-ever for a first-year Giants coach and helped him earn *Associated Press* coach of the year honors after helping the Giants improve from a 6-10 record in 1992. Reeves came to the Giants after spending 12 years as head coach of the Denver Broncos. His 138 career wins going into the 1995 season gives him the eleventh-most victories in NFL history and gives him the second-best among active head coaches in the NFL, behind Miami's Don Shula (337). He has participated in 45 NFL postseason games, 15 games as a head coach, 16 as an assistant coach, 6 as a player-coach, and 8 as a player. Reeves has played or coached in a record eight Super Bowls, including leading Denver to three Super Bowl appearances. He was the only AFC coach in the decade of the 1980s to lead his team to consecutive Super Bowl appearances as head coach (Super Bowls XXI, XXII, and XXIV), and he led Denver to seven 10-victory seasons in his 12 years there. Until taking the Denver post, Reeves had been a member of the Dallas coaching staff since 1970 when he spent two seasons as a player-coach. In 1977 when he was named offensive coordinator on Tom Landry's staff. Reeves began his professional football career as a free-agent running back for Dallas in 1965. Reeves was an all-purpose player during his eight seasons (1965-1972) with Dallas (1,900 yards rushing with 25 touchdowns and 129 pass receptions for 1,693 yards and 17 touchdowns) and he finished his playing career as the fifth all-time rusher in Dallas history. In addition, he completed 30 passes, including 2 for touchdowns, and he also returned punts and kickoffs at various times as he played in the 1966, 1967, and 1970 NFL Championship Games. Career record: 138-92-1.

Background: Quarterback at South Carolina from 1962-64. He was inducted into the school's Hall of Fame in 1978.

Personal: Born January 19, 1944, Americus, Ga. Dan and his wife, Pam, live in Ho-Ho-Kus, N.J., and have three children—Dana, Laura, and Lee. They also have two grandchildren—Caitlin and Ashley.

ASSISTANT COACHES

Don Blackmon, linebackers; born March 14, 1958, Pompano Beach, Fla., lives in Morristown, N.J. Linebacker Tulsa 1977-80. Pro linebacker New England Patriots 1981-87. Pro coach: New England Patriots 1988-90, Cleveland Browns 1991-92, joined Giants in 1993.

Dave Brazil, defensive quality control; born March 25, 1936, Detroit, Mich., lives in East Rutherford, N.J. No college or pro playing experience. College coach: Holy Cross 1968, Tulsa 1969-70, Eastern Michigan 1971-73, Boston College 1980, Kent State 1981-82. Pro coach: Detroit Wheels (WFL) 1974, Chicago Fire (WFL) 1975, Kansas City Chiefs 1984-88, Pittsburgh Steelers 1989-91, joined Giants in 1992.

James Daniel, tight ends; born January 17, 1953, Wetumpka, Ala., lives in Clifton, N.J. Offensive guard Alabama State 1970-73. No pro playing experience. College coach: Auburn 1981-92. Pro coach: Joined Giants in 1993.

1995 FIRST-YEAR ROSTER

Name	Pos.	Ht.	Wt.	Birthdate	College	Hometown	How Acq.
Allen, Derek	G	6-4	290	1/30/71	Illinois	Geneseo, Ill.	FA
Bender, Geoff	QB	6-3	210	8/14/71	North Carolina State	Pittsburgh, Pa.	FA
Burkett, Jeremy	WR	6-1	215	4/15/73	Colorado State	Denver, Colo.	FA
Davis, Mitch (1)	LB	6-3	238	7/7/71	Georgia	Mobile, Ala.	FA
Diehl, Bryne	P	6-1	220	12/20/71	Alabama	Oakman, Ala.	D7
Duff, Jamal	DE	6-7	259	3/11/72	San Diego State	Tustin, Calif.	D6a
Gragg, Scott	T	6-8	316	2/28/72	Montana	Silverton, Ore.	D2
Harrell, Gary (1)	WR	5-7	170	1/23/72	Howard	Miami, Fla.	FA
Jennings, Butch	RB	6-0	250	10/4/71	Liberty	Lynchburg, Va.	FA
Johnson, Akili	CB	6-0	185	5/10/72	Grambling State	Little Rock, Ark.	FA
Lawrence, Tyler (1)	LB	6-4	248	9/7/70	North Carolina State	Greensboro, N.C.	FA
Mazyck, Chris	DT	6-3	283	2/25/71	Penn State	Columbia, S.C.	FA
Mullen, Roderick	S	6-1	204	12/5/72	Grambling State	St. Francisville, La.	D5
Palacios, Jesse	G	6-5	292	2/23/70	Southeast Oklahoma	Sweetwater, Tex.	FA
Saxton, Brian	TE	6-6	256	3/13/72	Boston College	Whippany, N.J.	FA
Shufelt, Pete	LB	6-3	240	10/28/69	Texas-El Paso	Tucson, Ariz.	FA
Storm, Matt	DT	6-6	306	9/23/72	Georgia	Edmonds, Wash.	FA
Talley, Ben	LB	6-3	248	7/14/72	Tennessee	Griffin, Ga.	D4b
Thomas, Curtis	WR	6-2	185	12/12/72	Delaware State	Walkersville, Md.	FA
Way, Charles	RB	6-0	236	12/27/72	Virginia	Philadelphia, Pa.	D6b
Wheatley, Tyrone	RB	6-0	227	1/19/72	Michigan	Inkster, Mich.	D1
Yeaman, Todd	DT	6-5	280	1/7/71	Northeast Oklahoma	Ft. Worth, Tex.	FA
Young, Rodney	S	6-1	206	1/25/73	Louisiana State	Grambling, La.	D3
Zatechka, Bob	G	6-4	307	12/1/71	Nebraska	Lincoln, Neb.	D4a

The term NFL Rookie is defined as a player who is in his first season of professional football and has not been on the roster of another professional football team for any regular-season or postseason games. A Rookie is designated by an "R" on NFL rosters. Players who have been active in another professional football league or players who have NFL experience, including either preseason training camp or being on an Active List or Inactive List, or on Reserve/Injured or Reserve/Physically Unable to Perform for fewer than six regular-season games, are termed NFL First-Year Players. An NFL First-Year Player is designated by a "1" on NFL rosters. Thereafter, a player is credited with an additional year of experience for each season in which he accumulates six games on the Active List or Inactive List, or on Reserve/Injured or Reserve/Physically Unable to Perform.

NOTES

Steve DeBerg, quarterbacks; born January 19, 1954, Oakland, Calif., lives in East Rutherford, N.J. Quarterback San Jose State 1974-1977. Pro quarterback San Francisco 49ers 1978-80, Denver Broncos 1981-83, Tampa Bay Buccaneers 1984-87, Kansas City Chiefs 1988-1991, Tampa Bay Buccaneers 1992, Miami Dolphins 1993. Pro coach: Joined Giants in 1995.

Joe DeCamillis, special teams; born June 29, 1965, Arvada, Colo., lives in Morris Township, N.J. Wrestler Wyoming 1983-87. No pro playing experience. College coach: Wyoming 1988. Pro coach: Denver Broncos 1989-92, joined Giants 1993.

Kerry Goode, assistant strength and conditioning; born July 28, 1965, Town Creek, Ala., lives in Mahwah, N.J. Tailback Alabama 1983-87. Pro running back Tampa Bay Buccaneers 1988, Denver Broncos 1989, Miami Dolphins 1990. Pro coach: Joined Giants in 1993.

George Henshaw, offensive coordinator; born January 22, 1948, Midlothian, Va., lives in Smoke Rise, N.J. Defensive tackle West Virginia 1967-69. No pro playing experience. College coach: West Virginia 1970-75, Florida State 1976-82, Alabama 1983-86, Tulsa 1987 (head coach). Pro coach: Denver Broncos 1988-92, joined Giants in 1993.

Earl Leggett, defensive line, born March 5, 1935, Jacksonville, Fla., lives in Randolph, N.J. Tackle Hinds J.C. 1953-54, Louisiana State 1955-56. Pro defensive tackle Chicago Bears 1957-65, Los Angeles Rams 1966, New Orleans Saints 1967-68. College coach: Nicholls State 1971, Texas Christian 1972-73. Pro coach: Southern California Sun (WFL) 1974-75, Seattle Seahawks 1976-77, San Francisco 49ers 1978, Oakland/Los Angeles Raiders 1980-88, Denver Broncos 1989-92, joined Giants in 1993.

Pete Mangurian, offensive line; born June 17, 1955, Los Angeles, Calif., lives in Denville, N.J. Defensive lineman Louisiana State 1975-78. No pro playing experience. College coach: Southern Methodist 1979-80, New Mexico State 1981, Stanford 1982-83, Louisiana State 1984-87. Pro coach: Denver Broncos 1988-92, joined Giants in 1993.

Al Miller, strength and conditioning; born August 29, 1947, El Dorado, Ark., lives in Randolph, N.J. Wide receiver Northeast Louisiana 1965-69. No pro playing experience. College coach: Northwestern Louisiana 1974-78, Mississippi State 1980. Northeast Louisiana 1981, Alabama 1982-84. Pro coach: Denver Broncos 1987-92, joined Giants in 1993.

Mike Nolan, defensive coordinator, born March 7, 1959, Baltimore, Md., lives in Chatham, N.J. Safety Oregon 1977-80. No pro playing experience. College coach: Stanford 1982-83, Rice 1984-85, Louisiana State 1986. Pro coach: Denver Broncos 1987-92, joined Giants in 1993.

Dick Rehbein, wide receivers; born November 22, 1955, Green Bay, Wis., lives in Wayne, N.J. Center Ripon 1973-77. No pro playing experience. Pro coach: Green Bay Packers 1979-83, Los Angeles Express (USFL) 1984, Minnesota Vikings 1984-91, joined Giants in 1992.

George Sefcik, running backs, born December 27, 1939, Cleveland, Ohio, lives in Cranford, N.J. Halfback Notre Dame 1959-61. No pro playing experience. College coach: Notre Dame 1963-68, Kentucky 1969-72. Pro coach: Baltimore Colts 1973-74, Cleveland Browns 1975-77, 1989-90, Cincinnati Bengals 1978-83, Green Bay Packers 1984-87, Kansas City Chiefs 1988, joined Giants in 1991.

Zaven Yaralian, defensive backs, born February 5, 1952, lives in Mountain Lakes, N.J. Defensive back Nebraska 1972-73. Pro defensive back Green Bay Packers 1974, Philadelphia Bell (WFL) 1975. College coach: Nebraska 1975, Washington State 1976-77, Missouri 1978-83, Florida 1984-87, Colorado 1988-89. Pro coach: Chicago Bears 1990-92, joined Giants in 1993.

PHILADELPHIA EAGLES

National Football Conference
Eastern Division
Team Colors: Kelly Green, Silver, and White
Veterans Stadium
Broad Street and Pattison Avenue
Philadelphia, Pennsylvania 19148
Telephone: (215) 463-2500

CLUB OFFICIALS

Owner: Jeffrey Lurie
Director of Football Administration: Bob Ackles
Vice President-Business Development/ Broadcasting: Jeffrey Auerbach
Vice President: Joe Banner
Vice President-Chief Financial Officer: Mimi Box
Director of College Scouting: John Wooten
Director of Pro Personnel: Chuck Banker
General Counsel: Bob Wallace
Director of Marketing/Sponsorships: Karen Levine
Director of Corporate Sales: Scott O'Neil
Director of Penthouse Suites: Debbie Santore
Director of Public Relations: Ron Howard
Asst. Director of Public Relations: Michael Gilbert
Director of Alumni Relations/Traveling Secretary: Jim Gallagher
Director of Administration: Vicki Chatley
Ticket Manager: Leo Carlin
Asst. Director of Penthouse Sales: Ken Iman
Director of Penthouse Operations: Christiana Noyalas
Trainer: Otho Davis
Asst. Trainer: David Price
Peak Performance Specialist: Baron Baptiste
Equipment Manager: Rusty Sweeney
Video Director: Mike Dougherty
Stadium: Veterans Stadium • **Capacity:** 64,899
3501 South Broad Street
Philadelphia, Pennsylvania 19148
Playing Surface: AstroTurf-8
Training Camp: West Chester University
West Chester, Pennsylvania 19382

1995 SCHEDULE

PRESEASON

Aug. 5	**Atlanta**	7:30
Aug. 12	vs. New York Jets at Jackson, Miss.	8:00
Aug. 17	**New England**	8:00
Aug. 24	at Pittsburgh	8:00

REGULAR SEASON

Sept. 3	**Tampa Bay**	1:00
Sept. 10	at Arizona	5:00
Sept. 17	**San Diego**	1:00
Sept. 24	at Los Angeles	1:00
Oct. 1	at New Orleans	12:00
Oct. 8	**Washington**	1:00
Oct. 15	at New York Giants	1:00
Oct. 22	Open Date	
Oct. 29	**St. Louis**	1:00
Nov. 6	at Dallas (Monday)	8:00
Nov. 12	**Denver**	8:00
Nov. 19	**New York Giants**	1:00
Nov. 26	at Washington	1:00
Dec. 3	at Seattle	1:00
Dec. 10	**Dallas**	1:00
Dec. 17	**Arizona**	1:00
Dec. 24	at Chicago	12:00

RECORD HOLDERS

INDIVIDUAL RECORDS—CAREER

Category	Name	Performance
Rushing (Yds.)	Wilbert Montgomery, 1977-1984	6,538
Passing (Yds.)	Ron Jaworski, 1977-1986	26,963
Passing (TDs)	Ron Jaworski, 1977-1986	175
Receiving (No.)	Harold Carmichael, 1971-1983	589
Receiving (Yds.)	Harold Carmichael, 1971-1983	8,978
Interceptions	Bill Bradley, 1969-1976	34
Punting (Avg.)	Joe Muha, 1946-1950	42.9
Punt Return (Avg.)	Steve Van Buren, 1944-1951	13.9
Kickoff Return (Avg.)	Steve Van Buren, 1944-1951	26.7
Field Goals	Paul McFadden, 1984-87	91
Touchdowns (Tot.)	Harold Carmichael, 1971-1983	79
Points	Bobby Walston, 1951-1962	881

INDIVIDUAL RECORDS—SINGLE SEASON

Category	Name	Performance
Rushing (Yds.)	Wilbert Montgomery, 1979	1,512
Passing (Yds.)	Randall Cunningham, 1988	3,808
Passing (TDs)	Sonny Jurgensen, 1961	32
Receiving (No.)	Keith Jackson, 1988	81
	Keith Byars, 1990	81
Receiving (Yds.)	Mike Quick, 1983	1,409
Interceptions	Bill Bradley, 1971	11
Punting (Avg.)	Joe Muha, 1948	47.2
Punt Return (Avg.)	Steve Van Buren, 1944	15.3
Kickoff Return (Avg.)	Al Nelson, 1972	29.1
Field Goals	Paul McFadden, 1984	30
Touchdowns (Tot.)	Steve Van Buren, 1945	18
Points	Paul McFadden, 1984	116

INDIVIDUAL RECORDS—SINGLE GAME

Category	Name	Performance
Rushing (Yds.)	Steve Van Buren, 11-27-49	205
Passing (Yds.)	Randall Cunningham, 9-17-89	447
Passing (TDs)	Adrian Burk, 10-17-54	*7
Receiving (No.)	Don Looney, 12-1-40	14
Receiving (Yds.)	Tommy McDonald, 12-10-60	237
Interceptions	Russ Craft, 9-24-50	*4
Field Goals	Tom Dempsey, 11-12-72	6
Touchdowns (Tot.)	Many times.	4
	Last time by Wilbert Montgomery, 10-7-79	
Points	Bobby Walston, 10-17-54	25

*NFL Record

COACHING HISTORY

(370-443-24)

1933-35	Lud Wray	9-21-1
1936-40	Bert Bell	10-44-2
1941-50	Earle (Greasy) Neale*	66-44-5
1951	Alvin (Bo) McMillin**	2-0-0
1951	Wayne Millner	2-8-0
1952-55	Jim Trimble	25-20-3
1956-57	Hugh Devore	7-16-1
1958-60	Lawrence (Buck) Shaw	20-16-1
1961-63	Nick Skorich	15-24-3
1964-68	Joe Kuharich	28-41-1
1969-71	Jerry Williams***	7-22-2
1971-72	Ed Khayat	8-15-2
1973-75	Mike McCormack	16-25-1
1976-82	Dick Vermeil	57-51-0
1983-85	Marion Campbell****	17-29-1
1985	Fred Bruney	1-0-0
1986-90	Buddy Ryan	43-38-1
1991-94	Rich Kotite	37-29-0

*Co-coach with Walt Kiesling in Philadelphia-Pittsburgh merger in 1943
**Retired after two games in 1951
***Released after three games in 1971
****Released after 15 games in 1985

VETERANS STADIUM

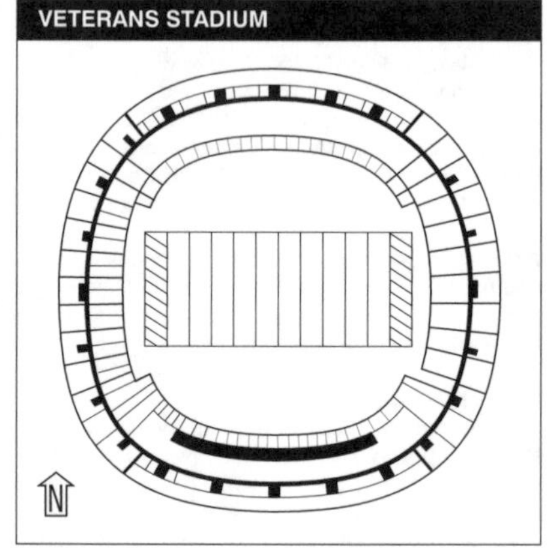

1994 TEAM RECORD

PRESEASON (1-3)

Date	Result		Opponents
8/5	L	6-12	at Chicago
8/13	L	24-34	N.Y. Jets
8/20	W	17-7	Cincinnati
8/26	L	12-20	at Atlanta

REGULAR SEASON (7-9)

Date	Result		Opponents	Att.
9/4	L	23-28	at N.Y. Giants	76,130
9/12	W	30-22	Chicago	64,890
9/18	W	13- 7	Green Bay	63,922
10/2	W	40- 8	at San Francisco	64,843
10/9	W	21-17	Washington	63,947
10/16	L	13-24	at Dallas	64,703
10/24	W	21- 6	Houston	65,233
10/30	W	31-29	at Washington	53,530
11/6	W	17- 7	Arizona	64,952
11/13	L	7-26	Cleveland	65,233
11/20	L	6-12	at Arizona	62,779
11/27	L	21-28	at Atlanta	60,008
12/4	L	19-31	Dallas	65,974
12/11	L	3-14	at Pittsburgh	55,474
12/18	L	13-16	N.Y. Giants	64,540
12/24	L	30-33	at Cincinnati	39,923

(OT) Overtime

SCORE BY PERIODS

Eagles	48	106	81	73	0	—	308
Opponents	65	73	65	105	0	—	308

ATTENDANCE

Home 518,691 Away 477,390 Total 996,081
Single-game home record, 72,111 (11-1-81)
Single-season home record, 557,325 (1980)

1994 TEAM STATISTICS

	Eagles	Opp.
Total First Downs	293	275
Rushing	103	94
Passing	168	151
Penalty	22	30
Third Down: Made/Att	101/243	78/214
Third Down Pct.	41.6	36.4
Fourth Down: Made/Att	6/17	4/9
Fourth Down Pct.	35.3	44.4
Total Net Yards	5125	4710
Avg. Per Game	320.3	294.4
Total Plays	1046	981
Avg. Per Play	4.9	4.8
Net Yards Rushing	1761	1616
Avg. Per Game	110.1	101.0
Total Rushes	432	449
Net Yards Passing	3364	3094
Avg. Per Game	210.3	193.4
Sacked/Yards Lost	48/372	42/265
Gross Yards	3736	3359
Att./Completions	566/316	490/251
Completion Pct.	55.8	51.2
Had Intercepted	14	21
Punts/Avg	92/40.5	90/39.7
Net Punting Avg.	92/35.4	90/32.8
Penalties/Yards Lost	138/1107	98/844
Fumbles/Ball Lost	23/12	29/14
Touchdowns	35	33
Rushing	14	11
Passing	18	20
Returns	3	2
Avg. Time of Possession	30:47	29:13

1994 INDIVIDUAL STATISTICS

PASSING	Att.	Comp.	Yds.	Pct.	TD	Int.	Tkld.	Rate
Cunningham	490	265	3229	54.1	16	13	43/333	74.4
Brister	76	51	507	67.1	2	1	5/39	89.1
Eagles	566	316	3736	55.8	18	14	48/372	76.4
Opponents	490	251	3359	51.2	20	21	42/265	69.1

SCORING	TD R	TD P	TD Rt	PAT	FG	Saf	PTS
Murray	0	0	0	33/33	21/25	0	96
Walker	5	2	1	0/0	0/0	0	48
Barnett	0	5	0	0/0	0/0	0	30
Bavaro	0	3	0	0/0	0/0	0	18
Cunningham	3	0	0	0/0	0/0	0	18
Garner	3	0	0	0/0	0/0	0	18
Joseph	1	2	0	0/0	0/0	0	18
C. Williams	0	3	0	0/0	0/0	0	18
Hebron	2	0	0	0/0	0/0	0	12
M. Johnson	0	2	0	0/0	0/0	0	12
Bailey	0	1	0	0/0	0/0	0	6
G. Jackson	0	0	1	0/0	0/0	0	6
Zordich	0	0	1	0/0	0/0	0	6
Fuller	0	0	0	0/0	0/0	1	2
Eagles	14	18	3	33/33	21/25	1	308
Opponents	11	20	2	27/28	25/26	0	308

2-Point conversions: 0. Team: 0-2.

RUSHING	Att.	Yds.	Avg.	LG	TD
Walker	113	528	4.7	91t	5
Garner	109	399	3.7	28t	3
Hebron	82	325	4.0	19	2
Cunningham	65	288	4.4	22	3
Joseph	60	203	3.4	34t	1
C. Williams	2	11	5.5	6	0
Brister	1	7	7.0	7	0
Eagles	432	1761	4.1	91t	14
Opponents	449	1616	3.6	33	11

RECEIVING	No.	Yds.	Avg.	LG	TD
Barnett	78	1127	14.4	54	5
C. Williams	58	813	14.0	53	3
Walker	50	500	10.0	93	2
Joseph	43	344	8.0	35t	2
M. Johnson	21	204	9.7	22	2
Bailey	20	311	15.6	61	1
Hebron	18	137	7.6	29	0
Bavaro	17	215	12.6	27t	3
Garner	8	74	9.3	28	0
Alexander	2	1	0.5	1	0
Sydner	1	10	10.0	10	0
Eagles	316	3736	11.8	93	18
Opponents	251	3359	13.4	85t	20

INTERCEPTIONS	No.	Yds.	Avg.	LG	TD
G. Jackson	6	86	14.3	55t	1
Zordich	4	39	9.8	18t	1
Allen	3	61	20.3	33	0
Romanowski	2	8	4.0	8	0
McMillian	2	2	1.0	5	0
Thomas	1	7	7.0	7	0
Evans	1	6	6.0	6	0
Hager	1	0	0.0	0	0
Harmon	1	0	0.0	0	0
Eagles	21	209	10.0	55t	2
Opponents	14	206	14.7	94t	1

PUNTING	No.	Yds.	Avg.	In 20	LG
Barker	66	2696	40.8	20	67
Berger	25	951	38.0	8	57
Cunningham	1	80	80.0	1	80
Eagles	92	3727	40.5	29	80
Opponents	90	3570	39.7	27	60

PUNT RETURNS	No.	FC	Yds.	Avg.	LG	TD
Sydner	40	17	381	9.5	49	0
O'Neal	1	0	0	0.0	0	0
Bailey	0	1	0	—	—	0
Eagles	41	18	381	9.3	49	0
Opponents	47	17	286	6.1	68t	1

KICKOFF RETURNS	No.	Yds.	Avg.	LG	TD
Walker	21	581	27.7	94t	1
Hebron	21	443	21.1	33	0
Sydner	20	392	19.6	34	0
Smith	1	14	14.0	14	0
Joseph	1	11	11.0	11	0
M. Johnson	1	0	0.0	0	0
O'Neal	1	0	0.0	0	0
Zordich	1	0	0.0	0	0
Eagles	67	1441	21.5	94t	1
Opponents	64	1425	22.3	68	0

SACKS	No.
Fuller	10.5
Harmon	9.0
Thomas	6.0
Grossman	5.5
Romanowski	2.5
Flores	2.0
Townsend	2.0
Hager	1.0
Jeter	1.0
Smith	1.0
Zordich	1.0
Evans	0.5
Eagles	42.0
Opponents	48.0

1995 DRAFT CHOICES

Round	Name	Pos.	College
1	Mike Mamula	DE	Boston College
2	Bobby Taylor	DB	Notre Dame
	Barrett Brooks	T	Kansas State
3	Greg Jefferson	DE	Central Florida
	Chris T. Jones	WR	Miami
4	Dave Barr	QB	California
6	Fred McCrary	RB	Mississippi State
7	Kevin Bouie	RB	Mississippi State
	Howard Smothers	T	Bethune-Cookman

PHILADELPHIA EAGLES

1995 VETERAN ROSTER

No.		Name	Pos.	Ht.	Wt.	Birthdate	NFL Exp.	College	Hometown	How Acq.	'94 Games/ Starts
72		Alexander, David	C	6-3	275	7/28/64	9	Tulsa	Broken Arrow, Okla.	D5-'87	16/16
24		Barlow, Corey	CB	5-9	182	11/1/70	3	Auburn	Atlanta, Ga.	D5-'92	0*
86		Barnett, Fred	WR	6-0	199	6/17/66	6	Arkansas State	Gunnison, Miss.	D3-'90	16/16
84	#	Bavaro, Mark	TE	6-4	245	4/28/63	10	Notre Dame	Danvers, Mass.	UFA(Clev)-'93	12/11
71		Chalenski, Mike	DE-DT	6-5	288	1/28/70	3	UCLA	Elizabeth, N.J.	FA-'93	0*
10		Conklin, Cary	QB	6-4	215	2/29/68	5	Washington	Yakima, Wash.	FA-'95	0*
12		Cunningham, Randall	QB	6-4	205	3/27/63	11	Nevada-Las Vegas	Santa Barbara, Calif.	D2-'85	14/14
78		Davis, Antone	T	6-4	325	2/28/67	5	Tennessee	Ft. Valley, Ga.	D1-'91	16/14
56	#	Evans, Byron	LB	6-2	235	2/23/64	9	Arizona	Phoenix, Ariz.	D4-'87	10/10
11		Fiedler, Jay	QB	6-1	215	12/29/71	2	Dartmouth	Oceanside, N.Y.	FA-'94	0*
83		Ford, Bernard	WR	5-9	168	2/27/66	4	Central Florida	Orlando, Fla.	FA-'95	0*
23		Frazier, Derrick	CB	5-10	178	4/29/70	3	Texas A&M	Sugar Land, Tex.	D3a-'93	12/0
95		Fuller, William	DE	6-3	274	3/8/62	10	North Carolina	Chesapeake, Va.	UFA(Hou)-'94	16/16
25		Garner, Charlie	RB	5-9	181	2/13/72	2	Tennessee	Falls Church, Va.	D2b-'94	10/8
22		Goodwin, Marvin	S	6-0	199	9/21/72	2	UCLA	Camden, N.J.	D5-'94	0*
54		Gouveia, Kurt	LB	6-1	233	9/14/64	10	Brigham Young	Honolulu, Hawaii	UFA(Wash)-'95	14/1*
69	#	Grossman, Burt	DE	6-4	275	4/10/67	7	Pittsburgh	Bala-Cynwyd, Pa.	T(SD)-'94	14/2
79		Gunn, Mark	DT	6-4	279	7/24/68	5	Pittsburgh	Cleveland, Ohio	UFA(NO)-'95	3/0*
97		Hall, Rhett	DT	6-2	260	12/5/68	5	California	Morgan Hill, Calif.	UFA(SF)-'95	11/2*
91		Harmon, Andy	DT	6-4	265	4/6/69	5	Kent State	Centerville, Ohio	D6-'91	16/16
45		Hebron, Vaughn	RB	5-8	196	10/7/70	3	Virginia Tech	Baltimore, Md.	FA-'93	16/2
26		Henderson, Jerome	CB	5-10	189	8/8/69	5	Clemson	Statesville, N.C.	UFA(Buff)-'95	12/0*
73		Holmes, Lester	G	6-3	301	9/27/69	3	Jackson State	Tylertown, Miss.	D1a-'93	16/16
66		Hudson, John	G-C	6-2	275	1/29/68	6	Auburn	Memphis, Tenn.	D11-'90	16/0
47		Jackson, Greg	S	6-1	210	8/20/66	7	Louisiana State	Miami, Fla.	FA-'94	16/16
98		Jeter, Tommy	DT	6-5	282	9/20/69	4	Texas	Nacogdoches, Tex.	D3-'92	14/0
87		Johnson, Maurice	TE	6-2	243	1/9/67	5	Temple	Washington, D.C.	FA-'91	16/10
80		Johnson, Reggie	TE	6-2	256	1/27/68	5	Florida State	Pensacola, Fla.	UFA(GB)-'95	9/2*
52	#	Johnson, Vaughan	LB	6-3	240	3/4/62	10	North Carolina State	Morehead City, N.C.	FA-'94	4/0
18		Lewis, Ron	WR	5-11	192	3/25/68	6	Florida State	Jacksonville, Fla.	FA-'95	6/1*
68	#	McHale, Tom	T	6-4	290	2/25/63	9	Cornell	Gaithersburg, Md.	FA-'95	13/2
62		McKenzie, Raleigh	G-C	6-2	277	2/8/63	11	Tennessee	Knoxville, Tenn.	UFA(Wash)-'95	16/16*
29		McMillian, Mark	CB	5-7	162	4/29/70	4	Alabama	Los Angeles, Calif.	D10-'92	16/16
3		Murray, Eddie	K	5-11	195	8/29/56	16	Tulane	Victoria, Canada	UFA(Dall)-'94	16/0
58		Oden, Derrick	LB	5-11	230	9/29/70	3	Alabama	Hillcrest, Ala.	D6-'93	11/0
63		Panos, Joe	G-C	6-2	296	1/24/71	2	Wisconsin	Brookfield, Wis.	D3a-'94	16/2
9		Peete, Rodney	QB	6-0	215	3/16/66	7	Southern California	Shawnee Mission, Kan.	UFA(Dall)-'95	7/1*
42		Reid, Mike	S	6-1	218	11/24/70	3	North Carolina State	Spartanburg, S.C.	D3b-'93	3/0
94		Renfro, Leonard	DT	6-2	291	6/29/70	3	Colorado	Detroit, Mich.	D1b-'93	9/0
53		Romanowski, Bill	LB	6-4	231	4/2/66	8	Boston College	Vernon, Conn.	T(SF)-'94	16/15
68		Sims, Joe	G	6-3	310	3/1/69	5	Nebraska	Sudbury, Mass.	UFA(GB)-'95	15/14*
93		Stubbs, Daniel	LB	6-4	264	1/3/65	7	Miami	Red Bank, N.J.	FA-'95	0*
85		Sydner, Jeff	WR	5-6	170	11/11/69	4	Hawaii	Columbus, Ohio	D6-'92	16/0
51		Thomas, William	LB	6-2	218	8/13/68	5	Texas A&M	Amarillo, Tex.	D4-'91	16/16
93	#	Townsend, Greg	DE	6-3	275	11/3/61	13	Texas Christian	Compton, Calif.	FA-'94	16/12
39		Turner, Kevin	RB	6-1	230	6/12/69	4	Alabama	Prattville, Ala.	RFA(NE)-'95	16/9*
32		Watters, Ricky	RB	6-1	212	4/7/69	5	Notre Dame	Harrisburg, Pa.	RFA(SF)-'95	16/16*
48		Wilburn, Barry	CB	6-2	190	12/9/63	7	Mississippi	Baltimore, Md.	FA-'95	0*
14		Wilkins, Jeff	K	6-1	180	4/19/72	2	Youngstown State	Austintown, Ohio	FA-'94	6/0
74		Williams, Bernard	T	6-8	317	7/18/72	2	Georgia	Memphis, Tenn.	D1-'94	16/16
89		Williams, Calvin	WR	5-11	190	3/3/67	6	Purdue	Baltimore, Md.	D5-'90	16/14
57		Woodard, Marc	LB	6-0	234	2/21/70	2	Mississippi State	Kosciusko, Miss.	FA-'94	16/0
27		Zomalt, Eric	S	5-11	197	8/9/72	2	California	Los Angeles, Calif.	D3b-'94	12/0
36		Zordich, Michael	S	6-1	201	10/12/63	9	Penn State	Youngstown, Ohio	FA-'94	16/16

* Barlow and Chalenski missed '94 season because of injury; Conklin last active with Washington in '93; Fiedler and Goodwin inactive for 16 games; Ford last active with Houston in '90; Gouveia played 14 games with Washington; Gunn played 3 games with N.Y. Jets in '94; Hall played 11 games with San Francisco; Henderson played 12 games with Buffalo; R. Johnson played 9 games with Green Bay; Lewis played 6 games with Green Bay; McKenzie played 16 games with Washington; Peete played 7 games with Dallas; Sims played 15 games with Green Bay; Stubbs last active with Cincinnati in '93; Turner played 16 games with New England; Watters played 16 games with San Francisco; Wilburn last active with Cleveland in '92.

\# Unrestricted free agent; subject to developments.

† Restricted free agent; subject to developments.

Retired—William Perry, 10-year defensive tackle, 16 games in '94.

Traded—WR Victor Bailey to Kansas City.

Players lost through free agency (8): CB Eric Allen (NO; 16 games in '94), P Bryan Barker (Jax; 11), QB Bubby Brister (NYJ; 7), DE Mike Flores (Cin; 15), LB Britt Hager (Den; 16), RB James Joseph (Cin; 14), S Rich Miano (Atl; 16), G Rob Selby (Atl; 2).

Players lost through Expansion Draft (2): CB-S Al Jackson (Jax; 11), RB Brian O'Neal (Car; 14).

Also played with Eagles in '94: WR Victor Bailey (16 games), P Mitch Berger (5), LB Ken Rose (16), CB Otis Smith (16), T Broderick Thompson (14), RB Herschel Walker (16).

COACHING STAFF

Head Coach

Ray Rhodes

Pro Career: Named the nineteenth head coach in Eagles history on February 2, 1995, after serving as the defensive coordinator for the San Francisco 49ers. Rhodes comes to Philadelphia after assisting George Seifert and the 49ers to that franchise's unprecedented fifth Super Bowl championship. In fact, Rhodes has been an assistant on each of the 49ers' championship teams, making him one of only four men in NFL history to have served on the staffs of five Super Bowl winners. Of San Francisco's 11 defensive starters in 1994, six were new to the team including free-agent acquisitions Ken Norton, Jr., Gary Plummer, Rickey Jackson, and Deion Sanders, as well as a pair of rookies, Lee Woodall and Bryant Young. This reshaped defense certainly had its share of favorable returns as Rhodes's unit ranked eighth in the NFL in overall defense and second against the run. Before his most recent stint with San Francisco, Rhodes served two seasons in Green Bay as defensive coordinator under ex-49ers assistant Mike Holmgren, where he elevated the Packers' defense to the second-ranked unit overall in just two seasons. Rhodes ended his seven-year NFL playing career with San Francisco in 1980 and then joined Bill Walsh's coaching staff as an assistant defensive backs coach the following season. In 1982, he was promoted to defensive backs coach and held that position through 1991. Over that period, he developed four Pro Bowl defenders, cornerbacks Ronnie Lott and Eric Wright, and safeties Dwight Hicks and Carlton Williamson.

Background: After spending two years at Texas Christian University, Rhodes finished his collegiate career at the University of Tulsa and was selected by the New York Giants in the tenth round of the 1974 NFL draft. He played wide receiver for his first three seasons with the Giants but was switched to defensive back in 1977. In 1979, he was traded to San Francisco in a deal that also saw 49ers defensive back Tony Dungy, presently the defensive coordinator of the Minnesota Vikings, sent to the Giants.

Personal: Born October 20, 1950 in Mexia, Tex. Rhodes and his wife Carmen have four daughters: Detra, Candra, Tynesha, and Raven, and reside in Philadelphia.

Assistant Coaches

Bill Callahan, offensive line; born July 31, 1956, Chicago, Ill., lives in Mt. Laurel, N.J. Quarterback Illinois Benedictine 1975-77. No pro playing experience. College coach: Illinois 1980-87, Northern Arizona 1987-88, Southern Illinois 1989, Wisconsin 1990-94. Pro coach: Joined Eagles in 1995.

Gerald Carr, wide receivers; born June 28, 1959, Davidson, N.C., lives in Siclerville, N.J. Quarterback Southern Illinois 1977-80. No pro playing experience. College coach: Southern Illinois 1982, Davidson 1983-85, Akron 1986-88, Washington State 1989-90, Arizona 1991, North Carolina 1992-94. Pro coach: Joined Eagles in 1995.

Juan Castillo, offensive assistant; born October 8, 1959, Port Isabel, Tex., lives in Moorestown, N.J. Linebacker Texas A&M-Kingsville (formerly Texas A&I) 1978-80. Pro linebacker San Antonio Gunslingers (USFL) 1984-85. College coach: Texas A&M-Kingsville 1982-85, 1990-94. Pro coach: Joined Eagles in 1995.

Jon Gruden, offensive coordinator; born August 17, 1963, Sandusky, Ohio, lives in Mt. Laurel, N.J. Quarterback Dayton 1983-85. No pro playing experience. College coach: Tennessee 1986-87, Southeast Missouri 1988, Pacific 1989, Pittsburgh 1991. Pro coach: San Francisco 49ers 1990, Green Bay Packers 1992-94, joined Eagles in 1995.

Dick Jamieson, running backs; born November 13, 1937, Streator, Ill., lives in Cherry Hill, N.J. Quarterback Bradley 1955-58. Pro quarterback Baltimore Colts 1959, New York Titans (AFL) 1960. College coach: Bradley 1962-64, Missouri 1972-77, Indiana State 1978-79, Northwestern 1990-91, Rutgers 1992-94. Pro coach: St. Louis Cardinals 1980-85, Houston Oilers 1986-87, joined Eagles in 1995.

Chuck Knox, Jr., defensive assistant; born June 19, 1965, Englewood, N.J., lives in Mt. Laurel, N.J. Running back Arizona 1984-85. No pro playing experience. Pro coach: Los Angeles Rams 1993-94, joined Eagles in 1995.

Danny Smith, special teams; born November 7, 1953, Pittsburgh, Pa., lives in Mt. Laurel, N.J. Defensive back Edinboro State 1972-75. No pro playing experience. College coach: Edinboro State 1976, Clemson 1979, William & Mary 1980-83, Citadel 1984-86, Georgia Tech 1987-94. Pro coach: Joined Eagles in 1995.

Emmitt Thomas, defensive coordinator; born June 3, 1943, Angleton, Tex., lives in Voorhees, N.J. Quarterback-wide receiver Bishop (Tex.) College 1963-65. Pro defensive back Kansas City Chiefs 1966-78. College coach: Central Missouri State 1979-80. Pro coach: St. Louis Cardinals 1981-85, Washington Redskins 1986-94, joined Eagles in 1995.

Mike Trgovac, defensive line; born Fenruary 27, 1959, Youngstown, Ohio, lives in Marlton, N.J. Defensive lineman Michigan 1977-80. No pro playing experience. College coach: Michigan 1984-85, Ball State 1986-88, Navy 1989, Colorado State 1990-91, Notre Dame 1992-94. Pro coach: Joined Eagles in 1995.

Joe Vitt, linebackers; born August 23, 1954, Camden, N.J., lives in Mt. Laurel, N.J. Linebacker Towson State 1973-75. No pro playing experience. Pro coach: Baltimore Colts 1979-81, Seattle Seahawks 1982-91, Los Angeles Rams 1992-94, joined Eagles in 1995.

Ted Williams, tight ends; born November 17, 1943, Lyons, Tex., lives in Siclerville, N.J. No college or pro playing experience. College coach: UCLA 1980-89, Washington State 1991-93, Arizona 1994. Pro coach: Joined Eagles in 1995.

Mike Wolf, strength and conditioning; born May 15, 1965, Allentown, Pa., lives in Marlton, N.J. Center Penn State 1983-87. No pro playing experience. College coach: Vanderbilt 1988-89, Lehigh 1990, Penn State 1991. Pro coach: Minnesota Vikings 1992-94, joined Eagles in 1995.

1995 FIRST-YEAR ROSTER

Name	Pos.	Ht.	Wt.	Birthdate	College	Hometown	How Acq.
Allen, Andre	LB	6-0	215	5/24/73	Northern Iowa	Iowa City, Iowa	FA
Barr, Dave	QB	6-3	210	5/9/72	California	Oakland, Calif.	D4
Baskin, Thomas	DT	6-0	288	12/9/72	Texas	Austin, Tex.	FA
Beckley, Jeff	P-K	6-1	195	2/8/71	Boston College	Tampa, Fla.	FA
Bouie, Kevin	RB	6-1	228	8/18/71	Mississippi State	Pahokee, Fla.	D7a
Brooks, Barrett	T	6-4	305	5/5/72	Kansas State	St. Louis, Mo.	D2b
Brown, Curt (1)	DT	6-5	260	4/5/70	North Carolina	Virginia Beach, Va.	FA
Burnett, Bryce (1)	TE	6-2	235	3/9/69	San Jose State	Flossmore, Ill.	FA
Canter, Andy	T	6-4	279	6/18/72	Ohio	Grove City, Ohio	FA
Dillon, Jerry (1)	LB	6-3	221	9/17/69	East Carolina	Lake Placid, Fla.	FA
Drake, Troy	T	6-6	268	5/15/72	Indiana	Byron, Ill.	FA
Ellis, Jamal	CB	5-10	192	6/21/72	Duke	Dallas, Tex.	FA
George, Chris	WR	5-10	188	11/27/71	Glenville State	Clarkesburg, W.Va.	FA
Henesey, Brian (1)	RB	5-10	215	12/10/69	Bucknell	Radnor, Pa.	FA
Hutton, Tom	P-K	6-1	186	7/8/72	Tennessee	Memphis, Tenn.	FA
Jefferson, Greg	DE	6-3	256	8/31/71	Central Florida	Orlando, Fla.	D3a
Johnson, George	CB	5-10	186	8/22/72	Bowling Green	Sarasota, Fla.	FA
Jones, Chris T.	WR	6-3	210	8/7/71	Miami	Palm Beach, Fla.	D3b
Jones, Kendrick	WR	5-8	185	12/1/72	Tennessee	Collierville, Tenn.	FA
Kearney, Jay (1)	WR	6-1	195	9/29/71	West Virginia	Piscataway, N.J.	FA
Lee, Reginald	LB	6-2	241	11/27/73	Youngstown State	Miami, Fla.	FA
Lillibridge, Marc	LB	6-1	232	2/18/72	Iowa State	Marion, Iowa	FA
Mamula, Mike	LB-DE	6-4	248	8/14/73	Boston College	Lackawanna, N.Y.	D1
Marshall, Malcom	RB	6-1	246	8/29/72	North Carolina	Winston-Salem, N.C.	FA
McCrary, Fred	RB	6-0	210	9/19/72	Mississippi State	Naples, Fla.	D6
Mundy, Aaron (1)	TE	6-5	252	12/9/71	Virginia	Hampton, Va.	FA
Nau, Jeremy	LB	6-4	233	1/28/72	Notre Dame	Hammond, Ind.	FA
O'Brien, Chris	T	6-5	291	8/23/72	Central Michigan	Northville, Mich.	FA
Owens, Gerald	DT	6-2	283	7/29/69	Florida State	Ft. Lauderdale, Fla.	FA
Pribnow, Kerry	T	6-5	290	7/30/72	Montana	Wolf Point, Mont.	FA
Rudolph, Joe	G	6-1	282	7/21/72	Wisconsin	Belle Vernon, Pa.	FA
Smothers, Howard	T	6-3	285	11/16/73	Bethune-Cookman	Jacksonville, Fla.	D7b
Sneathen, Bob	LB	6-1	224	5/22/71	Rutgers	Vineland, N.J.	FA
Solomon, Freddie	WR-KR	5-10	180	8/15/72	South Carolina State	Alachua, Fla.	FA
Taylor, Bobby	CB	6-3	208	12/28/73	Notre Dame	Houston, Tex.	D2a
Wills, Shawn	RB	5-10	185	6/22/70	UCLA	Hanford, Calif.	FA
Witherspoon, Derrick (1)	RB	5-10	197	2/14/71	Clemson	Sumter, S.C.	FA
Wright, Sylvester	LB	6-2	244	12/30/71	Kansas	Detroit, Mich.	FA

The term NFL Rookie is defined as a player who is in his first season of professional football and has not been on the roster of another professional football team for any regular-season or postseason games. A Rookie is designated by an "R" on NFL rosters. Players who have been active in another professional football league or players who have NFL experience, including either preseason training camp or being on an Active List or Inactive List, or on Reserve/Injured or Reserve/Physically Unable to Perform for fewer than six regular-season games, are termed NFL First-Year Players. An NFL First-Year Player is designated by a "1" on NFL rosters. Thereafter, a player is credited with an additional year of experience for each season in which he accumulates six games on the Active List or Inactive List, or on Reserve/Injured or Reserve/Physically Unable to Perform.

NOTES

ST. LOUIS RAMS

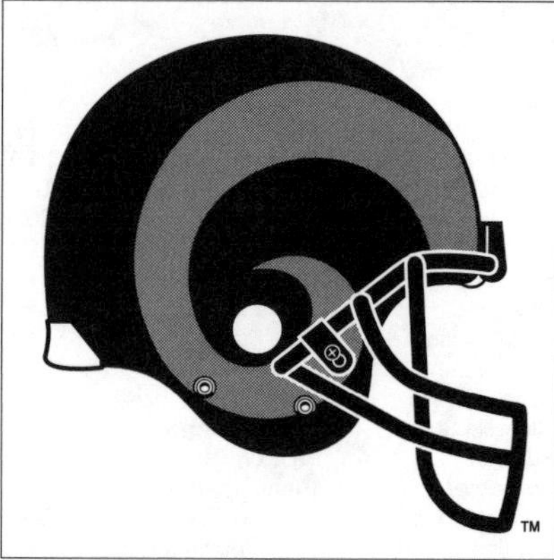

National Football Conference
Western Division
Team Colors: Royal Blue, Gold, and White
Business Address:
Matthews-Dickey Boys Club
4245 North Kingshighway
St. Louis, Missouri 63115-1276
Telephone: TBA

CLUB OFFICIALS

Owner/Chairman: Georgia Frontiere
President: John Shaw
Vice President-Football Operations: Steve Ortmayer
Vice President-Media and Community Relations: Marshall Klein
Director of Player Personnel: John Becker
Administrator of Pro Personnel: Jack Faulkner
Executive Director: Mary Olson-Kromolowski
Treasurer: Jeff Brewer
Director of Operations: John Oswald
Director of Public Relations: Rick Smith
Head Trainer: Jim Anderson
Equipment Manager: Todd Hewitt
Scouts: Lawrence McCutcheon, David Razzano, Pete Russell, Harley Sewell, Frank Trump, Ron Waller
Stadium: Busch Memorial Stadium
•**Capacity:** 57,191
200 Stadium Plaza
St. Louis, Missouri 63102
Playing Surface: AstroTurf
Training Camp: Maryville University
St. Louis, Missouri 63141

1995 SCHEDULE

PRESEASON

Aug. 5	at Seattle	7:00
Aug. 12	at Los Angeles	TBA
Aug. 18	at Jacksonville	7:00
Aug. 25	at San Diego	7:30

REGULAR SEASON

Sept. 3	at Green Bay	12:00
Sept. 10	**New Orleans**	12:00
Sept. 17	at Carolina	1:00
Sept. 24	**Chicago**	12:00
Oct. 1	at Indianapolis	12:00
Oct. 8	Open Date	
Oct. 12	**Atlanta** (Thursday)	7:00
Oct. 22	**San Francisco**	3:00
Oct. 29	at Philadelphia	1:00
Nov. 5	at New Orleans	12:00
Nov. 12	**Carolina**	12:00
Nov. 19	at Atlanta	1:00
Nov. 26	at San Francisco	1:00
Dec. 3	at New York Jets	1:00
Dec. 10	**Buffalo**	12:00
Dec. 17	**Washington**	12:00
Dec. 24	**Miami**	3:00

RECORD HOLDERS

INDIVIDUAL RECORDS—CAREER

Category	Name	Performance
Rushing (Yds.)	Eric Dickerson, 1983-87	7,245
Passing (Yds.)	Jim Everett, 1986-1993	23,758
Passing (TDs)	Roman Gabriel, 1962-1972	154
Receiving (No.)	Henry Ellard, 1983-1993	593
Receiving (Yds.)	Henry Ellard, 1983-1993	9,761
Interceptions	Ed Meador, 1959-1970	46
Punting (Avg.)	Danny Villanueva, 1960-64	44.2
Punt Return (Avg.)	Henry Ellard, 1983-1992	11.3
Kickoff Return (Avg.)	Tom Wilson, 1956-1961	27.1
Field Goals	Mike Lansford, 1982-1990	158
Touchdowns (Tot.)	Eric Dickerson, 1983-87	58
Points	Mike Lansford, 1982-1990	789

INDIVIDUAL RECORDS—SINGLE SEASON

Category	Name	Performance
Rushing (Yds.)	Eric Dickerson, 1984	*2,105
Passing (Yds.)	Jim Everett, 1989	4,310
Passing (TDs)	Jim Everett, 1988	31
Receiving (No.)	Henry Ellard, 1988	86
Receiving (Yds.)	Elroy (Crazylegs) Hirsch, 1951	1,425
Interceptions	Dick (Night Train) Lane, 1952	*14
Punting (Avg.)	Danny Villanueva, 1962	45.5
Punt Return (Avg.)	Woodley Lewis, 1952	18.5
Kickoff Return (Avg.)	Verda (Vitamin T) Smith, 1950	33.7
Field Goals	David Ray, 1973	30
Touchdowns (Tot.)	Eric Dickerson, 1983	20
Points	David Ray, 1973	130

INDIVIDUAL RECORDS—SINGLE GAME

Category	Name	Performance
Rushing (Yds.)	Eric Dickerson, 1-4-86	248
Passing (Yds.)	Norm Van Brocklin, 9-28-51	*554
Passing (TDs)	Many times.	5
	Last time by Jim Everett, 9-25-88	
Receiving (No.)	Tom Fears, 12-3-50	*18
Receiving (Yds.)	Willie Anderson, 11-26-89	*336
Interceptions	Many times.	3
	Last time by Pat Thomas, 10-7-79	
Field Goals	Bob Waterfield, 12-9-51	5
Touchdowns (Tot.)	Bob Shaw, 12-11-49	4
	Elroy (Crazylegs) Hirsch, 9-28-51	4
	Harold Jackson, 10-14-73	4
Points	Bob Shaw, 12-11-49	24
	Elroy (Crazylegs) Hirsch, 9-28-51	24
	Harold Jackson, 10-14-73	24

*NFL Record

COACHING HISTORY

Cleveland 1937-1945, Los Angeles 1946-1994 (411-369-20)

1937-38	Hugo Bezdek*	1-13-0
1938	Art Lewis	4-4-0
1939-42	Earl (Dutch) Clark	16-26-2
1944	Aldo (Buff) Donelli	4-6-0
1945-46	Adam Walsh	16-5-1
1947	Bob Snyder	6-6-0
1948-49	Clark Shaughnessy	14-8-3
1950-52	Joe Stydahar**	19-9-0
1952-54	Hamp Pool	23-11-2
1955-59	Sid Gillman	28-32-1
1960-62	Bob Waterfield***	9-24-1
1962-65	Harland Svare	14-31-3
1966-70	George Allen	49-19-4
1971-72	Tommy Prothro	14-12-2
1973-77	Chuck Knox	57-20-1
1978-82	Ray Malavasi	43-36-0
1983-91	John Robinson	79-74-0
1992-94	Chuck Knox	15-33-0

*Released after three games in 1938
**Resigned after one game in 1952
***Resigned after eight games in 1962

BUSCH MEMORIAL STADIUM

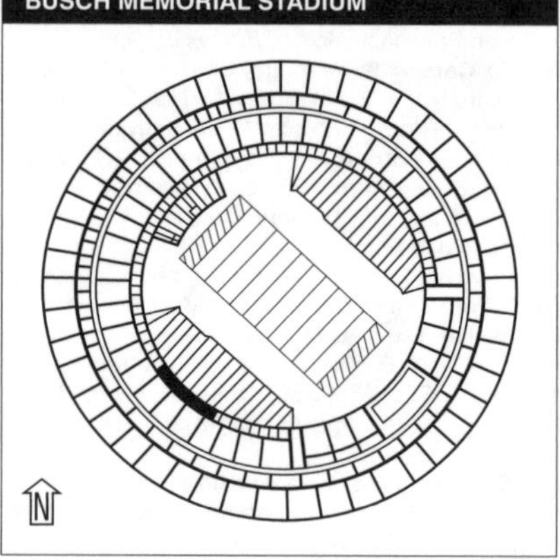

1994 TEAM RECORD

PRESEASON (0-4)

Date	Result		Opponents
8/6	L	6-14	vs. Green Bay at Madison
8/13	L	10-28	New England
8/20	L	20-29	L.A. Raiders
8/25	L	6-24	at San Diego

REGULAR SEASON (4-12)

Date	Result		Opponents	Att.
9/4	W	14-12	Arizona	32,969
9/11	L	13-31	at Atlanta	55,378
9/18	L	19-34	San Francisco	56,479
9/25	W	16-0	at Kansas City	78,184
10/2	L	5- 8	Atlanta	34,599
10/9	L	17-24	at Green Bay	58,911
10/16	W	17-10	N.Y. Giants	40,474
10/23	L	34-37	at New Orleans	47,908
11/6	W	27-21	Denver	48,103
11/13	L	17-20	L.A. Raiders	65,208
11/20	L	27-31	at San Francisco	62,774
11/27	L	17-31	at San Diego	59,579
12/4	L	15-31	New Orleans	34,960
12/11	L	14-24	at Tampa Bay	34,150
12/18	L	13-27	at Chicago	56,276
12/24	L	21-24	Washington	25,705

(OT) Overtime

SCORE BY PERIODS

Rams	79	100	36	71	0	—	286
Opponents	79	124	74	88	0	—	365

ATTENDANCE

Home 338,497 Away 453,160 Total 791,657
Single-game home record, 69,898 (11-9-92)
Single-season home record, 553,979 (1992)

1994 TEAM STATISTICS

	Rams	Opp.
Total First Downs	274	333
Rushing	80	103
Passing	163	198
Penalty	31	32
Third Down: Made/Att	80/204	101/221
Third Down Pct.	39.2	45.7
Fourth Down: Made/Att	6/14	5/11
Fourth Down Pct.	42.9	45.5
Total Net Yards	4747	5170
Avg. Per Game	296.7	323.1
Total Plays	944	1063
Avg. Per Play	5.0	4.9
Net Yards Rushing	1389	1781
Avg. Per Game	86.8	111.3
Total Rushes	397	496
Net Yards Passing	3358	3389
Avg. Per Game	209.9	211.8
Sacked/Yards Lost	35/239	26/159
Gross Yards	3597	3548
Att./Completions	512/291	541/320
Completion Pct.	56.8	59.1
Had Intercepted	18	14
Punts/Avg.	78/44.8	74/42.0
Net Punting Avg.	78/34.3	74/32.5
Penalties/Yards Lost	112/922	114/1015
Fumbles/Ball Lost	26/13	15/6
Touchdowns	33	42
Rushing	6	12
Passing	23	23
Returns	4	7
Avg. Time of Possession	27:59	32:01

1994 INDIVIDUAL STATISTICS

PASSING	Att.	Comp.	Yds.	Pct.	TD	Int.	Tkld.	Rate
Miller	317	173	2104	54.6	16	14	28/193	73.6
Chandler	176	108	1352	61.4	7	2	7/46	93.8
Maddox	19	10	141	52.6	0	2	0/0	37.3
Rams	512	291	3597	56.8	23	18	35/239	79.0
Opponents	541	320	3548	59.1	23	14	26/159	82.1

SCORING	TD R	TD P	TD Rt	PAT	FG	Saf	PTS
Zendejas	0	0	0	28/28	18/23	0	82
Drayton	0	6	0	0/0	0/0	0	36
Anderson	0	5	0	0/0	0/0	0	30
Bettis	3	1	0	0/0	0/0	0	28
Kinchen	1	3	0	0/0	0/0	0	24
Bruce	0	3	0	0/0	0/0	0	18
Hester	0	3	0	0/0	0/0	0	18
J. Bailey	1	0	0	0/0	0/0	0	6
R. Bailey	0	0	1	0/0	0/0	0	6
Chandler	1	0	0	0/0	0/0	0	6
Griffith	0	1	0	0/0	0/0	0	6
Lyght	0	0	1	0/0	0/0	0	6
Newman	0	0	1	0/0	0/0	0	6
Ross	0	1	0	0/0	0/0	0	6
Wright	0	0	1	0/0	0/0	0	6
Gilbert	0	0	0	0/0	0/0	1	2
Rams	6	23	4	28/28	18/23	1	286
Opponents	12	23	7	38/38	23/29	0	365

2-Point conversions: Bettis (2). Team: 2-5.

RUSHING	Att.	Yds.	Avg.	LG	TD
Bettis	319	1025	3.2	19	3
Miller	20	100	5.0	16	0
Chandler	18	61	3.4	22	1
Kinchen	1	44	44.0	44t	1
J. Bailey	11	35	3.2	9	1
Lang	6	34	5.7	17	0
Griffith	9	30	3.3	7	0
Hester	2	28	14.0	24	0
Lester	7	14	2.0	8	0
Anderson	1	11	11.0	11	0
Drayton	1	4	4.0	4	0
Bruce	1	2	2.0	2	0
Maddox	1	1	1.0	1	0
Rams	397	1389	3.5	44t	6
Opponents	496	1781	3.6	27t	12

RECEIVING	No.	Yds.	Avg.	LG	TD
J. Bailey	58	516	8.9	28	0
Anderson	46	945	20.5	72t	5
Hester	45	644	14.3	41	3
Drayton	32	276	8.6	22t	6
Bettis	31	293	9.5	34	1
Kinchen	23	352	15.3	43	3
Bruce	21	272	13.0	34t	3
Griffith	16	113	7.1	13	1
Lang	8	60	7.5	12	0
Buchanan	5	60	12.0	18	0
Brantley	4	29	7.3	10	0
Ross	1	36	36.0	36t	1
Lester	1	1	1.0	1	0
Rams	291	3597	12.4	72t	23
Opponents	320	3548	11.1	71t	23

INTERCEPTIONS	No.	Yds.	Avg.	LG	TD
Pope	3	66	22.0	51	0
Henley	3	46	15.3	23	0
Newman	2	46	23.0	24	1
Phifer	2	7	3.5	7	0
Lyle	2	1	0.5	1	0
Kelly	1	31	31.0	31	0
Lyght	1	14	14.0	14	0
Rams	14	211	15.1	51	1
Opponents	18	213	11.8	50t	2

PUNTING	No.	Yds.	Avg.	In 20	LG
Landeta	78	3494	44.8	23	62
Rams	78	3494	44.8	23	62
Opponents	74	3106	42.0	20	59

PUNT RETURNS	No.	FC	Yds.	Avg.	LG	TD
J. Bailey	19	4	153	8.1	24	0
Kinchen	16	5	158	9.9	40	0
Brantley	3	1	18	6.0	7	0
R. Bailey	1	0	103	103.0	103t	1
Lyght	1	0	29	29.0	27	0
Rams	40	10	461	11.5	103t	1
Opponents	47	8	637	13.6	85t	3

KICKOFF RETURNS	No.	Yds.	Avg.	LG	TD
Lang	27	626	23.2	57	0
Kinchen	21	510	24.3	46	0
J. Bailey	12	260	21.7	32	0
Brantley	7	150	21.4	33	0
Griffith	2	35	17.5	21	0
Farr	1	16	16.0	16	0
Lester	1	8	8.0	8	0
Rams	71	1605	22.6	57	0
Opponents	63	1446	23.0	98t	2

1995 DRAFT CHOICES

Round	Name	Pos.	College
1	Kevin Carter	DE	Florida
2	Zach Wiegert	T	Nebraska
	Jesse James	G	Mississippi State
3	Steve McLaughlin	K	Arizona
4	Lovell Pinkney	TE	Texas
5	Mike Scurlock	DB	Arizona
7	Gerald McBurrows	DB	Kansas
	Herman O'Berry	DB	Oregon
	Bronzell Miller	DE	Utah
	Johnny Thomas	WR	Arizona State

ST. LOUIS RAMS

1995 VETERAN ROSTER

No.	Name	Pos.	Ht.	Wt.	Birthdate	NFL Exp.	College	Hometown	How Acq.	'94 Games/ Starts
77	† Ashmore, Darryl	T	6-7	300	11/1/69	4	Northwestern	Peoria, Ill.	D7-'92	11/3
21	Bailey, Johnny	RB	5-8	180	3/17/67	6	Texas A&I	Houston, Tex.	FA-'94	14/0
28	Bailey, Robert	CB	5-9	176	9/3/68	5	Miami	Miami, Fla.	D4-'91	16/2
71	Belin, Chuck	G	6-2	312	10/27/70	3	Wisconsin	Milwaukee, Wis.	D5b-'93	14/6
36	Bettis, Jerome	RB	5-11	243	2/16/72	3	Notre Dame	Detroit, Mich.	D1-'93	16/16
33	Bostic, James	RB	5-11	230	3/13/72	2	Auburn	Ft. Lauderdale, Fla.	D3b-'94	0*
88	Brantley, Chris	WR	5-10	180	12/12/70	2	Rutgers	Teaneck, N.J.	D4-'94	15/0
61	Brostek, Bern	C	6-3	300	9/11/66	6	Washington	Honolulu, Hawaii	D1-'90	10/10
80	Bruce, Isaac	WR	6-0	178	11/10/72	2	Memphis State	Ft. Lauderdale, Fla.	D2a-'94	12/0
51	# Bush, Blair	C	6-3	275	11/25/56	18	Washington	Palos Verdes, Calif.	PB(GB)-'92	16/0
56	Conlan, Shane	LB	6-3	235	3/4/64	9	Penn State	Frewsburg, N.Y.	UFA(Buff)-'93	15/15
42	Cook, Marv	TE	6-4	234	2/24/66	7	Iowa	West Branch, Iowa	FA-'95	16/8*
29	# Davis, Dexter	CB	5-10	184	3/20/70	5	Clemson	Sumter, S.C.	FA-'93	4/0
46	Dorn, Torin	CB	6-0	190	2/29/68	5	North Carolina	Southfield, Mich.	FA-'95	0*
84	Drayton, Troy	TE	6-3	255	6/29/70	3	Penn State	Steelton, Pa.	D2-'93	16/16
67	Edwards, Ronald	T	6-5	311	9/18/71	2	North Carolina A&T	Temple Hill, Md.	W(Cin)-'94	0*
75	Farr, D'Marco	DT	6-1	270	6/9/71	2	Washington	Richmond, Calif.	FA-'94	10/3
70	Gandy, Wayne	T	6-4	289	2/10/71	2	Auburn	Haines City, Fla.	D1-'94	16/9
43	Gary, Cleveland	RB	6-0	235	5/4/66	7	Miami	Indiantown, Fla.	UFA(Mia)-'95	2/0*
90	Gilbert, Sean	DT	6-4	315	4/10/70	4	Pittsburgh	Aliquippa, Pa.	D1-'92	14/14
79	Goeas, Leo	G	6-4	300	8/15/66	6	Hawaii	Honolulu, Hawaii	T(SD)-'93	13/13
24	# Henderson, Wymon	CB	5-10	188	12/15/61	10	Nevada-Las Vegas	North Miami Beach, Fla.	FA-'93	15/1
86	Hester, Jessie	WR	5-11	175	1/21/63	10	Florida State	Belle Glade, Fla.	FA-'94	16/15
57	Homco, Thomas	LB	6-0	245	1/8/70	3	Northwestern	Highland, Ind.	FA-'92	15/0
31	Israel, Steve	CB	5-11	186	3/16/69	4	Pittsburgh	Lawnside, N.J.	D2-'92	10/2
50	Jenkins, Carlos	LB	6-3	217	7/12/68	5	Michigan State	Lantana, Fla.	UFA(Minn)-'95	16/16*
72	Jones, Clarence	T	6-6	280	5/6/68	5	Maryland	Long Island, N.Y.	FA-'94	16/16
94	Jones, Ernest	DE	6-2	270	4/1/71	2	Oregon	Utica, N.Y.	D3c-'94	0*
98	Jones, Jimmie	DT	6-4	276	1/9/66	8	Miami	Lake Okeechobee, Fla.	UFA(Dall)-'94	14/14
52	# Kelly, Joe	LB	6-2	235	12/11/64	10	Washington	Los Angeles, Calif.	FA-'94	16/14
81	† Kinchen, Todd	WR	5-11	187	1/7/69	4	Louisiana State	Baton Rouge, La.	D3b-'92	13/0
5	Landeta, Sean	P	6-0	210	1/6/62	11	Towson State	Baltimore, Md.	FA-'93	16/0
34	Lester, Tim	RB	5-9	215	6/15/68	4	Eastern Kentucky	Miami, Fla.	D10-'92	14/4
64	Loneker, Keith	G	6-3	330	6/21/71	3	Kansas	Roselle Park, N.J.	FA-'93	2/2
41	Lyght, Todd	CB	6-0	186	2/9/69	5	Notre Dame	Flint, Mich.	D1-'91	16/16
35	Lyle, Keith	S	6-2	204	4/17/72	2	Virginia	Vienna, Va.	D3a-'94	16/0
8	† Maddox, Tommy	QB	6-4	205	9/2/71	4	UCLA	Shreveport, La.	T(Den)-'94	5/0
9	Martin, Jamie	QB	6-2	215	2/8/70	2	Weber State	Arroyo Grande, Calif.	FA-'94	0*
91	McCants, Keith	DE	6-3	265	4/19/68	6	Alabama	Mobile, Ala.	UFA(Ariz)-'95	12/2*
87	# Middleton, Ron	TE	6-2	262	7/17/65	9	Auburn	Atmore, Ala.	FA-'94	16/3
12	Miller, Chris	QB	6-2	212	8/9/65	9	Oregon	Eugene, Ore.	UFA(Atl)-'94	13/10
26	Newman, Anthony	S	6-0	199	11/25/65	8	Oregon	Beaverton, Ore.	D2a-'88	16/14
95	Ottis, Brad	DE	6-4	272	8/2/72	2	Wayne State	Wahoo, Neb.	D2c-'94	13/0
27	Parker, Anthony	CB	5-10	181	2/11/66	5	Arizona State	Tempe, Ariz.	UFA(Minn)-'95	15/15*
58	Phifer, Roman	LB	6-2	230	3/5/68	5	UCLA	Pineville, N.C.	D2-'91	16/15
97	Robinson, Gerald	DE	6-3	280	5/4/63	9	Auburn	Notasulga, Ala.	PB(SD)-'91	13/0
92	# Rocker, David	DT	6-4	267	3/12/69	5	Auburn	Atlanta, Ga.	FA-'91	11/1
59	Rolling, Henry	LB	6-2	225	9/8/65	9	Nevada-Reno	Henderson, Nev.	UFA(SD)-'93	9/2
	Russell, Leonard	RB	6-2	235	11/17/69	5	Arizona State	Long Beach, Calif.	FA-'95	14/13*
11	Rypien, Mark	QB	6-4	234	10/2/62	10	Washington State	Spokane, Wash.	FA-'95	6/3*
78	Slater, Jackie	T	6-4	285	5/27/54	20	Jackson State	Jackson, Miss.	D3-'76	12/7
60	Stokes, Fred	DE	6-3	274	3/14/64	9	Georgia Southern	Vidalia, Ga.	UFA(Wash)-'93	16/15
69	White, Dwayne	G	6-2	315	2/10/67	6	Alcorn State	Philadelphia, Pa.	UFA(NYJ)-'95	16/16*
89	Wright, Alexander	WR	6-0	195	7/19/67	6	Auburn	Albany, Ga.	UFA(Raid)-'95	16/15*
32	Wright, Toby	S	5-11	203	11/19/70	2	Nebraska	Phoenix, Ariz.	D2b-'94	16/2
76	Young, Robert	DE	6-6	273	1/29/69	5	Mississippi State	Jackson, Miss.	D5-'91	16/16
10	Zendejas, Tony	K	5-8	165	5/15/60	11	Nevada-Reno	Chino, Calif.	PB(Hou)-'91	16/0
63	Zeno, Lance	G	6-4	279	4/15/67	3	UCLA	Fountain Valley, Calif.	FA-'95	0*

* Bostic inactive for 10 games in '94; Cook played 16 games with Chicago; Dorn last active with L.A. Raiders in '93; Edwards inactive for 7 games with Cincinnati, 6 games with L.A. Rams; Gary played 2 games with Miami; Jenkins played 16 games with Minnesota; E. Jones missed '94 season because of injury; J. Martin active for 1 game but did not play; McCants played 4 games with Houston, 8 games with Arizona; Parker played 15 games with Minnesota; Russell played 14 games with Denver; Rypien played 6 games with Cleveland; White played 16 games with N.Y. Jets; A. Wright played 16 games with L.A. Raiders; Zeno last active with Green Bay in '93.

\# Unrestricted free agent; subject to developments.

† Restricted free agent; subject to developments.

Players lost through free agency (5): WR Willie Anderson (Ind; 16 games in '94), QB Chris Chandler (Hou; 12), RB David Lang (Dall; 13), G Tom Newberry (Pitt; 15), CB-S Marquez Pope (SF; 16).

Players lost through Expansion Draft (2): WR Richard Buchanan (Car; 3 games in '94), RB Howard Griffith (Car; 16).

Also played with Rams in '94—TE Rickey Brady (1 game), LB Brett Collins (2), G Brad Fichtel (1), CB Darryl Henley (15), LB Chris Martin (14), WR Jermaine Ross (4).

COACHING STAFF

Head Coach,
Rich Brooks

Pro Career: Named nineteenth head coach of the Rams on February 10, 1995. Coached special teams and fundamentals in 1971-72 for the Los Angeles Rams under head coach Tommy Prothro. During that time, Rams kick returner Travis Williams led the NFL in 1971 with 29.72-yard average and set an NFL record with a 105-yard kickoff return versus New Orleans. Returned to the NFL in 1975 as defensive back and special teams coach with the San Francisco 49ers.

Background: Played single-wing tailback, defensive back, and quarterback for Tommy Prothro at Oregon State from 1959-1962. Was an assistant coach at Oregon State in 1963, then spent 1964 season at Norte Del Rio High School in Sacramento, Calif. In 1965, Brooks returned to his alma mater as a defensive end and line coach. Rejoined Prothro at UCLA in 1970 as linebackers coach. Returned to Oregon State in 1973 as defensive coordinator. Returned to UCLA as linebacker coach in 1976. Head coach at Oregon from 1977-1994.

Personal: Born August 10, 1941, in Forest, Calif. Graduated from Oregon State in 1963 with bachelor of science degree in physical education and earned a master's degree in education from Oregon State in 1964. Brooks and wife Karen have four children: Denny, Kasey, Kerri, and Brady.

Assistant Coaches

Nick Aliotti, secondary; born May 19, 1954, Pittsburg, Calif. Running back U.C.-Davis 1972-75. No pro playing experience. College coach: U.C.-Davis 1976-77, Oregon 1978-79, 1988-94, Oregon State 1980-83, Chico State 1984-87. Pro coach: Joined Rams in 1995.

Steve Brown, defensive assistant-quality control; born March 20, 1960, Sacramento, Calif. Defensive back Oregon 1978-1982. Pro cornerback Houston Oilers 1983-1990. Pro coach: Joined Rams in 1995.

Chris Clausen, strength and conditioning coordinator; born February 21, 1958, Evergreen Park, Ill. Cornerback Indiana 1976-79. No pro playing experience. College coach: San Diego State 1987-88. Pro coach: San Diego Chargers 1989-1991, joined Rams in 1992.

Steve Greatwood, offensive line-tight ends; born August 15, 1958, Portland, Ore. Guard Oregon 1976-79. No pro playing experience. College coach: Oregon 1982-1994. Pro coach: Joined Rams in 1995.

Mike Martz, receivers; born May 13, 1951, Sioux Falls, S.D. Tight end San Diego Mesa (Calif.) J.C. 1969-1970, U.C. Santa Barbara 1971, Fresno State 1972. No pro playing experience. College coach: San Diego Mesa (Calif.) J.C. 1974, 1976-77, San Jose State 1975, Santa Ana (Calif.) J.C. 1978-79, Fresno State 1979, Pacific 1980-81, Minnesota 1982-83, Arizona State 1984-1991. Pro coach: Joined Rams in 1992.

Don (Deek) Pollard, defensive line; born September 16, 1939, Roodhouse, Ill. Defensive back Western Illinois 1957-1961. No pro playing experience. College coach: Western Illinois 1971-73, Florida State 1974-75, Oklahoma State 1976-78, Central Florida 1990-93, Boston College 1994. Pro coach: New York Giants 1979-1981, Denver Gold (USFL) 1983, Arizona Wranglers (USFL) 1984-85, Cleveland Browns 1989, joined Rams in 1995.

Dan Radakovich, offensive line; born November 27, 1935, Duquesne, Pa. Center-linebacker Penn State 1953-56. No pro playing experience. College coach: Penn State 1957-1969, Cincinnati 1970, Colorado 1972-73, North Carolina State 1982, Robert Morris 1993-94. Pro coach: Pittsburgh Steelers 1971, 1974-77, San Francisco 49ers 1978, Los Angeles Rams 1979-1981, Denver Broncos 1983, Minnesota Vikings 1984, New York Jets 1985-88, Cleveland Browns 1989-90, rejoined Rams in 1995.

John Ramsdell, offensive assistant-quality control; born August 16, 1954, Lafayette, Ind. Running back Springfield (Mass.) College 1972-75. No pro playing experience. College coach: San Francisco State 1976-77, Long Beach State 1978, Pacific 1979-82, Oregon 1983-1994. Pro coach: Joined Rams in 1995.

Johnny Roland, assistant head coach-running backs; born May 21, 1943, Corpus Christi, Tex. Running back Missouri 1961-65. Pro running back St. Louis Cardinals 1966-1972, New York Giants 1973. College coach: Notre Dame 1975. Pro coach: Green Bay Packers 1974, Philadelphia Eagles 1976-78, Chicago Bears 1983-1992, New York Jets 1993-94, joined Rams in 1995.

Jack Reilly, offensive coordinator-quarterbacks; born May 22, 1945, Boston, Mass. Quarterback Washington State 1963, Santa Monica (Calif.) J.C. 1964, Long Beach State 1965-66. No pro playing experience. College coach: El Camino (Calif.) J.C. 1980-84 (head coach 1981-84), Utah 1985-89. Pro coach: San Diego Chargers 1990-93, Los Angeles Raiders 1994, joined Rams in 1995.

Dick Selcer, linebackers; born August 22, 1937, Cincinnati, Ohio. Running back Notre Dame 1955-58. No pro playing experience. College coach: Xavier, Ohio 1962-64, 1970-71 (head coach), Cincinnati 1965-66, Brown 1967-69, Wisconsin 1972-74, Kansas State 1975-77, Southwestern Louisiana 1978-1980. Pro coach: Houston Oilers 1981-83, Cincinnati Bengals 1984-1991, joined Rams in 1992.

Wayne Sevier, special teams; born July 3, 1941, San Diego, Calif. Quarterback Chaffey (Calif.) J.C. 1960, San Diego State 1961-62. No pro playing experience. College coach: California Western 1968-69. Pro coach: St. Louis Cardinals 1974-75, Atlanta Falcons 1976, San Diego Chargers 1979-1980, 1987-88, Washington Redskins 1981-86, 1989-1993, joined Rams in 1994.

Willie Shaw, defensive coordinator; born January 11, 1944, San Diego, Calif. Cornerback New Mexico 1966-68. No pro playing experience. College coach: San Diego City College 1970-73, Stanford 1974-76, 1989-91, Long Beach State 1977-78, Oregon 1979, Arizona State 1980-84. Pro coach: Detroit Lions 1985-88, Minnesota Vikings 1992-93, San Diego Chargers 1994, joined Rams in 1995.

1995 FIRST-YEAR ROSTER

Name	Pos.	Ht.	Wt.	Birthdate	College	Hometown	How Acq.
Brady, Rickey (1)	TE	6-4	246	11/19/71	Oklahoma	Oklahoma City, Okla.	D6a-'94
Brooks, Steve (1)	TE	6-5	245	6/2/71	Occidental	Ventura, Calif.	FA
Carter, Kevin	DE	6-5	274	9/21/73	Florida	Tallahassee, Fla.	D1
Jackson, Yonnie (1)	TE	6-2	260	2/28/71	Southern California	Stockton, Calif.	FA
James, Jesse	T	6-4	318	9/16/71	Mississippi State	Mobile, Ala.	D2b
McBurrows, Gerald	CB-S	5-11	188	10/7/73	Kansas	Detroit, Mich.	D7a
McLaughlin, Steve	K	6-0	167	10/2/71	Arizona	Tucson, Ariz.	D3
Miller, Bronzell	DE-LB	6-3	247	10/12/71	Utah	Federal Way, Wash.	D7c
Morris, Cree (1)	QB	6-7	230	12/17/70	St. Mary's	Escondido, Calif.	FA
Morris, Luther	TE	6-3	235	1/30/73	Northwestern	Chicago, Ill.	FA
O'Bannon, Turhon (1)	WR	6-0	195	3/23/70	New Mexico	Los Angeles, Calif.	FA
O'Berry, Herman	CB-S	5-9	195	10/7/73	Oregon	Highlands, Calif.	D7b
Patterson, Roosevelt (1)	G	6-3	315	6/12/70	Alabama	Mobile, Ala.	FA
Pinkney, Lovell	WR-TE	6-4	248	8/18/72	Texas	Washington, D.C.	D4
Ross, Jermaine (1)	WR	5-11	192	4/27/71	Purdue	Jeffersonville, Ind.	FA
Scurlock, Mike	CB-S	5-10	197	2/26/72	Arizona	Tucson, Ariz.	D5
Thomas, Johnny	WR	5-10	173	7/11/71	Arizona State	San Bernardino, Calif.	D7d
Wiegert, Zach	T	6-4	311	8/16/72	Nebraska	Fremont, Calif.	D2a
Williams, Jay (1)	DE	6-3	266	10/13/71	Wake Forest	Washington, D.C.	FA

The term NFL Rookie is defined as a player who is in his first season of professional football and has not been on the roster of another professional football team for any regular-season or postseason games. A Rookie is designated by an "R" on NFL rosters. Players who have been active in another professional football league or players who have NFL experience, including either preseason training camp or being on an Active List or Inactive List, or on Reserve/Injured or Reserve/Physically Unable to Perform for fewer than six regular-season games, are termed NFL First-Year Players. An NFL First-Year Player is designated by a "1" on NFL rosters. Thereafter, a player is credited with an additional year of experience for each season in which he accumulates six games on the Active List or Inactive List, or on Reserve/Injured or Reserve/Physically Unable to Perform.

NOTES

SAN FRANCISCO 49ERS

National Football Conference
Western Division
Team Colors: Forty Niners Gold and Scarlet
4949 Centennial Boulevard
Santa Clara, California 95054
Telephone: (408) 562-4949

CLUB OFFICIALS

Owner: Edward J. DeBartolo, Jr.
President: Carmen Policy
Vice President and Director of Football Operations: Dwight Clark
Vice President-Business Operations & C.F.O.: Keith Simon
Special Assistant to the President: John McVay
Director of Player Personnel: Vinny Cerrato
Coordinator of Pro Personnel-NFC: Allan Webb
Coordinator of Pro Personnel-AFC: Joe Collins
Director of Public/Community Relations: Rodney Knox
Director of Marketing/Promotions: Laurie Albrecht
Coordinator of Football Operations: Neal Dahlen
Ticket Manager: Lynn Carrozzi
Director of Stadium Operations: Murlan (Mo) Fowell
Video Director: Robert Yanagi
Trainer: Lindsy McLean
Equipment Manager: Bronco Hinek
Stadium: Candlestick Park • **Capacity:** 69,497
San Francisco, California 94124
Playing Surface: Grass
Training Camp: Sierra Community College
Rocklin, California 95677

1995 SCHEDULE

PRESEASON

July 29	at Denver	7:00
Aug. 5	vs. Denver at Tokyo	10:00
Aug. 13	at San Diego	5:00
Aug. 19	**Carolina**	5:00
Aug. 26	**Seattle**	5:00

REGULAR SEASON

Sept. 3	at New Orleans	12:00
Sept. 10	**Atlanta**	1:00
Sept. 17	**New England**	1:00
Sept. 25	at Detroit (Monday)	9:00
Oct. 1	**New York Giants**	1:00
Oct. 8	Open Date	
Oct. 15	at Indianapolis	12:00
Oct. 22	at St. Louis	3:00
Oct. 29	**New Orleans**	1:00
Nov. 5	**Carolina**	1:00
Nov. 12	at Dallas	3:00
Nov. 20	at Miami (Monday)	9:00
Nov. 26	**St. Louis**	1:00
Dec. 3	**Buffalo**	5:00
Dec. 10	at Carolina	1:00
Dec. 18	**Minnesota** (Monday)	6:00
Dec. 24	at Atlanta	1:00

RECORD HOLDERS

INDIVIDUAL RECORDS—CAREER

Category	Name	Performance
Rushing (Yds.)	Joe Perry, 1950-1960, 1963	7,344
Passing (Yds.)	Joe Montana, 1979-1992	35,124
Passing (TDs)	Joe Montana, 1979-1992	244
Receiving (No.)	Jerry Rice, 1985-1994	820
Receiving (Yds.)	Jerry Rice, 1985-1994	13,275
Interceptions	Ronnie Lott, 1981-1990	51
Punting (Avg.)	Tommy Davis, 1959-1969	44.7
Punt Return (Avg.)	Manfred Moore, 1974-75	14.7
Kickoff Return (Avg.)	Abe Woodson, 1958-1964	29.4
Field Goals	Ray Wersching, 1977-1987	190
Touchdowns (Tot.)	Jerry Rice, 1985-1994	*139
Points	Ray Wersching, 1977-1987	979

INDIVIDUAL RECORDS—SINGLE SEASON

Category	Name	Performance
Rushing (Yds.)	Roger Craig, 1988	1,502
Passing (Yds.)	Steve Young, 1993	4,023
Passing (TDs)	Steve Young, 1994	35
Receiving (No.)	Jerry Rice, 1994	112
Receiving (Yds.)	Jerry Rice, 1986	1,570
Interceptions	Dave Baker, 1960	10
	Ronnie Lott, 1986	10
Punting (Avg.)	Tommy Davis, 1965	45.8
Punt Return (Avg.)	Dana McLemore, 1982	22.3
Kickoff Return (Avg.)	Joe Arenas, 1953	34.4
Field Goals	Mike Cofer, 1989	29
Touchdowns (Tot.)	Jerry Rice, 1987	23
Points	Jerry Rice, 1987	138

INDIVIDUAL RECORDS—SINGLE GAME

Category	Name	Performance
Rushing (Yds.)	Delvin Williams, 10-31-76	194
Passing (Yds.)	Joe Montana, 10-14-90	476
Passing (TDs)	Joe Montana, 10-14-90	6
Receiving (No.)	Jerry Rice, 11-20-94	16
Receiving (Yds.)	John Taylor, 12-11-89	286
Interceptions	Dave Baker, 12-4-60	*4
Field Goals	Ray Wersching, 10-16-83	6
Touchdowns (Tot.)	Jerry Rice, 10-14-90	5
Points	Jerry Rice, 10-14-90	30

*NFL Record

COACHING HISTORY

(366-287-13)

1950-54	Lawrence (Buck) Shaw	33-25-2
1955	Norman (Red) Strader	4-8-0
1956-58	Frankie Albert	19-17-1
1959-63	Howard (Red) Hickey*	27-27-1
1963-67	Jack Christiansen	26-38-3
1968-75	Dick Nolan	56-56-5
1976	Monte Clark	8-6-0
1977	Ken Meyer	5-9-0
1978	Pete McCulley**	1-8-0
1978	Fred O'Connor	1-6-0
1979-88	Bill Walsh	102-63-1
1989-94	George Seifert	84-24-0

*Resigned after three games in 1963
**Released after nine games in 1978

CANDLESTICK PARK

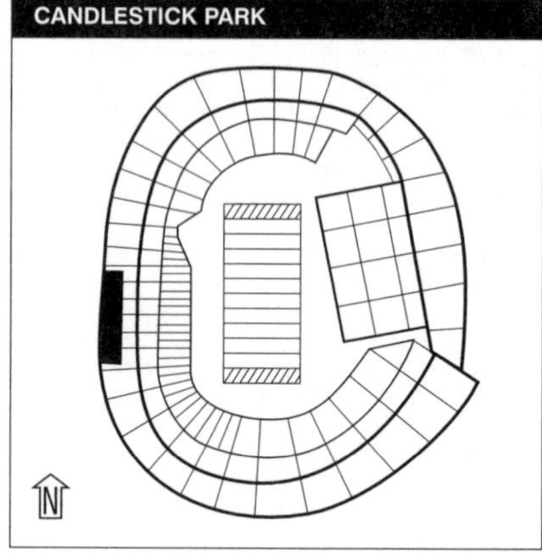

1994 TEAM RECORD

PRESEASON (3-1)

Date	Result		Opponents
8/5	L	7-17	at Arizona
8/12	W	20-3	Denver
8/18	W	30-24	at San Diego
8/26	W	13-9	Seattle

REGULAR SEASON (13-3)

Date	Result		Opponents	Att.
9/5	W	44-14	L.A. Raiders	68,032
9/11	L	17-24	at Kansas City	79,907
9/18	W	34-19	at L.A. Rams	56,479
9/25	W	24-13	New Orleans	63,971
10/2	L	8-40	Philadelphia	64,843
10/9	W	27-21	at Detroit	77,340
10/16	W	42- 3	at Atlanta	67,298
10/23	W	41-16	Tampa Bay	62,741
11/6	W	37-22	at Washington	54,335
11/13	W	21-14	Dallas	69,014
11/20	W	31-27	L.A. Rams	62,774
11/28	W	35-14	at New Orleans	61,304
12/4	W	50-14	Atlanta	60,549
12/11	W	38-15	at San Diego	62,105
12/17	W	42-19	Denver	64,884
12/26	L	14-21	at Minnesota	63,326

POSTSEASON (3-0)

1/7	W	44-15	Chicago	64,644
1/15	W	38-28	Dallas	69,125
1/29	W	49-26	San Diego	74,107

(OT) Overtime

SCORE BY PERIODS

49ers	106	173	103	123	0	—	505
Opponents	62	94	64	76	0	—	296

ATTENDANCE

Home 516,808 Away 522,094 Total 1,038,902

Single-game home record, 69,014 (11-13-94)

Single-season home record, 523,355 (1992)

1994 TEAM STATISTICS

	49ers	Opp.
Total First Downs	362	285
Rushing	122	82
Passing	210	182
Penalty	30	21
Third Down: Made/Att	102/200	87/221
Third Down Pct.	51.0	39.4
Fourth Down: Made/Att	11/18	11/19
Fourth Down Pct.	61.1	57.9
Total Net Yards	6060	4839
Avg. Per Game	378.8	302.4
Total Plays	1037	996
Avg. Per Play	5.8	4.9
Net Yards Rushing	1897	1338
Avg. Per Game	118.6	83.6
Total Rushes	491	375
Net Yards Passing	4163	3501
Avg. Per Game	260.2	218.8
Sacked/Yards Lost	35/199	38/255
Gross Yards	4362	3756
Att./Completions	511/359	583/329
Completion Pct.	70.3	56.4
Had Intercepted	11	23
Punts/Avg.	54/41.4	77/42.5
Net Punting Avg.	54/35.8	77/35.8
Penalties/Yards Lost	109/890	108/912
Fumbles/Ball Lost	25/13	25/12
Touchdowns	66	35
Rushing	23	16
Passing	37	15
Returns	6	4
Avg. Time of Possession	31:38	28:22

1994 INDIVIDUAL STATISTICS

PASSING	Att.	Comp.	Yds.	Pct.	TD	Int.	Tkld.	Rate
S. Young	461	324	3969	70.3	35	10	31/163	112.8
Grbac	50	35	393	70.0	2	1	4/36	98.2
49ers	511	359	4362	70.3	37	11	35/199	111.4
Opponents	583	329	3756	56.4	15	23	38/255	68.1

SCORING	TD R	TD P	TD Rt	PAT	FG	Saf	PTS
Brien	0	0	0	60/62	15/20	0	105
Rice	2	13	0	0/0	0/0	0	92
Watters	6	5	0	0/0	0/0	0	66
Jones	0	9	0	0/0	0/0	0	56
S. Young	7	0	0	0/0	0/0	0	42
Floyd	6	0	0	0/0	0/0	0	36
Taylor	0	5	0	0/0	0/0	0	30
Sanders	0	0	3	0/0	0/0	0	18
Logan	1	1	0	0/0	0/0	0	12
McCaffrey	0	2	0	0/0	0/0	0	12
McDonald	0	0	2	0/0	0/0	0	12
Singleton	0	2	0	0/0	0/0	0	12
Carter	0	0	1	0/0	0/0	0	6
Walker	1	0	0	0/0	0/0	0	6
49ers	23	37	6	60/62	15/20	0	505
Opponents	16	15	4	23/23	15/21	2	296

2-Point conversions: Jones, Rice. Team: 2-4.

RUSHING	Att.	Yds.	Avg.	LG	TD
Watters	239	877	3.7	23	6
Floyd	87	305	3.5	26	6
S. Young	58	293	5.1	27	7
Logan	33	143	4.3	22	1
Loville	31	99	3.2	13	0
Rice	7	93	13.3	28t	2
Walker	13	54	4.2	14	1
Carter	8	34	4.3	18	0
Grbac	13	1	0.1	6	0
Taylor	2	-2	-1.0	1	0
49ers	491	1897	3.9	28t	23
Opponents	375	1338	3.6	44t	16

RECEIVING	No.	Yds.	Avg.	LG	TD
Rice	112	1499	13.4	69t	13
Watters	66	719	10.9	65t	5
Jones	49	670	13.7	69t	9
Taylor	41	531	13.0	35	5
Singleton	21	294	14.0	43t	2
Floyd	19	145	7.6	15	0
Logan	16	97	6.1	15	1
Popson	13	141	10.8	24	0
McCaffrey	11	131	11.9	32	2
Carter	7	99	14.1	44	0
Loville	2	26	13.0	19	0
Carolan	2	10	5.0	6	0
49ers	359	4362	12.2	69t	37
Opponents	329	3756	11.4	90	15

INTERCEPTIONS	No.	Yds.	Avg.	LG	TD
Hanks	7	93	13.3	38	0
Sanders	6	303	50.5	93t	3
McDonald	2	79	39.5	73t	1
D. Hall	2	0	0.0	0	0
Cook	1	18	18.0	18	0
Davis	1	8	8.0	8	0
Drakeford	1	6	6.0	6	0
Plummer	1	1	1.0	1	0
Brown	1	0	0.0	0	0
Norton	1	0	0.0	0	0
49ers	23	508	22.1	93t	4
Opponents	11	107	9.7	36t	1

PUNTING	No.	Yds.	Avg.	In 20	LG
Wilmsmeyer	54	2235	41.4	18	60
49ers	54	2235	41.4	18	60
Opponents	77	3274	42.5	19	65

PUNT RETURNS	No.	FC	Yds.	Avg.	LG	TD
Carter	38	12	321	8.4	26	0
Singleton	2	1	13	6.5	8	0
49ers	40	13	334	8.4	26	0
Opponents	28	10	242	8.6	43	0

KICKOFF RETURNS	No.	Yds.	Avg.	LG	TD
Carter	48	1105	23.0	96t	1
Walker	6	82	13.7	19	0
Loville	2	34	17.0	19	0
Singleton	2	23	11.5	17	0
49ers	58	1244	21.4	96t	1
Opponents	89	1912	21.5	51	0

SACKS	No.
Stubblefield	8.5
B. Young	6.0
R. Hall	4.0
Jackson	3.5
Kelly	3.5
Brown	3.0
Dent	2.0
Harris	2.0
Wilson	2.0
Mann	1.0
Thomas	1.0
Woodall	1.0
Hanks	0.5
49ers	38.0
Opponents	35.0

1995 DRAFT CHOICES

Round	Name	Pos.	College
1	J.J. Stokes	WR	UCLA
4	Tim Hanshaw	G	Brigham Young
6	Antonio Armstrong	DE	Texas A&M
7	Herbert Coleman	DE	Trinity, Ill.

SAN FRANCISCO 49ERS

1995 VETERAN ROSTER

No.	Name	Pos.	Ht.	Wt.	Birthdate	NFL Exp.	College	Hometown	How Acq.	'94 Games/ Starts
60	Adams, Theo	G	6-5	300	4/24/66	3	Hawaii	Honolulu, Hawaii	FA-'95	0*
77	Barnett, Oliver	DE	6-3	285	4/9/66	6	Kentucky	Jefferson, Ky.	UFA(Buff)-'95	16/2*
79	Barton, Harris	G	6-4	286	4/19/64	9	North Carolina	Atlanta, Ga.	D1a-'87	9/9
4	Brien, Doug	K	5-11	177	11/24/70	2	California	Concord, Calif.	D3a-'94	16/0
96	Brown, Dennis	DE	6-4	280	11/6/67	6	Washington	Long Beach, Calif.	D2a-'90	16/14
86	Carolan, Brett	TE	6-3	241	3/10/71	2	Washington State	Novato, Calif.	FA-'94	4/0
76	Childs, Jason	T	6-4	292	1/6/69	2	North Dakota	Plymouth, Minn.	FA-'95	0*
91	t- Collins, Shane	DE	6-3	267	4/11/69	4	Arizona State	Bozeman, Mont.	T(Wash)-'95	7/0*
41	# Cook, Toi	CB	5-11	188	12/3/64	9	Stanford	Van Nuys, Calif.	FA-'94	16/2
67	Dalman, Chris	G-C	6-3	285	3/15/70	3	Stanford	Salinas, Calif.	D6-'93	16/4
25	Davis, Eric	CB	5-11	178	1/26/68	6	Jacksonville State	Anniston, Ala.	D2b-'90	16/16
63	Deese, Derrick	G	6-3	270	5/17/70	4	Southern California	Culver City, Calif.	FA-'92	16/15
33	Dodge, Dedrick	S	6-2	184	6/14/67	4	Florida State	Mulberry, Fla.	FA-'94	15/0
22	Drakeford, Tyronne	CB	5-9	185	6/21/71	2	Virginia Tech	Camden, S.C.	D2b-'94	13/0
40	Floyd, William	RB	6-1	242	2/17/72	2	Florida State	St. Petersburg, Fla.	D1b-'94	16/11
14	Gagliano, Bob	QB	6-3	205	9/5/58	10	Utah State	Los Angeles, Calif.	FA-'95	0*
98	Goss, Antonio	LB	6-4	228	8/11/66	6	North Carolina	Randleman, N.C.	FA-'94	16/1
18	Grbac, Elvis	QB	6-5	232	8/13/70	3	Michigan	Willoughby Hills, Ohio	D8-'93	11/0
36	Hanks, Merton	S-CB	6-2	185	3/12/68	5	Iowa	Dallas, Tex.	D5a-'91	16/16
99	# Harris, Tim	DE	6-6	265	9/10/64	9	Memphis State	Memphis, Tenn.	FA-'94	5/1
47	Hicks, Clifford	S-CB	5-10	187	8/18/64	9	Oregon	San Diego, Calif.	UFA(NYJ)-'95	16/0*
57	# Jackson, Rickey	LB	6-2	245	3/20/58	15	Pittsburgh	Pahokee, Fla.	FA-'94	16/14
84	Jones, Brent	TE	6-4	230	2/12/63	9	Santa Clara	San Jose, Calif.	FA-'87	15/15
90	Jordan, Darin	LB	6-2	245	12/4/64	5	Northeastern	Stoughton, Mass.	FA-'95	0*
58	Kelly, Todd	DE	6-2	259	11/27/70	3	Tennessee	Hampton, Va.	D1b-'93	11/1
20	Loville, Derek	RB	5-10	205	7/4/68	5	Oregon	San Francisco, Calif.	FA-'94	14/0
29	Lynn, Anthony	RB	6-3	230	12/21/68	2	Texas Tech	McKinney, Tex.	FA-'95	0*
46	McDonald, Tim	S	6-2	215	1/26/65	9	Southern California	Fresno, Calif.	FA-'93	16/16
69	Milstead, Rod	G	6-2	290	11/10/69	4	Delaware State	Bryans Road, Md.	FA-'94	5/0
55	Mitchell, Kevin	LB	6-1	260	1/1/71	2	Syracuse	Harrisburg, Pa.	D2a-'94	16/0
31	t- Moore, Derrick	RB	6-1	227	10/13/67	4	Northeast Oklahoma State	Albany, Ga.	T(Det)-'95	16/0*
51	Norton, Ken	LB	6-2	241	9/29/66	8	UCLA	Los Angeles, Calif.	UFA(Dall)-'94	16/16
66	Oates, Bart	C	6-3	278	12/16/58	11	Brigham Young	Albany, Ga.	FA-'94	16/15
53	Peterson, Anthony	LB	6-0	223	1/23/72	2	Notre Dame	Monongahela, Pa.	D5-'94	15/0
50	Plummer, Gary	LB	6-2	247	1/26/60	10	California	Fremont, Calif.	UFA(SD)-'94	16/16
75	Pollack, Frank	T	6-5	285	11/5/67	5	Northern Arizona	Phoenix, Ariz.	FA-'94	12/4
23	Pope, Marquez	CB-S	5-11	193	10/29/70	4	Fresno State	Long Beach, Calif.	RFA(Rams)-'95	16/16*
85	Popson, Ted	TE	6-4	250	9/10/66	2	Portland State	Lake Tahoe, Calif.	FA-'94	16/1
80	Rice, Jerry	WR	6-2	200	10/13/62	11	Mississippi Valley State	Crawford, Miss.	D1-'85	16/16
10	Rowe, Patrick	WR	6-1	195	2/17/69	3	San Diego State	San Diego, Calif.	FA-'95	0*
61	Sapolu, Jesse	C-G	6-4	278	3/10/61	13	Hawaii	Honolulu, Hawaii	D11-'83	13/13
76	Scrafford, Kirk	T	6-6	275	3/15/67	6	Montana	Billings, Mont.	UFA(Den)-'95	16/7*
88	Singleton, Nate	WR	5-11	190	7/5/68	3	Grambling State	Marrero, La.	FA-'93	16/1
94	Stubblefield, Dana	DT	6-2	302	11/14/70	3	Kansas	Cleves, Ohio	D1a-'93	14/14
82	Taylor, John	WR	6-1	185	3/31/62	10	Delaware State	Pennsauken, N.J.	D3c-'86	15/15
71	Wahler, Jim	DT	6-4	275	7/29/66	6	UCLA	San Jose, Calif.	FA-'95	0*
27	Walker, Adam	RB	6-1	210	6/7/68	3	Pittsburgh	Munhall, Pa.	FA-'94	8/0
74	Wallace, Steve	T	6-5	280	12/27/64	10	Auburn	Atlanta, Ga.	D4b-'86	15/15
92	Wilson, Troy	DE	6-4	235	11/20/70	3	Pittsburg State	Topeka, Kan.	D7-'93	11/0
54	Woodall, Lee	LB	6-0	220	10/31/69	2	West Chester, Pa.	Carlisle, Pa.	D6-'94	15/13
97	Young, Bryant	DT	6-2	276	1/27/72	2	Notre Dame	Chicago Heights, Ill.	D1a-'94	16/16
8	Young, Steve	QB	6-2	205	10/11/61	11	Brigham Young	Greenwich, Conn.	T(TB)-'87	16/16

* Adams last active with Tampa Bay in '93; Barnett played 16 games with Buffalo in '94; Childs last active with Seattle in '93; Collins played 7 games with Washington; Gagliano last active with Atlanta in '93; Hicks played 16 games with N.Y. Jets; Jordan last active with San Francisco in '93; Lynn last active with Denver in '93; Moore played 16 games with Detroit; Pope played 16 games with L.A. Rams; Rowe last active with Cleveland in '93; Scrafford played 16 games with Denver; Wahler last active with Washington in '93.

Unrestricted free agent; subject to developments.

† Restricted free agent; subject to developments.

t- 49ers traded for Collins (Washington), Moore (Detroit).

Players lost through free agency (6): RB Dexter Carter (NYJ; 16 games in '94), DT Rhett Hall (Phil; 11), DE Charles Mann (Wash; 14), WR Ed McCaffrey (Den; 16), QB Bill Musgrave (Den; 0), RB Ricky Watters (Phil; 16).

Players lost through Expansion Draft (2): T Harry Boatswain (Car; 13 games in '94), DE Mark Thomas (Car; 9).

Also played with 49ers in '94—T Brian Bollinger (7 games), DE Richard Dent (2), S Dana Hall (16), CB Adrian Hardy (2), RB Marc Logan (10), CB Deion Sanders (14), DE Artie Smith (2), G Ralph Tamm (1), P Klaus Wilmsmeyer (16).

COACHING STAFF

Head Coach,
George Seifert

Pro Career: In 1994, guided San Francisco to a record fifth Super Bowl championship, posting an NFL-best 16-3 record. Named 49ers' head coach on January 26, 1989, after serving as the team's defensive coordinator since 1983. Immediately earned a place in league history, winning a record 17 games his first year and becoming only the second rookie head coach to lead his team to a Super Bowl title (Don McCafferty of Baltimore in 1970 was the first). Recorded the NFL's best won-loss mark in 1990, posting a 14-2 record and guided San Francisco to its fifth consecutive NFC West title. In 1991, the 49ers recorded a 10-6 mark, missing the playoffs for the first time since 1982. Earned consecutive trips to the NFC Championship Game in 1992-93 winning the NFC West each season. Joined 49ers as secondary coach in 1980. In only his second season in the pro ranks, San Francisco had the second best defense in the league and won a Super Bowl (XVI) title, despite starting three rookies in the defensive backfield. Appointed the team's defensive coordinator in 1983. No pro playing experience. Career record: 84-24.

Background: Linebacker at University of Utah (1960-62). Served a six-month tour of duty with the U.S. Army following graduation. Returned to Utah as a graduate assistant in 1964. Named head coach at Westminster College in Salt Lake City in 1965. Assistant at Iowa (1966), Oregon (1967-71), and Stanford (1972-74). Left Stanford to become head coach at Cornell (1975-76). Joined Bill Walsh's staff at Stanford in 1977 and helped the Cardinal to a two-year mark of 17-7, including victories in the Sun and Bluebonnet Bowls. Received bachelor's degree in zoology (1963) and master's degree in physical education (1966) from Utah.

Personal: Born January 22, 1940, in San Francisco. He and his wife, Linda, have two children—Eve and Jason—and live in Los Altos, Calif.

ASSISTANT COACHES

Jerry Attaway, conditioning; born January 3, 1946, Susanville, Calif., lives in San Jose, Calif. Defensive back Yuba, Calif., J.C. 1964-65, Cal-Davis 1967. No pro playing experience. College coach: Cal-Davis 1970-71, Idaho 1972-74, Utah State 1975-77, Southern California 1978-82. Pro coach: Joined 49ers in 1983.

Mike Barnes, conditioning assistant; born March 13, 1966, Rochester N.Y., lives in Dublin, Calif. No college or pro playing experience. College coach: Texas A&M 1990, California 1991-93. Pro coach: Joined 49ers in 1994.

Dwaine Board, defensive line; born November 29, 1956, Rocky Mount, Va., lives in Redwood City, Calif. Defensive lineman North Carolina A&T 1974-77. Pro defensive lineman San Francisco 49ers 1979-87, New Orleans Saints 1988. Pro coach: Joined 49ers in 1991.

Pete Carroll, defensive coordinator; born September 15, 1951, San Francisco, Calif., lives in Santa Clara, Calif. Defensive back Pacific 1969-72. No pro playing experience. College coach: Arkansas 1977, Iowa State 1978, Ohio State 1979, North Carolina State 1980-82, Pacific 1983. Pro coach: Buffalo Bills 1984, Minnesota Vikings 1985-89, New York Jets 1990-94 (head coach 1994), joined 49ers in 1995.

Tom Holmoe, defensive backs; born March 7, 1960, Glendale, Calif., lives in Foster City, Calif. Defensive back Brigham Young 1979-82. Pro defensive back San Francisco 49ers 1983-89. College coach: Brigham Young 1990-91, Stanford 1992-93. Pro coach: Joined 49ers in 1994.

Carl Jackson, running backs; born August 16, 1940, Bay City, Tex., lives in San Jose, Calif. Quarterback Prairie View A&M 1959-62. No pro playing experience. College coach: North Texas State 1976-78, Iowa 1979-91. Pro coach: Joined 49ers in 1992.

Larry Kirksey, wide receivers; born January 6, 1951, Harlan, Ky., lives in Pleasanton, Calif. Wide receiver Eastern Kentucky 1970-72. No pro playing experience. College coach: Miami, Ohio 1974-76, Kentucky 1977-81, Kansas 1982, Kentucky State 1983 (head coach), Florida 1984-88, Pittsburgh 1989, Alabama 1990-93. Pro coach: Joined 49ers in 1994.

Greg Knapp, offensive assistant; born March 5, 1963, Long Beach, Calif., lives in Santa Clara, Calif. Quarterback Sacramento State 1982-85. No pro playing experience. College coach: Sacramento State 1986-94. Pro coach: Joined 49ers in 1995.

Alan Lowry, special teams; born November 21, 1950, Irving, Tex., lives in Danville, Calif. Defensive back-quarterback Texas 1970-72. No pro playing experience. College coach: Virginia Tech 1974, Wyoming 1975, Texas 1976-81. Pro coach: Dallas Cowboys 1982-90, Tampa Bay Buccaneers 1991, joined 49ers in 1992.

John Marshall, linebackers; born October 2, 1945, Arroyo Grande, Calif., lives in Pleasanton, Calif. Linebacker Washington State 1964. No pro playing experience. College coach: Oregon 1970-76, Southern California 1977-79. Pro coach: Green Bay Packers 1980-82, Atlanta Falcons 1983-85, Indianapolis Colts 1986-88, joined 49ers in 1989.

Bobb McKittrick, offensive line; born December 29, 1935, Baker, Ore., lives in San Mateo, Calif. Guard Oregon State 1955-57. No pro playing experience. College coach: Oregon State 1961-64, UCLA 1965-70. Pro coach: Los Angeles Rams 1971-72, San Diego Chargers 1974-78, joined 49ers in 1979.

Bill McPherson, assistant head coach; born October 24, 1931, Santa Clara, Calif., lives in San Jose, Calif. Tackle Santa Clara 1950-52. No pro playing experience. College coach: Santa Clara 1963-74, UCLA 1975-77. Pro coach: Philadelphia Eagles 1978, joined 49ers in 1979.

Bo Pellini, defensive assistant; born December 13, 1967, Youngstown, Ohio, lives in Sunnyvale, Calif. Defensive back Ohio State 1986-90. No pro playing experience. College coach: Iowa 1991-92. Pro coach: Joined 49ers in 1994.

Mike Solari, tight ends-offensive line assistant; born January 16, 1955, Daly City, Calif., lives in Pleasanton, Calif. Offensive lineman San Diego State 1975-76. No pro playing experience. College coach: Mira Vista (Calif.) Junior College 1977-78, U.S. International 1979, Boise State 1980, Cincinnati 1981-82, Kansas 1983-85, Pittsburgh 1986, Alabama 1990-91. Pro coach: Dallas Cowboys 1987-88, Phoenix Cardinals 1989, joined 49ers in 1992.

Marc Trestman, offensive coordinator; born January 15, 1956, Minneapolis, Minn., lives in Santa Clara, Calif. Quarterback Minnesota 1975-77, Moorhead (Minn.) State 1978. Pro quarterback Minnesota Vikings 1979. College coach: Miami 1981-84. Pro coach: Minnesota Vikings 1985-86, 1990-91, Tampa Bay Buccaneers 1987, Cleveland Browns 1988-89, joined 49ers in 1995.

1995 FIRST-YEAR ROSTER

Name	Pos.	Ht.	Wt.	Birthdate	College	Hometown	How Acq.
Allen, Brian	TE	6-4	240	9/18/70	UCLA	Newhall, Calif.	FA
Armstrong, Antonio	LB	6-1	285	10/15/73	Texas A&M	Houston, Tex.	D6
Browning, Alfonzo (1)	WR	6-2	203	7/27/72	Kentucky	San Francisco, Calif.	FA
Bryant, Junior (1)	DE	6-4	275	1/16/71	Notre Dame	Omaha, Neb.	FA
Caldwell, Mike (1)	WR	6-2	200	3/28/71	California	Danville, Calif.	FA
Calloway, Dominic (1)	CB	6-1	184	4/24/72	Memphis State	Anniston, Ala.	FA
Coleman, Herbert	DE	6-1	290	9/4/71	Trinity, Illinois	Country Club Hills, Ill.	D7
Cook, Mike (1)	WR	6-5	205	3/20/71	Stanford	Fountain Valley, Calif.	FA
Fountaine, Jamal (1)	DE	6-3	240	1/29/71	Washington	San Francisco, Calif.	FA
Gordon, Steve (1)	C	6-4	290	4/15/69	California	Nevada City, Calif.	FA
Hanshaw, Tim	G	6-5	300	4/27/70	Brigham Young	Spokane, Wash.	D4
Holland, Troy	DE	6-6	270	2/23/67	Navy	Warner Robins, Ga.	FA
Kellogg, Jackie (1)	CB	6-1	188	3/29/71	Eastern Washington	Tacoma, Wash.	FA
Kuehl, Ryan	DT	6-4	280	1/18/72	Virginia	Bethesda, Md.	FA
Mills, Troy (1)	RB	6-0	215	7/1/66	Sacramento State	Healdsburg, Calif.	FA
Pieri, Damon (1)	S	6-0	186	9/25/70	San Diego State	Phoenix, Ariz.	FA
Richardson, Mose (1)	CB	6-1	178	11/22/70	Indiana	Dayton, Ohio	FA
Stokes, J.J.	WR	6-4	217	10/6/72	UCLA	San Diego, Calif.	D1
Thompson, Tom (1)	P	5-10	192	4/27/72	Oregon	Lompoc, Calif.	FA
Williams, Michael	CB	5-10	185	5/28/70	UCLA	Los Angeles, Calif.	FA

The term NFL Rookie is defined as a player who is in his first season of professional football and has not been on the roster of another professional football team for any regular-season or postseason games. A Rookie is designated by an "R" on NFL rosters. Players who have been active in another professional football league or players who have NFL experience, including either preseason training camp or being on an Active List or Inactive List, or on Reserve/Injured or Reserve/Physically Unable to Perform for fewer than six regular-season games, are termed NFL First-Year Players. An NFL First-Year Player is designated by a "1" on NFL rosters. Thereafter, a player is credited with an additional year of experience for each season in which he accumulates six games on the Active List or Inactive List, or on Reserve/Injured or Reserve/Physically Unable to Perform.

NOTES

TAMPA BAY BUCCANEERS

National Football Conference
Central Division
Team Colors: Florida Orange, White, and Red
One Buccaneer Place
Tampa, Florida 33607
Telephone: (813) 870-2700

CLUB OFFICIALS

General Manager: Rich McKay
Director of Player Personnel: Jerry Angelo
Director of College Scouting: Tim Ruskell
Director of Ticket Sales and Operations: Rick Odioso
Director of Public Relations: Chip Namias
Director of Corporate Sales/Broadcasting: Jim Overton
Director of Sales & Advertising: Paul Sickmon
Controller: Patrick Smith
College Scouts: Mike Ackerley, Brian Gardner Ruston Webster, Mike Yowarsky
Pro Personnel Assistant: John Idzik
Asst. Director/Ticket Operations: Lori Grimm
Asst. Director/Public Relations: Scott Smith
Public Relations Assistant: Nelson Luis
Computer Services Coordinator: Terri Kimbell
Assistant Director/Sales & Advertising: Jayne Portnoy
Assistant Director/Sales & Fundraising: Sherry Gruden
Corporate Sales Assistant: Heidi Soderholm
Trainer: Chris Smith
Assistant Trainer: Joe Joe Petrone
Equipment Manager: Frank Pupello
Video Director: Davy Levy
Assistant Video Director: Pat Brazil
Stadium: Tampa Stadium •**Capacity:** 74,321 Tampa, Florida 33607
Playing Surface: Grass
Training Camp: University of Tampa Tampa, Florida 33606

1995 SCHEDULE

PRESEASON

Aug. 5	**New York Jets**	7:30
Aug. 11	at Cincinnati	7:30
Aug. 19	**Pittsburgh**	7:30
Aug. 25	vs. Miami at Orlando, Fla.	8:00

REGULAR SEASON

Sept. 3	at Philadelphia	1:00
Sept. 10	at Cleveland	1:00
Sept. 17	**Chicago**	4:00
Sept. 24	**Washington**	1:00
Oct. 1	at Carolina	1:00
Oct. 8	**Cincinnati**	1:00
Oct. 15	**Minnesota**	1:00
Oct. 22	**Atlanta**	1:00
Oct. 29	at Houston	3:00
Nov. 5	Open Date	
Nov. 12	at Detroit	1:00
Nov. 19	**Jacksonville**	1:00
Nov. 26	at Green Bay	12:00
Dec. 3	at Minnesota	12:00
Dec. 10	**Green Bay**	8:00
Dec. 17	at Chicago	12:00
Dec. 23	**Detroit** (Saturday)	4:00

RECORD HOLDERS

INDIVIDUAL RECORDS—CAREER

Category	Name	Performance
Rushing (Yds.)	James Wilder, 1981-89	5,957
Passing (Yds.)	Vinny Testaverde, 1987-1992	14,820
Passing (TDs)	Vinny Testaverde, 1987-1992	77
Receiving (No.)	James Wilder, 1981-89	430
Receiving (Yds.)	Mark Carrier, 1987-1992	5,018
Interceptions	Cedric Brown, 1977-1984	29
Punting (Avg.)	Frank Garcia, 1983-87	41.1
Punt Return (Avg.)	Willie Drewrey, 1989-1992	9.4
Kickoff Return (Avg.)	Isaac Hagins, 1976-1980	21.9
Field Goals	Donald Igwebuike, 1985-89	94
Touchdowns (Tot.)	James Wilder, 1981-89	46
Points	Donald Igwebuike, 1985-89	416

INDIVIDUAL RECORDS—SINGLE SEASON

Category	Name	Performance
Rushing (Yds.)	James Wilder, 1984	1,544
Passing (Yds.)	Doug Williams, 1981	3,563
Passing (TDs)	Doug Williams, 1980	20
	Vinny Testaverde, 1989	20
Receiving (No.)	Mark Carrier, 1989	86
Receiving (Yds.)	Mark Carrier, 1989	1,422
Interceptions	Cedric Brown, 1981	9
Punting (Avg.)	Larry Swider, 1981	42.7
Punt Return (Avg.)	Courtney Hawkins, 1993	11.1
Kickoff Return (Avg.)	Isaac Hagins, 1977	23.5
Field Goals	Steve Christie, 1990	23
	Michael Husted, 1994	23
Touchdowns (Tot.)	James Wilder, 1984	13
Points	Donald Igwebuike, 1989	99

INDIVIDUAL RECORDS—SINGLE GAME

Category	Name	Performance
Rushing (Yds.)	James Wilder, 11-6-83	219
Passing (Yds.)	Doug Williams, 11-16-80	486
Passing (TDs)	Steve DeBerg, 9-13-87	5
Receiving (No.)	James Wilder, 9-15-85	13
Receiving (Yds.)	Mark Carrier, 12-6-87	212
Interceptions	Many times	2
	Last time by Joe King and Milton Mack, 12-27-92	
Field Goals	Many times	4
	Last time by Steve Christie, 12-16-90	4
Touchdowns (Tot.)	Jimmie Giles, 10-20-85	4

COACHING HISTORY

(88-207-1)

1976-84	John McKay	45-91-1
1985-86	Leeman Bennett	4-28-0
1987-90	Ray Perkins*	19-41-0
1990-91	Richard Williamson	4-15-0
1992-94	Sam Wyche	16-32-0

*Released after 13 games in 1990

TAMPA STADIUM

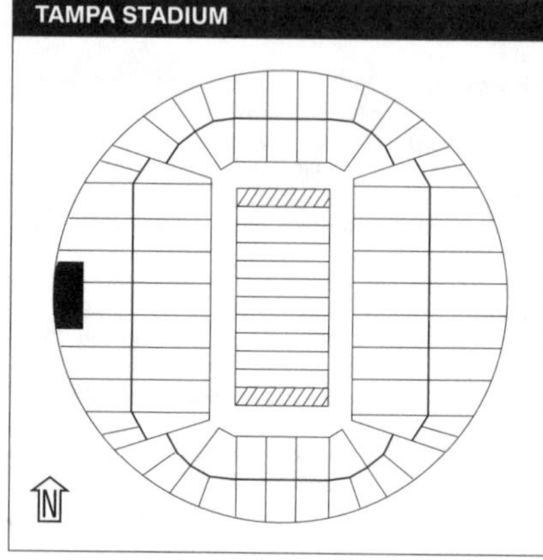

1994 TEAM RECORD

PRESEASON (2-2)

Date	Result		Opponents
8/6	W	17-16	Cincinnati
8/13	L	6-29	at Seattle
8/20	W	29-14	at Miami
8/26	L	9-10	N.Y. Jets

REGULAR SEASON (6-10)

Date	Result		Opponents	Att.
9/4	L	9-21	at Chicago	61,844
9/11	W	24-10	Indianapolis	36,631
9/18	L	7- 9	New Orleans	45,522
9/25	L	3-30	at Green Bay	58,551
10/2	W	24-14	Detroit	38,012
10/9	L	13-34	at Atlanta	52,633
10/23	L	16-41	at San Francisco	62,741
10/30	L	13-36	Minnesota	42,110
11/6	L	6-20	Chicago	60,821
11/13	L	9-14	at Detroit	50,814
11/20	L	21-22	at Seattle	37,466
11/27	W	20-17	at Minnesota (OT)	47,259
12/4	W	26-21	Washington	45,121
12/11	W	24-14	L.A. Rams	34,150
12/18	W	17-14	at Washington	47,315
12/24	L	19-34	Green Bay	65,076

(OT) Overtime

SCORE BY PERIODS

Buccaneers	30	94	35	89	3	—	251
Opponents	75	142	74	60	0	—	351

ATTENDANCE

Home 367,443 Away 418,623 Total 786,066
Single-game home record, 72,077 (10-8-89)
Single-season home record, 545,980 (1979)

1994 TEAM STATISTICS

	Buccaneers	Opp.
Total First Downs	276	298
Rushing	104	100
Passing	149	179
Penalty	23	19
Third Down: Made/Att	73/199	94/214
Third Down Pct.	36.7	43.9
Fourth Down: Made/Att	6/15	4/12
Fourth Down Pct.	40.0	33.3
Total Net Yards	4754	5336
Avg. Per Game	297.1	333.5
Total Plays	951	986
Avg. Per Play	5.0	5.4
Net Yards Rushing	1489	1964
Avg. Per Game	93.1	122.8
Total Rushes	430	468
Net Yards Passing	3265	3372
Avg. Per Game	204.1	210.8
Sacked/Yards Lost	30/171	20/114
Gross Yards	3436	3486
Att./Completions	491/271	498/303
Completion Pct.	55.2	60.8
Had Intercepted	16	9
Punts/Avg.	74/38.6	68/42.7
Net Punting Avg.	74/35.5	68/34.6
Penalties/Yards Lost	93/805	94/690
Fumbles/Ball Lost	18/7	21/12
Touchdowns	26	40
Rushing	8	13
Passing	17	25
Returns	1	2
Avg. Time of Possession	29:55	30:05

1994 INDIVIDUAL STATISTICS

PASSING	Att.	Comp.	Yds.	Pct.	TD	Int.	Tkld.	Rate
Erickson	399	225	2919	56.4	16	10	22/129	82.5
Dilfer	82	38	433	46.3	1	6	8/42	36.3
Weldon	9	7	63	77.8	0	0	0/0	95.8
Stryzinski	1	1	21	100.0	0	0	0/0	118.8
Buccaneers	491	271	3436	55.2	17	16	30/171	75.2
Opponents	498	303	3486	60.8	25	9	20/114	91.2

SCORING	TD R	TD P	TD Rt	PAT	FG	Saf	PTS
Husted	0	0	0	20/20	23/35	0	89
Rhett	7	0	0	0/0	0/0	0	44
C. Wilson	0	6	0	0/0	0/0	0	36
Hawkins	0	5	0	0/0	0/0	0	30
J. Harris	0	3	0	0/0	0/0	0	20
Armstrong	0	1	0	0/0	0/0	0	6
Dawsey	0	1	0	0/0	0/0	0	6
Erickson	1	0	0	0/0	0/0	0	6
McDowell	0	1	0	0/0	0/0	0	6
Turner	0	0	1	0/0	0/0	0	6
Copeland	0	0	0	0/0	0/0	0	2
Buccaneers	8	17	1	20/20	23/35	0	251
Opponents	13	25	2	38/38	23/26	0	351

2-Point conversions: Copeland, J. Harris, Rhett.
Team: 3-6.

RUSHING	Att.	Yds.	Avg.	LG	TD
Rhett	284	1011	3.6	27	7
Workman	79	291	3.7	18	0
Erickson	26	68	2.6	17	1
McDowell	21	58	2.8	8	0
Dilfer	2	27	13.5	15	0
C. Wilson	2	15	7.5	11	0
Turner	4	13	3.3	9	0
Royster	9	7	0.8	6	0
R. Harris	2	0	0.0	3	0
Armstrong	1	-1	-1.0	-1	0
Buccaneers	430	1489	3.5	27	8
Opponents	468	1964	4.2	85	13

RECEIVING	No.	Yds.	Avg.	LG	TD
Dawsey	46	673	14.6	46	1
Hawkins	37	438	11.8	32	5
C. Wilson	31	652	21.0	71t	6
McDowell	29	193	6.7	19	1
J. Harris	26	337	13.0	48t	3
Armstrong	22	265	12.0	29	1
Rhett	22	119	5.4	12	0
Copeland	17	308	18.1	65	0
Workman	11	82	7.5	23	0
W. Green	9	150	16.7	28	0
Thomas	7	94	13.4	27	0
Royster	7	36	5.1	12	0
Moore	4	57	14.3	18	0
R. Harris	2	11	5.5	8	0
Carter	1	21	21.0	21	0
Buccaneers	271	3436	12.7	71t	17
Opponents	303	3486	11.5	81t	25

INTERCEPTIONS	No.	Yds.	Avg.	LG	TD
Nickerson	2	9	4.5	10	0
Mayhew	2	4	2.0	4	0
Covington	1	38	38.0	38	0
Everett	1	26	26.0	26	0
Dimry	1	0	0.0	0	0
McGruder	1	0	0.0	0	0
Stargell	1	0	0.0	0	0
Buccaneers	9	77	8.6	38	0
Opponents	16	323	20.2	92t	2

PUNTING	No.	Yds.	Avg.	In 20	LG
Stryzinski	72	2800	38.9	20	53
Husted	2	53	26.5	2	32
Buccaneers	74	2853	38.6	22	53
Opponents	68	2902	42.7	18	65

PUNT RETURNS	No.	FC	Yds.	Avg.	LG	TD
Turner	21	4	218	10.4	80t	1
Hawkins	5	2	28	5.6	9	0
Everett	2	2	2	1.0	1	0
Buccaneers	28	8	248	8.9	80t	1
Opponents	19	42	103	5.4	40	0

KICKOFF RETURNS	No.	Yds.	Avg.	LG	TD
Turner	43	886	20.6	77	0
C. Wilson	10	251	25.1	41	0
Buckley	8	177	22.1	35	0
R. Green	2	33	16.5	18	0
Culpepper	2	30	15.0	18	0
Moore	2	27	13.5	16	0
R. Harris	1	12	12.0	12	0
Armstrong	1	6	6.0	6	0
Carter	1	0	0.0	0	0
Buccaneers	70	1422	20.3	77	0
Opponents	44	941	21.4	57	0

SACKS	No.
Culpepper	4.0
Curry	3.0
Dotson	3.0
Wheeler	3.0
K. Wilson	2.5
Bussey	1.5
Ahanotu	1.0
Carter	1.0
Nickerson	1.0
Buccaneers	20.0
Opponents	30.0

1995 DRAFT CHOICES

Round	Name	Pos.	College
1	Warren Sapp	DT	Miami
	Derrick Brooks	LB	Florida State
2	Melvin Johnson	DB	Kentucky
4	Jerry Wilson	DB	Southern
5	Clifton Abraham	DB	Florida State
6	Wardell Rouse	LB	Clemson
7	Steve Ingram	G	Maryland
	Jeff Rodgers	DE	Texas A&M-Kingsville

TAMPA BAY BUCCANEERS

1995 VETERAN ROSTER

No.	Name	Pos.	Ht.	Wt.	Birthdate	NFL Exp.	College	Hometown	How Acq.	'94 Games/ Starts
72	Ahanotu, Chidi	DE-DT	6-2	288	10/11/70	3	California	Berkeley, Calif.	D6-'93	16/16
86	Armstong, Tyji	TE	6-4	262	10/3/70	4	Mississippi	Inkster, Mich.	D3b-'92	16/9
62	Beckles, Ian	G	6-1	304	7/20/67	6	Indiana	Montreal, Canada	D5-'90	16/16
53	Brady, Ed	LB	6-2	238	6/17/62	12	Illinois	Morris, Ill.	PB(Cin)-'92	16/0
28	Buckley, Curtis	S	6-0	191	9/25/70	3	East Texas State	Silsbee, Tex.	FA-'93	13/0
27	Bussey, Barney	S	6-0	215	5/20/62	10	South Carolina State	Lincolnton, Ga.	UFA(Cin)-'93	16/15
88	Copeland, Horace	WR	6-3	202	1/2/71	3	Miami	Orlando, Fla.	D4b-'93	16/2
73	Culpepper, Brad	DT	6-1	270	5/8/69	4	Florida	Tallahassee, Fla.	W(Minn)-'94	16/15
75	Curry, Eric	DE	6-5	270	2/3/70	3	Alabama	Thomasville, Ga.	D1-'93	15/14
80	Dawsey, Lawrence	WR	6-0	192	11/16/67	5	Florida State	Dothan, Ala.	D3-'91	10/5
12	Dilfer, Trent	QB	6-4	235	3/13/72	2	Fresno State	Aptos, Calif.	D1-'94	5/2
76	Dill, Scott	G-T	6-5	295	4/5/66	8	Memphis State	Birmingham, Ala.	PB(Phx)-'90	16/16
39	Dimry, Charles	CB	6-0	176	1/31/66	8	Nevada-Las Vegas	Oceanside, Calif.	UFA(Den)-'94	16/16
71	† Dotson, Santana	DT-DE	6-5	276	12/19/69	4	Baylor	Houston, Tex.	D5b-'92	16/9
93	DuBose, Demetrius	LB	6-1	240	3/23/71	3	Notre Dame	Seattle, Wash.	D2-'93	16/1
41	Edmonds, Bobby Joe	RB-KR	5-11	186	9/26/64	5	Arkansas	St. Louis, Mo.	FA-'95	0*
22	Everett, Thomas	S	5-9	190	11/21/64	9	Baylor	Daingerfield, Tex.	T(Dall)-'94	15/15
29	Gant, Kenneth	S	5-11	189	4/18/67	6	Albany State	Lakeland, Fla.	UFA(Dall)-'95	16/0*
74	Gruber, Paul	T	6-5	296	2/24/65	8	Wisconsin	Prairie du Sac, Wis.	D1-'88	16/16
82	Harper, Alvin	WR	6-3	208	7/6/67	5	Tennessee	Frostproof, Fla.	UFA(Dall)-'95	16/14*
81	Harris, Jackie	TE	6-4	248	1/4/68	6	Northeast Louisiana	Pine Bluff, Ark.	RFA(GB)-'94	9/9
43	Harris, Rudy	RB	6-1	257	9/18/71	3	Clemson	Brockton, Mass.	D4a-'93	8/0
85	† Hawkins, Courtney	WR	5-9	183	12/12/69	4	Michigan State	Flint, Mich.	D2-'92	13/12
5	Husted, Michael	K	6-0	188	6/16/70	3	Virginia	Hampton, Va.	FA-'93	16/0
90	Jones, Milton	DE	6-5	270	3/24/71	2	Central State, Ohio	Detroit, Mich.	FA-'94	0*
79	Love, Sean	G	6-3	300	9/6/68	3	Penn State	Tamaqua, Pa.	FA-'93	6/0
47	Lynch, John	S	6-2	216	9/25/71	3	Stanford	Solana Beach, Calif.	D3b-'93	16/0
51	Marts, Lonnie	LB	6-1	236	11/10/68	6	Tulane	New Orleans, La.	UFA(KC)-'94	16/14
61	Mayberry, Tony	C	6-4	292	12/8/67	6	Wake Forest	Springfield, Va.	D4-'90	16/16
35	Mayhew, Martin	CB	5-8	178	10/8/65	8	Florida State	Tallahassee, Fla.	UFA(Wash)-'93	16/16
33	† McDowell, Anthony	RB	5-11	240	11/12/68	4	Texas Tech	Killeen, Tex.	D8-'92	14/11
21	McGruder, Mike	CB	5-10	182	5/6/64	6	Kent State	Cleveland Heights, Ohio	UFA(SF)-'94	15/3
94	McIntosh, Toddrick	DT-DE	6-3	277	1/22/72	2	Florida State	Richardson, Tex.	W(Dall)-'94	4/0
70	McRae, Charles	G-T	6-7	306	9/16/68	5	Tennessee	Clinton, Tenn.	D1-'91	15/10
83	Moore, Dave	TE	6-2	248	11/11/69	3	Pittsburgh	Roxbury, N.J.	FA-'92	15/5
56	Nickerson, Hardy	LB	6-2	228	9/1/65	9	California	Compton, Calif.	UFA(Pitt)-'93	14/14
95	Powe, Keith	DE	6-3	265	6/5/69	2	Texas-El Paso	Houston, Tex.	FA-'94	5/0
15	Philcox, Todd	QB	6-4	225	9/25/66	5	Syracuse	Norwalk, Conn.	FA-'95	0*
60	Pyne, Jim	C	6-2	282	11/23/71	2	Virginia Tech	Milford, Mass.	D7-'94	0*
32	Rhett, Errict	RB	5-11	211	12/11/70	2	Florida	Pembroke Pines, Fla.	D2-'94	16/8
1	Roby, Reggie	P	6-2	258	7/30/61	13	Iowa	East Waterloo, Iowa	UFA(Wash)-'95	16/0*
45	Stargell, Tony	CB	5-11	186	8/7/66	6	Tennessee State	La Grange, Ga.	UFA(Ind)-'94	10/2
98	Spindler, Marc	DT-DE	6-5	290	11/28/69	6	Pittsburgh	West Scranton, Pa.	UFA(Det)-'95	9/8*
67	Sullivan, Mike	G-C	6-3	292	12/22/67	4	Miami	Chicago, Ill.	FA-'92	16/1
87	Thomas, Lamar	WR	6-1	163	2/12/70	3	Miami	Gainesville, Fla.	D3a-'93	11/0
2	Verdin, Clarence	WR-KR	5-8	162	6/14/63	10	Southwestern Louisiana	Bourg, La.	UFA(Atl)-'95	12/0*
11	Weldon, Casey	QB	6-1	206	2/3/69	4	Florida State	Tallahassee, Fla.	FA-'93	2/0
77	Wheeler, Mark	DT	6-2	285	4/1/70	4	Texas A&M	San Marcos, Tex.	D3a-'92	15/8
4	Willis, Peter Tom	QB	6-2	204	1/4/67	5	Florida State	Morris, Ala.	FA-'95	0*
84	Wilson, Charles	WR	5-10	185	7/1/68	5	Memphis State	Tallahassee, Fla.	FA-'92	14/7
91	# Wilson, Karl	DE-DT	6-5	274	9/10/64	8	Louisiana State	Amite, La.	FA-'94	14/2
46	Workman, Vince	RB	5-10	205	5/9/68	7	Ohio State	Dublin, Ohio	RFA(GB)-'93	15/8

* Edmonds last active with L.A. Raiders in '89; Gant played 16 games with Dallas in '94; Harper played 16 games with Dallas; Jones inactive for 7 games; Philcox inactive for 2 games with Cincinnati; Pyne active for four games but did not play; Roby played 16 games with Washington; Spindler played 9 games with Detroit; Verdin played 12 games with Atlanta; Willis last active with Chicago in '93.

Unrestricted free agent; subject to developments.

† Restricted free agent; subject to developments.

Traded—TE Harold Bishop to Cleveland, QB Craig Erickson to Indianapolis.

Players lost through free agency (5): LB Jeff Brady (Minn; 16 games in '94), S Marty Carter (Chi; 16), S Tony Covington (Sea; 14), P Dan Stryzinski (Atl; 16), RB-KR Vernon Turner (Car; 12).

Players lost through Expansion Draft (3): CB Rogerick Green (Jax; 11 games in '94), DE Shawn Price (Car; 6), RB Mazio Royster (Jax; 14).

Also played with Buccaneers in '94—TE Harold Bishop (6 games), QB Craig Erickson (15), WR Willie Green (5), DE Jeff Hunter (1), T Tim Irwin (8), DT Bernard Wilson (1).

COACHING STAFF

Head Coach,
Sam Wyche

Pro Career: Became the Buccaneers' fifth head coach on January 10, 1992, after eight seasons as head coach of the Cincinnati Bengals. Led the Bengals to the AFC championship in 1988 and Super Bowl XXIII against the San Francisco 49ers. Played quarterback with the Bengals 1968-70, Washington Redskins 1971-73, Detroit Lions 1974, St. Louis Cardinals 1976, and Buffalo Bills 1976. Quarterback coach with the San Francisco 49ers 1979-82. Career record: 80-100.

Background: Attended North Fulton High School in Atlanta. Quarterback at Furman University from 1963-65. Assistant coach at South Carolina in 1967. Head coach at Indiana in 1983.

Personal: Born January 5, 1945, in Atlanta, Georgia. Sam and wife, Jane, live in Tampa, and have two children—Zak and Kerry.

ASSISTANT COACHES

Maxie Baughan, linebackers; born August 3, 1938, Forkland, Ala., lives in Tampa. Center-linebacker Georgia Tech 1957-60. Pro linebacker Philadelphia Eagles 1960-65, Los Angeles Rams 1966-70, Washington Redskins 1971, 1974. College coach: Georgia Tech 1972-73, Cornell 1983-88 (head coach). Pro coach: Baltimore Colts 1975-79, Detroit Lions 1980-82, Minnesota Vikings 1990-91, joined Buccaneers in 1992.

Kippy Brown, running backs; born March 6, 1955, Sweetwater, Tenn., lives in Tampa. Quarterback Memphis State 1975-77. No pro playing experience. College coach: Memphis State 1978-80, Louisville 1982, Tennessee 1983-89, 1993-94. Pro coach: New York Jets 1990-92, joined Buccaneers in 1995.

Ken Clarke, defensive line; born August 28, 1956, Savannah, Ga., lives in Tampa. Defensive tackle Syracuse 1974-77. Pro defensive tackle Philadelphia Eagles 1978-87, Seattle Seahawks 1988, Minnesota Vikings 1989-91. Pro coach: Joined Buccaneers in 1994.

David Culley, receivers; born September 17, 1955, Sparta, Tenn., lives in Tampa. Quarterback Vanderbilt 1973-77. No pro playing experience. College coach: Austin Peay 1978, Vanderbilt 1979-81, Middle Tennessee State 1982, Tennessee-Chattanooga 1983, Western Kentucky 1984, Southwestern Louisiana 1985-88, Texas-El Paso 1989-90, Texas A&M 1991-93. Pro coach: Joined Buccaneers in 1994.

Johnnie Lynn, defensive backs; born December 19, 1956, Los Angeles, Calif., lives in Tampa. Defensive back UCLA 1975-78. Pro defensive back New York Jets 1979-86. College coach: Arizona 1988-93. Pro coach: Joined Buccaneers in 1994.

Mike Mularkey, tight ends; born November 19, 1961, Ft. Lauderdale, Fla., lives in Palm Harbor, Fla. Tight end Florida 1979-82. Pro tight end Minnesota Vikings 1983-88, Pittsburgh Steelers 1989-91. College coach: Concordia 1993. Pro coach: Joined Buccaneers in 1994.

Tom Pratt, defensive line; born June 21, 1935, Edgerton, Wis., lives in Tampa. Linebacker Miami 1953-56. No pro playing experience. College coach: Miami 1957-60, Southern Mississippi 1961-62. Pro coach: Kansas City Chiefs 1963-77, 1989-94, New Orleans Saints 1978-80, Cleveland Browns 1981-88, joined Buccaneers in 1995.

Brad Roll, strength and conditioning; born July 4, 1958, Houston, Tex., lives in Tampa. Center Blinn (Tex.) J.C. 1976-77, Stephen F. Austin 1978-79. No pro playing experience. College coach: Southwestern Louisiana 1981-86, Kansas 1987-88, Miami 1989-92. Pro coach: Joined Buccaneers in 1993.

Turk Schonert, quarterbacks; born January 15, 1957, Placentia, Calif., lives in St. Petersburg, Fla. Quarterback Stanford 1976-79. Pro quarterback Cincinnati Bengals 1980-85, 1987-89, Atlanta Falcons 1986. Pro coach: Joined Buccaneers in 1992.

George Stewart, special teams; born December 29, 1958, Little Rock, Ark., lives in Odessa, Fla. Guard Arkansas 1977-80. No pro playing experience. College coach: Minnesota 1984-85, Notre Dame 1986-88. Pro coach: Pittsburgh Steelers 1989-91, joined Buccaneers in 1992.

Rusty Tillman, defensive coordinator; born February 27, 1946, Beloit, Wis., lives in Tampa. Linebacker Arizona 1966-67, Northern Arizona 1968-69. Pro linebacker Washington Redskins 1970-77. Pro coach: Seattle Seahawks 1979-94, joined Buccaneers in 1995.

Bob Wylie, offensive line; born February 16, 1951, Providence, R.I., lives in Tampa. Linebacker Colorado 1969-71. No pro playing experience. College coach: Brown 1981-82, Holy Cross 1983-84, Ohio University 1985-87, Colorado State 1988-89. Pro coach: New York Jets 1990-91, joined Buccaneers in 1992.

1995 FIRST-YEAR ROSTER

Name	Pos.	Ht.	Wt.	Birthdate	College	Hometown	How Acq.
Abraham, Clifton	CB	5-9	184	12/9/71	Florida State	Dallas, Tex.	D5
Bouie, Tony	S	5-10	187	8/7/72	Arizona	New Orleans, La.	FA
Brooks, Derrick	LB	6-0	229	4/18/73	Florida State	Pensacola, Fla.	D1b
Cosby, Carlos	G	6-2	306	8/19/72	Jackson State	Tuscaloosa, Ala.	FA
Crisman, Joel (1)	G	6-5	300	2/3/71	Southern California	Grundy Center, Iowa	FA
Davis, Tyree (1)	WR	5-9	175	9/23/70	Central Arkansas	Altheimer, Ark.	D7-'93
Duvic, Tim	K	5-10	170	1/27/72	Dayton	Chicago, Ill.	FA
Edge, Shayne	P	5-11	175	8/21/71	Florida	Lake City, Fla.	FA
Ellison, Jerry (1)	RB	5-10	194	12/20/71	Tenn.-Chattanooga	Augusta, Ga.	FA
Hammonds, Juan	DE	6-3	260	3/5/72	Michigan State	Louisville, Ky.	FA
Harris, Dwayne	LB	6-2	227	12/13/72	Nebraska	Bessemer, Ala.	FA
Hines, Harold	RB	5-10	240	5/29/72	Western Carolina	Charlotte, N.C.	FA
Holcomb, Kelly	QB	6-2	202	7/9/73	Middle Tennessee St.	Fayetteville, Tenn.	FA
Ingram, Stephen	T-G	6-4	311	5/8/71	Maryland	Seat Pleasant, Md.	D7a
Johnson, Melvin	S	6-0	195	4/15/72	Kentucky	Cincinnati, Ohio	D2
McMillon, Tiger	RB	5-8	185	2/26/72	Florida State	Kissimmee, Fla.	FA
Mock, Kerry	LB	6-1	232	8/17/73	North Carolina	Thomasville, N.C.	FA
Pierson, Pete (1)	T	6-5	295	2/4/71	Washington	Portland, Ore.	D5-'94
Rodgers, Jeffrey	DE	6-3	273	6/10/73	Texas A&M-Kingsville	Lufkin, Tex.	D7b
Rouse, Wardell	LB	6-2	231	6/9/72	Clemson	Clewiston, Fla.	D6
Sapp, Warren	DT	6-1	281	12/19/72	Miami	Apopka, Fla.	D1a
Saunders, Cedric (1)	TE	6-3	240	9/30/72	Ohio State	Sarasota, Fla.	FA
Stephens, Darnell	LB	5-11	253	1/29/73	Clemson	San Antonio, Tex.	FA
Stephens, Macey	S	6-1	190	12/19/71	South Carolina State	McBee, S.C.	FA
Thomas, Ryan	CB	5-9	184	9/24/71	Stephen F. Austin	Killeen, Tex.	FA
Ware, Moses	WR	6-4	191	8/12/73	North Carolina Central	Washington, D.C.	FA
Washington, Rodney	LB	6-2	235	1/27/71	Southeast Oklahoma	Independence, La.	FA
Willis, Dan	WR	6-3	205	12/1/72	Southeast Oklahoma	Belle Glade, Fla.	FA
Wilson, Jerry	CB	5-10	184	7/17/73	Southern	Lake Charles, La.	D4

The term NFL Rookie is defined as a player who is in his first season of professional football and has not been on the roster of another professional football team for any regular-season or postseason games. A Rookie is designated by an "R" on NFL rosters. Players who have been active in another professional football league or players who have NFL experience, including either preseason training camp or being on an Active List or Inactive List, or on Reserve/Injured or Reserve/Physically Unable to Perform for fewer than six regular-season games, are termed NFL First-Year Players. An NFL First-Year Player is designated by a "1" on NFL rosters. Thereafter, a player is credited with an additional year of experience for each season in which he accumulates six games on the Active List or Inactive List, or on Reserve/Injured or Reserve/Physically Unable to Perform.

NOTES

WASHINGTON REDSKINS

National Football Conference
Eastern Division
Team Colors: Burgundy and Gold
Redskin Park
P.O. Box 17247
Washington, D.C. 20041
Telephone: (703) 478-8900

CLUB OFFICIALS

Chairman of the Board-CEO: Jack Kent Cooke
Executive Vice President: John Kent Cooke
House Counsel: Stuart Haney
Controller: Gregory Dillon
Board of Directors: Jack Kent Cooke, John Kent Cooke, Ralph Kent Cooke
General Manager: Charley Casserly
Assistant General Manager: Bobby Mitchell
Director of Player Development: Joe Mendes
Director of Pro Player Personnel: Kirk Mee
Director of College Scouting: George Saimes
Scouts: Gene Bates, Larry Bryan, Scott Cohen, Mike Hagen, Reed Johnson, Mel Kaufman, Mike Maccagnan, Miller McCalmon
Director of Communications: Rick Vaughn
Director of Media Relations: Mike McCall
Director of Information: Chris Helein
Director of Stadium Operations/Club Promotions: John Kent Cooke, Jr.
Assistant Promotions/Advertising Director: John Wagner
Video Director: Donnie Schoenmann
Asst. Video Director: Hugh McPhillips
Video Analyst: Mike Bean
Ticket Manager: Jeff Ritter
Head Trainer: Bubba Tyer
Assistant Trainers: Al Bellamy, Kevin Bastin
Equipment Manager: Jay Brunetti
Asst. Equipment Manager: Jeff Parsons
Stadium: RFK Stadium • **Capacity:** 56,454
Washington, D.C. 20003
Playing Surface: Grass
Training Camp: Frostburg State University
Frostburg, Maryland 21532-1099

1995 SCHEDULE

PRESEASON

Aug. 5	at Kansas City	7:00
Aug. 12	vs. Houston at Knoxville, Tenn.	8:00
Aug. 19	at Miami	7:00
Aug. 25	at Green Bay	6:00

REGULAR SEASON

Sept. 3	**Arizona**	4:00
Sept. 10	**Los Angeles**	1:00
Sept. 17	at Denver	2:00
Sept. 24	at Tampa Bay	1:00
Oct. 1	**Dallas**	1:00
Oct. 8	at Philadelphia	1:00
Oct. 15	at Arizona	1:00
Oct. 22	**Detroit**	1:00
Oct. 29	**New York Giants**	8:00
Nov. 5	at Kansas City	12:00
Nov. 12	Open Date	
Nov. 19	**Seattle**	1:00
Nov. 26	**Philadelphia**	1:00
Dec. 3	at Dallas	3:00
Dec. 10	at New York Giants	4:00
Dec. 17	at St. Louis	12:00
Dec. 24	**Carolina**	4:00

RECORD HOLDERS

INDIVIDUAL RECORDS—CAREER

Category	Name	Performance
Rushing (Yds.)	John Riggins, 1976-79, 1981-85	7,472
Passing (Yds.)	Joe Theismann, 1974-1985	25,206
Passing (TDs)	Sammy Baugh, 1937-1952	187
Receiving (No.)	Art Monk, 1980-1993	*888
Receiving (Yds.)	Art Monk, 1980-1993	12,028
Interceptions	Darrell Green, 1983-1994	37
Punting (Avg.)	Sammy Baugh, 1937-1952	*45.1
Punt Return (Avg.)	Johnny Williams, 1952-53	12.8
Kickoff Return (Avg.)	Bobby Mitchell, 1962-68	28.5
Field Goals	Mark Moseley, 1974-1986	263
Touchdowns (Tot.)	Charley Taylor, 1964-1977	90
Points	Mark Moseley, 1974-1986	1,206

INDIVIDUAL RECORDS—SINGLE SEASON

Category	Name	Performance
Rushing (Yds.)	John Riggins, 1983	1,347
Passing (Yds.)	Jay Schroeder, 1986	4,109
Passing (TDs)	Sonny Jurgensen, 1967	31
Receiving (No.)	Art Monk, 1984	106
Receiving (Yds.)	Bobby Mitchell, 1963	1,436
Interceptions	Dan Sandifer, 1948	13
Punting (Avg.)	Sammy Baugh, 1940	*51.4
Punt Return (Avg.)	Johnny Williams, 1952	15.3
Kickoff Return (Avg.)	Mike Nelms, 1981	29.7
Field Goals	Mark Moseley, 1983	33
Touchdowns (Tot.)	John Riggins, 1983	*24
Points	Mark Moseley, 1983	161

INDIVIDUAL RECORDS—SINGLE GAME

Category	Name	Performance
Rushing (Yds.)	Gerald Riggs, 9-17-89	221
Passing (Yds.)	Sammy Baugh, 10-31-43	446
Passing (TDs)	Sammy Baugh, 10-31-43, 11-23-47	6
	Mark Rypien, 11-10-91	6
Receiving (No.)	Art Monk, 12-15-85	13
	Kelvin Bryant, 12-7-86	13
	Art Monk, 11-4-90	13
Receiving (Yds.)	Anthony Allen, 10-4-87	255
Interceptions	Sammy Baugh, 11-14-43	*4
	Dan Sandifer, 10-31-48	*4
Field Goals	Many times	5
	Last time by Chip Lohmiller, 10-25-92	
Touchdowns (Tot.)	Dick James, 12-17-61	4
	Larry Brown, 12-4-73	4
Points	Dick James, 12-17-61	24
	Larry Brown, 12-4-73	24

*NFL Record

COACHING HISTORY

Boston 1932-36
(453-390-26)

1932	Lud Wray	4-4-2
1933-34	William (Lone Star) Dietz	11-11-2
1935	Eddie Casey	2-8-1
1936-42	Ray Flaherty	56-23-3
1943	Arthur (Dutch) Bergman	7-4-1
1944-45	Dudley DeGroot	14-6-1
1946-48	Glen (Turk) Edwards	16-18-1
1949	John Whelchel*	3-3-1
1949-51	Herman Ball**	4-16-0
1951	Dick Todd	5-4-0
1952-53	Earl (Curly) Lambeau	10-13-1
1954-58	Joe Kuharich	26-32-2
1959-60	Mike Nixon	4-18-2
1961-65	Bill McPeak	21-46-3
1966-68	Otto Graham	17-22-3
1969	Vince Lombardi	7-5-2
1970	Bill Austin	6-8-0
1971-77	George Allen	69-35-1
1978-80	Jack Pardee	24-24-0
1981-92	Joe Gibbs	140-65-0
1993	Richie Petitbon	4-12-0
1994	Norv Turner	3-13-0

*Released after seven games in 1949
**Released after three games in 1951

ROBERT F. KENNEDY STADIUM

1994 TEAM RECORD

PRESEASON (1-3)

Date	Result		Opponents
8/8	L	11-13	at Buffalo
8/12	L	14-17	Kansas City
8/18	L	17-27	at New England
8/26	W	22-21	Pittsburgh

REGULAR SEASON (3-13)

Date	Result		Opponents	Att.
9/4	L	7-28	Seattle	52,930
9/11	W	38-24	at New Orleans	58,049
9/18	L	23-31	at N.Y. Giants	77,298
9/25	L	20-27	Atlanta	53,238
10/2	L	7-34	Dallas	55,394
10/9	L	17-21	at Philadelphia	63,947
10/16	L	16-19	Arizona (OT)	50,019
10/23	W	41-27	at Indianapolis	57,879
10/30	L	29-31	Philadelphia	53,530
11/6	L	22-37	San Francisco	54,335
11/20	L	7-31	at Dallas	64,644
11/27	L	19-21	N.Y. Giants	43,384
12/4	L	21-26	at Tampa Bay	45,121
12/11	L	15-17	at Arizona	53,790
12/18	L	14-17	Tampa Bay	47,315
12/24	W	24-21	at L.A. Rams	25,705

(OT) Overtime

SCORE BY PERIODS

Redskins	44	137	62	77	0	—	320
Opponents	95	128	81	105	3	—	412

ATTENDANCE

Home 410,145 Away 446,433 Total 856,578
Single-game home record, 56,345 (9-6-93)
Single-season home record, 443,678 (1992)

1994 TEAM STATISTICS

	Redskins	Opp.
Total First Downs	269	331
Rushing	79	129
Passing	166	182
Penalty	24	20
Third Down: Made/Att	75/209	87/223
Third Down Pct.	35.9	39.0
Fourth Down: Made/Att	4/13	5/10
Fourth Down Pct.	30.8	50.0
Total Net Yards	4793	5609
Avg. Per Game	299.6	350.6
Total Plays	974	1080
Avg. Per Play	4.9	5.2
Net Yards Rushing	1415	1975
Avg. Per Game	88.4	123.4
Total Rushes	407	556
Net Yards Passing	3378	3634
Avg. Per Game	211.1	227.1
Sacked/Yards Lost	21/146	28/165
Gross Yards	3524	3799
Att./Completions	546/271	496/300
Completion Pct.	49.6	60.5
Had Intercepted	27	17
Punts/Avg.	82/44.4	87/40.3
Net Punting Avg.	82/36.1	87/33.0
Penalties/Yards Lost	88/730	98/839
Fumbles/Ball Lost	21/13	21/6
Touchdowns	37	52
Rushing	5	24
Passing	25	22
Returns	7	6
Avg. Time of Possession	26:55	33:05

1994 INDIVIDUAL STATISTICS

PASSING	Att.	Comp.	Yds.	Pct.	TD	Int.	Tkld.	Rate
Shuler	265	120	1658	45.3	10	12	12/83	59.6
Friesz	180	105	1266	58.3	10	9	6/45	77.7
Frerotte	100	46	600	46.0	5	5	3/18	61.3
Mitchell	1	0	0	0.0	0	1	0/0	0.0
Redskins	546	271	3524	49.6	25	27	21/146	65.0
Opponents	496	300	3799	60.5	22	17	28/165	84.9

SCORING	TD R	TD P	TD Rt	PAT	FG	Saf	PTS
Lohmiller	0	0	0	30/32	20/28	0	90
Ellard	0	6	0	0/0	0/0	0	36
Howard	0	5	0	0/0	0/0	0	32
Ervins	3	1	0	0/0	0/0	0	24
Jenkins	0	4	0	0/0	0/0	0	24
Mitchell	0	1	2	0/0	0/0	0	20
Horton	0	3	0	0/0	0/0	0	18
Winans	0	2	0	0/0	0/0	0	14
Brooks	2	0	0	0/0	0/0	0	12
A. Collins	0	0	2	0/0	0/0	0	12
Bayless	0	0	1	0/0	0/0	0	6
Green	0	0	1	0/0	0/0	0	6
Morrison	0	0	1	0/0	0/0	0	6
C. Smith	0	1	0	0/0	0/0	0	6
Truitt	0	1	0	0/0	0/0	0	6
Wycheck	0	1	0	0/0	0/0	0	6
Redskins	5	25	7	30/32	20/28	1	320
Opponents	24	22	6	47/47	17/28	0	412

2-Point conversions: Howard, Mitchell, Winans. Team: 3-5.

RUSHING	Att.	Yds.	Avg.	LG	TD
Ervins	185	650	3.5	49	3
Mitchell	78	311	4.0	33	0
Brooks	100	297	3.0	15	2
Shuler	26	103	4.0	26	0
C. Smith	10	48	4.8	13	0
Winans	1	5	5.0	5	0
Howard	1	4	4.0	4	0
Friesz	1	1	1.0	1	0
Frerotte	4	1	0.3	2	0
Ellard	1	-5	-5.0	-5	0
Redskins	407	1415	3.5	49	5
Opponents	556	1975	3.6	38	24

RECEIVING	No.	Yds.	Avg.	LG	TD
Ellard	74	1397	18.9	73t	6
Ervins	51	293	5.7	21	1
Howard	40	727	18.2	81t	5
Mitchell	26	236	9.1	46t	1
Winans	19	344	18.1	51	2
Horton	15	157	10.5	20	3
C. Smith	15	118	7.9	28	1
Brooks	13	68	5.2	16	0
Jenkins	8	32	4.0	9	4
Wycheck	7	55	7.9	20	1
Truitt	2	89	44.5	77t	1
Shepherd	1	8	8.0	8	0
Redskins	271	3524	13.0	81t	25
Opponents	300	3799	12.7	85t	22

INTERCEPTIONS	No.	Yds.	Avg.	LG	TD
A. Collins	4	150	37.5	92t	2
Carter	3	58	19.3	40	0
Bayless	3	38	12.7	19	0
Green	3	32	10.7	27t	1
Hollinquest	1	39	39.0	39	0
Gouveia	1	7	7.0	7	0
Stowe	1	2	2.0	2	0
Grant	1	0	0.0	0	0
Redskins	17	326	19.2	92t	3
Opponents	27	482	17.9	73t	4

PUNTING	No.	Yds.	Avg.	In 20	LG
Roby	82	3639	44.4	21	65
Redskins	82	3639	44.4	21	65
Opponents	87	3506	40.3	27	59

PUNT RETURNS	No.	FC	Yds.	Avg.	LG	TD
Mitchell	32	24	452	14.1	78t	2
Redskins	32	24	452	14.1	78t	2
Opponents	45	11	441	9.8	83t	1

KICKOFF RETURNS	No.	Yds.	Avg.	LG	TD
Mitchell	58	1478	25.5	86	0
Wycheck	4	84	21.0	43	0
Rush	3	45	15.0	25	0
W. Bell	2	43	21.5	25	0
Ervins	1	17	17.0	17	0
Haws	1	10	10.0	10	0
Jenkins	1	4	4.0	4	0
A. Collins	1	0	0.0	0	0
Tr. Johnson	0	4	—	4	0
Redskins	71	1685	23.7	86	0
Opponents	62	1389	22.4	96t	1

SACKS	No.
Harvey	13.5
Woods	4.5
Wilson	2.5
Marshall	2.0
A. Collins	1.5
Ti. Johnson	1.0
Nottage	1.0
Palmer	1.0
Coleman	0.5
Hollinquest	0.5
Redskins	28.0
Opponents	21.0

1995 DRAFT CHOICES

Round	Name	Pos.	College
1	Michael Westbrook	WR	Colorado
2	Cory Raymer	C	Wisconsin
3	Darryl Pounds	DB	Nicholls State
4	Larry Jones	RB	Miami
5	Jamie Asher	TE	Louisville
	Rich Owens	DE	Lehigh
6	Brian Thure	T	California
7	Scott Turner	DB	Illinois

WASHINGTON REDSKINS

1995 VETERAN ROSTER

No.		Name	Pos.	Ht.	Wt.	Birthdate	NFL Exp.	College	Hometown	How Acq.	'94 Games/ Starts
56		Anderson, Erick	LB	6-1	240	10/7/68	3	Michigan	Glenview, Ill.	FA-'94	2/0
34	#	Bayless, Martin	S	6-2	213	10/11/62	12	Bowling Green	Dayton, Ohio	FA-'94	16/15
36		Bell, William	RB	5-11	203	7/22/71	2	Georgia Tech	Miami, Fla.	FA-'94	7/0
41		Bonner, Melvin	WR	6-3	207	2/18/70	3	Baylor	Hempstead, Tex.	W(Den)-'95	0*
93		Boutte, Marc	DT	6-4	296	7/26/69	4	Louisiana State	Lake Charles, La.	FA-'94	9/3
40		Brooks, Reggie	RB	5-8	202	1/19/71	3	Notre Dame	Tulsa, Okla.	D2-'93	13/5
67		Brown, Ray	T	6-5	312	12/12/62	10	Arkansas State	Marion, Ark.	PB(Phx)-'89	16/16
59		Brownlow, Darrick	LB	6-0	241	12/28/68	5	Illinois	Indianapolis, Ind.	UFA(Dall)-'95	16/0*
25		Carter, Tom	CB	5-11	181	9/5/72	3	Notre Dame	St. Petersburg, Fla.	D1-'93	16/16
51	#	Coleman, Monte	LB	6-2	242	11/4/57	17	Central Arkansas	Pine Bluff, Ark.	D11-'79	16/0
85		Ellard, Henry	WR	5-11	182	7/21/61	13	Fresno State	Fresno, Calif.	UFA(Rams)-'94	16/16
32	#	Ervins, Ricky	RB	5-7	195	12/7/68	5	Southern California	Pasadena, Calif.	D3-'91	16/10
55		Fichtel, Brad	C	6-2	285	3/10/70	2	Eastern Illinois	Oswego, Ill.	FA-'95	1/0*
12		Frerotte, Gus	QB	6-2	221	7/3/71	2	Tulsa	Ford Cliff, Pa.	D7-'94	4/4
45		Galbraith, Scott	TE	6-2	255	1/7/67	6	Southern California	Sacramento, Calif	UFA(Dall)-'95	16/2*
75		Gesek, John	C	6-5	282	2/18/63	9	Cal State-Sacramento	Danville, Calif.	UFA(Dall)-'94	15/12
26		Grant, Alan	CB	5-10	187	10/1/66	6	Stanford	La Cañada, Calif.	FA-'94	13/0
28		Green, Darrell	CB	5-8	170	2/15/60	13	Texas A&I	Houston, Tex.	D1-'83	16/16
10		Green, Trent	QB	6-3	212	7/9/70	2	Indiana	St. Louis, Mo.	FA-'95	0*
57		Harvey, Ken	LB	6-2	245	5/6/65	8	California	Austin, Tex.	UFA(Ariz)-'94	16/16
88	†	Jenkins, James	TE	6-2	241	8/17/67	4	Rutgers	Staten Island, N.Y.	FA-'91	16/3
47	#	Johnson, AJ	CB	5-8	175	6/22/67	6	Southwest Texas State	San Antonio, Tex.	D6-'89	11/0
78		Johnson, Tim	DT	6-3	275	1/29/65	9	Penn State	Sarasota, Fla.	T(Pitt)-'90	14/13
77		Johnson, Tré	T	6-2	315	8/30/71	2	Temple	Peekskill, N.Y.	D2-'94	14/1
79		Lachey, Jim	T	6-6	294	6/4/63	11	Ohio State	St. Henry, Ohio	T(Raid)-'88	13/13
20		Logan, Marc	RB	6-0	212	5/9/65	8	Kentucky	Lexington, Ky.	FA-'95	10/5*
8	†	Lohmiller, Chip	K	6-3	215	7/16/66	8	Minnesota	Woodbury, Minn.	D2-'88	16/0
59		Matich, Trevor	C	6-4	297	10/9/61	11	Brigham Young	Sacramento, Calif.	UFA(Ind)-'94	16/0
72		Mills, Lamar	DE	6-5	270	1/26/71	2	Indiana	Detroit, Mich.	FA-'94	13/4
30		Mitchell, Brian	RB	5-10	203	8/18/68	6	Southwestern Louisiana	Plaquemine, La.	D5-'90	16/7
37		Morrison, Darryl	CB	5-11	185	5/19/71	2	Arizona	Phoenix, Ariz.	D6a-'93	16/16
80		Newman, Patrick	WR	6-0	200	9/10/68	6	Utah State	San Diego, Calif.	FA-'95	1/0*
92		Nottage, Dexter	DE	6-4	273	11/14/70	2	Florida A&M	Miami, Fla.	D6-'94	15/1
41		Oliver, Muhammad	CB-S	5-11	180	3/12/69	4	Oregon	Brooklyn, N.Y.	FA-'95	13/2*
97		Palmer, Sterling	DE	6-5	256	2/4/71	3	Florida State	Ft. Lauderdale, Fla.	D4-'93	16/16
68		Patton, Joe	G	6-5	288	1/5/72	2	Alabama A&M	Birmingham, Ala.	D3b-'94	2/0
53		Patton, Marvcus	LB	6-2	240	5/1/67	6	UCLA	Lawndale, Calif.	UFA(Buff)-'95	16/16*
24		Richard, Stanley	S	6-2	197	10/21/67	5	Texas	Miniola, Tex.	UFA(SD)-'95	16/16*
39		Rush, Tyrone	RB	5-11	196	2/5/71	2	North Alabama	Philadelphia, Miss.	FA-'95	5/0
5		Shuler, Heath	QB	6-2	221	12/31/71	2	Tennessee	Bryson City, N.C.	D1-'94	11/8
76		Simmons, Ed	T	6-5	300	12/31/63	9	Eastern Washington	Seattle, Wash.	D6-'87	16/16
37		Smith, Cedric	RB	5-10	222	5/27/68	4	Florida	Enterprise, Ala.	FA-'94	14/8
61	#	Smith, Vernice	G	6-3	298	10/24/65	6	Florida A&M	Orlando, Fla.	FA-'93	4/0
99		Stephens, Rod	LB	6-1	237	6/15/66	6	Georgia Tech	Atlanta, Ga.	UFA(Sea)-'95	16/16*
27		Taylor, Keith	S	5-11	206	12/21/64	7	Illinois	Pennsauken, N.J.	UFA(NO)-'94	1/1
19		Thomas, Doug	WR	5-11	187	9/18/69	4	Clemson	Rockingham, N.C.	FA-'95	0*
84		Truitt, Olanda	WR	6-0	186	1/4/71	3	Mississippi State	Birmingham, Ala.	FA-'94	9/0
90		Vanderbeek, Matt	LB	6-3	243	8/16/67	6	Michigan State	Holland, Mich.	UFA(Dall)-'95	12/0*
35		Washington, James	S	6-1	209	1/10/65	8	UCLA	Los Angeles, Calif.	UFA(Dall)-'95	16/16*
94		Wilson, Bobby	DT	6-2	297	3/4/68	5	Michigan State	Chicago, Ill.	D1-'91	9/9
83		Winans, Tydus	WR	5-11	180	7/26/72	2	Fresno State	Los Angeles, Calif.	D3a-'95	15/0
98		Woods, Tony	DE	6-4	269	9/11/65	9	Pittsburgh	South Orange, N.J.	UFA(Rams)-'94	15/15
22		Wycheck, Frank	RB	6-3	235	10/14/71	3	Maryland	Philadelphia, Pa.	D6b-'93	9/1

* Bonner missed '94 season because of injury; Brownlow played 16 games with Dallas in '94; Fichtel played 1 game with L.A. Rams; Galbraith played 16 games with Dallas; T. Green last active with San Diego in '93; Logan played 10 games with San Francisco; Newman played 1 game with Cleveland; Oliver played 16 games with Miami; M. Patton played 16 games with Buffalo; Richard played 16 games with San Diego; Stephens played 16 games with Seattle; Thomas last active with Seattle in '93; Vanderbeek played 12 games with Dallas; Washington played 16 games with Dallas.

Unrestricted free agent; subject to developments.

† Restricted free agent; subject to developments.

Traded—DE Shane Collins to San Francisco.

Players lost through free agency (8): S Pat Eilers (Chi; 16 games in '94), QB John Friesz (Sea; 16), LB Kurt Gouveia (Phil; 14), CB-S Alvoid Mays (Pitt; 2), G-C Raleigh McKenzie (Phil; 16), P Reggie Roby (TB; 16), G Mark Schlereth (Den; 16), CB Johnny Thomas (Clev; 16).

Players lost through Expansion Draft (2): TE Kurt Haws (Car; 6 games in '94), WR Desmond Howard (Jax; 16).

Also played with Redskins in '94—S Deral Boykin (12 games), LB Andre Collins (16), DE Shane Collins (7), LB Rick Hamilton (1), LB Lamont Hollinquest (14), S Sebastian Savage (1), LB Tyronne Stowe (16).

COACHING STAFF

Head Coach,
Norv Turner

Pro Career: Enters his second seaon as head coach of the Washington Redskins after serving three years as the Dallas Cowboys' offensive coordinator. Turner guided the Cowboys' prolific offense during back-to-back Super Bowl championship seasons. He inherited a Cowboys offense that finished twenty-eighth in total offense in 1990, and a year later improved to ninth. The Cowboys finished fourth in the league offensively in 1992-93. In three seasons under Turner, quarterback Troy Aikman compiled a 91.7 rating, and running back Emmitt Smith won three consecutive NFL rushing titles. Prior to joining the Cowboys, Turner coached six seasons (1985-1990) with the Los Angeles Rams where he oversaw the passing game. Quarterback Jim Everett enjoyed his best seasons under Turner, while Willie Anderson led the NFL in yards per catch in 1989 and 1990, and Henry Ellard was the league's leading receiver in 1988. Career record: 3-13.

Background: Turner played quarterback for three seasons at the University of Oregon (1972-74). He began his coaching career as a graduate assistant at Oregon in 1975. A year later, he moved to the University of Southern California, where he coached from 1976-1984.

Personal: Born May 17, 1952, in LeJeune, N.C. Turner and his wife, Nancy, live in Oakton, Va., and have three children—Scott, Stephanie, and Drew.

1995 FIRST-YEAR ROSTER

Name	Pos.	Ht.	Wt.	Birthdate	College	Hometown	How Acq.
Abrams, Anthony (1)	DT	6-4	298	2/16/71	Clark	Warner Robins, Ga.	FA
Alexander, Patrise	LB	6-1	255	10/23/72	S.W. Louisiana	Galveston, Tex.	FA
Asher, Jamie	TE	6-3	243	10/31/72	Louisville	Indianapolis, Ind.	D5a
Bell, Coleman (1)	TE	6-2	243	4/22/70	Miami	Tampa, Fla.	FA
Blanton, Scott	K	6-2	223	7/1/73	Oklahoma	Norman, Okla.	FA
Burrest, Damon	DT	6-3	311	10/11/71	New Mexico	Tabb, Va.	FA
Dammann, Ken	G	6-5	285	1/17/72	Rutgers	Little Silver, N.J.	FA
Dillard, Barry	CB	5-10	176	2/14/73	Memphis State	McMinnville, Tenn.	FA
Dubose, Craig	LB	6-2	255	8/30/71	Clark	Decatur, Ga.	FA
Frazier, Joe	RB	6-0	212	4/13/72	Auburn	Montgomery, Ala.	FA
Henson, Don (1)	T	6-5	297	1/30/71	Sam Houston State	Aldine, Tex.	FA
Jones, Larry	RB	6-0	244	2/16/71	Miami	Gainesville, Fla.	D4
Jones, Reggie	WR	6-0	175	5/5/71	Louisiana State	Kansas City, Kan.	FA
Kalaniuvalu, Alai (1)	G	6-3	302	10/23/71	Oregon State	Seattle, Wash.	FA
Killian, P.J. (1)	LB	6-2	240	5/19/71	Virginia	Pittsburgh, Pa.	FA
Mahone, Elic	DE	6-4	260	3/7/72	Southern California	Pasadena, Calif.	FA
Owens, Rich	DE	6-6	255	5/22/72	Lehigh	Philadelphia, Pa.	D5b
Pounds, Darryl	CB	5-10	177	7/21/72	Nicholls State	Ft. Worth, Tex.	D3
Raymer, Cory	C	6-2	293	3/3/73	Wisconsin	Fond du Lac, Wis.	D2
Roberts, John	QB	6-3	190	6/20/72	Northern Colorado	Arvada, Colo.	FA
Savage, Sebastian (1)	S	5-10	187	12/12/69	North Carolina State	Union, S.C.	FA
Sheperd, Leslie (1)	WR	5-11	189	11/3/69	Temple	Forestville, Md.	FA
Talanoa, Ken	DE	6-4	271	12/14/72	Arizona State	El Segundo, Calif.	FA
Thompson, Ernie (1)	RB	6-0	260	10/25/69	Indiana	Terre Haute, Ind.	FA
Thure, Brian	T	6-5	300	9/3/73	Oklahoma	Downey, Calif.	D6
Turk, Matt (1)	P	6-5	230	6/16/68	Wis.-Whitewater	Greenfield, Wis.	FA
Turner, Scott	CB	5-10	178	2/26/72	Illinois	Richardson, Tex.	D7
Videtich, Steve	K	6-1	200	11/4/71	North Carolina State	Winston-Salem, N.C.	FA
Westbrook, Michael	WR	6-3	215	7/7/72	Colorado	Detroit, Mich.	D1

The term NFL Rookie is defined as a player who is in his first season of professional football and has not been on the roster of another professional football team for any regular-season or postseason games. A Rookie is designated by an "R" on NFL rosters. Players who have been active in another professional football league or players who have NFL experience, including either preseason training camp or being on an Active List or Inactive List, or on Reserve/Injured or Reserve/Physically Unable to Perform for fewer than six regular-season games, are termed NFL First-Year Players. An NFL First-Year Player is designated by a "1" on NFL rosters. Thereafter, a player is credited with an additional year of experience for each season in which he accumulates six games on the Active List or Inactive List, or on Reserve/Injured or Reserve/Physically Unable to Perform.

NOTES

ASSISTANT COACHES

Jason Arapoff, assistant conditioning; born July 8, 1965, Weymouth, Mass., lives in Centreville,Va. Defensive back Springfield College 1985-88. No pro playing experience. Pro coach: Joined Redskins in 1992.

Cam Cameron, quarterbacks; born February 6, 1961, Chapel Hill, N.C., lives in Ashburn, Va. Quarterback Indiana 1980-83. No pro playing experience. College coach: Michigan 1984-93. Pro coach: Joined Redskins in 1994.

Russ Grimm, tight ends; born May 2, 1959, Scottdale, Pa., lives in Fairfax, Va. Guard-center Pittsburgh 1977-80. Pro guard Washington Redskins 1981-91. Pro coach: Joined Redskins in 1992.

Mike Haluchak, linebackers; born November 28, 1949, Concord, Calif., lives in Ashburn, Va. Linebacker Southern California 1967-70. No pro playing experience. College coach: Southern California 1976-77, Cal State-Fullerton 1978, Pacific 1979-80, California 1981, North Carolina State 1982. Pro coach: Oakland Invaders (USFL) 1983-85, San Diego Chargers 1986-91, Cincinnati Bengals 1992-93, joined Redskins in 1994.

Jim Hanifan, offensive line; born September 21, 1933, Compton, Calif., lives in Ashburn, Va. Tight end California 1952-54. Pro tight end Toronto Argonauts (CFL) 1955. College coach: Glendale, Calif., J.C. 1964-66, Utah 1967-70, California 1971-72, San Diego State 1972-73. Pro coach: St. Louis Cardinals 1974-85 (head coach 1980-85), Atlanta Falcons 1987-89 (interim head coach last four games of 1989), joined Redskins in 1990.

Tom Hayes, defensive backs; born March 26, 1949, Keokuk, Iowa, lives in Ashburn, Va. Defensive back Iowa 1968-71. No pro playing experience. College coach: Coe College 1973, Iowa 1977-78, Cal State-Fullerton 1979, UCLA 1980-88, Texas A&M 1989, Oklahoma 1990-94. Pro coach: Joined Redskins in 1995.

Ray Horton, secondary assistant; born April 12, 1960, Tacoma, Wash., lives in Ashburn, Va. Defensive back Washington 1979-82. Pro defensive back Cincinnati Bengals 1983-88, Dallas Cowboys 1989-92. Pro coach: Joined Redskins in 1994.

Bobby Jackson, running backs; born February 16, 1940, Forsyth, Ga., lives in Sterling, Va. Linebacker-running back Samford (Ga.) 1959-62. No pro playing experience. College coach: Florida State 1965-69, Kansas State 1970-74, Louisville 1975-76, Tennessee 1977-82. Pro coach: Atlanta Falcons 1983-86, San Diego Chargers 1987-91, Phoenix Cardinals 1992-93, joined Redskins in 1994.

Bob Karmelowicz, defensive line; born July 22, 1949, New Britain, Conn., lives in Ashburn, Va. Nose tackle Bridgeport 1972. No pro playing experience. College coach: Arizona State 1974-79, Massachusetts 1979-80, Texas-El Paso 1980-81, Illinois 1982-87, Washington State 1987-89, Miami 1990-91. Pro coach: Cincinnati Bengals 1992-93, joined Redskins in 1994.

Ron Lynn, defensive coordinator, born December 6, 1944, Youngstown, Ohio, lives in Sterling, Va. Quarterback-defensive back Mt. Union (Ohio) 1963-65. No pro playing experience. College coach: Toledo 1966, Mt. Union (Ohio) 1967-73, Kent State 1974-76, San Jose State 1977-78, Pacific 1979, California 1980-82. Pro coach: Oakland Invaders (USFL) 1983-85, San Diego Chargers 1986-91, Cincinnati Bengals 1992-93, joined Redskins in 1994.

Dan Riley, conditioning; born October 19, 1949, Syracuse, N.Y., lives in Ashburn, Va. No college or pro playing experience. College coach: Army 1973-76, Penn State 1977-81. Pro coach: Joined Redskins in 1982.

Terry Robiskie, receivers; born November 12, 1954, New Orleans, La., lives in Clifton, Va. Running back Louisiana State 1973-76. Pro running back Oakland Raiders 1977-79, Miami Dolphins 1980-81. Pro coach: Oakland/Los Angeles Raiders 1982-1993, joined Redskins in 1994.

Pete Rodriguez, special teams; born July 25, 1940, Chicago, Ill., lives in Sterling, Va. Guard-linebacker Denver University 1959-60, Western State, Colo. 1961-63. No pro playing experience. College coach: Western State, Colo. 1964, Arizona 1968-69, Western Illinois 1970-73, 1979-82 (head coach), Florida State 1974-75, Iowa State 1976-78, Northern Iowa 1986. Pro coach: Michigan Panthers (USFL) 1983-84, Denver Gold (USFL) 1985, Jacksonville Bulls (USFL) 1986, Ottawa Rough Riders (CFL) 1987, Los Angeles Raiders 1988-89, Phoenix Cardinals 1990-93, joined Redskins in 1994.

1994 Season in Review

TRADES

1994 INTERCONFERENCE TRADES

Wide receiver **Reggie Barrett** from Detroit to Seattle for the Seahawks' fifth-round selection in 1995. (4/29)

Wide Receiver **Jeff Graham** from Pittsburgh to Chicago for the Bears' fifth-round selection in 1995. (5/2)

Quarterback **Steve Bono** from San Francisco to Kansas City for the Chiefs' fourth-round selection in 1995. (5/3)

Running back **Derrick Gainer** from Dallas to the Los Angeles Raiders for past considerations. (5/10)

Defensive back **William White** from Detroit to Kansas City for a 1996 draft choice. (7/12)

Defensive back **Darren Anderson** from Tampa Bay to Kansas City for the Chiefs' seventh-round selection in 1995. (8/23)

Quarterback **Tommy Maddox** from Denver to the Los Angeles Rams for Dallas's fourth-round selection in 1995. (8/27)

Wide receiver **Charles Jordan** from the Los Angeles Raiders to Green Bay for the Packers' fifth-round selection in 1995. (8/28)

Defensive back **Reginald Jones** from New Orleans to Cleveland for an unannounced selection in 1996. (10/11)

1995 INTERCONFERENCE TRADES

Wide receiver **Mark Ingram** from Miami to Green Bay for the Packers' fourth-round selection in 1995. (3/21)

Running back **Eric Metcalf** and the Browns' first-round selection in 1995 from Cleveland to Atlanta for the Falcons' first-round selection in 1995. (3/27)

Tight end **Keith Jackson** and Miami's fourth-round selection from Green Bay in 1995 from the Dolphins to Green Bay for the Packers' second-round selection in 1995. (3/29)

Wide receiver **Ricky Proehl** from Arizona to Seattle for the Seahawks' fourth-round selection in 1995. (4/3)

Defensive end **Trace Armstrong** from Chicago to Miami for the Dolphins' second- and third-round selections in 1995. (4/4)

Defensive back **Terrell Buckley** from Green Bay to Miami for past considerations. (4/4)

Quarterback **Mark Brunell** from Green Bay to Jacksonville for the Jaguars' third- and fifth-round selections in 1995. Green Bay selected running back **William Henderson** (North Carolina) and running back **Travis Jervey** (Citadel). (4/22)

Wide receiver **Rob Moore** from the New York Jets to Arizona for running back **Ron Moore**, the Cardinals' first-round selection in 1995 and fourth-round selection from Seattle in 1995. The Jets selected defensive end **Hugh Douglas** (Central State, Ohio) and tackle **Melvin Hayes** (Mississippi). (4/22)

Carolina's first-round selection in 1995 from the Panthers to Cincinnati for the Bengals' first- and second-round selections in 1995. Cincinnati selected running back **Ki-Jana Carter** (Penn State). Carolina selected quarterback **Kerry Collins** (Penn State) and defensive end **Shawn King** (Northeast Louisiana). (4/22)

Cleveland's first-round selection from Atlanta in 1995 from the Browns to San Francisco for the 49ers' first- and third-round selections in 1995, fourth-round selection from Kansas City in 1995, and the 49er's first-round selection in 1996. San Francisco selected wide receiver **J.J. Stokes** (UCLA). Cleveland selected linebacker **Craig Powell** (Ohio State) and defensive end **Mike Frederick** (Virginia). (4/22)

San Diego's first-round selection in 1995 from the Chargers to Carolina for the Panthers' second-round selection, third-round supplemental selection, and fourth-round selection in 1995. Carolina selected tackle **Blake Brockermeyer** (Texas). San Diego selected defensive back **Terrance Shaw** (Stephen F. Austin), linebacker **Preston Harrison** (Ohio State), and linebacker **Chris Cowart** (Florida State). (4/22)

Wide receiver **Victor Bailey** and Philadelphia's fourth-round selection in 1995 from the Eagles to Kansas City for the Chiefs' second-round selection in 1995 and the Chiefs' sixth-round selection in 1996. Philadelphia selected defensive back **Bobby Taylor** (Notre Dame). (4/22)

Detroit's second-round selection in 1995 from the Lions to San Diego for the Chargers' first-round selection in 1996. San Diego selected running back **Terrell Fletcher** (Wisconsin). (4/22)

Green Bay's third-round selection in 1995 from the Packers to Cleveland for the Browns' third- and fifth-round selections in 1995. Cleveland selected quarterback **Eric Zeier** (Georgia). Green Bay selected wide receiver **Antonio Freeman** (Virginia Tech) and quarterback **Jay Barker** (Alabama). (4/22)

Denver's fourth-round selection in 1995 from the Broncos to Minnesota for the Vikings' fourth- and sixth-round selections in 1995. Minnesota selected quarterback **Chad May** (Kansas State). Denver selected tackle **Jamie Brown** (Florida A&M) and running back **Terrell Davis** (Georgia). (4/23)

Kansas City's fourth-round selection in 1995 from Cleveland to Philadelphia for the Eagles' fifth-round selection in 1995 and the Eagles' fifth-round selection in 1996. Philadelphia selected quarterback **Dave Barr** (California). (4/23)

Washington's fifth-round selection in 1995 from the Redskins to the Los Angeles Raiders for the Raiders' fifth-round selection from Green Bay and seventh-round selection in 1995. The Raiders selected linebacker **Matt Dyson** (Michigan). Washington selected defensive end **Rich Owens** (Lehigh) and defensive back **Scott Turner** (Illinois). (4/23)

Philadelphia's fifth- and seventh-round selection in 1995 from the Eagles to Jacksonville for the Jaguars' sixth-round supplemental selection, seventh-round selection, and seventh-round supplemental selection in 1995. Jacksonville selected running back **Ryan Christopherson** (Wyoming) and wide receiver **Curtis Marsh** (Utah). Philadelphia selected running back **Fred McCrary** (Mississippi State), running back **Kevin Bouie** (Mississippi State), and tackle **Howard Smothers** (Bethune-Cookman). (4/23)

Kansas City's sixth-round selection in 1995 from the Chiefs to Carolina for the Panthers' sixth-round selection in 1996. Carolina selected quarterback **Jerry Colquitt** (Tennessee). (4/23)

Quarterback **Craig Erickson** from Tampa Bay to Indianapolis for the Colts' first-round selection in 1996. (4/27)

1994 AFC TRADES

Running back **Leroy Thompson** from Pittsburgh to New England for the Patriots' fourth-round selection in 1995. (8/10)

Defensive back **Darryl Wren** from New England to Seattle for the Seahawks' sixth-round selection in 1995 (condition not fulfilled). (8/19)

1995 AFC TRADES

Kansas City's first-round selection in 1995 from the Chiefs to Jacksonville for the Jaguars' first-round supplemental selection, third-round supplemental selection, and fourth-round supplemental selection in 1995, and the Jaguars' fourth-round supplemental selection in 1996. Jacksonville selected running back **James Stewart** (Tennessee). Kansas City selected tackle **Trezelle Jenkins** (Michigan), linebacker **Troy Dumas** (Nebraska), and quarterback **Steve Stenstrom** (Stanford). (4/22)

Jacksonville's second-round selection in 1995 from the Jaguars to the New York Jets for the Jets' second- and third-round selections in 1995. The Jets selected tackle **Matt O'Dwyer** (Northwestern). Jacksonville selected tackle **Brian DeMarco** (Michigan State) and defensive back **Chris Hudson** (Colorado). (4/22)

An unannounced selection in 1996 from the New England Patriots to Kansas City for the Chiefs' fourth-round selection from Philadelphia in 1995. New England selected center **Dave Wohlabaugh** (Syracuse). (4/23)

Cleveland's fourth-round selection in 1995 from the Browns to Jacksonville for the Jaguars' fifth-round selection in 1995 and an unannounced selection in 1996. Jacksonville selected defensive tackle **Mike Thompson** (Wisconsin). Cleveland selected defensive tackle **Tau Pupua** (Weber State). (4/23)

Cleveland's seventh-round selection in 1995 from the Browns to New England for the Patriots' seventh-round selection in 1995. New England selected defensive back **Carlos Yancy** (Georgia). Cleveland selected wide receiver **A.C. Tellison** (Miami). (4/23)

1994 NFC TRADES

Linebacker **Tyronne Stowe** from Arizona to Washington for the Redskins' seventh-round selection in 1995. (6/17)

Linebacker **Jim Schwantz** from Chicago to Dallas for an undisclosed selection in 1996. (8/28)

Tackle **Darryl Moore** from Washington to Green Bay for the Packers' seventh-round selection in 1995 (condition not fulfilled). (8/28)

1995 NFC TRADES

Punter **Harold Alexander** from Atlanta to Detroit for an undisclosed selection in 1996. (3/2)

Defensive end **Shane Collins** from Washington to San Francisco for an undisclosed selection in 1996. (4/7)

Running back **Derrick Moore** from Detroit to San Francisco for the 49ers' fifth-round selection in 1995. (4/18)

Tampa Bay's first- and third-round selections in 1995 from the Buccaneers to Philadelphia for the Eagles' first- and second-round selections and second-round Named Plaintiff compensatory selection in 1995. Philadelphia selected defensive end **Mike Mamula** (Boston College) and defensive end **Greg Jefferson** (Central Florida). Tampa Bay selected defensive tackle **Warren Sapp** (Miami) and defensive back **Melvin Johnson** (Kentucky). (4/22)

Green Bay's first- and sixth-round selections in 1995 from the Packers to Carolina for the Panthers' first-round supplemental selection, and third- and sixth-round selections in 1995. Carolina selected defensive back **Tyrone Poole** (Ft. Valley State) and defensive tackle **Steve Strahan** (Baylor). Green Bay selected defensive back **Craig Newsome** (Arizona State), defensive tackle **Darius Holland** (Colorado), and wide receiver **Charlie Simmons** (Georgia Tech). (4/22)

Tampa Bay's second-round selection and second-round Named Plaintiff compensatory selection from Philadelphia in 1995 from the Buccaneers to Dallas for the Cowboys' first-round selection in 1995. Dallas selected guard **Shane Hannah** (Michigan State). Tampa Bay selected linebacker **Derrick Brooks** (Florida State). (4/22)

Atlanta's second- and fourth-round selections in 1995 from the Falcons to Dallas for the Cowboys' second-round selections from Tampa Bay in 1995. Dallas selected running back **Sherman Williams** (Alabama) and wide receiver **Eric Bjornson** (Washington). Atlanta selected defensive back **Ronald Davis** (Tennessee). (4/22)

St. Louis's third-round selection in 1995 from the Rams to Detroit for the Lions' third- and fourth-round selections in 1995. Detroit selected tight end **David Sloan** (New Mexico). The Rams selected kicker **Steve McLaughlin** (Arizona) and tight end **Lovell Pinkney** (Texas). (4/22)

Defensive back **Vencie Glenn** from Minnesota to the New York Giants for the Giants' sixth-round selection in 1995. Minnesota selected linebacker **John Soloman** (Sam Houston State). (4/23)

FINAL STANDINGS

AMERICAN FOOTBALL CONFERENCE

Eastern Division	W	L	T	Pct.	Pts.	OP
Indianapolis	4	0	0	1.000	80	51
Buffalo	3	1	0	.750	62	57
New England	3	1	0	.750	99	57
N.Y. Jets	3	1	0	.750	70	69
Miami	3	2	0	.600	105	117
Central Division						
Cleveland	3	1	0	.750	75	53
Houston++	2	3	0	.400	93	69
Cincinnati	1	3	0	.250	82	74
Pittsburgh	1	3	0	.250	78	80
Western Division						
L.A. Raiders***	4	1	0	.800	122	113
Seattle	2	2	0	.500	77	51
Denver***	2	3	0	.400	102	116
Kansas City**	2	3	0	.400	71	93
San Diego*+	1	4	0	.200	88	116

NATIONAL FOOTBALL CONFERENCE

Eastern Division	W	L	T	Pct.	Pts.	OP
Dallas++	2	3	0	.400	80	80
Arizona	1	3	0	.250	54	77
Philadelphia	1	3	0	.250	59	73
Washington	1	3	0	.250	64	78
N.Y. Giants+	1	3	0	.250	93	104
Central Division						
Chicago	4	0	0	1.000	76	45
Green Bay	3	1	0	.750	75	67
Minnesota**	3	2	0	.600	97	89
Detroit	2	2	0	.500	71	83
Tampa Bay	2	2	0	.500	61	69
Western Division						
San Francisco	3	1	0	.750	70	53
Atlanta*	3	2	0	.600	91	101
New Orleans	1	3	0	.250	61	68
L.A. Rams	0	4	0	.000	42	95

** includes Hall of Fame Game*
*** includes American Bowl '94 in Tokyo*
**** includes American Bowl '94 in Barcelona*
+ includes American Bowl '94 in Berlin
++ includes American Bowl in '94 in Mexico City

AFC PRESEASON RECORDS—TEAM BY TEAM

Eastern Division

BUFFALO (3-1)		
13	*Washington	11
7	Atlanta	27
18	Houston (SA)	16
24	*Kansas City	3
62		57

INDIANAPOLIS (4-0)		
13	*Seattle	9
26	Cincinnati	21
17	Pittsburgh	14
24	*Cleveland	7
80		51

MIAMI (3-2)		
20	N.Y. Giants	19
24	*Pittsburgh	14
31	Green Bay (MIL)	24
14	*Tampa Bay	29
16	Minnesota	31
105		117

NEW ENGLAND (3-1)		
24	*New Orleans	6
28	L.A. Rams	10
27	*Washington	17
20	Green Bay	24
99		57

N.Y. JETS (3-1)		
13	Detroit	26
34	Philadelphia	24
13	*N.Y. Giants	10
10	Tampa Bay	9
70		69

Central Division

CINCINNATI (1-3)		
16	Tampa Bay	17
21	*Indianapolis	26
7	Philadelphia	17
38	*Detroit	14
82		74

CLEVELAND (3-1)		
24	N.Y. Giants	15
16	*Detroit	7
28	*Atlanta	7
7	Indianapolis	24
75		53

HOUSTON (2-3)		
17	Kansas City	24
31	San Diego (SA)	3
6	Dallas (ABM)	0
16	Buffalo (SA)	18
23	*L.A. Raiders	24
93		69

PITTSBURGH (1-3)		
14	Miami	24
29	*L.A. Raiders	17
14	*Indianapolis	17
21	Washington	22
78		80

Western Division

DENVER (2-3)		
22	L.A. Raiders (ABBa)	25
37	*Atlanta	16
3	San Francisco	20
10	Dallas	34
30	*Arizona	21
102		116

KANSAS CITY (2-3)		
24	*Houston	17
9	Minnesota (ABT)	17
17	Washington	14
18	*Chicago	21
3	Buffalo	24
71		93

L.A. RAIDERS (4-1)		
25	Denver (ABBa)	22
27	Dallas	19
17	Pittsburgh	29
29	L.A. Rams	20
24	Houston	23
122		113

SAN DIEGO (1-4)		
17	Atlanta (HOF)	21
3	Houston (SA)	31
20	N.Y. Giants (ABBe)	28
24	*San Francisco	30
24	*L.A. Rams	6
88		116

SEATTLE (2-2)		
9	Indianapolis	13
29	*Tampa Bay	6
30	*Minnesota	19
9	San Francisco	13
77		51

NFC PRESEASON RECORDS—TEAM BY TEAM

Eastern Division

ARIZONA (1-3)		
17	*San Francisco	7
0	*Chicago	16
16	Detroit	24
21	Denver	30
54		77

DALLAS (2-3)		
17	*Minnesota	9
19	*L.A. Raiders	27
0	Houston (ABM)	6
34	*Denver	10
10	New Orleans	28
80		80

N.Y. GIANTS (1-4)		
19	*Miami	20
15	*Cleveland	24
28	San Diego (ABBe)	20
10	N.Y. Jets	13
21	Chicago	27
93		104

PHILADELPHIA (1-3)		
6	Chicago	12
24	*N.Y. Jets	34
17	*Cincinnati	7
12	Atlanta	20
59		73

WASHINGTON (1-3)		
11	Buffalo	13
14	*Kansas City	17
17	New England	27
22	*Pittsburgh	21
64		78

Central Division

CHICAGO (4-0)		
12	*Philadelphia	6
16	Arizona	0
21	Kansas City	18
27	*N.Y. Giants	21
76		45

DETROIT (2-2)		
26	*N.Y. Jets	13
7	Cleveland	16
24	*Arizona	16
14	Cincinnati	38
71		83

GREEN BAY (3-1)		
14	L.A. Rams (MAD)	6
24	Miami (MIL)	31
13	New Orleans	10
24	*New England	20
75		67

MINNESOTA (3-2)		
9	Dallas	17
17	Kansas City (ABT)	9
21	*New Orleans	17
19	Seattle	30
31	*Miami	16
97		89

TAMPA BAY (2-2)		
17	*Cincinnati	16
6	Seattle	29
29	Miami	14
9	*N.Y. Jets	10
61		69

Western Division

ATLANTA (3-2)		
21	San Diego (HOF)	17
16	Denver	37
27	*Buffalo	7
7	Cleveland	28
20	*Philadelphia	12
91		101

L.A. RAMS (0-4)		
6	Green Bay (MAD)	14
10	*New England	28
20	*L.A. Raiders	29
6	San Diego	24
42		95

NEW ORLEANS (1-3)		
6	New England	24
17	Minnesota	21
10	*Green Bay	13
28	*Dallas	10
61		68

SAN FRANCISCO (3-1)		
7	Arizona	17
20	*Denver	3
30	San Diego	24
13	*Seattle	9
70		53

*denotes home game
(OT) denotes overtime
(HOF) denotes Hall of Fame Game
(ABBa) denotes American Bowl '94 in Barcelona
(ABBe) denotes American Bowl '94 in Berlin
(ABT) denotes American Bowl '94 in Tokyo
(ABM) denotes American Bowl '94 in Mexico City
(MAD) denotes game played in Madison, Wis.
(MIL) denotes game played in Milwaukee, Wis.
(SA) denotes game played in San Antonio, Tex.

1994 NFL STANDINGS/RESULTS

FINAL STANDINGS

AMERICAN FOOTBALL CONFERENCE

Eastern Division	W	L	T	Pct.	Pts.	OP
Miami	10	6	0	.625	389	327
*New England	10	6	0	.625	351	312
Indianapolis	8	8	0	.500	307	320
Buffalo	7	9	0	.438	340	356
N.Y. Jets	6	10	0	.375	264	320
Central Division						
Pittsburgh	12	4	0	.750	316	234
*Cleveland	11	5	0	.688	340	204
Cincinnati	3	13	0	.188	276	406
Houston	2	14	0	.125	226	352
Western Division						
San Diego	11	5	0	.688	381	306
*Kansas City	9	7	0	.563	319	298
L.A. Raiders	9	7	0	.563	303	327
Denver	7	9	0	.438	347	396
Seattle	6	10	0	.375	287	323

NATIONAL FOOTBALL CONFERENCE

Eastern Division	W	L	T	Pct.	Pts.	OP
Dallas	12	4	0	.750	414	248
N.Y. Giants	9	7	0	.563	279	305
Arizona	8	8	0	.500	235	267
Philadelphia	7	9	0	.438	308	308
Washington	3	13	0	.188	320	412
Central Division						
Minnesota	10	6	0	.625	356	314
*Green Bay	9	7	0	.563	382	287
*Detroit	9	7	0	.563	357	342
*Chicago	9	7	0	.563	271	307
Tampa Bay	6	10	0	.375	251	351
Western Division						
San Francisco	13	3	0	.813	505	296
New Orleans	7	9	0	.438	348	407
Atlanta	7	9	0	.438	317	385
L.A. Rams	4	12	0	.250	286	365

**Wild-Card qualifier for playoffs*

Miami finished ahead of New England based on a head-to-head sweep (2-0). Kansas City finished ahead of L.A. Raiders based on a head-to-head sweep (2-0). Green Bay was first Wild Card based on best head-to-head record (3-1) vs. Detroit (2-2) and Chicago (1-3) and better conference record (8-4) than N.Y. Giants (6-6). Detroit was second Wild Card based on better division record (4-4) than Chicago (3-5) and head-to-head sweep of N.Y. Giants (1-0). Chicago was third Wild Card based on better record vs. common opponents (4-4) than N.Y. Giants (3-5). New Orleans finished ahead of Atlanta based on a head-to-head sweep (2-0).

WILD CARD PLAYOFFS

AFC

Miami 27, Kansas City 17, December 31, at Miami
Cleveland 20, New England 13, January 1, at Cleveland

NFC

Green Bay 16, Detroit 12, December 31, at Green Bay
Chicago 35, Minnesota 18, January 1, at Minnesota

DIVISIONAL PLAYOFFS

AFC

Pittsburgh 29, Cleveland 9, January 7, at Pittsburgh
San Diego 22, Miami 21, January 8, at San Diego

NFC

San Francisco 44, Chicago 15, January 7, at San Francisco
Dallas 35, Green Bay 9, January 8, at Dallas

CHAMPIONSHIP GAMES

AFC

San Diego 17, Pittsburgh 13, January 15, at Pittsburgh

NFC

San Francisco 38, Dallas 28, January 15, at San Francisco

SUPER BOWL XXIX

San Francisco 49, San Diego 26, January 29, at Joe Robbie Stadium, Miami, Florida

AFC-NFC PRO BOWL

AFC 41, NFC 13, February 5, at Aloha Stadium, Honolulu, Hawaii

AFC SEASON RECORDS—TEAM BY TEAM

BUFFALO (7-9)		
3	*N.Y. Jets	23
38	at New England	35
15	at Houston	7
27	*Denver	20
13	at Chicago	20
21	*Miami	11
17	*Indianapolis	27
	OPEN DATE	
44	*Kansas City	10
17	at N.Y. Jets	22
10	at Pittsburgh	23
29	*Green Bay	20
21	at Detroit	35
42	at Miami	31
17	*Minnesota	21
17	*New England	41
9	at Indianapolis	10
340		356

CINCINNATI (3-13)		
20	*Cleveland	28
10	at San Diego	27
28	*New England	31
13	at Houston	20
7	*Miami	23
	OPEN DATE	
10	at Pittsburgh	14
13	at Cleveland	37
20	*Dallas	23
20	at Seattle (OT)	17
34	*Houston	31
13	*Indianapolis	17
13	at Denver	15
15	*Pittsburgh	38
20	at N.Y. Giants	27
7	at Arizona	28
33	*Philadelphia	30
276		406

CLEVELAND (11-5)		
28	at Cincinnati	20
10	*Pittsburgh	17
32	*Arizona	0
21	at Indianapolis	14
27	*N.Y. Jets	7
	OPEN DATE	
11	at Houston	8
37	*Cincinnati	13
14	at Denver	26
13	*New England	6
26	at Philadelphia	7
13	at Kansas City	20
34	*Houston	10
13	*N.Y. Giants	16
19	at Dallas	14
7	at Pittsburgh	17
35	*Seattle	9
340		204

DENVER (7-9)		
34	*San Diego	37
22	at N.Y. Jets (OT)	25
16	*L.A. Raiders	48
20	at Buffalo	27
	OPEN DATE	
16	at Seattle	9
28	*Kansas City	31
20	at San Diego	15
26	*Cleveland	14
21	at L.A. Rams	27
17	*Seattle	10
32	*Atlanta	28
15	*Cincinnati	13
20	at Kansas City (OT)	17
13	at L.A. Raiders	23
19	at San Francisco	42
28	*New Orleans	30
347		396

**denotes home games*
(OT) denotes overtime

HOUSTON (2-14)		
21	at Indianapolis	45
17	at Dallas	20
7	*Buffalo	15
20	*Cincinnati	13
14	at Pittsburgh	30
	OPEN DATE	
8	*Cleveland	11
6	at Philadelphia	21
14	at L.A. Raiders	17
9	*Pittsburgh (OT)	12
31	at Cincinnati	34
10	*N.Y. Giants	13
10	at Cleveland	34
12	*Arizona	30
14	*Seattle	16
9	at Kansas City	31
24	*N.Y. Jets	10
226		352

INDIANAPOLIS (8-8)		
45	*Houston	21
10	at Tampa Bay	24
21	at Pittsburgh	31
14	*Cleveland	21
17	*Seattle	15
6	at N.Y. Jets	16
27	at Buffalo	17
27	*Washington	41
28	*N.Y. Jets	25
21	at Miami	22
	OPEN DATE	
17	at Cincinnati	13
10	*New England	12
31	at Seattle	19
13	at New England	28
10	*Miami	6
10	*Buffalo	9
307		320

KANSAS CITY (9-7)		
30	at New Orleans	17
24	*San Francisco	17
30	at Atlanta	10
0	*L.A. Rams	16
	OPEN DATE	
6	at San Diego	20
31	at Denver	28
38	*Seattle	23
10	at Buffalo	44
13	*L.A. Raiders	3
13	*San Diego	14
20	*Cleveland	13
9	at Seattle	10
17	*Denver (OT)	20
28	at Miami	45
31	*Houston	9
19	at L.A. Raiders	9
319		298

L.A. RAIDERS (9-7)		
14	at San Francisco	44
9	*Seattle	38
48	at Denver	16
24	*San Diego	26
	OPEN DATE	
21	at New England	17
17	at Miami (OT)	20
30	*Atlanta	17
17	*Houston	14
3	at Kansas City	13
20	at L.A. Rams	17
24	*New Orleans	19
3	*Pittsburgh	21
24	at San Diego	17
23	*Denver	13
17	at Seattle	16
9	*Kansas City	19
303		327

MIAMI (10-6)		
39	*New England	35
24	at Green Bay	14
28	*N.Y. Jets	14
35	at Minnesota	38
23	at Cincinnati	7
11	at Buffalo	21
20	*L.A. Raiders (OT)	17
	OPEN DATE	
23	at New England	3
22	*Indianapolis	21
14	*Chicago	17
13	at Pittsburgh (OT)	16
28	at N.Y. Jets	24
31	*Buffalo	42
45	*Kansas City	28
6	at Indianapolis	10
27	*Detroit	20
389		327

NEW ENGLAND (10-6)		
35	at Miami	39
35	*Buffalo	38
31	at Cincinnati	28
23	at Detroit	17
17	*Green Bay	16
17	*L.A. Raiders	21
17	at N.Y. Jets	24
	OPEN DATE	
3	*Miami	23
6	at Cleveland	13
26	*Minnesota (OT)	20
23	*San Diego	17
12	at Indianapolis	10
24	*N.Y. Jets	13
28	*Indianapolis	13
41	at Buffalo	17
13	at Chicago	3
351		312

N.Y. JETS (6-10)		
23	at Buffalo	3
25	*Denver (OT)	22
14	at Miami	28
7	*Chicago	19
7	at Cleveland	27
16	*Indianapolis	6
24	*New England	17
	OPEN DATE	
25	at Indianapolis	28
22	*Buffalo	17
10	at Green Bay	17
31	at Minnesota	21
24	*Miami	28
13	at New England	24
7	*Detroit	18
6	*San Diego	21
10	at Houston	24
264		320

PITTSBURGH (12-4)		
9	*Dallas	26
17	at Cleveland	10
31	*Indianapolis	21
13	at Seattle	30
30	*Houston	14
	OPEN DATE	
14	*Cincinnati	10
10	at N.Y. Giants	6
17	at Arizona (OT)	20
12	at Houston (OT)	9
23	*Buffalo	10
16	*Miami (OT)	13
21	at L.A. Raiders	3
38	at Cincinnati	15
14	*Philadelphia	3
17	*Cleveland	7
34	at San Diego	37
316		234

SAN DIEGO (11-5)		
37	at Denver	34
27	*Cincinnati	10
24	at Seattle	10
26	at L.A. Raiders	24
	OPEN DATE	
20	*Kansas City	6
36	at New Orleans	22
15	*Denver	20
35	*Seattle	15
9	at Atlanta	10
14	at Kansas City	13
17	at New England	23
31	*L.A. Rams	17
17	*L.A. Raiders	24
15	*San Francisco	38
21	at N.Y. Jets	6
37	*Pittsburgh	34
381		306

SEATTLE (6-10)		
28	at Washington	7
38	at L.A. Raiders	9
10	*San Diego	24
30	*Pittsburgh	13
15	at Indianapolis	17
9	*Denver	16
	OPEN DATE	
23	at Kansas City	38
15	at San Diego	35
17	*Cincinnati (OT)	20
10	at Denver	17
22	*Tampa Bay	21
10	*Kansas City	9
19	*Indianapolis	31
16	at Houston	14
16	*L.A. Raiders	17
9	at Cleveland	35
287		323

NFC SEASON RECORDS—TEAM BY TEAM

ARIZONA (8-8)		
12	at L.A. Rams	14
17	*N.Y. Giants	20
0	at Cleveland	32
	OPEN DATE	
17	*Minnesota	7
3	at Dallas	38
19	at Washington (OT)	16
21	*Dallas	28
20	*Pittsburgh (OT)	17
7	at Philadelphia	17
10	at N.Y. Giants	9
12	*Philadelphia	6
16	*Chicago (OT)	19
30	at Houston	12
17	*Washington	15
28	*Cincinnati	7
6	at Atlanta	10
235		267

ATLANTA (7-9)		
28	at Detroit (OT)	31
31	*L.A. Rams	13
10	*Kansas City	30
27	at Washington	20
8	at L.A. Rams	5
34	*Tampa Bay	13
3	*San Francisco	42
17	at L.A. Raiders	30
	OPEN DATE	
10	*San Diego	9
32	at New Orleans	33
28	at Denver	32
28	*Philadelphia	21
14	at San Francisco	50
20	*New Orleans	29
17	at Green Bay	21
10	*Arizona	6
317		385

CHICAGO (9-7)		
21	*Tampa Bay	9
22	at Philadelphia	30
14	*Minnesota	42
19	at N.Y. Jets	7
20	*Buffalo	13
17	*New Orleans	7
	OPEN DATE	
16	at Detroit	21
6	*Green Bay	33
20	at Tampa Bay	6
17	at Miami	14
20	*Detroit	10
19	at Arizona (OT)	16
27	at Minnesota (OT)	33
3	at Green Bay	40
27	*L.A. Rams	13
3	*New England	13
271		307

DALLAS (12-4)		
26	at Pittsburgh	9
20	*Houston	17
17	*Detroit (OT)	20
	OPEN DATE	
34	at Washington	7
38	*Arizona	3
24	*Philadelphia	13
28	at Arizona	21
23	at Cincinnati	20
38	*N.Y. Giants	10
14	at San Francisco	21
31	*Washington	7
42	*Green Bay	31
31	at Philadelphia	19
14	*Cleveland	19
24	at New Orleans	16
10	at N.Y. Giants	15
414		248

**denotes home games*
(OT) denotes overtime

DETROIT (9-7)		
31	*Atlanta (OT)	28
3	at Minnesota	10
20	at Dallas (OT)	17
17	*New England	23
14	at Tampa Bay	24
21	*San Francisco	27
	OPEN DATE	
21	*Chicago	16
28	at N.Y. Giants (OT)	25
30	at Green Bay	38
14	*Tampa Bay	9
10	at Chicago	20
35	*Buffalo	21
34	*Green Bay	31
18	at N.Y. Jets	7
41	*Minnesota	19
20	at Miami	27
357		342

GREEN BAY (9-7)		
16	*Minnesota	10
14	*Miami	24
7	at Philadelphia	13
30	*Tampa Bay	3
16	at New England	17
24	*L.A. Rams	17
	OPEN DATE	
10	at Minnesota (OT)	13
33	at Chicago	6
38	*Detroit	30
17	*N.Y. Jets	10
20	at Buffalo	29
31	at Dallas	42
31	at Detroit	34
40	*Chicago	3
21	*Atlanta	17
34	at Tampa Bay	19
382		287

L.A. RAMS (4-12)		
14	*Arizona	12
13	at Atlanta	31
19	*San Francisco	34
16	at Kansas City	0
5	*Atlanta	8
17	at Green Bay	24
17	*N.Y. Giants	10
34	at New Orleans	37
	OPEN DATE	
27	*Denver	21
17	*L.A. Raiders	20
27	at San Francisco	31
17	at San Diego	31
15	*New Orleans	31
14	at Tampa Bay	24
13	at Chicago	27
21	*Washington	24
286		365

MINNESOTA (10-6)		
10	at Green Bay	16
10	*Detroit	3
42	at Chicago	14
38	*Miami	35
7	at Arizona	17
27	at N.Y. Giants	10
	OPEN DATE	
13	*Green Bay (OT)	10
36	at Tampa Bay	13
21	*New Orleans	20
20	at New England (OT)	26
21	*N.Y. Jets	31
17	*Tampa Bay (OT)	20
33	*Chicago (OT)	27
21	at Buffalo	17
19	at Detroit	41
21	*San Francisco	14
356		314

NEW ORLEANS (7-9)		
17	*Kansas City	30
24	*Washington	38
9	at Tampa Bay	7
13	at San Francisco	24
27	*N.Y. Giants	22
7	at Chicago	17
22	*San Diego	36
37	*L.A. Rams	34
	OPEN DATE	
20	at Minnesota	21
33	*Atlanta	32
19	at L.A. Raiders	24
14	*San Francisco	35
31	at L.A. Rams	15
29	at Atlanta	20
16	*Dallas	24
30	at Denver	28
348		407

N.Y. GIANTS (9-7)		
28	*Philadelphia	23
20	at Arizona	17
31	*Washington	23
	OPEN DATE	
22	at New Orleans	27
10	*Minnesota	27
10	at L.A. Rams	17
6	*Pittsburgh	10
25	*Detroit (OT)	28
10	at Dallas	38
9	*Arizona	10
13	at Houston	10
21	at Washington	19
16	at Cleveland	13
27	*Cincinnati	20
16	at Philadelphia	13
15	*Dallas	10
279		305

PHILADELPHIA (7-9)		
23	at N.Y. Giants	28
30	*Chicago	22
13	*Green Bay	7
	OPEN DATE	
40	at San Francisco	8
21	*Washington	17
13	at Dallas	24
21	*Houston	6
31	at Washington	29
17	*Arizona	7
7	*Cleveland	26
6	at Arizona	12
21	at Atlanta	28
19	*Dallas	31
3	at Pittsburgh	14
13	N.Y. Giants	16
30	at Cincinnati	33
308		308

SAN FRANCISCO (13-3)		
44	*L.A. Raiders	14
17	at Kansas City	24
34	at L.A. Rams	19
24	*New Orleans	13
8	*Philadelphia	40
27	at Detroit	21
42	at Atlanta	3
41	*Tampa Bay	16
	OPEN DATE	
37	at Washington	22
21	*Dallas	14
31	*L.A. Rams	27
35	at New Orleans	14
50	*Atlanta	14
38	at San Diego	15
42	*Denver	19
14	at Minnesota	21
505		296

TAMPA BAY (6-10)		
9	at Chicago	21
24	*Indianapolis	10
7	*New Orleans	9
3	at Green Bay	30
24	*Detroit	14
13	at Atlanta	34
	OPEN DATE	
16	at San Francisco	41
13	*Minnesota	36
6	*Chicago	20
9	at Detroit	14
21	at Seattle	22
20	at Minnesota (OT)	17
26	*Washington	21
24	*L.A. Rams	14
17	at Washington	14
19	*Green Bay	34
251		351

WASHINGTON (3-13)		
7	*Seattle	28
38	at New Orleans	24
23	at N.Y. Giants	31
20	*Atlanta	27
7	*Dallas	34
17	at Philadelphia	21
16	*Arizona (OT)	19
41	at Indianapolis	27
29	*Philadelphia	31
22	*San Francisco	37
	OPEN DATE	
7	at Dallas	31
19	*N.Y. Giants	21
21	at Tampa Bay	26
15	at Arizona	17
14	*Tampa Bay	17
24	at L.A. Rams	21
320		412

1994 WEEK BY WEEK

Attendance figures as they appear in the following, and in the club-by-club sections starting on page 26, are turnstile counts and not paid attendance. Paid attendance totals are on page 227.

FIRST WEEK SUMMARIES

AMERICAN FOOTBALL CONFERENCE

Eastern Division	W	L	T	Pct.	Pts.	OP
Indianapolis	1	0	0	1.000	45	21
Miami	1	0	0	1.000	39	35
N.Y. Jets	1	0	0	1.000	23	3
Buffalo	0	1	0	.000	3	23
New England	0	1	0	.000	35	39
Central Division						
Cleveland	1	0	0	1.000	28	20
Cincinnati	0	1	0	.000	20	28
Houston	0	1	0	.000	21	45
Pittsburgh	0	1	0	.000	9	26
Western Division						
Kansas City	1	0	0	1.000	30	17
San Diego	1	0	0	1.000	37	34
Seattle	1	0	0	1.000	28	7
Denver	0	1	0	.000	34	37
L.A. Raiders	0	1	0	.000	14	44

NATIONAL FOOTBALL CONFERENCE

Eastern Division	W	L	T	Pct.	Pts.	OP
Dallas	1	0	0	1.000	26	9
N.Y. Giants	1	0	0	1.000	28	23
Arizona	0	1	0	.000	12	14
Philadelphia	0	1	0	.000	23	28
Washington	0	1	0	.000	7	28
Central Division						
Chicago	1	0	0	1.000	21	9
Detroit	1	0	0	1.000	31	28
Green Bay	1	0	0	1.000	16	10
Minnesota	0	1	0	.000	10	16
Tampa Bay	0	1	0	.000	9	21
Western Division						
L.A. Rams	1	0	0	1.000	14	12
San Francisco	1	0	0	1.000	44	14
Atlanta	0	1	0	.000	28	31
New Orleans	0	1	0	.000	17	30

SUNDAY, SEPTEMBER 4

L.A. RAMS 14, ARIZONA 12—at Anaheim Stadium, attendance 32,969. The Rams parlayed turnovers into 2 touchdowns to win their first season opener since 1989 and spoil Buddy Ryan's debut as the Cardinals' coach. Los Angeles took a 7-0 lead midway through the first quarter when linebacker Joe Kelly forced a fumble that cornerback Todd Lyght picked out of the air and returned 74 yards for a touchdown. Arizona narrowed the lead to 7-6 at halftime on 2 field goals by Greg Davis. Early in the third quarter, after an interception by Marquez Pope, the Rams drove 55 yards for a touchdown on Jerome Bettis's 1-yard run. Arizona answered with a 12-play, 81-yard drive, capped by a 3-yard scoring toss from Steve Beuerlein to running back Larry Centers. But the ensuing two-point conversion attempt failed, and the Rams' defense shut down the Cardinals in the fourth quarter. Los Angeles limited Arizona to just 3 yards per play (230 total yards on 76 plays).

Arizona	0	6	6	0	—	12
L.A. Rams	7	0	7	0	—	14

Rams — Lyght 74 fumble return (Zendejas kick)
Ariz — FG Davis 37
Ariz — FG Davis 34
Rams — Bettis 1 run (Zendejas kick)
Ariz — Centers 3 pass from Beuerlein (pass failed)

DETROIT 31, ATLANTA 28—at Pontiac Silverdome, attendance 60,740. Jason Hanson made a game-saving tackle in regulation, then hobbled onto the field and kicked a 37-yard field goal in overtime to lift the Lions to victory. A 7-7 halftime tie turned into a shootout as both teams' passers threw for 3 scores in the second half. Atlanta, trailing 21-14 with 12:13 left in regulation, rallied to take a 28-21 lead with 3:57 left on scoring passes of 69 and 15 yards by Jeff George. The Lions answered with a 65-yard drive to tie the game on Scott Mitchell's 15-yard touchdown pass to Anthony Carter with 30 seconds left. Atlanta's Alton Montgomery returned the ensuing kickoff 37 yards before Hanson, the Lions' last man, finally made the stop. The Falcons' Norm Johnson missed a 52-yard field goal at the end of regulation. On its first possession in overtime, Detroit drove to Atlanta's 20 to set up Hanson, still smarting from making the tackle, for the winning kick with 5:14 gone in the extra period. George completed 29 of 37 passes for 281 yards. Atlanta's Andre Rison caught a career-best 14 passes for a team-record-tying 193 yards and 2 scores.

Atlanta	0	7	7	14	0	—	28
Detroit	7	0	7	14	3	—	31

Det — D. Moore 1 run (Hanson kick)
Atl — Pegram 1 run (Johnson kick)
Det — H. Moore 4 pass from Mitchell (Hanson kick)
Atl — Rison 2 pass from George (Johnson kick)
Det — Carter 9 pass from Mitchell (Hanson kick)
Atl — Rison 69 pass from George (Johnson kick)
Atl — Mathis 15 pass from George (Johnson kick)
Det — Carter 15 pass from Mitchell (Hanson kick)
Det — FG Hanson 37

CLEVELAND 28, CINCINNATI 20—at Riverfront Stadium, attendance 52,778. Two touchdowns on special teams propelled the Browns to victory. Cleveland, leading 3-0, upped its lead on an 11-yard scoring pass from Vinny Testaverde to running back Leroy Hoard. The Browns made it 11-0 on a two-point conversion by Tom Tupa, who lined up as a holder for a kick and instead ran the ball in for the first two-point conversion in an NFL game. The Bengals answered with a 73-yard drive that ended with a 1-yard touchdown run by Derrick Fenner to make it 11-7. But the Browns quickly restored their lead to 11, as Randy Baldwin returned the ensuing kickoff 85 yards for a score. Three minutes later, Eric Metcalf set a club record with a 92-yard punt return for a score, the first time in 17 years that a team had both a punt and kickoff return for touchdowns in a game. Cleveland led 25-7 at that point and coasted from there.

Cleveland	11	14	0	3	—	28
Cincinnati	0	10	3	7	—	20

Cleve — FG Stover 19
Cleve — Hoard 11 pass from Testaverde (Tupa run)
Cin — Fenner 1 run (Pelfrey kick)
Cleve — Baldwin 85 kickoff return (Stover kick)
Cleve — Metcalf 92 punt return (Stover kick)
Cin — FG Pelfrey 38
Cin — FG Pelfrey 49
Cleve — FG Stover 22
Cin — Scott 24 pass from Klingler (Pelfrey kick)

INDIANAPOLIS 45, HOUSTON 21—at RCA Dome, attendance 47,372. Marshall Faulk made a smashing NFL debut to lead the Colts' rout of the defending AFC Central Champs. Faulk ran 23 times for 143 yards and 3 scores, including 2 in the first half to help Indianapolis build a 35-0 lead. The Colts' first-half onslaught also featured 2 scoring passes from Jim Harbaugh to Floyd Turner, and a club-record 75-yard fumble return for a touchdown by linebacker Tony Bennett. The Colts' 28-point second quarter tied a club mark for most points in a period. Faulk finished his day in the third period with runs of 52 and 11 yards, the latter for a touchdown that upped the Colts' lead to 42-0.

Houston	0	0	0	21	—	21
Indianapolis	7	28	7	3	—	45

Ind — Faulk 1 run (Biasucci kick)
Ind — Bennett 75 fumble return (Biasucci kick)
Ind — Turner 4 pass from Harbaugh (Biasucci kick)
Ind — Turner 9 pass from Harbaugh (Biasucci kick)
Ind — Faulk 2 run (Biasucci kick)
Ind — Faulk 11 run (Biasucci kick)
Hou — Carter 2 pass from Richardson (Brown pass from Richardson)
Ind — FG Biasucci 42
Hou — Jeffires 16 pass from Richardson (pass failed)
Hou — Jeffires 15 pass from Richardson (Del Greco kick)

KANSAS CITY 30, NEW ORLEANS 17—at Louisiana Superdome, attendance 69,362. Joe Montana continued his mastery of the Saints with another superb performance in the Superdome. The Chiefs built a 17-3 halftime lead on a 13-yard touchdown pass from Montana to Willie Davis and Marcus Allen's 1-yard scoring run. New Orleans closed to 17-10 in the third quarter, but Kansas City answered by reeling off 13 straight points. Montana completed 24 of 33 passes for 315 yards and 2 touchdowns (with no interceptions). He ran his record against the Saints in the Superdome to 9-0. Allen rushed for 82 yards, and his touchdown moved him into sole possession of fifth place on the NFL's all-time list with 114. Jim Everett passed for 326 yards and 2 scores in his first game as a member of the Saints.

Kansas City	7	10	3	10	—	30
New Orleans	0	3	7	7	—	17

KC — Davis 13 pass from Montana (Elliott kick)
KC — Allen 1 run (Elliott kick)
NO — FG Andersen 48
KC — FG Elliott 24
NO — Walls 12 pass from Everett (Andersen kick)
KC — FG Elliott 22
KC — Cash 2 pass from Montana (Elliott kick)
KC — FG Elliott 27
NO — Brown 14 pass from Everett (Andersen kick)

GREEN BAY 16, MINNESOTA 10—at Lambeau Field, attendance 59,487. The Packers' defense intercepted 3 passes and limited the Vikings to 194 total yards in Green Bay's victory. The Packers built a 13-0 halftime lead on 2 field goals by Chris Jacke sandwiched around a 14-yard scoring pass from Brett Favre to Sterling Sharpe. Meanwhile, Minnesota's offense did not cross the Packers' 45 until late in the third quarter, when Fuad Reveiz got the Vikings on the board with a 28-yard field goal. Minnesota made a game of it early in the fourth quarter when James Harris returned a fumble 17 yards for a touchdown to shave Green Bay's lead to 13-10. But the Packers answered with a time-consuming drive that resulted in a field goal, and left it to their defense after that. Safety George Teague had 2 of the Packers' interceptions. Favre completed 22 of 36 passes for 185 yards and Sharpe had 7 catches for 53 yards.

Minnesota	0	0	3	7	—	10
Green Bay	3	10	0	3	—	16

GB — FG Jacke 25
GB — Sharpe 14 pass from Favre (Jacke kick)
GB — FG Jacke 39
Minn — FG Reveiz 28
Minn — Harris 17 fumble return (Reveiz kick)
GB — FG Jacke 49

N.Y. GIANTS 28, PHILADELPHIA 23—at Giants Stadium, attendance 76,130. David Meggett scored twice and recovered a fumble to set up another touchdown in the Giants' victory. Meggett's recovery of a fumbled punt return late in the first quarter gave New York the ball at the Eagles' 21. Three plays later, Rodney Hampton scored on a 1-yard run for a 7-0 lead. Meggett made it 14-0 less than three minutes later when he returned a punt 68 yards for a touchdown. After the Eagles cut the deficit to 14-3, Dave Brown, making his first start for New York, fired a 51-yard scoring strike to Chris Calloway for a 21-3 Giants lead. Philadelphia answered just before halftime on a 3-yard touchdown pass from Randall Cunningham to Mark Bavaro, which was set up by Herschel Walker's 93-yard reception. The Eagles cut the lead to 21-13 on a third-quarter field goal, only to be undone by Meggett, who ran 26 yards for a score to give New York a 28-13 lead. The Eagles added a field goal and a late touchdown to make the score close. Brown completed 10 of 20 passes for 171 yards. Cunningham was 20 of 39 for 344 yards, but was harassed all day by the Giants' defense, which recorded 5 sacks after switching from a 3-4 to a 4-3 format in the offseason.

Philadelphia	0	10	3	10	—	23
N.Y. Giants	14	7	7	0	—	28

Giants— Hampton 1 run (Treadwell kick)
Giants— Meggett 68 punt return (Treadwell kick)
Phil — FG Murray 21
Giants— Calloway 51 pass from Da. Brown (Treadwell kick)
Phil — Bavaro 3 pass from Cunningham (Murray kick)
Phil — FG Murray 39
Giants— Meggett 26 run (Treadwell kick)
Phil — FG Murray 36
Phil — Williams 10 pass from Cunningham (Murray kick)

SEATTLE 28, WASHINGTON 7—at RFK Stadium, attendance 56,454. The Seahawks played error-free football to give coach Tom Flores his 100th career victory. Washington took the opening kickoff and drove 82 yards for a touchdown on a 27-yard pass from John Friesz to Desmond Howard. It turned out to be the Redskins' lone highlight of the day. Later in the first period, Terry Wooden's fumble recovery gave Seattle the ball at the Redskins' 12, and on the next play Chris Warren ran in for the tying score. Seattle took a 21-7 halftime lead on a 69-yard interception return for a score by Wooden and a 5-yard touchdown pass from Rick Mirer to Brian Blades. Warren capped the scoring in the third quarter with a 4-yard touchdown run. Seattle gained 350 total yards, led by Warren (22 carries for 100 yards) and Mirer (17 of 28 for 183 yards). The Seahawks did not turn the ball over while forcing 3 turnovers.

Seattle	7	14	7	0	—	28
Washington	7	0	0	0	—	7

Wash — Howard 27 pass from Friesz (Lohmiller kick)
Sea — Warren 12 run (Kasay kick)
Sea — Wooden 69 interception return (Kasay kick)
Sea — Blades 5 pass from Mirer (Kasay kick)
Sea — Warren 4 run (Kasay kick)

CHICAGO 21, TAMPA BAY 9—at Soldier Field, attendance 61,844. Erik Kramer enjoyed a strong outing in his debut as the Bears' quarterback to lead Chicago to victory. Kramer, signed as a free agent in the offseason, led the Bears on a 68-yard scoring drive in his first possession, hitting tight end Chris Gedney for a 10-yard touchdown pass. Tampa Bay used a 21-play drive to position Michael Husted for a 31-yard field goal, but the Bears quickly responded with a 78-yard touchdown drive (capped by Lewis Tillman's 1-yard run) to take a 14-3 halftime lead. Two third-quarter field goals by Husted cut the deficit to 14-9, but Kramer clinched the victory with a 37-yard scoring pass to Gedney. Kramer completed 18 of 25 passes for 212 yards (with no interceptions), picking up the slack for a Bears' running attack that produced only 66 yards.

Tampa Bay	0	3	6	0	—	9
Chicago	7	7	0	7	—	21

Chi — Gedney 10 pass from Kramer (Butler kick)
TB — FG Husted 31
Chi — Tillman 1 run (Butler kick)
TB — FG Husted 49
TB — FG Husted 30
Chi — Gedney 37 pass from Kramer (Butler kick)

DALLAS 26, PITTSBURGH 9—at Three Rivers Stadium, attendance 60,156. The two-time defending Super Bowl-champion Cowboys began the defense of their Super Bowl XXVIII title with an impressive road victory over the Steelers, a preseason favorite to be the AFC's representative in the Super Bowl. Dallas dominated the game statistically and on the scoreboard to give Barry Switzer a victory in his debut as the Cowboys' coach. The Cowboys, who scored on six of their eight possessions, totaled 442 yards, led by Emmitt Smith (171 yards and a touchdown on 31 carries), Troy Aikman (245 passing yards and a score), and Michael Irvin (8 receptions for 139 yards). Dallas's defense limited the Steelers to 126 total yards, including only 71 through the air thanks to 9 sacks of Pittsburgh quarterback Neil O'Donnell.

Dallas	3	13	0	10	—	26
Pittsburgh	0	3	0	6	—	9

Dall — FG Boniol 40
Dall — FG Boniol 31
Pitt — FG Anderson 41
Dall — Johnston 2 pass from Aikman (Boniol kick)
Dall — FG Boniol 21
Dall — FG Boniol 32
Pitt — O'Donnell 2 run (pass failed)
Dall — E. Smith 2 run (Boniol kick)

MIAMI 39, NEW ENGLAND 35—at Joe Robbie Stadium, attendance 69,613. Dan Marino returned with a flourish to lead the Dolphins over the Patriots in an AFL-style shootout. Marino, making his first appearance in a regular-season game since an injured Achilles tendon sidelined him in the fifth game of the 1993 season, enjoyed the best single day of any passer in 1994, completing 23 of 42 attempts for 473 yards and 5 touchdowns. He rallied Miami from second-half deficits of 21-10, 28-18, and 35-32 with 4 touchdown passes—26 yards to tight end Keith Jackson, and 54, 50, and 35 yards to Irving Fryar. The 35-yard scoring pass to Fryar came on fourth and 5, and it gave the Dolphins a 39-35 lead with 3:19 left. New England's last gasp was snuffed out by a fumble at Miami's 26-yard line in the final minutes. Marino's output was the second-highest yardage total of his career, while Fryar had 5 catches for a career-high 211 yards. New England's Drew Bledsoe completed 32 of 51 passes for 421 yards and 4 scores. Patriots tight end Ben Coates had 8 receptions for 161 yards, including touchdowns of 16 and 63 yards.

New England	7	7	14	7	—	35
Miami	0	10	15	14	—	39

NE — Turner 1 run (Bahr kick)
Mia — Ingram 64 pass from Marino (Stoyanovich kick)
NE — Coates 16 pass from Bledsoe (Bahr kick)
Mia — FG Stoyanovich 42
NE — Coates 63 pass from Bledsoe (Bahr kick)
Mia — Jackson 26 pass from Marino (Kirby run)
NE — Timpson 5 pass from Bledsoe (Bahr kick)
Mia — Fryar 54 pass from Marino (Stoyanovich kick)
Mia — Fryar 50 pass from Marino (Stoyanovich kick)
NE — Crittenden 23 pass from Bledsoe (Bahr kick)
Mia — Fryar 35 pass from Marino (Stoyanovich kick)

N.Y. JETS 23, BUFFALO 3—at Rich Stadium, attendance 79,460. The Jets used a ball-control offense that consumed 37 minutes to stun the four-time defending AFC champion Bills. Buffalo took the opening kickoff and marched 65 yards to Steve Christie's 27-yard field goal. New York answered with a 70-yard drive that took nearly 10 minutes, culminating in Richie Anderson's 1-yard scoring run on fourth down. Johnny Johnson's 9-yard run and Nick Lowery's 27-yard field goal gave New York a 17-3 halftime lead. Lowery added 2 field goals in the second half while the Jets' defense bottled up the Bills, forcing 3 turnovers and limiting Buffalo to 216 total yards. Johnson ran for 75 yards and caught 4 passes for 33 more.

N.Y. Jets	0	17	3	3	—	23
Buffalo	3	0	0	0	—	3

Buff — FG Christie 27
Jets — Anderson 1 run (Lowery kick)
Jets — Johnson 9 run (Lowery kick)
Jets — FG Lowery 27
Jets — FG Lowery 42
Jets — FG Lowery 22

SUNDAY NIGHT, SEPTEMBER 4

SAN DIEGO 37, DENVER 34—at Mile High Stadium, attendance 74,032. The Chargers rallied from a 17-point deficit to overtake the Broncos, then hung on for victory thanks to a bizarre fumble. Denver built a 17-point first-quarter advantage, but San Diego rallied to take a 27-24 halftime lead on 3 scoring passes by Stan Humphries and Stanley Richard's 99-yard interception return for a touchdown as the first half ended. After the teams traded field goals in the third quarter, the Broncos took a 34-30 lead on John Elway's third scoring pass, a 5-yard toss to Shannon Sharpe. San Diego then embarked on an 89-yard, 19-play drive that consumed 11 minutes, retaking the lead at 37-34 on a 1-yard scoring run by Natrone Means with 3:01 to play. Another Elway comeback appeared in the offing, as the Broncos' quarterback swiftly led his team to San Diego's 3-yard line in the final minute. But it was not to be. As Elway rolled right and attempted to pass, the ball slipped out of his hands and popped into the waiting hands of Chargers linebacker Junior Seau. Elway completed 36 of 46 for 371 yards, including 5 for 119 yards to running back Glyn Milburn and 9 for 97 to Sharpe. Humphries completed 12 of 22 passes for 232 and Means ran for 96 yards.

San Diego	6	21	3	7	—	37
Denver	17	7	3	7	—	34

Den — Pritchard 50 pass from Elway (Elam kick)
Den — Russell 22 run (Elam kick)
Den — FG Elam 25
SD — Pupunu 22 pass from Humphries (run failed)
Den — Milburn 8 pass from Elway (Elam kick)
SD — Jefferson 47 pass from Humphries (Carney kick)
SD — Seay 29 pass from Humphries (pass failed)
SD — Richard 99 interception return (Harmon run)
Den — FG Elam 42
SD — FG Carney 27
Den — Sharpe 5 pass from Elway (Elam kick)
SD — Means 1 run (Carney kick)

MONDAY, SEPTEMBER 5

SAN FRANCISCO 44, L.A. RAIDERS 14—at Candlestick Park, attendance 68,032. Jerry Rice established an NFL standard for touchdowns as the 49ers coasted to victory. Rice entered the game with 124 career touchdowns, 2 short of Jim Brown's NFL mark. He quickly reduced that margin by catching a 69-yard scoring pass from Steve Young midway through the first quarter, helping San Francisco build a 23-14 lead at intermission. Rice tied Brown's mark in the fourth quarter on a 23-yard run, then broke it in fitting style—a leaping, 38-yard catch for the game's final score. Rice finished with 7 receptions for 169 yards. Young completed 19 of 32 passes for 308 yards and 4 scores, and also was game's top rusher with 51 yards.

L.A. Raiders	0	14	0	0	—	14
San Francisco	14	9	0	21	—	44

SF — Rice 69 pass from Young (Brien kick)
SF — Jones 15 pass from Young (Brien kick)
Raid — Brown 7 pass from Hostetler (Jaeger kick)
SF — Watters 1 run (kick failed)
Raid — McCallum 1 run (Jaeger kick)
SF — FG Brien 33
SF — Jones 8 pass from Young (Brien kick)
SF — Rice 23 run (Brien kick)
SF — Rice 38 pass from Young (Brien kick)

SECOND WEEK SUMMARIES

AMERICAN FOOTBALL CONFERENCE

Eastern Division	W	L	T	Pct.	Pts.	OP
Miami	2	0	0	1.000	63	49
N.Y. Jets	2	0	0	1.000	48	25
Buffalo	1	1	0	.500	41	58
Indianapolis	1	1	0	.500	55	45
New England	0	2	0	.000	70	77
Central Division						
Cleveland	1	1	0	.500	38	37
Pittsburgh	1	1	0	.500	26	36
Cincinnati	0	2	0	.000	30	55
Houston	0	2	0	.000	38	65
Western Division						
Kansas City	2	0	0	1.000	54	34
San Diego	2	0	0	1.000	64	44
Seattle	2	0	0	1.000	64	16
Denver	0	2	0	.000	56	62
L.A. Raiders	0	2	0	.000	23	82

NATIONAL FOOTBALL CONFERENCE

Eastern Division	W	L	T	Pct.	Pts.	OP
Dallas	2	0	0	1.000	46	26
N.Y. Giants	2	0	0	1.000	48	40
Philadelphia	1	1	0	.500	53	50
Washington	1	1	0	.500	45	52
Arizona	0	2	0	.000	29	34
Central Division						
Chicago	1	1	0	.500	43	39
Detroit	1	1	0	.500	34	38
Green Bay	1	1	0	.500	30	34
Minnesota	1	1	0	.500	20	19
Tampa Bay	1	1	0	.500	33	31
Western Division						
Atlanta	1	1	0	.500	59	44
L.A. Rams	1	1	0	.500	27	43
San Francisco	1	1	0	.500	61	38
New Orleans	0	2	0	.000	41	68

SUNDAY, SEPTEMBER 11

BUFFALO 38, NEW ENGLAND 35—at Foxboro Stadium, attendance 60,274. Steve Christie's 32-yard field goal with 52 seconds remaining lifted the Bills past the Patriots. Jim Kelly threw touchdown passes to four different receivers as Buffalo built a 28-14 halftime lead. And when nose tackle Mike Lodish fell on a fumble in the end zone 53 seconds into the fourth quarter, the Bills led 35-21. But New England rallied, converting Myron Guyton's interception and 15-yard return into a 21-yard touchdown pass from Drew Bledsoe to Michael Timpson with 9:17 to go, and then marching 69 yards to Marion Butts's game-tying 6-yard touchdown run with 4:22 left. Buffalo began the ensuing drive on its own 43, and Kelly led his team into field-goal range with a 19-yard completion to Andre Reed and a 12-yard toss to Don Beebe. Kelly finished with 25 completions in 41 attempts for 328 yards, with 3 interceptions. His 4 touchdown passes raised his career total to 183, a Bills record. Reed caught 7 passes for 142 yards, while Thurman Thomas rushed for 106 yards. Bledsoe completed 26 of 42 passes for 380 yards for the Patriots. Tight end Ben

Coates caught 9 passes for 124 yards and 2 touchdowns. New England amassed 467 total yards. Buffalo had 466.

Buffalo	14	14	0	10	—	38
New England	7	7	7	14	—	35

Buff — Reed 37 pass from Kelly (Christie kick)
Buff — Thomas 4 pass from Kelly (Christie kick)
NE — Coates 18 pass from Bledsoe (Bahr kick)
Buff — Bi. Brooks 12 pass from Kelly (Christie kick)
NE — Coates 5 pass from Bledsoe (Bahr kick)
Buff — Beebe 14 pass from Kelly (Christie kick)
NE — Butts 19 run (Bahr kick)
Buff — Lodish fumble recovery in end zone (Christie kick)
NE — Timpson 21 pass from Bledsoe (Bahr kick)
NE — Butts 6 run (Bahr kick)
Buff — FG Christie 32

SAN DIEGO 27, CINCINNATI 10—at San Diego Jack Murphy Stadium, attendance 53,217. Stan Humphries threw 2 touchdown passes and Natrone Means rushed for 107 yards and a touchdown as the Chargers opened the season 2-0 for the first time in 13 years. San Diego led 13-3 at halftime before breaking open the game with a five-play, 80-yard touchdown march late in the third quarter. Humphries completed a pair of passes on the drive to Mark Seay, including a 49-yard touchdown with 26 seconds left in the period. The pair teamed again on a 4-yard scoring play with 3:16 to go in the game. Humphries completed 18 of 29 passes for 299 yards in all. Seay caught 8 passes for 119 yards. David Klingler was 21 of 34 for 180 yards and 1 touchdown for the Bengals, but was intercepted once and lost a fumble.

Cincinnati	3	0	0	7	—	10
San Diego	3	10	7	7	—	27

SD — FG Carney 38
Cin — FG Pelfrey 19
SD — Means 3 run (Carney kick)
SD — FG Carney 20
SD — Seay 49 pass from Humphries (Carney kick)
Cin — Green 5 pass from Klingler (Pelfrey kick)
SD — Seay 4 pass from Humphries (Carney kick)

N.Y. JETS 25, DENVER 22—at Giants Stadium, attendance 73,436. Nick Lowery capped the opening possession in overtime with a 39-yard field goal to win it for the Jets. After winning the coin toss at the end of regulation, New York marched 45 yards in seven plays to Lowery's kick at the 3:57 mark. Boomer Esiason completed all 3 of his passes on the drive, including a 24-yard strike to Art Monk to move into Broncos' territory. Earlier, Esiason teamed with Rob Moore on a 35-yard touchdown pass and subsequent 2-point conversion to turn a 19-14 deficit into a 22-19 lead with 4:15 to go in the fourth quarter. But Denver rallied behind quarterback John Elway, who drove his team to Jason Elam's 29-yard field goal to tie the game at 22-22 with 1:46 left in regulation. Elway finished with 29 completions in 42 attempts for 319 yards. Anthony Miller had 105 yards on 6 receptions, while Mike Pritchard tallied 100 on his 9 catches. Esiason completed 26 of 37 passes for 297 yards for the Jets. Moore, playing with a cast to protect a broken wrist, caught 9 passes for 147 yards. The Broncos dropped to 0-2 for the first time since 1968.

Denver	0	13	6	3	0	—	22
N.Y. Jets	7	7	0	8	3	—	25

Jets — Lewis 67 interception return (Lowery kick)
Den — Miller 40 pass from Elway (Elam kick)
Den — FG Elam 42
Jets — F. Baxter 1 pass from Esiason (Lowery kick)
Den — FG Elam 21
Den — L. Russell 3 run (pass failed)
Jets — Moore 35 pass from Esiason (Lowery kick)
Den — FG Elam 29
Jets — FG Lowery 39

MINNESOTA 10, DETROIT 3—at Metrodome, attendance 57,349. Warren Moon threw a 30-yard touchdown pass to Qadry Ismail, but it was defense that paced the Vikings' victory. Defensive linemen John Randle, James Harris, and Roy Barker each contributed 2 sacks and harassed Lions quarterback Scott Mitchell into an interception and 3 fumbles, including 1 to snuff Detroit's final threat in Minnesota territory with 3:25 to play. The Vikings also limited Lions running back Barry Sanders to only 16 yards on 12 carries. Detroit managed only 212 total yards. The Vikings struggled themselves on offense, but got a 36-yard field goal from Fuad Reveiz late in the first quarter and drove 90 yards in 12 plays to the game's lone touchdown 5:08 into the second period. Moon completed 22 of 35 passes for 221 yards. Mitchell was 18 of 40 for 212 yards.

Detroit	0	0	0	3	—	3
Minnesota	3	7	0	0	—	10

Minn — FG Reveiz 36
Minn — Ismail 30 pass from Moon (Reveiz kick)
Det — FG Hanson 24

DALLAS 20, HOUSTON 17—at Texas Stadium, attendance 64,402. Troy Aikman threw a 53-yard touchdown pass to Alvin Harper late in the third quarter and the Cowboys held on to defeat their intrastate rivals. The game was tied 10-10 late in the second quarter until rookie Chris Boniol gave Dallas the lead for good with a 29-yard field goal on the final play of the first half. Aikman's bomb to Harper capped an 86-yard drive and made it 20-10 with 2:46 remaining in the third quarter. Houston made it close when Gary Brown ran for his second touchdown of the game, from 2 yards with 4:07 left in the game. Aikman passed for 228 yards for the Cowboys, who won their tenth consecutive game dating to last year. Bucky Richardson, subbing for the injured Cody Carlson, passed for 242 yards and scrambled for 37 more in his first NFL start. But Richardson also was intercepted twice and suffered 4 sacks. Dallas defensive end Charles Haley, who recorded 4 sacks in the Cowboys' season-opening victory over the Steelers, had 1½ sacks and an interception.

Houston	3	7	0	7	—	17
Dallas	7	6	7	0	—	20

Dall — E. Smith 1 run (Boniol kick)
Hou — FG Del Greco 41
Dall — FG Boniol 45
Hou — G. Brown 3 run (Del Greco kick)
Dall — FG Boniol 29
Dall — Harper 53 pass from Aikman (Boniol kick)
Hou — G. Brown 2 run (Del Greco kick)

TAMPA BAY 24, INDIANAPOLIS 10—at Tampa Stadium, attendance 36,631. Craig Erickson threw for 313 yards and 3 touchdowns to lead the Buccaneers past the Colts. Erickson, who completed 19 of 24 passes, had scoring bombs of 50 yards to Charles Wilson and 48 yards to tight end Jackie Harris as Tampa Bay built a 17-3 lead, then put the game away with a 3-yard touchdown pass to Courtney Hawkins in the fourth quarter. The latter came with 6:46 to play and capped a nine-play, 90-yard drive. The Buccaneers other touchdown marches covered 84 and 80 yards. Indianapolis rookie Marshall Faulk ran for more than 100 yards for the second consecutive week, gaining 104 on 18 carries. He also caught 7 passes for 82 yards.

Indianapolis	0	3	7	0	—	10
Tampa Bay	7	3	7	7	—	24

TB — Wilson 50 pass from Erickson (Husted kick)
Ind — FG Biasucci 26
TB — FG Husted 47
TB — Harris 48 pass from Erickson (Husted kick)
Ind — Potts 8 run (Biasucci kick)
TB — Hawkins 3 pass from Erickson (Husted kick)

ATLANTA 31, L.A. RAMS 13—at Georgia Dome, attendance 55,378. Andre Rison caught 12 passes for 123 yards and 2 touchdowns to key the Falcons' rout. Jeff George completed 29 of 38 passes for 3 touchdowns for the Falcons, who scored touchdowns on their first two possessions and went on to amass 428 total yards. The Rams had little trouble moving the ball themselves, and finished with 421 total yards. But Los Angeles stymied itself with 9 penalties, 3 interceptions, and a lost fumble. Cornerback D.J. Johnson had 2 interceptions for the Falcons. Cornerback Darnell Walker had the other, and returned it 44 yards for a touchdown to give Atlanta a 24-7 lead late in the third quarter. Rison, who caught a 16-yard touchdown pass in the first quarter and another 16-yarder to put the game out of reach in the fourth, became the Falcons' leading career receiver. Alfred Jenkins held the previous record with 359 catches; by game's end, Rison had 368. Jerome Bettis rushed for 102 yards for the Rams. Wide receiver Willie Anderson caught 5 passes for 154 yards.

L.A. Rams	0	7	0	6	—	13
Atlanta	14	3	7	7	—	31

Atl — Mathis 2 pass from George (Johnson kick)
Atl — Rison 16 pass from George (Johnson kick)
Rams — Bruce 34 pass from Miller (Zendejas kick)
Atl — FG Johnson 48
Atl — Walker 44 interception return (Johnson kick)
Atl — Rison 16 pass from George (Johnson kick)
Rams — Anderson 41 pass from Chandler (pass failed)

MIAMI 24, GREEN BAY 14—at Milwaukee County Stadium, attendance 55,011. Dan Marino threw 2 touchdown passes and the Dolphins scored on four of their first five possessions to build a 24-0 lead and coast to victory. Miami led 3-0 before breaking open the game with a pair of touchdowns late in the first half. Marino capped a 12-play, 86-yard drive by throwing 3 yards to tight end Keith Jackson on fourth-and-1 for a touchdown with 5:43 to go in the second quarter. Moments later, defensive end Jeff Cross recovered Packers quarterback Brett Favre's fumble at the Dolphins' 47, and Marino directed a 10-play march that culminated in his 3-yard touchdown pass to running back Keith Byars 27 seconds before halftime. Rookie running back Irving Spikes played a big role in both drives, carrying on three consecutive plays for 41 yards on the first drive, and rushing 5 times for 35 yards on the second. He left the game in the fourth quarter with a twisted knee after gaining 70 yards on 13 carries. Terry Kirby's 6-yard run midway through the third quarter made it 24-0. Green Bay's 2 touchdowns came long after the issue had been decided. Marino finished with 17 completions in 25 attempts, with no interceptions. Favre completed 31 of 51 passes for 362 yards and 2 touchdowns for the Packers.

Miami	3	14	7	0	—	24
Green Bay	0	0	0	14	—	14

Mia — FG Stoyanovich 48
Mia — Jackson 3 pass from Marino (Stoyanovich kick)
Mia — Byars 3 pass from Marino (Stoyanovich kick)
Mia — Kirby 6 run (Stoyanovich kick)
GB — West 2 pass from Favre (pass failed)
GB — Sharpe 9 pass from Favre (West pass from Favre)

PITTSBURGH 17, CLEVELAND 10—at Cleveland Stadium, attendance 77,774. Safety Darren Perry intercepted 3 passes, including a game-clinching theft at the Steelers' 10-yard line in the final minute. The Browns appeared to tie the game on their final drive when Vinny Testaverde threw 33 yards to Mark Carrier. But Cleveland was whistled for holding on the play, and four plays later, Perry secured the victory by intercepting a pass on fourth-and-16. To win, Pittsburgh had to rally from an early 10-point deficit. After Matt Stover kicked a 23-yard field goal to give the Browns a 10-0 lead 3:39 into the second quarter, Rod Woodson returned the ensuing kickoff 54 yards, and four plays later Neil O'Donnell threw a 31-yard touchdown pass to Yancey Thigpen. Barry Foster's 1-yard touchdown run 1:22 before halftime capped a 77-yard drive and gave the Steelers the lead for good. Pittsburgh won despite being penalized a whopping 15 times for 115 yards. The Steelers accumulated 9 penalties in the first quarter alone.

Pittsburgh	0	14	0	3	—	17
Cleveland	7	3	0	0	—	10

Cleve — Reeves 1 pass from Testaverde (Stover kick)
Cleve — FG Stover 23
Pitt — Thigpen 31 pass from O'Donnell (Anderson kick)
Pitt — Foster 1 run (Anderson kick)
Pitt — FG Anderson 25

KANSAS CITY 24, SAN FRANCISCO 17—at Arrowhead Stadium, attendance 79,907. Joe Montana threw 2 touchdown passes to lead the Chiefs to victory in his first game against his former teammates. Montana completed 19 of 31 passes for 203 yards. He capped Kansas City's first possession with a 1-yard touchdown pass to tackle-eligible Joe Valerio, and put the Chiefs ahead for good with an 8-yard touchdown pass to tight end Kerry Cash 6:17 into the second half. Trailing 24-14 in the fourth quarter, the 49ers tried to rally, marching to Kansas City's 2-yard line. But quarterback Steve Young was stopped short of the goal line on third down, and San Francisco had to settle for a 19-yard field goal by Doug Brien. The 49ers last chance ended when wide receiver John Taylor lost a fumble near midfield. Young completed 24 of 34 passes for 288 yards, but he was intercepted twice and was harassed by the Chiefs' defense most of the day. Derrick Thomas had 3 sacks for Kansas City, including 1 for a safety late in the first half.

San Francisco	0	14	0	3	—	17
Kansas City	7	2	15	0	—	24

KC — Valerio 1 pass from Montana (Elliott kick)
SF — Jones 5 pass from Young (Brien kick)
SF — Logan 1 run (Brien kick)
KC — Safety, Thomas tackled Young in end zone
KC — Cash 8 pass from Montana (Birden pass from Montana)
KC — Allen 4 run (Elliott kick)
SF — FG Brien 19

SEATTLE 38, L.A. RAIDERS 9—at Los Angeles Memorial Coliseum, attendance 47,319. Rick Mirer threw 3 touchdown passes in the second half as the Seahawks beat the Raiders for the first time in the last nine tries. Seattle led just 10-3 at halftime, but broke open the game by taking advantage of interceptions on three consecutive possessions in the second half. First, linebacker Terry Wooden intercepted Jeff Hostetler's pass at Los Angeles's 30-yard line, setting up Mirer's 5-yard touchdown pass to Brian Blades with 5:47 remaining in the third quarter. Moments later, cornerback Patrick Hunter intercepted a pass in the end zone and returned it 34 yards. The Seahawks' ensuing 67-yard drive was capped by Mirer's 40-yard touchdown pass to Michael Bates. Then, linebacker Bob Spitulski's interception and 7-yard return set up Mirer's 38-yard touchdown pass to running back Chris Warren, and Seattle led 31-3 4:16 into the fourth quarter. Mirer finished with 19 completions in 25 attempts for 242 yards.

Seattle	7	3	14	14	—	38
L.A. Raiders	3	0	0	6	—	9

Sea — Warren 4 run (Kasay kick)
Raid — FG Jaeger 26
Sea — FG Kasay 33
Sea — Blades 5 pass from Mirer (Kasay kick)
Sea — Bates 40 pass from Mirer (Kasay kick)
Sea — Warren 38 pass from Mirer (Kasay kick)
Raid — McDaniel 41 fumble return (pass failed)
Sea — Johnson 2 run (Kasay kick)

WASHINGTON 38, NEW ORLEANS 24—at Louisiana Superdome, attendance 58,049. John Friesz threw 4 touchdown passes and Brian Mitchell amassed 225 yards on kick returns to pace the Redskins' victory. Friesz gave his team the lead for good with a 14-yard touchdown pass to Henry Ellard 10:05 into the first quarter. Just 83 seconds later, Mitchell returned a punt 74 yards for a touchdown, and Washington led 14-3. The Redskins still had an 11-point lead at intermission, but Mitchell returned the second-half kickoff 86 yards to set up Friesz's 1-yard touchdown pass to Cedric Smith to help break open the game. Friesz, who completed 15 of 22 passes for 195 yards, added touchdown passes to Ellard (41 yards) and Desmond Howard (31 yards). Mitchell finished with 87 yards on 2 punt returns and 138 yards on 3 kickoff returns.

Washington	14	0	14	10	—	38
New Orleans	3	0	6	15	—	24

NO — FG Andersen 29
Wash — Ellard 14 pass from Friesz (Lohmiller kick)
Wash — Mitchell 74 punt return (Lohmiller kick)
Wash — Smith 1 pass from Friesz (Lohmiller kick)
NO — Haynes 17 pass from Everett (pass failed)
Wash — Ellard 41 pass from Friesz (Lohmiller kick)
Wash — FG Lohmiller 31
Wash — Howard 31 pass from Friesz (Lohmiller kick)
NO — Small 4 pass from Everett (Small pass from Everett)
NO — Muster 3 run (Andersen kick)

SUNDAY NIGHT, SEPTEMBER 11

N.Y. GIANTS 20, ARIZONA 17—at Sun Devil Stadium, attendance 60,066. Dave Brown's 2 touchdown passes to tight end Howard Cross made the difference in a defensive struggle between the Giants and the Cardinals. Cornerback Phillippi Sparks's interception set up Brown's 1-yard touchdown pass to Cross 3:05 into the game, and the pair teamed on another 1-yarder 15 seconds before halftime to give New York a 20-10 advantage. Jim McMahon relieved starting quarterback Steve Beuerlein late in the third quarter and completed 4 of 5 passes for 50 yards, including a 2-yard touchdown to running back Ron Moore with 10:52 remaining in the game. But the Cardinals last chance ended when McMahon was sacked by Michael Brooks and Keith Hamilton on consecutive plays in the fourth quarter. The Giants won despite totaling only 202 yards, including just 88 passing. But Arizona fared even worse, managing only 11 first downs, 39 rushing yards, and 174 total yards.

N.Y. Giants	6	14	0	0	—	20
Arizona	3	7	0	7	—	17

Giants— Cross 1 pass from Da. Brown (kick failed)
Ariz — FG Davis 21
Ariz — McAfee 2 run (Davis kick)
Giants— Hampton 3 run (Treadwell kick)
Giants— Cross 1 pass from Da. Brown (Treadwell kick)
Ariz — Moore 2 pass from McMahon (Davis kick)

MONDAY, SEPTEMBER 12

PHILADELPHIA 30, CHICAGO 22—at Veterans Stadium, attendance 64,890. Randall Cunningham threw 3 touchdown passes in the first half, and the Eagles held off a dramatic fourth-quarter surge by the Bears to hold on for the victory. Cunningham teamed with wide receiver Calvin Williams on a pair of touchdown passes and tight end Maurice Johnson on another, and by halftime had passed for 250 yards as Philadelphia led 24-0. A pair of field goals by Eddie Murray increased the advantage to 30-0 in the third period. Still, Chicago made a game of it. The Bears rallied by scoring 3 touchdowns in a span of 8:30 of the fourth quarter, the last on Erik Kramer's 16-yard touchdown pass to tight end Marv Cook with 3:35 remaining in the game. But Cunningham completed a third-down pass to running back Herschel Walker on the Eagles' ensuing possession, and Chicago never got the ball again. Cunningham finished with 24 completions in 36 attempts for 311 yards. Fred Barnett caught 8 passes for 102 yards. Kramer was 18 of 31 for 289 yards for the Bears. Curtis Conway caught 7 passes for 148 yards and 2 touchdowns.

Chicago	0	0	0	22	—	22
Philadelphia	7	17	6	0	—	30

Phil — C. Williams 9 pass from Cunningham (Murray kick)
Phil — C. Williams 14 pass from Cunningham (Murray kick)
Phil — M. Johnson 7 pass from Cunningham (Murray kick)
Phil — FG Murray 41
Phil — FG Murray 29
Phil — FG Murray 33
Chi — Conway 22 pass from Kramer (Butler kick)
Chi — Conway 85 pass from Kramer (Conway pass from Kramer)
Chi — Cook 16 pass from Kramer (Butler kick)

THIRD WEEK SUMMARIES

AMERICAN FOOTBALL CONFERENCE

Eastern Division	W	L	T	Pct.	Pts.	OP
Miami	3	0	0	1.000	91	63
Buffalo	2	1	0	.667	56	65
N.Y. Jets	2	1	0	.667	62	53
Indianapolis	1	2	0	.333	76	76
New England	1	2	0	.333	101	105
Central Division						
Cleveland	2	1	0	.667	70	37
Pittsburgh	2	1	0	.667	57	57
Cincinnati	0	3	0	.000	58	86
Houston	0	3	0	.000	45	80
Western Division						
Kansas City	3	0	0	1.000	84	44
San Diego	3	0	0	1.000	88	54
Seattle	2	1	0	.667	76	40
L.A. Raiders	1	2	0	.333	71	98
Denver	0	3	0	.000	72	110

NATIONAL FOOTBALL CONFERENCE

Eastern Division	W	L	T	Pct.	Pts.	OP
N.Y. Giants	3	0	0	1.000	79	63
Dallas	2	1	0	.667	63	46
Philadelphia	2	1	0	.667	66	57
Washington	1	2	0	.333	68	83
Arizona	0	3	0	.000	29	66
Central Division						
Detroit	2	1	0	.667	54	55
Minnesota	2	1	0	.667	62	33
Chicago	1	2	0	.333	57	81
Green Bay	1	2	0	.333	37	47
Tampa Bay	1	2	0	.333	40	40
Western Division						
San Francisco	2	1	0	.667	95	57
Atlanta	1	2	0	.333	69	74
L.A. Rams	1	2	0	.333	46	77
New Orleans	1	2	0	.333	50	75

SUNDAY, SEPTEMBER 18

CLEVELAND 32, ARIZONA 0—at Cleveland Stadium, attendance 62,818. Vinny Testaverde passed for 2 touchdowns and ran for another while the Browns' defense posted the club's first shutout at home since 1983. Cleveland, leading just 3-0 after a sluggish first half, took charge in the third quarter. Testaverde capped a 55-yard drive with a 1-yard touchdown run, then finished a 64-yard drive with a 16-yard scoring pass to running back Tommy Vardell. In the fourth quarter, Testaverde combined with rookie Derrick Alexander on an 81-yard touchdown pass, and safety Eric Turner finished the day with a 93-yard interception return for a touchdown. Testaverde completed 17 of 27 passes for 248 yards. Alexander had 6 catches for 136 yards. Jim McMahon, making his first start for Arizona, completed 19 of 38 passes for 169 yards before being relieved by Jay Schroeder, who threw the interception to Turner.

Arizona	0	0	0	0	—	0
Cleveland	0	3	15	14	—	32

Cleve — FG Stover 32
Cleve — Testaverde 1 run (Stover kick)
Cleve — Vardell 16 pass from Testaverde (Tupa run)
Cleve — Alexander 81 pass from Testaverde (Stover kick)
Cleve — Turner 93 interception return (Stover kick)

BUFFALO 15, HOUSTON 7—at Astrodome, attendance 55,424. Steve Christie kicked 5 field goals to provide the Bills' scoring and Bruce Smith posted 4 sacks to stymie the Oilers' offense. Three of Christie's field goals came in the second quarter as Buffalo took a 9-0 lead into intermission. The Bills built a 15-0 lead before Houston scored with 3:51 to play. Buffalo used a balanced offensive attack, led by Thurman Thomas (28 carries for 112 yards), Jim Kelly (18 of 28 for 190 yards), and Andre Reed (6 catches for 89 yards). Meanwhile, Smith spent most of the day in the Oilers' backfield, highlighted by a third-quarter sack that killed a Houston drive at the Bills' 27.

Buffalo	0	9	3	3	—	15
Houston	0	0	0	7	—	7

Buff — FG Christie 37
Buff — FG Christie 42
Buff — FG Christie 48
Buff — FG Christie 29
Buff — FG Christie 48
Hou — Coleman 22 pass from Richardson (Del Greco kick)

PHILADELPHIA 13, GREEN BAY 7—at Veterans Stadium, attendance 63,922. The Eagles' defense put on a show, sacking the Packers' Brett Favre 6 times and limiting the Packers to 37 rushing yards. Green Bay's only points came in the first quarter on a 37-yard touchdown pass from Favre to running back Reggie Cobb. Philadelphia cut the deficit to 7-3 at halftime, then used a fumble recovery to set up Randall Cunningham's 1-yard scoring run in the third period. Eddie Murray's second field goal made it 13-7, and the Eagles left the rest to their defense. The Packers had one last chance when they recovered a fumble at the Eagles' 16, but the Eagles stopped them at the 6-yard line in the final minutes. Favre completed 24 of 45 passes for 280 yards. Cunningham was 20 of 43 for 204 yards.

Green Bay	7	0	0	0	—	7
Philadelphia	0	3	10	0	—	13

GB — Cobb 37 pass from Favre (Jacke kick)
Phil — FG Murray 26
Phil — Cunningham 1 run (Murray kick)
Phil — FG Murray 26

PITTSBURGH 31, INDIANAPOLIS 21—at Three Rivers Stadium, attendance 54,040. Barry Foster enjoyed his best day in two seasons and lead the Steelers to victory. Indianapolis roared to a 14-0 lead on a 95-yard kickoff return by Ronald Humphrey and a club-record 78-yard fumble return by linebacker Quentin Coryatt. Pittsburgh responded with 17 points in the final 10 minutes of the first half, including a 29-yard scoring run by Foster. The Colts retook the lead in the third quarter, but the Steelers, behind Foster, scored twice in the fourth quarter to secure victory. Foster gained 179 yards on 31 carries, while Neil O'Donnell completed 22 of 35 passes for 254 yards and 2 touchdowns. Pittsburgh's defense limited the Colts to 181 total yards, while the Steelers' offense controlled the ball for 39 minutes 31 seconds and amassed 500 total yards.

Indianapolis	7	7	7	0	—	21
Pittsburgh	0	17	0	14	—	31

Ind — Humphrey 95 kickoff return (Biasucci kick)
Ind — Coryatt 78 fumble return (Biasucci kick)
Pitt — Green 27 pass from O'Donnell (Anderson kick)
Pitt — Foster 29 run (Anderson kick)
Pitt — FG Anderson 46
Ind — Dawkins 19 pass from Harbaugh (Biasucci kick)
Pitt — J.L. Williams 8 pass from O'Donnell (Anderson kick)
Pitt — Morris 1 run (Anderson kick)

L.A. RAIDERS 48, DENVER 16—at Mile High Stadium, attendance 75,764. Jeff Hostetler passed for 4 touchdowns as the Raiders blasted the Broncos. Los Angeles scored on its first four possessions to build a 28-3 halftime lead. Three of the possessions ended with scoring passes by Hostetler—65 yards to Ty Montgomery, 43 to Tim Brown, and 7 to Andrew Glover. Hostetler added a 5-yard touchdown pass to Harvey Williams in the third period, and cornerback Terry McDaniel completed the rout with a 15-yard interception return for a score. Hostetler completed 21 of 33 passes for 338 yards while leading the Raiders to their highest point output since 1979. The Broncos, who were wearing their 1966 uniforms as part of Throwbacks Weekend, suffered their worst loss at home since that season.

L.A. Raiders	21	7	10	10	—	48
Denver	3	0	13	0	—	16

Raid — H. Williams 2 run (Jaeger kick)
Den — FG Elam 43
Raid — Montgomery 65 pass from Hostetler (Jaeger kick)
Raid — Brown 43 pass from Hostetler (Jaeger kick)
Raid — Glover 7 pass from Hostetler (Jaeger kick)
Den — L. Russell 1 run (run failed)
Raid — H. Williams 5 pass from Hostetler (Jaeger kick)
Den — L. Russell 4 run (Elam kick)
Raid — FG Jaeger 42
Raid — FG Jaeger 33
Raid — McDaniel 15 interceptions return (Jaeger kick)

MINNESOTA 42, CHICAGO 14—at Soldier Field, attendance 61,073. The Vikings dominated the Bears in every phase of the game. Minnesota's offense, which had scored just 1 touchdown in the first two weeks, totaled 464 yards and put 4 touchdowns on the board. The Vikings led 10-0 at halftime thanks to a 12-yard run by Terry Allen and a 43-yard field goal by Fuad Reveiz, but the lead might have been 24-0 were it not for 2 costly turnovers inside the Bears' 10. No matter, for in the third quarter Reveiz kicked another field goal, Warren Moon hit Jake Reed for 18-yard touchdown pass, and rookie DeWayne Washington ran back an interception 81 yards for a score to give Minnesota a commanding 28-0 lead. Allen finished with 159 yards and 2 touchdowns on 22 carries. Moon completed 22 of 29 for 236 yards. Reed had 7 catches for 90 yards, and Cris Carter had a game-high 9 receptions for 86 yards.

Minnesota	0	10	18	14	—	42
Chicago	0	0	0	14	—	14

Minn — Allen 12 run (Reveiz kick)
Minn — FG Reveiz 43
Minn — FG Reveiz 24
Minn — Reed 18 pass from Moon (Reveiz kick)
Minn — Washington 81 interception return (Carter pass from Moon)
Minn — Allen 1 run (Reveiz kick)
Chi — Worley 1 run (pass failed)
Minn — Smith 14 run (Reveiz kick)
Chi — Waddle 8 pass from Kramer (Graham pass from Kramer)

NEW ENGLAND 31, CINCINNATI 28—at Riverfront Stadium, attendance 46,640. Drew Bledsoe completed 30 of 50 passes for 365 yards to lead the Patriots to their first victory of the year. The teams were tied 13-13 at halftime, but 2 fumble recoveries in the third quarter led to 2 field goals by the Patriots' Matt Bahr. After Bahr's second kick, Cincinnati drove 77 yards—the last 8 coming on Steve Broussard's second touchdown run of the day—to take a 20-19 lead. Bledsoe responded by directing New England on an 80-yard drive, hitting Michael Timpson with a perfect pass for a 34-yard scoring strike and a 25-20 lead. Marion Butts upped the Patriots' advantage to 31-20 in the fourth quarter on a 1-yard touchdown run, his second of the game. Cincinnati made it close, driving 99 yards for a late touchdown, but the Patriots recovered the ensuing onside kick-off to seal the win. Timpson (10 receptions for 125 yards) and tight end Ben Coates (8 for 108) led the Patriots' receivers. David Klingler completed 21 of 29 passes for 266 yards and 2 scores (with no interceptions) for the Bengals.

New England	7	6	12	6	—	31
Cincinnati	6	7	7	8	—	28

Cin — Broussard 37 run (kick failed)
NE — Butts 3 run (Bahr kick)
NE — FG Bahr 43
NE — FG Bahr 24
Cin — Pickens 7 pass from Klingler (Pelfrey kick)
NE — FG Bahr 28
NE — FG Bahr 35
Cin — Broussard 8 run (Pelfrey kick)
NE — Timpson 34 pass from Bledsoe (pass failed)
NE — Butts 1 run (pass failed)
Cin — Pickens 4 pass from Klingler (Broussard run)

NEW ORLEANS 9, TAMPA BAY 7—at Tampa Stadium, attendance 45,522. The Saints' defense returned to form with an outstanding performance in 87-degree Florida heat. New Orleans' offense managed just 235 yards and 3 first-half field goals. But the Saints' defense, after allowing more than 400 total yards in each of the team's first two games, limited the Buccaneers to 232 total yards and posted 5 sacks. Morten Andersen kicked 2 field goals to give New Orleans a 6-0 first-quarter lead. Craig Erickson found tight end Jackie Harris for a 10-yard scoring pass as Tampa Bay took a 7-6 lead in the second quarter, but the Saints quickly responded with another field goal just before halftime to reclaim the advantage. Neither team did much offensively in the second half until the final minute, when Tampa Bay advanced to the Saints' 36. But Michael Husted's potential winning field goal was wide right from 54 yards.

New Orleans	6	3	0	0	—	9
Tampa Bay	0	7	0	0	—	7

NO — FG Andersen 43
NO — FG Andersen 31
TB — J. Harris 10 pass from Erickson (Husted kick)
NO — FG Andersen 43

MIAMI 28, N.Y. JETS 14—at Joe Robbie Stadium, attendance 68,192. Terry Kirby totaled 135 yards in offense to lead the Dolphins to only their second victory in their last seven games against the Jets. Kirby caught 3 passes for 35 yards and ran 15 times for 100 yards, including a 1-yard touchdown run that helped Miami build a 14-0 halftime lead. Miami led 21-7 after three quarters thanks to an unusual play: Tight end Keith Jackson, about to be tackled at the Jets' 1, lateraled to teammate Irving Fryar, who ran 2 yards for the Dolphins' third touchdown. Bernie Parmalee clinched the win with a 5-yard touchdown run in the fourth quarter. Miami's Dan Marino completed 23 of 31 passes for 289 yards. Jackson had 6 receptions for 100 yards. New York's Boomer Esiason completed 22 of 37 passes for 293 yards and 2 scores, but he was intercepted 4 times.

N.Y. Jets	0	0	7	7	—	14
Miami	0	14	7	7	—	28

Mia — Kirby 1 run (Stoyanovich kick)
Mia — Byars 11 pass from Marino (Stoyanovich kick)
Jets — Anderson 27 pass from Esiason (Lowery kick)
Mia — Fryar 2 lateral from Jackson (Stoyanovich kick)
Mia — Parmalee 5 run (Stoyanovich kick)
Jets — J. Johnson 2 pass from Esiason (Lowery kick)

SAN DIEGO 24, SEATTLE 10—at Husky Stadium, attendance 65,536. The Chargers pulled away from the Seahawks thanks to three big plays in the third quarter, giving San Diego its first 3-0 start since 1981. Seattle, trailing 10-3, threatened to tie the game midway through the third period with a drive into San Diego territory. But Seahawks quarterback Rick Mirer, under pressure from blitzing linebacker Junior Seau, threw a pass that safety Stanley Richard intercepted and returned 73 yards for a score. It was Richard's second interception return for a touchdown in 1994. Five minutes later, San Diego made it 24-3 on an NFL-record-tying 99-yard touchdown pass from Stan Humphries to Tony Martin. Humphries finished with 19 completions in 29 attempts for 262 yards. Martin had 6 catches for 152 yards, and Natrone Means ran for 86 yards on 24 carries. The Chargers pressured Mirer all day, sacking him 6 times. The game was played in Husky Stadium because the Kingdome, the Seahawks' regular home field, was undergoing repairs for damaged roof tiles.

San Diego	0	10	14	0	—	24
Seattle	0	3	0	7	—	10

Sea — FG Kasay 39
SD — FG Carney 36
SD — Means 1 run (Carney kick)
SD — Richard 73 interception return (Carney kick)
SD — Martin 99 pass from Humphries (Carney kick)
Sea — Warren 11 run (Kasay kick)

SAN FRANCISCO 34, L.A. RAMS 19—at Anaheim Stadium, attendance 56,479. Steve Young enjoyed a fabulous day in leading the 49ers to their eighth consecutive victory at Anaheim Stadium. San Francisco overcame 14 penalties for a club-record 177 yards thanks to Young, who completed 31 of 39 passes for 355 yards and 2 touchdowns. The Rams stayed close early behind the running of Jerome Bettis, who gained nearly 100 yards in a first half that appeared was going to end with the teams tied. But Young, operating without any timeouts, hit Jerry Rice for 28 yards to the Rams' 1, then snuck in from 1 yard as the first half expired to give the 49ers a 17-10 halftime lead. San Francisco pulled away in the second half, keeping the ball away from Bettis (he had only 4 carries) while Young passed for 1 score and ran for another. Rice had 11 catches for 147 yards, and John Taylor had 7 receptions for 103 yards. Bettis finished with 21 carries for 104 yards.

San Francisco	10	7	3	14	—	34
L.A. Rams	7	3	0	9	—	19

SF — Taylor 3 pass from Young (Brien kick)
Rams — Drayton 4 pass from Miller (Zendejas kick)
SF — FG Brien 33
Rams — FG Zendejas 25
SF — Young 1 run (Brien kick)
SF — FG Brien 47
SF — Rice 1 pass from Young (Brien kick)
Rams — FG Zendejas 35
SF — Young 1 run (Brien kick)
Rams — Bettis 2 run (pass failed)

N.Y. GIANTS 31, WASHINGTON 23—at Giants Stadium, attendance 77,298. Running back David Meggett, replacing an injured Rodney Hampton, ran for 2 touchdowns and passed for another to pace the Giants. Meggett's 2-yard touchdown run was the game's first score, and his 16-yard touchdown pass to Aaron Pierce on a halfback option play gave New York a 24-20 third-quarter lead. After the Redskins pulled close at 24-23, Meggett provided breathing room with a 1-yard scoring run midway through the fourth period. Meggett finished with 82 yards on 26 carries, and also led the Giants with 4 receptions for 52 yards. The Giants' Dave Brown completed 14 of 19 passes for 221 yards. Washington's John Friesz went to the air 50 times, completing 32 passes for a career-high 381 yards and both of the Redskins' touchdowns. His favorite target was Henry Ellard, who caught 10 passes for 197 yards and 1 score. Ellard became the tenth player in NFL history to surpass 10,000 career receiving yards.

Washington	3	17	0	3	—	23
N.Y. Giants	10	7	7	7	—	31

Giants— Meggett 2 run (Treadwell kick)
Wash — FG Lohmiller 25
Giants— FG Treadwell 34

Wash — Ellard 3 pass from Friesz (Lohmiller kick)
Wash — FG Lohmiller 41
Giants— Sherrard 30 pass from Da. Brown (Treadwell kick)
Wash — Horton 4 pass from Friesz (Lohmiller kick)
Giants— Pierce 16 pass from Meggett (Treadwell kick)
Wash — FG Lohmiller 35
Giants— Meggett 1 run (Treadwell kick)

SUNDAY NIGHT, SEPTEMBER 18

KANSAS CITY 30, ATLANTA 10—at Georgia Dome, attendance 67,357. New uniform, similar result for Chiefs quarterback Joe Montana, who ran his record to 14-5 against the Falcons. Montana completed 28 of 39 passes for 361 yards and 2 touchdowns in leading Kansas City to its first 3-0 start since 1966, when the Chiefs won the AFL title and played in Super Bowl I. Montana found J.J. Birden for a 13-yard scoring strike in the first quarter as the Chiefs moved to a 10-0 lead. Two field goals and a 3-yard touchdown run by Donnell Bennett staked Kansas City to a 23-3 fourth-quarter lead. Atlanta pulled within 2 touchdowns when Jeff George hit Andre Rison on a 25-yard touchdown pass play. But Montana ended any of the Falcons' comeback hopes just two minutes later when he found Birden for a 34-yard touchdown pass. Birden had 7 catches for 99 yards, and tight end Keith Cash chipped in with 7 receptions for 73 yards. George was 29 of 45 for 299 yards, but his string of passes without an interception ended at 279, the third-longest streak in NFL history. The Chiefs sacked George 3 times and forced 6 turnovers by the Falcons.

Kansas City	7	3	7	13	—	30
Atlanta	0	0	3	7	—	10

KC — Birden 13 pass from Montana (Elliott kick)
KC — FG Elliott 48
KC — Bennett 3 run (Elliott kick)
Atl — FG Johnson 33
KC — FG Elliott 19
KC — FG Elliott 45
Atl — Rison 25 pass from George (Johnson kick)
KC — Birden 34 pass from Montana (Elliott kick)

MONDAY, SEPTEMBER 19

DETROIT 20, DALLAS 17—at Texas Stadium, attendance 64,102. Jason Hanson finally found a way to get a ball over Leon Lett, drilling a 44-yard field goal with just 27 seconds left in overtime to end the Cowboys' 10-game winning streak. The Lions were in control for much of regulation, behind the running of Barry Sanders and the passing of Scott Mitchell (scoring tosses of 25 and 9 yards) to take a 17-7 lead. But Dallas rallied, using a field goal late in the third quarter and Emmitt Smith's 6-yard touchdown with 4:09 left in regulation to tie the game at 17-17. The Lions had two longshot chances to win, but Lett, the Cowboys' defensive lineman, blocked Hanson's 57-yard field-goal attempt at the end of regulation, then blocked Hanson's 51-yard field-goal attempt 5½ minutes into overtime. Detroit got another chance with 1:55 to play in overtime when linebacker Pat Swilling sacked Troy Aikman, forcing a fumble that teammate Broderick Thomas recovered in Dallas territory. Mitchell's 17-yard pass to Brett Perriman positioned Hanson for the winning kick, his second overtime field goal of the year. In a duel of great running backs, Sanders ran for 194 yards on 40 carries to surpass 7,000 career yards, while Smith ran for 143 yards on 29 carries to surpass 6,000 career yards. Mitchell completed 13 of 27 passes for 174 yards, and Aikman was 26 of 39 for 223 yards.

Detroit	3	7	7	0	3	—	20
Dallas	7	0	3	7	0	—	17

Dall — Harper 17 pass from Aikman (Boniol kick)
Det — FG Hanson 32
Det — Perriman 25 pass from Mitchell (Hanson kick)
Det — H. Moore 9 pass from Mitchell (Hanson kick)
Dall — FG Boniol 19
Dall — E. Smith 6 run (Boniol kick)
Det — FG Hanson 44

FOURTH WEEK SUMMARIES

AMERICAN FOOTBALL CONFERENCE

Eastern Division	W	L	T	Pct.	Pts.	OP
Buffalo	3	1	0	.750	83	85
Miami	3	1	0	.750	126	101
New England	2	2	0	.500	124	122
N.Y. Jets	2	2	0	.500	69	72
Indianapolis	1	3	0	.250	90	97
Central Division						
Cleveland	3	1	0	.750	91	51
Pittsburgh	2	2	0	.500	70	87
Houston	1	3	0	.250	65	93
Cincinnati	0	4	0	.000	71	106
Western Division						
San Diego	4	0	0	1.000	114	78
Kansas City	3	1	0	.750	84	60
Seattle	3	1	0	.750	106	53
L.A. Raiders	1	3	0	.250	95	124
Denver	0	4	0	.000	92	137

NATIONAL FOOTBALL CONFERENCE

Eastern Division	W	L	T	Pct.	Pts.	OP
N.Y. Giants	3	0	0	1.000	79	63
Dallas	2	1	0	.667	63	46
Philadelphia	2	1	0	.667	66	57
Washington	1	3	0	.250	88	110
Arizona	0	3	0	.000	29	66
Central Division						
Minnesota	3	1	0	.750	100	68
Chicago	2	2	0	.500	76	88
Detroit	2	2	0	.500	71	78
Green Bay	2	2	0	.500	67	50
Tampa Bay	1	3	0	.250	43	70
Western Division						
San Francisco	3	1	0	.750	119	70
Atlanta	2	2	0	.500	96	94
L.A. Rams	2	2	0	.500	62	77
New Orleans	1	3	0	.250	63	99

SUNDAY, SEPTEMBER 25

ATLANTA 27, WASHINGTON 20—at RFK Stadium, attendance 53,238. Jeff George passed for 270 yards and 2 touchdowns to lead the Falcons to their first road victory over the Redskins in 11 tries. Atlanta took a 7-0 first-quarter lead on George's 4-yard touchdown pass to Terance Mathis, a score that was set up by George's 26-yard pass to Andre Rison on third-and-long. Early in the second quarter, however, George was intercepted by Redskins linebacker Andre Collins, who returned it 34 yards to the Falcons' 2. On the next play, Reggie Brooks ran for the tying touchdown. Later in the quarter, Washington's John Friesz and Henry Ellard combined on a 73-yard touchdown pass play that gave the Redskins a 13-7 halftime lead. But Atlanta reeled off 20 straight points in the second half to stake itself to a 27-13 lead, including a 17-point third quarter in which George hit rookie Bert Emanuel for a 31-yard score and a fumble recovery set up Craig Heyward's 1-yard touchdown run. George finished with 22 completions in 35 attempts despite being sacked 6 times. Mathis had 9 receptions for 92 yards and Rison had 4 for 74. Friesz completed 17 of 29 passes for 230 yards, but he was intercepted 3 times before being relieved in the fourth period. Atlanta had 5 takeaways while turning the ball over just once.

Atlanta	7	0	17	3	—	27
Washington	0	13	0	7	—	20

Atl — Mathis 4 pass from George (Johnson kick)
Wash — Brooks 2 run (Lohmiller kick)
Wash — Ellard 73 pass from Friesz (kick failed)
Atl — Emanuel 31 pass from George (Johnson kick)
Atl — FG Johnson 30
Atl — Heyward 1 run (Johnson kick)
Atl — FG Johnson 22
Wash — Ervins 3 run (Lohmiller kick)

HOUSTON 20, CINCINNATI 13—at Astrodome, attendance 44,253. The Oilers' defense buried the Bengals to provide Houston with its first victory of the year. Houston hammered Cincinnati quarterback David Klingler all day, sacking him 7 times and intercepting 3 of his passes. Gary Brown provided the Oilers with offense, catching a 20-yard touchdown pass from Cody Carlson in the first quarter and running 1 yard for another score in the second quarter, and Houston built a 17-0 halftime lead. Trailing 20-3, Cincinnati made a game of it in the fourth period on an 82-yard punt return for a score by Corey Sawyer and Doug Pelfrey's 48-yard field goal with 6:45 to play. But the Bengals' last gasp ended at midfield in the final minute when the Oilers' Ray Childress delivered the final sack of Klingler. Carlson, making his first start since he was injured in the season opener, passed for 211 yards before leaving in the third quarter with a broken nose. Brown had 87 yards on 19 carries and 2 catches for 37 yards. Klingler was 10 of 30 for 115 yards.

Cincinnati	0	0	3	10	—	13
Houston	7	10	3	0	—	20

Hou — G. Brown 20 pass from Carlson (Del Greco kick)
Hou — G. Brown 1 run (Del Greco kick)
Hou — FG Del Greco 45
Cin — FG Pelfrey 21
Hou — FG Del Greco 24
Cin — Sawyer 82 punt return (Pelfrey kick)
Cin — FG Pelfrey 49

CLEVELAND 21, INDIANAPOLIS 14—at RCA Dome, attendance 55,821. Vinny Testaverde passed for 3 touchdowns to lead the Browns. Testaverde entered the game as the AFC's lowest-rated passer, but he helped himself and his team by completing 16 of 28 passes for 266 yards. He hit running back Eric Metcalf for a 57-yard touchdown pass on the game's opening drive. After Indianapolis tied the game at 7-7, Testaverde and Metcalf hooked up again for a 15-yard scoring pass that gave Cleveland a 14-7 halftime lead. The Colts rallied once again, tying the game at 14-14 in the third quarter on Jim Harbaugh's 13-yard touchdown pass to running back Roosevelt Potts. In the fourth quarter, Testaverde answered again, passing to running back Leroy Hoard, who sidestepped a tackler and raced to the end zone to complete a 65-yard touchdown pass play. Metcalf had 5 catches for 74 yards and Hoard had 2 for 88. Harbaugh completed 16 of 26 passes for 194 yards and also was the game's leading rusher with 63 yards on 4 carries.

Cleveland	7	7	0	7	—	21
Indianapolis	7	0	7	0	—	14

Cleve — Metcalf 57 pass from Testaverde (Stover kick)
Ind — Faulk 1 run (Biasucci kick)
Cleve — Metcalf 15 pass from Testaverde (Stover kick)
Ind — Potts 13 pass from Harbaugh (Biasucci kick)
Cleve — Hoard 65 pass from Testaverde (Stover kick)

L.A. RAMS 16, KANSAS CITY 0—at Arrowhead Stadium, attendance 78,184. The Rams used a punishing running attack and stellar defensive play to post the first shutout of a Joe Montana-led team. Playing on a rain-soaked field, Los Angeles started fast, taking a 13-0 first-quarter lead on 2 field goals by Tony Zendejas sandwiched around a 72-yard scoring strike from Chris Chandler to Willie Anderson, with an assist from the intended receiver, Jessie Hester, who tipped the ball to Anderson. The Rams then turned the game over to Jerome Bettis, who ran 35 times for 132 yards and helped Los Angeles control the ball for 34 minutes. Meanwhile, the Rams' defense pressured Montana all day, sacking him once and forcing him into 3 interceptions. Montana was 18 of 37 for 175 yards, but he failed to lead his team to any points for the first time in his NFL career. The Rams' Chandler, starting in place of an injured Chris Miller, completed 13 of 21 for 207 yards with no interceptions. Los Angeles limited Kansas City to 242 total yards.

L.A. Rams	13	0	3	0	—	16
Kansas City	0	0	0	0	—	0

Rams — FG Zendejas 29
Rams — Anderson 72 pass from Chandler (Zendejas kick)
Rams — FG Zendejas 23
Rams — FG Zendejas 28

MINNESOTA 38, MIAMI 35—at Metrodome, attendance 64,035. The Vikings' Warren Moon outdueled the Dolphins' Dan Marino in a battle of two of the league's top quarterbacks. Minnesota built a 28-0 first-half lead behind Moon, who combined with Cris Carter on touchdown passes of 2, 44, and 8 yards. Miami finally got off the deck with a 3-play, 22-second drive that ended with Marino's 26-yard touchdown pass to O.J. McDuffie two seconds before halftime. In the third quarter, Marino's touchdown passes to tight ends Greg Baty (3 yards) and Keith Jackson (25 yards) pulled Miami to 28-21. Bernie Parmalee capped a furious Dolphins rally with a tying, 10-yard touchdown run 4½ minutes into the fourth quarter. Moon went back to work, hitting Jake Reed for 13 and 22 yards and getting a 30-yard scamper from Terry Allen en route to Scottie Graham's 3-yard touchdown run midway through the final period. The

Dolphins fumbled the ensuing kickoff to set up Fuad Reveiz's 38-yard field goal, which gave Minnesota a 10-point cushion with 3:37 to play. But Miami was not finished, scoring on Keith Byars's 1-yard run with 1:04 to play. Minnesota finally secured the victory when Chris Walsh recovered the ensuing onside kickoff. Moon completed 26 of 37 passes for 326 yards and 3 touchdowns, with no interceptions. Reed had 9 catches for 127 yards and Carter had 7 for 81. Marino added to his NFL record with his eleventh 400-yard game, completing 29 of 54 passes for 431 yards and 3 scores (with 3 interceptions). Byars had a game-high 10 catches for 79 yards, and Irving Fryar caught 6 passes for 160 yards. If Miami had won, it would have tied the NFL record for the greatest regular-season comeback.

Miami	0	6	15	14	—	35
Minnesota	14	14	0	10	—	38

Minn — Carter 2 pass from Moon (Reveiz kick)
Minn — Allen 8 run (Reveiz kick)
Minn — Carter 44 pass from Moon (Reveiz kick)
Minn — Carter 8 pass from Moon (Reveiz kick)
Mia — McDuffie 26 pass from Marino (run failed)
Mia — Baty 3 pass from Marino (Fryar pass from Marino)
Mia — Jackson 25 pass from Marino (Stoyanovich kick)
Mia — Parmalee 10 run (Stoyanovich kick)
Minn — Graham 3 run (Reveiz kick)
Minn — FG Reveiz 38
Mia — Byars 1 run (Stoyanovich kick)

NEW ENGLAND 23, DETROIT 17—at Pontiac Silverdome, attendance 59,618. The Patriots utilized a short-passing game to keep the ball out of the hands of Barry Sanders and defeat the Lions. New England controlled the football for nearly 35 minutes behind Drew Bledsoe, who completed 21 of 33 attempts for 251 yards. Sixteen of those completions went to running backs or tight ends. A failed fourth-and-1 conversion by Detroit set up the Patriots' first score, a 20-yard field goal by Matt Bahr. New England then went 89 yards, including passes of 32 and 43 yards by Bledsoe, to take a 10-0 lead on Marion Butts's 5-yard touchdown run. Sanders did not get many chances, but he made the most of them, running 35 yards for a touchdown that cut the Lions' deficit to 10-7. New England answered just before halftime with a 7-yard touchdown pass from Bledsoe to tight end Ben Coates, capping a 14-play drive. The Patriots upped their advantage to 20-7 in the third quarter on Bahr's second field goal, this one set up by a short punt. Sanders came right back, finishing an 80-yard drive with a 39-yard scoring run that made it 20-14. The teams traded field goals in the fourth quarter, but Patriots safety Myron Guyton ended the Lions' hopes with an interception in the final minutes. Sanders finished with 131 yards on only 18 carries.

New England	3	14	3	3	—	23
Detroit	0	7	7	3	—	17

NE — FG Bahr 20
NE — Butts 5 run (Bahr kick)
Det — Sanders 35 run (Hanson kick)
NE — Coates 7 pass from Bledsoe (Bahr kick)
NE — FG Bahr 28
Det — Sanders 39 run (Hanson kick)
NE — FG Bahr 21
Det — FG Hanson 27

SAN FRANCISCO 24, NEW ORLEANS 13—at Candlestick Park, attendance 63,971. Cornerback Deion Sanders, making his first start for his new club, returned an interception 74 yards for a touchdown to clinch the 49ers' victory. San Francisco struggled offensively, as the 49ers' injury-riddled line could not protect Steve Young nor provide a running attack. Young was sacked 5 times and intercepted twice, while the 49ers ran for just 74 yards. Tied 3-3, the 49ers drove 92 yards for a touchdown on Young's 28-yard pass to Jerry Rice early in the second quarter. But the Saints dominated the rest of the period, taking a 13-10 halftime lead on Jim Everett's 17-yard touchdown pass to tight end Irv Smith and Morten Andersen's 26-yard field goal. San Francisco reclaimed the lead at 17-13 late in the third period when Young, attempting to hit tight end Brent Jones, instead found Rice again, who caught the tip from Jones for a 6-yard score. Safety Merton Hanks's end-zone interception killed one of the Saints' fourth-quarter drives, only to have the Saints come right back and drive to San Francisco's 42 with 47 seconds remaining. But Everett's next pass, intended for Michael Haynes, was picked off along the right sideline by Sanders, who veered to the middle then returned to the outside and coasted the final 25 yards for the clinching score. Young completed 25 of 39 passes for 247 yards. Everett was 31 of 55 for 291 yards.

New Orleans	3	10	0	0	—	13
San Francisco	3	7	7	7	—	24

SF — FG Brien 43
NO — FG Andersen 22
SF — Rice 28 pass from Young (Brien kick)
NO — Smith 17 pass from Everett (Andersen kick)
NO — FG Andersen 26
SF — Rice 6 pass from Young (Brien kick)
SF — Sanders 74 interception return (Brien kick)

SEATTLE 30, PITTSBURGH 13—at Husky Stadium, attendance 59,637. The Seahawks used the running of Chris Warren, a third-quarter goal-line stand, and 4 interceptions to stun the Steelers. Seattle built a 20-6 halftime lead behind Warren, who ran 3 yards for a touchdown, and John Kasay, who kicked 2 field goals. The Seahawks' other score of the first half came on a 1-yard touchdown pass from Rick Mirer to tight end Trey Junkin that was set up by Warren's 28-yard run. The Steelers took the second-half kickoff and drove 68 yards to the Seahawks' 2. But four plays produced only 1 yard, as running back Barry Foster was wrapped up short of the goal line by safety Eugene Robinson on fourth down. Pittsburgh went to the air in the fourth quarter, with disastrous results—Neil O'Donnell was intercepted 3 times in the period, including 1 that rookie cornerback Orlando Watters, making his first start, returned 35 yards for a touchdown and a 27-6 Seattle lead. Warren finished with 26 carries for 100 yards. Pittsburgh outgained Seattle 452 to 297 yards, but the Steelers were undone by 4 turnovers and 9 penalties. O'Donnell was 21 of 43 for 282 yards, with 4 interceptions.

Pittsburgh	3	3	0	7	—	13
Seattle	7	13	0	10	—	30

Sea — Warren 3 run (Kasay kick)
Pitt — FG Anderson 31
Sea — FG Kasay 31
Sea — Junkin 1 pass from Mirer (Kasay kick)
Sea — FG Kasay 40
Pitt — FG Anderson 38
Sea — Watters 35 interception return (Kasay kick)
Pitt — C. Johnson 36 pass from O'Donnell (Anderson kick)
Sea — FG Kasay 31

SAN DIEGO 26, L.A. RAIDERS 24—at Los Angeles Memorial Coliseum, attendance 55,385. One good rally deserved another, as the Raiders came back from a 23-3 deficit to take a 24-23 lead only to watch the Chargers return the favor with a field goal in the final seconds. San Diego took a quick 7-0 lead on Darrien Gordon's 90-yard punt return, and the Chargers led 17-0 early in the second quarter after Natrone Means's 1-yard touchdown run. The Chargers' advantage reached 23-3 before the Raiders began their comeback in the third quarter. A long kickoff return set up Jeff Hostetler's 1-yard touchdown run, and then Hostetler hit Raghib Ismail for a 24-yard score to make it 23-17 at the end of three quarters. Los Angeles took its first lead with 7:01 to play when Lionel Washington returned an interception 31 yards for a score. But San Diego's Stan Humphries, who had been injured on the interception, hobbled back onto the field and directed the Chargers on a 65-yard, 14-play drive that ended with John Carney's 33-yard field goal with two seconds left. The key play on the winning drive came on fourth-and-1 from the Raiders' 32, where the Chargers, eschewing a long field-goal attempt, managed to convert on Humphries' 8-yard pass to running back Ronnie Harmon. Humphries completed 18 of 26 passes for 191 yards. Hostetler was 14 of 25 for 230 yards.

San Diego	10	10	3	3	—	26
L.A. Raiders	0	3	14	7	—	24

SD — Gordon 90 punt return (Carney kick)
SD — FG Carney 38
SD — Means 1 run (Carney kick)
Raid — FG Jaeger 43
SD — FG Carney 24
SD — FG Carney 27
Raid — Hostetler 1 run (Jaeger kick)
Raid — Ismail 24 pass from Hostetler (Jaeger kick)
Raid — Washington 31 interception return (Jaeger kick)
SD — FG Carney 33

GREEN BAY 30, TAMPA BAY 3—at Lambeau Field, attendance 58,551. Brett Favre worked the Packers' short-passing game to perfection to lead Green Bay to an easy victory. Favre completed 30 of 39 passes for 308 yards (with no interceptions). Seventeen of his completions went to running backs as the Packers controlled the football for 38 minutes 32 seconds. Green Bay got going in the second quarter, taking a 13-0 lead as Chris Jacke kicked 2 field goals sandwiched around Favre's 9-yard scoring toss to running back Edgar Bennett. Jacke added another field goal in the third period before Tampa Bay finally got on the board with Michael Husted's 34-yard field goal. But the Buccaneers' momentum did not last long, as Favre drove the Packers 64 yards to a touchdown on his 20-yard pass to tight end Ed West. Favre's third touchdown pass of the day, a 3-yard hookup with Sterling Sharpe, completed the scoring in the fourth quarter. Green Bay's defense limited Tampa Bay to 231 total yards while forcing 3 turnovers and sacking the Buccaneers' quarterbacks 4 times.

Tampa Bay	0	0	3	0	—	3
Green Bay	0	13	10	7	—	30

GB — FG Jacke 21
GB — Bennett 9 pass from Favre (Jacke kick)
GB — FG Jacke 20
GB — FG Jacke 22
TB — FG Husted 24
GB — West 20 pass from Favre (Jacke kick)
GB — Sharpe 3 pass from Favre (Jacke kick)

SUNDAY NIGHT, SEPTEMBER 25

CHICAGO 19, N.Y. JETS 7—at Giants Stadium, attendance 70,806. The Bears played mistake-free football to defeat the error-prone Jets. New York started fast, as Johnny Johnson ran in from 5 yards out for a 7-0 lead five minutes into the game. The Bears tied the game on Lewis Tillman's 2-yard touchdown run in the second quarter, capping a drive that was kept alive by a fake punt. Chicago took a 10-7 halftime lead on Kevin Butler's 44-yard field goal, then upped its advantage to 13-7 when Butler hit from 30 yards in the third period. The Jets self-destructed in the fourth quarter. First, quarterback Jack Trudeau, who replaced an injured Boomer Esiason earlier in the game, fumbled at New York's 22 and Chicago recovered. The Bears quickly converted that into Tillman's second touchdown, a 2-yard run. Then the Jets quickly answered, as Johnson's club-record 90-yard run put New York at the Bears' 7. But on fourth down, Trudeau's pass to an open Rob Moore was deflected by a teammate, and New York came away empty. The Jets finished with 3 turnovers and 2 missed field goals. Tillman gained 96 yards on 32 carries. Chicago's Steve Walsh, making his first start in place of an injured Erik Kramer, was 14 of 24 for 143 yards.

Chicago	0	10	3	6	—	19
N.Y. Jets	7	0	0	0	—	7

Jets — J. Johnson 5 run (Lowery kick)
Chi — Tillman 2 run (Butler kick)
Chi — FG Butler 44
Chi — FG Butler 30
Chi — Tillman 2 run (pass failed)

MONDAY, SEPTEMBER 26

BUFFALO 27, DENVER 20—at Rich Stadium, attendance 75,373. Thurman Thomas ran for 2 touchdowns in a driving rain as the Bills dropped the Broncos to 0-4. Buffalo, trailing 7-3, drove 68 yards for a touchdown late in the second quarter on Thomas's 16-yard run. The drive was kept alive by an offsides penalty against Denver on fourth down. On the Broncos' next possession, the Bills' Bruce Smith sacked John Elway, forcing a fumble that Buffalo recovered. On the next play, Thomas raced 27 yards for a touchdown with 18 seconds left in the first half to give Buffalo a 17-7 lead at intermission. Carwell Gardner's 3-yard touchdown run increased Buffalo's lead to 24-7 in the third quarter. The Broncos pulled close at 27-20 in the fourth quarter, and had a chance to tie the game, but Elway's fourth-down pass from the Bills' 4 fell incomplete with 21 seconds to play. Thomas gained 103 yards on 17 carries before leaving in the third quarter with an injury. Elway completed 26 of 46 passes for 280 yards for Denver, which committed 2 turnovers and 10 penalties.

Denver	0	7	10	3	—	20
Buffalo	3	14	7	3	—	27

Buff — FG Christie 36
Den — Miller 11 pass from Elway (Elam kick)
Buff — Thomas 16 run (Christie kick)
Buff — Thomas 27 run (Christie kick)
Buff — Gardner 3 run (Christie kick)
Den — L. Russell 2 run (Elam kick)
Den — FG Elam 28

Buff — FG Christie 28
Den — FG Elam 43

FIFTH WEEK SUMMARIES

AMERICAN FOOTBALL CONFERENCE

Eastern Division	W	L	T	Pct.	Pts.	OP
Miami	4	1	0	.800	149	108
Buffalo	3	2	0	.600	96	105
New England	3	2	0	.600	141	138
Indianapolis	2	3	0	.400	107	112
N.Y. Jets	2	3	0	.400	76	99
Central Division						
Cleveland	4	1	0	.800	118	58
Pittsburgh	3	2	0	.600	100	101
Houston	1	4	0	.200	79	123
Cincinnati	0	5	0	.000	78	129
Western Division						
San Diego	4	0	0	1.000	114	78
Kansas City	3	1	0	.750	84	60
Seattle	3	2	0	.600	121	70
L.A. Raiders	1	3	0	.250	95	124
Denver	0	4	0	.000	92	137

NATIONAL FOOTBALL CONFERENCE

Eastern Division	W	L	T	Pct.	Pts.	OP
Dallas	3	1	0	.750	97	53
N.Y. Giants	3	1	0	.750	101	90
Philadelphia	3	1	0	.750	106	65
Arizona	1	3	0	.250	46	73
Washington	1	4	0	.200	95	144
Central Division						
Chicago	3	2	0	.600	96	101
Minnesota	3	2	0	.600	107	85
Detroit	2	3	0	.400	85	102
Green Bay	2	3	0	.400	83	67
Tampa Bay	2	3	0	.400	67	84
Western Division						
Atlanta	3	2	0	.600	104	99
San Francisco	3	2	0	.600	127	110
L.A. Rams	2	3	0	.400	67	85
New Orleans	2	3	0	.400	90	121

SUNDAY, OCTOBER 2

ATLANTA 8, L.A. RAMS 5—at Anaheim Stadium, attendance 34,599. Backup quarterback Bobby Hebert threw a 13-yard touchdown pass to Ricky Sanders late in the fourth quarter to give the Falcons the victory. Hebert, in the game because starting quarterback Jeff George suffered a concussion in the third quarter, drove his team 89 yards in 11 plays on the winning drive, which began on Atlanta's 11-yard line with 7:30 to play and culminated in the touchdown pass to Sanders at the 3:14 mark. The Rams got as far as the Falcons' 27-yard line on their final drive, but safety Kevin Ross intercepted Tommy Maddox's pass with 1:37 to play to end the threat. Maddox entered the game in the second quarter when Chris Chandler had to leave the game with a severely sprained ankle. Chris Miller, the Rams' regular starting quarterback, was already out of the game with a shoulder injury. Maddox completed just 7 of 15 passes for 86 yards and was intercepted twice. Hebert was 10 of 14 for 122 yards. This was the first 8-5 game in NFL History.

Atlanta	0	0	0	8	—	8
L.A. Rams	0	2	3	0	—	5

Rams — Safety, Gilbert tackled George in end zone
Rams — FG Zendejas 28
Atl — Sanders 13 pass from Hebert (Mathis pass from Hebert)

CHICAGO 20, BUFFALO 13—at Soldier Field, attendance 62,406. Steve Walsh's 1-yard quarterback sneak 3:35 into the fourth quarter provided the Bears with the winning points. Chicago trailed 13-10 until Walsh, subbing for injured starter Erik Kramer, capped a 69-yard, 16-play drive that consumed more than nine minutes with the first touchdown of his five-year NFL career. Kevin Butler's 20-yard field goal with 3:08 to play provided the final margin of victory. The Bears used a ball-control offense and solid defense to forge the upset. Chicago maintained possession for 39:25 of the game's 60 minutes and limited the Bills' high-powered offense to only 204 total yards. Buffalo played without injured running back Thurman Thomas, who was out with a sprained knee. His backup, Kenneth Davis, rushed for 78 yards and caught 7 passes. He set up the Bills' lone touchdown with a 35-yard run in the third quarter.

Buffalo	3	3	7	0	—	13
Chicago	0	7	3	10	—	20

Buff — FG Christie 28
Chi — Gedney 13 pass from Walsh (Butler kick)
Buff — FG Christie 30
Chi — FG Butler 50
Buff — Metzelaars 15 pass from Kelly (Christie kick)
Chi — Walsh 1 run (Butler kick)
Chi — FG Butler 20

DALLAS 34, WASHINGTON 7—at RFK Stadium, attendance 55,394. The Cowboys built a 31-0 halftime lead en route to an easy victory, spoiling the starting debut of Redskins rookie quarterback Heath Shuler. Dallas scored on 5 of its 6 first-half possessions. Emmitt Smith scored on 2 touchdown runs and Washington helped by losing 3 fumbles. Shuler, the third overall pick in the 1994 draft, completed only 11 of 30 passes for 96 yards, including an 8-yard touchdown pass to running back Frank Wycheck. The Redskins managed only 110 total yards. Cowboys quarterback Troy Aikman was 20 of 28 for 181 yards and a touchdown. Smith ran for 48 yards but did not play in the second half because of a strained hamstring.

Dallas	7	24	3	0	—	34
Washington	0	0	7	0	—	7

Dall — E. Smith 4 run (Boniol kick)
Dall — E. Smith 6 run (Boniol kick)
Dall — FG Boniol 28
Dall — Novacek 3 pass from Aikman (Boniol kick)
Dall — Coleman 7 run (Boniol kick)
Dall — FG Boniol 47
Wash — Wycheck 8 pass from Shuler (Lohmiller kick)

TAMPA BAY 24, DETROIT 14—at Tampa Stadium, attendance 38,012. Two big plays on special teams—a punt return for a touchdown and a blocked punt—propelled the Buccaneers to the victory. Tampa Bay led 3-0 when Vernon Turner became the first player in franchise history to return a kick for a touchdown, taking Greg Montgomery's punt on the Buccaneers' 20-yard line and racing 80 yards for a touchdown. Tampa Bay increased its lead to 17-0 on a 35-yard touchdown pass from Craig Erickson to Charles Wilson. It was 17-14 midway through the third quarter when Rogerick Green blocked Montgomery's punt and teammate Jeff Brady recovered at the Lions' 2-yard line. Two plays later, rookie Errict Rhett ran 1 yard for his first NFL touchdown. Detroit threatened to rally but was turned away twice in the fourth quarter when Jason Hanson missed a 26-yard field-goal try and wide receiver Brett Perriman lost a fumble at Tampa Bay's 4-yard line. Lions running back Barry Sanders gained 166 yards on 20 carries and set a up a second-quarter touchdown with an 85-yard run, the longest of his career.

Detroit	0	14	0	0	—	14
Tampa Bay	10	7	7	0	—	24

TB — FG Husted 23
TB — Turner 80 punt return (Husted kick)
TB — Wilson 35 pass from Erickson (Husted kick)
Det — Mitchell 5 run (Hanson kick)
Det — D. Moore 5 run (Hanson kick)
TB — Rhett 1 run (Husted kick)

NEW ENGLAND 17, GREEN BAY 16—at Foxboro Stadium, attendance 57,522. Matt Bahr's 33-yard field goal with four seconds left won it for the Patriots. After New England rallied from a 10-0 halftime deficit to take a 14-10 lead on 2 touchdown passes from Drew Bledsoe to Vincent Brisby, the Packers regained the lead on Reggie Cobb's 1-yard touchdown run with 1:14 left in the game. But two failures on special teams cost Green Bay. First, the snap on the extra-point try following Cobb's touchdown was low, and Chris Jacke never got off a kick, leaving the Packers advantage at only 2 points. Jacke's ensuing kickoff then sailed out of bounds, giving the Patriots possession on their own 40-yard line. Bledsoe moved his team into Green Bay territory, and positioned Bahr for the winning kick by completing a 10-yard pass to Ray Crittendon on third-and-3 from the 25. Bledsoe finished with 29 completions in 53 attempts for 334 yards. Brisby caught 6 passes for 117 yards. Packers quarterback Brett Favre was 25 of 47 for 294 yards. Sterling Sharpe had 9 receptions for 132 yards, including a touchdown.

Green Bay	3	7	0	6	—	16
New England	0	0	7	10	—	17

GB — FG Jacke 27
GB — Sharpe 11 pass from Favre (Jacke kick)
NE — Brisby 10 pass from Bledsoe (Bahr kick)
NE — Brisby 37 pass from Bledsoe (Bahr kick)
GB — Cobb 1 run (kick failed)
NE — FG Bahr 33

ARIZONA 17, MINNESOTA 7—at Sun Devil Stadium, attendance 67,950. Buddy Ryan earned his first victory as Cardinals' head coach when Arizona broke a 7-7 tie with 10 points in the fourth quarter. Greg Davis's 46-yard field goal 51 seconds into the final period gave the Cardinals a 10-7 advantage, and Larry Centers ran 6 yards 3:11 later to close the scoring. Centers's touchdown came one play after quarterback Jay Schroeder teamed with Randal Hill on a 45-yard pass play. Schroeder, Arizona's third starting quarterback in three games, completed 20 of 36 passes for 221 yards. The Vikings' Warren Moon was 29 of 47 for 355 yards. But Moon also was intercepted twice and did not have the support of a rushing attack. Terry Allen's 18 yards on 12 carries was all Minnesota could muster on the ground. Vikings wide receiver Cris Carter caught 14 passes for 167 yards.

Minnesota	0	7	0	0	—	7
Arizona	7	0	0	10	—	17

Ariz — Ware 4 pass from Schroeder (Davis kick)
Minn — Reed 15 pass from Moon (Reveiz kick)
Ariz — FG Davis 46
Ariz — Centers 6 run (Davis kick)

NEW ORLEANS 27, N.Y. GIANTS 22—at Louisiana Superdome, attendance 55,076. The Saints scored 2 touchdowns less than a minute apart in the second quarter to turn a 10-point deficit into a 4-point lead at halftime, and went on to hand the Giants their first loss of the season. New Orleans trailed 13-3 until they marched 80 yards late in the second quarter to Jim Everett's 4-yard touchdown pass to Quinn Early 1:56 before halftime. Fifty-six seconds later, linebacker James Williams intercepted Dave Brown's pass and returned it 33 yards for a touchdown to give the Saints the lead for good at 17-13. New Orleans stretched the advantage to 27-13 before holding on to win. Everett completed 20 of 30 passes for 249 yards, but it was the Saints' defense that made the difference. New Orleans limited New York, hampered by the absence of injured Pro Bowl running back Rodney Hampton, to only 50 rushing yards and 202 total yards. Brown completed 20 of 35 passes for 180 yards and 2 touchdowns, but was intercepted twice and sacked 7 times.

N.Y. Giants	3	10	0	9	—	22
New Orleans	3	14	3	7	—	27

Giants— FG Treadwell 41
NO — FG Andersen 29
Giants— Sherrard 10 pass from Da. Brown (Treadwell kick)
Giants— FG Treadwell 32
NO — Early 4 pass from Everett (Andersen kick)
NO — J. Williams 33 interception return (Andersen kick)
NO — FG Andersen 32
NO — D. Brown 3 run (Andersen kick)
Giants— FG Treadwell 35
Giants— Sherrard 3 pass from Da. Brown (run failed)

CLEVELAND 27, N.Y. JETS 7—at Municipal Stadium, attendance 76,188. The Browns scored on four consecutive possessions to build a 24-0 lead in the first half en route to an easy victory. Vinny Testaverde passed for 257 yards and rookie Derrick Alexander caught 7 passes for 105 yards to lead Cleveland's offense, while safety Eric Turner keyed the defense with an interception, a sack, and a forced fumble. The Jets, without injured starting quarterback Boomer Esiason, managed little offensively. Jack Trudeau completed 28 of 46 passes for 288 yards, but much of it was long after the outcome was decided.

N.Y. Jets	0	0	0	7	—	7
Cleveland	7	17	3	0	—	27

Cleve — Metcalf 37 run (Stover kick)
Cleve — FG Stover 23
Cleve — Byner 1 run (Stover kick)
Cleve — Hoard 18 run (Stover kick)
Cleve — FG Stover 45
Jets — Moore 24 pass from Trudeau (Lowery kick)

PHILADELPHIA 40, SAN FRANCISCO 8—at Candlestick Park, attendance 64,771. Charlie Garner ran for 111 yards and 2 touchdowns in his NFL debut, sparking the Eagles to a stunning rout of the 49ers. Philadelphia dominated from the start, taking the opening kickoff and marching 75 yards in 11 plays to Garner's 1-yard run. Cornerback Eric Allen then intercepted Steve Young's pass on San Francisco's first play from scrimmage, returning it 11 yards to the 49ers' 28. Garner ran for another touchdown on the next play to make it 14-0 only 6:45 into the game. It was 23-0 before Young's 1-yard run and a 2-point conversion pulled San Francisco within 23-8 with 4:25 to go in the first half. But the Eagles eliminated any doubt about the outcome by countering with a 65-yard touchdown drive over the next 3:10 to make it 30-8 at halftime. Garner, a second-round draft choice who missed Philadelphia's first three games with a fractured rib, carried 16 times before leaving the game in the third quarter with a bruised back. Eagles quarterback Randall Cunningham completed 20 of 29 passes for 246 yards and 2 touchdowns. The 49ers' Young was only 11 of 23 for 99 yards, and was intercepted twice and sacked for a safety. Philadelphia finished with sizable advantages in first downs (26-11), total yards (437-189), and time of possession (39:16-20:44). It was San Francisco's worst regular-season defeat since a 59-14 drubbing at Dallas in 1980.

Philadelphia	14	16	3	7	—	40
San Francisco	0	8	0	0	—	8

Phil — Garner 1 run (Murray kick)
Phil — Garner 28 run (Murray kick)
Phil — Safety, Fuller tackled Young in end zone
Phil — Bailey 28 pass from Cunningham (Murray kick)
SF — Young 1 run (Jones pass from Young)
Phil — Walker 2 run (Murray kick)
Phil — FG Murray 36
Phil — Bavaro 18 pass from Cunningham (Murray kick)

INDIANAPOLIS 17, SEATTLE 15—at RCA Dome, attendance 49,876. Rookie Marshall Faulk's 2 touchdown runs helped the Colts snap a three-game losing streak. Faulk's 5-yard touchdown run late in the first quarter gave Indianapolis the lead for good, but it was his 1-yard score 9:11 into the second half that proved to be the game-winner. That gave the Colts a 17-8 lead, an advantage that held up despite a fourth-quarter rally by the Seahawks. Rick Mirer's 30-yard touchdown pass to Kelvin Martin 38 seconds into the final quarter pulled Seattle within 2 points, but the Seahawks eschewed a potential go-ahead field-goal attempt after reaching Indianapolis's 33-yard line with five minutes to go in the game. Instead, Mirer was sacked by nose tackle Tony Siragusa on fourth-and-4. Mirer finished with 20 completions in 36 attempts for 186 yards. Martin caught 8 passes for 104 yards. Colts quarterback Jim Harbaugh set up Faulk's touchdown runs with 49- and 36-yard pass completions to Sean Dawkins.

Seattle	5	3	0	7	—	15
Indianapolis	10	0	7	0	—	17

Sea — FG Kasay 42
Ind — FG Biasucci 45
Sea — Safety, Harbaugh called for intentional grounding in the end zone
Ind — Faulk 5 run (Biasucci kick)
Sea — FG Kasay 45
Ind — Faulk 1 run (Biasucci kick)
Sea — Martin 30 pass from Mirer (Kasay kick)

SUNDAY NIGHT, OCTOBER 2

MIAMI 23, CINCINNATI 7—at Riverfront Stadium, attendance 55,056. In a historic meeting, Don Shula's Dolphins outlasted Dave Shula's Bengals in the first father-son coaching matchup in major professional sports. It was the 331st career coaching victory for the elder Shula; his son's team remained winless in 1994. Still, it was Cincinnati that struck first, taking a 7-0 lead on David Klingler's 51-yard touchdown pass to Darnay Scott on the third play of the game. Miami took its first lead at 10-7 on Dan Marino's 11-yard touchdown pass to Keith Byars 1:14 before halftime. That capped an 80-yard drive, and was set up by Byars's 34-yard reception. The Dolphins gradually pulled away in the second half as the Bengals turned over the ball on five consecutive possessions.

Miami	0	10	7	6	—	23
Cincinnati	7	0	0	0	—	7

Cin — Scott 51 pass from Klingler (Pelfrey kick)
Mia — FG Stoyanovich 28
Mia — Byars 11 pass from Marino (Stoyanovich kick)
Mia — Ingram 4 pass from Marino (Stoyanovich kick)
Mia — FG Stoyanovich 27
Mia — FG Stoyanovich 32

MONDAY, OCTOBER 3

PITTSBURGH 30, HOUSTON 14—at Three Rivers Stadium, attendance 57,274. The Steelers scored on their first four possessions en route to an easy victory. After Gary Anderson staked Pittsburgh to a 6-0 lead with a pair of field goals, Steelers linebacker Kevin Greene recovered a fumble on a mishandled center snap at the Oilers' 3-yard line. Neil O'Donnell threw a 3-yard touchdown pass to tight end Eric Green on the next play to make it 13-0 9:18 into the game. Less than four minutes later, Barry Foster ran 1 yard for a touchdown set up by his own 26-yard run, and the rout began. Pittsburgh went on to build a 30-0 advantage before Houston's Bucky Richardson threw 2 touchdown passes in the fourth quarter. Content to nurse its big advantage, the Steelers kept the ball mostly on the ground, rushing for 215 of its 379 total yards. Foster had 115 yards on 21 carries, while rookie Byron (Bam) Morris added 70 yards. Greene recovered 2 fumbles and had 2 sacks.

Houston	0	0	0	14	—	14
Pittsburgh	20	3	0	7	—	30

Pitt — FG Anderson 42
Pitt — FG Anderson 25
Pitt — E. Green 3 pass from O'Donnell (Anderson kick)
Pitt — Foster 1 run (Anderson kick)
Pitt — FG Anderson 22
Pitt — Morris 2 run (Anderson kick)
Hou — Givins 76 pass from Richardson (Del Greco kick)
Hou — Jeffires 2 pass from Richardson (Del Greco kick)

SIXTH WEEK SUMMARIES

AMERICAN FOOTBALL CONFERENCE

Eastern Division	W	L	T	Pct.	Pts.	OP
Miami	4	2	0	.667	160	129
Buffalo	4	2	0	.667	117	116
New England	3	3	0	.500	158	159
N.Y. Jets	3	3	0	.500	92	105
Indianapolis	2	4	0	.333	113	128
Central Division						
Cleveland	4	1	0	.800	118	58
Pittsburgh	3	2	0	.600	100	101
Houston	1	4	0	.200	79	123
Cincinnati	0	5	0	.000	78	129
Western Division						
San Diego	5	0	0	1.000	134	84
Kansas City	3	2	0	.600	90	80
Seattle	3	3	0	.500	130	86
L.A. Raiders	2	3	0	.400	116	141
Denver	1	4	0	.200	108	146

NATIONAL FOOTBALL CONFERENCE

Eastern Division	W	L	T	Pct.	Pts.	OP
Dallas	4	1	0	.800	135	56
Philadelphia	4	1	0	.800	127	82
N.Y. Giants	3	2	0	.600	111	117
Arizona	1	4	0	.200	49	111
Washington	1	5	0	.167	112	165
Central Division						
Chicago	4	2	0	.667	113	108
Minnesota	4	2	0	.667	134	95
Green Bay	3	3	0	.500	107	84
Detroit	2	4	0	.333	106	129
Tampa Bay	2	4	0	.333	80	118
Western Division						
Atlanta	4	2	0	.667	138	112
San Francisco	4	2	0	.667	154	131
L.A. Rams	2	4	0	.333	84	109
New Orleans	2	4	0	.333	97	138

SUNDAY, OCTOBER 9

DALLAS 38, ARIZONA 3—at Texas Stadium, attendance 64,518. The Cowboys converted 3 first-half interceptions into 21 points and coasted to the victory. After Troy Aikman capped an 83-yard drive with a 2-yard touchdown pass to fullback Daryl Johnston 6:38 into the game, Dallas's defense took over. Rookie safety Darren Woodson intercepted Jay Schroeder's pass on the next possession, setting up the Cowboys at the Cardinals' 23-yard line. Three plays later, Emmitt Smith ran 3 yards for a touchdown and a 14-0 lead. Moments later, cornerback Larry Brown intercepted a pass and returned it 14 yards to Arizona's 18. It took four plays for Dallas to convert that into another short touchdown run by Smith and it was 21-0, still in the first quarter. Woodson intercepted another pass in the second quarter, setting up a 26-yard drive to Aikman's 12-yard touchdown pass to Michael Irvin. The Cardinals eventually fell behind 31-0 and managed only a 42-yard field goal by Greg Davis late in the third quarter. But to make matters worse, Davis injured his hamstring trying to chase down Kevin Williams when Williams returned the ensuing kickoff 87 yards for a touchdown. Schroeder also was hurt, leaving the game with a bruised elbow and shoulder following his third interception. Aikman finished with 16 completions in 22 attempts for 231 yards. Irvin caught 8 passes for 136 yards. The defeat was the worst ever for a Buddy Ryan-coached team.

Arizona	0	0	3	0	—	3
Dallas	21	7	10	0	—	38

Dall — Johnston 2 pass from Aikman (Boniol kick)
Dall — E. Smith 3 run (Boniol kick)
Dall — E. Smith 1 run (Boniol kick)
Dall — Irvin 12 pass from Aikman (Boniol kick)
Dall — FG Boniol 19
Ariz — FG Davis 42
Dall — K. Williams 87 kickoff return (Boniol kick)

DENVER 16, SEATTLE 9—at Husky Stadium, attendance 63,872. Leonard Russell rushed for 103 yards and quarterback John Elway ran 2 yards for the game's only touchdown as the Broncos broke into the win column for the first time this season. The game was tied 3-3 late in the first half when Denver safety Steve Atwater recovered a fumble by Seahawks wide receiver Michael Bates and returned it 17 yards to the Broncos' 30-yard line. From there, Elway directed a 70-yard touchdown drive to break the deadlock. The march featured Elway's 32-yard completion to Shannon Sharpe, and was kept alive by a defensive holding call that negated a third-down sack at Seattle's 12. Elway scored on the next play, 43 seconds before halftime. The teams traded field goals in the second half. The Seahawks outgained Denver 338 total yards to 278, but stymied themselves with 3 lost fumbles, 2 interceptions, and 8 penalties. They entered the game with a league-leading turnover ratio of plus-9, but were minus-5 on this day.

Denver	3	7	6	0	—	16
Seattle	0	3	3	3	—	9

Den — FG Elam 26
Sea — FG Kasay 37
Den — Elway 2 run (Elam kick)
Sea — FG Kasay 36
Den — FG Elam 33
Den — FG Elam 37
Sea — FG Kasay 42

N.Y. JETS 16, INDIANAPOLIS 6—at Giants Stadium, attendance 66,244. Nick Lowery broke a 6-6 tie by kicking a 37-yard field goal with 6:23 remaining, and the Jets went on to snap their three-game losing streak. Lowery's third field goal of the game gave him 336 for his career, lifting him past George Blanda and into second place on the NFL's all-time list (leader Jan Stenerud had 373 career field goals). With the kick, Lowery also became only the third player in league history to record 1,500 career points. New York cornerback James Hasty helped secure the game's outcome by forcing and recovering a fumble—1 of the Colts' 4 lost fumbles—at Indianapolis's 25-yard line with 5:36 remaining. Boomer Esiason, whose injured ankle kept him from starting the game, threw a 1-yard touchdown pass to tight end Johnny Mitchell with 2:26 left.

Indianapolis	3	3	0	0	—	6
N.Y. Jets	0	6	0	10	—	16

Ind — FG Biasucci 37
Jets — FG Lowery 27
Ind — FG Biasucci 44
Jets — FG Lowery 42
Jets — FG Lowery 37
Jets — Mitchell 1 pass from Esiason (Lowery kick)

SAN DIEGO 20, KANSAS CITY 6—at San Diego Jack Murphy Stadium, attendance 62,923. Natrone Means rushed for a career-high 125 yards and a touchdown as the Chargers remained the NFL's lone unbeaten team. San Diego led 6-3 late in the first half before Means carried 5 consecutive times on a 43-yard drive. His 9-yard touchdown run 2:56 before halftime increased the Chargers' advantage to 13-3. It was 13-6 in the fourth quarter when Means reeled off runs of 25 and 23 yards to highlight a 77-yard drive that was capped by Stan Humphries's 5-yard touchdown pass to Mark Seay with 7:47 left in the game. Means finished with a 6.6-yard average on his 19 rushing attempts. San Diego's defense, meanwhile, kept the Chiefs out of the end zone. Kansas City quarterback Joe Montana completed 37 of 55 passes for 310 yards, but was hampered by a running game that netted only 64 yards.

Kansas City	0	3	0	3	—	6
San Diego	3	10	0	7	—	20

SD — FG Carney 23
KC — FG Elliott 25
SD — FG Carney 32
SD — Means 9 run (Carney kick)
KC — FG Elliott 25
SD — Seay 5 pass from Humphries (Carney kick)

L.A. RAIDERS 21, NEW ENGLAND 17—at Foxboro Stadium, attendance 59,889. Cornerback Terry McDaniel intercepted 3 passes, returning 1 for a touchdown and setting up a touchdown with another, to lift the Raiders to the victory. McDaniel, who already had a fumble recovery and an interception for a touchdown earlier in the season, brought back Drew Bledsoe's pass 14 yards for a touchdown to give the Raiders a 7-3 lead 4:02 into the second quarter. But the Patriots drove 80 yards in nine plays to regain the lead on Bledsoe's 7-yard touchdown pass to running back Kevin Turner 6:09 before halftime. New England regained possession when Los Angeles mishandled the ensuing kickoff, and increased its advantage to 17-7 when Bledsoe threw 3 yards to running back Leroy Thompson for a touchdown with 1:55 left in the half. The Raiders countered with a 71-yard touchdown drive over the next 73 seconds, pulling within 17-14 on Jeff Hostetler's 27-yard touchdown pass to running back Harvey Williams. In the second half, McDaniel's interception set up Hostetler's 3-yard touchdown run 5:26 into the third quarter. That held up as the game-winner after the Raiders executed a goal-line stand late in the third quarter, recovering Turner's fumble at the 1, and thwarted another threat with McDaniel's third interception. The mistake-filled game featured 8 turnovers (4 by each team) and 18 penalties (11 on the Raiders). Hostetler passed for 250 yards but was intercepted 3 times inside the Patriots' 20. Bledsoe threw for 321 yards but completed only 23 of 55 passes and suffered McDaniel's 3 interceptions.

L.A. Raiders	0	14	7	0	—	21
New England	0	17	0	0	—	17

NE — FG Bahr 24
Raid — McDaniel 14 interception return (Jaeger kick)
NE — Turner 7 pass from Bledsoe (Bahr kick)
NE — Thompson 3 pass from Bledsoe (Bahr kick)
Raid — H. Williams 27 pass from Hostetler (Jaeger kick)
Raid — Hostetler 3 run (Jaeger kick)

GREEN BAY 24, L.A. RAMS 17—at Lambeau Field, attendance 58,911. The Packers rallied from a 14-point halftime deficit to beat the Rams. After trailing 17-3 at the intermission, Green Bay marched 62 yards on its first possession of the second half, cutting its deficit to seven points on Brett Favre's 8-yard touchdown pass to Sterling Sharpe 6:02 into the third quarter. On its next possession, Los Angeles was held without a first down, and the Packers' Robert Brooks returned the ensuing punt 85 yards for a touchdown to tie the game at 17-17. The winning score came 2:54 into the fourth quarter, when Edgar Bennett ran 1 yard for a touchdown. That capped a 40-yard drive that was set up when the Rams' Sean Landeta managed only a 13-yard punt. The Rams still had a chance to tie or go for a victory late in the game when they drove to Green Bay's 2-yard line with 1:04 remaining. But a holding penalty and a false start moved Los Angeles back to the 17, and rookie Lenny McGill intercepted Chris Miller's pass in the end zone to secure the victory for the Packers.

L.A. Rams	7	10	0	0	—	17
Green Bay	3	0	14	7	—	24

Rams — Drayton 2 pass from Miller (Zendejas kick)
GB — FG Jacke 25
Rams — Drayton 4 pass from Miller (Zendejas kick)
Rams — FG Zendejas 37
GB — Sharpe 8 pass from Favre (Jacke kick)
GB — Brooks 85 punt return (Jacke kick)
GB — Bennett 1 run (Jacke kick)

BUFFALO 21, MIAMI 11—at Rich Stadium, attendance 79,491. Thurman Thomas rushed for 125 yards and 2 touchdowns as the Bills turned to their ground game to beat the Dolphins. Thomas, who sat out Buffalo's game against Chicago the previous week with a strained hamstring, carried 31 times. As a team, the Bills finished with 48 attempts for 214 yards. Buffalo led 7-3 until late in the third period, when the Dolphins' O.J. McDuffie fumbled a punt. The Bills' Bucky Brooks recovered at Miami's 26-yard line, and Thomas scored on the next play to increase the advantage to 14-3 just 20 seconds before the end of the period. Kenneth Davis's 5-yard touchdown run midway through the fourth quarter put the game out of reach. Strong winds limited the effectiveness of each team's normally potent passing attack. Buffalo's Jim Kelly passed for only 130 yards. The Dolphins' Dan Marino threw for 212 yards, but completed only 20 of 43 passes.

Miami	3	0	0	8	—	11
Buffalo	0	7	7	7	—	21

Mia — FG Stoyanovich 40
Buff — Thomas 1 run (Christie kick)
Buff — Thomas 26 run (Christie kick)
Buff — Davis 5 run (Christie kick)
Mia — McDuffie 3 pass from Marino (Jackson pass from Marino)

CHICAGO 17, NEW ORLEANS 7—at Soldier Field, attendance 63,822. Bears quarterback Steve Walsh threw a third-quarter touchdown pass to help beat his former teammates. Walsh, who played three years for New Orleans but signed with Chicago as a free agent prior to the 1994 season, won his third consecutive start since replacing injured Erik Kramer as the Bears' quarterback. He capped an 8-play, 70-yard drive with a 21-yard touchdown pass to Jeff Graham for the touchdown that put Chicago ahead for good with 2:24 remaining in the third quarter. Lewis Tillman added some insurance by running 25 yards for a touchdown with 2:31 left in the game. Tillman finished the game with 100 yards on his 23 carries. The Saints' lone touchdown came on Jim Everett's 18-yard pass to Quinn Early 3:37 before halftime. New Orleans had 2 opportunities to extend its 7-0 lead thwarted by blocked field-goal attempts that were caused by a badly torn-up field.

New Orleans	0	7	0	0	—	7
Chicago	0	0	10	7	—	17

NO — Early 18 pass from Everett (Andersen kick)
Chi — FG Butler 46
Chi — Graham 21 pass from Walsh (Butler kick)
Chi — Tillman 25 run (Butler kick)

SAN FRANCISCO 27, DETROIT 21—at Pontiac Silverdome, attendance 77,340. Rookie fullback William Floyd scored 2 touchdowns in his first career start, helping the 49ers rally from a 14-point deficit to beat the Lions. San Francisco, coming off a 32-point drubbing at home by the Eagles one week earlier, fell behind 14-0 on Scott Mitchell's 33-yard touchdown pass to Brett Perriman and a 9-yard run by Barry Sanders, the latter 3:18 into the second quarter. But the 49ers countered Sanders's touchdown with a touchdown just 78 seconds later, when Floyd capped a 63-yard march with a 1-yard run. That touchdown was set up by Dexter Carter's 35-yard kickoff return, and when Carter returned a punt 21 yards later in the period, San Francisco had to march only 42 yards to the tying touchdown, a 4-yard run by Ricky Watters. Safety Merton Hanks intercepted Mitchell's pass on the first play of the second half, and returned it 38 yards to Detroit's 7-yard line. Three plays later, Floyd's 1-yard run gave the 49ers the lead for good.

San Francisco	0	14	7	6	—	27
Detroit	7	7	0	7	—	21

Det — Perriman 33 pass from Mitchell (Hanson kick)
Det — Sanders 9 run (Hanson kick)
SF — Floyd 1 run (Brien kick)
SF — Watters 4 run (Brien kick)
SF — Floyd 1 run (Brien kick)
SF — Singleton 5 pass from Young (kick failed)
Det — Moore 26 pass from Mitchell (Hanson kick)

ATLANTA 34, TAMPA BAY 13—at Georgia Dome, attendance 52,633. Craig Heyward ran for 2 touchdowns and Jeff George passed for 2 as the Falcons won their third consecutive game. Heyward capped a 74-yard drive on Atlanta's first possession with a 1-yard touchdown run 5:01 into the game. His 5-yard touchdown run 1:04 before halftime gave the Falcons a 24-0 advantage. George, who completed 23 of 35 passes for 269 yards, had scoring strikes of 36 yards to Andre Rison and 32 yards to Terance Mathis. Atlanta cornerback Vinnie Clark intercepted 2 of rookie quarterback Trent Dilfer's passes. He returned the first 21 yards to set up Heyward's second touchdown, and brought back another 74 yards to set up a field goal in the third quarter. The Buccaneers, who used three quarterbacks, amassed 288 yards through the air, but again were victimized by a nonexistent rushing attack. Tampa Bay ran for only 32 yards, 20 of that on scrambles by quarterback Craig Erickson.

Tampa Bay	0	3	0	10	—	13
Atlanta	14	10	3	7	—	34

Atl — Heyward 1 run (Johnson kick)
Atl — Rison 36 pass from George (Johnson kick)
Atl — FG Johnson 27
Atl — Heyward 5 run (Johnson kick)
TB — FG Husted 35
Atl — FG Johnson 29
TB — J. Harris 11 pass from Erickson (Husted kick)
Atl — Mathis 32 pass from George (Johnson kick)
TB — FG Husted 38

SUNDAY NIGHT, OCTOBER 9

PHILADELPHIA 21, WASHINGTON 17—at Veterans Stadium, attendance 63,947. Herschel Walker ran 2 yards for the go-ahead touchdown in the final quarter, and the Eagles held on to win their fourth in a row. Philadelphia trailed 17-14 before embarking on an 11-play, 80-yard drive to go in front. Walker had a 22-yard catch on third-and-10 from the Redskins' 45-yard line to keep the drive alive, then capped the march with his touchdown run with 9:46 left in the game. The outcome was in doubt, however, until the final minute, when safety Greg Jackson intercepted Heath Shuler's pass at the Eagles' 3 with 40 seconds to go. Earlier, Shuler had thrown touchdown passes of 27 and 41 yards to Tydus Winans. Those big plays kept Washington in the game despite a huge statistical disadvantage. Philadelphia amassed 431 total yards to only 226 for the Redskins, and the Eagles maintained possession for a whopping 43:11 of the game's 60 minutes. Philadelphia had 193 yards on the ground, 122 from Charlie Garner, who became the first rookie in club history to surpass the 100-yard mark in back-to-back games. Quarterback Randall Cunningham passed for 261 yards and a touchdown and scored on a 20-yard run.

Washington	0	6	11	0	—	17
Philadelphia	7	0	7	7	—	21

Phil — Cunningham 20 run (Murray kick)
Wash — Winans 27 pass from Shuler (kick failed)
Wash — Winans 41 pass from Shuler (Howard pass from Shuler)
Phil — Barnett 49 pass from Cunningham (Murray kick)
Wash — FG Lohmiller 47
Phil — Walker 2 run (Murray kick)

MONDAY, OCTOBER 10

MINNESOTA 27, N.Y. GIANTS 10—at Giants Stadium, attendance 77,294. Cornerback Anthony Parker returned an interception 44 yards for a touchdown to break a 10-10 tie in the third quarter, and the Vikings went on to defeat the Giants. New York quarterback Dave Brown completed 6 of 7 passes on a 94-yard touchdown drive shortly before halftime, capping the march with a 3-yard run to tie the score just seven seconds before halftime. But Parker quelled the momentum that drive created by stepping in front of Brown's pass just 1:44 into the third quarter and returning it for the tie-breaking touchdown. Late in the period, Warren Moon teamed with Cris Carter on a 20-yard touchdown pass to break open the game. Moon completed 23 of 34 passes for 299 yards. Minnesota wide receiver Qadry Ismail caught 7 passes for 117 yards. Brown passed for 226 yards but had 3 passes intercepted and was sacked 4 times. The Giants managed only 37 rushing yards despite the return of Pro Bowl running back Rodney Hampton, who had missed the previous two games because of a bruised kidney.

Minnesota	3	7	14	3	—	27
N.Y. Giants	0	10	0	0	—	10

Minn — FG Reveiz 44
Giants— FG Treadwell 22
Minn — Allen 1 run (Reveiz kick)
Giants— Da. Brown 3 run (Treadwell kick)
Minn — Parker 44 interception return (Reveiz kick)
Minn — Carter 20 pass from Moon (Reveiz kick)
Minn — FG Reveiz 24

SEVENTH WEEK SUMMARIES

AMERICAN FOOTBALL CONFERENCE

Eastern Division	W	L	T	Pct.	Pts.	OP
Miami	5	2	0	.714	180	146
Buffalo	4	3	0	.571	134	143
N.Y. Jets	4	3	0	.571	116	122
Indianapolis	3	4	0	.429	140	145
New England	3	4	0	.429	175	183
Central Division						
Cleveland	5	1	0	.833	129	66
Pittsburgh	4	2	0	.667	114	111
Houston	1	5	0	.167	87	134
Cincinnati	0	6	0	.000	88	143
Western Division						
San Diego	6	0	0	1.000	170	106
Kansas City	4	2	0	.667	121	108
Seattle	3	3	0	.500	130	86
L.A. Raiders	2	4	0	.333	133	161
Denver	1	5	0	.167	136	177

NATIONAL FOOTBALL CONFERENCE

Eastern Division	W	L	T	Pct.	Pts.	OP
Dallas	5	1	0	.833	159	69
Philadelphia	4	2	0	.667	140	106
N.Y. Giants	3	3	0	.500	121	134
Arizona	2	4	0	.333	68	127
Washington	1	6	0	.143	128	184
Central Division						
Chicago	4	2	0	.667	113	108
Minnesota	4	2	0	.667	134	95
Green Bay	3	3	0	.500	107	84
Detroit	2	4	0	.333	106	129
Tampa Bay	2	4	0	.333	80	118
Western Division						
San Francisco	5	2	0	.714	196	134
Atlanta	4	3	0	.571	141	154
L.A. Rams	3	4	0	.429	101	119
New Orleans	2	5	0	.286	119	174

THURSDAY, OCTOBER 13

CLEVELAND 11, HOUSTON 8—at Astrodome, attendance 50,364. The Browns improved to 5-1 for the first time since 1965 by beating the Oilers. Vinny Testaverde's 25-yard touchdown pass to Mark Carrier 6:39 into the second quarter and Matt Stover's 35-yard field goal on the final play of the first half was all the offense Cleveland could muster, but it was enough to hand Houston its fifth loss in six games. The Oilers did not score until Billy Joe Tolliver threw a 5-yard touchdown pass to running back Lorenzo White with 28 seconds left in the game. When Houston failed to cover the ensuing onside kick, the Browns held on to win.

Cleveland	0	11	0	0	—	11
Houston	0	0	0	8	—	8

Cleve — Carrier 25 pass from Testaverde (Tupa run)
Cleve — FG Stover 35
Hou — White 5 pass from Tolliver (Jeffires pass from Tolliver)

SUNDAY, OCTOBER 16

ARIZONA 19, WASHINGTON 16—at RFK Stadium, attendance 50,019. Todd Peterson's 29-yard field goal with 4:56 left in overtime gave the Cardinals the victory. Peterson, signed earlier in the week because regular kicker Greg Davis was out with a pulled hamstring, made his winning kick one play after Arizona safety Terry Hoage intercepted Heath Shuler's pass and returned it 23 yards to the Redskins' 12-yard line. It was the fifth time the rookie Shuler had been intercepted by the Cardinals' defense. Cornerback Aeneas Williams had 2 of the thefts, 1 of which he returned 43 yards to Washington's 22 with Arizona trailing 14-3 early in the fourth quarter. Four plays later, Ron Moore ran 10 yards for a touchdown to trim the Cardinals' deficit to 14-9. Rather than punting from his own end zone, Arizona's Jeff Feagles took an intentional safety that made it 16-9 with 4:47 left in regulation, but the Cardinals got the ball back at their own 28 with 3:03 to go. Quarterback Steve Beuerlein threw a 5-yard touchdown pass to Ricky Proehl to tie the game with 19 seconds remaining. Beuerlein, back in the starting lineup after losing his job to Jim McMahon and Jay Schroeder, completed only 16 of 34 passes for 194 yards and was intercepted 3 times. Shuler was 11 of 32 for 158 yards. Moore rushed for 118 yards on 28 carries.

Arizona	0	3	0	13	3	—	19
Washington	0	14	0	2	0	—	16

Wash — Mitchell 46 pass from Shuler (Lohmiller kick)
Wash — Green 27 interception return (Lohmiller kick)
Ariz — FG Peterson 35
Ariz — Moore 10 run (run failed)
Wash — Safety, Feagles stepped out of end zone
Ariz — Proehl 5 pass from Beuerlein (Peterson kick)
Ariz — FG Peterson 29

PITTSBURGH 14, CINCINNATI 10—at Three Rivers Stadium, attendance 55,353. Neil O'Donnell threw 2 second-quarter touchdown passes and the Steelers kept the Bengals winless in 1994. O'Donnell capped a 66-yard drive with a 13-yard touchdown pass to John L. Williams to break a scoreless tie 3:47 before halftime. Pittsburgh marched 32 yards to another touchdown on O'Donnell's 14-yard strike to Ernie Mills with 42 seconds left in the first half after Steelers linebacker Levon Kirkland intercepted Don Hollas's pass. The Steelers' offense, hampered by the loss of running back Barry Foster to a knee injury on the game's second play, managed little after that and finished with only 243 total yards. Still, it was enough to outlast the Bengals, who could muster only 241 total yards themselves. One bright spot for Cincinnati was its defense, which recorded 8 sacks, including 4 by linebacker Alfred Williams. The Bengals had only 3 sacks in their first five games.

Cincinnati	0	0	7	3	—	10
Pittsburgh	0	14	0	0	—	14

Pitt — J.L. Williams 13 pass from O'Donnell (Anderson kick)
Pitt — Mills 14 pass from O'Donnell (Anderson kick)
Cin — Cothran 7 pass from Johnson (Pelfrey kick)
Cin — FG Pelfrey 47

INDIANAPOLIS 27, BUFFALO 17—at Rich Stadium, attendance 79,404. Jim Harbaugh passed for 206 yards and 2 touchdowns to help the Colts forge an upset of the Bills. Indianapolis trailed 7-3 late in the first quarter before reeling off a 17-play, 98-yard drive that consumed 10:25 and culminated in Harbaugh's 6-yard touchdown pass to Floyd Turner. It was 10-10 at halftime, but the Colts opened the second half with another lengthy march—15 plays and 79 yards in 8:27—to take the lead for good on Harbaugh's 10-yard touchdown pass to tight end Kerry Cash. Harbaugh completed 18 of 22 passes before leaving the game with a bruised hand in the fourth quarter. Backup Don Majkowski came on and tossed a 19-yard touchdown to Turner on his first pass attempt, increasing the Colts' advantage to 24-10 with 8:14 left. Bills quarterback Jim Kelly completed 25 of 34 passes for 286 yards and became the leading passer in the club's history. Kelly finished the day at 27,788 career passing yards, surpassing the previous mark of 27,590 by Joe Ferguson.

Indianapolis	3	7	7	10	—	27
Buffalo	7	3	0	7	—	17

Buff — Davis 13 run (Christie kick)
Ind — FG Biasucci 43
Ind — Turner 6 pass from Harbaugh (Biasucci kick)
Buff — FG Christie 23
Ind — Cash 10 pass from Harbaugh (Biasucci kick)
Ind — Turner 19 pass from Majkowski (Biasucci kick)
Ind — FG Biasucci 33
Buff — Thomas 2 pass from Kelly (Christie kick)

MIAMI 20, L.A. RAIDERS 17—at Joe Robbie Stadium, attendance 69,380. Pete Stoyanovich's 29-yard field goal 5:46 into overtime lifted the Dolphins past the Raiders. Miami took the kickoff in the extra session and marched 65 yards, most of it on the ground, to the winning field goal on a wind-swept day that limited the effectiveness of each team's passing game. Quarterback Dan Marino passed only once in overtime, a 15-yard completion to Bobby Ingram, while running back Bernie Parmalee ran 5 times for 45 yards. Parmalee finished the game with 30 carries for a career-high 150 yards. He was a big factor on special teams, too, recovering a fumble by Los Angeles punt returner Tim Brown in the closing seconds of the third quarter. Six plays later, Marino passed 18 yards to running back Keith Byars to tie the score at 17-17 with 12:21 left in regulation. The Raiders, who managed only 86 passing yards and 210 total yards, nonetheless led by 10 points early in the game behind the strength of their defense. Tackle Nolan Harrison stripped Marino of the ball midway through the first quarter and Los Angeles nose tackle Jerry Ball recovered at the Dolphins' 41-yard line, setting up Jeff Jaeger's 19-yard field goal. Two plays later, Raiders defensive end Anthony Smith recovered Mark Higgs's fumble and returned it 25 yards for a touchdown. Miami's victory, coupled with the Bills loss to the Colts, moved the Dolphins into first place in the AFC Eastern Division.

L.A. Raiders	10	0	7	0	0	—	17
Miami	0	7	3	7	3	—	20

Raid — FG Jaeger 19
Raid — Smith 25 fumble return (Jaeger kick)
Mia — Jackson 15 pass from Marino (Stoyanovich kick)
Mia — FG Stoyanovich 21
Raid — Brown 7 pass from Hostetler (Jaeger kick)
Mia — Byars 18 pass from Marino (Stoyanovich kick)
Mia — FG Stoyanovich 29

N.Y. JETS 24, NEW ENGLAND 17—at Giants Stadium, attendance 71,123. Johnny Johnson rushed for 122 yards and Brad Baxter scored on a pair of short touchdown runs as the Jets beat the Patriots. New York took advantage of 4 turnovers, including one on New England's first play. Patriots quarterback Drew Bledsoe fumbled the snap, and Jets safety Ronnie Lott recovered at the 11-yard line. Three plays later, Baxter ran 1 yard for a touchdown and a 7-0 lead 7:45 into the game. Baxter's 2-yard touchdown run 1:57 before halftime broke a 7-7 tie and gave New York the lead for good. That came seven plays after Kyle Clifton recovered a fumbled punt at New England's 38. The Jets got the ball back a minute later and opened up a 21-7 lead on Boomer Esiason's 4-yard touchdown pass to Johnny Mitchell with 26 seconds left in the half. The Patriots outgained New York 324-242 but were stymied by the turnovers and a missed field goal, and converted only 3 of 7 fourth-down attempts. The 7 attempts on fourth down equaled the most tries in a single game since the statistic first was kept two decades ago.

New England	0	7	0	10	—	17
N.Y. Jets	7	14	0	3	—	24

Jets — B. Baxter 1 run (Lowery kick)
NE — Crittenden 3 pass from Bledsoe (Bahr kick)
Jets — B. Baxter 2 run (Lowery kick)
Jets — Mitchell 4 pass from Esiason (Lowery kick)
NE — Thomas 4 run (Bahr kick)
Jets — FG Lowery 37
NE — FG Bahr 40

L.A. RAMS 17, N.Y. GIANTS 10—at Anaheim Stadium, attendance 40,474. After the Rams' Chris Miller threw 2 first-half touchdown passes, its defense shut down the Giants in the second half to preserve the victory. Linebacker Joe Kelly's interception and 31-yard return set up Miller's first touchdown pass, 19 yards to rookie Isaac Bruce 4:19 into the game. Late in the first quarter, Miller teamed with tight end Troy Drayton on a 12-yard touchdown to break a 7-7 tie. In the second half, New York failed to advance past Los Angeles's 35-yard line. The Giants' last chance began with a possession at their own 20-yard line with 1:06 to go. But quarterback Dave Brown was intercepted by safety Anthony Newman on first down. New York lost its third consecutive game after beginning the season with three victories.

N.Y. Giants	7	3	0	0	—	10
L.A. Rams	14	3	0	0	—	17

Rams — Bruce 19 pass from Miller (Zendejas kick)
Giants— Hampton 27 run (Treadwell kick)
Rams — Drayton 12 pass from Miller (Zendejas kick)
Giants— FG Treadwell 24
Rams — FG Zendejas 22

DALLAS 24, PHILADELPHIA 13—at Texas Stadium, attendance 64,703. Troy Aikman threw 2 touchdown passes and the Cowboys overcame a sluggish start to beat the Eagles and take over sole possession of first place in the NFC East. Philadelphia's Jeff Sydner returned a punt 40 yards in the first quarter, setting up Randall Cunningham's 32-yard touchdown pass to Herschel Walker, and the Eagles led 7-0 9:31 into the game. Dallas, meanwhile, was having trouble getting on track, failing to make a first down and mustering only 6 total yards in the first quarter. But in the second quarter, the Cowboys marched 84 yards in 14 plays to a touchdown. Aikman completed all 4 of his pass attempts on the drive, and Emmitt Smith ran 2 yards to tie the score at 7-7 1:49 before halftime. For Smith, who ran for 106 yards in all, it was his team-record eighth consecutive game with a touchdown. Forty-one seconds later, Dallas took the lead for good on Aikman's 16-yard touchdown pass to Alvin Harper. That score was set up when safety Kenneth Gant intercepted Cunningham's pass at Philadelphia's 34-yard line. Interceptions played key roles in the second half as well. Safety Darren Woodson's theft and 26-yard return early in the third quarter preceded Aikman's 14-yard touchdown pass to tight end Jay Novacek as the Cowboys opened up a 21-7 advantage. And after the Eagles closed to 24-13 late in the game, then drove to Dallas's 1, they were thwarted when Cowboys cornerback Larry Brown secured the victory with an interception at the goal line.

Philadelphia	7	0	0	6	—	13
Dallas	0	14	7	3	—	24

Phil — Walker 32 pass from Cunningham (Murray kick)
Dall — E. Smith 2 run (Boniol kick)
Dall — Harper 16 pass from Aikman (Boniol kick)
Dall — Novacek 14 pass from Aikman (Boniol kick)
Dall — FG Boniol 37
Phil — Joseph 34 run (run failed)

SAN DIEGO 36, NEW ORLEANS 22—at Louisiana Superdome, attendance 50,565. Natrone Means rushed for 120 yards and 3 touchdowns as the Chargers routed the Saints to remain the NFL's lone unbeaten team. Except for a kneel-down to run out the clock in the first half, San Diego scored on its first seven possessions. Means, who carried 26 times, capped marches of 55 and 72 yards with touchdown runs as the Chargers built a 14-0 first-quarter lead. It was 27-7 at halftime, and San Diego kept the game out of reach with 3 second-half field goals. In all, kicker John Carney had 5 field goals without a miss. The Chargers' 6-0 start was their best since 1961, when they began the season 11-0 and advanced to the AFL Championship Game.

San Diego	14	13	6	3	—	36
New Orleans	0	7	7	8	—	22

SD — Means 16 run (Carney kick)
SD — Means 8 run (Carney kick)
SD — FG Carney 49
SD — Means 1 run (Carney kick)
NO — Early 18 pass from Everett (Andersen kick)
SD — FG Carney 31
SD — FG Carney 29
NO — Smith 1 pass from Everett (Andersen kick)
SD — FG Carney 29
NO — Neal 1 run (Walls pass from Everett)
SD — FG Carney 28

SAN FRANCISCO 42, ATLANTA 3—at Georgia Dome, attendance 67,298. Steve Young threw 4 touchdown passes and Deion Sanders returned an interception 93 yards for a touchdown as the 49ers routed the Falcons in a showdown for first place in the NFC West. Two of Young's scoring tosses went to running back Ricky Watters, the first from 10 yards to cap a 68-yard drive on the game's opening possession. Moments later, on Atlanta's third play from scrimmage, San Francisco safety Tim McDonald recovered Craig Heyward's fumble and returned it 49 yards for a touchdown and a 14-0 lead 7:11 into the game. It was 21-3 late in the first half when Sanders, the free-agent cornerback playing his first game against his former Falcons teammates, stepped in front of Jeff George's pass at the 49ers' 7-yard line and returned it for the touchdown that put the game out of reach. Atlanta turned over the ball twice on its first three plays of the second half, leading to San Francisco's final 2 touchdowns. Young, who completed his first 14 passes, finished 15 of 16 for 143 yards and gave way to backup Elvis Grbac after teaming with Watters on a 4-yard touchdown 5:25 into the second half for the game's final points. The 49ers had only 281 total yards, but intercepted 4 passes, recovered 2 fumbles, and recorded 6 sacks.

San Francisco	14	14	14	0	—	42
Atlanta	0	3	0	0	—	3

SF — Watters 10 pass from Young (Brien kick)
SF — McDonald 49 fumble return (Brien kick)
SF — Rice 1 pass from Young (Brien kick)
Atl — FG Johnson 34
SF — D. Sanders 93 interception return (Brien kick)
SF — B. Jones 7 pass from Young (Brien kick)
SF — Watters 4 pass from Young (Brien kick)

MONDAY, OCTOBER 17

KANSAS CITY 31, DENVER 28—at Mile High Stadium, attendance 75,151. Joe Montana's 5-yard touchdown pass to Willie Davis with eight seconds remaining gave the Chiefs a dramatic victory over the Broncos. Denver had taken a 28-24 lead on John Elway's 4-yard run with 1:29 remaining. But Kansas City countered with a 75-yard drive on which Montana completed 7 of 8 passes. His 19-yard toss to tight end Tracy Greene gave the Chiefs first-and-goal on the Broncos' 5-yard line with 13 seconds left. The game-winner came on the next play, capping a flurry of activity in the last 4:08 of the fourth quarter. It was at that point that Lin Elliott kicked a 19-yard field goal to give Kansas City a 24-21 lead. Denver wide receiver Shannon Sharpe lost a fumble at the 2:45 mark, but the Chiefs gave the ball back on the next play when Marcus Allen fumbled at Kansas City's 39 with 2:39 to go. Elway quickly marched his team to the go-ahead touchdown, only to see Montana's heroics prevail at the end. Montana, questionable for the game all week long because of bruised ribs, completed 34 of 54 passes for 393 yards and 3 touchdowns. Elway completed 18 of 29 attempts for 263 yards and 2 touchdowns. The Chiefs won in Denver for the first time since 1982.

Kansas City	0	14	7	10	—	31
Denver	0	14	7	7	—	28

Den — L. Russell 12 run (Elam kick)
KC — Allen 7 run (Elliott kick)
Den — Miller 27 pass from Elway (Elam kick)
KC — Birden 6 pass from Montana (Elliott kick)
KC — Valerio 4 pass from Montana (Elliott kick)
Den — Evans 20 pass from Elway (Elam kick)
KC — FG Elliott 19
Den — Elway 4 run (Elam kick)
KC — Davis 5 pass from Montana (Elliott kick)

EIGHTH WEEK SUMMARIES

AMERICAN FOOTBALL CONFERENCE

Eastern Division	W	L	T	Pct.	Pts.	OP
Miami	5	2	0	.714	180	146
Buffalo	4	3	0	.571	134	143
N.Y. Jets	4	3	0	.571	116	122
New England	3	4	0	.429	175	183
Indianapolis	3	5	0	.375	167	186
Central Division						
Cleveland	6	1	0	.857	166	79
Pittsburgh	5	2	0	.714	124	117
Houston	1	6	0	.143	93	155
Cincinnati	0	7	0	.000	101	180
Western Division						
San Diego	6	1	0	.857	185	126
Kansas City	5	2	0	.714	159	131
L.A. Raiders	3	4	0	.429	163	178
Seattle	3	4	0	.429	153	124
Denver	2	5	0	.286	156	192

NATIONAL FOOTBALL CONFERENCE

Eastern Division	W	L	T	Pct.	Pts.	OP
Dallas	6	1	0	.857	187	90
Philadelphia	5	2	0	.714	161	112
N.Y. Giants	3	4	0	.429	127	144
Arizona	2	5	0	.286	89	155
Washington	2	6	0	.250	169	211
Central Division						
Minnesota	5	2	0	.714	147	105
Chicago	4	3	0	.571	129	129
Detroit	3	4	0	.429	127	145
Green Bay	3	4	0	.429	117	97
Tampa Bay	2	5	0	.286	96	159
Western Division						
San Francisco	6	2	0	.750	237	150
Atlanta	4	4	0	.500	158	184
L.A. Rams	3	5	0	.375	135	156
New Orleans	3	5	0	.375	156	208

THURSDAY, OCTOBER 20

MINNESOTA 13, GREEN BAY 10—at Metrodome, attendance 63,041. Fuad Reveiz's 29-yard field goal tied the game with 17 seconds left in the fourth quarter and his 27-yarder won it 4:26 into overtime. The Vikings struggled offensively until taking over at their own 34-yard line with 5:32 left in the game and trailing 10-7. Warren Moon completed 7 of 10 passes on the ensuing 55-yard drive, including a 15-yard completion to Cris Carter to move into field-goal range. Then, on the first possession in overtime, Moon was 4 of 5 on the winning 62-yard drive. The veteran quarterback finished with 31 completions in 50 attempts for 271 yards. But he also was sacked 4 times, suffered 2 interceptions, and was supported by only 14 yards from Minnesota's running backs. Green Bay, meanwhile, fared little better on offense, managing only 158 total yards. Quarterback Brett Favre left the game in the first quarter with a hip pointer. His backup, Mark Brunell, completed 5 of 7 passes on a 69-yard drive that culminated in his 5-yard touchdown run shortly before halftime, but finished just 11 of 24 for 79 yards. Sean Jones had a pair of sacks for the Packers' defense.

Green Bay	0	10	0	0	0	—	10
Minnesota	7	0	0	3	3	—	13

Minn — Parker 23 fumble return (Reveiz kick)
GB — FG Jacke 50
GB — Brunell 5 run (Jacke kick)
Minn — FG Reveiz 29
Minn — FG Reveiz 27

SUNDAY, OCTOBER 23

L.A. RAIDERS 30, ATLANTA 17—at Los Angeles Memorial Coliseum, attendance 42,192. Jeff Hostetler passed for 204 yards, Harvey Williams rushed for 107, and the Raiders overcame an early 10-point deficit to beat the Falcons. Williams, making his first start for Los Angeles, carried 27 times and also caught 8 passes for 43 yards. He pulled the Raiders within 10-7 early in the second quarter by capping a 78-yard drive with a 1-yard touchdown run. Los Angeles forced Atlanta to punt on the next possession, and the 17-yard kick was partially blocked by Albert Lewis. That set up a 20-yard touchdown pass from Hostetler to Tim Brown to give the Raiders a lead they would not relinquish. The pair teamed again on a 31-yard touchdown pass 4:05 into the third quarter. Hostetler finished with 21 completions in 30 attempts, while Brown caught 8 passes for 130 yards. Jeff George completed 16 of 29 passes for 218 yards and a touchdown for the Falcons. Atlanta had taken a 10-0 lead in the first quarter by taking the opening kickoff and driving to a field goal and then taking advantage of Hostetler's fumble on the next series to march to Craig Heyward's 1-yard run.

Atlanta	10	0	0	7	—	17
L.A. Raiders	0	14	10	6	—	30

Atl — FG Johnson 23
Atl — Heyward 1 run (Johnson kick)
Raid — H. Williams 1 run (Jaeger kick)
Raid — Brown 20 pass from Hostetler (Jaeger kick)
Raid — Brown 31 pass from Hostetler (Jaeger kick)
Raid — FG Jaeger 46
Atl — Mathis 3 pass from George (Johnson kick)
Raid — FG Jaeger 31
Raid — FG Jaeger 24

DETROIT 21, CHICAGO 16—at Pontiac Silverdome, attendance 73,574. Barry Sanders rushed for 167 yards to help the Lions snap a three-game losing streak. Sanders carried 23 times, the longest an 84-yard run to set up Scott Mitchell's 6-yard touchdown pass 51 seconds into the second quarter. Eighteen seconds later, Detroit linebacker Chris Spielman returned a fumble 25 yards to give the Lions a 14-0 lead. Detroit's Mel Gray returned a kickoff 102 yards for the touchdown that proved decisive after the Bears closed within 14-10 late in the third period. Earlier in the game, Gray surpassed Ron Smith's NFL record for career yards on kickoff returns. Quarterback Erik Kramer pulled Chicago within five points on a 76-yard touchdown pass to Jeff Graham, but after marching his team 50 yards late in the game, his fourth-and-4 pass to Nate Lewis fell incomplete with 46 seconds to go, ending the Bears' last threat. Kramer, back in the starting lineup after missing three games with a separated shoulder, completed 29 of 48 passes for 309 yards and 2 touchdowns, with 3 interceptions. Graham caught 7 passes for 136 yards. Chicago had sizable advantages in first downs (22-8), total yards (402-232), and time of possession (36:36-23:24), but had its three-game winning streak snapped.

Chicago	0	7	9	0	—	16
Detroit	0	14	7	0	—	21

Det — Perriman 6 pass from Mitchell (Hanson kick)
Det — Spielman 25 fumble return (Hanson kick)
Chi — Lewis 5 pass from Kramer (Butler kick)
Chi — FG Butler 22
Det — Gray 102 kickoff return (Hanson kick)
Chi — Graham 76 pass from Kramer (pass failed)

CLEVELAND 37, CINCINNATI 13—at Cleveland Stadium, attendance 77,588. The Browns scored 17 points in a span of 3:20 of the third quarter to turn this game around. Cleveland's outburst was produced entirely by its special teams. Trailing the winless Bengals 13-10, Cleveland's rally began when Bennie Thompson recovered Corey Sawyer's fumbled punt return at Cincinnati's 15-yard line. That set up Matt Stover's 27-yard field goal to tie the game at 13-13. Moments later, the Browns' Gerald Dixon blocked Lee Johnson's punt and teammate Travis Hill recovered in the end zone to give Cleveland the lead. Eric Metcalf's 73-yard punt return on the last play of the third quarter increased the Browns' advantage to 27-13. With the victory, Cleveland improved its record to 6-1, its best start since 1963. The beleaguered Bengals, losers of eight consecutive regular-season games dating to the end of 1993, lost starting quarterback David Klingler (sprained knee) and backup Donald Hollas (separated shoulder) to injuries.

Cincinnati	10	3	0	0	—	13
Cleveland	3	7	17	10	—	37

Cleve — FG Stover 45
Cin — FG Pelfrey 36
Cin — Ti. McGee 11 pass from Klingler (Pelfrey kick)
Cleve — Hoard 11 pass from Testaverde (Stover kick)
Cin — FG Pelfrey 49
Cleve — FG Stover 27
Cleve — Hill recovered blocked punt in end zone (Stover kick)
Cleve — Metcalf 73 punt return (Stover kick)
Cleve — FG Stover 35
Cleve — Hoard 1 run (Stover kick)

DALLAS 28, ARIZONA 21—at Sun Devil Stadium, attendance 71,023. Reserve quarterback Rodney Peete came off the bench to throw 2 touchdown passes in the Cowboys' victory. Starting quarterback Troy Aikman suffered a concussion when hit by Cardinals linebacker Wilber Marshall on the game's opening drive, though he did stay in the game long enough to cap the 67-yard march with a 15-yard touchdown pass to Alvin Harper. Arizona countered with a pair of touchdowns in the second quarter, the latter on Ron Moore's 4-yard run to cap a 97-yard drive that gave the Cardinals a 14-7 advantage. But Dallas tied the game 55 seconds before halftime when Michael Irvin tipped Peete's high pass and caught it in the back of the end zone for a touchdown. After Arizona regained the advantage at 21-14, Peete and Irvin teamed again, this time on a 65-yard touchdown pass to tie the game at 21-21 1:42 into the fourth quarter. On their next possession, the Cowboys drove 79 yards to the winning touchdown, Emmitt Smith's 6-yard run with 5:13 to go. Peete's 39-yard pass to Alvin Harper was the big play on the drive. Peete, the former starting quarterback for the Lions who signed with Dallas as a free agent prior to the season, completed 12 of 19 passes for 186 yards, with no sacks or interceptions.

Dallas	7	7	0	14	—	28
Arizona	0	14	0	7	—	21

Dall — Harper 15 pass from Aikman (Boniol kick)
Ariz — Beuerlein 1 run (Peterson kick)
Ariz — Moore 4 run (Peterson kick)
Dall — Irvin 5 pass from Peete (Boniol kick)
Ariz — Proehl 9 pass from Beuerlein (Peterson kick)
Dall — Irvin 65 pass from Peete (Boniol kick)
Dall — E. Smith 6 run (Boniol kick)

DENVER 20, SAN DIEGO 15—at San Diego Jack Murphy Stadium, attendance 61,626. John Elway passed for 241 yards and a touchdown, and Jason Elam kicked a pair of fourth-quarter field goals as the Broncos handed the Chargers their first loss of the season. San Diego threatened to put the game out of reach in the first half, driving inside opposing territory on six of its seven possessions. But two of those marches were thwarted by interceptions and four resulted in field goals, forcing the Chargers to settle for a 12-7 lead at the intermission. Late in the third quarter, Denver's Glyn Milburn returned a punt 44 yards, and three plays later Elway gave the Broncos the lead for the first time with a 43-yard touchdown pass to Shannon Sharpe. John Carney's fifth field goal of the game, from 44 yards 3:49 into the fourth quarter, put San Diego ahead again 15-14. But Milburn's 23-yard kickoff return, plus a personal-foul penalty on the Chargers, positioned Elam for a 54-yard field goal just 1:09 later, giving Denver the lead for good. Elam's 25-yard field goal with 4:07 remaining proved important when San Diego drove to the Broncos' 31-yard line in the closing moments. The Chargers could get no closer to the end zone, however, when four consecutive passes by Gale Gilbert fell incomplete. Gilbert was in the game because starting quarterback Stan Humphries sprained his ankle in the fourth quarter. Humphries, who entered the game as the AFC's top-rated passer, completed only 17 of 33 passes for 142 yards, with 3 interceptions. Elway was 22 of 31, with 6 of his completions going to Sharpe for 121 yards. Natrone Means rushed for 100 yards on 19 carries for San Diego.

Denver	0	7	7	6	—	20
San Diego	6	6	0	3	—	15

SD — FG Carney 22
SD — FG Carney 39
SD — FG Carney 37
Den — L. Russell 3 run (Elam kick)
SD — FG Carney 26
Den — Sharpe 43 pass from Elway (Elam kick)
SD — FG Carney 44
Den — FG Elam 54
Den — FG Elam 25

NEW ORLEANS 37, L.A. RAMS 34—at Louisiana Superdome, attendance 47,908. Saints kick returner Tyrone Hughes set a pair of NFL records and tied another in a wild game punctuated by big plays on special teams and defense. Hughes returned 2 kickoffs for touchdowns, tying the league record shared by three others. His 304 yards on 7 kickoff returns established a record, as did his 347 yards on combined kick returns (he had 43 on 3 punt returns). The Rams' Robert Bailey also entered the record books with a 103-yard punt return, the longest in NFL history. That came with 4:08 remaining in the game and pulled Los Angeles within 3 points. New Orleans's Tommy Barnhardt punted into the end zone, and with players from both teams walking off the field, Bailey picked up the live ball and sprinted the length of the field. Earlier in the game, rookie safety Toby Wright returned a fumble 98 yards for a Rams' touchdown. The longest fumble return in franchise history brought Los Angeles within 17-14 midway through the second quarter, but Hughes took the ensuing kickoff 92 yards to put the Saints back up by 10. Hughes's 98-yard return on the final play of the third quarter opened up a 37-20 lead, which proved insurmountable. Though the Saints' and Rams' special teams finished with a whopping 797 yards on returns, the teams combined for a relatively modest 556 yards from scrimmage. Saints quarterback Jim Everett, playing against his former teammates for the first time, completed 17 of 26 passes for 206 yards.

L.A. Rams	0	17	3	14	—	34
New Orleans	14	13	10	0	—	37

NO — D. Brown 3 run (Andersen kick)
NO — Walls 30 pass from Everett (Andersen kick)
Rams — Bruce 19 pass from Miller (Zendejas kick)
NO — FG Andersen 21
Rams — Wright 98 fumble return (Zendejas kick)
NO — Hughes 92 kickoff return (Andersen kick)
Rams — FG Zendejas 47
NO — FG Andersen 40
NO — FG Andersen 37
Rams — FG Zendejas 32
NO — Hughes 98 kickoff return (Andersen kick)
Rams — J. Bailey 7 run (Zendejas kick)
Rams — R. Bailey 103 punt return (Zendejas kick)

PITTSBURGH 10, N.Y. GIANTS 6—at Giants Stadium, attendance 71,819. Byron (Bam) Morris ran for 146 yards and the game's lone touchdown in the fourth quarter as the Steelers handed the Giants their fourth consecutive defeat. Morris, a rookie filling in for injured starter Barry Foster, carried 29 times. His 6-yard touchdown run with 8:17 left in the game rallied Pittsburgh to the victory. That touchdown was set up by Steelers cornerback Rod Woodson, who intercepted New York quarterback Dave Brown and returned the ball 25 yards to the Giants' 34-yard line. Brown completed 13 of 25 passes for 206 yards, but suffered 5 sacks, was intercepted twice, and lost a fumble near Pittsburgh's goal line.

Pittsburgh	0	3	0	7	—	10
N.Y. Giants	3	3	0	0	—	6

Giants— FG Treadwell 19
Giants— FG Daluiso 49
Pitt — FG Anderson 29
Pitt — Morris 6 run (Anderson kick)

KANSAS CITY 38, SEATTLE 23—at Arrowhead Stadium, attendance 78,847. Joe Montana passed for 270 yards and 2 touchdowns in the Chiefs' rout. Montana, who completed 21 of 31 passes, tossed a 9-yard touchdown pass to running back Kimble Anders to open the scoring midway through the second quarter. His 21-yard touchdown pass to rookie Lake Dawson put the game out of reach at 28-7 early in the fourth quarter. Kansas City amassed 477 total yards, with 172 yards coming on the ground. Marcus Allen ran for 77 yards, including a 36-yard touchdown, while rookie running back Greg Hill added 74. Rick Mirer threw a pair of touchdown passes in the fourth quarter for the Seahawks. Seattle's Chris Warren ran for 117 yards on 19 carries.

Seattle	0	0	7	16	—	23
Kansas City	0	13	8	17	—	38

KC — Anders 9 pass from Montana (Elliott kick)
KC — FG Elliott 49
KC — FG Elliott 34
Sea — Vaughn 3 run (Kasay kick)
KC — Allen 36 run (Allen run)
KC — Dawson 21 pass from Montana (Elliott kick)
KC — FG Elliott 27
Sea — Blades 1 pass from Mirer (Blades pass from Mirer)
KC — E. Martin 32 pass from Bono (Elliott kick)
Sea — Blades 9 pass from Mirer (Vaughn run)

SAN FRANCISCO 41, TAMPA BAY 16—at Candlestick Park, attendance 62,741. Ricky Watters ran for 103 yards and 2 touchdowns as the 49ers routed the Buccaneers. It was the first individual 100-yard rushing performance this season for San Francisco, the offensive line of which was ravaged by injuries. Watters rushed 14 times, had a 13-yard touchdown run to open the scoring in the first quarter, and had a 2-yard touchdown run to make it 34-0 late in the third period. Quarterback Steve Young completed 20 of 26 passes for 255 yards and 1 touchdown as the 49ers amassed 451 total yards. Rookie quarterback Trent Dilfer made his first start for Tampa Bay but completed only 7 of 23 attempts for 45 yards. Craig Erickson came on to lead 2 touchdown drives in the fourth quarter.

Tampa Bay	0	0	0	16	—	16
San Francisco	7	10	17	7	—	41

SF — Watters 13 run (Brien kick)
SF — FG Brien 23
SF — McCaffrey 7 pass from Young (Brien kick)
SF — Floyd 1 run (Brien kick)
SF — FG Brien 35
SF — Watters 2 run (Brien kick)
TB — Rhett 1 run (Copeland pass from Erickson)
SF — Logan 1 pass from Grbac (Brien kick)
TB — Dawsey 34 pass from Erickson (Harris pass from Erickson)

WASHINGTON 41, INDIANAPOLIS 27—at RCA Dome, attendance 57,879. Rookie Gus Frerotte passed for 226 yards and 2 touchdowns in his NFL debut, leading the Redskins to the victory. Frerotte started in place of injured Heath Shuler and completed 17 of 32 passes. He was not intercepted or sacked, and he rallied his team from a 17-3 first-half deficit. The seventh-round draft pick threw for all the yards on a 59-yard drive to Chip Lohmiller's 27-yard field goal that trimmed the deficit to 17-6 with 6:28 left in the second quarter, then engineered a 14-play, 74-yard drive that culminated in his 1-yard touchdown pass to tight end James Jenkins, making it 17-13 seven seconds before halftime. Ricky Ervins ran 1 yard for a touchdown midway through the third quarter to give Washington the lead for the first time, and the Redskins pulled away by converting 3 interceptions the rest of the way into 21 points. Henry Ellard caught 6 passes for 108 yards for Washington. Colts rookie Marshall Faulk rushed for 86 yards and caught 8 passes for 127 yards, including an 85-yard touchdown.

Washington	0	13	14	14	—	41
Indianapolis	3	14	0	10	—	27

Ind — FG Biasucci 50
Ind — Dawkins 24 pass from Harbaugh (Biasucci kick)
Wash — FG Lohmiller 21
Ind — Faulk 85 pass from Harbaugh (Biasucci kick)
Wash — FG Lohmiller 27
Wash — Jenkins 1 pass from Frerotte (Lohmiller kick)
Wash — Ervins 1 run (Lohmiller kick)
Wash — Jenkins 5 pass from Frerotte (Lohmiller kick)
Ind — FG Biasucci 28

Wash — Collins 21 interception return (Lohmiller kick)
Wash — Ervins 3 run (Lohmiller kick)
Ind — Jackson 13 pass from Majkowski (Biasucci kick)

MONDAY, OCTOBER 24

PHILADELPHIA 21, HOUSTON 6—at Veterans Stadium, attendance 65,233. Randall Cunningham passed for 310 yards and 2 touchdowns to lead the Eagles over the struggling Oilers. Cunningham completed only 13 passes (in 24 attempts) but 3 were for more than 50 yards to wide receiver Fred Barnett, who caught 5 passes for 187 yards, including a 53-yarder that gave Philadelphia a 14-6 lead in the third quarter. Cunningham's 35-yard touchdown pass to running back James Joseph put the game out of reach with 2:18 remaining in the game. Houston quarterback Cody Carlson and running back Gary Brown returned to the lineup after bouts with injuries, but failed to spark the Oilers' offense, which managed only a pair of Al Del Greco field goals. Carlson completed 11 of 22 passes for 164 yards before being lifted after three quarters. Brown rushed for 67 yards but fumbled twice, once on a pitchout after Houston reached the Eagles' 2-yard line while trailing only 14-6 in the fourth quarter.

Houston	3	3	0	0	—	6
Philadelphia	0	7	7	7	—	21

Hou — FG Del Greco 21
Phil — Garner 1 run (Murray kick)
Hou — FG Del Greco 24
Phil — Barnett 53 pass from Cunningham (Murray kick)
Phil — Joseph 35 pass from Cunningham (Murray kick)

NINTH WEEK SUMMARIES

AMERICAN FOOTBALL CONFERENCE

Eastern Division	**W**	**L**	**T**	**Pct.**	**Pts.**	**OP**
Miami	6	2	0	.750	203	149
Buffalo	5	3	0	.625	178	153
N.Y. Jets	4	4	0	.500	141	150
Indianapolis	4	5	0	.444	195	211
New England	3	5	0	.375	178	206
Central Division						
Cleveland	6	2	0	.750	180	105
Pittsburgh	5	3	0	.625	141	137
Houston	1	7	0	.125	107	172
Cincinnati	0	8	0	.000	121	203
Western Division						
San Diego	7	1	0	.875	220	141
Kansas City	5	3	0	.625	169	175
L.A. Raiders	4	4	0	.500	180	192
Denver	3	5	0	.375	182	206
Seattle	3	5	0	.375	168	159

NATIONAL FOOTBALL CONFERENCE

Eastern Division	**W**	**L**	**T**	**Pct.**	**Pts.**	**OP**
Dallas	7	1	0	.875	210	110
Philadelphia	6	2	0	.750	192	141
Arizona	3	5	0	.375	109	172
N.Y. Giants	3	5	0	.375	152	172
Washington	2	7	0	.222	198	242
Central Division						
Minnesota	6	2	0	.750	183	118
Chicago	4	4	0	.500	135	162
Detroit	4	4	0	.500	155	170
Green Bay	4	4	0	.500	150	103
Tampa Bay	2	6	0	.250	109	195
Western Division						
San Francisco	6	2	0	.750	237	150
Atlanta	4	4	0	.500	158	184
L.A. Rams	3	5	0	.375	135	156
New Orleans	3	5	0	.375	156	208

SUNDAY, OCTOBER 30

DENVER 26, CLEVELAND 14—at Mile High Stadium, attendance 73,190. John Elway passed for 349 yards and 2 touchdowns as the Broncos snapped the Browns' five-game winning streak. Cleveland had allowed only 8.4 points per game during its streak, but Denver shattered that in the first half by marching 80 and 81 yards to touchdowns for a 14-6 advantage at intermission. Two third-quarter field goals by Jason Elam increased the Broncos' lead to 20-6. The Browns pulled within six points on Mark Rypien's 6-yard touchdown pass to Mark Carrier and a subsequent two-point conversion 1:41 into the fourth quarter, but Denver took only six plays to counter with Elway's 17-yard touchdown pass to running back Glyn Milburn with 11:35 remaining in the game. Elway was 18 of 20 in the first half and finished with 30 completions in 41 attempts, with no interceptions. Shannon Sharpe had 9 receptions for 85 yards and Milburn caught 8 passes for 76 yards as the Broncos amassed 457 total yards. Rypien replaced starting quarterback Vinny Testaverde late in the first half for Cleveland after Testaverde complained of dizziness, the result of a sack. Rypien passed for 210 yards in slightly more than two quarters.

Cleveland	0	6	0	8	—	14
Denver	7	7	6	6	—	26

Den — Evans 1 pass from Elway (Elam kick)
Cleve — FG Stover 43
Cleve — FG Stover 45
Den — L. Russell 1 run (Elam kick)
Den — FG Elam 27
Den — FG Elam 32
Cleve — Carrier 6 pass from Rypien (Alexander pass from Rypien)
Den — Milburn 17 pass from Elway (pass failed)

DALLAS 23, CINCINNATI 20—at Riverfront Stadium, attendance 57,096. Rookie Chris Boniol kicked 3 second-half field goals, including a 38-yarder with five minutes remaining, and the Cowboys survived a scare from the winless Bengals. Cincinnati jumped to a 14-0 lead eight seconds into the second quarter behind third-string quarterback Jeff Blake, who was making his first NFL start because of injuries to David Klingler and Donald Hollas. Blake forged the advantage by teaming with rookie Darnay Scott on touchdown bombs of 67 and 55 yards. It was 17-7 before a fourth-down, roughing-the-passer penalty kept Dallas's 55-yard touchdown drive alive shortly before halftime. Troy Aikman's 10-yard touchdown pass to Michael Irvin trimmed the Cowboys' deficit to 17-14 just 30 seconds before intermission. Emmitt Smith, who carried 25 times for 92 yards but failed to score a touchdown for the first time in 10 games, did most of the damage on the 60-yard drive to the winning field goal in the fourth quarter, rushing for 31 yards. Aikman completed 20 of 33 passes for 272 yards and 2 touchdowns. Alvin Harper caught 6 passes for 125 yards, including a 27-yard touchdown in the second quarter. Blake, whose previous experience included only 10 pass attempts in his three-year career, completed 14 of 32 passes for 247 yards, with no interceptions.

Dallas	0	14	6	3	—	23
Cincinnati	7	10	3	0	—	20

Cin — Scott 67 pass from Blake (Pelfrey kick)
Cin — Scott 55 pass from Blake (Pelfrey kick)
Dall — Harper 27 pass from Aikman (Boniol kick)
Cin — FG Pelfrey 22
Dall — Irvin 10 pass from Aikman (Boniol kick)
Dall — FG Boniol 37
Cin — FG Pelfrey 33
Dall — FG Boniol 43
Dall — FG Boniol 38

DETROIT 28, N.Y. GIANTS 25—at Giants Stadium, attendance 75,124. Barry Sanders rushed for 146 yards on 26 carries as the Lions became the first NFL team to win three games in overtime in a single season. Jason Hanson's 24-yard field goal 6:43 into the extra session capped a 70-yard drive to win it. Sanders kept the winning drive alive by catching a 9-yard pass on third-and-9 from Detroit's 25-yard line, and had a 16-yard run to move the ball into Giants' territory. Scott Mitchell's 29-yard pass to Herman Moore then positioned Hanson for the deciding field goal. Earlier, Sanders had a 62-yard run to set up Mitchell's 1-yard touchdown pass to Moore that gave the Lions a 25-18 lead with 8:48 left in the fourth quarter. But the Giants responded with a 15-play, 74-yard drive to tie the score on Dave Brown's 7-yard touchdown pass to tight end Aaron Pierce with 1:15 remaining. New York running back Rodney Hampton carried 30 times for 158 yards. David Meggett returned a punt 56 yards for a touchdown. Moore had 9 catches for 106 yards for the Lions. Linebacker Mike Johnson returned a third-quarter interception 48 yards for a touchdown. Sanders surpassed the 1,000-yard rushing mark for the season (he finished the game at 1,035) and joined Eric Dickerson as the only NFL players to reach that plateau in each of their first six years in the league.

Detroit	2	6	10	7	3	—	28
N.Y. Giants	0	10	0	15	0	—	25

Det — Safety, Da. Brown fumbled out of end zone
Giants— Hampton 4 run (Treadwell kick)
Giants— FG Treadwell 25
Det — Moore 14 pass from Mitchell (pass failed)
Det — FG Hanson 31
Det — Johnson 48 interception return (Hanson kick)
Giants— Meggett 56 punt return (Hampton run)
Det — Moore 1 pass from Mitchell (Hanson kick)
Giants— Pierce 7 pass from Da. Brown (Treadwell kick)
Det — FG Hanson 24

L.A. RAIDERS 17, HOUSTON 14—at Los Angeles Memorial Coliseum, attendance 40,473. Jeff Hostetler threw an 11-yard touchdown pass to Tim Brown with 1:49 left in the game, and the Raiders held on to win when Al Del Greco's 52-yard field goal attempt on the game's final play bounced off the crossbar. The Oilers had taken a 14-10 lead by driving 86 yards to Billy Joe Tolliver's 7-yard touchdown pass to Haywood Jeffires with 3:19 left in the game. But Los Angeles countered with a 67-yard march to the winning touchdown, covering most of the ground on Hostetler completions to running back Harvey Williams (18 and 14 yards) and Brown (16 yards and the 11-yard touchdown). Williams had his second 100-yard rushing game in as many weeks, gaining 128 yards on 29 carries. He also had a 2-yard touchdown run to cap an 80-yard drive in the first quarter. Tolliver got his first starting nod of the season and passed for 226 yards and a touchdown. He also ran for a touchdown but suffered 3 sacks and lost a pair of fumbles. Raiders defensive tackle Chester McGlockton had 2 sacks and forced 2 fumbles.

Houston	0	7	0	7	—	14
L.A. Raiders	7	0	3	7	—	17

Raid — H. Williams 2 run (Jaeger kick)
Hou — Tolliver 6 run (Del Greco kick)
Raid — FG Jaeger 35
Hou — Jeffires 7 pass from Tolliver (Del Greco kick)
Raid — T. Brown 11 pass from Hostetler (Jaeger kick)

BUFFALO 44, KANSAS CITY 10—at Rich Stadium, attendance 79,501. Jim Kelly threw 4 touchdown passes, and the Bills took advantage of 5 turnovers to rout the Chiefs. Buffalo led just 14-7 before putting the game away with 17 points in a three-minute span late in the first half. Thurman Thomas started the spurt with a 2-yard touchdown run 3:16 before halftime. Moments later, Kansas City quarterback Joe Montana and running back Marcus Allen failed to connect on a handoff and Bills linebacker Darryl Talley recovered at the Chiefs' 36, setting up Steve Christie's 49-yard field goal with one minute remaining in the second quarter. Montana was sacked on consecutive plays when Kansas City got the ball back, the latter resulting in a fumble that Buffalo defensive end Bruce Smith recovered at the Chiefs' 25. Kelly's 6-yard touchdown pass to Andre Reed with 11 seconds left in the half made it 31-7. Kelly completed 14 of 22 passes for 184 yards, while Reed caught 5 passes for 106 yards and 2 touchdowns. Running backs Kenneth Davis (83 yards) and Thomas (77) combined for 160 yards on the ground. Montana completed only 12 of 21 passes for 124 yards for the Chiefs before leaving the game with his team trailing by 24 points in the third quarter. He was intercepted once, sacked 3 times, and he fumbled twice.

Kansas City	7	0	3	0	—	10
Buffalo	14	17	3	10	—	44

Buff — Metzelaars 11 pass from Kelly (Christie kick)
KC — Allen 9 run (Elliott kick)
Buff — Reed 23 pass from Kelly (Christie kick)
Buff — Thomas 2 run (Christie kick)
Buff — FG Christie 49
Buff — Reed 6 pass from Kelly (Christie kick)
KC — FG Elliott 22
Buff — FG Christie 26
Buff — Metzelaars 3 pass from Kelly (Christie kick)
Buff — FG Christie 24

MIAMI 23, NEW ENGLAND 3—at Foxboro Stadium, attendance 59,167. Bernie Parmalee ran for 123 yards and Keith Byars scored twice to pace the Dolphins. Pete Stoyanovich added 3 long field goals for Miami, which maintained its one-game lead over Buffalo in the AFC Eastern Division. Stoyanovich kicked field goals of 44 and 50 yards in the second quarter to give the Dolphins a 6-3 lead, and Miami turned the game into a rout by scoring touchdowns on the final series of the first half and the first series of the second half. First, the Dolphins took advantage of an interception by defensive end Jeff Cross to open a 13-3 advantage at the intermission on Byars's 1-yard run with seven seconds left in the second quarter. Then Miami took the second-half kickoff and marched 73 yards to Dan Marino's 7-yard touchdown pass to Byars 6:12 into the third quarter. The Patriots, who managed only 188 total yards, never threatened to make it close after that. Quarterback Drew Bledsoe, the NFL leader in passing yards, completed only 16 of 33 attempts for 125 yards and was intercepted 3 times. Stoyanovich added a 48-yard field goal in the fourth quarter.

Miami	0	13	7	3	—	23
New England	3	0	0	0	—	3

NE — FG Bahr 48
Mia — FG Stoyanovich 44
Mia — FG Stoyanovich 50
Mia — Byars 1 run (Stoyanovich kick)
Mia — Byars 7 pass from Marino (Stoyanovich kick)
Mia — FG Stoyanovich 48

MINNESOTA 36, TAMPA BAY 13—at Tampa Stadium, attendance 42,110. Terry Allen rushed for a 113 yards and Fuad Reveiz kicked 5 field goals as the Vikings won their third in a row. Reveiz kicked his first field goal, from 36 yards, 7:18 into the game. Sixty-six seconds later, Minnesota cornerback Anthony Parker returned an interception 41 yards for a touchdown, and the rout began. It was the third touchdown in as many games for Parker, who had an interception return for a touchdown against the Giants and returned a fumble for a score against Green Bay. Allen had a 37-yard touchdown run early in the second quarter to make it 17-0. The Vikings went on to lead by as many as 29 points.

Minnesota	10	13	10	3	—	36
Tampa Bay	0	7	0	6	—	13

Minn — FG Reveiz 36
Minn — Parker 41 interception return (Reveiz kick)
Minn — Allen 37 run (Reveiz kick)
TB — Wilson 62 pass from Erickson (Husted kick)
Minn — FG Reveiz 21
Minn — FG Reveiz 48
Minn — Lee 8 pass from Moon (Reveiz kick)
Minn — FG Reveiz 38
Minn — FG Reveiz 35
TB — Hawkins 3 pass from Dilfer (pass failed)

INDIANAPOLIS 28, N.Y. JETS 25—at RCA Dome, attendance 44,350. Don Majkowski, making his first start in more than two years, threw 1 touchdown pass and ran for another to lead the Colts over the Jets. Majkowski, whose last starting assignment came with Green Bay in September, 1992, completed 14 of 22 passes for 159 yards. He gave Indianapolis a 14-0 lead 10:14 into the game with a 14-yard touchdown pass to Floyd Turner and his 3-yard run. After that, the Colts staved off New York, which recovered 3 fumbles and intercepted 2 passes but could not pull closer than 3 points. The Jets' last chance ended at Indianapolis's 38-yard line, when Boomer Esiason's fourth-and-1 completion to Rob Moore was stopped inches short of a first down. Rookie running back Marshall Faulk carried 24 times for 110 yards for the Colts. His 1-yard touchdown run midway through the third quarter increased Indianapolis's lead to 21-10 after New York had trimmed its 14-point deficit to four points at halftime, and his 29-yard touchdown run with 8:27 left in the game came after the Jets had pulled within three points. Esiason passed for 201 yards for the Jets. Moore caught 9 passes for 99 yards.

N.Y. Jets	0	10	8	7	—	25
Indianapolis	14	0	7	7	—	28

Ind — Turner 14 pass from Majkowski (Biasucci kick)
Ind — Majkowski 3 run (Biasucci kick)
Jets — Monk 22 pass from Esiason (Lowery kick)
Jets — FG Lowery 26
Ind — Faulk 1 run (Biasucci kick)
Jets — Lewis 18 interception return (Moore pass from Esiason)
Ind — Faulk 29 run (Biasucci kick)
Jets — Moore 41 pass from Esiason (Lowery kick)

PHILADELPHIA 31, WASHINGTON 29—at RFK Stadium, attendance 53,530. Eddie Murray's 30-yard field goal with 19 seconds left capped a wild fourth quarter and lifted the Eagles to the victory. Philadelphia trailed 17-7 at halftime and still faced a 20-14 deficit as the fourth quarter began. But Herschel Walker gave the Eagles the lead for the first time when he ran 1 yard for a touchdown on the first play of the final period, capping a 75-yard drive. Philadelphia marched 71 yards the next time it had the ball, with Vaughn Hebron's 6-yard run increasing the Eagles' advantage to 28-20. The Redskins took only four plays to answer, however, with a 34-yard pass interference penalty setting up Gus Frerotte's 1-yard touchdown pass to tight end James Jenkins with 8:29 left in the game. When Frerotte was stopped short of the goal line on the two-point conversion try, his team trailed 28-26. After stopping the Eagles, another quick drive—36 yards in 5 plays, most of it on Brian Mitchell's 34-yard run—led to Chip Lohmiller's 40-yard field goal and a 29-28 Redskins' lead with 3:58 to play. But Cunningham passed for 34 yards and ran for 8 yards on the ensuing 63-yard drive to the winning field goal. Frerotte, the seventh-round draft choice making his second consecutive start, was erratic, passing for 181 yards but completing only 13 of 30 passes. He threw 3 touchdown passes but was intercepted twice. Washington fell to 0-5 at home this season and dropped its twelfth consecutive game to an NFC East rival.

Philadelphia	0	7	7	17	—	31
Washington	7	10	3	9	—	29

Wash — Howard 13 pass from Frerotte (Lohmiller kick)
Wash — Horton 15 pass from Frerotte (Lohmiller kick)
Phil — Walker 11 pass from Cunningham (Murray kick)
Wash — FG Lohmiller 54
Phil — G. Jackson 55 interception return (Murray kick)
Wash — FG Lohmiller 23
Phil — Walker 1 run (Murray kick)
Phil — Hebron 6 run (Murray kick)
Wash — Jenkins 1 pass from Frerotte (run failed)
Wash — FG Lohmiller 40
Phil — FG Murray 30

SAN DIEGO 35, SEATTLE 15—at San Diego Jack Murphy Stadium, attendance 59,001. Natrone Means rushed for more than 100 yards for the fourth consecutive game and the Chargers rebounded from their first loss of the season to pound the Seahawks. Means carried 26 times for 104 yards and scored on a 5-yard run to give San Diego a 21-7 lead in the third quarter. That proved to be too much to overcome for Seattle, which managed only 76 total yards in the second half. The Seahawks did move the ball well in the first half (207 yards) and appeared on the verge of increasing their 7-3 lead when the Chargers' defense stopped Rick Mirer short of a first down on a fourth-and-1 quarterback sneak from San Diego's 39-yard line. The Chargers took possession and marched 40 yards to John Carney's 39-yard field goal 1:45 before halftime, then went ahead for good 30 seconds later after recovering Seattle running back Chris Warren's fumble on the next play from scrimmage. Ronnie Harmon's 15-yard run and two-point conversion made it 14-7 at the intermission, and when San Diego turned another fumble by Warren into Means's touchdown 4:48 into the second half, the Chargers were in command. San Diego's victory was not without cost, however. Chargers quarterback Stan Humphries dislocated his left elbow and came out of the game in the third quarter. Backup Gale Gilbert completed 11 of 14 passes for 125 yards, including touchdowns to tight end Alfred Pupunu (8 yards) and wide receiver Tony Martin (16 yards).

Seattle	0	7	0	8	—	15
San Diego	0	14	7	14	—	35

Sea — C. Warren 9 run (Kasay kick)
SD — FG Carney 25
SD — FG Carney 39
SD — Harmon 15 run (Harmon pass from Humphries)
SD — Means 5 run (Carney kick)
SD — Pupunu 8 pass from Gilbert (Carney kick)
SD — T. Martin 16 pass from Gilbert (Carney kick)
Sea — Vaughn 93 kickoff return (C. Warren run)

SUNDAY NIGHT, OCTOBER 30

ARIZONA 20, PITTSBURGH 17—at Sun Devil Stadium, attendance 73,400. Greg Davis kicked a 51-yard field goal just 1:40 into overtime as the Cardinals spoiled the Steelers' comeback. Pittsburgh trailed 17-14 before mounting a last-ditch, 78-yard drive to Gary Anderson's tying field goal from 23 yards with 47 seconds left. The key play came when Steelers quarterback Neil O'Donnell, about to be sacked, flipped a desperation pass to tight end Eric Green, who barreled 46 yards to Arizona's 5-yard line. Pittsburgh then won the toss in overtime, but rookie Charles Johnson fumbled the kickoff return and the Cardinals' David Merritt recovered at the Steelers' 32. Though Arizona lost a yard on the ensuing three plays, Davis came on to convert the game-winning field goal. The Cardinals entered the game with an offense ranked twenty-sixth in the league, but got big plays to set up 14 points in the first half. Steve Beuerlein's 63-yard pass to Ricky Proehl preceded Larry Centers's 4-yard touchdown run in the first quarter, and Beuerlein's 37-yard completion to Randal Hill led to Ron Moore's 1-yard touchdown run 1:10 before halftime. Beuerlein, who also teamed with Hill on a 51-yard pass play in the third quarter, completed 13 of 26 passes for 251 yards.

Pittsburgh	0	14	0	3	0	—	17
Arizona	7	10	0	0	3	—	20

Ariz — Centers 4 run (Davis kick)
Pitt — Morris 11 run (Anderson kick)
Ariz — FG Davis 20
Pitt — Thigpen 60 pass from O'Donnell (Anderson kick)
Ariz — Moore 1 run (Davis kick)
Pitt — FG Anderson 23
Ariz — FG Davis 51

MONDAY, OCTOBER 31

GREEN BAY 33, CHICAGO 6—at Soldier Field, attendance 47,381. Edgar Bennett rushed for 105 yards and scored 3 touchdowns as the Packers romped over the Bears in treacherous conditions in Chicago. Torrential rain, heavy winds that gusted up to 53 miles per hour, and a wind-chill of 8 degrees rendered Green Bay's passing attack ineffective, but the Packers did amass 223 yards on the ground. Bennett was the workhorse, carrying 26 times. His 3-yard touchdown run 4:20 into the second quarter gave Green Bay the lead, and six minutes later quarterback Brett Favre bootlegged 36 yards around right end to make it 14-0, an advantage that proved insurmountable. Favre, who failed to complete a pass in the first half, had a 13-yard touchdown pass to Bennett early in the fourth quarter and finished 6 of 15 for 82 yards. He also rushed twice for 58 yards. Bears starting quarterback Erik Kramer completed only 5 of 10 attempts for 34 yards and was intercepted twice. He was replaced in the second half by Steve Walsh, who threw for 140 yards, including a 5-yard touchdown to Jeff Graham in the fourth quarter. The Packers intercepted 3 passes and recovered 2 fumbles. Linebacker Bryce Paup had 2 interceptions and forced a fumble.

Green Bay	0	14	7	12	—	33
Chicago	0	0	0	6	—	6

GB — Bennett 3 run (Jacke kick)
GB — Favre 36 run (Jacke kick)
GB — Bennett 1 run (Jacke kick)
GB — Bennett 13 pass from Favre (run failed)
Chi — Graham 5 pass from Walsh (pass failed)
GB — Cobb 9 run (kick failed)

TENTH WEEK SUMMARIES

AMERICAN FOOTBALL CONFERENCE

Eastern Division	**W**	**L**	**T**	**Pct.**	**Pts.**	**OP**
Miami	7	2	0	.778	225	170
Buffalo	5	4	0	.556	195	175
N.Y. Jets	5	4	0	.556	163	167
Indianapolis	4	6	0	.400	216	233
New England	3	6	0	.333	184	219
Central Division						
Cleveland	7	2	0	.778	193	111
Pittsburgh	6	3	0	.667	153	146
Cincinnati	1	8	0	.111	141	220
Houston	1	8	0	.111	116	184
Western Division						
San Diego	7	2	0	.778	229	151
Kansas City	6	3	0	.667	182	178
L.A. Raiders	4	5	0	.444	183	205
Denver	3	6	0	.333	203	233
Seattle	3	6	0	.333	185	179

NATIONAL FOOTBALL CONFERENCE

Eastern Division	**W**	**L**	**T**	**Pct.**	**Pts.**	**OP**
Dallas	8	1	0	.889	248	120
Philadelphia	7	2	0	.778	209	148
Arizona	3	6	0	.333	116	189
N.Y. Giants	3	6	0	.333	162	210
Washington	2	8	0	.200	220	279
Central Division						
Minnesota	7	2	0	.778	204	138
Chicago	5	4	0	.556	155	168
Green Bay	5	4	0	.556	188	133
Detroit	4	5	0	.444	185	208
Tampa Bay	2	7	0	.222	115	215

Western Division

San Francisco	7	2	0	.778	274	172
Atlanta	5	4	0	.556	168	193
L.A. Rams	4	5	0	.444	162	177
New Orleans	3	6	0	.333	176	229

SUNDAY, NOVEMBER 6

PHILADELPHIA 17, ARIZONA 7—at Veterans Stadium, attendance 64,952. Fred Barnett caught 11 passes for 173 yards and 2 touchdowns as the Eagles beat the Cardinals in Buddy Ryan's return to Philadelphia. Ryan, who coached the Eagles from 1986-1990 and began at Arizona this season, saw his team get beat on a pair of touchdown bombs from Randall Cunningham to Barnett. The first covered 47 yards and gave Philadelphia a 10-0 advantage 3:41 into the second half. It came one play after Eagles defensive end Burt Grossman sacked Cardinals quarterback Steve Beuerlein, forcing a fumble that cornerback Mark McMillian recovered. Six minutes later, Cunningham and Barnett teamed again, this time on a 50-yard bomb to make it 17-0. That was more than enough cushion for Philadelphia's defense, which limited Arizona to 254 total yards and was working on a shutout until Beuerlein threw a 5-yard touchdown pass to Ricky Proehl with 1:51 left in the game. Beuerlein completed 19 of 30 passes for 219 yards, but suffered 5 sacks, 2 of them by defensive tackle Andy Harmon. Cunningham was 15 of 24 for 201 yards. He also had a game-high 63 rushing yards.

Arizona	0	0	0	7	—	7
Philadelphia	0	3	14	0	—	17

Phil — FG Murray 36
Phil — Barnett 47 pass from Cunningham (Murray kick)
Phil — Barnett 50 pass from Cunningham (Murray kick)
Ariz — Proehl 5 pass from Beuerlein (Davis kick)

N.Y. JETS 22, BUFFALO 17—at Giants Stadium, attendance 67,030. Boomer Esiason threw 2 touchdown passes to lead the Jets' first season sweep of the Bills since 1986. Esiason passed 5 yards to running back Johnny Johnson to trim a 14-3 deficit to 14-10 just 1:15 before halftime, then put New York ahead for good with a 4-yard touchdown pass to Rob Moore late in the third quarter. But the Jets, who beat Buffalo 23-3 in Rich Stadium to open the season, needed 2 field goals by Nick Lowery in the fourth quarter and had to withstand a Bills' rally at the end. Buffalo marched to a first down on the Jets' 30-yard line with a minute to go after Lowery's 41-yard field goal put New York ahead by five points with 3:24 remaining. But after two incompletions and a short run, Jim Kelly's fourth-down pass to running back Thurman Thomas was incomplete.

Buffalo	0	14	0	3	—	17
N.Y. Jets	3	7	6	6	—	22

Jets — FG Lowery 26
Buff — Thomas 2 run (Christie kick)
Buff — Beebe 37 pass from Kelly (Christie kick)
Jets — J. Johnson 5 pass from Esiason (Lowery kick)
Jets — Moore 4 pass from Esiason (kick failed)
Jets — FG Lowery 45
Buff — FG Christie 39
Jets — FG Lowery 41

CHICAGO 20, TAMPA BAY 6—at Tampa Stadium, attendance 60,821. Steve Walsh passed for 2 short touchdowns in the Bears' workmanlike victory. Chicago never trailed, and marched 78 and 64 yards to field goals in the first half and 62 and 80 yards to touchdowns in the second half. Walsh, back in the lineup after Erik Kramer was ineffective a week earlier against the Packers, won his fourth game without a defeat as the Bears' starting quarterback. He completed 19 of 32 passes for 205 yards and was complemented by a productive rushing attack. Running backs Raymont Harris (79 yards) and Lewis Tillman (54 yards) helped Chicago amass 178 yards on the ground and maintain possession for 39:28 of the game's 60 minutes. The Buccaneers managed only 9 first downs and 188 total yards en route to their fourth consecutive defeat.

Chicago	3	3	7	7	—	20
Tampa Bay	0	3	0	3	—	6

Chi — FG Butler 18
Chi — FG Butler 37
TB — FG Husted 33
Chi — Jennings 1 pass from Walsh (Butler kick)
TB — FG Husted 38
Chi — R. Green 4 pass from Walsh (Butler kick)

CINCINNATI 20, SEATTLE 17—at Kingdome, attendance 46,630. Doug Pelfrey kicked 6 field goals, including the game-winner from 26 yards 8:14 into overtime, to give the Bengals their first victory of the season. Pelfrey's winning kick came on first down, one play after quarterback Jeff Blake's 76-yard completion to rookie wide receiver Darnay Scott. Blake, who made the first start of his NFL career a week earlier and nearly engineered an upset of Dallas, completed 31 of 43 passes for 387 yards. Though Blake couldn't get his team into the end zone, he set up the win as Pelfrey made up for the lack of touchdowns by setting a club record for field goals in a game. His 44-yard kick on the last play of the first half gave the Bengals an 8-7 lead, and his 28-yard field goal with 4:27 to go in regulation forced the extra session. Cincinnati entered the game ranked twenty-seventh in the NFL in total offense, but rolled up 496 total yards against the Seahawks, who lost their fifth game in a row. Scott caught 7 passes for 157 yards, giving him 312 receiving yards in Blake's two starts. The game was the first played in the Kingdome in Seattle since the facility was closed July 19 for repairs to its roof.

Cincinnati	5	3	3	6	3	—	20
Seattle	7	0	3	7	0	—	17

Sea — T. Johnson 1 run (Kasay kick)
Cin — Safety, A. Williams sacked Mirer in end zone
Cin — FG Pelfrey 36
Cin — FG Pelfrey 44
Cin — FG Pelfrey 36
Sea — FG Kasay 23
Cin — FG Pelfrey 47
Sea — Smith 1 run (Kasay kick)
Cin — FG Pelfrey 28
Cin — FG Pelfrey 26

L.A. RAMS 27, DENVER 21—at Anaheim Stadium, attendance 48,103. Chris Chandler threw 2 touchdown passes as the Rams built a 24-3 lead and held on to defeat the Broncos. Chandler, starting because Chris Miller had not recovered fully from a concussion suffered two weeks earlier, completed 19 of 25 passes for 223 yards, including touchdowns of 3 yards to running back Howard Griffith and 30 yards to Willie Anderson, before leaving in the fourth quarter the result of a mild concussion of his own. The touchdown pass to Anderson put Los Angeles ahead by 21 points 4:26 into the second half, but Denver rallied behind quarterback John Elway. After throwing for only 40 yards in the first half, Elway passed for 201 in the second half. His 20-yard touchdown pass to running back Glyn Milburn pulled the Broncos within 24-14 one minute into the fourth quarter, and his 12-yard toss to Derek Russell narrowed the deficit to six points with 5:17 to play. After forcing a punt, Denver got the ball back on the Rams' 49-yard line with 2:28 to play, but the Broncos' last chance fizzled when they failed to make a first down.

Denver	0	3	3	15	—	21
L.A. Rams	7	10	7	3	—	27

Rams — Bettis 1 run (Zendejas kick)
Rams — Griffith 3 pass from Chandler (Zendejas kick)
Den — FG Elam 42
Rams — FG Zendejas 35
Rams — Anderson 30 pass from Chandler (Zendejas kick)
Den — FG Elam 29
Den — Milburn 20 pass from Elway (Sharpe pass from Elway)
Rams — FG Zendejas 18
Den — D. Russell 12 pass from Elway (Elam kick)

GREEN BAY 38, DETROIT 30—at Milwaukee County Stadium, attendance 54,995. Brett Favre threw 3 touchdown passes in the Packers' victory. Favre, who completed 24 of 36 attempts for 237 yards, tossed all of his scoring passes in the first half as Green Bay built a 31-7 advantage. Still, the Packers' win wasn't secured until cornerback Doug Evans knocked down a pass in the end zone in the final minute. Fifteen-year veteran Dave Krieg came on and rallied the Lions with starting quarterback Scott Mitchell out of the game because of a broken hand suffered in the second quarter. Krieg's 15-yard touchdown pass to Aubrey Matthews and subsequent two-point conversion pass to Brett Perriman pulled Detroit within 38-22 1:46 into the fourth quarter. After wide receiver Herman Moore recovered the ensuing onside kick, Krieg marched his team 58 yards in eight plays, culminating the drive with a 1-yard touchdown pass to Moore and another two-point conversion to Perriman. That reduced the deficit to only eight points with 8:31 to play. The Lions had a chance for the tying score after reaching Green Bay's 15-yard line in the final minute, but Krieg was sacked by Sean Jones on third down, and had his fourth-down pass broken up by Evans. Krieg completed 23 of 33 passes for 275 yards and 3 touchdowns in his relief role. Moore caught 8 passes for 151 yards and 2 scores. Favre, who threw all of his touchdown passes in a span for 5:02 of the second quarter, was 24 of 36 for 237 yards. The Packers recovered 3 fumbles, intercepted 2 passes, and scored their first 17 points following turnovers.

Detroit	0	7	7	16	—	30
Green Bay	10	21	7	0	—	38

GB — Paup 10 interception return (Jacke kick)
GB — FG Jacke 30
GB — Bennett 17 pass from Favre (Jacke kick)
GB — Brooks 12 pass from Favre (Jacke kick)
Det — Gray 91 kickoff return (Hanson kick)
GB — Brooks 28 pass from Favre (Jacke kick)
Det — H. Moore 28 pass from Krieg (Hanson kick)
GB — Cobb 10 run (Jacke kick)
Det — Matthews 15 pass from Krieg (Perriman pass from Krieg)
Det — H. Moore 1 pass from Krieg (Perriman pass from Krieg)

MIAMI 22, INDIANAPOLIS 21—at Joe Robbie Stadium, attendance 67,863. Pete Stoyanovich's 34-yard field goal with four seconds remaining capped a furious fourth-quarter rally and lifted the Dolphins to the victory. Miami entered the final 15 minutes trailing 14-6, and trimmed its deficit to two points on Irving Spikes's 7-yard touchdown run 2:56 into the period. Five minutes later, the Dolphins had the ball again, but Colts safety Ray Buchanan stepped in front of Marino's pass on the left sideline and returned the interception 28 yards for a touchdown to make it 21-12 with 7:32 left in the game. Marino responded by marching Miami 83 yards in 10 plays, the last his 28-yard touchdown pass to O.J. McDuffie with 3:52 to go. Indianapolis failed to make a first down on the next possession, and the Dolphins took over on their own 42-yard line at the 2:06 mark. Marino, who had completed 6 of his 7 attempts on the previous drive, completed 5 consecutive passes to reach the Colts' 22. Spikes's 5-yard run positioned Stoyanovich for the winning kick. Marino finished with 30 completions in 41 attempts for 261 yards. McDuffie had 108 yards on 7 receptions.

Indianapolis	7	0	7	7	—	21
Miami	3	0	3	16	—	22

Mia — FG Stoyanovich 33
Ind — Majkowski 1 run (Biasucci kick)
Mia — FG Stoyanovich 20
Ind — Faulk 1 run (Biasucci kick)
Mia — Spikes 7 run (pass failed)
Ind — Buchanan 28 interception return (Biasucci kick)
Mia — McDuffie 28 pass from Marino (Stoyanovich kick)
Mia — FG Stoyanovich 34

CLEVELAND 13, NEW ENGLAND 6—at Cleveland Stadium, attendance 73,878. Leroy Hoard rushed for 123 yards and caught a touchdown pass as the Browns dealt the Patriots their third consecutive defeat. Hoard's touchdown reception, on a 1-yard pass from Mark Rypien 2:18 into the fourth quarter, capped an 80-yard drive and broke a 3-3 tie. Cornerback Tim Jacobs intercepted Drew Bledsoe's pass on the next possession, and Matt Stover kicked a 41-yard field goal to increase Cleveland's advantage to 13-3 with 9:28 remaining. New England could not get closer than a touchdown after that. The Patriots' normally potent passing game was rendered ineffective by swirling winds that gusted to 45 miles per hour and intermittent rain. Bledsoe, who entered the game averaging more than 300 passing yards per game, completed 20 of 43 attempts for only 166 yards and was intercepted 4 times. Mark Rypien started for Cleveland in place of injured Vinny Testaverde and completed 14 of 28 passes for 164 yards.

New England	0	0	3	3	—	6
Cleveland	0	3	0	10	—	13

Cleve — FG Stover 33
NE — FG Bahr 20
Cleve — Hoard 1 pass from Rypien (Stover kick)
Cleve — FG Stover 41
NE — FG Bahr 39

MINNESOTA 21, NEW ORLEANS 20—at Metrodome, attendance 57,564. Warren Moon's 11-yard touchdown pass to Qadry Ismail with five seconds remaining gave the Vikings a dramatic victory. The winning pass capped a 13-play, 84-yard drive. Ismail caught the ball on the 7-yard line, sidestepped one defender, and dove over another for the winning points. Moon completed 33 of 57 passes for 420 yards in the game. Cris Carter caught 12 passes for 151 yards and Jake Reed had 8 receptions for 157 yards. Saints quarterback Jim Everett completed 24 of 36 passes for 256 yards and 2 touchdowns, including a 2-yarder to tight end Wesley Walls on the first play of the fourth quarter to tie the game at 14-14. Morten Andersen kicked 2 field goals in an 88-second span of the fourth quarter to give New Orleans a six-point lead. But the Vikings rallied to win their fourth consecutive game and maintain a two-game advantage in the NFC Central Division.

New Orleans	0	0	7	13	—	20
Minnesota	0	7	7	7	—	21

Minn — Lee 3 pass from Moon (Reveiz kick)
NO — Haynes 34 pass from Everett (Andersen kick)
Minn — Reed 13 pass from Moon (Reveiz kick)
NO — Walls 2 pass from Everett (Andersen kick)
NO — FG Andersen 44
NO — FG Andersen 26
Minn — Ismail 11 pass from Moon (Reveiz kick)

PITTSBURGH 12, HOUSTON 9—at Astrodome, attendance 47,822. In a battle of field goals, the Steelers' Gary Anderson outdueled the Oilers' Al Del Greco by kicking the game winner from 40 yards 11:24 into overtime. Anderson's fourth field goal of the game came two plays after safety Gary Jones recovered Gary Brown's fumble at Houston's 23-yard line. Del Greco had 3 field goals for the Oilers, including a 38-yarder to tie the game with seven seconds left. That capped a 61-yard drive highlighted by Cody Carlson's 26-yard completion to Ernest Givins on fourth-and-23 from Houston's 6. Carlson passed for 205 yards, but completed only 22 of 48 passes and was sacked 6 times. Defensive end Ray Seals had 3 of the sacks for Pittsburgh.

Pittsburgh	0	6	0	3	3	—	12
Houston	3	3	0	3	0	—	9

Hou — FG Del Greco 32
Pitt — FG Anderson 50
Pitt — FG Anderson 39
Hou — FG Del Greco 49
Pitt — FG Anderson 37
Hou — FG Del Greco 38
Pitt — FG Anderson 40

ATLANTA 10, SAN DIEGO 9—at Georgia Dome, attendance 59,217. Quarterback Jeff George and wide receiver Terance Mathis teamed for the game's only touchdown in the first quarter, and the Falcons edged the Chargers. Atlanta took the opening kickoff and marched 91 yards in 13 plays to George's 9-yard touchdown pass to Mathis 7:15 into the game. San Diego's John Carney kicked 3 field goals, the last from 49 yards 1:08 into the fourth quarter. That pulled the Chargers within one point and extended Carney's consecutive field-goal streak to 21. But the string ended when he missed from 47 yards with 8:01 to play in the game, and the Falcons held on to win. Natrone Means rushed for a game-high 102 yards on 25 carries for San Diego.

San Diego	0	3	3	3	—	9
Atlanta	7	0	3	0	—	10

Atl — Mathis 9 pass from George (Johnson kick)
SD — FG Carney 50
SD — FG Carney 33
Atl — FG Johnson 23
SD — FG Carney 49

SAN FRANCISCO 37, WASHINGTON 22—at RFK Stadium, attendance 54,335. The 49ers utilized a series of big plays to rout the Redskins. San Francisco led just 3-0 until Steve Young teamed with tight end Brent Jones on a 69-yard touchdown pass on the final play of the first quarter. Late in the first half, Young passed 55 yards to Jerry Rice, setting up Young's 1-yard touchdown run for a 17-3 advantage at halftime. Safety Tim McDonald's 73-yard interception return 9:27 into the second half increased San Francisco's lead to 24-3, and, following Chip Lohmiller's 23-yard field goal, Dexter Carter returned a kickoff 96 yards for a touchdown and an insurmountable 30-6 advantage. The 49ers finished with 421 total yards for the game. Young completed 15 of 25 passes for 291 yards, despite sitting out most of the fourth quarter.

San Francisco	10	7	13	7	—	37
Washington	0	3	3	16	—	22

SF — FG Brien 32
SF — Jones 69 pass from Young (Brien kick)
Wash — FG Lohmiller 22
SF — Young 1 run (Brien kick)
SF — McDonald 73 interception return (Brien kick)
Wash — FG Lohmiller 23
SF — D. Carter 96 kickoff return (kick failed)
SF — Rice 28 run (Brien kick)
Wash — Horton 4 pass from Friesz (Mitchell run)
Wash — Morrison 32 fumble return (Winans pass from Friesz)

SUNDAY NIGHT, NOVEMBER 6

KANSAS CITY 13, L.A. RAIDERS 3—at Arrowhead Stadium, attendance 78,709. Joe Montana threw a touchdown pass, and Lin Elliott kicked 2 field goals in the Chiefs' victory. Montana threw a 57-yard touchdown pass to tight end Derrick Walker on a 1-play drive 5:38 into the second quarter, and Kansas City never trailed. The Raiders posed little threat, gaining only 248 total yards and stopping themselves with 3 turnovers and 15 penalties for 115 yards. They also suffered 4 sacks. Montana completed 17 of 28 passes for 173 yards.

L.A. Raiders	0	3	0	0	—	3
Kansas City	0	7	3	3	—	13

KC — Walker 57 pass from Montana (Elliott kick)
Raid — FG Jaeger 50
KC — FG Elliott 19
KC — FG Elliott 27

MONDAY, NOVEMBER 7

DALLAS 38, N.Y. GIANTS 10—at Texas Stadium, attendance 64,836. Troy Aikman completed 19 of 24 passes for 241 yards as the Cowboys overwhelmed the Giants, handing New York its sixth consecutive defeat. Aikman teamed with wide receiver Alvin Harper on a 22-yard touchdown pass to break a scoreless tie on the first play of the second quarter, and had a 3-yard touchdown run in the third quarter to make it 28-3. In between, Emmitt Smith rushed for 2 touchdowns. Smith had 35 carries for 163 yards as Dallas amassed 209 yards on the ground and 450 in all. The Giants, meanwhile, managed only 183 total yards. Starting quarterback Dave Brown was limited to 4 completions in 17 attempts for 56 yards. Backup Kent Graham came on to account for New York's lone touchdown, a 9-yard pass to tight end Howard Cross in the fourth quarter. Cowboys wide receiver Michael Irvin caught 7 passes for 118 yards.

N.Y. Giants	0	3	0	7	—	10
Dallas	0	14	21	3	—	38

Dall — Harper 22 pass from Aikman (Boniol kick)
Giants— FG Treadwell 23
Dall — E. Smith 1 run (Boniol kick)
Dall — E. Smith 1 run (Boniol kick)
Dall — Aikman 3 run (Boniol kick)
Dall — Johnston 9 run (Boniol kick)
Dall — FG Boniol 45
Giants— Cross 9 pass from Graham (Treadwell kick)

ELEVENTH WEEK SUMMARIES

AMERICAN FOOTBALL CONFERENCE

Eastern Division	W	L	T	Pct.	Pts.	OP
Miami	7	3	0	.700	239	187
Buffalo	5	5	0	.500	205	198
N.Y. Jets	5	5	0	.500	173	184
Indianapolis	4	6	0	.400	216	233
New England	4	6	0	.400	210	239
Central Division						
Cleveland	8	2	0	.800	219	118
Pittsburgh	7	3	0	.700	176	156
Cincinnati	2	8	0	.200	175	251
Houston	1	9	0	.100	147	218
Western Division						
San Diego	8	2	0	.800	243	164
Kansas City	6	4	0	.600	195	192
L.A. Raiders	5	5	0	.500	203	222
Denver	4	6	0	.400	220	243
Seattle	3	7	0	.300	195	196

NATIONAL FOOTBALL CONFERENCE

Eastern Division	W	L	T	Pct.	Pts.	OP
Dallas	8	2	0	.800	262	141
Philadelphia	7	3	0	.700	216	174
Arizona	4	6	0	.400	126	198
N.Y. Giants	3	7	0	.300	171	220
Washington	2	8	0	.200	220	279
Central Division						
Minnesota	7	3	0	.700	224	164
Chicago	6	4	0	.600	172	182
Green Bay	6	4	0	.600	205	143
Detroit	5	5	0	.500	199	217
Tampa Bay	2	8	0	.200	124	229
Western Division						
San Francisco	8	2	0	.800	295	186
Atlanta	5	5	0	.500	200	226
L.A. Rams	4	6	0	.400	179	197
New Orleans	4	6	0	.400	209	261

SUNDAY, NOVEMBER 13

ARIZONA 10, N.Y. GIANTS 9—at Giants Stadium, attendance 71,719. Cardinals quarterback Steve Beuerlein, looking to throw the ball away, instead found Bryan Reeves for a 9-yard touchdown pass that lifted the Cardinals over the Giants. New York, which entered the game with a six-game losing streak, turned to backup quarterback Kent Graham. The strategy paid off early, as Graham directed the Giants on an 82-yard, 13-play drive that ended with his 4-yard touchdown pass to Aaron Pierce. The drive almost was a disaster, as Graham was sacked for a safety. But a Cardinals' penalty nullified the two-pointer, and New York went on to take a 7-0 lead. The Giants upped their advantage to 9-0 in the second quarter on a safety: Arizona was cited for holding in the end zone, after a Giants' punt was downed at the Cardinals' 1. Arizona finally got on the board with a 45-yard field goal by Greg Davis in the third quarter. But the Cardinals' frustration mounted in the fourth quarter as they drove 79 yards in 18 plays to the Giants' 1 only to be turned away by an incomplete pass on fourth down. But Beuerlein got Arizona back on track with passes of 25 and 9 yards to Randal Hill, positioning the Cardinals for the winning score, which came with 1:39 left. Beuerlein completed 17 of 33 passes for 180 yards. Graham was 9 of 26 for 92 yards. Rodney Hampton had 93 yards on 26 carries.

Arizona	0	0	3	7	—	10
N.Y. Giants	7	2	0	0	—	9

Giants— Pierce 4 pass from Graham (Treadwell kick)
Giants— Safety, Cardinals penalized for holding in end zone
Ariz — FG Davis 45
Ariz — Reeves 9 pass from Beuerlein (Davis kick)

NEW ORLEANS 33, ATLANTA 32—at Louisiana Superdome, attendance 60,313. The Saints overcame several deficits and mistakes to defeat the Falcons finally on Morten Andersen's 39-yard field goal with eight seconds remaining. It was Andersen's sixth game-winning field goal against Atlanta, and his fourth in the teams' previous five meetings. New Orleans, trailing 17-0 in the first quarter, pulled within 2 touchdowns by halftime at 23-10. In the third period, rookie running back Mario Bates took over, scoring on runs of 9 and 4 yards to give the Saints their first lead at 24-23. Atlanta responded in the fourth quarter with 2 field goals by Norm Johnson, but back came the Saints, retaking a one-point lead on Jim Everett's 21-yard touchdown pass to Wesley Walls (the two-point conversion attempt failed). Atlanta turned to Johnson once again, who gave Atlanta a 32-30 lead with 1:44 left on a 30-yard field goal, his sixth of the day. That proved to be too much time for Everett, who led the Saints 43 yards to the Falcons 22 to set up Andersen's winning kick. The Saints overcame 5 turnovers (the Falcons did not turn the ball over), thanks to Bates (22 carries for 141 yards, the first 100-yard game by a Saints' rusher in 1994) and Everett (19 of 25 for 204 yards in the second half). Atlanta's Jeff George completed 29 of 49 for 328 yards. His favorite targets were Terance Mathis (10 for 125) and Andre Rison (8 for 118).

Atlanta	17	6	0	9	—	32
New Orleans	3	7	14	9	—	33

Atl — FG Johnson 23
Atl — Rison 4 pass from George (Johnson kick)
Atl — Jack 27 fumble return (Johnson kick)
NO — FG Andersen 34
Atl — FG Johnson 33
NO — Smith 17 pass from Everett (Andersen kick)

Atl — FG Johnson 33
NO — Bates 9 run (Andersen kick)
NO — Bates 4 run (Andersen kick)
Atl — FG Johnson 31
Atl — FG Johnson 48
NO — Walls 21 pass from Everett (pass failed)
Atl — FG Johnson 30
NO — FG Andersen 39

CHICAGO 17, MIAMI 14—at Joe Robbie Stadium, attendance 65,006. A wacky touchdown pass on a fake field goal propelled the Bears over the Dolphins. Trailing 3-0 in the first quarter, Chicago lined up for an apparent attempt at a game-tying field goal. But the Bears switched to a formation stacked to the left, and wide receiver Curtis Conway (a quarterback in high school) took the snap and rolled to the right. The Dolphins quickly converged on Conway, who heaved ball into a crowd. Bears lineman Jerry Fontenot tipped the ball into the surprised hands of tight end Keith Jennings, who rambled 5 yards to complete the 23-yard touchdown pass play. Trailing 14-6, Miami finally got going late in the game, as Dan Marino found Keith Jackson for an 11-yard touchdown pass with 5:46 to play. Aaron Craver's two-point conversion run tied the game at 14-14. The Bears answered with a 47-yard drive that was capped by Kevin Butler's 40-yard field goal with 59 seconds left. Marino, working with no time outs, managed to position the Dolphins for a game-tying field-goal attempt, but Pete Stoyanovich's 45-yard kick was tipped and fell short with two seconds left. Marino passed for 289 yards, including 9 completions to Irving Fryar for 112 yards.

Chicago	7	0	0	10	—	17
Miami	3	3	0	8	—	14

Mia — FG Stoyanovich 29
Chi — Jennings 23 pass from Conway (Butler kick)
Mia — FG Stoyanovich 33
Chi — Tillman 1 run (Butler kick)
Mia — Jackson 11 pass from Marino (Craver run)
Chi — FG Butler 40

CLEVELAND 26, PHILADELPHIA 7—at Veterans Stadium, attendance 65,233. The Browns' defense was the story as Cleveland defeated the Eagles. The Browns limited the Eagles to 288 total yards and only 1 touchdown, handing Randall Cunningham his first loss in a home start in 21 games. Eric Metcalf's 22-yard punt return set up the Browns' first score, a 3-yard pass from Mark Rypien to Mark Carrier. Trailing 10-0, the Eagles got on the board on Vaughn Hebron's 15-yard touchdown run. But the Browns quickly reclaimed the momentum as Randy Baldwin returned the ensuing kickoff 60 yards. Baldwin's return set up Matt Stover's second field goal, and the Browns carried a 13-7 lead into intermission. Stover kicked 2 more field goals in the second half, and Earnest Byner added a 4-yard touchdown run. Meanwhile, the Browns' defense made 2 second-half takeaways, thwarting the Eagles' only scoring threat by forcing a fumble at the Browns' 13. Cleveland ran for 140 yards, led by Leroy Hoard (21 carries for 86 yards).

Cleveland	10	3	6	7	—	26
Philadelphia	0	7	0	0	—	7

Cleve — Carrier 3 pass from Rypien (Stover kick)
Cleve — FG Stover 35
Phil — Hebron 15 run (Murray kick)
Cleve — FG Stover 41
Cleve — FG Stover 22
Cleve — FG Stover 36
Cleve — Byner 4 run (Stover kick)

SAN FRANCISCO 21, DALLAS 14—at Candlestick Park, attendance 69,014. The 49ers, losers to Dallas in each of the previous two NFC Championship Games, exacted some revenge with a hard-fought victory. Dallas dominated the first half statistically, outgaining San Francisco 237 to 98 yards while throttling the 49ers' high-powered passing attack (Steve Young had more yards rushing than passing). But the teams were tied 7-7 at halftime, thanks to 2 interceptions and the 49ers' running game. San Francisco's passing attack recovered in the second half, as Young fired a 57-yard touchdown bomb to Jerry Rice for a 14-7 lead. Dallas answered by driving right down the field, but its attempt to tie the game went awry when Merton Hanks intercepted Troy Aikman's pass at the goal line. It was Hanks' second interception of the day. The 49ers then drove 87 yards in 11 plays, clinching the victory on a 13-yard touchdown pass from Young to tight end Brent Jones with 2:32 left. Smith added another touchdown to make it close at the end. Young completed 12 of 21 passes for 183 yards, and also ran 8 times for 60 yards as the 49ers' used the bootleg to slow down the Cowboys' aggressive pass rush. Aikman was 23 of 42 for 339 yards, with 3 interceptions.

Dallas	7	0	0	7	—	14
San Francisco	0	7	7	7	—	21

Dall — E. Smith 4 run (Boniol kick)
SF — Young 1 run (Brien kick)
SF — Rice 57 pass from Young (Brien kick)
SF — Jones 13 pass from Young (Brien kick)
Dall — E. Smith 2 run (Boniol kick)

CINCINNATI 34, HOUSTON 31—at Riverfront Stadium, attendance 54,908. Despite playing on a severely sprained ankle, Jeff Blake led the Bengals to 10 points in the final three minutes to rally them over the Oilers. Blake enjoyed a fantastic day, completing 23 of 33 passes for 354 yards and 4 touchdowns with no interceptions. He had 2 scoring tosses in the first half as the teams battled to a 17-17 halftime tie. Houston scored the only points of the third quarter, taking a 24-17 lead on Lorenzo White's 17-yard run. Blake was not finished, however, hitting Carl Pickens for his second score of the day, this one from 50 yards, to knot the game at 24-24 early in the fourth quarter. But Blake was injured on the play, and had to be carted off the field for X-rays. The Oilers reclaimed the lead at 31-24 on Billy Joe Tolliver's 5-yard touchdown pass to Webster Slaughter with 5:51 to play. But Blake returned on the cart, gingerly stepped on to the field, and led Cincinnati to a tying touchdown, hitting Pickens (21 yards) once again. After the Oilers were forced to punt, Blake went to work again. Another long pass to Pickens, this time for 33 yards, set up Doug Pelfrey for the winning 40-yard field goal as time expired. Pickens finished with 11 catches for 188 yards and 3 touchdowns.

Houston	10	7	7	7	—	31
Cincinnati	3	14	0	17	—	34

Cin — FG Pelfrey 50
Hou — Jeffires 11 pass from Tolliver (Del Greco kick)
Hou — FG Del Greco 34
Cin — Pickens 21 pass from Blake (Pelfrey kick)
Hou — Brown 1 run (Del Greco kick)
Cin — Fenner 14 pass from Blake (Pelfrey kick)
Hou — White 17 run (Del Greco kick)
Cin — Pickens 50 pass from Blake (Pelfrey kick)
Hou — Slaughter 5 pass from Tolliver (Del Greco kick)
Cin — Pickens 21 pass from Blake (Pelfrey kick)
Cin — FG Pelfrey 40

L.A. RAIDERS 20, L.A. RAMS 17—at Anaheim Stadium, attendance 65,208. The Raiders finally reached the .500 mark, thanks to 2 touchdown passes by Jeff Hostetler. It was the fifth meeting between the teams since the Raiders' move to Los Angeles in 1982, and it was the Raiders' fourth victory in the Battle of L.A. The Raiders went 80 yards in the first quarter, the last 27 on Hostetler's scoring pass to tight end Andrew Glover. Four minutes later, the Rams tied the game on Chris Chandler's 22-yard touchdown throw to Willie Anderson. The Raiders took the lead for good when Hostetler found Raghib Ismail for a 10-yard scoring strike to make it 14-7 at halftime. Jeff Jaeger added 2 field goals in the fourth quarter, although the Rams did make it close with a field goal and Todd Kinchen's 4-yard touchdown catch from Chris Miller with 1:27 to play. Hostetler completed 17 of 25 passes for 218 yards. Chandler was 10 of 11 for 171 yards before being knocked out with an injury. Miller, Chandler's replacement, threw on 21 straight plays at one point and ended up 13 of 26 for 131 yards.

L.A. Raiders	7	7	0	6	—	20
L.A. Rams	7	0	0	10	—	17

Raid — Glover 27 pass from Hostetler (Jaeger kick)
Rams — Anderson 22 pass from Chandler (Zendejas kick)
Raid — Ismail 10 pass from Hostetler (Jaeger kick)
Raid — FG Jaeger 44
Rams — FG Zendejas 22
Raid — FG Jaeger 47
Rams — Kinchen 4 pass from Miller (Zendejas kick)

NEW ENGLAND 26, MINNESOTA 20—at Foxboro Stadium, attendance 58,382. Drew Bledsoe set two NFL records while rallying the Patriots from a 20-0 deficit to an overtime victory over the Vikings. Bledsoe established NFL marks for attempts (70) and completions (45) in a game. Minnesota built a 20-0 lead on 2 field goals by Fuad Reveiz, a 2-yard touchdown run by Terry Allen, and Warren Moon's 65-yard touchdown pass to Qadry Ismail. New England finally got on board with a field goal as the first half expired, then turned to the No-Huddle Offense in the second half to change its fortunes. After halftime, Bledsoe went to the air 53 times, completing 37 for 354 yards. His 31-yard touchdown pass to Ray Crittenden shaved the Vikings' lead to 20-10 early in the third period. In the fourth quarter, Bledsoe drove the Patriots 87 yards to a touchdown on Leroy Thompson's 5-yard catch with 2:27 left. New England got the ball back, and Bledsoe led his team 56 yards to set up Matt Bahr's tying 23-yard field goal with 14 seconds remaining. The Patriots then took the overtime kickoff and marched 67 yards for the winning score, which came on a 14-yard touchdown pass from Bledsoe to Kevin Turner. Bledsoe finished with 426 passing yards, while his Vikings counterpart, Warren Moon, completed 26 of 42 passes for 349 yards (Moon had 234 yards in the first half alone). The Patriots and Vikings also set NFL records for most pass attempts by both teams in a game (112) and most completions by both teams in a game (71). Three receivers finished in double figures in receptions for New England: Leroy Thompson (11 catches for 74 yards), Michael Timpson (10 for 113), and Ben Coates (10 for 74).

Minnesota	10	10	0	0	0	—	20
New England	0	3	7	10	6	—	26

Minn — Allen 2 run (Reveiz kick)
Minn — FG Reveiz 40
Minn — Ismail 65 pass from Moon (Reveiz kick)
Minn — FG Reveiz 33
NE — FG Bahr 38
NE — Crittenden 31 pass from Bledsoe (Bahr kick)
NE — Thompson 5 pass from Bledsoe (Bahr kick)
NE — FG Bahr 23
NE — Turner 14 pass from Bledsoe

GREEN BAY 17, N.Y. JETS 10—at Lambeau Field, attendance 58,307. The Packers exploited a hole in the Jets' defense for 2 touchdown passes then hung on at the end for the victory. Safety Ronnie Lott, the Jets' leading tackler and defensive leader, was sidelined with a pinched nerve, and his absence did not go unnoticed. Both of Brett Favre's touchdown passes came in Lott's area, as he found Robert Brooks (11 yards) for the game's first score and then hit Anthony Morgan (17 yards) to give Green Bay a 14-10 third-quarter lead. New York threatened to tie the game, driving to the Packers' 9 with 1:04 to play after Chris Jacke kicked a 46-yard field goal to make it 17-10. But on fourth-and-3, wide receiver Rob Moore slipped on the wet turf, and he was unable to recover in time to catch Boomer Esiason's pass. Favre completed 20 of 28 for 183 yards. Esiason was 24 of 43 for 214 yards. Moore had 7 catches for 72 yards, including the Jets' only touchdown on an 11-yard catch.

N.Y. Jets	0	10	0	0	—	10
Green Bay	7	0	7	3	—	17

GB — Brooks 11 pass from Favre (Jacke kick)
Jets — FG Lowery 20
Jets — Moore 11 pass from Esiason (Lowery kick)
GB — Morgan 17 pass from Favre (Jacke kick)
GB — FG Jacke 46

SAN DIEGO 14, KANSAS CITY 13—at Arrowhead Stadium, attendance 76,997. The Chargers overcame their mistakes, but the Chiefs could not as San Diego won a showdown for the AFC West lead. The Chargers had an abysmal first half in the rain, making 4 turnovers, including 2 inside their 30, yet they trailed only 13-0 at halftime. Kansas City could only convert those mistakes into 2 field goals, and also used a long punt return to set up a 1-yard touchdown run by Kimble Anders. Roles reversed in the second half, as the Chiefs were called for a roughing-the-passer penalty to keep a Chargers' drive alive. On the next play, Stan Humphries went deep for a 52-yard touchdown pass to Shawn Jefferson that cut San Diego's deficit to 13-7 entering the final quarter. Midway through the quarter, the Chiefs' Joe Montana fired a pass over the middle that glanced off the hands of wide receiver Lake Dawson and into the hands of the Chargers' Darren Carrington, who returned the interception 19 yards to the Chiefs' 8. Three plays later, Humphries passed 5 yards to Duane Young for the winning score. Montana tried to pull off a miracle comeback, but time expired with the Chiefs on the Chargers' 30.

Humphries completed 21 of 36 for 208 yards. Montana was 20 of 46 for 178 yards with 2 interceptions.

San Diego	0	0	7	7	—	14
Kansas City	0	13	0	0	—	13

KC — FG Elliott 27
KC — Anders 1 run (Elliott kick)
KC — FG Elliott 34
SD — Jefferson 52 pass from Humphries (Carney kick)
SD — Young 5 pass from Humphries (Carney kick)

DENVER 17, SEATTLE 10—at Mile High Stadium, attendance 71,290. Leonard Russell ran for 109 yards and the winning touchdown as the Broncos escaped the AFC West cellar while handing Seattle its sixth consecutive loss. Both teams struggled offensively, as Denver carried a 7-0 lead into intermission on John Elway's 12-yard scoring run, which was set up by a fumble recovery. The teams swapped field goals in the third quarter, and after an interception, the Seahawks tied the game with 11:39 left on Chris Warren's 23-yard touchdown run right up the middle. The Broncos took the ensuing kickoff and drove 80 yards in 9 plays, the last 11 coming on Russell's touchdown run. Seattle had a chance to tie, but Rick Mirer's pass on fourth-and-2 from the Broncos' 22 fell incomplete with 1:26 left. Warren had 122 yards on 18 carries for Seattle.

Seattle	0	0	3	7	—	10
Denver	0	7	3	7	—	17

Den — Elway 12 run (Elam kick)
Den — FG Elam 42
Sea — FG Kasay 19
Sea — C. Warren 23 run (Kasay kick)
Den — L. Russell 11 run (Elam kick)

SUNDAY NIGHT, NOVEMBER 13

DETROIT 14, TAMPA BAY 9—at Pontiac Silverdome, attendance 50,814. Barry Sanders rushed for 237 yards to lead the Lions over the Buccaneers. A sluggish first half ended with Tampa Bay leading 3-0. But then Detroit turned to Sanders, who ran for 200 yards in the second half alone. His 23-yard run set up Derrick Moore's 1-yard touchdown run, which gave Detroit a 7-3 lead. After a Buccaneers' field goal cut it to 7-6, Sanders burst 69 yards to set up Dave Krieg's 9-yard scoring toss to Herman Moore. Sanders carried the ball 26 times, an average of 9.1 yards per attempt. His output was the NFL's top single-game performance in 1994 and tied Emmitt Smith for the sixth-highest single-game total in NFL history. Tampa Bay could not get into the end zone despite the performances of quarterback Craig Erickson (16 of 23 for 243 yards with no interceptions) and rookie running back Errict Rhett (25 carries for 112 yards.)

Tampa Bay	3	0	3	3	—	9
Detroit	0	0	14	0	—	14

TB — FG Husted 20
Det — D. Moore 1 run (Hanson kick)
TB — FG Husted 41
Det — H. Moore 9 pass from Krieg (Hanson kick)
TB — FG Husted 34

MONDAY, NOVEMBER 14

PITTSBURGH 23, BUFFALO 10—at Three Rivers Stadium, attendance 59,019. Cornerback Rod Woodson made 2 big plays as the Steelers won for the second consecutive week without scoring an offensive touchdown. Woodson gave Pittsburgh a 10-0 lead when he stepped in front of a Bills' receiver for an interception and returned it 37 yards for a touchdown. The Steelers led 16-3 at halftime, but Buffalo took the second-half kickoff and drove 74 yards for a touchdown on Jim Kelly's 19-yard pass to Andre Reed. After a Steelers' punt, the Bills got the ball back, only to have Woodson strike again. This time, he knocked the football loose from Kelly at the goal line, and teammate Gerald Williams fell on the fumble in the end zone to give the Steelers a 23-10 lead. Pittsburgh recorded 7 sacks, including 6 of Kelly, who was 22 of 43 for 212 yards.

Buffalo	0	3	7	0	—	10
Pittsburgh	10	6	7	0	—	23

Pitt — FG Anderson 39
Pitt — Woodson 37 interception return (Anderson kick)
Pitt — FG Anderson 39
Buff — FG Christie 52
Pitt — FG Anderson 30
Buff — Reed 19 pass from Kelly (Christie kick)
Pitt — G. Williams recovered fumble in end zone (Anderson kick)

TWELFTH WEEK SUMMARIES

AMERICAN FOOTBALL CONFERENCE

Eastern Division	W	L	T	Pct.	Pts.	OP
Miami	7	4	0	.636	252	203
Buffalo	6	5	0	.545	234	218
N.Y. Jets	6	5	0	.545	204	205
Indianapolis	5	6	0	.455	233	246
New England	5	6	0	.455	233	256
Central Division						
Cleveland	8	3	0	.727	232	138
Pittsburgh	8	3	0	.727	192	169
Cincinnati	2	9	0	.182	188	268
Houston	1	10	0	.091	157	231
Western Division						
San Diego	8	3	0	.727	260	187
Kansas City	7	4	0	.636	215	205
L.A. Raiders	6	5	0	.545	227	241
Denver	5	6	0	.455	252	271
Seattle	4	7	0	.364	217	217

NATIONAL FOOTBALL CONFERENCE

Eastern Division	W	L	T	Pct.	Pts.	OP
Dallas	9	2	0	.818	293	148
Philadelphia	7	4	0	.636	222	186
Arizona	5	6	0	.455	138	204
N.Y. Giants	4	7	0	.364	184	230
Washington	2	9	0	.182	227	310
Central Division						
Chicago	7	4	0	.636	192	192
Minnesota	7	4	0	.636	245	195
Green Bay	6	5	0	.545	225	172
Detroit	5	6	0	.455	209	237
Tampa Bay	2	9	0	.182	145	251
Western Division						
San Francisco	9	2	0	.818	326	213
Atlanta	5	6	0	.455	228	258
L.A. Rams	4	7	0	.364	206	228
New Orleans	4	7	0	.364	228	285

SUNDAY, NOVEMBER 20

DENVER 32, ATLANTA 28—at Mile High Stadium, attendance 70,594. John Elway led the Broncos to 2 fourth-quarter touchdowns to rally Denver past Atlanta. The Broncos raced to a 10-0 first-quarter lead on a 1-yard touchdown run by Reggie Rivers and Jason Elam's 35-yard field goal. But Atlanta answered with 2 second-quarter touchdown passes by Jeff George—6 yards to running back Craig Heyward (set up by Chris Doleman's interception) and 11 yards to wide receiver Bert Emanuel. Denver reclaimed the lead at 17-14 on Elway's 22-yard touchdown pass to Jeff Campbell in the third quarter. Back came George, who connected with Terance Mathis for a 47-yard scoring strike at the end of the third quarter. One minute into the fourth period, the same pair combined on a 49-yard touchdown pass to give Atlanta a 28-17 lead. Elway got rolling after that, driving the Broncos 72 yards, the last 32 on his touchdown pass to Anthony Miller (they also combined on the two-point conversion). Denver got the ball back with six minutes to play, and the Broncos went 57 yards, with Elway scoring the winning touchdown on a 4-yard run with 1:56 to play. Elway completed 27 of 42 passes for 382 yards. Cedric Tillman led Denver with 8 receptions for 175 yards, and Miller had 6 catches for 102 yards. George passed for 254 yards, and Mathis had 8 catches for 163 yards.

Atlanta	0	14	7	7	—	28
Denver	10	0	7	15	—	32

Den — Rivers 1 run (Elam kick)
Den — FG Elam 35
Atl — Heyward 6 pass from George (Johnson kick)
Atl — Emanuel 11 pass from George (Johnson kick)
Den — Campbell 22 pass from Elway (Elam kick)
Atl — Mathis 47 pass from George (Johnson kick)
Atl — Mathis 49 pass from George (Johnson kick)
Den — Miller 32 pass from Elway (Miller pass from Elway)
Den — Elway 4 run (Elam kick)

KANSAS CITY 20, CLEVELAND 13—at Arrowhead Stadium, attendance 66,129. The battered Chiefs, playing without seven injured starters, managed to hold off the Browns. With rain turning the field to mud, Kansas City got an early break when the Browns' Mark Rypien fumbled at the Chiefs' 6, wasting a 60-yard punt return by Cleveland's Mark Carrier. Both teams scored in the second quarter, but Kansas City led 7-6 at halftime because the Browns' two-point conversion attempt failed. Cleveland led 13-10 after three quarters thanks to Rypien's 15-yard touchdown pass to Michael Jackson. But Kansas City owned the fourth quarter, tying the game on Lin Elliott's 28-yard field goal early in the period and taking the lead with 7:46 to play on Kimble Anders' 1-yard touchdown run. The winning drive was set up by Dale Carter's interception at the Chiefs' 39. Cleveland had one last chance, but Chiefs linebacker Derrick Thomas ended it by sacking Rypien and forcing a fumble that defensive end Pellom McDaniels recovered in the final minute. Rypien, who was spelled by Vinny Testaverde in the first half, completed 10 of 24 for 114 yards. Kansas City's Joe Montana was 19 of 33 for 169 yards. Cleveland was undone by 4 turnovers and 15 penalties for 142 yards.

Cleveland	0	6	7	0	—	13
Kansas City	0	7	3	10	—	20

KC — Greene 6 pass from Montana (Elliott kick)
Cleve — Metcalf 15 pass from Testaverde (run failed)
KC — FG Elliott 22
Cleve — Jackson 15 pass from Rypien (Stover kick)
KC — FG Elliott 28
KC — Anders 1 run (Elliott kick)

CHICAGO 20, DETROIT 10—at Soldier Field, attendance 55,035. The Bears played keepaway from Barry Sanders, controlling the ball for 44 minutes 12 seconds to defeat the Lions. Sanders entered the game as the NFL's leading rusher, but he got only 11 carries (for 42 yards). Meanwhile, the Bears' Lewis Tillman ran for 126 yards on 32 carries. Tied 10-10 at halftime, Chicago took control in the second half. The Bears used nearly 12 minutes of the third quarter to drive to Kevin Butler's 23-yard field goal. Chicago then resorted to trickery, as Chris Gardocki attempted an onside kick and Bears cornerback John Mangum recovered the ball at Chicago's 42. Six plays later, Steve Walsh went deep for a 30-yard touchdown pass to Jeff Graham. Walsh completed 25 of 31 passes for 185 yards. The Bears ran 76 plays to the Lions' 36. Detroit had just 180 total yards, with 120 (on 6 receptions) from wide receiver Brett Perriman.

Detroit	0	10	0	0	—	10
Chicago	0	10	3	7	—	20

Chi — Tillman 1 run (Butler kick)
Det — H. Moore 9 pass from Krieg (Hanson kick)
Chi — FG Butler 28
Det — FG Hanson 29
Chi — FG Butler 23
Chi — Graham 30 pass from Walsh (Butler kick)

BUFFALO 29, GREEN BAY 20—at Rich Stadium, attendance 79,029. Jim Kelly passed for 365 yards and Andre Reed caught a club-record 15 passes to lead the Bills. Kelly and Reed combined on a 15-yard touchdown pass to give Buffalo a 14-0 first-quarter lead. The same tandem hooked up in the second quarter on a 10-yard touchdown pass that made it 24-0. Green Bay got on the board with Brett Favre's 29-yard touchdown pass to Sterling Sharpe, but the Bills went into halftime with a 27-6 lead thanks to Steve Christie's 51-yard field goal as time expired in the second quarter. Favre threw 2 more touchdown passes in the third period, but the Packers' final three possessions produced no more points. Kelly completed 32 of 44 passes, while Reed had 191 receiving yards.

Green Bay	0	6	14	0	—	20
Buffalo	14	13	0	2	—	29

Buff — Thomas 5 run (Christie kick)
Buff — Reed 15 pass from Kelly (Christie kick)
Buff — FG Christie 38
Buff — Reed 10 pass from Kelly (Christie kick)
GB — Sharpe 29 pass from Favre (kick blocked)
Buff — FG Christie 51
GB — Bennett 5 pass from Favre (Jacke kick)
GB — Sharpe 26 pass from Favre (Jacke kick)
Buff — Safety, Sims penalized for holding in end zone

INDIANAPOLIS 17, CINCINNATI 13—at Riverfront Stadium, attendance 55,566. Don Majkowski led the Colts to 10 fourth-quarter points and Ray Buchanan made a game-saving interception in the end zone to preserve the Colts' victory. A fumble recovery at the Bengals' 23 set up Indianapolis's first points, which came on Marshall Faulk's

1-yard touchdown run. Cincinnati closed to 7-6 at halftime on 2 field goals by Doug Pelfrey, and took a 13-7 lead in the third quarter on Jeff Blake's 15-yard scoring pass to Darnay Scott. Majkowski got going in the final period, completing passes of 29 and 13 yards to set up Dean Biasucci's 35-yard field goal. Later in the quarter, Majkowski led the Colts on a 62-yard drive, hitting Sean Dawkins for 24 and 8 yards, with the latter catch providing the go-ahead score with 1:52 remaining. One minute later, Buchanan outjumped Scott in the end zone to secure the victory. Majkowski completed 14 of 24 passes for 165 yards with no interceptions. Blake was 21 of 37 for 207 yards. The Bengals' Carl Pickens caught 6 passes for 103 yards, including a 53-yard bomb from Scott on a flanker-reverse pass.

Indianapolis	7	0	0	10	—	17
Cincinnati	3	3	7	0	—	13

Ind — Faulk 1 run (Biasucci kick)
Cin — FG Pelfrey 29
Cin — FG Pelfrey 46
Cin — Scott 15 pass from Blake (Pelfrey kick)
Ind — FG Biasucci 35
Ind — Dawkins 8 pass from Majkowski (Biasucci kick)

PITTSBURGH 16, MIAMI 13—at Three Rivers Stadium, attendance 59,148. Mike Tomczak, replacing an injured Neil O'Donnell, passed for 343 yards to lead the Steelers to an overtime victory over the Dolphins. Miami led 7-6 at halftime on Dan Marino's 2-yard touchdown pass to tight end Keith Jackson. Trailing 10-6 in the fourth quarter, Pittsburgh scored its first offensive touchdown in three weeks when Barry Foster ran 10 yards for a score with 8:35 left. Foster's run, which gave Pittsburgh a 13-10 lead, capped a 73-yard drive in which Tomczak had passes of 40 and 19 yards. That lead almost held up, but Marino's passing brought the Dolphins from their 6 to the Steelers' 31, where Pete Stoyanovich kicked a 48-yard field goal as regulation ended to tie the game. In overtime, Miami drove to the Steelers' 42, only to be stopped by a sack and was forced to punt. Tomczak then led the Steelers into field-goal range, using passes of 27, 23, and 13 yards to set up Gary Anderson's 39-yard field goal 10:19 into the extra period. Tomczak completed 26 of 42 passes. Marino was 31 of 45 for 312 yards.

Miami	0	7	3	3	0	—	13
Pittsburgh	3	3	0	7	3	—	16

Pitt — FG Anderson 19
Mia — Jackson 2 pass from Marino (Stoyanovich kick)
Pitt — FG Anderson 48
Mia — FG Stoyanovich 34
Pitt — Foster 10 run (Anderson kick)
Mia — FG Stoyanovich 48
Pitt — FG Anderson 39

L.A. RAIDERS 24, NEW ORLEANS 19—at Los Angeles Memorial Coliseum, attendance 41,722. Jeff Hostetler passed for 310 yards and 3 scores to pace the Raiders. Hostetler hit Tim Brown for a 12-yard score, and Jeff Jaeger made a 51-yard field goal at the halftime gun to give Los Angeles a 10-0 lead at intermission. Disaster struck on the opening possession of the second half, as Hostetler fumbled while being sacked and Tyrone Hughes picked up the loose ball and raced 42 yards for a touchdown. The Raiders recovered from that gaffe, as Hostetler threw touchdown passes of 17 yards (to Raghib Ismail) and 30 yards (to Brown) to give Los Angeles a comfortable 24-7 cushion. A long kickoff return and an interception set up 2 quick touchdowns by the Saints in the final four minutes, and New Orleans had a chance to win on the last play, but Jim Everett's "Hail Mary" pass fell incomplete. Hostetler completed 22 of 28 passes, including 8 to Brown for 132 yards. The Raiders held the Saints to 16 rushing yards.

New Orleans	0	0	7	12	—	19
L.A. Raiders	7	3	7	7	—	24

Raid — T. Brown 12 pass from Hostetler (Jaeger kick)
Raid — FG Jaeger 51
NO — Hughes 42 fumble return (Andersen kick)
Raid — Ismail 17 pass from Hostetler (Jaeger kick)
Raid — T. Brown 30 pass from Hostetler (Jaeger kick)
NO — Small 9 pass from Everett (pass failed)
NO — Small 14 pass from Everett (pass failed)

N.Y. JETS 31, MINNESOTA 21—at Metrodome, attendance 60,687. Reserve defensive back Marcus Turner intercepted 3 passes, including 1 he returned 90 yards for a score, to help the Jets defeat the Vikings. Turner picked a deflected pass out of the air and raced untouched for a touchdown and a 7-0 Jets lead. Minnesota claimed its only lead at 14-10 when Warren Moon hit Cris Carter for a 6-yard touchdown pass. But Boomer Esiason answered with 3 straight touchdown passes—11 yards to Ryan Yarborough in the second quarter, 5 yards to Rob Moore in the third, and 14 yards to Art Monk in the fourth—to give New York a 31-14 lead with 14:04 remaining in the game. The Vikings, after stopping themselves all day with interceptions, added a touchdown with 8:24 to play but never threatened after that. Moon was 33 of 50 for 400 yards, with 4 interceptions. The Vikings had three receivers with 100 yards—Carter (100 on 11 catches), tight end Adrian Cooper (101 on 7 catches), and Jake Reed (121 on 5). Esiason was 22 of 29 for 230 yards, connecting with tight end Johnny Mitchell for a career-best 11 receptions for 120 yards.

N.Y. Jets	10	7	7	7	—	31
Minnesota	7	7	0	7	—	21

Jets — Turner 90 interception return (Lowery kick)
Minn — Graham 4 run (Reveiz kick)
Jets — FG Lowery 38
Minn — Carter 6 pass from Moon (Reveiz kick)
Jets — Yarborough 11 pass from Esiason (Lowery kick)
Jets — Moore 5 pass from Esiason (Lowery kick)
Jets — Monk 14 pass from Esiason (Lowery kick)
Minn — Ismail 2 pass from Moon (Reveiz kick)

ARIZONA 12, PHILADELPHIA 6—at Sun Devil Stadium, attendance 62,779. The Cardinals won a battle of field goals to post consecutive victories for the first time in 1994. Greg Davis kicked 4 field goals for Arizona, following drives of 74, 72, 73, and 37 yards. The last drive was kept alive by an Eagles' penalty on fourth down. The game's only apparent touchdown—on a 96-yard kickoff return by the Eagles' Herschel Walker—was nullified by a holding penalty. Philadelphia could not muster much offense against the Cardinals, managing just 185 total yards and suffering 4 sacks. Despite their anemic offense, the Eagles had a chance to win in the final minutes, driving inside the Cardinals' 25. But Philadelphia was stopped there, losing 1 yard on first down and then throwing 3 consecutive incompletions.

Philadelphia	0	3	0	3	—	6
Arizona	3	3	3	3	—	12

Ariz — FG Davis 24
Ariz — FG Davis 24
Phil — FG Murray 26
Ariz — FG Davis 24
Phil — FG Murray 30
Ariz — FG Davis 39

NEW ENGLAND 23, SAN DIEGO 17—at Foxboro Stadium, attendance 59,690. Marion Butts, playing against his former team, ran for 88 yards and 1 touchdown on 28 carries, and the Patriots' defense played its best game of the year as New England stunned the AFC West-leading Chargers. Drew Bledsoe's passing led the Patriots to their first score, a 27-yard touchdown pass to Leroy Thompson. Butts's running set up Matt Bahr's 39-yard field goal, which gave New England a 10-0 halftime advantage. Bahr's second field goal made it 13-3 in the third quarter, but the Chargers made a game of it when Andre Coleman returned the ensuing kickoff 80 yards for a touchdown. The Patriots responded with 10 straight points via a 1-yard touchdown run by Butts and Bahr's 23-yard field goal with 6:17 left in the game. San Diego added a late touchdown to make it close. New England intercepted 3 passes and posted 5 sacks, including 3½ by linebacker Chris Slade, while limiting the Chargers to 241 total yards. Bledsoe was 21 of 36 for 224 yards.

San Diego	0	0	10	7	—	17
New England	7	3	3	10	—	23

NE — Thompson 27 pass from Bledsoe (Bahr kick)
NE — FG Bahr 39
SD — FG Carney 34
NE — FG Bahr 38
SD — Coleman 80 kickoff return (Carney kick)
NE — Butts 1 run (Bahr kick)
NE — FG Bahr 23
SD — Martin 2 pass from Humphries (Carney kick)

SEATTLE 22, TAMPA BAY 21—at Kingdome, attendance 37,466. The Seahawks blew a 15-point lead, then came back to win in the final minute on a 7-yard touchdown run by rookie Mack Strong. The victory ended Seattle's six-game losing streak. Rick Mirer's 2 touchdown passes propelled the Seahawks to a 15-0 lead two minutes into the second quarter, but then Seattle's offense went dormant until late in the game. Meanwhile, Tampa Bay used 2 touchdown passes from Craig Erickson to Courtney Hawkins and 2 field goals by Michael Husted, the last with 3:24 left in the game, to take a 21-15 lead. Seattle's offense awoke from its slumber and drove 77 yards in 12 plays, helped by 2 key penalties against the Buccaneers, to Strong's winning run with 42 seconds left. Chris Warren led Seattle with 116 yards on 16 carries. Errict Rhett had 24 carries for 111 yards for Tampa Bay. It was the first meeting since 1977 for the teams, both of which entered the league as expansion franchises in 1976.

Tampa Bay	0	7	3	11	—	21
Seattle	7	8	0	7	—	22

Sea — Warren 3 pass from Mirer (Kasay kick)
Sea — Vaughn 5 pass from Mirer (Tuten run)
TB — Hawkins 2 pass from Erickson (Husted kick)
TB — FG Husted 30
TB — Hawkins 13 pass from Erickson (Rhett run)
TB — FG Husted 35
Sea — Strong 7 run (Kasay kick)

DALLAS 31, WASHINGTON 7—at Texas Stadium, attendance 64,644. The Cowboys ripped the Redskins but suffered two costly losses in the process. Quarterback Troy Aikman left in the second quarter with a sprained knee, and Aikman's replacement, backup Rodney Peete, also was knocked out with a sprained thumb. Fortunately for Dallas, Emmitt Smith was not hurt. He ran for 2 first-quarter touchdowns to help Dallas build a 17-0 lead. After Washington scored to make it 17-7, Peete connected with Alvin Harper on a 15-yard touchdown pass just before halftime to make it 24-7. The Cowboys capped the scoring with Kevin Williams's 83-yard punt return for a touchdown in the third quarter. Smith ran for 85 yards on 21 carries. Dallas's defense did its part, forcing 5 turnovers.

Washington	0	7	0	0	—	7
Dallas	17	7	7	0	—	31

Dall — E. Smith 8 run (Boniol kick)
Dall — E. Smith 3 run (Boniol kick)
Dall — FG Boniol 32
Wash — Howard 19 pass from Friesz (Lohmiller kick)
Dall — Harper 15 pass from Peete (Boniol kick)
Dall — K. Williams 83 punt return (Boniol kick)

SUNDAY NIGHT, NOVEMBER 20

SAN FRANCISCO 31, L.A. RAMS 27—at Candlestick Park, attendance 62,774. Jerry Rice's third touchdown catch of the day gave the 49ers the lead with 1:56 to play, and Deion Sanders' deflection saved the victory over the pesky Rams. San Francisco appeared en route to an easy victory, building a 21-6 halftime lead on 3 touchdown passes by Steve Young—7 yards to John Taylor, and 7 and 5 yards to Rice. But the Rams rallied, using a 44-yard touchdown run on a reverse by receiver Todd Kinchen and touchdown passes of 50 and 22 yards by Chris Miller to take a 27-24 lead early in the fourth quarter. The 49ers went to the well once again, as Young and Rice combined for 3 passes on the winning drive, the last reception covering 18 yards and giving San Francisco a 31-27 lead with 1:56 left. Back came the Rams, as Miller drove Los Angeles to the 49ers' 38 in the final minute. The Rams' Willie Anderson raced past Sanders and Dana Hall, and Miller lofted a potential winning pass to the end zone. But Sanders recovered just enough to get his hand up and tip the ball away. Rice set a club record with 16 receptions for 165 yards. Young completed 30 of 44 passes for 325 yards and 4 touchdowns. Miller passed for 228 yards.

L.A. Rams	3	3	13	8	—	27
San Francisco	14	7	3	7	—	31

SF — Taylor 7 pass from Young (Brien kick)
Rams — FG Zendejas 31
SF — Rice 7 pass from Young (Brien kick)
Rams — FG Zendejas 27
SF — Rice 5 pass from Young (Brien kick)
Rams — Kinchen 44 run (pass failed)
SF — FG Brien 28

Rams — Anderson 50 pass from Miller (Zendejas kick)
Rams — Hester 22 pass from Miller (Bettis run)
SF — Rice 18 pass from Young (Brien kick)

MONDAY, NOVEMBER 21

N.Y. GIANTS 13, HOUSTON 10—at Astrodome, attendance 53,201. David Treadwell kicked a 37-yard field goal with two seconds remaining to end New York's seven-game losing streak and spoil Jeff Fisher's debut as Houston's head coach. After a scoreless first half in which the Oilers made three trips inside the Giants' territory, Houston took a 7-0 lead on Billy Joe Tolliver's 1-yard sneak in the third quarter. Kent Graham, who replaced an injured Dave Brown in the second quarter, got the Giants even with a 40-yard touchdown pass to Mike Sherrard. The teams traded field goals to make it 10-10, and then Graham led New York on a 47-yard drive to set up Treadwell's winning kick. Both teams ran well: Houston's Lorenzo White gained 156 yards on 27 carries, and New York's Rodney Hampton ran for 122 yards on 34 carries. Sherrard had 6 catches for 109 yards.

N.Y. Giants	0	0	7	6	—	13
Houston	0	0	7	3	—	10

Hou — Tolliver 1 run (Del Greco kick)
Giants— Sherrard 40 pass from Graham (Treadwell kick)
Giants— FG Treadwell 26
Hou — FG Del Greco 43
Giants— FG Treadwell 37

THIRTEENTH WEEK SUMMARIES

AMERICAN FOOTBALL CONFERENCE

Eastern Division	**W**	**L**	**T**	**Pct.**	**Pts.**	**OP**
Miami	8	4	0	.667	280	227
Buffalo	6	6	0	.500	255	253
New England	6	6	0	.500	245	266
N.Y. Jets	6	6	0	.500	228	233
Indianapolis	5	7	0	.417	243	258
Central Division						
Cleveland	9	3	0	.750	266	148
Pittsburgh	9	3	0	.750	213	172
Cincinnati	2	10	0	.167	201	283
Houston	1	11	0	.083	167	265
Western Division						
San Diego	9	3	0	.750	291	204
Kansas City	7	5	0	.583	224	215
Denver	6	6	0	.500	267	284
L.A. Raiders	6	6	0	.500	230	262
Seattle	5	7	0	.417	227	226

NATIONAL FOOTBALL CONFERENCE

Eastern Division	**W**	**L**	**T**	**Pct.**	**Pts.**	**OP**
Dallas	10	2	0	.833	335	179
Philadelphia	7	5	0	.583	243	214
Arizona	5	7	0	.417	154	223
N.Y. Giants	5	7	0	.417	205	249
Washington	2	10	0	.167	246	331
Central Division						
Chicago	8	4	0	.667	211	208
Minnesota	7	5	0	.583	262	215
Detroit	6	6	0	.500	244	258
Green Bay	6	6	0	.500	256	214
Tampa Bay	3	9	0	.250	165	268
Western Division						
San Francisco	10	2	0	.833	361	227
Atlanta	6	6	0	.500	256	279
L.A. Rams	4	8	0	.333	223	259
New Orleans	4	8	0	.333	242	320

THURSDAY, NOVEMBER 24

DETROIT 35, BUFFALO 21—at Pontiac Silverdome, attendance 75,672. Dave Krieg passed for 351 yards and 3 touchdowns in the Lions' victory. Krieg, who completed 20 of 25 passes, picked apart a Bills' defense that was keyed to stop running back Barry Sanders (he finished with 45 yards on 19 carries). He had 2 first-half scoring tosses to stake the Lions to a 21-7 halftime advantage. After Buffalo cut the Lions' lead to 21-14 in the second half, Krieg led Detroit on a 97-yard touchdown drive to increase the Lions' advantage to 28-14 with 7:01 remaining in the game. Krieg went 6 for 6 on the march, finishing with a 12-yard scoring pass to Brett Perriman. Jim Kelly's 15-yard touchdown run with 4:04 left brought the Bills back within striking distance, but Buffalo's hopes were dashed three minutes later when Kelly's interception was returned 28 yards for the clinching score by Willie Clay. Kelly was 29 of 35 for 273 yards and 2 scores. Detroit's Herman Moore had 7 receptions for 169 yards, including a 51-yard touchdown.

Buffalo	0	7	7	7	—	21
Detroit	7	14	0	14	—	35

Det — H. Moore 51 pass from Krieg (Hanson kick)
Det — Sanders 4 run (Hanson kick)
Buff — Copeland 20 pass from Kelly (Christie kick)
Det — Matthews 28 pass from Krieg (Hanson kick)
Buff — Metzelaars 27 pass from Kelly (Christie kick)
Det — Perriman 12 pass from Krieg (Hanson kick)
Buff — Kelly 15 run (Christie kick)
Det — Clay 28 interception return (Hanson kick)

DALLAS 42, GREEN BAY 31—at Texas Stadium, attendance 64,597. Third-string quarterback Jason Garrett led the Cowboys to a club-record 36 points in the second half as Dallas overcame a 17-6 halftime deficit to defeat the Packers. Two touchdown passes from Brett Favre to Sterling Sharpe and a field goal by Chris Jacke accounted for the Packers' first-half points, while the Cowboys managed only 2 field goals by Chris Boniol. Dallas started fast in the third quarter, as Kevin Williams returned the second-half kickoff 87 yards to set up Emmitt Smith's 5-yard touchdown run. Green Bay quickly retaliated with Favre and Sharpe's third touchdown collaboration of the day to rebuild its lead to 11 points at 24-13. Garrett then began raining bombs down on the Packers' defense, hitting Alvin Harper for a 45-yard touchdown pass to make it 24-19, then driving Dallas 81 yards to the go-ahead score on Daryl Johnston's 3-yard run. Garrett and Smith combined on a 68-yard pass play on the Cowboys' next drive, setting up Smith's 18-yard touchdown run that made it 32-24 in favor of the Cowboys. The onslaught continued, as Garrett threw the ball up and a soaring Michael Irvin brought it down in the end zone for 35-yard touchdown pass and a 39-24 lead. Favre and Sharpe combined on a fourth touchdown pass to cut Dallas's lead to 39-31, but the Cowboys concluded the scoring with another field goal by Boniol. Garrett completed 15 of 26 passes for 311 yards and 2 scores. Smith totaled 228 yards (133 rushing yards on 32 carries and 95 receiving yards on 6 catches). Favre was 27 of 40 for 257 yards. Sharpe caught 9 passes for 122 yards.

Green Bay	7	10	7	7	—	31
Dallas	0	6	19	17	—	42

GB — Sharpe 1 pass from Favre (Jacke kick)
GB — FG Jacke 28
Dall — FG Boniol 41
GB — Sharpe 36 pass from Favre (Jacke kick)
Dall — FG Boniol 37
Dall — E. Smith 5 run (Boniol kick)
GB — Sharpe 30 pass from Favre (Jacke kick)
Dall — Harper 45 pass from Garrett (run failed)
Dall — Johnston 3 run (run failed)
Dall — E. Smith 18 run (Boniol kick)
Dall — Irvin 35 pass from Garrett (Boniol kick)
GB — Sharpe 5 pass from Favre (Jacke kick)
Dall — FG Boniol 35

SUNDAY, NOVEMBER 27

CHICAGO 19, ARIZONA 16—at Sun Devil Stadium, attendance 65,922. Kevin Butler's fourth field goal, from 27 yards eight minutes into overtime, lifted the Bears into sole possession of first place in the NFC Central. Chicago scored its only touchdown in the first quarter on Steve Walsh's 2-yard pass to tight end Ryan Wetnight. The game then became a field-goal duel between Butler and Arizona's Greg Davis, with Butler kicking 3 and Davis 2 to give Chicago a 16-6 advantage entering the fourth quarter. But the Bears saw their grasp on the game slip away as Arizona defensive end Keith McCants batted Walsh's pass into the air, then collected the ball and ran 46 yards for a touchdown with 7:36 to play. The Cardinals got the ball back, and Jay Schroeder led them on a 13-play drive that culminated in Davis's tying 47-yard field goal with 58 seconds left in regulation. In overtime, Walsh's 44-yard bomb to Jeff Graham set up Butler's winning kick. Walsh completed 15 of 28 passes for 186 yards to run his record as a starter to 8-0 in 1994. Graham had 8 catches for 154 yards.

Chicago	7	3	6	0	3	—	19
Arizona	0	3	3	10	0	—	16

Chi — Wetnight 2 pass from Walsh (Butler kick)
Ariz — FG Davis 49
Chi — FG Butler 35
Chi — FG Butler 52
Ariz — FG Davis 22
Chi — FG Butler 31
Ariz — McCants 46 interception return (Davis kick)
Ariz — FG Davis 47
Chi — FG Butler 27

DENVER 15, CINCINNATI 13—at Mile High Stadium, attendance 69,714. The Broncos staked themselves to a 15-6 halftime lead, then barely held off the Bengals in the second half. Denver's first-half scoring was provided by Jason Elam (3 field goals) and by John Elway, who threw a 16-yard touchdown pass to Anthony Miller. After a scoreless third quarter, Cincinnati's Jeff Blake went deep, connecting with Carl Pickens on a 70-yard touchdown bomb in the opening minute of the final period. The Bengals had a chance to take the lead, driving to Denver's 20 with 3:50 left. But Broncos safety Steve Atwater hammered Bengals running back Harold Green, forcing a fumble that teammate Elijah Alexander recovered, and the Broncos' offense ran out the clock. Elway completed 21 of 38 passes for 239 yards. Blake was 15 of 33 for 215 yards, including 6 completions to Pickens for 132 yards. Denver won despite being outgained 328 to 256, thanks to 4 Bengals turnovers.

Cincinnati	0	6	0	7	—	13
Denver	6	9	0	0	—	15

Den — FG Elam 34
Den — FG Elam 33
Cin — FG Pelfrey 43
Den — Miller 16 pass from Elway (kick failed)
Den — FG Elam 37
Cin — FG Pelfrey 32
Cin — Pickens 70 pass from Blake (Pelfrey kick)

CLEVELAND 34, HOUSTON 10—at Cleveland Stadium, attendance 65,088. The Browns used a 17-point fourth quarter to blow open a close game and defeat the Oilers. Vinny Testaverde, playing his first full game in six weeks, passed for 2 second-quarter touchdowns as Cleveland took a 17-10 halftime lead. The score remained unchanged until the fourth quarter, when the Browns drove 88 yards to score on Leroy Hoard's 1-yard run early in the period. Houston then self-destructed, fumbling twice to set up Matt Stover's 23-yard field goal and Hoard's second touchdown run of the quarter. Hoard gained 103 yards on 23 carries, while Testaverde completed 15 of 28 passes for 199 yards. Houston managed only 182 total yards.

Houston	0	10	0	0	—	10
Cleveland	3	14	0	17	—	34

Cleve — FG Stover 37
Cleve — Hartley 1 pass from Testaverde (Stover kick)
Hou — White 1 run (Del Greco kick)
Cleve — Kinchen 11 pass from Testaverde (Stover kick)
Hou — FG Del Greco 42
Cleve — Hoard 1 run (Stover kick)
Cleve — FG Stover 23
Cleve — Hoard 5 run (Stover kick)

SEATTLE 10, KANSAS CITY 9—at Kingdome, attendance 54,120. First the Chiefs lost their quarterback, then they lost the game, virtually ending their hopes of winning the AFC West. Montana led Kansas City to 2 field goals before leaving the game in the third quarter with a foot injury. Those field goals stood up until the fourth quarter, when Seattle drove 66 yards leading to Steve Smith's 1-yard touchdown run with 13:02 remaining. Kansas City reclaimed the lead with 7:27 to play on Lin Elliott's 36-yard field goal, but it did not last. Kelvin Martin's punt return put the Seahawks at the Chiefs' 39, and Seattle drove 25 yards to set up John Kasay's winning 32-yard field goal with 1:42 left. The Chiefs' last hope ended with 1:01 left when receiver Lake Dawson fumbled and the Seahawks' Robert Blackmon recovered. Montana completed 19 of 35 passes for 163 yards, becoming only the fifth NFL quarterback to surpass 40,000 career yards. Brian Blades led Seattle with 141 yards on 7 receptions.

Kansas City	3	3	0	3	—	9
Seattle	0	0	0	10	—	10

KC — FG Elliott 32
KC — FG Elliott 23
Sea — S. Smith 2 run (Kasay kick)
KC — FG Elliott 38
Sea — FG Kasay 32

SAN DIEGO 31, L.A. RAMS 17—at San Diego Jack Murphy Stadium, attendance 59,579. Darrien Gordon's heroics helped the Chargers overcome a lackluster offensive performance and defeat the Rams. Los Angeles took a

14-6 halftime lead on 2 touchdown passes by Chris Miller. But in the third quarter, Gordon turned the game around with one play—a 75-yard punt return for a touchdown, that, when coupled with Ronnie Harmon's two-point conversion run, tied the game at 14-14. The Chargers took their first lead on Harmon's 11-yard touchdown reception, and Gordon made sure they kept the advantage by intercepting Miller in the end zone. Sean Vanhorse sealed the victory with a 50-yard interception return for a touchdown with 51 seconds left. Miller passed for 298 yards, but he was intercepted 4 times. Natrone Means gained 95 yards on 23 carries for San Diego. Los Angeles outgained San Diego 328 to 243.

L.A. Rams	0	14	0	3	—	17
San Diego	0	6	15	10	—	31

Rams — Hester 40 pass from Miller (Zendejas kick)
SD — FG Carney 31
Rams — Drayton 12 pass from Miller (Zendejas kick)
SD — FG Carney 48
SD — Gordon 75 punt return (Harmon run)
SD — Harmon 11 pass from Humphries (Carney kick)
SD — FG Carney 37
Rams — FG Zendejas 33
SD — Vanhorse 50 interception return (Carney kick)

MIAMI 28, N.Y. JETS 24—at Giants Stadium, attendance 75,606. The Dolphins stunned the Jets with 22 points in the final 16 minutes to take a two-game lead in the AFC East. The Jets dominated the game for most of the first three quarters. Boomer Esiason threw 2 touchdown passes to tight end Johnny Mitchell, and Brad Baxter ran 3 yards for a touchdown to give New York a 24-6 lead with 3:39 left in the third quarter. At that point, the Jets appeared headed to a victory and a first-place tie with Miami in the division race. But Dan Marino had other ideas. He hit Mark Ingram for a 17-yard score with 42 seconds remaining in the third period, then passed to Irving Fryar for a two-point conversion that made it 24-14. Troy Vincent's interception set up another Marino to Ingram touchdown pass, this one from 28 yards, to cut the Jets' lead to 24-21 with 10:13 left in the game. The Dolphins got the ball for the last time at their 16 with 2:34 remaining, and Marino led Miami to the Jets' 8 with time running out. Marino motioned that he was going to spike the ball to kill the clock. His feint fooled the Jets, who stood idly by while Marino took the snap and instead passed to Ingram for the winning score with 22 seconds left. Marino completed 31 of 44 passes for 359 yards, with 4 touchdown passes to Ingram, who had 9 catches for 117 yards. Fryar had 5 receptions for 103 yards. Esiason was 26 of 41 for 382 yards, hitting Rob Moore 7 times for 124 yards and Art Monk 5 times for 108 yards.

Miami	0	0	14	14	—	28
N.Y. Jets	3	7	14	0	—	24

Jets — FG Lowery 24
Jets — Mitchell 30 pass from Esiason (Lowery kick)
Jets — Baxter 3 run (Lowery kick)
Mia — Ingram 10 pass from Marino (pass failed)
Jets — Mitchell 14 pass from Esiason (Lowery kick)
Mia — Ingram 17 pass from Marino (Fryar pass from Marino)
Mia — Ingram 28 pass from Marino (Stoyanovich kick)
Mia — Ingram 8 pass from Marino (Stoyanovich kick)

N.Y. GIANTS 21, WASHINGTON 19—at RFK Stadium, attendance 43,384. Dave Brown passed for 2 touchdowns and ran for another score in the Giants' victory. Brown's 2-yard touchdown run gave New York a 7-3 first-quarter lead, and his 34-yard scoring strike to Chris Calloway helped the Giants take a 14-9 advantage into intermission. The Giants upped their lead to 21-9 on Brown's 6-yard scoring pass to Mike Sherrard. Brown completed 10 of 17 passes for 161 yards with no interceptions. Rodney Hampton led the Giants' ball-control offense with 34 carries for 106 yards. Washington's Ricky Ervins gained 92 yards on 14 carries.

N.Y. Giants	7	7	7	0	—	21
Washington	3	6	3	7	—	19

Wash — FG Lohmiller 43
Giants— Da. Brown 2 run (Treadwell kick)
Wash — FG Lohmiller 29
Giants— Calloway 34 pass from Da. Brown (Treadwell kick)
Wash — FG Lohmiller 29
Giants— Sherrard 6 pass from Da. Brown (Treadwell kick)
Wash — FG Lohmiller 46
Wash — Bayless 60 fumble return (Lohmiller kick)

ATLANTA 28, PHILADELPHIA 21—at Georgia Dome, attendance 60,008. Jeff George passed for 364 yards and 2 touchdowns to lead the Falcons over the Eagles. George hit Terance Mathis for the game's first score on a 9-yard pass. Atlanta led 13-7 at halftime, but its lead lasted just 1:14 into the second half as Herschel Walker raced 91 yards for a touchdown. George and Mathis combined on another touchdown pass, this time from 7 yards, to reclaim the lead for the Falcons at 21-14. Craig Heyward's 5-yard touchdown run made it 28-14, but Walker answered with a 2-yard scoring run that made it 28-21 with 4:22 left. Philadelphia got the ball back near midfield with 2:25 left, but the Eagles' final threat was snuffed out when rookie Anthony Phillips intercepted Randall Cunningham's pass. George completed 26 of 46 passes, with 10 completions to Mathis for 124 yards. Cunningham was 19 of 36 for 248 yards. Walker had 98 yards and 2 touchdowns on just 3 carries.

Philadelphia	0	7	7	7	—	21
Atlanta	7	6	8	7	—	28

Atl — Mathis 9 pass from George (Johnson kick)
Phil — Cunningham 1 run (Murray kick)
Atl — FG Johnson 50
Atl — FG Johnson 40
Phil — Walker 91 run (Murray kick)
Atl — Mathis 7 pass from George (Mathis pass from George)
Atl — Heyward 5 run (Johnson kick)
Phil — Walker 2 run (Murray kick)

PITTSBURGH 21, L.A. RAIDERS 3—at Los Angeles Memorial Coliseum, attendance 58,327. Mike Tomczak threw 2 touchdown passes to lead the Steelers to their fourth consecutive victory. Tomczak, making his second consecutive start in place of injured Neil O'Donnell, capped an 80-yard drive in the first quarter with a 27-yard touchdown pass to Yancey Thigpen. It was 7-3 early in the fourth quarter when defensive end Ray Seals recovered a fumble by Raiders quarterback Vince Evans at Pittsburgh's 46-yard line. Seven plays later, Tomczak teamed with tight end Eric Green on a 15-yard touchdown pass to give the Steelers a 14-3 lead with 9:22 left. That was more than enough to clinch the victory because the Steelers' stingy defense permitted Los Angeles only 179 total yards and registered 5 sacks. Raiders starting quarterback Jeff Hostetler completed only 8 of 17 passes for 85 yards and missed much of the second half after suffering a concussion. Tomczak completed just 12 of 27 passes for 131 yards, but Pittsburgh running backs Barry Foster, Byron (Bam) Morris, and John L. Williams combined for 172 rushing yards. Steelers linebacker Kevin Greene had 2 sacks.

Pittsburgh	7	0	0	14	—	21
L.A. Raiders	0	3	0	0	—	3

Pitt — Thigpen 27 pass from Tomczak (Anderson kick)
Raid — FG Jaeger 32
Pitt — Green 15 pass from Tomczak (Anderson kick)
Pitt — Morris 3 run (Anderson kick)

TAMPA BAY 20, MINNESOTA 17—at Metrodome, attendance 47,259. The Buccaneers recovered a fumbled punt return in overtime to set up Michael Husted's winning 22-yard field goal. Tampa Bay was in control almost from the start, as Tony Covington returned an interception 36 yards to set up Errict Rhett's 1-yard touchdown run. After the Vikings kicked 2 field goals to make it 7-6, Tampa Bay increased its lead on Craig Erickson's 14-yard touchdown pass to Courtney Hawkins. Fuad Reveiz's 51-yard field goal made it 14-9 at halftime, and it stayed that way until the fourth quarter when Husted kicked a 27-yard field goal to give Tampa Bay a 17-9 lead with 5:24 remaining. Minnesota, which never led, scrambled just to tie. The Vikings, needing a touchdown and a two-point conversion, got the former on Warren Moon's 40-yard touchdown pass to Qadry Ismail, who made a spectacular diving catch with 1:27 remaining, and they got the latter on Moon's pass to Cris Carter. But the Vikings' luck ran out in overtime when Eric Guliford fumbled a punt at Minnesota's 4, and the Buccaneers' Ed Brady recovered. Husted's winning kick came on the next play. Erickson was 20 of 38 for 254 yards, while Moon was 24 of 36 for 286 yards. Ismail had 6 catches for 101 yards.

Tampa Bay	7	7	0	3	3	—	20
Minnesota	0	9	0	8	0	—	17

TB — Rhett 1 run (Husted kick)
Minn — FG Reveiz 23
Minn — FG Reviez 21
TB — Hawkins 14 pass from Erickson (Husted kick)
Minn — FG Reveiz 51
TB — FG Husted 27
Minn — Ismail 40 pass from Moon (Carter pass from Moon)
TB — FG Husted 22

SUNDAY NIGHT, NOVEMBER 27

NEW ENGLAND 12, INDIANAPOLIS 10—at RCA Dome, attendance 43,839. Matt Bahr kicked 4 field goals to improve the Patriots' record to 6-6 and move them into a three-way tie for the AFC's final playoff spot. Quarterback Drew Bledsoe and tight end Ben Coates supplied most of New England's offense, combining on 12 passes for 119 yards. Bledsoe's passing set up 3 of Bahr's field goals, and a fumble recovery set up the other three-pointer. Bledsoe completed 26 of 36 passes for 271 yards. The Colts' Don Majkowski was 16 of 27 for 186 yards, including the game's only touchdown on a 23-yard pass to Sean Dawkins.

New England	3	0	3	6	—	12
Indianapolis	0	7	0	3	—	10

NE — FG Bahr 22
Ind — Dawkins 23 pass from Majkowski (Biasucci kick)
NE — FG Bahr 37
NE — FG Bahr 25
Ind — FG Biasucci 50
NE — FG Bahr 43

MONDAY, NOVEMBER 28

SAN FRANCISCO 35, NEW ORLEANS 14—at Louisiana Superdome, attendance 61,304. Steve Young threw 4 touchdown passes as the 49ers became the first team to secure a berth in the 1994 postseason. San Francisco's victory was its seventh in succession, and clinched the club's eleventh NFC Western Division title in the last 14 years. The 49ers also increased their record string of 10-win seasons to 12. Despite dominating most of the first two periods, San Francisco only led 20-14 at halftime because the Saints converted 2 fumble recoveries into touchdowns, including a franchise-record 86-yard fumble return by cornerback Tyrone Hughes to pull New Orleans within 17-14 just 34 seconds before halftime. But the 49ers countered by driving 46 yards leading to Doug Brien's 48-yard field goal with three seconds left in the half, then opened the second half with a 14-play, 78-yard drive that consumed 9:02. Young capped that march with a 6-yard touchdown pass to tight end Brent Jones, then put the game out of reach by teaming with Nate Singleton on a 43-yard scoring pass 3:03 into the fourth quarter. Young was 24 of 30 for 281 yards, and was supported by a running attack that accumulated 191 yards, including 105 from Ricky Watters. San Francisco amassed 28 first downs and 461 total yards while limiting the Saints to 13 first downs and 222 total yards. The 49ers maintained possession for 38 minutes 29 seconds.

San Francisco	10	10	8	7	—	35
New Orleans	0	14	0	0	—	14

SF — FG Brien 40
SF — Jones 4 pass from Young (Brien kick)
NO — Bates 3 run (Andersen kick)
SF — Taylor 4 pass from Young (Brien kick)
NO — Hughes 86 fumble return (Andersen kick)
SF — FG Brien 48
SF — Jones 6 pass from Young (Brien kick)
SF — Singleton 43 pass from Young (Brien kick)

FOURTEENTH WEEK SUMMARIES

AMERICAN FOOTBALL CONFERENCE

Eastern Division	W	L	T	Pct.	Pts.	OP
Miami	8	5	0	.615	311	269
Buffalo	7	6	0	.538	297	284
New England	7	6	0	.538	269	279
Indianapolis	6	7	0	.462	274	277
N.Y. Jets	6	7	0	.462	241	257

Central Division						
Pittsburgh	10	3	0	.769	251	187
Cleveland	9	4	0	.692	279	164
Cincinnati	2	11	0	.154	216	321
Houston	1	12	0	.077	179	295
Western Division						
San Diego	9	4	0	.692	308	228
Denver	7	6	0	.538	287	301
Kansas City	7	6	0	.538	241	235
L.A. Raiders	7	6	0	.538	254	279
Seattle	5	8	0	.385	246	257
NATIONAL FOOTBALL CONFERENCE						
Eastern Division	**W**	**L**	**T**	**Pct.**	**Pts.**	**OP**
Dallas	11	2	0	.846	366	198
Philadelphia	7	6	0	.538	262	245
Arizona	6	7	0	.462	184	235
N.Y. Giants	6	7	0	.462	221	262
Washington	2	11	0	.154	267	357
Central Division						
Chicago	8	5	0	.615	238	241
Minnesota	8	5	0	.615	295	242
Detroit	7	6	0	.538	278	289
Green Bay	6	7	0	.462	287	248
Tampa Bay	4	9	0	.308	191	289
Western Division						
San Francisco	11	2	0	.846	411	241
Atlanta	6	7	0	.462	270	329
New Orleans	5	8	0	.385	273	335
L.A. Rams	4	9	0	.308	238	290

THURSDAY, DECEMBER 1

MINNESOTA 33, CHICAGO 27—at Metrodome, attendance 61,483. Warren Moon's 65-yard touchdown pass to Cris Carter 5:46 into overtime gave the Vikings the victory and lifted them into a tie with the Bears for first place in the NFC Central. Chicago had a chance to win the game and hold onto its division lead, but kicker Kevin Butler missed a 40-yard field goal attempt only two plays before Moon teamed with Carter on the decisive play. Minnesota led 13-7 at halftime, but the lead changed hands four times in the second half, the first time when the Bears' Jeff Graham returned a punt 60 yards for a touchdown 2:05 into the third quarter. An exchange of field goals and Steve Walsh's 15-yard touchdown pass to Greg McMurtry gave Chicago a 24-16 lead, but the Vikings rallied behind Fuad Reveiz's 38-yard field goal and Moon's 1-yard touchdown pass to Carter with 4:12 left in regulation. The subsequent 2-point conversion pass from Moon to tight end Andrew Jordan gave Minnesota a 27-24 edge. The Bears forced overtime when Nate Lewis returned the ensuing kickoff 55 yards to position Butler for a 33-yard field goal with 1:55 left. Moon completed 27 of 48 passes for 306 yards for the Vikings, with 9 of his completions going to Carter for 124 yards. Walsh, who lost for the first time in eight games as Chicago's starting quarterback, was 24 of 33 for 233 yards. Each quarterback threw 2 touchdown passes.

Chicago	7	0	17	3	0	— 27
Minnesota	7	6	3	11	6	— 33

Minn — Washington 54 interception return (Reveiz kick)
Chi — Green 39 pass from Walsh (Butler kick)
Minn — FG Reveiz 45
Minn — FG Reveiz 41
Chi — Graham 60 punt return (Butler kick)
Minn — FG Reveiz 29
Chi — FG Butler 29
Chi — McMurtry 15 pass from Walsh (Butler kick)
Minn — FG Reveiz 38
Minn — Carter 1 pass from Moon (A. Jordan pass from Moon)
Chi — FG Butler 33
Minn — Carter 65 pass from Moon

SUNDAY, DECEMBER 4

ARIZONA 30, HOUSTON 12—at Astrodome, attendance 39,821. The Cardinals scored 18 points in a span of 4:53 of the fourth quarter to rally past the Oilers. Cris Dishman's 36-yard interception return late in the first quarter helped stake Houston to a 12-10 halftime lead. It remained that way until the first play of the final period, when Arizona quarterback Jay Schroeder threw a 13-yard touchdown pass to Gary Clark to give his team the lead for good. The touchdown—set up by Schroeder's 42-yard completion to Clark—and Ron Moore's 2-point conversion run gave the Cardinals an 18-12 lead. Moments later, linebacker Wilber Marshall stripped Oilers quarterback Bucky Richardson of the ball and safety Terry Hoage recovered at Houston's 10-yard line to set up Greg Davis's 23-yard field goal for a 21-12 advantage 1:58 into the fourth quarter. Hoage intercepted a pass on the Oilers' next possession and returned it 41 yards to Houston's 17. Four plays later, Larry Centers ran 4 yards for his second touchdown of the game, and the Cardinals had put the game out of reach. The game marked the return to the Astrodome of Arizona coach Buddy Ryan, the Oilers' defensive coordinator in 1993. Ryan also was coaching his first game against his former pupil, Houston coach Jeff Fisher, who was Ryan's defensive coordinator in Philadelphia. The Cardinals' defense wreaked havoc on the Oilers' quarterbacks, who were intercepted 5 times and lost a fumble. Starter Billy Joe Tolliver completed only 11 of 31 passes for 184 yards, with 4 interceptions and was sacked by defensive tackle Eric Swann for a safety. Richardson was 0 for 3 with an interception and a fumble. Clark caught 6 passes for 120 yards for the Cardinals, whose 30-point output easily exceeded their previous season high of 21. Hoage had 2 interceptions and the fumble recovery for Arizona.

Arizona	0	10	0	20	— 30
Houston	9	3	0	0	— 12

Hou — Safety, Lathon tackled Schroeder in end zone
Hou — Dishman 36 interception return (Del Greco kick)
Ariz — Centers 1 run (Davis kick)
Ariz — FG Davis 25
Hou — FG Del Greco 34
Ariz — Clark 13 pass from Schroeder (Moore run)
Ariz — FG Davis 23
Ariz — Centers 4 run (Davis kick)
Ariz — Safety, Swann tackled Tolliver in end zone

SAN FRANCISCO 50, ATLANTA 14—at Candlestick Park, attendance 60,549. Steve Young threw 3 touchdown passes and ran for 2 touchdowns as the 49ers blasted the Falcons to win their eighth consecutive game. Atlanta trailed only 17-14 after defensive end Chuck Smith intercepted Young's pass and returned it 36 yards for a touchdown 8:03 before halftime. But San Francisco responded with a 12-play, 74-yard drive. Young's 2-yard touchdown pass to running back Ricky Watters with 36 seconds left in the first half, and a fumble recovery on the ensuing kickoff led to Doug Brien's 36-yard field goal as time ran out for a 27-14 lead. Young, who completed 22 of 33 passes for 294 yards, ran 7 yards for a touchdown in the third quarter and passed 9 yards to Jerry Rice in the fourth period to break open the game. The 49ers, who beat Atlanta 42-3 earlier in the season, outgained the Falcons 476-249. Safety Merton Hanks intercepted 2 passes for San Francisco, which forced 5 turnovers that led to 17 points.

Atlanta	7	7	0	0	— 14
San Francisco	3	24	7	16	— 50

SF — FG Brien 24
Atl — Emanuel 11 pass from George (Johnson kick)
SF — Taylor 12 pass from Young (Brien kick)
SF — Young 1 run (Brien kick)
Atl — Smith 36 interception return (Johnson kick)
SF — Watters 2 pass from Young (Brien kick)
SF — FG Brien 36
SF — Young 7 run (Brien kick)
SF — Rice 9 pass from Young (run failed)
SF — FG Brien 32
SF — A. Walker 2 run (Brien kick)

DALLAS 31, PHILADELPHIA 19—at Veterans Stadium, attendance 65,974. Darren Woodson returned a fourth-quarter interception 94 yards for a touchdown to preserve the victory that gave the Cowboys their third consecutive NFC Eastern Division title. Philadelphia, which at one point trailed 21-6, had pulled within 24-19 on a pair of Randall Cunningham touchdown passes, including a 5-yard toss to tight end Maurice Johnson with 10:15 left in the game. The Eagles then forced a punt, which Jeff Sydner returned 49 yards to Dallas's 12-yard line. But on third-and-6 from the 8, Cunningham's pass for James Joseph in the right flat was intercepted by Woodson, who had only to beat the quarterback en route to the opposite end zone. Emmitt Smith rushed for 91 yards and 2 touchdowns for the Cowboys. Quarterback Rodney Peete, subbing for injured Troy Aikman, was efficient, completing 10 of 17 passes for 172 yards and a touchdown. Michael Irvin caught 4 passes for 117 yards. Cunningham, after passing for only 77 yards in the first half, finished 29 of 46 for 327 yards. But he also suffered 5 sacks, including 3 by defensive end Charles Haley.

Dallas	7	7	7	10	— 31
Philadelphia	0	6	7	6	— 19

Dall — Irvin 19 pass from Peete (Boniol kick)
Phil — FG Murray 22
Dall — E. Smith 4 run (Boniol kick)
Phil — FG Murray 19
Dall — E. Smith 3 run (Boniol kick)
Phil — Barnett 25 pass from Cunningham (Murray kick)
Dall — FG Boniol 19
Phil — Johnson 5 pass from Cunningham (pass failed)
Dall — Woodson 94 interception return (Boniol kick)

DENVER 20, KANSAS CITY 17—at Arrowhead Stadium, attendance 77,631. Jason Elam kicked a 34-yard field goal with 2:48 left in overtime to give the Broncos their seventh victory in nine games. After starting the season 0-4, Denver improved to 7-6 and drew even with the Chiefs and Raiders for second place in the AFC Western Division. Kansas City, which lost for the fourth time in six games, had a chance to win on the final play of regulation, but Broncos defensive end Shane Dronett blocked Lin Elliott's 37-yard field-goal try. The Chiefs had another chance to win after recovering a fumble at Denver's 35-yard line in overtime, but running back Marcus Allen lost a fumble at the 27 moments later. The Broncos led 14-3 after John Elway capped an 88-yard drive with a 24-yard touchdown pass to Shannon Sharpe with 5:33 remaining in the third quarter. But Kansas City took only 2:19 to counter, as quarterback Steve Bono completed 3 consecutive passes for 75 yards and Allen ran the final yard to trim the Chiefs' deficit to 14-9. After Denver maintained possession for nearly 11 minutes on an 18-play field-goal drive to make it 17-9, Kansas City answered quickly again, this time taking only 18 seconds. Bono's 62-yard touchdown pass to Willie Davis on the next play, and a subsequent 2-point conversion pass by the same combination, tied the game at 17-17 with 7:28 left in regulation. The Broncos' winning drive in overtime was kept alive when backup quarterback Matt Millen scrambled for 21 yards on third-and-17 from Denver's 35. Millen was in the game because John Elway injured his knee in the fourth quarter. Before leaving, Elway passed for 256 yards. Bono started for the Chiefs in place of injured Joe Montana and completed 18 of 37 passes for 323 yards. J.J. Birden caught 7 passes for 101 yards, and Davis had 3 receptions for 107 yards. Sharpe caught 10 passes for the Broncos, while Anthony Miller had 153 yards on his 6 receptions. The Chiefs amassed 401 total yards; Denver had 393.

Denver	7	0	7	3	3	— 20
Kansas City	0	3	6	8	0	— 17

Den — Rivers 1 run (Elam kick)
KC — FG Elliott 22
Den — Sharpe 24 pass from Elway (Elam kick)
KC — Allen 1 run (run failed)
Den — FG Elam 34
KC — Davis 62 pass from Bono (Davis pass from Bono)
Den — FG Elam 34

DETROIT 34, GREEN BAY 31—at Pontiac Silverdome, attendance 76,338. Barry Sanders ran for 188 yards and a touchdown on 20 carries as the Lions overcame an 11-point deficit to beat the Packers. Brett Favre's 26-yard touchdown pass to Anthony Morgan and a 96-yard kickoff return by Robert Brooks staked Green Bay to a 14-3 lead in the first quarter. But Detroit rallied for 3 second-quarter touchdowns, 1 on a 13-yard run by Sanders, to take a 24-21 lead at halftime. Favre, who passed for 366 yards and 3 touchdowns, teamed with Morgan for the second time on a 47-yard touchdown pass 8:15 into the second half to put Green Bay ahead again 31-24. But early in the fourth quarter, with his team trailing 31-27, Sanders broke off a 63-yard run to set up Derrick Moore's 1-yard run for the deciding touchdown with 9:02 left. Sanders's long run was his fifth of 60 or more yards this season. On it, he eclipsed his own club record for rushing yards in a season. He finished the game at an NFL-high 1,594 yards. Lions quarterback Dave Krieg passed for 196 yards and 2 touchdowns, including a 1-yard toss to tackle-eligible Scott Conover to give Detroit the lead 49 seconds before halftime. Favre completed 29 of 43 passes for the Packers, but was intercepted twice. Sterling Sharpe (115 yards on 10 catches) and Morgan (103 yards on 6 receptions) were his primary targets. The teams accounted for 804 total yards, including 417 by Green Bay.

Green Bay	14	7	10	0	— 31
Detroit	3	21	3	7	— 34

GB — Morgan 26 pass from Favre (Jacke kick)
Det — FG Hanson 27
GB — Brooks 96 kickoff return (Jacke kick)
Det — H. Moore 24 pass from Krieg (Hanson kick)
Det — Sanders 13 run (Hanson kick)
GB — Sharpe 22 pass from Favre (Jacke kick)
Det — Conover 1 pass from Krieg (Hanson kick)
GB — FG Jacke 24
GB — Morgan 47 pass from Favre (Jacke kick)
Det — FG Hanson 34
Det — D. Moore 1 run (Hanson kick)

INDIANAPOLIS 31, SEATTLE 19—at Kingdome, attendance 39,574. Marshall Faulk ran for 129 yards and a touchdown to pace the Colts' victory. A rookie first-round draft choice, Faulk surpassed the 1,000-yard mark for the season, finishing the game at 1,086. He had a key 45-yard touchdown run in the final minute of the first quarter, after the Seahawks had built a 10-0 lead. Midway through the second period, Indianapolis cornerback Ray Buchanan intercepted Rick Mirer's pass and returned it 37 yards for a touchdown to give his team the lead for good. Quarterback Don Majkowski ran for 1 touchdown and passed for another as the Colts broke open the game in the second half. Seattle was dealt a severe blow when quarterback Rick Mirer broke his left thumb on Buchanan's touchdown return and was lost for the rest of the season. Seahawks running back Chris Warren gained 81 yards on 23 carries despite playing with a pair of cracked ribs suffered in a serious car accident three nights before the game. The accident left Seattle defensive tackle Mike Frier seriously injured and the Seahawks organization shaken.

Indianapolis	7	7	7	10	—	31
Seattle	10	3	0	6	—	19

Sea — FG Kasay 37
Sea — Green 18 pass from Mirer (Kasay kick)
Ind — Faulk 45 run (Biasucci kick)
Ind — Buchanan 37 interception return (Biasucci kick)
Sea — FG Kasay 31
Ind — Majkowski 1 run (Biasucci kick)
Ind — Dawkins 16 pass from Majkowski (Biasucci kick)
Ind — FG Biasucci 21
Sea — S. Smith 1 pass from McGwire (pass failed)

NEW ORLEANS 31, L.A. RAMS 15—at Anaheim Stadium, attendance 34,960. Mario Bates ran for 3 touchdowns, and the Saints took advantage of 4 fumble recoveries to defeat the Rams. Bates scored all of his touchdowns in the first half, as New Orleans built a 28-7 lead and effectively put the game out of reach. The Saints set the tone for the day by marching 99 yards the first time they had the ball, an 11-play drive that culminated in Bates's 26-yard scamper 11:19 into the game. Moments later, Othello Henderson recovered Todd Kinchen's muffed punt at Los Angeles's 44-yard line. Quarterback Jim Everett completed a 33-yard pass to Michael Haynes on the next play and Bates ran 11 yards for a touchdown on the first play of the second quarter to make it 14-0. New Orleans broke open the game by converting fumble recoveries into touchdowns just 1:33 apart late in the first half after Chris Miller's 24-yard touchdown pass to Kinchen pulled the Rams within 14-7. Everett, making his return to Anaheim Stadium for the first time since being traded by the Rams for a seventh-round draft choice prior to the 1994 season, completed 13 of 22 passes for 161 yards and a touchdown before leaving the game with a sprained foot in the fourth quarter. Bates finished with 96 yards on 25 carries.

New Orleans	7	21	3	0	—	31
L.A. Rams	0	7	0	8	—	15

NO — Bates 26 run (Andersen kick)
NO — Bates 11 run (Andersen kick)
Rams — Kinchen 24 pass from Miller (Zendejas kick)
NO — Bates 1 run (Andersen kick)
NO — Haynes 30 pass from Everett (Andersen kick)
NO — FG Andersen 46
Rams — Bettis 5 pass from Miller (Bettis run)

N.Y. GIANTS 16, CLEVELAND 13—at Cleveland Stadium, attendance 72,068. Brad Daluiso kicked 3 field goals in the second half, including a 33-yarder with 19 seconds remaining, to lift the Giants to their third consecutive victory and knock the Browns from a first-place tie in the AFC Central Division. Daluiso normally is New York's long-range field-goal specialist. But after David Treadwell missed a 37-yard try late in the first half, Giants coach Dan Reeves lifted him in favor of Daluiso in the second half, and Daluiso responded by kicking field goals of 25 and 30 yards to give New York a 13-6 lead in the fourth quarter. Quarterback Vinny Testaverde rallied Cleveland with a 60-yard completion to Derrick Alexander, setting up Leroy Hoard's 5-yard touchdown run with 4:24 left to tie the game at 13-13. But the Giants converted three third downs on a 13-play, 59-yard march to the winning field goal. Quarterback Dave Brown passed for 2 of the first downs and ran for another on the drive. He threw for 226 yards in all. Testaverde passed for 238 yards but was intercepted twice. Alexander caught 7 passes for 171 yards.

N.Y. Giants	7	0	3	6	—	16
Cleveland	3	3	0	7	—	13

Cleve — FG Stover 41
Giants— Pierce 10 pass from Da. Brown (Treadwell kick)
Cleve — FG Stover 23
Giants— FG Daluiso 25
Giants— FG Daluiso 30
Cleve — Hoard 5 run (Stover kick)
Giants— FG Daluiso 33

NEW ENGLAND 24, N.Y. JETS 13—at Foxboro Stadium, attendance 60,138. With both teams in the thick of the playoff chase, the surging Patriots won their fourth consecutive game and dealt the Jets a major setback. New England dominated the first half, though the game was tied at 10-10 after New York took advantage of 2 turnovers in Patriots' territory to score all of its points. And when the Jets took the second-half kickoff and marched 62 yards to Nick Lowery's 26-yard field goal, New England found itself trailing 13-10 6:17 into the third quarter. But the Patriots turned the game around after their next drive stalled at New York's 31-yard line. Punter Pat O'Neill, who also tries long field goals, lined up in field-goal formation, took a direct snap from center, and placed a punt that was downed by tackle Todd Rucci at the 1-yard line. Three plays later, Boomer Esiason's pass in the flat was intercepted by cornerback Ricky Reynolds, whose 11-yard interception return gave New England the lead for good. Leroy Thompson's 2-yard touchdown run with 3:43 remaining provided insurance. Jets wide receiver Art Monk caught 4 passes for 61 yards, including a 15-yard touchdown in the second quarter. The veteran equaled Steve Largent's NFL record of 177 consecutive games with at least 1 reception.

N.Y. Jets	0	10	3	0	—	13
New England	3	7	7	7	—	24

NE — FG Bahr 33
Jets — Monk 15 pass from Esiason (Lowery kick)
NE — Brisby 16 pass from Bledsoe (Bahr kick)
Jets — FG Lowery 46
Jets — FG Lowery 26
NE — Reynolds 11 interception return (Bahr kick)
NE — Thompson 2 run (Bahr kick)

PITTSBURGH 38, CINCINNATI 15—at Riverfront Stadium, attendance 59,997. Rookie Byron (Bam) Morris rushed for 108 yards and 2 touchdowns as the Steelers moved into sole possession of first place in the AFC Central and clinched at least a wild-card playoff berth by winning their fifth consecutive game. Morris ran 1 yard for a touchdown to open the scoring in the first quarter and had an 8-yard touchdown run late in the third period to help Pittsburgh build a 21-7 advantage. Ahead 24-7 early in the fourth quarter, the Steelers put the game out of reach when cornerback Rod Woodson returned an interception 27 yards for a touchdown. Pittsburgh quarterback Neil O'Donnell returned after missing two games with ankle and hip injuries and threw 2 touchdown passes while Morris was subbing for injured starter Barry Foster. But the Steelers primarily kept the ball on the ground, relying on Morris and John L. Williams (60 yards) to maintain possession for 40 of the game's 60 minutes. Bengals quarterback Jeff Blake, who entered the game as the AFC's top-rated passer, completed only 8 of 19 attempts for 156 yards, was intercepted twice, and sacked 5 times. Pittsburgh linebacker Kevin Greene had 2 of the sacks.

Pittsburgh	7	7	7	17	—	38
Cincinnati	7	0	0	8	—	15

Pitt — Morris 1 run (Anderson kick)
Cin — Pickens 7 pass from Blake (Pelfrey kick)
Pitt — Green 5 pass from O'Donnell (Anderson kick)
Pitt — Morris 8 run (Anderson kick)
Pitt — FG Anderson 41
Pitt — Woodson 27 interception return (Anderson kick)
Cin — Blake 5 run (Blake run)
Pitt — Hayes 3 pass from O'Donnell (Anderson kick)

TAMPA BAY 26, WASHINGTON 21—at Tampa Stadium, attendance 45,121. Rookie Errict Rhett rushed for 192 yards on 40 carries as the Buccaneers won back-to-back games for the first time since the opening games of the 1992 season. Rhett's running offset the big plays the Redskins used to take a 21-17 lead at halftime despite the Buccaneers maintaining possession for only 5:40 of the first two quarters. Washington linebacker Andre Collins returned an interception 92 yards for a touchdown on the game's fourth play, and quarterback Heath Shuler teamed with Desmond Howard (81 yards) and Olanda Truitt (77 yards) on touchdown bombs, the latter coming just 28 seconds before halftime. But trailing 21-20 with 2:57 to go in the game, Tampa Bay marched 80 yards in 11 plays to quarterback Craig Erickson's 1-yard sneak with 32 seconds to play. Rhett, who broke Buccaneers' rookie records for rushing yards in a game and a season, kept the winning drive alive by running 4 yards for a first down on third-and-1 from the Redskins' 39-yard line, then broke off a 23-yard run to the 12. Erickson had a 19-yard pass to Courtney Hawkins on the march and finished with 18 completions in 35 attempts for 251 yards. Shuler completed 13 of 25 attempts for 278 yards, but Washington managed little offense outside of the long passes. The Redskins had only 10 yards on 12 rushing attempts.

Washington	7	14	0	0	—	21
Tampa Bay	3	14	0	9	—	26

Wash — Collins 92 interception return (Lohmiller kick)
TB — FG Husted 53
TB — Rhett 2 run (Husted kick)
Wash — Howard 81 pass from Shuler (Lohmiller kick)
TB — McDowell 13 pass from Erickson (Husted kick)
Wash — Truitt 77 pass from Shuler (Lohmiller kick)
TB — FG Husted 22
TB — Erickson 1 run (pass failed)

SUNDAY NIGHT, DECEMBER 4

BUFFALO 42, MIAMI 31—at Joe Robbie Stadium, attendance 69,358. Jim Kelly threw 4 touchdown passes, 3 in the second half as the Bills rallied from a 10-point halftime deficit, to keep Buffalo's playoff hopes alive. The Bills, winners of the last four AFC titles, were in danger of falling below .500 and three games behind the Dolphins in the AFC East with three to play after Miami jumped to a 17-7 lead at the intermission, largely on the strength of 2 touchdown passes from Dan Marino to Irving Fryar. But Buffalo quickly turned the game around in the second half. Two plays into the third period, Kelly's long pass was tipped by two Dolphins' defenders into the hands of Don Beebe, who completed a 72-yard scoring play to trim the deficit to 17-14. Safety Matt Darby intercepted a pass on Miami's next possession, and it took the Bills nine plays to convert the turnover into the go-ahead touchdown, as Kelly teamed with Andre Reed on a 21-yard pass 6:51 into the second half. The lead grew to 28-17 when Buffalo drove 67 yards the next time it had the ball to Carwell Gardner's 1-yard touchdown run. Miami tried to come back, pulling within 28-23 on Marino's 23-yard touchdown pass to tight end Keith Jackson in the first minute of the fourth quarter, but the Bills got another break on the ensuing kickoff to help put the game away. Yonel Jordain fumbled the return, but teammate Mike Dumas grabbed the loose ball and returned it to the Dolphins' 28-yard line. Four plays later, Gardner scored again from the 1. Kelly, who added an 83-yard touchdown bomb to Reed with 6:20 to go, completed 18 of 28 passes for 299 yards. Marino was 25 of 42 for 311 yards but was intercepted 3 times. The game featured 850 yards on offense, including 460 by Miami.

Buffalo	7	0	21	14	—	42
Miami	0	17	0	14	—	31

Buff — Brooks 8 pass from Kelly (Christie kick)
Mia — Fryar 3 pass from Marino (Stoyanovich kick)
Mia — FG Stoyanovich 23
Mia — Fryar 45 pass from Marino (Stoyanovich kick)
Buff — Beebe 72 pass from Kelly (Christie kick)

Buff — Reed 21 pass from Kelly (Christie kick)
Buff — Gardner 1 run (Christie kick)
Mia — K. Jackson 23 pass from Marino (pass failed)
Buff — Gardner 1 run (Christie kick)
Buff — Reed 83 pass from Kelly (Christie kick)
Mia — S. Miller 1 pass from Kosar (Parmalee run)

MONDAY, DECEMBER 5

L.A. RAIDERS 24, SAN DIEGO 17—at San Diego Jack Murphy Stadium, attendance 63,012. The Raiders kept their playoff hopes alive and prevented the Chargers from clinching the AFC Western Division title when Jeff Hostetler broke a fourth-quarter tie by teaming with Raghib Ismail on a 6-yard touchdown pass with 7:23 remaining. Hostetler, who tossed a 76-yard touchdown bomb to Alexander Wright on Los Angeles's first play from scrimmage, completed 22 of 29 passes for 319 yards. Backup Vince Evans came on to complete a 6-yard touchdown pass to Ismail to give the Raiders a 14-7 lead when Hostetler injured his left hand running for a first down early in the second quarter. The Chargers also got a touchdown pass from their backup quarterback to tie the game at 14-14 seven seconds before halftime. Gale Gilbert completed all 3 of his pass attempts for 34 yards, including a 16-yard touchdown to Tony Martin, after Stan Humphries injured the thumb on his throwing hand. Humphries returned in the second half, but was not as effective, and finished with 17 completions in 33 attempts for 202 yards. Los Angeles amassed 410 total yards despite hampering itself with 17 penalties for 146 yards. San Diego, which entered the game ranked third in the NFL with an average of more than 125 rushing yards per game, managed only 47 rushing yards and 261 total yards.

L.A. Raiders	7	7	0	10	—	24
San Diego	7	7	0	3	—	17

Raid — Wright 76 pass from Hostetler (Jaeger kick)
SD — Jefferson 29 pass from Humphries (Carney kick)
Raid — Ismail 6 pass from Evans (Jaeger kick)
SD — Martin 16 pass from Gilbert (Carney kick)
Raid — FG Jaeger 43
SD — FG Carney 24
Raid — Ismail 6 pass from Hostetler (Jaeger kick)

FIFTEENTH WEEK SUMMARIES

AMERICAN FOOTBALL CONFERENCE

Eastern Division	W	L	T	Pct.	Pts.	OP
Miami	9	5	0	.643	356	297
New England	8	6	0	.571	297	292
Buffalo	7	7	0	.500	314	305
Indianapolis	6	8	0	.429	287	305
N.Y. Jets	6	8	0	.429	248	275
Central Division						
Pittsburgh	11	3	0	.786	265	190
Cleveland	10	4	0	.714	298	178
Cincinnati	2	12	0	.143	236	348
Houston	1	13	0	.071	193	311
Western Division						
San Diego	9	5	0	.643	323	266
L.A. Raiders	8	6	0	.571	277	292
Denver	7	7	0	.500	300	324
Kansas City	7	7	0	.500	269	280
Seattle	6	8	0	.429	262	271

NATIONAL FOOTBALL CONFERENCE

Eastern Division	W	L	T	Pct.	Pts.	OP
Dallas	11	3	0	.786	380	217
Arizona	7	7	0	.500	201	250
N.Y. Giants	7	7	0	.500	248	282
Philadelphia	7	7	0	.500	265	259
Washington	2	12	0	.143	282	374
Central Division						
Minnesota	9	5	0	.643	316	259
Chicago	8	6	0	.571	241	281
Detroit	8	6	0	.571	296	296
Green Bay	7	7	0	.500	327	251
Tampa Bay	5	9	0	.357	215	303
Western Division						
San Francisco	12	2	0	.857	449	256
Atlanta	6	8	0	.429	290	358
New Orleans	6	8	0	.429	302	355
L.A. Rams	4	10	0	.286	252	314

SATURDAY, DECEMBER 10

CLEVELAND 19, DALLAS 14—at Texas Stadium, attendance 64,286. Matt Stover kicked 4 field goals, and the Browns held on to win when safety Eric Turner tackled Cowboys tight end Jay Novacek inches short of the goal line on the game's final play. Stover's fourth field goal, from 32 yards with 1:49 to play, gave Cleveland a five-point advantage. But Dallas's Kevin Williams returned the ensuing kickoff 42 yards to set up the Cowboys' last-ditch drive. Quarterback Troy Aikman, working without any timeouts, completed passes of 19 and 14 yards to Michael Irvin and 15 yards to Williams to move the ball to the Browns' 6-yard line with 10 seconds left. From there, he completed a pass near the goal line to Novacek, who tried to make his way to the end zone but was hit by Turner and time ran out. Aikman, playing for the first time after missing two weeks with a sprained knee, completed 21 of 36 passes for 188 yards but was intercepted twice and lost a fumble that led to the final field goal. Emmitt Smith rushed for 11 yards and a touchdown and also caught a touchdown pass. Cleveland's Leroy Hoard rushed for 99 yards. Coupled with Sunday's results, the victory clinched at least a wild-card playoff berth for the Browns.

Cleveland	7	3	0	9	—	19
Dallas	7	0	0	7	—	14

Dall — E. Smith 7 pass from Aikman (Boniol kick)
Cleve — Jackson 2 pass from Testaverde (Stover kick)
Cleve — FG Stover 34
Cleve — FG Stover 32
Cleve — FG Stover 43
Dall — E. Smith 4 run (Boniol kick)
Cleve — FG Stover 32

DETROIT 18, N.Y. JETS 7—at Giants Stadium, attendance 56,080. Barry Sanders rushed for 127 yards as the Lions dealt the Jets their third consecutive defeat. Sanders, who carried 23 times, also caught a 5-yard touchdown pass in the second quarter, and Jason Hanson's 4 field goals provided the rest of Detroit's points. New York never led and rarely threatened to score while managing only 261 total yards. Much of that came on an 80-yard drive late in the first half that led to the Jets' lone touchdown. Brad Baxter capped the 15-play march with a 1-yard touchdown run on fourth-and-goal 20 seconds before intermission. That trimmed New York's deficit to only 9-7 at halftime, but Hanson kept the Jets at bay with 3 field goals in the second half, including lengthy kicks of 49 and 48 yards. New York's Art Monk caught a 5-yard pass from Boomer Esiason on the game's first play. That gave the Jets' wide receiver a reception in an NFL-record 178th consecutive game.

Detroit	3	6	3	6	—	18
N.Y. Jets	0	7	0	0	—	7

Det — FG Hanson 37
Det — Sanders 5 pass from Krieg (kick blocked)
Jets — B. Baxter 1 run (Lowery kick)
Det — FG Hanson 49
Det — FG Hanson 48
Det — FG Hanson 23

SUNDAY, DECEMBER 11

GREEN BAY 40, CHICAGO 3—at Lambeau Field, attendance 57,927. Brett Favre threw 3 touchdown passes and the Packers snapped a three-game losing streak by routing the Bears. Chicago marched 92 yards to a field goal the first time it had the ball, then managed only 84 yards the rest of the game. Green Bay, meanwhile, amassed 516 total yards, including a season-high 257 on the ground. Favre completed 19 of 31 pass attempts for 250 yards. His 12-yard touchdown pass to Robert Brooks late in the first quarter put the Packers ahead for good, and 2 touchdown passes to Sterling Sharpe helped break open the game. Sharpe caught 7 passes for 86 yards, while Brooks added 6 receptions for 105 yards. Edgar Bennett rushed for 106 yards on 22 carries. It was his third career 100-yard game, all against the Bears. Chris Jacke kicked 4 field goals.

Chicago	3	0	0	0	—	3
Green Bay	7	17	10	6	—	40

Chi — FG Butler 25
GB — Brooks 12 pass from Favre (Jacke kick)
GB — FG Jacke 39
GB — Bennett 4 run (Jacke kick)
GB — Sharpe 13 pass from Favre (Jacke kick)
GB — Sharpe 22 pass from Favre (Jacke kick)
GB — FG Jacke 24
GB — FG Jacke 20
GB — FG Jacke 29

N.Y. GIANTS 27, CINCINNATI 20—at Giants Stadium, attendance 67,530. Rodney Hampton's 3-yard touchdown run with 40 seconds left gave the Giants the victory. After winning its first three games, and losing the next seven, New York won its fourth in a row to climb back to .500 and remain in the playoff hunt. The Bengals trailed 20-10 in the fourth quarter, then rallied to tie on Jeff Blake's 3-yard touchdown pass to Carl Pickens and Doug Pelfrey's 23-yard field goal with 1:47 left in the game. But the Giants marched 66 yards in only four plays to win the game. Dave Brown passed for 222 yards for New York.

Cincinnati	0	7	3	10	—	20
N.Y. Giants	0	17	3	7	—	27

Giants— Hampton 1 run (Daluiso kick)
Giants— FG Daluiso 52
Cin — Pickens 5 pass from Blake (Pelfrey kick)
Giants— Cross 8 pass from Da. Brown (Daluiso kick)
Cin — FG Pelfrey 38
Giants— FG Daluiso 33
Cin — Pickens 3 pass from Blake (Pelfrey kick)
Cin — FG Pelfrey 23
Giants— Hampton 3 run (Daluiso kick)

L.A. RAIDERS 23, DENVER 13—at Los Angeles Memorial Coliseum, attendance 60,016. Jeff Hostetler threw a touchdown pass and Jeff Jaeger kicked 5 field goals to lead the Raiders past the Broncos. Four of Jaeger's field goals staked Los Angeles to a 12-6 lead midway through the fourth quarter. Tim Brown then returned a punt 29 yards to set up a 17-yard drive to the Raiders' lone touchdown, which came on Hostetler's 5-yard pass to Harvey Williams with 5:59 to go in the game. Williams's two-point conversion run and another field goal by Jaeger with 2:21 to go put the game out of reach. Denver, playing without injured quarterback John Elway, got an effective performance from backup Hugh Millen, who completed 20 of 33 passes for 242 yards and a touchdown. But the Broncos were stymied by a pair of lost fumbles and two first-and-goal situations at Los Angeles's 1-yard line that only produced field goals. Defensive end Shane Dronett had 3 of Denver's 5 sacks of Hostetler. The Raiders beat the Broncos for the tenth time in their last 11 meetings.

Denver	0	3	3	7	—	13
L.A. Raiders	0	6	3	14	—	23

Raid — FG Jaeger 44
Raid — FG Jaeger 29
Den — FG Elam 20
Raid — FG Jaeger 47
Den — FG Elam 21
Raid — FG Jaeger 30
Raid — H. Williams 5 pass from Hostetler (H. Williams run)
Raid — FG Jaeger 28
Den — Tillman 1 pass from Millen (Elam kick)

NEW ENGLAND 28, INDIANAPOLIS 13—at Foxboro Stadium, attendance 57,656. Drew Bledsoe threw 2 touchdown passes and Leroy Thompson scored 2 touchdowns to lead the Patriots to their fifth consecutive victory. To win, New England had to overcome 5 turnovers and a 10-0 second-quarter deficit. Colts cornerback Ray Buchanan helped give his team that advantage when he returned an intercepted pass 90 yards for a touchdown 2:48 before halftime. But the Patriots rallied behind Bledsoe, whose 9-yard touchdown pass to Thompson capped a 78-yard drive that pulled New England within 10-7 42 seconds before halftime. In the third quarter, the Patriots went to a No-Huddle offense to take advantage of a strong wind, and Bledsoe put his team ahead for good with a 6-yard touchdown pass to tight end Ben Coates with 4:21 to go in the period. New England recovered a fumble on Indianapolis's 18-yard line on the ensuing kickoff, and seven plays later Marion Butts scored from the 1 to make it 21-10. Safety Harlon Barnett's interception and 21-yard return set up Thompson's game-clinching 6-yard touchdown run with 1:54 left in the game. Bledsoe completed 25 of 45 passes for 277 yards despite 4 interceptions. Indianapolis struggled on offense, managing only 212 total yards. Buchanan intercepted 2 passes for 113 yards for the Colts.

Indianapolis	0	10	0	3	—	13
New England	0	7	14	7	—	28

Ind — FG Biasucci 27
Ind — Buchanan 90 interception return (Biasucci kick)
NE — Thompson 9 pass from Bledsoe (Bahr kick)
NE — Coates 6 pass from Bledsoe (Bahr kick)
NE — Butts 1 run (Bahr kick)
Ind — FG Biasucci 47

NE — Thompson 6 run (Bahr kick)

TAMPA BAY 24, L.A. RAMS 14—at Tampa Stadium, attendance 34,150. Backup wide receiver Charles Wilson caught 4 passes for 176 yards and 2 touchdowns as the Buccaneers won three consecutive games in the same season for the first time since 1982. Wilson, in the game because Courtney Hawkins sprained a ligament in his knee in the first quarter, gave Tampa Bay a 10-0 lead with a 71-yard touchdown catch in the second quarter. His 44-yard touchdown catch clinched the victory with 1:34 to go in the game. He also had a 53-yard reception to set up a field goal. Buccaneers quarterback Craig Erickson completed only 10 of 22 passes, but the big plays to Wilson accounted for most of his 231 yards. Meanwhile, Errict Rhett was effective running the ball, gaining 119 yards on 31 carries. It was the rookie's fourth 100-yard rushing outing in the last five games. Tampa Bay's defense shut down the Rams' rushing attack, limiting Jerome Bettis to 23 yards on 13 carries. Chris Chandler passed for 199 yards and 2 touchdowns.

L.A. Rams	0	7	0	7	—	14
Tampa Bay	0	17	0	7	—	24

TB — FG Husted 20
TB — Wilson 71 pass from Erickson (Husted kick)
Rams — Drayton 22 pass from Chandler (Zendejas kick)
TB — Rhett 8 run (Husted kick)
Rams — Hester 12 pass from Chandler (Zendejas kick)
TB — Wilson 44 pass from Erickson (Husted kick)

MINNESOTA 21, BUFFALO 17—at Rich Stadium, attendance 66,501. The Vikings moved into first place in the NFC Central Division by rallying to beat the Bills. Jim Kelly's 2 touchdown passes helped stake Buffalo to a 17-9 lead early in the third quarter. Minnesota linebacker Jack Del Rio's interception led to a 74-yard drive that culminated in Terry Allen's 1-yard run for an 18-17 lead with 9:44 left in the game after Fuad Reveiz kicked a 25-yard field goal to trim the deficit to 17-12. Reveiz's club record-tying fifth field goal of the game, from 22 yards with 2:38 to go, increased the advantage to four points, and the Vikings held on to send the four-time AFC champions to the brink of playoff extinction. The defeat was particularly costly for the Bills, however, because Kelly sprained his knee with a minute remaining in the game and was expected to miss the final two games of the season. Vikings quarterback Warren Moon completed 21 of 34 passes for 261 yards. Wide receiver Cris Carter caught 9 passes for 111 yards and increased his season total to 111 receptions, just 1 short of the league record the Packers' Sterling Sharpe established in 1994.

Minnesota	3	6	3	9	—	21
Buffalo	7	3	7	0	—	17

Minn — FG Reveiz 30
Buff — Metzelaars 35 pass from Kelly (Christie kick)
Buff — FG Christie 41
Minn — FG Reveiz 38
Minn — FG Reveiz 30
Buff — Beebe 9 pass from Kelly (Christie kick)
Minn — FG Reveiz 25
Minn — Allen 1 run (pass failed)
Minn — FG Reveiz 22

PITTSBURGH 14, PHILADELPHIA 3—at Three Rivers Stadium, attendance 55,474. The Steelers won their sixth consecutive game by scoring touchdowns 1:48 apart in the fourth quarter and limiting the Eagles to 105 total yards. Philadelphia, which dropped its fifth game in a row after winning seven of its first nine, managed only 9 first downs and netted just 34 passing yards. Still, the Eagles, who scored after Herschel Walker's 58-yard return of the game's opening kickoff set up Eddie Murray's 21-yard field goal 3:46 into the game, took a 3-0 lead into the fourth quarter. But Pittsburgh quarterback Neil O'Donnell kept alive an 83-yard touchdown drive with a 27-yard completion to Andre Hastings on third-and-16, and capped the march by teaming with Hastings on an 18-yard touchdown pass with 10:04 to go in the game. Moments later, safety Darren Perry intercepted Cunningham's pass and returned it 37 yards to Philadelphia's 18, setting up John L. Williams's 3-yard touchdown run.

Philadelphia	3	0	0	0	—	3
Pittsburgh	0	0	0	14	—	14

Phil — FG Murray 21
Pitt — Hastings 18 pass from O'Donnell (Anderson kick)
Pitt — J. Williams 3 run (Anderson kick)

SAN FRANCISCO 38, SAN DIEGO 15—at San Diego Jack Murphy Stadium, attendance 62,105. Steve Young threw 2 touchdown passes to lead the 49ers to their ninth consecutive victory. The Chargers, meanwhile, missed a chance for the second consecutive week to clinch the AFC West title and lost for the fifth time in eight games since a 6-0 start. Young, who completed 25 of 32 passes for 304 yards, threw touchdown passes of 10 yards to tight end Brent Jones and 4 yards to wide receiver John Taylor as the 49ers built a 21-0 lead in the second quarter and never looked back. Cornerback Deion Sanders's 90-yard interception return for a touchdown in the final minute was the exclamation point to the rout. Jerry Rice caught 12 passes for 144 yards for the 49ers and became only the third player in NFL history to accumulate more than 13,000 receiving yards in his career. Tony Martin caught 9 passes for 172 yards for San Diego. Quarterback Stan Humphries completed 25 of 43 passes for 337 yards, most of it as the Chargers tried to play catch up in the second half.

San Francisco	7	14	3	14	—	38
San Diego	0	3	6	6	—	15

SF — Jones 10 pass from Young (Brien kick)
SF — Taylor 4 pass from Young (Brien kick)
SF — Watters 4 run (Brien kick)
SD — FG Carney 50
SD — Means 12 run (run failed)
SF — FG Brien 22
SF — Floyd 1 run (Brien kick)
SD — Martin 2 pass from Humphries (run failed)
SF — Sanders 90 interception return (Brien kick)

SEATTLE 16, HOUSTON 14—at Astrodome, attendance 31,453. Chris Warren rushed for a career-high 185 yards and the Seahawks withstood the Oilers' late charge to hand Houston its tenth consecutive defeat. Warren carried 30 times before sitting out the final 10 minutes of the game with ribs sore from the fractures he suffered in a car accident 10 days earlier. His 33-yard touchdown run in the second quarter helped stake Seattle to a 16-0 lead in the fourth quarter. But the Oilers' slumbering offense, last in the NFL in points scored, produced a 69-yard touchdown drive that culminated in Billy Joe Tolliver's 36-yard pass to Webster Slaughter with 4:23 remaining in the game. Tolliver's subsequent two-point conversion pass to Haywood Jeffires pulled Houston within 16-8. Ninety seconds later, the Oilers trimmed the deficit to two points when Ernest Givins returned a punt 78 yards for a touchdown. Houston was denied a tie on the conversion when safety Rolando Blackmon tackled running back Todd McNair on the 1-yard line after McNair caught a pass from Tolliver in the flat. Still, the Oilers had another chance after recovering the ensuing onside kick, only to have their hopes dashed by a sack and a penalty. Seahawks quarterback Dan McGwire, making his first start in two years because of the season-ending thumb injury suffered by Rick Mirer a week earlier, completed only 8 of 17 passes for 95 yards, but was supported by a running game that accounted for 266 yards and a defense that limited Houston to 208 total yards.

Seattle	3	7	6	0	—	16
Houston	0	0	0	14	—	14

Sea — FG Kasay 40
Sea — C. Warren 33 run (Kasay kick)
Sea — Strong 13 run (kick blocked)
Hou — Slaughter 36 pass from Tolliver (Jeffires pass from Tolliver)
Hou — Givins 78 punt return (pass failed)

ARIZONA 17, WASHINGTON 15—at Sun Devil Stadium, attendance 53,790. Greg Davis's 27-yard field goal as time expired kept the Cardinals' playoff hopes alive. It was the second time in 1994 that Arizona had beaten the Redskins with a field goal on the final play. Two months earlier, Arizona won 19-16 in overtime when Todd Peterson kicked a 29-yard field goal. The winning drive in this game was kept alive when the Cardinals gambled on fourth-and-1 from the Redskins' 35-yard line, going for the first down instead of attempting a 52-yard field goal. Running back Garrison Hearst took a short pass from Jay Schroeder and turned it into a 29-yard gain, and two plays later Davis converted his winning kick. Washington, which lost its sixth in a row, managed 406 total yards against the NFL's top-rated defense and used a 52-yard touchdown pass from Heath Shuler to Henry Ellard and Chip Lohmiller's 21-yard field goal with 2:54 remaining to take a 15-14 lead. Schroeder's 12-yard completion to Ricky Proehl and the pass to Hearst made up most of the 61 yards on Arizona's 10-play field-goal drive. Schroeder passed for 216 yards in all, and had a 48-yard touchdown strike to Proehl in the first quarter. Shuler threw for 286 yards for the Redskins. With the victory, the Cardinals moved into a three-way tie for second place in the NFC East.

Washington	3	3	0	9	—	15
Arizona	7	0	0	10	—	17

Ariz — Proehl 48 pass from Schroeder (Davis kick)
Wash — FG Lohmiller 34
Wash — FG Lohmiller 31
Ariz — Moore 1 run (Davis kick)
Wash — Ellard 52 pass from Shuler (run failed)
Wash — FG Lohmiller 21
Ariz — FG Davis 27

SUNDAY NIGHT, DECEMBER 11

NEW ORLEANS 29, ATLANTA 20—at Georgia Dome, attendance 61,307. Jim Everett threw 2 touchdown passes and Morten Andersen kicked 5 field goals to pace the Saints to the victory. Everett, who completed 18 of 31 passes for 273 yards, teamed with Michael Haynes on a 78-yard touchdown in the second quarter and tossed a 5-yard touchdown pass to Quinn Early in the fourth period. The latter gave New Orleans a 26-17 advantage with 3:58 to go in the game. Falcons quarterback Jeff George completed 25 of 42 passes for 284 yards. He was 10 of 10 in the first half, and his 1-yard touchdown pass to Andre Rison helped Atlanta to a 14-13 lead at the intermission. Andersen's fourth field goal, from 34 yards 3:49 into the fourth quarter, put the Saints ahead for good.

New Orleans	3	10	3	13	—	29
Atlanta	0	14	3	3	—	20

NO — FG Andersen 45
Atl — Heyward 9 run (Johnson kick)
NO — Haynes 78 pass from Everett (Andersen kick)
Atl — Rison 1 pass from George (Johnson kick)
NO — FG Andersen 33
NO — FG Andersen 31
Atl — FG Johnson 42
NO — FG Andersen 34
NO — Early 5 pass from Everett (Andersen kick)
Atl — FG Johnson 21
NO — FG Andersen 35

MONDAY, DECEMBER 12

MIAMI 45, KANSAS CITY 28—at Joe Robbie Stadium, attendance 71,578. Dan Marino threw 2 touchdown passes and ran for another as the Dolphins remained atop the AFC East and clinched at least a wild-card playoff berth. Marino completed 21 of 30 passes for 241 yards and kept Miami even at 14-14 at halftime by throwing touchdown passes to running back Bernie Parmalee (10 yards) and wide receiver Irving Fryar (4 yards). The Dolphins then broke the game open by scoring 3 touchdowns in a span of 5:21 late in the third quarter. Marino began the spurt with a 4-yard touchdown run 9:03 into the second half. Barely two minutes later, Miami safety Gene Atkins intercepted Steve Bono's pass at the Dolphins' 24, returned it 18 yards to the 42, and then lateraled to teammate Troy Vincent, who covered the remaining 58 yards for a touchdown and a 28-14 lead. Jon Vaughn returned the ensuing kickoff 91 yards for a touchdown to keep the Chiefs close, but Parmalee ended the wild stretch with a 47-yard touchdown run 36 seconds before the end of the third quarter to give Miami a 35-21 advantage. Parmalee finished with 127 yards on 19 carries, while Marino passed for 241 yards. Steve Bono completed 33 of 55 passes for 314 yards for Kansas City, but suffered 3 interceptions. J.J. Birden caught 10 passes for 131 yards.

Kansas City	7	7	7	7	—	28
Miami	0	14	21	10	—	45

KC — Birden 22 pass from Bono (Elliott kick)
Mia — Parmalee 10 pass from Marino (Stoyanovich kick)
KC — Allen 3 run (Elliott kick)
Mia — Fryar 4 pass from Marino (Stoyanovich kick)
Mia — Marino 4 run (Stoyanovich kick)
Mia — Vincent 58 lateral from Atkins (Stoyanovich kick)
KC — Vaughn 91 kickoff return (Elliott kick)
Mia — Parmalee 47 run (Stoyanovich kick)
Mia — FG Stoyanovich 21

KC — Davis 15 pass from Bono (Elliott kick)
Mia — Spikes 1 run (Stoyanovich kick)

SIXTEENTH WEEK SUMMARIES

AMERICAN FOOTBALL CONFERENCE

Eastern Division	W	L	T	Pct.	Pts.	OP
Miami	9	6	0	.600	362	307
New England	9	6	0	.600	338	309
Buffalo	7	8	0	.467	331	346
Indianapolis	7	8	0	.467	297	311
N.Y. Jets	6	9	0	.400	254	296
Central Division						
Pittsburgh	12	3	0	.800	282	197
Cleveland	10	5	0	.667	305	195
Cincinnati	2	13	0	.133	243	376
Houston	1	14	0	.067	202	342
Western Division						
San Diego	10	5	0	.667	344	272
L.A. Raiders	9	6	0	.600	294	308
Kansas City	8	7	0	.533	300	289
Denver	7	8	0	.467	319	366
Seattle	6	9	0	.400	278	288

NATIONAL FOOTBALL CONFERENCE

Eastern Division	W	L	T	Pct.	Pts.	OP
Dallas	12	3	0	.786	380	217
Arizona	8	7	0	.533	229	257
N.Y. Giants	8	7	0	.533	264	295
Philadelphia	7	8	0	.467	278	275
Washington	2	13	0	.133	296	391
Central Division						
Chicago	9	6	0	.600	268	294
Detroit	9	6	0	.600	337	315
Minnesota	9	6	0	.600	335	300
Green Bay	8	7	0	.533	348	268
Tampa Bay	6	9	0	.400	232	317
Western Division						
San Francisco	13	2	0	.867	491	275
New Orleans	6	9	0	.429	302	355
Atlanta	6	9	0	.400	307	379
L.A. Rams	4	11	0	.267	265	341

SATURDAY, DECEMBER 17

SAN FRANCISCO 42, DENVER 19—at Candlestick Park, attendance 64,884. The 49ers clinched home-field advantage throughout the NFC playoffs by crushing the Broncos. San Francisco was in command from start to finish, jumping to a 7-0 first-quarter lead on Steve Young's 12-yard touchdown pass to Ricky Watters. Twenty-two seconds later, after a fumble recovery, Young found Jerry Rice for a 23-yard touchdown pass and a 14-0 49ers lead. William Floyd ran for 2 second-quarter touchdowns as the 49ers went up 28-6 at intermission. Watters added 2 more touchdowns in the third period, including a 65-yard touchdown catch from Young that concluded the scoring. Young was 20 of 29 for 350 yards. Rice had 9 catches for 121 yards and Watters had 4 receptions for 106 yards. The 49ers' defense recorded 7 sacks, including 6 of John Elway.

Denver	0	6	13	0	—	19
San Francisco	14	14	14	0	—	42

SF — Watters 12 pass from Young (Brien kick)
SF — Rice 23 pass from Young (Brien kick)
SF — Floyd 11 run (Brien kick)
Den — FG Elam 28
SF — Floyd 1 run (Brien kick)
Den — FG Elam 45
Den — Milburn 11 run (Elam kick)
SF — Watters 9 run (Brien kick)
Den — Clark 1 run (run failed)
SF — Watters 65 pass from Young (Brien kick)

DETROIT 41, MINNESOTA 19—at Pontiac Silverdome, attendance 73,881. The Lions blasted the Vikings to win their fourth straight game and position themselves for a playoff berth. Mel Gray got Detroit going with a 98-yard kickoff return for a touchdown that broke a 3-3 first-quarter deadlock. Detroit took the lead for good on Dave Krieg's 18-yard scoring strike to rookie Johnnie Morton after the Vikings tied the game on Warren Moon's 20-yard touchdown pass to Jake Reed. The third quarter belonged to Barry Sanders, who had touchdown runs of 18 and 64 yards to increase the Lions' advantage to 34-19. Krieg capped the Lions' day with a 4-yard touchdown pass to former Vikings player Anthony Carter in the fourth period. Sanders gained 110 yards on 17 carries. Krieg completed 15 of 20 passes for 180 yards with no interceptions, giving him 13 touchdowns and only 1 interception since he became Detroit's starter in the ninth game. Gray's touchdown was his ninth, tying Ollie Matson's NFL mark for most career touchdowns on returns. Moon completed 15 of 22 passes for 186 yards before leaving with a knee injury in the third quarter.

Minnesota	3	10	6	0	—	19
Detroit	10	10	14	7	—	41

Det — FG Hanson 39
Minn — FG Reveiz 34
Det — Gray 98 kickoff return (Hanson kick)
Minn — Reed 20 pass from Moon (Reveiz kick)
Det — FG Hanson 41
Det — Morton 18 pass from Krieg (Hanson kick)
Minn — FG Reveiz 26
Det — Sanders 18 run (Hanson kick)
Minn — FG Reveiz 37
Minn — FG Reveiz 48
Det — Sanders 64 run (Hanson kick)
Det — A. Carter 4 pass from Krieg (Hanson kick)

SUNDAY, DECEMBER 18

GREEN BAY 21, ATLANTA 17—at Milwaukee County Stadium, attendance 54,885. Brett Favre's 9-yard touchdown run with 14 seconds remaining lifted the Packers over the Falcons and preserved Green Bay's playoff hopes. Favre's arm provided Green Bay's first 2 scores, on touchdown passes of 8 (to Sterling Sharpe) and 15 yards (to Anthony Morgan), which gave the Packers a 14-3 first-quarter lead. Atlanta closed to 14-9 by halftime, then drove 76 yards to take the lead on Bobby Hebert's 5-yard touchdown pass to Terance Mathis with 5:53 left in the game. Trailing 17-14, the Packers' last possession began at their 33 with 1:58 remaining. Favre's passing moved Green Bay to the Falcons' 9 with 21 seconds left. In position for a tying field goal, and with no timeouts left, it was essential that the Packers not be tackled in bounds. On third-and-2, Favre scrambled right and appeared to be headed for the sideline. But at the last instant he turned upfield and dived into the end zone for the winning score. Favre completed 29 of 44 passes for 321 yards. Hebert, who relieved an injured Jeff George in the first quarter, completed 20 of 41 passes for 221 yards.

Atlanta	3	6	0	8	—	17
Green Bay	14	0	0	7	—	21

GB — Sharpe 8 pass from Favre (Jacke kick)
Atl — FG Johnson 20
GB — Morgan 15 pass from Favre (Jacke kick)
Atl — Heyward 2 run (pass failed)
Atl — Mathis 5 pass from Hebert (Rison pass from Hebert)
GB — Favre 9 run (Jacke kick)

ARIZONA 28, CINCINNATI 7—at Sun Devil Stadium, attendance 50,110. The Cardinals dominated play on both sides of the football to defeat the Bengals. Arizona amassed 375 total yards while controlling the football for 41 minutes 31 seconds. Meanwhile, the Cardinals' defense limited the Bengals to 189 total yards while posting 4 sacks and forcing 3 turnovers. Garrison Hearst ran for a touchdown, then threw a 10-yard scoring pass to Larry Centers on a halfback option play to give Arizona a 14-0 first-quarter lead. Jay Schroeder made it 21-0 in the second quarter with a 15-yard touchdown pass to Ricky Proehl. Centers applied the finishing touches with a 10-yard touchdown run in the final period after the Bengals scored their only points in the third quarter. Hearst had 62 yards on 13 carries. Schroeder, who sat out the second half with a sore right knee, was 12 of 20 for 122 yards. Gary Clark led Arizona with 7 catches for 101 yards.

Cincinnati	0	0	7	0	—	7
Arizona	14	7	0	7	—	28

Ariz — Hearst 1 run (Davis kick)
Ariz — Centers 10 pass from Hearst (Davis kick)
Ariz — Proehl 15 pass from Schroeder (Davis kick)
Cin — Pickens 4 pass from Blake (Pelfrey kick)
Ariz — Centers 10 run (Davis kick)

PITTSBURGH 17, CLEVELAND 7—at Three Rivers Stadium, attendance 60,808. The Steelers, energized by a club-record crowd, swamped the Browns to secure the AFC Central title and home-field advantage throughout the AFC playoffs. Pittsburgh raced to an early lead, taking the opening kickoff and—helped by a Browns' penalty on fourth down—driving 69 yards to score on Neil O'Donnell's 40-yard touchdown pass to Yancey Thigpen. The Steelers went 84 yards on their next possession, with O'Donnell hitting passes of 42 and 17 yards to set up Barry Foster's 1-yard touchdown run and a 14-0 lead. The Browns then made three successive trips into Steelers' territory, only to be stopped twice on downs and once by an interception. Cleveland finally broke through in the second quarter on Vinny Testaverde's 14-yard touchdown pass to Mark Carrier. The Browns mounted just one more scoring threat after that (and that ended with a fourth-down incompletion at the Steelers' 2 in the final minute of the game), while Gary Anderson kicked a 49-yard field goal to give Pittsburgh a 10-point cushion with 9:50 remaining. Cleveland outgained Pittsburgh 331 to 278, but the Browns wilted in the face of unrelenting pressure from the Steelers' top-ranked defense, committing 3 turnovers and 10 penalties. The Steelers' Barry Foster gained 106 yards on 32 carries.

Cleveland	0	7	0	0	—	7
Pittsburgh	14	0	0	3	—	17

Pitt — Thigpen 40 pass from O'Donnell (Anderson kick)
Pitt — Foster 1 run (Anderson kick)
Cleve — Carrier 14 pass from Testaverde (Stover kick)
Pitt — FG Anderson 49

KANSAS CITY 31, HOUSTON 9—at Arrowhead Stadium, attendance 74,474. Joe Montana returned to the lineup to lead the Chiefs to victory and keep their playoff hopes alive. Montana, sidelined for two weeks with a foot injury, went right to work, hitting tight end Derrick Walker for a 10-yard touchdown pass in the first quarter. The score was set up by a fumble recovery. In the third period, Montana hit Lake Dawson for a 25-yard touchdown pass and Donnell Bennett ran 12 yards for a score to increase the Chiefs' lead to 21-3. Montana completed 16 of 27 passes for 235 yards, and Dawson caught 5 passes for 101 yards. Houston managed just 223 total yards and turned the ball over 5 times, including 4 lost fumbles.

Houston	3	0	0	6	—	9
Kansas City	7	0	14	10	—	31

KC — Walker 10 pass from Montana (Elliott kick)
Hou — FG Del Greco 48
KC — Dawson 25 pass from Montana (Elliott kick)
KC — Bennett 12 run (Elliott kick)
Hou — Jeffires 20 pass from Tolliver (pass failed)
KC — FG Elliott 21
KC — Hill 8 run (Elliott kick)

CHICAGO 27, L.A. RAMS 13—at Soldier Field, attendance 56,276. The Bears ran for 163 yards while their defense shut down the Rams' running attack in Chicago's victory. The Bears' run defense, coming off a game in which they allowed 247 rushing yards to Green Bay, held Los Angeles to 37 yards on 19 attempts. A hard-fought first half ended with Chicago leading 17-10, thanks to a 3-yard scoring pass from Steve Walsh to Keith Jennings and a 2-yard touchdown run by Raymont Harris. The Bears upped their lead to 10 points in the third quarter on Kevin Butler's 30-yard field goal, which was set up by a fumble recovery, then clinched the victory with 3:36 left in the game on Lewis Tillman's 1-yard scoring run. Walsh completed 12 of 25 passes for 135 yards, keeping several scoring drives alive with key third-down completions. Harris ran for 92 yards on 23 carries, and Tillman gained 69 yards on 14 carries.

L.A. Rams	7	3	0	3	—	13
Chicago	3	14	3	7	—	27

Rams — Chandler 1 run (Zendejas kick)
Chi — FG Butler 41
Rams — FG Zendejas 18
Chi — Jennings 3 pass from Walsh (Butler kick)
Chi — Harris 2 run (Butler kick)
Chi — FG Butler 30
Rams — FG Zendejas 21
Chi — Tillman 1 run (Butler kick)

INDIANAPOLIS 10, MIAMI 6—at RCA Dome, attendance 58,867. The Colts twice turned the Dolphins away inside the 10 to defeat Miami. The lone touchdown of the game came in the first quarter on a 75-yard punt return by Dewell Brewer that gave Indianapolis a 7-3 lead. Miami made a bid to take the lead at halftime, but Irving Fryar was tackled at the Colts' 2 as time expired in the first half. Pete Stoyanovich's second field goal pulled the Dolphins close at 7-6, but Dean Biasucci's 19-yard field goal with 8:10 remaining in the game gave the Colts a four-point advantage. Miami's Dan Marino then completed 4 passes to drive the Dolphins to the Colts' 4. Two runs by Bernie Parmalee gave the Dolphins a first down at the 2, but they advanced no farther. Parmalee was stopped on first down for no gain, and then Marino threw three straight incompletions. Marino's passes on third and fourth down were broken up by Colts defensive back Ashley Ambrose. Indianapolis then ran out the final 2:47 of the game.

Miami	3	0	3	0	—	6
Indianapolis	7	0	0	3	—	10

Mia — FG Stoyanovich 33
Ind — Brewer 75 punt return (Biasucci kick)
Mia — FG Stoyanovich 19
Ind — FG Biasucci 19

NEW ENGLAND 41, BUFFALO 17—at Rich Stadium, attendance 56,784. Drew Bledsoe passed for 3 touchdowns and the Patriots forced 5 turnovers to rout the Bills. The game represented a changing of the guard: The young Patriots won their sixth in a row as they closed in on their first playoff berth since 1986, while with the loss, the four-time defending AFC champion Bills were assured of missing the playoffs for the first time since 1987. Buffalo led early, taking a 17-3 lead two minutes into the second quarter. That was it for the Bills, however, as the Patriots reeled off 38 straight points. Bledsoe's touchdown passes to Ben Coates (4 yards) and Vincent Brisby (7 yards) tied the game at halftime. Buffalo lost its grasp on the ball and the game in the second half. On the opening drive, running back Carwell Gardner fumbled, and the Patriots' Ricky Reynolds picked up the loose ball and raced 25 yards for a score. Later in the third quarter, Buffalo's Andre Reed fumbled, and the Patriots drove 47 yards to take a 31-17 lead on Bledsoe's 6-yard touchdown throw to Brisby. Another fumble by Reed and Myron Guyton's 26-yard return set up the Patriots' last touchdown on a 1-yard run by Marion Butts. Bledsoe completed 22 of 31 passes for 276 yards, with no interceptions. Frank Reich, starting in place of an injured Jim Kelly, was 19 of 29 for 207 yards.

New England	3	14	14	10	—	41
Buffalo	10	7	0	0	—	17

NE — FG Bahr 33
Buff — Turner 26 pass from Reich (Christie kick)
Buff — FG Christie 24
Buff — Gardner 3 run (Christie kick)
NE — Coates 4 pass from Bledsoe (Bahr kick)
NE — Brisby 7 pass from Bledsoe (Bahr kick)
NE — Reynolds 25 fumble return (Bahr kick)
NE — Brisby 6 pass from Bledsoe (Bahr kick)
NE — Butts 1 run (Bahr kick)
NE — FG Bahr 20

N.Y. GIANTS 16, PHILADELPHIA 13—at Veterans Stadium, attendance 64,540. The Giants converted 2 turnovers into 10 points in the final four minutes to defeat the Eagles. Philadelphia took a 7-0 lead on Bubby Brister's 27-yard touchdown pass to Mark Bavaro late in the first quarter. The teams traded field goals after that, with the Giants pulling within a touchdown at 13-6 on Brad Daluiso's 19-yard kick late in the third period. The Eagles had the ball with eight minutes to play, but Giants rookie Thomas Randolph intercepted Brister at the Eagles' 44 with 7:36 remaining. Passes of 12 and 14 yards by Dave Brown set up the tying touchdown on David Meggett's 5-yard run with 3:54 to play. On the ensuing kickoff, Eagles return man Jeff Sydner fumbled after colliding with one of his blockers, and the Giants recovered at Philadelphia's 36. That turnover set up Daluiso for the winning field goal from 18 yards out with 54 seconds left. The Eagles had one last chance, driving to the Giants' 27, but Eddie Murray's 44-yard field-goal attempt was wide left. Brown completed 18 of 27 passes for 264 yards to lead New York to its fifth consecutive victory.

N.Y. Giants	0	3	3	10	—	16
Philadelphia	7	3	3	0	—	13

Phil — Bavaro 27 pass from Brister (Murray kick)
Phil — FG Murray 32
Giants— FG Daluiso 47
Phil — FG Murray 42
Giants— FG Daluiso 19
Giants— Meggett 5 run (Daluiso kick)
Giants— FG Daluiso 18

SAN DIEGO 21, N.Y. JETS 6—at Giants Stadium, attendance 48,213. The Chargers rolled over the Jets to clinch their second AFC West title in three seasons. New York scored its points in the first half on 2 field goals by Nick Lowery. The Chargers got moving after Lowery's second kick, driving 64 yards to take a 7-6 halftime lead on Stan Humphries 2-yard touchdown pass to Mark Seay. It was bombs away in the second half for San Diego, as Humphries hit Tony Martin on touchdown passes of 44 and 60 yards. Humphries completed 19 of 26 passes for 280 yards, with no interceptions. Martin had 3 catches for 116 yards, and Natrone Means gained 73 yards on 23 carries. The Chargers sacked the Jets' quarterbacks 5 times.

San Diego	0	7	7	7	—	21
N.Y. Jets	3	3	0	0	—	6

Jets — FG Lowery 38
Jets — FG Lowery 30
SD — Seay 2 pass from Humphries (Carney kick)
SD — Martin 44 pass from Humphries (Carney kick)
SD — Martin 60 pass from Humphries (Carney kick)

TAMPA BAY 17, WASHINGTON 14—at RFK Stadium, attendance 47,315. Craig Erickson passed for 267 yards to lead the Buccaneers to their fourth consecutive victory while the Redskins ended their home schedule without a victory for the first time in franchise history. After a scoreless first quarter, Washington got on the board with Heath Shuler's 15-yard touchdown pass to running back Ricky Ervins. Two 16-yard passes by Erickson set up a Buccaneers' field goal, and then Erickson found Lawrence Dawsey for a 46-yard pass to set up Errict Rhett's 1-yard touchdown run. Washington countered just before halftime with an 8-yard touchdown pass from Shuler to Henry Ellard to take a 14-10 lead. In the third quarter, a long punt return and 2 passes by Erickson set up the go-ahead score on Rhett's 3-yard run. Washington's only second-half scoring chance ended in a missed 44-yard field-goal attempt by Chip Lohmiller at the end of the third quarter. Erickson completed 19 of 34 passes, including 7 completions for 116 yards to Dawsey. Shuler was 17 of 35 for 201 yards.

Tampa Bay	0	10	0	7	—	17
Washington	0	14	0	0	—	14

Wash — Ervins 15 pass from Shuler (Lohmiller kick)
TB — FG Husted 42
TB — Rhett 1 run (Husted kick)
Wash — Ellard 8 pass from Shuler (Lohmiller kick)
TB — Rhett 3 run (Husted kick)

SUNDAY NIGHT, DECEMBER 18

L.A. RAIDERS 17, SEATTLE 16—at Kingdome, attendance 53,301. The Raiders escaped with a victory when the Seahawks' John Kasay barely missed a 43-yard field-goal attempt with nine seconds to play. Jeff Hostetler's 38-yard pass to Raghib Ismail set up the Raiders' first touchdown, a 5-yard run by Harvey Williams. After the teams swapped field goals, the Seahawks tied the game at 10-10 one minute before halftime on Chris Warren's 33-yard touchdown run. Warren's running set up 2 more field goals by Kasay, one from 50 yards and another from 33 yards with 9:35 to play that made it 16-10. The Raiders received the ensuing kickoff, and Hostetler immediately went deep, finding Tim Brown along the sideline in a seam in the Seahawks' zone. Brown caught the ball in stride and streaked down the field to complete a 77-yard touchdown pass. But the Seahawks were not done, as Dan McGwire completed passes of 19 and 32 yards to Kelvin Martin to position Kasay for the potential winning kick. But Kasay's kick just missed to the right. Hostetler was 17 of 29 for 235 yards, while Williams ran for 93 yards on 20 carries and Brown had 4 catches for 107 yards. Warren gained 122 yards on 24 carries for Seattle.

L.A. Raiders	0	10	0	7	—	17
Seattle	0	10	3	3	—	16

Raid — Williams 5 run (Jaeger kick)
Sea — FG Kasay 41
Raid — FG Jaeger 24
Sea — C. Warren 33 run (Kasay kick)
Sea — FG Kasay 50
Sea — FG Kasay 33
Raid — Brown 77 pass from Hostetler (Jaeger kick)

MONDAY, DECEMBER 19

DALLAS 24, NEW ORLEANS 16—at Louisiana Superdome, attendance 67,323. A meaningless game became very meaningful for the playoff-bound Cowboys, who lost running back Emmitt Smith to injury while defeating the Saints. Dallas's defense provided most of the Cowboys' scoring. Early in the game, defensive end Tony Tolbert gambled and won. He correctly guessed on a screen pass, and his 54-yard interception return gave Dallas a 7-0 lead early in the game. New Orleans tried to match Tolbert's feat, as Saints linebacker Darion Conner intercepted a tipped pass from Troy Aikman and took off for the end zone. But Conner, after running 50 yards, was stopped at the Cowboys' 15 by 330-pound tackle Larry Allen. The Saints had to settle for a 21-yard field goal by Morten Andersen. Dallas took a 17-6 lead in the third quarter on Smith's 1-yard touchdown run. Smith left with a pulled hamstring soon after, but his namesake picked up the slack—Cowboys linebacker Darrin Smith clinched the victory with a 13-yard interception return for a touchdown.

Dallas	7	3	7	7	—	24
New Orleans	0	6	3	7	—	16

Dall — Tolbert 54 interception return (Boniol kick)
NO — FG Andersen 21
NO — FG Andersen 32
Dall — FG Boniol 30
Dall — E. Smith 1 run (Boniol kick)
NO — FG Andersen 29
Dall — D. Smith 13 interception return (Boniol kick)
NO — D. Brown 4 run (Andersen kick)

SEVENTEENTH WEEK SUMMARIES

AMERICAN FOOTBALL CONFERENCE

Eastern Division	**W**	**L**	**T**	**Pct.**	**Pts.**	**OP**
Miami	10	6	0	.625	389	327
New England	10	6	0	.625	351	312
Indianapolis	8	8	0	.500	307	320
Buffalo	7	9	0	.438	340	356
N.Y. Jets	6	10	0	.375	264	320
Central Division						
Pittsburgh	12	4	0	.750	316	234
Cleveland	11	5	0	.688	340	204
Cincinnati	3	13	0	.188	276	406
Houston	2	14	0	.125	226	352
Western Division						
San Diego	11	5	0	.688	381	306
Kansas City	9	7	0	.563	319	298
L.A. Raiders	9	7	0	.563	303	327
Denver	7	9	0	.438	347	396
Seattle	6	10	0	.375	287	323

NATIONAL FOOTBALL CONFERENCE

Eastern Division	**W**	**L**	**T**	**Pct.**	**Pts.**	**OP**
Dallas	12	4	0	.750	414	248
N.Y. Giants	9	7	0	.563	279	305
Arizona	8	8	0	.500	235	267
Philadelphia	7	9	0	.438	308	308
Washington	3	13	0	.188	320	412
Central Division						
Minnesota	10	6	0	.625	356	314
Green Bay	9	7	0	.563	382	287
Detroit	9	7	0	.563	357	342
Chicago	9	7	0	.563	271	307
Tampa Bay	6	10	0	.375	251	351
Western Division						
San Francisco	13	3	0	.813	505	296
New Orleans	7	9	0	.438	348	407
Atlanta	7	9	0	.438	317	385
L.A. Rams	4	12	0	.250	286	365

SATURDAY, DECEMBER 24

ATLANTA 10, ARIZONA 6—at Georgia Dome, attendance 35,311. Linebacker Jessie Tuggle stopped the Cardinals' Ron Moore at the 1-yard line as time expired to preserve the Falcons' victory. The game's only touchdown came in the first quarter, when Atlanta's Jeff George lofted a long pass that Bert Emanuel hauled in at the Falcons' 40 and carried the rest of the way to complete an 85-yard touchdown. Atlanta led 7-3 at halftime, and then marched 90 yards to a field goal in the third quarter. Bobby Hebert, who replaced an injured George, completed passes of 40 and 23 yards to set up Norm Johnson's 24-yard field goal. Arizona's Jay Schroeder completed 26 of 42 passes for 317 yards, but he could not get the Cardinals into the end zone. Schroeder, operating without any timeouts, completed a 40-yard pass to the 2-yard line to Gary Clark and then raced downfield to spike the ball stopping the clock with 3 seconds remaining. The Cardinals' attempt to win failed, however, when Moore was denied by Tuggle in the middle of the line as time expired. Emanuel had 4 catches for 136 yards.

Arizona	0	3	0	3	—	6
Atlanta	7	0	3	0	—	10

Atl — Emanuel 85 pass from George (Johnson kick)
Ariz — FG Davis 22
Atl — FG Johnson 24
Ariz — FG Davis 49

INDIANAPOLIS 10, BUFFALO 9—at RCA Dome, attendance 38,458. Jim Harbaugh came off the bench to lead the Colts to 10 third-quarter points as Indianapolis won consecutive games for the only time in 1994. Browning Nagle started for the Colts, but he failed to generate much offense while setting up the Bills' 2 first-half field goals with an interception and a fumble. Harbaugh entered the game in the third period and led the Colts on a 50-yard drive, the last 13 coming on Harbaugh's touchdown pass to Floyd Turner. Later in the quarter, Ray Buchanan intercepted a pass from the Bills' Frank Reich, and Harbaugh marched the Colts 51 yards to a 22-yard field goal by Dean Biasucci. The key play on the drive was Marshall Faulk's 28-yard run on fourth-and-1. Buffalo's Steve Christie kicked his third field goal to make it 10-9 with 10:33 to play, and had a chance to win it in the final seconds, but missed a 46-yard field-goal attempt. Faulk gained 82 yards on 17 carries. Reich completed 26 of 45 passes for 258 yards, including 8 completions to Don Beebe for 111 yards.

Buffalo	0	6	0	3	—	9
Indianapolis	0	0	10	0	—	10

Buff — FG Christie 20
Buff — FG Christie 21
Ind — Turner 13 pass from Harbaugh (Biasucci kick)
Ind — FG Biasucci 22
Buff — FG Christie 24

N.Y. GIANTS 15, DALLAS 10—at Giants Stadium, attendance 66,943. The Giants ended the season the way they started it—with a winning streak. New York, which began the season with three consecutive victories, finished the year with six straight wins after defeating Dallas. Unfortunately for the Giants, they lost seven straight games in between to finish out of the playoffs. New York took a 10-3 halftime lead on Dave Brown's 49-yard touchdown pass to Mike Sherrard and Brad Daluiso's 38-yard field goal. Dallas tied the game in the third period on Blair Thomas's 1-yard touchdown run, which was set up by Kevin Williams's 52-yard punt return. The Giants reclaimed the lead thanks to their defense, as Jessie Armstead sacked Cowboys quarterback Rodney Peete at the goal line and the ball squirted out of the end zone for a safety. Daluiso added another field goal in the fourth quarter. Rodney Hampton ran for 91 yards, giving him 1,075 for the season and making him the first Giants running back with four 1,000-yard seasons. The Cowboys played without star running back Emmitt Smith, who injured his left hamstring the previous game.

Dallas	3	0	7	0	—	10
N.Y. Giants	0	10	2	3	—	15

Dall — FG Boniol 37
Giants— Sherrard 49 pass from Da. Brown (Daluiso kick)
Giants— FG Daluiso 38
Dall — B. Thomas 1 run (Boniol kick)
Giants— Safety, Peete fumbled ball out of end zone
Giants— FG Daluiso 30

GREEN BAY 34, TAMPA BAY 19—at Tampa Stadium, attendance 65,076. Brett Favre teamed with Sterling Sharpe on 3 scoring passes as the Packers clinched a wild-card berth. Green Bay scored twice in the first quarter on a 39-yard run by Edgar Bennett and Favre's 6-yard pass to Sharpe. The Buccaneers' Michael Husted kicked 2 second-quarter field goals to make it 14-6, but then Favre and Sharpe went back to work. Sharpe's 22-yard touchdown reception capped a 74-yard drive. Then Green Bay went 67 yards with Sharpe's 6-yard scoring catch 27 seconds before the half giving Green Bay a commanding 28-6 lead. The Packers coasted from there. Favre completed 24 of 36 passes for 291 yards. Sharpe had 9 catches for 132 yards. Bennett gained 100 yards on 21 carries. Tampa Bay rookie Errict Rhett gained 54 yards to finish with 1,011 rushing yards. The Buccaneers' 6-10 record marked the twelfth straight year that the club had double figures in defeats.

Green Bay	14	14	6	0	—	34
Tampa Bay	0	6	6	7	—	19

GB — Bennett 39 run (Jacke kick)
GB — Sharpe 6 pass from Favre (Jacke kick)
TB — FG Husted 38
TB — FG Husted 27
GB — Sharpe 22 pass from Favre (Jacke kick)
GB — Sharpe 6 pass from Favre (Jacke kick)
TB — Wilson 17 pass from Erickson (pass failed)
GB — FG Jacke 38
GB — FG Jacke 18
TB — Armstrong 1 pass from Erickson (Husted kick)

KANSAS CITY 19, L.A. RAIDERS 9—at Los Angeles Memorial Coliseum, attendance 64,130. With a playoff berth at stake for both teams, the Chiefs outplayed the Raiders to advance to the postseason. Kansas City took the opening kickoff and swiftly drove 77 yards for a touchdown. Joe Montana led the way, hitting Willie Davis with passes of 26 and 47 yards, the latter for a score that made it 7-0. Later in the first quarter, Los Angeles embarked on an 86-yard drive that took 22 plays and consumed 12 minutes 14 seconds—and produced only a field goal. The Raiders, who had been haunted by mistakes all year, then made a huge gaffe at the end of the first half. They had the ball in field-goal range at the Chiefs' 28 with 12 seconds left. Although they were out of timeouts, the Raiders tried to get it closer, and the Chiefs' Neil Smith made 'em pay, hitting Raiders quarterback Jeff Hostetler as he threw. The ball fluttered into the hands of streaking cornerback Mark Collins, who returned the interception 78 yards for a touchdown and a 14-3 lead as the first half expired. In the third quarter, Montana's passes of 30, 13, and 11 yards set up Lin Elliott's 22-yard field goal, which gave Kansas City a 17-3 advantage. After that, the Chiefs turned to former Raiders running back Marcus Allen, who gained 132 yards on 33 carries. Montana, who announced his retirement after the season, completed 15 of 24 passes for 214 yards in his final regular-season game. Kansas City amassed 424 total yards while controlling the ball for 38 minutes 24 seconds.

Kansas City	7	7	3	2	—	19
L.A. Raiders	0	3	0	6	—	9

KC — W. Davis 47 pass from Montana (Elliott kick)
Raid — FG Jaeger 30
KC — Collins 78 interception return (Elliott kick)
KC — FG Elliott 22
KC — Safety, Mosebar penalized for tripping in end zone
Raid — Wright 65 pass from Evans (pass failed)

NEW ENGLAND 13, CHICAGO 3—at Soldier Field, attendance 60,178. The Patriots' defense continued its stellar play as New England won its seventh consecutive game. The victory, coupled with the Raiders' loss, gave the Patriots their first playoff berth since 1986. Despite the loss, the Bears also advanced to the playoffs as a wild-card entrant. It was a day for the defenses, as neither team reached the end zone during the first three quarters. New England nursed a 6-3 lead into the fourth quarter. The Patriots' lead barely survived the third quarter, as Bears kicker Kevin Butler had a 38-yard field-goal attempt blocked and later missed a 36-yard attempt wide left. In the fourth quarter, quarterback Drew Bledsoe provided some breathing room, finding Vincent Brisby for a 31-yard pass to set up Bledsoe's clinching 3-yard touchdown pass to running back Leroy Thompson with 2:32 left in the game. Bledsoe completed 23 of 38 passes for 277 yards. He finished the season with an NFL record for most attempts (691). Brisby had 6 catches for 115 yards.

New England	3	3	0	7	—	13
Chicago	3	0	0	0	—	3

Chi — FG Butler 44
NE — FG Bahr 29
NE — FG Bahr 22
NE — Thompson 3 pass from Bledsoe (Bahr kick)

NEW ORLEANS 30, DENVER 28—at Mile High Stadium, attendance 64,445. Jim Everett passed for 343 yards and 3 touchdowns to lead the Saints over the Broncos. Everett had 2 scoring tosses in the second quarter—8 yards to Michael Haynes and 36 yards to Torrance Small—to help New Orleans take a 17-6 lead at intermission. Denver closed within 17-14 late in the third quarter, but Everett retaliated on the next possession, hitting Small for a 75-yard touchdown pass and a 24-14 Saints lead. Everett, who had bruised his elbow, then gave way to backup Wade Wilson, who led the Saints to 2 fourth-quarter field goals. Denver scored twice in the final period, but also committed 3 turnovers. Everett, who completed 23 of 27 passes, set a Saints' single-season record with 3,855 passing yards. Small had 6 catches for 200 yards. Denver's Hugh Millen, playing in place of an injured John Elway, completed 25 of 44 passes for 290 yards.

New Orleans	0	17	7	6	—	30
Denver	0	6	8	14	—	28

Den — FG Elam 32
NO — FG Andersen 26
NO — Haynes 8 pass from Everett (Andersen kick)
Den — FG Elam 30
NO — Small 36 pass from Everett (Andersen kick)
Den — D. Clark 4 run (Sharpe pass from Millen)
NO — Small 75 pass from Everett (Andersen kick)
Den — D. Clark 1 run (Elam kick)
NO — FG Andersen 37
NO — FG Andersen 40
Den — Sharpe 5 pass from Millen (Elam kick)

HOUSTON 24, N.Y. JETS 10—at Astrodome, attendance 31,176. The Oilers used a balanced offensive attack to defeat the Jets and end their 11-game losing streak. Bucky Richardson led the Oilers on a 70-yard scoring march in the first quarter, scoring from 1 yard out for a 7-0 Oilers lead. New York tied the game in the second period on Johnny Johnson's 1-yard scoring run, but Richardson countered with field-goal drives of 61 and 66 yards to give the Oilers a 13-7 advantage at intermission. Richardson's mistakes even turned in the Oilers' favor, as the Jets' Marvin Washington intercepted a pass from Richardson, only to fumble on the return. Running back Lorenzo White recovered Washington's fumble, and five plays later White ran in from 3 yards out to give the Oilers a 21-7 lead. Houston totaled 382 yards on offense, with 176 rushing yards and 206 through the air. White had 97 yards on 27 carries. Richardson completed 17 of 29 passes for 220 yards, including 8 completions to Webster Slaughter for 123 yards.

N.Y. Jets	0	7	3	0	—	10
Houston	7	6	8	3	—	24

Hou — Richardson 1 run (Del Greco kick)
Jets — Johnson 1 run (Lowery kick)
Hou — FG Del Greco 28
Hou — FG Del Greco 50
Hou — White 3 run (Jeffires pass from Richardson)
Jets — FG Lowery 49
Hou — FG Del Greco 42

CINCINNATI 33, PHILADELPHIA 30—at Riverfront Stadium, attendance 39,923. The Bengals rallied from a 17-point deficit to defeat the Eagles on 2 field goals in the game's final three seconds. Philadelphia's first-half lead of 20-10 included Herschel Walker's 94-yard kickoff return for a touchdown, which made Walker the only player in NFL history to have a rush, a reception, and a return of 90 or more yards in the same season. The Eagles upped their lead to 27-10 early in the second half when Michael Zordich returned an interception 18 yards for a score. The Bengals scored twice in the third period, but they still trailed 30-20 after Philadelphia's Eddie Murray kicked a 35-yard field goal with 5:13 remaining in the game. The Bengals then went 65 yards in four plays, with Jeff Blake passing 8 yards to Tony McGee to pull the Bengals within 30-27 with 3:32 to play. Cincinnati got the ball back and drove 73 yards to the tying field goal. Blake kept the drive alive with a 16-yard run on fourth-and-16, and Doug Pelfrey capped the march with a tying 22-yard field goal with three seconds left. The Bengals purposely squibbed the ensuing kickoff to prevent a return, and instead they came up with the ball at the Eagles' 37 with one second left when the Eagles' Bryan O'Neal muffed the kickoff. A surprised Pelfrey had to run back to the sideline to retrieve his helmet, then won the game with a 54-yard field goal as time expired. It was Pelfrey's fourth field goal of the day, and it tied the mark for the NFL's longest field goal in 1994. Philadelphia's Bubby Brister completed 26 of 37 passes for 325 yards, but it was not enough to prevent the Eagles' seventh consecutive loss. The Bengals' Carl Pickens had 9 catches for 135 yards, and the Eagles' Calvin Williams had 6 for 122.

Philadelphia	3	17	7	3	—	30
Cincinnati	7	3	10	13	—	33

Cin — Pickens 14 pass from Blake (Pelfrey kick)
Phil — FG Murray 34
Cin — FG Pelfrey 18
Phil — H. Walker 94 kickoff return (Murray kick)
Phil — Joseph 7 pass from Brister (Murray kick)
Phil — FG Murray 23
Phil — Zordich 18 interception return (Murray kick)
Cin — Green 5 run (Pelfrey kick)
Cin — FG Pelfrey 36
Phil — FG Murray 35

Cin — McGee 8 pass from Blake (Pelfrey kick)
Cin — FG Pelfrey 22
Cin — FG Pelfrey 54

SAN DIEGO 37, PITTSBURGH 34—at San Diego Jack Murphy Stadium, attendance 58,379. The Chargers scored 10 points in the final five minutes to defeat the Steelers and secure a first-round bye in the AFC playoffs. Pittsburgh had already clinched home-field advantage throughout the AFC playoffs. San Diego took a 10-3 second-quarter lead on Andre Coleman's 90-yard kickoff return for a touchdown. Both teams' two-minute offenses were in high gear, as the Steelers' Neil O'Donnell fired a 19-yard touchdown pass to Charles Johnson with one minute left in the half, and the Chargers answered by driving 73 yards in 34 seconds to Stan Humphries' 2-yard touchdown pass to Mark Seay. Pittsburgh, which trailed 24-13 after Natrone Means ran 2 yards for a touchdown in the third period, used touchdown drives of 83, 84, and 84 yards to take a 34-27 lead. Johnson had an 84-yard catch for 1 score and a 51-yard catch to set up Pittsburgh's final touchdown. But the game meant more to San Diego, and it showed in the final five minutes. The Chargers tied the game on Means's 20-yard touchdown run with 4:32 left, and, after a Steelers' punt, they drove 34 yards to set up John Carney's winning 32-yard field goal with three seconds left. Johnson had 4 catches for 165 yards for the Steelers. Tomczak was 10 of 16 for 248 yards after spelling O'Donnell. Humphries completed 21 of 35 passes for 249 yards for San Diego.

Pittsburgh	0	13	6	15	—	34
San Diego	3	14	7	13	—	37

SD — FG Carney 37
Pitt — FG Anderson 28
SD — Coleman 90 kickoff return (Carney kick)
Pitt — FG Anderson 28
Pitt — C. Johnson 19 pass from O'Donnell (Anderson kick)
SD — Seay 2 pass from Humphries (Carney kick)
SD — Means 2 run (Carney kick)
Pitt — McAfee 6 run (pass failed)
Pitt — C. Johnson 84 pass from Tomczak (Stone pass from Tomczak)
SD — FG Carney 40
Pitt — Hastings 11 pass from Tomczak (Anderson kick)
SD — Means 20 run (Carney kick)
SD — FG Carney 32

CLEVELAND 35, SEATTLE 9—at Cleveland Stadium, attendance 54,180. The Browns dominated the Seahawks to secure home-field advantage for an AFC first-round playoff game. Eric Metcalf's 6-yard touchdown run capped a 60-yard drive and gave the Browns a 7-0 first-quarter lead. It was 21-0 at halftime thanks to Vinny Testaverde, who threw a 35-yard touchdown pass to Mark Carrier and ran 1 yard for a touchdown. Seattle kicked a field goal on its first possession of the second half, but Cleveland countered with Testaverde's 3-yard touchdown pass to Derrick Alexander late in the third period. The outcome was never in doubt after that. Testaverde completed 16 of 22 passes for 228 yards. Carrier had 5 catches for 98 yards and also ran 14 yards for a touchdown on a reverse in the fourth quarter. The Browns allowed only 204 points, the fewest points permitted by an AFC team in a 16-game season since the Steelers (195) in 1978.

Seattle	0	0	3	6	—	9
Cleveland	7	14	7	7	—	35

Cleve — Metcalf 6 run (Stover kick)
Cleve — Carrier 35 pass from Testaverde (Stover kick)
Cleve — Testaverde 1 run (Stover kick)
Sea — FG Kasay 30
Cleve — Alexander 3 pass from Testaverde (Stover kick)
Cleve — Carrier 14 run (Stover kick)
Sea — McKnight 25 pass from Gelbaugh (pass failed)

WASHINGTON 24, L.A. RAMS 21—at Anaheim Stadium, attendance 25,705. The Redskins used a strong running game, a long punt return, and a solid performance from rookie quarterback Heath Shuler to defeat the Rams. Shuler's first effort went awry, as he was intercepted by the Rams' Anthony Newman, who returned it 22 yards for a touchdown. Shuler settled down after that, completing passes of 39 and 14 yards to lead the Redskins 80 yards to the tying touchdown. The Rams claimed a 14-7 lead on a 34-yard touchdown pass from Chris Miller to Todd Kinchen with 4:19 left in the first half. But the lead did not hold up, as Brian Mitchell fielded a punt at the Redskins' 22 and went 78 yards for a touchdown with 1:33 to go in the half. The Rams' next possession ended with an interception by Martin Bayles, which set up Chip Lohmiller's 37-yard field goal with 57 seconds left for a 17-14 Redskins lead. Back came the Rams, who drove 60 yards to score on Miller's 36-yard pass to Jermaine Ross with four seconds left in the half. It was Ross's first NFL reception, and it gave Los Angeles a 21-17 advantage at intermission. In the third quarter, Shuler led the Redskins on an 80-yard drive, which ended with Shuler's 1-yard touchdown toss to James Jenkins. The Rams had a chance to tie, but Tony Zendejas missed a 33-yard field goal with four minutes to play. The Redskins used four running backs to run for 150 yards. Shuler passed for 149 yards, hitting former Rams receiver Henry Ellard 5 times for 81 yards. Miller was 27 of 40 for 304 yards.

Washington	0	17	7	0	—	24
L.A. Rams	7	14	0	0	—	21

Rams — Newman 22 interception return (Zendejas kick)
Wash — Brooks 2 run (Lohmiller kick)
Rams — Kinchen 34 pass from Miller (Zendejas kick)
Wash — Mitchell 78 punt return (Lohmiller kick)
Wash — FG Lohmiller 37
Rams — Ross 36 pass from Miller (Zendejas kick)
Wash — Jenkins 1 pass from Shuler (Lohmiller kick)

SUNDAY NIGHT, DECEMBER 25

MIAMI 27, DETROIT 20—at Joe Robbie Stadium, attendance 70,980. The Dolphins defeated the Lions to win the AFC East title and give Don Shula his record 319th regular-season victory. Shula, already the NFL's winningest coach with 337 victories (including playoffs), surpassed George Halas's mark of 318 regular-season victories. Miami dominated the first half, as Dan Marino's passing set up 3 touchdown runs by Bernie Parmalee and 2 field goals by Pete Stoyanovich. The Lions' only salvation in the first 30 minutes was Johnnie Morton's 93-yard kickoff return for a touchdown, but Detroit still trailed 27-10 at intermission. The Lions finally made a game of it in the fourth quarter, when Dave Krieg fired a 5-yard scoring pass to Aubrey Matthews with 5:46 remaining to close the deficit to 27-20. But the Lions' attempt to tie was ended two minutes later when Gene Atkins intercepted Krieg's pass and Miami ran out the clock. Marino was 26 of 35 for 285 yards (222 in the first half). Barry Sanders, who entered the game needing 169 rushing yards to surpass 2,000, came up well short. He still totaled 110 yards from scrimmage (52 rushing and 58 receiving), and his NFL-leading total of 1,883 rushing yards was the fourth-best season in league history.

Detroit	3	7	3	7	—	20
Miami	7	20	0	0	—	27

Mia — Parmalee 1 run (Stoyanovich kick)
Det — FG Hanson 32
Mia — FG Stoyanovich 40
Mia — Parmalee 1 run (Stoyanovich kick)
Mia — Parmalee 6 run (Stoyanovich kick)
Det — Morton 93 kickoff return (Hanson kick)
Mia — FG Stoyanovich 45
Det — FG Hanson 40
Det — Matthews 5 pass from Krieg (Hanson kick)

MONDAY, DECEMBER 26

MINNESOTA 21, SAN FRANCISCO 14—at Metrodome, attendance 63,326. The Vikings' defense led the team to a victory over the 49ers, which clinched Minnesota's second NFC Central title in three seasons. The 49ers, who had already secured home-field advantage throughout the NFC playoffs, saw their 10-game winning streak end. Minnesota took a 7-0 lead in the first quarter on DeWayne Washington's 17-yard fumble return for a score. It was Washington's third touchdown of the year on a defensive return, which tied the rookie record held by Ronnie Lott and Lem Barney. San Francisco tied the game in the second quarter, as Steve Young capped a 91-yard drive with a 6-yard touchdown pass to Jerry Rice. Both Young and Rice left the game after that. The Vikings then reeled off 14 straight points on 2 field goals by Fuad Reveiz and Terry Allen's 1-yard touchdown run (and subsequent two-point conversion). The 49ers made it close in the fourth period on Elvis Grbac's 1-yard touchdown pass to Ed McCaffrey with 3:53 left, but never threatened after that. Young finished the season with an NFL-record passer rating of 112.8.

San Francisco	0	7	0	7	—	14
Minnesota	7	3	11	0	—	21

Minn — Washington 17 fumble return (Reveiz kick)
SF — Rice 6 pass from Young (Brien kick)
Minn — FG Reveiz 48
Minn — FG Reveiz 27
Minn — Allen 1 run (Allen run)
SF — McCaffrey 1 pass from Grbac (Brien kick)

EIGHTEENTH WEEK SUMMARIES

SATURDAY, DECEMBER 31, 1994
NFC WILD CARD PLAYOFF GAME

GREEN BAY 16, DETROIT 12—at Lambeau Field, attendance 58,125. The Packers won their first playoff game at home in 12 years by staving off the Lions in the closing minutes. Chris Jacke's third field goal of the game, from 28 yards with 5:35 to play in the fourth quarter, gave Green Bay a 16-10 lead. Detroit's Eric Lynch returned the ensuing kickoff 27 yards to the Packers' 49-yard line. The Lions reached the 11 at the two-minute warning, but linebacker Bryce Paup sacked Dave Krieg for a 6-yard loss, and on fourth-and-14 from the 17, Herman Moore caught Krieg's pass at the back of the end zone, only to come down past the end line with 1:45 to play. Green Bay ran out the rest of the clock, giving up a concession safety on the last play. Brett Favre passed for 262 yards for the Packers, but it was Green Bay's defense that made the difference. The Packers limited Barry Sanders, the NFL's leading rusher with 1,883 yards during the regular season, to minus-1 yard on 13 carries. Sanders, who caught 3 passes for 4 yards, was held to negative yardage eight of the 16 times he touched the ball. The Lions rushed for minus-4 yards as a team.

Detroit	0	0	3	9	—	12
Green Bay	7	3	3	3	—	16

GB — Levens 3 run (Jacke kick)
GB — FG Jacke 51
Det — FG Hanson 38
GB — FG Jacke 32
Det — Perriman 3 pass from Krieg (Hanson kick)
GB — FG Jacke 28
Det — Safety, Hentrich ran out of the end zone

AFC WILD CARD PLAYOFF GAME

MIAMI 27, KANSAS CITY 17—at Joe Robbie Stadium, attendance 67,487. Dan Marino threw 2 touchdown passes and the Dolphins' defense forced a pair of critical turnovers in the fourth quarter to preserve the victory. A wild first half ended in a 17-17 tie after Marino and Chiefs quarterback Joe Montana each had three possessions (excluding a Kansas City kneeldown on the final play) and produced a pair of touchdowns and a field goal. Marino picked up in the third quarter where he left off, directing a 64-yard touchdown drive following the second-half kickoff. He capped the six-play march with a 7-yard touchdown pass to Irving Fryar. Late in the quarter, Pete Stoyanovich kicked a 40-yard field goal to give Miami a 10-point lead, and the Dolphins' defense then took over. Cornerback J.B. Brown intercepted Montana at the goal line early in the fourth quarter, and safety Michael Stewart wrestled the ball from Kansas City running back Marcus Allen at Miami's 34-yard line with 7:31 left. Miami held onto the ball for nearly six minutes after that. Marino completed 22 of 29 passes for 257 yards for the Dolphins. Montana was 26 of 37 for 314 yards for the Chiefs. Kansas City running back Kimble Anders caught 6 passes for 103 yards, including a 57-yard touchdown.

Kansas City	14	3	0	0	—	17
Miami	7	10	10	0	—	27

KC — Walker 1 pass from Montana (Elliott kick)
Mia — Parmalee 1 run (Stoyanovich kick)
KC — Anders 57 pass from Montana (Elliott kick)
Mia — FG Stoyanovich 40
KC — FG Elliott 21
Mia — R. Williams 1 pass from Marino (Stoyanovich kick)
Mia — Fryar 7 pass from Marino (Stoyanovich kick)
Mia — FG Stoyanovich 40

SUNDAY, JANUARY 1, 1995
NFC WILD CARD PLAYOFF GAME

CHICAGO 35, MINNESOTA 18—at Metrodome, attendance 60,347. Steve Walsh threw 2 touchdowns passes as the Bears stunned the NFC Central Division-champion Vikings. Chicago, which didn't score more than 27 points in any game during the 1994 regular season, ended a six-game losing streak to the Vikings by shredding the NFL's fifth-ranked defense for 4 touchdowns. Despite turnovers on their first two possessions, the Bears forged a 14-3 lead in the second quarter on Lewis Tillman's 1-yard run and Walsh's 9-yard touchdown pass to tight end Keith Jennings. Minnesota pulled within 14-9 on Warren Moon's 4-yard touchdown pass to Cris Carter 19 seconds before halftime, but Chicago struck quickly in the third quarter to bolster its lead. Walsh teamed with Curtis Conway on a 23-yard completion and with Jeff Graham on an 18-yard gain before Raymont Harris ran 29 yards for a touchdown just 2:03 into the second half. It was the longest rushing play of the season for the Bears. Walsh's 21-yard touchdown pass to Graham early in the fourth quarter helped keep the game out of reach. He finished with 15 completions on 23 attempts for 221 yards. Graham caught 4 passes for 108 yards. Moon completed 29 of 52 passes for 292 yards, and running back Amp Lee caught 11 passes for 159 yards for the Vikings, who had sizeable advantages in plays (82-54) and total yards (389-308). But Minnesota was victimized by 4 turnovers and 11 penalties.

Chicago	0	14	7	14	—	35
Minnesota	3	6	3	6	—	18

Minn — FG Reveiz 29
Chi — Tillman 1 run (Butler kick)
Chi — Jennings 9 pass from Walsh (Butler kick)
Minn — Carter 4 pass from Moon (pass failed)
Chi — Harris 29 run (Butler kick)
Minn — FG Reveiz 48
Chi — Graham 21 pass from Walsh (Butler kick)
Minn — Lee 11 pass from Moon (pass failed)
Chi — Miniefield 48 fumble return (Butler kick)

AFC WILD CARD PLAYOFF GAME
CLEVELAND 20, NEW ENGLAND 13—at Cleveland Stadium, attendance 77,452. Vinny Testaverde threw for 268 yards and 1 touchdown, and the Browns survived a late scare to beat the Patriots. The Patriots marched from their own 22-yard line to the Browns' 15 after Matt Stover's 21-yard field goal with 3:36 remaining gave Cleveland a 20-10 advantage. The drive stalled there, and Matt Bahr trimmed New England's deficit to seven points with a 33-yard field goal at the 1:30 mark. The Patriots recovered the ensuing onside kick and picked up a first down before four consecutive incompletions from their 48-yard line ended their comeback hopes. Testaverde completed 20 of 30 passes for the Browns, including a 5-yard touchdown to Mark Carrier in the second quarter. Michael Jackson caught 7 passes for 122 yards. Drew Bledsoe completed only 21 of 50 passes for 235 yards for New England and was intercepted 3 times.

New England	0	10	0	3	—	13
Cleveland	3	7	7	3	—	20

Cleve — FG Stover 30
NE — Thompson 13 pass from Bledsoe (Bahr kick)
Cleve — Carrier 5 pass from Testaverde (Stover kick)
NE — FG Bahr 23
Cleve — Hoard 10 run (Stover kick)
Cleve — FG Stover 21
NE — FG Bahr 33

NINETEENTH WEEK SUMMARIES

SATURDAY, JANUARY 7, 1995
NFC DIVISIONAL PLAYOFF GAME
SAN FRANCISCO 44, CHICAGO 15—at Candlestick Park, attendance 64,644. William Floyd ran for 3 touchdowns and Steve Young ran for 1 and passed for 1 as the 49ers tuned up for the NFC Championship Game by routing the Bears. After turning over the ball on its first possession and spotting Chicago an early field goal, San Francisco scored on six consecutive possessions to turn the game into a rout. Floyd's 2-yard run with 3:41 left in the first quarter gave the 49ers the lead for good, and his 4-yard run midway through the second quarter increased their advantage to 20-3. Young, who tossed an 8-yard touchdown pass to tight end Brent Jones early in the second quarter, ran 6 yards for a score 1:17 before halftime to make it 30-3. Floyd's third touchdown, from 1 yard, capped a 70-yard drive on San Francisco's first possession of the second half, and many of the 49ers' starters, including Young, took the rest of the afternoon off. The Bears, limited to only 95 total yards behind starting quarterback Steve Walsh in the first half, turned to Erik Kramer in the second half. Kramer passed for 161 yards in his two quarters of play and generated 2 touchdowns in the fourth quarter, but they came long after the issue had been decided.

Chicago	3	0	0	12	—	15
San Francisco	7	23	7	7	—	44

Chi — FG Butler 39
SF — Floyd 2 run (Brien kick)
SF — Jones 8 pass from Young (kick failed)
SF — Floyd 4 run (Brien kick)
SF — FG Brien 36
SF — Young 6 run (Brien kick)
SF — Floyd 1 run (Brien kick)
Chi — Flanigan 2 pass from Kramer (pass failed)
SF — Walker 1 run (Brien kick)
Chi — Tillman 1 run (pass failed)

AFC DIVISIONAL PLAYOFF GAME
PITTSBURGH 29, CLEVELAND 9—at Three Rivers Stadium, attendance 58,185. The Steelers scored on their first three possession to open a 17-0 lead and went on to defeat the Browns for the third time this season. Pittsburgh dominated the first-ever playoff meeting between these long-time rivals (they've played each other twice a year in the regular season since 1950), rushing for 238 yards while amassing 424 total yards and maintaining possession for 42:27 of the game's 60 minutes. Barry Foster ran for 133 yards on 24 carries, and rookie Byron (Bam) Morris added 60 yards on 22 attempts. Quarterback Neil O'Donnell was efficient, completing 8 of his first 9 passes and finishing with 16 completions in 23 attempts for 186 yards. He threw a 2-yard touchdown pass to tight end Eric Green early in the second quarter and put the game out of reach with a 9-yard touchdown pass to Yancey Thigpen for a 24-3 lead just 16 seconds before halftime. That touchdown was set up by cornerback Tim McKyer's interception and 21-yard return to Cleveland's 6-yard line. It was 1 of 2 interceptions (safety Darren Perry had the other) of Browns quarterback Vinny Testaverde, who completed only 13 of 31 passes for 144 yards. Testaverde received little help from Cleveland's running game, which managed only 55 yards. Ernie Mills caught 5 passes for 117 yards for the Steelers.

Cleveland	0	3	0	6	—	9
Pittsburgh	3	21	3	2	—	29

Pitt — FG Anderson 39
Pitt — Green 2 pass from O'Donnell (Anderson kick)
Pitt — J. Williams 26 run (Anderson kick)
Cleve — FG Stover 22
Pitt — Thigpen 9 pass from O'Donnell (Anderson kick)
Pitt — FG Anderson 40
Cleve — McCardell 20 pass from Testaverde (pass failed)
Pitt — Safety, Lake sacked Testaverde in end zone

SUNDAY, JANUARY 8, 1995
NFC DIVISIONAL PLAYOFF GAME
DALLAS 35, GREEN BAY 9—at Texas Stadium, attendance 64,745. Troy Aikman passed for 337 yards and 2 touchdowns, including a 94-yard strike to Alvin Harper, to lead the Cowboys to an easy victory over the Packers. The win set the stage for the third consecutive NFC title game between Dallas and San Francisco. Aikman, who completed 23 of 30 passes, spread his passes around to tight end Jay Novacek and wide receivers Michael Irvin and Harper, each of whom garnered more than 100 receiving yards on the day. Novacek had 11 receptions for 104 yards, Irvin caught 6 passes for 111 yards, and Harper had a pair of receptions for 108 yards. His 94-yard touchdown catch gave the Cowboys a 14-3 lead late in the first quarter. It was the longest play from scrimmage in NFL postseason history. Dallas running back Emmitt Smith ran for 44 yards and a touchdown in the first quarter, but left the game after aggravating a hamstring injury. His backup, Blair Thomas, ran for 70 yards and 2 touchdowns, including a 1-yard score to help break open the game at 21-3 midway through the second quarter.

Green Bay	3	6	0	0	—	9
Dallas	14	14	0	7	—	35

Dall — E. Smith 5 run (Boniol kick)
GB — FG Jacke 50
Dall — Harper 94 pass from Aikman (Boniol kick)
Dall — B. Thomas 1 run (Boniol kick)
GB — Bennett 1 run (pass failed)
Dall — Galbraith 1 pass from Aikman (Boniol kick)
Dall — B. Thomas 2 run (Boniol kick)

AFC DIVISIONAL PLAYOFF GAME
SAN DIEGO 22, MIAMI 21—at San Diego Jack Murphy Stadium, attendance 63,381. Stan Humphries threw an 8-yard touchdown pass to Mark Seay with 35 seconds remaining, and the Chargers held on to win when Pete Stoyanovich's 48-yard field-goal try fell short and wide right with one second to play. To qualify for the AFC Championship Game for the first time since 1981, San Diego had to rally from a 21-6 halftime deficit. After having 2 drives stall inside Miami's 5-yard line in the first half, the Chargers opened the third quarter by marching 71 yards to the Dolphins' 1-yard line, only to be turned away on fourth down. But on the next play, defensive tackle Reuben Davis dropped Miami running back Bernie Parmalee in the end zone for a safety. San Diego took the ensuing free kick and marched 54 yards to a touchdown, pulling within 21-15 on Natrone Means's 24-yard run with 2:42 left in the third quarter. Late in the fourth quarter, Humphries drove his team from its own 39-yard line to the go-ahead touchdown. The Dolphins got one more chance when Chargers safety Eric Castle was whistled for a 32-yard pass interference penalty, but the snap was high on the strong-legged Stoyanovich's errant field-goal attempt. Humphries completed 28 of 43 passes for 276 yards, while Means rushed for 139 yards on 24 attempts for the Chargers. Miami quarterback Dan Marino was 24 of 38 for 262 yards and 2 touchdowns, but only 56 yards came after halftime, when the Dolphins were limited to five plays in the third quarter and 11 in the fourth quarter. Miami tight end Keith Jackson caught 8 passes for 109 yards and 2 touchdowns.

Miami	7	14	0	0	—	21
San Diego	0	6	9	7	—	22

Mia — K. Jackson 8 pass from Marino (Stoyanovich kick)
SD — FG Carney 20
Mia — K. Jackson 9 pass from Marino (Stoyanovich kick)
SD — FG Carney 21
Mia — M. Williams 16 pass from Marino (Stoyanovich kick)
SD — Safety, R. Davis tackled Parmalee in end zone
SD — Means 24 run (Carney kick)
SD — Seay 8 pass from Humphries (Carney kick)

TWENTIETH WEEK SUMMARIES

SUNDAY, JANUARY 15, 1995
NFC CHAMPIONSHIP GAME
SAN FRANCISCO 38, DALLAS 28—at Candlestick Park, attendance 69,125. The 49ers eliminated the two-time defending Super Bowl champions by racing to a 21-0 lead in the game's opening minutes and holding on for the victory. San Francisco, which lost to Dallas in each of the previous two NFC title games, thus qualified for its fifth Super Bowl and dashed the Cowboys' hopes of becoming the first team to win three consecutive Super Bowls. The 49ers took advantage of Dallas turnovers to build their early lead. Cornerback Eric Davis intercepted Troy Aikman's pass on the third play of the game and returned it 44 yards for a touchdown and a 7-0 lead with just 1:02 elapsed. Three plays later, Davis forced a fumble that teammate Tim McDonald recovered, and it took San Francisco five plays to convert that into Steve Young's 29-yard touchdown pass to running back Ricky Watters. Kevin Williams fumbled the ensuing kickoff and 49ers kicker Doug Brien recovered at the Cowboys' 35. Fullback William Floyd capped a seven-play drive with a 1-yard run for San Francisco's third touchdown in a span of 6:25. Dallas tried to rally, and pulled within 24-14 late in the first half on Brien's 34-yard field goal sandwiched between a 4-yard run by Emmitt Smith and a 44-yard pass from Aikman to Michael Irvin. But three incompletions that stopped the clock and John Jett's 23-yard punt positioned the 49ers for a back-breaking 28-yard touchdown pass from Young to Jerry Rice just eight seconds before halftime. The Cowboys closed within 10 points twice more in the second half, but were stopped on fourth down twice in the fourth quarter and could get no closer. Dallas finished with a sizeable advantage in total yards (451-294), but was undone by 5 turnovers. Aikman completed 30 of 53 passes for 380 yards and 2 touchdowns, but was intercepted twice. Smith rushed for 74 yards and 2 touchdowns despite nursing an injured hamstring. Irvin caught a club-record 12 passes for 192 yards and 2 touchdowns. Young passed for 2 touchdowns and ran for another for San Francisco.

Dallas	7	7	7	7	—	28
San Francisco	21	10	7	0	—	38

SF — Davis 44 interception return (Brien kick)

SF — Watters 29 pass from Young (Brien kick)
SF — Floyd 1 run (Brien kick)
Dall — Irvin 44 pass from Aikman (Boniol kick)
SF — FG Brien 34
Dall — E. Smith 4 run (Boniol kick)
SF — Rice 28 pass from Young (Brien kick)
Dall — E. Smith 1 run (Boniol kick)
SF — Young 3 run (Brien kick)
Dall — Irvin 10 pass from Aikman (Boniol kick)

AFC CHAMPIONSHIP GAME
SAN DIEGO 17, PITTSBURGH 13—at Three Rivers Stadium, attendance 61,545. Stan Humphries threw 2 second-half touchdown passes, and the Chargers turned back the Steelers with a goal-line stand late in the game to earn their first trip to the Super Bowl. Neil O'Donnell's 16-yard touchdown pass to running back John L. Williams and a pair of field goals by Gary Anderson staked Pittsburgh to a 13-3 lead early in the second half. But Humphries's 43-yard touchdown pass to tight end Alfred Pupunu pulled San Diego within 13-10 midway through the third quarter, and his 43-yard strike to Tony Martin with 5:13 left in the game gave the Chargers the lead. O'Donnell tried to rally the Steelers by completing 7 consecutive passes and marching his team from its own 17-yard line to a first-and-goal at San Diego's 9. Three plays later, it was fourth-and-goal from the 3, but O'Donnell's pass, intended for running back Barry Foster, was knocked down at the goal line by Chargers linebacker Dennis Gibson with 1:04 remaining. San Diego, which came from behind to win for the second consecutive week (the Chargers beat Miami 22-21 in the divisional playoffs after trailing 21-6 at halftime), snapped a six-game losing streak in Pittsburgh despite heavy deficits in total yards (415-226), plays (80-47), and time of possession (37:13-22:47). O'Donnell passed for 349 yards for the Steelers on AFC title-game records for attempts (54) and completions (32). Linebacker Junior Seau had 16 tackles for San Diego.

San Diego	0	3	7	7	—	17
Pittsburgh	7	3	3	0	—	13

Pitt — Williams 16 pass from O'Donnell (Anderson kick)
SD — FG Carney 20
Pitt — FG Anderson 39
Pitt — FG Anderson 23
SD — Pupunu 43 pass from Humphries (Carney kick)
SD — Martin 43 pass from Humphries (Carney kick)

TWENTY-FIRST WEEK SUMMARY

SUNDAY, JANUARY 29, 1995
SUPER BOWL XXIX
MIAMI, FLORIDA
SAN FRANCISCO 49, SAN DIEGO 26—at Joe Robbie Stadium Stadium, attendance 74,107. Steve Young threw a record 6 touchdown passes, and the 49ers became the first team to win five Super Bowls when they routed the Chargers. Young, the game's most valuable player, directed an explosive offense that generated 7 touchdowns, 28 first downs, and 449 total yards. He completed 24 of 36 passes for 325 yards, and broke former 49ers quarterback Joe Montana's previous record of 5 touchdown passes in Super Bowl XXIV. San Francisco wasted little time in this one, taking the lead for good on Young's 44-yard touchdown pass to Jerry Rice only three plays and 1:24 into the game. The next time they had the ball, the 49ers marched 79 yards in four plays, taking a 14-0 lead when Young teamed with running back Ricky Watters on a 51-yard touchdown pass with 10:05 still to play in the opening period. San Diego then put together its most impressive possession of the game, a 13-play, 78-yard drive that consumed more than 7 minutes and was capped by Natrone Means's 1-yard touchdown run, to cut its deficit to 14-7 late in the quarter. But San Francisco countered with a 70-yard drive of its own, and Young's 5-yard touchdown pass to fullback William Floyd made it 21-7. Young's fourth touchdown pass, of 8 yards to Watters 4:44 before halftime, increased the advantage to 28-7, and the Chargers could get no closer than 18 points after that. Watters, who ran 9 yards for a touchdown in the third quarter, equaled the Super Bowl record with 3 touchdowns. Rice also scored 3 touchdowns (the second time in his career he'd done that in a Super Bowl) while catching 10 passes for 149 yards. He established career records for receptions, yards, and touchdowns in a Super Bowl. Young, who scrambled 21 yards and 15 yards to set up touchdowns in the first half, was the game's leading rusher with 49 yards on 5 carries. San Diego's Means, who rushed for 1,350 yards during the regular season, was limited to 33 yards on 13 attempts. Chargers quarterback Stan Humphries completed 24 of 49 passes for 275 yards. Rookie Andre Coleman became only the third player in Super Bowl history to return a kickoff for a touchdown, going 98 yards in the third quarter. The 75 points scored by the two teams established another record, breaking the previous mark of 69 set in Dallas's 52-17 victory over Buffalo in XXVII. The 49ers' victory was the eleventh consecutive for NFC teams over AFC teams in the Super Bowl.

San Diego	7	3	8	8	—	26
San Francisco	14	14	14	7	—	49

SF — Rice 44 pass from Young (Brien kick)
SF — Watters 51 pass from Young (Brien kick)
SD — Means 1 run (Carney kick)
SF — Floyd 5 pass from Young (Brien kick)
SF — Watters 8 pass from Young (Brien kick)
SD — FG Carney 31
SF — Watters 9 run (Brien kick)
SF — Rice 15 pass from Young (Brien kick)
SD — Coleman 98 kickoff return (Seay pass from Humphries)
SF — Rice 7 pass from Young (Brien kick)
SD — Martin 30 pass from Humphries (Pupunu pass from Humphries)

TWENTY-SECOND WEEK SUMMARY

SUNDAY, FEBRUARY 5, 1995
PRO BOWL
HONOLULU, HAWAII
AFC 41, NFC 13—at Aloha Stadium, attendance 49,121. Colts rookie Marshall Faulk rushed for a Pro Bowl-record 180 yards to key the AFC's rout of the NFC. Faulk, who earned the Dan McGuire Trophy as the player of the game, averaged nearly 14 yards on his 13 carries and shattered the previous rushing mark of 112 yards set by O.J. Simpson in the 1973 game. Faulk's 49-yard touchdown run from punt formation in the fourth quarter was the longest in Pro Bowl history. The Seahawks' Chris Warren added 127 yards on 14 carries as the AFC amassed records for rushing yards (400) and total yards (552). Steelers tight end Eric Green caught 2 touchdown passes for the victors. The NFC managed only 196 total yards, a large chunk coming when 49ers quarterback Steve Young and Vikings wide receiver Cris Carter teamed on a 51-yard touchdown pass in the first quarter. That gave the NFC a 10-0 advantage, but the AFC rallied in the second quarter and took the lead for good when the Browns' Leroy Hoard scored on a 4-yard touchdown run 2:07 before halftime.

AFC	0	17	3	21	—	41
NFC	10	0	3	0	—	13

NFC — FG Reveiz 28
NFC — Carter 51 pass from Young (Reveiz kick)
AFC — Green 22 pass from Elway (Carney kick)
AFC — FG Carney 22
AFC — Hoard 4 run (Carney kick)
NFC — FG Reveiz 49
AFC — FG Carney 23
AFC — Warren 11 run (Carney kick)
AFC — Green 16 pass from Hostetler (Carney kick)
AFC — Faulk 49 run (Carney kick)

1994 PRO FOOTBALL AWARDS

	NFL	AFC	NFC
PRO FOOTBALL WRITERS OF AMERICA			
Most Valuable Player	Steve Young		
Rookie of the Year	Marshall Faulk		
Coach of the Year	Bill Parcells		
ASSOCIATED PRESS			
Most Valuable Player	Steve Young		
Offensive Player of the Year	Barry Sanders		
Defensive Player of the Year	Deion Sanders		
Offensive Rookie of the Year	Marshall Faulk		
Defensive Rookie of the Year	Tim Bowens		
Coach of the Year	Bill Parcells		
UNITED PRESS INTERNATIONAL			
Offensive Player of the Year		Dan Marino	Steve Young
Defensive Player of the Year		Greg Lloyd	Charles Haley
Rookie of the Year		Marshall Faulk	Bryant Young
Coach of the Year		Bill Parcells	Dave Wannstedt
THE SPORTING NEWS			
Player of the Year	Steve Young		
Rookie of the Year	Marshall Faulk		
Coach of the Year	George Seifert		
FOOTBALL NEWS			
Player of the Year		Dan Marino	Steve Young
Coach of the Year		Bill Cowher	Dave Wannstedt
PRO FOOTBALL WEEKLY			
Most Valuable Player	Steve Young		
Offensive Player of the Year	Steve Young		
Defensive Player of the Year	Deion Sanders		
Offensive Rookie of the Year	Marshall Faulk		
Defensive Rookie of the Year	Tim Bowens		
Coach of the Year	Bill Parcells		
FOOTBALL DIGEST			
Player of the Year	Barry Sanders		
Defensive Player of the Year	Charles Haley		
Offensive Rookie of the Year	Marshall Faulk		
Defensive Rookie of the Year	Antonio Langham		
Coach of the Year	Bill Parcells		
SPORTS ILLUSTRATED			
Player of the Year	Steve Young		
Rookie of the Year	Marshall Faulk		
Coach of the Year	Bobby Ross		
MAXWELL CLUB PLAYER OF THE YEAR (Bert Bell Trophy)	Steve Young		
MAXWELL CLUB COACH OF THE YEAR (Earle "Greasy" Neale Trophy)	Bill Parcells		
SUPER BOWL MOST VALUABLE PLAYER (Pete Rozelle Trophy)	Steve Young		
AFC-NFC PRO BOWL PLAYER OF THE GAME (Dan McGuire Award)	Marshall Faulk		

1994 AFC PLAYERS OF THE WEEK

		Offense		Defense		Special Teams
Week 1	QB	Dan Marino, Miami	LB	Junior Seau, San Diego	PR	Eric Metcalf, Cleveland
Week 2	QB	Joe Montana, Kansas City	LB	Derrick Thomas, Kansas City	P	Chris Mohr, Buffalo
Week 3	RB	Barry Foster, Pittsburgh	CB	Terry McDaniel, L.A. Raiders	K	Steve Christie, Buffalo
Week 4	RB	Chris Warren, Seattle	LB	Cornelius Bennett, Buffalo	K	John Carney, San Diego
Week 5	QB	Drew Bledsoe, New England	LB	Kevin Greene, Pittsburgh	P	Tom Tupa, Cleveland
Week 6	RB	Natrone Means, San Diego	CB	Terry McDaniel, L.A. Raiders	K	Nick Lowery, N.Y. Jets
Week 7	QB	Joe Montana, Kansas City	S	Brian Washington, N.Y. Jets	P	Tom Tupa, Cleveland
Week 8	WR	Tim Brown, L.A. Raiders	LB	Pepper Johnson, Cleveland	PR	Eric Metcalf, Cleveland
Week 9	QB	John Elway, Denver	DE	Bruce Smith, Buffalo	K	Pete Stoyanovich, Miami
Week 10	QB	Jeff Blake, Cincinnati	LB	Mo Lewis, N.Y. Jets	K	Doug Pelfrey, Cincinnati
Week 11	QB	Drew Bledsoe, New England	CB	Rod Woodson, Pittsburgh	K	Doug Pelfrey, Cincinnati
Week 12	WR	Andre Reed, Buffalo	CB	Marcus Turner, N.Y. Jets	PR	Tim Brown, L.A. Raiders
Week 13	WR	Mark Ingram, Miami	S	Robert Blackmon, Seattle	PR	Darrien Gordon, San Diego
Week 14	QB	Jeff Hostetler, L.A. Raiders	CB	Ray Buchanan, Indianapolis	ST	Shane Dronett, Denver
Week 15	RB	Bernie Parmalee, Miami	S	Eric Turner, Cleveland	K	Jeff Jaeger, L.A. Raiders
Week 16	QB	Stan Humphries, San Diego	DE	Neil Smith, Kansas City	P	Pat O'Neill, New England
Week 17	RB	Marcus Allen, Kansas City	S	Eric Turner, Clevland	KR	Andre Coleman, San Diego

1994 AFC PLAYERS OF THE MONTH

		Offense		Defense		Special Teams
September	QB	Stan Humphries, San Diego	DE	Bruce Smith, Buffalo	K	Steve Christie, Buffalo
October	RB	Natrone Means, San Diego	LB	Greg Lloyd, Pittsburgh	K	John Carney, San Diego
November	QB	Jeff Blake, Cincinnati	LB	Kevin Greene, Pittsburgh	ST	Bennie Thompson, Cleveland
December	QB	Drew Bledsoe, New England	S	Eric Turner, Cleveland	KR	Andre Coleman, San Diego

1994 NFC PLAYERS OF THE WEEK

		Offense		Defense		Special Teams
Week 1	WR	Jerry Rice, San Francisco	DE	Charles Haley, Dallas	KR-PR	David Meggett, N.Y. Giants
Week 2	WR	Andre Rison, Atlanta	LB	Hardy Nickerson, Tampa Bay	KR-PR	Brian Mitchell, Washington
Week 3	RB	Barry Sanders, Detroit	LB	Darion Conner, New Orleans	K	Doug Brien, San Francisco
Week 4	QB	Warren Moon, Minnesota	CB	Deion Sanders, San Francisco	P	Sean Landeta, L.A. Rams
Week 5	RB	Charlie Garner, Philadelphia	LB	James Williams, New Orleans	KR-PR	Vernon Turner, Tampa Bay
Week 6	QB	Troy Aikman, Dallas	S	Merton Hanks, San Francisco	PR	Robert Brooks, Green Bay
Week 7	QB	Steve Young, San Francisco	CB	Aeneas Williams, Arizona	ST	Bill Bates, Dallas
Week 8	QB	Gus Frerotte, Washington	LB	Chris Spielman, Detroit	KR-PR	Tyrone Hughes, New Orleans
Week 9	WR	Alvin Harper, Dallas	LB	Bryce Paup, Green Bay	K	Fuad Reveiz, Minnesota
Week 10	QB	Warren Moon, Minnesota	S	Kevin Ross, Atlanta	KR-PR	Dexter Carter, San Francisco
Week 11	RB	Barry Sanders, Detroit	S	Merton Hanks, San Francisco	P	Craig Hentrich, Green Bay
Week 12	WR	Jerry Rice, San Francisco	LB	Seth Joyner, Arizona	KR-PR	Kevin Williams, Dallas
Week 13	QB	Jason Garrett, Dallas	LB	Hardy Nickerson, Tampa Bay	K	Kevin Butler, Chicago
Week 14	WR	Cris Carter, Minnesota	S	Darren Woodson, Dallas	K	Brad Daluiso, N.Y. Giants
Week 15	QB	Steve Young, San Francisco	LB	Jack Del Rio, Minnesota	K	Morten Andersen, New Orleans
Week 16	RB	Barry Sanders, Detroit	LB	Darrin Smith, Dallas	KR	Mel Gray, Detroit
Week 17	WR	Sterling Sharpe, Green Bay	DT	John Randle, Minnesota	P	Tommy Barnhardt, New Orleans

1994 NFC PLAYERS OF THE MONTH

		Offense		Defense		Special Teams
September	RB	David Meggett, N.Y. Giants	LB	Jack Del Rio, Minnesota	P	Sean Landeta, L.A. Rams
October	RB	Barry Sanders, Detroit	CB	Anthony Parker, Minnesota	KR-PR	Tyrone Hughes, New Orleans
November	QB	Steve Young, San Francisco	LB	Bryce Paup, Green Bay	K	Kevin Butler, Chicago
December	QB	Steve Young, San Francisco	DT	John Randle, Minnesota	K	Fuad Reveiz, Minnesota

1994 ALL-PRO TEAMS

1994 PFWA ALL-PRO TEAM

Selected by the Professional Football Writers of America

Offense

Jerry Rice, San Francisco	Wide Receiver
Cris Carter, Minnesota	Wide Receiver
Ben Coates, New England	Tight End
William Roaf, New Orleans	Tackle
Richmond Webb, Miami	Tackle
Randall McDaniel, Minnesota	Guard
Nate Newton, Dallas	Guard
Dermontti Dawson, Pittsburgh	Center
Steve Young, San Francisco	Quarterback
Barry Sanders, Detroit	Running Back
Emmitt Smith, Dallas	Running Back

Defense

Bruce Smith, Buffalo	End
Charles Haley, Dallas	End
John Randle, Minnesota	Tackle
Chester McGlockton, Los Angeles Raiders	Tackle
Greg Lloyd, Pittsburgh	Linebacker
Kevin Greene, Pittsburgh	Linebacker
Junior Seau, San Diego	Linebacker
Chris Spielman, Detroit	Linebacker
Deion Sanders, San Francisco	Cornerback
Rod Woodson, Pittsburgh	Cornerback
Darren Woodson, Dallas	Safety
Eric Turner, Cleveland	Safety

Specialists

Fuad Reveiz, Minnesota	Kicker
Reggie Roby, Washington	Punter
Mel Gray, Detroit	Kick Returner
Brian Mitchell, Washington	Punt Returner
Steve Tasker, Buffalo	Special Teams Player

1994 ASSOCIATED PRESS ALL-PRO TEAM

Offense

Jerry Rice, San Francisco	Wide Receiver
Cris Carter, Minnesota	Wide Receiver
Ben Coates, New England	Tight End
William Roaf, New Orleans	Tackle
Richmond Webb, Miami	Tackle
Nate Newton, Dallas	Guard
Randall McDaniel, Minnesota	Guard
Dermontti Dawson, Pittsburgh	Center
Steve Young, San Francisco	Quarterback
Barry Sanders, Detroit	Running Back
Emmitt Smith, Dallas	Running Back

Defense

Charles Haley, Dallas	End
Bruce Smith, Buffalo	End
John Randle, Minnesota	Tackle
Cortez Kennedy, Seattle	Tackle
Greg Lloyd, Pittsburgh	Linebacker
Kevin Greene, Pittsburgh	Linebacker
Junior Seau, San Diego	Linebacker
Deion Sanders, San Francisco	Cornerback
Rod Woodson, Pittsburgh	Cornerback
Eric Turner, Cleveland	Safety
Darren Woodson, Dallas	Safety

Specialists

John Carney, San Diego	Kicker
Reggie Roby, Washington	Punter
Mel Gray, Detroit	Kick Returner

1994 ALL-NFL TEAM

Selected by the Associated Press and the Professional Football Writers of America

Offense

Jerry Rice, San Francisco (AP, PFWA)	Wide Receiver
Cris Carter, Minnesota (AP, PFWA)	Wide Receiver
Ben Coates, New England (AP, PFWA)	Tight End
William Roaf, New Orleans (AP, PFWA)	Tackle
Richmond Webb, Miami (AP, PFWA)	Tackle
Randall McDaniel, Minnesota (AP, PFWA)	Guard
Nate Newton, Dallas (AP, PFWA)	Guard
Dermontti Dawson, Pittsburgh (AP, PFWA)	Center
Steve Young, San Francisco (AP, PFWA)	Quarterback
Barry Sanders, Detroit (AP, PFWA)	Running Back
Emmitt Smith, Dallas (AP, PFWA)	Running Back

Defense

Bruce Smith, Buffalo (AP, PFWA)	End
Charles Haley, Dallas (AP, PFWA)	End
John Randle, Minnesota (AP, PFWA)	Tackle
Cortez Kennedy, Seattle (AP)	Tackle
Chester McGlockton, Los Angeles Raiders (PFWA)	Tackle
Greg Lloyd, Pittsburgh (AP, PFWA)	Linebacker
Kevin Greene, Pittsburgh (AP, PFWA)	Linebacker
Junior Seau, San Diego (AP, PFWA)	Linebacker
Chris Spielman, Detroit (PFWA)	Linebacker
Deion Sanders, San Francisco (AP, PFWA)	Cornerback
Rod Woodson, Pittsburgh (AP, PFWA)	Cornerback
Eric Turner, Cleveland (AP, PFWA)	Safety
Darren Woodson, Dallas (AP, PFWA)	Safety

Specialists

John Carney, San Diego (AP)	Kicker
Fuad Reveiz, Minnesota (PFWA)	Kicker
Reggie Roby, Washington (AP, PFWA)	Punter
Mel Gray, Detroit (AP, PFWA)	Kick Returner
Brian Mitchell, Washington (PFWA)	Punt Returner
Steve Tasker, Buffalo (PFWA)	Special Teams Player

1994 UPI ALL-AFC TEAM

Selected by United Press International

Offense

Andre Reed, Buffalo	Wide Receiver
Irving Fryar, Miami	Wide Receiver
Ben Coates, New England	Tight End
Bruce Armstrong, New England	Tackle
Richmond Webb, Miami	Tackle
Steve Wisniewski, Los Angeles Raiders	Guard
Keith Sims, Miami	Guard
Dermontti Dawson, Pittsburgh	Center
Dan Marino, Miami	Quarterback
Marshall Faulk, Indianapolis	Running Back
Chris Warren, Seattle	Running Back

Defense

Bruce Smith, Buffalo	End
Leslie O'Neal, San Diego	End
Michael Dean Perry, Cleveland	Tackle
Cortez Kennedy, Seattle	Tackle
Greg Lloyd, Pittsburgh	Linebacker
Derrick Thomas, Kansas City	Linebacker
Junior Seau, San Diego	Linebacker
Terry McDaniel, Los Angeles Raiders	Cornerback
Rod Woodson, Pittsburgh	Cornerback
Eric Turner, Cleveland	Safety
Carnell Lake, Pittsburgh	Safety

Specialists

John Carney, San Diego	Kicker
Rick Tuten, Seattle	Punter

1994 UPI ALL-NFC TEAM

Selected by United Press International

Offense

Jerry Rice, San Francisco	Wide Receiver
Cris Carter, Minnesota	Wide Receiver
Brent Jones, San Francisco	Tight End
William Roaf, New Orleans	Tackle
Lomas Brown, Detroit	Tackle
Nate Newton, Dallas	Guard
Randall McDaniel, Minnesota	Guard
Mark Stepnoski, Dallas	Center
Steve Young, San Francisco	Quarterback
Barry Sanders, Detroit	Running Back
Emmitt Smith, Dallas	Running Back

Defense

Charles Haley, Dallas	End
Reggie White, Green Bay	End
John Randle, Minnesota	Tackle
Leon Lett, Dallas	Tackle
Bryce Paup, Green Bay	Linebacker
Ken Harvey, Washington	Linebacker
Chris Spielman, Detroit	Linebacker
Deion Sanders, San Francisco	Cornerback
Aeneas Williams, Arizona	Cornerback
Darren Woodson, Dallas	Safety
Merton Hanks, San Francisco	Safety

Specialists

Fuad Reveiz, Minnesota	Kicker
Reggie Roby, Washington	Punter

1994 PFWA ALL-ROOKIE TEAM

Selected by the Professional Football Writers of America

Offense

Darnay Scott, Cincinnati	Wide Receiver
Derrick Alexander, Cleveland	Wide Receiver
Andrew Jordan, Minnesota	Tight End
Larry Allen, Dallas	Tackle
Todd Steussie, Minnesota	Tackle
Joe Panos, Philadelphia	Guard
Anthony Redmon, Arizona	Guard
Kevin Mawae, Seattle	Center
Heath Shuler, Washington	Quarterback
Marshall Faulk, Indianapolis	Running Back
Errict Rhett, Tampa Bay	Running Back

Defense

Sam Adams, Seattle	End
Joe Johnson, New Orleans	End
Tim Bowens, Miami	Tackle
Bryant Young, San Francisco	Tackle
Rob Fredrickson, Los Angeles Raiders	Linebacker
Lee Woodall, San Francisco	Linebacker
Willie McGinest, New England	Linebacker
Aubrey Beavers, Miami	Linebacker
Dewayne Washington, Minnesota	Cornerback
Antonio Langham, Cleveland	Cornerback
Darryl Morrison, Washington	Safety
Keith Lyle, Los Angeles Rams	Safety

Specialists

Chris Boniol, Dallas	Kicker
Pat O'Neill, New England	Punter
Andre Coleman, San Diego	Kick Returner
Jeff Burris, Buffalo	Punt Returner
Sam Rogers, Buffalo	Special Teams Player

1994 BEST PERFORMANCES

TEN BEST RUSHING PERFORMANCES, 1994

	Att.	Yards	TD
1. Barry Sanders Detroit vs. Tampa Bay, November 13	26	237	0
2. Barry Sanders Detroit vs. Dallas, September 19	40	194	0
3. Errict Rhett Tampa Bay vs. Washington, December 4	40	192	1
4. Barry Sanders Detroit vs. Green Bay, December 4	20	188	1
5. Chris Warren Seattle vs. Houston, December 11	30	185	1
6. Barry Foster Pittsburgh vs. Indianapolis, September 18	31	179	1
7. Emmitt Smith Dallas vs. Pittsburgh, September 4	31	171	1
8. Barry Sanders Detroit vs. Chicago, October 23	23	167	0
9. Barry Sanders Detroit vs. Tampa Bay, October 2	20	166	0
10. Emmitt Smith Dallas vs. N.Y. Giants, November 7	35	163	2

100-YARD RUSHING PERFORMANCES, 1994

First Week

Emmitt Smith, Dallas — 171 yards vs. Pittsburgh
Marshall Faulk, Indianapolis — 143 yards vs. Houston
Barry Sanders, Detroit — 120 yards vs. Atlanta
Chris Warren, Seattle — 100 yards vs. Washington

Second Week

Natrone Means, San Diego — 107 yards vs. Cincinnati
Thurman Thomas, Buffalo — 106 yards vs. New England
Marshall Faulk, Indianapolis — 104 yards vs. Tampa Bay
Jerome Bettis, L.A. Rams — 102 yards vs. Atlanta

Third Week

Barry Sanders, Detroit — 194 yards vs. Dallas
Barry Foster, Pittsburgh — 179 yards vs. Indianapolis
Terry Allen, Minnesota — 159 yards vs. Chicago
Emmitt Smith, Dallas — 143 yards vs. Detroit
Thurman Thomas, Buffalo — 112 yards vs. Houston
Jerome Bettis, L.A. Rams — 104 yards vs. San Francisco
Terry Kirby, Miami — 100 yards vs. N.Y. Jets

Fourth Week

Jerome Bettis, L.A. Rams — 132 yards vs. Kansas City
Barry Sanders, Detroit — 131 yards vs. New England
Johnny Johnson, N.Y. Jets — 126 yards vs. Chicago
Chris Warren, Seattle — 126 yards vs. Pittsburgh
Terry Allen, Minnesota — 113 yards vs. Miami
Thurman Thomas, Buffalo — 103 yards vs. Denver

Fifth Week

Barry Sanders, Detroit — 166 yards vs. Tampa Bay
Jerome Bettis, L.A. Rams — 117 yards vs. Atlanta
Barry Foster, Pittsburgh — 115 yards vs. Houston
Charlie Garner, Philadelphia — 111 yards vs. San Francisco

Sixth Week

Natrone Means, San Diego — 125 yards vs. Kansas City
Thurman Thomas, Buffalo — 125 yards vs. Miami
Charlie Garner, Philadelphia — 122 yards vs. Washington
Leonard Russell, Denver — 103 yards vs. Seattle
Lewis Tillman, Chicago — 100 yards vs. New Orleans

Seventh Week

Bernie Parmalee, Miami — 150 yards vs. L.A. Raiders
Johnny Johnson, N.Y. Jets — 122 yards vs. New England
Natrone Means, San Diego — 120 yards vs. New Orleans
Ron Moore, Arizona — 118 yards vs. Washington
Rodney Hampton, N.Y. Giants — 112 yards vs. L.A. Rams
Emmitt Smith, Dallas — 106 yards vs. Philadelphia

Eighth Week

Barry Sanders, Detroit — 167 yards vs. Chicago
Byron (Bam) Morris, Pittsburgh — 146 yards vs. N.Y. Giants
Chris Warren, Seattle — 117 yards vs. Kansas City
Harvey Williams, L.A. Raiders — 107 yards vs. Atlanta
Ricky Watters, San Francisco — 103 yards vs. Tampa Bay
Natrone Means, San Diego — 100 yards vs. Denver

Ninth Week

Barry Sanders, Detroit — 146 yards vs. N.Y. Giants
Rodney Hampton, N.Y. Giants — 138 yards vs. Detroit
Harvey Williams, L.A. Raiders — 128 yards vs. Houston
Bernie Parmalee, Miami — 123 yards vs. New England
Terry Allen, Minnesota — 113 yards vs. Tampa Bay
Marshall Faulk, Indianapolis — 110 yards vs. N.Y. Jets
Edgar Bennett, Green Bay — 105 yards vs. Chicago
Natrone Means, San Diego — 104 yards vs. Seattle

Tenth Week

Emmitt Smith, Dallas — 163 yards vs. N.Y. Giants
Leroy Hoard, Cleveland — 123 yards vs. New England
Natrone Means, San Diego — 102 yards vs. Atlanta

Eleventh Week

Barry Sanders, Detroit — 237 yards vs. Tampa Bay
Mario Bates, New Orleans — 141 yards vs. Atlanta
Chris Warren, Seattle — 122 yards vs. Denver
Errict Rhett, Tampa Bay — 112 yards vs. Detroit
Leonard Russell, Denver — 109 yards vs. Seattle

Twelfth Week

Lorenzo White, Houston — 156 yards vs. N.Y. Giants
Lewis Tillman, Chicago — 126 yards vs. Detroit
Rodney Hampton, N.Y. Giants — 122 yards vs. Houston
Chris Warren, Seattle — 116 yards vs. Tampa Bay
Errict Rhett, Tampa Bay — 111 yards vs. Seattle

Thirteenth Week

Emmitt Smith, Dallas — 133 yards vs. Green Bay
Rodney Hampton, N.Y. Giants — 106 yards vs. Washington
Ricky Watters, San Francisco — 105 yards vs. New Orleans
Leroy Hoard, Cleveland — 103 yards vs. Houston

Fourteenth Week

Errict Rhett, Tampa Bay — 192 yards vs. Washington
Barry Sanders, Detroit — 188 yards vs. Green Bay
Marshall Faulk, Indianapolis — 129 yards vs. Seattle
Byron (Bam) Morris, Pittsburgh — 108 yards vs. Cincinnati

Fifteenth Week

Chris Warren, Seattle — 185 yards vs. Houston
Bernie Parmalee, Miami — 127 yards vs. Kansas City
Barry Sanders, Detroit — 127 yards vs. N.Y. Jets
Errict Rhett, Tampa Bay — 119 yards vs. L.A. Rams
Emmitt Smith, Dallas — 112 yards vs. Cleveland
Edgar Bennett, Green Bay — 106 yards vs. Chicago

Sixteenth Week

Chris Warren, Seattle — 122 yards vs. L.A. Raiders
Barry Sanders, Detroit — 110 yards vs. Minnesota
Barry Foster, Pittsburgh — 106 yards vs. Cleveland

Seventeenth Week

Marcus Allen, Kansas City — 132 yards vs. L.A. Raiders
Edgar Bennett, Green Bay — 100 yards vs. Tampa Bay

Times 100 or More (82)

Sanders, 10; Warren, 7; Means, E. Smith, 6; Bettis, Faulk, Hampton, Rhett, Thomas, 4; T. Allen, Bennett, Foster, Parmalee, 3; Garner, Hoard, J. Johnson, Morris, Russell, Tillman, Watters, H. Williams, 2.

TEN BEST PASSING PERFORMANCES, 1994

	Att.	Comp.	Yards	TD
1. Dan Marino				
Miami vs. New England, September 4	42	23	473	5
2. Dan Marino				
Miami vs. Minnesota, September 25	54	29	431	3
3. Drew Bledsoe				
New England vs. Minnesota, November 13	70	45	426	3
4. Drew Bledsoe				
New England vs. Miami, September 4	51	32	421	4
5. Warren Moon				
Minnesota vs. New Orleans, November 6	57	33	420	3
6. Warren Moon				
Minnesota vs. N.Y. Jets, November 20	50	33	400	2
7. Joe Montana				
Kansas City vs. Denver, October 17	54	34	393	3
8. Jeff Blake				
Cincinnati vs. Seattle, November 6	43	31	387	0
9. John Elway				
Denver vs. Atlanta, November 20	42	27	382	2
Boomer Esiason				
N.Y. Jets vs. Miami, November 27	41	26	382	2

300-YARD PASSING PERFORMANCES, 1994

First Week	
Dan Marino, Miami	473 yards vs. New England
Drew Bledsoe, New England	421 yards vs. Miami
John Elway, Denver	371 yards vs. San Diego
Randall Cunningham, Philadelphia	344 yards vs. N.Y. Giants
Jim Everett, New Orleans	326 yards vs. Kansas City
Joe Montana, Kansas City	315 yards vs. New Orleans
Steve Young, San Francisco	308 yards vs. L.A. Raiders
Second Week	
Drew Bledsoe, New England	380 yards vs. Buffalo
Jim Everett, New Orleans	376 yards vs. Washington
Brett Favre, Green Bay	362 yards vs. Miami
Jim Kelly, Buffalo	328 yards vs. New England
John Elway, Denver	319 yards vs. N.Y. Jets
Craig Erickson, Tampa Bay	313 yards vs. Indianapolis
Randall Cunningham, Philadelphia	311 yards vs. Chicago
Third Week	
John Friesz, Washington	381 yards vs. N.Y. Giants
Drew Bledsoe, New England	365 yards vs. Cincinnati
Joe Montana, Kansas City	361 yards vs. Atlanta
Steve Young, San Francisco	355 yards vs. L.A. Rams
Jeff Hostetler, L.A. Raiders	338 yards vs. Denver
Fourth Week	
Dan Marino, Miami	431 yards vs. Minnesota
Warren Moon, Minnesota	326 yards vs. Miami
Brett Favre, Green Bay	306 yards vs. Tampa Bay
Fifth Week	
Warren Moon, Minnesota	355 yards vs. Arizona
Drew Bledsoe, New England	334 yards vs. Green Bay
Sixth Week	
Drew Bledsoe, New England	321 yards vs. L.A. Raiders
Joe Montana, Kansas City	310 yards vs. San Diego
Seventh Week	
Joe Montana, Kansas City	393 yards vs. Denver
Eighth Week	
Randall Cunningham, Philadelphia	310 yards vs. Houston
Erik Kramer, Chicago	309 yards vs. Detroit
Ninth Week	
John Elway, Denver	349 yards vs. Cleveland
Tenth Week	
Warren Moon, Minnesota	420 yards vs. New Orleans
Jeff Blake, Cincinnati	387 yards vs. Seattle
Eleventh Week	
Drew Bledsoe, New England	426 yards vs. Minnesota
Jeff Blake, Cincinnati	354 yards vs. Houston
Warren Moon, Minnesota	349 yards vs. New England
Troy Aikman, Dallas	339 yards vs. San Francisco
Jeff George, Atlanta	328 yards vs. New Orleans
Twelfth Week	
Warren Moon, Minnesota	400 yards vs. N.Y. Jets
John Elway, Denver	382 yards vs. Atlanta
Jim Kelly, Buffalo	365 yards vs. Green Bay
Mike Tomczak, Pittsburgh	343 yards vs. Miami
Steve Young, San Francisco	325 yards vs. L.A. Rams
Dan Marino, Miami	312 yards vs. Pittsburgh
Jeff Hostetler, L.A. Raiders	310 yards vs. New Orleans
Thirteenth Week	
Boomer Esiason, N.Y. Jets	382 yards vs. Miami
Jeff George, Atlanta	364 yards vs. Philadelphia
Dan Marino, Miami	359 yards vs. N.Y. Jets
Dave Krieg, Detroit	351 yards vs. Buffalo
Jason Garrett, Dallas	311 yards vs. Green Bay
Fourteenth Week	
Brett Favre, Green Bay	366 yards vs. Detroit
Randall Cunningham, Philadelphia	327 yards vs. Dallas
Steve Bono, Kansas City	323 yards vs. Denver
Jeff Hostetler, L.A. Raiders	319 yards vs. San Diego
Dan Marino, Miami	311 yards vs. Buffalo
Warren Moon, Minnesota	306 yards vs. Chicago
Fifteenth Week	
Stan Humphries, San Diego	337 yards vs. San Francisco
Steve Bono, Kansas City	314 yards vs. Miami
Steve Young, San Francisco	304 yards vs. San Diego
Sixteenth Week	
Steve Young, San Francisco	350 yards vs. Denver
Brett Favre, Green Bay	321 yards vs. Atlanta
Seventeenth Week	
Jim Everett, New Orleans	343 yards vs. Denver
Bubby Brister, Philadelphia	325 yards vs. Cincinnati
Jay Schroeder, Arizona	317 yards vs. Atlanta
Chris Miller, L.A. Rams	304 yards vs. Washington

Times 300 or More (64)
Bledsoe, Moon, 6; Marino, Young, 5; Cunningham, Elway, Favre, Montana, 4; Everett, Hostetler, 3; Blake, Bono, George, Kelly, 2.

1994 BEST PERFORMANCES

TEN BEST RECEIVING PERFORMANCES, 1994

		Yards	No.	TD
1.	Irving Fryar Miami vs. New England, September 4	211	5	3
2.	Torrance Small New Orleans vs. Denver, December 24	200	6	2
3.	Henry Ellard Washington vs. N.Y. Giants, September 18	197	10	1
4.	Andre Rison Atlanta vs. Detroit, September 4	193	14	2
5.	Henry Ellard Washington vs. Arizona, December 11	191	8	1
	Andre Reed Buffalo vs. Green Bay, November 20	191	15	2
7.	Carl Pickens Cincinnati vs. Houston, November 13	188	11	3
8.	Fred Barnett Philadelphia vs. Houston, October 24	187	5	1
9.	Charles Wilson Tampa Bay vs. L.A. Rams, December 11	176	4	2
10.	Cedric Tillman Denver vs. Atlanta, November 20	175	8	0

100-YARD RECEIVING PERFORMANCES, 1994

First Week

Irving Fryar, Miami — 211 yards vs. New England
Andre Rison, Atlanta — 193 yards vs. Detroit
Jerry Rice, San Francisco — 169 yards vs. L.A. Raiders
Ben Coates, New England — 161 yards vs. Miami
Michael Irvin, Dallas — 139 yards vs. Pittsburgh
Mike Pritchard, Denver — 119 yards vs. San Diego
Willie Davis, Kansas City — 109 yards vs. New Orleans
Henry Ellard, Washington — 105 yards vs. Seattle
Quinn Early, New Orleans — 101 yards vs. Kansas City

Second Week

Willie Anderson, L.A. Rams — 154 yards vs. Atlanta
Curtis Conway, Chicago — 148 yards vs. Philadelphia
Rob Moore, N.Y. Jets — 147 yards vs. Denver
Andre Reed, Buffalo — 142 yards vs. New England
Ben Coates, New England — 124 yards vs. Buffalo
Andre Rison, Atlanta — 123 yards vs. L.A. Rams
Mark Seay, San Diego — 119 yards vs. Cincinnati
Alvin Harper, Dallas — 109 yards vs. Houston
Anthony Miller, Denver — 105 yards vs. N.Y. Jets
Haywood Jeffires, Houston — 103 yards vs. Dallas
Fred Barnett, Philadelphia — 102 yards vs. Chicago
Michael Timpson, New England — 101 yards vs. Buffalo
Mike Pritchard, Denver — 100 yards vs. N.Y. Jets

Third Week

Henry Ellard, Washington — 197 yards vs. N.Y. Giants
Tony Martin, San Diego — 152 yards vs. Seattle
Jerry Rice, San Francisco — 147 yards vs. L.A. Rams
Derrick Alexander, Cleveland — 136 yards vs. Arizona
Tim Brown, L.A. Raiders — 136 yards vs. Denver
Michael Timpson, New England — 125 yards vs. Cincinnati
Terance Mathis, Atlanta — 123 yards vs. Kansas City
Webster Slaughter, Houston — 110 yards vs. Buffalo
Ben Coates, New England — 108 yards vs. Cincinnati
Sterling Sharpe, Green Bay — 108 yards vs. Philadelphia
John Taylor, San Francisco — 103 yards vs. L.A. Rams
Keith Jackson, Miami — 100 yards vs. N.Y. Jets

Fourth Week

Henry Ellard, Washington — 162 yards vs. Atlanta
Irving Fryar, Miami — 160 yards vs. Minnesota
Andre Reed, Minnesota — 127 yards vs. Miami
Pat Coleman, Houston — 112 yards vs. Cincinnati

Fifth Week

Cris Carter, Minnesota — 167 yards vs. Arizona
Sterling Sharpe, Green Bay — 132 yards vs. New England
Calvin Williams, Philadelphia — 122 yards vs. San Francisco
Vincent Brisby, New England — 117 yards vs. Green Bay
Derrick Alexander, Cleveland — 105 yards vs. N.Y. Jets
Kelvin Martin, Seattle — 104 yards vs. Indianapolis

Sixth Week

Michael Irvin, Dallas — 136 yards vs. Arizona
Ben Coates, New England — 123 yards vs. L.A. Raiders
Qadry Ismail, Minnesota — 117 yards vs. N.Y. Giants

Seventh Week

Sean Dawkins, Indianapolis — 105 yards vs. Buffalo

Eighth Week

Fred Barnett, Philadelphia — 187 yards vs. Houston
Jeff Graham, Chicago — 136 yards vs. Detroit
Tim Brown, L.A. Raiders — 130 yards vs. Atlanta
Marshall Faulk, Indianapolis — 127 yards vs. Washington
Shannon Sharpe, Denver — 121 yards vs. San Diego
Michael Irvin, Dallas — 115 yards vs. Arizona
Henry Ellard, Washington — 108 yards vs. Indianapolis

Ninth Week

Darnay Scott, Cincinnati — 155 yards vs. Dallas
Alvin Harper, Dallas — 125 yards vs. Cincinnati
Herman Moore, Detroit — 106 yards vs. N.Y. Giants
Andre Reed, Buffalo — 106 yards vs. Kansas City

Tenth Week

Fred Barnett, Philadelphia — 173 yards vs. Arizona
Jake Reed, Minnesota — 157 yards vs. New Orleans
Darnay Scott, Cincinnati — 157 yards vs. Seattle
Cris Carter, Minnesota — 151 yards vs. New Orleans
Herman Moore, Detroit — 151 yards vs. Green Bay
Michael Irvin, Dallas — 118 yards vs. N.Y. Giants
O.J. McDuffie, Miami — 108 yards vs. Indianapolis

Eleventh Week

Carl Pickens, Cincinnati — 188 yards vs. Houston
Alvin Harper, Dallas — 136 yards vs. San Francisco
Terance Mathis, Atlanta — 125 yards vs. New Orleans
Andre Rison, Atlanta — 118 yards vs. New Orleans
Michael Timpson, New England — 113 yards vs. Minnesota
Irving Fryar, Miami — 112 yards vs. Chicago
Willie Anderson, L.A. Rams — 105 yards vs. L.A. Raiders

Twelfth Week

Andre Reed, Buffalo — 191 yards vs. Green Bay
Cedric Tillman, Denver — 175 yards vs. Atlanta
Jerry Rice, San Francisco — 165 yards vs. L.A. Rams
Terance Mathis, Atlanta — 163 yards vs. Denver
Tim Brown, L.A. Raiders — 132 yards vs. New Orleans
Jake Reed, Minnesota — 121 yards vs. N.Y. Jets
Johnny Mitchell, N.Y. Jets — 120 yards vs. Minnesota
Brett Perriman, Detroit — 120 yards vs. Chicago
Irving Fryar, Miami — 113 yards vs. Pittsburgh
Mike Sherrard, N.Y. Giants — 109 yards vs. Houston
Desmond Howard, Washington — 107 yards vs. Dallas
Carl Pickens, Cincinnati — 103 yards vs. Indianapolis
Anthony Miller, Denver — 102 yards vs. Atlanta
Adrian Cooper, Minnesota — 101 yards vs. N.Y. Jets
Cris Carter, Minnesota — 100 yards vs. N.Y. Jets

Thirteenth Week

Herman Moore, Detroit — 169 yards vs. Buffalo
Jeff Graham, Chicago — 154 yards vs. Arizona
Brian Blades, Seattle — 141 yards vs. Kansas City
Carl Pickens, Cincinnati — 132 yards vs. Denver
Terance Mathis, Atlanta — 124 yards vs. Philadelphia
Rob Moore, N.Y. Jets — 124 yards vs. Miami
Sterling Sharpe, Green Bay — 122 yards vs. Dallas
Ben Coates, New England — 119 yards vs. Indianapolis

Mark Ingram, Miami	117 yards vs. N.Y. Jets
Anthony Miller, Denver	116 yards vs. Cincinnati
Art Monk, N.Y. Jets	108 yards vs. Miami
Irving Fryar, Miami	103 yards vs. N.Y. Jets
Qadry Ismail, Minnesota	101 yards vs. Tampa Bay
Fourteenth Week	
Derrick Alexander, Cleveland	171 yards vs. N.Y. Giants
Anthony Miller, Denver	153 yards vs. Kansas City
Desmond Howard, Washington	130 yards vs. Tampa Bay
Terance Mathis, Atlanta	128 yards vs. San Francisco
Cris Carter, Minnesota	124 yards vs. Chicago
Gary Clark, Arizona	120 yards vs. Houston
Michael Irvin, Dallas	117 yards vs. Philadelphia
Johnny Bailey, L.A. Rams	116 yards vs. New Orleans
Sterling Sharpe, Green Bay	115 yards vs. Detroit
Irving Fryar, Miami	110 yards vs. Buffalo
Willie Davis, Kansas City	107 yards vs. Denver
Andre Reed, Buffalo	106 yards vs. Miami
Carl Pickens, Cincinnati	105 yards vs. Pittsburgh
Anthony Morgan, Green Bay	103 yards vs. Detroit
J.J. Birden, Kansas City	101 yards vs. Denver
Mike Sherrard, N.Y. Giants	101 yards vs. Cleveland
Fifteenth Week	
Henry Ellard, Washington	191 yards vs. Arizona
Charles Wilson, Tampa Bay	176 yards vs. L.A. Rams
Tony Martin, San Diego	172 yards vs. San Francisco
Jerry Rice, San Francisco	144 yards vs. San Diego
J.J. Birden, Kansas City	131 yards vs. Miami
Cris Carter, Minnesota	111 yards vs. Buffalo
Robert Brooks, Green Bay	105 yards vs. Chicago
Michael Haynes, New Orleans	103 yards vs. Atlanta
Sixteenth Week	
Jerry Rice, San Francisco	121 yards vs. Denver
Anthony Miller, Denver	118 yards vs. San Francisco
Lawrence Dawsey, Tampa Bay	116 yards vs. Washington
Tony Martin, San Diego	116 yards vs. N.Y. Jets
Andre Reed, Buffalo	112 yards vs. New England
Tim Brown, L.A. Raiders	107 yards vs. Seattle
Ricky Watters, San Francisco	106 yards vs. Denver
Edgar Bennett, Green Bay	101 yards vs. Atlanta
Gary Clark, Arizona	101 yards vs. Cincinnati
Lake Dawson, Kansas City	101 yards vs. Houston
Seventeenth Week	
Torrance Small, New Orleans	200 yards vs. Denver
Charles Johnson, Pittsburgh	165 yards vs. San Diego
Bert Emanuel, Atlanta	136 yards vs. Arizona
Carl Pickens, Cincinnati	135 yards vs. Philadelphia
Sterling Sharpe, Green Bay	132 yards vs. Tampa Bay
Webster Slaughter, Houston	123 yards vs. N.Y. Jets
Calvin Williams, Philadelphia	122 yards vs. Cincinnati
Vincent Brisby, New England	115 yards vs. Chicago
Don Beebe, Buffalo	111 yards vs. Indianapolis

Times 100 or More (144)
Fryar, 6; Carter, Coates, Ellard, Irvin, Mathis, Miller, Pickens, Rice, A. Reed, St. Sharpe, 5; Brown, 4; Alexander, Barnett, Harper, T. Martin, H. Moore, J. Reed, Rison, Timpson, 3; Anderson, Birden, Brisby, Clark, Howard, W. Davis, Graham, Ismail, R. Moore, Pritchard, Scott, Sherrard, Slaughter, C. Williams, 2.

TOP QUARTERBACK SACK PERFORMANCES, 1994

(2.5 or More Sacks Per Game Needed to Qualify)

First Week	
Charles Haley, Dallas	4.0 vs. Pittsburgh
Jim Jeffcoat, Dallas	3.0 vs. Pittsburgh
Erik Howard, N.Y. Giants	2.5 vs. Philadelphia
Second Week	
Derrick Thomas, Kansas City	3.0 vs. San Francisco
Michael Bankston, Arizona	2.5 vs. N.Y. Giants
John Randle, Minnesota	2.5 vs. Detroit
Third Week	
Bruce Smith, Buffalo	4.0 vs. Houston
Darion Conner, New Orleans	3.0 vs. Tampa Bay
Leslie O'Neal, San Diego	3.0 vs. Seattle
Fourth Week	
Jeff Lageman, N.Y. Jets	2.5 vs. Chicago
Fifth Week	
Chris Slade, New England	2.5 vs. Green Bay
Sixth Week	
None	
Seventh Week	
Alfred Williams, Cincinnati	4.0 vs. Pittsburgh
Neil Smith, Kansas City	2.5 vs. Denver
Eighth Week	
None	
Ninth Week	
None	
Tenth Week	
Ray Seals, Pittsburgh	3.0 vs. Houston
Eleventh Week	
Kevin Greene, Pittsburgh	3.0 vs. Buffalo
Twelfth Week	
Chris Slade, New England	3.5 vs. San Diego
Jumpy Geathers, Atlanta	3.0 vs. Denver
Thirteenth Week	
Kelvin Pritchett, Detroit	3.0 vs. Buffalo
Chuck Smith, Atlanta	3.0 vs. Philadelphia
Fourteenth Week	
Charles Haley, Dallas	3.0 vs. Philadelphia
Fifteenth Week	
Shane Dronett, Denver	3.0 vs. L.A. Raiders
Sixteenth Week	
Rhett Hall, San Francisco	3.0 vs. Denver
Seventeenth Week	
Mo Lewis, N.Y. Jets	3.0 vs. Houston

1994 TEAM STATISTICS

AMERICAN FOOTBALL CONFERENCE OFFENSE

	Buff	Cin	Clev	Den	Hou	Ind	KC	Raid	Mia	NE	NYJ	Pitt	SD	Sea
First Downs	319	267	273	346	278	252	322	267	344	348	265	307	311	285
Rushing	107	84	80	101	97	108	97	87	109	83	90	138	102	114
Passing	181	158	161	202	158	126	211	158	220	243	164	148	181	143
Penalty	31	25	32	43	23	18	14	22	15	22	11	21	28	28
Rushes	483	404	449	431	417	495	464	428	433	478	416	546	482	480
Net Yds. Gained	1831	1556	1657	1470	1682	2060	1732	1512	1658	1332	1566	2180	1852	2084
Avg. Gain	3.8	3.9	3.7	3.4	4.0	4.2	3.7	3.5	3.8	2.8	3.8	4.0	3.8	4.3
Avg. Yds. per Game	114.4	97.3	103.6	91.9	105.1	128.8	108.3	94.5	103.6	83.3	97.9	136.3	115.8	130.3
Passes Attempted	542	542	507	626	554	376	615	488	627	699	539	463	522	498
Completed	342	289	266	388	274	217	366	281	392	405	310	266	305	253
% Completed	63.1	53.3	52.5	62.0	49.5	57.7	59.5	57.6	62.5	57.9	57.5	57.5	58.4	50.8
Total Yds. Gained	3714	3541	3269	4383	3216	2519	4092	3556	4533	4583	3323	3247	3619	2809
Times Sacked	41	44	14	55	65	28	19	50	18	22	28	39	29	40
Yds. Lost	301	305	94	366	417	166	132	289	113	139	186	283	251	241
Net Yds. Gained	3413	3236	3175	4017	2799	2353	3960	3267	4420	4444	3137	2964	3368	2568
Avg. Yds. per Game	213.3	202.3	198.4	251.1	174.9	147.1	247.5	204.2	276.3	277.8	196.1	185.3	210.5	160.5
Net Yds. per Pass Play	5.85	5.52	6.09	5.90	4.52	5.82	6.25	6.07	6.85	6.16	5.53	5.90	6.11	4.77
Yds. Gained per Comp.	10.86	12.25	12.29	11.30	11.74	11.61	11.18	12.65	11.56	11.32	10.72	12.21	11.87	11.10
Combined Net Yds. Gained	5244	4792	4832	5487	4481	4413	5692	4779	6078	5776	4703	5144	5220	4652
% Total Yds. Rushing	34.9	32.5	34.3	26.8	37.5	46.7	30.4	31.6	27.3	23.1	33.3	42.4	35.5	44.8
% Total Yds. Passing	65.1	67.5	65.7	73.2	62.5	53.3	69.6	68.4	72.7	76.9	66.7	57.6	64.5	55.2
Avg. Yds. per Game	327.8	299.5	302.0	342.9	280.1	275.8	355.8	298.7	379.9	361.0	293.9	321.5	326.3	290.8
Ball Control Plays	1066	990	970	1112	1036	899	1098	966	1078	1199	983	1048	1033	1018
Avg. Yds. per Play	4.9	4.8	5.0	4.9	4.3	4.9	5.2	4.9	5.6	4.8	4.8	4.9	5.1	4.6
Avg. Time of Poss.	29:21	27:11	28:44	30:58	29:06	28:31	30:55	29:30	31:46	32:08	29:54	31:58	30:19	28:43
Third Down Efficiency	43.2	31.0	33.8	37.7	34.8	35.4	39.5	39.4	46.1	41.2	34.7	39.0	39.5	37.9
Had Intercepted	21	19	21	13	17	14	14	16	18	27	18	9	14	9
Yds. Opp. Returned	262	176	225	288	188	174	217	202	190	252	232	106	233	210
Ret. by Opp. for TD	2	2	0	3	0	2	1	1	1	2	1	1	2	2
Punts	67	80	80	76	96	74	85	77	60	69	84	97	72	91
Yds. Punted	2799	3461	3211	3258	4115	3092	3582	3377	2412	2841	3534	3849	2951	3905
Avg. Yds. per Punt	41.8	43.3	40.1	42.9	42.9	41.8	42.1	43.9	40.2	41.2	42.1	39.7	41.0	42.9
Punt Returns	33	37	46	41	50	42	43	40	33	46	39	56	36	37
Yds. Returned	343	373	462	379	281	339	316	487	241	383	345	424	475	337
Avg. Yds. per Return	10.4	10.1	10.0	9.2	5.6	8.1	7.3	12.2	7.3	8.3	8.8	7.6	13.2	9.1
Returned for TD	0	1	2	0	1	1	0	0	0	0	0	0	2	0
Kickoff Returns	72	86	42	75	74	60	59	62	66	63	66	55	68	67
Yds. Returned	1345	1810	1031	1523	1436	1254	1300	1358	1294	1123	1282	1141	1636	1467
Avg. Yds. per Return	18.7	21.0	24.5	20.3	19.4	20.9	22.0	21.9	19.6	17.8	19.4	20.7	24.1	21.9
Returned for TD	0	0	1	0	0	1	1	0	0	0	0	0	2	1
Fumbles	30	31	26	27	42	30	21	22	28	28	28	18	19	31
Lost	13	22	14	18	25	17	12	14	14	11	10	8	9	19
Out of Bounds	4	1	3	1	2	1	1	1	2	3	3	2	2	1
Own Rec. for TD	0	0	0	0	0	0	0	0	0	0	0	0	0	0
Opp. Rec. by	12	8	13	14	12	10	26	13	9	18	21	14	15	11
Opp. Rec. for TD	1	0	0	0	0	2	0	2	0	1	0	1	0	0
Penalties	92	90	113	101	115	82	127	156	92	78	95	119	96	114
Yds. Penalized	631	618	969	865	959	658	911	1186	747	597	754	974	875	898
Total Points Scored	340	276	340	347	226	307	319	303	389	351	264	316	381	287
Total TDs	38	27	37	37	25	37	34	34	45	39	29	35	40	32
TDs Rushing	14	5	12	19	10	15	12	7	13	12	8	15	13	16
TDs Passing	23	21	20	18	13	15	20	22	31	25	18	17	20	13
TDs on Ret. and Rec.	1	1	5	0	2	7	2	5	1	2	3	3	7	3
Extra Points	38	26	36	32	22	37	33	32	41	36	28	33	36	29
Kicks Made	38	24	32	29	18	37	30	31	35	36	26	32	33	25
2Pt Conversions	0	2	4	3	4	0	3	1	6	0	2	1	3	4
Safeties	1	1	0	0	1	0	2	0	0	0	0	0	0	1
Field Goals Made	24	28	26	30	16	16	25	22	24	27	20	24	34	20
Field Goals Attempted	28	33	28	37	20	24	30	28	31	35	23	29	38	24
% Successful	85.7	84.8	92.9	81.1	80.0	66.7	83.3	78.6	77.4	77.1	87.0	82.8	89.5	83.3

AMERICAN FOOTBALL CONFERENCE DEFENSE

	Buff	Cin	Clev	Den	Hou	Ind	KC	Raid	Mia	NE	NYJ	Pitt	SD	Sea
First Downs	294	310	304	303	275	311	289	303	305	280	315	262	308	318
Rushing	82	126	98	103	112	98	93	94	85	86	105	76	89	122
Passing	199	168	173	182	132	192	164	176	195	173	189	156	191	178
Penalty	13	16	33	18	31	21	32	33	25	21	21	30	28	18
Rushes	447	517	465	432	540	463	446	444	394	422	463	421	385	511
Net Yds. Gained	1515	1906	1669	1752	2120	1646	1734	1543	1430	1760	1809	1452	1404	1952
Avg. Gain	3.4	3.7	3.6	4.1	3.9	3.6	3.9	3.5	3.6	4.2	3.9	3.4	3.6	3.8
Avg. Yds. per Game	94.7	119.1	104.3	109.5	132.5	102.9	108.4	96.4	89.4	110.0	113.1	90.8	87.8	122.0
Passes Attempted	535	505	587	568	400	598	504	564	577	545	522	532	577	537
Completed	314	294	325	322	221	354	300	306	334	298	333	280	363	313
% Completed	58.7	58.2	55.4	56.7	55.3	59.2	59.5	54.3	57.9	54.7	63.8	52.6	62.9	58.3
Total Yds. Gained	3812	3458	3425	4296	2963	3897	3500	3684	3954	3737	3730	3256	3911	3603
Times Sacked	25	31	38	23	31	29	39	38	29	39	29	55	43	29
Yds. Lost	152	210	268	141	168	218	234	284	160	290	201	382	253	206
Net Yds. Gained	3660	3248	3157	4155	2795	3679	3266	3400	3794	3447	3529	2874	3658	3397
Avg. Yds. per Game	228.8	203.0	197.3	259.7	174.7	229.9	204.1	212.5	237.1	215.4	220.6	179.6	228.6	212.3
Net Yds. per Pass Play	6.54	6.06	5.05	7.03	6.48	5.87	6.01	5.65	6.26	5.90	6.40	4.90	5.90	6.00
Yds. Gained per Comp.	12.14	11.76	10.54	13.34	13.41	11.01	11.67	12.04	11.84	12.54	11.20	11.63	10.77	11.51
Combined Net Yds. Gained	5175	5154	4826	5907	4915	5325	5000	4943	5224	5207	5338	4326	5062	5349
% Total Yds. Rushing	29.3	37.0	34.6	29.7	43.1	30.9	34.7	31.2	27.4	33.8	33.9	33.6	27.7	36.5
% Total Yds. Passing	70.7	63.0	65.4	70.3	56.9	69.1	65.3	68.8	72.6	66.2	66.1	66.4	72.3	63.5
Avg. Yds. per Game	323.4	322.1	301.6	369.2	307.2	332.8	312.5	308.9	326.5	325.4	333.6	270.4	316.4	334.3
Ball Control Plays	1007	1053	1090	1023	971	1090	989	1046	1000	1006	1014	1008	1005	1077
Avg. Yds. per Play	5.1	4.9	4.4	5.8	5.1	4.9	5.1	4.7	5.2	5.2	5.3	4.3	5.0	5.0
Avg. Time of Poss.	30:39	32:49	31:16	29:02	30:54	31:29	29:05	30:30	28:14	27:52	30:06	28:02	29:41	31:17
Third Down Efficiency	41.9	39.8	34.3	39.6	36.5	45.8	37.7	38.6	38.6	33.5	39.9	32.0	36.7	37.1
Intercepted By	16	10	18	12	14	18	12	12	23	22	17	17	17	19
Yds. Returned By	175	167	223	55	242	360	218	187	276	209	355	240	402	284
Returned for TD	0	0	1	0	1	3	1	3	1	1	3	2	3	2
Punts	69	87	97	76	82	72	85	84	68	83	62	97	76	78
Yds. Punted	2916	3528	3880	3303	3443	3039	3822	3414	2834	3333	2675	4096	3290	3188
Avg. Yds. per Punt	42.3	40.6	40.0	43.5	42.0	42.2	45.0	40.6	41.7	40.2	43.1	42.2	43.3	40.9
Punt Returns	38	43	38	39	50	40	50	38	32	34	38	39	38	43
Yds. Returned	324	459	220	275	438	366	506	366	324	260	260	263	348	426
Avg. Yds. per Return	8.5	10.7	5.8	7.1	8.8	9.2	10.1	9.6	10.1	7.6	6.8	6.7	9.2	9.9
Returned for TD	0	2	0	0	1	0	0	1	1	0	0	0	0	1
Kickoff Returns	72	61	71	70	48	65	66	65	74	63	61	68	79	61
Yds. Returned	1455	1408	1372	1396	832	1316	1447	1406	1549	1375	1195	1530	1740	1229
Avg. Yds. per Return	20.2	23.1	19.3	19.9	17.3	20.2	21.9	21.6	20.9	21.8	19.6	22.5	22.0	20.1
Returned for TD	0	2	0	0	0	0	0	0	2	1	0	2	1	0
Fumbles	23	26	26	24	20	21	36	26	29	34	30	31	29	21
Lost	12	8	13	14	12	10	26	13	9	18	21	14	15	11
Out of Bounds	1	2	1	1	1	1	1	1	5	1	2	3	0	2
Own Rec. for TD	0	0	0	0	0	0	0	0	0	0	0	0	0	0
Opp. Rec. by	13	22	14	18	25	17	12	14	14	11	10	8	9	19
Opp. Rec. for TD	2	0	0	0	1	0	0	1	1	1	0	1	0	1
Penalties	101	99	129	134	102	110	119	113	82	110	63	91	109	103
Yds. Penalized	770	861	1139	1031	807	824	925	823	653	795	489	763	989	773
Total Points Scored	356	406	204	396	352	320	298	327	327	312	320	234	306	323
Total TDs	40	45	22	43	37	34	35	38	42	36	37	23	34	34
TDs Rushing	10	16	9	12	17	8	11	11	14	11	17	7	11	15
TDs Passing	26	22	13	28	18	24	23	24	23	21	19	12	20	15
TDs on Ret. and Rec.	4	7	0	3	2	2	1	3	5	4	1	4	3	4
Total Extra Points	36	42	20	40	36	31	32	34	41	34	33	23	33	32
Kicks Made	34	41	19	35	34	29	30	34	40	32	31	22	30	28
2Pt Conversions	2	1	1	5	2	2	2	0	1	2	2	1	3	4
Safeties	0	0	0	0	1	1	0	1	0	0	0	0	0	1
Field Goals Made	26	31	17	31	30	27	18	21	11	20	21	24	22	27
Field Goals Attempted	30	35	26	37	31	34	23	29	18	25	27	29	27	33
% Successful	86.7	88.6	65.4	83.8	96.8	79.4	78.3	72.4	61.1	80.0	77.8	82.8	81.5	81.8

1994 TEAM STATISTICS

NATIONAL FOOTBALL CONFERENCE OFFENSE

	Ariz	Atl	Chi	Dall	Det	GB	Rams	Minn	NO	NYG	Phil	SF	TB	Wash
First Downs	287	302	274	322	280	314	274	325	308	263	293	362	276	269
Rushing	90	63	88	136	94	88	80	92	78	103	103	122	104	79
Passing	169	218	165	160	164	205	163	215	203	136	168	210	149	166
Penalty	28	21	21	26	22	21	31	18	27	24	22	30	23	24
Rushes	480	330	487	550	406	417	397	419	373	525	432	491	430	407
Net Yds. Gained	1560	1249	1588	1953	2080	1543	1389	1524	1336	1754	1761	1897	1489	1415
Avg. Gain	3.3	3.8	3.3	3.6	5.1	3.7	3.5	3.6	3.6	3.3	4.1	3.9	3.5	3.5
Avg. Yds. per Game	97.5	78.1	99.3	122.1	130.0	96.4	86.8	95.3	83.5	109.6	110.1	118.6	93.1	88.4
Passes Attempted	538	629	502	448	459	609	512	673	569	405	566	511	491	546
Completed	287	374	308	282	250	375	291	409	366	226	316	359	271	271
% Completed	53.3	59.5	61.4	62.9	54.5	61.6	56.8	60.8	64.3	55.8	55.8	70.3	55.2	49.6
Total Yds. Gained	3284	4344	3230	3461	3085	3977	3597	4570	4027	2847	3736	4362	3436	3524
Times Sacked	34	37	25	20	26	33	35	31	24	46	48	35	30	21
Yds. Lost	237	232	139	93	163	204	239	246	181	285	372	199	171	146
Net Yds. Gained	3047	4112	3091	3368	2922	3773	3358	4324	3846	2562	3364	4163	3265	3378
Avg. Yds. per Game	190.4	257.0	193.2	210.5	182.6	235.8	209.9	270.3	240.4	160.1	210.3	260.2	204.1	211.1
Net Yds. per Pass Play	5.33	6.17	5.87	7.20	6.02	5.88	6.14	6.14	6.49	5.68	5.48	7.62	6.27	5.96
Yds. Gained per Comp.	11.44	11.61	10.49	12.27	12.34	10.61	12.36	11.17	11.00	12.60	11.82	12.15	12.68	13.00
Combined Net Yds. Gained	4607	5361	4679	5321	5002	5316	4747	5848	5182	4316	5125	6060	4754	4793
% Total Yds. Rushing	33.9	23.3	33.9	36.7	41.6	29.0	29.3	26.1	25.8	40.6	34.4	31.3	31.3	29.5
% Total Yds. Passing	66.1	76.7	66.1	63.3	58.4	71.0	70.7	73.9	74.2	59.4	65.6	68.7	68.7	70.5
Avg. Yds. per Game	287.9	335.1	292.4	332.6	312.6	332.3	296.7	365.5	323.9	269.8	320.3	378.8	297.1	299.6
Ball Control Plays	1052	996	1014	1018	891	1059	944	1123	966	976	1046	1037	951	974
Avg. Yds. per Play	4.4	5.4	4.6	5.2	5.6	5.0	5.0	5.2	5.4	4.4	4.9	5.8	5.0	4.9
Avg. Time of Poss.	32:37	29:10	31:37	31:35	26:06	30:56	27:59	32:06	29:04	30:28	30:47	31:38	29:55	26:55
Third Down Efficiency	32.9	37.3	41.8	44.5	39.9	43.1	39.2	41.1	35.7	34.5	41.6	51.0	36.7	35.9
Had Intercepted	19	25	16	14	14	14	18	20	18	18	14	11	16	27
Yds. Opp. Returned	262	419	335	180	154	193	213	292	386	299	206	107	323	482
Ret. by Opp. for TD	3	1	3	0	1	0	2	1	3	3	1	1	2	4
Punts	98	79	76	70	64	81	78	77	67	89	92	54	74	82
Yds. Punted	3997	3121	2871	2935	2782	3351	3494	3301	2920	3578	3727	2235	2853	3639
Avg. Yds. per Punt	40.8	39.5	37.8	41.9	43.5	41.4	44.8	42.9	43.6	40.2	40.5	41.4	38.6	44.4
Punt Returns	42	31	27	44	25	49	40	39	25	32	41	40	28	32
Yds. Returned	286	188	218	404	256	414	461	238	152	388	381	334	248	452
Avg. Yds. per Return	6.8	6.1	8.1	9.2	10.2	8.4	11.5	6.1	6.1	12.1	9.3	8.4	8.9	14.1
Returned for TD	0	0	1	1	0	1	1	0	0	2	0	0	1	2
Kickoff Returns	57	75	66	50	71	56	71	60	82	73	67	58	70	71
Yds. Returned	1079	1627	1402	1284	1675	1168	1605	1296	1840	1328	1441	1244	1422	1685
Avg. Yds. per Return	18.9	21.7	21.2	25.7	23.6	20.9	22.6	21.6	22.4	18.2	21.5	21.4	20.3	23.7
Returned for TD	0	0	0	1	4	1	0	0	2	0	1	1	0	0
Fumbles	25	28	21	22	26	25	26	32	22	28	23	25	18	21
Lost	10	11	10	10	10	8	13	14	14	7	12	13	7	13
Out of Bounds	1	0	0	3	3	5	0	5	1	3	0	1	1	2
Own Rec. for TD	0	0	0	0	0	0	0	1	0	0	0	0	0	0
Opp. Rec. by	13	11	10	9	11	12	6	16	14	16	14	12	12	6
Opp. Rec. for TD	0	1	0	0	1	0	2	2	2	0	0	1	0	2
Penalties	128	119	65	100	109	85	112	112	88	92	138	109	93	88
Yds. Penalized	1090	934	503	895	781	760	922	880	678	818	1107	890	805	730
Total Points Scored	235	317	271	414	357	382	286	356	348	279	308	505	251	320
Total TDs	24	36	30	50	43	47	33	36	38	30	35	66	26	37
TDs Rushing	12	8	10	26	12	11	6	11	11	12	14	23	8	5
TDs Passing	11	25	19	19	24	33	23	18	22	16	18	37	17	25
TDs on Ret. and Rec.	1	3	1	5	7	3	4	7	5	2	3	6	1	7
Extra Points	22	35	26	48	41	42	30	34	34	28	33	62	23	33
Kicks Made	21	32	24	48	39	41	28	30	32	27	33	60	20	30
2Pt Conversions	1	3	2	0	2	1	2	4	2	1	0	2	3	3
Safeties	1	0	0	0	1	0	1	0	0	2	1	0	0	1
Field Goals Made	22	21	21	22	18	19	18	34	28	22	21	15	23	20
Field Goals Attempted	30	25	29	29	27	26	23	39	39	28	25	20	35	28
% Successful	73.3	84.0	72.4	75.9	66.7	73.1	78.3	87.2	71.8	78.6	84.0	75.0	65.7	71.4

NATIONAL FOOTBALL CONFERENCE DEFENSE

	Ariz	Atl	Chi	Dall	Det	GB	Rams	Minn	NO	NYG	Phil	SF	TB	Wash
First Downs	245	330	275	273	326	281	333	287	337	280	275	285	298	331
Rushing	71	107	100	86	131	82	103	65	106	92	94	82	100	129
Passing	144	201	163	157	169	182	198	195	208	166	151	182	179	182
Penalty	30	22	12	30	26	17	32	27	23	22	30	21	19	20
Rushes	409	426	432	437	511	381	496	355	458	447	449	375	468	556
Net Yds. Gained	1370	1693	1922	1561	1859	1363	1781	1090	1758	1728	1616	1338	1964	1975
Avg. Gain	3.3	4.0	4.4	3.6	3.6	3.6	3.6	3.1	3.8	3.9	3.6	3.6	4.2	3.6
Avg. Yds. per Game	85.6	105.8	120.1	97.6	116.2	85.2	111.3	68.1	109.9	108.0	101.0	83.6	122.8	123.4
Passes Attempted	465	580	522	522	547	605	541	597	559	500	490	583	498	496
Completed	234	364	295	269	370	337	320	368	353	289	251	329	303	300
% Completed	50.3	62.8	56.5	51.5	67.6	55.7	59.1	61.6	63.1	57.8	51.2	56.4	60.8	60.5
Total Yds. Gained	3310	4365	3262	3051	3745	3677	3548	3902	4007	3391	3359	3756	3486	3799
Times Sacked	35	32	28	47	28	37	26	36	36	26	42	38	20	28
Yds. Lost	272	229	175	299	199	276	159	250	196	169	265	255	114	165
Net Yds. Gained	3038	4136	3087	2752	3546	3401	3389	3652	3811	3222	3094	3501	3372	3634
Avg. Yds. per Game	189.9	258.5	192.9	172.0	221.6	212.6	211.8	228.3	238.2	201.4	193.4	218.8	210.8	227.1
Net Yds. per Pass Play	6.08	6.76	5.61	4.84	6.17	5.30	5.98	5.77	6.41	6.13	5.82	5.64	6.51	6.94
Yds. Gained per Comp.	14.15	11.99	11.06	11.34	10.12	10.91	11.09	10.60	11.35	11.73	13.38	11.42	11.50	12.66
Combined Net Yds. Gained	4408	5829	5009	4313	5405	4764	5170	4742	5569	4950	4710	4839	5336	5609
% Total Yds. Rushing	31.1	29.0	38.4	36.2	34.4	28.6	34.4	23.0	31.6	34.9	34.3	27.7	36.8	35.2
% Total Yds. Passing	68.9	71.0	61.6	63.8	65.6	71.4	65.6	77.0	68.4	65.1	65.7	72.3	63.2	64.8
Avg. Yds. per Game	275.5	364.3	313.1	269.6	337.8	297.8	323.1	296.4	348.1	309.4	294.4	302.4	333.5	350.6
Ball Control Plays	909	1038	982	1006	1086	1023	1063	988	1053	973	981	996	986	1080
Avg. Yds. per Play	4.8	5.6	5.1	4.3	5.0	4.7	4.9	4.8	5.3	5.1	4.8	4.9	5.4	5.2
Avg. Time of Poss.	27:23	30:50	28:23	28:25	33:54	29:04	32:01	27:54	30:56	29:32	29:13	28:22	30:05	33:05
Third Down Efficiency	27.8	41.0	37.2	39.7	48.5	35.6	45.7	36.3	43.3	41.1	36.4	39.4	43.9	39.0
Intercepted By	23	22	12	22	12	21	14	18	17	16	21	23	9	17
Yds. Returned By	297	322	127	297	144	232	211	338	197	128	209	508	77	326
Returned for TD	1	2	0	3	2	1	1	4	1	0	2	4	0	3
Punts	90	62	72	84	66	88	74	86	60	69	90	77	68	87
Yds. Punted	3677	2661	2808	3637	2963	3491	3106	3485	2558	2792	3570	3274	2902	3506
Avg. Yds. per Punt	40.9	42.9	39.0	43.3	44.9	39.7	42.0	40.5	42.6	40.5	39.7	42.5	42.7	40.3
Punt Returns	40	31	26	36	36	36	47	44	40	39	47	28	19	45
Yds. Returned	270	273	225	378	431	272	637	410	495	307	286	242	103	441
Avg. Yds. per Return	6.8	8.8	8.7	10.5	12.0	7.6	13.6	9.3	12.4	7.9	6.1	8.6	5.4	9.8
Returned for TD	0	0	0	0	2	0	3	1	2	0	1	0	0	1
Kickoff Returns	53	66	65	82	65	75	63	83	63	44	64	89	44	62
Yds. Returned	1214	1328	1271	1709	1572	1380	1446	1843	1493	923	1425	1912	941	1389
Avg. Yds. per Return	22.9	20.1	19.6	20.8	24.2	18.4	23.0	22.2	23.7	21.0	22.3	21.5	21.4	22.4
Returned for TD	1	0	1	0	1	1	2	1	0	0	0	0	0	1
Fumbles	28	20	29	15	34	32	15	25	28	25	29	25	21	21
Lost	13	11	10	9	11	12	6	16	14	16	14	12	12	6
Out of Bounds	2	1	4	2	7	6	0	1	0	2	1	0	3	1
Own Rec. for TD	0	0	0	0	0	1	0	0	0	0	0	0	0	0
Opp. Rec. by	10	11	10	10	10	8	13	14	14	7	12	13	7	13
Opp. Rec. for TD	1	1	1	0	0	1	0	0	2	1	0	3	0	0
Penalties	108	111	80	102	130	82	114	83	105	130	98	108	94	98
Yds. Penalized	800	853	645	826	1036	675	1015	614	922	1122	844	912	690	839
Total Points Scored	267	385	307	248	342	287	365	314	407	305	308	296	351	412
Total TDs	31	44	31	27	40	32	42	37	45	31	33	35	40	52
TDs Rushing	7	16	10	8	15	9	12	9	10	11	11	16	13	24
TDs Passing	19	26	16	19	21	20	23	25	28	16	20	15	25	22
TDs on Ret. and Rec.	5	2	5	0	4	3	7	3	7	4	2	4	2	6
Total Extra Points	29	40	28	24	38	27	41	33	44	30	31	30	40	48
Kicks Made	28	39	25	24	37	24	38	31	41	30	27	23	38	47
2Pt Conversions	1	1	3	0	1	3	3	2	3	0	4	7	2	1
Safeties	3	1	0	1	0	1	0	0	0	1	0	2	0	0
Field Goals Made	15	26	30	20	21	21	23	19	30	29	25	15	23	17
Field Goals Attempted	24	33	41	25	28	25	29	30	37	34	26	21	26	28
% Successful	62.5	78.8	73.2	80.0	75.0	84.0	79.3	63.3	81.1	85.3	96.2	71.4	88.5	60.7

1994 TEAM STATISTICS

AFC, NFC, AND NFL SUMMARY

	AFC Offense Total	AFC Offense Average	AFC Defense Total	AFC Defense Average	NFC Offense Total	NFC Offense Average	NFC Defense Total	NFC Defense Average	NFL Total	NFL Average
First Downs	4184	298.9	4177	298.4	4149	296.4	4156	296.9	8333	297.6
Rushing	1397	99.8	1369	97.8	1320	94.3	1348	96.3	2717	97.0
Passing	2454	175.3	2468	176.3	2491	177.9	2477	176.9	4945	176.6
Penalty	333	23.8	340	24.3	338	24.1	331	23.6	671	24.0
Rushes	6406	457.6	6350	453.6	6144	438.9	6200	442.9	12550	448.2
Net Yds. Gained	24172	1726.6	23692	1692.3	22538	1609.9	23018	1644.1	46710	1668.2
Avg. Gain	—	3.8	—	3.7	—	3.7	—	3.7	—	3.7
Avg. Yds. per Game	—	107.9	—	105.8	—	100.6	—	102.8	—	104.3
Passes Attempted	7598	542.7	7551	539.4	7458	532.7	7505	536.1	15056	537.7
Completed	4354	311.0	4357	311.2	4385	313.2	4382	313.0	8739	312.1
% Completed	—	57.3	—	57.7	—	58.8	—	58.4	—	58.0
Total Yds. Gained	50404	3600.3	51226	3659.0	51480	3677.1	50658	3618.4	101884	3638.7
Times Sacked	492	35.1	478	34.1	445	31.8	459	32.8	937	33.5
Yds. Lost	3283	234.5	3167	226.2	2907	207.6	3023	215.9	6190	221.1
Net Yds. Gained	47121	3365.8	48059	3432.8	48573	3469.5	47635	3402.5	95694	3417.6
Avg. Yds. per Game	—	210.4	—	214.5	—	216.8	—	212.7	—	213.6
Net Yds. per Pass Play	—	5.82	—	5.99	—	6.15	—	5.98	—	5.98
Yds. Gained per Comp.	—	11.58	—	11.76	—	11.74	—	11.56	—	11.66
Combined Net Yds. Gained	71293	5092.4	71751	5125.1	71111	5079.4	70653	5046.6	142404	5085.9
% Total Yds. Rushing	—	33.9	—	33.0	—	31.7	—	32.6	—	32.8
% Total Yds. Passing	—	66.1	—	67.0	—	68.3	—	67.4	—	67.2
Avg. Yds. per Game	—	318.3	—	320.3	—	317.5	—	315.4	—	317.9
Ball Control Plays	14496	1035.4	14379	1027.1	14047	1003.4	14164	1011.7	28543	1019.4
Avg. Yds. per Play	—	4.9	—	5.0	—	5.1	—	5.0	—	5.0
Third Down Efficiency	—	38.2	—	38.1	—	39.7	—	39.8	—	38.9
Interceptions	230	16.4	227	16.2	244	17.4	247	17.6	474	16.9
Yds. Returned	2955	211.1	3393	242.4	3851	275.1	3413	243.8	6806	243.1
Returned for TD	20	1.4	21	1.5	25	1.8	24	1.7	45	1.6
Punts	1108	79.1	1116	79.7	1081	77.2	1073	76.6	2189	78.2
Yds. Punted	46387	3313.4	46761	3340.1	44804	3200.3	44430	3173.6	91191	3256.8
Avg. Yds. per Punt	—	41.9	—	41.9	—	41.4	—	41.4	—	41.7
Punt Returns	579	41.4	560	40.0	495	35.4	514	36.7	1074	38.4
Yds. Returned	5185	370.4	4835	345.4	4420	315.7	4770	340.7	9605	343.0
Avg. Yds. per Return	—	9.0	—	8.6	—	8.9	—	9.3	—	8.9
Returned for TD	7	0.5	6	0.4	9	0.6	10	0.7	16	0.6
Kickoff Returns	915	65.4	924	66.0	927	66.2	918	65.6	1842	65.8
Yds. Returned	19000	1357.1	19250	1375.0	20096	1435.4	19846	1417.6	39096	1396.3
Avg. Yds. per Return	—	20.8	—	20.8	—	21.7	—	21.6	—	21.2
Returned for TD	6	0.4	8	0.6	10	0.7	8	0.6	16	0.6
Fumbles	381	27.2	376	26.9	342	24.4	347	24.8	723	25.8
Lost	206	14.7	196	14.0	152	10.9	162	11.6	358	12.8
Out of Bounds	27	1.9	22	1.6	25	1.8	30	2.1	52	1.9
Own Rec. for TD	0	0.0	0	0.0	1	0.1	1	0.1	1	0.0
Opp. Rec.	196	14.0	206	14.7	162	11.6	152	10.9	358	12.8
Opp. Rec. for TD	7	0.5	8	0.6	11	0.8	10	0.7	18	0.6
Penalties	1470	105.0	1465	104.6	1438	102.7	1443	103.1	2908	103.9
Yds. Penalized	11642	831.6	11642	831.6	11793	842.4	11793	842.4	23435	837.0
Total Points Scored	4446	317.6	4481	320.1	4629	330.6	4594	328.1	9075	324.1
Total TDs	489	34.9	500	35.7	531	37.9	520	37.1	1020	36.4
TDs Rushing	171	12.2	169	12.1	169	12.1	171	12.2	340	12.1
TDs Passing	276	19.7	288	20.6	307	21.9	295	21.1	583	20.8
TDs on Ret. and Rec.	42	3.0	43	3.1	55	3.9	54	3.9	97	3.5
Total Extra Points	459	32.8	467	33.4	491	35.1	483	34.5	950	33.9
Kicks Made	426	30.4	439	31.4	465	33.2	452	32.3	891	31.8
2Pt Conversions	33	2.4	28	2.0	26	1.9	31	2.2	59	2.1
Safeties	6	0.4	4	0.3	7	0.5	9	0.6	13	0.5
Field Goals Made	336	24.0	326	23.3	304	21.7	314	22.4	640	22.9
Field Goals Attempted	408	29.1	404	28.9	403	28.8	407	29.1	811	29.0
% Successful	—	82.4	—	80.7	—	75.4	—	77.1	—	78.9

CLUB LEADERS

	Offense	Defense
First Downs	S.F. 362	Ariz. 245
Rushing	Pitt. 138	Minn. 65
Passing	N.E. 243	Hou. 132
Penalty	Den. 43	Chi. 12
Rushes	Dall. 550	Minn. 355
Net Yds. Gained	Pitt. 2180	Minn. 1090
Avg. Gain	Det. 5.1	Minn. 3.1
Passes Attempted	N.E. 699	Hou. 400
Completed	Minn. 409	Hou. 221
% Completed	S.F. 70.3	Ariz. 50.3
Total Yds. Gained	N.E. 4583	Hou. 2963
Times Sacked	Clev. 14	Pitt. 55
Yds. Lost	Dall. 93	Pitt. 382
Net Yds. Gained	N.E. 4444	Dall. 2752
Net Yds. per Pass Play	S.F. 7.62	Dall. 4.84
Yds. Gained per Comp.	Wash. 13.00	Det. 10.12
Combined Net Yds. Gained	Mia. 6078	Dall. 4313
% Total Yds. Rushing	Ind. 46.7	Minn. 23.0
% Total Yds. Passing	N.E. 76.9	Hou. 56.9
Ball Control Plays	N.E. 1199	Ariz. 909
Avg. Yds. per Play	S.F. 5.80	Dall. 4.29
Avg. Time of Poss.	Ariz. 32:37	—
Third Down Efficiency	S.F. 51.0	Ariz. 27.8
Interceptions	—	Three tied with 23
Yds. Returned	—	S.F. 508
Returned for TD	—	Minn. & S.F. 4
Punts	Ariz. 98	—
Yds. Punted	Hou. 4115	—
Avg. Yds. per Punt	Rams 44.8	—
Punt Returns	Pitt. 56	T.B. 19
Yds. Returned	Raid. 487	T.B. 103
Avg. Yds. per Return	Wash. 14.1	T.B. 5.4
Returned for TD	Four with 2	—
Kickoff Returns	Cin. 86	N.Y.G. & T.B. 44
Yds. Returned	N.O. 1840	Hou. 832
Avg. Yds. per Return	Dall. 25.7	Hou. 17.3
Returned for TD	Det. 4	—
Total Points Scored	S.F. 505	Clev. 204
Total TDs	S.F. 66	Clev. 22
TDs Rushing	Dall. 26	Ariz. & Pitt. 7
TDs Passing	S.F. 37	Pitt. 12
TDs on Ret. and Rec.	Five with 7	Clev. & Dall. 0
Extra Points	S.F. 62	Clev. 20
Safeties	K.C. & N.Y.G. 2	—
Field Goals Made	Minn. & S.D. 34	Mia. 11
Field Goals Attempted	Minn. & N.O. 39	Mia. 18
% Successful	Clev. 92.9	Wash. 60.7

NFL CLUB RANKINGS BY YARDS

	Offense			Defense		
	Total	Rush	Pass	Total	Rush	Pass
Arizona	25	17	22	3	4	4
Atlanta	7	28	5	27	14	27
Buffalo	10	8	10	17	8	23
Chicago	23	15	21	13	24	5
Cincinnati	18	18	18	15	23	9
Cleveland	16	14	19	7	13	7
Dallas	8	5	12T	*1	10	*1
Denver	6	23	6	28	17	28
Detroit	15	3	24	24	22	19
Green Bay	9	19	9	6	3	15
Houston	26	12	25	9	28	2
Indianapolis	27	4	28	20	12	24
Kansas City	5	11	7	12	16	10
L.A. Raiders	19	21	16	10	9	14
L.A. Rams	21	25	15	16	20	12
Miami	*1	13	2	19	6	25
Minnesota	3	20	3	5	*1	21
New England	4	27	*1	18	19	16
New Orleans	12	26	8	25	18	26
N.Y. Giants	28	10	27	11	15	8
N.Y. Jets	22	16	20	22	21	18
Philadelphia	14	9	14	4	11	6
Pittsburgh	13	*1	23	2	7	3
San Diego	11	7	12T	14	5	22
San Francisco	2	6	4	8	2	17
Seattle	24	2	26	23	25	13
Tampa Bay	20	22	17	21	26	11
Washington	17	24	11	26	27	20

T = Tied for position
** = League Leader*

AFC TAKEAWAYS/GIVEAWAYS

	Takeaways			Giveaways			Net
	Int	Fum	Total	Int	Fum	Total	Diff.
Pittsburgh	17	14	31	9	8	17	+14
Kansas City	12	26	38	14	12	26	+12
N.Y. Jets	17	21	38	18	10	28	+10
San Diego	17	15	32	14	9	23	+9
New England	22	18	40	27	11	38	+2
Seattle	19	11	30	9	19	28	+2
Miami	23	9	32	18	14	32	0
Indianapolis	18	10	28	14	17	31	-3
Cleveland	18	13	31	21	14	35	-4
Denver	12	14	26	13	18	31	-5
L.A. Raiders	12	13	25	16	14	30	-5
Buffalo	16	12	28	21	13	34	-6
Houston	14	12	26	17	25	42	-16
Cincinnati	10	8	18	19	22	41	-23

NFC TAKEAWAYS/GIVEAWAYS

	Takeaways			Giveaways			Net
	Int	Fum	Total	Int	Fum	Total	Diff.
San Francisco	23	12	35	11	13	24	+11
Green Bay	21	12	33	14	8	22	+11
Philadelphia	21	14	35	14	12	26	+9
N.Y. Giants	16	16	32	18	7	25	+7
Arizona	23	13	36	19	10	29	+7
Dallas	22	9	31	14	10	24	+7
Minnesota	18	16	34	20	14	34	0
New Orleans	17	14	31	18	14	32	-1
Detroit	12	11	23	14	10	24	-1
Tampa Bay	9	12	21	16	7	23	-2
Atlanta	22	11	33	25	11	36	-3
Chicago	12	10	22	16	10	26	-4
L.A. Rams	14	6	20	18	13	31	-11
Washington	17	6	23	27	13	40	-17

1994 INDIVIDUAL STATISTICS

SCORING

Points

AFC: 135—John Carney, San Diego
NFC: 132—Fuad Reveiz, Minnesota

Touchdowns

NFC: 22—Emmitt Smith, Dallas
AFC: 12—Marshall Faulk, Indianapolis
Natrone Means, San Diego

Extra Points

NFC: 60—Doug Brien, San Francisco
AFC: 38—Steve Christie, Buffalo

Field Goals

AFC: 34—John Carney, San Diego
NFC: 34—Fuad Reveiz, Minnesota

Field Goal Attempts

NFC: 39—Morten Andersen, New Orleans
Fuad Reveiz, Minnesota
AFC: 38—John Carney, San Diego

Longest Field Goal

AFC: 54—Jason Elam, Denver at San Diego, October 23
Doug Pelfrey, Cincinnati vs. Philadelphia, December 24
NFC: 54—Chip Lohmiller, Washington vs. Philadelphia, October 3

Most Points, Game

AFC: 24—Mark Ingram, Miami at N.Y. Jets, November 27, (4 TD)
NFC: 24—Sterling Sharpe, Green Bay at Dallas, November 24, (4 TD)

Team Leaders, Points

AFC: BUFFALO: 110, Steve Christie; CINCINNATI: 108, Doug Pelfrey; CLEVELAND: 110, Matt Stover; DENVER: 119, Jason Elam; HOUSTON: 66, Al Del Greco; INDIANAPOLIS: 85, Dean Biasucci; KANSAS CITY: 105, Lin Elliott; L.A. RAIDERS: 97, Jeff Jaeger; MIAMI: 107, Pete Stoyanovich; NEW ENGLAND: 117, Matt Bahr; N.Y. JETS: 86, Nick Lowery; PITTSBURGH: 104, Gary Anderson; SAN DIEGO: 135, John Carney; SEATTLE: 85, John Kasay

NFC: ARIZONA: 77, Greg Davis; ATLANTA: 95, Norm Johnson; CHICAGO: 87, Kevin Butler; DALLAS: 132, Emmitt Smith; DETROIT: 93, Jason Hanson; GREEN BAY: 108, Sterling Sharpe; L.A. RAMS: 82, Tony Zendejas; MINNESOTA: 132, Fuad Reveiz; NEW ORLEANS: 116, Morten Andersen; N.Y. GIANTS: 55, David Treadwell; PHILADELPHIA: 96, Eddie Murray; SAN FRANCISCO: 105, Doug Brien; TAMPA BAY: 89, Michael Husted; WASHINGTON: 90, Chip Lohmiller

Team Champion

NFC: 505—San Francisco
AFC: 389—Miami

NFL TOP TEN SCORERS—NONKICKERS

	TD	TDR	TDP	TDM	X2G	PTS
Smith, Emmitt, Dall	22	21	1	0	0	132
Sharpe, Sterling, GB	18	0	18	0	0	108
Rice, Jerry, SF	15	2	13	0	1	92
Means, Natrone, SD	12	12	0	0	0	72
Faulk, Marshall, Ind	12	11	1	0	0	72
Mathis, Terance, Atl	11	0	11	0	2	70
Warren, Chris, Sea	11	9	2	0	1	68
Pickens, Carl, Cin	11	0	11	0	0	66
Watters, Ricky, SF	11	6	5	0	0	66
Moore, Herman, Det	11	0	11	0	0	66

NFL TOP TEN SCORERS—KICKERS

	XP	XPA	FG	FGA	PTS
Carney, John, SD	33	33	34	38	135
Reveiz, Fuad, Minn	30	30	34	39	132
Elam, Jason, Den	29	29	30	37	119
Bahr, Matt, NE	36	36	27	34	117
Andersen, Morten, NO	32	32	28	39	116
Boniol, Chris, Dall	48	48	22	29	114
Stover, Matt, Cle	32	32	26	28	110
Christie, Steve, Buff	38	38	24	28	110
Pelfrey, Doug, Cin	24	25	28	33	108
Stoyanovich, Pete, Mia	35	35	24	31	107

AFC SCORING—TEAM

	TD	TDR	TDP	TDM	XKG	X2G	X2A	XPA	FG	FGA	SAF	PTS
Miami	45	13	31	1	35	6	10	45	24	31	0	389
San Diego	40	13	20	7	33	3	7	40	34	38	0	381
New England	39	12	25	2	36	0	2	38	27	35	0	351
Denver	37	19	18	0	29	3	8	37	30	37	0	347
Cleveland	37	12	20	5	32	4	5	37	26	28	0	340
Buffalo	38	14	23	1	38	0	0	38	24	28	1	340
Kansas City	34	12	20	2	30	3	4	34	25	30	2	319
Pittsburgh	35	15	17	3	32	1	3	35	24	29	0	316
Indianapolis	37	15	15	7	37	0	0	37	16	24	0	307
L.A. Raiders	34	7	22	5	31	1	3	34	22	28	0	303
Seattle	32	16	13	3	25	4	6	32	20	24	1	287
Cincinnati	27	5	21	1	24	2	2	27	28	33	1	276
N.Y. Jets	29	8	18	3	26	2	2	29	20	23	0	264
Houston	25	10	13	2	18	4	7	25	16	20	1	226
AFC Total	489	171	276	42	426	33	59	488	336	408	6	4446
AFC Average	34.9	12.2	19.7	3.0	30.4	2.4	4.2	34.9	24.0	29.1	0.4	317.6

NFC SCORING—TEAM

	TD	TDR	TDP	TDM	XKG	X2G	X2A	XPA	FG	FGA	SAF	PTS
San Francisco	66	23	37	6	60	2	4	66	15	20	0	505
Dallas	50	26	19	5	48	0	2	50	22	29	0	414
Green Bay	47	11	33	3	41	1	4	47	19	26	0	382
Detroit	43	12	24	7	39	2	3	43	18	27	1	357
Minnesota	36	11	18	7	30	4	5	35	34	39	0	356
New Orleans	38	11	22	5	32	2	6	38	28	39	0	348
Washington	37	5	25	7	30	3	5	37	20	28	1	320
Atlanta	36	8	25	3	32	3	4	36	21	25	0	317
Philadelphia	35	14	18	3	33	0	2	35	21	25	1	308
L.A. Rams	33	6	23	4	28	2	5	33	18	23	1	286
N.Y. Giants	30	12	16	2	27	1	2	30	22	28	2	279
Chicago	30	10	19	1	24	2	6	30	21	29	0	271
Tampa Bay	26	8	17	1	20	3	6	26	23	35	0	251
Arizona	24	12	11	1	21	1	3	24	22	30	1	235
NFC Total	531	169	307	55	465	26	57	530	304	403	7	4629
NFC Average	37.9	12.1	21.9	3.9	33.2	1.9	4.1	37.9	21.7	28.8	0.5	330.6
NFL Total	1020	340	583	97	891	59	116	1018	640	811	13	9075
NFL Average	36.4	12.1	20.8	3.5	31.8	2.1	4.1	36.4	22.9	29.0	0.5	324.1

AFC SCORERS—INDIVIDUAL

Kickers

	XP	XPA	FG	FGA	PTS
Carney, John, SD	33	33	34	38	135
Elam, Jason, Den	29	29	30	37	119
Bahr, Matt, NE	36	36	27	34	117
Christie, Steve, Buff	38	38	24	28	110
Stover, Matt, Cle	32	32	26	28	110
Pelfrey, Doug, Cin	24	25	28	33	108
Stoyanovich, Pete, Mia	35	35	24	31	107
Elliott, Lin, KC	30	30	25	30	105
Anderson, Gary, Pitt	32	32	24	29	104
Jaeger, Jeff, LA Raid	31	31	22	28	97
Lowery, Nick, NYJ	26	27	20	23	86
Biasucci, Dean, Ind	37	37	16	24	85
Kasay, John, Sea	25	26	20	24	85
Del Greco, Al, Hou	18	18	16	20	66
O'Neill, Pat, NE	0	0	0	1	0

Nonkickers

	TD	TDR	TDP	TDM	X2G	PTS
Faulk, Marshall, Ind	12	11	1	0	0	72
Means, Natrone, SD	12	12	0	0	0	72
Warren, Chris, Sea	11	9	2	0	1	68
Pickens, Carl, Cin	11	0	11	0	0	66
Brown, Tim, LA Raid	9	0	9	0	0	54
Hoard, Leroy, Cle	9	5	4	0	0	54
Russell, Leonard, Den	9	9	0	0	0	54
Thomas, Thurman, Buff	9	7	2	0	0	54
Butts, Marion, NE	8	8	0	0	0	48
Reed, Andre, Buff	8	0	8	0	0	48
Fryar, Irving, Mia	7	0	7	0	2	46
Allen, Marcus, KC	7	7	0	0	1	44
Jackson, Keith, Mia	7	0	7	0	1	44
Parmalee, Bernie, Mia	7	6	1	0	1	44
Williams, Harvey, LA Raid	7	4	3	0	1	44
Byars, Keith, Mia	7	2	5	0	0	42
Coates, Ben, NE	7	0	7	0	0	42
Jeffires, Haywood, Hou	6	0	6	0	3	42
Martin, Tony, SD	7	0	7	0	0	42
Metcalf, Eric, Cle	7	2	3	2	0	42
Morris, Bam, Pitt	7	7	0	0	0	42
Thompson, Leroy, NE	7	2	5	0	0	42
Moore, Rob, NYJ	6	0	6	0	2	40
Carrier, Mark, Cle	6	1	5	0	0	36
Ingram, Mark, Mia	6	0	6	0	0	36
Seay, Mark, SD	6	0	6	0	0	36
Turner, Floyd, Ind	6	0	6	0	0	36
Davis, Willie, KC	5	0	5	0	1	32
Miller, Anthony, Den	5	0	5	0	1	32
Brisby, Vincent, NE	5	0	5	0	0	30
Brown, Gary, Hou	5	4	1	0	0	30
Dawkins, Sean, Ind	5	0	5	0	0	30
Foster, Barry, Pitt	5	5	0	0	0	30
Ismail, Raghib, LA Raid	5	0	5	0	0	30
Johnson, Johnny, NYJ	5	3	2	0	0	30
Metzelaars, Pete, Buff	5	0	5	0	0	30
Scott, Darnay, Cin	5	0	5	0	0	30
Sharpe, Shannon, Den	4	0	4	0	2	28
Birden, J. J., KC	4	0	4	0	1	26
Blades, Brian, Sea	4	0	4	0	1	26
Vaughn, Jon, Sea-KC	4	1	1	2	1	26
Baxter, Brad, NYJ	4	4	0	0	0	24
Beebe, Don, Buff	4	0	4	0	0	24
Elway, John, Den	4	4	0	0	0	24
Gardner, Carwell, Buff	4	4	0	0	0	24
Green, Eric, Pitt	4	0	4	0	0	24
Milburn, Glyn, Den	4	1	3	0	0	24
Mitchell, Johnny, NYJ	4	0	4	0	0	24
Thigpen, Yancey, Pitt	4	0	4	0	0	24
White, Lorenzo, Hou	4	3	1	0	0	24
Anders, Kimble, KC	3	2	1	0	0	18
Buchanan, Ray, Ind	3	0	0	3	0	18
Clark, Derrick, Den	3	3	0	0	0	18
Crittenden, Ray, NE	3	0	3	0	0	18
Harmon, Ronnie, SD	2	1	1	0	3	18
Jefferson, Shawn, SD	3	0	3	0	0	18
Johnson, Charles, Pitt	3	0	3	0	0	18
Majkowski, Don, Ind	3	3	0	0	0	18
McDaniel, Terry, LA Raid	3	0	0	3	0	18
McDuffie, O. J., Mia	3	0	3	0	0	18
Monk, Art, NYJ	3	0	3	0	0	18
Smith, Steve, Sea	3	2	1	0	0	18
Timpson, Michael, NE	3	0	3	0	0	18
Turner, Kevin, NE	3	1	2	0	0	18
Williams, John L., Pitt	3	1	2	0	0	18
Alexander, Derrick, Cle	2	0	2	0	1	14
Broussard, Steve, Cin	2	2	0	0	1	14
Kirby, Terry, Mia	2	2	0	0	1	14
Anderson, Richie, NYJ	2	1	1	0	0	12
Bennett, Donnell, KC	2	2	0	0	0	12
Brooks, Bill, Buff	2	0	2	0	0	12
Byner, Earnest, Cle	2	2	0	0	0	12
Cash, Keith, KC	2	0	2	0	0	12
Coleman, Andre, SD	2	0	0	2	0	12
Davis, Kenneth, Buff	2	2	0	0	0	12
Dawson, Lake, KC	2	0	2	0	0	12
Evans, Jerry, Den	2	0	2	0	0	12
Fenner, Derrick, Cin	2	1	1	0	0	12
Givins, Ernest, Hou	2	0	1	1	0	12
Glover, Andrew, LA Raid	2	0	2	0	0	12
Gordon, Darrien, SD	2	0	0	2	0	12
Green, Harold, Cin	2	1	1	0	0	12
Hastings, Andre, Pitt	2	0	2	0	0	12
Hostetler, Jeff, LA Raid	2	2	0	0	0	12
Jackson, Michael, Cle	2	0	2	0	0	12
Johnson, Tracy, Sea	2	2	0	0	0	12
Lewis, Mo, NYJ	2	0	0	2	0	12
McAfee, Fred, Ariz-Pitt	2	2	0	0	0	12
Potts, Roosevelt, Ind	2	1	1	0	0	12
Pupunu, Alfred, SD	2	0	2	0	0	12
Reynolds, Ricky, NE	2	0	0	2	0	12
Richard, Stanley, SD	2	0	0	2	0	12
Rivers, Reggie, Den	2	2	0	0	0	12
Slaughter, Webster, Hou	2	0	2	0	0	12
Spikes, Irving, Mia	2	2	0	0	0	12
Strong, Mack, Sea	2	2	0	0	0	12
Testaverde, Vinny, Cle	2	2	0	0	0	12
Tolliver, Billy Joe, Hou	2	2	0	0	0	12
Valerio, Joe, KC	2	0	2	0	0	12
Walker, Derrick, KC	2	0	2	0	0	12
Woodson, Rod, Pitt	2	0	0	2	0	12
Wright, Alexander, LA Raid	2	0	2	0	0	12
Blake, Jeff, Cin	1	1	0	0	1	8
Baldwin, Randy, Cle	1	0	0	1	0	6
Bates, Michael, Sea	1	0	1	0	0	6
Baty, Greg, Mia	1	0	1	0	0	6
Baxter, Fred, NYJ	1	0	1	0	0	6
Bennett, Tony, Ind	1	0	0	1	0	6
Brewer, Dewell, Ind	1	0	0	1	0	6
Campbell, Jeff, Den	1	0	1	0	0	6
Carter, Pat, Hou	1	0	1	0	0	6
Cash, Kerry, Ind	1	0	1	0	0	6
Coleman, Pat, Hou	1	0	1	0	0	6
Collins, Mark, KC	1	0	0	1	0	6
Copeland, Russell, Buff	1	0	1	0	0	6
Coryatt, Quentin, Ind	1	0	0	1	0	6
Cothran, Jeff, Cin	1	0	1	0	0	6
Dishman, Cris, Hou	1	0	0	1	0	6
Green, Paul, Sea	1	0	1	0	0	6
Greene, Tracy, KC	1	0	1	0	0	6
Hartley, Frank, Cle	1	0	1	0	0	6
Hayes, Jonathan, Pitt	1	0	1	0	0	6
Hill, Greg, KC	1	1	0	0	0	6
Hill, Travis, Cle	1	0	0	1	0	6
Humphrey, Ronald, Ind	1	0	0	1	0	6
Jackson, Mark, Ind	1	0	1	0	0	6
Junkin, Trey, Sea	1	0	1	0	0	6
Kelly, Jim, Buff	1	1	0	0	0	6
Kinchen, Brian, Cle	1	0	1	0	0	6
Lodish, Mike, Buff	1	0	0	1	0	6
Marino, Dan, Mia	1	1	0	0	0	6
Martin, Eric, KC	1	0	1	0	0	6
Martin, Kelvin, Sea	1	0	1	0	0	6
McCallum, Napoleon, Raid	1	1	0	0	0	6
McGee, Tim, Cin	1	0	1	0	0	6
McGee, Tony, Cin	1	0	1	0	0	6
McKnight, James, Sea	1	0	1	0	0	6
Miller, Scott, Mia	1	0	1	0	0	6
Mills, Ernie, Pitt	1	0	1	0	0	6
Montgomery, Tyrone, Raid	1	0	1	0	0	6
O'Donnell, Neil, Pitt	1	1	0	0	0	6
Pritchard, Mike, Den	1	0	1	0	0	6
Reeves, Walter, Cle	1	0	1	0	0	6
Richardson, Bucky, Hou	1	1	0	0	0	6
Russell, Derek, Den	1	0	1	0	0	6

1994 INDIVIDUAL STATISTICS

	TD	TDR	TDP	TDM	X2G	PTS
Sawyer, Corey, Cin	1	0	0	1	0	6
Smith, Anthony, LA Raid	1	0	0	1	0	6
Tillman, Cedric, Den	1	0	1	0	0	6
Tupa, Tom, Cle	0	0	0	0	3	6
Turner, Eric, Cle	1	0	0	1	0	6
Turner, Marcus, NYJ	1	0	0	1	0	6
Turner, Nate, Buff	1	0	1	0	0	6
Vanhorse, Sean, SD	1	0	0	1	0	6
Vardell, Tommy, Cle	1	0	1	0	0	6
Vincent, Troy, Mia	1	0	0	1	0	6
Washington, Lionel, LA Raid	1	0	0	1	0	6
Watters, Orlando, Sea	1	0	0	1	0	6
Williams, Gerald, Pitt	1	0	0	1	0	6
Wooden, Terry, Sea	1	0	0	1	0	6
Yarborough, Ryan, NYJ	1	0	1	0	0	6
Young, Duane, SD	1	0	1	0	0	6
Brown, Reggie, Hou	0	0	0	0	1	2
Craver, Aaron, Mia	0	0	0	0	1	2
Lathon, Lamar, Hou	0	0	0	0	0	*2
Stone, Dwight, Pitt	0	0	0	0	1	2
Thomas, Derrick, KC	0	0	0	0	0	*2
Tuten, Rick, Sea	0	0	0	0	1	2
Williams, Alfred, Cin	0	0	0	0	0	*2

** Safety*
Team Safeties credited to Buffalo, Kansas City, and Seattle.

NFC SCORERS—INDIVIDUAL

Kickers

	XP	XPA	FG	FGA	PTS
Reveiz, Fuad, Minn	30	30	34	39	132
Andersen, Morten, NO	32	32	28	39	116
Boniol, Chris, Dall	48	48	22	29	114
Brien, Doug, SF	60	62	15	20	105
Jacke, Chris, GB	41	43	19	26	98
Murray, Eddie, Phil	33	33	21	25	96
Johnson, Norm, Atl	32	32	21	25	95
Hanson, Jason, Det	39	40	18	27	93
Lohmiller, Chip, Wash	30	32	20	28	90
Husted, Michael, TB	20	20	23	35	89
Butler, Kevin, Chi	24	24	21	29	87
Zendejas, Tony, LA Rams	28	28	18	23	82
Davis, Greg, Ariz	17	17	20	26	77
Treadwell, David, NYG	22	23	11	17	55
Daluiso, Brad, NYG	5	5	11	11	38
Peterson, Todd, Ariz	4	4	2	4	10

Nonkickers

	TD	TDR	TDP	TDM	X2G	PTS
Smith, Emmitt, Dall	22	21	1	0	0	132
Sharpe, Sterling, GB	18	0	18	0	0	108
Rice, Jerry, SF	15	2	13	0	1	92
Mathis, Terance, Atl	11	0	11	0	2	70
Moore, Herman, Det	11	0	11	0	0	66
Watters, Ricky, SF	11	6	5	0	0	66
Jones, Brent, SF	9	0	9	0	1	56
Bennett, Edgar, GB	9	5	4	0	0	54
Allen, Terry, Minn	8	8	0	0	1	50
Rison, Andre, Atl	8	0	8	0	1	50
Harper, Alvin, Dall	8	0	8	0	0	48
Heyward, Craig, Atl	8	7	1	0	0	48
Sanders, Barry, Det	8	7	1	0	0	48
Walker, Herschel, Phil	8	5	2	1	0	48
Carter, Cris, Minn	7	0	7	0	2	46
Rhett, Errict, TB	7	7	0	0	1	44
Centers, Larry, Ariz	7	5	2	0	0	42
Tillman, Lewis, Chi	7	7	0	0	0	42
Young, Steve, SF	7	7	0	0	0	42
Hampton, Rodney, NYG	6	6	0	0	1	38
Bates, Mario, NO	6	6	0	0	0	36
Brooks, Robert, GB	6	0	4	2	0	36
Drayton, Troy, LA Rams	6	0	6	0	0	36
Ellard, Henry, Wash	6	0	6	0	0	36
Floyd, William, SF	6	6	0	0	0	36
Irvin, Michael, Dall	6	0	6	0	0	36
Meggett, David, NYG	6	4	0	2	0	36
Sherrard, Mike, NYG	6	0	6	0	0	36
Wilson, Charles, TB	6	0	6	0	0	36
Graham, Jeffrey, Chi	5	0	4	1	1	32
Howard, Desmond, Wash	5	0	5	0	1	32
Moore, Ron, Ariz	5	4	1	0	1	32
Small, Torrance, NO	5	0	5	0	1	32
Anderson, Willie, LA Rams	5	0	5	0	0	30
Barnett, Fred, Phil	5	0	5	0	0	30
Hawkins, Courtney, TB	5	0	5	0	0	30
Haynes, Michael, NO	5	0	5	0	0	30
Ismail, Qadry, Minn	5	0	5	0	0	30
Proehl, Ricky, Ariz	5	0	5	0	0	30
Taylor, John, SF	5	0	5	0	0	30
Bettis, Jerome, LA Rams	4	3	1	0	2	28
Perriman, Brett, Det	4	0	4	0	2	28
Walls, Wesley, NO	4	0	4	0	1	26
Brown, Derek, NO	4	3	1	0	0	24
Cobb, Reggie, GB	4	3	1	0	0	24
Cross, Howard, NYG	4	0	4	0	0	24
Early, Quinn, NO	4	0	4	0	0	24
Emanuel, Bert, Atl	4	0	4	0	0	24
Ervins, Ricky, Wash	4	3	1	0	0	24
Hughes, Tyrone, NO	4	0	0	4	0	24
Jenkins, James, Wash	4	0	4	0	0	24
Johnston, Daryl, Dall	4	2	2	0	0	24
Kinchen, Todd, LA Rams	4	1	3	0	0	24
Moore, Derrick, Det	4	4	0	0	0	24
Morgan, Anthony, GB	4	0	4	0	0	24
Pierce, Aaron, NYG	4	0	4	0	0	24
Reed, Jake, Minn	4	0	4	0	0	24
Harris, Jackie, TB	3	0	3	0	1	20
Mitchell, Brian, Wash	3	0	1	2	1	20
Bavaro, Mark, Phil	3	0	3	0	0	18
Bruce, Isaac, LA Rams	3	0	3	0	0	18
Carter, Anthony, Det	3	0	3	0	0	18
Cunningham, Randall, Phil	3	3	0	0	0	18
Garner, Charlie, Phil	3	3	0	0	0	18
Gedney, Chris, Chi	3	0	3	0	0	18
Gray, Mel, Det	3	0	0	3	0	18
Hester, Jessie, LA Rams	3	0	3	0	0	18
Horton, Ethan, Wash	3	0	3	0	0	18
Jennings, Keith, Chi	3	0	3	0	0	18
Joseph, James, Phil	3	1	2	0	0	18
Matthews, Aubrey, Det	3	0	3	0	0	18
Parker, Anthony, Minn	3	0	0	3	0	18
Sanders, Deion, SF	3	0	0	3	0	18
Smith, Irv, NO	3	0	3	0	0	18
Washington, DeWayne, Minn	3	0	0	3	0	18
Williams, Calvin, Phil	3	0	3	0	0	18
Conway, Curtis, Chi	2	0	2	0	1	14
West, Ed, GB	2	0	2	0	1	14
Winans, Tydus, Wash	2	0	2	0	1	14
Brooks, Reggie, Wash	2	2	0	0	0	12
Brown, Dave, NYG	2	2	0	0	0	12
Calloway, Chris, NYG	2	0	2	0	0	12
Collins, Andre, Wash	2	0	0	2	0	12
Favre, Brett, GB	2	2	0	0	0	12
Graham, Scottie, Minn	2	2	0	0	0	12
Green, Robert, Chi	2	0	2	0	0	12
Hebron, Vaughn, Phil	2	2	0	0	0	12
Johnson, Maurice, Phil	2	0	2	0	0	12
Lee, Amp, Minn	2	0	2	0	0	12
Logan, Marc, SF	2	1	1	0	0	12
McCaffrey, Ed, SF	2	0	2	0	0	12
McDonald, Tim, SF	2	0	0	2	0	12
Morton, Johnnie, Det	2	0	1	1	0	12
Novacek, Jay, Dall	2	0	2	0	0	12
Singleton, Nate, SF	2	0	2	0	0	12
Thomas, Blair, NE.-Dall	2	2	0	0	0	12
Williams, Kevin, Dall	2	0	0	2	0	12
Aikman, Troy, Dall	1	1	0	0	0	6
Armstrong, Tyji, TB	1	0	1	0	0	6
Bailey, Johnny, LA Rams	1	1	0	0	0	6
Bailey, Robert, LA Rams	1	0	0	1	0	6
Bailey, Victor, Phil	1	0	1	0	0	6
Bayless, Martin, Wash	1	0	0	1	0	6
Beuerlein, Steve, Ariz	1	1	0	0	0	6
Brunell, Mark, GB	1	1	0	0	0	6
Carter, Dexter, SF	1	0	0	1	0	6
Chandler, Chris, LA Rams	1	1	0	0	0	6
Clark, Gary, Ariz	1	0	1	0	0	6
Clay, Willie, Det	1	0	0	1	0	6
Coleman, Lincoln, Dall	1	1	0	0	0	6
Conover, Scott, Det	1	0	1	0	0	6
Cook, Marv, Chi	1	0	1	0	0	6
Dawsey, Lawrence, TB	1	0	1	0	0	6
Erickson, Craig, TB	1	1	0	0	0	6
Green, Darrell, Wash	1	0	0	1	0	6
Griffith, Howard, LA Rams	1	0	1	0	0	6
Harris, James, Minn	1	0	0	1	0	6

	TD	TDR	TDP	TDM	X2G	PTS
Harris, Raymont, Chi	1	1	0	0	0	6
Hearst, Garrison, Ariz	1	1	0	0	0	6
Jack, Eric, Atl	1	0	0	1	0	6
Jackson, Greg, Phil	1	0	0	1	0	6
Johnson, Mike, Det	1	0	0	1	0	6
Lewis, Nate, Chi	1	0	1	0	0	6
Lyght, Todd, LA Rams	1	0	0	1	0	6
McCants, Keith, Ariz	1	0	0	1	0	6
McDowell, Anthony, TB	1	0	1	0	0	6
McMurtry, Greg, Chi	1	0	1	0	0	6
Mitchell, Scott, Det	1	1	0	0	0	6
Morrison, Darryl, Wash	1	0	0	1	0	6
Muster, Brad, NO	1	1	0	0	0	6
Neal, Lorenzo, NO	1	1	0	0	0	6
Newman, Anthony, Rams	1	0	0	1	0	6
Paup, Bryce, GB	1	0	0	1	0	6
Pegram, Erric, Atl	1	1	0	0	0	6
Reeves, Bryan, Ariz	1	0	1	0	0	6
Ross, Jermaine, Rams	1	0	1	0	0	6
Sanders, Ricky, Atl	1	0	1	0	0	6
Smith, Cedric, Wash	1	0	1	0	0	6
Smith, Chuck, Atl	1	0	0	1	0	6
Smith, Darrin, Dall	1	0	0	1	0	6
Smith, Robert, Minn	1	1	0	0	0	6
Spielman, Chris, Det	1	0	0	1	0	6
Tolbert, Tony, Dall	1	0	0	1	0	6
Truitt, Olanda, Wash	1	0	1	0	0	6
Turner, Vernon, TB	1	0	0	1	0	6
Waddle, Tom, Chi	1	0	1	0	0	6
Walker, Adam, SF	1	1	0	0	0	6
Walker, Darnell, Atl	1	0	0	1	0	6
Walsh, Steve, Chi	1	1	0	0	0	6
Ware, Derek, Ariz	1	0	1	0	0	6
Wetnight, Ryan, Chi	1	0	1	0	0	6
Williams, James, NO	1	0	0	1	0	6
Woodson, Darren, Dall	1	0	0	1	0	6
Worley, Tim, Chi	1	1	0	0	0	6
Wright, Toby, LA Rams	1	0	0	1	0	6
Wycheck, Frank, Wash	1	0	1	0	0	6
Zordich, Mike, Phil	1	0	0	1	0	6
Copeland, Horace, TB	0	0	0	0	1	2
Fuller, William, Phil	0	0	0	0	0	*2
Gilbert, Sean, LA Rams	0	0	0	0	0	*2
Jordan, Andrew, Minn	0	0	0	0	1	2
Swann, Eric, Ariz	0	0	0	0	0	*2

** Safety*
Team Safeties credited to Detroit, New York Giants (2), and Washington.

FIELD GOALS

Field Goal Percentage
AFC: .929—Matt Stover, Cleveland
NFC: .872—Fuad Reveiz, Minnesota

Field Goals
AFC: 34—John Carney, San Diego
NFC: 34—Fuad Reveiz, Minnesota

Field Goal Attempts
NFC: 39—Morten Andersen, New Orleans
Fuad Reveiz, Minnesota
AFC: 38—John Carney, San Diego

Longest Field Goal
AFC: 54—Jason Elam, Denver at San Diego, October 23
Doug Pelfrey, Cincinnati vs. Philadelphia, December 24
NFC: 54—Chip Lohmiller, Washington vs. Philadelphia, October 3

Average Yards Made
AFC: 37.4—Al Del Greco, Houston
NFC: 34.3—Jason Hanson, Detroit

AFC FIELD GOALS—TEAM

	FG	FGA	Pct.	Long
Cleveland	26	28	.929	45
San Diego	34	38	.895	50
N.Y. Jets	20	23	.870	49
Buffalo	24	28	.857	52
Cincinnati	28	33	.848	54
Seattle	20	24	.833	50
Kansas City	25	30	.833	49
Pittsburgh	24	29	.828	50
Denver	30	37	.811	54
Houston	16	20	.800	50
L.A. Raiders	22	28	.786	51
Miami	24	31	.774	50
New England	27	35	.771	48
Indianapolis	16	24	.667	50
AFC Total	336	408	—	54
AFC Average	24.0	29.1	.824	—

NFC FIELD GOALS—TEAM

	FG	FGA	Pct.	Long
Minnesota	34	39	.872	51
Atlanta	21	25	.840	50
Philadelphia	21	25	.840	42
N.Y. Giants	22	28	.786	52
L.A. Rams	18	23	.783	47
Dallas	22	29	.759	47
San Francisco	15	20	.750	48
Arizona	22	30	.733	51
Green Bay	19	26	.731	50
Chicago	21	29	.724	52
New Orleans	28	39	.718	48
Washington	20	28	.714	54
Detroit	18	27	.667	49
Tampa Bay	23	35	.657	53
NFC Total	304	403	—	54
NFC Average	21.7	28.8	.754	—
League Total	640	811	—	54
League Average	22.9	29.0	.789	—

1994 INDIVIDUAL STATISTICS

AFC FIELD GOALS—INDIVIDUAL

	1-19 Yards	20-29 Yards	30-39 Yards	40-49 Yards	50 or Longer	Totals	Avg. Yds. Att.	Avg. Yds. Made	Avg. Yds. Miss	Long
Stover, Matt, Cle	1-1	7-7	10-11	8-8	0-1	26-28	33.9	33.3	41.0	45
	1.000	1.000	.909	1.000	.000	.929				
Carney, John, SD	0-0	12-12	15-15	5-9	2-2	34-38	35.4	34.1	46.3	50
	—	1.000	1.000	.556	1.000	.895				
Lowery, Nick, NYJ	0-0	8-8	6-7	6-8	0-0	20-23	34.9	34.1	40.0	49
	—	1.000	.857	.750	—	.870				
Christie, Steve, Buff	0-0	11-12	6-7	5-7	2-2	24-28	34.6	34.0	38.0	52
	—	.917	.857	.714	1.000	.857				
Pelfrey, Doug, Cin	1-1	8-8	8-10	9-10	2-4	28-33	37.5	36.5	43.0	54
	1.000	1.000	.800	.900	.500	.848				
Elliott, Lin, KC	3-3	15-17	4-6	3-4	0-0	25-30	29.1	28.0	34.2	49
	1.000	.882	.667	.750	—	.833				
Kasay, John, Sea	1-1	1-1	11-11	6-9	1-2	20-24	37.5	35.6	47.3	50
	1.000	1.000	1.000	.667	.500	.833				
Anderson, Gary, Pitt	1-1	7-8	8-9	7-9	1-2	24-29	36.4	35.3	41.6	50
	1.000	.875	.889	.778	.500	.828				
Elam, Jason, Den	0-0	11-11	11-11	7-12	1-3	30-37	36.0	33.4	47.0	54
	—	1.000	1.000	.583	.333	.811				
Del Greco, Al, Hou	0-0	4-5	4-4	7-8	1-3	16-20	39.2	37.4	46.0	50
	—	.800	1.000	.875	.333	.811				
Bahr, Matt, NE	0-0	14-14	9-12	4-8	0-0	27-34	32.9	30.6	41.9	48
	—	1.000	.750	.500	—	.794				
Jaeger, Jeff, LA Raid	1-1	5-5	6-9	8-11	2-2	22-28	37.1	36.3	40.2	51
	1.000	1.000	.667	.727	1.000	.786				
Stoyanovich, Pete, Mia	1-1	8-8	6-10	8-10	1-2	24-31	35.8	34.2	41.3	50
	1.000	1.000	.600	.800	.500	.774				
Biasucci, Dean, Ind	1-1	5-5	3-7	5-9	2-2	16-24	36.5	35.6	38.3	50
	1.000	1.000	.429	.556	1.000	.667				
Nonqualifiers:										
O'Neill, Pat, NE	0-0	0-0	0-0	0-1	0-0	0-1	47.0	—	47.0	0
	—	—	—	.000	—	.000				
AFC Totals	10-10	116-121	107-129	88-123	15-25	336-408	35.4	34.0	41.8	54
	1.000	.959	.829	.715	.600	.824				
League Totals	22-22	229-239	213-255	152-229	24-66	640-811	35.4	33.3	43.1	54
	1.000	.959	.835	.664	.364	.789				

Leader based on percentage, minimum 16 field goal attempts

NFC FIELD GOALS—INDIVIDUAL

	1-19 Yards	20-29 Yards	30-39 Yards	40-49 Yards	50 or Longer	Totals	Avg. Yds. Att.	Avg. Yds. Made	Avg. Yds. Miss	Long
Reveiz, Fuad, Minn	0-0	13-13	12-13	8-10	1-3	34-39	35.5	34.0	45.8	51
	—	1.000	.923	.800	.333	.872				
Johnson, Norm, Atl	0-0	9-9	7-7	4-4	1-5	21-25	34.7	31.5	51.5	50
	—	1.000	1.000	1.000	.200	.840				
Murray, Eddie, Phil	1-1	8-8	10-10	2-6	0-0	21-25	32.6	30.4	44.3	42
	1.000	1.000	1.000	.333	—	.840				
Zendejas, Tony, LA Rams	2-2	9-9	6-7	1-5	0-0	18-23	31.2	28.4	41.4	47
	1.000	1.000	.857	.200	—	.783				
Davis, Greg, Ariz	0-0	10-11	3-4	6-7	1-4	20-26	36.4	33.6	45.8	51
	—	.909	.750	.857	.250	.769				
Boniol, Chris, Dall	3-3	3-4	10-12	6-9	0-1	22-29	35.0	33.7	39.0	47
	1.000	.750	.833	.667	.000	.759				
Brien, Doug, SF	1-1	4-4	5-6	5-8	0-1	15-20	36.1	33.7	43.2	48
	1.000	1.000	.833	.625	.000	.750				
Jacke, Chris, GB	1-1	11-11	4-6	2-5	1-3	19-26	33.8	30.2	43.7	50
	1.000	1.000	.667	.400	.333	.731				
Butler, Kevin, Chi	1-1	7-7	6-9	5-8	2-4	21-29	36.1	33.6	42.9	52
	1.000	1.000	.667	.625	.500	.724				
Andersen, Morten, NO	0-0	9-9	11-14	8-10	0-6	28-39	37.3	34.0	45.5	48
	—	1.000	.786	.800	.000	.718				
Lohmiller, Chip, Wash	0-0	9-11	5-6	5-8	1-3	20-28	35.1	33.0	40.4	54
	—	.818	.833	.625	.333	.714				
Hanson, Jason, Det	0-0	6-7	7-7	5-8	0-5	18-27	38.4	34.3	46.6	49
	—	.857	1.000	.625	.000	.667				
Husted, Michael, TB	0-0	8-8	10-12	4-10	1-5	23-35	37.9	33.0	47.3	53
	—	1.000	.833	.400	.200	.657				
Treadwell, David, NYG	1-1	5-5	4-7	1-4	0-0	11-17	32.4	28.9	38.7	41
	1.000	1.000	.571	.250	—	.647				
Nonqualifiers										
Daluiso, Brad, NYG	2-2	1-1	5-5	2-2	1-1	11-11	34.0	34.0	—	52
	1.000	1.000	1.000	1.000	1.000	1.000				
Peterson, Todd, Ariz	0-0	1-1	1-1	0-2	0-0	2-4	38.0	32.0	44.0	35
	—	1.000	1.000	.000	—	.500				
NFC Totals	12-12	113-118	106-126	64-106	9-41	304-403	35.4	32.6	44.1	54
	1.000	.958	.841	.604	.220	.754				
League Totals	22-22	229-239	213-255	152-229	24-66	640-811	34.5	33.3	43.1	54
	1.000	.958	.835	.664	.364	.789				

Leader based on percentage, minimum 16 field goal attempts

RUSHING

Yards
- **NFC:** 1883—Barry Sanders, Detroit
- **AFC:** 1545—Chris Warren, Seattle

Yards, Game
- **NFC:** 237—Barry Sanders, Detroit vs. Tampa Bay, November 13, (26 attempts)
- **AFC:** 185—Chris Warren, Seattle at Houston, December 11, (30 attempts, TD)

Longest
- **NFC:** 91—Herschel Walker, Philadelphia at Atlanta, November 27 - TD
- **AFC:** 90—Johnny Johnson, N.Y. Jets vs. Chicago, September 25

Attempts
- **NFC:** 368—Emmitt Smith, Dallas
- **AFC:** 343—Natrone Means, San Diego

Attempts, Game
- **NFC:** 40—Barry Sanders, Detroit at Dallas, September 19 (194 yards) Errict Rhett, Tampa Bay vs. Washington, December 4 (192 yards)
- **AFC:** 33—Marcus Allen, Kansas City at L.A. Raiders, December 24 (132 yards)

Yards Per Attempt
- **NFC:** 5.7—Barry Sanders, Detroit
- **AFC:** 4.6—Chris Warren, Seattle

Touchdowns
- **NFC:** 21—Emmitt Smith, Dallas
- **AFC:** 12—Natrone Means, San Diego

Team Leaders, Yards

AFC: BUFFALO: 1093, Thurman Thomas; CINCINNATI: 468, Derrick Fenner; CLEVELAND: 890, Leroy Hoard; DENVER: 620, Leonard Russell; HOUSTON: 757, Lorenzo White; INDIANAPOLIS: 1282, Marshall Faulk; KANSAS CITY: 709, Marcus Allen; L.A. RAIDERS: 983, Harvey Williams; MIAMI: 868, Bernie Parmalee; NEW ENGLAND: 703, Marion Butts; N.Y. JETS: 931, Johnny Johnson; PITTSBURGH: 851, Barry Foster; SAN DIEGO: 1350, Natrone Means; SEATTLE: 1545, Chris Warren

NFC: ARIZONA: 780, Ron Moore; ATLANTA: 779, Craig Heyward; CHICAGO: 899, Lewis Tillman; DALLAS: 1484, Emmitt Smith; DETROIT: 1883, Barry Sanders; GREEN BAY: 623, Edgar Bennett; L.A. RAMS: 1025, Jerome Bettis; MINNESOTA: 1031, Terry Allen; NEW ORLEANS: 579, Mario Bates; N.Y. GIANTS: 1075, Rodney Hampton; PHILADELPHIA: 528, Herschel Walker; SAN FRANCISCO: 877, Ricky Watters; TAMPA BAY: 1011, Errict Rhett; WASHINGTON: 650, Ricky Ervins

Team Champion
- **AFC:** 2180—Pittsburgh
- **NFC:** 2080—Detroit

AFC RUSHING—TEAM

	Att	Yards	Avg	Long	TD
Pittsburgh	546	2180	4.0	29t	15
Seattle	480	2084	4.3	41	16
Indianapolis	495	2060	4.2	52	15
San Diego	482	1852	3.8	36	13
Buffalo	483	1831	3.8	60	14
Kansas City	464	1732	3.7	36t	12
Houston	417	1682	4.0	33	10
Miami	433	1658	3.8	47t	13
Cleveland	449	1657	3.7	39	12
N.Y. Jets	416	1566	3.8	90	8
Cincinnati	404	1556	3.9	37t	5
L.A. Raiders	428	1512	3.5	28	7
Denver	431	1470	3.4	24	19
New England	478	1332	2.8	26	12
AFC Total	6406	24172	3.8	90	171
AFC Average	457.6	1726.6	3.8	—	12.2

1994 INDIVIDUAL STATISTICS

NFC RUSHING—TEAM

	Att.	Yards	Avg.	Long	TD
Detroit	406	2080	5.1	85	12
Dallas	550	1953	3.6	46	26
San Francisco	491	1897	3.9	28t	23
Philadelphia	432	1761	4.1	91t	14
N.Y. Giants	525	1754	3.3	27t	12
Chicago	487	1588	3.3	25t	10
Arizona	480	1560	3.3	36	12
Green Bay	417	1543	3.7	43	11
Minnesota	419	1524	3.6	45	11
Tampa Bay	430	1489	3.5	27	8
Washington	407	1415	3.5	49	5
L.A. Rams	397	1389	3.5	44t	6
New Orleans	373	1336	3.6	40	11
Atlanta	330	1249	3.8	25	8
NFC Total	6144	22538	3.7	91t	169
NFC Average	438.9	1609.9	3.7	—	12.1
League Total	12550	46710	—	91t	340
League Average	448.2	1668.2	3.7	—	12.1

NFL TOP TEN RUSHERS

	Att.	Yards	Avg.	Long	TD
Sanders, Barry, Det	331	1883	5.7	85	7
Warren, Chris, Sea	333	1545	4.6	41	9
Smith, Emmitt, Dall	368	1484	4.0	46	21
Means, Natrone, SD	343	1350	3.9	25	12
Faulk, Marshall, Ind	314	1282	4.1	52	11
Thomas, Thurman, Buff	287	1093	3.8	29	7
Hampton, Rodney, NYG	327	1075	3.3	27t	6
Allen, Terry, Minn	255	1031	4.0	45	8
Bettis, Jerome, LA Rams	319	1025	3.2	19	3
Rhett, Errict, TB	284	1011	3.6	27	7

AFC RUSHERS—INDIVIDUAL

	Att.	Yards	Avg.	Long	TD
Warren, Chris, Sea	333	1545	4.6	41	9
Means, Natrone, SD	343	1350	3.9	25	12
Faulk, Marshall, Ind	314	1282	4.1	52	11
Thomas, Thurman, Buff	287	1093	3.8	29	7
Williams, Harvey, LA Raid	282	983	3.5	28	4
Johnson, Johnny, NYJ	240	931	3.9	90	3
Hoard, Leroy, Cle	209	890	4.3	39	5
Parmalee, Bernie, Mia	216	868	4.0	47t	6
Foster, Barry, Pitt	216	851	3.9	29t	5
Morris, Bam, Pitt	198	836	4.2	20	7
White, Lorenzo, Hou	191	757	4.0	33	3
Allen, Marcus, KC	189	709	3.8	36t	7
Butts, Marion, NE	243	703	2.9	26	8
Brown, Gary, Hou	169	648	3.8	18	4
Russell, Leonard, Den	190	620	3.3	22t	9
Hill, Greg, KC	141	574	4.1	20	1
Fenner, Derrick, Cin	141	468	3.3	21	1
Broussard, Steve, Cin	94	403	4.3	37t	2
Davis, Kenneth, Buff	91	381	4.2	60	2
Potts, Roosevelt, Ind	77	336	4.4	52	1
Metcalf, Eric, Cle	93	329	3.5	37t	2
Williams, John L., Pitt	68	317	4.7	23	1
Spikes, Irving, Mia	70	312	4.5	40	2
Thompson, Leroy, NE	102	312	3.1	13	2
Bieniemy, Eric, SD	73	295	4.0	36	0
Elway, John, Den	58	235	4.1	22	4
Kirby, Terry, Mia	60	233	3.9	30	2
Anders, Kimble, KC	62	231	3.7	19	2
Green, Harold, Cin	76	223	2.9	22	1
Harbaugh, Jim, Ind	39	223	5.7	41	0
Byner, Earnest, Cle	75	219	2.9	15	2
Richardson, Bucky, Hou	30	217	7.2	18	1
Anderson, Richie, NYJ	43	207	4.8	55	1
Blake, Jeff, Cin	37	204	5.5	16	1
Milburn, Glyn, Den	58	201	3.5	20	1
Bennett, Donnell, KC	46	178	3.9	17	2
Baxter, Brad, NYJ	60	170	2.8	13	4
Clark, Derrick, Den	56	168	3.0	12	3
Murrell, Adrian, NYJ	33	160	4.8	19	0
Hostetler, Jeff, LA Raid	46	159	3.5	14	2
Mirer, Rick, Sea	34	153	4.5	14	0
Gardner, Carwell, Buff	41	135	3.3	13	4
Rathman, Tom, LA Raid	28	118	4.2	14	0
Strong, Mack, Sea	27	114	4.2	14	2
Turner, Kevin, NE	36	111	3.1	13	1
Scott, Darnay, Cin	10	106	10.6	23	0
Montgomery, Tyrone, LA Raid	36	97	2.7	15	0
Vaughn, Jon, Sea	27	96	3.6	16	1
Harmon, Ronnie, SD	25	94	3.8	15t	1
Jones, Calvin, LA Raid	22	93	4.2	10	0
Bernstine, Rod, Den	17	91	5.4	24	0
Reed, Andre, Buff	10	87	8.7	20	0
Gash, Sam, NE	30	86	2.9	10	0
Cothran, Jeff, Cin	26	85	3.3	13	0
Humphrey, Ronald, Ind	18	85	4.7	27	0
Klingler, David, Cin	17	85	5.0	15	0
Rivers, Reggie, Den	43	83	1.9	11	2
O'Donnell, Neil, Pitt	31	80	2.6	18	1
Smith, Steve, Sea	26	80	3.1	12	2
Warren, Lamont, Ind	18	80	4.4	34	0
Baldwin, Randy, Cle	23	78	3.4	16	0
Kelly, Jim, Buff	25	77	3.1	18	1
Byars, Keith, Mia	19	64	3.4	12	2
Culver, Rodney, SD	8	63	7.9	22	0
Esiason, Boomer, NYJ	28	59	2.1	15	0
Millen, Hugh, Den	5	57	11.4	24	0
Jourdain, Yonel, Buff	17	56	3.3	16	0
McAfee, Fred, Ariz-Pitt	18	51	2.8	13	2
Vardell, Tommy, Cle	15	48	3.2	9	0
Johnson, Tracy, Sea	12	44	3.7	14	2
Craver, Aaron, Mia	6	43	7.2	19	0
Bledsoe, Drew, NE	44	40	0.9	7	0
Jefferson, Shawn, SD	3	40	13.3	22	0
Alexander, Derrick, Cle	4	38	9.5	25	0
Testaverde, Vinny, Cle	21	37	1.8	12	2
Tolliver, Billy Joe, Hou	12	37	3.1	10	2
Majkowski, Don, Ind	24	34	1.4	10	3
Blades, Brian, Sea	2	32	16.0	40	0
McDuffie, O.J., Mia	5	32	6.4	12	0
Ismail, Raghib, LA Raid	4	31	7.8	13	0
Trudeau, Jack, NYJ	6	30	5.0	15	0
Dawson, Lake, KC	3	24	8.0	13	0
Evans, Vince, LA Raid	6	24	4.0	23	0
Tomczak, Mike, Pitt	4	22	5.5	13	0
Humphries, Stan, SD	19	19	1.0	8	0
Mills, Ernie, Pitt	3	18	6.0	17	0
Carlson, Cody, Hou	10	17	1.7	6	0
Kosar, Bernie, Mia	1	17	17.0	17	0
Montana, Joe, KC	18	17	0.9	13	0
Saxon, James, Mia	8	16	2.0	7	0
Warren, Terrence, Sea	3	15	5.0	11	0
Carrier, Mark, Cle	1	14	14.0	14t	1
Timpson, Michael, NE	2	14	7.0	10	0
Johnson, Anthony, NYJ	5	12	2.4	5	0
Nagle, Browning, Ind	1	12	12.0	12	0
Tillman, Spencer, Hou	2	12	6.0	9	0
Beebe, Don, Buff	2	11	5.5	6	0
Gary, Cleveland, Mia	7	11	1.6	4	0
Toner, Ed, Ind	1	11	11.0	11	0
Gelbaugh, Stan, Sea	1	10	10.0	10	0
Stone, Dwight, Pitt	2	7	3.5	4	0
Bryant, Beno, Sea	1	6	6.0	6	0
Campbell, Jeff, Den	2	6	3.0	6	0
Russell, Derek, Den	1	6	6.0	6	0
McCallum, Napoleon, LA Raid	3	5	1.7	3	1
Avery, Steve, Pitt	2	4	2.0	5	0
Rypien, Mark, Cle	7	4	0.6	2	0
Turner, Nate, Buff	2	4	2.0	4	0
Anderson, Gary, Pitt	1	3	3.0	3	0
Hendrickson, Steve, SD	1	3	3.0	3	0
Miller, Anthony, Den	1	3	3.0	3	0
Reich, Frank, Buff	6	3	0.5	5	0
Coleman, Pat, Hou	1	2	2.0	2	0
Smith, Kevin, LA Raid	1	2	2.0	2	0
Ball, Eric, Cin	2	0	0.0	1	0
Coates, Ben, NE	1	0	0.0	0	0
Dickerson, Ron, KC	1	0	0.0	0	0
Jones, James, Cle	1	0	0.0	0	0
Bono, Steve, KC	4	-1	-.2	2	0
Johnson, Charles, Pitt	4	-1	-.2	7	0
Smith, Lamar, Sea	2	-1	-.5	0	0
Zolak, Scott, NE	1	-1	-1.0	-1	0
Gilbert, Gale, SD	8	-3	-.4	5	0
Moore, Rob, NYJ	1	-3	-3.0	-3	0
Turner, Floyd, Ind	3	-3	-1.0	5	0

	Att.	Yards	Avg.	Long	TD
Wellman, Gary, Hou	1	-3	-3.0	-3	0
Bates, Michael, Sea	2	-4	-2.0	7	0
Givins, Ernest, Hou	1	-5	-5.0	-5	0
Marino, Dan, Mia	22	-6	-.3	10	1
McGwire, Dan, Sea	10	-6	-.6	2	0
Copeland, Russell, Buff	1	-7	-7.0	-7	0
Martin, Tony, SD	2	-9	-4.5	4	0
Mohr, Chris, Buff	1	-9	-9.0	-9	0
Royals, Mark, Pitt	1	-13	-13.0	-13	0
McGee, Tim, Cin	1	-18	-18.0	-18	0

t = Touchdown
Leader based on most yards gained

NFC RUSHERS—INDIVIDUAL

	Att.	Yards	Avg.	Long	TD
Sanders, Barry, Det	331	1883	5.7	85	7
Smith, Emmitt, Dall	368	1484	4.0	46	21
Hampton, Rodney, NYG	327	1075	3.3	27t	6
Allen, Terry, Minn	255	1031	4.0	45	8
Bettis, Jerome, LA Rams	319	1025	3.2	19	3
Rhett, Errict, TB	284	1011	3.6	27	7
Tillman, Lewis, Chi	275	899	3.3	25t	7
Watters, Ricky, SF	239	877	3.7	23	6
Moore, Ron, Ariz	232	780	3.4	24	4
Heyward, Craig, Atl	183	779	4.3	17	7
Ervins, Ricky, Wash	185	650	3.5	49	3
Bennett, Edgar, GB	178	623	3.5	39t	5
Bates, Mario, NO	151	579	3.8	40	6
Cobb, Reggie, GB	153	579	3.8	30	3
Walker, Herschel, Phil	113	528	4.7	91t	5
Brown, Derek, NO	146	489	3.3	16	3
Harris, Raymont, Chi	123	464	3.8	13	1
Garner, Charlie, Phil	109	399	3.7	28t	3
Pegram, Erric, Atl	103	358	3.5	25	1
Centers, Larry, Ariz	115	336	2.9	17	5
Hebron, Vaughn, Phil	82	325	4.0	19	2
Mitchell, Brian, Wash	78	311	4.0	33	0
Floyd, William, SF	87	305	3.5	26	6
Meggett, David, NYG	91	298	3.3	26t	4
Brooks, Reggie, Wash	100	297	3.0	15	2
Young, Steve, SF	58	293	5.1	27	7
Workman, Vince, TB	79	291	3.7	18	0
Cunningham, Randall, Phil	65	288	4.4	22	3
Graham, Scottie, Minn	64	207	3.2	11	2
Joseph, James, Phil	60	203	3.4	34t	1
Favre, Brett, GB	42	202	4.8	36t	2
Brown, Dave, NYG	60	196	3.3	21	2
Higgs, Mark, Mia.-Ariz	62	195	3.1	21	0
Coleman, Lincoln, Dall	64	180	2.8	13	1
Hearst, Garrison, Ariz	37	169	4.6	36	1
Logan, Marc, SF	33	143	4.3	22	1
Johnston, Daryl, Dall	40	138	3.5	9t	2
Thomas, Blair, NE.-Dall	43	137	3.2	13	2
Green, Robert, Chi	25	122	4.9	14	0
Smith, Robert, Minn	31	106	3.4	14t	1
Lee, Amp, Minn	29	104	3.6	16	0
Shuler, Heath, Wash	26	103	4.0	26	0
Miller, Chris, LA Rams	20	100	5.0	16	0
Johnson, LeShon, GB	26	99	3.8	43	0
Loville, Derek, SF	31	99	3.2	13	0
Rice, Jerry, SF	7	93	13.3	28t	2
Neal, Lorenzo, NO	30	90	3.0	12	1
Perriman, Brett, Det	9	86	9.6	25	0
Calloway, Chris, NYG	8	77	9.6	20	0
Erickson, Craig, TB	26	68	2.6	17	1
George, Jeff, Atl	30	66	2.2	10	0
Aikman, Troy, Dall	30	62	2.1	13	1
Chandler, Chris, LA Rams	18	61	3.4	22	1
Schroeder, Jay, Ariz	16	59	3.7	16	0
McDowell, Anthony, TB	21	58	2.8	8	0
Moon, Warren, Minn	27	55	2.0	12	0
Walker, Adam, SF	13	54	4.2	14	1
Moore, Derrick, Det	27	52	1.9	12	4
Downs, Gary, NYG	15	51	3.4	8	0
Smith, Cedric, Wash	10	48	4.8	13	0
Kinchen, Todd, LA Rams	1	44	44.0	44t	1
Rasheed, Kenyon, NYG	17	44	2.6	6	0
Haynes, Michael, NO	4	43	10.8	15	0
Hebert, Bobby, Atl	9	43	4.8	20	0
Beuerlein, Steve, Ariz	22	39	1.8	19	1
Ned, Derrick, NO	11	36	3.3	15	0

	Att.	Yards	Avg.	Long	TD
Bailey, Johnny, LA Rams	11	35	3.2	9	1
Everett, Jim, NO	15	35	2.3	14	0
Krieg, Dave, Det	23	35	1.5	15	0
Carter, Dexter, SF	8	34	4.3	18	0
Lang, David, LA Rams	6	34	5.7	17	0
McMahon, Jim, Ariz	6	32	5.3	17	0
Conway, Curtis, Chi	6	31	5.2	12	0
Griffith, Howard, LA Rams	9	30	3.3	7	0
Christian, Bob, Chi	7	29	4.1	8	0
Hester, Jessie, LA Rams	2	28	14.0	24	0
Dilfer, Trent, TB	2	27	13.5	15	0
Hoge, Merril, Chi	6	24	4.0	8	0
Mitchell, Scott, Det	15	24	1.6	7	1
Barnhardt, Tommy, NO	1	21	21.0	21	0
Evans, Chuck, Minn	6	20	3.3	8	0
Williams, Kevin, Dall	6	20	3.3	8	0
Worley, Tim, Chi	9	17	1.9	4	1
Levens, Dorsey, GB	5	15	3.0	5	0
Levy, Chuck, Ariz	3	15	5.0	22	0
Sharpe, Sterling, GB	3	15	5.0	8	0
Wilson, Charles, TB	2	15	7.5	11	0
Wilson, Wade, NO	7	15	2.1	9	0
Lester, Tim, LA Rams	7	14	2.0	8	0
Turner, Vernon, TB	4	13	3.3	9	0
Anderson, Willie, LA Rams	1	11	11.0	11	0
Graham, Kent, NYG	2	11	5.5	9	0
Williams, Calvin, Phil	2	11	5.5	6	0
Early, Quinn, NO	2	10	5.0	8	0
Dunbar, Vaughn, NO	3	9	3.0	3	0
Feagles, Jeff, Ariz	2	8	4.0	12	0
Marshall, Arthur, NYG	2	8	4.0	6	0
Brister, Bubby, Phil	1	7	7.0	7	0
Brunell, Mark, GB	6	7	1.2	5t	1
Royster, Mazio, TB	9	7	0.8	6	0
Hughes, Tyrone, NO	2	6	3.0	7	0
Jordan, Charles, GB	1	5	5.0	5	0
Winans, Tydus, Wash	1	5	5.0	5	0
Agee, Tommie, Dall	5	4	0.8	3	0
Drayton, Troy, LA Rams	1	4	4.0	4	0
Elias, Keith, NYG	2	4	2.0	5	0
Emanuel, Bert, Atl	2	4	2.0	2	0
Howard, Desmond, Wash	1	4	4.0	4	0
Walsh, Steve, Chi	30	4	0.1	12	1
Muster, Brad, NO	1	3	3.0	3t	1
Bruce, Isaac, LA Rams	1	2	2.0	2	0
Salisbury, Sean, Minn	3	2	0.7	5	0
Frerotte, Gus, Wash	4	1	0.3	2	0
Friesz, John, Wash	1	1	1.0	1	0
Grbac, Elvis, SF	13	1	0.1	6	0
Maddox, Tommy, LA Rams	1	1	1.0	1	0
Palmer, David, Minn	1	1	1.0	1	0
Samuels, Terry, Ariz	1	1	1.0	1	0
Alexander, Harold, Atl	1	0	0.0	0	0
Brooks, Robert, GB	1	0	0.0	0	0
Harris, Rudy, TB	2	0	0.0	3	0
Lynch, Eric, Det	1	0	0.0	0	0
Saxon, Mike, Minn	1	0	0.0	0	0
Anderson, Jamal, Atl	2	-1	-.5	0	0
Armstrong, Tyji, TB	1	-1	-1.0	-1	0
Reeves, Bryan, Ariz	1	-1	-1.0	-1	0
Wilson, Robert, Dall	1	-1	-1.0	-1	0
Garrett, Jason, Dall	3	-2	-.7	0	0
Johnson, Brad, Minn	2	-2	-1.0	-1	0
Kramer, Erik, Chi	6	-2	-.3	2	0
Peete, Rodney, Dall	9	-2	-.2	2	0
Taylor, John, SF	2	-2	-1.0	1	0
Thompson, Darrell, GB	2	-2	-1.0	2	0
Ellard, Henry, Wash	1	-5	-5.0	-5	0
Sherrard, Mike, NYG	1	-10	-10.0	-10	0

t = Touchdown
Leader based on most yards gained

1994 INDIVIDUAL STATISTICS

PASSING

Highest Rating
NFC: 112.8—Steve Young, San Francisco
AFC: 89.2—Dan Marino, Miami

Completion Percentage
NFC: 70.3—Steve Young, San Francisco
AFC: 63.6—Jim Kelly, Buffalo

Attempts
AFC: 691—Drew Bledsoe, New England
NFC: 601—Warren Moon, Minnesota

Completions
AFC: 400—Drew Bledsoe, New England
NFC: 371—Warren Moon, Minnesota

Yards
AFC: 4555—Drew Bledsoe, New England
NFC: 4264—Warren Moon, Minnesota

Yards, Game
AFC: 473—Dan Marino, Miami vs. New England, September 4 (23-42, 5 TD)
NFC: 420—Warren Moon, Minnesota vs. New Orleans, November 6 (33-57, 3 TD)

Longest
AFC: 99—Stan Humphries (to Tony Martin), San Diego at Seattle, September 18 - TD
NFC: 93—Randall Cunningham (to Herschel Walker), Philadelphia at N.Y. Giants, September 4

Yards Per Attempt
NFC: 8.61—Steve Young, San Francisco
AFC: 7.33—Jeff Hostetler, L.A. Raiders

Touchdown Passes
NFC: 35—Steve Young, San Francisco
AFC: 30—Dan Marino, Miami

Touchdown Passes, Game
AFC: 5—Dan Marino, Miami vs. New England, September 4, (23-42, 456 yards)
NFC: 4—Steve Young, San Francisco vs. L.A. Raiders, September 5, (19-32, 292 yards)
John Friesz, Washington at New Orleans, September 11, (15-22, 190 yards)
Steve Young, San Francisco at Atlanta, October 16, (15-16, 138 yards)
Jeff George, Atlanta at Denver, November 20, (19-43, 254 yards)
Steve Young, San Francisco vs. L.A. Rams, November 20, (30-44, 325 yards)
Brett Favre, Green Bay at Dallas, November 24, (27-40, 248 yards)
Steve Young, San Francisco at New Orleans, November 28, (24-30, 270 yards)

Lowest Interception Percentage
AFC: 1.8—Joe Montana, Kansas City
NFC: 2.2—Steve Young, San Francisco

Team Champion (Most Net Yards)
AFC: 4444—New England
NFC: 4324—Minnesota

AFC PASSING—TEAM

	Att	Comp	Pct Comp	Gross Yards	Sacked	Yds Lost	Net Yards	Yds/ Att	Yds/ Comp	TD	Pct TD	Long	Int	Pct Int
New England	699	405	57.9	4583	22	139	4444	6.56	11.32	25	3.58	62t	27	3.9
Miami	627	392	62.5	4533	18	113	4420	7.23	11.56	31	4.94	64t	18	2.9
Denver	626	388	62.0	4383	55	366	4017	7.00	11.30	18	2.88	76	13	2.1
Kansas City	615	366	59.5	4092	19	132	3960	6.65	11.18	20	3.25	62t	14	2.3
Buffalo	542	342	63.1	3714	41	301	3413	6.85	10.86	23	4.24	83t	21	3.9
San Diego	522	305	58.4	3619	29	251	3368	6.93	11.87	20	3.83	99t	14	2.7
L.A. Raiders	488	281	57.6	3556	50	289	3267	7.29	12.65	22	4.51	77t	16	3.3
Cincinnati	542	289	53.3	3541	44	305	3236	6.53	12.25	21	3.87	76	19	3.5
N.Y. Jets	539	310	57.5	3323	28	186	3137	6.17	10.72	18	3.34	69	18	3.3
Cleveland	507	266	52.5	3269	14	94	3175	6.45	12.29	20	3.94	81t	21	4.1
Pittsburgh	463	266	57.5	3247	39	283	2964	7.01	12.21	17	3.67	84t	9	1.9
Houston	554	274	49.5	3216	65	417	2799	5.81	11.74	13	2.35	81	17	3.1
Seattle	498	253	50.8	2809	40	241	2568	5.64	11.10	13	2.61	51	9	1.8
Indianapolis	376	217	57.7	2519	28	166	2353	6.70	11.61	15	3.99	85t	14	3.7
AFC Total	7598	4354	—	50404	492	3283	47121	—	—	276	—	99t	230	—
AFC Average	542.7	311.0	57.3	3600.3	35.1	234.5	3365.8	6.63	11.58	19.7	3.6	—	16.4	3.0

NFC PASSING—TEAM

	Att	Comp	Pct Comp	Gross Yards	Sacked	Yds Lost	Net Yards	Yds/ Att	Yds/ Comp	TD	Pct TD	Long	Int	Pct Int
Minnesota	673	409	60.8	4570	31	246	4324	6.79	11.17	18	2.67	65t	20	3.0
San Francisco	511	359	70.3	4362	35	199	4163	8.54	12.15	37	7.24	69t	11	2.2
Atlanta	629	374	59.5	4344	37	232	4112	6.91	11.61	25	3.97	85t	25	4.0
New Orleans	569	366	64.3	4027	24	181	3846	7.08	11.00	22	3.87	78t	18	3.2
Green Bay	609	375	61.6	3977	33	204	3773	6.53	10.61	33	5.42	49	14	2.3
Philadelphia	566	316	55.8	3736	48	372	3364	6.60	11.82	18	3.18	93	14	2.5
L.A. Rams	512	291	56.8	3597	35	239	3358	7.03	12.36	23	4.49	72t	18	3.5
Washington	546	271	49.6	3524	21	146	3378	6.45	13.00	25	4.58	81t	27	4.9
Dallas	448	282	62.9	3461	20	93	3368	7.73	12.27	19	4.24	90	14	3.1
Tampa Bay	491	271	55.2	3436	30	171	3265	7.00	12.68	17	3.46	71t	16	3.3
Arizona	538	287	53.3	3284	34	237	3047	6.10	11.44	11	2.04	63	19	3.5
Chicago	502	308	61.4	3230	25	139	3091	6.43	10.49	19	3.78	85t	16	3.2
Detroit	459	250	54.5	3085	26	163	2922	6.72	12.34	24	5.23	51t	14	3.1
N.Y. Giants	405	226	55.8	2847	46	285	2562	7.03	12.60	16	3.95	55	18	4.4
NFC Total	7458	4385	—	51480	445	2907	48573	—	—	307	—	93	244	—
NFC Average	532.7	313.2	58.8	3677.1	31.8	207.6	3469.5	6.90	11.74	21.9	4.1	—	17.4	3.3
League Total	15056	8739	—	101884	937	6190	95694	—	—	583	—	99t	474	—
League Average	537.7	312.1	58.0	3638.7	33.5	221.1	3417.6	6.77	11.66	20.8	3.9	—	16.9	3.1

Leader based on net yards

NFL TOP TEN PASSERS

	Att.	Comp.	Pct. Comp.	Yds.	Avg. Gain	TD	Pct. TD	Long	Int.	Pct. Int.	Sack	Yds. Lost	Rating Points
Young, Steve, SF	461	324	70.3	3969	8.61	35	7.6	69t	10	2.2	31	163	112.8
Favre, Brett, GB	582	363	62.4	3882	6.67	33	5.7	49	14	2.4	31	188	90.7
Marino, Dan, Mia	615	385	62.6	4453	7.24	30	4.9	64t	17	2.8	18	113	89.2
Elway, John, Den	494	307	62.1	3490	7.06	16	3.2	63	10	2.0	46	303	85.7
Everett, Jim, NO	540	346	64.1	3855	7.14	22	4.1	78t	18	3.3	21	164	84.9
Aikman, Troy, Dall	361	233	64.5	2676	7.41	13	3.6	90	12	3.3	14	59	84.9
Kelly, Jim, Buff	448	285	63.6	3114	6.95	22	4.9	83t	17	3.8	34	244	84.6
Montana, Joe, KC	493	299	60.6	3283	6.66	16	3.2	57t	9	1.8	19	132	83.6
George, Jeff, Atl	524	322	61.5	3734	7.13	23	4.4	85t	18	3.4	32	206	83.3
Erickson, Craig, TB	399	225	56.4	2919	7.32	16	4.0	71t	10	2.5	22	129	82.5

AFC PASSING—INDIVIDUAL

	Att.	Comp.	Pct. Comp.	Yds.	Avg. Gain	TD	Pct. TD	Long	Int.	Pct. Int.	Sack	Yds. Lost	Rating Points
Marino, Dan, Mia	615	385	62.6	4453	7.24	30	4.9	64t	17	2.8	18	113	89.2
Elway, John, Den	494	307	62.1	3490	7.06	16	3.2	63	10	2.0	46	303	85.7
Kelly, Jim, Buff	448	285	63.6	3114	6.95	22	4.9	83t	17	3.8	34	244	84.6
Montana, Joe, KC	493	299	60.6	3283	6.66	16	3.2	57t	9	1.8	19	132	83.6
Humphries, Stan, SD	453	264	58.3	3209	7.08	17	3.8	99t	12	2.6	25	223	81.6
Hostetler, Jeff, LA Raid	455	263	57.8	3334	7.33	20	4.4	77t	16	3.5	41	232	80.8
O'Donnell, Neil, Pitt	370	212	57.3	2443	6.60	13	3.5	60t	9	2.4	35	250	78.9
Esiason, Boomer, NYJ	440	255	58.0	2782	6.32	17	3.9	69	13	3.0	19	134	77.3
Blake, Jeff, Cin	306	156	51.0	2154	7.04	14	4.6	76	9	2.9	19	120	76.9
Bledsoe, Drew, NE	691	400	57.9	4555	6.59	25	3.6	62t	27	3.9	22	139	73.6
Testaverde, Vinny, Cle	376	207	55.1	2575	6.85	16	4.3	81t	18	4.8	12	83	70.7
Mirer, Rick, Sea	381	195	51.2	2151	5.65	11	2.9	51	7	1.8	27	145	70.2
Klingler, David, Cin	231	131	56.7	1327	5.74	6	2.6	56	9	3.9	24	165	65.7
Tolliver, Billy Joe, Hou	240	121	50.4	1287	5.36	6	2.5	44	7	2.9	27	166	62.6
Nonqualifiers													
Gelbaugh, Stan, Sea	11	7	63.6	80	7.27	1	9.1	25t	0	0.0	0	0	115.7
Tomczak, Mike, Pitt	93	54	58.1	804	8.65	4	4.3	84t	0	0.0	4	33	100.8
Evans, Vince, LA Raid	33	18	54.5	222	6.73	2	6.1	65t	0	0.0	9	57	95.8
Gilbert, Gale, SD	67	41	61.2	410	6.12	3	4.5	26	1	1.5	4	28	87.3
Harbaugh, Jim, Ind	202	125	61.9	1440	7.13	9	4.5	85t	6	3.0	17	72	85.8
Millen, Hugh, Den	131	81	61.8	893	6.82	2	1.5	76	3	2.3	9	63	77.6
Bono, Steve, KC	117	66	56.4	796	6.80	4	3.4	62t	4	3.4	0	0	74.6
Kosar, Bernie, Mia	12	7	58.3	80	6.67	1	8.3	22	1	8.3	0	0	71.5
Richardson, Bucky, Hou	181	94	51.9	1202	6.64	6	3.3	76t	6	3.3	23	136	70.3
Majkowski, Don, Ind	152	84	55.3	1010	6.64	6	3.9	29	7	4.6	9	76	69.8
Rypien, Mark, Cle	128	59	46.1	694	5.42	4	3.1	43	3	2.3	2	11	63.7
Reich, Frank, Buff	93	56	60.2	568	6.11	1	1.1	47	4	4.3	7	57	63.4
McGwire, Dan, Sea	105	51	48.6	578	5.50	1	1.0	36	2	1.9	13	96	60.7
Trudeau, Jack, NYJ	91	50	54.9	496	5.45	1	1.1	24t	4	4.4	9	52	55.9
Carlson, Cody, Hou	132	59	44.7	727	5.51	1	0.8	81	4	3.0	15	115	52.2
Nagle, Browning, Ind	21	8	38.1	69	3.29	0	0.0	23	1	4.8	2	18	27.7
Fewer than 10 attempts													
Blundin, Matt, KC	5	1	20.0	13	2.60	0	0.0	13	1	20.0	0	0	0.0
Broussard, Steve, Cin	1	0	0.0	0	0.00	0	0.0	0	0	0.0	0	0	39.6
Camarillo, Rich, Hou	1	0	0.0	0	0.00	0	0.0	0	0	0.0	0	0	39.6
Foley, Glenn, NYJ	8	5	62.5	45	5.63	0	0.0	16	1	12.5	0	0	38.0
Hollas, Donald, Cin	2	0	0.0	0	0.00	0	0.0	0	1	50.0	1	20	0.0
Jackson, Michael, Cle	2	0	0.0	0	0.00	0	0.0	0	0	0.0	0	0	39.6
Johnson, Lee, Cin	1	1	100.0	7	7.00	1	100.0	7t	0	0.0	0	0	135.4
Martin, Tony, SD	1	0	0.0	0	0.00	0	0.0	0	1	100.0	0	0	0.0
Means, Natrone, SD	1	0	0.0	0	0.00	0	0.0	0	0	0.0	0	0	39.6
Metcalf, Eric, Cle	1	0	0.0	0	0.00	0	0.0	0	0	0.0	0	0	39.6
Reed, Andre, Buff	1	1	100.0	32	32.00	0	0.0	32	0	0.0	0	0	118.8
Rivers, Reggie, Den	1	0	0.0	0	0.00	0	0.0	0	0	0.0	0	0	39.6
Scott, Darnay, Cin	1	1	100.0	53	53.00	0	0.0	53	0	0.0	0	0	118.8
Tuten, Rick, Sea	1	0	0.0	0	0.00	0	0.0	0	0	0.0	0	0	39.6
Warren, Lamont, Ind	1	0	0.0	0	0.00	0	0.0	0	0	0.0	0	0	39.6
Zolak, Scott, NE	8	5	62.5	28	3.50	0	0.0	13	0	0.0	0	0	68.8

t = Touchdown
Leader based on rating points, minimum 224 attempts

1994 INDIVIDUAL STATISTICS

NFC PASSING—INDIVIDUAL

	Att.	Comp.	Pct. Comp.	Yds.	Avg. Gain	TD	Pct. TD	Long	Int.	Pct. Int.	Sack	Yds. Lost	Rating Points
Young, Steve, SF	461	324	70.3	3969	8.61	35	7.6	69t	10	2.2	31	163	112.8
Favre, Brett, GB	582	363	62.4	3882	6.67	33	5.7	49	14	2.4	31	188	90.7
Everett, Jim, NO	540	346	64.1	3855	7.14	22	4.1	78t	18	3.3	21	164	84.9
Aikman, Troy, Dall	361	233	64.5	2676	7.41	13	3.6	90	12	3.3	14	59	84.9
George, Jeff, Atl	524	322	61.5	3734	7.13	23	4.4	85t	18	3.4	32	206	83.3
Erickson, Craig, TB	399	225	56.4	2919	7.32	16	4.0	71t	10	2.5	22	129	82.5
Moon, Warren, Minn	601	371	61.7	4264	7.09	18	3.0	65t	19	3.2	29	235	79.9
Walsh, Steve, Chi	343	208	60.6	2078	6.06	10	2.9	50	8	2.3	11	52	77.9
Cunningham, Randall, Phil	490	265	54.1	3229	6.59	16	3.3	93	13	2.7	43	333	74.4
Miller, Chris, LA Rams	317	173	54.6	2104	6.64	16	5.0	54	14	4.4	28	193	73.6
Brown, Dave, NYG	350	201	57.4	2536	7.25	12	3.4	53	16	4.6	42	248	72.5
Schroeder, Jay, Ariz	238	133	55.9	1510	6.34	4	1.7	48t	7	2.9	11	85	68.4
Mitchell, Scott, Det	246	119	48.4	1456	5.92	10	4.1	34	11	4.5	12	63	62.0
Beuerlein, Steve, Ariz	255	130	51.0	1545	6.06	5	2.0	63	9	3.5	20	129	61.6
Shuler, Heath, Wash	265	120	45.3	1658	6.26	10	3.8	81t	12	4.5	12	83	59.6
Nonqualifiers													
Peete, Rodney, Dall	56	33	58.9	470	8.39	4	7.1	65t	1	1.8	4	21	102.5
Krieg, Dave, Det	212	131	61.8	1629	7.68	14	6.6	51t	3	1.4	14	100	101.7
Grbac, Elvis, SF	50	35	70.0	393	7.86	2	4.0	42	1	2.0	4	36	98.2
Garrett, Jason, Dall	31	16	51.6	315	10.16	2	6.5	68	1	3.2	2	13	95.5
Chandler, Chris, LA Rams	176	108	61.4	1352	7.68	7	4.0	72t	2	1.1	7	46	93.8
Brister, Bubby, Phil	76	51	67.1	507	6.67	2	2.6	53	1	1.3	5	39	89.1
Wilson, Wade, NO	28	20	71.4	172	6.14	0	0.0	16	0	0.0	3	17	87.2
Kramer, Erik, Chi	158	99	62.7	1129	7.15	8	5.1	85t	8	5.1	14	87	79.9
Friesz, John, Wash	180	105	58.3	1266	7.03	10	5.6	73t	9	5.0	6	45	77.7
Johnson, Brad, Minn	37	22	59.5	150	4.05	0	0.0	15	0	0.0	1	5	68.5
Graham, Kent, NYG	53	24	45.3	295	5.57	3	5.7	55	2	3.8	2	22	66.2
Frerotte, Gus, Wash	100	46	46.0	600	6.00	5	5.0	51	5	5.0	3	18	61.3
Brunell, Mark, GB	27	12	44.4	95	3.52	0	0.0	25	0	0.0	2	16	53.8
Hebert, Bobby, Atl	103	52	50.5	610	5.92	2	1.9	40	6	5.8	3	17	51.0
Salisbury, Sean, Minn	34	16	47.1	156	4.59	0	0.0	38	1	2.9	1	6	48.2
McMahon, Jim, Ariz	43	23	53.5	219	5.09	1	2.3	33	3	7.0	3	23	46.6
Maddox, Tommy, LA Rams	19	10	52.6	141	7.42	0	0.0	39	2	10.5	0	0	37.3
Dilfer, Trent, TB	82	38	46.3	433	5.28	1	1.2	42	6	7.3	8	42	36.3
Fewer than 10 attempts													
Barnhardt, Tommy, NO	1	0	0.0	0	0.00	0	0.0	0	0	0.0	0	0	39.6
Conway, Curtis, Chi	1	1	100.0	23	23.00	1	100.0	23t	0	0.0	0	0	158.3
Emanuel, Bert, Atl	1	0	0.0	0	0.00	0	0.0	0	1	100.0	0	0	0.0
Hearst, Garrison, Ariz	1	1	100.0	10	10.00	1	100.0	10t	0	0.0	0	0	147.9
Klein, Perry, Atl	1	0	0.0	0	0.00	0	0.0	0	0	0.0	2	9	39.6
Marshall, Arthur, NYG	0	0	—	0	—	0	—	—	0	—	1	8	-1.0
Meggett, David, NYG	2	1	50.0	16	8.00	1	50.0	16t	0	0.0	1	7	116.7
Mitchell, Brian, Wash	1	0	0.0	0	0.00	0	0.0	0	1	100.0	0	0	0.0
Moore, Ron, Ariz	1	0	0.0	0	0.00	0	0.0	0	0	0.0	0	0	39.6
Perriman, Brett, Det	1	0	0.0	0	0.00	0	0.0	0	0	0.0	0	0	39.6
Saxon, Mike, Minn	1	0	0.0	0	0.00	0	0.0	0	0	0.0	0	0	39.6
Stryzinski, Dan, TB	1	1	100.0	21	21.00	0	0.0	21	0	0.0	0	0	118.8
Weldon, Casey, TB	9	7	77.8	63	7.00	0	0.0	27	0	0.0	0	0	95.8

t = Touchdown
Leader based on rating points, minimum 224 attempts

PASS RECEIVING

Receptions
NFC: 122—Cris Carter, Minnesota
AFC: 96—Ben Coates, New England

Receptions, Game
NFC: 16—Jerry Rice, San Francisco vs. L.A. Rams, November 20, (165 yards - 3 TD)
AFC: 15—Andre Reed, Buffalo vs. Green Bay, November 20, (191 yards - 2 TD)

Yards
NFC: 1499—Jerry Rice, San Francisco
AFC: 1309—Tim Brown, L.A. Raiders

Yards, Game
AFC: 211—Irving Fryar, Miami vs. New England, September 4, (5 receptions - 3 TD)
NFC: 200—Torrance Small, New Orleans at Denver, December 24, (6 receptions - 2 TD)

Longest
AFC: 99—Tony Martin (from Stan Humphries), San Diego at Seattle, September 18 - TD
NFC: 93—Herschel Walker (from Randall Cunningham), Philadelphia at N.Y. Giants, September 4

Yards Per Reception
NFC: 24.9—Alvin Harper, Dallas
AFC: 18.8—Darnay Scott, Cincinnati

Touchdowns
NFC: 18—Sterling Sharpe, Green Bay
AFC: 11—Carl Pickens, Cincinnati

Team Leaders, Receptions
AFC: BUFFALO: 90, Andre Reed; CINCINNATI: 71, Carl Pickens; CLEVELAND: 48, Derrick Alexander; DENVER: 87, Shannon Sharpe; HOUSTON: 68, Webster Slaughter, Haywood Jeffires; INDIANAPOLIS: 52, Marshall Faulk, Floyd Turner; KANSAS CITY: 67, Kimble Anders; L.A. RAIDERS: 89, Tim Brown; MIAMI: 73, Irving Fryar; NEW ENGLAND: 96, Ben Coates; N.Y. JETS: 78, Rob Moore; PITTSBURGH: 51, John L. Williams; SAN DIEGO: 58, Ronnie Harmon, Mark Seay; SEATTLE: 81, Brian Blades
NFC: ARIZONA: 77, Larry Centers; ATLANTA: 111, Terance Mathis; CHICAGO: 68, Jeff Graham; DALLAS: 79, Michael Irvin; DETROIT: 72, Herman Moore; GREEN BAY: 94, Sterling Sharpe; L.A. RAMS: 58, Johnny Bailey; MINNESOTA: 122, Cris Carter; NEW ORLEANS: 82, Quinn Early; N.Y. GIANTS: 53, Mike Sherrard; PHILADELPHIA: 78, Fred Barnett; SAN FRANCISCO: 112, Jerry Rice; TAMPA BAY: 46, Lawrence Dawsey; WASHINGTON: 74, Henry Ellard

NFL TOP TEN PASS RECEIVERS

	No.	Yards	Avg.	Long	TD
Carter, Cris, Minn	122	1256	10.3	65t	7
Rice, Jerry, SF	112	1499	13.4	69t	13
Mathis, Terance, Atl	111	1342	12.1	81	11
Coates, Ben, NE	96	1174	12.2	62t	7
Sharpe, Sterling, GB	94	1119	11.9	49	18
Reed, Andre, Buff	90	1303	14.5	83t	8
Brown, Tim, LA Raid.	89	1309	14.7	77t	9
Sharpe, Shannon, Den	87	1010	11.6	44	4
Reed, Jake, Minn	85	1175	13.8	59	4
Early, Quinn, NO	82	894	10.9	33	4

NFL TOP TEN RECEIVERS BY YARDS

	Yards	No.	Avg.	Long	TD
Rice, Jerry, SF	1499	112	13.4	69t	13
Ellard, Henry, Wash	1397	74	18.9	73t	6
Mathis, Terance, Atl	1342	111	12.1	81	11
Brown, Tim, LA Raid	1309	89	14.7	77t	9
Reed, Andre, Buff	1303	90	14.5	83t	8
Fryar, Irving, Mia	1270	73	17.4	54t	7
Carter, Cris, Minn	1256	122	10.3	65t	7
Irvin, Michael, Dall	1241	79	15.7	65t	6
Reed, Jake, Minn	1175	85	13.8	59	4
Coates, Ben, NE	1174	96	12.2	62t	7

AFC RECEIVERS—INDIVIDUAL

	No.	Yards	Avg.	Long	TD
Coates, Ben, NE	96	1174	12.2	62t	7
Reed, Andre, Buff	90	1303	14.5	83t	8
Brown, Tim, LA Raid	89	1309	14.7	77t	9
Sharpe, Shannon, Den	87	1010	11.6	44	4
Blades, Brian, Sea	81	1086	13.4	45	4
Moore, Rob, NYJ	78	1010	12.9	41t	6
Milburn, Glyn, Den	77	549	7.1	33	3
Timpson, Michael, NE	74	941	12.7	37	3
Fryar, Irving, Mia	73	1270	17.4	54t	7
Pickens, Carl, Cin	71	1127	15.9	70t	11
Slaughter, Webster, Hou	68	846	12.4	57	2
Jeffires, Haywood, Hou	68	783	11.5	50	6
Anders, Kimble, KC	67	525	7.8	30	1
Thompson, Leroy, NE	65	465	7.2	27t	5
Miller, Anthony, Den	60	1107	18.5	76	5
Jackson, Keith, Mia	59	673	11.4	35	7
Brisby, Vincent, NE	58	904	15.6	43	5
Mitchell, Johnny, NYJ	58	749	12.9	55	4
Seay, Mark, SD	58	645	11.1	49t	6
Harmon, Ronnie, SD	58	615	10.6	35	1
Martin, Kelvin, Sea	56	681	12.2	32	1
Turner, Floyd, Ind	52	593	11.4	28	6
Faulk, Marshall, Ind	52	522	10.0	85t	1
Turner, Kevin, NE	52	471	9.1	32	2
Davis, Willie, KC	51	822	16.1	62t	5
Dawkins, Sean, Ind	51	742	14.5	49	5
Williams, John L., Pitt	51	378	7.4	23	2
Martin, Tony, SD	50	885	17.7	99t	7
Thomas, Thurman, Buff	50	349	7.0	28	2
Metzelaars, Pete, Buff	49	428	8.7	35t	5
Byars, Keith, Mia	49	418	8.5	34	5
Alexander, Derrick, Cle	48	828	17.3	81t	2
Birden, J. J., KC	48	637	13.3	44	4
Metcalf, Eric, Cle	47	436	9.3	57t	3
Williams, Harvey, LA Raid	47	391	8.3	27t	3
Scott, Darnay, Cin	46	866	18.8	76	5
Green, Eric, Pitt	46	618	13.4	46	4
Monk, Art, NYJ	46	581	12.6	69	3
Hoard, Leroy, Cle	45	445	9.9	65t	4
Ingram, Mark, Mia	44	506	11.5	64t	6
Jefferson, Shawn, SD	43	627	14.6	52t	3
Brooks, Bill, Buff	42	482	11.5	32	2
Allen, Marcus, KC	42	349	8.3	38	0
Johnson, Johnny, NYJ	42	303	7.2	24	2
Warren, Chris, Sea	41	323	7.9	51	2
Beebe, Don, Buff	40	527	13.2	72t	4
McGee, Tony, Cin	40	492	12.3	54	1
Means, Natrone, SD	39	235	6.0	22	0
Johnson, Charles, Pitt	38	577	15.2	84t	3
Russell, Leonard, Den	38	227	6.0	19	0
Dawson, Lake, KC	37	537	14.5	50	2
McDuffie, O. J., Mia	37	488	13.2	30	3
Thigpen, Yancey, Pitt	36	546	15.2	60t	4
Givins, Ernest, Hou	36	521	14.5	76t	1
Walker, Derrick, KC	36	382	10.6	57t	2
Fenner, Derrick, Cin	36	276	7.7	29	1
Ismail, Raghib, LA Raid	34	513	15.1	42	5
Parmalee, Bernie, Mia	34	249	7.3	22	1
Broussard, Steve, Cin	34	218	6.4	25	0
Glover, Andrew, LA Raid	33	371	11.2	27t	2
Green, Paul, Sea	30	208	6.9	20	1
Carrier, Mark, Cle	29	452	15.6	43	5
Tillman, Cedric, Den	28	455	16.3	63	1
Crittenden, Ray, NE	28	379	13.5	32	3
Green, Harold, Cin	27	267	9.9	34	1
Saxon, James, Mia	27	151	5.6	25	0
Potts, Roosevelt, Ind	26	251	9.7	30	1
Rathman, Tom, LA Raid	26	194	7.5	18	0
Russell, Derek, Den	25	342	13.7	43	1
Anderson, Richie, NYJ	25	212	8.5	27t	1
Craver, Aaron, Mia	24	237	9.9	28	0
Kinchen, Brian, Cle	24	232	9.7	38	1
Morris, Bam, Pitt	22	204	9.3	49	0
Martin, Eric, KC	21	307	14.6	61	1
Jackson, Michael, Cle	21	304	14.5	30	2
Copeland, Russell, Buff	21	255	12.1	35	1
Pupunu, Alfred, SD	21	214	10.2	25	2
White, Lorenzo, Hou	21	188	9.0	41	1
Coleman, Pat, Hou	20	298	14.9	81	1
Hastings, Andre, Pitt	20	281	14.1	46	2
Thornton, James, NYJ	20	171	8.6	25	0
Rivers, Reggie, Den	20	136	6.8	25	0
Foster, Barry, Pitt	20	124	6.2	27	0
Mills, Ernie, Pitt	19	384	20.2	43	1
Pritchard, Mike, Den	19	271	14.3	50t	1
Cash, Keith, KC	19	192	10.1	31	2
Brown, Gary, Hou	18	194	10.8	24	1
Davis, Kenneth, Buff	18	82	4.6	12	0
Young, Duane, SD	17	217	12.8	31	1
Wright, Alexander, LA Raid	16	294	18.4	76t	2
Cash, Kerry, Ind	16	190	11.9	24	1
Vardell, Tommy, Cle	16	137	8.6	19	1

1994 INDIVIDUAL STATISTICS

	No.	Yards	Avg.	Long	TD
Hill, Greg, KC	16	92	5.8	21	0
Jett, James, LA Raid	15	253	16.9	54	0
Williams, Mike, Mia	15	221	14.7	29	0
Kirby, Terry, Mia	14	154	11.0	26	0
McGee, Tim, Cin	13	175	13.5	25	1
Evans, Jerry, Den	13	127	9.8	20t	2
Smith, Steve, Sea	11	142	12.9	25	1
Mitchell, Shannon, SD	11	105	9.5	36	0
Byner, Earnest, Cle	11	102	9.3	30	0
Gardner, Carwell, Buff	11	89	8.1	21	0
Carter, Pat, Hou	11	74	6.7	19	1
Sadowski, Troy, Cin	11	54	4.9	11	0
McCardell, Keenan, Cle	10	182	18.2	34	0
Wellman, Gary, Hou	10	112	11.2	25	0
Johnson, Tracy, Sea	10	91	9.1	17	0
Jourdain, Yonel, Buff	10	56	5.6	18	0
Baxter, Brad, NYJ	10	40	4.0	7	0
Anderson, Steve, NYJ	9	90	10.0	17	0
Burke, John, NE	9	86	9.6	17	0
Bernstine, Rod, Den	9	70	7.8	16	0
Gash, Sam, NE	9	61	6.8	19	0
Butts, Marion, NE	9	54	6.0	15	0
Clark, Derrick, Den	9	47	5.2	10	0
Montgomery, Tyrone, LA Raid	8	126	15.8	65t	1
Jackson, Mark, Ind	8	97	12.1	22	1
McNair, Todd, Hou	8	78	9.8	21	0
Stone, Dwight, Pitt	7	81	11.6	25	0
Hughes, Danan, KC	7	80	11.4	22	0
Murrell, Adrian, NYJ	7	76	10.9	20	0
Bennett, Donnell, KC	7	53	7.6	15	0
Edmunds, Ferrell, Sea	7	43	6.1	8	0
Miller, Scott, Mia	6	94	15.7	27	1
Greene, Tracy, KC	6	69	11.5	20	1
Reeves, Walter, Cle	6	61	10.2	22	1
Yarborough, Ryan, NYJ	6	42	7.0	12	1
Bates, Michael, Sea	5	112	22.4	40t	1
Hobbs, Daryl, LA Raid	5	52	10.4	14	0
Hayes, Jonathan, Pitt	5	50	10.0	17	1
Bieniemy, Eric, SD	5	48	9.6	25	0
Marrow, Vince, Buff	5	44	8.8	14	0
Query, Jeff, Cin	5	44	8.8	14	0
Johnson, Anthony, NYJ	5	31	6.2	9	0
Thomas, Robb, Sea	4	70	17.5	35	0
Lewis, Roderick, Hou	4	48	12.0	19	0
Brown, Reggie, Hou	4	34	8.5	11	0
Cothran, Jeff, Cin	4	24	6.0	8	1
Spikes, Irving, Mia	4	16	4.0	9	0
Warren, Lamont, Ind	3	47	15.7	29	0
Johnson, Lonnie, Buff	3	42	14.0	21	0
Williams, Jamie, LA Raid	3	25	8.3	16	0
Hannah, Travis, Hou	3	24	8.0	11	0
Penn, Chris, KC	3	24	8.0	13	0
Humphrey, Ronald, Ind	3	19	6.3	12	0
Baldwin, Randy, Cle	3	15	5.0	15	0
Hartley, Frank, Cle	3	13	4.3	8	1
Baxter, Fred, NYJ	3	11	3.7	6	1
Strong, Mack, Sea	3	3	1.0	5	0
Smith, Rico, Cle	2	61	30.5	50	0
Thomas, Damon, Buff	2	31	15.5	17	0
Bailey, Aaron, Ind	2	30	15.0	23	0
Williams, Ronnie, Mia	2	26	13.0	17	0
Hawkins, Steve, NE	2	22	11.0	14	0
May, Deems, SD	2	22	11.0	18	0
Kimbrough, Tony, Den	2	20	10.0	12	0
Crumpler, Carlester, Sea	2	19	9.5	12	0
Gary, Cleveland, Mia	2	19	9.5	11	0
Baker, Shannon, Ind	2	15	7.5	10	0
Bender, Wes, LA Raid	2	14	7.0	7	0
Maston, Le'Shai, Hou	2	12	6.0	10	0
Baty, Greg, Mia	2	11	5.5	8	1
Dickerson, Ron, KC	2	11	5.5	6	0
Johnson, Jimmy, KC	2	7	3.5	5	0
Jones, Calvin, LA Raid	2	6	3.0	4	0
Valerio, Joe, KC	2	5	2.5	4t	2
Turner, Nate, Buff	1	26	26.0	26t	1
McKnight, James, Sea	1	25	25.0	25t	1
Campbell, Jeff, Den	1	22	22.0	22t	1
Harris, Ronnie, NE	1	11	11.0	11	0
Smith, Kevin, LA Raid	1	8	8.0	8	0
Arbuckle, Charles, Ind	1	7	7.0	7	0
Parker, Orlando, NYJ	1	7	7.0	7	0
Barnes, Johnnie, SD	1	6	6.0	6	0
Etheredge, Carlos, Ind	1	6	6.0	6	0
Vaughn, Jon, Sea	1	5	5.0	5t	1
Ball, Eric, Cin	1	4	4.0	4	0
Mills, John Henry, Hou	1	4	4.0	4	0
Avery, Steve, Pitt	1	2	2.0	2	0
Keith, Craig, Pitt	1	2	2.0	2	0
Jones, James, Cle	1	1	1.0	1	0
Junkin, Trey, Sea	1	1	1.0	1t	1
Klingler, David, Cin	1	-6	-6.0	-6	0

t = Touchdown
Leader based on receptions

NFC RECEIVERS—INDIVIDUAL

	No.	Yards	Avg.	Long	TD
Carter, Cris, Minn	122	1256	10.3	65t	7
Rice, Jerry, SF	112	1499	13.4	69t	13
Mathis, Terance, Atl	111	1342	12.1	81	11
Sharpe, Sterling, GB	94	1119	11.9	49	18
Reed, Jake, Minn	85	1175	13.8	59	4
Early, Quinn, NO	82	894	10.9	33	4
Rison, Andre, Atl	81	1088	13.4	69t	8
Irvin, Michael, Dall	79	1241	15.7	65t	6
Barnett, Fred, Phil	78	1127	14.4	54	5
Bennett, Edgar, GB	78	546	7.0	40	4
Haynes, Michael, NO	77	985	12.8	78t	5
Centers, Larry, Ariz	77	647	8.4	36	2
Ellard, Henry, Wash	74	1397	18.9	73t	6
Moore, Herman, Det	72	1173	16.3	51t	11
Graham, Jeffrey, Chi	68	944	13.9	76t	4
Sanders, Ricky, Atl	67	599	8.9	28	1
Watters, Ricky, SF	66	719	10.9	65t	5
Williams, Calvin, Phil	58	813	14.0	53	3
Brooks, Robert, GB	58	648	11.2	35	4
Bailey, Johnny, LA Rams	58	516	8.9	28	0
Perriman, Brett, Det	56	761	13.6	39	4
Sherrard, Mike, NYG	53	825	15.6	55	6
Proehl, Ricky, Ariz	51	651	12.8	63	5
Ervins, Ricky, Wash	51	293	5.7	21	1
Clark, Gary, Ariz	50	771	15.4	45	1
Walker, Herschel, Phil	50	500	10.0	93	2
Smith, Emmitt, Dall	50	341	6.8	68	1
Small, Torrance, NO	49	719	14.7	75t	5
Jones, Brent, SF	49	670	13.7	69t	9
Novacek, Jay, Dall	47	475	10.1	27	2
Anderson, Willie, LA Rams	46	945	20.5	72t	5
Dawsey, Lawrence, TB	46	673	14.6	46	1
Emanuel, Bert, Atl	46	649	14.1	85t	4
Ismail, Qadry, Minn	45	696	15.5	65t	5
Hester, Jessie, LA Rams	45	644	14.3	41	3
Lee, Amp, Minn	45	368	8.2	35	2
Brown, Derek, NO	44	428	9.7	37	1
Johnston, Daryl, Dall	44	325	7.4	24	2
Sanders, Barry, Det	44	283	6.4	22	1
Calloway, Chris, NYG	43	666	15.5	51t	2
Joseph, James, Phil	43	344	8.0	35t	2
Taylor, John, SF	41	531	13.0	35	5
Smith, Irv, NO	41	330	8.0	19	3
Howard, Desmond, Wash	40	727	18.2	81t	5
Conway, Curtis, Chi	39	546	14.0	85t	2
Harris, Raymont, Chi	39	236	6.1	18	0
Hill, Randal, Ariz	38	544	14.3	51	0
Walls, Wesley, NO	38	406	10.7	31	4
Hawkins, Courtney, TB	37	438	11.8	32	5
Jordan, Andrew, Minn	35	336	9.6	25	0
Cobb, Reggie, GB	35	299	8.5	37t	1
Harper, Alvin, Dall	33	821	24.9	90	8
Cooper, Adrian, Minn	32	363	11.3	34	0
Heyward, Craig, Atl	32	335	10.5	34	1
Meggett, David, NYG	32	293	9.2	34	0
Drayton, Troy, LA Rams	32	276	8.6	22t	6
Wilson, Charles, TB	31	652	21.0	71t	6
West, Ed, GB	31	377	12.2	26	2
Cross, Howard, NYG	31	364	11.7	40	4
Bettis, Jerome, LA Rams	31	293	9.5	34	1
Matthews, Aubrey, Det	29	359	12.4	33	3
McDowell, Anthony, TB	29	193	6.7	19	1
Morgan, Anthony, GB	28	397	14.2	47t	4
Tillman, Lewis, Chi	27	222	8.2	39	0
Harris, Jackie, TB	26	337	13.0	48t	3
Mitchell, Brian, Wash	26	236	9.1	46t	1
Waddle, Tom, Chi	25	244	9.8	22	1

	No.	Yards	Avg.	Long	TD
Green, Robert, Chi	24	199	8.3	39t	2
Kinchen, Todd, LA Rams	23	352	15.3	43	3
Armstrong, Tyji, TB	22	265	12.0	29	1
Rhett, Errict, TB	22	119	5.4	12	0
Singleton, Nate, SF	21	294	14.0	43t	2
Bruce, Isaac, LA Rams	21	272	13.0	34t	3
Cook, Marv, Chi	21	212	10.1	34	1
Johnson, Maurice, Phil	21	204	9.7	22	2
Bailey, Victor, Phil	20	311	15.6	61	1
Pierce, Aaron, NYG	20	214	10.7	29	4
Winans, Tydus, Wash	19	344	18.1	51	2
Floyd, William, SF	19	145	7.6	15	0
Hebron, Vaughn, Phil	18	137	7.6	29	0
Copeland, Horace, TB	17	308	18.1	65	0
Bavaro, Mark, Phil	17	215	12.6	27t	3
Ware, Derek, Ariz	17	171	10.1	33	1
Holman, Rodney, Det	17	163	9.6	18	0
Allen, Terry, Minn	17	148	8.7	31	0
Marshall, Arthur, NYG	16	219	13.7	34	0
Griffith, Howard, LA Rams	16	113	7.1	13	1
Pegram, Erric, Atl	16	99	6.2	28	0
Logan, Marc, SF	16	97	6.1	15	1
Horton, Ethan, Wash	15	157	10.5	20	3
Smith, Cedric, Wash	15	118	7.9	28	1
Smith, Robert, Minn	15	105	7.0	15	0
Reeves, Bryan, Ariz	14	202	14.4	33	1
Chmura, Mark, GB	14	165	11.8	27	0
Hampton, Rodney, NYG	14	103	7.4	17	0
Williams, Kevin, Dall	13	181	13.9	29	0
Johnson, LeShon, GB	13	168	12.9	33	0
Gedney, Chris, Chi	13	157	12.1	37t	3
Popson, Ted, SF	13	141	10.8	24	0
Ned, Derrick, NO	13	86	6.6	19	0
Hoge, Merril, Chi	13	79	6.1	11	0
Brooks, Reggie, Wash	13	68	5.2	16	0
Fann, Chad, Ariz	12	96	8.0	16	0
McCaffrey, Ed, SF	11	131	11.9	32	2
Wetnight, Ryan, Chi	11	104	9.5	19	1
Workman, Vince, TB	11	82	7.5	23	0
Jennings, Keith, Chi	11	75	6.8	23t	3
Hall, Ron, Det	10	106	10.6	18	0
Rasheed, Kenyon, NYG	10	97	9.7	22	0
Muster, Brad, NO	10	88	8.8	21	0
Green, Willie, TB	9	150	16.7	28	0
Harris, Leonard, Atl	9	113	12.6	26	0
McMurtry, Greg, Chi	8	112	14.0	30	1
Carter, Anthony, Det	8	97	12.1	18	3
Garner, Charlie, Phil	8	74	9.3	28	0
Bates, Mario, NO	8	62	7.8	14	0
Lang, David, LA Rams	8	60	7.5	12	0
Samuels, Terry, Ariz	8	57	7.1	17	0
Moore, Ron, Ariz	8	52	6.5	18	1
Coleman, Lincoln, Dall	8	46	5.8	14	0
Jenkins, James, Wash	8	32	4.0	9	4
Lewis, Ron, GB	7	108	15.4	38	0
Carter, Dexter, SF	7	99	14.1	44	0
Thomas, Lamar, TB	7	94	13.4	27	0
Johnson, Reggie, GB	7	79	11.3	24	0
Hallock, Ty, Det	7	75	10.7	21	0
Wycheck, Frank, Wash	7	55	7.9	20	1
Lyons, Mitch, Atl	7	54	7.7	10	0
Royster, Mazio, TB	7	36	5.1	12	0
Palmer, David, Minn	6	90	15.0	39	0
Hearst, Garrison, Ariz	6	49	8.2	29	0
Buchanan, Richard, LA Rams	5	60	12.0	18	0
Wilner, Jeff, GB	5	31	6.2	9	0
Moore, Dave, TB	4	57	14.3	18	0
Lewis, Thomas, NYG	4	46	11.5	23	0
Levy, Chuck, Ariz	4	35	8.8	15	0
Galbraith, Scott, Dall	4	31	7.8	15	0
Mickens, Terry, GB	4	31	7.8	11	0
Brantley, Chris, LA Rams	4	29	7.3	10	0
Thomas, Blair, NE.-Dall	4	16	4.0	9	0
Morton, Johnnie, Det	3	39	13.0	18t	1
Primus, Greg, Chi	3	25	8.3	12	0
Jordan, Steve, Minn	3	23	7.7	10	0
Mims, David, Atl	3	14	4.7	6	0
Truitt, Olanda, Wash	2	89	44.5	77t	1
Spencer, Darryl, Atl	2	51	25.5	40	0
Christian, Bob, Chi	2	30	15.0	21	0
Loville, Derek, SF	2	26	13.0	19	0
Lynch, Eric, Det	2	18	9.0	12	0
Downs, Gary, NYG	2	15	7.5	10	0
Lewis, Nate, Chi	2	13	6.5	8	1
Harris, Rudy, TB	2	11	5.5	8	0
Carolan, Brett, SF	2	10	5.0	6	0
Neal, Lorenzo, NO	2	9	4.5	5	0
Novoselsky, Brent, Minn	2	7	3.5	4	0
Alexander, David, Phil	2	1	0.5	1	0
Ross, Jermaine, LA Rams	1	36	36.0	36t	1
Carter, Antonio, Chi	1	24	24.0	24	0
Carter, Marty, TB	1	21	21.0	21	0
Mitchell, Derrell, NO	1	13	13.0	13	0
Moore, Derrick, Det	1	10	10.0	10	0
Sydner, Jeff, Phil	1	10	10.0	10	0
Levens, Dorsey, GB	1	9	9.0	9	0
Shepherd, Leslie, Wash	1	8	8.0	8	0
Worley, Tim, Chi	1	8	8.0	8	0
Williams, Willie, NO	1	7	7.0	7	0
Kozlowski, Brian, NYG	1	5	5.0	5	0
Robinson, Patrick, Ariz	1	5	5.0	5	0
McAfee, Fred, Ariz	1	4	4.0	4	0
Agee, Tommie, Dall	1	2	2.0	2	0
Evans, Chuck, Minn	1	2	2.0	2	0
Conover, Scott, Det	1	1	1.0	1t	1
Graham, Scottie, Minn	1	1	1.0	1	0
Lester, Tim, LA Rams	1	1	1.0	1	0
Kennard, Derek, Dall	1	-3	-3.0	-3	0

t = Touchdown
Leader based on receptions

INTERCEPTIONS

Interceptions
AFC: 9—Eric Turner, Cleveland
NFC: 9—Aeneas Williams, Arizona

Interceptions, Game
AFC: 3—Darren Perry, Pittsburgh at Cleveland, September 11
Terry McDaniel, L.A. Raiders at New England, October 9
Marcus Turner, N.Y. Jets at Minnesota, November 20
NFC: 2—George Teague, Green Bay vs. Minnesota, September 4
D.J. Johnson, Atlanta vs. L.A. Rams, September 11
Phillippi Sparks, N.Y. Giants at Arizona, September 11
Jack Del Rio, Minnesota vs. Miami, September 25
Larry Brown, Dallas vs. Arizona, October 9
Darren Woodson, Dallas vs. Arizona, October 9
Vinnie Clark, Atlanta vs. Tampa Bay, October 9
Darrell Green, Washington vs. Arizona, October 16 (OT)
Aeneas Williams, Arizona at Washington, October 16 (OT)
James Williams, Arizona at Washington, October 16 (OT)
Dana Hall, San Francisco at Atlanta, October 16
Jimmy Spencer, New Orleans vs. L.A. Rams, October 23
Bryce Paup, Green Bay at Chicago, October 31
Merton Hanks, San Francisco vs. Dallas, November 13
Kevin Smith, Dallas vs. Washington, November 20
Willie Clay, Detroit vs. Buffalo, November 24
Terry Hoage, Arizona at Houston, December 4
Merton Hanks, San Francisco vs. Atlanta, December 4
Darrin Smith, Dallas at New Orleans, December 19
Carl Lee, New Orleans at Denver, December 24

Yards
NFC: 303—Deion Sanders, San Francisco
AFC: 224—Stanley Richard, San Diego

Longest
AFC: 99—Stanley Richard, San Diego at Denver, September 4 - TD
NFC: 94—Darren Woodson, Dallas at Philadelphia, December 4 - TD

Touchdowns
NFC: 3—Deion Sanders, San Francisco
AFC: 3—Ray Buchanan, Indianapolis

Team Leaders, Interceptions
AFC: BUFFALO: 4, Matt Darby; CINCINNATI: 3, Louis Oliver; CLEVELAND: 9, Eric Turner; DENVER: 2, Ray Crockett, Randy Hilliard, Rondell Jones; HOUSTON: 5, Darryll Lewis; INDIANAPOLIS: 8, Ray Buchanan; KANSAS CITY: 3, Charles Mincy; L.A. RAIDERS: 7, Terry McDaniel; MIAMI: 5, Troy Vincent; NEW ENGLAND: 7, Maurice Hurst; N.Y. JETS: 5, James Hasty, Marcus Turner; PITTSBURGH: 7, Darren Perry; SAN DIEGO: 4, Darrien Gordon, Stanley Richard; SEATTLE: 3, Patrick Hunter, Orlando Watters, Terry Wooden

1994 INDIVIDUAL STATISTICS

NFC: ARIZONA: 9, Aeneas Williams; ATLANTA: 5, D.J. Johnson; CHICAGO: 5, Donnell Woolford; DALLAS: 5, James Washington, Darren Woodson; DETROIT: 4, Robert Massey; GREEN BAY: 5, Terrell Buckley; L.A. RAMS: 3, Darryl Henley, Marquez Pope; MINNESOTA: 4, Vencie Glenn, Anthony Parker; NEW ORLEANS: 5, Jimmy Spencer; N.Y. GIANTS: 3, John Booty, Phillippi Sparks; PHILADELPHIA: 6, Greg Jackson; SAN FRANCISCO : 7, Merton Hanks; TAMPA BAY: 2, Martin Mayhew, Hardy Nickerson; WASHINGTON: 4, Andre Collins

Team Champions

AFC: 23—Miami

NFC: 23—Arizona
San Francisco

AFC INTERCEPTIONS—TEAM

	No.	Yards	Avg.	Long	TD
Miami	23	276	12.0	76t	1
New England	22	209	9.5	24	1
Seattle	19	284	14.9	69t	2
Cleveland	18	223	12.4	93t	1
Indianapolis	18	360	20.0	90t	3
N.Y. Jets	17	355	20.9	90t	3
San Diego	17	402	23.6	99t	3
Pittsburgh	17	240	14.1	42	2
Buffalo	16	175	10.9	45	0
Houston	14	242	17.3	41	1
L.A. Raiders	12	187	15.6	35	3
Kansas City	12	218	18.2	78t	1
Denver	12	55	4.6	24	0
Cincinnati	10	167	16.7	49	0
AFC Total	227	3393	14.9	99t	21
AFC Average	16.2	242.4	14.9	—	1.5

NFC INTERCEPTIONS—TEAM

	No.	Yards	Avg.	Long	TD
Arizona	23	297	12.9	46t	1
San Francisco	23	508	22.1	93t	4
Atlanta	22	322	14.6	74	2
Dallas	22	297	13.5	94t	3
Philadelphia	21	209	10.0	55t	2
Green Bay	21	232	11.0	51	1
Minnesota	18	338	18.8	81t	4
New Orleans	17	197	11.6	56	1
Washington	17	326	19.2	92t	3
N.Y. Giants	16	128	8.0	36	0
L.A. Rams	14	211	15.1	51	1
Chicago	12	127	10.6	33	0
Detroit	12	144	12.0	48t	2
Tampa Bay	9	77	8.6	38	0
NFC Total	247	3413	13.8	94t	24
NFC Average	17.6	243.8	13.8	—	1.7
League Total	474	6806	—	99t	45
League Average	16.9	243.1	14.4	—	1.6

NFL TOP TEN INTERCEPTORS

	No.	Yards	Avg.	Long	TD
Turner, Eric, Cle	9	199	22.1	93t	1
Williams, Aeneas, Ariz	9	89	9.9	43	0
Buchanan, Ray, Ind	8	221	27.6	90t	3
Hanks, Merton, SF	7	93	13.3	38	0
Hurst, Maurice, NE	7	68	9.7	24	0
McDaniel, Terry, LA Raid	7	103	14.7	35	2
Perry, Darren, Pitt	7	112	16.0	42	0
Jackson, Greg, Phil	6	86	14.3	55t	1
Sanders, Deion, SF	6	303	50.5	93t	3

(11 players tied with 5)

AFC INTERCEPTIONS—INDIVIDUAL

	No.	Yards	Avg.	Long	TD
Turner, Eric, Cle	9	199	22.1	93t	1
Buchanan, Ray, Ind	8	221	27.6	90t	3
Perry, Darren, Pitt	7	112	16.0	42	0
McDaniel, Terry, LA Raid	7	103	14.7	35	2
Hurst, Maurice, NE	7	68	9.7	24	0
Turner, Marcus, NYJ	5	155	31.0	90t	1
Vincent, Troy, Mia	5	113	22.6	58t	1
Hasty, James, NYJ	5	90	18.0	40	0
Lewis, Darryll, Hou	5	57	11.4	20	0
Richard, Stanley, SD	4	224	56.0	99t	2
Woodson, Rod, Pitt	4	109	27.3	37t	2
Lewis, Mo, NYJ	4	106	26.5	67t	2
Dishman, Cris, Hou	4	74	18.5	38	1
Gordon, Darrien, SD	4	32	8.0	23	0
Darby, Matt, Buff	4	20	5.0	20	0
Robertson, Marcus, Hou	3	90	30.0	41	0
Hunter, Patrick, Sea	3	85	28.3	51	0
Brown, J. B., Mia	3	82	27.3	38	0
Wooden, Terry, Sea	3	78	26.0	69t	1
Washington, Lionel, LA Raid	3	65	21.7	31t	1
Washington, Mickey, Buff	3	63	21.0	36	0
Barnett, Harlon, NE	3	51	17.0	24	0
Carrington, Darren, SD	3	51	17.0	32	0
Tate, David, Ind	3	51	17.0	30	0
Mincy, Charles, KC	3	49	16.3	31	0
Watters, Orlando, Sea	3	39	13.0	35t	1
Oliver, Louis, Cin	3	36	12.0	19	0
Harper, Dwayne, SD	3	28	9.3	15	0
Atkins, Gene, Mia	3	24	8.0	18	0
Brown, Vincent, NE	3	22	7.3	12	0
Robinson, Eugene, Sea	3	18	6.0	18	0
Stewart, Michael, Mia	3	11	3.7	11	0
Collins, Mark, KC	2	83	41.5	78t	1
Brim, Michael, Cin	2	72	36.0	49	0
Vanhorse, Sean, SD	2	56	28.0	50t	1
Ambrose, Ashley, Ind	2	50	25.0	42	0
Jones, Henry, Buff	2	45	22.5	45	0
Williams, Darryl, Cin	2	45	22.5	33	0
Burris, Jeff, Buff	2	24	12.0	24	0
Carter, Dale, KC	2	24	12.0	24	0
Guyton, Myron, NE	2	18	9.0	15	0
Smith, Rod, NE	2	10	5.0	10	0
Jacobs, Tim, Cle	2	9	4.5	8	0
Jones, Rondell, Den	2	9	4.5	9	0
Hilliard, Randy, Den	2	8	4.0	8	0
Patton, Marvcus, Buff	2	8	4.0	8	0
Crockett, Ray, Den	2	6	3.0	6	0
Daniel, Eugene, Ind	2	6	3.0	6	0
Sabb, Dwayne, NE	2	6	3.0	5	0
Braxton, Tyrone, Mia	2	3	1.5	3	0
Griffin, Don, Cle	2	2	1.0	2	0
Langham, Antonio, Cle	2	2	1.0	2	0
Beavers, Aubrey, Mia	2	0	0.0	0	0
Gray, Carlton, Sea	2	0	0.0	0	0
Kirkland, Levon, Pitt	2	0	0.0	0	0
Sawyer, Corey, Cin	2	0	0.0	0	0
White, William, KC	2	0	0.0	0	0
Washington, Brian, NYJ	2	-3	-1.5	0	0
Smith, Neil, KC	1	41	41.0	41	0
Hollier, Dwight, Mia	1	36	36.0	36	0
Porter, Rufus, Sea	1	33	33.0	33	0
Belser, Jason, Ind	1	31	31.0	31	0
Atwater, Steve, Den	1	24	24.0	24	0
Blackmon, Robert, Sea	1	24	24.0	24	0
Bishop, Blaine, Hou	1	21	21.0	21	0
Grow, Monty, KC	1	21	21.0	21	0
Whigham, Larry, NE	1	21	21.0	21	0
Tovar, Steve, Cin	1	14	14.0	14	0
Biekert, Greg, LA Raid	1	11	11.0	11	0
Griggs, David, SD	1	11	11.0	11	0
Maddox, Mark, Buff	1	11	11.0	11	0
Reynolds, Ricky, NE	1	11	11.0	11t	1
Brown, Chad, Pitt	1	9	9.0	9	0
Frank, Donald, LA Raid	1	8	8.0	8	0
Lloyd, Greg, Pitt	1	8	8.0	8	0
Spitulski, Bob, Sea	1	7	7.0	7	0
Stams, Frank, Cle	1	7	7.0	7	0
Veasey, Craig, Mia	1	7	7.0	7	0
Washington, Marvin, NYJ	1	7	7.0	7	0
Washington, Ted, Den	1	5	5.0	5	0
Booth, Issac, Cle	1	4	4.0	4	0
Fletcher, Simon, Den	1	4	4.0	4	0
Smith, Thomas, Buff	1	4	4.0	4	0
Alexander, Elijah, Den	1	2	2.0	2	0
Lake, Carnell, Pitt	1	2	2.0	2	0
Ray, Terry, NE	1	2	2.0	2	0
Humphries, Leonard, Ind	1	1	1.0	1	0
Caldwell, Mike, Cle	1	0	0.0	0	0
Cross, Jeff, Mia	1	0	0.0	0	0
Jackson, Steve, Hou	1	0	0.0	0	0
Jones, Gary, Pitt	1	0	0.0	0	0

	No.	Yards	Avg.	Long	TD
Malone, Darrell, Mia	1	0	0.0	0	0
Oliver, Muhammad, Mia	1	0	0.0	0	0
Robinson, Rafael, Sea	1	0	0.0	0	0
Smith, Ben, Den	1	0	0.0	0	0
Smith, Bruce, Buff	1	0	0.0	0	0
Taylor, Jay, KC	1	0	0.0	0	0
Taylor, Terry, Sea	1	0	0.0	0	0
Watts, Damon, Ind	1	0	0.0	0	0
Williams, Dan, Den	1	-3	-3.0	-3	0

t = Touchdown
Leader based on interceptions

NFC INTERCEPTIONS—INDIVIDUAL

	No.	Yards	Avg.	Long	TD
Williams, Aeneas, Ariz	9	89	9.9	43	0
Hanks, Merton, SF	7	93	13.3	38	0
Sanders, Deion, SF	6	303	50.5	93t	3
Jackson, Greg, Phil	6	86	14.3	55t	1
Clark, Vinnie, Atl-NO	5	149	29.8	74	0
Woodson, Darren, Dall	5	140	28.0	94t	1
Washington, James, Dall	5	43	8.6	25	0
Buckley, Terrell, GB	5	38	7.6	26	0
Woolford, Donnell, Chi	5	30	6.0	25	0
Spencer, Jimmy, NO	5	24	4.8	11	0
Johnson, D. J., Atl	5	0	0.0	0	0
Collins, Andre, Wash	4	150	37.5	92t	2
Parker, Anthony, Minn	4	99	24.8	44t	2
Glenn, Vencie, Minn	4	55	13.8	32	0
Williams, James, Ariz	4	48	12.0	29	0
Zordich, Mike, Phil	4	39	9.8	18t	1
Massey, Robert, Det	4	25	6.3	17	0
Brown, Larry, Dall	4	21	5.3	14	0
Washington, DeWayne, Minn	3	135	45.0	81t	2
Walker, Darnell, Atl	3	105	35.0	44t	1
Booty, John, NYG	3	95	31.7	36	0
Butler, LeRoy, GB	3	68	22.7	51	0
Pope, Marquez, LA Rams	3	66	22.0	51	0
Hoage, Terry, Ariz	3	64	21.3	41	0
Allen, Eric, Phil	3	61	20.3	33	0
Carter, Tom, Wash	3	58	19.3	40	0
Clay, Willie, Det	3	54	18.0	28t	1
Paup, Bryce, GB	3	47	15.7	30	1
Henley, Darryl, LA Rams	3	46	15.3	23	0
Bayless, Martin, Wash	3	38	12.7	19	0
Teague, George, GB	3	33	11.0	16	0
Green, Darrell, Wash	3	32	10.7	27t	1
Ross, Kevin, Atl	3	26	8.7	16	0
Del Rio, Jack, Minn	3	5	1.7	5	0
Sparks, Phillippi, NYG	3	4	1.3	4	0
Joyner, Seth, Ariz	3	2	0.7	2	0
McDonald, Tim, SF	2	79	39.5	73t	1
Newman, Anthony, LA Rams	2	46	23.0	24	1
Williams, James, NO	2	42	21.0	33t	1
Lynch, Lorenzo, Ariz	2	35	17.5	23	0
Gayle, Shaun, Chi	2	33	16.5	33	0
Hughes, Tyrone, NO	2	31	15.5	31	0
Willis, James, GB	2	20	10.0	17	0
McGill, Lenny, GB	2	16	8.0	16	0
Smith, Darrin, Dall	2	13	6.5	13t	1
Case, Scott, Atl	2	12	6.0	12	0
Smith, Kevin, Dall	2	11	5.5	11	0
Carrier, Mark, Chi	2	10	5.0	7	0
Williams, Jarvis, NYG	2	10	5.0	10	0
Nickerson, Hardy, TB	2	9	4.5	10	0
Romanowski, Bill, Phil	2	8	4.0	8	0
Phifer, Roman, LA Rams	2	7	3.5	7	0
Miller, Corey, NYG	2	6	3.0	6	0
Mayhew, Martin, TB	2	4	2.0	4	0
Campbell, Jesse, NYG	2	3	1.5	2	0
Lee, Carl, NO	2	3	1.5	3	0
McMillian, Mark, Phil	2	2	1.0	5	0
Lyle, Keith, LA Rams	2	1	0.5	1	0
Hall, Dana, SF	2	0	0.0	0	0
Conner, Darion, NO	1	56	56.0	56	0
Tolbert, Tony, Dall	1	54	54.0	54t	1
Johnson, Mike, Det	1	48	48.0	48t	1
McCants, Keith, Ariz	1	46	46.0	46t	1
Hollinquest, Lamont, Wash	1	39	39.0	39	0
Covington, Tony, TB	1	38	38.0	38	0
Smith, Chuck, Atl	1	36	36.0	36t	1
Kelly, Joe, LA Rams	1	31	31.0	31	0
Spellman, Alonzo, Chi	1	31	31.0	31	0
Everett, Thomas, TB	1	26	26.0	26	0
Boyd, Malik, Minn	1	22	22.0	15	0
Harper, Roger, Atl	1	22	22.0	22	0
Harris, James, Minn	1	21	21.0	21	0
Cook, Toi, SF	1	18	18.0	18	0
Douglass, Maurice, Chi	1	18	18.0	18	0
Lyght, Todd, LA Rams	1	14	14.0	14	0
McNeil, Ryan, Det	1	14	14.0	14	0
Marion, Brock, Dall	1	11	11.0	11	0
Brooks, Michael, NYG	1	10	10.0	10	0
Mills, Sam, NO	1	10	10.0	10	0
Davis, Eric, SF	1	8	8.0	8	0
Gouveia, Kurt, Wash	1	7	7.0	7	0
Strickland, Fred, GB	1	7	7.0	7	0
Thomas, William, Phil	1	7	7.0	7	0
Drakeford, Tyronne, SF	1	6	6.0	6	0
Evans, Byron, Phil	1	6	6.0	6	0
Lincoln, Jeremy, Chi	1	5	5.0	5	0
Colon, Harry, Det	1	3	3.0	3	0
Johnson, Keshon, GB	1	3	3.0	3	0
Doleman, Chris, Atl	1	2	2.0	2	0
Stowe, Tyronne, Wash	1	2	2.0	2	0
Haley, Charles, Dall	1	1	1.0	1	0
Lumpkin, Sean, NO	1	1	1.0	1	0
McGriggs, Lamar, Minn	1	1	1.0	1	0
Plummer, Gary, SF	1	1	1.0	1	0
Armstead, Jessie, NYG	1	0	0.0	0	0
Blades, Bennie, Det	1	0	0.0	0	0
Brown, Dennis, SF	1	0	0.0	0	0
Buck, Vince, NO	1	0	0.0	0	0
Dimry, Charles, TB	1	0	0.0	0	0
Evans, Doug, GB	1	0	0.0	0	0
Gant, Kenneth, Dall	1	0	0.0	0	0
Grant, Alan, Wash	1	0	0.0	0	0
Hager, Britt, Phil	1	0	0.0	0	0
Harmon, Andy, Phil	1	0	0.0	0	0
Mack, Milton, Det	1	0	0.0	0	0
McDaniel, Ed, Minn	1	0	0.0	0	0
McGruder, Michael, TB	1	0	0.0	0	0
Norton, Ken, SF	1	0	0.0	0	0
Phillips, Anthony, Atl	1	0	0.0	0	0
Randolph, Thomas, NYG	1	0	0.0	0	0
Raymond, Corey, NYG	1	0	0.0	0	0
Stargell, Tony, TB	1	0	0.0	0	0
Swann, Eric, Ariz	1	0	0.0	0	0
Tubbs, Winfred, NO	1	0	0.0	0	0
Tuggle, Jessie, Atl	1	0	0.0	0	0
Marshall, Wilber, Ariz	0	13	—	13	0
Holmes, Clayton, Dall	0	3	—	3	0

t = Touchdown
Leader based on interceptions

1994 INDIVIDUAL STATISTICS

PUNTING

Average Yards Per Punt
- **NFC:** 44.8—Sean Landeta, L.A. Rams
- **AFC:** 43.9—Jeff Gossett, L.A. Raiders

Net Average Yards Per Punt
- **AFC:** 37.1—Tom Rouen, Denver
- **NFC:** 36.3—Bryan Barker, Philadelphia

Longest
- **NFC:** 80—Randall Cunningham, Philadelphia at Dallas, October 16
- **AFC:** 71—Chris Mohr, Buffalo at Indianapolis, December 24

Punts
- **NFC:** 98—Jeff Feagles, Arizona
- **AFC:** 97—Mark Royals, Pittsburgh

Punts, Game
- **AFC:** 11—Rich Camarillo, Houston vs. Pittsburgh, November 6, (OT) (502 yards); Mark Royals, Pittsburgh at Houston, November 6, (OT) (432 yards); Louie Aguiar, Kansas City vs. San Diego, November 13 (460 yards)
- **NFC:** 10—Reggie Roby, Washington vs. Arizona, October 16, (OT) (448 yards); Craig Hentrich, Green Bay at Minnesota, October 20, (OT) (460 yards); Mike Saxon, Minnesota vs. Green Bay, October 20, (OT) (396 yards); Bryan Barker, Philadelphia at Pittsburgh, December 11, (401 yards)

Team Champion
- **NFC:** 44.8—L.A. Rams
- **AFC:** 43.9—L.A. Raiders

AFC PUNTING—TEAM

	Total Punts	Yards	Long	Avg.	TB	Blk.	Opp. Ret.	Return Yards	Inside the 20	Net. Avg.
L.A. Raiders	77	3377	65	43.9	15	0	38	366	19	35.2
Cincinnati	80	3461	64	43.3	9	1	43	459	19	35.3
Seattle	91	3905	64	42.9	7	0	43	426	33	36.7
Denver	76	3258	59	42.9	8	0	39	275	23	37.1
Houston	96	4115	58	42.9	9	0	50	438	35	36.4
Kansas City	85	3582	61	42.1	7	0	50	506	15	34.5
N.Y. Jets	84	3534	64	42.1	12	0	38	260	25	36.1
Indianapolis	74	3092	60	41.8	10	1	40	366	22	34.1
Buffalo	67	2799	71	41.8	3	0	38	324	13	36.0
New England	69	2841	67	41.2	6	0	34	260	25	35.7
San Diego	72	2951	59	41.0	4	0	38	348	21	35.0
Miami	60	2412	58	40.2	7	0	32	324	16	32.5
Cleveland	80	3211	65	40.1	8	0	38	220	27	35.4
Pittsburgh	97	3849	64	39.7	6	0	39	263	35	35.7
AFC Total	1108	46387	71	—	111	2	560	4835	328	—
AFC Average	79.1	3313.4	—	41.9	7.9	0.1	40.0	345.4	23.4	35.5

NFC PUNTING—TEAM

	Total Punts	Yards	Long	Avg.	TB	Blk.	Opp. Ret.	Return Yards	Inside the 20	Net. Avg.
L.A. Rams	78	3494	62	44.8	9	0	47	637	23	34.3
Washington	82	3639	65	44.4	12	0	45	441	21	36.1
New Orleans	67	2920	57	43.6	9	0	40	495	14	33.5
Detroit	64	2782	64	43.5	8	1	36	431	19	34.2
Minnesota	77	3301	67	42.9	5	0	44	410	28	36.2
Dallas	70	2935	58	41.9	4	0	36	378	26	35.4
San Francisco	54	2235	60	41.4	3	0	28	242	18	35.8
Green Bay	81	3351	70	41.4	10	0	36	272	24	35.5
Arizona	98	3997	54	40.8	10	0	40	270	33	36.0
Philadelphia	92	3727	80	40.5	9	0	47	286	29	35.4
N.Y. Giants	89	3578	63	40.2	8	2	39	307	26	35.0
Atlanta	79	3121	61	39.5	6	0	31	273	14	34.5
Tampa Bay	74	2853	53	38.6	6	0	19	103	22	35.5
Chicago	76	2871	57	37.8	9	0	26	225	23	32.4
NFC Total	1081	44804	80	—	108	3	514	4770	320	—
NFC Average	77.2	3200.3	—	41.4	7.7	0.2	36.7	340.7	22.9	35.0
NFL Total	2189	91191	80	—	219	5	1074	9605	648	—
NFL Average	78.2	3256.8	—	41.7	7.8	0.2	38.4	343.0	23.1	35.3

NFL TOP TEN PUNTERS

	No.	Yards	Long	Avg.	Total Punts	TB	Blk.	Opp. Ret.	Ret. Yds.	In 20	Net. Avg.
Landeta, Sean, LA Rams	78	3494	62	44.8	78	9	0	47	637	23	34.3
Roby, Reggie, Wash	82	3639	65	44.4	82	12	0	45	441	21	36.1
Montgomery, Greg, Det	63	2782	64	44.2	64	8	1	36	431	19	34.2
Gossett, Jeff, LA Raid	77	3377	65	43.9	77	15	0	38	366	19	35.2
Johnson, Lee, Cin	79	3461	64	43.8	80	9	1	43	459	19	35.3
Barnhardt, Tommy, NO	67	2920	57	43.6	67	9	0	40	495	14	33.5
Tuten, Rick, Sea	91	3905	64	42.9	91	7	0	43	426	33	36.7
Saxon, Mike, Minn	77	3301	67	42.9	77	5	0	44	410	28	36.2
Rouen, Tom, Den	76	3258	59	42.9	76	8	0	39	275	23	37.1
Camarillo, Rich, Hou	96	4115	58	42.9	96	9	0	50	438	35	36.4

AFC PUNTERS—INDIVIDUAL

	No.	Yards	Long	Avg.	Total Punts	TB	Blk.	Opp. Ret.	Ret. Yds.	In 20	Net. Avg.
Gossett, Jeff, LA Raid	77	3377	65	43.9	77	15	0	38	366	19	35.2
Johnson, Lee, Cin	79	3461	64	43.8	80	9	1	43	459	19	35.3
Tuten, Rick, Sea	91	3905	64	42.9	91	7	0	43	426	33	36.7
Rouen, Tom, Den	76	3258	59	42.9	76	8	0	39	275	23	37.1
Camarillo, Rich, Hou	96	4115	58	42.9	96	9	0	50	438	35	36.4
Stark, Rohn, Ind	73	3092	60	42.4	74	10	1	40	366	22	34.1
Aguiar, Louie, KC	85	3582	61	42.1	85	7	0	50	506	15	34.5
Hansen, Brian, NYJ	84	3534	64	42.1	84	12	0	38	260	25	36.1
Mohr, Chris, Buff	67	2799	71	41.8	67	3	0	38	324	13	36.0
Wagner, Bryan, SD	65	2705	59	41.6	65	3	0	38	348	20	35.3
O'Neill, Pat, NE	69	2841	67	41.2	69	6	0	34	260	25	35.7
Tupa, Tom, Cle	80	3211	65	40.1	80	8	0	38	220	27	35.4
Royals, Mark, Pitt	97	3849	64	39.7	97	6	0	39	263	35	35.7
Arnold, Jim, Mia	46	1810	53	39.3	46	4	0	26	189	14	33.5
Nonqualifiers											
Kidd, John, SD-Mia	21	848	58	40.4	21	4	0	6	135	3	30.1

Leader based on average, minimum 40 punts

NFC PUNTERS—INDIVIDUAL

	No.	Yards	Long	Avg.	Total Punts	TB	Blk.	Opp. Ret.	Ret. Yds.	In 20	Net. Avg.
Landeta, Sean, LA Rams	78	3494	62	44.8	78	9	0	47	637	23	34.3
Roby, Reggie, Wash	82	3639	65	44.4	82	12	0	45	441	21	36.1
Montgomery, Greg, Det	63	2782	64	44.2	64	8	1	36	431	19	34.2
Barnhardt, Tommy, NO	67	2920	57	43.6	67	9	0	40	495	14	33.5
Saxon, Mike, Minn	77	3301	67	42.9	77	5	0	44	410	28	36.2

	No.	Yards	Long	Avg.	Total Punts	TB	Blk.	Opp. Ret.	Ret. Yds.	In 20	Net. Avg.
Jett, John, Dall	70	2935	58	41.9	70	4	0	36	378	26	35.4
Horan, Mike, NYG	85	3521	63	41.4	87	7	2	39	307	25	35.3
Wilmsmeyer, Klaus, SF	54	2235	60	41.4	54	3	0	28	242	18	35.8
Hentrich, Craig, GB	81	3351	70	41.4	81	10	0	36	272	24	35.5
Barker, Bryan, Phil	66	2696	67	40.8	66	7	0	37	158	20	36.3
Feagles, Jeff, Ariz	98	3997	54	40.8	98	10	0	40	270	33	36.0
Alexander, Harold, Atl	71	2836	61	39.9	71	6	0	27	242	12	34.8
Stryzinski, Dan, TB	72	2800	53	38.9	72	6	0	18	94	20	35.9
Gardocki, Chris, Chi	76	2871	57	37.8	76	9	0	26	225	23	32.4
Nonqualifiers											
Berger, Mitch, Phil	25	951	57	38.0	25	2	0	10	128	8	31.3
Tyner, Scott, Atl	8	285	46	35.6	8	0	0	4	31	2	31.8
Brown, Dave, NYG	2	57	33	28.5	2	1	0	0	0	1	18.5
Husted, Michael, TB	2	53	32	26.5	2	0	0	1	9	2	22.0
Cunningham, Randall, Phil	1	80	80	80.0	1	0	0	0	0	1	80.0

Leader based on average, minimum 40 punts

PUNT RETURNS

Yards Per Return
NFC: 14.1—Brian Mitchell, Washington
AFC: 13.2—Darrien Gordon, San Diego

Yards
AFC: 487—Tim Brown, L.A. Raiders
NFC: 452—Brian Mitchell, Washington

Yards, Game
AFC: 128—Darrien Gordon, San Diego vs. L.A. Rams, November 27, (6 returns - TD)
NFC: 122—Robert Brooks, Green Bay vs. L.A. Rams, October 9, (4 returns - TD)

Longest
NFC: 103—Robert Bailey, L.A. Rams at New Orleans, October 23 - TD
AFC: 92—Eric Metcalf, Cleveland at Cincinnati, September 4 - TD

Returns
AFC: 42—Dewell Brewer, Indianapolis
NFC: 41—Patrick Robinson, Arizona

Returns, Game
AFC: 7—Ray Crittenden, New England vs. Green Bay, October 2, (63 yards)
NFC: 7—Robert Brooks, Green Bay at New England, October 2, (34 yards)

Fair Catches
NFC: 24—Brian Mitchell, Washington
AFC: 20—Kelvin Martin, Seattle

Touchdowns
AFC: 2—Darrien Gordon, San Diego
Eric Metcalf, Cleveland
NFC: 2—David Meggett, N.Y. Giants
Brian Mitchell, Washington

Team Champion
NFC: 14.1—Washington
AFC: 13.2—San Diego

AFC PUNT RETURNS—TEAM

	No.	FC	Yards	Avg.	Long	TD
San Diego	36	19	475	13.2	90t	2
L.A. Raiders	40	14	487	12.2	48	0
Buffalo	33	8	343	10.4	57	0
Cincinnati	37	18	373	10.1	82t	1
Cleveland	46	7	462	10.0	92t	2
Denver	41	4	379	9.2	44	0
Seattle	37	23	337	9.1	31	0
N.Y. Jets	39	5	345	8.8	26	0
New England	46	16	383	8.3	38	0
Indianapolis	42	8	339	8.1	75t	1
Pittsburgh	56	16	424	7.6	42	0
Kansas City	43	13	316	7.3	43	0
Miami	33	17	241	7.3	26	0
Houston	50	12	281	5.6	78t	1
AFC Total	579	180	5185	9.0	92t	7
AFC Average	41.4	12.9	370.4	9.0	—	0.5

NFC PUNT RETURNS—TEAM

	No.	FC	Yards	Avg.	Long	TD
Washington	32	24	452	14.1	78t	2
N.Y. Giants	32	17	388	12.1	68t	2
L.A. Rams	40	10	461	11.5	103t	1
Detroit	25	12	256	10.2	24	0
Philadelphia	41	18	381	9.3	49	0
Dallas	44	14	404	9.2	83t	1
Tampa Bay	28	8	248	8.9	80t	1
Green Bay	49	18	414	8.4	85t	1
San Francisco	40	13	334	8.4	26	0
Chicago	27	20	218	8.1	61t	1
Arizona	42	13	286	6.8	23	0
Minnesota	39	16	238	6.1	25	0
New Orleans	25	10	152	6.1	35	0
Atlanta	31	16	188	6.1	29	0
NFC Total	495	209	4420	8.9	103t	9
NFC Average	35.4	14.9	315.7	8.9	—	0.6
League Total	1074	389	9605	—	103t	16
League Average	38.4	13.9	343.0	8.9	—	0.6

NFL TOP TEN PUNT RETURNERS

	No.	FC	Yards	Avg.	Long	TD
Mitchell, Brian, Wash	32	24	452	14.1	78t	2
Gordon, Darrien, SD	36	19	475	13.2	90t	2
Meggett, David, NYG	26	14	323	12.4	68t	2
Brown, Tim, LA Raid	40	14	487	12.2	48	0
Sawyer, Corey, Cin	26	16	307	11.8	82t	1
Gray, Mel, Det	21	12	233	11.1	24	0
Turner, Vernon, TB	21	4	218	10.4	80t	1
Burris, Jeff, Buff	32	6	332	10.4	57	0
Metcalf, Eric, Cle	35	6	348	9.9	92t	2
Sydner, Jeff, Phil	40	17	381	9.5	49	0

AFC - INDIVIDUAL PUNT RETURNERS

	No.	FC	Yards	Avg.	Long	TD
Gordon, Darrien, SD	36	19	475	13.2	90t	2
Brown, Tim, LA Raid	40	14	487	12.2	48	0
Sawyer, Corey, Cin	26	16	307	11.8	82t	1
Burris, Jeff, Buff	32	6	332	10.4	57	0
Metcalf, Eric, Cle	35	6	348	9.9	92t	2
Milburn, Glyn, Den	41	4	379	9.2	44	0
Hicks, Cliff, NYJ	38	5	342	9.0	26	0
Martin, Kelvin, Sea	33	20	280	8.5	23	0
Brown, Troy, NE	24	10	202	8.4	38	0
Woodson, Rod, Pitt	39	9	319	8.2	42	0
Brewer, Dewell, Ind	42	8	339	8.1	75t	1
McDuffie, O. J., Mia	32	15	228	7.1	26	0
Hughes, Danan, KC	27	9	192	7.1	43	0
Givins, Ernest, Hou	37	9	210	5.7	78t	1
Nonqualifiers						
Crittenden, Ray, NE	19	6	155	8.2	26	0
Carter, Dale, KC	16	4	124	7.8	42	0
Johnson, Charles, Pitt	15	7	90	6.0	15	0
Carrier, Mark, Cle	9	1	112	12.4	60	0
Pickens, Carl, Cin	9	2	62	6.9	16	0
Hannah, Travis, Hou	9	0	58	6.4	13	0
Harris, Ronnie, NE	3	0	26	8.7	12	0
McCloughan, Dave, Sea	3	3	26	8.7	16	0
Hastings, Andre, Pitt	2	0	15	7.5	12	0
Coleman, Pat, Hou	2	2	13	6.5	10	0
Bryant, Beno, Sea	1	0	31	31.0	31	0

1994 INDIVIDUAL STATISTICS

	No.	FC	Yards	Avg.	Long	TD
Miller, Scott, Mia	1	2	13	13.0	13	0
Copeland, Russell, Buff	1	2	11	11.0	11	0
Williams, Darryl, Cin	1	0	4	4.0	4	0
Johnson, Anthony, NYJ	1	0	3	3.0	3	0
Caldwell, Mike, Cle	1	0	2	2.0	2	0
Dishman, Cris, Hou	1	0	0	0.0	0	0
Jones, Roger, Cin	1	0	0	0.0	0	0
Robertson, Marcus, Hou	1	1	0	0.0	0	0
Turner, Eric, Cle	1	0	0	0.0	0	0

t = Touchdown
Leader based on average return, minimum 20 returns

NFC - INDIVIDUAL PUNT RETURNERS

	No.	FC	Yards	Avg.	Long	TD
Mitchell, Brian, Wash	32	24	452	14.1	78t	2
Meggett, David, NYG	26	14	323	12.4	68t	2
Gray, Mel, Det	21	12	233	11.1	24	0
Turner, Vernon, TB	21	4	218	10.4	80t	1
Sydner, Jeff, Phil	40	17	381	9.5	49	0
Williams, Kevin, Dall	39	13	349	8.9	83t	1
Brooks, Robert, GB	40	13	352	8.8	85t	1
Carter, Dexter, SF	38	12	321	8.4	26	0
Robinson, Patrick, Ariz	41	12	285	7.0	23	0
Hughes, Tyrone, NO	21	8	143	6.8	35	0
Palmer, David, Minn	30	9	193	6.4	20	0
Verdin, Clarence, Atl	23	13	113	4.9	29	0
Nonqualifiers						
Bailey, Johnny, LA Rams	19	4	153	8.1	24	0
Kinchen, Todd, LA Rams	16	5	158	9.9	40	0
Graham, Jeffrey, Chi	15	5	140	9.3	61t	1
Smith, Tony, Atl	8	3	75	9.4	20	0
Conway, Curtis, Chi	8	9	63	7.9	24	0
Prior, Mike, GB	8	4	62	7.8	16	0
Lewis, Thomas, NYG	5	2	64	12.8	35	0
Holmes, Clayton, Dall	5	1	55	11.0	19	0
Hawkins, Courtney, TB	5	2	28	5.6	9	0
Guliford, Eric, Minn	5	6	14	2.8	12	0
Parker, Anthony, Minn	4	1	31	7.8	25	0
Clay, Willie, Det	3	0	20	6.7	12	0
Brantley, Chris, LA Rams	3	1	18	6.0	7	0
Mitchell, Derrell, NO	3	2	9	3.0	5	0
Waddle, Tom, Chi	3	3	8	2.7	6	0
Singleton, Nate, SF	2	1	13	6.5	8	0
Everett, Thomas, TB	2	2	2	1.0	1	0
Bailey, Robert, LA Rams	1	0	103	103.0	103t	1
Lyght, Todd, LA Rams	1	0	29	29.0	27	0
Lewis, Nate, Chi	1	3	7	7.0	7	0
Massey, Robert, Det	1	0	3	3.0	3	0
Marshall, Arthur, NYG	1	1	1	1.0	1	0
Reeves, Bryan, Ariz	1	1	1	1.0	1	0
Jordan, Charles, GB	1	1	0	0.0	0	0
Legette, Tyrone, NO	1	0	0	0.0	0	0
O'Neal, Brian, Phil	1	0	0	0.0	0	0
Bailey, Victor, Phil	0	1	0	—	—	0

t = Touchdown
Leader based on average return, minimum 20 returns

KICKOFF RETURNS

Yards Per Return
- **NFC:** 28.4—Mel Gray, Detroit
- **AFC:** 26.9—Randy Baldwin, Cleveland

Yards
- **NFC:** 1556—Tyrone Hughes, New Orleans
- **AFC:** 1293—Andre Coleman, San Diego

Yards, Game
- **NFC:** 304—Tyrone Hughes, New Orleans vs. L.A. Rams, October 23, (7 returns - 2 TD)
- **AFC:** 251—Jon Vaughn, Kansas City at Miami, December 12, (8 returns - TD)

Longest
- **NFC:** 102—Mel Gray, Detroit vs. Chicago, October 23 - TD
- **AFC:** 95—Ronald Humphrey, Indianapolis at Pittsburgh, September 18 - TD

Returns
- **NFC:** 63—Tyrone Hughes, New Orleans
- **AFC:** 49—Andre Coleman, San Diego

Returns, Game
- **AFC:** 8—Jon Vaughn, Kansas City at Miami, December 12, (251 yards - TD)
- **NFC:** 8—Tyrone Hughes, New Orleans vs. San Diego, October 16, (196 yards)
  Vernon Turner, Tampa Bay vs. Minnesota, October 30, (242 yards)

Touchdowns
- **NFC:** 3—Mel Gray, Detroit
- **AFC:** 2—Andre Coleman, San Diego
  Jon Vaughn, Seattle-Kansas City

Team Champion
- **NFC:** 25.7—Dallas
- **AFC:** 24.5—Cleveland

AFC KICKOFF RETURNS—TEAM

	No.	Yards	Avg.	Long	TD
Cleveland	42	1031	24.5	85t	1
San Diego	68	1636	24.1	90t	2
Kansas City	59	1300	22.0	91t	1
L.A. Raiders	62	1358	21.9	55	0
Seattle	67	1467	21.9	93t	1
Cincinnati	86	1810	21.0	43	0
Indianapolis	60	1254	20.9	95t	1
Pittsburgh	55	1141	20.7	71	0
Denver	75	1523	20.3	41	0
Miami	66	1294	19.6	46	0
N.Y. Jets	66	1282	19.4	45	0
Houston	74	1436	19.4	44	0
Buffalo	72	1345	18.7	42	0
New England	63	1123	17.8	36	0
AFC Total	915	19000	20.8	95t	6
AFC Average	65.4	1357.1	20.8	—	0.4

NFC KICKOFF RETURNS—TEAM

	No.	Yards	Avg.	Long	TD
Dallas	50	1284	25.7	87t	1
Washington	71	1685	23.7	86	0
Detroit	71	1675	23.6	102t	4
L.A. Rams	71	1605	22.6	57	0
New Orleans	82	1840	22.4	98t	2
Atlanta	75	1627	21.7	69	0
Minnesota	60	1296	21.6	61	0
Philadelphia	67	1441	21.5	94t	1
San Francisco	58	1244	21.4	96t	1
Chicago	66	1402	21.2	55	0
Green Bay	56	1168	20.9	96t	1
Tampa Bay	70	1422	20.3	77	0
Arizona	57	1079	18.9	53	0
N.Y. Giants	73	1328	18.2	36	0
NFC Total	927	20096	21.7	102t	10
NFC Average	66.2	1435.4	21.7	—	0.7
League Total	1842	39096	—	102t	16
League Average	65.8	1396.3	21.2	—	0.6

TOP TEN KICKOFF RETURNERS

	No.	Yards	Avg.	Long	TD
Gray, Mel, Det	45	1276	28.4	102t	3
Walker, Herschel, Phil	21	581	27.7	94t	1
Baldwin, Randy, Cle	28	753	26.9	85t	1
Williams, Kevin, Dall	43	1148	26.7	87t	1
Coleman, Andre, SD	49	1293	26.4	90t	2
Mitchell, Brian, Wash	58	1478	25.5	86	0
Vaughn, Jon, Sea.-KC	33	829	25.1	93t	2
Lewis, Nate, Chi	35	874	25.0	55	0
Hughes, Tyrone, NO	63	1556	24.7	98t	2
Kinchen, Todd, LA Rams	21	510	24.3	46	0

AFC KICKOFF RETURNERS—INDIVIDUAL

	No.	Yards	Avg.	Long	TD
Baldwin, Randy, Cle	28	753	26.9	85t	1
Coleman, Andre, SD	49	1293	26.4	90t	2
Vaughn, Jon, Sea.-KC	33	829	25.1	93t	2
By'Not'e, Butler, Den	24	545	22.7	41	0
Dickerson, Ron, KC	21	472	22.5	62	0
Humphrey, Ronald, Ind	35	783	22.4	95t	1
Jourdain, Yonel, Buff	27	601	22.3	42	0
Ball, Eric, Cin	42	915	21.8	43	0
Glenn, Aaron, NYJ	27	582	21.6	45	0

	No.	Yards	Avg.	Long	TD
Ismail, Raghib, LA Raid	43	923	21.5	51	0
Milburn, Glyn, Den	37	793	21.4	40	0
McDuffie, O. J., Mia	36	767	21.3	46	0
McNair, Todd, Hou	23	481	20.9	44	0
Bates, Michael, Sea	26	508	19.5	38	0
Crittenden, Ray, NE	24	460	19.2	36	0
Nonqualifiers					
Spikes, Irving, Mia	19	434	22.8	34	0
Thompson, Leroy, NE	18	376	20.9	30	0
Brewer, Dewell, Ind	18	358	19.9	34	0
Johnson, Charles, Pitt	16	345	21.6	71	0
Prior, Anthony, NYJ	16	316	19.8	27	0
Woodson, Rod, Pitt	15	365	24.3	54	0
Scott, Darnay, Cin	15	342	22.8	34	0
Mills, John Henry, Hou	15	282	18.8	34	0
Warren, Terrence, Sea	14	350	25.0	47	0
Jackson, Steve, Hou	14	285	20.4	40	0
Murrell, Adrian, NYJ	14	268	19.1	37	0
Copeland, Russell, Buff	12	232	19.3	32	0
Beebe, Don, Buff	12	230	19.2	35	0
Stone, Dwight, Pitt	11	182	16.5	31	0
Wright, Alexander, LA Raid	10	282	28.2	55	0
Croom, Corey, NE	10	172	17.2	24	0
Metcalf, Eric, Cle	9	210	23.3	32	0
Penn, Chris, KC	9	194	21.6	34	0
Hughes, Danan, KC	9	190	21.1	32	0
Brooks, Bucky, Buff	9	162	18.0	25	0
Harmon, Ronnie, SD	9	157	17.4	25	0
Hardy, Adrian, Cin	8	185	23.1	42	0
Martin, Tony, SD	8	167	20.9	29	0
White, Lorenzo, Hou	8	167	20.9	28	0
Williams, Harvey, LA Raid	8	153	19.1	24	0
Bryant, Beno, Sea	7	136	19.4	38	0
Broussard, Steve, Cin	7	115	16.4	24	0
Turner, Nate, Buff	6	102	17.0	23	0
Thigpen, Yancey, Pitt	f5	121	24.2	31	0
Hannah, Travis, Hou	5	116	23.2	39	0
Green, Harold, Cin	5	113	22.6	31	0
Russell, Derek, Den	5	105	21.0	34	0
Morris, Bam, Pitt	4	114	28.5	45	0
Hill, Jeff, Cin	4	97	24.3	40	0
Tillman, Spencer, Hou	4	51	12.8	19	0
Anderson, Richie, NYJ	3	43	14.3	18	0
Thomas, Blair, NE	3	40	13.3	16	0
Kinchen, Brian, Cle	3	38	12.7	15	0
Clark, Derrick, Den	3	34	11.3	20	0
Campbell, Jeff, Den	f3	24	8.0	11	0
Burke, John, NE	3	11	3.7	6	0
Warren, Lamont, Ind	2	56	28.0	38	0
Anders, Kimble, KC	2	36	18.0	19	0
Hicks, Cliff, NYJ	2	30	15.0	16	0
Hoard, Leroy, Cle	f2	30	15.0	20	0
Martin, Kelvin, Sea	2	30	15.0	16	0
Williams, Ronnie, Mia	2	25	12.5	15	0
Etheredge, Carlos, Ind	2	23	11.5	14	0
Bishop, Blaine, Hou	2	18	9.0	11	0
Booker, Vaughn, KC	2	10	5.0	10	0
Pike, Mark, Buff	2	9	4.5	9	0
Teeter, Mike, Hou	f2	9	4.5	9	0
Williams, Mike, Mia	2	9	4.5	9	0
Zgonina, Jeff, Pitt	2	8	4.0	8	0
Mills, Ernie, Pitt	2	6	3.0	6	0
Parmalee, Bernie, Mia	2	0	0.0	0	0
Braxton, Tyrone, Mia	1	34	34.0	34	0
Timpson, Michael, NE	1	28	28.0	28	0
Givins, Ernest, Hou	1	27	27.0	27	0
Baxter, Fred, NYJ	1	20	20.0	20	0
Mitchell, Shannon, SD	1	18	18.0	18	0
Radecic, Scott, Ind	1	17	17.0	17	0
Stegall, Milt, Cin	1	16	16.0	16	0
Swann, Charles, Den	1	16	16.0	16	0
Brown, Troy, NE	1	14	14.0	14	0
DeOssie, Steve, NE	1	14	14.0	14	0
Sawyer, Corey, Cin	1	14	14.0	14	0
Clifton, Kyle, NYJ	1	13	13.0	13	0
Miller, Scott, Mia	1	13	13.0	13	0
Bennett, Donnell, KC	1	12	12.0	12	0
Saxon, James, Mia	1	12	12.0	12	0
Cadrez, Glenn, NYJ	1	10	10.0	10	0
Gash, Sam, NE	1	9	9.0	9	0
Toner, Ed, Ind	1	8	8.0	8	0
Tovar, Steve, Cin	1	8	8.0	8	0

	No.	Yards	Avg.	Long	TD
Evans, Jerry, Den	1	6	6.0	6	0
Gardner, Carwell, Buff	1	6	6.0	6	0
Jackson, Mark, Ind	1	5	5.0	5	0
McGee, Tony, Cin	1	4	4.0	4	0
Tasker, Steve, Buff	1	2	2.0	2	0
Parker, Vaughn, SD	1	1	1.0	1	0
Patton, James, Buff	1	1	1.0	1	0
Shaw, Eric, Cin	1	1	1.0	1	0
Baty, Greg, Mia	1	0	0.0	0	0
Carswell, Dwayne, Den	1	0	0.0	0	0
Davis, Kenneth, Buff	1	0	0.0	0	0
Ingram, Mark, Mia	1	0	0.0	0	0
Thornton, James, NYJ	1	0	0.0	0	0
Williams, Jamie, LA Raid	1	0	0.0	0	0
Guyton, Myron, NE	1	-1	-1.0	-1	0
Gray, Derwin, Ind	0	4	—	4	0

t = Touchdown
f = Fair Catch
Leader based on average return, minimum 20 returns

NFC KICKOFF RETURNERS—INDIVIDUAL

	No.	Yards	Avg.	Long	TD
Gray, Mel, Det	45	1276	28.4	102t	3
Walker, Herschel, Phil	21	581	27.7	94t	1
Williams, Kevin, Dall	43	1148	26.7	87t	1
Mitchell, Brian, Wash	58	1478	25.5	86	0
Lewis, Nate, Chi	35	874	25.0	55	0
Hughes, Tyrone, NO	63	1556	24.7	98t	2
Kinchen, Todd, LA Rams	21	510	24.3	46	0
Verdin, Clarence, Atl	44	1026	23.3	69	0
Lang, David, LA Rams	27	626	23.2	57	0
Ismail, Qadry, Minn	35	807	23.1	61	0
Carter, Dexter, SF	48	1105	23.0	96t	1
Harris, Corey, GB	29	618	21.3	59	0
Hebron, Vaughn, Phil	21	443	21.1	33	0
Turner, Vernon, TB	43	886	20.6	77	0
Levy, Chuck, Ariz	26	513	19.7	31	0
Sydner, Jeff, Phil	20	392	19.6	34	0
Lewis, Thomas, NYG	26	509	19.6	36	0
Meggett, David, NYG	29	548	18.9	30	0
Nonqualifiers					
Smith, Robert, Minn	16	419	26.2	45	0
Smith, Tony, Atl	16	333	20.8	31	0
Marshall, Arthur, NYG	15	249	16.6	30	0
Bailey, Johnny, LA Rams	12	260	21.7	32	0
Robinson, Patrick, Ariz	12	231	19.3	33	0
Wilson, Charles, TB	10	251	25.1	41	0
Conway, Curtis, Chi	10	228	22.8	34	0
Moore, Derrick, Det	10	113	11.3	19	0
Brooks, Robert, GB	9	260	28.9	96t	1
Pegram, Erric, Atl	9	145	16.1	35	0
Lynch, Eric, Det	9	105	11.7	16	0
Buckley, Curtis, TB	8	177	22.1	35	0
Brantley, Chris, LA Rams	7	150	21.4	33	0
McAfee, Fred, Ariz	7	113	16.1	29	0
Ned, Derrick, NO	7	77	11.0	19	0
Mitchell, Derrell, NO	6	129	21.5	30	0
Henesey, Brian, Ariz	6	108	18.0	25	0
Carter, Antonio, Chi	6	99	16.5	26	0
Walker, Adam, SF	6	82	13.7	19	0
Green, Robert, Chi	6	77	12.8	16	0
Jordan, Charles, GB	5	115	23.0	33	0
Morton, Johnnie, Det	4	143	35.8	93t	1
Holmes, Clayton, Dall	4	89	22.3	32	0
Wycheck, Frank, Wash	4	84	21.0	43	0
Thompson, Darrell, GB	4	67	16.8	19	0
Jurkovic, John, GB	4	57	14.3	16	0
Worley, Tim, Chi	4	52	13.0	25	0
Reeves, Bryan, Ariz	3	83	27.7	53	0
Rush, Tyrone, Wash	3	45	15.0	25	0
Lee, Amp, Minn	3	42	14.0	26	0
Malone, Van, Det	3	38	12.7	20	0
Montgomery, Alton, Atl	2	58	29.0	37	0
Harris, Leonard, Atl	2	47	23.5	30	0
Bell, William, Wash	2	43	21.5	25	0
Marion, Brock, Dall	2	39	19.5	21	0
Griffith, Howard, LA Rams	2	35	17.5	21	0
Loville, Derek, SF	2	34	17.0	19	0
Green, Rogerick, TB	2	33	16.5	18	0
Levens, Dorsey, GB	2	31	15.5	16	0
Culpepper, Brad, TB	2	30	15.0	18	0

1994 INDIVIDUAL STATISTICS

	No.	Yards	Avg.	Long	TD
Moore, Dave, TB	2	27	13.5	16	0
Flanigan, Jim, Chi	f2	26	13.0	14	0
Higgs, Mark, Ariz	2	25	12.5	17	0
Singleton, Nate, SF	2	23	11.5	17	0
Kozlowski, Brian, NYG	2	21	10.5	14	0
Wilson, Marcus, GB	2	14	7.0	14	0
Novoselsky, Brent, Minn	2	10	5.0	10	0
Smith, Irv, NO	2	10	5.0	10	0
Dunbar, Vaughn, NO	1	28	28.0	28	0
Woolford, Donnell, Chi	1	28	28.0	28	0
Bates, Mario, NO	1	20	20.0	26	0
Harris, Raymont, Chi	1	18	18.0	18	0
Ervins, Ricky, Wash	1	17	17.0	17	0
Neal, Lorenzo, NO	1	17	17.0	15	0
Farr, D'Marco, LA Rams	1	16	16.0	16	0
Smith, Otis, Phil	1	14	14.0	14	0
Harris, Rudy, TB	1	12	12.0	12	0
Anderson, Jamal, Atl	1	11	11.0	11	0
Joseph, James, Phil	1	11	11.0	11	0
Haws, Kurt, Wash	1	10	10.0	10	0
Jones, Robert, Dall	1	8	8.0	8	0
Jordan, Andrew, Minn	1	8	8.0	8	0
Lester, Tim, LA Rams	1	8	8.0	8	0
Heyward, Craig, Atl	1	7	7.0	7	0
Armstrong, Tyji, TB	1	6	6.0	6	0
Davey, Don, GB	1	6	6.0	6	0
Samuels, Terry, Ariz	1	6	6.0	6	0
Walsh, Chris, Minn	1	6	6.0	6	0
Evans, Chuck, Minn	1	4	4.0	4	0
Jenkins, James, Wash	1	4	4.0	4	0
Brown, Derek, NO	1	3	3.0	3	0
Brown, Derek, NYG	1	1	1.0	1	0
Carter, Marty, TB	1	0	0.0	0	0
Collins, Andre, Wash	1	0	0.0	0	0
Garnett, Dave, Minn	1	0	0.0	0	0
Johnson, Maurice, Phil	1	0	0.0	0	0
O'Neal, Brian, Phil	1	0	0.0	0	0
Thierry, John, Chi	1	0	0.0	0	0
Zordich, Mike, Phil	1	0	0.0	0	0
Johnson, Tre, Wash	0	4	—	4	0

t = Touchdown
f = Fair Catch
Leader based on average return, minimum 20 returns

FUMBLES

Most Fumbles
NFC: 12—Jeff George, Atlanta
AFC: 11—John Elway, Denver
Boomer Esiason, N.Y. Jets
Jim Kelly, Buffalo

Most Fumbles, Game
AFC: 4—Dan McGwire, Seattle vs. L.A. Raiders, December 18
NFC: 4—Steve Beuerlein, Arizona at Philadelphia, November 6
Randall Cunningham, Philadelphia vs. Cleveland, November 13

Own Fumbles Recovered
NFC: 6—Jeff George, Atlanta
AFC: 3—Drew Bledsoe, New England
Boomer Esiason, N.Y. Jets
Ernest Givins, Houston
Dan Marino, Miami
Dan McGwire, Seattle
Bucky Richardson, Houston

Most Own Fumbles Recovered, Game
NFC: 3—Jeff George, Atlanta vs. San Diego, November 6
AFC: 2—Jim Kelly, Buffalo at New England, September 11
Clifford Hicks, N.Y. Jets vs. New England, October 16
Dan McGwire, Seattle vs. L.A. Raiders, December 18

Opponents' Fumbles Recovered
AFC: 3—Cornelius Bennett, Buffalo
Robert Blackmon, Seattle
Kevin Greene, Pittsburgh
Don Griffin, Cleveland
Myron Guyton, New England
George Jamison, Kansas City
Aaron Jones, New England
Jeff Lageman, N.Y. Jets
Terry McDaniel, L.A. Raiders
Glenn Montgomery, Houston
Stevon Moore, Cleveland
Doug Terry, Kansas City
Derrick Thomas, Kansas City
Brian Washington, N.Y. Jets
NFC: 3—Michael Brooks, N.Y. Giants
James Harris, Minnesota
Sean Jones, Green Bay
Chris Spielman, Detroit
Mike Zordich, Philadelphia

Most Opponents' Fumbles Recovered, Game
AFC: 2—Terry McDaniel, L.A. Raiders at Denver, September 18
Derrick Thomas, Kansas City at Atlanta, September 18
Kevin Greene, Pittsburgh vs. Houston, October 3
Nolan Harrison, L.A. Raiders vs. Houston, October 30
Simon Fletcher, Denver vs. Cincinnati, November 27
Robert Blackmon, Seattle vs. Kansas City, November 27
Doug Terry, Kansas City vs. Houston, December 18
Ricky Reynolds, New England at Buffalo, December 18
Darryl Williams, Cincinnati vs. Philadelphia, December 24
NFC: 2—Othello Henderson, New Orleans at L.A. Rams, December 4
Chris Spielman, Detroit at Miami, December 25

Yards
NFC: 128—Tyrone Hughes, New Orleans
AFC: 78—Quentin Coryatt, Indianapolis

Longest
NFC: 98—Toby Wright, L.A. Rams at New Orleans, October 23 - TD
AFC: 78—Quentin Coryatt, Indianapolis at Pittsburgh, September 18 - TD

AFC FUMBLES—TEAM

	Fum.	Own. Rec.	Fum. OB	TD	Opp. Rec.	TD	Fum. Yards	Tot. Rec.
Pittsburgh	18	8	2	0	14	1	-1	22
San Diego	19	8	2	0	15	0	6	23
Kansas City	21	8	1	0	26	0	51	34
L.A. Raiders	22	7	1	0	13	2	109	20
Cleveland	26	9	3	0	13	0	29	22
Denver	27	8	1	0	14	0	63	22
New England	28	14	3	0	18	1	105	32
Miami	28	12	2	0	9	0	14	21
N.Y. Jets	28	15	3	0	21	0	3	36
Buffalo	30	13	4	0	12	1	18	25
Indianapolis	30	12	1	0	10	2	119	22
Seattle	31	11	1	0	11	0	3	22
Cincinnati	31	8	1	0	8	0	-4	16
Houston	42	15	2	0	12	0	12	27
AFC Total	381	148	27	0	196	7	527	344
AFC Average	27.2	10.6	1.9	0.0	14.0	0.5	37.6	24.6

NFC FUMBLES—TEAM

	Fum.	Own. Rec.	Fum. OB	TD	Opp. Rec.	TD	Fum. Yards	Tot. Rec.
Tampa Bay	18	10	1	0	12	0	1	22
Washington	21	6	2	0	6	2	95	12
Chicago	21	11	0	0	10	0	-9	21
Dallas	22	9	3	0	9	0	28	18
New Orleans	22	7	1	0	14	2	120	21
Philadelphia	23	11	0	0	14	0	47	25
San Francisco	25	11	1	0	12	1	45	23
Arizona	25	14	1	0	13	0	25	27
Green Bay	25	12	5	0	12	0	-3	24
L.A. Rams	26	13	0	0	6	2	164	19
Detroit	26	13	3	0	11	1	44	24
Atlanta	28	17	0	0	11	1	22	28
N.Y. Giants	28	18	3	0	16	0	-38	34
Minnesota	32	13	5	1	16	2	58	29
NFC Total	342	165	25	1	162	11	599	327
NFC Average	24.4	11.8	1.8	0.1	11.6	0.8	42.8	23.4
NFL Total	723	313	52	1	358	18	1126	671
NFL Average	25.8	11.2	1.9	0.0	12.8	0.6	40.2	24.0

Fum OB= Fumbled out of bounds, includes fumbled through the end zone.
Yards includes aborted plays, own recoveries, and opponents' recoveries.

AFC FUMBLES - INDIVIDUAL

	Fum.	Own Rec.	Opp. Rec.	Yards	Tot. Rec.
Alexander, Derrick, Cle	2	0	0	0	0
Alexander, Elijah, Den	0	0	1	9	1
Alipate, Tuineau, NYJ	0	0	1	0	1
Allen, Marcus, KC	3	0	0	0	0
Ambrose, Ashley, Ind	0	0	1	0	1
Anders, Kimble, KC	1	2	0	0	2
Anderson, Darren, KC	0	0	1	0	1
Anderson, Eddie, LA Raid	0	0	1	0	1
Anderson, Richie, NYJ	1	1	0	0	1
Arthur, Mike, NE	1	1	0	-2	1
Atwater, Steve, Den	0	0	2	17	2
Baldwin, Randy, Cle	1	1	0	0	1
Ball, Eric, Cin	1	1	0	0	1
Ball, Jerry, LA Raid	0	0	1	0	1
Barnett, Harlon, NE	0	0	2	7	2
Bates, Michael, Sea	3	0	0	0	0
Bates, Patrick, LA Raid	0	0	2	0	2
Baty, Greg, Mia	1	0	0	0	0
Baxter, Fred, NYJ	0	0	1	0	1
Beebe, Don, Buff	3	0	0	0	0
Bennett, Cornelius, Buff	0	0	3	14	3
Bennett, Donnell, KC	2	1	0	0	1
Bennett, Tony, Ind	0	0	1	75	1
Bieniemy, Eric, SD	1	1	0	0	1
Birden, J. J., KC	1	1	0	0	1
Bishop, Blaine, Hou	0	0	1	0	1
Blackmon, Robert, Sea	0	0	3	18	3
Blades, Brian, Sea	1	2	0	0	2
Blake, Jeff, Cin	6	0	0	-5	0
Bledsoe, Drew, NE	9	3	0	-5	3
Booker, Vaughn, KC	0	0	2	6	2
Bowens, Tim, Mia	0	0	1	0	1
Bradford, Ronnie, Den	0	1	1	0	2
Brewer, Dewell, Ind	3	1	0	0	1
Brilz, Darrick, Cin	0	1	0	0	1
Brim, Michael, Cin	0	0	1	1	1
Brisby, Vincent, NE	1	0	0	0	0
Brooks, Bucky, Buff	1	0	1	0	1
Brooks, Bill, Buff	1	0	0	0	0
Broussard, Steve, Cin	5	1	0	0	1
Brown, Gary, Hou	6	0	0	0	0
Brown, James, NYJ	0	1	0	0	1
Brown, Tim, LA Raid	3	0	0	0	0
Brown, Troy, NE	2	2	0	0	2
Brown, Vincent, NE	0	0	1	5	1
Buchanan, Ray, Ind	0	0	1	0	1
Buckner, Brentson, Pitt	0	0	1	0	1
Burnett, Rob, Cle	0	0	1	0	1
Burris, Jeff, Buff	2	1	0	0	1
Bush, Lewis, SD	0	0	1	0	1
Butts, Marion, NE	1	1	0	0	1
Cadrez, Glenn, NYJ.	0	1	0	0	1
Camarillo, Rich, Hou	1	1	0	0	1
Campbell, Jeff, Den	0	1	0	0	1
Carlson, Cody, Hou	6	1	0	0	1
Carrier, Mark, Cle	1	1	0	0	1
Carrington, Darren, SD	0	0	2	0	2
Carswell, Dwayne, Den	0	1	0	0	1
Carter, Dale, KC	1	1	0	0	1
Cash, Kerry, Ind	1	1	0	0	1
Christie, Steve, Buff	0	0	1	0	1
Clark, Derrick, Den	1	0	0	0	0
Clark, Reggie, Pitt	0	0	1	0	1
Clifton, Kyle, NYJ.	0	0	1	0	1
Coates, Ben, NE	2	2	0	0	2
Coleman, Andre, SD	3	1	0	0	1
Coleman, Marco, Mia	0	0	1	0	1
Collins, Mark, KC	0	0	2	0	2
Coryatt, Quentin, Ind	0	0	1	78	1
Crafts, Jerry, Buff	0	2	0	0	2
Craver, Aaron, Mia	1	1	0	0	1
Criswell, Jeff, NYJ	0	1	0	0	1
Crittenden, Ray, NE	1	1	0	0	1
Crockett, Ray, Den	0	0	2	43	2
Croom, Corey, NE	1	0	0	0	0
Cross, Jeff, Mia	0	0	1	0	1
Davis, Kenneth, Buff	3	0	0	0	0
Davis, Reuben, SD	0	0	1	0	1
Davis, Willie, KC	1	0	0	0	0
Dawkins, Sean, Ind	1	0	0	0	0
Dawson, Doug, Cle	0	1	0	0	1
Dawson, Lake, KC	1	0	0	0	0
Dellenbach, Jeff, Mia	1	0	0	-11	0
Dickerson, Ron, KC	1	0	0	0	0
Dishman, Cris, Hou	0	0	1	29	1
Donaldson, Ray, Sea	2	0	0	-3	0
Dumas, Mike, Buff	0	2	0	40	2
Edmunds, Ferrell, Sea	1	0	0	0	0
Elliott, Lin, KC	0	0	1	0	1
Elway, John, Den	11	2	0	-5	2
Emtman, Steve, Ind	0	0	1	0	1
Esiason, Boomer, NYJ	11	3	0	-11	3
Evans, Donald, NYJ.	0	0	1	0	1
Evans, Vince, LA Raid	2	1	0	0	1
Faulk, Marshall, Ind	5	1	0	0	1
Fenner, Derrick, Cin	6	1	0	0	1
Fields, Jaime, KC	0	0	1	0	1
Figures, Deon, Pitt	0	1	0	0	1
Flannery, John, Hou	0	2	0	0	2
Fletcher, Simon, Den	0	0	2	0	2
Frank, Donald, LA Raid	0	0	1	30	1
Frase, Paul, NYJ	0	0	1	0	1
Fryar, Irving, Mia	0	1	0	7	1
Gardner, Carwell, Buff	1	0	0	0	0
Gary, Cleveland, Mia	1	0	0	0	0
Gash, Sam, NE	1	1	0	0	1
Givins, Ernest, Hou	3	3	0	0	3
Glenn, Aaron, NYJ	2	1	0	0	1
Goad, Tim, NE	0	0	1	8	1
Gordon, Darrien, SD	2	1	2	15	3
Grant, Steve, Ind	0	0	1	2	1
Gray, Chris, Mia	0	1	0	0	1
Green, Eric, Pitt	2	0	0	0	0
Green, Harold, Cin	1	1	0	0	1
Green, Paul, Sea	1	1	0	0	1
Green, Victor, NYJ.	0	0	1	0	1
Greene, Kevin, Pitt	0	0	3	0	3
Griffin, Don, Cle	1	0	3	15	3
Grow, Monty, KC	1	0	0	0	0
Guyton, Myron, NE	0	0	3	34	3
Habib, Brian, Den	0	1	0	0	1
Hannah, Travis, Hou	1	0	0	0	0
Harbaugh, Jim, Ind	1	0	0	0	0
Hardy, Adrian, Cin	0	0	1	0	1
Harmon, Ronnie, SD	0	1	0	0	1
Harris, Ronnie, NE	1	0	0	0	0
Harrison, Nolan, LA Raid	0	0	2	0	2
Harrison, Rodney, SD	0	1	0	0	1
Harvey, Richard, Den	0	0	1	0	1
Hasty, James, NYJ	0	0	2	0	2
Hayes, Jonathan, Pitt	1	0	0	0	0
Hendrickson, Steve, SD	0	0	1	0	1
Henry, Kevin, Pitt	0	0	1	0	1
Hicks, Cliff, NYJ	5	2	0	0	2
Higgs, Mark, Mia	1	0	0	0	0
Hill, Greg, KC	1	0	0	0	0
Hoard, Leroy, Cle	8	0	0	0	0
Hopkins, Brad, Hou	0	1	0	0	1
Hoskins, Derrick, LA Raid	0	0	1	0	1
Hostetler, Jeff, LA Raid	10	0	0	-9	0
Houston, Bobby, NYJ	0	0	1	0	1
Hull, Kent, Buff	1	0	0	-19	0
Humphrey, Ronald, Ind	4	1	0	0	1
Humphries, Leonard, Ind	0	1	0	0	1
Humphries, Stan, SD	6	2	0	-9	2
Ingram, Mark, Mia	1	1	0	0	1
Jackson, John, Pitt	0	2	0	0	2
Jackson, Keith, Mia	2	1	0	0	1
Jackson, Tyoka, Mia	0	0	1	0	1
Jamison, George, KC	0	0	3	22	3
Jett, James, LA Raid	0	2	0	15	2
Johnson, Charles, Pitt	2	0	0	0	0
Johnson, Johnny, NYJ	4	0	0	0	0
Johnson, Pepper, Cle	0	0	1	10	1
Johnson, Tracy, Sea	1	0	0	0	0
Johnson, Bill, Cle	0	0	1	0	1
Jones, Aaron, NE	1	0	3	28	3
Jones, Gary, Pitt	0	0	1	0	1
Jones, Henry, Buff	0	0	1	0	1
Jones, James, Cle	0	0	2	0	2
Jones, Mike, NE	0	0	1	0	1

1994 INDIVIDUAL STATISTICS

	Fum.	Own Rec.	Opp. Rec.	Yards	Tot. Rec.
Jones, Roger, Cin	1	0	0	0	0
Jones, Rondell, Den	0	0	1	0	1
Jones, Tony, Cle	0	1	0	0	1
Jourdain, Yonel, Buff	1	0	0	0	0
Kelly, Jim, Buff	11	2	0	-19	2
Kennedy, Cortez, Sea	0	0	1	0	1
Kinchen, Brian, Cle	1	0	0	0	0
Kirby, Terry, Mia	2	0	0	0	0
Klingler, David, Cin	7	1	0	0	1
Lageman, Jeff, NYJ	0	0	3	0	3
Lake, Carnell, Pitt	0	0	1	0	1
Langham, Antonio, Cle	1	0	0	0	0
Lathon, Lamar, Hou	0	0	1	0	1
Lee, Shawn, SD	0	0	1	0	1
Lewis, Mo, NYJ	0	0	1	11	1
Lloyd, Greg, Pitt	0	0	1	0	1
Lodish, Mike, Buff	0	0	1	0	1
Lott, Ronnie, NYJ	0	0	1	0	1
Lowdermilk, Kirk, Ind	1	0	0	-4	0
Maddox, Mark, Buff	0	0	1	0	1
Majkowski, Don, Ind	5	2	0	-14	2
Manusky, Greg, KC	0	1	1	0	2
Marino, Dan, Mia	9	3	0	-4	3
Martin, Kelvin, Sea	2	1	0	0	1
Martin, Tony, SD	2	0	0	0	0
Matthews, Bruce, Hou	2	0	0	-9	0
Mawae, Kevin, Sea	0	1	0	0	1
McCoy, Tony, Ind	0	0	1	0	1
McDaniel, Terry, LA Raid	0	0	3	48	3
McDaniels, Pellom, KC	0	0	1	0	1
McDonald, Devon, Ind	0	1	0	0	1
McDowell, Bubba, Hou	0	0	1	0	1
McDuffie, O. J., Mia	3	1	0	0	1
McGinest, Willie, NE	0	0	2	0	2
McGlockton, Chester, LA Raid	0	0	1	0	1
McGwire, Dan, Sea	9	3	0	-7	3
McNair, Todd, Hou	0	0	1	0	1
Means, Natrone, SD	5	0	0	0	0
Mecklenburg, Karl, Den	0	0	2	0	2
Metcalf, Eric, Cle	6	0	0	0	0
Mickell, Darren, KC	0	0	1	0	1
Milburn, Glyn, Den	4	1	0	0	1
Millen, Hugh, Den	2	0	0	0	0
Mills, Ernie, Pitt	1	0	0	0	0
Mills, John Henry, Hou	1	0	0	0	0
Mims, Chris, SD	0	0	2	0	2
Mirer, Rick, Sea	2	1	0	-7	1
Mitchell, Johnny, NYJ	1	1	0	4	1
Montana, Joe, KC	7	1	0	-6	1
Montgomery, Glenn, Hou	0	0	3	-2	3
Montgomery, Tyrone, LA Raid	2	0	0	0	0
Moore, Rob, NYJ	0	1	0	0	1
Moore, Stevon, Cle	0	2	3	3	5
Morris, Bam, Pitt	3	1	0	0	1
Murrell, Adrian, NYJ	1	0	0	0	0
Nagle, Browning, Ind	2	0	0	0	0
O'Donnell, Neil, Pitt	4	1	0	0	1
Oliver, Louis, Cin	1	0	0	0	0
O'Neal, Leslie, SD	0	0	1	0	1
Parmalee, Bernie, Mia	5	2	1	20	3
Patton, Marvcus, Buff	1	0	0	0	1
Perry, Darren, Pitt	0	0	2	0	2
Phillips, Joe, KC	0	0	1	0	1
Pickens, Carl, Cin	1	1	0	0	1
Pitts, Mike, NE	0	0	2	8	2
Potts, Roosevelt, Ind	5	1	0	0	1
Pritchard, Mike, Den	1	0	0	0	0
Reed, Andre, Buff	3	2	0	0	2
Reich, Frank, Buff	1	1	0	0	1
Reynolds, Ricky, NE	0	1	2	25	3
Richardson, Bucky, Hou	7	3	0	-2	3
Rivers, Reggie, Den	1	0	1	0	1
Robertson, Marcus, Hou	1	1	0	0	1
Robinson, Ed, Pitt	0	1	0	0	1
Robinson, Eugene, Sea	0	0	1	0	1
Robinson, Rafael, Sea	0	0	1	0	1
Russell, Leonard, Den	4	0	0	0	0
Rypien, Mark, Cle	2	0	0	-1	0
Sadowski, Troy, Cin	0	1	0	0	1
Saleaumua, Dan, KC	0	0	1	0	1
Sawyer, Corey, Cin	2	0	1	0	1
Scrafford, Kirk, Den	0	1	0	0	1
Seals, Ray, Pitt	0	0	2	0	2
Seau, Junior, SD	0	0	3	0	3
Sharpe, Shannon, Den	1	0	0	0	0
Shields, Will, KC	0	1	0	0	1
Simien, Tracy, KC	0	0	2	0	2
Sims, Keith, Mia	0	1	1	0	2
Singleton, Chris, Mia	0	0	2	2	2
Siragusa, Tony, Ind	0	0	1	0	1
Slaughter, Webster, Hou	2	1	0	0	1
Smith, Al, Hou	0	0	1	0	1
Smith, Anthony, LA Raid	0	0	1	25	1
Smith, Bruce, Buff	0	0	2	0	2
Smith, Dennis, Den	0	0	1	0	1
Smith, Neil, KC	0	0	1	6	1
Spikes, Irving, Mia	1	0	0	0	0
Staysniak, Joe, Ind	1	2	0	-18	2
Stephens, Rod, Sea	0	0	2	0	2
Stewart, Michael, Mia	0	0	1	0	1
Strong, Mack, Sea	1	0	0	0	0
Sweeney, Jim, NYJ	0	1	0	0	1
Talley, Darryl, Buff	0	0	1	2	1
Taylor, Jay, KC	0	0	1	0	1
Teeter, Mike, Hou	1	0	0	0	0
Terry, Doug, KC	0	0	3	12	3
Testaverde, Vinny, Cle	3	2	0	2	2
Thomas, Derrick, KC	0	0	3	11	3
Thomas, Thurman, Buff	1	2	0	0	2
Thompson, Bennie, Cle	0	0	1	0	1
Thompson, Leroy, NE	2	1	0	0	1
Thornton, James, NYJ	0	0	2	0	2
Tillman, Cedric, Den	1	0	0	0	0
Tillman, Spencer, Hou	1	1	1	0	2
Tolliver, Billy Joe, Hou	7	0	0	-3	0
Tomczak, Mike, Pitt	2	0	0	-1	0
Toner, Ed, Ind	0	0	1	0	1
Tovar, Steve, Cin	0	0	2	0	2
Trudeau, Jack, NYJ	2	1	0	-1	1
Turner, Eric, Cle	0	0	1	0	1
Turner, Floyd, Ind	1	1	0	0	1
Turner, Marcus, NYJ	0	0	1	0	1
Turner, Kevin, NE	4	1	1	-3	2
Vaughn, Jon, Sea	3	0	0	0	0
Walker, Derrick, KC	1	0	0	0	0
Warren, Chris, Sea	5	2	0	0	2
Warren, Terrence, Sea	0	0	1	0	1
Washington, Brian, NYJ	0	0	3	0	3
Washington, Marvin, NYJ	1	0	1	0	1
Washington, Mickey, Buff	0	0	1	0	1
Wellman, Gary, Hou	1	0	0	0	0
Whigham, Larry, NE	1	0	0	0	0
White, Dwayne, NYJ	0	1	0	0	1
White, Lorenzo, Hou	2	0	1	-1	1
Whitley, Curtis, SD	0	1	0	0	1
Whitmore, David, KC	0	0	1	0	1
Widell, Dave, Den	1	0	0	-1	0
Wilkerson, Bruce, LA Raid	0	1	0	0	1
Williams, Alfred, Cin	0	0	1	0	1
Williams, Darryl, Cin	0	0	2	0	2
Williams, David W., Hou	0	1	0	0	1
Williams, Gerald, Pitt	0	0	1	0	1
Williams, Harvey, LA Raid	4	2	0	0	2
Williams, Jamie, LA Raid	1	0	0	0	0
Williams, Wally, Cle	0	1	0	0	1
Winter, Blaise, SD	0	0	1	0	1
Wolford, Will, Ind	0	0	1	0	1
Wooden, Terry, Sea	0	0	2	2	2
Woodson, Rod, Pitt	2	1	0	0	1
Wortham, Barron, Hou	0	0	1	0	1
Wright, Alexander, LA Raid	0	1	0	0	1
Zgonina, Jeff, Pitt	1	1	0	0	1

Yards includes aborted plays, own recoveries and opponents' recoveries.

NFC FUMBLES - INDIVIDUAL

	Fum.	Own Rec.	Opp. Rec.	Yards	Tot. Rec.
Adams, Scott, NO	0	1	0	0	1
Aikman, Troy, Dall	2	2	0	0	2
Alexander, David, Phil	0	1	0	0	1
Alexander, Harold, Atl	0	1	0	0	1

	Fum.	Own Rec.	Opp. Rec.	Yards	Tot. Rec.
Allen, Eric, Phil	0	0	1	30	1
Allen, Terry, Minn	3	2	0	4	2
Anderson, Willie, LA Rams	0	1	0	7	1
Armstrong, Tyji, TB	2	1	0	0	1
Bailey, Carlton, NYG	0	0	1	2	1
Bailey, Johnny, LA Rams	2	0	0	0	0
Bailey, Robert, LA Rams	0	1	0	0	1
Bankston, Michael, Ariz	0	0	1	2	1
Barker, Roy, Minn	0	0	1	0	1
Barnett, Fred, Phil	1	0	0	0	0
Bates, Mario, NO	3	1	0	0	1
Bayless, Martin, Wash	0	0	1	60	1
Beamon, Willie, NYG	0	0	2	0	2
Beckles, Ian, TB	0	1	1	0	2
Belin, Chuck, LA Rams	0	1	0	0	1
Bennett, Edgar, GB	1	1	0	0	1
Bettis, Jerome, LA Rams	5	3	0	0	3
Beuerlein, Steve, Ariz	8	3	0	-13	3
Bishop, Greg, NYG	0	1	1	0	2
Blades, Bennie, Det	0	1	1	0	2
Booty, John, NYG	0	1	1	5	2
Bouwens, Shawn, Det	1	3	0	0	3
Brady, Ed, TB	0	0	1	0	1
Brooks, Michael, NYG	1	0	3	0	3
Brooks, Reggie, Wash	3	0	0	0	0
Brooks, Robert, GB	4	1	0	0	1
Brown, Dave, NYG	11	4	0	-15	4
Brown, Derek, NO	4	2	0	0	2
Brown, Derek, NYG	0	0	1	0	1
Brown, Richard, Minn	0	1	0	0	1
Brunell, Mark, GB	1	0	0	-2	0
Buck, Vince, NO	0	0	1	0	1
Buckley, Curtis, TB	1	1	1	0	2
Buckley, Terrell, GB	0	0	1	0	1
Bussey, Barney, TB	0	0	1	0	1
Cain, Joseph, Chi	0	0	1	0	1
Calloway, Chris, NYG	1	0	0	0	0
Campbell, Jesse, NYG	0	0	2	3	2
Carter, Cris, Minn	4	0	0	0	0
Carter, Dexter, SF	2	2	0	0	2
Centers, Larry, Ariz	2	2	0	27	2
Chandler, Chris, LA Rams	3	0	0	-10	0
Cobb, Reggie, GB	1	0	0	0	0
Coleman, Lincoln, Dall	2	0	0	0	0
Collins, Andre, Wash	0	0	1	16	1
Conner, Darion, NO	0	0	1	0	1
Conway, Curtis, Chi	2	1	0	0	1
Cook, Marv, Chi	0	1	0	0	1
Cooper, Adrian, Minn	2	1	0	0	1
Cross, Howard, NYG	0	1	0	1	1
Culpepper, Brad, TB	0	0	1	0	1
Cunningham, Randall, Phil	10	2	0	-15	2
Dafney, Bernard, Minn	0	1	0	0	1
Dalman, Chris, SF	1	0	0	-3	0
Davis, Dexter, LA Rams	0	1	0	0	1
Davis, Eric, SF	1	0	2	0	2
Del Rio, Jack, Minn	0	0	2	0	2
Dilfer, Trent, TB	2	0	0	0	0
Dimry, Charles, TB	0	0	1	0	1
Douglass, Maurice, Chi	0	0	1	0	1
Downs, Gary, NYG	1	0	0	0	0
Dye, Ernest, Ariz	0	1	0	0	1
Edwards, Dixon, Dall	0	0	1	21	1
Ellard, Henry, Wash	1	0	0	0	0
Erickson, Craig, TB	6	1	0	-1	1
Ervins, Ricky, Wash	1	0	0	0	0
Evans, Byron, Phil	0	0	1	0	1
Evans, Doug, GB	0	0	1	3	1
Everett, Jim, NO	3	0	0	-2	0
Everett, Thomas, TB	0	0	1	0	1
Fann, Chad, Ariz	1	0	0	0	0
Favre, Brett, GB	7	1	0	-2	1
Flores, Mike, Phil	0	0	1	0	1
Frazier, Derrick, Phil	0	0	1	3	1
Frerotte, Gus, Wash	4	2	0	-4	2
Friesz, John, Wash	2	1	0	0	1
Fuller, William, Phil	0	0	1	0	1
Gardner, Moe, Atl	0	0	1	0	1
Garner, Charlie, Phil	3	0	0	0	0
Garnett, Dave, Minn	0	0	2	0	2
Garrett, Jason, Dall	0	1	0	0	1

	Fum.	Own Rec.	Opp. Rec.	Yards	Tot. Rec.
Gayle, Shaun, Chi	0	0	1	9	1
Gedney, Chris, Chi	1	0	0	0	0
George, Jeff, Atl	12	6	0	-12	6
George, Ron, Atl	0	0	1	0	1
Gesek, John, Wash	0	1	0	0	1
Goeas, Leo, LA Rams	0	1	0	0	1
Graham, Jeffrey, Chi	1	1	0	0	1
Graham, Kent, NYG	2	1	0	0	1
Gray, Mel, Det	3	2	0	13	2
Grbac, Elvis, SF	5	0	0	-2	0
Green, Robert, Chi	1	0	1	0	1
Gruber, Paul, TB	0	1	0	0	1
Guliford, Eric, Minn	1	0	0	0	0
Hager, Britt, Phil	0	0	1	0	1
Hall, Rhett, SF	0	0	1	0	1
Hall, Ron, Det	1	0	0	0	0
Hamilton, Keith, NYG	0	1	2	0	3
Hampton, Rodney, NYG	0	1	0	0	1
Hanks, Merton, SF	1	1	1	0	2
Harmon, Andy, Phil	0	0	2	0	2
Harper, Alvin, Dall	2	0	0	0	0
Harris, Corey, GB	1	1	0	0	1
Harris, James, Minn	2	0	3	18	3
Harris, Odie, Ariz	0	0	1	0	1
Harris, Rudy, TB	1	0	0	0	0
Harris, Raymont, Chi	1	2	1	0	3
Harvey, Ken, Wash	0	0	1	0	1
Haynes, Michael, NO	1	0	0	0	0
Hebert, Bobby, Atl	2	0	0	-5	0
Henderson, Othello, NO	0	0	2	0	2
Hennings, Chad, Dall	0	0	1	0	1
Hester, Jessie, LA Rams	1	0	0	0	0
Heyward, Craig, Atl	5	2	0	0	2
Hoage, Terry, Ariz	0	0	2	4	2
Hollinquest, Lamont, Wash	0	0	1	0	1
Holman, Rodney, Det	1	2	0	-4	2
Holmes, Clayton, Dall	1	0	0	0	0
Holmes, Lester, Phil	0	3	0	0	3
Holt, Pierce, Atl	0	0	1	0	1
Howard, Erik, NYG	0	0	1	0	1
Hughes, Tyrone, NO	7	1	2	128	3
Irving, Terry, Ariz	0	0	1	0	1
Ismail, Qadry, Minn	2	0	1	1	1
Jack, Eric, Atl	0	0	1	27	1
Jackson, Rickey, SF	0	0	2	5	2
Jenkins, Carlos, Minn	0	0	2	0	2
Johnson, D. J., Atl	0	0	2	15	2
Johnson, Joe, NO	0	0	1	0	1
Johnson, Keshon, GB	0	0	1	0	1
Johnson, Maurice, Phil	1	1	0	0	1
Johnson, Mike, Det	0	0	1	0	1
Johnston, Daryl, Dall	2	0	0	0	0
Jones, Brent, SF	1	1	0	0	1
Jones, Dante, Chi	0	0	2	0	2
Jones, Sean, GB	0	0	3	0	3
Jones, Jimmie, LA Rams	0	0	1	0	1
Jones, Robert, Dall	0	0	1	0	1
Jordan, Andrew, Minn	1	1	0	0	1
Jordan, Charles, GB	1	0	0	0	0
Joseph, James, Phil	1	1	0	0	1
Kelly, Joe, LA Rams	0	0	1	0	1
Kennard, Derek, Dall	1	0	0	0	0
Kennedy, Lincoln, Atl	0	1	0	0	1
Kinchen, Todd, LA Rams	5	0	0	0	0
Koonce, George, GB	0	0	2	0	2
Kramer, Erik, Chi	3	2	0	-5	2
Krieg, Dave, Det	4	2	0	-1	2
Lang, David, LA Rams	2	0	0	0	0
LeBel, Harper, Atl	1	0	0	-5	0
Lee, Amp, Minn	1	1	0	0	1
Lee, Carl, NO	0	0	1	0	1
Legette, Tyrone, NO	1	0	0	0	0
Lester, Tim, LA Rams	1	1	0	0	1
Levy, Chuck, Ariz	0	1	0	0	1
Lewis, Nate, Chi	1	0	0	0	0
Lewis, Thomas, NYG	2	2	0	0	2
Lumpkin, Sean, NO	0	0	1	0	1
Lyght, Todd, LA Rams	0	0	1	74	1
Malone, Van, Det	1	0	0	0	0
Mann, Charles, SF	0	0	1	0	1
Marshall, Arthur, NYG	1	0	0	0	0

1994 INDIVIDUAL STATISTICS

	Fum.	Own Rec.	Opp. Rec.	Yards	Tot. Rec.
Marshall, Wilber, Ariz	0	0	1	0	1
Marts, Lonnie, TB	0	0	2	0	2
Maryland, Russell, Dall	0	0	1	0	1
Massey, Robert, Det	1	0	0	0	0
Mathis, Terance, Atl	0	1	0	0	1
Matthews, Aubrey, Det	1	0	0	0	0
Mayberry, Tony, TB	0	1	0	0	1
Mayhew, Martin, TB	0	0	1	0	1
McAfee, Fred, Ariz	1	0	0	0	0
McCants, Keith, Ariz	0	0	1	0	1
McCleskey, J. J., NO	0	0	1	0	1
McDaniel, Randall, Minn	0	1	0	0	1
McDonald, Tim, SF	0	0	1	49	1
McDowell, Anthony, TB	0	1	0	0	1
McKenzie, Raleigh, Wash	0	1	0	0	1
McMahon, Jim, Ariz	1	0	0	0	0
McMichael, Steve, GB	0	0	1	0	1
McMillian, Mark, Phil	0	0	1	0	1
Meggett, David, NYG	6	4	1	0	5
Merritt, David, Ariz	0	0	1	0	1
Miller, Chris, LA Rams	7	3	0	-5	3
Miller, Corey, NYG	0	0	1	0	1
Mills, Sam, NO	0	0	1	0	1
Miniefield, Kevin, Chi	0	0	1	-5	1
Minter, Barry, Chi	0	0	1	0	1
Mitchell, Brian, Wash	4	0	0	0	0
Mitchell, Derrell, NO	0	0	1	0	1
Mitchell, Scott, Det	8	2	0	-5	2
Moon, Warren, Minn	9	2	0	-5	2
Moore, Derrick, Det	2	0	0	0	0
Moore, Herman, Det	1	0	0	0	0
Moore, Ron, Ariz	2	1	0	0	1
Morgan, Anthony, GB	1	0	0	0	0
Morrison, Darryl, Wash	0	0	2	32	2
Morton, Johnnie, Det	1	1	0	0	1
Neal, Lorenzo, NO	1	0	0	0	0
Ned, Derrick, NO	1	0	0	0	0
Newberry, Tom, LA Rams	0	1	0	0	1
Newman, Anthony, LA Rams	0	0	1	0	1
O'Neal, Brian, Phil	1	0	0	0	0
Palmer, David, Minn	2	0	0	0	0
Parker, Anthony, Minn	1	1	0	23	1
Paup, Bryce, GB	0	1	1	0	2
Peete, Rodney, Dall	3	2	0	-1	2
Pegram, Erric, Atl	2	1	0	2	1
Perriman, Brett, Det	1	0	0	0	0
Plummer, Gary, SF	0	0	1	0	1
Porcher, Robert, Det	0	0	1	0	1
Prior, Mike, GB	3	2	0	0	2
Pritchett, Kelvin, Det	0	0	1	0	1
Proehl, Ricky, Ariz	2	2	0	0	2
Randle, John, Minn	0	0	2	0	2
Rasheed, Kenyon, NYG	1	0	0	0	0
Reed, Jake, Minn	3	0	0	0	0
Reeves, Bryan, Ariz	1	1	1	0	2
Rhett, Errict, TB	2	1	0	0	1
Rice, Jerry, SF	1	0	0	0	0
Richards, David, Atl	0	1	0	0	1
Riesenberg, Doug, NYG	0	1	0	0	1
Rison, Andre, Atl	1	0	0	0	0
Roaf, Willie, NO	0	1	0	0	1
Robinson, Gerald, LA Rams	0	0	1	0	1
Robinson, Patrick, Ariz	1	1	0	0	1
Roby, Reggie, Wash	1	1	0	0	1
Romanowski, Bill, Phil	0	0	1	0	1
Royster, Mazio, TB	1	0	0	0	0
Ruettgers, Ken, GB	0	1	0	0	1
Sanders, Deion, SF	0	1	0	0	1
Sanders, Ricky, Atl	0	0	1	0	1
Sapolu, Jesse, SF	0	1	0	0	1
Saxon, Mike, Minn	1	0	0	0	0
Schroeder, Jay, Ariz	5	1	0	-5	1
Scroggins, Tracy, Det	0	0	1	0	1
Sharpe, Sterling, GB	1	0	0	0	0
Shelley, Elbert, Atl	0	1	0	0	1
Sheppard, Ashley, Minn	0	0	1	0	1
Shuler, Heath, Wash	3	0	0	-9	0
Sims, Joe, GB	0	1	0	0	1
Small, Torrance, NO	0	1	0	1	1
Smith, Cedric, Wash	1	0	0	0	0
Smith, Chuck, Atl	0	0	2	0	2
Smith, Darrin, Dall	0	0	2	11	2
Smith, Emmitt, Dall	1	0	0	0	0
Smith, Tony, Atl	1	0	0	0	0
Spencer, Jimmy, NO	0	0	1	0	1
Spielman, Chris, Det	0	0	3	25	3
Stargell, Tony, TB	0	0	1	2	1
Stepnoski, Mark, Dall	4	0	0	-3	0
Steussie, Todd, Minn	0	1	0	0	1
Stone, Ron, Dall	0	1	0	0	1
Stowe, Tyronne, Wash	1	0	0	0	0
Strickland, Fred, GB	0	0	1	0	1
Swann, Eric, Ariz	0	0	1	10	1
Swilling, Pat, Det	0	0	1	5	1
Sydner, Jeff, Phil	2	0	0	0	0
Taylor, John, SF	1	0	0	0	0
Thomas, Broderick, Det	0	0	2	11	2
Thomas, Henry, Minn	0	0	1	0	1
Thompson, Broderick, Phil	0	1	0	0	1
Tillman, Lewis, Chi	1	0	0	0	0
Tippins, Kenny, Atl	0	0	1	0	1
Tolbert, Tony, Dall	0	0	1	0	1
Townsend, Greg, Phil	0	0	1	24	1
Tuggle, Jessie, Atl	1	0	1	0	1
Turner, Vernon, TB	1	1	0	0	1
Verdin, Clarence, Atl	3	2	0	0	2
Waddle, Tom, Chi	1	1	0	0	1
Walker, Adam, SF	0	0	1	0	1
Walker, Herschel, Phil	4	1	0	0	1
Wallace, Steve, SF	0	2	0	0	2
Walsh, Steve, Chi	7	3	0	-8	3
Ware, Derek, Ariz	1	1	0	0	1
Warren, Frank, NO	0	0	1	0	1
Washington, Charles, Atl	0	1	0	0	1
Washington, DeWayne, Minn	0	1	1	17	2
Washington, James, Dall	0	0	1	0	1
Watters, Ricky, SF	8	2	0	0	2
West, Ed, GB	1	0	0	0	0
White, Reggie, GB	0	0	1	0	1
Williams, Aeneas, Ariz	0	0	1	0	1
Williams, Brian, NYG	2	1	0	-34	1
Williams, Calvin, Phil	0	1	0	0	1
Williams, James, Ariz	0	0	2	0	2
Williams, Kevin, Dall	4	3	0	0	3
Williams, Mark, GB	0	1	0	0	1
Willis, James, GB	1	1	0	0	1
Wilson, Wade, NO	1	0	0	-7	0
Wilson, Marcus, GB	1	0	0	0	0
Wilson, Karl, TB	0	0	1	0	1
Winters, Frank, GB	1	1	0	-2	1
Woodall, Lee, SF	0	0	1	0	1
Woodson, Darren, Dall	0	0	1	0	1
Woolford, Donnell, Chi	1	0	0	0	0
Workman, Vince, TB	2	1	0	0	1
Worley, Tim, Chi	1	0	0	0	0
Wright, Toby, LA Rams	0	0	1	98	1
Young, Bryant, SF	0	0	1	0	1
Young, Steve, SF	4	1	0	-4	1
Zordich, Mike, Phil	0	0	3	5	3
Zorich, Chris, Chi	0	0	1	0	1

Yards includes aborted plays, own recoveries and opponents' recoveries.

SACKS

Most Sacks

AFC: 14.0—Kevin Greene, Pittsburgh

NFC: 13.5—Ken Harvey, Washington
John Randle, Minnesota

Most Sacks, Game

AFC: 4.0—Bruce Smith, Buffalo at Houston, September 18
Alfred Williams, Cincinnati at Pittsburgh, October 16

NFC: 4.0—Charles Haley, Dallas at Pittsburgh, September 4

Team Champion

AFC: 55—Pittsburgh

NFC: 47—Dallas

AFC SACKS—TEAM

	Sacks	Yards
Pittsburgh	55	382
San Diego	43	253
New England	39	290
Kansas City	39	234

	Sacks	Yards
L.A. Raiders	38	284
Cleveland	38	268
Cincinnati	31	210
Houston	31	168
Miami	29	160
N.Y. Jets	29	201
Indianapolis	29	218
Seattle	29	206
Buffalo	25	152
Denver	23	141
AFC Total	478	3167
AFC Average	34.1	226.2

NFC SACKS—TEAM

	Sacks	Yards
Dallas	47	299
Philadelphia	42	265
San Francisco	38	255
Green Bay	37	276
New Orleans	36	196
Minnesota	36	250
Arizona	35	272
Atlanta	32	229
Detroit	28	199
Washington	28	165
Chicago	28	175
N.Y. Giants	26	169
L.A. Rams	26	159
Tampa Bay	20	114
NFC Total	459	3023
NFC Average	32.8	215.9
League Total	937	6190
League Average	33.5	221.1

NFL TOP TEN LEADERS - SACKS

	Total
Greene, Kevin, Pitt	14.0
Harvey, Ken, Wash	13.5
Randle, John, Minn	13.5
Haley, Charles, Dall	12.5
O'Neal, Leslie, SD	12.5
Smith, Neil, KC	11.5
Mims, Chris, SD	11.0
Smith, Chuck, Atl	11.0
Thomas, Derrick, KC	11.0
Conner, Darion, NO	10.5
Jones, Sean, GB	10.5

AFC SACKS—INDIVIDUAL

Greene, Kevin, Pitt	14.0
O'Neal, Leslie, SD	12.5
Smith, Neil, KC	11.5
Mims, Chris, SD	11.0
Thomas, Derrick, KC	11.0
Burnett, Rob, Cle	10.0
Lloyd, Greg, Pitt	10.0
Smith, Bruce, Buff	10.0
Cross, Jeff, Mia	9.5
McGlockton, Chester, LA Raid	9.5
Slade, Chris, NE	9.5
Williams, Alfred, Cin	9.5
Bennett, Tony, Ind	9.0
Brown, Chad, Pitt	8.5
Lathon, Lamar, Hou	8.5
Fletcher, Simon, Den	7.0
Mickell, Darren, KC	7.0
Seals, Ray, Pitt	7.0
Lageman, Jeff, NYJ	6.5
Lee, Shawn, SD	6.5
Childress, Ray, Hou	6.0
Coleman, Marco, Mia	6.0
Davidson, Kenny, Hou	6.0
Dronett, Shane, Den	6.0
Jones, Mike, NE	6.0
Lewis, Mo, NYJ	6.0
McCoy, Tony, Ind	6.0
Smith, Anthony, LA Raid	6.0
Hansen, Phil, Buff	5.5
Seau, Junior, SD	5.5
Wilkinson, Dan, Cin	5.5
Bennett, Cornelius, Buff	5.0
Harrison, Nolan, LA Raid	5.0
Siragusa, Tony, Ind	5.0
Francis, James, Cin	4.5
McGinest, Willie, NE	4.5
Pleasant, Anthony, Cle	4.5
Sinclair, Mike, Sea	4.5
Adams, Sam, Sea	4.0
Griffin, Don, Cle	4.0
Jones, Aaron, NE	4.0
Kennedy, Cortez, Sea	4.0
Perry, Michael Dean, Cle	4.0
Houston, Bobby, NYJ	3.5
Sabb, Dwayne, NE	3.5
Ball, Jerry, LA Raid	3.0
Bowens, Tim, Mia	3.0
Cox, Bryan, Mia	3.0
Fredrickson, Rob, LA Raid	3.0
Goad, Tim, NE	3.0
Hasty, James, NYJ	3.0
Jones, James, Cle	3.0
Kirkland, Levon, Pitt	3.0
Montgomery, Glenn, Hou	3.0
Phillips, Joe, KC	3.0
Spitulski, Bob, Sea	3.0
Tovar, Steve, Cin	3.0
Washington, Marvin, NYJ	3.0
Woodson, Rod, Pitt	3.0
Barrow, Micheal, Hou	2.5
Edwards, Antonio, Sea	2.5
Footman, Dan, Cle	2.5
Johnson, Pepper, Cle	2.5
Smith, Al, Hou	2.5
Stephens, Rod, Sea	2.5
Veasey, Craig, Mia	2.5
Washington, Ted, Den	2.5
Alberts, Trev, Ind	2.0
Anderson, Eddie, LA Raid	2.0
Buckner, Brentson, Pitt	2.0
Collins, Mark, KC	2.0
Gildon, Jason, Pitt	2.0
Hasselbach, Harald, Den	2.0
Hurst, Maurice, NE	2.0
McDaniels, Pellom, KC	2.0
Moss, Winston, LA Raid	2.0
Nash, Joe, Sea	2.0
Reynolds, Ricky, NE	2.0
Rucker, Keith, Cin	2.0
Singleton, Chris, Mia	2.0
Stams, Frank, Cle	2.0
Steed, Joel, Pitt	2.0
Wallace, Aaron, LA Raid	2.0
White, Alberto, LA Raid	2.0
White, Reggie, SD	2.0
Wright, Jeff, Buff	2.0
Banks, Carl, Cle	1.5
Biekert, Greg, LA Raid	1.5
Bishop, Blaine, Hou	1.5
Brown, Vincent, NE	1.5
Casillas, Tony, NYJ	1.5
Johnson, Raylee, SD	1.5
Jones, Roger, Cin	1.5
McCrary, Michael, Sea	1.5
Mecklenburg, Karl, Den	1.5
Porter, Rufus, Sea	1.5
Williams, Gerald, Pitt	1.5
Wooden, Terry, Sea	1.5
Alexander, Elijah, Den	1.0
Atkins, Gene, Mia	1.0
Barber, Kurt, NYJ	1.0
Barnett, Oliver, Buff	1.0
Barnett, Troy, NE	1.0
Bradford, Ronnie, Den	1.0
Buchanan, Ray, Ind	1.0
Copeland, John, Cin	1.0
Coryatt, Quentin, Ind	1.0
Dixon, Gerald, Cle	1.0
Emtman, Steve, Ind	1.0
Figures, Deon, Pitt	1.0
Frase, Paul, NYJ	1.0
Green, Victor, NYJ	1.0
Herrod, Jeff, Ind	1.0
Jackson, Steve, Hou	1.0
Jamison, George, KC	1.0
Johnson, Bill, Cle	1.0
Jones, Henry, Buff	1.0
Krumrie, Tim, Cin	1.0
Lake, Carnell, Pitt	1.0
Lewis, Albert, LA Raid	1.0
Lott, Ronnie, NYJ	1.0
McDonald, Devon, Ind	1.0
McDonald, Ricardo, Cin	1.0
Noga, Al, Ind	1.0
Nunn, Freddie Joe, Ind	1.0
Oliver, Louis, Cin	1.0
Parrella, John, SD	1.0
Pitts, Mike, NE	1.0
Robinson, Eugene, Sea	1.0
Robinson, Jeff, Den	1.0
Saleaumua, Dan, KC	1.0
Smith, Dennis, Den	1.0
Smith, Frankie, Mia	1.0
Thompson, Bennie, Cle	1.0
Trapp, James, LA Raid	1.0
Turner, Eric, Cle	1.0
Williams, Brent, Sea	1.0
Williams, Darryl, Cin	1.0
Young, Lonnie, SD	1.0
Agnew, Ray, NE	0.5
Davis, Reuben, SD	0.5
Evans, Donald, NYJ	0.5
Jones, Marvin, NYJ	0.5
Miller, Les, SD	0.5
Oglesby, Alfred, NYJ	0.5
Smith, Rod, NE	0.5
Washington, Mickey, Buff	0.5
Williams, Jerrol, KC	0.5

Team sacks credited to Miami and San Diego.

NFC SACKS—INDIVIDUAL

Harvey, Ken, Wash	13.5
Randle, John, Minn	13.5
Haley, Charles, Dall	12.5
Smith, Chuck, Atl	11.0
Conner, Darion, NO	10.5
Jones, Sean, GB	10.5
Martin, Wayne, NO	10.0
Fuller, William, Phil	9.5
Harmon, Andy, Phil	9.0
Stubblefield, Dana, SF	8.5
Geathers, Jumpy, Atl	8.0
Jeffcoat, Jim, Dall	8.0
White, Reggie, GB	8.0
Armstrong, Trace, Chi	7.5
Paup, Bryce, GB	7.5
Bankston, Michael, Ariz	7.0
Doleman, Chris, Atl	7.0
Hennings, Chad, Dall	7.0
Spellman, Alonzo, Chi	7.0
Swann, Eric, Ariz	7.0
Thomas, Broderick, Det	7.0
Thomas, Henry, Minn	7.0
Hamilton, Keith, NYG	6.5
Howard, Erik, NYG	6.5
Turnbull, Renaldo, NO	6.5
Young, Robert, LA Rams	6.5
Joyner, Seth, Ariz	6.0
Simmons, Clyde, Ariz	6.0
Thomas, William, Phil	6.0
Young, Bryant, SF	6.0
Grossman, Burt, Phil	5.5
Pritchett, Kelvin, Det	5.5
Tolbert, Tony, Dall	5.5
Zorich, Chris, Chi	5.5
Jones, Jimmie, LA Rams	5.0
Strahan, Michael, NYG	4.5
Woods, Tony, Wash	4.5
Culpepper, Brad, TB	4.0
Fontenot, Albert, Chi	4.0
Hall, Rhett, SF	4.0
Lett, Leon, Dall	4.0
Smith, Darrin, Dall	4.0
Warren, Frank, NO	4.0
Barker, Roy, Minn	3.5
Jackson, Rickey, SF	3.5
Kelly, Todd, SF	3.5
Swilling, Pat, Det	3.5
Armstead, Jessie, NYG	3.0
Brown, Dennis, SF	3.0
Brown, Gilbert, GB	3.0
Curry, Eric, TB	3.0
Dotson, Santana, TB	3.0
Flores, Mike, Phil	3.0
Gilbert, Sean, LA Rams	3.0
Harris, James, Minn	3.0
Maryland, Russell, Dall	3.0
Miller, Jamir, Ariz	3.0
Owens, Dan, Det	3.0
Porcher, Robert, Det	3.0
Wheeler, Mark, TB	3.0
McMichael, Steve, GB	2.5
Robinson, Gerald, LA Rams	2.5
Romanowski, Bill, Phil	2.5
Scroggins, Tracy, Det	2.5
Wilson, Bobby, Wash	2.5
Wilson, Karl, TB	2.5
Archambeau, Lester, Atl	2.0
Del Rio, Jack, Minn	2.0

Dent, Richard, SF	2.0
Harris, Robert, Minn	2.0
Harris, Tim, SF	2.0
Kelly, Joe, LA Rams	2.0
Marshall, Leonard, Wash	2.0
Stokes, Fred, LA Rams	2.0
Townsend, Greg, Phil	2.0
Wilson, Troy, SF	2.0
Bussey, Barney, TB	1.5
Collins, Andre, Wash	1.5
Davey, Don, GB	1.5
Dillard, Stacey, NYG	1.5
Douglass, Maurice, Chi	1.5
Hill, Eric, Ariz	1.5
Johnson, Mike, Det	1.5
McDaniel, Ed, Minn	1.5
Phifer, Roman, LA Rams	1.5
Ahanotu, Chidi, TB	1.0
Bates, Bill, Dall	1.0
Beamon, Willie, NYG	1.0
Blades, Bennie, Det	1.0
Brooks, Michael, NYG	1.0
Buck, Vince, NO	1.0
Butler, LeRoy, GB	1.0
Carter, Marty, TB	1.0
Conlan, Shane, LA Rams	1.0
Edwards, Dixon, Dall	1.0
Epps, Tory, Chi	1.0
Evans, Doug, GB	1.0
Farr, D'Marco, LA Rams	1.0
Fox, Mike, NYG	1.0
Glenn, Vencie, Minn	1.0
Hager, Britt, Phil	1.0
Harper, Roger, Atl	1.0
Hayworth, Tracy, Det	1.0
Hoage, Terry, Ariz	1.0
Jenkins, Carlos, Minn	1.0
Jeter, Tommy, Phil	1.0
Johnson, Joe, NO	1.0
Johnson, Tim, Wash	1.0
Koonce, George, GB	1.0
Legette, Tyrone, NO	1.0
Mann, Charles, SF	1.0
Marion, Brock, Dall	1.0
Marshall, Wilber, Ariz	1.0
Matthews, Clay, Atl	1.0
McCants, Keith, Ariz	1.0
Mills, Sam, NO	1.0
Nickerson, Hardy, TB	1.0
Nottage, Dexter, Wash	1.0
Ottis, Brad, LA Rams	1.0
Palmer, Sterling, Wash	1.0
Ross, Kevin, Atl	1.0
Smith, Otis, Phil	1.0
Smith, Vinson, Chi	1.0
Thomas, Mark, SF	1.0
Tubbs, Winfred, NO	1.0
Walker, Darnell, Atl	1.0
Widmer, Corey, NYG	1.0
Wilkins, Gabe, GB	1.0
Wilson, Bernard, Ariz	1.0
Woodall, Lee, SF	1.0
Zordich, Mike, Phil	1.0
Coleman, Monte, Wash	0.5
Evans, Byron, Phil	0.5
Hanks, Merton, SF	0.5
Hollinquest, Lamont, Wash	0.5
Lynch, Lorenzo, Ariz	0.5
Mangum, John, Chi	0.5
Rocker, David, LA Rams	0.5
Sheppard, Ashley, Minn	0.5

Team sack credited to Minnesota.

1994 NFL PAID ATTENDANCE BREAKDOWN

	Games	Attendance	Average
AFC Preseason	12	561,287	46,774
NFC Preseason	11	596,086	54,190
AFC-NFC Preseason, Interconference	38	2,042,718	53,756
NFL Preseason Total	**61**	**3,200,091**	**52,461**
AFC Regular Season	86	5,454,624	63,426
NFC Regular Season	86	5,281,866	61,417
AFC-NFC Regular Season, Interconference	52	3,293,945	63,345
NFL Regular Season Total	**224**	***14,030,435**	***62,636**
AFC Wild Card Playoffs	2		
Kansas at Miami		73,762	
New England at Cleveland		78,473	
AFC Divisional Playoffs	2		
Miami at San Diego		62,303	
Cleveland at Pittsburgh		60,478	
AFC Championship Game	1		
San Diego at Pittsburgh		60,654	
NFC Wild Card Playoffs	2		
Detroit at Green Bay		59,032	
Chicago at Minnesota		61,225	
NFC Divisional Playoffs	2		
Chicago at San Francisco		67,420	
Green Bay at Dallas		63,869	
NFC Championship Game	1		
Dallas at San Francisco		69,294	
Super Bowl XXIX at Miami, Florida	1		
San Diego vs. San Francisco		74,107	
AFC-NFC Pro Bowl at Honolulu, Hawaii	1	49,121	
NFL Postseason Total	**12**	**779,738**	
NFL All Games	**297**	***18,010,264**	**60,641**

**All-time record*

ONE MILLION PLUS CLUB

During the 1994 season, 14 clubs drew a combined home and away paid attendance of more than 1 million. The Kansas City Chiefs drew an NFL-leading 1,180,596 fans in 1994.

Team	Total Paid Home Attendance	Total Paid Visiting Attendance	Total Paid Attendance
Kansas City	626,612	553,984	1,180,596
New York Jets	614,281	496,302	1,110,583
Denver	577,101	525,562	1,102,663
Buffalo	586,539	510,544	1,097,083
Miami	585,195	510,389	1,095,584
New York Giants	615,321	479,709	1,095,030
Chicago	528,050	550,746	1,078,796
San Francisco	545,297	528,175	1,073,472
Cleveland	569,831	502,377	1,072,208
Detroit	555,957	511,252	1,067,209
Dallas	506,553	525,622	1,032,175
Philadelphia	518,027	506,572	1,024,599
Minnesota	502,079	515,414	1,017,493
Green Bay	459,003	542,242	1,001,245

Note: *For complete year-by-year paid attendance and attendance records,* *see page 350.*

Inside the Numbers

INSIDE THE NUMBERS

THE NFL, A THROUGH Z

Aeneas Williams of the Arizona Cardinals had 9 interceptions in 1994 to share the league lead with Cleveland's Eric Turner. Williams became the first Cardinals player to lead the NFL in that category since Pro Football Hall of Fame member Larry Wilson did it in 1966.

Brett Perriman of Detroit became the first player in NFL history to score a pair of two-point conversions in the same game when he did it against Green Bay on November 6, 1994.

Cris Carter's 122 receptions in 1994 not only set an individual one-season NFL record; he and Minnesota teammate Jake Reed (85 receptions) combined to set an all-time NFL record of 207 receptions by two teammates in one season.

Dallas's 35-9 victory over the Packers in an NFC Divisional Playoff Game last January extended the Cowboys' all-time record for postseason victories to 28. That's 7 more than the next-highest total of 21, shared by the Redskins, Raiders, and 49ers.

Eric Davis had at least 1 interception in each of San Francisco's three 1994 postseason games, becoming the first player to accomplish that since Washington linebacker Kurt Gouveia in the 1991 postseason.

Fuad Reveiz of Minnesota and John Carney of San Diego represented their respective conferences as the kickers in the 1995 AFC-NFC Pro Bowl this past February. Ironically, Carney replaced Reveiz as the Chargers' kicker during the 1990 season; Reveiz signed with the Vikings a month later.

George Seifert is the tenth head coach in NFL history to have won at least two Super Bowls. Those 10 head coaches have accounted for 24 of the 29 Super Bowl victories.

Hugh Millen of Denver completed 20 consecutive passes over a two-game span against the Raiders and the 49ers last December, the longest such streak since Joe Montana established the NFL record of 22 consecutive completions in 1987.

Irving Fryar of Miami gained 211 yards on receptions in the 1994 season opener against New England, which stood up as the highest one-game total in the NFL last season. Only three active receivers in the NFL in 1994 have had more than one 200-yard game: Jerry Rice has had three; Gary Clark and Art Monk, two each.

Jackie Slater played his nineteenth season with the Rams in 1994, tying the NFL record of 19 seasons with one team. That mark was set by Jim Marshall of the Minnesota Vikings from 1961 to 1979.

Ken Norton, Jr., is the only player in NFL history to play on a Super Bowl-winning team in each of three consecutive seasons (1992-93 with Dallas and 1994 with San Francisco).

Leslie O'Neal is one of three players to have at least three games of 4-or-more sacks since 1982, when the NFL began compiling individual sacks. The others are Derrick Thomas and Reggie White.

Morten Andersen has scored at least 1 point in his last 174 games, just 12 games shy of the NFL record held by Jim Breech. Andersen has not been blanked since December 4, 1983.

NFL teams made 59 of 116 two-point conversions (50.9 percent) during the 1994 regular season, with the Dolphins leading the league with 6 two-point conversions.

Only two of the 40 playoff teams that have been without a first-round bye have reached the AFC-NFC Championship Games during the 1990s—Buffalo reached the Super Bowl following the 1992 season; Kansas City reached the AFC Championship Game following the 1993 season.

Pittsburgh kicker Gary Anderson has made 13 consecutive field-goal attempts in postseason play, two shy of the all-time record held by former Dallas kicker Rafael Septien.

Qadry Ismail of Minnesota caught 23 of his total of 45 receptions on third-down plays last season, the highest such percentage by any NFL receiver (minimum of 32 receptions for the season).

Robert Bailey of the Rams scored a touchdown on a 103-yard punt return at New Orleans last October 23. That stands as the only punt return of his four-year NFL career.

San Diego became the first team in NFL history to reach the Super Bowl after trailing in the fourth quarter of each of its two previous playoff games.

Ten teams have played turnover-free Super Bowls, including the 49ers in Super Bowl XXIX. Excluding Super Bowl XXV, in which neither the Giants nor the Bills committed a turnover, each of the other eight turnover-free teams won Super Bowls.

Under the direction of Marv Levy, the Kansas City Chiefs and Buffalo Bills have won 117 regular-season games. That gives Levy the most wins by any coach in NFL history whose first win did not come until after his fiftieth birthday.

Vince Evans of the Los Angeles Raiders was the oldest active quarterback (39 years old) in the NFL last season, although he did not start any games. The oldest quarterback to start was Kansas City's Joe Montana, who was 38.

William Floyd scored 5 touchdowns in the 1994 postseason, the most postseason touchdowns scored by any rookie in NFL history.

XXIX Super Bowls have come and gone, but there still has not been a Super Bowl decided in overtime. Next chance for one: Super Bowl XXX at Sun Devil Stadium in Tempe, Arizona, on January 28, 1996.

Youngest player in the NFL in 1994 was Cincinnati linebacker Kevin Jefferson, who did not turn 21 years old until three weeks after the close of the season.

Zefross Moss of the Colts was the only player active in the NFL in 1994 whose first name starts with the letter "Z".

TEAMS THAT FINISHED IN FIRST PLACE IN THEIR DIVISION THE SEASON AFTER FINISHING IN LAST PLACE

Season	Team	Record	Previous Season
1967	Houston	9 - 4 - 1	*3 - 11
1968	Minnesota	8 - 6	3 - 8 - 3
1970	Cincinnati	8 - 6	4 - 9 - 1
1970	San Francisco	10 - 3 - 1	4 - 8 - 2
1972	Green Bay	10 - 4	4 - 8 - 2
1975	Baltimore	10 - 4	2 - 12
1979	Tampa Bay	10 - 6	5 - 11
1981	Cincinnati	12 - 4	6 - 10
1987	Indianapolis	9 - 6	3 - 13
1988	Cincinnati	12 - 4	4 - 11
1990	Cincinnati	9 - 7	8 - 8
1991	Denver	12 - 4	5 - 11
1992	San Diego	11 - 5	4 - 12
1993	Detroit	10 - 6	5 - 11

**tied for last place*

RECORDS OF NFL TEAMS, 1985-94

AFC	W - L - T	Pct.	Division Titles	Playoff Berths	Postseason Record	Super Bowl Record
Denver	92 - 66 - 1	.582	4	5	7-5	0-3
Miami	92 - 67 - 0	.579	3	4	4-4	0-0
Buffalo	90 - 69 - 0	.566	5	6	10-6	0-4
L.A. Raiders	87 - 72 - 0	.547	2	4	2-4	0-0
Kansas City	83 - 74 - 2	.528	1	6	3-6	0-0
Cleveland	83 - 75 - 1	.525	4	6	4-6	0-0
Pittsburgh	83 - 76 - 0	.522	2	4	2-4	0-0
Houston	82 - 77 - 0	.516	2	7	3-7	0-0
Seattle	73 - 86 - 0	.459	1	2	0-2	0-0
San Diego	72 - 87 - 0	.453	2	2	3-2	0-1
N.Y. Jets	71 - 87 - 1	.450	0	3	1-3	0-0
New England	68 - 91 - 0	.428	1	3	3-3	0-1
Cincinnati	64 - 95 - 0	.403	2	2	3-2	0-1
Indianapolis	63 - 96 - 0	.396	1	1	0-1	0-0
NFC	**W - L - T**	**Pct.**	**Division Titles**	**Playoff Berths**	**Postseason Record**	**Super Bowl Record**
San Francisco	118 - 40 - 1	.745	8	9	12-6	3-0
Chicago	101 - 58 - 0	.635	5	7	6-6	1-0
N.Y. Giants	99 - 60 - 0	.623	3	5	8-3	2-0
Washington	90 - 69 - 0	.566	2	5	10-3	2-0
Minnesota	89 - 70 - 0	.560	3	6	3-6	0-0
New Orleans	89 - 70 - 0	.560	1	4	0-4	0-0
Philadelphia	86 - 72 - 1	.544	1	4	1-4	0-0
Dallas	83 - 76 - 0	.522	4	5	8-3	2-0
L.A. Rams	71 - 88 - 0	.447	1	4	3-4	0-0
Detroit	69 - 90 - 0	.434	2	3	1-3	0-0
Green Bay	68 - 90 - 1	.431	0	2	2-2	0-0
Arizona	56 - 102 - 1	.355	0	0	0-0	0-0
Atlanta	56 - 102 - 1	.355	0	1	1-1	0-0
Tampa Bay	43 - 116 - 0	.270	0	0	0-0	0-0

Arizona totals include St. Louis, 1985-87, and Phoenix, 1988-93

HOME RECORDS, 1985-94

AFC	W-L-T	Pct.	NFC	W-L-T	Pct.
Denver	59-21-0	.738	San Francisco	60-19-0	.759
Kansas City	54-25-0	.684	Chicago	57-23-0	.713
Buffalo	54-26-0	.675	N.Y. Giants	57-23-0	.713
Houston	53-26-0	.671	Minnesota	52-28-0	.650
Miami	52-27-0	.658	Washington	49-30-0	.620
Pittsburgh	52-27-0	.658	New Orleans	47-32-0	.595
L.A. Raiders	48-32-0	.600	Philadelphia	47-32-1	.594
Cleveland	46-32-1	.589	Dallas	44-35-0	.557
Seattle	44-36-0	.550	Green Bay	40-39-1	.506
Cincinnati	41-39-0	.513	Detroit	39-40-0	.494
San Diego	40-39-0	.506	L.A. Rams	39-40-0	.494
N.Y. Jets	39-40-1	.494	Atlanta	37-42-1	.469
New England	39-41-0	.488	Arizona	34-45-0	.430
Indianapolis	35-45-0	.438	Tampa Bay	27-52-0	.342

Arizona totals include St. Louis, 1985-87, and Phoenix, 1988-93

ROAD RECORDS, 1985-94

AFC	W-L-T	Pct.	NFC	W-L-T	Pct.
Miami	40-40-0	.500	San Francisco	58-21-1	.731
L.A. Raiders	39-40-0	.494	Chicago	44-35-0	.557
Cleveland	37-43-0	.463	N.Y. Giants	42-37-0	.532
Buffalo	36-43-0	.456	New Orleans	42-38-0	.525
Denver	33-45-1	.424	Washington	41-39-0	.513
N.Y. Jets	32-47-0	.405	Philadelphia	39-40-0	.494
San Diego	32-48-0	.400	Dallas	39-41-0	.488

AFC	W-L-T	Pct.	NFC	W-L-T	Pct.
Pittsburgh	31-49-0	.388	Minnesota	37-42-0	.468
Kansas City	29-49-2	.375	L.A. Rams	32-48-0	.400
New England	29-50-0	.367	Detroit	30-50-0	.375
Seattle	29-50-0	.367	Green Bay	28-51-0	.354
Houston	29-51-0	.363	Arizona	22-57-1	.281
Indianapolis	28-51-0	.354	Atlanta	19-60-0	.241
Cincinnati	23-56-0	.291	Tampa Bay	16-64-0	.200

Arizona totals include St. Louis, 1985-87, and Phoenix, 1988-93

RECORDS BY MONTHS, 1985-94

AFC	Sept. W-L-T	Oct. W-L-T	Nov. W-L-T	Dec. W-L-T	Total W-L-T	Pct.
Denver	22-14-1	25-15	26-16	19-21	92-66-1	.582
Miami	20-16	26-14	25-18	21-19	92-67-0	.579
Buffalo	25-12	23-15	25-19	17-23	90-69-0	.566
L.A. Raiders	18-19	26-15	20-21	23-17	87-72-0	.547
Kansas City	23-14	14-26-1	21-19-1	25-15	83-74-2	.528
Cleveland	19-18	26-14	19-22-1	19-21	83-75-1	.525
Pittsburgh	16-21	20-20	24-19	23-16	83-76-0	.522
Houston	17-20	21-19	22-20	22-18	82-77-0	.516
Seattle	17-20	21-21	16-24	19-21	73-86-0	.459
San Diego	14-23	16-25	23-19	19-20	72-87-0	.453
N.Y. Jets	20-17	17-22-1	24-20	10-28	71-87-1	.450
New England	12-25	16-24	20-22	20-20	68-91-0	.428
Cincinnati	15-21	14-27	17-25	18-22	64-95-0	.403
Indianapolis	8-28	19-22	14-28	22-18	63-96-0	.396

NFC	Sept. W-L-T	Oct. W-L-T	Nov. W-L-T	Dec. W-L-T	Total W-L-T	Pct.
San Francisco	25-12	30-9-1	30-11	33-8	118-40-1	.745
Chicago	28-9	27-12	30-14	16-23	101-58-0	.635
N.Y. Giants	24-11	23-18	26-16	26-15	99-60-0	.623
Washington	21-15	23-17	22-21	24-16	90-69-0	.566
Minnesota	23-14	19-21	25-18	22-17	89-70-0	.560
New Orleans	21-16	22-18	24-18	22-18	89-70-0	.560
Philadelphia	18-17	22-19	24-19	22-17-1	86-72-1	.544
Dallas	19-16	24-18	21-24	19-18	83-76-0	.522
L.A. Rams	23-14	16-24	16-26	16-24	71-88-0	.447
Detroit	16-22	17-22	16-28	20-18	69-90-0	.434
Green Bay	10-26-1	18-21	21-22	19-21	68-90-1	.431
Arizona	13-23	14-28	15-28	14-23-1	56-102-1	.355
Atlanta	13-24	14-25-1	17-25	12-28	56-102-1	.355
Tampa Bay	12-25	9-31	11-32	11-28	43-116-0	.270

Arizona totals include St. Louis, 1985-87, and Phoenix, 1988-93
December totals include January

TAKEAWAYS/GIVEAWAYS IN 1985-94

AFC	Takeaways Int.	Takeaways Fum.	Takeaways Total	Giveaways Int.	Giveaways Fum.	Giveaways Total	Net.Diff.
Kansas City	194	181	375	157	143	300	75
Pittsburgh	214	156	370	171	141	312	58
N.Y. Jets	192	160	352	156	156	312	40
Denver	185	151	336	182	139	321	15
Cleveland	178	132	310	157	156	313	- 3
Seattle	185	162	347	197	157	354	- 7
Indianapolis	160	160	320	191	143	334	- 14
San Diego	197	133	330	209	135	344	- 14
Cincinnati	163	141	304	172	149	321	- 17
New England	176	170	346	220	149	369	- 23
Houston	198	155	353	211	172	383	- 30
Buffalo	188	146	334	196	175	371	- 37
L.A. Raiders	160	126	286	190	143	333	- 47
Miami	168	124	292	191	155	346	- 54

NFC	Takeaways Int.	Takeaways Fum.	Takeaways Total	Giveaways Int.	Giveaways Fum.	Giveaways Total	Net.Diff.
Philadelphia	234	167	401	174	145	319	82
San Francisco	213	137	350	138	139	277	73
Minnesota	235	148	383	193	132	325	58
N.Y. Giants	188	137	325	144	127	271	54
New Orleans	197	176	373	188	145	333	40
Chicago	222	133	355	190	157	347	8
Detroit	178	160	338	200	153	353	- 15
Washington	211	110	321	201	137	338	- 17
Green Bay	183	171	354	208	171	379	- 25
Dallas	166	139	305	194	137	331	- 26
L.A. Rams	182	129	311	177	160	337	- 26
Atlanta	185	132	317	205	149	354	- 37
Arizona	150	143	293	207	134	341	- 48
Tampa Bay	163	161	324	246	141	387	- 63

Arizona totals include St. Louis, 1985-87, and Phoenix, 1988-93

HIGH AND LOW SINGLE-GAME YARDAGE TOTALS, 1985-94

Most Total Yards, Game
676 Washington vs. Detroit, Nov. 4, 1990 (OT)
621 Cincinnati vs. N.Y. Jets, Dec. 21, 1986
598 San Francisco vs. Buffalo, Sept. 13, 1992
597 N.Y. Jets vs. Miami, Nov. 27, 1988
593 San Diego vs. L.A. Raiders, Nov. 10, 1985 (OT)

Fewest Total Yards, Game
53 Pittsburgh vs. Cleveland, Sept. 10, 1989
60 Detroit vs. Minnesota, Nov. 24, 1988
62 Seattle vs. Dallas, Oct. 11, 1992
65 Tampa Bay vs. Green Bay, Dec. 1, 1985
65 Seattle vs. New England, Dec. 4, 1988

Most Yards Rushing, Game
356 L.A. Raiders vs. Seattle, Nov. 30, 1987
315 Buffalo vs. Atlanta, Nov. 22, 1992
310 Kansas City vs. Detroit, Oct. 14, 1990
307 Washington vs. Atlanta, Nov. 3, 1985
305 Pittsburgh vs. Miami, Dec. 18, 1988

Fewest Yards Rushing, Game
0 Buffalo vs. Chicago, Oct. 2, 1988
1 Tampa Bay vs. Washington, Oct. 22, 1989
2 New England vs. New Orleans, Nov. 30, 1986
4 Indianapolis vs. Detroit, Sept. 22, 1991
6 N.Y. Giants vs. L.A. Rams, Nov. 12, 1989

Most Yards Passing, Game
521 Miami vs. N.Y. Jets, Oct. 23, 1988
505 Houston vs. Kansas City, Dec. 16, 1990
494 San Diego vs. Seattle, Sept. 15, 1985
483 Cincinnati vs. L.A. Rams, Oct. 7, 1990
482 Washington vs. Detroit, Nov. 4, 1990 (OT)

Fewest Yards Passing, Game
–22 Atlanta vs. Chicago, Nov. 24, 1985
–13 Cincinnati vs. San Diego, Oct. 4, 1987
4 St. Louis vs. New Orleans, Oct. 11, 1987
11 Tampa Bay vs. Green Bay, Dec. 1, 1985
15 New England vs. Atlanta, Nov. 29, 1992

NFL INDIVIDUAL LEADERS, 1985-94

Points
1,121 Morten Andersen
1,055 Gary Anderson
1,046 Nick Lowery
1,002 Kevin Butler
949 Norm Johnson

Touchdowns
139 Jerry Rice
80 Herschel Walker
76 Marcus Allen
75 Emmitt Smith
71 Neal Anderson

Field Goals
262 Morten Andersen
248 Gary Anderson
237 Nick Lowery
220 Kevin Butler
195 Norm Johnson

Rushes
2,227 Eric Dickerson
2,018 Thurman Thomas
1,907 Herschel Walker
1,784 Marcus Allen
1,763 Barry Sanders

Rushing Yards
9,346 Eric Dickerson
8,724 Thurman Thomas
8,672 Barry Sanders
7,996 Herschel Walker
7,183 Emmitt Smith

Rushing TDs
71 Emmitt Smith
65 Marcus Allen
62 Barry Sanders
60 Herschel Walker
58 Eric Dickerson

Passes
5,189 Dan Marino
4,745 John Elway
4,697 Warren Moon
4,189 Boomer Esiason
3,942 Jim Kelly

Completions
3,069 Dan Marino
2,744 Warren Moon
2,693 John Elway
2,397 Jim Kelly
2,389 Boomer Esiason

Passing Yards
37,879 Dan Marino
34,611 Warren Moon
33,475 John Elway
31,344 Boomer Esiason
29,527 Jim Kelly

TD Passes
260 Dan Marino
204 Boomer Esiason
202 Warren Moon
201 Jim Kelly
174 John Elway

Receptions
820 Jerry Rice
676 Andre Reed
662 Gary Clark
632 Art Monk
617 Henry Ellard

Reception Yards
13,275 Jerry Rice
10,331 Gary Clark
10,268 Henry Ellard
9,536 Andre Reed
8,484 Drew Hill

Receiving TDs
131 Jerry Rice
66 Andre Reed
65 Mark Clayton
65 Sterling Sharpe
63 Gary Clark

Interceptions
46 Ronnie Lott
41 Eugene Robinson
40 Dave Waymer
37 Gill Byrd
35 Deron Cherry

Sacks
145.0 Reggie White
116.0 Bruce Smith
106.0 Richard Dent
104.5 Lawrence Taylor
99.0 Kevin Greene

INSIDE THE NUMBERS

RECORDS FOR EACH CURRENT NFL TEAM FOR MOST POINTS IN A GAME (REGULAR SEASON ONLY)

***Note:** When the record has been achieved more than once, only the most recent game is shown; summaries are listed in alphabetical order by conference. Bold face indicates team holding record.*

BUFFALO BILLS
September 18, 1966, at Buffalo
Miami 3 7 0 14 — 24
Buffalo 21 27 3 7 — 58
TDs: Buff—Bobby Burnett 2, Butch Byrd 2, Jack Spikes 2, Bobby Crockett, Jack Kemp; Mia—Dave Kocourek, Bo Roberson, John Roderick. TD Passes: Buff—Jack Kemp, Daryle Lamonica; Mia—George Wilson 3. FGs: Buff—Booth Lusteg; Mia—Gene Mingo.

CINCINNATI BENGALS
December 17, 1989, at Cincinnati
Houston 0 0 0 7 — 7
Cincinnati 21 10 21 9 — 61
TDs: Cin—Eddie Brown 2, Eric Ball, James Brooks, Ira Hillary, Rodney Holman, Tim McGee, Craig Taylor; Hou—Lorenzo White. TD Passes: Cin—Boomer Esiason 4, Erik Wilhelm. FGs: Cin—Jim Breech 2.

CLEVELAND BROWNS
November 7, 1954, at Cleveland
Washington 0 3 0 0 — 3
Cleveland 13 14 21 14 — 62
TDs: Clev—Darrell Brewster 2, Mo Bassett, Ken Gorgal, Otto Graham, Dub Jones, Dante Lavelli, Curley Morrison. TD Passes: Clev—George Ratterman 3, Otto Graham. FGs: Clev—Lou Groza 2; Wash—Vic Janowicz.

DENVER BRONCOS
October 6, 1963, at Denver
San Diego 13 7 0 14 — 34
Denver 3 14 9 24 — 50
TDs: Den—Lionel Taylor 2, Goose Gonsoulin, Gene Prebola, Donnie Stone; SD—Keith Lincoln 2, Lance Alworth, Paul Lowe, Jacque MacKinnon. TD Passes: Den—John McCormick 3; SD—Tobin Rote 3, John Hadl 2. FGs: Den—Gene Mingo 5.

HOUSTON OILERS
December 9, 1990, at Houston
Cleveland 0 7 7 0 — 14
Houston 14 31 7 6 — 58
TDs: Hou—Lorenzo White 4, Ernest Givins, Leonard Harris, Tony Jones, Terry Kinard; Clev—Eric Metcalf 2. TD Passes: Hou—Warren Moon 2, Cody Carlson; Clev—Bernie Kosar. FG: Hou—Teddy Garcia.

INDIANAPOLIS COLTS
December 12, 1976, at Baltimore
Buffalo 3 3 7 7 — 20
Baltimore Colts 7 13 28 10 — 58
TDs: Balt—Roger Carr, Raymond Chester, Glenn Doughty, Roosevelt Leaks, Derrel Luce, Lydell Mitchell, Howard Stevens; Buff—Bob Chandler, O.J. Simpson. TD Passes: Balt—Bert Jones 3; Buff—Gary Marangi. FGs: Balt—Toni Linhart 3; Buff—George Jakowenko 2.

KANSAS CITY CHIEFS
September 7, 1963, at Denver
Kansas City 14 14 21 10 — 59
Denver 0 7 0 0 — 7
TDs: KC—Chris Burford 2, Frank Jackson 2, Dave Grayson, Abner Haynes, Sherrill Headrick, Curtis McClinton; Den—Lionel Taylor. TD Passes: KC—Len Dawson 4, Curtis McClinton; Den—Mickey Slaughter. FG: KC—Tommy Brooker.

LOS ANGELES RAIDERS
December 22, 1963, at Oakland
Houston 14 21 14 0 — 49
Oakland Raiders 7 28 7 10 — 52
TDs: Oak—Art Powell 4, Clem Daniels, Claude Gibson, Ken Herock; Hou—Willard Dewveall 2, Dave Smith 2, Charley Hennigan, Bob McLeod, Charley Tolar. TD Passes: Oak—Tom Flores 6; Hou—George Blanda 5. FG: Oak—Mike Mercer.

MIAMI DOLPHINS
November 24, 1977, at St. Louis
Miami 14 14 20 7 — 55
St. Louis 7 0 0 7 — 14
TDs: Mia—Nat Moore 3, Gary Davis, Duriel Harris, Leroy Harris, Benny Malone, Andre Tillman; StL—Ike Harris, Terry Metcalf. TD Passes: Mia—Bob Griese 6; StL—Jim Hart.

NEW ENGLAND PATRIOTS
September 9, 1979, at New England
New York Jets 3 0 0 0 — 3
New England 14 21 7 14 — 56
TDs: NE—Harold Jackson 3, Stanley Morgan 2, Allan Clark, Andy Johnson, Don Westbrook. TD Passes: NE—Steve Grogan 5, Tom Owen. FG: NYJ—Pat Leahy.

NEW YORK JETS
November 17, 1985, at New York
Tampa Bay 14 7 7 0 — 28
New York Jets 17 24 14 7 — 62
TDs: NYJ—Mickey Shuler 3, Johnny Hector 2, Tony Paige, Al Toon, Wesley Walker; TB—James Wilder 2, Kevin House, Calvin Magee. TD Passes: NYJ—Ken O'Brien 5; TB—Steve DeBerg 2. FGs: NYJ—Pat Leahy 2.

PITTSBURGH STEELERS
November 30, 1952, at Pittsburgh
New York Giants 0 0 7 0 — 7
Pittsburgh 14 14 7 28 — 63
TDs: Pitt—Lynn Chandnois 2, Dick Hensley 2, Jack Butler, George Hays, Ray Mathews, Ed Modzelewski, Elbie Nickel; NYG—Bill Stribling. TD Passes: Pitt—Jim Finks 4, Gary Kerkorian; NYG—Tom Landry.

SAN DIEGO CHARGERS
December 22, 1963, at San Diego
Denver 7 10 3 0 — 20
San Diego 10 16 10 22 — 58
TDs: SD—Paul Lowe 2, Chuck Allen, Bobby Jackson, Dave Kocourek, Keith Lincoln, Jacque MacKinnon; Den—Billy Joe, Donnie Stone. TD Passes: SD—John Hadl, Tobin Rote; Den—Don Breaux. FGs: SD—George Blair 3; Den—Gene Mingo 2.

SEATTLE SEAHAWKS
October 30, 1977, at Seattle
Buffalo 3 0 7 7 — 17
Seattle 14 28 7 7 — 56
TDs: Sea—Steve Largent 2, Duke Fergerson, Al Hunter, David Sims, Sherman Smith, Don Testerman, Jim Zorn; Buff—Joe Ferguson, John Kimbrough. TD Passes: Sea—Jim Zorn 4; Buff—Joe Ferguson. FG: Buff—Carson Long.

ARIZONA CARDINALS
November 13, 1949, at New York
Chicago Cardinals 7 31 14 13 — 65
New York Bulldogs 7 0 6 7 — 20
TDs: Chi—Red Cochran 2, Pat Harder 2, Bill Dewell, Mel Kutner, Bob Ravensburg, Vic Schwall, Charlie Trippi; NY—Joe Golding, Frank Muehlheuser, Johnny Rauch. TD Passes: Chi—Paul Christman 3, Jim Hardy 3; NY—Bobby Layne. FG: Chi—Pat Harder.

ATLANTA FALCONS
September 16, 1973, at New Orleans
Atlanta 0 24 21 17 — 62
New Orleans 0 0 7 0 — 7
TDs: Atl—Ken Burrow 2, Eddie Ray 2, Wes Chesson, Tom Hayes, Art Malone, Joe Profit; NO—Bill Butler. TD Passes: Atl—Dick Shiner 3, Bob Lee; NO—Archie Manning. FGs: Atl—Nick Mike-Mayer 2.

CHICAGO BEARS
December 7, 1980, at Chicago
Green Bay 0 7 0 0 — 7
Chicago 0 28 13 20 — 61
TDs: Chi—Walter Payton 3, Brian Baschnagel, Robin Earl, Roland Harper, Willie McClendon, Len Walterscheid, Rickey Watts; GB—James Lofton. TD Passes: Chi—Vince Evans 3; GB—Lynn Dickey.

DALLAS COWBOYS
October 12, 1980, at Dallas
San Francisco 0 7 0 7 — 14
Dallas 14 24 14 7 — 59
TDs: Dall—Drew Pearson 3, Ron Springs 2, Tony Dorsett, Billy Joe DuPree, Robert Newhouse; SF—Dwight Clark 2. TD Passes: Dall—Danny White 4; SF—Steve DeBerg 2. FG: Dall—Rafael Septien.

DETROIT LIONS
October 26, 1952, at Green Bay
Detroit 14 14 14 10 — 52
Green Bay 7 3 7 0 — 17
TDs: Det—Jug Girard 2, Bob Hoernschemeyer 2, Jack Christiansen, Jim Smith, Bill Swiacki; GB—Billy Howton, Jim Keane. TD Passes: Det—Bobby Layne 3; GB—Babe Parilli, Tobin Rote. FGs: Det—Pat Harder; GB—Bill Reichardt.

GREEN BAY PACKERS
October 7, 1945, at Milwaukee
Detroit 0 7 7 7 — 21
Green Bay 0 41 9 7 — 57
TDs: GB—Don Hutson 4, Charley Brock, Irv Comp, Ted Fritsch, Clyde Goodnight; Det—Chuck Fenenbock, John Greene, Bob Westfall. TD Passes: GB—Tex McKay 4, Lou Brock, Irv Comp; Det—Dave Ryan.

MINNESOTA VIKINGS
October 18, 1970, at Minnesota
Dallas 3 3 0 7 — 13
Minnesota 14 20 17 3 — 54
TDs: Minn—Clint Jones 2, Ed Sharockman 2, John Beasley, Dave Osborn; Dall—Calvin Hill. TD Pass: Minn—Gary Cuozzo. FGs: Minn—Fred Cox 4; Dall—Mike Clark 2.

NEW ORLEANS SAINTS
November 21, 1976, at Seattle
New Orleans 3 17 28 3 — 51
Seattle 6 0 7 14 — 27
TDs: NO—Bobby Douglass 2, Tony Galbreath, Chuck Muncie, Tom Myers, Elex Price; Sea—Sherman Smith 2, Steve Largent, Jim Zorn. TD Pass: Sea—Bill Munson. FGs: NO—Rich Szaro 3.

NEW YORK GIANTS
November 26, 1972, at New York
Philadelphia 3 7 0 0 — 10
New York Giants 14 24 10 14 — 62
TDs: NYG—Don Herrmann 2, Ron Johnson 2, Bob Tucker 2, Randy Johnson; Phil—Harold Jackson. TD Passes: NYG—Norm Snead 3, Randy Johnson 2; Phil—John Reaves. FGs: NYG—Pete Gogolak 2; Phil—Tom Dempsey.

PHILADELPHIA EAGLES
November 6, 1934, at Philadelphia
Cincinnati Reds 0 0 0 0 — 0
Philadelphia 26 6 12 20 — 64
TDs: Phil—Joe Carter 3, Swede Hanson 3, Marvin Ellstrom, Roger Kirkman, Ed Matesic, Ed Storm. TD Passes: Phil—Ed Matesic 2, Albert Weiner 2, Marvin Elstrom.

ST. LOUIS RAMS
October 22, 1950, at Los Angeles
Baltimore 13 0 7 7 — 27
Los Angeles 21 14 14 21 — 70
TDs: LA—Bob Boyd 2, Vitamin T. Smith 2, Tom Fears, Elroy (Crazylegs) Hirsch, Dick Hoerner, Ralph Pasquariello, Dan Towler, Bob Waterfield; Balt—Chet Mutryn 2, Adrian Burk, Billy Stone. TD Passes: LA—Norm Van Brocklin 2, Bob Waterfield 2, Glenn Davis; Balt—Adrian Burk 3.

SAN FRANCISCO 49ERS
October 18, 1992, at San Francisco
Atlanta 7 3 0 7 — 17
San Francisco 21 21 14 0 — 56
TDs: SF—Jerry Rice 3, Ricky Watters 3, Brent Jones, Tom Rathman; Atl—Michael Haynes, Jason Phillips. TD Passes: SF—Steve Young 3; Atl—Chris Miller, Wade Wilson. FG: Atl—Norm Johnson.

TAMPA BAY BUCCANEERS
September 13, 1987, at Tampa Bay
Atlanta 0 3 0 7 — 10
Tampa Bay 14 13 7 14 — 48
TDs: TB—Gerald Carter 2, Cliff Austin, Steve Bartalo, Mark Carrier, Phil Freeman, Calvin Magee; Atl—Stacey Bailey. TD Passes: TB—Steve DeBerg 5; Atl—Scott Campbell. FG: Atl—Mick Luckhurst.

WASHINGTON REDSKINS
November 27, 1966, at Washington
New York Giants 0 14 14 13 — 41
Washington 13 21 14 24 — 72
TDs: Wash—A.D. Whitfield 3, Brig Owens 2, Charley Taylor 2, Rickie Harris, Joe Don Looney, Bobby Mitchell; NYG—Allen Jacobs, Homer Jones, Dan Lewis, Joe Morrison, Aaron Thomas, Gary Wood. TD Passes: Wash—Sonny Jurgensen 3; NYG—Gary Wood 2, Tom Kennedy. FG: Wash—Charlie Gogolak.

NFL GAMES IN WHICH A TEAM HAS SCORED 60 OR MORE POINTS

(Home team in capitals)

Regular Season

WASHINGTON 72, New York Giants 41 .... November 27, 1966
LOS ANGELES RAMS 70, Baltimore 27 .... October 22, 1950
Chicago Cardinals 65, NEW YORK BULLDOGS 20 .... November 13, 1949
LOS ANGELES RAMS 65, Detroit 24 .... October 29, 1950
PHILADELPHIA 64, Cincinnati 0 .... November 6, 1934
CHICAGO CARDINALS 63, New York Giants 35 .... October 17, 1948
AKRON 62, Oorang 0 .... October 29,1922
PITTSBURGH 62, New York Giants 7 .... November 30, 1952
CLEVELAND 62, New York Giants 14 .... December 6, 1953
CLEVELAND 62, Washington 3 .... November 7, 1954
NEW YORK GIANTS 62, Philadelphia 10 .... November 26, 1972
Atlanta 62, NEW ORLEANS 7 .... September 16, 1973
NEW YORK JETS 62, Tampa Bay 28 .... November 17, 1985
CHICAGO 61, San Francisco 20 .... December 12, 1965
Cincinnati 61, HOUSTON 17 .... December 17, 1972
CHICAGO 61, Green Bay 7 .... December 7, 1980
CINCINNATI 61, Houston 7 .... December 17, 1989
ROCK ISLAND 60, Evansville 0 .... October 15, 1922
CHICAGO CARDINALS 60, Rochester 0 .... October 7, 1923

Postseason

Chicago Bears 73, WASHINGTON 0 .... December 8, 1940

YOUNGEST AND OLDEST PLAYERS IN NFL IN 1994

Ten Youngest Players	Birthdate	Games	Starts	Position
Kevin Jefferson, Cincinnati	1/14/74	6	0	LB
Jamir Miller, Arizona	11/19/73	16	0	LB
Sam Adams, Seattle	6/13/73	12	7	DE
Dan Wilkinson, Cincinnati	3/13/73	16	14	DT
Marshall Faulk, Indianapolis	2/26/73	16	16	RB
George Hegamin, Dallas	2/14/73	2	0	T
Tim Bowens, Miami	2/ 7/73	16	15	DT
Mario Bates, New Orleans	1/16/73	11	7	RB
Lamont Warren, Indianapolis	1/ 4/73	11	0	RB
Malcolm Seabron, Houston	12/29/72	13	0	WR

Ten Oldest Players	Birthdate	Games	Starts	Position
Jackie Slater, L.A. Rams	5/27/54	12	7	T
Vince Evans, L.A. Raiders	6/14/55	9	0	QB
Mike Kenn, Atlanta	2/ 9/56	15	15	T
Clay Matthews, Atlanta	3/15/56	15	15	LB
Max Montoya, L.A. Raiders	5/12/56	13	0	G
Nick Lowery, N.Y. Jets	5/27/56	16	0	K
Joe Montana, Kansas City	6/11/56	14	14	QB
Matt Bahr, New England	7/6/56	16	0	K
Eddie Murray, Philadelphia	8/29/56	16	0	K
Warren Moon, Minnesota	11/18/56	15	15	QB

YOUNGEST AND OLDEST REGULAR STARTERS BY POSITION IN 1994

Minimum: 8 Games Started

	Youngest		Oldest	
QB	2/14/72	Drew Bledsoe, N.E.	6/11/56	Joe Montana, K.C.
RB	2/26/73	Marshall Faulk, Ind.	3/26/60	Marcus Allen, K.C.
WR	7/7/72	Darnay Scott, Cin.	12/5/57	Art Monk, N.Y. Jets
TE	6/21/72	Andrew Jordan, Minn.	5/24/60	Pete Metzelaars, Buff.
C	8/21/70	Steve Everitt, Clev.	5/18/58	Ray Donaldson, Sea.
G	9/15/71	Will Shields, K.C.	2/12/61	Mark Bortz, Chi.
T	7/18/72	Bernard Williams, Phil.	2/9/56	Mike Kenn, Atl.
DE	7/11/72	Joe Johnson, N.O.	3/20/58	Rickey Jackson, S.F.
DT	3/13/73	Dan Wilkinson, Cin.	10/17/57	Steve McMichael, G.B.
LB	6/28/72	Marvin Jones, N.Y. Jets	3/15/56	Clay Matthews, Atl.
CB	12/27/72	DeWayne Washington, Minn.	2/15/60	Darrell Green, Wash.
S	9/29/71	Ray Buchanan, Ind.	2/3/59	Dennis Smith, Den.

MARCUS ALLEN'S CAREER RUSHING VS. EACH OPPONENT

Opponent	Games	Rushes	Yards	Yards Per Rush	Yards Per Game	TD
Arizona	2	22	96	4.4	48.0	1
Atlanta	4	55	241	4.4	60.3	1
Buffalo	8	128	439	3.4	54.9	5
Chicago	4	61	252	4.1	63.0	4
Cincinnati	8	101	363	3.6	45.4	5
Cleveland	4	55	224	4.1	56.0	0
Dallas	3	25	93	3.7	31.0	1
Denver	22	313	1,301	4.2	59.1	9
Detroit	3	46	153	3.3	51.0	2
Green Bay	4	75	269	3.6	67.3	5
Houston	6	84	323	3.8	53.8	3
Indianapolis	2	28	141	5.0	70.5	0
Kansas City	17	264	961	3.6	56.5	8
Los Angeles	4	82	303	3.7	75.8	2
Miami	7	94	470	5.0	67.1	7
Minnesota	4	44	150	3.4	37.5	1
New England	2	37	139	3.8	69.5	1
New Orleans	4	70	316	4.5	79.0	3
N.Y. Giants	4	30	117	3.9	29.3	1
N.Y. Jets	2	30	119	4.0	59.5	2
Philadelphia	2	30	82	2.7	41.0	0
Pittsburgh	2	24	82	3.4	41.0	1
St. Louis	4	78	328	4.2	82.0	3
San Diego	21	325	1,314	4.0	62.6	20
San Francisco	4	69	302	4.4	75.5	2
Seattle	23	274	1,217	4.4	52.9	11
Tampa Bay	1	13	79	6.1	79.0	0
Washington	3	28	144	5.1	48.0	0
Totals	174	2,485	10,018	4.0	57.6	98

Arizona totals include one game vs. St. Louis, one game vs. Phoenix

EMMITT SMITH'S CAREER RUSHING VS. EACH OPPONENT

Opponent	Games	Rushes	Yards	Yards Per Rush	Yards Per Game	TD
Arizona	10	192	814	4.2	81.4	14
Atlanta	4	73	369	5.1	92.3	4
Chicago	1	20	131	6.6	131.0	1
Cincinnati	2	44	154	3.5	77.0	1
Cleveland	2	58	224	3.9	112.0	1
Denver	1	26	62	2.4	62.0	1
Detroit	3	64	276	4.3	92.0	4
Green Bay	3	77	326	4.2	108.7	3
Houston	2	39	139	3.6	69.5	1
Indianapolis	1	25	104	4.2	104.0	1
Kansas City	1	24	95	4.0	95.0	1
Los Angeles	1	29	152	5.2	152.0	3
Miami	1	16	51	3.2	51.0	0
Minnesota	1	19	104	5.5	104.0	1
New Orleans	3	66	271	4.1	90.3	2
N.Y. Giants	9	184	860	4.7	95.6	8
N.Y. Jets	2	35	146	4.2	73.0	0
Philadelphia	10	219	1,068	4.9	106.8	5
Pittsburgh	2	63	280	4.4	140.0	2
St. Louis	2	40	134	3.4	67.0	1
San Diego	1	2	2	1.0	2.0	0
San Francisco	3	59	210	3.6	70.0	3
Seattle	1	22	78	3.5	78.0	2
Tampa Bay	2	39	169	4.3	84.5	1
Washington	9	195	964	4.9	107.1	11
Totals	77	1,630	7,183	4.4	93.3	71

Arizona totals include eight games vs. Phoenix

BARRY SANDERS'S CAREER RUSHING VS. EACH OPPONENT

Opponent	Games	Rushes	Yards	Yards Per Rush	Yards Per Game	TD
Arizona	2	32	161	5.0	80.5	1
Atlanta	4	91	423	4.6	105.8	5
Buffalo	2	45	153	3.4	76.5	2
Chicago	11	205	993	4.8	90.3	6
Cincinnati	2	47	265	5.6	132.5	2
Cleveland	2	58	232	4.0	116.0	1
Dallas	3	79	357	4.5	119.0	0
Denver	1	23	147	6.4	147.0	1
Green Bay	11	210	1,069	5.1	97.2	5
Houston	2	41	145	3.5	72.5	3
Indianapolis	1	30	179	6.0	179.0	2
Kansas City	1	16	90	5.6	90.0	1
Los Angeles	1	25	176	7.0	176.0	2
Miami	2	44	195	4.4	97.5	0
Minnesota	11	198	946	4.8	86.0	9
New England	2	50	279	5.6	139.5	2
New Orleans	4	57	194	3.4	48.5	2
N.Y. Giants	3	49	272	5.6	90.7	1
N.Y. Jets	2	43	241	5.6	120.5	2
Pittsburgh	2	26	95	3.7	47.5	1
St. Louis	2	52	148	2.8	74.0	1
San Francisco	3	48	225	4.7	75.0	1
Seattle	2	31	124	4.0	62.0	1
Tampa Bay	11	238	1,425	6.0	129.5	10
Washington	2	25	138	5.5	69.0	1
Totals	89	1,763	8,672	4.9	98.9	62

Arizona totals include two games vs. Phoenix

INSIDE THE NUMBERS

THURMAN THOMAS'S CAREER RUSHING VS. EACH OPPONENT

Opponent	Games	Rushes	Yards	Yards Per Rush	Yards Per Game	TD
Arizona	1	26	112	4.3	112.0	0
Atlanta	2	34	198	5.8	99.0	1
Chicago	2	30	129	4.3	64.5	1
Cincinnati	3	50	234	4.7	78.0	0
Cleveland	1	17	58	3.4	58.0	2
Dallas	1	25	75	3.0	75.0	0
Denver	4	67	297	4.4	74.3	3
Detroit	1	17	58	3.4	58.0	0
Green Bay	3	78	302	3.9	100.7	2
Houston	5	97	413	4.3	82.6	2
Indianapolis	14	239	1,023	4.3	73.1	6
Kansas City	3	49	153	3.1	51.0	1
Los Angeles	5	79	356	4.5	71.2	3
Miami	13	265	1,185	4.5	96.8	6
Minnesota	2	34	136	4.0	68.0	1
New England	14	303	1, 390	4.6	99.3	7
New Orleans	2	40	155	3.9	77.5	2
N.Y. Giants	2	47	182	3.9	91.0	1
N.Y. Jets	14	233	1,158	5.0	82.7	4
Philadelphia	2	31	84	2.7	42.0	0
Pittsburgh	5	102	442	4.3	88.4	1
St. Louis	2	46	208	4.5	104.0	3
San Francisco	2	25	92	3.7	46.0	1
Seattle	2	27	100	3.7	50.0	0
Tampa Bay	2	24	55	2.3	27.5	0
Washington	2	33	129	3.9	64.5	1
Totals	109	2,018	8,724	4.3	80.0	48

Arizona totals include one game vs. Phoenix

DAN MARINO'S CAREER PASSING VS. EACH OPPONENT

Opponent	Games	Att.	Cmp.	Pct.	Yards	Avg. Gain	TD	Int.	Sacked
Arizona	2	61	42	68.9	634	10.39	5	0	1/9
Atlanta	2	80	40	50.0	553	6.91	2	4	1/2
Buffalo	22	766	477	62.3	5,898	7.70	43	30	26/214
Chicago	4	117	63	53.8	855	7.31	6	4	8/50
Cincinnati	5	171	110	64.3	1,230	7.19	9	1	5/39
Cleveland	6	205	126	61.5	1,661	8.10	11	5	4/33
Dallas	3	115	66	57.4	860	7.48	6	3	4/36
Denver	1	43	25	58.1	390	9.07	3	0	3/25
Detroit	3	113	65	57.5	706	6.25	2	2	4/28
Green Bay	5	171	112	65.5	1,328	7.77	11	6	6/37
Houston	7	220	116	52.7	1,464	6.65	10	11	7/36
Indianapolis	23	765	463	60.5	5,594	7.31	38	13	19/133
Kansas City	5	178	105	59.0	1,272	7.15	10	3	2/20
Los Angeles	7	241	133	55.2	1,655	6.87	14	7	10/81
Minnesota	2	91	49	53.8	695	7.64	5	6	1/5
New England	21	727	420	57.8	5,215	7.17	36	32	15/118
New Orleans	3	105	65	61.9	650	6.19	5	2	6/42
N.Y. Giants	1	30	14	46.7	115	3.83	0	2	1/7
N.Y. Jets	21	787	471	59.8	6,372	8.10	55	25	28/153
Philadelphia	3	127	72	56.7	987	7.77	6	2	5/45
Pittsburgh	7	220	141	64.1	1,645	7.48	10	10	5/33
St. Louis	3	121	75	62.0	905	7.48	9	3	1/4
San Diego	4	163	103	63.2	1,243	7.63	9	2	6/42
San Francisco	3	106	61	57.5	687	6.48	3	4	4/36
Seattle	2	68	40	58.8	504	7.41	3	4	3/21
Tampa Bay	3	117	74	63.2	875	7.48	7	1	1/10
Washington	4	141	76	53.9	1,180	8.37	10	3	2/7
Totals	172	6,049	3,604	59.6	45,173	7.47	328	185	178/1,270

Arizona totals include one game vs. St. Louis, one game vs. Phoenix
Indianapolis totals include two games vs. Baltimore

JOHN ELWAY'S CAREER PASSING VS. EACH OPPONENT

Opponent	Games	Att.	Cmp.	Pct.	Yards	Avg. Gain	TD	Int.	Sacked
Arizona	2	62	39	62.9	492	7.94	3	5	3/16
Atlanta	3	106	62	58.5	908	8.57	6	3	9/72
Buffalo	5	155	81	52.3	1,019	6.57	6	5	12/90
Chicago	5	118	65	55.1	763	6.47	3	4	12/73
Cincinnati	4	113	69	61.1	856	7.58	7	1	6/46
Cleveland	9	251	147	58.6	2,005	7.99	14	7	16/126
Dallas	1	24	12	50.0	200	8.33	3	0	1/2
Detroit	3	88	56	63.6	699	7.94	2	2	7/72
Green Bay	4	153	88	57.5	913	5.97	2	5	5/38
Houston	3	98	54	55.1	749	7.64	6	4	11/109
Indianapolis	7	213	118	55.4	1,545	7.25	8	2	17/129
Kansas City	22	677	377	55.7	4,830	7.13	20	29	62/438
Los Angeles	20	593	320	54.0	3,962	6.68	22	24	54/438
Miami	1	37	18	48.6	250	6.76	0	1	3/24
Minnesota	5	130	84	64.6	923	7.10	10	2	13/100
New England	6	192	108	56.3	1,286	6.70	7	4	8/54
New Orleans	2	79	46	58.2	519	6.57	4	2	4/35
N.Y. Giants	3	103	58	56.3	724	7.03	2	3	3/19
N.Y. Jets	4	132	80	60.6	994	7.53	4	4	8/45
Philadelphia	4	102	52	51.0	626	6.14	4	6	16/119
Pittsburgh	7	192	105	54.7	1,366	7.11	6	5	14/109
St. Louis	3	119	63	52.9	742	6.24	7	2	4/29
San Diego	23	723	415	57.4	4,939	6.83	21	29	57/386
San Francisco	3	99	51	51.5	531	5.36	3	4	11/80
Seattle	22	717	401	55.9	5,260	7.34	28	22	51/365
Tampa Bay	1	41	26	63.4	225	5.49	0	0	1/0
Washington	2	67	35	52.2	410	6.12	1	2	8/59
Totals	174	5,384	3,030	56.3	37,736	7.01	199	177	416/3,073

Arizona totals include two games vs. Phoenix

BOOMER ESIASON'S CAREER PASSING VS. EACH OPPONENT

Opponent	Games	Att.	Cmp.	Pct.	Yards	Avg. Gain	TD	Int.	Sacked
Arizona	2	38	24	63.2	356	9.37	4	1	3/22
Atlanta	3	67	34	50.7	367	5.48	1	4	1/3
Buffalo	10	234	138	59.0	1,794	7.67	10	8	9/79
Chicago	4	115	59	51.3	680	5.91	5	5	11/101
Cincinnati	1	26	17	65.4	192	7.38	0	0	2/15
Cleveland	16	369	198	53.7	2,561	6.94	18	13	19/134
Dallas	4	122	69	56.6	855	7.01	6	3	5/35
Denver	4	127	87	68.5	1,180	9.29	8	7	6/47
Detroit	4	121	72	59.5	781	6.45	3	4	6/34
Green Bay	3	90	50	55.6	549	6.10	5	3	5/39
Houston	18	484	276	57.0	3,822	7.90	25	21	36/255
Indianapolis	8	213	115	54.0	1,338	6.28	9	7	10/74
Kansas City	4	121	67	55.4	940	7.77	5	3	7/71
Los Angeles	6	147	81	55.1	1,029	7.00	5	2	8/70
Miami	7	229	140	61.1	1,871	8.17	11	8	9/95
Minnesota	4	129	81	62.8	946	7.33	7	8	10/88
New England	10	298	161	54.0	2,230	7.48	15	8	17/116
New Orleans	3	75	33	44.0	309	4.12	3	2	9/71
N.Y. Giants	3	71	44	62.0	526	7.41	4	0	4/36
N.Y. Jets	7	180	93	51.7	1,410	7.83	12	8	16/123
Philadelphia	3	83	49	59.0	770	9.28	9	5	5/45
Pittsburgh	16	437	261	59.7	3,589	8.21	18	17	28/230
St. Louis	1	45	31	68.9	490	10.89	3	0	1/7
San Diego	4	109	65	59.6	844	7.74	8	5	11/88
San Francisco	2	49	26	53.1	294	6.00	2	2	5/28
Seattle	6	167	90	53.9	1,093	6.54	2	6	14/109
Tampa Bay	1	28	17	60.7	197	7.04	5	0	1/1
Washington	4	117	62	53.0	861	7.36	4	3	9/72
Totals	158	4,291	2,440	56.9	31,874	7.43	207	153	267/2,088

Arizona totals include one game vs. St. Louis, one game vs. Phoenix

WARREN MOON'S CAREER PASSING VS. EACH OPPONENT

Opponent	Games	Att.	Cmp.	Pct.	Yards	Avg. Gain	TD	Int.	Sacked
Arizona	3	108	60	55.6	808	7.48	5	4	4/36
Atlanta	4	156	87	55.8	1,189	7.62	9	5	9/43
Buffalo	8	206	117	56.8	1,528	7.42	7	9	12/94
Chicago	4	132	77	58.3	1,063	8.05	6	5	8/70
Cincinnati	19	606	357	58.9	4,608	7.60	35	22	36/301
Cleveland	18	561	316	56.3	4,048	7.22	23	21	41/308
Dallas	3	111	67	60.4	873	7.86	2	4	16/105
Denver	3	87	50	57.5	777	8.93	5	2	9/66
Detroit	4	133	88	66.2	1,150	8.65	5	6	3/30
Green Bay	3	108	65	60.2	655	6.06	2	6	7/61
Indianapolis	7	255	160	62.7	2,156	8.45	13	7	14/97
Kansas City	8	267	166	62.2	2,006	7.51	10	7	26/180
Los Angeles	4	138	68	49.3	1,004	7.28	6	5	13/115
Miami	6	148	102	68.9	1,236	8.35	8	6	11/112
Minnesota	3	95	58	61.1	592	6.23	2	2	14/106
New England	4	136	76	55.9	946	6.96	6	4	5/41
New Orleans	5	170	96	56.5	1,157	6.81	6	4	11/75
N.Y. Giants	3	117	71	60.7	865	7.39	4	3	6/53
N.Y. Jets	4	171	118	69.0	1,411	8.25	8	6	10/86
Philadelphia	1	46	24	52.2	262	5.70	0	0	4/36
Pittsburgh	19	591	333	56.3	4,208	7.12	22	27	41/315
St. Louis	4	157	85	54.1	1,163	7.41	4	7	10/71
San Diego	6	201	108	53.7	1,362	6.78	7	6	10/71
San Francisco	4	128	71	55.5	903	7.05	7	8	8/46
Seattle	3	115	73	63.5	783	6.81	4	4	5/34
Tampa Bay	3	102	57	55.9	617	6.05	4	2	5/40
Washington	3	102	53	52.0	579	5.68	4	3	6/46
Totals	156	5,147	3,003	58.3	37,949	7.37	214	185	344/2,638

Arizona totals include one game vs. St. Louis, one game vs. Phoenix

JIM KELLY'S CAREER PASSING VS. EACH OPPONENT

Opponent	Games	Att.	Cmp.	Pct.	Yards	Avg. Gain	TD	Int.	Sacked
Arizona	2	26	17	65.4	270	10.38	4	1	5/34
Atlanta	2	37	24	64.9	324	8.76	4	2	3/18
Chicago	3	99	58	58.6	692	6.99	4	3	11/96
Cincinnati	4	99	65	65.7	1,008	10.18	10	7	5/49
Cleveland	3	93	56	60.2	737	7.92	5	0	6/31
Dallas	1	27	16	59.3	155	5.74	1	1	4/26
Denver	5	150	87	58.0	991	6.61	3	8	10/70
Detroit	1	35	29	82.9	273	7.80	2	2	2/18
Green Bay	3	93	59	63.4	677	7.28	5	3	7/41
Houston	7	207	128	61.8	1,625	7.85	14	7	20/148
Indianapolis	16	441	266	60.3	3,301	7.49	27	10	18/148
Kansas City	5	153	95	62.1	1,068	6.98	7	7	13/105
Los Angeles	6	208	125	60.1	1,550	7.45	8	5	12/89
Miami	16	500	317	63.4	3,787	7.57	21	14	24/182
Minnesota	2	57	32	56.1	377	6.61	2	2	4/28
New England	16	467	277	59.3	3,563	7.63	24	22	43/335
New Orleans	2	63	30	47.6	346	5.49	2	4	3/16
N.Y. Giants	2	36	21	58.3	257	7.14	2	1	5/30
N.Y. Jets	17	538	320	59.5	3,946	7.33	27	20	31/213
Philadelphia	3	98	56	57.1	698	7.12	4	5	3/26
Pittsburgh	6	192	117	60.9	1,341	6.98	12	5	15/116
St. Louis	1	19	13	68.4	106	5.58	2	1	1/0
San Francisco	2	75	48	64.0	668	8.91	3	4	5/32
Seattle	2	48	26	54.2	324	6.75	1	2	2/21
Tampa Bay	3	114	72	63.2	913	8.01	4	3	5/54
Washington	2	67	43	64.2	530	7.91	3	4	3/33
Totals	132	3,942	2,397	60.8	29,527	7.49	201	143	260/1,959

Arizona totals include one game vs. St. Louis, one game vs. Phoenix

TROY AIKMAN'S CAREER PASSING VS. EACH OPPONENT

Opponent	Games	Att.	Cmp.	Pct.	Yards	Avg. Gain	TD	Int.	Sacked
Arizona	10	237	150	63.3	2,008	8.47	11	8	12/85
Atlanta	2	44	31	70.5	480	10.91	4	2	0/0
Buffalo	1	45	28	62.2	297	6.60	0	2	1/7
Chicago	1	20	10	50.0	78	3.90	0	0	1/2
Cincinnati	2	55	34	61.8	548	9.96	3	3	1/12
Cleveland	2	73	45	61.6	462	6.33	3	2	4/20
Denver	1	35	25	71.4	231	6.60	3	0	2/9
Detroit	3	106	70	66.0	765	7.22	3	3	4/30
Green Bay	3	92	67	72.8	729	7.92	2	4	4/29
Houston	2	64	38	59.4	488	7.63	2	1	6/22
Indianapolis	1	28	21	75.0	245	8.75	1	0	2/14
Kansas City	1	29	21	72.4	192	6.62	1	2	1/9
Los Angeles	1	25	16	64.0	234	9.36	0	0	5/27
Miami	2	76	53	69.7	442	5.82	2	2	0/0
Minnesota	1	29	19	65.5	208	7.17	1	0	0/0
New Orleans	3	84	53	63.1	532	6.33	1	4	4/46
N.Y. Giants	12	266	183	68.8	1,890	7.11	10	5	17/101
N.Y. Jets	2	67	46	68.7	501	7.48	2	5	6/40
Philadelphia	10	255	133	52.2	1,451	5.69	8	12	33/194
Pittsburgh	1	32	21	65.6	245	7.66	1	1	0/0
St. Louis	3	103	58	56.3	754	7.32	7	2	4/25
San Diego	1	29	13	44.8	193	6.66	1	1	5/32
San Francisco	3	98	53	54.1	678	6.92	1	4	7/47
Seattle	1	23	15	65.2	173	7.52	0	2	1/3
Tampa Bay	2	53	30	56.6	332	6.26	2	2	5/38
Washington	11	313	191	61.0	2,147	6.86	13	11	28/199
Totals	82	2,281	1,424	62.4	16,303	7.15	82	78	153/991

Arizona totals include eight games vs. Phoenix

STEVE YOUNG'S CAREER PASSING VS. EACH OPPONENT

Opponent	Games	Att.	Cmp.	Pct.	Yards	Avg. Gain	TD	Int.	Sacked
Arizona	5	131	69	52.7	885	6.76	5	2	10/71
Atlanta	12	277	179	64.6	2,559	9.24	24	10	15/98
Buffalo	3	80	49	61.3	808	10.10	4	3	8/66
Chicago	6	136	75	55.1	993	7.30	8	3	9/52
Cincinnati	1	25	13	52.0	179	7.16	0	2	1/6
Cleveland	3	34	19	55.9	274	8.06	0	3	1/8
Dallas	4	72	49	68.1	624	8.67	5	1	8/42
Denver	2	32	20	62.5	350	10.94	3	3	1/8
Detroit	7	160	111	69.4	1,320	8.25	9	2	14/105
Green Bay	5	109	59	54.1	668	6.13	2	6	24/177
Houston	2	29	15	51.7	178	6.14	0	2	2/10
Indianapolis	1	25	14	56.0	251	10.04	1	2	2/21
Kansas City	3	58	37	63.8	433	7.47	2	3	9/55
Los Angeles	2	67	37	55.2	525	7.84	4	3	4/20
Miami	1	27	19	70.4	220	8.15	2	1	0/0
Minnesota	8	194	124	63.9	1,513	7.80	9	7	27/129
New England	2	39	30	76.9	422	10.82	5	1	4/19
New Orleans	12	244	165	67.6	1,754	7.19	12	4	28/166
N.Y. Giants	4	47	27	57.4	304	6.47	2	1	5/26
N.Y. Jets	2	43	28	65.1	345	8.02	3	0	1/4
Philadelphia	4	92	60	65.2	702	7.63	5	2	8/52
Pittsburgh	2	36	24	66.7	240	6.67	3	3	1/0
St. Louis	12	281	189	67.3	2,466	8.78	17	2	17/82
San Diego	3	71	53	74.6	666	9.38	5	0	2/10
Seattle	1	6	4	66.7	49	8.17	1	0	0/0
Tampa Bay	4	87	62	71.3	850	9.77	8	0	5/28
Washington	2	27	15	55.6	291	10.78	1	2	2/8
Totals	113	2,429	1,546	63.6	19,869	8.18	140	68	208/1,263

Arizona totals include two games vs. St. Louis, three games vs. Phoenix

JERRY RICE'S CAREER RECEIVING VS. EACH OPPONENT

Opponent	Games	Rec.	Yards	Yards Per Rec.	Yards Per Game	TD
Arizona	5	25	465	18.6	93.0	5
Atlanta	19	102	1, 680	16.5	88.4	19
Buffalo	2	6	72	12.0	36.0	1
Chicago	5	24	424	17.7	84.8	7
Cincinnati	3	16	269	16.8	89.7	2
Cleveland	3	19	275	14.5	91.7	4
Dallas	5	33	461	14.0	92.2	3
Denver	3	16	266	16.6	88.7	1
Detroit	6	22	303	13.8	50.5	2
Green Bay	4	23	432	18.8	108.0	4
Houston	3	23	238	10.3	79.3	2
Indianapolis	2	12	335	27.9	167.5	4
Kansas City	3	13	178	13.7	59.3	2
Los Angeles	4	18	362	20.1	90.5	2
Miami	2	10	155	15.5	77.5	3
Minnesota	8	36	585	16.3	73.1	7
New England	3	13	207	15.9	69.0	3
New Orleans	20	98	1,423	14.5	71.2	11
N.Y. Giants	6	27	454	16.8	75.7	4
N.Y. Jets	3	15	265	17.7	88.3	2
Philadelphia	6	31	490	15.8	81.7	5
Pittsburgh	3	19	215	11.3	71.7	3
St. Louis	20	111	1,839	16.6	92.0	15
San Diego	3	27	465	17.2	155.0	4
Seattle	3	14	272	19.4	90.7	4
Tampa Bay	7	43	672	15.6	96.0	10
Washington	5	24	473	19.7	94.6	2
Totals	156	820	13,275	16.2	85.1	131

Arizona totals include one game vs. St. Louis, four games vs. Phoenix

ANDRE REED'S CAREER RECEIVING VS. EACH OPPONENT

Opponent	Games	Rec.	Yards	Yards Per Rec.	Yards Per Game	TD
Arizona	2	0	0	—	0.0	0
Atlanta	2	9	170	18.9	85.0	1
Chicago	3	14	156	11.1	52.0	0
Cincinnati	5	11	171	15.5	34.2	2
Cleveland	4	16	250	15.6	62.5	1
Dallas	1	1	10	10.0	10.0	0
Denver	5	26	341	13.1	68.2	1
Detroit	2	10	89	8.9	44.5	1
Green Bay	3	21	249	11.9	83.0	3
Houston	8	41	625	15.2	78.1	5
Indianapolis	19	87	1,193	13.7	62.8	13
Kansas City	5	26	368	14.2	73.6	4
Los Angeles	5	28	406	14.5	81.2	1
Miami	20	90	1,291	14.3	64.6	9
Minnesota	3	11	105	9.5	35.0	0
New England	18	80	1,295	16.2	71.9	6
New Orleans	2	6	54	9.0	27.0	0
N.Y. Giants	2	7	95	13.6	47.5	1
N.Y. Jets	20	82	1,115	13.6	55.8	8
Philadelphia	3	15	161	10.7	53.7	3
Pittsburgh	7	28	358	12.8	71.6	3
St. Louis	2	10	135	13.5	67.5	1
San Diego	2	9	138	15.3	69.0	0
San Francisco	2	20	259	13.0	129.5	0
Seattle	2	5	116	23.2	78.0	1
Tampa Bay	3	8	119	14.9	39.7	0
Washington	3	15	267	17.8	89.0	2
Totals	153	676	9,536	14.1	62.3	66

Arizona totals include one game vs. St. Louis, one game vs. Phoenix

INSIDE THE NUMBERS

MICHAEL IRVIN'S CAREER RECEIVING VS. EACH OPPONENT

Opponent	Games	Rec.	Yards	Yards Per Rec.	Yards Per Game	TD
Arizona	12	43	874	20.3	72.8	7
Atlanta	6	24	406	16.9	67.7	2
Buffalo	1	8	115	14.4	115.0	0
Chicago	1	5	46	9.2	46.0	0
Cincinnati	3	15	314	20.9	104.7	1
Cleveland	3	18	248	13.8	82.7	1
Denver	1	6	62	10.3	62.0	2
Detroit	3	16	304	19.0	101.3	1
Green Bay	4	21	360	17.1	90.0	3
Houston	3	11	141	12.8	47.0	1
Indianapolis	1	7	112	16.0	112.0	0
Kansas City	1	6	84	14.0	84.0	0
Los Angeles	1	3	54	18.0	54.0	0
Miami	1	3	31	10.3	31.0	0
Minnesota	2	10	167	16.7	83.5	1
New Orleans	5	17	268	15.8	53.6	0
N.Y. Giants	11	41	642	15.7	58.4	3
N.Y. Jets	2	10	184	18.4	92.0	2
Philadelphia	12	31	577	18.6	48.1	3
Pittsburgh	3	19	369	19.4	123.0	2
St. Louis	2	10	239	23.9	119.5	2
San Francisco	4	27	332	12.3	83.0	1
Seattle	1	6	113	18.8	113.0	0
Tampa Bay	2	2	42	21.0	21.0	1
Washington	11	57	851	14.9	77.4	7
Totals	96	416	6,935	16.7	73.0	40

Arizona totals include 10 games vs. Phoenix

ANDRE RISON'S CAREER RECEIVING VS. EACH OPPONENT

Opponent	Games	Rec.	Yards	Yards Per Rec.	Yards Per Game	TD
Arizona	5	20	310	15.5	62.0	2
Atlanta	1	2	36	18.0	36.0	0
Buffalo	3	14	180	12.9	60.0	0
Chicago	3	23	300	13.0	100.0	4
Cincinnati	3	13	140	10.8	46.7	1
Cleveland	3	16	313	19.6	104.3	2
Dallas	4	20	202	10.1	50.5	2
Denver	1	2	18	9.0	18.0	0
Detroit	3	24	330	13.8	110.0	4
Green Bay	3	20	297	14.9	99.0	4
Houston	2	10	140	14.0	70.0	2
Kansas City	2	5	83	16.6	41.5	1
Los Angeles	2	7	109	15.6	54.5	0
Miami	3	12	162	13.5	54.0	3
Minnesota	1	4	25	6.3	25.0	0
New England	3	11	183	16.6	61.0	1
New Orleans	11	55	704	12.8	64.0	5
N.Y. Jets	2	6	111	18.5	55.5	0
Philadelphia	2	11	180	16.4	90.0	1
Pittsburgh	2	8	104	13.0	52.0	0
St. Louis	11	57	854	15.0	77.6	10
San Diego	3	9	118	13.1	39.3	0
San Francisco	11	75	912	12.2	82.9	10
Seattle	1	3	35	11.7	35.0	0
Tampa Bay	5	32	404	12.6	80.8	7
Washington	4	16	203	12.7	50.8	1
Totals	94	475	6,453	13.6	68.6	60

Arizona totals include four games vs. Phoenix

CRIS CARTER'S CAREER RECEIVING VS. EACH OPPONENT

Opponent	Games	Rec.	Yards	Yards Per Rec.	Yards Per Game	TD
Arizona	9	30	513	17.1	57.0	7
Atlanta	2	9	179	19.9	89.5	4
Buffalo	2	10	121	12.1	60.5	0
Chicago	11	63	661	10.5	60.1	4
Cincinnati	2	13	144	11.1	72.0	2
Cleveland	2	4	42	10.5	21.0	0
Dallas	5	17	213	12.5	42.6	4
Denver	4	12	185	15.4	46.3	2
Detroit	10	43	473	11.0	47.3	2
Green Bay	9	41	486	11.9	54.0	4
Houston	2	5	96	19.2	48.0	1
Kansas City	2	5	88	17.6	44.0	2
Los Angeles	3	15	201	13.4	67.0	1
Miami	2	7	81	11.6	40.5	3
Minnesota	2	5	30	6.0	15.0	1
New England	3	16	160	10.0	53.3	0
New Orleans	5	19	225	11.8	45.0	1
N.Y. Giants	8	13	274	21.1	34.3	2
N.Y. Jets	2	12	114	9.5	57.0	2
Philadelphia	1	6	151	25.2	151.0	2
Pittsburgh	1	3	73	24.3	73.0	0
St. Louis	3	8	105	13.1	35.0	0
San Diego	2	9	122	13.6	61.0	0
San Francisco	5	16	152	9.5	30.4	1
Seattle	2	5	75	15.0	37.5	1
Tampa Bay	11	42	556	13.2	50.5	2
Washington	7	21	313	14.9	44.7	1
Totals	117	449	5,833	13.0	49.9	49

Arizona totals include two games vs. St. Louis, six games vs. Phoenix

STARTING RECORDS OF ACTIVE NFL QUARTERBACKS

Minimum: 10 starts

	W- L- T	Pct.
Jim McMahon	67- 30	.691
Stan Humphries	31- 14	.689
Steve Bono	7- 4	.636
Dan Marino	107- 63	.629
Jim Kelly	83- 49	.629
Mark Rypien	47- 28	.627
Jay Schroeder	62- 37	.626
Jeff Hostetler	35- 21	.625
John Elway	105- 66 -1	.613
Neil O'Donnell	30- 19	.612
Bobby Hebert	53- 34	.609
Randall Cunningham	62- 40 -1	.607
Dave Brown	9- 6	.600
Dave Krieg	88- 59	.599
Steve Young	52- 35	.598
Mike Tomczak	29- 20	.592
Troy Aikman	48- 34	.585
Cody Carlson	11- 8	.579
Brett Favre	26- 19	.578
Erik Kramer	12- 10	.545
Steve Walsh	19- 16	.543
Wade Wilson	35- 30	.538
Drew Bledsoe	15- 13	.536
Jim Harbaugh	39- 35	.527
Steve Beuerlein	21- 19	.525
Warren Moon	79- 75	.513
Rich Gannon	20- 19	.513
Bernie Kosar	53- 52 -1	.505
Boomer Esiason	71- 77	.480
Bubby Brister	32- 35	.478
Don Majkowski	25- 29 -1	.464
Rodney Peete	22- 26	.458
Jim Everett	53- 68	.438
Scott Mitchell	7- 9	.438
Vinny Testaverde	36- 55	.396
Jack Trudeau	19- 30	.388
Craig Erickson	11- 18	.379
Rick Mirer	11- 18	.379
Chris Chandler	17- 28	.378
Billy Joe Tolliver	13- 22	.371
Vince Evans	13- 23	.361
Chris Miller	25- 51	.329
Jeff George	21- 44	.323
Browning Nagle	4- 10	.286
Hugh Millen	7- 18	.280
John Friesz	7- 20	.259
Chuck Long	4- 17	.190
David Klingler	4- 20	.167
Stan Gelbaugh	0- 11	.000

ALL-TIME RANKINGS OF PLAYERS IN FOUR CATEGORIES THAT DETERMINE NFL PASSER RATING

Minimum: 1500 Attempts

COMPLETION PERCENTAGE	Pct.	Att.	Comp.
Steve Young	63.65	2429	1546
Joe Montana	63.24	5391	3409
Troy Aikman	62.43	2281	1424
Brett Favre	62.22	1580	983
Jim Kelly	60.81	3942	2397
Ken Stabler	59.85	3793	2270
Danny White	59.69	2950	1761
Dan Marino	59.58	6049	3604
Ken Anderson	59.31	4475	2654
Dan Fouts	58.83	5604	3297

TOUCHDOWN PERCENTAGE	Pct.	Att.	TD
Sid Luckman	7.86	1744	137
Frank Ryan	6.99	2133	149
Len Dawson	6.39	3741	239
Daryle Lamonica	6.31	2601	164
Sammy Baugh	6.24	2995	187
Charley Conerly	6.11	2833	173
Bob Waterfield	6.00	1617	97
Earl Morrall	5.99	2689	161
Sonny Jurgensen	5.98	4262	255
Norm Van Brocklin	5.98	2895	173

AVERAGE YARDS PER PASS	Avg.	Att.	Yards
Otto Graham	8.63	1565	13,499
Sid Luckman	8.42	1744	14,686
Steve Young	8.18	2429	19,869
Norm Van Brocklin	8.16	2895	23,611
Ed Brown	7.85	1987	15,600
Bart Starr	7.85	3149	24,718
Johnny Unitas	7.76	5186	40,239
Earl Morrall	7.74	2689	20,809
Dan Fouts	7.68	5604	43,040
Len Dawson	7.67	3741	28,711

INTERCEPTION PERCENTAGE	Pct.	Att.	Int.
Jeff Hostetler	2.52	1506	38
Bernie Kosar	2.54	3225	82
Joe Montana	2.58	5391	139
Ken O'Brien	2.72	3602	98
Steve Young	2.80	2429	68
Neil Lomax	2.85	3153	90
Dan Marino	3.06	6049	185
Randall Cunningham	3.09	3241	100
Jeff George	3.11	2056	64
Jim Harbaugh	3.16	1961	62
Tony Eason	3.26	1564	51

NFL INDIVIDUAL LEADERS OVER RECENT SEASONS

Last 2 Seasons	Last 3 Seasons	Last 4 Seasons
Points		
259 John Carney	372 John Carney	466 Morten Andersen
238 Jason Elam	353 Morten Andersen	461 Pete Stoyanovich
237 Fuad Reveiz	340 Pete Stoyanovich	460 John Carney
233 Morten Andersen	339 Fuad Reveiz	433 Gary Anderson
229 Jeff Jaeger	333 Gary Anderson	431 Chip Lohmiller
Touchdowns		
32 Emmitt Smith	51 Emmitt Smith	64 Emmitt Smith
31 Jerry Rice	42 Jerry Rice	56 Jerry Rice
29 Sterling Sharpe	42 Sterling Sharpe	46 Andre Rison
23 Andre Rison	34 Andre Rison	46 Sterling Sharpe
22 Marcus Allen	33 Ricky Watters	39 Thurman Thomas
22 Ricky Watters		

Last 2 Seasons	Last 3 Seasons	Last 4 Seasons
Field Goals		
65 John Carney	91 John Carney	110 Morten Andersen
60 Fuad Reveiz	85 Morten Andersen	110 John Carney
57 Jeff Jaeger	80 Gary Anderson	109 Pete Stoyanovich
56 Morten Andersen	79 Fuad Reveiz	103 Gary Anderson
56 Jason Elam	78 Pete Stoyanovich	101 Jeff Jaeger
Rushes		
651 Emmitt Smith	1,024 Emmitt Smith	1,389 Emmitt Smith
642 Thurman Thomas	954 Thurman Thomas	1,242 Thurman Thomas
619 Rodney Hampton	886 Barry Sanders	1,228 Barry Sanders
613 Jerome Bettis	876 Rodney Hampton	1,132 Rodney Hampton
606 Chris Warren	829 Chris Warren	880 Reggie Cobb
Rushing Yards		
2,998 Barry Sanders	4,683 Emmitt Smith	6,246 Emmitt Smith
2,970 Emmitt Smith	4,350 Barry Sanders	5,898 Barry Sanders
2,617 Chris Warren	3,895 Thurman Thomas	5,302 Thurman Thomas
2,454 Jerome Bettis	3,634 Chris Warren	4,352 Rodney Hampton
2,408 Thurman Thomas	3,293 Rodney Hampton	3,740 Barry Foster
Rushing TDs		
30 Emmitt Smith	48 Emmitt Smith	60 Emmitt Smith
20 Natrone Means	25 Rodney Hampton	35 Rodney Hampton
19 Marcus Allen	25 Ricky Watters	35 Barry Sanders
16 Leonard Russell	24 Barry Foster	29 Thurman Thomas
16 Chris Warren	22 Thurman Thomas	28 Brad Baxter
16 Ricky Watters		
Passes		
1,121 Warren Moon	1,575 Brett Favre	2,122 Warren Moon
1,120 Drew Bledsoe	1,467 Warren Moon	1,868 Dan Marino
1,104 Brett Favre	1,380 Jim Kelly	1,854 Jim Kelly
1,045 John Elway	1,361 John Elway	1,812 John Elway
931 Jeff George	1,325 Steve Young	1,779 Jim Everett
Completions		
681 Brett Favre	983 Brett Favre	1,302 Warren Moon
674 Warren Moon	906 Steve Young	1,146 Jim Kelly
655 John Elway	898 Warren Moon	1,124 Dan Marino
638 Steve Young	842 Jim Kelly	1,086 Steve Young
614 Drew Bledsoe	829 John Elway	1,071 John Elway
Passing Yards		
7,992 Steve Young	11,457 Steve Young	14,960 Warren Moon
7,749 Warren Moon	10,412 Brett Favre	13,974 Steve Young
7,520 John Elway	10,270 Warren Moon	13,797 Jim Kelly
7,185 Brett Favre	9,953 Jim Kelly	13,757 Dan Marino
7,049 Drew Bledsoe	9,787 Dan Marino	13,015 John Elway

HIGHEST NFL POSTSEASON PASSER RATINGS (MINIMUM: 150 ATTEMPTS)

	Games	Att.	Comp.	Pct.	Yds.	Avg. Gain	TD	Int.	Rating
Bart Starr	10	213	130	61.0	1753	8.23	15	3	104.8
Troy Aikman	9	270	186	68.9	2312	8.56	17	8	103.8
Steve Young	15	243	159	65.4	1884	7.75	14	5	99.5
Joe Montana	23	734	460	62.7	5772	7.86	45	21	95.6
Ken Anderson	6	166	110	66.3	1321	7.96	9	6	93.5
Joe Theismann	10	211	128	60.7	1782	8.45	11	7	91.4
Dan Marino	12	454	258	56.8	3178	7.00	27	14	85.6
Warren Moon	10	403	259	64.3	2870	7.12	17	14	84.9
Ken Stabler	13	351	203	57.8	2641	7.52	19	13	84.2
Bernie Kosar	9	269	151	56.1	1943	7.22	16	10	83.3

HIGHEST NFL POSTSEASON PASSER RATINGS, ACTIVE PLAYERS (MINIMUM: 150 ATTEMPTS)

	Games	Att.	Comp.	Pct.	Yds.	Avg.	TD	Int.	Rating
Troy Aikman	9	270	186	68.9	2312	8.56	17	8	103.8
Steve Young	15	243	159	65.4	1884	7.75	14	5	99.5
Joe Montana	23	734	460	62.7	5772	7.86	45	21	95.6
Dan Marino	12	454	258	56.8	3178	7.00	27	14	85.6
Warren Moon	10	403	259	64.3	2870	7.12	17	14	84.9
Bernie Kosar	9	269	151	56.1	1943	7.22	16	10	83.3
Jim McMahon	8	155	82	52.9	1112	7.17	5	4	76.1
John Elway	14	431	229	53.1	3321	7.71	19	18	75.8
Wade Wilson	6	185	99	53.5	1322	7.15	7	6	75.6
Jim Kelly	14	462	275	59.5	3294	7.13	18	22	74.5

NFL INDIVIDUAL LEADERS OVER RECENT SEASONS

Touchdown Passes

Last 2 Seasons	Last 3 Seasons	Last 4 Seasons
64 Steve Young	89 Steve Young	106 Steve Young
52 Brett Favre	70 Brett Favre	96 Jim Kelly
41 John Elway	63 Jim Kelly	87 Dan Marino
40 Drew Bledsoe	62 Dan Marino	80 Warren Moon
40 Jim Kelly	57 Warren Moon	70 Brett Favre

Receptions

Last 2 Seasons	Last 3 Seasons	Last 4 Seasons
210 Jerry Rice	314 Sterling Sharpe	383 Sterling Sharpe
208 Cris Carter	294 Jerry Rice	374 Jerry Rice
206 Sterling Sharpe	261 Cris Carter	341 Andre Rison
169 Tim Brown	260 Andre Rison	338 Michael Irvin
168 Shannon Sharpe	245 Michael Irvin	333 Cris Carter

Reception Yards

Last 2 Seasons	Last 3 Seasons	Last 4 Seasons
3,002 Jerry Rice	4,203 Jerry Rice	5,490 Michael Irvin
2,571 Michael Irvin	3,967 Michael Irvin	5,409 Jerry Rice
2,489 Tim Brown	3,854 Sterling Sharpe	4,815 Sterling Sharpe
2,393 Sterling Sharpe	3,449 Andre Rison	4,425 Andre Rison
2,342 Henry Ellard	3,329 Anthony Miller	4,183 Andre Reed

Receiving Touchdowns

Last 2 Seasons	Last 3 Seasons	Last 4 Seasons
29 Sterling Sharpe	42 Sterling Sharpe	52 Jerry Rice
28 Jerry Rice	38 Jerry Rice	46 Andre Rison
23 Andre Rison	34 Andre Rison	46 Sterling Sharpe
17 Herman Moore	23 Tim Brown	30 Michael Haynes
17 Carl Pickens	22 Cris Carter	28 three players

Interceptions

Last 2 Seasons	Last 3 Seasons	Last 4 Seasons
14 Eric Turner	19 Eugene Robinson	24 Eugene Robinson
13 Deion Sanders	17 Darren Perry	22 Deion Sanders
12 Ray Buchanan	16 Darren Carrington	20 Aeneas Williams
12 Terry McDaniel	16 Terry McDaniel	19 four players
12 Eugene Robinson	16 Deion Sanders	
12 Rod Woodson	16 Rod Woodson	

Sacks

Last 2 Seasons	Last 3 Seasons	Last 4 Seasons
26.5 Kevin Greene	41.5 Leslie O'Neal	50.5 Leslie O'Neal
26.5 Neil Smith	41.0 Neil Smith	50.0 Simon Fletcher
26.0 John Randle	38.0 Bruce Smith	50.0 Reggie White
24.5 Leslie O'Neal	37.5 John Randle	49.0 Neil Smith
24.0 Bruce Smith	36.5 Simon Fletcher	47.0 John Randle
	36.5 Kevin Greene	47.0 Derrick Thomas

NFL TEAM LEADERS OVER RECENT SEASONS

Highest Won-Lost Percentage

Last 2 Seasons	Last 3 Seasons	Last 4 Seasons
.750 Dallas	.771 Dallas	.750 Dallas
.719 San Francisco	.771 San Francisco	.734 San Francisco
.656 Pittsburgh	.667 Pittsburgh	.672 Buffalo
.625 Kansas City	.625 five teams	.625 Kansas City
.625 N.Y. Giants		.609 Pittsburgh

Most Points

Last 2 Seasons	Last 3 Seasons	Last 4 Seasons
978 San Francisco	1,409 San Francisco	1,802 San Francisco
790 Dallas	1,199 Dallas	1,541 Dallas
738 Miami	1,078 Miami	1,508 Buffalo
722 Green Bay	1,050 Buffalo	1,421 Miami
720 Denver	1,038 San Diego	1,336 New Orleans

Most Total Yards

Last 2 Seasons	Last 3 Seasons	Last 4 Seasons
12,495 San Francisco	18,690 San Francisco	24,548 San Francisco
11,887 Miami	17,387 Miami	22,649 Buffalo
10,948 Denver	16,542 Dallas	22,628 Miami
10,936 Dallas	16,397 Buffalo	21,781 Houston
10,841 New England	15,794 Houston	21,643 Dallas

Most Rushing Yards

Last 2 Seasons	Last 3 Seasons	Last 4 Seasons
4,183 Pittsburgh	6,345 San Francisco	8,591 Buffalo
4,114 Dallas	6,339 Pittsburgh	8,206 San Francisco
4,091 Seattle	6,235 Dallas	8,108 N.Y. Giants
4,030 San Francisco	6,210 Buffalo	7,966 Pittsburgh
4,024 Detroit	6,044 N.Y. Giants	7,946 Dallas

Most Passing Yards

Last 2 Seasons	Last 3 Seasons	Last 4 Seasons
8,762 Miami	12,737 Miami	16,626 Miami
8,465 San Francisco	12,345 San Francisco	16,342 San Francisco
7,779 Denver	11,265 Atlanta	15,315 Houston
7,729 New England	10,709 Denver	14,714 Atlanta
7,632 Atlanta	10,694 Houston	14,058 Buffalo

Fewest Turnovers

Last 2 Seasons	Last 3 Seasons	Last 4 Seasons
42 N.Y. Giants	65 N.Y. Giants	88 N.Y. Giants
42 San Diego	70 Dallas	94 Dallas
44 Pittsburgh	75 Kansas City	97 Kansas City
46 Dallas	75 San Diego	103 San Diego
54 Kansas City	76 Pittsburgh	106 Pittsburgh
54 San Francisco	76 San Francisco	

Fewest Points Allowed

Last 2 Seasons	Last 3 Seasons	Last 4 Seasons
477 Dallas	720 Dallas	1,030 Dallas
510 N.Y. Giants	740 Pittsburgh	1,066 San Francisco
511 Cleveland	786 Cleveland	1,084 Cleveland
515 Pittsburgh	827 San Francisco	1,084 Pittsburgh
536 Arizona	837 San Diego	1,099 Houston

Fewest Total Yards Allowed

Last 2 Seasons	Last 3 Seasons	Last 4 Seasons
8,854 Pittsburgh	13,011 Dallas	17,689 Philadelphia
9,080 Dallas	13,512 Pittsburgh	18,077 Dallas
9,148 Minnesota	13,663 Minnesota	18,273 New Orleans
9,246 Green Bay	14,000 Houston	18,679 Minnesota
9,575 Arizona	14,095 Kansas City	18,680 Pittsburgh

Fewest Rushing Yards Allowed

Last 2 Seasons	Last 3 Seasons	Last 4 Seasons
2,626 Minnesota	4,105 San Diego	5,771 San Diego
2,710 San Diego	4,359 Minnesota	6,027 Dallas
2,820 Pittsburgh	4,456 Dallas	6,068 San Francisco
2,945 Green Bay	4,556 San Francisco	6,196 Minnesota
3,095 Miami	4,661 Pittsburgh	6,243 Pittsburgh

Fewest Passing Yards Allowed

Last 2 Seasons	Last 3 Seasons	Last 4 Seasons
5,868 Dallas	8,555 Dallas	11,376 Philadelphia
5,905 Chicago	8,854 Pittsburgh	11,607 New Orleans
6,033 Philadelphia	8,887 New Orleans	11,836 Chicago
6,037 Pittsburgh	8,909 Chicago	12,050 Dallas
6,046 Cincinnati	8,948 Kansas City	12,176 Kansas City

Most Opponents' Turnovers

Last 2 Seasons	Last 3 Seasons	Last 4 Seasons
76 Kansas City	115 Kansas City	155 Philadelphia
75 Buffalo	114 N.Y. Jets	151 N.Y. Jets
75 N.Y. Jets	112 Pittsburgh	148 Kansas City
70 Philadelphia	110 Buffalo	147 Buffalo
69 Houston	110 Minnesota	147 New Orleans
69 Pittsburgh		

RECORDS OF TEAMS ON OPENING DAY, 1933-94

AFC	W	L	T	Pct.	Longest W Strk.	Longest L Strk.	Current Streak
Denver	21	13	1	.618	3	4	L-1
Cleveland	26	19	0	.578	5	5	W-2
Kansas City	20	15	0	.571	5	4	W-5
L.A. Raiders	20	15	0	.571	5	5	L-1
San Diego	20	15	0	.571	6	6	W-2
Indianapolis	22	20	0	.524	8	8	W-1
Pittsburgh	29	27	4	.518	4	3	L-2
Miami	14	14	1	.500	4	5	W-3
Houston	17	18	0	.486	4	3	L-3
Cincinnati	13	14	0	.481	4	4	L-2
New England	16	19	0	.457	6	3	L-3
Buffalo	15	20	0	.429	6	5	L-1
N.Y. Jets	15	20	0	.429	3	5	W-1
Seattle	5	14	0	.263	3	8	W-1

NFC	W	L	T	Pct.	Longest W Strk.	Longest L Strk.	Current Streak
Dallas	26	8	1	.765	17	3	W-1
N.Y. Giants	35	23	4	.603	4	3	W-2
Chicago	36	25	1	.590	9	6	W-1
Minnesota	18	15	1	.545	4	2	L-2
Detroit	32	28	2	.533	7	4	W-2
L.A. Rams	30	27	0	.526	5	6	W-1
Green Bay	31	28	3	.525	5	6	W-2
Atlanta	15	14	0	.517	5	3	L-2
Washington	30	28	4	.517	6	5	L-1
San Francisco	22	22	1	.500	4	3	W-3
Arizona	26	34	1	.433	6	6	L-3
Philadelphia	25	35	1	.417	5	9	L-1
Tampa Bay	7	12	0	.368	3	5	L-2
New Orleans	7	21	0	.250	1	6	L-1

NOTE: All tied games occurred prior to 1972, when calculation of ties in percentages as half-win, half-loss was begun.

OLDEST INDIVIDUAL SINGLE-SEASON OR SINGLE-GAME RECORDS IN NFL RECORD & FACT BOOK

Regular-Season Records That Have Not Been Surpassed or Tied

Most Points, Game—40, Ernie Nevers, Chi. Cardinals vs. Chi. Bears, Nov. 28, 1929 (6-td, 4-pat)
Most Touchdowns Rushing, Game—6, Ernie Nevers, Chi. Cardinals vs. Chi. Bears, Nov. 28, 1929
Highest Punting Average, Season (Qualifiers)—51.40, Sammy Baugh, Washington, 1940 (35-1,799)
Highest Punting Average, Game (minimum: 4 punts)—61.75, Bob Cifers, Detroit vs. Chi. Bears, Nov. 24, 1946 (4-247)
Highest Average Gain, Pass Receptions, Season (minimum: 24 receptions)—32.58, Don Currivan, Boston, 1947 (24-782)
Highest Average Gain, Passing, Game (minimum: 20 passes)—18.58, Sammy Baugh, Washington vs. Boston, Oct. 31, 1948 (24-446)
Most Touchdowns, Fumble Recoveries, Game—2, Fred (Dippy) Evans, Chi. Bears vs. Washington, Nov. 28, 1948
Most Yards Gained, Intercepted Passes, Rookie, Season—301, Don Doll, Detroit, 1949
Most Passes Had Intercepted, Game—8, Jim Hardy, Chi. Cardinals vs. Philadelphia, Sept. 24, 1950
Highest Average Gain, Rushing, Game (minimum: 10 attempts)—17.09, Marion Motley, Cleveland vs. Pittsburgh, Oct. 29, 1950 (11-188)
Most Yards Gained, Kickoff Returns, Game—294, Wally Triplett, Detroit vs. Los Angeles, Oct. 29, 1950
Highest Kickoff Return Average, Game (minimum: 3 returns)—73.50, Wally Triplett, Detroit vs. Los Angeles, Oct. 29, 1950 (4-294)
Most Pass Receptions, Game—18, Tom Fears, Los Angeles vs. Green Bay, Dec. 3, 1950
Highest Punt Return Average, Season (Qualifiers)—23.00, Herb Rich, Baltimore, 1950 (12-276)
Highest Punt Return Average, Rookie, Season (Qualifiers)—23.00, Herb Rich, Baltimore, 1950 (12-276)
Most Yards Passing, Game—554, Norm Van Brocklin, Los Angeles vs. N.Y. Yanks, Sept. 28, 1951
Most Touchdowns, Punt Returns, Rookie, Season—4, Jack Christiansen, Detroit, 1951
Most Interceptions By, Season—14, Dick (Night Train) Lane, Los Angeles, 1952
Most Interceptions By, Rookie, Season—14, Dick (Night Train) Lane, Los Angeles, 1952
Highest Average Gain, Passing, Season (Qualifiers)—11.17, Tommy O'Connell, Cleveland, 1957 (110-1,229)
Most Points, Season—176, Paul Hornung, Green Bay, 1960 (15-td, 41-pat,15-fg)
Most Yards Gained, Pass Receptions, Rookie, Season—1,473, Bill Groman, Houston, 1960

LARGEST TRADES IN NFL HISTORY

(Based on number of players or draft choices involved)

18—October 13, 1989—RB Herschel Walker from the Dallas Cowboys to Minnesota. Dallas also traded its third-round choice in 1990, its tenth-round choice in 1990, and its third-round choice in 1991 to Minnesota. Minnesota traded LB Jesse Solomon, LB David Howard, CB Issiac Holt, and DE Alex Stewart along with its first-round choice in 1990, its second-round choice in 1990, its sixth-round choice in 1990, its first-round choice in 1991, its second-round choice in 1991, its first-round choice in 1992, its second-round choice in 1992, and its third-round choice in 1992 to Dallas. Minnesota traded RB Darrin Nelson to Dallas, which traded Nelson to San Diego for the Chargers' fifth-round choice in 1990, which Dallas then sent to Minnesota.

15—March 26, 1953—T Mike McCormack, DT Don Colo, LB Tom Catlin, DB John Petitbon, and G Herschell Forester from Baltimore to Cleveland for DB Don Shula, DB Bert Rechichar, DB Carl Taseff, LB Ed Sharkey, E Gern Nagler, QB Harry Agganis, T Dick Batten, T Stu Sheets, G Art Spinney, and G Elmer Willhoite.

15—January 28, 1971—LB Marlin McKeever, first- and third-round choices in 1971, and third-, fourth-, fifth-, sixth-, and seventh-round choices in 1972 from Washington to the Los Angeles Rams for LB Maxie Baughan, LB Jack Pardee, LB Myron Pottios, RB Jeff Jordan, G John Wilbur, DT Diron Talbert, and a fifth-round choice in 1971.

12—June 13, 1952—Selection rights to Les Richter from the Dallas Texans to the Los Angeles Rams for RB Dick Hoerner, DB Tom Keane, DB George Sims, C Joe Reid, HB Billy Baggett, T Jack Halliday, FB Dick McKissack, LB Vic Vasicek, E Richard Wilkins, C Aubrey Phillips, and RB Dave Anderson.

10—March 23, 1959—HB Ollie Matson from the Chicago Cardinals to the Los Angeles Rams for T Frank Fuller, DE Glenn Holtzman, T Ken Panfil, DT Art Hauser, E John Tracey, FB Larry Hickman, HB Don Brown, the Rams second-round choice in 1960, and a player to be delivered during the 1959 training camp.

10—October 31, 1987—RB Eric Dickerson from the Los Angeles Rams to Indianapolis. The rights to LB Cornelius Bennett from Indianapolis to Buffalo. Indianapolis running back Owen Gill and the Colts' first- and second-round choices in 1988 and second-round choice in 1989, plus Bills running back Greg Bell and Buffalo's first-round choice in 1988 and first- and second-round choices in 1989 to the Rams.

RETIRED UNIFORM NUMBERS IN NFL

AFC

Buffalo:	None	
Cincinnati:	Bob Johnson	54
Cleveland:	Otto Graham	14
	Jim Brown	32
	Ernie Davis	45
	Don Fleming	46
	Lou Groza	76
Denver:	Frank Tripucka	18
	Floyd Little	44
Houston:	Earl Campbell	34
	Jim Norton	43
	Mike Munchak	63
	Elvin Bethea	65
Indianapolis:	Johnny Unitas	19
	Buddy Young	22
	Lenny Moore	24
	Art Donovan	70
	Jim Parker	77
	Raymond Berry	82
	Gino Marchetti	89
Kansas City:	Jan Stenerud	3
	Len Dawson	16
	Abner Haynes	28
	Stone Johnson	33
	Mack Lee Hill	36
	Willie Lanier	63
	Bobby Bell	78
	Buck Buchanan	86
Los Angeles:	None	
Miami:	Bob Griese	12
New England:	Gino Cappelletti	20
	Steve Nelson	57
	John Hannah	73
	Jim Hunt	79
	Bob Dee	89
New York Jets:	Joe Namath	12
	Don Maynard	13
Pittsburgh:	None	
San Diego:	Dan Fouts	14
Seattle:	"Fans/the twelfth man"	12

NFC

Arizona:	Larry Wilson	8
	Stan Mauldin	77
	J.V. Cain	88
	Marshall Goldberg	99
Atlanta:	Steve Bartowski	10
	William Andrews	31
	Jeff Van Note	57
	Tommy Nobis	60
Chicago:	Bronko Nagurski	3
	George McAfee	5
	George Halas	7
	Willie Galimore	28
	Walter Payton	34
	Gale Sayers	40
	Brian Piccolo	41
	Sid Luckman	42
	Dick Butkus	51
	Bill Hewitt	56
	Bill George	61
	Bulldog Turner	66
	Red Grange	77
Dallas:	None	
Detroit:	Dutch Clark	7
	Bobby Layne	22
	Doak Walker	37
	Joe Schmidt	56
	Chuck Hughes	85
	Charlie Sanders	88
Green Bay:	Tony Canadeo	3
	Don Hutson	14
	Bart Starr	15
	Ray Nitschke	66
Minnesota:	Fran Tarkenton	10
	Alan Page	88
New Orleans:	Jim Taylor	31
	Doug Atkins	81
New York Giants:	Ray Flaherty	1
	Mel Hein	7
	Y.A. Tittle	14
	Al Blozis	32

New York Giants:........................Joe Morrison 40
Charlie Conerly 42
Ken Strong 50
Lawrence Taylor 56
Philadelphia: ....Steve Van Buren 15
Tom Brookshier 40
Pete Retzlaff 44
Chuck Bednarik 60
Al Wistert 70
Jerome Brown..99
St. Louis: ....Bob Waterfield..7
Merlin Olsen 74
San Francisco: ....John Brodie..12
Joe Perry 34
Jimmy Johnson..37
Hugh McElhenny 39
Charlie Krueger 70
Leo Nomellini 73
Dwight Clark..87
Tampa Bay: ....Lee Roy Selmon..63
Washington: ....Sammy Baugh 33

1994 NFL SCORE BY QUARTERS

AFC Offense	1	2	3	4	OT	PTS
Miami	22	135	105	124	3	389
San Diego	52	134	95	100	0	381
New England	46	95	94	110	6	351
Denver	53	96	102	93	3	347
Cleveland	65	121	55	99	0	340
Buffalo	82	120	69	69	0	340
Kansas City	52	92	79	96	0	319
Pittsburgh	64	106	20	120	6	316
Indianapolis	82	86	73	66	0	307
L.A. Raiders	62	94	61	86	0	303
Seattle	53	74	49	111	0	287
Cincinnati	58	66	53	96	3	276
N.Y. Jets	40	112	51	58	3	264
Houston	45	56	25	100	0	226

NFC Offense	1	2	3	4	OT	PTS
San Francisco	106	173	103	123	0	505
Dallas	100	122	104	88	0	414
Green Bay	89	129	92	72	0	382
Detroit	45	130	82	91	9	357
Minnesota	74	116	75	82	9	356
New Orleans	42	132	77	97	0	348
Washington	44	137	62	77	0	320
Atlanta	93	76	61	87	0	317
Philadelphia	48	106	81	73	0	308
L.A. Rams	79	100	36	71	0	286
N.Y. Giants	64	106	39	70	0	279
Chicago	40	61	61	106	3	271
Tampa Bay	30	94	35	89	3	251
Arizona	41	66	18	104	6	235

AFC Defense	1	2	3	4	OT	PTS
Cleveland	52	58	28	66	0	204
Pittsburgh	50	86	31	64	3	234
Kansas City	40	84	72	99	3	298
San Diego	51	104	46	105	0	306
New England	53	133	56	70	0	312
Indianapolis	48	81	59	132	0	320
N.Y. Jets	54	111	72	83	0	320
Seattle	48	98	65	109	3	323
L.A. Raiders	72	87	52	113	3	327
Miami	85	52	87	100	3	327
Houston	57	122	60	110	3	352
Buffalo	46	115	87	108	0	356
Denver	64	148	77	104	3	396
Cincinnati	85	149	79	93	0	406

NFC Defense	1	2	3	4	OT	PTS
Dallas	34	93	46	72	3	248
Arizona	74	83	62	45	3	267
Green Bay	40	96	65	83	3	287
San Francisco	62	94	64	76	0	296
N.Y. Giants	44	100	77	81	3	305
Chicago	44	116	67	74	6	307
Philadelphia	65	73	65	105	0	308
Minnesota	51	80	74	100	9	314
Detroit	60	148	72	62	0	342
Tampa Bay	75	142	74	60	0	351
L.A. Rams	79	124	74	88	0	365
Atlanta	61	110	82	129	3	385
New Orleans	82	120	83	122	0	407
Washington	95	128	81	105	3	412

NFL Totals	1	2	3	4	OT	PTS
	1671	2935	1857	2558	54	9075

TEAM LEADERS

Offense	Most Scored	Fewest Scored
1st Quarter	106 San Francisco	22 Miami
2nd Quarter	173 San Francisco	56 Houston
3rd Quarter	105 Miami	18 Arizona
4th Quarter	124 Miami	58 N.Y. Jets

Defense	Most Allowed	Fewest Allowed
1st Quarter	95 Washington	34 Dallas
2nd Quarter	149 Cincinnati	52 Miami
3rd Quarter	87 Buffalo & Miami	28 Cleveland
4th Quarter	132 Indianapolis	45 Arizona

GREATEST COMEBACKS IN NFL HISTORY

(Most Points Overcome To Win Game)

REGULAR SEASON GAMES

FROM 28 POINTS BEHIND TO WIN:
December 7, 1980, at San Francisco

New Orleans	14	21	0	0	0	— 35
San Francisco	0	7	14	14	3	— 38

NO — Harris 33 pass from Manning (Ricardo kick)
NO — Childs 21 pass from Manning (Ricardo kick)
NO — Holmes 1 run (Ricardo kick)
SF — Solomon 57 punt return (Wersching kick)
NO — Holmes 1 run (Ricardo kick)
NO — Harris 41 pass from Manning (Ricardo kick)
SF — Montana 1 run (Wersching kick)
SF — Clark 71 pass from Montana (Wersching kick)
SF — Solomon 14 pass from Montana (Wersching kick)
SF — Elliott 7 run (Wersching kick)
SF — FG Wersching 36

	N.O.	S.F.
First Downs	27	24
Total Yards	519	430
Yards Rushing	143	176
Yards Passing	376	254
Turnovers	3	0

FROM 25 POINTS BEHIND TO WIN:
November 8, 1987, at St. Louis

Tampa Bay	7	7	14	0	— 28
St. Louis	0	3	0	28	— 31

TB — Carrier 5 pass from DeBerg (Igwebuike kick)
TB — Carter 3 pass from DeBerg (Igwebuike kick)
StL — FG Gallery 31
TB — Smith 34 pass from DeBerg (Igwebuike kick)
TB — Smith 3 run (Igwebuike kick)
StL — Awalt 4 pass from Lomax (Gallery kick)
StL — Noga 23 fumble recovery (Gallery kick)
StL — J. Smith 11 pass from Lomax (Gallery kick)
StL — J. Smith 17 pass from Lomax (Gallery kick)

	T.B.	St.L.
First Downs	26	26
Total Yards	377	415
Yards Rushing	83	137
Yards Passing	294	278
Turnovers	1	2

FROM 24 POINTS BEHIND TO WIN:
October 27, 1946, at Washington

Philadelphia	0	0	14	14	— 28
Washington	10	14	0	0	— 24

Wash — Rosato 2 run (Poillon kick)
Wash — FG Poillon 28
Wash — Rosato 4 run (Poillon kick)
Wash — Lapka recovered fumble in end zone (Poillon kick)
Phil — Steele 1 run (Lio kick)
Phil — Pritchard 45 pass from Thompson (Lio kick)
Phil — Steinke 7 pass from Thompson (Lio kick)
Phil — Ferrante 30 pass from Thompson (Lio kick)

	Phil.	Wash.
First Downs	14	8
Total Yards	262	127
Yards Rushing	34	66
Yards Passing	228	61
Turnovers	6	3

FROM 24 POINTS BEHIND TO WIN:
October 20, 1957, at Detroit

Baltimore	7	14	6	0	— 27
Detroit	0	3	7	21	— 31

Balt — Mutscheller 15 pass from Unitas (Rechichar kick)
Det — FG Martin 47
Balt — Moore 72 pass from Unitas (Rechichar kick)
Balt — Mutscheller 52 pass from Unitas (Rechichar kick)
Balt — Moore 4 pass from Unitas (kick failed)
Det — Junker 14 pass from Rote (Layne kick)
Det — Cassady 26 pass from Layne (Layne kick)
Det — Johnson 1 run (Layne kick)
Det — Cassady 29 pass from Layne (Layne kick)

	Balt.	Det.
First Downs	15	20
Total Yards	322	369
Yards Rushing	117	178
Yards Passing	205	191
Turnovers	6	4

FROM 24 POINTS BEHIND TO WIN:
October 25, 1959, at Minneapolis

Philadelphia	0	0	21	7	— 28
Chicago Cardinals	7	10	7	0	— 24

Cardinals — Crow 10 pass from Roach (Conrad kick)
Cardinals — J. Hill 77 blocked field goal return (Conrad kick)
Cardinals — FG Conrad 15
Cardinals — Lane 37 interception return (Conrad kick)
Phil — Barnes 1 run (Walston kick)
Phil — McDonald 29 pass from Van Brocklin (Walston kick)
Phil — Barnes 2 run (Walston kick)
Phil — McDonald 22 pass from Van Brocklin (Walston kick)

	Phil.	Cardinals
First Downs	22	14
Total Yards	399	313
Yards Rushing	168	163
Yards Passing	231	150
Turnovers	2	6

FROM 24 POINTS BEHIND TO WIN:
October 23, 1960, at Denver

Boston	10	7	7	0	— 24
Denver	0	0	14	17	— 31

Bos — FG Cappelletti 12
Bos — Colclough 10 pass from Songin (Cappelletti kick)
Bos — Wells 6 pass from Songin (Cappelletti kick)
Bos — Miller 47 pass from Songin (Cappelletti kick)
Den — Carmichael 21 pass from Tripucka (Mingo kick)
Den — Jessup 19 pass from Tripucka (Mingo kick)
Den — Carmichael 35 lateral from Taylor, pass from Tripucka (Mingo kick)
Den — Taylor 8 pass from Tripucka (Mingo kick)
Den — FG Mingo 9

	Bos.	Den.
First Downs	19	16
Total Yards	434	326
Yards Rushing	211	65
Yards Passing	223	261
Turnovers	7	4

FROM 24 POINTS BEHIND TO WIN:
December 15, 1974, at Miami

New England	21	3	0	3	— 27
Miami	0	17	7	10	— 34

NE — Hannah recovered fumble in end zone (J. Smith kick)
NE — Sanders 23 interception return (J. Smith kick)
NE — Herron 4 pass from Plunkett (J. Smith kick)
NE — FG J. Smith 46
Mia — Nottingham 1 run (Yepremian kick)
Mia — Baker 37 pass from Morrall (Yepremian kick)
Mia — FG Yepremian 28
Mia — Baker 46 pass from Morrall (Yepremian kick)
NE — FG J. Smith 34
Mia — Nottingham 2 run (Yepremian kick)
Mia — FG Yepremian 40

	N.E.	Mia.
First Downs	18	18
Total Yards	333	333
Yards Rushing	114	61
Yards Passing	219	272
Turnovers	3	4

FROM 24 POINTS BEHIND TO WIN:
December 4, 1977, at Minnesota

San Francisco	0	10	14	3	— 27
Minnesota	0	0	7	21	— 28

SF — Delvin Williams 2 run (Wersching kick)
SF — FG Wersching 31
SF — Dave Williams 80 kickoff return (Wersching kick)
SF — Delvin Williams 5 run (Wersching kick)
Minn— McClanahan 15 pass from Lee (Cox kick)
Minn— Rashad 8 pass from Kramer (Cox kick)
Minn— Tucker 9 pass from Kramer (Cox kick)
SF — FG Wersching 31
Minn— S. White 69 pass from Kramer (Cox kick)

	S.F.	Minn.
First Downs	19	18
Total Yards	243	309
Yards Rushing	196	52
Yards Passing	47	257
Turnovers	2	5

FROM 24 POINTS BEHIND TO WIN:
September 23, 1979, at Denver

Seattle	10	10	14	0	— 34
Denver	0	10	21	6	— 37

Sea — FG Herrera 28
Sea — Doornink 5 run (Herrera kick)
Den — FG Turner 27
Sea — Doornink 5 run (Herrera kick)
Den — Armstrong 2 run (Turner kick)
Sea — FG Herrera 22
Sea — McCullum 13 pass from Zorn (Herrera kick)
Sea — Smith 1 run (Herrera kick)
Den — Studdard 2 pass from Morton (Turner kick)
Den — Moses 11 pass from Morton (Turner kick)
Den — Upchurch 35 pass from Morton (Turner kick)
Den — Lytle 1 run (kick failed)

	Sea.	Den.
First Downs	22	23
Total Yards	350	344
Yards Rushing	153	90
Yards Passing	197	254
Turnovers	4	3

FROM 24 POINTS BEHIND TO WIN:
September 23, 1979, at Cincinnati

Houston	0	10	17	0	3	—30
Cincinnati	14	10	0	3	0	—27

Cin — Johnson 1 run (Bahr kick)
Cin — Alexander 2 run (Bahr kick)
Cin — Johnson 1 run (Bahr kick)
Cin — FG Bahr 52
Hou — Burrough 35 pass from Pastorini (Fritsch kick)
Hou — FG Fritsch 33
Hou — Campbell 8 run (Fritsch kick)
Hou — Caster 22 pass from Pastorini (Fritsch kick)
Hou — FG Fritsch 47
Cin — FG Bahr 55
Hou — FG Fritsch 29

	Hou.	Cin.
First Downs	19	21
Total Yards	361	265
Yards Rushing	177	165
Yards Passing	184	100
Turnovers	3	2

FROM 24 POINTS BEHIND TO WIN:
November 22, 1982, at Los Angeles

San Diego	10	14	0	0	— 24
L.A. Raiders	0	7	14	7	— 28

SD — FG Benirschke 19
SD — Scales 29 pass from Fouts (Benirschke kick)
SD — Muncie 2 run (Benirschke kick)
SD — Muncie 1 run (Benirschke kick)
Raiders — Christensen 1 pass from Plunkett (Bahr kick)

Raiders — Allen 3 run (Bahr kick)
Raiders — Allen 6 run (Bahr kick)
Raiders — Hawkins 1 run (Bahr kick)

	S.D.	Raiders
First Downs	26	23
Total Yards	411	326
Yards Rushing	72	181
Yards Passing	339	145
Turnovers	4	2

FROM 24 POINTS BEHIND TO WIN:
September 26, 1988, at Denver

L.A. Raiders	0	0	14	13	3 — 30
Denver	7	17	0	3	0 — 27

Den — Dorsett 1 run (Karlis kick)
Den — Dorsett 1 run (Karlis kick)
Den — Sewell 7 pass from Elway (Karlis kick)
Den — FG Karlis 39
Raiders — Smith 40 pass from Schroeder (Bahr kick)
Raiders — Smith 42 pass from Schroeder (Bahr kick)
Raiders — FG Bahr 28
Raiders — Allen 4 run (Bahr kick)
Den — FG Karlis 25
Raiders — FG Bahr 44
Raiders — FG Bahr 35

	Raiders	Den.
First Downs	20	23
Total Yards	363	398
Yards Rushing	128	189
Yards Passing	235	209
Turnovers	1	5

FROM 24 POINTS BEHIND TO WIN:
December 6, 1992, at Tampa

L.A. Rams	0	3	21	7 — 31
Tampa Bay	6	21	0	0 — 27

TB — FG Murray 34
TB — FG Murray 47
TB — Armstrong 81 pass from Testaverde (Murray kick)
TB — Jones 26 fumble recovery (Murray kick)
Rams — FG Zendejas 18
TB — Carrier 10 pass from Testaverde (Murray kick)
Rams — Anderson 40 pass from Everett (Zendejas kick)
Rams — Chadwick 27 pass from Everett (Zendejas kick)
Rams — Lang 1 run (Zendejas kick)
Rams — Carter 8 pass from Everett (Zendejas kick)

	Rams	T.B.
First Downs	21	16
Total Yards	405	313
Yards Rushing	63	150
Yards Passing	342	163
Turnovers	3	3

POSTSEASON GAMES

FROM 32 POINTS BEHIND TO WIN:
AFC First-Round Playoff Game
January 3, 1993, at Buffalo

Houston	7	21	7	3	0 — 38
Buffalo	3	0	28	7	3 — 41

Hou — Jeffires 3 pass from Moon (Del Greco kick)
Buff — FG Christie 36
Hou — Slaughter 7 pass from Moon (Del Greco kick)
Hou — Duncan 26 pass from Moon (Del Greco kick)
Hou — Jeffires 27 pass from Moon (Del Greco kick)
Hou — McDowell 58 interception return (Del Greco kick)
Buff — Davis 1 run (Christie kick)
Buff — Beebe 38 pass from Reich (Christie kick)
Buff — Reed 26 pass from Reich (Christie kick)
Buff — Reed 18 pass from Reich (Christie kick)
Buff — Reed 17 pass from Reich (Christie kick)
Hou — FG Del Greco 26
Buff — FG Christie 32

	Hou.	Buff.
First Downs	27	19
Total Yards	429	366
Yards Rushing	82	98
Yards Passing	347	268
Turnovers	2	1

FROM 20 POINTS BEHIND TO WIN:
Western Conference Playoff Game
December 22, 1957, at San Francisco

Detroit	0	7	14	10 — 31
San Francisco	14	10	3	0 — 27

SF — Owens 34 pass from Tittle (Soltau kick)
SF — McElhenny 47 pass from Tittle (Soltau kick)
Det — Junker 4 pass from Rote (Martin kick)
SF — Wilson 12 pass from Tittle (Soltau kick)
SF — FG Soltau 25
SF — FG Soltau 10
Det — Tracy 2 run (Martin kick)
Det — Tracy 58 run (Martin kick)
Det — Gedman 3 run (Martin kick)
Det — FG Martin 14

	Det.	S.F.
First Downs	22	20
Total Yards	324	351
Yards Rushing	129	127
Yards Passing	195	224
Turnovers	5	4

FROM 18 POINTS BEHIND TO WIN:
NFC Divisional Playoff Game
December 23, 1972, at San Francisco

Dallas	3	10	0	17 — 30
San Francisco	7	14	7	0 — 28

SF — Washington 97 kickoff return (Gossett kick)
Dall — FG Fritsch 37
SF — Schreiber 1 run (Gossett kick)
SF — Schreiber 1 run (Gossett kick)
Dall — FG Fritsch 45
Dall — Alworth 28 pass from Morton (Fritsch kick)
SF — Schreiber 1 run (Gossett kick)
Dall — FG Fritsch 27
Dall — Parks 20 pass from Staubach (Fritsch kick)
Dall — Sellers 10 pass from Staubach (Fritsch kick)

	Dall.	S.F.
First Downs	22	13
Total Yards	402	255
Yards Rushing	165	105
Yards Passing	237	150
Turnovers	5	3

FROM 18 POINTS BEHIND TO WIN:
AFC Divisional Playoff Game
January 4, 1986, at Miami

Cleveland	7	7	7	0 — 21
Miami	3	0	14	7 — 24

Mia — FG Reveiz 51
Clev — Newsome 16 pass from Kosar (Bahr kick)
Clev — Byner 21 run (Bahr kick)
Clev — Byner 66 run (Bahr kick)
Mia — Moore 6 pass from Marino (Reveiz kick)
Mia — Davenport 31 run (Reveiz kick)
Mia — Davenport 1 run (Reveiz kick)

	Clev.	Mia.
First Downs	17	20
Total Yards	313	330
Yards Rushing	251	92
Yards Passing	62	238
Turnovers	1	1

RECORDS OF NFL TEAMS SINCE 1970 AFL-NFL MERGER

AFC	W-L-T	Pct.	Division Titles	Playoff Berths	Post-season Record	Super Bowl Record
Miami	248-126-2	.663	11	15	17-13	2-3
Los Angeles	236-134-6	.637	9	15	18-12	3-0
Pittsburgh	224-151-1	.597	11	15	17-11	4-0
Denver	209-161-6	.564	7	10	9-10	0-4
Cleveland	189-184-3	.507	6	10	4-10	0-0
Kansas City	177-192-7	.480	2	7	3-7	0-0
Cincinnati	178-198-0	.473	5	7	5-7	0-2
Buffalo	176-198-2	.471	6	9	11-9	0-4
San Diego	170-201-5	.458	5	6	6-6	0-1
Seattle*	133-159-0	.455	1	4	3-4	0-0
New England	168-208-0	.447	2	6	3-6	0-1
Houston	166-208-2	.444	2	10	7-10	0-0
N.Y. Jets	158-216-2	.423	0	5	3-5	0-0
Indianapolis	156-218-2	.417	5	6	4-5	1-0

NFC	W-L-T	Pct.	Division Titles	Playoff Berths	Post-season Record	Super Bowl Record
Dallas	239-137-0	.636	12	18	27-14	4-3
Washington	228-147-1	.608	5	13	18-10	3-2
San Francisco	225-148-3	.603	14	15	21-10	5-0
Minnesota	220-154-2	.588	12	16	11-16	0-3
St. Louis	207-165-4	.556	8	14	10-14	0-1
Chicago	195-180-1	.520	6	10	7-9	1-0
Philadelphia	178-192-6	.481	2	8	4-8	0-1
N.Y. Giants	178-196-2	.476	3	7	10-5	2-0
Detroit	169-203-4	.455	3	6	1-6	0-0
Green Bay	159-209-8	.433	1	4	3-4	0-0
Arizona	159-211-6	.430	2	3	0-3	0-0
New Orleans	155-217-4	.417	1	4	0-4	0-0
Atlanta	151-221-4	.406	1	4	2-4	0-0
Tampa Bay*	87-204-1	.300	2	3	1-3	0-0

*entered NFL in 1976.
Indianapolis totals include Baltimore, 1970-83.
L.A. Raiders totals include Oakland, 1970-81.
Arizona totals include St. Louis, 1970-87, and Phoenix, 1988-93.
St. Louis totals include Los Angeles 1970-94
Tie games before 1972 are not calculated in won-lost percentage.
In 1982, because of players' strike, the divisional format was abandoned. (L.A. Raiders and Washington won regular-season conference titles, not included in "Division Titles" totals listed above. Sixteen teams were awarded playoff berths, included in totals listed above.)

LONGEST WINNING STREAKS SINCE 1970

Regular-season games

16	Miami, 1971-73	(1 in 1971, 14 in 1972, 1 in 1973)
16	Miami, 1983-84	(5 in 1983, 11 in 1984)
15	San Francisco, 1989-90	(5 in 1989, 10 in 1990)
14	Oakland, 1976-77	(10 in 1976, 4 in 1977)
13	Minnesota, 1974-75	(3 in 1974, 10 in 1975)
13	Chicago, 1984-85	(1 in 1984, 12 in 1985)
13	N.Y. Giants, 1989-90	(3 in 1989, 10 in 1990)
12	Washington, 1990-91	(1 in 1990, 11 in 1991)
11	Pittsburgh, 1975	
11	Baltimore, 1975-76	(9 in 1975, 2 in 1976)
11	Chicago, 1986-87	(7 in 1986, 4 in 1987)
11	Houston, 1993	
10	Miami, 1973	
10	Pittsburgh, 1976-77	(9 in 1976, 1 in 1977)
10	Denver, 1984	
10	San Francisco, 1994	

NFL PLAYOFF APPEARANCES BY SEASONS

Team	Number of Seasons in Playoffs
Cleveland	23
N.Y. Giants	23
Dallas	22
St. Louis	22
Chicago	21
Washington	19
Los Angeles	18
Minnesota	18
Pittsburgh	16
San Francisco	16
Green Bay	15
Houston	15
Miami	15
Buffalo	13
Philadelphia	12
Detroit	11
Indianapolis	11
Kansas City	11
San Diego	11
Denver	10
Cincinnati	7
New England	7
N.Y. Jets	7
Arizona	5
Atlanta	4
New Orleans	4
Seattle	4
Tampa Bay	3

TEAMS IN SUPER BOWL CONTENTION, 1978-94

	With 3 Weeks to Play	With 2 Weeks to Play	With 1 Week to Play
1994	*25	*22	15
1993	20	18	16
1992	20	16	14
1991	20	18	13
1990	23	20	15
1989	21	18	*17
1988	21	18	15
1987	19	19	15
1986	19	17	14
1985	21	18	13
1984	18	14	13
1983	24	19	15
1982	20	17	16
1981	21	20	16
1980	20	14	12
1979	19	15	13
1978	20	17	12

*NFL Record

GAMES DECIDED BY 7 POINTS OR LESS AND 3 POINTS OR LESS (1970-94)

	Games Decided by 7 Points or Less	Games Decided by 3 Points or Less
1970	59 of 182 (32.4%)	34 of 182 (18.7%)
1971	76 of 182 (41.8%)	35 of 182 (19.2%)
1972	71 of 182 (39.0%)	38 of 182 (20.9%)
1973	60 of 182 (32.9%)	28 of 182 (15.4%)
1974	91 of 182 (50.0%)	37 of 182 (20.3%)
1975	62 of 182 (34.1%)	35 of 182 (19.2%)
1976	73 of 196 (37.2%)	38 of 196 (19.4%)
1977	85 of 196 (43.4%)	36 of 196 (18.4%)
1978	108 of 224 (48.2%)	49 of 224 (21.9%)
1979	104 of 224 (46.4%)	51 of 224 (22.8%)
1980	108 of 224 (48.2%)	58 of 224 (25.9%)
1981	91 of 224 (40.6%)	**60 of 224 (26.8%)
1982	61 of 126 (48.4%)	33 of 126 (26.2%)
1983	106 of 224 (47.3%)	54 of 224 (24.1%)
1984	95 of 224 (42.4%)	58 of 224 (25.9%)
1985	87 of 224 (38.8%)	38 of 224 (17.0%)
1986	106 of 224 (47.3%)	48 of 224 (21.4%)
1987	99 of 210 (47.1%)	40 of 210 (19.0%)
1988	113 of 224 (50.4%)	*62 of 224 (27.7%)
1989	107 of 224 (47.8%)	55 of 224 (24.6%)
1990	97 of 224 (43.3%)	54 of 224 (24.1%)
1991	112 of 224 (50.0%)	57 of 224 (25.4%)
1992	88 of 224 (39.3%)	**48 of 224 (21.4%)
1993	*105 of 224 (46.9%)	53 of 224 (23.7%)
1994	115 of 224 (51.3%)	60 of 224 (26.8%)

*Week record: Dec. 11-13, 1993 (Week 15), 12 of 14 games (86%) decided by 7 points or less.
**Week Record: Nov. 8-9, 1981 (Week 10), 8 of 14 games (57%), and Nov. 15-16, 1992 (Week 11), 8 of 14 games (57%) decided by 3 points or less.

1994 RECORDS OF TEAMS IN CLOSE GAMES

AFC	Overall Record	Decided by 8 Pts. or Less	Decided By 3 Pts. or Less
Buffalo	7-9	3-4	1-1
Cincinnati	3-13	3-8	3-3
Cleveland	11-5	5-3	1-1
Denver	7-9	6-6	2-4
Houston	2-14	1-8	0-7
Indianapolis	8-8	5-3	3-2
Kansas City	9-7	3-3	1-3
L.A. Raiders	9-7	6-2	3-2
Miami	10-6	5-4	2-3
New England	10-6	6-5	3-1
N.Y. Jets	6-10	3-3	1-1
Pittsburgh	12-4	5-2	2-2
San Diego	11-5	4-4	4-1
Seattle	6-10	3-5	3-3
NFC	**Overall Record**	**Decided by 8 Pts. or Less**	**Decided By 3 Pts. or Less**
Arizona	8-8	5-5	4-3
Atlanta	7-9	5-4	2-2
Chicago	9-7	3-3	2-0
Dallas	12-4	4-4	2-1
Detroit	9-7	6-5	4-0
Green Bay	9-7	5-4	0-3
L.A. Rams	4-12	3-6	1-4
Minnesota	10-6	7-3	3-1
New Orleans	7-9	5-3	4-1
N.Y. Giants	9-7	9-5	5-2
Philadelphia	7-9	4-5	1-2
San Francisco	13-3	3-2	0-0
Tampa Bay	6-10	3-3	2-2
Washington	3-13	1-9	1-5

SUPER BOWL CHAMPIONS WHO DID NOT MAKE PLAYOFFS THE FOLLOWING YEAR

N.Y. Giants—Super Bowl XXV champions did not make playoffs in the 1991 season.

Washington—Super Bowl XXII champions did not make playoffs in the 1988 season.

N.Y. Giants—Super Bowl XXI champions did not make playoffs in the 1987 season.

San Francisco—Super Bowl XVI champions did not make playoffs in the 1982 season.

Oakland—Super Bowl XV champions did not make playoffs in the 1981 season.

Pittsburgh—Super Bowl XIV champions did not make playoffs in the 1980 season.

Kansas City—Super Bowl IV champions did not make playoffs in the 1970 season.

Green Bay—Super Bowl II champions did not make playoffs in the 1968 season.

WILD CARD TEAMS THAT MADE IT TO THE SUPER BOWL

1992	Buffalo Bills (Lost to Dallas, 52-17)	Super Bowl XXVII
1985	New England Patriots (Lost to Chicago, 46-10)	Super Bowl XX
1980	Oakland Raiders (Beat Philadelphia, 27-10)	Super Bowl XV
1975	Dallas Cowboys (Lost to Pittsburgh, 21-17)	Super Bowl X

.500 TEAMS IN PLAYOFFS (SINCE MERGER)

1991	New York Jets	8-8
1990	New Orleans Saints	8-8
1985	Cleveland Browns	8-8

COLDEST NFL GAMES ON RECORD

-13 degrees (-48 degree wind chill)—December 31, 1967, Lambeau Field, Green Bay, Wisconsin, NFL Championship (Green Bay 21, Dallas 17)

-9 degrees (-59 degree wind chill)—January 10, 1982, Riverfront Stadium, Cincinnati, Ohio, AFC Championship (Cincinnati 27, San Diego 7)

0 degrees (-32 degree wind chill)—January 15, 1994, Rich Stadium, Orchard Park, New York, AFC Divisional Playoff (Buffalo 29, Los Angeles Raiders 23)

1 degree (wind chill not recorded)—January 4, 1981, Cleveland Stadium, Cleveland, Ohio, AFC Divisional Playoff (Oakland 14, Cleveland 12)

ALL-TIME RECORDS OF CURRENT NFL TEAMS

AFC

BUFFALO BILLS

	All Games			Home Games			Road Games		
Season	W	L	T	W	L	T	W	L	T
1960	5	8	1	3	4		2	4	1
1961	6	8		2	5		4	3	
1962	7	6	1	3	3	1	4	3	
1963	7	6	1	4	2	1	3	4	
1964	12	2		6	1		6	1	
1965	10	3	1	5	2		5	1	1
1966	9	4	1	4	2	1	5	2	
1967	4	10		2	5		2	5	
1968	1	12	1	1	6		0	6	1
1969	4	10		4	3		0	7	
1970	3	10	1	1	6		2	4	1
1971	1	13		1	6		0	7	
1972	4	9	1	2	4	1	2	5	
1973	9	5		5	2		4	3	
1974	9	5		5	2		4	3	
1975	8	6		3	4		5	2	
1976	2	12		1	6		1	6	
1977	3	11		1	6		2	5	
1978	5	11		4	4		1	7	
1979	7	9		3	5		4	4	
1980	11	5		6	2		5	3	
1981	10	6		7	1		3	5	
1982	4	5		4	1		0	4	
1983	8	8		3	5		5	3	
1984	2	14		2	6		0	8	
1985	2	14		2	6		0	8	
1986	4	12		3	5		1	7	
1987	7	8		4	4		3	4	
1988	12	4		8	0		4	4	
1989	9	7		6	2		3	5	
1990	13	3		8	0		5	3	
1991	13	3		7	1		6	2	
1992	11	5		6	2		5	3	
1993	12	4		6	2		6	2	
1994	7	9		4	4		3	5	
Total	241	267	8	136	119	4	105	148	4

CINCINNATI BENGALS

	All Games			Home Games			Road Games		
Season	W	L	T	W	L	T	W	L	T
1968	3	11		2	5		1	6	
1969	4	9	1	4	3		0	6	1
1970	8	6		5	2		3	4	
1971	4	10		3	4		1	6	
1972	8	6		4	3		4	3	
1973	10	4		7	0		3	4	

	All Games			Home Games			Road Games		
Season	W	L	T	W	L	T	W	L	T
1974	7	7		4	3		3	4	
1975	11	3		6	1		5	2	
1976	10	4		6	1		4	3	
1977	8	6		5	2		3	4	
1978	4	12		3	5		1	7	
1979	4	12		4	4		0	8	
1980	6	10		3	5		3	5	
1981	12	4		6	2		6	2	
1982	7	2		4	0		3	2	
1983	7	9		4	4		3	5	
1984	8	8		5	3		3	5	
1985	7	9		5	3		2	6	
1986	10	6		6	2		4	4	
1987	4	11		1	7		3	4	
1988	12	4		8	0		4	4	
1989	8	8		5	3		3	5	
1990	9	7		5	3		4	4	
1991	3	13		3	5		0	8	
1992	5	11		3	5		2	6	
1993	3	13		3	5		0	8	
1994	3	13		2	6		1	7	
Total	185	218	1	116	86		69	132	1

CLEVELAND BROWNS

	All Games			Home Games			Road Games		
Season	W	L	T	W	L	T	W	L	T
1950	10	2		5	1		5	1	
1951	11	1		6	0		5	1	
1952	8	4		4	2		4	2	
1953	11	1		6	0		5	1	
1954	9	3		5	1		4	2	
1955	9	2	1	5	1		4	1	1
1956	5	7		1	5		4	2	
1957	9	2	1	6	0		3	2	1
1958	9	3		4	2		5	1	
1959	7	5		3	3		4	2	
1960	8	3	1	4	2		4	1	1
1961	8	5	1	4	3		4	2	1
1962	7	6	1	4	2	1	3	4	
1963	10	4		5	2		5	2	
1964	10	3	1	5	1	1	5	2	
1965	11	3		5	2		6	1	
1966	9	5		5	2		4	3	
1967	9	5		6	1		3	4	
1968	10	4		5	2		5	2	
1969	10	3	1	5	1	1	5	2	
1970	7	7		4	3		3	4	
1971	9	5		4	3		5	2	
1972	10	4		4	3		6	1	
1973	7	5	2	5	1	1	2	4	1
1974	4	10		3	4		1	6	
1975	3	11		3	4		0	7	
1976	9	5		6	1		3	4	
1977	6	8		2	5		4	3	
1978	8	8		5	3		3	5	
1979	9	7		5	3		4	4	
1980	11	5		6	2		5	3	
1981	5	11		3	5		2	6	
1982	4	5		2	2		2	3	
1983	9	7		6	2		3	5	
1984	5	11		2	6		3	5	
1985	8	8		5	3		3	5	
1986	12	4		6	2		6	2	
1987	10	5		5	2		5	3	
1988	10	6		6	2		4	4	
1989	9	6	1	5	2	1	4	4	
1990	3	13		2	6		1	7	
1991	6	10		3	5		3	5	
1992	7	9		4	4		3	5	
1993	7	9		4	4		3	5	
1994	11	5		6	2		5	3	
Total	369	255	10	199	112	5	170	143	5

DENVER BRONCOS

	All Games			Home Games			Road Games		
Season	W	L	T	W	L	T	W	L	T
1960	4	9	1	2	4	1	2	5	
1961	3	11		2	5		1	6	
1962	7	7		3	4		4	3	
1963	2	11	1	2	5		0	6	1
1964	2	11	1	2	4	1	0	7	

	All Games			Home Games			Road Games		
Season	W	L	T	W	L	T	W	L	T
1965	4	10		2	5		2	5	
1966	4	10		3	4		1	6	
1967	3	11		1	6		2	5	
1968	5	9		3	4		2	5	
1969	5	8	1	4	2	1	1	6	
1970	5	8	1	3	3	1	2	5	
1971	4	9	1	2	4	1	2	5	
1972	5	9		3	4		2	5	
1973	7	5	2	3	3	1	4	2	1
1974	7	6	1	3	3	1	4	3	
1975	6	8		5	2		1	6	
1976	9	5		6	1		3	4	
1977	12	2		6	1		6	1	
1978	10	6		6	2		4	4	
1979	10	6		6	2		4	4	
1980	8	8		4	4		4	4	
1981	10	6		8	0		2	6	
1982	2	7		1	4		1	3	
1983	9	7		6	2		3	5	
1984	13	3		7	1		6	2	
1985	11	5		6	2		5	3	
1986	11	5		7	1		4	4	
1987	10	4	1	7	1		3	3	1
1988	8	8		6	2		2	6	
1989	11	5		6	2		5	3	
1990	5	11		4	4		1	7	
1991	12	4		7	1		5	3	
1992	8	8		7	1		1	7	
1993	9	7		5	3		4	4	
1994	7	9		4	4		3	5	
Total	248	258	10	152	100	7	96	158	3

HOUSTON OILERS

	All Games			Home Games			Road Games		
Season	W	L	T	W	L	T	W	L	T
1960	10	4		6	1		4	3	
1961	10	3	1	6	1		4	2	1
1962	11	3		6	1		5	2	
1963	6	8		4	3		2	5	
1964	4	10		3	4		1	6	
1965	4	10		3	4		1	6	
1966	3	11		3	4		0	7	
1967	9	4	1	5	2		4	2	1
1968	7	7		3	4		4	3	
1969	6	6	2	4	2	1	2	4	1
1970	3	10	1	1	6		2	4	1
1971	4	9	1	3	3	1	1	6	
1972	1	13		1	6		0	7	
1973	1	13		0	7		1	6	
1974	7	7		3	4		4	3	
1975	10	4		5	2		5	2	
1976	5	9		3	4		2	5	
1977	8	6		5	2		3	4	
1978	10	6		5	3		5	3	
1979	11	5		6	2		5	3	
1980	11	5		6	2		5	3	
1981	7	9		5	3		2	6	
1982	1	8		1	4		0	4	
1983	2	14		2	6		0	8	
1984	3	13		2	6		1	7	
1985	5	11		4	4		1	7	
1986	5	11		4	4		1	7	
1987	9	6		5	2		4	4	
1988	10	6		7	1		3	5	
1989	9	7		6	2		3	5	
1990	9	7		6	2		3	5	
1991	11	5		7	1		4	4	
1992	10	6		5	3		5	3	
1993	12	4		7	1		5	3	
1994	2	14		2	6		0	8	
Total	236	274	6	144	112	2	92	162	4

INDIANAPOLIS COLTS*

	All Games			Home Games			Road Games		
Season	W	L	T	W	L	T	W	L	T
1953	3	9		2	4		1	5	
1954	3	9		2	4		1	5	
1955	5	6	1	4	1	1	1	5	
1956	5	7		4	2		1	5	
1957	7	5		4	2		3	3	
1958	9	3		6	0		3	3	

	All Games			Home Games			Road Games		
Season	W	L	T	W	L	T	W	L	T
1959	9	3		4	2		5	1	
1960	6	6		4	2		2	4	
1961	8	6		5	2		3	4	
1962	7	7		3	4		4	3	
1963	8	6		4	3		4	3	
1964	12	2		7	1		5	1	
1965	10	3	1	5	2		5	1	1
1966	9	5		5	2		4	3	
1967	11	1	2	6	0	1	5	1	1
1968	13	1		6	1		7	0	
1969	8	5	1	4	2	1	4	3	
1970	11	2	1	5	1	1	6	1	
1971	10	4		5	2		5	2	
1972	5	9		2	5		3	4	
1973	4	10		3	4		1	6	
1974	2	12		0	7		2	5	
1975	10	4		5	2		5	2	
1976	11	3		6	1		5	2	
1977	10	4		6	1		4	3	
1978	5	11		2	6		3	5	
1979	5	11		3	5		2	6	
1980	7	9		2	6		5	3	
1981	2	14		1	7		1	7	
1982	0	8	1	0	3	1	0	5	
1983	7	9		3	5		4	4	
1984	4	12		2	6		2	6	
1985	5	11		4	4		1	7	
1986	3	13		1	7		2	6	
1987	9	6		4	4		5	2	
1988	9	7		6	2		3	5	
1989	8	8		6	2		2	6	
1990	7	9		3	5		4	4	
1991	1	15		0	8		1	7	
1992	9	7		4	4		5	3	
1993	4	12		2	6		2	6	
1994	8	8		5	3		3	5	
Total	289	302	7	155	140	5	134	162	2

includes Baltimore Colts (1953-83).

KANSAS CITY CHIEFS*

	All Games			Home Games			Road Games		
Season	W	L	T	W	L	T	W	L	T
1960	8	6		5	2		3	4	
1961	6	8		4	3		2	5	
1962	11	3		6	1		5	2	
1963	5	7	2	4	3		1	4	2
1964	7	7		4	3		3	4	
1965	7	5	2	5	2		2	3	2
1966	11	2	1	4	2	1	7	0	
1967	9	5		4	3		5	2	
1968	12	2		6	1		6	1	
1969	11	3		6	1		5	2	
1970	7	5	2	4	1	2	3	4	
1971	10	3	1	7	0		3	3	1
1972	8	6		3	4		5	2	
1973	7	5	2	5	1	1	2	4	1
1974	5	9		1	6		4	3	
1975	5	9		3	4		2	5	
1976	5	9		1	6		4	3	
1977	2	12		1	6		1	6	
1978	4	12		3	5		1	7	
1979	7	9		3	5		4	4	
1980	8	8		3	5		5	3	
1981	9	7		5	3		4	4	
1982	3	6		2	2		1	4	
1983	6	10		5	3		1	7	
1984	8	8		5	3		3	5	
1985	6	10		5	3		1	7	
1986	10	6		6	2		4	4	
1987	4	11		3	4		1	7	
1988	4	11	1	4	4		0	7	1
1989	8	7	1	5	3		3	4	1
1990	11	5		6	2		5	3	
1991	10	6		6	2		4	4	
1992	10	6		7	1		3	5	
1993	11	5		7	1		4	4	
1994	9	7		5	3		4	4	
Total	264	240	12	153	100	4	111	140	8

includes Dallas Texans (1960-62).

LOS ANGELES RAIDERS*

	All Games			Home Games			Road Games		
Season	W	L	T	W	L	T	W	L	T
1960	6	8		3	4		3	4	
1961	2	12		1	6		1	6	
1962	1	13		1	6		0	7	
1963	10	4		6	1		4	3	
1964	5	7	2	5	2		0	5	2
1965	8	5	1	5	2		3	3	1
1966	8	5	1	3	3	1	5	2	
1967	13	1		7	0		6	1	
1968	12	2		6	1		6	1	
1969	12	1	1	7	0		5	1	1
1970	8	4	2	6	1		2	3	2
1971	8	4	2	5	1	1	3	3	1
1972	10	3	1	5	1	1	5	2	
1973	9	4	1	5	2		4	2	1
1974	12	2		6	1		6	1	
1975	11	3		6	1		5	2	
1976	13	1		7	0		6	1	
1977	11	3		6	1		5	2	
1978	9	7		4	4		5	3	
1979	9	7		6	2		3	5	
1980	11	5		6	2		5	3	
1981	7	9		4	4		3	5	
1982	8	1		4	0		4	1	
1983	12	4		6	2		6	2	
1984	11	5		6	2		5	3	
1985	12	4		7	1		5	3	
1986	8	8		3	5		5	3	
1987	5	10		3	5		2	5	
1988	7	9		3	5		4	4	
1989	8	8		7	1		1	7	
1990	12	4		6	2		6	2	
1991	9	7		5	3		4	4	
1992	7	9		5	3		2	6	
1993	10	6		5	3		5	3	
1994	9	7		4	4		5	3	
Total	313	192	11	174	81	3	139	111	8

**includes Oakland Raiders (1960-81).*

MIAMI DOLPHINS

	All Games			Home Games			Road Games		
Season	W	L	T	W	L	T	W	L	T
1966	3	11		2	5		1	6	
1967	4	10		4	3		0	7	
1968	5	8	1	1	5	1	4	3	
1969	3	10	1	2	4	1	1	6	
1970	10	4		6	1		4	3	
1971	10	3	1	6	1		4	2	1
1972	14	0		7	0		7	0	
1973	12	2		7	0		5	2	
1974	11	3		7	0		4	3	
1975	10	4		5	2		5	2	
1976	6	8		3	4		3	4	
1977	10	4		6	1		4	3	
1978	11	5		7	1		4	4	
1979	10	6		6	2		4	4	
1980	8	8		5	3		3	5	
1981	11	4	1	6	1	1	5	3	
1982	7	2		4	0		3	2	
1983	12	4		7	1		5	3	
1984	14	2		7	1		7	1	
1985	12	4		8	0		4	4	
1986	8	8		4	4		4	4	
1987	8	7		4	3		4	4	
1988	6	10		4	4		2	6	
1989	8	8		4	4		4	4	
1990	12	4		7	1		5	3	
1991	8	8		5	3		3	5	
1992	11	5		6	2		5	3	
1993	9	7		4	4		5	3	
1994	10	6		6	2		4	4	
Total	263	165	4	150	62	3	113	103	1

NEW ENGLAND PATRIOTS*

	All Games			Home Games			Road Games		
Season	W	L	T	W	L	T	W	L	T
1960	5	9		3	4		2	5	
1961	9	4	1	4	2	1	5	2	
1962	9	4	1	6	1		3	3	1
1963	7	6	1	5	1	1	2	5	
1964	10	3	1	4	2	1	6	1	
1965	4	8	2	1	4	2	3	4	
1966	8	4	2	4	2	1	4	2	1
1967	3	10	1	2	4		1	6	1
1968	4	10		2	5		2	5	
1969	4	10		2	5		2	5	
1970	2	12		1	6		1	6	
1971	6	8		5	2		1	6	
1972	3	11		2	5		1	6	
1973	5	9		3	4		2	5	
1974	7	7		3	4		4	3	
1975	3	11		2	5		1	6	
1976	11	3		6	1		5	2	
1977	9	5		6	1		3	4	
1978	11	5		5	3		6	2	
1979	9	7		6	2		3	5	
1980	10	6		6	2		4	4	
1981	2	14		2	6		0	8	
1982	5	4		3	1		2	3	
1983	8	8		5	3		3	5	
1984	9	7		5	3		4	4	
1985	11	5		7	1		4	4	
1986	11	5		4	4		7	1	
1987	8	7		5	3		3	4	
1988	9	7		7	1		2	6	
1989	5	11		3	5		2	6	
1990	1	15		0	8		1	7	
1991	6	10		4	4		2	6	
1992	2	14		1	7		1	7	
1993	5	11		3	5		2	6	
1994	10	6		5	3		5	3	
Total	231	276	9	132	119	6	99	157	3

**includes Boston Patriots (1960-70).*

NEW YORK JETS*

	All Games			Home Games			Road Games		
Season	W	L	T	W	L	T	W	L	T
1960	7	7		3	4		4	3	
1961	7	7		5	2		2	5	
1962	5	9		2	5		3	4	
1963	5	8	1	4	2	1	1	6	
1964	5	8	1	5	1	1	0	7	
1965	5	8	1	3	3	1	2	5	
1966	6	6	2	4	3		2	3	2
1967	8	5	1	4	2	1	4	3	
1968	11	3		6	1		5	2	
1969	10	4		5	2		5	2	
1970	4	10		2	5		2	5	
1971	6	8		4	3		2	5	
1972	7	7		4	3		3	4	
1973	4	10		2	4		2	6	
1974	7	7		3	4		4	3	
1975	3	11		1	6		2	5	
1976	3	11		2	5		1	6	
1977	3	11		1	6		2	5	
1978	8	8		4	4		4	4	
1979	8	8		6	2		2	6	
1980	4	12		2	6		2	6	
1981	10	5	1	6	2		4	3	1
1982	6	3		3	1		3	2	
1983	7	9		2	6		5	3	
1984	7	9		3	5		4	4	
1985	11	5		7	1		4	4	
1986	10	6		5	3		5	3	
1987	6	9		4	4		2	5	
1988	8	7	1	5	2	1	3	5	
1989	4	12		1	7		3	5	
1990	6	10		3	5		3	5	
1991	8	8		4	4		4	4	
1992	4	12		3	5		1	7	
1993	8	8		3	5		5	3	
1994	6	10		4	4		2	6	
Total	227	281	8	125	127	5	102	154	3

**includes New York Titans (1960-62).*

PITTSBURGH STEELERS*

	All Games			Home Games			Road Games		
Season	W	L	T	W	L	T	W	L	T
1933	3	6	2	2	3		1	3	2
1934	2	10		1	5		1	5	
1935	4	8		2	5		2	3	
1936	6	6		4	1		2	5	
1937	4	7		2	4		2	3	
1938	2	9		0	5		2	4	
1939	1	9	1	1	4		0	5	1
1940	2	7	2	1	2	2	1	5	
1941	1	9	1	1	4		0	5	1
1942	7	4		3	2		4	2	
1945	2	8		1	4		1	4	
1946	5	5	1	4	1		1	4	1
1947	8	4		5	1		3	3	
1948	4	8		4	2		0	6	
1949	6	5	1	3	2	1	3	3	
1950	6	6		2	4		4	2	
1951	4	7	1	1	4	1	3	3	
1952	5	7		2	4		3	3	
1953	6	6		3	3		3	3	
1954	5	7		4	2		1	5	
1955	4	8		3	2		1	6	
1956	5	7		3	3		2	4	
1957	6	6		4	2		2	4	
1958	7	4	1	5	1		2	3	1
1959	6	5	1	3	2	1	3	3	
1960	5	6	1	4	2		1	4	1
1961	6	8		4	3		2	5	
1962	9	5		4	3		5	2	
1963	7	4	3	5	0	2	2	4	1
1964	5	9		2	5		3	4	
1965	2	12		1	6		1	6	
1966	5	8	1	3	3	1	2	5	
1967	4	9	1	1	6		3	3	1
1968	2	11	1	1	6		1	5	1
1969	1	13		1	6		0	7	
1970	5	9		4	3		1	6	
1971	6	8		5	2		1	6	
1972	11	3		7	0		4	3	
1973	10	4		7	1		3	3	
1974	10	3	1	5	2		5	1	1
1975	12	2		6	1		6	1	
1976	10	4		6	1		4	3	
1977	9	5		6	1		3	4	
1978	14	2		7	1		7	1	
1979	12	4		8	0		4	4	
1980	9	7		6	2		3	5	
1981	8	8		5	3		3	5	
1982	6	3		4	0		2	3	
1983	10	6		4	4		6	2	
1984	9	7		6	2		3	5	
1985	7	9		5	3		2	6	
1986	6	10		4	4		2	6	
1987	8	7		4	3		4	4	
1988	5	11		4	4		1	7	
1989	9	7		4	4		5	3	
1990	9	7		6	2		3	5	
1991	7	9		5	3		2	6	
1992	11	5		7	1		4	4	
1993	9	7		6	2		3	5	
1994	12	4		7	1		5	3	
Total	381	404	19	228	162	8	153	242	11

**includes Pittsburgh Pirates (1933-40).*

SAN DIEGO CHARGERS*

	All Games			Home Games			Road Games		
Season	W	L	T	W	L	T	W	L	T
1960	10	4		5	2		5	2	
1961	12	2		6	1		6	1	
1962	4	10		3	4		1	6	
1963	11	3		6	1		5	2	
1964	8	5	1	4	3		4	2	1
1965	9	2	3	4	1	2	5	1	1
1966	7	6	1	5	2		2	4	1
1967	8	5	1	5	2	1	3	3	
1968	9	5		4	3		5	2	
1969	8	6		5	2		3	4	
1970	5	6	3	2	3	2	3	3	1
1971	6	8		6	1		0	7	
1972	4	9	1	2	5		2	4	1
1973	2	11	1	2	5		0	6	1
1974	5	9		3	4		2	5	
1975	2	12		1	6		1	6	
1976	6	8		3	4		3	4	
1977	7	7		3	4		4	3	
1978	9	7		5	3		4	4	

	All Games			Home Games			Road Games		
Season	W	L	T	W	L	T	W	L	T
1979	12	4		7	1		5	3	
1980	11	5		6	2		5	3	
1981	10	6		5	3		5	3	
1982	6	3		3	1		3	2	
1983	6	10		4	4		2	6	
1984	7	9		4	4		3	5	
1985	8	8		6	2		2	6	
1986	4	12		2	6		2	6	
1987	8	7		4	3		4	4	
1988	6	10		3	5		3	5	
1989	6	10		4	4		2	6	
1990	6	10		3	5		3	5	
1991	4	12		3	5		1	7	
1992	11	5		6	2		5	3	
1993	8	8		4	4		4	4	
1994	11	5		5	3		6	2	
Total	256	249	11	143	110	5	113	139	6

**includes Los Angeles Chargers (1960).*

SEATTLE SEAHAWKS

	All Games			Home Games			Road Games		
Season	W	L	T	W	L	T	W	L	T
1976	2	12		1	6		1	6	
1977	5	9		3	4		2	5	
1978	9	7		5	3		4	4	
1979	9	7		5	3		4	4	
1980	4	12		0	8		4	4	
1981	6	10		5	3		1	7	
1982	4	5		3	2		1	3	
1983	9	7		5	3		4	4	
1984	12	4		7	1		5	3	
1985	8	8		5	3		3	5	
1986	10	6		7	1		3	5	
1987	9	6		6	2		3	4	
1988	9	7		5	3		4	4	
1989	7	9		3	5		4	4	
1990	9	7		5	3		4	4	
1991	7	9		5	3		2	6	
1992	2	14		1	7		1	7	
1993	6	10		4	4		2	6	
1994	6	10		3	5		3	5	
Total	133	159		78	69		55	90	

NFC

ARIZONA CARDINALS*

	All Games			Home Games			Road Games		
Season	W	L	T	W	L	T	W	L	T
1920	6	2	2	5	1	1	1	1	1
1921	3	3	2	3	3	1	0	0	1
1922	8	3		8	3		0	0	
1923	8	4		8	3		0	1	
1924	5	4	1	5	3	1	0	1	
1925	11	2	1	11	2		0	0	1
1926	5	6	1	3	3		2	3	1
1927	3	7	1	2	3	1	1	4	
1928	1	5		1	1		0	4	
1929	6	6	1	3	2		3	4	1
1930	5	6	2	3	2		2	4	2
1931	5	4		3	0		2	4	
1932	2	6	2	1	2	1	1	4	1
1933	1	9	1	0	4	1	1	5	
1934	5	6		2	2		3	4	
1935	6	4	2	2	2		4	2	2
1936	3	8	1	3	1	1	0	7	
1937	5	5	1	1	3		4	2	1
1938	2	9		1	4		1	5	
1939	1	10		0	4		1	6	
1940	2	7	2	2	1	1	0	6	1
1941	3	7	1	0	3	1	3	4	
1942	3	8		2	2		1	6	
1943	0	10		0	3		0	7	
1945	1	9		0	3		1	6	
1946	6	5		2	2		4	3	
1947	9	3		5	0		4	3	
1948	11	1		5	1		6	0	
1949	6	5	1	2	3	1	4	2	
1950	5	7		3	3		2	4	
1951	3	9		1	5		2	4	
1952	4	8		2	4		2	4	
1953	1	10	1	0	5	1	1	5	
1954	2	10		2	4		0	6	
1955	4	7	1	3	2	1	1	5	
1956	7	5		4	2		3	3	
1957	3	9		0	6		3	3	
1958	2	9	1	1	4	1	1	5	
1959	2	10		2	4		0	6	
1960	6	5	1	3	2	1	3	3	
1961	7	7		3	4		4	3	
1962	4	9	1	2	4	1	2	5	
1963	9	5		3	4		6	1	
1964	9	3	2	4	1	1	5	2	1
1965	5	9		2	5		3	4	
1966	8	5	1	5	1	1	3	4	
1967	6	7	1	3	3	1	3	4	
1968	9	4	1	4	2	1	5	2	
1969	4	9	1	3	4		1	5	1
1970	8	5	1	6	1		2	4	1
1971	4	9	1	1	5	1	3	4	
1972	4	9	1	2	5		2	4	1
1973	4	9	1	2	4	1	2	5	
1974	10	4		5	2		5	2	
1975	11	3		6	1		5	2	
1976	10	4		6	1		4	3	
1977	7	7		4	3		3	4	
1978	6	10		3	5		3	5	
1979	5	11		3	5		2	6	
1980	5	11		2	6		3	5	
1981	7	9		5	3		2	6	
1982	5	4		1	3		4	1	
1983	8	7	1	4	3	1	4	4	
1984	9	7		5	3		4	4	
1985	5	11		4	4		1	7	
1986	4	11	1	3	5		1	6	1
1987	7	8		4	3		3	5	
1988	7	9		4	4		3	5	
1989	5	11		2	6		3	5	
1990	5	11		3	5		2	6	
1991	4	12		2	6		2	6	
1992	4	12		3	5		1	7	
1993	7	9		4	4		3	5	
1994	8	8		5	3		3	5	
Total	391	522	39	222	230	22	169	292	17

**includes Chicago Cardinals (1920-59), St. Louis Cardinals (1960-87), and Phoenix Cardinals (1988-1993).*

ATLANTA FALCONS

	All Games			Home Games			Road Games		
Season	W	L	T	W	L	T	W	L	T
1966	3	11		1	6		2	5	
1967	1	12	1	1	5	1	0	7	
1968	2	12		1	6		1	6	
1969	6	8		4	3		2	5	
1970	4	8	2	3	4		1	4	2
1971	7	6	1	4	3		3	3	1
1972	7	7		4	3		3	4	
1973	9	5		4	3		5	2	
1974	3	11		2	5		1	6	
1975	4	10		3	4		1	6	
1976	4	10		3	4		1	6	
1977	7	7		4	3		3	4	
1978	9	7		7	1		2	6	
1979	6	10		3	5		3	5	
1980	12	4		6	2		6	2	
1981	7	9		4	4		3	5	
1982	5	4		2	3		3	1	
1983	7	9		4	4		3	5	
1984	4	12		2	6		2	6	
1985	4	12		3	5		1	7	
1986	7	8	1	2	5	1	5	3	
1987	3	12		2	6		1	6	
1988	5	11		2	6		3	5	
1989	3	13		3	5		0	8	
1990	5	11		5	3		0	8	
1991	10	6		6	2		4	4	
1992	6	10		5	3		1	7	
1993	6	10		4	4		2	6	
1994	7	9		5	3		2	6	
Total	163	264	5	99	116	2	64	148	3

CHICAGO BEARS*

	All Games			Home Games			Road Games		
Season	W	L	T	W	L	T	W	L	T
1920	10	1	2	6	0	1	4	1	1
1921	9	1	1	9	1	1	0	0	
1922	9	3		7	1		2	2	
1923	9	2	1	7	1	1	2	1	
1924	6	1	4	5	0	3	1	1	1
1925	9	5	3	7	1	1	2	4	2
1926	12	1	3	10	0	2	2	1	1
1927	9	3	2	7	1	1	2	2	1
1928	7	5	1	6	3		1	2	1
1929	4	9	2	1	5	2	3	4	
1930	9	4	1	5	2	1	4	2	
1931	8	5		6	3		2	2	
1932	7	1	6	6	1	1	1	0	5
1933	10	2	1	6	0		4	2	1
1934	13	0		5	0		8	0	
1935	6	4	2	1	2	2	5	2	
1936	9	3		3	1		6	2	
1937	9	1	1	4	1		5	0	1
1938	6	5		2	3		4	2	
1939	8	3		4	1		4	2	
1940	8	3		5	0		3	3	
1941	10	1		5	1		5	0	
1942	11	0		6	0		5	0	
1943	8	1	1	5	0		3	1	1
1944	6	3	1	4	0	1	2	3	
1945	3	7		2	3		1	4	
1946	8	2	1	4	1	1	4	1	
1947	8	4		4	2		4	2	
1948	10	2		5	1		5	1	
1949	9	3		5	1		4	2	
1950	9	3		6	0		3	3	
1951	7	5		3	3		4	2	
1952	5	7		3	3		2	4	
1953	3	8	1	1	4	1	2	4	
1954	8	4		4	2		4	2	
1955	8	4		5	1		3	3	
1956	9	2	1	6	0		3	2	1
1957	5	7		2	4		3	3	
1958	8	4		5	1		3	3	
1959	8	4		4	2		4	2	
1960	5	6	1	4	2		1	4	1
1961	8	6		5	2		3	4	
1962	9	5		4	3		5	2	
1963	11	1	2	6	0	1	5	1	1
1964	5	9		2	5		3	4	
1965	9	5		5	2		4	3	
1966	5	7	2	4	1	2	1	6	
1967	7	6	1	3	3	1	4	3	
1968	7	7		2	5		5	2	
1969	1	13		1	6		0	7	
1970	6	8		3	4		3	4	
1971	6	8		4	3		2	5	
1972	4	9	1	1	5	1	3	4	
1973	3	11		1	6		2	5	
1974	4	10		4	3		0	7	
1975	4	10		3	4		1	6	
1976	7	7		4	3		3	4	
1977	9	5		5	2		4	3	
1978	7	9		4	4		3	5	
1979	10	6		6	2		4	4	
1980	7	9		5	3		2	6	
1981	6	10		4	4		2	6	
1982	3	6		2	2		1	4	
1983	8	8		5	3		3	5	
1984	10	6		6	2		4	4	
1985	15	1		8	0		7	1	
1986	14	2		7	1		7	1	
1987	11	4		6	2		5	2	
1988	12	4		7	1		5	3	
1989	6	10		4	4		2	6	
1990	11	5		7	1		4	4	
1991	11	5		6	2		5	3	
1992	5	11		4	4		1	7	
1993	7	9		3	5		4	4	
1994	9	7		5	3		4	4	
Total	582	378	42	341	158	24	241	220	18

**includes Decatur Staleys (1920) and Chicago Staleys (1921).*

DALLAS COWBOYS

	All Games			Home Games			Road Games		
Season	W	L	T	W	L	T	W	L	T
1960	0	11	1	0	6		0	5	1
1961	4	9	1	2	4	1	2	5	
1962	5	8	1	2	4	1	3	4	
1963	4	10		3	4		1	6	
1964	5	8	1	2	4	1	3	4	
1965	7	7		5	2		2	5	
1966	10	3	1	6	1		4	2	1
1967	9	5		5	2		4	3	
1968	12	2		5	2		7	0	
1969	11	2	1	6	0	1	5	2	
1970	10	4		6	1		4	3	
1971	11	3		6	1		5	2	
1972	10	4		5	2		5	2	
1973	10	4		6	1		4	3	
1974	8	6		5	2		3	4	
1975	10	4		5	2		5	2	
1976	11	3		6	1		5	2	
1977	12	2		6	1		6	1	
1978	12	4		7	1		5	3	
1979	11	5		6	2		5	3	
1980	12	4		8	0		4	4	
1981	12	4		8	0		4	4	
1982	6	3		3	2		3	1	
1983	12	4		6	2		6	2	
1984	9	7		5	3		4	4	
1985	10	6		7	1		3	5	
1986	7	9		3	5		4	4	
1987	7	8		3	4		4	4	
1988	3	13		1	7		2	6	
1989	1	15		0	8		1	7	
1990	7	9		5	3		2	6	
1991	11	5		6	2		5	3	
1992	13	3		7	1		6	2	
1993	12	4		6	2		6	2	
1994	12	4		6	2		6	2	
Total	306	202	6	168	85	4	138	117	2

DETROIT LIONS*

	All Games			Home Games			Road Games		
Season	W	L	T	W	L	T	W	L	T
1930	5	6	3	5	1	2	0	5	1
1931	11	3		8	0		3	3	
1932	6	2	4	3	0	2	3	2	2
1933	6	5		4	1		2	4	
1934	10	3		6	2		4	1	
1935	7	3	2	5	0	1	2	3	1
1936	8	4		5	1		3	3	
1937	7	4		4	2		3	2	
1938	7	4		4	3		3	1	
1939	6	5		4	2		2	3	
1940	5	5	1	3	3		2	2	1
1941	4	6	1	3	2		1	4	1
1942	0	11		0	7		0	4	
1943	3	6	1	2	2	1	1	4	
1944	6	3	1	4	2		2	1	1
1945	7	3		4	1		3	2	
1946	1	10		1	5		0	5	
1947	3	9		2	4		1	5	
1948	2	10		2	4		0	6	
1949	4	8		2	4		2	4	
1950	6	6		4	2		2	4	
1951	7	4	1	3	3	1	4	1	
1952	9	3		6	1		3	2	
1953	10	2		5	1		5	1	
1954	9	2	1	5	0	1	4	2	
1955	3	9		3	4		0	5	
1956	9	3		5	1		4	2	
1957	8	4		5	1		3	3	
1958	4	7	1	2	4		2	3	1
1959	3	8	1	2	4		1	4	1
1960	7	5		5	1		2	4	
1961	8	5	1	2	5		6	0	1
1962	11	3		7	0		4	3	
1963	5	8	1	3	3	1	2	5	
1964	7	5	2	3	3	1	4	2	1
1965	6	7	1	2	4	1	4	3	
1966	4	9	1	3	4		1	5	1
1967	5	7	2	3	4		2	3	2
1968	4	8	2	1	4	2	3	4	
1969	9	4	1	5	2		4	2	1
1970	10	4		6	1		4	3	
1971	7	6	1	3	4		4	2	1
1972	8	5	1	5	2		3	3	1
1973	6	7	1	4	3		2	4	1
1974	7	7		5	2		2	5	
1975	7	7		4	3		3	4	
1976	6	8		5	2		1	6	
1977	6	8		5	2		1	6	
1978	7	9		5	3		2	6	
1979	2	14		2	6		0	8	
1980	9	7		6	2		3	5	
1981	8	8		7	1		1	7	
1982	4	5		2	3		2	2	
1983	9	7		6	2		3	5	
1984	4	11	1	2	5	1	2	6	
1985	7	9		6	2		1	7	
1986	5	11		1	7		4	4	
1987	4	11		1	6		3	5	
1988	4	12		2	6		2	6	
1989	7	9		4	4		3	5	
1990	6	10		3	5		3	5	
1991	12	4		8	0		4	4	
1992	5	11		3	5		2	6	
1993	10	6		5	3		5	3	
1994	9	7		6	2		3	5	
Total	411	422	32	251	178	14	160	244	18

**includes Portsmouth Spartans (1930-33).*

GREEN BAY PACKERS

	All Games			Home Games			Road Games		
Season	W	L	T	W	L	T	W	L	T
1921	3	2	1	2	1		1	1	1
1922	4	3	3	4	1	1	0	2	2
1923	7	2	1	4	2	1	3	0	
1924	7	4		5	0		2	4	
1925	8	5		6	0		2	5	
1926	7	3	3	4	1	2	3	2	1
1927	7	2	1	6	1		1	1	1
1928	6	4	3	2	2	2	4	2	1
1929	12	0	1	5	0		7	0	1
1930	10	3	1	6	0		4	3	1
1931	12	2		8	0		4	2	
1932	10	3	1	5	0	1	5	3	
1933	5	7	1	3	2	1	2	5	
1934	7	6		4	2		3	4	
1935	8	4		5	2		3	2	
1936	10	1	1	5	1		5	0	1
1937	7	4		3	2		4	2	
1938	8	3		4	2		4	1	
1939	9	2		4	1		5	1	
1940	6	4	1	4	2		2	2	1
1941	10	1		4	1		6	0	
1942	8	2	1	4	1		4	1	1
1943	7	2	1	2	1	1	5	1	
1944	8	2		5	0		3	2	
1945	6	4		4	1		2	3	
1946	6	5		2	3		4	2	
1947	6	5	1	4	2		2	3	1
1948	3	9		2	4		1	5	
1949	2	10		1	5		1	5	
1950	3	9		3	3		0	6	
1951	3	9		2	4		1	5	
1952	6	6		3	3		3	3	
1953	2	9	1	1	5		1	4	1
1954	4	8		2	4		2	4	
1955	6	6		5	1		1	5	
1956	4	8		2	4		2	4	
1957	3	9		1	5		2	4	
1958	1	10	1	1	4	1	0	6	
1959	7	5		4	2		3	3	
1960	8	4		4	2		4	2	
1961	11	3		6	1		5	2	
1962	13	1		7	0		6	1	
1963	11	2	1	6	1		5	1	1
1964	8	5	1	4	3		4	2	1
1965	10	3	1	6	1		4	2	1
1966	12	2		6	1		6	1	
1967	9	4	1	4	2	1	5	2	
1968	6	7	1	2	5		4	2	1
1969	8	6		5	2		3	4	
1970	6	8		4	3		2	5	
1971	4	8	2	3	3	1	1	5	1
1972	10	4		4	3		6	1	
1973	5	7	2	3	2	2	2	5	
1974	6	8		4	3		2	5	
1975	4	10		3	4		1	6	
1976	5	9		4	3		1	6	
1977	4	10		2	5		2	5	
1978	8	7	1	5	2	1	3	5	
1979	5	11		4	4		1	7	
1980	5	10	1	4	4		1	6	1
1981	8	8		4	4		4	4	
1982	5	3	1	3	1		2	2	1
1983	8	8		5	3		3	5	
1984	8	8		5	3		3	5	
1985	8	8		5	3		3	5	
1986	4	12		1	7		3	5	
1987	5	9	1	2	5	1	3	4	
1988	4	12		2	6		2	6	
1989	10	6		6	2		4	4	
1990	6	10		3	5		3	5	
1991	4	12		2	6		2	6	
1992	9	7		6	2		3	5	
1993	9	7		6	2		3	5	
1994	9	7		7	1		2	6	
Total	503	429	36	288	179	16	215	250	20

MINNESOTA VIKINGS

	All Games			Home Games			Road Games		
Season	W	L	T	W	L	T	W	L	T
1961	3	11		3	4		0	7	
1962	2	11	1	1	5	1	1	6	
1963	5	8	1	3	4		2	4	1
1964	8	5	1	4	3		4	2	1
1965	7	7		2	5		5	2	
1966	4	9	1	2	5		2	4	1
1967	3	8	3	1	4	2	2	4	1
1968	8	6		4	3		4	3	
1969	12	2		7	0		5	2	
1970	12	2		7	0		5	2	
1971	11	3		5	2		6	1	
1972	7	7		3	4		4	3	
1973	12	2		7	0		5	2	
1974	10	4		4	3		6	1	
1975	12	2		7	0		5	2	
1976	11	2	1	6	0	1	5	2	
1977	9	5		5	2		4	3	
1978	8	7	1	5	3		3	4	1
1979	7	9		5	3		2	6	
1980	9	7		5	3		4	4	
1981	7	9		5	3		2	6	
1982	5	4		4	1		1	3	
1983	8	8		3	5		5	3	
1984	3	13		2	6		1	7	
1985	7	9		4	4		3	5	
1986	9	7		5	3		4	4	
1987	8	7		5	3		3	4	
1988	11	5		7	1		4	4	
1989	10	6		8	0		2	6	
1990	6	10		4	4		2	6	
1991	8	8		4	4		4	4	
1992	11	5		5	3		6	2	
1993	9	7		4	4		5	3	
1994	10	6		6	2		4	4	
Total	272	221	9	152	96	4	120	125	5

NEW ORLEANS SAINTS

	All Games			Home Games			Road Games		
Season	W	L	T	W	L	T	W	L	T
1967	3	11		2	5		1	6	
1968	4	9	1	3	4		1	5	1
1969	5	9		3	4		2	5	
1970	2	11	1	2	5		0	6	1
1971	4	8	2	2	4	1	2	4	1
1972	2	11	1	2	5		0	6	1
1973	5	9		5	2		0	7	
1974	5	9		4	3		1	6	
1975	2	12		2	5		0	7	
1976	4	10		2	5		2	5	
1977	3	11		2	5		1	6	
1978	7	9		3	5		4	4	
1979	8	8		3	5		5	3	

Season	All Games W	L	T	Home Games W	L	T	Road Games W	L	T
1980	1	15		0	8		1	7	
1981	4	12		2	6		2	6	
1982	4	5		2	3		2	2	
1983	8	8		5	3		3	5	
1984	7	9		3	5		4	4	
1985	5	11		3	5		2	6	
1986	7	9		4	4		3	5	
1987	12	3		6	1		6	2	
1988	10	6		5	3		5	3	
1989	9	7		5	3		4	4	
1990	8	8		5	3		3	5	
1991	11	5		6	2		5	3	
1992	12	4		6	2		6	2	
1993	8	8		4	4		4	4	
1994	7	9		3	5		4	4	
Total	167	246	5	94	114	1	73	132	4

NEW YORK GIANTS

Season	All Games W	L	T	Home Games W	L	T	Road Games W	L	T
1925	8	4		7	2		1	2	
1926	8	4	1	5	2	1	3	2	
1927	11	1	1	7	1		4	0	1
1928	4	7	2	1	2	2	3	5	
1929	13	1	1	7	1		6	0	1
1930	13	4		6	2		7	2	
1931	7	6	1	4	2	1	3	4	
1932	4	6	2	3	2	1	1	4	1
1933	11	3		7	0		4	3	
1934	8	5		5	1		3	4	
1935	9	3		4	2		5	1	
1936	5	6	1	3	3	1	2	3	
1937	6	3	2	4	2	1	2	1	1
1938	8	2	1	6	1		2	1	1
1939	9	1	1	6	0		3	1	1
1940	6	4	1	4	3		2	1	1
1941	8	3		5	2		3	1	
1942	5	5	1	3	2	1	2	3	
1943	6	3	1	4	2		2	1	1
1944	8	1	1	5	1		3	0	1
1945	3	6	1	2	4		1	2	1
1946	7	3	1	5	1	1	2	2	
1947	2	8	2	2	3	1	0	5	1
1948	4	8		2	4		2	4	
1949	6	6		2	4		4	2	
1950	10	2		5	1		5	1	
1951	9	2	1	5	1		4	1	1
1952	7	5		2	4		5	1	
1953	3	9		2	4		1	5	
1954	7	5		4	2		3	3	
1955	6	5	1	4	1	1	2	4	
1956	8	3	1	4	1	1	4	2	
1957	7	5		3	3		4	2	
1958	9	3		5	1		4	2	
1959	10	2		5	1		5	1	
1960	6	4	2	1	3	2	5	1	
1961	10	3	1	4	2	1	6	1	
1962	12	2		6	1		6	1	
1963	11	3		5	2		6	1	
1964	2	10	2	2	5		0	5	2
1965	7	7		3	4		4	3	
1966	1	12	1	1	6		0	6	1
1967	7	7		5	2		2	5	
1968	7	7		3	4		4	3	
1969	6	8		5	2		1	6	
1970	9	5		5	2		4	3	
1971	4	10		1	6		3	4	
1972	8	6		4	3		4	3	
1973	2	11	1	2	4	1	0	7	
1974	2	12		0	7		2	5	
1975	5	9		2	5		3	4	
1976	3	11		3	4		0	7	
1977	5	9		3	4		2	5	
1978	6	10		5	3		1	7	
1979	6	10		4	4		2	6	
1980	4	12		2	6		2	6	
1981	9	7		4	4		5	3	
1982	4	5		2	3		2	2	
1983	3	12	1	1	7		2	5	1
1984	9	7		6	2		3	5	
1985	10	6		6	2		4	4	
1986	14	2		8	0		6	2	
1987	6	9		5	3		1	6	
1988	10	6		5	3		5	3	
1989	12	4		7	1		5	3	
1990	13	3		7	1		6	2	
1991	8	8		5	3		3	5	
1992	6	10		4	4		2	6	
1993	11	5		6	2		5	3	
1994	9	7		4	4		5	3	
Total	502	403	32	284	186	16	218	217	16

PHILADELPHIA EAGLES

Season	All Games W	L	T	Home Games W	L	T	Road Games W	L	T
1933	3	5	1	2	3	1	1	2	
1934	4	7		2	4		2	3	
1935	2	9		0	5		2	4	
1936	1	11		1	6		0	5	
1937	2	8	1	0	5	1	2	3	
1938	5	6		2	3		3	3	
1939	1	9	1	1	3	1	0	6	
1940	1	10		1	4		0	6	
1941	2	8	1	1	4	1	1	4	
1942	2	9		0	5		2	4	
1944	7	1	2	3	1	2	4	0	
1945	7	3		6	0		1	3	
1946	6	5		3	2		3	3	
1947	8	4		6	1		2	3	
1948	9	2	1	6	0		3	2	1
1949	11	1		6	0		5	1	
1950	6	6		2	4		4	2	
1951	4	8		1	5		3	3	
1952	7	5		4	2		3	3	
1953	7	4	1	5	0	1	2	4	
1954	7	4	1	5	1		2	3	1
1955	4	7	1	4	2		0	5	1
1956	3	8	1	2	3	1	1	5	
1957	4	8		3	3		1	5	
1958	2	9	1	2	4		0	5	1
1959	6	5		4	1		2	4	
1960	10	2		5	1		5	1	
1961	10	4		5	2		5	2	
1962	3	10	1	2	5		1	5	1
1963	2	10	2	1	5	1	1	5	1
1964	6	8		3	4		3	4	
1965	5	9		2	5		3	4	
1966	9	5		5	2		4	3	
1967	6	7	1	5	2		1	5	1
1968	2	12		1	6		1	6	
1969	4	9	1	2	5		2	4	1
1970	3	10	1	3	3	1	0	7	
1971	6	7	1	3	4		3	3	1
1972	2	11	1	0	6	1	2	5	
1973	5	8	1	4	3		1	5	1
1974	7	7		5	2		2	5	
1975	4	10		2	5		2	5	
1976	4	10		2	5		2	5	
1977	5	9		4	3		1	6	
1978	9	7		5	3		4	4	
1979	11	5		5	3		6	2	
1980	12	4		7	1		5	3	
1981	10	6		6	2		4	4	
1982	3	6		1	4		2	2	
1983	5	11		1	7		4	4	
1984	6	9	1	5	3		1	6	1
1985	7	9		4	4		3	5	
1986	5	10	1	2	5	1	3	5	
1987	7	8		4	4		3	4	
1988	10	6		5	3		5	3	
1989	11	5		6	2		5	3	
1990	10	6		6	2		4	4	
1991	10	6		4	4		6	2	
1992	11	5		8	0		3	5	
1993	8	8		3	5		5	3	
1994	7	9		5	3		2	6	
Total	356	430	23	203	194	12	153	236	11

ST. LOUIS RAMS*

Season	All Games W	L	T	Home Games W	L	T	Road Games W	L	T
1937	1	10		0	5		1	5	
1938	4	7		2	2		2	5	
1939	5	5	1	3	2	1	2	3	
1940	4	6	1	3	1	1	1	5	
1941	2	9		1	4		1	5	
1942	5	6		3	2		2	4	
1944	4	6		1	2		3	4	
1945	9	1		4	0		5	1	
1946	6	4	1	3	2		3	2	1
1947	6	6		3	3		3	3	
1948	6	5	1	3	2	1	3	3	
1949	8	2	2	5	1		3	1	2
1950	9	3		5	1		4	2	
1951	8	4		5	2		3	2	
1952	9	3		5	1		4	2	
1953	8	3	1	5	1		3	2	1
1954	6	5	1	3	2	1	3	3	
1955	8	3	1	5	1		3	2	1
1956	4	8		4	2		0	6	
1957	6	6		5	1		1	5	
1958	8	4		4	2		4	2	
1959	2	10		0	6		2	4	
1960	4	7	1	2	3	1	2	4	
1961	4	10		4	3		0	7	
1962	1	12	1	0	7		1	5	1
1963	5	9		3	4		2	5	
1964	5	7	2	3	2	2	2	5	
1965	4	10		3	4		1	6	
1966	8	6		5	2		3	4	
1967	11	1	2	5	1	1	6	0	1
1968	10	3	1	5	2		5	1	1
1969	11	3		5	2		6	1	
1970	9	4	1	3	3	1	6	1	
1971	8	5	1	4	2	1	4	3	
1972	6	7	1	4	3		2	4	1
1973	12	2		7	0		5	2	
1974	10	4		6	1		4	3	
1975	12	2		6	1		6	1	
1976	10	3	1	5	2		5	1	1
1977	10	4		7	0		3	4	
1978	12	4		6	2		6	2	
1979	9	7		4	4		5	3	
1980	11	5		6	2		5	3	
1981	6	10		4	4		2	6	
1982	2	7		1	4		1	3	
1983	9	7		5	3		4	4	
1984	10	6		5	3		5	3	
1985	11	5		6	2		5	3	
1986	10	6		6	2		4	4	
1987	6	9		3	4		3	5	
1988	10	6		4	4		6	2	
1989	11	5		6	2		5	3	
1990	5	11		2	6		3	5	
1991	3	13		2	6		1	7	
1992	6	10		4	4		2	6	
1993	5	11		3	5		2	6	
1994	4	12		3	5		1	7	
Total	398	349	20	219	149	10	179	200	10

**includes Cleveland Rams (1937-42, 1944-45) and Los Angeles Rams (1946-94).*

SAN FRANCISCO 49ERS

Season	All Games W	L	T	Home Games W	L	T	Road Games W	L	T
1950	3	9		3	3		0	6	
1951	7	4	1	5	1		2	3	1
1952	7	5		3	3		4	2	
1953	9	3		5	1		4	2	
1954	7	4	1	4	2		3	2	1
1955	4	8		2	4		2	4	
1956	5	6	1	3	3		2	3	1
1957	8	4		5	1		3	3	
1958	6	6		4	2		2	4	
1959	7	5		4	2		3	3	
1960	7	5		3	3		4	2	
1961	7	6	1	5	1	1	2	5	
1962	6	8		1	6		5	2	
1963	2	12		2	5		0	7	
1964	4	10		3	4		1	6	
1965	7	6	1	4	2	1	3	4	
1966	6	6	2	4	2	1	2	4	1
1967	7	7		3	4		4	3	

Season	All Games W	L	T	Home Games W	L	T	Road Games W	L	T
1968	7	6	1	3	3	1	4	3	
1969	4	8	2	3	3	1	1	5	1
1970	10	3	1	5	1	1	5	2	
1971	9	5		4	3		5	2	
1972	8	5	1	4	2	1	4	3	
1973	5	9		3	4		2	5	
1974	6	8		3	4		3	4	
1975	5	9		2	5		3	4	
1976	8	6		4	3		4	3	
1977	5	9		3	4		2	5	
1978	2	14		2	6		0	8	
1979	2	14		2	6		0	8	
1980	6	10		4	4		2	6	
1981	13	3		7	1		6	2	
1982	3	6		0	5		3	1	
1983	10	6		4	4		6	2	
1984	15	1		7	1		8	0	
1985	10	6		5	3		5	3	
1986	10	5	1	6	2		4	3	1
1987	13	2		6	1		7	1	
1988	10	6		4	4		6	2	
1989	14	2		6	2		8	0	
1990	14	2		6	2		8	0	
1991	10	6		7	1		3	5	
1992	14	2		7	1		7	1	
1993	10	6		6	2		4	4	
1994	13	3		7	1		6	2	
Total	345	276	13	183	127	7	162	149	6

TAMPA BAY BUCCANEERS

Season	All Games W	L	T	Home Games W	L	T	Road Games W	L	T
1976	0	14		0	7		0	7	
1977	2	12		1	6		1	6	
1978	5	11		3	5		2	6	
1979	10	6		5	3		5	3	
1980	5	10	1	2	5	1	3	5	
1981	9	7		6	2		3	5	
1982	5	4		4	1		1	3	
1983	2	14		1	7		1	7	
1984	6	10		6	2		0	8	
1985	2	14		2	6		0	8	
1986	2	14		1	7		1	7	
1987	4	11		2	5		2	6	
1988	5	11		3	5		2	6	
1989	5	11		2	6		3	5	
1990	6	10		4	4		2	6	
1991	3	13		3	5		0	8	
1992	5	11		3	5		2	6	
1993	5	11		3	5		2	6	
1994	6	10		4	4		2	6	
Total	87	204	1	55	90	1	32	114	

WASHINGTON REDSKINS*

Season	All Games W	L	T	Home Games W	L	T	Road Games W	L	T
1932	4	4	2	2	3	1	2	1	1
1933	5	5	2	4	2		1	3	2
1934	6	6		4	3		2	3	
1935	2	8	1	2	5		0	3	1
1936	7	5		4	3		3	2	
1937	8	3		4	2		4	1	
1938	6	3	2	3	1	1	3	2	1
1939	8	2	1	5	0	1	3	2	
1940	9	2		6	0		3	2	
1941	6	5		4	2		2	3	
1942	10	1		5	1		5	0	
1943	6	3	1	4	2		2	1	1
1944	6	3	1	4	2		2	1	1
1945	8	2		6	0		2	2	
1946	5	5	1	3	2	1	2	3	
1947	4	8		4	2		0	6	
1948	7	5		4	2		3	3	
1949	4	7	1	3	3		1	4	1
1950	3	9		1	5		2	4	
1951	5	7		2	4		3	3	
1952	4	8		1	5		3	3	
1953	6	5	1	3	3		3	2	1
1954	3	9		3	3		0	6	
1955	8	4		3	3		5	1	
1956	6	6		4	2		2	4	
1957	5	6	1	2	3	1	3	3	
1958	4	7	1	3	2	1	1	5	
1959	4	8		2	4		2	4	
1960	1	9	2	1	4	1	0	5	1
1961	1	12	1	1	6		0	6	1
1962	5	7	2	3	4		2	3	2
1963	3	11		1	6		2	5	
1964	6	8		4	3		2	5	
1965	6	8		3	4		3	4	
1966	7	7		4	3		3	4	
1967	5	6	3	2	4	1	3	2	2
1968	5	9		3	4		2	5	
1969	7	5	2	4	2	1	3	3	1
1970	6	8		4	3		2	5	
1971	9	4	1	4	2	1	5	2	
1972	11	3		6	1		5	2	
1973	10	4		7	0		3	4	
1974	10	4		6	1		4	3	
1975	8	6		5	2		3	4	
1976	10	4		5	2		5	2	
1977	9	5		5	2		4	3	
1978	8	8		5	3		3	5	
1979	10	6		6	2		4	4	
1980	6	10		4	4		2	6	
1981	8	8		5	3		3	5	
1982	8	1		3	1		5	0	
1983	14	2		7	1		7	1	
1984	11	5		7	1		4	4	
1985	10	6		5	3		5	3	
1986	12	4		7	1		5	3	
1987	11	4		6	1		5	3	
1988	7	9		4	4		3	5	
1989	10	6		4	4		6	2	
1990	10	6		7	1		3	5	
1991	14	2		7	1		7	1	
1992	9	7		6	2		3	5	
1993	4	12		3	5		1	7	
1994	3	13		0	8		3	5	
Total	433	375	26	249	167	10	184	208	16

**includes Boston Braves (1932) and Boston Redskins (1933-36).*

History

PRO FOOTBALL HALL OF FAME

The Professional Football Hall of Fame is located in Canton, Ohio, site of the organizational meeting on September 17, 1920, from which the National Football League evolved. The NFL recognized Canton as the Hall of Fame site on April 27, 1961. Canton area individuals, foundations, and companies donated almost $400,000 in cash and services to provide funds for the construction of the original two-building complex, which was dedicated on September 7, 1963. Since that time, the Hall added two buildings and almost tripled its original size with major expansion projects in 1971 and 1978. The Hall's largest-ever expansion, an $8.6 million project scheduled for completion in early fall 1995, will add a fifth building and increase the Hall's size to 82,307-square feet, more than four times its original size.

After its newest expansion, the Hall will represent the sport of pro football in many ways—through (1) a dynamic two-part turntable theater featuring NFL action in Cinemascope for the first time, (2) a standard theater showing NFL films hourly, (3) six large exhibition areas where the history of pro football is detailed in memento, picture, and story form, (4) an extensive library and research center, and (5) a new and enlarged museum store.

In recent years, the Pro Football Hall of Fame has become an extremely popular tourist attraction. At the end of 1994, a total of 5,670,416 fans had visited the Hall of Fame.

New members of the Pro Football Hall of Fame are elected annually by a 34-member National Board of Selectors, made up of media representatives from every league city, 5 at-large representatives, and a representative of the Pro Football Writers of America. Between four and seven new members are elected each year. An affirmative vote of approximately 80 percent is needed for election.

Any fan may nominate any eligible player or contributor simply by writing to the Pro Football Hall of Fame. Players must be retired five years to be eligible, while a coach need only to be retired with no time limit specified. Contributors (administrators, owners, *et al.*) may be elected while they are still active.

The charter class of 17 enshrinees was elected in 1963 and the honor roll now stands at 180 with the election of a five-man class in 1995. That class consists of Jim Finks, Henry Jordan, Steve Largent, Lee Roy Selmon, and Kellen Winslow.

ROSTER OF MEMBERS

HERB ADDERLEY
Defensive back. 6-1, 200. Born in Philadelphia, Pennsylvania, June 8, 1939. Michigan State. Inducted in 1980. 1961-69 Green Bay Packers, 1970-72 Dallas Cowboys. **Highlights:** 48 interceptions, 7 touchdowns. Played in four Super Bowls, five Pro Bowls.

LANCE ALWORTH
Wide receiver. 6-0, 184. Born in Houston, Texas, August 3, 1940. Arkansas. Inducted in 1978. 1962-70 San Diego Chargers, 1971-72 Dallas Cowboys. **Highlights:** 542 receptions for 10,266 yards, 85 touchdowns. All-AFL seven times, seven All-Star games.

DOUG ATKINS
Defensive end. 6-8, 275. Born in Humboldt, Tennessee, May 8, 1930. Tennessee. Inducted in 1982. 1953-54 Cleveland Browns, 1955-66 Chicago Bears, 1967-69 New Orleans Saints. **Highlights:** Eight Pro Bowls, All-NFL three times. Played for 17 years, 205 games.

MORRIS (RED) BADGRO
End. 6-0, 190. Born in Orilla, Washington, December 1, 1902. Southern California. Inducted in 1981. 1927 New York Yankees, 1930-35 New York Giants, 1936 Brooklyn Dodgers. **Highlights:** All-NFL four times. Scored first touchdown in NFL championship game series.

LEM BARNEY
Cornerback. 6-0, 190. Born in Gulfport, Mississippi, September 9, 1945. Jackson State. Inducted in 1992. 1967-77 Detroit Lions. **Highlights:** 56 interceptions for 1,077 yards, 11 defensive touchdowns. Seven Pro Bowls, All-NFL/NFC three times.

CLIFF BATTLES
Halfback. 6-1, 201. Born in Akron, Ohio, May 1, 1910. Died April 28, 1981. West Virginia Wesleyan. Inducted in 1968. 1932 Boston Braves, 1933-36 Boston Redskins, 1937 Washington Redskins. **Highlights:** NFL rushing champion 1932, 1937. First to gain more than 200 yards in a game, 1933.

SAMMY BAUGH
Quarterback. 6-2, 180. Born in Temple, Texas, March 17, 1914. Texas Christian. Inducted in 1963. 1937-52 Washington Redskins. **Highlights:** Charter enshrinee. Six-time NFL passing leader. NFL passing, punting, interception champ, 1943.

CHUCK BEDNARIK
Center-linebacker. 6-3, 230. Born in Bethlehem, Pennsylvania, May 1, 1925. Pennsylvania. Inducted in 1967. 1949-62 Philadelphia Eagles. **Highlights:** Eight Pro Bowls. Missed three games in 14 years. Named NFL all-time center, 1969.

BERT BELL
Team owner. Commissioner. Born in Philadelphia, Pennsylvania, February 25, 1895. Died October 11, 1959. Pennsylvania. Inducted in 1963. 1933-40 Philadelphia Eagles, 1941-42 Pittsburgh Steelers, 1943 Phil-Pitt, 1944-46 Pittsburgh Steelers. Commissioner, 1946-59. **Highlights:** Charter enshrinee. Built NFL image as commissioner, 1946-1959. Set up long-term television policies.

BOBBY BELL
Linebacker. 6-4, 225. Born in Shelby, North Carolina, June 17, 1940. Minnesota. Inducted in 1983. 1963-74 Kansas City Chiefs. **Highlights:** 25 interceptions. All-AFL/AFC nine times. Eight career touchdowns, 1 on onside kick return.

RAYMOND BERRY
End. 6-2, 187. Born in Corpus Christi, Texas, February 27, 1933. Southern Methodist. Inducted in 1973. 1955-67 Baltimore Colts. **Highlights:** 631 receptions for 9,275 yards, 68 touchdowns. Set NFL title game mark with 12 catches for 178 yards, 1958.

CHARLES W. BIDWILL, SR.
Team owner. Born in Chicago, Illinois, September 16, 1895. Died April 19, 1947. Loyola of Chicago. Inducted in 1967. 1933-43 Chicago Cardinals, 1944 Card-Pitt, 1945-47 Chicago Cardinals. **Highlights:** Guiding light for NFL during depression years. Built famous "Dream Backfield."

FRED BILETNIKOFF
Wide receiver. 6-1, 190. Born in Erie, Pennsylvania, February 23, 1943. Florida State. Inducted in 1988. 1965-78 Oakland Raiders. **Highlights:** 589 receptions for 8,974 yards, 76 touchdowns. 40 catches 10 straight years. MVP, Super Bowl XI.

GEORGE BLANDA
Quarterback-kicker. 6-2, 215. Born in Youngwood, Pennsylvania, September 17, 1927. Kentucky. Inducted in 1981. 1949-58 Chicago Bears, 1950 Baltimore Colts, 1960-66 Houston Oilers, 1967-75 Oakland Raiders. **Highlights:** Record 2,002 career points. 26-season, 340-game career longest in NFL history.

MEL BLOUNT
Cornerback. 6-3, 205. Born in Vidalia, Georgia, April 10, 1948. Southern University. Inducted in 1989. 1970-83 Pittsburgh Steelers. **Highlights:** 57 interceptions for 736 yards. NFL defensive MVP, 1975. Played in five Pro Bowls.

TERRY BRADSHAW
Quarterback. 6-3, 210. Born in Shreveport, Louisiana, September 2, 1948. Louisiana Tech. Inducted in 1989. 1970-83 Pittsburgh Steelers. **Highlights:** 27,989 yards passing, 212 touchdowns. MVP in Super Bowls XIII, XIV.

JIM BROWN
Fullback. 6-2, 232. Born in St. Simons, Georgia, February 17, 1936. Syracuse. Inducted in 1971. 1957-65 Cleveland Browns. **Highlights:** 12,312 yards rushing, 756 points. Led NFL rushers eight years. Nine consecutive Pro Bowls.

PAUL BROWN
Coach. Born in Norwalk, Ohio, September 7, 1908. Died August 5, 1991. Miami, Ohio. Inducted in 1967. 1946-49 Cleveland Browns (AAFC), 1950-62 Cleveland Browns, 1968-75 Cincinnati Bengals. **Highlights:** Built Cleveland dynasty with 167-53-8 record, four AAFC titles, three NFL crowns.

ROOSEVELT BROWN
Tackle. 6-3, 255. Born in Charlottesville, Virginia, October 20, 1932. Morgan State. Inducted in 1975. 1953-65 New York Giants. **Highlights:** All-NFL eight consecutive years, nine Pro Bowls. NFL's Lineman of Year, 1956.

WILLIE BROWN
Defensive back. 6-1, 210. Born in Yazoo City, Mississippi, December 2, 1940. Grambling. Inducted in 1984. 1963-66 Denver Broncos, 1967-78 Oakland Raiders. **Highlights:** 54 interceptions for 472 yards. Scored on 75-yard interception in Super Bowl XI.

BUCK BUCHANAN
Defensive tackle. 6-7, 274. Born in Gainesville, Alabama, September 10, 1940. Grambling. Inducted in 1990. 1963-75 Kansas City Chiefs. **Highlights:** Led Chiefs defensive efforts in Super Bowl I, IV. Missed one game in 13 years.

DICK BUTKUS
Linebacker. 6-3, 245. Born in Chicago, Illinois, December 9, 1942. Illinois. Inducted in 1979. 1965-73 Chicago Bears. **Highlights:** All-NFL seven years, eight consecutive Pro Bowls. 25 fumble recoveries.

EARL CAMPBELL
Running back. 5-11, 233. Born in Tyler, Texas, March 29, 1955. Texas. Inducted in 1991. 1978-84 Houston Oilers, 1984-85 New Orleans Saints. **Highlights:** 9,407 yards rushing, 74 touchdowns. 1,934 yards rushing in 1980, including four games with at least 200 yards.

TONY CANADEO
Halfback. 5-11, 195. Born in Chicago, Illinois, May 5, 1919. Gonzaga. Inducted in 1974. 1941-44, 1946-52 Green Bay Packers. **Highlights:** Two-way player. Third player to rush for 1,000 yards in single season, 1949.

JOE CARR
NFL president. Born in Columbus, Ohio, October 22, 1880. Died May 20, 1939. Did not attend college. Inducted in 1963. President, 1921-39 National Football League. **Highlights:** Charter enshrinee. NFL co-organizer, 1920. Introduced standard player's contract.

GUY CHAMBERLIN
End. Coach. 6-2, 210. Born in Blue Springs, Nebraska, January 16, 1894. Died April 4, 1967. Nebraska. Inducted in 1965. 1920 Decatur Staleys, 1921 Chicago Staleys, player-coach 1922-23 Canton Bulldogs, 1924 Cleveland Bulldogs, 1925-26 Frankford Yellow Jackets, 1927 Chicago Cardinals. **Highlights:** Player-coach of four NFL championship teams. Six-year coaching record 56-14-5.

JACK CHRISTIANSEN
Defensive back. 6-1, 185. Born in Sublette, Kansas, December 20, 1928. Died June 29, 1986. Colorado State. Inducted in 1970. 1951-58 Detroit Lions. **Highlights:** 46 interceptions. NFL interception leader, 1953, 1957. NFL record 8 punt returns for touchdowns.

EARL (DUTCH) CLARK
Quarterback. 6-0, 185. Born in Fowler, Colorado, October 11, 1906. Died August 5, 1978. Colorado College.

Inducted in 1963. 1931-32 Portsmouth Spartans, 1934-38 Detroit Lions. **Highlights:** Charter enshrinee. NFL scoring champion three years. Led Lions to 1935 NFL title.

GEORGE CONNOR
Tackle-linebacker. 6-3, 240. Born in Chicago, Illinois, January 21, 1925. Holy Cross, Notre Dame. Inducted in 1975. 1948-55 Chicago Bears. **Highlights:** All-NFL at three positions—T, DT, LB. All-NFL five years. Played in first four Pro Bowls.

JIMMY CONZELMAN
Quarterback. Coach. Team owner. 6-0, 180. Born in St. Louis, Missouri, March 6, 1898. Died July 31, 1970. Washington, Missouri. Inducted in 1964. 1920 Decatur Staleys, 1921-22 Rock Island, Ill., Independents, 1923-24 Milwaukee Badgers; owner-coach, 1925-26 Detroit Panthers; player-coach 1927-29, coach 1930 Providence Steam Roller; coach, 1940-42 Chicago Cardinals, 1946-48 Chicago Cardinals. **Highlights:** Player-coach of four NFL teams in 1920's. Coached Cardinals to 1947 NFL crown.

LARRY CSONKA
Running back. 6-3, 235. Born in Stow, Ohio, December 25, 1946. Syracuse. Inducted in 1987. Miami Dolphins 1968-74, 1979, New York Giants 1976-78. **Highlights:** 8,081 yards rushing, 68 touchdowns. MVP Super Bowl VIII. Only 21 fumbles in 1,997 carries.

AL DAVIS
Team, League Administrator. Born in Brockton, Massachusetts, July 4, 1929. Wittenberg, Syracuse. Inducted in 1992. 1963-81 Oakland Raiders, 1982-92 Los Angeles Raiders, 1966 American Football League. **Highlights:** Only person to serve in pros as personnel assistant, scout, assistant coach, head coach, general manager, commissioner, team owner/CEO.

WILLIE DAVIS
Defensive end. 6-3, 245. Born in Lisbon, Louisiana, July 24, 1934. Grambling. Inducted in 1981. 1958-59 Cleveland Browns, 1960-69 Green Bay Packers. **Highlights:** All-NFL five seasons, five Pro Bowls. Did not miss game in 12-year career.

LEN DAWSON
Quarterback. 6-0, 190. Born in Alliance, Ohio, June 20, 1935. Purdue. Inducted in 1987. 1957-59 Pittsburgh Steelers, 1960-61 Cleveland Browns, 1962 Dallas Texans, 1963-75 Kansas City Chiefs. **Highlights:** 28,711 yards passing, 239 touchdowns. Four AFL passing crowns. MVP, Super Bowl IV.

MIKE DITKA
Tight end. 6-3, 225. Born in Carnegie, Pennsylvania, October 18, 1939. Pittsburgh. Inducted in 1988. 1961-66 Chicago Bears, 1967-68 Philadelphia Eagles, 1969-72 Dallas Cowboys. **Highlights:** 427 receptions for 5,812 yards, 43 touchdowns. First tight end selected to Hall of Fame. Five consecutive Pro Bowls.

ART DONOVAN
Defensive tackle. 6-3, 265. Born in Bronx, New York, June 5, 1925. Boston College. Inducted in 1968. 1950 Baltimore Colts, 1951 New York Yanks, 1952 Dallas Texans, 1953-61 Baltimore Colts. **Highlights:** Five Pro Bowls. Vital part of Baltimore's climb to powerhouse status in 1950s.

TONY DORSETT
Running back. 5-11, 184. Born in Rochester, Pennsylvania, April 7, 1954. Pittsburgh. Inducted in 1994. 1977-87 Dallas Cowboys, 1988 Denver Broncos. **Highlights:** 12,379 yards rushing, 398 receptions, 90 touchdowns. Ran record 99 yards for touchdown vs. Minnesota, 1983.

JOHN (PADDY) DRISCOLL
Quarterback. 5-11, 160. Born in Evanston, Illinois, January 11, 1896. Died June 29, 1968. Northwestern. Inducted in 1965. 1920 Decatur Staleys, 1920-25 Chicago Cardinals, 1926-29 Chicago Bears. Coach, 1956-57 Chicago Bears. **Highlights:** All-NFL six times. Dropkicked record 4 field goals in one game, 1925.

BILL DUDLEY
Halfback. 5-10, 176. Born in Bluefield, Virginia, December 24, 1921. Virginia. Inducted in 1966. 1942, 1945-46 Pittsburgh Steelers, 1947-49 Detroit Lions, 1950-51, 1953 Washington Redskins. **Highlights:** Won NFL rushing, interception, punt return titles, 1946. All-NFL 1942, 1946.

ALBERT GLEN (TURK) EDWARDS
Tackle. 6-2, 260. Born in Mold, Washington, September 28, 1907. Died January 12, 1973. Washington State. Inducted in 1969. 1932 Boston Braves, 1933-36 Boston Redskins, 1937-40 Washington Redskins. **Highlights:** All-NFL 1932-33, 1936, 1937. Steamrolling blocker, smothering tackler.

WEEB EWBANK
Coach. Born in Richmond, Indiana, May 6, 1907. Miami, Ohio. Inducted in 1978. 1954-62 Baltimore Colts, 1963-73 New York Jets. **Highlights:** Only coach to win championships in both NFL, AFL. Led both Colts(1958) and Jets (1968) to championships.

TOM FEARS
End. 6-2, 215. Born in Los Angeles, California, December 3, 1923. Santa Clara, UCLA. Inducted in 1970. 1948-56 Los Angeles Rams. **Highlights:** 400 receptions for 5,397 yards, 38 touchdowns. Led NFL receivers first three seasons. Record 18 receptions in single game.

JIM FINKS
Administrator. born in St. Louis, Missouri, August 31, 1927. Died May 8, 1994, Tulsa. Inducted 1995. 1964-73 Minnesota Vikings, 1974-82 Chicago Bears, 1986-93 New Orleans Saints. **Highlights:** Developed Vikings, Bears, Saints—all teams with losing records—into winners.

RAY FLAHERTY
End. Coach. Born in Spokane, Washington, September 1, 1904. Died July 19, 1994. Gonzaga. Inducted in 1976. 1926 Los Angeles Wildcats (AFL), 1927-28 New York Yankees, 1928-29, 1931-35 New York Giants. Coach, 1936 Boston Red-skins, 1937-42 Washington Redskins, 1946-48 New York Yankees (AAFC), 1949 Chicago Hornets (AAFC). **Highlights:** 80-37-5 coaching record. Introduced screen pass in 1937 title game and platoon system.

LEN FORD
Defensive End. 6-5, 260. Born in Washington, D.C., February 18, 1926. Died March 14, 1972. Morgan State, Michigan. Inducted in 1976. 1948-49 Los Angeles Dons (AAFC), 1950-57 Cleveland Browns, 1958 Green Bay Packers. **Highlights:** All-NFL five times, four Pro Bowls. Recovered 20 opponent's fumbles.

DAN FORTMANN
Guard. 6-0, 207. Born in Pearl River, New York, April 11, 1916. Colgate. Inducted in 1965. 1936-43 Chicago Bears. **Highlights:** At 19, became youngest starter in NFL. All-NFL six consecutive years.

DAN FOUTS
Quarterback. 6-3, 210. Born in San Francisco, California, June 10, 1951. Oregon. Inducted in 1993. 1973-1987 San Diego Chargers. **Highlights:** 43,040 passing yards, 254 touchdowns. Six-time Pro Bowler, NFL MVP, 1982.

FRANK GATSKI
Center. 6-3, 240. Born in Farmington, West Virginia, March 18, 1922. Marshall, Auburn. Inducted in 1985. 1946-49 Cleveland Browns (AAFC), 1950-56 Cleveland Browns, 1957 Detroit Lions. **Highlights:** Never missed game in high school, college, or pro football. Played 11 championship games, winning eight.

BILL GEORGE
Linebacker. 6-2, 230. Born in Waynesburg, Pennsylvania, October 27, 1930. Died September 30, 1982. Wake Forest. Inducted in 1974. 1952-65 Chicago Bears, 1966 Los Angeles Rams. **Highlights:** All-NFL eight years, eight consecutive Pro Bowls. 14 years of service longest of any Bears player.

FRANK GIFFORD
Halfback. 6-1, 195. Born in Santa Monica, California, August 16, 1930. Southern California. Inducted in 1977. 1952-60, 1962-64 New York Giants. **Highlights:** Starred on both offense and defense. Seven Pro Bowls, 1956 NFL Player of the Year.

SID GILLMAN
Coach. Born in Minneapolis, Minnesota, October 26, 1911. Ohio State. Inducted in 1983. 1955-59 Los Angeles Rams, 1960 Los Angeles Chargers, 1961-69, 1971 San Diego Chargers, 1973-74 Houston Oilers. **Highlights:** 123-104-7 coaching record. First to win division titles in both NFL, AFL.

OTTO GRAHAM
Quarterback. 6-1, 195. Born in Waukegan, Illinois, December 6, 1921. Northwestern. Inducted in 1965. 1946-49 Cleveland Browns (AAFC), 1950-55 Cleveland Browns. **Highlights:** 23,584 passing yards, 174 touchdowns. Guided Browns to 10 division or league crowns in 10 years.

HAROLD (RED) GRANGE
Halfback. 6-0, 185. Born in Forksville, Pennsylvania, June 13, 1903. Died January 28, 1991. Illinois. Inducted in 1963. 1925 Chicago Bears, 1926 New York Yankees (AFL), 1927 New York Yankees, 1929-34 Chicago Bears. **Highlights:** Nicknamed "Galloping Ghost." Name produced first huge pro football crowds.

BUD GRANT
Coach. Born in Superior, Wisconsin, May 20, 1927. Minnesota. Inducted in 1994. 1967-83, 1985 Minnesota Vikings. **Highlights:** 168-108-5 coaching record. Led Vikings to 11 division championships, four Super Bowls.

JOE GREENE
Defensive tackle. 6-4, 260. Born in Temple, Texas, September 24, 1946. North Texas State. Inducted in 1987. 1969-81 Pittsburgh Steelers. **Highlights:** NFL Defensive Player of the Year, 1972, 1974. Four-time Super Bowl champion, 10 Pro Bowls.

FORREST GREGG
Tackle. 6-4, 250. Born in Birthright, Texas, October 18, 1933. Southern Methodist. Inducted in 1977. 1956, 1958-70 Green Bay Packers, 1971 Dallas Cowboys. **Highlights:** Played 188 consecutive games. Nine Pro Bowls. Played on seven NFL championship teams, three Super Bowl winners.

BOB GRIESE
Quarterback. 6-1, 190. Born in Evansville, Indiana, February 3, 1945. Purdue. Inducted in 1990. 1967-80 Miami Dolphins. **Highlights:** 25,092 passing yards, 192 touchdowns. Led Miami to three AFC titles, Super Bowl VII, VIII wins.

LOU GROZA
Tackle-kicker. 6-3, 250. Born in Martin's Ferry, Ohio, January 25, 1924. Ohio State. Inducted in 1974. 1946-49 Cleveland Browns (AAFC), 1950-59, 1961-67 Cleveland Browns. **Highlights:** 1,608 points in 21 years. Nine Pro Bowls, All-NFL six years. NFL Player of the Year, 1954.

JOE GUYON
Halfback. 6-1, 180. Born in Mahnomen, Minnesota, November 26, 1892. Died November 27, 1971. Carlisle, Georgia Tech. Inducted in 1966. 1920 Canton Bulldogs, 1921 Cleveland Indians, 1922-23 Oorang Indians, 1924 Rock Island, Ill., Independents, 1924-25 Kansas City Cowboys, 1927 New York Giants. **Highlights:** Touchdown pass gave Giants win over Bears in 1927 NFL Championship Game.

PRO FOOTBALL HALL OF FAME

GEORGE HALAS
End. Coach. Team owner. Born in Chicago, Illinois, February 2, 1895. Died October 31, 1983. Illinois. Inducted in 1963. 1920 Decatur Staleys, 1921 Chicago Staleys, 1922-29 Chicago Bears; coach, 1933-42, 1946-55, 1958-67 Chicago Bears. **Highlights:** Charter enshrinee. 325 coaching wins. Only person associated with NFL throughout first 50 years. Coached Bears 40 seasons, won seven NFL titles.

JACK HAM
Linebacker. 6-1, 225. Born in Johnstown, Pennsylvania, December 23, 1948. Penn State. Inducted in 1988. 1971-82 Pittsburgh Steelers. **Highlights:** won four Super Bowls, 21 opponent's fumbles recovered, 32 interceptions. Eight consecutive Pro Bowls.

JOHN HANNAH
Guard. 6-3, 265. Born in Canton, Georgia, April 4, 1951. Alabama. Inducted in 1991. 1973-85 New England Patriots. **Highlights:** Renowned as premier guard of era. All-Pro 10 years, eight Pro Bowls.

FRANCO HARRIS
Running back. 6-2, 225. Born in Fort Dix, New Jersey, March 7, 1950. Penn State. Inducted in 1990. 1972-83 Pittsburgh Steelers, 1984 Seattle Seahawks. **Highlights:** 12,120 rushing yards, 100 total touchdowns. 1,556 rushing yards in 19 postseason games. MVP in Super Bowl IX.

ED HEALEY
Tackle. 6-3, 220. Born in Indian Orchard, Massachusetts, December 28, 1894. Died December 9, 1978. Dartmouth. Inducted in 1964. 1920-22 Rock Island, Ill., Independents, 1922-27 Chicago Bears. **Highlights:** Two-way star. Perennial all-pro with Bears.

MEL HEIN
Center. 6-2, 225. Born in Redding, California, August 22, 1909. Died January 31, 1992. Washington State. Inducted in 1963. 1931-45 New York Giants. **Highlights:** Charter enshrinee. 60-minute regular for 15 years. All-NFL eight consecutive years.

TED HENDRICKS
Linebacker. 6-7, 235. Born in Guatemala City, Guatemala, November 1, 1947. Miami. Inducted in 1990. 1969-73 Baltimore Colts, 1974 Green Bay Packers, 1975-81 Oakland Raiders, 1982-83 Los Angeles Raiders. **Highlights:** 25 blocked field goals or extra points, 26 interceptions. Played in 215 consecutive games.

WILBUR (PETE) HENRY
Tackle. 6-0, 250. Born in Mansfield, Ohio, October 31, 1897. Died February 7, 1952. Washington & Jefferson. Inducted in 1963. 1920-23, 1925-26 Canton Bulldogs, 1927 New York Giants, 1927-28 Pottsville Maroons. **Highlights:** Largest player of his time at 250 pounds. Bulwark of Canton's championship lines.

ARNIE HERBER
Quarterback. 6-1, 200. Born in Green Bay, Wisconsin, April 2, 1910. Died October 14, 1969. Wisconsin, Regis College. Inducted in 1966. 1930-40 Green Bay Packers, 1944-45 New York Giants. **Highlights:** NFL passing leader 1932, 1934, 1936. Left retirement to lead 1944 Giants to NFL Eastern crown.

BILL HEWITT
End. 5-11, 191. Born in Bay City,Michigan, October 8, 1909. Died January 14, 1947. Michigan. Inducted in 1971. 1932-36 Chicago Bears, 1937-39 Philadelphia Eagles, 1943 Phil-Pitt. **Highlights:** First to be named all-NFL with two teams—1933, 1934, 1936 Bears; 1937 Eagles.

CLARKE HINKLE
Fullback. 5-11, 201. Born in Toronto, Ohio, April 10, 1909. Died November 9, 1988. Bucknell. Inducted in 1964. 1932-41 Green Bay Packers. **Highlights:** 3,860 yards rushing, 373 points, 43.4 punting average. Fullback on offense, linebacker on defense.

ELROY (CRAZYLEGS) HIRSCH
Halfback-end. 6-2, 190. Born in Wausau, Wisconsin, June 17, 1923. Wisconsin, Michigan. Inducted in1968. 1946-48 Chicago Rockets (AAFC), 1949-57 Los Angeles Rams. **Highlights:** 387 receptions for 7,029 yards, 60 touchdowns. Key part of Rams' revolutionary "three end" offense, 1949.

PAUL HORNUNG
Halfback. 6-2, 220. Born in Louisville, Kentucky, December 23, 1935. Notre Dame. Inducted in 1986. 1957-62, 1964-66 Green Bay Packers. **Highlights:** 760 points. Led NFL scorers three years, including record 176 points, 1960. Record 19 points scored in 1961 NFL title game.

KEN HOUSTON
Safety. 6-3, 198. Born in Lufkin, Texas, November 12, 1944. Prairie View A&M. Inducted in 1986. 1967-72 Houston Oilers, 1973-80 Washington Redskins. **Highlights:** 49 interceptions, 898 yards, 9 touchdowns. NFL's premier strong safety of 1970s. 10 Pro Bowls.

CAL HUBBARD
Tackle. 6-5, 250. Born in Keytesville, Missouri, October 31, 1900. Died October 17, 1977. Centenary, Geneva. Inducted in 1963. 1927-28 New York Giants, 1929-33, 1935 Green Bay Packers, 1936 New York Giants, 1936 Pittsburgh Pirates. **Highlights:** Charter enshrinee. Most feared lineman of his time. All-NFL six years, 1928-33.

SAM HUFF
Linebacker. 6-1, 230. Born in Morgantown, West Virginia, October 4, 1934. West Virginia. Inducted in 1982. 1956-63 New York Giants, 1964-67, 1969 Washington Redskins. **Highlights:** 30 interceptions. Played in six NFL title games, five Pro Bowls. Redskins player-coach, 1969.

LAMAR HUNT
Team owner. Born in El Dorado, Arkansas, August 2, 1932. Southern Methodist. Inducted in 1972. 1960-62 Dallas Texans, 1963-90 Kansas City Chiefs. **Highlights:** Driving force behind organization of AFL. Spearheaded merger negotiations with NFL, 1966.

DON HUTSON
End. 6-1, 180. Born in Pine Bluff, Arkansas, January 31, 1913. Alabama. Inducted in 1963. 1935-45 Green Bay Packers. **Highlights:** 481 receptions for 7,991 yards, 99 touchdowns. NFL receiving champion eight years. NFL MVP, 1941, 1942.

JIMMY JOHNSON
Cornerback. 6-2, 187. Born in Dallas, Texas, March 31, 1938. UCLA. Inducted in 1994. 1961-76 San Francisco 49ers. **Highlights:** 47 interceptions for 615 yards. Five Pro Bowls. Opposing passers avoided throwing in his area.

JOHN HENRY JOHNSON
Fullback. 6-2, 225. Born in Waterproof, Louisiana, November 24, 1929. St. Mary's, Arizona State. Inducted in 1987. 1954-56 San Francisco 49ers, 1957-59 Detroit Lions, 1960-65 Pittsburgh Steelers, 1966 Houston Oilers. **Highlights:** 6,803 yards rushing, 48 touchdowns. Member of San Francisco's "Fabulous Foursome" backfield.

DAVID (DEACON) JONES
Defensive end. 6-5, 250. Born in Eatonville, Florida, December 9, 1938. Mississippi Vocational. Inducted in 1980. 1961-71 Los Angeles Rams, 1972-73 San Diego Chargers, 1974 Washington Redskins. **Highlights:** Specialized in quarterback 'sacks,' a name he invented. Unanimous all-league six consecutive years.

STAN JONES
Guard-defensive tackle. 6-1, 250. Born in Altoona, Pennsylvania, November 24, 1931. Maryland. Inducted in 1991. 1954-65 Chicago Bears, 1966 Washington Redskins. **Highlights:** Seven consecutive Pro Bowls. First to rely on weightlifting for football preparation.

HENRY JORDAN
Defensive tackle, 6-3, 240. Born in Emporia, Virginia, January 26, 1935. Died February 21, 1977. Virginia. Inducted in 1995. 1957-58 Cleveland Browns, 1959-69 Green Bay Packers. **Highlights:** 11-year fixture at DT. Played in four Pro Bowls, seven NFL title games, Super Bowls I, II.

SONNY JURGENSEN
Quarterback. 6-0, 203. Born in Wilmington, North Carolina, August 23, 1934. Duke. Inducted in 1983. 1957-63 Philadelphia Eagles, 1964-74 Washington Redskins. **Highlights:** 32,224 yards passing, 255 touchdowns, 82.63 passer rating. Surpassed 3,000 yards passing in five seasons.

LEROY KELLY
Running back. 6-0, 205. Born in Philadelphia, Pennsylvania, May 20, 1942. Morgan State. Inducted in 1994. 1964-73 Cleveland Browns. **Highlights:** 7,274 yards rushing, 90 total touchdowns, 1,000-yard rusher first three years. Two-time punt return champion.

WALT KIESLING
Guard. Coach. 6-2, 245. Born in St. Paul, Minnesota, March 27, 1903. Died March 2, 1962. St. Thomas (Minnesota). Inducted in 1966. 1926-27 Duluth Eskimos, 1928 Pottsville Maroons, 1929-33 Chicago Cardinals, 1934 Chicago Bears, 1935-36 Green Bay Packers, 1937-38 Pittsburgh Pirates; coach, 1939-42 Pittsburgh Steelers; co-coach, 1943 Phil-Pitt, 1944 Card-Pitt; coach, 1954-56 Pittsburgh Stellers. **Highlights:** 34-year career as pro player, assistant coach, head coach. Led Steelers to first winning season, 1942.

FRANK (BRUISER) KINARD
Tackle. 6-1, 210. Born in Pelahatchie, Mississippi, October 23, 1914. Died September 7, 1985. Mississippi. Inducted in 1971. 1938-44 Brooklyn Dodgers-Tigers, 1946-47 New York Yankees (AAFC). **Highlights:** First man to earn both All-NFL, All-AAFC honors. Out because of injury only once.

EARL (CURLY) LAMBEAU
Coach. Born in Green Bay, Wisconsin, April 9, 1898. Died June 1, 1965. Notre Dame. Inducted in 1963. 1919-49 Green Bay Packers, 1950-51 Chicago Cardinals, 1952-53 Washington Redskins. **Highlights:** 229-134-22 coaching record with six NFL championships. Founded pre-NFL Packers, 1919.

JACK LAMBERT
Linebacker. 6-4, 220. Born in Mantua, Ohio, July 8, 1952. Kent State. Inducted in 1990. 1974-84 Pittsburgh Steelers. **Highlights:** Prototype middle linebacker. Two-time NFL Defensive Player of Year, nine Pro Bowls.

TOM LANDRY
Coach. Born in Mission, Texas, September 11, 1924. Texas. Inducted in 1990. 1960-88 Dallas Cowboys. **Highlights:** 270-178-6 coaching record. 20 consecutive winning seasons. Perfected flex defense, shotgun offense.

DICK (NIGHT TRAIN) LANE
Defensive back. 6-2, 210. Born in Austin, Texas, April 16, 1928. Scottsbluff Junior College. Inducted in 1974. 1952-53 Los Angeles Rams, 1954-59 Chicago Cardinals, 1960-65 Detroit Lions. **Highlights:** 68 interceptions for 1,207 yards, 5 touchdowns. Record 14 interceptions as rookie. Six Pro Bowls.

JIM LANGER
Center. 6-2, 255. Born in Little Falls, Minnesota, May 16, 1948. South Dakota State. Inducted in 1987. 1970-79 Miami Dolphins, 1980-81 Minnesota Vikings. **Highlights:** Played every offensive down in Dolphins' perfect 1972 season. Six Pro Bowls.

WILLIE LANIER
Linebacker. 6-1, 245. Born in Clover, Virginia, August 21, 1945. Morgan State. Inducted in 1986. 1967-77 Kansas City Chiefs. **Highlights:** 27 interceptions. Defensive star in Super Bowl IV upset. Nicknamed 'contact' for ferocious tackling.

STEVE LARGENT
Wide receiver. 5-11, 191. Born in Tulsa, Oklahoma, September 28, 1954, Tulsa. Inducted in 1995. 1976-89 Seattle Seahawks. **Highlights:** 819 receptions for 13,089 yards, 100 touchdowns. Receptions in 177 consecutive games.

YALE LARY
Defensive back-punter. 5-11, 189. Born in Fort Worth, Texas, November 24, 1930. Texas A&M. Inducted in 1979. 1952-53, 1956-64 Detroit Lions. **Highlights:** 50 interceptions. Three NFL punting crowns, three touchdowns on punt returns. Nine Pro Bowls.

DANTE LAVELLI
End. 6-0, 199. Born in Hudson, Ohio, February 23, 1923. Ohio State. Inducted in 1975. 1946-49 Cleveland Browns (AAFC), 1950-56 Cleveland Browns. **Highlights:** 386 receptions for 6,488 yards, 62 touchdowns. 24 catches in six NFL title games.

BOBBY LAYNE
Quarterback. 6-2, 190. Born in Santa Anna, Texas, December 19, 1926. Died December 1, 1986. Texas. Inducted in 1967. 1948 Chicago Bears, 1949 New York Bulldogs, 1950-58 Detroit Lions, 1958-62 Pittsburgh Steelers. **Highlights:** 26,768 yards passing, 196 touchdowns, 2,451 yards rushing. Last-second touchdown pass won 1953 NFL title game.

ALPHONSE (TUFFY) LEEMANS
Fullback. 6-0, 200. Born in Superior, Wisconsin, November 12, 1912. Died January 19, 1979. George Washington. Inducted in 1978. 1936-43 New York Giants. **Highlights:** 3,142 yards rushing, 2,324 yards passing, 442 yards receiving. Led NFL rushers as rookie, 1936.

BOB LILLY
Defensive tackle. 6-5, 260. Born in Olney, Texas, July 26, 1939. Texas Christian. Inducted in 1980. 1961-74 Dallas Cowboys. **Highlights:** 11 Pro Bowls. Missed one game in 14 years. Foundation of great Dallas defensive units.

LARRY LITTLE
Guard. 6-1, 255. Born in Groveland, Georgia, November 2, 1945. Bethune-Cookman. Inducted in 1993. 1967-68 San Diego Chargers, 1969-80 Miami Dolphins. **Highlights:** Five Pro Bowls, started in three Super Bowls. Epitome of powerful Dolphins rushing game of 1970s.

VINCE LOMBARDI
Coach. Born in Brooklyn, New York, June 11, 1913. Died September 3, 1970. Fordham. Inducted in 1971. 1959-67 Green Bay Packers, 1969 Washington Redskins. **Highlights:** 105-35-6 coaching record in 10 years, including five NFL titles and victories in Super Bowl I and II.

SID LUCKMAN
Quarterback. 6-0, 195. Born in Brooklyn, New York, November 21, 1916. Columbia. Inducted in 1965. 1939-50 Chicago Bears. **Highlights:** 139 touchdown passes. All-NFL team five times. League MVP in 1943.

WILLIAM ROY (LINK) LYMAN
Tackle. 6-2, 252. Born in Table Rock, Nebraska, November 30, 1898. Died December 16, 1972. Nebraska. Inducted in 1964. 1922-23, 1925 Canton Bulldogs, 1924 Cleveland Bulldogs, 1925 Frankford Yellow Jackets, 1926-28, 1930-31, 1933-34 Chicago Bears. **Highlights:** Played for four NFL champions. In 16 seasons of college and pro football, played on one losing team.

JOHN MACKEY
Tight end. 6-2, 224. Born in New York, New York, September 24, 1941. Syracuse. Inducted in 1992. 1963-71 Baltimore Colts, 1972 San Diego Chargers. **Highlights:** 331 receptions for 5,236 yards, 38 touchdowns. Second tight end to enter Hall of Fame.

TIM MARA
Team owner. Born in New York, New York, July 29, 1887. Died February 17, 1959. Did not attend college. Inducted in 1963. 1925-59 New York Giants. **Highlights:** Charter enshrinee. Founder of New York Giants. Built team into powerhouse winning three NFL titles, eight division titles.

GINO MARCHETTI
Defensive end. 6-4, 245. Born in Smithers, West Virginia, January 2, 1927. San Francisco. Inducted in 1972. 1952 Dallas Texans, 1953-64, 1966 Baltimore Colts. **Highlights:** Named top defensive end of NFL's first 50 years. 11 consecutive Pro Bowls. All-NFL seven times.

GEORGE PRESTON MARSHALL
Team owner. Born in Grafton, West Virginia, October 11, 1897. Died August 9, 1969. Randolph-Macon. Inducted in 1963. 1932 Boston Braves, 1933-36 Boston Redskins, 1937-69 Washington Redskins. **Highlights:** Charter enshrinee. Sponsored progressive rules changes. Organized first team band, pioneered halftime shows.

OLLIE MATSON
Halfback. 6-2, 220. Born in Trinity, Texas, May 1, 1930. San Francisco. Inducted in 1972. 1952, 1954-58 Chicago Cardinals, 1959-62 Los Angeles Rams, 1963 Detroit Lions, 1964-66 Philadelphia Eagles. **Highlights:** NFL-record 9 touchdowns on kickoff, punt returns. Traded for nine players in 1959.

DON MAYNARD
Wide receiver. 6-1, 175. Born in Crosbyton, Texas, January 25, 1935. Texas Western. Inducted in 1987. 1958 New York Giants, 1960-62 New York Titans, 1963-72 New York Jets, 1973 St. Louis Cardinals. **Highlights:** 633 receptions for 11,834 yards, 88 touchdowns. At least 50 catches and 1,000 yards in five different seasons.

GEORGE McAFEE
Halfback. 6-0, 177. Born in Ironton, Ohio, March 13, 1918. Duke. Inducted in 1966. 1940-41, 1945-50 Chicago Bears. **Highlights:** Two-way star. 21 interceptions, 234 points. Career punt return record of 12.78 yards per return.

MIKE McCORMACK
Tackle. 6-4, 248. Born in Chicago, Illinois, June 21, 1930. Kansas. Inducted in 1984. 1951 New York Yanks, 1954-62 Cleveland Browns. **Highlights:** Excelled as offensive right tackle for eight years. Six Pro Bowls.

HUGH McELHENNY
Halfback. 6-1, 198. Born in Los Angeles, California, December 31, 1928. Washington. Inducted in 1970. 1952-60 San Francisco 49ers, 1961-62 Minnesota Vikings, 1963 New York Giants, 1964 Detroit Lions. **Highlights:** 5,281 rushing yards, 360 points. Scored 40-yard touchdown run on first pro play.

JOHNNY (BLOOD) McNALLY
Halfback. 6-0, 185. Born in New Richmond, Wisconsin, November 27, 1903. Died November 28, 1985. St. John's (Minnesota). Inducted in 1963. 1925-26 Milwaukee Badgers, 1926-27 Duluth Eskimos, 1928 Pottsville Maroons, 1929-33, 1935-36 Green Bay Packers, 1934 Pittsburgh Pirates; player-coach, 1937-39 Pittsburgh Pirates. **Highlights:** 37 touchdowns, 224 points in 15 seasons with five teams. Pittsburgh player-coach 1937-39.

MIKE MICHALSKE
Guard. 6-0, 209. Born in Cleveland, Ohio, April 24, 1903. Died October 26, 1983. Penn State. Inducted in 1964. 1926 New York Yankees (AFL), 1927-28 New York Yankees, 1929-35, 1937 Green Bay Packers. **Highlights:** Anchored Packers' championship lines, 1929-1931, 1935. First-ever guard enshrined in Canton.

WAYNE MILLNER
End. 6-0, 191. Born in Roxbury, Massachusetts, January 31, 1913. Died November 19, 1976. Notre Dame. Inducted in 1968. 1936 Boston Redskins, 1937-41, 1945 Washington Redskins. **Highlights:** Redskin's all-time leader with 124 catches when retired. 55- and 78-yard touchdown receptions in 1937 NFL championship.

BOBBY MITCHELL
Running back-wide receiver. 6-0, 195. Born in Hot Springs, Arkansas, June 6, 1935. Illinois. Inducted in 1983. 1958-61 Cleveland Browns, 1962-68 Washington Redskins. **Highlights:** 91 touchdowns, including 8 on kickoff and punt returns. 14,078 combined yards.

RON MIX
Tackle. 6-4, 250. Born in Los Angeles, California, March 10, 1938. Southern California. Inducted in 1979. 1960 Los Angeles Chargers, 1961-69 San Diego Chargers, 1971 Oakland Raiders. **Highlights:** All-AFL tackle eight times. Only two holding penalties in 10-year career.

LENNY MOORE
Back. 6-1, 198. Born in Reading, Pennsylvania, November 25, 1933. Penn State. Inducted in 1975. 1956-67 Baltimore Colts. **Highlights:** From 1963-65, scored touchdowns in record 18 consecutive games. 113 career touchdowns, 11,213 combined net yards.

MARION MOTLEY
Fullback. 6-1, 238. Born in Leesburg, Georgia, June 5, 1920. South Carolina State, Nevada. Inducted in 1968. 1946-49 Cleveland Browns (AAFC), 1950-53 Cleveland Browns, 1955 Pittsburgh Steelers. **Highlights:** AAFC's all-time rushing champion. Led league in rushing in first NFL season.

GEORGE MUSSO
Guard-tackle. 6-2, 270. Born in Collinsville, Illinois. April 8, 1910. Millikin. Inducted in 1982. 1933-44 Chicago Bears. **Highlights:** First player to achieve All-NFL status at two positions—tackle in 1935 and guard in 1937.

BRONKO NAGURSKI
Fullback. 6-2, 225. Born in Rainy River, Ontario, Canada, November 3, 1908. Died January 7, 1990. Minnesota. Inducted in 1963. 1930-37, 1943 Chicago Bears. **Highlights:** Charter enshrinee. 4,031 rushing yards in nine seasons. All-NFL three times.

JOE NAMATH
Quarterback. 6-2, 200. Born in Beaver Falls, Pennsylvania, May 31, 1943. Alabama. Inducted in 1985. 1965-76 New York Jets, 1977 Los Angeles Rams. **Highlights:** First quarterback to pass for more than 4,000 yards in season, 1967. Guaranteed, delivered victory over Colts in Super Bowl III.

EARLE (GREASY) NEALE
Coach. Born in Parkersburg, West Virginia, November 5, 1891. Died November 2, 1973. West Virginia Wesleyan. Inducted in 1969. 1941-42, 1944-50 Philadelphia Eagles; co-coach, Phil-Pitt 1943. **Highlights:** Turned Eagles into winners with three consecutive division crowns, NFL championships in 1948 and 1949.

ERNIE NEVERS
Fullback. 6-1, 205. Born in Willow River, Minnesota, June 11, 1903. Died May 3, 1976. Stanford. Inducted in 1963. 1926-27 Duluth Eskimos, 1929-31 Chicago Cardinals. **Highlights:** Charter enshrinee. Holds NFL's longest-standing record, 40 points in one game in 1929.

RAY NITSCHKE
Linebacker. 6-3, 235. Born in Elmwood Park, Illinois, December 29,

1936. Illinois. Inducted in 1978. 1958-72 Green Bay Packers. **Highlights:** MVP of 1962 title game. Named NFL's all-time linebacker in 1969.

CHUCK NOLL
Coach. Born in Cleveland, Ohio, January 5, 1932. Dayton. Inducted in 1993. 1969-91 Pittsburgh Steelers. **Highlights:** Coached for 23 years. Only coach to win four Super Bowl titles (IX, X, XIII, XIV).

LEO NOMELLINI
Defensive tackle. 6-3, 250. Born in Lucca, Italy, June 19, 1924. Minnesota. Inducted in 1969. 1950-63 San Francisco 49ers. **Highlights:** Played every 49ers game for 14 seasons. 10 Pro Bowls.

MERLIN OLSEN
Defensive tackle. 6-5, 270. Born in Logan, Utah, September 15, 1940. Utah State. Inducted in 1982. 1962-76 Los Angeles Rams. **Highlights:** Member of the Fearsome Foursome. Named to 14 consecutive Pro Bowls, Rams' all-time team.

JIM OTTO
Center. 6-2, 255. Born in Wausau, Wisconsin, January 5, 1938. Miami. Inducted in 1980. 1960-74 Oakland Raiders. **Highlights:** Named AFL's all-time center. Played in 308 games, 12 all-star games, six AFL/AFC title games.

STEVE OWEN
Tackle. Coach. 6-0, 235. Born in Cleo Springs, Oklahoma, April 21, 1898. Died May 17, 1964. Phillips. Inducted in 1966. 1924-25 Kansas City Cowboys, 1926-30 New York Giants; coach, 1931-53 New York Giants. **Highlights:** Both player and coach. Coached Giants to record of 153-108-17, eight divisional titles, two NFL championships.

ALAN PAGE
Defensive tackle. 6-4, 225. Born in Canton, Ohio, August 7, 1945. Notre Dame. Inducted in 1988. 1967-78 Minnesota Vikings, 1978-81 Chicago Bears. **Highlights:** NFL iron man. Played in 236 consecutive games, four Super Bowls. League MVP in 1971.

CLARENCE (ACE) PARKER
Quarterback. 5-11, 168. Born in Portsmouth, Virginia, May 17, 1912. Duke. Inducted in 1972. 1937-41 Brooklyn Dodgers, 1945 Boston Yanks, 1946 New York Yankees (AAFC). **Highlights:** Two-way threat. Two-time All-NFL performer, league MVP in 1940.

JIM PARKER
Guard-tackle. 6-3, 273. Born in Macon, Georgia, April 3, 1934. Ohio State. Inducted in 1973. 1957-67 Baltimore Colts. **Highlights:** First full-time offensive lineman elected to Hall of Fame. All-NFL eight consecutive years, eight Pro Bowls.

WALTER PAYTON
Running back. 5-10, 202. Born in Columbia, Mississippi, July 25, 1954. Jackson State. Inducted in 1993. 1975-87 Chicago Bears. **Highlights:** NFL's all-time leading rusher with 16,726 yards. Holds single-game rushing record of 275 yards.

JOE PERRY
Fullback. 6-0, 200. Born in Stevens, Arkansas, January 22, 1927. Compton Junior College. Inducted in 1969. 1948-49 San Francisco 49ers (AAFC), 1950-60, 1963 San Francisco 49ers, 1961-62 Baltimore Colts. **Highlights:** First player in NFL history to gain 1,000 yards two consecutive seasons. 12,505 combined yards.

PETE PIHOS
End. 6-1, 210. Born in Orlando, Florida, October 22, 1923. Indiana. Inducted in 1970. 1947-55 Philadelphia Eagles. **Highlights:** Three-time NFL receiving champion. Caught winning touchdown in 1949 NFL Championship Game.

HUGH (SHORTY) RAY
Supervisor of officials 1938-56. Born in Highland Park, Illinois, September 21, 1884. Died September 16, 1956. Illinois. Inducted in 1966. **Highlights:** Supervisor of Officials, 1938-1952. Streamlined rules to improve game tempo, player safety.

DAN REEVES
Team owner. Born in New York, New York, June 30, 1912. Died April 15, 1971. Georgetown. Inducted in 1967. 1941-45 Cleveland Rams, 1946-71 Los Angeles Rams. **Highlights:** Moved Rams to Los Angeles in 1946 and opened up west coast to pro football. First post-war owner to sign African-American player.

JOHN RIGGINS
Running back. 6-2, 240. Born in Seneca, Kansas, August 4, 1949. Kansas. Inducted in 1992. 1971-75 New York Jets, 1976-79, 1981-85 Washington Redskins. **Highlights:** 11,352 rushing yards, 104 touchdowns. MVP of Super Bowl XVII with 166 rushing yards including game-winning 43-yard touchdown.

JIM RINGO
Center. 6-1, 235. Born in Orange, New Jersey, November 21, 1931. Syracuse. Inducted in 1981. 1953-63 Green Bay Packers, 1964-67 Philadelphia Eagles. **Highlights:** Ten-time Pro Bowler, six-time All-NFL selection. Started in then-record 182 consecutive games.

ANDY ROBUSTELLI
Defensive end. 6-0, 230. Born in Stamford, Connecticut, December 6, 1925. Arnold College. Inducted in 1971. 1951-55 Los Angeles Rams, 1956-64 New York Giants. **Highlights:** Anchored Rams defense in eight championship games. Named NFL's top player in 1962.

ART ROONEY
Team owner. Born in Coulterville, Pennsylvania, January 27, 1901. Died August 25, 1988. Georgetown, Duquesne. Inducted in 1964. 1933-40 Pittsburgh Pirates, 1941-42, 1945-88 Pittsburgh Steelers, 1943 Phil-Pitt, 1944 Card-Pitt. **Highlights:** Bought Pittsburgh Pirates in 1933 and renamed them Steelers in 1940. Team won four Super Bowls in 1970s.

PETE ROZELLE
Commissioner. Born in South Gate, California, March 1, 1926. San Francisco. Inducted in 1985. Commissioner, 1960-89. **Highlights:** Negotiated first league-wide television contract in 1962. Generally recognized as premiere commissioner in all of sports. Credited with making NFL the nation's most popular sport.

BOB ST. CLAIR
Tackle. 6-9, 265. Born in San Francisco, California, February 18, 1931. San Francisco, Tulsa. Inducted in 1990. 1953-63 San Francisco 49ers. **Highlights:** Exceptional offensive lineman. Also played goal-line defense and had 10 career blocked field goals.

GALE SAYERS
Running back. 6-0, 200. Born in Wichita, Kansas, May 30, 1943. Kansas. Inducted in 1977. 1965-71 Chicago Bears. **Highlights:** Broke into league by scoring rookie-record 22 touchdowns. Led league in rushing in 1966, 1969. MVP of three Pro Bowls.

JOE SCHMIDT
Linebacker. 6-0, 222. Born in Pittsburgh, Pennsylvania, January 19,1932. Pittsburgh. Inducted in 1973. 1953-65 Detroit Lions. **Highlights:** 24 interceptions. Lions team captain for nine years. Mastered middle linebacker position which evolved in 1950s.

TEX SCHRAMM
Team president-general manager. Born in San Gabriel, California, June 2, 1920. Texas. Inducted in 1991. 1947-57 Los Angeles Rams. 1960-88 Dallas Cowboys. **Highlights:** Played prominent role in AFL-NFL merger. Chairman of Competition Committee from 1966-1988.

LEE ROY SELMON
Defensive end. 6-3, 250. Born in Eufaula, Oklahoma, October 20, 1954. Oklahoma. Inducted in 1995. 1976-84 Tampa Bay Buccaneers. **Highlights:** 78½ sacks, 380 quarterback pressures, forced 28 fumbles. Five consecutive Pro Bowls.

ART SHELL
Tackle. 6-5, 285. Born in Charleston, South Carolina, November 25, 1946. Maryland State-Eastern Shore. Inducted in 1989. 1968-81 Oakland Raiders, 1982 Los Angeles Raiders. **Highlights:** Cornerstone of Raiders' offensive line in 1970s. 207 regular-season games, 24 postseason games, 8 Pro Bowls.

O.J. SIMPSON
Running back. 6-1, 212. Born in San Francisco, California, July 9, 1947. Southern California. Inducted in 1985. 1969-77 Buffalo Bills, 1978-79 San Francisco 49ers. **Highlights:** In 1973, became first player to rush for 2,000 yards in season. Finished career with four rushing titles, 11,236 yards.

JACKIE SMITH
Tight end. 6-4, 232. Born in Columbia, Mississippi, February 23, 1940. Northwestern Louisiana. Inducted in 1994. 1963-77 St. Louis Cardinals, 1978 Dallas Cowboys. **Highlights:** 480 receptions for 7,918 yards, 40 touchdowns. Third tight end to be elected to Hall of Fame.

BART STARR
Quarterback. 6-1, 200. Born in Montgomery, Alabama, January 9, 1934. Alabama. Inducted in 1977. 1956-71 Green Bay Packers. **Highlights:** Quarterbacked Packers to six division titles, five NFL titles including first two Super Bowls in which he was MVP.

ROGER STAUBACH
Quarterback. 6-3, 202. Born in Cincinnati, Ohio, February 5, 1942. Navy Inducted in 1985. 1969-79 Dallas Cowboys. **Highlights:** Led Cowboys to four NFC titles and victories in Super Bowls VI, XII. When retired, 83.4 career passer rating was best of all time.

ERNIE STAUTNER
Defensive tackle. 6-2, 235. Born in Prinzing-by-Cham, Bavaria, Germany, April 20, 1925. Boston College. Inducted in 1969. 1950-63 Pittsburgh Steelers. **Highlights:** Played in nine Pro Bowls and won the best lineman award in 1957. Scored three safeties.

JAN STENERUD
Kicker. 6-2, 190. Born in Fetsund, Norway, November 26, 1942. Montana State. Inducted in 1991. 1967-79 Kansas City Chiefs, 1980-83 Green Bay Packers, 1984-85 Minnesota Vikings. **Highlights:** 1,699 points on 580 extra points, 373 field goals. First pure placekicker to enter Hall of Fame.

KEN STRONG
Halfback. 5-11, 210. Born in New Haven, Connecticut, August 6, 1906. Died October 5, 1979. New York University. Inducted in 1967. 1929-32 Staten Island Stapletons, 1933-35, 1939, 1944-47 New York Giants, 1936-37 New York Yanks (AFL). **Highlights:** In 1934, scored 17 points to lead Giants to victory in 1934 'Sneakers' game, led NFL with 64 points.

JOE STYDAHAR
Tackle. 6-4, 230. Born in Kaylor, Pennsylvania, March 3, 1912. Died March 23, 1977. West Virginia. Inducted in 1967. 1936-42, 1945-46 Chicago Bears. **Highlights:** One of stalwarts of Bears' 'Monsters of the Midway.' Played on five divisional, three NFL championship teams.

FRAN TARKENTON
Quarterback. 6-0, 185. Born in Richmond, Virginia, February 3, 1940. Georgia. Inducted in 1986. 1961-66, 1972-78 Minnesota Vikings, 1967-71 New York Giants. **Highlights:** Holds NFL records for attempts (6,467), completions (3,686), yards (47,003), and touchdowns (342). Four touchdowns passes in first NFL game.

CHARLEY TAYLOR
Running back-wide receiver. 6-3, 210. Born in Grand Prairie, Texas, September 28, 1941. Arizona State. Inducted in 1984. 1964-75, 1977 Washington Redskins. **Highlights:** Won Rookie of Year honors as running back. Switched to wide receiver and won receiving titles in 1966, 1967.

JIM TAYLOR
Fullback. 6-0, 216. Born in Baton Rouge, Louisiana, September 20, 1935. Louisiana State. Inducted in 1976. 1958-66 Green Bay Packers, 1967 New Orleans Saints. **Highlights:** 8,597 rushing yards, 558 points. In 1962, led league in rushing and scoring with 19 touchdowns.

JIM THORPE
Halfback. 6-1, 190. Born in Prague, Oklahoma, May 28, 1888. Died March 28, 1953. Carlisle. Inducted in 1963. 1915-17, 1919-20, 1926 Canton Bulldogs, 1921 Cleveland Indians, 1922-23 Oorang Indians, 1923 Toledo Maroons, 1924 Rock Island, Ill., Independents, 1925 New York Giants, 1928 Chicago Cardinals. **Highlights:** Charter enshrinee. First president of American Professional Football Association, 1920. Played for 13 seasons.

Y.A. TITTLE
Quarterback. 6-0, 200. Born in Marshall, Texas, October 24, 1926. Louisiana State. Inducted in 1971. 1948-49 Baltimore Colts (AAFC), 1950 Baltimore Colts, 1951-60 San Francisco 49ers, 1961-64 New York Giants. **Highlights:** 33,070 yards, 242 touchdowns. 33 touchdown passes in 1962 and 36 in 1963. Two-time league MVP.

GEORGE TRAFTON
Center. 6-2, 235. Born in Chicago, Illinois, December 6, 1896. Died September 5, 1971. Notre Dame. Inducted in 1964. 1920 Decatur Staleys, 1921 Chicago Staleys, 1922-32 Chicago Bears. **Highlights:** First center to snap with one hand. Named top NFL center of 1920s.

CHARLEY TRIPPI
Halfback. 6-0, 185. Born in Pittston, Pennsylvania, December 14, 1922. Georgia. Inducted in 1968. 1947-55 Chicago Cardinals. **Highlights:** One of football's most versatile performers. Played halfback five years, quarterback for two, defense for two.

EMLEN TUNNELL
Safety. 6-1, 200. Born in Bryn Mawr, Pennsylvania, March 29, 1925. Died July 23, 1975. Toledo, Iowa. Inducted in 1967. 1948-58 New York Giants, 1959-61 Green Bay Packers. **Highlights:** 79 interceptions. Gained more yards on kickoffs and interceptions (923) in 1952 than that season's NFL rushing leader.

CLYDE (BULLDOG) TURNER
Center. 6-2, 235. Born in Sweetwater, Texas, November 10, 1919. Hardin-Simmons. Inducted in 1966. 1940-52 Chicago Bears. **Highlights:** Anchored defense for four NFL championship teams. 4 interceptions in five title games.

JOHNNY UNITAS
Quarterback. 6-1, 195. Born in Pittsburgh, Pennsylvania, May 7, 1933. Louisville. Inducted in 1979. 1956-72 Baltimore Colts, 1973 San Diego Chargers. **Highlights:** 40,239 passing yards, 290 touchdowns. Led Colts to two NFL championships. Passed for at least one touchdown in 47 consecutive games.

GENE UPSHAW
Guard. 6-5, 255. Born in Robstown, Texas, August 15, 1945. Texas A & I. Inducted in 1987. 1967-81 Oakland Raiders. **Highlights:** Played in 10 AFL/AFC Championship Games, three Super Bowls, seven Pro Bowls—307 total games.

NORM VAN BROCKLIN
Quarterback. 6-1, 190. Born in Eagle Butte, South Dakota, March 15, 1926. Died May 2, 1983. Oregon. Inducted in 1971. 1949-57 Los Angeles Rams, 1958-60 Philadelphia Eagles. **Highlights:** NFL-record 554 yards passing in 1951 season opener. Guided Eagles to NFL crown as league MVP in 1960.

STEVE VAN BUREN
Halfback. 6-1, 200. Born in La Ceiba, Honduras, December 28, 1920. Louisiana State. Inducted in 1965. 1944-51 Philadelphia Eagles. **Highlights:** Four-time rushing champion. Won 1944 punt return title and was 1945 kick return champion.

DOAK WALKER
Halfback. 5-10, 172. Born in Dallas, Texas, January 1, 1927. Southern Methodist. Inducted in 1986. 1950-55 Detroit Lions. **Highlights:** 534 points. Won two NFL scoring titles. Had winning 62-yard scoring run in 1952 title game.

BILL WALSH
Coach. Born in Los Angeles, California, November 30, 1931. San Jose State. Inducted in 1993. 1979-88 San Francisco 49ers. **Highlights:** 102-63-1 coaching record. Guided 49ers to three Super Bowl titles (XVI, XIX, XXIII) in 10 years.

PAUL WARFIELD
Wide receiver. 6-0, 188. Born in Warren, Ohio, November 28, 1942. Ohio State. Inducted in 1983. 1964-69, 1976-77 Cleveland Browns, 1970-74 Miami Dolphins. **Highlights:** 8,565 yards receiving, 85 touchdowns. Eight-time Pro Bowler. Key to both Cleveland and Miami offenses.

BOB WATERFIELD
Quarterback. 6-2, 200. Born in Elmira, New York, July 26, 1920. Died March 25, 1983. UCLA. Inducted in 1965. 1945 Cleveland Rams, 1946-52 Los Angeles Rams. **Highlights:** NFL MVP as rookie in 1945 and led Rams to NFL title. 20 interceptions in limited defensive duties.

ARNIE WEINMEISTER
Defensive tackle. 6-4, 235. Born in Rhein, Saskatchewan, Canada, March 23, 1923. Washington. Inducted in 1984. 1948-49 New York Yankees (AAFC), 1950-53 New York Giants. **Highlights:** Dominant defensive tackle of his time. Four-time All-NFL selection, four Pro Bowls.

RANDY WHITE
Defensive tackle. 6-4, 265. Born in Wilmington, Delaware, January 15, 1953. Maryland. Inducted in 1994. 1975-88 Dallas Cowboys. **Highlights:** Missed only one game in 14 seasons. Co-MVP of Super Bowl XII. Nine-time Pro Bowler.

BILL WILLIS
Guard. 6-2, 215. Born in Columbus, Ohio, October 5, 1921. Ohio State. Inducted in 1977. 1946-49 Cleveland Browns (AAFC), 1950-53 Cleveland Browns. **Highlights:** Two-way player who excelled on defense. Four-time All-NFL player, three-time Pro Bowler.

LARRY WILSON
Safety. 6-0, 190. Born in Rigby, Idaho, March 24, 1938. Utah. Inducted in 1978. 1960-72 St. Louis Cardinals. **Highlights:** 52 interceptions. Had interception in seven consecutive games in 1966. Made "safety blitz" famous.

KELLEN WINSLOW
Tight End. 6-5, 250. Born in St. Louis, Missouri, November 5, 1957. Missouri. Inducted in 1995. 1979-87 San Diego Chargers **Highlights:** 541 receptions for 6,741 yards, 45 touchdowns. 13 catches, blocked field goal in 1981 playoff win over Miami.

ALEX WOJCIECHOWICZ
Center. 6-0, 235. Born in South River, New Jersey, August 12, 1915. Died July 13, 1992. Fordham. Inducted in 1968. 1938-46 Detroit Lions, 1946-50 Philadelphia Eagles. **Highlights:** One of league's first iron men. Played both ways for eight years with Lions.

WILLIE WOOD
Safety. 5-10, 190. Born in Washington, D.C., December 23, 1936. Southern California. Inducted in 1989. 1960-71 Green Bay Packers. **Highlights:** 48 interceptions. Competed in six NFL championship games including Super Bowls I and II.

CHRONOLOGY OF PROFESSIONAL FOOTBALL

1869
Rutgers and Princeton played a college soccer football game, the first ever, November 6. The game used modified London Football Association rules. During the next seven years, rugby gained favor with the major eastern schools over soccer, and modern football began to develop from rugby.

1876
At the Massasoit convention, the first rules for American football were written. Walter Camp, who would become known as the father of American football, first became involved with the game.

1892
In an era in which football was a major attraction of local athletic clubs, an intense competition between two Pittsburgh-area clubs, the Allegheny Athletic Association (AAA) and the Pittsburgh Athletic Club (PAC), led to the making of the first professional football player. Former Yale All-America guard William (Pudge) Heffelfinger was paid $500 by the AAA to play in a game against the PAC, becoming the first person to be paid to play football, November 12. The AAA won the game 4-0 when Heffelfinger picked up a PAC fumble and ran 25 yards for a touchdown.

1893
The Pittsburgh Athletic Club signed one of its players, probably halfback Grant Dibert, to the first known pro football contract, which covered all of the PAC's games for the year.

1895
John Brallier became the first football player to openly turn pro, accepting $10 and expenses to play for the Latrobe YMCA against the Jeannette Athletic Club.

1896
The Allegheny Athletic Association team fielded the first completely professional team for its abbreviated two-game season.

1897
The Latrobe Athletic Association football team went entirely professional, becoming the first team to play a full season with only professionals.

1898
A touchdown was changed from four points to five.

1899
Chris O'Brien formed a neighborhood team, which played under the name the Morgan Athletic Club, on the south side of Chicago. The team later became known as the Normals, then the Racine (for a street in Chicago) Cardinals, the Chicago Cardinals, the St. Louis Cardinals, the Phoenix Cardinals, and, in 1994, the Arizona Cardinals. The team remains the oldest continuing operation in pro football.

1900
William C. Temple took over the team payments for the Duquesne Country and Athletic Club, becoming the first known individual club owner.

1902
Baseball's Philadelphia Athletics, managed by Connie Mack, and the Philadelphia Phillies formed professional football teams, joining the Pittsburgh Stars in the first attempt at a pro football league, named the National Football League. The Athletics won the first night football game ever played, 39-0 over Kanaweola AC at Elmira, New York, November 21.

All three teams claimed the pro championship for the year, but the league president, Dave Berry, named the Stars the champions. Pitcher Rube Waddell was with the Athletics, and pitcher Christy Mathewson a fullback for Pittsburgh.

The first World Series of pro football, actually a five-team tournament, was played among a team made up of players from both the Athletics and the Phillies, but simply named New York; the New York Knickerbockers; the Syracuse AC; the Warlow AC; and the Orange (New Jersey) AC at New York's original Madison Square Garden. New York and Syracuse played the first indoor football game before 3,000, December 28. Syracuse, with Glen (Pop) Warner at guard, won 6-0 and went on to win the tournament.

1903
The Franklin (Pa.) Athletic Club won the second and last World Series of pro football over the Oreos AC of Asbury Park, New Jersey; the Watertown Red and Blacks; and the Orange AC.

Pro football was popularized in Ohio when the Massillon Tigers, a strong amateur team, hired four Pittsburgh pros to play in the season-ending game against Akron. At the same time, pro football declined in the Pittsburgh area, and the emphasis on the pro game moved west from Pennsylvania to Ohio.

1904
A field goal was changed from five points to four.

Ohio had at least seven pro teams, with Massillon winning the Ohio Independent Championship, that is, the pro title. Talk surfaced about forming a state-wide league to end spiraling salaries brought about by constant bidding for players and to write universal rules for the game. The feeble attempt to start the league failed.

Halfback Charles Follis signed a contract with the Shelby AC, making him the first known black pro football player.

1905
The Canton AC, later to become known as the Bulldogs, became a professional team. Massillon again won the Ohio League championship.

1906
The forward pass was legalized. The first authenticated pass completion in a pro game came on October 27, when George (Peggy) Parratt of Massillon threw a completion to Dan (Bullet) Riley in a victory over a combined Benwood-Moundsville team.

Arch-rivals Canton and Massillon, the two best pro teams in America, played twice, with Canton winning the first game but Massillon winning the second and the Ohio League championship. A betting scandal and the financial disaster wrought upon the two clubs by paying huge salaries caused a temporary decline in interest in pro football in the two cities and, somewhat, throughout Ohio.

1909
A field goal dropped from four points to three.

1912
A touchdown was increased from five points to six.

Jack Cusack revived a strong pro team in Canton.

1913
Jim Thorpe, a former football and track star at the Carlisle Indian School (Pa.) and a double gold medal winner at the 1912 Olympics in Stockholm, played for the Pine Village Pros in Indiana.

1915
Massillon again fielded a major team, reviving the old rivalry with Canton. Cusack signed Thorpe to play for Canton for $250 a game.

1916
With Thorpe and former Carlisle teammate Pete Calac starring, Canton went 9-0-1, won the Ohio League championship, and was acclaimed the pro football champion.

1917
Despite an upset by Massillon, Canton again won the Ohio League championship.

1919
Canton again won the Ohio League championship, despite the team having been turned over from Cusack to Ralph Hay. Thorpe and Calac were joined in the backfield by Joe Guyon.

Earl (Curly) Lambeau and George Calhoun organized the Green Bay Packers. Lambeau's employer at the Indian Packing Company provided $500 for equipment and allowed the team to use the company field for practices. The Packers went 10-1.

1920
Pro football was in a state of confusion due to three major problems: dramatically rising salaries; players continually jumping from one team to another following the highest offer; and the use of college players still enrolled in school. A league in which all the members would follow the same rules seemed the answer. An organizational meeting, at which the Akron Pros, Canton Bulldogs, Cleveland Indians, and Dayton Triangles were represented, was held at the Jordan and Hupmobile auto showroom in Canton, Ohio, August 20. This meeting resulted in the formation of the American Professional Football Conference.

A second organizational meeting was held in Canton, September 17. The teams were from four states—Akron, Canton, Cleveland, and Dayton from Ohio; the Hammond Pros and Muncie Flyers from Indiana; the Rochester Jeffersons from New York; and the Rock Island Independents, Decatur Staleys, and Racine Cardinals from Illinois. The name of the league was changed to the American Professional Football Association. Hoping to capitalize on his fame, the members elected Thorpe president; Stanley Cofall of Cleveland was elected vice president. A membership fee of $100 per team was charged to give an appearance of respectability, but no team ever paid it. Scheduling was left up to the teams, and there were wide variations, both in the overall number of games played and in the number played against APFA member teams.

Four other teams—the Buffalo All-Americans, Chicago Tigers, Columbus Panhandles, and Detroit Heralds—joined the league sometime during the year. On September 26, the first game featuring an APFA team was played at Rock Island's Douglas Park. A crowd of 800 watched the Independents defeat the St. Paul Ideals 48-0. A week later, October 3, the first game matching two APFA teams was held. At Triangle Park, Dayton defeated Columbus 14-0, with Lou Partlow of Dayton scoring the first touchdown in a game between Association teams. The same day, Rock Island defeated Muncie 45-0.

By the beginning of December, most of the teams in the APFA had abandoned their hopes for a championship, and some of them, including the Chicago Tigers and the Detroit Heralds, had finished their seasons, disbanded, and had their franchises canceled by the Association. Four teams—Akron, Buffalo, Canton, and Decatur—still had championship aspirations, but a series of late-season games among them left Akron as the only undefeated team in the Association. At one of these games, Akron sold tackle Bob Nash to Buffalo for $300 and five percent of the gate receipts—the first APFA player deal.

1921
At the league meeting in Akron, April 30, the championship of the 1920 season was awarded to the Akron Pros. The APFA was reorganized, with Joe Carr of the Columbus Panhandles named president and Carl Storck of Dayton secretary-treasurer. Carr moved the Association's headquarters to Columbus, drafted a league constitution and by-laws, gave teams territorial rights, restricted player movements, developed membership criteria for the franchises, and issued standings for the first time, so that the APFA would have a clear champion.

The Association's membership increased to 22 teams, including the Green Bay Packers, who were awarded to John Clair of the Acme Packing Company.

Thorpe moved from Canton to the Cleveland Indians, but he was hurt early in the season and played very little.

A.E. Staley turned the Decatur Staleys over to player-coach George Halas, who moved the team to Cubs

Park in Chicago. Staley paid Halas $5,000 to keep the name Staleys for one more year. Halas made halfback Ed (Dutch) Sternaman his partner.

The Staleys claimed the APFA championship with a 9-1-1 record, as did Buffalo at 9-1-2. Carr ruled in favor of the Staleys, giving Halas his first championship.

1922
After admitting the use of players who had college eligibility remaining during the 1921 season, Clair and the Green Bay management withdrew from the APFA, January 28. Curly Lambeau promised to obey league rules and then used $50 of his own money to buy back the franchise. Bad weather and low attendance plagued the Packers, and Lambeau went broke, but local merchants arranged a $2,500 loan for the club. A public nonprofit corporation was set up to operate the team, with Lambeau as head coach and manager.

The American Professional Football Association changed its name to the National Football League, June 24. The Chicago Staleys became the Chicago Bears.

The NFL fielded 18 teams, including the new Oorang Indians of Marion, Ohio, an all-Indian team featuring Thorpe, Joe Guyon, and Pete Calac, and sponsored by the Oorang dog kennels.

Canton, led by player-coach Guy Chamberlin and tackles Link Lyman and Wilbur (Pete) Henry, emerged as the league's first true powerhouse, going 10-0-2.

1923
For the first time, all of the franchises considered to be part of the NFL fielded teams. Thorpe played first for Oorang, then for the Toledo Maroons. Against the Bears, Thorpe fumbled, and Halas picked up the ball and returned it 98 yards for a touchdown, a record that would last until 1972.

Canton had its second consecutive undefeated season, going 11-0-1 for the NFL title.

1924
The league had 18 franchises, including new ones in Kansas City, Kenosha, and Frankford, a section of Philadelphia. League champion Canton, successful on the field but not at the box office, was purchased by the owner of the Cleveland franchise, who kept the Canton franchise inactive, while using the best players for his Cleveland team, which he renamed the Bulldogs. Cleveland won the title with a 7-1-1 record.

1925
Five new franchises were admitted to the NFL—the New York Giants, who were awarded to Tim Mara and Billy Gibson for $500; the Detroit Panthers, featuring Jimmy Conzelman as owner, coach, and tailback; the Providence Steam Roller; a new Canton Bulldogs team; and the Pottsville Maroons, who had been perhaps the most successful independent pro team. The NFL established its first player limit, at 16 players.

Late in the season, the NFL made its greatest coup in gaining national recognition. Shortly after the University of Illinois season ended in November, All-America halfback Harold (Red) Grange signed a contract to play with the Chicago Bears. On Thanksgiving Day, a crowd of 36,000—the largest in pro football history—watched Grange and the Bears play the Chicago Cardinals to a scoreless tie at Wrigley Field. At the beginning of December, the Bears left on a barnstorming tour that saw them play eight games in 12 days, in St. Louis, Philadelphia, New York City, Washington, Boston, Pittsburgh, Detroit, and Chicago. A crowd of 73,000 watched the game against the Giants at the Polo Grounds, helping assure the future of the troubled NFL franchise in New York. The Bears then played nine more games in the South and West, including a game in Los Angeles, in which 75,000 fans watched them defeat the Los Angeles Tigers in the Los Angeles Memorial Coliseum.

Pottsville and the Chicago Cardinals were the top contenders for the league title, with Pottsville winning a late-season meeting 21-7. Pottsville scheduled a game against a team of former Notre Dame players for Shibe Park in Philadelphia. Frankford lodged a protest not only because the game was in Frankford's protected territory, but because it was being played the same day as a Yellow Jackets home game. Carr gave three different notices forbidding Pottsville to play the game, but Pottsville played anyway, December 12. That day, Carr fined the club, suspended it from all rights and privileges (including the right to play for the NFL championship), and returned its franchise to the league. The Cardinals, who ended the season with the best record in the league, were named the 1925 champions.

1926
Grange's manager, C.C. Pyle, told the Bears that Grange wouldn't play for them unless he was paid a five-figure salary and given one-third ownership of the team. The Bears refused. Pyle leased Yankee Stadium in New York City, then petitioned for an NFL franchise. After he was refused, he started the first American Football League. It lasted one season and included Grange's New York Yankees and eight other teams. The AFL champion Philadelphia Quakers played a December game against the New York Giants, seventh in the NFL, and the Giants won 31-0. At the end of the season, the AFL folded.

Halas pushed through a rule that prohibited any team from signing a player whose college class had not graduated.

The NFL grew to 22 teams, including the Duluth Eskimos, who signed All-America fullback Ernie Nevers of Stanford, giving the league a gate attraction to rival Grange. The 15-member Eskimos, dubbed the Iron Men of the North, played 29 exhibition and league games, 28 on the road, and Nevers played in all but 29 minutes of them.

Frankford edged the Bears for the championship, despite Halas having obtained John (Paddy) Driscoll from the Cardinals. On December 4, the Yellow Jackets scored in the final two minutes to defeat the Bears 7-6 and move ahead of them in the standings.

1927
At a special meeting in Cleveland, April 23, Carr decided to secure the NFL's future by eliminating the financially weaker teams and consolidating the quality players onto a limited number of more successful teams. The new-look NFL dropped to 12 teams, and the center of gravity of the league left the Midwest, where the NFL had started, and began to emerge in the large cities of the East. One of the new teams was Grange's New York Yankees, but Grange suffered a knee injury and the Yankees finished in the middle of the pack. The NFL championship was won by the cross-town rival New York Giants, who posted 10 shutouts in 13 games.

1928
Grange and Nevers both retired from pro football, and Duluth disbanded, as the NFL was reduced to only 10 teams. The Providence Steam Roller of Jimmy Conzelman and Pearce Johnson won the championship, playing in the Cycledrome, a 10,000-seat oval that had been built for bicycle races.

1929
Chris O'Brien sold the Chicago Cardinals to David Jones, July 27.

The NFL added a fourth official, the field judge, July 28.

Grange and Nevers returned to the NFL. Nevers scored six rushing touchdowns and four extra points as the Cardinals beat Grange's Bears 40-6, November 28. The 40 points set a record that remains the NFL's oldest.

Providence became the first NFL team to host a game at night under floodlights, against the Cardinals, November 3.

The Packers added back Johnny Blood (McNally), tackle Cal Hubbard, and guard Mike Michalske, and won their first NFL championship, edging the Giants, who featured quarterback Benny Friedman.

1930
Dayton, the last of the NFL's original franchises, was purchased by William B. Dwyer and John C. Depler, moved to Brooklyn, and renamed the Dodgers. The Portsmouth, Ohio, Spartans entered the league.

The Packers edged the Giants for the title, but the most improved team was the Bears. Halas retired as a player and replaced himself as coach of the Bears with Ralph Jones, who refined the T-formation by introducing wide ends and a halfback in motion. Jones also introduced rookie All-America fullback-tackle Bronko Nagurski.

The Giants defeated a team of former Notre Dame players coached by Knute Rockne 22-0 before 55,000 at the Polo Grounds, December 14. The proceeds went to the New York Unemployment Fund to help those suffering because of the Great Depression, and the easy victory helped give the NFL credibility with the press and the public.

1931
The NFL decreased to 10 teams, and halfway through the season the Frankford franchise folded. Carr fined the Bears, Packers, and Portsmouth $1,000 each for using players whose college classes had not graduated.

The Packers won an unprecedented third consecutive title, beating out the Spartans, who were led by rookie backs Earl (Dutch) Clark and Glenn Presnell.

1932
George Preston Marshall, Vincent Bendix, Jay O'Brien, and M. Dorland Doyle were awarded a franchise for Boston, July 9. Despite the presence of two rookies—halfback Cliff Battles and tackle Glen (Turk) Edwards—the new team, named the Braves, lost money and Marshall was left as the sole owner at the end of the year.

NFL membership dropped to eight teams, the lowest in history. Official statistics were kept for the first time. The Bears and the Spartans finished the season in the first-ever tie for first place. After the season finale, the league office arranged for the first playoff game in NFL history. The game was moved indoors to Chicago Stadium because of bitter cold and heavy snow. The arena allowed only an 80-yard field that came right to the walls. The goal posts were moved from the end lines to the goal lines and, for safety, inbounds lines or hashmarks where the ball would be put in play were drawn 10 yards from the walls that butted against the sidelines. The Bears won 9-0, December 18, scoring the winning touchdown on a two-yard pass from Nagurski to Grange. The Spartans claimed Nagurski's pass was thrown from less than five yards behind the line of scrimmage, violating the existing passing rule, but the play stood.

1933
The NFL, which long had followed the rules of college football, made a number of significant changes from the college game for the first time and began to develop rules serving its needs and the style of play it preferred. The innovations from the 1932 championship game—inbounds line or hashmarks and goal posts on the goal lines—were adopted. Also the forward pass was legalized from anywhere behind the line of scrimmage, February 25.

Marshall and Halas pushed through a proposal that divided the NFL into two divisions, with the winners to meet in an annual championship game, July 8.

Three new franchises joined the league—the Pittsburgh Pirates of Art Rooney, the Philadelphia Eagles of Bert Bell and Lud Wray, and the Cincinnati Reds. The Staten Island Stapletons suspended operations for a year, but never returned to the league.

Halas bought out Sternaman, became sole owner of the Bears, and reinstated himself as head coach. Marshall changed the name of the Boston

Braves to the Redskins. David Jones sold the Chicago Cardinals to Charles W. Bidwill.

In the first NFL Championship Game scheduled before the season, the Western Division champion Bears defeated the Eastern Division champion Giants 23-21 at Wrigley Field, December 17.

1934

G.A. (Dick) Richards purchased the Portsmouth Spartans, moved them to Detroit, and renamed them the Lions.

Professional football gained new prestige when the Bears were matched against the best college football players in the first Chicago College All-Star Game, August 31. The game ended in a scoreless tie before 79,432 at Soldier Field.

The Cincinnati Reds lost their first eight games, then were suspended from the league for defaulting on payments. The St. Louis Gunners, an independent team, joined the NFL by buying the Cincinnati franchise and went 1-2 the last three weeks.

Rookie Beattie Feathers of the Bears became the NFL's first 1,000-yard rusher, gaining 1,004 on 101 carries. The Thanksgiving Day game between the Bears and the Lions became the first NFL game broadcast nationally, with Graham McNamee the announcer for NBC radio.

In the championship game, on an extremely cold and icy day at the Polo Grounds, the Giants trailed the Bears 13-3 in the third quarter before changing to basketball shoes for better footing. The Giants won 30-13 in what has come to be known as the Sneakers Game, December 9.

The player waiver rule was adopted, December 10.

1935

The NFL adopted Bert Bell's proposal to hold an annual draft of college players, to begin in 1936, with teams selecting in an inverse order of finish, May 19. The inbounds line or hashmarks were moved nearer the center of the field, 15 yards from the sidelines.

All-America end Don Hutson of Alabama joined Green Bay. The Lions defeated the Giants 26-7 in the NFL Championship Game, December 15.

1936

There were no franchise transactions for the first year since the formation of the NFL. It also was the first year in which all member teams played the same number of games.

The Eagles made University of Chicago halfback and Heisman Trophy winner Jay Berwanger the first player ever selected in the NFL draft, February 8. The Eagles traded his rights to the Bears, but Berwanger never played pro football. The first player selected to actually sign was the number-two pick, Riley Smith of Alabama, who was selected by Boston.

A rival league was formed, and it became the second to call itself the American Football League. The Boston Shamrocks were its champions.

Because of poor attendance, Marshall, the owner of the host team, moved the Championship Game from Boston to the Polo Grounds in New York. Green Bay defeated the Redskins 21-6, December 13.

1937

Homer Marshman was granted a Cleveland franchise, named the Rams, February 12. Marshall moved the Redskins to Washington, D.C., February 13. The Redskins signed TCU All-America tailback Sammy Baugh, who led them to a 28-21 victory over the Bears in the NFL Championship Game, December 12.

The Los Angeles Bulldogs had an 8-0 record to win the AFL title, but then the 2-year-old league folded.

1938

At the suggestion of Halas, Hugh (Shorty) Ray became a technical advisor on rules and officiating to the NFL. A new rule called for a 15-yard penalty for roughing the passer.

Rookie Byron (Whizzer) White of the Pittsburgh Pirates led the NFL in rushing. The Giants defeated the Packers 23-17 for the NFL title, December 11.

Marshall, *Los Angeles Times* sports editor Bill Henry, and promoter Tom Gallery established the Pro Bowl game between the NFL champion and a team of pro all-stars.

1939

The New York Giants defeated the Pro All-Stars 13-10 in the first Pro Bowl, at Wrigley Field, Los Angeles, January 15.

Carr, NFL president since 1921, died in Columbus, May 20. Carl Storck was named acting president, May 25.

An NFL game was televised for the first time when NBC broadcast the Brooklyn Dodgers-Philadelphia Eagles game from Ebbets Field to the approximately 1,000 sets then in New York.

Green Bay defeated New York 27-0 in the NFL Championship Game, December 10 at Milwaukee. NFL attendance exceeded 1 million in a season for the first time, reaching 1,071,200.

1940

A six-team rival league, the third to call itself the American Football League, was formed, and the Columbus Bullies won its championship.

Halas's Bears, with additional coaching by Clark Shaughnessy of Stanford, defeated the Redskins 73-0 in the NFL Championship Game, December 8. The game, which was the most decisive victory in NFL history, popularized the Bears' T-formation with a man-in-motion. It was the first championship carried on network radio, broadcast by Red Barber to 120 stations of the Mutual Broadcasting System, which paid $2,500 for the rights.

Art Rooney sold the Pittsburgh franchise to Alexis Thompson, December 9, then bought part interest in the Philadelphia Eagles.

1941

Elmer Layden was named the first Commissioner of the NFL, March 1; Storck, the acting president, resigned, April 5. NFL headquarters were moved to Chicago.

Bell and Rooney traded the Eagles to Thompson for the Pirates, then re-named their new team the Steelers. Homer Marshman sold the Rams to Daniel F. Reeves and Fred Levy, Jr.

The league by-laws were revised to provide for playoffs in case there were ties in division races, and sudden-death overtimes in case a playoff game was tied after four quarters. An official *NFL Record Manual* was published for the first time.

Columbus again won the championship of the AFL, but the two-year-old league then folded.

The Bears and the Packers finished in a tie for the Western Division championship, setting up the first divisional playoff game in league history. The Bears won 33-14, then defeated the Giants 37-9 for the NFL championship, December 21.

1942

Players departing for service in World War II depleted the rosters of NFL teams. Halas left the Bears in midseason to join the Navy, and Luke Johnsos and Heartley (Hunk) Anderson served as co-coaches as the Bears went 11-0 in the regular season. The Redskins defeated the Bears 14-6 in the NFL Championship Game, December 13.

1943

The Cleveland Rams, with co-owners Reeves and Levy in the service, were granted permission to suspend operations for one season, April 6. Levy transferred his stock in the team to Reeves, April 16.

The NFL adopted free substitution, April 7. The league also made the wearing of helmets mandatory and approved a 10-game schedule for all teams.

Philadelphia and Pittsburgh were granted permission to merge for one season, June 19. The team, known as Phil-Pitt (and called the Steagles by fans), divided home games between the two cities, and Earle (Greasy) Neale of Philadelphia and Walt Kiesling of Pittsburgh served as co-coaches. The merger automatically dissolved the last day of the season, December 5.

Ted Collins was granted a franchise for Boston, to become active in 1944.

Sammy Baugh led the league in passing, punting, and interceptions. He led the Redskins to a tie with the Giants for the Eastern Division title, and then to a 28-0 victory in a divisional playoff game. The Bears beat the Redskins 41-21 in the NFL Championship Game, December 26.

1944

Collins, who had wanted a franchise in Yankee Stadium in New York, named his new team in Boston the Yanks. Cleveland resumed operations. The Brooklyn Dodgers changed their name to the Tigers.

Coaching from the bench was legalized, April 20.

The Cardinals and the Steelers were granted permission to merge for one year under the name Card-Pitt, April 21. Phil Handler of the Cardinals and Walt Kiesling of the Steelers served as co-coaches. The merger automatically dissolved the last day of the season, December 3.

In the NFL Championship Game, Green Bay defeated the New York Giants 14-7, December 17.

1945

The inbounds lines or hashmarks were moved from 15 yards away from the sidelines to nearer the center of the field—20 yards from the sidelines.

Brooklyn and Boston merged into a team that played home games in both cities and was known simply as The Yanks. The team was coached by former Boston head coach Herb Kopf. In December, the Brooklyn franchise withdrew from the NFL to join the new All-America Football Conference; all the players on its active and reserve lists were assigned to The Yanks, who once again became the Boston Yanks.

Halas rejoined the Bears late in the season after service with the U.S. Navy. Although Halas took over much of the coaching duties, Anderson and Johnsos remained the coaches of record throughout the season.

Steve Van Buren of Philadelphia led the NFL in rushing, kickoff returns, and scoring.

After the Japanese surrendered ending World War II, a count showed that the NFL service roster, limited to men who had played in league games, totaled 638, 21 of whom had died in action.

Rookie quarterback Bob Waterfield led Cleveland to a 15-14 victory over Washington in the NFL Championship Game, December 16.

1946

The contract of Commissioner Layden was not renewed, and Bert Bell, the co-owner of the Steelers, replaced him, January 11. Bell moved the league headquarters from Chicago to the Philadelphia suburb of Bala-Cynwyd.

Free substitution was withdrawn and substitutions were limited to no more than three men at a time. Forward passes were made automatically incomplete upon striking the goal posts, January 11.

The NFL took on a truly national appearance for the first time when Reeves was granted permission by the league to move his NFL champion Rams to Los Angeles.

The rival All-America Football Conference began play with eight teams. The Cleveland Browns, coached by Paul Brown, won the AAFC's first championship, defeating the New York Yankees 14-9.

Bill Dudley of the Steelers led the NFL in rushing, interceptions, and punt returns, and won the league's most valuable player award.

Backs Frank Filchock and Merle Hapes of the Giants were questioned about an attempt by a New York man to fix the championship game with the Bears. Bell suspended Hapes but allowed Filchock to play; he played well, but Chicago won 24-14, December 15.

1947
The NFL added a fifth official, the back judge.

A bonus choice was made for the first time in the NFL draft. One team each year would select the special choice before the first round began. The Chicago Bears won a lottery and the rights to the first choice and drafted back Bob Fenimore of Oklahoma A&M.

The Cleveland Browns again won the AAFC title, defeating the New York Yankees 14-3.

Charles Bidwill, Sr., owner of the Cardinals, died April 19, but his wife and sons retained ownership of the team. On December 28, the Cardinals won the NFL Championship Game 28-21 over the Philadelphia Eagles, who had beaten Pittsburgh 21-0 in a playoff.

1948
Plastic helmets were prohibited. A flexible artificial tee was permitted at the kickoff. Officials other than the referee were equipped with whistles, not horns, January 14.

Fred Mandel sold the Detroit Lions to a syndicate headed by D. Lyle Fife, January 15.

Halfback Fred Gehrke of the Los Angeles Rams painted horns on the Rams' helmets, the first modern helmet emblems in pro football.

The Cleveland Browns won their third straight championship in the AAFC, going 14-0 and then defeating the Buffalo Bills 49-7.

In a blizzard, the Eagles defeated the Cardinals 7-0 in the NFL Championship Game, December 19.

1949
Alexis Thompson sold the champion Eagles to a syndicate headed by James P. Clark, January 15. The Boston Yanks became the New York Bulldogs, sharing the Polo Grounds with the Giants.

Free substitution was adopted for one year, January 20.

The NFL had two 1,000-yard rushers in the same season for the first time—Steve Van Buren of Philadelphia and Tony Canadeo of Green Bay.

The AAFC played its season with a one-division, seven-team format. On December 9, Bell announced a merger agreement in which three AAFC franchises—Cleveland, San Francisco, and Baltimore—would join the NFL in 1950. The Browns won their fourth consecutive AAFC title, defeating the 49ers 21-7, December 11.

In a heavy rain, the Eagles defeated the Rams 14-0 in the NFL Championship Game, December 18.

1950
Unlimited free substitution was restored, opening the way for the era of two platoons and specialization in pro football, January 20.

Curly Lambeau, founder of the franchise and Green Bay's head coach since 1921, resigned under fire, February 1.

The name National Football League was restored after about three months as the National-American Football League. The American and National conferences were created to replace the Eastern and Western divisions, March 3.

The New York Bulldogs became the Yanks and divided the players of the former AAFC Yankees with the Giants. A special allocation draft was held in which the 13 teams drafted the remaining AAFC players, with special consideration for Baltimore, which received 15 choices compared to 10 for other teams.

The Los Angeles Rams became the first NFL team to have all of its games—both home and away—televised. The Washington Redskins followed the Rams in arranging to televise their games; other teams made deals to put selected games on television.

In the first game of the season, former AAFC champion Cleveland defeated NFL champion Philadelphia 35-10. For the first time, deadlocks occurred in both conferences and playoffs were necessary. The Browns defeated the Giants in the American and the Rams defeated the Bears in the National. Cleveland defeated Los Angeles 30-28 in the NFL Championship Game, December 24.

1951
The Pro Bowl game, dormant since 1942, was revived under a new format matching the all-stars of each conference at the Los Angeles Memorial Coliseum. The American Conference defeated the National Conference 28-27, January 14.

Abraham Watner returned the Baltimore franchise and its player contracts back to the NFL for $50,000. Baltimore's former players were made available for drafting at the same time as college players, January 18.

A rule was passed that no tackle, guard, or center would be eligible to catch a forward pass, January 18.

The Rams reversed their television policy and televised only road games.

The NFL Championship Game was televised coast-to-coast for the first time, December 23. The DuMont Network paid $75,000 for the rights to the game, in which the Rams defeated the Browns 24-17.

1952
Ted Collins sold the New York Yanks' franchise back to the NFL, January 19. A new franchise was awarded to a group in Dallas after it purchased the assets of the Yanks, January 24. The new Texans went 1-11, with the owners turning the franchise back to the league in midseason. For the last five games of the season, the commissioner's office operated the Texans as a road team, using Hershey, Pennsylvania, as a home base. At the end of the season the franchise was canceled, the last time an NFL team failed.

The Pittsburgh Steelers abandoned the Single-Wing for the T-formation, the last pro team to do so.

The Detroit Lions won their first NFL championship in 17 years, defeating the Browns 17-7 in the title game, December 28.

1953
A Baltimore group headed by Carroll Rosenbloom was granted a franchise and was awarded the holdings of the defunct Dallas organization, January 23. The team, named the Colts, put together the largest trade in league history, acquiring 10 players from Cleveland in exchange for five.

The names of the American and National conferences were changed to the Eastern and Western conferences, January 24.

Jim Thorpe died, March 28.

Mickey McBride, founder of the Cleveland Browns, sold the franchise to a syndicate headed by Dave R. Jones, June 10.

The NFL policy of blacking out home games was upheld by Judge Allan K. Grim of the U.S. District Court in Philadelphia, November 12.

The Lions again defeated the Browns in the NFL Championship Game, winning 17-16, December 27.

1954
The Canadian Football League began a series of raids on NFL teams, signing quarterback Eddie LeBaron and defensive end Gene Brito of Washington and defensive tackle Arnie Weinmeister of the Giants, among others.

Fullback Joe Perry of the 49ers became the first player in league history to gain 1,000 yards rushing in consecutive seasons.

Cleveland defeated Detroit 56-10 in the NFL Championship Game, December 26.

1955
The sudden-death overtime rule was used for the first time in a preseason game between the Rams and Giants at Portland, Oregon, August 28. The Rams won 23-17 three minutes into overtime.

A rule change declared the ball dead immediately if the ball carrier touched the ground with any part of his body except his hands or feet while in the grasp of an opponent.

The Baltimore Colts made an 80-cent phone call to Johnny Unitas and signed him as a free agent. Another quarterback, Otto Graham, played his last game as the Browns defeated the Rams 38-14 in the NFL Championship Game, December 26. Graham had quarterbacked the Browns to 10 championship-game appearances in 10 years.

NBC replaced DuMont as the network for the title game, paying a rights fee of $100,000.

1956
The NFL Players Association was founded.

Grabbing an opponent's facemask (other than the ball carrier) was made illegal. Using radio receivers to communicate with players on the field was prohibited. A natural leather ball with white end stripes replaced the white ball with black stripes for night games.

The Giants moved from the Polo Grounds to Yankee Stadium.

Halas retired as coach of the Bears, and was replaced by Paddy Driscoll.

CBS became the first network to broadcast some NFL regular-season games to selected television markets across the nation.

The Giants routed the Bears 47-7 in the NFL Championship Game, December 30.

1957
Pete Rozelle was named general manager of the Rams. Anthony J. Morabito, founder and co-owner of the 49ers, died of a heart attack during a game against the Bears at Kezar Stadium, October 28. An NFL-record crowd of 102,368 saw the 49ers-Rams game at the Los Angeles Memorial Coliseum, November 10.

The Lions came from 20 points down to post a 31-27 playoff victory over the 49ers, December 22. Detroit defeated Cleveland 59-14 in the NFL Championship Game, December 29.

1958
The bonus selection in the draft was eliminated, January 29. The last selection was quarterback King Hill of Rice by the Chicago Cardinals.

Halas reinstated himself as coach of the Bears.

Jim Brown of Cleveland gained an NFL-record 1,527 yards rushing. In a divisional playoff game, the Giants held Brown to eight yards and defeated Cleveland 10-0.

Baltimore, coached by Weeb Ewbank, defeated the Giants 23-17 in the first sudden-death overtime in an NFL Championship Game, December 28. The game ended when Colts fullback Alan Ameche scored on a one-yard touchdown run after 8:15 of overtime.

1959
Vince Lombardi was named head coach of the Green Bay Packers, January 28. Tim Mara, the co-founder of the Giants, died, February 17.

Lamar Hunt of Dallas announced his intentions to form a second pro football league. The first meeting was held in Chicago, August 14, and consisted of Hunt representing Dallas; Bob Howsam, Denver; K.S. (Bud) Adams, Houston; Barron Hilton, Los Angeles; Max Winter and Bill Boyer, Minneapolis; and Harry Wismer, New York City. They made plans to begin play in 1960.

The new league was named the American Football League, August 22. Buffalo, owned by Ralph Wilson, became the seventh franchise, October 28. Boston, owned by William H. Sullivan, became the eighth team, November 22. The first AFL draft, lasting 33 rounds, was held, November 22. Joe Foss was named AFL Commissioner, November 30. An additional draft of 20 rounds was held by the AFL, December 2.

NFL Commissioner Bert Bell died of a heart attack suffered at Franklin Field, Philadelphia, during the last two minutes of a game between the Eagles and the Steelers, October 11. Treasurer Austin Gunsel was named president in the office of the commissioner, October 14.

The Colts again defeated the Giants in the NFL Championship Game, 31-16, December 27.

1960
Pete Rozelle was elected NFL Commissioner as a compromise choice on

the twenty-third ballot, January 26. Rozelle moved the league offices to New York City.

Hunt was elected AFL president for 1960, January 26. Minneapolis withdrew from the AFL, January 27, and the same ownership was given an NFL franchise for Minnesota (to start in 1961), January 28. Dallas received an NFL franchise for 1960, January 28. Oakland received an AFL franchise, January 30.

The AFL adopted the two-point option on points after touchdown, January 28. A no-tampering verbal pact, relative to players' contracts, was agreed to between the NFL and AFL, February 9.

The NFL owners voted to allow the transfer of the Chicago Cardinals to St. Louis, March 13.

The AFL signed a five-year television contract with ABC, June 9.

The Boston Patriots defeated the Buffalo Bills 28-7 before 16,000 at Buffalo in the first AFL preseason game, July 30. The Denver Broncos defeated the Patriots 13-10 before 21,597 at Boston in the first AFL regular-season game, September 9.

Philadelphia defeated Green Bay 17-13 in the NFL Championship Game, December 26.

1961
The Houston Oilers defeated the Los Angeles Chargers 24-16 before 32,183 in the first AFL Championship Game, January 1.

Detroit defeated Cleveland 17-16 in the first Playoff Bowl, or Bert Bell Benefit Bowl, between second-place teams in each conference in Miami, January 7.

End Willard Dewveall of the Bears played out his option and joined the Oilers, becoming the first player to move deliberately from one league to the other, January 14.

Ed McGah, Wayne Valley, and Robert Osborne bought out their partners in the ownership of the Raiders, January 17. The Chargers were transferred to San Diego, February 10. Dave R. Jones sold the Browns to a group headed by Arthur B. Modell, March 22. The Howsam brothers sold the Broncos to a group headed by Calvin Kunz and Gerry Phipps, May 26.

NBC was awarded a two-year contract for radio and television rights to the NFL Championship Game for $615,000 annually, $300,000 of which was to go directly into the NFL Player Benefit Plan, April 5.

Canton, Ohio, where the league that became the NFL was formed in 1920, was chosen as the site of the Pro Football Hall of Fame, April 27. Dick McCann, a former Redskins executive, was named executive director.

A bill legalizing single-network television contracts by professional sports leagues was introduced in Congress by Representative Emanuel Celler. It passed the House and Senate and was signed into law by President John F. Kennedy, September 30.

Houston defeated San Diego 10-3 for the AFL championship, December 24. Green Bay won its first NFL championship since 1944, defeating the New York Giants 37-0, December 31.

1962
The Western Division defeated the Eastern Division 47-27 in the first AFL All-Star Game, played before 20,973 in San Diego, January 7.

Both leagues prohibited grabbing any player's facemask. The AFL voted to make the scoreboard clock the official timer of the game.

The NFL entered into a single-network agreement with CBS for telecasting all regular-season games for $4.65 million annually, January 10.

Judge Roszel Thompson of the U.S. District Court in Baltimore ruled against the AFL in its antitrust suit against the NFL, May 21. The AFL had charged the NFL with monopoly and conspiracy in areas of expansion, television, and player signings. The case lasted two and a half years, the trial two months.

McGah and Valley acquired controlling interest in the Raiders, May 24. The AFL assumed financial responsibility for the New York Titans, November 8. With Commissioner Rozelle as referee, Daniel F. Reeves regained the ownership of the Rams, outbidding his partners in sealed-envelope bidding for the team, November 27.

The Dallas Texans defeated the Oilers 20-17 for the AFL championship at Houston after 17 minutes, 54 seconds of overtime on a 25-yard field goal by Tommy Brooker, December 23. The game lasted a record 77 minutes, 54 seconds.

Judge Edward Weinfeld of the U.S. District Court in New York City upheld the legality of the NFL's television blackout within a 75-mile radius of home games and denied an injunction that would have forced the championship game between the Giants and the Packers to be televised in the New York City area, December 28. The Packers beat the Giants 16-7 for the NFL title, December 30.

1963
The Dallas Texans transferred to Kansas City, becoming the Chiefs, February 8. The New York Titans were sold to a five-man syndicate headed by David (Sonny) Werblin, March 28. Weeb Ewbank became the Titans' new head coach and the team's name was changed to the Jets, April 15. They began play in Shea Stadium.

NFL Properties, Inc., was founded to serve as the licensing arm of the NFL.

Rozelle indefinitely suspended Green Bay halfback Paul Hornung and Detroit defensive tackle Alex Karras for placing bets on their own teams and on other NFL games; he also fined five other Detroit players $2,000 each for betting on one game in which they did not participate, and the Detroit Lions Football Company $2,000 on each of two counts for failure to report information promptly and for lack of sideline supervision.

Paul Brown, head coach of the Browns since their inception, was fired and replaced by Blanton Collier. Don Shula replaced Weeb Ewbank as head coach of the Colts.

The AFL allowed the Jets and Raiders to select players from other franchises in hopes of giving the league more competitive balance, May 11.

NBC was awarded exclusive network broadcasting rights for the 1963 AFL Championship Game for $926,000, May 23.

The Pro Football Hall of Fame was dedicated at Canton, Ohio, September 7.

The U.S. Fourth Circuit Court of Appeals reaffirmed the lower court's finding for the NFL in the $10-million suit brought by the AFL, ending three and a half years of litigation, November 21.

Jim Brown of Cleveland rushed for an NFL single-season record 1,863 yards.

Boston defeated Buffalo 26-8 in the first divisional playoff game in AFL history, December 28.

The Bears defeated the Giants 14-10 in the NFL Championship Game, a record sixth and last title for Halas in his thirty-sixth season as the Bears' coach, December 29.

1964
The Chargers defeated the Patriots 51-10 in the AFL Championship Game, January 5.

William Clay Ford, the Lions' president since 1961, purchased the team, January 10. A group representing the late James P. Clark sold the Eagles to a group headed by Jerry Wolman, January 21. Carroll Rosenbloom, the majority owner of the Colts since 1953, acquired complete ownership of the team, January 23.

The AFL signed a five-year, $36-million television contract with NBC to begin with the 1965 season, January 29.

Commissioner Rozelle negotiated an agreement on behalf of the NFL clubs to purchase Ed Sabol's Blair Motion Pictures, which was renamed NFL Films, March 5.

Hornung and Karras were reinstated by Rozelle, March 16.

CBS submitted the winning bid of $14.1 million per year for the NFL regular-season television rights for 1964 and 1965, January 24. CBS acquired the rights to the championship games for 1964 and 1965 for $1.8 million per game, April 17.

Pete Gogolak of Cornell signed a contract with Buffalo, becoming the first soccer-style kicker in pro football.

Buffalo defeated San Diego 20-7 in the AFL Championship Game, December 26. Cleveland defeated Baltimore 27-0 in the NFL Championship Game, December 27.

1965
The NFL teams pledged not to sign college seniors until completion of all their games, including bowl games, and empowered the Commissioner to discipline the clubs up to as much as the loss of an entire draft list for a violation of the pledge, February 15.

The NFL added a sixth official, the line judge, February 19. The color of the officials' penalty flags was changed from white to bright gold, April 5.

Atlanta was awarded an NFL franchise for 1966, with Rankin Smith, Sr., as owner, June 30. Miami was awarded an AFL franchise for 1966, with Joe Robbie and Danny Thomas as owners, August 16.

Green Bay defeated Baltimore 13-10 in sudden-death overtime in a Western Conference playoff game. Don Chandler kicked a 25-yard field goal for the Packers after 13 minutes, 39 seconds of overtime, December 26. The Packers then defeated the Browns 23-12 in the NFL Championship Game, January 2.

In the AFL Championship Game, the Bills again defeated the Chargers, 23-0, December 26.

CBS acquired the rights to the NFL regular-season games in 1966 and 1967, with an option for 1968, for $18.8 million per year, December 29.

1966
The AFL-NFL war reached its peak, as the leagues spent a combined $7 million to sign their 1966 draft choices. The NFL signed 75 percent of its 232 draftees, the AFL 46 percent of its 181. Of the 111 common draft choices, 79 signed with the NFL, 28 with the AFL, and 4 went unsigned.

The rights to the 1966 and 1967 NFL Championship Games were sold to CBS for $2 million per game, February 14.

Foss resigned as AFL Commissioner, April 7. Al Davis, the head coach and general manager of the Raiders, was named to replace him, April 8.

Goal posts offset from the goal line, painted bright yellow, and with uprights 20 feet above the cross-bar were made standard in the NFL, May 16.

A series of secret meetings regarding a possible AFL-NFL merger were held in the spring between Hunt of Kansas City and Tex Schramm of Dallas. Rozelle announced the merger, June 8. Under the agreement, the two leagues would combine to form an expanded league with 24 teams, to be increased to 26 in 1968 and to 28 by 1970 or soon thereafter. All existing franchises would be retained, and no franchises would be transferred outside their metropolitan areas. While maintaining separate schedules through 1969, the leagues agreed to play an annual AFL-NFL World Championship Game beginning in January, 1967, and to hold a combined draft, also beginning in 1967. Preseason games would be held between teams of each league starting in 1967. Official regular-season play would start in 1970 when the two leagues would officially merge to form one league with two conferences. Rozelle was named Commissioner of the expanded league setup.

Davis rejoined the Raiders, and Milt Woodard was named president of the AFL, July 25.

The St. Louis Cardinals moved into newly constructed Busch Memorial Stadium.

Barron Hilton sold the Chargers to a group headed by Eugene Klein and Sam Schulman, August 25.

Congress approved the AFL-NFL merger, passing legislation exempting the agreement itself from antitrust action, October 21.

New Orleans was awarded an NFL franchise to begin play in 1967, November 1. John Mecom, Jr., of Houston was designated majority stockholder and president of the franchise, December 15.

The NFL was realigned for the 1967-69 seasons into the Capitol and Century Divisions in the Eastern Conference and the Central and Coastal Divisions in the Western Conference, December 2. New Orleans and the New York Giants agreed to switch divisions in 1968 and return to the 1967 alignment in 1969.

The rights to the Super Bowl for four years were sold to CBS and NBC for $9.5 million, December 13.

1967

Green Bay earned the right to represent the NFL in the first AFL-NFL World Championship Game by defeating Dallas 34-27, January 1. The same day, Kansas City defeated Buffalo 31-7 to represent the AFL. The Packers defeated the Chiefs 35-10 before 61,946 fans at the Los Angeles Memorial Coliseum in the first game between AFL and NFL teams, January 15. The winning players' share for the Packers was $15,000 each, and the losing players' share for the Chiefs was $7,500 each. The game was televised by both CBS and NBC.

The "sling-shot" goal post and a six-foot-wide border around the field were made standard in the NFL, February 22.

Baltimore made Bubba Smith, a Michigan State defensive lineman, the first choice in the first combined AFL-NFL draft, March 14.

The AFL awarded a franchise to begin play in 1968 to Cincinnati, May 24. A group with Paul Brown as part owner, general manager, and head coach, was awarded the Cincinnati franchise, September 27.

Arthur B. Modell, the president of the Cleveland Browns, was elected president of the NFL, May 28.

An AFL team defeated an NFL team for the first time, when Denver beat Detroit 13-7 in a preseason game, August 5.

Green Bay defeated Dallas 21-17 for the NFL championship on a last-minute 1-yard quarterback sneak by Bart Starr in 13-below-zero temperature at Green Bay, December 31. The same day, Oakland defeated Houston 40-7 for the AFL championship.

1968

Green Bay defeated Oakland 33-14 in Super Bowl II at Miami, January 14. The game had the first $3-million gate in pro football history.

Vince Lombardi resigned as head coach of the Packers, but remained as general manager, January 28.

Werblin sold his shares in the Jets to his partners Don Lillis, Leon Hess, Townsend Martin, and Phil Iselin, May 21. Lillis assumed the presidency of the club, but then died July 23. Iselin was appointed president, August 6.

Halas retired for the fourth and last time as head coach of the Bears, May 27.

The Oilers left Rice Stadium for the Astrodome and became the first NFL team to play its home games in a domed stadium.

The movie *Heidi* became a footnote in sports history when NBC didn't show the last 1:05 of the Jets-Raiders game in order to permit the children's special to begin on time. The Raiders scored two touchdowns in the last 42 seconds to win 43-32, November 17.

Ewbank became the first coach to win titles in both the NFL and AFL when his Jets defeated the Raiders 27-23 for the AFL championship, December 29. The same day, Baltimore defeated Cleveland 34-0.

1969

The AFL established a playoff format for the 1969 season, with the winner in one division playing the runner-up in the other, January 11.

An AFL team won the Super Bowl for the first time, as the Jets defeated the Colts 16-7 at Miami, January 12 in Super Bowl III. The title Super Bowl was recognized by the NFL for the first time.

Vince Lombardi became part owner, executive vice-president, and head coach of the Washington Redskins, February 7.

Wolman sold the Eagles to Leonard Tose, May 1.

Baltimore, Cleveland, and Pittsburgh agreed to join the AFL teams to form the 13-team American Football Conference of the NFL in 1970, May 17. The NFL also agreed on a playoff format that would include one "wild-card" team per conference—the second-place team with the best record.

Monday Night Football was signed for 1970. ABC acquired the rights to televise 13 NFL regular-season Monday night games in 1970, 1971, and 1972.

George Preston Marshall, president emeritus of the Redskins, died at 72, August 9.

The NFL marked its fiftieth year by the wearing of a special patch by each of the 16 teams.

1970

Kansas City defeated Minnesota 23-7 in Super Bowl IV at New Orleans, January 11. The gross receipts of approximately $3.8 million were the largest ever for a one-day sports event.

Four-year television contracts, under which CBS would televise all NFC games and NBC all AFC games (except Monday night games) and the two would divide televising the Super Bowl and AFC-NFC Pro Bowl games, were announced, January 26.

Art Modell resigned as president of the NFL, March 12. Milt Woodard resigned as president of the AFL, March 13. Lamar Hunt was elected president of the AFC and George Halas was elected president of the NFC, March 19.

The merged 26-team league adopted rules changes putting names on the backs of players' jerseys, making a point after touchdown worth only one point, and making the scoreboard clock the official timing device of the game, March 18.

The Players Negotiating Committee and the NFL Players Association announced a four-year agreement guaranteeing approximately $4,535,000 annually to player pension and insurance benefits, August 3. The owners also agreed to contribute $250,000 annually to improve or implement items such as disability payments, widows' benefits, maternity benefits, and dental benefits. The agreement also provided for increased preseason game and per diem payments, averaging approximately $2.6 million annually.

The Pittsburgh Steelers moved into Three Rivers Stadium. The Cincinnati Bengals moved to Riverfront Stadium.

Lombardi died of cancer at 57, September 3.

Tom Dempsey of New Orleans kicked a game-winning NFL-record 63-yard field goal against Detroit, November 8.

1971

Baltimore defeated Dallas 16-13 on Jim O'Brien's 32-yard field goal with five seconds to go in Super Bowl V at Miami, January 17. The NBC telecast was viewed in an estimated 23,980,000 homes, the largest audience ever for a one-day sports event.

The NFC defeated the AFC 27-6 in the first AFC-NFC Pro Bowl at Los Angeles, January 24.

The Boston Patriots changed their name to the New England Patriots, March 25. Their new stadium, Schaefer Stadium, was dedicated in a 20-14 preseason victory over the Giants.

The Philadelphia Eagles left Franklin Field and played their games at the new Veterans Stadium.

The San Francisco 49ers left Kezar Stadium and moved their games to Candlestick Park.

Daniel F. Reeves, the president and general manager of the Rams, died at 58, April 15.

The Dallas Cowboys moved from the Cotton Bowl into their new home, Texas Stadium, October 24.

Miami defeated Kansas City 27-24 in sudden-death overtime in an AFC Divisional Playoff Game, December 25. Garo Yepremian kicked a 37-yard field goal for the Dolphins after 22 minutes, 40 seconds of overtime, as the game lasted 82 minutes, 40 seconds overall, making it the longest game in history.

1972

Dallas defeated Miami 24-3 in Super Bowl VI at New Orleans, January 16. The CBS telecast was viewed in an estimated 27,450,000 homes, the top-rated one-day telecast ever.

The inbounds lines or hashmarks were moved nearer the center of the field, 23 yards, 1 foot, 9 inches from the sidelines, March 23. The method of determining won-lost percentage in standings changed. Tie games, previously not counted in the standings, were made equal to a half-game won and a half-game lost, May 24.

Robert Irsay purchased the Los Angeles Rams and transferred ownership of the club to Carroll Rosenbloom in exchange for the Baltimore Colts, July 13.

William V. Bidwill purchased the stock of his brother Charles (Stormy) Bidwill to become the sole owner of the St. Louis Cardinals, September 2.

The National District Attorneys Association endorsed the position of professional leagues in opposing proposed legalization of gambling on professional team sports, September 28.

Franco Harris's "Immaculate Reception" gave the Steelers their first postseason win ever, 13-7 over the Raiders, December 23.

1973

Rozelle announced that all Super Bowl VII tickets were sold and that the game would be telecast in Los Angeles, the site of the game, on an experimental basis, January 3.

Miami defeated Washington 14-7 in Super Bowl VII at Los Angeles, completing a 17-0 season, the first perfect-record regular-season and postseason mark in NFL history, January 14. The NBC telecast was viewed by approximately 75 million people.

The AFC defeated the NFC 33-28 in the Pro Bowl in Dallas, the first time since 1942 that the game was played outside Los Angeles, January 21.

A jersey numbering system was adopted, April 5: 1-19 for quarterbacks and specialists, 20-49 for running backs and defensive backs, 50-59 for centers and linebackers, 60-79 for defensive linemen and interior offensive linemen other than centers, and 80-89 for wide receivers and tight ends. Players who had been in the NFL in 1972 could continue to use old numbers.

NFL Charities, a nonprofit organization, was created to derive an income from monies generated from NFL Properties' licensing of NFL trademarks and team names, June 26. NFL Charities was set up to support education and charitable activities and to supply economic support to persons formerly associated with professional football who were no longer able to support themselves.

Congress adopted experimental legislation (for three years) requiring any NFL game that had been declared a sellout 72 hours prior to kickoff to be made available for local televising, September 14. The legislation provided for an annual review to be made by the Federal Communications Commission.

The Buffalo Bills moved their home games from War Memorial Stadium to Rich Stadium in nearby Orchard Park. The Giants tied the Eagles 23-23 in the final game in Yankee Stadium, September 23. The Giants played the rest of their home games at the Yale Bowl in New Haven, Connecticut.

A rival league, the World Football League, was formed and was reported in operation, October 2. It had plans to start play in 1974.

O.J. Simpson of Buffalo became the first player to rush for more than 2,000 yards in a season, gaining 2,003.

1974

Miami defeated Minnesota 24-7 in Super Bowl VIII at Houston, the second consecutive Super Bowl championship for the Dolphins, January 13. The CBS telecast was viewed by approximately 75 million people.

Rozelle was given a 10-year contract effective January 1, 1973, February 27.

Tampa Bay was awarded a franchise to begin operation in 1976, April 24.

Sweeping rules changes were adopted to add action and tempo to games: one sudden-death overtime period was added for preseason and regular-season games; the goal posts were moved from the goal line to the end lines; kickoffs were moved from the 40- to the 35-yard line; after missed field goals from beyond the 20, the ball was to be returned to the line of scrimmage; restrictions were placed on members of the punting team to open up return possibilities; roll-blocking and cutting of wide receivers was eliminated; the extent of downfield contact a defender could have with an eligible receiver was restricted; the penalties for offensive holding, illegal use of the hands, and tripping were reduced from 15 to 10 yards; wide receivers blocking back toward the ball within three yards of the line of scrimmage were prevented from blocking below the waist, April 25.

The Toronto Northmen of the WFL signed Larry Csonka, Jim Kiick, and Paul Warfield of Miami, March 31.

Seattle was awarded an NFL franchise to begin play in 1976, June 4.

Lloyd W. Nordstrom, president of the Seattle Seahawks, and Hugh Culverhouse, president of the Tampa Bay Buccaneers, signed franchise agreements, December 5.

The Birmingham Americans defeated the Florida Blazers 22-21 in the WFL World Bowl, winning the league championship, December 5.

1975

Pittsburgh defeated Minnesota 16-6 in Super Bowl IX at New Orleans, the Steelers' first championship since entering the NFL in 1933. The NBC telecast was viewed by approximately 78 million people.

The divisional winners with the highest won-loss percentage were made the home team for the divisional playoffs, and the surviving winners with the highest percentage made home teams for the championship games, June 26.

Referees were equipped with wireless microphones for all preseason, regular-season, and playoff games.

The Lions moved to the new Pontiac Silverdome. The Giants played their home games in Shea Stadium. The Saints moved into the Louisiana Superdome.

The World Football League folded, October 22.

1976

Pittsburgh defeated Dallas 21-17 in Super Bowl X in Miami. The Steelers joined Green Bay and Miami as the only teams to win two Super Bowls; the Cowboys became the first wild-card team to play in the Super Bowl. The CBS telecast was viewed by an estimated 80 million people, the largest television audience in history.

Lloyd Nordstrom, the president of the Seahawks, died at 66, January 20. His brother Elmer succeeded him as majority representative of the team.

The owners awarded Super Bowl XII, to be played on January 15, 1978, to New Orleans. They also adopted the use of two 30-second clocks for all games, visible to both players and fans to note the official time between the ready-for-play signal and snap of the ball, March 16.

A veteran player allocation was held to stock the Seattle and Tampa Bay franchises with 39 players each, March 30-31. In the college draft, Seattle and Tampa Bay each received eight extra choices, April 8-9.

The Giants moved into new Giants Stadium in East Rutherford, New Jersey.

The Steelers defeated the College All-Stars in a storm-shortened Chicago College All-Star Game, the last of the series, July 23. St. Louis defeated San Diego 20-10 in a preseason game before 38,000 in Korakuen Stadium, Tokyo, in the first NFL game outside of North America, August 16.

1977

Oakland defeated Minnesota 32-14 before a record crowd of 100,421 in Super Bowl XI at Pasadena, January 9. The paid attendance was a pro record 103,438. The NBC telecast was viewed by 81.9 million people, the largest ever to view a sports event. The victory was the fifth consecutive for the AFC in the Super Bowl.

The NFL Players Association and the NFL Management Council ratified a collective bargaining agreement extending until 1982, covering five football seasons while continuing the pension plan—including years 1974, 1975, and 1976—with contributions totaling more than $55 million. The total cost of the agreement was estimated at $107 million. The agreement called for a college draft at least through 1986; contained a no-strike, no-suit clause; established a 43-man active player limit; reduced pension vesting to four years; provided for increases in minimum salaries and preseason and postseason pay; improved insurance, medical, and dental benefits; modified previous practices in player movement and control; and reaffirmed the NFL Commissioner's disciplinary authority. Additionally, the agreement called for the NFL member clubs to make payments totaling $16 million the next 10 years to settle various legal disputes, February 25.

The San Francisco 49ers were sold to Edward J. DeBartolo, Jr., March 28.

A 16-game regular season, 4-game preseason was adopted to begin in 1978, March 29. A second wild-card team was adopted for the playoffs beginning in 1978, with the wild-card teams to play each other and the winners advancing to a round of eight postseason series.

The Seahawks were permanently aligned in the AFC Western Division and the Buccaneers in the NFC Central Division, March 31.

The owners awarded Super Bowl XIII, to be played on January 21, 1979, to Miami, to be played in the Orange Bowl; Super Bowl XIV, to be played January 20, 1980, was awarded to Pasadena, to be played in the Rose Bowl, June 14.

Rules changes were adopted to open up the passing game and to cut down on injuries. Defenders were permitted to make contact with eligible receivers only once; the head slap was outlawed; offensive linemen were prohibited from thrusting their hands to an opponent's neck, face, or head; and wide receivers were prohibited from clipping, even in the legal clipping zone.

Rozelle negotiated contracts with the three television networks to televise all NFL regular-season and postseason games, plus selected preseason games, for four years beginning with the 1978 season. ABC was awarded yearly rights to 16 Monday night games, four prime-time games, the AFC-NFC Pro Bowl, and the Hall of Fame games. CBS received the rights to all NFC regular-season and postseason games (except those in the ABC package) and to Super Bowls XIV and XVI. NBC received the rights to all AFC regular-season and postseason games (except those in the ABC package) and to Super Bowls XIII and XV. Industry sources considered it the largest single television package ever negotiated, October 12.

Chicago's Walter Payton set a single-game rushing record with 275 yards (40 carries) against Minnesota, November 20.

1978

Dallas defeated Denver 27-10 in Super Bowl XII, held indoors for the first time, at the Louisiana Superdome in New Orleans, January 15. The CBS telecast was viewed by more than 102 million people, meaning the game was watched by more viewers than any other show of any kind in the history of television. Dallas's victory was the first for the NFC in six years.

According to a Louis Harris Sports Survey, 70 percent of the nation's sports fans said they followed football, compared to 54 percent who followed baseball. Football increased its lead as the country's favorite, 26 percent to 16 percent for baseball, January 19.

A seventh official, the side judge, was added to the officiating crew, March 14.

The NFL continued a trend toward opening up the game. Rules changes permitted a defender to maintain contact with a receiver within five yards of the line of scrimmage, but restricted contact beyond that point. The pass-blocking rule was interpreted to permit the extending of arms and open hands, March 17.

A study on the use of instant replay as an officiating aid was made during seven nationally televised preseason games.

The NFL played for the first time in Mexico City, with the Saints defeating the Eagles 14-7 in a preseason game, August 5.

Bolstered by the expansion of the regular-season schedule from 14 to 16 weeks, NFL paid attendance exceeded 12 million (12,771,800) for the first time. The per-game average of 57,017 was the third-highest in league history and the most since 1973.

1979

Pittsburgh defeated Dallas 35-31 in Super Bowl XIII at Miami to become the first team ever to win three Super Bowls, January 21. The NBC telecast was viewed in 35,090,000 homes, by an estimated 96.6 million fans.

The owners awarded three future Super Bowl sites: Super Bowl XV to the Louisiana Superdome in New Orleans, to be played on January 25, 1981; Super Bowl XVI to the Pontiac Silverdome in Pontiac, Michigan, to be played on January 24, 1982; and Super Bowl XVII to Pasadena's Rose Bowl, to be played on January 30, 1983, March 13.

NFL rules changes emphasized additional player safety. The changes prohibited players on the receiving team from blocking below the waist during kickoffs, punts, and field-goal attempts; prohibited the wearing of torn or altered equipment and exposed pads that could be hazardous; extended the zone in which there could be no crackback blocks; and instructed officials to quickly whistle a play dead when a quarterback was clearly in the grasp of a tackler, March 16.

Rosenbloom, the president of the Rams, drowned at 72, April 2. His widow, Georgia, assumed control of the club.

1980

Pittsburgh defeated the Los Angeles Rams 31-19 in Super Bowl XIV at Pasadena to become the first team to win four Super Bowls, January 20. The game was viewed in a record 35,330,000 homes.

The AFC-NFC Pro Bowl, won 37-27 by the NFC, was played before 48,060 fans at Aloha Stadium in Honolulu, Hawaii. It was the first time in the 30-year history of the Pro Bowl that the game was played in a non-NFL city.

Rules changes placed greater restrictions on contact in the area of the head, neck, and face. Under the heading of "personal foul," players were prohibited from directly striking, swinging, or clubbing on the head, neck, or face. Starting in 1980, a penalty could be called for such contact whether or not the initial contact was made below the neck area.

CBS, with a record bid of $12 million, won the national radio rights to 26 NFL regular-season games and all 10 postseason games for the 1980-83 seasons.

The Los Angeles Rams moved their home games to Anaheim Stadium in nearby Orange County, California.

The Oakland Raiders joined the Los Angeles Coliseum Commission's antitrust suit against the NFL. The suit contended the league violated antitrust laws in declining to approve a proposed move by the Raiders from Oakland to Los Angeles.

NFL regular-season attendance of nearly 13.4 million set a record for the third year in a row. The average paid attendance for the 224-game 1980 regular season was 59,787, the highest in the league's 61-year history. NFL games in 1980 were played before 92.4 percent of total stadium capacity.

Television ratings in 1980 were the second-best in NFL history, trailing only the combined ratings of the 1976 season. All three networks posted gains, and NBC's 15.0 rating was its best ever. CBS and ABC had their best ratings since 1977, with 15.3 and 20.8 ratings, respectively. CBS Radio reported a record audience of 7 million for Monday night and special games.

1981

Oakland defeated Philadelphia 27-10 in Super Bowl XV at the Louisiana Superdome in New Orleans, to become the first wild-card team to win a Super Bowl, January 25.

Edgar F. Kaiser, Jr., purchased the Denver Broncos from Gerald and Allan Phipps, February 26.

The owners adopted a disaster plan for re-stocking a team should the club be involved in a fatal accident, March 20.

The owners awarded Super Bowl XVIII to Tampa, to be played in Tampa Stadium on January 22, 1984, June 3.

A CBS-New York Times poll showed that 48 percent of sports fans preferred football to 31 percent for baseball.

The NFL teams hosted 167 representatives from 44 predominantly black colleges during training camps for a total of 289 days. The program was adopted for renewal during each training camp period.

NFL regular-season attendance—13.6 million for an average of 60,745—set a record for the fourth year in a row. It also was the first time the per-game average exceeded 60,000. NFL games in 1981 were played before 93.8 percent of total stadium capacity.

ABC and CBS set all-time rating highs. ABC finished with a 21.7 rating and CBS with a 17.5 rating. NBC was down slightly to 13.9.

1982

San Francisco defeated Cincinnati 26-21 in Super Bowl XVI at the Pontiac Silverdome, in the first Super Bowl held in the North, January 24. The CBS telecast achieved the highest rating of any televised sports event ever, 49.1 with a 73.0 share. The game was viewed by a record 110.2 million fans. CBS Radio reported a record 14 million listeners for the game.

The NFL signed a five-year contract with the three television networks (ABC, CBS, and NBC) to televise all NFL regular-season and postseason games starting with the 1982 season.

The owners awarded the 1983, 1984, and 1985 AFC-NFC Pro Bowls to Honolulu's Aloha Stadium.

A jury ruled against the NFL in the antitrust trial brought by the Los Angeles Coliseum Commission and the Oakland Raiders, May 7. The verdict cleared the way for the Raiders to move to Los Angeles, where they defeated Green Bay 24-3 in their first preseason game, August 29.

The 1982 season was reduced from a 16-game schedule to nine as the result of a 57-day players' strike. The strike was called by the NFLPA at midnight on Monday, September 20, following the Green Bay at New York Giants game. Play resumed November 21-22 following ratification of the Collective Bargaining Agreement by NFL owners, November 17 in New York.

Under the Collective Bargaining Agreement, which was to run through the 1986 season, the NFL draft was extended through 1992 and the veteran free-agent system was left basically unchanged. A minimum salary schedule for years of experience was established; training camp and postseason pay were increased; players' medical, insurance, and retirement benefits were increased; and a severance-pay system was introduced to aid in career transition, a first in professional sports.

Despite the players' strike, the average paid attendance in 1982 was 58,472, the fifth-highest in league history.

The owners awarded the sites of two Super Bowls, December 14: Super Bowl XIX, to be played on January 20, 1985, to Stanford University Stadium in Stanford, California, with San Francisco as host team; and Super Bowl XX, to be played on January 26, 1986, to the Louisiana Superdome in New Orleans.

1983

Because of the shortened season, the NFL adopted a format of 16 teams competing in a Super Bowl Tournament for the 1982 playoffs. The NFC's number-one seed, Washington, defeated the AFC's number-two seed, Miami, 27-17 in Super Bowl XVII at the Rose Bowl in Pasadena, January 30.

Super Bowl XVII was the second-highest rated live television program of all time, giving the NFL a sweep of the top 10 live programs in television history. The game was viewed in more than 40 million homes, the largest ever for a live telecast.

Halas, the owner of the Bears and the last surviving member of the NFL's second organizational meeting, died at 88, October 31.

1984

The Los Angeles Raiders defeated Washington 38-9 in Super Bowl XVIII at Tampa Stadium, January 22. The game achieved a 46.4 rating and 71.0 share.

An 11-man group headed by H.R. (Bum) Bright purchased the Dallas Cowboys from Clint Murchison, Jr., March 20. Club president Tex Schramm was designated as managing general partner.

Patrick Bowlen purchased a majority interest in the Denver Broncos from Edgar Kaiser, Jr., March 21.

The Colts relocated to Indianapolis, March 28. Their new home became the Hoosier Dome.

The owners awarded two Super Bowl sites at their May 23-25 meetings: Super Bowl XXI, to be played on January 25, 1987, to the Rose Bowl in Pasadena; and Super Bowl XXII, to be played on January 31, 1988, to San Diego Jack Murphy Stadium.

The New York Jets moved their home games to Giants Stadium in East Rutherford, New Jersey.

Alex G. Spanos purchased a majority interest in the San Diego Chargers from Eugene V. Klein, August 28.

Houston defeated Pittsburgh 23-20 to mark the one-hundredth overtime game in regular-season play since overtime was adopted in 1974, December 2.

On the field, many all-time records were set: Dan Marino of Miami passed for 5,084 yards and 48 touchdowns; Eric Dickerson of the Los Angeles Rams rushed for 2,105 yards; Art Monk of Washington caught 106 passes; and Walter Payton of Chicago broke Jim Brown's career rushing mark, finishing the season with 13,309 yards.

According to a CBS Sports/*New York Times* survey, 53 percent of the nation's sports fans said they most enjoyed watching football, compared to 18 percent for baseball, December 2-4.

NFL paid attendance exceeded 13 million for the fifth consecutive complete regular season when 13,398,112, an average of 59,813, attended games. The figure was the second-highest in league history. Teams averaged 42.4 points per game, the second-highest total since the 1970 merger.

1985

San Francisco defeated Miami 38-16 in Super Bowl XIX at Stanford Stadium in Stanford, California, January 20. The game was viewed on television by more people than any other live event in history. President Ronald Reagan, who took his second oath of office before tossing the coin for the game, was one of 115,936,000 viewers. The game drew a 46.4 rating and a 63.0 share. In addition, 6 million people watched the Super Bowl in the United Kingdom and a similar number in Italy. Super Bowl XIX had a direct economic impact of $113.5 million on the San Francisco Bay area.

NBC Radio and the NFL entered into a two-year agreement granting NBC the radio rights to a 37-game package in each of the 1985-86 seasons, March 6. The package included 27 regular-season games and 10 postseason games.

The owners awarded two Super Bowl sites at their annual meeting, March 10-15: Super Bowl XXIII, to be played on January 22, 1989, to the proposed Dolphins Stadium in Miami; and Super Bowl XXIV, to be played on January 28, 1990, to the Louisiana Superdome in New Orleans.

Norman Braman, in partnership with Edward Leibowitz, bought the Philadelphia Eagles from Leonard Tose, April 29.

Bruce Smith, a Virginia Tech defensive lineman selected by Buffalo, was the first player chosen in the fiftieth NFL draft, April 30.

A group headed by Tom Benson, Jr., was approved to purchase the New Orleans Saints from John W. Mecom, Jr., June 3.

The NFL owners adopted a resolution calling for a series of overseas preseason games, beginning in 1986, with one game to be played in England/Europe and/or one game in Japan each year. The game would be a fifth preseason game for the clubs involved and all arrangements and selection of the clubs would be under the control of the Commissioner, May 23.

The league-wide conversion to videotape from movie film for coaching study was approved.

Commissioner Rozelle was authorized to extend the commitment to Honolulu's Aloha Stadium for the AFC-NFC Pro Bowl for 1988, 1989, and 1990, October 15.

The NFL set a single-weekend paid attendance record when 902,657 tickets were sold for the weekend of October 27-28.

A Louis Harris poll in December revealed that pro football remained the sport most followed by Americans. Fifty-nine percent of those surveyed followed pro football, compared with 54 percent who followed baseball.

The Chicago-Miami Monday game had the highest rating, 29.6, and share, 46.0, of any prime-time game in NFL history, December 2. The game was viewed in more than 25 million homes.

The NFL showed a ratings increase on all three networks for the season, gaining 4 percent on NBC, 10 on CBS, and 16 on ABC.

1986

Chicago defeated New England 46-10 in Super Bowl XX at the Louisiana Superdome, January 26. The Patriots had earned the right to play the Bears by becoming the first wild-card team to win three consecutive games on the road. The NBC telecast replaced the final episode of *M*A*S*H* as the most-viewed television program in history, with an audience of 127 million viewers, according to A.C. Nielsen figures. In addition to drawing a 48.3 rating and a 70 percent share in the United States, Super Bowl XX was televised to 59 foreign countries and beamed via satellite to the QE II. An estimated 300 million Chinese viewed a tape delay of the game in March. NBC Radio figures indicated an audience of 10 million for the game.

Super Bowl XX injected more than $100 million into the New Orleans-area economy, and fans spent $250 per day and a record $17.69 per person on game day.

The owners adopted limited use of instant replay as an officiating aid, prohibited players from wearing or otherwise displaying equipment, apparel, or other items that carry commercial names, names of organizations, or personal messages of any type, March 11.

After an 11-week trial, a jury in U.S. District Court in New York awarded the United States Football League one dollar in its $1.7 billion antitrust suit against the NFL. The jury rejected all of the USFL's television-related claims, which were the self-proclaimed heart of the USFL's case, July 29.

Chicago defeated Dallas 17-6 at Wembley Stadium in London in the first American Bowl. The game drew a sellout crowd of 82,699 and the NBC national telecast in this country produced a 12.4 rating and 36 percent share, making it the second-highest-rated daytime preseason game and highest daytime preseason television audience ever with 10.65-million viewers, August 3.

Monday Night Football became the longest-running prime-time series in the history of the ABC network.

Instant replay was used to reverse two plays in 31 preseason games. During the regular season, 374 plays were closely reviewed by replay officials, leading to 38 reversals in 224 games. Eighteen plays were closely reviewed by instant replay in 10 postseason games with three reversals.

1987

The New York Giants defeated Denver 39-20 in Super Bowl XXI and captured their first NFL title since 1956. The game, played in Pasadena's Rose Bowl, drew a sellout crowd of 101,063. According to A.C. Nielsen figures, the CBS broadcast of the game was viewed in the U.S. on television by 122.64-million people, making the telecast the second most-watched television show of all-time behind Super Bowl XX. The game was watched live or on tape in 55 foreign countries and NBC Radio's broadcast of the game was heard by a record 10.1 million people.

The NFL set an all-time paid attendance mark of 17,304,463 for all games, including preseason, regular-season, and postseason. Average regular-season game attendance (60,663) exceeded the 60,000 figure for only the second time in league history.

New three-year TV contracts with ABC, CBS, and NBC were announced for 1987-89 at the NFL annual meeting in Maui, Hawaii, March 15. Commissioner Rozelle and Broadcast Committee Chairman Art Modell also announced a three-year contract with ESPN to televise 13 prime-time games each season. The ESPN contract was the first with a cable network. However, NFL games on ESPN also were scheduled for regular television in the city of the visiting team and in the home city if the game was sold out 72 hours in advance.

Owners also voted to continue in effect for one year the instant replay system used during the 1986 season.

A special payment program was adopted to benefit nearly 1,000 former NFL players who participated in the League before the current Bert Bell NFL Pension Plan was created and made retroactive to the 1959 season. Players covered by the new program spent at least five years in the League and played all or part of their career prior to 1959. Each vested player would receive $60 per month for each year of service in the League for life.

Possible sites for Super Bowl XXV were reduced to five locations by the NFL Super Bowl XXV Site Selection Committee: Anaheim Stadium, Los Angeles Memorial Coliseum, Joe Robbie Stadium, San Diego Jack Murphy Stadium, and Tampa Stadium.

NFL and CBS Radio jointly announced agreement granting CBS the radio rights to a 40-game package in each of the next three NFL seasons, 1987-89, April 7.

NFL owners awarded Super Bowl XXV, to be played on January 27, 1991, to Tampa Stadium, May 20.

Over 400 former NFL players from the pre-1959 era received first payments from NFL owners, July 1.

The NFL's debut on ESPN produced the two highest-rated and most-watched sports programs in basic cable history. The Chicago at Miami game on August 16 drew an 8.9 rating in 3.81 million homes. Those records fell two weeks later when the Los Angeles Raiders at Dallas game achieved a 10.2 cable rating in 4.36 million homes.

Fifty-eight preseason games drew a record paid attendance of 3,116,870.

The 1987 season was reduced from a 16-game season to 15 as the result of a 24-day players' strike. The strike was called by the NFLPA on Tuesday, September 22, following the New England at New York Jets game. Games scheduled for the third weekend were canceled but the games of weeks four, five, and six were played with replacement teams. Striking players returned for the seventh week of the season, October 25.

In a three-team deal involving 10 players and/or draft choices, the Los Angeles Rams traded running back Eric Dickerson to the Indianapolis Colts for six draft choices and two players. Buffalo obtained the rights to linebacker Cornelius Bennett from Indianapolis, sending Greg Bell and three draft choices to the Rams. The Colts added Owen Gill and three draft choices of their own to complete the deal with the Rams, October 31.

The Chicago at Minnesota game became the highest-rated and most-watched sports program in basic cable history when it drew a 14.4 cable rating in 6.5 million homes, December 6.

Instant replay was used to reverse eight plays in 52 preseason games. During the strike-shortened 210-game regular season, 490 plays were closely reviewed by replay officials, leading to 57 reversals. Eighteen plays were closely reviewed by instant replay in 10 postseason games, with three reversals.

1988

Washington defeated Denver 42-10 in Super Bowl XXII to earn its second victory this decade in the NFL Championship Game. The game, played for the first time in San Diego Jack Murphy Stadium, drew a sellout crowd of 73,302. According to A.C. Nielsen figures, the ABC broadcast of the game was viewed in the U.S. on television by 115,000,000 people. The game was seen live or on tape in 60 foreign countries, including the People's Republic of China, and CBS's radio broadcast of the game was heard by 13.7 million people.

A total of 811 players shared in the postseason pool of $16.9 million, the most ever distributed in a single season.

In a unanimous 3-0 decision, the 2nd Circuit Court of Appeals in New York upheld the verdict of the jury that in July, 1986, had awarded the United States Football League one dollar in its $1.7 billion antitrust suit against the NFL. In a 91-page opinion, Judge Ralph K. Winter said the USFL sought through court decree the success it failed to gain among football fans, March 10.

By a 23-5 margin, owners voted to continue the instant replay system for the third consecutive season with the Instant Replay Official to be assigned to a regular seven-man, on-the-field crew. At the NFL annual meeting in Phoenix, Arizona, a 45-second clock was also approved to replace the 30-second clock. For a normal sequence of plays, the interval between plays was changed to 45 seconds from the time the ball is signaled dead until it is snapped on the succeeding play.

NFL owners approved the transfer of the Cardinals' franchise from St. Louis to Phoenix; approved two supplemental drafts each year—one prior to training camp and one prior to the regular season; and voted to initiate an annual series of games in Japan/Asia as early as the 1989 preseason, March 14-18.

The NFL Annual Selection Meeting returned to a separate two-day format and for the first time originated on a Sunday. ESPN drew a 3.6 rating during their seven-hour coverage of the draft, which was viewed in 1.6 million homes, April 24-25.

Art Rooney, founder and owner of the Steelers, died at 87, August 25.

Paid and average attendance of 934,271 and 66,734 at 14 games on October 16-17 set single weekend records.

Commissioner Rozelle announced that two teams would play a preseason game as part of the American Bowl series on August 6, 1989, in the Korakuen Tokyo Dome in Japan, December 16.

NFL regular-season paid attendance of 13,535,335 and the average of 60,427 was the third highest all-time. Buffalo set an NFL team single-season, in-house attendance mark of 622,793.

1989

San Francisco defeated Cincinnati 20-16 in Super Bowl XXIII. The game, played for the first time at Joe Robbie Stadium in Miami, was attended by a sellout crowd of 75,129. NBC's telecast of the game was watched by an estimated 110,780,000 viewers, according to A.C. Nielsen, making it the sixth most-watched program in television history. The game was seen live or on tape in 60 foreign countries, including an estimated 300 million in China. The CBS Radio broadcast of the game was heard by 11.2 million people.

Commissioner Rozelle announced his retirement, pending the naming of a successor, March 22 at the NFL annual meeting in Palm Desert, California.

Following the announcement, AFC president Lamar Hunt and NFC president Wellington Mara announced the formation of a six-man search committee composed of Art Modell, Robert Parins, Dan Rooney, and Ralph Wilson. Hunt and Mara served as co-chairmen.

By a 24-4 margin, owners voted to continue the instant replay system for the fourth straight season. A strengthened policy regarding anabolic steroids and masking agents was announced by Commissioner Rozelle. NFL clubs called for strong disciplinary measures in cases of feigned injuries and adopted a joint proposal by the Long-Range Planning and Finance committees regarding player personnel rules, March 19-23.

Two hundred twenty-nine unconditional free agents signed with new teams under management's Plan B system, April 1.

Jerry Jones purchased a majority interest in the Dallas Cowboys from H.R. (Bum) Bright, April 18.

Tex Schramm was named president of the new World League of American Football to work with a six-man committee of Dan Rooney, chairman; Norman Braman, Lamar Hunt, Victor Kiam, Mike Lynn, and Bill Walsh, April 18.

NFL and CBS Radio jointly announced agreement extending CBS's radio rights to an annual 40-game package through the 1994 season, April 18.

NFL owners awarded Super Bowl XXVI, to be played on January 26, 1992, to Minneapolis, May 24.

As of opening day, September 10, of the 229 Plan B free agents, 111 were active and 23 others were on teams' reserve lists. Ninety-two others were waived and three retired.

Art Shell was named head coach of the Los Angeles Raiders making him the NFL's first black head coach since Fritz Pollard coached the Akron Pros in 1921, October 3.

The site of the New England Patriots at San Francisco 49ers game scheduled for Candlestick Park on October 22 was switched to Stanford Stadium in the aftermath of the Bay Area Earthquake of October 17. The change was announced on October 19.

Paul Tagliabue became the seventh chief executive of the NFL on October 26 when he was chosen to succeed Commissioner Pete Rozelle on the sixth ballot of a three-day meeting in Cleveland, Ohio.

In all, 12 ballots were required to select Tagliabue. Two were conducted at a meeting in Chicago on July 6, and four at a meeting in Dallas on October 10-11. On the twelfth ballot, with Seattle absent, Tagliabue received more than the 19 affirmative votes required for election from among the 27 clubs present.

The transfer from Commissioner Rozelle to Commissioner Tagliabue took place at 12:01 A.M. on Sunday, November 5.

NFL Charities donated $1 million through United Way to benefit Bay Area earthquake victims, November 6.

NFL paid attendance of 17,399,538 was the highest total in league history. This included a total of 13,625,662 for an average of 60,829—both NFL records—for the 224-game regular season.

1990

San Francisco defeated Denver 55-10 in Super Bowl XXIV at the Louisiana

Superdome, January 28. San Francisco joined Pittsburgh as the NFL's only teams to win four Super Bowls.

The NFL announced revisions in its 1990 draft eligibility rules. College juniors became eligible but must renounce their collegiate football eligibility before applying for the NFL Draft, February 16.

Commissioner Tagliabue announced NFL teams will play their 16-game schedule over 17 weeks in 1990 and 1991 and 16 games over 18 weeks in 1992 and 1993, February 27.

The NFL revised its playoff format to include two additional wild-card teams (one per conference).

Commissioner Tagliabue and Broadcast Committee Chairman Art Modell announced a four-year contract with Turner Broadcasting to televise nine Sunday-night games.

New four-year TV agreements were ratified for 1990-93 for ABC, CBS, NBC, ESPN, and TNT at the NFL annual meeting in Orlando, Florida, March 12. The contracts totaled $3.6 billion, the largest in TV history.

The NFL announced plans to expand its American Bowl series of preseason games. In addition to games in London and Tokyo, American Bowl games were scheduled for Berlin, Germany, and Montreal, Canada, in 1990.

For the fifth straight year, NFL owners voted to continue a limited system of Instant Replay. Beginning in 1990, the replay official will have a two-minute time limit to make a decision. The vote was 21-7, March 12.

Commissioner Tagliabue announced the formation of a Committee on Expansion and Realignment, March 13. He also named a Player Advisory Council, comprised of 12 former NFL players, March 14.

One-hundred eighty-four Plan B unconditional free agents signed with new teams, April 2.

Commissioner Tagliabue appointed Dr. John Lombardo as the League's Drug Advisor for Anabolic Steroids, April 25 and named Dr. Lawrence Brown as the League's Advisor for Drugs of Abuse, May 17.

NFL owners awarded Super Bowl XXVIII, to be played in 1994, to the proposed Georgia Dome, May 23.

Commissioner Tagliabue named NFL referee Jerry Seeman as NFL Director of Officiating, replacing Art McNally, who announced his retirement, July 12.

NFL International Week was celebrated with four preseason games in seven days in Tokyo, London, Berlin, and Montreal. More than 200,000 fans on three continents attended the four games, August 4-11.

Commissioner Tagliabue announced the NFL Teacher of the Month program in which the League furnishes grants and scholarships in recognition of teachers who provided a positive influence upon NFL players in elementary and secondary schools, September 20.

For the first time since 1957, every NFL club won at least one of its first four games, October 1.

NFL total paid attendance of 17,665,671 was the highest total in League history. The regular-season total paid attendance of 13,959,896 and average of 62,321 for 224 games were the highest ever, surpassing the previous records set in the 1989 season.

1991

The New York Giants defeated Buffalo 20-19 in Super Bowl XXV to capture their second title in five years. The game was played before a sellout crowd of 73,813 at Tampa Stadium and became the first Super Bowl decided by one point, January 26. The ABC broadcast of the game was seen by more than 112-million people in the United States and was seen live or taped in 60 other countries.

NFL playoff games earned the top television rating spot of the week for each week of the month-long playoffs, January 29.

A total of 693 players shared in the postseason pool of $14.9 million.

New York businessman Robert Tisch purchased a 50 percent interest in the New York Giants from Mrs. Helen Mara Nugent and her children, Tim Mara and Maura Mara Concannon, February 2.

Commissioner Tagliabue named Neil Austrian to the newly created position of President of the NFL to be chief operating officer for League-wide business and financial operations, February 27.

NFL clubs voted to continue a limited system of Instant Replay for the sixth consecutive year. The vote was 21-7, March 19.

The NFL launched the World League of American Football, the first sports league to operate on a weekly basis on two separate continents, March 23.

NFL Charities presented a $250,000 donation to the United Service Organization. The donation was the second largest single grant ever by NFL Charities, April 5.

Commissioner Tagliabue named Harold Henderson as Executive Vice President for Labor Relations and Chairman of the NFL Management Council Executive Committee, April 8.

Russell Maryland, a University of Miami defensive lineman, was selected by Dallas, becoming the first player chosen in the 1991 NFL draft, April 21.

NFL clubs approved a recommendation by the Expansion and Realignment Committee to add two teams for the 1994 season, resulting in six divisions of five teams each, May 22.

NFL clubs awarded Super Bowl XXIX, to be played on January 29, 1995, to Miami, May 23.

"NFL International Week" featured six 1990 playoff teams playing nationally televised games in London, Berlin, and Tokyo on July 28 and August 3-4. The games drew more than 150,000 fans.

Paul Brown, founder of the Cleveland Browns and Cincinnati Bengals, died at age 82, August 5.

NFL clubs approved a resolution establishing an international division, reporting to the President of the NFL. A three-year financial plan for the World League was approved by NFL clubs at a meeting in Dallas, October 23.

1992

The NFL agreed to provide a minimum of $2.5 million in financial support to the NFL Alumni Association and assistance to NFL Alumni-related programs. The agreement included contributions from NFL Charities to the Pre-59ers and Dire Need Programs for former players, January 25.

The Washington Redskins defeated the Buffalo Bills 37-24 in Super Bowl XXVI to capture their third world championship in 10 years, January 26. The game was played before a sellout crowd of 63,130 at the Hubert H. Humphrey Metrodome in Minneapolis and attracted the second largest television audience in Super Bowl history. The CBS broadcast was seen by more than 123 million people nationally, second only to the 127 million who viewed Super Bowl XX.

For the third consecutive season, NFL total paid attendance reached a record level. Total paid attendance was 17,752,139 for the 296 preseason, regular-season, and postseason games, February 3.

The use in officiating of a limited system of Instant Replay for a seventh consecutive year was not approved. The vote was 17-11 in favor of approval (21 votes were required), March 18.

Steve Emtman, a University of Washington defensive lineman, was selected by Indianapolis, becoming the first player chosen in the 1992 NFL draft, April 26.

St. Louis businessman James Orthwein purchased controlling interest in the New England Patriots from Victor Kiam, May 11.

In a Harris Poll taken during the NFL offseason, professional football again was declared the nation's most popular sport. Professional football finished atop similar surveys conducted by Harris in 1985 and 1989, May 23.

NFL clubs accepted the report of the Expansion Committee at a league meeting in Pasadena. The report names five cities as finalists for the two expansion teams—Baltimore, Charlotte, Jacksonville, Memphis, and St. Louis, May 19.

At a league meeting in Dallas, NFL clubs approved a proposal by the World League Board of Directors to restructure the World League and place future emphasis on its international success, September 17.

1993

The NFL and lawyers for the players announced a settlement of various lawsuits and an agreement on the terms of a seven-year deal that included a new player system to be in place through the 1999 season, January 6.

Commissioner Tagliabue announced the establishment of the "NFL World Partnership Program" to develop amateur football internationally through a series of clinics conducted by former NFL players and coaches, January 14.

As part of Super Bowl XXVII, the NFL announced the creation of the first NFL Youth Education Town, a facility located in south central Los Angeles for inner city youth. January 25.

The Dallas Cowboys defeated the Buffalo Bills 52-17 in Super Bowl XXVII to capture their first NFL title since 1978. The game was played before a crowd of 98,374 at the Rose Bowl in Pasadena, California. The NBC broadcast of the game was the most watched program in television history and was seen by 133,400,000 people in the United States. The game also was seen live or taped in 101 other countries. The rating for the game was 45.1, the tenth highest for any televised sports event, January 31.

A total of 695 players shared in the postseason pool of $14.9 million, February 15.

For the fourth consecutive season, the NFL total paid attendance reached a record level. Total paid attendance was 17,784,354 for the 296 preseason, regular-season, and postseason games, March 4.

NFL clubs awarded Super Bowl XXX to the city of Phoenix, to be played on January 28, 1996, at Sun Devil Stadium, March 23.

Drew Bledsoe, a quarterback from Washington State, was selected by New England, becoming the first player chosen in the 1993 NFL draft, April 25.

The NFL and the NFL Players Association officially signed a 7-year Collective Bargaining Agreement in Washington, D.C., which guarantees more than $1 billion in pension, health, and post-career benefits for current and retired players—the most extensive benefits plan in pro sports. It was the NFL's first CBA since the 1982 agreement expired in 1987, June 29.

Ron Bernard was named president of NFL Enterprises, a newly formed division of the NFL responsible for NFL Films, home video, and special domestic and international television programming, August 19.

NFL announced plans to allow fans, for the first time ever, to join players and coaches in selecting the annual AFC and NFC Pro Bowl teams, October 12.

NFL clubs unanimously awarded the league's twenty-ninth franchise to the Carolina Panthers at a meeting in Chicago. NFL clubs also awarded Super Bowl XXXI to New Orleans and Super Bowl XXXII to San Diego, October 26.

At the same meeting in Chicago, NFL clubs approved a plan to form a European league with joint venture partners, October 27.

Don Shula became the winningest coach in NFL history when Miami beat Philadelphia to give Shula his 325th victory, one more than George Halas, November 14.

NFL clubs awarded the league's thirtieth franchise to the Jacksonville Jaguars at a meeting in Chicago, November 30.

The NFL announced new 4-year television agreements with ABC, ESPN, TNT, and NFL newcomer FOX, which took over the NFC package from CBS, December 18.

The NFL completed its new TV agreements by announcing that NBC would retain the rights to the AFC package, December 20.

1994

The NFL announced that a regular-season paid attendance record was set in 1993. Attendance averaged 62,354, topping the previous record of 62,321 set in 1990, January 6.

The Dallas Cowboys defeated the Buffalo Bills 30-13 in Super Bowl XXVIII to become the fifth team to win back-to-back Super Bowl titles. The game was viewed by the largest U.S. audience in television history—134.8 million people. The game's 45.5 rating was the highest for a Super Bowl since 1987 and the tenth highest-rated Super Bowl ever, January 30.

NFL clubs unanimously approved the transfer of the New England Patriots from James Orthwein to Robert Kraft at a meeting in Orlando, February 22.

In an effort to increase offensive production, NFL clubs at the league's annual meeting in Orlando adopted a package of changes, including modifications in line play, chucking rules, and the roughing-the-passer rule, plus the adoption of the two-point conversion and moving the spot of the kickoff back to the 30-yard line, March 22.

NFL clubs approved the transfer of the majority interest in the Miami Dolphins from the Robbie family to H. Wayne Huizenga, March 23.

The NFL and FOX announced the formation of a joint venture to create a six-team World League to begin play in Europe in April, 1995, March 23.

The NFL announced a total paid attendance record for the fifth consecutive year, with 17,951,831 in paid attendance for all 1993 games, March 23.

Dan Wilkinson, a defensive tackle from Ohio State, was selected by Cincinnati as the first overall selection in the draft, April 24.

The Carolina Panthers earned the right to select first in the 1995 NFL draft by winning a coin toss with the Jacksonville Jaguars. The Jaguars received the second selection in the 1995 draft, April 24.

NFL clubs approved the transfer of the Philadelphia Eagles from Norman Braman to Jeffrey Lurie, May 6.

The NFL launched "NFL Sunday Ticket," a new season subscription service for satellite television dish owners, June 1.

Sara Levinson, president/business director of MTV, was named president of NFL Properties, July 12.

An all-time NFL record crowd of 112,376 attended the American Bowl game between Dallas and Houston in Mexico City. It concluded the biggest American Bowl series in NFL history with four games attracting a record 256,666 fans, August 15.

The NFL 75th Anniversary All-Time Team was announced at a press conference at Radio City Music Hall, August 30.

The NFL reached agreement on a new seven-year contract with its game officials, September 22.

The NFL Management Council and the NFL Players Association announced an agreement on the formulation and implementation of the most comprehensive drug and alcohol policy in sports, October 28.

At an NFL meeting in Chicago, Commissioner Tagliabue slotted the two new expansion teams into the AFC Central (Jacksonville Jaguars) and NFC West (Carolina Panthers) for the 1995 season only. He also appointed a special committee on realignment to make recommendations on the 1996 season and beyond, November 2.

The NFL set a regular-season paid attendance record for the second consecutive year, topping 14 million for the first time (14,034,977), December 27.

1995

The San Francisco 49ers became the first team to win five Super Bowls when they defeated the San Diego Chargers 49-26 in Super Bowl XXIX at Joe Robbie Stadium in Miami, January 29.

Carolina and Jacksonville stocked their expansion rosters with a total of 66 players from other NFL teams in a veteran player allocation draft in New York, February 16.

CBS Radio and the NFL agreed to a new four-year contract for an annual 53-game package of games, continuing a relationship that spanned 15 of the past 17 years, February 22.

NFL total paid attendance for all 1994 season games reached a record level for the sixth consecutive year, exceeding 18 million for the first time (18,010,264), March 9.

NFL clubs approved the transfer of the Tampa Bay Buccaneers from the estate of the late Hugh Culverhouse to South Florida businessman Malcolm Glazer, March 13.

A total of $20.3 million, the largest NFL postseason pool ever, was divided among 729 players who participated in the 1994 playoffs, March 13.

A series of safety-related rules changes were adopted at a league meeting in Phoenix, primarily related to the use of the helmet against defenseless players, March 14.

After a two-year hiatus, the World League of American Football returned to action with six teams in Europe, April 8.

The NFL became the first sports league to establish a site on the Internet system of on-line computer communication, April 10.

The transfer of the Rams from Los Angeles to St. Louis was approved by a vote of the NFL clubs at a meeting in Dallas, April 12.

ABC's *NFL Monday Night Football* finished the 1994-95 television season as the fifth highest-rated show out of 146 with a 17.8 average rating, the highest finish in the 25-year history of the series, April 18.

Ki-Jana Carter, a running back from Penn State, was selected by the Cincinnati Bengals as the first overall selection in the draft, April 22.

In an ABC News Poll taken during the NFL offseason, America's sports fans chose football as their favorite spectator sport by more than a 2-to-1 margin over basketball and baseball (35%-16%-12%), April 26.

NFL COMMISSIONERS AND PRESIDENTS*

1920.................Jim Thorpe, President
1921-39.................Joe Carr, President
1939-41 ....Carl Storck, President
1941-46 ....Elmer Layden, Commissioner
1946-59 ....Bert Bell, Commissioner
1960-89 ....Pete Rozelle, Commissioner
1989-present...............Paul Tagliabue, Commissioner

**NFL treasurer Austin Gunsel served as president in the office of the commissioner following the death of Bert Bell (Oct. 11, 1959) until the election of Pete Rozelle (Jan. 26, 1960).*

1994

AMERICAN CONFERENCE

Eastern Division

	W	L	T	Pct.	Pts.	OP
Miami	10	6	0	.625	389	327
New England*	10	6	0	.625	351	312
Indianapolis	8	8	0	.500	307	320
Buffalo	7	9	0	.438	340	356
N.Y. Jets	6	10	0	.375	264	320

Central Division

	W	L	T	Pct.	Pts.	OP
Pittsburgh	12	4	0	.750	316	234
Cleveland*	11	5	0	.688	340	204
Cincinnati	3	13	0	.188	276	406
Houston	2	14	0	.125	226	352

Western Division

	W	L	T	Pct.	Pts.	OP
San Diego	11	5	0	.688	381	306
Kansas City*	9	7	0	.563	319	298
L.A. Raiders	9	7	0	.563	303	327
Denver	7	9	0	.438	347	396
Seattle	6	10	0	.375	287	323

NATIONAL CONFERENCE

Eastern Division

	W	L	T	Pct.	Pts.	OP
Dallas	12	4	0	.750	414	248
N.Y. Giants	9	7	0	.563	279	305
Arizona	8	8	0	.500	235	267
Philadelphia	7	9	0	.438	308	308
Washington	3	13	0	.188	320	412

Central Division

	W	L	T	Pct.	Pts.	OP
Minnesota	10	6	0	.625	356	314
Green Bay*	9	7	0	.563	382	287
Detroit*	9	7	0	.563	357	342
Chicago*	9	7	0	.563	271	307
Tampa Bay	6	10	0	.375	251	351

Western Division

	W	L	T	Pct.	Pts.	OP
San Francisco	13	3	0	.813	505	296
New Orleans	7	9	0	.438	348	407
Atlanta	7	9	0	.438	317	385
L.A. Rams	4	12	0	.250	286	365

**Wild-Card qualifier for playoffs*

Miami finished ahead of New Engtland based on a head-to-head sweep (2-0). Kansas City finished ahead of L.A. Raiders based on a head-to-head sweep (2-0). Green Bay was first Wild Card based on best head-to-head record (3-1) vs. Detroit (2-2) and Chicago (1-3) and better conference record (8-4) than N.Y. Giants (6-6). Detroit was second Wild Card based on better division record (4-4) than Chicago (3-5) and head-to-head sweep of N.Y. Giants (1-0). Chicago was third Wild Card based on better record vs. common opponents (4-4) than N.Y. Giants (3-5). New Orleans finished ahead of Atlanta based on a head-to-head sweep (2-0).

Wild Card playoffs: MIAMI 27, Kansas City 17; CLEVELAND 20, New England 13
Divisional playoffs: PITTSBURGH 29, Cleveland 9; SAN DIEGO 22, Miami 21
AFC championship: San Diego 17, PITTSBURGH 13
Wild Card playoffs: GREEN BAY 16, Detroit 12; Chicago 35, MINNESOTA 18
Divisional playoffs: SAN FRANCISCO 44, Chicago 15; DALLAS 35, Green Bay 9
NFC championship: SAN FRANCISCO 38, Dallas 28
Super Bowl XXIX: San Francisco (NFC) 49, San Diego (AFC) 26, at Joe Robbie Stadium, Miami, Florida

In Past Standings section, home teams in playoff games are indicated by capital letters.

1993

AMERICAN CONFERENCE

Eastern Division

	W	L	T	Pct.	Pts.	OP
Buffalo	12	4	0	.750	329	242
Miami	9	7	0	.563	349	351
N.Y. Jets	8	8	0	.500	270	247
New England	5	11	0	.313	238	286
Indianapolis	4	12	0	.250	189	378

Central Division

	W	L	T	Pct.	Pts.	OP
Houston	12	4	0	.750	368	238
Pittsburgh*	9	7	0	.563	308	281
Cleveland	7	9	0	.438	304	307
Cincinnati	3	13	0	.188	187	319

Western Division

	W	L	T	Pct.	Pts.	OP
Kansas City	11	5	0	.688	328	291
L.A. Raiders*	10	6	0	.625	306	326
Denver*	9	7	0	.563	373	284
San Diego	8	8	0	.500	322	290
Seattle	6	10	0	.375	280	314

NATIONAL CONFERENCE

Eastern Division

	W	L	T	Pct.	Pts.	OP
Dallas	12	4	0	.750	376	229
N.Y. Giants*	11	5	0	.688	288	205
Philadelphia	8	8	0	.500	293	315
Phoenix	7	9	0	.438	326	269
Washington	4	12	0	.250	230	345

Central Division

	W	L	T	Pct.	Pts.	OP
Detroit	10	6	0	.625	298	292
Minnesota*	9	7	0	.563	277	290
Green Bay*	9	7	0	.563	340	282
Chicago	7	9	0	.438	234	230
Tampa Bay	5	11	0	.313	237	376

Western Division

	W	L	T	Pct.	Pts.	OP
San Francisco	10	6	0	.625	473	295
New Orleans	8	8	0	.500	317	343
Atlanta	6	10	0	.375	316	385
L.A. Rams	5	11	0	.313	221	367

**Wild-Card qualifier for playoffs*

Minnesota finished ahead of Green Bay based on a head-to-head sweep (2-0).

Wild Card playoffs: KANSAS CITY 27, Pittsburgh 24 (OT); L.A. RAIDERS 42, Denver 24
Divisional playoffs: BUFFALO 29, L.A. Raiders 23; Kansas City 28, HOUSTON 20
AFC championship: BUFFALO 30, Kansas City 13
Wild Card playoffs: Green Bay 28, DETROIT 24; N.Y. GIANTS 17, Minnesota 10
Divisional playoffs: SAN FRANCISCO 44, N.Y. Giants 3; DALLAS 27, Green Bay 17
NFC championship: DALLAS 38, San Francisco 21
Super Bowl XXVIII: Dallas (NFC) 30, Buffalo (AFC) 13, at Georgia Dome, Atlanta, Georgia

1992

AMERICAN CONFERENCE

Eastern Division

	W	L	T	Pct.	Pts.	OP
Miami	11	5	0	.688	340	281
Buffalo*	11	5	0	.688	381	283
Indianapolis	9	7	0	.563	216	302
N.Y. Jets	4	12	0	.250	220	315
New England	2	14	0	.125	205	363

Central Division

	W	L	T	Pct.	Pts.	OP
Pittsburgh	11	5	0	.688	299	225
Houston*	10	6	0	.625	352	258
Cleveland	7	9	0	.438	272	275
Cincinnati	5	11	0	.313	274	364

Western Division

	W	L	T	Pct.	Pts.	OP
San Diego	11	5	0	.688	335	241
Kansas City*	10	6	0	.625	348	282
Denver	8	8	0	.500	262	329
L.A. Raiders	7	9	0	.438	249	281
Seattle	2	14	0	.125	140	312

NATIONAL CONFERENCE

Eastern Division

	W	L	T	Pct.	Pts.	OP
Dallas	13	3	0	.813	409	243
Philadelphia*	11	5	0	.688	354	245
Washington*	9	7	0	.563	300	255
N.Y. Giants	6	10	0	.375	306	367
Phoenix	4	12	0	.250	243	332

Central Division

	W	L	T	Pct.	Pts.	OP
Minnesota	11	5	0	.688	374	249
Green Bay	9	7	0	.563	276	296
Tampa Bay	5	11	0	.313	267	365
Chicago	5	11	0	.313	295	361
Detroit	5	11	0	.313	273	332

Western Division

	W	L	T	Pct.	Pts.	OP
San Francisco	14	2	0	.875	431	236
New Orleans*	12	4	0	.750	330	202
Atlanta	6	10	0	.375	327	414
L.A. Rams	6	10	0	.375	313	383

**Wild-Card qualifier for playoffs*

Miami finished ahead of Buffalo based on better conference record (9-3 to 7-5). Tampa Bay finished ahead of Chicago and Detroit based on better conference record (5-9 to Bears' 4-8 and Lions' 3-9). Atlanta finished ahead of L.A. Rams based on better record versus common opponents (5-7 to 4-8).

Wild Card playoffs: SAN DIEGO 17, Kansas City 0; BUFFALO 41, Houston 38 (OT)
Divisional playoffs: Buffalo 24, PITTSBURGH 3; MIAMI 31, San Diego 0
AFC championship: Buffalo 29, MIAMI 10
Wild Card playoffs: Washington 24, MINNESOTA 7; Philadelphia 36, NEW ORLEANS 20
Divisional playoffs: SAN FRANCISCO 20, Washington 13; DALLAS 34, Philadelphia 10
NFC championship: Dallas 30, SAN FRANCISCO 20
Super Bowl XXVII: Dallas (NFC) 52, Buffalo (AFC) 17, at Rose Bowl, Pasadena, California.

1991

AMERICAN CONFERENCE

Eastern Division

	W	L	T	Pct.	Pts.	OP
Buffalo	13	3	0	.813	458	318
N.Y. Jets*	8	8	0	.500	314	293
Miami	8	8	0	.500	343	349
New England	6	10	0	.375	211	305
Indianapolis	1	15	0	.063	143	381

Central Division

	W	L	T	Pct.	Pts.	OP
Houston	11	5	0	.688	386	251
Pittsburgh	7	9	0	.438	292	344
Cleveland	6	10	0	.375	293	298
Cincinnati	3	13	0	.188	263	435

Western Division

	W	L	T	Pct.	Pts.	OP
Denver	12	4	0	.750	304	235
Kansas City*	10	6	0	.625	322	252
L.A. Raiders*	9	7	0	.563	298	297
Seattle	7	9	0	.438	276	261
San Diego	4	12	0	.250	274	342

NATIONAL CONFERENCE

Eastern Division

	W	L	T	Pct.	Pts.	OP
Washington	14	2	0	.875	485	224
Dallas*	11	5	0	.688	342	310
Philadelphia	10	6	0	.625	285	244
N.Y. Giants	8	8	0	.500	281	297
Phoenix	4	12	0	.250	196	344

Central Division

	W	L	T	Pct.	Pts.	OP
Detroit	12	4	0	.750	339	295
Chicago*	11	5	0	.688	299	269
Minnesota	8	8	0	.500	301	306
Green Bay	4	12	0	.250	273	313
Tampa Bay	3	13	0	.188	199	365

Western Division

	W	L	T	Pct.	Pts.	OP
New Orleans	11	5	0	.688	341	211
Atlanta*	10	6	0	.625	361	338
San Francisco	10	6	0	.625	393	239
L.A. Rams	3	13	0	.188	234	390

**Wild-Card qualifiers for playoffs*

New York Jets finished ahead of Miami based on head-to-head sweep (2-0). Atlanta finished ahead of San Francisco based on head-to-head sweep (2-0).

Wild Card playoffs: KANSAS CITY 10, L.A. Raiders 6; HOUSTON 17, N.Y. Jets 10
Divisional playoffs: DENVER 26, Houston 24; BUFFALO 37, Kansas City 14
AFC championship: BUFFALO 10, Denver 7
Wild Card playoffs: Atlanta 27, NEW ORLEANS 20; Dallas 17, CHICAGO 13
Divisional playoffs: WASHINGTON 24, Atlanta 7; DETROIT 38, Dallas 6
NFC championship: WASHINGTON 41, Detroit 10
Super Bowl XXVI: Washington (NFC) 37, Buffalo (AFC) 24, at Hubert H. Humphrey Metrodome, Minneapolis, Minnesota.

PAST STANDINGS

1990

AMERICAN CONFERENCE

Eastern Division

	W	L	T	Pct.	Pts.	OP
Buffalo	13	3	0	.813	428	263
Miami*	12	4	0	.750	336	242
Indianapolis	7	9	0	.438	281	353
N.Y. Jets	6	10	0	.375	295	345
New England	1	15	0	.063	181	446

Central Division

	W	L	T	Pct.	Pts.	OP
Cincinnati	9	7	0	.563	360	352
Houston*	9	7	0	.563	405	307
Pittsburgh	9	7	0	.563	292	240
Cleveland	3	13	0	.188	228	462

Western Division

	W	L	T	Pct.	Pts.	OP
L.A. Raiders	12	4	0	.750	337	268
Kansas City*	11	5	0	.688	369	257
Seattle	9	7	0	.563	306	286
San Diego	6	10	0	.375	315	281
Denver	5	11	0	.313	331	374

NATIONAL CONFERENCE

Eastern Division

	W	L	T	Pct.	Pts.	OP
N.Y. Giants	13	3	0	.813	335	211
Philadelphia*	10	6	0	.625	396	299
Washington*	10	6	0	.625	381	301
Dallas	7	9	0	.438	244	308
Phoenix	5	11	0	.313	268	396

Central Division

	W	L	T	Pct.	Pts.	OP
Chicago	11	5	0	.688	348	280
Tampa Bay	6	10	0	.375	264	367
Detroit	6	10	0	.375	373	413
Green Bay	6	10	0	.375	271	347
Minnesota	6	10	0	.375	351	326

Western Division

	W	L	T	Pct.	Pts.	OP
San Francisco	14	2	0	.875	353	239
New Orleans*	8	8	0	.500	274	275
L.A. Rams	5	11	0	.313	345	412
Atlanta	5	11	0	.313	348	365

**Wild-Card qualifiers for playoffs*

Cincinnati won AFC Central title based on best head-to-head record (3-1) vs. Houston (2-2) and Pittsburgh (1-3). Houston was Wild Card based on better conference record (8-4) than Seattle (7-5) and Pittsburgh (6-6). Philadelphia finished second in the NFC East based on better division record (5-3) than Washington (4-4). Tampa Bay was second in NFC Central based on 5-1 record vs. Detroit, Green Bay, and Minnesota. Detroit finished third based on best net division points (minus 8) vs. Green Bay (minus 40) in fourth. Minnesota was fifth based on 4-8 conference record. The Los Angeles Rams finished third in NFC West based on net points in division (plus 1) vs. Atlanta (minus 31).

Wild Card playoffs: MIAMI 17, Kansas City 16; CINCINNATI 41, Houston 14
Divisional playoffs: BUFFALO 44, Miami 34; L.A. RAIDERS 20, Cincinnati 10
AFC championship: BUFFALO 51, L.A. Raiders 3
Wild Card playoffs: Washington 20, PHILADELPHIA 6; CHICAGO 16, New Orleans 6
Divisional playoffs: SAN FRANCISCO 28, Washington 10; N.Y. GIANTS 31, Chicago 3
NFC championship: N.Y. Giants 15, SAN FRANCISCO 13
Super Bowl XXV: N.Y. Giants (NFC) 20, Buffalo (AFC) 19, at Tampa Stadium, Tampa, Florida.

1989

AMERICAN CONFERENCE

Eastern Division

	W	L	T	Pct.	Pts.	OP
Buffalo	9	7	0	.563	409	317
Indianapolis	8	8	0	.500	298	301
Miami	8	8	0	.500	331	379
New England	5	11	0	.313	297	391
N.Y. Jets	4	12	0	.250	253	411

Central Division

	W	L	T	Pct.	Pts.	OP
Cleveland	9	6	1	.594	334	254
Houston*	9	7	0	.563	365	412
Pittsburgh*	9	7	0	.563	265	326
Cincinnati	8	8	0	.500	404	285

Western Division

	W	L	T	Pct.	Pts.	OP
Denver	11	5	0	.688	362	226
Kansas City	8	7	1	.531	318	286
L.A. Raiders	8	8	0	.500	315	297
Seattle	7	9	0	.438	241	327
San Diego	6	10	0	.375	266	290

NATIONAL CONFERENCE

Eastern Division

	W	L	T	Pct.	Pts.	OP
N.Y. Giants	12	4	0	.750	348	252
Philadelphia*	11	5	0	.688	342	274
Washington	10	6	0	.625	386	308
Phoenix	5	11	0	.313	258	377
Dallas	1	15	0	.063	204	393

Central Division

	W	L	T	Pct.	Pts.	OP
Minnesota	10	6	0	.625	351	275
Green Bay	10	6	0	.625	362	356
Detroit	7	9	0	.438	312	364
Chicago	6	10	0	.375	358	377
Tampa Bay	5	11	0	.313	320	419

Western Division

	W	L	T	Pct.	Pts.	OP
San Francisco	14	2	0	.875	442	253
L.A. Rams*	11	5	0	.688	426	344
New Orleans	9	7	0	.563	386	301
Atlanta	3	13	0	.188	279	437

**Wild-Card qualifiers for playoffs*

Indianapolis finished ahead of Miami in AFC East because of better conference record (7-5 vs. 6-8). Houston finished ahead of Pittsburgh in AFC Central because of head-to-head sweep (2-0). Minnesota finished ahead of Green Bay in NFC Central because of better division record (6-2 vs. 5-3).

Wild Card playoff: Pittsburgh 26, HOUSTON 23 (OT)
Divisional playoffs: CLEVELAND 34, Buffalo 30; DENVER 24, Pittsburgh 23
AFC championship: DENVER 37, Cleveland 21
Wild Card playoff: L.A. Rams 21, PHILADELPHIA 7
Divisional playoffs: L.A. Rams 19, N.Y. GIANTS 13 (OT); SAN FRANCISCO 41, Minnesota 13
NFC championship: SAN FRANCISCO 30, L.A. Rams 3
Super Bowl XXIV: San Francisco (NFC) 55, Denver (AFC) 10, at Louisiana Superdome, New Orleans, Louisiana.

1988

AMERICAN CONFERENCE

Eastern Division

	W	L	T	Pct.	Pts.	OP
Buffalo	12	4	0	.750	329	237
Indianapolis	9	7	0	.563	354	315
New England	9	7	0	.563	250	284
N.Y. Jets	8	7	1	.531	372	354
Miami	6	10	0	.375	319	380

Central Division

	W	L	T	Pct.	Pts.	OP
Cincinnati	12	4	0	.750	448	329
Cleveland*	10	6	0	.625	304	288
Houston*	10	6	0	.625	424	365
Pittsburgh	5	11	0	.313	336	421

Western Division

	W	L	T	Pct.	Pts.	OP
Seattle	9	7	0	.563	339	329
Denver	8	8	0	.500	327	352
L.A. Raiders	7	9	0	.438	325	369
San Diego	6	10	0	.375	231	332
Kansas City	4	11	1	.281	254	320

NATIONAL CONFERENCE

Eastern Division

	W	L	T	Pct.	Pts.	OP
Philadelphia	10	6	0	.625	379	319
N.Y. Giants	10	6	0	.625	359	304
Washington	7	9	0	.438	345	387
Phoenix	7	9	0	.438	344	398
Dallas	3	13	0	.188	265	381

Central Division

	W	L	T	Pct.	Pts.	OP
Chicago	12	4	0	.750	312	215
Minnesota*	11	5	0	.688	406	233
Tampa Bay	5	11	0	.313	261	350
Detroit	4	12	0	.250	220	313
Green Bay	4	12	0	.250	240	315

Western Division

	W	L	T	Pct.	Pts.	OP
San Francisco	10	6	0	.625	369	294
L.A. Rams*	10	6	0	.625	407	293
New Orleans	10	6	0	.625	312	283
Atlanta	5	11	0	.313	244	315

**Wild-Card qualifiers for playoffs*

Indianapolis finished second in AFC East on basis of better record versus common opponents (7-5) over New England (6-6). Cleveland gained first AFC Wild-Card position based on better division record (4-2) over Houston (3-3). Philadelphia finished first in NFC East on basis of head-to-head sweep over New York Giants. Washington finished third in NFC East on basis of better division record (4-4) over Phoenix (3-5). Detroit finished fourth in NFC Central on basis of head-to-head sweep over Green Bay. San Francisco finished first in NFC West based on better head-to-head record (3-1) over Los Angeles Rams (2-2) and New Orleans (1-3). Los Angeles Rams finished second in NFC West on basis of better division record (4-2) over New Orleans (3-3) and earned Wild-Card position based on better conference record (8-4) over New York Giants (9-5) and New Orleans (6-6).

Wild Card playoff: Houston 24, CLEVELAND 23
Divisional playoffs: CINCINNATI 21, Seattle 13; BUFFALO 17, Houston 10
AFC championship: CINCINNATI 21, Buffalo 10
Wild Card playoff: MINNESOTA 28, Los Angeles Rams 17
Divisional playoffs: CHICAGO 20, Philadelphia 12; SAN FRANCISCO 34, Minnesota 9
NFC championship: San Francisco 28, CHICAGO 3
Super Bowl XXIII: San Francisco (NFC) 20, Cincinnati (AFC) 16, at Joe Robbie Stadium, Miami, Florida.

1987

AMERICAN CONFERENCE

Eastern Division

	W	L	T	Pct.	Pts.	OP
Indianapolis	9	6	0	.600	300	238
New England	8	7	0	.533	320	293
Miami	8	7	0	.533	362	335
Buffalo	7	8	0	.467	270	305
N.Y. Jets	6	9	0	.400	334	360

Central Division

	W	L	T	Pct.	Pts.	OP
Cleveland	10	5	0	.667	390	239
Houston*	9	6	0	.600	345	349
Pittsburgh	8	7	0	.533	285	299
Cincinnati	4	11	0	.267	285	370

Western Division

	W	L	T	Pct.	Pts.	OP
Denver	10	4	1	.700	379	288
Seattle*	9	6	0	.600	371	314
San Diego	8	7	0	.533	253	317
L.A. Raiders	5	10	0	.333	301	289
Kansas City	4	11	0	.267	273	388

NATIONAL CONFERENCE

Eastern Division

	W	L	T	Pct.	Pts.	OP
Washington	11	4	0	.733	379	285
Dallas	7	8	0	.467	340	348
St. Louis	7	8	0	.467	362	368
Philadelphia	7	8	0	.467	337	380
N.Y. Giants	6	9	0	.400	280	312

Central Division

	W	L	T	Pct.	Pts.	OP
Chicago	11	4	0	.733	356	282
Minnesota*	8	7	0	.533	336	335
Green Bay	5	9	1	.367	255	300
Tampa Bay	4	11	0	.267	286	360
Detroit	4	11	0	.267	269	384

Western Division

	W	L	T	Pct.	Pts.	OP
San Francisco	13	2	0	.867	459	253
New Orleans*	12	3	0	.800	422	283
L.A. Rams	6	9	0	.400	317	361
Atlanta	3	12	0	.200	205	436

**Wild-Card qualifiers for playoffs*

Houston gained first AFC Wild-Card position on better conference record (7-4) over Seattle (5-6).

Wild Card playoff: HOUSTON 23, Seattle 20 (OT)
Divisional playoffs: CLEVELAND 38, Indianapolis 21; DENVER 34, Houston 10
AFC championship: DENVER 38, Cleveland 33
Wild Card playoff: Minnesota 44, NEW ORLEANS 10
Divisional playoffs: Minnesota 36, SAN FRANCISCO 24; Washington 21, CHICAGO 17
NFC championship: WASHINGTON 17, Minnesota 10
Super Bowl XXII: Washington (NFC) 42, Denver (AFC) 10, at San Diego Jack Murphy Stadium, San Diego, California.

Note: 1987 regular season was reduced from 16 to 15 games for each team due to players' strike.

1986

AMERICAN CONFERENCE

Eastern Division

	W	L	T	Pct.	Pts.	OP
New England	11	5	0	.688	412	307
N.Y. Jets*	10	6	0	.625	364	386
Miami	8	8	0	.500	430	405
Buffalo	4	12	0	.250	287	348
Indianapolis	3	13	0	.188	229	400

Central Division

	W	L	T	Pct.	Pts.	OP
Cleveland	12	4	0	.750	391	310
Cincinnati	10	6	0	.625	409	394
Pittsburgh	6	10	0	.375	307	336
Houston	5	11	0	.313	274	329

Western Division

	W	L	T	Pct.	Pts.	OP
Denver	11	5	0	.688	378	327
Kansas City*	10	6	0	.625	358	326
Seattle	10	6	0	.625	366	293
L.A. Raiders	8	8	0	.500	323	346
San Diego	4	12	0	.250	335	396

NATIONAL CONFERENCE

Eastern Division

	W	L	T	Pct.	Pts.	OP
N.Y. Giants	14	2	0	.875	371	236
Washington*	12	4	0	.750	368	296
Dallas	7	9	0	.438	346	337
Philadelphia	5	10	1	.344	256	312
St. Louis	4	11	1	.281	218	351

Central Division

	W	L	T	Pct.	Pts.	OP
Chicago	14	2	0	.875	352	187
Minnesota	9	7	0	.563	398	273
Detroit	5	11	0	.313	277	326
Green Bay	4	12	0	.250	254	418
Tampa Bay	2	14	0	.125	239	473

Western Division

	W	L	T	Pct.	Pts.	OP
San Francisco	10	5	1	.656	374	247
L.A. Rams*	10	6	0	.625	309	267
Atlanta	7	8	1	.469	280	280
New Orleans	7	9	0	.438	288	287

**Wild-Card qualifiers for playoffs*

New York Jets gained first AFC Wild-Card position on better conference record (8-4) over Kansas City (9-5), Seattle (7-5), and Cincinnati (7-5). Kansas City gained second Wild Card based on better conference record (9-5) over Seattle (7-5) and Cincinnati (7-5).

Wild Card playoff: NEW YORK JETS 35, Kansas City 15

Divisional playoffs: CLEVELAND 23, New York Jets 20 (OT); DENVER 22, New England 17

AFC championship: Denver 23, CLEVELAND 20 (OT)

Wild Card playoff: WASHINGTON 19, Los Angeles Rams 7

Divisional playoffs: Washington 27, CHICAGO 13 NEW YORK GIANTS 49, San Francisco 3

NFC championship: NEW YORK GIANTS 17, Washington 0

Super Bowl XXI: New York Giants (NFC) 39, Denver (AFC) 20, at Rose Bowl, Pasadena, California.

1985

AMERICAN CONFERENCE

Eastern Division

	W	L	T	Pct.	Pts.	OP
Miami	12	4	0	.750	428	320
N.Y. Jets*	11	5	0	.688	393	264
New England*	11	5	0	.688	362	290
Indianapolis	5	11	0	.313	320	386
Buffalo	2	14	0	.125	200	381

Central Division

	W	L	T	Pct.	Pts.	OP
Cleveland	8	8	0	.500	287	294
Cincinnati	7	9	0	.438	441	437
Pittsburgh	7	9	0	.438	379	355
Houston	5	11	0	.313	284	412

Western Division

	W	L	T	Pct.	Pts.	OP
L.A. Raiders	12	4	0	.750	354	308
Denver	11	5	0	.688	380	329
Seattle	8	8	0	.500	349	303
San Diego	8	8	0	.500	467	435
Kansas City	6	10	0	.375	317	360

NATIONAL CONFERENCE

Eastern Division

	W	L	T	Pct.	Pts.	OP
Dallas	10	6	0	.625	357	333
N.Y. Giants*	10	6	0	.625	399	283
Washington	10	6	0	.625	297	312
Philadelphia	7	9	0	.438	286	310
St. Louis	5	11	0	.313	278	414

Central Division

	W	L	T	Pct.	Pts.	OP
Chicago	15	1	0	.938	456	198
Green Bay	8	8	0	.500	337	355
Minnesota	7	9	0	.438	346	359
Detroit	7	9	0	.438	307	366
Tampa Bay	2	14	0	.125	294	448

Western Division

	W	L	T	Pct.	Pts.	OP
L.A. Rams	11	5	0	.688	340	277
San Francisco*	10	6	0	.625	411	263
New Orleans	5	11	0	.313	294	401
Atlanta	4	12	0	.250	282	452

**Wild-Card qualifiers for playoffs*

New York Jets gained first AFC Wild-Card position on better conference record (9-3) over New England (8-4) and Denver (8-4). New England gained second AFC Wild-Card position based on better record vs. common opponents (4-2) than Denver (3-3). Dallas won NFC Eastern Division title based on better record (4-0) vs. New York Giants (1-3) and Washington (1-3). New York Giants gained first NFC Wild Card position based on better conference record (8-4) over San Francisco (7-5) and Washington (6-6). San Francisco gained second NFC Wild-Card position based on head-to-head victory over Washington.

Wild Card playoff: New England 26, NEW YORK JETS 14

Divisional playoffs: MIAMI 24, Cleveland 21; New England 27, LOS ANGELES RAIDERS 20

AFC championship: New England 31, MIAMI 14

Wild Card playoff: NEW YORK GIANTS 17, San Francisco 3

Divisional playoffs: LOS ANGELES RAMS 20, Dallas 0; CHICAGO 21, New York Giants 0

NFC championship: CHICAGO 24, Los Angeles Rams 0

Super Bowl XX: Chicago (NFC) 46, New England (AFC) 10, at Louisiana Superdome, New Orleans, Louisiana.

1984

AMERICAN CONFERENCE

Eastern Division

	W	L	T	Pct.	Pts.	OP
Miami	14	2	0	.875	513	298
New England	9	7	0	.563	362	352
N.Y. Jets	7	9	0	.438	332	364
Indianapolis	4	12	0	.250	239	414
Buffalo	2	14	0	.125	250	454

Central Division

	W	L	T	Pct.	Pts.	OP
Pittsburgh	9	7	0	.563	387	310
Cincinnati	8	8	0	.500	339	339
Cleveland	5	11	0	.313	250	297
Houston	3	13	0	.188	240	437

Western Division

	W	L	T	Pct.	Pts.	OP
Denver	13	3	0	.813	353	241
Seattle*	12	4	0	.750	418	282
L.A. Raiders*	11	5	0	.688	368	278
Kansas City	8	8	0	.500	314	324
San Diego	7	9	0	.438	394	413

NATIONAL CONFERENCE

Eastern Division

	W	L	T	Pct.	Pts.	OP
Washington	11	5	0	.688	426	310
N.Y. Giants*	9	7	0	.563	299	301
St. Louis	9	7	0	.563	423	345
Dallas	9	7	0	.563	308	308
Philadelphia	6	9	1	.406	278	320

Central Division

	W	L	T	Pct.	Pts.	OP
Chicago	10	6	0	.625	325	248
Green Bay	8	8	0	.500	390	309
Tampa Bay	6	10	0	.375	335	380
Detroit	4	11	1	.281	283	408
Minnesota	3	13	0	.188	276	484

Western Division

	W	L	T	Pct.	Pts.	OP
San Francisco	15	1	0	.938	475	227
L.A. Rams*	10	6	0	.625	346	316
New Orleans	7	9	0	.438	298	361
Atlanta	4	12	0	.250	281	382

**Wild-Card qualifiers for playoffs*

New York Giants clinched Wild-Card berth based on 3-1 record vs. St. Louis's 2-2 and Dallas's 1-3. St. Louis finished ahead of Dallas based on better division record (5-3 to 3-5).

Wild Card playoff: SEATTLE 13, Los Angeles Raiders 7

Divisional playoffs: MIAMI 31, Seattle 10; Pittsburgh 24, DENVER 17

AFC championship: MIAMI 45, Pittsburgh 28

Wild Card playoff: New York Giants 16, LOS ANGELES RAMS 13

Divisional playoffs: SAN FRANCISCO 21, New York Giants 10; Chicago 23, WASHINGTON 19

NFC championship: SAN FRANCISCO 23, Chicago 0

Super Bowl XIX: San Francisco (NFC) 38, Miami (AFC) 16, at Stanford Stadium, Stanford, California.

1983

AMERICAN CONFERENCE

Eastern Division

	W	L	T	Pct.	Pts.	OP
Miami	12	4	0	.750	389	250
New England	8	8	0	.500	274	289
Buffalo	8	8	0	.500	283	351
Baltimore	7	9	0	.438	264	354
N.Y. Jets	7	9	0	.438	313	331

Central Division

	W	L	T	Pct.	Pts.	OP
Pittsburgh	10	6	0	.625	355	303
Cleveland	9	7	0	.563	356	342
Cincinnati	7	9	0	.438	346	302
Houston	2	14	0	.125	288	460

Western Division

	W	L	T	Pct.	Pts.	OP
L.A. Raiders	12	4	0	.750	442	338
Seattle*	9	7	0	.563	403	397
Denver*	9	7	0	.563	302	327
San Diego	6	10	0	.375	358	462
Kansas City	6	10	0	.375	386	367

NATIONAL CONFERENCE

Eastern Division

	W	L	T	Pct.	Pts.	OP
Washington	14	2	0	.875	541	332
Dallas*	12	4	0	.750	479	360
St. Louis	8	7	1	.531	374	428
Philadelphia	5	11	0	.313	233	322
N.Y. Giants	3	12	1	.219	267	347

Central Division

	W	L	T	Pct.	Pts.	OP
Detroit	9	7	0	.563	347	286
Green Bay	8	8	0	.500	429	439
Chicago	8	8	0	.500	311	301
Minnesota	8	8	0	.500	316	348
Tampa Bay	2	14	0	.125	241	380

Western Division

	W	L	T	Pct.	Pts.	OP
San Francisco	10	6	0	.625	432	293
L.A. Rams*	9	7	0	.563	361	344
New Orleans	8	8	0	.500	319	337
Atlanta	7	9	0	.438	370	389

**Wild-Card qualifiers for playoffs*

Seattle and Denver gained Wild-Card berths over Cleveland because of their victories over the Browns.

Wild Card playoff: SEATTLE 31, Denver 7

Divisional playoffs: Seattle 27, MIAMI 20; LOS ANGELES RAIDERS 38, Pittsburgh 10

AFC championship: LOS ANGELES RAIDERS 30, Seattle 14

Wild Card playoff: Los Angeles Rams 24, DALLAS 17

Divisional playoffs: SAN FRANCISCO 24, Detroit 23; WASHINGTON 51, L.A. Rams 7

NFC championship: WASHINGTON 24, San Francisco 21

Super Bowl XVIII: Los Angeles Raiders (AFC) 38, Washington (NFC) 9, at Tampa Stadium, Tampa, Florida.

PAST STANDINGS

1982

AMERICAN CONFERENCE

	W	L	T	Pct.	Pts.	OP
L.A. Raiders	8	1	0	.889	260	200
Miami	7	2	0	.778	198	131
Cincinnati	7	2	0	.778	232	177
Pittsburgh	6	3	0	.667	204	146
San Diego	6	3	0	.667	288	221
N.Y. Jets	6	3	0	.667	245	166
New England	5	4	0	.556	143	157
Cleveland	4	5	0	.444	140	182
Buffalo	4	5	0	.444	150	154
Seattle	4	5	0	.444	127	147
Kansas City	3	6	0	.333	176	184
Denver	2	7	0	.222	148	226
Houston	1	8	0	.111	136	245
Baltimore	0	8	1	.056	113	236

NATIONAL CONFERENCE

	W	L	T	Pct.	Pts.	OP
Washington	8	1	0	.889	190	128
Dallas	6	3	0	.667	226	145
Green Bay	5	3	1	.611	226	169
Minnesota	5	4	0	.556	187	198
Atlanta	5	4	0	.556	183	199
St. Louis	5	4	0	.556	135	170
Tampa Bay	5	4	0	.556	158	178
Detroit	4	5	0	.444	181	176
New Orleans	4	5	0	.444	129	160
N.Y. Giants	4	5	0	.444	164	160
San Francisco	3	6	0	.333	209	206
Chicago	3	6	0	.333	141	174
Philadelphia	3	6	0	.333	191	195
L.A. Rams	2	7	0	.222	200	250

As the result of a 57-day players' strike, the 1982 NFL regular season schedule was reduced from 16 weeks to 9. At the conclusion of the regular season, the NFL conducted a 16-team postseason Super Bowl Tournament. Eight teams from each conference were seeded 1-8 based on their records during the season.

Miami finished ahead of Cincinnati based on better conference record (6-1 to 6-2). Pittsburgh won common games tie-breaker with San Diego (3-1 to 2-1) after New York Jets were eliminated from three-way tie based on conference record (Pittsburgh and San Diego 5-3 vs. Jets 2-3). Cleveland finished ahead of Buffalo and Seattle based on better conference record (4-3 to 3-3 to 3-5). Minnesota (4-1), Atlanta (4-3), St. Louis (5-4), Tampa Bay (3-3) seeds were determined by best won-lost record in conference games. Detroit finished ahead of New Orleans and the New York Giants based on better conference record (4-4 to 3-5 to 3-5).

First round playoff: MIAMI 28, New England 13
LOS ANGELES RAIDERS 27, Cleveland 10
New York Jets 44, CINCINNATI 17
San Diego 31, PITTSBURGH 28
Second round playoff: New York Jets 17, LOS ANGELES RAIDERS 14
MIAMI 34, San Diego 13
AFC championship: MIAMI 14, New York Jets 0
First round playoff: WASHINGTON 31, Detroit 7
GREEN BAY 41, St. Louis 16
MINNESOTA 30, Atlanta 24
DALLAS 30, Tampa Bay 17
Second round playoff: WASHINGTON 21, Minnesota 7
DALLAS 37, Green Bay 26
NFC championship: WASHINGTON 31, Dallas 17
Super Bowl XVII: Washington (NFC) 27, Miami (AFC) 17, at Rose Bowl, Pasadena, California.

1981

AMERICAN CONFERENCE

Eastern Division	W	L	T	Pct.	Pts.	OP
Miami	11	4	1	.719	345	275
N.Y. Jets*	10	5	1	.656	355	287
Buffalo*	10	6	0	.625	311	276
Baltimore	2	14	0	.125	259	533
New England	2	14	0	.125	322	370
Central Division	**W**	**L**	**T**	**Pct.**	**Pts.**	**OP**
Cincinnati	12	4	0	.750	421	304
Pittsburgh	8	8	0	.500	356	297
Houston	7	9	0	.438	281	355
Cleveland	5	11	0	.313	276	375
Western Division	**W**	**L**	**T**	**Pct.**	**Pts.**	**OP**
San Diego	10	6	0	.625	478	390
Denver	10	6	0	.625	321	289
Kansas City	9	7	0	.563	343	290
Oakland	7	9	0	.438	273	343
Seattle	6	10	0	.375	322	388

NATIONAL CONFERENCE

Eastern Division	W	L	T	Pct.	Pts.	OP
Dallas	12	4	0	.750	367	277
Philadelphia*	10	6	0	.625	368	221
N.Y. Giants*	9	7	0	.563	295	257
Washington	8	8	0	.500	347	349
St. Louis	7	9	0	.438	315	408
Central Division	**W**	**L**	**T**	**Pct.**	**Pts.**	**OP**
Tampa Bay	9	7	0	.563	315	268
Detroit	8	8	0	.500	397	322
Green Bay	8	8	0	.500	324	361
Minnesota	7	9	0	.438	325	369
Chicago	6	10	0	.375	253	324
Western Division	**W**	**L**	**T**	**Pct.**	**Pts.**	**OP**
San Francisco	13	3	0	.813	357	250
Atlanta	7	9	0	.438	426	355
Los Angeles	6	10	0	.375	303	351
New Orleans	4	12	0	.250	207	378

**Wild-Card qualifiers for playoffs*

San Diego won AFC Western title over Denver on the basis of a better division record (6-2 to 5-3). Buffalo won a Wild-Card playoff berth over Denver as the result of a 9-7 victory in head-to-head competition.

Wild Card playoff: Buffalo 31, NEW YORK JETS 27
Divisional playoffs: San Diego 41, MIAMI 38 (OT); CINCINNATI 28, Buffalo 21
AFC championship: CINCINNATI 27, San Diego 7
Wild Card playoff: New York Giants 27, PHILADELPHIA 21
Divisional playoffs: DALLAS 38, Tampa Bay 0; SAN FRANCISCO 38, New York Giants 24
NFC championship: SAN FRANCISCO 28, Dallas 27
Super Bowl XVI: San Francisco (NFC) 26, Cincinnati (AFC) 21, at Silverdome, Pontiac, Michigan.

1980

AMERICAN CONFERENCE

Eastern Division	W	L	T	Pct.	Pts.	OP
Buffalo	11	5	0	.688	320	260
New England	10	6	0	.625	441	325
Miami	8	8	0	.500	266	305
Baltimore	7	9	0	.438	355	387
N.Y. Jets	4	12	0	.250	302	395
Central Division	**W**	**L**	**T**	**Pct.**	**Pts.**	**OP**
Cleveland	11	5	0	.688	357	310
Houston*	11	5	0	.688	295	251
Pittsburgh	9	7	0	.563	352	313
Cincinnati	6	10	0	.375	244	312
Western Division	**W**	**L**	**T**	**Pct.**	**Pts.**	**OP**
San Diego	11	5	0	.688	418	327
Oakland*	11	5	0	.688	364	306
Kansas City	8	8	0	.500	319	336
Denver	8	8	0	.500	310	323
Seattle	4	12	0	.250	291	408

NATIONAL CONFERENCE

Eastern Division	W	L	T	Pct.	Pts.	OP
Philadelphia	12	4	0	.750	384	222
Dallas*	12	4	0	.750	454	311
Washington	6	10	0	.375	261	293
St. Louis	5	11	0	.313	299	350
N.Y. Giants	4	12	0	.250	249	425
Central Division	**W**	**L**	**T**	**Pct.**	**Pts.**	**OP**
Minnesota	9	7	0	.563	317	308
Detroit	9	7	0	.563	334	272
Chicago	7	9	0	.438	304	264
Tampa Bay	5	10	1	.344	271	341
Green Bay	5	10	1	.344	231	371
Western Division	**W**	**L**	**T**	**Pct.**	**Pts.**	**OP**
Atlanta	12	4	0	.750	405	272
Los Angeles*	11	5	0	.688	424	289
San Francisco	6	10	0	.375	320	415
New Orleans	1	15	0	.063	291	487

**Wild-Card qualifiers for playoffs*

Philadelphia won division title over Dallas on the basis of best net points in division games (plus 84 net points to plus 50). Minnesota won division title because of a better conference record than Detroit (8-4 to 9-5). Cleveland won division title because of a better conference record than Houston (8-4 to 7-5). San Diego won division title over Oakland on the basis of best net points in division games (plus 60 net points to plus 37).

Wild Card playoff: OAKLAND 27, Houston 7
Divisional playoffs: SAN DIEGO 20, Buffalo 14; Oakland 14, CLEVELAND 12
AFC championship: Oakland 34, SAN DIEGO 27
Wild Card playoff: DALLAS 34, Los Angeles 13
Divisional playoffs: PHILADELPHIA 31, Minnesota 16; Dallas 30, ATLANTA 27
NFC championship: PHILADELPHIA 20, Dallas 7
Super Bowl XV: Oakland (AFC) 27, Philadelphia (NFC) 10, at Louisiana Superdome, New Orleans, Louisiana.

1979

AMERICAN CONFERENCE

Eastern Division	W	L	T	Pct.	Pts.	OP
Miami	10	6	0	.625	341	257
New England	9	7	0	.563	411	326
N.Y. Jets	8	8	0	.500	337	383
Buffalo	7	9	0	.438	268	279
Baltimore	5	11	0	.313	271	351
Central Division	**W**	**L**	**T**	**Pct.**	**Pts.**	**OP**
Pittsburgh	12	4	0	.750	416	262
Houston*	11	5	0	.688	362	331
Cleveland	9	7	0	.563	359	352
Cincinnati	4	12	0	.250	337	421
Western Division	**W**	**L**	**T**	**Pct.**	**Pts.**	**OP**
San Diego	12	4	0	.750	411	246
Denver*	10	6	0	.625	289	262
Seattle	9	7	0	.563	378	372
Oakland	9	7	0	.563	365	337
Kansas City	7	9	0	.438	238	262

NATIONAL CONFERENCE

Eastern Division	W	L	T	Pct.	Pts.	OP
Dallas	11	5	0	.688	371	313
Philadelphia*	11	5	0	.688	339	282
Washington	10	6	0	.625	348	295
N.Y. Giants	6	10	0	.375	237	323
St. Louis	5	11	0	.313	307	358
Central Division	**W**	**L**	**T**	**Pct.**	**Pts.**	**OP**
Tampa Bay	10	6	0	.625	273	237
Chicago*	10	6	0	.625	306	249
Minnesota	7	9	0	.438	259	337
Green Bay	5	11	0	.313	246	316
Detroit	2	14	0	.125	219	365
Western Division	**W**	**L**	**T**	**Pct.**	**Pts.**	**OP**
Los Angeles	9	7	0	.563	323	309
New Orleans	8	8	0	.500	370	360
Atlanta	6	10	0	.375	300	388
San Francisco	2	14	0	.125	308	416

**Wild-Card qualifiers for playoffs*

Dallas won division title because of a better conference record than Philadelphia (10-2 to 9-3). Tampa Bay won division title because of a better division record than Chicago (6-2 to 5-3). Chicago won a Wild-Card berth over Washington on the basis of best net points in all games (plus 57 net points to plus 53).

Wild Card playoff: HOUSTON 13, Denver 7
Divisional playoffs: Houston 17, SAN DIEGO 14; PITTSBURGH 34, Miami 14
AFC championship: PITTSBURGH 27, Houston 13
Wild Card playoff: PHILADELPHIA 27, Chicago 17
Divisional playoffs: TAMPA BAY 24, Philadelphia 17; Los Angeles 21, DALLAS 19
NFC championship: Los Angeles 9, TAMPA BAY 0
Super Bowl XIV: Pittsburgh (AFC) 31, Los Angeles (NFC) 19, at Rose Bowl, Pasadena, California.

1978

AMERICAN CONFERENCE

Eastern Division

	W	L	T	Pct.	Pts.	OP
New England	11	5	0	.688	358	286
Miami*	11	5	0	.688	372	254
N.Y. Jets	8	8	0	.500	359	364
Buffalo	5	11	0	.313	302	354
Baltimore	5	11	0	.313	239	421

Central Division

	W	L	T	Pct.	Pts.	OP
Pittsburgh	14	2	0	.875	356	195
Houston*	10	6	0	.625	283	298
Cleveland	8	8	0	.500	334	356
Cincinnati	4	12	0	.250	252	284

Western Division

	W	L	T	Pct.	Pts.	OP
Denver	10	6	0	.625	282	198
Oakland	9	7	0	.563	311	283
Seattle	9	7	0	.563	345	358
San Diego	9	7	0	.563	355	309
Kansas City	4	12	0	.250	243	327

NATIONAL CONFERENCE

Eastern Division

	W	L	T	Pct.	Pts.	OP
Dallas	12	4	0	.750	384	208
Philadelphia*	9	7	0	.563	270	250
Washington	8	8	0	.500	273	283
St. Louis	6	10	0	.375	248	296
N.Y. Giants	6	10	0	.375	264	298

Central Division

	W	L	T	Pct.	Pts.	OP
Minnesota	8	7	1	.531	294	306
Green Bay	8	7	1	.531	249	269
Detroit	7	9	0	.438	290	300
Chicago	7	9	0	.438	253	274
Tampa Bay	5	11	0	.313	241	259

Western Division

	W	L	T	Pct.	Pts.	OP
Los Angeles	12	4	0	.750	316	245
Atlanta*	9	7	0	.563	240	290
New Orleans	7	9	0	.438	281	298
San Francisco	2	14	0	.125	219	350

**Wild-Card qualifiers for playoffs*

New England won division title on the basis of a better division record than Miami (6-2 to 5-3). Minnesota won division title because of a better head-to-head record against Green Bay (1-0-1).

Wild Card playoff: Houston 17, MIAMI 9

Divisional playoffs: Houston 31, NEW ENGLAND 14; PITTSBURGH 33, Denver 10

AFC championship: PITTSBURGH 34, Houston 5

Wild Card playoff: ATLANTA 14, Philadelphia 13

Divisional playoffs: DALLAS 27, Atlanta 20; LOS ANGELES 34, Minnesota 10

NFC championship: Dallas 28, LOS ANGELES 0

Super Bowl XIII: Pittsburgh (AFC) 35, Dallas (NFC) 31, at Orange Bowl, Miami, Florida.

1977

AMERICAN CONFERENCE

Eastern Division

	W	L	T	Pct.	Pts.	OP
Baltimore	10	4	0	.714	295	221
Miami	10	4	0	.714	313	197
New England	9	5	0	.643	278	217
N.Y. Jets	3	11	0	.214	191	300
Buffalo	3	11	0	.214	160	313

Central Division

	W	L	T	Pct.	Pts.	OP
Pittsburgh	9	5	0	.643	283	243
Houston	8	6	0	.571	299	230
Cincinnati	8	6	0	.571	238	235
Cleveland	6	8	0	.429	269	267

Western Division

	W	L	T	Pct.	Pts.	OP
Denver	12	2	0	.857	274	148
Oakland*	11	3	0	.786	351	230
San Diego	7	7	0	.500	222	205
Seattle	5	9	0	.357	282	373
Kansas City	2	12	0	.143	225	349

NATIONAL CONFERENCE

Eastern Division

	W	L	T	Pct.	Pts.	OP
Dallas	12	2	0	.857	345	212
Washington	9	5	0	.643	196	189
St. Louis	7	7	0	.500	272	287
Philadelphia	5	9	0	.357	220	207
N.Y. Giants	5	9	0	.357	181	265

Central Division

	W	L	T	Pct.	Pts.	OP
Minnesota	9	5	0	.643	231	227
Chicago*	9	5	0	.643	255	253
Detroit	6	8	0	.429	183	252
Green Bay	4	10	0	.286	134	219
Tampa Bay	2	12	0	.143	103	223

Western Division

	W	L	T	Pct.	Pts.	OP
Los Angeles	10	4	0	.714	302	146
Atlanta	7	7	0	.500	179	129
San Francisco	5	9	0	.357	220	260
New Orleans	3	11	0	.214	232	336

**Wild-Card qualifier for playoffs*

Baltimore won division title on the basis of a better conference record than Miami (9-3 to 8-4). Chicago won a Wild-Card berth over Washington on the basis of best net points in conference games (plus 48 net points to plus 4).

Divisional playoffs: DENVER 34, Pittsburgh 21; Oakland 37, BALTIMORE 31 (OT)

AFC championship: DENVER 20, Oakland 17

Divisional playoffs: DALLAS 37, Chicago 7; Minnesota 14, LOS ANGELES 7

NFC championship: DALLAS 23, Minnesota 6

Super Bowl XII: Dallas (NFC) 27, Denver (AFC) 10, at Louisiana Superdome, New Orleans, Louisiana.

1976

AMERICAN CONFERENCE

Eastern Division

	W	L	T	Pct.	Pts.	OP
Baltimore	11	3	0	.786	417	246
New England*	11	3	0	.786	376	236
Miami	6	8	0	.429	263	264
N.Y. Jets	3	11	0	.214	169	383
Buffalo	2	12	0	.143	245	363

Central Division

	W	L	T	Pct.	Pts.	OP
Pittsburgh	10	4	0	.714	342	138
Cincinnati	10	4	0	.714	335	210
Cleveland	9	5	0	.643	267	287
Houston	5	9	0	.357	222	273

Western Division

	W	L	T	Pct.	Pts.	OP
Oakland	13	1	0	.929	350	237
Denver	9	5	0	.643	315	206
San Diego	6	8	0	.429	248	285
Kansas City	5	9	0	.357	290	376
Tampa Bay	0	14	0	.000	125	412

NATIONAL CONFERENCE

Eastern Division

	W	L	T	Pct.	Pts.	OP
Dallas	11	3	0	.786	296	194
Washington*	10	4	0	.714	291	217
St. Louis	10	4	0	.714	309	267
Philadelphia	4	10	0	.286	165	286
N.Y. Giants	3	11	0	.214	170	250

Central Division

	W	L	T	Pct.	Pts.	OP
Minnesota	11	2	1	.821	305	176
Chicago	7	7	0	.500	253	216
Detroit	6	8	0	.429	262	220
Green Bay	5	9	0	.357	218	299

Western Division

	W	L	T	Pct.	Pts.	OP
Los Angeles	10	3	1	.750	351	190
San Francisco	8	6	0	.571	270	190
Atlanta	4	10	0	.286	172	312
New Orleans	4	10	0	.286	253	346
Seattle	2	12	0	.143	229	429

**Wild-Card qualifier for playoffs*

Baltimore won division title on the basis of a better division record than New England (7-1 to 6-2). Pittsburgh won division title because of a two-game sweep over Cincinnati. Washington won Wild-Card berth over St. Louis because of a two-game sweep over Cardinals.

Divisional playoffs: OAKLAND 24, New England 21; Pittsburgh 40, BALTIMORE 14

AFC championship: OAKLAND 24, Pittsburgh 7

Divisional playoffs: MINNESOTA 35, Washington 20; Los Angeles 14, DALLAS 12

NFC championship: MINNESOTA 24, Los Angeles 13

Super Bowl XI: Oakland (AFC) 32, Minnesota (NFC) 14, at Rose Bowl, Pasadena, California.

1975

AMERICAN CONFERENCE

Eastern Division

	W	L	T	Pct.	Pts.	OP
Baltimore	10	4	0	.714	395	269
Miami	10	4	0	.714	357	222
Buffalo	8	6	0	.571	420	355
New England	3	11	0	.214	258	358
N.Y. Jets	3	11	0	.214	258	433

Central Division

	W	L	T	Pct.	Pts.	OP
Pittsburgh	12	2	0	.857	373	162
Cincinnati*	11	3	0	.786	340	246
Houston	10	4	0	.714	293	226
Cleveland	3	11	0	.214	218	372

Western Division

	W	L	T	Pct.	Pts.	OP
Oakland	11	3	0	.786	375	255
Denver	6	8	0	.429	254	307
Kansas City	5	9	0	.357	282	341
San Diego	2	12	0	.143	189	345

NATIONAL CONFERENCE

Eastern Division

	W	L	T	Pct.	Pts.	OP
St. Louis	11	3	0	.786	356	276
Dallas*	10	4	0	.714	350	268
Washington	8	6	0	.571	325	276
N.Y. Giants	5	9	0	.357	216	306
Philadelphia	4	10	0	.286	225	302

Central Division

	W	L	T	Pct.	Pts.	OP
Minnesota	12	2	0	.857	377	180
Detroit	7	7	0	.500	245	262
Chicago	4	10	0	.286	191	379
Green Bay	4	10	0	.286	226	285

Western Division

	W	L	T	Pct.	Pts.	OP
Los Angeles	12	2	0	.857	312	135
San Francisco	5	9	0	.357	255	286
Atlanta	4	10	0	.286	240	289
New Orleans	2	12	0	.143	165	360

**Wild-Card qualifier for playoffs*

Baltimore won division title on the basis of a two-game sweep over Miami.

Divisional playoffs: PITTSBURGH 28, Baltimore 10; OAKLAND 31, Cincinnati 28

AFC championship: PITTSBURGH 16, Oakland 10

Divisional playoffs: LOS ANGELES 35, St. Louis 23; Dallas 17, MINNESOTA 14

NFC championship: Dallas 37, LOS ANGELES 7

Super Bowl X: Pittsburgh (AFC) 21, Dallas (NFC) 17, at Orange Bowl, Miami, Florida.

PAST STANDINGS

1974

AMERICAN CONFERENCE

Eastern Division

	W	L	T	Pct.	Pts.	OP
Miami	11	3	0	.786	327	216
Buffalo*	9	5	0	.643	264	244
New England	7	7	0	.500	348	289
N.Y. Jets	7	7	0	.500	279	300
Baltimore	2	12	0	.143	190	329

Central Division

	W	L	T	Pct.	Pts.	OP
Pittsburgh	10	3	1	.750	305	189
Cincinnati	7	7	0	.500	283	259
Houston	7	7	0	.500	236	282
Cleveland	4	10	0	.286	251	344

Western Division

	W	L	T	Pct.	Pts.	OP
Oakland	12	2	0	.857	355	228
Denver	7	6	1	.536	302	294
Kansas City	5	9	0	.357	233	293
San Diego	5	9	0	.357	212	285

NATIONAL CONFERENCE

Eastern Division

	W	L	T	Pct.	Pts.	OP
St. Louis	10	4	0	.714	285	218
Washington*	10	4	0	.714	320	196
Dallas	8	6	0	.571	297	235
Philadelphia	7	7	0	.500	242	217
N.Y. Giants	2	12	0	.143	195	299

Central Division

	W	L	T	Pct.	Pts.	OP
Minnesota	10	4	0	.714	310	195
Detroit	7	7	0	.500	256	270
Green Bay	6	8	0	.429	210	206
Chicago	4	10	0	.286	152	279

Western Division

	W	L	T	Pct.	Pts.	OP
Los Angeles	10	4	0	.714	263	181
San Francisco	6	8	0	.429	226	236
New Orleans	5	9	0	.357	166	263
Atlanta	3	11	0	.214	111	271

**Wild-Card qualifier for playoffs*

St. Louis won division title because of a two-game sweep over Washington.

Divisional playoffs: OAKLAND 28, Miami 26; PITTSBURGH 32, Buffalo 14

AFC championship: Pittsburgh 24, OAKLAND 13

Divisional playoffs: MINNESOTA 30, St. Louis 14; LOS ANGELES 19, Washington 10

NFC championship: MINNESOTA 14, Los Angeles 10

Super Bowl IX: Pittsburgh (AFC) 16, Minnesota (NFC) 6, at Tulane Stadium, New Orleans, Louisiana.

1973

AMERICAN CONFERENCE

Eastern Division

	W	L	T	Pct.	Pts.	OP
Miami	12	2	0	.857	343	150
Buffalo	9	5	0	.643	259	230
New England	5	9	0	.357	258	300
Baltimore	4	10	0	.286	226	341
N.Y. Jets	4	10	0	.286	240	306

Central Division

	W	L	T	Pct.	Pts.	OP
Cincinnati	10	4	0	.714	286	231
Pittsburgh*	10	4	0	.714	347	210
Cleveland	7	5	2	.571	234	255
Houston	1	13	0	.071	199	447

Western Division

	W	L	T	Pct.	Pts.	OP
Oakland	9	4	1	.679	292	175
Denver	7	5	2	.571	354	296
Kansas City	7	5	2	.571	231	192
San Diego	2	11	1	.179	188	386

NATIONAL CONFERENCE

Eastern Division

	W	L	T	Pct.	Pts.	OP
Dallas	10	4	0	.714	382	203
Washington*	10	4	0	.714	325	198
Philadelphia	5	8	1	.393	310	393
St. Louis	4	9	1	.321	286	365
N.Y. Giants	2	11	1	.179	226	362

Central Division

	W	L	T	Pct.	Pts.	OP
Minnesota	12	2	0	.857	296	168
Detroit	6	7	1	.464	271	247
Green Bay	5	7	2	.429	202	259
Chicago	3	11	0	.214	195	334

Western Division

	W	L	T	Pct.	Pts.	OP
Los Angeles	12	2	0	.857	388	178
Atlanta	9	5	0	.643	318	224
New Orleans	5	9	0	.357	163	312
San Francisco	5	9	0	.357	262	319

**Wild-Card qualifier for playoffs*

Cincinnati won division title on the basis of a better conference record than Pittsburgh (8-3 to 7-4). Dallas won division title on the basis of a better point differential vs. Washington (net 13 points).

Divisional playoffs: OAKLAND 33, Pittsburgh 14; MIAMI 34, Cincinnati 16

AFC championship: MIAMI 27, Oakland 10

Divisional playoffs: MINNESOTA 27, Washington 20; DALLAS 27, Los Angeles 16

NFC championship: Minnesota 27, DALLAS 10

Super Bowl VIII: Miami (AFC) 24, Minnesota (NFC) 7, at Rice Stadium, Houston, Texas.

1972

AMERICAN CONFERENCE

Eastern Division

	W	L	T	Pct.	Pts.	OP
Miami	14	0	0	1.000	385	171
N.Y. Jets	7	7	0	.500	367	324
Baltimore	5	9	0	.357	235	252
Buffalo	4	9	1	.321	257	377
New England	3	11	0	.214	192	446

Central Division

	W	L	T	Pct.	Pts.	OP
Pittsburgh	11	3	0	.786	343	175
Cleveland*	10	4	0	.714	268	249
Cincinnati	8	6	0	.571	299	229
Houston	1	13	0	.071	164	380

Western Division

	W	L	T	Pct.	Pts.	OP
Oakland	10	3	1	.750	365	248
Kansas City	8	6	0	.571	287	254
Denver	5	9	0	.357	325	350
San Diego	4	9	1	.321	264	344

NATIONAL CONFERENCE

Eastern Division

	W	L	T	Pct.	Pts.	OP
Washington	11	3	0	.786	336	218
Dallas*	10	4	0	.714	319	240
N.Y. Giants	8	6	0	.571	331	247
St. Louis	4	9	1	.321	193	303
Philadelphia	2	11	1	.179	145	352

Central Division

	W	L	T	Pct.	Pts.	OP
Green Bay	10	4	0	.714	304	226
Detroit	8	5	1	.607	339	290
Minnesota	7	7	0	.500	301	252
Chicago	4	9	1	.321	225	275

Western Division

	W	L	T	Pct.	Pts.	OP
San Francisco	8	5	1	.607	353	249
Atlanta	7	7	0	.500	269	274
Los Angeles	6	7	1	.464	291	286
New Orleans	2	11	1	.179	215	361

**Wild-Card qualifier for playoffs*

Divisional playoffs: PITTSBURGH 13, Oakland 7; MIAMI 20, Cleveland 14

AFC championship: Miami 21, PITTSBURGH 17

Divisional playoffs: Dallas 30, SAN FRANCISCO 28; WASHINGTON 16, Green Bay 3

NFC championship: WASHINGTON 26, Dallas 3

Super Bowl VII: Miami (AFC) 14, Washington (NFC) 7, at Memorial Coliseum, Los Angeles, California.

1971

AMERICAN CONFERENCE

Eastern Division

	W	L	T	Pct.	Pts.	OP
Miami	10	3	1	.769	315	174
Baltimore*	10	4	0	.714	313	140
New England	6	8	0	.429	238	325
N.Y. Jets	6	8	0	.429	212	299
Buffalo	1	13	0	.071	184	394

Central Division

	W	L	T	Pct.	Pts.	OP
Cleveland	9	5	0	.643	285	273
Pittsburgh	6	8	0	.429	246	292
Houston	4	9	1	.308	251	330
Cincinnati	4	10	0	.286	284	265

Western Division

	W	L	T	Pct.	Pts.	OP
Kansas City	10	3	1	.769	302	208
Oakland	8	4	2	.667	344	278
San Diego	6	8	0	.429	311	341
Denver	4	9	1	.308	203	275

NATIONAL CONFERENCE

Eastern Division

	W	L	T	Pct.	Pts.	OP
Dallas	11	3	0	.786	406	222
Washington*	9	4	1	.692	276	190
Philadelphia	6	7	1	.462	221	302
St. Louis	4	9	1	.308	231	279
N.Y. Giants	4	10	0	.286	228	362

Central Division

	W	L	T	Pct.	Pts.	OP
Minnesota	11	3	0	.786	245	139
Detroit	7	6	1	.538	341	286
Chicago	6	8	0	.429	185	276
Green Bay	4	8	2	.333	274	298

Western Division

	W	L	T	Pct.	Pts.	OP
San Francisco	9	5	0	.643	300	216
Los Angeles	8	5	1	.615	313	260
Atlanta	7	6	1	.538	274	277
New Orleans	4	8	2	.333	266	347

**Wild-Card qualifier for playoffs*

Divisional playoffs: Miami 27, KANSAS CITY 24 (OT); Baltimore 20, CLEVELAND 3

AFC championship: MIAMI 21, Baltimore 0

Divisional playoffs: Dallas 20, MINNESOTA 12; SAN FRANCISCO 24, Washington 20

NFC championship: DALLAS 14, San Francisco 3

Super Bowl VI: Dallas (NFC) 24, Miami (AFC) 3, at Tulane Stadium, New Orleans, Louisiana.

1970

AMERICAN CONFERENCE

Eastern Division

	W	L	T	Pct.	Pts.	OP
Baltimore	11	2	1	.846	321	234
Miami*	10	4	0	.714	297	228
N.Y. Jets	4	10	0	.286	255	286
Buffalo	3	10	1	.231	204	337
Boston Patriots	2	12	0	.143	149	361

Central Division

	W	L	T	Pct.	Pts.	OP
Cincinnati	8	6	0	.571	312	255
Cleveland	7	7	0	.500	286	265
Pittsburgh	5	9	0	.357	210	272
Houston	3	10	1	.231	217	352

Western Division

	W	L	T	Pct.	Pts.	OP
Oakland	8	4	2	.667	300	293
Kansas City	7	5	2	.583	272	244
San Diego	5	6	3	.455	282	278
Denver	5	8	1	.385	253	264

NATIONAL CONFERENCE

Eastern Division

	W	L	T	Pct.	Pts.	OP
Dallas	10	4	0	.714	299	221
N.Y. Giants	9	5	0	.643	301	270
St. Louis	8	5	1	.615	325	228
Washington	6	8	0	.429	297	314
Philadelphia	3	10	1	.231	241	332

Central Division

	W	L	T	Pct.	Pts.	OP
Minnesota	12	2	0	.857	335	143
Detroit*	10	4	0	.714	347	202
Chicago	6	8	0	.429	256	261
Green Bay	6	8	0	.429	196	293

Western Division

	W	L	T	Pct.	Pts.	OP
San Francisco	10	3	1	.769	352	267
Los Angeles	9	4	1	.692	325	202
Atlanta	4	8	2	.333	206	261
New Orleans	2	11	1	.154	172	347

**Wild-Card qualifier for playoffs*

Divisional playoffs: BALTIMORE 17, Cincinnati 0; OAKLAND 21, Miami 14
AFC championship: BALTIMORE 27, Oakland 17
Divisional playoffs: DALLAS 5, Detroit 0; San Francisco 17, MINNESOTA 14
NFC championship: Dallas 17, SAN FRANCISCO 10
Super Bowl V: Baltimore (AFC) 16, Dallas (NFC) 13, at Orange Bowl, Miami, Florida.

1969 NFL

EASTERN CONFERENCE

Capitol Division

	W	L	T	Pct.	Pts.	OP
Dallas	11	2	1	.846	369	223
Washington	7	5	2	.583	307	319
New Orleans	5	9	0	.357	311	393
Philadelphia	4	9	1	.308	279	377

Century Division

	W	L	T	Pct.	Pts.	OP
Cleveland	10	3	1	.769	351	300
N.Y. Giants	6	8	0	.429	264	298
St. Louis	4	9	1	.308	314	389
Pittsburgh	1	13	0	.071	218	404

WESTERN CONFERENCE

Coastal Division

	W	L	T	Pct.	Pts.	OP
Los Angeles	11	3	0	.786	320	243
Baltimore	8	5	1	.615	279	268
Atlanta	6	8	0	.429	276	268
San Francisco	4	8	2	.333	277	319

Central Division

	W	L	T	Pct.	Pts.	OP
Minnesota	12	2	0	.857	379	133
Detroit	9	4	1	.692	259	188
Green Bay	8	6	0	.571	269	221
Chicago	1	13	0	.071	210	339

Conference championships: Cleveland 38, DALLAS 14; MINNESOTA 23, Los Angeles 20
NFL championship: MINNESOTA 27, Cleveland 7
Super Bowl IV: Kansas City (AFL) 23, Minnesota (NFL) 7, at Tulane Stadium, New Orleans, Louisiana

1969 AFL

EASTERN DIVISION

	W	L	T	Pct.	Pts.	OP
N.Y. Jets	10	4	0	.714	353	269
Houston	6	6	2	.500	278	279
Boston Patriots	4	10	0	.286	266	316
Buffalo	4	10	0	.286	230	359
Miami	3	10	1	.231	233	332

WESTERN DIVISION

	W	L	T	Pct.	Pts.	OP
Oakland	12	1	1	.923	377	242
Kansas City	11	3	0	.786	359	177
San Diego	8	6	0	.571	288	276
Denver	5	8	1	.385	297	344
Cincinnati	4	9	1	.308	280	367

Divisional playoffs: Kansas City 13, N.Y. JETS 6; OAKLAND 56, Houston 7
AFL championship: Kansas City 17, OAKLAND 7

1968 NFL

EASTERN CONFERENCE

Capitol Division

	W	L	T	Pct.	Pts.	OP
Dallas	12	2	0	.857	431	186
N.Y. Giants	7	7	0	.500	294	325
Washington	5	9	0	.357	249	358
Philadelphia	2	12	0	.143	202	351

Century Division

	W	L	T	Pct.	Pts.	OP
Cleveland	10	4	0	.714	394	273
St. Louis	9	4	1	.692	325	289
New Orleans	4	9	1	.308	246	327
Pittsburgh	2	11	1	.154	244	397

WESTERN CONFERENCE

Coastal Division

	W	L	T	Pct.	Pts.	OP
Baltimore	13	1	0	.929	402	144
Los Angeles	10	3	1	.769	312	200
San Francisco	7	6	1	.538	303	310
Atlanta	2	12	0	.143	170	389

Central Division

	W	L	T	Pct.	Pts.	OP
Minnesota	8	6	0	.571	282	242
Chicago	7	7	0	.500	250	333
Green Bay	6	7	1	.462	281	227
Detroit	4	8	2	.333	207	241

Conference championships: CLEVELAND 31, Dallas 20; BALTIMORE 24, Minnesota 14
NFL championship: Baltimore 34, CLEVELAND 0
Super Bowl III: N.Y. Jets (AFL) 16, Baltimore (NFL) 7, at Orange Bowl, Miami, Florida.

1968 AFL

EASTERN DIVISION

	W	L	T	Pct.	Pts.	OP
N.Y. Jets	11	3	0	.786	419	280
Houston	7	7	0	.500	303	248
Miami	5	8	1	.385	276	355
Boston Patriots	4	10	0	.286	229	406
Buffalo	1	12	1	.077	199	367

WESTERN DIVISION

	W	L	T	Pct.	Pts.	OP
Oakland	12	2	0	.857	453	233
Kansas City	12	2	0	.857	371	170
San Diego	9	5	0	.643	382	310
Denver	5	9	0	.357	255	404
Cincinnati	3	11	0	.214	215	329

Western Division playoff: OAKLAND 41, Kansas City 6
AFL championship: N.Y. JETS 27, Oakland 23

1967 NFL

EASTERN CONFERENCE

Capitol Division

	W	L	T	Pct.	Pts.	OP
Dallas	9	5	0	.643	342	268
Philadelphia	6	7	1	.462	351	409
Washington	5	6	3	.455	347	353
New Orleans	3	11	0	.214	233	379

Century Division

	W	L	T	Pct.	Pts.	OP
Cleveland	9	5	0	.643	334	297
N.Y. Giants	7	7	0	.500	369	379
St. Louis	6	7	1	.462	333	356
Pittsburgh	4	9	1	.308	281	320

WESTERN CONFERENCE

Coastal Division

	W	L	T	Pct.	Pts.	OP
Los Angeles	11	1	2	.917	398	196
Baltimore	11	1	2	.917	394	198
San Francisco	7	7	0	.500	273	337
Atlanta	1	12	1	.077	175	422

Central Division

	W	L	T	Pct.	Pts.	OP
Green Bay	9	4	1	.692	332	209
Chicago	7	6	1	.538	239	218
Detroit	5	7	2	.417	260	259
Minnesota	3	8	3	.273	233	294

Los Angeles won division title on the basis of advantage in points (58-34) in two games vs. Baltimore.

Conference championships: DALLAS 52, Cleveland 14; GREEN BAY 28, Los Angeles 7
NFL championship: GREEN BAY 21, Dallas 17
Super Bowl II: Green Bay (NFL) 33, Oakland (AFL) 14, at Orange Bowl, Miami, Florida.

1967 AFL

EASTERN DIVISION

	W	L	T	Pct.	Pts.	OP
Houston	9	4	1	.692	258	199
N.Y. Jets	8	5	1	.615	371	329
Buffalo	4	10	0	.286	237	285
Miami	4	10	0	.286	219	407
Boston Patriots	3	10	1	.231	280	389

WESTERN DIVISION

	W	L	T	Pct.	Pts.	OP
Oakland	13	1	0	.929	468	233
Kansas City	9	5	0	.643	408	254
San Diego	8	5	1	.615	360	352
Denver	3	11	0	.214	256	409

AFL championship: OAKLAND 40, Houston 7

1966 NFL

EASTERN CONFERENCE

	W	L	T	Pct.	Pts.	OP
Dallas	10	3	1	.769	445	239
Cleveland	9	5	0	.643	403	259
Philadelphia	9	5	0	.643	326	340
St. Louis	8	5	1	.615	264	265
Washington	7	7	0	.500	351	355
Pittsburgh	5	8	1	.385	316	347
Atlanta	3	11	0	.214	204	437
N.Y. Giants	1	12	1	.077	263	501

WESTERN CONFERENCE

	W	L	T	Pct.	Pts.	OP
Green Bay	12	2	0	.857	335	163
Baltimore	9	5	0	.643	314	226
Los Angeles	8	6	0	.571	289	212
San Francisco	6	6	2	.500	320	325
Chicago	5	7	2	.417	234	272
Detroit	4	9	1	.308	206	317
Minnesota	4	9	1	.308	292	304

NFL championship: Green Bay 34, DALLAS 27
Super Bowl I: Green Bay (NFL) 35, Kansas City (AFL) 10, at Memorial Coliseum, Los Angeles, California.

1966 AFL

EASTERN DIVISION

	W	L	T	Pct.	Pts.	OP
Buffalo	9	4	1	.692	358	255
Boston Patriots	8	4	2	.677	315	283
N.Y. Jets	6	6	2	.500	322	312
Houston	3	11	0	.214	335	396
Miami	3	11	0	.214	213	362

WESTERN DIVISION

	W	L	T	Pct.	Pts.	OP
Kansas City	11	2	1	.846	448	276
Oakland	8	5	1	.615	315	288
San Diego	7	6	1	.538	335	284
Denver	4	10	0	.286	196	381

AFL championship: Kansas City 31, BUFFALO 7

1965 NFL

EASTERN CONFERENCE

	W	L	T	Pct.	Pts.	OP
Cleveland	11	3	0	.786	363	325
Dallas	7	7	0	.500	325	280
N.Y. Giants	7	7	0	.500	270	338
Washington	6	8	0	.429	257	301
Philadelphia	5	9	0	.357	363	359
St. Louis	5	9	0	.357	296	309
Pittsburgh	2	12	0	.143	202	397

WESTERN CONFERENCE

	W	L	T	Pct.	Pts.	OP
Green Bay	10	3	1	.769	316	224
Baltimore	10	3	1	.769	389	284
Chicago	9	5	0	.643	409	275
San Francisco	7	6	1	.538	421	402
Minnesota	7	7	0	.500	383	403
Detroit	6	7	1	.462	257	295
Los Angeles	4	10	0	.286	269	328

Western Conference playoff: GREEN BAY 13, Baltimore 10 (OT)
NFL championship: GREEN BAY 23, Cleveland 12

PAST STANDINGS

1965 AFL

EASTERN DIVISION

	W	L	T	Pct.	Pts.	OP
Buffalo	10	3	1	.769	313	226
N.Y. Jets	5	8	1	.385	285	303
Boston Patriots	4	8	2	.333	244	302
Houston	4	10	0	.286	298	429

WESTERN DIVISION

	W	L	T	Pct.	Pts.	OP
San Diego	9	2	3	.818	340	227
Oakland	8	5	1	.615	298	239
Kansas City	7	5	2	.583	322	285
Denver	4	10	0	.286	303	392

AFL championship: Buffalo 23, SAN DIEGO 0

1964 NFL

EASTERN CONFERENCE

	W	L	T	Pct.	Pts.	OP
Cleveland	10	3	1	.769	415	293
St. Louis	9	3	2	.750	357	331
Philadelphia	6	8	0	.429	312	313
Washington	6	8	0	.429	307	305
Dallas	5	8	1	.385	250	289
Pittsburgh	5	9	0	.357	253	315
N.Y. Giants	2	10	2	.167	241	399

WESTERN CONFERENCE

	W	L	T	Pct.	Pts.	OP
Baltimore	12	2	0	.857	428	225
Green Bay	8	5	1	.615	342	245
Minnesota	8	5	1	.615	355	296
Detroit	7	5	2	.583	280	260
Los Angeles	5	7	2	.417	283	339
Chicago	5	9	0	.357	260	379
San Francisco	4	10	0	.286	236	330

NFL championship: CLEVELAND 27, Baltimore 0

1964 AFL

EASTERN DIVISION

	W	L	T	Pct.	Pts.	OP
Buffalo	12	2	0	.857	400	242
Boston Patriots	10	3	1	.769	365	297
N.Y. Jets	5	8	1	.385	278	315
Houston	4	10	0	.286	310	355

WESTERN DIVISION

	W	L	T	Pct.	Pts.	OP
San Diego	8	5	1	.615	341	300
Kansas City	7	7	0	.500	366	306
Oakland	5	7	2	.417	303	350
Denver	2	11	1	.154	240	438

AFL championship: BUFFALO 20, San Diego 7

1963 NFL

EASTERN CONFERENCE

	W	L	T	Pct.	Pts.	OP
N.Y. Giants	11	3	0	.786	448	280
Cleveland	10	4	0	.714	343	262
St. Louis	9	5	0	.643	341	283
Pittsburgh	7	4	3	.636	321	295
Dallas	4	10	0	.286	305	378
Washington	3	11	0	.214	279	398
Philadelphia	2	10	2	.167	242	381

WESTERN CONFERENCE

	W	L	T	Pct.	Pts.	OP
Chicago	11	1	2	.917	301	144
Green Bay	11	2	1	.846	369	206
Baltimore	8	6	0	.571	316	285
Detroit	5	8	1	.385	326	265
Minnesota	5	8	1	.385	309	390
Los Angeles	5	9	0	.357	210	350
San Francisco	2	12	0	.143	198	391

NFL championship: CHICAGO 14, N.Y. Giants 10

1963 AFL

EASTERN DIVISION

	W	L	T	Pct.	Pts.	OP
Boston Patriots	7	6	1	.538	327	257
Buffalo	7	6	1	.538	304	291
Houston	6	8	0	.429	302	372
N.Y. Jets	5	8	1	.385	249	399

WESTERN DIVISION

	W	L	T	Pct.	Pts.	OP
San Diego	11	3	0	.786	399	256
Oakland	10	4	0	.714	363	288
Kansas City	5	7	2	.417	347	263
Denver	2	11	1	.154	301	473

Eastern Division playoff: Boston 26, BUFFALO 8
AFL championship: SAN DIEGO 51, Boston 10

1962 NFL

EASTERN CONFERENCE

	W	L	T	Pct.	Pts.	OP
N.Y. Giants	12	2	0	.857	398	283
Pittsburgh	9	5	0	.643	312	363
Cleveland	7	6	1	.538	291	257
Washington	5	7	2	.417	305	376
Dallas Cowboys	5	8	1	.385	398	402
St. Louis	4	9	1	.308	287	361
Philadelphia	3	10	1	.231	282	356

WESTERN CONFERENCE

	W	L	T	Pct.	Pts.	OP
Green Bay	13	1	0	.929	415	148
Detroit	11	3	0	.786	315	177
Chicago	9	5	0	.643	321	287
Baltimore	7	7	0	.500	293	288
San Francisco	6	8	0	.429	282	331
Minnesota	2	11	1	.154	254	410
Los Angeles	1	12	1	.077	220	334

NFL championship: Green Bay 16, N.Y. GIANTS 7

1962 AFL

EASTERN DIVISION

	W	L	T	Pct.	Pts.	OP
Houston	11	3	0	.786	387	270
Boston Patriots	9	4	1	.692	346	295
Buffalo	7	6	1	.538	309	272
N.Y. Titans	5	9	0	.357	278	423

WESTERN DIVISION

	W	L	T	Pct.	Pts.	OP
Dallas Texans	11	3	0	.786	389	233
Denver	7	7	0	.500	353	334
San Diego	4	10	0	.286	314	392
Oakland	1	13	0	.071	213	370

AFL championship: Dallas Texans 20, HOUSTON 17 (OT)

1961 NFL

EASTERN CONFERENCE

	W	L	T	Pct.	Pts.	OP
N.Y. Giants	10	3	1	.769	368	220
Philadelphia	10	4	0	.714	361	297
Cleveland	8	5	1	.615	319	270
St. Louis	7	7	0	.500	279	267
Pittsburgh	6	8	0	.429	295	287
Dallas Cowboys	4	9	1	.308	236	380
Washington	1	12	1	.077	174	392

WESTERN CONFERENCE

	W	L	T	Pct.	Pts.	OP
Green Bay	11	3	0	.786	391	223
Detroit	8	5	1	.615	270	258
Baltimore	8	6	0	.571	302	307
Chicago	8	6	0	.571	326	302
San Francisco	7	6	1	.538	346	272
Los Angeles	4	10	0	.286	263	333
Minnesota	3	11	0	.214	285	407

NFL championship: GREEN BAY 37, N.Y. Giants 0

1961 AFL

EASTERN DIVISION

	W	L	T	Pct.	Pts.	OP
Houston	10	3	1	.769	513	242
Boston Patriots	9	4	1	.692	413	313
N.Y. Titans	7	7	0	.500	301	390
Buffalo	6	8	0	.429	294	342

WESTERN DIVISION

	W	L	T	Pct.	Pts.	OP
San Diego	12	2	0	.857	396	219
Dallas Texans	6	8	0	.429	334	343
Denver	3	11	0	.214	251	432
Oakland	2	12	0	.143	237	458

AFL championship: Houston 10, SAN DIEGO 3

1960 NFL

EASTERN CONFERENCE

	W	L	T	Pct.	Pts.	OP
Philadelphia	10	2	0	.833	321	246
Cleveland	8	3	1	.727	362	217
N.Y. Giants	6	4	2	.600	271	261
St. Louis	6	5	1	.545	288	230
Pittsburgh	5	6	1	.455	240	275
Washington	1	9	2	.100	178	309

WESTERN CONFERENCE

	W	L	T	Pct.	Pts.	OP
Green Bay	8	4	0	.667	332	209
Detroit	7	5	0	.583	239	212
San Francisco	7	5	0	.583	208	205
Baltimore	6	6	0	.500	288	234
Chicago	5	6	1	.455	194	299
L.A. Rams	4	7	1	.364	265	297
Dallas Cowboys	0	11	1	.000	177	369

NFL championship: PHILADELPHIA 17, Green Bay 13

1960 AFL

EASTERN CONFERENCE

	W	L	T	Pct.	Pts.	OP
Houston	10	4	0	.714	379	285
N.Y. Titans	7	7	0	.500	382	399
Buffalo	5	8	1	.385	296	303
Boston	5	9	0	.357	286	349

WESTERN CONFERENCE

	W	L	T	Pct.	Pts.	OP
L.A. Chargers	10	4	0	.714	373	336
Dallas Texans	8	6	0	.571	362	253
Oakland	6	8	0	.429	319	388
Denver	4	9	1	.308	309	393

AFL championship: HOUSTON 24, L.A. Chargers 16

1959

EASTERN CONFERENCE

	W	L	T	Pct.	Pts.	OP
N.Y. Giants	10	2	0	.833	284	170
Cleveland	7	5	0	.583	270	214
Philadelphia	7	5	0	.583	268	278
Pittsburgh	6	5	1	.545	257	216
Washington	3	9	0	.250	185	350
Chi. Cardinals	2	10	0	.167	234	324

WESTERN CONFERENCE

	W	L	T	Pct.	Pts.	OP
Baltimore	9	3	0	.750	374	251
Chi. Bears	8	4	0	.667	252	196
Green Bay	7	5	0	.583	248	246
San Francisco	7	5	0	.583	255	237
Detroit	3	8	1	.273	203	275
Los Angeles	2	10	0	.167	242	315

NFL championship: BALTIMORE 31, N.Y. Giants 16

1958

EASTERN CONFERENCE

	W	L	T	Pct.	Pts.	OP
N.Y. Giants	9	3	0	.750	246	183
Cleveland	9	3	0	.750	302	217
Pittsburgh	7	4	1	.636	261	230
Washington	4	7	1	.364	214	268
Chi. Cardinals	2	9	1	.182	261	356
Philadelphia	2	9	1	.182	235	306

WESTERN CONFERENCE

	W	L	T	Pct.	Pts.	OP
Baltimore	9	3	0	.750	381	203
Chi. Bears	8	4	0	.667	298	230
Los Angeles	8	4	0	.667	344	278
San Francisco	6	6	0	.500	257	324
Detroit	4	7	1	.364	261	276
Green Bay	1	10	1	.091	193	382

Eastern Conference playoff: N.Y. GIANTS 10, Cleveland 0
NFL championship: Baltimore 23, N.Y. GIANTS 17 (OT)

1957

EASTERN CONFERENCE

	W	L	T	Pct.	Pts.	OP
Cleveland	9	2	1	.818	269	172
N.Y. Giants	7	5	0	.583	254	211
Pittsburgh	6	6	0	.500	161	178
Washington	5	6	1	.455	251	230
Philadelphia	4	8	0	.333	173	230
Chi. Cardinals	3	9	0	.250	200	299

WESTERN CONFERENCE

	W	L	T	Pct.	Pts.	OP
Detroit	8	4	0	.667	251	231
San Francisco	8	4	0	.667	260	264
Baltimore	7	5	0	.583	303	235
Los Angeles	6	6	0	.500	307	278
Chi. Bears	5	7	0	.417	203	211
Green Bay	3	9	0	.250	218	311

Western Conference playoff: Detroit 31, SAN FRANCISCO 27
NFL championship: DETROIT 59, Cleveland 14

1956

EASTERN CONFERENCE

	W	L	T	Pct.	Pts.	OP
N.Y. Giants	8	3	1	.727	264	197
Chi. Cardinals	7	5	0	.583	240	182
Washington	6	6	0	.500	183	225
Cleveland	5	7	0	.417	167	177
Pittsburgh	5	7	0	.417	217	250
Philadelphia	3	8	1	.273	143	215

WESTERN CONFERENCE

	W	L	T	Pct.	Pts.	OP
Chi. Bears	9	2	1	.818	363	246
Detroit	9	3	0	.750	300	188
San Francisco	5	6	1	.455	233	284
Baltimore	5	7	0	.417	270	322
Green Bay	4	8	0	.333	264	342
Los Angeles	4	8	0	.333	291	307

NFL championship: N.Y. GIANTS 47, Chi. Bears 7

1955

EASTERN CONFERENCE

	W	L	T	Pct.	Pts.	OP
Cleveland	9	2	1	.818	349	218
Washington	8	4	0	.667	246	222
N.Y. Giants	6	5	1	.545	267	223
Chi. Cardinals	4	7	1	.364	224	252
Philadelphia	4	7	1	.364	248	231
Pittsburgh	4	8	0	.333	195	285

WESTERN CONFERENCE

	W	L	T	Pct.	Pts.	OP
Los Angeles	8	3	1	.727	260	231
Chi. Bears	8	4	0	.667	294	251
Green Bay	6	6	0	.500	258	276
Baltimore	5	6	1	.455	214	239
San Francisco	4	8	0	.333	216	298
Detroit	3	9	0	.250	230	275

NFL championship: Cleveland 38, LOS ANGELES 14

1954

EASTERN CONFERENCE

	W	L	T	Pct.	Pts.	OP
Cleveland	9	3	0	.750	336	162
Philadelphia	7	4	1	.636	284	230
N.Y. Giants	7	5	0	.583	293	184
Pittsburgh	5	7	0	.417	219	263
Washington	3	9	0	.250	207	432
Chi. Cardinals	2	10	0	.167	183	347

WESTERN CONFERENCE

	W	L	T	Pct.	Pts.	OP
Detroit	9	2	1	.818	337	189
Chi. Bears	8	4	0	.667	301	279
San Francisco	7	4	1	.636	313	251
Los Angeles	6	5	1	.545	314	285
Green Bay	4	8	0	.333	234	251
Baltimore	3	9	0	.250	131	279

NFL championship: CLEVELAND 56, Detroit 10

1953

EASTERN CONFERENCE

	W	L	T	Pct.	Pts.	OP
Cleveland	11	1	0	.917	348	162
Philadelphia	7	4	1	.636	352	215
Washington	6	5	1	.545	208	215
Pittsburgh	6	6	0	.500	211	263
N.Y. Giants	3	9	0	.250	179	277
Chi. Cardinals	1	10	1	.091	190	337

WESTERN CONFERENCE

	W	L	T	Pct.	Pts.	OP
Detroit	10	2	0	.833	271	205
San Francisco	9	3	0	.750	372	237
Los Angeles	8	3	1	.727	366	236
Chi. Bears	3	8	1	.273	218	262
Baltimore	3	9	0	.250	182	350
Green Bay	2	9	1	.182	200	338

NFL championship: DETROIT 17, Cleveland 16

1952

AMERICAN CONFERENCE

	W	L	T	Pct.	Pts.	OP
Cleveland	8	4	0	.667	310	213
N.Y. Giants	7	5	0	.583	234	231
Philadelphia	7	5	0	.583	252	271
Pittsburgh	5	7	0	.417	300	273
Chi. Cardinals	4	8	0	.333	172	221
Washington	4	8	0	.333	240	287

NATIONAL CONFERENCE

	W	L	T	Pct.	Pts.	OP
Detroit	9	3	0	.750	344	192
Los Angeles	9	3	0	.750	349	234
San Francisco	7	5	0	.583	285	221
Green Bay	6	6	0	.500	295	312
Chi. Bears	5	7	0	.417	245	326
Dallas Texans	1	11	0	.083	182	427

National Conference playoff: DETROIT 31, Los Angeles 21

NFL championship: Detroit 17, CLEVELAND 7

1951

AMERICAN CONFERENCE

	W	L	T	Pct.	Pts.	OP
Cleveland	11	1	0	.917	331	152
N.Y. Giants	9	2	1	.818	254	161
Washington	5	7	0	.417	183	296
Pittsburgh	4	7	1	.364	183	235
Philadelphia	4	8	0	.333	234	264
Chi. Cardinals	3	9	0	.250	210	287

NATIONAL CONFERENCE

	W	L	T	Pct.	Pts.	OP
Los Angeles	8	4	0	.667	392	261
Detroit	7	4	1	.636	336	259
San Francisco	7	4	1	.636	255	205
Chi. Bears	7	5	0	.583	286	282
Green Bay	3	9	0	.250	254	375
N.Y. Yanks	1	9	2	.100	241	382

NFL championship: LOS ANGELES 24, Cleveland 17

1950

AMERICAN CONFERENCE

	W	L	T	Pct.	Pts.	OP
Cleveland	10	2	0	.833	310	144
N.Y. Giants	10	2	0	.833	268	150
Philadelphia	6	6	0	.500	254	141
Pittsburgh	6	6	0	.500	180	195
Chi. Cardinals	5	7	0	.417	233	287
Washington	3	9	0	.250	232	326

NATIONAL CONFERENCE

	W	L	T	Pct.	Pts.	OP
Los Angeles	9	3	0	.750	466	309
Chi. Bears	9	3	0	.750	279	207
N.Y. Yanks	7	5	0	.583	366	367
Detroit	6	6	0	.500	321	285
Green Bay	3	9	0	.250	244	406
San Francisco	3	9	0	.250	213	300
Baltimore	1	11	0	.083	213	462

American Conference playoff: CLEVELAND 8, N.Y. Giants 3

National Conference playoff: LOS ANGELES 24, Chi. Bears 14

NFL championship: CLEVELAND 30, Los Angeles 28

1949

EASTERN DIVISION

	W	L	T	Pct.	Pts.	OP
Philadelphia	11	1	0	.917	364	134
Pittsburgh	6	5	1	.545	224	214
N.Y. Giants	6	6	0	.500	287	298
Washington	4	7	1	.364	268	339
N.Y. Bulldogs	1	10	1	.091	153	365

WESTERN DIVISION

	W	L	T	Pct.	Pts.	OP
Los Angeles	8	2	2	.800	360	239
Chi. Bears	9	3	0	.750	332	218
Chi. Cardinals	6	5	1	.545	360	301
Detroit	4	8	0	.333	237	259
Green Bay	2	10	0	.167	114	329

NFL championship: Philadelphia 14, LOS ANGELES 0

1948

EASTERN DIVISION

	W	L	T	Pct.	Pts.	OP
Philadelphia	9	2	1	.818	376	156
Washington	7	5	0	.583	291	287
N.Y. Giants	4	8	0	.333	297	388
Pittsburgh	4	8	0	.333	200	243
Boston	3	9	0	.250	174	372

WESTERN DIVISION

	W	L	T	Pct.	Pts.	OP
Chi. Cardinals	11	1	0	.917	395	226
Chi. Bears	10	2	0	.833	375	151
Los Angeles	6	5	1	.545	327	269
Green Bay	3	9	0	.250	154	290
Detroit	2	10	0	.167	200	407

NFL championship: PHILADELPHIA 7, Chi. Cardinals 0

1947

EASTERN DIVISION

	W	L	T	Pct.	Pts.	OP
Philadelphia	8	4	0	.667	308	242
Pittsburgh	8	4	0	.667	240	259
Boston	4	7	1	.364	168	256
Washington	4	8	0	.333	295	367
N.Y. Giants	2	8	2	.200	190	309

WESTERN DIVISION

	W	L	T	Pct.	Pts.	OP
Chi. Cardinals	9	3	0	.750	306	231
Chi. Bears	8	4	0	.667	363	241
Green Bay	6	5	1	.545	274	210
Los Angeles	6	6	0	.500	259	214
Detroit	3	9	0	.250	231	305

Eastern Division playoff: Philadelphia 21, PITTSBURGH 0

NFL championship: CHI. CARDINALS 28, Philadelphia 21

1946

EASTERN DIVISION

	W	L	T	Pct.	Pts.	OP
N.Y. Giants	7	3	1	.700	236	162
Philadelphia	6	5	0	.545	231	220
Washington	5	5	1	.500	171	191
Pittsburgh	5	5	1	.500	136	117
Boston	2	8	1	.200	189	273

WESTERN DIVISION

	W	L	T	Pct.	Pts.	OP
Chi. Bears	8	2	1	.800	289	193
Los Angeles	6	4	1	.600	277	257
Green Bay	6	5	0	.545	148	158
Chi. Cardinals	6	5	0	.545	260	198
Detroit	1	10	0	.091	142	310

NFL championship: Chi. Bears 24, N.Y. GIANTS 14

1945

EASTERN DIVISION

	W	L	T	Pct.	Pts.	OP
Washington	8	2	0	.800	209	121
Philadelphia	7	3	0	.700	272	133
N.Y. Giants	3	6	1	.333	179	198
Boston	3	6	1	.333	123	211
Pittsburgh	2	8	0	.200	79	220

WESTERN DIVISION

	W	L	T	Pct.	Pts.	OP
Cleveland	9	1	0	.900	244	136
Detroit	7	3	0	.700	195	194
Green Bay	6	4	0	.600	258	173
Chi. Bears	3	7	0	.300	192	235
Chi. Cardinals	1	9	0	.100	98	228

NFL championship: CLEVELAND 15, Washington 14

1944

EASTERN DIVISION

	W	L	T	Pct.	Pts.	OP
N.Y. Giants	8	1	1	.889	206	75
Philadelphia	7	1	2	.875	267	131
Washington	6	3	1	.667	169	180
Boston	2	8	0	.200	82	233
Brooklyn	0	10	0	.000	69	166

WESTERN DIVISION

	W	L	T	Pct.	Pts.	OP
Green Bay	8	2	0	.800	238	141
Chi. Bears	6	3	1	.667	258	172
Detroit	6	3	1	.667	216	151
Cleveland	4	6	0	.400	188	224
Card-Pitt	0	10	0	.000	108	328

NFL championship: Green Bay 14, N.Y. GIANTS 7

1943

EASTERN DIVISION

	W	L	T	Pct.	Pts.	OP
Washington	6	3	1	.667	229	137
N.Y. Giants	6	3	1	.667	197	170
Phil-Pitt	5	4	1	.556	225	230
Brooklyn	2	8	0	.200	65	234

WESTERN DIVISION

	W	L	T	Pct.	Pts.	OP
Chi. Bears	8	1	1	.889	303	157
Green Bay	7	2	1	.778	264	172
Detroit	3	6	1	.333	178	218
Chi. Cardinals	0	10	0	.000	95	238

Eastern Division playoff: Washington 28, N.Y. GIANTS 0

NFL championship: CHI. BEARS 41, Washington 21

1942

EASTERN DIVISION

	W	L	T	Pct.	Pts.	OP
Washington	10	1	0	.909	227	102
Pittsburgh	7	4	0	.636	167	119
N.Y. Giants	5	5	1	.500	155	139
Brooklyn	3	8	0	.273	100	168
Philadelphia	2	9	0	.182	134	239

WESTERN DIVISION

	W	L	T	Pct.	Pts.	OP
Chi. Bears	11	0	0	1.000	376	84
Green Bay	8	2	1	.800	300	215
Cleveland	5	6	0	.455	150	207
Chi. Cardinals	3	8	0	.273	98	209
Detroit	0	11	0	.000	38	263

NFL championship: WASHINGTON 14, Chi. Bears 6

PAST STANDINGS

1941

EASTERN DIVISION

	W	L	T	Pct.	Pts.	OP
N.Y. Giants	8	3	0	.727	238	114
Brooklyn	7	4	0	.636	158	127
Washington	6	5	0	.545	176	174
Philadelphia	2	8	1	.200	119	218
Pittsburgh	1	9	1	.100	103	276

WESTERN DIVISION

	W	L	T	Pct.	Pts.	OP
Chi. Bears	10	1	0	.909	396	147
Green Bay	10	1	0	.909	258	120
Detroit	4	6	1	.400	121	195
Chi. Cardinals	3	7	1	.300	127	197
Cleveland	2	9	0	.182	116	244

Western Division playoff: CHI. BEARS 33, Green Bay 14
NFL championship: CHI. BEARS 37, N.Y. Giants 9

1940

EASTERN DIVISION

	W	L	T	Pct.	Pts.	OP
Washington	9	2	0	.818	245	142
Brooklyn	8	3	0	.727	186	120
N.Y. Giants	6	4	1	.600	131	133
Pittsburgh	2	7	2	.222	60	178
Philadelphia	1	10	0	.091	111	211

WESTERN DIVISION

	W	L	T	Pct.	Pts.	OP
Chi. Bears	8	3	0	.727	238	152
Green Bay	6	4	1	.600	238	155
Detroit	5	5	1	.500	138	153
Cleveland	4	6	1	.400	171	191
Chi. Cardinals	2	7	2	.222	139	222

NFL championship: Chi. Bears 73, WASHINGTON 0

1939

EASTERN DIVISION

	W	L	T	Pct.	Pts.	OP
N.Y. Giants	9	1	1	.900	168	85
Washington	8	2	1	.800	242	94
Brooklyn	4	6	1	.400	108	219
Philadelphia	1	9	1	.100	105	200
Pittsburgh	1	9	1	.100	114	216

WESTERN DIVISION

	W	L	T	Pct.	Pts.	OP
Green Bay	9	2	0	.818	233	153
Chi. Bears	8	3	0	.727	298	157
Detroit	6	5	0	.545	145	150
Cleveland	5	5	1	.500	195	164
Chi. Cardinals	1	10	0	.091	84	254

NFL championship: GREEN BAY 27, N.Y. Giants 0

1938

EASTERN DIVISION

	W	L	T	Pct.	Pts.	OP
N.Y. Giants	8	2	1	.800	194	79
Washington	6	3	2	.667	148	154
Brooklyn	4	4	3	.500	131	161
Philadelphia	5	6	0	.455	154	164
Pittsburgh	2	9	0	.182	79	169

WESTERN DIVISION

	W	L	T	Pct.	Pts.	OP
Green Bay	8	3	0	.727	223	118
Detroit	7	4	0	.636	119	108
Chi. Bears	6	5	0	.545	194	148
Cleveland	4	7	0	.364	131	215
Chi. Cardinals	2	9	0	.182	111	168

NFL championship: N.Y. GIANTS 23, Green Bay 17

1937

EASTERN DIVISION

	W	L	T	Pct.	Pts.	OP
Washington	8	3	0	.727	195	120
N.Y. Giants	6	3	2	.667	128	109
Pittsburgh	4	7	0	.364	122	145
Brooklyn	3	7	1	.300	82	174
Philadelphia	2	8	1	.200	86	177

WESTERN DIVISION

	W	L	T	Pct.	Pts.	OP
Chi. Bears	9	1	1	.900	201	100
Green Bay	7	4	0	.636	220	122
Detroit	7	4	0	.636	180	105
Chi. Cardinals	5	5	1	.500	135	165
Cleveland	1	10	0	.091	75	207

NFL championship: Washington 28, CHI. BEARS 21

1936

EASTERN DIVISION

	W	L	T	Pct.	Pts.	OP
Boston	7	5	0	.583	149	110
Pittsburgh	6	6	0	.500	98	187
N.Y. Giants	5	6	1	.455	115	163
Brooklyn	3	8	1	.273	92	161
Philadelphia	1	11	0	.083	51	206

WESTERN DIVISION

	W	L	T	Pct.	Pts.	OP
Green Bay	10	1	1	.909	248	118
Chi. Bears	9	3	0	.750	222	94
Detroit	8	4	0	.667	235	102
Chi. Cardinals	3	8	1	.273	74	143

NFL championship: Green Bay 21, Boston 6, at Polo Grounds, N.Y.

1935

EASTERN DIVISION

	W	L	T	Pct.	Pts.	OP
N. Y. Giants	9	3	0	.750	180	96
Brooklyn	5	6	1	.455	90	141
Pittsburgh	4	8	0	.333	100	209
Boston	2	8	1	.200	65	123
Philadelphia	2	9	0	.182	60	179

WESTERN DIVISION

	W	L	T	Pct.	Pts.	OP
Detroit	7	3	2	.700	191	111
Green Bay	8	4	0	.667	181	96
Chi. Bears	6	4	2	.600	192	106
Chi. Cardinals	6	4	2	.600	99	97

NFL championship: DETROIT 26, N.Y. Giants 7
One game between Boston and Philadelphia was canceled.

1934

EASTERN DIVISION

	W	L	T	Pct.	Pts.	OP
N.Y. Giants	8	5	0	.615	147	107
Boston	6	6	0	.500	107	94
Brooklyn	4	7	0	.364	61	153
Philadelphia	4	7	0	.364	127	85
Pittsburgh	2	10	0	.167	51	206

WESTERN DIVISION

	W	L	T	Pct.	Pts.	OP
Chi. Bears	13	0	0	1.000	286	86
Detroit	10	3	0	.769	238	59
Green Bay	7	6	0	.538	156	112
Chi. Cardinals	5	6	0	.455	80	84
St. Louis	1	2	0	.333	27	61
Cincinnati	0	8	0	.000	10	243

NFL championship: N.Y. GIANTS 30, Chi. Bears 13

1933

EASTERN DIVISION

	W	L	T	Pct.	Pts.	OP
N.Y. Giants	11	3	0	.786	244	101
Brooklyn	5	4	1	.556	93	54
Boston	5	5	2	.500	103	97
Philadelphia	3	5	1	.375	77	158
Pittsburgh	3	6	2	.333	67	208

WESTERN DIVISION

	W	L	T	Pct.	Pts.	OP
Chi. Bears	10	2	1	.833	133	82
Portsmouth	6	5	0	.545	128	87
Green Bay	5	7	1	.417	170	107
Cincinnati	3	6	1	.333	38	110
Chi. Cardinals	1	9	1	.100	52	101

NFL championship: CHI. BEARS 23, N.Y. Giants 21

1932

	W	L	T	Pct.
Chicago Bears	7	1	6	.875
Green Bay Packers	10	3	1	.769
Portsmouth Spartans	6	2	4	.750
Boston Braves	4	4	2	.500
New York Giants	4	6	2	.400
Brooklyn Dodgers	3	9	0	.250
Chicago Cardinals	2	6	2	.250
Staten Island Stapletons	2	7	3	.222

Chicago Bears and Portsmouth finished regularly scheduled games tied for first place. Bears won playoff game, which counted in standings, 9-0.

1931

	W	L	T	Pct.
Green Bay Packers	12	2	0	.857
Portsmouth Spartans	11	3	0	.786
Chicago Bears	8	5	0	.615
Chicago Cardinals	5	4	0	.556
New York Giants	7	6	1	.538
Providence Steam Roller	4	4	3	.500
Staten Island Stapletons	4	6	1	.400
Cleveland Indians	2	8	0	.200
Brooklyn Dodgers	2	12	0	.143
Frankford Yellow Jackets	1	6	1	.143

1930

	W	L	T	Pct.
Green Bay Packers	10	3	1	.769
New York Giants	13	4	0	.765
Chicago Bears	9	4	1	.692
Brooklyn Dodgers	7	4	1	.636
Providence Steam Roller	6	4	1	.600
Staten Island Stapletons	5	5	2	.500
Chicago Cardinals	5	6	2	.455
Portsmouth Spartans	5	6	3	.455
Frankford Yellow Jackets	4	13	1	.222
Minneapolis Red Jackets	1	7	1	.125
Newark Tornadoes	1	10	1	.091

1929

	W	L	T	Pct.
Green Bay Packers	12	0	1	1.000
New York Giants	13	1	1	.929
Frankford Yellow Jackets	9	4	5	.692
Chicago Cardinals	6	6	1	.500
Boston Bulldogs	4	4	0	.500
Orange Tornadoes	3	4	4	.429
Staten Island Stapletons	3	4	3	.429
Providence Steam Roller	4	6	2	.400
Chicago Bears	4	9	2	.308
Buffalo Bisons	1	7	1	.125
Minneapolis Red Jackets	1	9	0	.100
Dayton Triangles	0	6	0	.000

1928

	W	L	T	Pct.
Providence Steam Roller	8	1	2	.889
Frankford Yellow Jackets	11	3	2	.786
Detroit Wolverines	7	2	1	.778
Green Bay Packers	6	4	3	.600
Chicago Bears	7	5	1	.583
New York Giants	4	7	2	.364
New York Yankees	4	8	1	.333
Pottsville Maroons	2	8	0	.200
Chicago Cardinals	1	5	0	.167
Dayton Triangles	0	7	0	.000

1927

	W	L	T	Pct.
New York Giants	11	1	1	.917
Green Bay Packers	7	2	1	.778
Chicago Bears	9	3	2	.750
Cleveland Bulldogs	8	4	1	.667
Providence Steam Roller	8	5	1	.615
New York Yankees	7	8	1	.467
Frankford Yellow Jackets	6	9	3	.400
Pottsville Maroons	5	8	0	.385
Chicago Cardinals	3	7	1	.300
Dayton Triangles	1	6	1	.143
Duluth Eskimos	1	8	0	.111
Buffalo Bisons	0	5	0	.000

1926

	W	L	T	Pct.
Frankford Yellow Jackets	14	1	1	.933
Chicago Bears	12	1	3	.923
Pottsville Maroons	10	2	1	.833
Kansas City Cowboys	8	3	0	.727
Green Bay Packers	7	3	3	.700
Los Angeles Buccaneers	6	3	1	.667
New York Giants	8	4	1	.667
Duluth Eskimos	6	5	3	.545
Buffalo Rangers	4	4	2	.500
Chicago Cardinals	5	6	1	.455
Providence Steam Roller	5	7	1	.417
Detroit Panthers	4	6	2	.400
Hartford Blues	3	7	0	.300
Brooklyn Lions	3	8	0	.273
Milwaukee Badgers	2	7	0	.222
Akron Pros	1	4	3	.200
Dayton Triangles	1	4	1	.200
Racine Tornadoes	1	4	0	.200
Columbus Tigers	1	6	0	.143
Canton Bulldogs	1	9	3	.100
Hammond Pros	0	4	0	.000
Louisville Colonels	0	4	0	.000

1925

	W	L	T	Pct.
Chicago Cardinals	11	2	1	.846
Pottsville Maroons	10	2	0	.833
Detroit Panthers	8	2	2	.800
New York Giants	8	4	0	.667
Akron Indians	4	2	2	.667
Frankford Yellow Jackets	13	7	0	.650
Chicago Bears	9	5	3	.643
Rock Island Independents	5	3	3	.625
Green Bay Packers	8	5	0	.615
Providence Steam Roller	6	5	1	.545
Canton Bulldogs	4	4	0	.500
Cleveland Bulldogs	5	8	1	.385
Kansas City Cowboys	2	5	1	.286
Hammond Pros	1	4	0	.200
Buffalo Bisons	1	6	2	.143
Duluth Kelleys	0	3	0	.000
Rochester Jeffersons	0	6	1	.000
Milwaukee Badgers	0	6	0	.000
Dayton Triangles	0	7	1	.000
Columbus Tigers	0	9	0	.000

1924

	W	L	T	Pct.
Cleveland Bulldogs	7	1	1	.875
Chicago Bears	6	1	4	.857
Frankford Yellow Jackets	11	2	1	.846
Duluth Kelleys	5	1	0	.833
Rock Island Independents	6	2	2	.750
Green Bay Packers	7	4	0	.636
Racine Legion	4	3	3	.571
Chicago Cardinals	5	4	1	.556
Buffalo Bisons	6	5	0	.545
Columbus Tigers	4	4	0	.500
Hammond Pros	2	2	1	.500
Milwaukee Badgers	5	8	0	.385
Akron Indians	2	6	0	.250
Dayton Triangles	2	6	0	.250
Kansas City Blues	2	7	0	.222
Kenosha Maroons	0	5	1	.000
Minneapolis Marines	0	6	0	.000
Rochester Jeffersons	0	7	0	.000

1923

	W	L	T	Pct.
Canton Bulldogs	11	0	1	1.000
Chicago Bears	9	2	1	.818
Green Bay Packers	7	2	1	.778
Milwaukee Badgers	7	2	3	.778
Cleveland Indians	3	1	3	.750
Chicago Cardinals	8	4	0	.667
Duluth Kelleys	4	3	0	.571
Columbus Tigers	5	4	1	.556
Buffalo All-Americans	4	4	3	.500
Racine Legion	4	4	2	.500
Toledo Maroons	2	3	2	.400
Rock Island Independents	2	3	3	.400
Minneapolis Marines	2	5	2	.286
St. Louis All-Stars	1	4	2	.200
Hammond Pros	1	5	1	.167
Dayton Triangles	1	6	1	.143
Akron Indians	1	6	0	.143
Oorang Indians	1	10	0	.091
Rochester Jeffersons	0	2	0	.000
Louisville Brecks	0	3	0	.000

1922

	W	L	T	Pct.
Canton Bulldogs	10	0	2	1.000
Chicago Bears	9	3	0	.750
Chicago Cardinals	8	3	0	.727
Toledo Maroons	5	2	2	.714
Rock Island Independents	4	2	1	.667
Racine Legion	6	4	1	.600
Dayton Triangles	4	3	1	.571
Green Bay Packers	4	3	3	.571
Buffalo All-Americans	5	4	1	.556
Akron Pros	3	5	2	.375
Milwaukee Badgers	2	4	3	.333
Oorang Indians	2	6	0	.250
Minneapolis Marines	1	3	0	.250
Louisville Brecks	1	3	0	.250
Evansville Crimson Giants	0	3	0	.000
Rochester Jeffersons	0	4	1	.000
Hammond Pros	0	5	1	.000
Columbus Panhandles	0	7	0	.000

1921

	W	L	T	Pct.
Chicago Staleys	9	1	1	.900
Buffalo All-Americans	9	1	2	.900
Akron Pros	8	3	1	.727
Canton Bulldogs	5	2	3	.714
Rock Island Independents	4	2	1	.667
Evansville Crimson Giants	3	2	0	.600
Green Bay Packers	3	2	1	.600
Dayton Triangles	4	4	1	.500
Chicago Cardinals	3	3	2	.500
Rochester Jeffersons	2	3	0	.400
Cleveland Indians	3	5	0	.375
Washington Senators	1	2	0	.333
Cincinnati Celts	1	3	0	.250
Hammond Pros	1	3	1	.250
Minneapolis Marines	1	3	1	.250
Detroit Heralds	1	5	1	.167
Columbus Panhandles	1	8	0	.111
Tonawanda Kardex	0	1	0	.000
Muncie Flyers	0	2	0	.000
Louisville Brecks	0	2	0	.000
New York Giants	0	2	0	.000

1920*

	W	L	T	Pct.
Akron Pros	8	0	3	1.000
Decatur Staleys	10	1	2	.909
Buffalo All-Americans	9	1	1	.900
Chicago Cardinals	6	2	2	.750
Rock Island Independents	6	2	2	.750
Dayton Triangles	5	2	2	.714
Rochester Jeffersons	6	3	2	.667
Canton Bulldogs	7	4	2	.636
Detroit Heralds	2	3	3	.400
Cleveland Tigers	2	4	2	.333
Chicago Tigers	2	5	1	.286
Hammond Pros	2	5	0	.286
Columbus Panhandles	2	6	2	.250
Muncie Flyers	0	1	0	.000

**No official standing was maintained for the 1920 season, and the championship was awarded to the Akron Pros in a League meeting on April 30, 1921. Clubs played schedules which included games against non-league opponents. Records of clubs against all opponents are listed above.*

ALL-TIME TEAM VS. TEAM RESULTS

RS=REGULAR SEASON
PS=POSTSEASON
***ARIZONA vs. ATLANTA**
RS: Cardinals lead series, 11-6
1966—Falcons, 16-10 (A)
1968—Cardinals, 17-12 (StL)
1971—Cardinals, 26-9 (A)
1973—Cardinals, 32-10 (A)
1975—Cardinals, 23-20 (StL)
1978—Cardinals, 42-21 (StL)
1980—Falcons, 33-27 (StL) OT
1981—Falcons, 41-20 (A)
1982—Cardinals, 23-20 (A)
1986—Falcons, 33-13 (A)
1987—Cardinals, 34-21 (A)
1989—Cardinals, 34-20 (P)
1990—Cardinals, 24-13 (A)
1991—Cardinals, 16-10 (P)
1992—Falcons, 20-17 (A)
1993—Cardinals, 27-10 (A)
1994—Falcons, 10-6 (Atl)
(RS Pts.—Cardinals 391, Falcons 319)
**Franchise known as Phoenix prior to 1994 and in St. Louis prior to 1988*
***ARIZONA vs. BUFFALO**
RS: Series tied, 3-3
1971—Cardinals, 28-23 (B)
1975—Bills, 32-14 (StL)
1981—Cardinals, 24-0 (StL)
1984—Cardinals, 37-7 (StL)
1986—Bills, 17-10 (B)
1990—Bills, 45-14 (B)
(RS Pts.—Cardinals 127, Bills 124)
**Franchise known as Phoenix prior to 1994 and in St. Louis prior to 1988*
***ARIZONA vs. **CHICAGO**
RS: Bears lead series, 52-25-6
(NP denotes Normal Park;
Wr denotes Wrigley Field;
Co denotes Comiskey Park;
So denotes Soldier Field;
all Chicago)
1920—Cardinals, 7-6 (NP)
Staleys, 10-0 (Wr)
1921—Tie, 0-0 (Wr)
1922—Cardinals, 6-0 (Co)
Cardinals, 9-0 (Co)
1923—Bears, 3-0 (Wr)
1924—Bears, 6-0 (Wr)
Bears, 21-0 (Co)
1925—Cardinals, 9-0 (Co)
Tie, 0-0 (Wr)
1926—Bears, 16-0 (Wr)
Bears, 10-0 (So)
Tie, 0-0 (Wr)
1927—Bears, 9-0 (NP)
Cardinals, 3-0 (Wr)
1928—Bears, 15-0 (NP)
Bears, 34-0 (Wr)
1929—Tie, 0-0 (Wr)
Cardinals, 40-6 (Co)
1930—Bears, 32-6 (Co)
Bears, 6-0 (Wr)
1931—Bears, 26-13 (Wr)
Bears, 18-7 (Wr)
1932—Tie, 0-0 (Wr)
Bears, 34-0 (Wr)
1933—Bears, 12-9 (Wr)
Bears, 22-6 (Wr)
1934—Bears, 20-0 (Wr)
Bears, 17-6 (Wr)
1935—Tie, 7-7 (Wr)
Bears, 13-0 (Wr)
1936—Bears, 7-3 (Wr)
Cardinals, 14-7 (Wr)
1937—Bears, 16-7 (Wr)
Bears, 42-28 (Wr)
1938—Bears, 16-13 (So)
Bears, 34-28 (Wr)
1939—Bears, 44-7 (Wr)
Bears, 48-7 (Co)
1940—Cardinals, 21-7 (Co)
Bears, 31-23 (Wr)
1941—Bears, 53-7 (Wr)
Bears, 34-24 (Co)
1942—Bears, 41-14 (Wr)
Bears, 21-7 (Co)
1943—Bears, 20-0 (Wr)
Bears, 35-24 (Co)
1945—Cardinals, 16-7 (Wr)
Bears, 28-20 (Co)
1946—Bears, 34-17 (Co)
Cardinals, 35-28 (Wr)
1947—Cardinals, 31-7 (Co)
Cardinals, 30-21 (Wr)
1948—Bears, 28-17 (Co)
Cardinals, 24-21 (Wr)
1949—Bears, 17-7 (Co)
Bears, 52-21 (Wr)
1950—Bears, 27-6 (Wr)
Cardinals, 20-10 (Co)
1951—Cardinals, 28-14 (Co)
Cardinals, 24-14 (Wr)
1952—Cardinals, 21-10 (Co)
Bears, 10-7 (Wr)
1953—Cardinals, 24-17 (Wr)
1954—Bears, 29-7 (Co)
1955—Cardinals, 53-14 (Co)
1956—Bears, 10-3 (Wr)
1957—Bears, 14-6 (Co)
1958—Bears, 30-14 (Wr)
1959—Bears, 31-7 (So)
1965—Bears, 34-13 (Wr)
1966—Cardinals, 24-17 (StL)
1967—Bears, 30-3 (Wr)
1969—Cardinals, 20-17 (StL)
1972—Bears, 27-10 (StL)
1975—Cardinals, 34-20 (So)
1977—Cardinals, 16-13 (StL)
1978—Bears, 17-10 (So)
1979—Bears, 42-6 (So)
1982—Cardinals, 10-7 (So)
1984—Cardinals, 38-21 (StL)
1990—Bears, 31-21 (P)
1994—Bears, 19-16 (A) OT
(RS Pts.—Bears 1,567, Cardinals 1,014)
**Franchise known as Phoenix prior to 1994, in St. Louis prior to 1988, and in Chicago prior to 1960*
***Franchise in Decatur prior to 1921 and known as Staleys prior to 1922*
***ARIZONA vs. CINCINNATI**
RS: Bengals lead series, 3-2
1973—Bengals, 42-24 (C)
1979—Bengals, 34-28 (C)
1985—Cardinals, 41-27 (StL)
1988—Bengals, 21-14 (C)
1994—Cardinals, 28-7 (A)
(RS Pts.—Cardinals 135, Bengals 131)
**Franchise known as Phoenix prior to 1994 and in St. Louis prior to 1988*
***ARIZONA vs. CLEVELAND**
RS: Browns lead series, 32-10-3
1950—Browns, 34-24 (Cle)
Browns, 10-7 (Chi)
1951—Browns, 34-17 (Chi)
Browns, 49-28 (Cle)
1952—Browns, 28-13 (Cle)
Browns, 10-0 (Chi)
1953—Browns, 27-7 (Chi)
Browns, 27-16 (Cle)
1954—Browns, 31-7 (Cle)
Browns, 35-3 (Chi)
1955—Browns, 26-20 (Chi)
Browns, 35-24 (Cle)
1956—Cardinals, 9-7 (Chi)
Cardinals, 24-7 (Cle)
1957—Browns, 17-7 (Chi)
Browns, 31-0 (Cle)
1958—Browns, 35-28 (Cle)
Browns, 38-24 (Chi)
1959—Browns, 34-7 (Chi)
Browns, 17-7 (Cle)
1960—Browns, 28-27 (Cle)
Tie, 17-17 (StL)
1961—Browns, 20-17 (Cle)
Browns, 21-10 (StL)
1962—Browns, 34-7 (StL)
Browns, 38-14 (Cle)
1963—Cardinals, 20-14 (Cle)
Browns, 24-10 (StL)
1964—Tie, 33-33 (Cle)
Cardinals, 28-19 (StL)
1965—Cardinals, 49-13 (Cle)
Browns, 27-24 (StL)
1966—Cardinals, 34-28 (Cle)
Browns, 38-10 (StL)
1967—Browns, 20-16 (Cle)
Browns, 20-16 (StL)
1968—Cardinals, 27-21 (Cle)
Cardinals, 27-16 (StL)
1969—Tie, 21-21 (Cle)
Browns, 27-21 (StL)
1974—Cardinals, 29-7 (StL)
1979—Browns, 38-20 (StL)
1985—Cardinals, 27-24 (Cle) OT
1988—Browns, 29-21 (P)
1994—Browns, 32-0 (Cle)
(RS Pts.—Browns 1,141, Cardinals 797)
**Franchise known as Phoenix prior to 1994, in St. Louis prior to 1988, and in Chicago prior to 1960*
***ARIZONA vs. DALLAS**
RS: Cowboys lead series, 42-22-1
1960—Cardinals, 12-10 (StL)
1961—Cardinals, 31-17 (D)
Cardinals, 31-13 (StL)
1962—Cardinals, 28-24 (D)
Cardinals, 52-20 (StL)
1963—Cardinals, 34-7 (D)
Cowboys, 28-24 (StL)
1964—Cardinals, 16-6 (D)
Cowboys, 31-13 (StL)
1965—Cardinals, 20-13 (StL)
Cowboys, 27-13 (D)
1966—Tie, 10-10 (StL)
Cowboys, 31-17 (D)
1967—Cowboys, 46-21 (D)
1968—Cowboys, 27-10 (StL)
1969—Cowboys, 24-3 (D)
1970—Cardinals, 20-7 (StL)
Cardinals, 38-0 (D)
1971—Cowboys, 16-13 (StL)
Cowboys, 31-12 (D)
1972—Cowboys, 33-24 (D)
Cowboys, 27-6 (StL)
1973—Cowboys, 45-10 (D)
Cowboys, 30-3 (StL)
1974—Cardinals, 31-28 (StL)
Cowboys, 17-14 (D)
1975—Cowboys, 37-31 (D) OT
Cardinals, 31-17 (StL)
1976—Cardinals, 21-17 (StL)
Cowboys, 19-14 (D)
1977—Cowboys, 30-24 (StL)
Cardinals, 24-17 (D)
1978—Cowboys, 21-12 (D)
Cowboys, 24-21 (StL) OT
1979—Cowboys, 22-21 (StL)
Cowboys, 22-13 (D)
1980—Cowboys, 27-24 (StL)
Cowboys, 31-21 (D)
1981—Cowboys, 30-17 (D)
Cardinals, 20-17 (StL)
1982—Cowboys, 24-7 (StL)
1983—Cowboys, 34-17 (StL)
Cowboys, 35-17 (D)
1984—Cardinals, 31-20 (D)
Cowboys, 24-17 (StL)
1985—Cardinals, 21-10 (StL)
Cowboys, 35-17 (D)
1986—Cowboys, 31-7 (StL)
Cowboys, 37-6 (D)
1987—Cardinals, 24-13 (StL)
Cowboys, 21-16 (D)
1988—Cowboys, 17-14 (P)
Cardinals, 16-10 (D)
1989—Cardinals, 19-10 (D)
Cardinals, 24-20 (P)
1990—Cardinals, 20-3 (P)
Cowboys, 41-10 (D)
1991—Cowboys, 17-9 (P)
Cowboys, 27-7 (D)
1992—Cowboys, 31-20 (D)
Cowboys, 16-10 (P)
1993—Cowboys, 17-10 (P)
Cowboys, 20-15 (D)
1994—Cowboys, 38-3 (D)
Cowboys, 28-21 (A)
(RS Pts.—Cowboys 1,478, Cardinals 1,178)
**Franchise known as Phoenix prior to 1994 and in St. Louis prior to 1988*
***ARIZONA vs. DENVER**
RS: Broncos lead series, 3-0-1
1973—Tie, 17-17 (StL)
1977—Broncos, 7-0 (D)
1989—Broncos, 37-0 (P)
1991—Broncos, 24-19 (D)
(RS Pts.—Broncos 85, Cardinals 36)
**Franchise known as Phoenix prior to 1994 and in St. Louis prior to 1988*
***ARIZONA vs. **DETROIT**
RS: Lions lead series, 27-16-5
1930—Tie, 0-0 (Port)
Cardinals, 23-0 (C)
1931—Cardinals, 20-19 (C)
1932—Tie, 7-7 (Port)
1933—Spartans, 7-6 (Port)
1934—Lions, 6-0 (D)
Lions, 17-13 (C)
1935—Tie, 10-10 (D)
Lions, 7-6 (C)
1936—Lions, 39-0 (D)
Lions, 14-7 (C)
1937—Lions, 16-7 (C)
Lions, 16-7 (D)
1938—Lions, 10-0 (D)
Lions, 7-3 (C)
1939—Lions, 21-3 (D)
Lions, 17-3 (C)
1940—Tie, 0-0 (Buffalo)
Lions, 43-14 (C)
1941—Tie, 14-14 (C)
Lions, 21-3 (D)
1942—Cardinals, 13-0 (C)
Cardinals, 7-0 (D)
1943—Lions, 35-17 (D)
Lions, 7-0 (Buffalo)
1945—Lions, 10-0 (C)
Lions, 26-0 (D)
1946—Cardinals, 34-14 (C)
Cardinals, 36-14 (D)
1947—Cardinals, 45-21 (C)
Cardinals, 17-7 (D)
1948—Cardinals, 56-20 (C)
Cardinals, 28-14 (D)
1949—Lions, 24-7 (C)
Cardinals, 42-19 (D)
1959—Lions, 45-21 (D)
1961—Lions, 45-14 (StL)
1967—Cardinals, 38-28 (StL)
1969—Lions, 20-0 (D)
1970—Lions, 16-3 (D)
1973—Lions, 20-16 (StL)
1975—Cardinals, 24-13 (D)
1978—Cardinals, 21-14 (StL)
1980—Lions, 20-7 (D)
Cardinals, 24-23 (StL)
1989—Cardinals, 16-13 (D)
1993—Lions, 26-20 (D)
Lions, 21-14 (Phx)
(RS Pts.—Lions 806, Cardinals 676)
**Franchise known as Phoenix prior to 1994, in St. Louis prior to 1988, and in Chicago prior to 1960*
***Franchise in Portsmouth prior to 1934 and known as the Spartans*
***ARIZONA vs. GREEN BAY**
RS: Packers lead series, 39-21-4
PS: Packers lead series, 1-0
1921—Tie, 3-3 (C)
1922—Cardinals, 16-3 (C)

1924—Cardinals, 3-0 (C)
1925—Cardinals, 9-6 (C)
1926—Cardinals, 13-7 (GB)
Packers, 3-0 (C)
1927—Packers, 13-0 (GB)
Tie, 6-6 (C)
1928—Packers, 20-0 (GB)
1929—Packers, 9-2 (GB)
Packers, 7-6 (C)
Packers, 12-0 (C)
1930—Packers, 14-0 (GB)
Cardinals, 13-6 (C)
1931—Packers, 26-7 (GB)
Cardinals, 21-13 (C)
1932—Packers, 15-7 (GB)
Packers, 19-9 (C)
1933—Packers, 14-6 (C)
1934—Packers, 15-0 (GB)
Cardinals, 9-0 (Mil)
Cardinals, 6-0 (C)
1935—Cardinals, 7-6 (GB)
Cardinals, 3-0 (Mil)
Cardinals, 9-7 (C)
1936—Packers, 10-7 (GB)
Packers, 24-0 (Mil)
Tie, 0-0 (C)
1937—Cardinals, 14-7 (GB)
Packers, 34-13 (Mil)
1938—Packers, 28-7 (Mil)
Packers, 24-22 (Buffalo)
1939—Packers, 14-10 (GB)
Packers, 27-20 (Mil)
1940—Packers, 31-6 (Mil)
Packers, 28-7 (C)
1941—Packers, 14-13 (Mil)
Packers, 17-9 (GB)
1942—Packers, 17-13 (C)
Packers, 55-24 (GB)
1943—Packers, 28-7 (C)
Packers, 35-14 (Mil)
1945—Packers, 33-14 (GB)
1946—Packers, 19-7 (C)
Cardinals, 24-6 (GB)
1947—Cardinals, 14-10 (GB)
Cardinals, 21-20 (C)
1948—Cardinals, 17-7 (Mil)
Cardinals, 42-7 (C)
1949—Cardinals, 39-17 (Mil)
Cardinals, 41-21 (C)
1955—Packers, 31-14 (GB)
1956—Packers, 24-21 (C)
1962—Packers, 17-0 (Mil)
1963—Packers, 30-7 (StL)
1967—Packers, 31-23 (StL)
1969—Packers, 45-28 (GB)
1971—Tie, 16-16 (StL)
1973—Packers, 25-21 (GB)
1976—Cardinals, 29-0 (StL)
1982—**Packers, 41-16 (GB)
1984—Packers, 24-23 (GB)
1985—Cardinals, 43-28 (StL)
1988—Packers, 26-17 (P)
1990—Packers, 24-21 (P)
(RS Pts.—Packers 1,078, Cardinals 823)
(PS Pts.—Packers 41, Cardinals 16)
Franchise known as Phoenix prior to 1994, in St. Louis prior to 1988, and in Chicago prior to 1960
***NFC First-Round Playoff*

***ARIZONA vs. HOUSTON**
RS: Cardinals lead series, 4-2
1970—Cardinals, 44-0 (StL)
1974—Cardinals, 31-27 (H)
1979—Cardinals, 24-17 (H)
1985—Oilers, 20-10 (StL)
1988—Oilers, 38-20 (H)
1994—Cardinals, 30-12 (H)
(RS Pts.—Cardinals 159, Oilers 114)
Franchise known as Phoenix prior to 1994 and in St. Louis prior to 1988

***ARIZONA vs. **INDIANAPOLIS**
RS: Cardinals lead series, 6-5
1961—Colts, 16-0 (B)
1964—Colts, 47-27 (B)
1968—Colts, 27-0 (B)
1972—Cardinals, 10-3 (B)
1976—Cardinals, 24-17 (StL)
1978—Colts, 30-17 (StL)
1980—Cardinals, 17-10 (B)
1981—Cardinals, 35-24 (B)
1984—Cardinals, 34-33 (I)
1990—Cardinals, 20-17 (P)
1992—Colts, 16-13 (I)
(RS Pts.—Colts 240, Cardinals 197)
Franchise known as Phoenix prior to 1994 and in St. Louis prior to 1988
***Franchise in Baltimore prior to 1984*

***ARIZONA vs. KANSAS CITY**
RS: Chiefs lead series, 3-1-1
1970—Tie, 6-6 (KC)
1974—Chiefs, 17-13 (StL)
1980—Chiefs, 21-13 (StL)
1983—Chiefs, 38-14 (KC)
1986—Cardinals, 23-14 (StL)
(RS Pts.—Chiefs 96, Cardinals 69)
Franchise known as Phoenix prior to 1994 and in St. Louis prior to 1988

***ARIZONA vs. **LOS ANGELES**
RS: Raiders lead series, 2-1
1973—Raiders, 17-10 (StL)
1983—Cardinals, 34-24 (LA)
1989—Raiders, 16-14 (LA)
(RS Pts.—Cardinals 58, Raiders 57)
Franchise known as Phoenix prior to 1994 and in St. Louis prior to 1988
***Franchise in Oakland prior to 1982*

***ARIZONA vs. MIAMI**
RS: Dolphins lead series, 6-0
1972—Dolphins, 31-10 (M)
1977—Dolphins, 55-14 (StL)
1978—Dolphins, 24-10 (M)
1981—Dolphins, 20-7 (StL)
1984—Dolphins, 36-28 (StL)
1990—Dolphins, 23-3 (M)
(RS Pts.—Dolphins 189, Cardinals 72)
Franchise known as Phoenix prior to 1994 and in St. Louis prior to 1988

***ARIZONA vs. MINNESOTA**
RS: Cardinals lead series, 8-4
PS: Vikings lead series, 1-0
1963—Cardinals, 56-14 (M)
1967—Cardinals, 34-24 (M)
1969—Vikings, 27-10 (StL)
1972—Cardinals, 19-17 (M)
1974—Vikings, 28-24 (StL)
**Vikings, 30-14 (M)
1977—Cardinals, 27-7 (M)
1979—Cardinals, 37-7 (StL)
1981—Cardinals, 30-17 (StL)
1983—Cardinals, 41-31 (StL)
1991—Vikings, 34-7 (M)
Vikings, 28-0 (P)
1994—Cardinals, 17-7 (A)
(RS Pts.—Cardinals 302, Vikings 241)
(PS Pts.—Vikings 30, Cardinals 14)
Franchise known as Phoenix prior to 1994 and in St. Louis prior to 1988
***NFC Divisional Playoff*

***ARIZONA vs. **NEW ENGLAND**
RS: Cardinals lead series, 6-2
1970—Cardinals, 31-0 (StL)
1975—Cardinals, 24-17 (StL)
1978—Patriots, 16-6 (StL)
1981—Cardinals, 27-20 (NE)
1984—Cardinals, 33-10 (NE)
1990—Cardinals, 34-14 (P)
1991—Cardinals, 24-10 (P)
1993—Patriots, 23-21 (P)
(RS Pts.—Cardinals 200, Patriots 110)
Franchise known as Phoenix prior to 1994 and in St. Louis prior to 1988
***Franchise in Boston prior to 1971*

***ARIZONA vs. NEW ORLEANS**
RS: Cardinals lead series, 10-9
1967—Cardinals, 31-20 (StL)
1968—Cardinals, 21-20 (NO)
Cardinals, 31-17 (StL)
1969—Saints, 51-42 (StL)
1970—Cardinals, 24-17 (StL)
1974—Saints, 14-0 (NO)
1977—Cardinals, 49-31 (StL)
1980—Cardinals, 40-7 (NO)
1981—Cardinals, 30-3 (StL)
1982—Cardinals, 21-7 (NO)
1983—Saints, 28-17 (NO)
1984—Saints, 34-24 (NO)
1985—Cardinals, 28-16 (StL)
1986—Saints, 16-7 (StL)
1987—Cardinals, 24-19 (StL)
1990—Saints, 28-7 (NO)
1991—Saints, 27-3 (P)
1992—Saints, 30-21 (P)
1993—Saints, 20-17 (P)
(RS Pts.—Cardinals 437, Saints 405)
Franchise known as Phoenix prior to 1994 and in St. Louis prior to 1988

***ARIZONA vs. N.Y. GIANTS**
RS: Giants lead series, 66-36-2
1926—Giants, 20-0 (NY)
1927—Giants, 28-7 (NY)
1929—Giants, 24-21 (NY)
1930—Giants, 25-12 (NY)
Giants, 13-7 (C)
1935—Cardinals, 14-13 (NY)
1936—Giants, 14-6 (NY)
1938—Giants, 6-0 (NY)
1939—Giants, 17-7 (NY)
1941—Cardinals, 10-7 (NY)
1942—Giants, 21-7 (NY)
1943—Giants, 24-13 (NY)
1946—Giants, 28-24 (NY)
1947—Giants, 35-31 (NY)
1948—Cardinals, 63-35 (NY)
1949—Giants, 41-38 (C)
1950—Cardinals, 17-3 (C)
Giants, 51-21 (NY)
1951—Giants, 28-17 (NY)
Giants, 10-0 (C)
1952—Cardinals, 24-23 (NY)
Giants, 28-6 (C)
1953—Giants, 21-7 (NY)
Giants, 23-20 (C)
1954—Giants, 41-10 (C)
Giants, 31-17 (NY)
1955—Cardinals, 28-17 (C)
Giants, 10-0 (NY)
1956—Cardinals, 35-27 (C)
Giants, 23-10 (NY)
1957—Giants, 27-14 (NY)
Giants, 28-21 (C)
1958—Giants, 37-7 (Buffalo)
Cardinals, 23-6 (NY)
1959—Giants, 9-3 (NY)
Giants, 30-20 (Minn)
1960—Giants, 35-14 (StL)
Cardinals, 20-13 (NY)
1961—Cardinals, 21-10 (NY)
Giants, 24-9 (StL)
1962—Giants, 31-14 (StL)
Giants, 31-28 (NY)
1963—Giants, 38-21 (StL)
Cardinals, 24-17 (NY)
1964—Giants, 34-17 (NY)
Tie, 10-10 (StL)
1965—Giants, 14-10 (NY)
Giants, 28-15 (StL)
1966—Cardinals, 24-19 (StL)
Cardinals, 20-17 (NY)
1967—Giants, 37-20 (StL)
Giants, 37-14 (NY)
1968—Cardinals, 28-21 (NY)
1969—Cardinals, 42-17 (StL)
Giants, 49-6 (NY)
1970—Giants, 35-17 (NY)
Giants, 34-17 (StL)
1971—Giants, 21-20 (StL)
Cardinals, 24-7 (NY)
1972—Giants, 27-21 (NY)
Giants, 13-7 (StL)
1973—Cardinals, 35-27 (StL)
Giants, 24-13 (New Haven)
1974—Cardinals, 23-21 (New Haven)
Cardinals, 26-14 (StL)
1975—Cardinals, 26-14 (StL)
Cardinals, 20-13 (NY)
1976—Cardinals, 27-21 (StL)
Cardinals, 17-14 (NY)
1977—Cardinals, 28-0 (StL)
Giants, 27-7 (NY)
1978—Cardinals, 20-10 (StL)
Giants, 17-0 (NY)
1979—Cardinals, 27-14 (NY)
Cardinals, 29-20 (StL)
1980—Giants, 41-35 (StL)
Cardinals, 23-7 (NY)
1981—Giants, 34-14 (NY)
Giants, 20-10 (StL)
1982—Cardinals, 24-21 (StL)
1983—Tie, 20-20 (StL) OT
Cardinals, 10-6 (NY)
1984—Giants, 16-10 (NY)
Cardinals, 31-21 (StL)
1985—Giants, 27-17 (NY)
Giants, 34-3 (StL)
1986—Giants, 13-6 (StL)
Giants, 27-7 (NY)
1987—Giants, 30-7 (NY)
Cardinals, 27-24 (StL)
1988—Cardinals, 24-17 (P)
Giants, 44-7 (NY)
1989—Giants, 35-7 (NY)
Giants, 20-13 (P)
1990—Giants, 20-19 (NY)
Giants, 24-21 (P)
1991—Giants, 20-9 (NY)
Giants, 21-14 (P)
1992—Giants, 31-21 (NY)
Cardinals, 19-0 (P)
1993—Giants, 19-17 (NY)
Cardinals, 17-6 (P)
1994—Giants, 20-17 (A)
Cardinals, 10-9 (NY)
(RS Pts.—Giants 2,306, Cardinals 1,780)
Franchise known as Phoenix prior to 1994, in St. Louis prior to 1988, and in Chicago prior to 1960

***ARIZONA vs. N.Y. JETS**
RS: Cardinals lead series, 2-1
1971—Cardinals, 17-10 (StL)
1975—Cardinals, 37-6 (NY)
1978—Jets, 23-10 (NY)
(RS Pts.—Cardinals 64, Jets 39)
Franchise known as Phoenix prior to 1994 and in St. Louis prior to 1988

***ARIZONA vs. PHILADELPHIA**
RS: Cardinals lead series, 45-44-5
PS: Series tied, 1-1
1935—Cardinals, 12-3 (C)
1936—Cardinals, 13-0 (C)
1937—Tie, 6-6 (P)
1938—Eagles, 7-0 (Erie, Pa.)
1941—Eagles, 21-14 (P)
1945—Eagles, 21-6 (P)
1947—Cardinals, 45-21 (P)
**Cardinals, 28-21 (C)
1948—Cardinals, 21-14 (C)
**Eagles, 7-0 (P)
1949—Eagles, 28-3 (P)
1950—Eagles, 45-7 (C)
Cardinals, 14-10 (P)
1951—Eagles, 17-14 (C)
1952—Eagles, 10-7 (P)
Cardinals, 28-22 (C)
1953—Eagles, 56-17 (C)
Eagles, 38-0 (P)
1954—Eagles, 35-16 (C)
Eagles, 30-14 (P)
1955—Tie, 24-24 (C)
Eagles, 27-3 (P)
1956—Cardinals, 20-6 (P)
Cardinals, 28-17 (C)
1957—Eagles, 38-21 (C)

Cardinals, 31-27 (P)
1958—Tie, 21-21 (C)
Eagles, 49-21 (P)
1959—Eagles, 28-24 (Minn)
Eagles, 27-17 (P)
1960—Eagles, 31-27 (P)
Eagles, 20-6 (StL)
1961—Cardinals, 30-27 (P)
Eagles, 20-7 (StL)
1962—Cardinals, 27-21 (P)
Cardinals, 45-35 (StL)
1963—Cardinals, 28-24 (P)
Cardinals, 38-14 (StL)
1964—Cardinals, 38-13 (P)
Cardinals, 36-34 (StL)
1965—Eagles, 34-27 (P)
Eagles, 28-24 (StL)
1966—Cardinals, 16-13 (StL)
Cardinals, 41-10 (P)
1967—Cardinals, 48-14 (StL)
1968—Cardinals, 45-17 (P)
1969—Eagles, 34-30 (StL)
1970—Cardinals, 35-20 (P)
Cardinals, 23-14 (StL)
1971—Eagles, 37-20 (StL)
Eagles, 19-7 (P)
1972—Tie, 6-6 (P)
Cardinals, 24-23 (StL)
1973—Cardinals, 34-23 (P)
Eagles, 27-24 (StL)
1974—Cardinals, 7-3 (StL)
Cardinals, 13-3 (P)
1975—Cardinals, 31-20 (StL)
Cardinals, 24-23 (P)
1976—Cardinals, 33-14 (StL)
Cardinals, 17-14 (P)
1977—Cardinals, 21-17 (P)
Cardinals, 21-16 (StL)
1978—Cardinals, 16-10 (P)
Eagles, 14-10 (StL)
1979—Eagles, 24-20 (StL)
Eagles, 16-13 (P)
1980—Cardinals, 24-14 (StL)
Eagles, 17-3 (P)
1981—Eagles, 52-10 (StL)
Eagles, 38-0 (P)
1982—Cardinals, 23-20 (P)
1983—Cardinals, 14-11 (P)
Cardinals, 31-7 (StL)
1984—Cardinals, 34-14 (P)
Cardinals, 17-16 (StL)
1985—Eagles, 30-7 (P)
Eagles, 24-14 (StL)
1986—Cardinals, 13-10 (StL)
Tie, 10-10 (P) OT
1987—Eagles, 28-23 (StL)
Cardinals, 31-19 (P)
1988—Eagles, 31-21 (P)
Eagles, 23-17 (Phx)
1989—Eagles, 17-5 (Phx)
Eagles, 31-14 (P)
1990—Cardinals, 23-21 (P)
Eagles, 23-21 (Phx)
1991—Cardinals, 26-10 (P)
Eagles, 34-14 (Phx)
1992—Eagles, 31-14 (Phx)
Eagles, 7-3 (P)
1993—Eagles, 23-17 (P)
Cardinals, 16-3 (Phx)
1994—Eagles, 17-7 (P)
Cardinals, 12-6 (A)
(RS Pts.—Eagles 1,995, Cardinals 1,851)
(PS Pts.—Tie 28, 28)
Franchise known as Phoenix prior to 1994, in St. Louis prior to 1988, and in Chicago prior to 1960
***NFL Championship*

***ARIZONA vs. **PITTSBURGH**

RS: Steelers lead series, 29-22-3
1933—Pirates, 14-13 (C)
1935—Pirates, 17-13 (P)
1936—Cardinals, 14-6 (C)
1937—Cardinals, 13-7 (P)
1939—Cardinals, 10-0 (P)
1940—Tie, 7-7 (P)
1942—Steelers, 19-3 (P)
1945—Steelers, 23-0 (P)
1946—Steelers, 14-7 (P)
1948—Cardinals, 24-7 (P)
1950—Steelers, 28-17 (C)
Steelers, 28-7 (P)
1951—Steelers, 28-14 (C)
1952—Steelers, 34-28 (C)
Steelers, 17-14 (P)
1953—Steelers, 31-28 (P)
Steelers, 21-17 (C)
1954—Cardinals, 17-14 (C)
Steelers, 20-17 (P)
1955—Steelers, 14-7 (P)
Cardinals, 27-13 (C)
1956—Steelers, 14-7 (P)
Cardinals, 38-27 (C)
1957—Steelers, 29-20 (P)
Steelers, 27-2 (C)
1958—Steelers, 27-20 (C)
Steelers, 38-21 (P)
1959—Cardinals, 45-24 (C)
Steelers, 35-20 (P)
1960—Steelers, 27-14 (P)
Cardinals, 38-7 (StL)
1961—Steelers, 30-27 (P)
Cardinals, 20-0 (StL)
1962—Steelers, 26-17 (StL)
Steelers, 19-7 (P)
1963—Steelers, 23-10 (P)
Cardinals, 24-23 (StL)
1964—Cardinals, 34-30 (StL)
Cardinals, 21-20 (P)
1965—Cardinals, 20-7 (P)
Cardinals, 21-17 (StL)
1966—Steelers, 30-9 (P)
Cardinals, 6-3 (StL)
1967—Cardinals, 28-14 (P)
Tie, 14-14 (StL)
1968—Tie, 28-28 (StL)
Cardinals, 20-10 (P)
1969—Cardinals, 27-14 (P)
Cardinals, 47-10 (StL)
1972—Steelers, 25-19 (StL)
1979—Steelers, 24-21 (StL)
1985—Steelers, 23-10 (P)
1988—Cardinals, 31-14 (Phx)
1994—Cardinals, 20-17 (A) OT
(RS Pts.—Steelers 1,038, Cardinals 1,003)
Franchise known as Phoenix prior to 1994, in St. Louis prior to 1988, and in Chicago prior to 1960
***Steelers known as Pirates prior to 1941*

***ARIZONA vs. **ST. LOUIS**

RS: Rams lead series, 23-19-2
PS: Rams lead series, 1-0
1937—Cardinals, 6-0 (Clev)
Cardinals, 13-7 (Chi)
1938—Cardinals, 7-6 (Clev)
Cardinals, 31-17 (Chi)
1939—Rams, 24-0 (Chi)
Rams, 14-0 (Clev)
1940—Rams, 26-14 (Clev)
Cardinals, 17-7 (Chi)
1941—Rams, 10-6 (Clev)
Cardinals, 7-0 (Chi)
1942—Cardinals, 7-0 (Buffalo)
Rams, 7-3 (Clev)
1945—Rams, 21-0 (Clev)
Rams, 35-21 (Chi)
1946—Cardinals, 34-10 (Chi)
Rams, 17-14 (LA)
1947—Rams, 27-7 (LA)
Cardinals, 17-10 (Chi)
1948—Cardinals, 27-22 (LA)
Cardinals, 27-24 (Chi)
1949—Tie, 28-28 (Chi)
Cardinals, 31-27 (LA)
1951—Rams, 45-21 (LA)
1953—Tie, 24-24 (Chi)
1954—Rams, 28-17 (LA)
1958—Rams, 20-14 (Chi)
1960—Cardinals, 43-21 (LA)
1965—Rams, 27-3 (StL)
1968—Rams, 24-13 (StL)
1970—Rams, 34-13 (LA)
1972—Cardinals, 24-14 (StL)
1975—***Rams, 35-23 (LA)
1976—Cardinals, 30-28 (LA)
1979—Rams, 21-0 (LA)
1980—Rams, 21-13 (StL)
1984—Rams, 16-13 (StL)
1985—Rams, 46-14 (LA)
1986—Rams, 16-10 (StL)
1987—Rams, 27-24 (StL)
1988—Cardinals, 41-27 (LA)
1989—Rams, 37-14 (LA)
1991—Cardinals, 24-14 (LA)
1992—Cardinals, 20-14 (LA)
1993—Cardinals, 38-10 (P)
1994—Rams, 14-12 (LA)
(RS Pts.—Rams 867, Cardinals 742)
(PS Pts.—Rams 35, Cardinals 23)
Franchise known as Phoenix prior to 1994, in St. Louis prior to 1988, and in Chicago prior to 1960
***Franchise in Los Angeles prior to 1995 and in Cleveland prior to 1946*
****NFC Divisional Playoff*

***ARIZONA vs. SAN DIEGO**

RS: Chargers lead series, 5-1
1971—Chargers, 20-17 (SD)
1976—Chargers, 43-24 (SD)
1983—Cardinals, 44-14 (StL)
1987—Chargers, 28-24 (SD)
1989—Chargers, 24-13 (P)
1992—Chargers, 27-21 (P)
(RS Pts.—Chargers 156, Cardinals 143)
Franchise known as Phoenix prior to 1994, in St. Louis prior to 1988,

***ARIZONA vs. SAN FRANCISCO**

RS: 49ers lead series, 10-9
1951—Cardinals, 27-21 (SF)
1957—Cardinals, 20-10 (SF)
1962—49ers, 24-17 (StL)
1964—Cardinals, 23-13 (SF)
1968—49ers, 35-17 (SF)
1971—49ers, 26-14 (StL)
1974—Cardinals, 34-9 (SF)
1976—Cardinals, 23-20 (StL) OT
1978—Cardinals, 16-10 (SF)
1979—Cardinals, 13-10 (StL)
1980—49ers, 24-21 (SF) OT
1982—49ers, 31-20 (StL)
1983—49ers, 42-27 (StL)
1986—49ers, 43-17 (SF)
1987—49ers, 34-28 (SF)
1988—Cardinals, 24-23 (P)
1991—49ers, 14-10 (SF)
1992—Cardinals, 24-14 (P)
1993—49ers, 28-14 (SF)
(RS Pts.—49ers 431, Cardinals 389)
Franchise known as Phoenix prior to 1994, in St. Louis prior to 1988, and in Chicago prior to 1960

***ARIZONA vs. SEATTLE**

RS: Cardinals lead series, 4-0
1976—Cardinals, 30-24 (S)
1983—Cardinals, 33-28 (StL)
1989—Cardinals, 34-24 (S)
1993—Cardinals, 30-27 (S) OT
(RS Pts.—Cardinals 127, Seahawks 103)
Franchise known as Phoenix prior to 1994 and in St. Louis prior to 1988

***ARIZONA vs. TAMPA BAY**

RS: Series tied, 6-6
1977—Buccaneers, 17-7 (TB)
1981—Buccaneers, 20-10 (TB)
1983—Cardinals, 34-27 (TB)
1985—Buccaneers, 16-0 (TB)
1986—Cardinals, 30-19 (TB)
Cardinals, 21-17 (StL)
1987—Cardinals, 31-28 (StL)
Cardinals, 31-14 (TB)
1988—Cardinals, 30-24 (TB)
1989—Buccaneers, 14-13 (P)
1992—Buccaneers, 23-7 (TB)
Buccaneers, 7-3 (P)
(RS Pts.—Buccaneers 226, Cardinals 217)
Franchise known as Phoenix prior to 1994 and in St. Louis prior to 1988

***ARIZONA vs. **WASHINGTON**

RS: Redskins lead series, 61-38-2
1932—Cardinals, 9-0 (B)
Braves, 8-6 (C)
1933—Redskins, 10-0 (C)
Tie, 0-0 (B)
1934—Redskins, 9-0 (B)
1935—Cardinals, 6-0 (B)
1936—Redskins, 13-10 (B)
1937—Cardinals, 21-14 (W)
1939—Redskins, 28-7 (W)
1940—Redskins, 28-21 (W)
1942—Redskins, 28-0 (W)
1943—Redskins, 13-7 (W)
1945—Redskins, 24-21 (W)
1947—Redskins, 45-21 (W)
1949—Cardinals, 38-7 (C)
1950—Cardinals, 38-28 (W)
1951—Redskins, 7-3 (C)
Redskins, 20-17 (W)
1952—Redskins, 23-7 (C)
Cardinals, 17-6 (W)
1953—Redskins, 24-13 (C)
Redskins, 28-17 (W)
1954—Cardinals, 38-16 (C)
Redskins, 37-20 (W)
1955—Cardinals, 24-10 (W)
Redskins, 31-0 (C)
1956—Cardinals, 31-3 (W)
Redskins, 17-14 (C)
1957—Redskins, 37-14 (C)
Cardinals, 44-14 (W)
1958—Cardinals, 37-10 (C)
Redskins, 45-31 (W)
1959—Cardinals, 49-21 (C)
Redskins, 23-14 (W)
1960—Cardinals, 44-7 (StL)
Cardinals, 26-14 (W)
1961—Cardinals, 24-0 (W)
Cardinals, 38-24 (StL)
1962—Redskins, 24-14 (W)
Tie, 17-17 (StL)
1963—Cardinals, 21-7 (W)
Cardinals, 24-20 (StL)
1964—Cardinals, 23-17 (W)
Cardinals, 38-24 (StL)
1965—Cardinals, 37-16 (W)
Redskins, 24-20 (StL)
1966—Cardinals, 23-7 (StL)
Redskins, 26-20 (W)
1967—Cardinals, 27-21 (W)
1968—Cardinals, 41-14 (StL)
1969—Redskins, 33-17 (W)
1970—Cardinals, 27-17 (StL)
Redskins, 28-27 (W)
1971—Redskins, 24-17 (StL)
Redskins, 20-0 (W)
1972—Redskins, 24-10 (W)
Redskins, 33-3 (StL)
1973—Cardinals, 34-27 (StL)
Redskins, 31-13 (W)
1974—Cardinals, 17-10 (W)
Cardinals, 23-20 (StL)
1975—Redskins, 27-17 (W)
Cardinals, 20-17 (StL) OT
1976—Redskins, 20-10 (W)
Redskins, 16-10 (StL)
1977—Redskins, 24-14 (W)
Redskins, 26-20 (StL)
1978—Redskins, 28-10 (StL)
Cardinals, 27-17 (W)
1979—Redskins, 17-7 (StL)
Redskins, 30-28 (W)
1980—Redskins, 23-0 (W)
Redskins, 31-7 (StL)

1981—Cardinals, 40-30 (StL)
Redskins, 42-21 (W)
1982—Redskins, 12-7 (StL)
Redskins, 28-0 (W)
1983—Redskins, 38-14 (StL)
Redskins, 45-7 (W)
1984—Cardinals, 26-24 (StL)
Redskins, 29-27 (W)
1985—Redskins, 27-10 (W)
Redskins, 27-16 (StL)
1986—Redskins, 28-21 (W)
Redskins, 20-17 (StL)
1987—Redskins, 28-21 (W)
Redskins, 34-17 (StL)
1988—Cardinals, 30-21 (P)
Redskins, 33-17 (W)
1989—Redskins, 30-28 (W)
Redskins, 29-10 (P)
1990—Redskins, 31-0 (W)
Redskins, 38-10 (P)
1991—Redskins, 34-0 (W)
Redskins, 20-14 (P)
1992—Cardinals, 27-24 (P)
Redskins, 41-3 (W)
1993—Cardinals, 17-10 (W)
Cardinals, 36-6 (P)
1994—Cardinals, 19-16 (W) OT
Cardinals, 17-15 (A)
(RS Pts.—Redskins 2,192, Cardinals 1,862)
Franchise known as Phoenix prior to 1994, in St. Louis prior to 1988, and in Chicago prior to 1960
***Franchise in Boston prior to 1937 and known as Braves prior to 1933*

ATLANTA vs. ARIZONA
RS: Cardinals lead series, 11-6;
See Arizona vs. Atlanta
ATLANTA vs. BUFFALO
RS: Series tied, 3-3
1973—Bills, 17-6 (A)
1977—Bills, 3-0 (B)
1980—Falcons, 30-14 (B)
1983—Falcons, 31-14 (A)
1989—Falcons, 30-28 (A)
1992—Bills, 41-14 (B)
(RS Pts.—Bills 117, Falcons 111)
ATLANTA vs. CHICAGO
RS: Series tied, 9-9
1966—Bears, 23-6 (C)
1967—Bears, 23-14 (A)
1968—Falcons, 16-13 (C)
1969—Falcons, 48-31 (A)
1970—Bears, 23-14 (A)
1972—Falcons, 37-21 (C)
1973—Falcons, 46-6 (A)
1974—Falcons, 13-10 (A)
1976—Falcons, 10-0 (C)
1977—Falcons, 16-10 (C)
1978—Bears, 13-7 (C)
1980—Falcons, 28-17 (A)
1983—Falcons, 20-17 (C)
1985—Bears, 36-0 (C)
1986—Bears, 13-10 (A)
1990—Bears, 30-24 (C)
1992—Bears, 41-31 (C)
1993—Bears, 6-0 (C)
(RS Pts.—Falcons 340, Bears 333)
ATLANTA vs. CINCINNATI
RS: Bengals lead series, 6-2
1971—Falcons, 9-6 (C)
1975—Bengals, 21-14 (A)
1978—Bengals, 37-7 (C)
1981—Bengals, 30-28 (A)
1984—Bengals, 35-14 (C)
1987—Bengals, 16-10 (A)
1990—Falcons, 38-17 (A)
1993—Bengals, 21-17 (C)
(RS Pts.—Bengals 183, Falcons 137)
ATLANTA vs. CLEVELAND
RS: Browns lead series, 8-2
1966—Browns, 49-17 (A)
1968—Browns, 30-7 (C)
1971—Falcons, 31-14 (C)
1976—Browns, 20-17 (A)
1978—Browns, 24-16 (A)
1981—Browns, 28-17 (C)
1984—Browns, 23-7 (A)
1987—Browns, 38-3 (C)
1990—Browns, 13-10 (C)
1993—Falcons, 17-14 (A)
(RS Pts.—Browns 253, Falcons 142)
ATLANTA vs. DALLAS
RS: Cowboys lead series, 9-6
PS: Cowboys lead series, 2-0
1966—Cowboys, 47-14 (A)
1967—Cowboys, 37-7 (D)
1969—Cowboys, 24-17 (A)
1970—Cowboys, 13-0 (D)
1974—Cowboys, 24-0 (A)
1976—Falcons, 17-10 (A)
1978—*Cowboys, 27-20 (D)
1980—*Cowboys, 30-27 (A)
1985—Cowboys, 24-10 (D)
1986—Falcons, 37-35 (D)
1987—Falcons, 21-10 (D)
1988—Cowboys, 26-20 (D)
1989—Falcons 27-21 (A)
1990—Falcons, 26-7 (A)
1991—Cowboys, 31-27 (D)
1992—Cowboys, 41-17 (A)
1993—Falcons, 27-14 (A)
(RS Pts.—Cowboys 364, Falcons 267)
(PS Pts.—Cowboys 57, Falcons 47)
**NFC Divisional Playoff*
ATLANTA vs. DENVER
RS: Broncos lead series, 5-3
1970—Broncos, 24-10 (D)
1972—Falcons, 23-20 (A)
1975—Falcons, 35-21 (A)
1979—Broncos, 20-17 (A) OT
1982—Falcons, 34-27 (D)
1985—Broncos, 44-28 (A)
1988—Broncos, 30-14 (D)
1994—Broncos, 32-28 (D)
(RS Pts.—Broncos 218, Falcons 189)
ATLANTA vs. DETROIT
RS: Lions lead series, 18-5
1966—Lions, 28-10 (D)
1967—Lions, 24-3 (D)
1968—Lions, 24-7 (A)
1969—Lions, 27-21 (D)
1971—Lions, 41-38 (D)
1972—Lions, 26-23 (A)
1973—Lions, 31-6 (D)
1975—Lions, 17-14 (A)
1976—Lions, 24-10 (D)
1977—Falcons, 17-6 (A)
1978—Falcons, 14-0 (A)
1979—Lions, 24-23 (D)
1980—Falcons, 43-28 (A)
1983—Falcons, 30-14 (D)
1984—Lions, 27-24 (A) OT
1985—Lions, 28-27 (A)
1986—Falcons, 20-6 (D)
1987—Lions, 30-13 (A)
1988—Lions, 31-17 (D)
1989—Lions, 31-24 (A)
1990—Lions, 21-14 (D)
1993—Lions, 30-13 (D)
1994—Lions, 31-28 (D) OT
(RS Pts.—Lions 549, Falcons 439)
ATLANTA vs. GREEN BAY
RS: Packers lead series, 10-9
1966—Packers, 56-3 (Mil)
1967—Packers, 23-0 (Mil)
1968—Packers, 38-7 (A)
1969—Packers, 28-10 (GB)
1970—Packers, 27-24 (GB)
1971—Falcons, 28-21 (A)
1972—Falcons, 10-9 (Mil)
1974—Falcons, 10-3 (A)
1975—Packers, 22-13 (GB)
1976—Packers, 24-20 (A)
1979—Falcons, 25-7 (A)
1981—Falcons, 31-17 (GB)
1982—Packers, 38-7 (A)
1983—Falcons, 47-41 (A) OT
1988—Falcons, 20-0 (A)
1989—Packers, 23-21 (Mil)
1991—Falcons, 35-31 (A)
1992—Falcons, 24-10 (A)
1994—Packers, 21-17 (Mil)
(RS Pts.—Packers 439, Falcons 352)
ATLANTA vs. HOUSTON
RS: Falcons lead series, 5-3
1972—Falcons, 20-10 (A)
1976—Oilers, 20-14 (H)
1978—Falcons, 20-14 (A)
1981—Falcons, 31-27 (H)
1984—Falcons, 42-10 (A)
1987—Oilers, 37-33 (H)
1990—Falcons, 47-27 (A)
1993—Oilers, 33-17 (H)
(RS Pts.—Falcons 224, Oilers 178)
ATLANTA vs. *INDIANAPOLIS
RS: Colts lead series, 10-0
1966—Colts, 19-7 (A)
1967—Colts, 38-31 (B)
Colts, 49-7 (A)
1968—Colts, 28-20 (A)
Colts, 44-0 (B)
1969—Colts, 21-14 (A)
Colts, 13-6 (B)
1974—Colts, 17-7 (A)
1986—Colts, 28-23 (A)
1989—Colts, 13-9 (I)
(RS Pts.—Colts 270, Falcons 124)
**Franchise in Baltimore prior to 1984*
ATLANTA vs. KANSAS CITY
RS: Chiefs lead series, 4-0
1972—Chiefs, 17-14 (A)
1985—Chiefs, 38-10 (KC)
1991—Chiefs, 14-3 (KC)
1994—Chiefs, 30-10 (A)
(RS Pts.—Chiefs 99, Falcons 37)
ATLANTA vs. *LOS ANGELES
RS: Raiders lead series, 5-3
1971—Falcons, 24-13 (A)
1975—Raiders, 37-34 (O) OT
1979—Raiders, 50-19 (O)
1982—Raiders, 38-14 (A)
1985—Raiders, 34-24 (A)
1988—Falcons, 12-6 (LA)
1991—Falcons, 21-17 (A)
1994—Raiders, 30-17 (LA)
(RS Pts.—Raiders 225, Falcons 165)
**Franchise in Oakland prior to 1982*
ATLANTA vs. MIAMI
RS: Dolphins lead series, 5-1
1970—Dolphins, 20-7 (A)
1974—Dolphins, 42-7 (M)
1980—Dolphins, 20-17 (A)
1983—Dolphins, 31-24 (M)
1986—Falcons, 20-14 (M)
1992—Dolphins, 21-17 (M)
(RS Pts.—Dolphins 148, Falcons 92)
ATLANTA vs. MINNESOTA
RS: Vikings lead series, 11-6
PS: Vikings lead series, 1-0
1966—Falcons, 20-13 (M)
1967—Falcons, 21-20 (A)
1968—Vikings, 47-7 (M)
1969—Falcons, 10-3 (A)
1970—Vikings, 37-7 (A)
1971—Vikings, 24-7 (M)
1973—Falcons, 20-14 (A)
1974—Vikings, 23-10 (M)
1975—Vikings, 38-0 (M)
1977—Vikings, 14-7 (A)
1980—Vikings, 24-23 (M)
1981—Falcons, 31-30 (A)
1982—*Vikings, 30-24 (M)
1984—Vikings, 27-20 (M)
1985—Falcons, 14-13 (A)
1987—Vikings, 24-13 (M)
1989—Vikings, 43-17 (M)
1991—Vikings, 20-19 (A)
(RS Pts.—Vikings 414, Falcons 246)
(PS Pts.—Vikings 30, Falcons 24)
**NFC First-Round Playoff*
ATLANTA vs. NEW ENGLAND
RS: Falcons lead series, 4-3
1972—Patriots, 21-20 (NE)
1977—Patriots, 16-10 (A)
1980—Falcons, 37-21 (NE)
1983—Falcons, 24-13 (A)
1986—Patriots, 25-17 (NE)
1989—Falcons, 16-15 (A)
1992—Falcons, 34-0 (A)
(RS Pts.—Falcons 158, Patriots 111)
ATLANTA vs. NEW ORLEANS
RS: Falcons lead series, 27-24
PS: Falcons lead series, 1-0
1967—Saints, 27-24 (NO)
1969—Falcons, 45-17 (A)
1970—Falcons, 14-3 (NO)
Falcons, 32-14 (A)
1971—Falcons, 28-6 (A)
Falcons, 24-20 (NO)
1972—Falcons, 21-14 (NO)
Falcons, 36-20 (A)
1973—Falcons, 62-7 (NO)
Falcons, 14-10 (A)
1974—Saints, 14-13 (NO)
Saints, 13-3 (A)
1975—Falcons, 14-7 (A)
Saints, 23-7 (NO)
1976—Saints, 30-0 (NO)
Falcons, 23-20 (A)
1977—Saints, 21-20 (NO)
Falcons, 35-7 (A)
1978—Falcons, 20-17 (NO)
Falcons, 20-17 (A)
1979—Falcons, 40-34 (NO) OT
Saints, 37-6 (A)
1980—Falcons, 41-14 (NO)
Falcons, 31-13 (A)
1981—Falcons, 27-0 (A)
Falcons, 41-10 (NO)
1982—Falcons, 35-0 (A)
Saints, 35-6 (NO)
1983—Saints, 19-17 (A)
Saints, 27-10 (NO)
1984—Falcons, 36-28 (NO)
Saints, 17-13 (A)
1985—Falcons, 31-24 (A)
Falcons, 16-10 (NO)
1986—Falcons, 31-10 (NO)
Saints, 14-9 (A)
1987—Saints, 38-0 (A)
1988—Saints, 29-21 (A)
Saints, 10-9 (NO)
1989—Saints, 20-13 (NO)
Saints, 26-17 (A)
1990—Falcons, 28-27 (A)
Saints, 10-7 (NO)
1991—Saints, 27-6 (A)
Falcons, 23-20 (NO) OT
*Falcons, 27-20 (NO)
1992—Saints, 10-7 (A)
Saints, 22-14 (NO)
1993—Saints, 34-31 (A)
Falcons, 26-15 (NO)
1994—Saints, 33-32 (NO)
Saints, 29-20 (A)
(RS Pts.—Falcons 1,099, Saints 949)
(PS Pts.—Falcons 27, Saints 20)
**NFC First-Round Playoff*
ATLANTA vs. N.Y. GIANTS
RS: Series tied, 6-6
1966—Falcons, 27-16 (NY)
1968—Falcons, 24-21 (A)
1971—Giants, 21-17 (A)
1974—Falcons, 14-7 (New Haven)
1977—Falcons, 17-3 (A)
1978—Falcons, 23-20 (A)
1979—Giants, 24-3 (NY)
1981—Giants, 27-24 (A) OT
1982—Falcons, 16-14 (NY)
1983—Giants, 16-13 (A) OT
1984—Giants, 19-7 (A)

ALL-TIME TEAM VS. TEAM RESULTS

1988—Giants, 23-16 (A)
(RS Pts.—Giants 211, Falcons 201)
ATLANTA vs. N.Y. JETS
RS: Series tied, 3-3
1973—Falcons, 28-20 (NY)
1980—Jets, 14-7 (A)
1983—Falcons, 27-21 (NY)
1986—Jets, 28-14 (A)
1989—Jets, 27-7 (NY)
1992—Falcons, 20-17 (A)
(RS Pts.—Jets 127, Falcons 103)
ATLANTA vs. PHILADELPHIA
RS: Eagles lead series, 8-7-1
PS: Falcons lead series, 1-0
1966—Eagles, 23-10 (P)
1967—Eagles, 38-7 (A)
1969—Falcons, 27-3 (P)
1970—Tie, 13-13 (P)
1973—Falcons, 44-27 (P)
1976—Eagles, 14-13 (A)
1978—*Falcons, 14-13 (A)
1979—Falcons, 14-10 (P)
1980—Falcons, 20-17 (P)
1981—Eagles, 16-13 (P)
1983—Eagles, 28-24 (A)
1984—Falcons, 26-10 (A)
1985—Eagles, 23-17 (P) OT
1986—Eagles, 16-0 (A)
1988—Falcons, 27-24 (P)
1990—Eagles, 24-23 (A)
1994—Falcons, 28-21 (A)
(RS Pts.—Eagles 307, Falcons 306)
(PS Pts.—Falcons 14, Eagles 13)
**NFC First-Round Playoff*
ATLANTA vs. PITTSBURGH
RS: Steelers lead series, 9-1
1966—Steelers, 57-33 (A)
1968—Steelers, 41-21 (A)
1970—Falcons, 27-16 (A)
1974—Steelers, 24-17 (P)
1978—Steelers, 31-7 (P)
1981—Steelers, 34-20 (A)
1984—Steelers, 35-10 (P)
1987—Steelers, 28-12 (A)
1990—Steelers, 21-9 (P)
1993—Steelers, 45-17 (A)
(RS Pts.—Steelers 332, Falcons 173)
ATLANTA vs. *ST. LOUIS
RS: Rams lead series, 36-18-2
1966—Rams, 19-14 (A)
1967—Rams, 31-3 (A)
Rams, 20-3 (LA)
1968—Rams, 27-14 (LA)
Rams, 17-10 (A)
1969—Rams, 17-7 (LA)
Rams, 38-6 (A)
1970—Tie, 10-10 (LA)
Rams, 17-7 (A)
1971—Tie, 20-20 (LA)
Rams, 24-16 (A)
1972—Falcons, 31-3 (A)
Rams, 20-7 (LA)
1973—Rams, 31-0 (LA)
Falcons, 15-13 (A)
1974—Rams, 21-0 (LA)
Rams, 30-7 (A)
1975—Rams, 22-7 (LA)
Rams, 16-7 (A)
1976—Rams, 30-14 (A)
Rams, 59-0 (LA)
1977—Falcons, 17-6 (A)
Rams, 23-7 (LA)
1978—Rams, 10-0 (LA)
Falcons, 15-7 (A)
1979—Rams, 20-14 (LA)
Rams, 34-13 (A)
1980—Falcons, 13-10 (A)
Rams, 20-17 (LA) OT
1981—Rams, 37-35 (A)
Rams, 21-16 (LA)
1982—Falcons, 34-17 (A)
1983—Rams, 27-21 (LA)
Rams, 36-13 (A)
1984—Falcons, 30-28 (LA)
Rams, 24-10 (A)
1985—Rams, 17-6 (LA)
Falcons, 30-14 (A)
1986—Falcons, 26-14 (A)
Rams, 14-7 (LA)
1987—Falcons, 24-20 (A)
Rams, 33-0 (LA)
1988—Rams, 33-0 (A)
Rams, 22-7 (LA)
1989—Rams, 31-21 (A)
Rams, 26-14 (LA)
1990—Rams, 44-24 (LA)
Falcons, 20-13 (A)
1991—Falcons, 31-14 (A)
Falcons, 31-14 (LA)
1992—Falcons, 30-28 (A)
Rams, 38-27 (LA)
1993—Falcons, 30-24 (A)
Falcons, 13-0 (LA)
1994—Falcons, 31-13 (A)
Falcons, 8-5 (LA)
(RS Pts.—Rams 1,222, Falcons 833)
**Franchise in Los Angeles prior to 1995*
ATLANTA vs. SAN DIEGO
RS: Falcons lead series, 4-1
1973—Falcons, 41-0 (SD)
1979—Falcons, 28-26 (SD)
1988—Chargers, 10-7 (A)
1991—Falcons, 13-10 (SD)
1994—Falcons, 10-9 (A)
(RS Pts.—Falcons 99, Chargers 55)
ATLANTA vs. SAN FRANCISCO
RS: 49ers lead series, 34-21-1
1966—49ers, 44-7 (A)
1967—49ers, 38-7 (SF)
49ers, 34-28 (A)
1968—49ers, 28-13 (SF)
49ers, 14-12 (A)
1969—Falcons, 24-12 (A)
Falcons, 21-7 (SF)
1970—Falcons, 21-20 (A)
49ers, 24-20 (SF)
1971—Falcons, 20-17 (A)
49ers, 24-3 (SF)
1972—49ers, 49-14 (A)
49ers, 20-0 (SF)
1973—49ers, 13-9 (A)
Falcons, 17-3 (SF)
1974—49ers, 16-10 (A)
49ers, 27-0 (SF)
1975—Falcons, 17-3 (SF)
Falcons, 31-9 (A)
1976—49ers, 15-0 (SF)
Falcons, 21-16 (A)
1977—Falcons, 7-0 (SF)
49ers, 10-3 (A)
1978—Falcons, 20-17 (SF)
Falcons, 21-10 (A)
1979—49ers, 20-15 (SF)
Falcons, 31-21 (A)
1980—Falcons, 20-17 (SF)
Falcons, 35-10 (A)
1981—Falcons, 34-17 (A)
49ers, 17-14 (SF)
1982—Falcons, 17-7 (SF)
1983—49ers, 24-20 (SF)
Falcons, 28-24 (A)
1984—49ers, 14-5 (SF)
49ers, 35-17 (A)
1985—49ers, 35-16 (SF)
49ers, 38-17 (A)
1986—Tie, 10-10 (A) OT
49ers, 20-0 (SF)
1987—49ers, 25-17 (A)
49ers, 35-7 (SF)
1988—Falcons, 34-17 (SF)
49ers, 13-3 (A)
1989—49ers, 45-3 (SF)
49ers, 23-10 (A)
1990—49ers, 19-13 (SF)
49ers, 45-35 (A)
1991—Falcons, 39-34 (SF)
Falcons, 17-14 (A)
1992—49ers, 56-17 (SF)
49ers, 41-3 (A)
1993—49ers, 37-30 (SF)
Falcons, 27-24 (A)
1994—49ers, 42-3 (A)
49ers, 50-14 (SF)
(RS Pts.—49ers 1,299, Falcons 897)
ATLANTA vs. SEATTLE
RS: Seahawks lead series, 4-1
1976—Seahawks, 30-13 (S)
1979—Seahawks, 31-28 (A)
1985—Seahawks, 30-26 (S)
1988—Seahawks, 31-20 (A)
1991—Falcons, 26-13 (A)
(RS Pts.—Seahawks 135, Falcons 113)
ATLANTA vs. TAMPA BAY
RS: Falcons lead series, 7-6
1977—Falcons, 17-0 (TB)
1978—Buccaneers, 14-9 (TB)
1979—Falcons, 17-14 (A)
1981—Buccaneers, 24-23 (TB)
1984—Buccaneers, 23-6 (TB)
1986—Falcons, 23-20 (TB) OT
1987—Buccaneers, 48-10 (TB)
1988—Falcons, 17-10 (A)
1990—Buccaneers, 23-17 (TB)
1991—Falcons, 43-7 (A)
1992—Falcons, 35-7 (TB)
1993—Buccaneers, 31-24 (A)
1994—Falcons, 34-13 (A)
(RS Pts.—Falcons 275, Buccaneers 234)
ATLANTA vs. WASHINGTON
RS: Redskins lead series, 13-4-1
PS: Redskins lead series, 1-0
1966—Redskins, 33-20 (W)
1967—Tie, 20-20 (A)
1969—Redskins, 27-20 (W)
1972—Redskins, 24-13 (W)
1975—Redskins, 30-27 (A)
1977—Redskins, 10-6 (W)
1978—Falcons, 20-17 (A)
1979—Redskins, 16-7 (A)
1980—Falcons, 10-6 (A)
1983—Redskins, 37-21 (W)
1984—Redskins, 27-14 (W)
1985—Redskins, 44-10 (A)
1987—Falcons, 21-20 (A)
1989—Redskins, 31-30 (A)
1991—Redskins, 56-17 (W)
*Redskins, 24-7 (W)
1992—Redskins, 24-17 (W)
1993—Redskins, 30-17 (W)
1994—Falcons, 27-20 (W)
(RS Pts.—Redskins 472, Falcons 317)
(PS Pts.—Redskins 24, Falcons 7)
**NFC Divisional Playoff*

BUFFALO vs. ARIZONA
RS: Series tied, 3-3;
See Arizona vs. Buffalo
BUFFALO vs. ATLANTA
RS: Series tied 3-3;
See Atlanta vs. Buffalo
BUFFALO vs. CHICAGO
RS: Bears lead series, 4-2
1970—Bears, 31-13 (C)
1974—Bills, 16-6 (B)
1979—Bears, 7-0 (B)
1988—Bears, 24-3 (C)
1991—Bills, 35-20 (B)
1994—Bears, 20-13 (C)
(RS Pts.—Bears 108, Bills 80)
BUFFALO vs. CINCINNATI
RS: Bengals lead series, 9-7
PS: Bengals lead series, 2-0
1968—Bengals, 34-23 (C)
1969—Bills, 16-13 (B)
1970—Bengals, 43-14 (B)
1973—Bengals, 16-13 (B)
1975—Bengals, 33-24 (C)
1978—Bills, 5-0 (B)
1979—Bills, 51-24 (B)
1980—Bills, 14-0 (C)
1981—Bengals, 27-24 (C) OT
*Bengals, 28-21 (C)
1983—Bills, 10-6 (C)
1984—Bengals, 52-21 (C)
1985—Bengals, 23-17 (B)
1986—Bengals, 36-33 (C) OT
1988—Bengals, 35-21 (C)
**Bengals, 21-10 (C)
1989—Bills, 24-7 (B)
1991—Bills, 35-16 (B)
(RS Pts.—Bengals 365, Bills 345)
(PS Pts.—Bengals 49, Bills 31)
**AFC Divisional Playoff*
***AFC Championship*
BUFFALO vs. CLEVELAND
RS: Browns lead series, 7-3
PS: Browns lead series, 1-0
1972—Browns, 27-10 (C)
1974—Bills, 15-10 (C)
1977—Browns, 27-16 (B)
1978—Browns, 41-20 (C)
1981—Bills, 22-13 (B)
1984—Browns, 13-10 (B)
1985—Browns, 17-7 (C)
1986—Browns, 21-17 (B)
1987—Browns, 27-21 (C)
1989—*Browns, 34-30 (C)
1990—Bills, 42-0 (C)
(RS Pts.—Browns 196, Bills 180)
(PS Pts.—Browns 34, Bills 30)
**AFC Divisional Playoff*
BUFFALO vs. DALLAS
RS: Cowboys lead series, 3-2
PS: Cowboys lead series, 2-0
1971—Cowboys, 49-37 (B)
1976—Cowboys, 17-10 (D)
1981—Cowboys, 27-14 (D)
1984—Bills, 14-3 (B)
1992—*Cowboys, 52-17 (Pasadena)
1993—Bills, 13-10 (D)
**Cowboys, 30-13 (Atlanta)
(RS Pts.—Cowboys 106, Bills 88)
(PS Pts.—Cowboys 82, Bills 30)
**Super Bowl XXVII*
***Super Bowl XXVIII*
BUFFALO vs. DENVER
RS: Bills lead series, 17-10-1
PS: Bills lead series, 1-0
1960—Broncos, 27-21 (B)
Tie, 38-38 (D)
1961—Broncos, 22-10 (B)
Bills, 23-10 (D)
1962—Broncos, 23-20 (B)
Bills, 45-38 (D)
1963—Bills, 30-28 (D)
Bills, 27-17 (B)
1964—Bills, 30-13 (B)
Bills, 30-19 (D)
1965—Bills, 30-15 (D)
Bills, 31-13 (B)
1966—Bills, 38-21 (B)
1967—Bills, 17-16 (D)
Broncos, 21-20 (B)
1968—Broncos, 34-32 (D)
1969—Bills, 41-28 (B)
1970—Broncos, 25-10 (B)
1975—Bills, 38-14 (B)
1977—Broncos, 26-6 (D)
1979—Broncos, 19-16 (B)
1981—Bills, 9-7 (B)
1984—Broncos, 37-7 (B)
1987—Bills, 21-14 (B)
1989—Broncos, 28-14 (B)
1990—Bills, 29-28 (B)
1991—*Bills, 10-7 (B)
1992—Bills, 27-17 (B)
1994—Bills, 27-20 (B)
(RS Pts.—Bills 687, Broncos 618)
(PS Pts.—Bills 10, Broncos 7)
*AFC Championship
BUFFALO vs. DETROIT
RS: Lions lead series, 3-1-1

1972—Tie, 21-21 (B)
1976—Lions, 27-14 (D)
1979—Bills, 20-17 (D)
1991—Lions, 17-14 (B) OT
1994—Lions, 35-21 (D)
(RS Pts.—Lions 117, Bills 90)

BUFFALO vs. GREEN BAY
RS: Bills lead series, 5-1
1974—Bills, 27-7 (GB)
1979—Bills, 19-12 (B)
1982—Packers, 33-21 (Mil)
1988—Bills, 28-0 (B)
1991—Bills, 34-24 (Mil)
1994—Bills 29-20 (B)
(RS Pts.—Bills 158, Packers 96)

BUFFALO vs. HOUSTON
RS: Oilers lead series, 20-13
PS: Bills lead series, 2-0
1960—Bills, 25-24 (B)
Oilers, 31-23 (H)
1961—Bills, 22-12 (H)
Oilers, 28-16 (B)
1962—Oilers, 28-23 (B)
Oilers, 17-14 (H)
1963—Oilers, 31-20 (B)
Oilers, 28-14 (H)
1964—Bills, 48-17 (H)
Bills, 24-10 (B)
1965—Oilers, 19-17 (B)
Bills, 29-18 (H)
1966—Bills, 27-20 (B)
Bills, 42-20 (H)
1967—Oilers, 20-3 (B)
Oilers, 10-3 (H)
1968—Oilers, 30-7 (B)
Oilers, 35-6 (H)
1969—Oilers, 17-3 (B)
Oilers, 28-14 (H)
1971—Oilers, 20-14 (B)
1974—Oilers, 21-9 (B)
1976—Oilers, 13-3 (B)
1978—Oilers, 17-10 (H)
1983—Bills, 30-13 (B)
1985—Bills, 20-0 (B)
1986—Oilers, 16-7 (H)
1987—Bills, 34-30 (B)
1988—*Bills, 17-10 (B)
1989—Bills, 47-41 (H) OT
1990—Oilers, 27-24 (H)
1992—Oilers, 27-3 (H)
**Bills, 41-38 (B) OT
1993—Bills, 35-7 (B)
1994—Bills, 15-7 (H)
(RS Pts.—Oilers 682, Bills 631)
(PS Pts.—Bills 58, Oilers 48)
**AFC Divisional Playoff*
***AFC First-Round Game*

BUFFALO vs. *INDIANAPOLIS
RS: Bills lead series, 26-22-1
1970—Tie, 17-17 (Balt)
Colts, 20-14 (Buff)
1971—Colts, 43-0 (Buff)
Colts, 24-0 (Balt)
1972—Colts, 17-0 (Buff)
Colts, 35-7 (Balt)
1973—Bills, 31-13 (Buff)
Bills, 24-17 (Balt)
1974—Bills, 27-14 (Balt)
Bills, 6-0 (Buff)
1975—Bills, 38-31 (Balt)
Colts, 42-35 (Buff)
1976—Colts, 31-13 (Buff)
Colts, 58-20 (Balt)
1977—Colts, 17-14 (Balt)
Colts, 31-13 (Buff)
1978—Bills, 24-17 (Buff)
Bills, 21-14 (Balt)
1979—Bills, 31-13 (Balt)
Colts, 14-13 (Buff)
1980—Colts, 17-12 (Buff)
Colts, 28-24 (Balt)
1981—Bills, 35-3 (Balt)
Bills, 23-17 (Buff)
1982—Bills, 20-0 (Buff)
1983—Bills, 28-23 (Buff)
Bills, 30-7 (Balt)
1984—Colts, 31-17 (I)
Bills, 21-15 (Buff)
1985—Colts, 49-17 (I)
Bills, 21-9 (Buff)
1986—Bills, 24-13 (Buff)
Colts, 24-14 (I)
1987—Colts, 47-6 (Buff)
Bills, 27-3 (I)
1988—Bills, 34-23 (Buff)
Colts, 17-14 (I)
1989—Colts, 37-14 (I)
Bills, 30-7 (Buff)
1990—Bills, 26-10 (Buff)
Bills, 31-7 (I)
1991—Bills, 42-6 (Buff)
Bills, 35-7 (I)
1992—Bills, 38-0 (Buff)
Colts, 16-13 (I) OT
1993—Bills, 23-9 (Buff)
Bills, 30-10 (I)
1994—Colts, 27-17 (Buff)
Colts, 10-9 (I)
(RS Pts.—Bills 1,023, Colts 940)
**Franchise in Baltimore prior to 1984*

BUFFALO vs. *KANSAS CITY
RS: Bills lead series, 16-13-1
PS: Bills lead series, 2-1
1960—Texans, 45-28 (B)
Texans, 24-7 (D)
1961—Bills, 27-24 (B)
Bills, 30-20 (D)
1962—Texans, 41-21 (D)
Bills, 23-14 (B)
1963—Tie, 27-27 (B)
Bills, 35-26 (KC)
1964—Bills, 34-17 (B)
Bills, 35-22 (KC)
1965—Bills, 23-7 (KC)
Bills, 34-25 (B)
1966—Chiefs, 42-20 (B)
Bills, 29-14 (KC)
**Chiefs, 31-7 (B)
1967—Chiefs, 23-13 (KC)
1968—Chiefs, 18-7 (B)
1969—Chiefs, 29-7 (B)
Chiefs, 22-19 (KC)
1971—Chiefs, 22-9 (KC)
1973—Bills, 23-14 (B)
1976—Bills, 50-17 (B)
1978—Bills, 28-13 (B)
Chiefs, 14-10 (KC)
1982—Bills, 14-9 (B)
1983—Bills, 14-9 (KC)
1986—Chiefs, 20-17 (B)
Bills, 17-14 (KC)
1991—Chiefs, 33-6 (KC)
***Bills, 37-14 (B)
1993—Chiefs, 23-7 (KC)
****Bills, 30-13 (B)
1994—Bills, 44-10 (B)
(RS Pts.—Bills 653, Chiefs 643)
(PS Pts.—Bills 74, Chiefs 58)
**Franchise in Dallas prior to 1963 and known as Texans*
***AFL Championship*
****AFC Divisional Playoff*
*****AFC Championship*

BUFFALO vs. *LOS ANGELES
RS: Raiders lead series, 15-14
PS: Bills lead series, 2-0
1960—Bills, 38-9 (B)
Raiders, 20-7 (O)
1961—Raiders, 31-22 (B)
Bills, 26-21 (O)
1962—Bills, 14-6 (B)
Bills, 10-6 (O)
1963—Raiders, 35-17 (O)
Bills, 12-0 (B)
1964—Bills, 23-20 (B)
Raiders, 16-13 (O)
1965—Bills, 17-12 (B)
Bills, 17-14 (O)
1966—Bills, 31-10 (O)
1967—Raiders, 24-20 (B)
Raiders, 28-21 (O)
1968—Raiders, 48-6 (B)
Raiders, 13-10 (O)
1969—Raiders, 50-21 (O)
1972—Raiders, 28-16 (O)
1974—Bills, 21-20 (B)
1977—Raiders, 34-13 (O)
1980—Bills, 24-7 (B)
1983—Raiders, 27-24 (B)
1987—Raiders, 34-21 (LA)
1988—Bills, 37-21 (B)
1990—Bills, 38-24 (B)
**Bills, 51-3 (B)
1991—Bills, 30-27 (LA) OT
1992—Raiders, 20-3 (LA)
1993—Raiders, 25-24 (B)
***Bills, 29-23 (B)
(RS Pts.—Raiders 630, Bills 576)
(PS Pts.—Bills 80, Raiders 26)
**Franchise in Oakland prior to 1982*
***AFC Championship*
****AFC Divisional Playoff*

BUFFALO vs. MIAMI
RS: Dolphins lead series, 37-20-1
PS: Bills lead series, 2-0
1966—Bills, 58-24 (B)
Bills, 29-0 (M)
1967—Bills, 35-13 (B)
Dolphins, 17-14 (M)
1968—Tie, 14-14 (M)
Dolphins, 21-17 (B)
1969—Dolphins, 24-6 (M)
Bills, 28-3 (B)
1970—Dolphins, 33-14 (B)
Dolphins, 45-7 (M)
1971—Dolphins, 29-14 (B)
Dolphins, 34-0 (M)
1972—Dolphins, 24-23 (M)
Dolphins, 30-16 (B)
1973—Dolphins, 27-6 (M)
Dolphins, 17-0 (B)
1974—Dolphins, 24-16 (B)
Dolphins, 35-28 (M)
1975—Dolphins, 35-30 (B)
Dolphins, 31-21 (M)
1976—Dolphins, 30-21 (B)
Dolphins, 45-27 (M)
1977—Dolphins, 13-0 (B)
Dolphins, 31-14 (M)
1978—Dolphins, 31-24 (M)
Dolphins, 25-24 (B)
1979—Dolphins, 9-7 (B)
Dolphins, 17-7 (M)
1980—Bills, 17-7 (B)
Dolphins, 17-14 (M)
1981—Bills, 31-21 (B)
Dolphins, 16-6 (M)
1982—Dolphins, 9-7 (B)
Dolphins, 27-10 (M)
1983—Dolphins, 12-0 (B)
Bills, 38-35 (M) OT
1984—Dolphins, 21-17 (B)
Dolphins, 38-7 (M)
1985—Dolphins, 23-14 (B)
Dolphins, 28-0 (M)
1986—Dolphins, 27-14 (M)
Dolphins, 34-24 (B)
1987—Bills, 34-31 (M) OT
Bills, 27-0 (B)
1988—Bills, 9-6 (B)
Bills, 31-6 (M)
1989—Bills, 27-24 (M)
Bills, 31-17 (B)
1990—Dolphins, 30-7 (M)
Bills, 24-14 (B)
*Bills, 44-34 (B)
1991—Bills, 35-31 (B)
Bills, 41-27 (M)
1992—Dolphins, 37-10 (B)
Bills, 26-20 (M)
**Bills, 29-10 (M)
1993—Dolphins, 22-13 (B)
Bills, 47-34 (M)
1994—Bills, 21-11 (B)
Bills, 42-31 (M)
(RS Pts.—Dolphins 1,337, Bills 1,124)
(PS Pts.—Bills 73, Dolphins 44)
**AFC Divisional Playoff*
***AFC Championship*

BUFFALO vs. MINNESOTA
RS: Vikings lead series, 5-2
1971—Vikings, 19-0 (M)
1975—Vikings, 35-13 (B)
1979—Vikings, 10-3 (M)
1982—Bills, 23-22 (B)
1985—Vikings, 27-20 (B)
1988—Bills, 13-10 (B)
1994—Vikings, 21-17 (B)
(RS Pts.—Vikings 144, Bills 89)

BUFFALO vs. *NEW ENGLAND
RS: Series tied, 34-34-1
PS: Patriots lead series, 1-0
1960—Bills, 13-0 (Bos)
Bills, 38-14 (Buff)
1961—Patriots, 23-21 (Buff)
Patriots, 52-21 (Bos)
1962—Tie, 28-28 (Buff)
Patriots, 21-10 (Bos)
1963—Bills, 28-21 (Buff)
Patriots, 17-7 (Bos)
**Patriots, 26-8 (Buff)
1964—Patriots, 36-28 (Buff)
Bills, 24-14 (Bos)
1965—Bills, 24-7 (Buff)
Bills, 23-7 (Bos)
1966—Patriots, 20-10 (Buff)
Patriots, 14-3 (Bos)
1967—Patriots, 23-0 (Buff)
Bills, 44-16 (Bos)
1968—Patriots, 16-7 (Buff)
Patriots, 23-6 (Bos)
1969—Bills, 23-16 (Buff)
Patriots, 35-21 (Bos)
1970—Bills, 45-10 (Bos)
Patriots, 14-10 (Buff)
1971—Patriots, 38-33 (NE)
Bills, 27-20 (Buff)
1972—Bills, 38-14 (Buff)
Bills, 27-24 (NE)
1973—Bills, 31-13 (NE)
Bills, 37-13 (Buff)
1974—Bills, 30-28 (Buff)
Bills, 29-28 (NE)
1975—Bills, 45-31 (Buff)
Bills, 34-14 (NE)
1976—Patriots, 26-22 (Buff)
Patriots, 20-10 (NE)
1977—Bills, 24-14 (NE)
Patriots, 20-7 (Buff)
1978—Patriots, 14-10 (Buff)
Patriots, 26-24 (NE)
1979—Patriots, 26-6 (Buff)
Bills, 16-13 (NE) OT
1980—Bills, 31-13 (Buff)
Patriots, 24-2 (NE)
1981—Bills, 20-17 (Buff)
Bills, 19-10 (NE)
1982—Patriots, 30-19 (NE)
1983—Patriots, 31-0 (Buff)
Patriots, 21-7 (NE)
1984—Patriots, 21-17 (Buff)
Patriots, 38-10 (NE)
1985—Patriots, 17-14 (Buff)
Patriots, 14-3 (NE)
1986—Patriots, 23-3 (Buff)
Patriots, 22-19 (NE)
1987—Patriots, 14-7 (NE)
Patriots, 13-7 (Buff)
1988—Bills, 16-14 (NE)
Bills, 23-20 (Buff)
1989—Bills, 31-10 (Buff)
Patriots, 33-24 (NE)

ALL-TIME TEAM VS. TEAM RESULTS

1990—Bills, 27-10 (NE)
Bills, 14-0 (Buff)
1991—Bills, 22-17 (Buff)
Patriots, 16-13 (NE)
1992—Bills, 41-7 (NE)
Bills, 16-7 (Buff)
1993—Bills, 38-14 (Buff)
Bills, 13-10 (NE) OT
1994—Bills, 38-35 (NE)
Patriots, 41-17 (Buff)
(RS Pts.—Bills 1,395, Patriots 1,351)
(PS Pts.—Patriots 26, Bills 8)
Franchise in Boston prior to 1971
***Division Playoff*

BUFFALO vs. NEW ORLEANS
RS: Bills lead series, 3-2
1973—Saints, 13-0 (NO)
1980—Bills, 35-26 (NO)
1983—Bills, 27-21 (B)
1989—Saints, 22-19 (B)
1992—Bills, 20-16 (NO)
(RS Pts.—Bills 101, Saints 98)

BUFFALO vs. N.Y. GIANTS
RS: Bills lead series, 4-2
PS: Giants lead series, 1-0
1970—Giants, 20-6 (NY)
1975—Giants, 17-14 (B)
1978—Bills, 41-17 (B)
1987—Bills, 6-3 (B) OT
1990—Bills, 17-13 (NY)
*Giants, 20-19 (Tampa)
1993—Bills, 17-14 (B)
(RS Pts.—Bills 101, Giants 84)
(PS Pts.—Giants 20, Bills 19)
Super Bowl XXV

BUFFALO vs. *N.Y. JETS
RS: Bills lead series, 37-31
PS: Bills lead series, 1-0
1960—Titans, 27-3 (NY)
Titans, 17-13 (B)
1961—Bills, 41-31 (B)
Titans, 21-14 (NY)
1962—Titans, 17-6 (B)
Bills, 20-3 (NY)
1963—Bills, 45-14 (B)
Bills, 19-10 (NY)
1964—Bills, 34-24 (B)
Bills, 20-7 (NY)
1965—Bills, 33-21 (B)
Jets, 14-12 (NY)
1966—Bills, 33-23 (NY)
Bills, 14-3 (B)
1967—Bills, 20-17 (B)
Jets, 20-10 (NY)
1968—Bills, 37-35 (B)
Jets, 25-21 (NY)
1969—Jets, 33-19 (B)
Jets, 16-6 (NY)
1970—Bills, 34-31 (B)
Bills, 10-6 (NY)
1971—Jets, 28-17 (NY)
Jets, 20-7 (B)
1972—Jets, 41-24 (B)
Jets, 41-3 (NY)
1973—Bills, 9-7 (B)
Bills, 34-14 (NY)
1974—Bills, 16-12 (B)
Jets, 20-10 (NY)
1975—Bills, 42-14 (B)
Bills, 24-23 (NY)
1976—Jets, 17-14 (NY)
Jets, 19-14 (B)
1977—Jets, 24-19 (B)
Bills, 14-10 (NY)
1978—Jets, 21-20 (B)
Jets, 45-14 (NY)
1979—Bills, 46-31 (B)
Bills, 14-12 (NY)
1980—Bills, 20-10 (B)
Bills, 31-24 (NY)
1981—Bills, 31-0 (B)
Jets, 33-14 (NY)
**Bills, 31-27 (NY)
1983—Jets, 34-10 (B)
Bills, 24-17 (NY)
1984—Jets, 28-26 (B)
Jets, 21-17 (NY)
1985—Jets, 42-3 (NY)
Jets, 27-7 (B)
1986—Jets, 28-24 (B)
Jets, 14-13 (NY)
1987—Jets, 31-28 (B)
Bills, 17-14 (NY)
1988—Bills, 37-14 (NY)
Bills, 9-6 (B) OT
1989—Bills, 34-3 (B)
Bills, 37-0 (NY)
1990—Bills, 30-7 (NY)
Bills, 30-27 (B)
1991—Bills, 23-20 (NY)
Bills, 24-13 (B)
1992—Bills, 24-20 (NY)
Jets, 24-17 (B)
1993—Bills, 19-10 (NY)
Bills, 16-14 (B)
1994—Jets, 23-3 (B)
Jets, 22-17 (NY)
(RS Pts.—Bills, 1,390, Jets 1,340)
(PS Pts.—Bills 31, Jets 27)
Jets known as Titans prior to 1963
***AFC First-Round Playoff*

BUFFALO vs. PHILADELPHIA
RS: Eagles lead series, 4-3
1973—Bills, 27-26 (B)
1981—Eagles, 20-14 (B)
1984—Eagles, 27-17 (B)
1985—Eagles, 21-17 (P)
1987—Eagles, 17-7 (P)
1990—Bills, 30-23 (B)
1993—Bills, 10-7 (P)
(RS Pts.—Eagles 141, Bills 122)

BUFFALO vs. PITTSBURGH
RS: Series tied, 7-7
PS: Series tied, 1-1
1970—Steelers, 23-10 (P)
1972—Steelers, 38-21 (B)
1974—*Steelers, 32-14 (P)
1975—Bills, 30-21 (P)
1978—Steelers, 28-17 (B)
1979—Steelers, 28-0 (P)
1980—Bills, 28-13 (B)
1982—Bills, 13-0 (B)
1985—Steelers, 30-24 (P)
1986—Bills, 16-12 (B)
1988—Bills, 36-28 (B)
1991—Bills, 52-34 (B)
1992—Bills, 28-20 (B)
*Bills, 24-3 (P)
1993—Steelers, 23-0 (P)
1994—Steelers, 23-10 (P)
(RS Pts.—Steelers 321, Bills 285)
(PS Pts.—Bills 38, Steelers 35)
AFC Divisional Playoff

BUFFALO vs. *ST. LOUIS
RS: Series tied, 3-3
1970—Rams, 19-0 (B)
1974—Rams, 19-14 (LA)
1980—Bills, 10-7 (B) OT
1983—Rams, 41-17 (LA)
1989—Bills, 23-20 (B)
1992—Bills, 40-7 (B)
(RS Pts.—Rams 113, Bills 104)
Franchise in Los Angeles prior to 1995

BUFFALO vs. *SAN DIEGO
RS: Chargers lead series, 16-7-2
PS: Bills lead series, 2-1
1960—Chargers, 24-10 (B)
Bills, 32-3 (LA)
1961—Chargers, 19-11 (B)
Chargers, 28-10 (SD)
1962—Bills, 35-10 (B)
Bills, 40-20 (SD)
1963—Chargers, 14-10 (SD)
Chargers, 23-13 (B)
1964—Bills, 30-3 (B)
Bills, 27-24 (SD)
**Bills, 20-7 (B)
1965—Chargers, 34-3 (B)
Tie, 20-20 (SD)
**Bills, 23-0 (SD)
1966—Chargers, 27-7 (SD)
Tie, 17-17 (B)
1967—Chargers, 37-17 (B)
1968—Chargers, 21-6 (B)
1969—Chargers, 45-6 (SD)
1971—Chargers, 20-3 (SD)
1973—Chargers, 34-7 (SD)
1976—Chargers, 34-13 (B)
1979—Chargers, 27-19 (SD)
1980—Bills, 26-24 (SD)
***Chargers, 20-14 (SD)
1981—Bills, 28-27 (SD)
1985—Chargers, 14-9 (B)
Chargers, 40-7 (SD)
(RS Pts.—Chargers 589, Bills 406)
(PS Pts.—Bills 57, Chargers 27)
Franchise in Los Angeles prior to 1961
***AFL Championship*
****AFC Divisional Playoff*

BUFFALO vs. SAN FRANCISCO
RS: Bills lead series 3-2
1972—Bills, 27-20 (B)
1980—Bills, 18-13 (SF)
1983—49ers, 23-10 (B)
1989—49ers, 21-10 (SF)
1992—Bills, 34-31 (SF)
(RS Pts.—49ers 108, Bills 99)

BUFFALO vs. SEATTLE
RS: Seahawks lead series, 3-1
1977—Seahawks, 56-17 (S)
1984—Seahawks, 31-28 (S)
1988—Bills, 13-3 (S)
1989—Seahawks, 17-16 (S)
(RS Pts.—Seahawks 107, Bills 74)

BUFFALO vs. TAMPA BAY
RS: Buccaneers lead series, 4-2
1976—Bills, 14-9 (TB)
1978—Buccaneers, 31-10 (TB)
1982—Buccaneers, 24-23 (TB)
1986—Buccaneers, 34-28 (TB)
1988—Buccaneers, 10-5 (TB)
1991—Bills, 17-10 (TB)
(RS Pts.—Buccaneers 118, Bills 97)

BUFFALO vs. WASHINGTON
RS: Redskins lead series, 4-3
PS: Redskins lead series, 1-0
1972—Bills, 24-17 (W)
1977—Redskins, 10-0 (B)
1981—Bills, 21-14 (B)
1984—Redskins, 41-14 (W)
1987—Redskins, 27-7 (B)
1990—Redskins, 29-14 (W)
1991—*Redskins, 37-24 (Minneapolis)
1993—Bills, 24-10 (B)
(RS Pts.—Redskins 148, Bills 104)
(PS Pts.—Redskins 37, Bills 24)
Super Bowl XXVI

CHICAGO vs. ARIZONA
RS: Bears lead series, 52-25-6;
See Arizona vs. Chicago

CHICAGO vs. ATLANTA
RS: Series tied, 9-9;
See Atlanta vs. Chicago

CHICAGO vs. BUFFALO
RS: Bears lead series, 4-2;
See Buffalo vs. Chicago

CHICAGO vs. CINCINNATI
RS: Bengals lead series, 3-2
1972—Bengals, 13-3 (Chi)
1980—Bengals, 17-14 (Chi) OT
1986—Bears, 44-7 (Cin)
1989—Bears, 17-14 (Chi)
1992—Bengals, 31-28 (Chi) OT
(RS Pts.—Bears 106, Bengals 82)

CHICAGO vs. CLEVELAND
RS: Browns lead series, 8-3
1951—Browns, 42-21 (Cle)
1954—Browns, 39-10 (Chi)
1960—Browns, 42-0 (Cle)
1961—Bears, 17-14 (Chi)
1967—Browns, 24-0 (Cle)
1969—Browns, 28-24 (Chi)
1972—Bears, 17-0 (Cle)
1980—Browns, 27-21 (Cle)
1986—Bears, 41-31 (Chi)
1989—Browns, 27-7 (Cle)
1992—Browns, 27-14 (Cle)
(RS Pts.—Browns 301, Bears 172)

CHICAGO vs. DALLAS
RS: Cowboys lead series, 8-6
PS: Cowboys lead series, 2-0
1960—Bears, 17-7 (C)
1962—Bears, 34-33 (D)
1964—Cowboys, 24-10 (C)
1968—Cowboys, 34-3 (C)
1971—Bears, 23-19 (C)
1973—Cowboys, 20-17 (C)
1976—Cowboys, 31-21 (D)
1977—*Cowboys, 37-7 (D)
1979—Cowboys, 24-20 (D)
1981—Cowboys, 10-9 (D)
1984—Cowboys, 23-14 (C)
1985—Bears, 44-0 (D)
1986—Bears, 24-10 (D)
1988—Bears, 17-7 (C)
1991—**Cowboys, 17-13 (C)
1992—Cowboys, 27-14 (D)
(RS Pts.—Cowboys 269, Bears 267)
(PS Pts.—Cowboys 54, Bears 20)
NFC Divisional Playoff
***NFC First-Round Playoff*

CHICAGO vs. DENVER
RS: Series tied, 5-5
1971—Broncos, 6-3 (D)
1973—Bears, 33-14 (D)
1976—Broncos, 28-14 (C)
1978—Broncos, 16-7 (D)
1981—Bears, 35-24 (C)
1983—Bears, 31-14 (C)
1984—Bears, 27-0 (C)
1987—Broncos, 31-29 (D)
1990—Bears, 16-13 (D) OT
1993—Broncos, 13-3 (C)
(RS Pts.—Bears 198, Broncos 159)

CHICAGO vs. *DETROIT
RS: Bears lead series, 75-50-5
1930—Spartans, 7-6 (P)
Bears, 14-6 (C)
1931—Bears, 9-6 (C)
Spartans, 3-0 (P)
1932—Tie, 13-13 (C)
Tie, 7-7 (P)
Bears, 9-0 (C)
1933—Bears, 17-14 (C)
Bears, 17-7 (P)
1934—Bears, 19-16 (D)
Bears, 10-7 (C)
1935—Tie, 20-20 (C)
Lions, 14-2 (D)
1936—Bears, 12-10 (C)
Lions, 13-7 (D)
1937—Bears, 28-20 (C)
Bears, 13-0 (D)
1938—Lions, 13-7 (C)
Lions, 14-7 (D)
1939—Lions, 10-0 (C)
Bears, 23-13 (D)
1940—Bears, 7-0 (C)
Lions, 17-14 (D)
1941—Bears, 49-0 (C)
Bears, 24-7 (D)
1942—Bears, 16-0 (C)
Bears, 42-0 (D)
1943—Bears, 27-21 (D)
Bears, 35-14 (C)
1944—Tie, 21-21 (C)
Lions, 41-21 (D)
1945—Lions, 16-10 (D)
Lions, 35-28 (C)
1946—Bears, 42-6 (C)
Bears, 45-24 (D)

1947—Bears, 33-24 (C)
Bears, 34-14 (D)
1948—Bears, 28-0 (C)
Bears, 42-14 (D)
1949—Bears, 27-24 (C)
Bears, 28-7 (D)
1950—Bears, 35-21 (D)
Bears, 6-3 (C)
1951—Bears, 28-23 (D)
Lions, 41-28 (C)
1952—Bears, 24-23 (C)
Lions, 45-21 (D)
1953—Lions, 20-16 (C)
Lions, 13-7 (D)
1954—Lions, 48-23 (D)
Bears, 28-24 (C)
1955—Bears, 24-14 (D)
Bears, 21-20 (C)
1956—Lions, 42-10 (D)
Bears, 38-21 (C)
1957—Bears, 27-7 (D)
Lions, 21-13 (C)
1958—Bears, 20-7 (D)
Bears, 21-16 (C)
1959—Bears, 24-14 (D)
Bears, 25-14 (C)
1960—Bears, 28-7 (C)
Lions, 36-0 (D)
1961—Bears, 31-17 (D)
Lions, 16-15 (C)
1962—Lions, 11-3 (D)
Bears, 3-0 (C)
1963—Bears, 37-21 (D)
Bears, 24-14 (C)
1964—Lions, 10-0 (C)
Bears, 27-24 (D)
1965—Bears, 38-10 (C)
Bears, 17-10 (D)
1966—Lions, 14-3 (D)
Tie, 10-10 (C)
1967—Bears, 14-3 (C)
Bears, 27-13 (D)
1968—Lions, 42-0 (D)
Lions, 28-10 (C)
1969—Lions, 13-7 (D)
Lions, 20-3 (C)
1970—Lions, 28-14 (D)
Lions, 16-10 (C)
1971—Bears, 28-23 (D)
Lions, 28-3 (C)
1972—Lions, 38-24 (C)
Lions, 14-0 (D)
1973—Lions, 30-7 (C)
Lions, 40-7 (D)
1974—Bears, 17-9 (C)
Lions, 34-17 (D)
1975—Lions, 27-7 (D)
Bears, 25-21 (C)
1976—Bears, 10-3 (C)
Lions, 14-10 (D)
1977—Bears, 30-20 (C)
Bears, 31-14 (D)
1978—Bears, 19-0 (D)
Lions, 21-17 (C)
1979—Bears, 35-7 (C)
Lions, 20-0 (D)
1980—Bears, 24-7 (C)
Bears, 23-17 (D) OT
1981—Lions, 48-17 (D)
Lions, 23-7 (C)
1982—Lions, 17-10 (D)
Bears, 20-17 (C)
1983—Lions, 31-17 (D)
Lions, 38-17 (C)
1984—Bears, 16-14 (C)
Bears, 30-13 (D)
1985—Bears, 24-3 (C)
Bears, 37-17 (D)
1986—Bears, 13-7 (C)
Bears, 16-13 (D)
1987—Bears, 30-10 (C)
1988—Bears, 24-7 (D)
Bears, 13-12 (C)
1989—Bears, 47-27 (D)
Lions, 27-17 (C)
1990—Bears, 23-17 (C) OT
Lions, 38-21 (D)
1991—Bears, 20-10 (C)
Lions, 16-6 (D)
1992—Bears, 27-24 (C)
Lions, 16-3 (D)
1993—Bears, 10-6 (D)
Lions, 20-14 (C)
1994—Lions, 21-16 (D)
Bears, 20-10 (C)
(RS Pts.—Bears 2,422, Lions 2,187)
Franchise in Portsmouth prior to 1934 and known as the Spartans

***CHICAGO vs. GREEN BAY**
RS: Bears lead series, 81-61-6
PS: Bears lead series, 1-0
1921—Staleys, 20-0 (C)
1923—Bears, 3-0 (GB)
1924—Bears, 3-0 (C)
1925—Packers, 14-10 (GB)
Bears, 21-0 (C)
1926—Tie, 6-6 (GB)
Bears, 19-13 (C)
Tie, 3-3 (C)
1927—Bears, 7-6 (GB)
Bears, 14-6 (C)
1928—Tie, 12-12 (GB)
Packers, 16-6 (C)
Packers, 6-0 (C)
1929—Packers, 23-0 (GB)
Packers, 14-0 (C)
Packers, 25-0 (C)
1930—Packers, 7-0 (GB)
Packers, 13-12 (C)
Bears, 21-0 (C)
1931—Packers, 7-0 (GB)
Packers, 6-2 (C)
Bears, 7-6 (C)
1932—Tie, 0-0 (GB)
Packers, 2-0 (C)
Bears, 9-0 (C)
1933—Bears, 14-7 (GB)
Bears, 10-7 (C)
Bears, 7-6 (C)
1934—Bears, 24-10 (GB)
Bears, 27-14 (C)
1935—Packers, 7-0 (GB)
Packers, 17-14 (C)
1936—Bears, 30-3 (GB)
Packers, 21-10 (C)
1937—Bears, 14-2 (GB)
Packers, 24-14 (C)
1938—Bears, 2-0 (GB)
Packers, 24-17 (C)
1939—Packers, 21-16 (GB)
Bears, 30-27 (C)
1940—Bears, 41-10 (GB)
Bears, 14-7 (C)
1941—Bears, 25-17 (GB)
Packers, 16-14 (C)
**Bears, 33-14 (C)
1942—Bears, 44-28 (GB)
Bears, 38-7 (C)
1943—Tie, 21-21 (GB)
Bears, 21-7 (C)
1944—Packers, 42-28 (GB)
Bears, 21-0 (C)
1945—Packers, 31-21 (GB)
Bears, 28-24 (C)
1946—Bears, 30-7 (GB)
Bears, 10-7 (C)
1947—Packers, 29-20 (GB)
Bears, 20-17 (C)
1948—Bears, 45-7 (GB)
Bears, 7-6 (C)
1949—Bears, 17-0 (GB)
Bears, 24-3 (C)
1950—Packers, 31-21 (GB)
Bears, 28-14 (C)
1951—Bears, 31-20 (GB)
Bears, 24-13 (C)
1952—Bears, 24-14 (GB)
Packers, 41-28 (C)
1953—Bears, 17-13 (GB)
Tie, 21-21 (C)
1954—Bears, 10-3 (GB)
Bears, 28-23 (C)
1955—Packers, 24-3 (GB)
Bears, 52-31 (C)
1956—Bears, 37-21 (GB)
Bears, 38-14 (C)
1957—Packers, 21-17 (GB)
Bears, 21-14 (C)
1958—Bears, 34-20 (GB)
Bears, 24-10 (C)
1959—Packers, 9-6 (GB)
Bears, 28-17 (C)
1960—Bears, 17-14 (GB)
Packers, 41-13 (C)
1961—Packers, 24-0 (GB)
Packers, 31-28 (C)
1962—Packers, 49-0 (GB)
Packers, 38-7 (C)
1963—Bears, 10-3 (GB)
Bears, 26-7 (C)
1964—Packers, 23-12 (GB)
Packers, 17-3 (C)
1965—Packers, 23-14 (GB)
Bears, 31-10 (C)
1966—Packers, 17-0 (C)
Packers, 13-6 (GB)
1967—Packers, 13-10 (GB)
Packers, 17-13 (C)
1968—Bears, 13-10 (GB)
Packers, 28-27 (C)
1969—Packers, 17-0 (GB)
Packers, 21-3 (C)
1970—Packers, 20-19 (GB)
Bears, 35-17 (C)
1971—Packers, 17-14 (C)
Packers, 31-10 (GB)
1972—Packers, 20-17 (GB)
Packers, 23-17 (C)
1973—Bears, 31-17 (GB)
Packers, 21-0 (C)
1974—Bears, 10-9 (C)
Packers, 20-3 (Mil)
1975—Bears, 27-14 (C)
Packers, 28-7 (GB)
1976—Bears, 24-13 (C)
Bears, 16-10 (GB)
1977—Bears, 26-0 (GB)
Bears, 21-10 (C)
1978—Packers, 24-14 (GB)
Bears, 14-0 (C)
1979—Bears, 6-3 (C)
Bears, 15-14 (GB)
1980—Packers, 12-6 (GB) OT
Bears, 61-7 (C)
1981—Packers, 16-9 (C)
Packers, 21-17 (GB)
1983—Packers, 31-28 (GB)
Bears, 23-21 (C)
1984—Bears, 9-7 (GB)
Packers, 20-14 (C)
1985—Bears, 23-7 (C)
Bears, 16-10 (GB)
1986—Bears, 25-12 (GB)
Bears, 12-10 (C)
1987—Bears, 26-24 (GB)
Bears, 23-10 (C)
1988—Bears, 24-6 (GB)
Bears, 16-0 (C)
1989—Packers, 14-13 (GB)
Packers, 40-28 (C)
1990—Bears, 31-13 (GB)
Bears, 27-13 (C)
1991—Bears, 10-0 (GB)
Bears, 27-13 (C)
1992—Bears, 30-10 (GB)
Packers, 17-3 (C)
1993—Packers, 17-3 (GB)
Bears, 30-17 (C)
1994—Packers, 33-6 (C)
Packers, 40-3 (GB)
(RS Pts.—Bears 2,487, Packers 2,203)
(PS Pts.—Bears 33, Packers 14)
**Bears known as Staleys prior to 1922*
***Division Playoff*

CHICAGO vs. HOUSTON
RS: Oilers lead series, 4-2
1973—Bears, 35-14 (C)
1977—Oilers, 47-0 (H)
1980—Oilers, 10-6 (C)
1986—Bears, 20-7 (H)
1989—Oilers, 33-28 (C)
1992—Oilers, 24-7 (H)
(RS Pts.—Oilers 135, Bears 96)

CHICAGO vs. *INDIANAPOLIS
RS: Colts lead series, 21-16
1953—Colts, 13-9 (B)
Colts, 16-14 (C)
1954—Bears, 28-9 (C)
Bears, 28-13 (B)
1955—Colts, 23-17 (B)
Bears, 38-10 (C)
1956—Colts, 28-21 (B)
Bears, 58-27 (C)
1957—Colts, 21-10 (B)
Colts, 29-14 (C)
1958—Colts, 51-38 (B)
Colts, 17-0 (C)
1959—Bears, 26-21 (B)
Colts, 21-7 (C)
1960—Colts, 42-7 (B)
Colts, 24-20 (C)
1961—Bears, 24-10 (C)
Bears, 21-20 (B)
1962—Bears, 35-15 (C)
Bears, 57-0 (B)
1963—Bears, 10-3 (C)
Bears, 17-7 (B)
1964—Colts, 52-0 (B)
Colts, 40-24 (C)
1965—Colts, 26-21 (C)
Bears, 13-0 (B)
1966—Bears, 27-17 (C)
Colts, 21-16 (B)
1967—Colts, 24-3 (C)
1968—Colts, 28-7 (B)
1969—Colts, 24-21 (C)
1970—Colts, 21-20 (B)
1975—Colts, 35-7 (C)
1983—Colts, 22-19 (B) OT
1985—Bears, 17-10 (C)
1988—Bears, 17-13 (I)
1991—Bears, 31-17 (I)
(RS Pts.—Colts 770, Bears 742)
**Franchise in Baltimore prior to 1984*

CHICAGO vs. KANSAS CITY
RS: Bears lead series, 4-2
1973—Chiefs, 19-7 (KC)
1977—Bears, 28-27 (C)
1981—Bears, 16-13 (KC) OT
1987—Bears, 31-28 (C)
1990—Chiefs, 21-10 (C)
1993—Bears, 19-17 (KC)
(RS Pts.—Chiefs 125, Bears 111)

CHICAGO vs. *LOS ANGELES
RS: Raiders lead series, 5-3
1972—Raiders, 28-21 (O)
1976—Raiders, 28-27 (C)
1978—Raiders, 25-19 (C) OT
1981—Bears, 23-6 (O)
1984—Bears, 17-6 (C)
1987—Bears, 6-3 (LA)
1990—Raiders, 24-10 (LA)
1993—Raiders, 16-14 (C)
(RS Pts.—Bears 137, Raiders 136)
**Franchise in Oakland prior to 1982*

CHICAGO vs. MIAMI
RS: Dolphins lead series, 5-2
1971—Dolphins, 34-3 (M)
1975—Dolphins, 46-13 (C)
1979—Dolphins, 31-16 (M)
1985—Dolphins, 38-24 (M)
1988—Bears, 34-7 (C)

ALL-TIME TEAM VS. TEAM RESULTS

1991—Dolphins, 16-13 (C) OT
1994—Bears, 17-14 (M)
(RS Pts.—Dolphins 186, Bears 120)

CHICAGO vs. MINNESOTA
RS: Vikings lead series, 36-29-2
PS: Bears lead series, 1-0
1961—Vikings, 37-13 (M)
Bears, 52-35 (C)
1962—Bears, 13-0 (M)
Bears, 31-30 (C)
1963—Bears, 28-7 (M)
Tie, 17-17 (C)
1964—Bears, 34-28 (M)
Vikings, 41-14 (C)
1965—Bears, 45-37 (M)
Vikings, 24-17 (C)
1966—Bears, 13-10 (M)
Bears, 41-28 (C)
1967—Bears, 17-7 (M)
Tie, 10-10 (C)
1968—Bears, 27-17 (M)
Bears, 26-24 (C)
1969—Vikings, 31-0 (C)
Vikings, 31-14 (M)
1970—Vikings, 24-0 (C)
Vikings, 16-13 (M)
1971—Bears, 20-17 (M)
Vikings, 27-10 (C)
1972—Bears, 13-10 (C)
Vikings, 23-10 (M)
1973—Vikings, 22-13 (C)
Vikings, 31-13 (M)
1974—Vikings, 11-7 (M)
Vikings, 17-0 (C)
1975—Vikings, 28-3 (M)
Vikings, 13-9 (C)
1976—Vikings, 20-19 (M)
Bears, 14-13 (C)
1977—Vikings, 22-16 (M) OT
Bears, 10-7 (C)
1978—Vikings, 24-20 (C)
Vikings, 17-14 (M)
1979—Bears, 26-7 (C)
Vikings, 30-27 (M)
1980—Vikings, 34-14 (C)
Vikings, 13-7 (M)
1981—Vikings, 24-21 (M)
Bears, 10-9 (C)
1982—Vikings, 35-7 (M)
1983—Vikings, 23-14 (C)
Bears, 19-13 (M)
1984—Bears, 16-7 (C)
Bears, 34-3 (M)
1985—Bears, 33-24 (M)
Bears, 27-9 (C)
1986—Bears, 23-0 (C)
Vikings, 23-7 (M)
1987—Bears, 27-7 (C)
Bears, 30-24 (M)
1988—Vikings, 31-7 (C)
Vikings, 28-27 (M)
1989—Bears, 38-7 (C)
Vikings, 27-16 (M)
1990—Bears, 19-16 (C)
Vikings, 41-13 (M)
1991—Bears, 10-6 (C)
Bears, 34-17 (M)
1992—Vikings, 21-20 (M)
Vikings, 38-10 (C)
1993—Vikings, 10-7 (M)
Vikings, 19-12 (C)
1994—Vikings, 42-14 (C)
Vikings, 33-27 (M) OT
*Bears, 35-18 (M)
(RS Pts.—Vikings 1,377, Bears 1,212)
(PS Pts.—Bears 35, Vikings 18)
NFC First-Round Playoff

CHICAGO vs. NEW ENGLAND
RS: Patriots lead series, 4-2
PS: Bears lead series, 1-0
1973—Patriots, 13-10 (C)
1979—Patriots, 27-7 (C)
1982—Bears, 26-13 (C)
1985—Bears, 20-7 (C)
*Bears, 46-10 (New Orleans)
1988—Patriots, 30-7 (NE)
1994—Patriots, 13-3 (C)
(RS Pts.—Patriots 113, Bears 73)
(PS Pts.—Bears 46, Patriots 10)
Super Bowl XX

CHICAGO vs. NEW ORLEANS
RS: Bears lead series, 9-6
PS: Bears lead series, 1-0
1968—Bears, 23-17 (NO)
1970—Bears, 24-3 (NO)
1971—Bears, 35-14 (C)
1973—Saints, 21-16 (NO)
1974—Bears, 24-10 (C)
1975—Bears, 42-17 (NO)
1977—Saints, 42-24 (C)
1980—Bears, 22-3 (C)
1982—Saints, 10-0 (C)
1983—Saints, 34-31 (NO) OT
1984—Bears, 20-7 (C)
1987—Saints, 19-17 (C)
1990—*Bears, 16-6 (C)
1991—Bears, 20-17 (NO)
1992—Saints, 28-6 (NO)
1994—Bears, 17-7 (C)
(RS Pts.—Bears 321, Saints 249)
(PS Pts.—Bears 16, Saints 6)
NFC First-Round Playoff

CHICAGO vs. N.Y. GIANTS
RS: Bears lead series, 24-16-2
PS: Bears lead series, 5-3
1925—Bears, 19-7 (NY)
Giants, 9-0 (C)
1926—Bears, 7-0 (C)
1927—Giants, 13-7 (NY)
1928—Bears, 13-0 (C)
1929—Giants, 26-14 (C)
Giants, 34-0 (NY)
Giants, 14-9 (C)
1930—Giants, 12-0 (C)
Bears, 12-0 (NY)
1931—Bears, 6-0 (C)
Bears, 12-6 (NY)
Giants, 25-6 (C)
1932—Bears, 28-8 (NY)
Bears, 6-0 (C)
1933—Bears, 14-10 (C)
Giants, 3-0 (NY)
*Bears, 23-21 (C)
1934—Bears, 27-7 (C)
Bears, 10-9 (NY)
*Giants, 30-13 (NY)
1935—Bears, 20-3 (NY)
Giants, 3-0 (C)
1936—Bears, 25-7 (NY)
1937—Tie, 3-3 (NY)
1939—Giants, 16-13 (NY)
1940—Bears, 37-21 (NY)
1941—*Bears, 37-9 (C)
1942—Bears, 26-7 (NY)
1943—Bears, 56-7 (NY)
1946—Giants, 14-0 (NY)
*Bears, 24-14 (NY)
1948—Bears, 35-14 (C)
1949—Giants, 35-28 (NY)
1956—Tie, 17-17 (NY)
*Giants, 47-7 (NY)
1962—Giants, 26-24 (C)
1963—*Bears, 14-10 (C)
1965—Bears, 35-14 (NY)
1967—Bears, 34-7 (C)
1969—Giants, 28-24 (NY)
1970—Bears, 24-16 (NY)
1974—Bears, 16-13 (C)
1977—Bears, 12-9 (NY) OT
1985—**Bears, 21-0 (C)
1987—Bears, 34-19 (C)
1990—**Giants, 31-3 (NY)
1991—Bears, 20-17 (C)
1992—Giants, 27-14 (C)
1993—Giants, 26-20 (C)
(RS Pts.—Bears 707, Giants 532)
(PS Pts.—Giants 162, Bears 142)
NFL Championship
***NFC Divisional Playoff*

CHICAGO vs. N.Y. JETS
RS: Bears lead series, 4-1
1974—Jets, 23-21 (C)
1979—Bears, 23-13 (C)
1985—Bears, 19-6 (NY)
1991—Bears, 19-13 (C) OT
1994—Bears, 19-7 (NY)
(RS Pts.—Bears 101, Jets 62)

CHICAGO vs. PHILADELPHIA
RS: Bears lead series, 23-4-1
PS: Series tied, 1-1
1933—Tie, 3-3 (P)
1935—Bears, 39-0 (P)
1936—Bears, 17-0 (P)
Bears, 28-7 (P)
1938—Bears, 28-6 (P)
1939—Bears, 27-14 (C)
1941—Bears, 49-14 (P)
1942—Bears, 45-14 (C)
1944—Bears, 28-7 (P)
1946—Bears, 21-14 (C)
1947—Bears, 40-7 (C)
1948—Eagles, 12-7 (P)
1949—Bears, 38-21 (C)
1955—Bears, 17-10 (C)
1961—Eagles, 16-14 (P)
1963—Bears, 16-7 (C)
1968—Bears, 29-16 (P)
1970—Bears, 20-16 (C)
1972—Bears, 21-12 (P)
1975—Bears, 15-13 (C)
1979—*Eagles, 27-17 (P)
1980—Eagles, 17-14 (P)
1983—Bears, 7-6 (P)
Bears, 17-14 (C)
1986—Bears, 13-10 (C) OT
1987—Bears, 35-3 (P)
1988—**Bears, 20-12 (C)
1989—Bears, 27-13 (C)
1993—Bears, 17-6 (P)
1994—Eagles, 30-22 (P)
(RS Pts.—Bears 654, Eagles 308)
(PS Pts.—Eagles 39, Bears 37)
NFC First-Round Playoff
***NFC Divisional Playoff*

CHICAGO vs. *PITTSBURGH
RS: Bears lead series, 16-4-1
1934—Bears, 28-0 (P)
1935—Bears, 23-7 (P)
1936—Bears, 27-9 (P)
Bears, 26-6 (C)
1937—Bears, 7-0 (P)
1939—Bears, 32-0 (P)
1941—Bears, 34-7 (C)
1945—Bears, 28-7 (C)
1947—Bears, 49-7 (C)
1949—Bears, 30-21 (C)
1958—Steelers, 24-10 (P)
1959—Bears, 27-21 (C)
1963—Tie, 17-17 (P)
1967—Steelers, 41-13 (P)
1969—Bears, 38-7 (C)
1971—Bears, 17-15 (C)
1975—Steelers, 34-3 (P)
1980—Steelers, 38-3 (P)
1986—Bears, 13-10 (C) OT
1989—Bears, 20-0 (P)
1992—Bears, 30-6 (C)
(RS Pts.—Bears 475, Steelers 277)
Steelers known as Pirates prior to 1941

CHICAGO vs. *ST. LOUIS
RS: Bears lead series, 45-29-3
PS: Series tied, 1-1
1937—Bears, 20-2 (Clev)
Bears, 15-7 (C)
1938—Rams, 14-7 (C)
Rams, 23-21 (Clev)
1939—Bears, 30-21 (Clev)
Bears, 35-21 (C)
1940—Bears, 21-14 (Clev)
Bears, 47-25 (C)
1941—Bears, 48-21 (Clev)
Bears, 31-13 (C)
1942—Bears, 21-7 (Clev)
Bears, 47-0 (C)
1944—Rams, 19-7 (Clev)
Bears, 28-21 (C)
1945—Rams, 17-0 (Clev)
Rams, 41-21 (C)
1946—Tie, 28-28 (C)
Bears, 27-21 (LA)
1947—Bears, 41-21 (LA)
Rams, 17-14 (C)
1948—Bears, 42-21 (C)
Bears, 21-6 (LA)
1949—Rams, 31-16 (C)
Rams, 27-24 (LA)
1950—Bears, 24-20 (LA)
Bears, 24-14 (C)
**Rams, 24-14 (LA)
1951—Rams, 42-17 (C)
1952—Rams, 31-7 (LA)
Rams, 40-24 (C)
1953—Rams, 38-24 (LA)
Bears, 24-21 (C)
1954—Rams, 42-38 (LA)
Bears, 24-13 (C)
1955—Bears, 31-20 (LA)
Bears, 24-3 (C)
1956—Bears, 35-24 (LA)
Bears, 30-21 (C)
1957—Bears, 34-26 (C)
Bears, 16-10 (LA)
1958—Bears, 31-10 (C)
Rams, 41-35 (LA)
1959—Rams, 28-21 (C)
Bears, 26-21 (LA)
1960—Bears, 34-27 (C)
Tie, 24-24 (LA)
1961—Bears, 21-17 (LA)
Bears, 28-24 (C)
1962—Bears, 27-23 (LA)
Bears, 30-14 (C)
1963—Bears, 52-14 (LA)
Bears, 6-0 (C)
1964—Bears, 38-17 (C)
Bears, 34-24 (LA)
1965—Rams, 30-28 (LA)
Bears, 31-6 (C)
1966—Rams, 31-17 (LA)
Bears, 17-10 (C)
1967—Rams, 28-17 (C)
1968—Bears, 17-16 (LA)
1969—Rams, 9-7 (C)
1971—Rams, 17-3 (LA)
1972—Tie, 13-13 (C)
1973—Rams, 26-0 (C)
1975—Rams, 38-10 (LA)
1976—Rams, 20-12 (LA)
1977—Bears, 24-23 (C)
1979—Bears, 27-23 (C)
1981—Rams, 24-7 (C)
1982—Bears, 34-26 (LA)
1983—Rams, 21-14 (LA)
1984—Rams, 29-13 (LA)
1985—***Bears, 24-0 (C)
1986—Rams, 20-17 (C)
1988—Rams, 23-3 (LA)
1989—Bears, 20-10 (C)
1990—Bears, 38-9 (C)
1993—Rams, 20-6 (LA)
1994—Bears, 27-13 (C)
(RS Pts.—Bears 1,797, Rams 1,572)
(PS Pts.—Bears 38, Rams 24)
Franchise in Los Angeles prior to 1995 and in Cleveland prior to 1946
***Conference Playoff*
****NFC Championship*

CHICAGO vs. SAN DIEGO
RS: Chargers lead series, 4-2
1970—Chargers, 20-7 (C)
1974—Chargers, 28-21 (SD)
1978—Chargers, 40-7 (SD)

1981—Bears, 20-17 (C) OT
1984—Chargers, 20-7 (SD)
1993—Bears, 16-13 (SD)
(RS Pts.—Chargers 138, Bears 78)

CHICAGO vs. SAN FRANCISCO
RS: Series tied, 25-25-1
PS: 49ers lead series, 3-0
1950—Bears, 32-20 (SF)
Bears, 17-0 (C)
1951—Bears, 13-7 (C)
1952—49ers, 40-16 (C)
Bears, 20-17 (SF)
1953—49ers, 35-28 (C)
49ers, 24-14 (SF)
1954—49ers, 31-24 (C)
Bears, 31-27 (SF)
1955—49ers, 20-19 (C)
Bears, 34-23 (SF)
1956—Bears, 31-7 (C)
Bears, 38-21 (SF)
1957—49ers, 21-17 (C)
49ers, 21-17 (SF)
1958—Bears, 28-6 (C)
Bears, 27-14 (SF)
1959—49ers, 20-17 (SF)
Bears, 14-3 (C)
1960—Bears, 27-10 (C)
49ers, 25-7 (SF)
1961—Bears, 31-0 (C)
49ers, 41-31 (SF)
1962—Bears, 30-14 (SF)
49ers, 34-27 (C)
1963—49ers, 20-14 (SF)
Bears, 27-7 (C)
1964—49ers, 31-21 (SF)
Bears, 23-21 (C)
1965—49ers, 52-24 (SF)
Bears, 61-20 (C)
1966—Tie, 30-30 (C)
49ers, 41-14 (SF)
1967—Bears, 28-14 (SF)
1968—Bears, 27-19 (C)
1969—49ers, 42-21 (SF)
1970—49ers, 37-16 (C)
1971—49ers, 13-0 (SF)
1972—49ers, 34-21 (C)
1974—49ers, 34-0 (C)
1975—49ers, 31-3 (SF)
1976—Bears, 19-12 (SF)
1978—Bears, 16-13 (SF)
1979—Bears, 28-27 (SF)
1981—49ers, 28-17 (SF)
1983—Bears, 13-3 (C)
1984—*49ers, 23-0 (SF)
1985—Bears, 26-10 (SF)
1987—49ers, 41-0 (SF)
1988—Bears, 10-9 (C)
*49ers, 28-3 (C)
1989—49ers, 26-0 (SF)
1991—49ers, 52-14 (SF)
1994—**49ers, 44-15 (SF)
(RS Pts.—49ers 1,148, Bears 1,063)
(PS Pts.—49ers 95, Bears 18)
NFC Championship
***NFC Divisional Playoff*

CHICAGO vs. SEATTLE
RS: Seahawks lead series, 4-2
1976—Bears, 34-7 (S)
1978—Seahawks, 31-29 (C)
1982—Seahawks, 20-14 (S)
1984—Seahawks, 38-9 (S)
1987—Seahawks, 34-21 (C)
1990—Bears, 17-0 (C)
(RS Pts.—Seahawks 130, Bears 124)

CHICAGO vs. TAMPA BAY
RS: Bears lead series, 26-8
1977—Bears, 10-0 (TB)
1978—Buccaneers, 33-19 (TB)
Bears, 14-3 (C)
1979—Buccaneers, 17-13 (C)
Bears, 14-0 (TB)
1980—Bears, 23-0 (C)
Bears, 14-13 (TB)
1981—Bears, 28-17 (C)
Buccaneers, 20-10 (TB)
1982—Buccaneers, 26-23 (TB) OT
1983—Bears, 17-10 (C)
Bears, 27-0 (TB)
1984—Bears, 34-14 (C)
Bears, 44-9 (TB)
1985—Bears, 38-28 (C)
Bears, 27-19 (TB)
1986—Bears, 23-3 (TB)
Bears, 48-14 (C)
1987—Bears, 20-3 (C)
Bears, 27-26 (TB)
1988—Bears, 28-10 (C)
Bears, 27-15 (TB)
1989—Buccaneers, 42-35 (TB)
Buccaneers, 32-31 (C)
1990—Bears, 26-6 (TB)
Bears, 27-14 (C)
1991—Bears, 21-20 (TB)
Bears, 27-0 (C)
1992—Bears, 31-14 (C)
Buccaneers, 20-17 (TB)
1993—Bears, 47-17 (C)
Buccaneers, 13-10 (TB)
1994—Bears, 21-9 (C)
Bears, 20-6 (TB)
(RS Pts.—Bears 841, Buccaneers 473)

CHICAGO vs. *WASHINGTON
RS: Bears lead series, 18-12-1
PS: Redskins lead series, 4-3
1932—Tie, 7-7 (B)
1933—Bears, 7-0 (C)
Redskins, 10-0 (B)
1934—Bears, 21-0 (B)
1935—Bears, 30-14 (B)
1936—Bears, 26-0 (B)
1937—**Redskins, 28-21 (C)
1938—Bears, 31-7 (C)
1940—Redskins, 7-3 (W)
**Bears, 73-0 (W)
1941—Bears, 35-21 (C)
1942—**Redskins, 14-6 (W)
1943—Redskins, 21-7 (W)
**Bears, 41-21 (C)
1945—Redskins, 28-21 (W)
1946—Bears, 24-20 (C)
1947—Bears, 56-20 (W)
1948—Bears, 48-13 (C)
1949—Bears, 31-21 (W)
1951—Bears, 27-0 (W)
1953—Bears, 27-24 (W)
1957—Redskins, 14-3 (C)
1964—Redskins, 27-20 (W)
1968—Redskins, 38-28 (C)
1971—Bears, 16-15 (C)
1974—Redskins, 42-0 (W)
1976—Bears, 33-7 (C)
1978—Bears, 14-10 (W)
1980—Bears, 35-21 (C)
1981—Redskins, 24-7 (C)
1984—***Bears, 23-19 (W)
1985—Bears, 45-10 (C)
1986—***Redskins, 27-13 (C)
1987—***Redskins, 21-17 (C)
1988—Bears, 34-14 (W)
1989—Redskins, 38-14 (W)
1990—Redskins, 10-9 (W)
1991—Redskins, 20-7 (C)
(RS Pts.—Bears 666, Redskins 503)
(PS Pts.—Bears 194, Redskins 130)
**Franchise in Boston prior to 1937 and known as Braves prior to 1933*
***NFL Championship*
****NFC Divisional Playoff*

CINCINNATI vs. ARIZONA
RS: Bengals lead series, 3-2;
See Arizona vs. Cincinnati

CINCINNATI vs. ATLANTA
RS: Bengals lead series, 6-2;
See Atlanta vs. Cincinnati

CINCINNATI vs. BUFFALO
RS: Bengals lead series, 9-7
PS: Bengals lead series, 2-0;
See Buffalo vs. Cincinnati

CINCINNATI vs. CHICAGO
RS: Bengals lead series, 3-2;
See Chicago vs. Cincinnati

CINCINNATI vs. CLEVELAND
RS: Browns lead series, 25-24
1970—Browns, 30-27 (Cle)
Bengals, 14-10 (Cin)
1971—Browns, 27-24 (Cin)
Browns, 31-27 (Cle)
1972—Browns, 27-6 (Cle)
Browns, 27-24 (Cin)
1973—Browns, 17-10 (Cle)
Bengals, 34-17 (Cin)
1974—Bengals, 33-7 (Cin)
Bengals, 34-24 (Cle)
1975—Bengals, 24-17 (Cin)
Browns, 35-23 (Cle)
1976—Bengals, 45-24 (Cle)
Bengals, 21-6 (Cin)
1977—Browns, 13-3 (Cin)
Bengals, 10-7 (Cle)
1978—Browns, 13-10 (Cle) OT
Bengals, 48-16 (Cin)
1979—Browns, 28-27 (Cle)
Bengals, 16-12 (Cin)
1980—Browns, 31-7 (Cle)
Browns, 27-24 (Cin)
1981—Browns, 20-17 (Cin)
Bengals, 41-21 (Cle)
1982—Bengals, 23-10 (Cin)
1983—Browns, 17-7 (Cle)
Bengals, 28-21 (Cin)
1984—Bengals, 12-9 (Cin)
Bengals, 20-17 (Cle) OT
1985—Bengals, 27-10 (Cin)
Browns, 24-6 (Cle)
1986—Bengals, 30-13 (Cle)
Browns, 34-3 (Cin)
1987—Browns, 34-0 (Cin)
Browns, 38-24 (Cle)
1988—Bengals, 24-17 (Cin)
Browns, 23-16 (Cle)
1989—Bengals, 21-14 (Cin)
Bengals, 21-0 (Cle)
1990—Bengals, 34-13 (Cle)
Bengals, 21-14 (Cin)
1991—Browns, 14-13 (Cle)
Bengals, 23-21 (Cin)
1992—Bengals, 30-10 (Cin)
Browns, 37-21 (Cle)
1993—Browns, 27-14 (Cle)
Browns, 28-17 (Cin)
1994—Browns, 28-20 (Cin)
Browns, 37-13 (Cle)
(RS Pts.—Bengals 1,017, Browns 997)

CINCINNATI vs. DALLAS
RS: Cowboys lead series, 4-2
1973—Cowboys, 38-10 (D)
1979—Cowboys, 38-13 (D)
1985—Bengals, 50-24 (C)
1988—Bengals, 38-24 (D)
1991—Cowboys, 35-23 (D)
1994—Cowboys, 23-20 (C)
(RS Pts.—Cowboys 182, Bengals 154)

CINCINNATI vs. DENVER
RS: Broncos lead series, 11-6
1968—Bengals, 24-10 (C)
Broncos, 10-7 (D)
1969—Broncos, 30-23 (C)
Broncos, 27-16 (D)
1971—Bengals, 24-10 (D)
1972—Bengals, 21-10 (C)
1973—Broncos, 28-10 (D)
1975—Bengals, 17-16 (D)
1976—Bengals, 17-7 (C)
1977—Broncos, 24-13 (C)
1979—Broncos, 10-0 (D)
1981—Bengals, 38-21 (C)
1983—Broncos, 24-17 (D)
1984—Broncos, 20-17 (D)
1986—Broncos, 34-28 (D)
1991—Broncos, 45-14 (D)
1994—Broncos, 15-13 (D)
(RS Pts.—Broncos 341, Bengals 299)

CINCINNATI vs. DETROIT
RS: Series tied, 3-3
1970—Lions, 38-3 (D)
1974—Lions, 23-19 (C)
1983—Bengals, 17-9 (C)
1986—Bengals, 24-17 (D)
1989—Bengals, 42-7 (C)
1992—Lions, 19-13 (C)
(RS Pts.—Bengals 118, Lions 113)

CINCINNATI vs. GREEN BAY
RS: Bengals lead series, 4-3
1971—Packers, 20-17 (GB)
1976—Bengals, 28-7 (C)
1977—Bengals, 17-7 (Mil)
1980—Packers, 14-9 (GB)
1983—Bengals, 34-14 (C)
1986—Bengals, 34-28 (Mil)
1992—Packers, 24-23 (GB)
(RS Pts.—Bengals 162, Packers 114)

CINCINNATI vs. HOUSTON
RS: Oilers lead series, 26-25-1
PS: Bengals lead series, 1-0
1968—Oilers, 27-17 (C)
1969—Tie, 31-31 (H)
1970—Oilers, 20-13 (C)
Bengals, 30-20 (H)
1971—Oilers, 10-6 (H)
Bengals, 28-13 (C)
1972—Bengals, 30-7 (C)
Bengals, 61-17 (H)
1973—Bengals, 24-10 (C)
Bengals, 27-24 (H)
1974—Oilers, 34-21 (C)
Oilers, 20-3 (H)
1975—Bengals, 21-19 (H)
Bengals, 23-19 (C)
1976—Bengals, 27-7 (H)
Bengals, 31-27 (C)
1977—Bengals, 13-10 (C) OT
Oilers, 21-16 (H)
1978—Bengals, 28-13 (C)
Oilers, 17-10 (H)
1979—Oilers, 30-27 (C) OT
Oilers, 42-21 (H)
1980—Oilers, 13-10 (C)
Oilers, 23-3 (H)
1981—Oilers, 17-10 (H)
Bengals, 34-21 (C)
1982—Bengals, 27-6 (C)
Bengals, 35-27 (H)
1983—Bengals, 55-14 (H)
Bengals, 38-10 (C)
1984—Bengals, 13-3 (C)
Bengals, 31-13 (H)
1985—Oilers, 44-27 (H)
Bengals, 45-27 (C)
1986—Bengals, 31-28 (C)
Oilers, 32-28 (H)
1987—Oilers, 31-29 (C)
Oilers, 21-17 (H)
1988—Bengals, 44-21 (C)
Oilers, 41-6 (H)
1989—Oilers, 26-24 (H)
Bengals, 61-7 (C)
1990—Oilers, 48-17 (H)
Bengals, 40-20 (C)
*Bengals, 41-14 (C)
1991—Oilers, 30-7 (C)
Oilers, 35-3 (H)
1992—Oilers, 38-24 (C)
Oilers, 26-10 (H)
1993—Oilers, 28-12 (H)
Oilers, 38-3 (C)
1994—Oilers, 20-13 (H)
Bengals, 34-31 (C)
(RS Pts.—Bengals 1,239, Oilers 1,177)
(PS Pts.—Bengals 41, Oilers 14)
**AFC First Round Playoff*

CINCINNATI vs.*INDIANAPOLIS

ALL-TIME TEAM VS. TEAM RESULTS

RS: Colts lead series, 9-5
PS: Colts lead series, 1-0
1970—**Colts, 17-0 (B)
1972—Colts, 20-19 (C)
1974—Bengals, 24-14 (B)
1976—Colts, 28-27 (B)
1979—Colts, 38-28 (B)
1980—Bengals, 34-33 (C)
1981—Bengals, 41-19 (B)
1982—Bengals, 20-17 (B)
1983—Colts, 34-31 (C)
1987—Bengals, 23-21 (I)
1989—Colts, 23-12 (C)
1990—Colts, 34-20 (C)
1992—Colts, 21-17 (C)
1993—Colts, 9-6 (C)
1994—Colts, 17-13 (C)
(RS Pts.—Colts 328, Bengals 315)
(PS Pts.—Colts 17, Bengals 0)
Franchise in Baltimore prior to 1984
**AFC Divisional Playoff*

CINCINNATI vs. KANSAS CITY
RS: Chiefs lead series, 11-9
1968—Chiefs, 13-3 (KC)
Chiefs, 16-9 (C)
1969—Bengals, 24-19 (C)
Chiefs, 42-22 (KC)
1970—Chiefs, 27-19 (C)
1972—Bengals, 23-16 (KC)
1973—Bengals, 14-6 (C)
1974—Bengals, 33-6 (C)
1976—Bengals, 27-24 (KC)
1977—Bengals, 27-7 (KC)
1978—Chiefs, 24-23 (C)
1979—Chiefs, 10-7 (C)
1980—Bengals, 20-6 (KC)
1983—Chiefs, 20-15 (KC)
1984—Chiefs, 27-22 (C)
1986—Chiefs, 24-14 (KC)
1987—Bengals, 30-27 (C) OT
1988—Chiefs, 31-28 (KC)
1989—Bengals, 21-17 (KC)
1993—Chiefs, 17-15 (KC)
(RS Pts.—Bengals 396, Chiefs 379)

CINCINNATI vs. *LOS ANGELES
RS: Raiders lead series, 14-7
PS: Raiders lead series, 2-0
1968—Raiders, 31-10 (O)
Raiders, 34-0 (C)
1969—Bengals, 31-17 (C)
Raiders, 37-17 (O)
1970—Bengals, 31-21 (C)
1971—Raiders, 31-27 (O)
1972—Raiders, 20-14 (C)
1974—Raiders, 30-27 (O)
1975—Bengals, 14-10 (C)
**Raiders, 31-28 (O)
1976—Raiders, 35-20 (O)
1978—Raiders, 34-21 (C)
1980—Raiders, 28-17 (O)
1982—Bengals, 31-17 (C)
1983—Raiders, 20-10 (C)
1985—Raiders, 13-6 (LA)
1988—Bengals, 45-21 (LA)
1989—Raiders, 28-7 (LA)
1990—Raiders, 24-7 (LA)
**Raiders, 20-10 (LA)
1991—Raiders, 38-14 (C)
1992—Bengals, 24-21 (C) OT
1993—Bengals, 16-10 (C)
(RS Pts.—Raiders 520, Bengals 389)
(PS Pts.—Raiders 51, Bengals 38)
Franchise in Oakland prior to 1982
**AFC Divisional Playoff*

CINCINNATI vs. MIAMI
RS: Dolphins lead series, 10-3
PS: Dolphins lead series, 1-0
1968—Dolphins, 24-22 (C)
Bengals, 38-21 (M)
1969—Bengals, 27-21 (C)
1971—Dolphins, 23-13 (C)
1973—*Dolphins, 34-16 (M)
1974—Dolphins, 24-3 (M)
1977—Bengals, 23-17 (C)
1978—Dolphins, 21-0 (M)
1980—Dolphins, 17-16 (M)
1983—Dolphins, 38-14 (M)
1987—Dolphins, 20-14 (C)
1989—Dolphins, 20-13 (C)
1991—Dolphins, 37-13 (M)
1994—Dolphins, 23-7 (C)
(RS Pts.—Dolphins 340, Bengals 219)
(PS Pts.—Dolphins 34, Bengals 16)
AFC Divisional Playoff

CINCINNATI vs. MINNESOTA
RS: Vikings lead series, 4-3
1973—Bengals, 27-0 (C)
1977—Vikings, 42-10 (M)
1980—Bengals, 14-0 (C)
1983—Vikings, 20-14 (M)
1986—Bengals, 24-20 (C)
1989—Vikings, 29-21 (M)
1992—Vikings, 42-7 (C)
(RS Pts.—Vikings 153, Bengals 117)

CINCINNATI vs. *NEW ENGLAND
RS: Patriots lead series, 9-7
1968—Patriots, 33-14 (B)
1969—Patriots, 25-14 (C)
1970—Bengals, 45-7 (C)
1972—Bengals, 31-7 (NE)
1975—Bengals, 27-10 (C)
1978—Patriots, 10-3 (C)
1979—Patriots, 20-14 (C)
1984—Patriots, 20-14 (NE)
1985—Patriots, 34-23 (NE)
1986—Bengals, 31-7 (NE)
1988—Patriots, 27-21 (NE)
1990—Bengals, 41-7 (C)
1991—Bengals, 29-7 (C)
1992—Bengals, 20-10 (C)
1993—Patriots, 7-2 (NE)
1994—Patriots, 31-28 (C)
(RS Pts.—Bengals 357, Patriots 262)
Franchise in Boston prior to 1971

CINCINNATI vs. NEW ORLEANS
RS: Saints lead series, 5-3
1970—Bengals, 26-6 (C)
1975—Bengals, 21-0 (NO)
1978—Saints, 20-18 (C)
1981—Saints, 17-7 (NO)
1984—Bengals, 24-21 (NO)
1987—Saints, 41-24 (C)
1990—Saints, 21-7 (C)
1993—Saints, 20-13 (NO)
(RS Pts.—Saints 146, Bengals 140)

CINCINNATI vs. N.Y. GIANTS
RS: Bengals lead series, 4-1
1972—Bengals, 13-10 (C)
1977—Bengals, 30-13 (C)
1985—Bengals, 35-30 (C)
1991—Bengals, 27-24 (C)
1994—Giants, 27-20 (NY)
(RS Pts.—Bengals 125, Giants 104)

CINCINNATI vs. N.Y. JETS
RS: Jets lead series, 9-6
PS: Jets lead series, 1-0
1968—Jets, 27-14 (NY)
1969—Jets, 21-7 (C)
Jets, 40-7 (NY)
1971—Jets, 35-21 (NY)
1973—Bengals, 20-14 (C)
1976—Bengals, 42-3 (NY)
1981—Bengals, 31-30 (NY)
1982—*Jets, 44-17 (C)
1984—Jets, 43-23 (NY)
1985—Jets, 29-20 (C)
1986—Bengals, 52-21 (C)
1987—Jets, 27-20 (NY)
1988—Bengals, 36-19 (C)
1990—Bengals, 25-20 (C)
1992—Jets, 17-14 (NY)
1993—Jets, 17-12 (NY)
(RS Pts.—Jets 363, Bengals 344)
(PS Pts.—Jets 44, Bengals 17)
AFC First-Round Playoff

CINCINNATI vs. PHILADELPHIA
RS: Bengals lead series, 6-1
1971—Bengals, 37-14 (C)
1975—Bengals, 31-0 (P)
1979—Bengals, 37-13 (C)
1982—Bengals, 18-14 (P)
1988—Bengals, 28-24 (P)
1991—Eagles, 17-10 (P)
1994—Bengals, 33-30 (C)
(RS Pts.—Bengals 194, Eagles 112)

CINCINNATI vs. PITTSBURGH
RS: Steelers lead series, 28-21
1970—Steelers, 21-10 (P)
Bengals, 34-7 (C)
1971—Steelers, 21-10 (P)
Steelers, 21-13 (C)
1972—Bengals, 15-10 (C)
Steelers, 40-17 (P)
1973—Bengals, 19-7 (C)
Steelers, 20-13 (P)
1974—Bengals, 17-10 (C)
Steelers, 27-3 (P)
1975—Steelers, 30-24 (C)
Steelers, 35-14 (P)
1976—Steelers, 23-6 (P)
Steelers, 7-3 (C)
1977—Steelers, 20-14 (P)
Bengals, 17-10 (C)
1978—Steelers, 28-3 (C)
Steelers, 7-6 (P)
1979—Bengals, 34-10 (C)
Steelers, 37-17 (P)
1980—Bengals, 30-28 (C)
Bengals, 17-16 (P)
1981—Bengals, 34-7 (C)
Bengals, 17-10 (P)
1982—Steelers, 26-20 (P) OT
1983—Steelers, 24-14 (C)
Bengals, 23-10 (P)
1984—Steelers, 38-17 (P)
Bengals, 22-20 (C)
1985—Bengals, 37-24 (P)
Bengals, 26-21 (C)
1986—Bengals, 24-22 (C)
Steelers, 30-9 (P)
1987—Steelers, 23-20 (P)
Steelers, 30-16 (C)
1988—Bengals, 17-12 (P)
Bengals, 42-7 (C)
1989—Bengals, 41-10 (C)
Bengals, 26-16 (P)
1990—Bengals, 27-3 (C)
Bengals, 16-12 (P)
1991—Steelers, 33-27 (C) OT
Steelers, 17-10 (P)
1992—Steelers, 20-0 (P)
Steelers, 21-9 (C)
1993—Steelers, 34-7 (P)
Steelers, 24-16 (C)
1994—Steelers, 14-10 (P)
Steelers, 38-15 (C)
(RS Pts.—Steelers 981, Bengals 878)

CINCINNATI vs. *ST. LOUIS
RS: Bengals lead series, 5-2
1972—Rams, 15-12 (LA)
1976—Bengals, 20-12 (C)
1978—Bengals, 20-19 (LA)
1981—Bengals, 24-10 (C)
1984—Rams, 24-14 (C)
1990—Bengals, 34-31 (LA) OT
1993—Bengals, 15-3 (C)
(RS Pts.—Bengals 139, Rams 114)
Franchise in Los Angeles prior to 1995

CINCINNATI vs. SAN DIEGO
RS: Chargers lead series, 13-8
PS: Bengals lead series, 1-0
1968—Chargers, 29-13 (SD)
Chargers, 31-10 (C)
1969—Bengals, 34-20 (C)
Chargers, 21-14 (SD)
1970—Bengals, 17-14 (SD)
1971—Bengals, 31-0 (C)
1973—Bengals, 20-13 (SD)
1974—Chargers, 20-17 (C)
1975—Bengals, 47-17 (C)
1977—Chargers, 24-3 (SD)
1978—Chargers, 22-13 (SD)
1979—Chargers, 26-24 (C)
1980—Chargers, 31-14 (C)
1981—Bengals, 40-17 (SD)
*Bengals, 27-7 (C)
1982—Chargers, 50-34 (SD)
1985—Chargers, 44-41 (C)
1987—Chargers, 10-9 (C)
1988—Bengals, 27-10 (C)
1990—Bengals, 21-16 (SD)
1992—Chargers, 27-10 (SD)
1994—Chargers, 27-10 (SD)
(RS Pts.—Chargers 469, Bengals 449)
(PS Pts.—Bengals 27, Chargers 7)
AFC Championship

CINCINNATI vs. SAN FRANCISCO
RS: 49ers lead series, 6-1
PS: 49ers lead series, 2-0
1974—Bengals, 21-3 (SF)
1978—49ers, 28-12 (SF)
1981—49ers, 21-3 (C)
*49ers, 26-21 (Detroit)
1984—49ers, 23-17 (SF)
1987—49ers, 27-26 (C)
1988—**49ers, 20-16 (Miami)
1990—49ers, 20-17 (C)
1993—49ers, 21-8 (SF)
(RS Pts.—49ers 143, Bengals 104)
(PS Pts.—49ers 46, Bengals 37)
Super Bowl XVI
**Super Bowl XXIII*

CINCINNATI vs. SEATTLE
RS: Bengals lead series, 7-6
PS: Bengals lead series, 1-0
1977—Bengals, 42-20 (C)
1981—Bengals, 27-21 (C)
1982—Bengals, 24-10 (C)
1984—Seahawks, 26-6 (C)
1985—Seahawks, 28-24 (C)
1986—Bengals, 34-7 (C)
1987—Bengals, 17-10 (S)
1988—*Bengals, 21-13 (C)
1989—Seahawks, 24-17 (C)
1990—Seahawks, 31-16 (S)
1991—Seahawks, 13-7 (C)
1992—Bengals, 21-3 (S)
1993—Seahawks, 19-10 (C)
1994—Bengals, 20-17 (S) OT
(RS Pts.—Bengals 265, Seahawks 229)
(PS Pts.—Bengals 21, Seahawks 13)
AFC Divisional Playoff

CINCINNATI vs. TAMPA BAY
RS: Bengals lead series, 3-1
1976—Bengals, 21-0 (C)
1980—Buccaneers, 17-12 (C)
1983—Bengals, 23-17 (TB)
1989—Bengals, 56-23 (C)
(RS Pts.—Bengals 112, Buccaneers 57)

CINCINNATI vs. WASHINGTON
RS: Redskins lead series, 4-2
1970—Redskins, 20-0 (W)
1974—Bengals, 28-17 (C)
1979—Redskins, 28-14 (W)
1985—Redskins, 27-24 (W)
1988—Bengals, 20-17 (C) OT
1991—Redskins, 34-27 (C)
(RS Pts.—Redskins 143, Bengals 113)

CLEVELAND vs. ARIZONA
RS: Browns lead series, 32-10-3;
See Arizona vs. Cleveland

CLEVELAND vs. ATLANTA
RS: Browns lead series, 8-2;
See Atlanta vs. Cleveland

CLEVELAND vs. BUFFALO
RS: Browns lead series, 7-3
PS: Browns lead series, 1-0;
See Buffalo vs. Cleveland

CLEVELAND vs. CHICAGO
RS: Browns lead series, 8-3;
See Chicago vs. Cleveland

CLEVELAND vs. CINCINNATI
RS: Browns lead series, 25-24;
See Cincinnati vs. Cleveland
CLEVELAND vs. DALLAS
RS: Browns lead series, 15-9
PS: Browns lead series, 2-1
1960—Browns, 48-7 (D)
1961—Browns, 25-7 (C)
Browns, 38-17 (D)
1962—Browns, 19-10 (C)
Cowboys, 45-21 (D)
1963—Browns, 41-24 (D)
Browns, 27-17 (C)
1964—Browns, 27-6 (C)
Browns, 20-16 (D)
1965—Browns, 23-17 (C)
Browns, 24-17 (D)
1966—Browns, 30-21 (C)
Cowboys, 26-14 (D)
1967—Cowboys, 21-14 (C)
*Cowboys, 52-14 (D)
1968—Cowboys, 28-7 (C)
*Browns, 31-20 (C)
1969—Browns, 42-10 (C)
*Browns, 38-14 (D)
1970—Cowboys, 6-2 (C)
1974—Cowboys, 41-17 (D)
1979—Browns, 26-7 (C)
1982—Cowboys, 31-14 (D)
1985—Cowboys, 20-7 (D)
1988—Browns, 24-21 (C)
1991—Cowboys, 26-14 (C)
1994—Browns, 19-14 (D)
(RS Pts.—Browns 543, Cowboys 455)
(PS Pts.—Cowboys 86, Browns 83)
Conference Championship
CLEVELAND vs. DENVER
RS: Broncos lead series, 13-5
PS: Broncos lead series, 3-0
1970—Browns, 27-13 (D)
1971—Broncos, 27-0 (C)
1972—Browns, 27-20 (D)
1974—Browns, 23-21 (C)
1975—Broncos, 16-15 (D)
1976—Broncos, 44-13 (D)
1978—Broncos, 19-7 (C)
1980—Broncos, 19-16 (C)
1981—Broncos, 23-20 (D) OT
1983—Broncos, 27-6 (D)
1984—Broncos, 24-14 (C)
1986—*Broncos, 23-20 (C) OT
1987—*Broncos, 38-33 (D)
1988—Broncos, 30-7 (D)
1989—Browns, 16-13 (C)
*Broncos, 37-21 (D)
1990—Browns, 30-29 (D)
1991—Broncos, 17-7 (C)
1992—Broncos, 12-0 (C)
1993—Broncos, 29-14 (C)
1994—Broncos, 26-14 (D)
(RS Pts.—Broncos 409, Browns 256)
(PS Pts.—Broncos 98, Browns 74)
AFC Championship
CLEVELAND vs. DETROIT
RS: Lions lead series, 11-3
PS: Lions lead series, 3-1
1952—Lions, 17-6 (D)
*Lions, 17-7 (C)
1953—*Lions, 17-16 (D)
1954—Lions, 14-10 (C)
*Browns, 56-10 (C)
1957—Lions, 20-7 (D)
*Lions, 59-14 (D)
1958—Lions, 30-10 (C)
1963—Lions, 38-10 (D)
1964—Browns, 37-21 (C)
1967—Lions, 31-14 (D)
1969—Lions, 28-21 (C)
1970—Lions, 41-24 (C)
1975—Lions, 21-10 (D)
1983—Browns, 31-26 (D)
1986—Browns, 24-21 (C)
1989—Lions, 13-10 (D)
1992—Lions, 24-14 (D)
(RS Pts.—Lions 345, Browns 228)
(PS Pts.—Lions 103, Browns 93)
NFL Championship
CLEVELAND vs. GREEN BAY
RS: Packers lead series, 7-6
PS: Packers lead series, 1-0
1953—Browns, 27-0 (Mil)
1955—Browns, 41-10 (C)
1956—Browns, 24-7 (Mil)
1961—Packers, 49-17 (C)
1964—Packers, 28-21 (Mil)
1965—*Packers, 23-12 (GB)
1966—Packers, 21-20 (C)
1967—Packers, 55-7 (Mil)
1969—Browns, 20-7 (C)
1972—Packers, 26-10 (C)
1980—Browns, 26-21 (C)
1983—Packers, 35-21 (Mil)
1986—Packers, 17-14 (C)
1992—Browns, 17-6 (C)
(RS Pts.—Packers 282, Browns 265)
(PS Pts.—Packers 23, Browns 12)
NFL Championship
CLEVELAND vs. HOUSTON
RS: Browns lead series, 29-20
PS: Oilers lead series, 1-0
1970—Browns, 28-14 (C)
Browns, 21-10 (H)
1971—Browns, 31-0 (C)
Browns, 37-24 (H)
1972—Browns, 23-17 (H)
Browns, 20-0 (C)
1973—Browns, 42-13 (C)
Browns, 23-13 (H)
1974—Browns, 20-7 (C)
Oilers, 28-24 (H)
1975—Oilers, 40-10 (C)
Oilers, 21-10 (H)
1976—Browns, 21-7 (H)
Browns, 13-10 (C)
1977—Browns, 24-23 (H)
Oilers, 19-15 (C)
1978—Oilers, 16-13 (C)
Oilers, 14-10 (H)
1979—Oilers, 31-10 (H)
Browns, 14-7 (C)
1980—Oilers, 16-7 (C)
Browns, 17-14 (H)
1981—Oilers, 9-3 (C)
Oilers, 17-13 (H)
1982—Browns, 20-14 (H)
1983—Browns, 25-19 (C) OT
Oilers, 34-27 (H)
1984—Browns, 27-10 (C)
Browns, 27-20 (H)
1985—Browns, 21-6 (H)
Browns, 28-21 (C)
1986—Browns, 23-20 (H)
Browns, 13-10 (C) OT
1987—Oilers, 15-10 (C)
Browns, 40-7 (H)
1988—Oilers, 24-17 (H)
Browns, 28-23 (C)
*Oilers, 24-23 (C)
1989—Browns, 28-17 (C)
Browns, 24-20 (H)
1990—Oilers, 35-23 (C)
Oilers, 58-14 (H)
1991—Oilers, 28-24 (H)
Oilers, 17-14 (C)
1992—Browns, 24-14 (H)
Oilers, 17-14 (C)
1993—Oilers, 27-20 (C)
Oilers, 19-17 (H)
1994—Browns, 11-8 (H)
Browns, 34-10 (C)
(RS Pts.—Browns 1,002, Oilers 863)
(PS Pts.—Oilers 24, Browns 23)
AFC First-Round Playoff
CLEVELAND vs. *INDIANAPOLIS
RS: Browns lead series, 13-7
PS: Series tied, 2-2
1956—Colts, 21-7 (C)
1959—Browns, 38-31 (B)
1962—Colts, 36-14 (C)
1964—**Browns, 27-0 (C)
1968—Browns, 30-20 (B)
**Colts, 34-0 (C)
1971—Browns, 14-13 (B)
***Colts, 20-3 (C)
1973—Browns, 24-14 (C)
1975—Colts, 21-7 (B)
1978—Browns, 45-24 (B)
1979—Browns, 13-10 (C)
1980—Browns, 28-27 (B)
1981—Browns, 42-28 (C)
1983—Browns, 41-23 (C)
1986—Browns, 24-9 (I)
1987—Colts, 9-7 (C)
***Browns, 38-21 (C)
1988—Browns, 23-17 (C)
1989—Colts, 23-17 (I) OT
1991—Browns, 31-0 (I)
1992—Colts, 14-3 (I)
1993—Colts, 23-10 (I)
1994—Browns, 21-14 (I)
(RS Pts.—Browns 439, Colts 377)
(PS Pts.—Colts 75, Browns 68)
Franchise in Baltimore prior to 1984
**NFL Championship*
***AFC Divisional Playoff*
CLEVELAND vs. KANSAS CITY
RS: Series tied, 7-7-2
1971—Chiefs, 13-7 (KC)
1972—Chiefs, 31-7 (C)
1973—Tie, 20-20 (KC)
1975—Browns, 40-14 (C)
1976—Chiefs, 39-14 (KC)
1977—Browns, 44-7 (C)
1978—Chiefs, 17-3 (KC)
1979—Browns, 27-24 (KC)
1980—Browns, 20-13 (C)
1984—Chiefs, 10-6 (KC)
1986—Browns, 20-7 (C)
1988—Browns, 6-3 (KC)
1989—Tie, 10-10 (C) OT
1990—Chiefs, 34-0 (KC)
1991—Browns, 20-15 (C)
1994—Chiefs, 20-13 (KC)
(RS Pts.—Chiefs 277, Browns 257)
CLEVELAND vs. *LOS ANGELES
RS: Raiders lead series, 8-4
PS: Raiders lead series, 2-0
1970—Raiders, 23-20 (O)
1971—Raiders, 34-20 (C)
1973—Browns, 7-3 (O)
1974—Raiders, 40-24 (C)
1975—Raiders, 38-17 (O)
1977—Raiders, 26-10 (C)
1979—Raiders, 19-14 (O)
1980—**Raiders, 14-12 (C)
1982—***Raiders, 27-10 (LA)
1985—Raiders, 21-20 (C)
1986—Raiders, 27-14 (LA)
1987—Browns, 24-17 (LA)
1992—Browns, 28-16 (LA)
1993—Browns, 19-16 (LA)
(RS Pts.—Raiders 280, Browns 217)
(PS Pts.—Raiders 41, Browns 22)
Franchise in Oakland prior to 1982
**AFC Divisional Playoff*
***AFC First-Round Playoff*
CLEVELAND vs. MIAMI
RS: Dolphins lead series, 6-4
PS: Dolphins lead series, 2-0
1970—Browns, 28-0 (M)
1972—*Dolphins, 20-14 (M)
1973—Dolphins, 17-9 (C)
1976—Browns, 17-13 (C)
1979—Browns, 30-24 (C) OT
1985—*Dolphins, 24-21 (M)
1986—Browns, 26-16 (C)
1988—Dolphins, 38-31 (M)
1989—Dolphins, 13-10 (M) OT
1990—Dolphins, 30-13 (C)
1992—Dolphins, 27-23 (C)
1993—Dolphins, 24-14 (C)
(RS Pts.—Dolphins 202, Browns 201)
(PS Pts.—Dolphins 44, Browns 35)
AFC Divisional Playoff
CLEVELAND vs. MINNESOTA
RS: Vikings lead series, 7-3
PS: Vikings lead series, 1-0
1965—Vikings, 27-17 (C)
1967—Browns, 14-10 (C)
1969—Vikings, 51-3 (M)
*Vikings, 27-7 (M)
1973—Vikings, 26-3 (M)
1975—Vikings, 42-10 (C)
1980—Vikings, 28-23 (M)
1983—Vikings, 27-21 (C)
1986—Browns, 23-20 (M)
1989—Browns, 23-17 (C) OT
1992—Vikings, 17-13 (M)
(RS Pts.—Vikings 265, Browns 150)
(PS Pts.—Vikings 27, Browns 7)
NFL Championship
CLEVELAND vs. NEW ENGLAND
RS: Browns lead series, 10-3
PS: Browns lead series, 1-0
1971—Browns, 27-7 (C)
1974—Browns, 21-14 (NE)
1977—Browns, 30-27 (C) OT
1980—Patriots, 34-17 (NE)
1982—Browns, 10-7 (C)
1983—Browns, 30-0 (NE)
1984—Patriots, 17-16 (C)
1985—Browns, 24-20 (C)
1987—Browns, 20-10 (NE)
1991—Browns, 20-0 (NE)
1992—Browns, 19-17 (NE)
1993—Patriots, 20-17 (C)
1994—Browns, 13-6 (C)
*Browns, 20-13 (C)
(RS Pts.—Browns 264, Patriots 179)
(PS Pts.—Browns 20, Patriots 13)
AFC First-Round Playoff
CLEVELAND vs. NEW ORLEANS
RS: Browns lead series, 9-3
1967—Browns, 42-7 (NO)
1968—Browns, 24-10 (NO)
Browns, 35-17 (C)
1969—Browns, 27-17 (NO)
1971—Browns, 21-17 (NO)
1975—Browns, 17-16 (C)
1978—Browns, 24-16 (NO)
1981—Browns, 20-17 (C)
1984—Saints, 16-14 (C)
1987—Saints, 28-21 (NO)
1990—Saints, 25-20 (NO)
1993—Browns, 17-13 (C)
(RS Pts.—Browns 282, Saints 199)
CLEVELAND vs. N.Y. GIANTS
RS: Browns lead series, 25-17-2
PS: Series tied, 1-1
1950—Giants, 6-0 (C)
Giants, 17-13 (NY)
*Browns, 8-3 (C)
1951—Browns, 14-13 (C)
Browns, 10-0 (NY)
1952—Giants, 17-9 (C)
Giants, 37-34 (NY)
1953—Browns, 7-0 (NY)
Browns, 62-14 (C)
1954—Browns, 24-14 (C)
Browns, 16-7 (NY)
1955—Browns, 24-14 (C)
Tie, 35-35 (NY)
1956—Giants, 21-9 (C)
Browns, 24-7 (NY)
1957—Browns, 6-3 (C)
Browns, 34-28 (NY)
1958—Giants, 21-17 (C)
Giants, 13-10 (NY)
*Giants, 10-0 (NY)
1959—Giants, 10-6 (C)
Giants, 48-7 (NY)
1960—Giants, 17-13 (C)

ALL-TIME TEAM VS. TEAM RESULTS

Browns, 48-34 (NY)
1961—Giants, 37-21 (C)
Tie, 7-7 (NY)
1962—Browns, 17-7 (C)
Giants, 17-13 (NY)
1963—Browns, 35-24 (NY)
Giants, 33-6 (C)
1964—Browns, 42-20 (C)
Browns, 52-20 (NY)
1965—Browns, 38-14 (NY)
Browns, 34-21 (C)
1966—Browns, 28-7 (NY)
Browns, 49-40 (C)
1967—Giants, 38-34 (NY)
Browns, 24-14 (C)
1968—Browns, 45-10 (C)
1969—Browns, 28-17 (C)
Giants, 27-14 (NY)
1973—Browns, 12-10 (C)
1977—Browns, 21-7 (NY)
1985—Browns, 35-33 (NY)
1991—Giants, 13-10 (NY)
1994—Giants, 16-13 (C)
(RS Pts.—Browns 1,000, Giants 808)
(PS Pts.—Giants 13, Browns 8)
Conference Playoff

CLEVELAND vs. N.Y. JETS
RS: Browns lead series, 9-6
PS: Browns lead series, 1-0
1970—Browns, 31-21 (C)
1972—Browns, 26-10 (NY)
1976—Browns, 38-17 (C)
1978—Browns, 37-34 (C) OT
1979—Browns, 25-22 (NY) OT
1980—Browns, 17-14 (C)
1981—Jets, 14-13 (C)
1983—Browns, 10-7 (C)
1984—Jets, 24-20 (C)
1985—Jets, 37-10 (NY)
1986—*Browns, 23-20 (C) OT
1988—Jets, 23-3 (C)
1989—Browns, 38-24 (C)
1990—Jets, 24-21 (NY)
1991—Jets, 17-14 (C)
1994—Browns, 27-7 (C)
(RS Pts.—Browns 330, Jets 295)
(PS Pts.—Browns 23, Jets 20)
AFC Divisional Playoff

CLEVELAND vs. PHILADELPHIA
RS: Browns lead series, 31-12-1
1950—Browns, 35-10 (P)
Browns, 13-7 (C)
1951—Browns, 20-17 (C)
Browns, 24-9 (P)
1952—Browns, 49-7 (P)
Eagles, 28-20 (C)
1953—Browns, 37-13 (C)
Eagles, 42-27 (P)
1954—Eagles, 28-10 (P)
Browns, 6-0 (C)
1955—Browns, 21-17 (C)
Eagles, 33-17 (P)
1956—Browns, 16-0 (P)
Browns, 17-14 (C)
1957—Browns, 24-7 (C)
Eagles, 17-7 (P)
1958—Browns, 28-14 (C)
Browns, 21-14 (P)
1959—Browns, 28-7 (C)
Browns, 28-21 (P)
1960—Browns, 41-24 (P)
Eagles, 31-29 (C)
1961—Eagles, 27-20 (P)
Browns, 45-24 (C)
1962—Eagles, 35-7 (P)
Tie, 14-14 (C)
1963—Browns, 37-7 (C)
Browns, 23-17 (P)
1964—Browns, 28-20 (P)
Browns, 38-24 (C)
1965—Browns, 35-17 (P)
Browns, 38-34 (C)
1966—Browns, 27-7 (C)
Eagles, 33-21 (P)
1967—Eagles, 28-24 (P)
1968—Browns, 47-13 (C)
1969—Browns, 27-20 (P)
1972—Browns, 27-17 (P)
1976—Browns, 24-3 (C)
1979—Browns, 24-19 (P)
1982—Eagles, 24-21 (C)
1988—Browns, 19-3 (C)
1991—Eagles, 32-30 (C)
1994—Browns, 26-7 (P)
(RS Pts.—Browns 1,120, Eagles 785)

CLEVELAND vs. PITTSBURGH
RS: Browns lead series, 52-38
PS: Steelers lead series, 1-0
1950—Browns, 30-17 (P)
Browns, 45-7 (C)
1951—Browns, 17-0 (C)
Browns, 28-0 (P)
1952—Browns, 21-20 (P)
Browns, 29-28 (C)
1953—Browns, 34-16 (C)
Browns, 20-16 (P)
1954—Steelers, 55-27 (P)
Browns, 42-7 (C)
1955—Browns, 41-14 (C)
Browns, 30-7 (P)
1956—Browns, 14-10 (P)
Steelers, 24-16 (C)
1957—Browns, 23-12 (P)
Browns, 24-0 (C)
1958—Browns, 45-12 (P)
Browns, 27-10 (C)
1959—Steelers, 17-7 (P)
Steelers, 21-20 (C)
1960—Browns, 28-20 (C)
Steelers, 14-10 (P)
1961—Browns, 30-28 (P)
Steelers, 17-13 (C)
1962—Browns, 41-14 (P)
Browns, 35-14 (C)
1963—Browns, 35-23 (C)
Steelers, 9-7 (P)
1964—Steelers, 23-7 (C)
Browns, 30-17 (P)
1965—Browns, 24-19 (C)
Browns, 42-21 (P)
1966—Browns, 41-10 (C)
Steelers, 16-6 (P)
1967—Browns, 21-10 (C)
Browns, 34-14 (P)
1968—Browns, 31-24 (C)
Browns, 45-24 (P)
1969—Browns, 42-31 (C)
Browns, 24-3 (P)
1970—Browns, 15-7 (C)
Steelers, 28-9 (P)
1971—Browns, 27-17 (C)
Steelers, 26-9 (P)
1972—Browns, 26-24 (C)
Steelers, 30-0 (P)
1973—Steelers, 33-6 (P)
Browns, 21-16 (C)
1974—Steelers, 20-16 (P)
Steelers, 26-16 (C)
1975—Steelers, 42-6 (C)
Steelers, 31-17 (P)
1976—Steelers, 31-14 (P)
Browns, 18-16 (C)
1977—Steelers, 28-14 (C)
Steelers, 35-31 (P)
1978—Steelers, 15-9 (P) OT
Steelers, 34-14 (C)
1979—Steelers, 51-35 (C)
Steelers, 33-30 (P) OT
1980—Browns, 27-26 (C)
Steelers, 16-13 (P)
1981—Steelers, 13-7 (P)
Steelers, 32-10 (C)
1982—Browns, 10-9 (C)
Steelers, 37-21 (P)
1983—Steelers, 44-17 (P)
Browns, 30-17 (C)
1984—Browns, 20-10 (C)
Steelers, 23-20 (P)
1985—Browns, 17-7 (C)
Steelers, 10-9 (P)
1986—Browns, 27-24 (P)
Browns, 37-31 (C) OT
1987—Browns, 34-10 (C)
Browns, 19-13 (P)
1988—Browns, 23-9 (P)
Browns, 27-7 (C)
1989—Browns, 51-0 (P)
Steelers, 17-7 (C)
1990—Browns, 13-3 (C)
Steelers, 35-0 (P)
1991—Browns, 17-14 (C)
Steelers, 17-10 (P)
1992—Browns, 17-9 (C)
Steelers, 23-13 (P)
1993—Browns, 28-23 (C)
Steelers, 16-9 (P)
1994—Steelers, 17-10 (C)
Steelers, 17-7 (P)
*Steelers, 29-9 (P)
(RS Pts.—Browns 1,969, Steelers 1,716)
(PS Pts.—Steelers 29, Browns 9)
AFC Divisional Playoff

CLEVELAND vs. *ST. LOUIS
RS: Browns lead series, 8-7
PS: Browns lead series, 2-1
1950—**Browns, 30-28 (C)
1951—Browns, 38-23 (LA)
**Rams, 24-17 (LA)
1952—Browns, 37-7 (C)
1955—**Browns, 38-14 (LA)
1957—Browns, 45-31 (C)
1958—Browns, 30-27 (LA)
1963—Browns, 20-6 (C)
1965—Rams, 42-7 (LA)
1968—Rams, 24-6 (C)
1973—Rams, 30-17 (LA)
1977—Rams, 9-0 (C)
1978—Browns, 30-19 (C)
1981—Rams, 27-16 (LA)
1984—Rams, 20-17 (LA)
1987—Browns, 30-17 (C)
1990—Rams, 38-23 (C)
1993—Browns, 42-14 (LA)
(RS Pts.—Browns 358, Rams 334)
(PS Pts.—Browns 85, Rams 66)
Franchise in Los Angeles prior to 1995
***NFL Championship*

CLEVELAND vs. SAN DIEGO
RS: Chargers lead series, 8-6-1
1970—Chargers, 27-10 (C)
1972—Browns, 21-17 (SD)
1973—Tie, 16-16 (C)
1974—Chargers, 36-35 (SD)
1976—Browns, 21-17 (C)
1977—Chargers, 37-14 (SD)
1981—Chargers, 44-14 (C)
1982—Chargers, 30-13 (C)
1983—Browns, 30-24 (SD) OT
1985—Browns, 21-7 (SD)
1986—Browns, 47-17 (C)
1987—Chargers, 27-24 (SD) OT
1990—Chargers, 24-14 (C)
1991—Browns, 30-24 (SD) OT
1992—Chargers, 14-13 (C)
(RS Pts.—Chargers 361, Browns 323)

CLEVELAND vs. SAN FRANCISCO
RS: Browns lead series, 9-6
1950—Browns, 34-14 (C)
1951—49ers, 24-10 (SF)
1953—Browns, 23-21 (C)
1955—Browns, 38-3 (SF)
1959—49ers, 21-20 (C)
1962—Browns, 13-10 (SF)
1968—Browns, 33-21 (SF)
1970—49ers, 34-31 (SF)
1974—Browns, 7-0 (C)
1978—Browns, 24-7 (C)
1981—Browns, 15-12 (SF)
1984—49ers, 41-7 (C)
1987—49ers, 38-24 (SF)
1990—49ers, 20-17 (SF)
1993—Browns, 23-13 (C)
(RS Pts.—Browns 319, 49ers 279)

CLEVELAND vs. SEATTLE
RS: Seahawks lead series, 9-4
1977—Seahawks, 20-19 (S)
1978—Seahawks, 47-24 (S)
1979—Seahawks, 29-24 (C)
1980—Browns, 27-3 (S)
1981—Seahawks, 42-21 (S)
1982—Browns, 21-7 (S)
1983—Seahawks, 24-9 (C)
1984—Seahawks, 33-0 (S)
1985—Seahawks, 31-13 (S)
1988—Seahawks, 16-10 (C)
1989—Browns, 17-7 (S)
1993—Seahawks, 22-5 (S)
1994—Browns, 35-9 (C)
(RS Pts.—Seahawks 290, Browns 225)

CLEVELAND vs. TAMPA BAY
RS: Browns lead series, 4-0
1976—Browns, 24-7 (TB)
1980—Browns, 34-27 (TB)
1983—Browns, 20-0 (C)
1989—Browns, 42-31 (TB)
(RS Pts.—Browns 120, Buccaneers 65)

CLEVELAND vs. WASHINGTON
RS: Browns lead series, 32-9-1
1950—Browns, 20-14 (C)
Browns, 45-21 (W)
1951—Browns, 45-0 (C)
1952—Browns, 19-15 (C)
Browns, 48-24 (W)
1953—Browns, 30-14 (W)
Browns, 27-3 (C)
1954—Browns, 62-3 (C)
Browns, 34-14 (W)
1955—Redskins, 27-17 (C)
Browns, 24-14 (W)
1956—Redskins, 20-9 (W)
Redskins, 20-17 (C)
1957—Browns, 21-17 (C)
Tie, 30-30 (W)
1958—Browns, 20-10 (W)
Browns, 21-14 (C)
1959—Browns, 34-7 (C)
Browns, 31-17 (W)
1960—Browns, 31-10 (W)
Browns, 27-16 (C)
1961—Browns, 31-7 (C)
Browns, 17-6 (W)
1962—Redskins, 17-16 (C)
Redskins, 17-9 (W)
1963—Browns, 37-14 (C)
Browns, 27-20 (W)
1964—Browns, 27-13 (W)
Browns, 34-24 (C)
1965—Browns, 17-7 (W)
Browns, 24-16 (C)
1966—Browns, 38-14 (W)
Browns, 14-3 (C)
1967—Browns, 42-37 (C)
1968—Browns, 24-21 (W)
1969—Browns, 27-23 (C)
1971—Browns, 20-13 (W)
1975—Redskins, 23-7 (C)
1979—Redskins, 13-9 (C)
1985—Redskins, 14-7 (C)
1988—Browns, 17-13 (W)
1991—Redskins, 42-17 (W)
(RS Pts.—Browns 1,073, Redskins 667)

DALLAS vs. ARIZONA
RS: Cowboys lead series, 42-22-1;
See Arizona vs. Dallas

DALLAS vs. ATLANTA
RS: Cowboys lead series, 9-6
PS: Cowboys lead series, 2-0;
See Atlanta vs. Dallas

DALLAS vs. BUFFALO
RS: Cowboys lead series, 3-2
PS: Cowboys lead series, 2-0;

See Buffalo vs. Dallas

DALLAS vs. CHICAGO
RS: Cowboys lead series, 8-6
PS: Cowboys lead series, 2-0;
See Chicago vs. Dallas

DALLAS vs. CINCINNATI
RS: Cowboys lead series, 4-2;
See Cincinnati vs. Dallas

DALLAS vs. CLEVELAND
RS: Browns lead series, 15-9
PS: Browns lead series, 2-1;
See Cleveland vs. Dallas

DALLAS vs. DENVER
RS: Cowboys lead series, 3-2
PS: Cowboys lead series, 1-0
1973—Cowboys, 22-10 (Den)
1977—Cowboys, 14-6 (Dal)
*Cowboys, 27-10 (New Orleans)
1980—Broncos, 41-20 (Den)
1986—Broncos, 29-14 (Den)
1992—Cowboys, 31-27 (Den)
(RS Pts.—Broncos 113, Cowboys 101)
(PS Pts.—Cowboys 27, Broncos 10)
**Super Bowl XII*

DALLAS vs. DETROIT
RS: Cowboys lead series, 7-6
PS: Series tied, 1-1
1960—Lions, 23-14 (Det)
1963—Cowboys, 17-14 (Dal)
1968—Cowboys, 59-13 (Dal)
1970—*Cowboys, 5-0 (Dal)
1972—Cowboys, 28-24 (Dal)
1975—Cowboys, 36-10 (Det)
1977—Cowboys, 37-0 (Dal)
1981—Lions, 27-24 (Det)
1985—Lions, 26-21 (Det)
1986—Cowboys, 31-7 (Det)
1987—Lions, 27-17 (Det)
1991—Lions, 34-10 (Det)
*Lions, 38-6 (Det)
1992—Cowboys, 37-3 (Det)
1994—Lions, 20-17 (Dal) OT
(RS Pts.—Cowboys 348, Lions 228)
(PS Pts.—Lions 38, Cowboys 11)
**NFC Divisional Playoff*

DALLAS vs. GREEN BAY
RS: Packers lead series, 8-7
PS: Cowboys lead series, 3-2
1960—Packers, 41-7 (GB)
1964—Packers, 45-21 (D)
1965—Packers, 13-3 (Mil)
1966—*Packers, 34-27 (D)
1967—*Packers, 21-17 (GB)
1968—Packers, 28-17 (D)
1970—Cowboys, 16-3 (D)
1972—Packers, 16-13 (Mil)
1975—Packers, 19-17 (D)
1978—Cowboys, 42-14 (Mil)
1980—Cowboys, 28-7 (Mil)
1982—**Cowboys, 37-26 (D)
1984—Cowboys, 20-6 (D)
1989—Packers, 31-13 (GB)
Packers, 20-10 (D)
1991—Cowboys, 20-17 (Mil)
1993—Cowboys, 36-14 (D)
***Cowboys, 27-17 (D)
1994—Cowboys, 42-31 (D)
***Cowboys, 35-9 (D)
(RS Pts.—Cowboys 305, Packers 305)
(PS Pts.—Cowboys 143, Packers 107)
**NFL Championship*
***NFC Second-Round Playoff*
****NFC Divisional Playoff*

DALLAS vs. HOUSTON
RS: Cowboys lead series, 5-3
1970—Cowboys, 52-10 (D)
1974—Cowboys, 10-0 (H)
1979—Oilers, 30-24 (D)
1982—Cowboys, 37-7 (H)
1985—Cowboys, 17-10 (H)
1988—Oilers, 25-17 (D)
1991—Oilers, 26-23 (H) OT
1994—Cowboys, 20-17 (D)
(RS Pts.—Cowboys 200, Oilers 125)

DALLAS vs. *INDIANAPOLIS
RS: Cowboys lead series, 7-2
PS: Colts lead series, 1-0
1960—Colts, 45-7 (D)
1967—Colts, 23-17 (B)
1969—Cowboys, 27-10 (D)
1970—**Colts, 16-13 (Miami)
1972—Cowboys, 21-0 (B)
1976—Cowboys, 30-27 (D)
1978—Cowboys, 38-0 (D)
1981—Cowboys, 37-13 (B)
1984—Cowboys, 22-3 (D)
1993—Cowboys, 27-3 (I)
(RS Pts.—Cowboys 226, Colts 124)
(PS Pts.—Colts 16, Cowboys 13)
**Franchise in Baltimore prior to 1984*
***Super Bowl V*

DALLAS vs. KANSAS CITY
RS: Cowboys lead series, 3-2
1970—Cowboys, 27-16 (KC)
1975—Chiefs, 34-31 (D)
1983—Cowboys, 41-21 (D)
1989—Chiefs, 36-28 (KC)
1992—Cowboys, 17-10 (D)
(RS Pts.—Cowboys 144, Chiefs 117)

DALLAS vs. *LOS ANGELES
RS: Raiders lead series, 3-2
1974—Raiders, 27-23 (O)
1980—Cowboys, 19-13 (O)
1983—Raiders, 40-38 (D)
1986—Raiders, 17-13 (D)
1992—Cowboys, 28-13 (LA)
(RS Pts.—Cowboys 121, Raiders 110)
**Franchise in Oakland prior to 1982*

DALLAS vs. MIAMI
RS: Dolphins lead series, 6-1
PS: Cowboys lead series, 1-0
1971—*Cowboys, 24-3 (New Orleans)
1973—Dolphins, 14-7 (D)
1978—Dolphins, 23-16 (M)
1981—Cowboys, 28-27 (D)
1984—Dolphins, 28-21 (M)
1987—Dolphins, 20-14 (D)
1989—Dolphins, 17-14 (D)
1993—Dolphins, 16-14 (D)
(RS Pts.—Dolphins 145, Cowboys 114)
(PS Pts.—Cowboys 24, Dolphins 3)
**Super Bowl VI*

DALLAS vs. MINNESOTA
RS: Cowboys lead series, 8-6
PS: Cowboys lead series, 3-1
1961—Cowboys, 21-7 (D)
Cowboys, 28-0 (M)
1966—Cowboys, 28-17 (D)
1968—Cowboys, 20-7 (M)
1970—Vikings, 54-13 (M)
1971—*Cowboys, 20-12 (M)
1973—**Vikings, 27-10 (D)
1974—Vikings, 23-21 (D)
1975—*Cowboys, 17-14 (M)
1977—Cowboys, 16-10 (M) OT
**Cowboys, 23-6 (D)
1978—Vikings, 21-10 (D)
1979—Cowboys, 36-20 (M)
1982—Vikings, 31-27 (M)
1983—Cowboys, 37-24 (M)
1987—Vikings, 44-38 (D) OT
1988—Vikings, 43-3 (D)
1993—Cowboys, 37-20 (M)
(RS Pts.—Cowboys 335, Vikings 321)
(PS Pts.—Cowboys 70, Vikings 59)
**NFC Divisional Playoff*
***NFC Championship*

DALLAS vs. NEW ENGLAND
RS: Cowboys lead series, 6-0
1971—Cowboys, 44-21 (D)
1975—Cowboys, 34-31 (NE)
1978—Cowboys, 17-10 (D)
1981—Cowboys, 35-21 (NE)
1984—Cowboys, 20-17 (D)
1987—Cowboys, 23-17 (NE) OT
(RS Pts.—Cowboys 173, Patriots 117)

DALLAS vs. NEW ORLEANS
RS: Cowboys lead series, 14-3
1967—Cowboys, 14-10 (D)
Cowboys, 27-10 (NO)
1968—Cowboys, 17-3 (NO)
1969—Cowboys, 21-17 (NO)
Cowboys, 33-17 (D)
1971—Saints, 24-14 (NO)
1973—Cowboys, 40-3 (D)
1976—Cowboys, 24-6 (NO)
1978—Cowboys, 27-7 (D)
1982—Cowboys, 21-7 (D)
1983—Cowboys, 21-20 (D)
1984—Cowboys, 30-27 (D) OT
1988—Saints, 20-17 (NO)
1989—Saints, 28-0 (NO)
1990—Cowboys, 17-13 (D)
1991—Cowboys, 23-14 (D)
1994—Cowboys, 24-16 (NO)
(RS Pts.—Cowboys 370, Saints 242)

DALLAS vs. N.Y. GIANTS
RS: Cowboys lead series, 41-22-2
1960—Tie, 31-31 (NY)
1961—Giants, 31-10 (D)
Cowboys, 17-16 (NY)
1962—Giants, 41-10 (D)
Giants, 41-31 (NY)
1963—Giants, 37-21 (NY)
Giants, 34-27 (D)
1964—Tie, 13-13 (D)
Cowboys, 31-21 (NY)
1965—Cowboys, 31-2 (D)
Cowboys, 38-20 (NY)
1966—Cowboys, 52-7 (D)
Cowboys, 17-7 (NY)
1967—Cowboys, 38-24 (D)
1968—Giants, 27-21 (D)
Cowboys, 28-10 (NY)
1969—Cowboys, 25-3 (D)
1970—Cowboys, 28-10 (D)
Giants, 23-20 (NY)
1971—Cowboys, 20-13 (D)
Cowboys, 42-14 (NY)
1972—Cowboys, 23-14 (NY)
Giants, 23-3 (D)
1973—Cowboys, 45-28 (D)
Cowboys, 23-10 (New Haven)
1974—Giants, 14-6 (D)
Cowboys, 21-7 (New Haven)
1975—Cowboys, 13-7 (NY)
Cowboys, 14-3 (D)
1976—Cowboys, 24-14 (NY)
Cowboys, 9-3 (D)
1977—Cowboys, 41-21 (D)
Cowboys, 24-10 (NY)
1978—Cowboys, 34-24 (NY)
Cowboys, 24-3 (D)
1979—Cowboys, 16-14 (NY)
Cowboys, 28-7 (D)
1980—Cowboys, 24-3 (D)
Giants, 38-35 (NY)
1981—Cowboys, 18-10 (D)
Giants, 13-10 (NY) OT
1983—Cowboys, 28-13 (D)
Cowboys, 38-20 (NY)
1984—Giants, 28-7 (NY)
Giants, 19-7 (D)
1985—Cowboys, 30-29 (NY)
Cowboys, 28-21 (D)
1986—Cowboys, 31-28 (D)
Giants, 17-14 (NY)
1987—Cowboys, 16-14 (NY)
Cowboys, 33-24 (D)
1988—Giants, 12-10 (D)
Giants, 29-21 (NY)
1989—Giants, 30-13 (D)
Giants, 15-0 (NY)
1990—Giants, 28-7 (D)
Giants, 31-17 (NY)
1991—Cowboys, 21-16 (D)
Giants, 22-9 (NY)
1992—Cowboys, 34-28 (NY)
Cowboys, 30-3 (D)
1993—Cowboys, 31-9 (D)
Cowboys, 16-13 (NY) OT
1994—Cowboys, 38-10 (D)
Giants, 15-10 (NY)
(RS Pts.—Cowboys 1,475, Giants 1,165)

DALLAS vs. N.Y. JETS
RS: Cowboys lead series, 5-1
1971—Cowboys, 52-10 (D)
1975—Cowboys, 31-21 (NY)
1978—Cowboys, 30-7 (NY)
1987—Cowboys, 38-24 (NY)
1990—Jets, 24-9 (NY)
1993—Cowboys, 28-7 (NY)
(RS Pts.—Cowboys 188, Jets 93)

DALLAS vs. PHILADELPHIA
RS: Cowboys lead series, 42-26
PS: Series tied, 1-1
1960—Eagles, 27-25 (D)
1961—Eagles, 43-7 (D)
Eagles, 35-13 (P)
1962—Cowboys, 41-19 (D)
Eagles, 28-14 (P)
1963—Eagles, 24-21 (P)
Cowboys, 27-20 (D)
1964—Eagles, 17-14 (D)
Eagles, 24-14 (P)
1965—Eagles, 35-24 (D)
Cowboys, 21-19 (P)
1966—Cowboys, 56-7 (D)
Eagles, 24-23 (P)
1967—Eagles, 21-14 (P)
Cowboys, 38-17 (D)
1968—Cowboys, 45-13 (P)
Cowboys, 34-14 (D)
1969—Cowboys, 38-7 (P)
Cowboys, 49-14 (D)
1970—Cowboys, 17-7 (P)
Cowboys, 21-17 (D)
1971—Cowboys, 42-7 (P)
Cowboys, 20-7 (D)
1972—Cowboys, 28-6 (D)
Cowboys, 28-7 (P)
1973—Eagles, 30-16 (P)
Cowboys, 31-10 (D)
1974—Eagles, 13-10 (P)
Cowboys, 31-24 (D)
1975—Cowboys, 20-17 (P)
Cowboys, 27-17 (D)
1976—Cowboys, 27-7 (D)
Cowboys, 26-7 (P)
1977—Cowboys, 16-10 (P)
Cowboys, 24-14 (D)
1978—Cowboys, 14-7 (D)
Cowboys, 31-13 (P)
1979—Eagles, 31-21 (D)
Cowboys, 24-17 (P)
1980—Eagles, 17-10 (P)
Cowboys, 35-27 (D)
*Eagles, 20-7 (P)
1981—Cowboys, 17-14 (P)
Cowboys, 21-10 (D)
1982—Eagles, 24-20 (D)
1983—Cowboys, 37-7 (D)
Cowboys, 27-20 (P)
1984—Cowboys, 23-17 (D)
Cowboys, 26-10 (P)
1985—Eagles, 16-14 (P)
Cowboys, 34-17 (D)
1986—Cowboys, 17-14 (P)
Eagles, 23-21 (D)
1987—Cowboys, 41-22 (D)
Eagles, 37-20 (P)
1988—Eagles, 24-23 (P)
Eagles, 23-7 (D)
1989—Eagles, 27-0 (D)
Eagles, 20-10 (P)
1990—Eagles, 21-20 (D)
Eagles, 17-3 (P)
1991—Eagles, 24-0 (D)
Cowboys, 25-13 (P)
1992—Eagles, 31-7 (P)
Cowboys, 20-10 (D)
**Cowboys, 34-10 (D)

1993—Cowboys, 23-10 (P)
Cowboys, 23-17 (D)
1994—Cowboys, 24-13 (D)
Cowboys, 31-19 (P)
(RS Pts.—Cowboys 1,571, Eagles 1,220)
(PS Pts.—Cowboys 41, Eagles 30)
NFC Championship
**NFC Divisional Playoff*

DALLAS vs. PITTSBURGH
RS: Cowboys lead series, 13-11
PS: Steelers lead series, 2-0
1960—Steelers, 35-28 (D)
1961—Cowboys, 27-24 (D)
Steelers, 37-7 (P)
1962—Steelers, 30-28 (D)
Cowboys, 42-27 (P)
1963—Steelers, 27-21 (P)
Steelers, 24-19 (D)
1964—Steelers, 23-17 (P)
Cowboys, 17-14 (D)
1965—Steelers, 22-13 (P)
Cowboys, 24-17 (D)
1966—Cowboys, 52-21 (D)
Cowboys, 20-7 (P)
1967—Cowboys, 24-21 (P)
1968—Cowboys, 28-7 (D)
1969—Cowboys, 10-7 (P)
1972—Cowboys, 17-13 (D)
1975—*Steelers, 21-17 (Miami)
1977—Steelers, 28-13 (P)
1978—**Steelers, 35-31 (Miami)
1979—Steelers, 14-3 (P)
1982—Steelers, 36-28 (D)
1985—Cowboys, 27-13 (D)
1988—Steelers, 24-21 (P)
1991—Cowboys, 20-10 (D)
1994—Cowboys, 26-9 (P)
(RS Pts.—Cowboys 532, Steelers 490)
(PS Pts.—Steelers 56, Cowboys 48)
Super Bowl X
**Super Bowl XIII*

DALLAS vs. *ST. LOUIS
RS: Rams lead series, 9-8
PS: Series tied, 4-4
1960—Rams, 38-13 (D)
1962—Cowboys, 27-17 (LA)
1967—Rams, 35-13 (D)
1969—Rams, 24-23 (LA)
1971—Cowboys, 28-21 (D)
1973—Rams, 37-31 (LA)
**Cowboys, 27-16 (D)
1975—Cowboys, 18-7 (D)
***Cowboys, 37-7 (LA)
1976—**Rams, 14-12 (D)
1978—Rams, 27-14 (LA)
***Cowboys, 28-0 (LA)
1979—Cowboys, 30-6 (D)
**Rams, 21-19 (D)
1980—Rams, 38-14 (LA)
****Cowboys, 34-13 (D)
1981—Cowboys, 29-17 (D)
1983—****Rams, 24-17 (D)
1984—Cowboys, 20-13 (LA)
1985—**Rams, 20-0 (LA)
1986—Rams, 29-10 (LA)
1987—Cowboys, 29-21 (LA)
1989—Rams, 35-31 (D)
1990—Cowboys, 24-21 (LA)
1992—Rams, 27-23 (D)
(RS Pts.—Rams 413, Cowboys 377)
(PS Pts.—Cowboys 174, Rams 115)
Franchise in Los Angeles prior to 1995
**NFC Divisional Playoff*
***NFC Championship*
****NFC First-Round Playoff*

DALLAS vs. SAN DIEGO
RS: Cowboys lead series, 4-1
1972—Cowboys, 34-28 (SD)
1980—Cowboys, 42-31 (D)
1983—Chargers, 24-23 (SD)
1986—Cowboys, 24-21 (SD)
1990—Cowboys, 17-14 (D)
(RS Pts.—Cowboys 140, Chargers 118)

DALLAS vs. SAN FRANCISCO
RS: 49ers lead series, 10-6-1
PS: Cowboys lead series, 5-2
1960—49ers, 26-14 (D)
1963—49ers, 31-24 (SF)
1965—Cowboys, 39-31 (D)
1967—49ers, 24-16 (SF)
1969—Tie, 24-24 (D)
1970—*Cowboys, 17-10 (SF)
1971—*Cowboys, 14-3 (D)
1972—49ers, 31-10 (D)
**Cowboys, 30-28 (SF)
1974—Cowboys, 20-14 (D)
1977—Cowboys, 42-35 (SF)
1979—Cowboys, 21-13 (SF)
1980—Cowboys, 59-14 (D)
1981—49ers, 45-14 (SF)
*49ers, 28-27 (SF)
1983—49ers, 42-17 (SF)
1985—49ers, 31-16 (SF)
1989—49ers, 31-14 (D)
1990—49ers, 24-6 (D)
1992—*Cowboys, 30-20 (SF)
1993—Cowboys, 26-17 (D)
*Cowboys, 38-21 (D)
1994—49ers, 21-14 (SF)
*49ers, 38-28 (SF)
(RS Pts.—49ers 454, Cowboys 376)
(PS Pts.—Cowboys 184, 49ers 148)
NFC Championship
**NFC Divisional Playoff*

DALLAS vs. SEATTLE
RS: Cowboys lead series, 4-1
1976—Cowboys, 28-13 (S)
1980—Cowboys, 51-7 (D)
1983—Cowboys, 35-10 (S)
1986—Seahawks, 31-14 (D)
1992—Cowboys, 27-0 (D)
(RS Pts.—Cowboys 155, Seahawks 61)

DALLAS vs. TAMPA BAY
RS: Cowboys lead series, 6-0
PS: Cowboys lead series, 2-0
1977—Cowboys, 23-7 (D)
1980—Cowboys, 28-17 (D)
1981—*Cowboys, 38-0 (D)
1982—Cowboys, 14-9 (D)
**Cowboys, 30-17 (D)
1983—Cowboys, 27-24 (D) OT
1990—Cowboys, 14-10 (D)
Cowboys, 17-13 (TB)
(RS Pts.—Cowboys 123, Buccaneers 80)
(PS Pts.—Cowboys 68, Buccaneers 17)
NFC Divisional Playoff
**NFC First-Round Playoff*

DALLAS vs. WASHINGTON
RS: Cowboys lead series, 39-27-2
PS: Redskins lead series, 2-0
1960—Redskins, 26-14 (W)
1961—Tie, 28-28 (D)
Redskins, 34-24 (W)
1962—Tie, 35-35 (D)
Cowboys, 38-10 (W)
1963—Redskins, 21-17 (W)
Cowboys, 35-20 (D)
1964—Cowboys, 24-18 (D)
Redskins, 28-16 (W)
1965—Cowboys, 27-7 (D)
Redskins, 34-31 (W)
1966—Cowboys, 31-30 (W)
Redskins, 34-31 (D)
1967—Cowboys, 17-14 (W)
Redskins, 27-20 (D)
1968—Cowboys, 44-24 (W)
Cowboys, 29-20 (D)
1969—Cowboys, 41-28 (W)
Cowboys, 20-10 (D)
1970—Cowboys, 45-21 (W)
Cowboys, 34-0 (D)
1971—Redskins, 20-16 (D)
Cowboys, 13-0 (W)
1972—Redskins, 24-20 (W)
Cowboys, 34-24 (D)
*Redskins, 26-3 (W)
1973—Redskins, 14-7 (W)
Cowboys, 27-7 (D)
1974—Redskins, 28-21 (W)
Cowboys, 24-23 (D)
1975—Redskins, 30-24 (W) OT
Cowboys, 31-10 (D)
1976—Cowboys, 20-7 (W)
Redskins, 27-14 (D)
1977—Cowboys, 34-16 (D)
Cowboys, 14-7 (W)
1978—Redskins, 9-5 (W)
Cowboys, 37-10 (D)
1979—Redskins, 34-20 (W)
Cowboys, 35-34 (D)
1980—Cowboys, 17-3 (W)
Cowboys, 14-10 (D)
1981—Cowboys, 26-10 (W)
Cowboys, 24-10 (D)
1982—Cowboys, 24-10 (W)
*Redskins, 31-17 (W)
1983—Cowboys, 31-30 (W)
Redskins, 31-10 (D)
1984—Redskins, 34-14 (W)
Redskins, 30-28 (D)
1985—Cowboys, 44-14 (D)
Cowboys, 13-7 (W)
1986—Cowboys, 30-6 (D)
Redskins, 41-14 (W)
1987—Redskins, 13-7 (D)
Redskins, 24-20 (W)
1988—Redskins, 35-17 (D)
Cowboys, 24-17 (W)
1989—Redskins, 30-7 (D)
Cowboys, 13-3 (W)
1990—Redskins, 19-15 (W)
Cowboys, 27-17 (D)
1991—Redskins, 33-31 (D)
Cowboys, 24-21 (W)
1992—Cowboys, 23-10 (D)
Redskins, 20-17 (W)
1993—Redskins, 35-16 (W)
Cowboys, 38-3 (D)
1994—Cowboys, 34-7 (W)
Cowboys, 31-7 (D)
(RS Pts.—Cowboys, 1,630, Redskins 1,323)
(PS Pts.—Redskins 57, Cowboys 20)
NFC Championship

DENVER vs. ARIZONA
RS: Broncos lead series, 3-0-1;
See Arizona vs. Denver

DENVER vs. ATLANTA
RS: Broncos lead series, 5-3;
See Atlanta vs. Denver

DENVER vs. BUFFALO
RS: Bills lead series, 17-10-1
PS: Bills lead series, 1-0;
See Buffalo vs. Denver

DENVER vs. CHICAGO
RS: Series tied, 5-5;
See Chicago vs. Denver

DENVER vs. CINCINNATI
RS: Broncos lead series, 11-6;
See Cincinnati vs. Denver

DENVER vs. CLEVELAND
RS: Broncos lead series, 13-5
PS: Broncos lead series, 3-0;
See Cleveland vs. Denver

DENVER vs. DALLAS
RS: Cowboys lead series, 3-2
PS: Cowboys lead series, 1-0;
See Dallas vs. Denver

DENVER vs. DETROIT
RS: Broncos lead series, 4-3
1971—Lions, 24-20 (Den)
1974—Broncos, 31-27 (Det)
1978—Lions, 17-14 (Det)
1981—Broncos, 27-21 (Den)
1984—Broncos, 28-7 (Det)
1987—Broncos, 34-0 (Den)
1990—Lions, 40-27 (Det)
(RS Pts.—Broncos 181, Lions 136)

DENVER vs. GREEN BAY
RS: Broncos lead series, 4-2-1
1971—Packers, 34-13 (Mil)
1975—Broncos, 23-13 (D)
1978—Broncos, 16-3 (D)
1984—Broncos, 17-14 (D)
1987—Tie, 17-17 (Mil) OT
1990—Broncos, 22-13 (D)
1993—Packers, 30-27 (GB)
(RS Pts.—Broncos 135, Packers 124)

DENVER vs. HOUSTON
RS: Oilers lead series, 19-11-1
PS: Broncos lead series, 2-1
1960—Oilers, 45-25 (D)
Oilers, 20-10 (H)
1961—Oilers, 55-14 (D)
Oilers, 45-14 (H)
1962—Broncos, 20-10 (D)
Oilers, 34-17 (H)
1963—Oilers, 20-14 (H)
Oilers, 33-24 (D)
1964—Oilers, 38-17 (D)
Oilers, 34-15 (H)
1965—Broncos, 28-17 (D)
Broncos, 31-21 (H)
1966—Oilers, 45-7 (H)
Broncos, 40-38 (D)
1967—Oilers, 10-6 (H)
Oilers, 20-18 (D)
1968—Oilers, 38-17 (H)
1969—Oilers, 24-21 (H)
Tie, 20-20 (D)
1970—Oilers, 31-21 (H)
1972—Broncos, 30-17 (D)
1973—Broncos, 48-20 (H)
1974—Broncos, 37-14 (D)
1976—Oilers, 17-3 (H)
1977—Broncos, 24-14 (H)
1979—*Oilers, 13-7 (H)
1980—Oilers, 20-16 (D)
1983—Broncos, 26-14 (H)
1985—Broncos, 31-20 (D)
1987—Oilers, 40-10 (D)
**Broncos, 34-10 (D)
1991—Oilers, 42-14 (H)
**Broncos, 26-24 (D)
1992—Broncos, 27-21 (D)
(RS Pts.—Oilers 837, Broncos 645)
(PS Pts.—Broncos 67, Oilers 47)
AFC First-Round Playoff
**AFC Divisional Playoff*

DENVER vs. *INDIANAPOLIS
RS: Broncos lead series, 9-2
1974—Broncos, 17-6 (B)
1977—Broncos, 27-13 (D)
1978—Colts, 7-6 (B)
1981—Broncos, 28-10 (D)
1983—Broncos, 17-10 (B)
Broncos, 21-19 (D)
1985—Broncos, 15-10 (I)
1988—Colts, 55-23 (I)
1989—Broncos, 14-3 (D)
1990—Broncos, 27-17 (I)
1993—Broncos, 35-13 (D)
(RS Pts.—Broncos 230, Colts 163)
Franchise in Baltimore prior to 1984

DENVER vs. *KANSAS CITY
RS: Chiefs lead series, 39-30
1960—Texans, 17-14 (D)
Texans, 34-7 (Dal)
1961—Texans, 19-12 (D)
Texans, 49-21 (Dal)
1962—Texans, 24-3 (D)
Texans, 17-10 (Dal)
1963—Chiefs, 59-7 (D)
Chiefs, 52-21 (KC)
1964—Broncos, 33-27 (D)
Chiefs, 49-39 (KC)
1965—Chiefs, 31-23 (D)
Chiefs, 45-35 (KC)
1966—Chiefs, 37-10 (KC)
Chiefs, 56-10 (D)
1967—Chiefs, 52-9 (KC)
Chiefs, 38-24 (D)

1968—Chiefs, 34-2 (KC)
Chiefs, 30-7 (D)
1969—Chiefs, 26-13 (D)
Chiefs, 31-17 (KC)
1970—Broncos, 26-13 (D)
Chiefs, 16-0 (KC)
1971—Chiefs, 16-3 (D)
Chiefs, 28-10 (KC)
1972—Chiefs, 45-24 (D)
Chiefs, 24-21 (KC)
1973—Chiefs, 16-14 (KC)
Broncos, 14-10 (D)
1974—Broncos, 17-14 (KC)
Chiefs, 42-34 (D)
1975—Broncos, 37-33 (D)
Chiefs, 26-13 (KC)
1976—Broncos, 35-26 (KC)
Broncos, 17-16 (D)
1977—Broncos, 23-7 (D)
Broncos, 14-7 (KC)
1978—Broncos, 23-17 (KC) OT
Broncos, 24-3 (D)
1979—Broncos, 24-10 (KC)
Broncos, 20-3 (D)
1980—Chiefs, 23-17 (D)
Chiefs, 31-14 (KC)
1981—Chiefs, 28-14 (KC)
Broncos, 16-13 (D)
1982—Chiefs, 37-16 (D)
1983—Broncos, 27-24 (D)
Chiefs, 48-17 (KC)
1984—Broncos, 21-0 (D)
Chiefs, 16-13 (KC)
1985—Broncos, 30-10 (KC)
Broncos, 14-13 (D)
1986—Broncos, 38-17 (D)
Chiefs, 37-10 (KC)
1987—Broncos, 26-17 (KC)
Broncos, 20-17 (D)
1988—Chiefs, 20-13 (KC)
Broncos, 17-11 (D)
1989—Broncos, 34-20 (D)
Broncos, 16-13 (KC)
1990—Broncos, 24-23 (D)
Chiefs, 31-20 (KC)
1991—Broncos, 19-16 (D)
Broncos, 24-20 (KC)
1992—Broncos, 20-19 (D)
Chiefs, 42-20 (KC)
1993—Chiefs, 15-7 (KC)
Broncos, 27-21 (D)
1994—Chiefs, 31-28 (D)
Broncos, 20-17 (KC) OT
(RS Pts.—Chiefs 1,729, Broncos 1,292)
Franchise in Dallas prior to 1963 and known as Texans

DENVER vs. *LOS ANGELES
RS: Raiders lead series, 48-19-2
PS: Series tied, 1-1
1960—Broncos, 31-14 (D)
Raiders, 48-10 (O)
1961—Raiders, 33-19 (O)
Broncos, 27-24 (D)
1962—Broncos, 44-7 (D)
Broncos, 23-6 (O)
1963—Raiders, 26-10 (D)
Raiders, 35-31 (O)
1964—Raiders, 40-7 (O)
Tie, 20-20 (D)
1965—Raiders, 28-20 (D)
Raiders, 24-13 (O)
1966—Raiders, 17-3 (D)
Raiders, 28-10 (O)
1967—Raiders, 51-0 (O)
Raiders, 21-17 (D)
1968—Raiders, 43-7 (D)
Raiders, 33-27 (O)
1969—Raiders, 24-14 (D)
Raiders, 41-10 (O)
1970—Raiders, 35-23 (O)
Raiders, 24-19 (D)
1971—Raiders, 27-16 (D)
Raiders, 21-13 (O)
1972—Broncos, 30-23 (O)
Raiders, 37-20 (D)
1973—Tie, 23-23 (D)
Raiders, 21-17 (O)
1974—Raiders, 28-17 (D)
Broncos, 20-17 (O)
1975—Raiders, 42-17 (D)
Raiders, 17-10 (O)
1976—Raiders, 17-10 (D)
Raiders, 19-6 (O)
1977—Broncos, 30-7 (O)
Raiders, 24-14 (D)
**Broncos, 20-17 (D)
1978—Broncos, 14-6 (D)
Broncos, 21-6 (O)
1979—Raiders, 27-3 (O)
Raiders, 14-10 (D)
1980—Raiders, 9-3 (O)
Raiders, 24-21 (D)
1981—Broncos, 9-7 (D)
Broncos, 17-0 (O)
1982—Raiders, 27-10 (LA)
1983—Raiders, 22-7 (D)
Raiders, 22-20 (LA)
1984—Broncos, 16-13 (D)
Broncos, 22-19 (LA) OT
1985—Raiders, 31-28 (LA) OT
Raiders, 17-14 (D) OT
1986—Broncos, 38-36 (D)
Broncos, 21-10 (LA)
1987—Broncos, 30-14 (D)
Broncos, 23-17 (LA)
1988—Raiders, 30-27 (D) OT
Raiders, 21-20 (LA)
1989—Broncos, 31-21 (D)
Raiders, 16-13 (LA) OT
1990—Raiders, 14-9 (LA)
Raiders, 23-20 (D)
1991—Raiders, 16-13 (LA)
Raiders, 17-16 (D)
1992—Broncos, 17-13 (D)
Raiders, 24-0 (LA)
1993—Raiders, 23-20 (D)
Raiders, 33-30 (LA) OT
***Raiders, 42-24 (LA)
1994—Raiders, 48-16 (D)
Raiders, 23-13 (LA)
(RS Pts.—Raiders 1,588, Broncos 1,200)
(PS Pts.—Raiders 59, Broncos 44)
Franchise in Oakland prior to 1982
***AFC Championship*
****AFC First-Round Playoff*

DENVER vs. MIAMI
RS: Dolphins lead series, 5-2-1
1966—Dolphins, 24-7 (M)
Broncos, 17-7 (D)
1967—Dolphins, 35-21 (M)
1968—Broncos, 21-14 (D)
1969—Dolphins, 27-24 (M)
1971—Tie, 10-10 (D)
1975—Dolphins, 14-13 (M)
1985—Dolphins, 30-26 (D)
(RS Pts.—Dolphins 161, Broncos 139)

DENVER vs. MINNESOTA
RS: Vikings lead series, 5-3
1972—Vikings, 23-20 (D)
1978—Vikings, 12-9 (M) OT
1981—Broncos, 19-17 (D)
1984—Broncos, 42-21 (D)
1987—Vikings, 34-27 (M)
1990—Vikings, 27-22 (M)
1991—Broncos, 13-6 (M)
1993—Vikings, 26-23 (D)
(RS Pts.—Broncos 175, Vikings 166)

DENVER vs. *NEW ENGLAND
RS: Broncos lead series, 16-12
PS: Broncos lead series, 1-0
1960—Broncos, 13-10 (B)
Broncos, 31-24 (D)
1961—Patriots, 45-17 (B)
Patriots, 28-24 (D)
1962—Patriots, 41-16 (B)
Patriots, 33-29 (D)
1963—Broncos, 14-10 (D)
Patriots, 40-21 (B)
1964—Patriots, 39-10 (D)
Patriots, 12-7 (B)
1965—Broncos, 27-10 (B)
Patriots, 28-20 (D)
1966—Patriots, 24-10 (D)
Broncos, 17-10 (B)
1967—Broncos, 26-21 (D)
1968—Patriots, 20-17 (D)
Broncos, 35-14 (B)
1969—Broncos, 35-7 (D)
1972—Broncos, 45-21 (D)
1976—Patriots, 38-14 (NE)
1979—Broncos, 45-10 (D)
1980—Patriots, 23-14 (NE)
1984—Broncos, 26-19 (D)
1986—Broncos, 27-20 (D)
**Broncos, 22-17 (D)
1987—Broncos, 31-20 (D)
1988—Broncos, 21-10 (D)
1991—Broncos, 9-6 (NE)
Broncos, 20-3 (D)
(RS Pts.—Broncos 621, Patriots 586)
(PS Pts.—Broncos 22, Patriots 17)
Franchise in Boston prior to 1971
***AFC Divisional Playoff*

DENVER vs. NEW ORLEANS
RS: Broncos lead series, 4-2
1970—Broncos, 31-6 (NO)
1974—Broncos, 33-17 (D)
1979—Broncos, 10-3 (D)
1985—Broncos, 34-23 (D)
1988—Saints, 42-0 (NO)
1994—Saints, 30-28 (D)
(RS Pts.—Broncos 136, Saints 121)

DENVER vs. N.Y. GIANTS
RS: Series tied, 3-3
PS: Giants lead series, 1-0
1972—Giants, 29-17 (NY)
1976—Broncos, 14-13 (D)
1980—Broncos, 14-9 (NY)
1986—Giants, 19-16 (NY)
*Giants, 39-20 (Pasadena)
1989—Giants, 14-7 (D)
1992—Broncos, 27-13 (D)
(RS Pts.—Giants 97, Broncos 95)
(PS Pts.—Giants 39, Broncos 20)
Super Bowl XXI

DENVER vs. *N.Y. JETS
RS: Series tied, 12-12-1
1960—Titans, 28-24 (NY)
Titans, 30-27 (D)
1961—Titans, 35-28 (NY)
Broncos, 27-10 (D)
1962—Broncos, 32-10 (NY)
Titans, 46-45 (D)
1963—Tie, 35-35 (NY)
Jets, 14-9 (D)
1964—Jets, 30-6 (NY)
Broncos, 20-16 (D)
1965—Broncos, 16-13 (D)
Jets, 45-10 (NY)
1966—Jets, 16-7 (D)
1967—Jets, 38-24 (D)
Broncos, 33-24 (NY)
1968—Broncos, 21-13 (NY)
1969—Broncos, 21-19 (D)
1973—Broncos, 40-28 (NY)
1976—Broncos, 46-3 (D)
1978—Jets, 31-28 (D)
1980—Broncos, 31-24 (D)
1986—Jets, 22-10 (NY)
1992—Broncos, 27-16 (D)
1993—Broncos, 26-20 (NY)
1994—Jets, 25-22 (NY) OT
(RS Pts.—Broncos 615, Jets 591)
Jets known as Titans prior to 1963

DENVER vs. PHILADELPHIA
RS: Eagles lead series, 5-2
1971—Eagles, 17-16 (P)
1975—Broncos, 25-10 (D)
1980—Eagles, 27-6 (P)
1983—Eagles, 13-10 (D)
1986—Broncos, 33-7 (P)
1989—Eagles, 28-24 (D)
1992—Eagles, 30-0 (P)
(RS Pts.—Eagles 132, Broncos 114)

DENVER vs. PITTSBURGH
RS: Broncos lead series, 10-5-1
PS: Series tied, 2-2
1970—Broncos, 16-13 (D)
1971—Broncos, 22-10 (P)
1973—Broncos, 23-13 (P)
1974—Tie, 35-35 (D) OT
1975—Steelers, 20-9 (P)
1977—Broncos, 21-7 (D)
*Broncos, 34-21 (D)
1978—Steelers, 21-17 (D)
*Steelers, 33-10 (P)
1979—Steelers, 42-7 (P)
1983—Broncos, 14-10 (P)
1984—*Steelers, 24-17 (D)
1985—Broncos, 31-23 (P)
1986—Broncos, 21-10 (P)
1988—Steelers, 39-21 (P)
1989—Broncos, 34-7 (D)
*Broncos, 24-23 (D)
1990—Steelers, 34-17 (D)
1991—Broncos, 20-13 (D)
1993—Broncos, 37-13 (D)
(RS Pts.—Broncos 345, Steelers 310)
(PS Pts.—Steelers 101, Broncos 85)
AFC Divisional Playoff

DENVER vs. *ST. LOUIS
RS: Rams lead series, 4-3
1972—Broncos, 16-10 (LA)
1974—Rams, 17-10 (D)
1979—Rams, 13-9 (D)
1982—Broncos, 27-24 (LA)
1985—Rams, 20-16 (LA)
1988—Broncos, 35-24 (D)
1994—Rams, 27-21 (LA)
(RS Pts.—Rams 135, Broncos 134)
Franchise in Los Angeles prior to 1995

DENVER vs. *SAN DIEGO
RS: Broncos lead series, 36-33-1
1960—Chargers, 23-19 (D)
Chargers, 41-33 (LA)
1961—Chargers, 37-0 (SD)
Chargers, 19-16 (D)
1962—Broncos, 30-21 (D)
Broncos, 23-20 (SD)
1963—Broncos, 50-34 (D)
Chargers, 58-20 (SD)
1964—Chargers, 42-14 (SD)
Chargers, 31-20 (D)
1965—Chargers, 34-31 (SD)
Chargers, 33-21 (D)
1966—Chargers, 24-17 (SD)
Broncos, 20-17 (D)
1967—Chargers, 38-21 (D)
Chargers, 24-20 (SD)
1968—Chargers, 55-24 (SD)
Chargers, 47-23 (D)
1969—Broncos, 13-0 (D)
Chargers, 45-24 (SD)
1970—Chargers, 24-21 (SD)
Tie, 17-17 (D)
1971—Broncos, 20-16 (D)
Chargers, 45-17 (SD)
1972—Chargers, 37-14 (SD)
Broncos, 38-13 (D)
1973—Broncos, 30-19 (D)
Broncos, 42-28 (SD)
1974—Broncos, 27-7 (D)
Chargers, 17-0 (SD)
1975—Broncos, 27-17 (SD)
Broncos, 13-10 (D) OT
1976—Broncos, 26-0 (D)
Broncos, 17-0 (SD)
1977—Broncos, 17-14 (SD)
Broncos, 17-9 (D)
1978—Broncos, 27-14 (D)
Chargers, 23-0 (SD)
1979—Broncos, 7-0 (D)

Chargers, 17-7 (SD)
1980—Chargers, 30-13 (D)
Broncos, 20-13 (SD)
1981—Broncos, 42-24 (D)
Chargers, 34-17 (SD)
1982—Chargers, 23-3 (D)
Chargers, 30-20 (SD)
1983—Broncos, 14-6 (D)
Chargers, 31-7 (SD)
1984—Broncos, 16-13 (SD)
Broncos, 16-13 (D)
1985—Chargers, 30-10 (SD)
Broncos, 30-24 (D) OT
1986—Broncos, 31-14 (SD)
Chargers, 9-3 (D)
1987—Broncos, 31-17 (SD)
Broncos, 24-0 (D)
1988—Broncos, 34-3 (D)
Broncos, 12-0 (SD)
1989—Broncos, 16-10 (D)
Chargers, 19-16 (SD)
1990—Chargers, 19-7 (SD)
Broncos, 20-10 (D)
1991—Broncos, 27-19 (D)
Broncos, 17-14 (SD)
1992—Broncos, 21-13 (D)
Chargers, 24-21 (SD)
1993—Broncos, 34-17 (D)
Chargers, 13-10 (SD)
1994—Chargers, 37-34 (D)
Broncos, 20-15 (SD)
(RS Pts.—Chargers 1,494, Broncos 1,409)
Franchise in Los Angeles prior to 1961

DENVER vs. SAN FRANCISCO
RS: Broncos lead series, 4-3
PS: 49ers lead series, 1-0
1970—49ers, 19-14 (SF)
1973—49ers, 36-34 (D)
1979—Broncos, 38-28 (SF)
1982—Broncos, 24-21 (D)
1985—Broncos, 17-16 (D)
1988—Broncos, 16-13 (SF) OT
1989—*49ers, 55-10 (New Orleans)
1994—49ers, 42-19 (SF)
(RS Pts.—49ers 175, Broncos 162)
(PS Pts.—49ers 55, Broncos 10)
Super Bowl XXIV

DENVER vs. SEATTLE
RS: Broncos lead series, 22-13
PS: Seahawks lead series, 1-0
1977—Broncos, 24-13 (S)
1978—Broncos, 28-7 (D)
Broncos, 20-17 (S) OT
1979—Broncos, 37-34 (D)
Seahawks, 28-23 (S)
1980—Broncos, 36-20 (D)
Broncos, 25-17 (S)
1981—Seahawks, 13-10 (S)
Broncos, 23-13 (D)
1982—Seahawks, 17-10 (D)
Seahawks, 13-11 (S)
1983—Seahawks, 27-19 (S)
Broncos, 38-27 (D)
*Seahawks, 31-7 (S)
1984—Seahawks, 27-24 (D)
Broncos, 31-14 (S)
1985—Broncos, 13-10 (D) OT
Broncos, 27-24 (S)
1986—Broncos, 20-13 (D)
Seahawks, 41-16 (S)
1987—Broncos, 40-17 (D)
Seahawks, 28-21 (S)
1988—Seahawks, 21-14 (D)
Seahawks, 42-14 (S)
1989—Broncos, 24-21 (S) OT
Broncos, 41-14 (D)
1990—Broncos, 34-31 (D) OT
Seahawks, 17-12 (S)
1991—Broncos, 16-10 (D)
Seahawks, 13-10 (S)
1992—Seahawks, 16-13 (S) OT
Broncos, 10-6 (D)
1993—Broncos, 28-17 (D)
Broncos, 17-9 (S)
1994—Broncos, 16-9 (S)
Broncos, 17-10 (D)
(RS Pts.—Broncos 762, Seahawks 656)
(PS Pts.—Seahawks 31, Broncos 7)
AFC First-Round Playoff

DENVER vs. TAMPA BAY
RS: Broncos lead series, 2-1
1976—Broncos, 48-13 (D)
1981—Broncos, 24-7 (TB)
1993—Buccaneers, 17-10 (D)
(RS Pts.—Broncos 82, Buccaneers 37)

DENVER vs. WASHINGTON
RS: Series tied, 3-3
PS: Redskins lead series, 1-0
1970—Redskins, 19-3 (D)
1974—Redskins, 30-3 (W)
1980—Broncos, 20-17 (D)
1986—Broncos, 31-30 (D)
1987—*Redskins, 42-10 (San Diego)
1989—Broncos, 14-10 (W)
1992—Redskins, 34-3 (W)
(RS Pts.—Redskins 140, Broncos 74)
(PS Pts.—Redskins 42, Broncos 10)
Super Bowl XXII

DETROIT vs. ARIZONA
RS: Lions lead series, 27-16-5;
See Arizona vs. Detroit

DETROIT vs. ATLANTA
RS: Lions lead series, 18-5;
See Atlanta vs. Detroit

DETROIT vs. BUFFALO
RS: Lions lead series, 3-1-1;
See Buffalo vs. Detroit

DETROIT vs. CHICAGO
RS: Bears lead series, 75-50-5;
See Chicago vs. Detroit

DETROIT vs. CINCINNATI
RS: Series tied, 3-3;
See Cincinnati vs. Detroit

DETROIT vs. CLEVELAND
RS: Lions lead series, 11-3
PS: Lions lead series, 3-1;
See Cleveland vs. Detroit

DETROIT vs. DALLAS
RS: Cowboys lead series, 7-6
PS: Series tied, 1-1;
See Dallas vs. Detroit

DETROIT vs. DENVER
RS: Broncos lead series, 4-3;
See Denver vs. Detroit

***DETROIT vs. GREEN BAY**
RS: Packers lead series, 65-57-7
PS: Packers lead series, 2-0
1930—Packers, 47-13 (GB)
Tie, 6-6 (P)
1932—Packers, 15-10 (GB)
Spartans, 19-0 (P)
1933—Packers, 17-0 (GB)
Spartans, 7-0 (P)
1934—Lions, 3-0 (GB)
Packers, 3-0 (D)
1935—Packers, 13-9 (Mil)
Packers, 31-7 (GB)
Lions, 20-10 (D)
1936—Packers, 20-18 (GB)
Packers, 26-17 (D)
1937—Packers, 26-6 (GB)
Packers, 14-13 (D)
1938—Lions, 17-7 (GB)
Packers, 28-7 (D)
1939—Packers, 26-7 (GB)
Packers, 12-7 (D)
1940—Lions, 23-14 (GB)
Packers, 50-7 (D)
1941—Packers, 23-0 (GB)
Packers, 24-7 (D)
1942—Packers, 38-7 (Mil)
Packers, 28-7 (D)
1943—Packers, 35-14 (GB)
Packers, 27-6 (D)
1944—Packers, 27-6 (Mil)
Packers, 14-0 (D)
1945—Packers, 57-21 (Mil)
Lions, 14-3 (D)
1946—Packers, 10-7 (Mil)
Packers, 9-0 (D)
1947—Packers, 34-17 (GB)
Packers, 35-14 (D)
1948—Packers, 33-21 (GB)
Lions, 24-20 (D)
1949—Packers, 16-14 (Mil)
Lions, 21-7 (D)
1950—Lions, 45-7 (GB)
Lions, 24-21 (D)
1951—Lions, 24-17 (GB)
Lions, 52-35 (D)
1952—Lions, 52-17 (GB)
Lions, 48-24 (D)
1953—Lions, 14-7 (GB)
Lions, 34-15 (D)
1954—Lions, 21-17 (GB)
Lions, 28-24 (D)
1955—Packers, 20-17 (GB)
Lions, 24-10 (D)
1956—Lions, 20-16 (GB)
Packers, 24-20 (D)
1957—Lions, 24-14 (GB)
Lions, 18-6 (D)
1958—Tie, 13-13 (GB)
Lions, 24-14 (D)
1959—Packers, 28-10 (GB)
Packers, 24-17 (D)
1960—Packers, 28-9 (GB)
Lions, 23-10 (D)
1961—Lions, 17-13 (Mil)
Packers, 17-9 (D)
1962—Packers, 9-7 (GB)
Lions, 26-14 (D)
1963—Packers, 31-10 (Mil)
Tie, 13-13 (D)
1964—Packers, 14-10 (D)
Packers, 30-7 (GB)
1965—Packers, 31-21 (D)
Lions, 12-7 (GB)
1966—Packers, 23-14 (GB)
Packers, 31-7 (D)
1967—Tie, 17-17 (GB)
Packers, 27-17 (D)
1968—Lions, 23-17 (GB)
Tie, 14-14 (D)
1969—Packers, 28-17 (D)
Lions, 16-10 (GB)
1970—Lions, 40-0 (GB)
Lions, 20-0 (D)
1971—Lions, 31-28 (D)
Tie, 14-14 (Mil)
1972—Packers, 24-23 (D)
Packers, 33-7 (GB)
1973—Tie, 13-13 (GB)
Lions, 34-0 (D)
1974—Packers, 21-19 (Mil)
Lions, 19-17 (D)
1975—Lions, 30-16 (Mil)
Lions, 13-10 (D)
1976—Packers, 24-14 (GB)
Lions, 27-6 (D)
1977—Lions, 10-6 (D)
Packers, 10-9 (GB)
1978—Packers, 13-7 (D)
Packers, 35-14 (Mil)
1979—Packers, 24-16 (Mil)
Packers, 18-13 (D)
1980—Lions, 29-7 (Mil)
Lions, 24-3 (D)
1981—Lions, 31-27 (D)
Packers, 31-17 (GB)
1982—Lions, 30-10 (GB)
Lions, 27-24 (D)
1983—Lions, 38-14 (D)
Lions, 23-20 (Mil) OT
1984—Packers, 41-9 (GB)
Lions, 31-28 (D)
1985—Packers, 43-10 (GB)
Packers, 26-23 (D)
1986—Lions, 21-14 (GB)
Packers, 44-40 (D)
1987—Lions, 19-16 (GB) OT
Packers, 34-33 (D)
1988—Lions, 19-9 (Mil)
Lions, 30-14 (D)
1989—Packers, 23-20 (Mil) OT
Lions, 31-22 (D)
1990—Packers, 24-21 (D)
Lions, 24-17 (GB)
1991—Lions, 23-14 (D)
Lions, 21-17 (GB)
1992—Packers, 27-13 (D)
Packers, 38-10 (Mil)
1993—Packers, 26-17 (Mil)
Lions, 30-20 (D)
**Packers, 28-24 (D)
1994—Packers, 38-30 (Mil)
Lions, 34-31 (D)
**Packers, 16-12 (GB)
(RS Pts.—Packers 2,556, Lions 2,335)
(PS Pts.—Packers 44, Lions 36)
**Franchise in Portsmouth prior to 1934 and known as the Spartans*
***NFC First-Round Playoff*

DETROIT vs. HOUSTON
RS: Oilers lead series, 4-2
1971—Lions, 31-7 (H)
1975—Oilers, 24-8 (H)
1983—Oilers, 27-17 (H)
1986—Lions, 24-13 (D)
1989—Oilers, 35-31 (H)
1992—Oilers, 24-21 (D)
(RS Pts.—Lions 132, Oilers 130)

DETROIT vs. *INDIANAPOLIS
RS: Series tied, 17-17-2
1953—Lions, 27-17 (B)
Lions, 17-7 (D)
1954—Lions, 35-0 (D)
Lions, 27-3 (B)
1955—Colts, 28-13 (B)
Lions, 24-14 (D)
1956—Lions, 31-14 (B)
Lions, 27-3 (D)
1957—Colts, 34-14 (B)
Lions, 31-27 (D)
1958—Colts, 28-15 (B)
Colts, 40-14 (D)
1959—Colts, 21-9 (B)
Colts, 31-24 (D)
1960—Lions, 30-17 (D)
Lions, 20-15 (B)
1961—Lions, 16-15 (B)
Colts, 17-14 (D)
1962—Lions, 29-20 (B)
Lions, 21-14 (D)
1963—Colts, 25-21 (D)
Colts, 24-21 (B)
1964—Colts, 34-0 (D)
Lions, 31-14 (B)
1965—Colts, 31-7 (B)
Tie, 24-24 (D)
1966—Colts, 45-14 (B)
Lions, 20-14 (D)
1967—Colts, 41-7 (B)
1968—Colts, 27-10 (D)
1969—Tie, 17-17 (B)
1973—Colts, 29-27 (D)
1977—Lions, 13-10 (B)
1980—Colts, 10-9 (D)
1985—Colts, 14-6 (I)
1991—Lions, 33-24 (I)
(RS Pts.—Colts 748, Lions 698)
**Franchise in Baltimore prior to 1984*

DETROIT vs. KANSAS CITY
RS: Chiefs lead series, 4-3
1971—Lions, 32-21 (D)
1975—Chiefs, 24-21 (KC) OT
1980—Chiefs, 20-17 (KC)
1981—Lions, 27-10 (D)
1987—Chiefs, 27-20 (D)
1988—Lions, 7-6 (KC)
1990—Chiefs, 43-24 (KC)

(RS Pts.—Chiefs 151, Lions 148)
DETROIT vs. *LOS ANGELES
RS: Raiders lead series, 5-2
1970—Lions, 28-14 (D)
1974—Raiders, 35-13 (O)
1978—Raiders, 29-17 (O)
1981—Lions, 16-0 (D)
1984—Raiders, 24-3 (D)
1987—Raiders, 27-7 (LA)
1990—Raiders, 38-31 (D)
(RS Pts.—Raiders 167, Lions 115)
**Franchise in Oakland prior to 1982*
DETROIT vs. MIAMI
RS: Dolphins lead series, 3-2
1973—Dolphins, 34-7 (M)
1979—Dolphins, 28-10 (D)
1985—Lions, 31-21 (D)
1991—Lions, 17-13 (D)
1994—Dolphins, 27-20 (M)
(RS Pts.—Dolphins 123, Lions 85)
DETROIT vs. MINNESOTA
RS: Vikings lead series, 41-24-2
1961—Lions, 37-10 (M)
Lions, 13-7 (D)
1962—Lions, 17-6 (M)
Lions, 37-23 (D)
1963—Lions, 28-10 (D)
Vikings, 34-31 (M)
1964—Lions, 24-20 (M)
Tie, 23-23 (D)
1965—Lions, 31-29 (M)
Vikings, 29-7 (D)
1966—Lions, 32-31 (M)
Vikings, 28-16 (D)
1967—Tie, 10-10 (M)
Lions, 14-3 (D)
1968—Vikings, 24-10 (M)
Vikings, 13-6 (D)
1969—Vikings, 24-10 (M)
Vikings, 27-0 (D)
1970—Vikings, 30-17 (D)
Vikings, 24-20 (M)
1971—Vikings, 16-13 (D)
Vikings, 29-10 (M)
1972—Vikings, 34-10 (D)
Vikings, 16-14 (M)
1973—Vikings, 23-9 (D)
Vikings, 28-7 (M)
1974—Vikings, 7-6 (D)
Lions, 20-16 (M)
1975—Vikings, 25-19 (M)
Lions, 17-10 (D)
1976—Vikings, 10-9 (D)
Vikings, 31-23 (M)
1977—Vikings, 14-7 (M)
Vikings, 30-21 (D)
1978—Vikings, 17-7 (M)
Lions, 45-14 (D)
1979—Vikings, 13-10 (D)
Vikings, 14-7 (M)
1980—Lions, 27-7 (D)
Vikings, 34-0 (M)
1981—Vikings, 26-24 (M)
Lions, 45-7 (D)
1982—Vikings, 34-31 (D)
1983—Vikings, 20-17 (M)
Lions, 13-2 (D)
1984—Vikings, 29-28 (D)
Lions, 16-14 (M)
1985—Vikings, 16-13 (M)
Lions, 41-21 (D)
1986—Lions, 13-10 (M)
Vikings, 24-10 (D)
1987—Vikings, 34-19 (M)
Vikings, 17-14 (D)
1988—Vikings, 44-17 (M)
Vikings, 23-0 (D)
1989—Vikings, 24-17 (M)
Vikings, 20-7 (D)
1990—Lions, 34-27 (M)
Vikings, 17-7 (D)
1991—Lions, 24-20 (D)
Lions, 34-14 (M)
1992—Lions, 31-17 (D)
Vikings, 31-14 (M)
1993—Lions, 30-27 (M)
Vikings, 13-0 (D)
1994—Vikings, 10-3 (M)
Lions, 41-19 (D)
(RS Pts.—Vikings 1,356, Lions 1,207)
DETROIT vs. NEW ENGLAND
RS: Series tied, 3-3
1971—Lions, 34-7 (NE)
1976—Lions, 30-10 (D)
1979—Patriots, 24-17 (NE)
1985—Patriots, 23-6 (NE)
1993—Lions, 19-16 (NE) OT
1994—Patriots, 23-17 (D)
(RS Pts.—Lions 123, Patriots 103)
DETROIT vs. NEW ORLEANS
RS: Saints lead series, 7-6-1
1968—Tie, 20-20 (D)
1970—Saints, 19-17 (NO)
1972—Lions, 27-14 (D)
1973—Saints, 20-13 (NO)
1974—Lions, 19-14 (D)
1976—Saints, 17-16 (NO)
1977—Lions, 23-19 (D)
1979—Saints, 17-7 (NO)
1980—Lions, 24-13 (D)
1988—Saints, 22-14 (D)
1989—Lions, 21-14 (D)
1990—Lions, 27-10 (NO)
1992—Saints, 13-7 (D)
1993—Saints, 14-3 (NO)
(RS Pts.—Lions 238, Saints 226)
***DETROIT vs. N.Y. GIANTS**
RS: Lions lead series, 18-15-1
PS: Lions lead series, 1-0
1930—Giants, 19-6 (P)
1931—Spartans, 14-6 (P)
Giants, 14-0 (NY)
1932—Spartans, 7-0 (P)
Spartans, 6-0 (NY)
1933—Spartans, 17-7 (P)
Giants, 13-10 (NY)
1934—Lions, 9-0 (D)
1935—**Lions, 26-7 (D)
1936—Giants, 14-7 (NY)
Lions, 38-0 (D)
1937—Lions, 17-0 (NY)
1939—Lions, 18-14 (D)
1941—Giants, 20-13 (NY)
1943—Tie, 0-0 (D)
1945—Giants, 35-14 (NY)
1947—Lions, 35-7 (D)
1949—Lions, 45-21 (NY)
1953—Lions, 27-16 (NY)
1955—Giants, 24-19 (D)
1958—Giants, 19-17 (D)
1962—Giants, 17-14 (NY)
1964—Lions, 26-3 (D)
1967—Lions, 30-7 (NY)
1969—Lions, 24-0 (D)
1972—Lions, 30-16 (D)
1974—Lions, 20-19 (D)
1976—Giants, 24-10 (NY)
1982—Giants, 13-6 (D)
1983—Lions, 15-9 (D)
1988—Giants, 30-10 (NY)
Giants, 13-10 (D) OT
1989—Giants, 24-14 (NY)
1990—Giants, 20-0 (NY)
1994—Lions, 28-25 (NY) OT
(RS Pts.—Lions 556, Giants 449)
(PS Pts.—Lions 26, Giants 7)
**Franchise in Portsmouth prior to 1934 and known as the Spartans*
***NFL Championship*
DETROIT vs. N.Y. JETS
RS: Lions lead series, 4-3
1972—Lions, 37-20 (D)
1979—Jets, 31-10 (NY)
1982—Jets, 28-13 (D)
1985—Lions, 31-20 (D)
1988—Jets, 17-10 (D)
1991—Lions, 34-20 (D)
1994—Lions, 18-7 (NY)
(RS Pts.—Lions 153, Jets 143)
***DETROIT vs. PHILADELPHIA**
RS: Lions lead series, 12-9-2
1933—Spartans, 25-0 (P)
1934—Lions, 10-0 (P)
1935—Lions, 35-0 (D)
1936—Lions, 23-0 (P)
1938—Eagles, 21-7 (D)
1940—Lions, 21-0 (P)
1941—Lions, 21-17 (D)
1945—Lions, 28-24 (D)
1948—Eagles, 45-21 (P)
1949—Eagles, 22-14 (D)
1951—Lions, 28-10 (P)
1954—Tie, 13-13 (D)
1957—Lions, 27-16 (P)
1960—Eagles, 28-10 (P)
1961—Eagles, 27-24 (D)
1965—Lions, 35-28 (P)
1968—Eagles, 12-0 (D)
1971—Eagles, 23-20 (D)
1974—Eagles, 28-17 (P)
1977—Lions, 17-13 (D)
1979—Eagles, 44-7 (P)
1984—Tie, 23-23 (D) OT
1986—Lions, 13-11 (P)
(RS Pts.—Lions 439, Eagles 405)
**Franchise in Portsmouth prior to 1934 and known as the Spartans*
DETROIT vs. *PITTSBURGH
RS: Lions lead series, 13-11-1
1934—Lions, 40-7 (D)
1936—Lions, 28-3 (D)
1937—Lions, 7-3 (D)
1938—Lions, 16-7 (D)
1940—Pirates, 10-7 (D)
1942—Steelers, 35-7 (D)
1946—Lions, 17-7 (D)
1947—Steelers, 17-10 (P)
1948—Lions, 17-14 (D)
1949—Steelers, 14-7 (P)
1950—Lions, 10-7 (D)
1952—Lions, 31-6 (P)
1953—Lions, 38-21 (D)
1955—Lions, 31-28 (P)
1956—Lions, 45-7 (D)
1959—Tie, 10-10 (P)
1962—Lions, 45-7 (D)
1966—Steelers, 17-3 (P)
1967—Steelers, 24-14 (D)
1969—Steelers, 16-13 (P)
1973—Steelers, 24-10 (P)
1983—Lions, 45-3 (D)
1986—Steelers, 27-17 (P)
1989—Steelers, 23-3 (D)
1992—Steelers, 17-14 (P)
(RS Pts.—Lions 485, Steelers 354)
**Steelers known as Pirates prior to 1941*
DETROIT vs. *ST. LOUIS
RS: Rams lead series, 39-35-1
PS: Lions lead series, 1-0
1937—Lions, 28-0 (C)
Lions, 27-7 (D)
1938—Rams, 21-17 (C)
Lions, 6-0 (D)
1939—Lions, 15-7 (D)
Rams, 14-3 (C)
1940—Lions, 6-0 (D)
Rams, 24-0 (C)
1941—Lions, 17-7 (D)
Lions, 14-0 (C)
1942—Rams, 14-0 (D)
Rams, 27-7 (C)
1944—Rams, 20-17 (D)
Lions, 26-14 (C)
1945—Rams, 28-21 (D)
1946—Rams, 35-14 (LA)
Rams, 41-20 (D)
1947—Rams, 27-13 (D)
Rams, 28-17 (LA)
1948—Rams, 44-7 (LA)
Rams, 34-27 (D)
1949—Rams, 27-24 (LA)
Rams, 21-10 (D)
1950—Rams, 30-28 (D)
Rams, 65-24 (LA)
1951—Rams, 27-21 (D)
Lions, 24-22 (LA)
1952—Lions, 17-14 (LA)
Lions, 24-16 (D)
**Lions, 31-21 (D)
1953—Rams, 31-19 (D)
Rams, 37-24 (LA)
1954—Lions, 21-3 (D)
Lions, 27-24 (LA)
1955—Rams, 17-10 (D)
Rams, 24-13 (LA)
1956—Lions, 24-21 (D)
Lions, 16-7 (LA)
1957—Lions, 10-7 (D)
Rams, 35-17 (LA)
1958—Rams, 42-28 (D)
Lions, 41-24 (LA)
1959—Lions, 17-7 (LA)
Lions, 23-17 (D)
1960—Rams, 48-35 (LA)
Lions, 12-10 (D)
1961—Lions, 14-13 (D)
Lions, 28-10 (LA)
1962—Lions, 13-10 (D)
Lions, 12-3 (LA)
1963—Lions, 23-2 (LA)
Rams, 28-21 (D)
1964—Tie, 17-17 (LA)
Lions, 37-17 (D)
1965—Lions, 20-0 (D)
Lions, 31-7 (LA)
1966—Rams, 14-7 (D)
Rams, 23-3 (LA)
1967—Rams, 31-7 (D)
1968—Rams, 10-7 (LA)
1969—Lions, 28-0 (D)
1970—Lions, 28-23 (LA)
1971—Rams, 21-13 (D)
1972—Lions, 34-17 (LA)
1974—Rams, 16-13 (LA)
1975—Rams, 20-0 (D)
1976—Rams, 20-17 (D)
1980—Lions, 41-20 (LA)
1981—Rams, 20-13 (LA)
1982—Lions, 19-14 (LA)
1983—Rams, 21-10 (LA)
1986—Rams, 14-10 (LA)
1987—Rams, 37-16 (D)
1988—Rams, 17-10 (LA)
1991—Lions, 21-10 (D)
1993—Lions, 16-13 (LA)
(RS Pts.—Rams 1,436, Lions 1,340)
(PS Pts.—Lions 31, Rams 21)
**Franchise in Los Angeles prior to 1995 and in Cleveland prior to 1946*
***Conference Playoff*
DETROIT vs. SAN DIEGO
RS: Lions lead series, 3-2
1972—Lions, 34-20 (D)
1977—Lions, 20-0 (D)
1978—Lions, 31-14 (D)
1981—Chargers, 28-23 (SD)
1984—Chargers, 27-24 (SD)
(RS Pts.—Lions 132, Chargers 89)
DETROIT vs. SAN FRANCISCO
RS: 49ers lead series, 27-25-1
PS: Series tied, 1-1
1950—Lions, 24-7 (D)
49ers, 28-27 (SF)
1951—49ers, 20-10 (D)
49ers, 21-17 (SF)
1952—49ers, 17-3 (SF)
49ers, 28-0 (D)
1953—Lions, 24-21 (D)
Lions, 14-10 (SF)
1954—49ers, 37-31 (SF)
Lions, 48-7 (D)
1955—49ers, 27-24 (D)

49ers, 38-21 (SF)
1956—Lions, 20-17 (D)
Lions, 17-13 (SF)
1957—49ers, 35-31 (SF)
Lions, 31-10 (D)
*Lions, 31-27 (SF)
1958—49ers, 24-21 (SF)
Lions, 35-21 (D)
1959—49ers, 34-13 (D)
49ers, 33-7 (SF)
1960—49ers, 14-10 (D)
Lions, 24-0 (SF)
1961—49ers, 49-0 (D)
Tie, 20-20 (SF)
1962—Lions, 45-24 (D)
Lions, 38-24 (SF)
1963—Lions, 26-3 (D)
Lions, 45-7 (SF)
1964—Lions, 26-17 (SF)
Lions, 24-7 (D)
1965—49ers, 27-21 (D)
49ers, 17-14 (SF)
1966—49ers, 27-24 (SF)
49ers, 41-14 (D)
1967—Lions, 45-3 (SF)
1968—49ers, 14-7 (D)
1969—Lions, 26-14 (SF)
1970—Lions, 28-7 (D)
1971—49ers, 31-27 (SF)
1973—Lions, 30-20 (D)
1974—Lions, 17-13 (D)
1975—Lions, 28-17 (SF)
1977—49ers, 28-7 (SF)
1978—Lions, 33-14 (D)
1980—Lions, 17-13 (D)
1981—Lions, 24-17 (D)
1983—**49ers, 24-23 (SF)
1984—49ers, 30-27 (D)
1985—Lions, 23-21 (D)
1988—49ers, 20-13 (SF)
1991—49ers, 35-3 (SF)
1992—49ers, 24-6 (SF)
1993—49ers, 55-17 (D)
1994—49ers, 27-21 (D)
(RS Pts.—Lions 1,148, 49ers 1,128)
(PS Pts.—Lions 54, 49ers 51)
Conference Playoff
***NFC Divisional Playoff*

DETROIT vs. SEATTLE
RS: Seahawks lead series, 4-2
1976—Lions, 41-14 (S)
1978—Seahawks, 28-16 (S)
1984—Seahawks, 38-17 (S)
1987—Seahawks, 37-14 (D)
1990—Seahawks, 30-10 (S)
1993—Lions, 30-10 (D)
(RS Pts.—Seahawks 157, Lions 128)

DETROIT vs. TAMPA BAY
RS: Series tied, 17-17
1977—Lions, 16-7 (D)
1978—Lions, 15-7 (TB)
Lions, 34-23 (D)
1979—Buccaneers, 31-16 (TB)
Buccaneers, 16-14 (D)
1980—Lions, 24-10 (TB)
Lions, 27-14 (D)
1981—Buccaneers, 28-10 (TB)
Buccaneers, 20-17 (D)
1982—Buccaneers, 23-21 (TB)
1983—Lions, 11-0 (TB)
Lions, 23-20 (D)
1984—Buccaneers, 21-17 (TB)
Lions, 13-7 (D) OT
1985—Lions, 30-9 (D)
Buccaneers, 19-16 (TB) OT
1986—Buccaneers, 24-20 (D)
Lions, 38-17 (TB)
1987—Buccaneers, 31-27 (D)
Lions, 20-10 (TB)
1988—Buccaneers, 23-20 (D)
Buccaneers, 21-10 (TB)
1989—Lions, 17-16 (TB)
Lions, 33-7 (D)
1990—Buccaneers, 38-21 (D)
Buccaneers, 23-20 (TB)
1991—Lions, 31-3 (D)
Buccaneers, 30-21 (TB)
1992—Buccaneers, 27-23 (D)
Lions, 38-7 (TB)
1993—Buccaneers, 27-10 (TB)
Lions, 23-0 (D)
1994—Buccaneers, 24-14 (TB)
Lions, 14-9 (D)
(RS Pts.—Lions 704, Buccaneers 592)

***DETROIT vs. **WASHINGTON**
RS: Redskins lead series, 22-8
PS: Redskins lead series, 2-0
1932—Spartans, 10-0 (P)
1933—Spartans, 13-0 (B)
1934—Lions, 24-0 (D)
1935—Lions, 17-7 (B)
Lions, 14-0 (D)
1938—Redskins, 7-5 (D)
1939—Redskins, 31-7 (W)
1940—Redskins, 20-14 (D)
1942—Redskins, 15-3 (D)
1943—Redskins, 42-20 (W)
1946—Redskins, 17-16 (W)
1947—Lions, 38-21 (D)
1948—Redskins, 46-21 (W)
1951—Lions, 35-17 (D)
1956—Redskins, 18-17 (W)
1965—Lions, 14-10 (D)
1968—Redskins, 14-3 (W)
1970—Redskins, 31-10 (W)
1973—Redskins, 20-0 (D)
1976—Redskins, 20-7 (W)
1978—Redskins, 21-19 (D)
1979—Redskins, 27-24 (D)
1981—Redskins, 33-31 (W)
1982—***Redskins, 31-7 (W)
1983—Redskins, 38-17 (W)
1984—Redskins, 28-14 (W)
1985—Redskins, 24-3 (W)
1987—Redskins, 20-13 (W)
1990—Redskins, 41-38 (D)
1991—Redskins, 45-0 (W)
****Redskins, 41-10 (W)
1992—Redskins, 13-10 (W)
(RS Pts.—Redskins 626, Lions 457)
(PS Pts.—Redskins 72, Lions 17)
Franchise in Portsmouth prior to 1934 and known as the Spartans.
***Franchise in Boston prior to 1937*
****NFC First-Round Playoff*
*****NFC Championship*

GREEN BAY vs. ARIZONA
RS: Packers lead series, 39-21-4
PS: Packers lead series, 1-0;
See Arizona vs. Green Bay

GREEN BAY vs. ATLANTA
RS: Packers lead series, 10-9;
See Atlanta vs. Green Bay

GREEN BAY vs. BUFFALO
RS: Bills lead series, 5-1;
See Buffalo vs. Green Bay

GREEN BAY vs. CHICAGO
RS: Bears lead series, 81-61-6
PS: Bears lead series, 1-0;
See Chicago vs. Green Bay

GREEN BAY vs. CINCINNATI
RS: Bengals lead series, 4-3;
See Cincinnati vs. Green Bay

GREEN BAY vs. CLEVELAND
RS: Packers lead series, 7-6
PS: Packers lead series, 1-0;
See Cleveland vs. Green Bay

GREEN BAY vs. DALLAS
RS: Packers lead series, 8-7
PS: Cowboys lead series, 3-2;
See Dallas vs. Green Bay

GREEN BAY vs. DENVER
RS: Broncos lead series, 4-2-1;
See Denver vs. Green Bay

GREEN BAY vs. DETROIT
RS: Packers lead series, 65-57-7
PS: Packers lead series, 2-0;
See Detroit vs. Green Bay

GREEN BAY vs. HOUSTON
RS: Series tied, 3-3
1972—Packers, 23-10 (H)
1977—Oilers, 16-10 (GB)
1980—Oilers, 22-3 (GB)
1983—Packers, 41-38 (H) OT
1986—Oilers, 31-3 (GB)
1992—Packers, 16-14 (H)
(RS Pts.—Oilers 131, Packers 96)

GREEN BAY vs. *INDIANAPOLIS
RS: Series tied, 18-18-1
PS: Packers lead series, 1-0
1953—Packers, 37-14 (GB)
Packers, 35-24 (B)
1954—Packers, 7-6 (B)
Packers, 24-13 (Mil)
1955—Colts, 24-20 (Mil)
Colts, 14-10 (B)
1956—Packers, 38-33 (Mil)
Colts, 28-21 (B)
1957—Colts, 45-17 (Mil)
Packers, 24-21 (B)
1958—Colts, 24-17 (Mil)
Colts, 56-0 (B)
1959—Colts, 38-21 (B)
Colts, 28-24 (Mil)
1960—Packers, 35-21 (GB)
Colts, 38-24 (B)
1961—Packers, 45-7 (GB)
Colts, 45-21 (B)
1962—Packers, 17-6 (B)
Packers, 17-13 (GB)
1963—Packers, 31-20 (GB)
Packers, 34-20 (B)
1964—Colts, 21-20 (GB)
Colts, 24-21 (B)
1965—Packers, 20-17 (Mil)
Packers, 42-27 (B)
**Packers, 13-10 (GB) OT
1966—Packers, 24-3 (Mil)
Packers, 14-10 (B)
1967—Colts, 13-10 (B)
1968—Colts, 16-3 (GB)
1969—Colts, 14-6 (B)
1970—Colts, 13-10 (Mil)
1974—Packers, 20-13 (B)
1982—Tie, 20-20 (B) OT
1985—Colts, 37-10 (I)
1988—Colts, 20-13 (GB)
1991—Packers, 14-10 (Mil)
(RS Pts.—Colts 796, Packers 766)
(PS Pts.—Packers 13, Colts 10)
Franchise in Baltimore prior to 1984
***Conference Playoff*

GREEN BAY vs. KANSAS CITY
RS: Chiefs lead series, 4-1-1
PS: Packers lead series, 1-0
1966—*Packers, 35-10 (Los Angeles)
1973—Tie, 10-10 (Mil)
1977—Chiefs, 20-10 (KC)
1987—Packers, 23-3 (KC)
1989—Chiefs, 21-3 (GB)
1990—Chiefs, 17-3 (GB)
1993—Chiefs, 23-16 (KC)
(RS Pts.—Chiefs 94, Packers 65)
(PS Pts.—Packers 35, Chiefs 10)
Super Bowl I

GREEN BAY vs. *LOS ANGELES
RS: Raiders lead series, 5-2
PS: Packers lead series, 1-0
1967—**Packers, 33-14 (Miami)
1972—Raiders, 20-14 (GB)
1976—Raiders, 18-14 (O)
1978—Raiders, 28-3 (GB)
1984—Raiders, 28-7 (LA)
1987—Raiders, 20-0 (GB)
1990—Packers, 29-16 (LA)
1993—Packers, 28-0 (GB)
(RS Pts.—Raiders 130, Packers 95)
(PS Pts.—Packers 33, Raiders 14)
Franchise in Oakland prior to 1982
***Super Bowl II*

GREEN BAY vs. MIAMI
RS: Dolphins lead series, 8-0
1971—Dolphins, 27-6 (Mia)
1975—Dolphins, 31-7 (GB)
1979—Dolphins, 27-7 (Mia)
1985—Dolphins, 34-24 (GB)
1988—Dolphins, 24-17 (Mia)
1989—Dolphins, 23-20 (Mia)
1991—Dolphins, 16-13 (Mia)
1994—Dolphins, 24-14 (Mil)
(RS Pts.—Dolphins 206, Packers 108)

GREEN BAY vs. MINNESOTA
RS: Vikings lead series, 34-32-1
1961—Packers, 33-7 (Minn)
Packers, 28-10 (Mil)
1962—Packers, 34-7 (GB)
Packers, 48-21 (Minn)
1963—Packers, 37-28 (Minn)
Packers, 28-7 (GB)
1964—Vikings, 24-23 (GB)
Packers, 42-13 (Minn)
1965—Packers, 38-13 (Minn)
Packers, 24-19 (GB)
1966—Vikings, 20-17 (GB)
Packers, 28-16 (Minn)
1967—Vikings, 10-7 (Mil)
Packers, 30-27 (Minn)
1968—Vikings, 26-13 (Mil)
Vikings, 14-10 (Minn)
1969—Vikings, 19-7 (Minn)
Vikings, 9-7 (Mil)
1970—Packers, 13-10 (Mil)
Vikings, 10-3 (Minn)
1971—Vikings, 24-13 (GB)
Vikings, 3-0 (Minn)
1972—Vikings, 27-13 (GB)
Packers, 23-7 (Minn)
1973—Vikings, 11-3 (Minn)
Vikings, 31-7 (GB)
1974—Vikings, 32-17 (GB)
Packers, 19-7 (Minn)
1975—Vikings, 28-17 (GB)
Vikings, 24-3 (Minn)
1976—Vikings, 17-10 (Mil)
Vikings, 20-9 (Minn)
1977—Vikings, 19-7 (Minn)
Vikings, 13-6 (GB)
1978—Vikings, 21-7 (Minn)
Tie, 10-10 (GB) OT
1979—Vikings, 27-21 (Minn) OT
Packers, 19-7 (Mil)
1980—Packers, 16-3 (GB)
Packers, 25-13 (Minn)
1981—Vikings, 30-13 (Mil)
Packers, 35-23 (Minn)
1982—Packers, 26-7 (Mil)
1983—Vikings, 20-17 (GB) OT
Packers, 29-21 (Minn)
1984—Packers, 45-17 (Mil)
Packers, 38-14 (Minn)
1985—Packers, 20-17 (Mil)
Packers, 27-17 (Minn)
1986—Vikings, 42-7 (Minn)
Vikings, 32-6 (GB)
1987—Packers, 23-16 (Minn)
Packers, 16-10 (Mil)
1988—Packers, 34-14 (Minn)
Packers, 18-6 (GB)
1989—Vikings, 26-14 (Minn)
Packers, 20-19 (Mil)
1990—Packers, 24-10 (Mil)
Vikings, 23-7 (Minn)
1991—Vikings, 35-21 (GB)
Packers, 27-7 (Minn)
1992—Vikings, 23-20 (GB) OT
Vikings, 27-7 (Minn)
1993—Vikings, 15-13 (Minn)
Vikings, 21-17 (Mil)
1994—Packers, 16-10 (GB)
Vikings, 13-10 (M) OT
(RS Pts.—Packers 1,265, Vikings 1,169)

GREEN BAY vs. NEW ENGLAND
RS: Patriots lead series, 3-2
1973—Patriots, 33-24 (NE)
1979—Packers, 27-14 (GB)
1985—Patriots, 26-20 (NE)
1988—Packers, 45-3 (Mil)
1994—Patriots, 17-16 (NE)
(RS Pts.—Packers 132, Patriots 93)

GREEN BAY vs. NEW ORLEANS
RS: Packers lead series, 12-4
1968—Packers, 29-7 (Mil)
1971—Saints, 29-21 (Mil)
1972—Packers, 30-20 (NO)
1973—Packers, 30-10 (Mil)
1975—Saints, 20-19 (NO)
1976—Packers, 32-27 (Mil)
1977—Packers, 24-20 (NO)
1978—Packers, 28-17 (Mil)
1979—Packers, 28-19 (Mil)
1981—Packers, 35-7 (NO)
1984—Packers, 23-13 (NO)
1985—Packers, 38-14 (Mil)
1986—Saints, 24-10 (NO)
1987—Saints, 33-24 (NO)
1989—Packers, 35-34 (GB)
1993—Packers, 19-17 (NO)
(RS Pts.—Packers 425, Saints 311)

GREEN BAY vs. N.Y. GIANTS
RS: Packers lead series, 21-20-2
PS: Packers lead series, 4-1
1928—Giants, 6-0 (GB)
Packers, 7-0 (NY)
1929—Packers, 20-6 (NY)
1930—Packers, 14-7 (GB)
Giants, 13-6 (NY)
1931—Packers, 27-7 (GB)
Packers, 14-10 (NY)
1932—Packers, 13-0 (GB)
Giants, 6-0 (NY)
1933—Giants, 10-7 (Mil)
Giants, 17-6 (NY)
1934—Packers, 20-6 (Mil)
Giants, 17-3 (NY)
1935—Packers, 16-7 (GB)
1936—Packers, 26-14 (NY)
1937—Giants, 10-0 (NY)
1938—Giants, 15-3 (NY)
*Giants, 23-17 (NY)
1939—*Packers, 27-0 (Mil)
1940—Giants, 7-3 (NY)
1942—Tie, 21-21 (NY)
1943—Packers, 35-21 (NY)
1944—Giants, 24-0 (NY)
*Packers, 14-7 (NY)
1945—Packers, 23-14 (NY)
1947—Tie, 24-24 (NY)
1948—Giants, 49-3 (Mil)
1949—Giants, 30-10 (GB)
1952—Packers, 17-3 (NY)
1957—Giants, 31-17 (GB)
1959—Giants, 20-3 (NY)
1961—Packers, 20-17 (Mil)
*Packers, 37-0 (GB)
1962—*Packers, 16-7 (NY)
1967—Packers, 48-21 (NY)
1969—Packers, 20-10 (Mil)
1971—Giants, 42-40 (GB)
1973—Packers, 16-14 (New Haven)
1975—Packers, 40-14 (Mil)
1980—Giants, 27-21 (NY)
1981—Packers, 27-14 (NY)
Packers, 26-24 (Mil)
1982—Packers, 27-19 (NY)
1983—Giants, 27-3 (NY)
1985—Packers, 23-20 (GB)
1986—Giants, 55-24 (NY)
1987—Giants, 20-10 (NY)
1992—Giants, 27-7 (NY)
(RS Pts.—Giants 746, Packers 690)
(PS Pts.—Packers 111, Giants 37)
**NFL Championship*

GREEN BAY vs. N.Y. JETS
RS: Jets lead series, 5-2
1973—Packers, 23-7 (Mil)
1979—Jets, 27-22 (GB)
1981—Jets, 28-3 (NY)
1982—Jets, 15-13 (NY)
1985—Jets, 24-3 (Mil)
1991—Jets, 19-16 (NY) OT
1994—Packers, 17-10 (GB)
(RS Pts.—Jets 130, Packers 97)

GREEN BAY vs. PHILADELPHIA
RS: Packers lead series, 19-8
PS: Eagles lead series, 1-0
1933—Packers, 35-9 (GB)
Packers, 10-0 (P)
1934—Packers, 19-6 (GB)
1935—Packers, 13-6 (P)
1937—Packers, 37-7 (Mil)
1939—Packers, 23-16 (P)
1940—Packers, 27-20 (GB)
1942—Packers, 7-0 (P)
1946—Packers, 19-7 (P)
1947—Eagles, 28-14 (P)
1951—Packers, 37-24 (GB)
1952—Packers, 12-10 (Mil)
1954—Packers, 37-14 (P)
1958—Packers, 38-35 (GB)
1960—*Eagles, 17-13 (P)
1962—Packers, 49-0 (P)
1968—Packers, 30-13 (GB)
1970—Packers, 30-17 (Mil)
1974—Eagles, 36-14 (P)
1976—Packers, 28-13 (GB)
1978—Eagles, 10-3 (P)
1979—Eagles, 21-10 (GB)
1987—Packers, 16-10 (GB) OT
1990—Eagles, 31-0 (P)
1991—Eagles, 20-3 (GB)
1992—Packers, 27-24 (Mil)
1993—Eagles, 20-17 (GB)
1994—Eagles, 13-7 (P)
(RS Pts.—Packers 562, Eagles 410)
(PS Pts.—Eagles 17, Packers 13)
**NFL Championship*

GREEN BAY vs. *PITTSBURGH
RS: Packers lead series, 17-11
1933—Packers, 47-0 (GB)
1935—Packers, 27-0 (GB)
Packers, 34-14 (P)
1936—Packers, 42-10 (Mil)
1938—Packers, 20-0 (GB)
1940—Packers, 24-3 (Mil)
1941—Packers, 54-7 (P)
1942—Packers, 24-21 (Mil)
1946—Packers, 17-7 (GB)
1947—Steelers, 18-17 (Mil)
1948—Steelers, 38-7 (P)
1949—Steelers, 30-7 (Mil)
1951—Packers, 35-33 (Mil)
Steelers, 28-7 (P)
1953—Steelers, 31-14 (P)
1954—Steelers, 21-20 (GB)
1957—Packers, 27-10 (P)
1960—Packers, 19-13 (P)
1963—Packers, 33-14 (Mil)
1965—Packers, 41-9 (P)
1967—Steelers, 24-17 (GB)
1969—Packers, 38-34 (P)
1970—Packers, 20-12 (P)
1975—Steelers, 16-13 (Mil)
1980—Steelers, 22-20 (P)
1983—Steelers, 25-21 (GB)
1986—Steelers, 27-3 (P)
1992—Packers, 17-3 (GB)
(RS Pts.—Packers 665, Steelers 470)
**Steelers known as Pirates prior to 1941*

GREEN BAY vs. *ST. LOUIS
RS: Rams lead series, 42-37-2
PS: Packers lead series, 1-0
1937—Packers, 35-10 (C)
Packers, 35-7 (GB)
1938—Packers, 26-17 (GB)
Packers, 28-7 (C)
1939—Rams, 27-24 (GB)
Packers, 7-6 (C)
1940—Packers, 31-14 (GB)
Tie, 13-13 (C)
1941—Packers, 24-7 (Mil)
Packers, 17-14 (C)
1942—Packers, 45-28 (GB)
Packers, 30-12 (C)
1944—Packers, 30-21 (GB)
Packers, 42-7 (C)
1945—Rams, 27-14 (GB)
Rams, 20-7 (C)
1946—Rams, 21-17 (Mil)
Rams, 38-17 (LA)
1947—Packers, 17-14 (Mil)
Packers, 30-10 (LA)
1948—Packers, 16-0 (GB)
Rams, 24-10 (LA)
1949—Rams, 48-7 (GB)
Rams, 35-7 (LA)
1950—Rams, 45-14 (Mil)
Rams, 51-14 (LA)
1951—Rams, 28-0 (Mil)
Rams, 42-14 (LA)
1952—Rams, 30-28 (Mil)
Rams, 45-27 (LA)
1953—Rams, 38-20 (Mil)
Rams, 33-17 (LA)
1954—Packers, 35-17 (Mil)
Rams, 35-27 (LA)
1955—Packers, 30-28 (Mil)
Rams, 31-17 (LA)
1956—Packers, 42-17 (Mil)
Rams, 49-21 (LA)
1957—Rams, 31-27 (Mil)
Rams, 42-17 (LA)
1958—Rams, 20-7 (GB)
Rams, 34-20 (LA)
1959—Rams, 45-6 (Mil)
Packers, 38-20 (LA)
1960—Rams, 33-31 (Mil)
Packers, 35-21 (LA)
1961—Packers, 35-17 (GB)
Packers, 24-17 (LA)
1962—Packers, 41-10 (Mil)
Packers, 20-17 (LA)
1963—Packers, 42-10 (GB)
Packers, 31-14 (LA)
1964—Rams, 27-17 (Mil)
Tie, 24-24 (LA)
1965—Packers, 6-3 (Mil)
Rams, 21-10 (LA)
1966—Packers, 24-13 (GB)
Packers, 27-23 (LA)
1967—Rams, 27-24 (LA)
**Packers, 28-7 (Mil)
1968—Rams, 16-14 (Mil)
1969—Rams, 34-21 (LA)
1970—Rams, 31-21 (GB)
1971—Rams, 30-13 (LA)
1973—Rams, 24-7 (LA)
1974—Packers, 17-6 (Mil)
1975—Rams, 22-5 (LA)
1977—Rams, 24-6 (Mil)
1978—Rams, 31-14 (LA)
1980—Rams, 51-21 (LA)
1981—Rams, 35-23 (LA)
1982—Packers, 35-23 (Mil)
1983—Packers, 27-24 (Mil)
1984—Packers, 31-6 (Mil)
1985—Rams, 34-17 (LA)
1988—Rams, 34-7 (GB)
1989—Rams, 41-38 (LA)
1990—Packers, 36-24 (GB)
1991—Rams, 23-21 (LA)
1992—Packers, 28-13 (GB)
1993—Packers, 36-6 (Mil)
1994—Packers, 24-17 (GB)
(RS Pts.—Rams 1,934, Packers 1,803)
(PS Pts.—Packers 28, Rams 7)
**Franchise in Los Angeles prior to 1995 and in Cleveland prior to 1946*
***Conference Championship*

GREEN BAY vs. SAN DIEGO
RS: Packers lead series, 4-1
1970—Packers, 22-20 (SD)
1974—Packers, 34-0 (GB)
1978—Packers, 24-3 (SD)
1984—Chargers, 34-28 (GB)
1993—Packers, 20-13 (SD)
(RS Pts.—Packers 128, Chargers 70)

GREEN BAY vs. SAN FRANCISCO
RS: 49ers lead series, 25-21-1
1950—Packers, 25-21 (GB)
49ers, 30-14 (SF)
1951—49ers, 31-19 (SF)
1952—49ers, 24-14 (SF)
1953—49ers, 37-7 (Mil)
49ers, 48-14 (SF)
1954—49ers, 23-17 (Mil)
49ers, 35-0 (SF)
1955—Packers, 27-21 (Mil)
Packers, 28-7 (SF)
1956—49ers, 17-16 (GB)
49ers, 38-20 (SF)
1957—49ers, 24-14 (Mil)
49ers, 27-20 (SF)
1958—49ers, 33-12 (Mil)
49ers, 48-21 (SF)
1959—Packers, 21-20 (GB)
Packers, 36-14 (SF)
1960—Packers, 41-14 (Mil)
Packers, 13-0 (SF)
1961—Packers, 30-10 (GB)
49ers, 22-21 (SF)
1962—Packers, 31-13 (Mil)
Packers, 31-21 (SF)
1963—Packers, 28-10 (Mil)
Packers, 21-17 (SF)
1964—Packers, 24-14 (Mil)
49ers, 24-14 (SF)
1965—Packers, 27-10 (GB)
Tie, 24-24 (SF)
1966—49ers, 21-20 (SF)
Packers, 20-7 (Mil)
1967—Packers, 13-0 (GB)
1968—49ers, 27-20 (SF)
1969—Packers, 14-7 (Mil)
1970—49ers, 26-10 (SF)
1972—Packers, 34-24 (Mil)
1973—49ers, 20-6 (SF)
1974—49ers, 7-6 (SF)
1976—49ers, 26-14 (GB)
1977—Packers, 16-14 (Mil)
1980—Packers, 23-16 (Mil)
1981—49ers, 13-3 (Mil)
1986—49ers, 31-17 (Mil)
1987—49ers, 23-12 (GB)
1989—Packers, 21-17 (SF)
1990—49ers, 24-20 (GB)
(RS Pts.—49ers 980, Packers 899)

GREEN BAY vs. SEATTLE
RS: Series tied, 3-3
1976—Packers, 27-20 (Mil)
1978—Packers, 45-28 (Mil)
1981—Packers, 34-24 (GB)
1984—Seahawks, 30-24 (Mil)
1987—Seahawks, 24-13 (S)
1990—Seahawks, 20-14 (Mil)
(RS Pts.—Packers 157, Seahawks 146)

GREEN BAY vs. TAMPA BAY
RS: Packers lead series, 19-12-1
1977—Packers, 13-0 (TB)
1978—Packers, 9-7 (GB)
Packers, 17-7 (TB)
1979—Buccaneers, 21-10 (GB)
Buccaneers, 21-3 (TB)
1980—Tie, 14-14 (TB) OT
Buccaneers, 20-17 (Mil)
1981—Buccaneers, 21-10 (GB)
Buccaneers, 37-3 (TB)
1983—Packers, 55-14 (GB)
Packers, 12-9 (TB) OT
1984—Buccaneers, 30-27 (TB) OT
Packers, 27-14 (GB)
1985—Packers, 21-0 (GB)
Packers, 20-17 (TB)
1986—Packers, 31-7 (Mil)

Packers, 21-7 (TB)
1987—Buccaneers, 23-17 (Mil)
1988—Buccaneers, 13-10 (GB)
Buccaneers, 27-24 (TB)
1989—Buccaneers, 23-21 (GB)
Packers, 17-16 (TB)
1990—Buccaneers, 26-14 (TB)
Packers, 20-10 (Mil)
1991—Packers, 15-13 (GB)
Packers, 27-0 (TB)
1992—Buccaneers, 31-3 (TB)
Packers, 19-14 (Mil)
1993—Packers, 37-14 (TB)
Packers, 13-10 (GB)
1994—Packers, 30-3 (GB)
Packers, 34-19 (TB)
(RS Pts.—Packers 611, Buccaneers 488)

GREEN BAY vs. *WASHINGTON
RS: Packers lead series, 13-12-1
PS: Series tied, 1-1
1932—Packers, 21-0 (B)
1933—Tie, 7-7 (GB)
Redskins, 20-7 (B)
1934—Packers, 10-0 (B)
1936—Packers, 31-2 (GB)
Packers, 7-3 (B)
**Packers, 21-6 (New York)
1937—Redskins, 14-6 (W)
1939—Packers, 24-14 (Mil)
1941—Packers, 22-17 (W)
1943—Redskins, 33-7 (Mil)
1946—Packers, 20-7 (W)
1947—Packers, 27-10 (Mil)
1948—Redskins, 23-7 (Mil)
1949—Redskins, 30-0 (W)
1950—Packers, 35-21 (Mil)
1952—Packers, 35-20 (Mil)
1958—Redskins, 37-21 (W)
1959—Packers, 21-0 (GB)
1968—Packers, 27-7 (W)
1972—Redskins, 21-16 (W)
***Redskins, 16-3 (W)
1974—Redskins, 17-6 (GB)
1977—Redskins, 10-9 (W)
1979—Redskins, 38-21 (W)
1983—Packers, 48-47 (GB)
1986—Redskins, 16-7 (GB)
1988—Redskins, 20-17 (Mil)
(RS Pts.—Packers 459, Redskins 434)
(PS Pts.—Packers 24, Redskins 22)
Franchise in Boston prior to 1937 and known as Braves prior to 1933
***NFL Championship*
****NFC Divisional Playoff*

HOUSTON vs. ARIZONA
RS: Cardinals lead series, 4-2;
See Arizona vs. Houston

HOUSTON vs. ATLANTA
RS: Falcons lead series, 5-3;
See Atlanta vs. Houston

HOUSTON vs. BUFFALO
RS: Oilers lead series, 20-13
PS: Bills lead series, 2-0;
See Buffalo vs. Houston

HOUSTON vs. CHICAGO
RS: Oilers lead series, 4-2;
See Chicago vs. Houston

HOUSTON vs. CINCINNATI
RS: Oilers lead series, 26-25-1
PS: Bengals lead series, 1-0;
See Cincinnati vs. Houston

HOUSTON vs. CLEVELAND
RS: Browns lead series, 29-20
PS: Oilers lead series, 1-0;
See Cleveland vs. Houston

HOUSTON vs. DALLAS
RS: Cowboys lead series, 5-3;
See Dallas vs. Houston

HOUSTON vs. DENVER
RS: Oilers lead series, 19-11-1
PS: Broncos lead series, 2-1;
See Denver vs. Houston

HOUSTON vs. DETROIT
RS: Oilers lead series, 4-2;
See Detroit vs. Houston

HOUSTON vs. GREEN BAY
RS: Series tied, 3-3;
See Green Bay vs. Houston

HOUSTON vs. *INDIANAPOLIS
RS: Series tied, 7-7
1970—Colts, 24-20 (H)
1973—Oilers, 31-27 (B)
1976—Colts, 38-14 (B)
1979—Oilers, 28-16 (B)
1980—Oilers, 21-16 (H)
1983—Colts, 20-10 (B)
1984—Colts, 35-21 (H)
1985—Colts, 34-16 (I)
1986—Oilers, 31-17 (H)
1987—Colts, 51-27 (I)
1988—Oilers, 17-14 (I) OT
1990—Oilers, 24-10 (H)
1992—Oilers, 20-10 (I)
1994—Colts, 45-21 (I)
(RS Pts.—Colts 357, Oilers 301)
Franchise in Baltimore prior to 1984

HOUSTON vs. *KANSAS CITY
RS: Chiefs lead series, 22-17
PS: Chiefs lead series, 2-0
1960—Oilers, 20-10 (H)
Texans, 24-0 (D)
1961—Texans, 26-21 (D)
Oilers, 38-7 (H)
1962—Texans, 31-7 (H)
Oilers, 14-6 (D)
**Texans, 20-17 (H) OT
1963—Chiefs, 28-7 (KC)
Oilers, 28-7 (H)
1964—Chiefs, 28-7 (KC)
Chiefs, 28-19 (H)
1965—Chiefs, 52-21 (KC)
Oilers, 38-36 (H)
1966—Chiefs, 48-23 (KC)
1967—Chiefs, 25-20 (H)
Oilers, 24-19 (KC)
1968—Chiefs, 26-21 (H)
Chiefs, 24-10 (KC)
1969—Chiefs, 24-0 (KC)
1970—Chiefs, 24-9 (KC)
1971—Chiefs, 20-16 (H)
1973—Chiefs, 38-14 (KC)
1974—Chiefs, 17-7 (H)
1975—Oilers, 17-13 (KC)
1977—Oilers, 34-20 (H)
1978—Oilers, 20-17 (KC)
1979—Oilers, 20-6 (H)
1980—Chiefs, 21-20 (KC)
1981—Chiefs, 23-10 (KC)
1983—Chiefs, 13-10 (H) OT
1984—Oilers, 17-16 (KC)
1985—Oilers, 23-20 (H)
1986—Chiefs, 27-13 (KC)
1988—Oilers, 7-6 (H)
1989—Chiefs, 34-0 (KC)
1990—Oilers, 27-10 (KC)
1991—Oilers, 17-7 (H)
1992—Oilers, 23-20 (H) OT
1993—Oilers, 30-0 (H)
***Chiefs, 28-20 (H)
1994—Chiefs, 31-9 (KC)
(RS Pts.—Chiefs 832, Oilers 661)
(PS Pts.—Chiefs 48, Oilers 37)
Franchise in Dallas prior to 1963 and known as Texans
***AFL Championship*
****AFC Divisional Playoff*

HOUSTON vs. *LOS ANGELES
RS: Raiders lead series, 20-13
PS: Raiders lead series, 3-0
1960—Oilers, 37-22 (O)
Raiders, 14-13 (H)
1961—Oilers, 55-0 (H)
Oilers, 47-16 (O)
1962—Oilers, 28-20 (O)
Oilers, 32-17 (H)
1963—Raiders, 24-13 (H)
Raiders, 52-49 (O)
1964—Oilers, 42-28 (H)
Raiders, 20-10 (O)
1965—Raiders, 21-17 (O)
Raiders, 33-21 (H)
1966—Oilers, 31-0 (H)
Raiders, 38-23 (O)
1967—Raiders, 19-7 (H)
**Raiders, 40-7 (O)
1968—Raiders, 24-15 (H)
1969—Raiders, 21-17 (O)
***Raiders, 56-7 (O)
1971—Raiders, 41-21 (O)
1972—Raiders, 34-0 (H)
1973—Raiders, 17-6 (H)
1975—Oilers, 27-26 (O)
1976—Raiders, 14-13 (H)
1977—Raiders, 34-29 (O)
1978—Raiders, 21-17 (O)
1979—Oilers, 31-17 (H)
1980—****Raiders, 27-7 (O)
1981—Oilers, 17-16 (H)
1983—Raiders, 20-6 (LA)
1984—Raiders, 24-14 (H)
1986—Raiders, 28-17 (H)
1988—Oilers, 38-35 (H)
1989—Oilers, 23-7 (H)
1991—Oilers, 47-17 (H)
1994—Raiders, 17-14 (LA)
(RS Pts.—Oilers 777, Raiders 737)
(PS Pts.—Raiders 123, Oilers 21)
Franchise in Oakland prior to 1982
***AFL Championship*
****Inter-Divisional Playoff*
*****AFC First-Round Playoff*

HOUSTON vs. MIAMI
RS: Series tied, 11-11
PS: Oilers lead series, 1-0
1966—Dolphins, 20-13 (H)
Dolphins, 29-28 (M)
1967—Oilers, 17-14 (H)
Oilers, 41-10 (M)
1968—Oilers, 24-10 (M)
Dolphins, 24-7 (H)
1969—Oilers, 22-10 (H)
Oilers, 32-7 (M)
1970—Dolphins, 20-10 (H)
1972—Dolphins, 34-13 (M)
1975—Oilers, 20-19 (H)
1977—Dolphins, 27-7 (M)
1978—Oilers, 35-30 (H)
*Oilers, 17-9 (M)
1979—Oilers, 9-6 (M)
1981—Dolphins, 16-10 (H)
1983—Dolphins, 24-17 (H)
1984—Dolphins, 28-10 (M)
1985—Oilers, 26-23 (H)
1986—Dolphins, 28-7 (M)
1989—Oilers, 39-7 (H)
1991—Oilers, 17-13 (M)
1992—Dolphins, 19-16 (M)
(RS Pts.—Oilers 420, Dolphins 418)
(PS Pts.—Oilers 17, Dolphins 9)
AFC First Round Playoff

HOUSTON vs. MINNESOTA
RS: Series tied, 3-3
1974—Vikings, 51-10 (M)
1980—Oilers, 20-16 (H)
1983—Vikings, 34-14 (M)
1986—Oilers, 23-10 (H)
1989—Vikings, 38-7 (M)
1992—Oilers, 17-13 (M)
(RS Pts.—Vikings 162, Oilers 91)

HOUSTON vs. *NEW ENGLAND
RS: Patriots lead series, 17-14-1
PS: Oilers lead series, 1-0
1960—Oilers, 24-10 (B)
Oilers, 37-21 (H)
1961—Tie, 31-31 (B)
Oilers, 27-15 (H)
1962—Patriots, 34-21 (B)
Oilers, 21-17 (H)
1963—Patriots, 45-3 (B)
Patriots, 46-28 (H)
1964—Patriots, 25-24 (B)
Patriots, 34-17 (H)
1965—Oilers, 31-10 (H)
Patriots, 42-14 (B)
1966—Patriots, 27-21 (B)
Patriots, 38-14 (H)
1967—Patriots, 18-7 (B)
Oilers, 27-6 (H)
1968—Oilers, 16-0 (B)
Oilers, 45-17 (H)
1969—Patriots, 24-0 (B)
Oilers, 27-23 (H)
1971—Patriots, 28-20 (NE)
1973—Patriots, 32-0 (H)
1975—Oilers, 7-0 (NE)
1978—Oilers, 26-23 (NE)
**Oilers, 31-14 (NE)
1980—Oilers, 38-34 (H)
1981—Patriots, 38-10 (NE)
1982—Patriots, 29-21 (NE)
1987—Patriots, 21-7 (H)
1988—Oilers, 31-6 (H)
1989—Patriots, 23-13 (NE)
1991—Patriots, 24-20 (NE)
1993—Oilers, 28-14 (NE)
(RS Pts.—Patriots 755, Oilers 656)
(PS Pts.—Oilers 31, Patriots 14)
Franchise in Boston prior to 1971
***AFC Divisional Playoff*

HOUSTON vs. NEW ORLEANS
RS: Saints lead series, 4-3-1
1971—Tie, 13-13 (H)
1976—Oilers, 31-26 (NO)
1978—Oilers, 17-12 (NO)
1981—Saints, 27-24 (H)
1984—Saints, 27-10 (H)
1987—Saints, 24-10 (NO)
1990—Oilers, 23-10 (H)
1993—Saints, 33-21 (NO)
(RS Pts.—Saints 172, Oilers 149)

HOUSTON vs. N.Y. GIANTS
RS: Giants lead series, 5-0
1973—Giants, 34-14 (NY)
1982—Giants, 17-14 (NY)
1985—Giants, 35-14 (H)
1991—Giants, 24-20 (NY)
1994—Giants, 13-10 (H)
(RS Pts.—Giants 123, Oilers 72)

HOUSTON vs. *N.Y. JETS
RS: Oilers lead series, 18-12-1
PS: Oilers lead series, 1-0
1960—Oilers, 27-21 (H)
Oilers, 42-28 (NY)
1961—Oilers, 49-13 (H)
Oilers, 48-21 (NY)
1962—Oilers, 56-17 (H)
Oilers, 44-10 (NY)
1963—Jets, 24-17 (NY)
Oilers, 31-27 (H)
1964—Jets, 24-21 (NY)
Oilers, 33-17 (H)
1965—Oilers, 27-21 (H)
Jets, 41-14 (NY)
1966—Jets, 52-13 (NY)
Oilers, 24-0 (H)
1967—Tie, 28-28 (NY)
1968—Jets, 20-14 (H)
Jets, 26-7 (NY)
1969—Jets, 26-17 (NY)
Jets, 34-26 (H)
1972—Oilers, 26-20 (H)
1974—Oilers, 27-22 (NY)
1977—Oilers, 20-0 (H)
1979—Oilers, 27-24 (H) OT
1980—Jets, 31-28 (NY) OT
1981—Jets, 33-17 (NY)
1984—Oilers, 31-20 (H)
1988—Jets, 45-3 (NY)
1990—Jets, 17-12 (H)
1991—Oilers, 23-20 (NY)
**Oilers, 17-10 (H)

1993—Oilers, 24-0 (H)
1994—Oilers, 24-10 (H)
(RS Pts.—Oilers 800, Jets 692)
(PS Pts.—Oilers 17, Jets 10)
Jets known as Titans prior to 1963
***AFC First-Round Playoff*

HOUSTON vs. PHILADELPHIA
RS: Eagles lead series, 6-0
1972—Eagles, 18-17 (H)
1979—Eagles, 26-20 (H)
1982—Eagles, 35-14 (P)
1988—Eagles, 32-23 (P)
1991—Eagles, 13-6 (H)
1994—Eagles, 21-6 (P)
(RS Pts.—Eagles 145, Oilers 86)

HOUSTON vs. PITTSBURGH
RS: Steelers lead series, 31-18
PS: Steelers lead series, 3-0
1970—Oilers, 19-7 (P)
Steelers, 7-3 (H)
1971—Steelers, 23-16 (P)
Oilers, 29-3 (H)
1972—Steelers, 24-7 (P)
Steelers, 9-3 (H)
1973—Steelers, 36-7 (H)
Steelers, 33-7 (P)
1974—Steelers, 13-7 (H)
Oilers, 13-10 (P)
1975—Steelers, 24-17 (P)
Steelers, 32-9 (H)
1976—Steelers, 32-16 (P)
Steelers, 21-0 (H)
1977—Oilers, 27-10 (H)
Steelers, 27-10 (P)
1978—Oilers, 24-17 (P)
Steelers, 13-3 (H)
*Steelers, 34-5 (P)
1979—Steelers, 38-7 (P)
Oilers, 20-17 (H)
*Steelers, 27-13 (P)
1980—Steelers, 31-17 (P)
Oilers, 6-0 (H)
1981—Steelers, 26-13 (P)
Oilers, 21-20 (H)
1982—Steelers, 24-10 (H)
1983—Steelers, 40-28 (H)
Steelers, 17-10 (P)
1984—Steelers, 35-7 (P)
Oilers, 23-20 (H) OT
1985—Steelers, 20-0 (P)
Steelers, 30-7 (H)
1986—Steelers, 22-16 (H) OT
Steelers, 21-10 (P)
1987—Oilers, 23-3 (P)
Oilers, 24-16 (H)
1988—Oilers, 34-14 (P)
Steelers, 37-34 (H)
1989—Oilers, 27-0 (H)
Oilers, 23-16 (P)
**Steelers, 26-23 (H)
1990—Steelers, 20-9 (P)
Oilers, 34-14 (H)
1991—Steelers, 26-14 (P)
Oilers, 31-6 (H)
1992—Steelers, 29-24 (H)
Steelers, 21-20 (P)
1993—Oilers, 23-3 (H)
Oilers, 26-17 (P)
1994—Steelers, 30-14 (P)
Steelers, 12-9 (H) OT
(RS Pts.—Steelers 966, Oilers 781)
(PS Pts.—Steelers 87, Oilers 41)
**AFC Championship*
***AFC First-Round Playoff*

HOUSTON vs. *ST. LOUIS
RS: Rams lead series, 5-2
1973—Rams, 31-26 (H)
1978—Rams, 10-6 (H)
1981—Oilers, 27-20 (LA)
1984—Rams, 27-16 (LA)
1987—Oilers, 20-16 (H)
1990—Rams, 17-13 (LA)
1993—Rams, 28-13 (H)
(RS Pts.—Rams 149, Oilers 121)
**Franchise in Los Angeles prior to 1995*

HOUSTON vs. *SAN DIEGO
RS: Chargers lead series, 18-13-1
PS: Oilers lead series, 3-0
1960—Oilers, 38-28 (H)
Chargers, 24-21 (LA)
**Oilers, 24-16 (H)
1961—Chargers, 34-24 (SD)
Oilers, 33-13 (H)
**Oilers, 10-3 (SD)
1962—Oilers, 42-17 (SD)
Oilers, 33-27 (H)
1963—Chargers, 27-0 (SD)
Chargers 20-14 (H)
1964—Chargers, 27-21 (SD)
Chargers, 20-17 (H)
1965—Chargers, 31-14 (SD)
Chargers, 37-26 (H)
1966—Chargers, 28-22 (H)
1967—Chargers, 13-3 (SD)
Oilers, 24-17 (H)
1968—Chargers, 30-14 (SD)
1969—Chargers, 21-17 (H)
1970—Tie, 31-31 (SD)
1971—Oilers, 49-33 (H)
1972—Chargers, 34-20 (SD)
1974—Oilers, 21-14 (H)
1975—Oilers, 33-17 (H)
1976—Chargers, 30-27 (SD)
1978—Chargers, 45-24 (H)
1979—***Oilers, 17-14 (SD)
1984—Chargers, 31-14 (SD)
1985—Oilers, 37-35 (H)
1986—Chargers, 27-0 (SD)
1987—Oilers, 33-18 (H)
1989—Oilers, 34-27 (SD)
1990—Oilers, 17-7 (SD)
1992—Oilers, 27-0 (H)
1993—Chargers, 18-17 (SD)
(RS Pts.—Chargers 781, Oilers 747)
(PS Pts.—Oilers 51, Chargers 33)
**Franchise in Los Angeles prior to 1961*
***AFL Championship*
****AFC Divisional Playoff*

HOUSTON vs. SAN FRANCISCO
RS: 49ers lead series, 5-3
1970—49ers, 30-20 (H)
1975—Oilers, 27-13 (SF)
1978—Oilers, 20-19 (H)
1981—49ers, 28-6 (SF)
1984—49ers, 34-21 (H)
1987—49ers, 27-20 (SF)
1990—49ers, 24-21 (H)
1993—Oilers, 10-7 (SF)
(RS Pts.—49ers 182, Oilers 145)

HOUSTON vs. SEATTLE
RS: Seahawks lead series, 5-4
PS: Oilers lead series, 1-0
1977—Oilers, 22-10 (S)
1979—Seahawks, 34-14 (S)
1980—Seahawks, 26-7 (H)
1981—Oilers, 35-17 (H)
1982—Oilers, 23-21 (H)
1987—*Oilers, 23-20 (H) OT
1988—Seahawks, 27-24 (S)
1990—Seahawks, 13-10 (S) OT
1993—Oilers, 24-14 (H)
1994—Seahawks, 16-14 (H)
(RS Pts.—Seahawks 178, Oilers 173)
(PS Pts.—Oilers 23, Seahawks 20)
**AFC First-Round Playoff*

HOUSTON vs. TAMPA BAY
RS: Oilers lead series, 3-1
1976—Oilers, 20-0 (H)
1980—Oilers, 20-14 (H)
1983—Buccaneers, 33-24 (TB)
1989—Oilers, 20-17 (H)
(RS Pts.—Oilers 84, Buccaneers 64)

HOUSTON vs. WASHINGTON
RS: Series tied, 3-3
1971—Redskins, 22-13 (W)
1975—Oilers, 13-10 (H)
1979—Oilers, 29-27 (W)
1985—Redskins, 16-13 (W)
1988—Oilers, 41-17 (H)
1991—Redskins, 16-13 (W) OT
(RS Pts.—Oilers 122, Redskins 108)

INDIANAPOLIS vs. ARIZONA
RS: Cardinals lead series, 6-5;
See Arizona vs. Indianapolis

INDIANAPOLIS vs. ATLANTA
RS: Colts lead series, 10-0;
See Atlanta vs. Indianapolis

INDIANAPOLIS vs. BUFFALO
RS: Bills lead series, 26-22-1;
See Buffalo vs. Indianapolis

INDIANAPOLIS vs. CHICAGO
RS: Colts lead series, 21-16;
See Chicago vs. Indianapolis

INDIANAPOLIS vs. CINCINNATI
RS: Colts lead series, 9-5
PS: Colts lead series, 1-0;
See Cincinnati vs. Indianapolis

INDIANAPOLIS vs. CLEVELAND
RS: Browns lead series, 13-7
PS: Series tied, 2-2;
See Cleveland vs. Indianapolis

INDIANAPOLIS vs. DALLAS
RS: Cowboys lead series, 7-2
PS: Colts lead series, 1-0;
See Dallas vs. Indianapolis

INDIANAPOLIS vs. DENVER
RS: Broncos lead series, 9-2;
See Denver vs. Indianapolis

INDIANAPOLIS vs. DETROIT
RS: Series tied, 17-17-2;
See Detroit vs. Indianapolis

INDIANAPOLIS vs. GREEN BAY
RS: Series tied, 18-18-1
PS: Packers lead series, 1-0;
See Green Bay vs. Indianapolis

INDIANAPOLIS vs. HOUSTON
RS: Series tied, 7-7;
See Houston vs. Indianapolis

***INDIANAPOLIS vs. KANSAS CITY**
RS: Chiefs lead series, 6-4
1970—Chiefs, 44-24 (B)
1972—Chiefs, 24-10 (KC)
1975—Colts, 28-14 (B)
1977—Colts, 17-6 (KC)
1979—Chiefs, 14-0 (KC)
Chiefs, 10-7 (B)
1980—Colts, 31-24 (KC)
Chiefs, 38-28 (B)
1985—Chiefs, 20-7 (KC)
1990—Colts, 23-19 (I)
(RS Pts.—Chiefs 213, Colts 175)
**Franchise in Baltimore prior to 1984*

***INDIANAPOLIS vs **LOS ANGELES**
RS: Raiders lead series, 4-2
PS: Series tied, 1-1
1970—***Colts, 27-17 (B)
1971—Colts, 37-14 (O)
1973—Raiders, 34-21 (B)
1975—Raiders, 31-20 (B)
1977—****Raiders, 37-31 (B) OT
1984—Raiders, 21-7 (LA)
1986—Colts, 30-24 (LA)
1991—Raiders, 16-0 (LA)
(RS Pts.—Raiders 140, Colts 115)
(PS Pts.—Colts 58, Raiders 54)
**Franchise in Baltimore prior to 1984*
***Franchise in Oakland prior to 1982*
****AFC Championship*
*****AFC Divisional Playoff*

***INDIANAPOLIS vs. MIAMI**
RS: Dolphins lead series, 35-15
PS: Dolphins lead series, 1-0
1970—Colts, 35-0 (B)
Dolphins, 34-17 (M)
1971—Dolphins, 17-14 (M)
Colts, 14-3 (B)
**Dolphins, 21-0 (M)
1972—Dolphins, 23-0 (B)
Dolphins, 16-0 (M)
1973—Dolphins, 44-0 (M)
Colts, 16-3 (B)
1974—Dolphins, 17-7 (M)
Dolphins, 17-16 (B)
1975—Colts, 33-17 (M)
Colts, 10-7 (B) OT
1976—Colts, 28-14 (B)
Colts, 17-16 (M)
1977—Colts, 45-28 (B)
Dolphins, 17-6 (M)
1978—Dolphins, 42-0 (B)
Dolphins, 26-8 (M)
1979—Dolphins, 19-0 (M)
Dolphins, 28-24 (B)
1980—Colts, 30-17 (M)
Dolphins, 24-14 (B)
1981—Dolphins, 31-28 (B)
Dolphins, 27-10 (M)
1982—Dolphins, 24-20 (M)
Dolphins, 34-7 (B)
1983—Dolphins, 21-7 (B)
Dolphins, 37-0 (M)
1984—Dolphins, 44-7 (M)
Dolphins, 35-17 (I)
1985—Dolphins, 30-13 (M)
Dolphins, 34-20 (I)
1986—Dolphins, 30-10 (M)
Dolphins, 17-13 (I)
1987—Dolphins, 23-10 (I)
Colts, 40-21 (M)
1988—Colts, 15-13 (I)
Colts, 31-28 (M)
1989—Dolphins, 19-13 (M)
Colts, 42-13 (I)
1990—Dolphins, 27-7 (I)
Dolphins, 23-17 (M)
1991—Dolphins, 17-6 (M)
Dolphins, 10-6 (I)
1992—Colts, 31-20 (M)
Dolphins, 28-0 (I)
1993—Dolphins, 24-20 (I)
Dolphins, 41-27 (M)
1994—Dolphins, 22-21 (M)
Colts, 10-6 (I)
(RS Pts.—Dolphins 1,128, Colts 782)
(PS Pts.—Dolphins 21, Colts 0)
**Franchise in Baltimore prior to 1984*
***AFC Championship*

***INDIANAPOLIS vs. MINNESOTA**
RS: Colts lead series, 11-6-1
PS: Colts lead series, 1-0
1961—Colts, 34-33 (B)
Vikings, 28-20 (M)
1962—Colts, 34-7 (M)
Colts, 42-17 (B)
1963—Colts, 37-34 (M)
Colts, 41-10 (B)
1964—Vikings, 34-24 (M)
Colts, 17-14 (B)
1965—Colts, 35-16 (B)
Colts, 41-21 (M)
1966—Colts, 38-23 (M)
Colts, 20-17 (B)
1967—Tie, 20-20 (M)
1968—Colts, 21-9 (B)
**Colts, 24-14 (B)
1969—Vikings, 52-14 (M)
1971—Vikings, 10-3 (M)
1982—Vikings, 13-10 (M)
1988—Vikings, 12-3 (M)
(RS Pts.—Colts 454, Vikings 370)
(PS Pts.—Colts 24, Vikings 14)
**Franchise in Baltimore prior to 1984*
***Conference Championship*

***INDIANAPOLIS vs. **NEW ENGLAND**
RS: Patriots lead series, 29-20
1970—Colts, 14-6 (Bos)
Colts, 27-3 (Balt)
1971—Colts, 23-3 (NE)
Patriots, 21-17 (Balt)
1972—Colts, 24-17 (NE)
Colts, 31-0 (Balt)

1973—Patriots, 24-16 (NE)
Colts, 18-13 (Balt)
1974—Patriots, 42-3 (NE)
Patriots, 27-17 (Balt)
1975—Patriots, 21-10 (NE)
Colts, 34-21 (Balt)
1976—Colts, 27-13 (NE)
Patriots, 21-14 (Balt)
1977—Patriots, 17-3 (NE)
Colts, 30-24 (Balt)
1978—Colts, 34-27 (NE)
Patriots, 35-14 (Balt)
1979—Colts, 31-26 (Balt)
Patriots, 50-21 (NE)
1980—Patriots, 37-21 (Balt)
Patriots, 47-21 (NE)
1981—Colts, 29-28 (NE)
Colts, 23-21 (Balt)
1982—Patriots, 24-13 (Balt)
1983—Colts, 29-23 (NE) OT
Colts, 12-7 (Balt)
1984—Patriots, 50-17 (I)
Patriots, 16-10 (NE)
1985—Patriots, 34-15 (NE)
Patriots, 38-31 (I)
1986—Patriots, 33-3 (NE)
Patriots, 30-21 (I)
1987—Colts, 30-16 (I)
Patriots, 24-0 (NE)
1988—Patriots, 21-17 (NE)
Colts, 24-21 (I)
1989—Patriots, 23-20 (I) OT
Patriots, 22-16 (NE)
1990—Patriots, 16-14 (I)
Colts, 13-10 (NE)
1991—Patriots, 16-7 (I)
Patriots, 23-17 (NE) OT
1992—Patriots, 37-34 (I) OT
Colts, 6-0 (NE)
1993—Colts, 9-6 (I)
Patriots, 38-0 (NE)
1994—Patriots, 12-10 (I)
Patriots, 28-13 (NE)
(RS Pts.—Patriots 1,112, Colts 883)
Franchise in Baltimore prior to 1984
***Franchise in Boston prior to 1971*

***INDIANAPOLIS vs. NEW ORLEANS**
RS: Colts lead series, 3-2
1967—Colts, 30-10 (B)
1969—Colts, 30-10 (NO)
1973—Colts, 14-10 (B)
1986—Saints, 17-14 (I)
1989—Saints, 41-6 (NO)
(RS Pts.—Colts 94, Saints 88)
Franchise in Baltimore prior to 1984

***INDIANAPOLIS vs. N.Y. GIANTS**
RS: Series tied, 5-5
PS: Colts lead series, 2-0
1954—Colts, 20-14 (B)
1955—Giants, 17-7 (NY)
1958—Giants, 24-21 (NY)
**Colts, 23-17 (NY) OT
1959—**Colts, 31-16 (B)
1963—Giants, 37-28 (B)
1968—Colts, 26-0 (NY)
1971—Colts, 31-7 (NY)
1975—Colts, 21-0 (NY)
1979—Colts, 31-7 (NY)
1990—Giants, 24-7 (I)
1993—Giants, 20-6 (NY)
(RS Pts.—Colts 198, Giants 150)
(PS Pts.—Colts 54, Giants 33)
Franchise in Baltimore prior to 1984
***NFL Championship*

***INDIANAPOLIS vs. N.Y. JETS**
RS: Colts lead series, 28-21
PS: Jets lead series, 1-0
1968—**Jets 16-7 (Miami)
1970—Colts, 29-22 (NY)
Colts, 35-20 (B)
1971—Colts, 22-0 (B)
Colts, 14-13 (NY)
1972—Jets, 44-34 (B)
Jets, 24-20 (NY)
1973—Jets, 34-10 (B)
Jets, 20-17 (NY)
1974—Colts, 35-20 (NY)
Jets, 45-38 (B)
1975—Colts, 45-28 (NY)
Colts, 52-19 (B)
1976—Colts, 20-0 (NY)
Colts, 33-16 (B)
1977—Colts, 20-12 (NY)
Colts, 33-12 (B)
1978—Jets, 33-10 (B)
Jets, 24-16 (NY)
1979—Colts, 10-8 (B)
Jets, 30-17 (NY)
1980—Colts, 17-14 (NY)
Colts, 35-21 (B)
1981—Jets, 41-14 (B)
Jets, 25-0 (NY)
1982—Jets, 37-0 (NY)
1983—Colts, 17-14 (NY)
Jets, 10-6 (B)
1984—Jets, 23-14 (I)
Colts, 9-5 (NY)
1985—Jets, 25-20 (NY)
Jets, 35-17 (I)
1986—Jets, 26-7 (I)
Jets, 31-16 (NY)
1987—Colts, 6-0 (I)
Colts, 19-14 (NY)
1988—Colts, 38-14 (I)
Jets, 34-16 (NY)
1989—Colts, 17-10 (NY)
Colts, 27-10 (I)
1990—Colts, 17-14 (I)
Colts, 29-21 (NY)
1991—Jets, 17-6 (I)
Colts, 28-27 (NY)
1992—Colts, 6-3 (I) OT
Colts, 10-6 (NY)
1993—Jets, 31-17 (I)
Colts, 9-6 (NY)
1994—Jets, 16-6 (NY)
Colts, 28-25 (I)
(RS Pts.—Jets 979, Colts 961)
(PS Pts.—Jets 16, Colts 7)
Franchise in Baltimore prior to 1984
***Super Bowl III*

***INDIANAPOLIS vs. PHILADELPHIA**
RS: Series tied, 6-6
1953—Eagles, 45-14 (P)
1965—Colts, 34-24 (B)
1967—Colts, 38-6 (P)
1969—Colts, 24-20 (B)
1970—Colts, 29-10 (B)
1974—Eagles, 30-10 (P)
1978—Eagles, 17-14 (B)
1981—Eagles, 38-13 (P)
1983—Colts, 22-21 (P)
1984—Eagles, 16-7 (P)
1990—Colts, 24-23 (P)
1993—Eagles, 20-10 (I)
(RS Pts.—Eagles 270, Colts 239)
Franchise in Baltimore prior to 1984

***INDIANAPOLIS vs. PITTSBURGH**
RS: Steelers lead series, 11-4
PS: Steelers lead series, 2-0
1957—Steelers, 19-13 (B)
1968—Colts, 41-7 (P)
1971—Colts, 34-21 (B)
1974—Steelers, 30-0 (B)
1975—**Steelers, 28-10 (P)
1976—**Steelers, 40-14 (B)
1977—Colts, 31-21 (B)
1978—Steelers, 35-13 (P)
1979—Steelers, 17-13 (P)
1980—Steelers, 20-17 (B)
1983—Steelers, 24-13 (B)
1984—Colts, 17-16 (I)
1985—Steelers, 45-3 (P)
1987—Steelers, 21-7 (P)
1991—Steelers, 21-3 (I)
1992—Steelers, 30-14 (P)
1994—Steelers, 31-21 (P)
(RS Pts.—Steelers 358, Colts 240)
(PS Pts.—Steelers 68, Colts 24)
Franchise in Baltimore prior to 1984
***AFC Divisional Playoff*

***INDIANAPOLIS vs. **ST. LOUIS**
RS: Colts lead series, 20-16-2
1953—Rams, 21-13 (B)
Rams, 45-2 (LA)
1954—Rams, 48-0 (B)
Colts, 22-21 (LA)
1955—Tie, 17-17 (B)
Rams, 20-14 (LA)
1956—Colts, 56-21 (B)
Rams, 31-7 (LA)
1957—Colts, 31-14 (B)
Rams, 37-21 (LA)
1958—Colts, 34-7 (B)
Rams, 30-28 (LA)
1959—Colts, 35-21 (B)
Colts, 45-26 (LA)
1960—Colts, 31-17 (B)
Rams, 10-3 (LA)
1961—Colts, 27-24 (B)
Rams, 34-17 (LA)
1962—Colts, 30-27 (B)
Colts, 14-2 (LA)
1963—Rams, 17-16 (LA)
Colts, 19-16 (B)
1964—Colts, 35-20 (B)
Colts, 24-7 (LA)
1965—Colts, 35-20 (B)
Colts, 20-17 (LA)
1966—Colts, 17-3 (LA)
Rams, 23-7 (B)
1967—Tie, 24-24 (B)
Rams, 34-10 (LA)
1968—Colts, 27-10 (B)
Colts, 28-24 (LA)
1969—Rams, 27-20 (B)
Colts, 13-7 (LA)
1971—Colts, 24-17 (B)
1975—Rams, 24-13 (LA)
1986—Rams, 24-7 (I)
1989—Rams, 31-17 (LA)
(RS Pts.—Rams 818, Colts 803)
Franchise in Baltimore prior to 1984
***Franchise in Los Angeles prior to 1995*

***INDIANAPOLIS vs. SAN DIEGO**
RS: Chargers lead series, 9-5
1970—Colts, 16-14 (SD)
1972—Chargers, 23-20 (B)
1976—Colts, 37-21 (SD)
1981—Chargers, 43-14 (B)
1982—Chargers, 44-26 (SD)
1984—Chargers, 38-10 (I)
1986—Chargers, 17-3 (I)
1987—Chargers, 16-13 (I)
Colts, 20-7 (SD)
1988—Colts, 16-0 (SD)
1989—Colts, 10-6 (I)
1992—Chargers, 34-14 (I)
Chargers, 26-0 (SD)
1993—Chargers, 31-0 (I)
(RS Pts.—Chargers 320, Colts 199)
Franchise in Baltimore prior to 1984

***INDIANAPOLIS vs. SAN FRANCISCO**
RS: Colts lead series, 21-16
1953—49ers, 38-21 (B)
49ers, 45-14 (SF)
1954—Colts, 17-13 (B)
49ers, 10-7 (SF)
1955—Colts, 26-14 (B)
49ers, 35-24 (SF)
1956—49ers, 20-17 (B)
49ers, 30-17 (SF)
1957—Colts, 27-21 (B)
49ers, 17-13 (SF)
1958—Colts, 35-27 (B)
49ers, 21-12 (SF)
1959—Colts, 45-14 (B)
Colts, 34-14 (SF)
1960—49ers, 30-22 (B)
49ers, 34-10 (SF)
1961—Colts, 20-17 (B)
Colts, 27-24 (SF)
1962—49ers, 21-13 (B)
Colts, 22-3 (SF)
1963—Colts, 20-14 (SF)
Colts, 20-3 (B)
1964—Colts, 37-7 (B)
Colts, 14-3 (SF)
1965—Colts, 27-24 (B)
Colts, 34-28 (SF)
1966—Colts, 36-14 (B)
Colts, 30-14 (SF)
1967—Colts, 41-7 (B)
Colts, 26-9 (SF)
1968—Colts, 27-10 (B)
Colts, 42-14 (SF)
1969—49ers, 24-21 (B)
49ers, 20-17 (SF)
1972—49ers, 24-21 (SF)
1986—49ers, 35-14 (SF)
1989—49ers, 30-24 (I)
(RS Pts.—Colts 874, 49ers 728)
Franchise in Baltimore prior to 1984

***INDIANAPOLIS vs. SEATTLE**
RS: Colts lead series, 4-1
1977—Colts, 29-14 (S)
1978—Colts, 17-14 (S)
1991—Seahawks, 31-3 (S)
1994—Colts, 17-15 (I)
Colts, 31-19 (S)
(RS Pts.—Colts 97, Seahawks 93)
Franchise in Baltimore prior to 1984

***INDIANAPOLIS vs. TAMPA BAY**
RS: Colts lead series, 5-3
1976—Colts, 42-17 (B)
1979—Buccaneers, 29-26 (B) OT
1985—Colts, 31-23 (TB)
1987—Colts, 24-6 (I)
1988—Colts, 35-31 (I)
1991—Buccaneers, 17-3 (TB)
1992—Colts, 24-14 (TB)
1994—Buccaneers, 24-10 (TB)
(RS Pts.—Colts 195, Buccaneers 161)
Franchise in Baltimore prior to 1984

***INDIANAPOLIS vs. WASHINGTON**
RS: Colts lead series, 16-8
1953—Colts, 27-17 (B)
1954—Redskins, 24-21 (W)
1955—Redskins, 14-13 (B)
1956—Colts, 19-17 (B)
1957—Colts, 21-17 (W)
1958—Colts, 35-10 (B)
1959—Redskins, 27-24 (W)
1960—Colts, 20-0 (B)
1961—Colts, 27-6 (W)
1962—Colts, 34-21 (B)
1963—Colts, 36-20 (W)
1964—Colts, 45-17 (B)
1965—Colts, 38-7 (W)
1966—Colts, 37-10 (B)
1967—Colts, 17-13 (W)
1969—Colts, 41-17 (B)
1973—Redskins, 22-14 (W)
1977—Colts, 10-3 (B)
1978—Colts, 21-17 (B)
1981—Redskins, 38-14 (W)
1984—Redskins, 35-7 (I)
1990—Colts, 35-28 (I)
1993—Redskins, 30-24 (W)
1994—Redskins, 41-27 (I)
(RS Pts.—Colts 607, Redskins 451)
Franchise in Baltimore prior to 1984

KANSAS CITY vs. ARIZONA
RS: Chiefs lead series, 3-1-1;
See Arizona vs. Kansas City

KANSAS CITY vs. ATLANTA
RS: Chiefs lead series, 4-0;
See Atlanta vs. Kansas City

KANSAS CITY vs. BUFFALO
RS: Bills lead series, 16-13-1
PS: Bills lead series, 2-1;

See Buffalo vs. Kansas City
KANSAS CITY vs. CHICAGO
RS: Bears lead series, 4-2;
See Chicago vs. Kansas City
KANSAS CITY vs. CINCINNATI
RS: Chiefs lead series, 11-9;
See Cincinnati vs. Kansas City
KANSAS CITY vs. CLEVELAND
RS: Series tied, 7-7-2;
See Cleveland vs. Kansas City
KANSAS CITY vs. DALLAS
RS: Cowboys lead series, 3-2;
See Dallas vs. Kansas City
KANSAS CITY vs. DENVER
RS: Chiefs lead series, 39-30;
See Denver vs. Kansas City
KANSAS CITY vs. DETROIT
RS: Chiefs lead series, 4-3;
See Detroit vs. Kansas City
KANSAS CITY vs. GREEN BAY
RS: Chiefs lead series, 4-1-1
PS: Packers lead series, 1-0;
See Green Bay vs. Kansas City
KANSAS CITY vs. HOUSTON
RS: Chiefs lead series, 22-17
PS: Chiefs lead series, 2-0;
See Houston vs. Kansas City
KANSAS CITY vs. INDIANAPOLIS
RS: Chiefs lead series, 6-4;
See Indianapolis vs. Kansas City
***KANSAS CITY vs. **LOS ANGELES**
RS: Raiders lead series, 35-32-2
PS: Chiefs lead series, 2-1
1960—Texans, 34-16 (O)
Raiders, 20-19 (D)
1961—Texans, 42-35 (O)
Texans, 43-11 (D)
1962—Texans, 26-16 (O)
Texans, 35-7 (D)
1963—Raiders, 10-7 (O)
Raiders, 22-7 (KC)
1964—Chiefs, 21-9 (O)
Chiefs, 42-7 (KC)
1965—Raiders, 37-10 (O)
Chiefs, 14-7 (KC)
1966—Chiefs, 32-10 (O)
Raiders, 34-13 (KC)
1967—Raiders, 23-21 (O)
Raiders, 44-22 (KC)
1968—Chiefs, 24-10 (KC)
Raiders, 38-21 (O)
***Raiders, 41-6 (O)
1969—Raiders, 27-24 (KC)
Raiders, 10-6 (O)
****Chiefs, 17-7 (O)
1970—Tie, 17-17 (KC)
Raiders, 20-6 (O)
1971—Tie, 20-20 (O)
Chiefs, 16-14 (KC)
1972—Chiefs, 27-14 (KC)
Raiders, 26-3 (O)
1973—Chiefs, 16-3 (KC)
Raiders, 37-7 (O)
1974—Raiders, 27-7 (O)
Raiders, 7-6 (KC)
1975—Chiefs, 42-10 (KC)
Raiders, 28-20 (O)
1976—Raiders, 24-21 (KC)
Raiders, 21-10 (O)
1977—Raiders, 37-28 (KC)
Raiders, 21-20 (O)
1978—Raiders, 28-6 (O)
Raiders, 20-10 (KC)
1979—Chiefs, 35-7 (KC)
Chiefs, 24-21 (O)
1980—Raiders, 27-14 (KC)
Chiefs, 31-17 (O)
1981—Chiefs, 27-0 (KC)
Chiefs, 28-17 (O)
1982—Raiders, 21-16 (KC)
1983—Raiders, 21-20 (LA)
Raiders, 28-20 (KC)
1984—Raiders, 22-20 (KC)
Raiders, 17-7 (LA)
1985—Chiefs, 36-20 (KC)
Raiders, 19-10 (LA)
1986—Raiders, 24-17 (KC)
Chiefs, 20-17 (LA)
1987—Raiders, 35-17 (LA)
Chiefs, 16-10 (KC)
1988—Raiders, 27-17 (KC)
Raiders, 17-10 (LA)
1989—Chiefs, 24-19 (KC)
Raiders, 20-14 (LA)
1990—Chiefs, 9-7 (KC)
Chiefs, 27-24 (LA)
1991—Chiefs, 24-21 (KC)
Chiefs, 27-21 (LA)
†Chiefs, 10-6 (KC)
1992—Chiefs, 27-7 (KC)
Raiders, 28-7 (LA)
1993—Chiefs, 24-9 (KC)
Chiefs, 31-20 (LA)
1994—Chiefs, 13-3 (KC)
Chiefs, 19-9 (LA)
(RS Pts.—Chiefs 1,376, Raiders 1,322)
(PS Pts.—Raiders 54, Chiefs 33)
**Franchise in Dallas prior to 1963 and known as Texans*
***Franchise in Oakland prior to 1982*
****Division Playoff*
*****AFL Championship*
†AFC First-Round Playoff
KANSAS CITY vs. MIAMI
RS: Chiefs lead series, 10-8
PS: Dolphins lead series, 3-0
1966—Chiefs, 34-16 (KC)
Chiefs, 19-18 (M)
1967—Chiefs, 24-0 (M)
Chiefs, 41-0 (KC)
1968—Chiefs, 48-3 (M)
1969—Chiefs, 17-10 (KC)
1971—*Dolphins, 27-24 (KC) OT
1972—Dolphins, 20-10 (KC)
1974—Dolphins, 9-3 (M)
1976—Chiefs, 20-17 (M) OT
1981—Dolphins, 17-7 (KC)
1983—Dolphins, 14-6 (M)
1985—Dolphins, 31-0 (M)
1987—Dolphins, 42-0 (M)
1989—Chiefs, 26-21 (KC)
Chiefs, 27-24 (M)
1990—**Dolphins, 17-16 (M)
1991—Chiefs, 42-7 (KC)
1993—Dolphins, 30-10 (M)
1994—Dolphins, 45-28 (M)
**Dolphins, 27-17 (M)
(RS Pts.—Chiefs 362, Dolphins 324)
(PS Pts.—Dolphins 71, Chiefs 57)
**AFC Divisional Playoff*
***AFC First-Round Playoff*
KANSAS CITY vs. MINNESOTA
RS: Vikings lead series, 3-2
PS: Chiefs lead series, 1-0
1969—*Chiefs, 23-7 (New Orleans)
1970—Vikings, 27-10 (M)
1974—Vikings, 35-15 (KC)
1981—Chiefs, 10-6 (M)
1990—Chiefs, 24-21 (KC)
1993—Vikings, 30-10 (M)
(RS Pts.—Vikings 119, Chiefs 69)
(PS Pts.—Chiefs 23, Vikings 7)
**Super Bowl IV*
***KANSAS CITY vs. **NEW ENGLAND**
RS: Chiefs lead series, 13-7-3
1960—Patriots, 42-14 (B)
Texans, 34-0 (D)
1961—Patriots, 18-17 (D)
Patriots, 28-21 (B)
1962—Texans, 42-28 (D)
Texans, 27-7 (B)
1963—Tie, 24-24 (B)
Chiefs, 35-3 (KC)
1964—Patriots, 24-7 (B)
Patriots, 31-24 (KC)
1965—Chiefs, 27-17 (KC)
Tie, 10-10 (B)
1966—Chiefs, 43-24 (B)
Tie, 27-27 (KC)
1967—Chiefs, 33-10 (B)
1968—Chiefs, 31-17 (KC)
1969—Chiefs, 31-0 (B)
1970—Chiefs, 23-10 (KC)
1973—Chiefs, 10-7 (NE)
1977—Patriots, 21-17 (NE)
1981—Patriots, 33-17 (NE)
1990—Chiefs, 37-7 (NE)
1992—Chiefs, 27-20 (KC)
(RS Pts.—Chiefs 578, Patriots 408)
**Franchise located in Dallas prior to 1963 and known as Texans*
***Franchise in Boston prior to 1971*
KANSAS CITY vs. NEW ORLEANS
RS: Series tied, 3-3
1972—Chiefs, 20-17 (NO)
1976—Saints, 27-17 (KC)
1982—Saints, 27-17 (NO)
1985—Chiefs, 47-27 (NO)
1991—Saints, 17-10 (KC)
1994—Chiefs, 30-17 (NO)
(RS Pts.—Chiefs 141, Saints 132)
KANSAS CITY vs. N.Y. GIANTS
RS: Giants lead series, 6-1
1974—Giants, 33-27 (KC)
1978—Giants, 26-10 (NY)
1979—Giants, 21-17 (KC)
1983—Chiefs, 38-17 (KC)
1984—Giants, 28-27 (NY)
1988—Giants, 28-12 (NY)
1992—Giants, 35-21 (NY)
(RS Pts.—Giants 188, Chiefs 152)
***KANSAS CITY vs. **N.Y. JETS**
RS: Chiefs lead series, 14-12-1
PS: Series tied, 1-1
1960—Titans, 37-35 (D)
Titans, 41-35 (NY)
1961—Titans, 28-7 (NY)
Texans, 35-24 (D)
1962—Texans, 20-17 (D)
Texans, 52-31 (NY)
1963—Jets, 17-0 (NY)
Chiefs, 48-0 (KC)
1964—Jets, 27-14 (NY)
Chiefs, 24-7 (KC)
1965—Chiefs, 14-10 (NY)
Jets, 13-10 (KC)
1966—Chiefs, 32-24 (NY)
1967—Chiefs, 42-18 (KC)
Chiefs, 21-7 (NY)
1968—Jets, 20-19 (KC)
1969—Chiefs, 34-16 (NY)
***Chiefs, 13-6 (NY)
1971—Jets, 13-10 (NY)
1974—Chiefs, 24-16 (KC)
1975—Jets, 30-24 (KC)
1982—Chiefs, 37-13 (KC)
1984—Jets, 17-16 (KC)
Jets, 28-7 (NY)
1986—****Jets, 35-15 (NY)
1987—Jets, 16-9 (KC)
1988—Tie, 17-17 (NY)
Chiefs, 38-34 (KC)
1992—Chiefs, 23-7 (NY)
(RS Pts.—Chiefs 647, Jets 528)
(PS Pts.—Jets 41, Chiefs 28)
**Franchise in Dallas prior to 1963 and known as Texans*
***Jets known as Titans prior to 1963*
****Inter-Divisional Playoff*
*****AFC First-Round Playoff*
KANSAS CITY vs. PHILADELPHIA
RS: Series tied, 1-1
1972—Eagles, 21-20 (KC)
1992—Chiefs, 24-17 (KC)
(RS Pts.—Chiefs 44, Eagles 38)
KANSAS CITY vs. PITTSBURGH
RS: Steelers lead series, 13-5
PS: Chiefs lead series, 1-0
1970—Chiefs, 31-14 (P)
1971—Chiefs, 38-16 (KC)
1972—Steelers, 16-7 (P)
1974—Steelers, 34-24 (KC)
1975—Steelers, 28-3 (P)
1976—Steelers, 45-0 (KC)
1978—Steelers, 27-24 (P)
1979—Steelers, 30-3 (KC)
1980—Steelers, 21-16 (P)
1981—Chiefs, 37-33 (P)
1982—Steelers, 35-14 (P)
1984—Chiefs, 37-27 (P)
1985—Steelers, 36-28 (KC)
1986—Chiefs, 24-19 (P)
1987—Steelers, 17-16 (KC)
1988—Steelers, 16-10 (P)
1989—Steelers, 23-17 (P)
1992—Steelers, 27-3 (KC)
1993—*Chiefs, 27-24 (KC) OT
(RS Pts.—Steelers 464, Chiefs 332)
(PS Pts.—Chiefs 27, Steelers 24)
**AFC First-Round Playoff*
KANSAS CITY vs. *ST. LOUIS
RS: Rams lead series, 4-1
1973—Rams, 23-13 (KC)
1982—Rams, 20-14 (LA)
1985—Rams, 16-0 (KC)
1991—Chiefs, 27-20 (LA)
1994—Rams, 16-0 (KC)
(RS Pts.—Rams 95, Chiefs 54)
**Franchise in Los Angeles prior to 1995*
***KANSAS CITY vs. **SAN DIEGO**
RS: Chiefs lead series, 35-33-1
PS: Chargers lead series, 1-0
1960—Chargers, 21-20 (LA)
Texans, 17-0 (D)
1961—Chargers, 26-10 (D)
Chargers, 24-14 (SD)
1962—Chargers, 32-28 (SD)
Texans, 26-17 (D)
1963—Chargers, 24-10 (SD)
Chargers, 38-17 (KC)
1964—Chargers, 28-14 (KC)
Chiefs, 49-6 (SD)
1965—Tie, 10-10 (SD)
Chiefs, 31-7 (KC)
1966—Chiefs, 24-14 (KC)
Chiefs, 27-17 (SD)
1967—Chargers, 45-31 (SD)
Chargers, 17-16 (KC)
1968—Chiefs, 27-20 (KC)
Chiefs, 40-3 (SD)
1969—Chiefs, 27-9 (SD)
Chiefs, 27-3 (KC)
1970—Chiefs, 26-14 (KC)
Chargers, 31-13 (SD)
1971—Chargers, 21-14 (SD)
Chiefs, 31-10 (KC)
1972—Chiefs, 26-14 (SD)
Chargers, 27-17 (KC)
1973—Chiefs, 19-0 (SD)
Chiefs, 33-6 (KC)
1974—Chiefs, 24-14 (SD)
Chargers, 14-7 (KC)
1975—Chiefs, 12-10 (SD)
Chargers, 28-20 (KC)
1976—Chargers, 30-16 (KC)
Chiefs, 23-20 (SD)
1977—Chargers, 23-7 (KC)
Chiefs, 21-16 (SD)
1978—Chargers, 29-23 (SD) OT
Chiefs, 23-0 (KC)
1979—Chargers, 20-14 (KC)
Chargers, 28-7 (SD)
1980—Chargers, 24-7 (KC)
Chargers, 20-7 (SD)
1981—Chargers, 42-31 (KC)
Chargers, 22-20 (SD)
1982—Chiefs, 19-12 (KC)
1983—Chargers, 17-14 (KC)
Chargers, 41-38 (SD)
1984—Chiefs, 31-13 (KC)
Chiefs, 42-21 (SD)
1985—Chargers, 31-20 (SD)

Chiefs, 38-34 (KC)
1986—Chiefs, 42-41 (KC)
Chiefs, 24-23 (SD)
1987—Chiefs, 20-13 (KC)
Chargers, 42-21 (SD)
1988—Chargers, 24-23 (KC)
Chargers, 24-13 (SD)
1989—Chargers, 21-6 (SD)
Chargers, 20-13 (KC)
1990—Chiefs, 27-10 (KC)
Chiefs, 24-21 (SD)
1991—Chiefs, 14-13 (SD)
Chiefs, 20-17 (KC) OT
1992—Chiefs, 24-10 (SD)
Chiefs, 16-14 (KC)
***Chargers, 17-0 (SD)
1993—Chiefs, 17-14 (SD)
Chiefs, 28-24 (KC)
1994—Chargers, 20-6 (SD)
Chargers, 14-13 (KC)
(RS Pts.—Chiefs 1,459, Chargers 1,358)
(PS Pts.—Chargers 17, Chiefs 0)
**Franchise in Dallas prior to 1963 and known as Texans*
***Franchise in Los Angeles prior to 1961*
****AFC First-Round Playoff*

KANSAS CITY vs. SAN FRANCISCO
RS: 49ers lead series, 4-2
1971—Chiefs, 26-17 (SF)
1975—49ers, 20-3 (KC)
1982—49ers, 26-13 (KC)
1985—49ers, 31-3 (SF)
1991—49ers, 28-14 (SF)
1994—Chiefs, 24-17 (KC)
(RS Pts.—49ers 139, Chiefs 83)

KANSAS CITY vs. SEATTLE
RS: Chiefs lead series, 20-13
1977—Seahawks, 34-31 (KC)
1978—Seahawks, 13-10 (KC)
Seahawks, 23-19 (S)
1979—Chiefs, 24-6 (S)
Chiefs, 37-21 (KC)
1980—Seahawks, 17-16 (KC)
Chiefs, 31-30 (S)
1981—Chiefs, 20-14 (S)
Chiefs, 40-13 (KC)
1983—Chiefs, 17-13 (KC)
Seahawks, 51-48 (S) OT
1984—Seahawks, 45-0 (S)
Chiefs, 34-7 (KC)
1985—Chiefs, 28-7 (KC)
Seahawks, 24-6 (S)
1986—Seahawks, 23-17 (S)
Chiefs, 27-7 (KC)
1987—Seahawks, 43-14 (S)
Chiefs, 41-20 (KC)
1988—Seahawks, 31-10 (S)
Chiefs, 27-24 (KC)
1989—Chiefs, 20-16 (S)
Chiefs, 20-10 (KC)
1990—Seahawks, 19-7 (S)
Seahawks, 17-16 (KC)
1991—Chiefs, 20-13 (KC)
Chiefs, 19-6 (S)
1992—Chiefs, 26-7 (KC)
Chiefs, 24-14 (S)
1993—Chiefs, 31-16 (S)
Chiefs, 34-24 (KC)
1994—Chiefs, 38-23 (KC)
Seahawks, 10-9 (S)
(RS Pts.—Chiefs 761, Seahawks 641)

KANSAS CITY vs. TAMPA BAY
RS: Chiefs lead series, 5-2
1976—Chiefs, 28-19 (TB)
1978—Buccaneers, 30-13 (KC)
1979—Buccaneers, 3-0 (TB)
1981—Chiefs, 19-10 (KC)
1984—Chiefs, 24-20 (KC)
1986—Chiefs, 27-20 (KC)
1993—Chiefs, 27-3 (TB)
(RS Pts.—Chiefs 138, Buccaneers 105)

KANSAS CITY vs. WASHINGTON
RS: Chiefs lead series, 3-1
1971—Chiefs, 27-20 (KC)
1976—Chiefs, 33-30 (W)
1983—Redskins, 27-12 (W)
1992—Chiefs, 35-16 (KC)
(RS Pts.—Chiefs 107, Redskins 93)

LOS ANGELES vs. ARIZONA
RS: Raiders lead series, 2-1;
See Arizona vs. Los Angeles

LOS ANGELES vs. ATLANTA
RS: Raiders lead series, 5-3;
See Atlanta vs. Los Angeles

LOS ANGELES vs. BUFFALO
RS: Raiders lead series, 15-14
PS: Bills lead series, 2-0;
See Buffalo vs. Los Angeles

LOS ANGELES vs. CHICAGO
RS: Raiders lead series, 5-3;
See Chicago vs. Los Angeles

LOS ANGELES vs. CINCINNATI
RS: Raiders lead series, 14-7
PS: Raiders lead series, 2-0;
See Cincinnati vs. Los Angeles

LOS ANGELES vs. CLEVELAND
RS: Raiders lead series, 8-4
PS: Raiders lead series, 2-0;
See Cleveland vs. Los Angeles

LOS ANGELES vs. DALLAS
RS: Raiders lead series, 3-2;
See Dallas vs. Los Angeles

LOS ANGELES vs. DENVER
RS: Raiders lead series, 48-19-2
PS: Series tied, 1-1;
See Denver vs. Los Angeles

LOS ANGELES vs. DETROIT
RS: Raiders lead series, 5-2;
See Detroit vs. Los Angeles

LOS ANGELES vs. GREEN BAY
RS: Raiders lead series, 5-2
PS: Packers lead series, 1-0;
See Green Bay vs. Los Angeles

LOS ANGELES vs. HOUSTON
RS: Raiders lead series, 20-13
PS: Raiders lead series, 3-0;
See Houston vs. Los Angeles

LOS ANGELES vs. INDIANAPOLIS
RS: Raiders lead series, 4-2
PS: Series tied, 1-1;
See Indianapolis vs. Los Angeles

LOS ANGELES vs. KANSAS CITY
RS: Raiders lead series, 35-32-2
PS: Chiefs lead series, 2-1;
See Kansas City vs. Los Angeles

***LOS ANGELES vs. MIAMI**
RS: Raiders lead series, 14-5-1
PS: Raiders lead series, 2-1
1966—Raiders, 23-14 (M)
Raiders, 21-10 (O)
1967—Raiders, 31-17 (O)
1968—Raiders, 47-21 (M)
1969—Raiders, 20-17 (O)
Tie, 20-20 (M)
1970—Dolphins, 20-13 (M)
**Raiders, 21-14 (O)
1973—Raiders, 12-7 (O)
***Dolphins, 27-10 (M)
1974—**Raiders, 28-26 (O)
1975—Raiders, 31-21 (M)
1978—Dolphins, 23-6 (M)
1979—Raiders, 13-3 (O)
1980—Raiders, 16-10 (O)
1981—Raiders, 33-17 (M)
1983—Raiders, 27-14 (LA)
1984—Raiders, 45-34 (M)
1986—Raiders, 30-28 (M)
1988—Dolphins, 24-14 (LA)
1990—Raiders, 13-10 (M)
1992—Dolphins, 20-7 (M)
1994—Dolphins, 20-17 (M) OT
(RS Pts.—Raiders 439, Dolphins 350)
(PS Pts.—Dolphins 67, Raiders 59)
**Franchise in Oakland prior to 1982*
***AFC Divisional Playoff*
****AFC Championship*

***LOS ANGELES vs. MINNESOTA**
RS: Raiders lead series, 6-2
PS: Raiders lead series, 1-0
1973—Vikings, 24-16 (M)
1976—**Raiders, 32-14 (Pasadena)
1977—Raiders, 35-13 (O)
1978—Raiders, 27-20 (O)
1981—Raiders, 36-10 (M)
1984—Raiders, 23-20 (LA)
1987—Vikings, 31-20 (M)
1990—Raiders, 28-24 (M)
1993—Raiders, 24-7 (LA)
(RS Pts.—Raiders 209, Vikings 149)
(PS Pts.—Raiders 32, Vikings 14)
**Franchise in Oakland prior to 1982*
***Super Bowl XI*

***LOS ANGELES vs. **NEW ENGLAND**
RS: Raiders lead series, 13-12-1
PS: Series tied, 1-1
1960—Raiders, 27-14 (O)
Patriots, 34-28 (B)
1961—Patriots, 20-17 (B)
Patriots, 35-21 (O)
1962—Patriots, 26-16 (B)
Raiders, 20-0 (O)
1963—Patriots, 20-14 (O)
Patriots, 20-14 (B)
1964—Patriots, 17-14 (O)
Tie, 43-43 (B)
1965—Raiders, 24-10 (B)
Raiders, 30-21 (O)
1966—Patriots, 24-21 (B)
1967—Raiders, 35-7 (O)
Raiders, 48-14 (B)
1968—Raiders, 41-10 (O)
1969—Raiders, 38-23 (B)
1971—Patriots, 20-6 (NE)
1974—Raiders, 41-26 (O)
1976—Patriots, 48-17 (NE)
***Raiders, 24-21 (O)
1978—Patriots, 21-14 (O)
1981—Raiders, 27-17 (O)
1985—Raiders, 35-20 (NE)
***Patriots, 27-20 (LA)
1987—Patriots, 26-23 (NE)
1989—Raiders, 24-21 (LA)
1994—Raiders, 21-17 (NE)
(RS Pts.—Raiders 659, Patriots 554)
(PS Pts.—Patriots 48, Raiders 44)
**Franchise in Oakland prior to 1982*
***Franchise in Boston prior to 1971*
****AFC Divisional Playoff*

***LOS ANGELES vs. NEW ORLEANS**
RS: Raiders lead series, 4-2-1
1971—Tie, 21-21 (NO)
1975—Raiders, 48-10 (O)
1979—Raiders, 42-35 (NO)
1985—Raiders, 23-13 (LA)
1988—Saints, 20-6 (NO)
1991—Saints, 27-0 (NO)
1994—Raiders, 24-19 (LA)
(RS Pts.—Raiders 164, Saints 145)
**Franchise in Oakland prior to 1982*

***LOS ANGELES vs. N.Y. GIANTS**
RS: Raiders lead series, 4-2
1973—Raiders, 42-0 (O)
1980—Raiders, 33-17 (NY)
1983—Raiders, 27-12 (LA)
1986—Giants, 14-9 (LA)
1989—Giants, 34-17 (NY)
1992—Raiders, 13-10 (LA)
(RS Pts.—Raiders 141, Giants 87)
**Franchise in Oakland prior to 1982*

***LOS ANGELES vs. **N.Y. JETS**
RS: Raiders lead series, 14-9-2
PS: Jets lead series, 2-0
1960—Raiders, 28-27 (NY)
Titans, 31-28 (O)
1961—Titans, 14-6 (O)
Titans, 23-12 (NY)
1962—Titans, 28-17 (O)
Titans, 31-21 (NY)
1963—Jets, 10-7 (NY)
Raiders, 49-26 (O)
1964—Jets, 35-13 (NY)
Raiders, 35-26 (O)
1965—Tie, 24-24 (NY)
Raiders, 24-14 (O)
1966—Raiders, 24-21 (NY)
Tie, 28-28 (O)
1967—Jets, 27-14 (NY)
Raiders, 38-29 (O)
1968—Raiders, 43-32 (O)
***Jets, 27-23 (NY)
1969—Raiders, 27-14 (NY)
1970—Raiders, 14-13 (NY)
1972—Raiders, 24-16 (O)
1977—Raiders, 28-27 (NY)
1979—Jets, 28-19 (NY)
1982—****Jets, 17-14 (LA)
1985—Raiders, 31-0 (LA)
1989—Raiders, 14-7 (NY)
1993—Raiders, 24-20 (LA)
(RS Pts.—Raiders 592, Jets 551)
(PS Pts.—Jets 44, Raiders 37)
**Franchise in Oakland prior to 1982*
***Jets known as Titans prior to 1963*
****AFL Championship*
*****AFC Second-Round Playoff*

***LOS ANGELES vs. PHILADELPHIA**
RS: Eagles lead series, 4-2
PS: Raiders lead series, 1-0
1971—Raiders, 34-10 (O)
1976—Raiders, 26-7 (P)
1980—Eagles, 10-7 (P)
**Raiders, 27-10 (New Orleans)
1986—Eagles, 33-27 (LA) OT
1989—Eagles, 10-7 (P)
1992—Eagles, 31-10 (P)
(RS Pts.—Raiders 111, Eagles 101)
(PS Pts.—Raiders 27, Eagles 10)
**Franchise in Oakland prior to 1982*
***Super Bowl XV*

***LOS ANGELES vs. PITTSBURGH**
RS: Raiders lead series, 7-4
PS: Series tied, 3-3
1970—Raiders, 31-14 (O)
1972—Steelers, 34-28 (P)
**Steelers, 13-7 (P)
1973—Steelers, 17-9 (O)
**Raiders, 33-14 (O)
1974—Raiders, 17-0 (P)
***Steelers, 24-13 (O)
1975—***Steelers, 16-10 (P)
1976—Raiders, 31-28 (O)
***Raiders, 24-7 (O)
1977—Raiders, 16-7 (P)
1980—Raiders, 45-34 (P)
1981—Raiders, 30-27 (O)
1983—**Raiders, 38-10 (LA)
1984—Steelers, 13-7 (LA)
1990—Raiders, 20-3 (LA)
1994—Steelers, 21-3 (LA)
(RS Pts.—Raiders 237, Steelers 198)
(PS Pts.—Raiders 125, Steelers 84)
**Franchise in Oakland prior to 1982*
***AFC Divisional Playoff*
****AFC Championship*

***LOS ANGELES vs. **ST. LOUIS**
RS: Raiders lead series, 6-2
1972—Raiders, 45-17 (O)
1977—Rams, 20-14 (LA)
1979—Raiders, 24-17 (LA)
1982—Raiders, 37-31 (LA Raiders)
1985—Raiders, 16-6 (LA Rams)
1988—Rams, 22-17 (LA Raiders)
1991—Raiders, 20-17 (LA Raiders)
1994—Raiders, 20-17 (LA Rams)
(RS Pts.—Raiders 193, Rams 147)
**Franchise in Oakland prior to 1982*
***Franchise in Los Angeles prior to 1995*

***LOS ANGELES vs. **SAN DIEGO**
RS: Raiders lead series, 42-26-2
PS: Raiders lead series, 1-0

1960—Chargers, 52-28 (LA)
Chargers, 41-17 (O)
1961—Chargers, 44-0 (SD)
Chargers, 41-10 (O)
1962—Chargers, 42-33 (O)
Chargers, 31-21 (SD)
1963—Raiders, 34-33 (SD)
Raiders, 41-27 (O)
1964—Chargers, 31-17 (SD)
Raiders, 21-20 (O)
1965—Chargers, 17-6 (O)
Chargers, 24-14 (SD)
1966—Chargers, 29-20 (O)
Raiders, 41-19 (SD)
1967—Raiders, 51-10 (O)
Raiders, 41-21 (SD)
1968—Chargers, 23-14 (O)
Raiders, 34-27 (SD)
1969—Raiders, 24-12 (SD)
Raiders, 21-16 (O)
1970—Tie, 27-27 (SD)
Raiders, 20-17 (O)
1971—Raiders, 34-0 (SD)
Raiders, 34-33 (O)
1972—Tie, 17-17 (O)
Raiders, 21-19 (SD)
1973—Raiders, 27-17 (SD)
Raiders, 31-3 (O)
1974—Raiders, 14-10 (SD)
Raiders, 17-10 (O)
1975—Raiders, 6-0 (SD)
Raiders, 25-0 (O)
1976—Raiders, 27-17 (SD)
Raiders, 24-0 (O)
1977—Raiders, 24-0 (O)
Chargers, 12-7 (SD)
1978—Raiders, 21-20 (SD)
Chargers, 27-23 (O)
1979—Chargers, 30-10 (SD)
Raiders, 45-22 (O)
1980—Chargers, 30-24 (SD) OT
Raiders, 38-24 (O)
***Raiders, 34-27 (SD)
1981—Chargers, 55-21 (O)
Chargers, 23-10 (SD)
1982—Raiders, 28-24 (LA)
Raiders, 41-34 (SD)
1983—Raiders, 42-10 (SD)
Raiders, 30-14 (LA)
1984—Raiders, 33-30 (LA)
Raiders, 44-37 (SD)
1985—Raiders, 34-21 (LA)
Chargers, 40-34 (SD) OT
1986—Raiders, 17-13 (LA)
Raiders, 37-31 (SD) OT
1987—Chargers, 23-17 (LA)
Chargers, 16-14 (SD)
1988—Raiders, 24-13 (LA)
Raiders, 13-3 (SD)
1989—Raiders, 40-14 (LA)
Chargers, 14-12 (SD)
1990—Raiders, 24-9 (SD)
Raiders, 17-12 (LA)
1991—Chargers, 21-13 (LA)
Raiders, 9-7 (SD)
1992—Chargers, 27-3 (SD)
Chargers, 36-14 (LA)
1993—Chargers, 30-23 (LA)
Raiders, 12-7 (SD)
1994—Chargers, 26-24 (LA)
Raiders, 24-17 (SD)
(RS Pts.—Raiders 1,658, Chargers, 1,502)
(PS Pts.—Raiders 34, Chargers 27)
Franchise in Oakland prior to 1982
**Franchise in Los Angeles prior to 1961*
***AFC Championship*

***LOS ANGELES vs. SAN FRANCISCO**
RS: Raiders lead series, 5-3
1970—49ers, 38-7 (O)
1974—Raiders, 35-24 (SF)
1979—Raiders, 23-10 (O)
1982—Raiders, 23-17 (SF)
1985—49ers, 34-10 (LA)
1988—Raiders, 9-3 (SF)
1991—Raiders, 12-6 (LA)
1994—49ers, 44-14 (SF)
(RS Pts.—49ers 176, Raiders 133)
Franchise in Oakland prior to 1982

***LOS ANGELES vs. SEATTLE**
RS: Raiders lead series, 19-15
PS: Series tied, 1-1
1977—Raiders, 44-7 (O)
1978—Seahawks, 27-7 (S)
Seahawks, 17-16 (O)
1979—Seahawks, 27-10 (S)
Seahawks, 29-24 (O)
1980—Raiders, 33-14 (O)
Raiders, 19-17 (S)
1981—Raiders, 20-10 (O)
Raiders, 32-31 (S)
1982—Raiders, 28-23 (LA)
1983—Seahawks, 38-36 (S)
Seahawks, 34-21 (LA)
**Raiders, 30-14 (LA)
1984—Raiders, 28-14 (LA)
Seahawks, 17-14 (S)
***Seahawks, 13-7 (S)
1985—Seahawks, 33-3 (S)
Raiders, 13-3 (LA)
1986—Raiders, 14-10 (LA)
Seahawks, 37-0 (S)
1987—Seahawks, 35-13 (LA)
Raiders, 37-14 (S)
1988—Seahawks, 35-27 (S)
Seahawks, 43-37 (LA)
1989—Seahawks, 24-20 (LA)
Seahawks, 23-17 (S)
1990—Raiders, 17-13 (S)
Raiders, 24-17 (LA)
1991—Raiders, 23-20 (S) OT
Raiders, 31-7 (LA)
1992—Raiders, 19-0 (S)
Raiders, 20-3 (LA)
1993—Raiders, 17-13 (S)
Raiders, 27-23 (LA)
1994—Seahawks, 38-9 (LA)
Raiders, 17-16 (S)
(RS Pts.—Raiders 717, Seahawks 712)
(PS Pts.—Raiders 37, Seahawks 27)
Franchise in Oakland prior to 1982
**AFC Championship*
***AFC First-Round Playoff*

***LOS ANGELES vs. TAMPA BAY**
RS: Raiders lead series, 3-0
1976—Raiders, 49-16 (O)
1981—Raiders, 18-16 (O)
1993—Raiders, 27-20 (LA)
(RS Pts.—Raiders 94, Buccaneers 52)
Franchise in Oakland prior to 1982

***LOS ANGELES vs. WASHINGTON**
RS: Raiders lead series, 5-2
PS: Raiders lead series, 1-0
1970—Raiders, 34-20 (O)
1975—Raiders, 26-23 (W) OT
1980—Raiders, 24-21 (O)
1983—Redskins, 37-35 (W)
**Raiders, 38-9 (Tampa)
1986—Redskins, 10-6 (W)
1989—Raiders, 37-24 (LA)
1992—Raiders, 21-20 (W)
(RS Pts.—Raiders 183, Redskins 155)
(PS Pts.—Raiders 38, Redskins 9)
Franchise in Oakland prior to 1982
**Super Bowl XVIII*

MIAMI vs. ARIZONA
RS: Dolphins lead series, 6-0;
See Arizona vs. Miami

MIAMI vs. ATLANTA
RS: Dolphins lead series, 5-1;
See Atlanta vs. Miami

MIAMI vs. BUFFALO
RS: Dolphins lead series, 37-20-1
PS: Bills lead series, 2-0;
See Buffalo vs. Miami

MIAMI vs. CHICAGO
RS: Dolphins lead series, 5-2;
See Chicago vs. Miami

MIAMI vs. CINCINNATI
RS: Dolphins lead series, 10-3
PS: Dolphins lead series, 1-0;
See Cincinnati vs. Miami

MIAMI vs. CLEVELAND
RS: Dolphins lead series, 6-4
PS: Dolphins lead series, 2-0;
See Cleveland vs. Miami

MIAMI vs. DALLAS
RS: Dolphins lead series, 6-1
PS: Cowboys lead series, 1-0;
See Dallas vs. Miami

MIAMI vs. DENVER
RS: Dolphins lead series, 5-2-1;
See Denver vs. Miami

MIAMI vs. DETROIT
RS: Dolphins lead series, 3-2;
See Detroit vs. Miami

MIAMI vs. GREEN BAY
RS: Dolphins lead series, 8-0;
See Green Bay vs. Miami

MIAMI vs. HOUSTON
RS: Series tied, 11-11
PS: Oilers lead series, 1-0;
See Houston vs. Miami

MIAMI vs. INDIANAPOLIS
RS: Dolphins lead series, 35-15
PS: Dolphins lead series, 1-0;
See Indianapolis vs. Miami

MIAMI vs. KANSAS CITY
RS: Chiefs lead series, 10-8
PS: Dolphins lead series, 3-0;
See Kansas City vs. Miami

MIAMI vs. LOS ANGELES
RS: Raiders lead series, 14-5-1
PS: Raiders lead series, 2-1;
See Los Angeles vs. Miami

MIAMI vs. MINNESOTA
RS: Dolphins lead series, 4-2
PS: Dolphins lead series, 1-0
1972—Dolphins, 16-14 (Minn)
1973—*Dolphins, 24-7 (Houston)
1976—Vikings, 29-7 (Mia)
1979—Dolphins, 27-12 (Minn)
1982—Dolphins, 22-14 (Mia)
1988—Dolphins, 24-7 (Mia)
1994—Vikings, 38-35 (M)
(RS Pts.—Dolphins 131, Vikings 114)
(PS Pts.—Dolphins 24, Vikings 7)
Super Bowl VIII

MIAMI vs. *NEW ENGLAND
RS: Dolphins lead series, 35-21
PS: Series tied, 1-1
1966—Patriots, 20-14 (M)
1967—Patriots, 41-10 (B)
Dolphins, 41-32 (M)
1968—Dolphins, 34-10 (B)
Dolphins, 38-7 (M)
1969—Dolphins, 17-16 (B)
Patriots, 38-23 (Tampa)
1970—Patriots, 27-14 (B)
Dolphins, 37-20 (M)
1971—Dolphins, 41-3 (M)
Patriots, 34-13 (NE)
1972—Dolphins, 52-0 (M)
Dolphins, 37-21 (NE)
1973—Dolphins, 44-23 (M)
Dolphins, 30-14 (NE)
1974—Patriots, 34-24 (NE)
Dolphins, 34-27 (M)
1975—Dolphins, 22-14 (NE)
Dolphins, 20-7 (M)
1976—Patriots, 30-14 (NE)
Dolphins, 10-3 (M)
1977—Dolphins, 17-5 (M)
Patriots, 14-10 (NE)
1978—Patriots, 33-24 (NE)
Dolphins, 23-3 (M)
1979—Patriots, 28-13 (NE)
Dolphins, 39-24 (M)
1980—Patriots, 34-0 (NE)
Dolphins, 16-13 (M) OT
1981—Dolphins, 30-27 (NE) OT
Dolphins, 24-14 (M)
1982—Patriots, 3-0 (NE)
**Dolphins, 28-13 (M)
1983—Dolphins, 34-24 (M)
Patriots, 17-6 (NE)
1984—Dolphins, 28-7 (M)
Dolphins, 44-24 (NE)
1985—Patriots, 17-13 (NE)
Dolphins, 30-27 (M)
***Patriots, 31-14 (M)
1986—Patriots, 34-7 (NE)
Patriots, 34-27 (M)
1987—Patriots, 28-21 (NE)
Patriots, 24-10 (M)
1988—Patriots, 21-10 (NE)
Patriots, 6-3 (M)
1989—Dolphins, 24-10 (NE)
Dolphins, 31-10 (M)
1990—Dolphins, 27-24 (NE)
Dolphins, 17-10 (M)
1991—Dolphins, 20-10 (NE)
Dolphins, 30-20 (M)
1992—Dolphins, 38-17 (M)
Dolphins, 16-13 (NE) OT
1993—Dolphins, 17-13 (M)
Patriots, 33-27 (NE) OT
1994—Dolphins, 39-35 (M)
Dolphins, 23-3 (NE)
(RS Pts.—Dolphins 1,307, Patriots 1,080)
(PS Pts.—Patriots 44, Dolphins 42)
Franchise in Boston prior to 1971
**AFC First-Round Playoff*
***AFC Championship*

MIAMI vs. NEW ORLEANS
RS: Dolphins lead series, 4-2
1970—Dolphins, 21-10 (M)
1974—Dolphins, 21-0 (NO)
1980—Dolphins, 21-16 (M)
1983—Saints, 17-7 (NO)
1986—Dolphins, 31-27 (NO)
1992—Saints, 24-13 (NO)
(RS Pts.—Dolphins 114, Saints 94)

MIAMI vs. N.Y. GIANTS
RS: Giants lead series, 2-1
1972—Dolphins, 23-13 (NY)
1990—Giants, 20-3 (NY)
1993—Giants, 19-14 (M)
(RS Pts.—Giants 52, Dolphins 40)

MIAMI vs. N.Y. JETS
RS: Dolphins lead series, 29-28-1
PS: Dolphins lead series, 1-0
1966—Jets, 19-14 (M)
Jets, 30-13 (NY)
1967—Jets, 29-7 (NY)
Jets, 33-14 (M)
1968—Jets, 35-17 (NY)
Jets, 31-7 (M)
1969—Jets, 34-31 (NY)
Jets, 27-9 (M)
1970—Dolphins, 20-6 (NY)
Dolphins, 16-10 (M)
1971—Jets, 14-10 (M)
Dolphins, 30-14 (NY)
1972—Dolphins, 27-17 (NY)
Dolphins, 28-24 (M)
1973—Dolphins, 31-3 (M)
Dolphins, 24-14 (NY)
1974—Dolphins, 21-17 (M)
Jets, 17-14 (NY)
1975—Dolphins, 43-0 (NY)
Dolphins, 27-7 (M)
1976—Dolphins, 16-0 (M)
Dolphins, 27-7 (NY)
1977—Dolphins, 21-17 (M)
Dolphins, 14-10 (NY)
1978—Jets, 33-20 (NY)
Jets, 24-13 (M)
1979—Jets, 33-27 (NY)
Jets, 27-24 (M)
1980—Jets, 17-14 (NY)
Jets, 24-17 (M)

ALL-TIME TEAM VS. TEAM RESULTS

1981—Tie, 28-28 (M) OT
Jets, 16-15 (NY)
1982—Dolphins, 45-28 (NY)
Dolphins, 20-19 (M)
*Dolphins, 14-0 (M)
1983—Dolphins, 32-14 (NY)
Dolphins, 34-14 (M)
1984—Dolphins, 31-17 (NY)
Dolphins, 28-17 (M)
1985—Jets, 23-7 (NY)
Dolphins, 21-17 (M)
1986—Jets, 51-45 (NY) OT
Dolphins, 45-3 (M)
1987—Jets, 37-31 (NY) OT
Dolphins, 37-28 (M)
1988—Jets, 44-30 (M)
Jets, 38-34 (NY)
1989—Jets, 40-33 (M)
Dolphins, 31-23 (NY)
1990—Dolphins, 20-16 (M)
Dolphins, 17-3 (NY)
1991—Jets, 41-23 (NY)
Jets, 23-20 (M) OT
1992—Jets, 26-14 (NY)
Dolphins, 19-17 (M)
1993—Jets, 24-14 (M)
Jets, 27-10 (NY)
1994—Dolphins, 28-14 (M)
Dolphins, 28-24 (NY)
(RS Pts.—Dolphins 1,336, Jets 1,245)
(PS Pts.—Dolphins 14, Jets 0)
AFC Championship

MIAMI vs. PHILADELPHIA
RS: Dolphins lead series, 6-2
1970—Eagles, 24-17 (P)
1975—Dolphins, 24-16 (M)
1978—Eagles, 17-3 (P)
1981—Dolphins, 13-10 (M)
1984—Dolphins, 24-23 (M)
1987—Dolphins, 28-10 (P)
1990—Dolphins, 23-20 (M) OT
1993—Dolphins, 19-14 (P)
(RS Pts.—Dolphins 151, Eagles 134)

MIAMI vs. PITTSBURGH
RS: Dolphins lead series, 7-6
PS: Dolphins lead series, 2-1
1971—Dolphins, 24-21 (M)
1972—*Dolphins, 21-17 (P)
1973—Dolphins, 30-26 (M)
1976—Steelers, 14-3 (P)
1979—**Steelers, 34-14 (P)
1980—Steelers, 23-10 (P)
1981—Dolphins, 30-10 (M)
1984—Dolphins, 31-7 (P)
*Dolphins, 45-28 (M)
1985—Dolphins, 24-20 (M)
1987—Dolphins, 35-24 (M)
1988—Steelers, 40-24 (P)
1989—Steelers, 34-14 (M)
1990—Dolphins, 28-6 (P)
1993—Steelers, 21-20 (M)
1994—Steelers, 16-13 (P) OT
(RS Pts.—Dolphins 286, Steelers 262)
(PS Pts.—Dolphins 80, Steelers 79)
AFC Championship
***AFC Divisional Playoff*

MIAMI vs. *ST. LOUIS
RS: Dolphins lead series, 5-1;
1971—Dolphins, 20-14 (LA)
1976—Rams, 31-28 (M)
1980—Dolphins, 35-14 (LA)
1983—Dolphins, 30-14 (M)
1986—Dolphins, 37-31 (LA) OT
1992—Dolphins, 26-10 (M)
(RS Pts.—Dolphins 176, Rams 114)
Franchise in Los Angeles prior to 1995

MIAMI vs. SAN DIEGO
RS: Chargers lead series, 10-5
PS: Series tied, 2-2
1966—Chargers, 44-10 (SD)
1967—Chargers, 24-0 (SD)
Dolphins, 41-24 (M)
1968—Chargers, 34-28 (SD)
1969—Chargers, 21-14 (M)
1972—Dolphins, 24-10 (M)
1974—Dolphins, 28-21 (SD)
1977—Chargers, 14-13 (M)
1978—Dolphins, 28-21 (SD)
1980—Chargers, 27-24 (M) OT
1981—*Chargers, 41-38 (M) OT
1982—**Dolphins, 34-13 (M)
1984—Chargers, 34-28 (SD) OT
1986—Chargers, 50-28 (SD)
1988—Dolphins, 31-28 (M)
1991—Chargers, 38-30 (SD)
1992—*Dolphins, 31-0 (M)
1993—Chargers, 45-20 (SD)
1994—*Chargers, 22-21 (SD)
(RS Pts.—Chargers 435, Dolphins 347)
(PS Pts.—Dolphins 124, Chargers 76)
AFC Divisional Playoff
***AFC Second-Round Playoff*

MIAMI vs. SAN FRANCISCO
RS: Dolphins lead series, 4-2
PS: 49ers lead series, 1-0
1973—Dolphins, 21-13 (M)
1977—Dolphins, 19-15 (SF)
1980—Dolphins, 17-13 (M)
1983—Dolphins, 20-17 (SF)
1984—*49ers, 38-16 (Stanford)
1986—49ers, 31-16 (M)
1992—49ers, 27-3 (SF)
(RS Pts.—49ers 116, Dolphins 96)
(PS Pts.—49ers 38, Dolphins 16)
Super Bowl XIX

MIAMI vs. SEATTLE
RS: Dolphins lead series, 4-1
PS: Series tied, 1-1
1977—Dolphins, 31-13 (M)
1979—Dolphins, 19-10 (M)
1983—*Seahawks, 27-20 (M)
1984—*Dolphins, 31-10 (M)
1987—Seahawks, 24-20 (S)
1990—Dolphins, 24-17 (M)
1992—Dolphins, 19-17 (S)
(RS Pts.—Dolphins 113, Seahawks 81)
(PS Pts.—Dolphins 51, Seahawks 37)
AFC Divisional Playoff

MIAMI vs. TAMPA BAY
RS: Dolphins lead series, 4-1
1976—Dolphins, 23-20 (TB)
1982—Buccaneers, 23-17 (TB)
1985—Dolphins, 41-38 (M)
1988—Dolphins, 17-14 (TB)
1991—Dolphins, 33-14 (M)
(RS Pts.—Dolphins 131, Buccaneers 109)

MIAMI vs. WASHINGTON
RS: Dolphins lead series, 5-2
PS: Series tied, 1-1
1972—*Dolphins, 14-7 (Los Angeles)
1974—Redskins, 20-17 (W)
1978—Dolphins, 16-0 (W)
1981—Dolphins, 13-10 (M)
1982—**Redskins, 27-17 (Pasadena)
1984—Dolphins, 35-17 (W)
1987—Dolphins, 23-21 (M)
1990—Redskins, 42-20 (W)
1993—Dolphins, 17-10 (M)
(RS Pts.—Dolphins 141, Redskins 120)
(PS Pts.—Redskins 34, Dolphins 31)
Super Bowl VII
***Super Bowl XVII*

MINNESOTA vs. ARIZONA
RS: Cardinals lead series, 8-4
PS: Vikings lead series, 1-0;
See Arizona vs. Minnesota

MINNESOTA vs. ATLANTA
RS: Vikings lead series, 11-6
PS: Vikings lead series, 1-0;
See Atlanta vs. Minnesota

MINNESOTA vs. BUFFALO
RS: Vikings lead series, 5-2;
See Buffalo vs. Minnesota

MINNESOTA vs. CHICAGO
RS: Vikings lead series, 36-29-2
PS: Bears lead series, 1-0;
See Chicago vs. Minnesota

MINNESOTA vs. CINCINNATI
RS: Vikings lead series, 4-3;
See Cincinnati vs. Minnesota

MINNESOTA vs. CLEVELAND
RS: Vikings lead series, 7-3
PS: Vikings lead series, 1-0;
See Cleveland vs. Minnesota

MINNESOTA vs. DALLAS
RS: Cowboys lead series, 8-6
PS: Cowboys lead series, 3-1;
See Dallas vs. Minnesota

MINNESOTA vs. DENVER
RS: Vikings lead series, 5-3;
See Denver vs. Minnesota

MINNESOTA vs. DETROIT
RS: Vikings lead series, 41-24-2;
See Detroit vs. Minnesota

MINNESOTA vs. GREEN BAY
RS: Vikings lead series, 34-32-1;
See Green Bay vs. Minnesota

MINNESOTA vs. HOUSTON
RS: Series tied, 3-3;
See Houston vs. Minnesota

MINNESOTA vs. INDIANAPOLIS
RS: Colts lead series, 11-6-1
PS: Colts lead series, 1-0;
See Indianapolis vs. Minnesota

MINNESOTA vs. KANSAS CITY
RS: Vikings lead series, 3-2
PS: Chiefs lead series, 1-0;
See Kansas City vs. Minnesota

MINNESOTA vs. LOS ANGELES
RS: Raiders lead series, 6-2
PS: Raiders lead series, 1-0;
See Los Angeles vs. Minnesota

MINNESOTA vs. MIAMI
RS: Dolphins lead series, 4-2
PS: Dolphins lead series, 1-0;
See Miami vs. Minnesota

MINNESOTA vs. *NEW ENGLAND
RS: Patriots lead series, 4-2
1970—Vikings, 35-14 (B)
1974—Patriots, 17-14 (M)
1979—Patriots, 27-23 (NE)
1988—Vikings, 36-6 (M)
1991—Patriots, 26-23 (NE) OT
1994—Patriots, 26-20 (NE) OT
(RS Pts.—Vikings 151, Patriots 116)
Franchise in Boston prior to 1971

MINNESOTA vs. NEW ORLEANS
RS: Vikings lead series, 12-6
PS: Vikings lead series, 1-0
1968—Saints, 20-17 (NO)
1970—Vikings, 26-0 (M)
1971—Vikings, 23-10 (NO)
1972—Vikings, 37-6 (M)
1974—Vikings, 29-9 (M)
1975—Vikings, 20-7 (NO)
1976—Vikings, 40-9 (NO)
1978—Saints, 31-24 (NO)
1980—Vikings, 23-20 (NO)
1981—Vikings, 20-10 (M)
1983—Saints, 17-16 (NO)
1985—Saints, 30-23 (M)
1986—Vikings, 33-17 (M)
1987—*Vikings, 44-10 (NO)
1988—Vikings, 45-3 (M)
1990—Vikings, 32-3 (M)
1991—Saints, 26-0 (NO)
1993—Saints, 17-14 (M)
1994—Vikings, 21-20 (M)
(RS Pts.—Vikings 443, Saints 255)
(PS Pts.—Vikings 44, Saints 10)
NFC First-Round Playoff

MINNESOTA vs. N.Y. GIANTS
RS: Vikings lead series, 7-4
PS: Giants lead series, 1-0
1964—Vikings, 30-21 (NY)
1965—Vikings, 40-14 (M)
1967—Vikings, 27-24 (M)
1969—Giants, 24-23 (NY)
1971—Vikings, 17-10 (NY)
1973—Vikings, 31-7 (New Haven)
1976—Vikings, 24-7 (M)
1986—Giants, 22-20 (M)
1989—Giants, 24-14 (NY)
1990—Giants, 23-15 (NY)
1993—*Giants, 17-10 (NY)
1994—Vikings, 27-10 (NY)
(RS Pts.—Vikings 268, Giants 186)
(PS Pts.—Giants 17, Vikings 10)
NFC First-Round Playoff

MINNESOTA vs. N.Y. JETS
RS: Jets lead series, 4-1
1970—Jets, 20-10 (NY)
1975—Vikings, 29-21 (M)
1979—Jets, 14-7 (NY)
1982—Jets, 42-14 (M)
1994—Jets, 31-21 (M)
(RS Pts.—Jets 128, Vikings 81)

MINNESOTA vs. PHILADELPHIA
RS: Vikings lead series, 10-6
PS: Eagles lead series, 1-0
1962—Vikings, 31-21 (M)
1963—Vikings, 34-13 (P)
1968—Vikings, 24-17 (P)
1971—Vikings, 13-0 (P)
1973—Vikings, 28-21 (M)
1976—Vikings, 31-12 (P)
1978—Vikings, 28-27 (M)
1980—Eagles, 42-7 (M)
*Eagles, 31-16 (P)
1981—Vikings, 35-23 (M)
1984—Eagles, 19-17 (P)
1985—Vikings, 28-23 (P)
Eagles, 37-35 (M)
1988—Vikings, 23-21 (M)
1989—Eagles, 10-9 (P)
1990—Eagles, 32-24 (P)
1992—Eagles, 28-17 (P)
(RS Pts.—Vikings 384, Eagles 346)
(PS Pts.—Eagles 31, Vikings 16)
NFC Divisional Playoff

MINNESOTA vs. PITTSBURGH
RS: Vikings lead series, 7-4
PS: Steelers lead series, 1-0
1962—Steelers, 39-31 (P)
1964—Vikings, 30-10 (M)
1967—Vikings, 41-27 (P)
1969—Vikings, 52-14 (M)
1972—Steelers, 23-10 (P)
1974—*Steelers, 16-6 (New Orleans)
1976—Vikings, 17-6 (M)
1980—Steelers, 23-17 (M)
1983—Vikings, 17-14 (P)
1986—Vikings, 31-7 (M)
1989—Steelers, 27-14 (P)
1992—Vikings, 6-3 (P)
(RS Pts.—Vikings 266, Steelers 193)
(PS Pts.—Steelers 16, Vikings 6)
Super Bowl IX

MINNESOTA vs. *ST. LOUIS
RS: Vikings lead series, 15-11-2
PS: Vikings lead series, 5-1
1961—Rams, 31-17 (LA)
Vikings, 42-21 (M)
1962—Vikings, 38-14 (LA)
Tie, 24-24 (M)
1963—Rams, 27-24 (LA)
Vikings, 21-13 (M)
1964—Rams, 22-13 (LA)
Vikings, 34-13 (M)
1965—Vikings, 38-35 (LA)
Vikings, 24-13 (M)
1966—Vikings, 35-7 (M)
Rams, 21-6 (LA)
1967—Rams, 39-3 (LA)
1968—Rams, 31-3 (M)
1969—Vikings, 20-13 (LA)
**Vikings, 23-20 (M)
1970—Vikings, 13-3 (M)
1972—Vikings, 45-41 (LA)
1973—Vikings, 10-9 (M)

1974—Rams, 20-17 (LA)
***Vikings, 14-10 (M)
1976—Tie, 10-10 (M) OT
***Vikings, 24-13 (M)
1977—Rams, 35-3 (LA)
****Vikings, 14-7 (LA)
1978—Rams, 34-17 (M)
****Rams, 34-10 (LA)
1979—Rams, 27-21 (LA) OT
1985—Rams, 13-10 (LA)
1987—Vikings, 21-16 (LA)
1988—*****Vikings, 28-17 (M)
1989—Vikings, 23-21 (M) OT
1991—Vikings, 20-14 (M)
1992—Vikings, 31-17 (LA)
(RS Pts.—Rams 584, Vikings 583)
(PS Pts.—Vikings 113, Rams 101)
Franchise in Los Angeles prior to 1995
***Conference Championship*
****NFC Championship*
*****NFC Divisional Playoff*
******NFC First-Round Playoff*

MINNESOTA vs. SAN DIEGO
RS: Chargers lead series, 4-3
1971—Chargers, 30-14 (SD)
1975—Vikings, 28-13 (M)
1978—Chargers, 13-7 (M)
1981—Vikings, 33-31 (SD)
1984—Chargers, 42-13 (M)
1985—Vikings, 21-17 (M)
1993—Chargers, 30-17 (M)
(RS Pts.—Chargers 176, Vikings 133)

MINNESOTA vs. SAN FRANCISCO
RS: Vikings lead series, 16-15-1
PS: 49ers lead series, 3-1
1961—49ers, 38-24 (M)
49ers, 38-28 (SF)
1962—49ers, 21-7 (SF)
49ers, 35-12 (M)
1963—Vikings, 24-20 (SF)
Vikings, 45-14 (M)
1964—Vikings, 27-22 (SF)
Vikings, 24-7 (M)
1965—Vikings, 42-41 (SF)
49ers, 45-24 (M)
1966—Tie, 20-20 (SF)
Vikings, 28-3 (SF)
1967—49ers, 27-21 (M)
1968—Vikings, 30-20 (SF)
1969—Vikings, 10-7 (M)
1970—*49ers, 17-14 (M)
1971—49ers, 13-9 (M)
1972—49ers, 20-17 (SF)
1973—Vikings, 17-13 (SF)
1975—Vikings, 27-17 (M)
1976—49ers, 20-16 (SF)
1977—Vikings, 28-27 (M)
1979—Vikings, 28-22 (M)
1983—49ers, 48-17 (M)
1984—49ers, 51-7 (SF)
1985—Vikings, 28-21 (M)
1986—Vikings, 27-24 (SF) OT
1987—*Vikings, 36-24 (SF)
1988—49ers, 24-21 (SF)
*49ers, 34-9 (SF)
1989—*49ers, 41-13 (SF)
1990—49ers, 20-17 (M)
1991—Vikings, 17-14 (M)
1992—49ers, 20-17 (M)
1993—49ers, 38-19 (SF)
1994—Vikings, 21-14 (M)
(RS Pts.—49ers 764, Vikings 699)
(PS Pts.—49ers 116, Vikings 72)
**NFC Divisional Playoff*

MINNESOTA vs. SEATTLE
RS: Seahawks lead series, 3-2
1976—Vikings, 27-21 (M)
1978—Seahawks, 29-28 (S)
1984—Seahawks, 20-12 (M)
1987—Seahawks, 28-17 (S)
1990—Vikings, 24-21 (S)
(RS Pts.—Seahawks 119, Vikings 108)

MINNESOTA vs. TAMPA BAY
RS: Vikings lead series, 24-10
1977—Vikings, 9-3 (TB)
1978—Buccaneers, 16-10 (M)
Vikings, 24-7 (TB)
1979—Buccaneers, 12-10 (M)
Vikings, 23-22 (TB)
1980—Vikings, 38-30 (M)
Vikings, 21-10 (TB)
1981—Buccaneers, 21-13 (TB)
Vikings, 25-10 (M)
1982—Vikings, 17-10 (M)
1983—Vikings, 19-16 (TB) OT
Buccaneers, 17-12 (M)
1984—Buccaneers, 35-31 (TB)
Vikings, 27-24 (M)
1985—Vikings, 31-16 (TB)
Vikings, 26-7 (M)
1986—Vikings, 23-10 (TB)
Vikings, 45-13 (M)
1987—Buccaneers, 20-10 (TB)
Vikings, 23-17 (M)
1988—Vikings, 14-13 (M)
Vikings, 49-20 (TB)
1989—Vikings, 17-3 (M)
Vikings, 24-10 (TB)
1990—Buccaneers, 23-20 (M) OT
Buccaneers, 26-13 (TB)
1991—Vikings, 28-13 (M)
Vikings, 26-24 (TB)
1992—Vikings, 26-20 (M)
Vikings, 35-7 (TB)
1993—Vikings, 15-0 (M)
Buccaneers, 23-10 (TB)
1994—Vikings, 36-13 (TB)
Buccaneers, 20-17 (M) OT
(RS Pts.—Vikings 767, Buccaneers 531)

MINNESOTA vs. WASHINGTON
RS: Redskins lead series, 6-4
PS: Redskins lead series, 3-2
1968—Vikings, 27-14 (M)
1970—Vikings, 19-10 (W)
1972—Redskins, 24-21 (M)
1973—*Vikings, 27-20 (M)
1975—Redskins, 31-30 (W)
1976—*Vikings, 35-20 (M)
1980—Vikings, 39-14 (W)
1982—**Redskins, 21-7 (W)
1984—Redskins, 31-17 (M)
1986—Redskins, 44-38 (W) OT
1987—Redskins, 27-24 (M) OT
***Redskins, 17-10 (W)
1992—Redskins, 15-13 (M)
****Redskins, 24-7 (M)
1993—Vikings, 14-9 (W)
(RS Pts.—Vikings 242, Redskins 219)
(PS Pts.—Redskins 102, Vikings 86)
**NFC Divisional Playoff*
***NFC Second-Round Playoff*
****NFC Championship*
*****NFC First-Round Playoff*

NEW ENGLAND vs. ARIZONA
RS: Cardinals lead series, 6-2;
See Arizona vs. New England

NEW ENGLAND vs. ATLANTA
RS: Falcons lead series, 4-3;
See Atlanta vs. New England

NEW ENGLAND vs. BUFFALO
RS: Series tied, 34-34-1
PS: Patriots lead series, 1-0;
See Buffalo vs. New England

NEW ENGLAND vs. CHICAGO
RS: Patriots lead series, 4-2
PS: Bears lead series, 1-0;
See Chicago vs. New England

NEW ENGLAND vs. CINCINNATI
RS: Patriots lead series, 9-7;
See Cincinnati vs. New England

NEW ENGLAND vs. CLEVELAND
RS: Browns lead series, 10-3
PS: Browns lead series, 1-0;
See Cleveland vs. New England

NEW ENGLAND vs. DALLAS
RS: Cowboys lead series, 6-0;
See Dallas vs. New England

NEW ENGLAND vs. DENVER
RS: Broncos lead series, 16-12
PS: Broncos lead series, 1-0;
See Denver vs. New England

NEW ENGLAND vs. DETROIT
RS: Series tied, 3-3;
See Detroit vs. New England

NEW ENGLAND vs. GREEN BAY
RS: Patriots lead series, 3-2;
See Green Bay vs. New England

NEW ENGLAND vs. HOUSTON
RS: Patriots lead series, 17-14-1
PS: Oilers lead series, 1-0;
See Houston vs. New England

NEW ENGLAND vs. INDIANAPOLIS
RS: Patriots lead series, 29-20;
See Indianapolis vs. New England

NEW ENGLAND vs. KANSAS CITY
RS: Chiefs lead series, 13-7-3;
See Kansas City vs. New England

NEW ENGLAND vs. LOS ANGELES
RS: Raiders lead series, 13-12-1
PS: Series tied, 1-1;
See Los Angeles vs. New England

NEW ENGLAND vs. MIAMI
RS: Dolphins lead series, 35-21
PS: Series tied, 1-1;
See Miami vs. New England

NEW ENGLAND vs. MINNESOTA
RS: Patriots lead series, 4-2;
See Minnesota vs. New England

NEW ENGLAND vs. NEW ORLEANS
RS: Patriots lead series, 5-2
1972—Patriots, 17-10 (NO)
1976—Patriots, 27-6 (NE)
1980—Patriots, 38-27 (NO)
1983—Patriots, 7-0 (NE)
1986—Patriots, 21-20 (NO)
1989—Saints, 28-24 (NE)
1992—Saints, 31-14 (NE)
(RS Pts.—Patriots 148, Saints 122)

***NEW ENGLAND vs. N.Y. GIANTS**
RS: Giants lead series, 3-1
1970—Giants, 16-0 (B)
1974—Patriots, 28-20 (New Haven)
1987—Giants, 17-10 (NY)
1990—Giants, 13-10 (NE)
(RS Pts.—Giants 66, Patriots 48)
**Franchise in Boston prior to 1971*

***NEW ENGLAND vs. **N.Y. JETS**
RS: Jets lead series, 39-29-1
PS: Patriots lead series, 1-0
1960—Patriots, 28-24 (NY)
Patriots, 38-21 (B)
1961—Titans, 21-20 (B)
Titans, 37-30 (NY)
1962—Patriots, 43-14 (NY)
Patriots, 24-17 (B)
1963—Patriots, 38-14 (B)
Jets, 31-24 (NY)
1964—Patriots, 26-10 (B)
Jets, 35-14 (NY)
1965—Jets, 30-20 (B)
Patriots, 27-23 (NY)
1966—Tie, 24-24 (B)
Jets, 38-28 (NY)
1967—Jets, 30-23 (NY)
Jets, 29-24 (B)
1968—Jets, 47-31 (Birmingham)
Jets, 48-14 (NY)
1969—Jets, 23-14 (B)
Jets, 23-17 (NY)
1970—Jets, 31-21 (B)
Jets, 17-3 (NY)
1971—Patriots, 20-0 (NE)
Jets, 13-6 (NY)
1972—Jets, 41-13 (NE)
Jets, 34-10 (NY)
1973—Jets, 9-7 (NE)
Jets, 33-13 (NY)
1974—Patriots, 24-0 (NY)
Jets, 21-16 (NE)
1975—Jets, 36-7 (NY)
Jets, 30-28 (NE)
1976—Patriots, 41-7 (NE)
Patriots, 38-24 (NY)
1977—Jets, 30-27 (NY)
Patriots, 24-13 (NE)
1978—Patriots, 55-21 (NE)
Patriots, 19-17 (NY)
1979—Patriots, 56-3 (NE)
Jets, 27-26 (NY)
1980—Patriots, 21-11 (NY)
Patriots, 34-21 (NE)
1981—Jets, 28-24 (NY)
Jets, 17-6 (NE)
1982—Jets, 31-7 (NE)
1983—Patriots, 23-13 (NE)
Jets, 26-3 (NY)
1984—Patriots, 28-21 (NY)
Patriots, 30-20 (NE)
1985—Patriots, 20-13 (NE)
Jets, 16-13 (NY) OT
***Patriots, 26-14 (NY)
1986—Patriots, 20-6 (NY)
Jets, 31-24 (NE)
1987—Jets, 43-24 (NY)
Patriots, 42-20 (NE)
1988—Patriots, 28-3 (NE)
Patriots, 14-13 (NY)
1989—Patriots, 27-24 (NY)
Jets, 27-26 (NE)
1990—Jets, 37-13 (NE)
Jets, 42-7 (NY)
1991—Jets, 28-21 (NE)
Patriots, 6-3 (NY)
1992—Jets, 30-21 (NY)
Patriots, 24-3 (NE)
1993—Jets, 45-7 (NY)
Jets, 6-0 (NE)
1994—Jets, 24-17 (NY)
Patriots, 24-13 (NE)
(RS Pts.—Jets 1,561, Patriots 1,515)
(PS Pts.—Patriots 26, Jets 14)
**Franchise in Boston prior to 1971*
***Jets known as Titans prior to 1963*
****AFC First-Round Playoff*

NEW ENGLAND vs. PHILADELPHIA
RS: Eagles lead series, 5-2
1973—Eagles, 24-23 (P)
1977—Patriots, 14-6 (NE)
1978—Patriots, 24-14 (NE)
1981—Eagles, 13-3 (P)
1984—Eagles, 27-17 (P)
1987—Eagles, 34-31 (NE) OT
1990—Eagles, 48-20 (P)
(RS Pts.—Eagles 166, Patriots 132)

NEW ENGLAND vs. PITTSBURGH
RS: Steelers lead series, 9-3
1972—Steelers, 33-3 (P)
1974—Steelers, 21-17 (NE)
1976—Patriots, 30-27 (P)
1979—Steelers, 16-13 (NE) OT
1981—Steelers, 27-21 (P) OT
1982—Steelers, 37-14 (P)
1983—Patriots, 28-23 (P)
1986—Patriots, 34-0 (P)
1989—Steelers, 28-10 (P)
1990—Steelers, 24-3 (P)
1991—Steelers, 20-6 (P)
1993—Steelers, 17-14 (P)
(RS Pts.—Steelers 273, Patriots 193)

NEW ENGLAND vs. *ST. LOUIS
RS: Series tied, 3-3
1974—Patriots, 20-14 (NE)
1980—Rams, 17-14 (NE)
1983—Patriots, 21-7 (LA)
1986—Patriots, 30-28 (LA)
1989—Rams, 24-20 (NE)
1992—Rams, 14-0 (LA)
(RS Pts.—Patriots 105, Rams 104)
**Franchise in Los Angeles prior to 1995*

***NEW ENGLAND vs. **SAN DIEGO**
RS: Patriots lead series, 14-11-2

ALL-TIME TEAM VS. TEAM RESULTS

PS: Chargers lead series, 1-0
1960—Patriots, 35-0 (LA)
Chargers, 45-16 (B)
1961—Chargers, 38-27 (B)
Patriots, 41-0 (SD)
1962—Patriots, 24-20 (B)
Patriots, 20-14 (SD)
1963—Chargers, 17-13 (SD)
Chargers, 7-6 (B)
***Chargers, 51-10 (SD)
1964—Patriots, 33-28 (SD)
Chargers, 26-17 (B)
1965—Tie, 10-10 (B)
Patriots, 22-6 (SD)
1966—Chargers, 24-0 (SD)
Patriots, 35-17 (B)
1967—Chargers, 28-14 (SD)
Tie, 31-31 (SD)
1968—Chargers, 27-17 (B)
1969—Chargers, 13-10 (B)
Chargers, 28-18 (SD)
1970—Chargers, 16-14 (B)
1973—Patriots, 30-14 (NE)
1975—Patriots, 33-19 (SD)
1977—Patriots, 24-20 (SD)
1978—Patriots, 28-23 (NE)
1979—Patriots, 27-21 (NE)
1983—Patriots, 37-21 (NE)
1994—Patriots, 23-17 (NE)
(RS Pts.—Patriots 605, Chargers 530)
(PS Pts.—Chargers 51, Patriots 10)
Franchise in Boston prior to 1971
**Franchise in Los Angeles prior to 1961*
***AFL Championship*

NEW ENGLAND vs. SAN FRANCISCO
RS: 49ers lead series, 6-1
1971—49ers, 27-10 (SF)
1975—Patriots, 24-16 (NE)
1980—49ers, 21-17 (SF)
1983—49ers, 33-13 (NE)
1986—49ers, 29-24 (NE)
1989—49ers, 37-20 (SF)
1992—49ers, 24-12 (NE)
(RS Pts.—49ers 187, Patriots 120)

NEW ENGLAND vs. SEATTLE
RS: Seahawks lead series, 7-6
1977—Patriots, 31-0 (NE)
1980—Patriots, 37-31 (S)
1982—Patriots, 16-0 (S)
1983—Seahawks, 24-6 (S)
1984—Patriots, 38-23 (NE)
1985—Patriots, 20-13 (S)
1986—Seahawks, 38-31 (NE)
1988—Patriots, 13-7 (NE)
1989—Seahawks, 24-3 (NE)
1990—Seahawks, 33-20 (NE)
1992—Seahawks, 10-6 (NE)
1993—Seahawks, 17-14 (NE)
Seahawks, 10-9 (S)
(RS Pts.—Patriots 244, Seahawks 230)

NEW ENGLAND vs. TAMPA BAY
RS: Patriots lead series, 3-0
1976—Patriots, 31-14 (TB)
1985—Patriots, 32-14 (TB)
1988—Patriots, 10-7 (NE) OT
(RS Pts.—Patriots 73, Buccaneers 35)

NEW ENGLAND vs. WASHINGTON
RS: Redskins lead series, 4-1
1972—Patriots, 24-23 (NE)
1978—Redskins, 16-14 (NE)
1981—Redskins, 24-22 (W)
1984—Redskins, 26-10 (NE)
1990—Redskins, 25-10 (NE)
(RS Pts.—Redskins 114, Patriots 80)

NEW ORLEANS vs. ARIZONA
RS: Cardinals lead series, 10-9;
See Arizona vs. New Orleans

NEW ORLEANS vs. ATLANTA
RS: Falcons lead series, 27-24
PS: Falcons lead series, 1-0;
See Atlanta vs. New Orleans

NEW ORLEANS vs. BUFFALO
RS: Bills lead series, 3-2;
See Buffalo vs. New Orleans

NEW ORLEANS vs. CHICAGO
RS: Bears lead series, 9-6
PS: Bears lead series, 1-0;
See Chicago vs. New Orleans

NEW ORLEANS vs. CINCINNATI
RS: Saints lead series, 5-3;
See Cincinnati vs. New Orleans

NEW ORLEANS vs. CLEVELAND
RS: Browns lead series, 9-3;
See Cleveland vs. New Orleans

NEW ORLEANS vs. DALLAS
RS: Cowboys lead series, 14-3;
See Dallas vs. New Orleans

NEW ORLEANS vs. DENVER
RS: Broncos lead series, 4-2;
See Denver vs. New Orleans

NEW ORLEANS vs. DETROIT
RS: Saints lead series, 7-6-1;
See Detroit vs. New Orleans

NEW ORLEANS vs. GREEN BAY
RS: Packers lead series, 12-4;
See Green Bay vs. New Orleans

NEW ORLEANS vs. HOUSTON
RS: Saints lead series, 4-3-1;
See Houston vs. New Orleans

NEW ORLEANS vs. INDIANAPOLIS
RS: Colts lead series, 3-2;
See Indianapolis vs. New Orleans

NEW ORLEANS vs. KANSAS CITY
RS: Series tied, 3-3;
See Kansas City vs. New Orleans

NEW ORLEANS vs. LOS ANGELES
RS: Raiders lead series, 4-2-1;
See Los Angeles vs. New Orleans

NEW ORLEANS vs. MIAMI
RS: Dolphins lead series, 4-2;
See Miami vs. New Orleans

NEW ORLEANS vs. MINNESOTA
RS: Vikings lead series, 12-6
PS: Vikings lead series, 1-0;
See Minnesota vs. New Orleans

NEW ORLEANS vs. NEW ENGLAND
RS: Patriots lead series, 5-2;
See New England vs. New Orleans

NEW ORLEANS vs. N.Y. GIANTS
RS: Giants lead series, 9-7
1967—Giants, 27-21 (NY)
1968—Giants, 38-21 (NY)
1969—Saints, 25-24 (NY)
1970—Saints, 14-10 (NO)
1972—Giants, 45-21 (NY)
1975—Giants, 28-14 (NY)
1978—Saints, 28-17 (NO)
1979—Saints, 24-14 (NO)
1981—Giants, 20-7 (NY)
1984—Saints, 10-3 (NY)
1985—Giants, 21-13 (NO)
1986—Giants, 20-17 (NY)
1987—Saints, 23-14 (NO)
1988—Giants, 13-12 (NO)
1993—Giants, 24-14 (NO)
1994—Saints, 27-22 (NO)
(RS Pts.—Giants 340, Saints 291)

NEW ORLEANS vs. N.Y. JETS
RS: Jets lead series, 4-3
1972—Jets, 18-17 (NY)
1977—Jets, 16-13 (NO)
1980—Saints, 21-20 (NY)
1983—Jets, 31-28 (NO)
1986—Jets, 28-23 (NY)
1989—Saints, 29-14 (NO)
1992—Saints, 20-0 (NY)
(RS Pts.—Saints 151, Jets 127)

NEW ORLEANS vs. PHILADELPHIA
RS: Eagles lead series, 11-8
PS: Eagles lead series, 1-0
1967—Saints, 31-24 (NO)
Eagles, 48-21 (P)
1968—Eagles, 29-17 (P)
1969—Eagles, 13-10 (P)
Saints, 26-17 (NO)
1972—Saints, 21-3 (NO)
1974—Saints, 14-10 (NO)
1977—Eagles, 28-7 (P)
1978—Eagles, 24-17 (NO)
1979—Eagles, 26-14 (NO)
1980—Eagles, 34-21 (NO)
1981—Eagles, 31-14 (NO)
1983—Saints, 20-17 (P) OT
1985—Saints, 23-21 (NO)
1987—Eagles, 27-17 (P)
1989—Saints, 30-20 (NO)
1991—Saints, 13-6 (P)
1992—Eagles, 15-13 (P)
*Eagles, 36-20 (NO)
1993—Eagles, 37-26 (P)
(RS Pts.—Eagles 430, Saints 355)
(PS Pts.—Eagles 36, Saints 20)
NFC First-Round Playoff

NEW ORLEANS vs. PITTSBURGH
RS: Steelers lead series, 6-5
1967—Steelers, 14-10 (NO)
1968—Saints, 16-12 (P)
Saints, 24-14 (NO)
1969—Saints, 27-24 (NO)
1974—Steelers, 28-7 (NO)
1978—Steelers, 20-14 (P)
1981—Steelers, 20-6 (NO)
1984—Saints, 27-24 (NO)
1987—Saints, 20-16 (P)
1990—Steelers, 9-6 (NO)
1993—Steelers, 37-14 (P)
(RS Pts.—Steelers 218, Saints 171)

NEW ORLEANS vs. *ST. LOUIS
RS: Rams lead series, 27-23
1967—Rams, 27-13 (NO)
1969—Rams, 36-17 (LA)
1970—Rams, 30-17 (NO)
Rams, 34-16 (LA)
1971—Saints, 24-20 (NO)
Rams, 45-28 (LA)
1972—Rams, 34-14 (LA)
Saints, 19-16 (NO)
1973—Rams, 29-7 (LA)
Rams, 24-13 (NO)
1974—Rams, 24-0 (LA)
Saints, 20-7 (NO)
1975—Rams, 38-14 (LA)
Rams, 14-7 (NO)
1976—Rams, 16-10 (NO)
Rams, 33-14 (LA)
1977—Rams, 14-7 (LA)
Saints, 27-26 (NO)
1978—Rams, 26-20 (NO)
Saints, 10-3 (LA)
1979—Rams, 35-17 (NO)
Saints, 29-14 (LA)
1980—Rams, 45-31 (LA)
Rams, 27-7 (NO)
1981—Saints, 23-17 (NO)
Saints, 21-13 (LA)
1983—Rams, 30-27 (LA)
Rams, 26-24 (NO)
1984—Rams, 28-10 (NO)
Rams, 34-21 (LA)
1985—Rams, 28-10 (LA)
Saints, 29-3 (NO)
1986—Saints, 6-0 (NO)
Rams, 26-13 (LA)
1987—Saints, 37-10 (NO)
Saints, 31-14 (LA)
1988—Rams, 12-10 (NO)
Saints, 14-10 (LA)
1989—Saints, 40-21 (LA)
Rams, 20-17 (NO) OT
1990—Saints, 24-20 (LA)
Saints, 20-17 (NO)
1991—Saints, 24-7 (NO)
Saints, 24-17 (LA)
1992—Saints, 13-10 (NO)
Saints, 37-14 (LA)
1993—Saints, 37-6 (LA)
Rams, 23-20 (NO)
1994—Saints, 37-34 (NO)
Saints, 31-15 (LA)
(RS Pts.—Rams 1,072, Saints 981)
Franchise in Los Angeles prior to 1995

NEW ORLEANS vs. SAN DIEGO
RS: Chargers lead series, 5-1
1973—Chargers, 17-14 (SD)
1977—Chargers, 14-0 (NO)
1979—Chargers, 35-0 (NO)
1988—Saints, 23-17 (SD)
1991—Chargers, 24-21 (SD)
1994—Chargers, 36-22 (NO)
(RS Pts.—Chargers 143, Saints 80)

NEW ORLEANS vs. SAN FRANCISCO
RS: 49ers lead series, 35-14-2
1967—49ers, 27-13 (SF)
1969—Saints, 43-38 (NO)
1970—Tie, 20-20 (SF)
49ers, 38-27 (NO)
1971—49ers, 38-20 (NO)
Saints, 26-20 (SF)
1972—49ers, 37-2 (NO)
Tie, 20-20 (SF)
1973—49ers, 40-0 (SF)
Saints, 16-10 (NO)
1974—49ers, 17-13 (NO)
49ers, 35-21 (SF)
1975—49ers, 35-21 (SF)
49ers, 16-6 (NO)
1976—49ers, 33-3 (SF)
49ers, 27-7 (NO)
1977—49ers, 10-7 (NO) OT
49ers, 20-17 (SF)
1978—Saints, 14-7 (SF)
Saints, 24-13 (NO)
1979—Saints, 30-21 (SF)
Saints, 31-20 (NO)
1980—49ers, 26-23 (NO)
49ers, 38-35 (SF) OT
1981—49ers, 21-14 (SF)
49ers, 21-17 (NO)
1982—Saints, 23-20 (SF)
1983—49ers, 32-13 (NO)
49ers, 27-0 (SF)
1984—49ers, 30-20 (SF)
49ers, 35-3 (NO)
1985—Saints, 20-17 (SF)
49ers, 31-19 (NO)
1986—49ers, 26-17 (SF)
Saints, 23-10 (NO)
1987—49ers, 24-22 (NO)
Saints, 26-24 (SF)
1988—49ers, 34-33 (NO)
49ers, 30-17 (SF)
1989—49ers, 24-20 (NO)
49ers, 31-13 (SF)
1990—49ers, 13-12 (NO)
Saints, 13-10 (SF)
1991—Saints, 10-3 (NO)
49ers, 38-24 (SF)
1992—49ers, 16-10 (NO)
49ers, 21-20 (SF)
1993—Saints, 16-13 (NO)
49ers, 42-7 (SF)
1994—49ers, 24-13 (SF)
49ers, 35-14 (NO)
(RS Pts.—49ers, 1,258, Saints 878)

NEW ORLEANS vs. SEATTLE
RS: Saints lead series, 3-2
1976—Saints, 51-27 (S)
1979—Seahawks, 38-24 (S)
1985—Seahawks, 27-3 (NO)
1988—Saints, 20-19 (S)
1991—Saints, 27-24 (NO)
(RS Pts.—Seahawks 135, Saints 125)

NEW ORLEANS vs. TAMPA BAY
RS: Saints lead series, 12-4
1977—Buccaneers, 33-14 (NO)
1978—Saints, 17-10 (TB)
1979—Saints, 42-14 (TB)
1981—Buccaneers, 31-14 (NO)
1982—Buccaneers, 13-10 (NO)
1983—Saints, 24-21 (TB)
1984—Saints, 17-13 (NO)

1985—Saints, 20-13 (NO)
1986—Saints, 38-7 (NO)
1987—Saints, 44-34 (NO)
1988—Saints, 13-9 (NO)
1989—Buccaneers, 20-10 (TB)
1990—Saints, 35-7 (NO)
1991—Saints, 23-7 (NO)
1992—Saints, 23-21 (NO)
1994—Saints, 9-7, (TB)
(RS Pts.—Saints 353, Buccaneers 260)

NEW ORLEANS vs. WASHINGTON
RS: Redskins lead series, 12-5
1967—Redskins, 30-10 (NO)
Saints, 30-14 (W)
1968—Saints, 37-17 (NO)
1969—Redskins, 26-20 (NO)
Redskins, 17-14 (W)
1971—Redskins, 24-14 (W)
1973—Saints, 19-3 (NO)
1975—Redskins, 41-3 (W)
1979—Saints, 14-10 (W)
1980—Redskins, 22-14 (W)
1982—Redskins, 27-10 (NO)
1986—Redskins, 14-6 (NO)
1988—Redskins, 27-24 (W)
1989—Redskins, 16-14 (NO)
1990—Redskins, 31-17 (W)
1992—Saints, 20-3 (NO)
1994—Redskins, 38-24 (NO)
(RS Pts.—Redskins 360, Saints 290)

N.Y. GIANTS vs. ARIZONA
RS: Giants lead series, 66-36-2;
See Arizona vs. N.Y. Giants

N.Y. GIANTS vs. ATLANTA
RS: Series tied, 6-6;
See Atlanta vs. N.Y. Giants

N.Y. GIANTS vs. BUFFALO
RS: Bills lead series, 4-2
PS: Giants lead series, 1-0;
See Buffalo vs. N.Y. Giants

N.Y. GIANTS vs. CHICAGO
RS: Bears lead series, 24-16-2
PS: Bears lead series, 5-3;
See Chicago vs. N.Y. Giants

N.Y. GIANTS vs. CINCINNATI
RS: Bengals lead series, 4-1;
See Cincinnati vs. N.Y. Giants

N.Y. GIANTS vs. CLEVELAND
RS: Browns lead series, 25-17-2
PS: Series tied, 1-1;
See Cleveland vs. N.Y. Giants

N.Y. GIANTS vs. DALLAS
RS: Cowboys lead series, 41-22-2;
See Dallas vs. N.Y. Giants

N.Y. GIANTS vs. DENVER
RS: Series tied, 3-3
PS: Giants lead series, 1-0;
See Denver vs. N.Y. Giants

N.Y. GIANTS vs. DETROIT
RS: Lions lead series, 18-15-1
PS: Lions lead series, 1-0;
See Detroit vs. N.Y. Giants

N.Y. GIANTS vs. GREEN BAY
RS: Packers lead series, 21-20-2
PS: Packers lead series, 4-1;
See Green Bay vs. N.Y. Giants

N.Y. GIANTS vs. HOUSTON
RS: Giants lead series, 5-0;
See Houston vs. N.Y. Giants

N.Y. GIANTS vs. INDIANAPOLIS
RS: Series tied, 5-5
PS: Colts lead series, 2-0;
See Indianapolis vs. N.Y. Giants

N.Y. GIANTS vs. KANSAS CITY
RS: Giants lead series, 6-1;
See Kansas City vs. N.Y. Giants

N.Y. GIANTS vs. LOS ANGELES
RS: Raiders lead series, 4-2;
See Los Angeles vs. N.Y. Giants

N.Y. GIANTS vs. MIAMI
RS: Giants lead series, 2-1;
See Miami vs. N.Y. Giants

N.Y. GIANTS vs. MINNESOTA
RS: Vikings lead series, 7-4
PS: Giants lead series, 1-0;
See Minnesota vs. N.Y. Giants

N.Y. GIANTS vs. NEW ENGLAND
RS: Giants lead series, 3-1;
See New England vs. N.Y. Giants

N.Y. GIANTS vs. NEW ORLEANS
RS: Giants lead series, 9-7;
See New Orleans vs. N.Y. Giants

N.Y. GIANTS vs. N.Y. JETS
RS: Jets lead series, 4-3
1970—Giants, 22-10 (NYJ)
1974—Jets, 26-20 (New Haven) OT
1981—Jets, 26-7 (NYG)
1984—Giants, 20-10 (NYJ)
1987—Giants, 20-7 (NYG)
1988—Jets, 27-21 (NYJ)
1993—Jets, 10-6 (NYG)
(RS Pts.—Giants 116, Jets 116)

N.Y. GIANTS vs. PHILADELPHIA
RS: Giants lead series, 64-54-2
PS: Giants lead series, 1-0
1933—Giants, 56-0 (NY)
Giants, 20-14 (P)
1934—Giants, 17-0 (NY)
Eagles, 6-0 (P)
1935—Giants, 10-0 (NY)
Giants, 21-14 (P)
1936—Eagles, 10-7 (P)
Giants, 21-17 (NY)
1937—Giants, 16-7 (P)
Giants, 21-0 (NY)
1938—Eagles, 14-10 (P)
Giants, 17-7 (NY)
1939—Giants, 13-3 (P)
Giants, 27-10 (NY)
1940—Giants, 20-14 (P)
Giants, 17-7 (NY)
1941—Giants, 24-0 (P)
Giants, 16-0 (NY)
1942—Giants, 35-17 (NY)
Giants, 14-0 (P)
1944—Eagles, 24-17 (NY)
Tie, 21-21 (P)
1945—Eagles, 38-17 (P)
Giants, 28-21 (NY)
1946—Eagles, 24-14 (P)
Giants, 45-17 (NY)
1947—Eagles, 23-0 (P)
Eagles, 41-24 (NY)
1948—Eagles, 45-0 (P)
Eagles, 35-14 (NY)
1949—Eagles, 24-3 (NY)
Eagles, 17-3 (P)
1950—Giants, 7-3 (NY)
Giants, 9-7 (P)
1951—Giants, 26-24 (NY)
Giants, 23-7 (P)
1952—Giants, 31-7 (P)
Eagles, 14-10 (NY)
1953—Eagles, 30-7 (P)
Giants, 37-28 (NY)
1954—Giants, 27-14 (NY)
Eagles, 29-14 (P)
1955—Eagles, 27-17 (P)
Giants, 31-7 (NY)
1956—Giants, 20-3 (NY)
Giants, 21-7 (P)
1957—Giants, 24-20 (P)
Giants, 13-0 (NY)
1958—Eagles, 27-24 (P)
Giants, 24-10 (NY)
1959—Eagles, 49-21 (P)
Giants, 24-7 (NY)
1960—Eagles, 17-10 (NY)
Eagles, 31-23 (P)
1961—Giants, 38-21 (NY)
Giants, 28-24 (P)
1962—Giants, 29-13 (P)
Giants, 19-14 (NY)
1963—Giants, 37-14 (P)
Giants, 42-14 (NY)
1964—Eagles, 38-7 (P)
Eagles, 23-17 (NY)
1965—Giants, 16-14 (P)
Giants, 35-27 (NY)
1966—Eagles, 35-17 (P)
Eagles, 31-3 (NY)
1967—Giants, 44-7 (NY)
1968—Giants, 34-25 (P)
Giants, 7-6 (NY)
1969—Eagles, 23-20 (NY)
1970—Giants, 30-23 (NY)
Eagles, 23-20 (P)
1971—Eagles, 23-7 (P)
Eagles, 41-28 (NY)
1972—Giants, 27-12 (P)
Giants, 62-10 (NY)
1973—Tie, 23-23 (NY)
Eagles, 20-16 (P)
1974—Eagles, 35-7 (P)
Eagles, 20-7 (New Haven)
1975—Giants, 23-14 (P)
Eagles, 13-10 (NY)
1976—Eagles, 20-7 (P)
Eagles, 10-0 (NY)
1977—Eagles, 28-10 (NY)
Eagles, 17-14 (P)
1978—Eagles, 19-17 (NY)
Eagles, 20-3 (P)
1979—Eagles, 23-17 (P)
Eagles, 17-13 (NY)
1980—Eagles, 35-3 (P)
Eagles, 31-16 (NY)
1981—Eagles, 24-10 (NY)
Giants, 20-10 (P)
*Giants, 27-21 (P)
1982—Giants, 23-7 (NY)
Giants, 26-24 (P)
1983—Eagles, 17-13 (NY)
Giants, 23-0 (P)
1984—Giants, 28-27 (NY)
Eagles, 24-10 (P)
1985—Giants, 21-0 (NY)
Giants, 16-10 (P) OT
1986—Giants, 35-3 (NY)
Giants, 17-14 (P)
1987—Giants, 20-17 (P)
Giants, 23-20 (NY) OT
1988—Eagles, 24-13 (P)
Eagles, 23-17 (NY) OT
1989—Eagles, 21-19 (P)
Eagles, 24-17 (NY)
1990—Giants, 27-20 (NY)
Eagles, 31-13 (P)
1991—Eagles, 30-7 (P)
Eagles, 19-14 (NY)
1992—Eagles, 47-34 (NY)
Eagles, 20-10 (P)
1993—Giants, 21-10 (NY)
Giants, 7-3 (P)
1994—Giants, 28-23 (NY)
Giants, 16-13 (P)
(RS Pts.—Giants 2,292, Eagles 2,149)
(PS Pts.—Giants 27, Eagles 21)
NFC First-Round Playoff

N.Y. GIANTS vs. *PITTSBURGH
RS: Giants lead series, 42-27-3
1933—Giants, 23-2 (P)
Giants, 27-3 (NY)
1934—Giants, 14-12 (P)
Giants, 17-7 (NY)
1935—Giants, 42-7 (P)
Giants, 13-0 (NY)
1936—Pirates, 10-7 (P)
1937—Giants, 10-7 (P)
Giants, 17-0 (NY)
1938—Giants, 27-14 (P)
Pirates, 13-10 (NY)
1939—Giants, 14-7 (P)
Giants, 23-7 (NY)
1940—Tie, 10-10 (P)
Giants, 12-0 (NY)
1941—Giants, 37-10 (P)
Giants, 28-7 (NY)
1942—Steelers, 13-10 (P)
Steelers, 17-9 (NY)
1945—Giants, 34-6 (P)
Steelers, 21-7 (NY)
1946—Giants, 17-14 (P)
Giants, 7-0 (NY)
1947—Steelers, 38-21 (NY)
Steelers, 24-7 (P)
1948—Giants, 34-27 (NY)
Steelers, 38-28 (P)
1949—Steelers, 28-7 (P)
Steelers, 21-17 (NY)
1950—Giants, 18-7 (P)
Steelers, 17-6 (NY)
1951—Tie, 13-13 (P)
Giants, 14-0 (NY)
1952—Steelers, 63-7 (P)
1953—Steelers, 24-14 (P)
Steelers, 14-10 (NY)
1954—Giants, 30-6 (P)
Giants, 24-3 (NY)
1955—Steelers, 30-23 (P)
Steelers, 19-17 (NY)
1956—Giants, 38-10 (NY)
Giants, 17-14 (P)
1957—Giants, 35-0 (NY)
Steelers, 21-10 (P)
1958—Giants, 17-6 (NY)
Steelers, 31-10 (P)
1959—Giants, 21-16 (P)
Steelers, 14-9 (NY)
1960—Giants, 19-17 (P)
Giants, 27-24 (NY)
1961—Giants, 17-14 (P)
Giants, 42-21 (NY)
1962—Giants, 31-27 (P)
Steelers, 20-17 (NY)
1963—Steelers, 31-0 (P)
Giants, 33-17 (NY)
1964—Steelers, 27-24 (P)
Steelers, 44-17 (NY)
1965—Giants, 23-13 (P)
Giants, 35-10 (NY)
1966—Tie, 34-34 (P)
Steelers, 47-28 (NY)
1967—Giants, 27-24 (P)
Giants, 28-20 (NY)
1968—Giants, 34-20 (P)
1969—Giants, 10-7 (NY)
Giants, 21-17 (P)
1971—Steelers, 17-13 (P)
1976—Steelers, 27-0 (NY)
1985—Giants, 28-10 (NY)
1991—Giants, 23-20 (P)
1994—Steelers, 10-6 (NY)
(RS Pts.—Giants 1,399, Steelers 1,189)
Steelers known as Pirates prior to 1941

N.Y. GIANTS vs. *ST. LOUIS
RS: Rams lead series, 21-9
PS: Series tied, 1-1
1938—Giants, 28-0 (NY)
1940—Rams, 13-0 (NY)
1941—Giants, 49-14 (NY)
1945—Rams, 21-17 (NY)
1946—Rams, 31-21 (NY)
1947—Rams, 34-10 (LA)
1948—Rams, 52-37 (NY)
1953—Rams, 21-7 (LA)
1954—Rams, 17-16 (NY)
1959—Giants, 23-21 (LA)
1961—Giants, 24-14 (NY)
1966—Rams, 55-14 (LA)
1968—Rams, 24-21 (LA)
1970—Rams, 31-3 (NY)
1973—Rams, 40-6 (LA)
1976—Rams, 24-10 (LA)
1978—Rams, 20-17 (NY)
1979—Giants, 20-14 (LA)
1980—Rams, 28-7 (NY)
1981—Giants, 10-7 (NY)
1983—Rams, 16-6 (NY)
1984—Rams, 33-12 (LA)
**Giants, 16-13 (LA)

ALL-TIME TEAM VS. TEAM RESULTS

1985—Giants, 24-19 (NY)
1988—Rams, 45-31 (NY)
1989—Rams, 31-10 (LA)
***Rams, 19-13 (NY) OT
1990—Giants, 31-7 (LA)
1991—Rams, 19-13 (NY)
1992—Rams, 38-17 (LA)
1993—Giants, 20-10 (NY)
1994—Rams, 17-10 (LA)
(RS Pts.—Rams 716, Giants 514)
(PS Pts.—Rams 32, Giants 29)
Franchise in Los Angeles prior to 1995 and in Cleveland prior to 1946
***NFC First-Round Playoff*
****NFC Divisional Playoff*

N.Y. GIANTS vs. SAN DIEGO
RS: Giants lead series, 4-2
1971—Giants, 35-17 (NY)
1975—Giants, 35-24 (NY)
1980—Chargers, 44-7 (SD)
1983—Chargers, 41-34 (NY)
1986—Giants, 20-7 (NY)
1989—Giants, 20-13 (SD)
(RS Pts.—Giants 151, Chargers 146)

N.Y. GIANTS vs. SAN FRANCISCO
RS: Giants lead series, 11-10
PS: Series tied, 3-3
1952—Giants, 23-14 (NY)
1956—Giants, 38-21 (SF)
1957—49ers, 27-17 (NY)
1960—Giants, 21-19 (SF)
1963—Giants, 48-14 (NY)
1968—49ers, 26-10 (NY)
1972—Giants, 23-17 (SF)
1975—Giants, 26-23 (SF)
1977—Giants, 20-17 (NY)
1978—Giants, 27-10 (NY)
1979—Giants, 32-16 (NY)
1980—49ers, 12-0 (SF)
1981—49ers, 17-10 (SF)
*49ers, 38-24 (SF)
1984—49ers, 31-10 (NY)
*49ers, 21-10 (SF)
1985—**Giants, 17-3 (NY)
1986—Giants, 21-17 (SF)
*Giants, 49-3 (NY)
1987—49ers, 41-21 (NY)
1988—49ers, 20-17 (NY)
1989—49ers, 34-24 (SF)
1990—49ers, 7-3 (SF)
***Giants, 15-13 (SF)
1991—Giants, 16-14 (NY)
1992—49ers, 31-14 (NY)
1993—*49ers, 44-3 (SF)
(RS Pts.—49ers 431, Giants 421)
(PS Pts.—49ers 119, Giants 118)
**NFC Divisional Playoff*
***NFC First-Round Playoff*
****NFC Championship*

N.Y. GIANTS vs. SEATTLE
RS: Giants lead series, 5-2
1976—Giants, 28-16 (NY)
1980—Giants, 27-21 (S)
1981—Giants, 32-0 (S)
1983—Seahawks, 17-12 (NY)
1986—Seahawks, 17-12 (S)
1989—Giants, 15-3 (NY)
1992—Giants, 23-10 (NY)
(RS Pts.—Giants 149, Seahawks 84)

N.Y. GIANTS vs. TAMPA BAY
RS: Giants lead series, 8-3
1977—Giants, 10-0 (TB)
1978—Giants, 19-13 (TB)
Giants, 17-14 (NY)
1979—Giants, 17-14 (NY)
Buccaneers, 31-3 (TB)
1980—Buccaneers, 30-13 (TB)
1984—Giants, 17-14 (NY)
Buccaneers, 20-17 (TB)
1985—Giants, 22-20 (NY)
1991—Giants, 21-14 (TB)
1993—Giants, 23-7 (NY)
(RS Pts.—Giants 179, Buccaneers 177)

N.Y. GIANTS vs. *WASHINGTON
RS: Giants lead series, 71-50-3
PS: Series tied, 1-1
1932—Braves, 14-6 (B)
Tie, 0-0 (NY)
1933—Redskins, 21-20 (B)
Giants, 7-0 (NY)
1934—Giants, 16-13 (B)
Giants, 3-0 (NY)
1935—Giants, 20-12 (B)
Giants, 17-6 (NY)
1936—Giants, 7-0 (B)
Redskins, 14-0 (NY)
1937—Redskins, 13-3 (W)
Redskins, 49-14 (NY)
1938—Giants, 10-7 (W)
Giants, 36-0 (NY)
1939—Tie, 0-0 (W)
Giants, 9-7 (NY)
1940—Redskins, 21-7 (W)
Giants, 21-7 (NY)
1941—Giants, 17-10 (W)
Giants, 20-13 (NY)
1942—Giants, 14-7 (W)
Redskins, 14-7 (NY)
1943—Giants, 14-10 (NY)
Giants, 31-7 (W)
**Redskins, 28-0 (NY)
1944—Giants, 16-13 (NY)
Giants, 31-0 (W)
1945—Redskins, 24-14 (NY)
Redskins, 17-0 (W)
1946—Redskins, 24-14 (W)
Giants, 31-0 (NY)
1947—Redskins, 28-20 (W)
Giants, 35-10 (NY)
1948—Redskins, 41-10 (W)
Redskins, 28-21 (NY)
1949—Giants, 45-35 (W)
Giants, 23-7 (NY)
1950—Giants, 21-17 (W)
Giants, 24-21 (NY)
1951—Giants, 35-14 (W)
Giants, 28-14 (NY)
1952—Giants, 14-10 (W)
Redskins, 27-17 (NY)
1953—Redskins, 13-9 (W)
Redskins, 24-21 (NY)
1954—Giants, 51-21 (W)
Giants, 24-7 (NY)
1955—Giants, 35-7 (NY)
Giants, 27-20 (W)
1956—Redskins, 33-7 (W)
Giants, 28-14 (NY)
1957—Giants, 24-20 (W)
Redskins, 31-14 (NY)
1958—Giants, 21-14 (W)
Giants, 30-0 (NY)
1959—Giants, 45-14 (NY)
Giants, 24-10 (W)
1960—Tie, 24-24 (NY)
Giants, 17-3 (W)
1961—Giants, 24-21 (W)
Giants, 53-0 (NY)
1962—Giants, 49-34 (NY)
Giants, 42-24 (W)
1963—Giants, 24-14 (W)
Giants, 44-14 (NY)
1964—Giants, 13-10 (NY)
Redskins, 36-21 (W)
1965—Redskins, 23-7 (NY)
Giants, 27-10 (W)
1966—Giants, 13-10 (NY)
Redskins, 72-41 (W)
1967—Redskins, 38-34 (W)
1968—Giants, 48-21 (NY)
Giants, 13-10 (W)
1969—Redskins, 20-14 (W)
1970—Giants, 35-33 (NY)
Giants, 27-24 (W)
1971—Redskins, 30-3 (NY)
Redskins, 23-7 (W)
1972—Redskins, 23-16 (NY)
Redskins, 27-13 (W)
1973—Redskins, 21-3 (New Haven)
Redskins, 27-24 (W)
1974—Redskins, 13-10 (New Haven)
Redskins, 24-3 (W)
1975—Redskins, 49-13 (W)
Redskins, 21-13 (NY)
1976—Redskins, 19-17 (W)
Giants, 12-9 (NY)
1977—Giants, 20-17 (NY)
Giants, 17-6 (W)
1978—Giants, 17-6 (NY)
Redskins, 16-13 (W) OT
1979—Redskins, 27-0 (W)
Giants, 14-6 (NY)
1980—Redskins, 23-21 (NY)
Redskins, 16-13 (W)
1981—Giants, 17-7 (W)
Redskins, 30-27 (NY) OT
1982—Redskins, 27-17 (NY)
Redskins, 15-14 (W)
1983—Redskins, 33-17 (NY)
Redskins, 31-22 (W)
1984—Redskins, 30-14 (W)
Giants, 37-13 (NY)
1985—Giants, 17-3 (NY)
Redskins, 23-21 (W)
1986—Giants, 27-20 (NY)
Giants, 24-14 (W)
***Giants, 17-0 (NY)
1987—Redskins, 38-12 (NY)
Redskins, 23-19 (W)
1988—Giants, 27-20 (NY)
Giants, 24-23 (W)
1989—Giants, 27-24 (W)
Giants, 20-17 (NY)
1990—Giants, 24-20 (W)
Giants, 21-10 (NY)
1991—Redskins, 17-13 (NY)
Redskins, 34-17 (W)
1992—Giants, 24-7 (W)
Redskins, 28-10 (NY)
1993—Giants, 41-7 (W)
Giants, 20-6 (NY)
1994—Giants, 31-23 (NY)
Giants, 21-19 (W)
(RS Pts.—Giants 2,482, Redskins 2,209)
(PS Pts.—Redskins 28, Giants 17)
**Franchise in Boston prior to 1937 and known as Braves prior to 1933*
***Division Playoff*
****NFC Championship*

N.Y. JETS vs. ARIZONA
RS: Cardinals lead series, 2-1;
See Arizona vs. N.Y. Jets

N.Y. JETS vs. ATLANTA
RS: Series tied, 3-3;
See Atlanta vs. N.Y. Jets

N.Y. JETS vs. BUFFALO
RS: Bills lead series, 37-31
PS: Bills lead series, 1-0;
See Buffalo vs. N.Y. Jets

N.Y. JETS vs. CHICAGO
RS: Bears lead series, 4-1;
See Chicago vs. N.Y. Jets

N.Y. JETS vs. CINCINNATI
RS: Jets lead series, 9-6
PS: Jets lead series, 1-0;
See Cincinnati vs. N.Y. Jets

N.Y. JETS vs. CLEVELAND
RS: Browns lead series, 9-6
PS: Browns lead series, 1-0;
See Cleveland vs. N.Y. Jets

N.Y. JETS vs. DALLAS
RS: Cowboys lead series, 5-1;
See Dallas vs. N.Y. Jets

N.Y. JETS vs. DENVER
RS: Series tied, 12-12-1;
See Denver vs. N.Y. Jets

N.Y. JETS vs. DETROIT
RS: Lions lead series, 4-3;
See Detroit vs. N.Y. Jets

N.Y. JETS vs. GREEN BAY
RS: Jets lead series, 5-2;
See Green Bay vs. N.Y. Jets

N.Y. JETS vs. HOUSTON
RS: Oilers lead series, 18-12-1
PS: Oilers lead series, 1-0;
See Houston vs. N.Y. Jets

N.Y. JETS vs. INDIANAPOLIS
RS: Colts lead series, 28-21
PS: Jets lead series, 1-0;
See Indianapolis vs. N.Y. Jets

N.Y. JETS vs. KANSAS CITY
RS: Chiefs lead series, 14-12-1
PS: Series tied, 1-1;
See Kansas City vs. N.Y. Jets

N.Y. JETS vs. LOS ANGELES
RS: Raiders lead series, 14-9-2
PS: Jets lead series, 2-0;
See Los Angeles vs. N.Y. Jets

N.Y. JETS vs. MIAMI
RS: Dolphins lead series, 29-28-1
PS: Dolphins lead series, 1-0;
See Miami vs. N.Y. Jets

N.Y. JETS vs. MINNESOTA
RS: Jets lead series, 4-1;
See Minnesota vs. N.Y. Jets

N.Y. JETS vs. NEW ENGLAND
RS: Jets lead series, 39-29-1
PS: Patriots lead series, 1-0;
See New England vs. N.Y. Jets

N.Y. JETS vs. NEW ORLEANS
RS: Jets lead series, 4-3;
See New Orleans vs. N.Y. Jets

N.Y. JETS vs. N.Y. GIANTS
RS: Jets lead series, 4-3;
See N.Y. Giants vs. N.Y. Jets

N.Y. JETS vs. PHILADELPHIA
RS: Eagles lead series, 5-0
1973—Eagles, 24-23 (P)
1977—Eagles, 27-0 (P)
1978—Eagles, 17-9 (P)
1987—Eagles, 38-27 (NY)
1993—Eagles, 35-30 (NY)
(RS Pts.—Eagles 141, Jets 89)

N.Y. JETS vs. PITTSBURGH
RS: Steelers lead series, 12-1
1970—Steelers, 21-17 (P)
1973—Steelers, 26-14 (P)
1975—Steelers, 20-7 (NY)
1977—Steelers, 23-20 (NY)
1978—Steelers, 28-17 (NY)
1981—Steelers, 38-10 (P)
1983—Steelers, 34-7 (NY)
1984—Steelers, 23-17 (NY)
1986—Steelers, 45-24 (NY)
1988—Jets, 24-20 (NY)
1989—Steelers, 13-0 (NY)
1990—Steelers, 24-7 (NY)
1992—Steelers, 27-10 (P)
(RS Pts.—Steelers 342, Jets 174)

N.Y. JETS vs. *ST. LOUIS
RS: Rams lead series, 5-2
1970—Jets, 31-20 (LA)
1974—Rams, 20-13 (NY)
1980—Rams, 38-13 (LA)
1983—Jets, 27-24 (NY) OT
1986—Rams, 17-3 (NY)
1989—Rams, 38-14 (LA)
1992—Rams, 18-10 (LA)
(RS Pts.—Rams 175, Jets 111)
**Franchise in Los Angeles prior to 1995*

***N.Y. JETS vs. **SAN DIEGO**
RS: Chargers lead series, 17-9-1
1960—Chargers, 21-7 (NY)
Chargers, 50-43 (LA)
1961—Chargers, 25-10 (NY)
Chargers, 48-13 (SD)
1962—Chargers, 40-14 (SD)
Titans, 23-3 (NY)
1963—Chargers, 24-20 (SD)
Chargers, 53-7 (NY)
1964—Tie, 17-17 (NY)
Chargers, 38-3 (SD)

1965—Chargers, 34-9 (NY)
Chargers, 38-7 (SD)
1966—Jets, 17-16 (NY)
Chargers, 42-27 (SD)
1967—Jets, 42-31 (SD)
1968—Jets, 23-20 (NY)
Jets, 37-15 (SD)
1969—Chargers, 34-27 (SD)
1971—Chargers, 49-21 (SD)
1974—Jets, 27-14 (NY)
1975—Chargers, 24-16 (SD)
1983—Jets, 41-29 (SD)
1989—Jets, 20-17 (SD)
1990—Chargers, 39-3 (NY)
Chargers, 38-17 (SD)
1991—Jets, 24-3 (NY)
1994—Chargers, 21-6 (NY)
(RS Pts.—Chargers 783, Jets 521)
Jets known as Titans prior to 1963
***Franchise in Los Angeles prior to 1961*

N.Y. JETS vs. SAN FRANCISCO
RS: 49ers lead series, 6-1
1971—49ers, 24-21 (NY)
1976—49ers, 17-6 (SF)
1980—49ers, 37-27 (NY)
1983—Jets, 27-13 (SF)
1986—49ers, 24-10 (SF)
1989—49ers, 23-10 (NY)
1992—49ers, 31-14 (NY)
(RS Pts.—49ers 169, Jets 115)

N.Y. JETS vs. SEATTLE
RS: Seahawks lead series, 8-3
1977—Seahawks, 17-0 (NY)
1978—Seahawks, 24-17 (NY)
1979—Seahawks, 30-7 (S)
1980—Seahawks, 27-17 (NY)
1981—Seahawks, 19-3 (NY)
Seahawks, 27-23 (S)
1983—Seahawks, 17-10 (NY)
1985—Jets, 17-14 (NY)
1986—Jets, 38-7 (S)
1987—Jets, 30-14 (NY)
1991—Seahawks, 20-13 (S)
(RS Pts.—Seahawks 216, Jets 175)

N.Y. JETS vs. TAMPA BAY
RS: Jets lead series, 5-1
1976—Jets, 34-0 (NY)
1982—Jets, 32-17 (NY)
1984—Buccaneers, 41-21 (TB)
1985—Jets, 62-28 (NY)
1990—Jets, 16-14 (TB)
1991—Jets, 16-13 (NY)
(RS Pts.—Jets 181, Buccaneers 113)

N.Y. JETS vs. WASHINGTON
RS: Redskins lead series, 4-1
1972—Redskins, 35-17 (NY)
1976—Redskins, 37-16 (NY)
1978—Redskins, 23-3 (W)
1987—Redskins, 17-16 (W)
1993—Jets, 3-0 (W)
(RS Pts.—Redskins 112, Jets 55)

PHILADELPHIA vs. ARIZONA
RS: Cardinals lead series, 45-44-5
PS: Series tied, 1-1;
See Arizona vs. Philadelphia

PHILADELPHIA vs. ATLANTA
RS: Eagles lead series, 8-7-1
PS: Falcons lead series, 1-0;
See Atlanta vs. Philadelphia

PHILADELPHIA vs. BUFFALO
RS: Eagles lead series, 4-3;
See Buffalo vs. Philadelphia

PHILADELPHIA vs. CHICAGO
RS: Bears lead series, 23-4-1
PS: Series tied, 1-1;
See Chicago vs. Philadelphia

PHILADELPHIA vs. CINCINNATI
RS: Bengals lead series, 6-1;
See Cincinnati vs. Philadelphia

PHILADELPHIA vs. CLEVELAND
RS: Browns lead series, 31-12-1;
See Cleveland vs. Philadelphia

PHILADELPHIA vs. DALLAS
RS: Cowboys lead series, 42-26
PS: Series tied, 1-1;
See Dallas vs. Philadelphia

PHILADELPHIA vs. DENVER
RS: Eagles lead series, 5-2;
See Denver vs. Philadelphia

PHILADELPHIA vs. DETROIT
RS: Lions lead series, 12-9-2;
See Detroit vs. Philadelphia

PHILADELPHIA vs. GREEN BAY
RS: Packers lead series, 19-8
PS: Eagles lead series, 1-0;
See Green Bay vs. Philadelphia

PHILADELPHIA vs. HOUSTON
RS: Eagles lead series, 6-0;
See Houston vs. Philadelphia

PHILADELPHIA vs. INDIANAPOLIS
RS: Series tied, 6-6;
See Indianapolis vs. Philadelphia

PHILADELPHIA vs. KANSAS CITY
RS: Series tied, 1-1;
See Kansas City vs. Philadelphia

PHILADELPHIA vs. LOS ANGELES
RS: Eagles lead series, 4-2
PS: Raiders lead series, 1-0;
See Los Angeles vs. Philadelphia

PHILADELPHIA vs. MIAMI
RS: Dolphins lead series, 6-2;
See Miami vs. Philadelphia

PHILADELPHIA vs. MINNESOTA
RS: Vikings lead series, 10-6
PS: Eagles lead series, 1-0;
See Minnesota vs. Philadelphia

PHILADELPHIA vs. NEW ENGLAND
RS: Eagles lead series, 5-2;
See New England vs. Philadelphia

PHILADELPHIA vs. NEW ORLEANS
RS: Eagles lead series, 11-8
PS; Eagles lead series, 1-0;
See New Orleans vs. Philadelphia

PHILADELPHIA vs. N.Y. GIANTS
RS: Giants lead series, 64-54-2
PS: Giants lead series, 1-0;
See N.Y. Giants vs. Philadelphia

PHILADELPHIA vs. N.Y. JETS
RS: Eagles lead series, 5-0;
See N.Y. Jets vs. Philadelphia

PHILADELPHIA vs. *PITTSBURGH
RS: Eagles lead series, 43-26-3
PS: Eagles lead series, 1-0
1933—Eagles, 25-6 (Phila)
1934—Eagles, 17-0 (Pitt)
Pirates, 9-7 (Phila)
1935—Pirates, 17-7 (Phila)
Eagles, 17-6 (Pitt)
1936—Pirates, 17-0 (Pitt)
Pirates, 6-0 (Johnstown, Pa.)
1937—Pirates, 27-14 (Pitt)
Pirates, 16-7 (Pitt)
1938—Eagles, 27-7 (Buffalo)
Eagles, 14-7 (Charleston, W. Va.)
1939—Eagles, 17-14 (Phila)
Pirates, 24-12 (Pitt)
1940—Pirates, 7-3 (Pitt)
Eagles, 7-0 (Phila)
1941—Eagles, 10-7 (Pitt)
Tie, 7-7 (Phila)
1942—Eagles, 24-14 (Pitt)
Steelers, 14-0 (Phila)
1945—Eagles, 45-3 (Pitt)
Eagles, 30-6 (Phila)
1946—Steelers, 10-7 (Pitt)
Eagles, 10-7 (Phila)
1947—Steelers, 35-24 (Pitt)
Eagles, 21-0 (Phila)
**Eagles, 21-0 (Pitt)
1948—Eagles, 34-7 (Pitt)
Eagles, 17-0 (Phila)
1949—Eagles, 38-7 (Pitt)
Eagles, 34-17 (Phila)
1950—Eagles, 17-10 (Pitt)
Steelers, 9-7 (Phila)
1951—Eagles, 34-13 (Pitt)
Steelers, 17-13 (Phila)
1952—Eagles, 31-25 (Pitt)
Eagles, 26-21 (Phila)
1953—Eagles, 23-17 (Phila)
Eagles, 35-7 (Pitt)
1954—Eagles, 24-22 (Phila)
Steelers, 17-7 (Pitt)
1955—Steelers, 13-7 (Pitt)
Eagles, 24-0 (Phila)
1956—Eagles, 35-21 (Pitt)
Eagles, 14-7 (Phila)
1957—Steelers, 6-0 (Pitt)
Eagles, 7-6 (Phila)
1958—Steelers, 24-3 (Pitt)
Steelers, 31-24 (Phila)
1959—Eagles, 28-24 (Phila)
Steelers, 31-0 (Pitt)
1960—Eagles, 34-7 (Phila)
Steelers, 27-21 (Pitt)
1961—Eagles, 21-16 (Phila)
Eagles, 35-24 (Pitt)
1962—Steelers, 13-7 (Pitt)
Steelers, 26-17 (Phila)
1963—Tie, 21-21 (Phila)
Tie, 20-20 (Pitt)
1964—Eagles, 21-7 (Phila)
Eagles, 34-10 (Pitt)
1965—Steelers, 20-14 (Phila)
Eagles, 47-13 (Pitt)
1966—Eagles, 31-14 (Pitt)
Eagles, 27-23 (Phila)
1967—Eagles, 34-24 (Phila)
1968—Steelers, 6-3 (Pitt)
1969—Eagles, 41-27 (Phila)
1970—Eagles, 30-20 (Phila)
1974—Steelers, 27-0 (Pitt)
1979—Eagles, 17-14 (Phila)
1988—Eagles, 27-26 (Pitt)
1991—Eagles, 23-14 (Phila)
1994—Steelers, 14-3 (Pitt)
(RS Pts.—Eagles 1,362, Steelers 1,021)
(PS Pts.—Eagles 21, Steelers 0)
Steelers known as Pirates prior to 1941
***Division Playoff*

PHILADELPHIA vs. *ST. LOUIS
RS: Rams lead series, 15-11-1
PS: Series tied, 1-1
1937—Rams, 21-3 (P)
1939—Rams, 35-13 (Colorado Springs)
1940—Rams, 21-13 (C)
1942—Rams, 24-14 (Akron)
1944—Eagles, 26-13 (P)
1945—Eagles, 28-14 (P)
1946—Eagles, 25-14 (LA)
1947—Eagles, 14-7 (P)
1948—Tie, 28-28 (LA)
1949—Eagles, 38-14 (P)
**Eagles, 14-0 (LA)
1950—Eagles, 56-20 (P)
1955—Rams, 23-21 (P)
1956—Rams, 27-7 (LA)
1957—Rams, 17-13 (LA)
1959—Eagles, 23-20 (P)
1964—Rams, 20-10 (LA)
1967—Rams, 33-17 (LA)
1969—Rams, 23-17 (P)
1972—Rams, 34-3 (P)
1975—Rams, 42-3 (P)
1977—Rams, 20-0 (LA)
1978—Rams, 16-14 (P)
1983—Eagles, 13-9 (P)
1985—Rams, 17-6 (P)
1986—Eagles, 34-20 (P)
1988—Eagles, 30-24 (P)
1989—***Rams, 21-7 (P)
1990—Eagles, 27-21 (LA)
(RS Pts.—Rams 577, Eagles 496)
(PS Pts.—Rams 21, Eagles 21)
Franchise in Los Angeles prior to 1995 and in Cleveland prior to 1946
***NFL Championship*
****NFC First-Round Playoff*

PHILADELPHIA vs. SAN DIEGO
RS: Chargers lead series, 3-2
1974—Eagles, 13-7 (SD)
1980—Chargers, 22-21 (SD)
1985—Chargers, 20-14 (SD)
1986—Eagles, 23-7 (P)
1989—Chargers, 20-17 (SD)
(RS Pts.—Eagles 88, Chargers 76)

PHILADELPHIA vs. SAN FRANCISCO
RS: 49ers lead series, 13-6-1
1951—Eagles, 21-14 (P)
1953—49ers, 31-21 (SF)
1956—Tie, 10-10 (P)
1958—49ers, 30-24 (P)
1959—49ers, 24-14 (SF)
1964—49ers, 28-24 (P)
1966—Eagles, 35-34 (SF)
1967—49ers, 28-27 (P)
1969—49ers, 14-13 (SF)
1971—49ers, 31-3 (P)
1973—49ers, 38-28 (SF)
1975—Eagles, 27-17 (P)
1983—Eagles, 22-17 (SF)
1984—49ers, 21-9 (P)
1985—49ers, 24-13 (SF)
1989—49ers, 38-28 (P)
1991—49ers, 23-7 (P)
1992—49ers, 20-14 (SF)
1993—Eagles, 37-34 (SF) OT
1994—Eagles, 40-8 (SF)
(RS Pts.—49ers 484, Eagles 417)

PHILADELPHIA vs. SEATTLE
RS: Eagles lead series, 4-1
1976—Eagles, 27-10 (P)
1980—Eagles, 27-20 (S)
1986—Seahawks, 24-20 (S)
1989—Eagles, 31-7 (P)
1992—Eagles, 20-17 (S) OT
(RS Pts.—Eagles 125, Seahawks 78)

PHILADELPHIA vs. TAMPA BAY
RS: Eagles lead series, 3-1
PS: Buccaneers lead series, 1-0
1977—Eagles, 13-3 (P)
1979—*Buccaneers, 24-17 (TB)
1981—Eagles, 20-10 (P)
1988—Eagles, 41-14 (TB)
1991—Buccaneers, 14-13 (TB)
(RS Pts.—Eagles 87, Buccaneers 41)
(PS Pts.—Buccaneers 24, Eagles 17)
NFC Divisional Playoff

PHILADELPHIA vs. *WASHINGTON
RS: Redskins lead series, 66-48-5
PS: Redskins lead series, 1-0
1934—Redskins, 6-0 (B)
Redskins, 14-7 (P)
1935—Eagles, 7-6 (B)
1936—Redskins, 26-3 (P)
Redskins, 17-7 (B)
1937—Eagles, 14-0 (W)
Redskins, 10-7 (P)
1938—Redskins, 26-23 (P)
Redskins, 20-14 (W)
1939—Redskins, 7-0 (P)
Redskins, 7-6 (W)
1940—Redskins, 34-17 (P)
Redskins, 13-6 (W)
1941—Redskins, 21-17 (P)
Redskins, 20-14 (W)
1942—Redskins, 14-10 (P)
Redskins, 30-27 (W)
1944—Tie, 31-31 (P)
Eagles, 37-7 (W)
1945—Redskins, 24-14 (W)
Eagles, 16-0 (P)
1946—Eagles, 28-24 (W)
Redskins, 27-10 (P)
1947—Eagles, 45-42 (P)
Eagles, 38-14 (W)
1948—Eagles, 45-0 (W)
Eagles, 42-21 (P)
1949—Eagles, 49-14 (P)
Eagles, 44-21 (W)

ALL-TIME TEAM VS. TEAM RESULTS

1950—Eagles, 35-3 (P)
Eagles, 33-0 (W)
1951—Redskins, 27-23 (P)
Eagles, 35-21 (W)
1952—Eagles, 38-20 (P)
Redskins, 27-21 (W)
1953—Tie, 21-21 (P)
Redskins, 10-0 (W)
1954—Eagles, 49-21 (W)
Eagles, 41-33 (P)
1955—Redskins, 31-30 (P)
Redskins, 34-21 (W)
1956—Eagles, 13-9 (P)
Redskins, 19-17 (W)
1957—Eagles, 21-12 (P)
Redskins, 42-7 (W)
1958—Redskins, 24-14 (P)
Redskins, 20-0 (W)
1959—Eagles, 30-23 (P)
Eagles, 34-14 (W)
1960—Eagles, 19-13 (P)
Eagles, 38-28 (W)
1961—Eagles, 14-7 (P)
Eagles, 27-24 (W)
1962—Redskins, 27-21 (P)
Eagles, 37-14 (W)
1963—Eagles, 37-24 (W)
Redskins, 13-10 (P)
1964—Redskins, 35-20 (W)
Redskins, 21-10 (P)
1965—Redskins, 23-21 (W)
Eagles, 21-14 (P)
1966—Redskins, 27-13 (P)
Eagles, 37-28 (W)
1967—Eagles, 35-24 (P)
Tie, 35-35 (W)
1968—Redskins, 17-14 (W)
Redskins, 16-10 (P)
1969—Tie, 28-28 (W)
Redskins, 34-29 (P)
1970—Redskins, 33-21 (P)
Redskins, 24-6 (W)
1971—Tie, 7-7 (W)
Redskins, 20-13 (P)
1972—Redskins, 14-0 (W)
Redskins, 23-7 (P)
1973—Redskins, 28-7 (P)
Redskins, 38-20 (W)
1974—Redskins, 27-20 (P)
Redskins, 26-7 (W)
1975—Eagles, 26-10 (P)
Eagles, 26-3 (W)
1976—Redskins, 20-17 (P) OT
Redskins, 24-0 (W)
1977—Redskins, 23-17 (W)
Redskins, 17-14 (P)
1978—Redskins, 35-30 (W)
Eagles, 17-10 (P)
1979—Eagles, 28-17 (P)
Redskins, 17-7 (W)
1980—Eagles, 24-14 (P)
Eagles, 24-0 (W)
1981—Eagles, 36-13 (P)
Redskins, 15-13 (W)
1982—Redskins, 37-34 (P) OT
Redskins, 13-9 (W)
1983—Redskins, 23-13 (P)
Redskins, 28-24 (W)
1984—Redskins, 20-0 (W)
Eagles, 16-10 (P)
1985—Eagles, 19-6 (W)
Redskins, 17-12 (P)
1986—Redskins, 41-14 (W)
Redskins, 21-14 (P)
1987—Redskins, 34-24 (W)
Eagles, 31-27 (P)
1988—Redskins, 17-10 (W)
Redskins, 20-19 (P)
1989—Eagles, 42-37 (W)
Redskins, 10-3 (P)
1990—Redskins, 13-7 (W)
Eagles, 28-14 (P)
**Redskins, 20-6 (P)
1991—Redskins, 23-0 (W)
Eagles, 24-22 (P)
1992—Redskins, 16-12 (W)
Eagles, 17-13 (P)
1993—Eagles, 34-31 (P)
Eagles, 17-14 (W)
1994—Eagles, 21-17 (P)
Eagles, 31-29 (W)
(RS Pts.—Eagles 2,399, Redskins 2,370)
(PS Pts.—Redskins 20, Eagles 6)
Franchise in Boston prior to 1937
***NFC First-Round Playoff*

PITTSBURGH vs. ARIZONA
RS: Steelers lead series, 29-22-3;
See Arizona vs. Pittsburgh
PITTSBURGH vs. ATLANTA
RS: Steelers lead series, 9-1;
See Atlanta vs. Pittsburgh
PITTSBURGH vs. BUFFALO
RS: Series tied, 7-7
PS: Series tied, 1-1;
See Buffalo vs. Pittsburgh
PITTSBURGH vs. CHICAGO
RS: Bears lead series, 16-4-1;
See Chicago vs. Pittsburgh
PITTSBURGH vs. CINCINNATI
RS: Steelers lead series, 28-21;
See Cincinnati vs. Pittsburgh
PITTSBURGH vs. CLEVELAND
RS: Browns lead series, 52-38
PS: Steelers lead series, 1-0;
See Cleveland vs. Pittsburgh
PITTSBURGH vs. DALLAS
RS: Cowboys lead series, 13-11
PS: Steelers lead series, 2-0;
See Dallas vs. Pittsburgh
PITTSBURGH vs. DENVER
RS: Broncos lead series, 10-5-1
PS: Series tied, 2-2;
See Denver vs. Pittsburgh
PITTSBURGH vs. DETROIT
RS: Lions lead series, 13-11-1;
See Detroit vs. Pittsburgh
PITTSBURGH vs. GREEN BAY
RS: Packers lead series, 17-11;
See Green Bay vs. Pittsburgh
PITTSBURGH vs. HOUSTON
RS: Steelers lead series, 31-18
PS: Steelers lead series, 3-0;
See Houston vs. Pittsburgh
PITTSBURGH vs. INDIANAPOLIS
RS: Steelers lead series, 11-4
PS: Steelers lead series, 2-0;
See Indianapolis vs. Pittsburgh
PITTSBURGH vs. KANSAS CITY
RS: Steelers lead series, 13-5
PS: Chiefs lead series, 1-0;
See Kansas City vs. Pittsburgh
PITTSBURGH vs. LOS ANGELES
RS: Raiders lead series, 7-4
PS: Series tied, 3-3;
See Los Angeles vs. Pittsburgh
PITTSBURGH vs. MIAMI
RS: Dolphins lead series, 7-6
PS: Dolphins lead series, 2-1;
See Miami vs. Pittsburgh
PITTSBURGH vs. MINNESOTA
RS: Vikings lead series, 7-4
PS: Steelers lead series, 1-0;
See Minnesota vs. Pittsburgh
PITTSBURGH vs. NEW ENGLAND
RS: Steelers lead series, 9-3;
See New England vs. Pittsburgh
PITTSBURGH vs. NEW ORLEANS
RS: Steelers lead series, 6-5;
See New Orleans vs. Pittsburgh
PITTSBURGH vs. N.Y. GIANTS
RS: Giants lead series, 42-27-3;
See N.Y. Giants vs. Pittsburgh
PITTSBURGH vs. N.Y. JETS
RS: Steelers lead series, 12-1;
See N.Y. Jets vs. Pittsburgh

PITTSBURGH vs. PHILADELPHIA
RS: Eagles lead series, 43-26-3
PS: Eagles lead series, 1-0;
See Philadelphia vs. Pittsburgh
***PITTSBURGH vs. **ST. LOUIS**
RS: Rams lead series, 14-4-2
PS: Steelers lead series, 1-0
1938—Rams, 13-7 (New Orleans)
1939—Tie, 14-14 (C)
1941—Rams, 17-14 (Akron)
1947—Rams, 48-7 (P)
1948—Rams, 31-14 (LA)
1949—Tie, 7-7 (P)
1952—Rams, 28-14 (LA)
1955—Rams, 27-26 (LA)
1956—Steelers, 30-13 (P)
1961—Rams, 24-14 (LA)
1964—Rams, 26-14 (P)
1968—Rams, 45-10 (LA)
1971—Rams, 23-14 (P)
1975—Rams, 10-3 (LA)
1978—Rams, 10-7 (LA)
1979—***Steelers, 31-19 (Pasadena)
1981—Steelers, 24-0 (P)
1984—Steelers, 24-14 (P)
1987—Rams, 31-21 (LA)
1990—Steelers, 41-10 (P)
1993—Rams, 27-0 (LA)
(RS Pts.—Rams 418, Steelers 305)
(PS Pts.—Steelers 31, Rams 19)
**Steelers known as Pirates prior to 1941*
***Franchise in Los Angeles prior to 1995 and in Cleveland prior to 1946*
****Super Bowl XIV*
PITTSBURGH vs. SAN DIEGO
RS: Steelers lead series, 14-5
PS: Chargers lead series, 2-0
1971—Steelers, 21-17 (P)
1972—Steelers, 24-2 (SD)
1973—Steelers, 38-21 (P)
1975—Steelers, 37-0 (SD)
1976—Steelers, 23-0 (P)
1977—Steelers, 10-9 (SD)
1979—Chargers, 35-7 (SD)
1980—Chargers, 26-17 (SD)
1982—*Chargers, 31-28 (P)
1983—Steelers, 26-3 (P)
1984—Steelers, 52-24 (P)
1985—Chargers, 54-44 (SD)
1987—Steelers, 20-16 (SD)
1988—Chargers, 20-14 (SD)
1989—Steelers, 20-17 (P)
1990—Steelers, 36-14 (P)
1991—Steelers, 26-20 (P)
1992—Steelers, 23-6 (SD)
1993—Steelers,.16-3 (P)
1994—Chargers, 37-34 (SD)
**Chargers, 17-13 (P)
(RS Pts.—Steelers 488, Chargers 324)
(PS Pts.—Chargers 48, Steelers 41)
**AFC First-Round Playoff*
***AFC Championship*
PITTSBURGH vs. SAN FRANCISCO
RS: 49ers lead series, 8-7
1951—49ers, 28-24 (P)
1952—Steelers, 24-7 (SF)
1954—49ers, 31-3 (SF)
1958—49ers, 23-20 (SF)
1961—Steelers, 20-10 (P)
1965—49ers, 27-17 (SF)
1968—49ers, 45-28 (P)
1973—Steelers, 37-14 (SF)
1977—Steelers, 27-0 (P)
1978—Steelers, 24-7 (SF)
1981—49ers, 17-14 (P)
1984—Steelers, 20-17 (SF)
1987—Steelers, 30-17 (P)
1990—49ers, 27-7 (SF)
1993—49ers, 24-13 (P)
(RS Pts.—Steelers 308, 49ers 294)
PITTSBURGH vs. SEATTLE
RS: Seahawks lead series, 6-5
1977—Steelers, 30-20 (P)
1978—Steelers, 21-10 (P)
1981—Seahawks, 24-21 (S)
1982—Seahawks, 16-0 (S)
1983—Steelers, 27-21 (S)
1986—Seahawks, 30-0 (S)
1987—Steelers, 13-9 (P)
1991—Seahawks, 27-7 (P)
1992—Steelers, 20-14 (P)
1993—Seahawks, 16-6 (S)
1994—Seahawks, 30-13 (S)
(RS Pts.—Seahawks 217, Steelers 158)
PITTSBURGH vs. TAMPA BAY
RS: Steelers lead series, 4-0
1976—Steelers, 42-0 (P)
1980—Steelers, 24-21 (TB)
1983—Steelers, 17-12 (P)
1989—Steelers, 31-22 (TB)
(RS Pts.—Steelers 114, Buccaneers 55)
***PITTSBURGH vs. **WASHINGTON**
RS: Redskins lead series, 42-27-3
1933—Redskins, 21-6 (P)
Pirates, 16-14 (B)
1934—Redskins, 7-0 (P)
Redskins, 39-0 (B)
1935—Pirates, 6-0 (P)
Redskins, 13-3 (B)
1936—Pirates, 10-0 (P)
Redskins, 30-0 (B)
1937—Redskins, 34-20 (W)
Pirates, 21-13 (P)
1938—Redskins, 7-0 (P)
Redskins, 15-0 (W)
1939—Redskins, 44-14 (W)
Redskins, 21-14 (P)
1940—Redskins, 40-10 (P)
Redskins, 37-10 (W)
1941—Redskins, 24-20 (P)
Redskins, 23-3 (W)
1942—Redskins, 28-14 (W)
Redskins, 14-0 (P)
1945—Redskins, 14-0 (P)
Redskins, 24-0 (W)
1946—Tie, 14-14 (W)
Steelers, 14-7 (P)
1947—Redskins, 27-26 (W)
Steelers, 21-14 (P)
1948—Redskins, 17-14 (W)
Steelers, 10-7 (P)
1949—Redskins, 27-14 (P)
Redskins, 27-14 (W)
1950—Steelers, 26-7 (W)
Redskins, 24-7 (P)
1951—Redskins, 22-7 (P)
Steelers, 20-10 (W)
1952—Redskins, 28-24 (P)
Steelers, 24-23 (W)
1953—Redskins, 17-9 (P)
Steelers, 14-13 (W)
1954—Steelers, 37-7 (P)
Redskins, 17-14 (W)
1955—Redskins, 23-14 (P)
Redskins, 28-17 (W)
1956—Steelers, 30-13 (P)
Steelers, 23-0 (W)
1957—Steelers, 28-7 (P)
Redskins, 10-3 (W)
1958—Steelers, 24-16 (P)
Tie, 14-14 (W)
1959—Redskins, 23-17 (P)
Steelers, 27-6 (W)
1960—Tie, 27-27 (W)
Steelers, 22-10 (P)
1961—Steelers, 20-0 (P)
Steelers, 30-14 (W)
1962—Steelers, 23-21 (P)
Steelers, 27-24 (W)
1963—Steelers, 38-27 (P)
Steelers, 34-28 (W)
1964—Redskins, 30-0 (P)
Steelers, 14-7 (W)
1965—Redskins, 31-3 (P)
Redskins, 35-14 (W)
1966—Redskins, 33-27 (P)

Redskins, 24-10 (W)
1967—Redskins, 15-10 (P)
1968—Redskins, 16-13 (W)
1969—Redskins, 14-7 (P)
1973—Steelers, 21-16 (P)
1979—Steelers, 38-7 (P)
1985—Redskins, 30-23 (P)
1988—Redskins, 30-29 (W)
1991—Redskins, 41-14 (P)
(RS Pts.—Redskins 1,390, Steelers 1,117)
Steelers known as Pirates prior to 1941
***Franchise in Boston prior to 1937*

ST. LOUIS vs. ARIZONA
RS: Rams lead series, 23-19-2
PS: Rams lead series, 1-0;
See Arizona vs. St. Louis
ST. LOUIS vs. ATLANTA
RS: Rams lead series, 36-18-2;
See Atlanta vs. St. Louis
ST. LOUIS vs. BUFFALO
RS: Series tied, 3-3;
See Buffalo vs. St. Louis
ST. LOUIS vs. CHICAGO
RS: Bears lead series, 45-29-3
PS: Series tied, 1-1;
See Chicago vs. St. Louis
ST. LOUIS vs. CINCINNATI
RS: Bengals lead series, 5-2;
See Cincinnati vs. St. Louis
ST. LOUIS vs. CLEVELAND
RS: Browns lead series, 8-7
PS: Browns lead series, 2-1;
See Cleveland vs. St. Louis
ST. LOUIS vs. DALLAS
RS: Rams lead series, 9-8
PS: Series tied, 4-4;
See Dallas vs. St. Louis
ST. LOUIS vs. DENVER
RS: Rams lead series, 4-3;
See Denver vs. St. Louis
ST. LOUIS vs. DETROIT
RS: Rams lead series, 39-35-1
PS: Lions lead series, 1-0;
See Detroit vs. St. Louis
ST. LOUIS vs. GREEN BAY
RS: Rams lead series, 42-37-2
PS: Packers lead series, 1-0;
See Green Bay vs. St. Louis
ST. LOUIS vs. HOUSTON
RS: Rams lead series, 5-2;
See Houston vs. St. Louis
ST. LOUIS vs. INDIANAPOLIS
RS: Colts lead series, 20-16-2;
See Indianapolis vs. St. Louis
ST. LOUIS vs. KANSAS CITY
RS: Rams lead series, 4-1;
See Kansas City vs. St. Louis
ST. LOUIS vs. LOS ANGELES
RS: Raiders lead series, 6-2;
See Los Angeles vs. St. Louis
ST. LOUIS vs. MIAMI
RS: Dolphins lead series, 5-1;
See Miami vs. St. Louis
ST. LOUIS vs. MINNESOTA
RS: Vikings lead series, 15-11-2
PS: Vikings lead series, 5-1;
See Minnesota vs. St. Louis
ST. LOUIS vs. NEW ENGLAND
RS: Series tied, 3-3;
See New England vs. St. Louis
ST. LOUIS vs. NEW ORLEANS
RS: Rams lead series, 27-23;
See New Orleans vs. St. Louis
ST. LOUIS vs. N.Y. GIANTS
RS: Rams lead series, 21-9
PS: Series tied, 1-1;
See N.Y. Giants vs. St. Louis
ST. LOUIS vs. N.Y. JETS
RS: Rams lead series, 5-2;
See N.Y. Jets vs. St. Louis
ST. LOUIS vs. PHILADELPHIA
RS: Rams lead series, 15-11-1
PS: Series tied, 1-1;
See Philadelphia vs. St. Louis
ST. LOUIS vs. PITTSBURGH
RS: Rams lead series, 14-4-2
PS: Steelers lead series, 1-0;
See Pittsburgh vs. St. Louis
***ST. LOUIS vs. SAN DIEGO**
RS: Series tied, 3-3
1970—Rams, 37-10 (LA)
1975—Rams, 13-10 (SD) OT
1979—Chargers, 40-16 (LA)
1988—Chargers, 38-24 (LA)
1991—Rams, 30-24 (LA)
1994—Chargers, 31-17 (SD)
(RS Pts.—Chargers 153, Rams 137)
Franchise in Los Angeles prior to 1995
***ST. LOUIS vs. SAN FRANCISCO**
RS: Rams lead series, 48-40-2
PS: 49ers lead series, 1-0
1950—Rams, 35-14 (SF)
Rams, 28-21 (LA)
1951—49ers, 44-17 (SF)
Rams, 23-16 (LA)
1952—Rams, 35-9 (LA)
Rams, 34-21 (SF)
1953—49ers, 31-30 (SF)
49ers, 31-27 (LA)
1954—Tie, 24-24 (LA)
Rams, 42-34 (SF)
1955—Rams, 23-14 (SF)
Rams, 27-14 (LA)
1956—49ers, 33-30 (SF)
Rams, 30-6 (LA)
1957—49ers, 23-20 (SF)
Rams, 37-24 (LA)
1958—Rams, 33-3 (SF)
Rams, 56-7 (LA)
1959—49ers, 34-0 (SF)
49ers, 24-16 (LA)
1960—49ers, 13-9 (SF)
49ers, 23-7 (LA)
1961—49ers, 35-0 (SF)
Rams, 17-7 (LA)
1962—Rams, 28-14 (SF)
49ers, 24-17 (LA)
1963—Rams, 28-21 (LA)
Rams, 21-17 (SF)
1964—Rams, 42-14 (LA)
49ers, 28-7 (SF)
1965—49ers, 45-21 (LA)
49ers, 30-27 (SF)
1966—Rams, 34-3 (LA)
49ers, 21-13 (SF)
1967—49ers, 27-24 (LA)
Rams, 17-7 (SF)
1968—Rams, 24-10 (LA)
Tie, 20-20 (SF)
1969—Rams, 27-21 (SF)
Rams, 41-30 (LA)
1970—49ers, 20-6 (LA)
Rams, 30-13 (SF)
1971—Rams, 20-13 (SF)
Rams, 17-6 (LA)
1972—Rams, 31-7 (LA)
Rams, 26-16 (SF)
1973—Rams, 40-20 (SF)
Rams, 31-13 (LA)
1974—Rams, 37-14 (LA)
Rams, 15-13 (SF)
1975—Rams, 23-14 (SF)
49ers, 24-23 (LA)
1976—49ers, 16-0 (LA)
Rams, 23-3 (SF)
1977—Rams, 34-14 (LA)
Rams, 23-10 (SF)
1978—Rams, 27-10 (LA)
Rams, 31-28 (SF)
1979—Rams, 27-24 (LA)
Rams, 26-20 (SF)
1980—Rams, 48-26 (LA)
Rams, 31-17 (SF)
1981—49ers, 20-17 (SF)
49ers, 33-31 (LA)
1982—49ers, 30-24 (LA)
Rams, 21-20 (SF)
1983—Rams, 10-7 (SF)
49ers, 45-35 (LA)
1984—49ers, 33-0 (LA)
49ers, 19-16 (SF)
1985—49ers, 28-14 (LA)
Rams, 27-20 (SF)
1986—Rams, 16-13 (LA)
49ers, 24-14 (SF)
1987—49ers, 31-10 (LA)
49ers, 48-0 (SF)
1988—49ers, 24-21 (LA)
Rams, 38-16 (SF)
1989—Rams, 13-12 (SF)
49ers, 30-27 (LA)
**49ers, 30-3 (SF)
1990—Rams, 28-17 (SF)
49ers, 26-10 (LA)
1991—49ers, 27-10 (SF)
49ers, 33-10 (LA)
1992—49ers, 27-24 (SF)
49ers, 27-10 (LA)
1993—49ers, 40-17 (SF)
49ers, 35-10 (LA)
1994—49ers, 34-19 (LA)
49ers, 31-27 (SF)
(RS Pts.—Rams 2,059, 49ers 1,928)
(PS Pts.—49ers 30, Rams 3)
Franchise in Los Angeles prior to 1995
***NFC Championship*
***ST. LOUIS vs. SEATTLE**
RS: Rams lead series, 4-1
1976—Rams, 45-6 (LA)
1979—Rams, 24-0 (S)
1985—Rams, 35-24 (S)
1988—Rams, 31-10 (LA)
1991—Seahawks, 23-9 (S)
(RS Pts.—Rams 144, Seahawks 63)
Franchise in Los Angeles prior to 1995
***ST. LOUIS vs. TAMPA BAY**
RS: Rams lead series, 8-3
PS: Rams lead series, 1-0
1977—Rams, 31-0 (LA)
1978—Rams, 26-23 (LA)
1979—Buccaneers, 21-6 (TB)
**Rams, 9-0 (TB)
1980—Buccaneers, 10-9 (TB)
1984—Rams, 34-33 (TB)
1985—Rams, 31-27 (TB)
1986—Rams, 26-20 (LA) OT
1987—Rams, 35-3 (LA)
1990—Rams, 35-14 (TB)
1992—Rams, 31-27 (TB)
1994—Buccaneers, 24-14 (TB)
(RS Pts.—Rams 278, Buccaneers 202)
(PS Pts.—Rams 9, Buccaneers 0)
Franchise in Los Angeles prior to 1995
***NFC Championship*
***ST. LOUIS vs. WASHINGTON**
RS: Redskins lead series, 15-5-1
PS: Series tied, 2-2
1937—Redskins, 16-7 (C)
1938—Redskins, 37-13 (W)
1941—Redskins, 17-13 (W)
1942—Redskins, 33-14 (W)
1944—Redskins, 14-10 (W)
1945—**Rams, 15-14 (C)
1948—Rams, 41-13 (W)
1949—Rams, 53-27 (LA)
1951—Redskins, 31-21 (W)
1962—Redskins, 20-14 (W)
1963—Redskins, 37-14 (LA)
1967—Tie, 28-28 (LA)
1969—Rams, 24-13 (W)
1971—Redskins, 38-24 (LA)
1974—Redskins, 23-17 (LA)
***Rams, 19-10 (LA)
1977—Redskins, 17-14 (W)
1981—Redskins, 30-7 (LA)
1983—Redskins, 42-20 (LA)
***Redskins, 51-7 (W)
1986—****Redskins, 19-7 (W)
1987—Rams, 30-26 (W)
1991—Redskins, 27-6 (LA)
1993—Rams, 10-6 (LA)
1994—Redskins, 24-21 (LA)
(RS Pts.—Redskins 519, Rams 401)
(PS Pts.—Redskins 94, Rams 48)
Franchise in Los Angeles prior to 1995 and in Cleveland prior to 1946
***NFL Championship*
****NFC Divisional Playoff*
*****NFC First-Round Playoff*

SAN DIEGO vs. ARIZONA
RS: Chargers lead series, 5-1;
See Arizona vs. San Diego
SAN DIEGO vs. ATLANTA
RS: Falcons lead series, 4-1;
See Atlanta vs. San Diego
SAN DIEGO vs. BUFFALO
RS: Chargers lead series, 16-7-2
PS: Bills lead series, 2-1;
See Buffalo vs. San Diego
SAN DIEGO vs. CHICAGO
RS: Chargers lead series, 4-2;
See Chicago vs. San Diego
SAN DIEGO vs. CINCINNATI
RS: Chargers lead series, 13-8
PS: Bengals lead series, 1-0;
See Cincinnati vs. San Diego
SAN DIEGO vs. CLEVELAND
RS: Chargers lead series, 8-6-1;
See Cleveland vs. San Diego
SAN DIEGO vs. DALLAS
RS: Cowboys lead series, 4-1;
See Dallas vs. San Diego
SAN DIEGO vs. DENVER
RS: Broncos lead series, 36-33-1;
See Denver vs. San Diego
SAN DIEGO vs. DETROIT
RS: Lions lead series, 3-2;
See Detroit vs. San Diego
SAN DIEGO vs. GREEN BAY
RS: Packers lead series, 4-1;
See Green Bay vs. San Diego
SAN DIEGO vs. HOUSTON
RS: Chargers lead series, 18-13-1
PS: Oilers lead series, 3-0;
See Houston vs. San Diego
SAN DIEGO vs. INDIANAPOLIS
RS: Chargers lead series, 9-5;
See Indianapolis vs. San Diego
SAN DIEGO vs. KANSAS CITY
RS: Chiefs lead series, 35-33-1
PS: Chargers lead series, 1-0;
See Kansas City vs. San Diego
SAN DIEGO vs. LOS ANGELES
RS: Raiders lead series, 42-26-2
PS: Raiders lead series, 1-0;
See Los Angeles vs. San Diego
SAN DIEGO vs. MIAMI
RS: Chargers lead series, 10-5
PS: Series tied, 2-2;
See Miami vs. San Diego
SAN DIEGO vs. MINNESOTA
RS: Chargers lead series, 4-3;
See Minnesota vs. San Diego
SAN DIEGO vs. NEW ENGLAND
RS: Patriots lead series, 14-11-2
PS: Chargers lead series, 1-0;
See New England vs. San Diego
SAN DIEGO vs. NEW ORLEANS
RS: Chargers lead series, 5-1;
See New Orleans vs. San Diego
SAN DIEGO vs. N.Y. GIANTS
RS: Giants lead series, 4-2;
See N.Y. Giants vs. San Diego
SAN DIEGO vs. N.Y. JETS
RS: Chargers lead series, 17-9-1;
See N.Y. Jets vs. San Diego
SAN DIEGO vs. PHILADELPHIA
RS: Chargers lead series, 3-2;
See Philadelphia vs. San Diego
SAN DIEGO vs. PITTSBURGH

ALL-TIME TEAM VS. TEAM RESULTS

RS: Steelers lead series, 14-5
PS: Chargers lead series, 2-0;
See Pittsburgh vs. San Diego
SAN DIEGO vs. ST. LOUIS
RS: Series tied, 3-3
See St. Louis vs. San Diego
SAN DIEGO vs. SAN FRANCISCO
RS: 49ers lead series, 4-3
PS: 49ers lead series, 1-0;
1972—49ers, 34-3 (SF)
1976—Chargers, 13-7 (SD) OT
1979—Chargers, 31-9 (SD)
1982—Chargers, 41-37 (SF)
1988—49ers, 48-10 (SD)
1991—49ers, 34-14 (SF)
1994—49ers, 38-15 (SD)
*49ers, 49-26 (Miami)
(RS Pts.—49ers 207, Chargers 127)
(PS Pts.—49ers 49, Chargers 26)
**Super Bowl XXIX*
SAN DIEGO vs. SEATTLE
RS: Chargers lead series, 17-15
1977—Chargers, 30-28 (S)
1978—Chargers, 24-20 (S)
Chargers, 37-10 (SD)
1979—Chargers, 33-16 (S)
Chargers, 20-10 (SD)
1980—Chargers, 34-13 (S)
Chargers, 21-14 (SD)
1981—Chargers, 24-10 (SD)
Seahawks, 44-23 (S)
1983—Seahawks, 34-31 (S)
Chargers, 28-21 (SD)
1984—Seahawks, 31-17 (S)
Seahawks, 24-0 (SD)
1985—Seahawks, 49-35 (SD)
Seahawks, 26-21 (S)
1986—Seahawks, 33-7 (S)
Seahawks, 34-24 (SD)
1987—Seahawks, 34-3 (S)
1988—Chargers, 17-6 (SD)
Seahawks, 17-14 (S)
1989—Seahawks, 17-16 (SD)
Seahawks, 10-7 (S)
1990—Chargers, 31-14 (S)
Seahawks, 13-10 (SD) OT
1991—Seahawks, 20-9 (S)
Chargers, 17-14 (SD)
1992—Chargers, 17-6 (SD)
Chargers, 31-14 (S)
1993—Chargers, 18-12 (SD)
Seahawks, 31-14 (S)
1994—Chargers, 24-10 (S)
Chargers, 35-15 (SD)
(RS Pts.—Chargers 672, Seahawks 650)
SAN DIEGO vs. TAMPA BAY
RS: Chargers lead series, 6-0
1976—Chargers, 23-0 (TB)
1981—Chargers, 24-23 (TB)
1987—Chargers, 17-13 (TB)
1990—Chargers, 41-10 (SD)
1992—Chargers, 29-14 (SD)
1993—Chargers, 32-17 (TB)
(RS Pts.—Chargers 166, Buccaneers 77)
SAN DIEGO vs. WASHINGTON
RS: Redskins lead series, 5-0
1973—Redskins, 38-0 (W)
1980—Redskins, 40-17 (W)
1983—Redskins, 27-24 (SD)
1986—Redskins, 30-27 (SD)
1989—Redskins, 26-21 (W)
(RS Pts.—Redskins 161, Chargers 89)

SAN FRANCISCO vs. ARIZONA
RS: 49ers lead series, 10-9;
See Arizona vs. San Francisco
SAN FRANCISCO vs. ATLANTA
RS: 49ers lead series, 34-21-1;
See Atlanta vs. San Francisco
SAN FRANCISCO vs. BUFFALO
RS: Bills lead series, 3-2;
See Buffalo vs. San Francisco
SAN FRANCISCO vs. CHICAGO
RS: Series tied, 25-25-1
PS: 49ers lead series, 3-0;
See Chicago vs. San Francisco
SAN FRANCISCO vs. CINCINNATI
RS: 49ers lead series, 6-1
PS: 49ers lead series, 2-0;
See Cincinnati vs. San Francisco
SAN FRANCISCO vs. CLEVELAND
RS: Browns lead series, 9-6;
See Cleveland vs. San Francisco
SAN FRANCISCO vs. DALLAS
RS: 49ers lead series, 10-6-1
PS: Cowboys lead series, 5-2;
See Dallas vs. San Francisco
SAN FRANCISCO vs. DENVER
RS: Broncos lead series, 4-3
PS: 49ers lead series, 1-0;
See Denver vs. San Francisco
SAN FRANCISCO vs. DETROIT
RS: 49ers lead series, 27-25-1
PS: Series tied, 1-1;
See Detroit vs. San Francisco
SAN FRANCISCO vs. GREEN BAY
RS: 49ers lead series, 25-21-1;
See Green Bay vs. San Francisco
SAN FRANCISCO vs. HOUSTON
RS: 49ers lead series, 5-3;
See Houston vs. San Francisco
SAN FRANCISCO vs. INDIANAPOLIS
RS: Colts lead series, 21-16;
See Indianapolis vs. San Francisco
SAN FRANCISCO vs. KANSAS CITY
RS: 49ers lead series, 4-2;
See Kansas City vs. San Francisco
SAN FRANCISCO vs. LOS ANGELES
RS: Raiders lead series, 5-3;
See Los Angeles vs. San Francisco
SAN FRANCISCO vs. MIAMI
RS: Dolphins lead series, 4-2
PS: 49ers lead series, 1-0;
See Miami vs. San Francisco
SAN FRANCISCO vs. MINNESOTA
RS: Vikings lead series, 16-15-1
PS: 49ers lead series, 3-1;
See Minnesota vs. San Francisco
SAN FRANCISCO vs. NEW ENGLAND
RS: 49ers lead series, 6-1;
See New England vs. San Francisco
SAN FRANCISCO vs. NEW ORLEANS
RS: 49ers lead series, 35-14-2;
See New Orleans vs. San Francisco
SAN FRANCISCO vs. N.Y. GIANTS
RS: Giants lead series, 11-10
PS: Series tied, 3-3;
See N.Y. Giants vs. San Francisco
SAN FRANCISCO vs. N.Y. JETS
RS: 49ers lead series, 6-1;
See N.Y. Jets vs. San Francisco
SAN FRANCISCO vs. PHILADELPHIA
RS: 49ers lead series, 13-6-1;
See Philadelphia vs. San Francisco
SAN FRANCISCO vs. PITTSBURGH
RS: 49ers lead series, 8-7;
See Pittsburgh vs. San Francisco
SAN FRANCISCO vs. ST. LOUIS
RS: Rams lead series, 48-40-2
PS: 49ers lead series, 1-0;
See St. Louis vs. San Francisco
SAN FRANCISCO vs. SAN DIEGO
RS: 49ers lead series, 4-3
PS: 49ers lead series, 1-0;
See San Diego vs. San Francisco
SAN FRANCISCO vs. SEATTLE
RS: 49ers lead series, 4-1
1976—49ers, 37-21 (S)
1979—Seahawks, 35-24 (SF)
1985—49ers, 19-6 (SF)
1988—49ers, 38-7 (S)
1991—49ers, 24-22 (S)
(RS Pts.—49ers 142, Seahawks 91)
SAN FRANCISCO vs. TAMPA BAY
RS: 49ers lead series, 12-1
1977—49ers, 20-10 (SF)
1978—49ers, 6-3 (SF)
1979—49ers, 23-7 (SF)
1980—Buccaneers, 24-23 (SF)
1983—49ers, 35-21 (SF)
1984—49ers, 24-17 (SF)
1986—49ers, 31-7 (TB)
1987—49ers, 24-10 (TB)
1989—49ers, 20-16 (TB)
1990—49ers, 31-7 (SF)
1992—49ers, 21-14 (SF)
1993—49ers, 45-21 (TB)
1994—49ers, 41-16 (SF)
(RS. Pts.—49ers 344, Buccaneers 173)
SAN FRANCISCO vs. WASHINGTON
RS: 49ers lead series, 10-6-1
PS: 49ers lead series, 3-1
1952—49ers, 23-17 (W)
1954—49ers, 41-7 (SF)
1955—Redskins, 7-0 (W)
1961—49ers, 35-3 (SF)
1967—Redskins, 31-28 (W)
1969—Tie, 17-17 (SF)
1970—49ers, 26-17 (SF)
1971—*49ers, 24-20 (SF)
1973—Redskins, 33-9 (W)
1976—Redskins, 24-21 (SF)
1978—Redskins, 38-20 (W)
1981—49ers, 30-17 (W)
1983—**Redskins, 24-21 (W)
1984—49ers, 37-31 (SF)
1985—49ers, 35-8 (W)
1986—Redskins, 14-6 (W)
1988—49ers, 37-21 (SF)
1990—49ers, 26-13 (SF)
*49ers, 28-10 (SF)
1992—*49ers, 20-13 (SF)
1994—49ers, 37-22 (W)
(RS Pts.—49ers 428, Redskins 320)
(PS Pts.—49ers 93, Redskins 67)
**NFC Divisional Playoff*
***NFC Championship*

SEATTLE vs. ARIZONA
RS: Cardinals lead series, 4-0;
See Arizona vs. Seattle
SEATTLE vs. ATLANTA
RS: Seahawks lead series, 4-1;
See Atlanta vs. Seattle
SEATTLE vs. BUFFALO
RS: Seahawks lead series, 3-1;
See Buffalo vs. Seattle
SEATTLE vs. CHICAGO
RS: Seahawks lead series, 4-2;
See Chicago vs. Seattle
SEATTLE vs. CINCINNATI
RS: Bengals lead series, 7-6
PS: Bengals lead series, 1-0;
See Cincinnati vs. Seattle
SEATTLE vs. CLEVELAND
RS: Seahawks lead series, 9-4;
See Cleveland vs. Seattle
SEATTLE vs. DALLAS
RS: Cowboys lead series, 4-1;
See Dallas vs. Seattle
SEATTLE vs. DENVER
RS: Broncos lead series, 22-13
PS: Seahawks lead series, 1-0;
See Denver vs. Seattle
SEATTLE vs. DETROIT
RS: Seahawks lead series, 4-2;
See Detroit vs. Seattle
SEATTLE vs. GREEN BAY
RS: Series tied, 3-3;
See Green Bay vs. Seattle
SEATTLE vs. HOUSTON
RS: Seahawks lead series, 5-4
PS: Oilers lead series, 1-0;
See Houston vs. Seattle
SEATTLE vs. INDIANAPOLIS
RS: Colts lead series, 4-1;
See Indianapolis vs. Seattle
SEATTLE vs. KANSAS CITY
RS: Chiefs lead series, 20-13;
See Kansas City vs. Seattle
SEATTLE vs. LOS ANGELES
RS: Raiders lead series, 19-15
PS: Series tied, 1-1;
See Los Angeles vs. Seattle
SEATTLE vs. MIAMI
RS: Dolphins lead series, 4-1
PS: Series tied, 1-1;
See Miami vs. Seattle
SEATTLE vs. MINNESOTA
RS: Seahawks lead series, 3-2;
See Minnesota vs. Seattle
SEATTLE vs. NEW ENGLAND
RS: Seahawks lead series, 7-6;
See New England vs. Seattle
SEATTLE vs. NEW ORLEANS
RS: Saints lead series, 3-2;
See New Orleans vs. Seattle
SEATTLE vs. N.Y. GIANTS
RS: Giants lead series, 5-2;
See N.Y. Giants vs. Seattle
SEATTLE vs. N.Y. JETS
RS: Seahawks lead series, 8-3;
See N.Y. Jets vs. Seattle
SEATTLE vs. PHILADELPHIA
RS: Eagles lead series, 4-1;
See Philadelphia vs. Seattle
SEATTLE vs. PITTSBURGH
RS: Seahawks lead series, 6-5;
See Pittsburgh vs. Seattle
SEATTLE vs. ST. LOUIS
RS: Rams lead series, 4-1;
See St. Louis vs. Seattle
SEATTLE vs. SAN DIEGO
RS: Chargers lead series, 17-15;
See San Diego vs. Seattle
SEATTLE vs. SAN FRANCISCO
RS: 49ers lead series, 4-1;
See San Francisco vs. Seattle
SEATTLE vs. TAMPA BAY
RS: Seahawks lead series, 3-0
1976—Seahawks, 13-10 (TB)
1977—Seahawks, 30-23 (S)
1994—Seahawks, 22-21 (S)
(RS Pts.—Seahawks 65, Buccaneers 54)
SEATTLE vs. WASHINGTON
RS: Redskins lead series, 5-2
1976—Redskins, 31-7 (W)
1980—Seahawks, 14-0 (W)
1983—Redskins, 27-17 (S)
1986—Redskins, 19-14 (W)
1989—Redskins, 29-0 (S)
1992—Redskins, 16-3 (S)
1994—Seahawks, 28-7 (W)
(RS Pts.—Redskins 129, Seahawks 83)

TAMPA BAY vs. ARIZONA
RS: Series tied, 6-6;
See Arizona vs. Tampa Bay
TAMPA BAY vs. ATLANTA
RS: Falcons lead series, 7-6;
See Atlanta vs. Tampa Bay
TAMPA BAY vs. BUFFALO
RS: Buccaneers lead series, 4-2;
See Buffalo vs. Tampa Bay
TAMPA BAY vs. CHICAGO
RS: Bears lead series, 26-8;
See Chicago vs. Tampa Bay
TAMPA BAY vs. CINCINNATI
RS: Bengals lead series, 3-1;
See Cincinnati vs. Tampa Bay
TAMPA BAY vs. CLEVELAND
RS: Browns lead series, 4-0;
See Cleveland vs. Tampa Bay
TAMPA BAY vs. DALLAS
RS: Cowboys lead series, 6-0
PS: Cowboys lead series, 2-0;
See Dallas vs. Tampa Bay
TAMPA BAY vs. DENVER
RS: Broncos lead series, 2-1;
See Denver vs. Tampa Bay
TAMPA BAY vs. DETROIT
RS: Series tied, 17-17;

See Detroit vs. Tampa Bay
TAMPA BAY vs. GREEN BAY
RS: Packers lead series, 19-12-1;
See Green Bay vs. Tampa Bay
TAMPA BAY vs. HOUSTON
RS: Oilers lead series, 3-1;
See Houston vs. Tampa Bay
TAMPA BAY vs. INDIANAPOLIS
RS: Colts lead series, 5-3;
See Indianapolis vs. Tampa Bay
TAMPA BAY vs. KANSAS CITY
RS: Chiefs lead series, 5-2;
See Kansas City vs. Tampa Bay
TAMPA BAY vs. LOS ANGELES
RS: Raiders lead series, 3-0;
See Los Angeles vs. Tampa Bay
TAMPA BAY vs. MIAMI
RS: Dolphins lead series, 4-1;
See Miami vs. Tampa Bay
TAMPA BAY vs. MINNESOTA
RS: Vikings lead series, 24-10;
See Minnesota vs. Tampa Bay
TAMPA BAY vs. NEW ENGLAND
RS: Patriots lead series, 3-0;
See New England vs. Tampa Bay
TAMPA BAY vs. NEW ORLEANS
RS: Saints lead series, 12-4;
See New Orleans vs. Tampa Bay
TAMPA BAY vs. N.Y. GIANTS
RS: Giants lead series, 8-3;
See N.Y. Giants vs. Tampa Bay
TAMPA BAY vs. N.Y. JETS
RS: Jets lead series, 5-1;
See N.Y. Jets vs. Tampa Bay
TAMPA BAY vs. PHILADELPHIA
RS: Eagles lead series, 3-1
PS: Buccaneers lead series, 1-0;
See Philadelphia vs. Tampa Bay
TAMPA BAY vs. PITTSBURGH
RS: Steelers lead series, 4-0;
See Pittsburgh vs. Tampa Bay
TAMPA BAY vs. ST. LOUIS
RS: Rams lead series, 8-3
PS: Rams lead series, 1-0;
See St. Louis vs. Tampa Bay
TAMPA BAY vs. SAN DIEGO
RS: Chargers lead series, 6-0;
See San Diego vs. Tampa Bay
TAMPA BAY vs. SAN FRANCISCO
RS: 49ers lead series, 12-1;
See San Francisco vs. Tampa Bay
TAMPA BAY vs. SEATTLE
RS: Seahawks lead series, 3-0;
See Seattle vs. Tampa Bay
TAMPA BAY vs. WASHINGTON
RS: Redskins lead series, 4-2
1977—Redskins, 10-0 (TB)
1982—Redskins, 21-13 (TB)
1989—Redskins, 32-28 (W)
1993—Redskins, 23-17 (TB)
1994—Buccaneers, 26-21 (TB)
Buccaneers, 17-14 (W)
(RS Pts.—Redskins 121, Buccaneers 101)

WASHINGTON vs. ARIZONA
RS: Redskins lead series, 61-38-2;
See Arizona vs. Washington
WASHINGTON vs. ATLANTA
RS: Redskins lead series, 13-4-1
PS: Redskins lead series, 1-0;
See Atlanta vs. Washington
WASHINGTON vs. BUFFALO
RS: Redskins lead series, 4-3
PS: Redskins lead series, 1-0;
See Buffalo vs. Washington
WASHINGTON vs. CHICAGO
RS: Bears lead series, 18-12-1
PS: Redskins lead series, 4-3;
See Chicago vs. Washington
WASHINGTON vs. CINCINNATI
RS: Redskins lead series, 4-2;
See Cincinnati vs. Washington
WASHINGTON vs. CLEVELAND
RS: Browns lead series, 32-9-1;
See Cleveland vs. Washington
WASHINGTON vs. DALLAS
RS: Cowboys lead series, 39-27-2
PS: Redskins lead series, 2-0;
See Dallas vs. Washington
WASHINGTON vs. DENVER
RS: Series tied 3-3
PS: Redskins lead series, 1-0;
See Denver vs. Washington
WASHINGTON vs. DETROIT
RS: Redskins lead series, 22-8
PS: Redskins lead series, 2-0;
See Detroit vs. Washington
WASHINGTON vs. GREEN BAY
RS: Packers lead series, 13-12-1
PS: Series tied 1-1;
See Green Bay vs. Washington
WASHINGTON vs. HOUSTON
RS: Series tied 3-3;
See Houston vs. Washington
WASHINGTON vs. INDIANAPOLIS
RS: Colts lead series, 16-8;
See Indianapolis vs. Washington
WASHINGTON vs. KANSAS CITY
RS: Chiefs lead series, 3-1;
See Kansas City vs. Washington
WASHINGTON vs. LOS ANGELES
RS: Raiders lead series, 5-2
PS: Raiders lead series, 1-0;
See Los Angeles vs. Washington
WASHINGTON vs. MIAMI
RS: Dolphins lead series, 5-2
PS: Series tied 1-1;
See Miami vs. Washington
WASHINGTON vs. MINNESOTA
RS: Redskins lead series, 6-4
PS: Redskins lead series, 3-2;
See Minnesota vs. Washington
WASHINGTON vs. NEW ENGLAND
RS: Redskins lead series, 4-1;
See New England vs. Washington
WASHINGTON vs. NEW ORLEANS
RS: Redskins lead series, 12-5;
See New Orleans vs. Washington
WASHINGTON vs. N.Y. GIANTS
RS: Giants lead series, 71-50-3
PS: Series tied 1-1;
See N.Y. Giants vs. Washington
WASHINGTON vs. N.Y. JETS
RS: Redskins lead series, 4-1;
See N.Y. Jets vs. Washington
WASHINGTON vs. PHILADELPHIA
RS: Redskins lead series, 66-48-5
PS: Redskins lead series, 1-0;
See Philadelphia vs. Washington
WASHINGTON vs. PITTSBURGH
RS: Redskins lead series, 42-27-3;
See Pittsburgh vs. Washington
WASHINGTON vs. ST. LOUIS
RS: Redskins lead series, 15-5-1
PS: Series tied 2-2;
See St. Louis vs. Washington
WASHINGTON vs. SAN DIEGO
RS: Redskins lead series, 5-0;
See San Diego vs. Washington
WASHINGTON vs. SAN FRANCISCO
RS: 49ers lead series, 10-6-1
PS: 49ers lead series, 3-1;
See San Francisco vs. Washington
WASHINGTON vs. SEATTLE
RS: Redskins lead series, 5-2;
See Seattle vs. Washington
WASHINGTON vs. TAMPA BAY
RS: Redskins lead series, 4-2;
See Tampa Bay vs. Washington

SUPER BOWL SUMMARIES

RESULTS

Season	Date	Winner (Share)	Loser (Share)	Score	Site	Attendance
XXIX	1-29-95	San Francisco ($38,000)	San Diego ($23,500)	49-26	Miami	74,107
XXVIII	1-30-94	Dallas ($38,000)	Buffalo ($23,500)	30-13	Atlanta	72,817
XXVII	1-31-93	Dallas ($36,000)	Buffalo ($18,000)	52-17	Pasadena	98,374
XXVI	1-26-92	Washington ($36,000)	Buffalo ($18,000)	37-24	Minneapolis	63,130
XXV	1-27-91	N.Y. Giants ($36,000)	Buffalo ($18,000)	20-19	Tampa	73,813
XXIV	1-28-90	San Francisco ($36,000)	Denver ($18,000)	55-10	New Orleans	72,919
XXIII	1-22-89	San Francisco ($36,000)	Cincinnati ($18,000)	20-16	Miami	75,129
XXII	1-31-88	Washington ($36,000)	Denver ($18,000)	42-10	San Diego	73,302
XXI	1-25-87	N.Y. Giants ($36,000)	Denver ($18,000)	39-20	Pasadena	101,063
XX	1-26-86	Chicago ($36,000)	New England ($18,000)	46-10	New Orleans	73,818
XIX	1-20-85	San Francisco ($36,000)	Miami ($18,000)	38-16	Stanford	84,059
XVIII	1-22-84	L.A. Raiders ($36,000)	Washington ($18,000)	38-9	Tampa	72,920
XVII	1-30-83	Washington ($36,000)	Miami ($18,000)	27-17	Pasadena	103,667
XVI	1-24-82	San Francisco ($18,000)	Cincinnati ($9,000)	26-21	Pontiac	81,270
XV	1-25-81	Oakland ($18,000)	Philadelphia ($9,000)	27-10	New Orleans	76,135
XIV	1-20-80	Pittsburgh ($18,000)	Los Angeles ($9,000)	31-19	Pasadena	103,985
XIII	1-21-79	Pittsburgh ($18,000)	Dallas ($9,000)	35-31	Miami	79,484
XII	1-15-78	Dallas ($18,000)	Denver ($9,000)	27-10	New Orleans	75,583
XI	1-9-77	Oakland ($15,000)	Minnesota ($7,500)	32-14	Pasadena	103,438
X	1-18-76	Pittsburgh ($15,000)	Dallas ($7,500)	21-17	Miami	80,187
IX	1-12-75	Pittsburgh ($15,000)	Minnesota ($7,500)	16-6	New Orleans	80,997
VIII	1-13-74	Miami ($15,000)	Minnesota ($7,500)	24-7	Houston	71,882
VII	1-14-73	Miami ($15,000)	Washington ($7,500)	14-7	Los Angeles	90,182
VI	1-16-72	Dallas ($15,000)	Miami ($7,500)	24-3	New Orleans	81,023
V	1-17-71	Baltimore ($15,000)	Dallas ($7,500)	16-13	Miami	79,204
IV	1-11-70	Kansas City ($15,000)	Minnesota ($7,500)	23-7	New Orleans	80,562
III	1-12-69	N.Y. Jets ($15,000)	Baltimore ($7,500)	16-7	Miami	75,389
II	1-14-68	Green Bay ($15,000)	Oakland ($7,500)	33-14	Miami	75,546
I	1-15-67	Green Bay ($15,000)	Kansas City ($7,500)	35-10	Los Angeles	61,946

SUPER BOWL COMPOSITE STANDINGS

	W	L	Pct.	Pts.	OP
San Francisco 49ers	5	0	1.000	188	89
Pittsburgh Steelers	4	0	1.000	103	73
Green Bay Packers	2	0	1.000	68	24
New York Giants	2	0	1.000	59	39
Chicago Bears	1	0	1.000	46	10
New York Jets	1	0	1.000	16	7
Oakland/L.A. Raiders	3	1	.750	111	66
Washington Redskins	3	2	.600	122	103
Dallas Cowboys	4	3	.571	194	115
Baltimore Colts	1	1	.500	23	29
Kansas City Chiefs	1	1	.500	33	42
Miami Dolphins	2	3	.400	74	103
Los Angeles Rams	0	1	.000	19	31
New England Patriots	0	1	.000	10	46
Philadelphia Eagles	0	1	.000	10	27
San Diego Chargers	0	1	.000	26	49
Cincinnati Bengals	0	2	.000	37	46
Buffalo Bills	0	4	.000	73	139
Denver Broncos	0	4	.000	50	163
Minnesota Vikings	0	4	.000	34	95

SUPER BOWL MOST VALUABLE PLAYERS*

Super Bowl I — QB Bart Starr, Green Bay
Super Bowl II — QB Bart Starr, Green Bay
Super Bowl III — QB Joe Namath, N.Y. Jets
Super Bowl IV — QB Len Dawson, Kansas City
Super Bowl V — LB Chuck Howley, Dallas
Super Bowl VI — QB Roger Staubach, Dallas
Super Bowl VII — S Jake Scott, Miami
Super Bowl VIII — RB Larry Csonka, Miami
Super Bowl IX — RB Franco Harris, Pittsburgh
Super Bowl X — WR Lynn Swann, Pittsburgh
Super Bowl XI — WR Fred Biletnikoff, Oakland
Super Bowl XII — DT Randy White and DE Harvey Martin, Dallas
Super Bowl XIII — QB Terry Bradshaw, Pittsburgh
Super Bowl XIV — QB Terry Bradshaw, Pittsburgh
Super Bowl XV — QB Jim Plunkett, Oakland
Super Bowl XVI — QB Joe Montana, San Francisco
Super Bowl XVII — RB John Riggins, Washington
Super Bowl XVIII — RB Marcus Allen, L.A. Raiders
Super Bowl XIX — QB Joe Montana, San Francisco
Super Bowl XX — DE Richard Dent, Chicago
Super Bowl XXI — QB Phil Simms, N.Y. Giants
Super Bowl XXII — QB Doug Williams, Washington
Super Bowl XXIII — WR Jerry Rice, San Francisco
Super Bowl XXIV — QB Joe Montana, San Francisco
Super Bowl XXV — RB Ottis Anderson, N.Y. Giants
Super Bowl XXVI — QB Mark Rypien, Washington
Super Bowl XXVII — QB Troy Aikman, Dallas
Super Bowl XXVIII — RB Emmitt Smith, Dallas
Super Bowl XXIX — QB Steve Young, San Francisco

** Award named Pete Rozelle Trophy since Super Bowl XXV.*

SUPER BOWL XXIX

Joe Robbie Stadium, Miami, Florida
January 29, 1995, Attendance: 74,107

SAN FRANCISCO 49, SAN DIEGO 26—Steve Young threw a record 6 touchdown passes, and the 49ers became the first team to win five Super Bowls when they routed the Chargers. Young, the game's most valuable player, directed an explosive offense that generated 7 touchdowns, 28 first downs, and 455 total yards. He completed 24 of 36 passes for 325 yards, and broke former 49ers quarterback Joe Montana's previous record of 5 touchdown passes in Super Bowl XXIV. San Francisco wasted little time scoring, taking the lead for good on Young's 44-yard touchdown pass to Jerry Rice only three plays and 1:24 into the game. The next time they had the ball, the 49ers marched 79 yards in four plays, taking a 14-0 lead when Young teamed with running back Ricky Watters on a 51-yard touchdown pass with 10:05 still to play in the opening period. San Diego then put together its most impressive possession of the game, a 13-play, 78-yard drive that consumed more than 7 minutes and was capped by Natrone Means's 1-yard touchdown run, to cut its deficit to 14-7 late in the quarter. But San Francisco countered with a 70-yard drive of its own, and Young's 5-yard touchdown pass to fullback William Floyd made it 21-7. Young's fourth touchdown pass of the half, 8 yards to Watters 4:44 before halftime, increased the advantage to 28-7, and the Chargers could get no closer than 18 points after that. Watters, who ran 9 yards for a touchdown in the third quarter, equaled the Super Bowl record with 3 touchdowns. Rice also scored 3 touchdowns (the second time in his career he'd done that in a Super Bowl) while catching 10 passes for 149 yards. He established career records for receptions, yards, and touchdowns in a Super Bowl. Young, who scrambled 21 yards and 15 yards to set up touchdowns in the first half, was the game's leading rusher with 49 yards on 5 carries. San Diego's Means, who rushed for 1,350 yards during the regular season, was limited to 33 yards on 13 attempts. Chargers quarterback Stan Humphries completed 24 of 49 passes for 275 yards. Rookie Andre Coleman became only the third player in Super Bowl history to return a kickoff for a touchdown, going 98 yards in the third quarter. The 75 points scored by the two teams established another record, breaking the previous mark of 69 set in Dallas's 52-17 victory over Buffalo in XXVII. The 49ers' victory was the eleventh straight for NFC teams over AFC teams in the Super Bowl.

San Diego (26)	Offense	San Francisco (49)
Shawn Jefferson	WR	John Taylor
Harry Swane	LT	Steve Wallace
Isaac Davis	LG	Jesse Sapolu
Courtney Hall	C	Bart Oates
Joe Cocozzo	RG	Derrick Deese
Stan Brock	RT	Harris Barton
Duane Young	TE	Brent Jones
Mark Seay	WR	Jerry Rice
Stan Humphries	QB	Steve Young
Natrone Means	RB	Ricky Watters
Alfred Pupunu	TE-RB	William Floyd
	Defense	
Chris Mims	LE	Dennis Brown
Shawn Lee	LT	Bryant Young
Reuben Davis	RT	Dana Stubblefield
Leslie O'Neal	RE	Rickey Jackson
David Griggs	OLB-LLB	Lee Woodall
Dennis Gibson	ILB-MLB	Gary Plummer
Junior Seau	ILB-RLB	Ken Norton
Darrien Gordon	LCB	Eric Davis
Dwayne Harper	RCB	Deion Sanders
Darren Carrington	SS	Tim McDonald
Stanley Richard	FS	Merton Hanks

SUBSTITUTIONS

SAN DIEGO—Offense: K-John Carney. P-Bryan Wagner. QB-Gale Gilbert. RB-Eric Bieniemy, Rodney Culver, Ronnie Harmon. WR-Tony Martin. TE-David Binn, Shannon Mitchell. T-Eric Jonassen, Vaughn Parker. KR-Andre Coleman. Defense: DE-Raylee Johnson. DT-Les Miller, John Parrella. LB-Lewis

Bush, Steve Hendrickson, Doug Miller. CB-Willie Clark, Sean Vanhorse. S-Eric Castle, Rodney Harrison. DNP: C-Curtis Whitley.

SAN FRANCISCO—Offense: K-Doug Brien. P-Klaus Wilmsmeyer. QB-Elvis Grbac, Bill Musgrave. RB-Marc Logan, Derek Loville, Adam Walker. WR-Ed McCaffrey, Nate Singleton. TE-Ted Popson. T-Frank Pollack. G-Ralph Tamm. C-Chris Dalman. KR-Dexter Carter. Defense: DE-Tim Harris, Charles Mann, Troy Wilson. DT-Rhett Hall. LB-Antonio Goss, Darin Jordan, Kevin Mitchell. CB-Toi Cook, Tyronne Drakeford. S-Dana Hall. DNP: None.

OFFICIALS

Referee—Jerry Markbreit. Umpire-Ron Botchan. Head Linesman-Ron Phares. Line Judge-Ron Baynes. Back Judge-Timmie Millis. Field Judge-Jack Vaughan. Side Judge-Tom Fincken.

SCORING

San Diego (AFC)	7	3	8	8	—	26
San Francisco (NFC)	14	14	14	7	—	49

SF — Rice 44 pass from S. Young (Brien kick)
SF — Watters 51 pass from S. Young (Brien kick)
SD — Means 1 run (Carney kick)
SF — Floyd 5 pass from S. Young (Brien kick)
SF — Watters 8 pass from S. Young (Brien kick)
SD — FG Carney 31
SF — Watters 9 run (Brien kick)
SF — Rice 15 pass from S. Young (Brien kick)
SD — Coleman 98 kickoff return (Seay pass from Humphries)
SF — Rice 7 pass from S. Young (Brien kick)
SD — Martin 30 pass from Humphries (Pupunu pass from Humphries)

TEAM STATISTICS	San Diego	San Francisco
Total First Downs	20	28
Rushing	5	10
Passing	14	17
Penalty	1	1
Total Net Yardage	354	455
Total Offensive Plays	76	73
Average Gain per Offensive Play	4.7	6.2
Rushes	19	32
Yards Gained Rushing (Net)	67	139
Average Yards per Rush	3.5	4.3
Passes Attempted	55	38
Passes Completed	27	25
Had Intercepted	3	0
Tackled Attempting to Pass	2	3
Yards Lost Attempting to Pass	18	15
Yards Gained Passing (Net)	287	316
Punts	4	5
Average Distance	48.8	39.8
Punt Returns	3	2
Punt Return Yardage	1	12
Kickoff Returns	8	4
Kickoff Return Yardage	242	48
Interception Return Yardage	0	16
Total Return Yardage	243	76
Fumbles	1	2
Own Fumbles Recovered	1	2
Opponent Fumbles Recovered	0	0
Penalties	6	3
Yards Penalized	63	18
Total Points Scored	26	49
Touchdowns	3	7
Rushing	1	1
Passing	1	6
Returns	1	0
Extra Points	3	7
Field Goals	1	0
Field Goals Attempted	1	1
Safeties	0	0
Third-Down Efficiency	6/16	7/13
Fourth-Down Efficiency	0/4	0/0
Time of Possession	28:29	31:31

INDIVIDUAL STATISTICS

Rushing

San Diego	No.	Yds.	LG	TD
Means	13	33	11	1
Jefferson	1	10	10	0
Harmon	2	10	10	0
Gilbert	1	8	8	0
Bieniemy	1	3	3	0
Humphries	1	3	3	0
San Francisco	**No.**	**Yds.**	**LG**	**TD**
S. Young	5	49	21	0
Watters	15	47	13	1
Floyd	9	32	6	0
Rice	1	10	10	0
Carter	1	1	1	0
Grbac	1	0	0	0

Passing

San Diego	Att.	Comp.	Yds.	TD	Int.
Humphries	49	24	275	1	2
Gilbert	6	3	30	0	1
San Francisco	**Att.**	**Comp.**	**Yds.**	**TD**	**Int.**
S. Young	36	24	325	6	0
Musgrave	1	1	6	0	0
Grbac	1	0	0	0	0

Receiving

San Diego	No.	Yds.	LG	TD
Harmon	8	68	20	0
Seay	7	75	22	0
Pupunu	4	48	23	0
Martin	3	59	30t	1
Jefferson	2	15	9	0
Bieniemy	1	33	33	0
Means	1	4	4	0
D. Young	1	3	3	0
San Francisco	**No.**	**Yds.**	**LG**	**TD**
Rice	10	149	44t	3
Taylor	4	43	16	0
Floyd	4	26	9	1
Watters	3	61	51t	2
Jones	2	41	33	0
Popson	1	6	6	0
McCaffrey	1	5	5	0

Interceptions

San Diego	No.	Yds.	LG	TD
None				
San Francisco	**No.**	**Yds.**	**LG**	**TD**
Sanders	1	15	15	0
Cook	1	1	1	0
Davis	1	0	0	0

Punting

San Diego	No.	Avg.	LG	Blk.
Wagner	4	48.8	55	0
San Francisco	**No.**	**Avg.**	**LG**	**Blk.**
Wilmsmeyer	5	39.8	46	0

Punt Returns

San Diego	No.	FC	Yds.	LG	TD
Gordon	3	2	1	1	0
San Francisco	**No.**	**FC**	**Yds.**	**LG**	**TD**
Carter	2	0	12	11	0

Kickoff Returns

San Diego	No.	Yds.	LG	TD
Coleman	8	242	98t	1
San Francisco	**No.**	**Yds.**	**LG**	**TD**
Carter	4	48	18	0

SUPER BOWL XXVIII

Georgia Dome, Atlanta, Georgia
January 30, 1994, Attendance: 72,817

DALLAS 30, BUFFALO 13—Emmitt Smith rushed for 132 yards and 2 second-half touchdowns to power the Cowboys to their second consecutive NFL title. By winning, Dallas joined San Francisco and Pittsburgh as the only franchises with four Super Bowl victories. The Bills, meanwhile, extended a dubious string by losing in the Super Bowl for the fourth consecutive year. To win, the Cowboys had to rally from a 13-6 halftime deficit. Buffalo had forged its lead on Thurman Thomas's 4-yard touchdown run and a pair of field goals by Steve Christie, including a 54-yard kick, the longest in Super Bowl history. But just 55 seconds into the second half, Thomas was stripped of the ball by Dallas defensive tackle Leon Lett. Safety James Washington recovered and weaved his way 46 yards for a touchdown to tie the game at 13-13. After forcing the Bills to punt, the Cowboys began their next possession on their 36-yard line and Smith, the game's most valuable player, took over. He carried 7 times for 61 yards on the ensuing 8-play, 64-yard drive, capping the march with a 15-yard touchdown run to give Dallas the lead for good with 8:42 remaining in the third quarter. Early in the fourth quarter, Washington intercepted Jim Kelly's pass and returned it 12 yards to Buffalo's 34. A penalty moved the ball back to the 39, but Smith carried twice for 10 yards and caught a screen pass for 9, and quarterback Troy Aikman completed a 16-yard pass to Alvin Harper to give the Cowboys a first-and-goal at the 6. Smith took it from there, cracking the end zone on fourth-and-goal from the 1 to put Dallas ahead 27-13 with 9:50 remaining. Eddie Murray's third field goal, from 20 yards with 2:50 left, ended any doubt about the game's outcome. Smith had 30 carries in all, with 19 of his attempts and 92 yards coming after intermission. Washington, normally a reserve who played most of the game because the Cowboys used five defensive backs to combat the Bills' No-Huddle offense, had 11 tackles and forced another fumble by Thomas in the first quarter. Aikman completed 19 of 27 passes for 207 yards. Buffalo's Kelly completed a Super Bowl-record 31 passes in 50 attempts for 260 yards. Dallas, the first team in NFL history to begin the regular season 0-2 and go on to win the Super Bowl, also became the fifth to win back-to-back titles, following Green Bay, Miami, Pittsburgh (the Steelers did it twice), and San Francisco. Buffalo became the third team, along with Minnesota and Denver, to lose four Super Bowls. The Cowboys' victory was the tenth in succession for the NFC over the AFC.

Dallas (NFC)	6	0	14	10	—	30
Buffalo (AFC)	3	10	0	0	—	13

Dall — FG Murray 41
Buff — FG Christie 54
Dall — FG Murray 24
Buff — Thomas 4 run (Christie kick)
Buff — FG Christie 28
Dall — Washington 46 fumble return (Murray kick)
Dall — E. Smith 15 run (Murray kick)
Dall — E. Smith 1 run (Murray kick)
Dall — FG Murray 20

SUPER BOWL XXVII

Rose Bowl, Pasadena, California
January 31, 1993, Attendance: 98,374

DALLAS 52, BUFFALO 17—Troy Aikman threw 4 touchdown passes, Emmitt Smith rushed for 108 yards, and the Cowboys converted 9 turnovers into 35 points while coasting to the victory. Dallas's win was its third in its record sixth Super Bowl appearance; the Bills became the first team to drop three in succession. Buffalo led 7-0 until the first 2 of its record number of turnovers helped the Cowboys take the lead for good late in the opening quarter. First, Dallas safety James Washington intercepted a Jim Kelly pass and returned it 13 yards to the Bills' 47, setting up Aikman's 23-yard touchdown pass to tight end Jay Novacek with 1:36 remaining in the period. On the next play from scrimmage, Kelly was sacked by Charles Haley and fumbled at the Bills' 2-yard line where the Cowboys' Jimmie Jones picked up the loose ball and ran 2 yards for a touchdown. Dallas, which recovered 5 fumbles and intercepted 4 passes, struck just as quickly late in the first half, when Aikman tossed 19- and 18-yard touchdown passes to Michael Irvin 15 seconds apart to give the Cowboys a 28-10 lead at intermission. The second score was set up when Bills running back Thurman Thomas lost a fumble at his 19-yard line. Buffalo scored for the last time when backup quarterback Frank Reich, playing because Kelly was injured while attempting to pass midway through the second quarter, threw a 40-yard touchdown pass to Don Beebe on the final play of the third period to trim the deficit to 31-17. But Dallas put the game out of reach by scoring three times in a span of 2:33 of the fourth quarter. Aikman, the game's most valuable player, completed 22 of 30 passes for 273 yards and was not intercepted. The victory was the ninth in succession for the NFC over the AFC.

Buffalo (AFC)	7	3	7	0	—	17
Dallas (NFC)	14	14	3	21	—	52

Buff — Thomas 2 run (Christie kick)
Dall — Novacek 23 pass from Aikman (Elliott kick)
Dall — J. Jones 2 fumble recovery return (Elliott kick)
Buff — FG Christie 21
Dall — Irvin 19 pass from Aikman (Elliott kick)
Dall — Irvin 18 pass from Aikman (Elliott kick)
Dall — FG Elliott 20
Buff — Beebe 40 pass from Reich (Christie kick)
Dall — Harper 45 pass from Aikman (Elliott kick)
Dall — E. Smith 10 run (Elliott kick)
Dall — Norton 9 fumble recovery return (Elliott kick)

SUPER BOWL XXVI

Metrodome, Minneapolis, Minnesota
January 26, 1992, Attendance: 63,130

WASHINGTON 37, BUFFALO 24—Mark Rypien passed for 292 yards and 2 touchdowns as the Redskins overwhelmed the Bills to win their third Super Bowl in the past 10 years. Rypien, the game's most valuable player, completed 18 of 33 passes, including a 10-yard scoring strike to Earnest Byner and a 30-yard touchdown to Gary Clark. The latter came late in the third quarter after Buffalo had trimmed a 24-0 deficit to 24-10, and effectively put the game out of reach. Washington went on to lead by as much as 37-10 before the Bills made it close wih a pair of touchdowns in the final six minutes. Though the Redskins struggled early, converting their first three drives inside the Bills' 20-yard line into only 3 points, they built a 17-0 halftime lead. And they made it 24-0 just 16 seconds into the second half, after Kurt Gouveia intercepted Buffalo quarterback Jim Kelly's pass on the first play of the third quarter and returned it 23 yards to the Bills' 2. One play later, Gerald Riggs scored his second touchdown of the game to make it 24-0. Kelly, forced to bring Buffalo from behind, completed 28 of a Super Bowl-record 58 passes for 275 yards and 2 touchdowns, but was intercepted 4 times. Bills running back Thurman Thomas, who had an AFC-high 1,407 yards rushing and an NFL-best 2,038 total yards from scrimmage during the regular season, ran for only 13 yards on 10 carries and was limited to 27 yards on 4 receptions. Clark had 7 catches for 114 yards and Art Monk added 7 for 113 for the Redskins, who amassed 417 yards of total offense while limiting the explosive Bills to 283. Washington's Joe Gibbs became only the third head coach to win three Super Bowls.

Washington (NFC)	0	17	14	6	—	37
Buffalo (AFC)	0	0	10	14	—	24

Wash — FG Lohmiller 34
Wash — Byner 10 pass from Rypien (Lohmiller kick)
Wash — Riggs 1 run (Lohmiller kick)
Wash — Riggs 2 run (Lohmiller kick)
Buff — FG Norwood 21
Buff — Thomas 1 run (Norwood kick)
Wash — Clark 30 pass from Rypien(Lohmiller kick)
Wash — FG Lohmiller 25
Wash — FG Lohmiller 39
Buff — Metzelaars 2 pass from Kelly (Norwood kick)
Buff — Beebe 4 pass from Kelly (Norwood kick)

SUPER BOWL XXV

Tampa Stadium, Tampa, Florida
January 27, 1991, Attendance: 73,813

NEW YORK GIANTS 20, BUFFALO 19—The NFC champion New York Giants won their second Super Bowl in five years with a 20-19 victory over AFC titlist Buffalo. New York, employing its ball-control offense, had possession for 40 minutes, 33 seconds, a Super Bowl record. The Bills, who scored 95 points in their previous two playoff games leading to Super Bowl XXV, had the ball for less than eight minutes in the second half and just 19:27 for the game. Fourteen of New York's 73 plays came on its initial drive of the third quarter, which covered 75 yards and consumed a Super Bowl-record 9:29 before running back Ottis Anderson ran 1 yard for a touchdown. Giants quarterback Jeff Hostetler kept the long drive going by converting three third-down plays—an 11-yard pass to running back David Meggett on third-and-eight, a 14-yard toss to wide receiver Mark Ingram on third-and-13, and a 9-yard pass to Howard Cross on third-and-four—to give New York a 17-12 lead in the third quarter. Buffalo jumped to a 12-3 lead midway through the second quarter before Hostetler completed a 14-yard scoring strike to wide receiver Stephen Baker to close the score to 12-10 at halftime. Buffalo's Thurman Thomas ran 31 yards for a touchdown on the opening play of the fourth quarter to help Buffalo recapture the lead 19-17. Matt Bahr's 21-yard field goal gave the Giants a 20-19 lead, but Buffalo's Scott Norwood had a chance to win the game with seconds remaining before his 47-yard field-goal attempt sailed wide right. Hostetler completed 20 of 32 passes for 222 yards and 1 touchdown. Anderson rushed 21 times for 102 yards and 1 touchdown to capture the most-valuable-player honors. Thomas totaled 190 scrimmage yards, rushing 15 times for 135 yards and catching 5 passes for 55 yards.

Buffalo (AFC)	3	9	0	7	—	19
N.Y. Giants (NFC)	3	7	7	3	—	20

NYG — FG Bahr 28
Buff — FG Norwood 23
Buff — D. Smith 1 run (Norwood kick)
Buff — Safety, B. Smith tackled Hostetler in end zone
NYG — Baker 14 pass from Hostetler (Bahr kick)
NYG — Anderson 1 run (Bahr kick)
Buff — Thomas 31 run (Norwood kick)
NYG — FG Bahr 21

SUPER BOWL XXIV

Louisiana Superdome, New Orleans, Louisiana
January 28, 1990, Attendance: 72,919

SAN FRANCISCO 55, DENVER 10—NFC titlist San Francisco won its fourth Super Bowl championship with a 55-10 victory over AFC champion Denver. The 49ers, who also won Super Bowls XVI, XIX, and XXIII, tied the Pittsburgh Steelers for most Super Bowl victories. The Steelers captured Super Bowls IX, X, XIII, and XIV. San Francisco's 55 points broke the previous Super Bowl scoring mark of 46 points by Chicago in Super Bowl XX. San Francisco scored touchdowns on four of its six first-half possessions to hold a 27-3 lead at halftime. Interceptions by Michael Walter and Chet Brooks ended the Broncos' first two possessions of the second half. San Francisco quarterback Joe Montana was named the Super Bowl most valuable player for a record third time. Montana completed 22 of 29 passes for 297 yards and a Super Bowl-record 5 touchdowns. Jerry Rice, Super Bowl XXIII most valuable player, caught 7 passes for 148 yards and three touchdowns. The 49ers' domination included first downs (28 to 12), net yards (461 to 167), and time of possession (39:31 to 20:29).

San Francisco (NFC)	13	14	14	14	—	55
Denver (AFC)	3	0	7	0	—	10

SF — Rice 20 pass from Montana (Cofer kick)
Den — FG Treadwell 42
SF — Jones 7 pass from Montana (kick failed)
SF — Rathman 1 run (Cofer kick)
SF — Rice 38 pass from Montana (Cofer kick)
SF — Rice 28 pass from Montana (Cofer kick)
SF — Taylor 35 pass from Montana (Cofer kick)
Den — Elway 3 run (Treadwell kick)
SF — Rathman 3 run (Cofer kick)
SF — Craig 1 run (Cofer kick)

SUPER BOWL XXIII

Joe Robbie Stadium, Miami, Florida
January 22, 1989, Attendance: 75,129

SAN FRANCISCO 20, CINCINNATI 16—NFC champion San Francisco captured its third Super Bowl of the 1980s by defeating AFC champion Cincinnati 20-16. The 49ers, who also won Super Bowls XVI and XIX, are the first NFC team to win three Super Bowls. Pittsburgh, with four Super Bowl titles (IX, X, XIII, and XIV), and the Oakland/Los Angeles Raiders, with three (XI, XV, and XVIII), lead AFC franchises. Even though San Francisco held an advantage in total net yards (453 to 229), the 49ers found themselves trailing the Bengals late in the game. With the score 13-13, Cincinnati took a 16-13 lead on Jim Breech's 40-yard field goal with 3:20 remaining. It was Breech's third field goal of the day, following earlier successes from 34 and 43 yards. The 49ers started their winning drive at their 8-yard line. Over the next 11 plays, San Francisco covered 92 yards with the decisive score coming on a 10-yard pass from quarterback Joe Montana to wide receiver John Taylor with 34 seconds remaining. At halftime, the score was 3-3, the first time in Super Bowl history the game was tied at intermission. After the teams traded third-period field goals, the Bengals jumped ahead 13-6 on Stanford Jennings's 93-yard kickoff return for a touchdown with 34 seconds remaining in the quarter. The 49ers didn't waste any time coming back as they covered 85 yards in four plays, concluding with Montana's 14-yard scoring pass to Jerry Rice 57 seconds into the final stanza. Rice was named the game's most valuable player after compiling 11 catches for a Super Bowl-record 215 yards. Montana completed 23 of 36 passes for a Super Bowl-record 357 yards and 2 touchdowns.

Cincinnati (AFC)	0	3	10	3	—	16
San Francisco (NFC)	3	0	3	14	—	20

SF — FG Cofer 41
Cin — FG Breech 34
Cin — FG Breech 43
SF — FG Cofer 32
Cin — Jennings 93 kickoff return (Breech kick)
SF — Rice 14 pass from Montana (Cofer kick)
Cin — FG Breech 40
SF — Taylor 10 pass from Montana (Cofer kick)

SUPER BOWL XXII

San Diego Jack Murphy Stadium, San Diego, California
January 31, 1988, Attendance: 73,302

WASHINGTON 42, DENVER 10—NFC champion Washington won Super Bowl XXII and its second NFL championship of the 1980s with a 42-10 decision over AFC champion Denver. The Redskins, who also won Super Bowl XVII, enjoyed a record-setting second quarter en route to the victory. The Broncos broke in front 10-0 when quarterback John Elway threw a 56-yard touchdown pass to wide receiver Ricky Nattiel on the Broncos' first play from scrimmage. Following a Washington punt, Denver's Rich Karlis kicked a 24-yard field goal to cap a seven-play, 61-yard scoring drive. The Redskins then erupted for 35 points on five straight possessions in the second period and coasted thereafter. The 35 points established an NFL postseason mark for most points in a period, bettering the previous total of 21 by San Francisco in Super Bowl XIX and Chicago in Super Bowl XX. Redskins quarterback Doug Williams led the second-period explosion by throwing a Super Bowl record-tying 4 touchdown passes, including 80- and 50-yard passes to wide receiver Ricky Sanders, a 27-yard toss to wide receiver Gary Clark, and an 8-yard pass to tight end Clint Didier. Washington scored 5 touchdowns in 18 plays with total time of possession of only 5:47. Overall, Williams completed 18 of 29 passes for 340 yards and was named the game's most valuable player. His passyardage total eclipsed the Super Bowl record of 331 yards by Joe Montana of San Francisco in Super Bowl XIX. Sanders ended with 193 yards on 8 catches, breaking the previous Super Bowl yardage record of 161 yards by Lynn Swann of Pittsburgh in Game X. Rookie running back Timmy Smith was the game's leading rusher with 22 carries for a Super Bowl-record 204 yards, breaking the previous mark of 191 yards by Marcus Allen of the Raiders in Game XVIII. Smith also scored twice on runs of 58 and 4 yards. Washington's 6 touchdowns and 602 total yards gained also set Super Bowl records. Redskins cornerback Barry Wilburn had 2 of the team's 3 interceptions, and strong safety Alvin Walton had 2 of Washington's 5 sacks.

Washington (NFC)	0	35	0	7	— 42
Denver (AFC)	10	0	0	0	— 10

Den — Nattiel 56 pass from Elway (Karlis kick)
Den — FG Karlis 24
Wash — Sanders 80 pass from Williams (Haji-Sheikh kick)
Wash — Clark 27 pass from Williams (Haji-Sheikh kick)
Wash — Smith 58 run (Haji-Sheikh kick)
Wash — Sanders 50 pass from Williams (Haji-Sheikh kick)
Wash — Didier 8 pass from Williams (Haji-Sheikh kick)
Wash — Smith 4 run (Haji-Sheikh kick)

SUPER BOWL XXI

Rose Bowl, Pasadena, California
January 25, 1987, Attendance: 101,063

NEW YORK GIANTS 39, DENVER 20—The NFC champion New York Giants captured their first NFL title since 1956 when they downed the AFC champion Denver Broncos 39-20 in Super Bowl XXI. The victory marked the NFC's fifth NFL title in the past six seasons. The Broncos, behind the passing of quarterback John Elway, who was 13 of 20 for 187 yards in the first half, held a 10-9 lead at intermission, the narrowest halftime margin in Super Bowl history. Denver's Rich Karlis opened the scoring with a Super Bowl record-tying 48-yard field goal. New York drove 78 yards in nine plays on the next series to take a 7-3 lead on quarterback Phil Simms's 6-yard touchdown pass to tight end Zeke Mowatt. The Broncos came right back with a 58-yard scoring drive on six plays capped by Elway's 4-yard touchdown run. The only scoring in the second period was the sack of Elway in the end zone by defensive end George Martin for a New York safety. The Giants produced a key defensive stand early in the second quarter when the Broncos had a first down at the New York 1-yard line, but failed to score on three running plays and Karlis's 23-yard missed field-goal attempt. The Giants took command of the game in the third period en route to a 30-point second half, the most ever scored in one half of Super Bowl play. New York took the lead for good on tight end Mark Bavaro's 13-yard touchdown catch 4:52 into the third period. The nine-play, 63-yard scoring drive included the successful conversion of a fourth-and-1 play on the New York 46-yard line. Denver was limited to only 2 net yards on 10 offensive plays in the third period. Simms set Super Bowl records for most consecutive completions (10) and highest completion percentage (88 percent on 22 completions in 25 attempts). He also passed for 268 yards and 3 touchdowns and was named the game's most valuable player. New York running back Joe Morris was the game's leading rusher with 20 carries for 67 yards. Denver wide receiver Vance Johnson led all receivers with 5 catches for 121 yards. The Giants defeated their three playoff opponents by a cumulative total of 82 points (New York 105, opponents 23), the largest such margin by a Super Bowl winner.

Denver (AFC)	10	0	0	10	— 20
N.Y. Giants (NFC)	7	2	17	13	— 39

Den — FG Karlis 48
NYG — Mowatt 6 pass from Simms (Allegre kick)
Den — Elway 4 run (Karlis kick)
NYG — Safety, Martin tackled Elway in end zone
NYG — Bavaro 13 pass from Simms (Allegre kick)
NYG — FG Allegre 21
NYG — Morris 1 run (Allegre kick)
NYG — McConkey 6 pass from Simms (Allegre kick)
Den — FG Karlis 28
NYG — Anderson 2 run (kick failed)
Den — V. Johnson 47 pass from Elway (Karlis kick)

SUPER BOWL XX

Louisiana Superdome, New Orleans, Louisiana
January 26, 1986, Attendance: 73,818

CHICAGO 46, NEW ENGLAND 10—The NFC champion Chicago Bears, seeking their first NFL title since 1963, scored a Super Bowl-record 46 points in downing AFC champion New England 46-10 in Super Bowl XX. The previous record for most points in a Super Bowl was 38, shared by San Francisco in XIX and the Los Angeles Raiders in XVIII. The Bears' league-leading defense tied the Super Bowl record for sacks (7) and limited the Patriots to a record-low 7 rushing yards. New England took the quickest lead in Super Bowl history when Tony Franklin kicked a 36-yard field goal with 1:19 elapsed in the first period. The score came about because of Larry McGrew's fumble recovery at the Chicago 19-yard line. However, the Bears rebounded for a 23-3 first-half lead, while building a yardage advantage of 236 total yards to New England's minus 19. Running back Matt Suhey rushed 8 times for 37 yards, including an 11-yard touchdown run, and caught 1 pass for 24 yards in the first half. After the Patriots first drive of the second half ended with a punt to the Bears' 4-yard line, Chicago marched 96 yards in nine plays with quarterback Jim McMahon's 1-yard scoring run capping the drive. McMahon became the first quarterback in Super Bowl history to rush for a pair of touchdowns. The Bears completed their scoring via a 28-yard interception return by reserve cornerback Reggie Phillips, a 1-yard run by defensive tackle/fullback William Perry, and a safety when defensive end Henry Waechter tackled Patriots quarterback Steve Grogan in the end zone. Bears defensive end Richard Dent became the fourth defender to be named the game's most valuable player after contributing 1½ sacks. The Bears' victory margin of 36 points was the largest in Super Bowl history, bettering the previous mark of 29 by the Los Angeles Raiders when they topped Washington 38-9 in Game XVIII. McMahon completed 12 of 20 passes for 256 yards before leaving the game in the fourth period with a wrist injury. The NFL's all-time leading rusher, Bears running back Walter Payton, carried 22 times for 61 yards. Wide receiver Willie Gault caught 4 passes for 129 yards, the fourth-most receiving yards in a Super Bowl. Chicago coach Mike Ditka became the second man (Tom Flores of Raiders was the other) who played in a Super Bowl and coached a team to a victory in the game.

Chicago (NFC)	13	10	21	2	— 46
New England (AFC)	3	0	0	7	— 10

NE — FG Franklin 36
Chi — FG Butler 28
Chi — FG Butler 24
Chi — Suhey 11 run (Butler kick)
Chi — McMahon 2 run (Butler kick)
Chi — FG Butler 24
Chi — McMahon 1 run (Butler kick)
Chi — Phillips 28 interception return (Butler kick)
Chi — Perry 1 run (Butler kick)
NE — Fryar 8 pass from Grogan (Franklin kick)
Chi — Safety, Waechter tackled Grogan in end zone

SUPER BOWL XIX

Stanford Stadium, Stanford, California
January 20, 1985, Attendance: 84,059

SAN FRANCISCO 38, MIAMI 16—The San Francisco 49ers captured their second Super Bowl title with a dominating offense and a defense that tamed Miami's explosive passing attack. The Dolphins held a 10-7 lead at the end of the first period, which represented the most points scored by two teams in an opening quarter of a Super Bowl. However, the 49ers used excellent field position in the second period to build a 28-16 halftime lead. Running back Roger Craig set a Super Bowl record by scoring 3 touchdowns on pass receptions of 8 and 16 yards and a run of 2 yards. San Francisco's Joe Montana was voted the game's most valuable player. He joined Green Bay's Bart Starr and Pittsburgh's Terry Bradshaw as the only two-time Super Bowl most valuable players. Montana completed 24 of 35 passes for a Super Bowl-record 331 yards and 3 touchdowns, and rushed 5 times for 59 yards, including a 6-yard touchdown. Craig had 58 yards on 15 carries and caught 7 passes for 77 yards. Wendell Tyler rushed 13 times for 65 yards and had 4 catches for 70 yards. Dwight Clark had 6 receptions for 77 yards, while Russ Francis had 5 for 60. San Francisco's 537 total net yards bettered the previous Super Bowl record of 429 yards by Oakland in Super Bowl XI. The 49ers also held a time of possession advantage over the Dolphins of 37:11 to 22:49.

Miami (AFC)	10	6	0	0	— 16
San Francisco (NFC)	7	21	10	0	— 38

Mia — FG von Schamann 37
SF — Monroe 33 pass from Montana (Wersching kick)
Mia — D. Johnson 2 pass from Marino (von Schamann kick)
SF — Craig 8 pass from Montana (Wersching kick)
SF — Montana 6 run (Wersching kick)
SF — Craig 2 run (Wersching kick)
Mia — FG von Schamann 31
Mia — FG von Schamann 30
SF — FG Wersching 27
SF — Craig 16 pass from Montana (Wersching kick)

SUPER BOWL XVIII

Tampa Stadium, Tampa, Florida
January 22, 1984, Attendance: 72,920

LOS ANGELES RAIDERS 38, WASHINGTON 9—The Los Angeles Raiders dominated the Washington Redskins from the beginning in Super Bowl XVIII and achieved the most lopsided victory in Super Bowl history, surpassing Green Bay's 35-10 win over Kansas City in Super Bowl I. The Raiders took a 7-0 lead 4:52 into the game when Derrick Jensen blocked a Jeff Hayes punt and recovered it in the end zone for a touchdown. With 9:14 remaining in the first half, Raiders quarterback Jim Plunkett threw a 12-yard touchdown pass to wide receiver Cliff Branch to complete a three-play, 65-yard drive. Washington cut the Raiders' lead to 14-3 on a 24-yard field goal by Mark Moseley. With seven seconds left in the first half, Raiders linebacker Jack Squirek intercepted a Joe Theismann pass at the Redskins' 5-yard line and ran it in for a touchdown to give Los Angeles a 21-3 halftime lead. In the third period, running back Marcus Allen, who rushed for a Super Bowl-record 191 yards on 20 carries, increased the Raiders' lead to 35-9 on touchdown runs of 5 and 74 yards, the latter erasing the Super Bowl record of 58 yards set by Baltimore's Tom Matte in Game III. Allen was named the game's most valuable player. The victory over Washington raised Raiders coach Tom Flores' playoff record to 8-1, including a 27-10 win against Philadelphia in Super Bowl XV. The 38 points scored by the Raiders were the highest total by a Super Bowl team. The previous high was 35 points by Green Bay in Game I.

Washington (NFC)	0	3	6	0	— 9
L.A. Raiders (AFC)	7	14	14	3	— 38

Raiders — Jensen recovered blocked punt in end zone (Bahr kick)
Raiders — Branch 12 pass from Plunkett (Bahr kick)
Wash — FG Moseley 24
Raiders — Squirek 5 interception return (Bahr kick)
Wash — Riggins 1 run (kick blocked)
Raiders — Allen 5 run (Bahr kick)
Raiders — Allen 74 run (Bahr kick)
Raiders — FG Bahr 21

SUPER BOWL XVII

Rose Bowl, Pasadena, California
January 30, 1983, Attendance: 103,667

WASHINGTON 27, MIAMI 17—Fullback John Riggins ran for a Super Bowl-record 166 yards on 38 carries to spark Washington to a 27-17 victory over AFC champion Miami. It was Riggins's fourth straight 100-yard rushing game during the playoffs, also a record. The win marked Washington's first NFL title since 1942, and was only the second time in Super Bowl history NFL/NFC teams scored consecutive victories (Green Bay did it in Super Bowls I and II and San Francisco won Super Bowl XVI). The Redskins, under second-year head coach Joe Gibbs, used a balanced offense that accounted for 400 total yards (a Super Bowl-record 276 yards rushing and 124 passing), second in Super Bowl history to 429 yards by Oakland in Super Bowl XI. The Dolphins built a 17-10 halftime lead on a 76-yard touchdown pass from quarterback David Woodley to wide receiver Jimmy Cefalo 6:49 into the first period, a 20-yard field goal by Uwe von Schamann with 6:00 left in the half, and a Super Bowl-record 98-yard kickoff return by Fulton Walker with 1:38 remaining. Washington had tied the score at 10-10 with 1:51 left on a four-yard touchdown pass from Joe Theismann to wide receiver Alvin Garrett. Mark Moseley started the Redskins' scoring with a 31-yard field goal late in the first period, and added a 20-yarder midway through the third period to cut the Dolphins' lead to 17-13. Riggins, who was voted the game's most valuable player, gave Washington its first lead of the game with 10:01 left when he ran 43 yards off left tackle for a touchdown in a fourth-and-1 situation. Wide receiver Charlie Brown caught a six-yard scoring pass from Theismann with 1:55 left to complete the scoring. The Dolphins managed only 176 yards (142 in first half). Theismann completed 15 of 23 passes for 143 yards, with 2 touchdowns and 2 interceptions. For Miami, Woodley was 4 of 14 for 97 yards, with 1 touchdown, and 1 interception. Don Strock was 0 for 3 in relief.

Miami (AFC)	7	10	0	0	— 17
Washington (NFC)	0	10	3	14	— 27

Mia — Cefalo 76 pass from Woodley (von Schamann kick)
Wash — FG Moseley 31
Mia — FG von Schamann 20
Wash — Garrett 4 pass from Theismann (Moseley kick)
Mia — Walker 98 kickoff return (von Schamann kick)
Wash — FG Moseley 20
Wash — Riggins 43 run (Moseley kick)
Wash — Brown 6 pass from Theismann (Moseley kick)

SUPER BOWL XVI

Pontiac Silverdome, Pontiac, Michigan
January 24, 1982, Attendance: 81,270

SAN FRANCISCO 26, CINCINNATI 21—Ray Wersching's Super Bowl record-tying 4 field goals and Joe Montana's controlled passing helped lift the San Francisco 49ers to their first NFL championship with a 26-21 victory over Cincinnati. The 49ers built a game-record 20-0 halftime lead via Montana's 1-yard touchdown run, which capped an 11-play, 68-yard drive; fullback Earl Cooper's 11-yard scoring-pass from Montana, which climaxed a Super Bowl record 92-yard drive on 12 plays; and Wersching's 22- and 26-yard field goals. The Bengals rebounded in the second half, closing the gap to 20-14 on quarterback Ken Anderson's 5-yard run and Dan Ross's 4-yard reception from Anderson, who established Super Bowl passing records for completions (25) and completion percentage (73.5 percent on 25 of 34). Wersching added early fourth-period field goals of 40 and 23 yards to increase the 49ers' lead to 26-14. The Bengals managed to score on an Anderson-to-Ross 3-yard pass with only 16 seconds remaining. Ross set a Super Bowl record with 11 receptions for 104 yards. Montana, the game's most valuable player, completed 14 of 22 passes for 157 yards. Cincinnati compiled 356 yards to San Francisco's 275, which marked the first time in Super Bowl history that the team that gained the most yards from scrimmage lost the game.

San Francisco (NFC)	7	13	0	6	— 26
Cincinnati (AFC)	0	0	7	14	— 21

SF — Montana 1 run (Wersching kick)
SF — Cooper 11 pass from Montana (Wersching kick)
SF — FG Wersching 22
SF — FG Wersching 26
Cin — Anderson 5 run (Breech kick)
Cin — Ross 4 pass from Anderson (Breech kick)
SF — FG Wersching 40
SF — FG Wersching 23
Cin — Ross 3 pass from Anderson (Breech kick)

SUPER BOWL XV

Louisiana Superdome, New Orleans, Louisiana
January 25, 1981, Attendance: 76,135

OAKLAND 27, PHILADELPHIA 10—Jim Plunkett threw 3 touchdown passes, including an 80-yard strike to Kenny King, as the Raiders became the first wild-card team to win the Super Bowl. Plunkett's touchdown bomb to King—the longest play in Super Bowl history—gave Oakland a decisive 14-0 lead with nine seconds left in the first period. Linebacker Rod Martin had set up Oakland's first touchdown, a 2-yard reception by Cliff Branch, with a 17-yard interception return to the Eagles' 30-yard line. The Eagles never recovered from that early deficit, managing only a Tony Franklin field goal (30 yards) and an 8-yard touchdown pass from Ron Jaworski to Keith Krepfle. Plunkett, who became a starter in the sixth game of the season, completed 13 of 21 for 261 yards and was named the game's most valuable player. Oakland won 9 of 11 games with Plunkett starting, but that was good enough only for second place in the AFC West, although they tied division winner San Diego with an 11-5 record. The Raiders, who had previously won Super Bowl XI over Minnesota, had to win three playoff games to get to the championship game. Oakland defeated Houston 27-7 at home followed by road victories over Cleveland (14-12) and San Diego (34-27). Oakland's Mark van Eeghen was the game's leading rusher with 75 yards on 18 carries. Philadelphia's Wilbert Montgomery led all receivers with 6 receptions for 91 yards. Branch had 5 for 67 and Harold Carmichael of Philadelphia 5 for 83. Martin finished the game with 3 interceptions, a Super Bowl record.

Oakland (AFC)	14	0	10	3	— 27
Philadelphia (NFC)	0	3	0	7	— 10

Oak — Branch 2 pass from Plunkett (Bahr kick)
Oak — King 80 pass from Plunkett (Bahr kick)
Phil — FG Franklin 30
Oak — Branch 29 pass from Plunkett (Bahr kick)
Oak — FG Bahr 46
Phil — Krepfle 8 pass from Jaworski (Franklin kick)
Oak — FG Bahr 35

SUPER BOWL XIV

Rose Bowl, Pasadena, California
January 20, 1980, Attendance: 103,985

PITTSBURGH 31, LOS ANGELES 19—Terry Bradshaw completed 14 of 21 passes for 309 yards and set two passing records as the Steelers became the first team to win four Super Bowls. Despite 3 interceptions by the Rams, Bradshaw kept his poise and brought the Steelers from behind twice in the second half. Trailing 13-10 at halftime, Pittsburgh went ahead 17-13 when Bradshaw hit Lynn Swann with a 47-yard touchdown pass after 2:48 of the third quarter. On the Rams' next possession Vince Ferragamo, who completed 15 of 25 passes for 212 yards, responded with a 50-yard pass to Billy Waddy that moved Los Angeles from its 26 to the Steelers' 24. On the following play, Lawrence McCutcheon connected with Ron Smith on a halfback option pass that gave the Rams a 19-17 lead. On Pittsburgh's initial possession of the final period, Bradshaw lofted a 73-yard scoring pass to John Stallworth to put the Steelers in front to stay 24-19. Franco Harris scored on a 1-yard run later in the quarter to seal the verdict. A 45-yard pass from Bradshaw to Stallworth was the key play in the drive to Harris's score. Bradshaw, the game's most valuable player for the second straight year, set career Super Bowl records for most touchdown passes (9) and most passing yards (932). Larry Anderson gave the Steelers excellent field position throughout the game with 5 kickoff returns for a record 162 yards.

Los Angeles (NFC)	7	6	6	0	— 19
Pittsburgh (AFC)	3	7	7	14	— 31

Pitt — FG Bahr 41
LA — Bryant 1 run (Corral kick)
Pitt — Harris 1 run (Bahr kick)
LA — FG Corral 31
LA — FG Corral 45
Pitt — Swann 47 pass from Bradshaw (Bahr kick)
LA — Smith 24 pass from McCutcheon (kick failed)
Pitt — Stallworth 73 pass from Bradshaw (Bahr kick)
Pitt — Harris 1 run (Bahr kick)

SUPER BOWL XIII

Orange Bowl, Miami, Florida
January 21, 1979, Attendance: 79,484

PITTSBURGH 35, DALLAS 31—Terry Bradshaw threw a record 4 touchdown passes to lead the Steelers to victory. The Steelers became the first team to win three Super Bowls, mostly because of Bradshaw's accurate arm. Bradshaw, voted the game's most valuable player, completed 17 of 30 passes for 318 yards, a personal high. Four of those passes went for touchdowns—2 to John Stallworth and the third, with 26 seconds remaining in the second period, to Rocky Bleier for a 21-14 halftime lead. The Cowboys scored twice before intermission on Roger Staubach's 39-yard pass to Tony Hill and a 37-yard fumble return by linebacker Mike Hegman, who stole the ball from Bradshaw. The Steelers broke open the contest with 2 touchdowns in a span of 19 seconds midway through the final period. Franco Harris rambled 22 yards up the middle to give the Steelers a 28-17 lead with 7:10 left. Pittsburgh got the ball right back when Randy White fumbled the kickoff and Dennis Winston recovered for the Steelers. On first down, Bradshaw fired his fourth touchdown pass, an 18-yard pass to Lynn Swann to boost the Steelers' lead to 35-17 with 6:51 to play. The Cowboys refused to let the Steelers run away with the contest. Staubach connected with Billy Joe DuPree on a 7-yard scoring pass with 2:23 left. Then the Cowboys recovered an onside kick and Staubach took them in for another score, passing 4 yards to Butch Johnson with 22 seconds remaining. Bleier recovered another onside kick with 17 seconds left to seal the victory for the Steelers.

Pittsburgh (AFC)	7	14	0	14	— 35
Dallas (NFC)	7	7	3	14	— 31

Pitt — Stallworth 28 pass from Bradshaw (Gerela kick)
Dall — Hill 39 pass from Staubach (Septien kick)
Dall — Hegman 37 fumble recovery return (Septien kick)
Pitt — Stallworth 75 pass from Bradshaw (Gerela kick)
Pitt — Bleier 7 pass from Bradshaw (Gerela kick)
Dall — FG Septien 27
Pitt — Harris 22 run (Gerela kick)
Pitt — Swann 18 pass from Bradshaw (Gerela kick)
Dall — DuPree 7 pass from Staubach (Septien kick)
Dall — B. Johnson 4 pass from Staubach (Septien kick)

SUPER BOWL XII

Louisiana Superdome, New Orleans, Louisiana
January 15, 1978, Attendance: 75,583

DALLAS 27, DENVER 10—The Cowboys evened their Super Bowl record at 2-2 by defeating Denver before a sellout crowd of 75,583, plus 102,010,000 television viewers, the largest audience ever to watch a sporting event. Dallas converted 2 interceptions into 10 points and Efren Herrera added a 35-yard field goal for a 13-0 halftime advantage. In the third period Craig Morton engineered a drive to the Cowboys' 30 and Jim Turner's 47-yard field goal made the score 13-3. After an exchange of punts, Butch Johnson made a spectacular diving catch in the end zone to complete a 45-yard pass from Roger

Staubach and put the Cowboys ahead 20-3. Following Rick Upchurch's 67-yard kickoff return, Norris Weese guided the Broncos to a touchdown to cut the Dallas lead to 20-10. Dallas clinched the victory when running back Robert Newhouse threw a 29-yard touchdown pass to Golden Richards with 7:04 remaining in the game. It was the first pass thrown by Newhouse since 1975. Harvey Martin and Randy White, who were named co-most valuable players, led the Cowboys' defense, which recovered 4 fumbles and intercepted 4 passes.

Dallas (NFC)	10	3	7	7	— 27
Denver (AFC)	0	0	10	0	— 10

Dall — Dorsett 3 run (Herrera kick)
Dall — FG Herrera 35
Dall — FG Herrera 43
Den — FG Turner 47
Dall — Johnson 45 pass from Staubach (Herrera kick)
Den — Lytle 1 run (Turner kick)
Dall — Richards 29 pass from Newhouse (Herrera kick)

SUPER BOWL XI

Rose Bowl, Pasadena, California
January 9, 1977, Attendance: 103,438

OAKLAND 32, MINNESOTA 14—The Raiders won their first NFL championship before a record Super Bowl crowd plus 81 million television viewers, the largest audience ever to watch a sporting event. The Raiders gained a record-breaking 429 yards, including running back Clarence Davis's 137 rushing yards. Wide receiver Fred Biletnikoff made 4 key receptions, which earned him the game's most valuable player trophy. Oakland scored on three successive possessions in the second quarter to build a 16-0 halftime lead. Errol Mann's 24-yard field goal opened the scoring, then the AFC champions put together drives of 64 and 35 yards, scoring on a 1-yard pass from Ken Stabler to Dave Casper and a 1-yard run by Pete Banaszak. The Raiders increased their lead to 19-0 on a 40-yard field goal in the third quarter, but Minnesota responded with a 12-play, 58-yard drive late in the period, with Fran Tarkenton passing 8 yards to wide receiver Sammy White to cut the deficit to 19-7. Two fourth-quarter interceptions clinched the title for the Raiders. One set up Banaszak's second touchdown run, the other resulted in cornerback Willie Brown's Super Bowl-record 75-yard interception return.

Oakland (AFC)	0	16	3	13	— 32
Minnesota (NFC)	0	0	7	7	— 14

Oak — FG Mann 24
Oak — Casper 1 pass from Stabler (Mann kick)
Oak — Banaszak 1 run (kick failed)
Oak — FG Mann 40
Minn — S. White 8 pass from Tarkenton (Cox kick)
Oak — Banaszak 2 run (Mann kick)
Oak — Brown 75 interception return (kick failed)
Minn — Voigt 13 pass from Lee (Cox kick)

SUPER BOWL X

Orange Bowl, Miami, Florida
January 18, 1976, Attendance: 80,187

PITTSBURGH 21, DALLAS 17—The Steelers won the Super Bowl for the second year in a row on Terry Bradshaw's 64-yard touchdown pass to Lynn Swann and an aggressive defense that snuffed out a late rally by the Cowboys with an end-zone interception on the final play of the game. In the fourth quarter, Pittsburgh ran on fourth down and gave up the ball on the Cowboys' 39 with 1:22 to play. Roger Staubach ran and passed for 2 first downs but his last desperation pass was picked off by Glen Edwards. Dallas's scoring was the result of 2 touchdown passes by Staubach, one to Drew Pearson for 29 yards and the other to Percy Howard for 34 yards. Toni Fritsch had a 36-yard field goal. The Steelers scored on 2 touchdown passes by Bradshaw, 1 to Randy Grossman for 7 yards and the long bomb to Swann. Roy Gerela had 36- and 18-yard field goals. Reggie Harrison blocked a punt through the end zone for a safety. Swann set a Super Bowl record by gaining 161 yards on his 4 receptions.

Dallas (NFC)	7	3	0	7	— 17
Pittsburgh (AFC)	7	0	0	14	— 21

Dall — D. Pearson 29 pass from Staubach (Fritsch kick)
Pitt — Grossman 7 pass from Bradshaw (Gerela kick)
Dall — FG Fritsch 36
Pitt — Safety, Harrison blocked Hoopes's punt through end zone
Pitt — FG Gerela 36
Pitt — FG Gerela 18
Pitt — Swann 64 pass from Bradshaw (kick failed)
Dall — P. Howard 34 pass from Staubach (Fritsch kick)

SUPER BOWL IX

Tulane Stadium, New Orleans, Louisiana
January 12, 1975, Attendance: 80,997

PITTSBURGH 16, MINNESOTA 6—AFC champion Pittsburgh, in its initial Super Bowl appearance, and NFC champion Minnesota, making a third bid for its first Super Bowl title, struggled through a first half in which the only score was produced by the Steelers' defense when Dwight White downed Vikings' quarterback Fran Tarkenton in the end zone for a safety 7:49 into the second period. The Steelers forced another break and took advantage on the second-half kickoff when Minnesota's Bill Brown fumbled and Marv Kellum recovered for Pittsburgh on the Vikings' 30. After Rocky Bleier failed to gain on first down, Franco Harris carried 3 consecutive times for 24 yards, a loss of 3, and a 9-yard touchdown and a 9-0 lead. Though its offense was completely stymied by Pittsburgh's defense, Minnesota managed to move into a threatening position after 4:27 of the final period when Matt Blair blocked Bobby Walden's punt and Terry Brown recovered the ball in the end zone for a touchdown. Fred Cox's kick failed and the Steelers led 9-6. Pittsburgh wasted no time putting the victory away. The Steelers took the ensuing kickoff and marched 66 yards in 11 plays, climaxed by Terry Bradshaw's 4-yard scoring pass to Larry Brown with 3:31 left. Pittsburgh's defense permitted Minnesota only 119 yards total offense, including a Super Bowl low of 17 rushing yards. The Steelers, meanwhile, gained 333 yards, including Harris's record 158 yards on 34 carries.

Pittsburgh (AFC)	0	2	7	7	— 16
Minnesota (NFC)	0	0	0	6	— 6

Pitt — Safety, White downed Tarkenton in end zone
Pitt — Harris 9 run (Gerela kick)
Minn — T. Brown recovered blocked punt in end zone (kick failed)
Pitt — L. Brown 4 pass from Bradshaw (Gerela kick)

SUPER BOWL VIII

Rice Stadium, Houston, Texas
January 13, 1974, Attendance: 71,882

MIAMI 24, MINNESOTA 7—The defending NFL champion Dolphins, representing the AFC for the third straight year, scored the first two times they had possession on marches of 62 and 56 yards while the Miami defense limited the Vikings to only seven plays in the first period. Larry Csonka climaxed the initial 10-play drive with a 5-yard touchdown bolt through right guard after 5:27 had elapsed. Four plays later, Miami began another 10-play scoring drive, which ended with Jim Kiick bursting 1 yard through the middle for another touchdown after 13:38 of the period. Garo Yepremian added a 28-yard field goal midway in the second period for a 17-0 Miami lead. Minnesota then drove from its 20 to a second-and-2 situation on the Miami 7 yard line with 1:18 left in the half. But on two plays, Miami limited Oscar Reed to 1 yard. On fourth-and-1 from the 6, Reed went over right tackle, but Dolphins middle linebacker Nick Buoniconti jarred the ball loose and Jake Scott recovered for Miami to halt the Minnesota threat. The Vikings were unable to muster enough offense in the second half to threaten the Dolphins. Csonka rushed 33 times for a Super Bowl-record 145 yards. Bob Griese of Miami completed 6 of 7 passes for 73 yards.

Minnesota (NFC)	0	0	0	7	— 7
Miami (AFC)	14	3	7	0	— 24

Mia — Csonka 5 run (Yepremian kick)
Mia — Kiick 1 run (Yepremian kick)
Mia — FG Yepremian 28
Mia — Csonka 2 run (Yepremian kick)
Minn — Tarkenton 4 run (Cox kick)

SUPER BOWL VII

Memorial Coliseum, Los Angeles, California
January 14, 1973, Attendance: 90,182

MIAMI 14, WASHINGTON 7—The Dolphins played virtually perfect football in the first half as their defense permitted the Redskins to cross midfield only once and their offense turned good field position into 2 touchdowns. On its third possession, Miami opened its first scoring drive from the Dolphins' 37 yard line. An 18-yard pass from Bob Griese to Paul Warfield preceded by three plays Griese's 28-yard touchdown pass to Howard Twilley. After Washington moved from its 17 to the Miami 48 with two minutes remaining in the first half, Dolphins linebacker Nick Buoniconti intercepted a Billy Kilmer pass at the Miami 41 and returned it to the Washington 27. Jim Kiick ran for 3 yards, Larry Csonka for 3, Griese passed to Jim Mandich for 19, and Kiick gained 1 to the 1-yard line. With 18 seconds left until intermission, Kiick scored from the 1. Washington's only touchdown came with 2:07 left in the game and resulted from a misplayed field-goal attempt and fumble by Garo Yepremian, with the Redskins' Mike Bass picking the ball out of the air and running 49 yards for the score. Dolphins safety Jake Scott, who had 2 interceptions, including 1 in the end zone to kill a Redskins' drive, was voted the game's most valuable player.

Miami (AFC)	7	7	0	0	— 14
Washington (NFC)	0	0	0	7	— 7

Mia — Twilley 28 pass from Griese (Yepremian kick)
Mia — Kiick 1 run (Yepremian kick)
Wash — Bass 49 fumble recovery return (Knight kick)

SUPER BOWL VI

Tulane Stadium, New Orleans, Louisiana
January 16, 1972, Attendance: 81,023

DALLAS 24, MIAMI 3—The Cowboys rushed for a record 252 yards and their defense limited the Dolphins to a low of 185 yards while not permitting a touchdown for the first time in Super Bowl history. Dallas converted Chuck Howley's recovery of Larry Csonka's first fumble of the season into a 3-0 advantage and led at halftime 10-3. After Dallas received the second-half kickoff, Duane Thomas led a 71-yard march in eight plays for a 17-3 margin. Howley intercepted Bob Griese's pass at the 50 and returned it to the Miami 9 early in the fourth period, and three plays later Roger Staubach passed 7 yards to Mike Ditka for the final touchdown. Thomas rushed for 95 yards and Walt Garrison gained 74. Staubach, voted the game's most valuable player, completed 12 of 19 passes for 119 yards and 2 touchdowns.

Dallas (NFC)	3	7	7	7	— 24
Miami (AFC)	0	3	0	0	— 3

Dall — FG Clark 9
Dall — Alworth 7 pass from Staubach (Clark kick)
Mia — FG Yepremian 31
Dall — D. Thomas 3 run (Clark kick)
Dall — Ditka 7 pass from Staubach (Clark kick)

SUPER BOWL V

Orange Bowl, Miami, Florida
January 17, 1971, Attendance: 79,204

BALTIMORE 16, DALLAS 13—A 32-yard field goal by rookie kicker Jim O'Brien brought the Baltimore Colts a victory over the Dallas Cowboys in the final five seconds of Super Bowl V. The game between the champions of the AFC and NFC was played on artificial turf for the first time. Dallas led13-6 at the half but interceptions by Rick Volk and Mike Curtis set up a Baltimore touchdown and O'Brien's decisive kick in the fourth period. Earl Morrell relieved an injured Johnny Unitas late in the firsthalf, although Unitas completed the Colts' only scoring pass. It caromed off receiver Eddie Hinton's fingertips, off Dallas defensive back Mel Renfro, and finally settled into the grasp of John Mackey, who went 45 yards to score on a 75-yard play.

Baltimore (AFC)	0	6	0	10	— 16
Dallas (NFC)	3	10	0	0	— 13

Dall — FG Clark 14
Dall — FG Clark 30
Balt — Mackey 75 pass from Unitas (kick blocked)
Dall — Thomas 7 pass from Morton (Clark kick)
Balt — Nowatzke 2 run (O'Brien kick)
Balt — FG O'Brien 32

SUPER BOWL IV

Tulane Stadium, New Orleans, Louisiana
January 11, 1970, Attendance: 80,562

KANSAS CITY 23, MINNESOTA 7—The AFL squared the Super Bowl at two games apiece with the NFL, building a 16-0 halftime lead behind Len Dawson's superb quarterbacking and a powerful defense. Dawson, the fourth consecutive quarterback to be chosen the Super Bowl's top player, called an almost flawless game, completing 12 of 17 passes and hitting Otis Taylor on a 46-yard play for the final Chiefs touchdown. The Kansas City defense limited Minnesota's strong rushing game to 67 yards and had 3 interceptions and 2 fumble recoveries. The crowd of 80,562 set a Super Bowl record, as did the gross receipts of $3,817,872.69.

Minnesota (NFL)	0	0	7	0	— 7
Kansas City (AFL)	3	13	7	0	— 23

KC — FG Stenerud 48
KC — FG Stenerud 32
KC — FG Stenerud 25
KC — Garrett 5 run (Stenerud kick)
Minn — Osborn 4 run (Cox kick)
KC — Taylor 46 pass from Dawson (Stenerud kick)

SUPER BOWL III

Orange Bowl, Miami, Florida
January 12, 1969, Attendance: 75,389

NEW YORK JETS 16, BALTIMORE 7—Jets quarterback Joe Namath "guaranteed" victory on the Thursday before the game, then went out and led the AFL to its first Super Bowl victory over a Baltimore team that had lost only once in 16 games all season. Namath, chosen the outstanding player, completed 17 of 28 passes for 206 yards and directed a steady attack that dominated the NFL champions after the Jets' defense had intercepted Colts quarterback Earl Morrall 3 times in the first half. The Jets had 337 total yards, including 121 rushing yards by Matt Snell. Johnny Unitas, who had missed most of the season with a sore elbow, came off the bench and led Baltimore to its only touchdown late in the fourth quarter after New York led 16-0.

New York Jets (AFL)	0	7	6	3	— 16
Baltimore (NFL)	0	0	0	7	— 7

NYJ — Snell 4 run (Turner kick)
NYJ — FG Turner 32
NYJ — FG Turner 30
NYJ — FG Turner 9
Balt — Hill 1 run (Michaels kick)

SUPER BOWL II

Orange Bowl, Miami, Florida
January 14, 1968, Attendance: 75,546

GREEN BAY 33, OAKLAND 14—Green Bay, after winning its third consecutive NFL championship, won the Super Bowl title for the second straight year, defeating the AFL champion Raiders in a game that drew the first $3-million gate in football history. Bart Starr again was chosen the game's most valuable player as he completed 13 of 24 passes for 202 yards and 1 touchdown and directed a Packers attack that was in control all the way after building a 16-7 halftime lead. Don Chandler kicked 4 field goals and all-pro cornerback Herb Adderley capped the Green Bay scoring with a 60-yard interception return. The game marked the last for Vince Lombardi as Packers coach, ending nine years at Green Bay in which he won six Western Conference championships, five NFL championships, and two Super Bowls.

Green Bay (NFL)	3	13	10	7	— 33
Oakland (AFL)	0	7	0	7	— 14

GB — FG Chandler 39
GB — FG Chandler 20
GB — Dowler 62 pass from Starr (Chandler kick)
Oak — Miller 23 pass from Lamonica (Blanda kick)
GB — FG Chandler 43
GB — Anderson 2 run (Chandler kick)
GB — FG Chandler 31
GB — Adderley 60 interception return (Chandler kick)
Oak — Miller 23 pass from Lamonica (Blanda kick)

SUPER BOWL I

Memorial Coliseum, Los Angeles, California
January 15, 1967, Attendance: 61,946

GREEN BAY 35, KANSAS CITY 10—The Green Bay Packers opened the Super Bowl series by defeating the AFL champion Chiefs behind the passing of Bart Starr, the receiving of Max McGee, and a key interception by all-pro safety Willie Wood. Green Bay broke open the game with 3 second-half touchdowns, the first of which was set up by Wood's 50-yard return of an interception to the Chiefs' 5 yard line. McGee, filling in for ailing Boyd Dowler after having caught only 4 passes all season, caught 7 from Starr for 138 yards and 2 touchdowns. Elijah Pitts ran for two other scores. The Chiefs' 10 points came in the second quarter, the only touchdown on a 7-yard pass from Len Dawson to Curtis McClinton. Starr completed 16 of 23 passes for 250 yards and 2 touchdowns and was chosen the most valuable player. The Packers collected $15,000 per man and the Chiefs $7,500—the largest single-game shares in the history of team sports.

Kansas City (AFL)	0	10	0	0	— 10
Green Bay (NFL)	7	7	14	7	— 35

GB — McGee 37 pass from Starr (Chandler kick)
KC — McClinton 7 pass from Dawson (Mercer kick)
GB — Taylor 14 run (Chandler kick)
KC — FG Mercer 31
GB — Pitts 5 run (Chandler kick)
GB — McGee 13 pass from Starr (Chandler kick)
GB — Pitts 1 run (Chandler kick)

AFC CHAMPIONSHIP GAME RESULTS

Includes AFL Championship Games (1960-69)

Season	Date	Winner (Share)	Loser (Share)	Score	Site	Attendance
1994	Jan. 15	San Diego ($23,500)	Pittsburgh ($23,500)	17-13	Pittsburgh	61,545
1993	Jan. 23	Buffalo ($23,500)	Kansas City ($23,500)	30-13	Buffalo	76,642
1992	Jan. 17	Buffalo ($18,000)	Miami ($18,000)	29-10	Miami	72,703
1991	Jan. 12	Buffalo ($18,000)	Denver ($18,000)	10-7	Buffalo	80,272
1990	Jan. 20	Buffalo ($18,000)	L.A. Raiders ($18,000)	51-3	Buffalo	80,325
1989	Jan. 14	Denver ($18,000)	Cleveland ($18,000)	37-21	Denver	76,046
1988	Jan. 8	Cincinnati ($18,000)	Buffalo ($18,000)	21-10	Cincinnati	59,747
1987	Jan. 17	Denver ($18,000)	Cleveland ($18,000)	38-33	Denver	76,197
1986	Jan. 11	Denver ($18,000)	Cleveland ($18,000)	23-20*	Cleveland	79,973
1985	Jan. 12	New England ($18,000)	Miami ($18,000)	31-14	Miami	75,662
1984	Jan. 6	Miami ($18,000)	Pittsburgh ($18,000)	45-28	Miami	76,029
1983	Jan. 8	L.A. Raiders ($18,000)	Seattle ($18,000)	30-14	Los Angeles	91,445
1982	Jan. 23	Miami ($18,000)	N.Y. Jets ($18,000)	14-0	Miami	67,396
1981	Jan. 10	Cincinnati ($9,000)	San Diego ($9,000)	27-7	Cincinnati	46,302
1980	Jan. 11	Oakland ($9,000)	San Diego ($9,000)	34-27	San Diego	52,675
1979	Jan. 6	Pittsburgh ($9,000)	Houston ($9,000)	27-13	Pittsburgh	50,475
1978	Jan. 7	Pittsburgh ($9,000)	Houston ($9,000)	34-5	Pittsburgh	50,725
1977	Jan. 1	Denver ($9,000)	Oakland ($9,000)	20-17	Denver	75,044
1976	Dec. 26	Oakland ($8,500)	Pittsburgh ($5,500)	24-7	Oakland	53,821
1975	Jan. 4	Pittsburgh ($8,500)	Oakland ($5,500)	16-10	Pittsburgh	50,609
1974	Dec. 29	Pittsburgh ($8,500)	Oakland ($5,500)	24-13	Oakland	53,800
1973	Dec. 30	Miami ($8,500)	Oakland ($5,500)	27-10	Miami	79,325
1972	Dec. 31	Miami ($8,500)	Pittsburgh ($5,500)	21-17	Pittsburgh	50,845
1971	Jan. 2	Miami ($8,500)	Baltimore ($5,500)	21-0	Miami	76,622
1970	Jan. 3	Baltimore ($8,500)	Oakland ($5,500)	27-17	Baltimore	54,799
1969	Jan. 4	Kansas City ($7,755)	Oakland ($6,252)	17-7	Oakland	53,564
1968	Dec. 29	N.Y. Jets ($7,007)	Oakland ($5,349)	27-23	New York	62,627
1967	Dec. 31	Oakland ($6,321)	Houston ($4,996)	40-7	Oakland	53,330
1966	Jan. 1	Kansas City ($5,309)	Buffalo ($3,799)	31-7	Buffalo	42,080
1965	Dec. 26	Buffalo ($5,189)	San Diego ($3,447)	23-0	San Diego	30,361
1964	Dec. 26	Buffalo ($2,668)	San Diego ($1,738)	20-7	Buffalo	40,242
1963	Jan. 5	San Diego ($2,498)	Boston ($1,596)	51-10	San Diego	30,127
1962	Dec. 23	Dallas ($2,206)	Houston ($1,471)	20-17*	Houston	37,981
1961	Dec. 24	Houston ($1,792)	San Diego ($1,111)	10-3	San Diego	29,556
1960	Jan. 1	Houston ($1,025)	L.A. Chargers ($718)	24-16	Houston	32,183

**Sudden death overtime.*

AFC CHAMPIONSHIP GAME COMPOSITE STANDINGS

	W	L	Pct.	Pts.	OP
Cincinnati Bengals	2	0	1.000	48	17
Denver Broncos	4	1	.800	125	101
Buffalo Bills	6	2	.750	180	92
Kansas City Chiefs*	3	1	.750	81	61
Miami Dolphins	5	2	.714	152	115
Pittsburgh Steelers	4	4	.500	166	148
Baltimore Colts	1	1	.500	27	38
New England Patriots**	1	1	.500	41	65
New York Jets	1	1	.500	27	37
Houston Oilers	2	4	.333	76	140
Oakland/L.A. Raiders	4	8	.333	228	264
San Diego Chargers***	2	6	.250	128	161
Seattle Seahawks	0	1	.000	14	30
Cleveland Browns	0	3	.000	74	98

**One game played when franchise was in Dallas (Texans). (Won 20-17)*
***One game played when franchise was in Boston. (Lost 51-10)*
****One game played when franchise was in Los Angeles. (Lost 24-16)*

1994 AFC CHAMPIONSHIP GAME

Three Rivers Stadium, Pittsburgh, Pennsylvania
January 15, 1995, Attendance: 61,545

SAN DIEGO 17, PITTSBURGH 13—Stan Humphries threw 2 second-half touchdown passes and the Chargers turned back the Steelers with a goal-line stand late in the game to earn their first trip to the Super Bowl. Neil O'Donnell's 16-yard touchdown pass to running back John L. Williams and a pair of field goals by Gary Anderson staked Pittsburgh to a 13-3 lead early in the second half. But Humphries's 43-yard touchdown pass to tight end Alfred Pupunu pulled San Diego within 13-10 midway through the third quarter, and his 43-yard strike to Tony Martin with 5:13 left in the game gave the Chargers the lead. O'Donnell tried to rally the Steelers by completing 7 consecutive passes and marching his team from its own 17-yard line to a first-and-goal at San Diego's 9. Three plays later, it was fourth-and-goal from the 3, but O'Donnell's pass, intended for running back Barry Foster, was knocked down at the goal line by Chargers linebacker Dennis Gibson with 1:04 remaining. San Diego, which came from behind to win for the second consecutive week (the Chargers beat Miami 22-21 in the divisional playoffs after trailing 21-6 at halftime), snapped a six-game losing streak in Pittsburgh despite heavy deficits in total yards (415-226), plays (80-47), and time of possession (37:13-22:47). O'Donnell passed for 349 yards for the Steelers on AFC title-game records for attempts (54) and completions (32). Linebacker Junior Seau had 16 tackles for San Diego.

San Diego (17)	Offense	Pittsburgh (13)
Shawn Jefferson	WR	Yancey Thigpen
Harry Swayne	LT	John Jackson
Isaac Davis	LG	Duval Love
Courtney Hall	C	Dermontti Dawson
Joe Cocozzo	RG	Justin Strzelczyk
Stan Brock	RT	Leon Searcy
Duane Young	TE	Eric Green
Stan Humphries	QB	Neil O'Donnell
Natrone Means	RB	Barry Foster
Alfred Pupunu	TE-RB	John L. Williams
Mark Seay	WR	Ernie Mills
	Defense	
Chris Mims	LE	Brentson Buckner
John Parrella	LT-NT	Joel Steed
Reuben Davis	RT-RE	Ray Seals
Leslie O'Neal	RE-LOLB	Kevin Greene
David Griggs	OLB-LILB	Levon Kirkland
Dennis Gibson	ILB-RILB	Chad Brown
Junior Seau	ILB-ROLB	Greg Lloyd
Darrien Gordon	LCB	Rod Woodson
Dwayne Harper	RCB	Deon Figures
Darren Carrington	SS	Carnell Lake
Stanley Richard	FS	Darren Perry

SUBSTITUTIONS

San Diego—Offense: K—John Carney. P—Bryan Wagner. QB—Gale Gilbert. RB—Eric Bieniemy, Ronnie Harmon. WR—Tony Martin. TE—David Binn, Shannon Mitchell. KR—Andre Coleman. T—Eric Jonassen, Vaughn Parker. C—Curtis Whitley. Defense: DE—Raylee Johnson. DT—Reggie White. LB—Lewis Bush, Steve Hendrickson, Doug Miller. CB—Willie Clark, Sean Vanhorse. S—Eric Castle, Rodney Harrison. DNP: RB—Rodney Culver, DT—Les Miller.

Pittsburgh—Offense: K—Gary Anderson. P—Mark Royals. RB—Fred McAfee, Steve Avery, Byron (Bam) Morris. WR—Andre Hastings, Charles Johnson, Dwight Stone. TE—Jonathan Hayes, Walter Rasby. G—Tim Simpson. C—Kendall Gammon, Ariel Solomon. Defense: DE—Kevin Henry. DT—Jeff Zgonina. LB—Jason Gildon, Ed Robinson. CB—Tim McKyer, Willie Williams. S—Myron Bell, Fred Foggie. DNP: QB—Mike Tomczak, DE—Taase Faumui.

OFFICIALS

Referee—Gerry Austin. Umpire—Bob Boylston. Head Linesman—Dale Williams. Line Judge—Dick McKenzie. Back Judge—Jim Poole. Field Judge—Don Hakes. Side Judge—Mike Carey.

SCORING

San Diego	0	3	7	7	— 17
Pittsburgh	7	3	3	0	— 13

Pitt — J.L. Williams 16 pass from O'Donnell (Anderson kick)
SD — FG Carney 20
Pitt — FG Anderson 39
Pitt — FG Anderson 23
SD — Pupunu 43 pass from Humphries (Carney kick)
SD — Martin 43 pass from Humphries (Carney kick)

PLAYOFF GAMES SUMMARIES

TEAM STATISTICS

	S.D.	Pitt.
Total First Downs	13	22
Rushing	4	4
Passing	8	17
Penalty	1	1
Total Net Yardage	226	415
Total Offensive Plays	47	80
Average Gain per Offensive Play	4.8	5.2
Rushes	24	26
Yards Gained Rushing (Net)	66	66
Average Yards per Rush	2.8	2.5
Passes Attempted	22	54
Passes Completed	11	32
Had Intercepted	1	0
Tackled Attempting to Pass	1	0
Yards Lost Attempting to Pass	5	0
Yards Gained Passing (Net)	160	349
Punts	5	5
Average Distance	38.4	44.4
Punt Returns	2	2
Punt Return Yardage	2	10
Kickoff Returns	3	4
Kickoff Return Yardage	72	73
Interception Return Yardage	0	6
Total Return Yardage	74	89
Fumbles	0	3
Own Fumbles Recovered	0	2
Opponents Fumbles Recovered	1	0
Penalties	3	8
Yards Penalized	15	111
Total Points Scored	17	13
Touchdowns	2	1
Rushing	0	0
Passing	2	1
Returns	0	0
Extra Points	2	1
Field Goals	1	2
Field Goals Attempted	1	2
Safeties	0	0
Third-Down Efficiency	3/11	11/20
Fourth-Down Efficiency	0/0	2/3
Time of Possession	22:47	37:13

INDIVIDUAL STATISTICS

Rushing

San Diego	No.	Yds.	LG	TD
Means	20	69	17	0
Humphries	4	-3	0	0
Pittsburgh	**No.**	**Yds.**	**LG**	**TD**
Foster	20	47	11	0
J. Williams	3	16	11	0
Morris	2	2	1	0
O'Donnell	1	1	1	0

Passing

San Diego	Att.	Comp.	Yds.	TD	Int.
Humphries	22	11	165	2	1
Pittsburgh	**Att.**	**Comp.**	**Yds.**	**TD**	**Int.**
O'Donnell	54	32	349	1	0

Receiving

San Diego	No.	Yds.	LG	TD
Pupunu	4	76	43t	1
Means	2	19	15	0
Jefferson	2	16	11	0
Martin	1	43	43t	1
Mitchell	1	19	19	0
Harmon	1	-8	-8	0
Pittsburgh	**No.**	**Yds.**	**LG**	**TD**
Mills	8	106	19	0
J.L. Williams	7	45	16t	1
Hastings	5	55	18	0
Green	4	80	33	0
Thigpen	3	35	21	0
Foster	3	12	6	0
Hayes	1	16	16	0
Morris	1	0	0	0

Interceptions

San Diego	No.	Yds.	LG	TD
None	—	—	—	—
Pittsburgh	**No.**	**Yds.**	**LG**	**TD**
Woodson	1	6	6	0

Punting

San Diego	No.	Avg.	LG	Blk.
Wagner	5	38.4	45	0
Pittsburgh	**No.**	**Avg.**	**LG**	**Blk.**
Royals	5	44.4	55	0

Punt Returns

San Diego	No.	FC	Yds.	LG	TD
Gordon	2	0	2	6	0
Pittsburgh	**No.**	**FC**	**Yds.**	**LG**	**TD**
Woodson	2	1	10	10	0
Johnson	0	1	0	0	0

Kickoff Returns

San Diego	No.	Yds.	LG	TD
Coleman	2	49	32	0
Harmon	1	23	23	0
Pittsburgh	**No.**	**Yds.**	**LG**	**TD**
Johnson	4	73	24	0

NFC CHAMPIONSHIP GAME RESULTS

Includes NFL Championship Games (1933-69)

Season	Date	Winner (Share)	Loser (Share)	Score	Site	Attendance
1994	Jan. 15	San Francisco ($23,500)	Dallas ($23,500)	38-28	San Francisco	69,125
1993	Jan. 23	Dallas ($23,500)	San Francisco ($23,500)	38-21	Dallas	64,902
1992	Jan. 17	Dallas ($18,000)	San Francisco ($18,000)	30-20	San Francisco	64,920
1991	Jan. 12	Washington ($18,000)	Detroit ($18,000)	41-10	Washington	55,585
1990	Jan. 20	N.Y. Giants ($18,000)	San Francisco ($18,000)	15-13	San Francisco	65,750
1989	Jan. 14	San Francisco ($18,000)	L.A. Rams ($18,000)	30-3	San Francisco	65,634
1988	Jan. 8	San Francisco ($18,000)	Chicago ($18,000)	28-3	Chicago	66,946
1987	Jan. 17	Washington ($18,000)	Minnesota ($18,000)	17-10	Washington	55,212
1986	Jan. 11	New York Giants ($18,000)	Washington ($18,000)	17-0	East Rutherford	76,891
1985	Jan. 12	Chicago ($18,000)	L.A. Rams ($18,000)	24-0	Chicago	66,030
1984	Jan. 6	San Francisco ($18,000)	Chicago ($18,000)	23-0	San Francisco	61,336
1983	Jan. 8	Washington ($18,000)	San Francisco ($18,000)	24-21	Washington	55,363
1982	Jan. 22	Washington ($18,000)	Dallas ($18,000)	31-17	Washington	55,045
1981	Jan. 10	San Francisco ($9,000)	Dallas ($9,000)	28-27	San Francisco	60,525
1980	Jan. 11	Philadelphia ($9,000)	Dallas ($9,000)	20-7	Philadelphia	71,522
1979	Jan. 6	Los Angeles ($9,000)	Tampa Bay ($9,000)	9-0	Tampa Bay	72,033
1978	Jan. 7	Dallas ($9,000)	Los Angeles ($9,000)	28-0	Los Angeles	71,086
1977	Jan. 1	Dallas ($9,000)	Minnesota ($9,000)	23-6	Dallas	64,293
1976	Dec. 26	Minnesota ($8,500)	Los Angeles ($5,500)	24-13	Minnesota	48,379
1975	Jan. 4	Dallas ($8,500)	Los Angeles ($5,500)	37-7	Los Angeles	88,919
1974	Dec. 29	Minnesota ($8,500)	Los Angeles ($5,500)	14-10	Minnesota	48,444
1973	Dec. 30	Minnesota ($8,500)	Dallas ($5,500)	27-10	Dallas	64,422
1972	Dec. 31	Washington ($8,500)	Dallas ($5,500)	26-3	Washington	53,129
1971	Jan. 2	Dallas ($8,500)	San Francisco ($5,500)	14-3	Dallas	63,409
1970	Jan. 3	Dallas ($8,500)	San Francisco ($5,500)	17-10	San Francisco	59,364
1969	Jan. 4	Minnesota ($7,930)	Cleveland ($5,118)	27-7	Minnesota	46,503
1968	Dec. 29	Baltimore ($9,306)	Cleveland ($5,963)	34-0	Cleveland	78,410
1967	Dec. 31	Green Bay ($7,950)	Dallas ($5,299)	21-17	Green Bay	50,861
1966	Jan. 1	Green Bay ($9,813)	Dallas ($6,527)	34-27	Dallas	74,152
1965	Jan. 2	Green Bay ($7,819)	Cleveland ($5,288)	23-12	Green Bay	50,777
1964	Dec. 27	Cleveland ($8,052)	Baltimore ($5,571)	27-0	Cleveland	79,544
1963	Dec. 29	Chicago ($5,899)	New York ($4,218)	14-10	Chicago	45,801
1962	Dec. 30	Green Bay ($5,888)	New York ($4,166)	16-7	New York	64,892
1961	Dec. 31	Green Bay ($5,195)	New York ($3,339)	37-0	Green Bay	39,029
1960	Dec. 26	Philadelphia ($5,116)	Green Bay ($3,105)	17-13	Philadelphia	67,325
1959	Dec. 27	Baltimore ($4,674)	New York ($3,083)	31-16	Baltimore	57,545
1958	Dec. 28	Baltimore ($4,718)	New York ($3,111)	23-17*	New York	64,185
1957	Dec. 29	Detroit ($4,295)	Cleveland ($2,750)	59-14	Detroit	55,263
1956	Dec. 30	New York ($3,779)	Chi. Bears ($2,485)	47-7	New York	56,836
1955	Dec. 26	Cleveland ($3,508)	Los Angeles ($2,316)	38-14	Los Angeles	85,693
1954	Dec. 26	Cleveland ($2,478)	Detroit ($1,585)	56-10	Cleveland	43,827
1953	Dec. 27	Detroit ($2,424)	Cleveland ($1,654)	17-16	Detroit	54,577
1952	Dec. 28	Detroit ($2,274)	Cleveland ($1,712)	17-7	Cleveland	50,934
1951	Dec. 23	Los Angeles ($2,108)	Cleveland ($1,483)	24-17	Los Angeles	57,522

Season	Date	Winner (Share)	Loser (Share)	Score	Site	Attendance
1950	Dec. 24	Cleveland ($1,113)	Los Angeles ($686)	30-28	Cleveland	29,751
1949	Dec. 18	Philadelphia ($1,094)	Los Angeles ($739)	14-0	Los Angeles	27,980
1948	Dec. 19	Philadelphia ($1,540)	Chi. Cardinals ($874)	7-0	Philadelphia	36,309
1947	Dec. 28	Chi. Cardinals ($1,132)	Philadelphia ($754)	28-21	Chicago	30,759
1946	Dec. 15	Chi. Bears ($1,975)	New York ($1,295)	24-14	New York	58,346
1945	Dec. 16	Cleveland ($1,469)	Washington ($902)	15-14	Cleveland	32,178
1944	Dec. 17	Green Bay ($1,449)	New York ($814)	14-7	New York	46,016
1943	Dec. 26	Chi. Bears ($1,146)	Washington ($765)	41-21	Chicago	34,320
1942	Dec. 13	Washington ($965)	Chi. Bears ($637)	14-6	Washington	36,006
1941	Dec. 21	Chi. Bears ($430)	New York ($288)	37-9	Chicago	13,341
1940	Dec. 8	Chi. Bears ($873)	Washington ($606)	73-0	Washington	36,034
1939	Dec. 10	Green Bay ($703.97)	New York ($455.57)	27-0	Milwaukee	32,279
1938	Dec. 11	New York ($504.45)	Green Bay ($368.81)	23-17	New York	48,120
1937	Dec. 12	Washington ($225.90)	Chi. Bears ($127.78)	28-21	Chicago	15,870
1936	Dec. 13	Green Bay ($250)	Boston ($180)	21-6	New York	29,545
1935	Dec. 15	Detroit ($313.35)	New York ($200.20)	26-7	Detroit	15,000
1934	Dec. 9	New York ($621)	Chi. Bears ($414.02)	30-13	New York	35,059
1933	Dec. 17	Chi. Bears ($210.34)	New York ($140.22)	23-21	Chicago	26,000

Sudden death overtime.

NFC CHAMPIONSHIP GAME COMPOSITE STANDINGS

	W	L	Pct.	Pts.	OP
Green Bay Packers	8	2	.800	223	116
Philadelphia Eagles	4	1	.800	79	48
Baltimore Colts	3	1	.750	88	60
Detroit Lions	4	2	.667	139	141
Minnesota Vikings	4	2	.667	108	80
Washington Redskins*	7	5	.583	222	255
Chicago Bears	7	6	.538	286	245
Phoenix Cardinals**	1	1	.500	28	28
Dallas Cowboys	7	8	.467	323	292
San Francisco 49ers	5	6	.454	235	199
Cleveland Browns	4	7	.364	224	253
New York Giants	5	11	.313	240	322
Los Angeles Rams***	3	9	.250	123	270
Tampa Bay Buccaneers	0	1	.000	0	9

*One game played when franchise was in Boston. (Lost 21-6)

**Both games played when franchise was in Chicago. (Won 28-21, lost 7-0)

***One game played when franchise was in Cleveland. (Won 15-14)

1994 NFC CHAMPIONSHIP GAME

Candlestick Park, San Francisco, California

January 15, 1995, Attendance: 69,125

SAN FRANCISCO 38, DALLAS 28—The 49ers eliminated the two-time defending Super Bowl champions by racing to a 21-0 lead in the game's opening minutes and holding on for the victory. San Francisco, which lost to Dallas in each of the previous two NFC title games, thus qualified for its fifth Super Bowl and dashed the Cowboys' hopes of becoming the first team to win three consecutive Super Bowls. The 49ers took advantage of Dallas turnovers to build its early lead. Cornerback Eric Davis intercepted Troy Aikman's pass on the third play of the game and returned it 44 yards for a touchdown and a 7-0 lead with just 1:02 elapsed. Three plays later, Davis forced a fumble that teammate Tim McDonald recovered, and it took San Francisco five plays to convert that into Steve Young's 29-yard touchdown pass to running back Ricky Watters. Kevin Williams fumbled the ensuing kickoff and 49ers kicker Doug Brien recovered at the Cowboys' 35. Fullback William Floyd capped a seven-play drive with a 1-yard run for San Francisco's third touchdown in a span of 6:25. Dallas tried to rally, and pulled within 24-14 late in the first half on a 4-yard run by Emmitt Smith and a 44-yard pass from Aikman to Michael Irvin sandwiched around Brien's 34-yard field goal. But three incompletions that stopped the clock and John Jett's 23-yard punt positioned the 49ers for a back-breaking 28-yard touchdown pass from Young to Jerry Rice just eight seconds before halftime. The Cowboys closed within 10 points twice more in the second half, but were stopped on fourth down twice in the fourth quarter and could get no closer. Dallas finished with a sizeable advantage in total yards (451-294), but was undone by 5 turnovers. Aikman completed 30 of 53 passes for 380 yards and 2 touchdowns, but was intercepted twice. Smith rushed for 74 yards and 2 touchdowns despite nursing an injured hamstring. Irvin caught 12 passes for 192 yards and 2 touchdowns. Young passed for 2 touchdowns and ran for another for San Francisco.

Dallas (28)	Offense	San Francisco (38)
Alvin Harper	WR	John Taylor
Mark Tuinei	LT	Steve Wallace
Nate Newton	LG	Jesse Sapolu
Mark Stepnoski	C	Bart Oates
Derek Kennard	RG	Derrick Deese
Larry Allen	RT	Harris Barton
Jay Novacek	TE	Brent Jones
Michael Irvin	WR	Jerry Rice
Troy Aikman	QB	Steve Young
Emmitt Smith	RB	Ricky Watters
Daryl Johnston	FB	William Floyd
	Defense	
Tony Tolbert	LE	Dennis Brown
Russell Maryland	LT	Bryant Young
Leon Lett	RT	Dana Stubblefield
Charles Haley	RE	Rickey Jackson
Dixon Edwards	LLB	Lee Woodall
Robert Jones	MLB-ILB	Gary Plummer
Darrin Smith	RLB-ILB	Ken Norton
Kevin Smith	LCB	Eric Davis
Larry Brown	RCB	Deion Sanders
James Washington	SS	Tim McDonald
Darren Woodson	FS	Merton Hanks

SUBSTITUTIONS

Dallas—Offense: K—Chris Boniol. P—John Jett. RB—Tommie Agee, Blair Thomas. WR—Kevin Williams. TE—Scott Galbraith. G—Frank Cornish, Ron Stone. C—Dale Hellestrae. Defense: DE—Jim Jeffcoat. DT—Chad Hennings. LB—Darrick Brownlow, Godfrey Myles, Matt Vanderbeek. CB—Clayton Holmes, Dave Thomas. S—Bill Bates, Joe Fishback, Kenneth Gant, Brock Marion. DNP: QB—Rodney Peete, RB—Lincoln Coleman. DT—Hurvin McCormack.

San Francisco—Offense: K—Doug Brien. P—Klaus Wilmsmeyer. RB—Marc Logan, Derek Loville, Adam Walker. WR—Ed McCaffrey, Nate Singleton. TE—Ted Popson. KR—Dexter Carter. T—Harry Boatswain. G—Ralph Tamm. C—Chris Dalman. Defense: DE—Tim Harris, Charles Mann, Troy Wilson. DT—Rhett Hall. LB—Antonio Goss, Kevin Mitchell. CB—Toi Cook, Tyronne Drakeford. S—Dedrick Dodge, Dana Hall. DNP: QB—Elvis Grbac.

OFFICIALS

Referee—Dick Hantak. Umpire—Rex Stuart. Head Linesman—Sid Semon. Line Judge—Ben Montgomery. Back Judge—Ken Baker. Field Judge—Don Orr. Side Judge—Bill Carollo.

SCORING

Dallas	7	7	7	7	—	28
San Francisco	21	10	7	0	—	38

SF — Davis 44 interception (Brien kick)
SF — Watters 29 pass from Young (Brien kick)
SF — Floyd 1 run (Brien kick)
Dall — Irvin 44 pass from Aikman (Boniol kick)
SF — FG Brien 34
Dall — E. Smith 4 run (Boniol kick)
SF — Rice 28 pass from Young (Brien kick)
Dall — E. Smith 1 run (Boniol kick)
SF — Young 3 run (Brien kick)
Dall — Irvin 10 pass from Aikman (Boniol kick)

TEAM STATISTICS

	Dallas	S.F.
Total First Downs	29	19
Rushing	8	9
Passing	18	9
Penalty	3	1
Total Net Yardage	451	294
Total Offensive Plays	81	60
Average Gain per Offensive Play	5.6	4.9
Rushes	24	31
Yards Gained Rushing (Net)	99	139
Average Yards per Rush	4.1	4.5
Passes Attempted	53	29
Passes Completed	30	13
Had Intercepted	3	0
Tackled Attempting to Pass	4	0
Yards Lost Attempting to Pass	28	0
Yards Gained Passing (Net)	352	155
Punts	1	5
Average Distance	23.0	35.6
Punt Returns	1	0
Punt Return Yardage	10	0
Kickoff Returns	7	5
Kickoff Return Yardage	144	90
Interception Return Yardage	0	44
Total Return Yardage	154	134
Fumbles	2	1
Own Fumbles Recovered	0	0
Opponents Fumbles Recovered	1	2
Penalties	9	4
Yards Penalized	98	30
Total Points Scored	28	38
Touchdowns	4	5
Rushing	2	2
Passing	2	2
Returns	0	1
Extra Points	4	5
Field Goals	0	1
Field Goals Attempted	1	1
Safeties	0	0
Third-Down Efficiency	4/14	3/12
Fourth-Down Efficiency	3/5	2/2
Time of Possession	33:56	26:04

PLAYOFF GAMES SUMMARIES

INDIVIDUAL STATISTICS

Rushing

Dallas	**No.**	**Yds.**	**LG**	**TD**
E. Smith	20	74	14	2
Williams	2	12	8	0
Aikman	1	9	9	0
Johnston	1	4	4	0
San Francisco	**No.**	**Yds.**	**LG**	**TD**
Watters	14	72	15	0
Young	10	47	24	1
Floyd	7	20	4	1

Passing

Dallas	**Att.**	**Comp.**	**Yds.**	**TD**	**Int.**
Aikman	53	30	380	2	3
San Francisco	**Att.**	**Comp.**	**Yds.**	**TD**	**Int.**
Young	29	13	155	2	0

Receiving

Dallas	**No.**	**Yds.**	**LG**	**TD**
Irvin	12	192	44t	2
Williams	6	78	22	0
Novacek	5	72	20	0
Johnston	3	19	11	0
E. Smith	3	5	5	0
Harper	1	14	14	0
San Francisco	**No.**	**Yds.**	**LG**	**TD**
Jones	3	37	15	0
Floyd	3	16	7	0
Rice	2	36	28t	1
Taylor	2	31	17	0
Popson	2	6	4	0
Watters	1	29	29t	1

Interceptions

Dallas	**No.**	**Yds.**	**LG**	**TD**
None	—	—	—	—
San Francisco	**No.**	**Yds.**	**LG**	**TD**
E. Davis	2	44	44t	1
Sanders	1	0	0	0

Punting

Dallas	**No.**	**Avg.**	**LG**	**Blk.**
Jett	1	23.0	23	0
San Francisco	**No.**	**Avg.**	**LG**	**Blk.**
Wilmsmeyer	5	35.6	42	0

Punt Returns

Dallas	**No.**	**FC**	**Yds.**	**LG**	**TD**
Williams	1	1	10	10	0
San Francisco	**No.**	**FC**	**Yds.**	**LG**	**TD**
None	—	—	—	—	—

Kickoff Returns

Dallas	**No.**	**Yds.**	**LG**	**TD**
Williams	6	130	26	0
Marion	1	14	14	0
San Francisco	**No.**	**Yds.**	**LG**	**TD**
Carter	3	65	34	0
Sanders	1	25	25	0
Walker	1	0	0	0

AFC DIVISIONAL PLAYOFFS RESULTS

Includes Second-Round Playoff Games (1982), AFC Inter-Divisional Games (1969), and special playoff games to break ties for AFL Division Championships (1963, 1968)

Season	Date	Winner (Share)	Loser (Share)	Score	Site	Attendance
1994	Jan. 8	San Diego ($12,000)	Miami ($12,000)	22-21	San Diego	63,381
	Jan. 7	Pittsburgh ($12,000)	Cleveland ($12,000)	29-9	Pittsburgh	58,185
1993	Jan. 16	Kansas City ($12,000)	Houston ($12,000)	28-20	Houston	64,011
	Jan. 15	Buffalo ($12,000)	L.A. Raiders ($12,000)	29-23	Buffalo	61,923
1992	Jan. 10	Miami ($10,000)	San Diego ($10,000)	31-0	Miami	71,224
	Jan. 9	Buffalo ($10,000)	Pittsburgh ($10,000)	24-3	Pittsburgh	60,407
1991	Jan. 5	Buffalo ($10,000)	Kansas City ($10,000)	37-14	Buffalo	80,182
	Jan. 4	Denver ($10,000)	Houston ($10,000)	26-24	Denver	75,301
1990	Jan. 13	L.A. Raiders ($10,000)	Cincinnati ($10,000)	20-10	Los Angeles	92,045
	Jan. 12	Buffalo ($10,000)	Miami ($10,000)	44-34	Buffalo	77,087
1989	Jan. 7	Denver ($10,000)	Pittsburgh ($10,000)	24-23	Denver	75,477
	Jan. 6	Cleveland ($10,000)	Buffalo ($10,000)	34-30	Cleveland	78,921
1988	Jan. 1	Buffalo ($10,000)	Houston ($10,000)	17-10	Buffalo	79,532
	Dec. 31	Cincinnati ($10,000)	Seattle ($10,000)	21-13	Cincinnati	58,560
1987	Jan. 10	Denver ($10,000)	Houston ($10,000)	34-10	Denver	75,440
	Jan. 9	Cleveland ($10,000)	Indianapolis ($10,000)	38-21	Cleveland	79,372
1986	Jan. 4	Denver ($10,000)	New England ($10,000)	22-17	Denver	75,262
	Jan. 3	Cleveland ($10,000)	N.Y. Jets ($10,000)	23-20*	Cleveland	79,720
1985	Jan. 5	New England ($10,000)	L.A. Raiders ($10,000)	27-20	Los Angeles	87,163
	Jan. 4	Miami ($10,000)	Cleveland ($10,000)	24-21	Miami	74,667
1984	Dec. 30	Pittsburgh ($10,000)	Denver ($10,000)	24-17	Denver	74,981
	Dec. 29	Miami ($10,000)	Seattle ($10,000)	31-10	Miami	73,469
1983	Jan. 1	L.A. Raiders ($10,000)	Pittsburgh ($10,000)	38-10	Los Angeles	90,380
	Dec. 31	Seattle ($10,000)	Miami ($10,000)	27-20	Miami	74,136
1982	Jan. 16	Miami ($10,000)	San Diego ($10,000)	34-13	Miami	71,383
	Jan. 15	N.Y. Jets ($10,000)	L.A. Raiders ($10,000)	17-14	Los Angeles	90,038
1981	Jan. 3	Cincinnati ($5,000)	Buffalo ($5,000)	28-21	Cincinnati	55,420
	Jan. 2	San Diego ($5,000)	Miami ($5,000)	41-38*	Miami	73,735
1980	Jan. 4	Oakland ($5,000)	Cleveland ($5,000)	14-12	Cleveland	78,245
	Jan. 3	San Diego ($5,000)	Buffalo ($5,000)	20-14	San Diego	52,253
1979	Dec. 30	Pittsburgh ($5,000)	Miami ($5,000)	34-14	Pittsburgh	50,214
	Dec. 29	Houston ($5,000)	San Diego ($5,000)	17-14	San Diego	51,192
1978	Dec. 31	Houston ($5,000)	New England ($5,000)	31-14	New England	60,735
	Dec. 30	Pittsburgh ($5,000)	Denver ($5,000)	33-10	Pittsburgh	50,230
1977	Dec. 24	Oakland ($5,000)	Baltimore ($5,000)	37-31*	Baltimore	59,925
	Dec. 24	Denver ($5,000)	Pittsburgh ($5,000)	34-21	Denver	75,059
1976	Dec. 19	Pittsburgh ($)	Baltimore ($)	40-14	Baltimore	59,296
	Dec. 18	Oakland ($)	New England ($)	24-21	Oakland	53,050
1975	Dec. 28	Oakland ($)	Cincinnati ($)	31-28	Oakland	53,030
	Dec. 27	Pittsburgh ($)	Baltimore ($)	28-10	Pittsburgh	49,557
1974	Dec. 22	Pittsburgh ($)	Buffalo ($)	32-14	Pittsburgh	49,841
	Dec. 21	Oakland ($)	Miami ($)	28-26	Oakland	53,023
1973	Dec. 23	Miami ($)	Cincinnati ($)	34-16	Miami	78,928
	Dec. 22	Oakland ($)	Pittsburgh ($)	33-14	Oakland	52,646
1972	Dec. 24	Miami ($)	Cleveland ($)	20-14	Miami	78,916
	Dec. 23	Pittsburgh ($)	Oakland ($)	13-7	Pittsburgh	50,327
1971	Dec. 26	Baltimore ($)	Cleveland ($)	20-3	Cleveland	70,734
	Dec. 25	Miami ($)	Kansas City ($)	27-24*	Kansas City	45,822
1970	Dec. 27	Oakland ($)	Miami ($)	21-14	Oakland	52,594
	Dec. 26	Baltimore ($)	Cincinnati ($)	17-0	Baltimore	49,694
1969	Dec. 21	Oakland ($)	Houston ($)	56-7	Oakland	53,539
	Dec. 20	Kansas City ($)	N.Y. Jets ($)	13-6	New York	62,977
1968	Dec. 22	Oakland ($)	Kansas City ($)	41-6	Oakland	53,605
1963	Dec. 28	Boston ($)	Buffalo ($)	26-8	Buffalo	33,044

**Sudden Death Overtime.*

$ Players received 1/14 of annual salary for playoff appearances.

1994 AFC DIVISIONAL PLAYOFF GAMES

Three Rivers Stadium, Pittsburgh, Pennsylvania
January 7, 1995, Attendance: 58,185

PITTSBURGH 29, CLEVELAND 9—The Steelers scored on their first three possessions to open a 17-0 lead, and went on to defeat the Browns for the third time this season. Pittsburgh dominated the first playoff meeting ever between these long-time rivals (they've played each other twice a year in the regular season since 1950), rushing for 238 yards while amassing 424 total yards and maintaining possession for 42:27 of the game's 60 minutes. Barry Foster ran for 133 yards on 24 carries, and rookie Byron (Bam) Morris added 60 yards on 22 attempts. Quarterback Neil O'Donnell was efficient, completing 8 of his first 9 passes and finishing with 16 completions in 23 attempts for 186 yards. He threw a 2-yard touchdown pass to tight end Eric Green early in the second quarter, and put the game out of reach with a 9-yard touchdown pass to Yancey Thigpen for a 24-3 lead just 16 seconds before halftime. That touchdown was set up by cornerback Tim McKyer's interception and 21-yard return to Cleveland's 6-yard line. It was 1 of 2 interceptions (safety Darren Perry had the other) of Browns quarterback Vinny Testaverde, who completed only 13 of 31 passes for 144 yards. Testaverde received little help from Cleveland's running game, which managed only 55 yards. Ernie Mills caught 5 passes for 117 yards for the Steelers.

Cleveland	0	3	0	6	—	9
Pittsburgh	3	21	3	2	—	29

Pitt — FG Anderson 39
Pitt — Green 2 pass from O'Donnell (Anderson kick)
Pitt — J. Williams 26 run (Anderson kick)
Clev — FG Stover 22
Pitt — Thigpen 9 pass from O'Donnell (Anderson kick)
Pitt — FG Anderson 40
Clev — McCardell 20 pass from Testaverde (pass failed)
Pitt — Safety, Lake sacked Testaverde in end zone

San Diego Jack Murphy Stadium, San Diego, California
January 8, 1995, Attendance: 63,381

SAN DIEGO 22, MIAMI 21—Stan Humphries threw an 8-yard touchdown pass to Mark Seay with 35 seconds remaining, and the Chargers held on to win when Pete Stoyanovich's 48-yard field-goal try fell short and wide right with one second to play. To qualify for the AFC Championship Game for the first time since 1981, San Diego had to rally from a 21-6 halftime deficit. After having 2 drives stall inside Miami's 5-yard line in the first half, the Chargers opened the third quarter by marching 71 yards to the Dolphins' 1-yard line, only to be turned away on fourth down. But on the next play, defensive tackle Reuben Davis dropped Miami running back Bernie Parmalee in the end zone for a safety. San Diego took the ensuing free kick and marched 54 yards to a touchdown, pulling within 21-15 on Natrone Means's 24-yard run with 2:42 left in the third quarter. Late in the fourth quarter, Humphries drove his team from its own 39-yard line to the go-ahead touchdown. The Dolphins got one more chance when Chargers safety Eric Castle was whistled for a 32-yard pass interference penalty, but the snap was high on the strong-legged Stoyanovich's errant field-goal attempt. Humphries completed 28 of 43 passes for 276 yards, while Means rushed for 139 yards on 24 attempts for the Chargers. Miami quarterback Dan Marino was 24 of 38 for 262 yards and 2 touchdowns. But only 56 yards came after halftime, when the Dolphins were limited to five plays in the third quarter and 11 in the fourth quarter. Miami tight end Keith Jackson caught 8 passes for 109 yards and 2 touchdowns.

Miami	7	14	0	0	—	21
San Diego	0	6	9	7	—	22

Mia — K. Jackson 8 pass from Marino (Stoyanovich kick)
SD — FG Carney 20
Mia — K. Jackson 9 pass from Marino (Stoyanovich kick)
SD — FG Carney 21
Mia — M. Williams 16 pass from Marino (Stoyanovich kick)
SD — Safety, R. Davis tackled Parmalee in end zone
SD — Means 24 run (Carney kick)
SD — Seay 8 pass from Humphries (Carney kick)

NFC DIVISIONAL PLAYOFFS RESULTS

Includes Second-Round Playoff Games (1982), NFL Conference Championship Games (1967-69), and special playoff games to break ties for NFL Division or Conference Championships (1941, 1943, 1947, 1950, 1952, 1957, 1958, 1965)

Season	Date	Winner (Share)	Loser (Share)	Score	Site	Attendance
1994	Jan. 8	Dallas ($12,000)	Green Bay ($12,000)	35-9	Dallas	64,745
	Jan. 7	San Francisco ($12,000)	Chicago ($12,000)	44-15	San Francisco	64,644
1993	Jan. 16	Dallas ($12,000)	Green Bay ($12,000)	27-17	Dallas	64,790
	Jan. 15	San Francisco ($12,000)	N.Y. Giants ($12,000)	44-3	San Francisco	67,143
1992	Jan. 10	Dallas ($10,000)	Philadelphia ($10,000)	34-10	Dallas	63,721
	Jan. 9	San Francisco ($10,000)	Washington ($10,000)	20-13	San Francisco	64,991
1991	Jan. 5	Detroit ($10,000)	Dallas ($10,000)	38-6	Detroit	78,290
	Jan. 4	Washington ($10,000)	Atlanta ($10,000)	24-7	Washington	55,181
1990	Jan. 13	N.Y. Giants ($10,000)	Chicago ($10,000)	31-3	East Rutherford	77,025
	Jan. 12	San Francisco ($10,000)	Washington ($10,000)	28-10	San Francisco	65,292
1989	Jan. 7	L.A. Rams ($10,000)	N.Y. Giants ($10,000)	19-13*	East Rutherford	76,526
	Jan. 6	San Francisco ($10,000)	Minnesota ($10,000)	41-13	San Francisco	64,918
1988	Jan. 1	San Francisco ($10,000)	Minnesota ($10,000)	34-9	San Francisco	61,848
	Dec. 31	Chicago ($10,000)	Philadelphia ($10,000)	20-12	Chicago	65,534
1987	Jan. 10	Washington ($10,000)	Chicago ($10,000)	21-17	Chicago	65,268
	Jan. 9	Minnesota ($10,000)	San Francisco ($10,000)	36-24	San Francisco	63,008
1986	Jan. 4	N.Y. Giants ($10,000)	San Francisco ($10,000)	49-3	East Rutherford	75,691
	Jan. 3	Washington ($10,000)	Chicago ($10,000)	27-13	Chicago	65,524
1985	Jan. 5	Chicago ($10,000)	N.Y. Giants ($10,000)	21-0	Chicago	65,670
	Jan. 4	L.A. Rams ($10,000)	Dallas ($10,000)	20-0	Anaheim	66,581
1984	Dec. 30	Chicago ($10,000)	Washington ($10,000)	23-19	Washington	55,431
	Dec. 29	San Francisco ($10,000)	N.Y. Giants ($10,000)	21-10	San Francisco	60,303
1983	Jan. 1	Washington ($10,000)	L.A. Rams ($10,000)	51-7	Washington	54,440
	Dec. 31	San Francisco ($10,000)	Detroit ($10,000)	24-23	San Francisco	59,979
1982	Jan. 16	Dallas ($10,000)	Green Bay ($10,000)	37-26	Dallas	63,972
	Jan. 15	Washington ($10,000)	Minnesota ($10,000)	21-7	Washington	54,593
1981	Jan. 3	San Francisco ($5,000)	N.Y. Giants ($5,000)	38-24	San Francisco	58,360
	Jan. 2	Dallas ($5,000)	Tampa Bay ($5,000)	38-0	Dallas	64,848
1980	Jan. 4	Dallas ($5,000)	Atlanta ($5,000)	30-27	Atlanta	59,793
	Jan. 3	Philadelphia ($5,000)	Minnesota ($5,000)	31-16	Philadelphia	70,178
1979	Dec. 30	Los Angeles ($5,000)	Dallas ($5,000)	21-19	Dallas	64,792
	Dec. 29	Tampa Bay ($5,000)	Philadelphia ($5,000)	24-17	Tampa Bay	71,402
1978	Dec. 31	Los Angeles ($5,000)	Minnesota ($5,000)	34-10	Los Angeles	70,436
	Dec. 30	Dallas ($5,000)	Atlanta ($5,000)	27-20	Dallas	63,406
1977	Dec. 26	Dallas ($5,000)	Chicago ($5,000)	37-7	Dallas	63,260
	Dec. 26	Minnesota ($5,000)	Los Angeles ($5,000)	14-7	Los Angeles	70,203
1976	Dec. 19	Los Angeles ($)	Dallas ($)	14-12	Dallas	63,283
	Dec. 18	Minnesota ($)	Washington ($)	35-20	Minnesota	47,466
1975	Dec. 28	Dallas ($)	Minnesota ($)	17-14	Minnesota	48,050
	Dec. 27	Los Angeles ($)	St. Louis ($)	35-23	Los Angeles	73,459
1974	Dec. 22	Los Angeles ($)	Washington ($)	19-10	Los Angeles	77,925
	Dec. 21	Minnesota ($)	St. Louis ($)	30-14	Minnesota	48,150
1973	Dec. 23	Dallas ($)	Los Angeles ($)	27-16	Dallas	63,272
	Dec. 22	Minnesota ($)	Washington ($)	27-20	Minnesota	48,040
1972	Dec. 24	Washington ($)	Green Bay ($)	16-3	Washington	52,321
	Dec. 23	Dallas ($)	San Francisco ($)	30-28	San Francisco	59,746

PLAYOFF GAMES SUMMARIES

1971	Dec. 26	San Francisco ($)	Washington ($)	24-20	San Francisco	45,327
	Dec. 25	Dallas ($)	Minnesota ($)	20-12	Minnesota	47,307
1970	Dec. 27	San Francisco ($)	Minnesota ($)	17-14	Minnesota	45,103
	Dec. 26	Dallas ($)	Detroit ($)	5-0	Dallas	69,613
1969	Dec. 28	Cleveland ($)	Dallas ($)	38-14	Dallas	69,321
	Dec. 27	Minnesota ($)	Los Angeles ($)	23-20	Minnesota	47,900
1968	Dec. 22	Baltimore ($)	Minnesota ($)	24-14	Baltimore	60,238
	Dec. 21	Cleveland ($)	Dallas ($)	31-20	Cleveland	81,497
1967	Dec. 24	Dallas ($)	Cleveland ($)	52-14	Dallas	70,786
	Dec. 23	Green Bay ($)	Los Angeles ($)	28-7	Milwaukee	49,861
1965	Dec. 26	Green Bay ($)	Baltimore ($)	13-10*	Green Bay	50,484
1958	Dec. 21	N.Y. Giants (#)	Cleveland (#)	10-0	New York	61,274
1957	Dec. 22	Detroit (#)	San Francisco (#)	31-27	San Francisco	60,118
1952	Dec. 21	Detroit (#)	Los Angeles (#)	31-21	Detroit	47,645
1950	Dec. 17	Los Angeles (#)	Chicago Bears (#)	24-14	Los Angeles	83,501
	Dec. 17	Cleveland (#)	N.Y. Giants (#)	8-3	Cleveland	33,054
1947	Dec. 21	Philadelphia (#)	Pittsburgh (#)	21-0	Pittsburgh	35,729
1943	Dec. 19	Washington (¢)	N.Y. Giants (¢)	28-0	New York	42,800
1941	Dec. 14	Chicago Bears (¢)	Green Bay (¢)	33-14	Chicago	43,425

* *Sudden Death Overtime.*
$ Players received 1/14 of annual salary for playoff appearances.
 # Players received 1/12 of annual salary for playoff appearances.
¢ Players received 1/10 of annual salary for playoff appearances.

1994 NFC DIVISIONAL PLAYOFF GAMES

Texas Stadium, Irving, Texas
January 8, 1995, Attendance: 64,745

DALLAS 35, GREEN BAY 9—Troy Aikman passed for 337 yards and 2 touchdowns, including a 94-yard strike to Alvin Harper, to lead the Cowboys to an easy victory over the Packers. The win set the stage for the third consecutive NFC title game between Dallas and San Francisco. Aikman, who completed 23 of 30 passes, spread his passes around to tight end Jay Novacek and wide receivers Michael Irvin and Harper, each of whom caught passes for more than 100 yards. Novacek had a club playoff-record 11 receptions for 104 yards, Irvin caught 6 passes for 111 yards, and Harper had a pair of receptions for 108 yards. His 94-yard touchdown catch gave the Cowboys a 14-3 lead late in the first quarter. It was the longest play from scrimmage in NFL postseason history. Dallas running back Emmitt Smith ran for 44 yards and a touchdown in the first quarter, but left the game after aggravating a hamstring injury. His backup, Blair Thomas, ran for 70 yards and 2 touchdowns, including a 1-yard score to help break open the game at 21-3 midway through the second quarter.

Green Bay	3	6	0	0	—	9
Dallas	14	14	0	7	—	35

Dall — E. Smith 5 run (Boniol kick)
GB — FG Jacke 50
Dall — Harper 94 pass from Aikman (Boniol kick)
Dall — B.Thomas 1 run (Boniol kick)
GB — Bennett 1 run (pass failed)
Dall — Galbraith 1 pass from Aikman (Boniol kick)
Dall — B. Thomas 2 run (Boniol kick)

Candlestick Park, San Francisco, California
January 7, 1995, Attendance: 64,644

SAN FRANCISCO 44, CHICAGO 15—William Floyd ran for 3 touchdowns and Steve Young ran for 1 and passed for 1 as the 49ers tuned up for the NFC Championship Game by routing the Bears. After turning over the ball on its first possession and spotting Chicago an early field goal, San Francisco scored on six consecutive possessions to turn the game into a rout. Floyd's 2-yard run with 3:41 left in the first quarter gave the 49ers the lead for good, and his 4-yard run midway through the second quarter increased their advantage to 20-3. Young, who tossed an 8-yard touchdown pass to tight end Brent Jones early in the second quarter, ran 6 yards for a score 1:17 before halftime to make it 30-3. Floyd's third touchdown, from 1 yard, capped a 70-yard drive on San Francisco's first possession of the second half, and many of the 49ers' starters, including Young, took the rest of the afternoon off. The Bears, limited to only 95 total yards behind starting quarterback Steve Walsh in the first half, turned to Erik Kramer in the second half. Kramer passed for 161 yards in his two quarters of play and generated 2 touchdowns in the fourth quarter, but they came long after the game had been decided.

Chicago	3	0	0	12	—	15
San Francisco	7	23	7	7	—	44

Chi — FG Butler 39
SF — Floyd 2 run (Brien kick)
SF — Jones 8 pass from Young (kick failed)
SF — Floyd 4 run (Brien kick)
SF — FG Brien 36
SF — Young 6 run (Brien kick)
SF — Floyd 1 run (Brien kick)
Chi — Flanigan 2 pass from Kramer (pass failed)
SF — Walker 1 run (Brien kick)
Chi — Tillman 1 run (pass failed)

AFC WILD CARD PLAYOFF GAMES RESULTS

Season	Date	Winner (Share)	Loser (Share)	Score	Site	Attendance
1994	Jan. 1	Cleveland ($7,500)	New England ($7,500)	20-13	Cleveland	77,452
	Dec. 31	Miami ($12,000)	Kansas City ($7,500)	27-17	Miami	67,487
1993	Jan. 9	L.A. Raiders ($7,500)	Denver ($7,500)	42-24	Los Angeles	65,314
	Jan. 8	Kansas City ($12,000)	Pittsburgh ($7,500)	27-24*	Kansas City	74,515
1992	Jan. 3	Buffalo ($6,000)	Houston ($6,000)	41-38*	Buffalo	75,141
	Jan. 2	San Diego ($10,000)	Kansas City ($6,000)	17-0	San Diego	58,278
1991	Dec. 29	Houston ($10,000)	N.Y. Jets ($6,000)	17-10	Houston	61,485
	Dec. 28	Kansas City ($6,000)	L.A. Raiders ($6,000)	10-6	Kansas City	75,827
1990	Jan. 6	Cincinnati ($10,000)	Houston ($6,000)	41-14	Cincinnati	60,012
	Jan. 5	Miami ($6,000)	Kansas City ($6,000)	17-16	Miami	67,276
1989	Dec. 31	Pittsburgh ($6,000)	Houston ($6,000)	26-23*	Houston	59,406
1988	Dec. 26	Houston ($6,000)	Cleveland ($6,000)	24-23	Cleveland	75,896
1987	Jan. 3	Houston ($6,000)	Seattle ($6,000)	23-20*	Houston	50,519
1986	Dec. 28	N.Y. Jets ($6,000)	Kansas City ($6,000)	35-15	East Rutherford	75,210
1985	Dec. 28	New England ($6,000)	N.Y. Jets ($6,000)	26-14	East Rutherford	75,945
1984	Dec. 22	Seattle ($6,000)	L.A. Raiders ($6,000)	13-7	Seattle	62,049
1983	Dec. 24	Seattle ($6,000)	Denver ($6,000)	31-7	Seattle	64,275
1982	Jan. 9	N.Y. Jets ($6,000)	Cincinnati ($6,000)	44-17	Cincinnati	57,560
	Jan. 9	San Diego ($6,000)	Pittsburgh ($6,000)	31-28	Pittsburgh	53,546
	Jan. 8	L.A. Raiders ($6,000)	Cleveland ($6,000)	27-10	Los Angeles	56,555
	Jan. 8	Miami ($6,000)	New England ($6,000)	28-13	Miami	68,842
1981	Dec. 27	Buffalo ($3,000)	N.Y. Jets ($3,000)	31-27	New York	57,050
1980	Dec. 28	Oakland ($3,000)	Houston ($3,000)	27-7	Oakland	53,333
1979	Dec. 23	Houston ($3,000)	Denver ($3,000)	13-7	Houston	48,776
1978	Dec. 24	Houston ($3,000)	Miami ($3,000)	17-9	Miami	72,445

**Sudden death overtime.*

1994 AFC WILD CARD PLAYOFF GAMES

Cleveland Stadium, Cleveland, Ohio
January 1, 1995, Attendance: 77,452

CLEVELAND 20, NEW ENGLAND 13—Vinny Testaverde threw for 268 yards and 1 touchdown and the Browns survived a late scare to beat the Patriots. After Matt Stover's 21-yard field goal with 3:36 remaining gave Cleveland a 20-10 advantage, the Patriots marched from their own 22-yard line to the Browns' 15. The drive stalled there, and Matt Bahr trimmed New England's deficit to seven points with a 33-yard field goal at the 1:30 mark. The Patriots recovered the ensuing onside kick and picked up a first down before four consecutive incompletions from their 48-yard line ended their comeback hopes. Testaverde completed 20 of 30 passes for the Browns, including a 5-yard touchdown to Mark Carrier in the second quarter. Michael Jackson caught 7 passes for 122 yards. Drew Bledsoe completed only 21 of 50 passes for 235 yards for New England and was intercepted 3 times.

New England	0	10	0	3	—	13
Cleveland	3	7	7	3	—	20

Clev — FG Stover 30
NE — Thompson 13 pass from Bledsoe (Bahr kick)
Clev — Carrier 5 pass from Testaverde (Stover kick)
NE — FG Bahr 23
Clev — Hoard 10 run (Stover kick)
Clev — FG Stover 21
NE — FG Bahr 33

Joe Robbie Stadium, Miami, Florida
December 31, 1994, Attendance: 67,487

MIAMI 27, KANSAS CITY 17—Dan Marino threw 2 touchdown passes and the Dolphins' defense forced a pair of critical turnovers in the fourth quarter to preserve the victory. A wild first half ended in a 17-17 tie after Marino and Chiefs quarterback Joe Montana each had three possessions (excluding a Kansas City kneeldown on the final play) and produced a pair of touchdowns and a field goal. Marino picked up in the third quarter where he left off, directing a 64-yard touchdown drive following the second-half kickoff. He capped the six-play march with a 7-yard touchdown pass to Irving Fryar. Late in the quarter, Pete Stoyanovich kicked a 40-yard field goal to give Miami a 10-point lead, and the Dolphins' defense then took over. Cornerback J.B. Brown intercepted Montana at the goal line early in the fourth quarter, and safety Michael Stewart wrestled the ball from Kansas City running back Marcus Allen at Miami's 34-yard line with 7:31 left. Miami held onto the ball for nearly six minutes after that. Marino completed 22 of 29 passes for 257 yards for the Dolphins. Montana was 26 of 37 for 314 yards for the Chiefs. Kansas City running back Kimble Anders caught 6 passes for 103 yards, including a 57-yard touchdown.

Kansas City	14	3	0	0	—	17
Miami	7	10	10	0	—	27

KC — Walker 1 pass from Montana (Elliot kick)
Mia — Parmalee 1 run (Stoyanovich kick)
KC — Anders 57 pass from Montana (Elliot kick)
Mia — FG Stoyanovich 40
KC — FG Elliot 21
Mia — R. Williams 1 pass from Marino (Stoyanovich kick)
Mia — Fryar 7 pass from Marino (Stoyanovich kick)
Mia — FG Stoyanovich 40

NFC WILD CARD PLAYOFF GAMES RESULTS

Season	Date	Winner (Share)	Loser (Share)	Score	Site	Attendance
1994	Jan. 1	Chicago ($7,500)	Minnesota ($12,000)	35-18	Minneapolis	60,347
	Dec. 31	Green Bay ($7,500)	Detroit ($7,500)	16-12	Green Bay	58,125
1993	Jan. 9	N.Y. Giants ($7,500)	Minnesota ($7,500)	17-10	East Rutherford	75,089
	Jan. 8	Green Bay ($7,500)	Detroit ($12,000)	28-24	Detroit	68,479
1992	Jan. 3	Philadelphia ($6,000)	New Orleans ($6,000)	36-20	New Orleans	68,893
	Jan. 2	Washington ($6,000)	Minnesota ($10,000)	24-7	Minneapolis	57,353
1991	Dec. 29	Dallas ($6,000)	Chicago ($6,000)	17-13	Chicago	62,594
	Dec. 28	Atlanta ($6,000)	New Orleans ($10,000)	27-20	New Orleans	68,794
1990	Jan. 6	Chicago ($10,000)	New Orleans ($6,000)	16-6	Chicago	60,767
	Jan. 5	Washington ($6,000)	Philadelphia ($6,000)	20-6	Philadelphia	65,287
1989	Dec. 31	L.A. Rams ($6,000)	Philadelphia ($6,000)	21-7	Philadelphia	65,479
1988	Dec. 26	Minnesota ($6,000)	L.A. Rams ($6,000)	28-17	Minnesota	61,204
1987	Jan. 3	Minnesota ($6,000)	New Orleans ($6,000)	44-10	New Orleans	68,546
1986	Dec. 28	Washington ($6,000)	L.A. Rams ($6,000)	19-7	Washington	54,567
1985	Dec. 29	N.Y. Giants ($6,000)	San Francisco ($6,000)	17-3	East Rutherford	75,131
1984	Dec. 23	N.Y. Giants ($6,000)	L.A. Rams ($6,000)	16-3	Anaheim	67,037
1983	Dec. 26	L.A. Rams ($6,000)	Dallas ($6,000)	24-17	Dallas	62,118
1982	Jan. 9	Dallas ($6,000)	Tampa Bay ($6,000)	30-17	Dallas	65,042
	Jan. 9	Minnesota ($6,000)	Atlanta ($6,000)	30-24	Minnesota	60,560
	Jan. 8	Green Bay ($6,000)	St. Louis ($6,000)	41-16	Green Bay	54,282
	Jan. 8	Washington ($6,000)	Detroit ($6,000)	31-7	Washington	55,045
1981	Dec. 27	N.Y. Giants ($3,000)	Philadelphia ($3,000)	27-21	Philadelphia	71,611
1980	Dec. 28	Dallas ($3,000)	Los Angeles ($3,000)	34-13	Dallas	63,052
1979	Dec. 23	Philadelphia ($3,000)	Chicago ($3,000)	27-17	Philadelphia	69,397
1978	Dec. 24	Atlanta ($3,000)	Philadelphia ($3,000)	14-13	Atlanta	59,403

1994 NFC WILD CARD PLAYOFF GAMES

Metrodome, Minneapolis, Minnesota
January 1, 1995, Attendance: 60,347

CHICAGO 35, MINNESOTA 18—Steve Walsh threw 2 touchdowns passes as the Bears stunned the NFC Central Division-champion Vikings. Chicago, which didn't score more than 27 points in any game during the 1994 regular season, ended a six-game losing streak to the Vikings by shredding the NFL's fifth-ranked defense for 5 touchdowns. Despite turnovers on their first two possessions, the Bears forged a 14-3 lead in the second quarter on Lewis Tillman's 1-yard run and Walsh's 9-yard touchdown pass to tight end Keith Jennings. Minnesota pulled within 14-9 on Warren Moon's 4-yard touchdown pass to Cris Carter 19 seconds before halftime, but Chicago struck quickly in the third quarter to bolster its lead. Walsh teamed with Curtis Conway on a 23-yard completion and with Jeff Graham on an 18-yard gain before Raymont Harris ran 29 yards for a touchdown just 2:03 into the second half. It was the longest rushing play of the season for the Bears. Walsh's 21-yard touchdown pass to Graham early in the fourth quarter helped keep the game out of reach. He finished with 15 completions in 23 attempts for 221 yards. Graham caught 4 passes for 108 yards. Moon completed 29 of 52 passes for 292 yards and running back Amp Lee caught 11 passes for 159 yards for the Vikings, who had sizeable advantages in plays (82-54) and total yards (389-308). But Minnesota was victimized by 4 turnovers and 11 penalties.

Chicago	0	14	7	14	—	35
Minnesota	3	6	3	6	—	18

Minn — FG Reveiz 29
Chi — Tillman 1 run (Butler kick)
Chi — Jennings 9 pass from Walsh (Butler kick)
Minn — Carter 4 pass from Moon (pass failed)
Chi — Harris 29 run (Butler kick)
Minn — FG Reveiz 48
Chi — Graham 21 pass from Walsh (Butler kick)
Minn — Lee 11 pass from Moon (pass failed)
Chi — Miniefield 48 fumble return (Butler kick)

Lambeau Field, Green Bay, Wisconsin
December 31, 1994. Attendance: 58,125

GREEN BAY 16, DETROIT 12—The Packers won their first playoff game at home in 12 years by staving off the Lions in the closing minutes. After Chris Jacke's third field goal of the game, from 28 yards with 5:35 to play in the fourth quarter, gave Green Bay a 16-10 lead, Detroit's Eric Lynch returned the ensuing kickoff 27 yards to the Packers' 49-yard line. The Lions reached the 11 at the two-minute warning, but linebacker Bryce Paup sacked Dave Krieg for a 6-yard loss, and on fourth-and-14 from the 17, Herman Moore caught Krieg's pass at the back of the end zone, only to come down past the end line with 1:45 to play. Green Bay ran out the rest of the clock, giving up a concession safety on the last play. Brett Favre passed for 262 yards for the Packers, but it was Green Bay's defense that made the difference. The Packers limited Barry Sanders, the NFL's leading rusher with 1,883 yards during the regular season, to minus-1 yard on 13 carries. Sanders, who caught 3 passes for 4 yards, was held to negative yardage eight of the 16 times he touched the ball. The Lions rushed for minus-4 yards as a team.

Detroit	0	0	3	9	—	12
Green Bay	7	3	3	3	—	16

GB — Levens 3 run (Jacke kick)
GB — FG Jacke 51
Det — FG Hanson 38
GB — FG Jacke 32
Det — Perriman 3 pass from Krieg (Hanson kick)
GB — FG Jacke 28
Det — Safety, Hentrich ran out of the end zone

AFC-NFC PRO BOWL SUMMARIES

AFC-NFC PRO BOWL AT A GLANCE RESULTS (1971-1995)

NFC leads series, 14-11

Year	Date	Winner (Share)	Loser (Share)	Score	Site	Attendance
1995	Feb. 5	AFC ($20,000)	NFC ($10,000)	41-13	Honolulu	49,121
1994	Feb. 6	NFC ($20,000)	AFC ($10,000)	17-3	Honolulu	50,026
1993	Feb. 7	AFC ($10,000)	NFC ($5,000)	23-20 (OT)	Honolulu	50,007
1992	Feb. 2	NFC ($10,000)	AFC ($5,000)	21-15	Honolulu	50,209
1991	Feb. 3	AFC ($10,000)	NFC ($5,000)	23-21	Honolulu	50,345
1990	Feb. 4	NFC ($10,000)	AFC ($5,000)	27-21	Honolulu	50,445
1989	Jan. 29	NFC ($10,000)	AFC ($5,000)	34-3	Honolulu	50,113
1988	Feb. 7	AFC ($10,000)	NFC ($5,000)	15-6	Honolulu	50,113
1987	Feb. 1	AFC ($10,000)	NFC ($5,000)	10-6	Honolulu	50,101
1986	Feb. 2	NFC ($10,000)	AFC ($5,000)	28-24	Honolulu	50,101
1985	Jan. 27	AFC ($10,000)	NFC ($5,000)	22-14	Honolulu	50,385
1984	Jan. 29	NFC ($10,000)	AFC ($5,000)	45-3	Honolulu	50,445
1983	Feb. 6	NFC ($10,000)	AFC ($5,000)	20-19	Honolulu	49,883
1982	Jan. 31	AFC ($5,000)	NFC ($2,500)	16-13	Honolulu	50,402
1981	Feb. 1	NFC ($5,000)	AFC ($2,500)	21-7	Honolulu	50,360
1980	Jan. 27	NFC ($5,000)	AFC ($2,500)	37-27	Honolulu	49,800
1979	Jan. 29	NFC ($5,000)	AFC ($2,500)	13-7	Los Angeles	46,281
1978	Jan. 23	NFC ($5,000)	AFC ($2,500)	14-13	Tampa	51,337
1977	Jan. 17	AFC ($2,000)	NFC ($1,500)	24-14	Seattle	64,752
1976	Jan. 26	NFC ($2,000)	AFC ($1,500)	23-20	New Orleans	30,546
1975	Jan. 20	NFC ($2,000)	AFC ($1,500)	17-10	Miami	26,484
1974	Jan. 20	AFC ($2,000)	NFC ($1,500)	15-13	Kansas City	66,918
1973	Jan. 21	AFC ($2,000)	NFC ($1,500)	33-28	Dallas	37,091
1972	Jan. 23	AFC ($2,000)	NFC ($1,500)	26-13	Los Angeles	53,647
1971	Jan. 24	NFC ($2,000)	AFC ($1,500)	27-6	Los Angeles	48,222

1995 AFC-NFC PRO BOWL

Aloha Stadium, Honolulu, Hawaii
February 5, 1995, Attendance: 49,121

AFC 41, NFC 13—Colts rookie Marshall Faulk rushed for a Pro Bowl-record 180 yards to key the AFC's rout of the NFC. Faulk, who earned the Dan McGuire Trophy as the player of the game, averaged nearly 14 yards on his 13 carries and shattered the previous rushing mark of 112 yards set by O.J. Simpson in the 1973 game. Faulk's 49-yard touchdown run from punt formation in the fourth quarter was the longest in Pro Bowl history. The Seahawks' Chris Warren added 127 yards on 14 carries as the AFC amassed records for rushing yards (400) and total yards (552). Steelers tight end Eric Green caught 2 touchdown passes for the victors. The NFC managed only 196 total yards, a large chunk coming when 49ers quarterback Steve Young and Vikings wide receiver Cris Carter teamed on a 51-yard touchdown pass in the first quarter. That gave the NFC a 10-0 advantage, but the AFC rallied in the second quarter and took the lead for good when the Browns' Leroy Hoard scored on a 4-yard touchdown run 2:07 before halftime.

AFC (41)	Offense	NFC (33)
Tim Brown (L. A. Raiders)	WR	Michael Irvin (Dallas)
Richmond Webb (Miami)	LT	William Roaf (New Orleans)
Keith Sims (Miami)	LG	Nate Newton (Dallas)
Dermontti Dawson (Pittsburgh)	C	Mark Stepnoski (Dallas)
Duval Love (Pittsburgh)	RG	Randall McDaniel (Minnesota)
Bruce Armstrong (New England)	RT	Lomas Brown (Detroit)
Ben Coates (New England)	TE	Brent Jones (San Francisco)
Andre Reed (Buffalo)	WR	Cris Carter (Minnesota)
John Elway (Denver)	QB	Steve Young (San Francisco)
Marshall Faulk (Indianapolis)	RB	Barry Sanders (Detroit)
Natrone Means (San Diego)	RB	Daryl Johnston (Dallas)
	Defense	
Bruce Smith (Buffalo)	LE	Charles Haley (Dallas)
Michael Dean Perry (Cleveland)	IL	John Randle (Minnesota)
Cortez Kennedy (Seattle)	IL	Leon Lett (Dallas)
Leslie O'Neal (San Diego)	RE	William Fuller (Philadelphia)
Derrick Thomas (Kansas City)	LOLB	Ken Harvey (Washington)
Junior Seau (San Diego)	ILB	Chris Spielman (Detroit)
Greg Lloyd (Pittsburgh)	ROLB	Bryce Paup (Green Bay)
Rod Woodson (Pittsburgh)	LCB	Deion Sanders (San Francisco)
Terry McDaniel (L.A. Raiders)	RCB	Aeneas Williams (Arizona)
Carnell Lake (Pittsburgh)	SS	Darren Woodson (Dallas)
Eric Turner (Cleveland)	FS	Merton Hanks (San Francisco)

SUBSTITUTIONS

AFC—Offense: K-John Carney (San Diego). P-Rick Tuten (Seattle). QB-Drew Bledsoe (New England), Jeff Hostetler (L.A. Raiders). RB-Leroy Hoard (Cleveland), Chris Warren (Seattle). WR-Irving Fryar (Miami), Rob Moore (N.Y. Jets). TE- Eric Green (Steelers). ST-Steve Tasker (Buffalo). KR-Eric Metcalf (Cleveland). T-Gary Zimmerman (Denver). G-Kevin Gogan (L.A. Raiders). C-Bruce Matthews (Houston). Defense: E-Rob Burnett (Cleveland). T-Chester McGlockton (L.A. Raiders). LB-Bryan Cox (Miami), Kevin Greene (Pittsburgh), Pepper Johnson (Cleveland). CB-Dale Carter (Kansas City). S-Steve Atwater (Denver). DNP: None.

NFC—Offense: K-Fuad Reveiz (Minnesota). P-Reggie Roby (Washington). QB-Troy Aikman (Dallas), Warren Moon (Minnesota). RB-Jerome Bettis (L.A. Rams), Ricky Watters (San Francisco). WR-Terance Mathis (Atlanta), Herman Moore (Detroit). TE-Jay Novacek (Dallas). ST-Elbert Shelley (Atlanta). KR-Mel Gray (Detroit). T-Mark Tuinei (Dallas). G-Jesse Sapolu (San Francisco). C-Bart Oates (San Francisco). Defense: E-Wayne Martin (New Oreleans). T-Dana Stubblefield (San Francisco). LB-Jack Del Rio (Minnesota), Seth Joyner (Arizona), Jesse Tuggle (Atlanta). CB-Eric Allen (Philadelphia). S-Tim McDonald (San Francisco). DNP: None.

HEAD COACHES

AFC—Bill Cowher (Pittsburgh)
NFC—Barry Switzer (Dallas)

OFFICIALS

Referee–Larry Nemmers. Umpire–Jim Duke. Head Linesman–Jerry Bergman. Line Judge–Dale Orem. Back Judge–Banks Williams. Field Judge–Scott Green. Side Judge–Don Carlsen.

SCORING

AFC	0	17	3	21	—	41
NFC	10	0	3	0	—	13

NFC — FG Reveiz 28
NFC — Carter 51 pass from Young (Reveiz kick)
AFC — Green 22 pass from Elway (Carney kick)
AFC — FG Carney 22
AFC — Hoard 4 run (Carney kick)
NFC — FG Reveiz 49
AFC — FG Carney 23
AFC — Warren 11 run (Carney kick)
AFC — Green 16 pass from Hostetler (Carney kick)
AFC — Faulk 49 run (Carney kick)

TEAM STATISTICS	AFC	NFC
Total First Downs	27	10
Rushing	18	3
Passing	8	7
Penalty	1	0
Total Net Yardage	552	196
Total Offensive Plays	69	53
Average Gain per Offensive Play	8.0	3.7
Rushes	40	19
Yards Gained Rushing (Net)	400	41
Average Yards per Rush	10.0	2.2
Passes Attempted	28	32
Passes Completed	12	13
Had Intercepted	1	0
Tackled Attempting to Pass	1	2
Yards Lost Attempting to Pass	5	13
Yards Gained Passing (Net)	152	155
Punts	4	8
Average Distance	40.3	50.1
Punt Returns	7	2
Punt Return Yardage	105	47
Kickoff Returns	4	8
Kickoff Return Yardage	61	184
Interception Return Yardage	0	10
Total Return Yardage	166	241
Fumbles	0	0
Own Fumbles Recovered	0	0
Opponent Fumbles Recovered	0	0
Penalties	6	7
Yards Penalized	35	45
Total Points Scored	41	13

Touchdowns	5	1
Rushing	3	0
Passing	2	1
Returns	0	0
Extra Points	5	1
Field Goals	2	2
Field Goals Attempted	2	2
Safeties	0	0
Third-Down Efficiency	5/14	4/14
Fourth-Down Efficiency	2/2	0/0
Time of Possession	33:53	26:07

INDIVIDUAL STATISTICS

Rushing

AFC	No.	Yds.	LG	TD
Faulk	13	180	49t	1
Warren	14	127	28	1
Means	5	61	41	0
Hoard	4	20	11	1
Hostetler	1	10	10	0
Bledsoe	2	3	2	0
Reed	1	-1	-1	0
NFC	**No.**	**Yds.**	**LG**	**TD**
Bettis	6	22	9	0
B. Sanders	8	17	4	0
Johnston	2	6	5	0
Watters	1	2	2	0
Aikman	1	0	0	0
D. Sanders	1	-6	-6	0

Passing

AFC	Att.	Comp.	Yds.	TD	Int.
Bledsoe	13	5	43	0	1
Hostetler	8	4	83	1	0
Elway	7	3	31	1	0
NFC	**Att.**	**Comp.**	**Yds.**	**TD**	**Int.**
Young	15	8	129	1	0
Aikman	9	2	17	0	0
Moon	8	3	22	0	0

Receiving

AFC	No.	Yds.	LG	TD
Green	4	50	22t	2
Faulk	2	27	18	0
Coates	2	12	11	0
Brown	2	9	5	0
Fryar	1	35	35	0
Hoard	1	24	24	0
NFC	**No.**	**Yds.**	**LG**	**TD**
Carter	4	81	51t	1
Mathis	2	23	15	0
Johnston	2	17	12	0
Irvin	1	18	18	0
D. Sanders	1	15	15	0
Moore	1	13	13	0
B. Sanders	1	2	2	0
Bettis	1	-1	-1	0

Interceptions

AFC	No.	Yds.	LG	TD
None				
NFC	**No.**	**Yds.**	**LG**	**TD**
D. Sanders	1	10	10	0

Punting

AFC	No.	Avg.	LG	Blk.
Tuten	4	40.3	46	0
NFC	**No.**	**Avg.**	**LG**	**Blk.**
Roby	8	50.1	60	0

Punt Returns

AFC	No.	FC	Yds.	LG	TD
Metcalf	6	1	89	19	0
Brown	1	0	16	16	0
NFC	**No.**	**FC**	**Yds.**	**LG**	**TD**
Gray	2	0	47	40	0

Kickoff Returns

AFC	No.	Yds.	LG	TD
Faulk	2	37	26	0
Metcalf	2	24	21	0
NFC	**No.**	**Yds.**	**LG**	**TD**
Gray	7	162	27	0
Mathis	1	22	22	0

1994 AFC-NFC PRO BOWL

Aloha Stadium, Honolulu, Hawaii
February 6, 1994, Attendance: 50,026

NFC 17, AFC 3—The NFC converted a blocked punt and a fumble recovery into touchdowns just 2:20 apart in the second half of its victory over the AFC. With the score tied 3-3 late in the third quarter, Saints linebacker Renaldo Turnbull deflected a punt by the Oilers' Greg Montgomery, and the NFC took possession at the AFC's 48-yard line. A 32-yard pass from Bobby Hebert to Falcons teammate Andre Rison positioned Rams running back Jerome Bettis for a 4-yard touchdown run with 1:27 left in the third quarter. Moments later, Rams defensive tackle Sean Gilbert recovered a fumble by Oilers quarterback Warren Moon at the AFC's 19. Hebert then teamed with the Vikings' Cris Carter on a 15-yard touchdown pass 53 seconds into the fourth period. The NFC kept the AFC out of the end zone by maintaining possession for more than 38 minutes and forcing 6 turnovers. Rison earned the Dan McGuire Trophy as the player of the game by catching 6 passes for 86 yards. The victory was the fourth in the last six years for the NFC, which leads the series 14-10.

NFC	3	0	7	7	—	17
AFC	0	3	0	0	—	3

NFC — FG Johnson 35
AFC — FG Anderson 25
NFC — Bettis 4 run (Johnson kick)
NFC — Carter 15 pass from Hebert (Johnson kick)

1993 AFC-NFC PRO BOWL

Aloha Stadium, Honolulu, Hawaii
February 7, 1993, Attendance: 50,007

AFC 23, NFC 20—Nick Lowery's 33-yard field goal 4:09 into overtime gave the American Conference all-stars an unlikely 23-20 victory over the National Conference. Despite being overwhelmed by the NFC in first downs (30-9), total yards (471-114), and time of possession (10:19-23:50), the AFC won because it forced 6 turnovers, bocked a pair of field goals (1 of which was returned for a touchdown), and returned an interception for a score. Special-teams star Steve Tasker of the Bills earned the Dan McGuire Trophy as the player of the game for making 4 tackles, forcing a fumble, and blocking a field goal. The block came with eight minutes left in regulation and the game tied at 13-13. The Raiders' Terry McDaniel picked up the loose ball and ran 28 yards for a touchdown and a 20-13 AFC lead. The NFC rallied behind 49ers quarterback Steve Young, whose fourth-down, 23-yard touchdown pass to Giants running back Rodney Hampton tied the game at 20-20 with 10 seconds left in regulation. Young completed 18 of 32 passes for 196 yards but was intercepted 3 times and lost a fumble when sacked in overtime. Raiders defensive end Howie Long fell on that fumble at the NFC 28-yard line, and five plays later, Lowery converted the winning field goal.

AFC	0	10	3	7	3 — 23
NFC	3	10	0	7	0 — 20

NFC — FG Andersen 27
AFC — Seau 31 interception return (Lowery kick)
NFC — FG Andersen 37
NFC — Irvin 9 pass from Aikman (Andersen kick)
AFC — FG Lowery 42
AFC — FG Lowery 29
AFC — McDaniel 28 blocked field goal return (Lowery kick)
NFC — Hampton 23 pass from Young (Andersen kick)
AFC — FG Lowery 33

1992 AFC-NFC PRO BOWL

Aloha Stadium, Honolulu, Hawaii
February 2, 1992, Attendance: 50,209

NFC 21, AFC 15—Atlanta's Chris Miller threw an 11-yard touchdown pass to San Francisco's Jerry Rice with 4:04 remaining in the game to lift the NFC over the AFC. It was the NFC's thirteenth win in the 22-game series. The AFC had taken a 15-14 lead when the Raiders' Jeff Jaeger kicked a 27-yard field goal 1:49 into the fourth quarter. But the NFC, aided by a key roughing-the-passer penalty on a third-down incompletion from the AFC 24-yard line, drove 85 yards to the winning score. The Cowboys' Michael Irvin, playing in his first Pro Bowl, caught 8 passes for 125 yards, including a 13-yard touchdown in the first quarter, and was named the player of the game. Rice had 7 catches for 77 yards. Mark Rypien of Washington, the Super Bowl most valuable player one week earlier, completed 11 of 18 passes for 165 yards and 2 touchdowns for the NFC, including a 35-yard pass to Redskins teammate Gary Clark just 26 seconds before halftime. Miller completed 7 of his 10 attempts for 85 yards.

NFC	7	7	0	7	—	21
AFC	7	5	0	3	—	15

AFC — Clayton 4 pass from Kelly (Jaeger kick)
NFC — Irvin 13 pass from Rypien (Lohmiller kick)
AFC — Safety, Townsend tackled Byner in end zone
AFC — FG Jaeger 48
NFC — Clark 35 pass from Rypien (Lohmiller kick)
AFC — FG Jaeger 27
NFC — Rice 11 pass from Miller (Lohmiller kick)

1991 AFC-NFC PRO BOWL

Aloha Stadium, Honolulu, Hawaii
February 3, 1991, Attendance: 50,345

AFC 23, NFC 21—Buffalo's Jim Kelly and Houston's Ernest Givins combined for a 13-yard scoring pass late in the fourth quarter to rally the AFC over the NFC. Phoenix rookie Johnny Johnson scored on runs of 1 and 9 yards to put the NFC ahead 14-3 in the third quarter. Buffalo's Andre Reed, who led all receivers with 4 catches for 80 yards, caught a 20-yard scoring reception from Kelly early in the fourth quarter to move the AFC to within 1 point. Barry Sanders ran 22 yards for a touchdown to increase the NFC's lead to 21-13. Miami's Jeff Cross blocked a 46-yard field-goal attempt by New Orleans's Morten Andersen with seven seconds remaining to preserve the win. Buffalo's Bruce Smith recorded 3 sacks and also had a blocked field goal. Kelly, who completed 13 of 19 passes for 210 yards and 2 touchdowns, was presented the Dan McGuire Award as player of the game. The AFC's victory narrowed the NFC's Pro Bowl series lead to 12-9.

AFC	3	0	3	17	—	23
NFC	0	7	7	7	—	21

AFC — FG Lowery 26
NFC — J. Johnson 1 run (Andersen kick)
AFC — FG Lowery 43
NFC — J. Johnson 9 run (Andersen kick)
AFC — Reed 20 pass from Kelly (Lowery kick)
NFC — Sanders 22 run (Andersen kick)
AFC — FG Lowery 34
AFC — Givins 13 pass from Kelly (Lowery kick)

1990 AFC-NFC PRO BOWL

Aloha Stadium, Honolulu, Hawaii
February 4, 1990, Attendance: 50,445

NFC 27, AFC 21—The NFC captured its second straight Pro Bowl as the defense accounted for a pair of touchdowns and forced 5 turnovers before the eleventh consecutive sellout crowd at Aloha Stadium. The AFC held a 7-6 halftime edge on a 1-yard scoring run by Christian Okoye of the Chiefs. The NFC then rallied with 21 unanswered points in the third quarter. David Meggett of the Giants began the comeback with an 11-yard touchdown reception from Philadelphia's Randall Cunningham. The Rams' Jerry Gray followed with a 51-yard interception return for a score and the Vikings' Keith Millard added an 8-yard fumble return for a touchdown four minutes later to give the NFC a commanding 27-7 lead. Seattle's Dave Krieg rallied the AFC with a 5-yard touchdown pass to Miami's Ferrell Edmunds. Cleveland's Mike Johnson then returned an interception 22 yards for a score to pull the AFC to within 27-21. Gray, who was credited with 7 tackles, was given the Dan McGuire Award as player of the game. Krieg led all quarterbacks by completing 15 of 23 for 148 yards and 1 touchdown. Buffalo's Thurman Thomas topped all receivers with 5 catches for 47 yards, while Indianapolis's Eric Dickerson led all rushers with 46 yards on 15 carries. The win gave the NFC a 12-8 advantage in Pro Bowl games since 1971.

NFC	3	3	21	0	—	27
AFC	0	7	0	14	—	21

NFC — FG Murray 23
NFC — FG Murray 41
AFC — Okoye 1 run (Treadwell kick)
NFC — Meggett 11 pass from Cunningham (Murray kick)
NFC — Gray 51 interception return (Murray kick)
NFC — Millard 8 fumble recovery return (Murray kick)
AFC — Edmunds 5 pass from Krieg (Treadwell kick)
AFC — M. Johnson 22 interception return (Treadwell kick)

1989 AFC-NFC PRO BOWL

Aloha Stadium, Honolulu, Hawaii
January 29, 1989, Attendance: 50,113

NFC 34, AFC 3—The NFC scored 34 unanswered points to snap a two-game losing streak to the AFC before the tenth straight sellout crowd in Honolulu's Aloha Stadium. Bills kicker Scott Norwood provided the AFC's only points on a 38-yard field goal 6:23 into the game. Touchdown runs by Dallas's Herschel Walker (4 yards) and Atlanta's John Settle (1) brought the NFC a 14-3 halftime lead. Walker added a 7-yard scoring run, the Saints' Morten Andersen kicked field goals of 27 and 51 yards, and Los Angeles Rams' wide receiver Henry Ellard caught an 8-yard scoring pass from Minnesota quarterback Wade Wilson in the second half to complete the scoring. Chicago running back Neal Anderson and Philadelphia quarterback Randall Cunningham, who were both appearing in their first Pro Bowl, also played major roles in the NFC's victory. Anderson rushed 13 times for 85 yards and had 2 receptions for 17. Cunningham, who was voted the game's outstanding player, completed 10 of 14 passes for 63 yards and rushed for 49 yards. The NFC, which had 5 takeaways, outgained the AFC 355 yards to 167 and held a time-of-possession advantage of 35:18 to 24:42. Houston quarterback Warren Moon completed 13 of 20 passes for 134 yards for the AFC. The win gave the NFC an 11-8 advantage in Pro Bowl games.

AFC	3	0	0	0	—	3
NFC	7	7	10	10	—	34

AFC — FG Norwood 38
NFC — Walker 4 run (Andersen kick)
NFC — Settle 1 run (Andersen kick)
NFC — FG Andersen 27
NFC — Walker 7 run (Andersen kick)
NFC — FG Andersen 51
NFC — Ellard 8 pass from Wilson (Andersen kick)

1988 AFC-NFC PRO BOWL

Aloha Stadium, Honolulu, Hawaii
February 7, 1988, Attendance: 50,113

AFC 15, NFC 6—Led by a tenacious pass rush, the AFC defeated the NFC for the second consecutive year before the ninth straight sellout crowd in Honolulu's Aloha Stadium. Buffalo quarterback Jim Kelly scored the game's lone touchdown on a 1-yard run for a 7-6 halftime lead. Colts kicker Dean Biasucci added field goals from 37 and 30 yards to complete the AFC's scoring. Saints kicker Morten Andersen had 25- and 36-yard field goals to account for the NFC's points. AFC defenders held the NFC to 213 yards and recorded 8 sacks. Bills defensive end Bruce Smith, who had 2 sacks among his 5 tackles, was voted the game's outstanding player. Oilers running back Mike Rozier led all rushers with 49 yards on 9 carries. Jets wide receiver Al Toon had 5 receptions for 75 yards. The AFC generated 341 yards total offense and held a time-of-possession advantage of 34:14 to 25:46. By winning, the AFC cut the NFC's lead in the Pro Bowl series to 10-8.

NFC	0	6	0	0	—	6
AFC	0	7	6	2	—	15

NFC — FG Andersen 25
AFC — Kelly 1 run (Biasucci kick)
NFC — FG Andersen 36
AFC — FG Biasucci 37
AFC — FG Biasucci 30
AFC — Safety, Montana forced out of end zone

1987 AFC-NFC PRO BOWL

Aloha Stadium, Honolulu, Hawaii
February 1, 1987, Attendance: 50,101

AFC 10, NFC 6—The AFC defeated the NFC in the lowest-scoring game in AFC-NFC Pro Bowl history. The AFC took a 10-0 halftime lead on Broncos quarterback John Elway's 10-yard touchdown pass to Raiders tight end Todd Christensen and Patriots kicker Tony Franklin's 26-yard field goal. The AFC defense made the lead stand by forcing the NFC to settle for a pair of field goals from 38 and 19 yards by Saints kicker Morten Andersen after the NFC had first downs at the AFC 31-, 7-, 16-, 15-, 5-, and 7-yard lines. Both AFC scores were set up by fumble recoveries by Seahawks linebacker Fredd Young and Dolphins linebacker John Offerdahl, respectively. Eagles defensive end Reggie White, who tied a Pro Bowl record with 4 sacks among his 7 solo tackles, was voted the game's outstanding player. The AFC victory cut the NFC's lead in the Pro Bowl series to 10-7.

AFC	7	3	0	0	—	10
NFC	0	0	3	3	—	6

AFC — Christensen 10 pass from Elway (Franklin kick)
AFC — FG Franklin 26
NFC — FG Andersen 38
NFC — FG Andersen 19

1986 AFC-NFC PRO BOWL

Aloha Stadium, Honolulu, Hawaii
February 2, 1986, Attendance: 50,101

NFC 28, AFC 24—New York Giants quarterback Phil Simms brought the NFC back from a 24-7 halftime deficit to defeat the AFC. Simms, who completed 15 of 27 passes for 212 yards and 3 touchdowns, was named the most valuable player of the game. The AFC had taken its first-half lead behind a 2-yard run by Los Angeles Raiders running back Marcus Allen, who also threw a 51-yard scoring pass to San Diego wide receiver Wes Chandler, an 11-yard touchdown catch by Pittsburgh wide receiver Louis Lipps, and a 34-yard field goal by Steelers kicker Gary Anderson. Minnesota's Joey Browner accounted for the NFC's only score before halftime with a 48-yard interception return. After intermission, the NFC blanked the AFC while scoring 3 touchdowns via a 15-yard catch by Washington wide receiver Art Monk, a 2-yard reception by Dallas tight end Doug Cosbie, and a 15-yard catch by Tampa Bay tight end Jimmie Giles with 2:47 remaining in the game. The victory gave the NFC a 10-6 Pro Bowl record against the AFC.

NFC	0	7	7	14	—	28
AFC	7	17	0	0	—	24

AFC — Allen 2 run (Anderson kick)
NFC — Browner 48 interception return (Andersen kick)
AFC — Chandler 51 pass from Allen (Anderson kick)
AFC — FG Anderson 34
AFC — Lipps 11 pass from O'Brien (Anderson kick)
NFC — Monk 15 pass from Simms (Andersen kick)
NFC — Cosbie 2 pass from Simms (Andersen kick)
NFC — Giles 15 pass from Simms (Andersen kick)

1985 AFC-NFC PRO BOWL

Aloha Stadium, Honolulu, Hawaii
January 27, 1985, Attendance: 50,385

AFC 22, NFC 14—Defensive end Art Still of the Kansas City Chiefs recovered a fumble and returned it 83 yards for a touchdown to clinch the AFC's victory over the NFC. Still's touchdown came in the fourth period with the AFC trailing 14-12 and was one of several outstanding defensive plays in a Pro Bowl dominated by two record-breaking defenses. The teams combined for a Pro Bowl-record 17 sacks, including 4 by New York Jets defensive end Mark Gastineau, who was named the game's outstanding player. The AFC's first score came on a safety when Gastineau tackled running back Eric Dickerson of the Los Angeles Rams in the end zone. The AFC's second score, a 6-yard pass from Miami's Dan Marino to Los Angeles Raiders running back Marcus Allen, was set up by a partial block of a punt by Seahawks linebacker Fredd Young. The NFC leads the series 9-6.

AFC	0	9	0	13	—	22
NFC	0	0	7	7	—	14

AFC — Safety, Gastineau tackled Dickerson in end zone
AFC — Allen 6 pass from Marino (Johnson kick)
NFC — Lofton 13 pass from Montana (Stenerud kick)
NFC — Payton 1 run (Stenerud kick)
AFC — FG Johnson 33
AFC — Still 83 fumble recovery return (Johnson kick)
AFC — FG Johnson 22

1984 AFC-NFC PRO BOWL

Aloha Stadium, Honolulu, Hawaii
January 29, 1984, Attendance: 50,445

NFC 45, AFC 3—The NFC won its sixth Pro Bowl in the last seven seasons by routing the AFC. The NFC was led by the passing of most valuable player Joe Theismann of Washington, who completed 21 of 27 passes for 242 yards and 3 touchdowns. Theismann set Pro Bowl records for completions and touchdown passes. The NFC established Pro Bowl marks for most points scored and fewest points allowed. Running back William Andrews of Atlanta had 6 carries for 43 yards and caught 4 passes for 49 yards, including scoring receptions of 16 and 2 yards. Los Angeles Rams rookie Eric Dickerson gained 46 yards on 11 carries, including a 14-yard touchdown run, and had 45 yards on 5 catches. Rams safety Nolan Cromwell had a 44-yard interception return for a touchdown early in the third period to give the NFC a commanding 24-3 lead. Green Bay wide receiver James Lofton caught an 8-yard touchdown pass, while tight end teammate Paul Coffman had a 6-yard scoring catch.

NFC	3	14	14	14	—	45
AFC	0	3	0	0	—	3

NFC — FG Haji-Sheikh 23
NFC — Andrews 16 pass from Theismann (Haji-Sheikh kick)
NFC — Andrews 2 pass from Montana (Haji-Sheikh kick)
AFC — FG Anderson 43
NFC — Cromwell 44 interception return (Haji-Sheikh kick)
NFC — Lofton 8 pass from Theismann (Haji-Sheikh kick)
NFC — Coffman 6 pass from Theismann (Haji-Sheikh kick)
NFC — Dickerson 14 run (Haji-Sheikh kick)

1983 AFC-NFC PRO BOWL

Aloha Stadium, Honolulu, Hawaii
February 6, 1983, Attendance: 49,883

NFC 20, AFC 19—Dallas's Danny White threw an 11-yard touchdown pass to the Packers' John Jefferson with 35 seconds remaining to rally the NFC over the AFC. White, who completed 14 of 26 passes for 162 yards, kept the winning 65-yard drive alive with a 14-yard completion to Jefferson on a fourth-and-7 play at the AFC 25. The AFC was ahead 12-10 at halftime and increased the lead to 19-10 in the third period, when Marcus Allen scored on a 1-yard run. San Diego's Dan Fouts, who attempted 30 passes, set Pro Bowl records for most completions (17) and yards (274). Pittsburgh's John Stallworth was the AFC's leading receiver with 7 catches for 67 yards. William Andrews topped the NFC with 5 receptions for 48 yards. Fouts and Jefferson were co-winners of the player of the game award.

AFC	9	3	7	0	—	19
NFC	0	10	0	10	—	20

AFC — Walker 34 pass from Fouts (Benirschke kick)

AFC — Safety, Still tackled Theismann in end zone
NFC — Andrews 3 run (Moseley kick)
NFC — FG Moseley 35
AFC — FG Benirschke 29
AFC — Allen 1 run (Benirschke kick)
NFC — FG Moseley 41
NFC — Jefferson 11 pass from D. White (Moseley kick)

1982 AFC-NFC PRO BOWL

Aloha Stadium, Honolulu, Hawaii
January 31, 1982, Attendance: 50,402

AFC 16, NFC 13—Nick Lowery of Kansas City kicked a 23-yard field goal with three seconds remaining to give the AFC a last-second victory over the NFC. Lowery's kick climaxed a 69-yard drive directed by quarterback Dan Fouts. The NFC gained a 13-13 tie with 2:43 to go when Dallas's Tony Dorsett ran 4 yards for a touchdown. In the drive to the winning field goal, Fouts completed 3 passes, including a 23-yard toss to San Diego teammate Kellen Winslow that put the ball on the NFC's 5-yard line. Two plays later, Lowery kicked the field goal. Winslow, who caught 6 passes for 86 yards, was named co-player of the game along with Tampa Bay defensive end Lee Roy Selmon.

NFC	0	6	0	7	—	13
AFC	0	0	13	3	—	16

NFC — Giles 4 pass from Montana (kick blocked)
AFC — Muncie 2 run (kick failed)
AFC — Campbell 1 run (Lowery kick)
NFC — Dorsett 4 run (Septien kick)
AFC — FG Lowery 23

1981 AFC-NFC PRO BOWL

Aloha Stadium, Honolulu, Hawaii
February 1, 1981, Attendance: 50,360

NFC 21, AFC 7—Eddie Murray kicked 4 field goals and Steve Bartkowski fired a 55-yard scoring pass to Alfred Jenkins to lead the NFC to its fourth straight victory over the AFC and a 7-4 edge in the series. Murray was named the game's most valuable player and missed tying Garo Yepremian's Pro Bowl record of 5 field goals when a 37-yard attempt hit the crossbar with 22 seconds remaining. The AFC's only score came on a 9-yard pass from Brian Sipe to Stanley Morgan in the second period. Bartkowski completed 9 of 21 passes for 173 yards, while Sipe connected on 10 of 15 for 142 yards. Ottis Anderson led all rushers with 70 yards on 10 carries. Earl Campbell, the NFL's leading rusher in 1980, was limited to 24 yards on 8 attempts.

AFC	0	7	0	0	—	7
NFC	3	6	0	12	—	21

NFC — FG Murray 31
AFC — Morgan 9 pass from Sipe (J. Smith kick)
NFC — FG Murray 31
NFC — FG Murray 34
NFC — Jenkins 55 pass from Bartkowski (Murray kick)
NFC — FG Murray 36
NFC — Safety, Shell called for holding in end zone

1980 AFC-NFC PRO BOWL

Aloha Stadium, Honolulu, Hawaii
January 27, 1980, Attendance: 49,800

NFC 37, AFC 27—Running back Chuck Muncie of New Orleans ran for 2 touchdowns and threw a 25-yard option pass for another score to give the NFC its third consecutive victory over the AFC. Muncie, who was selected the game's most valuable player, snapped a 3-3 tie on a 1-yard touchdown run at 1:41 of the second quarter, then scored on an 11-yard run in the fourth quarter for the NFC's final touchdown. Two scoring records were set in the game— 37 points by the NFC, eclipsing the 33 by the AFC in 1973, and the 64 points by both teams, surpassing the 61 scored in 1973.

NFC	3	20	7	7	—	37
AFC	3	7	10	7	—	27

NFC — FG Moseley 37
AFC — FG Fritsch 19
NFC — Muncie 1 run (Moseley kick)
AFC — Pruitt 1 pass from Bradshaw (Fritsch kick)
NFC — D. Hill 13 pass from Manning (kick failed)
NFC — T. Hill 25 pass from Muncie (Moseley kick)
NFC — Henry 86 punt return (Moseley kick)
AFC — Campbell 2 run (Fritsch kick)
AFC — FG Fritsch 29
NFC — Muncie 11 run (Moseley kick)
AFC — Campbell 1 run (Fritsch kick)

1979 AFC-NFC PRO BOWL

Memorial Coliseum, Los Angeles, California
January 29, 1979, Attendance: 46,281

NFC 13, AFC 7—Roger Staubach completed 9 of 15 passes for 125 yards, including the winning touchdown on a 19-yard strike to Dallas Cowboys teammate Tony Hill in the third period. The winning drive began at the AFC's 45-yard line after a shanked punt. Staubach hit Ahmad Rashad with passes of 15 and 17 yards to set up Hill's decisive catch. The victory gave the NFC a 5-4 advantage in Pro Bowl games. Rashad, who accounted for 89 yards on 5 receptions, was named the player of the game. The AFC led 7-6 at halftime on Bob Griese's 8-yard scoring toss to Steve Largent late in the second quarter. Largent finished the game with 5 receptions for 75 yards. The NFC scored first as Archie Manning marched his team 70 yards in 11 plays, capped by Wilbert Montgomery's 2-yard touchdown run. The AFC's Earl Campbell was the game's leading rusher with 66 yards on 12 carries.

AFC	0	7	0	0	—	7
NFC	0	6	7	0	—	13

NFC — Montgomery 2 run (kick failed)
AFC — Largent 8 pass from Griese (Yepremian kick)
NFC — T. Hill 19 pass from Staubach (Corral kick)

1978 AFC-NFC PRO BOWL

Tampa Stadium, Tampa, Florida
January 23, 1978, Attendance: 51,337

NFC 14, AFC 13—Walter Payton, the NFL's leading rusher in 1977, sparked a second-half comeback to give the NFC the win and tie the series between the two conferences at four victories each. Payton, who was the game's most valuable player, gained 77 yards on 13 carries and scored the tying touchdown on a 1-yard burst with 7:37 left in the game. Efren Herrera kicked the winning extra point. The AFC dominated the first half of the game, taking a 13-0 lead on field goals of 21 and 39 yards by Toni Linhart and a 10-yard touchdown pass from Ken Stabler to Oakland teammate Cliff Branch. On the NFC's first possession of the second half, Pat Haden put together the first touchdown drive after Eddie Brown returned Ray Guy's punt to the AFC 46-yard line. Haden connected on all 4 of his passes on that drive, finally hitting Terry Metcalf with a 4-yard scoring toss. The NFC continued to rally and, with Jim Hart at quarterback, moved 63 yards in 12 plays for the go-ahead score. During the winning drive, Hart completed 5 of 6 passes for 38 yards and Payton picked up 20 more on the ground.

AFC	3	10	0	0	—	13
NFC	0	0	7	7	—	14

AFC — FG Linhart 21
AFC — Branch 10 pass from Stabler (Linhart kick)
AFC — FG Linhart 39
NFC — Metcalf 4 pass from Haden (Herrera kick)
NFC — Payton 1 run (Herrera kick)

1977 AFC-NFC PRO BOWL

Kingdome, Seattle, Washington
January 17, 1977, Attendance: 64,752

AFC 24, NFC 14—O.J. Simpson's 3-yard touchdown burst at 7:03 of the first quarter gave the AFC a lead it would not surrender, the victory breaking a two-game NFC win streak and giving the American Conference stars a 4-3 series lead. The AFC took a 17-7 lead midway through the second period on the first of 2 Ken Anderson touchdown passes, a 12-yard toss to Charlie Joiner. But the NFC mounted a 73-yard drive capped by Lawrence McCutcheon's 1-yard touchdown plunge to pull within 17-14 at the half. Following a scoreless third quarter, player of the game Mel Blount thwarted a possible NFC score when he intercepted Jim Hart's pass in the end zone. Less than three minutes later, Blount again picked off a Hart pass, returning it 16 yards to the NFC 27. That set up Anderson's 27-yard touchdown strike to the Raiders' Cliff Branch for the final score.

NFC	0	14	0	0	—	14
AFC	10	7	0	7	—	24

AFC — Simpson 3 run (Linhart kick)
AFC — FG Linhart 31
NFC — Thomas 15 run (Bakken kick)
AFC — Joiner 12 pass from Anderson (Linhart kick)
NFC — McCutcheon 1 run (Bakken kick)
AFC — Branch 27 pass from Anderson (Linhart kick)

1976 AFC-NFC PRO BOWL

Superdome, New Orleans, Louisiana
January 26, 1976, Attendance: 30,546

NFC 23, AFC 20—Mike Boryla, a late substitute who did not enter the game until 5:39 remained, lifted the National Football Conference to the victory over the American Football Conference with 2 touchdown passes in the final minutes. It was the second straight NFC win, squaring the series at 3-3. Until Boryla started firing the ball the AFC was in control, leading 13-0 at the half. Boryla entered the game after Billy Johnson had raced 90 yards with a punt to make the score 20-9 in favor of the AFC. He floated a 14-yard touchdown pass to Terry Metcalf and later fired an 8-yard scoring pass to Mel Gray for the winner.

AFC	0	13	0	7	—	20
NFC	0	0	9	14	—	23

AFC — FG Stenerud 20
AFC — FG Stenerud 35
AFC — Burrough 64 pass from Pastorini (Stenerud kick)
NFC — FG Bakken 42
NFC — Foreman 4 pass from Hart (kick blocked)
AFC — Johnson 90 punt return (Stenerud kick)
NFC — Metcalf 14 pass from Boryla (Bakken kick)
NFC — Gray 8 pass from Boryla (Bakken kick)

1975 AFC-NFC PRO BOWL

Orange Bowl, Miami, Florida
January 20, 1975, Attendance: 26,484

NFC 17, AFC 10—Los Angeles quarterback James Harris, who took over the NFC offense after Jim Hart of St. Louis suffered a laceration above his right eye in the second period, threw 2 touchdown passes early in the fourth period to pace the NFC to its second victory in the five-game Pro Bowl series. The NFC win snapped a three-game AFC victory string. Harris, who was named the player of the game, connected with St. Louis's Mel Gray for an 8-yard touchdown 2:03 into the final period. One minute and 24 seconds later, following a fumble recovery by Washington's Ken Houston, Harris tossed another 8-yard scoring pass to Washington's Charley Taylor for the decisive points.

NFC	0	3	0	14	—	17
AFC	0	0	10	0	—	10

NFC — FG Marcol 33
AFC — Warfield 32 pass from Griese (Gerela kick)
AFC — FG Gerela 33
NFC — Gray 8 pass from J. Harris (Marcol kick)
NFC — Taylor 8 pass from J. Harris (Marcol kick)

1974 AFC-NFC PRO BOWL

Arrowhead Stadium, Kansas City, Missouri
January 20, 1974, Attendance: 66,918

AFC 15, NFC 13—Miami's Garo Yepremian's fifth field goal—a 42-yard kick with 21 seconds remaining —gave the AFC its third straight victory since the NFC won the inaugural game following the 1970 season. The field goal by Yepremian, who was voted the game's outstanding player, offset a 21-yard field goal by Atlanta's Nick Mike-Mayer that had given the NFC a 13-12 advantage with 1:41 remaining. The only touchdown in the game was scored by the NFC on a 14-yard pass from Philadelphia's Roman Gabriel to Lawrence McCutcheon of the Los Angeles Rams.

NFC	0	10	0	3	—	13
AFC	3	3	3	6	—	15

AFC — FG Yepremian 16
NFC — FG Mike-Mayer 27
NFC — McCutcheon 14 pass from Gabriel (Mike-Mayer kick)
AFC — FG Yepremian 37
AFC — FG Yepremian 27
AFC — FG Yepremian 41
NFC — FG Mike-Mayer 21
AFC — FG Yepremian 42

1973 AFC-NFC PRO BOWL

Texas Stadium, Irving, Texas
January 21, 1973, Attendance: 37,091

AFC 33, NFC 28—Paced by the rushing and receiving of player of the game O.J. Simpson, the AFC erased a 14-0 first period deficit and built a commanding 33-14 lead midway through the fourth period before the NFC managed 2 touchdowns in the final minute of play. Simpson rushed for 112 yards and caught 3 passes for 58 more to gain unanimous recognition in the balloting for player of the game. John Brockington scored 3 touchdowns for the NFC.

AFC	0	10	10	13	—	33
NFC	14	0	0	14	—	28

NFC — Brockington 1 run (Marcol kick)
NFC — Brockington 3 pass from Kilmer (Marcol kick)
AFC — Simpson 7 run (Gerela kick)
AFC — FG Gerela 18
AFC — FG Gerela 22
AFC — Hubbard 11 run (Gerela kick)
AFC — O. Taylor 5 pass from Lamonica (kick failed)
AFC — Bell 12 interception return (Gerela kick)
NFC — Brockington 1 run (Marcol kick)
NFC — Kwalick 12 pass from Snead (Marcol kick)

1972 AFC-NFC PRO BOWL

Memorial Coliseum, Los Angeles, California
January 23, 1972, Attendance: 53,647

AFC 26, NFC 13—Kansas City's Jan Stenerud kicked 4 field goals to lead the AFC from a 6-0 deficit to victory. The AFC defense picked off 3 passes. Stenerud was selected as the outstanding offensive player and his Kansas City teammate, linebacker Willie Lanier, was the game's outstanding defensive player.

AFC	0	3	13	10	—	26
NFC	0	6	0	7	—	13

NFC — Grim 50 pass from Landry (kick failed)
AFC — FG Stenerud 25
AFC — FG Stenerud 23
AFC — FG Stenerud 48
AFC — Morin 5 pass from Dawson (Stenerud kick)
AFC — FG Stenerud 42
NFC — V. Washington 2 run (Knight kick)
AFC — F. Little 6 run (Stenerud kick)

1971 AFC-NFC PRO BOWL

Memorial Coliseum, Los Angeles, California
January 24, 1971, Attendance: 48,222

NFC 27, AFC 6—Mel Renfro of Dallas broke open the first meeting between the American Football Conference and National Football Conference all-star teams as he returned a pair of punts 82 and 56 yards for touchdowns in the final period to clinch the NFC victory over the AFC. Renfro was voted the game's outstanding back and linebacker Fred Carr of Green Bay the outstanding lineman.

AFC	0	3	3	0	—	6
NFC	0	3	10	14	—	27

AFC — FG Stenerud 37
NFC — FG Cox 13
NFC — Osborn 23 pass from Brodie (Cox kick)
NFC — FG Cox 35
AFC — FG Stenerud 16
NFC — Renfro 82 punt return (Cox kick)
NFC — Renfro 56 punt return (Cox kick)

PRO BOWL ALL-TIME RESULTS

Date	Result	Site (attendance)	Honored players
Jan. 15, 1939	New York Giants 13, Pro All-Stars 10	Wrigley Field, Los Angeles (20,000)	
Jan. 14, 1940	Green Bay 16, NFL All-Stars 7	Gilmore Stadium, Los Angeles (18,000)	
Dec. 29, 1940	Chicago Bears 28, NFL All-Stars 14	Gilmore Stadium, Los Angeles (21,624)	
Jan. 4, 1942	Chicago Bears 35, NFL All-Stars 24	Polo Grounds, New York (17,725)	
Dec. 27, 1942	NFL All-Stars 17, Washington 14	Shibe Park, Philadelphia (18,671)	
Jan. 14, 1951	American Conf. 28, National Conf. 27	Los Angeles Memorial Coliseum (53,676)	Otto Graham, Cleveland, player of the game
Jan. 12, 1952	National Conf. 30, American Conf. 13	Los Angeles Memorial Coliseum (19,400)	Dan Towler, Los Angeles, player of the game
Jan. 10, 1953	National Conf. 27, American Conf. 7	Los Angeles Memorial Coliseum (34,208)	Don Doll, Detroit, player of the game
Jan. 17, 1954	East 20, West 9	Los Angeles Memorial Coliseum (44,214)	Chuck Bednarik, Philadelphia, player of the game
Jan. 16, 1955	West 26, East 19	Los Angeles Memorial Coliseum (43,972)	Billy Wilson, San Francisco, player of the game
Jan. 15, 1956	East 31, West 30	Los Angeles Memorial Coliseum (37,867)	Ollie Matson, Chi. Cardinals, player of the game
Jan. 13, 1957	West 19, East 10	Los Angeles Memorial Coliseum (44,177)	Bert Rechichar, Baltimore, outstanding back Ernie Stautner, Pittsburgh, outstanding lineman
Jan. 12, 1958	West 26, East 7	Los Angeles Memorial Coliseum (66,634)	Hugh McElhenny, San Francisco, outstanding back Gene Brito, Washington, outstanding lineman
Jan. 11, 1959	East 28, West 21	Los Angeles Memorial Coliseum (72,250)	Frank Gifford, N.Y. Giants, outstanding back Doug Atkins, Chi. Bears, outstanding lineman
Jan. 17, 1960	West 38, East 21	Los Angeles Memorial Coliseum (56,876)	Johnny Unitas, Baltimore, outstanding back Gene (Big Daddy) Lipscomb, Baltimore, outstanding lineman
Jan. 15, 1961	West 35, East 31	Los Angeles Memorial Coliseum (62,971)	Johnny Unitas, Baltimore, outstanding back Sam Huff, N.Y. Giants, outstanding lineman
Jan. 7, 1962	AFL West 47, East 27	Balboa Stadium, San Diego (20,973)	Cotton Davidson, Dallas Texans, player of the game
Jan. 14, 1962	NFL West 31, East 30	Los Angeles Memorial Coliseum (57,409)	Jim Brown, Cleveland, outstanding back Henry Jordan, Green Bay, outstanding lineman
Jan. 13, 1963	AFL West 21, East 14	Balboa Stadium, San Diego (27,641)	Curtis McClinton, Dallas Texans, outstanding offensive player Earl Faison, San Diego, outstanding defensive player
Jan. 13, 1963	NFL East 30, West 20	Los Angeles Memorial Coliseum (61,374)	Jim Brown, Cleveland, outstanding back Gene (Big Daddy) Lipscomb, Pittsburgh, outstanding lineman
Jan. 12, 1964	NFL West 31, East 17	Los Angeles Memorial Coliseum (67,242)	Johnny Unitas, Baltimore, player of the game Gino Marchetti, Baltimore, outstanding lineman
Jan. 19, 1964	AFL West 27, East 24	Balboa Stadium, San Diego (20,016)	Keith Lincoln, San Diego, outstanding offensive player Archie Matsos, Oakland, outstanding defensive player
Jan. 10, 1965	NFL West 34, East 14	Los Angeles Memorial Coliseum (60,598)	Fran Tarkenton, Minnesota, outstanding back Terry Barr, Detroit, outstanding lineman
Jan. 16, 1965	AFL West 38, East 14	Jeppesen Stadium, Houston (15,446)	Keith Lincoln, San Diego, outstanding offensive player Willie Brown, Denver, outstanding defensive player
Jan. 15, 1966	AFL All-Stars 30, Buffalo 19	Rice Stadium, Houston (35,572)	Joe Namath, N.Y. Jets, most valuable player, offense Frank Buncom, San Diego, most valuable player, defense
Jan. 15, 1966	NFL East 36, West 7	Los Angeles Memorial Coliseum (60,124)	Jim Brown, Cleveland, outstanding back Dale Meinert, St. Louis, outstanding lineman
Jan. 21, 1967	AFL East 30, West 23	Oakland-Alameda County Coliseum (18,876)	Babe Parilli, Boston, outstanding offensive player Verlon Biggs, N.Y. Jets, outstanding defensive player
Jan. 22, 1967	NFL East 20, West 10	Los Angeles Memorial Coliseum (15,062)	Gale Sayers, Chicago, outstanding back Floyd Peters, Philadelphia, outstanding lineman
Jan. 21, 1968	AFL East 25, West 24	Gator Bowl, Jacksonville, Fla. (40,103)	Joe Namath and Don Maynard, N.Y. Jets, out. off. players Leslie (Speedy) Duncan, San Diego, out. def. player
Jan. 21, 1968	NFL West 38, East 20	Los Angeles Memorial Coliseum (53,289)	Gale Sayers, Chicago, outstanding back Dave Robinson, Green Bay, outstanding lineman
Jan. 19, 1969	AFL West 38, East 25	Gator Bowl, Jacksonville, Fla. (41,058)	Len Dawson, Kansas City, outstanding offensive player George Webster, Houston, outstanding defensive player
Jan. 19, 1969	NFL West 10, East 7	Los Angeles Memorial Coliseum (32,050)	Roman Gabriel, Los Angeles, outstanding back Merlin Olsen, Los Angeles, outstanding lineman
Jan. 17, 1970	AFL West 26, East 3	Astrodome, Houston (30,170)	John Hadl, San Diego, player of the game
Jan. 18, 1970	NFL West 16, East 13	Los Angeles Memorial Coliseum (57,786)	Gale Sayers, Chicago, outstanding back George Andrie, Dallas, outstanding lineman
Jan. 24, 1971	NFC 27, AFC 6	Los Angeles Memorial Coliseum (48,222)	Mel Renfro, Dallas, outstanding back Fred Carr, Green Bay, outstanding lineman
Jan. 23, 1972	AFC 26, NFC 13	Los Angeles Memorial Coliseum (53,647)	Jan Stenerud, Kansas City, outstanding offensive player Willie Lanier, Kansas City, outstanding defensive player
Jan. 21, 1973	AFC 33, NFC 28	Texas Stadium, Irving (37,091)	O.J. Simpson, Buffalo, player of the game
Jan. 20, 1974	AFC 15, NFC 13	Arrowhead Stadium, Kansas City (66,918)	Garo Yepremian, Miami, player of the game
Jan. 20, 1975	NFC 17, AFC 10	Orange Bowl, Miami (26,484)	James Harris, Los Angeles, player of the game
Jan. 26, 1976	NFC 23, AFC 20	Louisiana Superdome, New Orleans (30,546)	Billy Johnson, Houston, player of the game
Jan. 17, 1977	AFC 24, NFC 14	Kingdome, Seattle (64,752)	Mel Blount, Pittsburgh, player of the game
Jan. 23, 1978	NFC 14, AFC 13	Tampa Stadium (51,337)	Walter Payton, Chicago, player of the game
Jan. 29, 1979	NFC 13, AFC 7	Los Angeles Memorial Coliseum (46,281)	Ahmad Rashad, Minnesota, player of the game
Jan. 27, 1980	NFC 37, AFC 27	Aloha Stadium, Honolulu (49,800)	Chuck Muncie, New Orleans, player of the game
Feb. 1, 1981	NFC 21, AFC 7	Aloha Stadium, Honolulu (50,360)	Eddie Murray, Detroit, player of the game
Jan. 31, 1982	AFC 16, NFC 13	Aloha Stadium, Honolulu (50,402)	Kellen Winslow, San Diego, and Lee Roy Selmon, Tampa Bay, players of the game
Feb. 6, 1983	NFC 20, AFC 19	Aloha Stadium, Honolulu (49,883)	Dan Fouts, San Diego, and John Jefferson, Green Bay, players of the game
Jan. 29, 1984	NFC 45, AFC 3	Aloha Stadium, Honolulu (50,445)	Joe Theismann, Washington, player of the game
Jan. 27, 1985	AFC 22, NFC 14	Aloha Stadium, Honolulu (50,385)	Mark Gastineau, N.Y. Jets, player of the game
Feb. 2, 1986	NFC 28, AFC 24	Aloha Stadium, Honolulu (50,101)	Phil Simms, N.Y. Giants, player of the game
Feb. 1, 1987	AFC 10, NFC 6	Aloha Stadium, Honolulu (50,101)	Reggie White, Philadelphia, player of the game
Feb. 7, 1988	AFC 15, NFC 6	Aloha Stadium, Honolulu (50,113)	Bruce Smith, Buffalo, player of the game
Jan. 29, 1989	NFC 34, AFC 3	Aloha Stadium, Honolulu (50,113)	Randall Cunningham, Philadelphia, player of the game
Feb. 4, 1990	NFC 27, AFC 21	Aloha Stadium, Honolulu (50,445)	Jerry Gray, L.A. Rams, player of the game
Feb. 3, 1991	AFC 23, NFC 21	Aloha Stadium, Honolulu (50,345)	Jim Kelly, Buffalo, player of the game
Feb. 2, 1992	NFC 21, AFC 15	Aloha Stadium, Honolulu (50,209)	Michael Irvin, Dallas, player of the game
Feb. 7, 1993	AFC 23, NFC 20 (OT)	Aloha Stadium, Honolulu (50,007)	Steve Tasker, Buffalo, player of the game
Feb. 6, 1994	NFC 17, AFC 3	Aloha Stadium, Honolulu (50,026)	Andre Rison, Atlanta, player of the game
Feb. 5, 1995	AFC 41, NFC 13	Aloha Stadium, Honolulu (49,121)	Marshall Faulk, Indianapolis, player of the game

PRESEASON GAMES/PLAYOFF BOWLS

PRO FOOTBALL HALL OF FAME GAME

1962	New York Giants 21, St. Louis Cardinals 21
1963	Pittsburgh Steelers 16, Cleveland Browns 7
1964	Baltimore Colts 48, Pittsburgh Steelers 17
1965	Washington Redskins 20, Detroit Lions 3
1966	No game
1967	Philadelphia Eagles 28, Cleveland Browns 13
1968	Chicago Bears 30, Dallas Cowboys 24
1969	Green Bay Packers 38, Atlanta Falcons 24
1970	New Orleans Saints 14, Minnesota Vikings 13
1971	Los Angeles Rams (NFC) 17, Houston Oilers (AFC) 6
1972	Kansas City Chiefs (AFC) 23, New York Giants (NFC) 17
1973	San Francisco 49ers (NFC) 20, New England Patriots (AFC) 7
1974	St. Louis Cardinals (NFC) 21, Buffalo Bills (AFC) 13
1975	Washington Redskins (NFC) 17, Cincinnati Bengals (AFC) 9
1976	Denver Broncos (AFC) 10, Detroit Lions (NFC) 7
1977	Chicago Bears (NFC) 20, New York Jets (AFC) 6
1978	Philadelphia Eagles (NFC) 17, Miami Dolphins (AFC) 3
1979	Oakland Raiders (AFC) 20, Dallas Cowboys (NFC) 13
1980*	San Diego Chargers (AFC) 0, Green Bay Packers (NFC) 0
1981	Cleveland Browns (AFC) 24, Atlanta Falcons (NFC) 10
1982	Minnesota Vikings (NFC) 30, Baltimore Colts (AFC) 14
1983	Pittsburgh Steelers (AFC) 27, New Orleans Saints (NFC) 14
1984	Seattle Seahawks (AFC) 38, Tampa Bay Buccaneers (NFC) 0
1985	New York Giants (NFC) 21, Houston Oilers (AFC) 20
1986	New England Patriots (AFC) 21, St. Louis Cardinals (NFC) 16
1987	San Francisco 49ers (NFC) 20, Kansas City Chiefs (AFC) 7
1988	Cincinnati Bengals (AFC) 14, Los Angeles Rams (NFC) 7
1989	Washington Redskins (NFC) 31, Buffalo Bills (AFC) 6
1990	Chicago Bears (NFC) 13, Cleveland Browns (AFC) 0
1991	Detroit Lions (NFC) 14, Denver Broncos (AFC) 3
1992	New York Jets (AFC) 41, Philadelphia Eagles (NFC) 14
1993	Los Angeles Raiders (AFC) 19, Green Bay Packers (NFC) 3
1994	Atlanta Falcons (NFC) 21, San Diego Chargers (AFC) 17

Game called with 5:29 remaining due to severe thunder and lightning.

NFL INTERNATIONAL GAMES

Date	Site	Teams
Aug. 12, 1950	Ottawa, Canada	N.Y. Giants 27, Ottawa Roughriders 6
Aug. 11, 1951	Ottawa, Canada	N.Y. Giants 41, Ottawa Roughriders 18
Aug. 5, 1959	Toronto, Canada	Chi. Cardinals 55, Tor. Argonauts 26
Aug. 3, 1960	Toronto, Canada	Pittsburgh 43, Toronto Argonauts 16
Aug. 15, 1960	Toronto, Canada	Chicago 16, N.Y. Giants 7
Aug. 2, 1961	Toronto, Canada	St. Louis 36, Toronto Argonauts 7
Aug. 5, 1961	Montreal, Canada	Chicago 34, Montreal Allouettes 16
Aug. 8, 1961	Hamilton, Canada	Hamilton Tiger-Cats 38, Buffalo 21
Sept. 11, 1969	Montreal, Canada	Pittsburgh 17, N.Y. Giants 13
Aug. 25, 1969	Montreal, Canada	Detroit 22, Boston 9
Aug. 16, 1976	Tokyo, Japan	St. Louis 20, San Diego 10
Aug. 5, 1978	Mexico City, Mexico	New Orleans 14, Philadelphia 7
Aug. 6, 1983	London, England	Minnesota 28, St. Louis 10
*Aug. 3, 1986	London, England	Chicago 17, Dallas 6
*Aug. 9, 1987	London, England	L.A. Rams 28, Denver 27
*July 31, 1988	London, England	Miami 27, San Francisco 21
Aug. 14, 1988	Goteborg, Sweden	Minnesota 28, Chicago 21
Aug. 18, 1988	Montreal, Canada	N.Y. Jets 11, Cleveland 7
*Aug. 5, 1989	Tokyo, Japan	L.A. Rams 16, San Francisco 13 (OT)
*Aug. 6, 1989	London, England	Philadelphia 17, Cleveland 13
*Aug. 4, 1990	Tokyo, Japan	Denver 10, Seattle 7
*Aug. 5, 1990	London, England	New Orleans 17, L.A. Raiders 10
*Aug. 9, 1990	Montreal, Canada	Pittsburgh 30, New England 14
*Aug. 11, 1990	Berlin, Germany	L.A. Rams 19, Kansas City 3
*July 28, 1991	London, England	Buffalo 17, Philadelphia 13
*Aug. 3, 1991	Berlin, Germany	San Francisco 21, Chicago 7
*Aug. 3, 1991	Tokyo, Japan	Miami 19, L.A. Raiders 17
*Aug. 1, 1992	Tokyo, Japan	Houston 34, Dallas 23
*Aug. 15, 1992	Berlin, Germany	Miami 31, Denver 27
*Aug. 16, 1992	London, England	San Francisco 17, Washington 15
*July 31, 1993	Tokyo, Japan	New Orleans 28, Philadelphia 16
*Aug. 1, 1993	Barcelona, Spain	San Francisco 21, Pittsburgh 14
*Aug. 7, 1993	Berlin, Germany	Minnesota 20, Buffalo 6
*Aug. 8, 1993	London, England	Dallas 13, Detroit 13 (OT)
Aug. 14, 1993	Toronto, Canada	Cleveland 12, New England 9
*July 31, 1994	Barcelona, Spain	L.A. Raiders 25, Denver 22
*Aug. 6, 1994	Tokyo, Japan	Minnesota 17, Kansas City 9
*Aug. 13, 1994	Berlin, Germany	N.Y. Giants 28, San Diego 20
*Aug. 15, 1994	Mexico City, Mexico	Houston 6, Dallas 0

American Bowl Game

CHICAGO ALL-STAR GAME

Pro teams won 31, lost 9, and tied 2. The game was discontinued after 1976.

Year	Date	Winner	Loser	Attendance
1976*	July 23	Pittsburgh 24	All-Stars 0	52,895
1975	Aug. 1	Pittsburgh 21	All-Stars 14	54,103
1974		No game was played		
1973	July 27	Miami 14	All-Stars 3	54,103
1972	July 28	Dallas 20	All-Stars 7	54,162
1971	July 30	Baltimore 24	All-Stars 17	52,289
1970	July 31	Kansas City 24	All-Stars 3	69,940
1969	Aug. 1	N.Y. Jets 26	All-Stars 24	74,208
1968	Aug. 2	Green Bay 34	All-Stars 17	69,917
1967	Aug. 4	Green Bay 27	All-Stars 0	70,934
1966	Aug. 5	Green Bay 38	All-Stars 0	72,000
1965	Aug. 6	Cleveland 24	All-Stars 16	68,000
1964	Aug. 7	Chicago 28	All-Stars 17	65,000
1963	Aug. 2	All-Stars 20	Green Bay 17	65,000
1962	Aug. 3	Green Bay 42	All-Stars 20	65,000
1961	Aug. 4	Philadelphia 28	All-Stars 14	66,000
1960	Aug. 12	Baltimore 32	All-Stars 7	70,000
1959	Aug. 14	Baltimore 29	All-Stars 0	70,000
1958	Aug. 15	All-Stars 35	Detroit 19	70,000
1957	Aug. 9	N.Y. Giants 22	All-Stars 12	75,000
1956	Aug. 10	Cleveland 26	All-Stars 0	75,000
1955	Aug. 12	All-Stars 30	Cleveland 27	75,000
1954	Aug. 13	Detroit 31	All-Stars 6	93,470
1953	Aug. 14	Detroit 24	All-Stars 10	93,818
1952	Aug. 15	Los Angeles 10	All-Stars 7	88,316
1951	Aug. 17	Cleveland 33	All-Stars 0	92,180
1950	Aug. 11	All-Stars 17	Philadelphia 7	88,885
1949	Aug. 12	Philadelphia 38	All-Stars 0	93,780
1948	Aug. 20	Chi. Cardinals 28	All-Stars 0	101,220
1947	Aug. 22	All-Stars 16	Chi. Bears 0	105,840
1946	Aug. 23	All-Stars 16	Los Angeles 0	97,380
1945	Aug. 30	Green Bay 19	All-Stars 7	92,753
1944	Aug. 30	Chi. Bears 24	All-Stars 21	48,769
1943	Aug. 25	All-Stars 27	Washington 7	48,471
1942	Aug. 28	Chi. Bears 21	All-Stars 0	101,100
1941	Aug. 28	Chi. Bears 37	All-Stars 13	98,203
1940	Aug. 29	Green Bay 45	All-Stars 28	84,567
1939	Aug. 30	N.Y. Giants 9	All-Stars 0	81,456
1938	Aug. 31	All-Stars 28	Washington 16	74,250
1937	Sept. 1	All-Stars 6	Green Bay 0	84,560
1936	Sept. 3	All-Stars 7	Detroit 7 (tie)	76,000
1935	Aug. 29	Chi. Bears 5	All-Stars 0	77,450
1934	Aug. 31	Chi. Bears 0	All-Stars 0 (tie)	79,432

Game shortened due to thunderstorms.

NFL PLAYOFF BOWL

Western Conference won 8, Eastern Conference won 2.
All games played at Miami's Orange Bowl.

1970	Los Angeles Rams 31, Dallas Cowboys 0
1969	Dallas Cowboys 17, Minnesota Vikings 13
1968	Los Angeles Rams 30, Cleveland Browns 6
1967	Baltimore Colts 20, Philadelphia Eagles 14
1966	Baltimore Colts 35, Dallas Cowboys 3
1965	St. Louis Cardinals 24, Green Bay Packers 17
1964	Green Bay Packers 40, Cleveland Browns 23
1963	Detroit Lions 17, Pittsburgh Steelers 10
1962	Detroit Lions 28, Philadelphia Eagles 10
1961	Detroit Lions 17, Cleveland Browns 16

AFC VS. NFC (REGULAR SEASON), 1970-1994

	1970	1971	1972	1973	1974	1975	1976	1977	1978	1979	1980	1981	1982	1983	1984	1985	1986	1987	1988	1989	1990	1991	1992	1993	1994	Totals
Miami	2-1	3-0	3-0	3-0	2-1	3-0	0-2	2-0	3-1	4-0	4-0	3-1	1-1	3-1	4-0	3-1	2-2	3-0	3-1	2-0	2-2	3-1	2-2	3-1	2-2	65-20
Los Angeles	1-2	1-1-1	3-0	2-1	3-0	3-0	3-0	1-1	4-0	4-0	2-2	2-2	3-0	2-2	3-1	3-1	1-3	2-2	1-3	2-2	3-1	2-2	2-2	3-1	3-1	59-30-1
Pittsburgh	0-3	1-2	2-1	3-0	3-0	2-1	1-1	2-0	3-1	3-1	4-0	3-1	1-0	2-2	3-1	1-3	2-2	2-2	1-3	3-1	3-1	0-4	1-3	2-2	2-2	50-37
Cincinnati	1-2	1-2	2-1	2-1	2-1	3-0	2-0	2-1	2-2	2-2	2-2	2-2	1-0	3-1	2-2	2-2	3-1	1-2	4-0	2-2	1-3	1-3	1-3	2-2	1-3	47-40
Denver	2-2	1-3	1-3	0-3-1	2-2	2-1	2-0	1-1	2-2	3-1	3-1	3-1	2-1	0-2	3-1	3-1	3-1	2-1-1	3-1	2-2	1-3	2-0	1-3	1-3	1-3	46-42-2
Cleveland	0-3	2-1	1-2	1-2	1-2	1-3	2-0	1-1	4-0	3-1	3-1	3-1	0-2	2-2	1-3	1-3	2-2	2-2	4-0	3-1	1-3	0-4	2-2	3-1	3-1	46-43
Kansas City	0-2-1	2-1	2-1	1-1-1	1-2	2-1	1-1	1-1	0-2	0-2	2-0	2-2	0-3	2-2	1-1	2-2	1-1	1-2	0-2	2-0	4-0	2-2	2-2	2-2	3-1	36-36-2
San Diego	1-2	2-1	0-3	1-2	1-2	0-3	2-0	1-1	2-2	3-1	2-2	2-2	1-0	2-2	4-0	1-1	0-4	2-0	2-2	2-2	1-1	1-3	2-0	2-2	2-2	39-40
Seattle								1-0	3-1	3-1	1-3	0-2	1-0	1-3	4-0	2-2	3-1	4-0	1-3	0-4	2-2	1-3	0-4	0-2	2-0	29-31
Buffalo	0-3	0-3	2-0-1	2-1	2-1	1-2	0-2	1-1	1-1	2-2	3-1	1-3	1-2	1-3	1-3	0-2	1-1	1-2	2-2	1-3	3-1	3-1	4-0	4-0	1-3	38-43-1
New England	0-3	0-3	3-0	2-1	3-0	1-2	1-1	2-0	2-2	3-1	1-3	0-4	0-1	2-2	0-4	3-1	3-1	0-3	2-2	0-4	0-4	1-1	0-4	1-1	4-0	34-48
N.Y. Jets	2-1	0-3	1-2	0-3	2-1	0-3	0-2	1-1	1-3	3-1	1-3	2-0	4-0	3-1	0-2	2-2	2-2	0-4	2-0	1-3	2-0	2-2	0-4	2-2	1-3	34-48
Houston	0-3	0-2-1	0-3	0-3	0-3	3-0	2-0	2-0	2-2	2-2	4-0	1-3	0-3	1-3	0-4	1-3	2-2	2-2	3-1	3-1	1-3	1-3	3-1	2-2	0-4	35-53-1
Indianapolis	3-0	2-1	0-3	2-1	1-2	2-1	0-2	1-1	2-2	1-1	1-1	0-4	0-1-1	2-0	0-4	3-1	1-3	1-0	2-2	1-3	2-2	0-4	2-0	0-4	0-2	29-45-1
Tampa Bay							0-1																			0-1
TOTALS	12-27-1	15-23-2	20-19-1	19-19-2	23-17	23-17	16-12	19-9	31-21	36-16	33-19	24-28	15-14-1	26-26	26-26	27-25	26-26	23-22-1	30-22	24-28	26-26	19-33	22-30	27-25	25-27	587-557-8

NFC VS. AFC (REGULAR SEASON), 1970-1994

	1970	1971	1972	1973	1974	1975	1976	1977	1978	1979	1980	1981	1982	1983	1984	1985	1986	1987	1988	1989	1990	1991	1992	1993	1994	Totals
Dallas	3-0	3-0	3-0	2-1	2-1	2-1	2-0	1-1	3-1	1-3	3-1	4-0	2-1	2-2	2-2	3-1	1-3	2-1	0-4	0-2	1-1	3-1	4-0	2-2	3-1	54-30
San Francisco	4-0	2-1	2-1	1-2	0-3	1-2	1-1	0-2	1-3	0-4	2-2	3-1	1-3	2-2	3-1	3-1	4-0	3-1	2-2	4-0	4-0	3-1	3-1	2-2	3-1	54-37
Washington	2-1	1-2	1-2	2-1	2-1	1-2	1-1	1-1	2-2	2-2	1-3	2-2		4-0	3-1	4-0	3-1	2-1	1-3	2-2	3-1	4-0	2-2	1-3	1-1	48-35
Philadelphia	2-1	1-2	2-1	2-1	2-1	0-3	0-2	1-1	3-1	2-2	3-1	3-1	2-1	1-1	3-1	1-1	2-2	3-1	2-2	3-1	1-3	4-0	3-1	2-2	1-3	49-36
N.Y. Giants	3-0	1-2	1-2	1-2	1-2	2-1	0-2	0-2	1-1	1-1	1-3	1-1	1-0	0-4	2-0	2-2	3-1	2-1	1-1	4-0	3-1	3-1	2-2	2-2	3-1	41-35
St. Louis	2-1	1-2	1-2	3-0	3-1	3-0	1-1	2-0	2-2	2-2	2-2	1-3	1-2	1-3	3-1	3-1	2-2	1-2	2-2	3-1	2-2	1-3	2-2	2-2	2-2	48-41
Minnesota	2-1	2-1	1-2	2-1	2-1	4-0	2-0	1-1	1-3	1-3	1-3	1-3	1-3	4-0	0-4	2-0	1-3	2-1	2-2	2-2	2-2	0-2	3-1	2-2	2-2	43-43
Arizona	2-0-1	2-1	1-2	0-2-1	2-1	2-1	1-1	0-2	0-4	1-3	1-1	3-1		3-1	3-1	2-2	1-1	0-1	1-3	1-3	2-2	1-1	0-2	1-1	3-1	33-38-2
Chicago	1-2	1-2	1-2	2-2	0-3	0-3	0-2	1-1	0-4	2-2	0-4	4-0	1-1	1-1	2-2	3-1	4-0	2-2	3-1	2-2	2-2	2-2	1-3	2-2	3-1	40-47
Detroit	3-0	4-0	2-0-1	0-3	1-2	1-2	2-0	2-0	2-2	0-4	0-2	2-2	0-1	1-3	0-4	2-2	1-3	0-4	1-1	1-3	1-3	4-0	2-2	2-0	2-2	36-45-1
New Orleans	0-3	0-1-2	0-3	1-2	0-3	0-3	1-2	0-2	1-3	0-4	1-3	2-2	1-0	1-3	3-1	0-4	1-3	4-0	4-0	4-0	2-2	3-1	3-1	2-2	1-3	35-51-2
Atlanta	1-2	3-0	2-2	2-1	0-3	1-2	0-2	0-2	1-3	1-3	2-2	1-3	1-1	3-1	1-3	0-4	1-3	0-4	1-3	2-2	2-2	3-1	2-2	1-3	1-3	32-57
Green Bay	2-1	2-1	2-1	1-1-1	2-1	0-3	0-2	0-3	2-2	1-3	1-3	1-1	1-1-1	2-2	0-4	0-4	1-3	1-2-1	1-3	0-2	1-3	1-3	3-1	3-1	1-3	29-54-3
Tampa Bay								0-1	2-0	2-0	1-3	0-4	2-1	1-3	1-1	0-4	1-1	0-2	1-3	0-4	0-2	1-3	0-2	1-3	1-1	14-38
Seattle							1-0																			1-0
TOTALS	27-12-1	23-15-2	19-20-1	19-19-2	17-23	17-23	12-16	9-19	21-31	16-36	19-33	28-24	14-15-1	26-26	26-26	25-27	26-26	22-23-1	22-30	28-24	26-26	33-19	30-22	25-27	27-25	557-587-8

INTERCONFERENCE GAMES

1994 INTERCONFERENCE GAMES

(Home Team in capital letters)

NFC 27, AFC 25

AFC Victories

Kansas City 30, NEW ORLEANS 17
Seattle 28, WASHINGTON 7
Miami 24, GREEN BAY 14
KANSAS CITY 24, San Francisco 17
CLEVELAND 32, Arizona 0
Kansas City 30, ATLANTA 10
New England 23, DETROIT 17
NEW ENGLAND 17, Green Bay 16
San Diego 36, NEW ORLEANS 22
LOS ANGLES RAIDERS 30, Atlanta 17
Pittsburgh 10, NEW YORK GIANTS 6
Cleveland 26, PHILADELPHIA 7
Los Angeles Raiders 20, LOS ANGELES RAMS 17
NEW ENGLAND 26, Minnesota 20 (OT)
DENVER 32, Atlanta 28
BUFFALO 29, Green Bay 20
LOS ANGELES RAIDERS 24, New Orleans 19
New York Jets 31, MINNESOTA 21
SEATTLE 22, Tampa Bay 21
SAN DIEGO 31, Los Angeles Rams 17
Cleveland 19, DALLAS 14
PITTSBURGH 14, Philadelphia 3
New England 13, CHICAGO 3
CINCINATTI 33, Philadelphia 30
MIAMI 27, Detroit 20

NFC Victories

Dallas 26, PITTSBURGH 9
SAN FRANCISCO 44, Los Angeles Raiders 14
DALLAS 20, Houston 17
TAMPA BAY 24, Indianapolis 10
Los Angeles Rams 16, KANSAS CITY 0
MINNESOTA 38, Miami 35
Chicago 19, NEW YORK JETS 7
CHICAGO 20, Buffalo 13
Washington 41, INDIANAPOLIS 27
PHILADELPHIA 21, Houston 6
Dallas 23, CINCINNATI 20
ARIZONA 20, Pittsburgh 17 (OT)
LOS ANGELES RAMS 27, Denver 21
ATLANTA 10, San Diego 9
Chicago 17, MIAMI 14
GREEN BAY 17, New York Jets 10
New York Giants 13, HOUSTON 10
DETROIT 35, Buffalo 21
Arizona 30, HOUSTON 12
New York Giants 16, CLEVELAND 13
Detroit 18, NEW YORK JETS 7
NEW YORK GIANTS 27, Cincinnati 20
Minnesota 21, BUFFALO 17
San Francisco 38, SAN DIEGO 15
SAN FRANCISCO 42, Denver 19
ARIZONA 28, Cincinnati 7
New Orleans 30, DENVER 28

REGULAR SEASON INTERCONFERENCE RECORDS, 1970-1994

AMERICAN FOOTBALL CONFERENCE

Eastern Division	W	L	T	Pct.
Miami	65	20	0	.765
Buffalo	38	43	1	.470
New England	34	48	0	.415
New York Jets	34	48	0	.415
Indianapolis	29	45	1	.393
Central Division				
Pittsburgh	50	37	0	.575
Cincinnati	47	40	0	.540
Cleveland	46	43	0	.517
Houston	35	53	1	.399
Western Division				
Los Angeles	59	30	1	.661
Denver	46	42	2	.522
Kansas City	36	36	2	.500
San Diego	39	40	0	.494
Seattle	29	31	0	.483

NATIONAL FOOTBALL CONFERENCE

Eastern Division	W	L	T	Pct.
Dallas	54	30	0	.643
Washington	48	35	0	.578
Philadelphia	49	36	0	.576
New York Giants	41	35	0	.539
Arizona	33	38	2	.466
Central Division				
Minnesota	43	43	0	.500
Chicago	40	47	0	.460
Detroit	36	45	1	.445
Green Bay	29	54	3	.355
Tampa Bay	14	38	0	.269
Western Division				
San Francisco	54	37	0	.593
St. Louis	48	41	0	.539
New Orleans	35	51	2	.409
Atlanta	32	57	0	.360

INTERCONFERENCE VICTORIES, 1970-1994

REGULAR SEASON

	AFC	NFC	Tie
1970	12	27	1
1971	15	23	2
1972	20	19	1
1973	19	19	2
1974	23	17	0
1975	23	17	0
1976	16	12	0
1977	19	9	0
1978	31	21	0
1979	36	16	0
1980	33	19	0
1981	24	28	0
1982	15	14	1
1983	26	26	0
1984	26	26	0
1985	27	25	0
1986	26	26	0
1987	23	22	1
1988	30	22	0
1989	24	28	0
1990	26	26	0
1991	19	33	0
1992	22	30	0
1993	27	25	0
1994	25	27	0
Total	587	557	8

PRESEASON

	AFC	NFC	Tie
1970	21	28	1
1971	28	28	3
1972	27	25	4
1973	23	35	2
1974	35	25	0
1975	30	26	1
1976	30	31	0
1977	38	25	0
1978	20	19	0
1979	25	18	0
1980	22	20	1
1981	18	19	0
1982	25	16	0
1983	15	24	0
1984	16	19	0
1985	10	22	1
1986	22	17	0
1987	22	22	0
1988	23	16	1
1989	16	27	0
1990	15	29	0
1991	19	27	0
1992	30	22	0
1993	17	22	0
1994	22	16	0
Total	569	578	14

MONDAY NIGHT FOOTBALL, 1970-1994

(Home Team in capitals, games listed in chronological order.)

1994
SAN FRANCISCO 44, Los Angeles Raiders 14
PHILADELPHIA 30, Chicago 22
Detroit 20, DALLAS 17 (OT)
BUFFALO 27, Denver 20
PITTSBURGH 30, Houston 14
Minnesota 27, NEW YORK GIANTS 10
Kansas City 31, DENVER 28
PHILADELPHIA 21, Houston 6
Green Bay 33, CHICAGO 6
DALLAS 38, New York Giants 10
PITTSBURGH 23, Buffalo 10
New York Giants 13, HOUSTON 10
San Francisco 35, NEW ORLEANS 14
Los Angeles Raiders 24, SAN DIEGO 17
MIAMI 45, Kansas City 28
Dallas 24, NEW ORLEANS 16
MINNESOTA 21, San Francisco 14

1993
WASHINGTON 35, Dallas 16
CLEVELAND 23, San Francisco 13
KANSAS CITY 15, Denver 7
Pittsburgh 45, ATLANTA 17
MIAMI 17, Washington 10
BUFFALO 35, Houston 7
Los Angeles Raiders 23, DENVER 20
Minnesota 19, CHICAGO 12
BUFFALO 24, Washington 10
KANSAS CITY 23, Green Bay 16
PITTSBURGH 23, Buffalo 0
SAN FRANCISCO 42, New Orleans 7
San Diego 31, INDIANAPOLIS 0
DALLAS 23, Philadelphia 17
Pittsburgh 21, MIAMI 20
New York Giants 24, NEW ORLEANS 14
SAN DIEGO 45, Miami 20
Philadelphia 37, SAN FRANCISCO 34 (OT)

1992
DALLAS 23, Washington 10
Miami 27, CLEVELAND 23
New York Giants 27, CHICAGO 14
KANSAS CITY 27, Los Angeles Raiders 7
PHILADELPHIA 31, Dallas 7
WASHINGTON 34, Denver 3
PITTSBURGH 20, Cincinnati 0
Buffalo 24, NEW YORK JETS 20
Minnesota 38, CHICAGO 10
San Francisco 41, ATLANTA 3
Buffalo 26, MIAMI 20
NEW ORLEANS 20, Washington 3
SEATTLE 16, Denver 13 (OT)
HOUSTON 24, Chicago 7
MIAMI 20, Los Angeles Raiders 7
Dallas 41, ATLANTA 17
SAN FRANCISCO 24, Detroit 6

1991
NEW YORK GIANTS 16, San Francisco 14
Washington 33, DALLAS 31
HOUSTON 17, Kansas City 7
CHICAGO 19, New York Jets 13 (OT)
WASHINGTON 23, Philadelphia 0
KANSAS CITY 33, Buffalo 6
New York Giants 23, PITTSBURGH 20
BUFFALO 35, Cincinnati 16
KANSAS CITY 24, Los Angeles Raiders 21
PHILADELPHIA 30, New York Giants 7
Chicago 34, MINNESOTA 17
Buffalo 41, MIAMI 27
San Francisco 33, LOS ANGELES RAMS 10
Philadelphia 13, HOUSTON 6
MIAMI 37, Cincinnati 13
NEW ORLEANS 27, Los Angeles Raiders 0
SAN FRANCISCO 52, Chicago 14

1990
San Francisco 13, NEW ORLEANS 12
DENVER 24, Kansas City 23
Buffalo 30, NEW YORK JETS 7
SEATTLE 31, Cincinnati 16
Cleveland 30, DENVER 29
PHILADELPHIA 32, Minnesota 24
Cincinnati 34, CLEVELAND 13
PITTSBURGH 41, Los Angeles Rams 10
New York Giants 24, INDIANAPOLIS 7
PHILADELPHIA 28, Washington 14
Los Angeles Raiders 13, MIAMI 10
HOUSTON 27, Buffalo 24
SAN FRANCISCO 7, New York Giants 3
Los Angeles Raiders 38, DETROIT 31
San Francisco 26, LOS ANGELES RAMS 10
NEW ORLEANS 20, Los Angeles Rams 17

1989
New York Giants 27, WASHINGTON 24
Denver 28, BUFFALO 14
CINCINNATI 21, Cleveland 14
CHICAGO 27, Philadelphia 13
Los Angeles Raiders 14, NEW YORK JETS 7
BUFFALO 23, Los Angeles Rams 20
CLEVELAND 27, Chicago 7
NEW YORK GIANTS 24, Minnesota 14
SAN FRANCISCO 31, New Orleans 13
HOUSTON 26, Cincinnati 24
Denver 14, WASHINGTON 10
SAN FRANCISCO 34, New York Giants 24
SEATTLE 17, Buffalo 16
San Francisco 30, LOS ANGELES RAMS 27
NEW ORLEANS 30, Philadelphia 20
MINNESOTA 29, Cincinnati 21

1988
NEW YORK GIANTS 27, Washington 20
Dallas 17, PHOENIX 14
CLEVELAND 23, Indianapolis 17
Los Angeles Raiders 30, DENVER 27 (OT)
NEW ORLEANS 20, Dallas 17
PHILADELPHIA 24, New York Giants 13
Buffalo 37, NEW YORK JETS 14
CHICAGO 10, San Francisco 9
INDIANAPOLIS 55, Denver 23
HOUSTON 24, Cleveland 17
Buffalo 31, MIAMI 6
SAN FRANCISCO 37, Washington 21
SEATTLE 35, Los Angeles Raiders 27
LOS ANGELES RAMS 23, Chicago 3
MIAMI 38, Cleveland 31
MINNESOTA 28, Chicago 27

1987
CHICAGO 34, New York Giants 19
NEW YORK JETS 43, New England 24
San Francisco 41, NEW YORK GIANTS 21
DENVER 30, Los Angeles Raiders 14
Washington 13, DALLAS 7
CLEVELAND 30, Los Angeles Rams 17
MINNESOTA 34, Denver 27
DALLAS 33, New York Giants 24
NEW YORK JETS 30, Seattle 14
DENVER 31, Chicago 29
Los Angeles Rams 30, WASHINGTON 26
Los Angeles Raiders 37, SEATTLE 14
MIAMI 37, New York Jets 28
SAN FRANCISCO 41, Chicago 0
Dallas 29, LOS ANGELES RAMS 21
New England 24, MIAMI 10

1986
DALLAS 31, New York Giants 28
Denver 21, PITTSBURGH 10
Chicago 25, GREEN BAY 12
Dallas 31, ST. LOUIS 7
SEATTLE 33, San Diego 7
CINCINNATI 24, Pittsburgh 22
NEW YORK JETS 22, Denver 10
NEW YORK GIANTS 27, Washington 20
Los Angeles Rams 20, CHICAGO 17
CLEVELAND 26, Miami 16
WASHINGTON 14, San Francisco 6
MIAMI 45, New York Jets 3
New York Giants 21, SAN FRANCISCO 17
SEATTLE 37, Los Angeles Raiders 0
Chicago 16, DETROIT 13
New England 34, MIAMI 27

1985
DALLAS 44, Washington 14
CLEVELAND 17, Pittsburgh 7
Los Angeles Rams 35, SEATTLE 24
Cincinnati 37, PITTSBURGH 24
WASHINGTON 27, St. Louis 10
NEW YORK JETS 23, Miami 7
CHICAGO 23, Green Bay 7
LOS ANGELES RAIDERS 34, San Diego 21
ST. LOUIS 21, Dallas 10
DENVER 17, San Francisco 16
WASHINGTON 23, New York Giants 21
SAN FRANCISCO 19, Seattle 6
MIAMI 38, Chicago 24
Los Angeles Rams 27, SAN FRANCISCO 20
MIAMI 30, New England 27
L.A. Raiders 16, L.A. RAMS 6

1984
Dallas 20, LOS ANGELES RAMS 13
SAN FRANCISCO 37, Washington 31
Miami 21, BUFFALO 17
LOS ANGELES RAIDERS 33, San Diego 30
PITTSBURGH 38, Cincinnati 17
San Francisco 31, NEW YORK GIANTS 10
DENVER 17, Green Bay 14
Los Angeles Rams 24, ATLANTA 10
Seattle 24, SAN DIEGO 0
WASHINGTON 27, Atlanta 14
SEATTLE 17, Los Angeles Raiders 14
NEW ORLEANS 27, Pittsburgh 24
MIAMI 28, New York Jets 17
SAN DIEGO 20, Chicago 7
Los Angeles Raiders 24, DETROIT 3
MIAMI 28, Dallas 21

1983
Dallas 31, WASHINGTON 30
San Diego 17, KANSAS CITY 14
LOS ANGELES RAIDERS 27, Miami 14
NEW YORK GIANTS 27, Green Bay 3
New York Jets 34, BUFFALO 10
Pittsburgh 24, CINCINNATI 14
GREEN BAY 48, Washington 47
ST. LOUIS 20, New York Giants 20 (OT)
Washington 27, SAN DIEGO 24
DETROIT 15, New York Giants 9
Los Angeles Rams 36, ATLANTA 13
New York Jets 31, NEW ORLEANS 28
MIAMI 38, Cincinnati 14
DETROIT 13, Minnesota 2
Green Bay 12, TAMPA BAY 9 (OT)
SAN FRANCISCO 42, Dallas 17

1982
Pittsburgh 36, DALLAS 28
Green Bay 27, NEW YORK GIANTS 19
LOS ANGELES RAIDERS 28, San Diego 24
TAMPA BAY 23, Miami 17
New York Jets 28, DETROIT 13
Dallas 37, HOUSTON 7
SAN DIEGO 50, Cincinnati 34
MIAMI 27, Buffalo 10
MINNESOTA 31, Dallas 27

1981
San Diego 44, CLEVELAND 14
Oakland 36, MINNESOTA 10
Dallas 35, NEW ENGLAND 21
Los Angeles 24, CHICAGO 7
PHILADELPHIA 16, Atlanta 13
BUFFALO 31, Miami 21
DETROIT 48, Chicago 17
PITTSBURGH 26, Houston 13
DENVER 19, Minnesota 17
DALLAS 27, Buffalo 14
SEATTLE 44, San Diego 23
ATLANTA 31, Minnesota 30

MONDAY NIGHT FOOTBALL

MIAMI 13, Philadelphia 10
OAKLAND 30, Pittsburgh 27
LOS ANGELES 21, Atlanta 16
SAN DIEGO 23, Oakland 10

1980
Dallas 17, WASHINGTON 3
Houston 16, CLEVELAND 7
PHILADELPHIA 35, New York Giants 3
NEW ENGLAND 23, Denver 14
CHICAGO 23, Tampa Bay 0
DENVER 20, Washington 17
Oakland 45, PITTSBURGH 34
NEW YORK JETS 17, Miami 14
CLEVELAND 27, Chicago 21
HOUSTON 38, New England 34
Oakland 19, SEATTLE 17
Los Angeles 27, NEW ORLEANS 7
OAKLAND 9, Denver 3
MIAMI 16, New England 13 (OT)
LOS ANGELES 38, Dallas 14
SAN DIEGO 26, Pittsburgh 17

1979
Pittsburgh 16, NEW ENGLAND 13 (OT)
Atlanta 14, PHILADELPHIA 10
WASHINGTON 27, New York Giants 0
CLEVELAND 26, Dallas 7
GREEN BAY 27, New England 14
OAKLAND 13, Miami 3
NEW YORK JETS 14, Minnesota 7
PITTSBURGH 42, Denver 7
Seattle 31, ATLANTA 28
Houston 9, MIAMI 6
Philadelphia 31, DALLAS 21
LOS ANGELES 20, Atlanta 14
SEATTLE 30, New York Jets 7
Oakland 42, NEW ORLEANS 35
HOUSTON 20, Pittsburgh 17
SAN DIEGO 17, Denver 7

1978
DALLAS 38, Baltimore 0
MINNESOTA 12, Denver 9 (OT)
Baltimore 34, NEW ENGLAND 27
Minnesota 24, CHICAGO 20
WASHINGTON 9, Dallas 5
MIAMI 21, Cincinnati 0
DENVER 16, Chicago 7
Houston 24, PITTSBURGH 17
ATLANTA 15, Los Angeles 7
BALTIMORE 21, Washington 17
Oakland 34, CINCINNATI 21
HOUSTON 35, Miami 30
Pittsburgh 24, SAN FRANCISCO 7
SAN DIEGO 40, Chicago 7
Cincinnati 20, LOS ANGELES 19
MIAMI 23, New England 3

1977
PITTSBURGH 27, San Francisco 0
CLEVELAND 30, New England 27 (OT)
Oakland 37, KANSAS CITY 28
CHICAGO 24, Los Angeles 23
PITTSBURGH 20, Cincinnati 14
LOS ANGELES 35, Minnesota 3
ST. LOUIS 28, New York Giants 0
BALTIMORE 10, Washington 3
St. Louis 24, DALLAS 17
WASHINGTON 10, Green Bay 9
OAKLAND 34, Buffalo 13
MIAMI 17, Baltimore 6
Dallas 42, SAN FRANCISCO 35

1976
Miami 30, BUFFALO 21
Oakland 24, KANSAS CITY 21
Washington 20, PHILADELPHIA 17 (OT)
MINNESOTA 17, Pittsburgh 6
San Francisco 16, LOS ANGELES 0
NEW ENGLAND 41, New York Jets 7
WASHINGTON 20, St. Louis 10
BALTIMORE 38, Houston 14
CINCINNATI 20, Los Angeles 12
DALLAS 17, Buffalo 10
Baltimore 17, MIAMI 16
SAN FRANCISCO 20, Minnesota 16
OAKLAND 35, Cincinnati 20

1975
Oakland 31, MIAMI 21
DENVER 23, Green Bay 13
Dallas 36, DETROIT 10
WASHINGTON 27, St. Louis 17
New York Giants 17, BUFFALO 14
Minnesota 13, CHICAGO 9
Los Angeles 42, PHILADELPHIA 3
Kansas City 34, DALLAS 31
CINCINNATI 33, Buffalo 24
Pittsburgh 32, HOUSTON 9
MIAMI 20, New England 7
OAKLAND 17, Denver 10
SAN DIEGO 24, New York Jets 16

1974
BUFFALO 21, Oakland 20
PHILADELPHIA 13, Dallas 10
WASHINGTON 30, Denver 3
MIAMI 21, New York Jets 17
DETROIT 17, San Francisco 13
CHICAGO 10, Green Bay 9
PITTSBURGH 24, Atlanta 17
Los Angeles 15, SAN FRANCISCO 13
Minnesota 28, ST. LOUIS 24
Kansas City 42, DENVER 34
Pittsburgh 28, NEW ORLEANS 7
MIAMI 24, Cincinnati 3
Washington 23, LOS ANGELES 17

1973
GREEN BAY 23, New York Jets 7
DALLAS 40, New Orleans 3
DETROIT 31, Atlanta 6
WASHINGTON 14, Dallas 7
Miami 17, CLEVELAND 9
DENVER 23, Oakland 23
BUFFALO 23, Kansas City 14
PITTSBURGH 21, Washington 16
KANSAS CITY 19, Chicago 7
ATLANTA 20, Minnesota 14
SAN FRANCISCO 20, Green Bay 6
MIAMI 30, Pittsburgh 26
LOS ANGELES 40, New York Giants 6

1972
Washington 24, MINNESOTA 21
Kansas City 20, NEW ORLEANS 17
New York Giants 27, PHILADELPHIA 12
Oakland 34, HOUSTON 0
Green Bay 24, DETROIT 23
CHICAGO 13, Minnesota 10
DALLAS 28, Detroit 24
Baltimore 24, NEW ENGLAND 17
Cleveland 21, SAN DIEGO 17
WASHINGTON 24, Atlanta 13
MIAMI 31, St. Louis 10
Los Angeles 26, SAN FRANCISCO 16
OAKLAND 24, New York Jets 16

1971
Minnesota 16, DETROIT 13
ST. LOUIS 17, New York Jets 10
Oakland 34, CLEVELAND 20
DALLAS 20, New York Giants 13
KANSAS CITY 38, Pittsburgh 16
MINNESOTA 10, Baltimore 3
GREEN BAY 14, Detroit 14
BALTIMORE 24, Los Angeles 17
SAN DIEGO 20, St. Louis 17
ATLANTA 28, Green Bay 21
MIAMI 34, Chicago 3
Kansas City 26, SAN FRANCISCO 17
Washington 38, LOS ANGELES 24

1970
CLEVELAND 31, New York Jets 21
Kansas City 44, BALTIMORE 24
DETROIT 28, Chicago 14
Green Bay 22, SAN DIEGO 20
OAKLAND 34, Washington 20
MINNESOTA 13, Los Angeles 3
PITTSBURGH 21, Cincinnati 10
Baltimore 13, GREEN BAY 10
St. Louis 38, DALLAS 0
PHILADELPHIA 23, New York Giants 20
Miami 20, ATLANTA 7
Cleveland 21, HOUSTON 10
Detroit 28, LOS ANGELES 23

MONDAY NIGHT SYNDROME

1994

Of the 16 winning teams:
8 won the next week
6 lost the next week
0 tied the next week
2 had an Open Date the next week

Of the 16 losing teams:
6 won the next week
7 lost the next week
0 tied the next week
3 had an Open Date the next week

Of the 32 NFL teams:
14 won the next week
13 lost the next week
0 tied the next week
5 had an Open Date the next week

1970-1994

Of the 354 winning teams:
203 won the next week
138 lost the next week
3 tied the next week
10 had Open Dates the next week

Of the 354 losing teams:
188 won the next week
158 lost the next week
1 tied the next week
7 had Open Dates the next week

Of the 6 tying teams:
5 won the next week
1 lost the next week
0 tied the next week

Of the 714 NFL teams:
396 won the next week
297 lost the next week
4 tied the next week
17 had Open Dates the next week

MONDAY NIGHT WON-LOST RECORDS, 1970-1994

AMERICAN FOOTBALL CONFERENCE

	Buff.	Cin.	Clev.	Den.	Hou.	Ind.	K.C.	Raid.	Mia.	N.E.	N.Y.J.	Pitt.	S.D.	Sea.
Total	14-15	7-16	13-9	12-19-1	11-11	9-7	13-7	31-11-1	29-19	4-12	9-16	21-14	12-10	11-5
1994	1-1			0-2	0-3		1-1	1-1	1-0			2-0	0-1	
1993	2-1		1-0	0-2	0-1	0-1	2-0	1-0	1-2			3-0	2-0	
1992	2-0	0-1	0-1	0-2	1-0		1-0	0-2	2-1		0-1	1-0		1-0
1991	2-1	0-2			1-1		2-1	0-2	1-1		0-1	0-1		
1990	1-1	1-1	1-1	1-1	1-0	0-1	0-1	2-0	0-1		0-1	1-0		1-0
1989	1-2	1-2	1-1	2-0	1-0			1-0			0-1			1-0
1988	2-0		1-2	0-2	1-0	1-1		1-1	1-1		0-1			1-0
1987			1-0	2-1				1-1	1-1	1-1	2-1			0-2
1986		1-0	1-0	1-1				0-1	1-2	1-0	1-1	0-2	0-1	2-0
1985		1-0	1-0	1-0				2-0	2-1	0-1	1-0	0-2	0-1	0-2
1984	0-1	0-1		1-0				2-1	3-0		0-1	1-1	1-2	2-0
1983	0-1	0-2					0-1	1-0	1-1		2-0	1-0	1-1	
1982	0-1	0-1			0-1			1-0	1-1		1-0	1-0	1-1	
1981	1-1		0-1	1-0	0-1			2-1	1-1	0-1		1-1	2-1	1-0
1980			1-1	1-2	2-0			3-0	1-1	1-2	1-0	0-2	1-0	0-1
1979			1-0	0-2	2-0			2-0	0-2	0-2	1-1	2-1	1-0	2-0
1978		1-2		1-1	2-0	2-1		1-0	2-1	0-2		1-1	1-0	
1977	0-1	0-1	1-0			1-1	0-1	2-0	1-0	0-1		2-0		
1976	0-2	1-1			0-1	2-0	0-1	2-0	1-1	1-0	0-1	0-1		
1975	0-2	1-0		1-1	0-1		1-0	2-0	1-1	0-1	0-1	1-0	1-0	
1974	1-0	0-1		0-2			1-0	0-1	2-0		0-1	2-0		
1973	1-0		0-1	0-0-1			1-1	0-0-1	2-0		0-1	1-1		
1972			1-0		0-1	1-0	1-0	2-0	1-0	0-1	0-1		0-1	
1971			0-1			1-1	2-0	1-0	1-0		0-1	0-1	1-0	
1970		0-1	2-0		0-1	1-1	1-0	1-0	1-0		0-1	1-0	0-1	

NATIONAL FOOTBALL CONFERENCE

	Ariz.	Atl.	Chi.	Dall.	Det.	G.B.	Minn.	N.O.	N.Y.G.	Phil.	St. L.	S.F.	T.B.	Wash.
Total	5-8-1	5-14	12-25	24-20	8-9-1	8-11-1	6-13	6-12	14-20-1	14-9	17-20	23-15	1-2	22-21
1994			0-2	2-1	1-0	1-0	2-0	0-2	1-2	2-0		2-1		
1993		0-1	0-1	1-1		0-1	1-0	0-2	1-0	1-1		1-2		1-2
1992		0-2	0-3	2-1	0-1		1-0	1-0	1.0	1-0		2-0		1-2
1991			2-1	0-1			0-1	1-0	2-1	2-1	0-1	2-1		2-0
1990					0-1		0-1	1-1	1-1	2-0	0-3	3-0		0-1
1989			1-1				1-1	1-1	2-1	0-2	0-2	3-0		0-2
1988	0-1		1-2	1-1			1-0	1-0	1-0	1-1	1-0	1-1		0-2
1987			1-2	2-1			1-0		0-3		1-2	2-0		1-1
1986	0-1		2-1	2-0	0-1	0-1			2-1		1-0	0-2		1-1
1985	1-1		1-1	1-1		0-1			0-1		2-1	1-2		2-1
1984		0-2	0-1	1-1	0-1	0-1		1-0	0-1		1-1	2-0		1-1
1983	0-0-1	0-1		1-1	2-0	2-1	0-1	0-1	1-1-1		1-0	1-0	0-1	1-2
1982				1-2	0-1	1-0	1-0		0-1				1-0	
1981		1-2	0-2	2-0	1-0		0-3			1-1	2-0			
1980			1-1	1-1				0-1	0-1	1-0	2-0		0-1	0-2
1979		1-2		0-2		1-0	0-1	0-1	0-1	1-1	1-0			1-0
1978	2-0	1-0	0-3	1-1			2-0				0-2	0-1		1-1
1977	0-1		1-0	1-1		0-1	0-1		0-1		1-1	0-2		1-1
1976	0-1			1-0			1-1			0-1	0-2	2-0		2-0
1975	0-1		0-1	1-1	0-1	0-1	1-0		1-0	0-1	1-0			1-0
1974		0-1	1-0	0-1	1-0	0-1	1-0	0-1		1-0	1-1	0-2		2-0
1973	0-1	1-1	0-1	1-1	1-0	1-1	0-1	0-1	0-1		1-0	1-0		1-1
1972	1-1	0-1	1-0	1-0	0-2	1-0	0-2	0-1	1-0	0-1	1-0	0-1		2-0
1971	1-0	1-0	0-1	1-0	0-1-1	0-1-1	2-0		0-1		0-2	0-1		1-0
1970		0-1	0-1	0-1	2-0	1-1	1-0		0-1	1-0	0-2			0-1

THURSDAY-SUNDAY NIGHT FOOTBALL

THURSDAY-SUNDAY NIGHT FOOTBALL, 1974-1994

(Home Team in capitals, games listed in chronological order.)

1994
San Diego 17, DENVER 34 (Sun.)
New York Giants 20, ARIZONA 17 (Sun.)
Kansas City 30, ATLANTA 10 (Sun.)
Chicago 19, NEW YORK JETS 7 (Sun.)
Miami 23, CINCINNATI 7 (Sun.)
PHILADELPHIA 21, Washington 17 (Sun.)
Cleveland 11, HOUSTON 8 (Thurs.)
MINNESOTA 13, Green Bay 10 (OT) (Thurs.)
ARIZONA 20, Pittsburgh 17 (OT) (Sun.)
KANSAS CITY 13, Los Angeles Raiders 3 (Sun.)
DETROIT 14, Tampa Bay 9 (Sun.)
SAN FRANCISCO 31, Los Angeles Rams 27 (Sun.)
New England 12, INDIANAPOLIS 10 (Sun.)
MINNESOTA 33, Chicago 27 (OT) (Thurs.)
Buffalo 42, MIAMI 31 (Sun.)
New Orleans 29, ATLANTA 20 (Sun.)
Los Angeles Raiders 17, SEATTLE 16 (Sun.)
MIAMI 27, Detroit 20 (Sun.)

1993
NEW ORLEANS 33, Houston 21 (Sun.)
Los Angeles Raiders 17, SEATTLE 13 (Sun.)
Dallas 17, PHOENIX 10 (Sun.)
NEW YORK JETS 45, New England 7 (Sun.)
BUFFALO 17, New York Giants 14 (Sun.)
GREEN BAY 30, Denver 27 (Sun.)
ATLANTA 30, Los Angeles Rams 24 (Thurs.)
MIAMI 41, Indianapolis 27 (Sun.)
Detroit 30, MINNESOTA 27 (Sun.)
WASHINGTON 30, Indianapolis 24 (Sun.)
Chicago 16, SAN DIEGO 13 (Sun.)
TAMPA BAY 23, Minnesota 10 (Sun.)
HOUSTON 23, Pittsburgh 3 (Sun.)
SAN FRANCISCO 21, Cincinnati 8 (Sun.)
Green Bay 20, SAN DIEGO 13 (Sun.)
Philadelphia 20, INDIANAPOLIS 10 (Sun.)
MINNESOTA 30, Kansas City 10 (Sun.)
HOUSTON 24, New York Jets 0 (Sun.)

1992
DENVER 17, Los Angeles Raiders 13 (Sun.)
Philadelphia 31, PHOENIX 14 (Sun.)
BUFFALO 38, Indianapolis 0 (Sun.)
San Francisco 16, NEW ORLEANS 10 (Sun.)
NEW YORK JETS 30, New England 21 (Sun.)
NEW ORLEANS 13, Los Angeles Rams 10 (Sun.)
MINNESOTA 31, Detroit 14 (Thurs.)
Pittsburgh 27, KANSAS CITY 3 (Sun.)
New York Giants 24, WASHINGTON 7 (Sun.)
Cincinnati 31, CHICAGO 28 (OT) (Sun.)
DENVER 27, New York Giants 13 (Sun.)
Kansas City 24, SEATTLE 14 (Sun.)
SAN DIEGO 27, Los Angeles Raiders 3 (Sun.)
NEW ORLEANS 22, Atlanta 14 (Thurs.)
Los Angeles Rams 31, TAMPA BAY 27 (Sun.)
Green Bay 16, HOUSTON 14 (Sun.)
MIAMI 19, New York Jets 17 (Sun.)
HOUSTON 27, Buffalo 3 (Sun.)

1991
WASHINGTON 45, Detroit 0 (Sun.)
Houston 30, CINCINNATI 7 (Sun.)
NEW ORLEANS 24, Los Angeles Rams 7 (Sun.)
Dallas 17, PHOENIX 9 (Sun.)
Denver 13, MINNESOTA 6 (Sun.)
Pittsburgh 21, INDIANAPOLIS 3 (Sun.)
Los Angeles Raiders 23, SEATTLE 20 (Sun.)
Chicago 10, GREEN BAY 0 (Thurs.)
Washington 17, NEW YORK GIANTS 13 (Sun.)
DENVER 20, Pittsburgh 13 (Sun.)
MIAMI 30, New England 20 (Sun.)
HOUSTON 28, Cleveland 24 (Sun.)
Atlanta 23, NEW ORLEANS 20 (OT) (Sun.)
Los Angeles Raiders 9, SAN DIEGO 7 (Sun.)
Minnesota 26, TAMPA BAY 24 (Sun.)
Buffalo 35, INDIANAPOLIS 7 (Sun.)
SEATTLE 23, Los Angeles Rams 9 (Sun.)

1990
NEW YORK GIANTS 27, Philadelphia 20 (Sun.)
PITTSBURGH 20, Houston 9 (Sun.)
TAMPA BAY 23, Detroit 20 (Sun.)
Washington 38, PHOENIX 10 (Sun.)
BUFFALO 38, Los Angeles Raiders 24 (Sun.)
CHICAGO 38, Los Angeles Rams 9 (Sun.)
MIAMI 17, New England 10 (Thurs.)
ATLANTA 38, Cincinnati 17 (Sun.)
MINNESOTA 27, Denver 22 (Sun.)
San Francisco 24, DALLAS 6 (Sun.)
CINCINNATI 27, Pittsburgh 3 (Sun.)
Seattle 13, SAN DIEGO 10 (Sun.)
MINNESOTA 23, Green Bay 7 (Sun.)
MIAMI 23, Philadelphia 20 (Sun.)
DETROIT 38, Chicago 21 (Sun.)
INDIANAPOLIS 35, Washington 28 (Sat.)
SEATTLE 17, Denver 12 (Sun.)
HOUSTON 34, Pittsburgh 14 (Sun.)

1989
Dallas 13, WASHINGTON 3 (Sun.)
SAN DIEGO 14, Los Angeles Raiders 12 (Sun.)
INDIANAPOLIS 27, New York Jets 10 (Sun.)
Los Angeles Rams 20, NEW ORLEANS 17 (Sun.)
MINNESOTA 27, Chicago 16 (Sun.)
MIAMI 31, New England 10 (Sun.)
SEATTLE 23, Los Angeles Raiders 17 (Sun.)
Cleveland 24, HOUSTON 20 (Sat.)

1988
HOUSTON 41, Washington 17 (Sun.)
Los Angeles Raiders 13, SAN DIEGO 3 (Sun.)
Minnesota 34, DALLAS 3 (Sun.)
New England 6, MIAMI 3 (Sun.)
New York Giants 13, NEW ORLEANS 12 (Sun.)
Pittsburgh 37, HOUSTON 34 (Sun.)
SEATTLE 42, Denver 14 (Sun.)
Los Angeles Rams 38, SAN FRANCISCO 16 (Sun.)

1987
NEW YORK GIANTS 17, New England 10 (Sun.)
SAN DIEGO 16, Los Angeles Raiders 14 (Sun.)
Miami 20, DALLAS 14 (Sun.)
SAN FRANCISCO 38, Cleveland 24 (Sun.)
Chicago 30, MINNESOTA 24 (Sun.)
SEATTLE 28, Denver 21 (Sun.)
MIAMI 23, Washington 21 (Sun.)
SAN FRANCISCO 48, Los Angeles Rams 0 (Sun.)

1986
New England 20, NEW YORK JETS 6 (Thurs.)
Cincinnati 30, CLEVELAND 13 (Thurs.)
Los Angeles Raiders 37, SAN DIEGO 31 (OT) (Thurs.)
LOS ANGELES RAMS 29, Dallas 10 (Sun.)
SAN FRANCISCO 24, Los Angeles Rams 14 (Fri.)

1985
KANSAS CITY 36, Los Angeles Raiders 20 (Thurs.)
Chicago 33, MINNESOTA 24 (Thurs.)
Dallas 30, NEW YORK GIANTS 29 (Sun.)
SAN DIEGO 54, Pittsburgh 44 (Sun.)
Denver 27, SEATTLE 24 (Fri.)

1984
Pittsburgh 23, NEW YORK JETS 17 (Thurs.)
Denver 24, CLEVELAND 14 (Sun.)
DALLAS 30, New Orleans 27 (Sun.)
Washington 31, MINNESOTA 17 (Thurs.)
SAN FRANCISCO 19, Los Angeles Rams 16 (Fri.)

1983
San Francisco 48, MINNESOTA 17 (Thurs.)
CLEVELAND 17, Cincinnati 7 (Thurs.)
Los Angeles Raiders 40, DALLAS 38 (Sun.)
Los Angeles Raiders 42, SAN DIEGO 10 (Thurs.)
MIAMI 34, New York Jets 14 (Fri.)

1982
BUFFALO 23, Minnesota 22 (Thurs.)
SAN FRANCISCO 30, Los Angeles Rams 24 (Thurs.)
ATLANTA 17, San Francisco 7 (Sun.)

1981
MIAMI 30, Pittsburgh 10 (Thurs.)
Philadelphia 20, BUFFALO 14 (Thurs.)
DALLAS 29, Los Angeles 17 (Sun.)
HOUSTON 17, Cleveland 13 (Thurs.)

1980
TAMPA BAY 10, Los Angeles 9 (Thurs.)
DALLAS 42, San Diego 31 (Sun.)
San Diego 27, MIAMI 24 (OT) (Thurs.)
HOUSTON 6, Pittsburgh 0 (Thurs.)

1979
Los Angeles 13, DENVER 9 (Thurs.)
DALLAS 30, Los Angeles 6 (Sun.)
OAKLAND 45, San Diego 22 (Thurs.)
MIAMI 39, New England 24 (Thurs.)

1978
New England 21, OAKLAND 14 (Sun.)
Minnesota 21, DALLAS 10 (Thurs.)
LOS ANGELES 10, Pittsburgh 7 (Sun.)
Denver 21, OAKLAND 6 (Sun.)

1977
Minnesota 30, DETROIT 21 (Sat.)

1976
Los Angeles 20, DETROIT 17 (Sat.)

1975
LOS ANGELES 10, Pittsburgh 3 (Sat.)

1974
OAKLAND 27, Dallas 23 (Sat.)

HISTORY OF OVERTIME GAMES

PRESEASON

Aug. 28, 1955	Los Angeles 23, New York Giants 17, at Portland, Oregon
Aug. 24, 1962	Denver 27, Dallas Texans 24, at Fort Worth, Texas
Aug. 10, 1974	San Diego 20, New York Jets 14, at San Diego
Aug. 17, 1974	Pittsburgh 33, Philadelphia 30, at Philadelphia
Aug. 17, 1974	Dallas 19, Houston 13, at Dallas
Aug. 17, 1974	Cincinnati 13, Atlanta 7, at Atlanta
Sept. 6, 1974	Buffalo 23, New York Giants 17, at Buffalo
Aug. 9, 1975	Baltimore 23, Denver 20, at Denver
Aug. 30, 1975	New England 20, Green Bay 17, at Milwaukee
Sept. 13, 1975	Minnesota 14, San Diego 14, at San Diego
Aug. 1, 1976	New England 13, New York Giants 7, at New England
Aug. 2, 1976	Kansas City 9, Houston 3, at Kansas City
Aug. 20, 1976	New Orleans 26, Baltimore 20, at Baltimore
Sept. 4, 1976	Dallas 26, Houston 20, at Dallas
Aug. 13, 1977	Seattle 23, Dallas 17, at Seattle
Aug. 28, 1977	New England 13, Pittsburgh 10, at New England
Aug. 28, 1977	New York Giants 24, Buffalo 21, at East Rutherford, N.J.
Aug. 2, 1979	Seattle 12, Minnesota 9, at Minnesota
Aug. 4, 1979	Los Angeles 20, Oakland 14, at Los Angeles
Aug. 24, 1979	Denver 20, New England 17, at Denver
Aug. 23, 1980	Tampa Bay 20, Cincinnati 14, at Tampa Bay
Aug. 5, 1981	San Francisco 27, Seattle 24, at Seattle
Aug. 29, 1981	New Orleans 20, Detroit 17, at New Orleans
Aug. 28, 1982	Miami 17, Kansas City 17, at Kansas City
Sept. 3, 1982	Miami 16, New York Giants 13, at Miami
Aug. 6, 1983	L.A. Raiders 26, San Francisco 23, at Los Angeles
Aug. 6, 1983	Atlanta 13, Washington 10, at Atlanta
Aug. 13, 1983	St. Louis 27, Chicago 24, at St. Louis
Aug. 18, 1983	New York Jets 20, Cincinnati 17, at Cincinnati
Aug. 27, 1983	Chicago 20, Kansas City 17, at Chicago
Aug. 11, 1984	Pittsburgh 20, Philadelphia 17, at Pittsburgh
Aug. 9, 1985	Buffalo 10, Detroit 10, at Pontiac, Mich.
Aug. 10, 1985	Minnesota 16, Miami 13, at Miami
Aug. 17, 1985	Dallas 27, San Diego 24, at San Diego
Aug. 24, 1985	N.Y. Giants 34, N.Y. Jets 31, at East Rutherford, N.J.
Aug. 15, 1986	Washington 27, Pittsburgh 24, at Washington
Aug. 15, 1986	Detroit 30, Seattle 27, at Detroit
Aug. 23, 1986	Los Angeles Rams 20, San Diego 17, at Anaheim
Aug. 30, 1986	Minnesota 23, Indianapolis 20, at Indianapolis
Aug. 23, 1987	Philadelphia 19, New England 13, at New England
Sept. 5, 1987	Cleveland 30, Green Bay 24, at Milwaukee
Sept. 6, 1987	Kansas City 13, St. Louis 10, at Memphis, Tenn.
Aug. 11, 1988	Seattle 16, Detroit 13, at Detroit
Aug. 19, 1988	Miami 16, Denver 13, at Miami
Aug. 19, 1988	Green Bay 21, Kansas City 21, at Milwaukee
Aug. 20, 1988	Houston 20, Los Angeles Rams 17, at Anaheim
Aug. 21, 1988	Minnesota 19, Phoenix 16, at Phoenix
Aug. 5, 1989	Los Angeles Rams 16, San Francisco 13, at Tokyo, Japan
Aug. 26, 1989	Denver 24, Dallas 21, at Denver
Sept. 1, 1989	N.Y. Jets 15, Kansas City 13, at Kansas City
Aug. 24, 1990	Cincinnati 13, New England 10, at New England
Aug. 16, 1991	Cleveland 24, Washington 21, at Washington
Aug. 17, 1991	Cincinnati 27, Minnesota 24, at Cincinnati
Aug. 23, 1991	Dallas 20, Atlanta 17, at Dallas
Aug. 24, 1991	Cincinnati 19, Green Bay 16, at Green Bay
Aug. 22, 1992	Los Angeles Rams 16, Green Bay 13, at Anaheim
Aug. 8, 1993	Dallas 13, Detroit 13, at London, England

REGULAR SEASON

Sept. 22, 1974—Pittsburgh 35, Denver 35, at Denver; Steelers win toss. Gilliam's pass intercepted and returned by Rowser to Denver's 42. Turner misses 41-yard field goal. Walden punts and Greer returns to Broncos' 39. Van Heusen punts and Edwards returns to Steelers' 16. Game ends with Steelers on own 26.

Nov. 10, 1974—New York Jets 26, New York Giants 20, at New Haven, Conn.; Giants win toss. Gogolak misses 42-yard field goal. Namath passes to Boozer for five yards and touchdown at 6:53.

Sept. 28, 1975—Dallas 37, St. Louis 31, at Dallas; Cardinals win toss. Hart's pass intercepted and returned by Jordan to Cardinals' 37. Staubach passes to DuPree for three yards and touchdown at 7:53.

Oct. 12, 1975—Los Angeles 13, San Diego 10, at San Diego; Chargers win toss. Partee punts to Rams' 14. Dempsey kicks 22-yard field goal at 9:27.

Nov. 2, 1975—Washington 30, Dallas 24, at Washington; Cowboys win toss. Staubach's pass intercepted and returned by Houston to Cowboys' 35. Kilmer runs one yard for touchdown at 6:34.

Nov. 16, 1975—St. Louis 20, Washington 17, at St. Louis; Cardinals win toss. Bakken kicks 37-yard field goal at 7:00.

Nov. 23, 1975—Kansas City 24, Detroit 21, at Kansas City; Lions win toss. Chiefs take over on downs at own 38. Stenerud kicks 26-yard field goal at 6:44.

Nov. 23, 1975—Oakland 26, Washington 23, at Washington; Redskins win toss. Bragg punts to Raiders' 42. Blanda kicks 27-yard field goal at 7:13.

Nov. 30, 1975—Denver 13, San Diego 10, at Denver; Broncos win toss. Turner kicks 25-yard field goal at 4:13.

Nov. 30, 1975—Oakland 37, Atlanta 34, at Oakland; Falcons win toss. James punts to Raiders' 16. Guy punts and Herron returns to Falcons' 41. Nick Mike-Mayer misses 45-yard field goal. Guy punts into Falcons' end zone. James punts to Raiders' 39. Blanda kicks 36-yard field goal at 15:00.

Dec. 14, 1975—Baltimore 10, Miami 7, at Baltimore; Dolphins win toss. Seiple punts to Colts' 4. Linhart kicks 31-yard field goal at 12:44.

Sept. 19, 1976—Minnesota 10, Los Angeles 10, at Minnesota; Vikings win toss. Tarkenton's pass intercepted by Monte Jackson and returned to Minnesota 16. Allen blocks Dempsey's 30-yard field goal attempt, ball rolls into end zone for touchback. Clabo punts and Scribner returns to Rams' 20. Rusty Jackson punts to Vikings' 35. Tarkenton's pass intercepted by Kay at Rams' 1, no return. Game ends with Rams on own 3.

***Sept. 27, 1976—Washington 20, Philadelphia 17,** at Philadelphia; Eagles win toss. Jones punts and E. Brown loses one yard on return to Redskins' 40. Bragg punts 51 yards into end zone for touchback. Jones punts and E. Brown returns to Redskins' 42. Bragg punts and Marshall returns to Eagles' 41. Boryla's pass intercepted by Dusek at Redskins' 37, no return. Bragg punts and Bradley returns. Philadelphia holding penalty moves ball back to Eagles' 8. Boryla pass intercepted by E. Brown and returned to Eagles' 22. Moseley kicks 29-yard field goal at 12:49.

Oct. 17, 1976—Kansas City 20, Miami 17, at Miami; Chiefs win toss. Wilson punts into end zone for touchback. Bulaich fumbles into Kansas City end zone, Collier recovers for touchback. Stenerud kicks 34-yard field goal at 14:48.

Oct. 31, 1976—St. Louis 23, San Francisco 20, at St. Louis; Cardinals win toss. Joyce punts and Leonard fumbles on return, Jones recovers at 49ers' 43. Bakken kicks 21-yard field goal at 6:42.

Dec. 5, 1976—San Diego 13, San Francisco 7, at San Diego; Chargers win toss. Morris runs 13 yards for touchdown at 5:12.

Sept. 18, 1977—Dallas 16, Minnesota 10, at Minnesota; Vikings win toss. Dallas starts on Vikings' 47 after a punt early in the overtime period. Staubach scores seven plays later on a four-yard run at 6:14.

***Sept. 26, 1977—Cleveland 30, New England 27,** at Cleveland; Browns win toss. Sipe throws a 22-yard pass to Logan at Patriots' 19. Cockroft kicks 35-yard field goal at 4:45.

Oct. 16, 1977—Minnesota 22, Chicago 16, at Minnesota; Bears win toss. Parsons punts 53 yards to Vikings' 18. Minnesota drives to Bears' 11. On a first-and-10, Vikings fake a field goal and holder Krause hits Voigt with a touchdown pass at 6:45.

Oct. 30, 1977—Cincinnati 13, Houston 10, at Cincinnati; Bengals win toss. Bahr kicks a 22-yard field goal at 5:51.

Nov. 13, 1977—San Francisco 10, New Orleans 7, at New Orleans; Saints win toss. Saints fail to move ball and Blanchard punts to 49ers' 41. Wersching kicks a 33-yard field goal at 6:33.

Dec. 18, 1977—Chicago 12, New York Giants 9, at East Rutherford, N.J.; Giants win toss. The ball changes hands eight times before Thomas kicks a 28-yard field goal at 14:51.

Sept. 10, 1978—Cleveland 13, Cincinnati 10, at Cleveland; Browns win toss. Collins returns kickoff 41 yards to Browns' 47. Cockroft kicks 27-yard field goal at 4:30.

***Sept. 11, 1978—Minnesota 12, Denver 9,** at Minnesota; Vikings win toss. Danmeier kicks 44-yard field goal at 2:56.

Sept. 24, 1978—Pittsburgh 15, Cleveland 9, at Pittsburgh; Steelers win toss. Cunningham scores on a 37-yard "gadget" pass from Bradshaw at 3:43. Steelers start winning drive on their 21.

Sept. 24, 1978—Denver 23, Kansas City 17, at Kansas City; Broncos win toss. Dilts punts to Kansas City. Chiefs advance to Broncos' 40 where Reed fails to make first down on fourth-and-one situation. Broncos march downfield. Preston scores two-yard touchdown at 10:28.

Oct. 1, 1978—Oakland 25, Chicago 19, at Chicago; Bears win toss. Both teams punt on first possession. On Chicago's second offensive series, Colzie intercepts Avellini's pass and returns it to Bears' 3. Three plays later, Whittington runs two yards for a touchdown at 5:19.

Oct. 15, 1978—Dallas 24, St. Louis 21, at St. Louis; Cowboys win toss. Dallas drives from its 23 into field goal range. Septien kicks 27-yard field goal at 3:28.

Oct. 29, 1978—Denver 20, Seattle 17, at Seattle; Broncos win toss. Ball changes hands four times before Turner kicks 18-yard field goal at 12:59.

Nov. 12, 1978—San Diego 29, Kansas City 23, at San Diego; Chiefs win toss. Fouts hits Jefferson for decisive 14-yard touchdown pass on the last play (15:00) of overtime period.

Nov. 12, 1978—Washington 16, New York Giants 13, at Washington; Redskins win toss. Moseley kicks winning 45-yard field goal at 8:32 after missing first down field goal attempt of 35 yards at 4:50.

Nov. 26, 1978—Green Bay 10, Minnesota 10, at Green Bay; Packers win toss. Both teams have possession of the ball four times.

Dec. 9, 1978—Cleveland 37, New York Jets 34, at Cleveland; Browns win toss. Cockroft kicks 22-yard field goal at 3:07.

Sept. 2, 1979—Atlanta 40, New Orleans 34, at New Orleans; Falcons win toss. Bartkowski's pass intercepted by Myers and returned to Falcons' 46. Erxleben punts to Falcons' 4. James punts to Chandler on Saints' 43. Erxleben punts and Ryckman returns to Falcons' 28. James punts and Chandler returns to Saints' 36. Erxleben retrieves punt snap on Saints' 1 and attempts pass. Mayberry

OVERTIME GAMES

intercepts and returns six yards for touchdown at 8:22.

Sept. 2, 1979—Cleveland 25, New York Jets 22, at New York; Jets win toss. Leahy's 43-yard field goal attempt goes wide right at 4:41. Evans's punt blocked by Dykes is recovered by Newton. Ramsey punts into end zone for touchback. Evans punts and Harper returns to Jets' 24. Robinson's pass intercepted by Davis and returned 33 yards to Jets' 31. Cockroft kicks 27-yard field goal at 14:45.

***Sept. 3, 1979—Pittsburgh 16, New England 13,** at Foxboro; Patriots win toss. Hare punts to Swann at Steelers' 31. Bahr kicks 41-yard field goal at 5:10.

Sept. 9, 1979—Tampa Bay 29, Baltimore 26, at Baltimore; Colts win toss. Landry fumbles, recovered by Kollar at Colts' 14. O'Donoghue kicks 31-yard, first-down field goal at 1:41.

Sept. 16, 1979—Denver 20, Atlanta 17, at Atlanta; Broncos win toss. Broncos march 65 yards to Falcons' 7. Turner kicks 24-yard field goal at 6:15.

Sept. 23, 1979—Houston 30, Cincinnati 27, at Cincinnati; Oilers win toss. Parsley punts and Lusby returns to Bengals' 33. Bahr's 32-yard field goal attempt is wide right at 8:05. Parsley's punt downed on Bengals' 5. McInally punts and Ellender returns to Bengals' 42. Fritsch's third down, 29-yard field goal attempt hits left upright and bounces through at 14:28.

Sept. 23, 1979—Minnesota 27, Green Bay 21, at Minnesota; Vikings win toss. Kramer throws 50-yard touchdown pass to Rashad at 3:18.

Oct. 28, 1979—Houston 27, New York Jets 24, at Houston; Oilers win toss. Oilers march 58 yards to Jets' 18. Fritsch kicks 35-yard field goal at 5:10.

Nov. 18, 1979—Cleveland 30, Miami 24, at Cleveland; Browns win toss. Sipe passes 39 yards to Rucker for touchdown at 1:59.

Nov. 25, 1979—Pittsburgh 33, Cleveland 30, at Pittsburgh; Browns win toss. Sipe's pass intercepted by Blount on Steelers' 4. Bradshaw pass intercepted by Bolton on Browns' 12. Evans punts and Bell returns to Steelers' 17. Bahr kicks 37-yard field goal at 14:51.

Nov. 25, 1979—Buffalo 16, New England 13, at Foxboro; Patriots win toss. Hare's punt downed on Bills' 38. Jackson punts and Morgan returns to Patriots' 20. Grogan's pass intercepted by Haslett and returned to Bills' 42. Ferguson's 51-yard pass to Butler sets up N. Mike-Mayer's 29-yard field goal at 9:15.

Dec. 2, 1979—Los Angeles 27, Minnesota 21, at Los Angeles; Rams win toss. Clark punts and Miller returns to Vikings' 25. Kramer's pass intercepted by Brown and returned to Rams' 40. Cromwell, holding for 22-yard field goal attempt, runs around left end untouched for winning score at 6:53.

Sept. 7, 1980—Green Bay 12, Chicago 6, at Green Bay; Bears win toss. Parsons punts and Nixon returns 16 yards. Five plays later, Marcol returns own blocked field goal attempt 24 yards for touchdown at 6:00.

Sept. 14, 1980—San Diego 30, Oakland 24, at San Diego; Raiders win toss. Pastorini's first-down pass intercepted by Edwards. Millen intercepts Fouts' first-down pass and returns to San Diego 46. Bahr's 50-yard field goal attempt partially blocked by Williams and recovered on Chargers' 32. Eight plays later, Fouts throws 24-yard touchdown pass to Jefferson at 8:09.

Sept. 14, 1980—San Francisco 24, St. Louis 21, at San Francisco; Cardinals win toss. Swider punts and Robinson returns to 49ers' 32. San Francisco drives 52 yards to St. Louis 16, where Wersching kicks 33-yard field goal at 4:12.

Oct. 12, 1980—Green Bay 14, Tampa Bay 14, at Tampa Bay; Packers win toss. Teams trade punts twice. Lee returns second Tampa Bay punt to Green Bay 42. Dickey completes three passes to Buccaneers' 18, where Birney's 36-yard field goal attempt is wide right as time expires.

Nov. 9, 1980—Atlanta 33, St. Louis 27, at St. Louis; Falcons win toss. Strong runs 21 yards for touchdown at 4:20.

#Nov. 20, 1980—San Diego 27, Miami 24, at Miami; Chargers win toss. Partridge punts into end zone, Dolphins take over on their own 20. Woodley's pass for Nathan intercepted by Lowe and returned 28 yards to Dolphins' 12. Benirschke kicks 28-yard field goal at 7:14.

Nov. 23, 1980—New York Jets 31, Houston 28, at New York; Jets win toss. Leahy kicks 38-yard field goal at 3:58.

Nov. 27, 1980—Chicago 23, Detroit 17, at Detroit; Bears win toss. Williams returns kickoff 95 yards for touchdown at 0:21.

Dec. 7, 1980—Buffalo 10, Los Angeles 7, at Buffalo; Rams win toss. Corral punts and Hooks returns to Bills' 34. Ferguson's 30-yard pass to Lewis sets up N. Mike-Mayer's 30-yard field goal at 5:14.

Dec. 7, 1980—San Francisco 38, New Orleans 35, at San Francisco; Saints win toss. Erxleben's punt downed by Hardy on 49ers' 27. Wersching kicks 36-yard field goal at 7:40.

***Dec. 8, 1980—Miami 16, New England 13,** at Miami; Dolphins win toss. Von Schamann kicks 23-yard field goal at 3:20.

Dec. 14, 1980—Cincinnati 17, Chicago 14, at Chicago; Bengals win toss. Breech kicks 28-yard field goal at 4:23.

Dec. 21, 1980—Los Angeles 20, Atlanta 17, at Los Angeles; Rams win toss. Corral's punt downed at Rams' 37. James punts into end zone for touchback. Corral's punt downed on Falcons' 17. Bartkowski fumbles when hit by Harris, recovered by Delaney. Corral kicks 23-yard field goal on first play of possession at 7:00.

Sept. 27, 1981—Cincinnati 27, Buffalo 24, at Cincinnati; Bills win toss. Cater punts into end zone for touchback. Bengals drive to the Bills' 10 where Breech kicks 28-yard field goal at 9:33.

Sept. 27, 1981—Pittsburgh 27, New England 21, at Pittsburgh; Patriots win toss. Hubach punts and Smith returns five yards to midfield. Four plays later Bradshaw throws 24-yard touchdown pass to Swann at 3:19.

Oct. 4, 1981—Miami 28, New York Jets 28, at Miami; Jets win toss. Teams trade punts twice. Leahy's 48-yard field goal attempt is wide right as time expires.

Oct. 25, 1981—New York Giants 27, Atlanta 24, at Atlanta; Giants win toss. Jennings' punt goes out of bounds at New York 47. Bright returns Atlanta punt to Giants' 14. Woerner fair catches punt at own 28. Andrews fumbles on first play, recovered by Van Pelt. Danelo kicks 40-yard field goal four plays later at 9:20.

Oct. 25, 1981—Chicago 20, San Diego 17, at Chicago; Bears win toss. Teams trade punts. Bears' second punt returned by Brooks to Chargers' 33. Fouts pass intercepted by Fencik and returned 32 yards to San Diego 27. Roveto kicks 27-yard field goal seven plays later at 9:30.

Nov. 8, 1981—Chicago 16, Kansas City 13, at Kansas City; Bears win toss. Teams trade punts. Kansas City takes over on downs on its own 38. Fuller's fumble recovered by Harris on Chicago 36. Roveto's 37-yard field goal wide, but Chiefs penalized for leverage. Roveto's 22-yard field goal attempt three plays later is good at 13:07.

Nov. 8, 1981—Denver 23, Cleveland 20, at Denver; Browns win toss. D. Smith recovers Hill's fumble at Denver 48. Morton's 33-yard pass to Upchurch and 6-yard run by Preston set up Steinfort's 30-yard field goal at 4:10.

Nov. 8, 1981—Miami 30, New England 27, at New England; Dolphins win toss. Orosz punts and Morgan returns six yards to New England 26. Grogan's pass intercepted by Brudzinski who returns 19 yards to Patriots' 26. Von Schamann kicks 30-yard field goal on first down at 7:09.

Nov. 15, 1981—Washington 30, New York Giants 27, at New York; Giants win toss. Nelms returns Giants' punt 26 yards to New York 47. Five plays later Moseley kicks 48-yard field goal at 3:44.

Dec. 20, 1981—New York Giants 13, Dallas 10, at New York; Cowboys win toss and kick off. Jennings punts to Dallas 40. Taylor recovers Dorsett's fumble on second down. Danelo's 33-yard field goal attempt hits right upright and bounces back. White's pass for Pearson intercepted by Hunt and returned seven yards to Dallas 24. Four plays later Danelo kicks 35-yard field goal at 6:19.

Sept. 12, 1982—Washington 37, Philadelphia 34, at Philadelphia; Redskins win toss. Theismann completes five passes for 63 yards to set up Moseley's 26-yard field goal at 4:47.

Sept. 19, 1982—Pittsburgh 26, Cincinnati 20, at Pittsburgh; Bengals win toss. Anderson's pass intended for Kreider intercepted by Woodruff and returned 30 yards to Cincinnati 2. Bradshaw completes two-yard touchdown pass to Stallworth on first down at 1:08.

Dec. 19, 1982—Baltimore 20, Green Bay 20, at Baltimore; Packers win toss. K. Anderson intercepts Dickey's first-down pass and returns to Packers' 42. Miller's 44-yard field goal attempt blocked by G. Lewis. Teams trade punts before Stenerud's 47-yard field goal attempt is wide right. Teams trade punts again before time expires in Colts possession.

Jan. 2, 1983—Tampa Bay 26, Chicago 23, at Tampa; Bears win toss. Parsons punts to T. Bell at Buccaneers' 40. Capece kicks 33-yard field goal at 3:14.

Sept. 4, 1983—Baltimore 29, New England 23, at New England; Patriots win toss. Cooks runs 52 yards with fumble recovery three plays into overtime at 0:30.

Sept. 4, 1983—Green Bay 41, Houston 38, at Houston; Packers win toss. Stenerud kicks 42-yard field goal at 5:55.

Sept. 11, 1983—New York Giants 16, Atlanta 13, at Atlanta; Giants win toss. Dennis returns kickoff 54 yards to Atlanta 41. Haji-Sheikh kicks 30-yard field goal at 3:38.

Sept. 18, 1983—New Orleans 34, Chicago 31, at New Orleans; Bears win toss. Parsons punts and Groth returns five yards to New Orleans 34. Stabler pass intercepted by Schmidt at Chicago 47. Parsons punt downed by Gentry at New Orleans 2. Stabler gains 36 yards in four passes; Wilson 38 on six carries. Andersen kicks 41-yard field goal at 10:57.

Sept. 18, 1983—Minnesota 19, Tampa Bay 16, at Tampa; Vikings win toss. Coleman punts and Bell returns eight yards to Tampa Bay 47. Capece's 33-yard field goal attempt sails wide at 7:26. Dils and Young combine for 48-yard gain to Tampa Bay 27. Ricardo kicks 42-yard field goal at 9:27.

Sept. 25, 1983—Baltimore 22, Chicago 19, at Baltimore; Colts win toss. Allegre kicks 33-yard field goal nine plays later at 4:51.

Sept. 25, 1983—Cleveland 30, San Diego 24, at San Diego; Browns win toss. Walker returns kickoff 33 yards to Cleveland 37. Sipe completes 48-yard touchdown pass to Holt four plays later at 1:53.

Sept. 25, 1983—New York Jets 27, Los Angeles Rams 24, at New York; Jets win toss. Ramsey punts to Irvin who returns to 25 but penalty puts Rams on own 13. Holmes 30-yard interception return sets up Leahy's 26-yard field goal at 3:22.

Oct. 9, 1983—Buffalo 38, Miami 35, at Miami; Dolphins win toss. Von Schamann's 52-yard field goal attempt goes wide at 12:36. Cater punts to Clayton who loses 11 to own 13. Von Schamann's 43-yard field goal attempt sails wide at 5:15. Danelo kicks 36-yard field goal nine plays later at 13:58.

Oct. 9, 1983—Dallas 27, Tampa Bay 24, at Dallas; Cowboys win toss. Septien's 51-yard field goal attempt goes wide but Buccaneers penalized for roughing kicker. Septien kicks 42-yard field goal at 4:38.

Oct. 23, 1983—Kansas City 13, Houston 10, at Houston; Chiefs win toss. Lowery kicks 41-yard field goal 13 plays later at 7:41.

Oct. 23, 1983—Minnesota 20, Green Bay 17, at Green Bay; Packers win toss. Scribner's punt downed on Vikings' 42. Ricardo kicks 32-yard field goal eight plays later at 5:05.

***Oct. 24, 1983—New York Giants 20, St. Louis 20,** at St. Louis; Cardinals win toss. Teams trade punts before O'Donoghue's 44-yard field goal attempt is wide left. Jennings' punt returned by Bird to St. Louis 21. Lomax pass intercepted by Haynes who loses six yards to New York 33. Jennings' punt downed on St. Louis 17. O'Donoghue's 19-yard field goal attempt is wide right. Rutledge's pass intercepted by L. Washington who returns 25 yards to New York 25. O'Donoghue's 42-yard field goal attempt is wide right. Rutledge's pass intercepted by W. Smith at St. Louis 33 to end game.

Oct. 30, 1983—Cleveland 25, Houston 19, at Cleveland; Oilers win toss. Teams trade punts. Nielsen's pass intercepted by Whitwell who returns to Houston 20. Green runs 20 yards for touchdown on first down at 6:34.

Nov. 20, 1983—Detroit 23, Green Bay 20, at Milwaukee; Packers win toss. Scribner punts and Jenkins returns 14 yards to Green Bay 45. Murray's 33-yard field goal attempt is wide left at 9:32. Whitehurst's pass intercepted by Watkins and returned to Green Bay 27. Murray kicks 37-yard field goal four plays later at 8:30.

Nov. 27, 1983—Atlanta 47, Green Bay 41, at Atlanta; Packers win toss. K. Johnson returns interception 31 yards for touchdown at 2:13.

Nov. 27, 1983—Seattle 51, Kansas City 48, at Seattle; Seahawks win toss. Dixon's 47-yard kickoff return sets up N. Johnson's 42-yard field goal at 1:36.

Dec. 11, 1983—New Orleans 20, Philadelphia 17, at Philadelphia; Eagles win toss. Runager punts to Groth who fair catches on New Orleans 32. Stabler completes two passes for 36 yards to Goodlow to set up Andersen's 50-yard field goal at 5:30.

***Dec. 12, 1983—Green Bay 12, Tampa Bay 9,** at Tampa; Packers win toss. Stenerud kicks 23-yard field goal 11 plays later at 4:07.

Sept. 9, 1984—Detroit 27, Atlanta 24, at Atlanta; Lions win toss. Murray kicks 48-yard field goal nine plays later at 5:06.

Sept. 30, 1984—Tampa Bay 30, Green Bay 27, at Tampa; Packers win toss. Scribner punts 44 yards to Tampa Bay 2. Epps returns Garcia's punt three yards to Green Bay 27. Scribner's punt downed on Buccaneers' 33. Ariri kicks 46-yard field goal 11 plays later at 10:32.

Oct. 14, 1984—Detroit 13, Tampa Bay 7, at Detroit; Buccaneers win toss. Tampa Bay drives to Lions' 39 before Wilder fumbles. Five plays later Danielson hits Thompson with 37-yard touchdown pass at 4:34.

Oct. 21, 1984—Dallas 30, New Orleans 27, at Dallas; Cowboys win toss. Septien kicks 41-yard field goal eight plays later at 3:42.

Oct. 28, 1984—Denver 22, Los Angeles Raiders 19, at Los Angeles; Raiders win toss. Hawkins fumble recovered by Foley at Denver 7. Teams trade punts. Karlis's 42-yard field goal attempt is wide left. Teams trade punts. Wilson pass intercepted by R. Jackson at Los Angeles 45, returned 23 yards to Los Angeles 22. Karlis kicks 35-yard field goal two plays later at 15:00.

Nov. 4, 1984—Philadelphia 23, Detroit 23, at Detroit; Lions win toss. Lions drive to Eagles' 3 in eight plays. Murray's 21-yard field goal attempt hits right upright and bounces back. Jaworski's pass intercepted by Watkins at Detroit 5. Teams trade punts. Cooper returns Black's punt five yards to Eagles' 14. Time expires four plays later with Eagles on own 21.

Nov. 18, 1984—San Diego 34, Miami 28, at San Diego; Chargers win toss. McGee scores eight plays later on a 25-yard run at 3:17.

Dec. 2, 1984—Cincinnati 20, Cleveland 17, at Cleveland; Browns win toss. Simmons returns Cox's punt 30 yards to Cleveland 35. Breech kicks 35-yard field goal seven plays later at 4:34.

Dec. 2, 1984—Houston 23, Pittsburgh 20, at Houston; Oilers win toss. Cooper kicks 30-yard field goal 16 plays later at 5:53.

Sept. 8, 1985—St. Louis 27, Cleveland 24, at Cleveland; Cardinals win toss. O'Donoghue kicks 35-yard field goal nine plays later at 5:27.

Sept. 29, 1985—New York Giants 16, Philadelphia 10, at Philadelphia; Eagles win toss. Jaworski's pass tipped by Quick and intercepted by Patterson who returns 29 yards for touchdown at 0:55.

Oct. 20, 1985—Denver 13, Seattle 10, at Denver; Seahawks win toss. Teams trade punts twice. Krieg's pass intercepted by Hunter and returned to Seahawks' 15. Karlis kicks 24-yard field goal four plays later at 9:19.

Nov. 10, 1985—Philadelphia 23, Atlanta 17, at Philadelphia; Falcons win toss. Donnelly's 62-yard punt goes out of bounds at Eagles' 1. Jaworski completes 99-yard touchdown pass to Quick two plays later at 1:49.

Nov. 10, 1985—San Diego 40, Los Angeles Raiders 34, at San Diego; Chargers win toss. James scores on 17-yard run seven plays later at 3:44.

Nov. 17, 1985—Denver 30, San Diego 24, at Denver; Chargers win toss. Thomas' 40-yard field goal attempt blocked by Smith and returned 60 yards by Wright for touchdown at 4:45.

Nov. 24, 1985—New York Jets 16, New England 13, at New York; Jets win toss. Teams trade punts twice. Patriots' second punt returned 46 yards by Sohn to Patriots' 15. Leahy kicks 32-yard field goal one play later at 10:05.

Nov. 24, 1985—Tampa Bay 19, Detroit 16, at Tampa; Lions win toss. Teams trade punts. Lions' punt downed on Buccaneers' 38. Igwebuike kicks 24-yard field goal 11 plays later at 12:31.

Nov. 24, 1985—Los Angeles Raiders 31, Denver 28, at Los Angeles; Raiders win toss. Bahr kicks 32-yard field goal six plays later at 2:42.

Dec. 8, 1985—Los Angeles Raiders 17, Denver 14, at Denver; Broncos win toss. Teams trade punts twice. Elway's fumble recovered by Townsend at Broncos' 8. Bahr kicks 26-yard field goal one play later at 4:55.

Sept. 14, 1986—Chicago 13, Philadelphia 10, at Chicago; Eagles win toss. Crawford's fumble of kickoff recovered by Jackson at Eagles' 35. Butler kicks 23-yard field goal 10 plays later at 5:56.

Sept. 14, 1986—Cincinnati 36, Buffalo 33, at Cincinnati; Bills win toss. Zander intercepts Kelly's first-down pass and returns it to Bills' 17. Breech kicks 20-yard field goal two plays later at 0:56.

Sept. 21, 1986—New York Jets 51, Miami 45, at New York; Jets win toss. O'Brien completes 43-yard touchdown pass to Walker five plays later at 2:35.

Sept. 28, 1986—Pittsburgh 22, Houston 16, at Houston; Oilers win toss. Johnson's punt returned 41 yards by Woods to Oilers' 15. Abercrombie scores on three-yard run three plays later at 2:35.

Sept. 28, 1986—Atlanta 23, Tampa Bay 20, at Tampa; Falcons win toss. Teams trade punts. Luckhurst kicks 34-yard field goal 10 plays later at 12:35.

Oct. 5, 1986—Los Angeles Rams 26, Tampa Bay 20, at Anaheim; Rams win toss. Dickerson scores four plays later on 42-yard run at 2:16.

Oct. 12, 1986—Minnesota 27, San Francisco 24, at San Francisco; Vikings win toss. C. Nelson kicks 28-yard field goal nine plays later at 4:27.

Oct. 19, 1986—San Francisco 10, Atlanta 10, at Atlanta; Falcons win toss. Teams trade punts twice. Donnelly punts to 49ers' 27. The following play Wilson recovers Rice's fumble at 49ers' 46 as time expires.

Nov. 2, 1986—Washington 44, Minnesota 38, at Washington; Redskins win toss. Schroeder completes 38-yard touchdown pass to Clark four plays later at 1:46.

Nov. 20, 1986—Los Angeles Raiders 37, San Diego 31, at San Diego; Raiders win toss. Teams trade punts. Allen scores five plays later on 28-yard run at 8:33.

Nov. 23, 1986—Cleveland 37, Pittsburgh 31, at Cleveland; Browns win toss. Teams trade punts. Six plays later Kosar hits Slaughter with 36-yard touchdown pass at 6:37.

Nov. 30, 1986—Chicago 13, Pittsburgh 10, at Chicago; Bears win toss and kick off. Newsome's punt returned by Barnes to Chicago 49. Butler kicks 42-yard field goal five plays later at 3:55.

Nov. 30, 1986—Philadelphia 33, Los Angeles Raiders 27, at Los Angeles; Eagles win toss. Teams trade punts. Long recovers Cunningham's fumble at Philadelphia 42. Waters returns Allen's fumble 81 yards to Los Angeles 4. Cunningham scores on one-yard run two plays later at 6:53.

Nov. 30, 1986—Cleveland 13, Houston 10, at Cleveland; Oilers win toss and kick off. Gossett punts to Houston 39. Luck's pass intercepted by Minnifield at Cleveland 21. Gossett punts to Houston 34. Luck's pass intercepted by Minnifield at Cleveland 43 who returns 20 yards to Houston 37. Moseley kicks 29-yard field goal nine plays later at 14:44.

Dec. 7, 1986—St. Louis 10, Philadelphia 10, at Philadelphia; Cardinals win toss. White blocks Schubert's 40-yard field goal attempt. Teams trade punts. McFadden's 43-yard field goal attempt is wide left. Schubert's 37-yard field goal attempt is wide right. Cavanaugh's pass intercepted by Carter and returned to Eagles' 48 to end game.

Dec. 14, 1986—Miami 37, Los Angeles Rams 31, at Anaheim; Dolphins win toss. Marino completes 20-yard touchdown pass to Duper six plays later at 3:04.

Sept. 20, 1987—Denver 17, Green Bay 17, at Milwaukee; Packers win toss. Del Greco's 47-yard field goal attempt is short. Teams trade punts. Elway intercepted by Noble who returns 10 yards to Green Bay 34. Davis fumbles on next play and Smith recovers. Two plays later, Karlis's 40-yard field goal attempt is wide left. Time expires two plays later with Packers on own 23.

Oct. 11, 1987—Detroit 19, Green Bay 16, at Green Bay; Lions win toss. Prindle's 42-yard field goal attempt is wide left. Packers punt downed on Detroit 17. Prindle kicks 31-yard field goal 16 plays later at 12:26.

Oct. 18, 1987—New York Jets 37, Miami 31, at New York; Jets win toss. Teams trade punts. Ryan intercepted by Hooper at Jets' 47 who returns 11 yards. Mackey intercepted by Haslett at Jets' 37 who returns 9 yards. Jets punt. Mackey intercepted by Radachowsky who returns 45 yards to Miami 24. Ryan completes eight-yard touchdown pass to Hunter five plays later at 14:26.

Oct. 18, 1987—Green Bay 16, Philadelphia 10, at Green Bay; Packers win toss. Hargrove scores on seven-yard run 10 plays later at 5:04.

Oct. 18, 1987—Buffalo 6, New York Giants 3, at Buffalo; Bills win toss. Schlopy's 28-yard field goal attempt is wide left. Teams trade punts. Rutledge intercepted by Clark who returns 23 yards to Buffalo 40. Schlopy kicks 27-yard field goal nine plays later at 14:41.

Oct. 25, 1987—Buffalo 34, Miami 31, at Miami; Bills win toss. Norwood kicks 27-yard field goal seven plays later at 4:12.

Nov. 1, 1987—San Diego 27, Cleveland 24, at San Diego; Browns win toss. Kosar intercepted by Glenn who returns 20 yards to Browns' 25. Abbott kicks 33-yard field goal three plays later at 2:16.

Nov. 15, 1987—Dallas 23, New England 17, at New England; Cowboys win toss. Walker scores on 60-yard run four plays later at 1:50.

Nov. 26, 1987—Minnesota 44, Dallas 38, at Dallas; Vikings win toss. Coleman's punt downed by Hilton at Cowboys' 37. White intercepted by Studwell who returns 12 yards to Vikings' 37. D. Nelson scores on 24-yard run seven plays later at 7:51.

Nov. 29, 1987—Philadelphia 34, New England 31, at New England; Patriots win toss. Ramsey intercepted by Joyner who returns 29 yards to Eagles' 32. Fryar fair catches Teltschik's punt at Patriots' 13. Franklin's 46-yard field goal attempt is short. McFadden's 39-yard field goal attempt is wide left. Tatupu fumbles on next play and Cobb recovers. McFadden kicks 38-yard field goal four plays later at 12:16.

Dec. 6, 1987—New York Giants 23, Philadelphia 20, at New York; Giants win toss and kick off. Teams trade punts twice. Teltschik's punt is returned 16 yards by McConkey to Eagles' 33. Three plays later, Allegre's 50-yard field goal attempt is blocked by Joyner and returned 25 yards by Hoage to Eagles' 30. McConkey returns Teltschik's punt four yards to Giants' 44. Allegre kicks 28-yard field goal four plays later at 10:42.

OVERTIME GAMES

Dec. 6, 1987—Cincinnati 30, Kansas City 27, at Cincinnati; Bengals win toss. Teams trade punts. Breech kicks 32-yard field goal 16 plays later at 9:44.

Dec. 26, 1987—Washington 27, Minnesota 24, at Minnesota; Redskins win toss. Haji-Sheikh kicks 26-yard field goal six plays later at 2:09.

Sept. 4, 1988—Houston 17, Indianapolis 14, at Indianapolis; Colts win toss. Dickerson fumble recovered by Lyles who returns six yards to Colts' 42. Zendejas kicks 35-yard field goal six plays later at 3:51.

***Sept. 26, 1988—Los Angeles Raiders 30, Denver 27,** at Denver; Broncos win toss. Teams trade punts twice. Elway intercepted by Lee who returns 20 yards to Broncos' 31. Bahr kicks 35-yard field goal four plays later at 12:35.

Oct. 2, 1988—New York Jets 17, Kansas City 17, at New York; Chiefs win toss. Chiefs punt goes into end zone for touchback. Leahy's 44-yard field goal attempt is wide right. Chiefs punt is returned by Townsell to Jets' 26. Burruss recovers McNeil's fumble at Chiefs' 11. DeBerg intercepted by Humphery at Jets' 49. Three plays later, time expires.

Oct. 9, 1988—Denver 16, San Francisco 13, at San Francisco; Broncos win toss and kick off. Young intercepted by Haynes at Broncos' 32. Denver punt downed at 49ers' 5. Young intercepted by Wilson who returns seven yards to 49ers' 5. Karlis kicks 22-yard field goal two plays later at 8:11.

Oct. 30, 1988—New York Giants 13, Detroit 10, at Detroit; Lions win toss. James's fumble recovered by Taylor at Lions' 22. Three plays later, McFadden kicks 33-yard field goal at 1:13.

Nov. 20, 1988—Buffalo 9, New York Jets 6, at Buffalo; Jets win toss. Vick's fumble recovered by Bennett at Bills' 32. Norwood kicks 30-yard field goal five plays later at 3:47.

Nov. 20, 1988—Philadelphia 23, New York Giants 17, at New York; Eagles win toss. Philadelphia's punt goes into end zone for touchback. Hostetler intercepted by Hoage who returns 11 yards to Giants' 41. Six plays later, Zendejas's 30-yard field-goal attempt is blocked and ball is recovered behind line of scrimmage by Eagles' Simmons, who runs 15 yards for touchdown at 3:09.

Dec. 11, 1988—New England 10, Tampa Bay 7, at New England; Buccaneers win toss and kick off. Staurovsky kicks 27-yard field goal six plays later at 3:08.

Dec. 17, 1988—Cincinnati 20, Washington 17, at Cincinnati; Bengals win toss. Cincinnati's punt returned by Oliphant to Redskins' 16. Grant recovers Williams's fumble at Redskins' 17. Breech kicks 20-yard field goal three plays later at 7:01.

Sept. 24, 1989—Buffalo 47, Houston 41, at Houston; Oilers win toss. Johnson returns Brady's kickoff 17 yards to Oilers' 19. Oilers drive to Buffalo 25, Zendejas's 37-yard field goal blocked, but Bills offsides and Zendejas's second attempt is wide left. Bills' ball and Kelly completes series of passes, including 28-yard game-winner to Andre Reed, at 8:42.

Oct. 8, 1989—Miami 13, Cleveland 10, at Miami; Browns win toss. Metcalf returns Stoyanovich's kickoff 20 yards to Browns' 28. Browns drive ball 46 yards in eight plays; Bahr wide left on 44-yard field goal attempt. Dolphins ball. Browns called for pass interference on Marino pass to Banks at Cleveland 47. Two plays later, Banks's 20-yard reception at Browns' 23 sets up winning 35-yard field goal by Stoyanovich at 6:23.

Oct. 22, 1989—Denver 24, Seattle 21, at Seattle; Seahawks win toss. Treadwell's 56-yard kickoff returned 18 yards by Jefferson to Seahawks' 27. Seahawks drive to Broncos' 22 in 10 plays, but Johnson's 40-yard field goal attempt wide left. Smith intercepts a Krieg pass and returns it 28 yards to Seahawks' 10. Treadwell kicks winning 27-yard field goal at 7:46.

Oct. 29, 1989—New England 23, Indianapolis 20, at Indianapolis; Patriots win toss. Biasucci kickoff returned 13 yards to Patriots' 23 by Martin. Holding penalty brings ball back to Patriots' 13. After six plays, Feagles punt returned 11 yards by Verdin to Colts' 28. Six plays later, Colts punt to Martin at Patriots' 12. Grogan completes three straight passes to Patriots' 44. Five consecutive runs put New England on Colts' 33. Davis kicks a 51-yard winning field goal for Patriots at 9:46.

Oct. 29, 1989—Green Bay 23, Detroit 20, at Milwaukee; Lions win toss. Sanders touchback on Jacke kickoff. On first play, Murphy intercepts Lions' Peete and returns it three yards to Lions' 26. Fullwood gains five yards on three plays to set up Jacke's 38-yard field goal at 2:14.

Nov. 5, 1989—Minnesota 23, Los Angeles Rams 21, at Minneapolis; Rams win toss. Karlis's kick returned 18 yards by Delpino to Rams' 19. Drive stops at Rams' 28. Merriweather blocks Hatcher's punt at 12. Ball rolls out of end zone for safety.

Nov. 19, 1989—Cleveland 10, Kansas City 10, at Cleveland; Browns win toss. Browns punt three times; Chiefs twice; before Kansas City's Lowery misses 47-yard field goal with 17 seconds remaining in overtime. Kosar's pass intercepted as time expired.

Nov. 26, 1989—Los Angeles Rams 20, New Orleans 17, at New Orleans; Saints win toss. Lansford's kickoff returned 27 yards to Saints' 30. After four plays, Barnhardt punts to Rams' 15. Saints penalized 35 yards for interference to Rams' 43. Three plays later, Everett hits Anderson with 14-yard pass to Saints' 40, then 26-yarder to put Rams in field goal position. Lansford kicks 31-yard field goal at 6:38.

Dec. 3, 1989—Los Angeles Raiders 16, Denver 13, at Los Angeles; Broncos win toss. Bell returns Jaeger kickoff 14 yards to Broncos' 18. Broncos' penalized for illegal block to Broncos' 9. Elway completes three passes for two first downs. On third and eight Elway sacked for 10-yard loss. Horan punts, Adams calls for fair catch at Raiders' 29. Dyal's 26-yard reception moves Raiders to Denver 43. Raiders move ball 34 yards in three plays to set up Jaeger's 26-yard field goal at 7:02.

Dec. 10, 1989—Indianapolis 23, Cleveland 17, at Indianapolis; Browns win toss. Teams trade punts. McNeil returns Colts' punt 42 yards to 42. Seven plays later, Bahr misses 35-yard field goal attempt. Three plays later, Stark punts and McNeil returns ball to 50-yard line. Two plays later, Prior intercepts Kosar's pass at Colts' 42 and returns it 58 yards for touchdown at 10:54.

Dec. 17, 1989—Cleveland 23, Minnesota 17, at Cleveland; Browns win toss. Browns punt to Vikings' 18. Six plays later, Vikings punt to Browns' 22. Nine plays later, Bahr lines up to attempt 31-yard field goal. Holder Pagel takes snap and passes 14 yards to Waiters for touchdown at 9:30.

Sept. 23, 1990—Denver 34, Seattle 31, at Denver; Seahawks win toss. Loville returns kickoff 19 yards to Seahawks' 27. Seahawks drive to Broncos' 26, where Johnson misses 44-yard field goal wide right. Broncos take over and Elway completes series of passes to set up Treadwell's 25-yard field goal at 9:14.

Sept. 30, 1990—Tampa Bay 23, Minnesota 20, at Minnesota; Vikings win toss. Vikings drive to Buccaneers' 31; Igwebuike's 48-yard field goal attempt wide left. Buccaneers drive to Vikings' 43 and punt. Gannon's pass is intercepted at Vikings' 26 by Wayne Haddix. Buccaneers drive to Vikings' 19 to set up Christie's 36-yard field goal at 9:11.

Oct. 7, 1990—Cincinnati 34, Los Angeles Rams 31, at Anaheim; Rams win toss. Berry returns kickoff to Rams' 21. After 3 plays, English punts and Green downs ball at Bengals' 25. After 3 plays, Johnson punts and Sutton downs ball at Rams' 29-yard line. After 3 plays, English punts and Price signals fair catch at Bengals' 47. Esiason completes series of passes to 26-yard line to set up Breech's 44-yard field goal at 11:56.

Nov. 4, 1990—Washington 41, Detroit 38, at Detroit; Redskins win toss. Howard downs kickoff on Redskins' 15. After 3 plays, Mojsiejenko punts to Redskins' 45. After 3 plays, Arnold punts to Redskins' 10. Rutledge completes series of passes to set up Lohmiller's 34-yard field goal at 9:10.

Nov. 18, 1990—Chicago 16, Denver 13, at Denver; Broncos win toss. Ezor returns kickoff to Broncos' 12. Both teams have ball twice and have to punt after each possession. Broncos punt after third possession of overtime and Bailey returns 20 yards to Broncos' 34. Harbaugh completes 10-yard pass to Thornton to set up Butler's 44-yard field goal at 13:14.

Nov. 25, 1990—Seattle 13, San Diego 10, at San Diego; Chargers win toss. Lewis returns kickoff to Chargers' 22. After 2 plays, Cox fumbles and ball is recovered by Porter at Chargers' 23. After two plays, Johnson kicks 40-yard field goal at 3:01.

Dec. 2, 1990—Chicago 23, Detroit 17, at Chicago; Lions win toss. Gray returns kickoff to Lions' 35. After 10 plays, Murray misses 35-yard field goal. Bears take possession at Chicago 20. Harbaugh completes 50-yard game-winning pass to Anderson at 10:57.

Dec. 2, 1990—Seattle 13, Houston 10, at Seattle; Seahawks win toss. Warren returns kickoff to Seahawks' 13. After 5 plays, Donnelly punts to Oilers' 23-yard line. Ford's fumble recovered by Wyman. Seahawks take possession at Oilers' 27. After 2 plays, Johnson kicks 42-yard field goal at 4:25.

Dec. 9, 1990—Miami 23, Philadelphia 20, at Miami; Eagles win toss. After 11 plays, Feagles punts to Dolphins' 26. After 6 plays, Roby punts to Eagles' 14 and Harris returns to 25. After 3 plays, Feagles punts to Dolphins' 43. Marino completes series of passes to Eagles' 22. Stoyanovich kicks 39-yard field goal at 12:32.

Dec. 9, 1990—San Francisco 20, Cincinnati 17, at Cincinnati; 49ers win toss. Carter returns kickoff to 49ers' 19. After 10 plays, Cofer kicks 23-yard field goal at 6:12.

Sept. 24, 1991—Chicago 19, New York Jets 13, at Chicago; Jets win toss. Mathis returns kickoff seven yards to New York's 12. Jets drive to New York 26; Bailey returns punt to Chicago 39. Bears drive to Jets' 44-yard line and punt into the end zone. Jets drive to Bears' 11 where Leahy's 28-yard field goal attempt is wide left. Bears drive from 20 to Jets' 1 where Harbaugh runs for touchdown at 14:42.

Oct. 13, 1991—Los Angeles Raiders 23, Seattle 20, at Seattle. Seahawks win toss. Seahawks begin on 20. After 5 plays, Tuten punts and Brown signals fair catch at Raiders' 24. After 3 plays, Gossett punts and Land downs ball at Seattle 9. After 1 play, Lott intercepts at Seahawks' 19 to set up Jaeger's game-winning 37-yard field goal at 6:37.

Oct. 20, 1991—Cleveland 30, San Diego 24, at San Diego; Chargers win toss. After kickoff, Chargers drive to Browns' 45 and punt to Browns' 6 where Hendrickson downs ball. Browns drive to 38 and punt; Taylor fair catches on Chargers' 14. After 3 plays, Brandon intercepts at Chargers' 30 and scores at 5:58.

Oct. 20, 1991—New England 26, Minnesota 23, at New England; Patriots win toss. Martin returns kickoff 18 yards to New England 22. Patriots drive to Minnesota 19. Staurovsky's 36-yard field goal attempt is wide left. Minnesota drives to the 50 where Newsome punts into end zone. On first play, McMillian intercepts at the 40 for Minnesota. After 2 plays, Marion causes Jordan fumble and Pool recovers at New England 20. New England drives to Minnesota 24 where Staurovsky kicks 42-yard field goal as time expires.

Nov. 3, 1991—New York Jets 19, Green Bay 16, at New York; Packers win toss. Thompson returns kickoff 30 yards to Packers' 39. Green Bay drives to New York 24 where Jacke's 42-yard field goal attempt is wide right. Jets drive to 50. Aguiar's punt is fumbled by Sikahema and recovered by New York at Packers' 23. After 2 plays, Leahy kicks 37-yard field goal at 9:40.

Nov. 3, 1991—Washington 16, Houston 13, at Washington; Redskins win toss. Mitchell returns kickoff 9 yards to Washington 14. After 4 plays, Goodburn punts and Givins returns to Houston 31. After 1 play, Moon's pass is intercepted by Green at Oilers' 35. After 3 plays, Lohmiller kicks 41-yard field goal at 4:01.

Nov. 10, 1991—Houston 26, Dallas 23, at Houston; Oilers win toss. Pinkett returns kickoff 20 yards to Houston 24. After 6 plays, Montgomery punts and Martin returns to Dallas 24. Cowboys drive to Oilers' 24 where Smith fumbles and McDowell recovers at Oilers' 15. Houston drives to Dallas 5 where Del Greco kicks 23-yard field goal at 14:31.

Nov. 10, 1991—Pittsburgh 33, Cincinnati 27, at Cincinnati; Pittsburgh wins toss. Woodson downs kickoff for touchback. After 3 plays, Stryzinski punts and Barber returns 7 yards to Cincinnati 38. Bengals drive to Pittsburgh 37 where Woods fumbles and Lloyd returns recovery to Cincinnati 44. After 2 plays, O'Donnell passes to Green for 26-yard touchdown at 6:32.

Nov. 24, 1991—Atlanta 23, New Orleans 20, at New Orleans; Atlanta wins toss. Falcons begin at 20. After 3 plays, Fulhage punts and Fenerty signals fair catch at New Orleans 43. After 3 plays, Barnhardt punts and Thompson downs ball at Atlanta 23. After 3 plays, Fulhage punts and Fenerty fair catches at New Orleans 25. Saints drive to Atlanta 38 where Andersen misses 55-yard field-goal attempt. After 1 play, Rozier fumbles and Martin recovers on 50. Saints drive to Atlanta 38 where Barnhardt punts to Falcons' 2. Atlanta drives to New Orleans 33 where Johnson kicks 50-yard field goal at 13:03.

Nov. 24, 1991—Miami 16, Chicago 13, at Chicago; Miami wins toss. Butler kicks to Miami 20 where Paige returns kickoff 15 yards to 35. Miami drives to Chicago 9 where Stoyanovich kicks 27-yard field goal at 4:11.

Dec. 8, 1991—Buffalo 30, Los Angeles Raiders 27, at Los Angeles; Raiders win toss. Daluiso kicks into end zone for touchback. On third play, Kelso intercepts for Buffalo and returns ball to Bills' 36. Bills drive to Los Angeles 24 where Norwood kicks 42-yard field goal at 2:34.

Dec. 8, 1991—Kansas City 20, San Diego 17, at Kansas City; Chiefs win toss. Carney kicks to Kansas City 10 where Stradford returns 23 yards to 33. After 3 plays, Barker punts to San Diego 4. Chargers drive to 40 where Kidd punts 60 yards into end zone for touchback. Kansas City drives to San Diego 39 where Barker punts 38 yards to 1. After 3 plays, Kidd punts 41 yards to San Diego 42 where Stradford returns 12 yards to 30. Chiefs drive to San Diego 1 where Lowery kicks 18-yard field goal at 11:26.

Dec. 8, 1991—New England 23, Indianapolis 17, at New England; Indianapolis wins toss. Baumann kicks off to Indianapolis 2 where Martin returns 23 yards to 25. After 3 downs, Stark punts to New England 17 where Henderson returns 8 yards to 25. New England drives to 50 where McCarthy punts and Prior signals fair catch at Indianapolis 15. After 3 plays, Stark punts to New England 40 where Henderson returns 7 yards to 47. After 2 plays, Millen passes to Timpson for 45-yard touchdown at 8:55.

Dec. 22, 1991—Detroit 17, Buffalo 14, at Buffalo; Detroit wins toss. Daluiso kicks off to Detroit 20 where Dozier returns 15 yards to Lions 35. Lions drive to Bills' 3 where Murray kicks 21-yard field goal at 4:23.

Dec. 22, 1991—New York Jets 23, Miami 20, at Miami; Jets win toss. Aguiar kicks to Miami's 30 where Logan returns 3 yards to the 33. After 4 downs, Stoyanovich punts to Jets' 15 where Baty returns 8 yards to 23. Jets drive to Miami 12 where Allegre kicks 30-yard field goal at 6:33.

Sept. 6, 1992—Minnesota 23, Green Bay 20, at Green Bay. Vikings win toss. Nelson returns kickoff 14 yards to the Minnesota 23. After 5 plays, Newsome punts 49 yards to Green Bay 21 where Brooks returns 12 yards to the 33. After 2 plays, Glenn intercepts pass at the Vikings' 48. On first play, Allen fumbles and Billups recovers at Green Bay 35. After 3 plays, McJulien punts 33 yards to Vikings' 35. Vikings drive to Minnesota 48; Newsome punts 52 yards for touchback. After 3 plays, McJulien punts and Parker returns 10 yards to Green Bay 48. Vikings drive to Packers' 9 where Reveiz kicks 26-yard field goal at 10:20.

Sept. 13, 1992—Cincinnati 24, Los Angeles Raiders 21, at Cincinnati. Raiders win toss. Land returns kickoff 13 yards but fumbles at Los Angeles's 20; ball recovered by Bengals' Bennett at Raiders' 21. After 1 play, Breech kicks 34-yard field goal at 1:01.

Sept. 20, 1992—Houston 23, Kansas City 20, at Houston. Chiefs win toss. Carter returns kickoff 25 yards to Kansas City 28. On third play of drive, Birden fumbles at Kansas City 34; ball recovered by Houston's D. Smith at Chiefs' 23. After one play, Del Greco kicks 39-yard field goal at 1:55.

Oct. 11, 1992—Indianapolis 6, New York Jets 3, at Indianapolis. Colts win toss. Verdin returns kickoff 33 yards to Colts' 36. Colts drive to Jets' 30 where Biasucci kicks 47-yard field goal at 3:01.

Nov. 8, 1992—Cincinnati 31, Chicago 28, at Chicago. Bears win toss. Lewis returns kickoff 22 yards to Chicago's 29. Bears drive to Chicago's 46 where Gardocki punts; fair catch by Wright at the Cincinnati 17. Bengals drive to Bears' 18 where Breech kicks 36-yard field goal at 8:39.

Nov. 15, 1992—New England 37, Indianapolis 34, at Indianapolis. Colts win toss. Verdin returns kickoff 10 yards to Colts' 20; holding penalty brings ball back to Colts' 10. After two plays, Henderson intercepts pass at Colts' 38 and returns it 9 yards to the 29. In three plays, Patriots drive to 1 where Baumann kicks 18-yard field goal at 3:25.

Nov. 29, 1992—Indianapolis 16, Buffalo 13, at Indianapolis. Colts win toss. Verdin returns kickoff 24 yards to Colts' 22. Colts drive to Buffalo 22 where Biasucci kicks 40-yard field goal at 3:51.

***Nov. 30, 1992—Seattle 16, Denver 13,** at Seattle. Seahawks win toss. Daluiso kicks through end zone for touchback. After three plays, Tuten punts 53 yards to Denver 18 where Marshall returns for no gain. After three plays, Rodriguez punts 29 yards to Seattle 45 where Warren signals fair catch. Seahawks drive to Denver 15 where Kasay's 33-yard field goal attempt misses. Broncos take over at Denver 20. After three plays, Rodriguez punts 43 yards to Seattle 38 where Warren signals for fair catch. After four plays, Tuten punts 39 yards to Denver 4 where Daniels downs punt. After three plays, Rodriguez punts 46 yards to Denver 48 where Warren returns 10 yards to the 38. Seahawks drive to Denver 14 where Kasay kicks 32-yard field goal at 11:10.

Dec. 13, 1992—Philadelphia 20, Seattle 17, at Seattle. Eagles win toss. Sydner returns kick 12 yards to Eagles' 16; illegal block penalty brings ball back to 8. Eagles drive to Philadelphia 45 where Feagles punts for a touchback. After 6 plays, Tuten punts 45 yards to Philadelphia 22 where Sydner returns 7 yards to 29. After 6 plays, Feagles punts 44 yards to Seattle 26 where Warren returns 5 yards to 31. After 5 plays, Tuten punts 32 yards to Philadelphia 20 where Sydner signals for fair catch. Eagles drive to Seattle 27 where Ruzek kicks 44-yard field goal with no time remaining.

Dec. 27, 1992—Miami 16, New England 13, at New England. Patriots win toss. Lockwood returns kickoff 15 yards to Patriots' 21. After three plays, McCarthy punts 39 yards to Miami 33 where Miller returns 2 yards to the 35. Miami drives to New England 18 where Stoyanovich kicks 35-yard field goal at 8:17.

Sept. 12, 1993—Detroit 19, New England 16, at New England. Patriots win toss. Patriots begin at 20. After 3 plays, Saxon punts 42 yards to Detroit 29 where Gray returns 12 yards to the 41. After 3 plays, Arnold punts 41 yards to New England 12 where Brown returns 16 yards to the 28. Patriots drive to Detroit 44 where Saxon punts into the end zone for a touchback. Detroit drives to New England 20 where Hanson kicks 38-yard field goal at 11:04.

Nov. 7, 1993—Buffalo 13, New England 10, at New England. Patriots win toss. T. Brown returns kickoff 27 yards to Patriots 30. Patriots drive to Buffalo 48 where Bills take over on downs. Bills drive to New England 25 where Metzelaars fumbles, and C. Brown recovers. After 3 plays, Saxon punts 46 yards to Buffalo 24 where Copeland returns 11 yards to the 35. Bills drive to New England 14 where Christie kicks 32-yard field goal at 9:22.

Dec. 19, 1993—Phoenix 30, Seattle 27, at Seattle. Cardinals win toss. Bailey returns kickoff 14 yards to Cardinals 20. Cardinals drive to Seattle 23 where Davis kicks 41-yard field goal at 6:45.

Jan. 2, 1994—Dallas 16, New York Giants 13, at New York. Giants win toss. Meggett returns kickoff 19 yards to Giants 19. After 6 plays, Horan punts 45 yards to Cowboys 25 where Widmer downs punt. Cowboys drive to Giants' 23 where Murray kicks 41-yard field goal at 10:44.

Jan. 2, 1994—New England 33, Miami 27, at New England. Dolphins win toss. McDuffie returns kickoff 21 yards to Miami 27. After 3 plays, Hatcher punts 43 yards to New England 29 where Harris returns 6 yards to the 35. After 2 plays, Brown intercepts pass from Bledsoe and returns 3 yards to Miami 49. After 3 plays, Hatcher punts 37 yards to New England 14 where Harris returns 18 yards to the 32. After 2 plays, Bledsoe passes 36 yards to Timpson for touchdown at 4:44.

Jan. 2, 1994—Los Angeles Raiders 33, Denver 30, at Los Angeles. Broncos win toss. Delpino returns kickoff 12 yards to Denver 25. Broncos drive to Los Angeles 22 where Elam's 40-yard field goal attempt is wide left. Raiders drive to Denver 29 where Jaeger kicks 47-yard field goal at 7:10.

***Jan. 3, 1994—Philadelphia 37, San Francisco 34,** at San Francisco. 49ers win toss. Walker returns kickoff, 19 yards to San Francisco 27. 49ers drive to Philadelphia 14 where Cofer misses 32-yard field goal. Eagles start at their 20-yard line, and, after 3 plays, Feagles punts 48 yards to San Francisco 36 where Carter fumbles and 49ers recover. After 7 plays, Wilmsmeyer punts 57 yards to Philadelphia 6 where Sikahema returns 16 yards to the 22. Eagles drive to San Francisco 10 where Ruzek kicks 28-yard field goal with no time remaining.

Sept. 4, 1994—Detroit 31, Atlanta 28, at Detroit. Falcons win toss. Falcons start at their own 16 after holding penalty on kickoff. After 3 plays, Alexander punts 41 yards to Detroit 39 where Clay returns 12 yards to Atlanta 49. Detroit drives to Atlanta 20 where Hanson kicks 37-yard field goal with 9:46 remaining.

Sept. 11, 1994—New York Jets 25, Denver 22, at New York. Jets win toss. Murrell returns kickoff 24 yards to New York 33. Jets drive to Denver 22 where Lowery kicks 39-yard field goal with 11:03 remaining.

***Sept. 19, 1994—Detroit 20, Dallas 17,** at Dallas. Lions win toss. Gray returns kickoff 24 yards to Detroit 32. Lions drive to Dallas 34 where Hanson's 51-yard field-goal attempt is blocked by Lett. Cowboys take possession at Dallas 42. Cowboys drive to Detroit 37 where Kennard fumbles and Swilling recovers. Lions take possession at Detroit 45. After 6 plays, Montgomery punts 31 yards to Dallas 16. Cowboys drive to Dallas 49 where Aikman fumbles and Thomas recovers at Dallas 43. Lions drive to Dallas 26 where Hanson kicks 44-yard field goal with 27 seconds remaining.

Oct. 16, 1994—Arizona 19, Washington 16, at Washington. Redskins win toss. Mitchell returns kickoff 27 yards to Washington 41. Redskins drive to Arizona 34 where Lohmiller's 51-yard field-goal attempt is blocked by Joyner and recovered by Williams who returns it to the Washington 37. After 5 plays, Peterson's 45-yard field-goal attempt is wide right. Redskins take possession at the Washington 36. After 3 plays, Roby punts 36 yards to the Arizona 37 where Robinson returns 3 yards to the 40. After 3 plays, Feagles punts 51 yards for a touchback. After 1 play, Shuler's pass is intercepted by Hoage who returns it to the Washington 12. Peterson kicks 29-yard field goal with 5:00 remaining.

Oct. 16, 1994—Miami 20, Los Angeles Raiders 17, at Miami. Dolphins win toss. McDuffie returns kickoff 19 yards to Miami 23. Dolphins drive to Los Angeles 12 where Stoyanovich kicks 29-yard field goal with 9:14 remaining.

#Oct. 20, 1994—Minnesota 13, Green Bay 10, at Minnesota. Vikings win toss.

OVERTIME GAMES

Ismail returns kickoff 22 yards to Minnesota 29. Vikings drive to Green Bay 9 where Fuad Reveiz kicks 27-yard field goal with 10:34 remaining.

Oct. 30, 1994—Detroit 28, New York Giants 25, at New York. Giants win toss. Lewis returns kickoff 16 yards to New York 27. After 3 plays, Horan punts 42 yards to Detroit 24 where Gray calls for fair catch. Detroit drives to New York 6 where Hanson kicks 24-yard field goal with 8:17 remaining.

Oct. 30, 1994—Arizona 20, Pittsburgh 17, at Arizona. Steelers win toss. Johnson returns kickoff 24 yards to Pittsburgh 30 where he fumbles and Arizona's Merritt recovers at Pittsburgh 32. After 3 plays, Davis kicks 51-yard field goal with 13:20 remaining.

Nov. 6, 1994—Cincinnati 20, Seattle 17, at Seattle. Seahawks win toss. Warren returns kickoff 32 yards to Seattle 33. After 3 plays, Tuten punts 37 yards to Cincinnati 28 where Sawyer calls for fair catch. After 3 plays, Johnson punts 64 yards to Seattle 2 where Truitt downs ball. Seahawks drive to Seattle 38 where Tuten punts 50 yards to Cincinnati 12 and Sawyer returns 5 yards to 17. Blake passes to Scott for 76 yards to Seattle 7. Pelfrey kicks 26-yard field goal with 6:46 remaining.

Nov. 6, 1994—Pittsburgh 12, Houston 9, at Houston. Steelers win toss. Stone returns kickoff 15 yards to Pittsburgh 28. After 3 plays, Royals punts 53 yards to Houston 13 where Givins downs ball. After 3 plays, Camarillo punts 57 yards to Pittsburgh 31 where Woodson returns 20 yards to Houston 49. After 3 plays, Royals punts 43 yards to Houston 15 where Coleman returns 3 yards to 18. After 5 plays, Camarillo punts 57 yards to Pittsburgh 12 where Hastings returns 12 yards to 24. Steelers drive to Houston 41 where Royals punts 29 yards to Houston 12, and Coleman calls for fair catch. Brown fumbles on first play and Jones recovers at Houston 22. After 1 play, Anderson kicks 40-yard field goal with 3:36 remaining.

Nov. 13, 1994—New England 26, Minnesota 20, at New England. Patriots win toss. Thompson returns kickoff 27 yards to New England 33. Patriots drive to Minnesota 14 where Bledsoe passes 14 yards to Turner for touchdown with 10:50 remaining.

Nov. 20, 1994—Pittsburgh 16, Miami 13, at Pittsburgh. Steelers win toss. Stone returns kickoff 15 yards to Pittsburgh 16. Steelers drive to Miami 39 where they lose possession on downs. Dolphins drive to Pittsburgh 47 where Arnold punts 35 yards to Pittsburgh 12 and Oliver downs ball. Steelers drive to Miami 21 where Anderson kicks 39-yard field goal with 4:41 remaining.

Nov. 27, 1994—Chicago 19, Arizona 16, at Arizona. Cardinals win toss. Levy returns kickoff 31 yards to Arizona 45. After 5 plays, Feagles punts 38 yards to the end zone for a touchback. Bears drive to Arizona 10 where Butler kicks 27-yard field goal with 6:49 remaining.

Nov. 27, 1994—Tampa Bay 20, Minnesota 17, at Minnesota. Buccaneers win toss. Harris returns kickoff 12 yards to Tampa Bay 38. After 6 plays, Stryzinski punts 40 yards to Minnesota 4 where Guilford muffs punt and Buccaneers' Brady recovers. Husted kicks 22-yard field goal with 12:52 remaining.

#Dec. 1, 1994—Minnesota 33, Chicago 27, at Minnesota. Bears win toss. Lewis returns kickoff 23 yards to Chicago 33. Bears drive to Minnesota 22 where Butler's 40-yard field goal attempt is wide left. After 1 play, Moon passes 65 yards to Carter for touchdown with 9:14 remaining.

Dec. 4, 1994—Denver 20, Kansas City 17, at Kansas City. Broncos win toss. Milburn returns kickoff 24 yards to Denver 29. After 3 plays, Millen fumbles and Phillips recovers at Denver 35. After 4 plays, Allen fumbles and Smith recovers at Denver 27. After 6 plays, Rouen punts 45 yards to Kansas City 25 where Hughes calls for fair catch. After 3 plays, Aguiar punts 33 yards to Denver 42 where Chiefs down ball. Broncos drive to Kansas City 17 where Elam kicks 34-yard field goal with 2:48 remaining.

**indicates Monday night game*
#indicates Thursday night game

POSTSEASON

Dec. 28, 1958—Baltimore 23, New York Giants 17, at New York in NFL Championship Game. Giants win toss. Maynard returns kickoff to Giants' 20. Chandler punts and Taseff returns one yard to Colts' 20. Colts win at 8:15 on a 1-yard run by Ameche.

Dec. 23, 1962—Dallas Texans 20, Houston Oilers 17, at Houston in AFL Championship Game. Texans win toss and kick off. Jancik returns kickoff to Oilers' 33. Norton punts and Jackson makes fair catch on Texans' 22. Wilson punts and Jancik makes fair catch on Oilers' 45. Robinson intercepts Blanda's pass and returns 13 yards to Oilers' 47. Wilson's punt rolls dead at Oilers' 12. Hull intercepts Blanda's pass and returns 23 yards to midfield. Texans win at 17:54 on a 25-yard field goal by Brooker.

Dec. 26, 1965—Green Bay 13, Baltimore 10, at Green Bay in NFL Divisional Playoff Game. Packers win toss. Moore returns kickoff to Packers' 22. Chandler punts and Haymond returns nine yards to Colts' 41. Gilburg punts and Wood makes fair catch at Packers' 21. Chandler punts and Haymond returns one yard to Colts' 41. Michaels misses 47-yard field goal. Packers win at 13:39 on 25-yard field goal by Chandler.

Dec. 25, 1971—Miami 27, Kansas City 24, at Kansas City in AFC Divisional Playoff Game. Chiefs win toss. Podolak, after a lateral from Buchanan, returns kickoff to Chiefs' 46. Stenerud's 42-yard field goal is blocked. Seiple punts and Podolak makes fair catch at Chiefs' 17. Wilson punts and Scott returns 18 yards to Dolphins' 39. Yepremian misses 62-yard field goal. Scott intercepts Dawson's pass and returns 13 yards to Dolphins' 46. Seiple punts and Podolak loses one yard to Chiefs' 15. Wilson punts and Scott makes fair catch on Dolphins' 30. Dolphins win at 22:40 on a 37-yard field goal by Yepremian.

Dec. 24, 1977—Oakland 37, Baltimore 31, at Baltimore in AFC Divisional Playoff Game. Colts win toss. Raiders start on own 42 following a punt late in the first overtime. Oakland works way into field-goal range on Stabler's 19-yard pass to Branch at Colts' 26. Four plays later, on the second play of the second overtime, Stabler hits Casper with a 10-yard touchdown pass at 15:43.

Jan. 2, 1982—San Diego 41, Miami 38, at Miami in AFC Divisional Playoff Game. Chargers win toss. San Diego drives from its 13 to Miami 8. On second-and-goal, Benirschke misses 27-yard field goal attempt wide left at 9:15. Miami has the ball twice and San Diego twice more before the Dolphins get their third possession. Miami drives from the San Diego 46 to Chargers' 17 and on fourth-and-two, von Schamann's 34-yard field goal attempt is blocked by San Diego's Winslow after 11:27. Fouts then completes four of five passes, including a 39-yarder to Joiner that puts the ball on Dolphins' 10. On first down, Benirschke kicks a 29-yard field goal at 13:52. San Diego's winning drive covered 74 yards in six plays.

Jan. 3, 1987—Cleveland 23, New York Jets 20, at Cleveland in AFC Divisional Playoff Game. Jets win toss. Jets' punt downed at Browns' 26. Moseley's 23-yard field goal attempt is wide right. Teams trade punts. Jets' second punt downed at Browns' 31. First overtime period expires eight plays later with Browns in possession at Jets' 42. Moseley kicks 27-yard field goal four plays into second overtime at 17:02.

Jan. 11, 1987—Denver 23, Cleveland 20, at Cleveland in AFC Championship Game. Browns win toss. Broncos hold Browns on four downs. Browns' punt returned four yards to Denver's 25. Elway completes 22- and 28-yard passes to set up Karlis's 33-yard field goal nine plays into drive at 5:38.

Jan. 3, 1988—Houston 23, Seattle 20, at Houston in AFC Wild Card Game. Seahawks win toss. Rodriguez punts to K. Johnson who returns one yard to Houston 15. Zendejas kicks 32-yard field goal 12 plays later at 8:05.

Dec. 31, 1989—Pittsburgh 26, Houston 23, at Houston in AFC Wild Card Playoff Game. Steelers win toss. Steelers punt to Oilers. Oilers' fumble recovered by Woodson and returned three yards. Four plays and 13 yards later, Anderson kicks a 50-yard field goal at 3:26.

Jan. 7, 1990—Los Angeles Rams 19, New York Giants 13, at New York in NFC Wild Card Game. Rams win toss. Everett completes two passes to move ball to Giants' 48. White called for pass interference; ball spotted on Giants' 25. Everett hits Anderson with a 30-yard touchdown pass at 1:06.

Jan. 3, 1993—Buffalo 41, Houston 38, at Buffalo in AFC Wild Card Game. Houston wins toss. Oilers begin at 20. After 2 plays, Moon's pass is intercepted by Odomes who returns ball 2 yards to Houston 35. After 2 plays, Christie kicks 32-yard field goal at 3:06.

Jan. 8, 1994—Kansas City 27, Pittsburgh 24, at Kansas City. Kansas City wins toss. Hughes returns kickoff 20 yards to Kansas City 25. After 3 plays, Barker punts 48 yards to Pittsburgh 18 where Woodson returns 8 yards to the 26. After 6 plays, Royals punts 30 yards to Kansas City 20. Kansas City drives to Pittsburgh 14 where Lowery kicks 32-yard field goal at 11:03.

NFL POSTSEASON OVERTIME GAMES
(BY LENGTH OF GAME)

Date	Game	Length
Dec. 25, 1971	Miami 27, KANSAS CITY 24	82:40
Dec. 23, 1962	Dallas Texans 20, HOUSTON 17	77:54
Jan. 3, 1987	CLEVELAND 23, New York Jets 20	77:02
Dec. 24, 1977	Oakland 37, BALTIMORE 31	75:43
Jan. 2, 1982	San Diego 41, MIAMI 38	73:52
Dec. 26, 1965	GREEN BAY 13, Baltimore 10	73:39
Jan. 8, 1994	KANSAS CITY 27, Pittsburgh 24	71:03
Dec. 28, 1958	Baltimore 23, N.Y. GIANTS 17	68:15
Jan. 3, 1988	HOUSTON 23, Seattle 20	68:05
Jan. 11, 1987	Denver 23, CLEVELAND 20	65:38
Dec. 31, 1989	Pittsburgh 26, HOUSTON 23	63:26
Jan. 3, 1993	BUFFALO 41, Houston 38	63:06
Jan. 7, 1990	Los Angeles Rams 19, N.Y. GIANTS 13	61:06

Home team in CAPS

OVERTIME WON-LOST RECORDS, 1974-1994

(REGULAR SEASON)

AFC	W	L	T	Pct.
Buffalo	9	4	0	.692
Cincinnati	11	5	0	.688
Cleveland	11	8	1	.575
Denver	12	9	2	.565
Houston	6	11	0	.353
Indianapolis	6	5	1	.542
Kansas City	4	7	2	.385
Los Angeles	10	7	0	.588
Miami	8	12	1	.405
New England	7	13	0	.350
New York Jets	9	6	2	.588
Pittsburgh	9	4	1	.679
San Diego	7	9	0	.438
Seattle	4	8	0	.333

NFC	W	L	T	Pct.
Arizona	6	6	2	.500
Atlanta	5	8	1	.393
Chicago	11	10	0	.524
Dallas	7	5	0	.583
Detroit	9	7	1	.559
Green Bay	5	9	4	.389
Minnesota	11	10	2	.522
New Orleans	2	6	0	.250
New York Giants	6	8	1	.433
Philadelphia	6	8	2	.438
St. Louis	5	5	1	.500
San Francisco	4	5	1	.450
Tampa Bay	7	7	1	.500
Washington	9	4	0	.692

OVERTIME GAMES BY YEAR

(REGULAR SEASON)

1994-16	1988- 9	1982- 4	1976- 5
1993-7	1987-13	1981-10	1975- 9
1992-10	1986-16	1980-13	1974- 2
1991-15	1985-10	1979-12	
1990-10	1984- 9	1978-11	
1989-11	1983-19	1977- 6	

OVERTIME GAME SUMMARY—1974-1994

There have been 217 overtime games in regular-season play since the rule was adopted in 1974 (16 in 1994 season). Breakdown follows:

162 (12) times both teams had at least one possession (75%)
55 (4) times the team which won the toss drove for winning score (39 FG, 16 TD) (25%)
103 (9) times the team which won the toss won the game (47%)
101 (7) times the team which lost the toss won the game (47%)
149 (14) games were decided by a field goal (69%)
54 (2) games were decided by a touchdown (25%)
1 (0) game was decided by a safety (.5%)
13 (0) games ended tied (6.0%). Last time: Nov. 19, 1989, Cleveland 10, Kansas City 10, at Cleveland

Note: The number in parentheses represents the 1994 season total in each category.

MOST OVERTIME GAMES, SEASON

5 Green Bay Packers, 1983
4 Denver Broncos, 1985
Cleveland Browns, 1989
Minnesota Vikings, 1994
3 By many teams, last time: Arizona Cardinals, Detroit Lions, Pittsburgh Steelers, 1994

LONGEST CONSECUTIVE GAME STREAKS WITHOUT OVERTIME (Current)

76 St. Louis Rams (last OT game, 10/7/90 vs. Cincinnati)
57 Cleveland Browns (last OT game, 10/20/91 vs. San Diego)
52 New Orleans (last OT game, 11/24/91 vs. Atlanta)
(Record: 110, Phoenix Cardinals, 12/7/86-12/19/93)

SHORTEST OVERTIME GAMES

0:21 (Chicago 23, Detroit 17; 11/27/80)—only kickoff return for TD
0:30 (Baltimore 29, New England 23; 9/4/83)
0:55 (New York Giants 16, Philadelphia 10; 9/29/85)

There have been 13 overtime postseason games dating back to 1958. In 12 cases, both teams had at least one possession. Last time: 1/8/94, Kansas City 27, Pittsburgh 24.

LONGEST OVERTIME GAMES (All Postseason Games)

22:40 Miami 27, Kansas City 24; 12/25/71
17:54 Dallas Texans 20, Houston 17; 12/23/62
17:02 Cleveland 23, New York Jets 20; 1/3/87

OVERTIME SCORING SUMMARY

149 were decided by a field goal
24 were decided by a touchdown pass
17 were decided by a touchdown run
5 were decided by interceptions (Atlanta 40, New Orleans 34, 9/2/79; Atlanta 47, Green Bay 41, 11/27/83; New York Giants 16, Philadelphia 10, 9/29/85; Indianapolis 23, Cleveland 17, 12/10/89; Cleveland 30, San Diego 24, 10/20/91)
2 were decided on a fake field goal/touchdown pass (Minnesota 22, Chicago 16, 10/16/77; Cleveland 23, Minnesota 17, 12/17/89)
1 was decided by a kickoff return (Chicago 23, Detroit 17, 11/27/80)
1 was decided by a fumble recovery (Baltimore 29, New England 23, 9/4/83)
1 was decided on a fake field goal/touchdown run (Los Angeles Rams 27, Minnesota 21, 12/2/79)
1 was decided on a blocked field goal (Denver 30, San Diego 24, 11/17/85)
1 was decided on a blocked field goal/recovery by kicker (Green Bay 12, Chicago 6, 9/7/80)
1 was decided on a blocked field goal/recovery by kicking team (Philadelphia 23, New York Giants 17, 11/20/88)
1 was decided by a safety (Minnesota 23, Los Angeles Rams 21, 11/5/89)
13 ended tied

OVERTIME RECORDS

Longest Touchdown Pass

99 Yards — Ron Jaworski to Mike Quick, Philadelphia 23, Atlanta 17 (11/10/85)
65 Yards — Warren Moon to Cris Carter, Minnesota 33, Chicago 27 (12/1/94)
50 Yards — Tommy Kramer to Ahmad Rashad, Minnesota 27, Green Bay 21 (9/23/79)
50 Yards — Jim Harbaugh to Neal Anderson, Chicago 23, Detroit 17 (12/2/90)

Longest Touchdown Run

60 Yards — Herschel Walker, Dallas 23, New England 17 (11/15/87)
42 Yards — Eric Dickerson, Los Angeles Rams 26, Tampa Bay 20 (10/5/86)
28 Yards — Marcus Allen, Los Angeles Raiders 37, San Diego 31 (11/20/86)

Longest Field Goal

51 Yards — Greg Davis, New England 23, Indianapolis 20 (10/29/89)
Greg Davis, Arizona 20, Pittsburgh 17 (10/30/94)
50 Yards — Morten Andersen, New Orleans 20, Philadelphia 17 (12/11/83);
Norm Johnson, Atlanta 23, New Orleans 20 (11/24/91)
48 Yards — Eddie Murray, Detroit 27, Atlanta 24 (9/9/84);
Mark Moseley, Washington 30, New York Giants 27 (11/15/81)

Longest Touchdown Plays

99 Yards — (Pass) Ron Jaworski to Mike Quick, Philadelphia 23, Atlanta 17 (11/10/85)
65 Yards — (Pass) Warren Moon to Cris Carter, Minnesota 33, Chicago 27 (12/1/94)
60 Yards — (Blocked field goal return) Louis Wright, Denver 30, San Diego 24 (11/17/85)
(Run) Herschel Walker, Dallas 23, New England 17 (11/15/87)

PAID ATTENDANCE

NFL PAID ATTENDANCE

For detailed 1994 attendance, see page 227.

Year	Regular Season		Average	Postseason	Total
1994	#14,030,435	(224 games)	#62,636	779,738 (12)	#14,810,173
1993	13,966,843	(224 games)	62,352	814,607 (12)	14,781,450
1992	13,828,887	(224 games)	61,736	815,910 (12)	14,644,797
1991	13,841,459	(224 games)	61,792	813,247 (12)	14,654,706
1990	13,959,896	(224 games)	62,321	847,543 (12)	14,807,439
1989	13,625,662	(224 games)	60,829	685,771 (10)	14,311,433
1988	13,539,848	(224 games)	60,446	658,317 (10)	14,198,165
1987	*11,406,166	(210 games)	54,315	656,977 (10)	12,063,143
1986	13,588,551	(224 games)	60,663	734,002 (10)	14,322,553
1985	13,345,047	(224 games)	59,567	710,768 (10)	14,055,815
1984	13,398,112	(224 games)	59,813	665,194 (10)	14,063,306
1983	13,277,222	(224 games)	59,273	675,513 (10)	13,952,735
1982	**7,367,438	(126 games)	58,472	1,033,153 (16)	8,400,591
1981	13,606,990	(224 games)	60,745	637,763 (10)	14,244,753
1980	13,392,230	(224 games)	59,787	624,430 (10)	14,016,660
1979	13,182,039	(224 games)	58,848	630,326 (10)	13,812,365
1978	12,771,800	(224 games)	57,017	624,388 (10)	13,396,188
1977	11,018,632	(196 games)	56,218	534,925 (8)	11,553,557
1976	11,070,543	(196 games)	56,482	492,884 (8)	11,563,427
1975	10,213,193	(182 games)	56,116	475,919 (8)	10,689,112
1974	10,236,322	(182 games)	56,244	438,664 (8)	10,674,986
1973	10,730,933	(182 games)	58,961	525,433 (8)	11,256,366
1972	10,445,827	(182 games)	57,395	483,345 (8)	10,929,172
1971	10,076,035	(182 games)	55,363	483,891 (8)	10,559,926
1970	9,533,333	(182 games)	52,381	458,493 (8)	9,991,826
1969	6,096,127	(112 games)NFL	54,430	162,279 (3)	6,258,406
	2,843,373	(70 games) AFL	40,620	167,088 (3)	3,010,461
1968	5,882,313	(112 games)NFL	52,521	215,902 (3)	6,098,215
	2,635,004	(70 games) AFL	37,643	114,438 (2)	2,749,442
1967	5,938,924	(112 games)NFL	53,026	166,208 (3)	6,105,132
	2,295,697	(63 games) AFL	36,439	53,330 (1)	2,349,027
1966	5,337,044	(105 games)NFL	50,829	74,152 (1)	5,411,196
	2,160,369	(63 games) AFL	34,291	42,080 (1)	2,202,449
1965	4,634,021	(98 games)NFL	47,286	100,304 (2)	4,734,325
	1,782,384	(56 games) AFL	31,828	30,361 (1)	1,812,745
1964	4,563,049	(98 games)NFL	46,562	79,544 (1)	4,642,593
	1,447,875	(56 games) AFL	25,855	40,242 (1)	1,488,117
1963	4,163,643	(98 games)NFL	42,486	45,801 (1)	4,209,444
	1,208,697	(56 games) AFL	21,584	63,171 (2)	1,271,868
1962	4,003,421	(98 games)NFL	40,851	64,892 (1)	4,068,313
	1,147,302	(56 games) AFL	20,487	37,981 (1)	1,185,283
1961	3,986,159	(98 games)NFL	40,675	39,029 (1)	4,025,188
	1,002,657	(56 games) AFL	17,904	29,556 (1)	1,032,213
1960	3,128,296	(78 games)NFL	40,106	67,325 (1)	3,195,621
	926,156	(56 games) AFL	16,538	32,183 (1)	958,339
1959	3,140,000	(72 games)	43,617	57,545 (1)	3,197,545
1958	3,006,124	(72 games)	41,752	123,659 (2)	3,129,783
1957	2,836,318	(72 games)	39,393	119,579 (2)	2,955,897
1956	2,551,263	(72 games)	35,434	56,836 (1)	2,608,099
1955	2,521,836	(72 games)	35,026	85,693 (1)	2,607,529
1954	2,190,571	(72 games)	30,425	43,827 (1)	2,234,398
1953	2,164,585	(72 games)	30,064	54,577 (1)	2,219,162
1952	2,052,126	(72 games)	28,502	97,507 (2)	2,149,633
1951	1,913,019	(72 games)	26,570	57,522 (1)	1,970,541
1950	1,977,753	(78 games)	25,356	136,647 (3)	2,114,400
1949	1,391,735	(60 games)	23,196	27,980 (1)	1,419,715
1948	1,525,243	(60 games)	25,421	36,309 (1)	1,561,552
1947	1,837,437	(60 games)	30,624	66,268 (2)	1,903,705
1946	1,732,135	(55 games)	31,493	58,346 (1)	1,790,481
1945	1,270,401	(50 games)	25,408	32,178 (1)	1,302,579
1944	1,019,649	(50 games)	20,393	46,016 (1)	1,065,665
1943	969,128	(40 games)	24,228	71,315 (2)	1,040,443
1942	887,920	(55 games)	16,144	36,006 (1)	923,926
1941	1,108,615	(55 games)	20,157	55,870 (2)	1,164,485
1940	1,063,025	(55 games)	19,328	36,034 (1)	1,099,059
1939	1,071,200	(55 games)	19,476	32,279 (1)	1,103,479
1938	937,197	(55 games)	17,040	48,120 (1)	985,317
1937	963,039	(55 games)	17,510	15,878 (1)	978,917
1936	816,007	(54 games)	15,111	29,545 (1)	845,552
1935	638,178	(53 games)	12,041	15,000 (1)	653,178
1934	492,684	(60 games)	8,211	35,059 (1)	527,743

 # Record
**Players' 24-day strike reduced 224-game schedule to 210 games.*
***Players' 57-day strike reduced 224-game schedule to 126 games.*

NFL'S 10 BIGGEST ATTENDANCE WEEKENDS

(Paid Count)

Weekend	Games	Attendance
October 16-17, 1988	14	934,211
September 1-2, 1991	14	922,076
November 8-9, 1992	14	917,384
November 4-5, 1990	14	916,127
October 29-30, 1989	14	915,401
November 17-18, 1990	14	905,486
December 17-19, 1994	14	902,143
October 27-28, 1985	14	902,128
October 12-13, 1980	14	898,223
September 12-13, 1993	14	898,703

NFL'S 10 HIGHEST SCORING WEEKENDS

Point Total	Date	Weekend
761	October 16-17, 1983	7th
736	October 25-26, 1987	7th
732	November 9-10, 1980	10th
725	November 24, 27-28, 1983	13th
714	September 17-18, 1989	2nd
711	November 26, 29-30, 1987	12th
710	November 28, December 1-2, 1985	13th
696	October 2-3, 1983	5th
694	December 1, 4-5, 1994	14th
693	September 24-25, 1989	3rd

TOP 10 TELEVISED SPORTS EVENTS OF ALL-TIME

(Based on A.C. Nielsen Figures)

Program	Date	Network	Share	Rating
Super Bowl XVI	1/24/82	CBS	73.0	49.1
Super Bowl XVII	1/30/83	NBC	69.0	48.6
Winter Olympics	2/23/94	CBS	64.0	48.5
Super Bowl XX	1/26/86	NBC	70.0	48.3
Super Bowl XII	1/15/78	CBS	67.0	47.2
Super Bowl XIII	1/21/79	NBC	74.0	47.1
Super Bowl XVIII	1/22/84	CBS	71.0	46.4
Super Bowl XIX	1/20/85	ABC	63.0	46.4
Super Bowl XIV	1/20/80	CBS	67.0	46.3
Super Bowl XXI	1/25/87	CBS	66.0	45.8

TEN MOST WATCHED TV PROGRAMS & ESTIMATED TOTAL NUMBER OF VIEWERS

(Based on A.C. Nielsen Figures)

Program	Date	Network	*Total Viewers
Super Bowl XXVIII	Jan. 30, 1994	NBC	134,800,000
Super Bowl XXVII	Jan. 31, 1993	NBC	133,400,000
Super Bowl XX	Jan. 26, 1986	NBC	127,000,000
Winter Olympics	Feb. 23, 1994	CBS	126,686,000
Super Bowl XXIX	Jan. 29, 1995	ABC	125,216,000
Super Bowl XXI	Jan. 25, 1987	CBS	122,640,000
M*A*S*H (Special)	Feb. 28, 1983	CBS	121,624,000
Winter Olympics	Feb. 25, 1994	CBS	119,900,000
Super Bowl XXVI	Jan. 26, 1992	CBS	119,680,000
Super Bowl XIX	Jan. 20, 1985	ABC	115,936,000

**Watched some portion of the broadcast*

NFL'S 10 BIGGEST TEAM SINGLE-SEASON HOME ATTENDANCE TOTALS

(Paid Count)

Year	Club	Games	Attendance
1980	Detroit Lions	8	634,204
1988	Buffalo Bills	8	631,818
1991	Buffalo Bills	8	631,786
1992	Buffalo Bills	8	630,978
1994	Kansas City Chiefs	8	626,612
1989	Buffalo Bills	8	626,399
1989	Cleveland Browns	8	625,240
1993	Buffalo Bills	8	624,349
1988	Cleveland Browns	8	624,154
1980	Cleveland Browns	8	623,351

TOP FIVE PAID ATTENDANCE TOTALS FOR ALL GAMES (Includes Preseason)

Year	Preseason	Regular Season	Postseason	All Games
1994	3,200,091	14,030,435	779,738	18,010,264
1993	3,170,381	13,966,843	814,607	17,951,831
1992	3,139,557	13,828,887	815,910	17,784,354
1991	3,097,433	13,841,459	813,247	17,752,139
1990	2,858,302	13,959,896	847,543	17,665,671

TEN HIGHEST-RATED ABC NFL MONDAY NIGHT FOOTBALL GAMES OF ALL-TIME

(Based on A.C. Nielsen Figures)

Game	Date	Rating	Share
Chicago at Miami	12/2/85	29.6	46.0
N.Y. Giants at San Francisco	12/3/90	26.9	42.0
Dallas at Washington	10/2/78	26.8	43.0
Pittsburgh at San Diego	12/22/80	25.3	40.0
Philadelphia at Miami	11/30/81	25.3	40.0
Pittsburgh at Houston	12/10/79	25.1	40.0
Dallas at Miami	12/17/84	25.1	40.0
Pittsburgh at Dallas	9/13/82	24.9	42.0
Cincinnati at Oakland	12/6/76	24.7	40.0
Dallas at Washington	10/8/73	24.6	40.0
Minnesota at Atlanta	11/19/73	24.6	40.0

NFL'S TEN BIGGEST SINGLE-GAME ATTENDANCE TOTALS

Date	Site	Game	Teams	Attendance
August 22, 1947	Soldier Field	College All-Star	Bears vs. All-Stars	105,840
January 20, 1980	Rose Bowl	Super Bowl XIV	Steelers vs. Rams	103,985
January 30, 1983	Rose Bowl	Super Bowl XVII	Redskins vs. Dolphins	103,667
January 9, 1977	Rose Bowl	Super Bowl XI	Raiders vs. Vikings	103,438
November 10, 1957	L.A. Coliseum	Regular Season	49ers at Rams	102,368
January 25, 1987	Rose Bowl	Super Bowl XXI	Giants vs. Broncos	101,643
August 20, 1948	Soldier Field	College All-Star	Cardinals vs. All-Stars	101,220
August 28, 1942	Soldier Field	College All-Star	Bears vs. All-Stars	101,100
November 2, 1958	L.A. Coliseum	Regular Season	Bears at Rams	100,470
December 6, 1958	L.A. Coliseum	Regular Season	Colts at Rams	100,202

NUMBER-ONE DRAFT CHOICES

NUMBER-ONE DRAFT CHOICES

Season	Team	Player	Position	College
1995	Cincinnati	Ki-Jana Carter	RB	Penn State
1994	Cincinnati	Dan Wilkinson	DT	Ohio State
1993	New England	Drew Bledsoe	QB	Washington State
1992	Indianapolis	Steve Emtman	DT	Washington
1991	Dallas	Russell Maryland	DT	Miami
1990	Indianapolis	Jeff George	QB	Illinois
1989	Dallas	Troy Aikman	QB	UCLA
1988	Atlanta	Aundray Bruce	LB	Auburn
1987	Tampa Bay	Vinny Testaverde	QB	Miami
1986	Tampa Bay	Bo Jackson	RB	Auburn
1985	Buffalo	Bruce Smith	DE	Virginia Tech
1984	New England	Irving Fryar	WR	Nebraska
1983	Baltimore	John Elway	QB	Stanford
1982	New England	Kenneth Sims	DT	Texas
1981	New Orleans	George Rogers	RB	South Carolina
1980	Detroit	Billy Sims	RB	Oklahoma
1979	Buffalo	Tom Cousineau	LB	Ohio State
1978	Houston	Earl Campbell	RB	Texas
1977	Tampa Bay	Ricky Bell	RB	Southern California
1976	Tampa Bay	Lee Roy Selmon	DE	Oklahoma
1975	Atlanta	Steve Bartkowski	QB	California
1974	Dallas	Ed Jones	DE	Tennessee State
1973	Houston	John Matuszak	DE	Tampa
1972	Buffalo	Walt Patulski	DE	Notre Dame
1971	New England	Jim Plunkett	QB	Stanford
1970	Pittsburgh	Terry Bradshaw	QB	Louisiana Tech
1969	Buffalo (AFL)	O.J. Simpson	RB	Southern California
1968	Minnesota	Ron Yary	T	Southern California
1967	Baltimore	Bubba Smith	DT	Michigan State
1966	Atlanta	Tommy Nobis	LB	Texas
	Miami (AFL)	Jim Grabowski	RB	Illinois
1965	New York Giants	Tucker Frederickson	RB	Auburn
	Houston (AFL)	Lawrence Elkins	E	Baylor
1964	San Francisco	Dave Parks	E	Texas Tech
	Boston (AFL)	Jack Concannon	QB	Boston College
1963	Los Angeles	Terry Baker	QB	Oregon State
	Kansas City (AFL)	Buck Buchanan	DT	Grambling
1962	Washington	Ernie Davis	RB	Syracuse
	Oakland (AFL)	Roman Gabriel	QB	North Carolina State
1961	Minnesota	Tommy Mason	RB	Tulane
	Buffalo (AFL)	Ken Rice	G	Auburn
1960	Los Angeles	Billy Cannon	RB	Louisiana State
	(AFL had no formal first pick)			
1959	Green Bay	Randy Duncan	QB	Iowa
1958	Chicago Cardinals	King Hill	QB	Rice
1957	Green Bay	Paul Hornung	HB	Notre Dame
1956	Pittsburgh	Gary Glick	DB	Colorado A&M
1955	Baltimore	George Shaw	QB	Oregon
1954	Cleveland	Bobby Garrett	QB	Stanford
1953	San Francisco	Harry Babcock	E	Georgia
1952	Los Angeles	Bill Wade	QB	Vanderbilt
1951	New York Giants	Kyle Rote	HB	Southern Methodist
1950	Detroit	Leon Hart	E	Notre Dame
1949	Philadelphia	Chuck Bednarik	C	Pennsylvania
1948	Washington	Harry Gilmer	QB	Alabama
1947	Chicago Bears	Bob Fenimore	HB	Oklahoma A&M
1946	Boston	Frank Dancewicz	QB	Notre Dame
1945	Chicago Cardinals	Charley Trippi	HB	Georgia
1944	Boston	Angelo Bertelli	QB	Notre Dame
1943	Detroit	Frank Sinkwich	HB	Georgia
1942	Pittsburgh	Bill Dudley	HB	Virginia
1941	Chicago Bears	Tom Harmon	HB	Michigan
1940	Chicago Cardinals	George Cafego	HB	Tennessee
1939	Chicago Cardinals	Ki Aldrich	C	Texas Christian
1938	Cleveland	Corbett Davis	FB	Indiana
1937	Philadelphia	Sam Francis	FB	Nebraska
1936	Philadelphia	Jay Berwanger	HB	Chicago

Note: From 1947 through 1958, the first selection in the draft was a Bonus pick, awarded to the winner of a random draw. That club, in turn, forfeited its last-round draft choice. The winner of the Bonus choice was eliminated from future draws. The system was abolished after 1958, by which time all clubs had received a Bonus choice.

FIRST-ROUND SELECTIONS

If club had no first-round selection, first player drafted is listed with round in parentheses.

ARIZONA CARDINALS

Year	Player, College, Position
1936	Jim Lawrence, Texas Christian, B
1937	Ray Buivid, Marquette, B
1938	Jack Robbins, Arkansas, B
1939	Charles (Ki) Aldrich, Texas Christian, C
1940	George Cafego, Tennessee, B
1941	John Kimbrough, Texas A&M, B
1942	Steve Lach, Duke, B
1943	Glenn Dobbs, Tulsa, B
1944	Pat Harder, Wisconsin, B
1945	Charley Trippi, Georgia, B
1946	Dub Jones, Louisiana State, B
1947	DeWitt (Tex) Coulter, Army, T
1948	Jim Spavital, Oklahoma A&M, B
1949	Bill Fischer, Notre Dame, G
1950	Jack Jennings, Ohio State, T (2)
1951	Jerry Groom, Notre Dame, C
1952	Ollie Matson, San Francisco, B
1953	Johnny Olszewski, California, B
1954	Lamar McHan, Arkansas, B
1955	Max Boydston, Oklahoma, E
1956	Joe Childress, Auburn, B
1957	Jerry Tubbs, Oklahoma, C
1958	King Hill, Rice, B
	John David Crow, Texas A&M, B
1959	Bill Stacy, Mississippi State, B
1960	George Izo, Notre Dame, QB
1961	Ken Rice, Auburn, T
1962	Fate Echols, Northwestern, DT
	Irv Goode, Kentucky, C
1963	Jerry Stovall, Louisiana State, S
	Don Brumm, Purdue, DE
1964	Ken Kortas, Louisville, DT
1965	Joe Namath, Alabama, QB
1966	Carl McAdams, Oklahoma, LB
1967	Dave Williams, Washington, WR
1968	MacArthur Lane, Utah State, RB
1969	Roger Wehrli, Missouri, DB
1970	Larry Stegent, Texas A&M, RB
1971	Norm Thompson, Utah, CB
1972	Bobby Moore, Oregon, RB-WR
1973	Dave Butz, Purdue, DT
1974	J.V. Cain, Colorado, TE
1975	Tim Gray, Texas A&M, DB
1976	Mike Dawson, Arizona, DT
1977	Steve Pisarkiewicz, Missouri, QB
1978	Steve Little, Arkansas, K
	Ken Greene, Washington State, DB
1979	Ottis Anderson, Miami, RB
1980	Curtis Greer, Michigan, DE
1981	E.J. Junior, Alabama, LB
1982	Luis Sharpe, UCLA, T
1983	Leonard Smith, McNeese State, DB
1984	Clyde Duncan, Tennessee, WR
1985	Freddie Joe Nunn, Mississippi, LB
1986	Anthony Bell, Michigan State, LB
1987	Kelly Stouffer, Colorado State, QB
1988	Ken Harvey, California, LB
1989	Eric Hill, Louisiana State, LB
	Joe Wolf, Boston College, G
1990	Anthony Thompson, Indiana, RB (2)
1991	Eric Swann, No College, DE
1992	Tony Sacca, Penn State, QB (2)
1993	Garrison Hearst, Georgia, RB
	Ernest Dye, South Carolina, T
1994	Jamir Miller, UCLA, LB
1995	Frank Sanders, Auburn, WR (2)

ATLANTA FALCONS

Year	Player, College, Position
1966	Tommy Nobis, Texas, LB
	Randy Johnson, Texas A&I, QB
1967	Leo Carroll, San Diego State, DE (2)
1968	Claude Humphrey, Tennessee State, DE
1969	George Kunz, Notre Dame, T
1970	John Small, Citadel, LB
1971	Joe Profit, Northeast Louisiana, RB
1972	Clarence Ellis, Notre Dame, DB
1973	Greg Marx, Notre Dame, DT (2)
1974	Gerald Tinker, Kent State, WR (2)
1975	Steve Bartkowski, California, QB
1976	Bubba Bean, Texas A&M, RB
1977	Warren Bryant, Kentucky, T
	Wilson Faumuina, San Jose State, DT
1978	Mike Kenn, Michigan, T
1979	Don Smith, Miami, DE
1980	Junior Miller, Nebraska, TE
1981	Bobby Butler, Florida State, DB
1982	Gerald Riggs, Arizona State, RB
1983	Mike Pitts, Alabama, DE
1984	Rick Bryan, Oklahoma, DT
1985	Bill Fralic, Pittsburgh, T
1986	Tony Casillas, Oklahoma, NT
	Tim Green, Syracuse, LB
1987	Chris Miller, Oregon, QB
1988	Aundray Bruce, Auburn, LB
1989	Deion Sanders, Florida State, DB
	Shawn Collins, Northern Arizona, WR
1990	Steve Broussard, Washington State, RB
1991	Bruce Pickens, Nebraska, DB
	Mike Pritchard, Colorado, WR
1992	Bob Whitfield, Stanford, T
	Tony Smith, Southern Mississippi, RB
1993	Lincoln Kennedy, Washington, T
1994	Bert Emanuel, Rice, WR (2)
1995	Devin Bush, Florida State, DB

BUFFALO BILLS

Year	Player, College, Position
1960	Richie Lucas, Penn State, QB
1961	Ken Rice, Auburn, T
1962	Ernie Davis, Syracuse, RB
1963	Dave Behrman, Michigan State, C
1964	Carl Eller, Minnesota, DE
1965	Jim Davidson, Ohio State, T
1966	Mike Dennis, Mississippi, RB
1967	John Pitts, Arizona State, S
1968	Haven Moses, San Diego State, WR
1969	O.J. Simpson, Southern California, RB
1970	Al Cowlings, Southern California, DE
1971	J.D. Hill, Arizona State, WR
1972	Walt Patulski, Notre Dame, DE
1973	Paul Seymour, Michigan, TE
	Joe DeLamielleure, Michigan State, G
1974	Reuben Gant, Oklahoma State, TE
1975	Tom Ruud, Nebraska, LB
1976	Mario Clark, Oregon, DB
1977	Phil Dokes, Oklahoma State, DT
1978	Terry Miller, Oklahoma State, RB
1979	Tom Cousineau, Ohio State, LB
	Jerry Butler, Clemson, WR
1980	Jim Ritcher, North Carolina State, C
1981	Booker Moore, Penn State, RB
1982	Perry Tuttle, Clemson, WR
1983	Tony Hunter, Notre Dame, TE
	Jim Kelly, Miami, QB
1984	Greg Bell, Notre Dame, RB
1985	Bruce Smith, Virginia Tech, DE
	Derrick Burroughs, Memphis State, DB
1986	Ronnie Harmon, Iowa, RB
	Will Wolford, Vanderbilt, T
1987	Shane Conlan, Penn State, LB
1988	Thurman Thomas, Oklahoma State, RB (2)
1989	Don Beebe, Chadron, Neb., WR (3)
1990	James Williams, Fresno State, DB
1991	Henry Jones, Illinois, DB
1992	John Fina, Arizona, T
1993	Thomas Smith, North Carolina, DB
1994	Jeff Burris, Notre Dame, DB
1995	Ruben Brown, Pittsburgh, G

CAROLINA PANTHERS

Year	Player, College, Position
1995	Kerry Collins, Penn State, QB
	Tyrone Poole, Ft. Valley State, DB
	Blake Brockermeyer, Texas, T

CHICAGO BEARS

Year	Player, College, Position
1936	Joe Stydahar, West Virginia, T
1937	Les McDonald, Nebraska, E
1938	Joe Gray, Oregon State, B
1939	Sid Luckman, Columbia, QB
	Bill Osmanski, Holy Cross, B
1940	Clyde (Bulldog) Turner, Hardin-Simmons, C
1941	Tom Harmon, Michigan, B
	Norm Standlee, Stanford, B
	Don Scott, Ohio State, B
1942	Frankie Albert, Stanford, B
1943	Bob Steber, Missouri, B
1944	Ray Evans, Kansas, B
1945	Don Lund, Michigan, B
1946	Johnny Lujack, Notre Dame, QB
1947	Bob Fenimore, Oklahoma State, B
	Don Kindt, Wisconsin, B
1948	Bobby Layne, Texas, QB
	Max Bumgardner, Texas, E
1949	Dick Harris, Texas, C
1950	Chuck Hunsinger, Florida, B
	Fred Morrison, Ohio State, B
1951	Bob Williams, Notre Dame, B
	Billy Stone, Bradley, B
	Gene Schroeder, Virginia, E
1952	Jim Dooley, Miami, B
1953	Billy Anderson, Compton (Calif.) J.C., B
1954	Stan Wallace, Illinois, B
1955	Ron Drzewiecki, Marquette, B
1956	Menan (Tex) Schriewer, Texas, E
1957	Earl Leggett, Louisiana State, T
1958	Chuck Howley, West Virginia, G
1959	Don Clark, Ohio State, B
1960	Roger Davis, Syracuse, G
1961	Mike Ditka, Pittsburgh, E
1962	Ronnie Bull, Baylor, RB
1963	Dave Behrman, Michigan State, C
1964	Dick Evey, Tennessee, DT
1965	Dick Butkus, Illinois, LB
	Gale Sayers, Kansas, RB
	Steve DeLong, Tennessee, T
1966	George Rice, Louisiana State, DT
1967	Loyd Phillips, Arkansas, DE
1968	Mike Hull, Southern California, RB
1969	Rufus Mayes, Ohio State, T
1970	George Farmer, UCLA, WR (3)
1971	Joe Moore, Missouri, RB
1972	Lionel Antoine, Southern Illinois, T
	Craig Clemons, Iowa, DB
1973	Wally Chambers, Eastern Kentucky, DE
1974	Waymond Bryant, Tennessee State, LB
	Dave Gallagher, Michigan, DT
1975	Walter Payton, Jackson State, RB
1976	Dennis Lick, Wisconsin, T
1977	Ted Albrecht, California, T
1978	Brad Shearer, Texas, DT (3)
1979	Dan Hampton, Arkansas, DT
	Al Harris, Arizona State, DE
1980	Otis Wilson, Louisville, LB
1981	Keith Van Horne, Southern California, T
1982	Jim McMahon, Brigham Young, QB
1983	Jim Covert, Pittsburgh, T
	Willie Gault, Tennessee, WR
1984	Wilber Marshall, Florida, LB
1985	William Perry, Clemson, DT
1986	Neal Anderson, Florida, RB
1987	Jim Harbaugh, Michigan, QB
1988	Brad Muster, Stanford, RB
	Wendell Davis, Louisiana State, WR
1989	Donnell Woolford, Clemson, DB
	Trace Armstrong, Florida, DE
1990	Mark Carrier, Southern California, DB
1991	Stan Thomas, Texas, T
1992	Alonzo Spellman, Ohio State, DE
1993	Curtis Conway, Southern California, WR
1994	John Thierry, Alcorn State, DE
1995	Rashaan Salaam, Colorado, RB

CINCINNATI BENGALS

Year	Player, College, Position
1968	Bob Johnson, Tennessee, C
1969	Greg Cook, Cincinnati, QB
1970	Mike Reid, Penn State, DT
1971	Vernon Holland, Tennessee State, T
1972	Sherman White, California, DE
1973	Isaac Curtis, San Diego State, WR

FIRST-ROUND SELECTIONS

1974 Bill Kollar, Montana State, DT
1975 Glenn Cameron, Florida, LB
1976 Billy Brooks, Oklahoma, WR
Archie Griffin, Ohio State, RB
1977 Eddie Edwards, Miami, DT
Wilson Whitley, Houston, DT
Mike Cobb, Michigan State, TE
1978 Ross Browner, Notre Dame, DT
Blair Bush, Washington, C
1979 Jack Thompson, Washington State, QB
Charles Alexander, Louisiana State, RB
1980 Anthony Muñoz, Southern California, T
1981 David Verser, Kansas, WR
1982 Glen Collins, Mississippi State, DE
1983 Dave Rimington, Nebraska, C
1984 Ricky Hunley, Arizona, LB
Pete Koch, Maryland, DE
Brian Blados, North Carolina, T
1985 Eddie Brown, Miami, WR
Emanuel King, Alabama, LB
1986 Joe Kelly, Washington, LB
Tim McGee, Tennessee, WR
1987 Jason Buck, Brigham Young, DE
1988 Rickey Dixon, Oklahoma, DB
1989 Eric Ball, UCLA, RB (2)
1990 James Francis, Baylor, LB
1991 Alfred Williams, Colorado, LB
1992 David Klingler, Houston, QB
Darryl Williams, Miami, DB
1993 John Copeland, Alabama, DE
1994 Dan Wilkinson, Ohio State, DT
1995 Ki-Jana Carter, Penn State, RB

CLEVELAND BROWNS

Year Player, College, Position

1950 Ken Carpenter, Oregon State, B
1951 Ken Konz, Louisiana State, B
1952 Bert Rechichar, Tennessee, DB
Harry Agganis, Boston U., QB
1953 Doug Atkins, Tennessee, DE
1954 Bobby Garrett, Stanford, QB
John Bauer, Illinois, G
1955 Kurt Burris, Oklahoma, C
1956 Preston Carpenter, Arkansas, B
1957 Jim Brown, Syracuse, RB
1958 Jim Shofner, Texas Christian, DB
1959 Rich Kreitling, Illinois, DE
1960 Jim Houston, Ohio State, DE
1961 Bobby Crespino, Mississippi, TE
1962 Gary Collins, Maryland, WR
Leroy Jackson, Western Illinois, RB
1963 Tom Hutchinson, Kentucky, WR
1964 Paul Warfield, Ohio State, WR
1965 James Garcia, Purdue, T (2)
1966 Milt Morin, Massachusetts, TE
1967 Bob Matheson, Duke, LB
1968 Marvin Upshaw, Trinity, Tex., DT-DE
1969 Ron Johnson, Michigan, RB
1970 Mike Phipps, Purdue, QB
Bob McKay, Texas, T
1971 Clarence Scott, Kansas State, CB
1972 Thom Darden, Michigan, DB
1973 Steve Holden, Arizona State, WR
Pete Adams, Southern California, T
1974 Billy Corbett, Johnson C. Smith, T (2)
1975 Mack Mitchell, Houston, DE
1976 Mike Pruitt, Purdue, RB
1977 Robert Jackson, Texas A&M, LB
1978 Clay Matthews, Southern California, LB
Ozzie Newsome, Alabama, TE
1979 Willis Adams, Houston, WR
1980 Charles White, Southern California, RB
1981 Hanford Dixon, Southern Mississippi, DB
1982 Chip Banks, Southern California, LB
1983 Ron Brown, Arizona State, WR (2)
1984 Don Rogers, UCLA, DB
1985 Greg Allen, Florida State, RB (2)
1986 Webster Slaughter, San Diego State, WR (2)
1987 Mike Junkin, Duke, LB
1988 Clifford Charlton, Florida, LB
1989 Eric Metcalf, Texas, RB
1990 Leroy Hoard, Michigan, RB (2)
1991 Eric Turner, UCLA, DB
1992 Tommy Vardell, Stanford, RB
1993 Steve Everitt, Michigan, C
1994 Antonio Langham, Alabama, DB
Derrick Alexander, Michigan, WR
1995 Craig Powell, Ohio State, LB

DALLAS COWBOYS

Year Player, College, Position

1960 None
1961 Bob Lilly, Texas Christian, DT
1962 Sonny Gibbs, Texas Christian, QB (2)
1963 Lee Roy Jordan, Alabama, LB
1964 Scott Appleton, Texas, DT
1965 Craig Morton, California, QB
1966 John Niland, Iowa, G
1967 Phil Clark, Northwestern, DB (3)
1968 Dennis Homan, Alabama, WR
1969 Calvin Hill, Yale, RB
1970 Duane Thomas, West Texas State, RB
1971 Tody Smith, Southern California, DE
1972 Bill Thomas, Boston College, RB
1973 Billy Joe DuPree, Michigan State, TE
1974 Ed (Too Tall) Jones, Tennessee State, DE
Charley Young, North Carolina State, RB
1975 Randy White, Maryland, LB
Thomas Henderson, Langston, LB
1976 Aaron Kyle, Wyoming, DB
1977 Tony Dorsett, Pittsburgh, RB
1978 Larry Bethea, Michigan State, DE
1979 Robert Shaw, Tennessee, C
1980 Bill Roe, Colorado, LB (3)
1981 Howard Richards, Missouri, T
1982 Rod Hill, Kentucky State, DB
1983 Jim Jeffcoat, Arizona State, DE
1984 Billy Cannon, Jr., Texas A&M, LB
1985 Kevin Brooks, Michigan, DE
1986 Mike Sherrard, UCLA, WR
1987 Danny Noonan, Nebraska, DT
1988 Michael Irvin, Miami, WR
1989 Troy Aikman, UCLA, QB
1990 Emmitt Smith, Florida, RB
1991 Russell Maryland, Miami, DT
Alvin Harper, Tennessee, WR
Kelvin Pritchett, Mississippi, DT
1992 Kevin Smith, Texas A&M, DB
Robert Jones, East Carolina, LB
1993 Kevin Williams, Miami, WR (2)
1994 Shante Carver, Arizona State, DE
1995 Sherman Williams, Alabama, RB (2)

DENVER BRONCOS

Year Player, College, Position

1960 Roger LeClerc, Trinity, Conn., C
1961 Bob Gaiters, New Mexico State, RB
1962 Merlin Olsen, Utah State, DT
1963 Kermit Alexander, UCLA, CB
1964 Bob Brown, Nebraska, T
1965 Dick Butkus, Illinois, LB (2)
1966 Jerry Shay, Purdue, DT
1967 Floyd Little, Syracuse, RB
1968 Curley Culp, Arizona State, DE (2)
1969 Grady Cavness, Texas-El Paso, DB (2)
1970 Bob Anderson, Colorado, RB
1971 Marv Montgomery, Southern California, T
1972 Riley Odoms, Houston, TE
1973 Otis Armstrong, Purdue, RB
1974 Randy Gradishar, Ohio State, LB
1975 Louis Wright, San Jose State, DB
1976 Tom Glassic, Virginia, G
1977 Steve Schindler, Boston College, G
1978 Don Latimer, Miami, DT
1979 Kelvin Clark, Nebraska, T
1980 Rulon Jones, Utah State, DE (2)
1981 Dennis Smith, Southern California, DB
1982 Gerald Willhite, San Jose State, RB
1983 Chris Hinton, Northwestern, G
1984 Andre Townsend, Mississippi, DE (2)
1985 Steve Sewell, Oklahoma, RB
1986 Jim Juriga, Illinois, T (4)
1987 Ricky Nattiel, Florida, WR
1988 Ted Gregory, Syracuse, NT
1989 Steve Atwater, Arkansas, DB
1990 Alton Montgomery, Houston, DB (2)
1991 Mike Croel, Nebraska, LB
1992 Tommy Maddox, UCLA, QB
1993 Dan Williams, Toledo, DE
1994 Allen Aldridge, Houston, LB (2)
1995 Jamie Brown, Florida A&M, T (4)

DETROIT LIONS

Year Player, College, Position

1936 Sid Wagner, Michigan State, G
1937 Lloyd Cardwell, Nebraska, B
1938 Alex Wojciechowicz, Fordham, C
1939 John Pingel, Michigan State, B
1940 Doyle Nave, Southern California, B
1941 Jim Thomason, Texas A&M, B
1942 Bob Westfall, Michigan, B
1943 Frank Sinkwich, Georgia, B
1944 Otto Graham, Northwestern, B
1945 Frank Szymanski, Notre Dame, C
1946 Bill Dellastatious, Missouri, B
1947 Glenn Davis, Army, B
1948 Y.A. Tittle, Louisiana State, B
1949 John Rauch, Georgia, B
1950 Leon Hart, Notre Dame, E
Joe Watson, Rice, C
1951 Dick Stanfel, San Francisco, G (2)
1952 Yale Lary, Texas A&M, B (3)
1953 Harley Sewell, Texas, G
1954 Dick Chapman, Rice, T
1955 Dave Middleton, Auburn, B
1956 Hopalong Cassady, Ohio State, B
1957 Bill Glass, Baylor, G
1958 Alex Karras, Iowa, T
1959 Nick Pietrosante, Notre Dame, B
1960 John Robinson, Louisiana State, S
1961 Danny LaRose, Missouri, T (2)
1962 John Hadl, Kansas, QB
1963 Daryl Sanders, Ohio State, T
1964 Pete Beathard, Southern California, QB
1965 Tom Nowatzke, Indiana, RB
1966 Nick Eddy, Notre Dame, RB (2)
1967 Mel Farr, UCLA, RB
1968 Greg Landry, Massachusetts, QB
Earl McCullouch, Southern California, WR
1969 Altie Taylor, Utah State, RB (2)
1970 Steve Owens, Oklahoma, RB
1971 Bob Bell, Cincinnati, DT
1972 Herb Orvis, Colorado, DE
1973 Ernie Price, Texas A&I, DE
1974 Ed O'Neil, Penn State, LB
1975 Lynn Boden, South Dakota State, G
1976 James Hunter, Grambling, DB
Lawrence Gaines, Wyoming, RB
1977 Walt Williams, New Mexico State, DB (2)
1978 Luther Bradley, Notre Dame, DB
1979 Keith Dorney, Penn State, T
1980 Billy Sims, Oklahoma, RB
1981 Mark Nichols, San Jose State, WR
1982 Jimmy Williams, Nebraska, LB
1983 James Jones, Florida, RB
1984 David Lewis, California, TE
1985 Lomas Brown, Florida, T
1986 Chuck Long, Iowa, QB
1987 Reggie Rogers, Washington, DE
1988 Bennie Blades, Miami, DB
1989 Barry Sanders, Oklahoma State, RB
1990 Andre Ware, Houston, QB
1991 Herman Moore, Virginia, WR
1992 Robert Porcher, South Carolina State, DE
1993 Ryan McNeil, Miami, DB (2)
1994 Johnnie Morton, Southern California, WR
1995 Luther Elliss, Utah, DT

GREEN BAY PACKERS

Year Player, College, Position

1936 Russ Letlow, San Francisco, G
1937 Eddie Jankowski, Wisconsin, B
1938 Cecil Isbell, Purdue, B
1939 Larry Buhler, Minnesota, B
1940 Harold Van Every, Minnesota, B
1941 George Paskvan, Wisconsin, B
1942 Urban Odson, Minnesota, T
1943 Dick Wildung, Minnesota, T
1944 Merv Pregulman, Michigan, G

1945 Walt Schlinkman, Texas Tech, B
1946 Johnny (Strike) Strzykalski, Marquette, B
1947 Ernie Case, UCLA, B
1948 Earl (Jug) Girard, Wisconsin, B
1949 Stan Heath, Nevada, B
1950 Clayton Tonnemaker, Minnesota, C
1951 Bob Gain, Kentucky, T
1952 Babe Parilli, Kentucky, QB
1953 Al Carmichael, Southern California, B
1954 Art Hunter, Notre Dame, T
Veryl Switzer, Kansas State, B
1955 Tom Bettis, Purdue, G
1956 Jack Losch, Miami, B
1957 Paul Hornung, Notre Dame, B
Ron Kramer, Michigan, E
1958 Dan Currie, Michigan State, C
1959 Randy Duncan, Iowa, B
1960 Tom Moore, Vanderbilt, RB
1961 Herb Adderley, Michigan State, CB
1962 Earl Gros, Louisiana State, RB
1963 Dave Robinson, Penn State, LB
1964 Lloyd Voss, Nebraska, DT
1965 Donny Anderson, Texas Tech, RB
Lawrence Elkins, Baylor, E
1966 Jim Grabowski, Illinois, RB
Gale Gillingham, Minnesota, T
1967 Bob Hyland, Boston College, C
Don Horn, San Diego State, QB
1968 Fred Carr, Texas-El Paso, LB
Bill Lueck, Arizona, G
1969 Rich Moore, Villanova, DT
1970 Mike McCoy, Notre Dame, DT
Rich McGeorge, Elon, TE
1971 John Brockington, Ohio State, RB
1972 Willie Buchanon, San Diego State, DB
Jerry Tagge, Nebraska, QB
1973 Barry Smith, Florida State, WR
1974 Barty Smith, Richmond, RB
1975 Bill Bain, Southern California, G (2)
1976 Mark Koncar, Colorado, T
1977 Mike Butler, Kansas, DE
Ezra Johnson, Morris Brown, DE
1978 James Lofton, Stanford, WR
John Anderson, Michigan, LB
1979 Eddie Lee Ivery, Georgia Tech, RB
1980 Bruce Clark, Penn State, DE
George Cumby, Oklahoma, LB
1981 Rich Campbell, California, QB
1982 Ron Hallstrom, Iowa, G
1983 Tim Lewis, Pittsburgh, DB
1984 Alphonso Carreker, Florida State, DE
1985 Ken Ruettgers, Southern California, T
1986 Kenneth Davis, Texas Christian, RB (2)
1987 Brent Fullwood, Auburn, RB
1988 Sterling Sharpe, South Carolina, WR
1989 Tony Mandarich, Michigan State, T
1990 Tony Bennett, Mississippi, LB
Darrell Thompson, Minnesota, RB
1991 Vinnie Clark, Ohio State, DB
1992 Terrell Buckley, Florida State, DB
1993 Wayne Simmons, Clemson, LB
George Teague, Alabama, DB
1994 Aaron Taylor, Notre Dame, T
1995 Craig Newsome, Arizona State, DB

HOUSTON OILERS

Year Player, College, Position
1960 Billy Cannon, Louisiana State, RB
1961 Mike Ditka, Pittsburgh, E
1962 Ray Jacobs, Howard Payne, DT
1963 Danny Brabham, Arkansas, LB
1964 Scott Appleton, Texas, DT
1965 Lawrence Elkins, Baylor, WR
1966 Tommy Nobis, Texas, LB
1967 George Webster, Michigan State, LB
Tom Regner, Notre Dame, G
1968 Mac Haik, Mississippi, WR (2)
1969 Ron Pritchard, Arizona State, LB
1970 Doug Wilkerson, N. Carolina Central, G
1971 Dan Pastorini, Santa Clara, QB
1972 Greg Sampson, Stanford, DE
1973 John Matuszak, Tampa, DE
George Amundson, Iowa State, RB
1974 Steve Manstedt, Nebraska, LB (4)
1975 Robert Brazile, Jackson State, LB
Don Hardeman, Texas A&I, RB
1976 Mike Barber, Louisiana Tech, TE (2)
1977 Morris Towns, Missouri, T
1978 Earl Campbell, Texas, RB
1979 Mike Stensrud, Iowa State, DE (2)
1980 Angelo Fields, Michigan State, T (2)
1981 Michael Holston, Morgan State, WR (3)
1982 Mike Munchak, Penn State, G
1983 Bruce Matthews, Southern California, T
1984 Dean Steinkuhler, Nebraska, T
1985 Ray Childress, Texas A&M, DE
Richard Johnson, Wisconsin, DB
1986 Jim Everett, Purdue, QB
1987 Alonzo Highsmith, Miami, RB
Haywood Jeffires, North Carolina St., WR
1988 Lorenzo White, Michigan State, RB
1989 David Williams, Florida, T
1990 Lamar Lathon, Houston, LB
1991 Mike Dumas, Indiana, DB (2)
1992 Eddie Robinson, Alabama State, LB (2)
1993 Brad Hopkins, Illinois, T
1994 Henry Ford, Arkansas, DE
1995 Steve McNair, Alcorn State, QB

INDIANAPOLIS COLTS

Year Player, College, Position
1953 Billy Vessels, Oklahoma, B
1954 Cotton Davidson, Baylor, B
1955 George Shaw, Oregon, B
Alan Ameche, Wisconsin, FB
1956 Lenny Moore, Penn State, B
1957 Jim Parker, Ohio State, G
1958 Lenny Lyles, Louisville, B
1959 Jackie Burkett, Auburn, C
1960 Ron Mix, Southern California, T
1961 Tom Matte, Ohio State, RB
1962 Wendell Harris, Louisiana State, S
1963 Bob Vogel, Ohio State, T
1964 Marv Woodson, Indiana, CB
1965 Mike Curtis, Duke, LB
1966 Sam Ball, Kentucky, T
1967 Bubba Smith, Michigan State, DT
Jim Detwiler, Michigan, RB
1968 John Williams, Minnesota, G
1969 Eddie Hinton, Oklahoma, WR
1970 Norman Bulaich, Texas Christian, RB
1971 Don McCauley, North Carolina, RB
Leonard Dunlap, North Texas State, DB
1972 Tom Drougas, Oregon, T
1973 Bert Jones, Louisiana State, QB
Joe Ehrmann, Syracuse, DT
1974 John Dutton, Nebraska, DE
Roger Carr, Louisiana Tech, WR
1975 Ken Huff, North Carolina, G
1976 Ken Novak, Purdue, DT
1977 Randy Burke, Kentucky, WR
1978 Reese McCall, Auburn, TE
1979 Barry Krauss, Alabama, LB
1980 Curtis Dickey, Texas A&M, RB
Derrick Hatchett, Texas, DB
1981 Randy McMillan, Pittsburgh, RB
Donnell Thompson, North Carolina, DT
1982 Johnie Cooks, Mississippi State, LB
Art Schlichter, Ohio State, QB
1983 John Elway, Stanford, QB
1984 Leonard Coleman, Vanderbilt, DB
Ron Solt, Maryland, G
1985 Duane Bickett, Southern California, LB
1986 Jon Hand, Alabama, DE
1987 Cornelius Bennett, Alabama, LB
1988 Chris Chandler, Washington, QB (3)
1989 Andre Rison, Michigan State, WR
1990 Jeff George, Illinois, QB
1991 Shane Curry, Miami, DE (2)
1992 Steve Emtman, Washington, DT
Quentin Coryatt, Texas A&M, LB
1993 Sean Dawkins, California, WR
1994 Marshall Faulk, San Diego State, RB
Trev Alberts, Nebraska, LB
1995 Ellis Johnson, Florida, DT

JACKSONVILLE JAGUARS

Year Player, College, Position
1995 Tony Boselli, Southern California, T
James Stewart, Tennessee, RB

KANSAS CITY CHIEFS

Year Player, College, Position
1960 Don Meredith, Southern Methodist, QB
1961 E.J. Holub, Texas Tech, C
1962 Ronnie Bull, Baylor, RB
1963 Buck Buchanan, Grambling, DT
Ed Budde, Michigan State, G
1964 Pete Beathard, Southern California, QB
1965 Gale Sayers, Kansas, RB
1966 Aaron Brown, Minnesota, DE
1967 Gene Trosch, Miami, DE-DT
1968 Mo Moorman, Texas A&M, G
George Daney, Texas-El Paso, G
1969 Jim Marsalis, Tennessee State, CB
1970 Sid Smith, Southern California, T
1971 Elmo Wright, Houston, WR
1972 Jeff Kinney, Nebraska, RB
1973 Gary Butler, Rice, TE (2)
1974 Woody Green, Arizona State, RB
1975 Elmore Stephens, Kentucky, TE (2)
1976 Rod Walters, Iowa, G
1977 Gary Green, Baylor, DB
1978 Art Still, Kentucky, DE
1979 Mike Bell, Colorado State, DE
Steve Fuller, Clemson, QB
1980 Brad Budde, Southern California, G
1981 Willie Scott, South Carolina, TE
1982 Anthony Hancock, Tennessee, WR
1983 Todd Blackledge, Penn State, QB
1984 Bill Maas, Pittsburgh, DT
John Alt, Iowa, T
1985 Ethan Horton, North Carolina, RB
1986 Brian Jozwiak, West Virginia, T
1987 Paul Palmer, Temple, RB
1988 Neil Smith, Nebraska, DE
1989 Derrick Thomas, Alabama, LB
1990 Percy Snow, Michigan State, LB
1991 Harvey Williams, Louisiana State, RB
1992 Dale Carter, Tennessee, DB
1993 Will Shields, Nebraska, G (3)
1994 Greg Hill, Texas A&M, RB
1995 Trezelle Jenkins, Michigan, T

LOS ANGELES RAIDERS

Year Player, College, Position
1960 Dale Hackbart, Wisconsin, CB
1961 Joe Rutgens, Illinois, DT
1962 Roman Gabriel, North Carolina State, QB
1963 George Wilson, Alabama, RB (6)
1964 Tony Lorick, Arizona State, RB
1965 Harry Schuh, Memphis State, T
1966 Rodger Bird, Kentucky, S
1967 Gene Upshaw, Texas A&I, G
1968 Eldridge Dickey, Tennessee State, QB
1969 Art Thoms, Syracuse, DT
1970 Raymond Chester, Morgan State, TE
1971 Jack Tatum, Ohio State, S
1972 Mike Siani, Villanova, WR
1973 Ray Guy, Southern Mississippi, P
1974 Henry Lawrence, Florida A&M, T
1975 Neal Colzie, Ohio State, DB
1976 Charles Philyaw, Texas Southern, DT (2)
1977 Mike Davis, Colorado, DB (2)
1978 Dave Browning, Washington, DE (2)
1979 Willie Jones, Florida State, DE (2)
1980 Marc Wilson, Brigham Young, QB
1981 Ted Watts, Texas Tech, DB
Curt Marsh, Washington, T
1982 Marcus Allen, Southern California, RB
1983 Don Mosebar, Southern California, T
1984 Sean Jones, Northeastern, DE (2)
1985 Jessie Hester, Florida State, WR
1986 Bob Buczkowski, Pittsburgh, DE
1987 John Clay, Missouri, T
1988 Tim Brown, Notre Dame, WR
Terry McDaniel, Tennessee, DB
Scott Davis, Illinois, DE
1989 Jeff Francis, Tennessee, QB (6)

FIRST-ROUND SELECTIONS

1990 Anthony Smith, Arizona, DE
1991 Todd Marinovich, Southern California, QB
1992 Chester McGlockton, Clemson, DE
1993 Patrick Bates, Texas A&M, DB
1994 Rob Fredrickson, Michigan State, LB
1995 Napoleon Kaufman, Washington, RB

MIAMI DOLPHINS

Year	Player, College, Position
1966	Jim Grabowski, Illinois, RB
	Rick Norton, Kentucky, QB
1967	Bob Griese, Purdue, QB
1968	Larry Csonka, Syracuse, RB
	Doug Crusan, Indiana, T
1969	Bill Stanfill, Georgia, DE
1970	Jim Mandich, Michigan, TE (2)
1971	Otto Stowe, Iowa State, WR (2)
1972	Mike Kadish, Notre Dame, DT
1973	Chuck Bradley, Oregon, C (2)
1974	Donald Reese, Jackson State, DE
1975	Darryl Carlton, Tampa, T
1976	Larry Gordon, Arizona State, LB
	Kim Bokamper, San Jose State, LB
1977	A.J. Duhe, Louisiana State, DT
1978	Guy Benjamin, Stanford, QB (2)
1979	Jon Giesler, Michigan, T
1980	Don McNeal, Alabama, DB
1981	David Overstreet, Oklahoma, RB
1982	Roy Foster, Southern California, G
1983	Dan Marino, Pittsburgh, QB
1984	Jackie Shipp, Oklahoma, LB
1985	Lorenzo Hampton, Florida, RB
1986	John Offerdahl, Western Michigan, LB (2)
1987	John Bosa, Boston College, DE
1988	Eric Kumerow, Ohio State, DE
1989	Sammie Smith, Florida State, RB
	Louis Oliver, Florida, DB
1990	Richmond Webb, Texas A&M, T
1991	Randal Hill, Miami, WR
1992	Troy Vincent, Wisconsin, DB
	Marco Coleman, Georgia Tech, LB
1993	O.J. McDuffie, Penn State, WR
1994	Tim Bowens, Mississippi, DT
1995	Billy Milner, Houston, T

MINNESOTA VIKINGS

Year	Player, College, Position
1961	Tommy Mason, Tulane, RB
1962	Bill Miller, Miami, WR (3)
1963	Jim Dunaway, Mississippi, T
1964	Carl Eller, Minnesota, DE
1965	Jack Snow, Notre Dame, WR
1966	Jerry Shay, Purdue, DT
1967	Clint Jones, Michigan State, RB
	Gene Washington, Michigan State, WR
	Alan Page, Notre Dame, DT
1968	Ron Yary, Southern California, T
1969	Ed White, California, G (2)
1970	John Ward, Oklahoma State, DT
1971	Leo Hayden, Ohio State, RB
1972	Jeff Siemon, Stanford, LB
1973	Chuck Foreman, Miami, RB
1974	Fred McNeill, UCLA, LB
	Steve Riley, Southern California, T
1975	Mark Mullaney, Colorado State, DE
1976	James White, Oklahoma State, DT
1977	Tommy Kramer, Rice, QB
1978	Randy Holloway, Pittsburgh, DE
1979	Ted Brown, North Carolina State, RB
1980	Doug Martin, Washington, DT
1981	Mardye McDole, Mississippi State, WR (2)
1982	Darrin Nelson, Stanford, RB
1983	Joey Browner, Southern California, DB
1984	Keith Millard, Washington State, DE
1985	Chris Doleman, Pittsburgh, LB
1986	Gerald Robinson, Auburn, DE
1987	D.J. Dozier, Penn State, RB
1988	Randall McDaniel, Arizona State, G
1989	David Braxton, Wake Forest, LB (2)
1990	Mike Jones, Texas A&M, TE (3)
1991	Carlos Jenkins, Michigan State, LB (3)
1992	Robert Harris, Southern University, DE (2)
1993	Robert Smith, Ohio State, RB
1994	DeWayne Washington, N. Carolina St., DB
	Todd Steussie, California, T
1995	Derrick Alexander, Florida State, DE
	Korey Stringer, Ohio State, T

NEW ENGLAND PATRIOTS

Year	Player, College, Position
1960	Ron Burton, Northwestern, RB
1961	Tommy Mason, Tulane, RB
1962	Gary Collins, Maryland, WR
1963	Art Graham, Boston College, WR
1964	Jack Concannon, Boston College, QB
1965	Jerry Rush, Michigan State, DE
1966	Karl Singer, Purdue, T
1967	John Charles, Purdue, S
1968	Dennis Byrd, North Carolina State, DE
1969	Ron Sellers, Florida State, WR
1970	Phil Olsen, Utah State, DE
1971	Jim Plunkett, Stanford, QB
1972	Tom Reynolds, San Diego State, WR (2)
1973	John Hannah, Alabama, G
	Sam Cunningham, So. California, RB
	Darryl Stingley, Purdue, WR
1974	Steve Corbett, Boston College, G (2)
1975	Russ Francis, Oregon, TE
1976	Mike Haynes, Arizona State, DB
	Pete Brock, Colorado, C
	Tim Fox, Ohio State, DB
1977	Raymond Clayborn, Texas, DB
	Stanley Morgan, Tennessee, WR
1978	Bob Cryder, Alabama, G
1979	Rick Sanford, South Carolina, DB
1980	Roland James, Tennessee, DB
	Vagas Ferguson, Notre Dame, RB
1981	Brian Holloway, Stanford, T
1982	Kenneth Sims, Texas, DT
	Lester Williams, Miami, DT
1983	Tony Eason, Illinois, QB
1984	Irving Fryar, Nebraska, WR
1985	Trevor Matich, Brigham Young, C
1986	Reggie Dupard, Southern Methodist, RB
1987	Bruce Armstrong, Louisville, T
1988	John Stephens, Northwestern St., La., RB
1989	Hart Lee Dykes, Oklahoma State, WR
1990	Chris Singleton, Arizona, LB
	Ray Agnew, North Carolina State, DE
1991	Pat Harlow, Southern California, T
	Leonard Russell, Arizona State, RB
1992	Eugene Chung, Virginia Tech, T
1993	Drew Bledsoe, Washington State, QB
1994	Willie McGinest, Southern California, DE
1995	Ty Law, Michigan, DB

NEW ORLEANS SAINTS

Year	Player, College, Position
1967	Les Kelley, Alabama, RB
1968	Kevin Hardy, Notre Dame, DE
1969	John Shinners, Xavier, G
1970	Ken Burrough, Texas Southern, WR
1971	Archie Manning, Mississippi, QB
1972	Royce Smith, Georgia, G
1973	Derland Moore, Oklahoma, DE (2)
1974	Rick Middleton, Ohio State, LB
1975	Larry Burton, Purdue, WR
	Kurt Schumacher, Ohio State, T
1976	Chuck Muncie, California, RB
1977	Joe Campbell, Maryland, DE
1978	Wes Chandler, Florida, WR
1979	Russell Erxleben, Texas, P-K
1980	Stan Brock, Colorado, T
1981	George Rogers, South Carolina, RB
1982	Lindsay Scott, Georgia, WR
1983	Steve Korte, Arkansas, G (2)
1984	James Geathers, Wichita State, DE
1985	Alvin Toles, Tennessee, LB
1986	Jim Dombrowski, Virginia, T
1987	Shawn Knight, Brigham Young, DT
1988	Craig Heyward, Pittsburgh, RB
1989	Wayne Martin, Arkansas, DE
1990	Renaldo Turnbull, West Virginia, DE
1991	Wesley Carroll, Miami, WR (2)
1992	Vaughn Dunbar, Indiana, RB
1993	Willie Roaf, Louisiana Tech, T
	Irv Smith, Notre Dame, TE
1994	Joe Johnson, Louisville, DE
1995	Mark Fields, Washington State, LB

NEW YORK GIANTS

Year	Player, College, Position
1936	Art Lewis, Ohio U., T
1937	Ed Widseth, Minnesota, T
1938	George Karamatic, Gonzaga, B
1939	Walt Neilson, Arizona, B
1940	Grenville Lansdell, Southern California, B
1941	George Franck, Minnesota, B
1942	Merle Hapes, Mississippi, B
1943	Steve Filipowicz, Fordham, B
1944	Billy Hillenbrand, Indiana, B
1945	Elmer Barbour, Wake Forest, B
1946	George Connor, Notre Dame, T
1947	Vic Schwall, Northwestern, B
1948	Tony Minisi, Pennsylvania, B
1949	Paul Page, Southern Methodist, B
1950	Travis Tidwell, Auburn, B
1951	Kyle Rote, Southern Methodist, B
	Jim Spavital, Oklahoma A&M, B
1952	Frank Gifford, Southern California, B
1953	Bobby Marlow, Alabama, B
1954	Ken Buck, Pacific, C (2)
1955	Joe Heap, Notre Dame, B
1956	Henry Moore, Arkansas, B (2)
1957	Sam DeLuca, South Carolina, T (2)
1958	Phil King, Vanderbilt, B
1959	Lee Grosscup, Utah, B
1960	Lou Cordileone, Clemson, G
1961	Bruce Tarbox, Syracuse, G (2)
1962	Jerry Hillebrand, Colorado, LB
1963	Frank Lasky, Florida, T (2)
1964	Joe Don Looney, Oklahoma, RB
1965	Tucker Frederickson, Auburn, RB
1966	Francis Peay, Missouri, T
1967	Louis Thompson, Alabama, DT (4)
1968	Dick Buzin, Penn State, T (2)
1969	Fred Dryer, San Diego State, DE
1970	Jim Files, Oklahoma, LB
1971	Rocky Thompson, West Texas State, WR
1972	Eldridge Small, Texas A&I, DB
	Larry Jacobson, Nebraska, DE
1973	Brad Van Pelt, Michigan State, LB (2)
1974	John Hicks, Ohio State, G
1975	Al Simpson, Colorado State, T (2)
1976	Troy Archer, Colorado, DE
1977	Gary Jeter, Southern California, DT
1978	Gordon King, Stanford, T
1979	Phil Simms, Morehead State, QB
1980	Mark Haynes, Colorado, DB
1981	Lawrence Taylor, North Carolina, LB
1982	Butch Woolfolk, Michigan, RB
1983	Terry Kinard, Clemson, DB
1984	Carl Banks, Michigan State, LB
	William Roberts, Ohio State, T
1985	George Adams, Kentucky, RB
1986	Eric Dorsey, Notre Dame, DE
1987	Mark Ingram, Michigan State, WR
1988	Eric Moore, Indiana, T
1989	Brian Williams, Minnesota, C-G
1990	Rodney Hampton, Georgia, RB
1991	Jarrod Bunch, Michigan, RB
1992	Derek Brown, Notre Dame, TE
1993	Michael Strahan, Texas Southern, DE (2)
1994	Thomas Lewis, Indiana, WR
1995	Tyrone Wheatley, Michigan, RB

NEW YORK JETS

Year	Player, College, Position
1960	George Izo, Notre Dame, QB
1961	Tom Brown, Minnesota, G
1962	Sandy Stephens, Minnesota, QB
1963	Jerry Stovall, Louisiana State, S
1964	Matt Snell, Ohio State, RB
1965	Joe Namath, Alabama, QB
	Tom Nowatzke, Indiana, RB
1966	Bill Yearby, Michigan, DT
1967	Paul Seiler, Notre Dame, T
1968	Lee White, Weber State, RB
1969	Dave Foley, Ohio State, T

1970 Steve Tannen, Florida, CB
1971 John Riggins, Kansas, RB
1972 Jerome Barkum, Jackson State, WR
Mike Taylor, Michigan, LB
1973 Burgess Owens, Miami, DB
1974 Carl Barzilauskas, Indiana, DT
1975 Anthony Davis, Southern California, RB (2)
1976 Richard Todd, Alabama, QB
1977 Marvin Powell, Southern California, T
1978 Chris Ward, Ohio State, T
1979 Marty Lyons, Alabama, DE
1980 Johnny (Lam) Jones, Texas, WR
1981 Freeman McNeil, UCLA, RB
1982 Bob Crable, Notre Dame, LB
1983 Ken O'Brien, Cal-Davis, QB
1984 Russell Carter, Southern Methodist, DB
Ron Faurot, Arkansas, DE
1985 Al Toon, Wisconsin, WR
1986 Mike Haight, Iowa, T
1987 Roger Vick, Texas A&M, RB
1988 Dave Cadigan, Southern California, T
1989 Jeff Lageman, Virginia, LB
1990 Blair Thomas, Penn State, RB
1991 Browning Nagle, Louisville, QB (2)
1992 Johnny Mitchell, Nebraska, TE
1993 Marvin Jones, Florida State, LB
1994 Aaron Glenn, Texas A&M, DB
1995 Kyle Brady, Penn State, TE
Hugh Douglas, Central State, Ohio, DE

PHILADELPHIA EAGLES

Year	Player, College, Position
1936	Jay Berwanger, Chicago, B
1937	Sam Francis, Nebraska, B
1938	Jim McDonald, Ohio State, B
1939	Davey O'Brien, Texas Christian, B
1940	George McAfee, Duke, B
1941	Art Jones, Richmond, B (2)
1942	Pete Kmetovic, Stanford, B
1943	Joe Muha, Virginia Military, B
1944	Steve Van Buren, Louisiana State, B
1945	John Yonaker, Notre Dame, E
1946	Leo Riggs, Southern California, B
1947	Neill Armstrong, Oklahoma A&M, E
1948	Clyde (Smackover) Scott, Arkansas, B
1949	Chuck Bednarik, Pennsylvania, C
	Frank Tripucka, Notre Dame, B
1950	Harry (Bud) Grant, Minnesota, E
1951	Ebert Van Buren, Louisiana State, B
	Chet Mutryn, Xavier, B
1952	Johnny Bright, Drake, B
1953	Al Conway, Army, B (2)
1954	Neil Worden, Notre Dame, B
1955	Dick Bielski, Maryland, B
1956	Bob Pellegrini, Maryland, C
1957	Clarence Peaks, Michigan State, B
1958	Walt Kowalczyk, Michigan State, B
1959	J.D. Smith, Rice, T (2)
1960	Ron Burton, Northwestern, RB
1961	Art Baker, Syracuse, RB
1962	Pete Case, Georgia, G (2)
1963	Ed Budde, Michigan State, G
1964	Bob Brown, Nebraska, T
1965	Ray Rissmiller, Georgia, T (2)
1966	Randy Beisler, Indiana, DE
1967	Harry Jones, Arkansas, RB
1968	Tim Rossovich, Southern California, DE
1969	Leroy Keyes, Purdue, RB
1970	Steve Zabel, Oklahoma, TE
1971	Richard Harris, Grambling, DE
1972	John Reaves, Florida, QB
1973	Jerry Sisemore, Texas, T
	Charle Young, Southern California, TE
1974	Mitch Sutton, Kansas, DT (3)
1975	Bill Capraun, Miami, T (7)
1976	Mike Smith, Florida, DE (4)
1977	Skip Sharp, Kansas, DB (5)
1978	Reggie Wilkes, Georgia Tech, LB (3)
1979	Jerry Robinson, UCLA, LB
1980	Roynell Young, Alcorn State, DB
1981	Leonard Mitchell, Houston, DE
1982	Mike Quick, North Carolina State, WR
1983	Michael Haddix, Mississippi State, RB
1984	Kenny Jackson, Penn State, WR
1985	Kevin Allen, Indiana, T
1986	Keith Byars, Ohio State, RB
1987	Jerome Brown, Miami, DT
1988	Keith Jackson, Oklahoma, TE
1989	Jessie Small, Eastern Kentucky, LB (2)
1990	Ben Smith, Georgia, DB
1991	Antone Davis, Tennessee, T
1992	Siran Stacy, Alabama, RB (2)
1993	Lester Holmes, Jackson State, T
	Leonard Renfro, Colorado, DT
1994	Bernard Williams, Georgia, T
1995	Mike Mamula, Boston College, DE

PITTSBURGH STEELERS

Year	Player, College, Position
1936	Bill Shakespeare, Notre Dame, B
1937	Mike Basrak, Duquesne, C
1938	Byron (Whizzer) White, Colorado, B
1939	Bill Patterson, Baylor, B (3)
1940	Kay Eakin, Arkansas, B
1941	Chet Gladchuk, Boston College, C (2)
1942	Bill Dudley, Virginia, B
1943	Bill Daley, Minnesota, B
1944	Johnny Podesto, St. Mary's, Calif., B
1945	Paul Duhart, Florida, B
1946	Felix (Doc) Blanchard, Army, B
1947	Hub Bechtol, Texas, E
1948	Dan Edwards, Georgia, E
1949	Bobby Gage, Clemson, B
1950	Lynn Chandnois, Michigan State, B
1951	Butch Avinger, Alabama, B
1952	Ed Modzelewski, Maryland, B
1953	Ted Marchibroda, St. Bonaventure, B
1954	Johnny Lattner, Notre Dame, B
1955	Frank Varrichione, Notre Dame, T
1956	Gary Glick, Colorado A&M, B
	Art Davis, Mississippi State, B
1957	Len Dawson, Purdue, B
1958	Larry Krutko, West Virginia, B (2)
1959	Tom Barnett, Purdue, B (8)
1960	Jack Spikes, Texas Christian, RB
1961	Myron Pottios, Notre Dame, LB (2)
1962	Bob Ferguson, Ohio State, RB
1963	Frank Atkinson, Stanford, T (8)
1964	Paul Martha, Pittsburgh, S
1965	Roy Jefferson, Utah, WR (2)
1966	Dick Leftridge, West Virginia, RB
1967	Don Shy, San Diego State, RB (2)
1968	Mike Taylor, Southern California, T
1969	Joe Greene, North Texas State, DT
1970	Terry Bradshaw, Louisiana Tech, QB
1971	Frank Lewis, Grambling, WR
1972	Franco Harris, Penn State, RB
1973	J.T. Thomas, Florida State, DB
1974	Lynn Swann, Southern California, WR
1975	Dave Brown, Michigan, DB
1976	Bennie Cunningham, Clemson, TE
1977	Robin Cole, New Mexico, LB
1978	Ron Johnson, Eastern Michigan, DB
1979	Greg Hawthorne, Baylor, RB
1980	Mark Malone, Arizona State, QB
1981	Keith Gary, Oklahoma, DE
1982	Walter Abercrombie, Baylor, RB
1983	Gabriel Rivera, Texas Tech, DT
1984	Louis Lipps, Southern Mississippi, WR
1985	Darryl Sims, Wisconsin, DE
1986	John Rienstra, Temple, G
1987	Rod Woodson, Purdue, DB
1988	Aaron Jones, Eastern Kentucky, DE
1989	Tim Worley, Georgia, RB
	Tom Ricketts, Pittsburgh, T
1990	Eric Green, Liberty, TE
1991	Huey Richardson, Florida, DE
1992	Leon Searcy, Miami, T
1993	Deon Figures, Colorado, DB
1994	Charles Johnson, Colorado, WR
1995	Mark Bruener, Washington, TE

ST. LOUIS RAMS

Year	Player, College, Position
1937	Johnny Drake, Purdue, B
1938	Corbett Davis, Indiana, B
1939	Parker Hall, Mississippi, B
1940	Ollie Cordill, Rice, B
1941	Rudy Mucha, Washington, C
1942	Jack Wilson, Baylor, B
1943	Mike Holovak, Boston College, B
1944	Tony Butkovich, Illinois, B
1945	Elroy (Crazylegs) Hirsch, Wisconsin, B
1946	Emil Sitko, Notre Dame, B
1947	Herman Wedemeyer, St. Mary's, Calif., B
1948	Tom Keane, West Virginia, B (2)
1949	Bobby Thomason, Virginia Military, B
1950	Ralph Pasquariello, Villanova, B
	Stan West, Oklahoma, G
1951	Bud McFadin, Texas, G
1952	Bill Wade, Vanderbilt, QB
	Bob Carey, Michigan State, E
1953	Donn Moomaw, UCLA, C
	Ed Barker, Washington State, E
1954	Ed Beatty, Cincinnati, C
1955	Larry Morris, Georgia Tech, C
1956	Joe Marconi, West Virginia, B
	Charles Horton, Vanderbilt, B
1957	Jon Arnett, Southern California, B
	Del Shofner, Baylor, E
1958	Lou Michaels, Kentucky, T
	Jim Phillips, Auburn, E
1959	Dick Bass, Pacific, B
	Paul Dickson, Baylor, T
1960	Billy Cannon, Louisiana State, RB
1961	Marlin McKeever, So. California, E-LB
1962	Roman Gabriel, North Carolina State, QB
	Merlin Olsen, Utah State, DT
1963	Terry Baker, Oregon State, QB
	Rufus Guthrie, Georgia Tech, G
1964	Bill Munson, Utah State, QB
1965	Clancy Williams, Washington State, CB
1966	Tom Mack, Michigan, G
1967	Willie Ellison, Texas Southern, RB (2)
1968	Gary Beban, UCLA, QB (2)
1969	Larry Smith, Florida, RB
	Jim Seymour, Notre Dame, WR
	Bob Klein, Southern California, TE
1970	Jack Reynolds, Tennessee, LB
1971	Isiah Robertson, Southern, LB
	Jack Youngblood, Florida, DE
1972	Jim Bertelsen, Texas, RB (2)
1973	Cullen Bryant, Colorado, DB (2)
1974	John Cappelletti, Penn State, RB
1975	Mike Fanning, Notre Dame, DT
	Dennis Harrah, Miami, T
	Doug France, Ohio State, T
1976	Kevin McLain, Colorado State, LB
1977	Bob Brudzinski, Ohio State, LB
1978	Elvis Peacock, Oklahoma, RB
1979	George Andrews, Nebraska, LB
	Kent Hill, Georgia Tech, T
1980	Johnnie Johnson, Texas, DB
1981	Mel Owens, Michigan, LB
1982	Barry Redden, Richmond, RB
1983	Eric Dickerson, Southern Methodist, RB
1984	Hal Stephens, East Carolina, DE (5)
1985	Jerry Gray, Texas, DB
1986	Mike Schad, Queen's University, Canada, T
1987	Donald Evans, Winston-Salem, DE (2)
1988	Gaston Green, UCLA, RB
	Aaron Cox, Arizona State, WR
1989	Bill Hawkins, Miami, DE
	Cleveland Gary, Miami, RB
1990	Bern Brostek, Washington, C
1991	Todd Lyght, Notre Dame, DB
1992	Sean Gilbert, Pittsburgh, DE
1993	Jerome Bettis, Notre Dame, RB
1994	Wayne Gandy, Auburn, T
1995	Kevin Carter, Florida, DE

SAN DIEGO CHARGERS

Year	Player, College, Position
1960	Monty Stickles, Notre Dame, E
1961	Earl Faison, Indiana, DE
1962	Bob Ferguson, Ohio State, RB
1963	Walt Sweeney, Syracuse, G
1964	Ted Davis, Georgia Tech, LB
1965	Steve DeLong, Tennessee, DE

FIRST-ROUND SELECTIONS

1966 Don Davis, Cal State-Los Angeles, DT
1967 Ron Billingsley, Wyoming, DE
1968 Russ Washington, Missouri, DT
Jimmy Hill, Texas A&I, DB
1969 Marty Domres, Columbia, QB
Bob Babich, Miami, Ohio, LB
1970 Walker Gillette, Richmond, WR
1971 Leon Burns, Long Beach State, RB
1972 Pete Lazetich, Stanford, DE (2)
1973 Johnny Rodgers, Nebraska, WR
1974 Bo Matthews, Colorado, RB
Don Goode, Kansas, LB
1975 Gary Johnson, Grambling, DT
Mike Williams, Louisiana State, DB
1976 Joe Washington, Oklahoma, RB
1977 Bob Rush, Memphis State, C
1978 John Jefferson, Arizona State, WR
1979 Kellen Winslow, Missouri, TE
1980 Ed Luther, San Jose State, QB (4)
1981 James Brooks, Auburn, RB
1982 Hollis Hall, Clemson, DB (7)
1983 Billy Ray Smith, Arkansas, LB
Gary Anderson, Arkansas, WR
Gill Byrd, San Jose State, DB
1984 Mossy Cade, Texas, DB
1985 Jim Lachey, Ohio State, G
1986 Leslie O'Neal, Oklahoma State, DE
James FitzPatrick, Southern California, T
1987 Rod Bernstine, Texas A&M, TE
1988 Anthony Miller, Tennessee, WR
1989 Burt Grossman, Pittsburgh, DE
1990 Junior Seau, Southern California, LB
1991 Stanley Richard, Texas, DB
1992 Chris Mims, Tennessee, DE
1993 Darrien Gordon, Stanford, DB
1994 Isaac Davis, Arkansas, G (2)
1995 Terrance Shaw, Stephen F. Austin, DB (2)

SAN FRANCISCO 49ERS

Year Player, College, Position
1950 Leo Nomellini, Minnesota, T
1951 Y.A. Tittle, Louisiana State, B
1952 Hugh McElhenny, Washington, B
1953 Harry Babcock, Georgia, E
Tom Stolhandske, Texas, E
1954 Bernie Faloney, Maryland, B
1955 Dickie Moegle, Rice, B
1956 Earl Morrall, Michigan State, B
1957 John Brodie, Stanford, B
1958 Jim Pace, Michigan, B
Charlie Krueger, Texas A&M, T
1959 Dave Baker, Oklahoma, B
Dan James, Ohio State, C
1960 Monty Stickles, Notre Dame, E
1961 Jimmy Johnson, UCLA, CB
Bernie Casey, Bowling Green, WR
Bill Kilmer, UCLA, QB
1962 Lance Alworth, Arkansas, WR
1963 Kermit Alexander, UCLA, CB
1964 Dave Parks, Texas Tech, WR
1965 Ken Willard, North Carolina, RB
George Donnelly, Illinois, DB
1966 Stan Hindman, Mississippi, DE
1967 Steve Spurrier, Florida, QB
Cas Banaszek, Northwestern, T
1968 Forrest Blue, Auburn, C
1969 Ted Kwalick, Penn State, TE
Gene Washington, Stanford, WR
1970 Cedrick Hardman, North Texas State, DE
Bruce Taylor, Boston U., DB
1971 Tim Anderson, Ohio State, DB
1972 Terry Beasley, Auburn, WR
1973 Mike Holmes, Texas Southern, DB
1974 Wilbur Jackson, Alabama, RB
Bill Sandifer, UCLA, DT
1975 Jimmy Webb, Mississippi State, DT
1976 Randy Cross, UCLA, C (2)
1977 Elmo Boyd, Eastern Kentucky, WR (3)
1978 Ken MacAfee, Notre Dame, TE
Dan Bunz, Cal State-Long Beach, LB
1979 James Owens, UCLA, WR (2)
1980 Earl Cooper, Rice, RB
Jim Stuckey, Clemson, DT
1981 Ronnie Lott, Southern California, DB
1982 Bubba Paris, Michigan, T (2)
1983 Roger Craig, Nebraska, RB (2)
1984 Todd Shell, Brigham Young, LB
1985 Jerry Rice, Mississippi Valley State, WR
1986 Larry Roberts, Alabama, DE (2)
1987 Harris Barton, North Carolina, T
Terrence Flagler, Clemson, RB
1988 Danny Stubbs, Miami, DE (2)
1989 Keith DeLong, Tennessee, LB
1990 Dexter Carter, Florida State, RB
1991 Ted Washington, Louisville, DT
1992 Dana Hall, Washington, DB
1993 Dana Stubblefield, Kansas, DT
Todd Kelly, Tennessee, DE
1994 Bryant Young, Notre Dame, DT
William Floyd, Florida State, RB
1995 J.J. Stokes, UCLA, WR

SEATTLE SEAHAWKS

Year Player, College, Position
1976 Steve Niehaus, Notre Dame, DT
1977 Steve August, Tulsa, G
1978 Keith Simpson, Memphis State, DB
1979 Manu Tuiasosopo, UCLA, DT
1980 Jacob Green, Texas A&M, DE
1981 Ken Easley, UCLA, DB
1982 Jeff Bryant, Clemson, DE
1983 Curt Warner, Penn State, RB
1984 Terry Taylor, Southern Illinois, DB
1985 Owen Gill, Iowa, RB (2)
1986 John L. Williams, Florida, RB
1987 Tony Woods, Pittsburgh, LB
1988 Brian Blades, Miami, WR (2)
1989 Andy Heck, Notre Dame, T
1990 Cortez Kennedy, Miami, DT
1991 Dan McGwire, San Diego State, QB
1992 Ray Roberts, Virginia, T
1993 Rick Mirer, Notre Dame, QB
1994 Sam Adams, Texas A&M, DT
1995 Joey Galloway, Ohio State, WR

TAMPA BAY BUCCANEERS

Year Player, College, Position
1976 Lee Roy Selmon, Oklahoma, DT
1977 Ricky Bell, Southern California, RB
1978 Doug Williams, Grambling, QB
1979 Greg Roberts, Oklahoma, G (2)
1980 Ray Snell, Wisconsin, G
1981 Hugh Green, Pittsburgh, LB
1982 Sean Farrell, Penn State, G
1983 Randy Grimes, Baylor, C (2)
1984 Keith Browner, Southern California, LB (2)
1985 Ron Holmes, Washington, DE
1986 Bo Jackson, Auburn, RB
Roderick Jones, Southern Methodist, DB
1987 Vinny Testaverde, Miami, QB
1988 Paul Gruber, Wisconsin, T
1989 Broderick Thomas, Nebraska, LB
1990 Keith McCants, Alabama, LB
1991 Charles McRae, Tennessee, T
1992 Courtney Hawkins, Michigan State, WR (2)
1993 Eric Curry, Alabama, DE
1994 Trent Dilfer, Fresno State, QB
1995 Warren Sapp, Miami, DT
Derrick Brooks, Florida State, LB

WASHINGTON REDSKINS

Year Player, College, Position
1936 Riley Smith, Alabama, B
1937 Sammy Baugh, Texas Christian, B
1938 Andy Farkas, Detroit, B
1939 I.B. Hale, Texas Christian, T
1940 Ed Boell, New York U., B
1941 Forest Evashevski, Michigan, B
1942 Orban (Spec) Sanders, Texas, B
1943 Jack Jenkins, Missouri, B
1944 Mike Micka, Colgate, B
1945 Jim Hardy, Southern California, B
1946 Casl Rossi, UCLA, B*
1947 Casl Rossi, UCLA, B
1948 Harry Gilmer, Alabama, B
Lowell Tew, Alabama, B
1949 Rob Goode, Texas A&M, B
1950 George Thomas, Oklahoma, B
1951 Leon Heath, Oklahoma, B
1952 Larry Isbell, Baylor, B
1953 Jack Scarbath, Maryland, B
1954 Steve Meilinger, Kentucky, E
1955 Ralph Guglielmi, Notre Dame, B
1956 Ed Vereb, Maryland, B
1957 Don Bosseler, Miami, B
1958 Mike Sommer, George Washington, B (2)
1959 Don Allard, Boston College, B
1960 Richie Lucas, Penn State, QB
1961 Norman Snead, Wake Forest, QB
Joe Rutgens, Illinois, DT
1962 Ernie Davis, Syracuse, RB
1963 Pat Richter, Wisconsin, TE
1964 Charley Taylor, Arizona State, RB-WR
1965 Bob Breitenstein, Tulsa, T (2)
1966 Charlie Gogolak, Princeton, K
1967 Ray McDonald, Idaho, RB
1968 Jim Smith, Oregon, DB
1969 Eugene Epps, Texas-El Paso, DB (2)
1970 Bill Bundige, Colorado, DT (2)
1971 Cotton Speyrer, Texas, WR (2)
1972 Moses Denson, Maryland State, RB (8)
1973 Charles Cantrell, Lamar, G (5)
1974 Jon Keyworth, Colorado, TE (6)
1975 Mike Thomas, Nevada-Las Vegas, RB (6)
1976 Mike Hughes, Baylor, G (5)
1977 Duncan McColl, Stanford, DE (4)
1978 Tony Green, Florida, RB (6)
1979 Don Warren, San Diego State, TE (4)
1980 Art Monk, Syracuse, WR
1981 Mark May, Pittsburgh, T
1982 Vernon Dean, San Diego State, DB (2)
1983 Darrell Green, Texas A&I, DB
1984 Bob Slater, Oklahoma, DT (2)
1985 Tory Nixon, San Diego State, DB (2)
1986 Markus Koch, Boise State, DE (2)
1987 Brian Davis, Nebraska, DB (2)
1988 Chip Lohmiller, Minnesota, K (2)
1989 Tracy Rocker, Auburn, DT (3)
1990 Andre Collins, Penn State, LB (2)
1991 Bobby Wilson, Michigan State, DT
1992 Desmond Howard, Michigan, WR
1993 Tom Carter, Notre Dame, DB
1994 Heath Shuler, Tennessee, QB
1995 Michael Westbrook, Colorado, WR

**Choice lost due to ineligibility*

Records

ALL-TIME RECORDS

Compiled by Elias Sports Bureau

The following records reflect all available official information on the National Football League from its formation in 1920 to date. Also included are all applicable records from the American Football League, 1960-69.

Individuals eligible for Rookie records are players who were in their first season of professional football and had not been on the roster of another professional football team, including teams in other leagues, for any regular-season or postseason games in a previous season. Eligible players, therefore, include those who were under contract to a National Football League club for a previous season but were terminated prior to their club's first regular-season game and not re-signed, or who were placed on Reserve/Injured (or another category of the Reserve List) prior to their club's first regular-season game and were not activated during the rest of the regular season or postseason.

INDIVIDUAL RECORDS

SERVICE

Most Seasons

26 George Blanda, Chi. Bears, 1949, 1950-58; Baltimore, 1950; Houston, 1960-66; Oakland, 1967-75
21 Earl Morrall, San Francisco, 1956; Pittsburgh, 1957-58; Detroit, 1958-64; N.Y. Giants, 1965-67; Baltimore, 1968-71; Miami, 1972-76
20 Jim Marshall, Cleveland, 1960; Minnesota, 1961-79

Most Seasons, One Club

19 Jim Marshall, Minnesota, 1961-79
Jackie Slater, L.A. Rams, 1976-94
18 Jim Hart, St. Louis, 1966-83
Jeff Van Note, Atlanta, 1969-86
Pat Leahy, N.Y. Jets, 1974-91
17 Lou Groza, Cleveland, 1950-59, 1961-67
Johnny Unitas, Baltimore, 1956-72
John Brodie, San Francisco, 1957-73
Jim Bakken, St. Louis, 1962-78
Mick Tingelhoff, Minnesota, 1962-78
Mike Kenn, Atlanta, 1978-94

Most Games Played, Career

340 George Blanda, Chi. Bears, 1949, 1950-58; Baltimore, 1950; Houston, 1960-66; Oakland, 1967-75
282 Jim Marshall, Cleveland, 1960; Minnesota, 1961-79
263 Jan Stenerud, Kansas City, 1967-79; Green Bay, 1980-83; Minnesota, 1984-85

Most Consecutive Games Played, Career

282 Jim Marshall, Cleveland, 1960; Minnesota, 1961-79
240 Mick Tingelhoff, Minnesota, 1962-78
234 Jim Bakken, St. Louis, 1962-78

SCORING

Most Seasons Leading League

5 Don Hutson, Green Bay, 1940-44
Gino Cappelletti, Boston, 1961, 1963-66
3 Earl (Dutch) Clark, Portsmouth, 1932; Detroit, 1935-36
Pat Harder, Chi. Cardinals, 1947-49
Paul Hornung, Green Bay, 1959-61
2 Jack Manders, Chi. Bears, 1934, 1937
Gordy Soltau, San Francisco, 1952-53
Doak Walker, Detroit, 1950, 1955
Gene Mingo, Denver, 1960, 1962
Jim Turner, N.Y. Jets, 1968-69
Fred Cox, Minnesota, 1969-70
Chester Marcol, Green Bay, 1972, 1974
John Smith, New England, 1979-80

Most Consecutive Seasons Leading League

5 Don Hutson, Green Bay, 1940-44
4 Gino Cappelletti, Boston, 1963-66
3 Pat Harder, Chi. Cardinals, 1947-49
Paul Hornung, Green Bay, 1959-61

POINTS

Most Points, Career

2,002 George Blanda, Chi. Bears, 1949, 1950-58; Baltimore, 1950; Houston, 1960-66; Oakland, 1967-75 (9-td, 943-pat, 335-fg)
1,699 Jan Stenerud, Kansas City, 1967-79; Green Bay, 1980-83; Minnesota, 1984-85 (580-pat, 373-fg)
1,559 Nick Lowery, New England, 1978; Kansas City, 1980-93; N.Y. Jets, 1994

Most Points, Season

176 Paul Hornung, Green Bay, 1960 (15-td, 41-pat, 15-fg)
161 Mark Moseley, Washington, 1983 (62-pat, 33-fg)
155 Gino Cappelletti, Boston, 1964 (7-td, 38-pat, 25-fg)

Most Points, No Touchdowns, Season

161 Mark Moseley, Washington, 1983 (62-pat, 33-fg)
149 Chip Lohmiller, Washington, 1991 (56-pat, 31-fg)
145 Jim Turner, N.Y. Jets, 1968 (43-pat, 34-fg)

Most Seasons, 100 or More Points

11 Nick Lowery, Kansas City, 1981, 1983-86, 1988-93
9 Morten Andersen, New Orleans, 1985-89, 1991-94
8 Gary Anderson, Pittsburgh, 1983-85, 1988, 1991-94

Most Points, Rookie, Season

144 Kevin Butler, Chicago, 1985 (51-pat, 31-fg)
132 Gale Sayers, Chicago, 1965 (22-td)
128 Doak Walker, Detroit, 1950 (11-td, 38-pat, 8-fg)
Chester Marcol, Green Bay, 1972 (29-pat, 33-fg)

Most Points, Game

40 Ernie Nevers, Chi. Cardinals vs. Chi. Bears, Nov. 28, 1929 (6-td, 4-pat)
36 Dub Jones, Cleveland vs. Chi. Bears, Nov. 25, 1951 (6-td)
Gale Sayers, Chicago vs. San Francisco, Dec. 12, 1965 (6-td)
33 Paul Hornung, Green Bay vs. Baltimore, Oct. 8, 1961 (4-td, 6-pat, 1-fg)

Most Consecutive Games Scoring

186 Jim Breech, Oakland, 1979; Cincinnati, 1980-92
174 Morten Andersen, New Orleans, 1982-94 (current)
155 Ray Wersching, San Francisco, 1977-87

TOUCHDOWNS

Most Seasons Leading League

8 Don Hutson, Green Bay, 1935-38, 1941-44
3 Jim Brown, Cleveland, 1958-59, 1963
Lance Alworth, San Diego, 1964-66
2 By many players

Most Consecutive Seasons Leading League

4 Don Hutson, Green Bay, 1935-38, 1941-44
3 Lance Alworth, San Diego, 1964-66
2 By many players

Most Touchdowns, Career

139 Jerry Rice, San Francisco, 1985-94 (8-r, 131-p)
126 Jim Brown, Cleveland, 1957-65 (106-r, 20-p)
125 Walter Payton, Chicago, 1975-87 (110-r, 15-p)

Most Touchdowns, Season

24 John Riggins, Washington, 1983 (24-r)
23 O.J. Simpson, Buffalo, 1975 (16-r, 7-p)
Jerry Rice, San Francisco, 1987 (1-r, 22-p)
22 Gale Sayers, Chicago, 1965 (14-r, 6-p, 2-ret)
Chuck Foreman, Minnesota, 1975 (13-r, 9-p)
Emmitt Smith, Dallas, 1994 (21-r, 1-p)

Most Touchdowns, Rookie, Season

22 Gale Sayers, Chicago, 1965 (14-r, 6-p, 2-ret)
20 Eric Dickerson, L.A. Rams, 1983 (18-r, 2-p)
16 Billy Sims, Detroit, 1980 (13-r, 3-p)

Most Touchdowns, Game

6 Ernie Nevers, Chi. Cardinals vs. Chi. Bears, Nov. 28, 1929 (6-r)
Dub Jones, Cleveland vs. Chi. Bears, Nov. 25, 1951 (4-r, 2-p)
Gale Sayers, Chicago vs. San Francisco, Dec. 12, 1965 (4-r, 1-p, 1-ret)
5 Bob Shaw, Chi. Cardinals vs. Baltimore, Oct. 2, 1950 (5-p)
Jim Brown, Cleveland vs. Baltimore, Nov. 1, 1959 (5-r)
Abner Haynes, Dall. Texans vs. Oakland, Nov. 26, 1961 (4-r, 1-p)
Billy Cannon, Houston vs. N.Y. Titans, Dec. 10, 1961 (3-r, 2-p)
Cookie Gilchrist, Buffalo vs. N.Y. Jets, Dec. 8, 1963 (5-r)
Paul Hornung, Green Bay vs. Baltimore, Dec. 12, 1965 (3-r, 2-p)
Kellen Winslow, San Diego vs. Oakland, Nov. 22, 1981 (5-p)
Jerry Rice, San Francisco vs. Atlanta, Oct. 14, 1990 (5-p)
4 By many players. Last time: Mark Ingram, Miami vs. N.Y. Jets, Nov. 27, 1994 (4-p)

Most Consecutive Games Scoring Touchdowns

18 Lenny Moore, Baltimore, 1963-65
14 O.J. Simpson, Buffalo, 1975
13 John Riggins, Washington, 1982-83
George Rogers, Washington, 1985-86
Jerry Rice, San Francisco, 1986-87

POINTS AFTER TOUCHDOWN

Most Seasons Leading League

8 George Blanda, Chi. Bears, 1956; Houston, 1961-62; Oakland, 1967-69, 1972, 1974
4 Bob Waterfield, Cleveland, 1945; Los Angeles, 1946, 1950, 1952
3 Earl (Dutch) Clark, Portsmouth, 1932; Detroit, 1935-36
Jack Manders, Chi. Bears, 1933-35
Don Hutson, Green Bay, 1941-42, 1945

Most (Kicking) Points After Touchdown Attempted, Career

959 George Blanda, Chi. Bears, 1949, 1950-58; Baltimore, 1950; Houston, 1960-66; Oakland, 1967-75
657 Lou Groza, Cleveland, 1950-59, 1961-67
601 Jan Stenerud, Kansas City, 1967-79; Green Bay, 1980-83; Minnesota, 1984-85

Most (Kicking) Points After Touchdown Attempted, Season

70 Uwe von Schamann, Miami, 1984
65 George Blanda, Houston, 1961
63 Mark Moseley, Washington, 1983

Most (Kicking) Points After Touchdown Attempted, Game
10 Charlie Gogolak, Washington vs. N.Y. Giants, Nov. 27, 1966
9 Pat Harder, Chi. Cardinals vs. N.Y. Giants, Oct. 17, 1948; vs. N.Y. Bulldogs, Nov. 13, 1949
Bob Waterfield, Los Angeles vs. Baltimore, Oct. 22, 1950
Bob Thomas, Chicago vs. Green Bay, Dec. 7, 1980
8 By many players

Most (One-Point) Points After Touchdown, Career
943 George Blanda, Chi. Bears, 1949, 1950-58; Baltimore, 1950; Houston, 1960-66; Oakland, 1967-75
641 Lou Groza, Cleveland, 1950-59, 1961-67
580 Jan Stenerud, Kansas City, 1967-79; Green Bay, 1980-83; Minnesota, 1984-85

Most (One-Point) Points After Touchdown, Season
66 Uwe von Schamann, Miami, 1984
64 George Blanda, Houston, 1961
62 Mark Moseley, Washington, 1983

Most (One-Point) Points After Touchdown, Game
9 Pat Harder, Chi. Cardinals vs. N.Y. Giants, Oct. 17, 1948
Bob Waterfield, Los Angeles vs. Baltimore, Oct. 22, 1950
Charlie Gogolak, Washington vs. N.Y. Giants, Nov. 27, 1966
8 By many players

Most Consecutive (Kicking) Points After Touchdown
234 Tommy Davis, San Francisco, 1959-65
221 Jim Turner, N.Y. Jets, 1967-70; Denver, 1971-74
213 Chip Lohmiller, Washington, 1988-93

Highest (Kicking) Points After Touchdown Percentage, Career (200 points after touchdown)
99.43 Tommy Davis, San Francisco, 1959-69 (350-348)
99.05 Gary Anderson, Pittsburgh, 1982-94 (420-416)
99.03 Nick Lowery, New England, 1978; Kansas City, 1980-93; N.Y. Jets 1994 (517-512)

Most (Kicking) Points After Touchdown, No Misses, Season
56 Danny Villanueva, Dallas, 1966
Ray Wersching, San Francisco, 1984
Chip Lohmiller, Washington, 1991
54 Mike Clark, Dallas, 1968
George Blanda, Oakland, 1968
53 Pat Harder, Chi. Cardinals, 1948

Most (Kicking) Points After Touchdown, No Misses, Game
9 Pat Harder, Chi. Cardinals vs. N.Y. Giants, Oct. 17, 1948
Bob Waterfield, Los Angeles vs. Baltimore, Oct. 22, 1950
8 By many players

Most Two-Point Conversions, Career
4 Gino Cappelletti, Boston, 1960-69
3 Richie Lucas, Buffalo, 1960-61
Dave Kocourek, L.A. Chargers, 1960; San Diego, 1961-65; Miami, 1966; Oakland, 1967-68
Daryle Lamonica, Buffalo, 1963-66; Oakland, 1967-69
Bill Mathis, N.Y. Jets, 1960-69
Gene Prebola, Oakland, 1960; Denver, 1961-63
Ronnie Harmon, San Diego, 1994
Haywood Jeffires, Houston, 1994
Tom Tupa, Cleveland, 1994
2 By many players

Most Two-Point Conversions, Season
3 Gino Cappelletti, Boston, 1960
Richie Lucas, Buffalo, 1961
Ronnie Harmon, San Diego, 1994
Haywood Jeffires, Houston, 1994
Tom Tupa, Cleveland, 1994
2 By 12 players

Most Two-Point Conversions, Game
2 Brett Perriman, Detroit vs. Green Bay, Nov. 6, 1994

FIELD GOALS

Most Seasons Leading League
5 Lou Groza, Cleveland, 1950, 1952-54, 1957
4 Jack Manders, Chi. Bears, 1933-34, 1936-37
Ward Cuff, N.Y. Giants, 1938-39, 1943; Green Bay, 1947
Mark Moseley, Washington, 1976-77, 1979, 1982
3 Bob Waterfield, Los Angeles, 1947, 1949, 1951
Gino Cappelletti, Boston, 1961, 1963-64
Fred Cox, Minnesota, 1965, 1969-70
Jan Stenerud, Kansas City, 1967, 1970, 1975

Most Consecutive Seasons Leading League
3 Lou Groza, Cleveland, 1952-54
2 Jack Manders, Chi. Bears, 1933-34
Armand Niccolai, Pittsburgh, 1935-36
Jack Manders, Chi. Bears, 1936-37
Ward Cuff, N.Y. Giants, 1938-39
Clark Hinkle, Green Bay, 1940-41
Cliff Patton, Philadelphia, 1948-49
Gino Cappelletti, Boston, 1963-64
Jim Turner, N.Y. Jets, 1968-69
Fred Cox, Minnesota, 1969-70
Mark Moseley, Washington, 1976-77
Chip Lohmiller, Washington, 1991-92
Pete Stoyanovich, Miami, 1991-92

Most Field Goals Attempted, Career
637 George Blanda, Chi. Bears, 1949, 1950-58; Baltimore, 1950; Houston, 1960-66; Oakland, 1967-75
558 Jan Stenerud, Kansas City, 1967-79; Green Bay, 1980-83; Minnesota, 1984-85
488 Jim Turner, N.Y. Jets, 1964-70; Denver, 1971-79

Most Field Goals Attempted, Season
49 Bruce Gossett, Los Angeles, 1966
Curt Knight, Washington, 1971
48 Chester Marcol, Green Bay, 1972
47 Jim Turner, N.Y. Jets, 1969
David Ray, Los Angeles, 1973
Mark Moseley, Washington, 1983

Most Field Goals Attempted, Game
9 Jim Bakken, St. Louis vs. Pittsburgh, Sept. 24, 1967
8 Lou Michaels, Pittsburgh vs. St. Louis, Dec. 2, 1962
Garo Yepremian, Detroit vs. Minnesota, Nov. 13, 1966
Jim Turner, N.Y. Jets vs. Buffalo, Nov. 3, 1968
7 By many players

Most Field Goals, Career
373 Jan Stenerud, Kansas City, 1967-79; Green Bay, 1980-83; Minnesota, 1984-85
349 Nick Lowery, New England, 1978; Kansas City, 1980-93; N.Y. Jets, 1994
335 George Blanda, Chi. Bears, 1949, 1950-58; Baltimore, 1950; Houston, 1960-66; Oakland, 1967-75

Most Field Goals, Season
35 Ali Haji-Sheikh, N.Y. Giants, 1983
Jeff Jaeger, L.A. Raiders, 1993
34 Jim Turner, N.Y. Jets, 1968
Nick Lowery, Kansas City, 1990
Jason Hanson, Detroit, 1993
John Carney, San Diego, 1994
Fuad Reveiz, Minnesota, 1994
33 Chester Marcol, Green Bay, 1972
Mark Moseley, Washington, 1983
Gary Anderson, Pittsburgh, 1985

Most Field Goals, Rookie, Season
35 Ali Haji-Sheikh, N.Y. Giants, 1983
33 Chester Marcol, Green Bay, 1972
31 Kevin Butler, Chicago, 1985

Most Field Goals, Game
7 Jim Bakken, St. Louis vs. Pittsburgh, Sept. 24, 1967
Rich Karlis, Minnesota vs. L.A. Rams, Nov. 5, 1989 (OT)
6 Gino Cappelletti, Boston vs. Denver, Oct. 4, 1964
Garo Yepremian, Detroit vs. Minnesota, Nov. 13, 1966
Jim Turner, N.Y. Jets vs. Buffalo, Nov. 3, 1968
Tom Dempsey, Philadelphia vs. Houston, Nov. 12, 1972
Bobby Howfield, N.Y. Jets vs. New Orleans, Dec. 3, 1972
Jim Bakken, St. Louis vs. Atlanta, Dec. 9, 1973
Joe Danelo, N.Y. Giants vs. Seattle, Oct. 18, 1981
Ray Wersching, San Francisco vs. New Orleans, Oct. 16, 1983
Gary Anderson, Pittsburgh vs. Denver, Oct. 23, 1988
John Carney, San Diego vs. Seattle, Sept. 5, 1993
John Carney, San Diego vs. Houston, Sept. 19, 1993
Doug Pelfrey, Cincinnati vs. Seattle, Nov. 6, 1994 (OT)
Norm Johnson, Atlanta vs. New Orleans, Nov. 13, 1994
5 By many players

Most Field Goals, One Quarter
4 Garo Yepremian, Detroit vs. Minnesota, Nov. 13, 1966 (second quarter)
Curt Knight, Washington vs. N.Y. Giants, Nov. 15, 1970 (second quarter)
Roger Ruzek, Dallas vs. N.Y. Giants, Nov. 2, 1987 (fourth quarter)
3 By many players

Most Consecutive Games Scoring Field Goals
31 Fred Cox, Minnesota, 1968-70
28 Jim Turner, N.Y. Jets, 1970; Denver, 1971-72
Chip Lohmiller, Washington, 1988-90
23 Morten Andersen, New Orleans, 1986-88

Most Consecutive Field Goals
29 John Carney, San Diego, 1992-93
28 Fuad Reveiz, Minnesota, 1994 (current)
26 Norm Johnson, Atlanta, 1992-93

Longest Field Goal
63 Tom Dempsey, New Orleans vs. Detroit, Nov. 8, 1970
60 Steve Cox, Cleveland vs. Cincinnati, Oct. 21, 1984
Morten Andersen, New Orleans vs. Chicago, Oct. 27, 1991
59 Tony Franklin, Philadelphia vs. Dallas, Nov. 12, 1979

Pete Stoyanovich, Miami vs. N.Y. Jets, Nov. 12, 1989
Steve Christie, Buffalo vs. Miami, Sept. 26, 1993

Highest Field Goal Percentage, Career (100 field goals)
80.41 Nick Lowery, New England, 1978; Kansas City, 1980-93; N.Y. Jets 1994 (434-349)
79.56 Steve Christie, Tampa Bay, 1990-91; Buffalo, 1992-94 (137-109)
79.39 John Carney, Tampa Bay, 1988-89; L.A. Rams, 1990; San Diego, 1990-94 (165-131)

Highest Field Goal Percentage, Season (Qualifiers)
100.00 Tony Zendejas, L.A. Rams, 1991 (17-17)
96.30 Norm Johnson, Atlanta, 1993 (27-26)
95.24 Mark Moseley, Washington, 1982 (21-20)
Eddie Murray, Detroit, 1988 (21-20)
Eddie Murray, Detroit, 1989 (21-20)

Most Field Goals, No Misses, Game
7 Rich Karlis, Minnesota vs. L.A. Rams, Nov. 5, 1989 (OT)
6 Gino Cappelletti, Boston vs. Denver, Oct. 4, 1964
Joe Danelo, N.Y. Giants vs. Seattle, Oct. 18, 1981
Ray Wersching, San Francisco vs. New Orleans, Oct. 16, 1983
Gary Anderson, Pittsburgh vs. Denver, Oct. 23, 1988
John Carney, San Diego vs. Seattle, Sept. 5, 1993
John Carney, San Diego vs. Houston, Sept. 19, 1993
Doug Pelfrey, Cincinnati vs. Seattle, Nov. 6, 1994 (OT)
Norm Johnson, Atlanta vs. New Orleans, Nov. 13, 1994
5 By many players

Most Field Goals, 50 or More Yards, Career
22 Morten Andersen, New Orleans, 1982-94
20 Nick Lowery, New England, 1978; Kansas City, 1980-93; N.Y. Jets 1994
Eddie Murray, Detroit, 1980-91; Kansas City, 1992; Tampa Bay, 1992; Dallas, 1993; Philadelphia, 1994
18 Dean Biasucci, Indianapolis, 1984, 1986-94
Norm Johnson, Seattle, 1982-90; Atlanta, 1991-94

Most Field Goals, 50 or More Yards, Season
6 Dean Biasucci, Indianapolis, 1988
Chris Jacke, Green Bay, 1993
Tony Zendejas, L.A. Rams, 1993
5 Fred Steinfort, Denver, 1980
Norm Johnson, Seattle, 1986
Kevin Butler, Chicago, 1993
4 By many players

Most Field Goals, 50 or More Yards, Game
2 Jim Martin, Detroit vs. Baltimore, Oct. 23, 1960
Tom Dempsey, New Orleans vs. Los Angeles, Dec. 6, 1970
Chris Bahr, Cincinnati vs. Houston, Sept. 23, 1979
Nick Lowery, Kansas City vs. Seattle, Sept. 14, 1980
Mark Moseley, Washington vs. New Orleans, Oct. 26, 1980
Fred Steinfort, Denver vs. Seattle, Dec. 21, 1980
Mick Luckhurst, Atlanta vs. Denver, Dec. 5, 1982
Morten Andersen, New Orleans vs. Philadelphia, Dec. 11, 1983
Mick Luckhurst, Atlanta vs. L.A. Rams, Oct. 7, 1984
Paul McFadden, Philadelphia vs. Detroit, Nov. 4, 1984
Nick Lowery, Kansas City vs. New Orleans, Sept. 8, 1985
Pat Leahy, N.Y. Jets vs. New England, Oct. 20, 1985
Tony Zendejas, Houston vs. San Diego, Nov. 24, 1985
Norm Johnson, Seattle vs. L.A. Raiders, Dec. 8, 1986
Raul Allegre, N.Y. Giants vs. Philadelphia, Nov. 15, 1987
Nick Lowery, Kansas City vs. Detroit, Nov. 26, 1987
Dean Biasucci, Indianapolis vs. Miami, Sept. 25, 1988
Paul McFadden, Atlanta vs. Buffalo, Nov. 5, 1989
Kevin Butler, Chicago vs. Minnesota, Sept. 23, 1990
Kevin Butler, Chicago vs. Green Bay, Oct. 7, 1990
Chip Lohmiller, Washington vs. Indianapolis, Dec. 22, 1990
Chip Lohmiller, Washington vs. Dallas, Sept. 9, 1991
John Kasay, Seattle vs. San Diego, October 27, 1991
Fuad Reveiz, Minnesota vs. Tampa Bay, Dec. 8, 1991
John Carney, San Diego vs. Seattle, Sept. 5, 1993
Tony Zendejas, L.A. Rams vs. Pittsburgh, Sept. 12, 1993
Doug Pelfrey, Cincinnati vs. Houston, Oct. 24, 1993
Eddie Murray, Dallas vs. Minnesota, Dec. 12, 1993
Greg Davis, Phoenix vs. Seattle, Dec. 19, 1993 (OT)

SAFETIES

Most Safeties, Career
4 Ted Hendricks, Baltimore, 1969-73; Green Bay, 1974; Oakland, 1975-81; L.A. Raiders, 1982-83
Doug English, Detroit, 1975-79, 1981-85
3 Bill McPeak, Pittsburgh, 1949-57
Charlie Krueger, San Francisco, 1959-73
Ernie Stautner, Pittsburgh, 1950-63
Jim Katcavage, N.Y. Giants, 1956-68
Roger Brown, Detroit, 1960-66; Los Angeles, 1967-69
Bruce Maher, Detroit, 1960-67; N.Y. Giants, 1968-69
Ron McDole, St. Louis, 1961; Houston, 1962; Buffalo, 1963-70; Washington, 1971-78
Alan Page, Minnesota, 1967-78; Chicago, 1979-81
Lyle Alzado, Denver, 1971-78; Cleveland, 1979-81; L.A. Raiders, 1982-85
Rulon Jones, Denver, 1980-88
Steve McMichael, New England, 1980; Chicago, 1981-93; Green Bay, 1994
Kevin Greene, L.A. Rams, 1985-92; Pittsburgh, 1993-94
Burt Grossman, San Diego, 1989-93; Philadelphia, 1994
2 By many players

Most Safeties, Season
2 Tom Nash, Green Bay, 1932
Roger Brown, Detroit, 1962
Ron McDole, Buffalo, 1964
Alan Page, Minnesota, 1971
Fred Dryer, Los Angeles, 1973
Benny Barnes, Dallas, 1973
James Young, Houston, 1977
Tom Hannon, Minnesota, 1981
Doug English, Detroit, 1983
Don Blackmon, New England, 1985
Tim Harris, Green Bay, 1988
Brian Jordan, Atlanta, 1991
Burt Grossman, San Diego, 1992
Rod Stephens, Seattle, 1993

Most Safeties, Game
2 Fred Dryer, Los Angeles vs. Green Bay, Oct. 21, 1973

RUSHING

Most Seasons Leading League
8 Jim Brown, Cleveland, 1957-61, 1963-65
4 Steve Van Buren, Philadelphia, 1945, 1947-49
O.J. Simpson, Buffalo, 1972-73, 1975-76
Eric Dickerson, L.A. Rams, 1983-84, 1986; Indianapolis, 1988
3 Earl Campbell, Houston, 1978-80
Emmitt Smith, Dallas, 1991-93

Most Consecutive Seasons Leading League
5 Jim Brown, Cleveland, 1957-61
3 Steve Van Buren, Philadelphia, 1947-49
Jim Brown, Cleveland, 1963-65
Earl Campbell, Houston, 1978-80
Emmitt Smith, Dallas, 1991-93
2 Bill Paschal, N.Y. Giants, 1943-44
Joe Perry, San Francisco, 1953-54
Jim Nance, Boston, 1966-67
Leroy Kelly, Cleveland, 1967-68
O.J. Simpson, Buffalo, 1972-73; 1975-76
Eric Dickerson, L.A. Rams, 1983-84

ATTEMPTS

Most Seasons Leading League
6 Jim Brown, Cleveland, 1958-59, 1961, 1963-65
4 Steve Van Buren, Philadelphia, 1947-50
Walter Payton, Chicago, 1976-79
3 Cookie Gilchrist, Buffalo, 1963-64; Denver, 1965
Jim Nance, Boston, 1966-67, 1969
O.J. Simpson, Buffalo, 1973-75
Eric Dickerson, L.A. Rams, 1983, 1986; Indianapolis, 1988

Most Consecutive Seasons Leading League
4 Steve Van Buren, Philadelphia, 1947-50
Walter Payton, Chicago, 1976-79
3 Jim Brown, Cleveland, 1963-65
Cookie Gilchrist, Buffalo, 1963-64; Denver, 1965
O.J. Simpson, Buffalo, 1973-75
2 By many players

Most Attempts, Career
3,838 Walter Payton, Chicago, 1975-87
2,996 Eric Dickerson, L.A. Rams, 1983-87; Indianapolis, 1987-91; L.A. Raiders, 1992; Atlanta, 1993
2,949 Franco Harris, Pittsburgh, 1972-83; Seattle, 1984

Most Attempts, Season
407 James Wilder, Tampa Bay, 1984
404 Eric Dickerson, L.A. Rams, 1986
397 Gerald Riggs, Atlanta, 1985

Most Attempts, Rookie, Season
390 Eric Dickerson, L.A. Rams, 1983
378 George Rogers, New Orleans, 1981
335 Curt Warner, Seattle, 1983

Most Attempts, Game
45 Jamie Morris, Washington vs. Cincinnati, Dec. 17, 1988 (OT)
43 Butch Woolfolk, N.Y. Giants vs. Philadelphia, Nov. 20, 1983
James Wilder, Tampa Bay vs. Green Bay, Sept. 30, 1984 (OT)

42 James Wilder, Tampa Bay vs. Pittsburgh, Oct. 30, 1983

YARDS GAINED

Most Yards Gained, Career

16,726 Walter Payton, Chicago, 1975-87
13,259 Eric Dickerson, L.A. Rams, 1983-87; Indianapolis, 1987-91; L.A. Raiders, 1992; Atlanta, 1993
12,739 Tony Dorsett, Dallas, 1977-87; Denver, 1988

Most Seasons, 1,000 or More Yards Rushing

10 Walter Payton, Chicago, 1976-81, 1983-86
8 Franco Harris, Pittsburgh, 1972, 1974-79, 1983
Tony Dorsett, Dallas, 1977-81, 1983-85
7 Jim Brown, Cleveland, 1958-61, 1963-65
Eric Dickerson, L.A. Rams, 1983-86; L.A. Rams-Indianapolis, 1987; Indianapolis, 1988-89

Most Consecutive Seasons, 1,000 or More Yards Rushing

7 Eric Dickerson, L.A. Rams, 1983-86; L.A. Rams-Indianapolis, 1987; Indianapolis, 1988-89
6 Franco Harris, Pittsburgh, 1974-79
Walter Payton, Chicago, 1976-81
Barry Sanders, Detroit, 1989-94
Thurman Thomas, Buffalo, 1989-94
5 Jim Taylor, Green Bay, 1960-64
O.J. Simpson, Buffalo, 1972-76
Tony Dorsett, Dallas, 1977-81

Most Yards Gained, Season

2,105 Eric Dickerson, L.A. Rams, 1984
2,003 O.J. Simpson, Buffalo, 1973
1,934 Earl Campbell, Houston, 1980

Most Yards Gained, Rookie, Season

1,808 Eric Dickerson, L.A. Rams, 1983
1,674 George Rogers, New Orleans, 1981
1,605 Ottis Anderson, St. Louis, 1979

Most Yards Gained, Game

275 Walter Payton, Chicago vs. Minnesota, Nov. 20, 1977
273 O.J. Simpson, Buffalo vs. Detroit, Nov. 25, 1976
250 O.J. Simpson, Buffalo vs. New England, Sept. 16, 1973

Most Games, 200 or More Yards Rushing, Career

6 O.J. Simpson, Buffalo, 1969-77; San Francisco, 1978-79
4 Jim Brown, Cleveland, 1957-65
Earl Campbell, Houston, 1978-84; New Orleans, 1984-85
3 Eric Dickerson, L.A. Rams, 1983-87; Indianapolis, 1987-91; L.A. Raiders, 1992; Atlanta, 1993
Greg Bell, Buffalo, 1984-87; L.A. Rams, 1987-89; L.A. Raiders, 1990

Most Games, 200 or More Yards Rushing, Season

4 Earl Campbell, Houston, 1980
3 O.J. Simpson, Buffalo, 1973
2 Jim Brown, Cleveland, 1963
O.J. Simpson, Buffalo, 1976
Walter Payton, Chicago, 1977
Eric Dickerson, L.A. Rams, 1984
Greg Bell, L.A. Rams, 1989

Most Consecutive Games, 200 or More Yards Rushing

2 O.J. Simpson, Buffalo, 1973, 1976
Earl Campbell, Houston, 1980

Most Games, 100 or More Yards Rushing, Career

77 Walter Payton, Chicago, 1975-87
64 Eric Dickerson, L.A. Rams, 1983-87; Indianapolis, 1987-91; L.A. Raiders, 1992; Atlanta, 1993
58 Jim Brown, Cleveland, 1957-65

Most Games, 100 or More Yards Rushing, Season

12 Eric Dickerson, L.A. Rams, 1984
Barry Foster, Pittsburgh, 1992
11 O.J. Simpson, Buffalo, 1973
Earl Campbell, Houston, 1979
Marcus Allen, L.A. Raiders, 1985
Eric Dickerson, L.A. Rams, 1986
10 Walter Payton, Chicago, 1977, 1985
Earl Campbell, Houston, 1980
Barry Sanders, Detroit, 1994

Most Consecutive Games, 100 or More Yards Rushing

11 Marcus Allen, L.A. Raiders, 1985-86
9 Walter Payton, Chicago, 1985
7 O.J. Simpson, Buffalo, 1972-73
Earl Campbell, Houston, 1979

Longest Run From Scrimmage

99 Tony Dorsett, Dallas vs. Minnesota, Jan. 3, 1983 (TD)
97 Andy Uram, Green Bay vs. Chi. Cardinals, Oct. 8, 1939 (TD)
Bob Gage, Pittsburgh vs. Chi. Bears, Dec. 4, 1949 (TD)
96 Jim Spavital, Baltimore vs. Green Bay, Nov. 5, 1950 (TD)
Bob Hoernschemeyer, Detroit vs. N.Y. Yanks, Nov. 23, 1950 (TD)

AVERAGE GAIN

Highest Average Gain, Career (750 attempts)

5.22 Jim Brown, Cleveland, 1957-65 (2,359-12,312)
5.14 Eugene (Mercury) Morris, Miami, 1969-75; San Diego, 1976 (804-4,133)
5.00 Gale Sayers, Chicago, 1965-71 (991-4,956)

Highest Average Gain, Season (Qualifiers)

8.44 Beattie Feathers, Chi. Bears, 1934 (119-1,004)
7.98 Randall Cunningham, Philadelphia 1990 (118-942)
6.87 Bobby Douglass, Chicago, 1972 (141-968)

Highest Average Gain, Game (10 attempts)

17.09 Marion Motley, Cleveland vs. Pittsburgh, Oct. 29, 1950 (11-188)
16.70 Bill Grimes, Green Bay vs. N.Y. Yanks, Oct. 8, 1950 (10-167)
16.57 Bobby Mitchell, Cleveland vs. Washington, Nov. 15, 1959 (14-232)

TOUCHDOWNS

Most Seasons Leading League

5 Jim Brown, Cleveland, 1957-59, 1963, 1965
4 Steve Van Buren, Philadelphia, 1945, 1947-49
3 Abner Haynes, Dall. Texans, 1960-62
Cookie Gilchrist, Buffalo, 1962-64
Paul Lowe, L.A. Chargers, 1960; San Diego, 1961, 1965
Leroy Kelly, Cleveland, 1966-68

Most Consecutive Seasons Leading League

3 Steve Van Buren, Philadelphia, 1947-49
Jim Brown, Cleveland, 1957-59
Abner Haynes, Dall. Texans, 1960-62
Cookie Gilchrist, Buffalo, 1962-64
Leroy Kelly, Cleveland, 1966-68

Most Touchdowns, Career

110 Walter Payton, Chicago, 1975-87
106 Jim Brown, Cleveland, 1957-65
104 John Riggins, N.Y. Jets, 1971-75; Washington, 1976-79, 1981-85

Most Touchdowns, Season

24 John Riggins, Washington, 1983
21 Joe Morris, N.Y. Giants, 1985
Emmitt Smith, Dallas, 1994
19 Jim Taylor, Green Bay, 1962
Earl Campbell, Houston, 1979
Chuck Muncie, San Diego, 1981

Most Touchdowns, Rookie, Season

18 Eric Dickerson, L.A. Rams, 1983
15 Ickey Woods, Cincinnati, 1988
14 Gale Sayers, Chicago, 1965
Barry Sanders, Detroit, 1989

Most Touchdowns, Game

6 Ernie Nevers, Chi. Cardinals vs. Chi. Bears, Nov. 28, 1929
5 Jim Brown, Cleveland vs. Baltimore, Nov. 1, 1959
Cookie Gilchrist, Buffalo vs. N.Y. Jets, Dec. 8, 1963
4 By many players

Most Consecutive Games Rushing for Touchdowns

13 John Riggins, Washington, 1982-83
George Rogers, Washington, 1985-86
11 Lenny Moore, Baltimore, 1963-64
10 Greg Bell, L.A. Rams, 1988-89

PASSING

Most Seasons Leading League

6 Sammy Baugh, Washington, 1937, 1940, 1943, 1945, 1947, 1949
4 Len Dawson, Dall. Texans; 1962; Kansas City, 1964, 1966, 1968
Roger Staubach, Dallas, 1971, 1973, 1978-79
Ken Anderson, Cincinnati, 1974-75, 1981-82
Steve Young, San Francisco, 1991-94
3 Arnie Herber, Green Bay, 1932, 1934, 1936
Norm Van Brocklin, Los Angeles, 1950, 1952, 1954
Bart Starr, Green Bay, 1962, 1964, 1966

Most Consecutive Seasons Leading League

4 Steve Young, San Francisco, 1991-94
2 Cecil Isbell, Green Bay, 1941-42
Milt Plum, Cleveland, 1960-61
Ken Anderson, Cincinnati, 1974-75, 1981-82
Roger Staubach, Dallas, 1978-79

PASS RATING

Highest Pass Rating, Career (1,500 attempts)

96.8 Steve Young, Tampa Bay, 1985-86; San Francisco, 1987-94
92.3 Joe Montana, San Francisco, 1979-90, 1992; Kansas City, 1993-94
88.2 Dan Marino, Miami, 1983-94

Highest Pass Rating, Season (Qualifiers)

112.8 Steve Young, San Francisco, 1994
112.4 Joe Montana, San Francisco, 1989
110.4 Milt Plum, Cleveland, 1960

ALL-TIME RECORDS

Highest Pass Rating, Rookie, Season (Qualifiers)
96.0 Dan Marino, Miami, 1983
88.2 Greg Cook, Cincinnati, 1969
84.0 Charlie Conerly, N.Y. Giants, 1948

ATTEMPTS

Most Seasons Leading League
4 Sammy Baugh, Washington, 1937, 1943, 1947-48
Johnny Unitas, Baltimore, 1957, 1959-61
George Blanda, Chi. Bears, 1953; Houston, 1963-65
Dan Marino, Miami, 1984, 1986, 1988, 1992
3 Arnie Herber, Green Bay, 1932, 1934, 1936
Sonny Jurgensen, Washington, 1966-67, 1969
2 By many players

Most Consecutive Seasons Leading League
3 Johnny Unitas, Baltimore, 1959-61
George Blanda, Houston, 1963-65
2 By many players

Most Passes Attempted, Career
6,467 Fran Tarkenton, Minnesota, 1961-66, 1972-78; N.Y. Giants, 1967-71
6,049 Dan Marino, Miami, 1983-94
5,604 Dan Fouts, San Diego, 1973-87

Most Passes Attempted, Season
691 Drew Bledsoe, New England, 1994
655 Warren Moon, Houston, 1991
623 Dan Marino, Miami, 1986

Most Passes Attempted, Rookie, Season
486 Rick Mirer, Seattle, 1993
439 Jim Zorn, Seattle, 1976
429 Drew Bledsoe, New England, 1993

Most Passes Attempted, Game
70 Drew Bledsoe, New England vs. Minnesota, Nov. 13, 1994 (OT)
68 George Blanda, Houston vs. Buffalo, Nov. 1, 1964
66 Chris Miller, Atlanta vs. Detroit, Dec. 24, 1989

COMPLETIONS

Most Seasons Leading League
5 Sammy Baugh, Washington, 1937, 1943, 1945, 1947-48
Dan Marino, Miami, 1984-86, 1988, 1992
4 George Blanda, Chi. Bears, 1953; Houston, 1963-65
Sonny Jurgensen, Philadelphia, 1961; Washington, 1966-67, 1969
3 Arnie Herber, Green Bay, 1932, 1934, 1936
Johnny Unitas, Baltimore, 1959-60, 1963
John Brodie, San Francisco, 1965, 1968, 1970
Fran Tarkenton, Minnesota, 1975-76, 1978

Most Consecutive Seasons Leading League
3 George Blanda, Houston, 1963-65
Dan Marino, Miami, 1984-86
2 By many players

Most Passes Completed, Career
3,686 Fran Tarkenton, Minnesota, 1961-66, 1972-78; N.Y. Giants, 1967-71
3,604 Dan Marino, Miami, 1983-94
3,409 Joe Montana, San Francisco, 1979-90, 1992; Kansas City, 1993-94

Most Passes Completed, Season
404 Warren Moon, Houston, 1991
400 Drew Bledsoe, New England, 1994
385 Dan Marino, Miami, 1994

Most Passes Completed, Rookie, Season
274 Rick Mirer, Seattle, 1993
214 Drew Bledsoe, New England, 1993
208 Jim Zorn, Seattle, 1976

Most Passes Completed, Game
45 Drew Bledsoe, New England vs. Minnesota, Nov. 13, 1994 (OT)
42 Richard Todd, N.Y. Jets vs. San Francisco, Sept. 21, 1980
41 Warren Moon, Houston vs. Dallas, Nov. 10, 1991 (OT)

Most Consecutive Passes Completed
22 Joe Montana, San Francisco vs. Cleveland (5), Nov. 29, 1987; vs. Green Bay (17), Dec. 6, 1987
20 Ken Anderson, Cincinnati vs. Houston, Jan. 2, 1983
Hugh Millen, Denver vs. L.A. Raiders (7), Dec. 11, 1994; vs. San Francisco (13), Dec. 17, 1994
18 Steve DeBerg, Denver vs. L.A. Rams (17), Dec. 12, 1982; vs. Kansas City (1), Dec. 19, 1982
Lynn Dickey, Green Bay vs. Houston, Sept. 4, 1983
Joe Montana, San Francisco vs. L.A. Rams (13), Oct. 28, 1984; vs. Cincinnati (5), Nov. 4, 1984
Don Majkowski, Green Bay vs. New Orleans, Sept. 18, 1989
Boomer Esiason, N.Y. Jets vs. Miami (5), Sept. 12, 1993; vs. New England (13), Sept. 26, 1993

COMPLETION PERCENTAGE

Most Seasons Leading League
8 Len Dawson, Dall. Texans, 1962; Kansas City, 1964-69, 1975
7 Sammy Baugh, Washington, 1940, 1942-43, 1945, 1947-49
5 Joe Montana, San Francisco, 1980-81, 1985, 1987, 1989

Most Consecutive Seasons Leading League
6 Len Dawson, Kansas City, 1964-69
3 Sammy Baugh, Washington, 1947-49
Otto Graham, Cleveland, 1953-55
Milt Plum, Cleveland, 1959-61
2 By many players

Highest Completion Percentage, Career (1,500 attempts)
63.65 Steve Young, Tampa Bay, 1985-86; San Francisco, 1987-94 (2,429-1,546)
63.24 Joe Montana, San Francisco, 1979-90, 1992; Kansas City, 1993-94 (5,391-3,409)
62.43 Troy Aikman, Dallas, 1989-94 (2,281-1,424)

Highest Completion Percentage, Season (Qualifiers)
70.55 Ken Anderson, Cincinnati, 1982 (309-218)
70.33 Sammy Baugh, Washington, 1945 (182-128)
70.28 Steve Young, San Francisco, 1994 (461-324)

Highest Completion Percentage, Rookie, Season (Qualifiers)
58.45 Dan Marino, Miami, 1983 (296-173)
57.14 Jim McMahon, Chicago, 1982 (210-120)
56.38 Rick Mirer, Seattle, 1993 (486-274)

Highest Completion Percentage, Game (20 attempts)
91.30 Vinny Testaverde, Cleveland vs. L.A. Rams, Dec. 26, 1993 (23-21)
90.91 Ken Anderson, Cincinnati vs. Pittsburgh, Nov. 10, 1974 (22-20)
90.48 Lynn Dickey, Green Bay vs. New Orleans, Dec. 13, 1981 (21-19)

YARDS GAINED

Most Seasons Leading League
5 Sonny Jurgensen, Philadelphia, 1961-62; Washington, 1966-67, 1969
Dan Marino, Miami, 1984-86, 1988, 1992
4 Sammy Baugh, Washington, 1937, 1940, 1947-48
Johnny Unitas, Baltimore, 1957, 1959-60, 1963
Dan Fouts, San Diego, 1979-82
3 Arnie Herber, Green Bay, 1932, 1934, 1936
Sid Luckman, Chi. Bears, 1943, 1945-46
John Brodie, San Francisco, 1965, 1968, 1970
John Hadl, San Diego, 1965, 1968, 1971
Joe Namath, N.Y. Jets, 1966-67, 1972

Most Consecutive Seasons Leading League
4 Dan Fouts, San Diego, 1979-82
3 Dan Marino, Miami, 1984-86
2 By many players

Most Yards Gained, Career
47,003 Fran Tarkenton, Minnesota, 1961-66, 1972-78; N.Y. Giants, 1967-71
45,173 Dan Marino, Miami, 1983-94
43,040 Dan Fouts, San Diego, 1973-87

Most Seasons, 3,000 or More Yards Passing
10 Dan Marino, Miami, 1984-92, 1994
9 John Elway, Denver, 1985-91, 1993-94
8 Joe Montana, San Francisco, 1981, 1983-85, 1987, 1989-90; Kansas City, 1994

Most Yards Gained, Season
5,084 Dan Marino, Miami, 1984
4,802 Dan Fouts, San Diego, 1981
4,746 Dan Marino, Miami, 1986

Most Yards Gained, Rookie, Season
2,833 Rick Mirer, Seattle, 1993
2,571 Jim Zorn, Seattle, 1976
2,507 Dennis Shaw, Buffalo, 1970

Most Yards Gained, Game
554 Norm Van Brocklin, Los Angeles vs. N.Y. Yanks, Sept. 28, 1951
527 Warren Moon, Houston vs. Kansas City, Dec. 16, 1990
521 Dan Marino, Miami vs. N.Y. Jets, Oct. 23, 1988

Most Games, 400 or More Yards Passing, Career
12 Dan Marino, Miami, 1983-94
7 Joe Montana, San Francisco, 1979-90, 1992; Kansas City, 1993-94
6 Dan Fouts, San Diego, 1973-87
Warren Moon, Houston, 1984-93; Minnesota, 1994

Most Games, 400 or More Yards Passing, Season
4 Dan Marino, Miami, 1984
3 Dan Marino, Miami, 1986
2 By many players

Most Consecutive Games, 400 or More Yards Passing
2 Dan Fouts, San Diego, 1982
Dan Marino, Miami, 1984
Phil Simms, N.Y. Giants, 1985

Most Games, 300 or More Yards Passing, Career
51 Dan Fouts, San Diego, 1973-87
49 Dan Marino, Miami, 1983-94
44 Warren Moon, Houston, 1984-93; Minnesota, 1994

Most Games, 300 or More Yards Passing, Season
9 Dan Marino, Miami, 1984

Warren Moon, Houston, 1990
8 Dan Fouts, San Diego, 1980
7 Dan Fouts, San Diego, 1981
Bill Kenney, Kansas City, 1983
Neil Lomax, St. Louis, 1984
Dan Fouts, San Diego, 1985

Most Consecutive Games, 300 or More Yards Passing
5 Joe Montana, San Francisco, 1982
4 Dan Fouts, San Diego, 1979
Bill Kenney, Kansas City, 1983
Joe Montana, San Francisco, 1990
Warren Moon, Houston, 1990
Drew Bledsoe, New England, 1993-94
3 By many players

Longest Pass Completion (All TDs except as noted)
99 Frank Filchock (to Farkas), Washington vs. Pittsburgh, Oct. 15, 1939
George Izo (to Mitchell), Washington vs. Cleveland, Sept. 15, 1963
Karl Sweetan (to Studstill), Detroit vs. Baltimore, Oct. 16, 1966
Sonny Jurgensen (to Allen), Washington vs. Chicago, Sept. 15, 1968
Jim Plunkett (to Branch), L.A. Raiders vs. Washington, Oct. 2, 1983
Ron Jaworski (to Quick), Philadelphia vs. Atlanta, Nov. 10, 1985
Stan Humphries (to Martin), San Diego vs. Seattle, Sept. 18, 1994
98 Doug Russell (to Tinsley), Chi. Cardinals vs. Cleveland, Nov. 27, 1938
Ogden Compton (to Lane), Chi. Cardinals vs. Green Bay, Nov. 13, 1955
Bill Wade (to Farrington), Chicago Bears vs. Detroit, Oct. 8, 1961
Jacky Lee (to Dewveall), Houston vs. San Diego, Nov. 25, 1962
Earl Morrall (to Jones), N.Y. Giants vs. Pittsburgh, Sept. 11, 1966
Jim Hart (to Moore), St. Louis vs. Los Angeles, Dec. 10, 1972 (no TD)
Bobby Hebert (to Haynes), Atlanta vs. New Orleans, Sept. 12, 1993
97 Pat Coffee (to Tinsley), Chi. Cardinals vs. Chi. Bears, Dec. 5, 1937
Bobby Layne (to Box), Detroit vs. Green Bay, Nov. 26, 1953
George Shaw (to Tarr), Denver vs. Boston, Sept. 21, 1962
Bernie Kosar (to Slaughter), Cleveland vs. Chicago, Oct. 23, 1989
Steve Young (to Taylor), San Francisco vs. Atlanta, Nov. 3, 1991

AVERAGE GAIN

Most Seasons Leading League
7 Sid Luckman, Chi. Bears, 1939-43, 1946-47
4 Steve Young, San Francisco, 1991-94
3 Arnie Herber, Green Bay, 1932, 1934, 1936
Norm Van Brocklin, Los Angeles, 1950, 1952, 1954
Len Dawson, Dall. Texans, 1962; Kansas City, 1966, 1968
Bart Starr, Green Bay, 1966-68

Most Consecutive Seasons Leading League
5 Sid Luckman, Chi. Bears, 1939-43
4 Steve Young, San Francisco, 1991-94
3 Bart Starr, Green Bay, 1966-68

Highest Average Gain, Career (1,500 attempts)
8.63 Otto Graham, Cleveland, 1950-55 (1,565-13,499)
8.42 Sid Luckman, Chi. Bears, 1939-50 (1,744-14,686)
8.18 Steve Young, Tampa Bay, 1985-86; San Francisco, 1987-94 (2,429-19,869)

Highest Average Gain, Season (Qualifiers)
11.17 Tommy O'Connell, Cleveland, 1957 (110-1,229)
10.86 Sid Luckman, Chi. Bears, 1943 (202-2,194)
10.55 Otto Graham, Cleveland, 1953 (258-2,722)

Highest Average Gain, Rookie, Season (Qualifiers)
9.411 Greg Cook, Cincinnati, 1969 (197-1,854)
9.409 Bob Waterfield, Cleveland, 1945 (171-1,609)
8.36 Zeke Bratkowski, Chi. Bears, 1954 (130-1,087)

Highest Average Gain, Game (20 attempts)
18.58 Sammy Baugh, Washington vs. Boston, Oct. 31, 1948 (24-446)
18.50 Johnny Unitas, Baltimore vs. Atlanta, Nov. 12, 1967 (20-370)
17.71 Joe Namath, N.Y. Jets vs. Baltimore, Sept. 24, 1972 (28-496)

TOUCHDOWNS

Most Seasons Leading League
4 Johnny Unitas, Baltimore, 1957-60
Len Dawson, Dall. Texans, 1962; Kansas City, 1963, 1965-66
3 Arnie Herber, Green Bay, 1932, 1934, 1936
Sid Luckman, Chi. Bears, 1943, 1945-46
Y.A. Tittle, San Francisco, 1955; N.Y. Giants, 1962-63
Dan Marino, Miami, 1984-86
Steve Young, San Francisco, 1992-94
2 By many players

Most Consecutive Seasons Leading League
4 Johnny Unitas, Baltimore, 1957-60
3 Dan Marino, Miami, 1984-86
Steve Young, San Francisco, 1992-94
2 By many players

Most Touchdown Passes, Career
342 Fran Tarkenton, Minnesota, 1961-66, 1972-78; N.Y. Giants, 1967-71
328 Dan Marino, Miami, 1983-94
290 Johnny Unitas, Baltimore, 1956-72: San Diego, 1973

Most Touchdown Passes, Season
48 Dan Marino, Miami, 1984
44 Dan Marino, Miami, 1986
36 George Blanda, Houston, 1961
Y.A. Tittle, N.Y. Giants, 1963

Most Touchdown Passes, Rookie, Season
22 Charlie Conerly, N.Y. Giants, 1948
20 Dan Marino, Miami, 1983
19 Jim Plunkett, New England, 1971

Most Touchdown Passes, Game
7 Sid Luckman, Chi. Bears vs. N.Y. Giants, Nov. 14, 1943
Adrian Burk, Philadelphia vs. Washington, Oct. 17, 1954
George Blanda, Houston vs. N.Y. Titans, Nov. 19, 1961
Y.A. Tittle, N.Y. Giants vs. Washington, Oct. 28, 1962
Joe Kapp, Minnesota vs. Baltimore, Sept. 28, 1969
6 By many players. Last time: Mark Rypien, Washington vs. Atlanta, Nov. 10, 1991

Most Games, Four or More Touchdown Passes, Career
19 Dan Marino, Miami, 1983-94
17 Johnny Unitas, Baltimore, 1956-72; San Diego, 1973
13 George Blanda, Chi. Bears, 1949, 1950-58; Baltimore, 1950; Houston, 1960-66; Oakland, 1967-75

Most Games, Four or More Touchdown Passes, Season
6 Dan Marino, Miami, 1984
5 Dan Marino, Miami, 1986
4 George Blanda, Houston, 1961
Vince Ferragamo, Los Angeles, 1980

Most Consecutive Games, Four or More Touchdown Passes
4 Dan Marino, Miami, 1984
2 By many players

Most Consecutive Games, Touchdown Passes
47 Johnny Unitas, Baltimore, 1956-60
30 Dan Marino, Miami, 1985-87
28 Dave Krieg, Seattle, 1983-85

HAD INTERCEPTED

Most Consecutive Passes Attempted, None Intercepted
308 Bernie Kosar, Cleveland, 1990-91
294 Bart Starr, Green Bay, 1964-65
279 Jeff George, Indianapolis, 1993; Atlanta, 1994

Most Passes Had Intercepted, Career
277 George Blanda, Chi. Bears, 1949, 1950-58; Baltimore, 1950; Houston, 1960-66; Oakland, 1967-75
268 John Hadl, San Diego, 1962-72; Los Angeles, 1973-74; Green Bay, 1974-75; Houston, 1976-77
266 Fran Tarkenton, Minnesota, 1961-66, 1972-78; N.Y. Giants, 1967-71

Most Passes Had Intercepted, Season
42 George Blanda, Houston, 1962
35 Vinny Testaverde, Tampa Bay, 1988
34 Frank Tripucka, Denver, 1960

Most Passes Had Intercepted, Game
8 Jim Hardy, Chi. Cardinals vs. Philadelphia, Sept. 24, 1950
7 Parker Hall, Cleveland vs. Green Bay, Nov. 8, 1942
Frank Sinkwich, Detroit vs. Green Bay, Oct. 24, 1943
Bob Waterfield, Los Angeles vs. Green Bay, Oct. 17, 1948
Zeke Bratkowski, Chicago vs. Baltimore, Oct. 2, 1960
Tommy Wade, Pittsburgh vs. Philadelphia, Dec. 12, 1965
Ken Stabler, Oakland vs. Denver, Oct. 16, 1977
Steve DeBerg, Tampa Bay vs. San Francisco, Sept. 7, 1986
6 By many players

Most Attempts, No Interceptions, Game
70 Drew Bledsoe, New England vs. Minnesota, Nov. 13, 1994 (OT)
63 Rich Gannon, Minnesota vs. New England, Oct. 20, 1991 (OT)
60 Davey O'Brien, Philadelphia vs. Washington, Dec. 1, 1940

LOWEST PERCENTAGE, PASSES HAD INTERCEPTED

Most Seasons Leading League, Lowest Percentage, Passes Had Intercepted
5 Sammy Baugh, Washington, 1940, 1942, 1944-45, 1947
3 Charlie Conerly, N.Y. Giants, 1950, 1956, 1959
Bart Starr, Green Bay, 1962, 1964, 1966
Roger Staubach, Dallas, 1971, 1977, 1979
Ken Anderson, Cincinnati, 1972, 1981-82
Ken O'Brien, N.Y. Jets, 1985, 1987-88
2 By many players

Lowest Percentage, Passes Had Intercepted, Career (1,500 attempts)
2.52 Jeff Hostetler, N.Y. Giants, 1985-86, 1988-92; L.A. Raiders, 1993-94 (1,506-38)
2.54 Bernie Kosar, Cleveland, 1985-93; Dallas, 1993; Miami, 1994 (3,225-82)
2.58 Joe Montana, San Francisco, 1979-90, 1992; Kansas City, 1993-94 (5,391-139)

Lowest Percentage, Passes Had Intercepted, Season (Qualifiers)
0.66 Joe Ferguson, Buffalo, 1976 (151-1)
0.90 Steve DeBerg, Kansas City, 1990 (444-4)
1.16 Steve Bartkowski, Atlanta, 1983 (432-5)

Lowest Percentage, Passes Had Intercepted, Rookie, Season (Qualifiers)
2.03 Dan Marino, Miami, 1983 (296-6)
2.10 Gary Wood, N.Y. Giants, 1964 (143-3)
2.82 Bernie Kosar, Cleveland, 1985 (248-7)

TIMES SACKED
Times Sacked has been compiled since 1963.

Most Times Sacked, Career
483 Fran Tarkenton, Minnesota, 1961-66, 1972-78; N.Y. Giants, 1967-71
477 Phil Simms, N.Y. Giants, 1979-81, 1983-93
425 Dave Krieg, Seattle, 1980-91; Kansas City, 1992-93; Detroit, 1994

Most Times Sacked, Season
72 Randall Cunningham, Philadelphia, 1986
62 Ken O'Brien, N.Y. Jets, 1985
61 Neil Lomax, St. Louis, 1985

Most Times Sacked, Game
12 Bert Jones, Baltimore vs. St. Louis, Oct. 26, 1980
Warren Moon, Houston vs. Dallas, Sept. 29, 1985
11 Charley Johnson, St. Louis vs. N.Y. Giants, Nov. 1, 1964
Bart Starr, Green Bay vs. Detroit, Nov. 7, 1965
Jack Kemp, Buffalo vs. Oakland, Oct. 15, 1967
Bob Berry, Atlanta vs. St. Louis, Nov. 24, 1968
Greg Landry, Detroit vs. Dallas, Oct. 6, 1975
Ron Jaworski, Philadelphia vs. St. Louis, Dec. 18, 1983
Paul McDonald, Cleveland vs. Kansas City, Sept. 30, 1984
Archie Manning, Minnesota vs. Chicago, Oct. 28, 1984
Steve Pelluer, Dallas vs. San Diego, Nov. 16, 1986
Randall Cunningham, Philadelphia vs. L.A. Raiders, Nov. 30, 1986 (OT)
David Norrie, N.Y. Jets vs. Dallas, Oct. 4, 1987
Troy Aikman, Dallas vs. Philadelphia, Sept. 15, 1991
Bernie Kosar, Cleveland vs. Indianapolis, Sept. 6, 1992
10 By many players

PASS RECEIVING

Most Seasons Leading League
8 Don Hutson, Green Bay, 1936-37, 1939, 1941-45
5 Lionel Taylor, Denver, 1960-63, 1965
3 Tom Fears, Los Angeles, 1948-50
Pete Pihos, Philadelphia, 1953-55
Billy Wilson, San Francisco, 1954, 1956-57
Raymond Berry, Baltimore, 1958-60
Lance Alworth, San Diego, 1966, 1968-69
Sterling Sharpe, Green Bay, 1989, 1992-93

Most Consecutive Seasons Leading League
5 Don Hutson, Green Bay, 1941-45
4 Lionel Taylor, Denver, 1960-63
3 Tom Fears, Los Angeles, 1948-50
Pete Pihos, Philadelphia, 1953-55
Raymond Berry, Baltimore, 1958-60

Most Pass Receptions, Career
934 Art Monk, Washington, 1980-93; N.Y. Jets, 1994
820 Jerry Rice, San Francisco, 1985-94
819 Steve Largent, Seattle, 1976-89

Most Seasons, 50 or More Pass Receptions
10 Steve Largent, Seattle, 1976, 1978-81, 1983-87
Gary Clark, Washington, 1985-92; Phoenix, 1993; Arizona, 1994
9 Art Monk, Washington, 1980-81, 1984-86, 1988-91
James Lofton, Green Bay, 1979-81, 1983-86; Buffalo, 1991-92
Andre Reed, Buffalo, 1986-94
Jerry Rice, San Francisco, 1986-94
8 Earnest Givins, Houston, 1986-93
Henry Ellard, L.A. Rams, 1985, 1987-91, 1993; Washington, 1994

Most Pass Receptions, Season
122 Cris Carter, Minnesota, 1994
112 Sterling Sharpe, Green Bay, 1993
Jerry Rice, San Francisco, 1994
111 Terance Mathis, Atlanta, 1994

Most Pass Receptions, Rookie, Season
83 Earl Cooper, San Francisco, 1980
81 Keith Jackson, Philadelphia, 1988
75 Terry Kirby, Miami, 1993

Most Pass Receptions, Game
18 Tom Fears, Los Angeles vs. Green Bay, Dec. 3, 1950
17 Clark Gaines, N.Y. Jets vs. San Francisco, Sept. 21, 1980
16 Sonny Randle, St. Louis vs. N.Y. Giants, Nov. 4, 1962
Jerry Rice, San Francisco vs. L.A. Rams, Nov. 20, 1994

Most Consecutive Games, Pass Receptions
180 Art Monk, Washington, 1980-93; N.Y. Jets, 1994 (current)
177 Steve Largent, Seattle, 1977-89
150 Ozzie Newsome, Cleveland, 1979-89

YARDS GAINED

Most Seasons Leading League
7 Don Hutson, Green Bay, 1936, 1938-39, 1941-44
5 Jerry Rice, San Francisco, 1986, 1989-90, 1993-94
3 Raymond Berry, Baltimore, 1957, 1959-60
Lance Alworth, San Diego, 1965-66, 1968

Most Consecutive Seasons Leading League
4 Don Hutson, Green Bay, 1941-44
2 By many players

Most Yards Gained, Career
14,004 James Lofton, Green Bay, 1978-86; L.A. Raiders, 1987-88; Buffalo, 1989-92; L.A. Rams, 1993; Philadelphia, 1993
13,275 Jerry Rice, San Francisco, 1985-94
13,089 Steve Largent, Seattle, 1976-89

Most Seasons, 1,000 or More Yards, Pass Receiving
9 Jerry Rice, San Francisco, 1986-94
8 Steve Largent, Seattle, 1978-81, 1983-86
7 Lance Alworth, San Diego, 1963-69

Most Yards Gained, Season
1,746 Charley Hennigan, Houston, 1961
1,602 Lance Alworth, San Diego, 1965
1,570 Jerry Rice, San Francisco, 1986

Most Yards Gained, Rookie, Season
1,473 Bill Groman, Houston, 1960
1,231 Bill Howton, Green Bay, 1952
1,131 Bill Brooks, Indianapolis, 1986

Most Yards Gained, Game
336 Willie Anderson, L.A. Rams vs. New Orleans, Nov. 26, 1989 (OT)
309 Stephone Paige, Kansas City vs. San Diego, Dec. 22, 1985
303 Jim Benton, Cleveland vs. Detroit, Nov. 22, 1945

Most Games, 200 or More Yards Pass Receiving, Career
5 Lance Alworth, San Diego, 1962-70; Dallas, 1971-72
4 Don Hutson, Green Bay, 1935-45
Charley Hennigan, Houston, 1960-66
3 Don Maynard, N.Y. Giants, 1958; N.Y. Jets, 1960-72; St. Louis, 1973
Wes Chandler, New Orleans, 1978-81; San Diego, 1981-87; San Francisco, 1988
Jerry Rice, San Francisco, 1985-94

Most Games, 200 or More Yards Pass Receiving, Season
3 Charley Hennigan, Houston, 1961
2 Don Hutson, Green Bay, 1942
Gene Roberts, N.Y. Giants, 1949
Lance Alworth, San Diego, 1963
Don Maynard, N.Y. Jets, 1968

Most Games, 100 or More Yards Pass Receiving, Career
50 Don Maynard, N.Y. Giants, 1958; N.Y. Jets, 1960-72; St. Louis, 1973
49 Jerry Rice, San Francisco, 1985-94
43 James Lofton, Green Bay, 1978-86; L.A. Raiders, 1987-88; Buffalo, 1989-92; L.A. Rams, 1993; Philadelphia, 1993

Most Games, 100 or More Yards Pass Receiving, Season
10 Charley Hennigan, Houston, 1961
9 Elroy (Crazylegs) Hirsch, Los Angeles, 1951
Bill Groman, Houston, 1960
Lance Alworth, San Diego, 1965
Don Maynard, N.Y. Jets, 1967
Stanley Morgan, New England, 1986
Mark Carrier, Tampa Bay, 1989
8 Charley Hennigan, Houston, 1964
Lance Alworth, San Diego, 1967
Mark Duper, Miami, 1986
Jerry Rice, San Francisco, 1989

Most Consecutive Games, 100 or More Yards Pass Receiving
7 Charley Hennigan, Houston, 1961
Bill Groman, Houston, 1961
6 Raymond Berry, Baltimore, 1960
Pat Studstill, Detroit, 1966
5 Elroy (Crazylegs) Hirsch, Los Angeles, 1951
Bob Boyd, Los Angeles, 1954
Terry Barr, Detroit, 1963
Lance Alworth, San Diego, 1966
Harold Jackson, Philadelphia, 1971-72

Longest Pass Reception (All TDs except as noted)
99 Andy Farkas (from Filchock), Washington vs. Pittsburgh, Oct. 15, 1939
Bobby Mitchell (from Izo), Washington vs. Cleveland, Sept. 15, 1963
Pat Studstill (from Sweetan), Detroit vs. Baltimore, Oct. 16, 1966
Gerry Allen (from Jurgensen), Washington vs. Chicago, Sept. 15, 1968
Cliff Branch (from Plunkett), L.A. Raiders vs. Washington, Oct. 2, 1983
Mike Quick (from Jaworski), Philadelphia vs. Atlanta, Nov. 10, 1985
Tony Martin (from Humphries), San Diego vs. Seattle, Sept. 18, 1994
98 Gaynell Tinsley (from Russell), Chi. Cardinals vs. Cleveland, Nov. 17, 1938

Dick (Night Train) Lane (from Compton), Chi. Cardinals vs. Green Bay, Nov. 13, 1955
John Farrington (from Wade), Chicago vs. Detroit, Oct. 8, 1961
Willard Dewveall (from Lee), Houston vs. San Diego, Nov. 25, 1962
Homer Jones (from Morrall), N.Y. Giants vs. Pittsburgh, Sept. 11, 1966
Bobby Moore (from Hart), St. Louis vs. Los Angeles, Dec. 10, 1972 (no TD)
Michael Haynes (from Hebert), Atlanta vs. New Orleans, Sept. 12, 1993
97 Gaynell Tinsley (from Coffee), Chi. Cardinals vs. Chi. Bears, Dec. 5, 1937
Cloyce Box (from Layne), Detroit vs. Green Bay, Nov. 26, 1953
Jerry Tarr (from Shaw), Denver vs. Boston, Sept. 21, 1962
Webster Slaughter (from Kosar), Cleveland vs. Chicago, Oct. 23, 1989
John Taylor (from Young), San Francisco vs. Atlanta, Nov. 3, 1991

AVERAGE GAIN

Highest Average Gain, Career (200 receptions)
22.26 Homer Jones, N.Y. Giants, 1964-69; Cleveland, 1970 (224-4,986)
20.83 Buddy Dial, Pittsburgh, 1959-63; Dallas, 1964-66 (261-5,436)
20.25 Willie Anderson, L.A. Rams, 1988-94 (259-5,246)

Highest Average Gain, Season (24 receptions)
32.58 Don Currivan, Boston, 1947 (24-782)
31.44 Bucky Pope, Los Angeles, 1964 (25-786)
28.60 Bobby Duckworth, San Diego, 1984 (25-715)

Highest Average Gain, Game (3 receptions)
60.67 Bill Groman, Houston vs. Denver, Nov. 20, 1960 (3-182)
Homer Jones, N.Y. Giants vs. Washington, Dec. 12, 1965 (3-182)
60.33 Don Currivan, Boston vs. Washington, Nov. 30, 1947 (3-181)
59.67 Bobby Duckworth, San Diego vs. Chicago, Dec. 3, 1984 (3-179)

TOUCHDOWNS

Most Seasons Leading League
9 Don Hutson, Green Bay, 1935-38, 1940-44
6 Jerry Rice, San Francisco, 1986-87, 1989-91, 1993
3 Lance Alworth, San Diego, 1964-66

Most Consecutive Seasons Leading League
5 Don Hutson, Green Bay, 1940-44
4 Don Hutson, Green Bay, 1935-38
3 Lance Alworth, San Diego, 1964-66
Jerry Rice, San Francisco, 1989-91

Most Touchdowns, Career
131 Jerry Rice, San Francisco, 1985-94
100 Steve Largent, Seattle, 1976-89
99 Don Hutson, Green Bay, 1935-45

Most Touchdowns, Season
22 Jerry Rice, San Francisco, 1987
18 Mark Clayton, Miami, 1984
Sterling Sharpe, Green Bay, 1994
17 Don Hutson, Green Bay, 1942
Elroy (Crazylegs) Hirsch, Los Angeles, 1951
Bill Groman, Houston, 1961
Jerry Rice, San Francisco, 1989

Most Touchdowns, Rookie, Season
13 Bill Howton, Green Bay, 1952
John Jefferson, San Diego, 1979
12 Harlon Hill, Chi. Bears, 1954
Bill Groman, Houston, 1960
Mike Ditka, Chicago, 1961
Bob Hayes, Dallas, 1965
10 Bill Swiacki, N.Y. Giants, 1948
Bucky Pope, Los Angeles, 1964
Sammy White, Minnesota, 1976
Daryl Turner, Seattle, 1984

Most Touchdowns, Game
5 Bob Shaw, Chi. Cardinals vs. Baltimore, Oct. 2, 1950
Kellen Winslow, San Diego vs. Oakland, Nov. 22, 1981
Jerry Rice, San Francisco vs. Atlanta, Oct. 14, 1990
4 By many players. Last time: Mark Ingram, Miami vs. N.Y. Jets, Nov. 27, 1994

Most Consecutive Games, Touchdowns
13 Jerry Rice, San Francisco, 1986-87
11 Elroy (Crazylegs) Hirsch, Los Angeles, 1950-51
Buddy Dial, Pittsburgh, 1959-60
9 Lance Alworth, San Diego, 1963

INTERCEPTIONS BY

Most Seasons Leading League
3 Everson Walls, Dallas, 1981-82, 1985
2 Dick (Night Train) Lane, Los Angeles, 1952; Chi. Cardinals, 1954
Jack Christiansen, Detroit, 1953, 1957
Milt Davis, Baltimore, 1957, 1959
Dick Lynch, N.Y. Giants, 1961, 1963
Johnny Robinson, Kansas City, 1966, 1970
Bill Bradley, Philadelphia, 1971-72
Emmitt Thomas, Kansas City, 1969, 1974
Ronnie Lott, San Francisco, 1986; L.A. Raiders, 1991

Most Interceptions By, Career
81 Paul Krause, Washington, 1964-67; Minnesota, 1968-79
79 Emlen Tunnell, N.Y. Giants, 1948-58; Green Bay, 1959-61
68 Dick (Night Train) Lane, Los Angeles, 1952-53; Chi. Cardinals, 1954-59; Detroit, 1960-65

Most Interceptions By, Season
14 Dick (Night Train) Lane, Los Angeles, 1952
13 Dan Sandifer, Washington, 1948
Orban (Spec) Sanders, N.Y. Yanks, 1950
Lester Hayes, Oakland, 1980
12 By nine players

Most Interceptions By, Rookie, Season
14 Dick (Night Train) Lane, Los Angeles, 1952
13 Dan Sandifer, Washington, 1948
12 Woodley Lewis, Los Angeles, 1950
Paul Krause, Washington, 1964

Most Interceptions By, Game
4 Sammy Baugh, Washington vs. Detroit, Nov. 14, 1943
Dan Sandifer, Washington vs. Boston, Oct. 31, 1948
Don Doll, Detroit vs. Chi. Cardinals, Oct. 23, 1949
Bob Nussbaumer, Chi. Cardinals vs. N.Y. Bulldogs, Nov. 13, 1949
Russ Craft, Philadelphia vs. Chi. Cardinals, Sept. 24, 1950
Bobby Dillon, Green Bay vs. Detroit, Nov. 26, 1953
Jack Butler, Pittsburgh vs. Washington, Dec. 13, 1953
Austin (Goose) Gonsoulin, Denver vs. Buffalo, Sept. 18, 1960
Jerry Norton, St. Louis vs. Washington, Nov. 20, 1960; vs. Pittsburgh, Nov. 26, 1961
Dave Baker, San Francisco vs. L.A. Rams, Dec. 4, 1960
Bobby Ply, Dall. Texans vs. San Diego, Dec. 16, 1962
Bobby Hunt, Kansas City vs. Houston, Oct. 4, 1964
Willie Brown, Denver vs. N.Y. Jets, Nov. 15, 1964
Dick Anderson, Miami vs. Pittsburgh, Dec. 3, 1973
Willie Buchanon, Green Bay vs. San Diego, Sept. 24, 1978
Deron Cherry, Kansas City vs. Seattle, Sept. 29, 1985

Most Consecutive Games, Passes Intercepted By
8 Tom Morrow, Oakland, 1962-63
7 Paul Krause, Washington, 1964
Larry Wilson, St. Louis, 1966
Ben Davis, Cleveland, 1968
6 Dick (Night Train) Lane, Chi. Cardinals, 1954-55
Will Sherman, Los Angeles, 1954-55
Jim Shofner, Cleveland, 1960
Paul Krause, Minnesota, 1968
Willie Williams, N.Y. Giants, 1968
Kermit Alexander, San Francisco, 1968-69
Mel Blount, Pittsburgh, 1975
Lemar Parrish, Washington, 1978-79
Eric Harris, Kansas City, 1980
Lester Hayes, Oakland, 1980
Barry Wilburn, Washington, 1987

YARDS GAINED

Most Seasons Leading League
2 Dick (Night Train) Lane, Los Angeles, 1952; Chi. Cardinals, 1954
Herb Adderley, Green Bay, 1965, 1969
Dick Anderson, Miami, 1968, 1970

Most Yards Gained, Career
1,282 Emlen Tunnell, N.Y. Giants, 1948-58; Green Bay, 1959-61
1,207 Dick (Night Train) Lane, Los Angeles, 1952-53; Chi. Cardinals, 1954-59; Detroit, 1960-65
1,185 Paul Krause, Washington, 1964-67; Minnesota, 1968-79

Most Yards Gained, Season
349 Charlie McNeil, San Diego, 1961
303 Deion Sanders, San Francisco, 1994
301 Don Doll, Detroit, 1949

Most Yards Gained, Rookie, Season
301 Don Doll, Detroit, 1949
298 Dick (Night Train) Lane, Los Angeles, 1952
275 Woodley Lewis, Los Angeles, 1950

Most Yards Gained, Game
177 Charlie McNeil, San Diego vs. Houston, Sept. 24, 1961
170 Louis Oliver, Miami vs. Buffalo, Oct. 4, 1992
167 Dick Jauron, Detroit vs. Chicago, Nov. 18, 1973

Longest Return (All TDs)
103 Vencie Glenn, San Diego vs. Denver, Nov. 29, 1987
Louis Oliver, Miami vs. Buffalo, Oct. 4, 1992
102 Bob Smith, Detroit vs. Chi. Bears, Nov. 24, 1949
Erich Barnes, N.Y. Giants vs. Dall. Cowboys, Oct. 15, 1961
Gary Barbaro, Kansas City vs. Seattle, Dec. 11, 1977

Louis Breeden, Cincinnati vs. San Diego, Nov. 8, 1981
Eddie Anderson, L.A. Raiders vs. Miami, Dec. 14, 1992
Donald Frank, San Diego vs. L.A. Raiders, Oct. 31, 1993
101 Richie Petitbon, Chicago vs Los Angeles, Dec. 9, 1962
Henry Carr, N.Y. Giants vs. Los Angeles, Nov. 13, 1966
Tony Greene, Buffalo vs. Kansas City, Oct. 3, 1976
Tom Pridemore, Atlanta vs. San Francisco, Sept. 20, 1981

TOUCHDOWNS

Most Touchdowns, Career
9 Ken Houston, Houston, 1967-72; Washington, 1973-80
7 Herb Adderley, Green Bay, 1961-69; Dallas, 1970-72
Erich Barnes, Chi. Bears, 1958-60; N.Y. Giants, 1961-64; Cleveland, 1965-70
Lem Barney, Detroit, 1967-77
6 Tom Janik, Denver, 1963-64; Buffalo, 1965-68; Boston, 1969-70; New England, 1971
Miller Farr, Denver, 1965; San Diego, 1965-66; Houston, 1967-69; St. Louis, 1970-72; Detroit, 1973
Bobby Bell, Kansas City, 1963-74
Deion Sanders, Atlanta, 1989-93; San Francisco, 1994

Most Touchdowns, Season
4 Ken Houston, Houston, 1971
Jim Kearney, Kansas City, 1972
Eric Allen, Philadelphia, 1993
3 Dick Harris, San Diego, 1961
Dick Lynch, N.Y. Giants, 1963
Herb Adderley, Green Bay, 1965
Lem Barney, Detroit, 1967
Miller Farr, Houston, 1967
Monte Jackson, Los Angeles, 1976
Rod Perry, Los Angeles, 1978
Ronnie Lott, San Francisco, 1981
Lloyd Burruss, Kansas City, 1986
Wayne Haddix, Tampa Bay, 1990
Robert Massey, Phoenix, 1992
Ray Buchanan, Indianapolis, 1994
Deion Sanders, San Francisco, 1994
2 By many players

Most Touchdowns, Rookie, Season
3 Lem Barney, Detroit, 1967
Ronnie Lott, San Francisco, 1981
2 By many players

Most Touchdowns, Game
2 Bill Blackburn, Chi. Cardinals vs. Boston, Oct. 24, 1948
Dan Sandifer, Washington vs. Boston, Oct. 31, 1948
Bob Franklin, Cleveland vs. Chicago, Dec. 11, 1960
Bill Stacy, St. Louis vs. Dall. Cowboys, Nov. 5, 1961
Jerry Norton, St. Louis vs. Pittsburgh, Nov. 26, 1961
Miller Farr, Houston vs. Buffalo, Dec. 7, 1968
Ken Houston, Houston vs. San Diego, Dec. 19, 1971
Jim Kearney, Kansas City vs. Denver, Oct. 1, 1972
Lemar Parrish, Cincinnati vs. Houston, Dec. 17, 1972
Dick Anderson, Miami vs. Pittsburgh, Dec. 3, 1973
Prentice McCray, New England vs. N.Y. Jets, Nov. 21, 1976
Kenny Johnson, Atlanta vs. Green Bay, Nov. 27, 1983 (OT)
Mike Kozlowski, Miami vs. N.Y. Jets, Dec. 16, 1983
Dave Brown, Seattle vs. Kansas City, Nov. 4, 1984
Lloyd Burruss, Kansas City vs. San Diego, Oct. 19, 1986
Henry Jones, Buffalo vs. Indianapolis, Sept. 20, 1992
Robert Massey, Phoenix vs. Washington, Oct. 4, 1992
Eric Allen, Philadelphia vs. New Orleans, Dec. 26, 1993

PUNTING

Most Seasons Leading League
4 Sammy Baugh, Washington, 1940-43
Jerrel Wilson, Kansas City, 1965, 1968, 1972-73
3 Yale Lary, Detroit, 1959, 1961, 1963
Jim Fraser, Denver, 1962-64
Ray Guy, Oakland, 1974-75, 1977
Rohn Stark, Baltimore, 1983; Indianapolis, 1985-86
2 By many players

Most Consecutive Seasons Leading League
4 Sammy Baugh, Washington, 1940-43
3 Jim Fraser, Denver, 1962-64
2 By many players

PUNTS

Most Punts, Career
1,154 Dave Jennings, N.Y. Giants, 1974-84; N.Y. Jets, 1985-87
1,083 John James, Atlanta, 1972-81; Detroit, 1982, Houston, 1982-84
1,072 Jerrel Wilson, Kansas City, 1963-77; New England, 1978

Most Punts, Season
114 Bob Parsons, Chicago, 1981
109 John James, Atlanta, 1978
108 John Teltschik, Philadelphia, 1986
Rick Tuten, Seattle, 1992

Most Punts, Rookie, Season
108 John Teltschik, Philadelphia, 1986
99 Lewis Colbert, Kansas City, 1986
96 Mike Connell, San Francisco, 1978
Chris Norman, Denver, 1984

Most Punts, Game
15 John Teltschik, Philadelphia vs. N.Y. Giants, Dec. 6, 1987 (OT)
14 Dick Nesbitt, Chi. Cardinals vs. Chi. Bears, Nov. 30, 1933
Keith Molesworth, Chi. Bears vs. Green Bay, Dec. 10, 1933
Sammy Baugh, Washington vs. Philadelphia, Nov. 5, 1939
Carl Kinscherf, N.Y. Giants vs. Detroit, Nov. 7, 1943
George Taliaferro, N.Y. Yanks vs. Los Angeles, Sept. 28, 1951
12 By many players. Last time: Rick Tuten, Seattle vs. Denver, Nov. 28, 1993

Longest Punt
98 Steve O'Neal, N.Y. Jets vs. Denver, Sept. 21, 1969
94 Joe Lintzenich, Chi. Bears vs. N.Y. Giants, Nov. 16, 1931
93 Shawn McCarthy, New England vs. Buffalo, Nov. 3, 1991

AVERAGE YARDAGE

Highest Average, Punting, Career (250 punts)
45.10 Sammy Baugh, Washington, 1937-52 (338-15,245)
44.68 Tommy Davis, San Francisco, 1959-69 (511-22,833)
44.29 Yale Lary, Detroit, 1952-53, 1956-64 (503-22,279)

Highest Average, Punting, Season (Qualifiers)
51.40 Sammy Baugh, Washington, 1940 (35-1,799)
48.94 Yale Lary, Detroit, 1963 (35-1,713)
48.73 Sammy Baugh, Washington, 1941 (30-1,462)

Highest Average, Punting, Rookie, Season (Qualifiers)
45.92 Frank Sinkwich, Detroit, 1943 (12-551)
45.66 Tommy Davis, San Francisco, 1959 (59-2,694)
45.57 David Lee, Baltimore, 1966 (49-2,233)

Highest Average, Punting, Game (4 punts)
61.75 Bob Cifers, Detroit vs. Chi. Bears, Nov. 24, 1946 (4-247)
61.60 Roy McKay, Green Bay vs. Chi. Cardinals, Oct. 28, 1945 (5-308)
59.40 Sammy Baugh, Washington vs. Detroit, Oct. 27, 1940 (5-297)

PUNTS HAD BLOCKED

Most Consecutive Punts, None Blocked
623 Dave Jennings, N.Y. Giants, 1976-83
619 Ray Guy, Oakland, 1979-81; L.A. Raiders, 1982-86
578 Bobby Walden, Minnesota, 1964-67; Pittsburgh, 1968-72

Most Punts Had Blocked, Career
14 Herman Weaver, Detroit, 1970-76; Seattle, 1977-80
Harry Newsome, Pittsburgh, 1985-89; Minnesota, 1990-93
12 Jerrel Wilson, Kansas City, 1963-77; New England, 1978
Tom Blanchard, N.Y. Giants, 1971-73; New Orleans, 1974-78; Tampa Bay, 1979-81
11 David Lee, Baltimore, 1966-78

Most Punts Had Blocked, Season
6 Harry Newsome, Pittsburgh, 1988
4 Bryan Wagner, Cleveland, 1990
3 By many players

PUNT RETURNS

Most Seasons Leading League
3 Les (Speedy) Duncan, San Diego, 1965-66; Washington, 1971
Rick Upchurch, Denver, 1976, 1978, 1982
2 Dick Christy, N.Y. Titans, 1961-62
Claude Gibson, Oakland, 1963-64
Billy Johnson, Houston, 1975, 1977
Mel Gray, New Orleans, 1987; Detroit, 1991

PUNT RETURNS

Most Punt Returns, Career
292 Vai Sikahema, St. Louis, 1986-87; Phoenix, 1988-90; Green Bay, 1991; Philadelphia, 1992-93
282 Billy Johnson, Houston, 1974-80; Atlanta, 1982-87; Washington, 1988
267 J.T. Smith, Washington, 1978; Kansas City, 1978-84; St. Louis, 1985-87; Phoenix, 1988-90

Most Punt Returns, Season
70 Danny Reece, Tampa Bay, 1979
62 Fulton Walker, Miami-L.A. Raiders, 1985
58 J.T. Smith, Kansas City, 1979
Greg Pruitt, L.A. Raiders, 1983
Leo Lewis, Minnesota, 1988

Most Punt Returns, Rookie, Season
57 Lew Barnes, Chicago, 1986

54 James Jones, Dallas, 1980
53 Louis Lipps, Pittsburgh, 1984

Most Punt Returns, Game

11 Eddie Brown, Washington vs. Tampa Bay, Oct. 9, 1977
10 Theo Bell, Pittsburgh vs. Buffalo, Dec. 16, 1979
Mike Nelms, Washington vs. New Orleans, Dec. 26, 1982
Ronnie Harris, New England vs. Pittsburgh, Dec. 5, 1993
9 Rodger Bird, Oakland vs. Denver, Sept. 10, 1967
Ralph McGill, San Francisco vs. Atlanta, Oct. 29, 1972
Ed Podolak, Kansas City vs. San Diego, Nov. 10, 1974
Anthony Leonard, San Francisco vs. New Orleans, Oct. 17, 1976
Butch Johnson, Dallas vs. Buffalo, Nov. 15, 1976
Larry Marshall, Philadelphia vs. Tampa Bay, Sept. 18, 1977
Nesby Glasgow, Baltimore vs. Kansas City, Sept. 2, 1979
Mike Nelms, Washington vs. St. Louis, Dec. 21, 1980
Leon Bright, N.Y. Giants vs. Philadelphia, Dec. 11, 1982
Pete Shaw, N.Y. Giants vs. Philadelphia, Nov. 20, 1983
Cleotha Montgomery, L.A. Raiders vs. Detroit, Dec. 10, 1984
Phil McConkey, N.Y. Giants vs. Philadelphia, Dec. 6, 1987 (OT)

FAIR CATCHES

Most Fair Catches, Career

102 Willie Wood, Green Bay, 1960-71
99 Phil McConkey, N.Y. Giants, 1984-88; Green Bay, 1986; San Diego, 1989
98 Leo Lewis, Minnesota, 1981-90, 1991; Cleveland, 1990

Most Fair Catches, Season

27 Leo Lewis, Minnesota, 1989
25 Mark Konecny, Philadelphia, 1988
Phil McConkey, N.Y. Giants, 1988
Chris Warren, Seattle, 1992
24 Ken Graham, San Diego, 1969
Brian Mitchell, Washington, 1994

Most Fair Catches, Game

7 Lem Barney, Detroit vs. Chicago, Nov. 21, 1976
Bobby Morse, Philadelphia vs. Buffalo, Dec. 27, 1987
6 Jake Scott, Miami vs. Buffalo, Dec. 20, 1970
Greg Pruitt, L.A. Raiders vs. Seattle, Oct. 7, 1984
Phil McConkey, San Diego vs. Kansas City, Dec. 17, 1989
Gerald McNeil, Houston vs. Pittsburgh, Sept. 16, 1990
5 By many players

YARDS GAINED

Most Seasons Leading League

3 Alvin Haymond, Baltimore, 1965-66; Los Angeles, 1969
2 Bill Dudley, Pittsburgh, 1942, 1946
Emlen Tunnell, N.Y. Giants, 1951-52
Dick Christy, N.Y. Titans, 1961-62
Claude Gibson, Oakland, 1963-64
Rodger Bird, Oakland, 1966-67
J.T. Smith, Kansas City, 1979-80
Vai Sikahema, St. Louis, 1986-87
David Meggett, N.Y. Giants, 1989-90

Most Yards Gained, Career

3,317 Billy Johnson, Houston, 1974-80; Atlanta, 1982-87; Washington, 1988
3,169 Vai Sikahema, St. Louis, 1986-87; Phoenix, 1988-90; Green Bay, 1991; Philadelphia, 1992-93
3,008 Rick Upchurch, Denver, 1975-83

Most Yards Gained, Season

692 Fulton Walker, Miami-L.A. Raiders, 1985
666 Greg Pruitt, L.A. Raiders, 1983
656 Louis Lipps, Pittsburgh, 1984

Most Yards Gained, Rookie, Season

656 Louis Lipps, Pittsburgh, 1984
655 Neal Colzie, Oakland, 1975
608 Mike Haynes, New England, 1976

Most Yards Gained, Game

207 LeRoy Irvin, Los Angeles vs. Atlanta, Oct. 11, 1981
205 George Atkinson, Oakland vs. Buffalo, Sept. 15, 1968
184 Tom Watkins, Detroit vs. San Francisco, Oct. 6, 1963

Longest Punt Return (All TDs)

103 Robert Bailey, L.A. Rams vs. New Orleans, Oct. 23, 1994
98 Gil LeFebvre, Cincinnati vs. Brooklyn, Dec. 3, 1933
Charlie West, Minnesota vs. Washington, Nov. 3, 1968
Dennis Morgan, Dallas vs. St. Louis, Oct. 13, 1974
Terance Mathis, N.Y. Jets vs. Dallas, Nov. 4, 1990
97 Greg Pruitt, L.A. Raiders vs. Washington, Oct. 2, 1983

AVERAGE YARDAGE

Highest Average, Career (75 returns)

12.78 George McAfee, Chi. Bears, 1940-41, 1945-50 (112-1,431)
12.75 Jack Christiansen, Detroit, 1951-58 (85-1,084)
12.55 Claude Gibson, San Diego, 1961-62; Oakland, 1963-65 (110-1,381)

Highest Average, Season (Qualifiers)

23.00 Herb Rich, Baltimore, 1950 (12-276)
21.47 Jack Christiansen, Detroit, 1952 (15-322)
21.28 Dick Christy, N.Y. Titans, 1961 (18-383)

Highest Average, Rookie, Season (Qualifiers)

23.00 Herb Rich, Baltimore, 1950 (12-276)
20.88 Jerry Davis, Chi. Cardinals, 1948 (16-334)
20.73 Frank Sinkwich, Detroit, 1943 (11-228)

Highest Average, Game (3 returns)

47.67 Chuck Latourette, St. Louis vs. New Orleans, Sept. 29, 1968 (3-143)
47.33 Johnny Roland, St. Louis vs. Philadelphia, Oct. 2, 1966 (3-142)
45.67 Dick Christy, N.Y. Titans vs. Denver, Sept. 24, 1961 (3-137)

TOUCHDOWNS

Most Touchdowns, Career

8 Jack Christiansen, Detroit, 1951-58
Rick Upchurch, Denver, 1975-83
6 Billy Johnson, Houston, 1974-80; Atlanta, 1982-87; Washington, 1988
David Meggett, N.Y. Giants, 1989-94
5 Emlen Tunnell, N.Y. Giants, 1948-58; Green Bay, 1959-61
Brian Mitchell, Washington, 1990-94
Eric Metcalf, Cleveland, 1989-94

Most Touchdowns, Season

4 Jack Christiansen, Detroit, 1951
Rick Upchurch, Denver, 1976
3 Emlen Tunnell, N.Y. Giants, 1951
Billy Johnson, Houston, 1975
LeRoy Irvin, Los Angeles, 1981
2 By many players

Most Touchdowns, Rookie, Season

4 Jack Christiansen, Detroit, 1951
2 By 10 players

Most Touchdowns, Game

2 Jack Christiansen, Detroit vs. Los Angeles, Oct. 14, 1951; vs. Green Bay, Nov. 22, 1951
Dick Christy, N.Y. Titans vs. Denver, Sept. 24, 1961
Rick Upchurch, Denver vs. Cleveland, Sept. 26, 1976
LeRoy Irvin, Los Angeles vs. Atlanta, Oct. 11, 1981
Vai Sikahema, St. Louis vs. Tampa Bay, Dec. 21, 1986
Todd Kinchen, L.A. Rams vs. Atlanta, Dec. 27, 1992
Eric Metcalf, Cleveland vs. Pittsburgh, Oct. 24, 1993

KICKOFF RETURNS

Most Seasons Leading League

3 Abe Woodson, San Francisco, 1959, 1962-63
2 Lynn Chandnois, Pittsburgh, 1951-52
Bobby Jancik, Houston, 1962-63
Travis Williams, Green Bay, 1967; Los Angeles, 1971
Mel Gray, Detroit, 1991, 1994

KICKOFF RETURNS

Most Kickoff Returns, Career

309 Mel Gray, New Orleans, 1986-88; Detroit, 1989-94
275 Ron Smith, Chicago, 1965, 1970-72; Atlanta, 1966-67; Los Angeles, 1968-69; San Diego, 1973; Oakland, 1974
243 Bruce Harper, N.Y. Jets, 1977-84

Most Kickoff Returns, Season

63 Tyrone Hughes, New Orleans, 1994
60 Drew Hill, Los Angeles, 1981
58 Brian Mitchell, Washington, 1994

Most Kickoff Returns, Rookie, Season

55 Stump Mitchell, St. Louis, 1981
53 Buster Rhymes, Minnesota, 1985
50 Nesby Glasgow, Baltimore, 1979
Dino Hall, Cleveland, 1979

Most Kickoff Returns, Game

9 Noland Smith, Kansas City vs. Oakland, Nov. 23, 1967
Dino Hall, Cleveland vs. Pittsburgh, Oct. 7, 1979
Paul Palmer, Kansas City vs. Seattle, Sept. 20, 1987
8 By many players

YARDS GAINED

Most Seasons Leading League

3 Bruce Harper, N.Y. Jets, 1977-79
2 Marshall Goldberg, Chi. Cardinals, 1941-42
Woodley Lewis, Los Angeles, 1953-54
Al Carmichael, Green Bay, 1956-57
Timmy Brown, Philadelphia, 1961, 1963
Bobby Jancik, Houston, 1963, 1966
Ron Smith, Atlanta, 1966-67

Most Yards Gained, Career

7,650 Mel Gray, New Orleans, 1986-88; Detroit, 1989-94

6,922 Ron Smith, Chicago, 1965, 1970-72; Atlanta, 1966-67; Los Angeles, 1968-69; San Diego, 1973; Oakland, 1974
5,538 Abe Woodson, San Francisco, 1958-64; St. Louis, 1965-66

Most Yards Gained, Season
1,556 Tyrone Hughes, New Orleans, 1994
1,478 Brian Mitchell, Washington, 1994
1,345 Buster Rhymes, Minnesota, 1985

Most Yards Gained, Rookie, Season
1,345 Buster Rhymes, Minnesota, 1985
1,293 Andre Coleman, San Diego, 1994
1,292 Stump Mitchell, St. Louis, 1981

Most Yards Gained, Game
304 Tyrone Hughes, New Orleans vs. L.A. Rams, Oct. 23, 1994
294 Wally Triplett, Detroit vs. Los Angeles, Oct. 29, 1950
251 Jon Vaughn, Kansas City vs. Miami, Dec. 12, 1994

Longest Kickoff Return (All TDs)
106 Al Carmichael, Green Bay vs. Chi. Bears, Oct. 7, 1956
Noland Smith, Kansas City vs. Denver, Dec. 17, 1967
Roy Green, St. Louis vs. Dallas, Oct. 21, 1979
105 Frank Seno, Chi. Cardinals vs. N.Y. Giants, Oct. 20, 1946
Ollie Matson, Chi. Cardinals vs. Washington, Oct. 14, 1956
Abe Woodson, San Francisco vs. Los Angeles, Nov. 8, 1959
Timmy Brown, Philadelphia vs. Cleveland, Sept. 17, 1961
Jon Arnett, Los Angeles vs. Detroit, Oct. 29, 1961
Eugene (Mercury) Morris, Miami vs. Cincinnati, Sept. 14, 1969
Travis Williams, Los Angeles vs. New Orleans, Dec. 5, 1971
104 By many players

AVERAGE YARDAGE

Highest Average, Career (75 returns)
30.56 Gale Sayers, Chicago, 1965-71 (91-2,781)
29.57 Lynn Chandnois, Pittsburgh, 1950-56 (92-2,720)
28.69 Abe Woodson, San Francisco, 1958-64; St. Louis, 1965-66 (193-5,538)

Highest Average, Season (Qualifiers)
41.06 Travis Williams, Green Bay, 1967 (18-739)
37.69 Gale Sayers, Chicago, 1967 (16-603)
35.50 Ollie Matson, Chi. Cardinals, 1958 (14-497)

Highest Average, Rookie, Season (Qualifiers)
41.06 Travis Williams, Green Bay, 1967 (18-739)
33.08 Tom Moore, Green Bay, 1960 (12-397)
32.88 Duriel Harris, Miami, 1976 (17-559)

Highest Average, Game (3 returns)
73.50 Wally Triplett, Detroit vs. Los Angeles, Oct. 29, 1950 (4-294)
67.33 Lenny Lyles, San Francisco vs. Baltimore, Dec. 18, 1960 (3-202)
65.33 Ken Hall, Houston vs. N.Y. Titans, Oct. 23, 1960 (3-196)

TOUCHDOWNS

Most Touchdowns, Career
6 Ollie Matson, Chi. Cardinals, 1952, 1954-58; L.A. Rams, 1959-62; Detroit, 1963; Philadelphia, 1964
Gale Sayers, Chicago, 1965-71
Travis Williams, Green Bay, 1967-70; Los Angeles, 1971
Mel Gray, New Orleans, 1986-88; Detroit, 1989-94
5 Bobby Mitchell, Cleveland, 1958-61; Washington, 1962-68
Abe Woodson, San Francisco, 1958-64; St. Louis, 1965-66
Timmy Brown, Green Bay, 1959; Philadelphia, 1960-67; Baltimore, 1968
4 Cecil Turner, Chicago, 1968-73
Ron Brown, L.A. Rams, 1984-89, 1991; L.A. Raiders, 1990
Jon Vaughn, New England, 1991-92; Seattle, 1993-94; Kansas City, 1994

Most Touchdowns, Season
4 Travis Williams, Green Bay, 1967
Cecil Turner, Chicago, 1970
3 Verda (Vitamin T) Smith, Los Angeles, 1950
Abe Woodson, San Francisco, 1963
Gale Sayers, Chicago, 1967
Raymond Clayborn, New England, 1977
Ron Brown, L.A. Rams, 1985
Mel Gray, Detroit, 1994
2 By many players

Most Touchdowns, Rookie, Season
4 Travis Williams, Green Bay, 1967
3 Raymond Clayborn, New England, 1977
2 By eight players

Most Touchdowns, Game
2 Timmy Brown, Philadelphia vs. Dallas, Nov. 6, 1966
Travis Williams, Green Bay vs. Cleveland, Nov. 12, 1967
Ron Brown, L.A. Rams vs. Green Bay, Nov. 24, 1985
Tyrone Hughes, New Orleans vs. L.A. Rams, Oct. 23, 1994

COMBINED KICK RETURNS

Most Combined Kick Returns, Career
527 Vai Sikahema, St. Louis, 1986-87; Phoenix, 1988-90; Green Bay, 1991; Philadelphia, 1992-93 (p-292, k-235)
510 Ron Smith, Chicago, 1965, 1970-72; Atlanta, 1966-67; Los Angeles, 1968-69; San Diego, 1973; Oakland, 1974 (p-235, k-275)
490 Mel Gray, New Orleans, 1986-88; Detroit, 1989-94 (p-181, k-309)

Most Combined Kick Returns, Season
100 Larry Jones, Washington, 1975 (p-53, k-47)
97 Stump Mitchell, St. Louis, 1981 (p-42, k-55)
94 Nesby Glasgow, Baltimore, 1979 (p-44, k-50)

Most Combined Kick Returns, Game
13 Stump Mitchell, St. Louis vs. Atlanta, Oct. 18, 1981 (p-6, k-7)
Ronnie Harris, New England vs. Pittsburgh, Dec. 5, 1993 (p-10, k-3)
12 Mel Renfro, Dallas vs. Green Bay, Nov. 29, 1964 (p-4, k-8)
Larry Jones, Washington vs. Dallas, Dec. 13, 1975 (p-6, k-6)
Eddie Brown, Washington vs. Tampa Bay, Oct. 9, 1977 (p-11, k-1)
Nesby Glasgow, Baltimore vs. Denver, Sept. 2, 1979 (p-9, k-3)
11 By many players

YARDS GAINED

Most Yards Returned, Career
9,734 Mel Gray, New Orleans, 1986-88; Detroit, 1989-94 (p-2,084, k-7,650)
8,710 Ron Smith, Chicago, 1965, 1970-72; Atlanta, 1966-67; Los Angeles, 1968-69; San Diego, 1973; Oakland, 1974 (p-1,788, k-6,922)
8,102 Vai Sikahema, St. Louis, 1986-87; Phoenix, 1988-90; Green Bay, 1991; Philadelphia, 1992-93 (p-3,169, k-4,933)

Most Yards Returned, Season
1,930 Brian Mitchell, Washington, 1994 (p-452, k-1,478)
1,737 Stump Mitchell, St. Louis, 1981 (p-445, k-1,292)
1,699 Tyrone Hughes, New Orleans, 1994 (p-143, k-1,556)

Most Yards Returned, Game
347 Tyrone Hughes, New Orleans vs. L.A. Rams, Oct. 23, 1994 (p-43, k-304)
294 Wally Triplett, Detroit vs. Los Angeles, Oct. 29, 1950 (k-294)
Woodley Lewis, Los Angeles vs. Detroit, Oct. 18, 1953 (p-120, k-174)
289 Eddie Payton, Detroit vs. Minnesota, Dec. 17, 1977 (p-105, k-184)

TOUCHDOWNS

Most Touchdowns, Career
9 Ollie Matson, Chi. Cardinals, 1952, 1954-58; Los Angeles, 1959-62; Detroit, 1963; Philadelphia, 1964-66 (p-3, k-6)
Mel Gray, New Orleans, 1986-88; Detroit, 1989-94 (p-3, k-6)
8 Jack Christiansen, Detroit, 1951-58 (p-8)
Bobby Mitchell, Cleveland, 1958-61; Washington, 1962-68 (p-3, k-5)
Gale Sayers, Chicago, 1965-71 (p-2, k-6)
Rick Upchurch, Denver, 1975-83 (p-8)
Billy Johnson, Houston, 1974-80; Atlanta, 1982-87; Washington, 1988 (p-6, k-2)
7 Abe Woodson, San Francisco, 1958-64; St. Louis, 1965-66 (p-2, k-5)
Travis Williams, Green Bay, 1967-70; Los Angeles, 1971 (p-1, k-6)
David Meggett, N.Y. Giants, 1989-94 (p-6, k-1)
Eric Metcalf, Cleveland, 1989-94 (p-5, k-2)

Most Touchdowns, Season
4 Jack Christiansen, Detroit, 1951 (p-4)
Emlen Tunnell, N.Y. Giants, 1951 (p-3, k-1)
Gale Sayers, Chicago, 1967 (p-1, k-3)
Travis Williams, Green Bay, 1967 (k-4)
Cecil Turner, Chicago, 1970 (k-4)
Billy Johnson, Houston, 1975 (p-3, k-1)
Rick Upchurch, Denver, 1976 (p-4)
3 Verda (Vitamin T) Smith, Los Angeles, 1950 (k-3)
Abe Woodson, San Francisco, 1963 (k-3)
Raymond Clayborn, New England, 1977 (k-3)
Billy Johnson, Houston, 1977 (p-2, k-1)
LeRoy Irvin, Los Angeles, 1981 (p-3)
Ron Brown, L.A. Rams, 1985 (k-3)
Tyrone Hughes, New Orleans, 1993 (p-2, k-1)
Mel Gray, Detroit, 1994 (k-3)
2 By many players

Most Touchdowns, Game
2 Jack Christiansen, Detroit vs. Los Angeles, Oct. 14, 1951 (p-2); vs. Green Bay, Nov. 22, 1951 (p-2)
Jim Patton, N.Y. Giants vs. Washington, Oct. 30, 1955 (p-1, k-1)
Bobby Mitchell, Cleveland vs. Philadelphia, Nov. 23, 1958 (p-1, k-1)
Dick Christy, N.Y. Titans vs. Denver, Sept. 24, 1961 (p-2)
Al Frazier, Denver vs. Boston, Dec. 3, 1961 (p-1, k-1)
Timmy Brown, Philadelphia vs. Dallas, Nov. 6, 1966 (k-2)
Travis Williams, Green Bay vs. Cleveland, Nov. 12, 1967 (k-2); vs. Pittsburgh, Nov. 2, 1969 (p-1, k-1)
Gale Sayers, Chicago vs. San Francisco, Dec. 3, 1967 (p-1, k-1)
Rick Upchurch, Denver vs. Cleveland, Sept. 26, 1976 (p-2)
Eddie Payton, Detroit vs. Minnesota, Dec. 17, 1977 (p-1, k-1)

LeRoy Irvin, Los Angeles vs. Atlanta, Oct. 11, 1981 (p-2)
Ron Brown, L.A. Rams vs. Green Bay, Nov. 24, 1985 (k-2)
Vai Sikahema, St. Louis vs. Tampa Bay, Dec. 21, 1986 (p-2)
Eric Metcalf, Cleveland vs. Pittsburgh, Oct. 24, 1993 (p-2)
Tyrone Hughes, New Orleans vs. L.A. Rams, Oct. 23, 1994 (k-2)

FUMBLES

Most Fumbles, Career

128 Dave Krieg, Seattle, 1980-91; Kansas City, 1992-93; Detroit, 1994
125 Warren Moon, Houston, 1984-93; Minnesota, 1994
106 Dan Fouts, San Diego, 1973-87

Most Fumbles, Season

18 Dave Krieg, Seattle, 1989
Warren Moon, Houston, 1990
17 Dan Pastorini, Houston, 1973
Warren Moon, Houston, 1984
Randall Cunningham, Philadelphia, 1989
16 Don Meredith, Dallas, 1964
Joe Cribbs, Buffalo, 1980
Steve Fuller, Kansas City, 1980
Paul McDonald, Cleveland, 1984
Phil Simms, N.Y. Giants, 1985

Most Fumbles, Game

7 Len Dawson, Kansas City vs. San Diego, Nov. 15, 1964
6 Sam Etcheverry, St. Louis vs. N.Y. Giants, Sept, 17, 1961
Dave Krieg, Seattle vs. Kansas City, Nov. 5, 1989
5 Paul Christman, Chi. Cardinals vs. Green Bay, Nov. 10, 1946
Charlie Conerly, N.Y. Giants vs. San Francisco, Dec. 1, 1957
Jack Kemp, Buffalo vs. Houston, Oct. 29, 1967
Roman Gabriel, Philadelphia vs. Oakland, Nov. 21, 1976
Randall Cunningham, Philadelphia vs. L.A. Raiders, Nov. 30, 1986 (OT)
Willie Totten, Buffalo vs. Indianapolis, Oct. 4, 1987
Dave Walter, Cincinnati vs. Seattle, Oct. 11, 1987
Dave Krieg, Seattle vs. San Diego, Nov. 25, 1990 (OT)
Andre Ware, Detroit vs. Green Bay, Dec. 6, 1992

FUMBLES RECOVERED

Most Fumbles Recovered, Career, Own and Opponents'

46 Warren Moon, Houston, 1984-93; Minnesota, 1994 (46 own)
43 Fran Tarkenton, Minnesota, 1961-66, 1972-78; N.Y. Giants, 1967-71 (43 own)
40 Boomer Esiason, Cincinnati, 1984-92; N.Y. Jets, 1993-94 (40 own)

Most Fumbles Recovered, Season, Own and Opponents'

9 Don Hultz, Minnesota, 1963 (9 opp)
Dave Krieg, Seattle, 1989 (9 own)
8 Paul Christman, Chi. Cardinals, 1945 (8 own)
Joe Schmidt, Detroit, 1955 (8 opp)
Bill Butler, Minnesota, 1963 (8 own)
Kermit Alexander, San Francisco, 1965 (4 own, 4 opp)
Jack Lambert, Pittsburgh, 1976 (1 own, 7 opp)
Danny White, Dallas, 1981 (8 own)
Dan Marino, Miami, 1988 (7 own, 1 opp)
7 By many players

Most Fumbles Recovered, Game, Own and Opponents'

4 Otto Graham, Cleveland vs. N.Y. Giants, Oct. 25, 1953 (4 own)
Sam Etcheverry, St. Louis vs. N.Y. Giants, Sept. 17, 1961 (4 own)
Roman Gabriel, Los Angeles vs. San Francisco, Oct. 12, 1969 (4 own)
Joe Ferguson, Buffalo vs. Miami, Sept. 18, 1977 (4 own)
Randall Cunningham, Philadelphia vs. L.A. Raiders, Nov. 30, 1986 (OT) (4 own)
3 By many players

OWN FUMBLES RECOVERED

Most Own Fumbles Recovered, Career

46 Warren Moon, Houston, 1984-93; Minnesota, 1994
43 Fran Tarkenton, Minnesota, 1961-66, 1972-78; N.Y. Giants, 1967-71
40 Boomer Esiason, Cincinnati, 1984-92; N.Y. Jets, 1993-94

Most Own Fumbles Recovered, Season

9 Dave Krieg, Seattle, 1989
8 Paul Christman, Chi. Cardinals, 1945
Bill Butler, Minnesota, 1963
Danny White, Dallas, 1981
7 By many players

Most Own Fumbles Recovered, Game

4 Otto Graham, Cleveland vs. N.Y. Giants, Oct. 25, 1953
Sam Etcheverry, St. Louis vs. N.Y. Giants, Sept. 17, 1961
Roman Gabriel, Los Angeles vs. San Francisco, Oct. 12, 1969
Joe Ferguson, Buffalo vs. Miami, Sept. 18, 1977
Randall Cunningham, Philadelphia vs. L.A. Raiders, Nov. 30, 1986 (OT)
3 By many players

OPPONENTS' FUMBLES RECOVERED

Most Opponents' Fumbles Recovered, Career

29 Jim Marshall, Cleveland, 1960; Minnesota, 1961-79
28 Rickey Jackson, New Orleans, 1981-93; San Francisco, 1994
25 Dick Butkus, Chicago, 1965-73

Most Opponents' Fumbles Recovered, Season

9 Don Hultz, Minnesota, 1963
8 Joe Schmidt, Detroit, 1955
7 Alan Page, Minnesota, 1970
Jack Lambert, Pittsburgh, 1976
Ray Childress, Houston, 1988
Rickey Jackson, New Orleans, 1990

Most Opponents' Fumbles Recovered, Game

3 Corwin Clatt, Chi. Cardinals vs. Detroit, Nov. 6, 1949
Vic Sears, Philadelphia vs. Green Bay, Nov. 2, 1952
Ed Beatty, San Francisco vs. Los Angeles, Oct. 7, 1956
Ron Carroll, Houston vs. Cincinnati, Oct. 27, 1974
Maurice Spencer, New Orleans vs. Atlanta, Oct. 10, 1976
Steve Nelson, New England vs. Philadelphia, Oct. 8, 1978
Charles Jackson, Kansas City vs. Pittsburgh, Sept. 6, 1981
Willie Buchanon, San Diego vs. Denver, Sept. 27, 1981
Joey Browner, Minnesota vs. San Francisco, Sept. 8, 1985
Ray Childress, Houston vs. Washington, Oct. 30, 1988
2 By many players

YARDS RETURNING FUMBLES

Longest Fumble Run (All TDs)

104 Jack Tatum, Oakland vs. Green Bay, Sept. 24, 1972
100 Chris Martin, Kansas City vs. Miami, Oct. 13, 1991
99 Don Griffin, San Francisco vs. Chicago, Dec. 23, 1991

TOUCHDOWNS

Most Touchdowns, Career (Total)

4 Bill Thompson, Denver, 1969-81
Jessie Tuggle, Atlanta, 1987-94
3 Ralph Heywood, Detroit, 1947-48; Boston, 1948; N.Y. Bulldogs, 1949
Leo Sugar, Chi. Cardinals, 1954-59; St. Louis, 1960; Philadelphia, 1961; Detroit, 1962
Bud McFadin, Los Angeles, 1952-56; Denver, 1960-63; Houston, 1964-65
Doug Cline, Houston, 1960-66; San Diego, 1966
Bob Lilly, Dall. Cowboys, 1961-74
Chris Hanburger, Washington, 1965-78
Lemar Parrish, Cincinnati, 1970-77; Washington, 1978-81; Buffalo, 1982
Paul Krause, Washington, 1964-67; Minnesota, 1968-79
Brad Dusek, Washington, 1974-81
David Logan, Tampa Bay, 1979-86; Green Bay, 1987
Thomas Howard, Kansas City, 1977-83; St. Louis, 1984-85
Greg Townsend, L.A. Raiders, 1983-93; Philadelphia, 1994
Les Miller, San Diego, 1987-90, 1994; New Orleans, 1991-94
Chris Martin, New Orleans, 1983; Minnesota, 1984-88; Kansas City, 1989-92; L.A. Rams, 1993-94
Seth Joyner, Philadelphia, 1986-93; Arizona, 1994
Derrick Thomas, Kansas City, 1989-94
2 By many players

Most Touchdowns, Season (Total)

2 Harold McPhail, Boston, 1934
Harry Ebding, Detroit, 1937
John Morelli, Boston, 1944
Frank Maznicki, Boston, 1947
Fred (Dippy) Evans, Chi. Bears, 1948
Ralph Heywood, Boston, 1948
Art Tait, N.Y. Yanks, 1951
John Dwyer, Los Angeles, 1952
Leo Sugar, Chi. Cardinals, 1957
Doug Cline, Houston, 1961
Jim Bradshaw, Pittsburgh, 1964
Royce Berry, Cincinnati, 1970
Ahmad Rashad, Buffalo, 1974
Tim Gray, Kansas City, 1977
Charles Phillips, Oakland, 1978
Kenny Johnson, Atlanta, 1981
George Martin, N.Y. Giants, 1981
Del Rodgers, Green Bay, 1982
Mike Douglass, Green Bay, 1983
Shelton Robinson, Seattle, 1983
Erik McMillan, N.Y. Jets, 1989
Les Miller, San Diego, 1990
Seth Joyner, Philadelphia, 1991
Robert Goff, New Orleans, 1992
Willie Clay, Detroit, 1993
Tyrone Hughes, New Orleans, 1994

ALL-TIME RECORDS

Most Touchdowns, Career (Own recovered)
2 Ken Kavanaugh, Chi. Bears, 1940-41, 1945-50
Mike Ditka, Chicago, 1961-66; Philadelphia, 1967-68; Dallas, 1969-72
Gail Cogdill, Detroit, 1960-68; Baltimore, 1968; Atlanta, 1969-70
Ahmad Rashad, St. Louis, 1972-73; Buffalo, 1974; Minnesota, 1976-82
Jim Mitchell, Atlanta, 1969-79
Drew Pearson, Dallas, 1973-83
Del Rodgers, Green Bay, 1982, 1984; San Francisco, 1987-88

Most Touchdowns, Season (Own recovered)
2 Ahmad Rashad, Buffalo, 1974
Del Rodgers, Green Bay, 1982
1 By many players

Most Touchdowns, Career (Opponents' recovered)
4 Jessie Tuggle, Atlanta, 1987-94
3 Leo Sugar, Chi. Cardinals, 1954-59; St. Louis, 1960; Philadelphia, 1961; Detroit, 1962
Doug Cline, Houston, 1960-66; San Diego, 1966
Bud McFadin, Los Angeles, 1952-56; Denver, 1960-63; Houston, 1964-65
Bob Lilly, Dall. Cowboys, 1961-74
Chris Hanburger, Washington, 1965-78
Paul Krause, Washington, 1964-67; Minnesota, 1968-79
Lemar Parrish, Cincinnati, 1970-77; Washington, 1978-81; Buffalo, 1982
Bill Thompson, Denver, 1969-81
Brad Dusek, Washington, 1974-81
David Logan, Tampa Bay, 1979-86; Green Bay, 1987
Thomas Howard, Kansas City, 1977-83; St. Louis, 1984-85
Greg Townsend, L.A. Raiders, 1983-93; Philadelphia, 1994
Les Miller, San Diego, 1987-90, 1994; New Orleans, 1991-94
Chris Martin, New Orleans, 1983; Minnesota, 1984-88; Kansas City, 1989-92; L.A. Rams, 1993-94
Seth Joyner, Philadelphia, 1986-93; Arizona, 1994
Derrick Thomas, Kansas City, 1989-94
2 By many players

Most Touchdowns, Season (Opponents' recovered)
2 Harold McPhail, Boston, 1934
Harry Ebding, Detroit, 1937
John Morelli, Boston, 1944
Frank Maznicki, Boston, 1947
Fred (Dippy) Evans, Chi. Bears, 1948
Ralph Heywood, Boston, 1948
Art Tait, N.Y. Yanks, 1951
John Dwyer, Los Angeles, 1952
Leo Sugar, Chi. Cardinals, 1957
Doug Cline, Houston, 1961
Jim Bradshaw, Pittsburgh, 1964
Royce Berry, Cincinnati, 1970
Tim Gray, Kansas City, 1977
Charles Phillips, Oakland, 1978
Kenny Johnson, Atlanta, 1981
George Martin, N.Y. Giants, 1981
Mike Douglass, Green Bay, 1983
Shelton Robinson, Seattle, 1983
Erik McMillan, N.Y. Jets, 1989
Les Miller, San Diego, 1990
Seth Joyner, Philadelphia, 1991
Robert Goff, New Orleans, 1992
Willie Clay, Detroit, 1993
Tyrone Hughes, New Orleans, 1994

Most Touchdowns, Game (Opponents' recovered)
2 Fred (Dippy) Evans, Chi. Bears vs. Washington, Nov. 28, 1948

COMBINED NET YARDS GAINED

Rushing, receiving, interception returns, punt returns, kickoff returns, and fumble returns

Most Seasons Leading League
5 Jim Brown, Cleveland, 1958-61, 1964
3 Cliff Battles, Boston, 1932-33; Washington, 1937
Gale Sayers, Chicago, 1965-67
Eric Dickerson, L.A. Rams, 1983-84, 1986
Thurman Thomas, Buffalo, 1989, 1991-92
2 By many players

Most Consecutive Seasons Leading League
4 Jim Brown, Cleveland, 1958-61
3 Gale Sayers, Chicago, 1965-67
2 Cliff Battles, Boston, 1932-33
Charley Trippi, Chi. Cardinals, 1948-49
Timmy Brown, Philadelphia, 1962-63
• Floyd Little, Denver, 1967-68
James Brooks, San Diego, 1981-82
Eric Dickerson, L.A. Rams, 1983-84
Thurman Thomas, Buffalo, 1991-92

ATTEMPTS

Most Attempts, Career
4,368 Walter Payton, Chicago, 1975-87
3,351 Tony Dorsett, Dallas, 1977-87; Denver, 1988
3,293 Eric Dickerson, L.A. Rams, 1983-87; Indianapolis, 1987-91; L.A. Raiders, 1992; Atlanta, 1993

Most Attempts, Season
496 James Wilder, Tampa Bay, 1984
449 Marcus Allen, L.A. Raiders, 1985
442 Eric Dickerson, L.A. Rams, 1983

Most Attempts, Rookie, Season
442 Eric Dickerson, L.A. Rams, 1983
395 George Rogers, New Orleans, 1981
390 Joe Cribbs, Buffalo, 1980

Most Attempts, Game
48 James Wilder, Tampa Bay vs. Pittsburgh, Oct. 30, 1983
47 James Wilder, Tampa Bay vs. Green Bay, Sept. 30, 1984 (OT)
46 Gerald Riggs, Atlanta vs. L.A. Rams, Nov. 17, 1985

YARDS GAINED

Most Yards Gained, Career
21,803 Walter Payton, Chicago, 1975-87
16,326 Tony Dorsett, Dallas, 1977-87; Denver, 1988
15,459 Jim Brown, Cleveland, 1957-65

Most Yards Gained, Season
2,535 Lionel James, San Diego, 1985
2,477 Brian Mitchell, Washington, 1994
2,462 Terry Metcalf, St. Louis, 1975

Most Yards Gained, Rookie, Season
2,317 Tim Brown, L.A. Raiders, 1988
2,272 Gale Sayers, Chicago, 1965
2,212 Eric Dickerson, L.A. Rams, 1983

Most Yards Gained, Game
373 Billy Cannon, Houston vs. N.Y. Titans, Dec. 10, 1961
347 Tyrone Hughes, New Orleans vs. L.A. Rams, Oct. 23, 1994
345 Lionel James, San Diego vs. L.A. Raiders, Nov. 10, 1985 (OT)

SACKS

Sacks have been compiled since 1982.

Most Sacks, Career
145 Reggie White, Philadelphia, 1985-92; Green Bay, 1993-94
132.5 Lawrence Taylor, N.Y. Giants, 1982-93
126.5 Richard Dent, Chicago, 1983-93; San Francisco, 1994

Most Sacks, Season
22 Mark Gastineau, N.Y. Jets, 1984
21 Reggie White, Philadelphia, 1987
Chris Doleman, Minnesota, 1989
20.5 Lawrence Taylor, N.Y. Giants, 1986

Most Sacks, Rookie, Season
12.5 Leslie O'Neal, San Diego, 1986
12 Charles Haley, San Francisco, 1986
11 Vernon Maxwell, Baltimore, 1983

Most Sacks, Game
7 Derrick Thomas, Kansas City vs. Seattle, Nov. 11, 1990
6 Fred Dean, San Francisco vs. New Orleans, Nov. 13, 1983
5.5 William Gay, Detroit vs. Tampa Bay, Sept. 4, 1983

MISCELLANEOUS

Longest Return of Missed Field Goal (All TDs)
101 Al Nelson, Philadelphia vs. Dallas, Sept. 26, 1971
100 Al Nelson, Philadelphia vs. Cleveland, Dec. 11, 1966
Ken Ellis, Green Bay vs. N.Y. Giants, Sept. 19, 1971
99 Jerry Williams, Los Angeles vs. Green Bay, Dec. 16, 1951
Carl Taseff, Baltimore vs. Los Angeles, Dec. 12, 1959
Timmy Brown, Philadelphia vs. St. Louis, Sept. 16, 1962

TEAM RECORDS

CHAMPIONSHIPS

Most Seasons League Champion
11 Green Bay, 1929-31, 1936, 1939, 1944, 1961-62, 1965-67
9 Chi. Bears, 1921, 1932-33, 1940-41, 1943, 1946, 1963, 1985
6 N.Y. Giants, 1927, 1934, 1938, 1956, 1986, 1990

Most Consecutive Seasons League Champion
3 Green Bay, 1929-31
Green Bay, 1965-67
2 Canton, 1922-23
Chi. Bears, 1932-33
Chi. Bears, 1940-41
Philadelphia, 1948-49
Detroit, 1952-53
Cleveland, 1954-55
Baltimore, 1958-59

Houston, 1960-61
Green Bay, 1961-62
Buffalo, 1964-65
Miami, 1972-73
Pittsburgh, 1974-75
Pittsburgh, 1978-79
San Francisco, 1988-89
Dallas, 1992-93

Most Times Finishing First, Regular Season (Since 1933)
18 Clev. Browns, 1950-55, 1957, 1964-65, 1967-69, 1971, 1980, 1985-87, 1989
17 N.Y. Giants, 1933-35, 1938-39, 1941, 1944, 1946, 1956, 1958-59, 1961-63, 1986, 1989-90
16 Chi. Bears, 1933-34, 1937, 1940-43, 1946, 1956, 1963, 1984-88, 1990
Dallas, 1966-71, 1973, 1976-79, 1981, 1985, 1992-94

Most Consecutive Times Finishing First, Regular Season (Since 1933)
7 Los Angeles, 1973-79
6 Cleveland, 1950-55
Dallas, 1966-71
Minnesota, 1973-78
Pittsburgh, 1974-79
5 Oakland, 1972-76
Chicago, 1984-88
San Francisco, 1986-90

GAMES WON

Most Consecutive Games Won
17 Chi. Bears, 1933-34
16 Chi. Bears, 1941-42
Miami, 1971-73
Miami, 1983-84
15 L.A. Chargers/San Diego, 1960-61
San Francisco, 1989-90

Most Consecutive Games Without Defeat
25 Canton, 1921-23 (won 22, tied 3)
24 Chi. Bears, 1941-43 (won 23, tied 1)
23 Green Bay, 1928-30 (won 21, tied 2)

Most Games Won, Season
15 San Francisco, 1984
Chicago, 1985
14 Miami, 1972
Pittsburgh, 1978
Washington, 1983
Miami, 1984
Chicago, 1986
N.Y. Giants, 1986
San Francisco, 1989
San Francisco, 1990
Washington, 1991
San Francisco, 1992
13 By many teams

Most Consecutive Games Won, Season
14 Miami, 1972
13 Chi. Bears, 1934
12 Minnesota, 1969
Chicago, 1985

Most Consecutive Games Won, Start of Season
14 Miami, 1972, entire season
13 Chi. Bears, 1934, entire season
12 Chicago, 1985

Most Consecutive Games Won, End of Season
14 Miami, 1972, entire season
13 Chi. Bears, 1934, entire season
11 Chi. Bears, 1942, entire season
Cleveland, 1951
Houston, 1993

Most Consecutive Games Without Defeat, Season
14 Miami, 1972 (won 14)
13 Chi. Bears, 1926 (won 11, tied 2)
Green Bay, 1929 (won 12, tied 1)
Chi. Bears, 1934 (won 13)
Baltimore, 1967 (won 11, tied 2)
12 Canton, 1922 (won 10, tied 2)
Canton, 1923 (won 11, tied 1)
Minnesota, 1969 (won 12)
Chicago, 1985 (won 12)

Most Consecutive Games Without Defeat, Start of Season
14 Miami, 1972 (won 14), entire season
13 Chi. Bears, 1926 (won 11, tied 2)
Green Bay, 1929 (won 12, tied 1), entire season
Chi. Bears, 1934 (won 13), entire season
Baltimore, 1967 (won 11, tied 2)
12 Canton, 1922 (won 10, tied 2), entire season
Canton, 1923 (won 11, tied 1), entire season
Chicago, 1985 (won 12)

Most Consecutive Games Without Defeat, End of Season
14 Miami, 1972 (won 14), entire season
13 Green Bay, 1929 (won 12, tied 1), entire season
Chi. Bears, 1934 (won 13), entire season
12 Canton, 1922 (won 10, tied 2), entire season
Canton, 1923 (won 11, tied 1), entire season

Most Consecutive Home Games Won
27 Miami, 1971-74
20 Green Bay, 1929-32
18 Oakland, 1968-70
Dallas, 1979-81

Most Consecutive Home Games Without Defeat
30 Green Bay, 1928-33 (won 27, tied 3)
27 Miami, 1971-74 (won 27)
25 Chi. Bears, 1923-25 (won 19, tied 6)

Most Consecutive Road Games Won
18 San Francisco, 1988-90
11 L.A. Chargers/San Diego, 1960-61
San Francisco, 1987-88
10 Chi. Bears, 1941-42
Dallas, 1968-69
New Orleans, 1987-88

Most Consecutive Road Games Without Defeat
18 San Francisco, 1988-90 (won 18)
13 Chi. Bears, 1941-43 (won 12, tied 1)
12 Green Bay, 1928-30 (won 10, tied 2)

Most Shutout Games Won or Tied, Season
10 Pottsville, 1926 (won 9, tied 1)
N.Y. Giants, 1927 (won 9, tied 1)
9 Akron, 1921 (won 8, tied 1)
Canton, 1922 (won 7, tied 2)
Frankford, 1926 (won 9)
Frankford, 1929 (won 6, tied 3)
8 By many teams

Most Consecutive Shutout Games Won or Tied
13 Akron, 1920-21 (won 10, tied 3)
7 Pottsville, 1926 (won 6, tied 1)
Detroit, 1934 (won 7)
6 Buffalo, 1920-21 (won 5, tied 1)
Frankford, 1926 (won 6)
Detroit, 1926 (won 4, tied 2)
N.Y. Giants, 1926-27 (won 5, tied 1)

GAMES LOST

Most Consecutive Games Lost
26 Tampa Bay, 1976-77
19 Chi. Cardinals, 1942-43, 1945
Oakland, 1961-62
18 Houston, 1972-73

Most Consecutive Games Without Victory
26 Tampa Bay, 1976-77 (lost 26)
23 Rochester, 1922-25 (lost 21, tied 2)
Washington, 1960-61 (lost 20, tied 3)
19 Dayton, 1927-29 (lost 18, tied 1)
Chi. Cardinals, 1942-43, 1945 (lost 19)
Oakland, 1961-62 (lost 19)

Most Games Lost, Season
15 New Orleans, 1980
Dallas, 1989
New England, 1990
Indianapolis, 1991
14 By many teams

Most Consecutive Games Lost, Season
14 Tampa Bay, 1976
New Orleans, 1980
Baltimore, 1981
New England, 1990
13 Oakland, 1962
Pittsburgh, 1969
Indianapolis, 1986
12 Tampa Bay, 1977

Most Consecutive Games Lost, Start of Season
14 Tampa Bay, 1976, entire season
New Orleans, 1980
13 Oakland, 1962
Indianapolis, 1986
12 Tampa Bay, 1977

Most Consecutive Games Lost, End of Season
14 Tampa Bay, 1976, entire season
New England, 1990
13 Pittsburgh, 1969

11 Philadelphia, 1936
Detroit, 1942, entire season
Houston, 1972

Most Consecutive Games Without Victory, Season
14 Tampa Bay, 1976 (lost 14), entire season
New Orleans, 1980 (lost 14)
Baltimore, 1981 (lost 14)
New England, 1990 (lost 14)
13 Washington, 1961 (lost 12, tied 1)
Oakland, 1962 (lost 13)
Pittsburgh, 1969 (lost 13)
Indianapolis, 1986 (lost 13)
12 Dall. Cowboys, 1960 (lost 11, tied 1), entire season
Tampa Bay, 1977 (lost 12)

Most Consecutive Games Without Victory, Start of Season
14 Tampa Bay, 1976 (lost 14), entire season
New Orleans, 1980 (lost 14)
13 Washington, 1961 (lost 12, tied 1)
Oakland, 1962 (lost 13)
Indianapolis, 1986 (lost 13)
12 Dall. Cowboys, 1960 (lost 11, tied 1), entire season
Tampa Bay, 1977 (lost 12)

Most Consecutive Games Without Victory, End of Season
14 Tampa Bay, 1976, (lost 14), entire season
New England, 1990 (lost 14)
13 Pittsburgh, 1969 (lost 13)
12 Dall. Cowboys, 1960 (lost 11, tied 1), entire season

Most Consecutive Home Games Lost
14 Dallas, 1988-89
13 Houston, 1972-73
Tampa Bay, 1976-77
11 Oakland, 1961-62
Los Angeles, 1961-63

Most Consecutive Home Games Without Victory
14 Dallas, 1988-89 (lost 14)
13 Houston, 1972-73 (lost 13)
Tampa Bay, 1976-77 (lost 13)
12 Philadelphia, 1936-38 (lost 11, tied 1)

Most Consecutive Road Games Lost
23 Houston, 1981-84
22 Buffalo, 1983-86
19 Tampa Bay, 1983-85
Atlanta, 1988-91

Most Consecutive Road Games Without Victory
23 Houston, 1981-84 (lost 23)
22 Buffalo, 1983-86 (lost 22)
19 Tampa Bay, 1983-85 (lost 19)
Atlanta, 1988-91 (lost 19)

Most Shutout Games Lost or Tied, Season
8 Frankford, 1927 (lost 6, tied 2)
Brooklyn, 1931 (lost 8)
7 Dayton, 1925 (lost 6, tied 1)
Orange, 1929 (lost 4, tied 3)
Frankford, 1931 (lost 6, tied 1)
6 By many teams

Most Consecutive Shutout Games Lost or Tied
8 Rochester, 1922-24 (lost 8)
7 Hammond, 1922-23 (lost 6, tied 1)
6 Providence, 1926-27 (lost 5, tied 1)
Brooklyn, 1942-43 (lost 6)

TIE GAMES

Most Tie Games, Season
6 Chi. Bears, 1932
5 Frankford, 1929
4 Chi. Bears, 1924
Orange, 1929
Portsmouth, 1932

Most Consecutive Tie Games
3 Chi. Bears, 1932
2 By many teams

SCORING

Most Seasons Leading League
10 Chi. Bears, 1932, 1934-35, 1939, 1941-43, 1946-47, 1956
8 San Francisco, 1953, 1965, 1970, 1987, 1989, 1992-94
6 Green Bay, 1931, 1936-38, 1961-62
L.A. Rams, 1950-52, 1957, 1967, 1973

Most Consecutive Seasons Leading League
3 Green Bay, 1936-38
Chi. Bears, 1941-43
Los Angeles, 1950-52
Oakland, 1967-69
San Francisco, 1992-94

POINTS

Most Points, Season
541 Washington, 1983
513 Houston, 1961
Miami, 1984
505 San Francisco, 1994

Fewest Points, Season (Since 1932)
37 Cincinnati/St. Louis, 1934
38 Cincinnati, 1933
Detroit, 1942
51 Pittsburgh, 1934
Philadelphia, 1936

Most Points, Game
72 Washington vs. N.Y. Giants, Nov. 27, 1966
70 Los Angeles vs. Baltimore, Oct. 22, 1950
65 Chi. Cardinals vs. N.Y. Bulldogs, Nov. 13, 1949
Los Angeles vs. Detroit, Oct. 29, 1950

Most Points, Both Teams, Game
113 Washington (72) vs. N.Y. Giants (41), Nov. 27, 1966
101 Oakland (52) vs. Houston (49), Dec. 22, 1963
99 Seattle (51) vs. Kansas City (48), Nov. 27, 1983 (OT)

Fewest Points, Both Teams, Game
0 In many games. Last time: N.Y. Giants vs. Detroit, Nov. 7, 1943

Most Points, Shutout Victory, Game
64 Philadelphia vs. Cincinnati, Nov. 6, 1934
62 Akron vs. Oorang, Oct. 29, 1922
60 Rock Island vs. Evansville, Oct. 15, 1922
Chi. Cardinals vs. Rochester, Oct. 7, 1923

Fewest Points, Shutout Victory, Game
2 Green Bay vs. Chi. Bears, Oct. 16, 1932
Chi. Bears vs. Green Bay, Sept. 18, 1938

Most Points Overcome to Win Game
28 San Francisco vs. New Orleans, Dec. 7, 1980 (OT) (trailed 7-35, won 38-35)
25 St. Louis vs. Tampa Bay, Nov. 8, 1987 (trailed 3-28, won 31-28)
24 Philadelphia vs. Washington, Oct. 27, 1946 (trailed 0-24, won 28-24)
Detroit vs. Baltimore, Oct. 20, 1957 (trailed 3-27, won 31-27)
Philadelphia vs. Chi. Cardinals, Oct. 25, 1959 (trailed 0-24, won 28-24)
Denver vs. Boston, Oct. 23, 1960 (trailed 0-24, won 31-24)
Miami vs. New England, Dec. 15, 1974 (trailed 0-24, won 34-27)
Minnesota vs. San Francisco, Dec. 4, 1977 (trailed 0-24, won 28-27)
Denver vs. Seattle, Sept. 23, 1979 (trailed 10-34, won 37-34)
Houston vs. Cincinnati, Sept. 23, 1979 (OT) (trailed 0-24, won 30-27)
L.A. Raiders vs. San Diego, Nov. 22, 1982 (trailed 0-24, won 28-24)
L.A. Raiders vs. Denver, Sept. 26, 1988 (OT) (trailed 0-24, won 30-27)
L.A. Rams vs. Tampa Bay, Dec. 6, 1992 (trailed 3-27, won 31-27)

Most Points Overcome to Tie Game
31 Denver vs. Buffalo, Nov. 27, 1960 (trailed 7-38, tied 38-38)
28 Los Angeles vs. Philadelphia, Oct. 3, 1948 (trailed 0-28, tied 28-28)

Most Points, Each Half
1st: 49 Green Bay vs. Tampa Bay, Oct. 2, 1983
48 Buffalo vs. Miami, Sept. 18, 1966
45 Green Bay vs. Cleveland, Nov. 12, 1967
Indianapolis vs. Denver, Oct. 31, 1988
Houston vs. Cleveland, Dec. 9, 1990
2nd: 49 Chi. Bears vs. Philadelphia, Nov. 30, 1941
48 Chi. Cardinals vs. Baltimore, Oct. 2, 1950
N.Y. Giants vs. Baltimore, Nov. 19, 1950
45 Cincinnati vs. Houston, Dec. 17, 1972

Most Points, Both Teams, Each Half
1st: 70 Houston (35) vs. Oakland (35), Dec. 22, 1963
62 N.Y. Jets (41) vs. Tampa Bay (21), Nov. 17, 1985
59 St. Louis (31) vs. Philadelphia (28), Dec. 16, 1962
2nd: 65 Washington (38) vs. N.Y. Giants (27), Nov. 27, 1966
62 L.A. Raiders (31) vs. San Diego (31), Jan. 2, 1983
58 New England (37) vs. Baltimore (21), Nov. 23, 1980
N.Y. Jets (37) vs. New England (21), Sept. 21, 1987

Most Points, One Quarter
41 Green Bay vs. Detroit, Oct. 7, 1945 (second quarter)
Los Angeles vs. Detroit, Oct. 29, 1950 (third quarter)
37 Los Angeles vs. Green Bay, Sept. 21, 1980 (second quarter)
35 Chi. Cardinals vs. Boston, Oct. 24, 1948 (third quarter)
Green Bay vs. Cleveland, Nov. 12, 1967 (first quarter)
Green Bay vs. Tampa Bay, Oct. 2, 1983 (second quarter)

Most Points, Both Teams, One Quarter
49 Oakland (28) vs. Houston (21), Dec. 22, 1963 (second quarter)
48 Green Bay (41) vs. Detroit (7), Oct. 7, 1945 (second quarter)
Los Angeles (41) vs. Detroit (7), Oct. 29, 1950 (third quarter)
47 St. Louis (27) vs. Philadelphia (20), Dec. 13, 1964 (second quarter)

Most Points, Each Quarter
1st: 35 Green Bay vs. Cleveland, Nov. 12, 1967

31 Buffalo vs. Kansas City, Sept. 13, 1964
28 By seven teams
2nd: 41 Green Bay vs. Detroit, Oct. 7, 1945
37 Los Angeles vs. Green Bay, Sept. 21, 1980
35 Green Bay vs. Tampa Bay, Oct. 2, 1983
3rd: 41 Los Angeles vs. Detroit, Oct. 29, 1950
35 Chi. Cardinals vs. Boston, Oct. 24, 1948
28 By nine teams
4th: 31 Oakland vs. Denver, Dec. 17, 1960
Oakland vs. San Diego, Dec. 8, 1963
Atlanta vs. Green Bay, Sept. 13, 1981
28 By many teams

Most Points, Both Teams, Each Quarter
1st: 42 Green Bay (35) vs. Cleveland (7), Nov. 12, 1967
35 Dall. Texans (21) vs. N.Y. Titans (14), Nov. 11, 1962
Dallas (28) vs. Philadelphia (7), Oct. 19, 1969
Kansas City (21) vs. Seattle (14), Dec. 11, 1977
Detroit (21) vs. L.A. Raiders (14), Dec. 10, 1990
Dallas (21) vs. Atlanta (14), Dec. 22, 1991
34 Los Angeles (21) vs. Baltimore (13), Oct. 22, 1950
Oakland (21) vs. Atlanta (13), Nov. 30, 1975
2nd: 49 Oakland (28) vs. Houston (21), Dec. 22, 1963
48 Green Bay (41) vs. Detroit (7), Oct. 7, 1945
47 St. Louis (27) vs. Philadelphia (20), Dec. 13, 1964
3rd: 48 Los Angeles (41) vs. Detroit (7), Oct. 29, 1950
42 Washington (28) vs. Philadelphia (14), Oct. 1, 1955
41 Green Bay (21) vs. N.Y. Yanks (20), Oct. 8, 1950
4th: 42 Chi. Cardinals (28) vs. Philadelphia (14), Dec. 7, 1947
Green Bay (28) vs. Chi. Bears (14), Nov. 6, 1955
N.Y. Jets (28) vs. Boston (14), Oct. 27, 1968
Pittsburgh (21) vs. Cleveland (21), Oct. 18, 1969
41 Baltimore (27) vs. New England (14), Sept. 18, 1978
New England (27) vs. Baltimore (14), Nov. 23, 1980
40 Chicago (21) vs. Tampa Bay (19), Nov. 19, 1989

Most Consecutive Games Scoring
274 Cleveland, 1950-71
San Francisco, 1977-94 (current)
218 Dallas, 1970-85
217 Oakland, 1966-81

TOUCHDOWNS

Most Seasons Leading League, Touchdowns
13 Chi. Bears, 1932, 1934-35, 1939, 1941-44, 1946-48, 1956, 1965
7 Dallas, 1966, 1968, 1971, 1973, 1977-78, 1980
6 Oakland, 1967-69, 1972, 1974, 1977
San Diego, 1963, 1965, 1979, 1981-82, 1985

Most Consecutive Seasons Leading League, Touchdowns
4 Chi. Bears, 1941-44
Los Angeles, 1949-52
3 Chi. Bears, 1946-48
Baltimore, 1957-59
Oakland, 1967-69
San Francisco, 1992-94
2 By many teams

Most Touchdowns, Season
70 Miami, 1984
66 Houston, 1961
San Francisco, 1994
64 Los Angeles, 1950

Fewest Touchdowns, Season (Since 1932)
3 Cincinnati, 1933
4 Cincinnati/St. Louis, 1934
5 Detroit, 1942

Most Touchdowns, Game
10 Philadelphia vs. Cincinnati, Nov. 6, 1934
Los Angeles vs. Baltimore, Oct. 22, 1950
Washington vs. N.Y. Giants, Nov. 27, 1966
9 Chi. Cardinals vs. Rochester, Oct. 7, 1923
Chi. Cardinals vs. N.Y. Giants, Oct. 17, 1948
Chi. Cardinals vs. N.Y. Bulldogs, Nov. 13, 1949
Los Angeles vs. Detroit, Oct. 29, 1950
Pittsburgh vs. N.Y. Giants, Nov. 30, 1952
Chicago vs. San Francisco, Dec. 12, 1965
Chicago vs. Green Bay, Dec. 7, 1980
8 By many teams.

Most Touchdowns, Both Teams, Game
16 Washington (10) vs. N.Y. Giants (6), Nov. 27, 1966
14 Chi. Cardinals (9) vs. N.Y. Giants (5), Oct. 17, 1948
Los Angeles (10) vs. Baltimore (4), Oct. 22, 1950
Houston (7) vs. Oakland (7), Dec. 22, 1963
13 New Orleans (7) vs. St. Louis (6), Nov. 2, 1969
Kansas City (7) vs. Seattle (6), Nov. 27, 1983 (OT)
San Diego (8) vs. Pittsburgh (5), Dec. 8, 1985
N.Y. Jets (7) vs. Miami (6), Sept. 21, 1986 (OT)

Most Consecutive Games Scoring Touchdowns
166 Cleveland, 1957-69
97 Oakland, 1966-73
96 Kansas City, 1963-70

POINTS AFTER TOUCHDOWN

Most (One-Point) Points After Touchdown, Season
66 Miami, 1984
65 Houston, 1961
62 Washington, 1983

Fewest (One-Point) Points After Touchdown, Season
2 Chi. Cardinals, 1933
3 Cincinnati, 1933
Pittsburgh, 1934
4 Cincinnati/St. Louis, 1934

Most (One-Point) Points After Touchdown, Game
10 Los Angeles vs. Baltimore, Oct. 22, 1950
9 Chi. Cardinals vs. N.Y. Giants, Oct. 17, 1948
Pittsburgh vs. N.Y. Giants, Nov. 30, 1952
Washington vs. N.Y. Giants, Nov. 27, 1966
8 By many teams

Most (One-Point) Points After Touchdown, Both Teams, Game
14 Chi. Cardinals (9) vs. N.Y. Giants (5), Oct. 17, 1948
Houston (7) vs. Oakland (7), Dec. 22, 1963
Washington (9) vs. N.Y. Giants (5), Nov. 27, 1966
13 Los Angeles (10) vs. Baltimore (3), Oct. 22, 1950
12 In many games

Most Two-Point Conversions, Season
6 Miami, 1994
4 Boston, 1960
Buffalo, 1961
N.Y. Jets, 1967
Cleveland, 1994
Houston, 1994
Minnesota, 1994
Seattle, 1994
3 By many teams

Most Two-Point Conversions, Game
2 Denver vs. Oakland, Oct. 1, 1961
Oakland vs. San Diego, Sept. 30, 1962
Kansas City vs. Houston, Oct. 24, 1965
Houston vs. N.Y. Jets, Dec. 6, 1969
Seattle vs. Kansas City, Oct. 23, 1994
Tampa Bay vs. San Francisco, Oct. 23, 1994
Detroit vs. Green Bay, Nov. 6, 1994
Washington vs. San Francisco, Nov. 6, 1994

Most Two-Point Conversions, Both Teams, Game
3 Seattle (2) vs. Kansas City (1), Oct. 23, 1994
2 In many games

FIELD GOALS

Most Seasons Leading League, Field Goals
11 Green Bay, 1935-36, 1940-43, 1946-47, 1955, 1972, 1974
8 Washington, 1945, 1956, 1971, 1976-77, 1979, 1982, 1992
7 N.Y. Giants, 1933, 1937, 1939, 1941, 1944, 1959, 1983

Most Consecutive Seasons Leading League, Field Goals
4 Green Bay, 1940-43
3 Cleveland, 1952-54
2 By many teams

Most Field Goals Attempted, Season
49 Los Angeles, 1966
Washington, 1971
48 Green Bay, 1972
47 N.Y. Jets, 1969
Los Angeles, 1973
Washington, 1983

Fewest Field Goals Attempted, Season (Since 1938)
0 Chi. Bears, 1944
2 Cleveland, 1939
Card-Pitt, 1944
Boston, 1946
Chi. Bears, 1947
3 Chi. Bears, 1945
Cleveland, 1945

Most Field Goals Attempted, Game
9 St. Louis vs. Pittsburgh, Sept. 24, 1967
8 Pittsburgh vs. St. Louis, Dec. 2, 1962
Detroit vs. Minnesota, Nov. 13, 1966
N.Y. Jets vs. Buffalo, Nov. 3, 1968
7 By many teams

Most Field Goals Attempted, Both Teams, Game
11 St. Louis (6) vs. Pittsburgh (5), Nov. 13, 1966

Washington (6) vs. Chicago (5), Nov. 14, 1971
Green Bay (6) vs. Detroit (5), Sept. 29, 1974
Washington (6) vs. N.Y. Giants (5), Nov. 14, 1976
10 Denver (5) vs. Boston (5), Nov. 11, 1962
Boston (7) vs. San Diego (3), Sept. 20, 1964
Buffalo (7) vs. Houston (3), Dec. 5, 1965
St. Louis (7) vs. Atlanta (3), Dec. 11, 1966
Boston (7) vs. Buffalo (3), Sept. 24, 1967
Detroit (7) vs. Minnesota (3), Sept. 20, 1971
Washington (7) vs. Houston (3), Oct. 10, 1971
Green Bay (5) vs. St. Louis (5), Dec. 5, 1971
Kansas City (7) vs. Buffalo (3), Dec. 19, 1971
Kansas City (5) vs. San Diego (5), Oct. 29, 1972
Minnesota (6) vs. Chicago (4), Sept. 23, 1973
Cleveland (7) vs. Denver (3), Oct. 19, 1975
Cleveland (5) vs. Denver (5), Oct. 5, 1980
9 In many games

Most Field Goals, Season
35 N.Y. Giants, 1983
L.A. Raiders, 1993
34 N.Y. Jets, 1968
Kansas City, 1990
Detroit, 1993
Minnesota, 1994
San Diego, 1994
33 Green Bay, 1972
Washington, 1983
Pittsburgh, 1985
New Orleans, 1987
Miami, 1991

Fewest Field Goals, Season (Since 1932)
0 Boston, 1932, 1935
Chi. Cardinals, 1932, 1945
Green Bay, 1932, 1944
N.Y. Giants, 1932
Brooklyn, 1944
Card-Pitt, 1944
Chi. Bears, 1944, 1947
Boston, 1946
Baltimore, 1950
Dallas, 1952

Most Field Goals, Game
7 St. Louis vs. Pittsburgh, Sept. 24, 1967
Minnesota vs. L.A. Rams, Nov. 5, 1989 (OT)
6 Boston vs. Denver, Oct. 4, 1964
Detroit vs. Minnesota, Nov. 13, 1966
N.Y. Jets vs. Buffalo, Nov. 3, 1968
Philadelphia vs. Houston, Nov. 12, 1972
N.Y. Jets vs. New Orleans, Dec. 3, 1972
St. Louis vs. Atlanta, Dec. 9, 1973
N.Y. Giants vs. Seattle, Oct. 18, 1981
San Francisco vs. New Orleans, Oct. 16, 1983
Pittsburgh vs. Denver, Oct. 23, 1988
San Diego vs. Seattle, Sept. 5, 1993
San Diego vs. Houston, Sept. 19, 1993
Cincinnati vs. Seattle, Nov. 6, 1994
Atlanta vs. New Orleans, Nov. 13, 1994
5 By many teams

Most Field Goals, Both Teams, Game
8 Cleveland (4) vs. St. Louis (4), Sept. 20, 1964
Chicago (5) vs. Philadelphia (3), Oct. 20, 1968
Washington (5) vs. Chicago (3), Nov. 14, 1971
Kansas City (5) vs. Buffalo (3), Dec. 19, 1971
Detroit (4) vs. Green Bay (4), Sept. 29, 1974
Cleveland (5) vs. Denver (3), Oct. 19, 1975
New England (4) vs. San Diego (4), Nov. 9, 1975
San Francisco (6) vs. New Orleans (2), Oct. 16, 1983
Seattle (5) vs. L.A. Raiders (3), Dec. 18, 1988
Atlanta (6) vs. New Orleans (2), Nov. 13, 1994
7 In many games

Most Consecutive Games Scoring Field Goals
31 Minnesota, 1968-70
28 Washington, 1988-90
22 San Francisco, 1988-89

SAFETIES

Most Safeties, Season
4 Cleveland, 1927
Detroit, 1962
3 By many teams

Most Safeties, Game
3 L.A. Rams vs. N.Y. Giants, Sept. 30, 1984
2 N.Y. Giants vs. Pottsville, Oct. 30, 1927
Chi. Bears vs. Pottsville, Nov. 13, 1927
Detroit vs. Brooklyn, Dec. 1, 1935
N.Y. Giants vs. Pittsburgh, Sept. 17, 1950
N.Y. Giants vs. Washington, Nov. 5, 1961
Chicago vs. Pittsburgh, Nov. 9, 1969
Dallas vs. Philadelphia, Nov. 19, 1972
Los Angeles vs. Green Bay, Oct. 21, 1973
Oakland vs. San Diego, Oct. 26, 1975
Denver vs. Seattle, Jan. 2, 1983
New Orleans vs. Cleveland, Sept. 13, 1987
Buffalo vs. Denver, Nov. 8, 1987

Most Safeties, Both Teams, Game
3 L.A. Rams (3) vs. N.Y. Giants (0), Sept. 30, 1984
2 Chi. Cardinals (1) vs. Frankford (1), Nov. 19, 1927
Chi. Cardinals (1) vs. Cincinnati (1), Nov. 12, 1933
Chi. Bears (1) vs. San Francisco (1), Oct. 19, 1952
Cincinnati (1) vs. Los Angeles (1), Oct. 22, 1972
Chi. Bears (1) vs. San Francisco (1), Sept. 19, 1976
Baltimore (1) vs. Miami (1), Oct. 29, 1978
Atlanta (1) vs. Detroit (1), Oct. 5, 1980
Houston (1) vs. Philadelphia (1), Oct. 2, 1988
Cleveland (1) vs. Seattle (1), Nov. 14, 1993
Arizona (1) vs. Houston (1), Dec. 4, 1994
(Also see previous record)

FIRST DOWNS

Most Seasons Leading League
9 Chi. Bears, 1935, 1939, 1941, 1943, 1945, 1947-49, 1955
7 San Diego, 1965, 1969, 1980-83, 1985
6 L.A. Rams, 1946, 1950-51, 1954, 1957, 1973

Most Consecutive Seasons Leading League
4 San Diego, 1980-83
3 Chi. Bears, 1947-49
2 By many teams

Most First Downs, Season
387 Miami, 1984
380 San Diego, 1985
379 San Diego, 1981

Fewest First Downs, Season
51 Cincinnati, 1933
64 Pittsburgh, 1935
67 Philadelphia, 1937

Most First Downs, Game
39 N.Y. Jets vs. Miami, Nov. 27, 1988
Washington vs. Detroit, Nov. 4, 1990 (OT)
38 Los Angeles vs. N.Y. Giants, Nov. 13, 1966
37 Green Bay vs. Philadelphia, Nov. 11, 1962

Fewest First Downs, Game
0 N.Y. Giants vs. Green Bay, Oct. 1, 1933
Pittsburgh vs. Boston, Oct. 29, 1933
Philadelphia vs. Detroit, Sept. 20, 1935
N.Y. Giants vs. Washington, Sept. 27, 1942
Denver vs. Houston, Sept. 3, 1966

Most First Downs, Both Teams, Game
62 San Diego (32) vs. Seattle (30), Sept. 15, 1985
59 Miami (31) vs. Buffalo (28), Oct. 9, 1983 (OT)
Seattle (33) vs. Kansas City (26), Nov. 27, 1983 (OT)
N.Y. Jets (32) vs. Miami (27), Sept. 21, 1986 (OT)
N.Y. Jets (39) vs. Miami (20), Nov. 27, 1988
58 Los Angeles (30) vs. Chi. Bears (28), Oct. 24, 1954
Denver (34) vs. Kansas City (24), Nov. 18, 1974
Atlanta (35) vs. New Orleans (23), Sept. 2, 1979 (OT)
Pittsburgh (36) vs. Cleveland (22), Nov. 25, 1979 (OT)
San Diego (34) vs. Miami (24), Nov. 18, 1984 (OT)
Cincinnati (32) vs. San Diego (26), Sept. 22, 1985

Fewest First Downs, Both Teams, Game
7 Chi. Cardinals (2) vs. Detroit (5), Sept. 15, 1940
9 Pittsburgh (1) vs. Boston (8), Oct. 27, 1935
Boston (4) vs. Brooklyn (5), Nov. 24, 1935
N.Y. Giants (3) vs. Detroit (6), Nov. 7, 1943
Pittsburgh (4) vs. Chi. Cardinals (5), Nov. 11, 1945
N.Y. Bulldogs (1) vs. Philadelphia (8), Sept. 22, 1949
10 N.Y. Giants (4) vs. Washington (6), Dec. 11, 1960

Most First Downs, Rushing, Season
181 New England, 1978
177 Los Angeles, 1973
176 Chicago, 1985

Fewest First Downs, Rushing, Season
36 Cleveland, 1942
Boston, 1944
39 Brooklyn, 1943
40 Philadelphia, 1940
Detroit, 1945

Most First Downs, Rushing, Game
25 Philadelphia vs. Washington, Dec. 2, 1951
23 St. Louis vs. New Orleans, Oct. 5, 1980
21 Cleveland vs. Philadelphia, Dec. 13, 1959
Green Bay vs. Philadelphia, Nov. 11, 1962
Los Angeles vs. New Orleans, Nov. 25, 1973
Pittsburgh vs. Kansas City, Nov. 7, 1976
New England vs. Denver, Nov. 28, 1976
Oakland vs. Green Bay, Sept. 17, 1978

Fewest First Downs, Rushing, Game
0 By many teams. Last time: Chicago vs. Green Bay, Dec. 11, 1994

Most First Downs, Rushing, Both Teams, Game
36 Philadelphia (25) vs. Washington (11), Dec. 2, 1951
31 Detroit (18) vs. Washington (13), Sept. 30, 1951
30 Los Angeles (17) vs. Minnesota (13), Nov. 5, 1961
New Orleans (17) vs. Green Bay (13), Sept. 9, 1979
New Orleans (16) vs. San Francisco (14), Nov. 11, 1979
New England (16) vs. Kansas City (14), Oct. 4, 1981

Fewest First Downs, Rushing, Both Teams, Game
2 Houston (0) vs. Denver (2), Dec. 2, 1962
3 Philadelphia (1) vs. Pittsburgh (2), Oct. 27, 1957
Boston (1) vs. Buffalo (2), Nov. 15, 1964
Los Angeles (0) vs. San Francisco (3), Dec. 6, 1964
Pittsburgh (1) vs. St. Louis (2), Nov. 13, 1966
Seattle (1) vs. New Orleans (2), Sept. 1, 1991
4 In many games

Most First Downs, Passing, Season
259 San Diego, 1985
251 Houston, 1990
250 Miami, 1986

Fewest First Downs, Passing, Season
18 Pittsburgh, 1941
23 Brooklyn, 1942
N.Y. Giants, 1944
24 N.Y. Giants, 1943

Most First Downs, Passing, Game
29 N.Y. Giants vs. Cincinnati, Oct. 13, 1985
27 San Diego vs. Seattle, Sept. 15, 1985
26 Miami vs. Cleveland, Dec. 12, 1988

Fewest First Downs, Passing, Game
0 By many teams. Last time: Houston vs. Kansas City, Oct. 9, 1988

Most First Downs, Passing, Both Teams, Game
43 San Diego (23) vs. Cincinnati (20), Dec. 20, 1982
Miami (24) vs. N.Y. Jets (19), Sept. 21, 1986 (OT)
42 San Francisco (22) vs. San Diego (20), Dec. 11, 1982
41 San Diego (27) vs. Seattle (14), Sept. 15, 1985
Miami (26) vs. Cleveland (15), Dec. 12, 1988

Fewest First Downs, Passing, Both Teams, Game
0 Brooklyn vs. Pittsburgh, Nov. 29, 1942
1 Green Bay (0) vs. Cleveland (1), Sept. 21, 1941
Pittsburgh (0) vs. Brooklyn (1), Oct. 11, 1942
N.Y. Giants (0) vs. Detroit (1), Nov. 7, 1943
Pittsburgh (0) vs. Chi. Cardinals (1), Nov. 11, 1945
N.Y. Bulldogs (0) vs. Philadelphia (1), Sept. 22, 1949
Chicago (0) vs. Buffalo (1), Oct. 7, 1979
2 In many games

Most First Downs, Penalty, Season
43 Denver, 1994
42 Chicago, 1987
41 Denver, 1986

Fewest First Downs, Penalty, Season
2 Brooklyn, 1940
4 Chi. Cardinals, 1940
N.Y. Giants, 1942, 1944
Washington, 1944
Cleveland, 1952
Kansas City, 1969
5 Brooklyn, 1939
Chi. Bears, 1939
Detroit, 1953
Los Angeles, 1953
Houston, 1982

Most First Downs, Penalty, Game
11 Denver vs. Houston, Oct. 6, 1985
9 Chi. Bears vs. Cleveland, Nov. 25, 1951
Baltimore vs. Pittsburgh, Oct. 30, 1977
N.Y. Jets vs. Houston, Sept. 18, 1988
8 Philadelphia vs. Detroit, Dec. 2, 1979
Cincinnati vs. N.Y. Jets, Oct. 6, 1985
Buffalo vs. Houston, Sept. 20, 1987
Houston vs. Atlanta, Sept. 9, 1990
Kansas City vs. L.A. Raiders, Oct. 3, 1993

Most First Downs, Penalty, Both Teams, Game
11 Chi. Bears (9) vs. Cleveland (2), Nov. 25, 1951
Cincinnati (8) vs. N.Y. Jets (3), Oct. 6, 1985
Denver (11) vs. Houston (0), Oct. 6, 1985
Detroit (6) vs. Dallas (5), Nov. 8, 1987
N.Y. Jets (9) vs. Houston (2), Sept. 18, 1988
Kansas City (8) vs. L.A. Raiders (3), Oct. 3, 1993
10 In many games

NET YARDS GAINED RUSHING AND PASSING

Most Seasons Leading League
12 Chi. Bears, 1932, 1934-35, 1939, 1941-44, 1947, 1949, 1955-56
7 San Diego, 1963, 1965, 1980-83, 1985
6 L.A. Rams, 1946, 1950-51, 1954, 1957, 1973
Baltimore, 1958-60, 1964, 1967, 1976
Dall. Cowboys, 1966, 1968-69, 1971, 1974, 1977

Most Consecutive Seasons Leading League
4 Chi. Bears, 1941-44
San Diego, 1980-83
3 Baltimore, 1958-60
Houston, 1960-62
Oakland, 1968-70
2 By many teams

Most Yards Gained, Season
6,936 Miami, 1984
6,744 San Diego, 1981
6,535 San Diego, 1985

Fewest Yards Gained, Season
1,150 Cincinnati, 1933
1,443 Chi. Cardinals, 1934
1,486 Chi. Cardinals, 1933

Most Yards Gained, Game
735 Los Angeles vs. N.Y. Yanks, Sept. 28, 1951
683 Pittsburgh vs. Chi. Cardinals, Dec. 13, 1958
682 Chi. Bears vs. N.Y. Giants, Nov. 14, 1943

Fewest Yards Gained, Game
–7 Seattle vs. Los Angeles, Nov. 4, 1979
–5 Denver vs. Oakland, Sept. 10, 1967
14 Chi. Cardinals vs. Detroit, Sept. 15, 1940

Most Yards Gained, Both Teams, Game
1,133 Los Angeles (636) vs. N.Y. Yanks (497), Nov. 19, 1950
1,102 San Diego (661) vs. Cincinnati (441), Dec. 20, 1982
1,087 St. Louis (589) vs. Philadelphia (498), Dec. 16, 1962

Fewest Yards Gained, Both Teams, Game
30 Chi. Cardinals (14) vs. Detroit (16), Sept. 15, 1940
136 Chi. Cardinals (50) vs. Green Bay (86), Nov. 18, 1934
154 N.Y. Giants (51) vs. Washington (103), Dec. 11, 1960

Most Consecutive Games, 400 or More Yards Gained
11 San Diego, 1982-83
6 Houston, 1961-62
San Diego, 1981
San Francisco, 1987
5 Chi. Bears, 1947
Philadelphia, 1953
Chi. Bears, 1955
Oakland, 1968
New England, 1981
Cincinnati, 1986
San Francisco, 1994

Most Consecutive Games, 300 or More Yards Gained
29 Los Angeles, 1949-51
26 Miami, 1983-85
23 Miami, 1993-94 (current)

RUSHING

Most Seasons Leading League
16 Chi. Bears, 1932, 1934-35, 1939-42, 1951, 1955-56, 1968, 1977, 1983-86
7 Buffalo, 1962, 1964, 1973, 1975, 1982, 1991-92
6 Cleveland, 1958-59, 1963, 1965-67

Most Consecutive Seasons Leading League
4 Chi. Bears, 1939-42
Chi. Bears, 1983-86
3 Detroit, 1936-38
San Francisco, 1952-54
Cleveland, 1965-67
2 By many teams

ATTEMPTS

Most Rushing Attempts, Season
681 Oakland, 1977
674 Chicago, 1984
671 New England, 1978

Fewest Rushing Attempts, Season
211 Philadelphia, 1982
219 San Francisco, 1982
225 Houston, 1982

Most Rushing Attempts, Game
72 Chi. Bears vs. Brooklyn, Oct. 20, 1935
70 Chi. Cardinals vs. Green Bay, Dec. 5, 1948
69 Chi. Cardinals vs. Green Bay, Dec. 6, 1936
Kansas City vs. Cincinnati, Sept. 3, 1978

Fewest Rushing Attempts, Game
6 Chi. Cardinals vs. Boston, Oct. 29, 1933
7 Oakland vs. Buffalo, Oct. 15, 1963
Houston vs. N.Y. Giants, Dec. 8, 1985
Seattle vs. L.A. Raiders, Nov. 17, 1991
Green Bay vs. Miami, Sept. 11, 1994
8 Denver vs. Oakland, Dec. 17, 1960
Buffalo vs. St. Louis, Sept. 9, 1984
Detroit vs. San Francisco, Oct. 20, 1991
Atlanta vs. Detroit, Sept. 5, 1993

Most Rushing Attempts, Both Teams, Game
108 Chi. Cardinals (70) vs. Green Bay (38), Dec. 5, 1948
105 Oakland (62) vs. Atlanta (43), Nov. 30, 1975 (OT)
104 Chi. Bears (64) vs. Pittsburgh (40), Oct. 18, 1936

Fewest Rushing Attempts, Both Teams, Game
34 Atlanta (12) vs. Houston (22), Dec. 5, 1993
35 Seattle (15) vs. New Orleans (20), Sept. 1, 1991
36 Houston (15) vs. N.Y. Jets (21), Oct. 13, 1991

YARDS GAINED

Most Yards Gained Rushing, Season
3,165 New England, 1978
3,088 Buffalo, 1973
2,986 Kansas City, 1978

Fewest Yards Gained Rushing, Season
298 Philadelphia, 1940
467 Detroit, 1946
471 Boston, 1944

Most Yards Gained Rushing, Game
426 Detroit vs. Pittsburgh, Nov. 4, 1934
423 N.Y. Giants vs. Baltimore, Nov. 19, 1950
420 Boston vs. N.Y. Giants, Oct. 8, 1933

Fewest Yards Gained Rushing, Game
–53 Detroit vs. Chi. Cardinals, Oct. 17, 1943
–36 Philadelphia vs. Chi. Bears, Nov. 19, 1939
–33 Phil-Pitt vs. Brooklyn, Oct. 2, 1943

Most Yards Gained Rushing, Both Teams, Game
595 Los Angeles (371) vs. N.Y. Yanks (224), Nov. 18, 1951
574 Chi. Bears (396) vs. Pittsburgh (178), Oct. 10, 1934
558 Boston (420) vs. N.Y. Giants (138), Oct. 8, 1933

Fewest Yards Gained Rushing, Both Teams, Game
–15 Detroit (–53) vs. Chi. Cardinals (38), Oct. 17, 1943
4 Detroit (–10) vs. Chi. Cardinals (14), Sept. 15, 1940
62 L.A. Rams (15) vs. San Francisco (47), Dec. 6, 1964

AVERAGE GAIN

Highest Average Gain, Rushing, Season
5.74 Cleveland, 1963
5.65 San Francisco, 1954
5.56 San Diego, 1963

Lowest Average Gain, Rushing, Season
0.94 Philadelphia, 1940
1.45 Boston, 1944
1.55 Pittsburgh, 1935

TOUCHDOWNS

Most Touchdowns, Rushing, Season
36 Green Bay, 1962
33 Pittsburgh, 1976
30 Chi. Bears, 1941
New England, 1978
Washington, 1983

Fewest Touchdowns, Rushing, Season
1 Brooklyn, 1934
2 Chi. Cardinals, 1933
Cincinnati, 1933
Pittsburgh, 1934
Philadelphia, 1935
Philadelphia, 1936
Philadelphia, 1937
Philadelphia, 1938
Pittsburgh, 1940
Philadelphia, 1972
3 By many teams

Most Touchdowns, Rushing, Game
7 Los Angeles vs. Atlanta, Dec. 4, 1976
6 By many teams

Most Touchdowns, Rushing, Both Teams, Game
8 Los Angeles (6) vs. N.Y. Yanks (2), Nov. 18, 1951
Chi. Bears (5) vs. Green Bay (3), Nov. 6, 1955
Cleveland (6) vs. Los Angeles (2), Nov. 24, 1957
7 In many games

PASSING

ATTEMPTS

Most Passes Attempted, Season
709 Minnesota, 1981
699 New England, 1994
673 Minnesota, 1994

Fewest Passes Attempted, Season
102 Cincinnati, 1933
106 Boston, 1933
120 Detroit, 1937

Most Passes Attempted, Game
70 New England vs. Minnesota, Nov. 13, 1994
68 Houston vs. Buffalo, Nov 1, 1964
66 Atlanta vs. Detroit, Dec. 24, 1989

Fewest Passes Attempted, Game
0 Green Bay vs. Portsmouth, Oct. 8, 1933
Detroit vs. Cleveland, Sept. 10, 1937
Pittsburgh vs. Brooklyn, Nov. 16, 1941
Pittsburgh vs. Los Angeles, Nov. 13, 1949
Cleveland vs. Philadelphia, Dec. 3, 1950

Most Passes Attempted, Both Teams, Game
112 New England (70) vs. Minnesota (42), Nov. 13, 1994
104 Miami (55) vs. N.Y. Jets (49), Oct. 18, 1987 (OT)
102 San Francisco (57) vs. Atlanta (45), Oct. 6, 1985

Fewest Passes Attempted, Both Teams, Game
4 Chi. Cardinals (1) vs. Detroit (3), Nov. 3, 1935
Detroit (0) vs. Cleveland (4), Sept. 10, 1937
6 Chi. Cardinals (2) vs. Detroit (4), Sept. 15, 1940
8 Brooklyn (2) vs. Philadelphia (6), Oct. 1, 1939

COMPLETIONS

Most Passes Completed, Season
411 Houston, 1991
409 Minnesota, 1994
405 New England, 1994

Fewest Passes Completed, Season
25 Cincinnati, 1933
33 Boston, 1933
34 Chi. Cardinals, 1934
Detroit, 1934

Most Passes Completed, Game
45 New England vs. Minnesota, Nov. 13, 1994 (OT)
42 N.Y. Jets vs. San Francisco, Sept. 21, 1980
41 Houston vs. Dallas, Nov. 10, 1991 (OT)

Fewest Passes Completed, Game
0 By many teams. Last time: Buffalo vs. N.Y. Jets, Sept. 29, 1974

Most Passes Completed, Both Teams, Game
71 New England (45) vs. Minnesota (26), Nov. 13, 1994
68 San Francisco (37) vs. Atlanta (31), Oct. 6, 1985
66 Cincinnati (40) vs. San Diego (26), Dec. 20, 1982

Fewest Passes Completed, Both Teams, Game
1 Chi. Cardinals (0) vs. Philadelphia (1), Nov. 8, 1936
Detroit (0) vs. Cleveland (1), Sept. 10, 1937
Chi. Cardinals (0) vs. Detroit (1), Sept. 15, 1940
Brooklyn (0) vs. Pittsburgh (1), Nov. 29, 1942
2 Chi. Cardinals (0) vs. Detroit (2), Nov. 3, 1935
Buffalo (0) vs. N.Y. Jets (2), Sept. 29, 1974
Chi. Cardinals (0) vs. Green Bay (2), Nov. 18, 1934
3 In seven games

YARDS GAINED

Most Seasons Leading League, Passing Yardage
10 San Diego, 1965, 1968, 1971, 1978-83, 1985
8 Chi. Bears, 1932, 1939, 1941, 1943, 1945, 1949, 1954, 1964
Washington, 1938, 1940, 1944, 1947-48, 1967, 1974, 1989
7 Houston, 1960-61, 1963-64, 1990-92

Most Consecutive Seasons Leading League, Passing Yardage
6 San Diego, 1978-83
4 Green Bay, 1934-37
3 Miami, 1986-88
Houston, 1990-92

Most Yards Gained, Passing, Season
5,018 Miami, 1984
4,870 San Diego, 1985
4,805 Houston, 1990

Fewest Yards Gained, Passing, Season
302 Chi. Cardinals, 1934
357 Cincinnati, 1933
459 Boston, 1934

Most Yards Gained, Passing, Game
554 Los Angeles vs. N.Y. Yanks, Sept. 28, 1951
530 Minnesota vs. Baltimore, Sept. 28, 1969
521 Miami vs. N.Y. Jets, Oct. 23, 1988

Fewest Yards Gained, Passing, Game
–53 Denver vs. Oakland, Sept. 10, 1967
–52 Cincinnati vs. Houston, Oct. 31, 1971
–39 Atlanta vs. San Francisco, Oct. 23, 1976

Most Yards Gained, Passing, Both Teams, Game
884 N.Y. Jets (449) vs. Miami (435), Sept. 21, 1986 (OT)
883 San Diego (486) vs. Cincinnati (397), Dec. 20, 1982
874 Miami (456) vs. New England (418), Sept. 4, 1994

Fewest Yards Gained, Passing, Both Teams, Game
–11 Green Bay (–10) vs. Dallas (–1), Oct. 24, 1965
1 Chi. Cardinals (0) vs. Philadelphia (1), Nov. 8, 1936
7 Brooklyn (0) vs. Pittsburgh (7), Nov. 29, 1942

TIMES SACKED

Most Seasons Leading League, Fewest Times Sacked
10 Miami, 1973, 1982-90
4 San Diego, 1963-64, 1967-68
San Francisco, 1964-65, 1970-71
N.Y. Jets, 1965-66, 1968, 1993
3 Houston, 1961-62, 1978
St. Louis, 1974-76
Washington, 1966-67, 1991

Most Consecutive Seasons Leading League, Fewest Times Sacked
9 Miami, 1982-90
3 St. Louis, 1974-76
2 By many teams

Most Times Sacked, Season
104 Philadelphia, 1986
72 Philadelphia, 1987
70 Atlanta, 1968

Fewest Times Sacked, Season
7 Miami, 1988
8 San Francisco, 1970
St. Louis, 1975
9 N.Y. Jets, 1966
Washington, 1991

Most Times Sacked, Game
12 Pittsburgh vs. Dallas, Nov. 20, 1966
Baltimore vs. St. Louis, Oct. 26, 1980
Detroit vs. Chicago, Dec. 16, 1984
Houston vs. Dallas, Sept. 29, 1985
11 St. Louis vs. N.Y. Giants, Nov. 1, 1964
Los Angeles vs. Baltimore, Nov. 22, 1964
Denver vs. Buffalo, Dec. 13, 1964
Green Bay vs. Detroit, Nov. 7, 1965
Buffalo vs. Oakland, Oct. 15, 1967
Denver vs. Oakland, Nov. 5, 1967
Atlanta vs. St. Louis, Nov. 24, 1968
Detroit vs. Dallas, Oct. 6, 1975
Philadelphia vs. St. Louis, Dec. 18, 1983
Cleveland vs. Kansas City, Sept. 30, 1984
Minnesota vs. Chicago, Oct. 28, 1984
Atlanta vs. Cleveland, Nov. 18, 1984
Dallas vs. San Diego, Nov. 16, 1986
Philadelphia vs. Detroit, Nov. 16, 1986
Philadelphia vs. L.A. Raiders, Nov. 30, 1986 (OT)
L.A. Raiders vs. Seattle, Dec. 8, 1986
N.Y. Jets vs. Dallas, Oct. 4, 1987
Philadelphia vs. Chicago, Oct. 4, 1987
Dallas vs. Philadelphia, Sept. 15, 1991
Cleveland vs. Indianapolis, Sept. 6, 1992
10 By many teams

Most Times Sacked, Both Teams, Game
18 Green Bay (10) vs. San Diego (8), Sept. 24, 1978
17 Buffalo (10) vs. N.Y. Titans (7), Nov. 23, 1961
Pittsburgh (12) vs. Dallas (5), Nov. 20, 1966
Atlanta (9) vs. Philadelphia (8), Dec. 16, 1984
Philadelphia (11) vs. L.A. Raiders (6), Nov. 30, 1986 (OT)
16 Los Angeles (11) vs. Baltimore (5), Nov. 22, 1964
Buffalo (11) vs. Oakland (5), Oct. 15, 1967

COMPLETION PERCENTAGE

Most Seasons Leading League, Completion Percentage
11 Washington, 1937, 1939-40, 1942-45, 1947-48, 1969-70
San Francisco, 1952, 1957-58, 1965, 1981, 1983, 1987, 1989, 1992-94
7 Green Bay, 1936, 1941, 1961-62, 1964, 1966, 1968
6 Cleveland, 1951, 1953-55, 1959-60

Most Consecutive Seasons Leading League, Completion Percentage
4 Washington, 1942-45
Kansas City, 1966-69
3 Cleveland, 1953-55
San Francisco, 1992-94
2 By many teams

Highest Completion Percentage, Season
70.65 Cincinnati, 1982 (310-219)
70.25 San Francisco, 1994 (511-359)
70.19 San Francisco, 1989 (483-339)

Lowest Completion Percentage, Season
22.9 Philadelphia, 1936 (170-39)
24.5 Cincinnati, 1933 (102-25)
25.0 Pittsburgh, 1941 (168-42)

TOUCHDOWNS

Most Touchdowns, Passing, Season
49 Miami, 1984
48 Houston, 1961
46 Miami, 1986

Fewest Touchdowns, Passing, Season
0 Cincinnati, 1933
Pittsburgh, 1945
1 Boston, 1932
Boston, 1933
Chi. Cardinals, 1934
Cincinnati/St. Louis, 1934
Detroit, 1942
2 Chi. Cardinals, 1932
Stapleton, 1932
Chi. Cardinals, 1935
Brooklyn, 1936
Pittsburgh, 1942

Most Touchdowns, Passing, Game
7 Chi. Bears vs. N.Y. Giants, Nov. 14, 1943
Philadelphia vs. Washington, Oct. 17, 1954
Houston vs. N.Y. Titans, Nov. 19, 1961
Houston vs. N.Y. Titans, Oct. 14, 1962
N.Y. Giants vs. Washington, Oct. 28, 1962
Minnesota vs. Baltimore, Sept. 28, 1969
San Diego vs. Oakland, Nov. 22, 1981
6 By many teams.

Most Touchdowns, Passing, Both Teams, Game
12 New Orleans (6) vs. St. Louis (6), Nov. 2, 1969
11 N.Y. Giants (7) vs. Washington (4), Oct. 28, 1962
Oakland (6) vs. Houston (5), Dec. 22, 1963
10 San Diego (5) vs. Seattle (5), Sept. 15, 1985
Miami (6) vs. N.Y. Jets (4), Sept. 21, 1986 (OT)

PASSES HAD INTERCEPTED

Most Passes Had Intercepted, Season
48 Houston, 1962
45 Denver, 1961
41 Card-Pitt, 1944

Fewest Passes Had Intercepted, Season
5 Cleveland, 1960
Green Bay, 1966
Kansas City, 1990
N.Y. Giants, 1990
6 Green Bay, 1964
St. Louis, 1982
Dallas, 1993
7 Los Angeles, 1969

Most Passes Had Intercepted, Game
9 Detroit vs. Green Bay, Oct. 24, 1943
Pittsburgh vs. Philadelphia, Dec. 12, 1965
8 Green Bay vs. N.Y. Giants, Nov. 21, 1948
Chi. Cardinals vs. Philadelphia, Sept. 24, 1950
N.Y. Yanks vs. N.Y. Giants, Dec. 16, 1951
Denver vs. Houston, Dec. 2, 1962
Chi. Bears vs. Detroit, Sept. 22, 1968
Baltimore vs. N.Y. Jets, Sept. 23, 1973
7 By many teams. Last time: Green Bay vs. New Orleans, Sept. 14, 1986

Most Passes Had Intercepted, Both Teams, Game
13 Denver (8) vs. Houston (5), Dec. 2, 1962

11 Philadelphia (7) vs. Boston (4), Nov. 3, 1935
Boston (6) vs. Pittsburgh (5), Dec. 1, 1935
Cleveland (7) vs. Green Bay (4), Oct. 30, 1938
Green Bay (7) vs. Detroit (4), Oct. 20, 1940
Detroit (7) vs. Chi. Bears (4), Nov. 22, 1942
Detroit (7) vs. Cleveland (4), Nov. 26, 1944
Chi. Cardinals (8) vs. Philadelphia (3), Sept. 24, 1950
Washington (7) vs. N.Y. Giants (4), Dec. 8, 1963
Pittsburgh (9) vs. Philadelphia (2), Dec 12, 1965
10 In many games

PUNTING

Most Seasons Leading League (Average Distance)
7 Denver, 1962-64, 1966-67, 1982, 1988
6 Washington, 1940-43, 1945, 1958
Kansas City, 1968, 1971-73, 1979, 1984
5 L.A. Rams, 1946, 1949, 1955-56, 1994

Most Consecutive Seasons Leading League (Average Distance)
4 Washington, 1940-43
3 Cleveland, 1950-52
Denver, 1962-64
Kansas City, 1971-73

Most Punts, Season
114 Chicago, 1981
113 Boston, 1934
Brooklyn, 1934
112 Boston, 1935

Fewest Punts, Season
23 San Diego, 1982
31 Cincinnati, 1982
32 Chi. Bears, 1941

Most Punts, Game
17 Chi. Bears vs. Green Bay, Oct. 22, 1933
Cincinnati vs. Pittsburgh, Oct. 22, 1933
16 Cincinnati vs. Portsmouth, Sept. 17, 1933
Chi. Cardinals vs. Chi. Bears, Nov. 30, 1933
Chi. Cardinals vs. Detroit, Sept. 15, 1940
15 N.Y. Giants vs. Chi. Bears, Nov. 17, 1935
Philadelphia vs. N.Y. Giants, Dec. 6, 1987 (OT)

Fewest Punts, Game
0 By many teams. Last time: Minnesota vs. Chicago, Sept. 18, 1994

Most Punts, Both Teams, Game
31 Chi. Bears (17) vs. Green Bay (14), Oct. 22, 1933
Cincinnati (17), vs. Pittsburgh (14), Oct. 22, 1933
29 Chi. Cardinals (15) vs. Cincinnati (14), Nov. 12, 1933
Chi. Cardinals (16) vs. Chi. Bears (13), Nov. 30, 1933
Chi. Cardinals (16) vs. Detroit (13), Sept. 15, 1940
28 Philadelphia (14) vs. Washington (14), Nov. 5, 1939

Fewest Punts, Both Teams, Game
0 Buffalo vs. San Francisco, Sept. 13, 1992
1 Baltimore (0) vs. Cleveland (1), Nov. 1, 1959
Dall. Cowboys (0) vs. Cleveland (1), Dec. 3, 1961
Chicago (0) vs. Detroit (1), Oct. 1, 1972
San Francisco (0) vs. N.Y. Giants (1), Oct. 15, 1972
Green Bay (0) vs. Buffalo (1), Dec. 5, 1982
Miami (0) vs. Buffalo (1), Oct. 12, 1986
Green Bay (0) vs. Chicago (1), Dec. 17, 1989
2 In many games

AVERAGE YARDAGE

Highest Average Distance, Punting, Season
47.6 Detroit, 1961 (56-2,664)
47.0 Pittsburgh, 1961 (73-3,431)
46.9 Pittsburgh, 1953 (80-3,752)

Lowest Average Distance, Punting, Season
32.7 Card-Pitt, 1944 (60-1,964)
33.8 Cincinnati, 1986 (59-1,996)
33.9 Detroit, 1969 (74-2,510)

PUNT RETURNS

Most Seasons Leading League (Average Return)
9 Detroit, 1943-45, 1951-52, 1962, 1966, 1969, 1991
7 Chi. Cardinals/St. Louis, 1948-49, 1955-56, 1959, 1986-87
5 Cleveland, 1958, 1960, 1964-65, 1967
Green Bay, 1950, 1953-54, 1961, 1972
Dall. Texans/Kansas City, 1960, 1968, 1970, 1979-80

Most Consecutive Seasons Leading League (Average Return)
3 Detroit, 1943-45
2 By many teams

Most Punt Returns, Season
71 Pittsburgh, 1976
Tampa Bay, 1979
L.A. Raiders, 1985
67 Pittsburgh, 1974
Los Angeles, 1978
L.A. Raiders, 1984
65 San Francisco, 1976

Fewest Punt Returns, Season
12 Baltimore, 1981
San Diego, 1982
14 Los Angeles, 1961
Philadelphia, 1962
Baltimore, 1982
15 Houston, 1960
Washington, 1960
Oakland, 1961
N.Y. Giants, 1969
Philadelphia, 1973
Kansas City, 1982

Most Punt Returns, Game
12 Philadelphia vs. Cleveland, Dec. 3, 1950
11 Chi. Bears vs. Chi. Cardinals, Oct. 8, 1950
Washington vs. Tampa Bay, Oct. 9, 1977
10 Philadelphia vs. N.Y. Giants, Nov. 26, 1950
Philadelphia vs. Tampa Bay, Sept. 18, 1977
Pittsburgh vs. Buffalo, Dec. 16, 1979
Washington vs. New Orleans, Dec. 26, 1982
Philadelphia vs. Seattle, Dec. 13, 1992 (OT)
New England vs. Pittsburgh, Dec. 5, 1993

Most Punt Returns, Both Teams, Game
17 Philadelphia (12) vs. Cleveland (5), Dec. 3, 1950
16 N.Y. Giants (9) vs. Philadelphia (7), Dec. 12, 1954
Washington (11) vs. Tampa Bay (5), Oct. 9, 1977
15 Detroit (8) vs. Cleveland (7), Sept. 27, 1942
Los Angeles (8) vs. Baltimore (7), Nov. 27, 1966
Pittsburgh (8) vs. Houston (7), Dec. 1, 1974
Philadelphia (10) vs. Tampa Bay (5), Sept. 18, 1977
Baltimore (9) vs. Kansas City (6), Sept. 2, 1979
Washington (10) vs. New Orleans (5), Dec. 26, 1982
L.A. Raiders (8) vs. Cleveland (7), Nov. 16, 1986

FAIR CATCHES

Most Fair Catches, Season
34 Baltimore, 1971
32 San Diego, 1969
30 St. Louis, 1967
Minnesota, 1971

Fewest Fair Catches, Season
0 San Diego, 1975
New England, 1976
Tampa Bay, 1976
Pittsburgh, 1977
Dallas, 1982
1 Cleveland, 1974
San Francisco, 1975
Kansas City, 1976
St. Louis, 1976
San Diego, 1976
L.A. Rams, 1982
St. Louis, 1982
Tampa Bay, 1982
2 By many teams

Most Fair Catches, Game
7 Minnesota vs. Dallas, Sept. 25, 1966
Detroit vs. Chicago, Nov. 21, 1976
Philadelphia vs. Buffalo, Dec. 27, 1987
6 By many teams

YARDS GAINED

Most Yards, Punt Returns, Season
785 L.A. Raiders, 1985
781 Chi. Bears, 1948
774 Pittsburgh, 1974

Fewest Yards, Punt Returns, Season
27 St. Louis, 1965
35 N.Y. Giants, 1965
37 New England, 1972

Most Yards, Punt Returns, Game
231 Detroit vs. San Francisco, Oct. 6, 1963
225 Oakland vs. Buffalo, Sept. 15, 1968
219 Los Angeles vs. Atlanta, Oct. 11, 1981

Fewest Yards, Punt Returns, Game
-28 Washington vs. Dallas, Dec. 11, 1966
-23 N.Y. Giants vs. Buffalo, Oct. 20, 1975
Pittsburgh vs. Houston, Sept. 20, 1970
-20 New Orleans vs. Pittsburgh, Oct. 20, 1968

Most Yards, Punt Returns, Both Teams, Game
282 Los Angeles (219) vs. Atlanta (63), Oct. 11, 1981
245 Detroit (231) vs. San Francisco (14), Oct. 6, 1963
244 Oakland (225) vs. Buffalo (19), Sept. 15, 1968

Fewest Yards, Punt Returns, Both Teams, Game
-18 Buffalo (-18) vs. Pittsburgh (0), Oct. 29, 1972
-14 Miami (-14) vs. Boston (0), Nov. 30, 1969
-13 N.Y. Giants (-13) vs. Cleveland (0), Nov. 14, 1965

AVERAGE YARDS RETURNING PUNTS

Highest Average, Punt Returns, Season
20.2 Chi. Bears, 1941 (27-546)
19.1 Chi. Cardinals, 1948 (35-669)
18.2 Chi. Cardinals, 1949 (30-546)

Lowest Average, Punt Returns, Season
1.2 St. Louis, 1965 (23-27)
1.5 N.Y. Giants, 1965 (24-35)
1.7 Washington, 1970 (27-45)

TOUCHDOWNS RETURNING PUNTS

Most Touchdowns, Punt Returns, Season
5 Chi. Cardinals, 1959
4 Chi. Cardinals, 1948
Detroit, 1951
N.Y. Giants, 1951
Denver, 1976
3 Washington, 1941
Detroit, 1952
Pittsburgh, 1952
Houston, 1975
Los Angeles, 1981
Cleveland, 1993

Most Touchdowns, Punt Returns, Game
2 Detroit vs. Los Angeles, Oct. 14, 1951
Detroit vs. Green Bay, Nov. 22, 1951
Chi. Cardinals vs. Pittsburgh, Nov. 1, 1959
Chi. Cardinals vs. N.Y. Giants, Nov. 22, 1959
N.Y. Titans vs. Denver, Sept. 24, 1961
Denver vs. Cleveland, Sept. 26, 1976
Los Angeles vs. Atlanta, Oct. 11, 1981
St. Louis vs. Tampa Bay, Dec. 21, 1986
L.A. Rams vs. Atlanta, Dec. 27, 1992
Cleveland vs. Pittsburgh, Oct. 24, 1993

Most Touchdowns, Punt Returns, Both Teams, Game
2 Philadelphia (1) vs. Washington (1), Nov. 9, 1952
Kansas City (1) vs. Buffalo (1), Sept. 11, 1966
Baltimore (1) vs. New England (1), Nov. 18, 1979
L.A. Raiders (1) vs. Philadelphia (1), Nov. 30, 1986 (OT)
Cincinnati (1) vs. Green Bay (1), Sept. 20, 1992
(Also see previous record)

KICKOFF RETURNS

Most Seasons Leading League (Average Return)
7 Washington, 1942, 1947, 1962-63, 1973-74, 1981
6 Chicago Bears, 1943, 1948, 1958, 1966, 1972, 1985
5 N.Y. Giants, 1944, 1946, 1949, 1951, 1953

Most Consecutive Seasons Leading League (Average Return)
3 Denver, 1965-67
2 By many teams

Most Kickoff Returns, Season
88 New Orleans, 1980
86 Minnesota, 1984
Cincinnati, 1994
84 Baltimore, 1981

Fewest Kickoff Returns, Season
17 N.Y. Giants, 1944
20 N.Y. Giants, 1941, 1943
Chi. Bears, 1942
23 Washington, 1942

Most Kickoff Returns, Game
12 N.Y. Giants vs. Washington, Nov. 27, 1966
10 By many teams

Most Kickoff Returns, Both Teams, Game
19 N.Y. Giants (12) vs. Washington (7), Nov. 27, 1966
18 Houston (10) vs. Oakland (8), Dec. 22, 1963
17 Washington (9) vs. Green Bay (8), Oct. 17, 1983
San Diego (9) vs. Pittsburgh (8), Dec. 8, 1985
Detroit (9) vs. Green Bay (8), Nov. 27, 1986
L.A. Raiders (9) vs. Seattle (8), Dec. 18, 1988

YARDS GAINED

Most Yards, Kickoff Returns, Season
1,973 New Orleans, 1980
1,840 New Orleans, 1994
1,824 Houston, 1963

Fewest Yards, Kickoff Returns, Season
282 N.Y. Giants, 1940
381 Green Bay, 1940
424 Chicago, 1963

Most Yards, Kickoff Returns, Game
362 Detroit vs. Los Angeles, Oct. 29, 1950
304 Chi. Bears vs. Green Bay, Nov. 9, 1952
New Orleans vs. L.A. Rams, Oct. 23, 1994
295 Denver vs. Boston, Oct. 4, 1964

Most Yards, Kickoff Returns, Both Teams, Game
560 Detroit (362) vs. Los Angeles (198), Oct. 29, 1950
501 New Orleans (304) vs. L.A. Rams (197), Oct. 23, 1994
453 Washington (236) vs. Philadelphia (217), Sept. 28, 1947

AVERAGE YARDAGE

Highest Average, Kickoff Returns, Season
29.4 Chicago, 1972 (52-1,528)
28.9 Pittsburgh, 1952 (39-1,128)
28.2 Washington, 1962 (61-1,720)

Lowest Average, Kickoff Returns, Season
14.7 N.Y. Jets, 1993 (46-675)
15.8 N.Y. Giants, 1993 (32-507)
15.9 Tampa Bay, 1993 (58-922)

TOUCHDOWNS

Most Touchdowns, Kickoff Returns, Season
4 Green Bay, 1967
Chicago, 1970
Detroit, 1994
3 Los Angeles, 1950
Chi. Cardinals, 1954
San Francisco, 1963
Denver, 1966
Chicago, 1967
New England, 1977
L.A. Rams, 1985
2 By many teams

Most Touchdowns, Kickoff Returns, Game
2 Chi. Bears vs. Green Bay, Sept. 22, 1940
Chi. Bears vs. Green Bay, Nov. 9, 1952
Philadelphia vs. Dallas, Nov. 6, 1966
Green Bay vs. Cleveland, Nov. 12, 1967
L.A. Rams vs. Green Bay, Nov. 24, 1985
New Orleans vs. L.A. Rams, Oct. 23, 1994

Most Touchdowns, Kickoff Returns, Both Teams, Game
2 Washington (1) vs. Philadelphia (1), Nov. 1, 1942
Washington (1) vs. Philadelphia (1), Sept. 28, 1947
Los Angeles (1) vs. Detroit (1), Oct. 29, 1950
N.Y. Yanks (1) vs. N.Y. Giants (1), Nov. 4, 1951 (consecutive)
Baltimore (1) vs. Chi. Bears (1), Oct. 4, 1958
Buffalo (1) vs. Boston (1), Nov. 3, 1962
Pittsburgh (1) vs. Dallas (1), Oct. 30, 1966
St. Louis (1) vs. Washington (1), Sept. 23, 1973 (consecutive)
Atlanta (1) vs. San Francisco (1), Dec. 20, 1987 (consecutive)
Houston (1) vs. Pittsburgh (1), Dec. 4, 1988
(Also see previous record)

FUMBLES

Most Fumbles, Season
56 Chi. Bears, 1938
San Francisco, 1978
54 Philadelphia, 1946
51 New England, 1973

Fewest Fumbles, Season
8 Cleveland, 1959
11 Green Bay, 1944
12 Brooklyn, 1934
Detroit, 1943
Cincinnati, 1982
Minnesota, 1982

Most Fumbles, Game
10 Phil-Pitt vs. N.Y. Giants, Oct. 9, 1943
Detroit vs. Minnesota, Nov. 12, 1967
Kansas City vs. Houston, Oct. 12, 1969
San Francisco vs. Detroit, Dec. 17, 1978
9 Philadelphia vs. Green Bay, Oct. 13, 1946
Kansas City vs. San Diego, Nov. 15, 1964
N.Y. Giants vs. Buffalo, Oct. 20, 1975
St. Louis vs. Washington, Oct. 25, 1976
San Diego vs. Green Bay, Sept. 24, 1978
Pittsburgh vs. Cincinnati, Oct. 14, 1979

Cleveland vs. Seattle, Dec. 20, 1981
Cleveland vs. Pittsburgh, Dec. 23, 1990
8 By many teams

Most Fumbles, Both Teams, Game
14 Washington (8) vs. Pittsburgh (6), Nov. 14, 1937
Chi. Bears (7) vs. Cleveland (7), Nov. 24, 1940
St. Louis (8) vs. N.Y. Giants (6), Sept. 17, 1961
Kansas City (10) vs. Houston (4), Oct. 12, 1969
13 Washington (8) vs. Pittsburgh (5), Nov. 14, 1937
Philadelphia (7) vs. Boston (6), Dec. 8, 1946
N.Y. Giants (7) vs. Washington (6), Nov. 5, 1950
Kansas City (9) vs. San Diego (4), Nov. 15, 1964
Buffalo (7) vs. Denver (6), Dec. 13, 1964
N.Y. Jets (7) vs. Houston (6), Sept. 12, 1965
Houston (8) vs. Pittsburgh (5), Dec. 9, 1973
St. Louis (9) vs. Washington (4), Oct. 25, 1976
Cleveland (9) vs. Seattle (4), Dec. 20, 1981
Green Bay (7) vs. Detroit (6), Oct. 6, 1985
12 In many games

FUMBLES LOST

Most Fumbles Lost, Season
36 Chi. Cardinals, 1959
31 Green Bay, 1952
29 Chi. Cardinals, 1946
Pittsburgh, 1950

Fewest Fumbles Lost, Season
3 Philadelphia, 1938
Minnesota, 1980
4 San Francisco, 1960
Kansas City, 1982
5 Chi. Cardinals, 1943
Detroit, 1943
N.Y. Giants, 1943
Cleveland, 1959
Minnesota, 1982
San Diego, 1993

Most Fumbles Lost, Game
8 St. Louis vs. Washington, Oct. 25, 1976
Cleveland vs. Pittsburgh, Dec. 23, 1990
7 Cincinnati vs. Buffalo, Nov. 30, 1969
Pittsburgh vs. Cincinnati, Oct. 14, 1979
Cleveland vs. Seattle, Dec. 20, 1981
6 By many teams

FUMBLES RECOVERED

Most Fumbles Recovered, Season, Own and Opponents'
58 Minnesota, 1963 (27 own, 31 opp)
51 Chi. Bears, 1938 (37 own, 14 opp)
San Francisco, 1978 (24 own, 27 opp)
50 Philadelphia, 1987 (23 own, 27 opp)

Fewest Fumbles Recovered, Season, Own and Opponents'
9 San Francisco, 1982 (5 own, 4 opp)
11 Cincinnati, 1982 (5 own, 6 opp)
12 Washington, 1994 (6 own, 6 opp)

Most Fumbles Recovered, Game, Own and Opponents'
10 Denver vs. Buffalo, Dec. 13, 1964 (5 own, 5 opp)
Pittsburgh vs. Houston, Dec. 9, 1973 (5 own, 5 opp)
Washington vs. St. Louis, Oct. 25, 1976 (2 own, 8 opp)
9 St. Louis vs. N.Y. Giants, Sept. 17, 1961 (6 own, 3 opp)
Houston vs. Cincinnati, Oct. 27, 1974 (4 own, 5 opp)
Kansas City vs. Dallas, Nov. 10, 1975 (4 own, 5 opp)
Green Bay vs. Detroit, Oct. 6, 1985 (5 own, 4 opp)
8 By many teams

Most Own Fumbles Recovered, Season
37 Chi. Bears, 1938
28 Pittsburgh, 1987
27 Philadelphia, 1946
Minnesota, 1963

Fewest Own Fumbles Recovered, Season
2 Washington, 1958
3 Detroit, 1956
Cleveland, 1959
Houston, 1982
4 By many teams

Most Opponents' Fumbles Recovered, Season
31 Minnesota, 1963
29 Cleveland, 1951
28 Green Bay, 1946
Houston, 1977
Seattle, 1983

Fewest Opponents' Fumbles Recovered, Season
3 Los Angeles, 1974
4 Philadelphia, 1944
San Francisco, 1982
5 Baltimore, 1982

Most Opponents' Fumbles Recovered, Game
8 Washington vs. St. Louis, Oct. 25, 1976
Pittsburgh vs. Cleveland, Dec. 23, 1990
7 Buffalo vs. Cincinnati, Nov. 30, 1969
Cincinnati vs. Pittsburgh, Oct. 14, 1979
Seattle vs. Cleveland, Dec. 20, 1981
6 By many teams

TOUCHDOWNS

Most Touchdowns, Fumbles Recovered, Season, Own and Opponents'
5 Chi. Bears, 1942 (1 own, 4 opp)
Los Angeles, 1952 (1 own, 4 opp)
San Francisco, 1965 (1 own, 4 opp)
Oakland, 1978 (2 own, 3 opp)
4 Chi. Bears, 1948 (1 own, 3 opp)
Boston, 1948 (4 opp)
Denver, 1979 (1 own, 3 opp)
Atlanta, 1981 (1 own, 3 opp)
Denver, 1984 (4 opp)
St. Louis, 1987 (4 opp)
Minnesota, 1989 (4 opp)
Atlanta, 1991 (4 opp)
3 By many teams

Most Touchdowns, Own Fumbles Recovered, Season
2 Chi. Bears, 1953
New England, 1973
Buffalo, 1974
Denver, 1975
Oakland, 1978
Green Bay, 1982
New Orleans, 1983
Cleveland, 1986
Green Bay, 1989

Most Touchdowns, Opponents' Fumbles Recovered, Season
4 Detroit, 1937
Chi. Bears, 1942
Boston, 1948
Los Angeles, 1952
San Francisco, 1965
Denver, 1984
St. Louis, 1987
Minnesota, 1989
Atlanta, 1991
3 By many teams

Most Touchdowns, Fumbles Recovered, Game, Own and Opponents'
2 By many teams

Most Touchdowns, Fumbled Recovered, Game, Both Teams, Own and Opponents'
3 Detroit (2) vs. Minnesota (1), Dec. 9, 1962 (2 own, 1 opp)
Green Bay (2) vs. Dallas (1), Nov. 29, 1964 (3 opp)
Oakland (2) vs. Buffalo (1), Dec. 24, 1967 (3 opp)

Most Touchdowns, Own Fumbles Recovered, Game
1 By many teams

Most Touchdowns, Opponents' Fumbles Recovered, Game
2 Detroit vs. Cleveland, Nov. 7, 1937
Philadelphia vs. N.Y. Giants, Sept. 25, 1938
Chi. Bears vs. Washington, Nov. 28, 1948
N.Y. Giants vs. Pittsburgh, Sept. 17, 1950
Cleveland vs. Dall. Cowboys, Dec. 3, 1961
Cleveland vs. N.Y. Giants, Oct. 25, 1964
Green Bay vs. Dallas, Nov. 29, 1964
San Francisco vs. Detroit, Nov. 14, 1965
Oakland vs. Buffalo, Dec. 24, 1967
N.Y. Giants vs. Green Bay, Sept. 19, 1971
Washington vs. San Diego, Sept. 16, 1973
New Orleans vs. San Francisco, Oct. 19, 1975
Cincinnati vs. Pittsburgh, Oct. 14, 1979
Atlanta vs. Detroit, Oct. 5, 1980
Kansas City vs. Oakland, Oct. 5, 1980
New England vs. Baltimore, Nov. 23, 1980
Denver vs. Green Bay, Oct. 15, 1984
Miami vs. Kansas City, Oct. 11, 1987
St. Louis vs. New Orleans, Oct. 11, 1987
Minnesota vs. Atlanta, Dec. 10, 1989
Philadelphia vs. Phoenix, Nov. 24, 1991
Cincinnati vs. Seattle, Sept. 6, 1992

Most Touchdowns, Opponents' Fumbled Recovered, Game, Both Teams
3 Green Bay (2) vs. Dallas (1), Nov. 29, 1964
Oakland (2) vs. Buffalo (1), Dec. 24, 1967

TURNOVERS

(Number of times losing the ball on interceptions and fumbles.)

Most Turnovers, Season

63 San Francisco, 1978
58 Chi. Bears, 1947
Pittsburgh, 1950
N.Y. Giants, 1983
57 Green Bay, 1950
Houston, 1962, 1963
Pittsburgh, 1965

Fewest Turnovers, Season

12 Kansas City, 1982
14 N.Y. Giants, 1943
Cleveland, 1959
N.Y. Giants, 1990
16 San Francisco, 1960
Cincinnati, 1982
St. Louis, 1982
Washington, 1982

Most Turnovers, Game

12 Detroit vs. Chi. Bears, Nov. 22, 1942
Chi. Cardinals vs. Philadelphia, Sept. 24, 1950
Pittsburgh vs. Philadelphia, Dec. 12, 1965
11 San Diego vs. Green Bay, Sept. 24, 1978
10 Washington vs. N.Y. Giants, Dec. 4, 1938
Pittsburgh vs. Green Bay, Nov. 23, 1941
Detroit vs. Green Bay, Oct. 24, 1943
Chi. Cardinals vs. Green Bay, Nov. 10, 1946
Chi. Cardinals vs. N.Y. Giants, Nov. 2, 1952
Minnesota vs. Detroit, Dec. 9, 1962
Houston vs. Oakland, Sept. 7, 1963
Washington vs. N.Y. Giants, Dec. 8, 1963
Chicago vs. Detroit, Sept. 22, 1968
St. Louis vs. Washington, Oct. 25, 1976
N.Y. Jets vs. New England, Nov. 21, 1976
San Francisco vs. Dallas, Oct. 12, 1980
Cleveland vs. Seattle, Dec. 20, 1981
Detroit vs. Denver, Oct. 7, 1984

Most Turnovers, Both Teams, Game

17 Detroit (12) vs. Chi. Bears (5), Nov. 22, 1942
Boston (9) vs. Philadelphia (8), Dec. 8, 1946
16 Chi. Cardinals (12) vs. Philadelphia (4), Sept. 24, 1950
Chi. Cardinals (8) vs. Chi. Bears (8), Dec. 7, 1958
Minnesota (10) vs. Detroit (6), Dec. 9, 1962
Houston (9) vs. Kansas City (7), Oct. 12, 1969
15 Philadelphia (8) vs. Chi. Cardinals (7), Oct. 3, 1954
Denver (9) vs. Houston (6), Dec. 2, 1962
Washington (10) vs. N.Y. Giants (5), Dec. 8, 1963
St. Louis (9) vs. Kansas City (6), Oct. 2, 1983

PENALTIES

Most Seasons Leading League, Fewest Penalties

13 Miami, 1968, 1976-84, 1986, 1990-91
9 Pittsburgh, 1946-47, 1950-52, 1954, 1963, 1965, 1968
7 Boston/New England, 1962, 1964-65, 1973, 1987, 1989, 1993

Most Consecutive Seasons Leading League, Fewest Penalties

9 Miami, 1976-84
3 Pittsburgh, 1950-52
2 By many teams

Most Seasons Leading League, Most Penalties

16 Chi. Bears, 1941-44, 1946-49, 1951, 1959-61, 1963, 1965, 1968, 1976
10 Oakland/L.A. Raiders, 1963, 1966, 1968-69, 1975, 1982, 1984, 1991, 1993-94
6 L.A. Rams, 1950, 1952, 1962, 1969, 1978, 1980

Most Consecutive Seasons Leading League, Most Penalties

4 Chi. Bears, 1941-44, 1946-49
3 Chi. Cardinals, 1954-56
Chi. Bears, 1959-61
Houston, 1988-90

Fewest Penalties, Season

19 Detroit, 1937
21 Boston, 1935
24 Philadelphia, 1936

Most Penalties, Season

156 L.A. Raiders, 1994
149 Houston, 1989
148 L.A. Raiders, 1993

Fewest Penalties, Game

0 By many teams. Last time: Indianapolis vs. N.Y. Jets, Oct. 30, 1994

Most Penalties, Game

22 Brooklyn vs. Green Bay, Sept. 17, 1944
Chi. Bears vs. Philadelphia, Nov. 26, 1944
21 Cleveland vs. Chi. Bears, Nov. 25, 1951
20 Tampa Bay vs. Seattle, Oct. 17, 1976

Fewest Penalties, Both Teams, Game

0 Brooklyn vs. Pittsburgh, Oct. 28, 1934
Brooklyn vs. Boston, Sept. 28, 1936
Cleveland vs. Chi. Bears, Oct. 9, 1938
Pittsburgh vs. Philadelphia, Nov. 10, 1940

Most Penalties, Both Teams, Game

37 Cleveland (21) vs. Chi. Bears (16), Nov. 25, 1951
35 Tampa Bay (20) vs. Seattle (15), Oct. 17, 1976
33 Brooklyn (22) vs. Green Bay (11), Sept. 17, 1944

YARDS PENALIZED

Most Seasons Leading League, Fewest Yards Penalized

13 Miami, 1967-68, 1973, 1977-84, 1990-91
8 Boston/Washington, 1935, 1953-54, 1956-58, 1970, 1985
7 Pittsburgh, 1946-47, 1950, 1952, 1962, 1965, 1968
Boston/New England, 1962, 1964-66, 1987, 1989, 1993

Most Consecutive Seasons Leading League, Fewest Yards Penalized

8 Miami, 1977-84
3 Washington, 1956-58
Boston, 1964-66
2 By many teams

Most Seasons Leading League, Most Yards Penalized

15 Chi. Bears, 1935, 1937, 1939-44, 1946-47, 1949, 1951, 1961-62, 1968
10 Oakland/L.A. Raiders, 1963-64, 1968-69, 1975, 1982, 1984, 1991, 1993-94
6 Buffalo, 1962, 1967, 1970, 1972, 1981, 1983
Houston, 1961, 1985-86, 1988-90

Most Consecutive Seasons Leading League, Most Yards Penalized

6 Chi. Bears, 1939-44
3 Cleveland, 1976-78
Houston, 1988-90
2 By many teams

Fewest Yards Penalized, Season

139 Detroit, 1937
146 Philadelphia, 1937
159 Philadelphia, 1936

Most Yards Penalized, Season

1,274 Oakland, 1969
1,239 Baltimore, 1979
1,209 L.A. Raiders, 1984

Fewest Yards Penalized, Game

0 By many teams. Last time: Indianapolis vs. N.Y. Jets, Oct. 30, 1994

Most Yards Penalized, Game

209 Cleveland vs. Chi. Bears, Nov. 25, 1951
191 Philadelphia vs. Seattle, Dec. 13, 1992 (OT)
190 Tampa Bay vs. Seattle, Oct. 17, 1976

Fewest Yards Penalized, Both Teams, Game

0 Brooklyn vs. Pittsburgh, Oct. 28, 1934
Brooklyn vs. Boston, Sept. 28, 1936
Cleveland vs. Chi. Bears, Oct. 9, 1938
Pittsburgh vs. Philadelphia, Nov. 10, 1940

Most Yards Penalized, Both Teams, Game

374 Cleveland (209) vs. Chi. Bears (165), Nov. 25, 1951
310 Tampa Bay (190) vs. Seattle (120), Oct. 17, 1976
309 Green Bay (184) vs. Boston (125), Oct. 21, 1945

DEFENSE

SCORING

Most Seasons Leading League, Fewest Points Allowed

10 N.Y. Giants, 1935, 1938-39, 1941, 1944, 1958-59, 1961, 1990, 1993
9 Chi. Bears, 1932, 1936-37, 1942, 1948, 1963, 1985-86, 1988
7 Cleveland, 1951, 1953-57, 1994

Most Consecutive Seasons Leading League, Fewest Points Allowed

5 Cleveland, 1953-57
3 Buffalo, 1964-66
Minnesota, 1969-71
2 By many teams

Fewest Points Allowed, Season (Since 1932)

44 Chi. Bears, 1932
54 Brooklyn, 1933
59 Detroit, 1934

Most Points Allowed, Season

533 Baltimore, 1981
501 N.Y. Giants, 1966
487 New Orleans, 1980

Fewest Touchdowns Allowed, Season (Since 1932)

6 Chi. Bears, 1932
Brooklyn, 1933
7 Detroit, 1934
8 Green Bay, 1932

Most Touchdowns Allowed, Season
68 Baltimore, 1981
66 N.Y. Giants, 1966
63 Baltimore, 1950

FIRST DOWNS

Fewest First Downs Allowed Season
77 Detroit, 1935
79 Boston, 1935
82 Washington, 1937

Most First Downs Allowed, Season
406 Baltimore, 1981
371 Seattle, 1981
366 Green Bay, 1983

Fewest First Downs Allowed, Rushing, Season
35 Chi. Bears, 1942
40 Green Bay, 1939
41 Brooklyn, 1944

Most First Downs Allowed, Rushing, Season
179 Detroit, 1985
178 New Orleans, 1980
175 Seattle, 1981

Fewest First Downs Allowed, Passing, Season
33 Chi. Bears, 1943
34 Pittsburgh, 1941
Washington, 1943
35 Detroit, 1940
Philadelphia, 1940, 1944

Most First Downs Allowed, Passing, Season
218 San Diego, 1985
216 San Diego, 1981
N.Y. Jets, 1986
214 Baltimore, 1981

Fewest First Downs Allowed, Penalty, Season
1 Boston, 1944
3 Philadelphia, 1940
Pittsburgh, 1945
Washington, 1957
4 Cleveland, 1940
Green Bay, 1943
N.Y. Giants, 1943

Most First Downs Allowed, Penalty, Season
48 Houston, 1985
46 Houston, 1986
43 L.A. Raiders, 1984

NET YARDS ALLOWED RUSHING AND PASSING

Most Seasons Leading League, Fewest Yards Allowed
8 Chi. Bears, 1942-43, 1948, 1958, 1963, 1984-86
6 N.Y. Giants, 1938, 1940-41, 1951, 1956, 1959
Philadelphia, 1944-45, 1949, 1953, 1981, 1991
Minnesota, 1969-70, 1975, 1988-89, 1993
5 Boston/Washington, 1935-37, 1939, 1946

Most Consecutive Seasons Leading League, Fewest Yards Allowed
3 Boston/Washington, 1935-37
Chicago, 1984-86
2 By many teams

Fewest Yards Allowed, Season
1,539 Chi. Cardinals, 1934
1,703 Chi. Bears, 1942
1,789 Brooklyn, 1933

Most Yards Allowed, Season
6,793 Baltimore, 1981
6,403 Green Bay, 1983
6,352 Minnesota, 1984

RUSHING

Most Seasons Leading League, Fewest Yards Allowed
10 Chi. Bears, 1937, 1939, 1942, 1946, 1949, 1963, 1984-85, 1987-88
7 Detroit, 1938, 1950, 1952, 1962, 1970, 1980-81
Philadelphia, 1944-45, 1947-48, 1953, 1990-91
Dallas, 1966-69, 1972, 1978, 1992
5 N.Y. Giants, 1940, 1951, 1956, 1959, 1986

Most Consecutive Seasons Leading League, Fewest Yards Allowed
4 Dallas, 1966-69
2 By many teams

Fewest Yards Allowed, Rushing, Season
519 Chi. Bears, 1942
558 Philadelphia, 1944
762 Pittsburgh, 1982

Most Yards Allowed, Rushing, Season
3,228 Buffalo, 1978
3,106 New Orleans, 1980
3,010 Baltimore, 1978

Fewest Touchdowns Allowed, Rushing, Season
2 Detroit, 1934
Dallas, 1968
Minnesota, 1971
3 By many teams

Most Touchdowns Allowed, Rushing, Season
36 Oakland, 1961
31 N.Y. Giants, 1980
Tampa Bay, 1986
30 Baltimore, 1981

PASSING

Most Seasons Leading League, Fewest Yards Allowed
8 Green Bay, 1947-48, 1962, 1964-68
7 Washington, 1939, 1942, 1945, 1952-53, 1980, 1985
6 Chi. Bears, 1938, 1943-44, 1958, 1960, 1963
Minnesota, 1969-70, 1972, 1975-76, 1989
Pittsburgh, 1941, 1946, 1951, 1955, 1974, 1990
Philadelphia, 1934, 1936, 1940, 1949, 1981, 1991

Most Consecutive Seasons Leading League, Fewest Yards Allowed
5 Green Bay, 1964-68
2 By many teams

Fewest Yards Allowed, Passing, Season
545 Philadelphia, 1934
558 Portsmouth, 1933
585 Chi. Cardinals, 1934

Most Yards Allowed, Passing, Season
4,389 N.Y. Jets, 1986
4,311 San Diego, 1981
4,293 San Diego, 1985

Fewest Touchdowns Allowed, Passing, Season
1 Portsmouth, 1932
Philadelphia, 1934
2 Brooklyn, 1933
Chi. Bears, 1934
3 Chi. Bears, 1932
Green Bay, 1932
Green Bay, 1934
Chi. Bears, 1936
New York, 1939
New York, 1944

Most Touchdowns Allowed, Passing, Season
40 Denver, 1963
38 St. Louis, 1969
37 Washington, 1961
Baltimore, 1981

SACKS

Most Seasons Leading League
5 Oakland/L.A. Raiders, 1966-68, 1982, 1986
4 Boston/New England, 1961, 1963, 1977, 1979
Dallas, 1966, 1968-69, 1978
Dallas/Kansas City, 1960, 1965, 1969, 1990
3 San Francisco, 1967, 1972, 1976
L.A. Rams, 1968, 1970, 1988

Most Consecutive Seasons Leading League
3 Oakland, 1966-68
2 Dallas, 1968-69

Most Sacks, Season
72 Chicago, 1984
71 Minnesota, 1989
70 Chicago, 1987

Fewest Sacks, Season
11 Baltimore, 1982
12 Buffalo, 1982
13 Baltimore, 1981

Most Sacks, Game
12 Dallas vs. Pittsburgh, Nov. 20, 1966
St. Louis vs. Baltimore, Oct. 26, 1980
Chicago vs. Detroit, Dec. 16, 1984
Dallas vs. Houston, Sept. 29, 1985
11 N.Y. Giants vs. St. Louis, Nov. 1, 1964
Baltimore vs. Los Angeles, Nov. 22, 1964
Buffalo vs. Denver, Dec. 13, 1964
Detroit vs. Green Bay, Nov. 7, 1965
Oakland vs. Buffalo, Oct. 15, 1967
Oakland vs. Denver, Nov. 5, 1967
St. Louis vs. Atlanta, Nov. 24, 1968
Dallas vs. Detroit, Oct. 6, 1975
St. Louis vs. Philadelphia, Dec. 18, 1983
Kansas City vs. Cleveland, Sept. 30, 1984
Chicago vs. Minnesota, Oct. 28, 1984

Cleveland vs. Atlanta, Nov. 18, 1984
Detroit vs. Philadelphia, Nov. 16, 1986
San Diego vs. Dallas, Nov. 16, 1986
L.A. Raiders vs. Philadelphia, Nov. 30, 1986 (OT)
Seattle vs. L.A. Raiders, Dec. 8, 1986
Chicago vs. Philadelphia, Oct. 4, 1987
Dallas vs. N.Y. Jets, Oct. 4, 1987
Indianapolis vs. Cleveland, Sept. 6, 1992
10 By many teams

Most Opponents Yards Lost Attempting to Pass, Season
666 Oakland, 1967
583 Chicago, 1984
573 San Francisco, 1976

Fewest Opponents Yards Lost Attempting to Pass, Season
75 Green Bay, 1956
77 N.Y. Bulldogs, 1949
78 Green Bay, 1958

INTERCEPTIONS BY

Most Seasons Leading League
9 N.Y. Giants, 1933, 1937-39, 1944, 1948, 1951, 1954, 1961
8 Green Bay, 1940, 1942-43, 1947, 1955, 1957, 1962, 1965
Chi. Bears, 1935-36, 1941-42, 1946, 1963, 1985, 1990
6 Kansas City, 1966-70, 1974

Most Consecutive Seasons Leading League
5 Kansas City, 1966-70
3 N.Y. Giants, 1937-39
2 By many teams

Most Passes Intercepted By, Season
49 San Diego, 1961
42 Green Bay, 1943
41 N.Y. Giants, 1951

Fewest Passes Intercepted By, Season
3 Houston, 1982
5 Baltimore, 1982
6 Houston, 1972
St. Louis, 1982

Most Passes Intercepted By, Game
9 Green Bay vs. Detroit, Oct. 24, 1943
Philadelphia vs. Pittsburgh, Dec. 12, 1965
8 N.Y. Giants vs. Green Bay, Nov. 21, 1948
Philadelphia vs. Chi. Cardinals, Sept. 24, 1950
N.Y. Giants vs. N.Y. Yanks, Dec. 16, 1951
Houston vs. Denver, Dec. 2, 1962
Detroit vs. Chicago, Sept. 22, 1968
N.Y. Jets vs. Baltimore, Sept. 23, 1973
7 By many teams. Last time: New Orleans vs. Green Bay, Sept. 14, 1986

Most Consecutive Games, One or More Interceptions By
46 L.A. Chargers/San Diego, 1960-63
37 Detroit, 1960-63
36 Boston, 1944-47

Most Yards Returning Interceptions, Season
929 San Diego, 1961
712 Los Angeles, 1952
697 Seattle, 1984

Fewest Yards Returning Interceptions, Season
5 Los Angeles, 1959
37 Dallas, 1989
42 Philadelphia, 1982

Most Yards Returning Interceptions, Game
325 Seattle vs. Kansas City, Nov. 4, 1984
314 Los Angeles vs. San Francisco, Oct. 18, 1964
245 Houston vs. N.Y. Jets, Oct. 15, 1967

Most Yards Returning Interceptions, Both Teams, Game
356 Seattle (325) vs. Kansas City (31), Nov. 4, 1984
338 Los Angeles (314) vs. San Francisco (24), Oct. 18, 1964
308 Dallas (182) vs. Los Angeles (126), Nov. 2, 1952

Most Touchdowns, Returning Interceptions, Season
9 San Diego, 1961
7 Seattle, 1984
6 Cleveland, 1960
Green Bay, 1966
Detroit, 1967
Houston, 1967

Most Touchdowns Returning Interceptions, Game
4 Seattle vs. Kansas City, Nov. 4, 1984
3 Baltimore vs. Green Bay, Nov. 5, 1950
Cleveland vs. Chicago, Dec. 11, 1960
Philadelphia vs. Pittsburgh, Dec. 12, 1965
Baltimore vs. Pittsburgh, Sept. 29, 1968
Buffalo vs. N.Y. Jets, Sept. 29, 1968
Houston vs. San Diego, Dec. 19, 1971
Cincinnati vs. Houston, Dec. 17, 1972
Tampa Bay vs. New Orleans, Dec. 11, 1977
2 By many teams

Most Touchdown Returning Interceptions, Both Teams, Game
4 Philadelphia (3) vs. Pittsburgh (1), Dec. 12, 1965
Seattle (4) vs. Kansas City (0), Nov. 4, 1984
3 Los Angeles (2) vs. Detroit (1), Nov. 1, 1953
Cleveland (2) vs. N.Y. Giants (1), Dec. 18, 1960
Pittsburgh (2) vs. Cincinnati (1), Oct. 10, 1983
Kansas City (2) vs. San Diego (1), Oct. 19, 1986
(Also see previous record)

PUNT RETURNS

Fewest Opponents Punt Returns, Season
7 Washington, 1962
San Diego, 1982
10 Buffalo, 1982
11 Boston, 1962

Most Opponents Punt Returns, Season
71 Tampa Bay, 1976, 1977
69 N.Y. Giants, 1953
68 Cleveland, 1974

Fewest Yards Allowed, Punt Returns, Season
22 Green Bay, 1967
34 Washington, 1962
39 Cleveland, 1959
Washington, 1972

Most Yards Allowed, Punt Returns, Season
932 Green Bay, 1949
913 Boston, 1947
906 New Orleans, 1974

Lowest Average Allowed, Punt Returns, Season
1.20 Chi. Cardinals, 1954 (46-55)
1.22 Cleveland, 1959 (32-39)
1.55 Chi. Cardinals, 1953 (44-68)

Highest Average Allowed, Punt Returns, Season
18.6 Green Bay, 1949 (50-932)
18.0 Cleveland, 1977 (31-558)
17.9 Boston, 1960 (20-357)

Most Touchdowns Allowed, Punt Returns, Season
4 New York, 1959
Atlanta, 1992
3 Green Bay, 1949
Chi. Cardinals, 1951
L.A. Rams, 1951, 1994
Washington, 1952
Dallas, 1952
Pittsburgh, 1959, 1993
N.Y. Jets, 1968
Cleveland, 1977
Atlanta, 1986
Tampa Bay, 1986
2 By many teams

KICKOFF RETURNS

Fewest Opponents Kickoff Returns, Season
10 Brooklyn, 1943
13 Denver, 1992
15 Detroit, 1942
Brooklyn, 1944

Most Opponents Kickoff Returns, Season
91 Washington, 1983
89 New England, 1980
San Francisco, 1994
88 San Diego, 1981

Fewest Yards Allowed, Kickoff Returns, Season
225 Brooklyn, 1943
254 Denver, 1992
293 Brooklyn, 1944

Most Yards Allowed, Kickoff Returns, Season
2,045 Kansas City, 1966
1,912 San Francisco, 1994
1,843 Minnesota, 1994

Lowest Average Allowed, Kickoff Returns, Season
14.3 Cleveland, 1980 (71-1,018)
14.9 Indianapolis, 1993 (37-551)
15.0 Seattle, 1982 (24-361)

Highest Average Allowed, Kickoff Returns, Season
29.5 N.Y. Jets, 1972 (47-1,386)
29.4 Los Angeles, 1950 (48-1,411)
29.1 New England, 1971 (49-1,427)

Most Touchdowns Allowed, Kickoff Returns, Season

3 Minnesota, 1963, 1970
Dallas, 1966
Detroit, 1980
Pittsburgh, 1986
2 By many teams

FUMBLES

Fewest Opponents Fumbles, Season

11 Cleveland, 1956
Baltimore, 1982
13 Los Angeles, 1956
Chicago, 1960
Cleveland, 1963
Cleveland, 1965
Detroit, 1967
San Diego, 1969
14 Baltimore, 1970
Oakland, 1975
Buffalo, 1982
St. Louis, 1982
San Francisco, 1982

Most Opponents Fumbles, Season

50 Minnesota, 1963
San Francisco, 1978
48 N.Y. Giants, 1980
N.Y. Jets, 1986
47 N.Y. Giants, 1977
Seattle, 1984

TURNOVERS

(Number of times losing the ball on interceptions and fumbles.)

Fewest Opponents Turnovers, Season

11 Baltimore, 1982
13 San Francisco, 1982
15 St. Louis, 1982

Most Opponents Turnovers, Season

66 San Diego, 1961
63 Seattle, 1984
61 Washington, 1983

Most Opponents Turnovers, Game

12 Chi. Bears vs. Detroit, Nov. 22, 1942
Philadelphia vs. Chi. Cardinals, Sept. 24, 1950
Philadelphia vs. Pittsburgh, Dec. 12, 1965
11 Green Bay vs. San Diego, Sept. 24, 1978
10 By 14 teams

1,000 YARDS RUSHING IN A SEASON

Year	Player, Team	Att.	Yards	Avg.	Long	TD
1994	Barry Sanders, Detroit[6]	331	1,883	5.7	85	7
	Chris Warren, Seattle[3]	333	1,545	4.6	41	9
	Emmitt Smith, Dallas[4]	368	1,484	4.0	46	21
	Natrone Means, San Diego	343	1,350	3.9	25	12
	*Marshall Faulk, Indianapolis	314	1,282	4.1	52	11
	Thurman Thomas, Buffalo[6]	287	1,093	3.8	29	7
	Rodney Hampton, N.Y. Giants[4]	327	1,075	3.3	27	6
	Terry Allen, Minnesota[2]	255	1,031	4.0	45	8
	Jerome Bettis, L.A. Rams[2]	319	1,025	3.2	19	3
	*Errict Rhett, Tampa Bay	284	1,011	3.6	27	7
1993	Emmitt Smith, Dallas[3]	283	1,486	5.3	62	9
	*Jerome Bettis, L.A. Rams	294	1,429	4.9	71	7
	Thurman Thomas, Buffalo[5]	355	1,315	3.7	27	6
	Erric Pegram, Atlanta	292	1,185	4.1	29	3
	Barry Sanders, Detroit[5]	243	1,115	4.6	42	3
	Leonard Russell, New England	300	1,088	3.6	21	7
	Rodney Hampton, N.Y. Giants[3]	292	1,077	3.7	20	5
	Chris Warren, Seattle[2]	273	1,072	3.9	45	7
	*Reggie Brooks, Washington	223	1,063	4.8	85	3
	*Ron Moore, Phoenix	263	1,018	3.9	20	9
	Gary Brown, Houston	195	1,002	5.1	26	6
1992	Emmitt Smith, Dallas[2]	373	1,713	4.6	68	18
	Barry Foster, Pittsburgh	390	1,690	4.3	69	11
	Thurman Thomas, Buffalo[4]	312	1,487	4.8	44	9
	Barry Sanders, Detroit[4]	312	1,352	4.3	55	9
	Lorenzo White, Houston	265	1,226	4.6	44	7
	Terry Allen, Minnesota	266	1,201	4.5	51	13
	Reggie Cobb, Tampa Bay	310	1,171	3.8	25	9
	Harold Green, Cincinnati	265	1,170	4.4	53	2
	Rodney Hampton, N.Y. Giants[2]	257	1,141	4.4	63	14
	Cleveland Gary, L.A. Rams	279	1,125	4.0	63	7
	Herschel Walker, Philadelphia[2]	267	1,070	4.0	38	8
	Chris Warren, Seattle	223	1,017	4.6	52	3
	*Ricky Watters, San Francisco	206	1,013	4.9	43	9
1991	Emmitt Smith, Dallas	365	1,563	4.3	75	12
	Barry Sanders, Detroit[3]	342	1,548	4.5	69	16
	Thurman Thomas, Buffalo[3]	288	1,407	4.9	33	7
	Rodney Hampton, N.Y. Giants	256	1,059	4.1	44	10
	Earnest Byner, Washington[3]	274	1,048	3.8	32	5
	Gaston Green, Denver	261	1,037	4.0	63	4
	Christian Okoye, Kansas City[2]	225	1,031	4.6	48	9
1990	Barry Sanders, Detroit[2]	255	1,304	5.1	45	13
	Thurman Thomas, Buffalo[2]	271	1,297	4.8	80	11
	Marion Butts, San Diego	265	1,225	4.6	52	8
	Earnest Byner, Washington[2]	297	1,219	4.1	22	6
	Bobby Humphrey, Denver[2]	288	1,202	4.2	37	7
	Neal Anderson, Chicago[3]	260	1,078	4.1	52	10
	Barry Word, Kansas City	204	1,015	5.0	53	4
	James Brooks, Cincinnati[3]	195	1,004	5.1	56	5
1989	Christian Okoye, Kansas City	370	1,480	4.0	59	12
	*Barry Sanders, Detroit	280	1,470	5.3	34	14
	Eric Dickerson, Indianapolis[7]	314	1,311	4.2	21	7
	Neal Anderson, Chicago[2]	274	1,275	4.7	73	11
	Dalton Hilliard, New Orleans	344	1,262	3.7	40	13
	Thurman Thomas, Buffalo	298	1,244	4.2	38	6
	James Brooks, Cincinnati[2]	221	1,239	5.6	65	7
	*Bobby Humphrey, Denver	294	1,151	3.9	40	7
	Greg Bell, L.A. Rams[3]	272	1,137	4.2	47	15
	Roger Craig, San Francisco[3]	271	1,054	3.9	27	6
	Ottis Anderson, N.Y. Giants[6]	325	1,023	3.1	36	14
1988	Eric Dickerson, Indianapolis[6]	388	1,659	4.3	41	14
	Herschel Walker, Dallas	361	1,514	4.2	38	5
	Roger Craig, San Francisco[2]	310	1,502	4.8	46	9
	Greg Bell, L.A. Rams[2]	288	1,212	4.2	44	16
	*John Stephens, New England	297	1,168	3.9	52	4
	Gary Anderson, San Diego	225	1,119	5.0	36	3
	Neal Anderson, Chicago	249	1,106	4.4	80	12
	Joe Morris, N.Y. Giants[3]	307	1,083	3.5	27	5
	*Ickey Woods, Cincinnati	203	1,066	5.3	56	15
	Curt Warner, Seattle[4]	266	1,025	3.9	29	10
	John Settle, Atlanta	232	1,024	4.4	62	7
	Mike Rozier, Houston	251	1,002	4.0	28	10
1987	Charles White, L.A. Rams	324	1,374	4.2	58	11
	Eric Dickerson, L.A. Rams-Indianapolis[5]	283	1,288	4.6	57	6
1986	Eric Dickerson, L.A. Rams[4]	404	1,821	4.5	42	11
	Joe Morris, N.Y. Giants[2]	341	1,516	4.4	54	14
	Curt Warner, Seattle[3]	319	1,481	4.6	60	13
	*Rueben Mayes, New Orleans	286	1,353	4.7	50	8
	Walter Payton, Chicago[10]	321	1,333	4.2	41	8
	Gerald Riggs, Atlanta[3]	343	1,327	3.9	31	9
	George Rogers, Washington[4]	303	1,203	4.0	42	18
	James Brooks, Cincinnati	205	1,087	5.3	56	5
1985	Marcus Allen, L.A. Raiders[3]	390	1,759	4.6	61	11
	Gerald Riggs, Atlanta[2]	397	1,719	4.3	50	10
	Walter Payton, Chicago[9]	324	1,551	4.8	40	9
	Joe Morris, N.Y. Giants	294	1,336	4.5	65	21
	Freeman McNeil, N.Y. Jets[2]	294	1,331	4.5	69	3
	Tony Dorsett, Dallas[8]	305	1,307	4.3	60	7
	James Wilder, Tampa Bay[2]	365	1,300	3.6	28	10
	Eric Dickerson, L.A. Rams[3]	292	1,234	4.2	43	12
	Craig James, New England	263	1,227	4.7	65	5
	Kevin Mack, Cleveland	222	1,104	5.0	61	7
	Curt Warner, Seattle[2]	291	1,094	3.8	38	8
	George Rogers, Washington[3]	231	1,093	4.7	35	7
	Roger Craig, San Francisco	214	1,050	4.9	62	9
	Earnest Jackson, Philadelphia[2]	282	1,028	3.6	59	5
	Stump Mitchell, St. Louis	183	1,006	5.5	64	7
	Earnest Byner, Cleveland	244	1,002	4.1	36	8
1984	Eric Dickerson, L.A. Rams[2]	379	2,105	5.6	66	14
	Walter Payton, Chicago[8]	381	1,684	4.4	72	11
	James Wilder, Tampa Bay	407	1,544	3.8	37	13
	Gerald Riggs, Atlanta	353	1,486	4.2	57	13
	Wendell Tyler, San Francisco[3]	246	1,262	5.1	40	7
	John Riggins, Washington[5]	327	1,239	3.8	24	14
	Tony Dorsett, Dallas[7]	302	1,189	3.9	31	6
	Earnest Jackson, San Diego	296	1,179	4.0	32	8
	Ottis Anderson, St. Louis[5]	289	1,174	4.1	24	6
	Marcus Allen, L.A. Raiders[2]	275	1,168	4.2	52	13
	Sammy Winder, Denver	296	1,153	3.9	24	4
	*Greg Bell, Buffalo	262	1,100	4.2	85	7
	Freeman McNeil, N.Y. Jets	229	1,070	4.7	53	5
1983	*Eric Dickerson, L.A. Rams	390	1,808	4.6	85	18
	William Andrews, Atlanta[4]	331	1,567	4.7	27	7
	*Curt Warner, Seattle	335	1,449	4.3	60	13
	Walter Payton, Chicago[7]	314	1,421	4.5	49	6
	John Riggins, Washington[4]	375	1,347	3.6	44	24
	Tony Dorsett, Dallas[6]	289	1,321	4.6	77	8
	Earl Campbell, Houston[5]	322	1,301	4.0	42	12
	Ottis Anderson, St. Louis[4]	296	1,270	4.3	43	5
	Mike Pruitt, Cleveland[4]	293	1,184	4.0	27	10
	George Rogers, New Orleans[2]	256	1,144	4.5	76	5
	Joe Cribbs, Buffalo[3]	263	1,131	4.3	45	3
	Curtis Dickey, Baltimore	254	1,122	4.4	56	4
	Tony Collins, New England	219	1,049	4.8	50	10
	Billy Sims, Detroit[3]	220	1,040	4.7	41	7
	Marcus Allen, L.A. Raiders	266	1,014	3.8	19	9
	Franco Harris, Pittsburgh[8]	279	1,007	3.6	19	5
1981	*George Rogers, New Orleans	378	1,674	4.4	79	13
	Tony Dorsett, Dallas[5]	342	1,646	4.8	75	4
	Billy Sims, Detroit[2]	296	1,437	4.9	51	13
	Wilbert Montgomery, Philadelphia[3]	286	1,402	4.9	41	8
	Ottis Anderson, St. Louis[3]	328	1,376	4.2	28	9
	Earl Campbell, Houston[4]	361	1,376	3.8	43	10
	William Andrews, Atlanta[3]	289	1,301	4.5	29	10
	Walter Payton, Chicago[6]	339	1,222	3.6	39	6
	Chuck Muncie, San Diego[2]	251	1,144	4.6	73	19
	*Joe Delaney, Kansas City	234	1,121	4.8	82	3
	Mike Pruitt, Cleveland[3]	247	1,103	4.5	21	7
	Joe Cribbs, Buffalo[2]	257	1,097	4.3	35	3
	Pete Johnson, Cincinnati	274	1,077	3.9	39	12
	Wendell Tyler, Los Angeles[2]	260	1,074	4.1	69	12
	Ted Brown, Minnesota	274	1,063	3.9	34	6
1980	Earl Campbell, Houston[3]	373	1,934	5.2	55	13
	Walter Payton, Chicago[5]	317	1,460	4.6	69	6
	Ottis Anderson, St. Louis[2]	301	1,352	4.5	52	9
	William Andrews, Atlanta[2]	265	1,308	4.9	33	4
	*Billy Sims, Detroit	313	1,303	4.2	52	13
	Tony Dorsett, Dallas[4]	278	1,185	4.3	56	11
	*Joe Cribbs, Buffalo	306	1,185	3.9	48	11
	Mike Pruitt, Cleveland[2]	249	1,034	4.2	56	6
1979	Earl Campbell, Houston[2]	368	1,697	4.6	61	19
	Walter Payton, Chicago[4]	369	1,610	4.4	43	14
	*Ottis Anderson, St. Louis	331	1,605	4.8	76	8
	Wilbert Montgomery, Philadelphia[2]	338	1,512	4.5	62	9
	Mike Pruitt, Cleveland	264	1,294	4.9	77	9
	Ricky Bell, Tampa Bay	283	1,263	4.5	49	7
	Chuck Muncie, New Orleans	238	1,198	5.0	69	11
	Franco Harris, Pittsburgh[7]	267	1,186	4.4	71	11
	John Riggins, Washington[3]	260	1,153	4.4	66	9
	Wendell Tyler, Los Angeles	218	1,109	5.1	63	9
	Tony Dorsett, Dallas[3]	250	1,107	4.4	41	6
	*William Andrews, Atlanta	239	1,023	4.3	23	3
1978	*Earl Campbell, Houston	302	1,450	4.8	81	13
	Walter Payton, Chicago[3]	333	1,395	4.2	76	11

	Tony Dorsett, Dallas[2]	290	1,325	4.6	63	7
	Delvin Williams, Miami[2]	272	1,258	4.6	58	8
	Wilbert Montgomery, Philadelphia	259	1,220	4.7	47	9
	Terdell Middleton, Green Bay	284	1,116	3.9	76	11
	Franco Harris, Pittsburgh[6]	310	1,082	3.5	37	8
	Mark van Eeghen, Oakland[3]	270	1,080	4.0	34	9
	*Terry Miller, Buffalo	238	1,060	4.5	60	7
	Tony Reed, Kansas City	206	1,053	5.1	62	5
	John Riggins, Washington[2]	248	1,014	4.1	31	5
1977	Walter Payton, Chicago[2]	339	1,852	5.5	73	14
	Mark van Eeghen, Oakland[2]	324	1,273	3.9	27	7
	Lawrence McCutcheon, Los Angeles[4]	294	1,238	4.2	48	7
	Franco Harris, Pittsburgh[5]	300	1,162	3.9	61	11
	Lydell Mitchell, Baltimore[3]	301	1,159	3.9	64	3
	Chuck Foreman, Minnesota[3]	270	1,112	4.1	51	6
	Greg Pruitt, Cleveland[3]	236	1,086	4.6	78	3
	Sam Cunningham, New England	270	1,015	3.8	31	4
	*Tony Dorsett, Dallas	208	1,007	4.8	84	12
1976	O.J. Simpson, Buffalo[5]	290	1,503	5.2	75	8
	Walter Payton, Chicago	311	1,390	4.5	60	13
	Delvin Williams, San Francisco	248	1,203	4.9	80	7
	Lydell Mitchell, Baltimore[2]	289	1,200	4.2	43	5
	Lawrence McCutcheon, Los Angeles[3]	291	1,168	4.0	40	9
	Chuck Foreman, Minnesota[2]	278	1,155	4.2	46	13
	Franco Harris, Pittsburgh[4]	289	1,128	3.9	30	14
	Mike Thomas, Washington	254	1,101	4.3	28	5
	Rocky Bleier, Pittsburgh	220	1,036	4.7	28	5
	Mark van Eeghen, Oakland	233	1,012	4.3	21	3
	Otis Armstrong, Denver[2]	247	1,008	4.1	31	5
	Greg Pruitt, Cleveland[2]	209	1,000	4.8	64	4
1975	O.J. Simpson, Buffalo[4]	329	1,817	5.5	88	16
	Franco Harris, Pittsburgh[3]	262	1,246	4.8	36	10
	Lydell Mitchell, Baltimore	289	1,193	4.1	70	11
	Jim Otis, St. Louis	269	1,076	4.0	30	5
	Chuck Foreman, Minnesota	280	1,070	3.8	31	13
	Greg Pruitt, Cleveland	217	1,067	4.9	50	8
	John Riggins, N.Y. Jets	238	1,005	4.2	42	8
	Dave Hampton, Atlanta	250	1,002	4.0	22	5
1974	Otis Armstrong, Denver	263	1,407	5.3	43	9
	*Don Woods, San Diego	227	1,162	5.1	56	7
	O.J. Simpson, Buffalo[3]	270	1,125	4.2	41	3
	Lawrence McCutcheon, Los Angeles[2]	236	1,109	4.7	23	3
	Franco Harris, Pittsburgh[2]	208	1,006	4.8	54	5
1973	O.J. Simpson, Buffalo[2]	332	2,003	6.0	80	12
	John Brockington, Green Bay[3]	265	1,144	4.3	53	3
	Calvin Hill, Dallas[2]	273	1,142	4.2	21	6
	Lawrence McCutcheon, Los Angeles	210	1,097	5.2	37	2
	Larry Csonka, Miami[3]	219	1,003	4.6	25	5
1972	O.J. Simpson, Buffalo	292	1,251	4.3	94	6
	Larry Brown, Washington[2]	285	1,216	4.3	38	8
	Ron Johnson, N.Y. Giants[2]	298	1,182	4.0	35	9
	Larry Csonka, Miami[2]	213	1,117	5.2	45	6
	Marv Hubbard, Oakland	219	1,100	5.0	39	4
	*Franco Harris, Pittsburgh	188	1,055	5.6	75	10
	Calvin Hill, Dallas	245	1,036	4.2	26	6
	Mike Garrett, San Diego[2]	272	1,031	3.8	41	6
	John Brockington, Green Bay[2]	274	1,027	3.7	30	8
	Eugene (Mercury) Morris, Miami	190	1,000	5.3	33	12
1971	Floyd Little, Denver	284	1,133	4.0	40	6
	*John Brockington, Green Bay	216	1,105	5.1	52	4
	Larry Csonka, Miami	195	1,051	5.4	28	7
	Steve Owens, Detroit	246	1,035	4.2	23	8
	Willie Ellison, Los Angeles	211	1,000	4.7	80	4
1970	Larry Brown, Washington	237	1,125	4.7	75	5
	Ron Johnson, N.Y. Giants	263	1,027	3.9	68	8
1969	Gale Sayers, Chicago[2]	236	1,032	4.4	28	8
1968	Leroy Kelly, Cleveland[3]	248	1,239	5.0	65	16
	*Paul Robinson, Cincinnati	238	1,023	4.3	87	8
1967	Jim Nance, Boston[2]	269	1,216	4.5	53	7
	Leroy Kelly, Cleveland[2]	235	1,205	5.1	42	11
	Hoyle Granger, Houston	236	1,194	5.1	67	6
	Mike Garrett, Kansas City	236	1,087	4.6	58	9
1966	Jim Nance, Boston	299	1,458	4.9	65	11
	Gale Sayers, Chicago	229	1,231	5.4	58	8
	Leroy Kelly, Cleveland	209	1,141	5.5	70	15
	Dick Bass, Los Angeles[2]	248	1,090	4.4	50	8
1965	Jim Brown, Cleveland[7]	289	1,544	5.3	67	17
	Paul Lowe, San Diego[2]	222	1,121	5.0	59	7
1964	Jim Brown, Cleveland[6]	280	1,446	5.2	71	7
	Jim Taylor, Green Bay[5]	235	1,169	5.0	84	12
	John Henry Johnson, Pittsburgh[2]	235	1,048	4.5	45	7
1963	Jim Brown, Cleveland[5]	291	1,863	6.4	80	12
	Clem Daniels, Oakland	215	1,099	5.1	74	3
	Jim Taylor, Green Bay[4]	248	1,018	4.1	40	9
	Paul Lowe, San Diego	177	1,010	5.7	66	8
1962	Jim Taylor, Green Bay[3]	272	1,474	5.4	51	19
	John Henry Johnson, Pittsburgh	251	1,141	4.5	40	7
	Cookie Gilchrist, Buffalo	214	1,096	5.1	44	13
	Abner Haynes, Dall. Texans	221	1,049	4.7	71	13
	Dick Bass, Los Angeles	196	1,033	5.3	57	6
	Charlie Tolar, Houston	244	1,012	4.1	25	7
1961	Jim Brown, Cleveland[4]	305	1,408	4.6	38	8
	Jim Taylor, Green Bay[2]	243	1,307	5.4	53	15
1960	Jim Brown, Cleveland[3]	215	1,257	5.8	71	9
	Jim Taylor, Green Bay	230	1,101	4.8	32	11
	John David Crow, St. Louis	183	1,071	5.9	57	6
1959	Jim Brown, Cleveland[2]	290	1,329	4.6	70	14
	J.D. Smith, San Francisco	207	1,036	5.0	73	10
1958	Jim Brown, Cleveland	257	1,527	5.9	65	17
1956	Rick Casares, Chi. Bears	234	1,126	4.8	68	12
1954	Joe Perry, San Francisco[2]	173	1,049	6.1	58	8
1953	Joe Perry, San Francisco	192	1,018	5.3	51	10
1949	Steve Van Buren, Philadelphia[2]	263	1,146	4.4	41	11
	Tony Canadeo, Green Bay	208	1,052	5.1	54	4
1947	Steve Van Buren, Philadelphia	217	1,008	4.6	45	13
1934	*Beattie Feathers, Chi. Bears	119	1,004	8.4	82	8

First season of professional football.

200 YARDS RUSHING IN A GAME

Date	Player, Team, Opponent	Att.	Yards	TD
Nov. 13, 1994	Barry Sanders, Detroit vs. Tampa Bay	26	237	0
Dec. 12, 1993	*Jerome Bettis, L.A. Rams vs. New Orleans	28	212	1
Oct. 31, 1993	Emmitt Smith, Dallas vs. Philadelphia	30	237	1
Nov. 24, 1991	Barry Sanders, Detroit vs. Minnesota	23	220	4
Dec. 23, 1990	James Brooks, Cincinnati vs. Houston	20	201	1
Oct. 14, 1990	Barry Word, Kansas City vs. Detroit	18	200	2
Sept. 24, 1990	Thurman Thomas, Buffalo vs. N.Y. Jets	18	214	0
Dec. 24, 1989	Greg Bell, L.A. Rams vs. New England	26	210	1
Sept. 24, 1989	Greg Bell, L.A. Rams vs. Green Bay	28	221	2
Sept. 17, 1989	Gerald Riggs, Washington vs. Philadelphia	29	221	1
Dec. 18, 1988	Gary Anderson, San Diego vs. Kansas City	34	217	1
Nov. 30, 1987	*Bo Jackson, L.A. Raiders vs. Seattle	18	221	2
Nov. 15, 1987	Charles White, L.A. Rams vs. St. Louis	34	213	1
Dec. 7, 1986	Rueben Mayes, New Orleans vs. Miami	28	203	2
Oct. 5, 1986	Eric Dickerson, L.A. Rams vs. Tampa Bay (OT)	30	207	2
Dec. 21, 1985	George Rogers, Washington vs. St. Louis	34	206	1
Dec. 21, 1985	Joe Morris, N.Y. Giants vs. Pittsburgh	36	202	3
Dec. 9, 1984	Eric Dickerson, L.A. Rams vs. Houston	27	215	2
Nov. 18, 1984	*Greg Bell, Buffalo vs. Dallas	27	206	1
Nov. 4, 1984	Eric Dickerson, L.A. Rams vs. St. Louis	21	208	0
Sept. 2, 1984	Gerald Riggs, Atlanta vs. New Orleans	35	202	2
Nov. 27, 1983	*Curt Warner, Seattle vs. Kansas City (OT)	32	207	3
Nov. 6, 1983	James Wilder, Tampa Bay vs. Minnesota	31	219	1
Sept. 18, 1983	Tony Collins, New England vs. N.Y. Jets	23	212	3
Sept. 4, 1983	George Rogers, New Orleans vs. St. Louis	24	206	2
Dec. 21, 1980	Earl Campbell, Houston vs. Minnesota	29	203	1
Nov. 16, 1980	Earl Campbell, Houston vs. Chicago	31	206	0
Oct. 26, 1980	Earl Campbell, Houston vs. Cincinnati	27	202	2
Oct. 19, 1980	Earl Campbell, Houston vs. Tampa Bay	33	203	0
Nov. 26, 1978	*Terry Miller, Buffalo vs. N.Y. Giants	21	208	2
Dec. 4, 1977	*Tony Dorsett, Dallas vs. Philadelphia	23	206	2
Nov. 20, 1977	Walter Payton, Chicago vs. Minnesota	40	275	1
Oct. 30, 1977	Walter Payton, Chicago vs. Green Bay	23	205	2
Dec. 5, 1976	O.J. Simpson, Buffalo vs. Miami	24	203	1
Nov. 25, 1976	O.J. Simpson, Buffalo vs. Detroit	29	273	2
Oct. 24, 1976	Chuck Foreman, Minnesota vs. Philadelphia	28	200	2
Dec. 14, 1975	Greg Pruitt, Cleveland vs. Kansas City	26	214	3
Sept. 28, 1975	O.J. Simpson, Buffalo vs. Pittsburgh	28	227	1
Dec. 16, 1973	O.J. Simpson, Buffalo vs. N.Y. Jets	34	200	1
Dec. 9, 1973	O.J. Simpson, Buffalo vs. New England	22	219	1
Sept. 16, 1973	O.J. Simpson, Buffalo vs. New England	29	250	2
Dec. 5, 1971	Willie Ellison, Los Angeles vs. New Orleans	26	247	1
Dec. 20, 1970	John (Frenchy) Fuqua, Pittsburgh vs. Philadelphia	20	218	2
Nov. 3, 1968	Gale Sayers, Chicago vs. Green Bay	24	205	0
Oct. 30, 1966	Jim Nance, Boston vs. Oakland	38	208	2
Oct. 10, 1964	John Henry Johnson, Pittsburgh vs. Cleveland	30	200	3
Dec. 8, 1963	Cookie Gilchrist, Buffalo vs. N.Y. Jets	36	243	5
Nov. 3, 1963	Jim Brown, Cleveland vs. Philadelphia	28	223	1
Oct. 20, 1963	Clem Daniels, Oakland vs. N.Y. Jets	27	200	2
Sept. 22, 1963	Jim Brown, Cleveland vs. Dallas	20	232	2
Dec. 10, 1961	Billy Cannon, Houston vs. N.Y. Titans	25	216	3
Nov. 19, 1961	Jim Brown, Cleveland vs. Philadelphia	34	237	4
Dec. 18, 1960	John David Crow, St. Louis vs. Pittsburgh	24	203	0
Nov. 15, 1959	Bobby Mitchell, Cleveland vs. Washington	14	232	3
Nov. 24, 1957	*Jim Brown, Cleveland vs. Los Angeles	31	237	4
Dec. 16, 1956	*Tom Wilson, Los Angeles vs. Green Bay	23	223	0

Nov. 22, 1953	Dan Towler, Los Angeles vs. Baltimore	14	205	1
Nov. 12, 1950	Gene Roberts, N.Y. Giants vs. Chi. Cardinals	26	218	2
Nov. 27, 1949	Steve Van Buren, Philadelphia vs. Pittsburgh	27	205	0
Oct. 8, 1933	Cliff Battles, Boston vs. N.Y. Giants	16	215	1

**First season of professional football.*

TIMES 200 OR MORE

60 times by 41 players...Simpson 6; Brown, Campbell 4; Bell, Dickerson 3; Payton, Riggs, Rogers, Sanders 2.

4,000 YARDS PASSING IN A SEASON

Year	Player, Team	Att.	Comp.	Pct.	Yards	TD	Int.
1994	Drew Bledsoe, New England	691	400	57.9	4,555	25	27
	Dan Marino, Miami[6]	615	385	62.6	4,453	30	17
	Warren Moon, Minnesota[3]	601	371	61.7	4,264	18	19
1993	John Elway, Denver	551	348	63.2	4,030	25	10
	Steve Young, San Francisco	462	314	68.0	4,023	29	16
1992	Dan Marino, Miami[5]	554	330	59.6	4,116	24	16
1991	Warren Moon, Houston[2]	655	404	61.7	4,690	23	21
1990	Warren Moon, Houston	584	362	62.0	4,689	33	13
1989	Don Majkowski, Green Bay	599	353	58.9	4,318	27	20
	Jim Everett, L.A. Rams	518	304	58.7	4,310	29	17
1988	Dan Marino, Miami[4]	606	354	58.4	4,434	28	23
1986	Dan Marino, Miami[3]	623	378	60.7	4,746	44	23
	Jay Schroeder, Washington	541	276	51.0	4,109	22	22
1985	Dan Marino, Miami[2]	567	336	59.3	4,137	30	21
1984	Dan Marino, Miami	564	362	64.2	5,084	48	17
	Neil Lomax, St. Louis	560	345	61.6	4,614	28	16
	Phil Simms, N.Y. Giants	533	286	53.7	4,044	22	18
1983	Lynn Dickey, Green Bay	484	289	59.7	4,458	32	29
	Bill Kenney, Kansas City	603	346	57.4	4,348	24	18
1981	Dan Fouts, San Diego[3]	609	360	59.1	4,802	33	17
1980	Dan Fouts, San Diego[2]	589	348	59.1	4,715	30	24
	Brian Sipe, Cleveland	554	337	60.8	4,132	30	14
1979	Dan Fouts, San Diego	530	332	62.6	4,082	24	24
1967	Joe Namath, N.Y. Jets	491	258	52.5	4,007	26	28

400 YARDS PASSING IN A GAME

Date	Player, Team, Opponent	Att.	Comp.	Yards	TD
Sept. 4, 1994	Dan Marino, Miami vs. New England (OT)	42	23	473	5
Sept. 4, 1994	Drew Bledsoe, New England vs. Miami (OT)	51	32	421	4
Sept. 25, 1994	Dan Marino, Miami vs. Minnesota	54	29	431	3
Nov. 6, 1994	Warren Moon, Minnesota vs. New Orleans	57	33	420	3
Nov. 13, 1994	Drew Bledsoe, New England vs. Minnesota (OT)	70	45	426	3
Nov. 20, 1994	Warren Moon, Minnesota vs. N.Y. Jets	50	33	400	2
Dec. 19, 1993	Steve Beuerlein, Phoenix vs. Seattle	53	34	431	3
Dec. 5, 1993	Brett Favre, Green Bay vs. Chicago	54	36	402	2
Nov. 28, 1993	Steve Young, San Francisco vs. L.A. Rams	32	26	462	4
Oct. 31, 1993	Jeff Hostetler, L.A. Raiders vs. San Diego	32	20	424	2
Sept. 13, 1992	Steve Young, San Francisco vs. Buffalo	37	26	449	3
Sept. 13, 1992	Jim Kelly, Buffalo vs. San Francisco	33	22	403	3
Nov. 10, 1991	Warren Moon, Houston vs. Dallas (OT)	56	41	432	0
Nov. 10, 1991	Mark Rypien, Washington vs. Atlanta	31	16	442	6
Oct. 13, 1991	Warren Moon, Houston vs. N.Y. Jets	50	35	423	2
Dec. 16, 1990	Warren Moon, Houston vs. Kansas City	45	27	527	3
Nov. 4, 1990	Joe Montana, San Francisco vs. Green Bay	40	25	411	3
Oct. 14, 1990	Joe Montana, San Francisco vs. Atlanta	49	32	476	6
Oct. 7, 1990	Boomer Esiason, Cincinnati vs. L.A. Rams (OT)	45	31	490	3
Dec. 23, 1989	Warren Moon, Houston vs. Cleveland	51	32	414	2
Dec. 11, 1989	Joe Montana, San Francisco vs. L.A. Rams	42	30	458	3
Nov. 26, 1989	Jim Everett, L.A. Rams vs. New Orleans (OT)	51	29	454	1
Nov. 26, 1989	Mark Rypien, Washington vs. Chicago	47	30	401	4
Oct. 2, 1989	Randall Cunningham, Philadelphia vs. Chicago	62	32	401	1
Sept. 24, 1989	Joe Montana, San Francisco vs. Philadelphia	34	25	428	5
Sept. 24, 1989	Dan Marino, Miami vs. N.Y. Jets	55	33	427	3
Sept. 17, 1989	Randall Cunningham, Phil. vs. Washington	46	34	447	5
Dec. 18, 1988	Dave Krieg, Seattle vs. L.A. Raiders	32	19	410	4
Dec. 12, 1988	Dan Marino, Miami vs. Cleveland	50	30	404	4
Oct. 23, 1988	Dan Marino, Miami vs. N.Y. Jets	60	35	521	3
Oct. 16, 1988	Vinny Testaverde, Tampa Bay vs. Indianapolis	42	25	469	2
Sept. 11, 1988	Doug Williams, Washington vs. Pittsburgh	52	30	430	2
Nov. 29, 1987	Tom Ramsey, New England vs. Philadelphia	53	34	402	3
Nov. 22, 1987	Boomer Esiason, Cincinnati vs. Pittsburgh	53	30	409	0
Sept. 20, 1987	Neil Lomax, St. Louis vs. San Diego	61	32	457	3
Dec. 21, 1986	Boomer Esiason, Cincinnati vs. N.Y. Jets	30	23	425	5
Dec. 14, 1986	Dan Marino, Miami vs. L.A. Rams (OT)	46	29	403	5
Nov. 23, 1986	Bernie Kosar, Cleveland vs. Pittsburgh (OT)	46	28	414	2
Nov. 17, 1986	Joe Montana, San Francisco vs. Washington	60	33	441	0
Nov. 16, 1986	Dan Marino, Miami vs. Buffalo	54	39	404	4
Nov. 10, 1986	Bernie Kosar, Cleveland vs. Miami	50	32	401	0
Nov. 2, 1986	Tommy Kramer, Minnesota vs. Washington (OT)	35	20	490	4
Nov. 2, 1986	Ken O'Brien, N.Y. Jets vs. Seattle	32	26	431	4
Oct. 27, 1986	Jay Schroeder, Washington vs. N.Y. Giants	40	22	420	1
Oct. 12, 1986	Steve Grogan, New England vs. N.Y. Jets	42	23	401	3
Sept. 21, 1986	Ken O'Brien, N.Y. Jets vs. Miami (OT)	43	29	479	4
Sept. 21, 1986	Dan Marino, Miami vs. N.Y. Jets (OT)	50	30	448	6
Sept. 21, 1986	Tony Eason, New England vs. Seattle	45	26	414	3
Dec. 20, 1985	John Elway, Denver vs. Seattle	42	24	432	1
Nov. 10, 1985	Dan Fouts, San Diego vs. L.A. Raiders (OT)	41	26	436	4
Oct. 13, 1985	Phil Simms, N.Y. Giants vs. Cincinnati	62	40	513	1
Oct. 13, 1985	Dave Krieg, Seattle vs. Atlanta	51	33	405	4
Oct. 6, 1985	Phil Simms, N.Y. Giants vs. Dallas	36	18	432	3
Oct. 6, 1985	Joe Montana, San Francisco vs. Atlanta	57	37	429	5
Sept. 19, 1985	Tommy Kramer, Minnesota vs. Chicago	55	28	436	3
Sept. 15, 1985	Dan Fouts, San Diego vs. Seattle	43	29	440	4
Dec. 16, 1984	Neil Lomax, St. Louis vs. Washington	46	37	468	2
Dec. 9, 1984	Dan Marino, Miami vs. Indianapolis	41	29	404	4
Dec. 2, 1984	Dan Marino, Miami vs. L.A. Raiders	57	35	470	4
Nov. 25, 1984	Dave Krieg, Seattle vs. Denver	44	30	406	3
Nov. 4, 1984	Dan Marino, Miami vs. N.Y. Jets	42	23	422	2
Oct. 21, 1984	Dan Fouts, San Diego vs. L.A. Raiders	45	24	410	3
Sept. 30, 1984	Dan Marino, Miami vs. St. Louis	36	24	429	3
Sept. 2, 1984	Phil Simms, N.Y. Giants vs. Philadelphia	30	23	409	4
Dec. 11, 1983	Bill Kenney, Kansas City vs. San Diego	41	31	411	4
Nov. 20, 1983	Dave Krieg, Seattle vs. Denver	42	31	418	3
Oct. 9, 1983	Joe Ferguson, Buffalo vs. Miami (OT)	55	38	419	5
Oct. 2, 1983	Joe Theismann, Washington vs. L.A. Raiders	39	23	417	3
Sept. 25, 1983	Richard Todd, N.Y. Jets vs. L.A. Rams (OT)	50	37	446	2
Dec. 26, 1982	Vince Ferragamo, L.A. Rams vs. Chicago	46	30	509	3
Dec. 20, 1982	Dan Fouts, San Diego vs. Cincinnati	40	25	435	1
Dec. 20, 1982	Ken Anderson, Cincinnati vs. San Diego	56	40	416	2
Dec. 11, 1982	Dan Fouts, San Diego vs. San Francisco	48	33	444	5
Nov. 21, 1982	Joe Montana, San Francisco vs. St. Louis	39	26	408	3
Nov. 15, 1981	Steve Bartkowski, Atlanta vs. Pittsburgh	50	33	416	2
Oct. 25, 1981	Brian Sipe, Cleveland vs. Baltimore	41	30	444	4
Oct. 25, 1981	David Woodley, Miami vs. Dallas	37	21	408	3
Oct. 11, 1981	Tommy Kramer, Minnesota vs. San Diego	43	27	444	4
Dec. 14, 1980	Tommy Kramer, Minnesota vs. Cleveland	49	38	456	4
Nov. 16, 1980	Doug Williams, Tampa Bay vs. Minnesota	55	30	486	4
Oct. 19, 1980	Dan Fouts, San Diego vs. N.Y. Giants	41	26	444	3
Oct. 12, 1980	Lynn Dickey, Green Bay vs. Tampa Bay (OT)	51	35	418	1
Sept. 21, 1980	Richard Todd, N.Y. Jets vs. San Francisco	60	42	447	3
Oct. 3, 1976	James Harris, Los Angeles vs. Miami	29	17	436	2
Nov. 17, 1975	Ken Anderson, Cincinnati vs. Buffalo	46	30	447	2
Nov. 18, 1974	Charley Johnson, Denver vs. Kansas City	42	28	445	2
Dec. 11, 1972	Joe Namath, N.Y. Jets vs. Oakland	46	25	403	1
Sept. 24, 1972	Joe Namath, N.Y. Jets vs. Baltimore	28	15	496	6
Dec. 21, 1969	Don Horn, Green Bay vs. St. Louis	31	22	410	5
Sept. 28, 1969	Joe Kapp, Minnesota vs. Baltimore	43	28	449	7
Sept. 9, 1968	Pete Beathard, Houston vs. Kansas City	48	23	413	2
Nov. 26, 1967	Sonny Jurgensen, Washington vs. Cleveland	50	32	418	3
Oct. 1, 1967	Joe Namath, N.Y. Jets vs. Miami	39	23	415	3
Sept. 17, 1967	Johnny Unitas, Baltimore vs. Atlanta	32	22	401	2
Nov. 13, 1966	Don Meredith, Dallas vs. Washington	29	21	406	2
Nov. 28, 1965	Sonny Jurgensen, Washington vs. Dallas	43	26	411	3
Oct. 24, 1965	Fran Tarkenton, Minnesota vs. San Francisco	35	21	407	3
Nov. 1, 1964	Len Dawson, Kansas City vs. Denver	38	23	435	6
Oct. 25, 1964	Cotton Davidson, Oakland vs. Denver	36	23	427	5
Oct. 16, 1964	Babe Parilli, Boston vs. Oakland	47	25	422	4
Dec. 22, 1963	Tom Flores, Oakland vs. Houston	29	17	407	6
Nov. 17, 1963	Norm Snead, Washington vs. Pittsburgh	40	23	424	2
Nov. 10, 1963	Don Meredith, Dallas vs. San Francisco	48	30	460	3
Oct. 13, 1963	Charley Johnson, St. Louis vs. Pittsburgh	41	20	428	2
Dec. 16, 1962	Sonny Jurgensen, Philadelphia vs. St. Louis	34	15	419	5
Nov. 18, 1962	Bill Wade, Chicago vs. Dall. Cowboys	46	28	466	2
Oct. 28, 1962	Y.A. Tittle, N.Y. Giants vs. Washington	39	27	505	7
Sept. 15, 1962	Frank Tripucka, Denver vs. Buffalo	56	29	447	2
Dec. 17, 1961	Sonny Jurgensen, Philadelphia vs. Detroit	42	27	403	3
Nov. 19, 1961	George Blanda, Houston vs. N.Y. Titans	32	20	418	7
Oct. 29, 1961	George Blanda, Houston vs. Buffalo	32	18	464	4
Oct. 29, 1961	Sonny Jurgensen, Philadelphia vs. Washington	41	27	436	3
Oct. 13, 1961	Jacky Lee, Houston vs. Boston	41	27	457	2
Dec. 13, 1958	Bobby Layne, Pittsburgh vs. Chi. Cardinals	49	23	409	2
Nov. 8, 1953	Bobby Thomason, Philadelphia vs. N.Y. Giants	44	22	437	4
Oct. 4, 1952	Otto Graham, Cleveland vs. Pittsburgh	49	21	401	3
Sept. 28, 1951	Norm Van Brocklin, Los Angeles vs. N.Y. Yanks	41	27	554	5
Dec. 11, 1949	Johnny Lujack, Chi. Bears vs. Chi. Cardinals	39	24	468	6
Oct. 31, 1948	Sammy Baugh, Washington vs. Boston	24	17	446	4
Oct. 31, 1948	Jim Hardy, Los Angeles vs. Chi. Cardinals	53	28	406	3
Nov. 14, 1943	Sid Luckman, Chi. Bears vs. N.Y. Giants	32	21	433	7

OUTSTANDING PERFORMERS

TIMES 400 OR MORE

119 times by 63 players...Marino 12; Montana 7; Fouts, Moon 6; Jurgensen 5; Kramer, Krieg, 4; Esiason, Namath, Simms 3; Anderson, Blanda, Bledsoe, Cunningham, Johnson, Kosar, Lomax, Meredith, O'Brien, Rypien, Todd, Williams, Young 2.

1,000 YARDS PASS RECEIVING IN A SEASON

Year	Player, Team	No.	Yards	Avg.	Long	TD
1994	Jerry Rice, San Francisco[9]	112	1,499	13.4	69	13
	Henry Ellard, Washington[5]	74	1,397	18.9	73	6
	Terance Mathis, Atlanta	111	1,342	12.1	81	11
	Tim Brown, L.A. Raiders[2]	89	1,309	14.7	77	9
	Andre Reed, Buffalo[2]	90	1,303	14.5	83	8
	Irving Fryar, Miami[3]	73	1,270	17.4	54	7
	Cris Carter, Minnesota[2]	122	1,256	10.3	65	7
	Michael Irvin, Dallas[4]	79	1,241	15.7	65	6
	Jake Reed, Minnesota	85	1,175	13.8	59	4
	Ben Coates, New England	96	1,174	12.2	62	7
	Herman Moore, Detroit	72	1,173	16.3	51	11
	Fred Barnett, Philadelphia[2]	78	1,127	14.4	54	5
	Carl Pickens, Cincinnati	71	1,127	15.9	70	11
	Sterling Sharpe, Green Bay[4]	94	1,119	11.9	49	18
	Anthony Miller, Denver[4]	60	1,107	18.5	76	5
	Andre Rison, Atlanta[3]	81	1,088	13.4	69	8
	Brian Blades, Seattle[3]	81	1,088	13.4	45	4
	Rob Moore, N.Y. Jets	78	1,010	12.9	41	6
	Shannon Sharpe, Denver	87	1,010	11.6	44	4
1993	Jerry Rice, San Francisco[8]	98	1,503	15.3	80	15
	Michael Irvin, Dallas[3]	88	1,330	15.1	61	7
	Sterling Sharpe, Green Bay[4]	112	1,274	11.4	54	11
	Andre Rison, Atlanta[3]	86	1,242	14.4	53	15
	Tim Brown, L.A. Raiders	80	1,180	14.8	71	7
	Anthony Miller, San Diego[3]	84	1,162	13.8	66	7
	Cris Carter, Minnesota	86	1,071	12.5	58	9
	Reggie Langhorne, Indianapolis	85	1,038	12.2	72	3
	Irving Fryar, Miami[2]	64	1,010	15.8	65	5
1992	Sterling Sharpe, Green Bay[3]	108	1,461	13.5	76	13
	Michael Irvin, Dallas[2]	78	1,396	17.9	87	7
	Jerry Rice, San Francisco[7]	84	1,201	14.3	80	10
	Andre Rison, Atlanta[2]	93	1,119	12.0	71	11
	Fred Barnett, Philadelphia	67	1,083	16.2	71	6
	Anthony Miller, San Diego[2]	72	1,060	14.7	67	7
	Eric Martin, New Orleans[3]	68	1,041	15.3	52	5
1991	Michael Irvin, Dallas	93	1,523	16.4	66	8
	Gary Clark, Washington[5]	70	1,340	19.1	82	10
	Jerry Rice, San Francisco[6]	80	1,206	15.1	73	14
	Haywood Jeffires, Houston[2]	100	1,181	11.8	44	7
	Michael Haynes, Atlanta	50	1,122	22.4	80	11
	Andre Reed, Buffalo[2]	81	1,113	13.7	55	10
	Drew Hill, Houston[5]	90	1,109	12.3	61	4
	Mark Duper, Miami[4]	70	1,085	15.5	43	5
	James Lofton, Buffalo[6]	57	1,072	18.8	77	8
	Mark Clayton, Miami[5]	70	1,053	15.0	43	12
	Henry Ellard, L.A. Rams[4]	64	1,052	16.4	38	3
	Art Monk, Washington[5]	71	1,049	14.8	64	8
	Irving Fryar, New England	68	1,014	14.9	56	3
	John Taylor, San Francisco[2]	64	1,011	15.8	97	9
	Brian Blades, Seattle[2]	70	1,003	14.3	52	2
1990	Jerry Rice, San Francisco[5]	100	1,502	15.0	64	13
	Henry Ellard, L.A. Rams[3]	76	1,294	17.0	50	4
	Andre Rison, Atlanta	82	1,208	14.7	75	10
	Gary Clark, Washington[4]	75	1,112	14.8	53	8
	Sterling Sharpe, Green Bay[2]	67	1,105	16.5	76	6
	Willie Anderson, L.A. Rams[2]	51	1,097	21.5	55	4
	Haywood Jeffires, Houston	74	1,048	14.2	87	8
	Stephone Paige, Kansas City	65	1,021	15.7	86	5
	Drew Hill, Houston[4]	74	1,019	13.8	57	5
	Anthony Carter, Minnesota[3]	70	1,008	14.4	56	8
1989	Jerry Rice, San Francisco[4]	82	1,483	18.1	68	17
	Sterling Sharpe, Green Bay	90	1,423	15.8	79	12
	Mark Carrier, Tampa Bay	86	1,422	16.5	78	9
	Henry Ellard, L.A. Rams[2]	70	1,382	19.7	53	8
	Andre Reed, Buffalo	88	1,312	14.9	78	9
	Anthony Miller, San Diego	75	1,252	16.7	69	10
	Webster Slaughter, Cleveland	65	1,236	19.0	97	6
	Gary Clark, Washington[3]	79	1,229	15.6	80	9
	Tim McGee, Cincinnati	65	1,211	18.6	74	8
	Art Monk, Washington[4]	86	1,186	13.8	60	8
	Willie Anderson, L.A. Rams	44	1,146	26.0	78	5
	Ricky Sanders, Washington[2]	80	1,138	14.2	68	4
	Vance Johnson, Denver	76	1,095	14.4	69	7
	Richard Johnson, Detroit	70	1,091	15.6	75	8
	Eric Martin, New Orleans[2]	68	1,090	16.0	53	8
	John Taylor, San Francisco	60	1,077	18.0	95	10
	Mervyn Fernandez, L.A. Raiders	57	1,069	18.8	75	9
	Anthony Carter, Minnesota[2]	65	1,066	16.4	50	4
	Brian Blades, Seattle	77	1,063	13.8	60	5
	Mark Clayton, Miami[4]	64	1,011	15.8	78	9
1988	Henry Ellard, L.A. Rams	86	1,414	16.4	68	10
	Jerry Rice, San Francisco[3]	64	1,306	20.4	96	9
	Eddie Brown, Cincinnati	53	1,273	24.0	86	9
	Anthony Carter, Minnesota	72	1,225	17.0	67	6
	Ricky Sanders, Washington	73	1,148	15.7	55	12
	Drew Hill, Houston[3]	72	1,141	15.8	57	10
	Mark Clayton, Miami[3]	86	1,129	13.1	45	14
	Roy Green, Phoenix[3]	68	1,097	16.1	52	7
	Eric Martin, New Orleans	85	1,083	12.7	40	7
	Al Toon, N.Y. Jets[2]	93	1,067	11.5	42	5
	Bruce Hill, Tampa Bay	58	1,040	17.9	42	9
	Lionel Manuel, N.Y. Giants	65	1,029	15.8	46	4
1987	J.T. Smith, St. Louis[2]	91	1,117	12.3	38	8
	Jerry Rice, San Francisco[2]	65	1,078	16.6	57	22
	Gary Clark, Washington[2]	56	1,066	19.0	84	7
	Carlos Carson, Kansas City[3]	55	1,044	19.0	81	7
1986	Jerry Rice, San Francisco	86	1,570	18.3	66	15
	Stanley Morgan, New England[3]	84	1,491	17.8	44	10
	Mark Duper, Miami[3]	67	1,313	19.6	85	11
	Gary Clark, Washington	74	1,265	17.1	55	7
	Al Toon, N.Y. Jets	85	1,176	13.8	62	8
	Todd Christensen, L.A. Raiders[3]	95	1,153	12.1	35	8
	Mark Clayton, Miami[2]	60	1,150	19.2	68	10
	*Bill Brooks, Indianapolis	65	1,131	17.4	84	8
	Drew Hill, Houston[2]	65	1,112	17.1	81	5
	Steve Largent, Seattle[8]	70	1,070	15.3	38	9
	Art Monk, Washington[3]	73	1,068	14.6	69	4
	*Ernest Givins, Houston	61	1,062	17.4	60	3
	Cris Collinsworth, Cincinnati[4]	62	1,024	16.5	46	10
	Wesley Walker, N.Y. Jets[2]	49	1,016	20.7	83	12
	J.T. Smith, St. Louis	80	1,014	12.7	45	6
	Mark Bavaro, N.Y. Giants	66	1,001	15.2	41	4
1985	Steve Largent, Seattle[7]	79	1,287	16.3	43	6
	Mike Quick, Philadelphia[3]	73	1,247	17.1	99	11
	Art Monk, Washington[2]	91	1,226	13.5	53	2
	Wes Chandler, San Diego[4]	67	1,199	17.9	75	10
	Drew Hill, Houston	64	1,169	18.3	57	9
	James Lofton, Green Bay[5]	69	1,153	16.7	56	4
	Louis Lipps, Pittsburgh	59	1,134	19.2	51	12
	Cris Collinsworth, Cincinnati[3]	65	1,125	17.3	71	5
	Tony Hill, Dallas[3]	74	1,113	15.0	53	7
	Lionel James, San Diego	86	1,027	11.9	67	6
	Roger Craig, San Francisco	92	1,016	11.0	73	6
1984	Roy Green, St. Louis[2]	78	1,555	19.9	83	12
	John Stallworth, Pittsburgh[3]	80	1,395	17.4	51	11
	Mark Clayton, Miami	73	1,389	19.0	65	18
	Art Monk, Washington	106	1,372	12.9	72	7
	James Lofton, Green Bay[4]	62	1,361	22.0	79	7
	Mark Duper, Miami[2]	71	1,306	18.4	80	8
	Steve Watson, Denver[3]	69	1,170	17.0	73	7
	Steve Largent, Seattle[6]	74	1,164	15.7	65	12
	Tim Smith, Houston[2]	69	1,141	16.5	75	4
	Stacey Bailey, Atlanta	67	1,138	17.0	61	6
	Carlos Carson, Kansas City[2]	57	1,078	18.9	57	4
	Mike Quick, Philadelphia[2]	61	1,052	17.2	90	9
	Todd Christensen, L.A. Raiders[2]	80	1,007	12.6	38	7
	Kevin House, Tampa Bay[2]	76	1,005	13.2	55	5
	Ozzie Newsome, Cleveland[2]	89	1,001	11.2	52	5
1983	Mike Quick, Philadelphia	69	1,409	20.4	83	13
	Carlos Carson, Kansas City	80	1,351	16.9	50	7
	James Lofton, Green Bay[3]	58	1,300	22.4	74	8
	Todd Christensen, L.A. Raiders	92	1,247	13.6	45	12
	Roy Green, St. Louis	78	1,227	15.7	71	14
	Charlie Brown, Washington	78	1,225	15.7	75	8
	Tim Smith, Houston	83	1,176	14.2	47	6
	Kellen Winslow, San Diego[3]	88	1,172	13.3	46	8
	Earnest Gray, N.Y. Giants	78	1,139	14.6	62	5
	Steve Watson, Denver[2]	59	1,133	19.2	78	5
	Cris Collinsworth, Cincinnati[2]	66	1,130	17.1	63	5
	Steve Largent, Seattle[5]	72	1,074	14.9	46	11
	Mark Duper, Miami	51	1,003	19.7	85	10
1982	Wes Chandler, San Diego[3]	49	1,032	21.1	66	9
1981	Alfred Jenkins, Atlanta[2]	70	1,358	19.4	67	13
	James Lofton, Green Bay[2]	71	1,294	18.2	75	8
	Steve Watson, Denver	60	1,244	20.7	95	13
	Frank Lewis, Buffalo[2]	70	1,244	17.8	33	4

Year	Player, Team	No.	Yards	Avg.	Long	TD
	Steve Largent, Seattle[4]	75	1,224	16.3	57	9
	Charlie Joiner, San Diego[4]	70	1,188	17.0	57	7
	Kevin House, Tampa Bay	56	1,176	21.0	84	9
	Wes Chandler, N.O.-San Diego[2]	69	1,142	16.6	51	6
	Dwight Clark, San Francisco	85	1,105	13.0	78	4
	John Stallworth, Pittsburgh[2]	63	1,098	17.4	55	5
	Kellen Winslow, San Diego[2]	88	1,075	12.2	67	10
	Pat Tilley, St. Louis	66	1,040	15.8	75	3
	Stanley Morgan, New England[2]	44	1,029	23.4	76	6
	Harold Carmichael, Philadelphia[3]	61	1,028	16.9	85	6
	Freddie Scott, Detroit	53	1,022	19.3	48	5
	*Cris Collinsworth, Cincinnati	67	1,009	15.1	74	8
	Joe Senser, Minnesota	79	1,004	12.7	53	8
	Ozzie Newsome, Cleveland	69	1,002	14.5	62	6
	Sammy White, Minnesota	66	1,001	15.2	53	3
1980	John Jefferson, San Diego[3]	82	1,340	16.3	58	13
	Kellen Winslow, San Diego	89	1,290	14.5	65	9
	James Lofton, Green Bay	71	1,226	17.3	47	4
	Charlie Joiner, San Diego[3]	71	1,132	15.9	51	4
	Ahmad Rashad, Minnesota[2]	69	1,095	15.9	76	5
	Steve Largent, Seattle[3]	66	1,064	16.1	67	6
	Tony Hill, Dallas[2]	60	1,055	17.6	58	8
	Alfred Jenkins, Atlanta	57	1,026	18.0	57	6
1979	Steve Largent, Seattle[2]	66	1,237	18.7	55	9
	John Stallworth, Pittsburgh	70	1,183	16.9	65	8
	Ahmad Rashad, Minnesota	80	1,156	14.5	52	9
	John Jefferson, San Diego[2]	61	1,090	17.9	65	10
	Frank Lewis, Buffalo	54	1,082	20.0	55	2
	Wes Chandler, New Orleans	65	1,069	16.4	85	6
	Tony Hill, Dallas	60	1,062	17.7	75	10
	Drew Pearson, Dallas[2]	55	1,026	18.7	56	8
	Wallace Francis, Atlanta	74	1,013	13.7	42	8
	Harold Jackson, New England[3]	45	1,013	22.5	59	7
	Charlie Joiner, San Diego[2]	72	1,008	14.0	39	4
	Stanley Morgan, New England	44	1,002	22.8	63	12
1978	Wesley Walker, N.Y. Jets	48	1,169	24.4	77	8
	Steve Largent, Seattle	71	1,168	16.5	57	8
	Harold Carmichael, Philadelphia[2]	55	1,072	19.5	56	8
	*John Jefferson, San Diego	56	1,001	17.9	46	13
1976	Roger Carr, Baltimore	43	1,112	25.9	79	11
	Cliff Branch, Oakland[2]	46	1,111	24.2	88	12
	Charlie Joiner, San Diego	50	1,056	21.1	81	7
1975	Ken Burrough, Houston	53	1,063	20.1	77	8
1974	Cliff Branch, Oakland	60	1,092	18.2	67	13
	Drew Pearson, Dallas	62	1,087	17.5	50	2
1973	Harold Carmichael, Philadelphia	67	1,116	16.7	73	9
1972	Harold Jackson, Philadelphia[2]	62	1,048	16.9	77	4
	John Gilliam, Minnesota	47	1,035	22.0	66	7
1971	Otis Taylor, Kansas City[2]	57	1,110	19.5	82	7
1970	Gene Washington, San Francisco	53	1,100	20.8	79	12
	Marlin Briscoe, Buffalo	57	1,036	18.2	48	8
	Dick Gordon, Chicago	71	1,026	14.5	69	13
	Gary Garrison, San Diego[2]	44	1,006	22.9	67	12
1969	Warren Wells, Oakland[2]	47	1,260	26.8	80	14
	Harold Jackson, Philadelphia	65	1,116	17.2	65	9
	Roy Jefferson, Pittsburgh[2]	67	1,079	16.1	63	9
	Dan Abramowicz, New Orleans	73	1,015	13.9	49	7
	Lance Alworth, San Diego[7]	64	1,003	15.7	76	4
1968	Lance Alworth, San Diego[6]	68	1,312	19.3	80	10
	Don Maynard, N.Y. Jets[5]	57	1,297	22.8	87	10
	George Sauer, N.Y. Jets[3]	66	1,141	17.3	43	3
	Warren Wells, Oakland	53	1,137	21.5	94	11
	Gary Garrison, San Diego	52	1,103	21.2	84	10
	Roy Jefferson, Pittsburgh	58	1,074	18.5	62	11
	Paul Warfield, Cleveland	50	1,067	21.3	65	12
	Homer Jones, N.Y. Giants[3]	45	1,057	23.5	84	7
	Fred Biletnikoff, Oakland	61	1,037	17.0	82	6
	Lance Rentzel, Dallas	54	1,009	18.7	65	6
1967	Don Maynard, N.Y. Jets[4]	71	1,434	20.2	75	10
	Ben Hawkins, Philadelphia	59	1,265	21.4	87	10
	Homer Jones, N.Y. Giants[2]	49	1,209	24.7	70	13
	Jackie Smith, St. Louis	56	1,205	21.5	76	9
	George Sauer, N.Y. Jets[2]	75	1,189	15.9	61	6
	Lance Alworth, San Diego[5]	52	1,010	19.4	71	9
1966	Lance Alworth, San Diego[4]	73	1,383	18.9	78	13
	Otis Taylor, Kansas City	58	1,297	22.4	89	8
	Pat Studstill, Detroit	67	1,266	18.9	99	5
	Bob Hayes, Dallas[2]	64	1,232	19.3	95	13
	Charlie Frazier, Houston	57	1,129	19.8	79	12
	Charley Taylor, Washington	72	1,119	15.5	86	12
	George Sauer, N.Y. Jets	63	1,081	17.2	77	5
	Homer Jones, N.Y. Giants	48	1,044	21.8	98	8
	Art Powell, Oakland[5]	53	1,026	19.4	46	11
1965	Lance Alworth, San Diego[3]	69	1,602	23.2	85	14
	Dave Parks, San Francisco	80	1,344	16.8	53	12
	Don Maynard, N.Y. Jets[3]	68	1,218	17.9	56	14
	Pete Retzlaff, Philadelphia	66	1,190	18.0	78	10
	Lionel Taylor, Denver[4]	85	1,131	13.3	63	6
	Tommy McDonald, Los Angeles[3]	67	1,036	15.5	51	9
	*Bob Hayes, Dallas	46	1,003	21.8	82	12
1964	Charley Hennigan, Houston[3]	101	1,546	15.3	53	8
	Art Powell, Oakland[4]	76	1,361	17.9	77	11
	Lance Alworth, San Diego[2]	61	1,235	20.2	82	13
	Johnny Morris, Chicago	93	1,200	12.9	63	10
	Elbert Dubenion, Buffalo	42	1,139	27.1	72	10
	Terry Barr, Detroit[2]	57	1,030	18.1	58	9
1963	Bobby Mitchell, Washington[2]	69	1,436	20.8	99	7
	Art Powell, Oakland[3]	73	1,304	17.9	85	16
	Buddy Dial, Pittsburgh[2]	60	1,295	21.6	83	9
	Lance Alworth, San Diego	61	1,205	19.8	85	11
	Del Shofner, N.Y. Giants[4]	64	1,181	18.5	70	9
	Lionel Taylor, Denver[3]	78	1,101	14.1	72	10
	Terry Barr, Detroit	66	1,086	16.5	75	13
	Charley Hennigan, Houston[2]	61	1,051	17.2	83	10
	Sonny Randle, St. Louis[2]	51	1,014	19.9	68	12
	Bake Turner, N.Y. Jets	71	1,009	14.2	53	6
1962	Bobby Mitchell, Washington	72	1,384	19.2	81	11
	Sonny Randle, St. Louis	63	1,158	18.4	86	7
	Tommy McDonald, Philadelphia[2]	58	1,146	19.8	60	10
	Del Shofner, N.Y. Giants[3]	53	1,133	21.4	69	12
	Art Powell, N.Y. Titans[2]	64	1,130	17.7	80	8
	Frank Clarke, Dall. Cowboys	47	1,043	22.2	66	14
	Don Maynard, N.Y. Titans[2]	56	1,041	18.6	86	8
1961	Charley Hennigan, Houston	82	1,746	21.3	80	12
	Lionel Taylor, Denver[2]	100	1,176	11.8	52	4
	Bill Groman, Houston[2]	50	1,175	23.5	80	17
	Tommy McDonald, Philadelphia	64	1,144	17.9	66	13
	Del Shofner, N.Y. Giants[2]	68	1,125	16.5	46	11
	Jim Phillips, Los Angeles	78	1,092	14.0	69	5
	*Mike Ditka, Chicago	56	1,076	19.2	76	12
	Dave Kocourek, San Diego	55	1,055	19.2	76	4
	Buddy Dial, Pittsburgh	53	1,047	19.8	88	12
	R.C. Owens, San Francisco	55	1,032	18.8	54	5
1960	*Bill Groman, Houston	72	1,473	20.5	92	12
	Raymond Berry, Baltimore	74	1,298	17.5	70	10
	Don Maynard, N.Y. Titans	72	1,265	17.6	65	6
	Lionel Taylor, Denver	92	1,235	13.4	80	12
	Art Powell, N.Y. Titans	69	1,167	16.9	76	14
1958	Del Shofner, Los Angeles	51	1,097	21.5	92	8
1956	Bill Howton, Green Bay[2]	55	1,188	21.6	66	12
	Harlon Hill, Chi. Bears[2]	47	1,128	24.0	79	11
1954	Bob Boyd, Los Angeles	53	1,212	22.9	80	6
	*Harlon Hill, Chi. Bears	45	1,124	25.0	76	12
1953	Pete Pihos, Philadelphia	63	1,049	16.7	59	10
1952	*Bill Howton, Green Bay	53	1,231	23.2	90	13
1951	Elroy (Crazylegs) Hirsch, Los Angeles	66	1,495	22.7	91	17
1950	Tom Fears, Los Angeles[2]	84	1,116	13.3	53	7
	Cloyce Box, Detroit	50	1,009	20.2	82	11
1949	Bob Mann, Detroit	66	1,014	15.4	64	4
	Tom Fears, Los Angeles	77	1,013	13.2	51	9
1945	Jim Benton, Cleveland	45	1,067	23.7	84	8
1942	Don Hutson, Green Bay	74	1,211	16.4	73	17

First season of professional football.

250 YARDS PASS RECEIVING IN A GAME

Date	Player, Team, Opponent	No.	Yards	TD
Dec. 11, 1989	John Taylor, San Francisco vs. L.A. Rams	11	286	2
Nov. 26, 1989	Willie Anderson, L.A. Rams vs. New Orleans (OT)	15	336	1
Oct. 18, 1987	Steve Largent, Seattle vs. Detroit	15	261	3
Oct. 4, 1987	Anthony Allen, Washington vs. St. Louis	7	255	3
Dec. 22, 1985	Stephone Paige, Kansas City vs. San Diego	8	309	2
Dec. 20, 1982	Wes Chandler, San Diego vs. Cincinnati	10	260	2
Sept. 23, 1979	*Jerry Butler, Buffalo vs. N.Y. Jets	10	255	4
Nov. 4, 1962	Sonny Randle, St. Louis vs. N.Y. Giants	16	256	1
Oct. 28, 1962	Del Shofner, N.Y. Giants vs. Washington	11	269	1
Oct. 13, 1961	Charley Hennigan, Houston vs. Boston	13	272	1
Oct. 21, 1956	Billy Howton, Green Bay vs. Los Angeles	7	257	2
Dec. 3, 1950	Cloyce Box, Detroit vs. Baltimore	12	302	4
Nov. 22, 1945	Jim Benton, Cleveland vs. Detroit	10	303	1

First season of professional football.

2,000 COMBINED NET YARDS GAINED IN A SEASON

Year	Player, Team	Rushing Att.-Yds.	Pass Rec.	Punt Ret.	Kickoff Ret.	Fum. Runs	Total Yds.
1994	Brian Mitchell, Wash.	78-311	26-236	32-452	58-1,478	0-0	194-2,477
	Barry Sanders, Detroit	331-1,883	44-283	0-0	0-0	0-0	375-2,166

Year	Player						
1992	Thurman Thomas, Buffalo	312-1,487	58-626	0-0	0-0	1-0	371-2,113
	Emmitt Smith, Dallas	373-1,713	59-335	0-0	0-0	1-0	433-2,048
	Barry Foster, Pittsburgh	390-1,690	36-344	0-0	0-0	2-(–20)	428-2,014
1991	Thurman Thomas, Buffalo	288-1,407	62-631	0-0	0-0	0-0	350-2,038
1990	Herschel Walker, Minnesota	184-770	35-315	0-0	44-966	4-0	267-2,051
1988	*Tim Brown, L.A. Raiders	14-50	43-725	49-444	41-1,098	7-0	154-2,317
	Roger Craig, San Fran.	310-1,502	76-534	0-0	2-32	2-0	390-2,068
	Eric Dickerson, Indianapolis	388-1,659	36-377	0-0	0-0	1-0	425-2,036
	Herschel Walker, Dallas	361-1,514	53-505	0-0	0-0	3-0	417-2,019
1986	Eric Dickerson, L.A. Rams	404-1,821	26-205	0-0	0-0	2-0	432-2,026
	Gary Anderson, San Diego	127-442	80-871	25-227	24-482	2-0	258-2,022
1985	Lionel James, San Diego	105-516	86-1,027	25-213	36-779	1-0	253-2,535
	Marcus Allen, L.A. Raiders	380-1,759	67-555	0-0	0-0	2-(–6)	449-2,308
	Roger Craig, San Fran.	214-1,050	92-1,016	0-0	0-0	0-0	306-2,066
	Walter Payton, Chicago	324-1,551	49-483	0-0	0-0	1-0	374-2,034
1984	Eric Dickerson, L.A. Rams	379-2,105	21-139	0-0	0-0	4-15	404-2,259
	James Wilder, Tampa Bay	407-1,544	85-685	0-0	0-0	4-0	496-2,229
	Walter Payton, Chicago	381-1,684	45-368	0-0	0-0	1-0	427-2,052
1983	*Eric Dickerson, L.A. Rams	390-1,808	51-404	0-0	0-0	1-0	442-2,212
	William Andrews, Atlanta	331-1,567	59-609	0-0	0-0	2-0	392-2,176
	Walter Payton, Chicago	314-1,421	53-607	0-0	0-0	2-0	369-2,028
1981	*James Brooks, San Diego	109-525	46-329	22-290	40-949	2-0	219-2,093
	William Andrews, Atlanta	289-1,301	81-735	0-0	0-0	0-0	370-2,036
1980	Bruce Harper, N.Y. Jets	45-126	50-634	28-242	49-1,070	3-0	175-2,072
1979	Wilbert Montgomery, Phil.	338-1,512	41-494	0-0	1-6	2-0	382-2,012
1978	Bruce Harper, N.Y. Jets	58-303	13-196	30-378	55-1,280	1-0	157-2,157
1977	Walter Payton, Chicago	339-1,852	27-269	0-0	2-95	5-0	373-2,216
	Terry Metcalf, St. Louis	149-739	34-403	14-108	32-772	1-0	230-2,022
1975	Terry Metcalf, St. Louis	165-816	43-378	23-285	35-960	2-23	268-2,462
	O.J. Simpson, Buffalo	329-1,817	28-426	0-0	0-0	1-0	358-2,243
1974	Mack Herron, New England	231-824	38-474	35-517	28-629	3-0	335-2,444
	Otis Armstrong, Denver	263-1,407	38-405	0-0	16-386	1-0	318-2,198
	Terry Metcalf, St. Louis	152-718	50-377	26-340	20-623	7-0	255-2,058
1973	O.J. Simpson, Buffalo	332-2,003	6-70	0-0	0-0	0-0	338-2,073
1966	Gale Sayers, Chicago	229-1,231	34-447	6-44	23-718	3-0	295-2,440
	Leroy Kelly, Cleveland	209-1,141	32-366	13-104	19-403	0-0	273-2,014
1965	*Gale Sayers, Chicago	166-867	29-507	16-238	21-660	4-0	236-2,272
1963	Timmy Brown, Philadelphia	192-841	36-487	16-152	33-945	2-3	279-2,428
	Jim Brown, Cleveland	291-1,863	24-268	0-0	0-0	0-0	315-2,131
1962	Timmy Brown, Philadelphia	137-545	52-849	6-81	30-831	4-0	229-2,306
	Dick Christy, N.Y. Titans	114-535	62-538	15-250	38-824	2-0	231-2,147
1961	Billy Cannon, Houston	200-948	43-586	9-70	18-439	2-0	272-2,043
1960	*Abner Haynes, Dall. Texans	156-875	55-576	14-215	19-434	4-0	248-2,100

**First season of professional football.*

300 COMBINED NET YARDS GAINED IN A GAME

Date	Player, Team, Opponent	No.	Yards	TD
Oct. 23, 1994	Tyrone Hughes, New Orleans vs. L.A. Rams	11	347	2
Dec. 11, 1989	John Taylor, San Francisco vs. L.A. Rams	14	321	2
Nov. 26, 1989	Willie Anderson, L.A. Rams vs. New Orleans (OT)	15	336	1
Nov. 28, 1988	*Tim Brown, L.A. Raiders vs. Seattle	12	308	1
Dec. 22, 1985	Stephone Paige, Kansas City vs. San Diego	8	309	2
Nov. 10, 1985	Lionel James, San Diego vs. L.A. Raiders (OT)	23	345	0
Sept. 22, 1985	Lionel James, San Diego vs. Cincinnati	20	316	2
Dec. 21, 1975	*Walter Payton, Chicago vs. New Orleans	32	300	1
Nov. 23, 1975	Greg Pruitt, Cleveland vs. Cincinnati	28	304	2
Nov. 1, 1970	Eugene (Mercury) Morris, Miami vs. Baltimore	17	302	0
Oct. 4, 1970	O.J. Simpson, Buffalo vs. N.Y. Jets	26	303	2
Dec. 6, 1969	Jerry LeVias, Houston vs. N.Y. Jets	18	329	1
Nov. 2, 1969	Travis Williams, Green Bay vs. Pittsburgh	11	314	3
Dec. 18, 1966	Gale Sayers, Chicago vs. Minnesota	20	339	2
Dec. 12, 1965	*Gale Sayers, Chicago vs. San Francisco	17	336	6
Nov. 17, 1963	Gary Ballman, Pittsburgh vs. Washington	12	320	2
Dec. 16, 1962	Timmy Brown, Philadelphia vs. St. Louis	19	341	2
Dec. 10, 1961	Billy Cannon, Houston vs. N.Y. Titans	32	373	5
Nov. 19, 1961	Jim Brown, Cleveland vs. Philadelphia	38	313	4
Dec. 3, 1950	Cloyce Box, Detroit vs. Baltimore	13	302	4
Oct. 29, 1950	Wally Triplett, Detroit vs. Los Angeles	11	331	1
Nov. 22, 1945	Jim Benton, Cleveland vs. Detroit	10	303	1

**First season of professional football.*

TOP 20 SCORERS

Player	Years	TD	FG	PAT	TP
George Blanda	26	9	335	943	2,002
Jan Stenerud	19	0	373	580	1,699
Nick Lowery	16	0	349	512	1,559
Pat Leahy	18	0	304	558	1,470
Jim Turner	16	1	304	521	1,439
Mark Moseley	16	0	300	482	1,382
Jim Bakken	17	0	282	534	1,380
Fred Cox	15	0	282	519	1,365
Eddie Murray	17	0	298	465	1,359
Lou Groza	17	1	234	641	1,349
Gary Anderson	13	0	309	416	1,343
Matt Bahr	16	0	277	495	1,326
Morten Andersen	13	0	302	412	1,318
Jim Breech	14	0	243	517	1,246
Chris Bahr	14	0	241	490	1,213
Norm Johnson	13	0	243	476	1,213
Gino Cappelletti	11	42	176	350	1,130
Ray Wersching	15	0	222	456	1,122
Don Cockroft	13	0	216	432	1,080
Garo Yepremian	14	0	210	444	1,074

Cappelletti's total includes 4 two-point conversions.

TOP 20 TOUCHDOWN SCORERS

Player	Years	Rush	Rec.	Returns	Total TD
Jerry Rice	10	8	131	0	139
Jim Brown	9	106	20	0	126
Walter Payton	13	110	15	0	125
Marcus Allen	13	98	21	1	120
John Riggins	14	104	12	0	116
Lenny Moore	12	63	48	2	113
Don Hutson	11	3	99	3	105
Steve Largent	14	1	100	0	101
Franco Harris	13	91	9	0	100
Eric Dickerson	11	90	6	0	96
Jim Taylor	10	83	10	0	93
Tony Dorsett	12	77	13	1	91
Bobby Mitchell	11	18	65	8	91
Leroy Kelly	10	74	13	3	90
Charley Taylor	13	11	79	0	90
Don Maynard	15	0	88	0	88
Lance Alworth	11	2	85	0	87
Ottis Anderson	14	81	5	0	86
Paul Warfield	13	1	85	0	86
Mark Clayton	11	0	84	1	85
Tommy McDonald	12	0	84	1	85

TOP 20 RUSHERS

Player	Years	Att.	Yards	Avg.	Long	TD
Walter Payton	13	3,838	16,726	4.4	76	110
Eric Dickerson	11	2,996	13,259	4.4	85	90
Tony Dorsett	12	2,936	12,739	4.3	99	77
Jim Brown	9	2,359	12,312	5.2	80	106
Franco Harris	13	2,949	12,120	4.1	75	91
John Riggins	14	2,916	11,352	3.9	66	104
O.J. Simpson	11	2,404	11,236	4.7	94	61
Ottis Anderson	14	2,562	10,273	4.0	76	81
Marcus Allen	13	2,485	10,018	4.0	61	98
Earl Campbell	8	2,187	9,407	4.3	81	74
Thurman Thomas	7	2,018	8,724	4.3	80	48
Barry Sanders	6	1,763	8,672	4.9	85	62
Jim Taylor	10	1,941	8,597	4.4	84	83
Joe Perry	14	1,737	8,378	4.8	78	53
Roger Craig	11	1,991	8,189	4.1	71	56
Gerald Riggs	10	1,989	8,188	4.1	58	69
Larry Csonka	11	1,891	8,081	4.3	54	64
Freeman McNeil	12	1,798	8,074	4.5	69	38
Herschel Walker	9	1,907	7,996	4.2	91	60
James Brooks	12	1,685	7,962	4.7	65	49

TOP 20 COMBINED YARDS GAINED

	Years	Tot.	Rush.	Rec.	Int. Ret.	Punt Ret.	Kickoff Ret.	Fumble Ret.
Walter Payton	13	21,803	16,726	4,538	0	0	539	0
Tony Dorsett	12	16,326	12,739	3,554	0	0	0	33
Jim Brown	9	15,459	12,312	2,499	0	0	648	0
Eric Dickerson	11	15,411	13,259	2,137	0	0	0	15
James Brooks	12	14,910	7,962	3,621	0	565	2,762	0
Marcus Allen	13	14,857	10,018	4,845	0	0	0	–6
Herschel Walker	9	14,640	7,996	4,387	0	0	2,257	0
Franco Harris	13	14,622	12,120	2,287	0	0	233	–18
O.J. Simpson	11	14,368	11,236	2,142	0	0	990	0
James Lofton	16	14,277	246	14,004	0	0	0	27
Bobby Mitchell	11	14,078	2,735	7,954	0	699	2,690	0
Jerry Rice	10	13,792	511	13,275	0	0	6	0
John Riggins	14	13,435	11,352	2,090	0	0	0	–7
Steve Largent	14	13,396	83	13,089	0	68	156	0
Ottis Anderson	14	13,364	10,273	3,062	0	0	0	29
Drew Hill	14	13,337	19	9,831	0	22	3,460	5
Greg Pruitt	12	13,262	5,672	3,069	0	2,007	2,514	0
Roger Craig	11	13,143	8,189	4,911	0	0	43	0
Henry Ellard	12	13,099	50	11,158	0	1,527	364	0
Art Monk	15	12,949	332	12,607	0	0	10	0

TOP 20 PASSERS

Player	Years	Att.	Comp.	Pct. Comp.	Yards	TD	Pct. TD	Int.	Pct. Int.	Avg. Gain	Rating
Steve Young	10	2,429	1,546	63.6	19,869	140	5.8	68	2.8	8.18	96.8
Joe Montana	15	5,391	3,409	63.2	40,551	273	5.1	139	2.6	7.52	92.3
Dan Marino	12	6,049	3,604	59.6	45,173	328	5.4	185	3.1	7.47	88.2
Jim Kelly	9	3,942	2,397	60.8	29,527	201	5.1	143	3.6	7.49	85.8
R. Staubach	11	2,958	1,685	57.0	22,700	153	5.2	109	3.7	7.67	83.4
Dave Krieg	15	4,390	2,562	58.4	32,114	231	5.3	166	3.8	7.32	83.0
Neil Lomax	8	3,153	1,817	57.6	22,771	136	4.3	90	2.9	7.22	82.7
S. Jurgensen	18	4,262	2,433	57.1	32,224	255	6.0	189	4.4	7.56	82.6
Len Dawson	19	3,741	2,136	57.1	28,711	239	6.4	183	4.9	7.67	82.6
Brett Favre	4	1,580	983	62.2	10,412	70	4.4	53	3.4	6.59	82.2
Ken Anderson	16	4,475	2,654	59.3	32,838	197	4.4	160	3.6	7.34	81.9
Bernie Kosar	10	3,225	1,896	58.8	22,394	120	3.7	82	2.5	6.94	81.8
Jeff Hostetler	9	1,506	864	57.4	10,985	54	3.6	38	2.5	7.29	81.7
Danny White	13	2,950	1,761	59.7	21,959	155	5.3	132	4.5	7.44	81.7
B. Esiason	11	4,291	2,440	56.9	31,874	207	4.8	153	3.6	7.43	81.6
Troy Aikman	6	2,281	1,424	62.4	16,303	82	3.6	78	3.4	7.15	81.6
Bart Starr	16	3,149	1,808	57.4	24,718	152	4.8	138	4.4	7.85	80.5
Ken O'Brien	10	3,602	2,110	58.6	25,094	128	3.6	98	2.7	6.97	80.4
F. Tarkenton	18	6,467	3,686	57.0	47,003	342	5.3	266	4.1	7.27	80.4
Warren Moon	11	5,147	3,003	58.3	37,949	214	4.2	185	3.6	7.37	80.3

1,500 or more attempts. The passing ratings are based on performance standards established for completion percentage, interception percentage, touchdown percentage, and average gain. Passers are allocated points according to how their marks compare with those standards.

TOP 20 LEADERS IN PASSES COMPLETED

Fran Tarkenton 3,686
Dan Marino 3,604
Joe Montana 3,409
Dan Fouts 3,297
John Elway 3,030
Warren Moon 3,003
Steve DeBerg 2,844
Johnny Unitas 2,830
Ken Anderson 2,654
Jim Hart 2,593
Phil Simms 2,576
Dave Krieg 2,562
John Brodie 2,469
Boomer Esiason 2,440
Sonny Jurgensen 2,433
Jim Kelly 2,397
Joe Ferguson 2,369
Roman Gabriel 2,366
John Hadl 2,363
Norm Snead 2,276

TOP 20 LEADERS IN PASSING YARDS

Fran Tarkenton 47,003
Dan Marino 45,173
Dan Fouts 43,040
Joe Montana 40,551
Johnny Unitas 40,239
Warren Moon 37,949
John Elway 37,736
Jim Hart 34,665
Steve DeBerg 33,872
John Hadl 33,503
Phil Simms 33,462
Ken Anderson 32,838
Sonny Jurgensen 32,224
Dave Krieg 32,114
Boomer Esiason 31,874
John Brodie 31,548
Norm Snead 30,797
Joe Ferguson 29,817
Jim Kelly 29,527
Roman Gabriel 29,444

TOP 20 LEADERS IN TOUCHDOWN PASSES

Fran Tarkenton 342
Dan Marino 328
Johnny Unitas 290
Joe Montana 273
Sonny Jurgensen 255
Dan Fouts 254
John Hadl 244
Len Dawson 239
George Blanda 236
Dave Krieg 231
John Brodie 214
Warren Moon 214
Terry Bradshaw 212
Y.A. Tittle 212
Jim Hart 209
Boomer Esiason 207
Roman Gabriel 201
Jim Kelly 201
John Elway 199
Phil Simms 199

TOP 20 PASS RECEIVERS

Player	Years	No.	Yards	Avg.	Long	TD
Art Monk	15	934	12,607	13.5	79	68
Jerry Rice	10	820	13,275	16.2	96	131
Steve Largent	14	819	13,089	16.0	74	100
James Lofton	16	764	14,004	18.3	80	75
Charlie Joiner	18	750	12,146	16.2	87	65
Andre Reed	10	676	9,536	14.1	83	66
Henry Ellard	12	667	11,158	16.7	81	54
Gary Clark	10	662	10,331	15.6	84	63
Ozzie Newsome	13	662	7,980	12.1	74	47
Charley Taylor	13	649	9,110	14.0	88	79
Drew Hill	14	634	9,831	15.5	81	60
Don Maynard	15	633	11,834	18.7	87	88
Raymond Berry	13	631	9,275	14.7	70	68
Sterling Sharpe	7	595	8,134	13.7	79	65
Harold Carmichael	14	590	8,985	15.2	85	79
Fred Biletnikoff	14	589	8,974	15.2	82	76
Mark Clayton	11	582	8,974	15.4	78	84
Harold Jackson	16	579	10,372	17.9	79	76
Lionel Taylor	10	567	7,195	12.7	80	45
Roger Craig	11	566	4,911	8.7	73	17

TOP 20 LEADERS IN RECEPTION YARDS

James Lofton 14,004
Jerry Rice 13,275
Steve Largent 13,089
Art Monk 12,607
Charlie Joiner 12,146
Don Maynard 11,834
Henry Ellard 11,158
Stanley Morgan 10,716
Harold Jackson 10,372
Gary Clark 10,331
Lance Alworth 10,266
Drew Hill 9,831
Andre Reed 9,536
Raymond Berry 9,275
Charley Taylor 9,110
Harold Carmichael 8,985
Fred Biletnikoff 8,974
Mark Clayton 8,974
Wes Chandler 8,966
Roy Green 8,965

TOP 20 INTERCEPTORS

Player	Years	No.	Yards	Avg.	Long	TD
Paul Krause	16	81	1,185	14.6	81	3
Emlen Tunnell	14	79	1,282	16.2	55	4
Dick (Night Train) Lane	14	68	1,207	17.8	80	5
Ken Riley	15	65	596	9.2	66	5
Ronnie Lott	14	63	730	11.6	83	5
Dick LeBeau	13	62	762	12.3	70	3
Dave Brown	15	62	698	11.3	90	5
Emmitt Thomas	13	58	937	16.2	73	5
Bobby Boyd	9	57	994	17.4	74	4
Johnny Robinson	12	57	741	13.0	57	1
Mel Blount	14	57	736	12.9	52	2
Everson Walls	13	57	504	8.8	40	1
Lem Barney	11	56	1,077	19.2	71	7
Pat Fischer	17	56	941	16.8	69	4
Willie Brown	16	54	472	8.7	45	2
Bobby Dillon	8	52	976	18.8	61	5
Jack Butler	9	52	826	15.9	52	4
Larry Wilson	13	52	800	15.4	96	5
Jim Patton	12	52	712	13.7	51	2
Mel Renfro	14	52	626	12.0	90	3

OUTSTANDING PERFORMERS

TOP 20 PUNTERS

Player	Years	No.	Yards	Avg.	Long	Blk.
Sammy Baugh	16	338	15,245	45.1	85	9
Tommy Davis	11	511	22,833	44.7	82	2
Yale Lary	11	503	22,279	44.3	74	4
Bob Scarpitto	8	283	12,408	43.8	87	4
Horace Gillom	7	385	16,872	43.8	80	5
Rohn Stark	13	985	43,162	43.8	72	7
Jerry Norton	11	358	15,671	43.8	78	2
Greg Montgomery	7	373	16,311	43.7	77	7
David Lewis	4	285	12,447	43.7	63	0
Sean Landeta	10	646	28,125	43.5	71	4
Reggie Roby	12	715	31,122	43.5	77	3
Don Chandler	12	660	28,678	43.5	90	4
Rick Tuten	6	398	17,141	43.1	65	1
Jerrel Wilson	16	1,072	46,139	43.0	72	12
Tommy Barnhardt	8	454	19,482	42.9	65	2
Rich Camarillo	14	950	40,730	42.9	76	5
Norm Van Brocklin	12	523	22,413	42.9	72	3
Danny Villanueva	8	488	20,862	42.8	68	2
Bobby Joe Green	14	970	41,317	42.6	75	3
Sam Baker	15	703	29,938	42.6	72	2

250 or more punts

TOP 20 PUNT RETURNERS

Player	Years	No.	Yards	Avg.	Long	TD
George McAfee	8	112	1,431	12.8	74	2
Jack Christiansen	8	85	1,084	12.8	89	8
Claude Gibson	5	110	1,381	12.6	85	3
Bill Dudley	9	124	1,515	12.2	96	3
Rick Upchurch	9	248	3,008	12.1	92	8
Billy Johnson	14	282	3,317	11.8	87	6
Mack Herron	3	84	982	11.7	66	0
Billy Thompson	13	157	1,814	11.6	60	0
Mel Gray	9	181	2,084	11.5	80	3
Henry Ellard	12	135	1,527	11.3	83	4
Rodger Bird	3	94	1,063	11.3	78	0
Bosh Pritchard	6	95	1,072	11.3	81	2
Bobby Joe Edmonds	4	105	1,178	11.2	75	1
Terry Metcalf	6	84	936	11.1	69	1
Bob Hayes	11	104	1,158	11.1	90	3
Brian Mitchell	5	147	1,623	11.0	84	5
David Meggett	6	202	2,230	11.0	76	6
Floyd Little	9	81	893	11.0	72	2
Louis Lipps	9	112	1,234	11.0	76	3
Les (Speedy) Duncan	11	202	2,201	10.9	95	4

75 or more returns

TOP 20 KICKOFF RETURNERS

Player	Years	No.	Yards	Avg.	Long	TD
Gale Sayers	7	91	2,781	30.6	103	6
Lynn Chandnois	7	92	2,720	29.6	93	3
Abe Woodson	9	193	5,538	28.7	105	5
Claude (Buddy) Young	6	90	2,514	27.9	104	2
Travis Williams	5	102	2,801	27.5	105	6
Joe Arenas	7	139	3,798	27.3	96	1
Clarence Davis	8	79	2,140	27.1	76	0
Steve Van Buren	8	76	2,030	26.7	98	3
Lenny Lyles	12	81	2,161	26.7	103	3
Eugene (Mercury) Morris	8	111	2,947	26.5	105	3
Bobby Jancik	6	158	4,185	26.5	61	0
Mel Renfro	14	85	2,246	26.4	100	2
Bobby Mitchell	11	102	2,690	26.4	98	5
Ollie Matson	14	143	3,746	26.2	105	6
Alvin Haymond	10	170	4,438	26.1	98	2
Noland Smith	3	82	2,137	26.1	106	1
Al Nelson	9	101	2,625	26.0	78	0
Tim Brown	10	184	4,781	26.0	105	5
Vic Washington	6	129	3,341	25.9	98	1
Dave Hampton	8	113	2,923	25.9	101	3

75 or more returns

ANNUAL SCORING LEADERS

Year	Player, Team	TD	FG	PAT	TP
1994	John Carney, San Diego, AFC	0	34	33	135
	Fuad Reveiz, Minnesota, NFC	0	34	30	132
1993	Jeff Jaeger, L.A. Raiders, AFC	0	35	27	132
	Jason Hanson, Detroit, NFC	0	34	28	130
1992	Pete Stoyanovich, Miami, AFC	0	30	34	124
	Morten Andersen, New Orleans, NFC	0	29	33	120
	Chip Lohmiller, Washington, NFC	0	30	30	120
1991	Chip Lohmiller, Washington, NFC	0	31	56	149
	Pete Stoyanovich, Miami, AFC	0	31	28	121
1990	Nick Lowery, Kansas City, AFC	0	34	37	139
	Chip Lohmiller, Washington, NFC	0	30	41	131
1989	Mike Cofer, San Francisco, NFC	0	29	49	136
	*David Treadwell, Denver, AFC	0	27	39	120
1988	Scott Norwood, Buffalo, AFC	0	32	33	129
	Mike Cofer, San Francisco, NFC	0	27	40	121
1987	Jerry Rice, San Francisco, NFC	23	0	0	138
	Jim Breech, Cincinnati, AFC	0	24	25	97
1986	Tony Franklin, New England, AFC	0	32	44	140
	Kevin Butler, Chicago, NFC	0	28	36	120
1985	*Kevin Butler, Chicago, NFC	0	31	51	144
	Gary Anderson, Pittsburgh, AFC	0	33	40	139
1984	Ray Wersching, San Francisco, NFC	0	25	56	131
	Gary Anderson, Pittsburgh, AFC	0	24	45	117
1983	Mark Moseley, Washington, NFC	0	33	62	161
	Gary Anderson, Pittsburgh, AFC	0	27	38	119
1982	*Marcus Allen, L.A. Raiders, AFC	14	0	0	84
	Wendell Tyler, L.A. Rams, NFC	13	0	0	78
1981	Ed Murray, Detroit, NFC	0	25	46	121
	Rafael Septien, Dallas, NFC	0	27	40	121
	Jim Breech, Cincinnati, AFC	0	22	49	115
	Nick Lowery, Kansas City, AFC	0	26	37	115
1980	John Smith, New England, AFC	0	26	51	129
	*Ed Murray, Detroit, NFC	0	27	35	116
1979	John Smith, New England, AFC	0	23	46	115
	Mark Moseley, Washington, NFC	0	25	39	114
1978	*Frank Corral, Los Angeles, NFC	0	29	31	118
	Pat Leahy, N.Y. Jets, AFC	0	22	41	107
1977	Errol Mann, Oakland, AFC	0	20	39	99
	Walter Payton, Chicago, NFC	16	0	0	96
1976	Toni Linhart, Baltimore, AFC	0	20	49	109
	Mark Moseley, Washington, NFC	0	22	31	97
1975	O.J. Simpson, Buffalo, AFC	23	0	0	138
	Chuck Foreman, Minnesota, NFC	22	0	0	132
1974	Chester Marcol, Green Bay, NFC	0	25	19	94
	Roy Gerela, Pittsburgh, AFC	0	20	33	93
1973	David Ray, Los Angeles, NFC	0	30	40	130
	Roy Gerela, Pittsburgh, AFC	0	29	36	123
1972	*Chester Marcol, Green Bay, NFC	0	33	29	128
	Bobby Howfield, N.Y. Jets, AFC	0	27	40	121
1971	Garo Yepremian, Miami, AFC	0	28	33	117
	Curt Knight, Washington, NFC	0	29	27	114
1970	Fred Cox, Minnesota, NFC	0	30	35	125
	Jan Stenerud, Kansas City, AFC	0	30	26	116
1969	Jim Turner, N.Y. Jets, AFL	0	32	33	129
	Fred Cox, Minnesota, NFL	0	26	43	121
1968	Jim Turner, N.Y. Jets, AFL	0	34	43	145
	Leroy Kelly, Cleveland, NFL	20	0	0	120
1967	Jim Bakken, St. Louis, NFL	0	27	36	117
	George Blanda, Oakland, AFL	0	20	56	116
1966	Gino Cappelletti, Boston, AFL	6	16	35	119
	Bruce Gossett, Los Angeles, NFL	0	28	29	113
1965	*Gale Sayers, Chicago, NFL	22	0	0	132
	Gino Cappelletti, Boston, AFL	9	17	27	132
1964	Gino Cappelletti, Boston, AFL	7	25	36	#155
	Lenny Moore, Baltimore, NFL	20	0	0	120
1963	Gino Cappelletti, Boston, AFL	2	22	35	113
	Don Chandler, N.Y. Giants, NFL	0	18	52	106
1962	Gene Mingo, Denver, AFL	4	27	32	137
	Jim Taylor, Green Bay, NFL	19	0	0	114
1961	Gino Cappelletti, Boston, AFL	8	17	48	147
	Paul Hornung, Green Bay, NFL	10	15	41	146
1960	Paul Hornung, Green Bay, NFL	15	15	41	176
	*Gene Mingo, Denver, AFL	6	18	33	123
1959	Paul Hornung, Green Bay	7	7	31	94
1958	Jim Brown, Cleveland	18	0	0	108
1957	Sam Baker, Washington	1	14	29	77
	Lou Groza, Cleveland	0	15	32	77
1956	Bobby Layne, Detroit	5	12	33	99
1955	Doak Walker, Detroit	7	9	27	96
1954	Bobby Walston, Philadelphia	11	4	36	114
1953	Gordy Soltau, San Francisco	6	10	48	114
1952	Gordy Soltau, San Francisco	7	6	34	94
1951	Elroy (Crazylegs) Hirsch, Los Angeles	17	0	0	102
1950	*Doak Walker, Detroit	11	8	38	128
1949	Pat Harder, Chi. Cardinals	8	3	45	102
	Gene Roberts, N.Y. Giants	17	0	0	102
1948	Pat Harder, Chi. Cardinals	6	7	53	110
1947	Pat Harder, Chi. Cardinals	7	7	39	102
1946	Ted Fritsch, Green Bay	10	9	13	100
1945	Steve Van Buren, Philadelphia	18	0	2	110
1944	Don Hutson, Green Bay	9	0	31	85
1943	Don Hutson, Green Bay	12	3	36	117
1942	Don Hutson, Green Bay	17	1	33	138
1941	Don Hutson, Green Bay	12	1	20	95
1940	Don Hutson, Green Bay	7	0	15	57
1939	Andy Farkas, Washington	11	0	2	68
1938	Clarke Hinkle, Green Bay	7	3	7	58
1937	Jack Manders, Chi. Bears	5	8	15	69
1936	Earl (Dutch) Clark, Detroit	7	4	19	73
1935	Earl (Dutch) Clark, Detroit	6	1	16	55
1934	Jack Manders, Chi. Bears	3	10	31	79
1933	Ken Strong, N.Y. Giants	6	5	13	64
	Glenn Presnell, Portsmouth	6	6	10	64
1932	Earl (Dutch) Clark, Portsmouth	6	3	10	55

**First season of professional football.*
#Cappelletti's total includes a two-point conversion.

ANNUAL TOUCHDOWN LEADERS

Year	Player, Team	TD	Rush	Pass	Ret.
1994	Emmitt Smith, Dallas, NFC	22	21	1	0
	*Marshall Faulk, Indianapolis, AFC	12	11	1	0
	Natrone Means, San Diego, AFC	12	12	0	0
1993	Jerry Rice, San Francisco, NFC	16	1	15	0
	Marcus Allen, Kansas City, AFC	15	12	3	0
1992	Emmitt Smith, Dallas, NFC	19	18	1	0
	Thurman Thomas, Buffalo, AFC	12	9	3	0
1991	Barry Sanders, Detroit, NFC	17	16	1	0
	Mark Clayton, Miami, AFC	12	0	12	0
	Thurman Thomas, Buffalo, AFC	12	7	5	0
1990	Barry Sanders, Detroit, NFC	16	13	3	0
	Derrick Fenner, Seattle, AFC	15	14	1	0
1989	Dalton Hilliard, New Orleans, NFC	18	13	5	0
	Christian Okoye, Kansas City, AFC	12	12	0	0
	Thurman Thomas, Buffalo, AFC	12	6	6	0
1988	Greg Bell, L.A. Rams, NFC	18	16	2	0
	Eric Dickerson, Indianapolis, AFC	15	14	1	0
	*Ickey Woods, Cincinnati, AFC	15	15	0	0
1987	Jerry Rice, San Francisco, NFC	23	1	22	0
	Johnny Hector, N.Y. Jets, AFC	11	11	0	0
1986	George Rogers, Washington, NFC	18	18	0	0
	Sammy Winder, Denver, AFC	14	9	5	0
1985	Joe Morris, N.Y. Giants, NFC	21	21	0	0
	Louis Lipps, Pittsburgh, AFC	15	1	12	2
1984	Marcus Allen, L.A. Raiders, AFC	18	13	5	0
	Mark Clayton, Miami, AFC	18	0	18	0
	Eric Dickerson, L.A. Rams, NFC	14	14	0	0
	John Riggins, Washington, NFC	14	14	0	0
1983	John Riggins, Washington, NFC	24	24	0	0
	Pete Johnson, Cincinnati, AFC	14	14	0	0
	*Curt Warner, Seattle, AFC	14	13	1	0
1982	*Marcus Allen, L.A. Raiders, AFC	14	11	3	0
	Wendell Tyler, L.A. Rams, NFC	13	9	4	0
1981	Chuck Muncie, San Diego, AFC	19	19	0	0
	Wendell Tyler, Los Angeles, NFC	17	12	5	0
1980	*Billy Sims, Detroit, NFC	16	13	3	0
	Earl Campbell, Houston, AFC	13	13	0	0
	*Curtis Dickey, Baltimore, AFC	13	11	2	0
	John Jefferson, San Diego, AFC	13	0	13	0
1979	Earl Campbell, Houston, AFC	19	19	0	0
	Walter Payton, Chicago, NFC	16	14	2	0
1978	David Sims, Seattle, AFC	15	14	1	0
	Terdell Middleton, Green Bay, NFC	12	11	1	0
1977	Walter Payton, Chicago, NFC	16	14	2	0
	Nat Moore, Miami, AFC	13	1	12	0
1976	Chuck Foreman, Minnesota, NFC	14	13	1	0
	Franco Harris, Pittsburgh, AFC	14	14	0	0
1975	O.J. Simpson, Buffalo, AFC	23	16	7	0
	Chuck Foreman, Minnesota, NFC	22	13	9	0
1974	Chuck Foreman, Minnesota, NFC	15	9	6	0
	Cliff Branch, Oakland, AFC	13	0	13	0
1973	Larry Brown, Washington, NFC	14	8	6	0
	Floyd Little, Denver, AFC	13	12	1	0
1972	Emerson Boozer, N.Y. Jets, AFC	14	11	3	0
	Ron Johnson, N.Y. Giants, NFC	14	9	5	0

YEARLY STATISTICAL LEADERS

1971	Duane Thomas, Dallas, NFC	13	11	2	0
	Leroy Kelly, Cleveland, AFC	12	10	2	0
1970	Dick Gordon, Chicago, NFC	13	0	13	0
	MacArthur Lane, St. Louis, NFC	13	11	2	0
	Gary Garrison, San Diego, AFC	12	0	12	0
1969	Warren Wells, Oakland, AFL	14	0	14	0
	Tom Matte, Baltimore, NFL	13	11	2	0
	Lance Rentzel, Dallas, NFL	13	0	12	1
1968	Leroy Kelly, Cleveland, NFL	20	16	4	0
	Warren Wells, Oakland, AFL	12	1	11	0
1967	Homer Jones, N.Y. Giants, NFL	14	1	13	0
	Emerson Boozer, N.Y. Jets, AFL	13	10	3	0
1966	Leroy Kelly, Cleveland, NFL	16	15	1	0
	Dan Reeves, Dallas, NFL	16	8	8	0
	Lance Alworth, San Diego, AFL	13	0	13	0
1965	*Gale Sayers, Chicago, NFL	22	14	6	2
	Lance Alworth, San Diego, AFL	14	0	14	0
	Don Maynard, N.Y. Jets, AFL	14	0	14	0
1964	Lenny Moore, Baltimore, NFL	20	16	3	1
	Lance Alworth, San Diego, AFL	15	2	13	0
1963	Art Powell, Oakland, AFL	16	0	16	0
	Jim Brown, Cleveland, NFL	15	12	3	0
1962	Abner Haynes, Dallas, AFL	19	13	6	0
	Jim Taylor, Green Bay, NFL	19	19	0	0
1961	Bill Groman, Houston, AFL	18	1	17	0
	Jim Taylor, Green Bay, NFL	16	15	1	0
1960	Paul Hornung, Green Bay, NFL	15	13	2	0
	Sonny Randle, St. Louis, NFL	15	0	15	0
	Art Powell, N.Y. Titans, AFL	14	0	14	0
1959	Raymond Berry, Baltimore	14	0	14	0
	Jim Brown, Cleveland	14	14	0	0
1958	Jim Brown, Cleveland	18	17	1	0
1957	Lenny Moore, Baltimore	11	3	7	1
1956	Rick Casares, Chi. Bears	14	12	2	0
1955	*Alan Ameche, Baltimore	9	9	0	0
	Harlon Hill, Chi. Bears	9	0	9	0
1954	*Harlon Hill, Chi. Bears	12	0	12	0
1953	Joseph Perry, San Francisco	13	10	3	0
1952	Cloyce Box, Detroit	15	0	15	0
1951	Elroy (Crazylegs) Hirsch, Los Angeles	17	0	17	0
1950	Bob Shaw, Chi. Cardinals	12	0	12	0
1949	Gene Roberts, N.Y. Giants	17	9	8	0
1948	Mal Kutner, Chi. Cardinals	15	1	14	0
1947	Steve Van Buren, Philadelphia	14	13	0	1
1946	Ted Fritsch, Green Bay	10	9	1	0
1945	Steve Van Buren, Philadelphia	18	15	2	1
1944	Don Hutson, Green Bay	9	0	9	0
	Bill Paschal, N.Y. Giants	9	9	0	0
1943	Don Hutson, Green Bay	12	0	11	1
	*Bill Paschal, N.Y. Giants	12	10	2	0
1942	Don Hutson, Green Bay	17	0	17	0
1941	Don Hutson, Green Bay	12	2	10	0
	George McAfee, Chi. Bears	12	6	3	3
1940	John Drake, Cleveland	9	9	0	0
	Richard Todd, Washington	9	4	4	1
1939	Andrew Farkas, Washington	11	5	5	1
1938	Don Hutson, Green Bay	9	0	9	0
1937	Cliff Battles, Washington	7	5	1	1
	Clarke Hinkle, Green Bay	7	5	2	0
	Don Hutson, Green Bay	7	0	7	0
1936	Don Hutson, Green Bay	9	0	8	1
1935	*Don Hutson, Green Bay	7	0	6	1
1934	*Beattie Feathers, Chi. Bears	9	8	1	0
1933	*Charlie (Buckets) Goldenberg, Green Bay	7	4	1	2
	John (Shipwreck) Kelly, Brooklyn	7	2	3	2
	*Elvin (Kink) Richards, N.Y. Giants	7	4	3	0
1932	Earl (Dutch) Clark, Portsmouth	6	3	3	0
	Red Grange, Chi. Bears	6	3	3	0

First season of professional football.

ANNUAL LEADERS—MOST FIELD GOALS MADE

Year	Player, Team	Att.	Made	Pct.
1994	John Carney, San Diego, AFC	38	34	89.5
	Fuad Reveiz, Minnesota, NFC	39	34	87.2
1993	Jeff Jaeger, L.A. Raiders, AFC	44	35	79.5
	Jason Hanson, Detroit, NFC	43	34	79.1
1992	Pete Stoyanovich, Miami, AFC	37	30	81.1
	Chip Lohmiller, Washington, NFC	40	30	75.0
1991	Pete Stoyanovich, Miami, AFC	37	31	83.8
	Chip Lohmiller, Washington, NFC	43	31	72.1
1990	Nick Lowery, Kansas City, AFC	37	34	91.9
	Chip Lohmiller, Washington, NFC	40	30	75.0
1989	Rich Karlis, Minnesota, NFC	39	31	79.5
	*David Treadwell, Denver, AFC	33	27	81.8
1988	Scott Norwood, Buffalo, AFC	37	32	86.5
	Mike Cofer, San Francisco, NFC	38	27	71.1
1987	Morten Andersen, New Orleans, NFC	36	28	77.8
	Dean Biasucci, Indianapolis, AFC	27	24	88.9
	Jim Breech, Cincinnati, AFC	30	24	80.0
1986	Tony Franklin, New England, AFC	41	32	78.0
	Kevin Butler, Chicago, NFC	41	28	68.3
1985	Gary Anderson, Pittsburgh, AFC	42	33	78.6
	Morten Andersen, New Orleans, NFC	35	31	88.6
	*Kevin Butler, Chicago, NFC	37	31	83.8
1984	*Paul McFadden, Philadelphia, NFC	37	30	81.1
	Gary Anderson, Pittsburgh, AFC	32	24	75.0
	Matt Bahr, Cleveland, AFC	32	24	75.0
1983	*Ali-Haji-Sheikh, N.Y. Giants, NFC	42	35	83.3
	*Raul Allegre, Baltimore, AFC	35	30	85.7
1982	Mark Moseley, Washington, NFC	21	20	95.2
	Nick Lowery, Kansas City, AFC	24	19	79.2
1981	Rafael Septien, Dallas, NFC	35	27	77.1
	Nick Lowery, Kansas City, AFC	36	26	72.2
1980	*Ed Murray, Detroit, NFC	42	27	64.3
	John Smith, New England, AFC	34	26	76.5
	Fred Steinfort, Denver, AFC	34	26	76.5
1979	Mark Moseley, Washington, NFC	33	25	75.8
	John Smith, New England, AFC	33	23	69.7
1978	*Frank Corral, Los Angeles, NFC	43	29	67.4
	Pat Leahy, N.Y. Jets, AFC	30	22	73.3
1977	Mark Moseley, Washington, NFC	37	21	56.8
	Errol Mann, Oakland, AFC	28	20	71.4
1976	Mark Moseley, Washington, NFC	34	22	64.7
	Jan Stenerud, Kansas City, AFC	38	21	55.3
1975	Jan Stenerud, Kansas City, AFC	32	22	68.8
	Toni Fritsch, Dallas, NFC	35	22	62.9
1974	Chester Marcol, Green Bay, NFC	39	25	64.1
	Roy Gerela, Pittsburgh, AFC	29	20	69.0
1973	David Ray, Los Angeles, NFC	47	30	63.8
	Roy Gerela, Pittsburgh, AFC	43	29	67.4
1972	*Chester Marcol, Green Bay, NFC	48	33	68.8
	Roy Gerela, Pittsburgh, AFC	41	28	68.3
1971	Curt Knight, Washington, NFC	49	29	59.2
	Garo Yepremian, Miami, AFC	40	28	70.0
1970	Jan Stenerud, Kansas City, AFC	42	30	71.4
	Fred Cox, Minnesota, NFC	46	30	65.2
1969	Jim Turner, N.Y. Jets, AFL	47	32	68.1
	Fred Cox, Minnesota, NFL	37	26	70.3
1968	Jim Turner, N.Y. Jets, AFL	46	34	73.9
	Mac Percival, Chicago, NFL	36	25	69.4
1967	Jim Bakken, St. Louis, NFL	39	27	69.2
	Jan Stenerud, Kansas City, AFL	36	21	58.3
1966	Bruce Gossett, Los Angeles, NFL	49	28	57.1
	Mike Mercer, Oakland-Kansas City, AFL	30	21	70.0
1965	Pete Gogolak, Buffalo, AFL	46	28	60.9
	Fred Cox, Minnesota, NFL	35	23	65.7
1964	Jim Bakken, St. Louis, NFL	38	25	65.8
	Gino Cappelletti, Boston, AFL	39	25	64.1
1963	Jim Martin, Baltimore, NFL	39	24	61.5
	Gino Cappelletti, Boston, AFL	38	22	57.9
1962	Gene Mingo, Denver, AFL	39	27	69.2
	Lou Michaels, Pittsburgh, NFL	42	26	61.9
1961	Steve Myhra, Baltimore, NFL	39	21	53.8
	Gino Cappelletti, Boston, AFL	32	17	53.1
1960	Tommy Davis, San Francisco, NFL	32	19	59.4
	*Gene Mingo, Denver, AFL	28	18	64.3
1959	Pat Summerall, N.Y. Giants	29	20	69.0
1958	Paige Cothren, Los Angeles	25	14	56.0
	*Tom Miner, Pittsburgh	28	14	50.0
1957	Lou Groza, Cleveland	22	15	68.2
1956	Sam Baker, Washington	25	17	68.0
1955	Fred Cone, Green Bay	24	16	66.7
1954	Lou Groza, Cleveland	24	16	66.7
1953	Lou Groza, Cleveland	26	23	88.5
1952	Lou Groza, Cleveland	33	19	57.6
1951	Bob Waterfield, Los Angeles	23	13	56.5
1950	Lou Groza, Cleveland	19	13	68.4
1949	Cliff Patton, Philadelphia	18	9	50.0
	Bob Waterfield, Los Angeles	16	9	56.3
1948	Cliff Patton, Philadelphia	12	8	66.7
1947	Ward Cuff, Green Bay	16	7	43.8
	Pat Harder, Chi. Cardinals	10	7	70.0
	Bob Waterfield, Los Angeles	16	7	43.8
1946	Ted Fritsch, Green Bay	17	9	52.9
1945	Joe Aguirre, Washington	13	7	53.8
1944	Ken Strong, N.Y. Giants	12	6	50.0

1943	Ward Cuff, N.Y. Giants	9	3	33.3
	Don Hutson, Green Bay	5	3	60.0
1942	Bill Daddio, Chi. Cardinals	10	5	50.0
1941	Clarke Hinkle, Green Bay	14	6	42.9
1940	Clarke Hinkle, Green Bay	14	9	64.3
1939	Ward Cuff, N.Y. Giants	16	7	43.8
1938	Ward Cuff, N.Y. Giants	9	5	55.6
	Ralph Kercheval, Brooklyn	13	5	38.5
1937	Jack Manders, Chi. Bears		8	
1936	Jack Manders, Chi. Bears		7	
	Armand Niccolai, Pittsburgh		7	
1935	Armand Niccolai, Pittsburgh		6	
	Bill Smith, Chi. Cardinals		6	
1934	Jack Manders, Chi. Bears		10	
1933	*Jack Manders, Chi. Bears		6	
	Glenn Presnell, Portsmouth		6	
1932	Earl (Dutch) Clark, Portsmouth		3	

**First season of professional football.*

ANNUAL RUSHING LEADERS

Year	Player, Team	Att.	Yards	Avg.	TD
1994	Barry Sanders, Detroit, NFC	331	1,883	5.7	7
	Chris Warren, Seattle, AFC	333	1,545	4.6	9
1993	Emmitt Smith, Dallas, NFC	283	1,486	5.3	9
	Thurman Thomas, Buffalo, AFC	355	1,315	3.7	6
1992	Emmitt Smith, Dallas, NFC	373	1,713	4.6	18
	Barry Foster, Pittsburgh, AFC	390	1,690	4.3	11
1991	Emmitt Smith, Dallas, NFC	365	1,563	4.3	12
	Thurman Thomas, Buffalo, AFC	288	1,407	4.9	7
1990	Barry Sanders, Detroit, NFC	255	1,304	5.1	13
	Thurman Thomas, Buffalo, AFC	271	1,297	4.8	11
1989	Christian Okoye, Kansas City, AFC	370	1,480	4.0	12
	*Barry Sanders, Detroit, NFC	280	1,470	5.3	14
1988	Eric Dickerson, Indianapolis, AFC	388	1,659	4.3	14
	Herschel Walker, Dallas, NFC	361	1,514	4.2	5
1987	Charles White, L.A. Rams, NFC	324	1,374	4.2	11
	Eric Dickerson, Indianapolis, AFC	223	1,011	4.5	5
1986	Eric Dickerson, L.A. Rams, NFC	404	1,821	4.5	11
	Curt Warner, Seattle, AFC	319	1,481	4.6	13
1985	Marcus Allen, L.A. Raiders, AFC	380	1,759	4.6	11
	Gerald Riggs, Atlanta, NFC	397	1,719	4.3	10
1984	Eric Dickerson, L.A. Rams, NFC	379	2,105	5.6	14
	Earnest Jackson, San Diego, AFC	296	1,179	4.0	8
1983	*Eric Dickerson, L.A. Rams, NFC	390	1,808	4.6	18
	*Curt Warner, Seattle, AFC	335	1,449	4.3	13
1982	Freeman McNeil, N.Y. Jets, AFC	151	786	5.2	6
	Tony Dorsett, Dallas, NFC	177	745	4.2	5
1981	*George Rogers, New Orleans, NFC	378	1,674	4.4	13
	Earl Campbell, Houston, AFC	361	1,376	3.8	10
1980	Earl Campbell, Houston, AFC	373	1,934	5.2	13
	Walter Payton, Chicago, NFC	317	1,460	4.6	6
1979	Earl Campbell, Houston, AFC	368	1,697	4.6	19
	Walter Payton, Chicago, NFC	369	1,610	4.4	14
1978	*Earl Campbell, Houston, AFC	302	1,450	4.8	13
	Walter Payton, Chicago, NFC	333	1,395	4.2	11
1977	Walter Payton, Chicago, NFC	339	1,852	5.5	14
	Mark van Eeghen, Oakland, AFC	324	1,273	3.9	7
1976	O.J. Simpson, Buffalo, AFC	290	1,503	5.2	8
	Walter Payton, Chicago, NFC	311	1,390	4.5	13
1975	O.J. Simpson, Buffalo, AFC	329	1,817	5.5	16
	Jim Otis, St. Louis, NFC	269	1,076	4.0	5
1974	Otis Armstrong, Denver, AFC	263	1,407	5.3	9
	Lawrence McCutcheon, Los Angeles, NFC	236	1,109	4.7	3
1973	O.J. Simpson, Buffalo, AFC	332	2,003	6.0	12
	John Brockington, Green Bay, NFC	265	1,144	4.3	3
1972	O.J. Simpson, Buffalo, AFC	292	1,251	4.3	6
	Larry Brown, Washington, NFC	285	1,216	4.3	8
1971	Floyd Little, Denver, AFC	284	1,133	4.0	6
	*John Brockington, Green Bay, NFC	216	1,105	5.1	4
1970	Larry Brown, Washington, NFC	237	1,125	4.7	5
	Floyd Little, Denver, AFC	209	901	4.3	3
1969	Gale Sayers, Chicago, NFL	236	1,032	4.4	8
	Dickie Post, San Diego, AFL	182	873	4.8	6
1968	Leroy Kelly, Cleveland, NFL	248	1,239	5.0	16
	*Paul Robinson, Cincinnati, AFL	238	1,023	4.3	8
1967	Jim Nance, Boston, AFL	269	1,216	4.5	7
	Leroy Kelly, Cleveland, NFL	235	1,205	5.1	11
1966	Jim Nance, Boston, AFL	299	1,458	4.9	11
	Gale Sayers, Chicago, NFL	229	1,231	5.4	8
1965	Jim Brown, Cleveland, NFL	289	1,544	5.3	17
	Paul Lowe, San Diego, AFL	222	1,121	5.0	7
1964	Jim Brown, Cleveland, NFL	280	1,446	5.2	7
	Cookie Gilchrist, Buffalo, AFL	230	981	4.3	6
1963	Jim Brown, Cleveland, NFL	291	1,863	6.4	12
	Clem Daniels, Oakland, AFL	215	1,099	5.1	3
1962	Jim Taylor, Green Bay, NFL	272	1,474	5.4	19
	Cookie Gilchrist, Buffalo, AFL	214	1,096	5.1	13
1961	Jim Brown, Cleveland, NFL	305	1,408	4.6	8
	Billy Cannon, Houston, AFL	200	948	4.7	6
1960	Jim Brown, Cleveland, NFL	215	1,257	5.8	9
	*Abner Haynes, Dall. Texans, AFL	156	875	5.6	9
1959	Jim Brown, Cleveland	290	1,329	4.6	14
1958	Jim Brown, Cleveland	257	1,527	5.9	17
1957	*Jim Brown, Cleveland	202	942	4.7	9
1956	Rick Casares, Chi. Bears	234	1,126	4.8	12
1955	*Alan Ameche, Baltimore	213	961	4.5	9
1954	Joe Perry, San Francisco	173	1,049	6.1	8
1953	Joe Perry, San Francisco	192	1,018	5.3	10
1952	Dan Towler, Los Angeles	156	894	5.7	10
1951	Eddie Price, N.Y. Giants	271	971	3.6	7
1950	Marion Motley, Cleveland	140	810	5.8	3
1949	Steve Van Buren, Philadelphia	263	1,146	4.4	11
1948	Steve Van Buren, Philadelphia	201	945	4.7	10
1947	Steve Van Buren, Philadelphia	217	1,008	4.6	13
1946	Bill Dudley, Pittsburgh	146	604	4.1	3
1945	Steve Van Buren, Philadelphia	143	832	5.8	15
1944	Bill Paschal, N.Y. Giants	196	737	3.8	9
1943	*Bill Paschal, N.Y. Giants	147	572	3.9	10
1942	*Bill Dudley, Pittsburgh	162	696	4.3	5
1941	Clarence (Pug) Manders, Brooklyn	111	486	4.4	5
1940	Byron (Whizzer) White, Detroit	146	514	3.5	5
1939	*Bill Osmanski, Chicago	121	699	5.8	7
1938	*Byron (Whizzer) White, Pittsburgh	152	567	3.7	4
1937	Cliff Battles, Washington	216	874	4.0	5
1936	*Alphonse (Tuffy) Leemans, N.Y. Giants	206	830	4.0	2
1935	Doug Russell, Chi. Cardinals	140	499	3.6	0
1934	*Beattie Feathers, Chi. Bears	119	1,004	8.4	8
1933	Jim Musick, Boston	173	809	4.7	5
1932	*Cliff Battles, Boston	148	576	3.9	3

**First season of professional football.*

ANNUAL PASSING LEADERS

(Current rating system implemented in 1973)

Year	Player, Team	Att.	Comp.	Yards	TD	Int.	Rating
1994	Steve Young, San Francisco, NFC	461	324	3,969	35	10	112.8
	Dan Marino, Miami, AFC	615	385	4,453	30	17	89.2
1993	Steve Young, San Francisco, NFC	462	314	4,023	29	16	101.5
	John Elway, Denver, AFC	551	348	4,030	25	10	92.8
1992	Steve Young, San Francisco, NFC	402	268	3,465	25	7	107.0
	Warren Moon, Houston, AFC	346	224	2,521	18	12	89.3
1991	Steve Young, San Francisco, NFC	279	180	2,517	17	8	101.8
	Jim Kelly, Buffalo, AFC	474	304	3,844	33	17	97.6
1990	Jim Kelly, Buffalo, AFC	346	219	2,829	24	9	101.2
	Phil Simms, N.Y. Giants, NFC	311	184	2,284	15	4	92.7
1989	Joe Montana, San Francisco, NFC	386	271	3,521	26	8	112.4
	Boomer Esiason, Cincinnati, AFC	455	258	3,525	28	11	92.1
1988	Boomer Esiason, Cincinnati, AFC	388	223	3,572	28	14	97.4
	Wade Wilson, Minnesota, NFC	332	204	2,746	15	9	91.5
1987	Joe Montana, San Francisco, NFC	398	266	3,054	31	13	102.1
	Bernie Kosar, Cleveland, AFC	389	241	3,033	22	9	95.4
1986	Tommy Kramer, Minnesota, NFC	372	208	3,000	24	10	92.6
	Dan Marino, Miami, AFC	623	378	4,746	44	23	92.5
1985	Ken O'Brien, N.Y. Jets, AFC	488	297	3,888	25	8	96.2
	Joe Montana, San Francisco, NFC	494	303	3,653	27	13	91.3
1984	Dan Marino, Miami, AFC	564	362	5,084	48	17	108.9
	Joe Montana, San Francisco, NFC	432	279	3,630	28	10	102.9
1983	Steve Bartkowski, Atlanta, NFC	432	274	3,167	22	5	97.6
	*Dan Marino, Miami, AFC	296	173	2,210	20	6	96.0
1982	Ken Anderson, Cincinnati, AFC	309	218	2,495	12	9	95.5
	Joe Theismann, Washington, NFC	252	161	2,033	13	9	91.3
1981	Ken Anderson, Cincinnati, AFC	479	300	3,754	29	10	98.5
	Joe Montana, San Francisco, NFC	488	311	3,565	19	12	88.2
1980	Brian Sipe, Cleveland, AFC	554	337	4,132	30	14	91.4
	Ron Jaworski, Philadelphia, NFC	451	257	3,529	27	12	90.9
1979	Roger Staubach, Dallas, NFC	461	267	3,586	27	11	92.4
	Dan Fouts, San Diego, AFC	530	332	4,082	24	24	82.6
1978	Roger Staubach, Dallas, NFC	413	231	3,190	25	16	84.9
	Terry Bradshaw, Pittsburgh, AFC	368	207	2,915	28	20	84.8
1977	Bob Griese, Miami, AFC	307	180	2,252	22	13	88.0
	Roger Staubach, Dallas, NFC	361	210	2,620	18	9	87.1
1976	Ken Stabler, Oakland, AFC	291	194	2,737	27	17	103.4
	James Harris, Los Angeles, NFC	158	91	1,460	8	6	89.8
1975	Ken Anderson, Cincinnati, AFC	377	228	3,169	21	11	94.1
	Fran Tarkenton, Minnesota, NFC	425	273	2,994	25	13	91.7
1974	Ken Anderson, Cincinnati, AFC	328	213	2,667	18	10	95.9
	Sonny Jurgensen, Washington, NFC	167	107	1,185	11	5	94.6

YEARLY STATISTICAL LEADERS

1973	Roger Staubach, Dallas, NFC	286	179	2,428	23	15	94.6
	Ken Stabler, Oakland, AFC	260	163	1,997	14	10	88.5
1972	Norm Snead, N.Y. Giants, NFC	325	196	2,307	17	12	
	Earl Morrall, Miami, AFC	150	83	1,360	11	7	
1971	Roger Staubach, Dallas, NFC	211	126	1,882	15	4	
	Bob Griese, Miami, AFC	263	145	2,089	19	9	
1970	John Brodie, San Francisco, NFC	378	223	2,941	24	10	
	Daryle Lamonica, Oakland, AFC	356	179	2,516	22	15	
1969	Sonny Jurgensen, Washington, NFL	442	274	3,102	22	15	
	*Greg Cook, Cincinnati, AFL	197	106	1,854	15	11	
1968	Len Dawson, Kansas City, AFL	224	131	2,109	17	9	
	Earl Morrall, Baltimore, NFL	317	182	2,909	26	17	
1967	Sonny Jurgensen, Washington, NFL	508	288	3,747	31	16	
	Daryle Lamonica, Oakland, AFL	425	220	3,228	30	20	
1966	Bart Starr, Green Bay, NFL	251	156	2,257	14	3	
	Len Dawson, Kansas City, AFL	284	159	2,527	26	10	
1965	Rudy Bukich, Chicago, NFL	312	176	2,641	20	9	
	John Hadl, San Diego, AFL	348	174	2,798	20	21	
1964	Len Dawson, Kansas City, AFL	354	199	2,879	30	18	
	Bart Starr, Green Bay, NFL	272	163	2,144	15	4	
1963	Y.A. Tittle, N.Y. Giants, NFL	367	221	3,145	36	14	
	Tobin Rote, San Diego, AFL	286	170	2,510	20	17	
1962	Len Dawson, Dall. Texans, AFL	310	189	2,759	29	17	
	Bart Starr, Green Bay, NFL	285	178	2,438	12	9	
1961	George Blanda, Houston, AFL	362	187	3,330	36	22	
	Milt Plum, Cleveland, NFL	302	177	2,416	18	10	
1960	Milt Plum, Cleveland, NFL	250	151	2,297	21	5	
	Jack Kemp, L.A. Chargers, AFL	406	211	3,018	20	25	
1959	Charlie Conerly, N.Y. Giants	194	113	1,706	14	4	
1958	Eddie LeBaron, Washington	145	79	1,365	11	10	
1957	Tommy O'Connell, Cleveland	110	63	1,229	9	8	
1956	Ed Brown, Chi. Bears	168	96	1,667	11	12	
1955	Otto Graham, Cleveland	185	98	1,721	15	8	
1954	Norm Van Brocklin, Los Angeles	260	139	2,637	13	21	
1953	Otto Graham, Cleveland	258	167	2,722	11	9	
1952	Norm Van Brocklin, Los Angeles	205	113	1,736	14	17	
1951	Bob Waterfield, Los Angeles	176	88	1,566	13	10	
1950	Norm Van Brocklin, Los Angeles	233	127	2,061	18	14	
1949	Sammy Baugh, Washington	255	145	1,903	18	14	
1948	Tommy Thompson, Philadelphia	246	141	1,965	25	11	
1947	Sammy Baugh, Washington	354	210	2,938	25	15	
1946	Bob Waterfield, Los Angeles	251	127	1,747	18	17	
1945	Sammy Baugh, Washington	182	128	1,669	11	4	
	Sid Luckman, Chi. Bears	217	117	1,725	14	10	
1944	Frank Filchock, Washington	147	84	1,139	13	9	
1943	Sammy Baugh, Washington	239	133	1,754	23	19	
1942	Cecil Isbell, Green Bay	268	146	2,021	24	14	
1941	Cecil Isbell, Green Bay	206	117	1,479	15	11	
1940	Sammy Baugh, Washington	177	111	1,367	12	10	
1939	*Parker Hall, Cleveland	208	106	1,227	9	13	
1938	Ed Danowski, N.Y. Giants	129	70	848	7	8	
1937	*Sammy Baugh, Washington	171	81	1,127	8	14	
1936	Arnie Herber, Green Bay	173	77	1,239	11	13	
1935	Ed Danowski, N.Y. Giants	113	57	794	10	9	
1934	Arnie Herber, Green Bay	115	42	799	8	12	
1933	*Harry Newman, N.Y. Giants	136	53	973	11	17	
1932	Arnie Herber, Green Bay	101	37	639	9	9	

**First season of professional football.*

ANNUAL PASSING TOUCHDOWN LEADERS

Year	Player, Team	TD
1994	Steve Young, San Francisco, NFC	35
	Dan Marino, Miami, AFC	30
1993	Steve Young, San Francisco, NFC	29
	John Elway, Denver, AFC	25
1992	Steve Young, San Francisco, NFC	25
	Dan Marino, Miami, AFC	24
1991	Jim Kelly, Buffalo, AFC	33
	Mark Rypien, Washington, NFC	28
1990	Warren Moon, Houston, AFC	33
	Randall Cunningham, Philadelphia, NFC	30
1989	Jim Everett, L.A. Rams, NFC	29
	Boomer Esiason, Cincinnati, AFC	28
1988	Jim Everett, L.A. Rams, NFC	31
	Boomer Esiason, Cincinnati, AFC	28
	Dan Marino, Miami, AFC	28
1987	Joe Montana, San Francisco, NFC	31
	Dan Marino, Miami, AFC	26
1986	Dan Marino, Miami, AFC	44
	Tommy Kramer, Minnesota, NFC	24
1985	Dan Marino, Miami, AFC	30
	Joe Montana, San Francisco, NFC	27
1984	Dan Marino, Miami, AFC	48
	Neil Lomax, St. Louis, NFC	28
	Joe Montana, San Francisco, NFC	28
1983	Lynn Dickey, Green Bay, NFC	32
	Joe Ferguson, Buffalo, AFC	26
	Brian Sipe, Cleveland, AFC	26
1982	Terry Bradshaw, Pittsburgh, AFC	17
	Dan Fouts, San Diego, AFC	17
	Joe Montana, San Francisco, NFC	17
1981	Dan Fouts, San Diego, AFC	33
	Steve Bartkowski, Atlanta, NFC	30
1980	Steve Bartkowski, Atlanta, NFC	31
	Dan Fouts, San Diego, AFC	30
	Brian Sipe, Cleveland, AFC	30
1979	Steve Grogan, New England, AFC	28
	Brian Sipe, Cleveland, AFC	28
	Roger Staubach, Dallas, NFC	27
1978	Terry Bradshaw, Pittsburgh, AFC	28
	Roger Staubach, Dallas, NFC	25
	Fran Tarkenton, Minnesota, NFC	25
1977	Bob Griese, Miami, AFC	22
	Ron Jaworski, Philadelphia, NFC	18
	Roger Staubach, Dallas, NFC	18
1976	Ken Stabler, Oakland, AFC	27
	Jim Hart, St. Louis, NFC	18
1975	Joe Ferguson, Buffalo, AFC	25
	Fran Tarkenton, Minnesota, NFC	25
1974	Ken Stabler, Oakland, AFC	26
	Jim Hart, St. Louis, NFC	20
1973	Roman Gabriel, Philadelphia, NFC	23
	Roger Staubach, Dallas, NFC	23
	Charley Johnson, Denver, AFC	20
1972	Billy Kilmer, Washington, NFC	19
	Joe Namath, N.Y. Jets, AFC	19
1971	John Hadl, San Diego, AFC	21
	John Brodie, San Francisco, NFC	18
1970	John Brodie, San Francisco, NFC	24
	John Hadl, San Diego, AFC	22
	Daryle Lamonica, Oakland, AFC	22
1969	Daryle Lamonica, Oakland, AFL	34
	Roman Gabriel, Los Angeles, NFL	24
1968	John Hadl, San Diego, AFL	27
	Earl Morrall, Baltimore, NFL	26
1967	Sonny Jurgensen, Washington, NFL	31
	Daryle Lamonica, Oakland, AFL	30
1966	Frank Ryan, Cleveland, NFL	29
	Len Dawson, Kansas City, AFL	26
1965	John Brodie, San Francisco, NFL	30
	Len Dawson, Kansas City, AFL	21
1964	Babe Parilli, Boston, AFL	31
	Frank Ryan, Cleveland, NFL	25
1963	Y.A. Tittle, N.Y. Giants, NFL	36
	Len Dawson, Kansas City, AFL	26
1962	Y.A. Tittle, N.Y. Giants, NFL	33
	Len Dawson, Dallas, AFL	29
1961	George Blanda, Houston, AFL	36
	Sonny Jurgensen, Philadelphia, NFL	32
1960	Al Dorow, N.Y. Titans, AFL	26
	Johnny Unitas, Baltimore, NFL	25
1959	Johnny Unitas, Baltimore	32
1958	Johnny Unitas, Baltimore	19
1957	Johnny Unitas, Baltimore	24
1956	Tobin Rote, Green Bay	18
1955	Tobin Rote, Green Bay	17
	Y.A. Tittle, San Francisco	17
1954	Adrian Burk, Philadelphia	23
1953	Robert Thomason, Philadelphia	21
1952	Jim Finks, Pittsburgh	20
	Otto Graham, Cleveland	20
1951	Bobby Layne, Detroit	26
1950	George Ratterman, N.Y. Yanks	22
1949	Johnny Lujack, Chi. Bears	23
1948	Tommy Thompson, Philadelphia	25
1947	Sammy Baugh, Washington	25
1946	Sid Luckman, Chi. Bears	17
	Bob Waterfield, Los Angeles	17
1945	Sid Luckman, Chi. Bears	14
	*Bob Waterfield, Cleveland	14
1944	Frank Filchock, Washington	13
1943	Sid Luckman, Chi. Bears	28
1942	Cecil Isbell, Green Bay	24
1941	Cecil Isbell, Green Bay	15
1940	Sammy Baugh, Washington	12
1939	Frank Filchock, Washington	11

Year	Player, Team	
1938	Bob Monnett, Green Bay	9
1937	Bernie Masterson, Chi. Bears	9
1936	Arnie Herber, Green Bay	11
1935	Ed Danowski, N.Y. Giants	10
1934	Arnie Herber, Green Bay	8
1933	*Harry Newman, N.Y. Giants	11
1932	Arnie Herber, Green Bay	9

First season of professional football.

ANNUAL PASS RECEIVING LEADERS

Year	Player, Team	No.	Yards	Avg.	TD
1994	Cris Carter, Minnesota, NFC	122	1,256	10.3	7
	Ben Coates, New England, AFC	96	1,174	12.2	7
1993	Sterling Sharpe, Green Bay, NFC	112	1,274	11.4	11
	Reggie Langhorne, Indianapolis, AFC	85	1,038	12.2	3
1992	Sterling Sharpe, Green Bay, NFC	108	1,461	13.5	13
	Haywood Jeffires, Houston, AFC	90	913	10.1	9
1991	Haywood Jeffires, Houston, AFC	100	1,181	11.8	7
	Michael Irvin, Dallas, NFC	93	1,523	16.4	8
1990	Jerry Rice, San Francisco, NFC	100	1,502	15.0	13
	Haywood Jeffires, Houston, AFC	74	1,048	14.2	8
	Drew Hill, Houston, AFC	74	1,019	13.8	5
1989	Sterling Sharpe, Green Bay, NFC	90	1,423	15.8	12
	Andre Reed, Buffalo, AFC	88	1,312	14.9	9
1988	Al Toon, N.Y. Jets, AFC	93	1,067	11.5	5
	Henry Ellard, L.A. Rams, NFC	86	1,414	16.4	10
1987	J.T. Smith, St. Louis, NFC	91	1,117	12.3	8
	Al Toon, N.Y. Jets, AFC	68	976	14.4	5
1986	Todd Christensen, L.A. Raiders, AFC	95	1,153	12.1	8
	Jerry Rice, San Francisco, NFC	86	1,570	18.3	15
1985	Roger Craig, San Francisco, NFC	92	1,016	11.0	6
	Lionel James, San Diego, AFC	86	1,027	11.9	6
1984	Art Monk, Washington, NFC	106	1,372	12.9	7
	Ozzie Newsome, Cleveland, AFC	89	1,001	11.2	5
1983	Todd Christensen, L.A. Raiders, AFC	92	1,247	13.6	12
	Roy Green, St. Louis, NFC	78	1,227	15.7	14
	Charlie Brown, Washington, NFC	78	1,225	15.7	8
	Earnest Gray, N.Y. Giants, NFC	78	1,139	14.6	5
1982	Dwight Clark, San Francisco, NFC	60	913	15.2	5
	Kellen Winslow, San Diego, AFC	54	721	13.4	6
1981	Kellen Winslow, San Diego, AFC	88	1,075	12.2	10
	Dwight Clark, San Francisco, NFC	85	1,105	13.0	4
1980	Kellen Winslow, San Diego, AFC	89	1,290	14.5	9
	*Earl Cooper, San Francisco, NFC	83	567	6.8	4
1979	Joe Washington, Baltimore, AFC	82	750	9.1	3
	Ahmad Rashad, Minnesota, NFC	80	1,156	14.5	9
1978	Rickey Young, Minnesota, NFC	88	704	8.0	5
	Steve Largent, Seattle, AFC	71	1,168	16.5	8
1977	Lydell Mitchell, Baltimore, AFC	71	620	8.7	4
	Ahmad Rashad, Minnesota, NFC	51	681	13.4	2
1976	MacArthur Lane, Kansas City, AFC	66	686	10.4	1
	Drew Pearson, Dallas, NFC	58	806	13.9	6
1975	Chuck Foreman, Minnesota, NFC	73	691	9.5	9
	Reggie Rucker, Cleveland, AFC	60	770	12.8	3
	Lydell Mitchell, Baltimore, AFC	60	544	9.1	4
1974	Lydell Mitchell, Baltimore, AFC	72	544	7.6	2
	Charles Young, Philadelphia, NFC	63	696	11.0	3
1973	Harold Carmichael, Philadelphia, NFC	67	1,116	16.7	9
	Fred Willis, Houston, AFC	57	371	6.5	1
1972	Harold Jackson, Philadelphia, NFC	62	1,048	16.9	4
	Fred Biletnikoff, Oakland, AFC	58	802	13.8	7
1971	Fred Biletnikoff, Oakland, AFC	61	929	15.2	9
	Bob Tucker, N.Y. Giants, NFC	59	791	13.4	4
1970	Dick Gordon, Chicago, NFC	71	1,026	14.5	13
	Marlin Briscoe, Buffalo, AFC	57	1,036	18.2	8
1969	Dan Abramowicz, New Orleans, NFL	73	1,015	13.9	7
	Lance Alworth, San Diego, AFL	64	1,003	15.7	4
1968	Clifton McNeil, San Francisco, NFL	71	994	14.0	7
	Lance Alworth, San Diego, AFL	68	1,312	19.3	10
1967	George Sauer, N.Y. Jets, AFL	75	1,189	15.9	6
	Charley Taylor, Washington, NFL	70	990	14.1	9
1966	Lance Alworth, San Diego, AFL	73	1,383	18.9	13
	Charley Taylor, Washington, NFL	72	1,119	15.5	12
1965	Lionel Taylor, Denver, AFL	85	1,131	13.3	6
	Dave Parks, San Francisco, NFL	80	1,344	16.8	12
1964	Charley Hennigan, Houston, AFL	101	1,546	15.3	8
	Johnny Morris, Chicago, NFL	93	1,200	12.9	10
1963	Lionel Taylor, Denver, AFL	78	1,101	14.1	10
	Bobby Joe Conrad, St. Louis, NFL	73	967	13.2	10
1962	Lionel Taylor, Denver, AFL	77	908	11.8	4
	Bobby Mitchell, Washington, NFL	72	1,384	19.2	11
1961	Lionel Taylor, Denver, AFL	100	1,176	11.8	4
	Jim (Red) Phillips, Los Angeles, NFL	78	1,092	14.0	5
1960	Lionel Taylor, Denver, AFL	92	1,235	13.4	12
	Raymond Berry, Baltimore, NFL	74	1,298	17.5	10
1959	Raymond Berry, Baltimore	66	959	14.5	14
1958	Raymond Berry, Baltimore	56	794	14.2	9
	Pete Retzlaff, Philadelphia	56	766	13.7	2
1957	Billy Wilson, San Francisco	52	757	14.6	6
1956	Billy Wilson, San Francisco	60	889	14.8	5
1955	Pete Pihos, Philadelphia	62	864	13.9	7
1954	Pete Pihos, Philadelphia	60	872	14.5	10
	Billy Wilson, San Francisco	60	830	13.8	5
1953	Pete Pihos, Philadelphia	63	1,049	16.7	10
1952	Mac Speedie, Cleveland	62	911	14.7	5
1951	Elroy (Crazylegs) Hirsch, Los Angeles	66	1,495	22.7	17
1950	Tom Fears, Los Angeles	84	1,116	13.3	7
1949	Tom Fears, Los Angeles	77	1,013	13.2	9
1948	*Tom Fears, Los Angeles	51	698	13.7	4
1947	Jim Keane, Chi. Bears	64	910	14.2	10
1946	Jim Benton, Los Angeles	63	981	15.6	6
1945	Don Hutson, Green Bay	47	834	17.7	9
1944	Don Hutson, Green Bay	58	866	14.9	9
1943	Don Hutson, Green Bay	47	776	16.5	11
1942	Don Hutson, Green Bay	74	1,211	16.4	17
1941	Don Hutson, Green Bay	58	738	12.7	10
1940	*Don Looney, Philadelphia	58	707	12.2	4
1939	Don Hutson, Green Bay	34	846	24.9	6
1938	Gaynell Tinsley, Chi. Cardinals	41	516	12.6	1
1937	Don Hutson, Green Bay	41	552	13.5	7
1936	Don Hutson, Green Bay	34	536	15.8	8
1935	*Tod Goodwin, N.Y. Giants	26	432	16.6	4
1934	Joe Carter, Philadelphia	16	238	14.9	4
	Morris (Red) Badgro, N.Y. Giants	16	206	12.9	1
1933	John (Shipwreck) Kelly, Brooklyn	22	246	11.2	3
1932	Ray Flaherty, N.Y. Giants	21	350	16.7	3

First season of professional football.

ANNUAL PASS RECEIVING LEADERS (YARDS)

Year	Player, Team	No.	Yards	Avg.	TD
1994	Jerry Rice, San Francisco, NFC	112	1,499	13.4	13
	Tim Brown, L.A. Raiders, AFC	89	1,309	14.7	9
1993	Jerry Rice, San Francisco, NFC	98	1,503	15.3	15
	Tim Brown, L.A. Raiders, AFC	80	1,180	14.8	7
1992	Sterling Sharpe, Green Bay, NFC	108	1,461	13.5	13
	Anthony Miller, San Diego, AFC	72	1,060	14.7	7
1991	Michael Irvin, Dallas, NFC	93	1,523	16.4	8
	Haywood Jeffires, Houston, AFC	100	1,181	11.8	7
1990	Jerry Rice, San Francisco, NFC	100	1,502	15.0	13
	Haywood Jeffires, Houston, AFC	74	1,048	14.2	8
1989	Jerry Rice, San Francisco, NFC	82	1,483	18.1	17
	Andre Reed, Buffalo, AFC	88	1,312	14.9	9
1988	Henry Ellard, L.A. Rams, NFC	86	1,414	16.4	10
	Eddie Brown, Cincinnati, AFC	53	1,273	24.0	9
1987	J.T. Smith, St. Louis, NFC	91	1,117	12.3	8
	Carlos Carson, Kansas City, AFC	55	1,044	19.0	7
1986	Jerry Rice, San Francisco, NFC	86	1,570	18.3	15
	Stanley Morgan, New England, AFC	84	1,491	17.8	10
1985	Steve Largent, Seattle, AFC	79	1,287	16.3	6
	Mike Quick, Philadelphia, NFC	73	1,247	17.1	11
1984	Roy Green, St. Louis, NFC	78	1,555	19.9	12
	John Stallworth, Pittsburgh, AFC	80	1,395	17.4	11
1983	Mike Quick, Philadelphia, NFC	69	1,409	20.4	13
	Carlos Carson, Kansas City, AFC	80	1,351	16.9	7
1982	Wes Chandler, San Diego, AFC	49	1,032	21.1	9
	Dwight Clark, San Francisco, NFC	60	913	15.2	5
1981	Alfred Jenkins, Atlanta, NFC	70	1,358	19.4	13
	Frank Lewis, Buffalo, AFC	70	1,244	17.8	4
	Steve Watson, Denver, AFC	60	1,244	20.7	13
1980	John Jefferson, San Diego, AFC	82	1,340	16.3	13
	James Lofton, Green Bay, NFC	71	1,226	17.3	4
1979	Steve Largent, Seattle, AFC	66	1,237	18.7	9
	Ahmad Rashad, Minnesota, NFC	80	1,156	14.5	9
1978	Wesley Walker, N.Y. Jets, AFC	48	1,169	24.4	8
	Harold Carmichael, Philadelphia, NFC	55	1,072	19.5	8
1977	Drew Pearson, Dallas, NFC	48	870	18.1	2
	Ken Burrough, Houston, AFC	43	816	19.0	8
1976	Roger Carr, Baltimore, AFC	43	1,112	25.9	11
	*Sammy White, Minnesota, NFC	51	906	17.8	10
1975	Ken Burrough, Houston, AFC	53	1,063	20.1	8
	Mel Gray, St. Louis, NFC	48	926	19.3	11
1974	Cliff Branch, Oakland, AFC	60	1,092	18.2	13
	Drew Pearson, Dallas, NFC	62	1,087	17.5	2
1973	Harold Carmichael, Philadelphia, NFC	67	1,116	16.7	9
	*Isaac Curtis, Cincinnati, AFC	45	843	18.7	9
1972	Harold Jackson, Philadelphia, NFC	62	1,048	16.9	4

YEARLY STATISTICAL LEADERS

	Rich Caster, N.Y. Jets, AFC	39	833	21.4	10
1971	Otis Taylor, Kansas City, AFC	57	1,110	19.5	7
	Gene Washington, San Francisco, NFC	46	884	19.2	4
1970	Gene Washington, San Francisco, NFC	53	1,100	20.8	12
	Marlin Briscoe, Buffalo, AFC	57	1,036	18.2	8
1969	Warren Wells, Oakland, AFL	47	1,260	26.8	14
	Harold Jackson, Philadelphia, NFL	65	1,116	17.2	9
1968	Lance Alworth, San Diego, AFL	68	1,312	19.3	10
	Roy Jefferson, Pittsburgh, NFL	58	1,074	18.5	11
1967	Don Maynard, N.Y. Jets, AFL	71	1,434	20.3	10
	Ben Hawkins, Philadelphia, NFL	59	1,265	21.4	10
1966	Lance Alworth, San Diego, AFL	73	1,383	18.9	13
	Pat Studstill, Detroit, NFL	67	1,266	18.9	5
1965	Lance Alworth, San Diego, AFL	69	1,602	23.2	14
	Dave Parks, San Francisco, NFL	80	1,344	16.8	12
1964	Charley Hennigan, Houston, AFL	101	1,546	15.3	8
	Johnny Morris, Chicago, NFL	93	1,200	12.9	10
1963	Bobby Mitchell, Washington, NFL	69	1,436	20.8	7
	Art Powell, Oakland, AFL	73	1,304	17.8	16
1962	Bobby Mitchel, Washington, NFL	72	1,384	19.2	11
	Art Powell, N.Y. Titans, AFL	64	1,130	17.6	8
1961	Charley Hennigan, Houston, AFL	82	1,746	21.3	12
	Tommy McDonald, Philadelphia, NFL	64	1,144	17.9	13
1960	*Bill Groman, Houston, AFL	72	1,473	20.5	12
	Raymond Berry, Baltimore, NFL	74	1,298	17.5	10
1959	Raymond Berry, Baltimore	66	959	14.5	14
1958	Del Shofner, Los Angeles	51	1,097	21.5	8
1957	Raymond Berry, Baltimore	47	800	17.0	6
1956	Billy Howton, Green Bay	55	1,188	21.6	12
1955	Pete Pihos, Philadelphia	62	864	13.9	7
1954	Bob Boyd, Los Angeles	53	1,212	22.9	6
1953	Pete Pihos, Philadelphia	63	1,049	16.7	10
1952	*Bill Howton, Green Bay	53	1,231	23.2	13
1951	Elroy (Crazylegs) Hirsch, Los Angeles	66	1,495	22.7	17
1950	Tom Fears, Los Angeles	84	1,116	13.3	7
1949	Bob Mann, Detroit	66	1,014	15.4	4
1948	Mal Kutner, Chi. Cardinals	41	943	23.0	14
1947	Mal Kutner, Chi. Cardinals	43	944	21.9	7
1946	Jim Benton, Los Angeles	63	981	15.5	6
1945	Jim Benton, Cleveland	45	1,067	23.7	8
1944	Don Hutson, Green Bay	58	866	14.6	9
1943	Don Hutson, Green Bay	47	776	16.5	11
1942	Don Hutson, Green Bay	74	1,211	16.4	17
1941	Don Hutson, Green Bay	58	738	12.7	10
1940	*Don Looney, Philadelphia	58	707	12.2	4
1939	Don Hutson, Green Bay	34	846	24.9	6
1938	Don Hutson, Green Bay	32	548	17.1	9
1937	*Gaynell Tinsley, Chi. Cardinals	36	675	18.8	5
1936	Don Hutson, Green Bay	34	526	15.5	8
1935	Charley Malone, Boston	22	433	19.7	2
1934	Harry Ebding, Detroit	9	257	28.6	2
1933	*Paul Moss, Pittsburgh	18	383	21.3	2
1932	Johnny Blood (McNally), Green Bay	19	326	17.2	3

**First season of professional football.*

ANNUAL INTERCEPTION LEADERS

Year	Player, Team	No.	Yards	TD
1994	Eric Turner, Cleveland, AFC	9	199	1
	Aeneas Williams, Arizona, NFC	9	89	0
1993	Eugene Robinson, Seattle, AFC	9	80	0
	Nate Odomes, Buffalo, AFC	9	65	0
	Deion Sanders, Atlanta, NFC	7	91	0
1992	Henry Jones, Buffalo, AFC	8	263	2
	Audray McMillan, Minnesota, NFC	8	157	2
1991	Ronnie Lott, L.A. Raiders, AFC	8	52	0
	Ray Crockett, Detroit, NFC	6	141	1
	Deion Sanders, Atlanta, AFC	6	119	1
	*Aeneas Williams, Phoenix, NFC	6	60	0
	Tim McKyer, Atlanta, NFC	6	24	0
1990	*Mark Carrier, Chicago, NFC	10	39	0
	Richard Johnson, Houston, AFC	8	100	1
1989	Felix Wright, Cleveland, AFC	9	91	1
	Eric Allen, Philadelphia, NFC	8	38	0
1988	Scott Case, Atlanta, NFC	10	47	0
	Erik McMillan, N.Y. Jets, AFC	8	168	2
1987	Barry Wilburn, Washington, NFC	9	135	1
	Mike Prior, Indianapolis, AFC	6	57	0
	Mark Kelso, Buffalo, AFC	6	25	0
	Keith Bostic, Houston, AFC	6	-14	0
1986	Ronnie Lott, San Francisco, NFC	10	134	1
	Deron Cherry, Kansas City, AFC	9	150	0
1985	Everson Walls, Dallas, NFC	9	31	0
	Albert Lewis, Kansas City, AFC	8	59	0
	Eugene Daniel, Indianapolis, AFC	8	53	0
1984	Ken Easley, Seattle, AFC	10	126	2
	*Tom Flynn, Green Bay, NFC	9	106	0
1983	Mark Murphy, Washington, NFC	9	127	0
	Ken Riley, Cincinnati, AFC	8	89	2
	Vann McElroy, L.A. Raiders, AFC	8	68	0
1982	Everson Walls, Dallas, NFC	7	61	0
	Ken Riley, Cincinnati, AFC	5	88	1
	Bobby Jackson, N.Y Jets, AFC	5	84	1
	Dwayne Woodruff, Pittsburgh, AFC	5	53	0
	Donnie Shell, Pittsburgh, AFC	5	27	0
1981	*Everson Walls, Dallas, NFC	11	133	0
	John Harris, Seattle, AFC	10	155	2
1980	Lester Hayes, Oakland, AFC	13	273	1
	Nolan Cromwell, Los Angeles, NFC	8	140	1
1979	Mike Reinfeldt, Houston, AFC	12	205	0
	Lemar Parrish, Washiongton, NFC	9	65	0
1978	Thom Darden, Cleveland, AFC	10	200	0
	Ken Stone, St. Louis, NFC	9	139	0
	Willie Buchanon, Green Bay, NFC	9	93	1
1977	Lyle Blackwood, Baltimore, AFC	10	163	0
	Rolland Lawrence, Atlanta, NFC	7	138	0
1976	Monte Jackson, Los Angeles, NFC	10	173	3
	Ken Riley, Cincinnati, AFC	9	141	1
1975	Mel Blount, Pittsburgh, AFC	11	121	0
	Paul Krause, Minnesota, NFC	10	201	0
1974	Emmitt Thomas, Kansas City, AFC	12	214	2
	Ray Brown, Atlanta, NFC	8	164	1
1973	Dick Anderson, Miami, AFC	8	163	2
	Mike Wagner, Pittsburgh, AFC	8	134	0
	Bobby Bryant, Minnesota, NFC	7	105	1
1972	Bill Bradley, Philadelphia, NFC	9	73	0
	Mike Sensibaugh, Kansas City, AFC	8	65	0
1971	Bill Bradley, Philadelphia, NFC	11	248	0
	Ken Houston, Houston, AFC	9	220	4
1970	Johnny Robinson, Kansas City, AFC	10	155	0
	Dick LeBeau, Detroit, NFC	9	96	0
1969	Mel Renfro, Dallas, NFL	10	118	0
	Emmitt Thomas, Kansas City, AFL	9	146	1
1968	Dave Grayson, Oakland, AFL	10	195	1
	Willie Williams, N.Y. Giants, NFL	10	103	0
1967	Miller Farr, Houston, AFL	10	264	3
	*Lem Barney, Detroit, NFL	10	232	3
	Tom Janik, Buffalo, AFL	10	222	2
	Dave Whitsell, New Orleans, NFL	10	178	2
	Dick Westmoreland, Miami, AFL	10	127	1
1966	Larry Wilson, St. Louis, NFL	10	180	2
	Johnny Robinson, Kansas City, AFL	10	136	1
	Bobby Hunt, Kansas City, AFL	10	113	0
1965	W.K. Hicks, Houston, AFL	9	156	0
	Bobby Boyd, Baltimore, NFL	9	78	1
1964	Dainard Paulson, N.Y. Jets, AFL	12	157	1
	*Paul Krause, Washington, NFL	12	140	1
1963	Fred Glick, Houston, AFL	12	180	1
	Dick Lynch, N.Y. Giants, NFL	9	251	3
	Roosevelt Taylor, Chicago, NFL	9	172	1
1962	Lee Riley, N.Y. Titans, AFL	11	122	0
	Willie Wood, Green Bay, NFL	9	132	0
1961	Billy Atkins, Buffalo, AFL	10	158	0
	Dick Lynch, N.Y. Giants, NFL	9	60	0
1960	*Austin (Goose) Gonsoulin, Denver, AFL	11	98	0
	Dave Baker, San Francisco, NFL	10	96	0
	Jerry Norton, St. Louis, NFL	10	96	0
1959	Dean Derby, Pittsburgh	7	127	0
	Milt Davis, Baltimore	7	119	1
	Don Shinnick, Baltimore	7	70	0
1958	Jim Patton, N.Y. Giants	11	183	0
1957	Milt Davis, Baltimore	10	219	2
	Jack Christiansen, Detroit	10	137	1
	Jack Butler, Pittsburgh	10	85	0
1956	Linden Crow, Chi. Cardinals	11	170	0
1955	Will Sherman, Los Angeles	11	101	0
1954	Dick (Night Train) Lane, Chi. Cardinals	10	181	0
1953	Jack Christiansen, Detroit	12	238	1
1952	*Dick (Night Train) Lane, Los Angeles	14	298	2
1951	Otto Schnellbacher, N.Y. Giants	11	194	2
1950	Orban (Spec) Sanders, N.Y. Yanks	13	199	0
1949	Bob Nussbaumer, Chi. Cardinals	12	157	0
1948	*Dan Sandifer, Washington	13	258	2
1947	Frank Reagan, N.Y. Giants	10	203	0
	Frank Seno, Boston	10	100	0
1946	Bill Dudley, Pittsburgh	10	242	1
1945	Roy Zimmerman, Philadelphia	7	90	0

1944	*Howard Livingston, N.Y. Giants	9	172	1
1943	Sammy Baugh, Washington	11	112	0
1942	Clyde (Bulldog) Turner, Chi. Bears	8	96	1
1941	Marshall Goldberg, Chi. Cardinals	7	54	0
	*Art Jones, Pittsburgh	7	35	0
1940	Clarence (Ace) Parker, Brooklyn	6	146	1
	Kent Ryan, Detroit	6	65	0
	Don Hutson, Green Bay	6	24	0

First season of professional football.

ANNUAL PUNTING LEADERS

Year	Player, Team	No.	Avg.	Long
1994	Sean Landeta, L.A. Rams, NFC	78	44.8	62
	Jeff Gossett, L.A. Raiders, AFC	77	43.9	65
1993	Greg Montgomery, Houston, AFC	54	45.6	77
	Jim Arnold, Detroit, NFC	72	44.5	68
1992	Greg Montgomery, Houston, AFC	53	46.9	66
	Harry Newsome, Minnesota, NFC	72	45.0	84
1991	Reggie Roby, Miami, AFC	54	45.7	64
	Harry Newsome, Minnesota, AFC	68	45.5	65
1990	Mike Horan, Denver, AFC	58	44.4	67
	Sean Landeta, N.Y. Giants, NFC	75	44.1	67
1989	Rich Camarillo, Phoenix, NFC	76	43.4	58
	Greg Montgomery, Hounton, AFC	56	43.3	63
1988	Harry Newsome, Pittsburgh, AFC	65	45.4	62
	Jim Arnold, Detroit, NFC	97	42.4	69
1987	Rick Donnelly, Atlanta, NFC	61	44.0	62
	Ralf Mojsiejenko, San Diego, AFC	67	42.9	57
1986	Rohn Stark, Indianapolis, AFC	76	45.2	63
	Sean Landeta, N.Y. Giants, NFC	79	44.8	61
1985	Rohn Stark, Indianapolis, AFC	78	45.9	68
	*Rick Donnelly, Atlanta, NFC	59	43.6	68
1984	Jim Arnold, Kansas City, AFC	98	44.9	63
	*Brian Hansen, New Orleans, NFC	69	43.8	66
1983	Rohn Stark, Baltimore, AFC	91	45.3	68
	Frank Garcia, Tampa Bay, NFC	95	42.2	64
1982	Luke Prestridge, Denver, AFC	45	45.0	65
	Carl Birdsong, St. Louis, NFC	54	43.8	65
1981	Pat McInally, Cincinnati, AFC	72	45.4	62
	Tom Skladany, Detroit, NFC	64	43.5	74
1980	Dave Jennings, N.Y. Giants, NFC	94	44.8	63
	Luke Prestridge, Denver, AFC	70	43.9	57
1979	*Bob Grupp, Kansas City, AFC	89	43.6	74
	Dave Jennings, N.Y. Giants, NFC	104	42.7	72
1978	Pat McInally, Cincinnati, AFC	91	43.1	65
	*Tom Skladany, Detroit, NFC	86	42.5	63
1977	Ray Guy, Oakland, AFC	59	43.3	74
	Tom Blanchard, New Orleans, NFC	82	42.4	66
1976	Marv Bateman, Buffalo, AFC	86	42.8	78
	John James, Atlanta, NFC	101	42.1	67
1975	Ray Guy, Oakland, AFC	68	43.8	64
	Herman Weaver, Detroit, NFC	80	42.0	61
1974	Ray Guy, Oakland, AFC	74	42.2	66
	Tom Blanchard, New Orleans, NFC	88	42.1	71
1973	Jerrel Wilson, Kansas City, AFC	80	45.5	68
	*Tom Wittum, San Francisco, NFC	79	43.7	62
1972	Jerrel Wilson, Kansas City, AFC	66	44.8	69
	Dave Chapple, Los Angeles, NFC	53	44.2	70
1971	Dave Lewis, Cincinnati, AFC	72	44.8	56
	Tom McNeill, Philadelphia, NFC	73	42.0	64
1970	Dave Lewis, Cincinnati, AFC	79	46.2	63
	*Julian Fagan, New Orleans, NFC	77	42.5	64
1969	David Lee, Baltimore, NFL	57	45.3	66
	Dennis Partee, San Diego, AFL	71	44.6	62
1968	Jerrel Wilson, Kansas City, AFL	63	45.1	70
	Billy Lothridge, Atlanta, NFL	75	44.3	70
1967	Bob Scarpitto, Denver, AFL	105	44.9	73
	Billy Lothridge, Atlanta, NFL	87	43.7	62
1966	Bob Scarpitto, Denver, AFL	76	45.8	70
	*David Lee, Baltimore, NFL	49	45.6	64
1965	Gary Collins, Cleveland, NFL	65	46.7	71
	Jerrel Wilson, Kansas City, AFL	69	45.4	64
1964	Bobby Walden, Minnesota, NFL	72	46.4	73
	Jim Fraser, Denver, AFL	73	44.2	67
1963	Yale Lary, Detroit, NFL	35	48.9	73
	Jim Fraser, Denver, AFL	81	44.4	66
1962	Tommy Davis, San Francisco, NFL	48	45.6	82
	Jim Fraser, Denver, AFL	55	43.6	75
1961	Yale Lary, Detroit, NFL	52	48.4	71
	Billy Atkins, Buffalo, AFL	85	44.5	70
1960	Jerry Norton, St. Louis, NFL	39	45.6	62
	*Paul Maguire, L.A. Chargers, AFL	43	40.5	61
1959	Yale Lary, Detroit	45	47.1	67
1958	Sam Baker, Washington	48	45.4	64
1957	Don Chandler, N.Y. Giants	60	44.6	61
1956	Norm Van Brocklin, Los Angeles	48	43.1	72
1955	Norm Van Brocklin, Los Angeles	60	44.6	61
1954	Pat Brady, Pittsburgh	66	43.2	72
1953	Pat Brady, Pittsburgh	80	46.9	64
1952	Horace Gillom, Cleveland	61	45.7	73
1951	Horace Gillom, Cleveland	73	45.5	66
1950	*Fred (Curly) Morrison, Chi. Bears	57	43.3	65
1949	*Mike Boyda, N.Y. Bulldogs	56	44.2	61
1948	Joe Muha, Philadelphia	57	47.3	82
1947	Jack Jacobs, Green Bay	57	43.5	74
1946	Roy McKay, Green Bay	64	42.7	64
1945	Roy McKay, Green Bay	44	41.2	73
1944	Frank Sinkwich, Detroit	45	41.0	73
1943	Sammy Baugh, Washington	50	45.9	81
1942	Sammy Baugh, Washington	37	48.2	74
1941	Sammy Baugh, Washington	30	48.7	75
1940	Sammy Baugh, Washington	35	51.4	85
1939	*Parker Hall, Cleveland	58	40.8	80

First season of professional football.

ANNUAL PUNT RETURN LEADERS

Year	Player, Team	No.	Yards	Avg.	Long	TD
1994	Brian Mitchell, Washington, NFC	32	452	14.1	78	2
	Darrien Gordon, San Diego, AFC	36	475	13.2	90	2
1993	*Tyrone Hughes, New Orleans, NFC	37	503	13.6	83	2
	Eric Metcalf, Cleveland, AFC	36	464	12.9	91	2
1992	Johnny Bailey, Phoenix, NFC	20	263	13.2	65	0
	Rod Woodson, Pittsburgh, AFC	32	364	11.4	80	1
1991	Mel Gray, Detroit, NFC	25	385	15.4	78	1
	Rod Woodson, Pittsburgh, AFC	28	320	11.4	40	0
1990	Clarence Verdin, Indianapolis, AFC	31	396	12.8	36	0
	*Johnny Bailey, Chicago, NFC	36	399	11.1	95	1
1989	Walter Stanley, Detroit, NFC	36	496	13.8	74	0
	Clarence Verdin, Indianapolis, AFC	23	296	12.9	49	1
1988	John Taylor, San Francisco, NFC	44	556	12.6	95	2
	JoJo Townsell, N.Y. Jets, AFC	35	409	11.7	59	1
1987	Mel Gray, New Orleans, NFC	24	352	14.7	80	0
	Bobby Joe Edmonds, Seattle, AFC	20	251	12.6	40	0
1986	*Bobby Joe Edmonds, Seattle, AFC	34	419	12.3	75	1
	*Vai Sikahema, St. Louis, NFC	43	522	12.1	71	2
1985	Irving Fryar, New England, AFC	37	520	14.1	85	2
	Henry Ellard, L.A. Rams, NFC	37	501	13.5	80	1
1984	Mike Martin, Cincinnati, AFC	24	376	15.7	55	0
	Henry Ellard, L.A. Rams, NFC	30	403	13.4	83	2
1983	*Henry Ellard, L.A. Rams, NFC	16	217	13.6	72	1
	Kirk Springs, N.Y. Jets, AFC	23	287	12.5	76	1
1982	Rick Upchurch, Denver, AFC	15	242	16.1	78	2
	Billy Johnson, Atlanta, NFC	24	273	11.4	71	0
1981	LeRoy Irvin, Los Angeles, NFC	46	615	13.4	84	3
	*James Brooks, San Diego, AFC	22	290	13.2	42	0
1980	J.T. Smith, Kansas City, AFC	40	581	14.5	75	2
	*Kenny Johnson, Atlanta, NFC	23	281	12.2	56	0
1979	John Sciarra, Philadelphia, NFC	16	182	11.4	38	0
	*Tony Nathan, Miami, AFC	28	306	10.9	86	1
1978	Rick Upchurch, Denver, AFC	36	493	13.7	75	1
	Jackie Wallace, Los Angeles, NFC	52	618	11.9	58	0
1977	Billy Johnson, Houston, AFC	35	539	15.4	87	2
	Larry Marshall, Philadelphia, NFC	46	489	10.6	48	0
1976	Rick Upchurch, Denver, AFC	39	536	13.7	92	4
	Eddie Brown, Washington, NFC	48	646	13.5	71	1
1975	Billy Johnson, Houston, AFC	40	612	15.3	83	3
	Terry Metcalf, St. Louis, NFC	23	285	12.4	69	1
1974	Lemar Parrish, Cincinnati, AFC	18	338	18.8	90	2
	Dick Jauron, Detroit, NFC	17	286	16.8	58	0
1973	Bruce Taylor, San Francisco, NFC	15	207	13.8	61	0
	Ron Smith, San Diego, AFC	27	352	13.0	84	2
1972	Ken Ellis, Green Bay, NFC	14	215	15.4	80	1
	Chris Farasopoulos, N.Y. Jets, AFC	17	179	10.5	65	1
1971	Les (Speedy) Duncan, Washington, NFC	22	233	10.6	33	0
	Leroy Kelly, Cleveland, AFC	30	292	9.7	74	0
1970	Ed Podolak, Kansas City, AFC	23	311	13.5	60	0
	*Bruce Taylor, San Francisco, NFC	43	516	12.0	76	0
1969	Alvin Haymond, Los Angeles, NFL	33	435	13.2	52	0
	*Bill Thompson, Denver, AFL	25	288	11.5	40	0
1968	Bob Hayes, Dallas, NFL	15	312	20.8	90	2
	Noland Smith, Kansas City, AFL	18	270	15.0	80	1
1967	Floyd Little, Denver, AFL	16	270	16.9	72	1
	Ben Davis, Cleveland, NFL	18	229	12.7	52	1
1966	Les (Speedy) Duncan, San Diego, AFL	18	238	13.2	81	1
	Johnny Roland, St. Louis, NFL	20	221	11.1	86	1
1965	Leroy Kelly, Cleveland, NFL	17	265	15.6	67	2

YEARLY STATISTICAL LEADERS

Year	Player, Team	No.	Yards	Avg.	Long	TD
	Les (Speedy) Duncan, San Diego, AFL	30	464	15.5	66	2
1964	Bobby Jancik, Houston, AFL	12	220	18.3	82	1
	Tommy Watkins, Detroit, NFL	16	238	14.9	68	2
1963	Dick James, Washington, NFL	16	214	13.4	39	0
	Claude (Hoot) Gibson, Oakland, AFL	26	307	11.8	85	2
1962	Dick Christy, N.Y. Titans, AFL	15	250	16.7	73	2
	Pat Studstill, Detroit, NFL	29	457	15.8	44	0
1961	Dick Christy, N.Y. Titans, AFL	18	383	21.3	70	2
	Willie Wood, Green Bay, NFL	14	225	16.1	72	2
1960	*Abner Haynes, Dall. Texans, AFL	14	215	15.4	46	0
	Abe Woodson, San Francisco, NFL	13	174	13.4	48	0
1959	Johnny Morris, Chi. Bears	14	171	12.2	78	1
1958	Jon Arnett, Los Angeles	18	223	12.4	58	0
1957	Bert Zagers, Washington	14	217	15.5	76	2
1956	Ken Konz, Cleveland	13	187	14.4	65	1
1955	Ollie Matson, Chi. Cardinals	13	245	18.8	78	2
1954	*Veryl Switzer, Green Bay	24	306	12.8	93	1
1953	Charley Trippi, Chi. Cardinals	21	239	11.4	38	0
1952	Jack Christiansen, Detroit	15	322	21.5	79	2
1951	Claude (Buddy) Young, N.Y. Yanks	12	231	19.3	79	1
1950	*Herb Rich, Baltimore	12	276	23.0	86	1
1949	Verda (Vitamin T) Smith, Los Angeles	27	427	15.8	85	1
1948	George McAfee, Chi. Bears	30	417	13.9	60	1
1947	*Walt Slater, Pittsburgh	28	435	15.5	33	0
1946	Bill Dudley, Pittsburgh	27	385	14.3	52	0
1945	*Dave Ryan, Detroit	15	220	14.7	56	0
1944	*Steve Van Buren, Philadelphia	15	230	15.3	55	1
1943	Andy Farkas, Washington	15	168	11.2	33	0
1942	Merlyn Condit, Brooklyn	21	210	10.0	23	0
1941	Byron (Whizzer) White, Detroit	19	262	13.8	64	0

First season of professional football.

ANNUAL KICKOFF RETURN LEADERS

Year	Player, Team	No.	Yards	Avg.	Long	TD
1994	Mel Gray, Detroit, NFC	45	1,276	28.4	102	3
	Randy Baldwin, Cleveland, AFC	28	753	26.9	85	1
1993	Robert Brooks, Green Bay, NFC	23	611	26.6	95	1
	*Raghib Ismail, L.A. Raiders, AFC	25	605	24.2	66	0
1992	Jon Vaughn, New England, AFC	20	564	28.2	100	1
	Deion Sanders, Atlanta, NFC	40	1,067	26.7	99	2
1991	Mel Gray, Detroit, NFC	36	929	25.8	71	0
	Nate Lewis, San Diego, AFC	23	578	25.1	95	1
1990	Kevin Clark, Denver, AFC	20	505	25.3	75	0
	David Meggett, N.Y. Giants, NFC	21	492	23.4	58	0
1989	Rod Woodson, Pittsburgh, AFC	36	982	27.3	84	1
	Mel Gray, Detroit, NFC	24	640	26.7	57	0
1988	*Tim Brown, L.A. Raiders, AFC	41	1,098	26.8	97	1
	Donnie Elder, Tampa Bay, NFC	34	772	22.7	51	0
1987	Sylvester Stamps, Atlanta, NFC	24	660	27.5	97	1
	Paul Palmer, Kansas City, AFC	38	923	24.3	95	2
1986	Dennis Gentry, Chicago, NFC	20	576	28.8	91	1
	Lupe Sanchez, Pittsburgh, AFC	25	591	23.6	64	0
1985	Ron Brown, L.A. Rams, NFC	28	918	32.8	98	3
	Glen Young, Cleveland, AFC	35	898	25.7	63	0
1984	*Bobby Humphery, N.Y. Jets, AFC	22	675	30.7	97	1
	Barry Redden, L.A. Rams, NFC	23	530	23.0	40	0
1983	Fulton Walker, Miami, AFC	36	962	26.7	78	0
	Darrin Nelson, Minnesota, NFC	18	445	24.7	50	0
1982	*Mike Mosley, Buffalo, AFC	18	487	27.1	66	0
	Alvin Hall, Detroit, NFC	16	426	26.6	96	1
1981	Mike Nelms, Washington, NFC	37	1,099	29.7	84	0
	Carl Roaches, Houston, AFC	28	769	27.5	96	1
1980	Horace Ivory, New England, AFC	36	992	27.6	98	1
	Rich Mauti, New Orleans, NFC	31	798	25.7	52	0
1979	Larry Brunson, Oakland, AFC	17	441	25.9	89	0
	Jimmy Edwards, Minnesota, NFC	44	1,103	25.1	83	0
1978	Steve Odom, Green Bay, NFC	25	677	27.1	95	1
	*Keith Wright, Cleveland, AFC	30	789	26.3	86	0
1977	*Raymond Clayborn, New England, AFC	28	869	31.0	101	3
	*Wilbert Montgomery, Philadelphia, NFC	23	619	26.9	99	1
1976	*Duriel Harris, Miami, AFC	17	559	32.9	69	0
	Cullen Bryant, Los Angeles, NFC	16	459	28.7	90	1
1975	*Walter Payton, Chicago, NFC	14	444	31.7	70	0
	Harold Hart, Oakland, AFC	17	518	30.5	102	1
1974	Terry Metcalf, St. Louis, NFC	20	623	31.2	94	1
	Greg Pruitt, Cleveland, AFC	22	606	27.5	88	1
1973	Carl Garrett, Chicago, NFC	16	486	30.4	67	0
	*Wallace Francis, Buffalo, AFC	23	687	29.9	101	2
1972	Ron Smith, Chicago, NFC	30	924	30.8	94	1
	*Bruce Laird, Baltimore, AFC	29	843	29.1	73	0
1971	Travis Williams, Los Angeles, NFC	25	743	29.7	105	1
	Eugene (Mercury) Morris, Miami, AFC	15	423	28.2	94	1
1970	Jim Duncan, Baltimore, AFC	20	707	35.4	99	1
	Cecil Turner, Chicago, NFC	23	752	32.7	96	4
1969	Bobby Williams, Detroit, NFL	17	563	33.1	96	1
	*Bill Thompson, Denver, AFL	18	513	28.5	63	0
1968	Preston Pearson, Baltimore, NFL	15	527	35.1	102	2
	*George Atkinson, Oakland, AFL	32	802	25.1	60	0
1967	*Travis Williams, Green Bay, NFL	18	739	41.1	104	4
	*Zeke Moore, Houston, AFL	14	405	28.9	92	1
1966	Gale Sayers, Chicago, NFL	23	718	31.2	93	2
	*Goldie Sellers, Denver, AFL	19	541	28.5	100	2
1965	Tommy Watkins, Detroit, NFL	17	584	34.4	94	0
	Abner Haynes, Denver, AFL	34	901	26.5	60	0
1964	*Clarence Childs, N.Y. Giants, NFL	34	987	29.0	100	1
	Bo Roberson, Oakland, AFL	36	975	27.1	59	0
1963	Abe Woodson, San Francisco, NFL	29	935	32.2	103	3
	Bobby Jancik, Houston, AFL	45	1,317	29.3	53	0
1962	Abe Woodson, San Francisco, NFL	37	1,157	31.3	79	0
	*Bobby Jancik, Houston, AFL	24	826	30.3	61	0
1961	Dick Bass, Los Angeles, NFL	23	698	30.3	64	0
	*Dave Grayson, Dall. Texans, AFL	16	453	28.3	73	0
1960	*Tom Moore, Green Bay, NFL	12	397	33.1	84	0
	Ken Hall, Houston, AFL	19	594	31.3	104	1
1959	Abe Woodson, San Francisco	13	382	29.4	105	1
1958	Ollie Matson, Chi. Cardinals	14	497	35.5	101	2
1957	*Jon Arnett, Los Angeles	18	504	28.0	98	1
1956	*Tom Wilson, Los Angeles	15	477	31.8	103	1
1955	Al Carmichael, Green Bay	14	418	29.9	100	1
1954	Billy Reynolds, Cleveland	14	413	29.5	51	0
1953	Joe Arenas, San Francisco	16	551	34.4	82	0
1952	Lynn Chandnois, Pittsburgh	17	599	35.2	93	2
1951	Lynn Chandnois, Pittsburgh	12	390	32.5	55	0
1950	Verda (Vitamin T) Smith, Los Angeles	22	742	33.7	97	3
1949	*Don Doll, Detroit	21	536	25.5	56	0
1948	*Joe Scott, N.Y. Giants	20	569	28.5	99	1
1947	Eddie Saenz, Washington	29	797	27.5	94	2
1946	Abe Karnofsky, Boston	21	599	28.5	97	1
1945	Steve Van Buren, Philadelphia	13	373	28.7	98	1
1944	Bob Thurbon, Card.-Pitt.	12	291	24.3	55	0
1943	Ken Heineman, Brooklyn	16	444	27.8	69	0
1942	Marshall Goldberg, Chi. Cardinals	15	393	26.2	95	1
1941	Marshall Goldberg, Chi. Cardinals	12	290	24.2	41	0

First season of professional football.

ANNUAL LEADERS IN SACKS (SINCE 1982)

Year	Player, Team	Sacks
1994	Kevin Greene, Pittsburgh, AFC	14
	Ken Harvey, Washington, NFC	13.5
1993	Neil Smith, Kansas City, AFC	15
	Renaldo Turnbull, New Orleans, NFC	13
	Reggie White, Green Bay, NFC	13
1992	Clyde Simmons, Philadelphia, NFC	19
	Leslie O'Neal, San Diego, AFC	17
1991	Pat Swilling, New Orleans, NFC	17
	William Fuller, Houston, AFC	15
1990	Derrick Thomas, Kansas City, AFC	20
	Charles Haley, San Francisco, NFC	16
1989	Chris Doleman, Minnesota, NFC	21
	Lee Williams, San Diego, AFC	14
1988	Reggie White, Philadelphia, NFC	18
	G. Townsend, L.A. Raiders, AFC	11.5
1987	Reggie White, Philadelphia, NFC	21
	Andre Tippett, New England, AFC	12.5
1986	Lawrence Taylor, N.Y. Giants, NFC	20.5
	Sean Jones, L.A. Raiders, AFC	15.5
1985	Richard Dent, Chicago, NFC	17
	Andre Tippett, New England, AFC	16.5
1984	Mark Gastineau, N.Y. Jets, AFC	22
	Richard Dent, Chicago, NFC	17.5
1983	Mark Gastineau, N.Y. Jets, AFC	19
	Fred Dean, San Francisco, NFC	17.5
1982	Doug Martin, Minnesota, NFC	11.5
	Jesse Baker, Houston, AFC	7.5

POINTS SCORED

Year	Team	Points
1994	San Francisco, NFC	505
	Miami, AFC	389
1993	San Francisco, NFC	473
	Denver, AFC	373
1992	San Francisco, NFC	431
	Buffalo, AFC	381
1991	Washington, NFC	485
	Buffalo, AFC	458
1990	Buffalo, AFC	428
	Philadelphia, NFC	396
1989	San Francisco, NFC	442
	Buffalo, AFC	409
1988	Cincinnati, AFC	448
	L.A. Rams, NFC	407
1987	San Francisco, NFC	459
	Cleveland, AFC	390
1986	Miami, AFC	430
	Minnesota, NFC	398
1985	San Diego, AFC	467
	Chicago, NFC	456
1984	Miami, AFC	513
	San Francisco, NFC	475
1983	Washington, NFC	541
	L.A. Raiders, AFC	442
1982	San Diego, AFC	288
	Dallas, NFC	226
	Green Bay, NFC	226
1981	San Diego, AFC	478
	Atlanta, NFC	426
1980	Dallas, NFC	454
	New England, AFC	441
1979	Pittsburgh, AFC	416
	Dallas, NFC	371
1978	Dallas, NFC	384
	Miami, AFC	372
1977	Oakland, AFC	351
	Dallas, NFC	345
1976	Baltimore, AFC	417
	Los Angeles, NFC	351
1975	Buffalo, AFC	420
	Minnesota, NFC	377
1974	Oakland, AFC	355
	Washington, NFC	320
1973	Los Angeles, NFC	388
	Denver, AFC	354
1972	Miami, AFC	385
	San Francisco, NFC	353
1971	Dallas, NFC	406
	Oakland, AFC	344
1970	San Francisco, NFC	352
	Baltimore, AFC	321
1969	Minnesota, NFL	379
	Oakland, AFL	377
1968	Oakland, AFL	453
	Dallas, NFL	431
1967	Oakland, AFL	468
	Los Angeles, NFL	398
1966	Kansas City, AFL	448
	Dallas, NFL	445
1965	San Francisco, NFL	421
	San Diego, AFL	340
1964	Baltimore, NFL	428
	Buffalo, AFL	400
1963	N.Y. Giants, NFL	448
	San Diego, AFL	399
1962	Green Bay, NFL	415
	Dall. Texans, AFL	389
1961	Houston, AFL	513
	Green Bay, NFL	391
1960	N.Y. Titans, AFL	382
	Cleveland, NFL	362
1959	Baltimore	374
1958	Baltimore	381
1957	Los Angeles	307
1956	Chi. Bears	363
1955	Cleveland	349
1954	Detroit	337
1953	San Francisco	372
1952	Los Angeles	349
1951	Los Angeles	392
1950	Los Angeles	466
1949	Philadelphia	364
1948	Chi. Cardinals	395
1947	Chi. Bears	363
1946	Chi. Bears	289
1945	Philadelphia	272
1944	Philadelphia	267
1943	Chi. Bears	303
1942	Chi. Bears	376
1941	Chi. Bears	396
1940	Washington	245
1939	Chi. Bears	298
1938	Green Bay	223
1937	Green Bay	220
1936	Green Bay	248
1935	Chi. Bears	192
1934	Chi. Bears	286
1933	N.Y. Giants	244
1932	Chicago Bears	160

TOTAL YARDS GAINED

Year	Team	Yards
1994	Miami, AFC	6,078
	San Francisco, NFC	6,060
1993	San Francisco, NFC	6,435
	Miami, AFC	5,812
1992	San Francisco, NFC	6,195
	Buffalo, AFC	5,893
1991	Buffalo, AFC	6,252
	San Francisco, NFC	5,858
1990	Houston, AFC	6,222
	San Francisco, NFC	5,895
1989	San Francisco, NFC	6,268
	Cincinnati, AFC	6,101
1988	Cincinnati, AFC	6,057
	San Francisco, NFC	5,900
1987	San Francisco, NFC	5,987
	Denver, AFC	5,624
1986	Cincinnati, AFC	6,490
	San Francisco, NFC	6,082
1985	San Diego, AFC	6,535
	San Francisco, NFC	5,920
1984	Miami, AFC	6,936
	San Francisco, NFC	6,366
1983	San Diego, AFC	6,197
	Green Bay, NFC	6,172
1982	San Diego, AFC	4,048
	San Francisco, NFC	3,242
1981	San Diego, AFC	6,744
	Detroit, NFC	5,933
1980	San Diego, AFC	6,410
	Los Angeles, NFC	6,006
1979	Pittsburgh, AFC	6,258
	Dallas, NFC	5,968
1978	New England, AFC	5,965
	Dallas, NFC	5,959
1977	Dallas, NFC	4,812
	Oakland, AFC	4,736
1976	Baltimore, AFC	5,236
	St. Louis, NFC	5,136
1975	Buffalo, AFC	5,467
	Dallas, NFC	5,025
1974	Dallas, NFC	4,983
	Oakland, AFC	4,718
1973	Los Angeles, NFC	4,906
	Oakland, AFC	4,773
1972	Miami, AFC	5,036
	N.Y. Giants, NFC	4,483
1971	Dallas, NFC	5,035
	San Diego, AFC	4,738
1970	Oakland, AFC	4,829
	San Francisco, NFC	4,503
1969	Dallas, NFL	5,122
	Oakland, AFL	5,036
1968	Oakland, AFL	5,696
	Dallas, NFL	5,117
1967	N.Y. Jets, AFL	5,152
	Baltimore, NFL	5,008
1966	Dallas, NFL	5,145
	Kansas City, AFL	5,114
1965	San Francisco, NFL	5,270
	San Diego, AFL	5,188
1964	Buffalo, AFL	5,206
	Baltimore, NFL	4,779
1963	San Diego, AFL	5,153
	N.Y. Giants, NFL	5,024
1962	N.Y. Giants, NFL	5,005
	Houston, AFL	4,971
1961	Houston, AFL	6,288
	Philadelphia, NFL	5,112
1960	Houston, AFL	4,936
	Baltimore, NFL	4,245
1959	Baltimore	4,458
1958	Baltimore	4,539
1957	Los Angeles	4,143
1956	Chi. Bears	4,537
1955	Chi. Bears	4,316
1954	Los Angeles	5,187
1953	Philadelphia	4,811
1952	Cleveland	4,352
1951	Los Angeles	5,506
1950	Los Angeles	5,420
1949	Chi. Bears	4,873
1948	Chi. Cardinals	4,705
1947	Chi. Bears	5,053
1946	Los Angeles	3,793
1945	Washington	3,549
1944	Chi. Bears	3,239
1943	Chi. Bears	4,045
1942	Chi. Bears	3,900
1941	Chi. Bears	4,265
1940	Green Bay	3,400
1939	Chi. Bears	3,988
1938	Green Bay	3,037
1937	Green Bay	3,201
1936	Detroit	3,703
1935	Chi. Bears	3,454
1934	Chi. Bears	3,900
1933	N.Y. Giants	2,973
1932	Chi. Bears	2,755

YARDS RUSHING

Year	Team	Yards
1994	Pittsburgh, AFC	2,180
	Detroit, NFC	2,080
1993	N.Y. Giants, NFC	2,210
	Seattle, AFC	2,015
1992	Buffalo, AFC	2,436
	Philadelphia, NFC	2,388
1991	Buffalo, AFC	2,381
	Minnesota, NFC	2,201
1990	Philadelphia, NFC	2,556
	San Diego, AFC	2,257
1989	Cincinnati, AFC	2,483
	Chicago, NFC	2,287
1988	Cincinnati, AFC	2,710
	San Francisco, NFC	2,523
1987	San Francisco, NFC	2,237
	L.A. Raiders, AFC	2,197
1986	Chicago, NFC	2,700
	Cincinnati, AFC	2,533
1985	Chicago, NFC	2,761
	Indianapolis, AFC	2,439
1984	Chicago, NFC	2,974
	N.Y. Jets, AFC	2,189
1983	Chicago, NFC	2,727
	Baltimore, AFC	2,695
1982	Buffalo, AFC	1,371
	Dallas, NFC	1,313
1981	Detroit, NFC	2,795
	Kansas City, AFC	2,633
1980	Los Angeles, NFC	2,799
	Houston, AFC	2,635
1979	N.Y. Jets, AFC	2,646
	St. Louis, NFC	2,582
1978	New England, AFC	3,165
	Dallas, NFC	2,783
1977	Chicago, NFC	2,811
	Oakland, AFC	2,627
1976	Pittsburgh, AFC	2,971
	Los Angeles, NFC	2,528
1975	Buffalo, AFC	2,974
	Dallas, NFC	2,432
1974	Dallas, NFC	2,454
	Pittsburgh, AFC	2,417
1973	Buffalo, AFC	3,088
	Los Angeles, NFC	2,925
1972	Miami, AFC	2,960
	Chicago, NFC	2,360
1971	Miami, AFC	2,429
	Detroit, NFC	2,376
1970	Dallas, NFC	2,300
	Miami, AFC	2,082
1969	Dallas, NFL	2,276
	Kansas City, AFL	2,220
1968	Chicago, NFL	2,377
	Kansas City, AFL	2,227
1967	Cleveland, NFL	2,139
	Houston, AFL	2,122
1966	Kansas City, AFL	2,274
	Cleveland, NFL	2,166
1965	Cleveland, NFL	2,331
	San Diego, AFL	2,085
1964	Green Bay, NFL	2,276
	Buffalo, AFL	2,040
1963	Cleveland, NFL	2,639
	San Diego, AFL	2,203
1962	Buffalo, AFL	2,480
	Green Bay, NFL	2,460
1961	Green Bay, NFL	2,350
	Dall. Texans, AFL	2,189
1960	St. Louis, NFL	2,356
	Oakland, AFL	2,056
1959	Cleveland	2,149
1958	Cleveland	2,526
1957	Los Angeles	2,142
1956	Chi. Bears	2,468
1955	Chi. Bears	2,388
1954	San Francisco	2,498
1953	San Francisco	2,230
1952	San Francisco	1,905
1951	Chi. Bears	2,408
1950	N.Y. Giants	2,336
1949	Philadelphia	2,607
1948	Chi. Cardinals	2,560
1947	Los Angeles	2,171
1946	Green Bay	1,765
1945	Cleveland	1,714
1944	Philadelphia	1,661
1943	Phil-Pitt	1,730
1942	Chi. Bears	1,881
1941	Chi. Bears	2,263
1940	Chi. Bears	1,818
1939	Chi. Bears	2,043
1938	Detroit	1,893
1937	Detroit	2,074
1936	Detroit	2,885
1935	Chi. Bears	2,096
1934	Chi. Bears	2,847
1933	Boston	2,260
1932	Chi. Bears	1,770

YARDS PASSING

Leadership in this category has been based on net yards since 1952.

Year	Team	Yards
1994	New England, AFC	4,444
	Minnesota, NFC	4,324
1993	Miami, AFC	4,353
	San Francisco, NFC	4,302
1992	Houston, AFC	4,029
	San Francisco, NFC	3,880
1991	Houston, AFC	4,621
	San Francisco, NFC	3,997
1990	Houston, AFC	4,805
	San Francisco, NFC	4,177
1989	Washington, NFC	4,349
	Miami, AFC	4,216
1988	Miami, AFC	4,516
	Washington, NFC	4,136
1987	Miami, AFC	3,876
	San Francisco, NFC	3,750
1986	Miami, AFC	4,779
	San Francisco, NFC	4,096
1985	San Diego, AFC	4,870
	Dallas, NFC	3,861
1984	Miami, AFC	5,018
	St. Louis, NFC	4,257
1983	San Diego, AFC	4,661
	Green Bay, NFC	4,365

YEARLY STATISTICAL LEADERS

Year	Team	Yards
1982	San Diego, AFC	2,927
	San Francisco, NFC	2,502
1981	San Diego, AFC	4,739
	Minnesota, NFC	4,333
1980	San Diego, AFC	4,531
	Minnesota, NFC	3,688
1979	San Diego, AFC	3,915
	San Francisco, NFC	3,641
1978	San Diego, AFC	3,375
	Minnesota, NFC	3,243
1977	Buffalo, AFC	2,530
	St. Louis, NFC	2,499
1976	Baltimore, AFC	2,933
	Minnesota, NFC	2,855
1975	Cincinnati, AFC	3,241
	Washington, NFC	2,917
1974	Washington, NFC	2,978
	Cincinnati, AFC	2,804
1973	Philadelphia, NFC	2,998
	Denver, AFC	2,519
1972	N.Y. Jets, AFC	2,777
	San Francisco, NFC	2,735
1971	San Diego, AFC	3,134
	Dallas, NFC	2,786
1970	San Francisco, NFC	2,923
	Oakland, AFC	2,865
1969	Oakland, AFL	3,271
	San Francisco, NFL	3,158
1968	San Diego, AFL	3,623
	Dallas, NFL	3,026
1967	N.Y. Jets, AFL	3,845
	Washington, NFL	3,730
1966	N.Y. Jets, AFL	3,464
	Dallas, NFL	3,023
1965	San Francisco, NFL	3,487
	San Diego, AFL	3,103
1964	Houston, AFL	3,527
	Chicago, NFL	2,841
1963	Baltimore, NFL	3,296
	Houston, AFL	3,222
1962	Denver, AFL	3,404
	Philadelphia, NFL	3,385
1961	Houston, AFL	4,392
	Philadelphia, NFL	3,605
1960	Houston, AFL	3,203
	Baltimore, NFL	2,956
1959	Baltimore	2,753
1958	Pittsburgh	2,752
1957	Baltimore	2,388
1956	Los Angeles	2,419
1955	Philadelphia	2,472
1954	Chi. Bears	3,104
1953	Philadelphia	3,089
1952	Cleveland	2,566
1951	Los Angeles	3,296
1950	Los Angeles	3,709
1949	Chi. Bears	3,055
1948	Washington	2,861
1947	Washington	3,336
1946	Los Angeles	2,080
1945	Chi. Bears	1,857
1944	Washington	2,021
1943	Chi. Bears	2,310
1942	Green Bay	2,407
1941	Chi. Bears	2,002
1940	Washington	1,887
1939	Chi. Bears	1,965
1938	Washington	1,536
1937	Green Bay	1,398
1936	Green Bay	1,629
1935	Green Bay	1,449
1934	Green Bay	1,165
1933	N.Y. Giants	1,348
1932	Chi. Bears	1,013

FEWEST POINTS ALLOWED

Year	Team	Points
1994	Cleveland, AFC	204
	Dallas, NFC	248
1993	N.Y. Giants, NFC	205
	Houston, AFC	238
1992	New Orleans, NFC	202
	Pittsburgh, AFC	225
1991	New Orleans, NFC	211
	Denver, AFC	235
1990	N.Y. Giants, NFC	211
	Pittsburgh, AFC	240
1989	Denver, AFC	226
	N.Y. Giants, NFC	252
1988	Chicago, NFC	215
	Buffalo, AFC	237
1987	Indianapolis, AFC	238
	San Francisco, NFC	253
1986	Chicago, NFC	187
	Seattle, AFC	293
1985	Chicago, NFC	198
	N.Y. Jets, AFC	264
1984	San Francisco, NFC	227
	Denver, AFC	241
1983	Miami, AFC	250
	Detroit, NFC	286
1982	Washington, NFC	128
	Miami, AFC	131
1981	Philadelphia, NFC	221
	Miami, AFC	275
1980	Philadelphia, NFC	222
	Houston, AFC	251
1979	Tampa Bay, NFC	237
	San Diego, AFC	246
1978	Pittsburgh, AFC	195
	Dallas, NFC	208
1977	Atlanta, NFC	129
	Denver, AFC	148
1976	Pittsburgh, AFC	138
	Minnesota, NFC	176
1975	Los Angeles, NFC	135
	Pittsburgh, AFC	162
1974	Los Angeles, NFC	181
	Pittsburgh, AFC	189
1973	Miami, AFC	150
	Minnesota, NFC	168
1972	Miami, AFC	171
	Washington, NFC	218
1971	Minnesota, NFC	139
	Baltimore, AFC	140
1970	Minnesota, NFC	143
	Miami, AFC	228
1969	Minnesota, NFL	133
	Kansas City, AFL	177
1968	Baltimore, NFL	144
	Kansas City, AFL	170
1967	Los Angeles, NFL	196
	Houston, AFL	199
1966	Green Bay, NFL	163
	Buffalo, AFL	255
1965	Green Bay, NFL	224
	Buffalo, AFL	226
1964	Baltimore, NFL	225
	Buffalo, AFL	242
1963	Chicago, NFL	144
	San Diego, AFL	255
1962	Green Bay, NFL	148
	Dall. Texans, AFL	233
1961	San Diego, AFL	219
	N.Y. Giants, NFL	220
1960	San Francisco, NFL	205
	Dall. Texans, AFL	253
1959	N.Y. Giants	170
1958	N.Y. Giants	183
1957	Cleveland	172
1956	Cleveland	177
1955	Cleveland	218
1954	Cleveland	162
1953	Cleveland	162
1952	Detroit	192
1951	Cleveland	152
1950	Philadelphia	141
1949	Philadelphia	134
1948	Chi. Bears	151
1947	Green Bay	210
1946	Pittsburgh	117
1945	Washington	121
1944	N.Y. Giants	75
1943	Washington	137
1942	Chi. Bears	84
1941	N.Y. Giants	114
1940	Brooklyn	120
1939	N.Y. Giants	85
1938	N.Y. Giants	79
1937	Chi. Bears	100
1936	Chi. Bears	94
1935	Green Bay	96
	N.Y. Giants	96
1934	Detroit	59
1933	Brooklyn	54
1932	Chi. Bears	44

FEWEST TOTAL YARDS ALLOWED

Year	Team	Yards
1994	Dallas, NFC	4,313
	Pittsburgh, AFC	4,326
1993	Minnesota, NFC	4,406
	Pittsburgh, AFC	4,531
1992	Dallas, NFC	3,931
	Houston, AFC	4,211
1991	Philadelphia, NFC	3,549
	Denver, AFC	4,549
1990	Pittsburgh, AFC	4,115
	N.Y. Giants, NFC	4,206
1989	Minnesota, NFC	4,184
	Kansas City, AFC	4,293
1988	Minnesota, NFC	4,091
	Buffalo, AFC	4,578
1987	San Francisco, NFC	4,095
	Cleveland, AFC	4,264
1986	Chicago, NFC	4,130
	L.A. Raiders, AFC	4,804
1985	Chicago, NFC	4,135
	L.A. Raiders, AFC	4,603
1984	Chicago, NFC	3,863
	Cleveland, AFC	4,641
1983	Cincinnati, AFC	4,327
	New Orleans, NFC	4,691
1982	Miami, AFC	2,312
	Tampa Bay, NFC	2,442
1981	Philadelphia, NFC	4,447
	N.Y. Jets, AFC	4,871
1980	Buffalo, AFC	4,101
	Philadelphia, NFC	4,443
1979	Tampa Bay, NFC	3,949
	Pittsburgh, AFC	4,270
1978	Los Angeles, NFC	3,893
	Pittsburgh, AFC	4,168
1977	Dallas, NFC	3,213
	New England, AFC	3,638
1976	Pittsburgh, AFC	3,323
	San Francisco, NFC	3,562
1975	Minnesota, NFC	3,153
	Oakland, AFC	3,629
1974	Pittsburgh, AFC	3,074
	Washington, NFC	3,285
1973	Los Angeles, NFC	2,951
	Oakland, AFC	3,160
1972	Miami, AFC	3,297
	Green Bay, NFC	3,474
1971	Baltimore, AFC	2,852
	Minnesota, NFC	3,406
1970	Minnesota, NFC	2,803
	N.Y. Jets, AFC	3,655
1969	Minnesota, NFL	2,720
	Kansas City, AFL	3,163
1968	Los Angeles, NFL	3,118
	N.Y. Jets, AFL	3,363
1967	Oakland, AFL	3,294
	Green Bay, NFL	3,300
1966	St. Louis, NFL	3,492
	Oakland, AFL	3,910
1965	San Diego, AFL	3,262
	Detroit, NFL	3,557
1964	Green Bay, NFL	3,179
	Buffalo, AFL	3,878
1963	Chicago, NFL	3,176
	Boston, AFL	3,834
1962	Detroit, NFL	3,217
	Dall. Texans, AFL	3,951
1961	San Diego, AFL	3,726
	Baltimore, NFL	3,782
1960	St. Louis, NFL	3,029
	Buffalo, AFL	3,866
1959	N.Y. Giants	2,843
1958	Chi. Bears	3,066
1957	Pittsburgh	2,791
1956	N.Y. Giants	3,081
1955	Cleveland	2,841
1954	Cleveland	2,658
1953	Philadelphia	2,998
1952	Cleveland	3,075
1951	N.Y. Giants	3,250
1950	Cleveland	3,154
1949	Philadelphia	2,831
1948	Chi. Bears	2,931
1947	Green Bay	3,396
1946	Washington	2,451
1945	Philadelphia	2,073
1944	Philadelphia	1,943
1943	Chi. Bears	2,262
1942	Chi. Bears	1,703
1941	N.Y. Giants	2,368
1940	N.Y. Giants	2,219
1939	Washington	2,116
1938	N.Y. Giants	2,029
1937	Washington	2,123
1936	Boston	2,181
1935	Boston	1,996
1934	Chi. Cardinals	1,539
1933	Brooklyn	1,789

FEWEST RUSHING YARDS ALLOWED

Year	Team	Yards
1994	Minnesota, NFC	1,090
	San Diego, AFC	1,404
1993	Houston, AFC	1,273
	Minnesota, NFC	1,536
1992	Dallas, NFC	1,244
	Buffalo, AFC	1,395
	San Diego, AFC	1,395
1991	Philadelphia, NFC	1,136
	N.Y. Jets, AFC	1,442
1990	Philadelphia, NFC	1,169
	San Diego, AFC	1,515
1989	New Orleans, NFC	1,326
	Denver, AFC	1,580
1988	Chicago, NFC	1,326
	Houston, AFC	1,592
1987	Chicago, NFC	1,413
	Cleveland, AFC	1,433
1986	N.Y. Giants, NFC	1,284
	Denver, AFC	1,651
1985	Chicago, NFC	1,319
	N.Y. Jets, AFC	1,516
1984	Chicago, NFC	1,377
	Pittsburgh, AFC	1,617
1983	Washington, NFC	1,289
	Cincinnati, AFC	1,499
1982	Pittsburgh, AFC	762
	Detroit, NFC	854
1981	Detroit, NFC	1,623
	Kansas City, AFC	1,747
1980	Detroit, NFC	1,599
	Cincinnati, AFC	1,680
1979	Denver, AFC	1,693
	Tampa Bay, NFC	1,873
1978	Dallas, NFC	1,721
	Pittsburgh, AFC	1,774
1977	Denver, AFC	1,531
	Dallas, NFC	1,651
1976	Pittsburgh, AFC	1,457
	Los Angeles, NFC	1,564
1975	Minnesota, NFC	1,532
	Houston, AFC	1,680
1974	Los Angeles, NFC	1,302
	New England, AFC	1,587
1973	Los Angeles, NFC	1,270
	Oakland, AFC	1,470
1972	Dallas, NFC	1,515
	Miami, AFC	1,548
1971	Baltimore, AFC	1,113
	Dallas, NFC	1,144
1970	Detroit, NFC	1,152

Year	Team	Yards
	N.Y. Jets, AFC	1,283
1969	Dallas, NFL	1,050
	Kansas City, AFL	1,091
1968	Dallas, NFL	1,195
	N.Y. Jets, AFL	1,195
1967	Dallas, NFL	1,081
	Oakland, AFL	1,129
1966	Buffalo, AFL	1,051
	Dallas, NFL	1,176
1965	San Diego, AFL	1,094
	Los Angeles, NFL	1,409
1964	Buffalo, AFL	913
	Los Angeles, NFL	1,501
1963	Boston, AFL	1,107
	Chicago, NFL	1,442
1962	Detroit, NFL	1,231
	Dall. Texans, AFL	1,250
1961	Boston, AFL	1,041
	Pittsburgh, NFL	1,463
1960	St. Louis, NFL	1,212
	Dall. Texans, AFL	1,338
1959	N.Y. Giants	1,261
1958	Baltimore	1,291
1957	Baltimore	1,174
1956	N.Y. Giants	1,443
1955	Cleveland	1,189
1954	Cleveland	1,050
1953	Philadelphia	1,117
1952	Detroit	1,145
1951	N.Y. Giants	913
1950	Detroit	1,367
1949	Chi. Bears	1,196
1948	Philadelphia	1,209
1947	Philadelphia	1,329
1946	Chi. Bears	1,060
1945	Philadelphia	817
1944	Philadelphia	558
1943	Phil-Pitt	793
1942	Chi. Bears	519
1941	Washington	1,042
1940	N.Y. Giants	977
1939	Chi. Bears	812
1938	Detroit	1,081
1937	Chi. Bears	933
1936	Boston	1,148
1935	Boston	998
1934	Chi. Cardinals	954
1933	Brooklyn	964

FEWEST PASSING YARDS ALLOWED

Leadership in this category has been based on net yards since 1952.

Year	Team	Yards
1994	Dallas, NFC	2,752
	Houston, AFC	2,795
1993	New Orleans, NFC	2,606
	Cincinnati, AFC	2,798
1992	New Orleans, NFC	2,470
	Kansas City, AFC	2,537
1991	Philadelphia, NFC	2,413
	Denver, AFC	2,755
1990	Pittsburgh, AFC	2,500
	Dallas, NFC	2,639
1989	Minnesota, NFC	2,501
	Kansas City, AFC	2,527
1988	Kansas City, AFC	2,434
	Minnesota, NFC	2,489
1987	San Francisco, NFC	2,484
	L.A. Raiders, AFC	2,727
1986	St. Louis, NFC	2,637
	New England, AFC	2,978
1985	Washington, NFC	2,746
	Pittsburgh, AFC	2,783
1984	New Orleans, NFC	2,453
	Cleveland, AFC	2,696
1983	New Orleans, NFC	2,691
	Cincinnati, AFC	2,828
1982	Miami, AFC	1,027
	Tampa Bay, NFC	1,384
1981	Philadelphia, NFC	2,696
	Buffalo, AFC	2,870
1980	Washington, NFC	2,171
	Buffalo, AFC	2,282
1979	Tampa Bay, NFC	2,076
	Buffalo, AFC	2,530
1978	Buffalo, AFC	1,960
	Los Angeles, NFC	2,048
1977	Atlanta, NFC	1,384
	San Diego, AFC	1,725
1976	Minnesota, NFC	1,575
	Cincinnati, AFC	1,758
1975	Minnesota, NFC	1,621
	Cincinnati, AFC	1,729
1974	Pittsburgh, AFC	1,466
	Atlanta, NFC	1,572
1973	Miami, AFC	1,290
	Atlanta, NFC	1,430
1972	Minnesota, NFC	1,699
	Cleveland, AFC	1,736
1971	Atlanta, NFC	1,638
	Baltimore, AFC	1,739
1970	Minnesota, NFC	1,438
	Kansas City, AFC	2,010
1969	Minnesota, NFL	1,631
	Kansas City, AFL	2,072
1968	Houston, AFL	1,671
	Green Bay, NFL	1,796
1967	Green Bay, NFL	1,377
	Buffalo, AFL	1,825
1966	Green Bay, NFL	1,959
	Oakland, AFL	2,118
1965	Green Bay, NFL	1,981
	San Diego, AFL	2,168
1964	Green Bay, NFL	1,647
	San Diego, AFL	2,518
1963	Chicago, NFL	1,734
	Oakland, AFL	2,589
1962	Green Bay, NFL	1,746
	Oakland, AFL	2,306
1961	Baltimore, NFL	1,913
	San Diego, AFL	2,363
1960	Chicago, NFL	1,388
	Buffalo, AFL	2,124
1959	N.Y. Giants	1,582
1958	Chi. Bears	1,769
1957	Cleveland	1,300
1956	Cleveland	1,103
1955	Pittsburgh	1,295
1954	Cleveland	1,608
1953	Washington	1,751
1952	Washington	1,580
1951	Pittsburgh	1,687
1950	Cleveland	1,581
1949	Philadelphia	1,607
1948	Green Bay	1,626
1947	Green Bay	1,790
1946	Pittsburgh	939
1945	Washington	1,121
1944	Chi. Bears	1,052
1943	Chi. Bears	980
1942	Washington	1,093
1941	Pittsburgh	1,168
1940	Philadelphia	1,012
1939	Washington	1,116
1938	Chi. Bears	897
1937	Detroit	804
1936	Philadelphia	853
1935	Chi. Cardinals	793
1934	Philadelphia	545
1933	Portsmouth	558

SUPER BOWL RECORDS

Compiled by Elias Sports Bureau

1967: Super Bowl I	1977: Super Bowl XI	1987: Super Bowl XXI
1968: Super Bowl II	1978: Super Bowl XII	1988: Super Bowl XXII
1969: Super Bowl III	1979: Super Bowl XIII	1989: Super Bowl XXIII
1970: Super Bowl IV	1980: Super Bowl XIV	1990: Super Bowl XXIV
1971: Super Bowl V	1981: Super Bowl XV	1991: Super Bowl XXV
1972: Super Bowl VI	1982: Super Bowl XVI	1992: Super Bowl XXVI
1973: Super Bowl VII	1983: Super Bowl XVII	1993: Super Bowl XXVII
1974: Super Bowl VIII	1984: Super Bowl XVIII	1994: Super Bowl XXVIII
1975: Super Bowl IX	1985: Super Bowl XIX	1995: Super Bowl XXIX
1976: Super Bowl X	1986: Super Bowl XX	

INDIVIDUAL RECORDS

SERVICE

Most Games

5 Marv Fleming, Green Bay, 1967-68; Miami, 1972-74
Larry Cole, Dallas, 1971-72, 1976, 1978-79
Cliff Harris, Dallas, 1971-72, 1976, 1978-79
D.D. Lewis, Dallas, 1971-72, 1976, 1978-79
Preston Pearson, Baltimore, 1969; Pittsburgh, 1975; Dallas, 1976, 1978-79
Charlie Waters, Dallas, 1971-72, 1976, 1978-79
Rayfield Wright, Dallas, 1971-72, 1976, 1978-79
4 By many players

Most Games, Winning Team

4 By many players

Most Games, Coach

6 Don Shula, Baltimore, 1969; Miami, 1972-74, 1983, 1985
5 Tom Landry, Dallas, 1971-72, 1976, 1978-79
4 Bud Grant, Minnesota, 1970, 1974-75, 1977
Chuck Noll, Pittsburgh, 1975-76, 1979-80
Joe Gibbs, Washington, 1983-84, 1988, 1992
Marv Levy, Buffalo, 1991-94

Most Games, Winning Team, Coach

4 Chuck Noll, Pittsburgh, 1975-76, 1979-80
3 Bill Walsh, San Francisco, 1982, 1985, 1989
Joe Gibbs, Washington, 1983, 1988, 1992
2 Vince Lombardi, Green Bay, 1967-68
Tom Landry, Dallas, 1972, 1978
Don Shula, Miami, 1973-74
Tom Flores, Oakland, 1981; L.A. Raiders, 1984
Bill Parcells, N.Y. Giants, 1987, 1991
Jimmy Johnson, Dallas, 1993-94
George Seifert, San Francisco, 1990, 1995

Most Games, Losing Team, Coach

4 Bud Grant, Minnesota, 1970, 1974-75, 1977
Don Shula, Baltimore, 1969; Miami, 1972, 1983, 1985
Marv Levy, Buffalo, 1991-94
3 Tom Landry, Dallas, 1971, 1976, 1979
Dan Reeves, Denver, 1987-88, 1990

SCORING

POINTS

Most Points, Career

42 Jerry Rice, San Francisco, 3 games (7-td)
24 Franco Harris, Pittsburgh, 4 games (4-td)
Roger Craig, San Francisco, 3 games (4-td)
Thurman Thomas, Buffalo, 4 games (4-td)
22 Ray Wersching, San Francisco, 2 games (7-pat, 5-fg)

Most Points, Game

18 Roger Craig, San Francisco vs. Miami, 1985 (3-td)
Jerry Rice, San Francisco vs. Denver, 1990 (3-td); vs. San Diego, 1995 (3-td)
Ricky Watters, San Francisco vs. San Diego, 1995 (3-td)
15 Don Chandler, Green Bay vs. Oakland, 1968 (3-pat, 4-fg)
14 Ray Wersching, San Francisco vs. Cincinnati, 1982 (2-pat, 4-fg)
Kevin Butler, Chicago vs. New England, 1986 (5-pat, 3-fg)

TOUCHDOWNS

Most Touchdowns, Career

7 Jerry Rice, San Francisco, 3 games (7-p)
4 Franco Harris, Pittsburgh, 4 games (4-r)
Roger Craig, San Francisco, 3 games (2-r, 2-p)
Thurman Thomas, Buffalo, 4 games (4-r)
3 John Stallworth, Pittsburgh, 4 games (3-p)
Lynn Swann, Pittsburgh, 4 games (3-p)
Cliff Branch, Oakland-L.A. Raiders, 3 games (3-p)
Emmitt Smith, Dallas, 2 games (3-r)
Ricky Watters, San Francisco, 1 game (1-r, 2-p)

Most Touchdowns, Game

3 Roger Craig, San Francisco vs. Miami, 1985 (1-r, 2-p)
Jerry Rice, San Francisco. vs. Denver, 1990 (3-p); vs. San Diego, 1995 (3-p)
Ricky Watters, San Francisco vs. San Diego, 1995 (1-r, 2-p)
2 Max McGee, Green Bay vs. Kansas City, 1967 (2-p)
Elijah Pitts, Green Bay vs. Kansas City, 1967 (2-r)
Bill Miller, Oakland vs. Green Bay, 1968 (2-p)
Larry Csonka, Miami vs. Minnesota, 1974 (2-r)
Pete Banaszak, Oakland vs. Minnesota, 1977 (2-r)
John Stallworth, Pittsburgh vs. Dallas, 1979 (2-p)
Franco Harris, Pittsburgh vs. Los Angeles, 1980 (2-r)
Cliff Branch, Oakland vs. Philadelphia, 1981 (2-p)
Dan Ross, Cincinnati vs. San Francisco, 1982 (2-p)
Marcus Allen, L.A. Raiders vs. Washington, 1984 (2-r)
Jim McMahon, Chicago vs. New England, 1986 (2-r)
Ricky Sanders, Washington vs. Denver, 1988 (2-p)
Timmy Smith, Washington vs. Denver, 1988 (2-r)
Tom Rathman, San Francisco vs. Denver, 1990 (2-r)
Gerald Riggs, Washington vs. Buffalo, 1992 (2-r)
Michael Irvin, Dallas vs. Buffalo, 1993 (2-p)
Emmitt Smith, Dallas vs. Buffalo, 1994 (2-r)

POINTS AFTER TOUCHDOWN

Most (One-Point) Points After Touchdown, Career

9 Mike Cofer, San Francisco, 2 games (10 att)
8 Don Chandler, Green Bay, 2 games (8 att)
Roy Gerela, Pittsburgh, 3 games (9 att)
Chris Bahr, Oakland-L.A. Raiders, 2 games (8 att)
7 Ray Wersching, San Francisco, 2 games (7 att)
Lin Elliott, Dallas, 1 game (7 att)
Doug Brien, San Francisco, 1 game (7 att)

Most (One-Point) Points After Touchdown, Game

7 Mike Cofer, San Francisco vs. Denver, 1990 (8 att)
Lin Elliott, Dallas vs. Buffalo, 1993 (7 att)
Doug Brien, San Francisco vs. San Diego, 1995 (7 att)
6 Ali Haji-Sheikh, Washington vs. Denver, 1988 (6 att)
5 Don Chandler, Green Bay vs. Kansas City, 1967 (5 att)
Roy Gerela, Pittsburgh vs. Dallas, 1979 (5 att)
Chris Bahr, L.A. Raiders vs. Washington, 1984 (5 att)
Ray Wersching, San Francisco vs. Miami, 1985 (5 att)
Kevin Butler, Chicago vs. New England, 1986 (5 att)

Most Two-Point Conversions, Game

1 Mark Seay, San Diego vs. San Francisco, 1995
Alfred Pupunu, San Diego vs. San Francisco, 1995

FIELD GOALS

Field Goals Attempted, Career

6 Jim Turner, N.Y. Jets-Denver, 2 games
Roy Gerela, Pittsburgh, 3 games
Rich Karlis, Denver, 2 games
5 Efren Herrera, Dallas, 1 game
Ray Wersching, San Francisco, 2 games

Most Field Goals Attempted, Game

5 Jim Turner, N.Y. Jets vs. Baltimore, 1969
Efren Herrera, Dallas vs. Denver, 1978
4 Don Chandler, Green Bay vs. Oakland, 1968
Roy Gerela, Pittsburgh vs. Dallas, 1976
Ray Wersching, San Francisco vs. Cincinnati, 1982
Rich Karlis, Denver vs. N.Y. Giants, 1987
Mike Cofer, San Francisco vs. Cincinnati, 1989

Most Field Goals, Career

5 Ray Wersching, San Francisco, 2 games (5 att)
4 Don Chandler, Green Bay, 2 games (4 att)
Jim Turner, N.Y. Jets-Denver, 2 games (6 att)
Uwe von Schamann, Miami, 2 games (4 att)
3 Mike Clark, Dallas, 2 games (3 att)
Jan Stenerud, Kansas City, 1 game (3 att)
Chris Bahr, Oakland-L.A. Raiders, 2 games (4 att)
Mark Moseley, Washington, 2 games (4 att)
Kevin Butler, Chicago, 1 game (3 att)
Rich Karlis, Denver, 2 games (6 att)
Jim Breech, Cincinnati, 2 games (3 att)
Matt Bahr, Pittsburgh-N.Y. Giants, 2 games (3 att)
Chip Lohmiller, Washington, 1 game (3 att)
Steve Christie, Buffalo, 2 games (3 att)
Eddie Murray, Dallas, 1 game (3 att)

Most Field Goals, Game

4 Don Chandler, Green Bay vs. Oakland, 1968
Ray Wersching, San Francisco vs. Cincinnati, 1982
3 Jim Turner, N.Y. Jets vs. Baltimore, 1969
Jan Stenerud, Kansas City vs. Minnesota, 1970
Uwe von Schamann, Miami vs. San Francisco, 1985
Kevin Butler, Chicago vs. New England, 1986

Jim Breech, Cincinnati vs. San Francisco, 1989
Chip Lohmiller, Washington vs. Buffalo, 1992
Eddie Murray, Dallas vs. Buffalo, 1994

Longest Field Goal
54 Steve Christie, Buffalo vs. Dallas, 1994
48 Jan Stenerud, Kansas City vs. Minnesota, 1970
Rich Karlis, Denver vs. N.Y. Giants, 1987
47 Jim Turner, Denver vs. Dallas, 1978

SAFETIES

Most Safeties, Game
1 Dwight White, Pittsburgh vs. Minnesota, 1975
Reggie Harrison, Pittsburgh vs. Dallas, 1976
Henry Waechter, Chicago vs. New England, 1986
George Martin, N.Y. Giants vs. Denver, 1987
Bruce Smith, Buffalo vs. N.Y. Giants, 1991

RUSHING

ATTEMPTS

Most Attempts, Career
101 Franco Harris, Pittsburgh, 4 games
64 John Riggins, Washington, 2 games
57 Larry Csonka, Miami, 3 games

Most Attempts, Game
38 John Riggins, Washington vs. Miami, 1983
34 Franco Harris, Pittsburgh vs. Minnesota, 1975
33 Larry Csonka, Miami vs. Minnesota, 1974

YARDS GAINED

Most Yards Gained, Career
354 Franco Harris, Pittsburgh, 4 games
297 Larry Csonka, Miami, 3 games
240 Emmitt Smith, Dallas, 2 games

Most Yards Gained, Game
204 Timmy Smith, Washington vs. Denver, 1988
191 Marcus Allen, L.A. Raiders vs. Washington, 1984
166 John Riggins, Washington vs. Miami, 1983

Longest Run From Scrimmage
74 Marcus Allen, L.A. Raiders vs. Washington, 1984 (TD)
58 Tom Matte, Baltimore vs. N.Y. Jets, 1969
Timmy Smith, Washington vs. Denver, 1988 (TD)
49 Larry Csonka, Miami vs. Washington, 1973

AVERAGE GAIN

Highest Average Gain, Career (20 attempts)
9.6 Marcus Allen, L.A. Raiders, 1 game (20-191)
9.3 Timmy Smith, Washington, 1 game (22-204)
5.3 Walt Garrison, Dallas, 2 games (26-139)

Highest Average Gain, Game (10 attempts)
10.5 Tom Matte, Baltimore vs. N.Y. Jets, 1969 (11-116)
9.6 Marcus Allen, L.A. Raiders vs. Washington, 1984 (20-191)
9.3 Timmy Smith, Washington vs. Denver, 1988 (22-204)

TOUCHDOWNS

Most Touchdowns, Career
4 Franco Harris, Pittsburgh, 4 games
Thurman Thomas, Buffalo, 4 games
3 Emmitt Smith, Dallas, 2 games
2 Elijah Pitts, Green Bay, 1 game
Jim Kiick, Miami, 3 games
Larry Csonka, Miami, 3 games
Pete Banaszak, Oakland, 2 games
Marcus Allen, L.A. Raiders, 1 game
John Riggins, Washington, 2 games
Jim McMahon, Chicago, 1 game
Timmy Smith, Washington, 1 game
Roger Craig, San Francisco, 3 games
Tom Rathman, San Francisco, 2 games
John Elway, Denver, 3 games
Ottis Anderson, N.Y. Giants, 2 games
Gerald Riggs, Washington, 1 game
Joe Montana, San Francisco, 4 games

Most Touchdowns, Game
2 Elijah Pitts, Green Bay vs. Kansas City, 1967
Larry Csonka, Miami vs. Minnesota, 1974
Pete Banaszak, Oakland vs. Minnesota, 1977
Franco Harris, Pittsburgh vs. Los Angeles, 1980
Marcus Allen, L.A. Raiders vs. Washington, 1984
Jim McMahon, Chicago vs. New England, 1986
Timmy Smith, Washington vs. Denver, 1988
Tom Rathman, San Francisco vs. Denver, 1990
Gerald Riggs, Washington vs. Buffalo, 1992
Emmitt Smith, Dallas vs. Buffalo, 1994

PASSING

PASSER RATING

Highest Passer Rating, Career (40 attempts)
127.8 Joe Montana, San Francisco, 4 games
122.8 Jim Plunkett, Oakland-L.A. Raiders, 2 games
113.2 Troy Aikman, Dallas, 2 games

ATTEMPTS

Most Passes Attempted, Career
145 Jim Kelly, Buffalo, 4 games
122 Joe Montana, San Francisco, 4 games
101 John Elway, Denver, 3 games

Most Passes Attempted, Game
58 Jim Kelly, Buffalo vs. Washington, 1992
50 Dan Marino, Miami vs. San Francisco, 1985
Jim Kelly, Buffalo vs. Dallas, 1994
49 Stan Humphries, San Diego vs. San Francisco, 1995

COMPLETIONS

Most Passes Completed, Career
83 Joe Montana, San Francisco, 4 games
81 Jim Kelly, Buffalo, 4 games
61 Roger Staubach, Dallas, 4 games

Most Passes Completed, Game
31 Jim Kelly, Buffalo vs. Dallas, 1994
29 Dan Marino, Miami vs. San Francisco, 1985
28 Jim Kelly, Buffalo vs. Washington, 1992

Most Consecutive Completions, Game
13 Joe Montana, San Francisco vs. Denver, 1990
10 Phil Simms, N.Y. Giants vs. Denver, 1987
9 Jim Kelly, Buffalo vs. Dallas, 1994

COMPLETION PERCENTAGE

Highest Completion Percentage, Career (40 attempts)
71.9 Troy Aikman, Dallas, 2 games (57-41)
68.0 Joe Montana, San Francisco, 4 games (122-83)
63.6 Len Dawson, Kansas City, 2 games (44-28)

Highest Completion Percentage, Game (20 attempts)
88.0 Phil Simms, N.Y. Giants vs. Denver, 1987 (25-22)
75.9 Joe Montana, San Francisco vs. Denver, 1990 (29-22)
73.5 Ken Anderson, Cincinnati vs. San Francisco, 1982 (34-25)

YARDS GAINED

Most Yards Gained, Career
1,142 Joe Montana, San Francisco, 4 games
932 Terry Bradshaw, Pittsburgh, 4 games
829 Jim Kelly, Buffalo, 4 games

Most Yards Gained, Game
357 Joe Montana, San Francisco vs. Cincinnati, 1989
340 Doug Williams, Washington vs. Denver, 1988
331 Joe Montana, San Francisco vs. Miami, 1985

Longest Pass Completion
80 Jim Plunkett (to King), Oakland vs. Philadelphia, 1981 (TD)
Doug Williams (to Sanders), Washington vs. Denver, 1988 (TD)
76 David Woodley (to Cefalo), Miami vs. Washington, 1983 (TD)
75 Johnny Unitas (to Mackey), Baltimore vs. Dallas, 1971 (TD)
Terry Bradshaw (to Stallworth), Pittsburgh vs. Dallas, 1979 (TD)

AVERAGE GAIN

Highest Average Gain, Career (40 attempts)
11.10 Terry Bradshaw, Pittsburgh, 4 games (84-932)
9.62 Bart Starr, Green Bay, 2 games (47-452)
9.41 Jim Plunkett, Oakland-L.A. Raiders, 2 games (46-433)

Highest Average Gain, Game (20 attempts)
14.71 Terry Bradshaw, Pittsburgh vs. Los Angeles, 1980 (21-309)
12.80 Jim McMahon, Chicago vs. New England, 1986 (20-256)
12.43 Jim Plunkett, Oakland vs. Philadelphia, 1981 (21-261)

TOUCHDOWNS

Most Touchdown Passes, Career
11 Joe Montana, San Francisco, 4 games
9 Terry Bradshaw, Pittsburgh, 4 games
8 Roger Staubach, Dallas, 4 games

Most Touchdown Passes, Game
6 Steve Young, San Francisco vs. San Diego, 1995
5 Joe Montana, San Francisco vs. Denver, 1990
4 Terry Bradshaw, Pittsburgh vs. Dallas, 1979
Doug Williams, Washington vs. Denver, 1988
Troy Aikman, Dallas vs. Buffalo, 1993

SUPER BOWL RECORDS

HAD INTERCEPTED

Lowest Percentage, Passes Had Intercepted, Career (40 attempts)

0.00 Jim Plunkett, Oakland-L.A. Raiders, 2 games (46-0)
Joe Montana, San Francisco, 4 games (122-0)
1.75 Troy Aikman, Dallas, 2 games (57-1)
2.13 Bart Starr, Green Bay, 2 games (47-1)

Most Attempts, Without Interception, Game

36 Joe Montana, San Francisco vs. Cincinnati, 1989
Steve Young, San Francisco vs. San Diego, 1995
35 Joe Montana, San Francisco vs. Miami, 1985
32 Jeff Hostetler, N.Y. Giants vs. Buffalo, 1991

Most Passes Had Intercepted, Career

7 Craig Morton, Dallas-Denver, 2 games
Jim Kelly, Buffalo, 4 games
6 Fran Tarkenton, Minnesota, 3 games
John Elway, Denver, 3 games
4 Earl Morrall, Baltimore-Miami, 4 games
Roger Staubach, Dallas, 4 games
Terry Bradshaw, Pittsburgh, 4 games
Joe Theismann, Washington, 2 games

Most Passes Had Intercepted, Game

4 Craig Morton, Denver vs. Dallas, 1978
Jim Kelly, Buffalo vs. Washington, 1992
3 By eight players

PASS RECEIVING

RECEPTIONS

Most Receptions, Career

28 Jerry Rice, San Francisco, 3 games
27 Andre Reed, Buffalo, 4 games
20 Roger Craig, San Francisco, 3 games
Thurman Thomas, Buffalo, 4 games

Most Receptions, Game

11 Dan Ross, Cincinnati vs. San Francisco, 1982
Jerry Rice, San Francisco vs. Cincinnati, 1989
10 Tony Nathan, Miami vs. San Francisco, 1985
Jerry Rice, San Francisco vs. San Diego, 1995
9 Ricky Sanders, Washington vs. Denver, 1988

YARDS GAINED

Most Yards Gained, Career

512 Jerry Rice, San Francisco, 3 games
364 Lynn Swann, Pittsburgh, 4 games
323 Andre Reed, Buffalo, 4 games

Most Yards Gained, Game

215 Jerry Rice, San Francisco vs. Cincinnati, 1989
193 Ricky Sanders, Washington vs. Denver, 1988
161 Lynn Swann, Pittsburgh vs. Dallas, 1976

Longest Reception

80 Kenny King (from Plunkett), Oakland vs. Philadelphia, 1981 (TD)
Ricky Sanders (from Williams), Washington vs. Denver, 1988 (TD)
76 Jimmy Cefalo (from Woodley), Miami vs. Washington, 1983 (TD)
75 John Mackey (from Unitas), Baltimore vs. Dallas, 1971 (TD)
John Stallworth (from Bradshaw), Pittsburgh vs. Dallas, 1979 (TD)

AVERAGE GAIN

Highest Average Gain, Career (8 receptions)

24.4 John Stallworth, Pittsburgh, 4 games (11-268)
23.4 Ricky Sanders, Washington, 2 games (10-234)
22.8 Lynn Swann, Pittsburgh, 4 games (16-364)

Highest Average Gain, Game (3 receptions)

40.33 John Stallworth, Pittsburgh vs. Los Angeles, 1980 (3-121)
40.25 Lynn Swann, Pittsburgh vs. Dallas, 1979 (4-161)
38.33 John Stallworth, Pittsburgh vs. Dallas, 1979 (3-115)

TOUCHDOWNS

Most Touchdowns, Career

7 Jerry Rice, San Francisco, 3 games
3 John Stallworth, Pittsburgh, 4 games
Lynn Swann, Pittsburgh, 4 games
Cliff Branch, Oakland-L.A. Raiders, 3 games
2 Max McGee, Green Bay, 2 games
Bill Miller, Oakland, 1 game
Butch Johnson, Dallas, 2 games
Dan Ross, Cincinnati, 1 game
Roger Craig, San Francisco, 3 games
Ricky Sanders, Washington, 2 games
John Taylor, San Francisco, 3 games
Gary Clark, Washington, 2 games
Don Beebe, Buffalo, 3 games
Michael Irvin, Dallas, 2 games
Ricky Watters, San Francisco, 1 game

Most Touchdowns, Game

3 Jerry Rice, San Francisco vs. San Diego, 1995; vs. Denver, 1990
2 Max McGee, Green Bay vs. Kansas City, 1967
Bill Miller, Oakland vs. Green Bay, 1968
John Stallworth, Pittsburgh vs. Dallas, 1979
Cliff Branch, Oakland vs. Philadelphia, 1981
Dan Ross, Cincinnati vs. San Francisco, 1982
Roger Craig, San Francisco vs. Miami, 1985
Ricky Sanders, Washington vs. Denver, 1988
Michael Irvin, Dallas vs. Buffalo, 1993
Ricky Watters, San Francisco vs. San Diego, 1995

INTERCEPTIONS BY

Most Interceptions By, Career

3 Chuck Howley, Dallas, 2 games
Rod Martin, Oakland-L.A. Raiders, 2 games
2 Randy Beverly, N.Y. Jets, 1 game
Jake Scott, Miami, 3 games
Mike Wagner, Pittsburgh, 3 games
Mel Blount, Pittsburgh, 4 games
Eric Wright, San Francisco, 4 games
Barry Wilburn, Washington, 1 game
Brad Edwards, Washington, 1 game
Thomas Everett, Dallas, 2 games
James Washington, Dallas, 2 games

Most Interceptions By, Game

3 Rod Martin, Oakland vs. Philadelphia, 1981
2 Randy Beverly, N.Y. Jets vs. Baltimore, 1969
Chuck Howley, Dallas vs. Baltimore, 1971
Jake Scott, Miami vs. Washington, 1973
Barry Wilburn, Washington vs. Denver, 1988
Brad Edwards, Washington vs. Buffalo, 1992
Thomas Everett, Dallas vs. Buffalo, 1993

YARDS GAINED5

Most Yards Gained, Career

75 Willie Brown, Oakland, 2 games
63 Chuck Howley, Dallas, 2 games
Jake Scott, Miami, 3 games
60 Herb Adderley, Green Bay-Dallas, 4 games

Most Yards Gained, Game

75 Willie Brown, Oakland vs. Minnesota, 1977
63 Jake Scott, Miami vs. Washington, 1973
60 Herb Adderley, Green Bay vs. Oakland, 1968

Longest Return

75 Willie Brown, Oakland vs. Minnesota, 1977 (TD)
60 Herb Adderley, Green Bay vs. Oakland, 1968 (TD)
55 Jake Scott, Miami vs. Washington, 1973

TOUCHDOWNS

Most Touchdowns, Game

1 Herb Adderley, Green Bay vs. Oakland, 1968
Willie Brown, Oakland vs. Minnesota, 1977
Jack Squirek, L.A. Raiders vs. Washington, 1984
Reggie Phillips, Chicago vs. New England, 1986

PUNTING

Most Punts, Career

17 Mike Eischeid, Oakland-Minnesota, 3 games
15 Larry Seiple, Miami, 3 games
Mike Horan, Denver, 3 games
14 Ron Widby, Dallas, 2 games
Ray Guy, Oakland-L.A. Raiders, 3 games
Chris Mohr, Buffalo, 3 games

Most Punts, Game

9 Ron Widby, Dallas vs. Baltimore, 1971
7 By eight players

Longest Punt

63 Lee Johnson, Cincinnati vs. San Francisco, 1989
62 Rich Camarillo, New England vs. Chicago, 1986
61 Jerrel Wilson, Kansas City vs. Green Bay, 1967

AVERAGE YARDAGE

Highest Average, Punting, Career (10 punts)

46.5 Jerrel Wilson, Kansas City, 2 games (11-511)
41.9 Ray Guy, Oakland-L.A. Raiders, 3 games (14-587)
41.3 Larry Seiple, Miami, 3 games (15-620)

Highest Average, Punting, Game (4 punts)

48.8 Bryan Wagner, San Diego vs. San Francisco, 1995 (4-195)
48.5 Jerrel Wilson, Kansas City vs. Minnesota, 1970 (4-194)
46.3 Jim Miller, San Francisco vs. Cincinnati, 1982 (4-185)

PUNT RETURNS

Most Punt Returns, Career

6 Willie Wood, Green Bay, 2 games
Jake Scott, Miami, 3 games
Theo Bell, Pittsburgh, 2 games
Mike Nelms, Washington, 1 game
John Taylor, San Francisco, 3 games
5 Dana McLemore, San Francisco, 1 game
4 By eight players

Most Punt Returns, Game

6 Mike Nelms, Washington vs. Miami, 1983
5 Willie Wood, Green Bay vs. Oakland, 1968
Dana McLemore, San Francisco vs. Miami, 1985
4 By six players

Most Fair Catches, Game

3 Ron Gardin, Baltimore vs. Dallas, 1971
Golden Richards, Dallas vs. Pittsburgh, 1976
Greg Pruitt, L.A. Raiders vs. Washington, 1984
Al Edwards, Buffalo vs. N.Y. Giants, 1991
David Meggett, N.Y. Giants vs. Buffalo, 1991

YARDS GAINED

Most Yards Gained, Career

94 John Taylor, San Francisco, 3 games
52 Mike Nelms, Washington, 1 game
51 Dana McLemore, San Francisco, 1 game

Most Yards Gained, Game

56 John Taylor, San Francisco vs. Cincinnati, 1989
52 Mike Nelms, Washington vs. Miami, 1983
51 Dana McLemore, San Francisco vs. Miami, 1985

Longest Return

45 John Taylor, San Francisco vs. Cincinnati, 1989
34 Darrell Green, Washington vs. L.A. Raiders, 1984
31 Willie Wood, Green Bay vs. Oakland, 1968

AVERAGE YARDAGE

Highest Average, Career (4 returns)

15.7 John Taylor, San Francisco, 3 games (6-94)
10.8 Neal Colzie, Oakland, 1 game (4-43)
10.2 Dana McLemore, San Francisco, 1 game (5-51)

Highest Average, Game (3 returns)

18.7 John Taylor, San Francisco vs. Cincinnati, 1989 (3-56)
12.7 John Taylor, San Francisco vs. Denver, 1990 (3-38)
11.7 Kelvin Martin, Dallas vs. Buffalo, 1993 (3-35)

TOUCHDOWNS

Most Touchdowns, Game

None

KICKOFF RETURNS

Most Kickoff Returns, Career

10 Ken Bell, Denver, 3 games
8 Larry Anderson, Pittsburgh, 2 games
Fulton Walker, Miami, 2 games
Andre Coleman, San Diego, 1 game
7 Preston Pearson, Baltimore-Pittsburgh-Dallas, 5 games
Stephen Starring, New England, 1 game

Most Kickoff Returns, Game

8 Andre Coleman, San Diego vs. San Francisco, 1995
7 Stephen Starring, New England vs. Chicago, 1986
6 Darren Carrington, Denver vs. San Francisco, 1990

YARDS GAINED

Most Yards Gained, Career

283 Fulton Walker, Miami, 2 games
242 Andre Coleman, San Diego, 1 game
207 Larry Anderson, Pittsburgh, 2 games

Most Yards Gained, Game

242 Andre Coleman, San Diego vs. San Francisco, 1995
190 Fulton Walker, Miami vs. Washington, 1983
162 Larry Anderson, Pittsburgh vs. Los Angeles, 1980

Longest Return

98 Fulton Walker, Miami vs. Washington, 1983 (TD)
Andre Coleman, San Diego vs. San Francisco, 1995 (TD)
93 Stanford Jennings, Cincinnati vs. San Francisco, 1989 (TD)
67 Rick Upchurch, Denver vs. Dallas, 1978

AVERAGE YARDAGE

Highest Average, Career (4 returns)

35.4 Fulton Walker, Miami, 2 games (8-283)
30.3 Andre Coleman, San Diego, 1 game (8-242)
25.9 Larry Anderson, Pittsburgh, 2 games (8-207)

Highest Average, Game (3 returns)

47.5 Fulton Walker, Miami vs. Washington, 1983 (4-190)
32.4 Larry Anderson, Pittsburgh vs. Los Angeles, 1980 (5-162)
31.3 Rick Upchurch, Denver vs. Dallas, 1978 (3-94)

TOUCHDOWNS

Most Touchdowns, Game

1 Fulton Walker, Miami vs. Washington, 1983
Stanford Jennings, Cincinnati vs. San Francisco, 1989
Andre Coleman, San Diego vs. San Francisco, 1995

FUMBLES

Most Fumbles, Career

5 Roger Staubach, Dallas, 4 games
4 Jim Kelly, Buffalo, 4 games
3 Franco Harris, Pittsburgh, 4 games
Terry Bradshaw, Pittsburgh, 4 games
John Elway, Denver, 3 games
Frank Reich, Buffalo, 4 games
Thurman Thomas, Buffalo, 4 games

Most Fumbles, Game

3 Roger Staubach, Dallas vs. Pittsburgh, 1976
Jim Kelly, Buffalo vs. Washington, 1992
Frank Reich, Buffalo vs. Dallas, 1993
2 Franco Harris, Pittsburgh vs. Minnesota, 1975
Butch Johnson, Dallas vs. Denver, 1978
Terry Bradshaw, Pittsburgh vs. Dallas, 1979
Joe Montana, San Francisco vs. Cincinnati, 1989
John Elway, Denver vs. San Francisco, 1990
Thurman Thomas, Buffalo vs. Dallas, 1994

RECOVERIES

Most Fumbles Recovered, Career

2 Jake Scott, Miami, 3 games (1 own, 1 opp)
Fran Tarkenton, Minnesota, 3 games (2 own)
Franco Harris, Pittsburgh, 4 games (2 own)
Roger Staubach, Dallas, 4 games (2 own)
Bobby Walden, Pittsburgh, 2 games (2 own)
John Fitzgerald, Dallas, 4 games (2 own)
Randy Hughes, Dallas, 3 games (2 opp)
Butch Johnson, Dallas, 2 games (2 own)
Mike Singletary, Chicago, 1 game (2 opp)
John Elway, Denver, 3 games (2 own)
Jimmie Jones, Dallas, 2 games (2 opp)
Kenneth Davis, Buffalo, 4 games (2 own)

Most Fumbles Recovered, Game

2 Jake Scott, Miami vs. Minnesota, 1974 (1 own, 1 opp)
Roger Staubach, Dallas vs. Pittsburgh, 1976 (2 own)
Randy Hughes, Dallas vs. Denver, 1978 (2 opp)
Butch Johnson, Dallas vs. Denver, 1978 (2 own)
Mike Singletary, Chicago vs. New England, 1986 (2 opp)
Jimmie Jones, Dallas vs. Buffalo, 1993 (2 opp)

YARDS GAINED

Most Yards Gained, Game

64 Leon Lett, Dallas vs. Buffalo, 1993 (opp)
49 Mike Bass, Washington vs. Miami, 1973 (opp)
46 James Washington, Dallas vs. Buffalo, 1994 (opp)

Longest Return

64 Leon Lett, Dallas vs. Buffalo, 1993
49 Mike Bass, Washington vs. Miami, 1973 (TD)
46 James Washington, Dallas vs. Buffalo, 1994 (TD)

TOUCHDOWNS

Most Touchdowns, Game

1 Mike Bass, Washington vs. Miami, 1973 (opp 49 yds)
Mike Hegman, Dallas vs. Pittsburgh, 1979 (opp 37 yds)
Jimmie Jones, Dallas vs. Buffalo, 1993 (opp 2 yds)
Ken Norton, Dallas vs. Buffalo, 1993 (opp 9 yds)
James Washington, Dallas vs. Buffalo, 1994 (opp 46 yds)

COMBINED NET YARDS GAINED

(Rushing, receiving, interception returns, punt returns, kickoff returns, and fumble returns)

ATTEMPTS

Most Attempts, Career

108 Franco Harris, Pittsburgh, 4 games
72 Roger Craig, San Francisco, 3 games
Thurman Thomas, Buffalo, 4 games
66 John Riggins, Washington, 2 games

Most Attempts, Game

39 John Riggins, Washington vs. Miami, 1983
35 Franco Harris, Pittsburgh vs. Minnesota, 1975

34 Matt Snell, N.Y. Jets vs. Baltimore, 1969
Emmitt Smith, Dallas vs. Buffalo, 1994

YARDS GAINED

Most Yards Gained, Career
527 Jerry Rice, San Francisco, 3 games
468 Franco Harris, Pittsburgh, 4 games
410 Roger Craig, San Francisco, 3 games

Most Yards Gained, Game
235 Ricky Sanders, Washington vs. Denver, 1988
220 Jerry Rice, San Francisco vs. Cincinnati, 1989
213 Timmy Smith, Washington vs. Denver, 1988

SACKS

Sacks have been compiled since 1983.

Most Sacks, Career
3.5 Charles Haley, San Francisco-Dallas, 4 games
3 Danny Stubbs, San Francisco, 2 games
Leonard Marshall, N.Y. Giants, 2 games
Jeff Wright, Buffalo, 4 games
2.5 Dexter Manley, Washington, 3 games

Most Sacks, Game
2 Dwaine Board, San Francisco vs. Miami, 1985
Dennis Owens, New England vs. Chicago, 1986
Otis Wilson, Chicago vs. New England, 1986
Leonard Marshall, N.Y. Giants vs. Denver, 1987
Alvin Walton, Washington vs. Denver, 1988
Charles Haley, San Francisco vs. Cincinnati, 1989
Danny Stubbs, San Francisco vs. Denver, 1990
Jeff Wright, Buffalo vs. Dallas, 1994
Raylee Johnson, San Diego vs. San Francisco, 1995

TEAM RECORDS

GAMES, VICTORIES, DEFEATS

Most Games
7 Dallas, 1971-72, 1976, 1978-79, 1993-94
5 Miami, 1972-74, 1983, 1985
Washington, 1973, 1983-84, 1988, 1992
San Francisco, 1982, 1985, 1989-90, 1995
4 Minnesota, 1970, 1974-75, 1977
Pittsburgh, 1975-76, 1979-80
Oakland/L.A. Raiders, 1968, 1977, 1981, 1984
Denver, 1978, 1987-88, 1990
Buffalo, 1991-94

Most Consecutive Games
4 Buffalo, 1991-94
3 Miami, 1972-74
2 Green Bay, 1967-68
Dallas, 1971-72; 1978-79; 1993-94
Minnesota, 1974-75
Pittsburgh, 1975-76, 1979-80
Washington, 1983-84
Denver, 1987-88
San Francisco 1989-90

Most Games Won
5 San Francisco, 1982, 1985, 1989-90, 1995
4 Pittsburgh, 1975-76, 1979-80
Dallas, 1972, 1978, 1993-94
3 Oakland/L.A. Raiders, 1977, 1981, 1984
Washington, 1983, 1988, 1992

Most Consecutive Games Won
2 Green Bay, 1967-68
Miami, 1973-74
Pittsburgh, 1975-76, 1979-80
San Francisco, 1989-90
Dallas, 1993-94

Most Games Lost
4 Minnesota, 1970, 1974-75, 1977
Denver, 1978, 1987-88, 1990
Buffalo, 1991-94
3 Dallas, 1971, 1976, 1979
Miami, 1972, 1983, 1985
2 Washington, 1973, 1984
Cincinnati, 1982, 1989

Most Consecutive Games Lost
4 Buffalo, 1991-94
2 Minnesota, 1974-75
Denver, 1987-88

SCORING

Most Points, Game
55 San Francisco vs. Denver, 1990
52 Dallas vs. Buffalo, 1993
49 San Francisco vs. San Diego, 1995

Fewest Points, Game
3 Miami vs. Dallas, 1972
6 Minnesota vs. Pittsburgh, 1975
7 By four teams

Most Points, Both Teams, Game
75 San Francisco (49) vs. San Diego (26), 1995
69 Dallas (52) vs. Buffalo (17), 1993
66 Pittsburgh (35) vs. Dallas (31), 1979

Fewest Points, Both Teams, Game
21 Washington (7) vs. Miami (14), 1973
22 Minnesota (6) vs. Pittsburgh (16), 1975
23 Baltimore (7) vs. N.Y. Jets (16), 1969

Largest Margin of Victory, Game
45 San Francisco vs. Denver, 1990 (55-10)
36 Chicago vs. New England, 1986 (46-10)
35 Dallas vs. Buffalo, 1993 (52-17)

Most Points, Each Half
1st: 35 Washington vs. Denver, 1988
2nd: 30 N.Y. Giants vs. Denver, 1987

Most Points, Each Quarter
1st: 14 Miami vs. Minnesota, 1974
Oakland vs. Philadelphia, 1981
Dallas vs. Buffalo, 1993
San Francisco vs. San Diego, 1995
2nd: 35 Washington vs. Denver, 1988
3rd: 21 Chicago vs. New England, 1986
4th: 21 Dallas vs. Buffalo, 1993

Most Points, Both Teams, Each Half
1st: 45 Washington (35) vs. Denver (10), 1988
2nd: 44 Buffalo (24) vs. Washington (20), 1992

Fewest Points, Both Teams, Each Half
1st: 2 Minnesota (0) vs. Pittsburgh (2), 1975
2nd: 7 Miami (0) vs. Washington (7), 1973
Denver (0) vs. Washington (7), 1988

Most Points, Both Teams, Each Quarter
1st: 21 Dallas (14) vs. Buffalo (7), 1993
San Francisco (14) vs. San Diego (7), 1995
2nd: 35 Washington (35) vs. Denver (0), 1988
3rd: 24 Washington (14) vs. Buffalo (10), 1992
4th: 28 Dallas (14) vs. Pittsburgh (14), 1979

TOUCHDOWNS

Most Touchdowns, Game
8 San Francisco vs. Denver, 1990
7 Dallas vs. Buffalo, 1993
San Francisco vs. San Diego, 1995
6 Washington vs. Denver, 1988

Fewest Touchdowns, Game
0 Miami vs. Dallas, 1972
1 By 17 teams

Most Touchdowns, Both Teams, Game
10 San Francisco (7) vs. San Diego (3), 1995
9 Pittsburgh (5) vs. Dallas (4), 1979
San Francisco (8) vs. Denver (1), 1990
Dallas (7) vs. Buffalo (2), 1993
7 N.Y. Giants (5) vs. Denver (2), 1987
Washington (6) vs. Denver (1), 1988
Washington (4) vs. Buffalo (3), 1992

Fewest Touchdowns, Both Teams, Game
2 Baltimore (1) vs. N.Y. Jets (1), 1969
3 In six games

POINTS AFTER TOUCHDOWN

Most (One-Point) Points After Touchdown, Game
7 San Francisco vs. Denver, 1990
Dallas vs. Buffalo, 1993
San Francisco vs. San Diego, 1995
6 Washington vs. Denver, 1988
5 Green Bay vs. Kansas City, 1967
Pittsburgh vs. Dallas, 1979
L.A. Raiders vs. Washington, 1984
San Francisco vs. Miami, 1985
Chicago vs. New England, 1986

Most (One-Point) Points After Touchdown, Both Teams, Game
9 Pittsburgh (5) vs. Dallas (4), 1979
Dallas (7) vs. Buffalo (2), 1993
8 San Francisco (7) vs. Denver (1), 1990
San Francisco (7) vs. San Diego (1), 1995
7 Washington (6) vs. Denver (1), 1988
Washington (4) vs. Buffalo (3), 1992

Fewest (One-Point) Points After Touchdown, Both Teams, Game
2 Baltimore (1) vs. N.Y. Jets (1), 1969
Baltimore (1) vs. Dallas (1), 1971
Minnesota (0) vs. Pittsburgh (2), 1975

Most Two-Point Conversions, Game
2 San Diego vs. San Francisco, 1995

Most Two-Point Conversions, Both Teams, Game
2 San Diego (2) vs. San Francisco (0), 1995

FIELD GOALS

Most Field Goals Attempted, Game
5 N.Y. Jets vs. Baltimore, 1969
Dallas vs. Denver, 1978
4 Green Bay vs. Oakland, 1968
Pittsburgh vs. Dallas, 1976
San Francisco vs. Cincinnati, 1982; 1989
Denver vs. N.Y. Giants, 1987

Most Field Goals Attempted, Both Teams, Game
7 N.Y. Jets (5) vs. Baltimore (2), 1969
San Francisco (4) vs. Cincinnati (3), 1989
6 Dallas (5) vs. Denver (1), 1978
5 Green Bay (4) vs. Oakland (1), 1968
Pittsburgh (4) vs. Dallas (1), 1976
Oakland (3) vs. Philadelphia (2), 1981
Denver (4) vs. N.Y. Giants (1), 1987
Dallas (3) vs. Buffalo (2), 1994

Fewest Field Goals Attempted, Both Teams, Game
1 Minnesota (0) vs. Miami (1), 1974
San Francisco (0) vs. Denver (1), 1990
2 Green Bay (0) vs. Kansas City (2), 1967
Miami (1) vs. Washington (1), 1973
Dallas (1) vs. Pittsburgh (1), 1979
Dallas (1) vs. Buffalo (1), 1993
San Diego (1) vs. San Francisco (1), 1995

Most Field Goals, Game
4 Green Bay vs. Oakland, 1968
San Francisco vs. Cincinnati, 1982
3 N.Y. Jets vs. Baltimore, 1969
Kansas City vs. Minnesota, 1970
Miami vs. San Francisco, 1985
Chicago vs. New England, 1986
Cincinnati vs. San Francisco, 1989
Washington vs. Buffalo, 1992
Dallas vs. Buffalo, 1994

Most Field Goals, Both Teams, Game
5 Cincinnati (3) vs. San Francisco (2), 1989
Dallas (3) vs. Buffalo (2), 1994
4 Green Bay (4) vs. Oakland (0), 1968
San Francisco (4) vs. Cincinnati (0), 1982
Miami (3) vs. San Francisco (1), 1985
Chicago (3) vs. New England (1), 1986
Buffalo (2) vs. N.Y. Giants (2), 1991
Washington (3) vs. Buffalo (1), 1992
3 In eight games

Fewest Field Goals, Both Teams, Game
0 Miami vs. Washington, 1973
Pittsburgh vs. Minnesota, 1975
1 Green Bay (0) vs. Kansas City (1), 1967
Minnesota (0) vs. Miami (1), 1974
Pittsburgh (0) vs. Dallas (1), 1979
Washington (0) vs. Denver (1), 1988
San Francisco (0) vs. Denver (1), 1990
San Francisco (0) vs. San Diego (1), 1995

SAFETIES

Most Safeties, Game
1 Pittsburgh vs. Minnesota, 1975; vs. Dallas, 1976
Chicago vs. New England, 1986
N.Y. Giants vs. Denver, 1987
Buffalo vs. N.Y. Giants, 1991

FIRST DOWNS

Most First Downs, Game
31 San Francisco vs. Miami, 1985
28 San Francisco vs. Denver, 1990
San Francisco vs. San Diego, 1995
25 Washington vs. Denver, 1988
Buffalo vs. Washington, 1992

Fewest First Downs, Game
9 Minnesota vs. Pittsburgh, 1975
Miami vs. Washington, 1983
10 Dallas vs. Baltimore, 1971
Miami vs. Dallas, 1972
11 Denver vs. Dallas, 1978

Most First Downs, Both Teams, Game
50 San Francisco (31) vs. Miami (19), 1985
49 Buffalo (25) vs. Washington (24), 1992
48 San Francisco (28) vs. San Diego (20), 1995

Fewest First Downs, Both Teams, Game
24 Dallas (10) vs. Baltimore (14), 1971
26 Minnesota (9) vs. Pittsburgh (17), 1975
27 Pittsburgh (13) vs. Dallas (14), 1976

RUSHING

Most First Downs, Rushing, Game
16 San Francisco vs. Miami, 1985
15 Dallas vs. Miami, 1972
14 Washington vs. Miami, 1983
San Francisco vs. Denver, 1990

Fewest First Downs, Rushing, Game
1 New England vs. Chicago, 1986
2 Minnesota vs. Kansas City, 1970; vs. Pittsburgh, 1975; vs. Oakland, 1977
Pittsburgh vs. Dallas, 1979
Miami vs. San Francisco, 1985
3 Miami vs. Dallas, 1972
Philadelphia vs. Oakland, 1981

Most First Downs, Rushing, Both Teams, Game
21 Washington (14) vs. Miami (7), 1983
19 Washington (13) vs. Denver (6), 1988
San Francisco (14) vs. Denver (5), 1990
18 Dallas (15) vs. Miami (3), 1972
Miami (13) vs. Minnesota (5), 1974
San Francisco (16) vs. Miami (2), 1985
N.Y. Giants (10) vs. Buffalo (8), 1991

Fewest First Downs, Rushing, Both Teams, Game
8 Baltimore (4) vs. Dallas (4), 1971
Pittsburgh (2) vs. Dallas (6), 1979
9 Philadelphia (3) vs. Oakland (6), 1981
10 Minnesota (2) vs. Kansas City (8), 1970

PASSING

Most First Downs, Passing, Game
18 Buffalo vs. Washington, 1992
17 Miami vs. San Francisco, 1985
San Francisco vs. San Diego, 1995
16 Denver vs. N.Y. Giants, 1987
San Francisco vs. Cincinnati, 1989

Fewest First Downs, Passing, Game
1 Denver vs. Dallas, 1978
2 Miami vs. Washington, 1983
4 Miami vs. Minnesota, 1974

Most First Downs, Passing, Both Teams, Game
32 Miami (17) vs. San Francisco (15), 1985
31 San Francisco (17) vs. San Diego (14), 1995
30 Buffalo (18) vs. Washington (12), 1992

Fewest First Downs, Passing, Both Teams, Game
9 Denver (1) vs. Dallas (8), 1978
10 Minnesota (5) vs. Pittsburgh (5), 1975
11 Dallas (5) vs. Baltimore (6), 1971
Miami (2) vs. Washington (9), 1983

PENALTY

Most First Downs, Penalty, Game
4 Baltimore vs. Dallas, 1971
Miami vs. Minnesota, 1974
Cincinnati vs. San Francisco, 1982
Buffalo vs. Dallas, 1993
3 Kansas City vs. Minnesota, 1970
Minnesota vs. Oakland, 1977
Buffalo vs. Washington, 1992

Most First Downs, Penalty, Both Teams, Game
6 Cincinnati (4) vs. San Francisco (2), 1982
5 Baltimore (4) vs. Dallas (1), 1971
Miami (4) vs. Minnesota (1), 1974
Buffalo (3) vs. Washington (2), 1992
4 Kansas City (3) vs. Minnesota (1), 1970
Buffalo (4) vs. Dallas (0), 1993

Fewest First Downs, Penalty, Both Teams, Game
0 Dallas vs. Miami, 1972
Miami vs. Washington, 1973
Dallas vs. Pittsburgh, 1976
Miami vs. San Francisco, 1985
1 Green Bay (0) vs. Kansas City (1), 1967
Miami (0) vs. Washington (1), 1983
Cincinnati (0) vs. San Francisco (1), 1989

San Francisco (0) vs. Denver (1), 1990
Dallas (0) vs. Buffalo (1), 1994

NET YARDS GAINED RUSHING AND PASSING

Most Yards Gained, Game
602 Washington vs. Denver, 1988
537 San Francisco vs. Miami, 1985
461 San Francisco vs. Denver, 1990

Fewest Yards Gained, Game
119 Minnesota vs. Pittsburgh, 1975
123 New England vs. Chicago, 1986
156 Denver vs. Dallas, 1978

Most Yards Gained, Both Teams, Game
929 Washington (602) vs. Denver (327), 1988
851 San Francisco (537) vs. Miami (314), 1985
809 San Francisco (455) vs. San Diego (354), 1995

Fewest Yards Gained, Both Teams, Game
452 Minnesota (119) vs. Pittsburgh (333), 1975
481 Washington (228) vs. Miami (253), 1973
Denver (156) vs. Dallas (325), 1978
497 Minnesota (238) vs. Miami (259), 1974

RUSHING

ATTEMPTS

Most Attempts, Game
57 Pittsburgh vs. Minnesota, 1975
53 Miami vs. Minnesota, 1974
52 Oakland vs. Minnesota, 1977
Washington vs. Miami, 1983

Fewest Attempts, Game
9 Miami vs. San Francisco, 1985
11 New England vs. Chicago, 1986
17 Denver vs. Washington, 1988; vs. San Francisco, 1990

Most Attempts, Both Teams, Game
81 Washington (52) vs. Miami (29), 1983
78 Pittsburgh (57) vs. Minnesota (21), 1975
Oakland (52) vs. Minnesota (26), 1977
77 Miami (53) vs. Minnesota (24), 1974
Pittsburgh (46) vs. Dallas (31), 1976

Fewest Attempts, Both Teams, Game
49 Miami (9) vs. San Francisco (40), 1985
51 San Diego (19) vs. San Francisco (32), 1995
53 Kansas City (19) vs. Green Bay (34), 1967

YARDS GAINED

Most Yards Gained, Game
280 Washington vs. Denver, 1988
276 Washington vs. Miami, 1983
266 Oakland vs. Minnesota, 1977

Fewest Yards Gained, Game
7 New England vs. Chicago, 1986
17 Minnesota vs. Pittsburgh, 1975
25 Miami vs. San Francisco, 1985

Most Yards Gained, Both Teams, Game
377 Washington (280) vs. Denver (97), 1988
372 Washington (276) vs. Miami (96), 1983
338 N.Y. Giants (172) vs. Buffalo (166), 1991

Fewest Yards Gained, Both Teams, Game
168 Buffalo (43) vs. Washington (125), 1992
171 Baltimore (69) vs. Dallas (102), 1971
174 New England (7) vs. Chicago (167), 1986

AVERAGE GAIN

Highest Average Gain, Game
7.00 L.A. Raiders vs. Washington, 1984 (33-231)
Washington vs. Denver, 1988 (40-280)
6.64 Buffalo vs. N.Y. Giants, 1991 (25-166)
6.22 Baltimore vs. N.Y. Jets, 1969 (23-143)

Lowest Average Gain, Game
0.64 New England vs. Chicago, 1986 (11-7)
0.81 Minnesota vs. Pittsburgh, 1975 (21-17)
2.23 Baltimore vs. Dallas, 1971 (31-69)

TOUCHDOWNS

Most Touchdowns, Game
4 Chicago vs. New England, 1986
3 Green Bay vs. Kansas City, 1967
Miami vs. Minnesota, 1974
San Francisco vs. Denver, 1990
2 Oakland vs. Minnesota, 1977
Pittsburgh vs. Los Angeles, 1980
L.A. Raiders vs. Washington, 1984
San Francisco vs. Miami, 1985
N.Y. Giants vs. Denver, 1987
Washington vs. Denver, 1988; vs. Buffalo, 1992
Buffalo vs. N.Y. Giants, 1991

Fewest Touchdowns, Game
0 By 17 teams

Most Touchdowns, Both Teams, Game
4 Miami (3) vs. Minnesota (1), 1974
Chicago (4) vs. New England (0), 1986
San Francisco (3) vs. Denver (1), 1990
3 Green Bay (3) vs. Kansas City (0), 1967
Pittsburgh (2) vs. Los Angeles (1), 1980
L.A. Raiders (2) vs. Washington (1), 1984
N.Y. Giants (2) vs. Denver (1), 1987
Buffalo (2) vs. N.Y. Giants (1), 1991
Washington (2) vs. Buffalo (1), 1992
Dallas (2) vs. Buffalo (1), 1994

Fewest Touchdowns, Both Teams, Game
0 Pittsburgh vs. Dallas, 1976
Oakland vs. Philadelphia, 1981
Cincinnati vs. San Francisco, 1989
1 In seven games

PASSING

ATTEMPTS

Most Passes Attempted, Game
59 Buffalo vs. Washington, 1992
55 San Diego vs. San Francisco, 1995
50 Miami vs. San Francisco, 1985
Buffalo vs. Dallas, 1994

Fewest Passes Attempted, Game
7 Miami vs. Minnesota, 1974
11 Miami vs. Washington, 1973
14 Pittsburgh vs. Minnesota, 1975

Most Passes Attempted, Both Teams, Game
93 San Diego (55) vs. San Francisco (38), 1995
92 Buffalo (59) vs. Washington (33), 1992
85 Miami (50) vs. San Francisco (35), 1985

Fewest Passes Attempted, Both Teams, Game
35 Miami (7) vs. Minnesota (28), 1974
39 Miami (11) vs. Washington (28), 1973
40 Pittsburgh (14) vs. Minnesota (26), 1975
Miami (17) vs. Washington (23), 1983

COMPLETIONS

Most Passes Completed, Game
31 Buffalo vs. Dallas, 1994
29 Miami vs. San Francisco, 1985
Buffalo vs. Washington, 1992
27 San Diego vs. San Francisco, 1995

Fewest Passes Completed, Game
4 Miami vs. Washington, 1983
6 Miami vs. Minnesota, 1974
8 Miami vs. Washington, 1973
Denver vs. Dallas, 1978

Most Passes Completed, Both Teams, Game
53 Miami (29) vs. San Francisco (24), 1985
52 San Diego (27) vs. San Francisco (25), 1995
50 Buffalo (31) vs. Dallas (19), 1994

Fewest Passes Completed, Both Teams, Game
19 Miami (4) vs. Washington (15), 1983
20 Pittsburgh (9) vs. Minnesota (11), 1975
22 Miami (8) vs. Washington (14), 1973

COMPLETION PERCENTAGE

Highest Completion Percentage, Game (20 attempts)
88.0 N.Y. Giants vs. Denver, 1987 (25-22)
75.0 San Francisco vs. Denver, 1990 (32-24)
73.5 Cincinnati vs. San Francisco, 1982 (34-25)

Lowest Completion Percentage, Game (20 attempts)
32.0 Denver vs. Dallas, 1978 (25-8)
37.9 Denver vs. San Francisco, 1990 (29-11)
38.5 Denver vs. Washington, 1988 (39-15)

YARDS GAINED

Most Yards Gained, Game
341 San Francisco vs. Cincinnati, 1989
326 San Francisco vs. Miami, 1985
322 Washington vs. Denver, 1988

Fewest Yards Gained, Game
35 Denver vs. Dallas, 1978
63 Miami vs. Minnesota, 1974
69 Miami vs. Washington, 1973

Most Yards Gained, Both Teams, Game
615 San Francisco (326) vs. Miami (289), 1985
603 San Francisco (316) vs. San Diego (287), 1995
583 Denver (320) vs. N.Y. Giants (263), 1987

Fewest Yards Gained, Both Teams, Game
156 Miami (69) vs. Washington (87), 1973
186 Pittsburgh (84) vs. Minnesota (102), 1975
205 Dallas (100) vs. Miami (105), 1972

TIMES SACKED

Most Times Sacked, Game
7 Dallas vs. Pittsburgh, 1976
New England vs. Chicago, 1986
6 Kansas City vs. Green Bay, 1967
Washington vs. L.A. Raiders, 1984
Denver vs. San Francisco, 1990
5 Dallas vs. Denver, 1978; vs. Pittsburgh, 1979
Cincinnati vs. San Francisco, 1982; 1989
Denver vs. Washington, 1988
Buffalo vs. Washington, 1992

Fewest Times Sacked, Game
0 Baltimore vs. N.Y. Jets, 1969; vs. Dallas, 1971
Minnesota vs. Pittsburgh, 1975
Pittsburgh vs. Los Angeles, 1980
Philadelphia vs. Oakland, 1981
Washington vs. Buffalo, 1992
1 By 11 teams

Most Times Sacked, Both Teams, Game
10 New England (7) vs. Chicago (3), 1986
9 Kansas City (6) vs. Green Bay (3), 1967
Dallas (7) vs. Pittsburgh (2), 1976
Dallas (5) vs. Denver (4), 1978
Dallas (5) vs. Pittsburgh (4), 1979
Cincinnati (5) vs. San Francisco (4), 1989
8 Washington (6) vs. L.A. Raiders (2), 1984

Fewest Times Sacked, Both Teams, Game
1 Philadelphia (0) vs. Oakland (1), 1981
2 Baltimore (0) vs. N.Y. Jets (2), 1969
Baltimore (0) vs. Dallas (2), 1971
Minnesota (0) vs. Pittsburgh (2), 1975
3 In four games

TOUCHDOWNS

Most Touchdowns, Game
6 San Francisco vs. San Diego, 1995
5 San Francisco vs. Denver, 1990
4 Pittsburgh vs. Dallas, 1979
Washington vs. Denver, 1988
Dallas vs. Buffalo, 1993

Fewest Touchdowns, Game
0 By 16 teams

Most Touchdowns, Both Teams, Game
7 Pittsburgh (4) vs. Dallas (3), 1979
San Francisco (6) vs. San Diego (1), 1995
5 Washington (4) vs. Denver (1), 1988
San Francisco (5) vs. Denver (0), 1990
Dallas (4) vs. Buffalo (1), 1993
4 Dallas (2) vs. Pittsburgh (2), 1976
Oakland (3) vs. Philadelphia (1), 1981
San Francisco (3) vs. Miami (1), 1985
N.Y. Giants (3) vs. Denver (1), 1987
Washington (2) vs. Buffalo (2), 1992

Fewest Touchdowns, Both Teams, Game
0 N.Y. Jets vs. Baltimore, 1969
Miami vs. Minnesota, 1974
Buffalo vs. Dallas, 1994
1 In six games

INTERCEPTIONS BY

Most Interceptions By, Game
4 N.Y. Jets vs. Baltimore, 1969
Dallas vs. Denver, 1978
Washington vs. Buffalo, 1992
Dallas vs. Buffalo, 1993
3 By 10 teams

Most Interceptions By, Both Teams, Game
6 Baltimore (3) vs. Dallas (3), 1971
5 Washington (4) vs. Buffalo (1), 1992
4 In seven games

Fewest Interceptions By, Both Teams, Game
0 Buffalo vs. N.Y. Giants, 1991
1 Oakland (0) vs. Green Bay (1), 1968
Miami (0) vs. Dallas (1), 1972
Minnesota (0) vs. Miami (1), 1974
N.Y. Giants (0) vs. Denver (1), 1987
Cincinnati (0) vs. San Francisco (1), 1989

YARDS GAINED

Most Yards Gained, Game
95 Miami vs. Washington, 1973
91 Oakland vs. Minnesota, 1977
89 Pittsburgh vs. Dallas, 1976

Most Yards Gained, Both Teams, Game
95 Miami (95) vs. Washington (0), 1973
91 Oakland (91) vs. Minnesota (0), 1977
89 Pittsburgh (89) vs. Dallas (0), 1976

TOUCHDOWNS

Most Touchdowns, Game
1 Green Bay vs. Oakland, 1968
Oakland vs. Minnesota, 1977
L.A. Raiders vs. Washington, 1984
Chicago vs. New England, 1986

PUNTING

Most Punts, Game
9 Dallas vs. Baltimore, 1971
8 Washington vs. L.A. Raiders, 1984
7 By seven teams

Fewest Punts, Game
2 Pittsburgh vs. Los Angeles, 1980
Denver vs. N.Y. Giants, 1987
3 By 10 teams

Most Punts, Both Teams, Game
15 Washington (8) vs. L.A. Raiders (7), 1984
13 Dallas (9) vs. Baltimore (4), 1971
Pittsburgh (7) vs. Minnesota (6), 1975
12 In three games

Fewest Punts, Both Teams, Game
5 Denver (2) vs. N.Y. Giants (3), 1987
6 Oakland (3) vs. Philadelphia (3), 1981
7 In five games

AVERAGE YARDAGE

Highest Average, Game (4 punts)
48.75 San Diego vs. San Francisco, 1995 (4-195)
48.50 Kansas City vs. Minnesota, 1970 (4-194)
46.25 San Francisco vs. Cincinnati, 1982 (4-185)

Lowest Average, Game (4 punts)
31.20 Washington vs. Miami, 1973 (5-156)
32.38 Washington vs. L.A. Raiders, 1984 (8-259)
32.40 Oakland vs. Minnesota, 1977 (5-162)

PUNT RETURNS

Most Punt Returns, Game
6 Washington vs. Miami, 1983
5 By five teams

Fewest Punt Returns, Game
0 Minnesota vs. Miami, 1974
Buffalo vs. N.Y. Giants, 1991
Washington vs. Buffalo, 1992
1 By 12 teams

Most Punt Returns, Both Teams, Game
9 Pittsburgh (5) vs. Minnesota (4), 1975
8 Green Bay (5) vs. Oakland (3), 1968
Baltimore (5) vs. Dallas (3), 1971
Washington (6) vs. Miami (2), 1983
7 Green Bay (4) vs. Kansas City (3), 1967
Oakland (4) vs. Minnesota (3), 1977
San Francisco (5) vs. Miami (2), 1985

Fewest Punt Returns, Both Teams, Game
2 Dallas (1) vs. Miami (1), 1972
Denver (1) vs. N.Y. Giants (1), 1987
Buffalo (0) vs. N.Y. Giants (2), 1991
Buffalo (1) vs. Dallas (1), 1994
3 Kansas City (1) vs. Minnesota (2), 1970
Minnesota (0) vs. Miami (3), 1974
Washington (1) vs. Denver (2), 1988
Washington (0) vs. Buffalo (3), 1992
4 L.A. Raiders (2) vs. Washington (2), 1984
Chicago (2) vs. New England (2), 1986
Buffalo (1) vs. Dallas (3), 1993

YARDS GAINED

Most Yards Gained, Game
56 San Francisco vs. Cincinnati, 1989

52 Washington vs. Miami, 1983
51 San Francisco vs. Miami, 1985

Fewest Yards Gained, Game
–1 Dallas vs. Miami, 1972
0 By eight teams

Most Yards Gained, Both Teams, Game
74 Washington (52) vs. Miami (22), 1983
66 San Francisco (51) vs. Miami (15), 1985
61 San Francisco (56) vs. Cincinnati (5), 1989

Fewest Yards Gained, Both Teams, Game
9 Washington (0) vs. Bufffalo (9), 1992
10 Buffalo (5) vs. Dallas (5), 1994
13 Miami (4) vs. Washington (9), 1973
San Diego (1) vs. San Francisco (12), 1995

AVERAGE RETURN
Highest Average, Game (3 returns)
18.7 San Francisco vs. Cincinnati, 1989 (3-56)
12.7 San Francisco vs. Denver, 1990 (3-38)
11.7 Dallas vs. Buffalo, 1993 (3-35)

TOUCHDOWNS
Most Touchdowns, Game
None

KICKOFF RETURNS
Most Kickoff Returns, Game
9 Denver vs. San Francisco, 1990
8 San Diego vs. San Francisco, 1995
7 Oakland vs. Green Bay, 1968
Minnesota vs. Oakland, 1977
Cincinnati vs. San Francisco, 1982
Washington vs. L.A. Raiders, 1984
Miami vs. San Francisco, 1985
New England vs. Chicago, 1986

Fewest Kickoff Returns, Game
1 N.Y. Jets vs. Baltimore, 1969
L.A. Raiders vs. Washington, 1984
Washington vs. Buffalo, 1992
2 By seven teams

Most Kickoff Returns, Both Teams, Game
12 Denver (9) vs. San Francisco (3), 1990
San Diego (8) vs. San Francisco (4), 1995
11 Los Angeles (6) vs. Pittsburgh (5), 1980
Miami (7) vs. San Francisco (4), 1985
New England (7) vs. Chicago (4), 1986
10 Oakland (7) vs. Green Bay (3), 1968

Fewest Kickoff Returns, Both Teams, Game
5 N.Y. Jets (1) vs. Baltimore (4), 1969
Miami (2) vs. Washington (3), 1973
Washington (1) vs. Buffalo (4), 1992
6 In three games

YARDS GAINED
Most Yards Gained, Game
242 San Diego vs. San Francisco, 1995
222 Miami vs. Washington, 1983
196 Denver vs. San Francisco, 1990

Fewest Yards Gained, Game
16 Washington vs. Buffalo, 1992
17 L.A. Raiders vs. Washington, 1984
25 N.Y. Jets vs. Baltimore, 1969

Most Yards Gained, Both Teams, Game
290 San Diego (242) vs. San Francisco (48), 1995
279 Miami (222) vs. Washington (57), 1983
245 Denver (196) vs. San Francisco (49), 1990

Fewest Yards Gained, Both Teams, Game
78 Miami (33) vs. Washington (45), 1973
82 Pittsburgh (32) vs. Minnesota (50), 1975
92 San Francisco (40) vs. Cincinnati (52), 1982

AVERAGE GAIN
Highest Average, Game (3 returns)
44.0 Cincinnati vs. San Francisco, 1989 (3-132)
37.0 Miami vs. Washington, 1983 (6-222)
32.4 Pittsburgh vs. Los Angeles, 1980 (5-162)

TOUCHDOWNS
Most Touchdowns, Game
1 Miami vs. Washington, 1983
Cincinnati vs. San Francisco, 1989
San Diego vs. San Francisco, 1995

PENALTIES
Most Penalties, Game
12 Dallas vs. Denver, 1978
10 Dallas vs. Baltimore, 1971
9 Dallas vs. Pittsburgh, 1979

Fewest Penalties, Game
0 Miami vs. Dallas, 1972
Pittsburgh vs. Dallas, 1976
Denver vs. San Francisco, 1990
1 Green Bay vs. Oakland, 1968
Miami vs. Minnesota, 1974; vs. San Francisco, 1985
Buffalo vs. Dallas, 1994
2 By four teams

Most Penalties, Both Teams, Game
20 Dallas (12) vs. Denver (8), 1978
16 Cincinnati (8) vs. San Francisco (8), 1982
14 Dallas (10) vs. Baltimore (4), 1971
Dallas (9) vs. Pittsburgh (5), 1979

Fewest Penalties, Both Teams, Game
2 Pittsburgh (0) vs. Dallas (2), 1976
3 Miami (0) vs. Dallas (3), 1972
Miami (1) vs. San Francisco (2), 1985
4 Denver (0) vs. San Francisco (4), 1990

YARDS PENALIZED
Most Yards Penalized, Game
133 Dallas vs. Baltimore, 1971
122 Pittsburgh vs. Minnesota, 1975
94 Dallas vs. Denver, 1978

Fewest Yards Penalized, Game
0 Miami vs. Dallas, 1972
Pittsburgh vs. Dallas, 1976
Denver vs. San Francisco, 1990
4 Miami vs. Minnesota, 1974
10 Miami vs. San Francisco, 1985
San Francisco vs. Miami, 1985
Buffalo vs. Dallas, 1994

Most Yards Penalized, Both Teams, Game
164 Dallas (133) vs. Baltimore (31), 1971
154 Dallas (94) vs. Denver (60), 1978
140 Pittsburgh (122) vs. Minnesota (18), 1975

Fewest Yards Penalized, Both Teams, Game
15 Miami (0) vs. Dallas (15), 1972
20 Pittsburgh (0) vs. Dallas (20), 1976
Miami (10) vs. San Francisco (10), 1985
38 Denver (0) vs. San Francisco (38), 1990

FUMBLES
Most Fumbles, Game
8 Buffalo vs. Dallas, 1993
6 Dallas vs. Denver, 1978
Buffalo vs. Washington, 1992
5 Baltimore vs. Dallas, 1971

Fewest Fumbles, Game
0 By 11 teams

Most Fumbles, Both Teams, Game
12 Buffalo (8) vs. Dallas (4), 1993
10 Dallas (6) vs. Denver (4), 1978
8 Dallas (4) vs. Pittsburgh (4), 1976

Fewest Fumbles, Both Teams, Game
0 Los Angeles vs. Pittsburgh, 1980
1 Oakland (0) vs. Minnesota (1), 1977
Oakland (0) vs. Philadelphia (1), 1981
Denver (0) vs. Washington (1), 1988
N.Y. Giants (0) vs. Buffalo (1), 1991
2 In four games

Most Fumbles Lost, Game
5 Buffalo vs. Dallas, 1993
4 Baltimore vs. Dallas, 1971
Denver vs. Dallas, 1978
New England vs. Chicago, 1986
2 In many games

Most Fumbles Lost, Both Teams, Game
7 Buffalo (5) vs. Dallas (2), 1993
6 Denver (4) vs. Dallas (2), 1978
New England (4) vs. Chicago (2), 1986
5 Baltimore (4) vs. Dallas (1), 1971

Fewest Fumbles Lost, Both Teams, Game
0 Green Bay vs. Kansas City, 1967
Dallas vs. Pittsburgh, 1976
Los Angeles vs. Pittsburgh, 1980
Denver vs. N.Y. Giants, 1987
Denver vs. Washington, 1988

Buffalo vs. N.Y. Giants, 1991
San Diego vs. San Francisco, 1995

Most Fumbles Recovered, Game

8 Dallas vs. Denver, 1978 (4 own, 4 opp.)
6 Dallas vs. Buffalo, 1993 (1 own, 5 opp.)
5 Chicago vs. New England, 1986 (1 own, 4 opp.)

TURNOVERS

(Number of times losing the ball on interceptions and fumbles.)

Most Turnovers, Game

9 Buffalo vs. Dallas, 1993
8 Denver vs. Dallas, 1978
7 Baltimore vs. Dallas, 1971

Fewest Turnovers, Game

0 Green Bay vs. Oakland, 1968
Miami vs. Minnesota, 1974
Pittsburgh vs. Dallas, 1976
Oakland vs. Minnesota, 1977; vs. Philadelphia, 1981
N.Y. Giants vs. Denver, 1987; vs. Buffalo, 1991
San Francisco vs. Denver, 1990; vs. San Diego, 1995
Buffalo vs. N.Y. Giants, 1991
1 By many teams

Most Turnovers, Both Teams, Game

11 Baltimore (7) vs. Dallas (4), 1971
Buffalo (9) vs. Dallas (2), 1993
10 Denver (8) vs. Dallas (2), 1978
8 New England (6) vs. Chicago (2), 1986

Fewest Turnovers, Both Teams, Game

0 Buffalo vs. N.Y. Giants, 1991
1 N.Y. Giants (0) vs. Denver (1), 1987
2 Green Bay (1) vs. Kansas City (1), 1967
Miami (0) vs. Minnesota (2), 1974
Cincinnati (1) vs. San Francisco (1), 1989

POSTSEASON GAME RECORDS

Compiled by Elias Sports Bureau

Throughout this all-time postseason record section, the following abbreviations are used to indicate various levels of postseason games:

SB Super Bowl (1966 to date)

AFC AFC Championship Game (1970 to date) or AFL Championship Game (1960-69)

NFC NFC Championship Game (1970 to date) or NFL Championship Game (1933-69)

AFC-D AFC Divisional Playoff Game (1970 to date), AFC Second-Round Playoff Game (1982), AFL Inter-Divisional Playoff Game (1969), or special playoff game to break tie for AFL Division Championship (1963, 1968)

NFC-D NFC Divisional Playoff Game (1970 to date), NFC Second-Round Playoff Game (1982), NFL Conference Championship Game (1967-69), or special playoff game to break tie for NFL Division or Conference Championship (1941, 1943, 1947, 1950, 1952, 1957, 1958, 1965)

AFC-FR AFC First-Round Playoff Game (1978 to date)

NFC-FR NFC First-Round Playoff Game (1978 to date)

POSTSEASON GAME COMPOSITE STANDINGS

	W	L	PCT.	PTS.	OP
Green Bay Packers	15	7	.682	486	357
San Francisco 49ers	21	11	.656	843	605
Dallas Cowboys	28	18	.609	1102	836
Washington Redskins*	21	14	.600	738	625
Pittsburgh Steelers	17	12	.586	651	571
Los Angeles Raiders**	21	15	.583	855	659
Miami Dolphins	17	13	.567	675	596
Buffalo Bills	13	11	.542	563	520
Chicago Bears	14	14	.500	579	552
Detroit Lions	7	7	.500	305	299
Indianapolis Colts***	8	8	.500	285	300
Denver Broncos	9	10	.474	380	502
Kansas City Chiefs****	8	9	.471	284	360
Philadelphia Eagles	8	9	.471	290	288
New York Jets	5	6	.455	216	200
New York Giants	14	18	.438	529	593
Seattle Seahawks	3	4	.429	128	139
Minnesota Vikings	13	18	.419	553	646
Cincinnati Bengals	5	7	.417	246	257
San Diego Chargers†	7	10	.412	312	393
Houston Oilers	9	13	.409	371	533
St. Louis Rams††	13	20	.394	501	697
Cleveland Browns	11	19	.367	596	692
New England Patriots†††	4	7	.364	208	278
Atlanta Falcons	2	4	.333	119	144
Tampa Bay Buccaneers	1	3	.250	41	94
Arizona Cardinals††††	1	4	.200	81	134
New Orleans Saints	0	4	.000	56	123

**One game played when franchise was in Boston (lost 21-6).*

***24 games played when franchise was in Oakland (won 15, lost 9, 587 points scored, 435 points allowed).*

****15 games played when franchise was in Baltimore (won 8, lost 7, 264 points scored, 262 points allowed).*

*****One game played when franchise was Dallas Texans (won 20-17).*

†One game played when franchise was in Los Angeles (lost 24-16).

††One game played when franchise was in Cleveland (won 15-14), 32 games played when franchise was in Los Angeles (won 12, lost 20, 486 points scored, 683 points allowed).

†††Two games played when franchise was in Boston (won 26-8, lost 51-10).

††††Two games played when franchise was in Chicago (won 28-21, lost 7-0), three games played when franchise was in St. Louis (lost 30-14, lost 35-23, lost 41-16).

INDIVIDUAL RECORDS

SERVICE

Most Games, Career

27 D.D. Lewis, Dallas (SB 5, NFC 9, NFC-D 12, NFC-FR 1)
26 Larry Cole, Dallas (SB 5, NFC 8, NFC-D 12, NFC-FR 1)
25 Charlie Waters, Dallas (SB 5, NFC 9, NFC-D 10, NFC-FR 1)

Most Games, Head Coach

36 Tom Landry, Dallas
35 Don Shula, Baltimore-Miami
24 Chuck Noll, Pittsburgh

Most Games Won, Head Coach

20 Tom Landry, Dallas
19 Don Shula, Baltimore-Miami
16 Chuck Noll, Pittsburgh
Joe Gibbs, Washington

Most Games Lost, Head Coach

16 Tom Landry, Dallas
Don Shula, Baltimore-Miami
12 Bud Grant, Minnesota
11 Chuck Knox, L.A. Rams-Buffalo-Seattle

SCORING

POINTS

Most Points, Career

115 George Blanda, Chi. Bears-Houston-Oakland, 19 games (49-pat, 22-fg)
103 Matt Bahr, Pittsburgh-Cleveland-N.Y. Giants-New England, 14 games (40-pat, 21-fg)
102 Franco Harris, Pittsburgh, 19 games (17-td)
Jerry Rice, San Francisco, 18 games (17-td)

Most Points, Game

30 Ricky Watters, NFC-D:San Francisco vs. N.Y. Giants, 1993 (5-td)
19 Pat Harder, NFC-D: Detroit vs. Los Angeles, 1952 (2-td, 4-pat, 1-fg)
Paul Hornung, NFC: Green Bay vs. N.Y. Giants, 1961 (1-td, 4-pat, 3-fg)
18 By 25 players

Most Consecutive Games Scoring

19 George Blanda, Chi. Bears-Houston-Oakland, 1956-75
15 Roy Gerela, Houston-Pittsburgh, 1969-78
14 Toni Fritsch, Dallas-Houston, 1972-80
Rafael Septien, L.A. Rams-Dallas, 1977-83
Matt Bahr, Pittsburgh-Cleveland-N.Y. Giants-New England, 1979-94 (current)

TOUCHDOWNS

Most Touchdowns, Career

17 Franco Harris, Pittsburgh, 19 games (16-r, 1-p)
Jerry Rice, San Francisco, 18 games (17-p)
15 Thurman Thomas, Buffalo, 16 games (12-r, 3-p)
13 Marcus Allen, L.A. Raiders-Kansas City, 14 games (11-r, 2-p)

Most Touchdowns, Game

5 Ricky Watters, NFC-D:San Francisco vs. N.Y. Giants, 1993 (5-r)
3 Andy Farkas, NFC-D: Washington vs. N.Y. Giants, 1943 (3-r)
Tom Fears, NFC-D: Los Angeles vs. Chi. Bears, 1950 (3-p)
Otto Graham, NFC: Cleveland vs. Detroit, 1954 (3-r)
Gary Collins, NFC: Cleveland vs. Baltimore, 1964 (3-p)
Craig Baynham, NFC-D: Dallas vs. Cleveland, 1967 (2-r, 1-p)
Fred Biletnikoff, AFC-D: Oakland vs. Kansas City, 1968 (3-p)
Tom Matte, NFC: Baltimore vs. Cleveland, 1968 (3-r)
Larry Schreiber, NFC-D: San Francisco vs. Dallas, 1972 (3-r)
Larry Csonka, AFC: Miami vs. Oakland, 1973 (3-r)
Franco Harris, AFC-D: Pittsburgh vs. Buffalo, 1974 (3-r)
Preston Pearson, NFC: Dallas vs. Los Angeles, 1975 (3-p)
Dave Casper, AFC-D: Oakland vs. Baltimore, 1977 (OT) (3-p)
Alvin Garrett, NFC-FR: Washington vs. Detroit, 1982 (3-p)
John Riggins, NFC-D: Washington vs. L.A. Rams, 1983 (3-r)
Roger Craig, SB: San Francisco vs. Miami, 1984 (1-r, 2-p)
Jerry Rice, NFC-D: San Francisco vs. Minnesota, 1988 (3-p)
Jerry Rice, SB: San Francisco vs. Denver, 1989 (3-p)
Kenneth Davis, AFC: Buffalo vs. L.A. Raiders, 1990 (3-r)
Andre Reed, AFC-FR: Buffalo vs. Houston, 1992 (OT) (3-p)
Sterling Sharpe, NFC-FR: Green Bay vs. Detroit, 1993 (3-p)
Napoleon McCallum, AFC-FR: L.A. Raiders vs. Denver, 1993 (3-r)
Thurman Thomas, AFC: Buffalo vs. Kansas City, 1993 (3-r)
William Floyd, NFC-D: San Francisco vs. Chicago, 1994 (3-r)
Ricky Watters, SB: San Francisco vs. San Diego, 1994 (1-r, 2-p)
Jerry Rice, SB: San Francisco vs. San Diego, 1994 (3-p)

Most Consecutive Games Scoring Touchdowns

8 John Stallworth, Pittsburgh, 1978-83
7 John Riggins, Washington, 1982-84
Marcus Allen, L.A. Raiders, 1982-85
5 Duane Thomas, Dallas, 1970-71
Franco Harris, Pittsburgh, 1974-75
Franco Harris, Pittsburgh, 1977-79
James Lofton, Green Bay-Buffalo, 1982-90
Thurman Thomas, Buffalo, 1992-93 (current)

POINTS AFTER TOUCHDOWN

Most (One-Point) Points After Touchdown, Career

49 George Blanda, Chi. Bears-Houston-Oakland, 19 games (49 att)
42 Mike Cofer, San Francisco, 12 games (46 att)
41 Rafael Septien, L.A. Rams-Dallas, 15 games (41 att)

Most (One-Point) Points After Touchdown, Game

8 Lou Groza, NFC: Cleveland vs. Detroit, 1954 (8 att)
Jim Martin, NFC: Detroit vs. Cleveland, 1957 (8 att)
George Blanda, AFC-D: Oakland vs. Houston, 1969 (8 att)
7 Danny Villanueva, NFC-D: Dallas vs. Cleveland, 1967 (7 att)
Raul Allegre, NFC-D: N.Y. Giants vs. San Francisco, 1986 (7 att)
Mike Cofer, SB: San Francisco vs. Denver, 1989 (8 att)
Lin Elliott, SB: Dallas vs. Buffalo, 1992 (7 att)
Doug Brien, SB: San Francisco vs. San Diego, 1994 (7 att)

6 George Blair, AFC: San Diego vs. Boston, 1963 (6 att)
Mark Moseley, NFC-D: Washington vs. L.A. Rams, 1983 (6 att)
Uwe von Schamann, AFC: Miami vs. Pittsburgh, 1984 (6 att)
Ali Haji-Sheikh, SB: Washington vs. Denver, 1987 (6 att)
Scott Norwood, AFC: Buffalo vs. L.A. Raiders, 1990 (7 att)
Jeff Jaeger, AFC-FR: L.A. Raiders vs. Denver, 1993 (6 att)

Most (Kicking) Points After Touchdown, No Misses, Career
49 George Blanda, Chi. Bears-Houston-Oakland, 19 games
41 Rafael Septien, L.A. Rams-Dallas, 14 games
40 Matt Bahr, Pittsburgh-Cleveland-N.Y. Giants-New England, 14 games

Most Two-Point Conversions, Game
1 John Tracey, AFC-D: Buffalo vs. Boston, 1963
Mark Seay, SB: San Diego vs. San Francisco, 1994
Alfred Pupunu, SB: San Diego vs. San Francisco, 1994

FIELD GOALS

Most Field Goals Attempted, Career
39 George Blanda, Chi. Bears-Houston-Oakland, 19 games
31 Mark Moseley, Washington-Cleveland, 11 games
26 Roy Gerela, Houston-Pittsburgh, 15 games

Most Field Goals Attempted, Game
6 George Blanda, AFC: Oakland vs. Houston, 1967
David Ray, NFC-D: Los Angeles vs. Dallas, 1973
Mark Moseley, AFC-D: Cleveland vs. N.Y. Jets, 1986 (OT)
Matt Bahr, NFC: N.Y. Giants vs. San Francisco, 1990
Steve Christie, AFC: Buffalo vs. Miami, 1992
5 Jerry Kramer, NFC: Green Bay vs. N.Y. Giants, 1962
Gino Cappelletti, AFC-D: Boston vs. Buffalo, 1963
Pete Gogolak, AFC: Buffalo vs. San Diego, 1965
Jim Turner, SB: N.Y. Jets vs. Baltimore, 1968
Jan Stenerud, AFC-D: Kansas City vs. N.Y. Jets, 1969
George Blanda, AFC-D: Oakland vs. Pittsburgh, 1973
Ed Murray, NFC-D: Detroit vs. San Francisco, 1983
Mark Moseley, NFC: Washington vs. San Francisco, 1983
Tony Franklin, AFC-FR: New England vs. N.Y. Jets, 1985
Tony Zendejas, AFC-FR: Houston vs. Seattle, 1987 (OT)
Chuck Nelson, NFC-D: Minnesota vs. San Francisco, 1987
Luis Zendejas, NFC-D: Philadelphia vs. Chicago, 1988
4 By many players

Most Field Goals, Career
22 George Blanda, Chi. Bears-Houston-Oakland, 19 games
21 Matt Bahr, Pittsburgh-Cleveland-N.Y. Giants-New England, 14 games
20 Toni Fritsch, Dallas-Houston, 14 games

Most Field Goals, Game
5 Chuck Nelson, NFC-D: Minnesota vs. San Francisco, 1987
Matt Bahr, NFC: N.Y. Giants vs. San Francisco, 1990
Steve Christie, AFC: Buffalo vs. Miami, 1992
4 Gino Cappelletti, AFC-D: Boston vs. Buffalo, 1963
George Blanda, AFC: Oakland vs. Houston, 1967
Don Chandler, SB: Green Bay vs. Oakland, 1967
Curt Knight, NFC: Washington vs. Dallas, 1972
George Blanda, AFC-D: Oakland vs. Pittsburgh, 1973
Ray Wersching, SB: San Francisco vs. Cincinnati, 1981
Tony Franklin, AFC-FR: New England vs. N.Y. Jets, 1985
Jess Atkinson, NFC-FR: Washington vs. L.A. Rams, 1986
Luis Zendejas, NFC-D: Philadelphia vs. Chicago, 1988
Gary Anderson, AFC-FR: Pittsburgh vs. Houston, 1989 (OT)
3 By many players

Most Consecutive Games Scoring Field Goals
13 Toni Fritsch, Dallas-Houston, 1972-79
9 Kevin Butler, Chicago, 1985-91
Scott Norwood, Buffalo, 1988-91
8 Mark Moseley, Washington-Cleveland, 1982-86
Rich Karlis, Denver-Minnesota, 1984-89

Most Consecutive Field Goals
15 Rafael Septien, Dallas, 1978-82
13 Gary Anderson, Pittsburgh, 1989-94 (current)
9 Chuck Nelson, Minnesota, 1987

Longest Field Goal
58 Pete Stoyanovich, AFC-FR: Miami vs. Kansas City, 1990
54 Ed Murray, NFC-D: Detroit vs. San Francisco, 1983
Steve Christie, SB: Buffalo vs. Dallas, 1993
53 Al Del Greco, AFC-FR: Houston vs. N.Y. Jets, 1991

Highest Field Goal Percentage, Career (10 field goals)
90.9 Chuck Nelson, L.A. Rams-Minnesota, 6 games (10-11)
88.2 Steve Christie, Buffalo, 7 games (15-17)
85.7 Rafael Septien, L.A. Rams-Dallas, 15 games (18-21)

SAFETIES

Most Safeties, Game
1 Bill Willis, NFC-D: Cleveland vs. N.Y. Giants, 1950
Carl Eller, NFC-D: Minnesota vs. Los Angeles, 1969
George Andrie, NFC-D: Dallas vs. Detroit, 1970
Alan Page, NFC-D: Minnesota vs. Dallas, 1971
Dwight White, SB: Pittsburgh vs. Minnesota, 1974
Reggie Harrison, SB: Pittsburgh vs. Dallas, 1975
Jim Jensen, NFC-D: Dallas vs. Los Angeles, 1976
Ted Washington, AFC: Houston vs. Pittsburgh, 1978
Randy White, NFC-D: Dallas vs. Los Angeles, 1979
Henry Waechter, SB: Chicago vs. New England, 1985
Rulon Jones, AFC-FR: Denver vs. New England, 1986
George Martin, SB: N.Y. Giants vs. Denver, 1986
D.D. Hoggard, AFC: Cleveland vs. Denver, 1987
Bruce Smith, SB: Buffalo vs. N.Y. Giants, 1990
Reggie White, NFC-FR: Philadelphia vs. New Orleans, 1992
Willie Clay, NFC-FR: Detroit vs. Green Bay, 1994
Carnell Lake, AFC-D: Pittsburgh vs. Cleveland, 1994
Reuben Davis, AFC-D: San Diego vs. Miami, 1994

RUSHING

ATTEMPTS

Most Attempts, Career
400 Franco Harris, Pittsburgh, 19 games
302 Tony Dorsett, Dallas, 17 games
275 Thurman Thomas, Buffalo, 16 games

Most Attempts, Game
38 Ricky Bell, NFC-D: Tampa Bay vs. Philadelphia, 1979
John Riggins, SB: Washington vs. Miami, 1982
37 Lawrence McCutcheon, NFC-D: Los Angeles vs. St. Louis, 1975
John Riggins, NFC-D: Washington vs. Minnesota, 1982
36 John Riggins, NFC: Washington vs. Dallas, 1982
John Riggins, NFC: Washington vs. San Francisco, 1983

YARDS GAINED

Most Yards Gained, Career
1,556 Franco Harris, Pittsburgh, 19 games
1,383 Tony Dorsett, Dallas, 17 games
1,216 Marcus Allen, L.A. Raiders-Kansas City, 14 games

Most Yards Gained, Game
248 Eric Dickerson, NFC-D: L.A. Rams vs. Dallas, 1985
206 Keith Lincoln, AFC: San Diego vs. Boston, 1963
204 Timmy Smith, SB: Washington vs. Denver, 1987

Most Games, 100 or More Yards Rushing, Career
6 John Riggins, Washington, 9 games
5 Franco Harris, Pittsburgh, 19 games
Marcus Allen, L.A. Raiders-Kansas City, 14 games
Thurman Thomas, Buffalo, 16 games
Emmitt Smith, Dallas, 10 games
4 Larry Csonka, Miami, 12 games
Chuck Foreman, Minnesota, 13 games

Most Consecutive Games, 100 or More Yards Rushing
6 John Riggins, Washington, 1982-83
4 Thurman Thomas, Buffalo, 1990-91
3 Larry Csonka, Miami, 1973-74
Franco Harris, Pittsburgh, 1974-75
Marcus Allen, L.A. Raiders, 1983
Emmitt Smith, Dallas, 1992

Longest Run From Scrimmage
80 Roger Craig, NFC-D: San Francisco vs. Minnesota, 1988 (TD)
74 Marcus Allen, SB: L.A. Raiders vs. Washington, 1983 (TD)
71 Hugh McElhenny, NFC-D: San Francisco vs. Detroit, 1957
James Lofton, NFC-D: Green Bay vs. Dallas, 1982 (TD)

AVERAGE GAIN

Highest Average Gain, Career (75 attempts)
5.68 Roger Staubach, Dallas, 20 games (76-432)
5.20 Marcus Allen, L.A. Raiders-Kansas City, 14 games (234-1,216)
4.89 Eric Dickerson, L.A. Rams-Indianapolis, 7 games (148-724)

Highest Average Gain, Game (10 attempts)
15.90 Elmer Angsman, NFC: Chi. Cardinals vs. Philadelphia, 1947 (10-159)
15.85 Keith Lincoln, AFC: San Diego vs. Boston, 1963 (13-206)
10.90 Bill Osmanski, NFC: Chi. Bears vs. Washington, 1940 (10-109)

TOUCHDOWNS

Most Touchdowns, Career
16 Franco Harris, Pittsburgh, 19 games
12 John Riggins, Washington, 9 games
Thurman Thomas, Buffalo, 16 games
11 Marcus Allen, L.A. Raiders-Kansas City, 14 games

Most Touchdowns, Game
5 Ricky Watters, NFC-D: San Francisco vs. N.Y. Giants, 1993
3 Andy Farkas, NFC-D: Washington vs. N.Y. Giants, 1943
Otto Graham, NFC: Cleveland vs. Detroit, 1954
Tom Matte, NFC: Baltimore vs. Cleveland, 1968
Larry Schreiber, NFC-D: San Francisco vs. Dallas, 1972
Larry Csonka, AFC: Miami vs. Oakland, 1973

Franco Harris, AFC-D: Pittsburgh vs. Buffalo, 1974
John Riggins, NFC-D: Washington vs. L.A. Rams, 1983
Kenneth Davis, AFC: Buffalo vs. L.A. Raiders, 1990
Napoleon McCallum, AFC-FR: L.A. Raiders vs. Denver, 1993
Thurman Thomas, AFC: Buffalo vs. Kansas City, 1993
William Floyd, NFC-D: San Francisco vs. Chicago, 1994

Most Consecutive Games Rushing for Touchdowns
7 John Riggins, Washington, 1982-84
5 Franco Harris, Pittsburgh, 1974-75
Franco Harris, Pittsburgh, 1977-79
4 Thurman Thomas, Buffalo, 1992-93 (current)
Emmitt Smith, Dallas, 1993-94 (current)

PASSING

PASSER RATING

Highest Passer Rating, Career (150 attempts)
104.8 Bart Starr, Green Bay, 10 games
103.8 Troy Aikman, Dallas, 9 games
99.5 Steve Young, San Francisco, 15 games

ATTEMPTS

Most Passes Attempted, Career
734 Joe Montana, San Francisco-Kansas City, 23 games
462 Jim Kelly, Buffalo, 14 games
456 Terry Bradshaw, Pittsburgh, 19 games

Most Passes Attempted, Game
64 Bernie Kosar, AFC-D: Cleveland vs. N.Y. Jets, 1986 (OT)
58 Jim Kelly, SB: Buffalo vs. Washington, 1991
54 Randall Cunningham, NFC-D: Philadelphia vs. Chicago, 1988
Jim Kelly, AFC-D: Buffalo vs. Cleveland, 1989
Neil O'Donnell, AFC: Pittsburgh vs. San Diego, 1994

COMPLETIONS

Most Passes Completed, Career
460 Joe Montana, San Francisco-Kansas City, 23 games
275 Jim Kelly, Buffalo, 14 games
261 Terry Bradshaw, Pittsburgh, 19 games

Most Passes Completed, Game
36 Warren Moon, AFC-FR: Houston vs. Buffalo, 1992 (OT)
33 Dan Fouts, AFC-D: San Diego vs. Miami, 1981 (OT)
Bernie Kosar, AFC-D: Cleveland vs. N.Y. Jets, 1986 (OT)
32 Neil Lomax, NFC-FR: St. Louis vs. Green Bay, 1982
Danny White, NFC-FR: Dallas vs. L.A. Rams, 1983
Warren Moon, AFC-D: Houston vs. Kansas City, 1993
Neil O'Donnell, AFC: Pittsburgh vs. San Diego, 1994

COMPLETION PERCENTAGE

Highest Completion Percentage, Career (150 attempts)
68.9 Troy Aikman, Dallas, 9 games (270-186)
66.3 Ken Anderson, Cincinnati, 6 games (166-110)
65.4 Steve Young, San Francisco, 15 games (243-159)

Highest Completion Percentage, Game (15 completions)
88.0 Phil Simms, SB: N.Y. Giants vs. Denver, 1986 (25-22)
86.7 Joe Montana, NFC: San Francisco vs. L.A. Rams, 1989 (30-26)
84.2 David Woodley, AFC-FR: Miami vs. New England, 1982 (19-16)

YARDS GAINED

Most Yards Gained, Career
5,772 Joe Montana, San Francisco-Kansas City, 23 games
3,833 Terry Bradshaw, Pittsburgh, 19 games
3,321 John Elway, Denver, 14 games

Most Yards Gained, Game
489 Bernie Kosar, AFC-D: Cleveland vs. N.Y. Jets, 1986 (OT)
433 Dan Fouts, AFC-D: San Diego vs. Miami, 1981 (OT)
421 Dan Marino, AFC: Miami vs. Pittsburgh, 1984

Most Games, 300 or More Yards Passing, Career
6 Joe Montana, San Francisco-Kansas City, 23 games
5 Dan Fouts, San Diego, 7 games
4 Warren Moon, Houston-Minnesota, 10 games
Troy Aikman, Dallas, 9 games

Most Consecutive Games, 300 or More Yards Passing
4 Dan Fouts, San Diego, 1979-81
3 Jim Kelly, Buffalo, 1989-90
Warren Moon, Houston, 1991-93
2 Daryle Lamonica, Oakland, 1968
Ken Anderson, Cincinnati, 1981-82
Terry Bradshaw, Pittsburgh, 1979-82
Joe Montana, San Francisco, 1983-84
Dan Marino, Miami, 1984
Troy Aikman, Dallas, 1994

Longest Pass Completion
94 Troy Aikman (to Harper), NFC-D: Dallas vs. Green Bay, 1994 (TD)
93 Daryle Lamonica (to Dubenion), AFC-D: Buffalo vs. Boston, 1963 (TD)
88 George Blanda (to Cannon), AFC: Houston vs. L.A. Chargers, 1960 (TD)

AVERAGE GAIN

Highest Average Gain, Career (150 attempts)
8.56 Troy Aikman, Dallas, 9 games (270-2,312)
8.45 Joe Theismann, Washington, 10 games (211-1,782)
8.43 Jim Plunkett, Oakland-L.A. Raiders, 10 games (272-2,293)

Highest Average Gain, Game (20 attempts)
14.71 Terry Bradshaw, SB: Pittsburgh vs. Los Angeles, 1979 (21-309)
13.33 Bob Waterfield, NFC-D: Los Angeles vs. Chi. Bears, 1950 (21-280)
13.16 Dan Marino, AFC: Miami vs. Pittsburgh, 1984 (32-421)

TOUCHDOWNS

Most Touchdown Passes, Career
45 Joe Montana, San Francisco-Kansas City, 23 games
30 Terry Bradshaw, Pittsburgh, 19 games
27 Dan Marino, Miami, 12 games

Most Touchdown Passes, Game
6 Daryle Lamonica, AFC-D: Oakland vs. Houston, 1969
Steve Young, SB: San Francisco vs. San Diego, 1994
5 Sid Luckman, NFC: Chi. Bears vs. Washington, 1943
Daryle Lamonica, AFC-D: Oakland vs. Kansas City, 1968
Joe Montana, SB: San Francisco vs. Denver, 1989
4 Otto Graham, NFC: Cleveland vs. Los Angeles, 1950
Tobin Rote, NFC: Detroit vs. Cleveland, 1957
Bart Starr, NFC: Green Bay vs. Dallas, 1966
Ken Stabler, AFC-D: Oakland vs. Miami, 1974
Roger Staubach, NFC: Dallas vs. Los Angeles, 1975
Terry Bradshaw, SB: Pittsburgh vs. Dallas, 1978
Don Strock, AFC-D: Miami vs. San Diego, 1981 (OT)
Lynn Dickey, NFC-FR: Green Bay vs. St. Louis, 1982
Dan Marino, AFC: Miami vs. Pittsburgh, 1984
Phil Simms, NFC-D: N.Y. Giants vs. San Francisco, 1986
Doug Williams, SB: Washington vs. Denver, 1987
Jim Kelly, AFC-D: Buffalo vs. Cleveland, 1989
Joe Montana, NFC-D: San Francisco vs. Minnesota, 1989
Warren Moon, AFC-FR: Houston vs. Buffalo, 1992 (OT)
Frank Reich, AFC-FR: Buffalo vs. Houston, 1992 (OT)
Troy Aikman, SB: Dallas vs. Buffalo, 1992

Most Consecutive Games, Touchdown Passes
12 Dan Marino, Miami, 1983-94 (current)
10 Ken Stabler, Oakland, 1973-77
Joe Montana, San Francisco-Kansas City, 1988-93
9 John Elway, Denver, 1984-89

HAD INTERCEPTED

Lowest Percentage, Passes Had Intercepted, Career (150 attempts)
1.41 Bart Starr, Green Bay, 10 games (213-3)
2.06 Steve Young, San Francisco, 15 games (243-5)
2.15 Phil Simms, N.Y. Giants, 10 games (279-6)

Most Attempts Without Interception, Game
54 Neil O'Donnell, AFC: Pittsburgh vs. San Diego, 1994
48 Warren Moon, AFC-FR: Houston vs. Pittsburgh, 1989 (OT)
47 Daryle Lamonica, AFC: Oakland vs. N.Y. Jets, 1968

Most Passes Had Intercepted, Career
26 Terry Bradshaw, Pittsburgh, 19 games
22 Jim Kelly, Buffalo, 14 games
21 Joe Montana, San Francisco-Kansas City, 23 games

Most Passes Had Intercepted, Game
6 Frank Filchock, NFC: N.Y. Giants vs. Chi. Bears, 1946
Bobby Layne, NFC: Detroit vs. Cleveland, 1954
Norm Van Brocklin, NFC: Los Angeles vs. Cleveland, 1955
5 Frank Filchock, NFC: Washington vs. Chi. Bears, 1940
George Blanda, AFC: Houston vs. San Diego, 1961
George Blanda, AFC: Houston vs. Dall. Texans, 1962 (OT)
Y.A. Tittle, NFC: N.Y. Giants vs. Chicago, 1963
Mike Phipps, AFC-D: Cleveland vs. Miami, 1972
Dan Pastorini, AFC: Houston vs. Pittsburgh, 1978
Dan Fouts, AFC-D: San Diego vs. Houston, 1979
Tommy Kramer, NFC-D: Minnesota vs. Philadelphia, 1980
Dan Fouts, AFC-D: San Diego vs. Miami, 1982
Richard Todd, AFC: N.Y. Jets vs Miami, 1982
Gary Danielson, NFC-D: Detroit vs. San Francisco, 1983
Jay Schroeder, AFC: L.A. Raiders vs. Buffalo, 1990
4 By many players

PASS RECEIVING

RECEPTIONS

Most Receptions, Career
100 Jerry Rice, San Francisco, 18 games
75 Andre Reed, Buffalo, 16 games
73 Cliff Branch, Oakland-L.A. Raiders, 22 games

Most Receptions, Game

13 Kellen Winslow, AFC-D: San Diego vs. Miami, 1981 (OT)
Thurman Thomas, AFC-D: Buffalo vs. Cleveland, 1989
Shannon Sharpe, AFC-FR: Denver vs. L.A. Raiders, 1993
12 Raymond Berry, NFC: Baltimore vs. N.Y. Giants, 1958
Michael Irvin, NFC: Dallas vs. San Francisco, 1994
11 Dante Lavelli, NFC: Cleveland vs. Los Angeles, 1950
Dan Ross, SB: Cincinnati vs. San Francisco, 1981
Franco Harris, AFC-FR: Pittsburgh vs. San Diego, 1982
Steve Watson, AFC-D: Denver vs. Pittsburgh, 1984
John L. Williams, AFC-D: Seattle vs. Cincinnati, 1988
Jerry Rice, SB: San Francisco vs. Cincinnati, 1988
Ernest Givins, AFC-FR: Houston vs. Pittsburgh, 1989 (OT)
Amp Lee, NFC-D: Minnesota vs. Chicago, 1994
Jay Novacek, NFC-D: Dallas vs. Green Bay, 1994

Most Consecutive Games, Pass Receptions

22 Drew Pearson, Dallas, 1973-83
18 Paul Warfield, Cleveland-Miami, 1964-74
Cliff Branch, Oakland-L.A. Raiders, 1974-83
Jerry Rice, San Francisco, 1985-94 (current)
17 John Stallworth, Pittsburgh, 1974-84

YARDS GAINED

Most Yards Gained, Career

1,539 Jerry Rice, San Francisco, 18 games
1,289 Cliff Branch, Oakland-L.A. Raiders, 22 games
1,167 Fred Biletnikoff, Oakland, 19 games

Most Yards Gained, Game

227 Anthony Carter, NFC-D: Minnesota vs. San Francisco, 1987
215 Jerry Rice, SB: San Francisco vs. Cincinnati, 1988
198 Tom Fears, NFC-D: Los Angeles vs. Chi. Bears, 1950

Most Games, 100 or More Yards Receiving, Career

6 Jerry Rice, San Francisco, 18 games
5 John Stallworth, Pittsburgh, 18 games
Andre Reed, Buffalo, 16 games
4 Fred Biletnikoff, Oakland, 19 games
Dwight Clark, San Francisco, 7 games
Art Monk, Washington, 15 games
Michael Irvin, Dallas, 10 games

Most Consecutive Games, 100 or More Yards Receiving, Career

3 Tom Fears, Los Angeles, 1950-51
Jerry Rice, San Francisco, 1988-89
2 Lenny Moore, Baltimore, 1958-59
Fred Biletnikoff, Oakland, 1968
Paul Warfield, Miami, 1971
Charlie Joiner, San Diego, 1980-81
Dwight Clark, San Francisco, 1981
Cris Collinsworth, Cincinnati, 1981-82
John Stallworth, Pittsburgh, 1979-82
Wesley Walker, N.Y. Jets, 1982
Charlie Brown, Washington, 1983
Steve Largent, Seattle, 1984-87
Vance Johnson, Denver, 1986-87
Andre Reed, Buffalo, 1989-90
James Lofton, Buffalo, 1990
Ernest Givins, Houston, 1991-92
Michael Irvin, Dallas, 1992-93
Sterling Sharpe, Green Bay, 1993
Ernie Mills, Pittsburgh, 1994 (current)
Michael Irvin, Dallas, 1994 (current)

Longest Reception

94 Alvin Harper (from Aikman), NFC-D: Dallas vs. Green Bay, 1994 (TD)
93 Elbert Dubenion (from Lamonica), AFC-D: Buffalo vs. Boston, 1963 (TD)
88 Billy Cannon (from Blanda), AFC: Houston vs. L.A. Chargers, 1960 (TD)

AVERAGE GAIN

Highest Average Gain, Career (20 receptions)

27.3 Alvin Harper, Dallas, 10 games (24-655)
23.7 Willie Gault, Chicago-L.A. Raiders, 10 games (21-497)
22.8 Harold Jackson, L.A. Rams-New England-Minnesota-Seattle, 14 games (24-548)

Highest Average Gain, Game (3 receptions)

46.3 Harold Jackson, NFC: Los Angeles vs. Minnesota, 1974 (3-139)
42.7 Billy Cannon, AFC: Houston vs. L.A. Chargers, 1960 (3-128)
42.0 Lenny Moore, NFC: Baltimore vs. N.Y. Giants, 1959 (3-126)

TOUCHDOWNS

Most Touchdowns, Career

17 Jerry Rice, San Francisco, 18 games
12 John Stallworth, Pittsburgh, 18 games
10 Fred Biletnikoff, Oakland, 19 games

Most Touchdowns, Game

3 Tom Fears, NFC-D: Los Angeles vs. Chi. Bears, 1950
Gary Collins, NFC: Cleveland vs. Baltimore, 1964
Fred Biletnikoff, AFC-D: Oakland vs. Kansas City, 1968
Preston Pearson, NFC: Dallas vs. Los Angeles, 1975
Dave Casper, AFC-D: Oakland vs. Baltimore, 1977 (OT)
Alvin Garrett, NFC-FR: Washington vs. Detroit, 1982
Jerry Rice, NFC-D: San Francisco vs. Minnesota, 1988
Jerry Rice, SB: San Francisco vs. Denver, 1989
Andre Reed, AFC-FR: Buffalo vs. Houston, 1992 (OT)
Sterling Sharpe, NFC-FR: Green Bay vs. Detroit, 1993
Jerry Rice, SB: San Francisco vs. San Diego, 1994

Most Consecutive Games, Touchdown Passes Caught

8 John Stallworth, Pittsburgh, 1978-83
5 James Lofton, Green Bay-Buffalo, 1982-90
4 Lynn Swann, Pittsburgh, 1978-79
Harold Carmichael, Philadelphia, 1978-80
Fred Solomon, San Francisco, 1983-84
Jerry Rice, San Francisco, 1988-89
John Taylor, San Francisco, 1988-89

INTERCEPTIONS BY

Most Interceptions, Career

9 Charlie Waters, Dallas, 25 games
Bill Simpson, Los Angeles-Buffalo, 11 games
Ronnie Lott, San Francisco-L.A. Raiders, 20 games
8 Lester Hayes, Oakland-L.A. Raiders, 13 games
7 Willie Brown, Oakland, 17 games
Dennis Thurman, Dallas, 14 games

Most Interceptions, Game

4 Vernon Perry, AFC-D: Houston vs. San Diego, 1979
3 Joe Laws, NFC: Green Bay vs. N.Y. Giants, 1944
Charlie Waters, NFC-D: Dallas vs. Chicago, 1977
Rod Martin, SB: Oakland vs. Philadelphia, 1980
Dennis Thurman, NFC-D: Dallas vs. Green Bay, 1982
A.J. Duhe, AFC: Miami vs. N.Y. Jets, 1982
2 By many players

Most Consecutive Games, Interceptions

3 Warren Lahr, Cleveland, 1950-51
Ken Gorgal, Cleveland, 1950-53
Joe Schmidt, Detroit, 1954-57
Emmitt Thomas, Kansas City, 1969
Mel Renfro, Dallas, 1970
Rick Volk, Baltimore, 1970-71
Mike Wagner, Pittsburgh, 1975-76
Randy Hughes, Dallas, 1977-78
Vernon Perry, Houston, 1979-80
Lester Hayes, Oakland, 1980
Gerald Small, Miami, 1982
Lester Hayes, L.A. Raiders, 1982-83
Fred Marion, New England, 1985
John Harris, Seattle-Minnesota, 1984-87
Felix Wright, Cleveland, 1987-88
Kurt Gouveia, Washington, 1991
Eric Davis, San Francisco, 1994 (current)

YARDS GAINED

Most Yards Gained, Career

196 Willie Brown, Oakland, 17 games
187 Ronnie Lott, San Francisco-L.A. Raiders, 20 games
151 Glen Edwards, Pittsburgh-San Diego, 17 games

Most Yards Gained, Game

101 George Teague, NFC-FR: Green Bay vs. Detroit, 1993
98 Darrol Ray, AFC-FR: N.Y. Jets vs. Cincinnati, 1982
94 LeRoy Irvin, NFC-FR: L.A. Rams vs. Dallas, 1983

Longest Return

101 George Teague, NFC-FR: Green Bay vs. Detroit, 1993 (TD)
98 Darrol Ray, AFC-FR: N.Y. Jets vs. Cincinnati, 1982 (TD)
94 LeRoy Irvin, NFC-FR: L.A. Rams vs. Dallas, 1983

TOUCHDOWNS

Most Touchdowns, Career

3 Willie Brown, Oakland, 17 games
2 Lester Hayes, Oakland-L.A. Raiders, 13 games
Ronnie Lott, San Francisco-L.A. Raiders, 20 games
Darrell Green, Washington, 16 games
Melvin Jenkins, Seattle-Detroit, 5 games

Most Touchdowns, Game

1 By many players.

PUNTING

Most Punts, Career

111 Ray Guy, Oakland-L.A. Raiders, 22 games
84 Danny White, Dallas, 18 games
73 Mike Eischeid, Oakland-Minnesota, 14 games

POSTSEASON GAME RECORDS

Most Punts, Game

14 Dave Jennings, AFC-D: N.Y. Jets vs. Cleveland, 1986 (OT)
12 David Lee, AFC-D: Baltimore vs. Oakland, 1977 (OT)
11 Ken Strong, NFC: N.Y. Giants vs. Chi. Bears, 1933
Jim Norton, AFC: Houston vs. Oakland, 1967
Ode Burrell, AFC-D: Houston vs. Oakland, 1969
Dale Hatcher, NFC: L.A. Rams vs. Chicago, 1985

Longest Punt

76 Ed Danowski, NFC: N.Y. Giants vs. Detroit, 1935
Mike Horan, AFC: Denver vs. Buffalo, 1991
72 Charlie Conerly, NFC-D: N.Y. Giants vs. Cleveland, 1950
Yale Lary, NFC: Detroit vs. Cleveland, 1953
71 Ray Guy, AFC: Oakland vs. San Diego, 1980

AVERAGE YARDAGE

Highest Average, Career (25 punts)

44.5 Rich Camarillo, New England, 6 games (35-1,559)
44.4 Lee Johnson, Cleveland-Cincinnati, 7 games (28-1,244)
44.0 John Kidd, Buffalo-San Diego-Miami, 7 games (34-1,495)

Highest Average, Game (4 punts)

56.0 Ray Guy, AFC: Oakland vs. San Diego, 1980 (4-224)
52.5 Sammy Baugh, NFC: Washington vs. Chi. Bears, 1942 (6-315)
51.6 Lee Johnson, AFC-D: Cincinnati vs. L.A. Raiders, 1990 (5-258)

PUNT RETURNS

Most Punt Returns, Career

25 Theo Bell, Pittsburgh-Tampa Bay, 10 games
21 Gerald McNeil, Cleveland-Houston, 8 games
19 Willie Wood, Green Bay, 10 games
Butch Johnson, Dallas-Denver, 18 games
Phil McConkey, N.Y. Giants, 5 games

Most Punt Returns, Game

7 Ron Gardin, AFC-D: Baltimore vs. Cincinnati, 1970
Carl Roaches, AFC-FR: Houston vs. Oakland, 1980
Gerald McNeil, AFC-D: Cleveland vs. N.Y. Jets, 1986 (OT)
Phil McConkey, NFC-D: N.Y. Giants vs. San Francisco, 1986
6 George McAfee, NFC-D: Chi. Bears vs. Los Angeles, 1950
Eddie Brown, NFC-D: Washington vs. Minnesota, 1976
Theo Bell, AFC: Pittsburgh vs. Houston, 1978
Eddie Brown, NFC: Los Angeles vs. Tampa Bay, 1979
John Sciarra, NFC: Philadelphia vs. Dallas, 1980
Kurt Sohn, AFC: N.Y. Jets vs. Miami, 1982
Mike Nelms, SB: Washington vs. Miami, 1982
Anthony Carter, NFC-FR: Minnesota vs. New Orleans, 1987
5 By many players

YARDS GAINED

Most Yards Gained, Career

259 Anthony Carter, Minnesota-Detroit, 9 games
221 Neal Colzie, Oakland-Miami-Tampa Bay, 10 games
211 Gerald McNeil, Cleveland-Houston, 8 games

Most Yards Gained, Game

143 Anthony Carter, NFC-FR: Minnesota vs. New Orleans, 1987
141 Bob Hayes, NFC-D: Dallas vs. Cleveland, 1967
102 Charley Trippi, NFC: Chi. Cardinals vs. Philadelphia, 1947

Longest Return

84 Anthony Carter, NFC-FR: Minnesota vs. New Orleans, 1987 (TD)
81 Hugh Gallarneau, NFC-D: Chi. Bears vs. Green Bay, 1941 (TD)
79 Bosh Pritchard, NFC-D: Philadelphia vs. Pittsburgh, 1947 (TD)

AVERAGE YARDAGE

Highest Average, Career (10 returns)

15.2 Anthony Carter, Minnesota-Detroit, 9 games (17-259)
12.9 Brian Mitchell, Washington, 7 games (11-142)
12.6 Bob Hayes, Dallas, 15 games (12-151)

Highest Average Gain, Game (3 returns)

47.0 Bob Hayes, NFC-D: Dallas vs. Cleveland, 1967 (3-141)
29.0 George (Butch) Byrd, AFC: Buffalo vs. San Diego, 1965 (3-87)
25.3 Bosh Pritchard, NFC-D: Philadelphia vs. Pittsburgh, 1947 (4-101)

TOUCHDOWNS

Most Touchdowns

1 Hugh Gallarneau, NFC-D: Chicago Bears vs. Green Bay, 1941
Bosh Pritchard, NFC-D: Philadelphia vs. Pittsburgh, 1947
Charley Trippi, NFC: Chicago Cardinals vs. Philadelphia, 1947
Verda (Vitamin T) Smith, NFC-D: Los Angeles vs. Detroit, 1952
George (Butch) Byrd, AFC: Buffalo vs. San Diego, 1965
Golden Richards, NFC: Dallas vs. Minnesota, 1973
Wes Chandler, AFC-D: San Diego vs. Miami, 1981 (OT)
Shaun Gayle, NFC-D: Chicago vs. N.Y. Giants, 1985
Anthony Carter, NFC-FR: Minnesota vs. New Orleans, 1987
Darrell Green, NFC-D: Washington vs. Chicago, 1987

KICKOFF RETURNS

Most Kickoff Returns, Career

29 Fulton Walker, Miami-L.A. Raiders, 10 games
21 Ken Bell, Denver, 9 games
19 Preston Pearson, Baltimore-Pittsburgh-Dallas, 22 games
James Brooks, San Diego-Cincinnati, 9 games

Most Kickoff Returns, Game

8 Marc Logan, AFC-D: Miami vs. Buffalo, 1990
Andre Coleman, SB: San Diego vs. San Francisco, 1994
7 Don Bingham, NFC: Chi. Bears vs. N.Y. Giants, 1956
Reggie Brown, NFC-FR: Atlanta vs. Minnesota, 1982
David Verser, AFC-FR: Cincinnati vs. N.Y. Jets, 1982
Del Rodgers, NFC-D: Green Bay vs. Dallas, 1982
Henry Ellard, NFC-D: L.A. Rams vs. Washington, 1983
Stephen Starring, SB: New England vs. Chicago, 1985
6 By many players

YARDS GAINED

Most Yards Gained, Career

677 Fulton Walker, Miami-L.A. Raiders, 10 games
481 Carl Garrett, Oakland, 5 games
435 Dennis Gentry, Chicago, 12 games

Most Yards Gained, Game

242 Andre Coleman, SB: San Diego vs. San Francisco, 1994
190 Fulton Walker, SB: Miami vs. Washington, 1982
170 Les (Speedy) Duncan, NFC-D: Washington vs. San Francisco, 1971

Longest Return

98 Fulton Walker, SB: Miami vs. Washington, 1982 (TD)
Andre Coleman, SB: San Diego vs. San Francisco, 1994 (TD)
97 Vic Washington, NFC-D: San Francisco vs. Dallas, 1972 (TD)
93 Stanford Jennings, SB: Cincinnati vs. San Francisco, 1988 (TD)

AVERAGE YARDAGE

Highest Average, Career (10 returns)

30.1 Carl Garrett, Oakland, 5 games (16-481)
27.9 George Atkinson, Oakland, 16 games (12-335)
26.8 Andre Coleman, San Diego, 3 games (13-348)

Highest Average, Game (3 returns)

56.7 Les (Speedy) Duncan, NFC-D: Washington vs. San Francisco, 1971 (3-170)
51.3 Ed Podolak, AFC-D: Kansas City vs. Miami, 1971 (OT) (3-154)
49.0 Les (Speedy) Duncan, AFC: San Diego vs. Buffalo, 1964 (3-147)

TOUCHDOWNS

Most Touchdowns

1 Vic Washington, NFC-D: San Francisco vs. Dallas, 1972
Nat Moore, AFC-D: Miami vs. Oakland, 1974
Marshall Johnson, AFC-D: Baltimore vs. Oakland, 1977 (OT)
Fulton Walker, SB: Miami vs. Washington, 1982
Stanford Jennings, SB: Cincinnati vs. San Francisco, 1988
Eric Metcalf, AFC-D: Cleveland vs. Buffalo, 1989
Andre Coleman, SB: San Diego vs. San Francisco, 1994

FUMBLES

Most Fumbles, Career

16 Warren Moon, Houston-Minnesota, 10 games
13 Tony Dorsett, Dallas, 17 games
10 Franco Harris, Pittsburgh, 19 games
Terry Bradshaw, Pittsburgh, 19 games
Roger Staubach, Dallas, 20 games

Most Fumbles, Game

5 Warren Moon, AFC-D: Houston vs. Kansas City, 1993
4 Brian Sipe, AFC-D: Cleveland vs. Oakland, 1980
3 By many players

RECOVERIES

Most Own Fumbles Recovered, Career

8 Warren Moon, Houston-Minnesota, 10 games
6 John Elway, Denver, 14 games
5 Roger Staubach, Dallas, 20 games

Most Opponents' Fumbles Recovered, Career

4 Cliff Harris, Dallas, 21 games
Harvey Martin, Dallas, 22 games
Ted Hendricks, Baltimore-Oakland-L.A. Raiders, 21 games
Alvin Walton, Washington, 9 games
Monte Coleman, Washington, 21 games
3 Paul Krause, Minnesota, 19 games
Jack Lambert, Pittsburgh, 18 games
Fred Dryer, Los Angeles, 14 games
Charlie Waters, Dallas, 25 games
Jack Ham, Pittsburgh, 16 games
Mike Hegman, Dallas, 16 games
Tom Jackson, Denver, 10 games
Rich Milot, Washington, 13 games

Mike Singletary, Chicago, 12 games
Darryl Grant, Washington, 16 games
Wes Hopkins, Philadelphia, 3 games
Wilber Marshall, Chicago-Washington, 15 games
2 By many players

Most Fumbles Recovered, Game, Own and Opponents'
3 Jack Lambert, AFC: Pittsburgh vs. Oakland, 1975 (3 opp)
Ron Jaworski, NFC-FR: Philadelphia vs. N.Y. Giants, 1981 (3 own)
2 By many players

YARDS GAINED

Longest Return
93 Andy Russell, AFC-D: Pittsburgh vs. Baltimore, 1975 (opp, TD)
64 Leon Lett, SB: Dallas vs. Buffalo, 1992 (opp)
60 Mike Curtis, NFC-D: Baltimore vs. Minnesota, 1968 (opp, TD)
Hugh Green, NFC-FR: Tampa Bay vs. Dallas, 1982 (opp, TD)

TOUCHDOWNS

Most Touchdowns
1 By many players

COMBINED NET YARDS GAINED

Rushing, receiving, interception returns, punt returns, kickoff returns, and fumble returns.

ATTEMPTS

Most Attempts, Career
454 Franco Harris, Pittsburgh, 19 games
350 Tony Dorsett, Dallas, 17 games
342 Thurman Thomas, Buffalo, 16 games

Most Attempts, Game
40 Lawrence McCutcheon, NFC-D: Los Angeles vs. St. Louis, 1975
39 John Riggins, SB: Washington vs. Miami, 1982
Rodney Hampton, NFC-FR: N.Y. Giants vs. Minnesota, 1993
38 Ricky Bell, NFC-D: Tampa Bay vs. Philadelphia, 1979
Rob Carpenter, NFC-FR: N.Y. Giants vs. Philadelphia, 1981

YARDS GAINED

Most Yards Gained, Career
2,060 Franco Harris, Pittsburgh, 19 games
1,786 Tony Dorsett, Dallas, 17 games
1,736 Thurman Thomas, Buffalo, 16 games

Most Yards Gained, Game
350 Ed Podolak, AFC-D: Kansas City vs. Miami, 1971 (OT)
329 Keith Lincoln, AFC: San Diego vs. Boston, 1963
285 Bob Hayes, NFC-D: Dallas vs. Cleveland, 1967

SACKS

Sacks have been compiled since 1982.

Most Sacks, Career
12 Bruce Smith, Buffalo, 16 games
10.5 Richard Dent, Chicago-San Francisco, 11 games
10 Charles Mann, Washington-San Francisco, 19 games
Charles Haley, San Francisco-Dallas, 18 games

Most Sacks, Game
3.5 Rich Milot, NFC-D: Washington vs. Chicago, 1984
Richard Dent, NFC-D: Chicago vs. N.Y. Giants, 1985
3 Richard Dent, NFC-D: Chicago vs. Washington, 1984
Garin Veris, AFC-FR: New England vs. N.Y. Jets, 1985
Gary Jeter, NFC-D: L.A. Rams vs. Dallas, 1985
Carl Hairston, AFC-D: Cleveland vs. N.Y. Jets, 1986 (OT)
Charles Mann, NFC-D: Washington vs. Chicago, 1987
Kevin Greene, NFC-FR: L.A. Rams vs. Minnesota, 1988
Greg Townsend, AFC-D: L.A. Raiders vs. Cincinnati, 1990
Wilber Marshall, NFC: Washington vs. Detroit, 1991
Fred Stokes, NFC-FR: Washington vs. Minnesota, 1992
Pierce Holt, NFC-D: San Francisco vs. Washington, 1992
Tony Casillas, NFC: Dallas vs. San Francisco, 1992
Gerald Williams, AFC-FR: Pittsburgh vs. Kansas City, 1993
2.5 Lyle Alzado, AFC-D: L.A. Raiders vs. Pittsburgh, 1983
Jacob Green, AFC-FR: Seattle vs. L.A. Raiders, 1984
Larry Roberts, NFC-D: San Francisco vs. Minnesota, 1988
Leslie O'Neal, AFC-FR: San Diego vs. Kansas City, 1992

TEAM RECORDS

GAMES, VICTORIES, DEFEATS

Most Seasons Participating in Postseason Games
23 N.Y. Giants, 1933-35, 1938-39, 1941, 1943-44, 1946, 1950, 1956, 1958-59,1961-63, 1981, 1984-86, 1989-90, 1993
Cleveland, 1950-55, 1957-58, 1964-65, 1967-69, 1971-72, 1980, 1982, 1985-89, 1994
22 Cleveland/L.A. Rams, 1945, 1949-52, 1955, 1967, 1969, 1973-80, 1983-86, 1988-89
Dallas, 1966-73, 1975-83, 1985, 1991-94
21 Chicago, 1933-34, 1937, 1940-43, 1946, 1950, 1956, 1963, 1977, 1979, 1984-88, 1990-91, 1994

Most Consecutive Seasons Participating in Postseason Games
9 Dallas, 1975-83
8 Dallas, 1966-73
Pittsburgh, 1972-79
Los Angeles, 1973-80
San Francisco, 1983-90
7 Houston, 1987-93

Most Games
46 Dallas, 1966-73, 1975-83, 1985, 1991-94
36 Oakland/L.A. Raiders, 1967-70, 1973-77, 1980, 1982-85, 1990-91, 1993
35 Boston/Washington, 1936-37, 1940, 1942-43, 1945, 1971-74, 1976-77, 1982-84, 1986-87, 1990-92

Most Games Won
28 Dallas, 1967, 1970-73, 1975, 1977-78, 1980-82, 1991-94
21 Washington, 1937, 1942-43, 1972, 1982-83, 1986-87, 1990-92
Oakland/L.A. Raiders, 1967-70, 1973-77, 1980, 1982-83, 1990, 1993
San Francisco, 1970-71, 1981, 1983-84, 1988-90, 1992-94
17 Miami, 1971-73, 1982, 1984-85, 1990, 1992, 1994
Pittsburgh, 1972, 1974-76, 1978-79, 1984, 1989, 1994

Most Consecutive Games Won
9 Green Bay, 1961-62, 1965-67
7 Pittsburgh, 1974-76
San Francisco, 1988-90
Dallas, 1992-94
6 Miami, 1972-73
Pittsburgh, 1978-79
Washington, 1982-83

Most Games Lost
20 L.A. Rams, 1949-50, 1952, 1955, 1967, 1969, 1973-80, 1983-86, 1988-89
19 Cleveland, 1951-53, 1957-58, 1965, 1967-69, 1971-72, 1980, 1982, 1985-89, 1994
18 N.Y. Giants, 1933, 1935, 1939, 1941, 1943-44, 1946, 1950, 1958-59, 1961-63, 1981, 1984-85, 1989, 1993
Minnesota, 1968-71, 1973-78, 1980, 1982, 1987-89, 1992-94
Dallas, 1966-70, 1972-73, 1975-76, 1978-83, 1985, 1991, 1994

Most Consecutive Games Lost
6 N.Y. Giants, 1939, 1941, 1943-44, 1946, 1950
Cleveland, 1969, 1971-72, 1980, 1982, 1985
5 N.Y. Giants, 1958-59, 1961-63
Los Angeles, 1952, 1955, 1967, 1969, 1973
Denver, 1977-79, 1983-84
Baltimore/Indianapolis, 1971, 1975-77, 1987 (current)
Philadelphia, 1980-81, 1988-90
Minnesota, 1988-89, 1992-94 (current)
4 Washington, 1972-74, 1976
Miami, 1974, 1978-79, 1981
Chi. Cardinals/St. Louis, 1948, 1974-75, 1982 (current)
Boston/New England, 1963, 1976, 1978, 1982
New Orleans, 1987, 1990-92 (current)

SCORING

Most Points, Game
73 NFC: Chi. Bears vs. Washington, 1940
59 NFC: Detroit vs. Cleveland, 1957
56 NFC: Cleveland vs. Detroit, 1954
AFC-D: Oakland vs. Houston, 1969

Most Points, Both Teams, Game
79 AFC-D: San Diego (41) vs. Miami (38), 1981 (OT)
AFC-FR: Buffalo (41) vs. Houston (38), 1992 (OT)
78 AFC-D: Buffalo (44) vs. Miami (34), 1990
75 SB: San Francisco (49) vs. San Diego (26), 1994

Fewest Points, Both Teams, Game
5 NFC-D: Detroit (0) vs. Dallas (5), 1970
7 NFC: Chi. Cardinals (0) vs. Philadelphia (7), 1948
9 NFC: Tampa Bay (0) vs. Los Angeles (9), 1979

Largest Margin of Victory, Game
73 NFC: Chi. Bears vs. Washington, 1940 (73-0)
49 AFC-D: Oakland vs. Houston, 1969 (56-7)
48 AFC: Buffalo vs. L.A. Raiders, 1990 (51-3)

Most Points, Shutout Victory, Game
73 NFC: Chi. Bears vs. Washington, 1940
38 NFC-D: Dallas vs. Tampa Bay, 1981
37 NFC: Green Bay vs. N.Y. Giants, 1961

Most Points Overcome to Win Game
32 AFC-FR: Buffalo vs. Houston, 1992 (trailed 3-35, won 41-38) (OT)
20 NFC-D: Detroit vs. San Francisco, 1957 (trailed 7-27, won 31-27)
18 NFC-D: Dallas vs. San Francisco, 1972 (trailed 3-21, won 30-28)
AFC-D: Miami vs. Cleveland, 1985 (trailed 3-21, won 24-21)

POSTSEASON GAME RECORDS

Most Points, Each Half

1st: 41 AFC: Buffalo vs. L.A. Raiders, 1990
38 NFC-D: Washington vs. L.A. Rams, 1983
35 NFC: Cleveland vs. Detroit, 1954
AFC-D: Oakland vs. Houston, 1969
SB: Washington vs. Denver, 1987
2nd: 45 NFC: Chi. Bears vs. Washington, 1940
35 AFC-FR: Buffalo vs. Houston, 1992
30 SB: N.Y. Giants vs. Denver, 1986
AFC: Cleveland vs. Denver, 1987

Most Points, Each Quarter

1st: 28 AFC-D: Oakland vs. Houston, 1969
24 AFC-D: San Diego vs. Miami, 1981
21 NFC: Chi. Bears vs. Washington, 1940
AFC: San Diego vs. Boston, 1963
AFC-D: Oakland vs. Kansas City, 1968
AFC: Oakland vs. San Diego, 1980
AFC: Buffalo vs. L.A. Raiders, 1990
NFC: San Francisco vs. Dallas, 1994
2nd: 35 SB: Washington vs. Denver, 1987
26 AFC-D: Pittsburgh vs. Buffalo, 1974
24 NFC-D: Chi. Bears vs. Green Bay, 1941
NFC: Green Bay vs. N.Y. Giants, 1961
3rd: 28 AFC-FR: Buffalo vs. Houston, 1992
26 NFC: Chi. Bears vs. Washington, 1940
21 NFC-D: Dallas vs. Cleveland, 1967
NFC-D: Dallas vs. Tampa Bay, 1981
AFC-D: L.A. Raiders vs. Pittsburgh, 1983
SB: Chicago vs. New England, 1985
NFC-D: N.Y. Giants vs. San Francisco, 1986
AFC: Cleveland vs. Denver, 1987
AFC: Cleveland vs. Denver, 1989
4th: 27 NFC: N.Y. Giants vs. Chi. Bears, 1934
26 NFC-FR: Philadelphia vs. New Orleans, 1992
24 NFC: Baltimore vs. N.Y. Giants, 1959
OT: 6 NFC: Baltimore vs. N.Y. Giants, 1958
AFC-D: Oakland vs. Baltimore, 1977
NFC-D: L.A. Rams vs. N.Y. Giants, 1989

TOUCHDOWNS

Most Touchdowns, Game

11 NFC: Chi. Bears vs. Washington, 1940
8 NFC: Cleveland vs. Detroit, 1954
NFC: Detroit vs. Cleveland, 1957
AFC-D: Oakland vs. Houston, 1969
SB: San Francisco vs. Denver, 1989
7 AFC: San Diego vs. Boston, 1963
NFC-D: Dallas vs. Cleveland, 1967
NFC-D: N.Y. Giants vs. San Francisco, 1986
AFC: Buffalo vs. L.A. Raiders, 1990
SB: Dallas vs. Buffalo, 1992
SB: San Francisco vs. San Diego, 1994

Most Touchdowns, Both Teams, Game

11 NFC: Chi. Bears (11) vs. Washington (0), 1940
10 NFC: Detroit (8) vs. Cleveland (2), 1957
AFC-D: Miami (5) vs. San Diego (5), 1981 (OT)
AFC: Miami (6) vs. Pittsburgh (4), 1984
AFC-FR: Buffalo (5) vs. Houston (5), 1992 (OT)
SB: San Francisco (7) vs. San Diego (3), 1994
9 NFC: Chi. Bears (6) vs. Washington (3), 1943
NFC: Cleveland (8) vs. Detroit (1), 1954
NFC-D: Dallas (7) vs. Cleveland (2), 1967
AFC-D: Oakland (8) vs. Houston (1), 1969
AFC-D: Oakland (5) vs. Baltimore (4), 1977 (OT)
SB: Pittsburgh (5) vs. Dallas (4), 1978
AFC: Denver (5) vs. Cleveland (4), 1987
SB: San Francisco (8) vs. Denver (1), 1989
AFC-D: Buffalo (5) vs. Miami (4), 1990
SB: Dallas (7) vs. Buffalo (2), 1992
AFC-FR: L.A. Raiders (6) vs. Denver (3), 1993
NFC: San Francisco (5) vs. Dallas (4), 1994

Fewest Touchdowns, Both Teams, Game

0 NFC-D: N.Y. Giants vs. Cleveland, 1950
NFC-D: Dallas vs. Detroit, 1970
NFC: Los Angeles vs. Tampa Bay, 1979
1 NFC: Chi. Cardinals (0) vs. Philadelphia (1), 1948
NFC-D: Cleveland (0) vs. N.Y. Giants (1), 1958
AFC: San Diego (0) vs. Houston (1), 1961
AFC-D: N.Y. Jets (0) vs. Kansas City (1), 1969
NFC-D: Green Bay (0) vs. Washington (1), 1972
NFC-FR: New Orleans (0) vs. Chicago (1), 1990
NFC: N.Y. Giants (0) vs. San Francisco (1), 1990
AFC-FR: L.A. Raiders (0) vs. Kansas City (1), 1991
2 In many games

POINTS AFTER TOUCHDOWN

Most (One-Point) Points After Touchdown, Game

8 NFC: Cleveland vs. Detroit, 1954
NFC: Detroit vs. Cleveland, 1957
AFC-D: Oakland vs. Houston, 1969
7 NFC: Chi. Bears vs. Washington, 1940
NFC-D: Dallas vs. Cleveland, 1967
NFC-D: N.Y. Giants vs. San Francisco, 1986
SB: San Francisco vs. Denver, 1989
SB: Dallas vs. Buffalo, 1992
SB: San Francisco vs. San Diego, 1994
6 AFC: San Diego vs. Boston, 1963
NFC-D: Washington vs. L.A. Rams, 1983
AFC: Miami vs. Pittsburgh, 1984
SB: Washington vs. Denver, 1987
AFC: Buffalo vs. L.A. Raiders, 1990
AFC-FR: L.A. Raiders vs. Denver, 1993

Most (One-Point) Points After Touchdown, Both Teams, Game

10 NFC: Detroit (8) vs. Cleveland (2), 1957
AFC-D: Miami (5) vs. San Diego (5), 1981 (OT)
AFC: Miami (6) vs. Pittsburgh (4), 1984
AFC-FR: Buffalo (5) vs. Houston (5), 1992 (OT)
9 In many games

Fewest (One-Point) Points After Touchdown, Both Teams, Game

0 NFC-D: N.Y. Giants vs. Cleveland, 1950
NFC-D: Dallas vs. Detroit, 1970
NFC: Los Angeles vs. Tampa Bay, 1979

Most Two-Point Conversions, Game

2 SB: San Diego vs. San Francisco, 1994
1 AFC-D: Buffalo vs. Boston, 1963

FIELD GOALS

Most Field Goals, Game

5 NFC-D: Minnesota vs. San Francisco, 1987
NFC: N.Y. Giants vs. San Francisco, 1990
AFC: Buffalo vs. Miami, 1992
4 AFC-D: Boston vs. Buffalo, 1963
AFC: Oakland vs. Houston, 1967
SB: Green Bay vs. Oakland, 1967
NFC: Washington vs. Dallas, 1972
AFC-D: Oakland vs. Pittsburgh, 1973
SB: San Francisco vs. Cincinnati, 1981
AFC-FR: New England vs. N.Y. Jets, 1985
NFC-FR: Washington vs. L.A. Rams, 1986
NFC-D: Philadelphia vs. Chicago, 1988
AFC-FR: Pittsburgh vs. Houston, 1989 (OT)
3 By many teams

Most Field Goals, Both Teams, Game

7 AFC-FR: Pittsburgh (4) vs. Houston (3), 1989 (OT)
NFC: N.Y. Giants (5) vs. San Francisco (2), 1990
6 NFC-D: Minnesota (5) vs. San Francisco (1), 1987
NFC-D: Philadelphia (4) vs. Chicago (2), 1988
AFC: Buffalo (5) vs. Miami (1), 1992
5 In many games

Most Field Goals Attempted, Game

6 AFC: Oakland vs. Houston, 1967
NFC-D: Los Angeles vs. Dallas, 1973
AFC-D: Cleveland vs. N.Y. Jets, 1986 (OT)
NFC: N.Y. Giants vs. San Francisco, 1990
5 By many teams

Most Field Goals Attempted, Both Teams, Game

9 NFC-D: Philadelphia (5) vs. Chicago (4), 1988
8 NFC-D: Los Angeles (6) vs. Dallas (2), 1973
NFC-D: Detroit (5) vs. San Francisco (3), 1983
AFC-D: Cleveland (6) vs. N.Y. Jets (2), 1986 (OT)
NFC-D: Minnesota (5) vs. San Francisco (3), 1987
AFC-FR: Houston (4) vs. Pittsburgh (4), 1989 (OT)
NFC-FR: Chicago (4) vs. New Orleans (4), 1990
NFC: N.Y. Giants (6) vs. San Francisco (2), 1990
7 In many games

SAFETIES

Most Safeties, Game

1 By many teams

Most Safeties, Both Teams, Game

1 In many games

FIRST DOWNS

Most First Downs, Game

34 AFC-D: San Diego vs. Miami, 1981 (OT)
33 AFC-D: Cleveland vs. N.Y. Jets, 1986 (OT)

31 SB: San Francisco vs. Miami, 1984

Fewest First Downs, Game

6 NFC: N.Y. Giants vs. Green Bay, 1961
7 NFC: Green Bay vs. Boston, 1936
NFC-D: Pittsburgh vs. Philadelphia, 1947
NFC: Chi. Cardinals vs. Philadelphia, 1948
NFC: Los Angeles vs. Philadelphia, 1949
NFC-D: Cleveland vs. N.Y. Giants, 1958
AFC-D: Cincinnati vs. Baltimore, 1970
NFC-D: Detroit vs. Dallas, 1970
NFC: Tampa Bay vs. Los Angeles, 1979
8 By many teams

Most First Downs, Both Teams, Game

59 AFC-D: San Diego (34) vs. Miami (25), 1981 (OT)
55 AFC-FR: San Diego (29) vs. Pittsburgh (26), 1982
51 AFC: Buffalo (30) vs. L.A. Raiders (21), 1990
AFC: Buffalo (29) vs. Kansas City (22), 1993

Fewest First Downs, Both Teams, Game

15 NFC: Green Bay (7) vs. Boston (8), 1936
19 NFC: N.Y. Giants (9) vs. Green Bay (10), 1939
NFC: Washington (9) vs. Chi. Bears (10), 1942
20 NFC-D: Cleveland (9) vs. N.Y. Giants (11), 1950

RUSHING

Most First Downs, Rushing, Game

19 NFC-FR: Dallas vs. Los Angeles, 1980
18 AFC-D: Miami vs. Cincinnati, 1973
AFC: Miami vs. Oakland, 1973
AFC-D: Pittsburgh vs. Buffalo, 1974
17 AFC-D: Cincinnati vs. Seattle, 1988
AFC: Buffalo vs. Kansas City, 1993

Fewest First Downs, Rushing, Game

0 NFC: Los Angeles vs. Philadelphia, 1949
AFC-D: Buffalo vs. Boston, 1963
AFC: Oakland vs. Pittsburgh, 1974
NFC-FR: New Orleans vs. Minnesota, 1987
NFC: L.A. Rams vs. San Francisco, 1989
NFC-D: Chicago vs. N.Y. Giants, 1990
1 By many teams

Most First Downs, Rushing, Both Teams, Game

26 AFC: Buffalo (14) vs. L.A. Raiders (12), 1990
25 NFC-FR: Dallas (19) vs. Los Angeles (6), 1980
23 NFC: Cleveland (15) vs. Detroit (8), 1952
AFC-D: Miami (18) vs. Cincinnati (5), 1973
AFC-D: Pittsburgh (18) vs. Buffalo (5), 1974

Fewest First Downs, Rushing, Both Teams, Game

5 AFC-D: Buffalo (0) vs. Boston (5), 1963
6 NFC: Green Bay (2) vs. Boston (4), 1936
NFC-D: Baltimore (2) vs. Minnesota (4), 1968
AFC-D: Houston (1) vs. Oakland (5), 1969
AFC-FR: N.Y. Jets (1) vs. Houston (5), 1991
7 NFC-D: Washington (2) vs. N.Y. Giants (5), 1943
NFC: Baltimore (3) vs. N.Y. Giants (4), 1959
NFC: Washington (3) vs. Dallas (4), 1972
AFC-FR: N.Y. Jets (3) vs. Buffalo (4), 1981
NFC-D: Detroit (3) vs. Dallas (4), 1991
AFC-D: Kansas City (3) vs. Houston (4), 1993
NFC-FR: Detroit (1) vs. Green Bay (6), 1994

PASSING

Most First Downs, Passing, Game

21 AFC-D: Miami vs. San Diego, 1981 (OT)
AFC-D: San Diego vs. Miami, 1981 (OT)
AFC-D: Cleveland vs. N.Y. Jets, 1986 (OT)
NFC-D: Philadelphia vs. Chicago, 1988
20 NFC-FR: Dallas vs. L.A. Rams, 1983
AFC-D: Buffalo vs. Cleveland, 1989
19 NFC-FR: St. Louis vs. Green Bay, 1982
NFC-FR: Dallas vs. Tampa Bay, 1982
AFC-FR: Pittsburgh vs. San Diego, 1982
AFC-FR: San Diego vs. Pittsburgh, 1982
NFC: Dallas vs. Washington, 1982
NFC-D: Detroit vs. Dallas, 1991
AFC-FR: Kansas City vs. Pittsburgh, 1993 (OT)

Fewest First Downs, Passing, Game

0 NFC: Philadelphia vs. Chi. Cardinals, 1948
1 NFC-D: N.Y. Giants vs. Washington, 1943
NFC: Cleveland vs. Detroit, 1953
SB: Denver vs. Dallas, 1977
2 By many teams

Most First Downs, Passing, Both Teams, Game

42 AFC-D: Miami (21) vs. San Diego (21), 1981 (OT)
38 AFC-FR: Pittsburgh (19) vs. San Diego (19), 1982
34 NFC-FR: Washington (18) vs. San Francisco (16), 1990
AFC-FR: Kansas City (19) vs. Pittsburgh (15), 1993 (OT)

Fewest First Downs, Passing, Both Teams, Game

2 NFC: Philadelphia (0) vs. Chi. Cardinals (2), 1948
4 NFC-D: Cleveland (2) vs. N.Y. Giants (2), 1950
5 NFC: Detroit (2) vs. N.Y. Giants (3), 1935
NFC: Green Bay (2) vs. N.Y. Giants (3), 1939

PENALTY

Most First Downs, Penalty, Game

7 AFC-D: New England vs. Oakland, 1976
6 AFC-D: Cleveland vs. N.Y. Jets, 1986 (OT)
5 AFC-FR: Cleveland vs. L. A. Raiders, 1982

Most First Downs, Penalty, Both Teams, Game

9 AFC-D: New England (7) vs. Oakland (2), 1976
8 NFC-FR: Atlanta (4) vs. Minnesota (4), 1982
7 AFC-D: Baltimore (4) vs. Oakland (3), 1977 (OT)
AFC-FR: Denver (4) vs. L.A. Raiders (3), 1993

NET YARDS GAINED RUSHING AND PASSING

Most Yards Gained, Game

610 AFC: San Diego vs. Boston, 1963
602 SB: Washington vs. Denver, 1987
569 AFC: Miami vs. Pittsburgh, 1984

Fewest Yards Gained, Game

86 NFC-D: Cleveland vs. N.Y. Giants, 1958
99 NFC: Chi. Cardinals vs. Philadelphia, 1948
114 NFC-D: N.Y. Giants vs. Washington, 1943

Most Yards Gained, Both Teams, Game

1,036 AFC-D: San Diego (564) vs. Miami (472), 1981 (OT)
1,024 AFC: Miami (569) vs. Pittsburgh (455), 1984
929 SB: Washington (602) vs. Denver (327), 1987

Fewest Yards Gained, Both Teams, Game

331 NFC: Chi. Cardinals (99) vs. Philadelphia (232), 1948
332 NFC-D: N.Y. Giants (150) vs. Cleveland (182), 1950
336 NFC: Boston (116) vs. Green Bay (220), 1936

RUSHING

ATTEMPTS

Most Attempts, Game

65 NFC: Detroit vs. N.Y. Giants, 1935
61 NFC: Philadelphia vs. Los Angeles, 1949
59 AFC: New England vs. Miami, 1985

Fewest Attempts, Game

8 AFC-D: Miami vs. San Diego, 1994
9 SB: Miami vs. San Francisco, 1984
10 NFC: L.A. Rams vs. San Francisco, 1989

Most Attempts, Both Teams, Game

109 NFC: Detroit (65) vs. N.Y. Giants (44), 1935
97 AFC-D: Baltimore (50) vs. Oakland (47), 1977 (OT)
91 NFC: Philadelphia (57) vs. Chi. Cardinals (34), 1948

Fewest Attempts, Both Teams, Game

32 AFC-D: Houston (14) vs. Kansas City (18), 1993
38 NFC-D: Detroit (16) vs. Dallas (22), 1991
40 NFC-D: Green Bay (13) vs. Dallas (27), 1993

YARDS GAINED

Most Yards Gained, Game

382 NFC: Chi. Bears vs. Washington, 1940
338 NFC-FR: Dallas vs. Los Angeles, 1980
318 AFC: San Diego vs. Boston, 1963

Fewest Yards Gained, Game

–4 NFC-FR: Detroit vs. Green Bay, 1994
7 AFC-D: Buffalo vs. Boston, 1963
SB: New England vs. Chicago, 1985
17 SB: Minnesota vs. Pittsburgh, 1974

Most Yards Gained, Both Teams, Game

430 NFC-FR: Dallas (338) vs. Los Angeles (92), 1980
426 NFC: Cleveland (227) vs. Detroit (199), 1952
404 NFC: Chi. Bears (382) vs. Washington (22), 1940

Fewest Yards Gained, Both Teams, Game

77 NFC-FR: Detroit (–4) vs. Green Bay (81), 1994
90 AFC-D: Buffalo (7) vs. Boston (83), 1963
106 NFC: Boston (39) vs. Green Bay (67), 1936

AVERAGE GAIN

Highest Average Gain, Game

9.94 AFC: San Diego vs. Boston, 1963 (32-318)
9.29 NFC-D: Green Bay vs. Dallas, 1982 (17-158)
7.35 NFC-FR: Dallas vs. Los Angeles, 1980 (46-338)

Lowest Average Gain, Game

–0.27 NFC-FR: Detroit vs. Green Bay, 1994 (15-(–4))
0.58 AFC-D: Buffalo vs. Boston, 1963 (12-7)

0.64 SB: New England vs. Chicago, 1985 (11-7)

TOUCHDOWNS
Most Touchdowns, Game
7 NFC: Chi. Bears vs. Washington, 1940
6 NFC-D: San Francisco vs. N.Y. Giants, 1993
5 NFC: Cleveland vs. Detroit, 1954
NFC-D: San Francisco vs. Chicago, 1994
Most Touchdowns, Both Teams, Game
7 NFC: Chi. Bears (7) vs. Washington (0), 1940
6 NFC: Cleveland (5) vs. Detroit (1), 1954
NFC-D: San Francisco (6) vs. N.Y. Giants (0), 1993
NFC-D: San Francisco (5) vs. Chicago (1), 1994
5 NFC: Chi. Cardinals (3) vs. Philadelphia (2), 1947
AFC: San Diego (4) vs. Boston (1), 1963
AFC-D: Cincinnati (3) vs. Buffalo (2), 1981

PASSING
ATTEMPTS
Most Attempts, Game
65 AFC-D: Cleveland vs. N.Y. Jets, 1986 (OT)
61 NFC-FR: Minnesota vs. Chicago, 1994
59 SB: Buffalo vs. Washington, 1991
Fewest Attempts, Game
5 NFC: Detroit vs. N.Y. Giants, 1935
6 AFC: Miami vs. Oakland, 1973
7 SB: Miami vs. Minnesota, 1973
Most Attempts, Both Teams, Game
102 AFC-D: San Diego (54) vs. Miami (48), 1981 (OT)
96 AFC: N.Y. Jets (49) vs. Oakland (47), 1968
95 AFC-D: Cleveland (65) vs. N.Y. Jets (30), 1986 (OT)
Fewest Attempts, Both Teams, Game
18 NFC: Detroit (5) vs. N.Y. Giants (13), 1935
23 NFC: Chi. Cardinals (11) vs. Philadelphia (12), 1948
24 NFC-D: Cleveland (9) vs. N.Y. Giants (15), 1950

COMPLETIONS
Most Completions, Game
36 AFC-FR: Houston vs. Buffalo, 1992 (OT)
34 AFC-D: Cleveland vs. N.Y. Jets, 1986 (OT)
33 AFC-D: San Diego vs. Miami, 1981 (OT)
NFC-FR: Minnesota vs. Chicago, 1994
Fewest Completions, Game
2 NFC: Detroit vs. N.Y. Giants, 1935
NFC: Philadelphia vs. Chi. Cardinals, 1948
3 NFC: N.Y. Giants vs. Chi. Bears, 1941
NFC: Green Bay vs. N.Y. Giants, 1944
NFC: Chi. Cardinals vs. Philadelphia, 1947
NFC: Chi. Cardinals vs. Philadelphia, 1948
NFC-D: Cleveland vs. N.Y. Giants, 1950
NFC-D: N.Y. Giants vs. Cleveland, 1950
NFC: Cleveland vs. Detroit, 1953
AFC: Miami vs. Oakland, 1973
4 NFC: N.Y. Giants vs. Detroit, 1935
NFC-D: N.Y. Giants vs. Washington, 1943
NFC-D: Pittsburgh vs. Philadelphia, 1947
NFC-D: Dallas vs. Detroit, 1970
AFC: Miami vs. Baltimore, 1971
SB: Miami vs. Washington, 1982
AFC-FR: Seattle vs. L.A. Raiders, 1984
Most Completions, Both Teams, Game
64 AFC-D: San Diego (33) vs. Miami (31), 1981 (OT)
57 AFC-FR: Houston (36) vs. Buffalo (21), 1992 (OT)
56 NFC-D: Dallas (28) vs. Green Bay (28), 1993
Fewest Completions, Both Teams, Game
5 NFC: Philadelphia (2) vs. Chi. Cardinals (3), 1948
6 NFC: Detroit (2) vs. N.Y. Giants (4), 1935
NFC-D: Cleveland (3) vs. N.Y. Giants (3), 1950
11 NFC: Green Bay (3) vs. N.Y. Giants (8), 1944
NFC-D: Dallas (4) vs. Detroit (7), 1970

COMPLETION PERCENTAGE
Highest Completion Percentage, Game (20 attempts)
88.0 SB: N.Y. Giants vs. Denver, 1986 (25-22)
87.1 NFC: San Francisco vs. L.A. Rams, 1989 (31-27)
80.0 NFC-D: Washington vs. L.A. Rams, 1983 (25-20)
Lowest Completion Percentage, Game (20 attempts)
18.5 NFC: Tampa Bay vs. Los Angeles, 1979 (27-5)
20.0 NFC-D: N.Y. Giants vs. Washington, 1943 (20-4)
25.8 NFC: Chi. Bears vs. Washington, 1937 (31-8)

YARDS GAINED
Most Yards Gained, Game
483 AFC-D: Cleveland vs. N.Y. Jets, 1986 (OT)
435 AFC: Miami vs. Pittsburgh, 1984
415 AFC-D: San Diego vs. Miami, 1981 (OT)
Fewest Yards Gained, Game
3 NFC: Chi. Cardinals vs. Philadelphia, 1948
7 NFC: Philadelphia vs. Chi. Cardinals, 1948
9 NFC-D: N.Y. Giants vs. Cleveland, 1950
NFC: Cleveland vs. Detroit, 1953
Most Yards Gained, Both Teams, Game
809 AFC-D: San Diego (415) vs. Miami (394), 1981 (OT)
747 AFC: Miami (435) vs. Pittsburgh (312), 1984
666 AFC-D: Cleveland (483) vs. N.Y. Jets (183), 1986 (OT)
Fewest Yards Gained, Both Teams, Game
10 NFC: Chi. Cardinals (3) vs. Philadelphia (7), 1948
38 NFC-D: N.Y. Giants (9) vs. Cleveland (29), 1950
102 NFC-D: Dallas (22) vs. Detroit (80), 1970

TIMES SACKED
Most Times Sacked, Game
9 AFC: Kansas City vs. Buffalo, 1966
NFC: Chicago vs. San Francisco, 1984
AFC-D: N.Y. Jets vs. Cleveland, 1986 (OT)
AFC-D: Houston vs. Kansas City, 1993
8 NFC: Green Bay vs. Dallas, 1967
NFC: Minnesota vs. Washington, 1987
7 NFC-D: Dallas vs. Los Angeles, 1973
SB: Dallas vs. Pittsburgh, 1975
AFC-FR: Houston vs. Oakland, 1980
NFC-D: Washington vs. Chicago, 1984
SB: New England vs. Chicago, 1985
AFC-FR: Kansas City vs. San Diego, 1992
AFC-D: Pittsburgh vs. Buffalo, 1992
Most Times Sacked, Both Teams, Game
13 AFC: Kansas City (9) vs. Buffalo (4), 1966
AFC-D: N.Y. Jets (9) vs. Cleveland (4), 1986 (OT)
12 NFC-D: Dallas (7) vs. Los Angeles (5), 1973
NFC-D: Washington (7) vs. Chicago (5), 1984
NFC: Chicago (9) vs. San Francisco (3), 1984
AFC-FR: Kansas City (7) vs. San Diego (5), 1992
11 AFC-D: Houston (9) vs. Kansas City (2), 1993
Fewest Times Sacked, Both Teams, Game
0 AFC-D: Buffalo vs. Pittsburgh, 1974
AFC-FR: Pittsburgh vs. San Diego, 1982
AFC: Miami vs. Pittsburgh, 1984
AFC-D: Buffalo vs. Miami, 1990
AFC-D: Denver vs. Houston, 1991
1 In many games

TOUCHDOWNS
Most Touchdowns, Game
6 AFC-D: Oakland vs. Houston, 1969
SB: San Francisco vs. San Diego, 1994
5 NFC: Chi. Bears vs. Washington, 1943
NFC: Detroit vs. Cleveland, 1957
AFC-D: Oakland vs. Kansas City, 1968
SB: San Francisco vs. Denver, 1989
4 By many teams
Most Touchdowns, Both Teams, Game
8 AFC-FR: Buffalo (4) vs. Houston (4), 1992 (OT)
7 NFC: Chi. Bears (5) vs. Washington (2), 1943
AFC-D: Oakland (6) vs. Houston (1), 1969
SB: Pittsburgh (4) vs. Dallas (3), 1978
AFC-D: Miami (4) vs. San Diego (3), 1981 (OT)
AFC: Miami (4) vs. Pittsburgh (3), 1984
AFC-D: Buffalo (4) vs. Cleveland (3), 1989
SB: San Francisco (6) vs. San Diego (1), 1994
6 NFC-FR: Green Bay (4) vs. St. Louis (2), 1982
AFC: Cleveland (3) vs. Denver (3), 1987
AFC-D: Buffalo (3) vs. Miami (3), 1990
AFC-FR: Denver (3) vs. L.A. Raiders (3), 1993

INTERCEPTIONS BY
Most Interceptions By, Game
8 NFC: Chi. Bears vs. Washington, 1940
7 NFC: Cleveland vs. Los Angeles, 1955
6 NFC: Green Bay vs. N.Y. Giants, 1939
NFC: Chi. Bears vs. N.Y. Giants, 1946
NFC: Cleveland vs. Detroit, 1954
AFC: San Diego vs. Houston, 1961
AFC: Buffalo vs. L.A. Raiders, 1990

Most Interceptions By, Both Teams, Game

10 NFC: Cleveland (7) vs. Los Angeles (3), 1955
AFC: San Diego (6) vs. Houston (4), 1961
9 NFC: Green Bay (6) vs. N.Y. Giants (3), 1939
8 NFC: Chi. Bears (8) vs. Washington (0), 1940
NFC: Chi. Bears (6) vs. N.Y. Giants (2), 1946
NFC: Cleveland (6) vs. Detroit (2), 1954
AFC-FR: Buffalo (4) vs. N.Y. Jets (4), 1981
AFC: Miami (5) vs. N.Y. Jets (3), 1982

YARDS GAINED

Most Yards Gained, Game

138 AFC-FR: N.Y. Jets vs. Cincinnati, 1982
136 AFC: Dall. Texans vs. Houston, 1962 (OT)
130 NFC-D: Los Angeles vs. St. Louis, 1975

Most Yards Gained, Both Teams, Game

156 NFC: Green Bay (123) vs. N.Y. Giants (33), 1939
149 NFC: Cleveland (103) vs. Los Angeles (46), 1955
141 AFC-FR: Buffalo (79) vs. N.Y. Jets (62), 1981

TOUCHDOWNS

Most Touchdowns, Game

3 NFC: Chi. Bears vs. Washington, 1940
2 NFC-D: Los Angeles vs. St. Louis, 1975
1 In many games

Most Touchdowns, Both Teams, Game

3 NFC: Chi. Bears (3) vs. Washington (0), 1940
2 NFC-D: Los Angeles (2) vs. St. Louis(0), 1975
NFC-D: Dallas (1) vs. Green Bay (1), 1982
NFC-D: Minnesota (1) vs. San Francisco (1), 1987
NFC-FR: Detroit (1) vs. Green Bay (1), 1993
1 In many games

PUNTING

Most Punts, Game

14 AFC-D: N.Y. Jets vs. Cleveland, 1986 (OT)
13 NFC: N.Y. Giants vs. Chi. Bears, 1933
AFC-D: Baltimore vs. Oakland, 1977 (OT)
11 AFC: Houston vs. Oakland, 1967
AFC-D: Houston vs. Oakland, 1969
NFC: L.A. Rams vs. Chicago, 1985

Fewest Punts, Game

0 NFC-FR: St. Louis vs. Green Bay, 1982
AFC-FR: N.Y. Jets vs. Cincinnati, 1982
1 NFC-D: Cleveland vs. Dallas, 1969
AFC: Miami vs. Oakland, 1973
AFC-D: Oakland vs. Cincinnati, 1975
AFC-D: Pittsburgh vs. Baltimore, 1976
AFC: Pittsburgh vs. Houston, 1978
NFC-FR: Green Bay vs. St. Louis, 1982
AFC-FR: Miami vs. New England, 1982
AFC-FR: San Diego vs. Pittsburgh, 1982
AFC-D: Cleveland vs. Indianapolis, 1987
AFC-D: Buffalo vs. Miami, 1990
AFC-FR: L.A. Raiders vs. Kansas City, 1991
NFC-FR: Atlanta vs. New Orleans, 1991
NFC-FR: Chicago vs. Dallas, 1991
AFC-D: Houston vs. Denver, 1991
NFC: San Francisco vs. Dallas, 1992
NFC: Dallas vs. San Francisco, 1994
2 In many games

Most Punts, Both Teams, Game

23 NFC: N.Y. Giants (13) vs. Chi. Bears (10), 1933
22 AFC-D: N.Y. Jets (14) vs. Cleveland (8), 1986 (OT)
21 AFC-D: Baltimore (13) vs. Oakland (8), 1977 (OT)
NFC: L.A. Rams (11) vs. Chicago (10), 1985

Fewest Punts, Both Teams, Game

1 NFC-FR: St. Louis (0) vs. Green Bay (1), 1982
2 AFC-FR: N.Y. Jets (0) vs. Cincinnati (2), 1982
3 AFC: Miami (1) vs. Oakland (2), 1973
AFC-FR: San Diego (1) vs. Pittsburgh (2), 1982
AFC-D: Buffalo (1) vs. Miami (2), 1990
AFC-FR: L.A. Raiders (1) vs. Kansas City (2), 1991
AFC-D: Houston (1) vs. Denver (2), 1991

AVERAGE YARDAGE

Highest Average, Punting, Game (4 punts)

56.0 AFC: Oakland vs. San Diego, 1980
52.5 NFC: Washington vs. Chi. Bears, 1942
51.6 AFC-D: Cincinnati vs. L.A. Raiders, 1990

Lowest Average, Punting, Game (4 punts)

24.9 NFC: Washington vs. Chi. Bears, 1937
25.3 AFC-FR: Pittsburgh vs. Houston, 1989
25.5 NFC: Green Bay vs. N.Y. Giants, 1962

PUNT RETURNS

Most Punt Returns, Game

8 NFC: Green Bay vs. N.Y. Giants, 1944
7 By eight teams

Most Punt Returns, Both Teams, Game

13 AFC-FR: Houston (7) vs. Oakland (6), 1980
11 NFC: Green Bay (8) vs. N.Y. Giants (3), 1944
NFC-D: Green Bay (6) vs. Baltimore (5), 1965
10 In many games

Fewest Punt Returns, Both Teams, Game

0 NFC: Chi. Bears vs. N.Y. Giants, 1941
AFC: Boston vs. San Diego, 1963
NFC-FR: Green Bay vs. St. Louis, 1982
AFC-FR: Houston vs. N.Y. Jets, 1991
AFC-D: Denver vs. Houston, 1991
NFC-D: San Francisco vs. Washington, 1992
1 In many games

YARDS GAINED

Most Yards Gained, Game

155 NFC-D: Dallas vs. Cleveland, 1967
150 NFC: Chi. Cardinals vs. Philadelphia, 1947
143 NFC-FR: Minnesota vs. New Orleans, 1987

Fewest Yards Gained, Game

−10 NFC: Green Bay vs. Cleveland, 1965
−9 NFC: Dallas vs. Green Bay, 1966
AFC-D: Kansas City vs. Oakland, 1968
−5 AFC-D: Miami vs. Oakland, 1970
NFC-D: San Francisco vs. Dallas, 1972
NFC: Dallas vs. Washington, 1972

Most Yards Gained, Both Teams, Game

166 NFC-D: Dallas (155) vs. Cleveland (11), 1967
160 NFC: Chi. Cardinals (150) vs. Philadelphia (10), 1947
146 NFC-D: Philadelphia (112) vs. Pittsburgh (34), 1947

Fewest Yards Gained, Both Teams, Game

−9 NFC: Dallas (−9) vs. Green Bay (0), 1966
−6 AFC-D: Miami (−5) vs. Oakland (−1), 1970
−3 NFC-D: San Francisco (−5) vs. Dallas (2), 1972

TOUCHDOWNS

Most Touchdowns, Game

1 By 10 teams

KICKOFF RETURNS

Most Kickoff Returns, Game

10 NFC-D: L.A. Rams vs. Washington, 1983
9 NFC: Chi. Bears vs. N.Y. Giants, 1956
AFC: Boston vs. San Diego, 1963
AFC: Houston vs. Oakland, 1967
SB: Denver vs. San Francisco, 1989
AFC-D: Miami vs. Buffalo, 1990
AFC: L.A. Raiders vs. Buffalo, 1990
8 By many teams

Most Kickoff Returns, Both Teams, Game

15 AFC-D: Miami (9) vs. Buffalo (6), 1990
13 NFC-D: Green Bay (7) vs. Dallas (6), 1982
12 In many games

Fewest Kickoff Returns, Both Teams, Game

1 NFC: Green Bay (0) vs. Boston (1), 1936
AFC-FR: San Diego (0) vs. Kansas City (1), 1992
2 NFC-D: Los Angeles (0) vs. Chi. Bears (2), 1950
AFC: Houston (0) vs. San Diego (2), 1961
AFC-D: Oakland (1) vs. Pittsburgh (1), 1972
AFC-D: N.Y. Jets (0) vs. L.A. Raiders (2), 1982
AFC: Miami (1) vs. N.Y. Jets (1), 1982
NFC: N.Y. Giants (0) vs. Washington (2), 1986
3 In many games

YARDS GAINED

Most Yards Gained, Game

242 SB: San Diego vs. San Francisco, 1994
225 NFC: Washington vs. Chi. Bears, 1940
222 SB: Miami vs. Washington, 1982

Most Yards Gained, Both Teams, Game

379 AFC-D: Baltimore (193) vs. Oakland (186), 1977 (OT)
321 NFC-D: Dallas (173) vs. Green Bay (148), 1982
318 AFC-D: Miami (183) vs. Oakland (135), 1974

Fewest Yards Gained, Both Teams, Game

5 AFC-FR: San Diego (0) vs. Kansas City (5), 1992
15 NFC: N.Y. Giants (0) vs. Washington (15), 1986
31 NFC-D: Los Angeles (0) vs. Chi. Bears (31), 1950

POSTSEASON GAME RECORDS

TOUCHDOWNS

Most Touchdowns, Game

1 NFC-D: San Francisco vs. Dallas, 1972
AFC-D: Miami vs. Oakland, 1974
AFC-D: Baltimore vs. Oakland, 1977 (OT)
SB: Miami vs. Washington, 1982
SB: Cincinnati vs. San Francisco, 1988
AFC-D: Cleveland vs. Buffalo, 1989
SB: San Diego vs. San Francisco, 1994

PENALTIES

Most Penalties, Game

17 AFC-FR: L.A. Raiders vs. Denver, 1993
14 AFC-FR: Oakland vs. Houston, 1980
NFC-D: San Francisco vs. N.Y. Giants, 1981
13 AFC-FR: Houston vs. Cleveland, 1988
AFC-D: Houston vs. Denver, 1991

Fewest Penalties, Game

0 NFC: Philadelphia vs. Green Bay, 1960
NFC-D: Detroit vs. Dallas, 1970
AFC-D: Miami vs. Oakland, 1970
SB: Miami vs. Dallas, 1971
NFC-D: Washington vs. Minnesota, 1973
SB: Pittsburgh vs. Dallas, 1975
NFC: San Francisco vs. Chicago, 1988
SB: Denver vs. San Francisco, 1989
AFC-D: L.A. Raiders vs. Cincinnati, 1990
AFC-D: Miami vs. San Diego, 1992
1 By many teams

Most Penalties, Both Teams, Game

27 AFC-FR: L.A. Raiders (17) vs. Denver (10), 1993
22 AFC-FR: Oakland (14) vs. Houston (8), 1980
NFC-D: San Francisco (14) vs. N.Y. Giants (8), 1981
AFC-FR: Houston (13) vs. Cleveland (9), 1988
21 AFC-D: Oakland (11) vs. New England (10), 1976

Fewest Penalties, Both Teams, Game

1 AFC-D: L.A. Raiders (0) vs. Cincinnati (1), 1990
2 NFC: Washington (1) vs. Chi. Bears (1), 1937
NFC-D: Washington (0) vs. Minnesota (2), 1973
SB: Pittsburgh (0) vs. Dallas (2), 1975
3 AFC: Miami (1) vs. Baltimore (2), 1971
NFC: San Francisco (1) vs. Dallas (2), 1971
SB: Miami (0) vs. Dallas (3), 1971
AFC-D: Pittsburgh (1) vs. Oakland (2), 1972
AFC-D: Miami (1) vs. Cincinnati (2), 1973
SB: Miami (1) vs. San Francisco (2), 1984
NFC: San Francisco (0) vs. Chicago (3), 1988

YARDS PENALIZED

Most Yards Penalized, Game

145 NFC-D: San Francisco vs. N.Y. Giants, 1981
133 SB: Dallas vs. Baltimore, 1970
130 AFC-FR: L.A. Raiders vs. Denver, 1993

Fewest Yards Penalized, Game

0 By 10 teams

Most Yards Penalized, Both Teams, Game

227 AFC-FR: L.A. Raiders (130) vs. Denver (97), 1993
206 NFC-D: San Francisco (145) vs. N.Y. Giants (61), 1981
193 AFC-FR: Houston (118) vs. Cleveland (75), 1988

Fewest Yards Penalized, Both Teams, Game

5 AFC-D: L.A. Raiders (0) vs. Cincinnati (5), 1990
9 NFC-D: Washington (0) vs. Minnesota (9), 1973
15 SB: Miami (0) vs. Dallas (15), 1971

FUMBLES

Most Fumbles, Game

8 SB: Buffalo vs. Dallas, 1992
7 AFC-D: Houston vs. Kansas City, 1993
6 By 11 teams

Most Fumbles, Both Teams, Game

12 AFC: Houston (6) vs. Pittsburgh (6), 1978
SB: Buffalo (8) vs. Dallas (4), 1992
10 NFC: Chi. Bears (5) vs. N.Y. Giants (5), 1934
SB: Dallas (6) vs. Denver (4), 1977
9 NFC-D: San Francisco (6) vs. Detroit (3), 1957
NFC-D: San Francisco (5) vs. Dallas (4), 1972
NFC: Dallas (5) vs. Philadelphia (4), 1980

Most Fumbles Lost, Game

5 SB: Buffalo vs. Dallas, 1992
4 NFC: N.Y. Giants vs. Baltimore, 1958 (OT)
AFC: Kansas City vs. Oakland, 1969
SB: Baltimore vs. Dallas, 1970
AFC: Pittsburgh vs. Oakland, 1975
SB: Denver vs. Dallas, 1977
AFC: Houston vs. Pittsburgh, 1978
AFC: Miami vs. New England, 1985
SB: New England vs. Chicago, 1985
NFC-FR: L.A. Rams vs. Washington, 1986
3 By many teams

Fewest Fumbles, Both Teams, Game

0 NFC: Green Bay vs. Cleveland, 1965
AFC-D: Houston vs. San Diego, 1979
NFC-D: Dallas vs. Los Angeles, 1979
SB: Los Angeles vs. Pittsburgh, 1979
AFC-D: Buffalo vs. Cincinnati, 1981
NFC-D: San Francisco vs. Washington, 1990
1 In many games

RECOVERIES

Most Total Fumbles Recovered, Game

8 SB: Dallas vs. Denver, 1977 (4 own, 4 opp)
7 NFC: Chi. Bears vs. N.Y. Giants, 1934 (5 own, 2 opp)
NFC-D: San Francisco vs. Detroit, 1957 (4 own, 3 opp)
NFC-D: San Francisco vs. Dallas, 1972 (4 own, 3 opp)
AFC: Pittsburgh vs. Houston, 1978 (3 own, 4 opp)
6 AFC: Houston vs. San Diego, 1961 (4 own, 2 opp)
AFC-D: Cleveland vs. Baltimore, 1971 (4 own, 2 opp)
AFC-D: Cleveland vs. Oakland, 1980 (5 own, 1 opp)
NFC: Philadelphia vs. Dallas, 1980 (3 own, 3 opp)
SB: Dallas vs. Buffalo, 1992 (1 own, 5 opp)

Most Own Fumbles Recovered, Game

5 NFC: Chi. Bears vs. N.Y. Giants, 1934
AFC-D: Cleveland vs. Oakland, 1980
4 By many teams

TURNOVERS

(Numbers of times losing the ball on interceptions and fumbles.)

Most Turnovers, Game

9 NFC: Washington vs. Chi. Bears, 1940
NFC: Detroit vs. Cleveland, 1954
AFC: Houston vs. Pittsburgh, 1978
SB: Buffalo vs. Dallas, 1992
8 NFC: N.Y. Giants vs. Chi. Bears, 1946
NFC: Los Angeles vs. Cleveland, 1955
NFC: Cleveland vs. Detroit, 1957
SB: Denver vs. Dallas, 1977
NFC-D: Minnesota vs. Philadelphia, 1980
7 AFC: Houston vs. San Diego, 1961
SB: Baltimore vs. Dallas, 1970
AFC: Pittsburgh vs. Oakland, 1975
NFC-D: Chicago vs. Dallas, 1977
NFC: Los Angeles vs. Dallas, 1978
AFC-D: San Diego vs. Miami, 1982
AFC: Buffalo vs. L.A. Raiders, 1990

Fewest Turnovers, Game

0 By many teams

Most Turnovers, Both Teams, Game

14 AFC: Houston (9) vs. Pittsburgh (5), 1978
13 NFC: Detroit (9) vs. Cleveland (4), 1954
AFC: Houston (7) vs. San Diego (6), 1961
12 AFC: Pittsburgh (7) vs. Oakland (5), 1975

Fewest Turnovers, Both Teams, Game

0 SB: Buffalo vs. N.Y. Giants, 1990
FR: Kansas City vs Pittsburgh, 1993 (OT)
NFC-FR: Detroit vs. Green Bay, 1994
1 AFC-D: Baltimore (0) vs. Cincinnati (1), 1970
AFC-D: Pittsburgh (0) vs. Buffalo (1), 1974
AFC: Oakland (0) vs. Pittsburgh (1), 1976
NFC-D: Minnesota (0) vs. Washington (1), 1982
NFC-D: Chicago (0) vs. N.Y. Giants (1), 1985
SB: N.Y. Giants (0) vs. Denver (1), 1986
NFC: Washington (0) vs. Minnesota (1), 1987
AFC-D: Cincinnati (0) vs. L.A. Raiders (1), 1990
NFC: N.Y. Giants (0) vs. San Francisco (1), 1990
NFC-FR: N.Y. Giants (0) vs. Minnesota (1), 1993
AFC-FR: L.A. Raiders (0) vs. Denver (1), 1993
NFC: Dallas (0) vs. San Francisco (1), 1993
2 In many games

Compiled by Elias Sports Bureau

INDIVIDUAL RECORDS

SERVICE

Most Games

10 Lawrence Taylor, N.Y. Giants, 1982-91
Ronnie Lott, San Francisco, 1982-85, 1987-91; L.A. Raiders 1992
Mike Singletary, Chicago, 1984-93
9 *Ken Houston, Houston, 1971-73; Washington, 1974-79
Joe Greene, Pittsburgh, 1971-77, 1979-80
Jack Lambert, Pittsburgh, 1976-84
Walter Payton, Chicago, 1977-81, 1984-87
Harry Carson, N.Y. Giants, 1979-80, 1982-88
Mike Webster, Pittsburgh, 1979-86, 1988
**Anthony Muñoz, Cincinnati, 1982-87, 1989-90, 1992
8 Tom Mack, Los Angeles, 1971-76, 1978-79
*Franco Harris, Pittsburgh, 1973-76, 1978-81
Lemar Parrish, Cincinnati, 1971-72, 1975-77; Washington, 1978, 1980-81
Art Shell, Oakland, 1973-79, 1981
Ted Hendricks, Baltimore, 1972-74; Green Bay, 1975; Oakland, 1981-82; L.A. Raiders, 1983-84
*John Hannah, New England, 1977, 1979-83, 1985-86
*Randy White, Dallas, 1978, 1980-86
*Mike Haynes, New England, 1978-81, 1983; L.A. Raiders, 1985-87
James Lofton, Green Bay, 1979, 1981-86; Buffalo 1992
*Mike Munchak, Houston, 1985-86, 1988-93
Howie Long, L.A. Raiders, 1984-88, 1990, 1993-94
Reggie White, Philadelphia, 1987-93; Green Bay, 1994
**Also selected, but did not play, in one additional game*
***Also selected, but did not play, in two additional games*

SCORING

POINTS

Most Points, Career

37 Morten Andersen, New Orleans, 1986-89, 1991, 1993 (13-pat, 8-fg)
30 Jan Stenerud, Kansas City, 1971-72, 1976; Green Bay, 1985 (6-pat, 8-fg)
26 Nick Lowery, Kansas City, 1982, 1991, 1993 (5 pat, 7 fg)

Most Points, Game

18 John Brockington, Green Bay, 1973 (3-td)
15 Garo Yepremian, Miami, 1974 (5-fg)
14 Jan Stenerud, Kansas City, 1972 (2-pat, 4-fg)

TOUCHDOWNS

Most Touchdowns, Career

3 John Brockington, Green Bay, 1972-74 (2-r, 1-p)
Earl Campbell, Houston, 1979-82, 1984 (3-r)
Chuck Muncie, New Orleans, 1980; San Diego, 1982-83 (3-r)
William Andrews, Atlanta, 1981-84 (1-r, 2-p)
Marcus Allen, L.A. Raiders, 1983, 1985-86, 1988; Kansas City, 1994 (2-r, 1-p)
2 By 15 players

Most Touchdowns, Game

3 John Brockington, Green Bay, 1973 (2-r, 1-p)
2 Mel Renfro, Dallas, 1971 (2-ret)
Earl Campbell, Houston, 1980 (2-r)
Chuck Muncie, New Orleans, 1980 (2-r)
William Andrews, Atlanta, 1984 (2-p)
Herschel Walker, Dallas, 1989 (2-r)
Johnny Johnson, Phoenix, 1991 (2-r)
Eric Green, Pittsburgh, 1995 (2-p)

POINTS AFTER TOUCHDOWN

Most Points After Touchdown, Career

13 Morten Andersen, New Orleans, 1986-89, 1991, 1993 (13 att)
6 Chester Marcol, Green Bay, 1973, 1975 (6 att)
Mark Moseley, Washington, 1980, 1983 (7 att)
Ali Haji-Sheikh, N.Y. Giants, 1984 (6 att)
Jan Stenerud, Kansas City, 1971-72, 1976; Green Bay, 1985 (6 att)
5 Nick Lowery, Kansas City, 1982, 1991, 1993 (5 att)
John Carney, San Diego, 1995 (5 att)

Most Points After Touchdown, Game

6 Ali Haji-Sheikh, N.Y. Giants, 1984 (6 att)
5 John Carney, San Diego, 1995 (5 att)
4 Chester Marcol, Green Bay, 1973 (4 att)
Mark Moseley, Washington, 1980 (5 att)
Morten Andersen, New Orleans, 1986 (4 att), 1989 (4 att)

FIELD GOALS

Most Field Goals Attempted, Career

15 Jan Stenerud, Kansas City, 1971-72, 1976; Green Bay, 1985
Morten Andersen, New Orleans, 1986-89, 1991, 1993
10 Nick Lowery, Kansas City, 1982, 1991, 1993
9 Eddie Murray, Detroit, 1980, 1989

Most Field Goals Attempted, Game

6 Jan Stenerud, Kansas City, 1972
Eddie Murray, Detroit, 1981
Mark Moseley, Washington, 1983
5 Garo Yepremian, Miami, 1974
4 Jan Stenerud, Kansas City, 1976
Nick Lowery, Kansas City, 1991, 1993
Morten Andersen, New Orleans, 1993

Most Field Goals, Career

8 Jan Stenerud, Kansas City, 1971-72, 1976; Green Bay, 1985
Morten Andersen, New Orleans, 1986-89, 1991, 1993
7 Nick Lowery, Kansas City, 1982, 1991, 1993
6 Eddie Murray, Detroit, 1980, 1989

Most Field Goals, Game

5 Garo Yepremian, Miami, 1974 (5 att)
4 Jan Stenerud, Kansas City, 1972 (6 att)
Eddie Murray, Detroit, 1981 (6 att)
3 Nick Lowery, Kansas City, 1991 (4 att)
Nick Lowery, Kansas City, 1993 (4 att)

Longest Field Goal

51 Morten Andersen, New Orleans, 1989
49 Fuad Reveiz, Minnesota, 1995
48 Jan Stenerud, Kansas City, 1972
Jeff Jaeger, L.A. Raiders, 1992

SAFETIES

Most Safeties, Game

1 Art Still, Kansas City, 1983
Mark Gastineau, N.Y. Jets, 1985
Greg Townsend, L.A. Raiders, 1992

RUSHING

ATTEMPTS

Most Attempts, Career

81 Walter Payton, Chicago, 1977-81, 1984-87
68 O.J. Simpson, Buffalo, 1973-77
63 Eric Dickerson, L.A. Rams, 1984-85, 1987; Indianapolis, 1988-90

Most Attempts, Game

19 O.J. Simpson, Buffalo, 1974
17 Marv Hubbard, Oakland, 1974
16 O.J. Simpson, Buffalo, 1973
Marcus Allen, L.A. Raiders, 1986

YARDS GAINED

Most Yards Gained, Career

368 Walter Payton, Chicago, 1977-81, 1984-87
356 O.J. Simpson, Buffalo, 1973-77
220 Earl Campbell, Houston, 1979-82, 1984

Most Yards Gained, Game

180 Marshall Faulk, Indianapolis, 1995
127 Chris Warren, Seattle, 1995
112 O. J. Simpson, Buffalo, 1973

Longest Run From Scrimmage

49 Marshall Faulk, Indianapolis, 1995 (TD)
41 Lawrence McCutcheon, Los Angeles, 1976
Natrone Means, San Diego, 1995
Marshall Faulk, Indianapolis, 1995
39 Chris Warren, Seattle, 1994

AVERAGE GAIN

Highest Average Gain, Career (20 attempts)

5.81 Marv Hubbard, Oakland, 1972-74 (36-209)
5.71 Wilbert Montgomery, Philadelphia, 1979-80 (21-120)
5.36 Larry Csonka, Miami, 1971-72, 1975 (22-118)

Highest Average Gain, Game (10 attempts)

13.85 Marshall Faulk, Indianapolis, 1995 (13-180)
9.07 Chris Warren, Seattle, 1995 (14-127)
7.00 O.J. Simpson, Buffalo, 1973 (16-112)
Ottis Anderson, St. Louis, 1981 (10-70)

TOUCHDOWNS

Most Touchdowns, Career

3 Earl Campbell, Houston, 1979-82, 1984
Chuck Muncie, New Orleans, 1980; San Diego, 1982-83
2 John Brockington, Green Bay, 1972-74
O.J. Simpson, Buffalo, 1973-77
Walter Payton, Chicago, 1977-81, 1984-87
Marcus Allen, L.A. Raiders, 1983, 1985-86, 1988; Kansas City, 1994
Herschel Walker, Dallas, 1988-89
Johnny Johnson, Phoenix, 1991

AFC-NFC PRO BOWL RECORDS

Most Touchdowns, Game

2 John Brockington, Green Bay, 1973
Earl Campbell, Houston, 1980
Chuck Muncie, New Orleans, 1980
Herschel Walker, Dallas, 1989
Johnny Johnson, Phoenix, 1991

PASSING

ATTEMPTS

Most Attempts, Career

120 Dan Fouts, San Diego, 1980-84, 1986
88 Bob Griese, Miami, 1971-72, 1974-75, 1977, 1979
76 Warren Moon, Houston, 1989-94; Minnesota, 1995

Most Attempts, Game

32 Bill Kenney, Kansas City, 1984
Steve Young, San Francisco, 1993
30 Dan Fouts, San Diego, 1983
28 Jim Hart, St. Louis, 1976

COMPLETIONS

Most Completions, Career

63 Dan Fouts, San Diego, 1980-84, 1986
44 Bob Griese, Miami, 1971-72, 1974-75, 1977, 1979
37 Warren Moon, Houston, 1989-94; Minnesota, 1995

Most Completions, Game

21 Joe Theismann, Washington, 1984
18 Steve Young, San Francisco, 1993
17 Dan Fouts, San Diego, 1983

COMPLETION PERCENTAGE

Highest Completion Percentage, Career (40 attempts)

68.9 Joe Theismann, Washington, 1983-84 (45-31)
64.4 Jim Kelly, Buffalo, 1988, 1991-92 (45-29)
58.9 Ken Anderson, Cincinnati, 1976-77, 1982-83 (56-33)

Highest Completion Percentage, Game (10 attempts)

90.0 Archie Manning, New Orleans, 1980 (10-9)
77.8 Joe Theismann, Washington, 1984 (27-21)
72.2 Jim Everett, L.A. Rams, 1991 (18-13)

YARDS GAINED

Most Yards Gained, Career

890 Dan Fouts, San Diego, 1980-84, 1986
554 Bob Griese, Miami, 1971-72, 1974-75, 1977, 1979
398 Ken Anderson, Cincinnati, 1976-77, 1982-83

Most Yards Gained, Game

274 Dan Fouts, San Diego, 1983
242 Joe Theismann, Washington, 1984
212 Phil Simms, N.Y. Giants, 1986

Longest Completion

64 Dan Pastorini, Houston (to Burrough, Houston), 1976 (TD)
59 Randall Cunningham, Philadelphia (to Jackson, Philadelphia [19 yards] lateral to Byner, Washington [40 yards]), 1991
57 James Harris, Los Angeles (to Gray, St. Louis), 1975
Ken Anderson, Cincinnati (to G. Pruitt, Cleveland), 1977

AVERAGE GAIN

Highest Average Gain, Career (40 attempts)

8.02 Jim Kelly, Buffalo, 1988, 1991-92 (45-361)
7.91 Randall Cunningham, Philadelphia, 1989-91 (44-348)
7.64 Joe Theismann, Washington, 1983-84 (45-344)

Highest Average Gain, Game (10 attempts)

15.27 Randall Cunningham, Philadelphia, 1991 (11-168)
11.40 Ken Anderson, Cincinnati, 1977 (10-114)
11.20 Archie Manning, New Orleans, 1980 (10-112)

TOUCHDOWNS

Most Touchdowns, Career

3 Joe Theismann, Washington, 1983-84
Joe Montana, San Francisco, 1982, 1984-85, 1988
Phil Simms, N.Y. Giants, 1986
Jim Kelly, Buffalo, 1988, 1991-92
2 James Harris, Los Angeles, 1975
Mike Boryla, Philadelphia, 1976
Ken Anderson, Cincinnati, 1976-77, 1982-83
Bob Griese, Miami, 1971-72, 1974-75, 1977, 1979
Mark Rypien, Washington, 1990, 1992
John Elway, Denver, 1987-88, 1994-95
Steve Young, San Francisco, 1993-95

Most Touchdowns, Game

3 Joe Theismann, Washington, 1984
Phil Simms, N.Y. Giants, 1986
2 James Harris, Los Angeles, 1975
Mike Boryla, Philadelphia, 1976
Ken Anderson, Cincinnati, 1977
Jim Kelly, Buffalo, 1991
Mark Rypien, Washington, 1992

HAD INTERCEPTED

Most Passes Had Intercepted, Career

8 Dan Fouts, San Diego, 1980-84, 1986
6 Jim Hart, St. Louis, 1975-78
5 Ken Stabler, Oakland, 1974-75, 1978

Most Passes Had Intercepted, Game

5 Jim Hart, St. Louis, 1977
4 Ken Stabler, Oakland, 1974
3 Dan Fouts, San Diego, 1986
Mark Rypien, Washington, 1990
Steve Young, San Francisco, 1993

Most Attempts, Without Interception, Game

27 Joe Theismann, Washington, 1984
Phil Simms, N.Y. Giants, 1986
26 John Brodie, San Francisco, 1971
Danny White, Dallas, 1983
21 Roman Gabriel, Philadelphia, 1974
Dan Marino, Miami, 1985

PERCENTAGE, PASSES HAD INTERCEPTED

Lowest Percentage, Passes Had Intercepted, Career (40 attempts)

0.00 Joe Theismann, Washington, 1983-84 (45-0)
2.13 Dave Krieg, Seattle, 1985, 1989-90 (47-1)
2.22 Jim Kelly, Buffalo, 1988, 1991-92 (45-1)

PASS RECEIVING

RECEPTIONS

Most Receptions, Career

22 Jerry Rice, San Francisco, 1987-88, 1990-94
18 Walter Payton, Chicago, 1977-81, 1984-87
17 Steve Largent, Seattle, 1979, 1982, 1985-88

Most Receptions, Game

8 Steve Largent, Seattle, 1986
Michael Irvin, Dallas, 1992
Andre Rison, Atlanta, 1993
7 John Stallworth, Pittsburgh, 1983
Jerry Rice, San Francisco, 1992
6 John Stallworth, Pittsburgh, 1980
Kellen Winslow, San Diego, 1982
Gary Clark, Washington, 1991
Keith Byars, Miami, 1994
Andre Rison, Atlanta, 1994

YARDS GAINED

Most Yards Gained, Career

317 Jerry Rice, San Francisco, 1987-88, 1990-94
236 Steve Largent, Seattle, 1979, 1982, 1985-88
226 Wes Chandler, New Orleans, 1980; San Diego, 1983-84, 1986

Most Yards Gained, Game

125 Michael Irvin, Dallas, 1992
114 Wes Chandler, San Diego, 1986
96 Ken Burrough, Houston, 1976

Longest Reception

64 Ken Burrough, Houston (from Pastorini, Houston), 1976 (TD)
59 Keith Jackson, Philadelphia (19 yards) lateral to Earnest Byner, Washington (40 yards) (from Cunningham, Philadelphia), 1991
57 Mel Gray, St. Louis (from Harris, Los Angeles), 1975
Greg Pruitt, Cleveland (from Anderson, Cincinnati), 1977

TOUCHDOWNS

Most Touchdowns, Career

2 Mel Gray, St. Louis, 1975-78
Cliff Branch, Oakland, 1975-78
Terry Metcalf, St. Louis, 1975-76, 1978
Tony Hill, Dallas, 1979-80, 1986
William Andrews, Atlanta, 1981-84
James Lofton, Green Bay, 1979, 1981-86; Buffalo 1992
Jimmie Giles, Tampa Bay, 1981-83, 1986
Michael Irvin, Dallas, 1992-95
Cris Carter, Minnesota, 1994-95
Eric Green, Pittsburgh, 1994-95

Most Touchdowns, Game

2 William Andrews, Atlanta, 1984
Eric Green, Pittsburgh, 1995

INTERCEPTIONS BY

Most Interceptions By, Career

4 Everson Walls, Dallas, 1982-84, 1986
3 Ken Houston, Houston, 1971-73; Washington, 1974-79

Jack Lambert, Pittsburgh, 1976-84
Ted Hendricks, Baltimore, 1972-74; Green Bay, 1975; Oakland, 1981-82; L.A. Raiders, 1983-84
Mike Haynes, New England, 1978-81, 1983; L.A. Raiders, 1985-87
Deion Sanders, Atlanta, 1992-94; San Francisco, 1995
2 By eight players

Most Interceptions By, Game
2 Mel Blount, Pittsburgh, 1977
Everson Walls, Dallas, 1982, 1983
LeRoy Irvin, L.A. Rams, 1986
David Fulcher, Cincinnati, 1990

YARDS GAINED

Most Yards Gained, Career
77 Ted Hendricks, Baltimore, 1972-74; Green Bay, 1975; Oakland, 1981-82; L.A. Raiders, 1983-84
73 Rod Woodson, Pittsburgh, 1990-94
51 Jerry Gray, L.A. Rams, 1987-90

Most Yards Gained, Game
73 Rod Woodson, Pittsburgh, 1994
65 Ted Hendricks, Baltimore, 1973
51 Jerry Gray, L.A. Rams, 1990

Longest Gain
73 Rod Woodson, Pittsburgh, 1994 (lateral)
65 Ted Hendricks, Baltimore, 1973
51 Jerry Gray, L.A. Rams, 1990 (TD)

TOUCHDOWNS

Most Touchdowns, Game
1 Bobby Bell, Kansas City, 1973
Nolan Cromwell, L.A. Rams, 1984
Joey Browner, Minnesota, 1986
Jerry Gray, L.A. Rams, 1990
Mike Johnson, Cleveland, 1990
Junior Seau, San Diego, 1993

PUNTING

Most Punts, Career
33 Ray Guy, Oakland, 1974-79, 1981
23 Rohn Stark, Indianapolis, 1986-87, 1991, 1993
22 Reggie Roby, Miami, 1985, 1990; Washington, 1995

Most Punts, Game
10 Reggie Roby, Miami, 1985
9 Tom Wittum, San Francisco, 1974
Rohn Stark, Indianapolis, 1987
8 Jerrel Wilson, Kansas City, 1971
Tom Skladany, Detroit, 1982
Reggie Roby, Washington, 1995

Longest Punt
64 Tom Wittum, San Francisco, 1974
61 Reggie Roby, Miami, 1985
60 Ron Widby, Dallas, 1972
Reggie Roby, Washington, 1995

AVERAGE YARDAGE

Highest Average, Career (10 punts)
46.73 Reggie Roby, Miami, 1985, 1990; Washington, 1995 (22-1,028)
45.25 Jerrel Wilson, Kansas City, 1971-73 (16-724)
44.65 Rohn Stark, Indianapolis, 1986-87, 1991, 1993 (23-1,027)

Highest Average, Game (4 punts)
50.13 Reggie Roby, Washington, 1995 (8-401)
49.57 Jim Arnold, Detroit, 1988 (7-347)
49.00 Ray Guy, Oakland, 1974 (4-196)

PUNT RETURNS

Most Punt Returns, Career
13 Rick Upchurch, Denver, 1977, 1979-80, 1983
11 Vai Sikahema, St. Louis, 1987-88
10 Mike Nelms, Washington, 1981-83

Most Punt Returns, Game
7 Vai Sikahema, St. Louis, 1987
6 Henry Ellard, L.A. Rams, 1985
Gerald McNeil, Cleveland, 1988
Eric Metcalf, Cleveland, 1995
5 Rick Upchurch, Denver, 1980
Mike Nelms, Washington, 1981
Carl Roaches, Houston, 1982
Johnny Bailey, Phoenix, 1993

Most Fair Catches, Game
2 Jerry Logan, Baltimore, 1971
Dick Anderson, Miami, 1974
Henry Ellard, L.A. Rams, 1985

YARDS GAINED

Most Yards Gained, Career
183 Billy Johnson, Houston, 1976, 1978; Atlanta, 1984
138 Mel Renfro, Dallas, 1971-72, 1974
Rick Upchurch, Denver, 1977, 1979-80, 1983
125 Eric Metcalf, Cleveland, 1994-95

Most Yards Gained, Game
159 Billy Johnson, Houston, 1976
138 Mel Renfro, Dallas, 1971
117 Wally Henry, Philadelphia, 1980

Longest Punt Return
90 Billy Johnson, Houston, 1976 (TD)
86 Wally Henry, Philadelphia, 1980 (TD)
82 Mel Renfro, Dallas, 1971 (TD)

AVERAGE YARDAGE

Highest Average, Career (4 returns)
22.88 Billy Johnson, Houston, 1976, 1978; Atlanta, 1984 (8-183)
21.50 Tony Green, Washington, 1979 (4-86)
14.00 Mel Gray, Detroit, 1991-92, 1995 (5-70)

Highest Average, Game (3 returns)
39.75 Billy Johnson, Houston, 1976 (4-159)
39.00 Wally Henry, Philadelphia, 1980 (3-117)
21.50 Tony Green, Washington, 1979 (4-86)

TOUCHDOWNS

Most Touchdowns, Game
2 Mel Renfro, Dallas, 1971
1 Billy Johnson, Houston, 1976
Wally Henry, Philadelphia, 1980

KICKOFF RETURNS

Most Kickoff Returns, Career
14 Mel Gray, Detroit, 1991-92, 1995
10 Rick Upchurch, Denver, 1977, 1979-80, 1983
Greg Pruitt, Cleveland, 1974-75, 1977-78; L.A. Raiders, 1984
8 Mike Nelms, Washington, 1981-83

Most Kickoff Returns, Game
7 Mel Gray, Detroit, 1995
6 Greg Pruitt, L.A. Raiders, 1984
5 Les (Speedy) Duncan, Washington, 1972
Ron Smith, Chicago, 1973
Herb Mul-Key, Washington, 1974
Mel Gray, Detroit, 1991

YARDS GAINED

Most Yards Gained, Career
309 Greg Pruitt, Cleveland, 1974-75, 1977-78; L.A. Raiders, 1984
294 Mel Gray, Detroit, 1991-92, 1995
222 Rick Upchurch, Denver, 1977, 1979-80, 1983

Most Yards Gained, Game
192 Greg Pruitt, L.A. Raiders, 1984
175 Les (Speedy) Duncan, Washington, 1972
162 Mel Gray, Detroit, 1995

Longest Kickoff Return
62 Greg Pruitt, L.A. Raiders, 1984
61 Eugene (Mercury) Morris, Miami, 1972
55 Ron Smith, Chicago, 1973

AVERAGE YARDAGE

Highest Average, Career (4 returns)
35.00 Les (Speedy) Duncan, Washington, 1972 (5-175)
31.25 Eugene (Mercury) Morris, Miami, 1972 (3-93)
30.90 Greg Pruitt, Cleveland, 1974-75, 1977-78; L.A. Raiders, 1984 (6-192)

Highest Average, Game (3 returns)
35.00 Les (Speedy) Duncan, Washington, 1972 (5-175)
32.00 Greg Pruitt, L.A. Raiders, 1984 (6-192)
31.00 Eugene (Mercury) Morris, Miami, 1972 (3-93)

TOUCHDOWNS

Most Touchdowns, Game
None

FUMBLES

Most Fumbles, Career
6 Dan Fouts, San Diego, 1980-84, 1986
4 Lawrence McCutcheon, Los Angeles, 1974-78
Franco Harris, Pittsburgh, 1973-76, 1978-81
Jay Schroeder, Washington, 1987
Vai Sikahema, St. Louis, 1987-88
3 O.J. Simpson, Buffalo, 1973-77
William Andrews, Atlanta, 1981-84
Joe Montana, San Francisco, 1982, 1984-85, 1988

Walter Payton, Chicago, 1977-81, 1984-87
Neil Lomax, St. Louis, 1985, 1988
Jim Kelly, Buffalo, 1988, 1991-92

Most Fumbles, Game
4 Jay Schroeder, Washington, 1987
3 Dan Fouts, San Diego, 1982
Vai Sikahema, St. Louis, 1987
2 By 11 players

RECOVERIES

Most Fumbles Recovered, Career
3 Harold Jackson, Philadelphia, 1973; Los Angeles, 1974, 1976, 1978 (3-own)
Dan Fouts, San Diego, 1980-84, 1986 (3-own)
Randy White, Dallas, 1978, 1980-86 (3-opp)
2 By many players

Most Fumbles Recovered, Game
2 Dick Anderson, Miami, 1974 (1-own, 1-opp)
Harold Jackson, Los Angeles, 1974 (2-own)
Dan Fouts, San Diego, 1982 (2-own)
Joey Browner, Minnesota, 1990 (2-opp)

YARDAGE

Longest Fumble Return
83 Art Still, Kansas City, 1985 (TD, opp)
51 Phil Villapiano, Oakland, 1974 (opp)
37 Sam Mills, New Orleans, 1988 (opp)

TOUCHDOWNS

Most Touchdowns, Game
1 Art Still, Kansas City, 1985
Keith Millard, Minnesota, 1990

SACKS

Sacks have been compiled since 1983.

Most Sacks, Career
9.5 Reggie White, Philadelphia, 1987-93; Green Bay, 1994
9 Howie Long, L.A. Raiders, 1984-88, 1990, 1993-1994
7 Mark Gastineau, N.Y. Jets, 1983-86

Most Sacks, Game
4 Mark Gastineau, N.Y. Jets, 1985
Reggie White, Philadelphia, 1987
3 Richard Dent, Chicago, 1985
Bruce Smith, Buffalo, 1991
2 By many players

TEAM RECORDS

SCORING

Most Points, Game
45 NFC, 1984

Fewest Points, Game
3 AFC, 1984, 1989, 1994

Most Points, Both Teams, Game
64 NFC (37) vs. AFC (27), 1980

Fewest Points, Both Teams, Game
16 NFC (6) vs. AFC (10), 1987

TOUCHDOWNS

Most Touchdowns, Game
6 NFC, 1984

Fewest Touchdowns, Game
0 AFC, 1971, 1974, 1984, 1989, 1994
NFC, 1987, 1988

Most Touchdowns, Both Teams, Game
8 AFC (4) vs. NFC (4), 1973
NFC (5) vs. AFC (3), 1980

Fewest Touchdowns, Both Teams, Game
1 AFC (0) vs. NFC (1), 1974
NFC (0) vs. AFC (1), 1987
NFC (0) vs. AFC (1), 1988

POINTS AFTER TOUCHDOWN

Most Points After Touchdown, Game
6 NFC, 1984

Most Points After Touchdown, Both Teams, Game
7 NFC (4) vs. AFC (3), 1973
NFC (4) vs. AFC (3), 1980
NFC (4) vs. AFC (3), 1986

FIELD GOALS

Most Field Goals Attempted, Game
6 AFC, 1972
NFC, 1981, 1983

Most Field Goals Attempted, Both Teams, Game
9 NFC (6) vs. AFC (3), 1983

Most Field Goals, Game
5 AFC, 1974

Most Field Goals, Both Teams, Game
7 AFC (5) vs. NFC (2), 1974

NET YARDS GAINED RUSHING AND PASSING

Most Yards Gained, Game
552 AFC, 1995

Fewest Yards Gained, Game
114 AFC, 1993

Most Yards Gained, Both Teams, Game
811 AFC (466) vs. NFC (345), 1983

Fewest Yards Gained, Both Teams, Game
424 AFC (202) vs. NFC (222), 1987

RUSHING

ATTEMPTS

Most Attempts, Game
50 AFC, 1974

Fewest Attempts, Game
14 AFC, 1994

Most Attempts, Both Teams, Game
80 AFC (50) vs. NFC (30), 1974

Fewest Attempts, Both Teams, Game
48 AFC (20) vs. NFC (28), 1991

YARDS GAINED

Most Yards Gained, Game
400 AFC, 1995

Fewest Yards Gained, Game
28 NFC, 1992

Most Yards Gained, Both Teams, Game
441 AFC (400) vs. NFC (41), 1995

Fewest Yards Gained, Both Teams, Game
131 NFC (28) vs. AFC (103), 1992

TOUCHDOWNS

Most Touchdowns, Game
3 NFC, 1989, 1991
AFC, 1995

Most Touchdowns, Both Teams, Game
4 AFC (2) vs. NFC (2), 1973
AFC (2) vs. NFC (2), 1980

PASSING

ATTEMPTS

Most Attempts, Game
55 NFC, 1993

Fewest Attempts, Game
17 NFC, 1972

Most Attempts, Both Teams, Game
94 AFC (50) vs. NFC (44), 1983

Fewest Attempts, Both Teams, Game
42 NFC (17) vs. AFC (25), 1972

COMPLETIONS

Most Completions, Game
32 NFC, 1993

Fewest Completions, Game
7 NFC, 1972, 1982

Most Completions, Both Teams, Game
55 AFC (31) vs. NFC (24), 1983

Fewest Completions, Both Teams, Game
18 NFC (7) vs. AFC (11), 1972

YARDS GAINED

Most Yards Gained, Game
387 AFC, 1983

Fewest Yards Gained, Game
42 NFC, 1982

Most Yards Gained, Both Teams, Game
608 AFC (387) vs. NFC (221), 1983

Fewest Yards Gained, Both Teams, Game
215 NFC (89) vs. AFC (126), 1972

TIMES SACKED

Most Times Sacked, Game
9 NFC, 1985

Fewest Times Sacked, Game
0 NFC, 1971

Most Times Sacked, Both Teams, Game
17 NFC (9) vs. AFC (8), 1985
Fewest Times Sacked, Both Teams, Game
3 AFC (1) vs. NFC (2), 1995

TOUCHDOWNS
Most Touchdowns, Game
4 NFC, 1984
Most Touchdowns, Both Teams, Game
5 NFC (3) vs. AFC (2), 1986

INTERCEPTIONS BY
Most Interceptions By, Game
6 AFC, 1977
Most Interceptions By, Both Teams, Game
7 AFC (6) vs. NFC (1), 1977

YARDS GAINED
Most Yards Gained, Game
103 AFC, 1994
Most Yards Gained, Both Teams, Game
116 AFC (103) vs. NFC (13), 1994

TOUCHDOWNS
Most Touchdowns, Game
1 AFC, 1973, 1990, 1993
NFC, 1984, 1986, 1990

PUNTING
Most Punts, Game
10 AFC, 1985
Fewest Punts, Game
0 NFC, 1989
Most Punts, Both Teams, Game
16 AFC (10) vs. NFC (6), 1985
Fewest Punts, Both Teams, Game
4 NFC (1) vs. AFC (3), 1992

PUNT RETURNS
Most Punt Returns, Game
7 NFC, 1985, 1987
AFC, 1995
Fewest Punt Returns, Game
0 AFC, 1984, 1989
Most Punt Returns, Both Teams, Game
11 NFC (7) vs. AFC (4), 1985
Fewest Punt Returns, Both Teams, Game
3 AFC (0) vs. NFC (3), 1984
AFC (0) vs. NFC (3), 1989
NFC (1) vs. AFC (2), 1991
AFC (1) vs. NFC (2), 1992

YARDS GAINED
Most Yards Gained, Game
177 AFC, 1976
Fewest Yards Gained, Game
–1 NFC, 1991
Most Yards Gained, Both Teams, Game
263 AFC (177) vs. NFC (86), 1976
Fewest Yards Gained, Both Teams, Game
16 AFC (0) vs. NFC (16), 1984

TOUCHDOWNS
Most Touchdowns, Game
2 NFC, 1971

KICKOFF RETURNS
Most Kickoff Returns, Game
8 NFC, 1995
Fewest Kickoff Returns, Game
1 NFC, 1971, 1984, 1994
AFC, 1988, 1991
Most Kickoff Returns, Both Teams, Game
12 NFC (8) vs. AFC (4), 1995
Fewest Kickoff Returns, Both Teams, Game
5 NFC (2) vs. AFC (3), 1979
AFC (1) vs. NFC (4), 1988
NFC (2) vs. AFC (3), 1992
NFC (1) vs. AFC (4), 1994

YARDS GAINED
Most Yards Gained, Game
215 AFC, 1984
Fewest Yards Gained, Game
6 NFC, 1971
Most Yards Gained, Both Teams, Game
293 NFC (200) vs. AFC (93), 1972
Fewest Yards Gained, Both Teams, Game
99 NFC (48) vs. AFC (51), 1987

TOUCHDOWNS
Most Touchdowns, Game
None

FUMBLES
Most Fumbles, Game
10 NFC, 1974
Most Fumbles, Both Teams, Game
15 NFC (10) vs. AFC (5), 1974

RECOVERIES
Most Fumbles Recovered, Game
10 NFC, 1974 (6 own, 4 opp)
Most Fumbles Lost, Game
4 AFC, 1974, 1988
NFC, 1974

YARDS GAINED
Most Yards Gained, Game
87 AFC, 1985

TOUCHDOWNS
Most Touchdowns, Game
1 AFC, 1985
NFC, 1990

TURNOVERS
(Number of times losing the ball on interceptions and fumbles.)
Most Turnovers, Game
8 AFC, 1974
Fewest Turnovers, Game
0 AFC, 1991
NFC, 1991, 1995
Most Turnovers, Both Teams, Game
12 AFC (8) vs. NFC (4), 1974
Fewest Turnovers, Both Teams, Game
0 AFC vs. NFC, 1991

Rules

OFFICIALS

1995 NFL ROSTER OF OFFICIALS

Jerry Seeman, Director of Officiating
Leo Miles, Supervisor of Officials
Jack Reader, Supervisor of Officials
Ron DeSouza, Supervisor of Officials

No.	Name	Position	College
25	Alderton, John	Line Judge	Portland State
115	Ancich, Hendi	Umpire	Harbor College
81	Anderson, Dave	Line Judge	Salem College
34	Austin, Gerald	Referee	Western Carolina
22	Baetz, Paul	Back Judge	Heidelberg
91	Baker, Ken	Field Judge	Eastern Illinois
26	Baltz, Mark	Head Linesman	Ohio University
55	Barnes, Tom	Line Judge	Minnesota
56	Baynes, Ron	Line Judge	Auburn
32	Bergman, Jeff	Line Judge	Robert Morris
17	Bergman, Jerry	Head Linesman	Duquesne
40	Bible, Jon	Side Judge	Texas
7	Blum, Ron	Referee	Marin College
90	Borgard, Mike	Side Judge	St. Louis
18	Boston, Byron	Line Judge	Austin
110	Botchan, Ron	Umpire	Occidental
101	Boylston, Bob	Umpire	Alabama
31	Brown, Chad	Umpire	East Texas State
126	Carey, Don	Field Judge	U.C.-Riverside
94	Carey, Mike	Referee	Santa Clara
39	Carlsen, Don	Side Judge	Cal State-Chico
63	Carollo, Bill	Side Judge	Wisconsin
11	Carroll, Rob	Back Judge	Ithaca
43	Cashion, Red	Referee	Texas A&M
45	Coleman, George	Umpire	Bishop College
65	Coleman, Walt	Line Judge	Arkansas
27	Conway, Al	Umpire	Army
99	Corrente, Tony	Back Judge	Cal State-Fullerton
71	Coukart, Ed	Umpire	Northwestern
61	Creed, Dick	Back Judge	Louisville
75	Daopoulos, Jim	Back Judge	Kentucky
70	Dawson, Scott	Umpire	Virginia Tech
78	Demmas, Art	Umpire	Vanderbilt
113	Dorkowski, Don	Field Judge	Cal State-Los Angeles
6	Dornan, Kirk	Line Judge	Central Washington
74	Duke, James	Umpire	Howard
89	Dunn, Neely	Side Judge	South Carolina State
57	Fiffick, Ed	Umpire	Marquette
47	Fincken, Tom	Side Judge	Kansas State
111	Frantz, Earnie	Head Linesman	No College
50	Gereb, Neil	Umpire	California
72	Gierke, Terry	Head Linesman	Portland State
3	Golmont, Van	Back Judge	Miami
19	Green, Scott	Field Judge	Delaware
23	Grier, Johnny	Referee	University of D.C.
96	Hakes, Don	Field Judge	Bradley
104	Hamer, Dale	Referee	California, Pa.
105	Hantak, Dick	Referee	Southeast Missouri
125	Hayes, Laird	Side Judge	Princeton
54	Hayward, George	Head Linesman	Missouri Western
85	Hochuli, Ed	Back Judge	Texas-El Paso
114	Johnson, Tom	Head Linesman	Miami, Ohio
97	Jones, Nate	Side Judge	Lewis & Clark
106	Jury, Al	Back Judge	San Bernardino Valley
67	Keck, John	Umpire	Cornell College
14	Knight, Jim	Back Judge	Wake Forest
86	Kukar, Bernie	Referee	St. John's
120	Lane, Gary	Referee	Missouri
127	Leavy, Bill	Field Judge	San Jose State
76	Liebsack, Ron	Side Judge	Western State
49	Look, Dean	Side Judge	Michigan State
98	Lovett, Bill	Back Judge	Maryland
59	Luckett, Phil	Field Judge	Texas-El Paso
9	Markbreit, Jerry	Referee	Illinois
38	Maurer, Bruce	Line Judge	Ohio State
48	McCarter, Gordon	Referee	Western Reserve
95	McElwee, Bob	Referee	Navy
35	McGrath, Bob	Head Linesman	Western Kentucky
64	McPeters, Lloyd	Line Judge	Oklahoma State
80	Millis, Timmie	Back Judge	Millsaps
117	Montgomery, Ben	Line Judge	Morehouse
36	Moore, Bob	Back Judge	Dayton
60	Moore, Tommy	Side Judge	Stephen F. Austin
20	Nemmers, Larry	Referee	Upper Iowa
51	Orem, Dale	Line Judge	Louisville
77	Orr, Don	Field Judge	Vanderbilt
10	Phares, Ron	Head Linesman	Virginia Tech
79	Pointer, Aaron	Head Linesman	Pacific Lutheran
92	Poole, Jim	Back Judge	San Diego State
5	Quirk, Jim	Umpire	Delaware
83	Reels, Richard	Field Judge	No College
53	Reynolds, Bill	Line Judge	West Chester State
68	Richard, Louis	Back Judge	Southwest Louisiana
121	Rivers, Sanford	Head Linesman	Youngstown State
46	Robison, John	Field Judge	Utah
33	Roe, Howard	Referee	Wichita State
58	Saracino, Jim	Back Judge	Northern Colorado
21	Schleyer, John	Head Linesman	Millersville
122	Schmitz, Bill	Field Judge	Colorado State
109	Semon, Sid	Head Linesman	Southern California
118	Sifferman, Tom	Back Judge	Seattle
73	Skelton, Bobby	Field Judge	Alabama
29	Slavin, Howard	Side Judge	Southern California
2	Smith, Billy	Field Judge	East Carolina
124	Speight, Leslie	Side Judge	No College
119	Spitler, Ron	Field Judge	Panhandle State
24	Stabile, Tom	Head Linesman	Slippery Rock
88	Steenson, Scott	Back Judge	North Texas
84	Steinkerchner, Mark	Field Judge	Akron
62	Stewart, Charles	Line Judge	Long Beach State
103	Stuart, Rex	Umpire	Appalachian State
4	Toole, Doug	Side Judge	Utah State
37	Upson, Larry	Line Judge	Prince George C.C.
93	Vaughan, Jack	Field Judge	Mississippi State
52	Veteri, Tony	Head Linesman	Manhattan College
100	Wagner, Bob	Umpire	Penn State
28	Wedge, Don	Side Judge	Ohio Wesleyan
87	Weidner, Paul	Head Linesman	Cincinnati
123	White, Tom	Referee	Temple
8	Williams, Dale	Head Linesman	Cal State-Northridge
82	Winter, Ron	Line Judge	Michigan State
16	Wyant, David	Side Judge	Virginia

NUMERICAL ROSTER

No.	Name	Position
2	Billy Smith	FJ
3	Van Golmont	BJ
4	Doug Toole	SJ
5	Jim Quirk	U
6	Kirk Dornan	LJ
7	Ron Blum	R
8	Dale Williams	HL
9	Jerry Markbreit	R
10	Ron Phares	HL
11	Rob Carroll	BJ
14	Jim Knight	BJ
16	David Wyant	SJ
17	Jerry Bergman	HL
18	Byron Boston	LJ
19	Scott Green	FJ
20	Larry Nemmers	R
21	John Schleyer	HL
22	Paul Baetz	BJ
23	Johnny Grier	R
24	Tom Stabile	HL
25	John Alderton	LJ
26	Mark Baltz	HL
27	Al Conway	U
28	Don Wedge	SJ
29	Howard Slavin	SJ
31	Chad Brown	U
32	Jeff Bergman	LJ
33	Howard Roe	R
34	Gerry Austin	R
35	Bob McGrath	HL
36	Bob Moore	BJ
37	Larry Upson	LJ
38	Bruce Maurer	LJ
39	Don Carlsen	SJ
40	Jon Bible	SJ
43	Red Cashion	R
45	George Coleman	U
46	John Robison	FJ
47	Tom Fincken	SJ
48	Gordon McCarter	R
49	Dean Look	SJ
50	Neil Gereb	U
51	Dale Orem	LJ
52	Tony Veteri	HL
53	Bill Reynolds	LJ
54	George Hayward	HL
55	Tom Barnes	LJ
56	Ron Baynes	LJ
57	Ed Fiffick	U
58	Jim Saracino	BJ
59	Phil Luckett	FJ
60	Tommy Moore	SJ
61	Dick Creed	BJ
62	Charles Stewart	LJ
63	Bill Carollo	SJ
64	Lloyd McPeters	LJ
65	Walt Coleman	LJ
67	John Keck	U
68	Louis Richard	BJ
70	Scott Dawson	U
71	Ed Coukart	U
72	Terry Gierke	HL
73	Bobby Skelton	FJ
74	James Duke	U
75	Jim Daopoulos	BJ
76	Ron Liebsack	SJ
77	Don Orr	FJ
78	Art Demmas	U
79	Aaron Pointer	HL
80	Timmie Millis	BJ
81	Dave Anderson	LJ
82	Ron Winter	LJ
83	Richard Reels	FJ
84	Mark Steinkerchner	FJ
85	Ed Hochuli	BJ
86	Bernie Kukar	R
87	Paul Weidner	HL
88	Scott Steenson	BJ
89	Neely Dunn	SJ
90	Mike Borgard	SJ
91	Ken Baker	FJ
92	Jim Poole	BJ
93	Jack Vaughan	FJ
94	Mike Carey	R
95	Bob McElwee	R
96	Don Hakes	FJ
97	Nate Jones	SJ
98	Bill Lovett	BJ
99	Tony Corrente	BJ
100	Bob Wagner	U
101	Bob Boylston	U
103	Rex Stuart	U
104	Dale Hamer	R
105	Dick Hantak	R
106	Al Jury	BJ
109	Sid Semon	HL
110	Ron Botchan	U
111	Earnie Frantz	HL
113	Don Dorkowski	FJ
114	Tom Johnson	HL
115	Hendi Ancich	U
117	Ben Montgomery	LJ
118	Tom Sifferman	BJ
119	Ron Spitler	FJ
120	Gary Lane	R
121	Sanford Rivers	HL
122	Bill Schmitz	FJ
123	Tom White	R
124	Leslie Speight	SJ
125	Laird Hayes	SJ
126	Don Carey	FJ
127	Bill Leavy	FJ

1995 OFFICIALS AT A GLANCE

REFEREES

Gerry Austin, No. **34,** Western Carolina, president, leadership development group, 14th year.
Ron Blum, No. **7,** Marin College, professional golfer, 11th year.
Mike Carey, No. **94,** Santa Clara, owner, skiing accessories, 6th year.
Red Cashion, No. **43,** Texas A&M, chairman, insurance company, 24th year.
Johnny Grier, No. **23,** University of D.C., planning engineer, 15th year.
Dale Hamer, No. **104,** California (Pa.) University, consultant, 18th year.
Dick Hantak, No. **105,** Southeast Missouri, educator, 18th year.
Ed Hochuli, No. **85,** Texas-El Paso, attorney, 6th year.
Bernie Kukar, No. **86,** St. John's, sales representative, employees benefit plan, 12th year.
Gary Lane, No. **120,** Missouri, vice president, medical supplies, former NFL player, 14th year.
Jerry Markbreit, No. **9,** Illinois, corporate consultant, 20th year.
Gordon McCarter, No. **48,** Western Reserve, retired sales manager, 29th year.
Bob McElwee, No. **95,** Navy, owner, heavy construction firm, 20th year.
Larry Nemmers, No. **20,** Upper Iowa, speaking consultant, 11th year.
Howard Roe, No. **33,** Wichita State, director, administration and finance, 12th year.
Tom White, No. **123,** Temple, president, athletic sportswear, 7th year.

UMPIRES

Hendi Ancich, No. **115,** Harbor, longshoreman, 14th year.
Ron Botchan, No. **110,** Occidental, college professor, former AFL player, 16th year.
Bob Boylston, No. **101,** Alabama, stockbroker, 18th year.
Chad Brown, No. **31,** East Texas State, director, intramural/sports clubs, 4th year.
George Coleman, No. **45,** Bishop College, executive director YMCA, 3rd year.
Al Conway, No. **27,** Army, director of manufacturing, 27th year.
Ed Coukart, No. **71,** Northwestern, president, commercial bank, 7th year.
Scott Dawson, No. **70,** Virginia Tech, owner, commercial construction company, 1st year.
Art Demmas, No. **78,** Vanderbilt, Southern coordinator, National Football Foundation and College Hall of Fame, 28th year.
James Duke, No. **74,** Howard, Ward manager, department of parks and recreation, 3rd year.
Ed Fiffick, No. **57,** Marquette, podiatric physician, 17th year.
Neil Gereb, No. **50,** California, project manager, aircraft company, 15th year.
John Keck, No. **67,** Cornell, petroleum distributor, 24th year.
Jim Quirk, No. **5,** Delaware, senior vice president, foreign sales government securities, 8th year.
Rex Stuart, No. **103,** Appalachian State, insurance agent, 12th year.
Bob Wagner, No. **100,** Penn State, executive director, cardiovascular institute, 11th year.

HEAD LINESMEN

Mark Baltz, No. **26,** Ohio University, manufacturer's representative, 7th year.
Jerry Bergman, No. **17,** Duquesne, executive director, pension fund, 30th year.
Earnie Frantz, No. **111,** no college, vice president and manager, insurance company, 15th year.
Terry Gierke, No. **72,** Portland State, real estate broker, 15th year.
George Hayward, No. **54,** Missouri Western, vice president and manager, warehouse company, 5th year.
Tom Johnson, No. **114,** Miami, Ohio, educator, president, security company, 14th year.
Bob McGrath, No. **35,** Western Kentucky, sales representative, fund raiser, 3rd year.
Ron Phares, No. **10,** Virginia Tech, president, construction company, 11th year.
Aaron Pointer, No. **79,** Pacific Lutheran, park department administrator, 9th year.
Sanford Rivers, No. **121,** Youngstown State, assistant vice president, school administration, 7th year.
John Schleyer, No. **21,** Millersville, medical sales, 6th year.
Sid Semon, No. **109,** Southern California, chairman, physical education department, 18th year.
Tom Stabile, No. **24,** Slippery Rock, teacher, 1st year.
Tony Veteri, No. **52,** Manhattan, director of athletics, 4th year.
Paul Weidner, No. **87,** Cincinnati, marketing manager, 10th year.
Dale Williams, No. **8,** Cal State-Northridge, owner, coin-op laundromats, 16th year.

LINE JUDGES

John Alderton, No. **25,** Portland State, vice president, insurance, 7th year.
Dave Anderson, No. **81,** Salem, insurance executive, 12th year.
Tom Barnes, No. **55,** Minnesota, manufacturing representative, 10th year.
Ron Baynes, No. **56,** Auburn, school administrator, coach, 9th year.
Jeff Bergman, No. **32,** Robert Morris, president and chief executive officer, medical services, 5th year.
Byron Boston, No. **18,** Austin, trucking management, 1st year.
Walt Coleman, No. **65,** Arkansas, president, dairy processor, 7th year.
Bruce Maurer, No. **38,** Ohio State, administrator and associate director, recreational sports, 9th year.
Lloyd McPeters, No. **64,** Oklahoma State, business insurance sales, 3rd year.
Ben Montgomery, No. **117,** Morehouse, school administrator, 14th year.
Dale Orem, No. **51,** Louisville, executive director, community foundation, 16th year.
Bill Reynolds, No. **53,** West Chester State, educator, 21st year.
Mark Steinkerchner, No. **84,** Akron, vice president, 2nd year.
Charles Stewart, No. **62,** Long Beach State, administrative deputy director, 4th year.
Larry Upson, No. **37,** Prince George City College, senior personnel management specialist, 5th year.
Ron Winter, No. **82,** Michigan State, associate professor, 1st year.

BACK JUDGES

Paul Baetz, No. **22,** Heidelberg, financial consultant, 18th year.
Rob Carroll, No. **11,** Ithaca, insurance sales, 1st year.
Roy Clymer, No. **24,** New Mexico State, district marketing manager, gas company, 16th year.
Tony Corrente, No. **99,** Cal State-Fullerton, educator, coach, 1st year.
Richard Creed, No. **61,** Louisville, manager, real estate, 18th year.
Jim Daopoulos, No. **75,** Kentucky, mortgage broker, 7th year.
Van Golmont, No. **3,** Miami, regional manager, marketing development, 5th year.
Al Jury, No. **106,** San Bernardino Valley, state traffic officer, 18th year.
Jim Knight, No. **14,** Wake Forest, manufacturer's representative, 2nd year.
Bill Lovett, No. **98,** Maryland, managing partner, financial sales, 6th year.
Timmie Millis, No. **80,** Millsaps, financial investigative consultant, 7th year.
Bob Moore, No. **36,** Dayton, attorney, 12th year.
Jim Poole, No. **92,** San Diego State, college professor, 21st year.
Louis Richard, No. **68,** Southwestern Louisiana, sales manager, 10th year.
Jim Saracino, No. **58,** Northern Colorado, secondary educator, 1st year.
Tom Sifferman, No. **118,** Seattle, manufacturer's representative, 10th year.
Scott Steenson, No. **88,** North Texas State, real estate broker, 5th year.

SIDE JUDGES

Jon Bible, No. **40,** Texas, attorney/college educator, 2nd year.
Mike Borgard, No. **90,** St. Louis, president/owner, advertising specialties, 6th year.
Don Carlsen, No. **39,** Cal State-Chico, budget analyst, comptroller, 7th year.
Bill Carollo, No. **63,** Wisconsin, marketing executive, 7th year.
Neely Dunn, No. **89,** South Carolina State, principal, 1st year.
Tom Fincken, No. **47,** Emporia State, retired educator, 12th year.
Laird Hayes, No. **125,** Princeton, associate professor, physical education/ athletics, 1st year.
Nate Jones, No. **97,** Lewis and Clark, high school principal, 19th year.
Ron Liebsack, No. **76,** Regis, manager, telecommunications, 1st year.
Dean Look, No. **49,** Michigan State, director, medical manufacturing, former AFL player, 23rd year.
Tommy Moore, No. **60,** Stephen F. Austin, marketing, manufacturing, representative, 4th year.
Howard Slavin, No. **29,** Southern California, attorney, 9th year.
Leslie Speight, No. **124,** No college, high school teacher, 1st year.
Doug Toole, No. **4,** Utah State, physical therapist, orthopedic and sports medicine, 8th year.
Don Wedge, No. **28,** Ohio Wesleyan, executive account manager, 24th year.
David Wyant, No. **16,** Virginia, director, technology transfer center, 5th year.

FIELD JUDGES

Ken Baker, No. **91,** Eastern Illinois, college educator, 5th year.
Don Carey, No. **126,** California-Riverside, contract manager, Dept. of Defense, 1st year.
Don Dorkowski, No. **113,** Cal State-Los Angeles, department head, health and safety, 10th year.
Kirk Dornan, No. **6,** Central Washington, managing partner, 2nd year.
Scott Green, No. **19,** Delaware, vice president, government relations, 5th year.
Don Hakes, No. **96,** Bradley, retired educator, 19th year.
Bill Leavy, No. **127** San Jose State, firefighter, 1st year.
Phil Luckett, No. **59,** Texas-El Paso, computer program analyst, federal civil services, 5th year.
Don Orr, No. **77,** Vanderbilt, mechanical contractor, 25th year.
Richard Reels, No. **83,** Chicago State, director of security, court services, 3rd year.
John Robison, No. **46,** Utah, junior high school counselor, 8th year.
Bill Schmitz, No. **122,** Colorado State, general sales manager, 7th year.
Bobby Skelton, No. **73,** Alabama, industrial representative, 11th year.
Billy Smith, No. **2,** East Carolina, Federal government, 2nd year.
Ron Spitler, No. **119,** Panhandle State, owner, service center, 14th year.
Jack Vaughan, No. **93,** Mississippi State, financial services, 20th year.

OFFICIAL SIGNALS

1

TOUCHDOWN, FIELD GOAL, or SUCCESSFUL TRY
Both arms extended above head.

2

SAFETY
Palms together above head.

3

FIRST DOWN
Arm pointed toward defensive team's goal.

4

CROWD NOISE, DEAD BALL, or NEUTRAL ZONE ESTABLISHED
One arm above head with an open hand.
With fist closed: **Fourth Down.**

5

BALL ILLEGALLY TOUCHED, KICKED OR BATTED
Fingertips tap both shoulders.

6

TIME OUT
Hands crisscrossed above head.
Same signal followed by placing one hand on top of cap: **Referee's Time Out.**
Same signal followed by arm swung at side: **Touchback.**

7

NO TIME OUT or TIME IN WITH WHISTLE
Full arm circled to simulate moving clock.

8

DELAY OF GAME, ILLEGAL SUBSTITUTION, or EXCESS TIME OUT
Folded arms.

9

FALSE START, ILLEGAL SHIFT, ILLEGAL FORMATION, or KICKOFF OR SAFETY KICK OUT OF BOUNDS
Forearms rotated over and over in front of body.

10

PERSONAL FOUL
One wrist striking the other above head.

Same signal followed by swinging leg: **Roughing the Kicker.**

Same signal followed by raised arm swinging forward: **Roughing the Passer.**

Same signal followed by hand striking back of calf: **Clipping.**

11

HOLDING
Grasping one wrist, the fist clenched, in front of chest.

12

ILLEGAL USE OF HANDS, ARMS, OR BODY
Grasping one wrist, the hand open and facing forward, in front of chest.

13

PENALTY REFUSED, INCOMPLETE PASS, PLAY OVER, or MISSED FIELD GOAL OR EXTRA POINT
Hands shifted in horizontal plane.

14

PASS JUGGLED INBOUNDS AND CAUGHT OUT OF BOUNDS
Hands up and down in front of chest (following incomplete pass signal).

15

ILLEGAL FORWARD PASS
One hand waved behind back followed by loss of down signal (23).

16

INTENTIONAL GROUNDING OF PASS
Parallel arms waved in a diagonal plane across body. Followed by loss of down signal (23).

OFFICIAL SIGNALS

17

INTERFERENCE WITH FORWARD PASS OR FAIR CATCH
Hands open and extended forward from shoulders with hands vertical.

18

INVALID FAIR-CATCH SIGNAL
One hand waved above head.

19

INELIGIBLE RECEIVER OR INELIGIBLE MEMBER OF KICKING TEAM DOWNFIELD
Right hand touching top of cap.

20

ILLEGAL CONTACT
One open hand extended forward.

21

OFFSIDE, ENCROACHING, or NEUTRAL ZONE INFRACTION
Hands on hips.

22

ILLEGAL MOTION AT SNAP
Horizontal arc with one hand.

23

LOSS OF DOWN
Both hands held behind head.

24

CRAWLING, INTERLOCKING INTERFERENCE, PUSHING, or HELPING RUNNER
Pushing movement of hands to front with arms downward.

25

TOUCHING A FORWARD PASS OR SCRIMMAGE KICK
Diagonal motion of one hand across another.

26

UNSPORTSMANLIKE CONDUCT
Arms outstretched, palms down. (Same signal means continuous-action fouls are disregarded.) Chop block.

27

ILLEGAL CUT or BLOCKING BELOW THE WAIST
Hand striking front of thigh preceded by personal-foul signal (10).

28

ILLEGAL CRACKBACK
Strike of an open right hand against the right mid-thigh preceded by personal foul signal (10).

29

PLAYER DISQUALIFIED
Ejection signal.

30

TRIPPING
Repeated action of right foot in back of left heel.

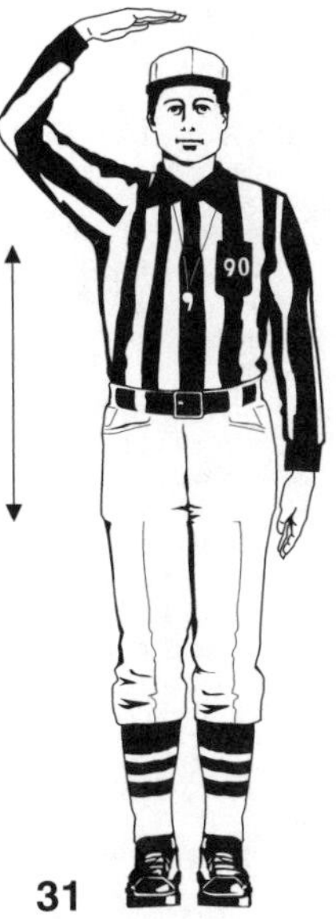

31

UNCATCHABLE FORWARD PASS
Palm of right hand held parallel to ground above head and moved back and forth.

32

ILLEGAL SUBSTITUTION or TOO MANY MEN ON THE FIELD
Both hands on top of head.

DIGEST OF RULES

NFL DIGEST OF RULES

This Digest of Rules of the National Football League has been prepared to aid players, fans, and members of the press, radio, and television media in their understanding of the game.

It is not meant to be a substitute for the official rule book. In any case of conflict between these explanations and the official rules, the rules always have precedence.

In order to make it easier to coordinate the information in this digest, the topics discussed generally follow the order of the rule book.

OFFICIALS' JURISDICTIONS, POSITIONS, AND DUTIES

Referee—General oversight and control of game. Gives signals for all fouls and is final authority for rule interpretations. Takes a position in backfield 10 to 12 yards behind line of scrimmage, favors right side (if quarterback is right-handed passer). Determines legality of snap, observes deep back(s) for legal motion. On running play, observes quarterback during and after handoff, remains with him until action has cleared away, then proceeds downfield, checking on runner and contact behind him. When runner is downed, Referee determines forward progress from wing official and, if necessary, adjusts final position of ball.

On pass plays, drops back as quarterback begins to fade back, picks up legality of blocks by near linemen. Changes to complete concentration on quarterback as defenders approach. Primarily responsible to rule on possible roughing action on passer and if ball becomes loose, rules whether ball is free on a fumble or dead on an incomplete pass.

During kicking situations, Referee has primary responsibility to rule on kicker's actions and whether or not any subsequent contact by a defender is legal. The Referee will announce on the microphone when each period is ended.

Umpire—Primary responsibility to rule on players' equipment, as well as their conduct and actions on scrimmage line. Lines up approximately four to five yards downfield, varying position from in front of weakside tackle to strongside guard. Looks for possible false start by offensive linemen. Observes legality of contact by both offensive linemen while blocking and by defensive players while they attempt to ward off blockers. Is prepared to call rule infractions if they occur on offense or defense. Moves forward to line of scrimmage when pass play develops in order to insure that interior linemen do not move illegally downfield. If offensive linemen indicate screen pass is to be attempted, Umpire shifts his attention toward screen side, picks up potential receiver in order to insure that he will legally be permitted to run his pattern and continues to rule on action of blockers. Umpire is to assist in ruling on incomplete or trapped passes when ball is thrown overhead or short.

Head Linesman—Primarily responsible for ruling on offside, encroachment, and actions pertaining to scrimmage line prior to or at snap. Keys on closest setback on his side of the field. On pass plays, Linesman is responsible to clear his receiver approximately seven yards downfield as he moves to a point five yards beyond the line. Linesman's secondary responsibility is to rule on any illegal action taken by defenders on any delay receiver moving downfield. Has full responsibility for ruling on sideline plays on his side, e.g., pass receiver or runner in or out of bounds. Together with Referee, Linesman is responsible for keeping track of number of downs and is in charge of mechanics of his chain crew in connection with its duties.

Linesman must be prepared to assist in determining forward progress by a runner on play directed toward middle or into his side zone. He, in turn, is to signal Referee or Umpire what forward point ball has reached. Linesman is also responsible to rule on legality of action involving any receiver who approaches his side zone. He is to call pass interference when the infraction occurs and is to rule on legality of blockers and defenders on plays involving ball carriers, whether it is entirely a running play, a combination pass and run, or a play involving a kick.

Line Judge—Straddles line of scrimmage on side of field opposite Linesman. Keeps time of game as a backup for clock operator. Along with Linesman is responsible for offside, encroachment, and actions pertaining to scrimmage line prior to or at snap. Line Judge keys on closest setback on his side of field. Line Judge is to observe his receiver until he moves at least seven yards downfield. He then moves toward backfield side, being especially alert to rule on any back in motion and on flight of ball when pass is made (he must rule whether forward or backward). Line Judge has primary responsibility to rule whether or not passer is behind or beyond line of scrimmage when pass is made. He also assists in observing actions by blockers and defenders who are on his side of field. After pass is thrown, Line Judge directs attention toward activities that occur in back of Umpire. During punting situations, Line Judge remains at line of scrimmage to be sure that only the end men move downfield until kick has been made. He also rules whether or not the kick crossed line and then observes action by members of the kicking team who are moving downfield to cover the kick. The Line Judge will advise the Referee when time has expired at the end of each period.

Back Judge—Operates on same side of field as Line Judge, 20 yards deep. Keys on wide receiver on his side. Concentrates on path of end or back, observing legality of his potential block(s) or of actions taken against him. Is prepared to rule from deep position on holding or illegal use of hands by end or back or on defensive infractions committed by player guarding him. Has primary responsibility to make decisions involving sideline on his side of field, e.g., pass receiver or runner in or out of bounds.

Back Judge makes decisions involving catching, recovery, or illegal touching of a loose ball beyond line of scrimmage; rules on plays involving pass receiver, including legality of catch or pass interference; assists in covering actions of runner, including blocks by teammates and that of defenders; calls clipping on punt returns; and, together with Field Judge, rules whether or not field goal attempts are successful.

Side Judge—Operates on same side of field as Linesman, 20 yards deep. Keys on wide receiver on his side. Concentrates on path of end or back, observing legality of his potential block(s) or of actions taken against him. Is prepared to rule from deep position on holding or illegal use of hands by end or back or on defensive infractions committed by player guarding him. Has primary responsibility to make decisions involving sideline on his side of field, e.g., pass receiver or runner in or out of bounds.

Side Judge makes decisions involving catching, recovery, or illegal touching of a loose ball beyond line of scrimmage; rules on plays involving pass receiver, including legality of catch or pass interference; assists in covering actions of runner, including blocks by teammates and that of defenders; and calls clipping on punt returns. On field goals and point after touchdown attempts, he becomes a double umpire.

Field Judge—Takes a position 25 yards downfield. In general, favors the tight end's side of field. Keys on tight end, concentrates on his path and observes legality of tight end's potential block(s) or of actions taken against him. Is prepared to rule from deep position on holding or illegal use of hands by end or back or on defensive infractions committed by player guarding him.

Field Judge times interval between plays on 40/25-second clock plus intermission between two periods of each half; makes decisions involving catching, recovery, or illegal touching of a loose ball beyond line of scrimmage; is responsible to rule on plays involving end line; calls pass interference, fair catch infractions, and clipping on kick returns; and, together with Back Judge, rules whether or not field goals and conversions are successful.

DEFINITIONS

1. **Chucking:** Warding off an opponent who is in front of a defender by contacting him with a quick extension of arm or arms, followed by the return of arm(s) to a flexed position, thereby breaking the original contact.
2. **Clipping:** Throwing the body across the back of an opponent's leg or hitting him from the back below the waist while moving up from behind unless the opponent is a runner or the action is in close line play.
3. **Close Line Play:** The area between the positions normally occupied by the offensive tackles, extending three yards on each side of the line of scrimmage.
4. **Crackback:** Eligible receivers who take or move to a position more than two yards outside the tackle may not block an opponent below the waist if they then move back inside to block.
5. **Dead Ball:** Ball not in play.
6. **Double Foul:** A foul by each team during the same down.
7. **Down:** The period of action that starts when the ball is put in play and ends when it is dead.
8. **Encroachment:** When a player enters the neutral zone and makes contact with an opponent before the ball is snapped.
9. **Fair Catch:** An unhindered catch of a kick by a member of the receiving team who must raise one arm a full length above his head while the kick is in flight.
10. **Foul:** Any violation of a playing rule.
11. **Free Kick:** A kickoff, kick after a safety, or kick after a fair catch. It may be a placekick, dropkick, or punt, except a punt may not be used on a kickoff.
12. **Fumble:** The loss of possession of the ball.
13. **Game Clock:** Scoreboard game clock.
14. **Impetus:** The action of a player that gives momentum to the ball.
15. **Live Ball:** A ball legally free kicked or snapped. It continues in play until the down ends.
16. **Loose Ball:** A live ball not in possession of any player.
17. **Muff:** The touching of a loose ball by a player in an unsuccessful attempt to obtain possession.
18. **Neutral Zone:** The space the length of a ball between the two scrimmage lines. The offensive team and defensive team must remain behind their end of the ball.
    Exception: The offensive player who snaps the ball.
19. **Offside:** A player is offside when any part of his body is beyond his scrimmage or free kick line when the ball is snapped.
20. **Own Goal:** The goal a team is guarding.
21. **Play Clock:** 40/25 second clock.
22. **Pocket Area:** Applies from a point two yards outside of either offensive tackle and includes the tight end if he drops off the line of scrimmage to pass protect. Pocket extends longitudinally behind the line back to offensive team's own end line.
23. **Possession:** When a player controls the ball throughout the act of clearly touching both feet, or any other part of his body other than his hand(s), to the ground inbounds.
24. **Post-Possession Foul:** A foul by the receiving team that occurs after a ball is legally kicked from scrimmage prior to possession changing. The ball must cross the line of scrimmage and the receiving team must retain possession of the kicked ball.
25. **Punt:** A kick made when a player drops the ball and kicks it while it is in flight.
26. **Safety:** The situation in which the ball is dead on or behind a team's own goal if the impetus comes from a player on that team. Two points are scored for the opposing team.
27. **Shift:** The movement of two or more offensive players at the same time before the snap.
28. **Striking:** The act of swinging, clubbing, or propelling the arm or forearm in contacting an opponent.

29. **Sudden Death:** The continuation of a tied game into sudden death overtime in which the team scoring first (by safety, field goal, or touchdown) wins.
30. **Touchback:** When a ball is dead on or behind a team's own goal line, provided the impetus came from an opponent and provided it is not a touchdown or a missed field goal.
31. **Touchdown:** When any part of the ball, legally in possession of a player inbounds, is on, above, or over the opponent's goal line, provided it is not a touchback.
32. **Unsportsmanlike Conduct:** Any act contrary to the generally understood principles of sportsmanship.

SUMMARY OF PENALTIES

Automatic First Down

1. Awarded to offensive team on all defensive fouls with these exceptions:
   (a) Offside.
   (b) Encroachment.
   (c) Delay of game.
   (d) Illegal substitution.
   (e) Excessive time out(s).
   (f) Incidental grasp of facemask.
   (g) Neutral zone infraction.
   (h) Running into the kicker.

Loss of Down (No yardage)

1. Second forward pass behind the line.
2. Forward pass strikes ground, goal post, or crossbar.
3. Forward pass goes out of bounds.
4. Forward pass is first touched by eligible receiver who has gone out of bounds and returned.
5. Forward pass touches or is caught by an ineligible receiver on or behind line.
6. Forward pass thrown from behind line of scrimmage after ball once crossed the line.

Five Yards

1. Defensive holding or illegal use of hands (automatic first down).
2. Delay of game.
3. Delay of kickoff.
4. Encroachment.
5. Excessive time out(s).
6. False start.
7. Illegal formation.
8. Illegal shift.
9. Illegal motion.
10. Illegal substitution.
11. First onside kickoff out of bounds between goal lines and not touched.
12. Invalid fair catch signal.
13. More than 11 players on the field at snap for either team.
14. Less than seven men on offensive line at snap.
15. Offside.
16. Failure to pause one second after shift or huddle.
17. Running into kicker.
18. More than one man in motion at snap.
19. Grasping facemask of the ball carrier or quarterback.
20. Player out of bounds at snap.
21. Ineligible member(s) of kicking team going beyond line of scrimmage before ball is kicked.
22. Illegal return.
23. Failure to report change of eligibility.
24. Neutral zone infraction.
25. Loss of team time out(s) or five-yard penalty on the defense for excessive crowd noise.
26. Ineligible player downfield during passing down.

10 Yards

1. Offensive pass interference.
2. Holding, illegal use of hands, arms, or body by offense.
3. Tripping by a member of either team.
4. Helping the runner.
5. Deliberately batting or punching a loose ball.
6. Deliberately kicking a loose ball.

15 Yards

1. Chop block.
2. Clipping below the waist.
3. Fair catch interference.
4. Illegal crackback block by offense.
5. Piling on (automatic first down).
6. Roughing the kicker (automatic first down).
7. Roughing the passer (automatic first down).
8. Twisting, turning, or pulling an opponent by the facemask.
9. Unnecessary roughness.
10. Unsportsmanlike conduct.
11. Delay of game at start of either half.
12. Illegal low block.
13. A tackler using his helmet to butt, spear, or ram an opponent.
14. Any player who uses the top of his helmet unnecessarily.
15. A punter, placekicker, or holder who simulates being roughed by a defensive player.
16. A defender who takes a running start from beyond the line of scrimmage in an attempt to block a field goal or point after touchdown and lands on players at the line of scrimmage.

Five Yards and Loss of Down

1. Forward pass thrown from beyond line of scrimmage.

10 Yards and Loss of Down

1. Intentional grounding of forward pass (safety if passer is in own end zone). If foul occurs more than 10 yards behind line, play results in loss of down at spot of foul.

15 Yards and Loss of Coin Toss Option

1. Team's late arrival on the field prior to scheduled kickoff.
2. Captains not appearing for coin toss.

15 Yards (and disqualification if flagrant)

1. Striking opponent with fist.
2. Kicking or kneeing opponent.
3. Striking opponent on head or neck with forearm, elbow, or hands whether or not the initial contact is made below the neck area.
4. Roughing kicker.
5. Roughing passer.
6. Malicious unnecessary roughness.
7. Unsportsmanlike conduct.
8. Palpably unfair act. (Distance penalty determined by the Referee after consultation with other officials.)

15 Yards and Automatic Disqualification

1. Using a helmet (not worn) as a weapon.

Suspension From Game For One Down

1. Illegal equipment. (Player may return after one down when legally equipped.)

Touchdown Awarded (Palpably Unfair Act)

1. When Referee determines a palpably unfair act deprived a team of a touchdown. (Example: Player comes off bench and tackles runner apparently en route to touchdown.)

FIELD

1. Sidelines and end lines are out of bounds. The goal line is actually in the end zone. A player with the ball in his possession scores when the ball is on, above, or over the goal line.
2. The field is rimmed by a white border, six feet wide, along the sidelines. All of this is out of bounds.
3. The hashmarks (inbound lines) are 70 feet, 9 inches from each sideline.
4. Goal posts must be single-standard type, offset from the end line and painted bright gold. The goal posts must be 18 feet, 6 inches wide and the top face of the crossbar must be 10 feet above the ground. Vertical posts extend at least 30 feet above the crossbar. A ribbon 4 inches by 42 inches long is to be attached to the top of each post. The actual goal is the plane extending indefinitely above the crossbar and between the outer edges of the posts.
5. The field is 360 feet long and 160 feet wide. The end zones are 30 feet deep. The line used in try-for-point plays is two yards out from the goal line.
6. Chain crew members and ball boys must be uniformly identifiable.
7. All clubs must use standardized sideline markers. Pylons must be used for goal line and end line markings.
8. End zone markings and club identification at 50 yard line must be approved by the Commissioner to avoid any confusion as to delineation of goal lines, sidelines, and end lines.

BALL

1. Twenty-four approved footballs will be used in each game (12 each half).

COIN TOSS

1. The toss of coin will take place within three minutes of kickoff in center of field. The toss will be called by the visiting captain. The winner may choose one of two privileges and the loser gets the other:
   (a) Receive or kick
   (b) Goal his team will defend
2. Immediately prior to the start of the second half, the captains of both teams must inform the officials of their respective choices. The loser of the original coin toss gets first choice.

TIMING

1. The stadium game clock is official. In case it stops or is operating incorrectly, the Line Judge takes over the official timing on the field.
2. Each period is 15 minutes. The intermission between the periods is two minutes. Halftime is 12 minutes, unless otherwise specified.
3. On charged team time outs, the Field Judge starts watch and blows whistle after 1 minute 50 seconds, unless television does not utilize the time for commercial. In this case the length of the time out is reduced to 40 seconds.
4. The Referee will allow necessary time to attend to an injured player, or repair a legal player's equipment.
5. Each team is allowed three time outs each half.
6. Time between plays will be 40 seconds from the end of a given play until the snap of the ball for the next play, or a 25-second interval after certain adminis-

trative stoppages and game delays.
7. Clock will start running when ball is snapped following all changes of team possession.
8. With the exception of the last two minutes of the first half and the last five minutes of the second half, the game clock will be restarted following a kickoff return, a player going out of bounds on a play from scrimmage, or after declined penalties when appropriate on the referee's signal.
9. Consecutive team time outs can be taken by opposing teams but the length of the second time out will be reduced to 40 seconds.
10. When, in the judgment of the Referee, the level of crowd noise prevents the offense from hearing its signals, he can institute a series of procedures which can result in a loss of team time outs or a five-yard penalty against the defensive team.

SUDDEN DEATH

1. The sudden death system of determining the winner shall prevail when score is tied at the end of the regulation playing time of all NFL games. The team scoring first during overtime play shall be the winner and the game automatically ends upon any score (by safety, field goal, or touchdown) or when a score is awarded by Referee for a palpably unfair act.
2. At the end of regulation time the Referee will immediately toss coin at center of field in accordance with rules pertaining to the usual pregame toss. The captain of the visiting team will call the toss.
3. Following a three-minute intermission after the end of the regulation game, play will be continued in 15-minute periods or until there is a score. There is a two-minute intermission between subsequent periods. The teams change goals at the start of each period. Each team has three time outs per half and all general timing provisions apply as during a regular game. Disqualified players are not allowed to return.
   Exception: In preseason and regular season games there shall be a maximum of 15 minutes of sudden death with two time outs instead of three. General provisions that apply for the fourth quarter will prevail.

TIMING IN FINAL TWO MINUTES OF EACH HALF

1. On kickoff, clock does not start until the ball has been legally touched by player of either team in the field of play. (In all other cases, clock starts with kickoff.)
2. A team cannot buy an excess time out for a penalty. However, a fourth time out is allowed without penalty for an injured player, who must be removed immediately. A fifth time out or more is allowed for an injury and a five-yard penalty is assessed if the clock was running. Additionally, if the clock was running and the score is tied or the team in possession is losing, the ball cannot be put in play for at least 10 seconds on the fourth or more time out. The half or game can end while those 10 seconds are run off on the clock.
3. If the defensive team is behind in the score and commits a foul when it has no time outs left in the final 30 seconds of either half, the offensive team can decline the penalty for the foul and have the time on the clock expire.
4. Fouls that occur in the last five minutes of the fourth quarter as well as the last two minutes of the first half will result in the clock starting on the snap.

TRY

1. After a touchdown, the scoring team is allowed a try during one scrimmage down. The ball may be spotted anywhere between the inbounds lines, two or more yards from the goal line. The successful conversion counts one point by kick; two points for a successful conversion by touchdown; or one point for a safety.
2. The defensive team never can score on a try. As soon as defense gets possession or the kick is blocked or a touchdown is not scored, the try is over.
3. Any distance penalty for fouls committed by the defense that prevent the try from being attempted can be enforced on the succeeding try or succeeding kickoff. Any foul committed on a successful try will result in a distance penalty being assessed on the ensuing kickoff.
4. Only the fumbling player can recover and advance a fumble during a try.

PLAYERS-SUBSTITUTIONS

1. Each team is permitted 11 men on the field at the snap.
2. Unlimited substitution is permitted. However, players may enter the field only when the ball is dead. Players who have been substituted for are not permitted to linger on the field. Such lingering will be interpreted as unsportsmanlike conduct.
3. Players leaving the game must be out of bounds on their own side, clearing the field between the end lines, before a snap or free kick. If player crosses end line leaving field, it is delay of game (five-yard penalty).
4. Substitutes who remain in the game must move onto the field as far as the inside of the field numerals before moving to a wide position.
5. With the exception of the last two minutes of either half, the offensive team, while in the process of substitution or simulated substitution, is prohibited from rushing quickly to the line and snapping the ball with the obvious attempt to cause a defensive foul; i.e., too many men on the field.

KICKOFF

1. The kickoff shall be from the kicking team's 30-yard line at the start of each half and after a field goal and try-for-point. A kickoff is one type of free kick.
2. A one-inch tee may be used (no tee permitted for field goal or try attempt) on a kickoff. The ball is put in play by a placekick or dropkick.
3. If the kickoff clears the opponent's goal posts it is not a field goal.
4. A kickoff is illegal unless it travels 10 yards OR is touched by the receiving team. Once the ball is touched by the receiving team it is a free ball. Receivers may recover and advance. Kicking team may recover but NOT advance UNLESS receiver had possession and lost the ball.
5. When a kickoff goes out of bounds between the goal lines without being touched by the receiving team, the ball belongs to the receivers 30 yards from the spot of the kick or at the out-of-bounds spot unless the ball went out-of-bounds the first time an onside kick was attempted. In this case the kicking team is to be penalized five yards and the ball must be kicked again.
6. When a kickoff goes out of bounds between the goal lines and is touched last by receiving team, it is receiver's ball at out-of-bounds spot.

FREE KICK

1. In addition to a kickoff, the other free kicks are a kick after a safety and a kick after a fair catch. In both cases, a dropkick, placekick, or punt may be used (a punt may not be used on a kickoff).
2. On a free kick after a fair catch, captain of receiving team has the option to put ball in play by punt, dropkick, or placekick without a tee, or by snap. If the placekick or dropkick goes between the uprights a field goal is scored.
3. On a free kick after a safety, the team scored upon puts ball in play by a punt, dropkick, or placekick without tee. No score can be made on a free kick following a safety, even if a series of penalties places team in position. (A field goal can be scored only on a play from scrimmage or a free kick after a fair catch.)

FIELD GOAL

1. All field goals attempted (kicker) and missed from beyond the 20-yard line will result in the defensive team taking possession of the ball at the spot of the kick. On any field goal attempted and missed where the spot of the kick is on or inside the 20-yard line, ball will revert to defensive team at the 20-yard line.

SAFETY

1. The important factor in a safety is impetus. Two points are scored for the opposing team when the ball is dead on or behind a team's own goal line if the impetus came from a player on that team.

Examples of Safety:

(a) Blocked punt goes out of kicking team's end zone. Impetus was provided by punting team. The block only changes direction of ball, not impetus.
(b) Ball carrier retreats from field of play into his own end zone and is downed. Ball carrier provides impetus.
(c) Offensive team commits a foul and spot of enforcement is behind its own goal line.
(d) Player on receiving team muffs punt and, trying to get ball, forces or illegally kicks (creating new impetus) it into end zone where it goes out of the end zone or is recovered by a member of the receiving team in the end zone.

Examples of Non-Safety:

(a) Player intercepts a pass with both feet inbounds in the field of play and his momentum carries him into his own end zone. Ball is put in play at spot of interception.
(b) Player intercepts a pass in his own end zone and is downed in the end zone, even after recovering in the end zone. Impetus came from passing team, not from defense. (Touchback)
(c) Player passes from behind his own goal line. Opponent bats down ball in end zone. (Incomplete pass)

MEASURING

1. The forward point of the ball is used when measuring.

POSITION OF PLAYERS AT SNAP

1. Offensive team must have at least seven players on line.
2. Offensive players, not on line, must be at least one yard back at snap. **(Exception:** player who takes snap.)
3. No interior lineman may move after taking or simulating a three-point stance.
4. No player of either team may invade neutral zone before snap.
5. No player of offensive team may charge or move, after assuming set position, in such manner as to lead defense to believe snap has started.
6. If a player changes his eligibility, the Referee must alert the defensive captain after player has reported to him.
7. All players of offensive team must be stationary at snap, except one back who may be in motion parallel to scrimmage line or backward (not forward).
8. After a shift or huddle all players on offensive team must come to an absolute stop for at least one second with no movement of hands, feet, head, or swaying of body.
9. Quarterbacks can be called for a false start penalty (five yards) if their actions are judged to be an obvious attempt to draw an opponent offside.

USE OF HANDS, ARMS, AND BODY

1. No player on offense may assist a runner except by blocking for him. There shall be no interlocking interference.

2. A runner may ward off opponents with his hands and arms but no other player on offense may use hands or arms to obstruct an opponent by grasping with hands, pushing, or encircling any part of his body during a block. Hands (open or closed) can be thrust forward to initially contact an opponent on or outside the opponent's frame, but the blocker must work to bring his hands on or inside the frame.
   Note: Pass blocking: Hand(s) thrust forward that slip outside the body of the defender will be legal if blocker worked to bring them back inside. Hand(s) or arm(s) that encircle a defender—i.e., hook an opponent—are to be considered illegal and officials are to call a foul for holding.
   Blocker cannot use his hands or arms to push from behind, hang onto, or encircle an opponent in a manner that restricts his movement as the play develops.
3. Hands cannot be thrust forward above the frame to contact an opponent on the neck, face or head.
   Note: The frame is defined as the part of the opponent's body below the neck that is presented to the blocker.
4. A defensive player may not tackle or hold an opponent other than a runner. Otherwise, he may use his hands, arms, or body only:
   (a) To defend or protect himself against an obstructing opponent.
   Exception: An eligible receiver is considered to be an obstructing opponent ONLY to a point five yards beyond the line of scrimmage unless the player who receives the snap clearly demonstrates no further intention to pass the ball. Within this five-yard zone, a defensive player may make contact with an eligible receiver that may be maintained as long as it is continuous and unbroken up until a point when the receiver is beyond the defender. The defensive player cannot use his hands or arms to push from behind, hang onto, or encircle an eligible receiver in a manner that restricts movement as the play develops. Beyond this five-yard limitation, a defender may use his hands or arms ONLY to defend or protect himself against impending contact caused by a receiver. In such reaction, the defender may not contact a receiver who attempts to take a path to evade him.
   (b) To push or pull opponent out of the way on line of scrimmage.
   (c) In actual attempt to get at or tackle runner.
   (d) To push or pull opponent out of the way in a legal attempt to recover a loose ball.
   (e) During a legal block on an opponent who is not an eligible pass receiver.
   (f) When legally blocking an eligible pass receiver above the waist.
   Exception: Eligible receivers lined up within two yards of the tackle, whether on or immediately behind the line, may be blocked below the waist at or behind the line of scrimmage. NO eligible receiver may be blocked below the waist after he goes beyond the line. (Illegal cut)
   Note: Once the quarterback hands off or pitches the ball to a back, or if the quarterback leaves the pocket area, the restrictions (illegal chuck, illegal cut) on the defensive team relative to the offensive receivers will end, provided the ball is not in the air.
5. A defensive player may not contact an opponent above the shoulders with the palm of his hand except to ward him off on the line. This exception is permitted only if it is not a repeated act against the same opponent during any one contact. In all other cases the palms may be used on head, neck, or face only to ward off or push an opponent in legal attempt to get at the ball.
6. Any offensive player who pretends to possess the ball or to whom a teammate pretends to give the ball may be tackled provided he is crossing his scrimmage line between the ends of a normal tight offensive line.
7. An offensive player who lines up more than two yards outside his own tackle or a player who, at the snap, is in a backfield position and subsequently takes a position more than two yards outside a tackle may not clip an opponent anywhere nor may he contact an opponent below the waist if the blocker is moving toward the ball and if contact is made within an area five yards on either side of the line.
8. A player of either team may block at any time provided it is not pass interference, fair catch interference, or unnecessary roughness.
9. A player may not bat or punch:
   (a) A loose ball (in field of play) toward his opponent's goal line or in any direction in either end zone.
   (b) A ball in player possession.
   Note: If there is any question as to whether a defender is stripping or batting a ball in player possession, the official(s) will rule the action as a legal act (stripping the ball).
   Exception: A forward or backward pass may be batted, tipped, or deflected in any direction at any time by either the offense or the defense.
   Note: A pass in flight that is controlled or caught may only be thrown backward, if it is thrown forward it is considered an illegal bat.
10. No player may deliberately kick any ball except as a punt, dropkick, or placekick.

FORWARD PASS

1. A forward pass may be touched or caught by any eligible receiver. All members of the defensive team are eligible. Eligible receivers on the offensive team are players on either end of line (other than center, guard, or tackle) or players at least one yard behind the line at the snap. A T-formation quarterback is not eligible to receive a forward pass during a play from scrimmage.
   Exception: T-formation quarterback becomes eligible if pass is previously touched by an eligible receiver.
2. An offensive team may make only one forward pass during each play from scrimmage (Loss of down).
3. The passer must be behind his line of scrimmage (Loss of down and five yards, enforced from the spot of pass).
4. Any eligible offensive player may catch a forward pass. If a pass is touched by one offensive player and touched or caught by a second eligible offensive player, pass completion is legal. Further, all offensive players become eligible once a pass is touched by an eligible receiver or any defensive player.
5. The rules concerning a forward pass and ineligible receivers:
   (a) If ball is touched accidentally by an ineligible receiver on or behind his line: loss of down.
   (b) If ineligible receiver is illegally downfield: loss of five yards.
   (c) If touched or caught (intentionally or accidentally) by ineligible receiver beyond the line: loss of 10 yards or loss of down.
6. The player who first controls and continues to maintain control of a pass will be awarded the ball even though his opponent later establishes joint control of the ball.
7. Any forward pass becomes incomplete and ball is dead if:
   (a) Pass hits the ground or goes out of bounds.
   (b) Hits the goal post or the crossbar of either team.
   (c) Is caught by offensive player after touching ineligible receiver.
   (d) An illegal pass is caught by the passer.
8. A forward pass is complete when a receiver clearly possesses the pass and touches the ground with both feet inbounds while in possession of the ball. If a receiver would have landed inbounds with both feet but is carried or pushed out of bounds while maintaining possession of the ball, pass is complete at the out-of-bounds spot.
9. If an eligible receiver goes out of bounds accidentally or is forced out by a defender and returns to first touch and catch a pass, the play is regarded as a pass caught out of bounds. (Loss of down, no yardage.)
10. On a fourth down pass—when the offensive team is inside the opposition's 20-yard line—an incomplete pass results in a loss of down at the line of scrimmage.
11. If a personal foul is committed by the defense prior to the completion of a pass, the penalty is 15 yards from the spot where ball becomes dead.
12. If a personal foul is committed by the offense prior to the completion of a pass, the penalty is 15 yards from the previous line of scrimmage.

INTENTIONAL GROUNDING OF FORWARD PASS

1. Intentional grounding of a forward pass is a foul: loss of down and 10 yards from previous spot if passer is in the field of play or loss of down at the spot of the foul if it occurs more than 10 yards behind the line or safety if passer is in his own end zone when ball is released.
2. Intentional grounding will be called when a passer, facing an imminent loss of yardage due to pressure from the defense, throws a forward pass without a realistic chance of completion.
3. Intentional grounding will not be called when a passer, while out of the pocket and facing an imminent loss of yardage, throws a pass that lands beyond the line of scrimmage, even if no offensive player(s) have a realistic chance to catch the ball (including if the ball lands out of bounds over the sideline or end line).

PROTECTION OF PASSER

1. By interpretation, a pass begins when the passer—with possession of ball—starts to bring his hand forward. If ball strikes ground after this action has begun, play is ruled an incomplete pass. If passer loses control of ball prior to his bringing his hand forward, play is ruled a fumble.
2. No defensive player may run into a passer of a legal forward pass after the ball has left his hand (15 yards). The Referee must determine whether opponent had a reasonable chance to stop his momentum during an attempt to block the pass or tackle the passer while he still had the ball.
3. No defensive player who has an unrestricted path to the quarterback may hit him flagrantly in the area of the knee(s) when approaching in any direction.
4. Officials are to blow the play dead as soon as the quarterback is clearly in the grasp and control of any tackler, and his safety is in jeopardy.

PASS INTERFERENCE

1. There shall be no interference with a forward pass thrown from behind the line. The restriction for the passing team starts with the snap. The restriction on the defensive team starts when the ball leaves the passer's hand. Both restrictions end when the ball is touched by anyone.
2. The penalty for defensive pass interference is an automatic first down at the spot of the foul. If interference is in the end zone, it is first down for the offense on the defense's 1-yard line. If previous spot was inside the defense's 1-yard line, penalty is half the distance to the goal line.
3. The penalty for offensive pass interference is 10 yards from the previous spot.
4. It is pass interference by either team when any player movement beyond the offensive line significantly hinders the progress of an eligible player or such player's opportunity to catch the ball during a legal forward pass. When players are competing for position to make a play on the ball, any contact by hands, arms, or body shall be considered incidental unless prohibited. Prohib-

ited conduct shall be when a player physically restricts or impedes the opponent in such a manner that is visually evident and materially affects the opponent's opportunity to gain position or retain his position to catch the ball. If a player has gained position, he shall not be considered to have impeded or restricted his opponent in a prohibited manner if all of his actions are a bona fide effort to go to and catch the ball. Provided an eligible player is not interfered with in such a manner, the following exceptions to pass interference will prevail:

(a) If neither player is looking for the ball and there is incidental contact in the act of moving to the ball that does not materially affect the route of an eligible player, there is no interference. If there is any question whether the incidental contact materially affects the route, the ruling shall be no interference.
Note: Inadvertent tripping is not a foul in this situation.
(b) Any eligible player looking for and intent on playing the ball who initiates contact, however severe, while attempting to move to the spot of comple tion or interception will not be called for interference.
(c) Any eligible player who makes contact, however severe, with one or more eligible players while looking for and making a genuine attempt to catch or bat a reachable ball, will not be called for interference.
(d) It must be remembered that defensive players have as much right to the ball as offensive eligible receivers.
(e) Pass interference by the defense is not to be called when the forward pass is clearly uncatchable.
(f) Note: There is no defensive pass interference behind the line.

BACKWARD PASS

1. Any pass not forward is regarded as a backward pass or lateral. A pass parallel to the line is a backward pass. A runner may pass backward at any time. Any player on either team may catch the pass or recover the ball after it touches the ground.
2. A backward pass that strikes the ground can be recovered and advanced by either team.
3. A backward pass caught in the air can be advanced by either team.
4. A backward pass in flight may not be batted forward by an offensive player.

FUMBLE

1. The distinction between a fumble and a muff should be kept in mind in considering rules about fumbles. A fumble is the loss of possession of the ball. A muff is the touching of a loose ball by a player in an unsuccessful attempt to obtain possession.
2. A fumble may be advanced by any player on either team regardless of whether recovered before or after ball hits the ground.
3. A fumble that goes forward and out of bounds will return to the fumbling team at the spot of the fumble unless the ball goes out of bounds in the opponent's end zone. In this case, it is a touchback.
4. On a play from scrimmage, if an offensive player fumbles anywhere on the field during fourth down, only the fumbling player is permitted to recover and/or advance the ball. If any player fumbles after the two-minute warning in a half, only the fumbling player is permitted to recover and/or advance the ball. If recovered by any other offensive player, the ball is dead at the spot of the fumble unless it is recovered behind the spot of the fumble. In that case, the ball is dead at the spot of recovery. Any defensive player may recover and/or advance any fumble at any time.

KICKS FROM SCRIMMAGE

1. Any kick from scrimmage must be made from behind the line to be legal.
2. Any punt or missed field goal that touches a goal post is dead.
3. During a kick from scrimmage, only the end men, as eligible receivers on the line of scrimmage at the time of the snap, are permitted to go beyond the line before the ball is kicked.
Exception: An eligible receiver who, at the snap, is aligned or in motion behind the line and more than one yard outside the end man on his side of the line, clearly making him the outside receiver, replaces that end man as the player eligible to go downfield after the snap. All other members of the kicking team must remain at the line of scrimmage until the ball has been kicked.
4. Any punt that is blocked and does not cross the line of scrimmage can be recovered and advanced by either team. However, if offensive team recovers it must make the yardage necessary for its first down to retain possession if punt was on fourth down.
5. The kicking team may never advance its own kick even though legal recovery is made beyond the line of scrimmage. Possession only.
6. A member of the receiving team may not run into or rough a kicker who kicks from behind his line unless contact is:
(a) Incidental to and after he had touched ball in flight.
(b) Caused by kicker's own motions.
(c) Occurs during a quick kick, or a kick made after a run, or after kicker recovers a loose ball. Ball is loose when kicker muffs snap or snap hits ground.
(d) Defender is blocked into kicker.
The penalty for running into the kicker is 5 yards. For roughing the kicker: 15 yards, an automatic first down and disqualification if flagrant.
7. If a member of the kicking team attempting to down the ball on or inside opponent's 5-yard line carries the ball into the end zone, it is a touchback.
8. Fouls during a punt are enforced from the previous spot (line of scrimmage).
Exception: Illegal touching, illegal fair catch, invalid fair catch signal, and fouls by the receiving team during loose ball after ball is kicked.
9. While the ball is in the air or rolling on the ground following a punt or field goal attempt and receiving team commits a foul before gaining possession, receiving team will retain possession and will be penalized for its foul.
10. It will be illegal for a defensive player to jump or stand on any player, or be picked up by a teammate or to use a hand or hands on a teammate to gain additional height in an attempt to block a kick (Penalty: 15 yards, unsportsmanlike conduct).
11. A punted ball remains a kicked ball until it is declared dead or in possession of either team.
12. Any member of the punting team may down the ball anywhere in the field of play. However, it is illegal touching (Official's time out and receiver's ball at spot of illegal touching). This foul does not offset any foul by receivers during the down.
13. Defensive team may advance all kicks from scrimmage (including unsuccessful field goal) whether or not ball crosses defensive team's goal line. Rules pertaining to kicks from scrimmage apply until defensive team gains possession.

FAIR CATCH

1. The member of the receiving team must raise one arm a full length above his head and wave it from side to side while kick is in flight. (Failure to give proper sign: receivers' ball five yards behind spot of signal.) **Note:** It is legal for the receiver to shield his eyes from the sun by raising one hand no higher than the helmet.
2. No opponent may interfere with the fair catcher, the ball, or his path to the ball. Penalty: 15 yards from spot of foul and fair catch is awarded.
3. A player who signals for a fair catch is not required to catch the ball. However, if a player signals for a fair catch, he may not block or initiate contact with any player on the kicking team until the ball touches a player. Penalty: snap 15 yards behind spot of foul.
4. If ball hits ground or is touched by member of kicking team in flight, fair catch signal is off and all rules for a kicked ball apply.
5. Any undue advance by a fair catch receiver is delay of game. No specific distance is specified for undue advance as ball is dead at spot of catch. If player comes to a reasonable stop, no penalty. For violation, five yards.
6. If time expires while ball is in play and a fair catch is awarded, receiving team may choose to extend the period with one free kick down. However, placekicker may not use tee.

FOUL ON LAST PLAY OF HALF OR GAME

1. On a foul by defense on last play of half or game, the down is replayed if penalty is accepted.
2. On a foul by the offense on last play of half or game, the down is not replayed and the play in which the foul is committed is nullified.
Exception: Fair catch interference, foul following change of possession, illegal touching. No score by offense counts.
3. On double foul on last play of half or game, down is replayed.

SPOT OF ENFORCEMENT OF FOUL

1. There are four basic spots at which a penalty for a foul is enforced:
(a) Spot of foul: The spot where the foul is committed.
(b) Previous spot: The spot where the ball was put in play.
(c) Spot of snap, pass, fumble, return kick, or free kick: The spot where the act connected with the foul occurred.
(d) Succeeding spot: The spot where the ball next would be put in play if no distance penalty were to be enforced.
Exception: If foul occurs after a touchdown and before the whistle for a try-for-point, succeeding spot is spot of next kickoff.
2. All fouls committed by offensive team behind the line of scrimmage and in the field of play shall be penalized from the previous spot.
3. When spot of enforcement for fouls involving defensive holding or illegal use of hands by the defense is behind the line of scrimmage, any penalty yardage to be assessed on that play shall be measured from the line if the foul occurred beyond the line.

DOUBLE FOUL

1. If there is a double foul during a down in which there is a change of possession, the team last gaining possession may keep the ball unless its foul was committed prior to the change of possession.
2. If double foul occurs after a change of possession, the defensive team retains the ball at the spot of its foul or dead ball spot.
3. If one of the fouls of a double foul involves disqualification, that player must be removed, but no penalty yardage is to be assessed.
4. If the kickers foul during a kick before possession changes and the receivers foul after possession changes, the receivers will retain the ball after enforcement of its foul.

PENALTY ENFORCED ON FOLLOWING KICKOFF

1. When a team scores by touchdown, field goal, extra point, or safety and either team commits a personal foul, unsportsmanlike conduct, or obvious unfair act during the down, the penalty will be assessed on the following kickoff.

PROCEDURES TO TERMINATE OR TEMPORARILY DELAY COMPLETION OF A GAME

The National Football League holds to the position that all games should be played to their conclusion. However, if in the opinion of appropriate League authorities, it is impossible to begin or continue a game due to an emergency, or a game is deemed to be imminently threatened by any such emergency—e.g., severely inclement weather, lightning, flooding, power failure, interference by spectators, or other non-participants—then the following procedures will serve as guidelines for the Commissioner and/or his duly appointed representatives. The Commissioner will have the power to review the circumstances of each emergency and to adjust the following procedures in whatever manner he deems appropriate. If, in the Commissioner's opinion, it is reasonable to project that the resumption of an interrupted game would not change its ultimate result, he will be empowered to terminate the game.

1. The League employees vested with the authority to define emergencies under these procedures are the Commissioner, his representatives, and the game Referee. In cases where neither the Commissioner nor his representatives are present, the Referee shall have sole authority, but he must make every effort to contact the Commissioner or representative for consultation. In all cases of significant delay, the League authorities will consult with the management of the participating clubs.
2. If, due to an emergency, a regular-season or postseason game is not started at its scheduled time and cannot be played at any later time that same day, the game, nevertheless, must be played on a subsequent date to be determined by the Commissioner.
3. If there is deemed to be a threat of an emergency (e.g., incoming tropical storm) that may occur during the playing of a game, the starting time of such game will not be moved to an earlier time unless there is clearly sufficient time to make an orderly change.
4. If an interrupted regular-season or postseason game cannot be completed on the same day, such game will be rescheduled by the Commissioner and resumed at that point.
5. In instances which require the Commissioner to reschedule a regular-season game, he will make every effort to set the game for no later than two days after its originally scheduled date, and if possible, at its original site. If unable to do so, he will schedule it at the nearest available facility. If it is impossible to schedule the game within two days after its original date, the Commissioner will attempt to schedule it on the Tuesday of the next calendar week in which the two involved clubs play other clubs no earlier than Sunday.
6. If an emergency interrupts a postseason game and such game cannot be resumed on that same date, the Commissioner will make every effort to arrange for its completion as soon as possible. If unable to schedule the game at the same site, he will select an appropriate alternate site. He will terminate the game short of completion only if in his judgment the continuation of the game would not be normally expected to alter the ultimate outcome.
7. In all instances where a game is resumed after interruption, the resumption will begin at the point at which the game was interrupted. The referee will call time out when it is necessary to declare an emergency interruption, and he will make a record of the team possessing the ball, position of the ball on the field, down, distance, time remaining in the period, and any other pertinent information required for an efficient and equitable resumption of play.

Note: In recent history, only two games, both preseason, have been terminated. In 1976, the Chicago College All-Star game was terminated due to thunderstorms with the Steelers leading the All-Stars 24-0, and the 1980 Pro Football Hall of Fame Game at Canton, Ohio, was called with 5:29 remaining due to severe thunder and lightning with the Chargers and Packers tied 0-0.

NOTES

NOTES

NOTES